The Middle Ages · SIMPSON

The Sixteenth Century · GREENBLATT / LOGAN

The Early Seventeenth Century
MAUS

The Restoration and the Eighteenth Century
NOGGLE

The Romantic Period · LYNCH

The Victorian Age · ROBSON

The Twentieth and Twenty-First Centuries
RAMAZANI

THE NORTON ANTHOLOGY OF

ENGLISH

LITERATURE

TENTH EDITION

VOLUME F

THE TWENTIETH AND TWENTY-FIRST CENTURIES

THE NORTON ANTHOLOGY OF
ENGLISH
LITERATURE

TENTH EDITION

Stephen Greenblatt, *General Editor*
COGAN UNIVERSITY PROFESSOR OF THE HUMANITIES
HARVARD UNIVERSITY

VOLUME F

THE TWENTIETH AND TWENTY-FIRST CENTURIES
Jahan Ramazani

W·W·NORTON & COMPANY
NEW YORK · LONDON

W. W. Norton & Company has been independent since its founding in 1923, when William Warder Norton and Mary D. Herter Norton first published lectures delivered at the People's Institute, the adult education division of New York City's Cooper Union. The firm soon expanded its program beyond the Institute, publishing books by celebrated academics from America and abroad. By midcentury, the two major pillars of Norton's publishing program—trade books and college texts—were firmly established. In the 1950s, the Norton family transferred control of the company to its employees, and today—with a staff of four hundred and a comparable number of trade, college, and professional titles published each year—W. W. Norton & Company stands as the largest and oldest publishing house owned wholly by its employees.

Editors: Julia Reidhead and Marian Johnson
Assistant Editor, Print: Rachel Taylor
Manuscript Editors: Michael Fleming, Katharine Ings, Candace Levy
Media Editor: Carly Fraser Doria
Assistant Editor, Media: Ava Bramson
Marketing Manager, Literature: Kimberly Bowers
Managing Editor, College Digital Media: Kim Yi
Production Manager: Sean Mintus
Text design: Jo Anne Metsch
Art director: Rubina Yeh
Photo Editor: Nelson Colon
Permissions Manager: Megan Jackson Schindel
Permissions Clearing: Nancy J. Rodwan
Cartographer: Adrian Kitzinger
Composition: Westchester Book Company
Manufacturing: LSC Crawfordsville

ISBN: 978-0-393-60307-1

W. W. Norton & Company, Inc., 500 Fifth Avenue, New York, NY 10110
wwnorton.com

W. W. Norton & Company Ltd., 15 Carlisle Street, London W1D 3BS

1 2 3 4 5 6 7 8 9 0

Contents*

PREFACE TO THE TENTH EDITION xvii

ACKNOWLEDGMENTS xxvii

The Twentieth and Twenty-First Centuries

INTRODUCTION 3

TIMELINE 31

THOMAS HARDY (1840–1928)   34
    On the Western Circuit 36
    Hap 52
    Neutral Tones 52
    Drummer Hodge 53
    The Darkling Thrush 53
    The Ruined Maid 54
    A Trampwoman's Tragedy 55
    One We Knew 58
    Channel Firing 59
    The Convergence of the Twain 60
    Ah, Are You Digging on My Grave? 62
    Under the Waterfall 63
    The Walk 64
    The Voice 64
    During Wind and Rain 65
    In Time of 'The Breaking of Nations' 66
    He Never Expected Much 66

JOSEPH CONRAD (1857–1924)   67
    Preface to The Nigger of the "Narcissus" 69
        [The Task of the Artist] 69
    Heart of Darkness 71

A. E. HOUSMAN (1859–1936)   131
    Loveliest of Trees 132
    When I Was One-and-Twenty 132

---

* Additional readings are available on the NAEL Archive (digital.wwnorton.com/englishlit10def).

To an Athlete Dying Young 133
Terence, This Is Stupid Stuff 134
Epitaph on an Army of Mercenaries 135

VOICES FROM WORLD WAR I   136

RUPERT BROOKE   139
The Soldier 139
ROBERT SERVICE   140
Only a Boche 140
EDWARD THOMAS   142
Adlestrop 142
The Owl 143
Rain 143
The Cherry Trees 144
As the Team's Head Brass 144
MARY BORDEN   145
Belgium 145
The Song of the Mud 147
SIEGFRIED SASSOON   148
'They' 149
The Rear-Guard 150
The General 150
Glory of Women 151
Everyone Sang 151
On Passing the New Menin Gate 151
Memoirs of an Infantry Officer 152
[The Opening of the Battle of the Somme] 152
IVOR GURNEY   153
To His Love 154
The Silent One 155
ISAAC ROSENBERG   155
Break of Day in the Trenches 156
Louse Hunting 158
Returning, We Hear the Larks 158
Dead Man's Dump 159
WILFRED OWEN   161
Anthem for Doomed Youth 161
Apologia Pro Poemate Meo 162
Miners 163
Dulce Et Decorum Est 164
Strange Meeting 166
Futility 167
Disabled 167
From Owen's Letters to His Mother 168
Preface 170

MAY WEDDERBURN CANNAN   170
  Rouen 171
ROBERT GRAVES   172
  Goodbye to All That 173
    [The Attack on High Wood] 173
  Recalling War 176
DAVID JONES   177
  In Parenthesis 178
    From Preface 178
    From Part 7: The Five Unmistakable Marks 179

MODERNIST MANIFESTOS   183

T. E. HULME: *From* Romanticism and Classicism (w. 1911–12)   185
F. S. FLINT AND EZRA POUND: Imagisme (1913)   191
  A Few Don'ts by an Imagiste (1913) 192
AN IMAGIST CLUSTER   195
  T. E. Hulme: Autumn 196
  Ezra Pound: In a Station of the Metro 196
  H.D.: Oread 196
    Sea Rose 197
BLAST   197
  Long Live the Vortex! (1914) 199
  Blast 6 (1914) 201
MINA LOY   204
  Feminist Manifesto (w. 1914) 205
  Songs to Joannes 208
    I 208
    III 208
    XIV 208
    XXVI 209

WILLIAM BUTLER YEATS (1865–1939)   209
  The Stolen Child 212
  Down by the Salley Gardens 214
  The Rose of the World 214
  The Lake Isle of Innisfree 215
  The Sorrow of Love 215
  When You Are Old 216
  Who Goes with Fergus? 216
  The Man Who Dreamed of Faeryland 216
  Adam's Curse 218
  No Second Troy 219
  The Fascination of What's Difficult 219

A Coat 219
September 1913 220
Easter, 1916 221
The Wild Swans at Coole 223
In Memory of Major Robert Gregory 223
An Irish Airman Foresees His Death 226
The Second Coming 227
A Prayer for My Daughter 227
Leda and the Swan 229
Sailing to Byzantium 230
Among School Children 231
A Dialogue of Self and Soul 233
Byzantium 234
Crazy Jane Talks with the Bishop 235
Lapis Lazuli 236
Under Ben Bulben 237
Man and the Echo 240
The Circus Animals' Desertion 241
From Introduction [A General Introduction for My Work] 242

E. M. FORSTER (1879–1970)   248
The Other Boat 249

VIRGINIA WOOLF (1882–1941)   270
The Mark on the Wall 272
Modern Fiction 277
Mrs. Dalloway 282
A Room of One's Own 392
        [Shakespeare's Sister] 392
Professions for Women 400

JAMES JOYCE (1882–1941)   404
Araby 407
The Dead 411
A Portrait of the Artist as a Young Man 440
Ulysses 602
        [*From* Penelope] 604

D. H. LAWRENCE (1885–1930)   611
Odour of Chrysanthemums 611
The Horse Dealer's Daughter 626
Why the Novel Matters 637
Love on the Farm 642
Piano 643
Bavarian Gentians 644
Snake 644

How Beastly the Bourgeois Is 646
The Ship of Death 647

T. S. ELIOT (1888–1965)   651
The Love Song of J. Alfred Prufrock 654
Sweeney among the Nightingales 657
The Waste Land 659
The Hollow Men 673
Journey of the Magi 676
Four Quartets 677
      Little Gidding 677
Tradition and the Individual Talent 684
The Metaphysical Poets 690

KATHERINE MANSFIELD (1888–1923)   697
The Daughters of the Late Colonel 698
The Garden Party 711

JEAN RHYS (1890–1979)   721
The Day They Burned the Books 722
On Not Shooting Sitting Birds 726

STEVIE SMITH (1902–1971)   728
Sunt Leones 729
Our Bog Is Dood 730
Not Waving but Drowning 731
Thoughts About the Person from Porlock 732
Pretty 733

GEORGE ORWELL (1903–1950)   734
Shooting an Elephant 735
Politics and the English Language 740

SAMUEL BECKETT (1906–1989)   749
Waiting for Godot 751

W. H. AUDEN (1907–1973)   807
Petition 808
On This Island 809
Lullaby 809
Spain 810
As I Walked Out One Evening 813
Musée des Beaux Arts 815
In Memory of W. B. Yeats 815
The Unknown Citizen 818
September 1, 1939 818

In Praise of Limestone 821
The Shield of Achilles 823
[Poetry as Memorable Speech] 825

DYLAN THOMAS (1914–1953)   827
The Force That Through the Green Fuse Drives the Flower 828
The Hunchback in the Park 829
Poem in October 830
Fern Hill 832
Do Not Go Gentle into That Good Night 833

VOICES FROM WORLD WAR II   834

VIRGINIA WOOLF   836
Three Guineas 836
[As a Woman I Have No Country] 836
PABLO PICASSO   841
Guernica 842
EDITH SITWELL   843
Still Falls the Rain 843
HENRY REED   844
Lessons of the War 845
1. Naming of Parts 845
KEITH DOUGLAS   846
Vergissmeinnicht 846
Aristocrats 847

NATION, RACE, AND LANGUAGE   848

CLAUDE McKAY   853
Old England 854
If We Must Die 855
LOUISE BENNETT   855
Jamaica Language 856
Dry-Foot Bwoy 857
Colonization in Reverse 858
Jamaica Oman 859
KAMAU BRATHWAITE   861
[Nation Language] 861
Calypso 866
NGŨGĨ WA THIONG'O   867
Decolonising the Mind 868
From The Language of African Literature 868
M. NOURBESE PHILIP   872
Discourse on the Logic of Language 873

SALMAN RUSHDIE   876
   [The British Indian Writer and a Dream-England]   877
   [English Is an Indian Literary Language]   880
GRACE NICHOLS   882
   Epilogue   882
   The Fat Black Woman Goes Shopping   882
   Wherever I Hang   883
LINTON KWESI JOHNSON   885
   Inglan Is a Bitch   885
HANIF KUREISHI   887
   [You Will Always Be a Paki]   887
BERNARDINE EVARISTO   891
   The Emperor's Babe   891
     Amo Amas Amat   891
PATIENCE AGBABI   893
   Prologue   894
DALJIT NAGRA   896
   A Black History of the English-Speaking Peoples   896

—————

DORIS LESSING (1919–2013)   900
   To Room Nineteen   901

PHILIP LARKIN (1922–1985)   923
   Church Going   924
   MCMXIV   925
   Talking in Bed   926
   Ambulances   926
   High Windows   927
   Sad Steps   928
   Homage to a Government   928
   The Explosion   929
   This Be The Verse   930
   Aubade   930

NADINE GORDIMER (1923–2014)   931
   The Moment before the Gun Went Off   932

A. K. RAMANUJAN (1929–1993)   936
   Self-Portrait   936
   Elements of Composition   936

THOM GUNN (1929–2004)   938
   Black Jackets   939
   My Sad Captains   940

From the Wave 940
Still Life 941
The Missing 942

DEREK WALCOTT (1930–2017)   942
A Far Cry from Africa 943
The Schooner *Flight* 944
    1 Adios, Carenage 944
The Season of Phantasmal Peace 946
Omeros 947
    1.3.3 ("*Mais qui ça qui rivait-'ous, Philoctete?*") 947
    6.49.1–2 ("She bathed him in the brew of the root. The basin") 948

TED HUGHES (1930–1998)   950
Wind 951
Relic 951
Pike 952
Out 953
Theology 954
Crow's Last Stand 955
Daffodils 955

HAROLD PINTER (1930–2008)   957
The Dumb Waiter 958

CHINUA ACHEBE (1930–2013)   978
Civil Peace 980

ALICE MUNRO (b. 1931)   984
Walker Brothers Cowboy 985

GEOFFREY HILL (1932–2016)   995
In Memory of Jane Fraser 995
Requiem for the Plantagenet Kings 996
September Song 996
Broken Hierarchies 997

V. S. NAIPAUL (b. 1932)   998
One Out of Many 999

TOM STOPPARD (b. 1937)   1021
Arcadia 1022

LES MURRAY (b. 1938)   1090
Morse 1091
Corniche 1092
The Kitchen Grammars 1092

SEAMUS HEANEY (1939–2013)   1093
   Digging 1095
   The Forge 1095
   The Grauballe Man 1096
   Punishment 1097
   Casualty 1099
   The Skunk 1101
   Station Island 1102
      12 ("Like a convalescent, I took the hand") 1102
   Clearances 1104
   The Sharping Stone 1107
   Anything Can Happen 1109
   A Kite for Aibhín 1109

MARGARET ATWOOD (b. 1939)   1110
   Death by Landscape 1111
   Miss July Grows Older 1123

J. M. COETZEE (b. 1940)   1124
   From Waiting for the Barbarians 1126

EAVAN BOLAND (b. 1944)   1139
   Fond Memory 1139
   The Dolls Museum in Dublin 1140
   The Lost Land 1141

SALMAN RUSHDIE (b. 1947)   1142
   The Prophet's Hair 1144

IAN McEWAN (b. 1948)   1154
   From Enduring Love 1155

ANNE CARSON (b. 1950)   1168
   From The Glass Essay 1169

PAUL MULDOON (b. 1951)   1173
   Anseo 1174
   Meeting the British 1175
   7, Middagh Street 1176
      ("And were Yeats living at this hour") 1176
   Milkweed and Monarch 1177
   The Loaf 1178
   Turtles 1179

HILARY MANTEL (b. 1952)   1179
   Sorry to Disturb 1181

KAZUO ISHIGURO (b. 1954)   1192
    A Village after Dark 1193

HANIF KUREISHI (b. 1954)   1200
    My Son the Fanatic 1202

CAROL ANN DUFFY (b. 1955)   1209
    Warming Her Pearls 1210
    Valentine 1211
    Medusa 1211
    Mrs Lazarus 1212
    The Christmas Truce 1213

CARYL PHILLIPS (b. 1958)   1216
    Growing Pains 1217

SIMON ARMITAGE (b. 1963)   1221
    The Tyre 1221
    Horses, M62 1223
    The English Astronaut 1224
    Beck 1225

KIRAN DESAI (b. 1971)   1225
    The Sermon in the Guava Tree 1227

ZADIE SMITH (b. 1975)   1236
    The Waiter's Wife 1238

CHIMAMANDA NGOZI ADICHIE (b. 1977)   1249
    Checking Out 1250

APPENDIXES   A1
    General Bibliography A3
    Literary Terminology A11
    Geographic Nomenclature A32
    MAP: London in the Nineteenth and Twentieth Centuries A34
    British Money A35
    The British Baronage A40
        The Royal Lines of England and Great Britain A43
    Religions in Great Britain A46

PERMISSIONS ACKNOWLEDGMENTS A51

INDEX A57

Preface to the Tenth Edition

For centuries the study of literature has occupied a central place in the Humanities curriculum. The power of great literature to reach across time and space, its exploration of the expressive potential of language, and its ability to capture the whole range of experiences from the most exalted to the everyday have made it an essential part of education. But there are significant challenges to any attempt to derive the full measure of enlightenment and pleasure from this precious resource. In a world in which distraction reigns, savoring works of literature requires quiet focus. In a society in which new media clamor for attention, attending to words on the page can prove difficult. And in a period obsessed with the present at its most instantaneous, it takes a certain effort to look at anything penned earlier than late last night.

The Norton Anthology of English Literature is designed to meet these challenges. It is deeply rewarding to enter the sensibility of a different place, to hear a new voice, to be touched by an unfamiliar era. It is critically important to escape the narrow boundaries of our immediate preoccupations and to respond with empathy to lives other than our own. It is moving, even astonishing, to feel that someone you never met is speaking directly to you. But for any of this to happen requires help. The overarching goal of the Norton Anthology—as it has been for over fifty-five years and ten editions—is to help instructors energize their classrooms, engage their students, and bring literature to life.* At a time when the Humanities are under great pressure, we are committed to facilitating the special joy that comes with encountering significant works of art.

The works anthologized in these six volumes generally form the core of courses designed to introduce students to English literature. The selections reach back to the earliest moments of literary creativity in English, when the language itself was still molten, and extend to some of the most recent experiments, when, once again, English seems remarkably fluid and open. That openness—a recurrent characteristic of a language that has never been officially regulated and that has constantly renewed itself—helps to account for the sense of freshness that characterizes the works brought together here.

One of the joys of literature in English is its spectacular abundance. Even within the geographical confines of England, Scotland, Wales, and

---

* For more on the help we offer and how to access it, see "Additional Resources for Instructors and Students," p. xxiv.

Ireland, where the majority of texts in this collection originated, one can find more than enough distinguished and exciting works to fill the pages of this anthology many times over. But English literature is not confined to the British Isles; it is a global phenomenon. This border-crossing is not a consequence of modernity alone. It is fitting that among the first works here is *Beowulf*, a powerful epic written in the Germanic language known as Old English about a singularly restless Scandinavian hero. *Beowulf*'s remarkable translator in *The Norton Anthology of English Literature*, Seamus Heaney, was one of the great contemporary masters of English literature— he was awarded the Nobel Prize for Literature in 1995—but it would be potentially misleading to call him an "English poet" for he was born in Northern Ireland and was not in fact English. It would be still more misleading to call him a "British poet," as if the British Empire were the most salient fact about the language he spoke and wrote in or the culture by which he was shaped. What matters is that the language in which Heaney wrote is English, and this fact links him powerfully with the authors assembled in these volumes, a linguistic community that stubbornly refuses to fit comfortably within any firm geographical or ethnic or national boundaries. So too, to glance at other authors and writings in the anthology, in the twelfth century, the noblewoman Marie de France wrote her short stories in an Anglo-Norman dialect at home on both sides of the channel; in the sixteenth century William Tyndale, in exile in the Low Countries and inspired by German religious reformers, translated the New Testament from Greek and thereby changed the course of the English language; in the seventeenth century Aphra Behn touched readers with a story that moves from Africa, where its hero is born, to South America, where Behn herself may have witnessed some of the tragic events she describes; and early in the twentieth century Joseph Conrad, born in Ukraine of Polish parents, wrote in eloquent English a celebrated novella whose ironic vision of European empire gave way by the century's end to the voices of those over whom the empire, now in ruins, had once hoped to rule: the Caribbean-born Claude McKay, Louise Bennett, Derek Walcott, Kamau Brathwaite, V. S. Naipaul, and Grace Nichols; the African-born Chinua Achebe, J. M. Coetzee, Ngũgĩ Wa Thiong'o, and Chimamanda Ngozi Adichie; and the Indian-born A. K. Ramanujan and Salman Rushdie.

A vital literary culture is always on the move. This principle was the watchword of M. H. Abrams, the distinguished literary critic who first conceived *The Norton Anthology of English Literature*, brought together the original team of editors, and, with characteristic insight, diplomacy, and humor, oversaw seven editions. Abrams wisely understood that new scholarly discoveries and the shifting interests of readers constantly alter the landscape of literary history. To stay vital, the anthology, therefore, would need to undergo a process of periodic revision, guided by advice from teachers, as well as students, who view the anthology with a loyal but critical eye. As with past editions, we have benefited from detailed information on the works actually assigned and suggestions for improvements from 273 reviewers. Their participation has been crucial as the editors grapple with the task of strengthening the selection of more traditional texts while adding texts that reflect the expansion of the field of English studies.

With each edition, *The Norton Anthology of English Literature* has offered a broadened canon without sacrificing major writers and a selection of complete longer texts in which readers can immerse themselves. Perhaps the most emblematic of these great texts are the epics *Beowulf* and *Paradise Lost*. Among the many other complete longer works in the Tenth Edition are *Sir Gawain and the Green Knight* (in Simon Armitage's spectacular translation), Sir Thomas More's *Utopia*, Sir Philip Sidney's *Defense of Poesy*, William Shakespeare's *Twelfth Night* and *Othello*, Samuel Johnson's *Rasselas*, Aphra Behn's *Oroonoko*, Jonathan Swift's *Gulliver's Travels*, Laurence Sterne's *A Sentimental Journey through France and Italy*, Charles Dickens's *A Christmas Carol*, Robert Louis Stevenson's *The Strange Case of Dr. Jekyll and Mr. Hyde*, Rudyard Kipling's *The Man Who Would Be King*, Joseph Conrad's *Heart of Darkness*, Virginia Woolf's *Mrs. Dalloway*, James Joyce's *Portrait of the Artist as a Young Man*, Samuel Beckett's *Waiting for Godot*, Harold Pinter's *The Dumb Waiter*, and Tom Stoppard's *Arcadia*. To augment the number of complete longer works instructors can assign, and—a special concern—better to represent the achievements of novelists, the publisher is making available the full list of Norton Critical Editions, more than 240 titles, including such frequently assigned novels as Jane Austen's *Pride and Prejudice*, Mary Shelley's *Frankenstein*, Charles Dickens's *Hard Times*, and Chinua Achebe's *Things Fall Apart*. A Norton Critical Edition may be included with either package (volumes A, B, C and volumes D, E, F) or any individual volume at a discounted price (contact your Norton representative for details).

We have in this edition continued to expand the selection of writing by women in several historical periods. The sustained work of scholars in recent years has recovered dozens of significant authors who had been marginalized or neglected by a male-dominated literary tradition and has deepened our understanding of those women writers who had managed, against considerable odds, to claim a place in that tradition. The First Edition of the Norton Anthology included 6 women writers; this Tenth Edition includes 83, of whom 13 are newly added and 10 are reselected or expanded. Poets and dramatists whose names were scarcely mentioned even in the specialized literary histories of earlier generations—Aemilia Lanyer, Lady Mary Wroth, Margaret Cavendish, Mary Leapor, Anna Letitia Barbauld, Charlotte Smith, Letitia Elizabeth Landon, Mary Elizabeth Coleridge, Mina Loy, and many others—now appear in the company of their male contemporaries. There are in addition four complete long prose works by women— Aphra Behn's *Oroonoko*, Eliza Haywood's *Fantomina*, Jane Austen's *Love and Friendship,* and Virginia Woolf's *Mrs. Dalloway*—along with selections from such celebrated fiction writers as Maria Edgeworth, Jean Rhys, Katherine Mansfield, Doris Lessing, Margaret Atwood, Kiran Desai, Zadie Smith, and new authors Hilary Mantel and Chimamanda Ngozi Adichie.

Building on an innovation introduced in the First Edition, the editors have expanded the array of topical clusters that gather together short texts illuminating the cultural, historical, intellectual, and literary concerns of each of the periods. We have designed these clusters with three aims: to make them lively and accessible, to ensure that they can be taught effectively in a class meeting or two, and to make clear their relevance to the surrounding works of literature. Hence, for example, in the Sixteenth Century, a new cluster, "The Wider World," showcases the English fascination with narratives of adventure, exploration, trade, and reconnaissance. New in the Eighteenth Century, "Print Culture and the Rise of the Novel" offers statements on the emergence of what would become English literature's most popular form as well as excerpts from *Robinson Crusoe* and *Evelina*. And in the Romantic Period, a new cluster on "The Romantic Imagination and the 'Oriental Nations'" joins contemporary discussion of the literature of those nations with selections from William Beckford's *Vathek* and Byron's *The Giaour*, among other texts. Across the volumes the clusters provide an exciting way to broaden the field of the literary and to set masterpieces in a wider cultural, social, and historical framework

Now, as in the past, cultures define themselves by the songs they sing and the stories they tell. But the central importance of visual media in contemporary culture has heightened our awareness of the ways in which songs and stories have always been closely linked to the images that societies have fashioned and viewed. The Tenth Edition of *The Norton Anthology of English Literature* features fifty-six pages of color plates (in seven color inserts) and more than 120 black-and-white illustrations throughout the volumes, including six new maps. In selecting visual material—from the Sutton Hoo treasure of the seventh century to Yinka Shonibare's *Nelson's Ship in a Bottle* in the twenty-first century—the editors sought to provide images that conjure up, whether directly or indirectly, the individual writers in each section; that relate specifically to individual works in the anthology; and that shape and illuminate the culture of a particular literary period. We have tried to choose visually striking images that will interest students and provoke discussion, and our captions draw attention to important details and cross-reference related texts in the anthology.

Period-by-Period Revisions

The Middle Ages. Edited by James Simpson, this period, huge in its scope and immensely varied in its voices, continues to offer exciting surprises. The heart of the Anglo-Saxon portion is the great epic *Beowulf*, in the acclaimed translation by Seamus Heaney. Now accompanied by a map of England at the time, the Anglo-Saxon texts include the haunting poems "Wulf and Eadwacer" and "The Ruin" as well as an intriguing collection of Anglo-Saxon riddles. These new works join verse translations of the *Dream of the Rood*, the *Wanderer*, and *The Wife's Lament*. An Irish Literature selection features a tale from *The Tain* and a group of ninth-century lyrics. The Anglo-Norman section—a key bridge between the Anglo-Saxon period and the time of Chaucer—offers a new pairing of texts about the tragic story of Tristan and Ysolt; an illuminating cluster on the Romance, with three stories by Marie de France (in award-winning translations); and *Sir Orfeo*, a comic version of the Orpheus and Eurydice story. The Middle English section centers, as always, on Chaucer, with a generous selection of tales and poems glossed and annotated so as to heighten their accessibility. Simon Armitage's brilliant verse translation of *Sir Gawain and the Green Knight* appears once again, and we offer newly modernized versions both of Thomas Hoccleve's *My Complaint*, a startlingly personal account of the speaker's attempt to reenter society after a period of mental instability, and of the playfully ironic and spiritually moving *Second Shepherds' Play.* "Talking Animals," a delightful new cluster, presents texts by Marie de France, Chaucer, and Robert Henryson that show how medieval writers used animals in stories that reveal much about humankind.

The Sixteenth Century, edited by Stephen Greenblatt and George Logan, features eight extraordinary longer texts in their entirety: More's *Utopia* (with two letters from More to Peter Giles); Book 1 of Spenser's *Faerie Queene* and, new to this edition, the posthumously published *Mutabilitie Cantos,* which arguably offer some of Spenser's finest poetry; Marlowe's *Hero and Leander* and *Doctor Faustus,* Sidney's *Defense of Poesy;* and Shakespeare's *Twelfth Night* and *Othello,* which has been added to the Tenth Edition by instructor request. Two exciting new topical clusters join the section. "An Elizabethan Miscellany" is a full, richly teachable grouping of sixteenth-century poems in English, by writers from George Gascoigne to Michael Drayton to Thomas Campion, among others, and provides access the period's explosion of lyric genius. "The Wider World" showcases the English Renaissance fascination with narratives of adventure, exploration, trade, and reconnaissance. Ranging from Africa to the Muslim East to the New World, the texts are compelling reading in our contemporary global context and offer particularly suggestive insights into the world of Shakespeare's *Othello.*

The Early Seventeenth Century. At the heart of this period, edited by Katharine Eisaman Maus, is John Milton's *Paradise Lost,* presented in its entirety. New to the Tenth Edition are the Arguments to each book, which are especially helpful for students first reading this magnificent, compelling epic. Along with Milton's "Lycidas" and *Samson Agonistes,* which is new to this edition, other complete longer works include John Donne's *Satire 3* and *The Anatomy of the World: The First Anniversary;* Aemilia Lanyer's country-house poem "The Description of Cookham"; Ben Jonson's *Volpone* and the moving Cary-Morison ode; and John Webster's tragedy *The Duchess of Malfi.* Generous selections from Donne, Mary Wroth, George Herbert, Katherine Philips, Andrew Marvell, and others, as well as the clusters "Inquiry and Experience," "Gender Relations," and "Crisis of Authority," together make for an exciting and thorough representation of the period.

The Restoration and the Eighteenth Century. The impressive array of complete longer texts in this period, edited by James Noggle, includes Dryden's *Absalom and Achitophel* and *MacFlecknoe;* Aphra Behn's *Oroonoko* (now with its dedicatory epistle); Congreve's comedy *The Way of the World;* Swift's *Gulliver's Travels* (newly complete, with illustrations from the first edition); Pope's *Essay on Criticism, The Rape of the Lock,* and *Epistle to Dr. Arbuthnot;* Gay's *Beggar's Opera;* Eliza Haywood's novella of sexual role-playing, *Fantomina;* Hogarth's graphic satire "Marriage A-la-Mode"; Johnson's *Vanity of Human Wishes* and *Rasselas;* Laurence Sterne's *A Sentimental Journey through France and Italy* (new to this edition); Gray's "Elegy Written in a Country Churchyard"; and Goldsmith's "The Deserted Village." An exciting new topical cluster, "Print Culture and the Rise of the Novel," with selections by Daniel Defoe, Henry Fielding, Samuel Richardson, Frances Burney, Clara Reeve, and others, enables readers to explore the origins of English literature's most popular form.

The Romantic Period. Edited by Deidre Shauna Lynch, this period again offers many remarkable additions. Chief among them are two topical clusters: "Romantic Literature and Wartime," which, through texts by Godwin, Wordsworth, Coleridge, Barbauld, Byron, De Quincey, and others, explores the varied ways in which war's violence came home to English literature; and "The Romantic Imagination and the 'Oriental Nations,'" which shows how English writers of the late eighteenth and early nineteenth centuries looked eastward for new, often contradictory themes of cultural identity and difference and for "exotic" subjects that were novel and enticing to the English audience. Also new to this period are poems by Barbauld, Robinson, Charlotte Smith, Wordsworth, Shelley, Hemans, and Landon. We are excited to include an excerpt from *The History of Mary Prince, a West Indian Slave*— the first slave narrative by a woman. John Clare, the increasingly appreciated "natural poet," receives four new texts.

The Victorian Age, edited by Catherine Robson, offers an impressive array of complete longer works. New to the prose selections is Charles Dickens's *A Christmas Carol*, complete with its original illustrations. Dickens's celebrated tale, which entertains at the same time that it deals brilliantly with matters social, economic, and spiritual, joins Robert Louis Stevenson's *The Strange Case of Dr. Jekyll and Mr. Hyde*, Arthur Conan Doyle's *The Speckled Band*, Elizabeth Gaskell's *The Old Nurse's Story*, and Rudyard Kipling's *The Man Who Would Be King*. Authors with significant longer poems include Elizabeth Barrett Browning, Alfred, Lord Tennyson, Robert Browning, Dante Gabriel Rossetti, Christina Rossetti, Algernon Charles Swinburne, and Gerard Manley Hopkins. Plays include Oscar Wilde's *The Importance of Being Earnest* and George Bernard Shaw's controversial drama on prostitution, *Mrs Warren's Profession*. And, continuing the tradition of enabling readers to grapple with the period's most resonant and often fiercely contentious issues, the Tenth Edition offers an exciting new cluster, "Beacons of the Future? Education in Victorian Britain," which brings together powerful reflections by John Stuart Mill and others, government reports on the nature of education, and illuminating excerpts from *Hard Times*, *Alice's Adventures in Wonderland*, *Tom Brown's School Days*, and *Jude the Obscure*.

The Twentieth and Twenty-first Centuries. The editor, Jahan Ramazani, continues his careful revision of this, the most rapidly changing period in the anthology. Once again its core is three modernist masterpieces: Virginia Woolf's *Mrs. Dalloway*, James Joyce's *Portrait of the Artist as a Young Man*, and Samuel Beckett's *Waiting for Godot*, all complete. These works are surrounded by a dazzling array of other fiction and drama. New to the Tenth Edition are the recent recipient of the Nobel Prize for Literature, Kazuo Ishiguro, along with Hilary Mantel, Caryl Phillips, and Chimamanda Ngozi Adichie. Their works join Joseph Conrad's *Heart of Darkness*, Harold Pinter's *The Dumb Waiter*, Tom Stoppard's *Arcadia*, and stories by D. H. Lawrence,

Katherine Mansfield, Jean Rhys, Doris Lessing, Nadine Gordimer, Kiran Desai, and Zadie Smith. A generous representation of poetry centers on substantial selections from Thomas Hardy, William Butler Yeats, and T. S. Eliot, and extends out to a wide range of other poets, from A. E. Housman, Wilfred Owen, and W. H. Auden to Philip Larkin, Derek Walcott, and Seamus Heaney. Two new poets, frequently requested by our readers, join the anthology: Anne Carson and Simon Armitage; and there are new poems by Yeats, Heaney, Geoffrey Hill, and Carol Ann Duffy. Visual aids have proved very helpful in teaching this period, and new ones include facsimile manuscript pages of poems by Isaac Rosenberg and Wilfred Owen, plus five new maps, which illustrate, among other things, the dramatic changes in the British Empire from 1891 to the late twentieth century, the movement of peoples to and from England during this time, and the journeys around London of the central characters in Woolf's *Mrs. Dalloway*. Linton Kwesi Johnson, Bernardine Evaristo, Patience Agbabi, and Dajlit Nagra join Claude McKay, Louise Bennett, Kamau Brathwaite, Ngũgĩ Wa Thiong'o, M. NourbeSe Philip, Salman Rushdie, and Grace Nichols in the much-praised cluster "Nation, Race, and Language"—together they bear witness to the global diffusion of English, the urgency of issues of nation and identity, and the rich complexity of literary history.

Editorial Procedures and Format

The Tenth Edition adheres to the principles that have always characterized *The Norton Anthology of English Literature*. Period introductions, headnotes, and annotations are designed to enhance students' reading and, without imposing an interpretation, to give students the information they need to understand each text. The aim of these editorial materials is to make the anthology self-sufficient, so that it can be read anywhere—in a coffeeshop, on a bus, under a tree.

The Norton Anthology of English Literature prides itself on both the scholarly accuracy and the readability of its texts. To ease students' encounter with some works, we have normalized spelling and capitalization in texts up to and including the Romantic period—for the most part they now follow the conventions of modern English. We leave unaltered, however, texts in which such modernizing would change semantic or metrical qualities. From the Victorian period onward, we have used the original spelling and punctuation. We continue other editorial procedures that have proved useful in the past. After each work, we cite the date of first publication on the right; in some instances, this date is followed by the date of a revised edition for which the author was responsible. Dates of composition, when they differ from those of publication and when they are known, are provided on the left. We use square brackets to indicate titles supplied by the editors for the convenience of readers. Whenever a portion of a text is omitted, we indicate that omission with three asterisks. If the omitted portion is important for following the plot or argument, we provide a brief summary within the text or in a footnote. Finally, we have reconsidered annotations throughout and increased the number of marginal glosses for archaic, dialect, or unfamiliar words.

The Tenth Edition includes the useful "Literary Terminology" appendix, a quick-reference alphabetical glossary with examples from works in the anthology. We have also updated the General Bibliography that appears in the print volumes, as well as the period and author bibliographies, which appear online, where they can be easily searched and updated.

Additional Resources for Instructors and Students

The idea that a vital literary culture is always on the move applies not only to the print anthology but also to the resources that accompany it. For the Tenth Edition, we have added exciting new resources and improved and updated existing resources to make them more useful and easy to find.

We are pleased to launch the new NAEL Archive site, found at digital. wwnorton.com/englishlit10abc (for volumes A, B, C) and digital.wwnorton .com/englishlit10def (for volumes D, E, F). This searchable and sortable site contains thousands of resources for students and instructors in one centralized place at no additional cost. Following are some highlights:

- A series of twenty brand-new video modules designed to enhance classroom presentation of the literary works. These videos, conceived of and narrated by the anthology editors, bring various texts from the anthology to life by providing a closer look at a rarely seen manuscript, visiting a place of literary significance, or offering a conversation with a living writer.
- Over 1,000 additional readings from the Middle Ages to the turn of the twentieth century, edited, glossed, and annotated to the scholarly standards and with the sensitivity to classroom use for which the Norton Anthology is renowned. Teachers who wish to add to the selections in the print anthology will find numerous exciting works, including Wycherley's *The Country Wife*, Joanna Baillie's "A Mother to Her Waking Infant," and Edward Lear's "The Jumblies." In addition, there are many fascinating topical clusters—"The First Crusade: Sanctifying War," "Genius," and "The Satanic and Byronic Hero," to name only a few—all designed to draw readers into larger cultural contexts and to expose them to a wide spectrum of voices.
- Hundreds of images—maps, author portraits, literary places, and manuscripts—available for student browsing or instructor download for in-class presentation.
- Several hours of audio recordings.
- Annotated bibliographies for all periods and authors in the anthology.

The NAEL Archive also provides a wealth of teaching resources that are unlocked on instructor log-in:

- "Quick read" summaries, teaching notes, and discussion questions for every work in the anthology, from the much-praised *Teaching with The Norton Anthology of English Literature: A Guide for Instructors* by Naomi Howell (University of Exeter), Philip Schwyzer (University of Exeter), Judyta Frodyma (University of Northern British Columbia), and Sondra Archimedes (University of California–Santa Cruz).

- Downloadable PowerPoints featuring images and audio for in-class presentation

In addition to the wealth of resources in the NAEL Archive, Norton offers a downloadable coursepack that allows instructors to easily add high-quality Norton digital media to online, hybrid, or lecture courses—all at no cost. Norton Coursepacks work within existing learning management systems; there's no new system to learn, and access is free and easy. Content is customizable and includes over seventy-four reading-comprehension quizzes, short-answer questions with suggested answers, links to the video modules, and more.

The editors are deeply grateful to the hundreds of teachers worldwide who have helped us to improve *The Norton Anthology of English Literature*. A list of the instructors who replied to a detailed questionnaire follows, under Acknowledgments. The editors would like to express appreciation for their assistance to Lara Bovilsky (University of Oregon), Gordon Braden (University of Virginia), Dympna Callaghan (Syracuse University), Ariel Churchill (Harvard University), Joseph Connors (Harvard University), Taylor Cowdery (University of North Carolina at Chapel Hill), Maria Devlin (Harvard University), Lars Engel (University of Tulsa), James Engell (Harvard University), Aubrey Everett (Harvard University), Kevis Goodman (University of California, Berkeley), Alexander Gourlay (Rhode Island School of Design), John Hale (University of Otago), Stephen Hequembourg (University of Virginia), Seth Herbst (United States Military Academy, West Point), Rhema Hokama (Singapore University of Technology and Design), Jean Howard (Columbia University), Robert Irvine (University of Edinburgh), Thomas Keirstead (University of Toronto), Mario Menendez (Harvard University), John Miller (University of Virginia), Peter Miller (University of Virginia), A. J. Odasso (Wellesley College, Robert Pinsky (Boston University), Will Porter (Harvard University), Mark Rankin (James Madison University), Josephine Reece (Harvard University), Jessica Rosenberg (University of Miami), Suparna Roychoudhury (Mount Holyoke College), Peter Sacks (Harvard University), Ray Siemens (University of Victoria), Kim Simpson (University of Southampton), Bailey Sincox (Harvard University), Ramie Targoff (Brandeis University), Misha Teramura (Reed College), Gordon Teskey (Harvard University), Katie Trumpener (Yale University), Paul Westover (Brigham Young University), Katy Woodring (Harvard University), and Faye Zhang (Harvard University).

We also thank the many people at Norton, an employee-owned publishing house with a commitment to excellence, who contributed to the Tenth Edition. In planning this edition, Julia Reidhead served, as she has done in the past, as our wise and effective collaborator. In addition, we are now working with Marian Johnson, literature editor and managing editor for college books, a splendid new collaborator who has helped us bring the Tenth Edition to fruition. With admirable equanimity and skill, Carly Frasier Doria, electronic media editor and course guide editor, fashioned the new video modules and brought together the dazzling array of web resources and other pedagogical aids. We also have debts of gratitude to Katharine Ings, Candace Levy, and Michael Fleming, manuscript editors; Sean Mintus, senior production manager; Kimberly Bowers, marketing manager for litera-ture; Megan Jackson Schindel and Nancy Rodwan, permissions; Jo Anne Metsch, designer; Nelson Colon, photo editor; and Rachel Taylor and Ava Bramson, assistant editor and assistant media editor, respectively. All these friends provided the editors with indispensable help in meeting the challenge of representing the unparalleled range and variety of English literature.

STEPHEN GREENBLATT

Acknowledgments

The editors would like to express appreciation and thanks to the hundreds of teachers who provided reviews:

Michel Aaij (Auburn University at Montgomery), Jerry J. Alexander (Presbyterian College), Sarah Alexander (The University of Vermont), Marshall N. Armintor (University of North Texas), Marilyn Judith Atlas (Ohio University), Alison Baker (California State Polytechnic University, Pomona), Reid Barbour (University of North Carolina, Chapel Hill), Jessica Barnes-Pietruszynski (West Virginia State University), Jessica Barr (Eureka College), Chris Barrett (Louisiana State University), Craig Barrette (Brescia University), Carol Beran (St. Mary's College), Peter Berek (Amherst College), David Bergman (Towson University), Scott Black (University of Utah), William R. "Beau" Black III (Weatherford College), Justin Blessinger (Dakota State University), William E. Bolton (La Salle University), Wyatt Bonikowski (Suffolk University), Rebecca Bossie (University of Texas at El Paso), Bruce Brandt (South Dakota State University), Heather Braun (University of Akron), Mark Brown (University of Jamestown), Logan D. Browning (Rice University), Monica Brzezinski Potkay (College of William and Mary), Rebecca Bushnell (University of Pennsylvania), Claire Busse (La Salle University), Thomas Butler (Eastern Kentucky University), Jim Casey (Arcadia University), Susan P. Cerasano (Colgate University), Maria Chappell (University of Georgia), Brinda Charry (Keene State College), Susannah Chewning (Union County College), Lin Chih-hsin (National Chengchi University), Kathryn Chittick (Trent University), Nora Corrigan (Mississippi University for Women), David Cowart (University of South Carolina), Catherine Craft-Fairchild (University of St. Thomas), Susan Crisafulli (Franklin College), Jenny Crisp (Dalton State College), Ashley Cross (Manhattan College), James P. Crowley (Bridgewater State University), Susie Crowson (Del Mar College), Rebecca Crump (Louisiana State University), Cyrus Mulready (SUNY New Paltz), Lisa Darien (Hartwick College), Sean Dempsey (University of Arkansas), Anthony Ding (Grossmont Community College), Lorraine Eadie (Hillsdale College), Schuyler Eastin (San Diego Christian College), Gary Eddy (Winona State University), J. Craig Eller (Louisburg College), Robert Ellison (Marshall University), Nikolai Endres (Western Kentucky University), Robert Epstein (Fairfield University), Richard Erable (Franklin College), Simon C. Estok (Sungkyunkwan University), Michael Faitell (Mohawk Valley Community College), Jonathan Farina (Seton Hall University), Tyler Farrell (Marquette University), Jennifer

Feather (The University of North Carolina Greensboro), Annette Federico (James Madison University), Kerstin Feindert (Cosumnes River College), Maryanne Felter (Cayuga Community College), Benjamin Fischer (Northwest Nazarene University), Matthew Fisher (University of California, Los Angeles), Chris Fletcher (North Central University), Michael J. Flynn (The University of North Dakota), James E. Foley (Worcester State University), Walter C. Foreman (University of Kentucky), Ann Frank Wake (Elmhurst College), Michael D. Friedman (University of Scranton), Lee Garver (Butler University), Paul L. Gaston (Kent State University), Sara E. Gerend (Aurora University), Avilah Getzler (Grand View University), Edward Gieskes (University of South Carolina), Elaine Glanz (Immaculata University), Adam Golaski (Brown University), Rachel Goldberg (Northeastern CPS), Augusta Gooch (University of Alabama–Huntsville), Nathan Gorelick (Utah Valley University), Robert Gorsch (Saint Mary's College of California), Carey Goyette (Clinton Community College), Richard J. Grande (Pennsylvania State University–Abington), David A. Grant (Columbus State Community College), Sian Griffiths (Weber State University), Ann H. Guess (Alvin Community College), Audley Hall (NorthWest Arkansas Community College), Jenni Halpin (Savannah State University), Brian Harries (Concordia University Wisconsin), Samantha Harvey (Boise State University), Raychel Haugrud Reiff (University of Wisconsin–Superior), Erica Haugtvedt (The Ohio State University), Mary Hayes (University of Mississippi), Joshua R. Held (Indiana University, Bloomington), Roze Hentschell (Colorado State University), Erich Hertz (Siena College), Natalie Hewitt (Hope International University), Lisa Hinrichsen (University of Arkansas), Lorretta Holloway (Framingham State University), Catherine Howard (University of Houston), Chia-Yin Huang (Chinese Culture University), Sister Marie Hubert Kealy (Immaculata University), Elizabeth Hutcheon (Huntingdon College), Peter Hyland (Huron University College, Western University), Eileen Jankowski (Chapman University), Alan Johnson (Idaho State University), Brian Jukes (Yuba College), Kari Kalve (Earlham College), Parmita Kapadia (Northern Kentucky University), Deborah Kennedy (Saint Mary's University), Mark Kipperman (Northern Illinois University), Cindy Klestinec (Miami University–Ohio), Neal W. Kramer (Brigham Young University), Kathryn Laity (College of Saint Rose), Jameela Lares (University of Southern Mississippi), Caroline Levine (University of Wisconsin–Madison), Melinda Linscott (Idaho State University), Janet Madden (El Camino College), Gerald Margolis (Temple University), Elizabeth Mazzola (The City College of New York), Keely McCarthy (Chestnut Hill College), Cathryn McCarthy Donahue (College of Mount Saint Vincent), Mary H. McMurran (University of Western Ontario), Josephine A. McQuail (Tennessee Technological University), Brett Mertins (Metropolitan Community College), Christian Michener (Saint Mary's University), Brook Miller (University of Minnesota, Morris), Kristine Miller (Utah State University), Jacqueline T. Miller (Rutgers University), Richard J. Moll (University of Western Ontario), Lorne Mook (Taylor University), Rod Moore (Los Angeles Valley College), Rory Moore (University of California, Riverside), Grant Moss (Utah Valley University), Nicholas D. Nace (Hampden-Sydney College), Jonathan Naito (St. Olaf College), Mary Nelson (Dallas Baptist University), Mary Anne Nunn (Central Connecticut State University), John

O'Brien (University of Virginia), Onno Oerlemans (Hamilton College), Michael Oishi (Leeward Community College), Sylvia Pamboukian (Robert Morris University), Adam Parkes (University of Georgia), Michelle Parkinson (University of Wisconsin–River Falls), Geoffrey Payne (Macquarie University), Anna Peak (Temple University), Dan Pearce (Brigham Young University–Idaho), Christopher Penna (University of Delaware), Zina Petersen (Brigham Young University), Kaara L. Peterson (Miami University of Ohio), Keith Peterson (Brigham Young University–Hawaii), Professor Maggie Piccolo (Rowan University), Ann Pleiss Morris (Ripon College), Michael Pogach (Northampton Community College), Matthew Potolsky (The University of Utah), Miguel Powers (Fullerton College), Gregory Priebe (Harford Community College), Jonathan Purkiss (Pulaski Technical College), Kevin A. Quarmby (Oxford College of Emory University), Mark Rankin (James Madison University), Tawnya Ravy (The George Washington University), Professor Joan Ray (University of Colorado, Colorado Springs), Helaine Razovsky (Northwestern State University of Louisiana), Vince Redder (Dakota Wesleyan University), Elizabeth Rich (Saginaw Valley State University), Patricia Rigg (Acadia University), Albert J. Rivero (Marquette University), Phillip Ronald Stormer (Culver-Stockton College), Kenneth Rooney (University College Cork, Ireland), David Ruiter (University of Texas at El Paso), Kathryn Rummell (California Polytechnic State University), Richard Ruppel (Chapman University), Jonathan Sachs (Concordia University), David A. Salomon (Russell Sage College), Abigail Scherer (Nicholls State University), Roger Schmidt (Idaho State University), William Sheldon (Hutchinson Community College), Christian Sheridan (Bridgewater College), Nicole Sidhu (East Carolina University), Lisa Siefker Bailey (Indiana University–Purdue University Columbus), Samuel Smith (Messiah College), Cindy Soldan (Lakehead University), Diana Solomon (Simon Fraser University), Vivasvan Soni (Northwestern University), Timothy Spurgin (Lawrence University), Felicia Jean Steele (The College of New Jersey), Carole Lynn Stewart (Brock University), Judy Suh (Duquesne University), Dean Swinford (Fayetteville State University), Allison Symonds (Cecil College), Brenda Tuberville (Rogers State University), Verne Underwood (Rogue Community College), Janine Utell (Widener University), Paul Varner (Abilene Christian University), Deborah Vause (York College of Pennsylvania), Nicholas Wallerstein (Black Hills State University), Rod Waterman (Central Connecticut State University), Eleanor Welsh (Chesapeake College), Paul Westover (Brigham Young University), Christopher Wheatley (The Catholic University of America), Miranda Wilcox (Brigham Young University), Brett D. Wilson (College of William & Mary), Lorraine Wood (Brigham Young University), Nicholas A. Wright (Marist College), Michael Wutz (Weber State University).

THE NORTON ANTHOLOGY OF

ENGLISH

LITERATURE

TENTH EDITION

VOLUME F

THE TWENTIETH AND TWENTY-FIRST CENTURIES

The Twentieth and Twenty-First Centuries

1914–18: World War I
1922: James Joyce's *Ulysses*; T. S. Eliot's *The Waste Land*
1929: Stock market crash; Great Depression begins
1939–45: World War II
1947: India and Pakistan become independent nations
1953: Premiere of Samuel Beckett's *Waiting for Godot*
1957–62: Ghana, Nigeria, Uganda, Jamaica, and Trinidad and Tobago become independent nations
1981: Salman Rushdie's *Midnight's Children*
1991: Collapse of the Soviet Union
2001: Attacks destroy World Trade Center in New York
2016: United Kingdom votes to leave European Union

HISTORICAL BACKGROUND

The roots of modern literature are in the late nineteenth century. The aesthetic movement, with its insistence on "art for art's sake," assaulted middle-class assumptions about the nature and function of art. Rejecting Victorian notions of the artist's moral and educational duties, aestheticism helped widen the breach between writers and the general public, resulting in the "alienation" of the modern artist from society. This alienation is evident in the lives and work of the French symbolists and other late-nineteenth-century bohemians who repudiated conventional

The Merry-Go-Round (detail), 1916, Mark Gertler. For more information about this image, see the color insert in this volume.

Ascot Race Track. Spectators segregated by class at the track,
England, June 1, 1907. Top hats and dress distinguish the upper class
in the top rows. Working-class men are barred from the stands and
wear cloth caps. Middle-class men wear bowlers and straw hats.
Virginia Woolf critically inspects the British class system in
Mrs. Dalloway, a novel that mentions Ascot, among other London
athletic and social venues (pp. 285 and 292).

notions of respectability, and it underlies key works of modern literature,
such as James Joyce's *A Portrait of the Artist as a Young Man* and T. S. Eliot's
The Waste Land.

The growth of public education in England as a result of the Education Act
of 1870, which finally made elementary schooling compulsory and universal, led to the rapid emergence of a mass literate population, toward whom
a new mass-produced popular literature and new cheap journalism (the "yellow
press") were directed. The audience for literature split up into "highbrows,"
"middlebrows," and "lowbrows," and the segmentation of the reading public, developing with unprecedented speed and to an unprecedented degree,
helped widen the gap between popular art and art esteemed only by the sophisticated and the expert. This breach yawned ever wider with the twentieth-
century emergence of modernist iconoclasm and avant-garde experiments in
literature, music, and the visual arts.

To Queen Victoria's contemporaries, her Jubilee in 1887 and, even more,
her Diamond Jubilee in 1897 marked the end of an era. The reaction against
middle-class Victorian attitudes that is central to modernism was already
under way in the two decades before the queen's death in 1901. Samuel
Butler attacked the Victorian conceptions of the family, education, and religion in his novel *The Way of All Flesh* (completed in 1884, published posthumously in 1903), the bitterest indictment in English literature of Victorian
conventions. And the high tide of anti-Victorianism was marked by the publication in 1918 of a classic of ironic debunking, Lytton Strachey's collection of biographical essays, *Eminent Victorians*.

A pivotal figure between Victorianism and modernism, Thomas Hardy marked the end of the Victorian period and the dawn of the new age in "The Darkling Thrush," a poem originally titled "By the Century's Deathbed" and postdated December 31, 1900, the last day of the nineteenth century. The poem marks the demise of a century of relative conviction and optimism, and it intimates the beginnings of a new era in its skeptical irresolution and its bleak sense of the modern world as "hard and dry"—favorite adjectives of later writers such as Ezra Pound and T. E. Hulme:

> The land's sharp features seemed to be
>   The Century's corpse outleant,
> His crypt the cloudy canopy,
>   The wind his death-lament.
> The ancient pulse of germ and birth
>   Was shrunken hard and dry,
> And every spirit upon earth
>   Seemed fervourless as I.

This poem and other works by Hardy, A. E. Housman, and Joseph Conrad exemplify the pessimism of imaginative writing in the last decade of the nineteenth century and the first decade of the twentieth. Stoicism—a stiff-upper-lip determination to endure whatever fate may bring—also characterizes the literature written in the transitional period between the Victorian era and modernism, including the work of popular middlebrow authors such as Robert Louis Stevenson and Rudyard Kipling.

By the dawn of the twentieth century, traditional stabilities of society, religion, and culture seemed to have weakened, the pace of change to be accelerating. The unsettling force of modernity profoundly challenged traditional ways of structuring and making sense of human experience. Because of the rapid pace of social and technological change; because of the mass dislocation of populations by war, empire, and economic migration; and because of the mixing in close quarters of cultures and classes in rapidly expanding cities, modernity disrupted the old order, upended ethical and social codes, and cast into doubt previously stable assumptions about self, community, the world, and the divine.

Early-twentieth-century writers were keenly aware that powerful concepts and vocabularies were emerging in anthropology, psychology, philosophy, and the visual arts that reimagined human identity in radically new ways. Sigmund Freud's seminal book, *The Interpretation of Dreams*, was published in 1900; soon psychoanalysis was changing how people saw and described rationality, the self, and personal development. In his prose and poetry, D. H. Lawrence adapted Freud's concept of the Oedipus complex to interpret and represent his relationships with his parents, though Lawrence rejected Freud's negative definition of the unconscious. By the time of his death in 1939, Freud had become, as W. H. Auden wrote in an elegy for him, "a whole climate of opinion // under whom we conduct our different lives." Also in the early twentieth century, Sir James Frazer's *Golden Bough* (1890–1915) and other works of anthropology were altering basic conceptions of culture, religion, and myth. Eliot observed that Frazer's work "influenced our generation profoundly," and the critic Lionel Trilling suggested that "perhaps no book has had so decisive an effect upon modern literature as Frazer's." For both anthropologists and modern writers, Western religion was now decentered by being placed in a comparative context as one of numerous related mythologies, with Jesus Christ linked to "primitive" fertility gods thought to die and revive in concert with the seasons. Furthering this challenge to religious doctrine were the writings of Friedrich Nietzsche, the nineteenth-century German philosopher who declared the death of God, repudiated Christianity, and offered instead a harshly tragic conception of life: people look "deeply into the true nature of things" and realize "that no action of theirs can work any change," but they nevertheless laugh and stoically affirm their fate. W. B. Yeats, who remarks in a 1902 letter that his eyes are exhausted from reading "that strong enchanter," greets death and destruction in a Nietzschean spirit of tragic exultation.

These profound changes in modern intellectual history coincided with changes of a more mundane sort, for everyday life was also undergoing rapid transformation during the first years of the twentieth century. The use of electricity was spreading, cinema and radio were proliferating, and new pharmaceuticals such as aspirin were being developed. As labor was increasingly managed and rationalized, as more and more people crowded into cities, as modern communication and transportation compressed global space and accelerated time, literature could not stand still, and modern writers sought to create forms that could register these profound alterations in human experience. This was a period of scientific revolution, as exemplified in physics by the German Max Planck's quantum theory (1900) and Planck's countryman Albert Einstein's theory of relativity (1905). Their Anglo-American contemporary T. S. Eliot reflects the increasing dominance of science when he argues that the poet surrenders to tradition and thus extinguishes rather than expresses personality: "It is in this depersonalization that art may be said to approach the condition of science," he claims, adding that "the mind of the poet is the shred of platinum" that catalyzes change but itself remains "inert, neutral, and unchanged" ("Tradition and the Individual Talent").

The early twentieth century also brought countless advances in technology: the first wireless communication across the Atlantic occurred in 1901, the Wright brothers flew the first airplane in 1903, and Henry Ford introduced the first mass-produced car, the Model T or "Tin Lizzie," in 1913. Not that modern writers unequivocally embraced such changes. Although some were more sanguine, many modern writers were paradoxically repulsed by aspects of modernization. Mass-produced appliances and products, such as the "gramophone" and canned goods ("tins"), are objects of revulsion in Eliot's *Waste Land*, for example. Because scientific materialism and positivism, according to which empirical explanations could be found for everything, were weakening the influence of organized religion, many writers looked to literature as an alternative. Finding his "simple-minded" Protestantism spoiled by science, Yeats says in his autobiography, he "made a new religion, almost an infallible church of poetic tradition." Whether or not they welcomed the demise of tradition, habit, and certitude in favor of the new, modern writers articulated the effects of modernity's relentless change, loss, and destabilization. "Things fall apart," Yeats wrote, "the centre cannot hold." In *Four Quartets* Eliot describes his quest for the "still point of the turning world." The modernist drive to "make it new"—in Ezra Pound's famous slogan—thus arises in part out of an often ambivalent consciousness of the relentless mutations brought by modernization.

The position of women, too, was rapidly changing during this period. The Married Woman's Property Act of 1882 allowed wives to own property in their own right, and universities began to admit women during the latter part of the century. Since the days of Mary Wollstonecraft, women in Great Britain had been arguing and lobbying for the right to vote, but in the first decades of the twentieth century, Emmeline Pankhurst and her daughter Christabel encouraged suffragettes, as they were known, to take a more militant approach, which included boycotts, bombings, and hunger strikes. The long fight for women's suffrage was finally won in 1918 for women thirty and over, and in 1928 for women twenty-one and over. These shifts in attitudes toward women, in the roles women played in the national

Women's Suffrage. Emmeline Pankhurst being arrested at a demonstration outside Buckingham Palace, London, January 5, 1914. A leader in Britain of the movement for women's right to vote, she and other militant "suffragettes" were repeatedly jailed. During their hunger strikes they were force-fed.

life, and in the relations between the sexes are reflected in a variety of ways in the literature of the period.

Britain's modern political history begins with the Anglo-Boer War (1899–1902), fought by the British to establish political and economic control over the Boer republics (self-governing states) of the Dutch-descended South African Afrikaners. It was an imperial war against which many British intellectuals protested and one that the British in the end were slightly ashamed of having won. The war spanned the reign of Queen Victoria, who died in 1901, and Edward VII, who held the throne from 1901 to 1910. This latter decade is known as the Edwardian period, and the king stamped his extroverted and self-indulgent character upon it. The wealthy made it a vulgar age of conspicuous enjoyment, but most writers and artists kept well away from involvement in high society; in general this period had no equivalent to Queen Victoria's friendship with Tennyson. The alienation of artists and intellectuals from political rulers and middle-class society was proceeding apace. From 1910 (when George V came to the throne) until World War I broke out in August 1914, Britain achieved a temporary equilibrium between Victorian earnestness and Edwardian flashiness; in retrospect the Georgian period seems peculiarly golden, the last phase of assurance and stability before the old order throughout Europe broke up in violence. Yet even still, under the surface, there was restlessness and experimentation. The age of Rupert Brooke's idyllic sonnets on the English countryside was also the age of T. S. Eliot's first experiments in a radically new kind of poetry, James Joyce's and Virginia Woolf's in radically new forms of fiction.

Edwardian as a term applied to English cultural history suggests a period in which the social and economic stabilities of the Victorian age—country houses with numerous servants, a flourishing and confident middle class, a strict hierarchy of social classes—remained unimpaired, though on the level of ideas a

Hindu Serving Tea to Colonial Woman, 1891. A symbol of
upper-class leisure, tea was also a lucrative commodity of the
East India Company in an increasingly global capitalist
economy. The British preference for sweetened tea buoyed
demand for sugar from West Indian slave plantations and
colonies, adding to the human toll of this seemingly innocu-
ous beverage. From the early twentieth century, India and
other colonies intensified their struggle against subordination
to the British Crown.

sense of change and liberation existed. *Georgian* refers largely to the lull before
the storm of World War I. That war, as the bitterly skeptical and antiheroic
work of Wilfred Owen, Siegfried Sassoon, Isaac Rosenberg, and other war
poets makes clear, produced major shifts in attitude toward Western myths of
progress and civilization. The postwar disillusion of the 1920s resulted, in
part, from the sense of utter social and political collapse during a war in
which unprecedented millions were killed.

By the beginning of World War I, nearly a quarter of the earth's surface and
more than a quarter of the world's population were under British dominion,
including the vast African territories mostly acquired in the late nineteenth
century. Some of the colonies in the empire were settler nations with large
European populations, such as Canada, Australia, and New Zealand, and in
1907 the empire granted them the new status of dominions, recognizing their
relative control over internal affairs. Over time these largely independent nations came to be known as the British Commonwealth, an association
of self-governing countries. The twentieth century witnessed the emergence
of internationally acclaimed literary voices from these dominions, from the
early-century New Zealander Katherine Mansfield to the late-century and
twenty-first-century Australian Les Murray and Canadians Alice Munro, Margaret Atwood, and Anne Carson. The rest of the colonies in the British Empire
consisted primarily of indigenous populations that had little or no political

power, but nationalist movements were gaining strength in the early years of the century— as when, in 1906, the Congress movement in India first demanded *swaraj* ("self-rule"), soon to become the mantra of Indian nationalism. In Britain imperialist and anti-imperialist sentiments often met head-on in Parliament and the press, the debate involving writers as far apart as Rudyard Kipling and E. M. Forster.

A steadily rising Irish nationalism resulted in increasingly violent protests against the cultural, economic, and political subordination of Ireland

The Easter Rising. Dublin buildings destroyed during the Easter Rising of 1916. In revolt against British rule of Ireland, rebels took over key positions on April 24 until the British crushed the insurrection a week later and then executed fifteen leaders. (See Yeats's "Easter, 1916," p. 221.)

to the British Crown and government. During the Easter Rising of 1916, Irish rebels in Dublin staged a revolt against British rule, and by executing fifteen Irish leaders, the British inadvertently intensified the drive for independence, finally achieved in 1921–22 when the southern counties were declared the Irish Free State. (The six counties of Northern Ireland remained, however, part of Great Britain.) No one can fully understand Yeats or Joyce without some awareness of the Irish struggle for independence and the way in which the Irish literary revival of the late nineteenth and early twentieth centuries (with Yeats at the forefront) reflected a determination to achieve a vigorous national life culturally even if the road seemed blocked politically.

Depression and unemployment in the early 1930s, followed by the rise of Hitler and the shadow of fascism and Nazism over Europe, with its threat of another war, deeply affected the emerging poets and novelists of the time. Feminism, pacifism, and liberal attitudes regarding sexuality and gender relations were espoused by some members of the Bloomsbury Group, named after the London district where its adherents congregated, including the writers Virginia Woolf and E. M. Forster, as well as the economist John Maynard Keynes. But many other prominent literary figures of this older generation, such as Eliot, Lawrence, Wyndham Lewis, Yeats, and Pound, turned to the political right. Meanwhile, the impotence of capitalist governments in the face of fascism combined with economic dislocation to turn the majority of young intellectuals (and not only intellectuals) to the political left in the 1930s—the so-called red decade, because only the left seemed to offer any solution in various forms of socialism, communism, and liberalism. The early poetry of W. H. Auden and his contemporaries cried out for "the death of the old gang" (in Auden's phrase) and a clean sweep politically and economically, while in Spain the right-wing army's rebellion against the left-wing republican government, which started in the summer of 1936 and soon led to full-scale civil war, was regarded as a rehearsal for an inevitable second international conflict and thus further emphasized the inadequacy of politicians. Yet, though the younger writers of the period expressed the up-to-date, radical political views of the left, they were less technically inventive than the first-generation modernists, such as Eliot, Joyce, and Woolf. The outbreak of World War II in September 1939—following shortly after Hitler's pact with the Soviet Union, which so shocked and disillusioned many of the young left-wing writers that they subsequently moved politically to the center—marked the sudden end of the red decade. What was from the beginning expected to be a long and costly war brought inevitable exhaustion. The diminution of British political power, its secondary status in relation to the United States as a player in the Cold War, led to a painful reappraisal of Britain's place in the world, even as countries that had lost the war—West Germany and Japan—were, in economic terms, winning the peace that followed.

In winning a war, Great Britain lost an empire. The largest, most powerful, best organized of the modern European empires, it had expropriated enormous quantities of land, raw materials, and labor from its widely scattered overseas territories. India, long the jewel in the imperial crown, won its independence in 1947, along with the newly formed Muslim state of Pakistan. The postwar wave of decolonization that began in South Asia spread to Africa and the Caribbean: in 1957 Ghana was the first nation in sub-Saharan Africa to become independent, unleashing an unstoppable wave of liberation from British rule that freed Nigeria in 1960, Sierra Leone in 1961, Uganda in 1962, and Kenya in 1963; in the Caribbean, Jamaica and Trinidad and Tobago in 1962, Barbados and Guyana in 1966, and Saint Lucia in 1979. India and Pakistan elected to remain within a newly expanded and reconceived British Commonwealth, but other former colonies did not. The Irish Republic withdrew from the Commonwealth in 1949; the Republic of South Africa, in 1961. Postwar decolonization coincided with and encouraged the efflorescence of postcolonial writing that would bring about the most dramatic geographic shift in literature in English since its inception. Writers from Britain's former colonies published influential and innovative novels, plays, and poems, hybridizing their local traditions and varieties of English with those of the empire. The names of the Nobel Prize winners Wole Soyinka, Nadine Gordimer, Derek Walcott, V. S. Naipaul, J. M. Coetzee, Doris Lessing, and Alice Munro were added to the annals of literature in English.

While Britain was decolonizing its empire, the former empire was colonizing Britain, as Louise Bennett wryly suggests in her poem "Colonization in Reverse." Encouraged by the postwar labor shortage in England and the scarcity of work at home, waves of Caribbean migrants journeyed to and settled in "the motherland," the first group on the *Empire Windrush* that sailed from Jamaica to Tilbury Docks, near London, in 1948. Migrants followed from India, Pakistan, Bangladesh, Africa, and other regions of the "New Commonwealth." Even as immigration laws became more restrictive in the late 1960s, relatives of earlier migrants and refugees from these and other nations continued to arrive, transforming Britain into an increasingly multiracial society and energizing British arts and literature. But people of Caribbean, African, and South Asian origin, who brought distinctive vernaculars and cultural traditions with them, painfully discovered that their official status as British subjects often did not mean that they were welcomed as full-fledged members of British society. Many of them experienced racial discrimination in jobs and housing, and bigotry sometimes erupted into violent attacks on them, such as race riots in Nottingham and London's Notting Hill in 1958.

Decolonization. Dancers celebrate on the eve of Ghana's creation and independence in March 1957. After India and Pakistan won independence from Britain in 1947, Ghana was the first sub-Saharan nation to gain its freedom, beginning a wave of decolonization that swept through most of Britain's remaining colonies.

Conservative Member of Parliament Enoch Powell delivered his infamous "Rivers of Blood" speech in 1968, foreseeing deadly interracial strife and warning against further immigration. The collision between the Anglo-Saxon conception of Englishness and the emerging multiracial reality of British society prompted a large-scale, ongoing rethinking of national identity in Britain. Among the new arrivals were many who journeyed to Britain to study in the late 1940s and 1950s and eventually became prominent writers, such as Bennett, Soyinka, Kamau (then Edward) Brathwaite, and Chinua Achebe. In the 1970s and 1980s a younger generation of black and Asian British writers emerged—some born in the United Kingdom, some in the former empire—including Salman Rushdie, Hanif Kureishi, Grace Nichols, and Caryl Phillips, and in the 1990s and the first decade of the new millennium, still younger writers including Zadie Smith, Bernardine Evaristo, and Patience Agbabi.

London, as the capital of the empire, had long dominated the culture as well as the politics and the economy of the British Isles. London spoke for Britain in the impeccable southern English intonations of the radio announcers of the state-owned British Broadcasting Corporation (known as the BBC), but from the end of World War II this changed. Regional dialects and multicultural accents were admitted to the airwaves. Regional radio and television stations sprang up. In the 1940s and 1950s the BBC produced a weekly program called "Caribbean Voices," which, broadcast through the Overseas Service, proved an important stimulus to Caribbean anglophone writing both in London and in the West Indies. The Arts Council, which had subsidized the nation's drama, literature, music, painting, and plastic arts from London, delegated much of its grant-giving responsibility to regional arts

Extent of the BRITISH EMPIRE,
the Late Nineteenth and the Twentieth Centuries

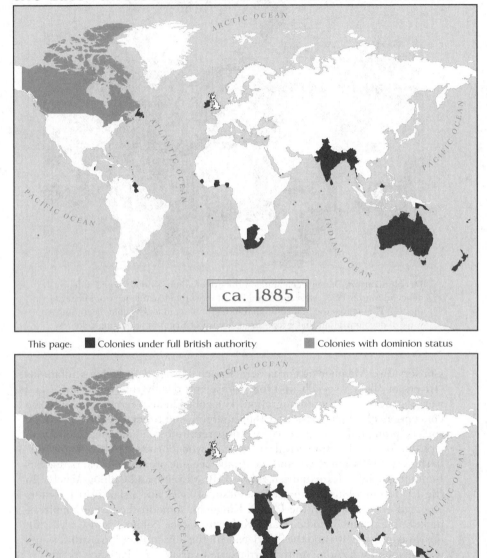

This page: ■ Colonies under full British authority   ■ Colonies with dominion status

ca. 1885

ca. 1919

Britain and other European powers greatly expanded their rule during the "Scramble for Africa," from 1881 to 1914. The white settler colonies, such as Canada, Australia, and New Zealand, were recognized as self-governing dominions in the early twentieth century. By the beginning of World War I, the British Empire included nearly a quarter of the world's population and total land area. After World War II, the independence of India and Pakistan

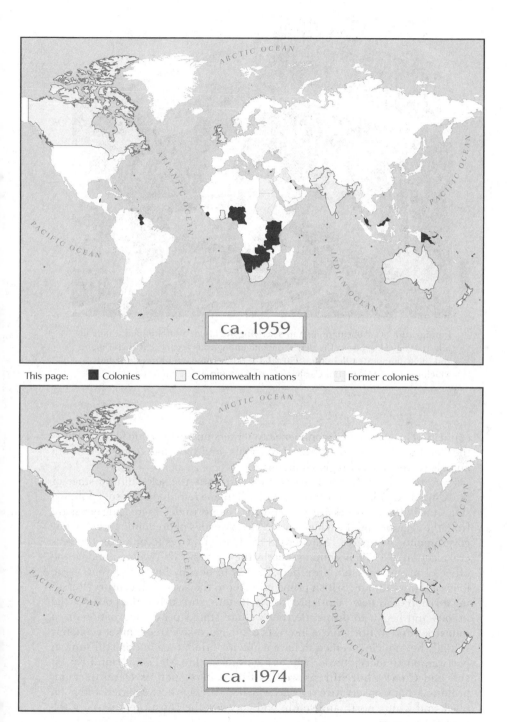

ca. 1959

This page: ■ Colonies ☐ Commonwealth nations ☐ Former colonies

ca. 1974

in 1947, followed by Ghana in 1957, began a wave of decolonization that spread across South Asia, Africa, the Caribbean, and elsewhere. By 1965 the number of people under British rule outside the United Kingdom had fallen from over 500 million to 5 million. After independence, many of these nations became members of the Commonwealth, an association of sovereign states under the symbolic leadership of the British monarch.

Immigration. Caribbean immigrants arriving by ship in Southampton, England, July 1, 1962. The waves of largely economic immigrants from the British Empire and the Commonwealth in the 1950s and 1960s created a multiracial Britain, which included substantial Caribbean, African, and Asian minorities.

councils. This gave a new confidence to writers and artists outside London—the Beatles were launched from Liverpool—and has since contributed to a notable renaissance of regional literature.

From the 1960s, London ceased to be virtually the sole cultural stage of the United Kingdom, and though its Parliament remained the sole political stage until 1999, successive governments came under increasing pressure from the regions and the wider world. After decades of predominantly Labour governments, Margaret Thatcher led the Conservatives to power in the general election of 1979, becoming thereby the country's first woman to hold the office of prime minister, an office she was to occupy for twelve years—the longest tenure for any British prime minister in the twentieth century. Pursuing a vision of a "new," more productive Britain, she curbed the power of the unions and began to dismantle the "welfare state," privatizing nationalized industries and utilities in the interests of an aggressive free-market economy. Initially her policies seemed to have a bracing effect on a nation still sunk in postwar, postimperial torpor, but writers such as Ian McEwan, Hanif Kureishi, and Caryl Churchill, as well as filmmakers such as Derek Jarman, protested that Conservative reforms widened the gaps between rich and poor, black and white, north and south, and between the constituent parts of the United Kingdom.

From the late 1960s, the Irish Republican Army waged a bloody campaign for a united Ireland and against continued British rule in Northern Ireland.

Boys in Belfast, Northern Ireland, May 16, 1976. They run toward a British armored vehicle to throw bottles and rocks as part of a campaign against British rule. From the late 1960s to the 1990s, members of the Irish Catholic minority in Northern Ireland protested discrimination by the Protestant Unionist majority, backed by the British military.

The mainly Roman Catholic IRA was met by violent suppression by the British Army and reprisals by Protestant Unionists, who sought to keep Northern Ireland a part of the United Kingdom. In the 1990s, politics finally took precedence over armed struggle in the Republican movement. In 1998 the Good Friday Agreement, also known as the Belfast Agreement, led to elections for a Northern Ireland Assembly, which convened for the first time in 1999, and the leaders of the main Catholic and Protestant parties were jointly awarded the Nobel Peace Prize.

Thatcher was deposed by her own party in 1990, and the Conservatives were routed in the election of 1997. The electorate's message was clear, and Tony Blair, the new Labour prime minister, moved to restore the run-down Health Service and system of state education. Honoring other of his campaign pledges, he offered Scotland its own parliament and Wales its own assembly, each with tax-raising powers and a substantial budget for the operation of its social services, and each holding its first elections in 1999. Blair and his Labour party successor Gordon Brown faced increasing skepticism over their justification for joining forces with the U.S.-led invasion and occupation of Iraq in 2003 and over their handling of the economy. In 2010, David Cameron, the first Conservative prime minister in thirteen years, headed a coalition government with the Liberal Democrats, the first formal coalition government since World War II. He instituted controversial austerity measures to reduce the budget deficit. In 2016, after losing the referendum he introduced on the United Kingdom's continued membership in the European Union, he resigned and was succeeded by Theresa May.

The UK Votes for Brexit. A journalist displays the *London Evening Standard* in a television broadcast outside the Bank of England on June 24, 2016. The day before, a narrow majority had voted for a British exit, or Brexit, from the European Union. Britain had been a member of the European community since 1973, but anti-immigration feeling and skepticism toward European governance helped propel the Brexit vote.

POETRY

The years leading up to World War I saw the start of a poetic revolution. The imagist movement, influenced by the philosopher-poet T. E. Hulme's insistence on hard, clear, precise images, arose in reaction to what it saw as Romantic fuzziness and facile emotionalism in poetry. (Like other modernists, the imagists somewhat oversimplified the nineteenth-century aesthetic against which they defined their own artistic ideal, while scanting underlying continuities.) The movement developed initially in London, where the American modernist poet Ezra Pound was living, and quickly migrated across the Atlantic; its early members included Hulme, Pound, H. D. (Hilda Doolittle), Amy Lowell, Richard Aldington, John Gould Fletcher, and F. S. Flint. As Flint explained in March 1913 in an article, partly dictated by Pound, imagists insisted on "direct treatment of the 'thing,' whether subjective or objective," on the avoidance of all words "that did not contribute to the presentation," and on a freer metrical movement than a strict adherence to the "sequence of a metronome" could allow. Inveighing in manifestos against Victorian discursiveness, the imagists wrote short, sharply etched, descriptive lyrics, but they lacked a technique for the production of longer and more complex poems.

Other new ideas about poetry helped provide this technique, many of them associated with another American in London, T. S. Eliot. Sir Herbert Grierson's 1912 edition of John Donne's poems both reflected and encouraged a new enthusiasm for seventeenth-century Metaphysical poetry. The revived interest in Metaphysical "wit" brought with it a desire on the part of pioneering poets to introduce into their work a much higher degree of intellectual complexity than had been found among the Victorians or the Georgians. The full subtlety of French symbolist poetry also now came to be appreciated; it had been admired in the 1890s, but more for its dreamy suggestiveness than for its imagistic precision and complexity. At the same time, modernist writers wanted to bring poetic language and rhythms closer to those of conversation, or at least they wanted to spice the formalities of poetic utterance with echoes of the colloquial and even the slangy. Irony, which made possible several levels of discourse simultaneously, and wit, with the use of puns (banished from serious poetry for more than two hundred years), helped achieve that union of thought and passion that Eliot, in his review of Grierson's anthology of Metaphysical poetry (1921), saw as characteristic of the Metaphysicals and wished to bring back into poetry. A new critical movement and a new creative movement in poetry went hand in hand, with Eliot the high priest of both. He extended the scope of imagism by bringing the English Metaphysicals and the French symbolists (as well as the English Jacobean dramatists) to the rescue, thus adding new possibilities of complexity and allusiveness to the criteria of concreteness and precision stressed by the imagists. Eliot also introduced into modern English and American poetry the kind of irony achieved by shifting suddenly from the formal to the colloquial, or by alluding obliquely to objects or ideas that contrasted sharply with the surface meaning of the poem. Nor were Eliot and the imagists alone in their efforts to reinvent poetry. By 1912 D. H. Lawrence had begun writing poems freer in form and emotion, wanting to unshackle verse from the constraints of the "gem-like" lyric and to approach even the "insurgent naked throb of the instant moment." From 1915 the self-declared "Anglo-Mongrel" Mina Loy "mongrelized" the diction of English-language poetry and desentimentalized Anglo-American love poetry. Thus between, say, 1911 (the first year covered by Edward Marsh's anthologies of Georgian poetry) and 1922 (the year of the publication of *The Waste Land*), a major revolution occurred in English—and for that matter American—poetic theory and practice, one that would determine the way in which many poets think about their art to this day.

This modernist revolution was by no means an isolated literary phenomenon. Writers on both sides of the English Channel were influenced by the French impressionist, postimpressionist, and cubist painters' radical reexamination of the nature of reality. The influence of Italian futurism was likewise strong on the painter and writer Wyndham Lewis, whose short-lived journal *Blast* was meant to be as shocking in its visual design as in its violent rhetoric. Mina Loy shared the futurist fascination with modernity and speed, while repudiating its misogyny and jingoism, as evidenced by her "Feminist Manifesto." Pound wrote books about the French sculptor Henri Gaudier-Brzeska and the American composer George Antheil, and indeed the jagged rhythms and wrenching dissonances of modern music influenced a range of writers. Wilfred Owen wrote in 1918: "I suppose I am doing in poetry what the advanced composers are doing in music"; and Eliot, while writing *The Waste Land* three years later, was so impressed by a performance of the composer Igor Stravinsky's *Le Sacre du Printemps* (*The Rite of Spring*) that he stood up at the end and cheered.

The posthumous 1918 publication by Robert Bridges of Gerard Manley Hopkins's poetry encouraged experimentation in language and rhythms, as evidenced by the verse's influence on Eliot, Auden, and the Welshman Dylan Thomas. Hopkins combined precision of the individual image with a complex ordering of images and a new kind of metrical patterning he named "sprung rhythm," in which the stresses of a line could be more freely distributed.

Meanwhile Yeats's remarkable oeuvre, stretching across the whole modern period, reflected varying developments of the age yet maintained an unmistakably individual accent. Beginning with the ideas of the aesthetes, turning to a tougher and sparer ironic language without losing its characteristic verbal magic, working out its author's idiosyncratic notions of symbolism, developing in its full maturity into a richly symbolic and Metaphysical poetry with its own curiously haunting cadences and with imagery both shockingly realistic and movingly suggestive, Yeats's work encapsulates a history of English poetry between 1890 and 1939.

In his poem "Remembering the 'Thirties," Donald Davie declared: "A neutral tone is nowadays preferred." That tone—Auden's coolly clinical tone—dominated the poetry of the decade. The young poets of the early 1930s—Auden, Stephen Spender, C. Day Lewis, Louis MacNeice—were the first generation to grow up in the shadow of the first-generation modern poets. Hopkins's attention to sonorities, Hardy's experiments in stanzaic patterns, Yeats's ambivalent meditations on public themes, Eliot's satiric treatment of a mechanized and urbanized world, and Owen's slant-rhymed enactments of pity influenced Auden and the other poets in his circle. But these younger poets also had to distinguish themselves from the still-living eminences in poetry, and they did so by writing poems more low-pitched and ironic than Yeats's, for example, or more individually responsive to and active in the social world than Eliot's. Stevie Smith's poetry, though largely independent of the period style, shared its progressive politics, conversational idiom, and ironic (if often whimsical) tone, as well as an interest in adapting oral forms such as ballads, folk songs, and even nursery rhymes.

As World War II began, the Auden group's neutral tone gave way to an increasingly direct and humane voice, as in Auden's own work, and to the vehemence of what came to be known as the New Apocalypse. The poets of this movement, most notably Dylan Thomas, owed something of their imagistic audacity and rhetorical violence to the French surrealists, whose poetry was introduced to English readers in translations and in *A Short Survey of Surrealism* (1936) by David Gascoyne, one of the New Apocalypse poets. Many of the surrealists, such as Salvador Dalí and André Breton, were both poets and painters, and in their verbal as well as their visual art they sought to express, often by free association, the operation of the unconscious mind.

With the coming of the 1950s, however, the pendulum swung back. A new generation of poets, including Donald Davie, Thom Gunn, and Philip Larkin, reacted against what seemed to them the verbal excesses and extravagances of Dylan Thomas and Edith Sitwell, as well as the arcane myths and knotty allusiveness of Yeats, Eliot, and Pound. "The Movement," as this new group came to be called, aimed once again for a neutral tone, a purity of diction, in which to render an unpretentious fidelity to mundane experience. Larkin, its most notable exponent, rejected the intimidating gestures of an imported modernism in favor of a more civil and accessible "native" tradition that went back to Hardy, Housman, and the Georgian pastoralists of the 1910s.

Not everyone in England followed the lead of Larkin and the Movement, some rejecting the Movement's notion of a limited, rationalist, polished poetics. In the late 1950s and the 1960s, Ted Hughes began to write poems in which predators and victims in the natural world suggest the violence and irrationality of modern history, particularly the carnage of World War I, in which his father had fought. Geoffrey Hill also saw a rationalist humanism as inadequate to the ethical and religious challenges of twentieth-century war, genocide, and atrocity, which he evoked in a strenuous language built on the traditions of high modernism and Metaphysical poetry.

Since the 1980s, the spectrum of Britain's poets has become more diverse in class, ethnicity, gender, and region than ever before, introducing a range of voices into the English literary tradition. Born in the northern English district of West Yorkshire, Tony Harrison and Simon Armitage brought the local vernacular rhythms into contact with traditional English and classical verse. The daughter of an Irish mother, Carol Ann Duffy was raised in Scotland in a left-wing, working-class Catholic family and grew up amid Irish, Scottish, and Standard varieties of English; this youthful experience helped equip her to speak in the different voices that characterize her feminist monologues.

Post–World War II Ireland—both north and south—was among the most productive spaces for poetry in the second half of the twentieth century. Born just two and a half weeks after Yeats died, Seamus Heaney, his most celebrated successor, responded to the horrors of sectarian bloodshed in Northern Ireland with subtlety and acute ethical sensitivity in poems that drew on both Irish genres and sonorities as well as the English literary tradition of Wordsworth, Hopkins, and Ted Hughes. Paul Muldoon, one of Heaney's former students in Belfast, has also written about the "troubles" in Northern Ireland but through eerily distorted fixed forms and multiple screens of irony, combining experimental zaniness with formal reserve. A native of the Irish Republic, Eavan Boland has made a space within the largely male tradition of Irish verse—with its standard, mythical emblems of femininity—for Irish women's historical experiences of suffering and survival.

The massive postwar change in the geographical contours of poetry written in English involved, in part, the emergence of new voices and styles from the "Old Commonwealth," or dominions, such as Canada and Australia. Self-conscious about being at the margins of the former empire, Les Murray fashions a brash, playful, overbrimming poetry that mines the British and classical traditions while remaking them in what he styles his "redneck" Australian manner. Anne Carson continues Canadian poetry's dialogue with its British literary origins, imaginatively transporting, for example, the Victorian writers Charlotte and Emily Brontë into a Canadian landscape, but she also illustrates a heightened interest in American poetry and popular culture, bringing into the literary mix influences that range from ancient Greek poetry to Ezra Pound and Sylvia Plath, television and video. Deliberately Canadian and feminist, Margaret Atwood writes out of the "inescapable doubleness," isolation, and alienation she ascribes to Canadian writing: "We are all immigrants to this place," she says, "even if we were born here."

From the former colonies of the British Empire in the so-called developing world came some of the most important innovations in the language and thematic reach of poetry in English. Born under British rule and educated in colonial schools that repressed or denigrated native languages and traditions, these postcolonial poets grew up with an acute awareness of the riches of their own cultural inheritances, as well as a deep knowledge of the British literary canon. They expanded the range of possibilities in English-language poetry by hybridizing traditions of the British Isles with their indigenous images and speech rhythms, creoles, and genres. Some of these writers, such as the Nobel laureate Derek Walcott, the most eminent West Indian poet, drew largely on British, American, and classical European models, though Walcott creolized the rhythms, diction, and sensibility of English-language poetry. "I have Dutch, nigger, and English in me," declares the mulatto hero of "The Schooner *Flight*," "and either I'm nobody, or I'm a nation." Other poets emphasized even more strongly their African Caribbean inheritances in speech and culture. When colonial prejudices still branded West Indian English, or Creole, as a backward language, a "corruption" of English, the African Jamaican poets Claude McKay and Louise Bennett claimed its wit, vibrancy, and proverbial richness for poetry. In the late 1960s the Barbadian Kamau (then Edward) Brathwaite revalued the linguistic, musical, and mythic survivals of Africa in the Caribbean—resources long repressed because of colonial attitudes. In poetry as well as fiction, Nigeria was the most prolific anglophone African nation around the time of independence, which was said to be the "golden age" of letters in sub-Saharan Africa. Wole Soyinka, later the first black African to win the Nobel Prize, stretched English syntax and figurative language in poems dense with Yoruba-inspired wordplay and myth. At the same time, poets from India were bringing its great variety of indigenous cultures into English-language poetry. A. K. Ramanujan's sharply etched poems interfused Anglo-modernist principles with the south Indian legacies of Tamil and Kannada poetry. All of these poets responded with emotional ambivalence and linguistic versatility to the experience of living after colonialism, between non-Western traditions and globalist modernity, in a period of explosive change in the relation between Western and "native" cultures.

A century that began with a springtime of poetic innovation drew to its close with the full flowering of older poets such as Walcott, Hill, and Heaney, and the twenty-first century opened with welcome signs of fresh growth in English-language poetry, including new books by Paul Muldoon, elected Oxford Professor of Poetry from 1999 to 2004, Carol Ann Duffy, appointed poet laureate from 2009 to 2019 (the first woman and first Scot to hold the position), and Simon Armitage, elected Oxford Professor of Poetry from 2015 to 2019.

FICTION

Novels—"loose baggy monsters," in Henry James's phrase—can be, can do, can include anything at all. The form defies prescriptions and limits. Yet its variety converges on persistent issues such as the construction of the self within society, the reproduction of the real world, and the temporality of human experience and of narrative. The novel's flexibility and porousness, its omnivorousness and multivoicedness have enabled writers to take advantage of modernity's global dislocation and mixture of peoples, while meeting the challenges to the imagination of mass death and world war, of the relentless and rapid mutations in modern cultures and societies, in evolving knowledge and beliefs.

The twentieth century's novels may be divided roughly into three main sub-periods: high modernism through the 1920s, celebrating personal and textual inwardness, complexity, and difficulty; the reaction against modernism, involving a return to social realism, moralism, and assorted documentary endeavors, in the 1930s, 1940s, and 1950s; and the period after the collapse of the British Empire (especially from the time of the countercultural revolution of the 1960s), in which the fictional claims of various realisms—urban, proletarian, provincial English (e.g., northern), regional (e.g., Scottish and Irish), immigrant, postcolonial, feminist, gay—are asserted alongside, but also through, a continuing self-consciousness about language and form and meaning that is, in effect, the enduring legacy of modernism. By the end of the century, modernism had given way to the striking pluralism of postmodernism and postcolonialism. Yet the roots of the late-century panoramic mix of voices and styles lay in the early part of the century, when writers on the margins of "Englishness"—a Pole, Joseph Conrad; an Irishman, James Joyce; an American, Henry James; an Englishwoman, Virginia Woolf; and a working-class Englishman, D. H. Lawrence—were the most instrumental inventors of the modernist "English" novel.

The high modernists wrote in the wake of the First World War's shattering of confidence in the old certainties about the deity and the Christian faith, about the person, knowledge, materialism, history, the old grand narratives, which had, more or less, sustained the Western novel through the nineteenth century. They boldly ventured into this general shaking of belief in the novel's founding assumptions—that the world, things, and selves were knowable, that language was a reliably revelatory instrument, that the author's story gave history meaning and moral shape, that narratives should fall into ethically instructive beginnings, middles, and endings. Trying to be true to the new skepticisms and hesitations, the modernists also attempted to construct credible new alternatives to the old belief systems.

The once-prevailing nineteenth-century notions of ordinary reality came under serious attack. In her famous essay "Modern Fiction" (1919, revised 1925), Virginia Woolf explicitly assaulted the "materialism" of the realistic Edwardian heirs of Victorian naturalist confidence, Arnold Bennett, H. G. Wells, and John Galsworthy. For Woolf, as for other modernists, what was knowable, and thus representable, could not be thought of as some given, fixed, transcribable essence. Reality existed, rather, only as it was perceived. Hence the introduction of the impressionistic, flawed, even utterly unreliable narrator—a substitute for the classic nineteenth-century authoritative narrating voice, usually the voice of the author or some close stand-in. Even a relatively reliable narrator, such as Conrad's Marlow, the main narrating voice of *Heart of Darkness* and *Lord Jim*, dramatized the struggle to know, penetrate, and interpret reality, with his large rhetoric of the invisible, inaudible, impossible, unintelligible, and thus unsayable. The real was offered, then, as refracted and reflected in the novel's representative consciousness. "Look within," Woolf urged the novelist. Reality and its truth had gone inward.

Woolf's subject would be "an ordinary mind on an ordinary day." The life that mattered most would now be mental life. And so the modernist novel turned resolutely inward, its concern being now with consciousness—a flow of reflections, momentary impressions, disjunctive bits of recall and half-memory, simultaneously revealing both the past and the way the past is repressed. Psychoanalysis helped to enable this concentration: to narrate the reality of persons as the life of the mind in all its complexity and inner tumult—consciousness, unconsciousness, id, libido, and so on. And the apparent truths of this inward life were, of course, utterly tricky, scattered, fragmentary, spotty, now illuminated, now twilit, now quite occluded. For Woolf, Joyce's *Ulysses* was a prime expression of this desired impressionistic agenda: "he is concerned at all costs to reveal the flickerings of that inner-most flame which flashes its messages through the brain."

The characters of Joyce and Woolf are caught, then, as they are immersed in the so-called stream of consciousness; and some version of an interior flow of thought becomes the main modernist access to "character." The reader overhears the characters speaking, so to say, from within their particular consciousnesses, but not always directly. The modernists felt free also to enter their characters' minds, to speak as though on their behalf, in the technique known as "free indirect style" (*style indirect libre* in French).

A marked feature of the new fictional selfhood was a fraught condition of existential loneliness. Conrad's Lord Jim, Joyce's Leopold Bloom and Stephen Dedalus, Lawrence's Paul Morel and Birkin, and Woolf's Mrs. Dalloway were people on their own, individuals bereft of the old props (Church, Bible, ideological consensus), and so doomed to make their own puzzled way through life's labyrinths without much confidence in belief, in the knowable solidity of the world, and above all in language as a tool of knowledge about self and other. Jacob of Woolf's *Jacob's Room* remains stubbornly unknowable to his closest friends and loved ones, above all to his novelist. The walls and cupboards of Rhoda's room in *The Waves*, also by Woolf, bend disconcertingly around her bed; she tries in vain to restore her sense of the solidity of things by touching the bottom bed rail with her toes; her mind "pours" out of her; the very boundaries of her self soften, slip, dissolve. The old conclusive plots—everything resolved on the novel's last page, on the model of the detective story—gave place to irresolute open endings: the unending vista of the last paragraph in Lawrence's *Sons and Lovers*; the jump from third-person narration to a fragmentary diary at the conclusion of Joyce's *Portrait of the Artist as a Young Man*; the melancholy of regret and unfulfilled desire at the end of Woolf's *Mrs. Dalloway*.

Novelists built modern myths on the dry bones of the old Christian ones. In his review of *Ulysses* ("*Ulysses*, Order, and Myth," 1923), T. S. Eliot famously praised the novel for replacing the old "narrative method" by a new "mythical method": Joyce's Irish Jew, Bloom, is mythicized as a modern Ulysses, his day's odyssey often ironically reviving episodes in Homer's *Odyssey*. This manipulation of "a continuous parallel between contemporaneity and antiquity" was, Eliot thought, "a step toward making the modern world possible for art," much in keeping with the new anthropology and psychology as well as with what Yeats was doing in verse. In Joyce's *Portrait of the Artist*, Stephen Dedalus's last name sets up (sometimes ironic) parallels between the mythical Greek past and the aspirations of a contemporary young Irishman. Modernism's private mythmaking could, of course, take worrying turns. The "religion of the blood" that D. H. Lawrence celebrated led directly to the fascist sympathies of his *Aaron's Rod* and the revived Aztec blood cult of *The Plumed Serpent*.

Language and textuality, reading and writing were now central to these highly metafictional novels, which are often about writers and artists, and surrogates for artists, such as Woolf's Mrs. Ramsay with her dinners and Mrs. Dalloway with her party, producers of what Woolf called the "unpublished works of women." But this self-reflexivity was not necessarily consoling—Mrs. Flanders's vision blurs and an inkblot spreads across the postcard we find her writing in the opening page of *Jacob's Room*. Joyce's *Finnegans Wake*, perhaps the greatest modernist example of language gone rampant, taxes even its most dedicated readers and verges on unreadability for others.

The skeptical modernist linguistic turn, the rejection of materialist externality and of the Victorians' realist project, left ineradicable traces on later fiction, but modernism's revolutions were not absolute or permanent. *Ulysses* and *Finnegans Wake* were influential but also unrepeatable. And even within the greatest modernist fictions, the worldly and the material, political and moral questions never dried up. Woolf and Joyce, for example, celebrate the perplexities of urban life in London and Dublin, and, indeed, modernist fiction is largely an art of the great city. Lawrence was preoccupied with the condition of England, industrialism, provincial life. Satire was one of modernism's recurrent notes. So it was not odd for the right-wing novelists who came through in the 1920s, such as Wyndham Lewis and Evelyn Waugh, to resort to the social subject and the satiric stance, nor for their left-leaning contemporaries such as Graham Greene and George Orwell—who came to be seen as even more characteristic of the red decade of the 1930s—to engage with the human condition in ways that Dickens or Balzac, let alone Bennett-Wells-Galsworthy, would have recognized as not all that distant from their own spirit.

Despite the turn to documentary realism in the 1930s, the modernist emphasis on linguistic self-consciousness did not disappear. Instead, the new writers politicized the modern novel's linguistic self-consciousness: they deployed the discourse of the unemployed or of the West Midlands' proletariat, for example, for political ends. The comically chaotic meeting of English and German languages in Christopher Isherwood's *Berlin Stories* is central to the fiction's dire warning about Anglo-German politics; Newspeak in George Orwell's *Nineteen Eighty-Four* is the culmination of the author's nearly two decades of politically motivated engagement with the ways of English speakers at home and abroad. In this politicized aftermath of the modernist experiment, novelists such as Aldous Huxley in *Brave New World* satirically engage the socio-politico-moral matter of the 1930s in part through reflections on the corruptions of language.

Where World War I was a great engine of modernism, endorsing the chaos of shattered belief, the fragility of language and of the human subject, the Spanish Civil War and then World War II confirmed the English novel in its return to registering the social scene and the historical event. World War II provoked whole series of more or less realist fictions, including Evelyn Waugh's *Sword of Honour* trilogy, as well as powerful singletons such as Graham Greene's *Ministry of Fear* and Waugh's *Brideshead Revisited*. The new fictions of the post–World War II period spoke with the satirical energies of the young demobilized officer class (Kingsley Amis's *Lucky Jim* set the disgruntled tone), and of the ordinary provincial citizen finding a fictional voice yet again in the new Welfare State atmosphere of the 1950s, as in Alan Sillitoe's proletarian Nottingham novel *Saturday Night and Sunday Morning*.

Questing for new moral foundations for the post-Holocaust nuclear age, William Golding published the first of many intense post-Christian moral fables with *The Lord of the Flies*, and Iris Murdoch released the first of many novels of moral philosophy with *Under the Net*, both in 1954. Murdoch espoused the "sovereignty of good" and the importance of the novel's loving devotion to "the otherness of the other person." Murdoch and Golding were consciously retrospective (as were the contemporary Roman Catholic novelists Greene, Waugh, and Muriel Spark) in their investment in moral form. But even such firmly grounded determinations could not calm the anxieties of belatedness. As the century drew on, British fiction struggled with a disconcertingly pervasive sense of posteriority—postwar flatness, postimperial diminution of power and influence, and the sense of the grand narratives now losing their force as never before.

Some younger novelists, such as Ian McEwan and Martin Amis (son of Kingsley), became obsessed with Germany (the now accusingly prosperous old foe) and with the lingering ghosts of the *Hitlerzeit*—and not least after 1989, when the Berlin Wall came down and wartime European horrors stirred into vivid focus. The dereliction of the once-grand imperial center, London, became a main topic for McEwan and for Amis, as well as for the later Kingsley Amis and the ex-Rhodesian Doris Lessing. Whereas Conrad, E. M. Forster (*A Passage to India*), and Jean Rhys (*Wide Sargasso Sea*) had been harshly accusatory about Britain's overseas behavior, now nostalgia for old imperial days shrouded the pages of Lawrence Durrell's *Alexandria Quartet* and Paul Scott's *Raj Quartet* and *Staying On*. Observers of English fiction worried that the only tasks left for it were to ruminate over past history and rehash old stories. The modernist Joycean strategy of resurrecting ancient narratives to revitalize present consciousness had given way to a fear that the postmodern novelist was condemned to a disabled career of parroting old stuff. *On est parlé*, "one is spoken," rather than speaking for oneself, thinks the main character of Julian Barnes's *Flaubert's Parrot*, reflecting with dismay on this dilemma. Ventriloquial reproduction of old voices became Peter Ackroyd's trademark. Worries about being merely possessed by the past came to seem central to late-twentieth-century English fiction, as in A. S. Byatt's *Possession*, which is about the magnetism of past (Victorian) writers and writings.

Yet this was also a time for the spectacular emergence of many robust voices, particularly from assorted margins—writers for whom the enervation at the English center represented an opportunity for telling their untold stories. After a sensational trial in 1960, the ban on D. H. Lawrence's erotically explicit *Lady Chatterley's Lover* was finally lifted, ensuring greater freedom in the narrative exploration of sexuality. Relaxing views on gender roles, the influx of women into the workplace, and the collapse of the grand patriarchal narratives also gave impetus to feminist revisionary narratives of history, and to the remaking of narrative technique as more fluid and free. In the 1980s and 1990s, prominent and inventive women's voices included those of Jeanette Winterson, celebrator of women's arts and bodiliness, and Angela Carter, feminist neomythographer, reviser of fairy tales, rewriter of the Marquis de Sade, espouser of raucous and rebellious heroines. Among the chorus of voices seeking to express experiences once held taboo with new intimacy and vividness were those of uncloseted gay writers, such as Alan Hollinghurst, pioneer of the openly male-homosexual literary novel of the post–World War II period, and Adam Mars-Jones, short-story chronicler of the HIV/AIDS crisis. The literary counterpart for political decolonization and devolution within the British Isles was the emergence of a multitude of regional and national voices outside the south of England, many deploying a vigorously local idiom, such as the Scottish novelist Irvine Welsh and the Irish writer Roddy Doyle, who reached mass international audiences through 1990s film versions of their novels *Trainspotting* (Welsh) and *The Commitments* (Doyle). Hilary Mantel, who grew up in a working-class Irish Catholic immigrant family in the north of England, brought an acute sensitivity to the outsider's perspective, even when she was writing historical fiction about the Tudor court, as in her novels *Wolf Hall* (2009) and *Bring up the Bodies* (2012).

While postimperial anxieties and exhaustion seemed to beset many post-war English writers, postcolonial novelists were energetically claiming for literature in English untold histories, hybrid identities, and vibrantly creolized vocabularies. A major phase in the huge geographic shift in the center of gravity of English-language fiction occurred during the postwar decolonization of much of South Asia, Africa, and the Caribbean, when Chinua Achebe's *Things Fall Apart* (1958) was published, just two years before Nigerian independence. Retelling the story of colonial incursion from an indigenous viewpoint, Achebe's influential novel intricately represents an African community before and after the arrival of whites, in a language made up of English and Igbo words, encompassed by a narrative that enmeshes African proverbs and oral tales with English realism and modernist reflexivity. A few years later and on the eve of his natal island's independence, the Trinidad-born writer V. S. Naipaul published his first major novel, *A House for Mr. Biswas* (1961), one of many works that brilliantly develop the potential of a translucent realist fiction to explore issues such as migrant identities, cross-cultural mimicry, and the spaces of colonialism. The Indian-born Salman Rushdie, more restive than Naipaul in relation to Englishness and English literary traditions, has exuberantly championed hybrid narrative forms made out of the fresh convergence of modern European fiction and "Third World" orality, magical realism, and polyglossia. In novels such as *Midnight's Children* (1981) and *The Satanic Verses* (1988), Rushdie wryly offer a "chutnification of history" in South Asia and in an Asianized England. The colonies where English literature had once been a means of imposing imperial models of "civilization" now gave rise to novelists who, ironically, outstripped in lively imagination, cultural energy, and narrative inventiveness their counterparts from the seat of the empire. A younger generation of novelists who published their groundbreaking work after the turn of the millennium, including the Indian Kiran Desai, the Jamaican Marlon James, and the Nigerian Chimamanda Ngozi Adichie, have ensured the continued vibrancy of the "postcolonial" or "global" novel into the twenty-first century.

White fiction writers from the colonies and dominions, many of them women, and many of them resident in England, such as Katherine Mansfield, Doris Lessing, and Jean Rhys, had long brought fresh perspectives to the novel from the outposts of empire, each of these eminent writers sharply etching a feminist critique of women's lives diminished by subordination to the colonial order. South Africa, not least because of its fraught racial and political history, can count among its progeny some of the most celebrated fiction writers of the late twentieth century. Nadine Gordimer has extended the potential of an ethical narrative realism to probe the fierce moral challenges of apartheid and its aftermath, whereas J. M. Coetzee has used self-reflexively postmodern and allegorical forms to inquire into the tangled complexities and vexed complicities of white South African experience.

Late-twentieth-century and early-twenty-first-century "English" fiction would have looked startlingly thin and poverty-stricken were it not for the large presence in Britain of writers of non-European origin. Like the first modern novelists, many of the writers who have most enriched English-language fiction in recent decades are migrants, émigrés, and expatriates, such as Naipaul and Rushdie, as well as the delicately ironic realist Kazuo Ishiguro, from Japan, the postsurreal fabulist Wilson Harris, from Guyana, and the chronicler of transatlantic slavery, Caryl Phillips, from Saint Kitts. Still others are the sons and daughters of non-European immigrants to Britain, including two of the most visible exemplars of the often comically cross-cultural fiction of a new multiracial England, Hanif Kureishi and Zadie Smith, both born on the peripheries of London, Kureishi to a Pakistani father and English mother, Smith to a Jamaican mother and English father. Their first novels, both set in London—Kureishi's *The Buddha of Suburbia* (1990) and Smith's *White Teeth* (2000)—helped establish a paradigm for the vibrantly cross-cultural and interethnic novel. These and other "British" novelists of color, giving voice to new and emergent experiences of immigration, hybridization, and cross-racial encounter, take advantage of the novel's fecund polymorphousness with little anxiety about belatedness, no fright over parroting, and no neomodernist worries about attempting realistic encounters with the world.

DRAMA

Late Victorians from one perspective, Oscar Wilde and Bernard Shaw can also be seen as early moderns, forerunners of the twentieth century's renovators of dramatic form. The wit of Wilde's drawing-room comedies is combative and generative of paradoxes, but beneath the glitter of his verbal play are serious—if heavily coded—reflections on social, political, and feminist issues. Shaw brought still another kind of wit into drama—not Wilde's lighthearted sparkle but the provocative paradox that was meant to tease and disturb, to challenge the complacency of the audience. Over time the desire to unsettle, to shock, even to alienate the audience became one hallmark of modern drama.

Wilde and Shaw were both born in Ireland, and it was in Dublin that the century's first major theatrical movement originated. To nourish Irish poetic drama and foster the Irish literary renaissance, Yeats and Lady Augusta Gregory founded the Irish Literary Theatre in 1899, with Yeats's early nationalist play *The Countess Cathleen* as its first production. In 1902 the Irish Literary Theatre was able to maintain a permanent all-Irish company and changed its name to the Irish National Theatre, which moved in 1904 to the Abbey Theatre, by which name it has been known ever since. J. M. Synge brought the speech and imagination of Irish country people into theater, but the Abbey's 1907 staging of his play *The Playboy of the Western World* so offended orthodox religious and nationalist sentiment that the audience rioted. While defending Synge and other pioneers of Irish drama, Yeats continued to write his own plays, which drew themes from old Irish legend and which, after 1913, stylized and ritualized theatrical performance on the model of Japanese Noh drama. In the 1920s, Sean O'Casey brought new vitality to the Abbey Theatre, using the Easter Rising and Irish civil war as a background for controversial plays (one of which again sparked riots) that combined tragic melodrama, humor of character, and irony of circumstance. In England, T. S. Eliot attempted with considerable success to revive a ritual poetic drama with his *Murder in the Cathedral* (1935), though his later attempts to combine religious symbolism with the chatter of entertaining society comedy, as in *The Cocktail Party* (1950), were uneven.

Despite the achievements of Yeats, Synge, O'Casey, and Eliot, it cannot be said of Irish and British drama, as it can of poetry and fiction in the first half of the century, that a technical revolution changed the whole course of literary history. The major innovations in drama in the first half of the twentieth century were on the Continent. German expressionist drama developed out of the dark, psychological focus of the later plays of the Swedish dramatist August Strindberg (1849–1912). Another worldwide influence was the "epic" drama of the leftist German dramatist Bertolt Brecht (1898–1956): to foster ideological awareness, he rejected the idea that the audience should identify with a play's characters and become engrossed in its plot; instead, the playwright should break the illusion of reality through the alienation effect (*Verfremdungseffekt*) and foreground the play's theatrical constructedness and historical specificity. The French dramatist Antonin Artaud (1896–1948) also defied realism and rationalism, but unlike Brecht, his theory of the theater of cruelty sought a transformative, mystical communion with the audience through incantations and sounds, physical gestures and strange scenery. Another French dramatist, the Romanian-born Eugène Ionesco (1909–1994), helped inaugurate the theater of the absurd just after World War II, in plays that enact people's hopeless efforts to communicate and that comically intimate a tragic vision of life devoid of meaning or purpose. In such Continental drama the influences of symbolism (on the later Strindberg), Marxism (on Brecht), and surrealism (on Artaud and Ionesco) contributed to the shattering of naturalistic convention in drama, making the theater a space where linear plot gave way to fractured scenes and circular action, transparent conversation was displaced by misunderstanding and verbal opacity, a predictable and knowable universe was unsettled by eruptions of the irrational and the absurd.

In Britain, the impact of these Continental innovations was delayed by a conservative theater establishment until the late 1950s and 1960s, when they converged with the countercultural revolution to transform the nature of English-language theater. Meanwhile the person who played the most significant role in the anglophone absorption of modernist experiment was the Irishman Samuel Beckett. He changed the history of drama with his first produced play, written in French in 1948 and translated by the author as *Waiting for Godot* (premiered in Paris in 1953, in London in 1955). The play astonishingly did away with plot altogether ("Nothing happens—twice," as one critic put it), as did *Endgame* (1958) and Beckett's later plays, such as *Not I* (1973) and *That Time* (1976). In the shadow of the mass death of World War II, the plotlessness, the minimal characterization and setting, the absurdist intimation of an existential darkness without redemption, and the tragicomic melding of anxiety, circular wordplay, and slapstick action in Beckett's plays gave impetus to a seismic shift in British writing for the theater.

The epicenter of the new developments in British drama was the Royal Court Theatre, symbolically located a little away from London's West End "theater land" (the rough equivalent of Broadway in New York). From 1956 the Royal Court was the home of the English Stage Company. Together they provided a venue and a vision that provoked and enabled a new wave of writers. John Osborne's *Look Back in Anger* (1956), the hit of the ESC's first season (significantly helped by the play's television broadcast), offered the audience "lessons in feeling" through a searing depiction of class-based indignation, emotional cruelty, and directionless angst, all in a surprisingly nonmetropolitan setting. At the Royal Court, the working-class naturalism of the so-called kitchen-sink dramatists and other "angry young men" of the 1950s, such as Arnold Wesker, author of the trilogy *Chicken Soup with Barley* (1958), also broke with the genteel proprieties and narrowly upper-class set designs that, in one unadventurous drawing-room comedy after another, had dominated the British stage for decades. The political consciousness of the new theater was still more evident in John Arden's plays produced expressly for the Royal Court, such as *Sergeant Musgrave's Dance* (1959), which, in the stylized setting of an isolated mining town, explores colonial oppression, communal guilt for wartime atrocities, and pacifism. By the later 1960s, the influence of the counterculture on British theater was unavoidable. Joe Orton challenged bourgeois sentiment in a series of classically precise, blackly comic, and sexually ambiguous parodies—for example, his farce *What the Butler Saw* (1969).

While plays of social and political critique were one response to the postwar period, Beckett and the theater of the absurd inspired another group of Royal Court writers to refocus theater on language, symbolism, and existential realities. Informed by kitchen-sink naturalism and absurdism, Harold Pinter's "comedies of menace" map out a social trajectory from his early study of working-class stress and inarticulate anxiety, *The Room* (1957), through the film-noirish black farce of *The Dumb Waiter* (1960) and the emotional power plays of *The Caretaker* (1960), to the savagely comic study of middle-class escape from working-class mores in *The Homecoming* (1965). Later plays reflect on patrician suspicion and betrayal, though in the 1980s his work acquired a more overtly political voice. Though less bleak than Pinter, Tom Stoppard is no less indebted to Beckett's wordplay, skewed conversations, and theatrical technique, as evidenced by *Rosencrantz and Guildenstern Are Dead* (1967) and other plays, many of which embed within themselves earlier literary works (such as *Godot* and *Hamlet*) and thus offer virtuoso postmodernist reflections on art, language, and performance. This enjoyment and exploitation of self-conscious theatricality arises partly out of the desire to show theater as different from film and television and is also apparent in the 1970s productions of another playwright: the liturgical stylization of Peter Shaffer's *Equus* (1973) and the bleak mental landscape of his Antonio Salieri in *Amadeus* (1979) emphasize the stage as battleground and site of struggle (an effect lost in their naturalistic film versions). Stoppard's time shifts and memory lapses in *Travesties* (1974) allow a nonnaturalistic study of the role of memory and imagination in the creative process, a theme he returns to in *Arcadia* (1993), a stunning double-exposure account of a Romantic poet and his modern critical commentators occupying the same physical space but never reaching intellectual common ground.

Legal reform intensified the postwar ferment in British theater. Following the Theatres Act of 1843, writers for the public stage had been required to submit their playscripts to the Lord Chamberlain's office for state censorship, but in 1968 a new Theatres Act abolished that office. With this new freedom from conservative mores and taste, Howard Brenton, Howard Barker, Edward Bond, and David Hare were able to write challenging studies of violence, social deprivation, and political and sexual aggression, often using mythical settings and epic stories to construct austere tableaux of power and oppression. Bond's *Lear* (1971) typifies his ambitious combination of soaring lyrical language and alienatingly realistic violence. Directors such as Peter Brook took advantage of the new freedom in plays that emphasized, as had Artaud's theater of cruelty, physical gesture, bodily movement, and ritualized spectacle. The post-1968 liberalization also encouraged the emergence of new theater groups addressing specific political agendas, many of them inspired by Brecht's "epic" theater's discontinuous, distancing, and socially critical style. Companies such as Monstrous Regiment, Gay Sweatshop, Joint Stock, and

John McGrath's 7:84 worked collaboratively with dramatists who were invited to help devise and develop shows. Increasingly in the 1970s, published plays were either transcriptions of the first production or "blueprints for the alchemy of live performance" (Micheline Wandor). In Ireland, the founding of the Field Day Theatre Company in 1980 by the well-established playwright Brian Friel and actor Stephen Rea had similar motives of collaborative cultural catalysis. Their first production, Friel's *Translations* (1980), exploring linguistic colonialism and the fragility of cultural identity in nineteenth-century Ireland, achieved huge international success.

This ethos of collaboration and group development helped foster the first major cohort of women dramatists to break through onto mainstream stages. Working with Joint Stock and Monstrous Regiment in the late 1970s on plays such as the gender-bending anticolonial *Cloud Nine* (1979), Caryl Churchill developed plays out of workshops exploring gender, class, and colonialism. She carefully transcribes and overlaps the speech of her characters to create a seamlessly interlocking web of discourse, a streamlined version of the ebb and flow of normal speech. In *Top Girls* (1982) and *Serious Money* (1987), plays that anatomize the market-driven ethos of the 1980s, she explores modern society with the wit and detachment of Restoration comedy. Pam Gems studies the social and sexual politics of misogyny and feminism in her campy theatrical explorations of strong women—*Queen Cristina* (1977), *Piaf* (1978), *Camille* (1984)—while Sarah Daniels reinterprets the naturalism of kitchen-sink drama by adding to it the linguistic stylization of Churchill.

Massive strides in the diversification of English-language theater occurred during the era of decolonization, when two eminent poets, Derek Walcott and Wole Soyinka, helped breathe new life into anglophone drama. As early as the 1950s, Derek Walcott was writing and directing plays about Caribbean history and experience, re-creating in his drama a West Indian "oral culture, of chants, jokes, folk-songs, and fables," at a time when theater in the Caribbean tended to imitate European themes and styles. After moving to Trinidad in 1958, he founded what came to be known as the Trinidad Theatre Workshop, and for much of the next twenty years devoted himself to directing and writing plays that included *Dream on Monkey Mountain*, first produced in 1967, in which Eurocentric and Afrocentric visions of Caribbean identity collide. Since then, a notable breakthrough in Caribbean theater has been the collaborative work of the Sistren Theatre Collective in Jamaica, which, following the lead of Louise Bennett and other West Indian poets, draws on women's personal histories in dramatic performances that make vivid use of Jamaican speech, expression, and rhythm. Meanwhile in Africa, Wole Soyinka, who had been involved with the Royal Court Theatre in the late 1950s when Brecht's influence was first being absorbed, returned to Nigeria in the year of its independence to write and direct plays that fused Euromodernist dramatic techniques with conventions from Yoruba popular and traditional drama. His play *Death and the King's Horseman*, premiered in Nigeria in 1976, represents a tragic confrontation between colonial officials and the guardians of Yoruba rituals and beliefs. While Soyinka has been a towering presence in sub-Saharan Africa, other playwrights, such as the fellow Nigerian Femi Osofisan and the South African Athol Fugard, have used the stage to probe issues of class, race, and the often violent legacy of colonialism. In England, playwrights of Caribbean, African, and Asian origin or descent, such as Mustapha Matura, Caryl Phillips, and

Hanif Kureishi, the latter of whom is best known internationally for his screenplays for the films *My Beautiful Laundrette* (1985), *Sammy and Rosie Get Laid* (1988), *My Son the Fanatic* (1998), *The Mother* (2004), *Venus* (2006), and *Weddings and Beheadings* (2007), have revitalized British drama with a host of new vocabularies, new techniques, new visions of identity in an increasingly cross-ethnic and transnational world. The century that began with its first great dramatic movement in Ireland was followed by a century that began with English-language drama more diverse in its accents and styles, more international in its bearings and vision than ever before.

The Twentieth and Twenty-First Centuries

TEXTS	CONTEXTS
1899, 1902 Joseph Conrad, *Heart of Darkness*	
	1900 Max Planck, quantum theory
	1901 First wireless communication across the Atlantic
	1901–10 Reign of Edward VII
	1902 End of the Anglo-Boer War
	1903 Henry Ford introduces the first mass-produced car. Wright Brothers make the first successful airplane flight
	1905 Albert Einstein, theory of special relativity. Impressionist exhibition, London
1910 George Bernard Shaw, *Pygmalion*	1910 Postimpressionist exhibition, London
	1910–36 Reign of George V
1913 Ezra Pound, "A Few Don'ts by an Imagiste"	
1914 James Joyce, *Dubliners.* Thomas Hardy, *Satires of Circumstance*	1914–18 World War I
1914–15 *Blast*	
1916 Joyce, *A Portrait of the Artist as a Young Man*	1916 Easter Rising in Dublin
1917 T. S. Eliot, "The Love Song of J. Alfred Prufrock"	
1918 Gerard Manley Hopkins, *Poems*	1918 Armistice. Franchise Act grants vote to women thirty and over
1920 D. H. Lawrence, *Women in Love.* Wilfred Owen, *Poems*	1920 Treaty of Versailles. League of Nations formed
1921 William Butler Yeats, *Michael Robartes and the Dancer*	1921–22 Formation of Irish Free State with Northern Ireland (Ulster) remaining part of Great Britain
1922 Katherine Mansfield, *The Garden Party and Other Stories.* Joyce, *Ulysses.* Eliot, *The Waste Land*	
1924 E. M. Forster, *A Passage to India*	
1925 Virginia Woolf, *Mrs. Dalloway*	
1927 Woolf, *To the Lighthouse*	
1928 Yeats, *The Tower*	1928 Women twenty-one and over granted voting rights
1929 Woolf, *A Room of One's Own.* Robert Graves, *Goodbye to All That*	1929 Stock market crash; Great Depression begins
	1933 Hitler comes to power in Germany
1935 Eliot, *Murder in the Cathedral*	
	1936 Edward VIII succeeds George V, but abdicates in favor of his brother, crowned as George VI
	1936–39 Spanish Civil War
1937 David Jones, *In Parenthesis*	
1939 Joyce, *Finnegans Wake.* Yeats, *Last Poems and Two Plays*	1939–45 World War II

TEXTS	CONTEXTS
1940 W. H. Auden, *Another Time*	1940 Fall of France. Battle of Britain
	1941–45 The Holocaust
1943 Eliot, *Four Quartets*	
1945 Auden, *Collected Poems*. George Orwell, *Animal Farm*	1945 First atomic bombs dropped, on Japan
1946 Dylan Thomas, *Deaths and Entrances*	
	1947 India and Pakistan become independent nations
	1948 *Empire Windrush* brings West Indians to U.K.
1949 Orwell, *Nineteen Eighty-Four*	
	1950 Apartheid laws passed in South Africa
1953 Premiere of Samuel Beckett's *Waiting for Godot*	
	1956 Suez crisis
	1957 Ghana becomes independent
1958 Chinua Achebe, *Things Fall Apart*	
	1960 Nigeria becomes independent
	1961 Berlin Wall erected
1962 Doris Lessing, *The Golden Notebook*	1962 Cuban missile crisis. Uganda, Jamaica, Trinidad and Tobago become independent
1964 Philip Larkin, *The Whitsun Weddings*	
	1965 U.S. troops land in South Vietnam
1966 Nadine Gordimer, *The Late Bourgeois World*. Tom Stoppard, *Rosencrantz and Guildenstern Are Dead*. Jean Rhys, *Wide Sargasso Sea*	1966 Barbados and Guyana become independent
	1969 *Apollo* moon landing
1971 V. S. Naipaul, *In a Free State*	1971 Indo-Pakistan War, leading to creation of Bangladesh
	1972 Britain enters European Common Market
	1973 U.S. troops leave Vietnam
1975 Seamus Heaney, *North*	
1979 Caryl Churchill, *Cloud Nine*	1979 Islamic Revolution in Iran; the shah flees. Soviets invade Afghanistan
	1979–90 Margaret Thatcher is British prime minister
1980 J. M. Coetzee, *Waiting for the Barbarians*	1980–88 Iran-Iraq War
1981 Salman Rushdie, *Midnight's Children*. Brian Friel, *Translations*	
	1982 Falklands War

TEXTS	CONTEXTS
1985 Production of Hanif Kureishi's *My Beautiful Laundrette*. Margaret Atwood, *The Handmaid's Tale*	
1988 Rushdie, *The Satanic Verses*	
1989 Kazuo Ishiguro, *The Remains of the Day*	1989 Fall of the Berlin Wall. Tiananmen Square, Beijing, demonstration and massacre
1990 Derek Walcott, *Omeros*	
1991 Caryl Phillips, *Cambridge*	1991 Collapse of the Soviet Union
1992 Thom Gunn, *The Man with Night Sweats*	
1993 Tom Stoppard, *Arcadia*	
	1994 Democracy comes to South Africa
1997 Arundhati Roy, *The God of Small Things*	1997 Labour party victory in the U.K. ends eighteen years of Conservative government
	1998 British handover of Hong Kong to China. Northern Ireland Assembly established
1999 Carol Ann Duffy, *The World's Wife*	
2000 Zadie Smith, *White Teeth*	
2001 Ian McEwan, *Atonement*	2001 September 11 attacks destroy World Trade Center
2002 Paul Muldoon, *Moy Sand and Gravel*	2002 Euro becomes sole currency in most of European Union
	2003 Invasion of Iraq led by U.S. and U.K.
	2005 Bombings of London transport system
2006 Kiran Desai, *The Inheritance of Loss*	
2009 Hilary Mantel, *Wolf Hall*	2010 David Cameron is first Conservative party prime minister in 13 years
2013 Chimamanda Ngozi Adichie, *Americanah*	
	2016 U.K. votes to leave European Union. David Cameron resigns, replaced by Theresa May

THOMAS HARDY
1840–1928

Thomas Hardy was born in the Dorset hamlet of Higher Bockhampton, in that area of southwest England that he was to make the "Wessex" of his fiction and poetry. The son of a stonemason, the young Hardy was kept mostly at home, where he closely observed and came to love the surrounding countryside, the rhythms of the seasons and the songs, stories, and folk beliefs of a still predominantly oral culture. He attended local schools until the age of sixteen, when he was apprenticed to a Dorchester architect in whose office he remained for six years. In 1862 he moved to London and found a position as a draftsman in the office of Arthur Blomfield, a leading architect of Gothic-style buildings. Meanwhile, as Hardy was completing his general education informally through his eclectic reading, he began to study and write poetry. His first novel, seen as an attack on upper-class pretensions, was rejected by publishers in 1868, though one of the readers, George Meredith, advised Hardy to write another work of fiction, with a more complicated plot. The result was the sensational novel *Desperate Remedies* (1871), which was followed by a tale of rural life, *Under the Greenwood Tree* (1872). The serialization of his next two novels, *A Pair of Blue Eyes* (1872–73) and *Far from the Madding Crowd* (1874), provided him with sufficient income to abandon architecture for literature. He continued to write novels until the sexual frankness and irreligiousness of his last novel, *Jude the Obscure* (1895), resulted in a hostile critical reception, including reviews headed "Jude the Obscene" and "Hardy the Degenerate." Financial security finally enabled Hardy to make his long-desired return to poetry. Straddling the Victorian and modern periods, he published all his novels in the nineteenth century, and all but the first of his poetry collections, *Wessex Poems and Other Verses* (1898), in the twentieth. His remarkable epic drama of the Napoleonic Wars, *The Dynasts*, came out in three parts between 1903 and 1908, and he continued to write verse until his death, at age eighty-seven.

In Hardy's fiction, set in the predominantly rural "Wessex," acutely observed and richly detailed, the forces of nature outside and inside individuals combine to shape human destiny. Against a background of immemorial agricultural labor, with ancient monuments such as Stonehenge or a Roman amphitheater reminding us of the past, he presents characters at the mercy of elements beyond their control: their emotions or sexual impulses, and the barriers of social class and restrictions of social mores. Men and women in Hardy's fiction are rarely masters of their fates; walking long distances across a landscape that dwarfs them, they may be subjected to the indifferent forces that manipulate their behavior and their relations with others. They can achieve dignity, however, through endurance, heroism, or simple strength of character. Most of his fiction is tragic or at least tragicomic, observing humanity with a mixture of cold detachment and searching empathy, and exploring the bitter ironies of life with an almost malevolent staging of coincidence to emphasize the disparity between human desire and ambition, on the one hand, and, on the other, what fate—often determined by the character's very nature—has in store. One of the darkest of Hardy's novels, *Tess of the d'Urbervilles* (1891), is the story of an intelligent and sensitive young woman, daughter of a poor family, who is driven to murder, and thus to death by hanging, by a painfully ironic concatenation of events and circumstances. Published in the same year as *Tess*, the story anthologized here, "On the Western Circuit," similarly has at its center a young country woman deceived by a sophisticated city man; her "ruin" (see also Hardy's poem

"The Ruined Maid") leads—contrary to the good intentions of the three protagonists, and again as the result of bitter irony—to *his* ruin and a lifetime of misery for all concerned.

Hardy denied that he was a pessimist, calling himself a "meliorist"—that is, one who believes that the world can be made better by human effort. But there is little sign of meliorism in either his fiction or his poetry. A number of his poems, such as the one he wrote about the *Titanic* disaster, "The Convergence of the Twain," illustrate the perversity of fate, the disastrous or ironic coincidence of events. Other poems go beyond this mood to present, with quiet gravity and a carefully controlled elegiac feeling, some aspect of human sorrow, loss, frustration, or regret, always grounded in a particular, fully realized situation. "Hap" shows Hardy in the characteristic mood of complaining about the irony of human destiny in a universe ruled by chance, while "The Walk" (one of a group of poems written after the death of his first wife in 1912) gives, with remarkable power, concrete embodiment to a sense of loss.

Hardy's verse, like his prose, often has a self-taught air about it; both can seem, on first reading, roughly hewn. He said he wanted to avoid "the jewelled line," and like many modern and contemporary poets, he sought instead what he called "dissonances, and other irregularities" in his art, because they convey more authenticity and spontaneity. "Art is a disproportioning . . . of realities," he declared. While adhering to the metered line, Hardy roughens prosody and contorts syntax, and he creates irregular and complex stanza forms. His diction includes archaisms and deliberately awkward coinages (e.g., "Powerfuller" and "unblooms" in "Hap"). He distorts, vigorously revises, and sometimes forces together conventions of traditional genres such as the sonnet, the ballad, the love poem, the war poem, and the elegy. Though rooted in the Victorian period, Hardy thus looks ahead to the dislocations of poetic form carried out by subsequent poets of the twentieth century.

The sadness in Hardy—his skepticism about the existence of a benevolent God, his sense of the waste and frustration involved in human life, his insistent irony when faced with moral or metaphysical questions—is part of the late Victorian mood, found also, say, in A. E. Housman's poetry and, earlier, in Edward FitzGerald's *Rubáiyát of Omar Khayyám*, published when Hardy was eighteen. Although his attitudes toward the sacred remained tangled and vexed, what has been termed "the disappearance of God" affected him more deeply than it did many of his contemporaries, not least because as a young man he seriously considered becoming a Church of England priest. Yet his characteristic themes and attitudes cannot be viewed simply as the reaction to the scientific and philosophical developments (Darwin's theory of evolution, for example) that we see in many forms in late nineteenth-century literature. The favorite poetic mood of both Tennyson and Matthew Arnold was also elegiac (e.g., in Tennyson's "Break, Break, Break" and Arnold's "Dover Beach"), but the mood of Hardy's poetry differs from Victorian sorrow; it is sterner, more skeptical, as though braced by a long look at the worst. It is this sternness, this ruggedness of his poetry, together with its verbal and emotional integrity, its formal variety and tonal complexity, its quietly searching individual accent and even occasional playfulness, that helped bring about the steady rise in Hardy's reputation as a poet. Ezra Pound remarked in a 1934 letter: "Nobody has taught me anything about writing since Thomas Hardy died." W. H. Auden begins an essay with this testament to the effect of Hardy's verse: "I cannot write objectively about Thomas Hardy because I was once in love with him." And Hardy appears as the major figure—with more poems than either Yeats or Eliot—in Philip Larkin's influential *Oxford Book of Twentieth-Century English Verse* (1973).

On the Western Circuit[1]

I

The man who played the disturbing part in the two quiet feminine lives here-under depicted—no great man, in any sense, by the way—first had knowledge of them on an October evening, in the city of Melchester. He had been standing in the Close,[2] vainly endeavouring to gain amid the darkness a glimpse of the most homogeneous pile of mediæval architecture in England, which towered and tapered from the damp and level sward[3] in front of him. While he stood the presence of the Cathedral walls was revealed rather by the ear than by the eyes; he could not see them, but they reflected sharply a roar of sound which entered the Close by a street leading from the city square, and, falling upon the building, was flung back upon him.

He postponed till the morrow his attempt to examine the deserted edifice, and turned his attention to the noise. It was compounded of steam barrel-organs, the clanging of gongs, the ringing of hand-bells, the clack of rattles, and the undistinguishable shouts of men. A lurid light hung in the air in the direction of the tumult. Thitherward he went, passing under the arched gateway, along a straight street, and into the square.

He might have searched Europe over for a greater contrast between juxta-posed scenes. The spectacle was that of the eighth chasm of the Inferno as to colour and flame, and, as to mirth, a development of the Homeric heaven. A smoky glare, of the complexion of brass-filings, ascended from the fiery tongues of innumerable naphtha lamps affixed to booths, stalls, and other temporary erections which crowded the spacious market-square. In front of this irradiation scores of human figures, more or less in profile, were darting athwart and across, up, down, and around, like gnats against a sunset.

Their motions were so rhythmical that they seemed to be moved by machinery. And it presently appeared that they were moved by machinery indeed; the figures being those of the patrons of swings, see-saws, flying-leaps, above all of the three steam roundabouts[4] which occupied the centre of the position. It was from the latter that the din of steam-organs came.

Throbbing humanity in full light was, on second thoughts, better than architecture in the dark. The young man, lighting a short pipe, and putting his hat on one side and one hand in his pocket, to throw himself into harmony with his new environment, drew near to the largest and most patronized of the steam circuses, as the roundabouts were called by their owners. This was one of brilliant finish, and it was now in full revolution. The musical instrument around which and to whose tones the riders revolved, directed its trumpet-mouths of brass upon the young man, and the long plate-glass mirrors set at angles, which revolved with the machine, flashed the gyrating person-ages and hobby-horses kaleidoscopically into his eyes.

---

1. When first published in magazine form in England and America in 1891, "On the Western Circuit" was altered to minimize its illicit sexuality. References to Anna's seduction and pregnancy were eliminated, and Mrs. Harnham was made a widow rather than a wife. When Hardy published the story in his collection *Life's Little Ironies* (1894), he restored it to its original form.

The Western Circuit was the subdivision of England's High Court of Justice with jurisdiction over the southwestern counties. In Hardy's literary landscape Melchester is Salisbury, which has a particularly beautiful cathedral.
2. Closed yard surrounding a church.
3. Grassy surface of ground.
4. Carousels.

It could now be seen that he was unlike the majority of the crowd. A gentlemanly young fellow, one of the species found in large towns only, and London particularly, built on delicate lines, well, though not fashionably dressed, he appeared to belong to the professional class; he had nothing square or practical about his look, much that was curvilinear and sensuous. Indeed, some would have called him a man not altogether typical of the middle-class male of a century wherein sordid ambition is the master-passion that seems to be taking the time-honoured place of love.

The revolving figures passed before his eyes with an unexpected and quiet grace in a throng whose natural movements did not suggest gracefulness or quietude as a rule. By some contrivance there was imparted to each of the hobby-horses a motion which was really the triumph and perfection of roundabout inventiveness—a galloping rise and fall, so timed that, of each pair of steeds, one was on the spring while the other was on the pitch. The riders were quite fascinated by these equine undulations in this most delightful holiday-game of our times. There were riders as young as six, and as old as sixty years, with every age between. At first it was difficult to catch a personality, but by and by the observer's eyes centred on the prettiest girl out of the several pretty ones revolving.

It was not that one with the light frock and light hat whom he had been at first attracted by; no, it was the one with the black cape, grey skirt, light gloves and—no, not even she, but the one behind her; she with the crimson skirt, dark jacket, brown hat and brown gloves. Unmistakably that was the prettiest girl.

Having finally selected her, this idle spectator studied her as well as he was able during each of her brief transits across his visual field. She was absolutely unconscious of everything save the act of riding: her features were rapt in an ecstatic dreaminess; for the moment she did not know her age or her history or her lineaments, much less her troubles. He himself was full of vague latter-day glooms and popular melancholies, and it was a refreshing sensation to behold this young thing then and there, absolutely as happy as if she were in a Paradise.

Dreading the moment when the inexorable stoker, grimily lurking behind the glittering rococo-work,[5] should decide that this set of riders had had their pennyworth, and bring the whole concern of steam-engine, horses, mirrors, trumpets, drums, cymbals, and such-like to pause and silence, he waited for her every reappearance, glancing indifferently over the intervening forms, including the two plainer girls, the old woman and child, the two youngsters, the newly-married couple, the old man with a clay pipe, the sparkish youth with a ring, the young ladies in the chariot, the pair of journeyman[6] carpenters, and others, till his select country beauty followed on again in her place. He had never seen a fairer product of nature, and at each round she made a deeper mark in his sentiments. The stoppage then came, and the sighs of the riders were audible.

He moved round to the place at which he reckoned she would alight; but she retained her seat. The empty saddles began to refill, and she plainly was deciding to have another turn. The young man drew up to the side of her steed, and pleasantly asked her if she had enjoyed her ride.

5. Florid ornamentation. "Stoker": man who stokes the furnace powering the "steam circus." 6. Craftsman who has completed an apprentice- ship but not yet attained mastership of his craft or guild.

'O yes!' she said, with dancing eyes. 'It has been quite unlike anything I have ever felt in my life before!'

It was not difficult to fall into conversation with her. Unreserved—too unreserved—by nature, she was not experienced enough to be reserved by art, and after a little coaxing she answered his remarks readily. She had come to live in Melchester from a village on the Great Plain,[7] and this was the first time that she had ever seen a steam-circus; she could not understand how such wonderful machines were made. She had come to the city on the invitation of Mrs Harnham, who had taken her into her household to train her as a servant, if she showed any aptitude. Mrs Harnham was a young lady who before she married had been Miss Edith White, living in the country near the speaker's cottage; she was now very kind to her through knowing her in childhood so well. She was even taking the trouble to educate her. Mrs Harnham was the only friend she had in the world, and being without children had wished to have her near her in preference to anybody else, though she had only lately come; allowed her to do almost as she liked, and to have a holiday whenever she asked for it. The husband of this kind young lady was a rich wine-merchant of the town, but Mrs Harnham did not care much about him. In the daytime you could see the house from where they were talking. She, the speaker, liked Melchester better than the lonely country, and she was going to have a new hat for next Sunday that was to cost fifteen and ninepence.[8]

Then she inquired of her acquaintance where he lived, and he told her in London, that ancient and smoky city, where everybody lived who lived at all, and died because they could not live there. He came into Wessex two or three times a year for professional reasons; he had arrived from Wintoncester yesterday, and was going on into the next county in a day or two. For one thing he did like the country better than the town, and it was because it contained such girls as herself.

Then the pleasure-machine started again, and, to the light-hearted girl, the figure of the handsome young man, the market-square with its lights and crowd, the houses beyond, and the world at large, began moving round as before, countermoving in the revolving mirrors on her right hand, she being as it were the fixed point in an undulating, dazzling, lurid universe, in which loomed forward most prominently of all the form of her late interlocutor. Each time that she approached the half of her orbit that lay nearest him they gazed at each other with smiles, and with that unmistakable expression which means so little at the moment, yet so often leads up to passion, heart-ache, union, disunion, devotion, overpopulation, drudgery, content, resignation, despair.

When the horses slowed anew he stepped to her side and proposed another heat. 'Hang the expense for once,' he said. 'I'll pay!'

She laughed till the tears came.

'Why do you laugh, dear?' said he.

'Because—you are so genteel that you must have plenty of money, and only say that for fun!' she returned.

'Ha-ha!' laughed the young man in unison, and gallantly producing his money she was enabled to whirl on again.

---

7. In Hardy's Wessex the Salisbury Plain, a large plateau on which stands Stonehenge.

8. Approximately one dollar.

As he stood smiling there in the motley crowd, with his pipe in his hand, and clad in the rough pea-jacket and wideawake[9] that he had put on for his stroll, who would have supposed him to be Charles Bradford Raye, Esquire, stuff-gownsman,[1] educated at Wintoncester, called to the Bar at Lincoln's-Inn[2] now going the Western Circuit, merely detained in Melchester by a small arbitration after his brethren had moved on to the next county-town?

II

The square was overlooked from its remoter corner by the house of which the young girl had spoken, a dignified residence of considerable size, having several windows on each floor. Inside one of these, on the first floor, the apartment being a large drawing-room, sat a lady, in appearance from twenty-eight to thirty years of age. The blinds were still undrawn, and the lady was absently surveying the weird scene without, her cheek resting on her hand. The room was unlit from within, but enough of the glare from the market-place entered it to reveal the lady's face. She was what is called an interesting creature rather than a handsome woman; dark-eyed, thoughtful, and with sensitive lips.

A man sauntered into the room from behind and came forward.

'O, Edith, I didn't see you,' he said. 'Why are you sitting here in the dark?'

'I am looking at the fair,' replied the lady in a languid voice.

'Oh? Horrid nuisance every year! I wish it could be put a stop to.'

'I like it.'

'H'm. There's no accounting for taste.'

For a moment he gazed from the window with her, for politeness sake, and then went out again.

In a few minutes she rang.

'Hasn't Anna come in?' asked Mrs Harnham.

'No m'm.'

'She ought to be in by this time. I meant her to go for ten minutes only.'

'Shall I go and look for her, m'm?' said the house-maid alertly.

'No. It is not necessary: she is a good girl and will come soon.'

However, when the servant had gone Mrs Harnham arose, went up to her room, cloaked and bonneted herself, and proceeded downstairs, where she found her husband.

'I want to see the fair,' she said; 'and I am going to look for Anna. I have made myself responsible for her, and must see she comes to no harm. She ought to be indoors. Will you come with me?'

'Oh, she's all right. I saw her on one of those whirligig things, talking to her young man as I came in. But I'll go if you wish, though I'd rather go a hundred miles the other way.'

'Then please do so. I shall come to no harm alone.'

She left the house and entered the crowd which thronged the market-place, where she soon discovered Anna, seated on the revolving horse. As

9. Soft felt hat.
1. A junior counsel, who wears a gown of "stuff" rather than silk; qualified to plead cases in court but not appointed to a senior position.
2. One of the four London Inns of Court, at which lawyers must be trained to qualify for the bar and to which they afterward must belong to practice law. "Wintoncester": Winchester College, the oldest English public school (the equivalent in the American system of an elite private secondary boarding school).

soon as it stopped Mrs Harnham advanced and said severely, 'Anna, how can you be such a wild girl? You were only to be out for ten minutes.'

Anna looked blank, and the young man, who had dropped into the background, came to help her alight.

'Please don't blame her,' he said politely. 'It is my fault that she has stayed. She looked so graceful on the horse that I induced her to go round again. I assure you that she has been quite safe.'

'In that case I'll leave her in your hands,' said Mrs Harnham, turning to retrace her steps.

But this for the moment it was not so easy to do. Something had attracted the crowd to a spot in their rear, and the wine-merchant's wife, caught by its sway, found herself pressed against Anna's acquaintance without power to move away. Their faces were within a few inches of each other, his breath fanned her cheek as well as Anna's. They could do no other than smile at the accident; but neither spoke, and each waited passively. Mrs Harnham then felt a man's hand clasping her fingers, and from the look of consciousness on the young fellow's face she knew the hand to be his: she also knew that from the position of the girl he had no other thought than that the imprisoned hand was Anna's. What prompted her to refrain from undeceiving him she could hardly tell. Not content with holding the hand, he playfully slipped two of his fingers inside her glove, against her palm. Thus matters continued till the pressure lessened; but several minutes passed before the crowd thinned sufficiently to allow Mrs Harnham to withdraw.

'How did they get to know each other, I wonder?' she mused as she retreated. 'Anna is really very forward—and he very wicked and nice.'

She was so gently stirred with the stranger's manner and voice, with the tenderness of his idle touch, that instead of re-entering the house she turned back again and observed the pair from a screened nook. Really she argued (being little less impulsive than Anna herself) it was very excusable in Anna to encourage him, however she might have contrived to make his acquaintance; he was so gentlemanly, so fascinating, had such beautiful eyes. The thought that he was several years her junior produced a reasonless sigh.

At length the couple turned from the roundabout towards the door of Mrs Harnham's house, and the young man could be heard saying that he would accompany her home. Anna, then, had found a lover, apparently a very devoted one. Mrs Harnham was quite interested in him. When they drew near the door of the wine-merchant's house, a comparatively deserted spot by this time, they stood invisible for a little while in the shadow of a wall, where they separated, Anna going on to the entrance, and her acquaintance returning across the square.

'Anna,' said Mrs Harnham, coming up. 'I've been looking at you! That young man kissed you at parting, I am almost sure.'

'Well,' stammered Anna; 'he said, if I didn't mind—it would do me no harm, and, and, him a great deal of good!'

'Ah, I thought so! And he was a stranger till tonight?'

'Yes ma'am.'

'Yet I warrant you told him your name and everything about yourself?'

'He asked me.'

'But he didn't tell you his?'

'Yes ma'am, he did!' cried Anna victoriously. 'It is Charles Bradford, of London.'

'Well, if he's respectable, of course I've nothing to say against your knowing him,' remarked her mistress, prepossessed, in spite of general principles, in the young man's favour. 'But I must reconsider all that, if he attempts to renew your acquaintance. A country-bred girl like you, who has never lived in Melchester till this month, who had hardly ever seen a black-coated man till you came here, to be so sharp as to capture a young Londoner like him!'

'I didn't capture him. I didn't do anything,' said Anna, in confusion.

When she was indoors and alone Mrs Harnham thought what a well-bred and chivalrous young man Anna's companion had seemed. There had been a magic in his wooing touch of her hand; and she wondered how he had come to be attracted by the girl.

The next morning the emotional Edith Harnham went to the usual week-day service in Melchester cathedral. In crossing the Close through the fog she again perceived him who had interested her the previous evening, gazing up thoughtfully at the high-piled architecture of the nave: and as soon as she had taken her seat he entered and sat down in a stall opposite hers.

He did not particularly heed her; but Mrs Harnham was continually occupying her eyes with him, and wondered more than ever what had attracted him in her unfledged maid-servant. The mistress was almost as unaccustomed as the maiden herself to the end-of-the-age young man, or she might have wondered less. Raye, having looked about him awhile, left abruptly, without regard to the service that was proceeding; and Mrs Harnham— lonely, impressionable creature that she was—took no further interest in praising the Lord. She wished she had married a London man who knew the subtleties of lovemaking as they were evidently known to him who had mistakenly caressed her hand.

III

The calendar at Melchester had been light, occupying the court only a few hours; and the assizes[3] at Casterbridge, the next county-town on the Western Circuit, having no business for Raye, he had not gone thither. At the next town after that they did not open till the following Monday, trials to begin on Tuesday morning. In the natural order of things Raye would have arrived at the latter place on Monday afternoon; but it was not till the middle of Wednesday that his gown and grey wig, curled in tiers, in the best fashion of Assyrian bas-reliefs, were seen blowing and bobbing behind him as he hastily walked up the High Street from his lodgings. But though he entered the assize building there was nothing for him to do, and sitting at the blue baize table in the well of the court, he mended pens with a mind far away from the case in progress. Thoughts of unpremeditated conduct, of which a week earlier he would not have believed himself capable, threw him into a mood of dissatisfied depression.

He had contrived to see again the pretty rural maiden Anna, the day after the fair, had walked out of the city with her to the earthworks[4] of Old Melchester, and feeling a violent fancy for her, had remained in Melchester all Sunday, Monday, and Tuesday; by persuasion obtaining walks and

3. Sessions of the superior court. "Calendar": list of cases to be tried.

4. Banks of earth constructed as fortifications in ancient times.

meetings with the girl six or seven times during the interval; had in brief won her, body and soul.

He supposed it must have been owing to the seclusion in which he had lived of late in town that he had given way so unrestrainedly to a passion for an artless creature whose inexperience had, from the first, led her to place herself unreservedly in his hands. Much he deplored trifling with her feelings for the sake of a passing desire; and he could only hope that she might not live to suffer on his account.

She had begged him to come to her again; entreated him; wept. He had promised that he would do so, and he meant to carry out that promise. He could not desert her now. Awkward as such unintentional connections were, the interspace of a hundred miles—which to a girl of her limited capabilities was like a thousand—would effectually hinder this summer fancy from greatly encumbering his life; while thought of her simple love might do him the negative good of keeping him from idle pleasures in town when he wished to work hard. His circuit journeys would take him to Melchester three or four times a year; and then he could always see her.

The pseudonym, or rather partial name, that he had given her as his before knowing how far the acquaintance was going to carry him, had been spoken on the spur of the moment, without any ulterior intention whatever. He had not afterwards disturbed Anna's error, but on leaving her he had felt bound to give her an address at a stationer's not far from his chambers, at which she might write to him under the initials 'C. B'.

In due time Raye returned to his London abode, having called at Melchester on his way and spent a few additional hours with his fascinating child of nature. In town he lived monotonously every day. Often he and his rooms were enclosed by a tawny fog from all the world besides, and when he lighted the gas to read or write by, his situation seemed so unnatural that he would look into the fire and think of that trusting girl at Melchester again and again. Often, oppressed by absurd fondness for her, he would enter the dim religious nave of the Law Courts by the north door, elbow other juniors habited like himself, and like him unretained; edge himself into this or that crowded court where a sensational case was going on, just as if he were in it, though the police officers at the door knew as well as he knew himself that he had no more concern with the business in hand than the patient idlers at the gallery-door outside, who had waited to enter since eight in the morning because, like him, they belonged to the classes that live on expectation. But he would do these things to no purpose, and think how greatly the characters in such scenes contrasted with the pink and breezy Anna.

An unexpected feature in that peasant maiden's conduct was that she had not as yet written to him, though he had told her she might do so if she wished. Surely a young creature had never before been so reticent in such circumstances. At length he sent her a brief line, positively requesting her to write. There was no answer by the return post, but the day after a letter in a neat feminine hand, and bearing the Melchester post-mark, was handed to him by the stationer.

The fact alone of its arrival was sufficient to satisfy his imaginative sentiment. He was not anxious to open the epistle, and in truth did not begin to read it for nearly half-an-hour, anticipating readily its terms of passionate retrospect and tender adjuration. When at last he turned his feet to the fireplace and unfolded the sheet, he was surprised and pleased to find that neither extravagance nor vulgarity was there. It was the most charming little missive he had ever received from woman. To be sure the language was simple and the ideas were slight; but it was so self-possessed; so purely that of a young girl who felt her womanhood to be enough for her dignity that he read it through twice. Four sides were filled, and a few lines written across, after the fashion of former days; the paper, too, was common, and not of the latest shade and surface. But what of those things? He had received letters from women who were fairly called ladies, but never so sensible, so human a letter as this. He could not single out any one sentence and say it was at all remarkable or clever; the *ensemble* of the letter it was which won him; and beyond the one request that he would write or come to her again soon there was nothing to show her sense of a claim upon him.

To write again and develop a correspondence was the last thing Raye would have preconceived as his conduct in such a situation; yet he did send a short, encouraging line or two, signed with his pseudonym, in which he asked for another letter, and cheeringly promised that he would try to see her again on some near day, and would never forget how much they had been to each other during their short acquaintance.

IV

To return now to the moment at which Anna, at Melchester, had received Raye's letter.

It had been put into her own hand by the postman on his morning rounds. She flushed down to her neck on receipt of it, and turned it over and over. 'It is mine?' she said.

'Why, yes, can't you see it is?' said the postman, smiling as he guessed the nature of the document and the cause of the confusion.

'O yes, of course!' replied Anna, looking at the letter, forcedly tittering, and blushing still more.

Her look of embarrassment did not leave her with the postman's departure. She opened the envelope, kissed its contents, put away the letter in her pocket, and remained musing till her eyes filled with tears.

A few minutes later she carried up a cup of tea to Mrs Harnham in her bedchamber. Anna's mistress looked at her, and said: 'How dismal you seem this morning, Anna. What's the matter?'

'I'm not dismal, I'm glad; only I—' She stopped to stifle a sob.

'Well?'

'I've got a letter—and what good is it to me, if I can't read a word in it!'

'Why, I'll read it, child, if necessary.'

'But this is from somebody—I don't want anybody to read it but myself!' Anna murmured.

'I shall not tell anybody. Is it from that young man?'

'I think so.' Anna slowly produced the letter, saying: 'Then will you read it to me, ma'am?'

This was the secret of Anna's embarrassment and flutterings. She could neither read nor write. She had grown up under the care of an aunt by marriage, at one of the lonely hamlets on the Great Mid-Wessex Plain where, even in days of national education, there had been no school within a distance of two miles. Her aunt was an ignorant woman; there had been nobody to investigate Anna's circumstances, nobody to care about her learning the rudiments; though, as often in such cases, she had been well fed and clothed and not unkindly treated. Since she had come to live at Melchester with Mrs Harnham, the latter, who took a kindly interest in the girl, had taught her to speak correctly, in which accomplishment Anna showed considerable readiness, as is not unusual with the illiterate; and soon became quite fluent in the use of her mistress's phraseology. Mrs Harnham also insisted upon her getting a spelling and copy book, and beginning to practise in these. Anna was slower in this branch of her education, and meanwhile here was the letter.

Edith Harnham's large dark eyes expressed some interest in the contents, though, in her character of mere interpreter, she threw into her tone as much as she could of mechanical passiveness. She read the short epistle on to its concluding sentence, which idly requested Anna to send him a tender answer.

'Now—you'll do it for me, won't you, dear mistress?' said Anna eagerly. 'And you'll do it as well as ever you can, please? Because I couldn't bear him to think I am not able to do it myself. I should sink into the earth with shame if he knew that!'

From some words in the letter Mrs Harnham was led to ask questions, and the answers she received confirmed her suspicions. Deep concern filled Edith's heart at perceiving how the girl had committed her happiness to the issue of this new-sprung attachment. She blamed herself for not interfering in a flirtation which had resulted so seriously for the poor little creature in her charge; though at the time of seeing the pair together she had a feeling that it was hardly within her province to nip young affection in the bud. However, what was done could not be undone, and it behoved her now, as Anna's only protector, to help her as much as she could. To Anna's eager request that she, Mrs Harnham, should compose and write the answer to this young London man's letter, she felt bound to accede, to keep alive his attachment to the girl if possible; though in other circumstances she might have suggested the cook as an amanuensis.[5]

A tender reply was thereupon concocted, and set down in Edith Harnham's hand. This letter it had been which Raye had received and delighted in. Written in the presence of Anna it certainly was, and on Anna's humble notepaper, and in a measure indited by the young girl; but the life, the spirit, the individuality, were Edith Harnham's.

'Won't you at least put your name yourself?' she said. 'You can manage to write that by this time?'

'No, no,' said Anna, shrinking back. 'I should do it so bad. He'd be ashamed of me, and never see me again!'

The note, so prettily requesting another from him, had, as we have seen, power enough in its pages to bring one. He declared it to be such a pleasure to hear from her that she must write every week. The same process of manufacture was accordingly repeated by Anna and her mistress, and continued for several weeks in succession; each letter being penned and suggested by Edith, the girl standing by; the answer read and commented on by Edith, Anna standing by and listening again.

Late on a winter evening, after the dispatch of the sixth letter, Mrs Harnham was sitting alone by the remains of her fire. Her husband had retired to bed, and she had fallen into that fixity of musing which takes no count of hour or temperature. The state of mind had been brought about in Edith by

5. Secretary.

a strange thing which she had done that day. For the first time since Raye's visit Anna had gone to stay over a night or two with her cottage friends on the Plain, and in her absence had arrived, out of its time, a letter from Raye. To this Edith had replied on her own responsibility, from the depths of her own heart, without waiting for her maid's collaboration. The luxury of writing to him what would be known to no consciousness but his was great, and she had indulged herself therein.

Why was it a luxury?

Edith Harnham led a lonely life. Influenced by the belief of the British parent that a bad marriage with its aversions is better than free woman-hood with its interests, dignity, and leisure, she had consented to marry the elderly wine-merchant as a *pis aller*,[6] at the age of seven-and-twenty—some three years before this date—to find afterwards that she had made a mis-take. That contract had left her still a woman whose deeper nature had never been stirred.

She was now clearly realising that she had become possessed to the bottom of her soul with the image of a man to whom she was hardly so much as a name. From the first he had attracted her by his looks and voice; by his tender touch; and, with these as generators, the writing of letter after letter and the reading of their soft answers had insensibly developed on her side an emotion which fanned his; till there had resulted a magnetic reciprocity between the correspondents, notwithstanding that one of them wrote in a character not her own. That he had been able to seduce another woman in two days was his crowning though unrecognised fascination for her as the she-animal.

They were her own impassioned and pent-up ideas—lowered to monosyl-labic phraseology in order to keep up the disguise—that Edith put into let-ters signed with another name, much to the shallow Anna's delight, who, unassisted, could not for the world have conceived such pretty fancies for winning him, even had she been able to write them. Edith found that it was these, her own foisted-in sentiments, to which the young barrister mainly responded. The few sentences occasionally added from Anna's own lips made apparently no impression upon him.

The letter-writing in her absence Anna never discovered; but on her return the next morning she declared she wished to see her lover about something at once, and begged Mrs Harnham to ask him to come.

There was a strange anxiety in her manner which did not escape Mrs Harnham, and ultimately resolved itself into a flood of tears. Sinking down at Edith's knees, she made confession that the result of her relations with her lover it would soon become necessary to disclose.

Edith Harnham was generous enough to be very far from inclined to cast Anna adrift at this conjuncture. No true woman ever is so inclined from her own personal point of view, however prompt she may be in taking such steps to safeguard those dear to her. Although she had written to Raye so short a time previously, she instantly penned another Anna-note hinting clearly though delicately the state of affairs.

Raye replied by a hasty line to say how much he was concerned at her news: he felt that he must run down to see her almost immediately.

But a week later the girl came to her mistress's room with another note, which on being read informed her that after all he could not find time for

6. Last resort (French).

the journey. Anna was broken with grief; but by Mrs Harnham's counsel strictly refrained from hurling at him the reproaches and bitterness customary from young women so situated. One thing was imperative: to keep the young man's romantic interest in her alive. Rather therefore did Edith, in the name of her *protégée*, request him on no account to be distressed about the looming event, and not to inconvenience himself to hasten down. She desired above everything to be no weight upon him in his career, no clog upon his high activities. She had wished him to know what had befallen: he was to dismiss it again from his mind. Only he must write tenderly as ever, and when he should come again on the spring circuit it would be soon enough to discuss what had better be done.

It may well be supposed that Anna's own feelings had not been quite in accord with these generous expressions; but the mistress's judgment had ruled, and Anna had acquiesced. 'All I want is that *niceness* you can so well put into your letters, my dear, dear mistress, and that I can't for the life o' me make up out of my own head; though I mean the same thing and feel it exactly when you've written it down!'

When the letter had been sent off, and Edith Harnham was left alone, she bowed herself on the back of her chair and wept.

'I wish his child was mine—I wish it was!' she murmured. 'Yet how can I say such a wicked thing!'

V

The letter moved Raye considerably when it reached him. The intelligence itself had affected him less than her unexpected manner of treating him in relation to it. The absence of any word of reproach, the devotion to his interests, the self-sacrifice apparent in every line, all made up a nobility of character that he had never dreamt of finding in womankind.

'God forgive me!' he said tremulously. 'I have been a wicked wretch. I did not know she was such a treasure as this!'

He reassured her instantly; declaring that he would not of course desert her, that he would provide a home for her somewhere. Meanwhile she was to stay where she was as long as her mistress would allow her.

But a misfortune supervened in this direction. Whether an inkling of Anna's circumstances reached the knowledge of Mrs Harnham's husband or not cannot be said, but the girl was compelled, in spite of Edith's entreaties, to leave the house. By her own choice she decided to go back for a while to the cottage on the Plain. This arrangement led to a consultation as to how the correspondence should be carried on; and in the girl's inability to continue personally what had been begun in her name, and in the difficulty of their acting in concert as heretofore, she requested Mrs Harnham—the only well-to-do friend she had in the world—to receive the letters and reply to them off-hand, sending them on afterwards to herself on the Plain, where she might at least get some neighbour to read them to her, if a trustworthy one could be met with. Anna and her box then departed for the Plain.

Thus it befell that Edith Harnham found herself in the strange position of having to correspond, under no supervision by the real woman, with a man not her husband, in terms which were virtually those of a wife, concerning a corporeal condition that was not Edith's at all; the man being one for whom, mainly through the sympathies involved in playing this part, she secretly cherished a predilection, subtle and imaginative truly, but strong and absorbing. She opened each letter, read it as if intended for herself, and replied from the promptings of her own heart and no other.

Throughout this correspondence, carried on in the girl's absence, the high-strung Edith Harnham lived in the ecstasy of fancy; the vicarious intimacy engendered such a flow of passionateness as was never exceeded. For conscience' sake Edith at first sent on each of his letters to Anna, and even rough copies of her replies; but later on these so-called copies were much abridged, and many letters on both sides were not sent on at all.

Though sensuous, and, superficially at least, infested with the self-indulgent vices of artificial society, there was a substratum of honesty and fairness in Raye's character. He had really a tender regard for the country girl, and it grew more tender than ever when he found her apparently capable of expressing the deepest sensibilities in the simplest words. He meditated, he wavered; and finally resolved to consult his sister, a maiden lady much older than himself, of lively sympathies and good intent. In making this confidence he showed her some of the letters.

'She seems fairly educated,' Miss Raye observed. 'And bright in ideas. She expresses herself with a taste that must be innate.'

'Yes. She writes very prettily, doesn't she, thanks to these elementary schools?'

'One is drawn out towards her, in spite of one's self, poor thing.'

The upshot of the discussion was that though he had not been directly advised to do it, Raye wrote, in his real name, what he would never have decided to write on his own responsibility; namely that he could not live without her, and would come down in the spring and shelve her looming difficulty by marrying her.

This bold acceptance of the situation was made known to Anna by Mrs Harnham driving out immediately to the cottage on the Plain. Anna jumped for joy like a little child. And poor, crude directions for answering appropriately were given to Edith Harnham, who on her return to the city carried them out with warm intensifications.

'O!' she groaned, as she threw down the pen. 'Anna—poor good little fool—hasn't intelligence enough to appreciate him! How should she? While I—don't bear his child!'

It was now February. The correspondence had continued altogether for four months; and the next letter from Raye contained incidentally a statement of his position and prospects. He said that in offering to wed her he had, at first, contemplated the step of retiring from a profession which hitherto had brought him very slight emolument, and which, to speak plainly, he had thought might be difficult of practice after his union with her. But the unexpected mines of brightness and warmth that her letters had disclosed to be lurking in her sweet nature had led him to abandon that somewhat sad prospect. He felt sure that, with her powers of development, after a little private training in the social forms of London under his supervision, and a little help from a governess if necessary, she would make as good a professional man's wife as could be desired, even if he should rise to the woolsack.[7] Many a Lord Chancellor's wife had been less intuitively a lady than she had shown herself to be in her lines to him.

7. Seat of the Lord Chancellor in the House of Lords, formerly made of a sack of wool.

'O—poor fellow, poor fellow!' mourned Edith Harnham.

Her distress now raged as high as her infatuation. It was she who had wrought him to this pitch—to a marriage which meant his ruin; yet she could not, in mercy to her maid, do anything to hinder his plan. Anna was coming to Melchester that week, but she could hardly show the girl this last reply from the young man; it told too much of the second individuality that had usurped the place of the first.

Anna came, and her mistress took her into her own room for privacy. Anna began by saying with some anxiety that she was glad the wedding was so near.

'O Anna!' replied Mrs Harnham. 'I think we must tell him all—that I have been doing your writing for you?—lest he should not know it till after you become his wife, and it might lead to dissension and recriminations—'

'O mis'ess, dear mis'ess—please don't tell him now!' cried Anna in distress. 'If you were to do it, perhaps he would not marry me; and what should I do then? It would be terrible what would come to me! And I am getting on with my writing, too. I have brought with me the copybook you were so good as to give me, and I practise every day, and though it is so, so hard, I shall do it well at last, I believe, if I keep on trying.'

Edith looked at the copybook. The copies had been set by herself, and such progress as the girl had made was in the way of grotesque facsimile of her mistress's hand. But even if Edith's flowing calligraphy were reproduced the inspiration would be another thing.

'You do it so beautifully,' continued Anna, 'and say all that I want to say so much better than I could say it, that I do hope you won't leave me in the lurch just now!'

'Very well,' replied the other. 'But I—but I thought I ought not to go on!'

'Why?'

Her strong desire to confide her sentiments led Edith to answer truly:

'Because of its effect upon me.'

'But it *can't* have any!'

'Why, child?'

'Because you are married already!' said Anna with lucid simplicity.

'Of course it can't,' said her mistress hastily; yet glad, despite her conscience, that two or three out-pourings still remained to her. 'But you must concentrate your attention on writing your name as I write it here.'

VI

Soon Raye wrote about the wedding. Having decided to make the best of what he feared was a piece of romantic folly, he had acquired more zest for the grand experiment. He wished the ceremony to be in London, for greater privacy. Edith Harnham would have preferred it at Melchester; Anna was passive. His reasoning prevailed, and Mrs Harnham threw herself with mournful zeal into the preparations for Anna's departure. In a last desperate feeling that she must at every hazard be in at the death of her dream, and see once again the man who by a species of telepathy had exercised such an influence on her, she offered to go up with Anna and be with her through the ceremony—'to see the end of her,' as her mistress put it with forced gaiety; an offer which the girl gratefully accepted; for she had no other friend capable of playing the part of companion and witness, in the presence of a gentlemanly bridegroom, in such a way as not to hasten an opinion that he had made an irremediable social blunder.

It was a muddy morning in March when Raye alighted from a four-wheel cab at the door of a registry-office in the S.W. district of London, and carefully handed down Anna and her companion Mrs Harnham. Anna looked attractive in the somewhat fashionable clothes which Mrs Harnham had helped her to buy, though not quite so attractive as, an innocent child, she had appeared in her country gown on the back of the wooden horse at Melchester Fair.

Mrs Harnham had come up this morning by an early train, and a young man—a friend of Raye's—having met them at the door, all four entered the registry-office together. Till an hour before this time Raye had never known the wine-merchant's wife, except at that first casual encounter, and in the flutter of the performance before them he had little opportunity for more than a brief acquaintance. The contract of marriage at a registry is soon got through; but somehow, during its progress, Raye discovered a strange and secret gravitation between himself and Anna's friend.

The formalities of the wedding—or rather ratification of a previous union—being concluded, the four went in one cab to Raye's lodgings, newly taken in a new suburb in preference to a house, the rent of which he could ill afford just then. Here Anna cut the little cake which Raye had bought at a pastry-cook's on his way home from Lincoln's Inn the night before. But she did not do much besides. Raye's friend was obliged to depart almost immediately, and when he had left the only ones virtually present were Edith and Raye, who exchanged ideas with much animation. The conversation was indeed theirs only, Anna being as a domestic animal who humbly heard but understood not. Raye seemed startled in awakening to this fact, and began to feel dissatisfied with her inadequacy.

At last, more disappointed than he cared to own, he said, 'Mrs Harnham, my darling is so flurried that she doesn't know what she is doing or saying. I see that after this event a little quietude will be necessary before she gives tongue to that tender philosophy which she used to treat me to in her letters.'

They had planned to start early that afternoon for Knollsea, to spend the few opening days of their married life there, and as the hour for departure was drawing near Raye asked his wife if she would go to the writing-desk in the next room and scribble a little note to his sister, who had been unable to attend through indisposition, informing her that the ceremony was over, thanking her for her little present, and hoping to know her well now that she was the writer's sister as well as Charles's.

'Say it in the pretty poetical way you know so well how to adopt,' he added, 'for I want you particularly to win her, and both of you to be dear friends.'

Anna looked uneasy, but departed to her task, Raye remaining to talk to their guest. Anna was a long while absent, and her husband suddenly rose and went to her.

He found her still bending over the writing-table, with tears brimming up in her eyes; and he looked down upon the sheet of note-paper with some interest, to discover with what tact she had expressed her good-will in the delicate circumstances. To his surprise she had progressed but a few lines, in the characters and spelling of a child of eight, and with the ideas of a goose.

'Anna,' he said, staring; 'what's this?'

'It only means—that I can't do it any better!' she answered, through her tears.

'Eh? Nonsense!'

'I can't!' she insisted, with miserable, sobbing hardihood. 'I—I—didn't write those letters, Charles! I only told *her* what to write! And not always that! But I am learning, O so fast, my dear, dear husband! And you'll forgive me, won't you, for not telling you before?' She slid to her knees, abjectly clasped his waist and laid her face against him.

He stood a few moments, raised her, abruptly turned, and shut the door upon her, rejoining Edith in the drawing-room. She saw that something untoward had been discovered, and their eyes remained fixed on each other.

'Do I guess rightly?' he asked, with wan quietude. '*You* were her scribe through all this?'

'It was necessary,' said Edith.

'Did she dictate every word you ever wrote to me?'

'Not every word.'

'In fact, very little?'

'Very little.'

'You wrote a great part of those pages every week from your own conceptions, though in her name!'

'Yes.'

'Perhaps you wrote many of the letters when you were alone, without communication with her?'

'I did.'

He turned to the bookcase, and leant with his hand over his face; and Edith, seeing his distress, became white as a sheet.

'You have deceived me—ruined me!' he murmured.

'O, don't say it!' she cried in her anguish, jumping up and putting her hand on his shoulder. 'I can't bear that!'

'Delighting me deceptively! Why did you do it—*why* did you!'

'I began doing it in kindness to her! How could I do otherwise than try to save such a simple girl from misery? But I admit that I continued it for pleasure to myself.'

Raye looked up. 'Why did it give you pleasure?' he asked.

'I must not tell,' said she.

He continued to regard her, and saw that her lips suddenly began to quiver under his scrutiny, and her eyes to fill and droop. She started aside, and said that she must go to the station to catch the return train: could a cab be called immediately?

But Raye went up to her, and took her unresisting hand. 'Well, to think of such a thing as this!' he said. 'Why, you and I are friends—lovers—devoted lovers—by correspondence!'

'Yes; I suppose.'

'More.'

'More?'

'Plainly more. It is no use blinking that. Legally I have married her—God help us both!—in soul and spirit I have married you, and no other woman in the world!'

'Hush!'

'But I will not hush! Why should you try to disguise the full truth, when you have already owned half of it? Yes, it is between you and me that the bond is—not between me and her! Now I'll say no more. But, O my cruel one, I think I have one claim upon you!'

She did not say what, and he drew her towards him, and bent over her. 'If it was all pure invention in those letters,' he said emphatically, 'give me your cheek only. If you meant what you said, let it be lips. It is for the first and last time, remember!'

She put up her mouth, and he kissed her long. 'You forgive me?' she said, crying.

'Yes.'

'But you are ruined!'

'What matter!' he said, shrugging his shoulders. 'It serves me right!'

She withdrew, wiped her eyes, entered and bade good-bye to Anna, who had not expected her to go so soon, and was still wrestling with the letter. Raye followed Edith downstairs, and in three minutes she was in a hansom driving to the Waterloo station.

He went back to his wife. 'Never mind the letter, Anna, to-day,' he said gently. 'Put on your things. We, too, must be off shortly.'

The simple girl, upheld by the sense that she was indeed married, showed her delight at finding that he was as kind as ever after the disclosure. She did not know that before his eyes he beheld as it were a galley, in which he, the fastidious urban, was chained to work for the remainder of his life, with her, the unlettered peasant, chained to his side.

Edith travelled back to Melchester that day with a face that showed the very stupor of grief, her lips still tingling from the desperate pressure of his kiss. The end of her impassioned dream had come. When at dusk she reached the Melchester station her husband was there to meet her, but in his perfunctoriness and her preoccupation they did not see each other, and she went out of the station alone.

She walked mechanically homewards without calling a fly.[8] Entering, she could not bear the silence of the house, and went up in the dark to where Anna had slept, where she remained thinking awhile. She then returned to the drawing-room, and not knowing what she did, crouched down upon the floor.

'I have ruined him!' she kept repeating. 'I have ruined him; because I would not deal treacherously towards her!'

In the course of half an hour a figure opened the door of the apartment.

'Ah—who's that?' she said, starting up, for it was dark.

'Your husband—who should it be?' said the worthy merchant.

'Ah—my husband!—I forgot I had a husband!' she whispered to herself.

'I missed you at the station,' he continued. 'Did you see Anna safely tied up? I hope so, for 'twas time.'

'Yes—Anna is married.'

Simultaneously with Edith's journey home Anna and her husband were sitting at the opposite windows of a second-class carriage which sped along to Knollsea. In his hand was a pocket-book full of creased sheets closely written over. Unfolding them one after another he read them in silence, and sighed.

'What are you doing, dear Charles?' she said timidly from the other window, and drew nearer to him as if he were a god.

'Reading over all those sweet letters to me signed "Anna,"' he replied with dreary resignation.

1891

8. Carriage.

Hap[1]

If but some vengeful god would call to me
From up the sky, and laugh: 'Thou suffering thing,
Know that thy sorrow is my ecstasy,
That thy love's loss is my hate's profiting!'

5   Then would I bear it, clench myself, and die,
Steeled by the sense of ire unmerited;
Half-eased in that a Powerfuller than I
Had willed and meted me the tears I shed.

But not so. How arrives it joy lies slain,
10 And why unblooms the best hope ever sown?
—Crass Casualty obstructs the sun and rain,
And dicing Time for gladness casts a moan. . . .
These purblind Doomsters[2] had as readily strown
Blisses about my pilgrimage as pain.

1866   1898

Neutral Tones

We stood by a pond that winter day,
And the sun was white, as though chidden of° God,   *rebuked by*
And a few leaves lay on the starving sod;
   —They had fallen from an ash, and were gray.

5   Your eyes on me were as eyes that rove
Over tedious riddles of years ago;
And some words played between us to and fro
   On which lost the more by our love.

The smile on your mouth was the deadest thing
10 Alive enough to have strength to die;
And a grin of bitterness swept thereby
   Like an ominous bird a-wing . . .

Since then, keen lessons that love deceives,
And wrings with wrong, have shaped to me
15 Your face, and the God-curst sun, and a tree,
   And a pond edged with grayish leaves.

1867   1898

---

1. I.e., chance (as also "Casualty," line 11).
2. Half-blind judges.

Drummer Hodge

1

They throw in Drummer Hodge, to rest
    Uncoffined—just as found:
His landmark is a kopje-crest
    That breaks the veldt[1] around;
5   And foreign constellations[2] west°   *set*
    Each night above his mound.

2

Young Hodge the Drummer never knew—
    Fresh from his Wessex home—
The meaning of the broad Karoo,[3]
10   The Bush,[4] the dusty loam,
And why uprose to nightly view
    Strange stars amid the gloam.

3

Yet portion of that unknown plain
    Will Hodge for ever be;
15   His homely Northern breast and brain
    Grow to some Southern tree,
And strange-eyed constellations reign
    His stars eternally.

1899, 1901

The Darkling[1] Thrush

I leant upon a coppice gate[2]
    When Frost was spectre-gray,
And Winter's dregs made desolate
    The weakening eye of day.
5   The tangled bine-stems[3] scored the sky
    Like strings of broken lyres,
And all mankind that haunted nigh°   *near*
    Had sought their household fires.

The land's sharp features seemed to be
10   The Century's corpse outleant,[4]
    His crypt the cloudy canopy,

---

1. South African Dutch (Afrikaans) word for a plain or prairie. "Kopje-crest": Afrikaans for a small hill. The poem is a lament for an English soldier killed in the Anglo-Boer War (1899–1902).
2. Those visible only in the Southern Hemisphere.
3. A dry tableland region in South Africa (usually spelled "Karroo").

4. British colonial word for an uncleared area of land.
1. In the dark.
2. Gate leading to a small wood or thicket.
3. Twining stems of shrubs.
4. Leaning out (of its coffin); i.e., the 19th century was dead. This poem was dated December 31, 1900.

        The wind his death-lament.
      The ancient pulse of germ and birth
        Was shrunken hard and dry,
15   And every spirit upon earth
        Seemed fervourless as I.

      At once a voice arose among
        The bleak twigs overhead
      In a full-hearted evensong
20   Of joy illimited;
      An aged thrush, frail, gaunt, and small,
        In blast-beruffled plume,
      Had chosen thus to fling his soul
        Upon the growing gloom.

25   So little cause for carolings
        Of such ecstatic sound
      Was written on terrestrial things
        Afar or nigh around,
      That I could think there trembled through
30   His happy good-night air
      Some blessed Hope, whereof he knew
        And I was unaware.

                     1900, 1901

The Ruined Maid

'O 'Melia,[1] my dear, this does everything crown!
Who could have supposed I should meet you in Town?
And whence such fair garments, such prosperi-ty?'—
'O didn't you know I'd been ruined?' said she.

5   —'You left us in tatters, without shoes or socks,
Tired of digging potatoes, and spudding up docks;[2]
And now you've gay bracelets and bright feathers three!'—
'Yes: that's how we dress when we're ruined,' said she.

    —'At home in the barton° you said "thee" and "thou",   *farmyard*
10 And "thik oon", and "theäs oon", and "t'other"; but now
Your talking quite fits 'ee° for high compa-ny!'—   *thee*
'Some polish is gained with one's ruin,' said she.

    —'Your hands were like paws then, your face blue and bleak
But now I'm bewitched by your delicate cheek,
15 And your little gloves fit as on any la-dy!'—
'We never do work when we're ruined,' said she.

    —'You used to call home-life a hag-ridden dream,
And you'd sigh, and you'd sock;° but at present you seem   *sigh*

---

1. Diminutive form of Amelia.   2. Digging up a species of thick-rooted weed.

To know not of megrims° or melancho-ly!'—   *low spirits*
20   'True. One's pretty lively when ruined,' said she.

—'I wish I had feathers, a fine sweeping gown,
And a delicate face, and could strut about Town!'—
'My dear—a raw country girl, such as you be,
Cannot quite expect that. You ain't ruined,' said she.

1866   1901

A Trampwoman's Tragedy

(182–)

I

From Wynyard's Gap¹ the livelong day,
        The livelong day,
We beat afoot the northward way
        We had travelled times before.
5   The sun-blaze burning on our backs,
Our shoulders sticking to our packs,
By fosseway,² fields, and turnpike tracks
        We skirted sad Sedge-Moor³

2

Full twenty miles we jaunted on,
10   We jaunted on,—
My fancy-man, and jeering John,
        And Mother Lee, and I.
And, as the sun drew down to west,
We climbed the toilsome Poldon crest,
15   And saw, of landskip° sights the best,   *landscape*
        The inn that beamed thereby.

3

For months we had padded side by side,
        Ay, side by side
Through the Great Forest, Blackmoor wide,
20   And where the Parret ran,
We'd faced the gusts on Mendip ridge,
Had crossed the Yeo unhelped by bridge,
Been stung by every Marshwood midge,
        I and my fancy-man.

1. The places named are in Somerset, in south-west England on the northern edge of the area that Hardy called "Wessex" and of which his native Dorset, the county south and southwest of Somerset, reaching to the English Channel, was the major part.

2. Path running along a ditch.
3. Sad because of the Battle of Sedgemoor (1685), when the rebellion of the duke of Monmouth against James II was crushed with excessive cruelty.

4

25 Lone inns we loved, my man and I,
  My man and I;
'King's Stag', 'Windwhistle'⁴ high and dry,
  'The Horse' on Hintock Green,
The cozy house at Wynyard's Gap,
30 'The Hut' renowned on Bredy Knap,
And many another wayside tap°   *taproom, inn*
  Where folk might sit unseen.

5

Now as we trudged—O deadly day,
  O deadly day!—
35 I teased my fancy-man in play
  And wanton idleness.
I walked alongside jeering John,
I laid his hand my waist upon;
I would not bend my glances on
40   My lover's dark distress.

6

Thus Poldon top at last we won,
  At last we won,
And gained the inn at sink of sun
  Far-famed as 'Marshal's Elm'⁵
45 Beneath us figured tor and lea,⁶
From Mendip to the western sea—
I doubt if finer sight there be
  Within this royal realm.

7

Inside the settle all a-row—
50   All four a-row
We sat, I next to John, to show
  That he had wooed and won.
And then he took me on his knee,
And swore it was his turn to be
55 My favoured mate, and Mother Lee
  Passed to my former one.

---

4. The highness and dryness of Windwhistle Inn was impressed upon the writer two or three years ago, when, after climbing on a hot afternoon to the beautiful spot near which it stands and entering the inn for tea, he was informed by the landlady that none could be had, unless he would fetch water from a valley half a mile off, the house containing not a drop, owing to its situation. However, a tantalizing row of full barrels behind her back testified to a wetness of a certain sort, which was not at that time desired [Hardy's note].

5. "Marshal's Elm," so picturesquely situated, is no longer an inn, though the house, or part of it, still remains. It used to exhibit a fine old swinging sign [Hardy's note].

6. Rocky hill and tract of open ground.

8

Then in a voice I had never heard,
  I had never heard,
My only Love to me: 'One word,
60   My lady, if you please!
Whose is the child you are like to bear?—
His? After all my months o' care?'
God knows 'twas not! But, O despair!
  I nodded—still to tease.

9

65 Then up he sprung, and with his knife—
  And with his knife
He let out jeering Johnny's life,
  Yes; there, at set of sun.
The slant ray through the window nigh
70 Gilded John's blood and glazing eye,
Ere scarcely Mother Lee and I
  Knew that the deed was done.

10

The taverns tell the gloomy tale,
  The gloomy tale,
75 How that at Ivel-chester jail
  My Love, my sweetheart swung;
Though stained till now by no misdeed
Save one horse ta'en in time o' need;
(Blue Jimmy stole right many a steed
80 Ere his last fling he flung).[7]

11

Thereaft I walked the world alone,
  Alone, alone!
On his death-day I gave my groan
  And dropt his dead-born child.
85 'Twas nigh° the jail, beneath a tree,   *near*
None tending me; for Mother Lee
Had died at Glaston, leaving me
  Unfriended on the wild.

---

7. "Blue Jimmy" was a notorious horse stealer of Wessex in those days, who appropriated more than a hundred horses before he was caught, among others one belonging to a neighbor of the writer's grandfather. He was hanged at the now demolished Ivel-chester or Ilchester jail above mentioned—that building formerly of so many sinister associations in the minds of the local peasantry, and the continual haunt of fever, which at last led to its condemnation. Its site is now an innocent-looking green meadow [Hardy's note].

12

And in the night as I lay weak,
90   As I lay weak,
The leaves a-falling on my cheek,
        The red moon low declined—
The ghost of him I'd die to kiss
Rose up and said: 'Ah, tell me this!
95 Was the child mine, or was it his?
        Speak, that I rest may find!'

13

O doubt not but I told him then,
        I told him then,
That I had kept me from all men
100   Since we joined lips and swore.
Whereat he smiled, and thinned away
As the wind stirred to call up day . . .
—'Tis past! And here alone I stray
        Haunting the Western Moor.

Apr. 1902   1909

One We Knew

(M. H.[1] 1772–1857)

She told how they used to form for the country dances—
    'The Triumph,' 'The New-rigged Ship'—
To the light of the guttering wax in the panelled manses,
    And in cots to the blink of a dip.[2]

5 She spoke of the wild 'poussetting' and 'allemanding'[3]
    On carpet, on oak, and on sod;°   turf
And the two long rows of ladies and gentlemen standing,
    And the figures the couples trod.

She showed us the spot where the maypole was yearly planted,
10   And where the bandsmen stood
While breeched and kerchiefed partners whirled, and panted
    To choose each other for good.[4]

She told of that far-back day when they learnt astounded
    Of the death of the King of France:
15 Of the Terror; and then of Bonaparte's unbounded
    Ambition and arrogance.

1. Hardy's grandmother.
2. I.e., in cottages by the light of a candle.
3. Allemande is the name of a dance originating
in Germany. To pousette is to dance round with
hands joined.

4. A tall pole, gaily painted and decorated with
flowers and ribbons ("the maypole"), was danced
around on May 1 by men (wearing "breeches," or
trousers) and women (wearing "kerchiefs," or
headscarves).

Of how his threats woke warlike preparations
    Along the southern strand,
And how each night brought tremors and trepidations
20   Lest morning should see him land.

She said she had often heard the gibbet creaking
    As it swayed in the lightning flash,
Had caught from the neighbouring town a small child's shrieking
    At the cart-tail under the lash. . . .

25 With cap-framed face and long gaze into the embers—
        We seated around her knees—
    She would dwell on such dead themes, not as one who remembers,
        But rather as one who sees.

    She seemed one left behind of a band gone distant
30   So far that no tongue could hail:
    Past things retold were to her as things existent,
        Things present but as a tale.

May 20, 1902   1909

Channel Firing[1]

That night your great guns, unawares,
Shook all our coffins as we lay,
And broke the chancel[2] window-squares,
We thought it was the Judgement-day

5   And sat upright. While drearisome
    Arose the howl of wakened hounds:
    The mouse let fall the altar-crumb,
    The worms drew back into the mounds,

    The glebe cow[3] drooled. Till God called, 'No;
10 It's gunnery practise out at sea
    Just as before you went below;
    The world is as it used to be:

    'All nations striving strong to make
    Red war yet redder. Mad as hatters[4]
15 They do no more for Christès[5] sake
    Than you who are helpless in such matters.

---

1. Written in April 1914, when Anglo-German naval rivalry was growing steadily more acute; the title refers to gunnery practice in the English Channel. Four months later (August 4), World War I broke out.
2. Part of church nearest to the altar.
3. I.e., cow on a small plot of land belonging to a church (a "glebe" is a small field).
4. Cf. the Mad Hatter in Lewis Carroll's *Alice's Adventures in Wonderland* (1865).
5. The archaic spelling and pronunciation suggest a ballad note of doom.

'That this is not the judgement-hour
For some of them's a blessed thing,
For if it were they'd have to scour
20   Hell's floor for so much threatening. . . .

'Ha, ha. It will be warmer when
I blow the trumpet (if indeed
I ever do; for you are men,
And rest eternal sorely need).'

25   So down we lay again. 'I wonder,
Will the world ever saner be,'
Said one, 'than when He sent us under
In our indifferent century!'

And many a skeleton shook his head.
30   'Instead of preaching forty year,'
My neighbour Parson Thirdly said,
'I wish I had stuck to pipes and beer.'

Again the guns disturbed the hour,
Roaring their readiness to avenge,
35   As far inland as Stourton Tower,
And Camelot, and starlit Stonehenge.[6]

1914   1914

The Convergence of the Twain

(*Lines on the loss of the* Titanic)[1]

I

In a solitude of the sea
Deep from human vanity,
And the Pride of Life that planned her, stilly couches she.

2

Steel chambers, late the pyres
5   Of her salamandrine[2] fires,
Cold currents thrid,[3] and turn to rhythmic tidal lyres.

6. The sound of guns preparing for war across the Channel reaches Alfred's ("Stourton") Tower (near Stourton in Dorset), commemorating King Alfred's defeat of a Danish invasion in 878; also the site of King Arthur's court at Camelot (supposedly near Glastonbury) and the famous prehistoric stone circle of Stonehenge on Salisbury Plain.
1. The *Titanic* was the largest and most luxurious ocean liner of the day. Considered unsinkable, it sank with great loss of life on April 15, 1912, on the ship's maiden voyage, from Southampton to the United States, after colliding with an iceberg. "Twain": two.
2. I.e., destructive. The salamander was supposed to be able to survive fire.
3. A variant form of the verb *thread*.

3

Over the mirrors meant
To glass the opulent
The sea-worm crawls—grotesque, slimed, dumb, indifferent.

4

10   Jewels in joy designed
To ravish the sensuous mind
Lie lightless, all their sparkles bleared and black and blind.

5

Dim moon-eyed fishes near
Gaze at the gilded gear
15   And query: 'What does this vaingloriousness down here?' . . .

6

Well: while was fashioning
This creature of cleaving wing,
The Immanent Will[4] that stirs and urges everything

7

Prepared a sinister mate
20   For her—so gaily great—
A Shape of Ice, for the time far and dissociate.

8

And as the smart ship grew
In stature, grace, and hue,
In shadowy silent distance grew the Iceberg too.

9

25   Alien they seemed to be:
No mortal eye could see
The intimate welding of their later history,

10

Or sign that they were bent
By paths coincident
30   On being anon° twin halves of one august° event,   *soon / important*

---

4. The force (blind, but slowly gaining consciousness throughout history) that drives the world, according to Hardy's philosophy.

II

Till the Spinner of the Years
        Said 'Now!' And each one hears,
And consummation comes, and jars two hemispheres.

1912   1912, 1914

Ah, Are You Digging on My Grave?

'Ah, are you digging on my grave
        My loved one?—planting rue?'[1]
—'No: yesterday he went to wed
One of the brightest wealth has bred.
5   'It cannot hurt her now,' he said,
        "That I should not be true."'

'Then who is digging on my grave?
        My nearest dearest kin?'
—'Ah, no; they sit and think, "What use!
10   What good will planting flowers produce?
No tendance of her mound can loose
        Her spirit from Death's gin."°   *trap*

'But some one digs upon my grave?
        My enemy?—prodding sly?'
15   —'Nay: when she heard you had passed the Gate
That shuts on all flesh soon or late,
She thought you no more worth her hate,
        And cares not where you lie.'

'Then, who is digging on my grave?
20   Say—since I have not guessed!'
—'O it is I, my mistress dear,
Your little dog, who still lives near,
And much I hope my movements here
        Have not disturbed your rest?'

25   'Ah, yes! *You* dig upon my grave . . .
        Why flashed it not on me
That one true heart was left behind!
What feeling do we ever find
To equal among human kind
30   A dog's fidelity!'

'Mistress, I dug upon your grave
        To bury a bone, in case
I should be hungry near this spot

---

1. A yellow-flowered herb, traditionally an emblem of sorrow (*rue* is also an archaic word for "sorrow").

When passing on my daily trot.
35   I am sorry, but I quite forgot
      It was your resting-place.'

1914

Under the Waterfall

'Whenever I plunge my arm, like this,
In a basin of water, I never miss
The sweet sharp sense of a fugitive day
Fetched back from its thickening shroud of gray.
5   Hence the only prime
           And real love-rhyme
           That I know by heart,
           And that leaves no smart,
Is the purl° of a little valley fall   *rippling flow*
10 About three spans wide and two spans tall
Over a table of solid rock,
And into a scoop of the self-same block;
The purl of a runlet that never ceases
In stir of kingdoms, in wars, in peaces;
15 With a hollow boiling voice it speaks
And has spoken since hills were turfless peaks.'

'And why gives this the only prime
Idea to you of a real love-rhyme?
And why does plunging your arm in a bowl
20 Full of spring water, bring throbs to your soul?'

'Well, under the fall, in a crease of the stone,
Though where precisely none ever has known,
Jammed darkly, nothing to show how prized,
And by now with its smoothness opalized,
25   Is a drinking-glass:
           For, down that pass
           My lover and I
           Walked under a sky
Of blue with a leaf-wove awning of green,
30 In the burn of August, to paint the scene,
And we placed our basket of fruit and wine
By the runlet's rim, where we sat to dine;
And when we had drunk from the glass together,
Arched by the oak-copse from the weather,
35 I held the vessel to rinse in the fall,
Where it slipped, and sank, and was past recall,
Though we stooped and plumbed the little abyss
With long bared arms. There the glass still is.
And, as said, if I thrust my arm below
40 Cold water in basin or bowl, a throe°   *violent pang*
From the past awakens a sense of that time,
And the glass we used, and the cascade's rhyme.

The basin seems the pool, and its edge
The hard smooth face of the brook-side ledge,
45 And the leafy pattern of china-ware
The hanging plants that were bathing there.

'By night, by day, when it shines or lours,
There lies intact that chalice of ours,
And its presence adds to the rhyme of love
50 Persistently sung by the fall above.
No lip has touched it since his and mine
In turns therefrom sipped lovers' wine.'

1914

The Walk

You did not walk with me
Of late to the hill-top tree
      By the gated ways,
      As in earlier days;
5   You were weak and lame,
      So you never came,
And I went alone, and I did not mind,
Not thinking of you as left behind.

I walked up there to-day
10   Just in the former way:
      Surveyed around
      The familiar ground
      By myself again:
      What difference, then?
15 Only that underlying sense
Of the look of a room on returning thence.

1912–13   1914

The Voice

Woman much missed, how you call to me, call to me,
Saying that now you are not as you were
When you had changed from the one who was all to me,
But as at first, when our day was fair.

5 Can it be you that I hear? Let me view you, then,
Standing as when I drew near to the town
Where you would wait for me: yes, as I knew you then,
Even to the original air-blue gown!

Or is it only the breeze, in its listlessness
10 Travelling across the wet mead° to me here,   *meadow*
You being ever dissolved to wan wistlessness,°   *inattention*
Heard no more again far or near?

Thus I; faltering forward,
Leaves around me falling,
15 Wind oozing thin through the thorn from norward,°   *northward*
And the woman calling.

Dec. 1912   1914

During Wind and Rain

They sing their dearest songs—
He, she, all of them—yea,
Treble and tenor and bass,
    And one to play;
5 With the candles mooning° each face. . . .   *lighting*
    Ah, no; the years O!
How the sick leaves reel down in throngs!

They clear the creeping moss—
Elders and juniors—aye,
10 Making the pathways neat
    And the garden gay;
And they build a shady seat. . . .
    Ah, no; the years, the years;
See, the white storm-birds wing across.

15 They are blithely breakfasting all—
Men and maidens—yea,
Under the summer tree,
    With a glimpse of the bay,
While pet fowl come to the knee. . . .
20   Ah, no; the years O!
And the rotten rose is ript from the wall.

They change to a high new house,
He, she, all of them—aye,
Clocks and carpets and chairs
25   On the lawn all day,
And brightest things that are theirs. . . .
    Ah, no; the years, the years;
Down their carved names the rain-drop ploughs.

1917

In Time of 'The Breaking of Nations'[1]

1

Only a man harrowing clods
    In a slow silent walk
With an old horse that stumbles and nods
    Half asleep as they stalk.

2

5   Only thin smoke without flame
    From the heaps of couch-grass;
Yet this will go onward the same
    Though Dynasties pass.

3

Yonder a maid and her wight°   *man*
10   Come whispering by:
War's annals will cloud into night
    Ere their story die.

1915   1916, 1917

He Never Expected Much

[or]

A CONSIDERATION

(A reflection) On my Eighty-Sixth Birthday

Well, World, you have kept faith with me,
    Kept faith with me;
Upon the whole you have proved to be
    Much as you said you were.
5   Since as a child I used to lie
Upon the leaze° and watch the sky,   *pasture*
Never, I own, expected I
    That life would all be fair.

'Twas then you said, and since have said,
10   Times since have said,
In that mysterious voice you shed
    From clouds and hills around:
'Many have loved me desperately,
Many with smooth serenity,
15 While some have shown contempt of me
    Till they dropped underground.

---

1. Cf. "Thou art my battle axe and weapon of war: for with thee will I break in pieces the nations" (Jeremiah 51.20). The poem was written during World War I.

'I do not promise overmuch,
  Child; overmuch;
Just neutral-tinted haps° and such,'   *happenings*
20   You said to minds like mine.
Wise warning for your credit's sake!
Which I for one failed not to take,
And hence could stem such strain and ache
    As each year might assign.

1926   1928

JOSEPH CONRAD
1857–1924

Joseph Conrad was born Józef Teodor Konrad Korzeniowski in Poland (then under Russian rule), son of a Polish patriot who suffered exile in Russia for his Polish nationalist activities and died in 1869, leaving Conrad to be brought up by a maternal uncle. At the age of fifteen he amazed his family and friends by announcing his passionate desire to go to sea; he was eventually allowed to go to Marseilles, France, in 1874, and from there he made a number of voyages on French merchant ships to Martinique and other islands in the Caribbean. In 1878 he signed on an English ship that brought him to the east coast English port of Lowestoft, where (still as an ordinary seaman) he joined the crew of a small coasting vessel plying between Lowestoft and Newcastle. In six voyages between these two ports he learned English. Thus launched on a career in the British merchant service, Conrad sailed on a variety of British ships to East Asia, Australia, India, South America, and Africa, eventually gaining his master's certificate in 1886, the year he became a naturalized British subject. He received his first command in 1888, and in 1890 took a steamboat up the Congo River in nightmarish circumstances (described in *Heart of Darkness*, 1899) that permanently afflicted his health and his imagination.

In the early 1890s he was already thinking of turning some of his Malayan experiences into English fiction, and in 1892–93, when serving as first mate on the *Torrens* sailing from London to Adelaide, he revealed to a sympathetic passenger that he had begun a novel (*Almayer's Folly*), while on the return journey he impressed the young novelist John Galsworthy, who was on board, with his conversation. Conrad found it difficult to obtain a command, and this disappointment, together with the interest aroused by *Almayer's Folly* when it was published in 1895, helped turn him away from the sea to a career as a writer. He settled in London and in 1896 married an Englishwoman. This son of a Polish patriot turned merchant seaman turned writer was henceforth—after twenty years at sea—an English novelist.

In his travels through the Asian, African, and Caribbean landscapes that eventually made their way into his fiction, Conrad witnessed at close range the workings of European empires, including the British, French, Belgian, Dutch, and German, that at the time controlled most of the earth's surface and were extracting from it vast quantities of raw materials and profiting from forced or cheap labor. In the essay "Geography and Some Explorers," Conrad describes the imperial exploitation he observed in Africa as "the vilest scramble for loot that ever disfigured the history of human conscience and geographical exploration." What he saw of the uses and abuses of imperial power helped make him deeply skeptical. Marlow, the intermediate narrator of *Heart of Darkness*, reflects: "The conquest of the earth, which mostly means the taking it away from those who have a different complexion or slightly flatter noses than ourselves, is not a pretty thing when you look into it too much. What redeems it is the idea only. An idea at the back of it. . . ." And yet in this novella, the ideas at the back of colonialism's ruthless greed and violence are hardly shown to redeem anything at all.

Conrad's questioning of the ethics of empire, perhaps harkening back to his childhood experience as a Pole under Russian occupation, is part of his many-faceted exploration of the ethical ambiguities in human experience. In his great novel *Lord Jim* (1900), which like *Heart of Darkness* uses the device of an intermediate narrator (again, it is Marlow), he probes the meaning of a gross failure of duty on the part of a romantic and idealistic young sailor, and by presenting the hero's history from a series of different points of view, he sustains the ethical questioning to the end. By deploying intermediate narrators and multiple points of view in his fiction, Conrad suggests the complexity of experience and the difficulty of judging human actions.

Although Conrad's plots and exotic settings recall imperial romance and Victorian tales of adventure, he helped develop modern narrative strategies—frame narration, fragmented perspective, flashbacks and flash-forwards, psychologically laden symbolism—that disrupt chronology, render meaning indeterminate, reveal unconscious drives, blur boundaries between civilization and barbarism, and radically cast in doubt epistemological and ethical certainties. Another indication of Conrad's modernist proclivities is the alienation of his characters. Many of his works expose the difficulty of true communion, while also paradoxically exposing how communication is sometimes unexpectedly forced on us, often with someone who may be on the surface our moral opposite, so that we are compelled into a mysterious recognition of our opposite as our true self. Other stories and novels—and Conrad wrote prolifically despite his late start—explore the ways in which the codes we live by are tested in moments of crisis, revealing either their inadequacy or our own. Imagination can corrupt (as with Lord Jim) or save (as in *The Shadow-Line*, 1917), and a total lack of it can either see a person through (Captain MacWhirr in *Typhoon*, 1902) or render a person comically ridiculous (Captain Mitchell in *Nostromo*, 1904). Set in an imaginary Latin American republic, *Nostromo* subtly studies the corrupting effects of politics and "material interests" on personal relationships. Conrad wrote two other political novels—*The Secret Agent* (1906) and *Under Western Eyes* (1911). The latter is a story of Dostoyevskian power about a Russian student who becomes involuntarily associated with anti-government violence in czarist Russia and is maneuvered by circumstances into a position where, although a government spy, he has to pretend to be a revolutionary among revolutionaries. Having to pretend consistently to be the opposite of what he is, this character, like others in Conrad's fiction, is alienated, trapped, unable to communicate. Conrad was as much a pessimist as Hardy, but Conrad aesthetically embodied his pessimism in subtler ways.

He was also a great master of English prose, an astonishing fact given that English was his third language, after Polish and French; that he was twenty-one before he learned English; and that to the end of his life he spoke English with a strong foreign accent. He approached English's linguistic and literary conventions aslant, but the seeming handicap of his foreignness helped him bring to the English novel a fresh geopolitical understanding, a formal seriousness, and a psychological depth, all of which opened up new possibilities for imaginative literature in English, as indicated by his profound, if vexed, influence on later writers as different from himself as the Nigerian Chinua Achebe and the Anglo-Trinidadian V. S. Naipaul.

Preface to *The Nigger of the "Narcissus"*[1]

[THE TASK OF THE ARTIST]

A work that aspires, however humbly, to the condition of art should carry its justification in every line. And art itself may be defined as a single-minded attempt to render the highest kind of justice to the visible universe, by bringing to light the truth, manifold and one, underlying its every aspect. It is an attempt to find in its forms, in its colours, in its light, in its shadows, in the aspects of matter and in the facts of life what of each is fundamental, what is enduring and essential—their one illuminating and convincing quality—the very truth of their existence. The artist, then, like the thinker or the scientist, seeks the truth and makes his appeal. Impressed by the aspect of the world the thinker plunges into ideas, the scientist into facts—whence, presently, emerging they make their appeal to those qualities of our being that fit us best for the hazardous enterprise of living. They speak authoritatively to our common-sense, to our intelligence, to our desire of peace or to our desire of unrest; not seldom to our prejudices, sometimes to our fears, often to our egoism—but always to our credulity. And their words are heard with reverence, for their concern is with weighty matters: with the cultivation of our minds and the proper care of our bodies, with the attainment of our ambitions, with the perfection of the means and the glorification of our precious aims.

It is otherwise with the artist.

Confronted by the same enigmatical spectacle the artist descends within himself, and in that lonely region of stress and strife, if he be deserving and fortunate, he finds the terms of his appeal. His appeal is made to our less obvious capacities: to that part of our nature which, because of the warlike conditions of existence, is necessarily kept out of sight within the more resisting and hard qualities—like the vulnerable body within a steel armour. His appeal is less loud, more profound, less distinct, more stirring—and sooner forgotten. Yet its effect endures forever. The changing wisdom of successive generations discards ideas, questions facts, demolishes theories. But the artist appeals to that part of our being which is not dependent on wisdom; to that in us which is a gift and not an acquisition—and, therefore, more permanently enduring. He speaks to our capacity for delight and wonder, to the sense of mystery surrounding our lives; to our sense of pity, and beauty, and pain; to the latent feeling of fellowship with all creation—and to the subtle but invincible conviction of solidarity that knits together the loneliness of innumerable hearts, to the solidarity in dreams, in joy, in sorrow, in aspirations, in illusions, in hope, in fear, which binds men to each other, which binds together all humanity—the dead to the living and the living to the unborn.

It is only some such train of thought, or rather of feeling, that can in a measure explain the aim of the attempt, made in the tale which follows,[2] to present an unrestful episode in the obscure lives of a few individuals out of

---

1. Conrad wrote *The Nigger of the "Narcissus"* in 1896–97, shortly after his marriage; it was published first in *The New Review*, August–December 1897, and then in book form in 1898. Conrad took particular pleasure in writing the novel and later called it "the story by which, as a creative artist, I stand or fall." A few months after finishing it, feeling that he was now wholly dedicated to writing and had "done with the sea," he wrote this preface, which first appeared in the 1898 edition.

2. *The Nigger of the "Narcissus."*

all the disregarded multitude of the bewildered, the simple and the voiceless. For, if any part of truth dwells in the belief confessed above, it becomes evident that there is not a place of splendour or a dark corner of the earth that does not deserve, if only a passing glance of wonder and pity. The motive then, may be held to justify the matter of the work; but this preface, which is simply an avowal of endeavour, cannot end here—for the avowal is not yet complete.

Fiction—if it at all aspires to be art—appeals to temperament. And in truth it must be, like painting, like music, like all art, the appeal of one temperament to all the other innumerable temperaments whose subtle and resistless power endows passing events with their true meaning, and creates the moral, the emotional atmosphere of the place and time. Such an appeal to be effective must be an impression conveyed through the senses; and, in fact, it cannot be made in any other way, because temperament, whether individual or collective, is not amenable to persuasion. All art, therefore, appeals primarily to the senses, and the artistic aim when expressing itself in written words must also make its appeal through the senses, if its high desire is to reach the secret spring of responsive emotions. It must strenuously aspire to the plasticity of sculpture, to the colour of painting, and to the magic suggestiveness of music—which is the art of arts. And it is only through complete, unswerving devotion to the perfect blending of form and substance; it is only through an unremitting never-discouraged care for the shape and ring of sentences that an approach can be made to plasticity, to colour, and that the light of magic suggestiveness may be brought to play for an evanescent instant over the commonplace surface of words: of the old, old words, worn thin, defaced by ages of careless usage.

The sincere endeavour to accomplish that creative task, to go as far on that road as his strength will carry him, to go undeterred by faltering, weariness or reproach, is the only valid justification for the worker in prose. And if his conscience is clear, his answer to those who in the fulness of a wisdom which looks for immediate profit, demand specifically to be edified, consoled, amused; who demand to be promptly improved, or encouraged, or frightened, or shocked, or charmed, must run thus:—My task which I am trying to achieve is, by the power of the written word to make you hear, to make you feel—it is, before all, to make you *see*. That—and no more, and it is everything. If I succeed, you shall find there according to your deserts: encouragement, consolation, fear, charm—all you demand—and, perhaps, also that glimpse of truth for which you have forgotten to ask.

To snatch in a moment of courage, from the remorseless rush of time, a passing phase of life, is only the beginning of the task. The task approached in tenderness and faith is to hold up unquestioningly, without choice and without fear, the rescued fragment before all eyes in the light of a sincere mood. It is to show its vibration, its colour, its form; and through its movement, its form, and its colour, reveal the substance of its truth—disclose its inspiring secret: the stress and passion within the core of each convincing moment. In a single-minded attempt of that kind, if one be deserving and fortunate, one may perchance attain to such clearness of sincerity that at last the presented vision of regret or pity, of terror or mirth, shall awaken in the hearts of the beholders that feeling of unavoidable solidarity; of the solidarity in mysterious origin, in toil, in joy, in hope, in uncertain fate, which binds men to each other and all mankind to the visible world.

It is evident that he who, rightly or wrongly, holds by the convictions expressed above cannot be faithful to any one of the temporary formulas of his craft. The enduring part of them—the truth which each only imperfectly veils—should abide with him as the most precious of his possessions, but they all: Realism, Romanticism, Naturalism, even the unofficial sentimentalism (which like the poor, is exceedingly difficult to get rid of),[3] all these gods must, after a short period of fellowship, abandon him—even on the very threshold of the temple—to the stammerings of his conscience and to the outspoken consciousness of the difficulties of his work. In that uneasy solitude the supreme cry of Art for Art itself, loses the exciting ring of its apparent immorality. It sounds far off. It has ceased to be a cry, and is heard only as a whisper, often incomprehensible, but at times and faintly encouraging.

Sometimes, stretched at ease in the shade of a roadside tree, we watch the motions of a labourer in a distant field, and after a time, begin to wonder languidly as to what the fellow may be at. We watch the movements of his body, the waving of his arms, we see him bend down, stand up, hesitate, begin again. It may add to the charm of an idle hour to be told the purpose of his exertions. If we know he is trying to lift a stone, to dig a ditch, to uproot a stump, we look with a more real interest at his efforts; we are disposed to condone the jar of his agitation upon the restfulness of the landscape; and even, if in a brotherly frame of mind, we may bring ourselves to forgive his failure. We understood his object, and, after all, the fellow has tried, and perhaps he had not the strength—and perhaps he had not the knowledge. We forgive, go on our way—and forget.

And so it is with the workman of art. Art is long and life is short,[4] and success is very far off. And thus, doubtful of strength to travel so far, we talk a little about the aim—the aim of art, which, like life itself, is inspiring, difficult—obscured by mists. It is not in the clear logic of a triumphant conclusion; it is not in the unveiling of one of those heartless secrets which are called the Laws of Nature. It is not less great, but only more difficult.

To arrest, for the space of a breath, the hands busy about the work of the earth, and compel men entranced by the sight of distant goals to glance for a moment at the surrounding vision of form and colour, of sunshine and shadows; to make them pause for a look, for a sigh, for a smile—such is the aim, difficult and evanescent, and reserved only for a very few to achieve. But sometimes, by the deserving and the fortunate, even that task is accomplished. And when it is accomplished—behold!—all the truth of life is there: a moment of vision, a sigh, a smile—and the return to an eternal rest.

1897   1898

Heart of Darkness

Heart of Darkness   This story is derived from Conrad's experience in the Congo in 1890. Like Marlow, the narrator of the story, Conrad had as a child determined one day to visit the heart of Africa. "It was in 1868, when nine years old or thereabouts, that while looking at a map of Africa at the time and putting my finger on the blank space then representing the unsolved mystery of that continent, I said

3. "For the poor always ye have with you" (John 12.8).
4. *Ars longa, vita brevis*: a Latin proverb, deriving from a dictum of the Greek physician Hippocrates.

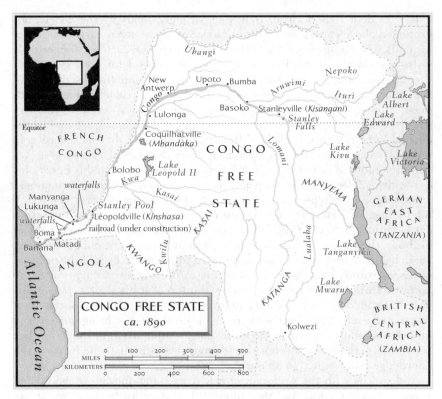

CONGO FREE STATE
ca. 1890

Heart of Darkness describes a voyage up the Congo River (now the Zaire River) into the Congo Free State, then ruled by the despotic King Leopold II of Belgium. The river, the second longest in Africa, is compared in the novel to an uncoiled snake with its head in the Atlantic. Making his way upriver, the protagonist, Marlow, must detour overland on a "two-hundred mile tramp" from the Company Station (Matadi) to the Central Station (Kinshasa), before proceeding by river to the Inner Station (Kisangani).

to myself with absolute assurance and an amazing audacity which are no longer in my character now: 'When I grow up I shall go *there*'" (*A Personal Record*, 1912).

Conrad was promised a job as a Congo River pilot through the influence of his distant cousin Marguerite Poradowska, who lived in Brussels and knew important officials of the Belgian company that exploited the Congo. At this time the Congo, although nominally an independent state, the Congo Free State (État Indépendent du Congo), was virtually the personal property of Leopold II, king of Belgium, who made a fortune out of it. Later, the appalling abuses involved in the naked colonial exploitation that went on in the Congo were exposed to public view, and international criticism compelled the setting up of a committee of inquiry in 1904. From 1885 to 1908, masses of Congolese men were worked to death, women were raped, hands were cut off, villages were looted and burned. What Conrad saw in 1890 shocked him profoundly and shook his view of the moral basis of colonialism, of exploration and trade in newly discovered countries, indeed of civilization in general. "*Heart of Darkness* is experience, too," Conrad wrote in his 1917 "Author's Note," "but it is experience pushed a little (and only very little) beyond the actual facts of the case for the perfectly legitimate, I believe, purpose of bringing it home to the minds and bosoms of the readers." And later he told Edward Garnett: "Before the Congo I was just a mere animal."

A Village on the Kasai River. Indigenous inhabitants of a village on the Kasai River, a tributary of the Congo, in 1888. They are visiting the *Roi des Belges*, the steamship on which Conrad served two years later as second-in-command. Under King Leopold II's rule of the Congo Free State, the local people suffered violent abuse and exploitation.

Conrad arrived in Africa in May 1890 and made his way up the Congo River very much as described in *Heart of Darkness*. At Kinshasa (which Conrad spells Kinchassa) on Stanley Pool, which he reached after an exhausting two-hundred-mile trek from Matadi, near the mouth of the river, Conrad was taken aback to learn that the steamer of which he was to be captain had been damaged and was undergoing repairs. He was sent as supernumerary on another steamer to learn the river. This steamer was sent to Stanley Falls to collect and bring back to Kinshasa one Georges Antoine Klein, an agent of the company who had fallen so gravely ill that he died on board. Conrad himself then fell seriously ill and eventually returned to London in January 1891 without ever having served as a Congo River pilot. The Congo experience permanently impaired his health; it also permanently haunted his imagination. The nightmare atmosphere of *Heart of Darkness* is an accurate reflection of Conrad's response to his traumatic experience.

The theme of the story is partly the "choice of nightmares" facing whites in the Congo—either to become like the commercially minded manager, who sees Africa, its people, and its resources solely as instruments of financial gain, or to become like Kurtz, the self-tortured and corrupted idealist (inspired by Klein). The manager is a "hollow man" (T. S. Eliot used a quotation from this story as one epigraph for his poem "The Hollow Men"); his only objections to Kurtz are commercial, not moral: Kurtz's methods are "unsound" and would therefore lose the company money. At the last Kurtz seems to recognize the moral horror of his having succumbed to the dark temptations that African life posed for the European. "He had summed up—he had judged." But the story also has other levels of meaning, and the counterpointing of Western civilization in Europe with what that civilization has done in Africa (see the concluding interview between Marlow and Kurtz's "intended"—based on an interview between Conrad and the dead Klein's fiancée) illuminates several of these. The story first appeared in *Blackwood's Magazine* in 1899 and was revised for book publication in 1902 as part of *Youth: A Narrative, and Two Other Stories*.

Heart of Darkness

1

The *Nellie*, a cruising yawl,[1] swung to her anchor without a flutter of the sails, and was at rest. The flood had made, the wind was nearly calm, and being bound down the river, the only thing for it was to come to and wait for the turn of the tide.

The sea-reach of the Thames stretched before us like the beginning of an interminable waterway. In the offing the sea and the sky were welded together without a joint, and in the luminous space the tanned sails of the barges drifting up with the tide seemed to stand still in red clusters of canvas sharply peaked, with gleams of varnished sprits. A haze rested on the low shores that ran out to sea in vanishing flatness. The air was dark above Gravesend,[2] and farther back still seemed condensed into a mournful gloom, brooding motionless over the biggest, and the greatest, town on earth.

The Director of Companies was our captain and our host. We four affectionately watched his back as he stood in the bows looking to seaward. On the whole river there was nothing that looked half so nautical. He resembled a pilot, which to a seaman is trustworthiness personified. It was difficult to realise his work was not out there in the luminous estuary, but behind him, within the brooding gloom.

Between us there was, as I have already said somewhere, the bond of the sea. Besides holding our hearts together through long periods of separation, it had the effect of making us tolerant of each other's yarns—and even convictions. The Lawyer—the best of old fellows—had, because of his many years and many virtues, the only cushion on deck, and was lying on the only rug. The Accountant had brought out already a box of dominoes, and was toying architecturally with the bones. Marlow sat cross-legged right aft, leaning against the mizzenmast. He had sunken cheeks, a yellow complexion, a straight back, an ascetic aspect, and, with his arms dropped, the palms of hands outwards, resembled an idol. The Director, satisfied the anchor had good hold, made his way aft and sat down amongst us. We exchanged a few words lazily. Afterwards there was silence on board the yacht. For some reason or other we did not begin that game of dominoes. We felt meditative, and fit for nothing but placid staring. The day was ending in a serenity of still and exquisite brilliance. The water shone pacifically; the sky, without a speck, was a benign immensity of unstained light; the very mist on the Essex marshes was like a gauzy and radiant fabric, hung from the wooded rises inland, and draping the low shores in diaphanous folds. Only the gloom to the west, brooding over the upper reaches, became more sombre every minute, as if angered by the approach of the sun.

And at last, in its curved and imperceptible fall, the sun sank low, and from glowing white changed to a dull red without rays and without heat, as if about to go out suddenly, stricken to death by the touch of that gloom brooding over a crowd of men.

Forthwith a change came over the waters, and the serenity became less brilliant but more profound. The old river in its broad reach rested unruffled at the decline of day, after ages of good service done to the race that peopled its

---

1. Two-masted boat.
2. River port on the south bank of the Thames twenty-four miles east (downriver) of London.

banks, spread out in the tranquil dignity of a waterway leading to the uttermost ends of the earth. We looked at the venerable stream not in the vivid flush of a short day that comes and departs for ever, but in the august light of abiding memories. And indeed nothing is easier for a man who has, as the phrase goes, "followed the sea" with reverence and affection, than to evoke the great spirit of the past upon the lower reaches of the Thames. The tidal current runs to and fro in its unceasing service, crowded with memories of men and ships it has borne to the rest of home or to the battles of the sea. It had known and served all the men of whom the nation is proud, from Sir Francis Drake to Sir John Franklin,[3] knights all, titled and untitled—the great knights-errant of the sea. It had borne all the ships whose names are like jewels flashing in the night of time, from the *Golden Hind* returning with her round flanks full of treasure, to be visited by the Queen's Highness and thus pass out of the gigantic tale, to the *Erebus* and *Terror*, bound on other conquests—and that never returned. It had known the ships and the men. They had sailed from Deptford, from Greenwich, from Erith—the adventurers and the settlers; kings' ships and the ships of men on 'Change; captains, admirals, the dark "interlopers"[4] of the Eastern trade, and the commissioned "generals" of East India fleets. Hunters for gold or pursuers of fame, they all had gone out on that stream, bearing the sword, and often the torch, messengers of the might within the land, bearers of a spark from the sacred fire. What greatness had not floated on the ebb of that river into the mystery of an unknown earth! . . . The dreams of men, the seed of commonwealths, the germs of empires.

The sun set; the dusk fell on the stream, and lights began to appear along the shore. The Chapman lighthouse, a three-legged thing erect on a mud-flat, shone strongly. Lights of ships moved in the fairway[5]—a great stir of lights going up and going down. And farther west on the upper reaches the place of the monstrous town was still marked ominously on the sky, a brooding gloom in sunshine, a lurid glare under the stars.

"And this also," said Marlow suddenly, "has been one of the dark places of the earth."

He was the only man of us who still "followed the sea." The worst that could be said of him was that he did not represent his class. He was a seaman, but he was a wanderer too, while most seamen lead, if one may so express it, a sedentary life. Their minds are of the stay-at-home order, and their home is always with them—the ship; and so is their country—the sea. One ship is very much like another, and the sea is always the same. In the immutability of their surroundings the foreign shores, the foreign faces, the changing immensity of life, glide past, veiled not by a sense of mystery but by a slightly disdainful ignorance; for there is nothing mysterious to a seaman unless it be the sea itself, which is the mistress of his existence and as inscrutable as Destiny. For the rest, after his hours of work, a casual stroll or a casual spree on shore suffices to unfold for him the secret of a whole

3. Sir John Franklin (1786–1847), Arctic explorer who in 1845 commanded an expedition consisting of the ships *Erebus* and *Terror* in search of the Northwest Passage. The ships never returned. Sir Francis Drake (ca. 1540–1596), Elizabethan naval hero and explorer, sailed around the world on his ship *The Golden Hind*. Upon his return to England in 1580, Queen Elizabeth knighted Drake aboard his ship, loaded with captured Spanish treasure.
4. Private ships muscling in on the monopoly of

the East India Company, which was founded in 1600, lost its trading monopoly in 1813, and transferred its governmental functions to the Crown in 1858. Deptford, on the south bank of the Thames, on the eastern edge of London, was once an important dockyard. Greenwich is on the south bank of the Thames immediately east of Deptford. Erith is eight miles farther east. "'Change": the Stock Exchange.
5. Navigable part of a river, through which ships enter and depart.

continent, and generally he finds the secret not worth knowing. The yarns of seamen have a direct simplicity, the whole meaning of which lies within the shell of a cracked nut. But Marlow was not typical (if his propensity to spin yarns be excepted), and to him the meaning of an episode was not inside like a kernel but outside, enveloping the tale which brought it out only as a glow brings out a haze, in the likeness of one of these misty halos that sometimes are made visible by the spectral illumination of moonshine.

His remark did not seem at all surprising. It was just like Marlow. It was accepted in silence. No one took the trouble to grunt even; and presently he said, very slow:

"I was thinking of very old times, when the Romans first came here, nineteen hundred years ago—the other day. . . . Light came out of this river since—you say Knights? Yes; but it is like a running blaze on a plain, like a flash of lightning in the clouds. We live in the flicker—may it last as long as the old earth keeps rolling! But darkness was here yesterday. Imagine the feelings of a commander of a fine—what d'ye call 'em?—trireme[6] in the Mediterranean, ordered suddenly to the north; run overland across the Gauls in a hurry; put in charge of one of these craft the legionaries—a wonderful lot of handy men they must have been too—used to build, apparently by the hundred, in a month or two, if we may believe what we read. Imagine him here—the very end of the world, a sea the colour of lead, a sky the colour of smoke, a kind of ship about as rigid as a concertina—and going up this river with stores, or orders, or what you like. Sandbanks, marshes, forests, savages—precious little to eat fit for a civilised man, nothing but Thames water to drink. No Falernian wine[7] here, no going ashore. Here and there a military camp lost in a wilderness, like a needle in a bundle of hay—cold, fog, tempests, disease, exile, and death—death skulking in the air, in the water, in the bush. They must have been dying like flies here. Oh yes—he did it. Did it very well, too, no doubt, and without thinking much about it either, except afterwards to brag of what he had gone through in his time, perhaps. They were men enough to face the darkness. And perhaps he was cheered by keeping his eye on a chance of promotion to the fleet at Ravenna[8] by and by, if he had good friends in Rome and survived the awful climate. Or think of a decent young citizen in a toga—perhaps too much dice, you know—coming out here in the train of some prefect, or tax-gatherer, or trader, even, to mend his fortunes. Land in a swamp, march through the woods, and in some inland post feel the savagery, the utter savagery, had closed round him—all that mysterious life of the wilderness that stirs in the forest, in the jungles, in the hearts of wild men. There's no initiation either into such mysteries. He has to live in the midst of the incomprehensible, which is also detestable. And it has a fascination, too, that goes to work upon him. The fascination of the abomination—you know. Imagine the growing regrets, the longing to escape, the powerless disgust, the surrender, the hate."

He paused.

"Mind," he began again, lifting one arm from the elbow, the palm of the hand outwards, so that, with his legs folded before him, he had the pose of a Buddha preaching in European clothes and without a lotus-flower—"Mind, none of us would feel exactly like this. What saves us is efficiency—the devotion to efficiency. But these chaps were not much account, really. They were

---

6. Ancient Greek and Roman galley with three ranks of oars.
7. Wine from a famed wine-making district in Campania (Italy).

8. A city in northern Italy once directly on the Adriatic Sea and an important naval station in Roman times. It is now about six miles from the sea, connected with it by a canal.

no colonists; their administration was merely a squeeze, and nothing more, I suspect. They were conquerors, and for that you want only brute force—nothing to boast of, when you have it, since your strength is just an accident arising from the weakness of others. They grabbed what they could get for the sake of what was to be got. It was just robbery with violence, aggravated murder on a great scale, and men going at it blind—as is very proper for those who tackle a darkness. The conquest of the earth, which mostly means the taking it away from those who have a different complexion or slightly flatter noses than ourselves, is not a pretty thing when you look into it too much. What redeems it is the idea only. An idea at the back of it; not a sentimental pretence but an idea; and an unselfish belief in the idea—something you can set up, and bow down before, and offer a sacrifice to. . . ."

He broke off. Flames glided in the river, small green flames, red flames, white flames, pursuing, overtaking, joining, crossing each other—then separating slowly or hastily. The traffic of the great city went on in the deepening night upon the sleepless river. We looked on, waiting patiently—there was nothing else to do till the end of the flood; but it was only after a long silence, when he said, in a hesitating voice, "I suppose you fellows remember I did once turn fresh-water sailor for a bit," that we knew we were fated, before the ebb began to run, to hear about one of Marlow's inconclusive experiences.

"I don't want to bother you much with what happened to me personally," he began, showing in this remark the weakness of many tellers of tales who seem so often unaware of what their audience would best like to hear; "yet to understand the effect of it on me you ought to know how I got out there, what I saw, how I went up that river to the place where I first met the poor chap. It was the farthest point of navigation and the culminating point of my experience. It seemed somehow to throw a kind of light on everything about me—and into my thoughts. It was sombre enough too—and pitiful—not extraordinary in any way—not very clear either. No, not very clear. And yet it seemed to throw a kind of light.

"I had then, as you remember, just returned to London after a lot of Indian Ocean, Pacific, China Seas—a regular dose of the East—six years or so, and I was loafing about, hindering you fellows in your work and invading your homes, just as though I had got a heavenly mission to civilise you. It was very fine for a time, but after a bit I did get tired of resting. Then I began to look for a ship—I should think the hardest work on earth. But the ships wouldn't even look at me. And I got tired of that game too.

"Now when I was a little chap I had a passion for maps. I would look for hours at South America, or Africa, or Australia, and lose myself in all the glories of exploration. At that time there were many blank spaces on the earth, and when I saw one that looked particularly inviting on a map (but they all look that) I would put my finger on it and say, When I grow up I will go there. The North Pole was one of these places, I remember. Well, I haven't been there yet, and shall not try now. The glamour's off. Other places were scattered about the Equator, and in every sort of latitude all over the two hemispheres. I have been in some of them, and . . . well, we won't talk about that. But there was one yet—the biggest, the most blank, so to speak—that I had a hankering after.

"True, by this time it was not a blank space any more. It had got filled since my boyhood with rivers and lakes and names. It had ceased to be a blank space of delightful mystery—a white patch for a boy to dream gloriously over. It had become a place of darkness. But there was in it one river especially, a mighty big river, that you could see on the map, resembling an immense snake uncoiled, with its head in the sea, its body at rest curving afar over a vast country, and its tail lost in the depths of the land. And as I looked at the map of it in a shop-window, it fascinated me as a snake would a bird—a silly little bird. Then I remembered there was a big concern, a Company for trade on that river. Dash it all! I thought to myself, they can't trade without using some kind of craft on that lot of fresh water—steamboats! Why shouldn't I try to get charge of one? I went on along Fleet Street,[9] but could not shake off the idea. The snake had charmed me.

"You understand it was a Continental concern, that Trading Society; but I have a lot of relations living on the Continent, because it's cheap and not so nasty as it looks, they say.

"I am sorry to own I began to worry them. This was already a fresh departure for me. I was not used to get things that way, you know. I always went my own road and on my own legs where I had a mind to go. I wouldn't have believed it of myself; but, then—you see—I felt somehow I must get there by hook or by crook. So I worried them. The men said, 'My dear fellow,' and did nothing. Then—would you believe it?—I tried the women. I, Charlie Marlow, set the women to work—to get a job. Heavens! Well, you see, the notion drove me. I had an aunt, a dear enthusiastic soul. She wrote: 'It will be delightful. I am ready to do anything, anything for you. It is a glorious idea. I know the wife of a very high personage in the Administration, and also a man who has lots of influence with,' etc. etc. She was determined to make no end of fuss to get me appointed skipper of a river steamboat, if such was my fancy.

"I got my appointment—of course; and I got it very quick. It appears the Company had received news that one of their captains had been killed in a scuffle with the natives. This was my chance, and it made me the more anxious to go. It was only months and months afterwards, when I made the attempt to recover what was left of the body, that I heard the original quarrel arose from a misunderstanding about some hens. Yes, two black hens. Fresleven—that was the fellow's name, a Dane—thought himself wronged somehow in the bargain, so he went ashore and started to hammer the chief of the village with a stick. Oh, it didn't surprise me in the least to hear this, and at the same time to be told that Fresleven was the gentlest, quietest creature that ever walked on two legs. No doubt he was; but he had been a couple of years already out there engaged in the noble cause, you know, and he probably felt the need at last of asserting his self-respect in some way. Therefore he whacked the old nigger mercilessly, while a big crowd of his people watched him, thunderstruck, till some man—I was told the chief's son—in desperation at hearing the old chap yell, made a tentative jab with a spear at the white man—and of course it went quite easy between the shoulder-blades. Then the whole population cleared into the forest, expecting all kinds of calamities to happen, while, on the other hand, the steamer Fresleven commanded left also in a bad panic, in charge of the engineer, I believe. Afterwards nobody seemed to trouble much about Fresleven's remains, till I got out and stepped into his shoes. I couldn't let it rest, though; but when an opportunity offered at last to meet my predecessor, the grass growing through his ribs was tall enough to hide his bones. They were all there. The supernatural being had not been touched after he fell. And the village was deserted, the huts gaped black, rotting, all askew within the fallen enclosures. A calam-

---

9. Street in central London.

ity had come to it, sure enough. The people had vanished. Mad terror had scattered them, men, women, and children, through the bush, and they had never returned. What became of the hens I don't know either. I should think the cause of progress got them, anyhow. However, through this glorious affair I got my appointment, before I had fairly begun to hope for it.

"I flew around like mad to get ready, and before forty-eight hours I was crossing the Channel to show myself to my employers, and sign the contract. In a very few hours I arrived in a city that always makes me think of a whited sepulchre. Prejudice no doubt. I had no difficulty in finding the Company's offices. It was the biggest thing in the town, and everybody I met was full of it. They were going to run an over-sea empire, and make no end of coin by trade.

"A narrow and deserted street in deep shadow, high houses, innumerable windows with Venetian blinds, a dead silence, grass sprouting between the stones, imposing carriage archways right and left, immense double doors standing ponderously ajar. I slipped through one of these cracks, went up a swept and ungarnished staircase, as arid as a desert, and opened the first door I came to. Two women, one fat and the other slim, sat on straw-bottomed chairs, knitting black wool. The slim one got up and walked straight at me— still knitting with downcast eyes—and only just as I began to think of getting out of her way, as you would for a somnambulist, stood still, and looked up. Her dress was as plain as an umbrella-cover, and she turned round without a word and preceded me into a waiting-room. I gave my name, and looked about. Deal table in the middle, plain chairs all round the walls, on one end a large shining map, marked with all the colours of a rainbow. There was a vast amount of red—good to see at any time, because one knows that some real work is done in there, a deuce of a lot of blue, a little green, smears of orange, and, on the East Coast, a purple patch, to show where the jolly pioneers of progress drink the jolly lager-beer. However, I wasn't going into any of these. I was going into the yellow. Dead in the centre. And the river was there—fascinating—deadly—like a snake. Ough! A door opened, a white-haired secretarial head, but wearing a compassionate expression, appeared, and a skinny forefinger beckoned me into the sanctuary. Its light was dim, and a heavy writing desk squatted in the middle. From behind that structure came out an impression of pale plumpness in a frockcoat. The great man himself. He was five feet six, I should judge, and had his grip on the handle-end of ever so many millions. He shook hands, I fancy, murmured vaguely, was satisfied with my French. *Bon voyage.*

"In about forty-five seconds I found myself again in the waiting-room with the compassionate secretary, who, full of desolation and sympathy, made me sign some document. I believe I undertook amongst other things not to disclose any trade secrets. Well, I am not going to.

"I began to feel slightly uneasy. You know I am not used to such ceremonies, and there was something ominous in the atmosphere. It was just as though I had been let into some conspiracy—I don't know—something not quite right; and I was glad to get out. In the outer room the two women knitted black wool feverishly. People were arriving, and the younger one was walking back and forth introducing them. The old one sat on her chair. Her flat cloth slippers were propped up on a foot-warmer, and a cat reposed on her lap. She wore a starched white affair on her head, had a wart on one cheek, and silver-rimmed spectacles hung on the tip of her nose. She glanced at me above the glasses. The swift and indifferent placidity of that look troubled me. Two youths with foolish and cheery countenances were being piloted over, and she threw at them the same quick glance of unconcerned wisdom. She seemed to know all about them and about me too. An eerie feeling came over me. She seemed uncanny and fateful. Often far away there I thought of these two, guarding the door of Darkness, knitting black wool as for a warm pall, one introducing, introducing continuously to the unknown, the other scrutinising the cheery and foolish faces with unconcerned old eyes. *Ave!* Old knitter of black wool. *Morituri te salutant.*[1] Not many of those she looked at ever saw her again—not half, by a long way.

"There was yet a visit to the doctor. 'A simple formality,' assured me the secretary, with an air of taking an immense part in all my sorrows. Accordingly a young chap wearing his hat over the left eyebrow, some clerk I suppose—there must have been clerks in the business, though the house was as still as a house in a city of the dead—came from somewhere upstairs, and led me forth. He was shabby and careless, with ink-stains on the sleeves of his jacket, and his cravat was large and billowy, under a chin shaped like the toe of an old boot. It was a little too early for the doctor, so I proposed a drink, and thereupon he developed a vein of joviality. As we sat over our vermuths he glorified the Company's business, and by and by I expressed casually my surprise at him not going out there. He became very cool and collected all at once. 'I am not such a fool as I look, quoth Plato to his disciples,' he said sententiously, emptied his glass with great resolution, and we rose.

"The old doctor felt my pulse, evidently thinking of something else the while. 'Good, good for there,' he mumbled, and then with a certain eagerness asked me whether I would let him measure my head. Rather surprised, I said Yes, when he produced a thing like callipers and got the dimensions back and front and every way, taking notes carefully. He was an unshaven little man in a threadbare coat like a gaberdine, with his feet in slippers, and I thought him a harmless fool. 'I always ask leave, in the interests of science, to measure the crania of those going out there,' he said. 'And when they come back too?' I asked. 'Oh, I never see them,' he remarked; 'and, moreover, the changes take place inside, you know.' He smiled, as if at some quiet joke. 'So you are going out there. Famous. Interesting too.' He gave me a searching glance, and made another note. 'Ever any madness in your family?' he asked, in a matter-of-fact tone. I felt very annoyed. 'Is that question in the interests of science too?' 'It would be,' he said, without taking notice of my irritation, 'interesting for science to watch the mental changes of individuals, on the spot, but . . .' 'Are you an alienist?'[2] I interrupted. 'Every doctor should be—a little,' answered that original[3] imperturbably. 'I have a little theory which you Messieurs who go out there must help me to prove. This is my share in the advantages my country shall reap from the possession of such a magnificent dependency. The mere wealth I leave to others. Pardon my questions, but you are the first Englishman coming under my observation . . .' I hastened to assure him I was not in the least typical. 'If I were,' said I, 'I wouldn't be talking like this with you.' 'What you say is rather profound, and probably erroneous,' he said, with a laugh. 'Avoid irritation more than exposure to the sun. Adieu. How do you English say, eh? Good-bye. Ah! Good-bye. Adieu. In the tropics one must before everything keep calm.' . . . He lifted a warning forefinger. . . . '*Du calme, du calme. Adieu.*'

1. "Hail! . . . Those who are about to die salute you" (Latin). The Roman gladiators' salute to the emperor on entering the arena.

2. Doctor who treats mental diseases. (The term has now been replaced by *psychiatrist*.)

3. Eccentric person.

"One thing more remained to do—say good-bye to my excellent aunt. I found her triumphant. I had a cup of tea—the last decent cup of tea for many days—and in a room that most soothingly looked just as you would expect a lady's drawing-room to look, we had a long quiet chat by the fireside. In the course of these confidences it became quite plain to me I had been represented to the wife of the high dignitary, and goodness knows to how many more people besides, as an exceptional and gifted creature—a piece of good fortune for the Company—a man you don't get hold of every day. Good heavens! and I was going to take charge of a two-penny-halfpenny river-steamboat with a penny whistle attached! It appeared, however, I was also one of the Workers, with a capital—you know. Something like an emissary of light, something like a lower sort of apostle. There had been a lot of such rot let loose in print and talk just about that time, and the excellent woman, living right in the rush of all that humbug, got carried off her feet. She talked about 'weaning those ignorant millions from their horrid ways,' till, upon my word, she made me quite uncomfortable. I ventured to hint that the Company was run for profit.

"'You forget, dear Charlie, that the labourer is worthy of his hire,' she said brightly. It's queer how out of touch with truth women are. They live in a world of their own, and there had never been anything like it, and never can be. It is too beautiful altogether, and if they were to set it up it would go to pieces before the first sunset. Some confounded fact we men have been living contentedly with ever since the day of creation would start up and knock the whole thing over.

"After this I got embraced, told to wear flannel, be sure to write often, and so on—and I left. In the street—I don't know why—a queer feeling came to me that I was an impostor. Odd thing that I, who used to clear out for any part of the world at twenty-four hours' notice, with less thought than most men give to the crossing of a street, had a moment—I won't say of hesitation, but of startled pause, before this commonplace affair. The best way I can explain it to you is by saying that, for a second or two, I felt as though, instead of going to the centre of a continent, I were about to set off for the centre of the earth.

"I left in a French steamer, and she called in every blamed port they have out there, for, as far as I could see, the sole purpose of landing soldiers and custom-house officers. I watched the coast. Watching a coast as it slips by the ship is like thinking about an enigma. There it is before you—smiling, frowning, inviting, grand, mean, insipid, or savage, and always mute with an air of whispering, Come and find out. This one was almost featureless, as if still in the making, with an aspect of monotonous grimness. The edge of a colossal jungle, so dark green as to be almost black, fringed with white surf, ran straight, like a ruled line, far, far away along a blue sea whose glitter was blurred by a creeping mist. The sun was fierce, the land seemed to glisten and drip with steam. Here and there greyish-whitish specks showed up clustered inside the white surf, with a flag flying above them perhaps—settlements some centuries old, and still no bigger than pin-heads on the untouched expanse of their background. We pounded along, stopped, landed soldiers; went on, landed custom-house clerks to levy toll in what looked like a God-forsaken wilderness, with a tin shed and a flag-pole lost in it; landed more soldiers—to take care of the custom-house clerks presumably. Some, I heard, got drowned in the surf; but whether they did or not, nobody seemed particularly to care. They were just flung out there, and on we went. Every day the coast looked the same, as though we had not moved; but we passed various places—trading places—with names like Gran' Bassam, Little Popo; names that seemed to belong to some sordid farce acted in front of a sinister back-cloth. The idleness of a passenger, my isolation amongst all these men with whom I had no point of contact, the oily and languid sea, the uniform sombreness of the coast, seemed to keep me away from the truth of things, within the toil of a mournful and senseless delusion. The voice of the surf heard now and then was a positive pleasure, like the speech of a brother. It was something natural, that had its reason, that had a meaning. Now and then a boat from the shore gave one a momentary contact with reality. It was paddled by black fellows. You could see from afar the white of their eyeballs glistening. They shouted, sang; their bodies streamed with perspiration; they had faces like grotesque masks—these chaps; but they had bone, muscle, a wild vitality, an intense energy of movement, that was as natural and true as the surf along their coast. They wanted no excuse for being there. They were a great comfort to look at. For a time I would feel I belonged still to a world of straightforward facts; but the feeling would not last long. Something would turn up to scare it away. Once, I remember, we came upon a man-of-war anchored off the coast. There wasn't even a shed there, and she was shelling the bush. It appears the French had one of their wars going on thereabouts. Her ensign dropped limp like a rag; the muzzles of the long six-inch guns stuck out all over the low hull; the greasy, slimy swell swung her up lazily and let her down, swaying her thin masts. In the empty immensity of earth, sky, and water, there she was, incomprehensible, firing into a continent. Pop, would go one of the six-inch guns; a small flame would dart and vanish, a little white smoke would disappear, a tiny projectile would give a feeble screech— and nothing happened. Nothing could happen. There was a touch of insanity in the proceeding, a sense of lugubrious drollery in the sight; and it was not dissipated by somebody on board assuring me earnestly there was a camp of natives—he called them enemies!—hidden out of sight somewhere.

"We gave her her letters (I heard the men in that lonely ship were dying of fever at the rate of three a day) and went on. We called at some more places with farcical names, where the merry dance of death and trade goes on in a still and earthy atmosphere as of an overheated catacomb; all along the formless coast bordered by dangerous surf, as if Nature herself had tried to ward off intruders; in and out of rivers, streams of death in life, whose banks were rotting into mud, whose waters, thickened into slime, invaded the contorted mangroves,[4] that seemed to writhe at us in the extremity of an impotent despair. Nowhere did we stop long enough to get a particularised impression, but the general sense of vague and oppressive wonder grew upon me. It was like a weary pilgrimage amongst hints for nightmares.

"It was upward of thirty days before I saw the mouth of the big river. We anchored off the seat of the government. But my work would not begin till some two hundred miles farther on. So as soon as I could I made a start for a place thirty miles higher up.

"I had my passage on a little sea-going steamer. Her captain was a Swede, and knowing me for a seaman, invited me on the bridge. He was a young man, lean, fair, and morose, with lanky hair and a shuffling gait. As we left the miserable little wharf, he tossed his head contemptuously at the shore.

4. Tropical evergreen trees or shrubs with roots and stems forming dense thickets along riverbanks.

'Been living there?' he asked. I said, 'Yes.' 'Fine lot these government chaps—are they not?' he went on, speaking English with great precision and considerable bitterness. 'It is funny what some people will do for a few francs a month. I wonder what becomes of that kind when it goes up country?' I said to him I expected to see that soon. 'So-o-o!' he exclaimed. He shuffled athwart, keeping one eye ahead vigilantly. 'Don't be too sure,' he continued. 'The other day I took up a man who hanged himself on the road. He was a Swede, too.' 'Hanged himself! Why, in God's name?' I cried. He kept on looking out watchfully. 'Who knows? The sun too much for him, or the country perhaps.'

"At last we opened a reach. A rocky cliff appeared, mounds of turned-up earth by the shore, houses on a hill, others with iron roofs, amongst a waste of excavations, or hanging to the declivity. A continuous noise of the rapids above hovered over this scene of inhabited devastation. A lot of people, mostly black and naked, moved about like ants. A jetty[5] projected into the river. A blinding sunlight drowned all this at times in a sudden recrudescence of glare. "There's your Company's station,' said the Swede, pointing to three wooden barrack-like structures on the rocky slope. 'I will send your things up. Four boxes did you say? So. Farewell.'

"I came upon a boiler wallowing in the grass, then found a path leading up the hill. It turned aside for the boulders, and also for an undersized railway truck lying there on its back with its wheels in the air. One was off. The thing looked as dead as the carcass of some animal. I came upon more pieces of decaying machinery, a stack of rusty nails. To the left a clump of trees made a shady spot, where dark things seemed to stir feebly. I blinked, the path was steep. A horn tooted to the right, and I saw the black people run. A heavy and dull detonation shook the ground, a puff of smoke came out of the cliff, and that was all. No change appeared on the face of the rock. They were building a railway. The cliff was not in the way or anything; but this objectless blasting was all the work going on.

"A slight clinking behind me made me turn my head. Six black men advanced in a file, toiling up the path. They walked erect and slow, balancing small baskets full of earth on their heads, and the clink kept time with their footsteps. Black rags were wound round their loins, and the short ends behind waggled to and fro like tails. I could see every rib, the joints of their limbs were like knots in a rope; each had an iron collar on his neck, and all were connected together with a chain whose bights swung between them, rhythmically clinking. Another report from the cliff made me think suddenly of that ship of war I had seen firing into a continent. It was the same kind of ominous voice; but these men could by no stretch of imagination be called enemies. They were called criminals, and the outraged law, like the bursting shells, had come to them, an insoluble mystery from the sea. All their meagre breasts panted together, the violently dilated nostrils quivered, the eyes stared stonily uphill. They passed me within six inches, without a glance, with that complete, deathlike indifference of unhappy savages. Behind this raw matter one of the reclaimed, the product of the new forces at work, strolled despondently, carrying a rifle by its middle. He had a uniform jacket with one button off, and seeing a white man on the path, hoisted his weapon to his shoulder with alacrity. This was simple prudence, white men being so much alike at a distance that he could not tell who I might be. He was speedily reassured, and with a large, white, rascally grin, and a glance at his charge,

5. Wharf or pier.

seemed to take me into partnership in his exalted trust. After all, I also was a part of the great cause of these high and just proceedings.

"Instead of going up, I turned and descended to the left. My idea was to let that chain-gang get out of sight before I climbed the hill. You know I am not particularly tender; I've had to strike and to fend off. I've had to resist and to attack sometimes—that's only one way of resisting—without counting the exact cost, according to the demands of such sort of life as I had blundered into. I've seen the devil of violence, and the devil of greed, and the devil of hot desire; but, by all the stars! these were strong, lusty, red-eyed devils, that swayed and drove men—men, I tell you. But as I stood on this hillside, I foresaw that in the blinding sunshine of that land I would become acquainted with a flabby, pretending, weak-eyed devil of a rapacious and pitiless folly. How insidious he could be, too, I was only to find out several months later and a thousand miles farther. For a moment I stood appalled, as though by a warning. Finally I descended the hill, obliquely, towards the trees I had seen.

"I avoided a vast artificial hole somebody had been digging on the slope, the purpose of which I found it impossible to divine. It wasn't a quarry or a sandpit, anyhow. It was just a hole. It might have been connected with the philanthropic desire of giving the criminals something to do. I don't know. Then I nearly fell into a very narrow ravine, almost no more than a scar in the hillside. I discovered that a lot of imported drainage-pipes for the settlement had been tumbled in there. There wasn't one that was not broken. It was a wanton smash-up. At last I got under the trees. My purpose was to stroll into the shade for a moment; but no sooner within than it seemed to me I had stepped into the gloomy circle of some Inferno. The rapids were near, and an uninterrupted, uniform, headlong, rushing noise filled the mournful stillness of the grove, where not a breath stirred, not a leaf moved, with a mysterious sound—as though the tearing pace of the launched earth had suddenly become audible.

"Black shapes crouched, lay, sat between the trees, leaning against the trunks, clinging to the earth, half coming out, half effaced within the dim light, in all the attitudes of pain, abandonment, and despair. Another mine on the cliff went off, followed by a slight shudder of the soil under my feet. The work was going on. The work! And this was the place where some of the helpers had withdrawn to die.

"They were dying slowly—it was very clear. They were not enemies, they were not criminals, they were nothing earthly now—nothing but black shadows of disease and starvation, lying confusedly in the greenish gloom. Brought from all the recesses of the coast in all the legality of time contracts, lost in uncongenial surroundings, fed on unfamiliar food, they sickened, became inefficient, and were then allowed to crawl away and rest. These moribund shapes were free as air—and nearly as thin. I began to distinguish the gleam of eyes under the trees. Then, glancing down, I saw a face near my hand. The black bones reclined at full length with one shoulder against the tree, and slowly the eyelids rose and the sunken eyes looked up at me, enormous and vacant, a kind of blind, white flicker in the depths of the orbs, which died out slowly. The man seemed young—almost a boy—but you know with them it's hard to tell. I found nothing else to do but to offer him one of my good Swede's ship's biscuits I had in my pocket. The fingers closed slowly on it and held—there was no other movement and no other glance. He had tied a bit of white worsted[6] round his neck—Why? Where did he get it? Was

---

6. Fine wool fabric.

it a badge—an ornament—a charm—a propitiatory act? Was there any idea at all connected with it? It looked startling round his black neck, this bit of white thread from beyond the seas.

"Near the same tree two more bundles of acute angles sat with their legs drawn up. One, with his chin propped on his knees, stared at nothing, in an intolerable and appalling manner: his brother phantom rested its forehead, as if overcome with a great weariness; and all about others were scattered in every pose of contorted collapse, as in some picture of a massacre or a pestilence. While I stood horror-struck, one of these creatures rose to his hands and knees, and went off on all-fours towards the river to drink. He lapped out of his hand, then sat up in the sunlight, crossing his shins in front of him, and after a time let his woolly head fall on his breastbone.

"I didn't want any more loitering in the shade, and I made haste towards the station. When near the buildings I met a white man, in such an unexpected elegance of get-up that in the first moment I took him for a sort of vision. I saw a high starched collar, white cuffs, a light alpaca[7] jacket, snowy trousers, a clear necktie, and varnished boots. No hat. Hair parted, brushed, oiled, under a green-lined parasol held in a big white hand. He was amazing, and had a penholder behind his ear.

"I shook hands with this miracle, and I learned he was the Company's chief accountant, and that all the book-keeping was done at this station. He had come out for a moment, he said, 'to get a breath of fresh air.' The expression sounded wonderfully odd, with its suggestion of sedentary desk-life. I wouldn't have mentioned the fellow to you at all, only it was from his lips that I first heard the name of the man who is so indissolubly connected with the memories of that time. Moreover, I respected the fellow. Yes; I respected his collars, his vast cuffs, his brushed hair. His appearance was certainly that of a hairdresser's dummy; but in the great demoralisation of the land he kept up his appearance. That's backbone. His starched collars and got-up shirt-fronts were achievements of character. He had been out nearly three years; and, later, I could not help asking him how he managed to sport such linen. He had just the faintest blush, and said modestly, 'I've been teaching one of the native women about the station. It was difficult. She had a distaste for the work.' Thus this man had verily accomplished something. And he was devoted to his books, which were in apple-pie order.

"Everything else in the station was in a muddle,—heads, things, buildings. Strings of dusty niggers with splay feet arrived and departed; a stream of manufactured goods, rubbishy cottons, beads, and brass-wire set into the depths of darkness, and in return came a precious trickle of ivory.

"I had to wait in the station for ten days—an eternity. I lived in a hut in the yard, but to be out of the chaos I would sometimes get into the accountant's office. It was built of horizontal planks, and so badly put together that, as he bent over his high desk, he was barred from neck to heels with narrow strips of sunlight. There was no need to open the big shutter to see. It was hot there too; big flies buzzed fiendishly, and did not sting, but stabbed. I sat generally on the floor, while, of faultless appearance (and even slightly scented), perching on a high stool, he wrote, he wrote. Sometimes he stood up for exercise. When a truckle-bed with a sick man (some invalided agent from up country) was put in there, he exhibited a gentle annoyance. 'The groans of this sick person' he said, 'distract my attention.

---

7. Made from the wool of a South American animal by that name.

And without that it is extremely difficult to guard against clerical errors in this climate.'

"One day he remarked, without lifting his head, 'In the interior you will no doubt meet Mr Kurtz.' On my asking who Mr Kurtz was, he said he was a first-class agent; and seeing my disappointment at this information, he added slowly, laying down his pen, 'He is a very remarkable person.' Further questions elicited from him that Mr Kurtz was at present in charge of a trading-post, a very important one, in the true ivory-country, at 'the very bottom of there. Sends in as much ivory as all the others put together . . .' He began to write again. The sick man was too ill to groan. The flies buzzed in a great peace.

"Suddenly there was a growing murmur of voices and a great tramping of feet. A caravan had come in. A violent babble of uncouth sounds burst out on the other side of the planks. All the carriers were speaking together, and in the midst of the uproar the lamentable voice of the chief agent was heard 'giving it up' tearfully for the twentieth time that day. . . . He rose slowly. 'What a frightful row,' he said. He crossed the room gently to look at the sick man, and returning, said to me, 'He does not hear.' 'What! Dead?' I asked, startled. 'No, not yet,' he answered, with great composure. Then, alluding with a toss of the head to the tumult in the station-yard, 'When one has got to make correct entries, one comes to hate those savages—hate them to the death.' He remained thoughtful for a moment. 'When you see Mr Kurtz,' he went on, 'tell him from me that everything here'—he glanced at the desk—'is very satisfactory. I don't like to write to him—with those messengers of ours you never know who may get hold of your letter—at that Central Station.' He stared at me for a moment with his mild, bulging eyes. 'Oh, he will go far, very far,' he began again. 'He will be a somebody in the Administration before long. They, above—the Council in Europe, you know—mean him to be.'

"He turned to his work. The noise outside had ceased, and presently in going out I stopped at the door. In the steady buzz of flies the homeward-bound agent was lying flushed and insensible; the other, bent over his books, was making correct entries of perfectly correct transactions; and fifty feet below the doorstep I could see the still tree-tops of the grove of death.

"Next day I left that station at last, with a caravan of sixty men, for a two-hundred-mile tramp.

"No use telling you much about that. Paths, paths, everywhere; a stamped-in network of paths spreading over the empty land, through long grass, through burnt grass, through thickets, down and up chilly ravines, up and down stony hills ablaze with heat; and a solitude, a solitude, nobody, not a hut. The population had cleared out a long time ago. Well, if a lot of mysterious niggers armed with all kinds of fearful weapons suddenly took to travelling on the road between Deal and Gravesend, catching the yokels right and left to carry heavy loads for them, I fancy every farm and cottage thereabouts would get empty very soon. Only here the dwellings were gone too. Still, I passed through several abandoned villages. There's something pathetically childish in the ruins of grass walls. Day after day, with the stamp and shuffle of sixty pair of bare feet behind me, each pair under a 60-lb. load. Camp, cook, sleep, strike camp, march. Now and then a carrier dead in harness, at rest in the long grass near the path, with an empty water-gourd and his long staff lying by his side. A great silence around and above. Perhaps on some quiet night the tremor of far-off drums, sinking, swelling, a tremor vast, faint; a sound weird, appealing, suggestive, and wild—and perhaps with as profound a meaning as the sound of bells in a Christian country. Once a white man in an unbuttoned uniform, camping on the path with an armed escort of lank Zanzibaris,[8] very hospitable and festive—not to say drunk. Was looking after the upkeep of the road, he declared. Can't say I saw any road or any upkeep, unless the body of a middle-aged negro, with a bullet-hole in the forehead, upon which I absolutely stumbled three miles farther on, may be considered as a permanent improvement. I had a white companion too, not a bad chap, but rather too fleshy and with the exasperating habit of fainting on the hot hillsides, miles away from the least bit of shade and water. Annoying, you know, to hold your own coat like a parasol over a man's head while he is coming-to. I couldn't help asking him once what he meant by coming there at all. 'To make money, of course. What do you think?' he said scornfully. Then he got fever, and had to be carried in a hammock slung under a pole. As he weighed sixteen stone[9] I had no end of rows with the carriers. They jibbed, ran away, sneaked off with their loads in the night—quite a mutiny. So, one evening, I made a speech in English with gestures, not one of which was lost to the sixty pairs of eyes before me, and the next morning I started the hammock off in front all right. An hour afterwards I came upon the whole concern wrecked in a bush—man, hammock, groans, blankets, horrors. The heavy pole had skinned his poor nose. He was very anxious for me to kill somebody, but there wasn't the shadow of a carrier near. I remembered the old doctor—'It would be interesting for science to watch the mental changes of individuals, on the spot.' I felt I was becoming scientifically interesting. However, all that is to no purpose. On the fifteenth day I came in sight of the big river again, and hobbled into the Central Station. It was on a back water surrounded by scrub and forest, with a pretty border of smelly mud on one side, and on the three others enclosed by a crazy fence of rushes. A neglected gap was all the gate it had, and the first glance at the place was enough to let you see the flabby devil was running that show. White men with long staves in their hands appeared languidly from amongst the buildings, strolling up to take a look at me, and then retired out of sight somewhere. One of them, a stout, excitable chap with black moustaches, informed me with great volubility and many digressions, as soon as I told him who I was, that my steamer was at the bottom of the river. I was thunderstruck. What, how, why? Oh, it was 'all right.' The 'manager himself was there. All quite correct. 'Everybody had behaved splendidly! splendidly!'—'You must,' he said in agitation, 'go and see the general manager at once. He is waiting!'

"I did not see the real significance of that wreck at once. I fancy I see it now, but I am not sure—not at all. Certainly the affair was too stupid—when I think of it—to be altogether natural. Still . . . But at the moment it presented itself simply as a confounded nuisance. The steamer was sunk. They had started two days before in a sudden hurry up the river with the manager on board, in charge of some volunteer skipper, and before they had been out three hours they tore the bottom out of her on stones, and she sank near the south bank. I asked myself what I was to do there, now my boat was lost. As a matter of fact, I had plenty to do in fishing my command out of the river. I had to set about it the very next day. That, and the repairs when I brought the pieces to the station, took some months.

---

8. Natives of Zanzibar, an island off the east coast of Africa, once part of the sultanate of Zanzibar and a British protectorate, now part of the independent state of Tanzania. Zanzibaris were used as mercenaries throughout Africa.
9. One stone equals 14 pounds. The man weighed 224 pounds.

"My first interview with the manager was curious. He did not ask me to sit down after my twenty-mile walk that morning. He was commonplace in complexion, in feature, in manners, and in voice. He was of middle size and of ordinary build. His eyes, of the usual blue, were perhaps remarkably cold, and he certainly could make his glance fall on one as trenchant and heavy as an axe. But even at these times the rest of his person seemed to disclaim the intention. Otherwise there was only an indefinable, faint expression of his lips, something stealthy—a smile—not a smile—I remember it, but I can't explain. It was unconscious, this smile was, though just after he had said something it got intensified for an instant. It came at the end of his speeches like a seal applied on the words to make the meaning of the commonest phrase appear absolutely inscrutable. He was a common trader, from his youth up employed in these parts—nothing more. He was obeyed, yet he inspired neither love nor fear, nor even respect. He inspired uneasiness. That was it! Uneasiness. Not a definite mistrust—just uneasiness—nothing more. You have no idea how effective such a . . . a . . . faculty can be. He had no genius for organising, for initiative, or for order even. That was evident in such things as the deplorable state of the station. He had no learning, and no intelligence. His position had come to him—why? Perhaps because he was never ill . . . He had served three terms of three years out there . . . Because triumphant health in the general rout of constitutions is a kind of power in itself. When he went home on leave he rioted on a large scale—pompously. Jack ashore—with a difference—in externals only. This one could gather from his casual talk. He originated nothing, he could keep the routine going—that's all. But he was great. He was great by this little thing that it was impossible to tell what could control such a man. He never gave that secret away. Perhaps there was nothing within him. Such a suspicion made one pause—for out there there were no external checks. Once when various tropical diseases had laid low almost every 'agent' in the station, he was heard to say, 'Men who come out here should have no entrails.' He sealed the utterance with that smile of his, as though it had been a door opening into a darkness he had in his keeping. You fancied you had seen things—but the seal was on. When annoyed at meal-times by the constant quarrels of the white men about precedence, he ordered an immense round table to be made, for which a special house had to be built. This was the station's mess-room. Where he sat was the first place—the rest were nowhere. One felt this to be his unalterable conviction. He was neither civil nor uncivil. He was quiet. He allowed his 'boy'—an overfed young negro from the coast—to treat the white men, under his very eyes, with provoking insolence.

"He began to speak as soon as he saw me. I had been very long on the road. He could not wait. Had to start without me. The up-river stations had to be relieved. There had been so many delays already that he did not know who was dead and who was alive, and how they got on—and so on, and so on. He paid no attention to my explanations, and, playing with a stick of sealing-wax, repeated several times that the situation was 'very grave, very grave.' There were rumours that a very important station was in jeopardy, and its chief, Mr Kurtz, was ill. Hoped it was not true. Mr Kurtz was . . . I felt weary and irritable. Hang Kurtz, I thought. I interrupted him by saying I had heard of Mr Kurtz on the coast. 'Ah! So they talk of him down there,' he murmured to himself. Then he began again, assuring me Mr Kurtz was the best agent he had, an exceptional man, of the greatest importance to the Company; therefore I could understand his anxiety. He was, he said, 'very, very uneasy.' Certainly he fidgeted on his chair a good deal, exclaimed, 'Ah, Mr Kurtz!' broke the stick of sealing-wax and seemed dumbfounded by the accident. Next thing he wanted to know 'how long it would take to' . . . I interrupted him again. Being hungry, you know, and kept on my feet too, I was getting savage. 'How can I tell?' I said, 'I haven't even seen the wreck yet—some months, no doubt.' All this talk seemed to me so futile. 'Some months,' he said. 'Well, let us say three months before we can make a start. Yes. That ought to do the affair.' I flung out of his hut (he lived all alone in a clay hut with a sort of verandah) muttering to myself my opinion of him. He was a chattering idiot. Afterwards I took it back when it was borne in upon me startlingly with what extreme nicety he had estimated the time requisite for the 'affair.'

"I went to work the next day, turning, so to speak, my back on that station. In that way only it seemed to me I could keep my hold on the redeeming facts of life. Still, one must look about sometimes; and then I saw this station, these men strolling aimlessly about in the sunshine of the yard. I asked myself sometimes what it all meant. They wandered here and there with their absurd long staves in their hands, like a lot of faithless pilgrims bewitched inside a rotten fence. The word 'ivory' rang in the air, was whispered, was sighed. You would think they were praying to it. A taint of imbecile rapacity blew through it all, like a whiff from some corpse. By Jove! I've never seen anything so unreal in my life. And outside, the silent wilderness surrounding this cleared speck on the earth struck me as something great and invincible, like evil or truth, waiting patiently for the passing away of this fantastic invasion.

"Oh, these months! Well, never mind. Various things happened. One evening a grass shed full of calico, cotton prints, beads, and I don't know what else, burst into a blaze so suddenly that you would have thought the earth had opened to let an avenging fire consume all that trash. I was smoking my pipe quietly by my dismantled steamer, and saw them all cutting capers in the light, with their arms lifted high, when the stout man with moustaches came tearing down to the river, a tin pail in his hand, assured me that everybody was 'behaving splendidly, splendidly,' dipped about a quart of water and tore back again. I noticed there was a hole in the bottom of his pail.

"I strolled up. There was no hurry. You see the thing had gone off like a box of matches. It had been hopeless from the very first. The flame had leaped high, driven everybody back, lighted up everything—and collapsed. The shed was already a heap of embers glowing fiercely. A nigger was being beaten near by. They said he had caused the fire in some way; be that as it may, he was screeching most horribly. I saw him, later, for several days, sitting in a bit of shade looking very sick and trying to recover himself: afterwards he arose and went out—and the wilderness without a sound took him into its bosom again. As I approached the glow from the dark I found myself at the back of two men, talking. I heard the name of Kurtz pronounced, then the words, 'take advantage of this unfortunate accident.' One of the men was the manager. I wished him a good evening. 'Did you ever see anything like it—eh? it is incredible,' he said, and walked off. The other man remained. He was a first-class agent, young, gentlemanly, a bit reserved, with a forked little beard and a hooked nose. He was standoffish with the other agents, and they on their side said he was the manager's spy upon them. As to me, I had hardly ever spoken to him before. We got into talk, and by and by we strolled away from the hissing ruins. Then he asked me to his room, which was in the main building of the station. He struck a match, and I perceived that this young aristocrat had not only a silver-mounted dressing-case but also a whole candle all to himself. Just at that time the manager was the only man supposed to have any right to candles. Native mats covered the clay walls; a collection of spears, assegais,[1] shields, knives, was hung up in trophies. The business entrusted to this fellow was the making of bricks—so I had been informed; but there wasn't a fragment of a brick anywhere in the station, and he had been there more than a year—waiting. It seems he could not make bricks without something, I don't know what—straw maybe. Anyway, it could not be found there, and as it was not likely to be sent from Europe, it did not appear clear to me what he was waiting for. An act of special creation perhaps. However, they were all waiting—all the sixteen or twenty pilgrims of them—for something; and upon my word it did not seem an uncongenial occupation, from the way they took it, though the only thing that ever came to them was disease—as far as I could see. They beguiled the time by backbiting and intriguing against each other in a foolish kind of way. There was an air of plotting about that station, but nothing came of it, of course. It was as unreal as everything else—as the philanthropic pretence of the whole concern, as their talk, as their government, as their show of work. The only real feeling was a desire to get appointed to a trading-post where ivory was to be had, so that they could earn percentages. They intrigued and slandered and hated each other only on that account—but as to effectually lifting a little finger—oh no. By heavens! there is something after all in the world allowing one man to steal a horse while another must not look at a halter. Steal a horse straight out. Very well. He has done it. Perhaps he can ride. But there is a way of looking at a halter that would provoke the most charitable of saints into a kick.

"I had no idea why he wanted to be sociable, but as we chatted in there it suddenly occurred to me the fellow was trying to get at something—in fact, pumping me. He alluded constantly to Europe, to the people I was supposed to know there—putting leading questions as to my acquaintances in the sepulchral city, and so on. His little eyes glittered like mica[2] discs—with curiosity—though he tried to keep up a bit of superciliousness. At first I was astonished, but very soon I became awfully curious to see what he would find out from me. I couldn't possibly imagine what I had in me to make it worth his while. It was very pretty to see how he baffled himself, for in truth my body was full only of chills, and my head had nothing in it but that wretched steamboat business. It was evident he took me for a perfectly shameless prevaricator. At last he got angry, and, to conceal a movement of furious annoyance, he yawned. I rose. Then I noticed a small sketch in oils, on a panel, representing a woman, draped and blindfolded, carrying a lighted torch. The background was sombre—almost black. The movement of the woman was stately, and the effect of the torchlight on the face was sinister.

"It arrested me, and he stood by civilly, holding an empty half-pint champagne bottle (medical comforts) with the candle stuck in it. To my question he said Mr Kurtz had painted this—in this very station more than a year ago—while waiting for means to go to his trading-post. 'Tell me, pray,' said I, 'who is this Mr Kurtz?'

---

1. Slender iron-tipped spears.   2. Glassy mineral.

"'The chief of the Inner Station,' he answered in a short tone, looking away. 'Much obliged,' I said, laughing. 'And you are the brickmaker of the Central Station. Every one knows that.' He was silent for a while. 'He is a prodigy,' he said at last. 'He is an emissary of pity, and science, and progress, and devil knows what else. We want,' he began to declaim suddenly, 'for the guidance of the cause entrusted to us by Europe, so to speak, higher intelligence, wide sympathies, a singleness of purpose.' 'Who says that?' I asked. 'Lots of them,' he replied. 'Some even write that; and so *he* comes here, a special being, as you ought to know.' 'Why ought I to know?' I interrupted, really surprised. He paid no attention. 'Yes. To-day he is chief of the best station, next year he will be assistant-manager, two years more and . . . but I daresay you know what he will be in two years' time. You are of the new gang—the gang of virtue. The same people who sent him specially also recommended you. Oh, don't say no. I've my own eyes to trust.' Light dawned upon me. My dear aunt's influential acquaintances were producing an unexpected effect upon that young man. I nearly burst into a laugh. 'Do you read the Company's confidential correspondence?' I asked. He hadn't a word to say. It was great fun. 'When Mr Kurtz,' I continued severely, 'is General Manager, you won't have the opportunity.'

"He blew the candle out suddenly, and we went outside. The moon had risen. Black figures strolled about listlessly, pouring water on the glow, whence proceeded a sound of hissing; steam ascended in the moonlight; the beaten nigger groaned somewhere. 'What a row the brute makes!' said the indefatigable man with the moustaches, appearing near us. 'Serve him right. Transgression—punishment—bang! Pitiless, pitiless. That's the only way. This will prevent all conflagrations for the future. I was just telling the manager . . .' He noticed my companion, and became crestfallen all at once. 'Not in bed yet,' he said, with a kind of servile heartiness; 'it's so natural. Ha! Danger—agitation.' He vanished. I went on to the river-side, and the other followed me. I heard a scathing murmur at my ear, 'Heap of muffs—go to.' The pilgrims could be seen in knots gesticulating, discussing. Several had still their staves in their hands. I verily believe they took these sticks to bed with them. Beyond the fence the forest stood up spectrally in the moonlight, and through the dim stir, through the faint sounds of that lamentable courtyard, the silence of the land went home to one's very heart—its mystery, its greatness, the amazing reality of its concealed life. The hurt nigger moaned feebly somewhere near by, and then fetched a deep sigh that made me mend my pace away from there. I felt a hand introducing itself under my arm. 'My dear sir,' said the fellow, 'I don't want to be misunderstood, and especially by you, who will see Mr Kurtz long before I can have that pleasure. I wouldn't like him to get a false idea of my disposition. . . .'

"I let him run on, this papier-mâché Mephistopheles, and it seemed to me that if I tried I could poke my forefinger through him, and would find nothing inside but a little loose dirt, maybe. He, don't you see, had been planning to be assistant-manager by and by under the present man, and I could see that the coming of that Kurtz had upset them both not a little. He talked precipitately, and I did not try to stop him. I had my shoulders against the wreck of my steamer, hauled up on the slope like a carcass of some big river animal. The smell of mud, of primeval mud, by Jove! was in my nostrils, the high stillness of primeval forest was before my eyes; there were shiny patches on the black creek. The moon had spread over everything a thin layer of silver—over the rank grass, over the mud, upon the wall of matted vegetation standing higher than the wall of a temple, over the great river I could see through a sombre gap glittering, glittering, as it flowed broadly by without a murmur. All this was great, expectant, mute, while the man jabbered about himself. I wondered whether the stillness on the face of the immensity looking at us two were meant as an appeal or as a menace. What were we who had strayed in here? Could we handle that dumb thing, or would it handle us? I felt how big, how confoundedly big, was that thing that couldn't talk and perhaps was deaf as well. What was in there? I could see a little ivory coming out from there, and I had heard Mr Kurtz was in there. I had heard enough about it too—God knows! Yet somehow it didn't bring any image with it—no more than if I had been told an angel or a fiend was in there. I believed it in the same way one of you might believe there are inhabitants in the planet Mars. I knew once a Scotch sailmaker who was certain, dead sure, there were people in Mars. If you asked him for some idea how they looked and behaved, he would get shy and mutter something about 'walking on all-fours.' If you as much as smiled, he would—though a man of sixty—offer to fight you. I would not have gone so far as to fight for Kurtz, but I went for him near enough to a lie. You know I hate, detest, and can't bear a lie, not because I am straighter than the rest of us, but simply because it appals me. There is a taint of death, a flavour of mortality in lies—which is exactly what I hate and detest in the world—what I want to forget. It makes me miserable and sick, like biting something rotten would do. Temperament, I suppose. Well, I went near enough to it by letting the young fool there believe anything he liked to imagine as to my influence in Europe. I became in an instant as much of a pretence as the rest of the bewitched pilgrims. This simply because I had a notion it somehow would be of help to that Kurtz whom at the time I did not see—you understand. He was just a word for me. I did not see the man in the name any more than you do. Do you see him? Do you see the story? Do you see anything? It seems to me I am trying to tell you a dream—making a vain attempt, because no relation of a dream can convey the dream-sensation, that commingling of absurdity, surprise, and bewilderment in a tremor of struggling revolt, that notion of being captured by the incredible which is of the very essence of dreams. . . ."

He was silent for a while.

". . . No, it is impossible; it is impossible to convey the life-sensation of any given epoch of one's existence—that which makes its truth, its meaning—its subtle and penetrating essence. It is impossible. We live, as we dream—alone. . . ."

He paused again as if reflecting, then added:

"Of course in this you fellows see more than I could then. You see me, whom you know. . . ."

It had become so pitch dark that we listeners could hardly see one another. For a long time already he, sitting apart, had been no more to us than a voice. There was not a word from anybody. The others might have been asleep, but I was awake. I listened, I listened on the watch for the sentence, for the word, that would give me the clue to the faint uneasiness inspired by this narrative that seemed to shape itself without human lips in the heavy night-air of the river.

". . . Yes—I let him run on," Marlow began again, "and think what he pleased about the powers that were behind me. I did! And there was nothing behind me! There was nothing but that wretched, old, mangled steamboat I was leaning against, while he talked fluently about 'the necessity for every man to get on.' 'And when one comes out here, you conceive, it is not to gaze at the moon.' Mr Kurtz was a 'universal genius,' but even a genius would find it easier to work with 'adequate tools—intelligent men.' He did not make bricks—why, there was a physical impossibility in the way—as I was well aware; and if he did secretarial work for the manager, it was because 'no sensible man rejects wantonly the confidence of his superiors.' Did I see it? I saw it. What more did I want? What I really wanted was rivets, by heaven! Rivets. To get on with the work—to stop the hole. Rivets I wanted. There were cases of them down at the coast—cases—piled up—burst— split! You kicked a loose rivet at every second step in that station yard on the hillside. Rivets had rolled into the grove of death. You could fill your pockets with rivets for the trouble of stooping down—and there wasn't one rivet to be found where it was wanted. We had plates that would do, but nothing to fasten them with. And every week the messenger, a lone negro, letter-bag on shoulder and staff in hand, left our station for the coast. And several times a week a coast caravan came in with trade goods—ghastly glazed calico that made you shudder only to look at it, glass beads value about a penny a quart, confounded spotted cotton handkerchiefs. And no rivets. Three carriers could have brought all that was wanted to set that steamboat afloat.

"He was becoming confidential now, but I fancy my unresponsive attitude must have exasperated him at last, for he judged it necessary to inform me he feared neither God nor devil, let alone any mere man. I said I could see that very well, but what I wanted was a certain quantity of rivets—and rivets were what really Mr Kurtz wanted, if he had only known it. Now letters went to the coast every week. . . . 'My dear sir,' he cried, 'I write from dictation.' I demanded rivets. There was a way—for an intelligent man. He changed his manner; became very cold, and suddenly began to talk about a hippopotamus; wondered whether sleeping on board the steamer (I stuck to my salvage night and day) I wasn't disturbed. There was an old hippo that had the bad habit of getting out on the bank and roaming at night over the station grounds. The pilgrims used to turn out in a body and empty every rifle they could lay hands on at him. Some even had sat up o' nights for him. All this energy was wasted, though. 'That animal has a charmed life,' he said; 'but you can say this only of brutes in this country. No man—you apprehend me?—no man here bears a charmed life.' He stood there for a moment in the moonlight with his delicate hooked nose set a little askew, and his mica eyes glittering without a wink, then, with a curt Good-night, he strode off. I could see he was disturbed and considerably puzzled, which made me feel more hopeful than I had been for days. It was a great comfort to turn from that chap to my influential friend, the battered, twisted, ruined, tinpot steamboat. I clambered on board. She rang under my feet like an empty Huntley & Palmer biscuit-tin kicked along a gutter; she was nothing so solid in make, and rather less pretty in shape, but I had expended enough hard work on her to make me love her. No influential friend would have served me better. She had given me a chance to come out a bit—to find out what I could do. No, I don't like work. I had rather laze about and think of all the fine things that can be done. I don't like work—no man does—but I like what is in the work—the chance to find yourself. Your own reality—for yourself, not for others—what no other man can ever know. They can only see the mere show, and never can tell what it really means.

"I was not surprised to see somebody sitting aft, on the deck, with his legs dangling over the mud. You see I rather chummed with the few mechanics there were in that station, whom the other pilgrims naturally despised—on account of their imperfect manners, I suppose. This was the foreman—a boiler-maker by trade—a good worker. He was a lank, bony, yellow-faced man, with big intense eyes. His aspect was worried, and his head was as bald as the palm of my hand; but his hair in falling seemed to have stuck to his chin, and had prospered in the new locality, for his beard hung down to his waist. He was a widower with six young children (he had left them in charge of a sister of his to come out there), and the passion of his life was pigeon-flying. He was an enthusiast and a connoisseur. He would rave about pigeons. After work hours he used sometimes to come over from his hut for a talk about his children and his pigeons; at work, when he had to crawl in the mud under the bottom of the steamboat, he would tie up that beard of his in a kind of white serviette[3] he brought for the purpose. It had loops to go over his ears. In the evening he could be seen squatted on the bank rinsing that wrapper in the creek with great care, then spreading it solemnly on a bush to dry.

"I slapped him on the back and shouted 'We shall have rivets!' He scrambled to his feet exclaiming 'No! Rivets!' as though he couldn't believe his ears. Then in a low voice, 'You . . . eh?' I don't know why we behaved like lunatics. I put my finger to the side of my nose and nodded mysteriously. 'Good for you!' he cried, snapped his fingers above his head, lifting one foot. I tried a jig. We capered on the iron deck. A frightful clatter came out of that hulk, and the virgin forest on the other bank of the creek sent it back in a thundering roll upon the sleeping station. It must have made some of the pilgrims sit up in their hovels. A dark figure obscured the lighted doorway of the manager's hut, vanished, then, a second or so after, the doorway itself vanished too. We stopped, and the silence driven away by the stamping of our feet flowed back again from the recesses of the land. The great wall of vegetation, an exuberant and entangled mass of trunks, branches, leaves, boughs, festoons, motionless in the moonlight, was like a rioting invasion of soundless life, a rolling wave of plants, piled up, crested, ready to topple over the creek, to sweep every little man of us out of his little existence. And it moved not. A deadened burst of mighty splashes and snorts reached us from afar, as though an ichthyosaurus[4] had been taking a bath of glitter in the great river. 'After all,' said the boiler-maker in a reasonable tone, 'why shouldn't we get the rivets?' Why not, indeed! I did not know of any reason why we shouldn't. 'They'll come in three weeks,' I said confidently.

"But they didn't. Instead of rivets there came an invasion, an infliction, a visitation. It came in sections during the next three weeks, each section headed by a donkey carrying a white man in new clothes and tan shoes, bowing from that elevation right and left to the impressed pilgrims. A quarrelsome band of footsore sulky niggers trod on the heels of the donkey; a lot of tents, campstools, tin boxes, white cases, brown bales would be shot down in the courtyard, and the air of mystery would deepen a little over the muddle of the station. Five such instalments came, with their absurd air of disorderly flight with the loot of innumerable outfit shops and provision stores, that, one would think, they were lugging, after a raid, into the wil-

3. Table napkin.   4. Large prehistoric marine creature.

derness for equitable division. It was an inextricable mess of things decent in themselves but that human folly made look like the spoils of thieving.

"This devoted band called itself the Eldorado[5] Exploring Expedition, and I believe they were sworn to secrecy. Their talk, however, was the talk of sordid buccaneers: it was reckless without hardihood, greedy without audacity, and cruel without courage; there was not an atom of foresight or of serious intention in the whole batch of them, and they did not seem aware these things are wanted for the work of the world. To tear treasure out of the bowels of the land was their desire, with no more moral purpose at the back of it than there is in burglars breaking into a safe. Who paid the expenses of the noble enterprise I don't know; but the uncle of our manager was leader of that lot.

"In exterior he resembled a butcher in a poor neighbourhood, and his eyes had a look of sleepy cunning. He carried his fat paunch with ostentation on his short legs, and during the time his gang infested the station spoke to no one but his nephew. You could see these two roaming about all day long with their heads close together in an everlasting confab.[6]

"I had given up worrying myself about the rivets. One's capacity for that kind of folly is more limited than you would suppose. I said Hang!—and let things slide. I had plenty of time for meditation, and now and then I would give some thought to Kurtz. I wasn't very interested in him. No. Still, I was curious to see whether this man, who had come out equipped with moral ideas of some sort, would climb to the top after all, and how he would set about his work when there."

2

"One evening as I was lying flat on the deck of my steamboat, I heard voices approaching—and there were the nephew and the uncle strolling along the bank. I laid my head on my arm again, and had nearly lost myself in a doze, when somebody said in my ear, as it were: 'I am as harmless as a little child, but I don't like to be dictated to. Am I the manager—or am I not? I was ordered to send him there. It's incredible.' . . . I became aware that the two were standing on the shore alongside the forepart of the steamboat, just below my head. I did not move; it did not occur to me to move: I was sleepy. 'It *is* unpleasant,' grunted the uncle. 'He has asked the Administration to be sent there,' said the other, 'with the idea of showing what he could do; and I was instructed accordingly. Look at the influence that man must have. Is it not frightful?' They both agreed it was frightful, then made several bizarre remarks: 'Make rain and fine weather—one man—the Council—by the nose'—bits of absurd sentences that got the better of my drowsiness, so that I had pretty near the whole of my wits about me when the uncle said, 'The climate may do away with this difficulty for you. Is he alone there?' 'Yes,' answered the manager; 'he sent his assistant down the river with a note to me in these terms: "Clear this poor devil out of the country, and don't bother sending more of that sort. I had rather be alone than have the kind of men you can dispose of with me." It was more than a year ago. Can you imagine such impudence?' 'Anything since then?' asked the other hoarsely. 'Ivory,' jerked the nephew; 'lots of it—prime sort—lots—most annoying, from him.'

5. Fabled land of gold (*el dorado*, Spanish for "the gilded") imagined by the Spanish conquis-

tadors to exist in South America.
6. Confabulation, talk.

'And with that?' questioned the heavy rumble. 'Invoice,' was the reply fired out, so to speak. Then silence. They had been talking about Kurtz.

"I was broad awake by this time, but, lying perfectly at ease, remained still, having no inducement to change my position. 'How did that ivory come all this way?' growled the elder man, who seemed very vexed. The other explained that it had come with a fleet of canoes in charge of an English half-caste clerk Kurtz had with him; that Kurtz had apparently intended to return himself, the station being by that time bare of goods and stores, but after coming three hundred miles, had suddenly decided to go back, which he started to do alone in a small dugout with four paddlers, leaving the half-caste to continue down the river with the ivory. The two fellows there seemed astounded at anybody attempting such a thing. They were at a loss for an adequate motive. As for me, I seemed to see Kurtz for the first time. It was a distinct glimpse: the dugout, four paddling savages, and the lone white man turning his back suddenly on the headquarters, on relief, on thoughts of home—perhaps; setting his face towards the depths of the wilderness, towards his empty and desolate station. I did not know the motive. Perhaps he was just simply a fine fellow who stuck to his work for its own sake. His name, you understand, had not been pronounced once. He was 'that man.' The half-caste, who, as far as I could see, had conducted a difficult trip with great prudence and pluck, was invariably alluded to as 'that scoundrel.' The 'scoundrel' had reported that the 'man' had been very ill—had recovered imperfectly. . . . The two below me moved away then a few paces, and stroked back and forth at some little distance. I heard: 'Military post—doctor—two hundred miles—quite alone now—unavoidable delays—nine months—no news—strange rumours.' They approached again, just as the manager was saying, 'No one, as far as I know, unless a species of wandering trader—a pestilential fellow, snapping ivory from the natives.' Who was it they were talking about now? I gathered in snatches that this was some man supposed to be in Kurtz's district, and of whom the manager did not approve. 'We will not be free from unfair competition till one of these fellows is hanged for an example,' he said. 'Certainly,' grunted the other; 'get him hanged! Why not? Anything—anything can be done in this country. That's what I say; nobody here, you understand, *here*, can endanger your position. And why? You stand the climate—you outlast them all. The danger is in Europe; but there before I left I took care to—' They moved off and whispered, then their voices rose again. 'The extraordinary series of delays is not my fault. I did my possible.'[7] The fat man sighed, 'Very sad.' 'And the pestiferous absurdity of his talk,' continued the other; 'he bothered me enough when he was here. "Each station should be like a beacon on the road towards better things, a centre for trade of course, but also for humanising, improving, instructing." Conceive you—that ass! And he wants to be manager! No, it's—' Here he got choked by excessive indignation, and I lifted my head the least bit. I was surprised to see how near they were—right under me. I could have spat upon their hats. They were looking on the ground, absorbed in thought. The manager was switching his leg with a slender twig: his sagacious relative lifted his head. 'You have been well since you came out this

---

7. Literal rendering of the French *J'ai fait mon possible* (I have done all I could). Conrad sprinkles the conversation of his Belgian characters with Gallicisms to remind us that their words, though reported in English, were spoken in French. Other examples are "a species of wandering trader" (above), "Conceive you" (below), "I would be desolated" (p. 104).

time?' he asked. The other gave a start. 'Who? I? Oh! Like a charm—like a charm. But the rest—oh, my goodness! All sick. They die so quick, too, that I haven't the time to send them out of the country—it's incredible!' 'H'm. Just so,' grunted the uncle. 'Ah! my boy, trust to this—I say, trust to this.' I saw him extend his short flipper of an arm for a gesture that took in the forest, the creek, the mud, the river—seemed to beckon with a dishonouring flourish before the sunlit face of the land a treacherous appeal to the lurking death, to the hidden evil, to the profound darkness of its heart. It was so startling that I leaped to my feet and looked back at the edge of the forest, as though I had expected an answer of some sort to that black display of confidence. You know the foolish notions that come to one sometimes. The high stillness confronted these two figures with its ominous patience, waiting for the passing away of a fantastic invasion.

"They swore aloud together—out of sheer fright, I believe—then, pretending not to know anything of my existence, turned back to the station. The sun was low; and leaning forward side by side, they seemed to be tugging painfully uphill their two ridiculous shadows of unequal length, that trailed behind them slowly over the tall grass without bending a single blade.

"In a few days the Eldorado Expedition went into the patient wilderness, that closed upon it as the sea closes over a diver. Long afterwards the news came that all the donkeys were dead. I know nothing as to the fate of the less valuable animals. They, no doubt, like the rest of us, found what they deserved. I did not inquire. I was then rather excited at the prospect of meeting Kurtz very soon. When I say very soon I mean it comparatively. It was just two months from the day we left the creek when we came to the bank below Kurtz's station.

"Going up that river was like travelling back to the earliest beginnings of the world, when vegetation rioted on the earth and the big trees were kings. An empty stream, a great silence, an impenetrable forest. The air was warm, thick, heavy, sluggish. There was no joy in the brilliance of sunshine. The long stretches of the waterway ran on, deserted, into the gloom of overshadowed distances. On silvery sandbanks hippos and alligators sunned themselves side by side. The broadening waters flowed through a mob of wooded islands; you lost your way on that river as you would in a desert, and butted all day long against shoals, trying to find the channel, till you thought yourself bewitched and cut off for ever from everything you had known once— somewhere—far away—in another existence perhaps. There were moments when one's past came back to one, as it will sometimes when you have not a moment to spare to yourself; but it came in the shape of an unrestful and noisy dream, remembered with wonder amongst the overwhelming realities of this strange world of plants, and water, and silence. And this stillness of life did not in the least resemble a peace. It was the stillness of an implacable force brooding over an inscrutable intention. It looked at you with a vengeful aspect. I got used to it afterwards; I did not see it any more; I had no time. I had to keep guessing at the channel; I had to discern, mostly by inspiration, the signs of hidden banks; I watched for sunken stones; I was learning to clap my teeth smartly before my heart flew out, when I shaved by a fluke some infernal sly old snag that would have ripped the life out of the tin-pot steamboat and drowned all the pilgrims; I had to keep a lookout for the signs of dead wood we could cut up in the night for next day's steaming. When you have to attend to things of that sort, to the mere incidents of the surface, the reality—the reality, I tell you—fades. The inner truth is hidden—luckily, luckily. But I felt it all the same; I felt often its mysterious stillness watching me at my monkey tricks, just as it watches you fellows performing on your respective tight-ropes for—what is it? half a crown a tumble—"

"Try to be civil, Marlow," growled a voice, and I knew there was at least one listener awake besides myself.

"I beg your pardon. I forgot the heartache which makes up the rest of the price. And indeed what does the price matter, if the trick be well done? You do your tricks very well. And I didn't do badly either, since I managed not to sink that steamboat on my first trip. It's a wonder to me yet. Imagine a blindfolded man set to drive a van over a bad road. I sweated and shivered over that business considerably, I can tell you. After all, for a seaman, to scrape the bottom of the thing that's supposed to float all the time under his care is the unpardonable sin. No one may know of it, but you never forget the thump—eh? A blow on the very heart. You remember it, you dream of it, you wake up at night and think of it—years after—and go hot and cold all over. I don't pretend to say that steamboat floated all the time. More than once she had to wade for a bit, with twenty cannibals splashing around and pushing. We had enlisted some of these chaps on the way for a crew. Fine fellows—cannibals—in their place. They were men one could work with, and I am grateful to them. And, after all, they did not eat each other before my face: they had brought along a provision of hippo-meat which went rotten, and made the mystery of the wilderness stink in my nostrils. Phoo! I can sniff it now. I had the manager on board and three or four pilgrims with their staves—all complete. Sometimes we came upon a station close by the bank, clinging to the skirts of the unknown, and the white men rushing out of a tumble-down hovel, with great gestures of joy and surprise and welcome, seemed very strange—had the appearance of being held there captive by a spell. The word 'ivory' would ring in the air for a while—and on we went again into the silence, along empty reaches, round the still bends, between the high walls of our winding way, reverberating in hollow claps the ponderous beat of the stern-wheel. Trees, trees, millions of trees, massive, immense, running up high; and at their foot, hugging the bank against the stream, crept the little begrimed steamboat, like a sluggish beetle crawling on the floor of a lofty portico. It made you feel very small, very lost, and yet it was not altogether depressing, that feeling. After all, if you were small, the grimy beetle crawled on—which was just what you wanted it to do. Where the pilgrims imagined it crawled to I don't know. To some place where they expected to get something, I bet! For me it crawled towards Kurtz—exclusively; but when the steam-pipes started leaking we crawled very slow. The reaches opened before us and closed behind, as if the forest had stepped leisurely across the water to bar the way for our return. We penetrated deeper and deeper into the heart of darkness. It was very quiet there. At night sometimes the roll of drums behind the curtain of trees would run up the river and remain sustained faintly, as if hovering in the air high over our heads, till the first break of day. Whether it meant war, peace, or prayer we could not tell. The dawns were heralded by the descent of a chill stillness; the woodcutters slept, their fires burned low; the snapping of a twig would make you start. We were wanderers on a prehistoric earth, on an earth that wore the aspect of an unknown planet. We could have fancied ourselves the first of men taking possession of an accursed inheritance, to be subdued at the cost of profound anguish and of excessive toil. But suddenly, as we struggled round a bend, there would be a glimpse of rush walls, of peaked grass-roofs, a burst of yells, a whirl of black limbs, a mass of hands clapping, of feet stamping, of bodies swaying, of eyes rolling, under the droop of heavy and motionless foliage. The steamer toiled along slowly on the edge of a black and incomprehensible frenzy. The prehistoric man was cursing us, praying to us, welcoming us—who could tell? We were cut off from the comprehension of our surroundings; we glided past like phantoms, wondering and secretly appalled, as sane men would be before an enthusiastic outbreak in a madhouse. We could not understand because we were too far and could not remember, because we were travelling in the night of first ages, of those ages that are gone, leaving hardly a sign—and no memories.

"The earth seemed unearthly. We are accustomed to look upon the shackled form of a conquered monster, but there—there you could look at a thing monstrous and free. It was unearthly, and the men were—No, they were not inhuman. Well, you know, that was the worst of it—this suspicion of their not being inhuman. It would come slowly to one. They howled and leaped, and spun, and made horrid faces; but what thrilled you was just the thought of their humanity—like yours—the thought of your remote kinship with this wild and passionate uproar. Ugly. Yes, it was ugly enough; but if you were man enough you would admit to yourself that there was in you just the faintest trace of a response to the terrible frankness of that noise, a dim suspicion of there being a meaning in it which you—you so remote from the night of first ages—could comprehend. And why not? The mind of man is capable of anything—because everything is in it, all the past as well as all the future. What was there after all? Joy, fear, sorrow, devotion, valour, rage—who can tell?—but truth—truth stripped of its cloak of time. Let the fool gape and shudder—the man knows, and can look on without a wink. But he must at least be as much of a man as these on the shore. He must meet that truth with his own true stuff—with his own inborn strength. Principles? Principles won't do. Acquisitions, clothes, pretty rags—rags that would fly off at the first good shake. No; you want a deliberate belief. An appeal to me in this fiendish row—is there? Very well; I hear; I admit, but I have a voice too, and for good or evil mine is the speech that cannot be silenced. Of course, a fool, what with sheer fright and fine sentiments, is always safe. Who's that grunting? You wonder I didn't go ashore for a howl and a dance? Well, no—I didn't. Fine sentiments, you say? Fine sentiments be hanged! I had no time. I had to mess about with white-lead and strips of woollen blanket helping to put bandages on those leaky steam-pipes—I tell you. I had to watch the steering, and circumvent those snags, and get the tin-pot along by hook or by crook. There was surface-truth enough in these things to save a wiser man. And between whiles I had to look after the savage who was fireman. He was an improved specimen; he could fire up a vertical boiler. He was there below me, and, upon my word, to look at him was as edifying as seeing a dog in a parody of breeches and a feather hat, walking on his hind legs. A few months of training had done for that really fine chap. He squinted at the steam-gauge and at the water-gauge with an evident effort of intrepidity—and he had filed teeth too, the poor devil, and the wool of his pate shaved into queer patterns, and three ornamental scars on each of his cheeks. He ought to have been clapping his hands and stamping his feet on the bank, instead of which he was hard at work, a thrall to strange witchcraft, full of improving knowledge. He was useful because he had been instructed; and what he knew was this—that should the water in that transparent thing disappear, the evil spirit inside the boiler would get angry through the greatness of his thirst, and take a terrible vengeance. So he sweated and fired up and watched the glass fearfully (with an impromptu charm, made of rags, tied to his arm, and a piece of polished bone, as big as a watch, stuck flatways through his lower lip), while the wooded banks slipped past us slowly, the short noise was left behind, the interminable miles of silence—and we crept on, towards Kurtz. But the snags were thick, the water was treacherous and shallow, the boiler seemed indeed to have a sulky devil in it, and thus neither that fireman nor I had any time to peer into our creepy thoughts.

"Some fifty miles below the Inner Station we came upon a hut of reeds, an inclined and melancholy pole, with the unrecognisable tatters of what had been a flag of some sort flying from it, and a neatly stacked wood-pile. This was unexpected. We came to the bank, and on the stack of firewood found a flat piece of board with some faded pencil-writing on it. When deciphered it said: 'Wood for you. Hurry up. Approach cautiously.' There was a signature, but it was illegible—not Kurtz—a much longer word. Hurry up. Where? Up the river? 'Approach cautiously.' We had not done so. But the warning could not have been meant for the place where it could be only found after approach. Something was wrong above. But what—and how much? That was the question. We commented adversely upon the imbecility of that telegraphic style. The bush around said nothing, and would not let us look very far, either. A torn curtain of red twill hung in the doorway of the hut, and flapped sadly in our faces. The dwelling was dismantled; but we could see a white man had lived there not very long ago. There remained a rude table—a plank on two posts; a heap of rubbish reposed in a dark corner, and by the door I picked up a book. It had lost its covers, and the pages had been thumbed into a state of extremely dirty softness; but the back had been lovingly stitched afresh with white cotton thread, which looked clean yet. It was an extraordinary find. Its title was, *An Inquiry into some Points of Seamanship*, by a man Towser, Towson—some such name— Master in His Majesty's Navy. The matter looked dreary reading enough, with illustrative diagrams and repulsive tables of figures, and the copy was sixty years old. I handled this amazing antiquity with the greatest possible tenderness, lest it should dissolve in my hands. Within, Towson or Towser was inquiring earnestly into the breaking strain of ships' chains and tackle, and other such matters. Not a very enthralling book; but at the first glance you could see there a singleness of intention, an honest concern for the right way of going to work, which made these humble pages, thought out so many years ago, luminous with another than a professional light. The simple old sailor, with his talk of chains and purchases, made me forget the jungle and the pilgrims in a delicious sensation of having come upon something unmistakably real. Such a book being there was wonderful enough; but still more astounding were the notes pencilled in the margin, and plainly referring to the text. I couldn't believe my eyes! They were in cipher! Yes, it looked like cipher. Fancy a man lugging with him a book of that description into this nowhere and studying it—and making notes—in cipher at that! It was an extravagant mystery.

"I had been dimly aware for some time of a worrying noise, and when I lifted my eyes I saw the wood-pile was gone, and the manager, aided by all the pilgrims, was shouting at me from the river-side. I slipped the book into my pocket. I assure you to leave off reading was like tearing myself away from the shelter of an old and solid friendship.

"I started the lame engine ahead. 'It must be this miserable trader—this intruder,' exclaimed the manager, looking back malevolently at the place we had left. 'He must be English,' I said. 'It will not save him from getting into trouble if he is not careful,' muttered the manager darkly. I observed with assumed innocence that no man was safe from trouble in this world.

"The current was more rapid now, the steamer seemed at her last gasp, the stern-wheel flopped languidly, and I caught myself listening on tiptoe for the next beat of the float,[8] for in sober truth I expected the wretched thing to give up every moment. It was like watching the last flickers of a life. But still we crawled. Sometimes I would pick out a tree a little way ahead to measure our progress towards Kurtz by, but I lost it invariably before we got abreast. To keep the eyes so long on one thing was too much for human patience. The manager displayed a beautiful resignation. I fretted and fumed and took to arguing with myself whether or no I would talk openly with Kurtz; but before I could come to any conclusion it occurred to me that my speech or my silence, indeed any action of mine, would be a mere futility. What did it matter what any one knew or ignored? What did it matter who was manager? One gets sometimes such a flash of insight. The essentials of this affair lay deep under the surface, beyond my reach, and beyond my power of meddling.

"Towards the evening of the second day we judged ourselves about eight miles from Kurtz's station. I wanted to push on; but the manager looked grave, and told me the navigation up there was so dangerous that it would be advisable, the sun being very low already, to wait where we were till next morning. Moreover, he pointed out that if the warning to approach cautiously were to be followed, we must approach in daylight—not at dusk, or in the dark. This was sensible enough. Eight miles meant nearly three hours' steaming for us, and I could also see suspicious ripples at the upper end of the reach. Nevertheless, I was annoyed beyond expression at the delay, and most unreasonably too, since one night more could not matter much after so many months. As we had plenty of wood, and caution was the word, I brought up in the middle of the stream. The reach was narrow, straight, with high sides like a railway cutting. The dusk came gliding into it long before the sun had set. The current ran smooth and swift, but a dumb immobility sat on the banks. The living trees, lashed together by the creepers and every living bush of the undergrowth, might have been changed into stone, even to the slenderest twig, to the lightest leaf. It was not sleep—it seemed unnatural, like a state of trance. Not the faintest sound of any kind could be heard. You looked on amazed, and began to suspect yourself of being deaf—then the night came suddenly, and struck you blind as well. About three in the morning some large fish leaped, and the loud splash made me jump as though a gun had been fired. When the sun rose there was

8. Automatic water-level regulator opening and closing a water-supply valve.

a white fog, very warm and clammy, and more blinding than the night. It did not shift or drive; it was just there, standing all round you like something solid. At eight or nine, perhaps, it lifted as a shutter lifts. We had a glimpse of the towering multitude of trees, of the immense matted jungle, with the blazing little ball of the sun hanging over it—all perfectly still—and then the white shutter came down again, smoothly, as if sliding in greased grooves. I ordered the chain, which we had begun to heave in, to be paid out again. Before it stopped running with a muffled rattle, a cry, a very loud cry, as of infinite desolation, soared slowly in the opaque air. It ceased. A complaining clamour, modulated in savage discords, filled our ears. The sheer unexpectedness of it made my hair stir under my cap. I don't know how it struck the others: to me it seemed as though the mist itself had screamed, so suddenly, and apparently from all sides at once, did this tumultuous and mournful uproar arise. It culminated in a hurried outbreak of almost intolerably excessive shrieking, which stopped short, leaving us stiffened in a variety of silly attitudes, and obstinately listening to the nearly as appalling and excessive silence. 'Good God! What is the meaning—?' stammered at my elbow one of the pilgrims—a little fat man, with sandy hair and red whiskers, who wore side-spring boots, and pink pyjamas tucked into his socks. Two others remained open-mouthed a whole minute, then dashed into the little cabin, to rush out incontinently and stand darting scared glances, with Winchesters at 'ready' in their hands. What we could see was just the steamer we were on, her outlines blurred as though she had been on the point of dissolving, and a misty strip of water, perhaps two feet broad, around her—and that was all. The rest of the world was nowhere, as far as our eyes and ears were concerned. Just nowhere. Gone, disappeared; swept off without leaving a whisper or a shadow behind.

"I went forward, and ordered the chain to be hauled in short, so as to be ready to trip the anchor and move the steamboat at once if necessary. 'Will they attack?' whispered an awed voice. 'We will all be butchered in this fog,' murmured another. The faces twitched with the strain, the hands trembled slightly, the eyes forgot to wink. It was very curious to see the contrast of expressions of the white men and of the black fellows of our crew, who were as much strangers to that part of the river as we, though their homes were only eight hundred miles away. The whites, of course greatly discomposed, had besides a curious look of being painfully shocked by such an outrageous row. The others had an alert, naturally interested expression; but their faces were essentially quiet, even those of the one or two who grinned as they hauled at the chain. Several exchanged short, grunting phrases, which seemed to settle the matter to their satisfaction. Their headman, a young, broad-chested black, severely draped in dark-blue fringed cloths, with fierce nostrils and his hair all done up artfully in oily ringlets, stood near me. 'Aha!' I said, just for good fellowship's sake. 'Catch 'im,' he snapped, with a bloodshot widening of his eyes and a flash of sharp teeth—'catch 'im. Give 'im to us.' 'To you, eh?' I asked; 'what would you do with them?' 'Eat 'im!' he said curtly, and, leaning his elbow on the rail, looked out into the fog in a dignified and profoundly pensive attitude. I would no doubt have been properly horrified, had it not occurred to me that he and his chaps must be very hungry: that they must have been growing increasingly hungry for at least this month past. They had been engaged for six months (I don't think a single one of them had any clear idea of time, as we at the end of countless ages

have. They still belonged to the beginnings of time—had no inherited experience to teach them, as it were), and of course, as long as there was a piece
of paper written over in accordance with some farcical law or other made
down the river, it didn't enter anybody's head to trouble how they would live.
Certainly they had brought with them some rotten hippo-meat, which
couldn't have lasted very long, anyway, even if the pilgrims hadn't, in the
midst of a shocking hullabaloo, thrown a considerable quantity of it overboard. It looked like a high-handed proceeding; but it was really a case of
legitimate self-defence. You can't breathe dead hippo waking, sleeping, and
eating, and at the same time keep your precarious grip on existence. Besides
that, they had given them every week three pieces of brass wire, each about
nine inches long; and the theory was they were to buy their provisions with
that currency in river-side villages. You can see how *that* worked. There were
either no villages, or the people were hostile, or the director, who like the
rest of us fed out of tins, with an occasional old he-goat thrown in, didn't
want to stop the steamer for some more or less recondite reasons. So, unless
they swallowed the wire itself, or made loops of it to snare the fishes with, I
don't see what good their extravagant salary could be to them. I must say it
was paid with a regularity worthy of a large and honourable trading company. For the rest, the only thing to eat—though it didn't look eatable in the
least—I saw in their possession was a few lumps of some stuff like half-
cooked dough, of a dirty lavender colour, they kept wrapped in leaves, and
now and then swallowed a piece of, but so small that it seemed done more
for the look of the thing than for any serious purpose of sustenance. Why in
the name of all the gnawing devils of hunger they didn't go for us—they
were thirty to five—and have a good tuck-in for once, amazes me now when
I think of it. They were big powerful men, with not much capacity to weigh
the consequences, with courage, with strength, even yet, though their skins
were no longer glossy and their muscles no longer hard. And I saw that
something restraining, one of those human secrets that baffle probability,
had come into play there. I looked at them with a swift quickening of
interest—not because it occurred to me I might be eaten by them before
very long, though I own to you that just then I perceived—in a new light, as
it were—how unwholesome the pilgrims looked, and I hoped, yes, I positively hoped, that my aspect was not so—what shall I say?—so—unappetis-
ing: a touch of fantastic vanity which fitted well with the dream-sensation
that pervaded all my days at that time. Perhaps I had a little fever too. One
can't live with one's finger everlastingly on one's pulse. I had often 'a little
fever,' or a little touch of other things—the playful paw-strokes of the wilderness, the preliminary trifling before the more serious onslaught which
came in due course. Yes; I looked at them as you would on any human being,
with a curiosity of their impulses, motives, capacities, weaknesses, when
brought to the test of an inexorable physical necessity. Restraint! What possible restraint? Was it superstition, disgust, patience, fear—or some kind of
primitive honour? No fear can stand up to hunger, no patience can wear it
out, disgust simply does not exist where hunger is; and as to superstition,
beliefs, and what you may call principles, they are less than chaff in a breeze.
Don't you know the devilry of lingering starvation, its exasperating torment,
its black thoughts, its sombre and brooding ferocity? Well, I do. It takes a
man all his inborn strength to fight hunger properly. It's really easier to face
bereavement, dishonour, and the perdition of one's soul—than this kind of

prolonged hunger. Sad, but true. And these chaps too had no earthly reason for any kind of scruple. Restraint! I would just as soon have expected restraint from a hyena prowling amongst the corpses of a battlefield. But there was the fact facing me—the fact dazzling, to be seen, like the foam on the depths of the sea, like a ripple on an unfathomable enigma, a mystery greater—when I thought of it—than the curious, inexplicable note of desperate grief in this savage clamour that had swept by us on the river-bank, behind the blind whiteness of the fog.

"Two pilgrims were quarrelling in hurried whispers as to which bank. 'Left.' 'No, no; how can you? Right, right, of course.' 'It is very serious,' said the manager's voice behind me; 'I would be desolated if anything should happen to Mr Kurtz before we came up.' I looked at him, and had not the slightest doubt he was sincere. He was just the kind of man who would wish to preserve appearances. That was his restraint. But when he muttered something about going on at once, I did not even take the trouble to answer him. I knew, and he knew, that it was impossible. Were we to let go our hold of the bottom, we would be absolutely in the air—in space. We wouldn't be able to tell where we were going to—whether up or down stream, or across— till we fetched against one bank or the other—and then we wouldn't know at first which it was. Of course I made no move. I had no mind for a smash-up. You couldn't imagine a more deadly place for a shipwreck. Whether drowned at once or not, we were sure to perish speedily in one way or another. 'I authorise you to take all the risks,' he said, after a short silence. 'I refuse to take any,' I said shortly; which was just the answer he expected, though its tone might have surprised him. 'Well, I must defer to your judgment. You are captain,' he said, with marked civility. I turned my shoulder to him in sign of my appreciation, and looked into the fog. How long would it last? It was the most hopeless lookout. The approach to this Kurtz grubbing for ivory in the wretched bush was beset by as many dangers as though he had been an enchanted princess sleeping in a fabulous castle. 'Will they attack, do you think?' asked the manager, in a confidential tone.

"I did not think they would attack, for several obvious reasons. The thick fog was one. If they left the bank in their canoes they would get lost in it, as we would be if we attempted to move. Still, I had also judged the jungle of both banks quite impenetrable—and yet eyes were in it, eyes that had seen us. The river-side bushes were certainly very thick; but the undergrowth behind was evidently penetrable. However, during the short lift I had seen no canoes anywhere in the reach—certainly not abreast of the steamer. But what made the idea of attack inconceivable to me was the nature of the noise—of the cries we had heard. They had not the fierce character boding of immediate hostile intention. Unexpected, wild, and violent as they had been, they had given me an irresistible impression of sorrow. The glimpse of the steamboat had for some reason filled those savages with unrestrained grief. The danger, if any, I expounded, was from our proximity to a great human passion let loose. Even extreme grief may ultimately vent itself in violence—but more generally takes the form of apathy. . . .

"You should have seen the pilgrims stare! They had no heart to grin, or even to revile me; but I believe they thought me gone mad—with fright, maybe. I delivered a regular lecture. My dear boys, it was no good bothering. Keep a look-out? Well, you may guess I watched the fog for the signs of lifting as a cat watches a mouse; but for anything else our eyes were of no more use to us than if we had been buried miles deep in a heap of cotton-wool. It felt like it too—choking, warm, stifling. Besides, all I said, though it sounded extravagant, was absolutely true to fact. What we afterwards alluded to as an attack was really an attempt at repulse. The action was very far from being aggressive—it was not even defensive, in the usual sense: it was undertaken under the stress of desperation, and in its essence was purely protective.

"It developed itself, I should say, two hours after the fog lifted, and its commencement was at a spot, roughly speaking, about a mile and a half below Kurtz's station. We had just floundered and flopped round a bend, when I saw an islet, a mere grassy hummock of bright green, in the middle of the stream. It was the only thing of the kind; but as we opened the reach more, I perceived it was the head of a long sandbank, or rather of a chain of shallow patches stretching down the middle of the river. They were discoloured, just awash, and the whole lot was seen just under the water, exactly as a man's backbone is seen running down the middle of his back under the skin. Now, as far as I did see, I could go to the right or to the left of this. I didn't know either channel, of course. The banks looked pretty well alike, the depth appeared the same; but as I had been informed the station was on the west side, I naturally headed for the western passage.

"No sooner had we fairly entered it than I became aware it was much narrower than I had supposed. To the left of us there was the long uninterrupted shoal,[9] and to the right a high steep bank heavily overgrown with bushes. Above the bush the trees stood in serried ranks. The twigs overhung the current thickly, and from distance to distance a large limb of some tree projected rigidly over the stream. It was then well on in the afternoon, the face of the forest was gloomy, and a broad strip of shadow had already fallen on the water. In this shadow we steamed up—very slowly, as you may imagine. I sheered her well inshore—the water being deepest near the bank, as the sounding-pole informed me.

"One of my hungry and forbearing friends was sounding in the bows just below me. This steamboat was exactly like a decked scow. On the deck there were two little teak-wood houses, with doors and windows. The boiler was in the fore-end, and the machinery right astern. Over the whole there was a light roof, supported on stanchions. The funnel projected through that roof, and in front of the funnel a small cabin built of light planks served for a pilot-house. It contained a couch, two camp-stools, a loaded Martini-Henry[1] leaning in one corner, a tiny table, and the steering-wheel. It had a wide door in front and a broad shutter at each side. All these were always thrown open, of course. I spent my days perched up there on the extreme fore-end of that roof, before the door. At night I slept, or tried to, on the couch. An athletic black belonging to some coast tribe, and educated by my poor predecessor, was the helmsman. He sported a pair of brass earrings, wore a blue cloth wrapper from the waist to the ankles, and thought all the world of himself. He was the most unstable kind of fool I had ever seen. He steered with no end of a swagger while you were by; but if he lost sight of you, he became instantly the prey of an abject funk, and would let that cripple of a steamboat get the upper hand of him in a minute.

9. Sandbank.
1. Rifle combining the seven-grooved barrel of the Scottish gun maker A. Henry with the block-action breech mechanism introduced by the Swiss inventor F. Martini.

"I was looking down at the sounding-pole, and feeling much annoyed to
see at each try a little more of it stick out of that river, when I saw my pole-
man give up the business suddenly, and stretch himself flat on the deck,
without even taking the trouble to haul his pole in. He kept hold on it
though, and it trailed in the water. At the same time the fireman, whom I
could also see below me, sat down abruptly before his furnace and ducked
his head. I was amazed. Then I had to look at the river mighty quick, because
there was a snag in the fairway. Sticks, little sticks, were flying about—
thick; they were whizzing before my nose, dropping below me, striking
behind me against my pilot-house. All this time the river, the shore, the
woods, were very quiet—perfectly quiet. I could only hear the heavy splashing thump of the stern-wheel and the patter of these things. We cleared the
snag clumsily. Arrows, by Jove! We were being shot at! I stepped in quickly
to close the shutter on the landside. That fool-helmsman, his hands on the
spokes, was lifting his knees high, stamping his feet, champing his mouth,
like a reined-in horse. Confound him! And we were staggering within ten
feet of the bank. I had to lean right out to swing the heavy shutter, and I saw
a face amongst the leaves on the level with my own, looking at me very fierce
and steady; and then suddenly, as though a veil had been removed from my
eyes, I made out, deep in the tangled gloom, naked breasts, arms, legs, glaring eyes—the bush was swarming with human limbs in movement, glistening, of bronze colour. The twigs shook, swayed, and rustled, the arrows flew
out of them, and then the shutter came to. 'Steer her straight,' I said to the
helmsman. He held his head rigid, face forward; but his eyes rolled, he kept
on lifting and setting down his feet gently, his mouth foamed a little. 'Keep
quiet!' I said in a fury. I might just as well have ordered a tree not to sway in
the wind. I darted out. Below me there was a great scuffle of feet on the iron
deck; confused exclamations; a voice screamed, 'Can you turn back?' I
caught sight of a V-shaped ripple on the water ahead. What? Another snag!
A fusillade burst out under my feet. The pilgrims had opened with their
Winchesters, and were simply squirting lead into that bush. A deuce of a lot
of smoke came up and drove slowly forward. I swore at it. Now I couldn't see
the ripple or the snag either. I stood in the doorway, peering, and the arrows
came in swarms. They might have been poisoned, but they looked as though
they wouldn't kill a cat. The bush began to howl. Our wood-cutters raised a
warlike whoop; the report of a rifle just at my back deafened me. I glanced
over my shoulder, and the pilot-house was yet full of noise and smoke when
I made a dash at the wheel. The fool-nigger had dropped everything, to
throw the shutter open and let off that Martini-Henry. He stood before the
wide opening, glaring, and I yelled at him to come back, while I straightened
the sudden twist out of that steamboat. There was no room to turn even if I
had wanted to, the snag was somewhere very near ahead in that confounded
smoke, there was no time to lose, so I just crowded her into the bank—right
into the bank, where I knew the water was deep.

"We tore slowly along the overhanging bushes in a whirl of broken twigs
and flying leaves. The fusillade below stopped short, as I had foreseen it
would when the squirts got empty. I threw my head back to a glinting whizz
that traversed the pilot-house, in at one shutter-hole and out at the other.
Looking past that mad helmsman, who was shaking the empty rifle and
yelling at the shore, I saw vague forms of men running bent double, leaping,
gliding, distinct, incomplete, evanescent. Something big appeared in the air

before the shutter, the rifle went overboard, and the man stepped back swiftly, looked at me over his shoulder in an extraordinary, profound, familiar manner, and fell upon my feet. The side of his head hit the wheel twice, and the end of what appeared a long cane clattered round and knocked over a little camp-stool. It looked as though after wrenching that thing from somebody ashore he had lost his balance in the effort. The thin smoke had blown away, we were clear of the snag, and looking ahead I could see that in another hundred yards or so I would be free to sheer off, away from the bank; but my feet felt so very warm and wet that I had to look down. The man had rolled on his back and stared straight up at me; both his hands clutched that cane. It was the shaft of a spear that, either thrown or lunged through the opening, had caught him in the side just below the ribs; the blade had gone in out of sight, after making a frightful gash; my shoes were full; a pool of blood lay very still, gleaming dark-red under the wheel; his eyes shone with an amazing lustre. The fusillade burst out again. He looked at me anxiously, gripping the spear like something precious, with an air of being afraid I would try to take it away from him. I had to make an effort to free my eyes from his gaze and attend to the steering. With one hand I felt above my head for the line of the steam whistle, and jerked out screech after screech hurriedly. The tumult of angry and warlike yells was checked instantly, and then from the depths of the woods went out such a tremulous and prolonged wail of mournful fear and utter despair as may be imagined to follow the flight of the last hope from the earth. There was a great commotion in the bush; the shower of arrows stopped, a few dropping shots rang out sharply—then silence, in which the languid beat of the stern-wheel came plainly to my ears. I put the helm hard a-starboard at the moment when the pilgrim in pink pyjamas, very hot and agitated, appeared in the doorway. 'The manager sends me—' he began in an official tone, and stopped short. 'Good God!' he said, glaring at the wounded man.

"We two whites stood over him, and his lustrous and inquiring glance enveloped us both. I declare it looked as though he would presently put to us some question in an understandable language; but he died without uttering a sound, without moving a limb, without twitching a muscle. Only in the very last moment, as though in response to some sign we could not see, to some whisper we could not hear, he frowned heavily, and that frown gave to his black death-mask an inconceivably sombre, brooding, and menacing expression. The lustre of inquiring glance faded swiftly into vacant glassiness. 'Can you steer?' I asked the agent eagerly. He looked very dubious; but I made a grab at his arm, and he understood at once I meant him to steer whether or no. To tell you the truth, I was morbidly anxious to change my shoes and socks. 'He is dead,' murmured the fellow, immensely impressed. 'No doubt about it,' said I, tugging like mad at the shoe-laces. 'And by the way, I suppose Mr Kurtz is dead as well by this time.'

"For the moment that was the dominant thought. There was a sense of extreme disappointment, as though I had found out I had been striving after something altogether without a substance. I couldn't have been more disgusted if I had travelled all this way for the sole purpose of talking with Mr Kurtz. Talking with . . . I flung one shoe overboard, and became aware that that was exactly what I had been looking forward to—a talk with Kurtz. I made the strange discovery that I had never imagined him as doing, you know, but as discoursing. I didn't say to myself, 'Now I will never see him,' or 'Now I will never shake him by the hand,' but, 'Now I will never hear him.' The man presented himself as a voice. Not of course that I did not connect him with some sort of action. Hadn't I been told in all the tones of jealousy and admiration that he had collected, bartered, swindled, or stolen more ivory than all the other agents together? That was not the point. The point was in his being a gifted creature, and that of all his gifts the one that stood out pre-eminently, that carried with it a sense of real presence, was his ability to talk, his words—the gift of expression, the bewildering, the illuminating, the most exalted and the most contemptible, the pulsating stream of light, or the deceitful flow from the heart of an impenetrable darkness.

"The other shoe went flying unto the devil-god of that river. I thought, By Jove! it's all over. We are too late; he has vanished—the gift has vanished, by means of some spear, arrow, or club. I will never hear that chap speak after all—and my sorrow had a startling extravagance of emotion, even such as I had noticed in the howling sorrow of these savages in the bush. I couldn't have felt more of lonely desolation somehow, had I been robbed of a belief or had missed my destiny in life. . . . Why do you sigh in this beastly way, somebody? Absurd? Well, absurd. Good Lord! mustn't a man ever— Here, give me some tobacco." . . .

There was a pause of profound stillness, then a match flared, and Marlow's lean face appeared, worn, hollow, with downward folds and dropped eyelids, with an aspect of concentrated attention; and as he took vigorous draws at his pipe, it seemed to retreat and advance out of the night in the regular flicker of the tiny flame. The match went out.

"Absurd!" he cried. "This is the worst of trying to tell . . . Here you all are, each moored with two good addresses, like a hulk with two anchors, a butcher round one corner, a policeman round another, excellent appetites, and temperature normal—you hear—normal from year's end to year's end. And you say, Absurd! Absurd be—exploded! Absurd! My dear boys, what can you expect from a man who out of sheer nervousness had just flung overboard a pair of new shoes? Now I think of it, it is amazing I did not shed tears. I am, upon the whole, proud of my fortitude. I was cut to the quick at the idea of having lost the inestimable privilege of listening to the gifted Kurtz. Of course I was wrong. The privilege was waiting for me. Oh yes, I heard more than enough. And I was right, too. A voice. He was very little more than a voice. And I heard—him—it—this voice—other voices—all of them were so little more than voices—and the memory of that time itself lingers around me, impalpable, like a dying vibration of one immense jabber, silly, atrocious, sordid, savage, or simply mean, without any kind of sense. Voices, voices— even the girl herself—now—"

He was silent for a long time.

"I laid the ghost of his gifts at last with a lie," he began suddenly. "Girl! What? Did I mention a girl? Oh, she is out of it—completely. They—the women I mean—are out of it—should be out of it. We must help them to stay in that beautiful world of their own, lest ours gets worse. Oh, she had to be out of it. You should have heard the disinterred body of Mr Kurtz saying, 'My Intended.' You would have perceived directly then how completely she was out of it. And the lofty frontal bone of Mr Kurtz! They say the hair goes on growing sometimes, but this—ah—specimen was impressively bald. The wilderness had patted him on the head, and, behold, it was like a ball—an ivory ball; it had caressed him, and—lo!—he had withered; it had taken him, loved him, embraced him, got into his veins, consumed his flesh, and sealed his soul to its own by the inconceivable ceremonies of some devilish initiation. He was its spoiled and pampered favourite. Ivory? I should think so. Heaps of it, stacks of it. The old mud shanty was bursting with it. You would think there was not a single tusk left either above or below the ground in the whole country. 'Mostly fossil,' the manager had remarked disparagingly. It was no more fossil than I am; but they call it fossil when it is dug up. It appears these niggers do bury the tusks sometimes—but evidently they couldn't bury this parcel deep enough to save the gifted Mr Kurtz from his fate. We filled the steamboat with it, and had to pile a lot on the deck. Thus he could see and enjoy as long as he could see, because the appreciation of this favour had remained with him to the last. You should have heard him say, 'My ivory.' Oh yes, I heard him. 'My Intended, my ivory, my station, my river, my—' everything belonged to him. It made me hold my breath in expectation of hearing the wilderness burst into a prodigious peal of laughter that would shake the fixed stars in their places. Everything belonged to him—but that was a trifle. The thing was to know what he belonged to, how many powers of darkness claimed him for their own. That was the reflection that made you creepy all over. It was impossible—it was not good for one either—trying to imagine. He had taken a high seat amongst the devils of the land—I mean literally. You can't understand. How could you?—with solid pavement under your feet, surrounded by kind neighbours ready to cheer you or to fall on you, stepping delicately between the butcher and the policeman, in the holy terror of scandal and gallows and lunatic asylums—how can you imagine what particular region of the first ages a man's untrammelled feet may take him into by the way of solitude—utter solitude without a policeman—by the way of silence—utter silence, where no warning voice of a kind neighbour can be heard whispering of public opinion? These little things make all the great difference. When they are gone you must fall back upon your own innate strength, upon your own capacity for faithfulness. Of course you may be too much of a fool to go wrong—too dull even to know you are being assaulted by the powers of darkness. I take it, no fool ever made a bargain for his soul with the devil: the fool is too much of a fool, or the devil too much of a devil—I don't know which. Or you may be such a thunderingly exalted creature as to be altogether deaf and blind to anything but heavenly sights and sounds. Then the earth for you is only a standing place—and whether to be like this is your loss or your gain I won't pretend to say. But most of us are neither one nor the other. The earth for us is a place to live in, where we must put up with sights, with sounds, with smells, too, by Jove!—breathe dead hippo, so to speak, and not be contaminated. And there, don't you see? your strength comes in, the faith in your ability for the digging of unostentatious holes to bury the stuff in—your power of devotion, not to yourself, but to an obscure, back-breaking business. And that's difficult enough. Mind, I am not trying to excuse or even explain—I am trying to account to myself for—for—Mr Kurtz—for the shade of Mr Kurtz. This initiated wraith from the back of Nowhere honoured me with its amazing confidence before it vanished altogether. This was because it could speak English to me. The original Kurtz had been educated partly in England, and—as he was good enough to say himself—his sympathies were in the right place. His mother was half-English, his father was half-French.

All Europe contributed to the making of Kurtz; and by and by I learned that, most appropriately, the International Society for the Suppression of Savage Customs had entrusted him with the making of a report, for its future guidance. And he had written it too. I've seen it. I've read it. It was eloquent, vibrating with eloquence, but too high-strung, I think. Seventeen pages of close writing he had found time for! But this must have been before his—let us say—nerves went wrong, and caused him to preside at certain midnight dances ending with unspeakable rites, which—as far as I reluctantly gathered from what I heard at various times—were offered up to him—do you understand?—to Mr Kurtz himself. But it was a beautiful piece of writing. The opening paragraph, however, in the light of later information, strikes me now as ominous. He began with the argument that we whites, from the point of development we had arrived at, 'must necessarily appear to them [savages] in the nature of supernatural beings—we approach them with the might as of a deity,' and so on, and so on. 'By the simple exercise of our will we can exert a power for good practically unbounded,' etc. etc. From that point he soared and took me with him. The peroration was magnificent, though difficult to remember, you know. It gave me the notion of an exotic Immensity ruled by an august Benevolence. It made me tingle with enthusiasm. This was the unbounded power of eloquence—of words—of burning noble words. There were no practical hints to interrupt the magic current of phrases, unless a kind of note at the foot of the last page, scrawled evidently much later, in an unsteady hand, may be regarded as the exposition of a method. It was very simple, and at the end of that moving appeal to every altruistic sentiment it blazed at you, luminous and terrifying, like a flash of lightning in a serene sky: 'Exterminate all the brutes!' The curious part was that he had apparently forgotten all about that valuable postscriptum, because, later on, when he in a sense came to himself, he repeatedly entreated me to take good care of 'my pamphlet' (he called it), as it was sure to have in the future a good influence upon his career. I had full information about all these things, and, besides, as it turned out, I was to have the care of his memory. I've done enough for it to give me the indisputable right to lay it, if I choose, for an everlasting rest in the dust-bin of progress, amongst all the sweepings and, figuratively speaking, all the dead cats of civilisation. But then, you see, I can't choose. He won't be forgotten. Whatever he was, he was not common. He had the power to charm or frighten rudimentary souls into an aggravated witchdance in his honour; he could also fill the small souls of the pilgrims with bitter misgivings: he had one devoted friend at least, and he had conquered one soul in the world that was neither rudimentary nor tainted with self-seeking. No; I can't forget him, though I am not prepared to affirm the fellow was exactly worth the life we lost in getting to him. I missed my late helmsman awfully—I missed him even while his body was still lying in the pilot-house. Perhaps you will think it passing strange this regret for a savage who was no more account than a grain of sand in a black Sahara. Well, don't you see, he had done something, he had steered; for months I had him at my back—a help—an instrument. It was a kind of partnership. He steered for me—I had to look after him, I worried about his deficiencies, and thus a subtle bond had been created, of which I only became aware when it was suddenly broken. And the intimate profundity of that look he gave me when he received his hurt remains to this day in my memory—like a claim of distant kinship affirmed in a supreme moment.

"Poor fool! If he had only left that shutter alone. He had no restraint, no restraint—just like Kurtz—a tree swayed by the wind. As soon as I had put on a dry pair of slippers, I dragged him out, after first jerking the spear out of his side, which operation I confess I performed with my eyes shut tight. His heels leaped together over the little doorstep; his shoulders were pressed to my breast; I hugged him from behind desperately. Oh! he was heavy, heavy; heavier than any man on earth, I should imagine. Then without more ado I tipped him overboard. The current snatched him as though he had been a wisp of grass, and I saw the body roll over twice before I lost sight of it for ever. All the pilgrims and the manager were then congregated on the awning-deck about the pilot-house, chattering at each other like a flock of excited magpies, and there was a scandalised murmur at my heartless promptitude. What they wanted to keep that body hanging about for I can't guess. Embalm it, maybe. But I had also heard another, and a very ominous, murmur on the deck below. My friends the wood-cutters were likewise scandalised, and with a better show of reason—though I admit that the reason itself was quite inadmissible. Oh, quite! I had made up my mind that if my late helmsman was to be eaten, the fishes alone should have him. He had been a very second-rate helmsman while alive, but now he was dead he might have become a first-class temptation, and possibly cause some startling trouble. Besides, I was anxious to take the wheel, the man in pink pyjamas showing himself a hopeless duffer at the business.

"This I did directly the simple funeral was over. We were going half-speed, keeping right in the middle of the stream, and I listened to the talk about me. They had given up Kurtz, they had given up the station; Kurtz was dead, and the station had been burnt—and so on—and so on. The red-haired pilgrim was beside himself with the thought that at least this poor Kurtz had been properly revenged. 'Say! We must have made a glorious slaughter of them in the bush. Eh? What do you think? Say?' He positively danced, the bloodthirsty little gingery beggar.[2] And he had nearly fainted when he saw the wounded man! I could not help saying, 'You made a glorious lot of smoke, anyhow.' I had seen, from the way the tops of the bushes rustled and flew, that almost all the shots had gone too high. You can't hit anything unless you take aim and fire from the shoulder; but these chaps fired from the hip with their eyes shut. The retreat, I maintained—and I was right—was caused by the screeching of the steam-whistle. Upon this they forgot Kurtz, and began to howl at me with indignant protests.

"The manager stood by the wheel murmuring confidentially about the necessity of getting well away down the river before dark at all events, when I saw in the distance a clearing on the river-side and the outlines of some sort of building. 'What's this?' I asked. He clapped his hands in wonder. 'The station!' he cried. I edged in at once, still going half-speed.

"Through my glasses I saw the slope of a hill interspersed with rare trees and perfectly free from undergrowth. A long decaying building on the summit was half buried in the high grass; the large holes in the peaked roof gaped black from afar; the jungle and the woods made a background. There was no enclosure or fence of any kind; but there had been one apparently, for near the house half a dozen slim posts remained in a row, roughly trimmed, and with their upper ends ornamented with round carved balls. The rails, or

2. Little redheaded rascal.

whatever there had been between, had disappeared. Of course the forest surrounded all that. The river-bank was clear, and on the water side I saw a white man under a hat like a cart-wheel beckoning persistently with his whole arm. Examining the edge of the forest above and below, I was almost certain I could see movements—human forms gliding here and there. I steamed past prudently, then stopped the engines and let her drift down. The man on the shore began to shout, urging us to land. 'We have been attacked,' screamed the manager. 'I know—I know. It's all right,' yelled back the other, as cheerful as you please. 'Come along. It's all right. I am glad.'

"His aspect reminded me of something I had seen—something funny I had seen somewhere. As I manœuvred to get alongside, I was asking myself, 'What does this fellow look like?' Suddenly I got it. He looked like a harlequin.[3] His clothes had been made of some stuff that was brown holland[4] probably, but it was covered with patches all over, with bright patches, blue, red, and yellow—patches on the back, patches on the front, patches on elbows, on knees; coloured binding round his jacket, scarlet edging at the bottom of his trousers; and the sunshine made him look extremely gay and wonderfully neat withal, because you could see how beautifully all this patching had been done. A beardless, boyish face, very fair, no features to speak of, nose peeling, little blue eyes, smiles and frowns chasing each other over that open countenance like sunshine and shadow on a wind-swept plain. 'Look out, captain!' he cried; 'there's a snag lodged in here last night.' What! Another snag? I confess I swore shamefully. I had nearly holed my cripple, to finish off that charming trip. The harlequin on the bank turned his little pug nose up to me. 'You English?' he asked, all smiles. 'Are you?' I shouted from the wheel. The smiles vanished, and he shook his head as if sorry for my disappointment. Then he brightened up. 'Never mind!' he cried encouragingly. 'Are we in time?' I asked. 'He is up there,' he replied, with a toss of the head up the hill, and becoming gloomy all of a sudden. His face was like the autumn sky, overcast one moment and bright the next.

"When the manager, escorted by the pilgrims, all of them armed to the teeth, had gone to the house, this chap came on board. 'I say, I don't like this. These natives are in the bush,' I said. He assured me earnestly it was all right. 'They are simple people,' he added; 'well, I am glad you came. It took me all my time to keep them off.' 'But you said it was all right,' I cried. 'Oh, they meant no harm,' he said; and as I stared he corrected himself, 'Not exactly.' Then vivaciously, 'My faith, your pilot-house wants a clean up!' In the next breath he advised me to keep enough steam on the boiler to blow the whistle in case of any trouble. 'One good screech will do more for you than all your rifles. They are simple people,' he repeated. He rattled away at such a rate he quite overwhelmed me. He seemed to be trying to make up for lots of silence, and actually hinted, laughing, that such was the case. 'Don't you talk with Mr Kurtz?' I said. 'You don't talk with that man—you listen to him,' he exclaimed with severe exaltation. 'But now—' He waved his arm, and in the twinkling of an eye was in the uttermost depths of despondency. In a moment he came up again with a jump, possessed himself of both my hands, shook them continuously, while he gabbled: 'Brother sailor . . . honour . . . pleasure . . . delight . . . introduce myself . . .

---

3. Character from Italian comedy traditionally dressed in multicolored clothes.   4. Coarse linen fabric.

Russian . . . son of an arch-priest . . . Government of Tambov . . . What? Tobacco! English tobacco; the excellent English tobacco! Now, that's brotherly. Smoke? Where's a sailor that does not smoke?'

"The pipe soothed him, and gradually I made out he had run away from school, had gone to sea in a Russian ship; ran away again; served some time in English ships; was now reconciled with the arch-priest. He made a point of that. 'But when one is young one must see things, gather experience, ideas; enlarge the mind.' 'Here!' I interrupted. 'You can never tell! Here I met Mr Kurtz,' he said, youthfully solemn and reproachful. I held my tongue after that. It appears he had persuaded a Dutch trading-house on the coast to fit him out with stores and goods, and had started for the interior with a light heart, and no more idea of what would happen to him than a baby. He had been wandering about that river for nearly two years alone, cut off from everybody and everything. 'I am not so young as I look. I am twenty-five,' he said. 'At first old Van Shuyten would tell me to go to the devil,' he narrated with keen enjoyment; 'but I stuck to him, and talked and talked, till at last he got afraid I would talk the hind-leg off his favourite dog, so he gave me some cheap things and a few guns, and told me he hoped he would never see my face again. Good old Dutchman, Van Shuyten. I sent him one small lot of ivory a year ago, so that he can't call me a little thief when I get back. I hope he got it. And for the rest I don't care. I had some wood stacked for you. That was my old house. Did you see?'

"I gave him Towson's book. He made as though he would kiss me, but restrained himself. 'The only book I had left, and I thought I had lost it,' he said, looking at it ecstatically. 'So many accidents happen to a man going about alone, you know. Canoes get upset sometimes—and sometimes you've got to clear out so quick when the people get angry.' He thumbed the pages. 'You made notes in Russian?' I asked. He nodded. 'I thought they were written in cipher,' I said. He laughed, then became serious. 'I had lots of trouble to keep these people off,' he said. 'Did they want to kill you?' I asked. 'Oh no!' he cried, and checked himself. 'Why did they attack us?' I pursued. He hesitated, then said shamefacedly, 'They don't want him to go.' 'Don't they?' I said curiously. He nodded a nod full of mystery and wisdom. 'I tell you,' he cried, 'this man has enlarged my mind.' He opened his arms wide, staring at me with his little blue eyes that were perfectly round."

3

"I looked at him, lost in astonishment. There he was before me, in motley, as though he had absconded from a troupe of mimes, enthusiastic, fabulous. His very existence was improbable, inexplicable, and altogether bewildering. He was an insoluble problem. It was inconceivable how he had existed, how he had succeeded in getting so far, how he had managed to remain—why he did not instantly disappear. 'I went a little farther,' he said, 'then still a little farther—till I had gone so far that I don't know how I'll ever get back. Never mind. Plenty time. I can manage. You take Kurtz away quick—quick—I tell you.' The glamour of youth enveloped his particoloured rags, his destitution, his loneliness, the essential desolation of his futile wanderings. For months— for years—his life hadn't been worth a day's purchase; and there he was gallantly, thoughtlessly alive, to all appearance indestructible solely by the virtue of his few years and of his unreflecting audacity. I was seduced into something like admiration—like envy. Glamour urged him on, glamour kept him unscathed. He surely wanted nothing from the wilderness but space to breathe in and to push on through. His need was to exist, and to move onwards at the greatest possible risk, and with a maximum of privation. If the absolutely pure, uncalculating, unpractical spirit of adventure had ever ruled a human being, it ruled this be-patched youth. I almost envied him the possession of this modest and clear flame. It seemed to have consumed all thought of self so completely, that, even while he was talking to you, you forgot that it was he—the man before your eyes—who had gone through these things. I did not envy him his devotion to Kurtz, though. He had not meditated over it. It came to him, and he accepted it with a sort of eager fatalism. I must say that to me it appeared about the most dangerous thing in every way he had come upon so far.

"They had come together unavoidably, like two ships becalmed near each other, and lay rubbing sides at last. I suppose Kurtz wanted an audience, because on a certain occasion, when encamped in the forest, they had talked all night, or more probably Kurtz had talked. 'We talked of everything,' he said, quite transported at the recollection. 'I forgot there was such a thing as sleep. The night did not seem to last an hour. Everything! Everything! . . . Of love too.' 'Ah, he talked to you of love!' I said, much amused. 'It isn't what you think,' he cried, almost passionately. 'It was in general. He made me see things—things.'

"He threw his arms up. We were on deck at the time, and the head-man of my wood-cutters, lounging near by, turned upon him his heavy and glittering eyes. I looked around, and I don't know why, but I assure you that never, never before, did this land, this river, this jungle, the very arch of this blazing sky, appear to me so hopeless and so dark, so impenetrable to human thought, so pitiless to human weakness. 'And, ever since, you have been with him, of course?' I said.

"On the contrary. It appears their intercourse had been very much broken by various causes. He had, as he informed me proudly, managed to nurse Kurtz through two illnesses (he alluded to it as you would to some risky feat), but as a rule Kurtz wandered alone, far in the depths of the forest. 'Very often coming to this station, I had to wait days and days before he would turn up,' he said. 'Ah, it was worth waiting for!—sometimes.' 'What was he doing? exploring or what?' I asked. 'Oh yes, of course'; he had discovered lots of villages, a lake too—he did not know exactly in what direction; it was dangerous to inquire too much—but mostly his expeditions had been for ivory. 'But he had no goods to trade with by that time,' I objected. 'There's a good lot of cartridges left even yet,' he answered, looking away. 'To speak plainly, he raided the country,' I said. He nodded. 'Not alone, surely!' He muttered something about the villages round that lake. 'Kurtz got the tribe to follow him, did he?' I suggested. He fidgeted a little. 'They adored him,' he said. The tone of these words was so extraordinary that I looked at him searchingly. It was curious to see his mingled eagerness and reluctance to speak of Kurtz. The man filled his life, occupied his thoughts, swayed his emotions. 'What can you expect?' he burst out; 'he came to them with thunder and lightning, you know—and they had never seen anything like it—and very terrible. He could be very terrible. You can't judge Mr Kurtz as you would an ordinary man. No, no, no! Now—just to give you an idea—I don't mind telling you, he wanted to shoot me too one day—but I don't judge him.'

'Shoot you!' I cried. 'What for?' 'Well, I had a small lot of ivory the chief of that village near my house gave me. You see I used to shoot game for them. Well, he wanted it, and wouldn't hear reason. He declared he would shoot me unless I gave him the ivory and then cleared out of the country, because he could do so, and had a fancy for it, and there was nothing on earth to prevent him killing whom he jolly well pleased. And it was true too. I gave him the ivory. What did I care! But I didn't clear out. No, no. I couldn't leave him. I had to be careful, of course, till we got friendly again for a time. He had his second illness then. Afterwards I had to keep out of the way; but I didn't mind. He was living for the most part in those villages on the lake. When he came down to the river, sometimes he would take to me, and some-times it was better for me to be careful. This man suffered too much. He hated all this, and somehow he couldn't get away. When I had a chance I begged him to try and leave while there was time; I offered to go back with him. And he would say yes, and then he would remain; go off on another ivory hunt; disappear for weeks; forget himself amongst these people—forget himself—you know.' 'Why! he's mad,' I said. He protested indignantly. Mr Kurtz couldn't be mad. If I had heard him talk, only two days ago, I wouldn't dare hint at such a thing. . . . I had taken up my binoculars while we talked, and was looking at the shore, sweeping the limit of the forest at each side and at the back of the house. The consciousness of there being people in that bush, so silent, so quiet—as silent and quiet as the ruined house on the hill—made me uneasy. There was no sign on the face of nature of this amazing tale that was not so much told as suggested to me in desolate exclamations, completed by shrugs, in interrupted phrases, in hints ending in deep sighs. The woods were unmoved, like a mask—heavy, like the closed door of a prison—they looked with their air of hidden knowledge, of patient expectation, of unapproachable silence. The Russian was explaining to me that it was only lately that Mr Kurtz had come down to the river, bringing along with him all the fighting men of that lake tribe. He had been absent for several months—getting himself adored, I suppose—and had come down unexpectedly, with the intention to all appearance of making a raid either across the river or down stream. Evidently the appetite for more ivory had got the better of the—what shall I say?—less material aspirations. However, he had got much worse suddenly. 'I heard he was lying helpless, and so I came up—took my chance,' said the Russian. 'Oh, he is bad, very bad.' I directed my glass to the house. There were no signs of life, but there was the ruined roof, the long mud wall peeping above the grass, with three little square window-holes, no two of the same size; all this brought within reach of my hand, as it were. And then I made a brusque movement, and one of the remaining posts of that vanished fence leaped up in the field of my glass. You remember I told you I had been struck at the distance by certain attempts at ornamentation, rather remarkable in the ruinous aspect of the place. Now I had suddenly a nearer view, and its first result was to make me throw my head back as if before a blow. Then I went carefully from post to post with my glass, and I saw my mistake. These round knobs were not orna-mental but symbolic; they were expressive and puzzling, striking and disturbing—food for thought and also for the vultures if there had been any looking down from the sky; but at all events for such ants as were industri-ous enough to ascend the pole. They would have been even more impressive, those heads on the stakes, if their faces had not been turned to the house.

Only one, the first I had made out, was facing my way. I was not so shocked as you may think. The start back I had given was really nothing but a movement of surprise. I had expected to see a knob of wood there, you know. I returned deliberately to the first I had seen—and there it was, black, dried, sunken, with closed eyelids—a head that seemed to sleep at the top of that pole, and, with the shrunken dry lips showing a narrow white line of the teeth, was smiling too, smiling continuously at some endless and jocose dream of that eternal slumber.

"I am not disclosing any trade secrets. In fact the manager said afterwards that Mr Kurtz's methods had ruined the district. I have no opinion on that point, but I want you clearly to understand that there was nothing exactly profitable in these heads being there. They only show that Mr Kurtz lacked restraint in the gratification of his various lusts, that there was something wanting in him—some small matter which, when the pressing need arose, could not be found under his magnificent eloquence. Whether he knew of this deficiency himself I can't say. I think the knowledge came to him at last—only at the very last. But the wilderness had found him out early, and had taken on him a terrible vengeance for the fantastic invasion. I think it had whispered to him things about himself which he did not know, things of which he had no conception till he took counsel with this great solitude—and the whisper had proved irresistibly fascinating. It echoed loudly within him because he was hollow at the core. . . . I put down the glass, and the head that had appeared near enough to be spoken to seemed at once to have leaped away from me into inaccessible distance.

"The admirer of Mr Kurtz was a bit crestfallen. In a hurried, indistinct voice he began to assure me he had not dared to take these—say, symbols—down. He was not afraid of the natives; they would not stir till Mr Kurtz gave the word. His ascendancy was extraordinary. The camps of these people surrounded the place, and the chiefs came every day to see him. They would crawl . . . 'I don't want to know anything of the ceremonies used when approaching Mr Kurtz,' I shouted. Curious, this feeling that came over me that such details would be more intolerable than those heads drying on the stakes under Mr Kurtz's windows. After all, that was only a savage sight, while I seemed at one bound to have been transported into some lightless region of subtle horrors, where pure, uncomplicated savagery was a positive relief, being something that had a right to exist—obviously—in the sunshine. The young man looked at me with surprise. I suppose it did not occur to him that Mr Kurtz was no idol of mine. He forgot I hadn't heard any of these splendid monologues on, what was it? on love, justice, conduct of life—or what not. If it had come to crawling before Mr Kurtz, he crawled as much as the veriest savage of them all. I had no idea of the conditions, he said: these heads were the heads of rebels. I shocked him excessively by laughing. Rebels! What would be the next definition I was to hear? There had been enemies, criminals, workers—and these were rebels. Those rebellious heads looked very subdued to me on their sticks. 'You don't know how such a life tries a man like Kurtz,' cried Kurtz's last disciple. 'Well, and you?' I said. 'I! I! I am a simple man. I have no great thoughts. I want nothing from anybody. How can you compare me to . . . ?' His feelings were too much for speech, and suddenly he broke down. 'I don't understand,' he groaned. 'I've been doing my best to keep him alive, and that's enough. I had no hand in all this. I have no abilities. There hasn't been a drop of medicine or a mouthful of invalid food for months here. He was shamefully abandoned. A man like this, with such ideas. Shamefully! Shamefully! I—I—haven't slept for the last ten nights. . . .'

"His voice lost itself in the calm of the evening. The long shadows of the forest had slipped down hill while we talked, had gone far beyond the ruined hovel, beyond the symbolic row of stakes. All this was in the gloom, while we down there were yet in the sunshine, and the stretch of the river abreast of the clearing glittered in a still and dazzling splendour, with a murky and overshadowed bend above and below. Not a living soul was seen on the shore. The bushes did not rustle.

"Suddenly round the corner of the house a group of men appeared, as though they had come up from the ground. They waded waist-deep in the grass, in a compact body, bearing an improvised stretcher in their midst. Instantly, in the emptiness of the landscape, a cry arose whose shrillness pierced the still air like a sharp arrow flying straight to the very heart of the land; and, as if by enchantment, streams of human beings—of naked human beings—with spears in their hands, with bows, with shields, with wild glances and savage movements, were poured into the clearing by the dark-faced and pensive forest. The bushes shook, the grass swayed for a time, and then everything stood still in attentive immobility.

"'Now, if he does not say the right thing to them we are all done for,' said the Russian at my elbow. The knot of men with the stretcher had stopped too, half-way to the steamer, as if petrified. I saw the man on the stretcher sit up, lank and with an uplifted arm, above the shoulders of the bearers. 'Let us hope that the man who can talk so well of love in general will find some particular reason to spare us this time,' I said. I resented bitterly the absurd danger of our situation, as if to be at the mercy of that atrocious phantom had been a dishonouring necessity. I could not hear a sound, but through my glasses I saw the thin arm extended commandingly, the lower jaw moving, the eyes of that apparition shining darkly far in its bony head that nodded with grotesque jerks. Kurtz—Kurtz—that means 'short' in German—don't it? Well, the name was as true as everything else in his life—and death. He looked at least seven feet long. His covering had fallen off, and his body emerged from it pitiful and appalling as from a winding-sheet. I could see the cage of his ribs all astir, the bones of his arm waving. It was as though an animated image of death carved out of old ivory had been shaking its hand with menaces at a motionless crowd of men made of dark and glittering bronze. I saw him open his mouth wide—it gave him a weirdly voracious aspect, as though he had wanted to swallow all the air, all the earth, all the men before him. A deep voice reached me faintly. He must have been shouting. He fell back suddenly. The stretcher shook as the bearers staggered forward again, and almost at the same time I noticed that the crowd of savages was vanishing without any perceptible movement of retreat, as if the forest that had ejected these beings so suddenly had drawn them in again as the breath is drawn in a long aspiration.

"Some of the pilgrims behind the stretcher carried his arms—two shotguns, a heavy rifle, and a light revolver-carbine—the thunderbolts of that pitiful Jupiter. The manager bent over him murmuring as he walked beside his head. They laid him down in one of the little cabins—just a room for a bedplace and a camp-stool or two, you know. We had brought his belated correspondence, and a lot of torn envelopes and open letters littered his bed. His hand roamed feebly amongst these papers. I was struck by the fire of his eyes and the composed languor of his expression. It was not so much the exhaustion of disease. He did not seem in pain. This shadow looked satiated and calm, as though for the moment it had had its fill of all the emotions.

"He rustled one of the letters, and looking straight in my face said, 'I am glad.' Somebody had been writing to him about me. These special recommendations were turning up again. The volume of tone he emitted without effort, almost without the trouble of moving his lips, amazed me. A voice! a voice! It was grave, profound, vibrating, while the man did not seem capable of a whisper. However, he had enough strength in him—factitious no doubt—to very nearly make an end of us, as you shall hear directly.

"The manager appeared silently in the doorway; I stepped out at once and he drew the curtain after me. The Russian, eyed curiously by the pilgrims, was staring at the shore. I followed the direction of his glance.

"Dark human shapes could be made out in the distance, flitting indistinctly against the gloomy border of the forest, and near the river two bronze figures, leaning on tall spears, stood in the sunlight under fantastic head-dresses of spotted skins, warlike and still in statuesque repose. And from right to left along the lighted shore moved a wild and gorgeous apparition of a woman.

"She walked with measured steps, draped in striped and fringed cloths, treading the earth proudly, with a slight jingle and flash of barbarous ornaments. She carried her head high; her hair was done in the shape of a helmet; she had brass leggings to the knee, brass wire gauntlets to the elbow, a crimson spot on her tawny cheek, innumerable necklaces of glass beads on her neck; bizarre things, charms, gifts of witch-men, that hung about her, glittered and trembled at every step. She must have had the value of several elephant tusks upon her. She was savage and superb, wild-eyed and magnificent; there was something ominous and stately in her deliberate progress. And in the hush that had fallen suddenly upon the whole sorrowful land, the immense wilderness, the colossal body of the fecund and mysterious life seemed to look at her, pensive, as though it had been looking at the image of its own tenebrous and passionate soul.

"She came abreast of the steamer, stood still, and faced us. Her long shadow fell to the water's edge. Her face had a tragic and fierce aspect of wild sorrow and of dumb pain mingled with the fear of some struggling, half-shaped resolve. She stood looking at us without a stir, and like the wilderness itself, with an air of brooding over an inscrutable purpose. A whole minute passed, and then she made a step forward. There was a low jingle, a glint of yellow metal, a sway of fringed draperies, and she stopped as if her heart had failed her. The young fellow by my side growled. The pilgrims murmured at my back. She looked at us all as if her life had depended upon the unswerving steadiness of her glance. Suddenly she opened her bared arms and threw them up rigid above her head, as though in an uncontrollable desire to touch the sky, and at the same time the swift shadows darted out on the earth, swept around on the river, gathering the steamer into a shadowy embrace. A formidable silence hung over the scene.

"She turned away slowly, walked on, following the bank, and passed into the bushes to the left. Once only her eyes gleamed back at us in the dusk of the thickets before she disappeared.

"'If she had offered to come aboard I really think I would have tried to shoot her,' said the man of patches nervously. 'I had been risking my life every day for the last fortnight to keep her out of the house. She got in one day and kicked up a row about those miserable rags I picked up in the store-room to mend my clothes with. I wasn't decent. At least it must have been that, for she talked like a fury to Kurtz for an hour, pointing at me now and then. I don't understand the dialect of this tribe. Luckily for me, I fancy Kurtz felt too ill that day to care, or there would have been mischief. I don't understand. . . . No—it's too much for me. Ah, well, it's all over now.'

"At this moment I heard Kurtz's deep voice behind the curtain: 'Save me!—save the ivory, you mean. Don't tell me. Save *me*! Why, I've had to save you. You are interrupting my plans now. Sick! Sick! Not so sick as you would like to believe. Never mind. I'll carry my ideas out yet—I will return. I'll show you what can be done. You with your little peddling notions—you are interfering with me. I will return. I . . .'

"The manager came out. He did me the honour to take me under the arm and lead me aside. 'He is very low, very low,' he said. He considered it neces-sary to sigh, but neglected to be consistently sorrowful. 'We have done all we could for him—haven't we? But there is no disguising the fact, Mr Kurtz has done more harm than good to the Company. He did not see the time was not ripe for vigorous action. Cautiously, cautiously—that's my principle. We must be cautious yet. The district is closed to us for a time. Deplorable! Upon the whole, the trade will suffer. I don't deny there is a remarkable quantity of ivory—mostly fossil. We must save it, at all events—but look how precarious the position is—and why? Because the method is unsound.' 'Do you,' said I, looking at the shore, 'call it "unsound method"?' 'Without doubt,' he exclaimed hotly, 'Don't you?' . . . 'No method at all,' I murmured after a while. 'Exactly,' he exulted. 'I anticipated this. Shows a complete want of judgment. It is my duty to point it out in the proper quarter.' 'Oh,' said I, 'that fellow—what's his name?—the brickmaker, will make a read-able report for you.' He appeared confounded for a moment. It seemed to me I had never breathed an atmosphere so vile, and I turned mentally to Kurtz for relief—positively for relief. 'Nevertheless, I think Mr Kurtz is a remarkable man,' I said with emphasis. He started, dropped on me a cold heavy glance, said very quietly, 'He *was*,' and turned his back on me. My hour of favour was over; I found myself lumped along with Kurtz as a parti-san of methods for which the time was not ripe: I was unsound! Ah! but it was something to have at least a choice of nightmares.

"I had turned to the wilderness really, not to Mr Kurtz, who, I was ready to admit, was as good as buried. And for a moment it seemed to me as if I also were buried in a vast grave full of unspeakable secrets. I felt an intoler-able weight oppressing my breast, the smell of the damp earth, the unseen presence of victorious corruption, the darkness of an impenetrable night. . . . The Russian tapped me on the shoulder. I heard him mumbling and stammering something about 'brother seaman—couldn't conceal—knowledge of matters that would affect Mr Kurtz's reputation.' I waited. For him evidently Mr Kurtz was not in his grave; I suspect that for him Mr Kurtz was one of the immortals. 'Well!' said I at last, 'speak out. As it hap-pens, I am Mr Kurtz's friend—in a way.'

"He stated with a good deal of formality that had we not been 'of the same profession,' he would have kept the matter to himself without regard to conse-quences. He suspected 'there was an active ill-will towards him on the part of these white men that—' 'You are right,' I said, remembering a certain conver-sation I had overheard. 'The manager thinks you ought to be hanged.' He showed a concern at this intelligence which amused me at first. 'I had better get out of the way quietly,' he said earnestly. 'I can do no more for Kurtz now, and they would soon find some excuse. What's to stop them? There's a military post three hundred miles from here.' 'Well, upon my word,' said I, 'perhaps you had better go if you have any friends amongst the savages near by.' 'Plenty,' he said. 'They are simple people—and I want nothing, you know.' He stood biting his lip, then: 'I don't want any harm to happen to these whites here, but of course I was thinking of Mr Kurtz's reputation—but you are a brother seaman and—' 'All right,' said I, after a time. 'Mr Kurtz's reputation is safe with me.' I did not know how truly I spoke.

"He informed me, lowering his voice, that it was Kurtz who had ordered the attack to be made on the steamer. 'He hated sometimes the idea of being taken away—and then again . . . But I don't understand these matters. I am a simple man. He thought it would scare you away—that you would give it up, thinking him dead. I could not stop him. Oh, I had an awful time of it this last month.' 'Very well,' I said. 'He is all right now.' 'Ye-e-es,' he muttered, not very convinced apparently. 'Thanks,' said I; 'I shall keep my eyes open.' 'But quiet—eh?' he urged anxiously. 'It would be awful for his reputation if anybody here—' I promised a complete discretion with great gravity. 'I have a canoe and three black fellows waiting not very far. I am off. Could you give me a few Martini-Henry cartridges?' I could, and did, with proper secrecy. He helped himself, with a wink at me, to a handful of my tobacco. 'Between sailors—you know—good English tobacco.' At the door of the pilot-house he turned round—'I say, haven't you a pair of shoes you could spare?' He raised one leg. 'Look.' The soles were tied with knotted strings sandal-wise under his bare feet. I rooted out an old pair, at which he looked with admiration before tucking it under his left arm. One of his pockets (bright red) was bulging with cartridges, from the other (dark blue) peeped 'Towson's Inquiry,' etc. etc. He seemed to think himself excellently well equipped for a renewed encounter with the wilderness. 'Ah! I'll never, never meet such a man again. You ought to have heard him recite poetry—his own too it was, he told me. Poetry!' He rolled his eyes at the recollection of these delights. 'Oh, he enlarged my mind!' 'Good-bye,' said I. He shook hands and vanished in the night. Sometimes I ask myself whether I had ever really seen him—whether it was possible to meet such a phenomenon! . . .

"When I woke up shortly after midnight his warning came to my mind with its hint of danger that seemed, in the starred darkness, real enough to make me get up for the purpose of having a look round. On the hill a big fire burned, illuminating fitfully a crooked corner of the station-house. One of the agents with a picket of a few of our blacks, armed for the purpose, was keeping guard over the ivory; but deep within the forest, red gleams that wavered, that seemed to sink and rise from the ground amongst confused columnar shapes of intense blackness, showed the exact position of the camp where Mr Kurtz's adorers were keeping their uneasy vigil. The monotonous beating of a big drum filled the air with muffled shocks and a lingering vibration. A steady droning sound of many men chanting each to himself some weird incantation came out from the black, flat wall of the woods as the humming of bees comes out of a hive, and had a strange narcotic effect upon my half-awake senses. I believe I dozed off leaning over the rail, till an abrupt burst of yells, an overwhelming outbreak of a pent-up and mysterious frenzy, woke me up in a bewildered wonder. It was cut short all at once, and the low droning went on with an effect of audible and soothing silence. I glanced casually into the little cabin. A light was burning within, but Mr Kurtz was not there.

"I think I would have raised an outcry if I had believed my eyes. But I didn't believe them at first—the thing seemed so impossible. The fact is I was completely unnerved by a sheer blank fright, pure abstract terror, unconnected with any distinct shape of physical danger. What made this emotion so overpowering was—how shall I define it?—the moral shock I received, as if something altogether monstrous, intolerable to thought and odious to the soul, had been thrust upon me unexpectedly. This lasted of course the merest fraction of a second, and then the usual sense of commonplace, deadly danger, the possibility of a sudden onslaught and massacre, or something of the kind, which I saw impending, was positively welcome and composing. It pacified me, in fact, so much, that I did not raise an alarm.

"There was an agent buttoned up inside an ulster[5] and sleeping on a chair on deck within three feet of me. The yells had not awakened him; he snored very slightly; I left him to his slumbers and leaped ashore. I did not betray Mr Kurtz—it was ordered I should never betray him—it was written I should be loyal to the nightmare of my choice. I was anxious to deal with this shadow by myself alone—and to this day I don't know why I was so jealous of sharing with any one the peculiar blackness of that experience.

"As soon as I got on the bank I saw a trail—a broad trail through the grass. I remember the exultation with which I said to myself, 'He can't walk—he is crawling on all-fours—I've got him.' The grass was wet with dew. I strode rapidly with clenched fists. I fancy I had some vague notion of falling upon him and giving him a drubbing. I don't know. I had some imbecile thoughts. The knitting old woman with the cat obtruded herself upon my memory as a most improper person to be sitting at the other end of such an affair. I saw a row of pilgrims squirting lead in the air out of Winchesters held to the hip. I thought I would never get back to the steamer, and imagined myself living alone and unarmed in the woods to an advanced age. Such silly things—you know. And I remember I confounded the beat of the drum with the beating of my heart, and was pleased at its calm regularity.

"I kept to the track though—then stopped to listen. The night was very clear; a dark blue space, sparkling with dew and starlight, in which black things stood very still. I thought I could see a kind of motion ahead of me. I was strangely cocksure of everything that night. I actually left the track and ran in a wide semicircle (I verily believe chuckling to myself) so as to get in front of that stir, of that motion I had seen—if indeed I had seen anything. I was circumventing Kurtz as though it had been a boyish game.

"I came upon him, and, if he had not heard me coming, I would have fallen over him too, but he got up in time. He rose, unsteady, long, pale, indistinct, like a vapour exhaled by the earth, and swayed slightly, misty and silent before me; while at my back the fires loomed between the trees, and the murmur of many voices issued from the forest. I had cut him off cleverly; but when actually confronting him I seemed to come to my senses, I saw the danger in its right proportion. It was by no means over yet. Suppose he began to shout? Though he could hardly stand, there was still plenty of vigour in his voice. 'Go away—hide yourself,' he said, in that

5. Long overcoat.

profound tone. It was very awful. I glanced back. We were within thirty yards of the nearest fire. A black figure stood up, strode on long black legs, waving long black arms, across the glow. It had horns—antelope horns, I think—on its head. Some sorcerer, some witch-man no doubt: it looked fiend-like enough. 'Do you know what you are doing?' I whispered. 'Perfectly,' he answered, raising his voice for that single word: it sounded to me far off and yet loud, like a hail through a speaking-trumpet. If he makes a row we are lost, I thought to myself. This clearly was not a case for fisticuffs, even apart from the very natural aversion I had to beat that Shadow— this wandering and tormented thing. 'You will be lost,' I said—'utterly lost.' One gets sometimes such a flash of inspiration, you know. I did say the right thing, though indeed he could not have been more irretrievably lost than he was at this very moment, when the foundations of our intimacy were being laid—to endure—to endure—even to the end—even beyond.

"'I had immense plans,' he muttered irresolutely. 'Yes,' said I; 'but if you try to shout I'll smash your head with—' There was not a stick or a stone near. 'I will throttle you for good,' I corrected myself. 'I was on the threshold of great things,' he pleaded, in a voice of longing, with a wistfulness of tone that made my blood run cold. 'And now for this stupid scoundrel—' 'Your success in Europe is assured in any case,' I affirmed steadily. I did not want to have the throttling of him, you understand—and indeed it would have been very little use for any practical purpose. I tried to break the spell—the heavy, mute spell of the wilderness—that seemed to draw him to its pitiless breast by the awakening of forgotten and brutal instincts, by the memory of gratified and monstrous passions. This alone, I was convinced, had driven him out to the edge of the forest, to the bush, towards the gleam of fires, the throb of drums, the drone of weird incantations; this alone had beguiled his unlawful soul beyond the bounds of permitted aspirations. And, don't you see, the terror of the position was not in being knocked on the head—though I had a very lively sense of that danger too—but in this, that I had to deal with a being to whom I could not appeal in the name of anything high or low. I had, even like the niggers, to invoke him—himself— his own exalted and incredible degradation. There was nothing either above or below him, and I knew it. He had kicked himself loose of the earth. Confound the man! he had kicked the very earth to pieces. He was alone, and I before him did not know whether I stood on the ground or floated in the air. I've been telling you what we said—repeating the phrases we pronounced— but what's the good? They were common everyday words—the familiar, vague sounds exchanged on every waking day of life. But what of that? They had behind them, to my mind, the terrific suggestiveness of words heard in dreams, of phrases spoken in nightmares. Soul! If anybody had ever struggled with a soul, I am the man. And I wasn't arguing with a lunatic either. Believe me or not, his intelligence was perfectly clear—concentrated, it is true, upon himself with horrible intensity, yet clear; and therein was my only chance—barring, of course, the killing him there and then, which wasn't so good, on account of unavoidable noise. But his soul was mad. Being alone in the wilderness, it had looked within itself, and, by heavens! I tell you, it had gone mad. I had—for my sins, I suppose, to go through the ordeal of looking into it myself. No eloquence could have been so withering to one's belief in mankind as his final burst of sincerity. He struggled with himself too. I saw it—I heard it. I saw the inconceivable mystery of a soul that knew no restraint, no faith, and no fear, yet struggling blindly with itself. I kept my head pretty well; but when I had him at last stretched on the couch, I wiped my forehead, while my legs shook under me as though I had carried half a ton on my back down that hill. And yet I had only supported him, his bony arm clasped round my neck—and he was not much heavier than a child.

"When next day we left at noon, the crowd, of whose presence behind the curtain of trees I had been acutely conscious all the time, flowed out of the woods again, filled the clearing, covered the slope with a mass of naked, breathing, quivering, bronze bodies. I steamed up a bit, then swung downstream, and two thousand eyes followed the evolutions of the splashing, thumping, fierce river-demon beating the water with its terrible tail and breathing black smoke into the air. In front of the first rank, along the river, three men, plastered with bright red earth from head to foot, strutted to and fro restlessly. When we came abreast again, they faced the river, stamped their feet, nodded their horned heads, swayed their scarlet bodies; they shook towards the fierce river-demon a bunch of black feathers, a mangy skin with a pendent tail—something that looked like a dried gourd; they shouted periodically together strings of amazing words that resembled no sounds of human language; and the deep murmurs of the crowd, interrupted suddenly, were like the responses of some satanic litany.

"We had carried Kurtz into the pilot-house: there was more air there. Lying on the couch, he stared through the open shutter. There was an eddy in the mass of human bodies, and the woman with helmeted head and tawny cheeks rushed out to the very brink of the stream. She put out her hands, shouted something, and all that wild mob took up the shout in a roaring chorus of articulated, rapid, breathless utterance.

"'Do you understand this?' I asked.

"He kept on looking out past me with fiery, longing eyes, with a mingled expression of wistfulness and hate. He made no answer, but I saw a smile, a smile of indefinable meaning, appear on his colourless lips that a moment after twitched convulsively. 'Do I not?' he said slowly, gasping, as if the words had been torn out of him by a supernatural power.

"I pulled the string of the whistle, and I did this because I saw the pilgrims on deck getting out their rifles with an air of anticipating a jolly lark. At the sudden screech there was a movement of abject terror through that wedged mass of bodies. 'Don't! don't you frighten them away,' cried some one on deck disconsolately. I pulled the string time after time. They broke and ran, they leaped, they crouched, they swerved, they dodged the flying terror of the sound. The three red chaps had fallen flat, face down on the shore, as though they had been shot dead. Only the barbarous and superb woman did not so much as flinch, and stretched tragically her bare arms after us over the sombre and glittering river.

"And then that imbecile crowd down on the deck started their little fun, and I could see nothing more for smoke.

"The brown current ran swiftly out of the heart of darkness, bearing us down towards the sea with twice the speed of our upward progress; and Kurtz's life was running swiftly too, ebbing, ebbing out of his heart into the sea of inexorable time. The manager was very placid, he had no vital anxieties now, he took us both in with a comprehensive and satisfied glance: the 'affair' had come off as well as could be wished. I saw the time approaching when I would be left alone of the party of 'unsound method.' The pilgrims looked upon me with disfavour. I was, so to speak, numbered with the dead. It is strange how I accepted this unforeseen partnership, this choice of nightmares forced upon me in the tenebrous land invaded by these mean and greedy phantoms.

"Kurtz discoursed. A voice! a voice! It rang deep to the very last. It survived his strength to hide in the magnificent folds of eloquence the barren darkness of his heart. Oh, he struggled! he struggled! The wastes of his weary brain were haunted by shadowy images now—images of wealth and fame revolving obsequiously round his unextinguishable gift of noble and lofty expression. My Intended, my station, my career, my ideas—these were the subjects for the occasional utterances of elevated sentiments. The shade of the original Kurtz frequented the bedside of the hollow sham, whose fate it was to be buried presently in the mould of primeval earth. But both the diabolic love and the unearthly hate of the mysteries it had penetrated fought for the possession of that soul satiated with primitive emotions, avid of lying fame, of sham distinction, of all the appearances of success and power.

"Sometimes he was contemptibly childish. He desired to have kings meet him at railway stations on his return from some ghastly Nowhere, where he intended to accomplish great things. 'You show them you have in you something that is really profitable, and then there will be no limits to the recognition of your ability,' he would say. 'Of course you must take care of the motives—right motives—always.' The long reaches that were like one and the same reach, monotonous bends that were exactly alike, slipped past the steamer with their multitude of secular[6] trees looking patiently after this grimy fragment of another world, the forerunner of change, of conquest, of trade, of massacres, of blessings. I looked ahead—piloting. 'Close the shutter,' said Kurtz suddenly one day; 'I can't bear to look at this.' I did so. There was a silence. 'Oh, but I will wring your heart yet!' he cried at the invisible wilderness.

"We broke down—as I had expected—and had to lie up for repairs at the head of an island. This delay was the first thing that shook Kurtz's confidence. One morning he gave me a packet of papers and a photograph—the lot tied together with a shoe-string. 'Keep this for me,' he said. 'This noxious fool' (meaning the manager) 'is capable of prying into my boxes when I am not looking.' In the afternoon I saw him. He was lying on his back with closed eyes, and I withdrew quietly, but I heard him mutter, 'Live rightly, die, die . . .' I listened. There was nothing more. Was he rehearsing some speech in his sleep, or was it a fragment of a phrase from some newspaper article? He had been writing for the papers and meant to do so again, 'for the furthering of my ideas. It's a duty.'

"His was an impenetrable darkness. I looked at him as you peer down at a man who is lying at the bottom of a precipice where the sun never shines. But I had not much time to give him, because I was helping the engine-driver to take to pieces the leaky cylinders, to straighten a bent connecting-rod, and in other such matters. I lived in an infernal mess of rust, filings, nuts, bolts, spanners, hammers, ratchet-drills—things I abominate, because I don't get on with them. I tended the little forge we fortunately had aboard; I toiled wearily in a wretched scrap-heap—unless I had the shakes too bad to stand.

6. Centuries old.

"One evening coming in with a candle I was startled to hear him say a little tremulously, 'I am lying here in the dark waiting for death.' The light was within a foot of his eyes. I forced myself to murmur, 'Oh, nonsense!' and stood over him as if transfixed.

"Anything approaching the change that came over his features I have never seen before, and hope never to see again. Oh, I wasn't touched. I was fascinated. It was as though a veil had been rent. I saw on that ivory face the expression of sombre pride, of ruthless power, of craven terror—of an intense and hopeless despair. Did he live his life again in every detail of desire, temptation, and surrender during that supreme moment of complete knowledge? He cried in a whisper at some image, at some vision—he cried out twice, a cry that was no more than a breath:

"'The horror! The horror!'

"I blew the candle out and left the cabin. The pilgrims were dining in the mess-room, and I took my place opposite the manager, who lifted his eyes to give me a questioning glance, which I successfully ignored. He leaned back, serene, with that peculiar smile of his sealing the unexpressed depths of his meanness. A continuous shower of small flies streamed upon the lamp, upon the cloth, upon our hands and faces. Suddenly the manager's boy put his insolent black head in the doorway, and said in a tone of scathing contempt:

"'Mistah Kurtz—he dead.'

"All the pilgrims rushed out to see. I remained, and went on with my dinner. I believe I was considered brutally callous. However, I did not eat much. There was a lamp in there—light, don't you know—and outside it was so beastly, beastly dark. I went no more near the remarkable man who had pronounced a judgement upon the adventures of his soul on this earth. The voice was gone. What else had been there? But I am of course aware that next day the pilgrims buried something in a muddy hole.

"And then they very nearly buried me.

"However, as you see, I did not go to join Kurtz there and then. I did not. I remained to dream the nightmare out to the end, and to show my loyalty to Kurtz once more. Destiny. My destiny! Droll thing life is—that mysterious arrangement of merciless logic for a futile purpose. The most you can hope from it is some knowledge of yourself—that comes too late—a crop of unextinguishable regrets. I have wrestled with death. It is the most unexciting contest you can imagine. It takes place in an impalpable greyness, with nothing underfoot, with nothing around, without spectators, without clamour, without glory, without the great desire of victory, without the great fear of defeat, in a sickly atmosphere of tepid scepticism, without much belief in your own right, and still less in that of your adversary. If such is the form of ultimate wisdom, then life is a greater riddle than some of us think it to be. I was within a hair's-breadth of the last opportunity for pronouncement, and I found with humiliation that probably I would have nothing to say. This is the reason why I affirm that Kurtz was a remarkable man. He had something to say. He said it. Since I had peeped over the edge myself, I understand better the meaning of his stare, that could not see the flame of the candle, but was wide enough to embrace the whole universe, piercing enough to penetrate all the hearts that beat in the darkness. He had summed up—he had judged. 'The horror!' He was a remarkable man. After all, this was the expression of some sort of belief; it had candour, it had conviction, it had a vibrating note of revolt in its whisper, it had the appalling face of a glimpsed truth—the strange commingling of desire and hate. And it is not my own extremity I remember best—a vision of greyness without form filled with physical pain, and a careless contempt for the evanescence of all things—even of this pain itself. No! It is his extremity that I seem to have lived through. True, he had made that last stride, he had stepped over the edge, while I had been permitted to draw back my hesitating foot. And perhaps in this is the whole difference; perhaps all the wisdom, and all truth, and all sincerity, are just compressed into that inappreciable moment of time in which we step over the threshold of the invisible. Perhaps! I like to think my summing-up would not have been a word of careless contempt. Better his cry—much better. It was an affirmation, a moral victory paid for by innumerable defeats, by abominable terrors, by abominable satisfactions. But it was a victory! That is why I have remained loyal to Kurtz to the last, and even beyond, when a long time after I heard once more, not his own voice, but the echo of his magnificent eloquence thrown to me from a soul as translucently pure as a cliff of crystal.

"No, they did not bury me, though there is a period of time which I remember mistily, with a shuddering wonder, like a passage through some inconceivable world that had no hope in it and no desire. I found myself back in the sepulchral city resenting the sight of people hurrying through the streets to filch a little money from each other, to devour their infamous cookery, to gulp their unwholesome beer, to dream their insignificant and silly dreams. They trespassed upon my thoughts. They were intruders whose knowledge of life was to me an irritating pretence, because I felt so sure they could not possibly know the things I knew. Their bearing, which was simply the bearing of commonplace individuals going about their business in the assurance of perfect safety, was offensive to me like the outrageous flauntings of folly in the face of a danger it is unable to comprehend. I had no particular desire to enlighten them, but I had some difficulty in restraining myself from laughing in their faces, so full of stupid importance. I daresay I was not very well at that time. I tottered about the streets—there were various affairs to settle—grinning bitterly at perfectly respectable persons. I admit my behaviour was inexcusable, but then my temperature was seldom normal in these days. My dear aunt's endeavours to 'nurse up my strength' seemed altogether beside the mark. It was not my strength that wanted nursing, it was my imagination that wanted soothing. I kept the bundle of papers given me by Kurtz, not knowing exactly what to do with it. His mother had died lately, watched over, as I was told, by his Intended. A clean-shaven man, with an official manner and wearing gold-rimmed spectacles, called on me one day and made inquiries, at first circuitous, afterwards suavely pressing, about what he was pleased to denominate certain 'documents.' I was not surprised, because I had had two rows with the manager on the subject out there. I had refused to give up the smallest scrap out of that package, and I took the same attitude with the spectacled man. He became darkly menacing at last, and with much heat argued that the Company had the right to every bit of information about its 'territories.' And, said he, 'Mr Kurtz's knowledge of unexplored regions must have been necessarily extensive and peculiar—owing to his great abilities and to the deplorable circumstances in which he had been placed: therefore—' I assured him Mr Kurtz's knowledge, however extensive, did not bear upon the problems of commerce or administration. He invoked then the name of science. 'It would be an incalculable loss if,' etc. etc. I offered him the report on the 'Suppression of Savage Customs,' with the postscriptum torn off. He took it up eagerly, but ended by sniffing at it with an air of contempt. 'This is not what we had a right to expect,' he remarked. 'Expect nothing else,' I said. 'There are only private letters.' He withdrew upon some threat of legal proceedings, and I saw him no more; but another fellow, calling himself Kurtz's cousin, appeared two days later, and was anxious to hear all the details about his dear relative's last moments. Incidentally he gave me to understand that Kurtz had been essentially a great musician. 'There was the making of an immense success,' said the man, who was an organist, I believe, with lank grey hair flowing over a greasy coat-collar. I had no reason to doubt his statement; and to this day I am unable to say what was Kurtz's profession, whether he ever had any—which was the greatest of his talents. I had taken him for a painter who wrote for the papers, or else for a journalist who could paint—but even the cousin (who took snuff during the interview) could not tell me what he had been—exactly. He was a universal genius—on that point I agreed with the old chap, who thereupon blew his nose noisily into a large cotton handkerchief and withdrew in senile agitation, bearing off some family letters and memoranda without importance. Ultimately a journalist anxious to know something of the fate of his 'dear colleague' turned up. This visitor informed me Kurtz's proper sphere ought to have been politics 'on the popular side.' He had furry straight eyebrows, bristly hair cropped short, an eyeglass on a broad ribbon, and, becoming expansive, confessed his opinion that Kurtz really couldn't write a bit—'but heavens! how that man could talk! He electrified large meetings. He had faith—don't you see?—he had the faith. He could get himself to believe anything—anything. He would have been a splendid leader of an extreme party.' 'What party?' I asked. 'Any party,' answered the other. 'He was an—an—extremist.' Did I not think so? I assented. Did I know, he asked, with a sudden flash of curiosity, 'what it was that had induced him to go out there?' 'Yes,' said I, and forthwith handed him the famous Report for publication, if he thought fit. He glanced through it hurriedly, mumbling all the time, judged 'it would do,' and took himself off with this plunder.

"Thus I was left at last with a slim packet of letters and the girl's portrait. She struck me as beautiful—I mean she had a beautiful expression. I know that the sunlight can be made to lie too, yet one felt that no manipulation of light and pose could have conveyed the delicate shade of truthfulness upon those features. She seemed ready to listen without mental reservation, without suspicion, without a thought for herself. I concluded I would go and give her back her portrait and those letters myself. Curiosity? Yes; and also some other feeling perhaps. All that had been Kurtz's had passed out of my hands: his soul, his body, his station, his plans, his ivory, his career. There remained only his memory and his Intended—and I wanted to give that up too to the past, in a way—to surrender personally all that remained of him with me to that oblivion which is the last word of our common fate. I don't defend myself. I had no clear perception of what it was I really wanted. Perhaps it was an impulse of unconscious loyalty, or the fulfilment of one of those ironic necessities that lurk in the facts of human existence. I don't know. I can't tell. But I went.

"I thought his memory was like the other memories of the dead that accumulate in every man's life—a vague impress on the brain of shadows that had fallen on it in their swift and final passage; but before the high and ponderous door, between the tall houses of a street as still and decorous as a well-kept alley in a cemetery, I had a vision of him on the stretcher, opening his mouth voraciously, as if to devour all the earth with all its mankind. He lived then before me; he lived as much as he had ever lived—a shadow insatiable of splendid appearances, of frightful realities; a shadow darker than the shadow of the night, and draped nobly in the folds of a gorgeous eloquence. The vision seemed to enter the house with me—the stretcher, the phantom-bearers, the wild crowd of obedient worshippers, the gloom of the forests, the glitter of the reach between the murky bends, the beat of the drum, regular and muffled like the beating of a heart—the heart of a conquering darkness. It was a moment of triumph for the wilderness, an invading and vengeful rush which, it seemed to me, I would have to keep back alone for the salvation of another soul. And the memory of what I had heard him say afar there, with the horned shapes stirring at my back, in the glow of fires, within the patient woods, those broken phrases came back to me, were heard again in their ominous and terrifying simplicity. I remembered his abject pleading, his abject threats, the colossal scale of his vile desires, the meanness, the torment, the tempestuous anguish of his soul. And later on I seemed to see his collected languid manner, when he said one day, 'This lot of ivory now is really mine. The Company did not pay for it. I collected it myself at a very great personal risk. I am afraid they will try to claim it as theirs though. H'm. It is a difficult case. What do you think I ought to do—resist? Eh? I want no more than justice.' . . . He wanted no more than justice—no more than justice. I rang the bell before a mahogany door on the first floor, and while I waited he seemed to stare at me out of the glossy panel—stare with that wide and immense stare embracing, condemning, loathing all the universe. I seemed to hear the whispered cry, "The horror! The horror!'

"The dusk was falling. I had to wait in a lofty drawing-room with three long windows from floor to ceiling that were like three luminous and bedraped columns. The bent gilt legs and backs of the furniture shone in indistinct curves. The tall marble fireplace had a cold and monumental whiteness. A grand piano stood massively in a corner; with dark gleams on the flat surfaces like a sombre and polished sarcophagus. A high door opened—closed. I rose.

"She came forward, all in black, with a pale head, floating towards me in the dusk. She was in mourning. It was more than a year since his death, more than a year since the news came; she seemed as though she would remember and mourn for ever. She took both my hands in hers and murmured, 'I had heard you were coming.' I noticed she was not very young—I mean not girlish. She had a mature capacity for fidelity, for belief, for suffering. The room seemed to have grown darker, as if all the sad light of the cloudy evening had taken refuge on her forehead. This fair hair, this pale visage, this pure brow, seemed surrounded by an ashy halo from which the dark eyes looked out at me. Their glance was guileless, profound, confident, and trustful. She carried her sorrowful head as though she were proud of that sorrow, as though she would say, I—I alone know how to mourn for him as he deserves. But while we were still shaking hands, such a look of awful desolation came upon her face that I perceived she was one of those creatures that are not the playthings of Time. For her he had died only yesterday. And, by Jove! the impression was so powerful that for me too he seemed to have died only yesterday—nay, this very minute. I saw her and him in the same instant of time—his death and her sorrow—I saw her sorrow in the very moment of his death. Do you understand? I saw them together—I heard them together. She had said, with a deep catch of the breath, 'I have survived'; while my strained ears seemed to hear distinctly, mingled with her tone of despairing regret, the summing-up whisper of his eternal condemnation. I asked myself what I was doing there, with a sensation of panic in my heart as though I had blundered into a place of cruel and absurd mysteries not fit for a human being to behold. She motioned me to a chair. We sat down. I laid the packet gently on the little table, and she put her hand over it. . . . 'You knew him well,' she murmured, after a moment of mourning silence.

"'Intimacy grows quickly out there,' I said. 'I knew him as well as it is possible for one man to know another.'

"'And you admired him,' she said. 'It was impossible to know him and not to admire him. Was it?'

"'He was a remarkable man,' I said unsteadily. Then before the appealing fixity of her gaze, that seemed to watch for more words on my lips, I went on, 'It was impossible not to—'

"'Love him,' she finished eagerly, silencing me into an appalled dumbness. 'How true! how true! But when you think that no one knew him so well as I! I had all his noble confidence. I knew him best.'

"'You knew him best,' I repeated. And perhaps she did. But with every word spoken the room was growing darker, and only her forehead, smooth and white, remained illumined by the unextinguishable light of belief and love.

"'You were his friend,' she went on. 'His friend,' she repeated, a little louder. 'You must have been, if he had given you this, and sent you to me. I feel I can speak to you—and oh! I must speak. I want you—you who have heard his last words—to know I have been worthy of him. . . . It is not pride. . . . Yes! I am proud to know I understood him better than any one on earth—he told me so himself. And since his mother died I have had no one—no one—to—to—'

"I listened. The darkness deepened. I was not even sure whether he had given me the right bundle. I rather suspect he wanted me to take care of another batch of his papers which, after his death, I saw the manager examining under the lamp. And the girl talked, easing her pain in the certitude of my sympathy; she talked as thirsty men drink. I had heard that her engagement with Kurtz had been disapproved by her people. He wasn't rich enough or something. And indeed I don't know whether he had not been a pauper all his life. He had given me some reason to infer that it was his impatience of comparative poverty that drove him out there.

"'. . . Who was not his friend who had heard him speak once?' she was saying. 'He drew men towards him by what was best in them.' She looked at me with intensity. 'It is the gift of the great,' she went on, and the sound of her low voice seemed to have the accompaniment of all the other sounds, full of mystery, desolation, and sorrow, I had ever heard—the ripple of the river, the soughing of the trees swayed by the wind, the murmurs of the crowds, the faint ring of incomprehensible words cried from afar, the whisper of a voice speaking from beyond the threshold of an eternal darkness. 'But you have heard him! You know!' she cried.

"'Yes, I know,' I said with something like despair in my heart, but bowing my head before the faith that was in her, before that great and saving illusion that shone with an unearthly glow in the darkness, in the triumphant darkness from which I could not have defended her—from which I could not even defend myself.

"'What a loss to me—to us!'—she corrected herself with beautiful generosity; then added in a murmur, 'To the world.' By the last gleams of twilight I could see the glitter of her eyes, full of tears—of tears that would not fall.

"'I have been very happy—very fortunate—very proud,' she went on. 'Too fortunate. Too happy for a little while. And now I am unhappy for—for life.'

"She stood up; her fair hair seemed to catch all the remaining light in a glimmer of gold. I rose too.

"'And of all this,' she went on mournfully, 'of all his promise, and of all his greatness, of his generous mind, of his noble heart, nothing remains—nothing but a memory. You and I—'

"'We shall always remember him,' I said hastily.

"'No!' she cried. 'It is impossible that all this should be lost—that such a life should be sacrificed to leave nothing—but sorrow. You know what vast plans he had. I knew of them too—I could not perhaps understand—but others knew of them. Something must remain. His words, at least, have not died.'

"'His words will remain,' I said.

"'And his example,' she whispered to herself. 'Men looked up to him—his goodness shone in every act. His example—'

"'True,' I said; 'his example too. Yes, his example. I forgot that.'

"'But I do not. I cannot—I cannot believe—not yet. I cannot believe that I shall never see him again, that nobody will see him again, never, never, never.'

"She put out her arms as if after a retreating figure, stretching them black and with clasped pale hands across the fading and narrow sheen of the window. Never see him! I saw him clearly enough then. I shall see this eloquent phantom as long as I live, and I shall see her too, a tragic and familiar Shade, resembling in this gesture another one, tragic also, and bedecked with powerless charms, stretching bare brown arms over the glitter of the infernal stream, the stream of darkness. She said suddenly very low, 'He died as he lived.'

"'His end,' said I, with dull anger stirring in me, 'was in every way worthy of his life.'

"'And I was not with him,' she murmured. My anger subsided before a feeling of infinite pity.

"'Everything that could be done—' I mumbled.

"'Ah, but I believed in him more than any one on earth—more than his own mother, more than—himself. He needed me! Me! I would have treasured every sigh, every word, every sign, every glance.'

"I felt like a chill grip on my chest. 'Don't,' I said, in a muffled voice.

"'Forgive me. I—I—have mourned so long in silence—in silence. . . . You were with him—to the last? I think of his loneliness. Nobody near to understand him as I would have understood. Perhaps no one to hear. . . .'

"'To the very end,' I said shakily. 'I heard his very last words. . . .' I stopped in a fright.

"'Repeat them,' she murmured in a heart-broken tone. 'I want—I want—something—something—to—to live with.'

"I was on the point of crying at her, 'Don't you hear them?' The dusk was repeating them in a persistent whisper all around us, in a whisper that seemed to swell menacingly like the first whisper of a rising wind. 'The horror! The horror!'

"'His last word—to live with,' she insisted. 'Don't you understand I loved him—I loved him—I loved him!'

"I pulled myself together and spoke slowly.

"'The last word he pronounced was—your name.'

"I heard a light sigh and then my heart stood still, stopped dead short by an exulting and terrible cry, by the cry of inconceivable triumph and of unspeakable pain. 'I knew it—I was sure!' . . . She knew. She was sure. I heard her weeping; she had hidden her face in her hands. It seemed to me that the house would collapse before I could escape, that the heavens would fall upon my head. But nothing happened. The heavens do not fall for such a trifle. Would they have fallen, I wonder, if I had rendered Kurtz that justice which was his due? Hadn't he said he wanted only justice? But I couldn't. I could not tell her. It would have been too dark—too dark altogether. . . ."[7]

Marlow ceased, and sat apart, indistinct and silent, in the pose of a meditating Buddha. Nobody moved for a time. "We have lost the first of the ebb," said the Director suddenly. I raised my head. The offing was barred by a black bank of clouds, and the tranquil waterway leading to the uttermost ends of the earth flowed sombre under an overcast sky—seemed to lead into the heart of an immense darkness.

1898–99   1899, 1902

7. Writing to William Blackwood (editor of *Blackwood's Magazine*, where the story first appeared) in May 1902, Conrad referred to "the last pages of Heart of Darkness where the interview of the man and the girl locks in—as it were—the whole 30,000 words of narrative description into one suggestive view of a whole phase of life, and makes of that story something quite on another plane than an anecdote of a man who went mad in the Centre of Africa" (Joseph Conrad, *Letters to William Blackwood and David S. Meldrum*, ed. William Blackburn, 1958).

A. E. HOUSMAN
1859–1936

Alfred Edward Housman was born in Fockbury, Worcestershire (close to the Shropshire border), and attended school at the nearby town of Bromsgrove. He studied classics and philosophy at Oxford and in 1881 shocked his friends and teachers by failing his final examinations (he was at the time in a state of psychological turmoil resulting from his suppressed homosexual love for a fellow student). He obtained a civil service job and pursued his classical studies alone, gradually building up a reputation as a great textual critic of Latin literature. In 1892 he was appointed to the chair of Latin at University College, London, and from 1911 until his death he was professor of Latin at Cambridge.

Housman's classical studies consisted of meticulous, impersonal textual investigations; both his scholarship and his life were reserved and solitary. Yet his feeling for literature ran strong and deep, and in his lecture "The Name and Nature of Poetry" (1933) he says that poetry should be "more physical than intellectual," having a skin-bristling, spine-shivering effect on the reader. His own poetry was limited both in quantity and in range, but—stark, lucid, elegant—it exemplifies the "superior terseness" he prized in verse. Two "slim volumes"—*A Shropshire Lad* (1896) and *Last Poems* (1922)—were all that appeared during his lifetime, and after his death his brother Laurence brought out another small book, *More Poems* (1936).

As a poet Housman aimed not to expand or develop the resources of English poetry but by limitation and concentration to achieve an utterance both compact and moving. He was influenced by Greek and Latin lyric poetry, by the traditional ballad, and by the lyrics of the early nineteenth-century German poet Heinrich Heine. His favorite theme is that of the doomed youth acting out the tragedy of his brief life; the context is agricultural activity in England, with the land bearing visual reminders of humanity's long history. Nature is beautiful but indifferent and is to be enjoyed while we are still able to savor it. Love, friendship, and conviviality cannot last and may well result in betrayal or death, but are likewise to be relished while there is time. Wryly ironic in tone, stoic in temperament, Housman sounds a note of resigned wisdom with quiet poignancy. He avoids self-pity by projecting emotion through an imagined character, notably the "Shropshire lad," so that even the first-person poems seem to be distanced in some degree. At the same time the poems are distinguished from the "gather ye rosebuds" (or carpe diem) tradition by the undertones of fatalism and even doom.

Loveliest of Trees

Loveliest of trees, the cherry now
Is hung with bloom along the bough,
And stands about the woodland ride
Wearing white for Eastertide.

5   Now, of my threescore years and ten,
Twenty will not come again,
And take from seventy springs a score,
It only leaves me fifty more.

And since to look at things in bloom
10   Fifty springs are little room,
About the woodlands I will go
To see the cherry hung with snow.

1896

When I Was One-and-Twenty

When I was one-and-twenty
    I heard a wise man say,
"Give crowns and pounds and guineas
    But not your heart away;
5   Give pearls away and rubies
    But keep your fancy free."
But I was one-and-twenty,
    No use to talk to me.

When I was one-and-twenty
10   I heard him say again,
"The heart out of the bosom
    Was never given in vain;

'Tis paid with sighs a plenty
     And sold for endless rue."°   *repentance*
15 And I am two-and-twenty,
     And oh, 'tis true, 'tis true.

1896

To an Athlete Dying Young

The time you won your town the race
We chaired you through the market-place;
Man and boy stood cheering by,
And home we brought you shoulder-high.

5   Today, the road all runners come,
Shoulder-high we bring you home,
And set you at your threshold down,
Townsman of a stiller town.

Smart lad, to slip betimes away
10 From fields where glory does not stay,
And early though the laurel[1] grows
It withers quicker than the rose.

Eyes the shady night has shut
Cannot see the record cut,°   *broken*
15 And silence sounds no worse than cheers
After earth has stopped the ears:

Now you will not swell the rout°   *crowd*
Of lads that wore their honours out,
Runners whom renown outran
20 And the name died before the man.

So set, before its echoes fade,
The fleet foot on the sill of shade,
And hold to the low lintel up
The still-defended challenge-cup.

25 And round that early laurelled head
Will flock to gaze the strengthless dead
And find unwithered on its curls
The garland briefer than a girl's.

1896

---

1. In ancient Greece and Rome victorious athletes were crowned with laurel wreaths.

Terence,[1] This Is Stupid Stuff

"Terence, this is stupid stuff:
You eat your victuals fast enough;
There can't be much amiss, 'tis clear,
To see the rate you drink your beer.
5   But oh, good Lord, the verse you make,
It gives a chap the belly-ache.
The cow, the old cow, she is dead;
It sleeps well, the hornèd head:
We poor lads, 'tis our turn now
10   To hear such tunes as killed the cow.
Pretty friendship 'tis to rhyme
Your friends to death before their time
Moping melancholy mad:
Come, pipe a tune to dance to, lad."

15   Why, if 'tis dancing you would be,
There's brisker pipes than poetry.
Say, for what were hop-yards meant,
Or why was Burton built on Trent?[2]
Oh many, a peer[3] of England brews
20   Livelier liquor than the Muse,
And malt does more than Milton can
To justify God's ways to man.[4]
Ale, man, ale's the stuff to drink
For fellows whom it hurts to think:
25   Look into the pewter pot
To see the world as the world's not.
And faith, 'tis pleasant till 'tis past:
The mischief is that 'twill not last.
Oh I have been to Ludlow[5] Fair
30   And left my necktie God knows where,
And carried half-way home, or near,
Pints and quarts of Ludlow beer:
Then the world seemed none so bad,
And I myself a sterling lad;
35   And down in lovely muck I've lain,
Happy till I woke again.
Then I saw the morning sky:
Heigho, the tale was all a lie;
The world, it was the old world yet,
40   I was I, my things were wet,
And nothing now remained to do
But begin the game anew.

Therefore, since the world has still
Much good, but much less good than ill,

---

1. *The Poems of Terence Hearsay* was Housman's intended title for *The Shropshire Lad*.
2. Burton-on-Trent is the most famous of all English brewing towns.
3. A reference to the "beer barons," brewery magnates raised to the peerage (i.e., made nobles).
4. Cf. Milton's promise in *Paradise Lost* (1.17–26) to "justify the ways of God to men."
5. A market town in Shropshire.

45 And while the sun and moon endure
Luck's a chance, but trouble's sure,
I'd face it as a wise man would,
And train for ill and not for good.
'Tis true the stuff I bring for sale
50 Is not so brisk a brew as ale:
Out of a stem that scored° the hand   cut
I wrung it in a weary land.
But take it: if the smack is sour,
The better for the embittered hour;
55 It should do good to heart and head
When your soul is in my soul's stead;
And I will friend you, if I may,
In the dark and cloudy day.

There was a king reigned in the East:
60 There, when kings will sit to feast,
They get their fill before they think
With poisoned meat and poisoned drink.
He gathered all that springs to birth
From the many-venomed earth;
65 First a little, thence to more,
He sampled all her killing store;
And easy, smiling, seasoned sound,
Sate the king when healths went round.
They put arsenic in his meat
70 And stared aghast to watch him eat;
They poured strychnine in his cup
And shook to see him drink it up:
They shook, they stared as white's their shirt:
Them it was their poison hurt.
75 —I tell the tale that I heard told.
Mithridates, he died old.[6]

1896

Epitaph on an Army of Mercenaries[1]

These, in the day when heaven was falling,
    The hour when earth's foundations fled,
Followed their mercenary calling
    And took their wages and are dead.

5 Their shoulders held the sky suspended;
    They stood, and earth's foundations stay;
What God abandoned, these defended,
    And saved the sum of things for pay.

1917, 1922

6. The story of Mithridates, king of Pontus, who made himself immune to poison by taking small doses daily, is told in Pliny's *Natural History*.
1. To honor the heroism of the professional soldiers of the British Regular Army in the First Battle of Ypres (1914), Housman published this poem in *The Times* on the third anniversary of the turning point of that battle, October 31, 1917.

Voices from World War I

The original spark that set off what proved to be the bloodiest and most widespread war that had yet been fought was the assassination of the Archduke Ferdinand of Austria in the Balkan state of Serbia on June 28, 1914. Austria, supported by Germany, used the murder as a pretext for declaring war on Serbia, which in turn was supported by its fellow-Slav country Russia. Because Russia was bound by a treaty obligation to both France and Britain, Russia and France were soon at war with Germany and Austria. The most effective way for Germany to attack France was to go through Belgium, though all the powers had guaranteed Belgian neutrality. The attack on Belgium impelled Britain to declare war on Germany on August 4, but rival imperialisms, an international armaments race, France's desire to regain Alsace-Lorraine (which it had lost to Germany in 1870), and German and Austrian ambitions in the Balkans were some of the many other factors that brought about the four-year conflict, a struggle that shook the world. Turkey sided with Germany and Austria in October 1914, and Bulgaria allied itself with them the following year. Britain and France were joined by Japan late in August 1914, by Italy (although Italy had in 1882 joined the "Triple Alliance" with Germany and Austria directed against France and Russia) in May 1915, and by the United States in April 1917.

Before the collapse of Germany followed by the armistice of November 11, 1918, some 8,700,000 lives had been lost (including 780,000 British—virtually a whole generation of young men) and the prolonged horrors of trench warfare had seared themselves into the minds of the survivors. For three years the battle line, "the Western Front," was stabilized between northwest France and Switzerland, with both sides dug in and making repeated, costly, and generally useless attempts to advance. The German use of poison gas at the Second Battle of Ypres in 1915, the massive German attack at Verdun in 1916, and the British

(*Left*) British soldiers cross no-man's-land. The terrain has been scorched and laid waste by battle. (*Right*) Allied soldiers follow the lead of an officer out of a trench, April 7, 1918. German shells burst around them during the Arras and Cambrai offensive on the Western Front in France. The phrase "going over the top" was used to describe infantry rising up out of their trenches to attack the enemy. Soldiers were at grave risk as they came into the open and crossed into no-man's-land.

WORLD WAR I
Western Front, 1914–1918

GERMAN ADVANCE
ALLIED ADVANCE
✕ Major battle

The Western Front was the primary site of military conflict during World War I, although the war also extended to Africa, Asia, and elsewhere. Following the outbreak of war in August 1914, Germany opened the front by invading Luxembourg and Belgium, then gaining control of important industrial regions in France. The two sides bogged down for years, erecting fortified trenches along a line that changed little for most of the war. In major offenses along the front, massive infantry advances and artillery bombardments resulted in unprecedented casualties.

introduction of tanks on the Somme in the same year failed to produce the breakthrough each side desired. Desolate, war-scarred landscapes with blasted trees and mud everywhere, trenches half-filled with water and infested with rats, miles of protective barbed wire requiring individual "volunteers" to crawl through machinegun fire and cut it so an advance could begin, long-continued massive bombardments by heavy artillery, and a sense of stalemate that suggested to the soldiers involved that this living hell could go on forever—all this was long kept from the knowledge of the civilians at home, who continued to use the old patriotic slogans and write in old-fashioned romantic terms about glorious cavalry charges and the noble pursuit of heroic ideals. But those poets who were involved on the front, however romantically they may have felt about the cause when they joined up, soon realized the full horror of war, and this realization affected both their imaginations and their poetic techniques. They had to find a way of expressing the terrible truths they had experienced, and even when they did not express them directly, the underlying knowledge affected the way they wrote.

The poetry that was in vogue when war broke out, and that some poets continued to write for some years afterward, was named "Georgian" in honor of King George V, who had succeeded Edward VII in 1910. The term was first used of poets when Edward Marsh brought out in 1912 the first of a series of five anthologies called *Georgian Poetry*. The work therein represented an attempt to wall in the garden of English poetry against the disruptive forces of modern civilization. Cultured meditations of the English countryside ("I love the mossy quietness / That grows upon the great stone flags") alternated with self-conscious exercises in the exotic ("When I was but thirteen or so / I went into a golden land, / Chimporazo, Cotopaxi / Took me by the hand"). Sometimes the magical note was authentic, as in many of Walter de la Mare's poems, and sometimes the meditative strain was original and impressive, as in Edward Thomas's poetry. But as World War I went on, with more and more poets killed and the survivors increasingly

"**Women of Britain Say—'Go!'**" The women in this British recruiting poster from 1915 are represented as having sent off their men to fight for the domestic harmony of home and the idyllic beauty of a countryside glimpsed through the open window.

disillusioned, the whole world on which the Georgian imagination rested came to appear unreal. A patriotic poem such as Rupert Brooke's "The Soldier" became a ridiculous anachronism in the face of the realities of trench warfare, and the even more blatantly patriotic note sounded by other Georgian poems (as in John Freeman's "Happy Is England Now," which claimed that "there's not a nobleness of heart, hand, brain / But shines the purer; happiest is England now / In those that fight") seemed obscene. The savage ironies of Siegfried Sassoon's war poems and the combination of pity and irony in Wilfred Owen's work portrayed a world undreamed of in the golden years from 1910 to 1914.

World War I left throughout Europe a sense that the bases of civilization had been destroyed, that all traditional values had been wiped out. We see this sense reflected in the years immediately after the war in different ways in, for example, T. S. Eliot's *The Waste Land* and Aldous Huxley's early fiction. But the poets who wrote during the war most directly reflected the impact of the war experience.

Returning to the Trenches, 1916, by C. R. W. Nevinson. In this English war artist's painting, influenced by the Italian futurist emphasis on movement and machines, the soldiers' bodies seem propelled by an unstoppable force, their feet blurred by the rapidity of the march.

RUPERT BROOKE

Rupert Brooke (1887–1915) was educated at Rugby School and at King's College, Cambridge. When World War I began he was commissioned as an officer into the Royal Naval Division and took part in its brief and abortive expedition to Antwerp. On leave in December 1914 he wrote the "war sonnets" that were to make him famous; five months later he died of dysentery and blood poisoning on a troopship destined for Gallipoli.

Brooke was the most popular of the Georgians, pastoral poets who infused nature with nationalist feeling. His early death symbolized the death of a whole generation of patriotic Englishmen. Shortly before then the dean of St. Paul's read "The Soldier" in a sermon from the Cathedral pulpit, and in a 1915 valediction in the London *Times*, Winston Churchill sounded a note that swelled over the following months and years: "Joyous, fearless, versatile, deeply instructed, with classic symmetry of mind and body, he was all that one would wish England's noblest sons to be in days when no sacrifice but the most precious is acceptable, and the most precious is that which is most freely proffered." Brooke's *1914 and Other Poems* was published in June 1915, and during the next decade this and his *Collected Poems* sold three hundred thousand copies.

The Soldier

If I should die, think only this of me:
    That there's some corner of a foreign field
That is forever England. There shall be
    In that rich earth a richer dust concealed;

5 A dust whom England bore, shaped, made aware,
    Gave, once, her flowers to love, her ways to roam,
A body of England's, breathing English air,
    Washed by the rivers, blest by suns of home.

And think, this heart, all evil shed away,
10   A pulse in the Eternal mind, no less
      Gives somewhere back the thoughts by England given,
Her sights and sounds; dreams happy as her day;
    And laughter, learnt of friends; and gentleness,
      In hearts at peace, under an English heaven.

1914   1915

ROBERT SERVICE

B orn in Preston, England, to Scottish parents, Robert Service (1874–1958) lived a life that crossed national borders. He moved to Scotland at the age of five and was educated in Glasgow before moving to Canada in his early twenties. Working on farms and then as a banker in western Canada, he won popular acclaim with his first volume of verse, *Songs of a Sourdough* (1907), including his narrative poems about the Yukon Gold Rush of 1898, "The Shooting of Dan McGrew" and "The Ballad of Sam McGee." These early ballads established his reputation as the "Canadian Kipling" or "Bard of the Yukon," though Service never gave up his British citizenship. Before the First World War, he married a Frenchwoman, Germaine Bourgoin. During the war, he was a war reporter for Canadian newspapers, writing gritty accounts of the suffering on the front. He was also able to observe wounded combatants at close hand while serving as an ambulance driver and stretcher bearer for the American Red Cross. After the war he lived mostly in France.

Service's wartime collection of poetry, *Rhymes of a Red Cross Man* (1916), was dedicated to his brother, killed while fighting in 1916 in the Canadian infantry. These poems show a deep empathy for the lot of the common soldier. The oral, folk style of his poetic ballads is unlike the Keats-inspired (if soured) Romanticism of wartime lyrics by a contemporary like Wilfred Owen. Cast in boisterous rhythms and rhymes, many of them are dramatic monologues voiced in the language of the working-class soldier. In "Only a Boche," Service represents in engrossing detail a French soldier's imagining his way across wartime division into a German soldier's experience. The poem is one of the war's most vivid dramatizations of a soldier's tentative breakthrough into the shared humanity of the enemy other.

Only a Boche[1]

We brought him in from between the lines: we'd better have let him lie;
For what's the use of risking one's skin for a *tyke*[2] that's going to die?
What's the use of tearing him loose under a gruelling fire,
When he's shot in the head, and worse than dead, and all messed up on
     the wire?[3]

5   However, I say, we brought him in. *Diable!*[4] The mud was bad;
The trench was crooked and greasy and high, and oh, what a time we had!
And often we slipped, and often we tripped, but never he made a moan;
And how we were wet with blood and with sweat! but we carried him in
     like our own.

Now there he lies in the dug-out dim, awaiting the ambulance,
10   And the doctor shrugs his shoulders at him, and remarks, "he hasn't a chance."
And we squat and smoke at our game of bridge on the glistening, straw-
     packed floor,
And above our oaths we can hear his breath deep-drawn in a kind of snore.

1. A German, especially a soldier (derogatory).
2. Uncouth fellow.
3. Barbed wire protecting entrenchments from infantry attack.
4. Devil! (French)

For the dressing station is long and low, and the candles gutter dim,
And the mean light falls on the cold clay walls and our faces bristly and grim;
15   And we flap our cards on the lousy straw, and we laugh and jibe as we play,
And you'd never know that the cursed foe was less than a mile away.
As we con[5] our cards in the rancid gloom, oppresse by that snoring breath,
You'd never dream that our broad roof-beam was swept by the broom of death.

Heigh-ho! My turn for the dummy hand;[6] I rise and I stretch a bit;
20   The fetid air is making me yawn, and my cigarette's unlit,
So I go to the nearest candle flame, and the man we brought is there,
And his face is white in the shabby light, and I stand at his feet and stare.
Stand for awhile, and quietly stare, for strange though it seems to be,
The dying Boche on the stretcher there has a queer resemblance to me.

25   It gives one a kind of a turn, you know, to come on a thing like that.
It's just as if I were lying there, with a turban of blood for a hat,
Lying there in a coat grey-green instead of a coat grey-blue,[7]
With one of my eyes all shot away, and my brain half tumbling through;
Lying there with a chest that heaves like a bellows up and down,
30   And a cheek as white as snow on a grave, and lips that are coffee brown.

And confound him, too! He wears like me on his finger a wedding ring,
And around his neck, as around my own, by a greasy bit of string,
A locket hangs with a woman's face, and I turn it about to see:
Just as I thought . . . on the other side the faces of children three;
35   Clustered together cherub-like three little laughing girls,
With the usual tiny rosebud mouths and the usual silken curls.
"*Zut!*"[8] I say. "He has beaten me; for me, I have only two,"
And I push the locket beneath his shirt, feeling a little blue.

Oh, it isn't cheerful to see a man, the marvellous work of God,
40   Crushed in the mutilation mill, crushed to a smeary clod;
Oh, it isn't cheerful to hear him moan; but it isn't that I mind,
It isn't the anguish that goes with him, it's the anguish he leaves behind.
For his going opens a tragic door that gives on a world of pain,
And the death he dies, those who live and love, will die again and again.

45   So here I am at my cards once more, but it's kind of spoiling my play,
Thinking of those three brats of his so many a mile away.
War is war, and he's only a Boche, and we all of us take our chance;
But all the same I'll be mighty glad when I'm hearing the ambulance.
One foe the less, but all the same I'm heartily glad I'm not
50   The man who gave him his broken head, the sniper who fired the shot.

No trumps you make it, I think you said? You'll pardon me if I err;
For a moment I thought of other things . . . *Mon Dieu! Quelle vache de guerre.*[9]

1916

5. Study.
6. In bridge, a hand of cards displayed for all to see; its holder does not play that round.
7. German soldiers wore gray-green uniforms;

French soldiers wore gray-blue.
8. "Damn!" (French).
9. My God! What a cow the war is (French); i.e., this war sucks.

EDWARD THOMAS

E dward Thomas (1878–1917) was born of Welsh parents in London and was educated there and at Lincoln College, Oxford, which he left with a wife, a baby, and
high literary ambitions. Despite his chronic depression, which became more marked
over the difficult years that followed, he reviewed up to fifteen books a week, published thirty books between 1897 and 1917, and during those twenty years edited
sixteen anthologies and editions. His great gifts as a literary critic appeared to best
advantage in his reviewing of poetry, and he was the first to salute new stars in the
literary firmament such as Robert Frost and Ezra Pound.

Although he had long been conscientiously reviewing poetry, which he regarded as
the highest form of literature, he apparently made no serious attempt to write poems
until the autumn of 1914. Then, as he faced the stress of deciding whether to enlist,
poems began to pour out of him: five between December 3 and 7, and ten more before
the end of the month. His friend Frost offered to find him work in the United States,
but feelings of patriotism, and the attraction of a salary that would support his growing family, led him to enlist in July 1915. His awareness of the natural world, its richness and beauty, was then intensified by a sense of impending loss and the certainty of
death—his own and others'. In the long sentences that make up his verse, he ruminates with great delicacy on beauty and nature, but he also demonstrates an unsentimental toughness. In "Rain," for example, he compares the dead to "Myriads of broken
reeds all still and stiff." As violence to the natural order of things, war indirectly but
persistently shadows Thomas's poems. In January 1917 he was sent to the Western
Front and, on Easter Monday, was killed by a shell blast.

Adlestrop[1]

Yes, I remember Adlestrop—
The name, because one afternoon
Of heat the express-train drew up there
Unwontedly. It was late June.

5   The steam hissed. Someone cleared his throat.
No one left and no one came
On the bare platform. What I saw
Was Adlestrop—only the name

And willows, willow-herb, and grass,
10   And meadowsweet, and haycocks dry,
No whit less still and lonely fair
Than the high cloudlets in the sky.

And for that minute a blackbird sang
Close by, and round him, mistier,
15   Farther and farther, all the birds
Of Oxfordshire and Gloucestershire.

Jan. 1915   1917

1. A village in Gloucestershire.

The Owl

Downhill I came, hungry, and yet not starved;
Cold, yet had heat within me that was proof
Against the North wind; tired, yet so that rest
Had seemed the sweetest thing under a roof.

5   Then at the inn I had food, fire, and rest,
Knowing how hungry, cold, and tired was I.
All of the night was quite barred out except
An owl's cry, a most melancholy cry

Shaken out long and clear upon the hill,
10   No merry note, nor cause of merriment,
But one telling me plain what I escaped
And others could not, that night, as in I went.

And salted° was my food, and my repose,   *flavored (as with salt)*
Salted and sobered, too, by the bird's voice
15   Speaking for all who lay under the stars,
Soldiers and poor, unable to rejoice.

1915   1917

Rain[1]

Rain, midnight rain, nothing but the wild rain
On this bleak hut, and solitude, and me
Remembering again that I shall die
And neither hear the rain nor give it thanks
5   For washing me cleaner than I have been
Since I was born into this solitude.
Blessed are the dead that the rain rains upon:
But here I pray that none whom once I loved
Is dying tonight or lying still awake
10   Solitary, listening to the rain,
Either in pain or thus in sympathy
Helpless among the living and the dead,
Like a cold water among broken reeds,
Myriads of broken reeds all still and stiff,
15   Like me who have no love which this wild rain
Has not dissolved except the love of death,

---

1. Cf. Thomas's account of an English walking tour, *The Icknield Way* (1913): "In the heavy, black rain falling straight from invisible, dark sky to invisible, dark earth the heat of summer is annihilated, the splendour is dead, the summer is gone. The midnight rain buries it away where it has buried all sound but its own. I am alone in the dark still night, and my ear listens to the rain piping in the gutters and roaring softly in the trees of the world. Even so will the rain fall darkly upon the grass over the grave when my ears can hear it no more. . . . Black and monotonously sounding is the midnight and solitude of the rain. In a little while or in an age—for it is all one—I shall know the full truth of the words I used to love, I knew not why, in my days of nature, in the days before the rain: 'Blessed are the dead that the rain rains on.'"

If love it be towards what is perfect and
Cannot, the tempest tells me, disappoint.

Jan. 1916   1917

The Cherry Trees

The cherry trees bend over and are shedding
On the old road where all that passed are dead,
Their petals, strewing the grass as for a wedding
This early May morn when there is none to wed.

May 1916   1917

As the Team's Head Brass[1]

As the team's head brass flashed out on the turn
The lovers disappeared into the wood.
I sat among the boughs of the fallen elm
That strewed an angle of the fallow,[2] and
5 Watched the plough narrowing a yellow square
Of charlock.° Every time the horses turned   *wild mustard*
Instead of treading me down, the ploughman leaned
Upon the handles to say or ask a word,
About the weather, next about the war.
10 Scraping the share° he faced towards the wood,   *plowshare*
And screwed along the furrow till the brass flashed
Once more.
          The blizzard felled the elm whose crest
I sat in, by a woodpecker's round hole,
The ploughman said. "When will they take it away?"
15 "When the war's over." So the talk began—
One minute and an interval of ten,
A minute more and the same interval.
"Have you been out?" "No." "And don't want to, perhaps?"
"If I could only come back again, I should.
20 I could spare an arm. I shouldn't want to lose
A leg. If I should lose my head, why, so,
I should want nothing more. . . . Have many gone
From here?" "Yes." "Many lost?" "Yes, a good few.
Only two teams work on the farm this year.
25 One of my mates is dead. The second day
In France they killed him. It was back in March,
The very night of the blizzard, too. Now if
He had stayed here we should have moved the tree."
"And I should not have sat here. Everything
30 Would have been different. For it would have been

---

1. Also known as horse brass: a decorative brass medallion or emblem attached to a horse's harness.

2. Ground plowed and harrowed but left uncropped for a year or more.

Another world." "Ay, and a better, though
If we could see all all might seem good." Then
The lovers came out of the wood again:
The horses started and for the last time
35   I watched the clods crumble and topple over
After the ploughshare and the stumbling team.

May 1916   1917

MARY BORDEN

Born in Chicago and educated at Vassar College, Mary Borden (1886–1968) lived most of her life in England and Europe. While traveling in India she met her first husband, Douglas Turner, a Scottish missionary, and they settled in London in 1913. There she was part of a literary circle that included Ezra Pound and Wyndham Lewis. She was also a stone-throwing feminist activist, or "suffragette," for which she was briefly jailed. At the start of World War I, her husband enlisted and Borden volunteered as a nurse. During the war their marriage fell apart, and Borden met her second husband, Louis Spears, an English officer who later became a member of Parliament and diplomat. Having begun the war as a nurse for the French Red Cross, Borden eventually ran French field hospitals near the front line, for which she won British and French military medals for bravery. Having lived in England between the wars and published a spate of novels, she again ran French military hospitals during World War II. But the memories of her close encounters with the gruesome carnage of World War I made the most enduring impression on her literary work.

These memories feature in the sketches, short stories, and poems that make up *The Forbidden Zone* (1929)—an earlier version of which she had tried to publish during the war but could not because of censorship. In prose sketches such as "Belgium," she observes in acute detail the war's fragmentation of lives and its erasing of meaningful social distinctions. "Belgium" begins with the all-engulfing mud that is also the subject of her most innovative poem, "Song of the Mud," originally the middle of a poetic trilogy, "The Somme," published during the war. Few poems capture as vividly the ecological disaster of the World War I: the military destruction turned vast tracts of the Earth's surface into mud, and many soldiers were swallowed whole by it. In the free-verse repetitions of Borden's poem, the mud becomes a devouring monster that is covering, spreading, coating, caking, soaking, mixing, crawling, filling, sucking. Her ever-expanding and contracting lines seem to embody the mudlike force of the war's human and environmental catastrophe.

Belgium[1]

Mud: and a thin rain coming down to make more mud.

    Mud: with scraps of iron lying in it and the straggling fragment of a nation, lolling, hanging about in the mud on the edge of disaster.

---

1. Germany invaded and occupied Belgium to gain a positional advantage against France near the beginning of World War I. The occupa- tion, which included widespread violence against civilians, is often referred to as "the Rape of Belgium."

It is quiet here. The rain and the mud muffle the voice of the war that is growling beyond the horizon. But if you listen you can hear cataracts of iron pouring down channels in the sodden land, and you feel the earth trembling.

Back there is France, just behind the windmill. To the north, the coast; a coast without a port, futile. On our right? That's the road to Ypres.[2] The less said about that road the better: no one goes down it for choice—it's British now. Ahead of us, then? No, you can't get out that way. No, there's no frontier, just a bleeding edge, trenches. That's where the enemy took his last bite, fastened his iron teeth, and stuffed to bursting, stopped devouring Belgium, left this strip, these useless fields, these crumpled dwellings.

Cities? None. Towns? No whole ones. Yes, there are half a dozen villages. But there is plenty of mud, and a thin silent rain falling to make more mud—mud with things lying in it, wheels, broken motors, parts of houses, graves.

This is what is left of Belgium. Come, I'll show you. Here are trees drooping along a canal, ploughed fields, roads leading into sand-dunes, roofless houses. There's a farm, an old woman with a crooked back feeding chickens,[3] a convoy of motor lorries[3] round a barn; they squat like elephants. And here is a village crouching in the mud: the cobblestone street is slippery and smeared with refuse, and there is a yellow cat sitting in a window. This is the headquarters of the Belgian Army. You see those men, lolling in the doorways—uncouth, dishevelled, dirty? They are soldiers. You can read on their heavy jowls, in their stupefied, patient, hopeless eyes, how boring it is to be a hero.

The King[4] is here. His office is in the schoolroom down the street, a little way past the church, just beyond the dung heap. If we wait we may see him. Let's stand with these people in the rain and wait.

A band is going to play to the army. Yes, I told you, this is the army—these stolid men standing aimlessly in the drizzle, and these who come stumbling along the slippery ditches, and those leaning in degraded doorways. They fought their way out of Liége and Namur,[5] followed the King here; they are what is left of plucky little Belgium's heroic army.

And the song of the nation that comes from the horns in the front of the wine shop, the song that sounds like the bleating of sheep, can it help them? Can it deceive them? Can it whisk from their faces the stale despair, and unutterable boredom, and brighten their disappointed eyes? They are so few, and they have nothing to do but stand in the rain waiting. When the band stops they will disappear into the *estaminet*[6] to warm their stomachs with wine and cuddle the round-cheeked girls. What else can they do? The French are on one side of them, the British on the other, and the enemy in front. They cannot go back; to go back is to retreat, and they have been retreating ever since they can remember. They can retreat no farther. This village is where they stop. At one end of it is a pigsty, at the other end is a grave-yard, and all about are flats of mud. Can the noise, the rhythmical beating of the drum, the piping, the hoarse shrieking, help these men, make them believe, make them glad to be heroes? They have nowhere to go now and nothing to

2 Key Belgian city during the war, between France and Germany's planned course of attack.
3. Trucks.
4. Albert I reigned as king of the Belgians from

1909 to 1934. He took personal command of the Belgian army during the war.
5. Belgian cities fortified against German invasion.
6. Café (French).

do. There is nothing but mud all about, and a soft fine rain coming down to make more mud—mud with a broken fragment of a nation lolling in it, hanging about waiting in it behind the shelter of a disaster that has been accomplished.

Come away, for God's sake—come away. Let's go back to Dunkerque.[7] The King? Didn't you see him? He came out of the schoolhouse some time ago and drove away toward the sand-dunes—a big fair man in uniform. You didn't notice? Never mind. Come away.

1914–18   1929

The Song of the Mud

This is the song of the mud,
The pale yellow glistening mud that covers the naked hills like satin,
The grey gleaming silvery mud that is spread like enamel over the valleys,
The frothing, squirting, spurting liquid mud that gurgles along the
    road-beds,
5 The thick elastic mud that is kneaded and pounded and squeezed under
    the hoofs of horses,
The invincible, inexhaustible mud of the War Zone.

This is the song of the mud, the uniform of the *poilu*.[1]
His coat is of mud, his poor great flapping coat that is too big for him and
    too heavy,
His coat that once was blue, and now is grey and stiff with the mud that
    cakes it.
10 This is the mud that clothes him—
His trousers and boots are of mud—
And his skin is of mud—
And there is mud in his beard.
His head is crowned with a helmet of mud,
15 And he wears it—oh, he wears it well!
He wears it as a King wears the ermine[2] that bores him—
He has set a new style in clothing,
He has introduced the *chic*° of mud.   *stylishness (French)*

This is the song of the mud that wriggles its way into battle,
20 The impertinent, the intrusive, the ubiquitous, the unwelcome,
The slimy, inveterate nuisance,
That fills the trenches,
That mixes in with the food of the soldiers,
That spoils the working of motors and crawls into their secret parts,
25 That spreads itself over the guns,
That sucks the guns down and holds them fast in its slimy, voluminous
    lips,
That has no respect for destruction and muzzles the bursting of shells,
And slowly, softly, easily,

---

7. Dunkirk, a city on the northern coast of France.
1. Informal term for French infantryman.

2. The white winter coat of the stoat; a highly
valuable fur traditionally associated with royalty.

Soaks up the fire, the noise, soaks up the energy and the courage,
30 Soaks up the power of armies,
Soaks up the battle—
Just soaks it up and thus stops it.

This is the song of the mud, the obscene, the filthy, the putrid,
The vast liquid grave of our Armies—
35 It has drowned our men—
Its monstrous distended belly reeks with the undigested dead—
Our men have gone down into it, sinking slowly, and struggling and slowly
    disappearing.
Our fine men, our brave, strong young men,
Our glowing, red, shouting, brawny men,
40 Slowly, inch by inch, they have gone down into it.
Into its darkness, its thickness, its silence,
Relentlessly it drew them down, sucking them down,
They have been drowned there in thick, bitter, heaving mud—
It hides them—oh, so many of them!
45 Under its smooth glistening surface it is hiding them blandly,
There is not a trace of them—
There is no mark where they went down.
The mute, enormous mouth of the mud has closed over them.

This is the song of the mud,
50 The beautiful, glistening, golden mud that covers the hills like satin;
The mysterious, gleaming, silvery mud that is spread like enamel over the
    valleys.
Mud, the fantastic disguise of the War Zone;
Mud, the extinguishing mantle of battles;
Mud, the smooth, fluid grave of our soldiers.
55 This is the song of the mud.

1917

SIEGFRIED SASSOON

Siegfried Sassoon (1886–1967) was educated at Marlborough College and Clare College, Cambridge (which he left without taking a degree). His father came from a prosperous family of Sephardic Jews, his mother from Anglican English gentry. As a young man he divided his time between literary London and the life of a country gentleman. These worlds and the brutally different one of the trenches, in which he found himself in 1914, are memorably described in his classic *Memoirs of a Fox-Hunting Man* (1928) and its sequel, *Memoirs of an Infantry Officer* (1930).

He fought at Mametz Wood and in the Somme Offensive of July 1916 with such conspicuous courage that he acquired the Military Cross and the nickname Mad Jack. After a sniper's bullet went through his chest, however, he was sent back to England at the beginning of April 1917, and he began to take a different view of the war. Eventually, with courage equal to any he had shown in action, he made public a letter he sent to his commanding officer: "I am making this statement as an act of wilful defiance of military authority, because I believe that the war is being deliberately prolonged by those who have the power to end it." Sassoon continued: "I am a soldier, convinced that I am acting on behalf of soldiers. I believe that this war, upon which I entered as a war of defence and liberation, has now become a war of aggression and conquest." The military authorities, rather than make a martyr of him, announced that he was suffering from shell shock and sent him to a hospital near Edinburgh, where he met and befriended Wilfred Owen.

Sassoon's public protest may have been smothered, but his poems, with their shock tactics, bitter irony, and masterly use of direct speech (learned from Thomas Hardy), continued to attack the old men of the army, Church, and government, whom he held responsible for the miseries and murder of the young. His poems satirically play on contrasts between romanticized notions of war and the grim realities. They angrily flaunt the grisly effects of violence: in "The Rear-Guard" a corpse is "a soft unanswering heap" whose "fists of fingers clutched a blackening wound."

Sassoon returned to the Western Front in 1918, was wounded again, and was again sent home. An increasingly reclusive country gentleman, he continued to write poetry, but his style never regained the satiric pungency of the war poems that made him famous. His 1933 marriage failed because of his homosexuality; and after he became a Roman Catholic in 1957, he wrote mainly devotional poems.

'They'

The Bishop tells us: 'When the boys come back
They will not be the same; for they'll have fought
In a just cause: they lead the last attack
On Anti-Christ; their comrades' blood has bought
5   New right to breed an honourable race,
They have challenged Death and dared him face to face.'

'We're none of us the same!' the boys reply.
'For George lost both his legs; and Bill's stone blind;
Poor Jim's shot through the lungs and like to die;
10   And Bert's gone syphilitic: you'll not find
A chap who's served that hasn't found *some* change.'
And the Bishop said: 'The ways of God are strange!'

Oct. 31, 1916   1917

The Rear-Guard

(Hindenburg Line, April 1917)[1]

Groping along the tunnel, step by step,
He winked his prying torch with patching glare
From side to side, and sniffed the unwholesome air.
Tins, boxes, bottles, shapes too vague to know;
5   A mirror smashed, the mattress from a bed;
And he, exploring fifty feet below
The rosy gloom of battle overhead.

Tripping, he grabbed the wall; saw some one lie
Humped at his feet, half-hidden by a rug,
10   And stooped to give the sleeper's arm a tug.
'I'm looking for headquarters.' No reply.
'God blast your neck!' (For days he'd had no sleep)
'Get up and guide me through this stinking place.'
Savage, he kicked a soft unanswering heap,
15   And flashed his beam across the livid face
Terribly glaring up, whose eyes yet wore
Agony dying hard ten days before;
And fists of fingers clutched a blackening wound.

Alone he staggered on until he found
20   Dawn's ghost that filtered down a shafted stair
To the dazed, muttering creatures underground
Who hear the boom of shells in muffled sound.
At last, with sweat of horror in his hair,
He climbed through darkness to the twilight air,
25   Unloading hell behind him step by step.

Apr. 22, 1917   1918

The General

'Good-morning; good-morning!' the General said
When we met him last week on our way to the line.
Now the soldiers he smiled at are most of 'em dead,
And we're cursing his staff for incompetent swine.
5   'He's a cheery old card,' grunted Harry to Jack
As they slogged up to Arras[1] with rifle and pack.

• • •

But he did for them both by his plan of attack.

Apr. 1917   1918

---

1. In 1916 Field Marshal Paul von Hindenburg (1847–1934) became commander in chief of the German armies and, for a time, blocked the Allied advance in western France with the massive defensive "line" named after him. Its barbed-wire entanglements, deep trenches, and gun emplacements ran from Lens to Rheims.

1. A city in northern France, in the front line through much of the war. The British assault on the Western Front that began on April 9, 1917, was known as the Battle of Arras.

Glory of Women

You love us when we're heroes, home on leave,
Or wounded in a mentionable place.
You worship decorations; you believe
That chivalry redeems the war's disgrace.
5 You make us shells.[1] You listen with delight,
By tales of dirt and danger fondly thrilled.
You crown our distant ardours while we fight,
And mourn our laurelled[2] memories when we're killed.
You can't believe that British troops 'retire'
10 When hell's last horror breaks them, and they run,
Trampling the terrible corpses—blind with blood.
　　O German mother dreaming by the fire,
While you are knitting socks to send your son
His face is trodden deeper in the mud.

1917   1918

Everyone Sang

Everyone suddenly burst out singing;
And I was filled with such delight
As prisoned birds must find in freedom,
Winging wildly across the white
5 Orchards and dark-green fields; on—on—and out of sight.

Everyone's voice was suddenly lifted;
And beauty came like the setting sun:
My heart was shaken with tears; and horror
Drifted away . . . O, but Everyone
10 Was a bird; and the song was wordless; the singing will never be done.

Apr. 1919   1919

On Passing the New Menin Gate[1]

Who will remember, passing through this Gate,
The unheroic Dead who fed the guns?
Who shall absolve the foulness of their fate,—
Those doomed, conscripted, unvictorious ones?
5 　Crudely renewed, the Salient[2] holds its own.
Paid are its dim defenders by this pomp;
Paid, with a pile of peace-complacent stone,
The armies who endured that sullen swamp.

---

1. Many women were recruited into munitions factories during the war.
2. In ancient Greece and Rome, victorious generals were crowned with laurel wreaths.
1. The names of 54,889 men are engraved on this war memorial outside Brussels.
2. Protruding part of fortifications or, as here, lines of defensive trenches. Salients are particularly vulnerable, being exposed to enemy fire from the front and both sides.

Here was the world's worst wound. And here with pride
10 'Their name liveth for ever,' the Gateway claims.
Was ever an immolation so belied
As these intolerably nameless names?
Well might the Dead who struggled in the slime
Rise and deride this sepulchre° of crime.   *tomb*

1927–28   1928

From Memoirs of an Infantry Officer

[THE OPENING OF THE BATTLE OF THE SOMME]

On July [1916] the first the weather, after an early morning mist, was of the kind commonly called heavenly. Down in our frowsty cellar we breakfasted at six, unwashed and apprehensive. Our table, appropriately enough, was an empty ammunition box. At six-forty-five the final bombardment began, and there was nothing for us to do except sit round our candle until the tornado ended. For more than forty minutes the air vibrated and the earth rocked and shuddered. Through the sustained uproar the tap and rattle of machine-guns could be identified; but except for the whistle of bullets no retaliation came our way until a few 5.9[1] shells shook the roof of our dug-out. Barton and I sat speechless, deafened and stupefied by the seismic state of affairs, and when he lit a cigarette the match flame staggered crazily. Afterwards I asked him what he had been thinking about. His reply was 'Carpet slippers and Kettle-holders'. My own mind had been working in much the same style, for during that cannonading cataclysm the following refrain was running in my head:

> *They come as a boon and a blessing to men,*
> *The Something, the Owl, and the Waverley Pen.*

For the life of me I couldn't remember what the first one was called. Was it the Shakespeare? Was it the Dickens? Anyhow it was an advertisement which I'd often seen in smoky railway stations. Then the bombardment lifted and lessened, our vertigo abated, and we looked at one another in dazed relief. Two Brigades of our Division were now going over the top on our right. Our Brigade was to attack 'when the main assault had reached its final objective'. In our fortunate rôle of privileged spectators Barton and I went up the stairs to see what we could from Kingston Road Trench. We left Jenkins crouching in a corner, where he remained most of the day. His haggard blinking face haunts my memory. He was an example of the paralysing effect which such an experience could produce on a nervous system sensitive to noise, for he was a good officer both before and afterwards. I felt no sympathy for him at the time, but I do now. From the support-trench, which Barton called 'our opera box', I observed as much of the battle as the formation of the country allowed, the rising ground on the right making it impossible to see anything of the attack towards Mametz. A small shiny black note-book contains my pencilled particulars, and nothing will be gained by embroidering them with afterthoughts. I cannot turn my field-glasses on to the past.[2]

---

1. I.e., 5.9-caliber (5.9-inch diameter).
2. The extracts that follow are edited versions of the actual entries in Sassoon's diary. (See *Sieg-*

fried Sassoon: Diaries 1915–1918, ed. Rupert Hart-Davis, 1983, pp. 82–83.)

7.45.   The barrage is now working to the right of Fricourt and beyond. I can see the 21st Division advancing about three-quarters of a mile away on the left and a few Germans coming to meet them, apparently surrendering. Our men in small parties (not extended in line) go steadily on to the German front-line. Brilliant sunshine and a haze of smoke drifting along the landscape. Some Yorkshires[3] a little way below on the left, watching the show and cheering as if at a football match. The noise almost as bad as ever.

9.30.   Came back to dug-out and had a shave. 21st Division still going across the open, apparently without casualties. The sunlight flashes on bayonets as the tiny figures move quietly forward and disappear beyond mounds of trench debris. A few runners come back and ammunition parties go across. Trench-mortars are knocking hell out of Sunken Road trench and the ground where the Manchesters[4] will attack soon. Noise not so bad now and very little retaliation.

9.50.   Fricourt half-hidden by clouds of drifting smoke, blue, pinkish and grey. Shrapnel bursting in small bluish-white puffs with tiny flashes. The birds seem bewildered; a lark begins to go up and then flies feebly along, thinking better of it. Others flutter above the trench with querulous cries, weak on the wing. I can see seven of our balloons,[5] on the right. On the left our men still filing across in twenties and thirties. Another huge explosion in Fricourt and a cloud of brown-pink smoke. Some bursts are yellowish.

10.5.   I can see the Manchesters down in New Trench, getting ready to go over. Figures filing down the trench. Two of them have gone out to look at our wire gaps![6] Have just eaten my last orange. . . . I am staring at a sunlit picture of Hell, and still the breeze shakes the yellow weeds, and the poppies glow under Crawley Ridge where some shells fell a few minutes ago. Manchesters are sending forward some scouts. A bayonet glitters. A runner comes back across the open to their Battalion Headquarters, close here on the right. 21st Division still trotting along the sky line toward La Boisselle. Barrage going strong to the right of Contalmaison Ridge. Heavy shelling toward Mametz.

1916   1930

---

3. Men of a Yorkshire regiment.
4. Men of the Manchester regiment.
5. Long cables, tethering such balloons, pre-

vented attacks by low-flying aircraft.
6. Holes, made by shell fire, in the long coils of barbed wire protecting the trenches.

IVOR GURNEY

I vor Bertie Gurney (1890–1937) was born in Gloucester and showed an early aptitude for music. After five years at the King's School, Gloucester, he won a scholarship to the Royal College of Music. He first acquired a modest reputation as a composer. After war broke out in August 1914, he enlisted; his battalion was sent to France the following year, and Gurney experienced the horrors of the Western Front. He was wounded in April 1917, and when in the hospital in Rouen, he sent some of his poems to friends in London. The resultant volume, *Severn and Somme*, was published that year. (The Severn is the English river at the head of whose estuary Gloucester is situated; it appears often in his poetry. The Somme is the northern French river that was the scene of some of the most murderous fighting in the war.) Gurney was returned to the front in time to take part in the grim Passchendaele offensive of the summer of 1917. He suffered the effects of a poison-gas attack on August 22 and was sent home, where he moved from hospital to hospital. He returned to the Royal College of Music to study under the composer Ralph Vaughan Williams (1872–1958) and continued also to write poetry. His second book of poems, *War's Embers*, appeared in 1919. Gurney, now believed to have been schizophrenic, spent the last fifteen years of his life in mental asylums.

Gurney was a mere private in the war, unlike officers such as Wilfred Owen and Siegfried Sassoon, and his poems recapture with immediacy particular scenes and moments in the trenches. He was influenced by the poetry of Edward Thomas, with whom he shares a limpid directness, and Gerard Manley Hopkins, whose "terrible" sonnets are racked by despair. Though ruminating on traditional subjects such as landscape, nature, and mortality, Gurney dislocates these Georgian conventions through the compression, disharmony, and unredemptive language of his poetry. His "modern" techniques include syntactic contortions, colloquial diction, shifting rhythms and rhymes, and enjambments that accentuate the jarring experience of war (a body described as "that red wet / Thing" in "To His Love").

To His Love

He's gone, and all our plans
    Are useless indeed.
We'll walk no more on Cotswold[1]
    Where the sheep feed
5   Quietly and take no heed.

His body that was so quick
    Is not as you
Knew it, on Severn river°   *a British river*
    Under the blue
10   Driving our small boat through.

You would not know him now . . .
    But still he died
Nobly, so cover him over
    With violets of pride
15   Purple from Severn side.

Cover him, cover him soon!
    And with thick-set
Masses of memoried flowers—
    Hide that red wet
20   Thing I must somehow forget.

1919

---

1. Range of hills in Gloucestershire and Oxfordshire, in south central England.

The Silent One

Who died on the wires,[1] and hung there, one of two—
Who for his hours of life had chattered through
Infinite lovely chatter of Bucks[2] accent:
Yet faced unbroken wires; stepped over, and went
A noble fool, faithful to his stripes—and ended.
But I weak, hungry, and willing only for the chance
Of line—to fight in the line, lay down under unbroken
Wires, and saw the flashes and kept unshaken,
Till the politest voice—a finicking accent, said:
"Do you think you might crawl through there: there's a hole."
Darkness, shot at: I smiled, as politely replied—
"I'm afraid not, Sir." There was no hole no way to be seen
Nothing but chance of death, after tearing of clothes.
Kept flat, and watched the darkness, hearing bullets whizzing—
And thought of music—and swore deep heart's deep oaths
(Polite to God) and retreated and came on again,
Again retreated—and a second time faced the screen.

1954

1. The barbed wire protecting the front from infantry attack.
2. Buckinghamshire, in southern England.

ISAAC ROSENBERG

Isaac Rosenberg (1890–1918) was born in Bristol to a poor Jewish family that moved to London in 1897. There, at Stepney, he attended elementary schools until the age of fourteen, when he became apprenticed as an engraver in a firm of art publishers and attended evening classes at the Art School of Birkbeck College. His first ambition was to be a painter, and in 1911, when his apprenticeship was over, a group of three Jewish women provided the means for his studying at the Slade School of Art. His interest in writing poetry steadily developed, and with his sister's encouragement he circulated copies of his poems among members of London's literary set and gained a certain reputation, though neither his poetry nor his painting won him any material success. In 1912 he brought out *Night and Day*, the first of three pamphlets of poetry published at his own expense. The other two were *Youth* (1915) and *Moses, A Play* (1916).

In 1915 Rosenberg enlisted in the army, and he was killed in action on April 1, 1918. After his death his reputation steadily grew as an unusually interesting and original poet, who, though he did not live to maturity, nevertheless broke new ground in imagery, rhythms, and the handling of dramatic effects. His poetry strangely amalgamates acerbic irony (the sardonic grin of a rat in "Break of Day in the Trenches") with lush, resonant, even biblical diction and imagery ("shrieking iron and flame / Hurled through still heavens"). The fierce apprehension of the physical reality of war, the exclamatory directness of the language, and the vivid sense of involvement distinguish his poems. Perhaps Rosenberg's working-class background had something to do with this vividness: like Ivor Gurney and David Jones, he served in the ranks.

Break of Day in the Trenches

The darkness crumbles away.
It is the same old druid[1] Time as ever,
Only a live thing leaps my hand,
A queer sardonic rat,
5 As I pull the parapet's[2] poppy
To stick behind my ear.
Droll rat, they would shoot you if they knew
Your cosmopolitan sympathies.
Now you have touched this English hand
10 You will do the same to a German
Soon, no doubt, if it be your pleasure
To cross the sleeping green between.
It seems you inwardly grin as you pass
Strong eyes, fine limbs, haughty athletes,
15 Less chanced than you for life,
Bonds to the whims of murder,
Sprawled in the bowels of the earth,
The torn fields of France.
What do you see in our eyes
20 At the shrieking iron and flame
Hurled through still heavens?
What quaver—what heart aghast?
Poppies whose roots are in man's veins
Drop, and are ever dropping;
25 But mine in my ear is safe—
Just a little white with the dust.

June 1916   1922

---

1. Ancient Celtic priest.
2. Wall protecting a trench.

In the Trenches

The darkness crumbles away,
It is the same old Druid Time as ever,
Only a live thing leaps my hand,
A queer ~~uncanny~~ sardonic rat
As I pull a poppy from the parapet
To stick behind my ear,
~~Queer~~ Droll ~~rat they~~ subterranean!
They would shoot you if they knew
Your cosmopolitan sympathies
(And Lord knows what antipathies)
For you have touched an English hand,
And will do the same to a German
Soon, no doubt, if it be your pleasure
To cross the poppy blooded field between
Our hands will touch through your feet,
It seems odd thing, you grin as you pass
Strong eyes, fine limbs, haughty athletes
Less chanced than you for life,
Helpless whims of Murder,
Sprawled in the bowels of the earth
p.T.o.

Manuscript page, "Break of Day in the Trenches." Rosenberg wrote poems on scraps of paper he found while fighting in World War I. His manuscript papers still have mud on them from the trenches. This early draft page of one of the war's most famous poems includes words and lines that Rosenberg subsequently revised or omitted. Rosenberg changed, for example, "queer uncanny rat" to "queer sardonic rat" and deleted the line "(and Lord knows what antipathies)," once rhymed with the rat's "cosmopolitan sympathies."

Louse Hunting

Nudes—stark and glistening,
Yelling in lurid glee. Grinning faces
And raging limbs
Whirl over the floor one fire.
5   For a shirt verminously busy
Yon soldier tore from his throat, with oaths
Godhead might shrink at, but not the lice.
And soon the shirt was aflare
Over the candle he'd lit while we lay.

10   Then we all sprang up and stript
To hunt the verminous brood.
Soon like a demons' pantomime
The place was raging.
See the silhouettes agape,
15   See the gibbering shadows
Mixed with the battled arms on the wall.
See gargantuan hooked fingers
Pluck in supreme flesh
To smutch° supreme littleness.   *blacken, besmirch*
20   See the merry limbs in hot Highland fling[1]
Because some wizard vermin
Charmed from the quiet this revel
When our ears were half lulled
By the dark music
25   Blown from Sleep's trumpet.

1917   1922

Returning, We Hear the Larks

Sombre the night is.
And though we have our lives, we know
What sinister threat lurks there.

Dragging these anguished limbs, we only know
5   This poison-blasted track opens on our camp—
On a little safe sleep.

But hark! joy—joy—strange joy.
Lo! heights of night ringing with unseen larks.
Music showering on our upturned list'ning faces.

10   Death could drop from the dark
As easily as song—
But song only dropped,

1. In wild Scottish dance.

Like a blind man's dreams on the sand
By dangerous tides,
15 Like a girl's dark hair for she dreams no ruin lies there,
Or her kisses where a serpent hides.

1917   1922

Dead Man's Dump

The plunging limbers[1] over the shattered track
Racketed with their rusty freight,
Stuck out like many crowns of thorns,
And the rusty stakes like sceptres old
5 To stay the flood of brutish men
Upon our brothers dear.

The wheels lurched over sprawled dead
But pained them not, though their bones crunched,
Their shut mouths made no moan.
10 They lie there huddled, friend and foeman,
Man born of man, and born of woman,
And shells go crying over them
From night till night and now.

Earth has waited for them,
15 All the time of their growth
Fretting for their decay:
Now she has them at last!
In the strength of their strength
Suspended—stopped and held.

20 What fierce imaginings their dark souls lit?
Earth! have they gone into you?
Somewhere they must have gone,
And flung on your hard back
Is their soul's sack,
25 Emptied of God-ancestralled essences.
Who hurled them out? Who hurled?

None saw their spirits' shadow shake the grass,
Or stood aside for the half-used life to pass
Out of those doomed nostrils and the doomed mouth,
30 When the swift iron burning bee
Drained the wild honey of their youth.

What of us who, flung on the shrieking pyre,
Walk, our usual thoughts untouched,
Our lucky limbs as on ichor[2] fed,

---

1. Two-wheeled carts, here carrying barbed wire.
2. In Greek mythology, the ethereal fluid that flowed in the veins of the gods.

35 Immortal seeming ever?
Perhaps when the flames beat loud on us,
A fear may choke in our veins
And the startled blood may stop.

The air is loud with death,
40 The dark air spurts with fire,
The explosions ceaseless are.
Timelessly now, some minutes past,
These dead strode time with vigorous life,
Till the shrapnel called "An end!"
45 But not to all. In bleeding pangs
Some borne on stretchers dreamed of home,
Dear things, war-blotted from their hearts.

A man's brains splattered on
A stretcher-bearer's face;
50 His shook shoulders slipped their load,
But when they bent to look again
The drowning soul was sunk too deep
For human tenderness.

They left this dead with the older dead,
55 Stretched at the crossroads.

Burnt black by strange decay
Their sinister faces lie;
The lid over each eye,
The grass and coloured clay
60 More motion have than they,
Joined to the great sunk silences.

Here is one not long dead;
His dark hearing caught our far wheels,
And the choked soul stretched weak hands
65 To reach the living word the far wheels said,
The blood-dazed intelligence beating for light,
Crying through the suspense of the far torturing wheels
Swift for the end to break,
Or the wheels to break,
70 Cried as the tide of the world broke over his sight.

Will they come? Will they ever come?
Even as the mixed hoofs of the mules,
The quivering-bellied mules,
And the rushing wheels all mixed
75 With his tortured upturned sight.
So we crashed round the bend,
We heard his weak scream,
We heard his very last sound,
And our wheels grazed his dead face.

1917   1922

WILFRED OWEN

Wilfred Owen (1893–1918) was brought up in the backstreets of Birkenhead and Shrewsbury, and on leaving school he took up a post as lay assistant to a country vicar. Removed from the influence of a devout mother, he became increasingly critical of the Church's role in society. His letters and poems of this period show an emerging awareness of the poor's sufferings and the first stirrings of the compassion that was to characterize his later poems about the Western Front. In 1913 he broke with the vicar and went to teach English in France.

For more than a year after the outbreak of war, Owen could not decide whether he ought to enlist. Finally he did, and from January to May 1917 he fought as an officer in the Battle of the Somme. Then, suffering from shell shock, he was sent to a hospital near Edinburgh, where he had the good fortune to meet Siegfried Sassoon, whose first fiercely realistic war poems had just appeared. The influence of Sassoon's satiric realism was a useful tonic to Owen's lush, Keatsian Romanticism. Throughout his months in the hospital, Owen suffered from the horrendous nightmares symptomatic of shell shock. The experience of battle, banished from his waking mind, erupted into his dreams and then into poems haunted with obsessive images of blinded eyes ("Dulce et Decorum Est") and the mouth of hell ("Miners" and "Strange Meeting"). The distinctive music of such later poems owes much of its power to Owen's mastery of alliteration, onomatopoeia, assonance, half-rhyme, and the pararhyme that he pioneered. This last technique, the rhyming of two words with identical or similar consonants but differing, stressed vowels (such as *groined / groaned, killed / cold, hall / hell*), of which the second is usually the lower in pitch, produces effects of dissonance, failure, and unfulfillment that subtly reinforce his themes.

Echoing Dante, Shakespeare, Shelley, Keats, and the Bible, Owen puts literary and religious language into jarring new relationships with the absurdities of modern war experience. He recuperates but distorts the conventions of pastoral elegy, relocating them to scenes of terror, extreme pain, and irredeemable mass death.

In the year of life left to him after leaving the hospital in November 1917, Owen matured rapidly. Success as a soldier, marked by the award of the Military Cross, and as a poet, which had won him the recognition of his peers, gave him a new confidence. He wrote eloquently of the tragedy of young men killed in battle. In his later elegies a disciplined sensuality and a passionate intelligence find their fullest, most moving, and most memorable expression.

Owen was killed in action a week before the war ended.

Anthem for Doomed Youth

What passing-bells for these who die as cattle?
　　—Only the monstrous anger of the guns.
　　Only the stuttering rifles' rapid rattle
Can patter out their hasty orisons.°　　　　　　　　　　　*prayers*
5　No mockeries now for them; no prayers nor bells;
　　Nor any voice of mourning save the choirs,—
　　The shrill, demented choirs of wailing shells;
　　　And bugles calling for them from sad shires.°　　　*counties*

What candles may be held to speed them all?
10   Not in the hands of boys but in their eyes
Shall shine the holy glimmers of goodbyes.
    The pallor of girls' brows shall be their pall;
Their flowers the tenderness of patient minds,
And each slow dusk a drawing-down of blinds.

Sept.–Oct. 1917   1920

Apologia Pro Poemate Meo[1]

I, too, saw God through mud,—
    The mud that cracked on cheeks when wretches smiled.
War brought more glory to their eyes than blood,
    And gave their laughs more glee than shakes a child.

5   Merry it was to laugh there—
    Where death becomes absurd and life absurder.
For power was on us as we slashed bones bare
    Not to feel sickness or remorse of murder.

I, too, have dropped off Fear—
10   Behind the barrage, dead as my platoon,
And sailed my spirit surging light and clear
    Past the entanglement where hopes lay strewn;

And witnessed exultation—[2]
    Faces that used to curse me, scowl for scowl,
15   Shine and lift up with passion of oblation,[3]
    Seraphic° for an hour; though they were foul.   *ecstatic*

I have made fellowships—
    Untold of happy lovers in old song.
For love is not the binding of fair lips
20   With the soft silk of eyes that look and long,

By Joy, whose ribbon slips,—
    But wound with war's hard wire whose stakes are strong;
Bound with the bandage of the arm that drips;
    Knit in the webbing of the rifle-thong.

25   I have perceived much beauty
    In the hoarse oaths that kept our courage straight;
Heard music in the silentness of duty;
    Found peace where shell-storms spouted reddest spate.

1. This Latin title, meaning "Apology for My Poem," may have been prompted by that of Cardinal Newman's *Apologia Pro Vita Sua*, "Apology for His Life." Here an apology is a written vindication rather than a remorseful account.
2. Cf. Shelley, *A Defence of Poetry*: "Poetry is a mirror which makes beautiful that which is distorted. . . . It exalts the beauty of that which is most beautiful, and it adds beauty to that which is most deformed; it marries exultation and horror."
3. Sacrifice offered to God.

Nevertheless, except you share
30   With them in hell the sorrowful dark of hell,
        Whose world is but the trembling of a flare
        And heaven but as the highway for a shell,

    You shall not hear their mirth:
        You shall not come to think them well content
35   By any jest of mine. These men are worth
        Your tears. You are not worth their merriment.

Nov.–Dec. 1917   1920

Miners[1]

        There was a whispering in my hearth,
            A sigh of the coal,
        Grown wistful of a former earth
            It might recall.

5   I listened for a tale of leaves
            And smothered ferns,
        Frond-forests, and the low sly lives
            Before the fauns.

        My fire might show steam-phantoms simmer
10   From Time's old cauldron,
        Before the birds made nests in summer,
            Or men had children.

        But the coals were murmuring of their mine,
            And moans down there
15   Of boys that slept wry sleep, and men
            Writhing for air.

        And I saw white bones in the cinder-shard,
            Bones without number.
        Many the muscled bodies charred,
20   And few remember.

        I thought of all that worked dark pits
            Of war,[2] and died
        Digging the rock where Death reputes
            Peace lies indeed.

25   Comforted years will sit soft-chaired,
            In rooms of amber;
        The years will stretch their hands, well-cheered
            By our life's ember;

1. Wrote a poem on the Colliery Disaster [of Jan. 12, 1918, at Halmerend]: but I get mixed up with the War at the end. It is short, but oh! sour [Owen's Jan. 14 letter to his mother]. The explo-sion killed about 150 miners.
2. Miners who dug tunnels under no-man's-land in which to detonate mines beneath the enemy trenches.

The centuries will burn rich loads
30   With which we groaned,
Whose warmth shall lull their dreaming lids,
        While songs are crooned;
But they will not dream of us poor lads,
        Left in the ground.

Jan. 1918   1931

Dulce Et Decorum Est[1]

Bent double, like old beggars under sacks,
Knock-kneed, coughing like hags, we cursed through sludge,
Till on the haunting flares we turned our backs
And towards our distant rest began to trudge.
5   Men marched asleep. Many had lost their boots
But limped on, blood-shod. All went lame; all blind;
Drunk with fatigue; deaf even to the hoots
Of tired, outstripped Five-Nines[2] that dropped behind.

Gas! GAS! Quick, boys!—An ecstasy of fumbling,
10   Fitting the clumsy helmets just in time;
But someone still was yelling out and stumbling,
And flound'ring like a man in fire or lime . . .
Dim, through the misty panes[3] and thick green light,
As under a green sea, I saw him drowning.

15   In all my dreams, before my helpless sight,
He plunges at me, guttering, choking, drowning.

If in some smothering dreams you too could pace
Behind the wagon that we flung him in,
And watch the white eyes writhing in his face,
20   His hanging face, like a devil's sick of sin;
If you could hear, at every jolt, the blood
Come gargling from the froth-corrupted lungs,
Obscene as cancer, bitter as the cud
Of vile, incurable sores on innocent tongues,—
25   My friend,[4] you would not tell with such high zest
To children ardent for some desperate glory,
The old Lie: Dulce et decorum est
Pro patria mori.

Oct. 1917–Mar. 1918   1920

1. The famous Latin tag [from Horace, *Odes* 3.2.13] means, of course, *It is sweet and meet to die for one's country. Sweet!* And *decorous!* [Owen's Oct. 16, 1917, letter to his mother].
2. I.e., 5.9-caliber shells.
3. Of the gas mask's celluloid window.
4. Jessie Pope, to whom the poem was originally to have been dedicated, published jingoistic war poems urging young men to enlist.

Dulce et Decorum est.

~~To Jessie Pope etc~~. To a certain Poetess.

Bent double, like old beggars under sacks,
Knock-kneed, coughing like hags, we cursed through sludge,
Till on the ~~haunting~~ ~~glowing~~ flares we turned our backs.
And towards our distant rest began to trudge.
Dead slow we moved. Many had lost their boots,
But limped on, blood-shod. All went lame; all blind;
Drunk with fatigue; deaf even to the hoots
~~Of disappointed shells that dropped behind.~~
~~Of tired-voices~~ five-nines that dropped behind.
~~Two, outstripped~~

Then somewhere near in front: Whew... fup... fop... fup...
Gas-shells or duds? We loosened masks, in case —
And listened.... Nothing... Far rumouring of Krupp;...
Then ~~smartly~~ stinging poison hit us in the face.

Gas! GAS! ~~An instant~~ Quick, boys! An ecstasy of fumbling,
Fitting the clumsy helmets just in time.
But someone still was yelling out, and stumbling,
And floundering like a man in fire or lime. —
Dim, through the misty panes and ~~thick~~ green light,
As under a dark sea, I saw him drowning.

In all my dreams, before my helpless sight,
He plunges at me, ~~gargling~~, choking, drowning.
~~gargling~~
~~gargling~~
guttering

Manuscript page, "Dulce et Decorum Est." This manuscript draft page of Owen's famous poem includes four lines at the beginning of the second stanza that introduce the horrific gas attack. The poem becomes more powerful when, in its final version, Owen deletes this transitional material, confronting the reader with the terror-stricken cry "Gas! GAS! Quick, boys!" Owen tries out several different participles to describe the gassed soldier before settling on "guttering."

Strange Meeting[1]

It seemed that out of battle I escaped
Down some profound dull tunnel,[2] long since scooped
Through granites which titanic wars had groined.°   grooved

Yet also there encumbered sleepers groaned,
5   Too fast in thought or death to be bestirred.
Then, as I probed them, one sprang up, and stared
With piteous recognition in fixed eyes,
Lifting distressful hands, as if to bless.
And by his smile, I knew that sullen hall,—
10   By his dead smile I knew we stood in Hell.

With a thousand pains that vision's face was grained;
Yet no blood reached there from the upper ground,
And no guns thumped, or down the flues made moan.
"Strange friend," I said, "here is no cause to mourn."
15   "None," said that other, "save the undone years,
The hopelessness. Whatever hope is yours,
Was my life also; I went hunting wild
After the wildest beauty in the world,
Which lies not calm in eyes, or braided hair,
20   But mocks the steady running of the hour,
And if it grieves, grieves richlier than here.
For by my glee might many men have laughed,
And of my weeping something had been left,
Which must die now. I mean the truth untold,
25   The pity of war, the pity war distilled.[3]
Now men will go content with what we spoiled,
Or, discontent, boil bloody, and be spilled.
They will be swift with swiftness of the tigress.
None will break ranks, though nations trek from progress.
30   Courage was mine, and I had mystery,
Wisdom was mine, and I had mastery:
To miss the march of this retreating world
Into vain citadels that are not walled.
Then, when much blood had clogged their chariot-wheels,
35   I would go up and wash them from sweet wells.
Even with truths that lie too deep for taint,[4]
I would have poured my spirit without stint
But not through wounds; not on the cess[5] of war.
Foreheads of men have bled where no wounds were.

---

1. Cf. Shelley, *The Revolt of Islam*, lines 1828–32:

   And one whose spear had pierced me, leaned
     beside,
     With quivering lips and humid eyes;—and all
   Seemed like some brothers on a journey
     wide
     Gone forth, whom now strange meeting did
     befall
     In a strange land.

The speaker of Owen's poem imagines his victim a poet like himself.

2. Cf. Sassoon's "The Rear-Guard" (p. 150).
3. My subject is War, and the pity of War. The Poetry is in the pity [Owen's draft preface to his poems].
4. Cf. "Thoughts that do often lie too deep for tears," line 203 of William Wordsworth's "Ode: Intimations of Immortality" (1807).
5. Luck, as in the phrase *bad cess to you* (may evil befall you), and muck or excrement, as in the word *cesspool*.

40   "I am the enemy you killed, my friend.
     I knew you in this dark: for so you frowned
     Yesterday through me as you jabbed and killed.
     I parried; but my hands were loath and cold.
     Let us sleep now. . . ."

May [?] 1918   1920

Futility

Move him into the sun—
Gently its touch awoke him once,
At home, whispering of fields half-sown.
Always it woke him, even in France,
5   Until this morning and this snow.
If anything might rouse him now
The kind old sun will know.

Think how it wakes the seeds—
Woke once the clays of a cold star.
10   Are limbs, so dear achieved, are sides
Full-nerved, still warm, too hard to stir?
Was it for this the clay grew tall?
—O what made fatuous sunbeams toil
To break earth's sleep at all?

May 1918   1920

Disabled

He sat in a wheeled chair, waiting for dark,
And shivered in his ghastly suit of grey,
Legless, sewn short at elbow. Through the park
Voices of boys rang saddening like a hymn,
5   Voices of play and pleasure after day,
Till gathering sleep had mothered them from him.

• • •

About this time Town used to swing so gay
When glow-lamps budded in the light blue trees,
And girls glanced lovelier as the air grew dim,—
10   In the old times, before he threw away his knees.
Now he will never feel again how slim
Girls' waists are, or how warm their subtle hands.
All of them touch him like some queer disease.

• • •

There was an artist silly for his face,
15   For it was younger than his youth, last year.
Now, he is old; his back will never brace;
He's lost his colour very far from here,
Poured it down shell-holes till the veins ran dry,

And half his lifetime lapsed in the hot race
20   And leap of purple spurted from his thigh.

• • •

One time he liked a blood-smear down his leg,
After the matches, carried shoulder-high.[1]
It was after football, when he'd drunk a peg,[2]
He thought he'd better join.—He wonders why.
25   Someone had said he'd look a god in kilts,
That's why; and maybe, too, to please his Meg,
Aye, that was it, to please the giddy jilts[3]
He asked to join. He didn't have to beg;
Smiling they wrote his lie: aged nineteen years[4]
30   Germans he scarcely thought of; all their guilt,
And Austria's, did not move him. And no fears
Of Fear came yet. He thought of jewelled hilts
For daggers in plaid socks;[5] of smart salutes;
And care of arms; and leave; and pay arrears;
35   Esprit de corps;[6] and hints for young recruits.
And soon, he was drafted out with drums and cheers.

• • •

Some cheered him home, but not as crowds cheer Goal.
Only a solemn man who brought him fruits
Thanked him; and then enquired about his soul.

• • •

40   Now, he will spend a few sick years in institutes,
And do what things the rules consider wise,
And take whatever pity they may dole.
Tonight he noticed how the women's eyes
Passed from him to the strong men that were whole.
45   How cold and late it is! Why don't they come
And put him into bed? Why don't they come?

Oct. 1917–July 1918   1920

From Owen's Letters to His Mother

16 January 1917

*   *   *

I can see no excuse for deceiving you about these last 4 days. I have suffered seventh hell.
  I have not been at the front.
  I have been in front of it.

---

1. Cf. Housman's "To an Athlete Dying Young" (p. 133, lines 1–4).
2. Slang for a drink, usually brandy and soda.
3. Capricious women.
4. The recruiting officers entered on his enlistment form his lie that he was nineteen years old and, therefore, above the minimum age for military service.
5. Kilted Scottish Highlanders used to carry a small ornamental dagger in the top of a stocking.
6. Regard for the honor and interests of an organization or, as here, a military unit (French). "Pay arrears": back pay.

I held an advanced post, that is, a 'dug-out' in the middle of No Man's Land.

We had a march of 3 miles over shelled road then nearly 3 along a flooded trench. After that we came to where the trenches had been blown flat out and had to go over the top. It was of course dark, too dark, and the ground was not mud, not sloppy mud, but an octopus of sucking clay, 3, 4, and 5 feet deep, relieved only by craters full of water. Men have been known to drown in them. Many stuck in the mud & only got on by leaving their waders, equipment, and in some cases their clothes.

High explosives were dropping all around out, and machine guns spluttered every few minutes. But it was so dark that even the German flares did not reveal us.

Three quarters dead, I mean each of us ¾ dead, we reached the dug-out, and relieved the wretches therein. I then had to go forth and find another dugout for a still more advanced post where I left 18 bombers. I was responsible for other posts on the left but there was a junior officer in charge.

My dug-out held 25 men tight packed. Water filled it to a depth of 1 or 2 feet, leaving say 4 feet of air.

One entrance had been blown in & blocked.

So far, the other remained.

The Germans knew we were staying there and decided we shouldn't.

Those fifty hours were the agony of my happy life.

Every ten minutes on Sunday afternoon seemed an hour.

I nearly broke down and let myself drown in the water that was now slowly rising over my knees.

Towards 6 o'clock, when, I suppose, you would be going to church, the shelling grew less intense and less accurate: so that I was mercifully helped to do my duty and crawl, wade, climb and flounder over No Man's Land to visit my other post. It took me half an hour to move about 150 yards.

I was chiefly annoyed by our own machine guns from behind. The seeng-seeng-seeng of the bullets reminded me of Mary's canary. On the whole I can support[1] the canary better.

In the Platoon on my left the sentries over the dug-out were blown to nothing. One of these poor fellows was my first servant whom I rejected. If I had kept him he would have lived, for servants don't do Sentry Duty. I kept my own sentries half way down the stairs during the more terrific bombardment. In spite of this one lad was blown down and, I am afraid, blinded.[2]

31 December 1917

Last year, at this time, (it is just midnight, and now is the intolerable instant of the Change) last year I lay awake in a windy tent in the middle of a vast, dreadful encampment. It seemed neither France nor England, but a kind of paddock where the beasts are kept a few days before the shambles.[3] I heard the revelling of the Scotch troops, who are now dead, and who knew they would be dead. I thought of this present night, and whether I should indeed—whether we should indeed—whether you would indeed—but I thought neither long nor deeply, for I am a master of elision.

But chiefly I thought of the very strange look on all faces in that camp; an incomprehensible look, which a man will never see in England, though

1. Tolerate. Mary: Owen's sister.
2. This incident prompted Owen's poem "The Sentry."
3. Slaughterhouse.

wars should be in England; nor can it be seen in any battle. But only in Étaples.[4]

It was not despair, or terror, it was more terrible than terror, for it was a blindfold look, and without expression, like a dead rabbit's.

It will never be painted, and no actor will ever seize it. And to describe it, I think I must go back and be with them.

Preface[1]

This book is not about heroes. English poetry is not yet fit to speak of them.

Nor is it about deeds, or lands, nor anything about glory, honour, might, majesty, dominion, or power, except War.[2]

Above all I am not concerned with Poetry.

My subject is War, and the pity of War.

The Poetry is in the pity.

Yet these elegies are to this generation in no sense consolatory. They may be to the next. All a poet can do today is warn. That is why the true Poets must be truthful.

(If I thought the letter of this book would last, I might have used proper names; but if the spirit of it survives—survives Prussia[3]—my ambition and those names will have achieved fresher fields than Flanders.[4] . . .)

1918   1920

4. Until 1914, a fishing port of 5,800 inhabitants, Étaples and its surrounding hills housed 100,000 soldiers on their way to and from the front in 1917.
1. In May 1918 Wilfred Owen was posted in Ripon, North Yorkshire, England, and was preparing a book of his war poems. Around this time he drafted this unfinished preface, which was published posthumously, along with most of his poems, in *Poems* (1920), edited by his friend the poet Siegfried Sassoon. The text is reprinted from *The Poems of Wil-*

fred Owen (1985), ed. Jon Stallworthy.
2. Cf. Jude 1.25: "To the only wise God our Saviour, be glory and majesty, dominion and power, both now and ever."
3. Dominant region of the German Empire until the end of World War I.
4. In western Belgium, site of the front line. The Canadian poet John McCrae (1872–1918) memorialized one devastating 1915 battle in his famous poem "In Flanders Fields."

MAY WEDDERBURN CANNAN

Born and educated in Oxford, May Wedderburn Cannan (1893–1973) was the daughter of the secretary to the delegates (or chief executive) of the Oxford University Press. At eighteen, she joined the Red Cross Voluntary Aid Detachment, and when England entered the war three years later, she was active in the Red Cross mobilization, setting up a hospital in a local school. During the early part of the war, she worked at Oxford University Press, continued her volunteer nursing, and spent a month as a volunteer worker in a soldiers' canteen in Rouen, France. In 1918 she joined the War Office in Paris to work in intelligence. Her fiancé, Bevil Quiller-Couch, survived the devastating Battle of the Somme and the remainder of the war, only to die of pneumonia several months after the armistice. Cannan later worked at King's College, London, and at the Athenaeum Club as assistant librarian. She wrote three books of poems—*In War Time* (1917), *The Splendid Days* (1919), and *The House of*

Hope (1923)—as well as a novel, *The Lonely Generation* (1934). Her unfinished auto-biography, *Grey Ghosts and Voices*, was published posthumously in 1976.

"Rouen," with its echoes of G. K. Chesterton's incantatory "Tarantella" (beginning "Do you remember an Inn, / Miranda?"), voices emotions closer to those of Rupert Brooke's "The Soldier" than to any given expression by the other soldier poets in this section. In 1917, however, Cannan and Brooke spoke for what was then the majority. As she noted in her autobiography: "Siegfried Sassoon wrote to the Press from France saying that the war was now a war of conquest and without justification, and declared himself to be a conscientious objector. . . . A saying went round, 'Went to the war with Rupert Brooke and came home with Siegfried Sassoon.'" Her own poems pose an alternative to protest and despair: "I had much admired some of Sassoon's verse but I was not coming home with him. Someone must go on writing for those who were still convinced of the right of the cause for which they had taken up arms."

Rouen

26 April–25 May 1915

Early morning over Rouen, hopeful, high, courageous morning,
And the laughter of adventure and the steepness of the stair,
And the dawn across the river, and the wind across the bridges,
And the empty littered station and the tired people there.

5 Can you recall those mornings and the hurry of awakening,
And the long-forgotten wonder if we should miss the way,
And the unfamiliar faces, and the coming of provisions,
And the freshness and the glory of the labour of the day?

Hot noontide over Rouen, and the sun upon the city,
10 Sun and dust unceasing, and the glare of cloudless skies,
And the voices of the Indians and the endless stream of soldiers,
And the clicking of the tatties,[1] and the buzzing of the flies.

Can you recall those noontides and the reek of steam and coffee,
Heavy-laden noontides with the evening's peace to win,
15 And the little piles of Woodbines,[2] and the sticky soda bottles,
And the crushes[3] in the "Parlour," and the letters coming in?

Quiet night-time over Rouen, and the station full of soldiers,
All the youth and pride of England from the ends of all the earth;
And the rifles piled together, and the creaking of the sword-belts,
20 And the faces bent above them, and the gay, heart-breaking mirth.

Can I forget the passage from the cool white-bedded Aid Post
Past the long sun-blistered coaches of the khaki Red Cross train
To the truck train full of wounded, and the weariness and laughter,
And "Good-bye, and thank-you, Sister,"[4] and the empty yards again?

25 Can you recall the parcels that we made them for the railroad,
Crammed and bulging parcels held together by their string,

1. Screens or mats hung in a doorway and kept wet to cool and freshen the air.
2. Popular brand of cheap cigarette.
3. Crowded social gatherings.
4. Nurse.

And the voices of the sergeants who called the Drafts[5] together,
And the agony and splendour when they stood to save the King?[6]

Can you forget their passing, the cheering and the waving,
30   The little group of people at the doorway of the shed,
The sudden awful silence when the last train swung to darkness,
And the lonely desolation, and the mocking stars o'erhead?

Can you recall the midnights, and the footsteps of night watchers,
Men who came from darkness and went back to dark again,
35   And the shadows on the rail-lines and the all-inglorious labour,
And the promise of the daylight firing blue the window-pane?

Can you recall the passing through the kitchen door to morning,
Morning very still and solemn breaking slowly on the town,
And the early coastways engines that had met the ships at daybreak,
40   And the Drafts just out from England, and the day shift coming down?

Can you forget returning slowly, stumbling on the cobbles,
And the white-decked Red Cross barges dropping seawards for the tide,
And the search for English papers, and the blessed cool of water,
And the peace of half-closed shutters that shut out the world outside?

45   Can I forget the evenings and the sunsets on the island,
And the tall black ships at anchor far below our balcony,
And the distant call of bugles, and the white wine in the glasses,
And the long line of the street lamps, stretching Eastwards to the sea?

. . . When the world slips slow to darkness, when the office fire burns lower,
50   My heart goes out to Rouen, Rouen all the world away;
When other men remember I remember our Adventure
And the trains that go from Rouen at the ending of the day.

1916

---

5. Groups of soldiers.
6. I.e., to sing the British national anthem, "God Save the King."

ROBERT GRAVES

Robert von Ranke Graves (1895–1985) was born in London of partly Anglo-Irish and partly German descent—his great-uncle was the distinguished German historian Leopold von Ranke. He left Charterhouse School to go immediately into the army, serving in World War I until he was invalided out in 1917. After the war he went to Oxford, took a B.Litt. degree, and in 1929 published *Goodbye to All That*, a vivid account of his experiences in the war, including his almost dying from severe chest wounds. His autobiography, as he put it, "paid my debts and enabled me to set up in Majorca as a writer." He lived on that Spanish island with the American poet Laura Riding—his muse and mentor—until in 1936 the outbreak of the Spanish Civil War forced them to leave. Their relationship soon ended, and after World War II he returned to Majorca, where he remained for the rest of his life.

Graves began as a Georgian poet, but he was a Georgian with a difference. The mingling of the colloquial and the visionary in his vocabulary, the accent of conversation underlying the regular rhythms of his stanzas, the tension between a Romantic indulgence in emotion and a cool appraisal of its significance—these are qualities found even in his early poetry. His best work combines the ironic and the imaginative in a highly individual manner, and he is also capable of a down-to-earth poetry, often mocking in tone and dealing with simple domestic facts or even the more annoying of personal relationships. He admired Thomas Hardy but chided Yeats, Pound, and Eliot for their obscurity and slovenliness, preferring that poetry be lucid, orderly, and civil.

Graves made his living by his prose, which is extensive and varied and includes, in addition to *Goodbye to All That*, a number of historical novels in which characters and events from the classical or biblical past are reconstructed in a modern idiom: the most notable of his historical novels are *I, Claudius* (1934), *Claudius the God* (1934), and *King Jesus* (1946). In *The White Goddess* (1948), a study of mythology drawn from a variety of sources and devoted to what he considered the female inspirational principle, Graves argued that only a return to goddess worship and an abandonment of patriarchal for matriarchal society could help modern poetry recover its lost force, clarity, and mythic wisdom.

From Goodbye to All That

[THE ATTACK ON HIGH WOOD]

Next evening, July 19th, we were relieved and told that we would be attacking High Wood,[1] which could be seen a thousand yards away to the right at the top of a slope. High Wood, which the French called 'Raven Wood', formed part of the main German battle-line that ran along the ridge, with Delville Wood not far off on the German left. Two British brigades had already attempted it; in both cases a counter-attack drove them out again. The Royal Welch[2] were now reduced by casualties to about four hundred strong, including transport, stretcher-bearers, cooks and other non-combatants. I took command of 'B' Company.

The German batteries were handing out heavy stuff, six- and eight-inch, and so much of it that we decided to move back fifty yards at a rush. As we did so, an eight-inch shell burst three paces behind me. I heard the explosion, and felt as though I had been punched rather hard between the shoulder-blades, but without any pain. I took the punch merely for the shock of the explosion; but blood trickled into my eye and, turning faint, I called to Moodie: 'I've been hit.' Then I fell. A minute or two before I had got two very small wounds on my left hand; and in exactly the same position as the two that drew blood from my right hand during the preliminary bombardment at Loos.[3] This I took as a lucky sign, and for further security repeated to myself a line of Nietzsche's, in French translation:

Non, tu ne me peus pas tuer![4]

One piece of shell went through my left thigh, high up, near the groin; I must have been at the full stretch of my stride to escape emasculation. The

1. The battle for High Wood, one of the bloodiest fights of the Somme Offensive, began on July 14, 1916, and was won by the British on September 15, 1916.

2. Royal Welch Fusiliers.
3. The Battle of Loos, September 1915.
4. No, you cannot kill me. Friedrich Nietzsche (1844–1900), German philosopher.

wound over the eye was made by a little chip of marble, possibly from one of the Bazentin[5] cemetery headstones. [Later, I had it cut out, but a smaller piece has since risen to the surface under my right eyebrow, where I keep it for a souvenir.] This, and a finger-wound which split the bone, probably came from another shell bursting in front of me. But a piece of shell had also gone in two inches below the point of my right shoulder-blade and came out through my chest two inches above the right nipple.

My memory of what happened then is vague. Apparently Dr Dunn came up through the barrage with a stretcher-party, dressed my wound, and got me down to the old German dressing-station at the north end of Mametz Wood.[6] I remember being put on the stretcher, and winking at the stretcher-bearer sergeant who had just said: 'Old Gravy's got it, all right!' They laid my stretcher in a corner of the dressing-station, where I remained unconscious for more than twenty-four hours.

Late that night, Colonel Crawshay came back from High Wood and visited the dressing-station; he saw me lying in the corner, and they told him I was done for. The next morning, July 21st, clearing away the dead, they found me still breathing and put me on an ambulance for Heilly, the nearest field hospital. The pain of being jolted down the Happy Valley, with a shell hole at every three or four yards of the road, woke me up. I remember screaming. But back on the better roads I became unconscious again. That morning, Crawshay wrote the usual formal letters of condolence to the next-of-kin of the six or seven officers who had been killed. This was his letter to my mother:

22.7.16

Dear Mrs Graves,

I very much regret to have to write and tell you your son has died of wounds. He was very gallant, and was doing so well and is a great loss.

He was hit by a shell and very badly wounded, and died on the way down to the base I believe. He was not in bad pain, and our doctor managed to get across and attend to him at once.

We have had a very hard time, and our casualties have been large. Believe me you have all our sympathy in your loss, and we have lost a very gallant soldier.

Please write to me if I can tell you or do anything.

Yours sincerely,
C. Crawshay, Lt.-Col.

Then he made out the official casualty list—a long one, because only eighty men were left in the battalion—and reported me 'died of wounds'. Heilly lay on the railway; close to the station stood the hospital tents with the red cross prominently painted on the roofs, to discourage air-bombing. Fine July weather made the tents insufferably hot. I was semi-conscious now, and aware of my lung-wound through a shortness of breath. It amused me to watch the little bubbles of blood, like scarlet soap-bubbles, which my breath made in escaping through the opening of the wound. The doctor came over

5. The Battle of Bazentin Ridge, July 14–17, 1916, part of the Somme Offensive.
6. Recently captured by the British.

to my bed. I felt sorry for him; he looked as though he had not slept for days.

I asked him: 'Can I have a drink?'

'Would you like some tea?'

I whispered: 'Not with condensed milk.'

He said, most apologetically: 'I'm afraid there's no fresh milk.'

Tears of disappointment pricked my eyes; I expected better of a hospital behind the lines.

'Will you have some water?'

'Not if it's boiled.'

'It is boiled. And I'm afraid I can't give you anything alcoholic in your present condition.'

'Some fruit then?'

'I have seen no fruit for days.'

Yet a few minutes later he returned with two rather unripe greengages.[7] In whispers I promised him a whole orchard when I recovered.

The nights of the 22nd and 23rd were horrible. Early on the morning of the 24th, when the doctor came round the ward, I said: 'You must send me away from here. This heat will kill me.' It was beating on my head through the canvas.

'Stick it out. Your best chance is to lie here and not to be moved. You'd not reach the Base alive.'

'Let me risk the move. I'll be all right, you'll see.'

Half an hour later he returned. 'Well, you're having it your way. I've just got orders to evacuate every case in the hospital. Apparently the Guards have been in it up at Delville Wood, and they'll all be coming down tonight.' I did not fear that I would die, now—it was enough to be honourably wounded and bound for home.

A brigade-major, wounded in the leg, who lay in the next bed, gave me news of the battalion. He looked at my label and said: 'I see you're in the Second Royal Welch. I watched your High Wood show through field-glasses. The way your battalion shook out into artillery formation, company by company—with each section of four or five men in file at fifty yards interval and distance— going down into the hollow and up the slope through the barrage, was the most beautiful bit of parade-ground drill I've ever seen. Your company officers must have been superb.' Yet one company at least had started without a single officer. When I asked whether they had held the wood, he told me: 'They hung on to the near end. I believe what happened was that the Public Schools Battalion came away at dark; and so did most of the Scotsmen. Your chaps were left there more or less alone for some time. They steadied themselves by singing. Afterwards the chaplain—R. C.[8] of course—Father McCabe, brought the Scotsmen back. Being Glasgow Catholics, they would follow a priest where they wouldn't follow an officer. The centre of the wood was impossible for either the Germans or your fellows to hold—a terrific concentration of artillery on it. The trees were splintered to matchwood. Late that night a brigade of the Seventh Division relieved the survivors; it included your First Battalion.'

1929, 1957

7. Type of plum.
8. Roman Catholic.

Recalling War

Entrance and exit wounds are silvered clean,
The track aches only when the rain reminds.
The one-legged man forgets his leg of wood,
The one-armed man his jointed wooden arm.
5   The blinded man sees with his ears and hands
As much or more than once with both his eyes.
Their war was fought these twenty years ago
And now assumes the nature-look of time,
As when the morning traveller turns and views
10   His wild night-stumbling carved into a hill.

What, then, was war? No mere discord of flags
But an infection of the common sky
That sagged ominously upon the earth
Even when the season was the airiest May.
15   Down pressed the sky, and we, oppressed, thrust out
Boastful tongue, clenched fist and valiant yard.
Natural infirmities were out of mode,
For Death was young again: patron alone
Of healthy dying, premature fate-spasm.

20   Fear made fine bed-fellows. Sick with delight
At life's discovered transitoriness,
Our youth became all-flesh and waived the mind.
Never was such antiqueness of romance,
Such tasty honey oozing from the heart.
25   And old importances came swimming back—
Wine, meat, log-fires, a roof over the head,
A weapon at the thigh, surgeons at call.
Even there was a use again for God—
A word of rage in lack of meat, wine, fire,
30   In ache of wounds beyond all surgeoning.

War was return of earth to ugly earth,
War was foundering° of sublimities,   *collapsing*
Extinction of each happy art and faith
By which the world had still kept head in air,
35   Protesting logic or protesting love,
Until the unendurable moment struck—
The inward scream, the duty to run mad.

And we recall the merry ways of guns—
Nibbling the walls of factory and church
40   Like a child, piecrust; felling groves of trees
Like a child, dandelions with a switch.
Machine-guns rattle toy-like from a hill,
Down in a row the brave tin-soldiers fall:
A sight to be recalled in elder days
45   When learnedly the future we devote
To yet more boastful visions of despair.

1935   1938

DAVID JONES

David Jones (1895–1974) was born in Brockley, Kent, the son of a Welsh father and an English mother. He studied at the Camberwell School of Art before joining the army in January 1915; he served as a private soldier until the end of World War I—service that provided the material for his modern epic of war, *In Parenthesis*. He attended Westminster Art School after the war and subsequently made a name for himself as an illustrator, engraver, and watercolorist. In 1921 he joined the Roman Catholic Church and a few months later began working with the Catholic stone carver and engraver Eric Gill. Jones's Welsh and English origins, his visual sensitivity as an artist, and his interest in Catholic liturgy and ritual can be seen in his literary work, which includes the obscure but powerful long religious poem *The Anathémata* (1952) and *The Sleeping Lord and Other Fragments* (1973).

In Parenthesis, Jones's first literary work, was published in 1937 and won the Hawthornden Prize. Its seven parts, combining prose and poetry, evoke the activities of a British infantry unit from its training in England to its participation in the Somme Offensive of July 1916. The work proceeds chronologically, beginning with a battalion parade in England before embarkation for France, moving to the preparation for the offensive, and concluding when the protagonist Private John Ball's platoon is destroyed. Far from a straightforward narrative, since every contemporary detail is associated with the heroic past, the poem echoes in carefully patterned moments Shakespeare's history plays, Malory's accounts of Arthurian quests, Welsh epics of heroic and futile battles, the Bible, and Catholic liturgy. Even so, *In Parenthesis* avoids the traditional epic concentration on high-ranking heroes and builds its narrative around ordinary characters, both English and Welsh. Identified with historical or mythological figures, they—Mr. Jenkins, Sergeant Snell, Corporal Quilter, Lance-Corporal Lewis, and John Ball, who is wounded in the leg, as Jones was at the First Battle of the Somme—are presented in vivid silhouettes and sudden stabs of personal memory.

Begun a decade after the armistice, *In Parenthesis* could not have been written when Wilfred Owen and Siegfried Sassoon wrote their war poems. Jones profits from the ways in which James Joyce's *Ulysses* and T. S. Eliot's *The Waste Land* drew on mythology and ritual and thus gained depth and scope. He has combined the pity for and irony of the soldier that we see in Owen with the distanced, more elaborately illustrated, less immediately personal style of Eliot's long poem. And like Eliot, he introduces notes to help the reader follow the mythological and literary references. Unique among the soldier poets, Jones combines the immediacy of war poetry with high modernism's strategies of formal discontinuity and rich allusiveness. The poem conveys the texture of war experience through comic or sardonic references to popular soldiers' songs, to follies and vices and vanities and every kind of trivial behavior. At the same time the poem is multilayered and densely textured, its complex allusions to history, ritual, and heroic myth infusing the characters and the war with mysterious meaning.

The extracts printed here are, first, from Jones's preface, in which he explains his intention and method, and, second, from part 7, describing events during and after the attack. At the beginning of the last section quoted, Ball is wounded and crawling toward the rear through the mingled bodies of British and German soldiers. In his fevered imagination he sees the Queen of the Woods distributing flowers to the dead. He wonders whether he can continue carrying his rifle, which he finally leaves under an oak tree. (At the end of the medieval French epic *Chanson de Roland* [*Song of Roland*], the dying Roland tries in vain to shatter his sword, Durendal, to prevent its being taken as a trophy by the Saracens; he finally puts it under his body.) In the end Ball lies still under the oak beside a dead German and a dead Englishman, hearing the reserves coming forward to continue the battle.

From In Parenthesis

From *Preface*

This writing has to do with some things I saw, felt, & was part of. The period covered begins early in December 1915 and ends early in July 1916. The first date corresponds to my going to France. The latter roughly marks a change in the character of our lives in the Infantry on the West Front. From then onward things hardened into a more relentless, mechanical affair, took on a more sinister aspect. The wholesale slaughter of the later years, the conscripted levies filling the gaps in every file of four, knocked the bottom out of the intimate, continuing, domestic life of small contingents of men, within whose structure Roland could find, and, for a reasonable while, enjoy, his Oliver.[1] In the earlier months there was a certain attractive amateurishness, and elbowroom for idiosyncrasy that connected one with a less exacting past. The period of the individual rifle-man, of the "old sweat" of the Boer campaign, the "Bairns-father"[2] war, seemed to terminate with the Somme battle. There were, of course, glimpses of it long after—all through in fact—but it seemed never quite the same. * * *

My companions in the war were mostly Londoners with an admixture of Welshmen, so that the mind and folk-life of those two differing racial groups are an essential ingredient to my theme. Nothing could be more representative. These came from London. Those from Wales. Together they bore in their bodies the genuine tradition of the Island of Britain, from Bendigeid Vran to Jingle and Marie Lloyd. These were the children of Doll Tearsheet. Those are before Caractacus[3] was. Both speak in parables, the wit of both is quick, both are natural poets; yet no two groups could well be more dissimilar. It was curious to know them harnessed together, and together caught in the toils of "good order and military discipline"; to see them shape together to the remains of an antique regimental tradition, to see them react to the few things that united us—the same jargon, the same prejudice against "other arms" and against the Staff, the same discomforts, the same grievances, the same maims, the same deep fears, the same pathetic jokes; to watch them, oneself part of them, respond to the war landscape; for I think the day by day in the Waste Land, the sudden violences and the long stillnesses, the sharp contours and unformed voids of that mysterious existence, profoundly affected the imaginations of those who suffered it. It was a place of enchantment. It is perhaps best described in Malory,[4] book iv, chapter 15—that landscape spoke "with a grimly voice."

I suppose at no time did one so much live with a consciousness of the past, the very remote, and the more immediate and trivial past, both superficially and more subtly. No one, I suppose, however much not given to association, could see infantry in tin-hats, with ground-sheets over their shoulders, with sharpened pine-stakes in their hands, and not recall

---

1. Roland's close friend and companion-at-arms in the medieval French epic *Chanson de Roland* (*Song of Roland*).
2. Bruce Bairnsfather (1888–1959), English cartoonist and journalist, best known for his sketches of life in the trenches during World War I.
3. Caractacus or Caradoc, king of the Silures in the west of Britain during the reign of Roman emperor Claudius. He was taken to Rome as a prisoner in 51 C.E., but was pardoned by Claudius, who was impressed by his nobility of spirit. Bendigeid Vran, hero in Welsh heroic legend. Alfred Jingle, character in Dickens's *Pickwick Papers*. Marie Lloyd (real name Matilda Alice Victoria Wood), English music-hall comedienne. Doll Tearsheet, prostitute in Shakespeare's *2 Henry IV*.
4. Sir Thomas Malory, author of *Morte Darthur*.

> . . . or may we cram,
> Within this wooden O . . . [5]

But there were deeper complexities of sight and sound to make ever present

the pibble pabble in Pompey's camp.[6]

Every man's speech and habit of mind were a perpetual showing: now of Napier's expedition, now of the Legions at the Wall, now of "train-band captain," now of Jack Cade, of John Ball, of the commons in arms. Now of *High Germany*, of *Dolly Gray*, of Bullcalf, Wart and Poins; of Jingo largenesses, of things as small as the Kingdom of Elmet; of Wellington's raw shire recruits, of ancient border antipathies, of our contemporary, less intimate, larger unities, of *John Barleycorn*, of "sweet Sally Frampton." Now of Coel Hên—of the Celtic cycle that lies, a subterranean influence as a deep water troubling, under every tump[7] in this Island, like Merlin[8] complaining under his big rock.[9]

*   *   *

This writing is called *In Parenthesis* because I have written it in a kind of space between—I don't know between quite what—but as you turn aside to do something; and because for us amateur soldiers (and especially for the writer, who was not only amateur, but grotesquely incompetent, a knocker-over of piles, a parade's despair) the war itself was a parenthesis—how glad we thought we were to step outside its brackets at the end of '18—and also because our curious type of existence here is altogether in parenthesis.

D. J.

From *Part 7: The Five Unmistakable Marks*[1]

> Gododdin I demand thy support.
> It is our duty to sing: a meeting
> place has been found.[2]

*   *   *

The gentle slopes are green to remind you
of South English places, only far wider and flatter spread and grooved and
harrowed criss-cross whitely and the disturbed subsoil heaped up albescent.[3]

---

5. Shakespeare's *Henry V*, prologue, lines 12–13. The "wooden O" is the stage of the theater.
6. Cf. *Henry V* 4.1.71.
7. Mound or tumulus.
8. The powerful enchanter of the Arthurian legends.
9. The mass of references here provide a wide area of historical and literary association, beginning with *Henry V* and going on to refer to Sir William Napier, who fought in the Peninsular War and later wrote a famous history of that campaign; to the Roman legions who manned the Great Wall built by the Romans in Britain; to Jack Cade, who led an unsuccessful popular revolt against the misrule of Henry VI in 1450, and John Ball, a leader of the Peasants' Revolt of 1381; to a number of English ballads and popular songs and to characters in *Henry IV*; to the ancient British kingdom of Elmet in southwest Yorkshire, finally overthrown by Anglo-Saxon invaders early in the 7th century; to Wellington's "raw shire recruits," who helped win the Battle of Waterloo; and concluding with a reference to the old Celtic British myths that lie beneath everything.

1. Carroll's *Hunting of the Snark*, Fit the 2nd verse 15 [Jones's note]. Lewis Carroll's mock-heroic nonsense poem concerns the hunting of the elusive animal Snark, which may be known by "five unmistakable marks." A reference to the five wounds of the crucified Christ may also be intended.
2. From *Y Gododdin*, early Welsh epical poem attributed to Aneirin (6th century); commemorates raid of 300 Welsh of Gododdin (the territory of the Otadini located near the Firth of Forth) into English kingdom of Deira. Describes the ruin of this 300 in battle at Catraeth (perhaps Catterick in Yorkshire). Three men alone escaped death, including the poet, who laments his friends [Jones's note].
3. Becoming white.

Across upon this undulated board of verdure[4] chequered bright
when you look to left and right
small, drab, bundled pawns severally make effort
moved in tenuous line
and if you looked behind—the next wave came slowly, as successive surfs creep
in to dissipate on flat shore;
and to your front, stretched long laterally,
and receded deeply,
the dark wood.

And now the gradient runs more flatly toward the separate scarred saplings,
where they make fringe for the interior thicket and you take notice.
    There between the thinning uprights
at the margin
straggle tangled oak and flayed sheeny beech-bole, and fragile birch
  whose silver queenery is draggled and ungraced
and June shoots lopt
and fresh stalks bled
          runs the Jerry[5] trench.
And cork-screw stapled trip-wire
to snare among the briars
and iron warp with bramble weft[6]
with meadow-sweet and lady-smock
for a fair camouflage.

Mr Jenkins half inclined his head to them—he walked just barely in advance
of his platoon and immediately to the left of Private Ball.
    He makes the conventional sign
and there is the deeply inward effort of spent men who would make response
for him,
and take it at the double.
He sinks on one knee
and now on the other,
his upper body tilts in rigid inclination
this way and back;
weighted lanyard[7] runs out to full tether,
        swings like a pendulum
         and the clock run down.
Lurched over, jerked iron saucer over tilted brow,
clampt unkindly over lip and chin
nor no ventaille[8] to this darkening
       and masked face lifts to grope the air
and so disconsolate;
enfeebled fingering at a paltry strap—
buckle holds,
holds him blind against the morning.
    Then stretch still where weeds pattern the chalk predella[9]—
where it rises to his wire[1]—and Sergeant T. Quilter takes over.

* * *

---

4. Green vegetation.
5. British army slang for "German" in both world wars.
6. Warp and weft are the horizontal and vertical threads of woven cloth.
7. Short cord (here "weighted" by a whistle).
8. Hinged visor of a helmet.
9. A platform or shelf below or behind an altar.
1. The approach to the German trenches here rose slightly, in low chalk ridges [Jones's note].

It's difficult with the weight of the rifle.
Leave it—under the oak.
Leave it for a salvage-bloke[2]
let it lie bruised for a monument
dispense the authenticated fragments to the faithful.
It's the thunder-besom for us
it's the bright bough borne
it's the tensioned yew for a Genoese jammed arbalest[3] and a scarlet square
for a mounted *mareschal*,[4] it's that county-mob back to back.[5] Majuba mountain and Mons Cherubim[6] and spreaded mats for Sydney Street East,[7] and
come to Bisley for a Silver Dish.[8] It's R.S.M. O'Grady[9] says, it's the soldier's
best friend if you care for the working parts and let us be 'aving those springs
released smartly in Company billets on wet forenoons and clickerty-click
and one up the spout and you men must really cultivate the habit of treating
this weapon with the very greatest care and there should be a healthy rivalry
among you—it should be a matter of very proper pride and
     Marry it man! Marry it!
Cherish her, she's your very own.
     Coax it man coax it—it's delicately and ingeniously made—it's an instru-
ment of precision—it costs us tax-payers, money—I want you men to remember that.
     Fondle it like a granny—talk to it—consider it as you would a friend—
and when you ground these arms she's not a rooky's gas-pipe for greenhorns
to tarnish.[1]
You've known her hot and cold.
You would choose her from among many.
You know her by her bias, and by her exact error at 300, and by the deep scar
at the small, by the fair flaw in the grain, above the lower sling-swivel—
but leave it under the oak.

✻   ✻   ✻

The secret princes between the leaning trees have diadems given them.
     Life the leveller hugs her impudent equality—she may proceed at once
to less discriminating zones.

The Queen of the Woods has cut bright boughs of various flowering.
     These knew her influential eyes. Her awarding hands can pluck for each
their fragile prize.
     She speaks to them according to precedence. She knows what's due to
this elect society. She can choose twelve gentle-men. She knows who is most
lord between the high trees and on the open down.

2. Man (slang).
3. A powerful medieval crossbow.
4. Marshal (French).
5. The Gloucestershire Regiment, during, an action near Alexandria, in 1801, about-turned their rear rank and engaged the enemy back to back [Jones's note].
6. The British were defeated by the Boers on Majuba Hill on February 27, 1881. The "Angels of Mons" were angels (varying in number from two to a platoon) widely believed to have helped the British repel an attack at Mons by superior German forces on August 23, 1914.
7. In what became known as the Siege or Battle of Sydney Street, Winston Churchill, when he was home secretary in 1911, directed military operations in London against a group of anarchists. "It

is said that in 'The Battle of Sydney Street' under Mr. Churchill's Home Secretaryship mats were spread on the pavement for troops firing from the prone position" [Jones's note].
8. At Bisley marksmen compete annually in rifle shooting for trophies such as "a Silver Dish."
9. "R.S.M.": regimental sergeant major. "R.S.M. O'Grady;" according to Jones's note, "refers to mythological personage figuring in Army exercises, the precise describing of which would be tedious. Anyway these exercises were supposed to foster alertness in dull minds—and were a curious blend of the parlour game and military drill."
1. I have employed here only such ideas as were common to the form of speech affected by Instructors in Musketry [Jones's note].

Some she gives white berries
          some she gives brown
Emil has a curious crown it's
          made of golden saxifrage.
Fatty wears sweet-briar,
he will reign with her for a thousand years.
     For Balder she reaches high to fetch his.
     Ulrich smiles for his myrtle wand.
     That swine Lillywhite has daisies to his chain—you'd hardly credit it.
     She plaits torques[2] of equal splendour for Mr Jenkins and Billy Crower.
     Hansel with Gronwy share dog-violets for a palm, where they lie in
serious embrace beneath the twisted tripod.
     Siôn gets St John's Wort—that's fair enough.
     Dai Great-coat,[3] she can't find him anywhere—she calls both high and
low, she had a very special one for him.
     Among this July noblesse she is mindful of December wood—when the
trees of the forest beat against each other because of him.
     She carries to Aneirin-in-the-nullah[4] a rowan[5] sprig, or the glory of
Guenedota.[6] You couldn't hear what she said to him, because she was careful
for the Disciplines of the Wars.

At the gate of the wood you try a last adjustment, but slung so, it's an
impediment, it's of detriment to your hopes, you had best be rid of it—the
sagging webbing and all and what's left of your two fifty[7]—but it were wise
to hold on to your mask.

     You're clumsy in your feebleness, you implicate your tin-hat rim with the
slack sling of it.
     Let it lie for the dews to rust it, or ought you to decently cover the work-
ing parts.
     Its dark barrel, where you leave it under the oak, reflects the solemn star
that rises urgently from Cliff Trench.
     It's a beautiful doll for us
it's the Last Reputable Arm.
     But leave it—under the oak.
leave it for a Cook's tourist to the Devastated Areas and crawl as far
     as you can and wait for the bearers.[8]

1937

---

2. Collars, like those of gold worn by warriors of
Y Gododdin.
3. Character whose first name is the familiar
Welsh form of David, alluding to a figure in Malory's *Morte Darthur.*
4. A river, stream, or riverbed.
5. Also called mountain ash, a tree with magical
properties in Celtic folklore.
6. The northwest parts of Wales. The last king of
Wales, Llywelyn, was killed there in 1282. Jones
refers to his death in another note on this part of
Wales. He adds: "His [Llywelyn's] contemporary,
Gruffydd ap yr Ynad Côch, sang of his death: 'The
voice of lamentation is heard in everyplace . . .

the course of nature is changed . . . the trees of
the forest furiously rush against each other.'"
7. Two hundred and fifty rounds of ammunition.
8. This may appear to be an anachronism, but I
remember in 1917 discussing with a friend the
possibilities of tourist activity if peace ever came.
I remember we went into details and wondered if
the unexploded projectile lying near us would go
up under a holiday-maker, and how people would
stand up to be photographed on our parapets. I
recall feeling very angry about this, as you do if
you think of strangers ever occupying a house you
live in, and which has, for you, particular associations [Jones's note].

Modernist Manifestos

At the beginning of the twentieth century, traditions and boundaries of many kinds were under assault across the Western world. Rapid developments in science and technology were transforming the texture of everyday life and conceptions of the universe; psychology, anthropology, and philosophy were challenging old ways of conceiving the human mind and religion; empire, migration, and city life were forcing together peoples of diverse origins. This dizzying pace of change, this break with tradition, this eruption of modernity can also be seen in the cutting-edge art and literature of the time. Avant-garde modernism caught fire in Europe in the decade before World War I. The Spanish expatriate artist Pablo Picasso's landmark cubist painting of 1907, *Les Demoiselles d'Avignon* (see the color insert), shattered centuries of artistic convention. Two years later the Italian poet F. T. Marinetti published his first futurist manifesto in the French journal *Le Figaro*, blasting the dead weight of "museums, libraries, and academies" while glorifying "the beauty of speed." Written from 1911 to 1913, the Russian-born composer Igor Stravinsky's ballet *Le Sacre du Printemps* (*The Rite of Spring*) marked such a daring departure from harmonic and rhythmic traditions in Western classical music that its first performance, in Paris, sparked a riot. Like Picasso, Marinetti, and Stravinsky, other avant-garde modernists—advocates of radical newness in the arts—exploded conventions in music, painting, fiction, poetry, and other genres, opening up new formal and thematic possibilities for the twentieth and twenty-first centuries.

In just a few years modernism's rebellious energies and convention-defying activities swept through the major European cities, from Moscow and Milan to Munich, Paris, and London. Some of the leading modernists published manifestos, public declarations explaining, justifying, and promoting their ambitions and revolutionary views. They were not the first artists to adapt the manifesto from the political sphere, but they used manifestos widely and vociferously, trumpeting iconoclastic ideas in terms that were meant not only to rally but also, in some cases, to shock. These documents were so influential that they have become an integral part of the history of modernism.

London, where the startling impact of cubism and futurism was felt almost immediately, became a central site in the formation of anglophone modernism. London's publishing opportunities and literary ferment attracted an array of visiting and expatriate writers. The American poet Ezra Pound arrived there in 1908, at twenty-three, and soon ignited London's literary avant-garde, his apartment in Kensington a magnet for like-minded innovators. He befriended the English philosopher-poet T. E. Hulme, who led an avant-garde literary group. Like the cubists and futurists, these modernists advocated a radical break with artistic convention. In lectures Hulme influentially denounced Romanticism as so much moaning and whining, and proposed a "hard, dry" literature in its stead—a notion Pound echoed in his call for "harder and saner" verse, "like granite." After T. S. Eliot came to England in 1914, astonishing Pound by his having "modernized himself *on his own*," Eliot also composed essays marked by Hulme's influence. Aggressively asserting new form and subject matter while holding up the standard of classic texts, the modernists repudiated what they saw as the slushy, self-indulgent literature of the nineteenth century—"blurry, messy," and "sentimentalistic," in Pound's words. This desire to break decisively with Romanticism and Victorianism—often realized more in theory than in practice—became a recurrent feature in their public declarations. The 1914 manifesto of the journal *Blast* thunders, "**BLAST** / years **1837** to **1900**": like other avant-garde statements of intentions, this one damns the middle class for perpetuating Victorian taste and conventional mores.

The agitations, declarations, and poetic experiments of Hulme, Pound, and others resulted in the formation of imagism. Leaders of this London-born movement advocated clear and immediate images, exact and efficient diction, inventive and musical rhythms. The imagist poem was to be brief and stripped down, presenting an image in as few words as possible without commenting on it. In his lecture "Romanticism and Classicism" Hulme said the poet must render "the exact curve of what he sees whether it be an object or an idea in the mind." Having arranged for the nascent movement to be announced by the English poet and critic F. S. Flint in a brief article/interview entitled "Imagisme" (spelled in the French manner), Pound demanded, through Flint's introductory synopsis of imagism's precepts, "Direct treatment of the 'thing,' whether subjective or objective." The principles of imagism and Pound's further recommendations in "A Few Don'ts by an Imagiste" had a profound transatlantic influence long after the movement had petered out.

Red Stone Dancer, ca. 1913, by Henri Gaudier-Brzeska. This vorticist work by the French-born sculptor, based in London and killed early in World War I, combines organic movement with abstract form. Ezra Pound described it as "almost a thesis of his ideas upon the use of pure form."

The American poet H.D. (then called Hilda Doolittle) arrived in London in 1911, just in time to become a major figure in the imagist movement. Her poems, written under the influence of ancient Greek lyrical fragments, so impressed Pound that he sent them, signed "H.D. Imagiste" at his insistence, to Harriet Monroe, the founding editor of *Poetry,* a Chicago clearinghouse for modern verse. He told Monroe that H.D.'s poems were "modern" and "laconic," though classical in subject: "Objective—no slither; direct—no excessive use of adjectives, no metaphors that won't permit examination. It's straight talk, straight as the Greek!" Eventually H.D. and Pound wrote ambitious long poems that broke the mold of the imagist lyric, but even in their more capacious work, imagist compression, immediacy, and juxtaposition remained generative principles.

As early as 1914 Pound was tiring of imagism as static and insufficiently rigorous. Together with the London-based English painter and writer Wyndham Lewis, he helped found a new modernist movement in the arts, vorticism, which emphasized dynamism of content. Pound conceived the vortex—an image of whirling, intensifying, encompassing energy—as the movement's emblem. Like imagism, vorticism lasted for only a few years. Its most raucous embodiment was the 1914 vorticist manifesto in Wyndham Lewis's journal *Blast,* and its main aesthetic achievements were Lewis's paintings and the London-based French artist Henri Gaudier-Brzeska's sculptures.

The *Blast* manifesto is clearly influenced by Continental modernism, most visibly Italian futurism in the experimental layout and the fire-breathing rhetoric of destruction: the vorticists blast conventions, dull people, and middle-class attitudes. The English-born poet Mina Loy became closely involved with the leaders of the futurist movement, including Marinetti, while in Florence from 1906 to 1916. She was excited by futurism's embrace of modernity and its violent rebuke of tradition, but her typographically experimental "Feminist Manifesto" and her

Newcastle, 1914, by Edward Wadsworth. The work appeared as an illustration in the first issue of the journal *Blast*. The vorticist fascination with machines and abstraction, influenced by the Italian futurists, is seen in this woodcut, named after the English industrial city.

sexually defiant poetry also mark a break with the movement's misogyny and jingoism. Marinetti, Pound, and Lewis—despite their progressive prewar views on many social and artistic matters—later embraced fascism, believing it would help advance their cultural ideals.

Modernist manifestos take on a variety of different forms. Some are individual statements, such as Hulme's lecture "Romanticism and Classicism." Others are meant to be declarations on behalf of an emergent group or movement, such as "A Few Don'ts by an Imagiste" or the *Blast* manifesto. Occasionally, and paradoxically, a manifesto is a nonpublic declaration, unpublished in the author's lifetime, as in the case of Loy's "Feminist Manifesto." Although the manifesto is not an art form in the same sense as a poem or painting is, manifestos became an important literary genre in the modernist era, and some are more than mere declarations of doctrine. The vorticist manifesto and Loy's "Feminist Manifesto," for example, cross poetry with poster art, creatively manipulating words on the page for maximum effect. In their jagged typography, wild energy, and radical individualism turned to a collective purpose, these modernist manifestos helped advance and now exemplify elements of innovative art through the twentieth century and into the twenty-first.

T. E. HULME

Although he published only six poems during his brief life, T. E. Hulme (1883–1917), English poet, philosopher, and critic, was one of the strongest intellectual forces behind the development of modernism. In this essay, probably composed in either 1911 or 1912 and probably delivered as a lecture in 1912, Hulme prophesies a "dry, hard, classical verse" that exhibits precision, clarity, and freshness. He sharply repudiates the "spilt religion" of Romanticism, responsible for vagueness in the arts. Hulme sees human beings as limited and capable of improvement only through the influence of tradition. These ideas were an important influence on the thought and poetry of T. S. Eliot. Hulme's views of conventional language, the visual image, and verbal exactitude also shaped the imagism and vorticism of Ezra Pound and others.

Hulme was born in Staffordshire, England, and attended St. John's College, Cambridge, from which he was expelled for rebellious behavior in 1904 without finishing his degree. He lived mainly in London, where, befriending Pound and other poets and artists, he became a central figure of the prewar avant-garde. A critic of pacifism, Hulme enlisted as a private in the army when World War I broke out in 1914, and was killed in battle in 1917. First published posthumously in *Speculations* (1924), this essay is excerpted from *The Collected Writings of T. E. Hulme* (1994), ed. Karen Csengeri.

From Romanticism and Classicism

I want to maintain that after a hundred years of romanticism, we are in for a classical revival, and that the particular weapon of this new classical spirit, when it works in verse, will be fancy. * * *

I know that in using the words 'classic' and 'romantic' I am doing a dangerous thing. They represent five or six different kinds of antitheses, and while I may be using them in one sense you may be interpreting them in another. In this present connection I am using them in a perfectly precise and limited sense. I ought really to have coined a couple of new words, but I prefer to use the ones I have used, as I then conform to the practice of the group of polemical writers who make most use of them at the present day, and have almost succeeded in making them political catchwords. I mean Maurras, Lasserre and all the group connected with *l'Action Fran-çaise*.[1]

At the present time this is the particular group with which the distinction is most vital. Because it has become a party symbol. If you asked a man of a certain set whether he preferred the classics or the romantics, you could deduce from that what his politics were.

The best way of gliding into a proper definition of my terms would be to start with a set of people who are prepared to fight about it—for in them you will have no vagueness. (Other people take the infamous attitude of the person with catholic tastes who says he likes both.)

About a year ago, a man whose name I think was Fauchois gave a lecture at the Odéon on Racine,[2] in the course of which he made some disparaging remarks about his dullness, lack of invention and the rest of it. This caused an immediate riot: fights took place all over the house; several people were arrested and imprisoned, and the rest of the series of lectures took place with hundreds of gendarmes[3] and detectives scattered all over the place. These people interrupted because the classical ideal is a living thing to them and Racine is the great classic. That is what I call a real vital interest in literature. They regard romanticism as an awful disease from which France had just recovered.

1. Charles Maurras (1868–1952) and Pierre Lasserre (1867–1930) were intellectuals associated with *l'Action Française*, a reactionary political movement that denigrated Romanticism and supported the Catholic Church as a force for order. (T. S. Eliot also fell under the movement's influence.)

2. Jean Racine (1639–1699), French tragic playwright associated with classicism. The riot occurred at a lecture delivered by French playwright René Fauchois (1882–1962) at the Odéon Theater, Paris, on November 3, 1910.
3. Police officers (French).

The thing is complicated in their case by the fact that it was romanticism that made the revolution.[4] They hate the revolution, so they hate romanticism.

I make no apology for dragging in politics here; romanticism both in England and France is associated with certain political views, and it is in taking a concrete example of the working out of a principle in action that you can get its best definition.

What was the positive principle behind all the other principles of '89? I am talking here of the revolution in as far as it was an idea; I leave out material causes—they only produce the forces. The barriers which could easily have resisted or guided these forces had been previously rotted away by ideas. This always seems to be the case in successful changes; the privileged class is beaten only when it has lost faith in itself, when it has itself been penetrated with the ideas which are working against it.

It was not the rights of man—that was a good solid practical war-cry. The thing which created enthusiasm, which made the revolution practically a new religion, was something more positive than that. People of all classes, people who stood to lose by it, were in a positive ferment about the idea of liberty. There must have been some idea which enabled them to think that something positive could come out of so essentially negative a thing. There was, and here I get my definition of romanticism. They had been taught by Rousseau[5] that man was by nature good, that it was only bad laws and customs that had suppressed him. Remove all these and the infinite possibilities of man would have a chance. This is what made them think that something positive could come out of disorder, this is what created the religious enthusiasm. Here is the root of all romanticism: that man, the individual, is an infinite reservoir of possibilities; and if you can so rearrange society by the destruction of oppressive order then these possibilities will have a chance and you will get Progress.

One can define the classical quite clearly as the exact opposite to this. Man is an extraordinarily fixed and limited animal whose nature is absolutely constant. It is only by tradition and organisation that anything decent can be got out of him.

*　　*　　*

Put shortly, these are the two views, then. One, that man is intrinsically good, spoilt by circumstance; and the other that he is intrinsically limited, but disciplined by order and tradition to something fairly decent. To the one party man's nature is like a well, to the other like a bucket. The view which regards man as a well, a reservoir full of possibilities, I call the romantic; the one which regards him as a very finite and fixed creature, I call the classical.

One may note here that the Church has always taken the classical view since the defeat of the Pelagian heresy[6] and the adoption of the sane classical dogma of original sin.

It would be a mistake to identify the classical view with that of materialism. On the contrary it is absolutely identical with the normal religious attitude. I should put it in this way: That part of the fixed nature of man is the

---

4. The French Revolution (1789–99).
5. Jean-Jacques Rousseau (1712–1778), Swiss-born French writer and philosopher whose ideas greatly influenced the leaders of the French Rev-

olution and the development of Romanticism.
6. Controversial Church doctrine denying the transmission of original sin, named after the theologian Pelagius (ca. 354–after 418).

belief in the Deity. This should be as fixed and true for every man as belief in the existence of matter and in the objective world. It is parallel to appetite, the instinct of sex, and all the other fixed qualities. Now at certain times, by the use of either force or rhetoric, these instincts have been suppressed—in Florence under Savonarola, in Geneva under Calvin, and here under the Roundheads.[7] The inevitable result of such a process is that the repressed instinct bursts out in some abnormal direction. So with religion. By the perverted rhetoric of Rationalism, your natural instincts are suppressed and you are converted into an agnostic. Just as in the case of the other instincts, Nature has her revenge. The instincts that find their right and proper outlet in religion must come out in some other way. You don't believe in a God, so you begin to believe that man is a god. You don't believe in Heaven, so you begin to believe in a heaven on earth. In other words, you get romanticism. The concepts that are right and proper in their own sphere are spread over, and so mess up, falsify and blur the clear outlines of human experience. It is like pouring a pot of treacle[8] over the dinner table. Romanticism then, and this is the best definition I can give of it, is spilt religion.

I must now shirk the difficulty of saying exactly what I mean by romantic and classical in verse. I can only say that it means the result of these two attitudes towards the cosmos, towards man, in so far as it gets reflected in verse. The romantic, because he thinks man infinite, must always be talking about the infinite; and as there is always the bitter contrast between what you think you ought to be able to do and what man actually can, it always tends, in its later stages at any rate, to be gloomy. I really can't go any further than to say it is the reflection of these two temperaments, and point out examples of the different spirits. On the one hand I would take such diverse people as Horace, most of the Elizabethans and the writers of the Augustan age, and on the other side Lamartine, Hugo, parts of Keats, Coleridge, Byron, Shelley and Swinburne.[9]

* * *

What I mean by classical in verse, then, is this. That even in the most imaginative flights there is always a holding back, a reservation. The classical poet never forgets this finiteness, this limit of man. He remembers always that he is mixed up with earth. He may jump, but he always returns back; he never flies away into the circumambient gas.

You might say if you wished that the whole of the romantic attitude seems to crystallise in verse round metaphors of flight. Hugo is always flying, flying over abysses, flying up into the eternal gases. The word infinite in every other line.

---

7. Puritan members of the Parliamentary Party during the English Civil War (1642–51), named for their short haircuts. Girolamo Savonarola (1452–1498), Dominican monk who denounced the extravagance of the Renaissance. John Calvin (1509–1564), Protestant theologian who stressed the predestination and the depravity of humankind.
8. Molasses (British).
9. Horace (65–8 B.C.E.), Roman poet. "The Elizabethans": English poets and playwrights (such as Shakespeare) writing during the reign of Queen Elizabeth I (1558–1603). "The Augustan age": the late seventeenth and early eighteenth centuries, when English writers such as John Dryden (1631–1700) and Alexander Pope (1688–1744) embraced a classicism likened to the Augustan Age of Rome. Alphonse Lamartine (1790–1869), French poet and politician. Victor Hugo (1802–1885), French poet and novelist. John Keats (1795–1821), Samuel Taylor Coleridge (1772–1834), George Gordon (Lord) Byron (1788–1824), Percy Bysshe Shelley (1792–1822), Algernon Charles Swinburne (1837–1909), English poets.

In the classical attitude you never seem to swing right along to the infinite nothing. If you say an extravagant thing which does exceed the limits inside which you know man to be fastened, yet there is always conveyed in some way at the end an impression of yourself standing outside it, and not quite believing it, or consciously putting it forward as a flourish. You never go blindly into an atmosphere more than the truth, an atmosphere too rarefied for man to breathe for long. You are always faithful to the conception of a limit. It is a question of pitch; in romantic verse you move at a certain pitch of rhetoric which you know, man being what he is, to be a little highfalutin. The kind of thing you get in Hugo or Swinburne. In the coming classical reaction that will feel just wrong.

* * *

I object even to the best of the romantics. I object still more to the receptive attitude.[1] I object to the sloppiness which doesn't consider that a poem is a poem unless it is moaning or whining about something or other. I always think in this connection of the last line of a poem of John Webster's which ends with a request I cordially endorse:
'End your moan and come away.'[2]
The thing has got so bad now that a poem which is all dry and hard, a properly classical poem, would not be considered poetry at all. How many people now can lay their hands on their hearts and say they like either Horace or Pope? They feel a kind of chill when they read them.

The dry hardness which you get in the classics is absolutely repugnant to them. Poetry that isn't damp isn't poetry at all. They cannot see that accurate description is a legitimate object of verse. Verse to them always means a bringing in of some of the emotions that are grouped round the word infinite.

The essence of poetry to most people is that it must lead them to a beyond of some kind. Verse strictly confined to the earthly and the definite (Keats is full of it) might seem to them to be excellent writing, excellent craftsmanship, but not poetry. So much has romanticism debauched us, that, without some form of vagueness, we deny the highest.

In the classic it is always the light of ordinary day, never the light that never was on land or sea. It is always perfectly human and never exaggerated: man is always man and never a god.

But the awful result of romanticism is that, accustomed to this strange light, you can never live without it. Its effect on you is that of a drug.

* * *

It is essential to prove that beauty may be in small, dry things.
The great aim is accurate, precise and definite description. The first thing is to recognise how extraordinarily difficult this is. It is no mere matter of carefulness; you have to use language, and language is by its very nature a communal thing; that is, it expresses never the exact thing but a compromise—that which is common to you, me and everybody. But each man sees a little differently, and to get out clearly and exactly what he does

1. Elsewhere in the essay, Hulme claims that every sort of verse has an accompanying receptive attitude by which readers come to expect certain qualities from poetry. These receptive attitudes, he explains, sometimes outlast the poetry from which they develop.
2. From *The Duchess of Malfi* (1623) 4.2, by the English dramatist John Webster (ca. 1580–ca. 1625).

see, he must have a terrific struggle with language, whether it be with words or the technique of other arts. Language has its own special nature, its own conventions and communal ideas. It is only by a concentrated effort of the mind that you can hold it fixed to your own purpose. I always think that the fundamental process at the back of all the arts might be represented by the following metaphor. You know what I call architect's curves— flat pieces of wood with all different kinds of curvature. By a suitable selection from these you can draw approximately any curve you like. The artist I take to be the man who simply can't bear the idea of that 'approximately'. He will get the exact curve of what he sees whether it be an object or an idea in the mind. I shall here have to change my metaphor a little to get the process in his mind. Suppose that instead of your curved pieces of wood you have a springy piece of steel of the same types of curvature as the wood. Now the state of tension or concentration of mind, if he is doing anything really good in this struggle against the ingrained habit of the technique, may be represented by a man employing all his fingers to bend the steel out of its own curve and into the exact curve which you want. Something different to what it would assume naturally.

*　*　*

This is the point I aim at, then, in my argument. I prophesy that a period of dry, hard, classical verse is coming. I have met the preliminary objection founded on the bad romantic aesthetic that in such verse, from which the infinite is excluded, you cannot have the essence of poetry at all.

*　*　*

Poetry * * * is a compromise for a language of intuition which would hand over sensations bodily. It always endeavours to arrest you, and to make you continuously see a physical thing, to prevent you gliding through an abstract process. It chooses fresh epithets and fresh metaphors, not so much because they are new, and we are tired of the old, but because the old cease to convey a physical thing and become abstract counters. A poet says a ship 'coursed the seas' to get a physical image, instead of the counter word 'sailed'. Visual meanings can only be transferred by the new bowl of metaphor; prose is an old pot that lets them leak out. Images in verse are not mere decoration, but the very essence of an intuitive language. Verse is a pedestrian taking you over the ground, prose—a train which delivers you at a destination.

*　*　*

The point is that exactly the same activity is at work as in the highest verse. That is the avoidance of conventional language in order to get the exact curve of the thing.

*　*　*

A powerfully imaginative mind seizes and combines at the same instant all the important ideas of its poem or picture, and while it works with one of them, it is at the same instant working with and modifying all in their relation to it and never losing sight of their bearings on each other—as the motion of a snake's body goes through all parts at once and its volition acts at the same instant in coils which go contrary ways.

A romantic movement must have an end of the very nature of the thing. It may be deplored, but it can't be helped—wonder must cease to be wonder.

I guard myself here from all the consequences of the analogy, but it expresses at any rate the inevitableness of the process. A literature of wonder must have an end as inevitably as a strange land loses its strangeness when one lives in it. Think of the lost ecstasy of the Elizabethans. 'Oh my America, my new found land,'[3] think of what it meant to them and of what it means to us. Wonder can only be the attitude of a man passing from one stage to another, it can never be a permanently fixed thing.

1911–12   1924

3. Line 27 of John Donne's "To His Mistress Going to Bed."

F. S. FLINT AND EZRA POUND

I n the March 1913 issue of *Poetry* magazine, the English poet and translator F. S. Flint published an article summarizing an interview with an unidentified "imagiste"—surely Ezra Pound. The article, partly dictated and rewritten by Pound, famously states the three principles of imagism—directness, economy, musical rhythm—which Pound later said he and the poets H.D. and Richard Aldington had agreed on in 1912. Flint's prefatory piece was followed in the same issue by Pound's manifesto, "A Few Don'ts by an Imagiste." There Pound defines the image and issues injunctions and admonitions to help poets strip their verse of unnecessary rhetoric and abstraction. Poets, he argues, should write direct, musically cadenced, image-grounded verse.

Born in London, F. S. Flint (1885–1960) worked in the British civil service, translated poetry (mostly French), and eventually published volumes of his own imagist poetry. Ezra Pound (1885–1972) was born in Hailey, Idaho, and was educated at the University of Pennsylvania and Hamilton College. During his twelve years in London, from 1908 to 1920, where he became closely associated with W. B. Yeats and T. E. Hulme, he was the most vigorous entrepreneur of literary modernism, helping James Joyce, T. S. Eliot, and other writers launch their careers. In London he also began producing material for his major work, the massive poem *The Cantos*. Living briefly in Paris and then for twenty years in Italy as an ardent supporter of the fascist regime, he was arrested for treason in 1945, having made Rome Radio broadcasts against the U.S. war effort. He spent twelve years, from 1946 to 1958, in a Washington, D.C., asylum for the criminally insane before returning to Italy, where he fell into an almost complete public silence until the end of his life.

Imagisme[1]

Some curiosity has been aroused concerning *Imagisme*, and as I was unable to find anything definite about it in print, I sought out an *imagiste*, with

1. In response to many requests for information regarding *Imagism* and the *Imagistes*, we publish this note by Mr. Flint, supplementing it with further exemplification by Mr. Pound. It will be seen from these that *Imagism* is not necessarily associated with Hellenic subjects, or with *vers libre* as a prescribed form ["Editor's Note" from original]. "*Vers libre*": free verse (French).

intent to discover whether the group itself knew anything about the "movement." I gleaned these facts.

The *imagistes* admitted that they were contemporaries of the Post Impressionists and the Futurists; but they had nothing in common with these schools. They had not published a manifesto. They were not a revolutionary school; their only endeavor was to write in accordance with the best tradition, as they found it in the best writers of all time,—in Sappho, Catullus, Villon.[2] They seemed to be absolutely intolerant of all poetry that was not written in such endeavor, ignorance of the best tradition forming no excuse. They had a few rules, drawn up for their own satisfaction only, and they had not published them. They were:

1. Direct treatment of the "thing," whether subjective or objective.

2. To use absolutely no word that did not contribute to the presentation.

3. As regarding rhythm: to compose in sequence of the musical phrase, not in sequence of a metronome.

By these standards they judged all poetry, and found most of it wanting. They held also a certain 'Doctrine of the Image,' which they had not committed to writing; they said that it did not concern the public, and would provoke useless discussion.

The devices whereby they persuaded approaching poetasters to attend their instruction were:

1. They showed him his own thought already splendidly expressed in some classic (and the school musters altogether a most formidable erudition).

2. They re-wrote his verses before his eyes, using about ten words to his fifty.

Even their opponents admit of them—ruefully—"At least they do keep bad poets from writing!"

I found among them an earnestness that is amazing to one accustomed to the usual London air of poetic dilettantism. They consider that Art is all science, all religion, philosophy and metaphysic. It is true that *snobisme* may be urged against them; but it is at least *snobisme* in its most dynamic form, with a great deal of sound sense and energy behind it; and they are stricter with themselves than with any outsider.

F. S. Flint

A Few Don'ts by an Imagiste

An "Image" is that which presents an intellectual and emotional complex in an instant of time. I use the term "complex" rather in the technical sense employed by the newer psychologists, such as Hart,[1] though we might not agree absolutely in our application.

It is the presentation of such a "complex" instantaneously which gives that sense of sudden liberation; that sense of freedom from time limits and space limits; that sense of sudden growth, which we experience in the presence of the greatest works of art.

---

2. François Villon (1431–after 1463), French poet. Sappho (fl. ca. 610–ca. 580 B.C.E.), Greek poet. Catullus (ca. 84–ca. 54 B.C.E.), Roman poet.
1. British psychologist Bernard Hart (1879–

1966) discusses "the complex" in *The Psychology of Insanity* (1912), a book that helped popularize psychoanalysis.

It is better to present one Image in a lifetime than to produce voluminous works.

All this, however, some may consider open to debate. The immediate necessity is to tabulate A LIST OF DONT's for those beginning to write verses. But I can not put all of them into Mosaic negative.[2]

To begin with, consider the three rules recorded by Mr. Flint, not as dogma—never consider anything as dogma—but as the result of long contemplation, which, even if it is some one else's contemplation, may be worth consideration.

Pay no attention to the criticism of men who have never themselves written a notable work. Consider the discrepancies between the actual writing of the Greek poets and dramatists, and the theories of the Graeco-Roman grammarians, concocted to explain their metres.

Language

Use no superflous word, no adjective, which does not reveal something.

Don't use such an expression as "dim lands of *peace*." It dulls the image. It mixes an abstraction with the concrete. It comes from the writer's not realizing that the natural object is always the *adequate* symbol.

Go in fear of abstractions. Don't retell in mediocre verse what has already been done in good prose. Don't think any intelligent person is going to be deceived when you try to shirk all the difficulties of the unspeakably difficult art of good prose by chopping your composition into line lengths.

What the expert is tired of today the public will be tired of tomorrow.

Don't imagine that the art of poetry is any simpler than the art of music, or that you can please the expert before you have spent at least as much effort on the art of verse as the average piano teacher spends on the art of music.

Be influenced by as many great artists as you can, but have the decency either to acknowledge the debt outright, or to try to conceal it.

Don't allow "influence" to mean merely that you mop up the particular decorative vocabulary of some one or two poets whom you happen to admire. A Turkish war correspondent was recently caught red-handed babbling in his dispatches of "dove-gray" hills, or else it was "pearl-pale," I can not remember.

Use either no ornament or good ornament.

Rhythm and Rhyme

Let the candidate fill his mind with the finest cadences he can discover, preferably in a foreign language so that the meaning of the words may be less likely to divert his attention from the movement; e.g., Saxon charms, Hebridean Folk Songs, the verse of Dante, and the lyrics of Shakespeare—if he can dissociate the vocabulary from the cadence. Let him dissect the lyrics of Goethe[3] coldly into their component sound values, syllables long and short, stressed and unstressed, into vowels and consonants.

It is not necessary that a poem should rely on its music, but if it does rely on its music that music must be such as will delight the expert.

---

2. Reference to the Ten Commandments delivered to Moses (Exodus 20).

3. Johann Wolfgang von Goethe (1749–1832), German Romantic poet, playwright, and novelist.

Let the neophyte know assonance and alliteration, rhyme immediate and delayed, simple and polyphonic, as a musician would expect to know harmony and counterpoint and all the minutiae of his craft. No time is too great to give to these matters or to any one of them, even if the artist seldom have need of them.

Don't imagine that a thing will "go" in verse just because it's too dull to go in prose.

Don't be "viewy"—leave that to the writers of pretty little philosophic essays. Don't be descriptive; remember that the painter can describe a landscape much better than you can, and that he has to know a deal more about it.

When Shakespeare talks of the "Dawn in russet mantle clad"[4] he presents something which the painter does not present. There is in this line of his nothing that one can call description; he presents.

Consider the way of the scientists rather than the way of an advertising agent for a new soap.

The scientist does not expect to be acclaimed as a great scientist until he has *discovered* something. He begins by learning what has been discovered already. He goes from that point onward. He does not bank on being a charming fellow personally. He does not expect his friends to applaud the results of his freshman class work. Freshmen in poetry are unfortunately not confined to a definite and recognizable class room. They are "all over the shop." Is it any wonder "the public is indifferent to poetry?"

Don't chop your stuff into separate *iambs.* Don't make each line stop dead at the end, and then begin every next line with a heave. Let the beginning of the next line catch the rise of the rhythm wave, unless you want a definite longish pause.

In short, behave as a musician, a good musician, when dealing with that phase of your art which has exact parallels in music. The same laws govern, and you are bound by no others.

Naturally, your rhythmic structure should not destroy the shape of your words, or their natural sound, or their meaning. It is improbable that, at the start, you will be able to get a rhythm-structure strong enough to affect them very much, though you may fall a victim to all sorts of false stopping due to line ends and caesurae.

The musician can rely on pitch and the volume of the orchestra. You can not. The term harmony is misapplied to poetry; it refers to simultaneous sounds of different pitch. There is, however, in the best verse a sort of residue of sound which remains in the ear of the hearer and acts more or less as an organ-base. A rhyme must have in it some slight element of surprise if it is to give pleasure; it need not be bizarre or curious, but it must be well used if used at all.

Vide further Vildrac and Duhamel's notes on rhyme in "*Technique Poétique.*"[5]

That part of your poetry which strikes upon the imaginative *eye* of the reader will lose nothing by translation into a foreign tongue; that which appeals to the ear can reach only those who take it in the original.

4. From Horatio's speech in the opening scene of Shakespeare's *Hamlet*: "But look, the morn in russet mantle clad / Walks o'er the dew of yon high eastern hill" (1.1.147–48).
5. Charles Vildrac (1882–1971), French poet, playwright, and critic, and Georges Duhamel (1884–1966), French novelist and critic, cowrote *Notes sur la Technique Poétique* (1910). "Vide": consider (Latin).

Consider the definiteness of Dante's presentation, as compared with Milton's rhetoric. Read as much of Wordsworth[6] as does not seem too unutterably dull.

If you want the gist of the matter go to Sappho, Catullus, Villon, Heine when he is in the vein, Gautier when he is not too frigid; or, if you have not the tongues, seek out the leisurely Chaucer.[7] Good prose will do you no harm, and there is good discipline to be had by trying to write it.

Translation is likewise good training, if you find that your original matter "wobbles" when you try to rewrite it. The meaning of the poem to be translated can not "wobble."

If you are using a symmetrical form, don't put in what you want to say and then fill up the remaining vacuums with slush.

Don't mess up the perception of one sense by trying to define it in terms of another. This is usually only the result of being too lazy to find the exact word. To this clause there are possibly exceptions.

The first three simple proscriptions[8] will throw out nine-tenths of all the bad poetry now accepted as standard and classic; and will prevent you from many a crime of production.

". . . *Mais d'abord il faut etre un poete*,"[9] as MM. Duhamel and Vildrac have said at the end of their little book, "*Notes sur la Technique Poetique*"; but in an American one takes that at least for granted, otherwise why does one get born upon that august continent!

Ezra Pound

1913

6. John Milton (1608–1674) and William Words-worth (1770–1850), English poets.
7. Geoffrey Chaucer (ca. 1342–1400), English poet. Heinrich Heine (1797–1856), German poet.

Théophile Gautier (1811–1872), French poet.
8. Noted by Mr. Flint [Pound's note].
9. But first it is necessary to be a poet (French).

AN IMAGIST CLUSTER:
T. E. HULME, EZRA POUND, H.D.

At the inception of imagism in London, its key proponents included the English poet-philosopher T. E. Hulme and the expatriate American poets Ezra Pound and H.D. The paths of these three writers were densely interconnected at this juncture. In his poetry volume *Ripostes* (1912), Pound published an appendix of five poems, "The Complete Poetical Works of T. E. Hulme," prefaced by a note that printed the term *imagistes* for the first time. That year, in a London teashop, Pound had announced to the English poet Richard Aldington and the American poet H.D. that they were "imagistes," and two years later he included their and his work in the first anthology of such poetry, *Des Imagistes*. Although the movement began in London, with a French-styled name, the American poet Amy Lowell (1874–1925), derided by Pound for watering down its principles and helped disseminate its ideas in the United States, where she publicized and promoted the form in anthologies, lectures, and readings.

In spare, hard-edged poems, the imagists sought to turn verse away from what they saw as the slack sentimentality, fuzzy abstraction, explanatory excess, and metrical predictability of Victorian poetry. Imagism owed a debt to the symbolism of Yeats and nineteenth-century French poets, but it shifted the emphasis from the musical to the visual, the mysterious to the actual, the ambiguously suggestive symbol to the clear-cut natural image. Adherents looked to models from East Asia (haiku for Pound's "In a Station in the Metro") and classical Europe (Greek verse for H.D.'s "Oread"). Their poetry is compressed, achieving a maximum effect with a minimum of words. It is often centered in a single figurative juxtaposition, conjoining tenor and vehicle without explanation. And it typically relies not on strict meters but on informal rhythms or cadences.

H.D. (1886–1961) was born Hilda Doolittle in Bethlehem, Pennsylvania, and educated at Bryn Mawr College. In 1911 she went to Europe for what she thought would be a brief visit but became a lifelong stay, mainly in England and in Switzerland. After her initial imagist phase she wrote more expansive works, including the three long, meditative poems that make up *Trilogy* (1973), precipitated by the experience of the London bombings in World War II.

T. E. HULME: Autumn

A touch of cold in the Autumn night—
I walked abroad,
And saw the ruddy moon lean over a hedge
Like a red-faced farmer.
5   I did not stop to speak, but nodded,
And round about were the wistful stars
With white faces like town children.

1912

EZRA POUND: In a Station of the Metro

The apparition of these faces in the crowd;
Petals on a wet, black bough.[1]

1913, 1916

H.D.: Oread[1]

Whirl up, sea—
Whirl your pointed pines,
Splash your great pines
On our rocks,
5   Hurl your green over us,
Cover us with your pools of fir.

1914

1. Pound describes this poem's genesis in *Gaudier-Brzeska* (1916): "Three years ago in Paris I got out of a 'metro' train at La Concorde, and saw suddenly a beautiful face, and then another and another, and then a beautiful child's face, and then another beautiful woman, and I tried all that day to find words for what this had meant to me, and I could not find any words that seemed to me worthy, or as lovely as that sudden emotion. And that evening . . . I was still trying and I found, suddenly, the expression. I do not mean that I found words, but there came an equation . . . not in speech, but in little splotches of colour. . . . The 'one-image poem' is a form of super-position, that is to say, it is one idea getting out of the impasse in which I had been left by my metro emotion. I wrote a thirty-line poem, and destroyed it. . . . Six months later I made a poem half that length; a year later I made the following *hokku*-like sentence." "*Hokku*": another term for haiku.

1. Greek nymph of the mountains.

H.D.: Sea Rose

Rose, harsh rose,
marred and with stint of petals,
meagre flower, thin,
sparse of leaf,

5   more precious
than a wet rose,
single on a stem—
you are caught in the drift.

Stunted, with small leaf,
10 you are flung on the sands,
you are lifted
in the crisp sand
that drives in the wind.

Can the spice-rose
15 drip such acrid fragrance
hardened in a leaf?

1916

BLAST

The journal *Blast* was published only twice—on June 20, 1914, though released on July 2, one month before Great Britain entered World War I, and a year later, during the war that would bring its short life to an end. But its initial preface and two-part manifesto, printed in the first pages of the first number and excerpted below, are among the most important documents in the history of modernism. They rhetorically and typographically embody the violent iconoclasm of vorticism, an avant-garde movement in the literary and visual arts centered in London. The English writer and painter Wyndham Lewis founded and edited *Blast*, whose title he said, "means the blowing away of dead ideas and worn-out notions" (it also suggests *fire, explosion,* and *damn!*). He drafted much of the vorticist manifesto and fashioned its shocking visual design, likening *Blast* to a "battering ram." Ezra Pound became a vorticist after abandoning imagism, because he felt that the *vortex,* "the point of maximum energy," offered a more dynamic model for art than the static image of the imagists. The French sculptor Henri Gaudier-Brzeska (1891–1915), killed in World War I and memorialized both in the "War Number" of *Blast* and in Pound's book named for him, was another key vorticist leader. In the pages of *Blast* 1 and 2, artworks by Lewis, Gaudier-Brzeska, and other visual artists appeared alongside writings by Lewis, Pound, T. S. Eliot, and other avant-gardists.

The vorticist manifesto, signed by Lewis, Pound, and Gaudier-Brzeska, among others, reflects the London modernists' competitive anxiety about European avant-garde movements such as cubism and especially futurism. Under the charismatic leadership of F. T. Marinetti, the futurists celebrated speed, modernization, and the machine, while calling for the destruction of the museums, the libraries, and

Cover, *Blast 2*, 1915. The second and final issue of the journal *Blast* featured a woodcut, "Before Antwerp," by the vorticist artist Wyndham Lewis. Vorticism embraced machine-age modernity, as evident in this woodcut's sharp angles, geometric forms, and dynamic movement. The mechanistic soldiers tilt forward to suggest their forward march, juxtaposed against abstract urban architecture.

all such bastions of the past. The vorticists—in lists of things and people to "**BLAST**" and "**BLESS**," which they compiled at group meetings—similarly blast convention, standardization, the middle class, even the "years **1837** to **1900**." And yet despite their cosmopolitan enthusiasms, the vorticists also assert their independence, repeatedly criticizing the futurists. For all their antipathy toward England, they also "**BLESS**" it, revaluing, for example, English mobility (via the sea) and inventiveness (as the engine of the Industrial Revolution).

Wyndham Lewis (1882–1957) studied for several years at London's Slade School of Art before exploring the avant-garde visual arts in Paris. On returning to London in 1909, he began to write fiction and exhibit his paintings. During World War I he served as an artillery officer and then as a war artist, and afterward he continued to paint and publish essays, poetry, and fiction, including his first novel, *Tarr* (1918). Like Ezra Pound, he alienated many friends when he subsequently supported fascism.

The excerpts below are taken from *Blast: Review of the Great English Vortex*, No. 1 (1914).

Long Live the Vortex!

Long live the great art vortex sprung up in the centre of this town![1]

We stand for the Reality of the Present—not for the sentimental Future, or the sacripant[2] Past.

We want to leave Nature and Men alone.

We do not want to make people wear Futurist Patches, or fuss men to take to pink and sky-blue trousers.[3]

We are not their wives or tailors.

The only way Humanity can help artists is to remain independent and work unconsciously.

WE NEED THE UNCONSCIOUSNESS OF HUMANITY— their stupidity, animalism and dreams.

We believe in no perfectibility except our own.

Intrinsic beauty is in the Interpreter and Seer, not in the object or content.

We do not want to change the appearance of the world, because we are not Naturalists, Impressionists or Futurists (the latest form of Impressionism),[4] and do not depend on the appearance of the world for our art.

WE ONLY WANT THE WORLD TO LIVE, and to feel its crude energy flowing through us.

It may be said that great artists in England are always revolutionary, just as in France any really great artist had a strong traditional vein.

Blast sets out to be an avenue for all those vivid and violent ideas that could reach the Public in no other way.

Blast will be popular, essentially. It will not appeal to any particular class, but to the fundamental and popular instincts in every class and description of people, TO THE INDIVIDUAL. The moment a man feels or realizes himself as an artist, he ceases to belong to any milieu or time. Blast is created for this timeless, fundamental Artist that exists in everybody.

The Man in the Street and the Gentleman are equally ignored.

Popular art does not mean the art of the poor people, as it is usually supposed to. It means the art of the individuals.

Education (art education and general education) tends to destroy the creative instinct Therefore it is in times when education has been non-existant that art chiefly flourished.

1. London
2. Boastful of valor.
3. The futurists celebrated the technology, power, and dynamism of the modern age and sought to break with the past and traditional forms.
4. Naturalism, a late-nineteenth-century school of realism, claimed that all human life was governed by natural laws. Impressionism emphasized the subjectivity of perspective over any inherent quality in a represented object.

But it is nothing to do with "the People."

It is a mere accident that that is the most favourable time for the individual to appear.

To make the rich of the community shed their education skin, to destroy politeness, standardization and academic, that is civilized, vision, is the task we have set ourselves.

We want to make in England not a popular art, not a revival of lost folk art, or a romantic fostering of such unactual conditions, but to make individuals, wherever found.

We will convert the King[5] if possible.

A VORTICIST KING! WHY NOT?

DO YOU THINK LLOYD GEORGE[6] HAS THE VORTEX IN HIM?

MAY WE HOPE FOR ART FROM LADY MOND?[7]

We are against the glorification of "the People," as we are against snobbery. It is not necessary to be an outcast bohemian, to be unkempt or poor, any more than it is necessary to be rich or handsome, to be an artist. Art is nothing to do with the coat you wear. A top-hat can well hold the Sixtine. A cheap cap could hide the image of Kephren.[8]

AUTOMOBILISM (Marinetteism)[9] bores us. We don't want to go about making a hullo-bulloo about motor cars, anymore than about knives and forks, elephants or gas-pipes.

Elephants are VERY BIG. Motor cars go quickly.

Wilde gushed twenty years ago about the beauty of machinery. Gissing,[1] in his romantic delight with modern lodging houses was futurist in this sense.

The futurist is a sensational and sentimental mixture of the aesthete of 1890 and the realist of 1870.

The "Poor" are detestable animals! They are only picturesque and amusing for the sentimentalist or the romantic! The "Rich" are bores without a single exception, *en tant que riches!*[2]

We want those simple and great people found everywhere.

Blast presents an art of Individuals.

---

5. George V ascended the British throne in 1910 and remained the king until 1936.
6. David Lloyd George (1863–1945), British politician, prime minister 1916–22.
7. Wife of wealthy industrialist Sir Robert Mond, and a prominent member of fashionable London society.
8. Ancient Egyptian pharaoh buried in one of the great pyramids at Giza. "The Sixtine": the Sistine Chapel, in the Vatican.
9. Filippo Tommaso Marinetti (1876–1944), Italian writer and founder of futurism, glorified war and technology and invented a "drama of objects" in which human actors play no parts.
1. George Gissing (1837–1903), naturalist English novelist. Oscar Wilde (1854–1900), Irish writer and critic; in his 1891 essay "The Soul of Man under Socialism," he writes: "All unintellectual labour, all monotonous, dull labour, all labour that deals with dreadful things, and involves unpleasant conditions, must be done by machinery. . . . At present machinery competes against man. Under proper conditions machinery will serve man."
2. Insofar as they are rich (French).

6

BLAST

years **1837** to **1900**[1]

Curse abysmal inexcusable middle-class
(also Aristocracy and Proletariat).

BLAST

pasty shadow cast by gigantic **Boehm**[2]

(Imagined at introduction of **BOURGEOIS VICTORIAN VISTAS**).

WRING THE NECK OF all sick inventions born in that progressive white wake.

BLAST their weeping whiskers—hirsute[3]
RHETORIC of EUNUCH and STYLIST—
SENTIMENTAL HYGIENICS
ROUSSEAUISMS[4] (wild Nature cranks)
FRATERNIZING WITH MONKEYS
DIABOLICS—raptures and roses
of the erotic bookshelves
culminating in
PURGATORY OF PUTNEY.[5]

CHAOS OF ENOCH ARDENS

laughing Jennys
Ladies with Pains
good-for-nothing Guineveres.[6]

1. Queen Victoria reigned from 1837 to 1901. This sixth list of items in the "BLAST" section comes last, before the "BLESS" section.
2. Joseph Edgar Boehm (1834–1890) sculpted a colossal marble statue of Queen Victoria.
3. Hairy.
4. Jean-Jacques Rousseau (1712–1778), Swiss-born French philosopher who argued that humans

are good and noble in their natural state, before society and civilization corrupt them.
5. A middle-class London suburb.
6. In late medieval romance, King Arthur's queen in Camelot; also, the title character in two narrative poems by the English poet Alfred, Lord Tennyson (1809–1892). "Enoch Arden" (1864) is another narrative poem by Tennyson, rejected

SNOBBISH BORROVIAN running after
GIPSY KINGS and **ESPADAS**[7]

bowing the knee to
wild Mother Nature,
her feminine contours,
Unimaginative insult to
MAN.

DAMN

all those to-day who have taken on that Rotten Menagerie,
and still crack their whips and tumble in Piccadilly Circus,
as though London were a provincial town.

WE WHISPER IN YOUR EAR A GREAT SECRET.

LONDON IS NOT A PROVINCIAL TOWN.

We will allow Wonder Zoos. But we do not want the
GLOOMY VICTORIAN CIRCUS[8] in
Piccadilly Circus.

IT IS PICCADILLY'S CIRCUS!

NOT MEANT FOR MENAGERIES trundling

out of Sixties **DICKENSIAN CLOWNS,**
CORELLI LADY RIDERS,[9]
TROUPS OF PERFORMING
GIPSIES (who complain

---

here for its sentimentalism. Jenny is the title character of another sentimental poem (1870), by the English poet Dante Gabriel Rossetti (1828–1882).
7. Swords (Spanish). "Borrovian": from George Henry Borrow (1803–1881), English writer of popular gypsy romances, such as *The Zincali: An Account of the Gypsies of Spain* (1843).
8. "Circus": here, traveling entertainment act with animals and acrobats; also British traffic circle (e.g., Piccadilly Circus in central London). "Wonder Zoos": traveling exhibition of exotic animals.
9. Marie Corelli, pseudonym of Mary Mackay (1855–1924), best-selling (and royal favorite) English writer of romances and religious novels in which she aimed to reform social ills. "Dickensian clowns": from the novels of English writer Charles Dickens (1812–1870).

besides that 1/6 a night
does not pay fare back to
Clapham).[1]

BLAST[2]

The Post Office   **Frank Brangwyn**   **Robertson Nicol**

Rev. Pennyfeather   **Galloway Kyle**
(Bells)   (Cluster of Grapes)

Bishop of London and all his posterity

Galsworthy   **Dean Inge**   **Croce**   **Matthews**

Rev Meyer   **Seymour Hicks**

Lionel Cust   **C. B. Fry**   **Bergson**   **Abdul Bahai**

Hawtrey   **Edward Elgar**   **Sardlea**

Filson Young   **Marie Gorelli**   **Geddes**

Codliver Oil   **St. Loe Strachey**   **Lyceum Club**

Rhabindraneth Tagore   **Lord Glenconner of Glen**

Weiniger   **Norman Angel**   **Ad. Mahon**

Mr. and Mrs. Dearmer   **Beecham**   **Ella**

A. C. Benson   (Pills, Opera, Thomas)   **Sydney Webb**

British Academy   **Messrs. Chapell**

Countess of Warwick   **George Edwards**

1. Suburban district of London. "1/6": 18d, or a shilling and sixpence, then equivalent to about thirty-five cents.
2. Those blasted here range from individuals, such as Charles Burgess Fry, England's star cricket player and a tireless self-promoter, to things mocked seemingly for the thrill of doing so, such as codliver oil. Blasted, too, are institutions or members of the national, literary, or cultural establishment (e.g., the post office, a much-lauded model of Victorian efficiency, and the British Academy, established in 1902 by Royal Charter as the national institute for humanities and social sciences), including various clergy and public leaders (e.g., bishop of London; William Ralph Inge, dean of St. Paul's Cathedral; the Reverends Pennyfeather and Meyer; R. J. Campbell, English Congregationalist minister in the City Temple of London, and a Pantheist; Cardinal Herbert Vaughan, archbishop of Westminster and superior of the Catholic Missionary Society; Norman Angell, pacifist British economist; Arthur Christopher Benson, schoolmaster at Eton College,

author of Edward VII's coronation ode). Critics unfriendly to the avant-garde are also included (e.g., William Archer, drama critic for the *Nation*; Sir William Robertson Nicoll, biblical editor and sometime literary critic; Lionel Cust, director of the National Portrait Gallery and contributor to the *Dictionary of National Biography*, etc.). Also ridiculed are artists and writers whom the vorticists believed were meager talents in spite of their popularity (e.g., painter Frank Brangwyn, poet Ella Wheeler Wilcox, actors George Grossmith and Seymour Hicks, composers Joseph Holbrooke and Edward Elgar, etc.), as well as those associated with fads (e.g., Sir Abdul Baha Bahai, leader of the Baha'i faith) or idealistic social reform (e.g., author Marie Corelli; Sidney Webb, a leader of the Fabian Socialist organization; Annie Besant, theosophist and suffragist). Some names (e.g., Indian poet Rabindranath Tagore) are misspelled. For a detailed discussion of the cursing and blessing in Blast, see William C. Wees, *Vorticism and the English Avant-Garde* (1972).

Willie Ferraro   **Captain Cook**   **R. J. Campbell**
Clan Thesiger   **Martin Harvey**   **William Archer**
George Grossmith   **R. H. Benson**
Annie Besant   **Chenil**   **Clan Meynell**
Father Vaughan   **Joseph Holbrooke**   **Clan Strachey**

1914

MINA LOY

M ina Loy (1882–1966) was born in London to a Protestant mother and a Jewish father. She began her artistic career in the visual arts, but she later became an experimental poet, writing lyrics and long poems that created a stir because of their literary, linguistic, and sexual iconoclasm. Among them were the scandalous "Songs to Joannes," in which she risks de-idealizing and desentimentalizing sex while freeing poetry of conventional diction, syntax, and punctuation. From 1899 to 1916 she lived and worked mostly in Munich, Paris, and especially Florence. She moved to New York in 1916 and to Paris in 1923, then settled in the United States in 1936.

Loy composed this manifesto, which she considered a rough draft and never published, in November 1914 and sent it to her friend Mabel Dodge (1879–1962), American author and celebrated patron of the arts. In the decade before Loy wrote it, feminist activism had intensified in England, particularly the militant civil disobedience of Christabel Pankhurst and other suffragettes in the Women's Social and Political Union. Loy's piece, which bears fruitful comparison with the masculine *Blast* manifesto published a few months earlier, was partly the result of Loy's quarrels with the Italian futurists, with whom she was closely associated despite the movement's misogyny. In the manifesto Loy tries to harness for feminism the radicalism and individualism of the avant-garde, calling for nothing less than a revolution in gender relations. She abandons the suffragette movement's central issue of equality and insists instead on an adversarial model of gender, claiming that women should not look to men for a standard of value but should find it within themselves. First published in the posthumous collection *The Last Lunar Baedeker* (1982), the manifesto is reprinted from *The Lost Lunar Baedeker* (1996); both volumes were edited by Roger L. Conover.

Feminist Manifesto

The feminist movement as at present instituted is

Inadequate

Women if you want to realise yourselves—you are on the eve of a devastating psychological upheaval—all your pet illusions must be unmasked—the lies of centuries have got to go— are you prepared for the **Wrench**—? There is no half- measure—NO scratching on the surface of the rubbish heap of tradition, will bring about **Reform**, the only method is **Absolute Demolition**

Cease to place your confidence in economic legislation, vice- crusades & uniform education—you are glossing over **Reality**. Professional & commercial careers are opening up for you—

Is that all you want ?

And if you honestly desire to find your level without preju- dice—be **Brave** & deny at the outset—that pa- thetic clap-trap war cry **Woman is the equal of man**—

She is **NOT!** for

The man who lives a life in which his activities conform to a social code which is a protectorate of the feminine element— ——is no longer **masculine** The women who adapt themselves to a theoretical valuation of their sex as a **relative impersonality** , are not yet **Feminine** Leave off looking to men to find out what you are **not** —seek within yourselves to find out what you **are**

As conditions are at present constituted—you have the choice between **<u>Parasitism</u>, & <u>Prostitu-tion</u>**—or Negation

Men & women are enemies, with the enmity of the exploited for the parasite, the parasite for the exploited—at present they are at the mercy of the advantage that each can take of the others sexual dependence—. The only point at which the interests of the sexes merge—is the sexual embrace.

The first illusion it is to your interest to demolish is the division of women into two classes   **<u>the mistress,</u> & <u>the mother</u>** every well-balanced & developed woman knows that is not true, Nature has endowed the complete woman with a faculty for expressing herself through <u>all</u> her functions—there are **<u>no restrictions</u>** the woman who is so incompletely evolved as to be un-self-conscious in sex, will prove a restrictive influence on the temperamental expansion of the next generation; the woman who is a poor mistress will be an incompetent mother—an inferior mentality—& will enjoy an inadequate apprehension of **<u>Life</u>** .

To obtain results you must make sacrifices & the first & greatest sacrifice you have to make is of your "<u>virtue</u>" The fictitious value of woman as identified with her physical purity—is too easy a stand-by——rendering her lethargic in the acquisition of intrinsic merits of character by which she could obtain a concrete value— therefore, the first self-enforced law for the female sex, as a protection against the man made bogey of virtue—which is the principle instrument of her subjection, would be the <u>unconditional</u> surgical <u>destruction</u> <u>of</u> <u>virginity</u> through-out the female population at puberty—.

The value of man is assessed entirely according to his use or interest to the community, the value of woman, depends entirely on <u>chance</u>, her success or insuccess in manoeuvering a man into taking the life-long responsibility of her—

The advantages of marriage of too ridiculously ample—
compared to all other trades—for under modern conditions a
woman can accept preposterously luxurious support from a
man (with-out return of any sort—even offspring)—as a thank
offering for her virginity
The woman who has not succeeded in striking that
advantageous bargain—is prohibited from any but
surreptitious re-action to Life-stimuli—& entirely
debarred maternity.
Every woman has a right to maternity—
Every woman of superior intelligence should realize her race-
responsibility, in producing children in adequate proportion to
the unfit or degenerate members of her sex—

Each child of a superior woman should be the result of a
definite period of psychic development in her life—& not
necessarily of a possibly irksome & outworn continuance of an
alliance—spontaneously adapted for vital creation in the
beginning but not necessarily harmoniously balanced as the
parties to it—follow their individual lines of personal
evolution—
For the harmony of the race, each individual should be the
expression of an easy & ample interpenetration of the male &
female temperaments—free of stress
Woman must become more responsible for the child than man—
Women must destroy in themselves, the desire to be loved—

The feeling that it is a personal insult when a man transfers
his attentions from her to another woman
The desire for comfortable protection instead of an intelligent
curiosity & courage in meeting & resisting the pressure of life
sex or so called love must be reduced to its initial element,
honour, grief, sentimentality, pride & consequently jealousy
must be detached from it.
Woman for her happiness must retain her deceptive fragility of
appearance, combined with indomitable will, irreducible
courage, & abundant health the outcome of sound nerves—
Another great illusion that woman must use all her
introspective clear-sightedness & unbiassed bravery to
destroy—for the sake of her self respect is the impurity of sex

the realisation in defiance of superstition that there is <u>nothing</u> <u>impure</u> <u>in</u> <u>sex</u>—except in the mental attitude to it—will constitute an incalculable & wider social regeneration than it is possible for our generation to imagine.

1914   1982

From Songs to Joannes[1]

I

Spawn   of   Fantasies
Silting the appraisable
Pig Cupid   his rosy snout
Rooting garbage
5   "Once upon a time"
Pulls a weed   white star-topped
Among wild oats   sown in mucous-membrane

I would   an   eye in a Bengal light[2]
Eternity in a sky-rocket
10   Constellations in an ocean
Whose rivers run no fresher
Than a trickle of saliva

These   are suspect places

I must live in my lantern
15   Trimming subliminal flicker
Virginal   to the bellows
Of Experience   Coloured   glass

III

We might have coupled
In the bed-ridden monopoly of a moment
Or broken flesh with one another
At the profane communion table
5   Where wine is spill'd on promiscuous lips

We might have given birth to a butterfly
With the daily news
Printed in blood on its wings

XIV

Today
Everlasting   passing   apparent   imperceptible
To you

---

1. Loy's pseudonym for her difficult lover, the Italian poet Giovanni Papini (1881–1956).   2. Flare used for signaling or illumination.

I bring the nascent virginity of
5 —Myself   for the moment

No love   or the other thing
Only the impact of lighted bodies
Knocking sparks off each other
In chaos

XXVI

Shedding our petty pruderies
From slit eyes

We sidle up
To Nature
5 — — — that irate pornographist

1915–17

WILLIAM BUTLER YEATS
1865–1939

William Butler Yeats was born to an Anglo-Irish family in Dublin. His father, J. B. Yeats, had abandoned law to take up painting, at which he made a somewhat precarious living. His mother came from the Pollexfen family that lived near Sligo, in the west of Ireland, where Yeats spent much of his childhood. The Yeatses moved to London in 1874, then returned to Dublin in 1880. Yeats attended first high school and then art school, which he soon left to concentrate on poetry.

Yeats's father was a religious skeptic, but he believed in the "religion of art." Yeats, religious by temperament but unable to believe in Christian orthodoxy, sought all his life to compensate for his lost religion. This search led him to various kinds of mysticism, to folklore, theosophy, spiritualism, and neoplatonism. He said he "made a new religion, almost an infallible church of poetic tradition."

Yeats's childhood and young manhood were spent between Dublin, London, and Sligo, and each of these places contributed something to his poetic development. In London in the 1890s he met the important poets of the day, founded the Irish Literary Society, and acquired late-Romantic, Pre-Raphaelite ideas of poetry: he believed, in this early stage of his career, that a poet's language should be dreamy, evocative, and ethereal. From the countryside around Sligo he gained a knowledge of the life of the peasantry and of their folklore. In Dublin, where he founded the National Literary Society, he was influenced by Irish nationalism and, although often disagreeing with those who wished to use literature for political ends, he nevertheless came to see his poetry as contributing to the rejuvenation of Irish culture.

Yeats's poetry began in the tradition of self-conscious Romanticism, strongly influenced by the English poets Edmund Spenser, Percy Shelley, and, a little later, William Blake, whose works he edited. About the same time, he was writing poems (e.g., "The Stolen Child") derived from his Sligo experience, with quietly precise nature imagery, Irish place-names, and themes from Irish folklore. A little later he drew on the great stories of the heroic age of Irish history and translations of Gaelic poetry into "that dialect which gets from Gaelic its syntax and keeps its still partly Tudor vocabulary." The heroic legends of ancient Ireland and the folk traditions of the modern Irish countryside helped brace his early dreamlike imagery. "The Lake Isle of Innisfree"—"my first lyric with anything in its rhythm of my own music," said Yeats—is both a Romantic evocation of escape into dream, art, and the imagination, and a specifically Irish reverie on freedom and self-reliance.

Yeats vigorously hybridizes Irish and English traditions, and eventually draws into this potent intercultural mix East and South Asian cultural resources, including Japanese Noh theater and Indian meditative practices. Resolutely Irish, he imaginatively reclaims a land colonized by the British; imposes Irish rhythms, images, genres, and syntax on English-language poetry; and revives native myths, place-names, and consciousness. Yet he is also cosmopolitan, insisting on the transnationalism of the collective storehouse of images he calls "Spiritus Mundi" or "Anima Mundi," spending much of his life in England, and cross-pollinating forms, ideas, and images from Ireland and England, Europe and Asia.

Irish nationalism first sent Yeats in search of a consistently simpler and more popular style, to express the elemental facts about Irish life and aspirations. This led him to the concrete image, as did translations from Gaelic folk songs, in which "nothing . . . was abstract, nothing worn-out." But other forces were also working on him. In 1902 a friend gave him the works of the German philosopher Friedrich Nietzsche, to which he responded with great excitement, and it would seem that, in persuading the passive love poet to get off his knees, Nietzsche's books intensified his search for a more active stance, a more vigorous style. At the start of the twentieth century, Yeats wearied of his early languid aesthetic, declaring his intentions, in a 1901 letter, to make "everything hard and clear" and, in another of 1904, to leave behind "sentiment and sentimental sadness." He wished for poems that did not reach for disembodied beauty but that could "carry the normal, passionate, reasoning self, the personality as a whole." In poems of his middle period, such as "Adam's Curse" and "A Coat," Yeats combines the colloquial with the formal, enacting in his more austere diction, casual rhythms, and passionate syntax his will to leave behind the poetic "embroideries" of his youth and walk "naked." The American poet Ezra Pound, who spent winters from 1913 to 1916 with Yeats in a stone cottage in Sussex, strengthened Yeats's resolve to develop a less mannered, more stripped-down style.

In 1889 Yeats had met the beautiful actor and Irish nationalist Maud Gonne, with whom he was desperately in love for many years, but who persistently refused to marry him. She became the subject of many of his early love poems, and in later poems, such as "No Second Troy" and "A Prayer for My Daughter," he expresses anger over her self-sacrifice to political activism. He had also met Augusta, Lady Gregory, an Anglo-Irish writer and promoter of Irish literature, in 1896, and Yeats spent many holidays at her aristocratic country house, Coole Park. Disliking the moneygrubbing and prudery of the middle classes, as indicated in "September 1913," he looked for his ideal characters either below, to peasants and beggars, or above, to the aristocracy, for each of these had their own traditions and lived according to them. Under Lady Gregory's influence, Yeats began to organize the Irish dramatic movement in 1899 and, with her help, founded the Abbey Theatre in 1904. His active participation in theatrical production—confronting political censorship, economic problems of paying carpenters and actors, and other aspects of "theatre business, management of men"—also helped toughen his style, as he demonstrates in "The Fascination of What's Difficult." Yeats's long-cherished hope had been to "bring the halves together"—Protestant and Catholic—through a literature infused with Ireland's ancient myths and cultural riches before the divisions between rival Christianities. But in a string of national controversies, he ran afoul of both the Roman Catholic middle class and the Anglo-Irish Protestant ascendancy, and at last, bitterly turning his back on Ireland, moved to England.

Then came the Easter Rising of 1916, led by men and women he had long known, some of whom were executed or imprisoned by the British. Persuaded by Gonne (whose estranged husband was one of the executed leaders) that "tragic dignity had returned to Ireland," Yeats returned. His culturally nationalist work had helped inspire the poet revolutionaries, and so he asked himself, as he put it in the late poem "Man and the Echo," did his work "send out / Certain men the English shot?" Yeats's nationalism and antinationalism, his divided loyalties to Ireland and to England, find powerfully ambivalent expression in "Easter, 1916" and other poems. Throughout his poetry he brilliantly mediates between contending aspects of himself—late-Romantic visionary and astringent modern skeptic, Irish patriot and irreverent antinationalist, shrewd man of action and esoteric dreamer. As he said: "We make out of the quarrel with others, rhetoric, but of the quarrel with ourselves, poetry." Conceiving consciousness as conflict, he fashioned a kind of poetry that could embody the contradictory feelings and ideas of his endless inner debate.

To mark his recommitment to Ireland, Yeats refurbished and renamed Thoor (Castle) Ballylee, the Norman tower on Lady Gregory's land, in which he lived off and on, and which became, along with its inner winding stair, a central symbol in his later poetry. In 1922 he was appointed a senator of the recently established Irish Free State, and he served until 1928, playing an active part not only

The Tower. Yeats commissioned the artist Thomas Sturge Moore to create the cover of his collection *The Tower* (1928). He praised Moore's stylized gold and green woodcut design for its visual accuracy and symbolic potency in depicting Thoor Ballylee. Yeats restored the fifteenth-century Norman tower in the west of Ireland and made it an emblem of his poetry. He wrote and lived there with his family during summers from 1921 to 1929.

in promoting the arts but also in mediating general political affairs, in which he supported the views of the minority Protestant landed class. At the same time, he was continuing his esoteric studies. He married Georgie (changed by Yeats to George) Hyde Lees in 1917, when he was fifty-two, and she proved so sympathetic to his imaginative needs that the automatic writing she produced for several years (believed by Yeats to have been dictated by spirits) gave him the elements of a symbolic system that he later worked out in his book *A Vision* (1925, 1937). The system was a theory of the movements of history and of the different types of personality, each movement and type being related to a different phase of the moon. At the center of the symbolic system were the interpenetrating cones, or "gyres," that represented the movement through major cycles of history and across antitheses of human personality.

He compressed and embodied his personal mythology in visionary poems of great scope, linguistic force, and incantatory power, such as "The Second Coming" and "Leda and the Swan." In poems of the 1920s and 1930s, winding stairs, spinning tops, "gyres," spirals of all kinds, are important symbols, serving as a means of resolving some of the contraries that had arrested him from the beginning—paradoxes of time and eternity, change and continuity, spirit and the body, life and art. If his earliest poetry was sometimes static, a beautifully stitched tapestry laden with symbols of inner states, his late poetry became more dynamic, its propulsive syntax and muscular rhythms more suited to his themes of lust, rage, and the body. He had once screened these out of his verse as unpoetic, along with war, violence, "the mire of human veins." Now he embraced the mortal world intensely. In "A Dialogue of Self and Soul," the self defies the soul's injunction to leave the world behind: "I am content to live it all again / And yet again, if it be life to pitch / Into the frog-spawn of a blind man's ditch." Yeats no longer sought transcendence of the human, but instead aimed for the active interpenetration of the corporeal and the visionary. In his Nietzsche-inspired poems of "tragic joy," such as "Lapis Lazuli," he affirmed ruin and destruction as necessary to imaginative creation.

One key to Yeats's greatness is that there are many different Yeatses: a hard-nosed skeptic and an esoteric idealist, a nativist and a cosmopolitan, an Irish nationalist and an ironic antinationalist, a Romantic brooding on loss and unrequited desire and a modernist mocking idealism, nostalgia, and contemporary society. Similarly, in his poetic innovations and consolidations, he is both a conservative and a radical. That is, he is a literary traditionalist, working within such inherited genres as love poetry, the elegy, the self-elegy, the sonnet, and the occasional poem on public themes. But he is also a restless innovator who disrupts generic conventions, breaking up the coherence of the sonnet, de-idealizing the dead mourned in elegies, and bringing into public poems an intense personal ambivalence. In matters of form, too, he rhymes but often in off-rhyme, uses standard meters but bunches or scatters their stresses, employs an elegant syntax that nevertheless has the passionate urgency of colloquial speech; his diction, tone, enjambments, and stanzas intermix ceremony with contortion, controlled artifice with wayward unpredictability. A difficulty in reading Yeats— but also one of the great rewards—is comprehending his many-sidedness.

Like Pound, T. S. Eliot, and Windham Lewis, Yeats was attracted to right-wing politics, and in the 1930s he was briefly drawn to fascism. His late interest in authoritarian politics arose in part from his desire for a feudal, aristocratic society that, unlike middle-class culture, in his view, might allow the imagination to flourish, and in part from his anticolonialism, since he thought a fascist Spain, for example, would "weaken the British Empire." But eventually he was appalled by all political ideologies, and the grim prophecy of "The Second Coming" seemed to him increasingly apt.

Written in a rugged, colloquial, and concrete language, Yeats's last poems have a controlled yet startling wildness. His return to life, to "the foul rag-and-bone shop of the heart," is one of the most impressive final phases of any poet's career. In one of his last letters he wrote: "When I try to put all into a phrase I say, 'Man can embody truth but he cannot know it.' . . . The abstract is not life and everywhere draws out its contradictions. You can refute Hegel but not the Saint or the Song of Sixpence." He died in southern France just before the beginning of World War II. His grave is, as his poem directed, near Sligo, "under Ben Bulben." He left behind a body of verse that, in variety and power, has been an enduring influence for English-language poets around the globe, from W. H. Auden and Seamus Heaney to Derek Walcott and A. K. Ramanujan.

The Stolen Child[1]

Where dips the rocky highland
Of Sleuth Wood[2] in the lake,
There lies a leafy island
Where flapping herons wake
5   The drowsy water-rats;

1. I.e., a child stolen by fairies to be their companion, as in Irish folklore.
2. This and other places mentioned in the poem are in County Sligo, in the west of Ireland, where Yeats spent much of his childhood.

There we've hid our faery vats,
Full of berries
And of reddest stolen cherries.
Come away, O human child!
To the waters and the wild
With a faery, hand in hand,
For the world's more full of weeping than you can understand.

Where the wave of moonlight glosses
The dim grey sands with light,
Far off by furthest Rosses
We foot it all the night,
Weaving olden dances,
Mingling hands and mingling glances
Till the moon has taken flight;
To and fro we leap
And chase the frothy bubbles,
While the world is full of troubles
And is anxious in its sleep.
Come away, O human child!
To the waters and the wild
With a faery, hand in hand,
For the world's more full of weeping than you can understand.

Where the wandering water gushes
From the hills above Glen-Car,
In pools among the rushes
That scarce could bathe a star,
We seek for slumbering trout
And whispering in their ears
Give them unquiet dreams;
Leaning softly out
From ferns that drop their tears
Over the young streams.
Come away, O human child!
To the waters and the wild
With a faery, hand in hand,
For the world's more full of weeping than you can understand.

Away with us he's going,
The solemn-eyed:
He'll hear no more the lowing
Of the calves on the warm hillside
Or the kettle on the hob
Sing peace into his breast,
Or see the brown mice bob
Round and round the oatmeal-chest.
For he comes, the human child,
To the waters and the wild
With a faery, hand in hand,
From a world more full of weeping than he can understand.

1886, 1889

Down by the Salley Gardens[1]

Down by the salley gardens my love and I did meet;
She passed the salley gardens with little snow-white feet.
She bid me take love easy, as the leaves grow on the tree;
But I, being young and foolish, with her would not agree.

5   In a field by the river my love and I did stand,
And on my leaning shoulder she laid her snow-white hand.
She bid me take life easy, as the grass grows on the weirs;°   *dams*
But I was young and foolish, and now am full of tears.

1889

The Rose of the World[1]

Who dreamed that beauty passes like a dream?
For these red lips, with all their mournful pride,
Mournful that no new wonder may betide,
Troy[2] passed away in one high funeral gleam,
5   And Usna's children died.[3]

We and the labouring world are passing by:
Amid men's souls, that waver and give place
Like the pale waters in their wintry race,
Under the passing stars, foam of the sky,
10   Lives on this lonely face.

Bow down, archangels, in your dim abode:
Before you were, or any hearts to beat,
Weary and kind one lingered by His seat;
He made the world to be a grassy road
15   Before her wandering feet.

1892, 1895

1. Originally titled "An Old Song Resung," with Yeats's footnote: "This is an attempt to reconstruct an old song from three lines imperfectly remembered by an old peasant woman in the village of Ballysodare, Sligo, who often sings them to herself." "Salley": a variant of *sallow*, a species of willow tree.

1. The Platonic idea of eternal beauty. "I notice upon reading these poems for the first time for several years that the quality symbolized as The Rose differs from the Intellectual Beauty of Shelley and of Spenser in that I have imagined it as suffering with man and not as something pursued and seen from afar" [Yeats, in 1925]. Yeats wrote this poem to Maud Gonne.

2. Ancient city destroyed by the Greeks, according to legend, after the abduction of the beautiful Helen.

3. In Old Irish legend the Ulster warrior Naoise, son of Usna or Usnach (pronounced *Úskna*), eloped with the beautiful Deirdre, whom King Conchubar of Ulster had intended to marry, and with his two brothers took her to Scotland. Eventually Conchubar lured the four of them back to Ireland and killed the three brothers.

The Lake Isle of Innisfree[1]

I will arise and go now, and go to Innisfree,
And a small cabin build there, of clay and wattles[2] made:
Nine bean-rows will I have there, a hive for the honey-bee,
And live alone in the bee-loud glade.

5   And I shall have some peace there, for peace comes dropping slow,
Dropping from the veils of the morning to where the cricket sings;
There midnight's all a glimmer, and noon a purple glow,
And evening full of the linnet's wings.

I will arise and go now, for always night and day
10   I hear lake water lapping with low sounds by the shore;
While I stand on the roadway, or on the pavements grey,
I hear it in the deep heart's core.

1890   1890, 1892

The Sorrow of Love[1]

The brawling of a sparrow in the eaves,
The brilliant moon and all the milky sky,
And all that famous harmony of leaves,
Had blotted out man's image and his cry.

5   A girl arose that had red mournful lips
And seemed the greatness of the world in tears,
Doomed like Odysseus and the labouring ships
And proud as Priam murdered with his peers;[2]

Arose, and on the instant clamorous eaves,
10   A climbing moon upon an empty sky,
And all that lamentation of the leaves,
Could but compose man's image and his cry.

1891   1892, 1925

1. Inis Fraoigh (Heather Island) is a small island in Lough Gill, near Sligo, in the west of Ireland. In his autobiography Yeats writes: "I had still the ambition, formed in Sligo in my teens, of living in imitation of Thoreau on Innisfree . . . and when walking through Fleet Street [in London] very homesick I heard a little tinkle of water and saw a fountain in a shop-window which balanced a little ball upon its jet, and began to remember lake water. From the sudden remembrance came my poem *Innisfree*, my first lyric with anything in its rhythm of my own music."
2. Stakes interwoven with twigs or branches.
1. For earlier versions of this poem, go to the NAEL Archive.
2. Odysseus (whom the Romans called Ulysses) is the hero of Homer's *Odyssey*, which describes how, after having fought in the siege of Troy, he wandered for ten years before reaching his home, the Greek island of Ithaca. Priam was king of Troy at the time of the siege and was killed when the Greeks captured the city.

When You Are Old[1]

When you are old and grey and full of sleep,
And nodding by the fire, take down this book,
And slowly read, and dream of the soft look
Your eyes had once, and of their shadows deep;

5   How many loved your moments of glad grace,
And loved your beauty with love false or true,
But one man loved the pilgrim soul in you,
And loved the sorrows of your changing face;

And bending down beside the glowing bars,[2]
10   Murmur, a little sadly, how Love fled
And paced upon the mountains overhead
And hid his face amid a crowd of stars.

1891   1892, 1899

Who Goes with Fergus?[1]

Who will go drive with Fergus now,
And pierce the deep wood's woven shade,
And dance upon the level shore?
Young man, lift up your russet brow,
5   And lift your tender eyelids, maid,
And brood on hopes and fear no more.

And no more turn aside and brood
Upon love's bitter mystery;
For Fergus rules the brazen cars,°   *bronze chariots*
10   And rules the shadows of the wood,
And the white breast of the dim sea
And all dishevelled wandering stars.

1893

The Man Who Dreamed of Faeryland

He stood among a crowd at Drumahair;[1]
His heart hung all upon a silken dress,
And he had known at last some tenderness,

---

1. A poem suggested by a sonnet by the French poet Pierre de Ronsard (1524–1585); it begins: "Quand vous serez bien vieille, au soir, à la chandelle" (When you are quite old, in the evening by candlelight).
2. I.e., of the fireplace grate.
1. In a late version of this Irish heroic legend,

Fergus, "king of the proud Red Branch Kings," gave up his throne voluntarily to King Conchubar of Ulster to learn by dreaming and meditating the bitter wisdom of the poet and philosopher.
1. This and other place-names in the poem refer to locations in County Sligo.

Before earth took him to her stony care;
5   But when a man poured fish into a pile,
It seemed they raised their little silver heads,
And sang what gold morning or evening sheds
Upon a woven world-forgotten isle
Where people love beside the ravelled² seas;
10   That Time can never mar a lover's vows
Under that woven changeless roof of boughs:
The singing shook him out of his new ease.

He wandered by the sands of Lissadell;
His mind ran all on money cares and fears,
15   And he had known at last some prudent years
Before they heaped his grave under the hill;
But while he passed before a plashy place,
A lug-worm with its grey and muddy mouth
Sang that somewhere to north or west or south
20   There dwelt a gay, exulting, gentle race
Under the golden or the silver skies;
That if a dancer stayed his hungry foot
It seemed the sun and moon were in the fruit:
And at that singing he was no more wise.

25   He mused beside the well of Scanavin,
He mused upon his mockers: without fail
His sudden vengeance were a country tale,
When earthy night had drunk his body in;
But one small knot-grass growing by the pool
30   Sang where—unnecessary cruel voice—
Old silence bids its chosen race rejoice,
Whatever ravelled waters rise and fall
Or stormy silver fret the gold of day,
And midnight there enfold them like a fleece
35   And lover there by lover be at peace.
The tale drove his fine angry mood away.

He slept under the hill of Lugnagall;
And might have known at last unhaunted sleep
Under that cold and vapour-turbaned steep,
40   Now that the earth had taken man and all:
Did not the worms that spired about his bones
Proclaim with that unwearied, reedy cry
That God has laid His fingers on the sky,
That from those fingers glittering summer runs
45   Upon the dancer by the dreamless wave.
Why should those lovers that no lovers miss
Dream, until God burn Nature with a kiss?
The man has found no comfort in the grave.

1891, 1930

---

2. Tangled; here, turbulent.

Adam's Curse[1]

We sat together at one summer's end,
That beautiful mild woman, your close friend,
And you and I,[2] and talked of poetry.
I said, "A line will take us hours maybe;
5   Yet if it does not seem a moment's thought,
Our stitching and unstitching has been naught.
Better go down upon your marrow-bones
And scrub a kitchen pavement, or break stones
Like an old pauper, in all kinds of weather;
10   For to articulate sweet sounds together
Is to work harder than all these, and yet
Be thought an idler by the noisy set
Of bankers, schoolmasters, and clergymen
The martyrs call the world."

                        And thereupon
15   That beautiful mild woman for whose sake
There's many a one shall find out all heartache
On finding that her voice is sweet and low
Replied, "To be born woman is to know—
Although they do not talk of it at school—
20   That we must labour to be beautiful."

I said, "It's certain there is no fine thing
Since Adam's fall but needs much labouring.
There have been lovers who thought love should be
So much compounded of high courtesy
25   That they would sigh and quote with learned looks
Precedents out of beautiful old books;
Yet now it seems an idle trade enough."

We sat grown quiet at the name of love;
We saw the last embers of daylight die,
30   And in the trembling blue-green of the sky
A moon, worn as if it had been a shell
Washed by time's waters as they rose and fell
About the stars and broke in days and years.

I had a thought for no one's but your ears:
35   That you were beautiful, and that I strove
To love you in the old high way of love;
That it had all seemed happy, and yet we'd grown
As weary-hearted as that hollow moon.

Nov. 1902   1902, 1922

---

1. When Adam was evicted from the Garden of Eden, God cursed him with a life of toil and labor (Genesis 3.17–19).

2. The two women in the poem are modeled on Maud Gonne and her sister, Kathleen Pilcher (1868–1919).

No Second Troy

Why should I blame her[1] that she filled my days
With misery, or that she would of late
Have taught to ignorant men most violent ways,
Or hurled the little streets upon the great,
5   Had they but courage equal to desire?
What could have made her peaceful with a mind
That nobleness made simple as a fire,
With beauty like a tightened bow, a kind
That is not natural in an age like this,
10   Being high and solitary and most stern?
Why, what could she have done, being what she is?
Was there another Troy for her to burn?[2]

Dec. 1908   1910

The Fascination of What's Difficult[1]

The fascination of what's difficult
Has dried the sap out of my veins, and rent
Spontaneous joy and natural content
Out of my heart. There's something ails our colt[2]
5   That must, as if it had not holy blood
Nor on Olympus[3] leaped from cloud to cloud,
Shiver under the lash, strain, sweat and jolt
As though it dragged road metal. My curse on plays
That have to be set up in fifty ways,
10   On the day's war with every knave and dolt,
Theatre business, management of men.
I swear before the dawn comes round again
I'll find the stable and pull out the bolt.

Sept. 1909–Mar. 1910   1910

A Coat

I made my song a coat
Covered with embroideries
Out of old mythologies
From heel to throat;
5   But the fools caught it,

---

1. Maud Gonne, whose revolutionary activities are at issue in the poem.
2. Helen of Troy was the legendary cause of the Trojan War and thus of Troy's destruction.
1. Written when Yeats was director-manager of the Abbey Theatre. "Subject. To complain of the fascination of what's difficult. It spoils spontane-

ity and pleasure, and wastes time. Repeat the line ending difficult three times and rhyme on bolt, exalt, colt, jolt" [Yeats's diary for September 1909].
2. Pegasus, in Greek mythology a winged horse associated with poetry.
3. A mountain in Greece; the home of the gods.

Wore it in the world's eyes
As though they'd wrought it.
Song, let them take it,
For there's more enterprise
10   In walking naked.

1912   1914

September 1913

What need you,[1] being come to sense,
But fumble in a greasy till°   cash register
And add the halfpence to the pence
And prayer to shivering prayer, until
5   You have dried the marrow from the bone;
For men were born to pray and save:
Romantic Ireland's dead and gone,
It's with O'Leary[2] in the grave.

Yet they were of a different kind,
10   The names that stilled your childish play,
They have gone about the world like wind,
But little time had they to pray
For whom the hangman's rope was spun,
And what, God help us, could they save?
15   Romantic Ireland's dead and gone,
It's with O'Leary in the grave.

Was it for this the wild geese[3] spread
The grey wing upon every tide,
For this that all that blood was shed,
20   For this Edward Fitzgerald died,
And Robert Emmet and Wolfe Tone,[4]
All that delirium of the brave?
Romantic Ireland's dead and gone,
It's with O'Leary in the grave.

25   Yet could we turn the years again,
And call those exiles as they were
In all their loneliness and pain,
You'd cry, "Some woman's yellow hair

1. Members of the new, largely Roman Catholic middle class. When the art dealer Hugh Lane (d. 1915) offered to give his collection of French impressionist paintings to the city of Dublin, provided they were permanently housed in a suitable gallery, Yeats became angry over fierce public opposition to funding the project.
2. John O'Leary (1830–1907), Irish nationalist, who, after five years' imprisonment and fifteen years' exile, returned to Dublin in 1885; he rallied the young Yeats to the cause of literary nationalism.
3. Popular name for the Irish who, because of the penal laws against Catholics (1695–1727), were forced to flee to the Continent.
4. Theobald Wolfe Tone (1763–1798), one of the chief founders of the United Irishmen (an Irish nationalist organization) and leader of the 1798 Irish Rising, committed suicide in prison. Lord Edward Fitzgerald (1763–1798), British officer who, after being dismissed from the army for disloyal activities, joined the United Irishmen, helped lead the 1798 Irish Rising, and died in prison. Robert Emmet (1778–1803), a leader of the abortive 1803 Irish Nationalist Revolt, was hanged for treason.

Has maddened every mother's son":
30   They weighed so lightly what they gave.
But let them be, they're dead and gone,
They're with O'Leary in the grave.

Sept. 1913   1913

Easter, 1916[1]

I have met them at close of day
Coming with vivid faces
From counter or desk among grey
Eighteenth-century houses.
5   I have passed with a nod of the head
Or polite meaningless words,
Or have lingered awhile and said
Polite meaningless words,
And thought before I had done
10 Of a mocking tale or a gibe
To please a companion
Around the fire at the club,
Being certain that they and I
But lived where motley[2] is worn:
15 All changed, changed utterly:
A terrible beauty is born.

That woman's days were spent
In ignorant good-will,
Her nights in argument
20 Until her voice grew shrill.
What voice more sweet than hers
When, young and beautiful,
She rode to harriers?[3]
This man had kept a school
25 And rode our wingèd horse;[4]
This other his helper and friend[5]
Was coming into his force;
He might have won fame in the end,
So sensitive his nature seemed,
30 So daring and sweet his thought.
This other man I had dreamed
A drunken, vainglorious lout.[6]
He had done most bitter wrong

1. During the Easter Rising of 1916, Irish nationalists revolted against the British government and proclaimed an Irish Republic. Nearly sixteen hundred Irish Volunteers and two hundred members of the Citizen Army seized buildings and a park in Dublin. The rebellion began on Easter Monday, April 24, 1916, and was crushed in six days. Over the next two weeks fifteen of the leaders were executed by firing squad. Yeats knew the chief nationalist leaders personally.
2. The multicolored clothes of a jester.
3. Constance Gore-Booth (1868–1927), afterward Countess Markievicz, took a prominent role in the uprising. Her death sentence was reduced to imprisonment. The other rebel leaders to whom Yeats refers were executed.
4. Padraic Pearse (1879–1916), founder of a boys' school in Dublin and poet—hence the "winged horse," or Pegasus, the horse of the Muses.
5. Thomas MacDonagh (1878–1916), poet and dramatist.
6. Major John MacBride (1865–1916), Irish revolutionary and estranged husband of Maud Gonne.

To some who are near my heart,
35 Yet I number him in the song;
He, too, has resigned his part
In the casual comedy;
He, too, has been changed in his turn,
Transformed utterly:
40 A terrible beauty is born.

Hearts with one purpose alone
Through summer and winter seem
Enchanted to a stone
To trouble the living stream.
45 The horse that comes from the road,
The rider, the birds that range
From cloud to tumbling cloud,
Minute by minute they change;
A shadow of cloud on the stream
50 Changes minute by minute;
A horse-hoof slides on the brim,
And a horse plashes within it;
The long-legged moor-hens dive,
And hens to moor-cocks call;
55 Minute by minute they live:
The stone's in the midst of all.

Too long a sacrifice
Can make a stone of the heart.
O when may it suffice?
60 That is Heaven's part, our part
To murmur name upon name,
As a mother names her child
When sleep at last has come
On limbs that had run wild.
65 What is it but nightfall?
No, no, not night but death;
Was it needless death after all?
For England may keep faith
For all that is done and said.[7]
70 We know their dream; enough
To know they dreamed and are dead;
And what if excess of love
Bewildered them till they died?
I write it out in a verse—
75 MacDonagh and MacBride
And Connolly[8] and Pearse
Now and in time to be,
Wherever green is worn,
Are changed, changed utterly:
80 A terrible beauty is born.

May–Sept. 1916   1916, 1920

7. In 1914 the English government had passed Home Rule for Ireland into law, but because of World War I had suspended it, promising to implement it later.
8. James Connolly (1870–1916), a trade-union organizer and military commander of the rebellion.

The Wild Swans at Coole[1]

The trees are in their autumn beauty,
The woodland paths are dry,
Under the October twilight the water
Mirrors a still sky;
5   Upon the brimming water among the stones
Are nine-and-fifty swans.

The nineteenth autumn has come upon me
Since I first made my count[2]
I saw, before I had well finished,
10   All suddenly mount
And scatter wheeling in great broken rings
Upon their clamorous wings.

I have looked upon those brilliant creatures,
And now my heart is sore.
15   All's changed since I, hearing at twilight,
The first time on this shore,
The bell-beat of their wings above my head,
Trod with a lighter tread.

Unwearied still, lover by lover,
20   They paddle in the cold
Companionable streams or climb the air;
Their hearts have not grown old;
Passion or conquest, wander where they will,
Attend upon them still.

25   But now they drift on the still water,
Mysterious, beautiful;
Among what rushes will they build,
By what lake's edge or pool
Delight men's eyes when I awake some day
30   To find they have flown away?

Oct. 1916   1917

In Memory of Major Robert Gregory[1]

I

Now that we're almost settled in our house
I'll name the friends that cannot sup with us
Beside a fire of turf° in th' ancient tower,[2]   *peat*

1. Coole Park, in County Galway, was the estate of the Irish playwright Lady Augusta Gregory (1852–1932).
2. Yeats made his first long visit to Coole in 1897; from then on he spent summers there, often staying into the fall.
1. Robert Gregory (1881–1918) was the only child

of Lady Augusta Gregory. The first printing of this elegy included the following note: "(Major Robert Gregory, R.F.C. [Royal Flying Corps], M.C. [Military Cross], Legion of Honour, was killed in action on the Italian Front, January 23, 1918)."
2. In 1917 Yeats purchased the Norman tower Thoor Ballylee, near Lady Gregory's home in

And having talked to some late hour
5 Climb up the narrow winding stair to bed:
Discoverers of forgotten truth
Or mere companions of my youth,
All, all are in my thoughts to-night being dead.

2

Always we'd have the new friend meet the old
10 And we are hurt if either friend seem cold,
And there is salt to lengthen out the smart
In the affections of our heart,
And quarrels are blown up upon that head;
But not a friend that I would bring
15 This night can set us quarrelling,
For all that come into my mind are dead.

3

Lionel Johnson[3] comes the first to mind,
That loved his learning better than mankind,
Though courteous to the worst; much falling he
20 Brooded upon sanctity
Till all his Greek and Latin learning seemed
A long blast upon the horn that brought
A little nearer to his thought
A measureless consummation that he dreamed.

4

25 And that enquiring man John Synge[4] comes next,
That dying chose the living world for text
And never could have rested in the tomb
But that, long travelling, he had come
Towards nightfall upon certain set apart
30 In a most desolate stony place,
Towards nightfall upon a race
Passionate and simple like his heart.

5

And then I think of old George Pollexfen,[5]
In muscular youth well known to Mayo[6] men
35 For horsemanship at meets or at racecourses,
That could have shown how pure-bred horses
And solid men, for all their passion, live
But as the outrageous stars incline
By opposition, square and trine;[7]
40 Having grown sluggish and contemplative.

Coole Park. While that residence was being reno-
vated, Yeats and his wife were living in a house
that Lady Gregory had lent them.
3. English poet and scholar (1867–1902); he was
"much falling" (line 19) because of his drinking.
4. Irish playwright (1871–1909), associated with
the Irish literary renaissance and the Abbey
Theatre. When Yeats first met Synge, in 1896, he
encouraged him to travel to the Aran Islands ("a
most desolate and stony place") and write about
its rural residents.
5. Yeats's maternal uncle (1839–1910), with whom
he had spent holidays in Sligo as a young man.
6. County in western Ireland.
7. Terms from astrology, in which both Yeats
and his uncle were interested.

6

They were my close companions many a year,
A portion of my mind and life, as it were,
And now their breathless faces seem to look
Out of some old picture-book;
45   I am accustomed to their lack of breath,
But not that my dear friend's dear son,
Our Sidney[8] and our perfect man,
Could share in that discourtesy of death.

7

For all things the delighted eye now sees
50   Were loved by him:[9] the old storm-broken trees
That cast their shadows upon road and bridge;
The tower set on the stream's edge;
The ford where drinking cattle make a stir
Nightly, and startled by that sound
55   The water-hen must change her ground;
He might have been your heartiest welcomer.

8

When with the Galway foxhounds he would ride
From Castle Taylor to the Roxborough side[1]
Or Esserkelly plain, few kept his pace;
60   At Mooneen he had leaped a place
So perilous that half the astonished meet
Had shut their eyes; and where was it
He rode a race without a bit?
And yet his mind outran the horses' feet.

9

65   We dreamed that a great painter had been born[2]
To cold Clare[3] rock and Galway rock and thorn,
To that stern colour and that delicate line
That are our secret discipline
Wherein the gazing heart doubles her might.
70   Soldier, scholar, horseman, he,
And yet he had the intensity
To have published all to be a world's delight.

10

What other could so well have counselled us
In all lovely intricacies of a house
75   As he that practised or that understood
All work in metal or in wood,

8. Sir Philip Sidney (1554–1586), English poet and exemplar of the "Renaissance man"; like Gregory, he was killed in battle.
9. Robert Gregory encouraged Yeats to buy the tower.
1. Big country houses in County Galway. Roxborough was Lady Gregory's childhood home.
2. "Robert Gregory painted the Burren Hills and thereby found what promised to grow into a great style, but he had hardly found it before he was killed" (Yeats, "Ireland and the Arts").
3. County south of Galway.

In moulded plaster or in carven stone?
Soldier, scholar, horseman, he,
And all he did done perfectly
80 As though he had but that one trade alone.

11

Some burn damp faggots,[4] others may consume
The entire combustible world in one small room
As though dried straw, and if we turn about
The bare chimney is gone black out
85 Because the work had finished in that flare.
Soldier, scholar, horseman, he,
As 'twere all life's epitome,
What made us dream that he could comb grey hair?

12

I had thought, seeing how bitter is that wind
90 That shakes the shutter, to have brought to mind
All those that manhood tried, or childhood loved
Or boyish intellect approved,
With some appropriate commentary on each;
Until imagination brought
95 A fitter welcome; but a thought
Of that late death took all my heart for speech.

June 1918   1918

An Irish Airman Foresees His Death[1]

I know that I shall meet my fate
Somewhere among the clouds above;
Those that I fight I do not hate,
Those that I guard I do not love;
5 My country is Kiltartan Cross,[2]
My countrymen Kiltartan's poor,
No likely end could bring them loss
Or leave them happier than before.
Nor law, nor duty bade me fight,
10 Nor public men, nor cheering crowds,
A lonely impulse of delight
Drove to this tumult in the clouds;
I balanced all, brought all to mind,
The years to come seemed waste of breath,
15 A waste of breath the years behind
In balance with this life, this death.

1919   1920

---

4. Bundles of sticks.
1. Robert Gregory (1881–1918), the only child of Yeats's close friend and patroness Augusta, Lady Gregory, was killed on the Italian front as a member of the British Royal Flying Corps.
2. Crossroads village in County Galway, near Coole Park.

The Second Coming

Turning and turning in the widening gyre[1]
The falcon cannot hear the falconer;
Things fall apart; the centre cannot hold;
Mere anarchy is loosed upon the world,
5   The blood-dimmed tide is loosed, and everywhere
The ceremony of innocence is drowned;
The best lack all conviction, while the worst
Are full of passionate intensity.[2]

Surely some revelation is at hand;
10 Surely the Second Coming is at hand.
The Second Coming![3] Hardly are those words out
When a vast image out of *Spiritus Mundi*[4]
Troubles my sight: somewhere in sands of the desert
A shape with lion body and the head of a man,
15 A gaze blank and pitiless as the sun,
Is moving its slow thighs, while all about it
Reel shadows of the indignant desert birds.
The darkness drops again; but now I know
That twenty centuries of stony sleep
20 Were vexed to nightmare by a rocking cradle,
And what rough beast, its hour come round at last,
Slouches towards Bethlehem[5] to be born?

Jan. 1919   1920, 1921

A Prayer for My Daughter

Once more the storm is howling, and half hid
Under this cradle-hood and coverlid
My child sleeps on.[1] There is no obstacle
But Gregory's wood[2] and one bare hill
5   Whereby the haystack- and roof-levelling wind,
Bred on the Atlantic, can be stayed;
And for an hour I have walked and prayed
Because of the great gloom that is in my mind.

I have walked and prayed for this young child an hour
10 And heard the sea-wind scream upon the tower,

1. Yeats's term (pronounced with a hard g) for a spiraling motion in the shape of a cone. He envisions the two-thousand-year cycle of the Christian age as spiraling toward its end and the next historical cycle as beginning after a violent reversal: "the end of an age, which always receives the revelation of the character of the next age, is represented by the coming of one gyre to its place of greatest expansion and of the other to that of its greatest contraction" [Yeats's note].
2. The poem was written in January 1919, in the aftermath of World War I and the Russian Revolution and on the eve of the Anglo-Irish War.
3. Christ's second coming is heralded by the com-

ing of the Beast of the Apocalypse, or Antichrist (1 John 2.18).
4. World spirit, or universal spirit (Latin); i.e., Yeats said, "a general storehouse of images," a collective unconscious or memory, in which the human race preserves its past memories.
5. Jesus's birthplace.
1. Yeats's daughter and first child, Anne Butler Yeats, was born on February 26, 1919, in Dublin and brought home to Yeats's refitted Norman tower of Thoor Ballylee in Galway.
2. Lady Gregory's wood at Coole, only a few miles from Thoor Ballylee.

And under the arches of the bridge, and scream
In the elms above the flooded stream;
Imagining in excited reverie
That the future years had come,
15 Dancing to a frenzied drum,
Out of the murderous innocence of the sea.

May she be granted beauty and yet not
Beauty to make a stranger's eye distraught,
Or hers before a looking-glass, for such,
20 Being made beautiful overmuch,
Consider beauty a sufficient end,
Lose natural kindness and maybe
The heart-revealing intimacy
That chooses right, and never find a friend.

25 Helen being chosen found life flat and dull
And later had much trouble from a fool[3]
While that great Queen, that rose out of the spray,[4]
Being fatherless could have her way
Yet chose a bandy-leggèd smith for man.
30 It's certain that fine women eat
A crazy salad with their meat
Whereby the Horn of Plenty[5] is undone.

In courtesy I'd have her chiefly learned;
Hearts are not had as a gift but hearts are earned
35 By those that are not entirely beautiful;
Yet many, that have played the fool
For beauty's very self, has charm made wise,
And many a poor man that has roved,
Loved and thought himself beloved,
40 From a glad kindness cannot take his eyes.

May she become a flourishing hidden tree
That all her thoughts may like the linnet° be,   *small songbird*
And have no business but dispensing round
Their magnanimities of sound,
45 Not but in merriment begin a chase,
Nor but in merriment a quarrel.
O may she live like some green laurel
Rooted in one dear perpetual place.

My mind, because the minds that I have loved,
50 The sort of beauty that I have approved,
Prosper but little, has dried up of late,
Yet knows that to be choked with hate
May well be of all evil chances chief.
If there's no hatred in a mind
55 Assault and battery of the wind
Can never tear the linnet from the leaf.

---

3. Menelaus, Helen's husband. Her abduction by
Paris precipitated the Trojan War.
4. Venus, born from the sea, was the Roman goddess of love; her husband, Vulcan, was the lame

god of fire and metalwork (line 29).
5. In Greek mythology, the goat's horn that suck-
led the god Zeus flowed with nectar and ambrosia;
the cornucopia thus became a symbol of plenty.

An intellectual hatred is the worst,
So let her think opinions are accursed.
Have I not seen the loveliest woman[6] born
60 Out of the mouth of Plenty's horn,
Because of her opinionated mind
Barter that horn and every good
By quiet natures understood
For an old bellows full of angry wind?

65 Considering that, all hatred driven hence,
The soul recovers radical innocence
And learns at last that it is self-delighting,
Self-appeasing, self-affrighting,
And that its own sweet will is Heaven's will;
70 She can, though every face should scowl
And every windy quarter howl
Or every bellows burst, be happy still.

And may her bridegroom bring her to a house
Where all's accustomed, ceremonious;
75 For arrogance and hatred are the wares
Peddled in the thoroughfares.
How but in custom and in ceremony
Are innocence and beauty born?
Ceremony's a name for the rich horn,
80 And custom for the spreading laurel tree.

Feb.–June 1919   1919, 1921

Leda and the Swan[1]

A sudden blow: the great wings beating still
Above the staggering girl, her thighs caressed
By the dark webs, her nape caught in his bill,
He holds her helpless breast upon his breast.

5 How can those terrified vague fingers push
The feathered glory from her loosening thighs?
And how can body, laid in that white rush,
But feel the strange heart beating where it lies?

A shudder in the loins engenders there
10 The broken wall, the burning roof and tower[2]
And Agamemnon dead.
                        Being so caught up,

6. Maud Gonne.
1. In Greek mythology the god Zeus, in the form of a swan, raped Leda, a mortal. Helen, Clytemnestra, Castor, and Pollux were the children of this union. Yeats saw Leda's rape as the beginning of a new age, analogous with the dove's annunciation to Mary of Jesus's conception: "I imagine the annunciation that founded Greece as made to Leda, remembering that they showed in a Spartan temple, strung up to the roof as a holy relic, an unhatched egg of hers, and that from one of her eggs came love and from the other war" (A Vision). For the author's revisions while composing the poem, go to the NAEL Archive.
2. I.e., the destruction of Troy, caused by Helen's abduction by Paris. Agamemnon, the leader of the Greek army that besieged Troy, was murdered by his wife, Clytemnestra, the other daughter of Leda and the swan.

So mastered by the brute blood of the air,
Did she put on his knowledge with his power
Before the indifferent beak could let her drop?

Sept. 1923   1924, 1928

Sailing to Byzantium[1]

I

That is no country for old men. The young
In one another's arms, birds in the trees,
—Those dying generations—at their song,
The salmon-falls, the mackerel-crowded seas,
Fish, flesh, or fowl, commend all summer long
Whatever is begotten, born, and dies.
Caught in that sensual music all neglect
Monuments of unageing intellect.

2

An aged man is but a paltry thing,
A tattered coat upon a stick, unless
Soul clap its hands and sing,[2] and louder sing
For every tatter in its mortal dress,
Nor is there singing school but studying
Monuments of its own magnificence;
And therefore I have sailed the seas and come
To the holy city of Byzantium.

3

O sages standing in God's holy fire
As in the gold mosaic of a wall,[3]
Come from the holy fire, perne in a gyre,[4]
And be the singing-masters of my soul.
Consume my heart away; sick with desire
And fastened to a dying animal
It knows not what it is; and gather me
Into the artifice of eternity.

4

Once out of nature I shall never take
My bodily form from any natural thing,
But such a form as Grecian goldsmiths make

---

1. Yeats wrote in *A Vision*: "I think that if I could be given a month of Antiquity and leave to spend it where I chose, I would spend it in Byzantium [now Istanbul] a little before Justinian opened St. Sophia and closed the Academy of Plato [in the 6th century C.E.]. . . . I think that in early Byzantium, maybe never before or since in recorded history, religious, aesthetic and practical life were one, that architect and artificers . . . spoke to the multitude and the few alike. The painter, the mosaic worker, the worker in gold and silver, the illuminator of sacred books, were almost impersonal, almost perhaps without the consciousness of individual design, absorbed in their subject-matter and that the vision of a whole people."
2. The poet William Blake (1757–1827) saw the soul of his dead brother rising to heaven, "clapping his hands for joy."
3. The mosaics in San Apollinaire Nuovo, in Ravenna, Italy, depict rows of Christian saints on a gold background; Yeats saw them in 1907.
4. I.e., whirl in a spiral.

Of hammered gold and gold enamelling
To keep a drowsy Emperor awake;[5]
30 Or set upon a golden bough to sing
To lords and ladies of Byzantium
Of what is past, or passing, or to come.

Sept. 1926   1927

Among School Children

1

I walk through the long schoolroom questioning;
A kind old nun in a white hood replies;
The children learn to cipher° and to sing,   *do arithmetic*
To study reading-books and history,
5 To cut and sew, be neat in everything
In the best modern way—the children's eyes
In momentary wonder stare upon
A sixty-year-old smiling public man.[1]

2

I dream of a Ledaean[2] body, bent
10 Above a sinking fire, a tale that she
Told of a harsh reproof, or trivial event
That changed some childish day to tragedy—
Told, and it seemed that our two natures blent
Into a sphere from youthful sympathy,
15 Or else, to alter Plato's parable,
Into the yolk and white of the one shell.[3]

3

And thinking of that fit of grief or rage
I look upon one child or t'other there
And wonder if she stood so at that age—
20 For even daughters of the swan can share
Something of every paddler's heritage—
And had that colour upon cheek or hair,
And thereupon my heart is driven wild:
She stands before me as a living child.

4

25 Her present image floats into the mind—
Did Quattrocento finger[4] fashion it
Hollow of cheek as though it drank the wind
And took a mess of shadows for its meat?

---

5. I have read somewhere that in the Emperor's palace at Byzantium was a tree made of gold and silver, and artificial birds that sang [Yeats's note].
1. Yeats, as part of his work in the Irish Senate, visited a Montessori school in Waterford in 1926.
2. A body like Leda's. Yeats associated her daughter, Helen of Troy, with Maud Gonne.
3. In the *Symposium*, by the Greek philosopher Plato (ca. 428–ca. 348 B.C.E.), Aristophanes argues that "the primeval man" was both male and female but was divided (like an egg separated into yoke and white); the resulting two beings come together in love to become one again.
4. I.e., the skill of a 15th-century Italian painter.

And I though never of Ledaean kind
30   Had pretty plumage once—enough of that,
Better to smile on all that smile, and show
There is a comfortable kind of old scarecrow.

5

What youthful mother, a shape upon her lap
Honey of generation had betrayed,
35   And that must sleep, shriek, struggle to escape
As recollection or the drug decide,[5]
Would think her son, did she but see that shape
With sixty or more winters on its head,
A compensation for the pang of his birth,
40   Or the uncertainty of his setting forth?

6

Plato thought nature but a spume that plays
Upon a ghostly paradigm of things;[6]
Solider Aristotle played the taws
Upon the bottom of a king of kings;[7]
45   World-famous golden-thighed Pythagoras[8]
Fingered upon a fiddle-stick or strings
What a star sang and careless Muses heard:
Old clothes upon old sticks to scare a bird.

7

Both nuns and mothers worship images,
50   But those the candles light are not as those
That animate a mother's reveries,
But keep a marble or a bronze repose.
And yet they too break hearts—O Presences
That passion, piety or affection knows,
55   And that all heavenly glory symbolise—
O self-born mockers of man's enterprise;

8

Labour is blossoming or dancing where
The body is not bruised to pleasure soul,
Nor beauty born out of its own despair,
60   Nor blear-eyed wisdom out of midnight oil.
O chestnut tree, great-rooted blossomer,
Are you the leaf, the blossom or the bole?°   *trunk*
O body swayed to music, O brightening glance,
How can we know the dancer from the dance?

June 1926   1927

5. I have taken the "honey of generation" from
Porphyry's essay on "The Cave of Nymphs"
[Yeats's note]. Porphyry (ca. 234–ca. 305 C.E.)
was a Neo-platonic philosopher.
6. As he explained in the famed "Allegory of the
Cave" in his *Republic,* Plato thought nature merely
an image of an ideal world that exists elsewhere.
7. Plato's student Aristotle (384–322 B.C.E.) was
"solider" because he regarded this world as the
authentic one. He tutored Alexander the Great
(356–323 B.C.E.), the "king of kings," and disciplined him with the "taws," or leather strap.
8. Greek philosopher (ca. 580–500 B.C.E.), known
for his doctrine of the harmony of the spheres and
his discovery of the mathematical basis of musical
intervals. His disciples, the Pythagoreans, venerated their master as a god with a golden thigh.

A Dialogue of Self and Soul[1]

I

My Soul. I summon to the winding ancient stair;
    Set all your mind upon the steep ascent,
    Upon the broken, crumbling battlement,
    Upon the breathless starlit air,
5   Upon the star that marks the hidden pole;
    Fix every wandering thought upon
    That quarter where all thought is done:
    Who can distinguish darkness from the soul?

My Self. The consecrated blade upon my knees
10   Is Sato's ancient blade, still as it was,
    Still razor-keen, still like a looking-glass
    Unspotted by the centuries;
    That flowering, silken, old embroidery, torn
    From some court-lady's dress and round
15   The wooden scabbard bound and wound,
    Can, tattered, still protect, faded adorn.

My Soul. Why should the imagination of a man
    Long past his prime remember things that are
    Emblematical of love and war?
20   Think of ancestral night that can,
    If but imagination scorn the earth
    And intellect its wandering
    To this and that and t'other thing,
    Deliver from the crime of death and birth.

25 *My Self.* Montashigi, third of his family, fashioned it
    Five hundred years ago, about it lie
    Flowers from I know not what embroidery—
    Heart's purple—and all these I set
    For emblems of the day against the tower
30   Emblematical of the night,
    And claim as by a soldier's right
    A charter to commit the crime once more.

My Soul. Such fullness in that quarter overflows
    And falls into the basin of the mind
35   That man is stricken deaf and dumb and blind,
    For intellect no longer knows
    Is from the *Ought*, or *Knower* from the *Known*—
    That is to say, ascends to Heaven;
    Only the dead can be forgiven;
40   But when I think of that my tongue's a stone.

1. In a letter of October 2, 1923, Yeats wrote: "I am writing a new tower poem 'Sword and Tower,' which is a choice of rebirth rather than deliverance from birth. I make my Japanese sword and its silk covering my symbol of life." Junzo Sato, a friend, had given him the ceremonial sword in 1920.

2

My Self. A living man is blind and drinks his drop.
What matter if the ditches are impure?
What matter if I live it all once more?
Endure that toil of growing up;
45 The ignominy of boyhood; the distress
Of boyhood changing into man;
The unfinished man and his pain
Brought face to face with his own clumsiness;

The finished man among his enemies?—
50 How in the name of Heaven can he escape
That defiling and disfigured shape
The mirror of malicious eyes
Casts upon his eyes until at last
He thinks that shape must be his shape?
55 And what's the good of an escape
If honour find him in the wintry blast?

I am content to live it all again
And yet again, if it be life to pitch
Into the frog-spawn of a blind man's ditch,
60 A blind man battering blind men;
Or into that most fecund ditch of all,
The folly that man does
Or must suffer, if he woos
A proud woman not kindred of his soul.

65 I am content to follow to its source
Every event in action or in thought;
Measure the lot; forgive myself the lot!
When such as I cast out remorse
So great a sweetness flows into the breast
70 We must laugh and we must sing,
We are blest by everything,
Everything we look upon is blest.

July–Dec. 1927   1929

Byzantium[1]

The unpurged images of day recede;
The Emperor's drunken soldiery are abed;
Night resonance recedes, night-walkers' song
After great cathedral gong;
5 A starlit or a moonlit dome[2] disdains

1. On October 4, 1930, Yeats sent his friend Sturge Moore a copy of this poem, saying: "The poem originates from a criticism of yours. You objected to the last verse of 'Sailing to Byzantium' because a bird made by a goldsmith was just as natural as anything else. That showed me that the idea needed exposition." The previous April, Yeats had noted in his diary: "Subject for a poem": "Describe Byzantium as it is in the system towards the end of the first Christian millennium. A walking mummy. Flames at the street corners where the soul is purified, birds of hammered gold singing in the golden trees, in the harbour [dolphins] offering their backs to the wailing dead that they may carry them to Paradise." 2. Of the great church of St. Sophia.

All that man is,
All mere complexities,
The fury and the mire° of human veins.   *deep mud*

Before me floats an image, man or shade,
10   Shade more than man, more image than a shade;
For Hades' bobbin[3] bound in mummy-cloth
May unwind the winding path;[4]
A mouth that has no moisture and no breath
Breathless mouths may summon;
15   I hail the superhuman;
I call it death-in-life and life-in-death.[5]

Miracle, bird or golden handiwork,
More miracle than bird or handiwork,
Planted on the starlit golden bough,
20   Can like the cocks of Hades crow,
Or, by the moon embittered, scorn aloud
In glory of changeless metal
Common bird or petal
And all complexities of mire or blood.

25   At midnight on the Emperor's pavement flit
Flames that no faggot° feeds, nor steel has lit,   *bundle of sticks*
Nor storm disturbs, flames begotten of flame,
Where blood-begotten spirits come
And all complexities of fury leave,
30   Dying into a dance,
An agony of trance,
An agony of flame that cannot singe a sleeve.

Astraddle on the dolphin's mire and blood,[6]
Spirit after spirit! The smithies break the flood,
35   The golden smithies of the Emperor!
Marbles of the dancing floor
Break bitter furies of complexity,
Those images that yet
Fresh images beget,
40   That dolphin-torn, that gong-tormented sea.

Sept. 1930   1932

Crazy Jane Talks with the Bishop[1]

I met the Bishop on the road
And much said he and I.
"Those breasts are flat and fallen now
Those veins must soon be dry;

---

3. Spool. Hades was the Greek god of the underworld, the realm of the dead.
4. I.e., the spool of people's fate, which spins their
destiny and which is wound like a mummy, may be
unwound and lead to the timeless world of pure
spirit.
5. On Roman tombstones the cock is a herald of

rebirth, thus of the continuing cycle of human life.
6. In ancient mythology dolphins were thought to
carry the souls of the dead to the Isles of the
Blessed.
1. One of a series of poems about an old woman
partly modeled on Cracked Mary, an old woman
who lived near Lady Gregory.

5   Live in a heavenly mansion,
       Not in some foul sty."

       "Fair and foul are near of kin,
       And fair needs foul," I cried.
       "My friends are gone, but that's a truth
10   Nor grave nor bed denied,
       Learned in bodily lowliness
       And in the heart's pride.

       "A woman can be proud and stiff
       When on love intent;
15   But Love has pitched his mansion in
       The place of excrement;
       For nothing can be sole or whole
       That has not been rent."

Nov. 1931   1932

Lapis Lazuli

(For Harry Clifton)[1]

I have heard that hysterical women say
They are sick of the palette and fiddle-bow,
Of poets that are always gay,
For everybody knows or else should know
5   That if nothing drastic is done[2]
Aeroplane and Zeppelin[3] will come out,
Pitch like King Billy[4] bomb-balls in
Until the town lie beaten flat.

All perform their tragic play,
10   There struts Hamlet, there is Lear,
That's Ophelia, that Cordelia;
Yet they, should the last scene be there,
The great stage curtain about to drop,
If worthy their prominent part in the play,
15   Do not break up their lines to weep.
They know that Hamlet and Lear are gay;
Gaiety transfiguring all that dread.
All men have aimed at, found and lost;
Black out; Heaven blazing into the head:
20   Tragedy wrought to its uttermost.
Though Hamlet rambles and Lear rages,
And all the drop scenes drop at once
Upon a hundred thousand stages,
It cannot grow by an inch or an ounce.

1. The English writer Harry Clifton (1908–1978) gave Yeats for his seventieth birthday a piece of lapis lazuli, a deep blue stone, "carved by some Chinese sculptor into the semblance of a mountain with temple, trees, paths, and an ascetic and pupil about to climb the mountain. Ascetic, pupil, hard stone, eternal theme of the sensual east. The heroic cry in the midst of despair. But no, I am wrong, the east has its solutions always and therefore knows nothing of tragedy. It is we, not the east, that must raise the heroic cry" [Yeats to Dorothy Wellesley, July 6, 1935].
2. Because Europe was (in 1936) close to war.
3. German zeppelins, or airships, bombed London during World War I.
4. King William III (William of Orange), who defeated the army of King James II at the Battle of the Boyne, in Ireland, in 1690. In a popular ballad, "King William he threw his bomb-balls in, / And set them on fire."

25 On their own feet they came, or on shipboard,
Camel-back, horse-back, ass-back, mule-back,
Old civilisations put to the sword.
Then they and their wisdom went to rack:
No handiwork of Callimachus[5]
30 Who handled marble as if it were bronze,
Made draperies that seemed to rise
When sea-wind swept the corner, stands;
His long lamp chimney shaped like the stem
Of a slender palm, stood but a day;
35 All things fall and are built again
And those that build them again are gay.

Two Chinamen, behind them a third,
Are carved in Lapis Lazuli,
Over them flies a long-legged bird
40 A symbol of longevity;
The third, doubtless a serving-man,
Carries a musical instrument.

Every discolouration of the stone,
Every accidental crack or dent
45 Seems a water-course or an avalanche,
Or lofty slope where it still snows
Though doubtless plum or cherry-branch
Sweetens the little half-way house
Those Chinamen climb towards, and I
50 Delight to imagine them seated there;
There, on the mountain and the sky,
On all the tragic scene they stare.
One asks for mournful melodies;
Accomplished fingers begin to play.
55 Their eyes mid many wrinkles, their eyes,
Their ancient, glittering eyes, are gay.

July 1936   1938

Under Ben Bulben[1]

1

Swear by what the Sages spoke
Round the Mareotic Lake[2]
That the Witch of Atlas knew,
Spoke and set the cocks a-crow.

---

5. Athenian sculptor (5th century B.C.E.), supposedly the originator of the Corinthian column and of the use of the running drill to imitate folds in drapery in statues. Yeats wrote of him: "With Callimachus pure Ionic revives again . . . and upon the only example of his work known to us, a marble chair, a Persian is represented, and may one not discover a Persian symbol in that bronze lamp, shaped like a palm . . . ? But he was an archaistic workman, and those who set him to work brought back public life to an older form" (*A Vision*).
1. A mountain near Sligo; Yeats's grave is in sight of it, in Drumcliff churchyard.

2. Lake Mareotis, near Alexandria, Egypt, was an ancient center of Christian Neoplatonism and of neo-Pythagorean philosophy. The lake is mentioned in Percy Bysshe Shelley's poem "The Witch of Atlas." In an essay on Shelley, Yeats interprets the witch as a symbol of timeless, absolute beauty; passing in a boat by this and another lake, she "sees all human life shadowed upon its waters . . . and because she can see the reality of things she is described as journeying 'in the calm depths' of 'the wide lake' we journey over unpiloted."

5   Swear by those horsemen, by those women,
   Complexion and form prove superhuman,[3]
   That pale, long visaged company
   That airs an immortality
   Completeness of their passions won;
10   Now they ride the wintry dawn
   Where Ben Bulben sets the scene.

   Here's the gist of what they mean.

2

   Many times man lives and dies
   Between his two eternities,
15   That of race and that of soul,
   And ancient Ireland knew it all.
   Whether man dies in his bed
   Or the rifle knocks him dead,
   A brief parting from those dear
20   Is the worst man has to fear.
   Though grave-diggers' toil is long,
   Sharp their spades, their muscle strong,
   They but thrust their buried men
   Back in the human mind again.

3

25   You that Mitchel's prayer have heard
   "Send war in our time, O Lord!"[4]
   Know that when all words are said
   And a man is fighting mad,
   Something drops from eyes long blind
30   He completes his partial mind,
   For an instant stands at ease,
   Laughs aloud, his heart at peace,
   Even the wisest man grows tense
   With some sort of violence
35   Before he can accomplish fate,
   Know his work or choose his mate.

4

   Poet and sculptor do the work
   Nor let the modish painter shirk
   What his great forefathers did,
40   Bring the soul of man to God,
   Make him fill the cradles right.
   Measurement began our might:
   Forms a stark Egyptian thought,
   Forms that gentler Phidias[5] wrought.

---

3. Superhuman beings or fairies, like the Sidhe, believed to ride through the countryside near Ben Bulben.

4. From *Jail Journal*, by the Irish nationalist John Mitchel (1815–1875).

5. Greek sculptor (fl. ca. 490–430 B.C.E.).

45 Michael Angelo left a proof
On the Sistine Chapel roof,
Where but half-awakened Adam
Can disturb globe-trotting Madam
Till her bowels are in heat,
50 Proof that there's a purpose set
Before the secret working mind:
Profane perfection of mankind.

Quattrocento[6] put in paint,
On backgrounds for a God or Saint,
55 Gardens where a soul's at ease;
Where everything that meets the eye
Flowers and grass and cloudless sky
Resemble forms that are, or seem
When sleepers wake and yet still dream,
60 And when it's vanished still declare,
With only bed and bedstead there,
That Heavens had opened.

                  Gyres[7] run on;
When that greater dream had gone
Calvert and Wilson, Blake and Claude[8]
65 Prepared a rest for the people of God,
Palmer's[9] Phrase, but after that
Confusion fell upon our thought.

5

Irish poets learn your trade
Sing whatever is well made,
70 Scorn the sort now growing up
All out of shape from toe to top,
Their unremembering hearts and heads
Base-born products of base beds.
Sing the peasantry, and then
75 Hard-riding country gentlemen,
The holiness of monks, and after
Porter-drinkers'[1] randy laughter;
Sing the lords and ladies gay
That were beaten into the clay
80 Through seven heroic centuries;[2]
Cast your mind on other days
That we in coming days may be
Still the indomitable Irishry.

---

6. 15th-century Italian art.
7. Yeats's term for conelike spirals or cycles of history.
8. Edward Calvert (1799–1883), English visionary artist and follower of William Blake (1757–1827), English mystical poet and artist. Richard Wilson (1714–1782), English landscape painter and disciple of Claude Lorraine (1600–1682), French artist.
9. Samuel Palmer (1805–1881), English landscape painter who admired Blake.
1. Drinkers of dark brown bitter beer.
2. Since the Norman conquest of Ireland, in the 12th century.

6

Under bare Ben Bulben's head
85   In Drumcliff churchyard Yeats is laid,
An ancestor was rector there[3]
Long years ago; a church stands near,
By the road an ancient Cross.
No marble, no conventional phrase,
On limestone quarried near the spot
By his command these words are cut:

Cast a cold eye
On life, on death.
Horseman, pass by!

Sept. 1938   1939

Man and the Echo

Man. In a cleft that's christened Alt
        Under broken stone I halt
        At the bottom of a pit
        That broad noon has never lit,
5   And shout a secret to the stone.
        All that I have said and done,
        Now that I am old and ill,
        Turns into a question till
        I lie awake night after night
10   And never get the answers right.
        Did that play of mine[1] send out
        Certain men the English shot?
        Did words of mine put too great strain
        On that woman's reeling brain?[2]
15   Could my spoken words have checked
        That whereby a house[3] lay wrecked?
        And all seems evil until I
        Sleepless would lie down and die.

Echo. Lie down and die.

Man.   That were to shirk
20   The spiritual intellect's great work
        And shirk it in vain. There is no release
        In a bodkin[4] or disease,

3. Yeats's great-grandfather, the Reverend John Yeats (1774–1846), was rector of Drumcliff Church, Sligo.
1. *Cathleen ni Houlihan*, a nationalist play Yeats wrote with Lady Gregory and in which Maud Gonne played the title role in 1902. It helped inspire the Easter Rising of 1916.
2. Margot Ruddock (1907–1951), a young poet

with whom Yeats had a brief affair in the 1930s and to whom he offered financial support when she suffered a nervous breakdown.
3. Coole Park, Lady Gregory's home, in disrepair after her death in 1932.
4. Dagger. Cf. *Hamlet* 3.1.77–78: "When he himself might his quietus make / With a bare bodkin."

Nor can there be a work so great
As that which cleans man's dirty slate.
25 While man can still his body keep
Wine or love drug him to sleep,
Waking he thanks the Lord that he
Has body and its stupidity,
But body gone he sleeps no more
30 And till his intellect grows sure
That all's arranged in one clear view
Pursues the thoughts that I pursue,
Then stands in judgment on his soul,
And, all work done, dismisses all
35 Out of intellect and sight
And sinks at last into the night.

Echo. Into the night.

Man.   O rocky voice
Shall we in that great night rejoice?
What do we know but that we face
40 One another in this place?
But hush, for I have lost the theme
Its joy or night seem but a dream;
Up there some hawk or owl has struck
Dropping out of sky or rock,
45 A stricken rabbit is crying out
And its cry distracts my thought.

1938   1939

The Circus Animals' Desertion

1

I sought a theme and sought for it in vain,
I sought it daily for six weeks or so.
Maybe at last being but a broken man,
I must be satisfied with my heart, although
5 Winter and summer till old age began
My circus animals were all on show,
Those stilted boys, that burnished chariot,
Lion and woman and the Lord knows what.[1]

2

What can I but enumerate old themes,
10 First that sea-rider Oisin[2] led by the nose
Through three enchanted islands, allegorical dreams,

1. Yeats refers to the ancient Irish heroes of his early work ("Those stilted boys"), the gilded carriage of his play *The Unicorn from the Stars* (1908), and the lion in several of his poems, including "The Second Coming."
2. In the long title poem of Yeats's first successful book, *The Wanderings of Oisin and Other Poems* (1889), the legendary poet warrior Oisin (pronounced *Ushēēn*) is enchanted by the beautiful fairy woman Niamh (pronounced *Neeve*), who leads him to the Islands of Delight, of Many Fears, and of Forgetfulness.

Vain gaiety, vain battle, vain repose,
Themes of the embittered heart, or so it seems,
That might adorn old songs or courtly shows;
15 But what cared I that set him on to ride,
I, starved for the bosom of his fairy bride.

And then a counter-truth filled out its play,
"The Countess Cathleen"[3] was the name I gave it,
She, pity-crazed, had given her soul away,
20 But masterful Heaven had intervened to save it.
I thought my dear must her own soul destroy
So did fanaticism and hate enslave it,
And this brought forth a dream and soon enough
This dream itself had all my thought and love.

25 And when the Fool and Blind Man stole the bread
Cuchulain fought the ungovernable sea;[4]
Heart mysteries there, and yet when all is said
It was the dream itself enchanted me:
Character isolated by a deed
30 To engross the present and dominate memory.
Players and painted stage took all my love
And not those things that they were emblems of.

3

Those masterful images because complete
Grew in pure mind but out of what began?
35 A mound of refuse or the sweepings of a street,
Old kettles, old bottles, and a broken can,
Old iron, old bones, old rags, that raving slut
Who keeps the till. Now that my ladder's gone
I must lie down where all the ladders start
40 In the foul rag and bone shop of the heart.

1939

From Introduction
[A General Introduction for My Work][1]

I. The First Principle

A poet writes always of his personal life, in his finest work out of its tragedies, whatever it be, remorse, lost love or mere loneliness; he never speaks directly as to someone at the breakfast table, there is always a phantasmagoria. Dante and Milton had mythologies, Shakespeare the characters of English history,

3. A play (published in 1892) about an Irish countess (an idealized version of Maud Gonne) who sells her soul to the devil to buy food for the starving Irish poor but is taken up to heaven (for God "Looks always on the motive, not the deed"). 4. In Yeats's play *On Baile's Strand* (1904), the legendary warrior Cuchulain (pronounced *CuHOOlin* by Yeats, *KooHULLin* in Irish), crazed

by his discovery that he has killed his son, fights with the sea.
1. Written in 1937 and originally printed as "A General Introduction for My Work" in *Essays and Introductions* (1961), the text is excerpted from *Later Essays,* ed. William H. O'Donnell (1994), vol. 5 of *The Collected Works of W. B. Yeats.*

of traditional romance; even when the poet seems most himself, when Raleigh and gives potentates the lie,[2] or Shelley 'a nerve o'er which do creep the else unfelt oppressions of mankind',[3] or Byron when 'the heart wears out the breast as the sword wears out the sheath',[4] he is never the bundle of accident and incoherence that sits down to breakfast; he has been re-born as an idea, something intended, complete. A novelist might describe his accidence, his incoherence, he must not, he is more type than man, more passion than type. He is Lear, Romeo, Oedipus, Tiresias; he has stepped out of a play and even the woman he loves is Rosalind, Cleopatra, never The Dark Lady.[5] He is part of his own phantasmagoria and we adore him because nature has grown intelligible, and by so doing a part of our creative power. 'When mind is lost in the light of the Self', says the Prashna Upanishad,[6] 'it dreams no more; still in the body it is lost in happiness.' 'A wise man seeks in Self', says the Chāndôgya Upanishad, 'those that are alive and those that are dead and gets what the world cannot give.' The world knows nothing because it has made nothing, we know everything because we have made everything.

II. Subject-Matter

* * *

I am convinced that in two or three generations it will become generally known that the mechanical theory[7] has no reality, that the natural and supernatural are knit together, that to escape a dangerous fanaticism we must study a new science; at that moment Europeans may find something attractive in a Christ posed against a background not of Judaism but of Druidism, not shut off in dead history, but flowing, concrete, phenomenal.

I was born into this faith, have lived in it, and shall die in it; my Christ, a legitimate deduction from the Creed of St Patrick[8] as I think, is that Unity of Being Dante compared to a perfectly proportioned human body, Blake's 'Imagination',[9] what the Upanishads have named 'Self': nor is this unity distant and therefore intellectually understandable, but imminent,[1] differing from man to man and age to age, taking upon itself pain and ugliness, 'eye of newt, and leg of frog'.[2]

Subconscious preoccupation with this theme brought me A Vision,[3] its harsh geometry an incomplete interpretation. The 'Irishry' have preserved their ancient 'deposit' through wars which, during the sixteenth and seventeenth centuries, became wars of extermination; no people, Lecky said at

2. From "The Lie," by the English writer and explorer Sir Walter Ralegh (1552–1618): "Tell potentates, they live / Acting by others' action; / Not loved unless they give, / Not strong but by a faction: / If potentates' reply, / Give potentates the lie."
3. From "Julian and Maddalo," by the English poet Percy Bysshe Shelley (1792–1822).
4. Cf. "So, we'll go no more a roving," by the English poet George Gordon, Lord Byron.
5. The woman to whom many of Shakespeare's de-idealizing sonnets are addressed. The rest of the names refer to characters in Shakespeare's plays and in Sophocles' ancient Greek drama Oedipus the King.
6. One of a series of ancient philosophical dialogues in Sanskrit. From Ten Principal Upanishads (1937), translated by Yeats and the Indian monk Shri Purohit Swami (1882–1941).

7. Theory explaining the universe in strictly naturalistic, Newtonian terms.
8. From the second paragraph of "The Confession of St. Patrick, or His Epistle to the Irish," by the 5th-century saint, the apostle of Ireland.
9. In Jerusalem the English poet William Blake (1757–1827) describes imagination as the "Divine body of the lord Jesus." Yeats's ideas about the Unity of Being are drawn from his reading of Dante's Il Convito.
1. In manuscript Yeats wrote "imanent" (a misspelling of "immanent"), but he allowed "imminent" to stand in the typescript.
2. Yeats's paraphrase of the ingredients of the witches' cauldron in Shakespeare's Macbeth 4.1.
3. Yeats's mystical writings (1925, 1937), in which he sketches out and schematizes many of his theories.

the opening of his *Ireland in the Eighteenth Century*,[4] have undergone greater persecution, nor did that persecution altogether cease up to our own day. No people hate as we do in whom that past is always alive; there are moments when hatred poisons my life and I accuse myself of effeminacy because I have not given it adequate expression. It is not enough to have put it into the mouth of a rambling peasant poet. Then I remind myself that, though mine is the first English marriage I know of in the direct line, all my family names are English and that I owe my soul to Shakespeare, to Spenser and to Blake, perhaps to William Morris,[5] and to the English language in which I think, speak and write, that everything I love has come to me through English; my hatred tortures me with love, my love with hate. I am like the Tibetan monk who dreams at his initiation that he is eaten by a wild beast and learns on waking that he himself is eater and eaten. This is Irish hatred and solitude, the hatred of human life that made Swift write *Gulliver*[6] and the epitaph upon his tomb, that can still make us wag between extremes and doubt our sanity.

Again and again I am asked why I do not write in Gaelic; some four or five years ago I was invited to dinner by a London society and found myself among London journalists, Indian students and foreign political refugees. An Indian paper says it was a dinner in my honour, I hope not; I have forgotten though I have a clear memory of my own angry mind. I should have spoken as men are expected to speak at public dinners; I should have paid and been paid conventional compliments; then they would speak of the refugees, from that on all would be lively and topical, foreign tyranny would be arraigned, England seem even to those confused Indians the protector of liberty; I grew angrier and angrier; Wordsworth, that typical Englishman, had published his famous sonnet to François Dominique Toussaint, a Santo Domingo negro:

> There's not a breathing of the common wind
> That will forget thee[7]

in the year when Emmet conspired and died, and he remembered that rebellion as little as the half hanging and the pitch cap that preceded it by half a dozen years.[8] That there might be no topical speeches I denounced the oppression of the people of India; being a man of letters, not a politician, I told how they had been forced to learn everything, even their own Sanscrit, through the vehicle of English till the first discoverers of wisdom had become bywords for vague abstract facility. I begged the Indian writers present to remember that no man can think or write with music and vigour except in his mother tongue. I turned a friendly audience hostile, yet when I think of that scene I am unrepentant and angry.

I could no more have written in Gaelic than can those Indians write in English; Gaelic is my national language, but it is not my mother tongue.

---

4. *A History of Ireland in the Eighteenth Century*, by the Irish historian William Edward Hartpole Lecky (1838–1903).
5. English poet and designer (1834–1896). Edmund Spenser (1552–1599), English poet who, in addition to poetic works such as *The Faerie Queene*, wrote a treatise proposing the extermination of the Irish.
6. *Gulliver's Travels*, by the Irish satirist Jonathan Swift (1667–1745). Yeats's poem "Swift's Epitaph," a loose translation of the Latin on Swift's tomb,

claims that "Swift has sailed into his rest; / Savage indignation there / Cannot lacerate his breast."
7. From "To Toussaint L'Ouverture," by the English poet William Wordsworth (1770–1850). L'Ouverture (1743–1803) died in prison after rebelling against France's rule in Haiti.
8. Paper caps filled with burning pitch were used for torture during the martial law preceding and following the Irish Rising of 1798. Robert Emmet (1778–1803), Irish nationalist executed after the Irish rebellion of 1803.

III. Style and Attitude

Style is almost unconscious. I know what I have tried to do, little what I have done. Contemporary lyric poems, even those that moved me—'The Stream's Secret', 'Dolores'[9]—seemed too long, but an Irish preference for a swift current might be mere indolence, yet Burns may have felt the same when he read Thomson and Cowper.[1] The English mind is meditative, rich, deliberate; it may remember the Thames[2] valley. I planned to write short lyrics or poetic drama where every speech [would] be short and concentrated, knit by dramatic tension, and I did so with more confidence because young English poets were at that time writing out of emotion at the moment of crisis, though their old slow-moving meditation returned almost at once. Then, and in this English poetry has followed my lead, I tried to make the language of poetry coincide with that of passionate, normal speech. I wanted to write in whatever language comes most naturally when we soliloquise, as I do all day long, upon the events of our own lives or of any life where we can see ourselves for the moment. I sometimes compare myself with the mad old slum women I hear denouncing and remembering; 'how dare you,' I heard one say of some imaginary suitor, 'and you without health or a home'. If I spoke my thoughts aloud they might be as angry and as wild. It was a long time before I had made a language to my liking; I began to make it when I discovered some twenty years ago that I must seek, not as Wordsworth thought words in common use,[3] but a powerful and passionate syntax, and a complete coincidence between period and stanza. Because I need a passionate syntax for passionate subject-matter I compel myself to accept those traditional metres that have developed with the language. Ezra Pound, Turner, Lawrence, wrote admirable free verse, I could not.[4] I would lose myself, become joyless like those mad old women. The translators of the Bible, Sir Thomas Browne,[5] certain translators from the Greek when translators still bothered about rhythm, created a form midway between prose and verse that seems natural to impersonal meditation; but all that is personal soon rots; it must be packed in ice or salt. Once when I was in delirium from pneumonia I dictated a letter to George Moore[6] telling him to eat salt because it was a symbol of eternity; the delirium passed, I had no memory of that letter, but I must have meant what I now mean. If I wrote of personal love or sorrow in free verse, or in any rhythm that left it unchanged, amid all its accident, I would be full of self-contempt because of my egotism and indiscretion, and I foresee the boredom of my reader. I must choose a traditional stanza, even what I alter must seem traditional. I commit my emotion to shepherds, herdsmen, camel-drivers, learned men, Milton's or Shelley's Platonist, that tower Palmer drew.[7] Talk to me of originality and I will turn on you with rage. I am a crowd, I am a lonely man, I am nothing. Ancient salt is

9. Long poems by Dante Gabriel Rossetti (1828–1882) and Algernon Charles Swinburne (1837–1909), respectively.
1. James Thomson (1700–1748) and William Cowper (1731–1800), poets most famous for their long poems. Robert Burns (1759–1796), Scottish poet of short lyrics.
2. River that runs through London.
3. In the preface to *Lyrical Ballads* (1800), Wordsworth says that poetry should be written in "language really used by men."
4. In his *Oxford Book of Modern Verse* (1936), Yeats included free verse by the American poet

Ezra Pound (1885–1972), the English poet Walter Turner (1889–1946), and the English poet and novelist D. H. Lawrence (1885–1930).
5. English physician and author (1605–1682) with an elaborate prose style.
6. Irish novelist (1852–1933).
7. The English artist Samuel Palmer (1805–1881) drew "The Lonely Tower" (1879) as an illustration of Milton's poem about the pensive man, "Il Penseroso" (1645), in which a scholar in a "high lonely tower" is dedicated to uncovering Plato's insights; in Shelley's "Prince Athanase," the idealistic hero searches for love.

best packing. The heroes of Shakespeare convey to us through their looks, or through the metaphorical patterns of their speech, the sudden enlargement of their vision, their ecstasy at the approach of death, 'She should have died hereafter', 'Of many million kisses, the poor last', 'Absent thee from felicity awhile'; they have become God or Mother Goddess, the pelican, 'My baby at my breast',[8] but all must be cold; no actress has ever sobbed when she played Cleopatra, even the shallow brain of a producer has never thought of such a thing. The supernatural is present, cold winds blow across our hands, upon our faces, the thermometer falls, and because of that cold we are hated by journalists and groundlings. There may be in this or that detail painful tragedy, but in the whole work none. I have heard Lady Gregory say, rejecting some play in the modern manner sent to the Abbey Theatre, 'Tragedy must be a joy to the man who dies.' Nor is it any different with lyrics, songs, narrative poems; neither scholars nor the populace have sung or read anything generation after generation because of its pain. The maid of honour whose tragedy they sing must be lifted out of history with timeless pattern, she is one of the four Maries,[9] the rhythm is old and familiar, imagination must dance, must be carried beyond feeling into the aboriginal ice. Is ice the correct word? I once boasted, copying the phrase from a letter of my father's, that I would write a poem 'cold and passionate as the dawn'.[1]

When I wrote in blank verse I was dissatisfied; my vaguely mediaeval *Countess Cathleen* fitted the measure, but our Heroic Age went better, or so I fancied, in the ballad metre of *The Green Helmet*.[2] There was something in what I felt about Deirdre, about Cuchulain,[3] that rejected the Renaissance and its characteristic metres, and this was a principal reason why I created in dance plays the form that varies blank verse with lyric metres. When I speak blank verse and analyse my feelings I stand at a moment of history when instinct, its traditional songs and dances, its general agreement, is of the past. I have been cast up out of the whale's belly though I still remember the sound and sway that came from beyond its ribs,[4] and, like the Queen in Paul Fort's ballad,[5] I smell of the fish of the sea. The contrapuntal structure of the verse, to employ a term adopted by Robert Bridges,[6] combines the past and present. If I repeat the first line of *Paradise Lost* so as to emphasise its five feet I am among the folk singers, 'Of mán's first dísobédience ánd the frúit', but speak it as I should I cross it with another emphasis, that of passionate prose, 'Of mán's first disobédience and the frúit', or 'Of mán's fírst dísobedience and the frúit', the folk song is still there, but a ghostly voice, an unvariable possibility, an unconscious norm. What moves me and my hearer is a vivid speech that has no laws except that it must not exorcise the ghostly voice. I am awake and asleep, at my moment of revelation, self-possessed in self-surrender; there is no rhyme, no echo of the beaten drum, the dancing foot, that would overset my balance. When I was a boy I

8. From *Macbeth* 5.4, *Anthony and Cleopatra* 4.15, *Hamlet* 5.2, respectively. "Pelican": thought to feed its babies with its blood and thus often a symbol of self-sacrifice.
9. Mary, Queen of Scots (1542–1587), was served by four women named Mary.
1. From "The Fisherman" (1916): "Before I am old / I shall have written him one / Poem maybe as cold / And passionate as the dawn."
2. *The Countess Cathleen* (1892, later revised) is written in blank verse; *The Green Helmet* (1910), in iambic heptameter, which resembles the meter of a ballad (alternating between four- and three-stress lines).

3. The warrior hero of the Irish mythological Ulster Cycle; he also appears in Yeats's "dance" plays, derived from Japanese Noh drama. "Deirdre": in the Ulster Cycle, woman chosen to be queen of Ulster before she elopes with Naoise (pronounced *Neesha*).
4. Cf. Jonah 2.10: "And the Lord spake unto the fish, and it vomited out Jonah upon the dry land."
5. "La Reine à la Mer" ("The Queen of the Sea," 1894–96), by the French poet Paul Fort (1872–1960).
6. English poet (1844–1930), who stressed the poetic tension of the counterpoint between regular meters and the rhythm of poetry as actually spoken.

wrote a poem upon dancing that had one good line: 'They snatch with their hands at the sleep of the skies.' If I sat down and thought for a year I would discover that but for certain syllabic limitations, a rejection or acceptance of certain elisions, I must wake or sleep.

The Countess Cathleen could speak a blank verse which I had loosened, almost put out of joint, for her need, because I thought of her as mediaeval and thereby connected her with the general European movement. For Deirdre and Cuchulain and all the other figures of Irish legend are still in the whale's belly.

IV. Whither?

The young English poets reject dream and personal emotion; they have thought out opinions that join them to this or that political party; they employ an intricate psychology, action in character, not as in the ballads character in action, and all consider that they have a right to the same close attention that men pay to the mathematician and the metaphysician. One of the more distinguished has just explained that man has hitherto slept but must now awake.[7] They are determined to express the factory, the metropolis, that they may be modern. Young men teaching school in some picturesque cathedral town, or settled for life in Capri or in Sicily, defend their type of metaphor by saying that it comes naturally to a man who travels to his work by Tube.[8] I am indebted to a man of this school who went through my work at my request, crossing out all conventional metaphors,[9] but they seem to me to have rejected also those dream associations which were the whole art of Mallarmé.[1] He had topped a previous wave. As they express not what the Upanishads call 'that ancient Self' but individual intellect, they have the right to choose the man in the Tube because of his objective importance. They attempt to kill the whale, push the Renaissance higher yet, outthink Leonardo;[2] their verse kills the folk ghost and yet would remain verse. I am joined to the 'Irishry' and I expect a counter-Renaissance. No doubt it is part of the game to push that Renaissance; I make no complaint; I am accustomed to the geometrical arrangement of history in A Vision, but I go deeper than 'custom' for my convictions. When I stand upon O'Connell Bridge[3] in the half-light and notice that discordant architecture, all those electric signs, where modern heterogeneity has taken physical form, a vague hatred comes up out of my own dark and I am certain that wherever in Europe there are minds strong enough to lead others the same vague hatred rises; in four or five or in less generations this hatred will have issued in violence and imposed some kind of rule of kindred. I cannot know the nature of that rule, for its opposite fills the light; all I can do to bring it nearer is to intensify my hatred. I am no Nationalist, except in Ireland for passing reasons; State and Nation are the work of intellect, and when you consider what comes before and after them they are, as Victor Hugo said of something or other, not worth the blade of grass God gives for the nest of the linnet.[4]

1937   1961

7. Perhaps W. H. Auden (1907–1973) or C. Day Lewis (1904–1972).
8. London's underground railway. Lewis taught in the spa town of Cheltenham in the early 1930s. D. H. Lawrence lived in Capri and Sicily in the early 1920s.
9. Ezra Pound did this circa 1910.

1. Stéphane Mallarmé (1842–1898), French poet.
2. Leonardo da Vinci (1452–1519), Italian artist and inventor.
3. Over Dublin's river Liffey.
4. Small finch. Victor Hugo (1802–1885), French writer.

E. M. FORSTER
1879–1970

B orn in London, Edward Morgan Forster was an infant when his father, an architect of Welsh extraction, died of consumption. An only child, Forster was raised by his paternal great-aunt and his mother, a member of a family distinguished over several generations for its evangelical religion and its philanthropic reformist activities. He was educated at Tonbridge School (the "Sawston" of his novel *The Longest Journey*), where he suffered from the cruelty of his classmates and other tribulations of being a day boy at a boarding school. As a student at King's College, Cambridge, he found an intellectual companionship that influenced his entire life. The friends he made were to become, with Forster, members of the Bloomsbury Group—so called because some of its prominent figures lived in the Bloomsbury district of London—which included the writers Lytton Strachey and Virginia Woolf, the art historians Clive Bell and Roger Fry, and the economist John Maynard Keynes. Forster's main interest was always in personal relations, the "little society" we make for ourselves with our friends. He cast a wary eye on society at large, his point of view being that of the independent liberal, suspicious of political slogans and catchwords, critical of Victorian attitudes and British imperialism.

After graduating from Cambridge, Forster visited Greece and spent some time in Italy in 1901, and this experience influenced him permanently; throughout his life he tended to set Greek and Italian peasant life in symbolic contrast to the stuffy and repressed life of middle-class England. Both Greek mythology and Italian Renaissance art opened up to him a world of vital exuberance, and most of his work is concerned with ways of discovering such a quality in personal relationships amid the complexities and distortions of modern life. He began writing as a contributor to the newly founded liberal *Independent Review* in 1903, and in 1905 published his first novel, *Where Angels Fear to Tread*, a tragicomic projection of conflicts between refined English gentility and coarse Italian vitality.

Forster's second novel, *The Longest Journey* (1907), examines the differences between living and dead relationships with much incidental satire of English public-school education and English notions of respectability. *A Room with a View* (1908) explores the nature of love with a great deal of subtlety, using (as with his first novel) Italy as a liberating agent for the British tourists whom he also satirizes. *Howards End* (1910) involves a conflict between two families, one interested in art and literature and the other only in money and business, and probes the relation between inward feeling and outward action, between the kinds of reality in which people live. "Only connect!" exclaims one of the characters. "Only connect the prose and the passion, and both will be exalted, and human love will soon be at its height." But no one knew better than Forster that this is more easily said than done and that false or premature connections, connections made by rule and not achieved through total realization of the personality, can destroy and corrupt.

A pacifist, Forster refused to fight in World War I and instead served in the International Red Cross in Egypt. In Alexandria he had his first significant sexual relationship, with Mohammed el Adl, an Egyptian tram conductor; he feared social disapproval less there than in England, where, not long after Oscar Wilde's infamous prosecution for homosexual offenses, he hid his personal life from public scrutiny.

He traveled to India in 1912 and 1922, and in his last (for Forster published no more fiction during his life) and best-known novel, *A Passage to India* (1924), he takes the fraught relations between British and colonized Indians in the subcontinent as a background for the most searching and complex of all his explorations of the possibilities and limitations, the promises and pitfalls, of human relationships. Published posthumously was another novel, *Maurice*, written more than fifty years before and circulated privately during his life, in which he tried to define and do justice to homosexual love, which had played an important part in his life. In addition to fiction Forster wrote critical, autobiographical, and descriptive prose, notably *Aspects of the Novel* (1927), which, as a discussion of the techniques of fiction by a practicing novelist, has become a minor classic of criticism.

"The Other Boat," which concerns cross-ethnic homosexual attraction that collides with the sexual taboos and racial hierarchies of empire, is an unusually long and rich short story that Forster originally intended to turn into a novel, beginning it around 1913 but not completing it until 1957–58, and it was not published until after his death, first appearing in *The Life to Come and Other Stories* (1972). The first part of the story tells of a British family's journey by ship from India to England, and the rest of the story, set some years later, reverses direction, the journey into the Mediterranean and on toward India becoming the backdrop for the loosening—and then drastic reassertion—of British, imperial norms of order, discipline, racial superiority, and heterosexuality. As in other of Forster's works, the passage into another cultural geography calls into question British middle-class values, which exact a high price in repression, tragically conflict with the protagonist's sensual and emotional desires, and ultimately explode into violence.

The Other Boat

I

'Cocoanut, come and play at soldiers.'

'I cannot, I am beesy.'

'But you must, Lion wants you.'

'Yes come along, man,' said Lionel, running up with some paper cocked hats[1] and a sash. It was long long ago, and little boys still went to their deaths stiffly, and dressed in as many clothes as they could find.

'I cannot, I am beesy,' repeated Cocoanut.

'But man, what are you busy about?'

'I have soh many things to arrange, man.'

'Let's leave him and play by ourselves,' said Olive. 'We've Joan and Noel and Baby and Lieutenant Bodkin. Who wants Cocoanut?'

'Oh, shut up! *I* want him. We must have him. He's the only one who falls down when he's killed. All you others go on fighting long too long. The battle this morning was a perfect fast. Mother said so.'

'Well, I'll die.'

'So you say beforehand, but when it comes to the point you won't. Noel won't. Joan won't. Baby doesn't do anything properly—of course he's too little—and you can't expect Lieutenant Bodkin to fall down. Cocoanut, man, do.'

'I—weel—not.'

'Cocoanut cocoanut cocoanut cocoanut cocoanut cocoanut,' said Baby.

The little boy rolled on the deck screaming happily. He liked to be pressed by these handsome good-natured children. 'I must go and see the m'm m'm m'm,' he said.

---

1. Triangular hats worn in navy and army.

'The what?'

'The m'm m'm m'm. They live—oh, so many of them—in the thin part of the ship.'

'He means the bow,'[2] said Olive. 'Oh, come along, Lion. He's hopeless.'

'What are m'm m'm m'm?'

'M'm.' He whirled his arms about, and chalked some marks on the planks.

'What are those?'

'M'm.'

'What's their name?'

'They have no name.'

'What do they do?'

'They just go so and oh! and so—ever—always——'

'Flying fish? . . . Fairies? . . . Noughts and crosses?'[3]

'They have no name.'

'Mother!' said Olive to a lady who was promenading with a gentleman, 'hasn't everything a name?'

'I suppose so.'

'Who's this?' asked the lady's companion.

'He's always hanging on to my children. I don't know.'

'Touch of the tar-brush,[4] eh?'

'Yes, but it doesn't matter on a voyage home. I would never allow it going to India.' They passed on, Mrs March calling back, 'Shout as much as you like, boys, but don't scream, don't scream.'

'They must have a name,' said Lionel, recollecting, 'because Adam named all the animals when the Bible was beginning.'

'They weren't in the Bible, m'm m'm m'm; they were all the time up in the thin part of the sheep, and when you pop out they pop in, so how could Adam have?'

'Noah's ark is what he's got to now.'

Baby said 'Noah's ark, Noah's ark, Noah's ark,' and they all bounced up and down and roared. Then, without any compact, they drifted from the saloon[5] deck on to the lower, and from the lower down the staircase that led to the forecastle,[6] much as the weeds and jellies were drifting about outside in the tropical sea. Soldiering was forgotten, though Lionel said, 'We may as well wear our cocked hats.' They played with a fox-terrier, who was in the charge of a sailor, and asked the sailor himself if a roving life was a happy one. Then drifting forward again, they climbed into the bows, where the m'm m'm m'm were said to be.

Here opened a glorious country, much the best in the boat. None of the March children had explored there before, but Cocoanut, having few domesticities, knew it well. That bell that hung in the very peak—it was the ship's bell and if you rang it the ship would stop. Those big ropes were tied into knots—twelve knots an hour. This paint was wet, but only as far as there. Up that hole was coming a Lascar.[7] But of the m'm m'm he said nothing until asked. Then he explained in offhand tones that if you popped out they popped in, so that you couldn't expect to see them.

---

2. Forward part of the ship.
3. Tic-tac-toe.
4. Appearance of having non-European ancestry, i.e., of having brown skin.

5. Deck with large cabin(s) for passenger use.
6. Raised deck at the forward part of the ship.
7. An Indian sailor.

What treachery! How disappointing! Yet so ill-balanced were the children's minds that they never complained. Olive, in whom the instincts of a lady were already awaking, might have said a few well-chosen words, but when she saw her brothers happy she forgot too, and lifted Baby up on to a bollard[8] because he asked her to. They all screamed. Into their midst came the Lascar and laid down a mat for his three-o'clock prayer. He prayed as if he was still in India, facing westward, not knowing that the ship had rounded Arabia so that his holy places now lay behind him.[9] They continued to scream.

Mrs March and her escort remained on the saloon deck, inspecting the approach to Suez.[1] Two continents were converging with great magnificence of mountains and plain. At their junction, nobly placed, could be seen the smoke and the trees of the town. In addition to her more personal problems, she had become anxious about Pharaoh. 'Where exactly was Pharaoh drowned?'[2] she asked Captain Armstrong. 'I shall have to show my boys.' Captain Armstrong did not know, but he offered to ask Mr Hotblack, the Moravian[3] missionary. Mr Hotblack knew—in fact he knew too much. Somewhat snubbed by the military element in the earlier part of the voyage, he now bounced to the surface, became authoritative and officious, and undertook to wake Mrs March's little ones when they were passing the exact spot. He spoke of the origins of Christianity in a way that made her look down her nose, saying that the Canal was one long genuine Bible picture gallery, that donkeys could still be seen going down into Egypt carrying Holy Families,[4] and naked Arabs wading into the water to fish; 'Peter and Andrew by Galilee's shore, why, it hits the truth plumb.'[5] A clergyman's daughter and a soldier's wife, she could not admit that Christianity had ever been oriental. What good thing can come out of the Levant,[6] and is it likely that the apostles[7] ever had a touch of the tar-brush? Still, she thanked Mr Hotblack (for, having asked a favour of him, she had contracted an obligation towards him), and she resigned herself to greeting him daily until Southampton,[8] when their paths would part.

Then she observed, against the advancing land, her children playing in the bows without their topis[9] on. The sun in those far-off days was a mighty power and hostile to the Ruling Race.[1] Officers staggered at a touch of it, Tommies[2] collapsed. When the regiment was under canvas, it wore helmets at tiffin,[3] lest the rays penetrated the tent. She shouted at her doomed off-spring, she gesticulated, Captain Armstrong and Mr Hotblack shouted, but the wind blew their cries backwards. Refusing company, she hurried forward alone; the children were far too excited and covered with paint.

'Lionel! Olive! Olive! What are you doing?'

'M'm m'm m'm, mummy—it's a new game.'

8. A thick post for securing ropes to.
9. Muslims pray facing Mecca.
1. Egyptian city at the south end of the Suez Canal (the shortest maritime route between Europe and India; it separates Asia and Africa).
2. In Exodus 14.21–23 Moses parts the Red Sea, but after the Israelites have passed, the sea closes, drowning Pharoah and his army.
3. Member of a Protestant denomination, originally from a 15th-century reform religious movement in Moravia and Bohemia.
4. In Matthew 2.13–15 the family of the baby Jesus, fleeing from King Herod, travels from Bethlehem into Egypt; the journey is often depicted as taking place by donkey.
5. Peter and Andrew, Jesus's disciples, were fishermen on the Sea of Galilee.
6. Historical term for region of the eastern Mediterranean.
7. Jesus's disciples.
8. Major port on the English Channel.
9. Pith helmets worn for protection from sun and heat.
1. I.e., the British.
2. Nickname for British soldiers.
3. Lunch (Anglo-Indian).

'Go back and play properly under the awning at once—it's far too hot. You'll have sunstroke every one of you. Come, Baby!'

'M'm m'm m'm.'

'Now, you won't want me to carry a great boy like you, surely.'

Baby flung himself round the bollard and burst into tears.

'It always ends like this,' said Mrs March as she detached him. 'You all behave foolishly and selfishly and then Baby cries. No, Olive—don't help me. Mother would rather do everything herself.'

'Sorry,' said Lionel gruffly. Baby's shrieks rent the air. Thoroughly naughty, he remained clasping an invisible bollard. As she bent him into a portable shape, another mishap occurred. A sailor—an Englishman—leapt out of the hatchway with a piece of chalk and drew a little circle round her where she stood. Cocoanut screamed, 'He's caught you. He's come.'

'You're on dangerous ground, lady,' said the sailor respectfully. 'Men's quarters. Of course we leave it to your generosity.'

Tired with the voyage and the noise of the children, worried by what she had left in India and might find in England, Mrs March fell into a sort of trance. She stared at the circle stupidly, unable to move out of it, while Cocoanut danced round her and gibbered.

'Men's quarters—just to keep up the old custom.'

'I don't understand.'

'Passengers are often kind enough to pay their footing,' he said, feeling awkward; though rapacious he was independent. 'But of course there's no compulsion, lady. Ladies and gentlemen do as they feel.'

'I will certainly do what is customary—Baby, *be* quiet.'

'Thank you, lady. We divide whatever you give among the crew. Of course not those chaps.' He indicated the Lascar.

'The money shall be sent to you. I have no purse.'

He touched his forelock[4] cynically. He did not believe her. She stepped out of the circle and as she did so Cocoanut sprang into it and squatted grinning.

'You're a silly little boy and I shall complain to the stewardess about you,' she told him with unusual heat. 'You never will play any game properly and you stop the others. You're a silly idle useless unmanly little boy.'

II

S. S. Normannia
Red Sea
October, 191–

Hullo the Mater!

You may be thinking it is about time I wrote you a line, so here goes, however you should have got my wire sent before leaving Tilbury[5] with the glad news that I got a last minute passage on this boat when it seemed quite impossible I should do so. The Arbuthnots are on it too all right, so is a Lady Manning who claims acquaintance with Olive, not to mention several remarkably cheery subalterns,[6] poor devils, don't know what they are in for

---

4. Lock of hair growing from the front of the head.

5. Port on the river Thames estuary.
6. Junior officers.

in the tropics. We make up two Bridge tables every night besides hanging together at other times, and get called the Big Eight, which I suppose must be regarded as a compliment. How I got my passage is curious. I was coming away from the S.S.[7] office after my final try in absolute despair when I ran into an individual whom you may or may not remember—he was a kid on that other boat when we cleared all out of India on that unlikely occasion over ten years ago—got called Cocoanut because of his peculiar shaped head. He has now turned into an equally weird youth, who has however managed to become influential in shipping circles, I can't think how some people manage to do things. He duly recognized me—dagoes[8] sometimes have marvellous memories—and on learning my sad plight fixed me up with a (single berth) cabin, so all is well. He is on board too, but our paths seldom cross. He has more than a touch of the tar-brush, so consorts with his own dusky fraternity, no doubt to their mutual satisfaction.

The heat is awful and I fear this is but a dull letter in consequence. Bridge I have already mentioned, and there are the usual deck games, betting on the ship's log, etc., still I think everyone will be glad to reach Bombay and get into harness.[9] Colonel and Mrs Arbuthnot are very friendly, and speaking confidentially I don't think it will do my prospects any harm having got to know them better. Well I will now conclude this screed[1] and I will write again when I have rejoined the regiment and contacted Isabel. Best love to all which naturally includes yourself from

Your affectionate first born,
Lionel March

PS. Lady Manning asks to be remembered to Olive, nearly forgot.

When Captain March had posted this epistle he rejoined the Big Eight. Although he had spent the entire day with them they were happy to see him, for he exactly suited them. He was what any rising young officer ought to be—clean-cut, athletic, good-looking without being conspicuous. He had had wonderful professional luck, which no one grudged him: he had got into one of the little desert wars that were becoming too rare, had displayed dash and decision, had been wounded, and had been mentioned in despatches and got his captaincy early. Success had not spoiled him, nor was he vain of his personal appearance, although he must have known that thick fairish hair, blue eyes, glowing cheeks and strong white teeth constitute, when broad shoulders support them, a combination irresistible to the fair sex. His hands were clumsier than the rest of him, but bespoke hard honest work, and the springy gleaming hairs on them suggested virility. His voice was quiet, his demeanour assured, his temper equable. Like his brother officers he wore a mess[2] uniform slightly too small for him, which accentuated his physique—the ladies accentuating theirs by wearing their second best frocks and reserving their best ones for India.

Bridge proceeded without a hitch, as his mother had been given to understand it might. She had not been told that on either side of the players, violet darkening into black, rushed the sea, nor would she have been interested.

---

7. Steamship.
8. Disparaging term for foreigners.
9. I.e., get to work, especially with military undertakings.
1. Gossipy letter.
2. Mealtime.

Her son gazed at it occasionally, his forehead furrowed. For despite his out-standing advantages he was a miserable card-player, and he was having wretched luck. As soon as the Normannia entered the Mediterranean he had begun to lose, and the 'better luck after Port Said,[3] always the case' that had been humorously promised him had never arrived. Here in the Red Sea he had lost the maximum the Big Eight's moderate stakes allowed. He couldn't afford it, he had no private means and he ought to be saving up for the future, also it was humiliating to let down his partner: Lady Manning herself. So he was thankful when play terminated and the usual drinks cir-culated. They sipped and gulped while the lighthouses on the Arabian coast winked at them and slid northwards. 'Bedfordshire!'[4] fell pregnantly from the lips of Mrs Arbuthnot. And they dispersed, with the certainty that the day which was approaching would exactly resemble the one that had died.

In this they were wrong.

Captain March waited until all was quiet, still frowning at the sea. Then with something alert and predatory about him, something disturbing and disturbed, he went down to his cabin.

'Come een,' said a sing-song voice.

For it was not a single cabin, as he had given his mother to understand. There were two berths, and the lower one contained Cocoanut. Who was naked. A brightly coloured scarf lay across him and contrasted with his blackish-grayish skin, and an aromatic smell came off him, not at all unpleas-ant. In ten years he had developed into a personable adolescent, but still had the same funny-shaped head. He had been doing his accounts and now he laid them down and gazed at the British officer adoringly.

'Man, I thought you was never coming,' he said, and his eyes filled with tears.

'It's only those bloody Arbuthnots and their blasted bridge,' replied Lionel and closed the cabin door.

'I thought you was dead.'

'Well, I'm not.'

'I thought I should die.'

'So you will.' He sat down on the berth, heavily and with deliberate heavi-ness. The end of the chase was in sight. It had not been a long one. He had always liked the kid, even on that other boat, and now he liked him more than ever. Champagne in an ice-bucket too. An excellent kid. They couldn't associate on deck with that touch of the tar-brush, but it was a very different business down here, or soon would be. Lowering his voice, he said: 'The trouble is we're not supposed to do this sort of thing under any circum-stances whatsoever, which you never seem to understand. If we got caught there'd be absolute bloody hell to pay, yourself as well as me, so for God's sake don't make a noise.'

'Lionel, O Lion of the Night, love me.'

'All right. Stay where you are.' Then he confronted the magic that had been worrying him on and off the whole evening and had made him inattentive at cards. A tang of sweat spread as he stripped and a muscle thickened up out of gold. When he was ready he shook off old Cocoanut, who was now climbing about like a monkey, and put him where he had to be, and manhandled him,

---

3. Egyptian city at the northern entrance to the Suez Canal.

4. County in the southeastern Midlands of England.

gently, for he feared his own strength and was always gentle, and closed on him, and they did what they both wanted to do.

Wonderful, wonnerful . . .

They lay entwined, Nordic warrior and subtle supple boy, who belonged to no race and always got what he wanted. All his life he had wanted a toy that would not break, and now he was planning how he would play with Lionel for ever. He had longed for him ever since their first meeting, embraced him in dreams when only that was possible, met him again as the omens foretold, and marked him down, spent money to catch him and lime[5] him, and here he lay, caught, and did not know it.

There they lay caught, both of them, and did not know it, while the ship carried them inexorably towards Bombay.

III

It had not always been so wonderful, wonnerful. Indeed the start of the affair had been grotesque and nearly catastrophic. Lionel had stepped on board at Tilbury entirely the simple soldier man, without an inkling of his fate. He had thought it decent of a youth whom he had only known as a child to fix him up with a cabin, but had not expected to find the fellow on board too—still less to have to share the cabin with him. This gave him a nasty shock. British officers are never stabled with dagoes, never, it was too damn awkward for words. However, he could not very well protest under the circumstances, nor did he in his heart want to, for his colour-prejudices were tribal rather than personal, and only worked when an observer was present. The first half-hour together went most pleasantly, they were unpacking and sorting things out before the ship started, he found his childhood's acquaintance friendly and quaint, exchanged reminiscences, and even started teasing and bossing him as in the old days, and got him giggling delightedly. He sprang up to his berth and sat on its edge, swinging his legs. A hand touched them, and he thought no harm until it approached their junction. Then he became puzzled, scared and disgusted in quick succession, leapt down with a coarse barrack-room oath and a brow of thunder and went straight to the Master at Arms[6] to report an offence against decency. Here he showed the dash and decision that had so advantaged him in desert warfare: in other words he did not know what he was doing.

The Master at Arms could not be found, and during the delay Lionel's rage abated somewhat, and he reflected that if he lodged a formal complaint he would have to prove it, which he could not do, and might have to answer questions, at which he was never good. So he went to the Purser[7] instead, and he demanded to be given alternative accommodation, without stating any reason for the change. The Purser stared: the boat was chockablock full already, as Captain March must have known. 'Don't speak to me like that,' Lionel stormed, and shouldered his way to the gunwale[8] to see England recede. Here was the worst thing in the world, the thing for which Tommies got given the maximum, and here was he bottled up with it for a fortnight.

---

5. Ensnare.
6. Officer in charge of enforcing discipline on a ship.

7. Ship's officer who keeps accounts and manages provisions.
8. Upper edge of a ship's side.

What the hell was he to do? Go forward with the charge or blow his own brains out or what?

On to him thus desperately situated the Arbuthnots descended. They were slight acquaintances, their presence calmed him, and before long his light military guffaw rang out as if nothing had happened. They were pleased to see him, for they were hurriedly forming a group of sahibs[9] who would hang together during the voyage and exclude outsiders. With his help the Big Eight came into being, soon to be the envy of less happy passengers; introductions; drinks; jokes; difficulties of securing a berth. At this point Lionel made a shrewd move: everything gets known on a boat and he had better anticipate discovery. 'I got a passage all right,' he brayed, 'but at the cost of sharing my cabin with a wog.'[1] All condoled, and Colonel Arbuthnot in the merriest of moods exclaimed, 'Let's hope the blacks don't come off on the sheets,' and Mrs Arbuthnot, wittier still, cried, 'Of course they won't, dear, if it's a wog it'll be the coffees.' Everyone shouted with laughter, the good lady basked in the applause, and Lionel could not understand why he suddenly wanted to throw himself into the sea. It was so unfair, he was the aggrieved party, yet he felt himself in the wrong and almost a cad. If only he had found out the fellow's tastes in England he would never have touched him, no, not with tongs. But could he have found out? You couldn't tell by just looking. Or could you? Dimly, after ten years' forgetfulness, something stirred in that faraway boat of his childhood and he saw his mother . . . Well, she was always objecting to something or other, the poor Mater. No, he couldn't possibly have known.

The Big Eight promptly reserved tables for lunch and all future meals, and Cocoanut and his set were relegated to a second sitting—for it became evident that he too was in a set: the tagrag and coloured bobtail[2] stuff that accumulates in corners and titters and whispers, and may well be influential, but who cares? Lionel regarded it with distaste and looked for a touch of the hangdog[3] in his unspeakable cabin-mate, but he was skipping and gibbering on the promenade deck as if nothing had occurred. He himself was safe for the moment, eating curry by the side of Lady Manning, and amusing her by his joke about the various names which the cook would give the same curry on successive days. Again something stabbed him and he thought: 'But what shall I do, *do*, when night comes? There will have to be some sort of showdown.' After lunch the weather deteriorated. England said farewell to her children with her choppiest seas, her gustiest winds, and the banging of invisible pots and pans in the empyrean.[4] Lady Manning thought she might do better in a deckchair. He squired her to it and then collapsed and re-entered his cabin as rapidly as he had left it a couple of hours earlier.

It now seemed full of darkies, who rose to their feet as he retched,[5] assisted him up to his berth and loosened his collar, after which the gong summoned them to their lunch. Presently Cocoanut and his elderly Parsee[6] secretary looked in to inquire and were civil and helpful and he could not but thank them. The showdown must be postponed. Later in the day he felt better and less inclined for it, and the night did not bring its dreaded perils or indeed anything at all. It was almost as if nothing had happened—almost but not

---

9. Respectful term for Europeans in colonial India.
1. Offensive term for a foreign person of color.
2. "Tagrag and bobtail" is another version of "rag, tag, and bobtail," meaning the riffraff, or rabble.

3. I.e., abashedness, shame.
4. Sky.
5. Stretched.
6. Indian follower of Zoroastrianism, an ancient religion originating in Iran.

quite. Master Cocoanut had learned his lesson, for he pestered no more, yet he skilfully implied that the lesson was an unimportant one. He was like someone who has been refused a loan and indicates that he will not apply again. He seemed positively not to mind his disgrace—incomprehensibly to Lionel, who expected either repentance or terror. Could it be that he himself had made too much fuss?

In this uneventful atmosphere the voyage across the Bay of Biscay[7] proceeded. It was clear that his favours would not again be asked, and he could not help wondering what would have happened if he had granted them. Propriety was re-established, almost monotonously; if he and Cocoanut ever overlapped in the cabin and had to settle (for instance) who should wash first, they solved the problem with mutual tact.

And then the ship entered the Mediterranean.

Resistance weakened under the balmier sky, curiosity increased. It was an exquisite afternoon—their first decent weather. Cocoanut was leaning out of the porthole to see the sunlit rock of Gibraltar.[8] Lionel leant against him to look too and permitted a slight, a very slight familiarity with his person. The ship did not sink nor did the heavens fall. The contact started something whirling about inside his head and all over him, he could not concentrate on after-dinner bridge, he felt excited, frightened and powerful all at once and kept looking at the stars. Cocoa, who said weird things sometimes, declared that the stars were moving into a good place and could be kept there.

That night champagne appeared in the cabin, and he was seduced. He never could resist champagne. Curse, oh curse! How on earth had it happened? Never again. More happened off the coast of Sicily, more, much more at Port Said, and here in the Red Sea they slept together as a matter of course.

IV

And this particular night they lay motionless for longer than usual, as though something in the fall of their bodies had enchanted them. They had never been so content with each other before, and only one of them realized that nothing lasts, that they might be more happy or less happy in the future, but would never again be exactly thus. He tried not to stir, not to breathe, not to live even, but life was too strong for him and he sighed.

'All right?' whispered Lionel.

'Yes.'

'Did I hurt?'

'Yes.'

'Sorry.'

'Why?'

'Can I have a drink?'

'You can have the whole world.'

'Lie still and I'll get you one too, not that you deserve it after making such a noise.'

'Was I again a noise?'

---

7. Arm of the Atlantic bordered by the west coast of France and the north coast of Spain.
8. Limestone promontory at the southern tip of Spain; since 1713 Gibraltar has been a British territory.

'You were indeed. Never mind, you shall have a nice drink.' Half Gany-mede, half Goth,[9] he jerked a bottle out of the ice-bucket. Pop went a cork and hit the partition wall. Sounds of feminine protest became audible, and they both laughed. 'Here, hurry up, scuttle up and drink.' He offered the goblet, received it back, drained it, refilled. His eyes shone, any depths through which he might have passed were forgotten. 'Let's make a night of it,' he suggested. For he was of the conventional type who once the conven-tions are broken breaks them into little pieces, and for an hour or two there was nothing he wouldn't say or do.

Meanwhile the other one, the deep one, watched. To him the moment of ecstasy was sometimes the moment of vision, and his cry of delight when they closed had wavered into fear. The fear passed before he could under-stand what it meant or against what it warned him, against nothing perhaps. Still, it seemed wiser to watch. As in business, so in love, precautions are desirable, insurances must be effected. 'Man, shall we now perhaps have our cigarette?' he asked.

This was an established ritual, an assertion deeper than speech that they belonged to each other and in their own way. Lionel assented and lit the thing, pushed it between dusky lips, pulled it out, pulled at it, replaced it, and they smoked it alternately with their faces touching. When it was fin-ished Cocoa refused to extinguish the butt in an ashtray but consigned it through the porthole into the flying waters with incomprehensible words. He thought the words might protect them, though he could not explain how, or what they were.

'That reminds me . . .' said Lionel, and stopped. He had been reminded, and for no reason, of his mother. He did not want to mention her in his pres-ent state, the poor old Mater, especially after all the lies she had been told.

'Yes, of what did it remind you, our cigarette? Yes and please? I should know.'

'Nothing.' And he stretched himself, flawless except for a scar down in the groin.

'Who gave you that?'

'One of your fuzzy-wuzzy cousins.'

'Does it hurt?'

'No.' It was a trophy from the little desert war. An assegai[1] had nearly unmanned him, nearly but not quite, which Cocoa said was a good thing. A dervish,[2] a very holy man, had once told him that what nearly destroys may bring strength and can be summoned in the hour of revenge. 'I've no use for revenge,' Lionel said.

'Oh Lion, why not when it can be so sweet?'

He shook his head and reached up for his pyjamas, a sultan's gift. It was presents all the time in these days. His gambling debts were settled through the secretary, and if he needed anything, or was thought to need it, some-thing or other appeared. He had ceased to protest and now accepted indis-criminately. He could trade away the worst of the junk later on—some impossible jewelry for instance which one couldn't be seen dead in. He did

9. An uncouth or uncivilized person. "Gany-mede": in Greek mythology a Trojan boy whom Zeus, attracted by his great beauty, carried away to be the gods' cupbearer.

1. Slender spear.
2. Member of any of various Muslim ascetic orders.

wish, though, that he could have given presents in return, for he was anything but a sponger. He had made an attempt two nights previously, with dubious results. 'I seem always taking and never giving,' he had said. 'Is there nothing of mine you'd fancy? I'd be so glad if there was.' To receive the reply: 'Yes. Your hairbrush'—'My *hairbrush*?'—and he was not keen on parting with this particular object, for it had been a coming-of-age gift from Isabel. His hesitation brought tears to the eyes, so he had to give in. 'You're welcome to my humble brush if you want it, of course. I'll just comb it out for you first'—'No, no, as it is uncombed,' and it was snatched away fanatically. Almost like a vulture snatching. Odd little things like this did happen occasionally, m'm m'm m'ms he called them, for they reminded him of oddities on the other boat. They did no one any harm, so why worry? Enjoy yourself while you can. He lolled at his ease and let the gifts rain on him as they would—a Viking at a Byzantine court, spoiled, adored and not yet bored.

This was certainly the life, and sitting on one chair with his feet on another he prepared for their usual talk, which might be long or short but was certainly the life. When Cocoanut got going it was fascinating. For all the day he had slipped around the ship, discovering people's weaknesses. More than that, he and his cronies were cognizant of financial possibilities that do not appear in the City columns,[3] and could teach one how to get rich if one thought it worth while. More than that, he had a vein of fantasy. In the midst of something ribald and scandalous—the discovery of Lady Manning, for instance: Lady Manning of all people in the cabin of the Second Engineer—he imagined the discovery being made by a flying fish who had popped through the Engineer's porthole, and he indicated the expression on the fish's face.

Yes, this was the life, and one that he had never experienced in his austere apprenticeship: luxury, gaiety, kindness, unusualness, and delicacy that did not exclude brutal pleasure. Hitherto he had been ashamed of being built like a brute: his preceptors had condemned carnality or had dismissed it as a waste of time, and his mother had ignored its existence in him and all her children; being hers, they had to be pure.

What to talk about this pleasurable evening? How about the passport scandal? For Cocoanut possessed two passports, not one like most people, and they confirmed a growing suspicion that he might not be altogether straight. In England Lionel would have sheered off at once from such a subject, but since Gibraltar they had become so intimate and morally so relaxed that he experienced nothing but friendly curiosity. The information on the passports was conflicting, so that it was impossible to tell the twister's[4] age, or where he had been born or indeed what his name was. 'You could get into serious trouble over this,' Lionel had warned him, to be answered by irresponsible giggles. 'You could, you know. However, you're no better than a monkey, and I suppose a monkey can't be expected to know it's own name.' To which the reply had been 'Lion, he don't know nothing at all. Monkey's got to come along to tell a Lion he's alive.' It was never easy to score. He had picked up his education, if that was the word for it, in London, and his financial beginnings in Amsterdam, one of the passports was Portuguese, the other Danish, and half the blood must be Asiatic, unless a drop was Negro.

3. Newspapers of the City of London, the financial district.
4. One who speaks or acts to evade the truth.

'Now come along, tell me the truth and nothing but the truth for a change,' he began. 'Ah, that reminds me I've at last got off that letter to the Mater. She adores news. It was a bit difficult to think of anything to interest her, however I filled it up with tripe about the Arbuthnots, and threw you in at the end as a sort of makeweight.'

'To make what sort of weight?'

'Well, naturally I didn't say what we do. I'm not stark staring raving mad. I merely mentioned I'd run into you in the London office, and got a cabin through you, that is to say single-berth one. I threw dust in her eyes all right.'

'Dear Lionel, you don't know how to throw dust or even where it is. Of mud you know a little, good, but not dust. Why bring me into the matter at all?'

'Oh, for the sake of something to say.'

'Did you say I too was on board?'

'I did in passing,' he said irritably, for he now realized he had better not have. 'I was writing that damned epistle, not you, and I had to fill it up. Don't worry—she's forgotten your very existence by this time.'

The other was certain she hadn't. If he had foreseen this meeting and had worked towards it through dreams, why should not an anxious parent have foreseen it too? She had valid reasons for anxiety, for things had actually started on that other boat. A trivial collision between children had alerted them towards each other as men. Thence had their present happiness sprung, thither might it wither, for the children had been disturbed. That vengeful onswishing of skirts . . . ! 'What trick can I think of this time that will keep him from her? I love him, I am clever, I have money. I will try.' The first step was to contrive his exit from the Army. The second step was to dispose of that English girl in India, called Isabel, about whom too little was known. Marriage or virginity or concubinage for Isabel? He had no scruples at perverting Lionel's instincts in order to gratify his own, or at endangering his prospects of paternity. All that mattered was their happiness, and he thought he knew what that was. Much depended on the next few days: he had to work hard and to work with the stars. His mind played round approaching problems, combining them, retreating from them, and aware all the time of a further problem, of something in the beloved which he did not understand. He half-closed his eyes and watched, and listened through half-closed ears. By not being too much on the spot and sacrificing shrewd-ness to vision he sometimes opened a door. And sure enough Lionel said, 'As a matter of fact the Mater never liked you,' and a door opened, slowly.

'Man, how should she? Oh, when the chalk went from the hand of the sailor round the feet of the lady and she could not move and we all knew it, and oh man how we mocked her.'

'I don't remember—well, I do a little. It begins to come back to me and does sound like the sort of thing that would put her off. She certainly went on about you after we landed, and complained that you made things inter-esting when they weren't, funny thing to say, still the Mater is pretty funny. So we put our heads together as children sometimes do——'

'Do they? Oh yes.'

'—and Olive who's pretty bossy herself decreed we shouldn't mention you again as it seemed to worry her extra and she had just had a lot of worry. He actually—I hadn't meant to tell you this, it's a dead secret.'

'It shall be. I swear. By all that is without me and within me I swear.' He became incomprehensible in his excitement and uttered words in that unknown tongue. Nearly all tongues were unknown to Lionel, and he was impressed.

'Well, he actually——'

'Man, of whom do you now speak?'

'Oh yes, the Mater's husband, my Dad. He was in the Army too, in fact he attained the rank of major, but a quite unspeakable thing happened—he went native somewhere out East and got cashiered[5]—deserted his wife and left her with five young children to bring up, and no money. She was taking us all away from him when you met us and still had a faint hope that he might pull himself together and follow her. Not he. He never even wrote—remember, this is absolutely secret.'

'Yes, yes,' but he thought the secret a very tame one: how else should a middle-aged husband behave? 'But, Lionel, one question to you the more. For whom did the Major desert the Mater?'

'He went native.'

'With a girl or with a boy?'

'A boy? Good God! Well, I mean to say, with a girl, naturally—I mean, it was somewhere right away in the depths of Burma.'

'Even in Burma there are boys. At least I once heard so. But the Dad went native with a girl. Ver' well. Might not therefore there be offspring?'

'If there were, they'd be half-castes.[6] Pretty depressing prospect. Well, you know what I mean. My family—Dad's, that's to say—can trace itself back nearly two hundred years, and the Mater's goes back to the War of the Roses. It's really pretty awful, Cocoa.'

The half-caste smiled as the warrior floundered. Indeed he valued him most when he fell full length. And the whole conversation—so unimportant in itself—gave him a sense of approaching victory which he had not so far entertained. He had a feeling that Lionel knew that he was in the net or almost in it, and did not mind. Cross-question him further! Quick! Rattle him! 'Is Dad dead?' he snapped.

'I couldn't very well come East if he wasn't. He has made our name stink in these parts. As it is I've had to change my name, or rather drop half of it. He called himself Major Corrie March. We were all proud of the "Corrie" and had reason to be. Try saying "Corrie March" to the Big Eight here, and watch the effect.'

'You must get two passports, must you not, one with and one without a "Corrie" on it. I will fix it, yes? At Bombay?'

'So as I can cheat like you? No, thank you. My name is Lionel March and that's my name.' He poured out some more champagne.

'Are you like him?'

'I should hope not. I hope I'm not cruel and remorseless and selfish and self-indulgent and a liar as he was.'

'I don't mean unimportant things like that. I mean are you like him to look at?'

'You have the strangest ideas of what is important.'

'Was his body like yours?'

'How should I know?'—and he was suddenly shy. 'I was only a kid and the Mater's torn up every photograph of him she could lay her hands on. He

---

5. Dishonorably discharged.
6. Offensive term for people of mixed racial descent.

was a hundred per cent Aryan all right and there was plenty of him as there certainly is of me—indeed there'll be too much of me if I continue swilling at this rate. Suppose we talk about your passports for a change.'

'Was he one in whom those who sought rest found fire, and fire rest?'

'I've not the least idea what you're talking about. Do you mean I'm such a one myself?'

'I do.'

'I've not the least idea——' Then he hesitated. 'Unless . . . no, you're daft[7] as usual, and in any case we've spent more than enough time in dissecting my unfortunate parent. I brought him up to show you how much the Mater has to put up with, one has to make endless allowances for her and you mustn't take it amiss if she's unreasonable about you. She'd probably like you if she got the chance. There was something else that upset her at the time . . . I seem to be bringing out all the family skeletons in a bunch, still they won't go any further, and I feel like chattering to someone about everything, once in a way. I've never had anyone to talk to like you. Never, and don't suppose I ever shall. Do you happen to remember the youngest of us all, the one we called Baby?'

'Ah, that pretty Baby!'

'Well, a fortnight after we landed and while we were up at my grandfather's looking for a house, that poor kid died.'

'Die what of?' he exclaimed, suddenly agitated. He raised his knees and rested his chin on them. With his nudity and his polished duskiness and his strange-shaped head, he suggested an image crouched outside a tomb.

'Influenza, quite straightforward. It was going through the parish and he caught it. But the worst of it was the Mater wouldn't be reasonable. She would insist that it was sunstroke, and that he got it running about with no topi on when she wasn't looking after him properly in this very same Red Sea.'

'Her poor pretty Baby. So I killed him for her.'

'Cocoa! How ever did you guess that? It's exactly what she twisted it round to. We had quite a time with her. Olive argued, grandfather prayed . . . and I could only hang around and do the wrong thing, as I generally do.'

'But she—she saw me only, running in the sun with my devil's head, and m'm m'm m'm all you follow me till the last one the tiny one dies, and she, she talking to an officer, a handsome one, oh to sleep in his arms as I shall in yours, so she forgets the sun and it strikes the tiny one. I see.'

'Yes, you see in a wrong sort of way'; every now and then came these outbursts which ought to be rubbish yet weren't. Wrong of course about his mother, who was the very soul of purity, and over Captain Armstrong, who had become their valued family adviser. But right over Baby's death: she actually had declared that the idle unmanly imp had killed him, and designedly. Of recent years she had not referred to the disaster, and might have forgotten it. He was more than ever vexed with himself for mentioning Cocoanut in the letter he had recently posted to her.

'Did I kill him for you also?'

'For me? Of course not. I know the difference between influenza and sunstroke, and you don't develop the last-named after a three weeks' interval.'

'Did I kill him for anyone—or for anything?'

---

7. Foolish.

Lionel gazed into eyes that gazed through him and through cabin walls into the sea. A few days ago he would have ridiculed the question, but tonight he was respectful. This was because his affection, having struck earthward, was just trying to flower. 'Something's worrying you? Why not tell me about it?' he said.

'Did you love pretty Baby?'

'No, I was accustomed to see him around but he was too small to get interested in and I haven't given him a thought for years. So all's well.'

'There is nothing between us then?'

'Why should there be?'

'Lionel—dare I ask you one more question?'

'Yes, of course.'

'It is about blood. It is the last of all the questions. Have you ever shed blood?'

'No—oh, sorry, I should have said yes. I forgot that little war of mine. It goes clean out of my head between times. A battle's such a mess-up, you wouldn't believe, and this one had a miniature sandstorm raging to make confusion more confounded. Yes, I shed blood all right, or so the official report says. I didn't know at the time.' He was suddenly silent. Vividly and unexpectedly the desert surged up, and he saw it as a cameo,[8] from outside. The central figure—a grotesque one—was himself going berserk, and close to him was a dying savage who had managed to wound him and was trying to speak.

'I hope I never shed blood,' the other said. 'I do not blame others, but for me never.'

'I don't expect you ever will. You're not exactly cut out for a man of war. All the same, I've fallen for you.'

He had not expected to say this, and it was the unexpectedness that so delighted the boy. He turned away his face. It was distorted with joy and suffused with the odd purplish tint that denoted violent emotion. Everything had gone fairly right for a long time. Each step in the stumbling confession had brought him nearer to knowing what the beloved was like. But an open avowal—he had not hoped for so much. 'Before morning I shall have enslaved him,' he thought, 'and he will begin doing whatever I put into his mind.' Even now he did not exult, for he knew by experience that though he always got what he wanted he seldom kept it, also that too much adoration can develop a flaw in the jewel. He remained impassive, crouched like a statue, chin on knees, hands round ankles, waiting for words to which he could safely reply.

'It seemed just a bit of foolery at first,' he went on. 'I woke up properly ashamed of myself after Gib, I don't mind telling you. Since then it's been getting so different, and now it's nothing but us. I tell you one thing though, one silly mistake I've made. I ought never to have mentioned you in that letter to the Mater. There's no advantage in putting her on the scent of something she can't understand; it's all right what we do, I don't mean that.'

'So you want the letter back?'

'But it's posted! Not much use wanting it.'

'Posted?' He was back to his normal and laughed gaily, his sharp teeth gleaming. 'What is posting? Nothing at all, even in a red English pillar-box.

8. Vividly carved stone.

Even thence you can get most things out, and here is a boat. No! My secretary comes to you tomorrow morning: 'Excuse me, Captain March, sir, did you perhaps drop this unposted letter upon the deck?' You thank secretary, you take letter, you write Mater a better letter. Does anything trouble you now?'

'Not really. Except——'

'Except what?'

'Except I'm—I don't know. I'm fonder of you than I know how to say.'

'Should that trouble you?'

O calm mutual night, to one of them triumphant and promising both of them peace! O silence except for the boat throbbing gently! Lionel sighed, with a happiness he couldn't understand. 'You ought to have someone to look after you,' he said tenderly. Had he said this before to a woman and had she responded? No such recollection disturbed him, he did not even know that he was falling in love. 'I wish I could stay with you myself, but of course that's out of the question. If only things were a little different I——Come along, let's get our sleep.'

'You shall sleep and you shall awake.' For the moment was upon them at last, the flower opened to receive them, the appointed star mounted the sky, the beloved leaned against him to switch off the light over by the door. He closed his eyes to anticipate divine darkness. He was going to win. All was happening as he had planned, and when morning came and practical life had to be re-entered he would have won.

'Damn!'

The ugly stupid little word rattled out. 'Damn and blast,' Lionel muttered. As he stretched towards the switch, he had noticed the bolt close to it, and he discovered that he had left the door unbolted. The consequences could have been awkward. 'Pretty careless of me,' he reflected, suddenly wide awake. He looked round the cabin as a general might at a battlefield nearly lost by his own folly. The crouched figure was only a unit in it, and no longer the centre of desire. 'Cocoa, I'm awfully sorry,' he went on. 'As a rule it's you who take the risks, this time it's me. I apologize.'

The other roused himself from the twilight where he had hoped to be joined, and tried to follow the meaningless words. Something must have miscarried, but what? The sound of an apology was odious. He had always loathed the English trick of saying 'It's all my fault'; and if he encountered it in business it provided an extra incentive to cheat, and it was contemptible on the lips of a hero. When he grasped what the little trouble was and what the empty 'damns' signified, he closed his eyes again and said, 'Bolt the door therefore.'

'I have.'

'Turn out the light therefore.'

'I will. But a mistake like this makes one feel all insecure. It could have meant a courtmartial.'

'Could it, man?' he said sadly—sad because the moment towards which they were moving might be passing, because the chances of their convergence might be lost. What could he safely say? 'You was not to blame over the door, dear Lion,' he said. 'I mean we was both to blame. I knew it was unlocked all the time.' He said this hoping to console the beloved and to recall him to the entrance of night. He could not have made a more disastrous remark.

'You knew. But why didn't you say?'

'I had not the time.'

'Not the time to say "Bolt the door"?'

'No, I had not the time. I did not speak because there was no moment for such a speech.'

'No moment when I've been here for ages?'

'And when in that hour? When you come in first? Then? When you embrace me and summon my heart's blood. Is that the moment to speak? When I rest in your arms and you in mine, when your cigarette burns us, when we drink from one glass? When you are smiling? Do I interrupt then? Do I then say, "Captain March, sir, you have however forgotten to bolt the cabin door?" And when we talk of our faraway boat and of poor pretty Baby whom I never killed and I did not want to kill, and I never dreamt to kill—of what should we talk but of things far away? Lionel, no, no. Lion of the Night, come back to me before our hearts cool. Here is our place and we have so far no other and only we can guard each other. The door shut, the door unshut, is nothing, and is the same.'

'It wouldn't be nothing if the steward had come in,' said Lionel grimly.

'What harm if he did come in?'

'Give him the shock of his life, to say the least of it.'

'No shock at all. Such men are accustomed to far worse. He would be sure of a larger tip and therefore pleased. "Excuse me, gentlemen . . ." Then he goes and tomorrow my secretary tips him.'

'Cocoa, for God's sake, the things you sometimes say . . .' The cynicism repelled him. He noticed that it sometimes came after a bout of high faluting. It was a sort of backwash.[9] 'You never seem to realize the risks we run, either. Suppose I got fired from the Army through this.'

'Yes, suppose?'

'Well, what else could I do?'

'You could be my assistant manager at Basra.'[1]

'Not a very attractive alternative.' He was not sure whether he was being laughed at or not, which always rattled him, and the incident of the unbolted door increased in importance. He apologized again 'for my share in it' and added, 'You've not told that scruffy Parsee of yours about us, I do trust.'

'No. Oh no no no no and oh no. Satisfied?'

'Nor the Goanese[2] steward?'

'Not told. Only tipped. Tip all. Of what other use is money?'

'I shall think you've tipped me next.'

'So I have.'

'That's not a pretty thing to say.'

'I am not pretty. I am not like you.' And he burst into tears. Lionel knew that nerves were on edge, but the suggestion that he was a hireling hurt him badly. He whose pride and duty it was to be independent and command! Had he been regarded as a male prostitute? 'What's upset you?' he said as kindly as possible. 'Don't take on so, Cocoa, there's no occasion for it.'

The sobs continued. He was weeping because he had planned wrongly. Rage rather than grief convulsed him. The bolt unbolted, the little snake not driven back into its hole—he had foreseen everything else and ignored the enemy at the gate. Bolt and double-bolt now—they would never complete

9. Motion of a receding wave.   2. From Goa, India.
1. City in what is now southeast Iraq.

the movement of love. As sometimes happened to him when he was unhinged, he could foretell the immediate future, and he knew before Lionel spoke exactly what he was going to say.

'I think I'll go on deck for a smoke.'

'Go.'

'I've a bit of a headache with this stupid misunderstanding, plus too much booze. I want a breath of fresh air. Then I'll come back.'

'When you come back you will not be you. And I may not be I.'

Further tears. Snivellings. 'We're both to blame,' said Lionel patiently, taking up the cigarette-case. 'I'm not letting myself off. I was careless. But why you didn't tell me at once I shall never understand, not if you talk till you're blue. I've explained to you repeatedly that this game we've been playing's a risky one, and honestly I think we'd better never have started it. However, we'll talk about that when you're not so upset.' Here he remembered that the cigarette-case was one of his patron's presents to him, so he substituted for it a favourite old pipe. The change was observed and it caused a fresh paroxysm. Like many men of the warm-blooded type, he was sympathetic to a few tears but exasperated when they persisted. Fellow crying and not trying to stop. Fellow crying as if he had the right to cry. Repeating 'I'll come back' as cordially as he could, he went up on deck to think the whole situation over. For there were several things about it he didn't like at all.

Cocoanut stopped weeping as soon as he was alone. Tears were a method of appeal which had failed, and he must seek comfort for his misery and desolation elsewhere. What he longed to do was to climb up into Lionel's berth above him and snuggle down there and dream that he might be joined. He dared not. Whatever else he ventured, it must not be that. It was forbidden to him, although nothing had ever been said. It was the secret place, the sacred place whence strength issued, as he had learned during the first half-hour of the voyage. It was the lair of a beast who might retaliate. So he remained down in his own berth, the safe one, where his lover would certainly never return. It was wiser to work and make money, and he did so for a time. It was still wiser to sleep, and presently he put his ledger aside and lay motionless. His eyes closed. His nostrils occasionally twitched as if responding to something which the rest of his body ignored. The scarf covered him. For it was one of his many superstitions that it is dangerous to lie unclad when alone. Jealous of what she sees, the hag comes with her scimitar,[3] and she . . . Or she lifts up a man when he feels lighter than air.

V

Up on deck, alone with his pipe, Lionel began to recover his poise and his sense of leadership. Not that he and his pipe were really alone, for the deck was covered with passengers who had had their bedding carried up and now slept under the stars. They lay prone in every direction, and he had to step carefully between them on his way to the railing. He had forgotten that this migration happened nightly as soon as a boat entered the Red Sea; his nights had passed otherwise and elsewhere. Here lay a guileless subaltern, cherry-cheeked; there lay Colonel Arbuthnot, his bottom turned. Mrs Arbuthnot lay parted from her lord in the ladies' section. In the morning,

3. Curved Asian sword.

very early, the Goanese stewards would awake the sahibs and carry their bedding back to their cabins. It was an old ritual—not practised in the English Channel or the Bay of Biscay or even in the Mediterranean—and on previous voyages he had taken part in it.

How decent and reliable they looked, the folk to whom he belonged! He had been born one of them, he had his work with them, he meant to marry into their caste. If he forfeited their companionship he would become nobody and nothing. The widened expanse of the sea, the winking lighthouse, helped to compose him, but what really recalled him to sanity was this quiet sleeping company of his peers. He liked his profession, and was rising in it thanks to that little war; it would be mad to jeopardize it, which he had been doing ever since he drank too much champagne at Gibraltar.

Not that he had ever been a saint. No—he had occasionally joined a brothel expedition, so as not to seem better than his fellow officers. But he had not been so much bothered by sex as were some of them. He hadn't had the time, what with his soldiering duties and his obligations at home as eldest son, and the doc said an occasional wet dream was nothing to worry about. Don't sleep on your back, though. On this simple routine he had proceeded since puberty. And during the past few months he had proceeded even further. Learning that he was to be posted to India, where he would contact Isabel, he had disciplined himself more severely and practised chastity even in thought. It was the least he could do for the girl he hoped to marry. Sex had entirely receded— only to come charging back like a bull. That infernal Cocoa—the mischief he had done. He had woken up so much that might have slept.

For Isabel's sake, as for his profession's, their foolish relationship must stop at once. He could not think how he had yielded to it, or why it had involved him so deeply. It would have ended at Bombay, it would have to end now, and Cocoanut must cry his eyes out if he thought it worth while. So far all was clear. But behind Isabel, behind the Army, was another power, whom he could not consider calmly; his mother, blind-eyed in the midst of the enormous web she had spun—filaments drifting everywhere, strands catching. There was no reasoning with her or about her, she understood nothing and controlled everything. She had suffered too much and was too high-minded to be judged like other people, she was outside carnality and incapable of pardoning it. Earlier in the evening, when Cocoa mentioned her, he had tried to imagine her with his father, enjoying the sensations he was beginning to find so pleasant, but the attempt was sacrilegious and he was shocked at himself. From the great blank country she inhabited came a voice condemning him and all her children for sin, but condemning him most. There was no parleying[4] with her—she was a voice. God had not granted her ears—nor could she see, mercifully: the sight of him stripping[5] would have killed her. He, her first-born, set apart for the redemption of the family name. His surviving brother was too much a bookworm to be of any use, and the other two were girls.

He spat into the sea. He promised her 'Never again'. The words went out into the night like other enchantments. He said them aloud, and Colonel Arbuthnot, who was a light sleeper, woke up and switched on his torch.

'Hullo, who's that, what's there?'

'March, sir, Lionel March. I'm afraid I've disturbed you.'

---

4. Mutual conversation.
5. Forster's substitution for his original phrase, "topping a dago." ("Topping": copulating with).

'No, no, Lionel, that's all right, I wasn't asleep. Ye gods, what gorgeous pyjamas the fellow's wearing. What's he going about like a lone wolf for? Eh?'

'Too hot in my cabin, sir. Nothing sinister.'

'How goes the resident wog?'

'The resident wog he sleeps.'

'By the way, what's his name?'

'Moraes, I believe.'

'Exactly. Mr Moraes is in for trouble.'

'Oh. What for, sir?'

'For being on board. Lady Manning has just heard the story. It turns out that he gave someone in the London office a fat bribe to get him a passage though the boat was full, and as an easy way out they put him into your cabin. I don't care who gives or takes bribes. Doesn't interest me. But if the Company thinks it can treat a British officer like that it's very much mistaken. I'm going to raise hell at Bombay.'

'He's not been any particular nuisance,' said Lionel after a pause.

'I daresay not. It's the question of our prestige in the East, and it is also very hard luck on you, very hard. Why don't you come and sleep on deck like the rest of the gang?'

'Sound idea, I will.'

'We've managed to cordon off this section of the deck, and woe betide anything black that walks this way, if it's only a beetle. Good night.'

'Good night, sir.' Then something snapped and he heard himself shouting, 'Bloody rubbish, leave the kid alone.'

'Wh—what's that, didn't catch,' said the puzzled Colonel.

'Nothing sir, sorry sir.' And he was back in the cabin.

Why on earth had he nearly betrayed himself just as everything was going right? There seemed a sort of devil around. At the beginning of the voyage he had tempted him to throw himself overboard for no reason, but this was something more serious. 'When you come back to the cabin you will not be you,' Cocoa had said; and was it so?

However, the lower berth was empty, that was something, the boy must have gone to the lav, and he slipped out of his effeminate pyjamas and prepared to finish the night where he belonged—a good sleep there would steady him. His forearm was already along the rail, his foot poised for the upspring, when he saw what had happened.

'Hullo, Cocoanut, up in my berth for a change?' he said in clipped officer-tones, for it was dangerous to get angry. 'Stay there if you want to, I've just decided to sleep on deck.' There was no reply, but his own remarks pleased him and he decided to go further. 'As a matter of fact I shan't be using our cabin again except when it is absolutely necessary,' he continued. 'It's scarcely three days to Bombay, so I can easily manage, and I shan't, we shan't be meeting again after disembarkation. As I said earlier on, the whole thing has been a bit of a mistake. I wish we . . .' He stopped. If only it wasn't so difficult to be kind! But his talk with the Colonel and his communion with the Mater prevented it. He must keep with his own people, or he would perish. He added, 'Sorry to have to say all this.'

'Kiss me.'

The words fell quietly after his brassiness and vulgarity and he could not answer them. The face was close to his now, the body curved away seductively into darkness.

'Kiss me.'

'No.'

'Noah? No? Then I kiss you.' And he lowered his mouth on to the muscular forearm and bit it.

Lionel yelped with the pain.

'Bloody bitch, wait till I . . .' Blood oozed between the gold-bright hairs. 'You wait . . .' And the scar in his groin reopened. The cabin vanished. He was back in a desert fighting savages. One of them asked for mercy, stumbled, and found none.

The sweet act of vengeance followed, sweeter than ever for both of them, and as ecstasy hardened into agony his hands twisted the throat. Neither of them knew when the end came, and he when he realized it felt no sadness, no remorse. It was part of a curve that had long been declining, and had nothing to do with death. He covered again with his warmth and kissed the closed eyelids tenderly and spread the bright-coloured scarf. Then he burst out of the stupid cabin on to the deck, and naked and with the seeds of love on him he dived into the sea.

The scandal was appalling. The Big Eight did their best, but it was soon all over the boat that a British officer had committed suicide after murdering a half-caste. Some of the passengers recoiled from such news. Others snuffled for more. The secretary of Moraes was induced to gossip and hint at proclivities, the cabin steward proved to have been overtipped, the Master at Arms had had complaints which he had managed to stifle, the Purser had been suspicious throughout, and the doctor who examined the injuries divulged that strangulation was only one of them, and that March had been a monster in human form, of whom the earth was well rid. The cabin was sealed up for further examination later, and the place where the two boys had made love and the tokens they had exchanged in their love went on without them to Bombay. For Lionel had been only a boy.

His body was never recovered—the blood on it quickly attracted the sharks. The body of his victim was consigned to the deep with all possible speed. There was a slight disturbance at the funeral. The native crew had become interested in it, no one understood why, and when the corpse was lowered were heard betting which way it would float. It moved northwards— contrary to the prevailing current—and there were clappings of hands and some smiles.

Finally Mrs March had to be informed. Colonel Arbuthnot and Lady Manning were deputed for the thankless task. Colonel Arbuthnot assured her that her son's death had been accidental, whatever she heard to the contrary; that he had stumbled overboard in the darkness during a friendly talk they had had together on deck. Lady Manning spoke with warmth and affection of his good looks and good manners and his patience 'with us old fogies at our Bridge.' Mrs March thanked them for writing but made no comment. She also received a letter from Lionel himself—the one that should have been intercepted in the post—and she never mentioned his name again.

1913–58   1972

VIRGINIA WOOLF
1882–1941

Virginia Woolf was born in London, the daughter of Julia Jackson Duckworth, a member of the Duckworth publishing family, and Leslie (later Sir Leslie) Stephen, the Victorian critic, philosopher, biographer, and scholar. She grew up within a large and talented family, educating herself in her father's magnificent library, meeting in childhood many eminent Victorians, and learning Greek from the essayist and critic Walter Pater's sister. Writing and the intellectual life thus came naturally to her. But her youth was shadowed by suffering: her older half-brother sexually abused her; her mother died in 1895, precipitating the first of her mental breakdowns; a beloved half-sister died in childbirth two years later; her father died of cancer in 1904; and a brother died of typhoid in 1906.

After her father's death she settled with her sister and two brothers in Bloomsbury, the district of London that later became associated with the group among whom she moved. The Bloomsbury Group was an intellectual coterie frequented at various times by the biographer Lytton Strachey, the economist John Maynard Keynes, the art critic Roger Fry, and the novelist E. M. Forster. When her sister, Vanessa, a notable painter, married Clive Bell, an art critic, in 1907, Woolf and her brother Adrian took another house in Bloomsbury, and there they entertained their literary and artistic friends at evening gatherings, where the conversation sparkled. The Bloomsbury Group thrived at the center of the middle-class and upper-middle-class London intelligentsia. Their intelligence was equaled by their frankness, notably on sexual topics, and the sexual life of Bloomsbury provided ample material for discussion and contributed to Woolf's freedom of thinking about gender relations. The painter Duncan Grant, for example, was at different times the lover of Keynes, Woolf's brother Adrian, and her sister, whose daughter, Angelica, he fathered. Woolf too was bisexual; and thirteen years after her marriage to the journalist and essayist Leonard Woolf, she fell passionately in love with the poet Vita (Victoria) Sackville-West, wife of the bisexual diplomat and author Harold Nicolson. Woolf's relationship with this aristocratic lesbian inspired the most lighthearted and scintillating of her books, *Orlando* (1928), a novel about a transhistorical androgynous protagonist, whose identity shifts from masculine to feminine over centuries.

Underneath Woolf's liveliness and wit—qualities so well known among the Bloomsbury Group—lay psychological tensions created partly by her childhood wounds and partly by her perfectionism, she being her own most exacting critic. The public was unaware until her death that she had been subject to periods of severe depression, particularly after finishing a book. In March 1941 she drowned herself in a river, an act influenced by her dread of World War II (had the Nazis invaded England, she and Leonard would have been arrested by the Gestapo because Leonard was Jewish) and her fear that she was about to lose her mind and become a burden on her husband, who had supported her emotionally and intellectually. (In 1917 the Woolfs had founded the Hogarth Press, which published some of the most interesting literature of their time, including T. S. Eliot's *Poems* [1919], fiction by Maxim Gorky, Katherine Mansfield, and E. M. Forster, the English translations of Freud, and Virginia's novels.)

As a fiction writer Woolf rebelled against what she called the "materialism" of novelists such as her contemporaries Arnold Bennett and John Galsworthy, who depicted suffering and social injustice through gritty realism, and she sought to render more intricately those aspects of consciousness in which she felt the truth of human experience lay. In her essay "Modern Fiction" she defines the task of the novelist as looking within, as conveying the mind receiving "a myriad impressions," as representing the "luminous halo" or "semi-transparent envelope surrounding us from the beginning of consciousness to the end." In her novels she abandoned linear narratives in favor of interior monologues and stream-of-consciousness narration, exploring with great subtlety problems of personal identity and personal relationships as well as the significance of time, change, loss, and memory for human personality. After two conventionally realistic novels, *The Voyage Out* (1915) and *Night and Day* (1919), she developed her own style, a carefully modulated flow that brought into prose fiction something of the rhythms and imagery of lyric poetry. While intensely psychological and interior, her novels also found inspiration and material in the physical realities of the body and in the heavily trafficked and populated streets of London. In *Monday or Tuesday* (1921), a series of sketches, she explored the possibilities of moving between action and contemplation, between retrospection and anticipation, between specific external events and delicate tracings of the flow of consciousness. These technical experiments made possible those later novels in which her characteristic method is fully developed—the elegiac *Jacob's Room* (1922); *Mrs. Dalloway* (1925), the first completely successful realization of her style; *To the Lighthouse* (1927), which in part memorializes her parents; *The Waves* (1931), the most experimental and difficult of her novels; and *Between the Acts* (1941), which includes a discontinuous pageant of English history and was published after her death.

Woolf was also a prodigious reviewer and essayist. She began to write criticism in 1905 for the *Times Literary Supplement* and published some five hundred reviews and essays for it and other periodicals, collected in *The Common Reader* (1925) and *The Second Common Reader* (1932); her prose presents itself as suggestive rather than authoritative and has an engaging air of spontaneity. In marked contrast to the formal language of the lecture hall or philosophical treatise, arenas and forms of learning from which women were historically barred, she writes in an informal, personal, playfully polemical tone, which is implicitly linked to her identity as a female writer. In her essays she is equally concerned with her own craft as a writer and with what it was like to be a quite different person living in a different age. At once more informal and more revealing are the six volumes of her *Letters* (1975–80) and five volumes of her *Diary* (1977–84), which she began to write in 1917. These, with their running commentary on her life and work, resemble a painter's sketchbooks and serve as a reminder that her writings, for all their variety, have the coherence found only in the work of the greatest literary artists.

Over the course of her career, Woolf grew increasingly concerned with the position of women, especially professional women, and the constrictions under which they suffered. She wrote several cogent essays on the subject, and women's social subjection also figures in her fiction. Her novel *The Years* (1937) was originally to have reflections on the position of women interspersed amid the action, but she later decided to publish them as a separate book, *Three Guineas* (1938), which also includes an incisive meditation on war (see the excerpt in "Voices from World War II," later in this volume). In *A Room of One's Own* (1929), an essay based on two lectures on "Women and Fiction" delivered to female students at Cambridge, Woolf discusses various male institutions that historically either were denied to or oppressed women. Refused access to education, wealth, and property ownership, women such as Shakespeare's imaginary sister lacked the conditions necessary to write and were unable to develop a literature of their own. Woolf advocated the creation of a literature that would include women's experience and ways of thinking, but instead of encouraging an exclusively female perspective, she proposed literature that would be "androgynous in mind" and resonate equally with men and women.

The Mark on the Wall

Perhaps it was the middle of January in the present year that I first looked up and saw the mark on the wall. In order to fix a date it is necessary to remember what one saw. So now I think of the fire; the steady film of yellow light upon the page of my book; the three chrysanthemums in the round glass bowl on the mantelpiece. Yes, it must have been the winter time, and we had just finished our tea, for I remember that I was smoking a cigarette when I looked up and saw the mark on the wall for the first time. I looked up through the smoke of my cigarette and my eye lodged for a moment upon the burning coals, and that old fancy of the crimson flag flapping from the castle tower came into my mind, and I thought of the cavalcade of red knights riding up the side of the black rock. Rather to my relief the sight of the mark interrupted the fancy, for it is an old fancy, an automatic fancy, made as a child perhaps. The mark was a small round mark, black upon the white wall, about six or seven inches above the mantelpiece.

How readily our thoughts swarm upon a new object, lifting it a little way, as ants carry a blade of straw so feverishly, and then leave it. . . . If that mark was made by a nail, it can't have been for a picture, it must have been for a miniature—the miniature of a lady with white powdered curls, powder-dusted cheeks, and lips like red carnations. A fraud of course, for the people who had this house before us would have chosen pictures in that way—an old picture for an old room. That is the sort of people they were—very interesting people, and I think of them so often, in such queer places, because one will never see them again, never know what happened next. They wanted to leave this house because they wanted to change their style of furniture, so he said, and he was in process of saying that in his opinion art should have ideas behind it when we were torn asunder, as one is torn from the old lady about to pour out tea and the young man about to hit the tennis ball in the back garden of the suburban villa as one rushes past in the train.

But for that mark, I'm not sure about it; I don't believe it was made by a nail after all; it's too big, too round, for that. I might get up, but if I got up and looked at it, ten to one I shouldn't be able to say for certain; because once a thing's done, no one ever knows how it happened. Oh! dear me, the mystery of life; the inaccuracy of thought! The ignorance of humanity! To show how very little control of our possessions we have—what an accidental affair this living is after all our civilisation—let me just count over a few of the things lost in one lifetime, beginning, for that seems always the most mysterious of losses—what cat would gnaw, what rat would nibble—three pale blue canisters of book-binding tools? Then there were the bird cages, the iron hoops, the steel skates, the Queen Anne coal-scuttle, the bagatelle[1] board, the hand organ—all gone, and jewels, too. Opals and emeralds, they lie about the roots of turnips. What a scraping paring affair it is to be sure! The wonder is that I've any clothes on my back, that I sit surrounded by solid furniture at this moment. Why, if one wants to compare life to anything, one must liken it to being blown through the Tube[2] at fifty miles an hour—landing at the other end without a single hairpin in one's hair! Shot

---

1. Game played on oblong table with cue and balls. "Coal-scuttle": metal pail for carrying coal.   2. The London underground railway, or subway.

out at the feet of God entirely naked! Tumbling head over heels in the asphodel meadows[3] like brown paper parcels pitched down a shoot in the post
office! With one's hair flying back like the tail of a race-horse. Yes, that seems
to express the rapidity of life, the perpetual waste and repair; all so casual, all
so haphazard. . . .

But after life. The slow pulling down of thick green stalks so that the cup
of the flower, as it turns over, deluges one with purple and red light. Why,
after all, should one not be born there as one is born here, helpless, speechless, unable to focus one's eyesight, groping at the roots of the grass, at the
toes of the Giants? As for saying which are trees, and which are men and
women, or whether there are such things, that one won't be in a condition
to do for fifty years or so. There will be nothing but spaces of light and dark,
intersected by thick stalks, and rather higher up perhaps, rose-shaped blots
of an indistinct colour—dim pinks and blues—which will, as time goes on,
become more definite, become—I don't know what. . . .

And yet that mark on the wall is not a hole at all. It may even be caused
by some round black substance, such as a small rose leaf, left over from the
summer, and I, not being a very vigilant housekeeper—look at the dust on
the mantelpiece, for example, the dust which, so they say, buried Troy[4] three
times over, only fragments of pots utterly refusing annihilation, as one can
believe.

The tree outside the window taps very gently on the pane. . . . I want to
think quietly, calmly, spaciously, never to be interrupted, never to have to
rise from my chair, to slip easily from one thing to another, without any
sense of hostility, or obstacle. I want to sink deeper and deeper, away from
the surface, with its hard separate facts. To steady myself, let me catch hold
of the first idea that passes . . . Shakespeare. . . . Well, he will do as well as
another. A man who sat himself solidly in an arm-chair, and looked into the
fire, so— A shower of ideas fell perpetually from some very high Heaven
down through his mind. He leant his forehead on his hand, and people, looking in through the open door—for this scene is supposed to take place on a
summer's evening— But how dull this is, this historical fiction! It doesn't
interest me at all. I wish I could hit upon a pleasant track of thought, a track
indirectly reflecting credit upon myself, for those are the pleasantest thoughts,
and very frequent even in the minds of modest mouse-coloured people, who
believe genuinely that they dislike to hear their own praises. They are not
thoughts directly praising oneself; that is the beauty of them; they are
thoughts like this:

"And then I came into the room. They were discussing botany. I said how
I'd seen a flower growing on a dust heap on the site of an old house in Kings-
way.[5] The seed, I said, must have been sown in the reign of Charles the First.
What flowers grew in the reign of Charles the First?" I asked—(but I don't
remember the answer). Tall flowers with purple tassels to them perhaps. And
so it goes on. All the time I'm dressing up the figure of myself in my own
mind, lovingly, stealthily, not openly adoring it, for if I did that, I should
catch myself out, and stretch my hand at once for a book in self-protection.
Indeed, it is curious how instinctively one protects the image of oneself from
idolatry or any other handling that could make it ridiculous, or too unlike the

---

3. I.e., heaven, the next world (in Greek mythology asphodel flowers grow in the Elysian fields).
4. Legendary site of ancient war chronicled in

Homer's Greek epic *The Iliad*.
5. Street in London.

original to be believed in any longer. Or is it not so very curious after all? It is a matter of great importance. Suppose the looking-glass smashes, the image disappears, and the romantic figure with the green of forest depths all about it is there no longer, but only that shell of a person which is seen by other people—what an airless, shallow, bald, prominent world it becomes! A world not to be lived in. As we face each other in omnibuses and underground railways we are looking into the mirror; that accounts for the vagueness, the gleam of glassiness, in our eyes. And the novelists in future will realise more and more the importance of these reflections, for of course there is not one reflection but an almost infinite number; those are the depths they will explore, those the phantoms they will pursue, leaving the description of reality more and more out of their stories, taking a knowledge of it for granted, as the Greeks did and Shakespeare perhaps—but these generalisations are very worthless. The military sound of the word is enough. It recalls leading articles, cabinet ministers—a whole class of things indeed which, as a child, one thought the thing itself, the standard thing, the real thing, from which one could not depart save at the risk of nameless damnation. Generalisations bring back somehow Sunday in London, Sunday afternoon walks, Sunday luncheons, and also ways of speaking of the dead, clothes, and habits—like the habit of sitting all together in one room until a certain hour, although nobody liked it. There was a rule for everything. The rule for tablecloths at that particular period was that they should be made of tapestry with little yellow compartments marked upon them, such as you may see in photographs of the carpets in the corridors of the royal palaces. Tablecloths of a different kind were not real tablecloths. How shocking, and yet how wonderful it was to discover that these real things, Sunday luncheons, Sunday walks, country houses, and tablecloths were not entirely real, were indeed half phantoms, and the damnation which visited the disbeliever in them was only a sense of illegitimate freedom. What now takes the place of those things I wonder, those real standard things? Men perhaps, should you be a woman; the masculine point of view which governs our lives, which sets the standard, which establishes Whitaker's Table of Precedency,[6] which has become, I suppose, since the war, half a phantom to many men and women, which soon, one may hope, will be laughed into the dustbin where the phantoms go, the mahogany sideboards and the Landseer[7] prints, Gods and Devils, Hell and so forth, leaving us all with an intoxicating sense of illegitimate freedom—if freedom exists. . . .

In certain lights that mark on the wall seems actually to project from the wall. Nor is it entirely circular. I cannot be sure, but it seems to cast a perceptible shadow, suggesting that if I ran my finger down that strip of the wall it would, at a certain point, mount and descend a small tumulus, a smooth tumulus like those barrows on the South Downs[8] which are, they say, either tombs or camps. Of the two I should prefer them to be tombs, desiring melancholy like most English people, and finding it natural at the end of a walk to think of the bones stretched beneath the turf. . . . There must be some book about it. Some antiquary must have dug up those bones and given them a name. . . . What sort of a man is an antiquary, I wonder? Retired

6. *Whitaker's Almanack*, an annual compendium of information, prints a "Table of Precedency," which shows the order in which the various ranks in public life and society proceed on formal occasions.
7. Sir Edwin Henry Landseer (1802–1873),

English painter, reproductions of whose *Stag at Bay, Monarch of the Glen*, and similar animal paintings were often found in Victorian homes.
8. A range of low hills in southeastern England. "Barrows": mounds of earth or stones erected by prehistoric peoples, usually as burial places.

Colonels for the most part, I daresay, leading parties of aged labourers to the top here, examining clods of earth and stone, and getting into correspondence with the neighbouring clergy, which, being opened at breakfast time, gives them a feeling of importance, and the comparison of arrow-heads necessitates cross-country journeys to the country towns, an agreeable necessity both to them and to their elderly wives, who wish to make plum jam or to clean out the study, and have every reason for keeping that great question of the camp or the tomb in perpetual suspension, while the Colonel himself feels agreeably philosophic in accumulating evidence on both sides of the question. It is true that he does finally incline to believe in the camp; and, being opposed, indites a pamphlet which he is about to read at the quarterly meeting of the local society when a stroke lays him low, and his last conscious thoughts are not of wife or child, but of the camp and that arrowhead there, which is now in the case at the local museum, together with the foot of a Chinese murderess, a handful of Elizabethan nails, a great many Tudor clay pipes, a piece of Roman pottery, and the wineglass that Nelson[9] drank out of—proving I really don't know what.

No, no, nothing is proved, nothing is known. And if I were to get up at this very moment and ascertain that the mark on the wall is really—what shall we say?—the head of a gigantic old nail, driven in two hundred years ago, which has now, owing to the patient attrition of many generations of housemaids, revealed its head above the coat of paint, and is taking its first view of modern life in the sight of a white-walled fire-lit room, what should I gain?— Knowledge? Matter for further speculation? I can think sitting still as well as standing up. And what is knowledge? What are our learned men save the descendants of witches and hermits who crouched in caves and in woods brewing herbs, interrogating shrew-mice and writing down the language of the stars? And the less we honour them as our superstitions dwindle and our respect for beauty and health of mind increases. . . . Yes, one could imagine a very pleasant world. A quiet, spacious world, with the flowers so red and blue in the open fields. A world without professors or specialists or house-keepers with the profiles of policemen, a world which one could slice with one's thought as a fish slices the water with his fin, grazing the stems of the water-lilies, hanging suspended over nests of white sea eggs. . . . How peaceful it is down here, rooted in the centre of the world and gazing up through the grey waters, with their sudden gleams of light, and their reflections—if it were not for Whitaker's Almanack—if it were not for the Table of Precedency!

I must jump up and see for myself what that mark on the wall really is—a nail, a rose-leaf, a crack in the wood?

Here is Nature once more at her old game of self-preservation. This train of thought, she perceives, is threatening mere waste of energy, even some collision with reality, for who will ever be able to lift a finger against Whitaker's Table of Precedency? The Archbishop of Canterbury is followed by the Lord High Chancellor; the Lord High Chancellor is followed by the Archbishop of York. Everybody follows somebody, such is the philosophy of Whitaker; and the great thing is to know who follows whom. Whitaker knows, and let that, so Nature counsels, comfort you, instead of enraging you; and if you can't be comforted, if you must shatter this hour of peace, think of the mark on the wall.

9. Horatio Nelson (1758–1805), celebrated British admiral. "Tudor": 15th-century English.

I understand Nature's game—her prompting to take action as a way of ending any thought that threatens to excite or to pain. Hence, I suppose, comes our slight contempt for men of action—men, we assume, who don't think. Still, there's no harm in putting a full stop to one's disagreeable thoughts by looking at a mark on the wall.

Indeed, now that I have fixed my eyes upon it, I feel that I have grasped a plank in the sea; I feel a satisfying sense of reality which at once turns the two Archbishops and the Lord High Chancellor to the shadows of shades. Here is something definite, something real. Thus, waking from a midnight dream of horror, one hastily turns on the light and lies quiescent, worshipping the chest of drawers, worshipping solidity, worshipping reality, worshipping the impersonal world which is a proof of some existence other than ours. That is what one wants to be sure of. . . . Wood is a pleasant thing to think about. It comes from a tree; and trees grow, and we don't know how they grow. For years and years they grow, without paying any attention to us, in meadows, in forests, and by the side of rivers—all things one likes to think about. The cows swish their tails beneath them on hot afternoons; they paint rivers so green that when a moorhen dives one expects to see its feathers all green when it comes up again. I like to think of the fish balanced against the stream like flags blown out; and of water-beetles slowly raising domes of mud upon the bed of the river. I like to think of the tree itself: first of the close dry sensation of being wood; then the grinding of the storm; then the slow, delicious ooze of sap; I like to think of it, too, on winter's nights standing in the empty field with all leaves close-furled, nothing tender exposed to the iron bullets of the moon, a naked mast upon an earth that goes tumbling, tumbling, all night long. The song of birds must sound very loud and strange in June; and how cold the feet of insects must feel upon it, as they make laborious progresses up the creases of the bark, or sun themselves upon the thin green awning of the leaves, and look straight in front of them with diamond-cut red eyes. . . . One by one the fibres snap beneath the immense cold pressure of the earth, then the last storm comes and, falling, the highest branches drive deep into the ground again. Even so, life isn't done with; there are a million patient, watchful lives still for a tree, all over the world, in bedrooms, in ships, on the pavement, living rooms, where men and women sit after tea, smoking cigarettes. It is full of peaceful thoughts, happy thoughts, this tree. I should like to take each one separately—but something is getting in the way. . . . Where was I? What has it all been about? A tree? A river? The Downs?[1] Whitaker's Almanack? The fields of asphodel? I can't remember a thing. Everything's moving, falling, slipping, vanishing. . . . There is a vast upheaval of matter. Someone is standing over me and saying:

"I'm going out to buy a newspaper."

"Yes?"

"Though it's no good buying newspapers. . . . Nothing ever happens. Curse this war; God damn this war! . . . All the same, I don't see why we should have a snail on our wall."

Ah, the mark on the wall! It was a snail.

1921

---

1. Part of the sea off the east coast of Kent (or perhaps a reference to the South Downs, the hills mentioned earlier in "The Mark on the Wall").

Modern Fiction

In making any survey, even the freest and loosest, of modern fiction, it is difficult not to take it for granted that the modern practice of the art is somehow an improvement upon the old. With their simple tools and primitive materials, it might be said, Fielding[1] did well and Jane Austen even better, but compare their opportunities with ours! Their masterpieces certainly have a strange air of simplicity. And yet the analogy between literature and the process, to choose an example, of making motor cars scarcely holds good beyond the first glance. It is doubtful whether in the course of the centuries, though we have learnt much about making machines, we have learnt anything about making literature. We do not come to write better; all that we can be said to do is to keep moving, now a little in this direction, now in that, but with a circular tendency should the whole course of the track be viewed from a sufficiently lofty pinnacle. It need scarcely be said that we make no claim to stand, even momentarily, upon that vantage-ground. On the flat, in the crowd, half blind with dust, we look back with envy to those happier warriors, whose battle is won and whose achievements wear so serene an air of accomplishment that we can scarcely refrain from whispering that the fight was not so fierce for them as for us. It is for the historian of literature to decide; for him to say if we are now beginning or ending or standing in the middle of a great period of prose fiction, for down in the plain little is visible. We only know that certain gratitudes and hostilities inspire us; that certain paths seem to lead to fertile land, others to the dust and the desert; and of this perhaps it may be worth while to attempt some account.

Our quarrel, then, is not with the classics, and if we speak of quarrelling with Mr Wells, Mr Bennett, and Mr Galsworthy;[2] it is partly that by the mere fact of their existence in the flesh their work has a living, breathing, everyday imperfection which bids us take what liberties with it we choose. But it is also true, that, while we thank them for a thousand gifts, we reserve our unconditional gratitude for Mr Hardy, for Mr Conrad, and in much lesser degree for the Mr Hudson of *The Purple Land, Green Mansions*, and *Far Away and Long Ago*.[3] Mr Wells, Mr Bennett, and Mr Galsworthy have excited so many hopes and disappointed them so persistently that our gratitude largely takes the form of thanking them for having shown us what they might have done but have not done; what we certainly could not do, but as certainly, perhaps, do not wish to do. No single phrase will sum up the charge or grievance which we have to bring against a mass of work so large in its volume and embodying so many qualities, both admirable and the reverse. If we tried to formulate our meaning in one word we should say that these three writers are materialists. It is because they are concerned not with the spirit but with the body that they have disappointed us, and left us with the feeling that the sooner English fiction turns its back upon them, as politely as may be, and marches, if only into the desert, the better for its soul. Naturally, no single word reaches the centre of three separate targets.

1. Henry Fielding (1707–1754), English novelist.
2. H. G. Wells (1866–1946), Arnold Bennett (1867–1931), John Galsworthy (1867–1933), English novelists.
3. W. H. Hudson (1841–1922), naturalist and writer, was born in Argentina, although he later lived in London. *The Purple Land* (1885) is about South America; *Green Mansions* (1904), a novel set in South America, was his first real success.

In the case of Mr Wells it falls notably wide of the mark. And yet even with him it indicates to our thinking the fatal alloy in his genius, the great clod of clay that has got itself mixed up with the purity of his inspiration. But Mr Bennett is perhaps the worst culprit of the three, inasmuch as he is by far the best workman. He can make a book so well constructed and solid in its craftsmanship that it is difficult for the most exacting of critics to see through what chink or crevice decay can creep in. There is not so much as a draught between the frames of the windows, or a crack in the boards. And yet—if life should refuse to live there? That is a risk which the creator of *The Old Wives' Tale*, George Cannon, Edwin Clayhanger,[4] and hosts of other figures, may well claim to have surmounted. His characters live abundantly, even unexpectedly, but it remains to ask how do they live, and what do they live for? More and more they seem to us, deserting even the well-built villa in the Five Towns,[5] to spend their time in some softly padded first-class railway carriage, pressing bells and buttons innumerable; and the destiny to which they travel so luxuriously becomes more and more unquestionably an eternity of bliss spent in the very best hotel in Brighton.[6] It can scarcely be said of Mr Wells that he is a materialist in the sense that he takes too much delight in the solidity of his fabric. His mind is too generous in its sympathies to allow him to spend much time in making things shipshape and substantial. He is a materialist from sheer goodness of heart, taking upon his shoulders the work that ought to have been discharged by Government officials, and in the plethora of his ideas and facts scarcely having leisure to realize, or forgetting to think important, the crudity and coarseness of his human beings. Yet what more damaging criticism can there be both of his earth and of his Heaven than that they are to be inhabited here and hereafter by his Joans and his Peters?[7] Does not the inferiority of their natures tarnish whatever institutions and ideals may be provided for them by the generosity of their creator? Nor, profoundly though we respect the integrity and humanity of Mr Galsworthy, shall we find what we seek in his pages.

If we fasten, then, one label on all these books, on which is one word, materialists, we mean by it that they write of unimportant things; that they spend immense skill and immense industry making the trivial and the transitory appear the true and the enduring.

We have to admit that we are exacting, and, further, that we find it difficult to justify our discontent by explaining what it is that we exact. We frame our question differently at different times. But it reappears most persistently as we drop the finished novel on the crest of a sigh—Is it worth while? What is the point of it all? Can it be that, owing to one of those little deviations which the human spirit seems to make from time to time, Mr Bennett has come down with his magnificent apparatus for catching life just an inch or two on the wrong side? Life escapes; and perhaps without life nothing else is worth while. It is a confession of vagueness to have to make use of such a figure as this, but we scarcely better the matter by speaking, as critics are prone to do, of reality. Admitting the vagueness which afflicts all criticism of novels, let us hazard the opinion that for us at this moment the form of

---

4. Characters in Arnold Bennett's novels; *The Old Wives' Tale* (1908) is the best known.
5. The pottery towns of Staffordshire in which much of Bennett's fiction was set.
6. Once-fashionable seaside resort on the south-

west coast of England.
7. In his novel *Joan and Peter: The Story of an Education* (1918), Wells advocates education to address social problems.

fiction most in vogue more often misses than secures the thing we seek. Whether we call it life or spirit, truth or reality, this, the essential thing, has moved off, or on, and refuses to be contained any longer in such ill-fitting vestments as we provide. Nevertheless, we go on perseveringly, conscientiously, constructing our two and thirty chapters after a design which more and more ceases to resemble the vision in our minds. So much of the enormous labour of proving the solidity, the likeness to life, of the story is not merely labour thrown away but labour misplaced to the extent of obscuring and blotting out the light of the conception. The writer seems constrained, not by his own free will but by some powerful and unscrupulous tyrant who has him in thrall, to provide a plot, to provide comedy, tragedy, love interest, and an air of probability embalming the whole so impeccable that if all his figures were to come to life they would find themselves dressed down to the last button of their coats in the fashion of the hour. The tyrant is obeyed; the novel is done to a turn. But sometimes, more and more often as time goes by, we suspect a momentary doubt, a spasm of rebellion, as the pages fill themselves in the customary way. Is life like this? Must novels be like this?

Look within and life, it seems, is very far from being "like this." Examine for a moment an ordinary mind on an ordinary day. The mind receives a myriad impressions—trivial, fantastic, evanescent, or engraved with the sharpness of steel. From all sides they come, an incessant shower of innumerable atoms; and as they fall, as they shape themselves into the life of Monday or Tuesday,[8] the accent falls differently from of old; the moment of importance came not here but there; so that, if a writer were a free man and not a slave, if he could write what he chose, not what he must, if he could base his work upon his own feeling and not upon convention, there would be no plot, no comedy, no tragedy, no love interest or catastrophe in the accepted style, and perhaps not a single button sewn on as the Bond Street[9] tailors would have it. Life is not a series of gig-lamps[1] symmetrically arranged; life is a luminous halo, a semi-transparent envelope surrounding us from the beginning of consciousness to the end. Is it not the task of the novelist to convey this varying, this unknown and uncircumscribed spirit, whatever aberration or complexity it may display, with as little mixture of the alien and external as possible? We are not pleading merely for courage and sincerity; we are suggesting that the proper stuff of fiction is a little other than custom would have us believe it.

It is, at any rate, in some such fashion as this that we seek to define the quality which distinguishes the work of several young writers, among whom Mr James Joyce is the most notable, from that of their predecessors. They attempt to come closer to life, and to preserve more sincerely and exactly what interests and moves them, even if to do so they must discard most of the conventions which are commonly observed by the novelist. Let us record the atoms as they fall upon the mind in the order in which they fall, let us trace the pattern, however disconnected and incoherent in appearance, which each sight or incident scores upon the consciousness. Let us not take it for granted that life exists more fully in what is commonly thought big than in what is commonly thought small. Anyone who has read *The Portrait of the Artist as a Young Man* or, what promises to be a far more interesting

---

8. *Monday or Tuesday* was Woolf's 1921 collection of experimental stories and sketches.

9. Fashionable shopping street in London.
1. Carriage lamps.

work, Ulysses,[2] now appearing in the Little Review, will have hazarded some theory of this nature as to Mr Joyce's intention. On our part, with such a fragment before us, it is hazarded rather than affirmed; but whatever the intention of the whole, there can be no question but that it is of the utmost sincerity and that the result, difficult or unpleasant as we may judge it, is undeniably important. In contrast with those whom we have called materialists, Mr Joyce is spiritual; he is concerned at all costs to reveal the flickerings of that innermost flame which flashes its messages through the brain, and in order to preserve it he disregards with complete courage whatever seems to him adventitious, whether it be probability, or coherence, or any other of these signposts which for generations have served to support the imagination of a reader when called upon to imagine what he can neither touch nor see. The scene in the cemetery,[3] for instance, with its brilliancy, its sordidity, its incoherence, its sudden lightning flashes of significance, does undoubtedly come so close to the quick of the mind that, on a first reading at any rate, it is difficult not to acclaim a masterpiece. If we want life itself, here surely we have it. Indeed, we find ourselves fumbling rather awkwardly if we try to say what else we wish, and for what reason a work of such originality yet fails to compare, for we must take high examples, with Youth or The Mayor of Casterbridge.[4] It fails because of the comparative poverty of the writer's mind, we might say simply and have done with it. But it is possible to press a little further and wonder whether we may not refer our sense of being in a bright yet narrow room, confined and shut in, rather than enlarged and set free, to some limitation imposed by the method as well as by the mind. Is it the method that inhibits the creative power? Is it due to the method that we feel neither jovial nor magnanimous, but centred in a self which, in spite of its tremor of susceptibility, never embraces or creates what is outside itself and beyond? Does the emphasis laid, perhaps didactically, upon indecency contribute to the effect of something angular and isolated? Or is it merely that in any effort of such originality it is much easier, for contemporaries especially, to feel what it lacks than to name what it gives? In any case it is a mistake to stand outside examining "methods". Any method is right, every method is right, that expresses what we wish to express, if we are writers; that brings us closer to the novelist's intention if we are readers. This method has the merit of bringing us closer to what we were prepared to call life itself; did not the reading of Ulysses suggest how much of life is excluded or ignored, and did it not come with a shock to open Tristram Shandy or even Pendennis[5] and be by them convinced that there are not only other aspects of life, but more important ones into the bargain.

However this may be, the problem before the novelist at present, as we suppose it to have been in the past, is to contrive means of being free to set down what he chooses. He has to have the courage to say that what interests him is no longer "this" but "that": out of "that" alone must he construct his work. For the moderns "that", the point of interest, lies very likely in the dark places of psychology. At once, therefore, the accent falls a little differently; the emphasis is upon something hitherto ignored; at once a different outline of form becomes necessary, difficult for us to grasp, incomprehensible

2. Written April, 1919 [Woolf's note].
3. The sixth episode ("Hades") of Ulysses, where Bloom goes to Paddy Dignam's funeral.
4. A story and a novel by, respectively, Joseph

Conrad and Thomas Hardy.
5. Novels by, respectively, the English writers Laurence Sterne (1713–1768) and William Makepeace Thackeray (1811–1863).

to our predecessors. No one but a modern, no one perhaps but a Russian, would have felt the interest of the situation which Tchekov has made into the short story which he calls "Gusev."[6] Some Russian soldiers lie ill on board a ship which is taking them back to Russia. We are given a few scraps of their talk and some of their thoughts; then one of them dies and is carried away; the talk goes on among the others for a time, until Gusev himself dies, and looking "like a carrot or a radish" is thrown overboard. The emphasis is laid upon such unexpected places that at first it seems as if there were no emphasis at all; and then, as the eyes accustom themselves to twilight and discern the shapes of things in a room we see how complete the story is, how profound, and how truly in obedience to his vision Tchekov has chosen this, that, and the other, and placed them together to compose something new. But it is impossible to say "this is comic," or "that is tragic," nor are we certain, since short stories, we have been taught, should be brief and conclusive, whether this, which is vague and inconclusive, should be called a short story at all.

The most elementary remarks upon modern English fiction can hardly avoid some mention of the Russian influence, and if the Russians are mentioned one runs the risk of feeling that to write of any fiction save theirs is waste of time. If we want understanding of the soul and heart where else shall we find it of comparable profundity? If we are sick of our own materialism the least considerable of their novelists has by right of birth a natural reverence for the human spirit. "Learn to make yourself akin to people. . . . But let this sympathy be not with the mind—for it is easy with the mind— but with the heart, with love towards them." In every great Russian writer we seem to discern the features of a saint, if sympathy for the sufferings of others, love towards them, endeavour to reach some goal worthy of the most exacting demands of the spirit constitute saintliness. It is the saint in them which confounds us with a feeling of our own irreligious triviality, and turns so many of our famous novels to tinsel and trickery. The conclusions of the Russian mind, thus comprehensive and compassionate, are inevitably, perhaps, of the utmost sadness. More accurately indeed we might speak of the inconclusiveness of the Russian mind. It is the sense that there is no answer, that if honestly examined life presents question after question which must be left to sound on and on after the story is over in hopeless interrogation that fills us with a deep, and finally it may be with a resentful, despair. They are right perhaps; unquestionably they see further than we do and without our gross impediments of vision. But perhaps we see something that escapes them, or why should this voice of protest mix itself with our gloom? The voice of protest is the voice of another and an ancient civilisation which seems to have bred in us the instinct to enjoy and fight rather than to suffer and understand. English fiction from Sterne to Meredith[7] bears witness to our natural delight in humour and comedy, in the beauty of earth, in the activities of the intellect, and in the splendour of the body. But any deductions that we may draw from the comparison of two fictions so immeasurably far apart are futile save indeed as they flood us with a view of the infinite possibilities of the art and remind us that there is no limit to the horizon, and that nothing—no "method," no experiment, even of the wildest—is forbidden, but only falsity

6. 1890 story by the Russian writer Anton Pavlovich Chekhov (1860–1904).

7. George Meredith (1828–1909), English novelist.

and pretence. "The proper stuff of fiction" does not exist; everything is the proper stuff of fiction, every feeling, every thought; every quality of brain and spirit is drawn upon; no perception comes amiss. And if we can imagine the art of fiction come alive and standing in our midst, she would undoubtedly bid us break her and bully her, as well as honour and love her, for so her youth is renewed and her sovereignty assured.

1925

Mrs. Dalloway   "Look within," Virginia Woolf urges in her essay "Modern Fiction" (1919, revised 1925): "Examine for a moment an ordinary mind on an ordinary day. The mind receives a myriad impressions—trivial, fantastic, evanescent, or engraved with the sharpness of steel." Her 1925 novel *Mrs. Dalloway* looks deep within the consciousness of a middle-aged woman planning an evening party on a fine London day in the middle of June 1923. In exploring the events of a single day, Woolf's novel recalls James Joyce's day-long narrative in *Ulysses* (1922), which, despite her reservations about its form and "indecency," she admired for revealing "the flickering of that innermost flame which flashes its messages through the brain."

In Woolf's more intimately scaled novel, Clarissa Dalloway's "ordinary mind on an ordinary day" is revealed to contain extraordinary riches, and so too, Woolf suggests, might any mind on any day, at least for the sufficiently attentive novelist. As Clarissa walks through London's streets, reacting to the flood of sights and sounds around her, her exhilarated if fleeting impressions of the present often give way to steel-engraved memories of her young adulthood in an idyllic countryside home in Bourton. Following her there through thoughts conveyed in rich metaphors, precise rhythms, and finely spun syntax, we learn of her disappointed suitor Peter Walsh, alluring but too demanding, now a civil servant in India, though he has made a surprising return; the victorious but predictable suitor Richard Dalloway, still her husband and a Conservative member of Parliament; her independent-minded socialist friend Sally Seton, who once planted a burning kiss on her lips, and many years later will unexpectedly appear at Clarissa's party. Thoughts of more-recent events surge just below the surface, such as her daughter Elizabeth's disturbing infatuation with her zealous history tutor. Dismissing more realist novelists' preoccupation with the externalities of plot, Woolf wrote in her diary: "I dig out beautiful caves behind my characters: I think that gives exactly what I want; humanity, humour, depth."

However isolated in its cavelike interiority, each mind in *Mrs. Dalloway* intersects with many others. "The idea is that the caves shall connect," said Woolf, elaborating her metaphor, "and each comes to daylight at the present moment." When a car loudly backfires, the shock of the sound and the mystery of the opulent car's occupants form a hinge between Clarissa Dalloway's consciousness and that of her double, Septimus Warren Smith, a veteran traumatized by his experience on the Western Front in World War I. The two characters never directly meet in the novel, but the narrative weaves back and forth between their minds—"the world seen by the sane and the insane side by side," in Woolf's words. Showing Septimus to be a casualty of modern warfare, class stratification, and the mental health profession, her novel questions the solidity of the dividing line between the sane and the insane. Like many thousands of young men, such as the war poets included in the section "Voices of World War I," Septimus had volunteered to fight for a Britain idealized as Shakespeare and English culture; but the carnage of the war, including the irrepressible memory of his dear friend Evans's death, has demolished all hope for, and faith in, English civilization.

In plumbing the depths of her characters' minds, Woolf's narrative subtly glides from one character to another, and from one narrative method to another, including

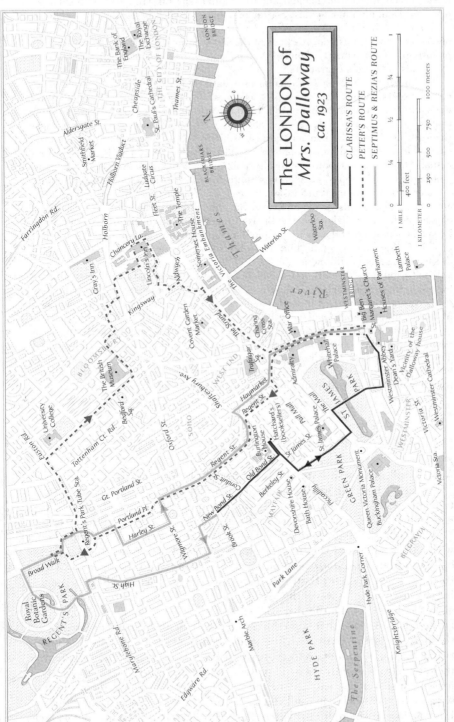

Mrs. Dalloway traces the movement of Woolf's characters through London, including the near misses and intersections of modern city life. Both distinctive and overlapping in their mental experience, characters as unlike as Clarissa Dalloway and Septimus Smith share both physical and psychological space. This map highlights some of the novel's London landmarks and the approximate routes taken by the main characters on a single day in mid-June 1923.

direct speech, interior monologue, and free indirect speech. The events of the day are refracted from an almost cubistic array of angles, as when bystanders speculate on who is in that mysterious car. When an airplane writes a brand name in the sky, observers arrive at different readings of the airy inscription. The passage of time, as hauntingly and insistently signaled by Big Ben's chimes, assumes various forms in the minds of Woolf's characters.

But for all her interest in focusing on what Woolf called the "radiant halo" of consciousness, things happen in *Mrs. Dalloway*—sometimes violent things. Woolf wrote of her intentions for her novel, "I want to criticise the social system, & to show it at work, at its most intense." She observes Clarissa's class position both sympathetically and critically, a society hostess arranging her all-important party with the labor of less privileged household workers. The British class system is shown to perpetuate the wealth and power of royalty, politicians, and doctors, while putting enormous pressure on people like Septimus Smith and Elizabeth's ill-fated history tutor of German descent. Medical professionals, such as Septimus Smith's doctors, seem to advance themselves above all and to miss the reflection, in some psychiatric illnesses, of a deeply flawed social order. The British Empire demands obeisance to nationalistic symbols of itself and crushes people like Septimus who are summoned to fulfill its will. Barriers along gender lines block the social advancement of women, as well as same-sex sexual fulfillment.

Woolf's ability to "dig out" both the human mind and the social structures and strictures that shape it has helped to make *Mrs. Dalloway* one of the most influential novels of the twentieth century; the work has been rewritten in various novels, including Michael Cunningham's *The Hours* (1998), and adapted for film. In conveying, as part of a larger social mix, the intricacies of Clarissa Dalloway's thoughts and feelings on a summer's day—her exultation in flowers, her longings and regrets in friendship and love, her anxieties about the hovering threat of despondency and death—Woolf fulfills her aspiration to portray life as "a luminous halo, a semi-transparent envelope surrounding us from the beginning of consciousness to the end."

Mrs. Dalloway

Mrs. Dalloway said she would buy the flowers herself.

For Lucy[1] had her work cut out for her. The doors would be taken off their hinges; Rumpelmayer's men[2] were coming. And then, thought Clarissa Dalloway, what a morning—fresh as if issued to children on a beach.

What a lark! What a plunge! For so it had always seemed to her, when, with a little squeak of the hinges, which she could hear now, she had burst open the French windows and plunged at Bourton[3] into the open air. How fresh, how calm, stiller than this of course, the air was in the early morning; like the flap of a wave; the kiss of a wave; chill and sharp and yet (for a girl of eighteen as she then was) solemn, feeling as she did, standing there at the open window, that something awful was about to happen; looking at the flowers, at the trees with the smoke winding off them and the rooks rising, falling; standing and looking until Peter Walsh said, "Musing among the vegetables?"—was that it?—"I prefer men to cauliflowers"—was that it? He must have said it at breakfast one morning when she had gone out on to the terrace—Peter Walsh. He would be back from India one of these days, June or July, she forgot which, for his letters were awfully dull; it was his sayings one

---

1. Clarissa Dalloway's maid.
2. Caterers.

3. Village in western England and Mrs. Dalloway's childhood home.

remembered; his eyes, his pocket-knife, his smile, his grumpiness and, when millions of things had utterly vanished—how strange it was!—a few sayings like this about cabbages.

She stiffened a little on the kerb, waiting for Durtnall's van[4] to pass. A charming woman, Scrope Purvis thought her (knowing her as one does know people who live next door to one in Westminster[5]); a touch of the bird about her, of the jay, blue-green, light, vivacious, though she was over fifty, and grown very white since her illness. There she perched, never seeing him, waiting to cross, very upright.

For having lived in Westminster—how many years now? over twenty,—one feels even in the midst of the traffic, or waking at night, Clarissa was positive, a particular hush, or solemnity; an indescribable pause; a suspense (but that might be her heart, affected, they said, by influenza[6]) before Big Ben strikes. There! Out it boomed. First a warning, musical; then the hour, irrevocable. The leaden circles dissolved in the air. Such fools we are, she thought, crossing Victoria Street.[7] For Heaven only knows why one loves it so, how one sees it so, making it up, building it round one, tumbling it, creating it every moment afresh; but the veriest frumps,[8] the most dejected of miseries sitting on door-steps (drink their downfall) do the same; can't be dealt with, she felt positive, by Acts of Parliament for that very reason: they love life. In people's eyes, in the swing, tramp, and trudge; in the bellow and the uproar; the carriages, motor cars, omnibuses, vans, sandwich men shuffling and swinging; brass bands; barrel organs; in the triumph and the jingle and the strange high singing of some aeroplane overhead was what she loved; life; London; this moment of June.

For it was the middle of June. The War[9] was over, except for some one like Mrs. Foxcroft at the Embassy last night eating her heart out because that nice boy was killed and now the old Manor House must go to a cousin; or Lady Bexborough who opened a bazaar[1] they said, with the telegram in her hand, John, her favourite, killed; but it was over; thank Heaven—over. It was June. The King and Queen were at the Palace.[2] And everywhere, though it was still so early, there was a beating, a stirring of galloping ponies, tapping of cricket bats; Lords, Ascot, Ranelagh[3] and all the rest of it; wrapped in the soft mesh of the grey-blue morning air, which, as the day wore on, would unwind them, and set down on their lawns and pitches the bouncing ponies whose forefeet just struck the ground and up they sprung, the whirling young men, and laughing girls in their transparent muslins who, even now, after dancing all night, were taking their absurd woolly dogs for a run; and even now, at this hour, discreet old dowagers were shooting out in their motor cars on errands of mystery; and the shopkeepers were fidgeting in their windows with their paste and diamonds, their lovely old sea-green brooches in eighteenth-century settings to tempt Americans (but one must economise, not buy things rashly for Elizabeth), and she, too, loving it as she

---

4. A warehouse van.
5. London borough that includes Buckingham Palace, the Houses of Parliament, and Westminster Abbey.
6. The 1918–19 worldwide influenza pandemic had killed over 20 million people.
7. Clarissa is walking north. "Big Ben": the name for the Great Bell in the clock tower above the Houses of Parliament.
8. Grumpy, shabbily dressed people.
9. World War I (1914–18).

1. Street fair with many stalls selling a variety of goods to benefit a charitable organization.
2. Buckingham Palace, where King George V (1865–1936) and Queen Mary (1867–1953) resided.
3. The Hurlingham Club in Ranelagh Gardens in southwest London, where polo is played. "Lords": the cricket ground at St John's Wood in north London. "Ascot": a town west of London with an annual horse race. Summer sporting events at all three locations have long been fixtures of the London social season.

did with an absurd and faithful passion, being part of it, since her people were courtiers once in the time of the Georges,[4] she, too, was going that very night to kindle and illuminate; to give her party. But how strange, on entering the Park,[5] the silence; the mist; the hum; the slow-swimming happy ducks; the pouched birds waddling; and who should be coming along with his back against the Government buildings, most appropriately, carrying a despatch box stamped with the Royal Arms,[6] who but Hugh Whitbread; her old friend Hugh—the admirable Hugh!

"Good-morning to you, Clarissa!" said Hugh, rather extravagantly, for they had known each other as children. "Where are you off to?"

"I love walking in London," said Mrs. Dalloway. "Really it's better than walking in the country."

They had just come up—unfortunately—to see doctors. Other people came to see pictures; go to the opera; take their daughters out; the Whitbreads came "to see doctors." Times without number Clarissa had visited Evelyn Whitbread in a nursing home. Was Evelyn ill again? Evelyn was a good deal out of sorts, said Hugh, intimating by a kind of pout or swell of his very well-covered, manly, extremely handsome, perfectly upholstered body (he was almost too well dressed always, but presumably had to be, with his little job at Court) that his wife had some internal ailment, nothing serious, which, as an old friend, Clarissa Dalloway would quite understand without requiring him to specify. Ah yes, she did of course; what a nuisance; and felt very sisterly and oddly conscious at the same time of her hat. Not the right hat for the early morning, was that it? For Hugh always made her feel, as he bustled on, raising his hat rather extravagantly and assuring her that she might be a girl of eighteen, and of course he was coming to her party to-night, Evelyn absolutely insisted, only a little late he might be after the party at the Palace to which he had to take one of Jim's boys,—she always felt a little skimpy beside Hugh; schoolgirlish; but attached to him, partly from having known him always, but she did think him a good sort in his own way, though Richard was nearly driven mad by him, and as for Peter Walsh, he had never to this day forgiven her for liking him.

She could remember scene after scene at Bourton—Peter furious; Hugh not, of course, his match in any way, but still not a positive imbecile as Peter made out; not a mere barber's block. When his old mother wanted him to give up shooting or to take her to Bath[7] he did it, without a word; he was really unselfish, and as for saying, as Peter did, that he had no heart, no brain, nothing but the manners and breeding of an English gentleman, that was only her dear Peter at his worst; and he could be intolerable; he could be impossible; but adorable to walk with on a morning like this.

(June had drawn out every leaf on the trees. The mothers of Pimlico[8] gave suck to their young. Messages were passing from the Fleet to the Admiralty.[9] Arlington Street and Piccadilly[1] seemed to chafe the very air in the Park and lift its leaves hotly, brilliantly, on waves of that divine vitality which Clarissa loved. To dance, to ride, she had adored all that.)

4. Era of the combined reigns of the Kings George I–IV (1714–1830).
5. St. James's Park, home to many kinds of water birds and a frequent haunt of politicians.
6. Sign indicating that the box contains papers to or from the royal family.
7. Spa town in southwest England.
8. Modest London borough southwest of West-minster.
9. Since 1909 a wireless antenna on the Admiralty building in Whitehall had enabled communication by telegraph with British ships at sea.
1. Intersection at the northeast corner of Green Park, part of a luxurious district containing the Ritz Hotel.

For they might be parted for hundreds of years, she and Peter; she never wrote a letter and his were dry sticks; but suddenly it would come over her, If he were with me now what would he say?—some days, some sights bringing him back to her calmly, without the old bitterness; which perhaps was the reward of having cared for people; they came back in the middle of St. James's Park on a fine morning—indeed they did. But Peter—however beautiful the day might be, and the trees and the grass, and the little girl in pink—Peter never saw a thing of all that. He would put on his spectacles, if she told him to; he would look. It was the state of the world that interested him; Wagner, Pope's poetry,[2] people's characters eternally, and the defects of her own soul. How he scolded her! How they argued! She would marry a Prime Minister and stand at the top of a staircase; the perfect hostess he called her (she had cried over it in her bedroom), she had the makings of the perfect hostess, he said.

So she would still find herself arguing in St. James's Park, still making out that she had been right—and she had too—not to marry him. For in marriage a little licence, a little independence there must be between people living together day in day out in the same house; which Richard gave her, and she him. (Where was he this morning for instance? Some committee, she never asked what.) But with Peter everything had to be shared; everything gone into. And it was intolerable, and when it came to that scene in the little garden by the fountain, she had to break with him or they would have been destroyed, both of them ruined, she was convinced; though she had borne about with her for years like an arrow sticking in her heart the grief, the anguish; and then the horror of the moment when some one told her at a concert that he had married a woman met on the boat going to India! Never should she forget all that! Cold, heartless, a prude, he called her. Never could she understand how he cared. But those Indian women did presumably—silly, pretty, flimsy nincompoops. And she wasted her pity. For he was quite happy, he assured her—perfectly happy, though he had never done a thing that they talked of; his whole life had been a failure. It made her angry still.

She had reached the Park gates.[3] She stood for a moment, looking at the omnibuses in Piccadilly.

She would not say of any one in the world now that they were this or were that. She felt very young; at the same time unspeakably aged. She sliced like a knife through everything; at the same time was outside, looking on. She had a perpetual sense, as she watched the taxi cabs, of being out, out, far out to sea and alone; she always had the feeling that it was very, very dangerous to live even one day. Not that she thought herself clever, or much out of the ordinary. How she had got through life on the few twigs of knowledge Fräulein Daniels[4] gave them she could not think. She knew nothing; no language, no history; she scarcely read a book now, except memoirs in bed; and yet to her it was absolutely absorbing; all this; the cabs passing; and she would not say of Peter, she would not say of herself, I am this, I am that.

Her only gift was knowing people almost by instinct, she thought, walking on. If you put her in a room with some one, up went her back like a cat's; or she purred. Devonshire House, Bath House, the house with the china cockatoo,[5] she had seen them all lit up once; and remembered Sylvia, Fred, Sally

2. Works by English poet Alexander Pope (1688–1744). "Wagner": Richard Wilhelm Wagner (1813–1883), German composer famous for his grandly staged operas.

3. Green Park's northeast gate on Piccadilly.
4. Her governess.
5. Private homes near Piccadilly.

Seton—such hosts of people; and dancing all night; and the waggons plod-
ding past to market; and driving home across the Park. She remembered
once throwing a shilling into the Serpentine.[6] But every one remembered;
what she loved was this, here, now, in front of her; the fat lady in the cab.
Did it matter then, she asked herself, walking towards Bond Street,[7] did it
matter that she must inevitably cease completely; all this must go on without
her; did she resent it; or did it not become consoling to believe that death
ended absolutely? but that somehow in the streets of London, on the ebb and
flow of things, here, there, she survived, Peter survived, lived in each other,
she being part, she was positive, of the trees at home; of the house there,
ugly, rambling all to bits and pieces as it was; part of people she had never
met; being laid out like a mist between the people she knew best, who lifted
her on their branches as she had seen the trees lift the mist, but it spread
ever so far, her life, herself. But what was she dreaming as she looked into
Hatchards'[8] shop window? What was she trying to recover? What image of
white dawn in the country, as she read in the book spread open:

> Fear no more the heat o' the sun
> Nor the furious winter's rages.[9]

This late age of the world's experience had bred in them all, all men and
women, a well of tears. Tears and sorrows; courage and endurance; a perfectly
upright and stoical bearing. Think, for example, of the woman she admired
most, Lady Bexborough, opening the bazaar.

There were Jorrocks' *Jaunts and Jollities*; there were *Soapy Sponge* and
Mrs. Asquith's *Memoirs* and *Big Game Shooting in Nigeria*,[1] all spread open.
Ever so many books there were; but none that seemed exactly right to take to
Evelyn Whitbread in her nursing home. Nothing that would serve to amuse
her and make that indescribably dried-up little woman look, as Clarissa came
in, just for a moment cordial; before they settled down for the usual interminable talk of women's ailments. How much she wanted it—that people should
look pleased as she came in, Clarissa thought and turned and walked back
towards Bond Street, annoyed, because it was silly to have other reasons for
doing things. Much rather would she have been one of those people like
Richard who did things for themselves, whereas, she thought, waiting to
cross, half the time she did things not simply, not for themselves; but to make
people think this or that; perfect idiocy she knew (and now the policeman
held up his hand) for no one was ever for a second taken in. Oh if she could
have had her life over again! she thought, stepping on to the pavement, could
have looked even differently!

She would have been, in the first place, dark like Lady Bexborough, with
a skin of crumpled leather and beautiful eyes. She would have been, like
Lady Bexborough, slow and stately; rather large; interested in politics like a
man; with a country house; very dignified, very sincere. Instead of which she
had a narrow pea-stick figure; a ridiculous little face, beaked like a bird's.
That she held herself well was true; and had nice hands and feet; and dressed

---

6. A large, winding pond in Hyde Park.
7. Important shopping street in northwest London.
8. A bookstore.
9. From a song bidding farewell to the supposedly dead heroine of Shakespeare's *Cymbeline*
(4.2.258–81).
1. Book invented by Woolf. "Jorrocks' *Jaunts and
Jollities*": 1838 collection of stories about a Cock-
ney grocer named Jorrocks by English sporting
novelist Robert Smith Surtees (1805–1864).
"*Soapy Sponge*": character in another novel by
Surtees, *Mr Sponge's Sporting Tour* (1853). Mrs.
Asquith's *Memoirs*" two-volume autobiography
(1920–1922) of Emma Alice Margaret (Margot)
Asquith (1864–1945), wife of Prime Minister
Herbert Henry Asquith (served 1908–16).

well, considering that she spent little. But often now this body she wore (she stopped to look at a Dutch picture), this body, with all its capacities, seemed nothing—nothing at all. She had the oddest sense of being herself invisible, unseen; unknown; there being no more marrying, no more having of children now, but only this astonishing and rather solemn progress with the rest of them, up Bond Street, this being Mrs. Dalloway; not even Clarissa any more; this being Mrs. Richard Dalloway.

Bond Street fascinated her; Bond Street early in the morning in the season; its flags flying; its shops; no splash; no glitter; one roll of tweed in the shop where her father had bought his suits for fifty years; a few pearls; salmon on an iceblock.

"That is all," she said, looking at the fishmonger's. "That is all," she repeated, pausing for a moment at the window of a glove shop where, before the War, you could buy almost perfect gloves. And her old Uncle William used to say a lady is known by her shoes and her gloves. He had turned on his bed one morning in the middle of the War. He had said, "I have had enough." Gloves and shoes; she had a passion for gloves; but her own daughter, her Elizabeth, cared not a straw for either of them.

Not a straw, she thought, going on up Bond Street to a shop where they kept flowers for her when she gave a party. Elizabeth really cared for her dog most of all. The whole house this morning smelt of tar. Still, better poor Grizzle than Miss Kilman; better distemper and tar[2] and all the rest of it than sitting mewed in a stuffy bedroom with a prayer book! Better anything, she was inclined to say. But it might be only a phase, as Richard said, such as all girls go through. It might be falling in love. But why with Miss Kilman? who had been badly treated of course; one must make allowances for that, and Richard said she was very able, had a really historical mind. Anyhow they were inseparable, and Elizabeth, her own daughter, went to Communion; and how she dressed, how she treated people who came to lunch she did not care a bit, it being her experience that the religious ecstasy made people callous (so did causes); dulled their feelings, for Miss Kilman would do anything for the Russians, starved herself for the Austrians,[3] but in private inflicted positive torture, so insensitive was she, dressed in a green mackintosh coat.[4] Year in year out she wore that coat; she perspired; she was never in the room five minutes without making you feel her superiority, your inferiority; how poor she was; how rich you were; how she lived in a slum without a cushion or a bed or a rug or whatever it might be, all her soul rusted with that grievance sticking in it, her dismissal from school during the War—poor embittered unfortunate creature! For it was not her one hated but the idea of her, which undoubtedly had gathered in to itself a great deal that was not Miss Kilman; had become one of those spectres with which one battles in the night; one of those spectres who stand astride us and suck up half our life-blood, dominators and tyrants; for no doubt with another throw of the dice, had the black been uppermost and not the white, she would have loved Miss Kilman! But not in this world. No.

It rasped her, though, to have stirring about in her this brutal monster! to hear twigs cracking and feel hooves planted down in the depths of that leaf-encumbered forest, the soul; never to be content quite, or quite secure, for

2. Used for dog grooming. "Distemper": an animal disease characterized by cough, loss of strength, and a discharge from the nose or eyes.

3. Peoples suffering poor economies after World War I and the Russian Revolution.
4. Raincoat.

at any moment the brute would be stirring, this hatred, which, especially since her illness, had power to make her feel scraped, hurt in her spine; gave her physical pain, and made all pleasure in beauty, in friendship, in being well, in being loved and making her home delightful rock, quiver, and bend as if indeed there were a monster grubbing at the roots, as if the whole panoply of content were nothing but self love! this hatred!

Nonsense, nonsense! she cried to herself, pushing through the swing doors of Mulberry's the florists.

She advanced, light, tall, very upright, to be greeted at once by button-faced Miss Pym, whose hands were always bright red, as if they had been stood in cold water with the flowers.

There were flowers: delphiniums, sweet peas, bunches of lilac; and carnations, masses of carnations. There were roses; there were irises. Ah yes—so she breathed in the earthy garden sweet smell as she stood talking to Miss Pym who owed her help, and thought her kind, for kind she had been years ago; very kind, but she looked older, this year, turning her head from side to side among the irises and roses and nodding tufts of lilac with her eyes half closed, snuffing in, after the street uproar, the delicious scent, the exquisite coolness. And then, opening her eyes, how fresh like frilled linen clean from a laundry laid in wicker trays the roses looked; and dark and prim the red carnations, holding their heads up; and all the sweet peas spreading in their bowls, tinged violet, snow white, pale—as if it were the evening and girls in muslin frocks came out to pick sweet peas and roses after the superb summer's day, with its almost blue-black sky, its delphiniums, its carnations, its arum lilies was over; and it was the moment between six and seven when every flower—roses, carnations, irises, lilac—glows; white, violet, red, deep orange; every flower seems to burn by itself, softly, purely in the misty beds; and how she loved the grey-white moths spinning in and out, over the cherry pie,[5] over the evening primroses!

And as she began to go with Miss Pym from jar to jar, choosing, nonsense, nonsense, she said to herself, more and more gently, as if this beauty, this scent, this colour, and Miss Pym liking her, trusting her, were a wave which she let flow over her and surmount that hatred, that monster, surmount it all; and it lifted her up and up when—oh! a pistol shot in the street outside!

"Dear, those motor cars,"[6] said Miss Pym, going to the window to look, and coming back and smiling apologetically with her hands full of sweet peas, as if those motor cars, those tyres of motor cars, were all *her* fault.

The violent explosion which made Mrs. Dalloway jump and Miss Pym go to the window and apologise came from a motor car which had drawn to the side of the pavement precisely opposite Mulberry's shop window. Passers-by who, of course, stopped and stared, had just time to see a face of the very greatest importance against the dove-grey upholstery, before a male hand drew the blind and there was nothing to be seen except a square of dove grey.

Yet rumours were at once in circulation from the middle of Bond Street to Oxford Street on one side, to Atkinson's scent[7] shop on the other, passing invisibly, inaudibly, like a cloud, swift, veil-like upon hills, falling indeed with something of a cloud's sudden sobriety and stillness upon faces which a sec-

5. Nickname for valerian, an herb with white or pink flowers.

6. A car has backfired.

7. I.e., perfume.

ond before had been utterly disorderly. But now mystery had brushed them with her wing; they had heard the voice of authority; the spirit of religion was abroad with her eyes bandaged tight and her lips gaping wide. But nobody knew whose face had been seen. Was it the Prince of Wales's, the Queen's, the Prime Minister's? Whose face was it? Nobody knew.

Edgar J. Watkiss, with his roll of lead piping round his arm, said audibly, humorously of course: "The Proime Minister's kyar."

Septimus Warren Smith, who found himself unable to pass, heard him.

Septimus Warren Smith, aged about thirty, pale-faced, beak-nosed, wearing brown shoes and a shabby overcoat, with hazel eyes which had that look of apprehension in them which makes complete strangers apprehensive too. The world has raised its whip; where will it descend?

Everything had come to a standstill. The throb of the motor engines sounded like a pulse irregularly drumming through an entire body. The sun became extraordinarily hot because the motor car had stopped outside Mulberry's shop window; old ladies on the tops of omnibuses spread their black parasols; here a green, here a red parasol opened with a little pop. Mrs. Dalloway, coming to the window with her arms full of sweet peas, looked out with her little pink face pursed in enquiry. Every one looked at the motor car. Septimus looked. Boys on bicycles sprang off. Traffic accumulated. And there the motor car stood, with drawn blinds, and upon them a curious pattern like a tree, Septimus thought, and this gradual drawing together of everything to one centre before his eyes, as if some horror had come almost to the surface and was about to burst into flames, terrified him. The world wavered and quivered and threatened to burst into flames. It is I who am blocking the way, he thought. Was he not being looked at and pointed at; was he not weighted there, rooted to the pavement, for a purpose? But for what purpose?

"Let us go on, Septimus," said his wife, a little woman, with large eyes in a sallow pointed face; an Italian girl.

But Lucrezia herself could not help looking at the motor car and the tree pattern on the blinds. Was it the Queen in there—the Queen going shopping?

The chauffeur, who had been opening something, turning something, shutting something, got on to the box.[8]

"Come on," said Lucrezia.

But her husband, for they had been married four, five years now, jumped, started, and said, "All right!" angrily, as if she had interrupted him.

People must notice; people must see. People, she thought, looking at the crowd staring at the motor car; the English people, with their children and their horses and their clothes, which she admired in a way; but they were "people" now, because Septimus had said, "I will kill myself"; an awful thing to say. Suppose they had heard him? She looked at the crowd. Help, help! she wanted to cry out to butchers' boys and women. Help! Only last autumn she and Septimus had stood on the Embankment[9] wrapped in the same cloak and, Septimus reading a paper instead of talking, she had snatched it from him and laughed in the old man's face who saw them! But failure one conceals. She must take him away into some park.

8. Because the car stalled, the driver has to crank its starting handle before returning to his seat and continuing to drive.

9. Road running along the River Thames between Westminster and Blackfriars Bridges.

"Now we will cross," she said.

She had a right to his arm, though it was without feeling. He would give her, who was so simple, so impulsive, only twenty-four, without friends in England, who had left Italy for his sake, a piece of bone.

The motor car with its blinds drawn and an air of inscrutable reserve proceeded towards Piccadilly, still gazed at, still ruffling the faces on both sides of the street with the same dark breath of veneration whether for Queen, Prince, or Prime Minister nobody knew. The face itself had been seen only once by three people for a few seconds. Even the sex was now in dispute. But there could be no doubt that greatness was seated within; greatness was passing, hidden, down Bond Street, removed only by a hand's-breadth from ordinary people who might now, for the first and last time, be within speaking distance of the majesty of England, of the enduring symbol of the state which will be known to curious antiquaries, sifting the ruins of time, when London is a grass-grown path and all those hurrying along the pavement this Wednesday morning are but bones with a few wedding rings mixed up in their dust and the gold stoppings of innumerable decayed teeth. The face in the motor car will then be known.

It is probably the Queen, thought Mrs. Dalloway, coming out of Mulberry's with her flowers; the Queen. And for a second she wore a look of extreme dignity standing by the flower shop in the sunlight while the car passed at a foot's pace, with its blinds drawn. The Queen going to some hospital; the Queen opening some bazaar, thought Clarissa.

The crush was terrific for the time of day. Lords, Ascot, Hurlingham,[1] what was it? she wondered, for the street was blocked. The British middle classes sitting sideways on the tops of omnibuses with parcels and umbrellas, yes, even furs on a day like this, were, she thought, more ridiculous, more unlike anything there has ever been than one could conceive; and the Queen herself held up; the Queen herself unable to pass. Clarissa was suspended on one side of Brook Street;[2] Sir John Buckhurst, the old Judge on the other, with the car between them (Sir John had laid down the law for years and liked a well-dressed woman) when the chauffeur, leaning ever so slightly, said or showed something to the policeman, who saluted and raised his arm and jerked his head and moved the omnibus to the side and the car passed through. Slowly and very silently it took its way.

Clarissa guessed; Clarissa knew of course; she had seen something white, magical, circular, in the footman's hand, a disc inscribed with a name,—the Queen's, the Prince of Wales's, the Prime Minister's?—which, by force of its own lustre, burnt its way through (Clarissa saw the car diminishing, disappearing), to blaze among candelabras, glittering stars, breasts stiff with oak leaves,[3] Hugh Whitbread and all his colleagues, the gentlemen of England, that night in Buckingham Palace. And Clarissa, too, gave a party. She stiffened a little; so she would stand at the top of her stairs.

The car had gone, but it had left a slight ripple which flowed through glove shops and hat shops and tailors' shops on both sides of Bond Street. For thirty seconds all heads were inclined the same way—to the window. Choosing a pair of gloves—should they be to the elbow or above it, lemon or pale grey?—ladies stopped; when the sentence was finished something had

---

1. Exclusive club in Ranelagh Gardens (cf. p. 285, n. 3).
2. Street in Mayfair that crosses Bond Street. From here, Clarissa turns south again and walks

home to Westminster.
3. Worn on King Charles II's birthday (May 29) to commemorate his restoration in 1660.

happened. Something so trifling in single instances that no mathematical instrument, though capable of transmitting shocks in China, could register the vibration; yet in its fulness rather formidable and in its common appeal emotional; for in all the hat shops and tailors' shops strangers looked at each other and thought of the dead; of the flag; of Empire. In a public house[4] in a back street a Colonial[5] insulted the House of Windsor[6] which led to words, broken beer glasses, and a general shindy,[7] which echoed strangely across the way in the ears of girls buying white underlinen threaded with pure white ribbon for their weddings. For the surface agitation of the passing car as it sunk grazed something very profound.

Gliding across Piccadilly, the car turned down St. James's Street. Tall men, men of robust physique, well-dressed men with their tail-coats and their white slips[8] and their hair raked back who, for reasons difficult to discriminate, were standing in the bow window of Brooks's[9] with their hands behind the tails of their coats, looking out, perceived instinctively that greatness was passing, and the pale light of the immortal presence fell upon them as it had fallen upon Clarissa Dalloway. At once they stood even straighter, and removed their hands, and seemed ready to attend their Sovereign, if need be, to the cannon's mouth, as their ancestors had done before them. The white busts and the little tables in the background covered with copies of the *Tatler*[1] and syphons of soda water seemed to approve; seemed to indicate the flowing corn and the manor houses of England; and to return the frail hum of the motor wheels as the walls of a whispering gallery return a single voice expanded and made sonorous by the might of a whole cathedral.[2] Shawled Moll Pratt with her flowers on the pavement wished the dear boy well (it was the Prince of Wales for certain) and would have tossed the price of a pot of beer—a bunch of roses—into St. James's Street out of sheer light-heartedness and contempt of poverty had she not seen the constable's eye upon her, discouraging an old Irishwoman's loyalty. The sentries at St. James's saluted; Queen Alexandra's policeman[3] approved.

A small crowd meanwhile had gathered at the gates of Buckingham Palace. Listlessly, yet confidently, poor people all of them, they waited; looked at the Palace itself with the flag flying; at Victoria, billowing on her mound,[4] admired her shelves of running water, her geraniums; singled out from the motor cars in the Mall[5] first this one, then that; bestowed emotion, vainly, upon commoners out for a drive; recalled their tribute to keep it unspent while this car passed and that; and all the time let rumour accumulate in their veins and thrill the nerves in their thighs at the thought of Royalty looking at them; the Queen bowing; the Prince saluting; at the thought of the heavenly life divinely bestowed upon Kings; of the equerries[6] and deep curtsies; of the Queen's old doll's house;[7] of Princess Mary married to an

4. Pub.
5. Someone from one of the colonies of the British Empire.
6. I.e., the British royal family.
7. Uproar, fracas.
8. Light garment showing under a waistcoat.
9. Aristocratic gentlemen's club on St. James's Street.
1. Journal reporting high-society news.
2. Acoustical effect whereby a curved wall, ceiling, or doorframe carries a soft sound, such as the whispering gallery in the dome of St. Paul's Cathedral.
3. Guard on duty at Marlborough House, the

residence of Queen Alexandra (1844–1925), the widow of King Edward VII. "Sentries at St. James's": guards at St. James's Palace. Both the palace and the house are within view of the car's route down St. James's Street.
4. Queen Victoria's statue outside the entrance to Buckingham Palace.
5. Wide avenue that leads from the Admiralty Arch along St. James's Park to Buckingham Palace.
6. Officers of the royal household.
7. Doll house designed by British architect Sir Edwin Lutyens (1869–1944) in 1923 for Queen Mary.

Englishman, and the Prince—ah! the Prince! who took wonderfully, they said, after old King Edward,[8] but was ever so much slimmer. The Prince lived at St. James's; but he might come along in the morning to visit his mother.

So Sarah Bletchley said with her baby in her arms, tipping her foot up and down as though she were by her own fender in Pimlico, but keeping her eyes on the Mall, while Emily Coates ranged over the Palace windows and thought of the housemaids, the innumerable housemaids, the bedrooms, the innumerable bedrooms. Joined by an elderly gentleman with an Aberdeen terrier, by men without occupation, the crowd increased. Little Mr. Bowley, who had rooms in the Albany[9] and was sealed with wax over the deeper sources of life but could be unsealed suddenly, inappropriately, sentimentally, by this sort of thing—poor women waiting to see the Queen go past—poor women, nice little children, orphans, widows, the War—tut-tut—actually had tears in his eyes. A breeze flaunting ever so warmly down the Mall through the thin trees, past the bronze heroes,[1] lifted some flag flying in the British breast of Mr. Bowley and he raised his hat as the car turned into the Mall and held it high as the car approached; and let the poor mothers of Pimlico press close to him, and stood very upright. The car came on.

Suddenly Mrs. Coates looked up into the sky. The sound of an aeroplane bored ominously into the ears of the crowd. There it was coming over the trees, letting out white smoke from behind, which curled and twisted, actually writing something! making letters in the sky![2] Every one looked up.

Dropping dead down the aeroplane soared straight up, curved in a loop, raced, sank, rose, and whatever it did, wherever it went, out fluttered behind it a thick ruffled bar of white smoke which curled and wreathed upon the sky in letters. But what letters? A C was it? an E, then an L? Only for a moment did they lie still; then they moved and melted and were rubbed out up in the sky, and the aeroplane shot further away and again, in a fresh space of sky, began writing a K, an E, a Y perhaps?

"Glaxo,"[3] said Mrs. Coates in a strained, awe-stricken voice, gazing straight up, and her baby, lying stiff and white in her arms, gazed straight up.

"Kreemo," murmured Mrs. Bletchley, like a sleepwalker. With his hat held out perfectly still in his hand, Mr. Bowley gazed straight up. All down the Mall people were standing and looking up into the sky. As they looked the whole world became perfectly silent, and a flight of gulls crossed the sky, first one gull leading, then another, and in this extraordinary silence and peace, in this pallor, in this purity, bells struck eleven times, the sound fading up there among the gulls.

The aeroplane turned and raced and swooped exactly where it liked, swiftly, freely, like a skater—

"That's an E," said Mrs. Bletchley—or a dancer—

"It's toffee," murmured Mr. Bowley—(and the car went in at the gates and nobody looked at it), and, shutting off the smoke, away and away it

8. The Prince of Wales, the future Edward VIII (1894–1972), is compared to his grandfather, King Edward VII (1841–1910). Princess Mary (1897–1965), the only daughter of King George V and Queen Mary, married Viscount Lascelles (1882–1947) in 1922.
9. Apartment complex in Piccadilly, housing politicians.
1. The Royal Marines Memorial, completed in 1903 in memory of those who served in artillery and light infantry regiments and died in wars in South Africa and China (1889–1902). The memorial is located in St. James's Park near the Admiralty Arch.
2. The first demonstration of skywriting for advertising, in which Major Cyril Turner wrote the words "Daily Mail," occurred over Epsom Downs, a racecourse southwest of London, in 1922.
3. Name of a baby formula and the firm that produced it.

rushed, and the smoke faded and assembled itself round the broad white shapes of the clouds.

It had gone; it was behind the clouds. There was no sound. The clouds to which the letters E, G, or L had attached themselves moved freely, as if destined to cross from West to East on a mission of the greatest importance which would never be revealed, and yet certainly so it was—a mission of the greatest importance. Then suddenly, as a train comes out of a tunnel, the aeroplane rushed out of the clouds again, the sound boring into the ears of all people in the Mall, in the Green Park,[4] in Piccadilly, in Regent Street, in Regent's Park, and the bar of smoke curved behind and it dropped down, and it soared up and wrote one letter after another—but what word was it writing?

Lucrezia Warren Smith, sitting by her husband's side on a seat in Regent's Park in the Broad Walk,[5] looked up.

"Look, look, Septimus!" she cried. For Dr. Holmes had told her to make her husband (who had nothing whatever seriously the matter with him but was a little out of sorts) take an interest in things outside himself.

So, thought Septimus, looking up, they are signalling to me. Not indeed in actual words; that is, he could not read the language yet; but it was plain enough, this beauty, this exquisite beauty, and tears filled his eyes as he looked at the smoke words languishing and melting in the sky and bestowing upon him in their inexhaustible charity and laughing goodness one shape after another of unimaginable beauty and signalling their intention to provide him, for nothing, for ever, for looking merely, with beauty, more beauty! Tears ran down his cheeks.

It was toffee; they were advertising toffee, a nursemaid told Rezia. Together they began to spell t . . . o . . . f . . .

"K . . . R . . ." said the nursemaid, and Septimus heard her say "Kay Arr" close to his ear, deeply, softly, like a mellow organ, but with a roughness in her voice like a grasshopper's, which rasped his spine deliciously and sent running up into his brain waves of sound which, concussing, broke. A marvellous discovery indeed—that the human voice in certain atmospheric conditions (for one must be scientific, above all scientific) can quicken trees into life! Happily Rezia put her hand with a tremendous weight on his knee so that he was weighted down, transfixed, or the excitement of the elm trees rising and falling, rising and falling with all their leaves alight and the colour thinning and thickening from blue to the green of a hollow wave, like plumes on horses' heads, feathers on ladies', so proudly they rose and fell, so superbly, would have sent him mad. But he would not go mad. He would shut his eyes; he would see no more.

But they beckoned; leaves were alive; trees were alive. And the leaves being connected by millions of fibres with his own body, there on the seat, fanned it up and down; when the branch stretched he, too, made that statement. The sparrows fluttering, rising, and falling in jagged fountains were part of the pattern; the white and blue, barred with black branches. Sounds made harmonies with premeditation; the spaces between them were as significant as the sounds. A child cried. Rightly far away a horn sounded. All taken together meant the birth of a new religion—

"Septimus!" said Rezia. He started violently. People must notice.

---

4. Royal park north of St. James's Park.
5. North–south pedestrian avenue in Regent's Park in north London.

"I am going to walk to the fountain and back," she said.

For she could stand it no longer. Dr. Holmes might say there was nothing the matter. Far rather would she that he were dead! She could not sit beside him when he stared so and did not see her and made everything terrible; sky and tree, children playing, dragging carts, blowing whistles, falling down; all were terrible. And he would not kill himself; and she could tell no one. "Septimus has been working too hard"—that was all she could say to her own mother. To love makes one solitary, she thought. She could tell nobody, not even Septimus now, and looking back, she saw him sitting in his shabby overcoat alone on the seat, hunched up, staring. And it was cowardly for a man to say he would kill himself, but Septimus had fought;[6] he was brave; he was not Septimus now. She put on her lace collar. She put on her new hat and he never noticed; and he was happy without her. Nothing could make her happy without him! Nothing! He was selfish. So men are. For he was not ill. Dr. Holmes said there was nothing the matter with him. She spread her hand before her. Look! Her wedding ring slipped—she had grown so thin. It was she who suffered—but she had nobody to tell.

Far was Italy and the white houses and the room where her sisters sat making hats, and the streets crowded every evening with people walking, laughing out loud, not half alive like people here, huddled up in Bath chairs,[7] looking at a few ugly flowers stuck in pots!

"For you should see the Milan gardens,"[8] she said aloud. But to whom?

There was nobody. Her words faded. So a rocket fades. Its sparks, having grazed their way into the night, surrender to it, dark descends, pours over the outlines of houses and towers; bleak hillsides soften and fall in. But though they are gone, the night is full of them; robbed of colour, blank of windows, they exist more ponderously, give out what the frank daylight fails to transmit—the trouble and suspense of things conglomerated there in the darkness; huddled together in the darkness; reft of the relief which dawn brings when, washing the walls white and grey, spotting each windowpane, lifting the mist from the fields, showing the red brown cows peacefully grazing, all is once more decked out to the eye; exists again. I am alone; I am alone! she cried, by the fountain in Regent's Park (staring at the Indian and his cross[9]), as perhaps at midnight, when all boundaries are lost, the country reverts to its ancient shape, as the Romans[1] saw it, lying cloudy, when they landed, and the hills had no names and rivers wound they knew not where— such was her darkness; when suddenly, as if a shelf were shot forth and she stood on it, she said how she was his wife, married years ago in Milan, his wife, and would never, never tell that he was mad! Turning, the shelf fell; down, down she dropped. For he was gone, she thought—gone, as he threatened, to kill himself—to throw himself under a cart! But no; there he was; still sitting alone on the seat, in his shabby overcoat, his legs crossed, staring, talking aloud.

Men must not cut down trees. There is a God. (He noted such revelations on the backs of envelopes.) Change the world. No one kills from hatred. Make it known (he wrote it down). He waited. He listened. A sparrow

6. In World War I (1914–18).
7. Wheeled chairs for invalids.
8. In Italy.
    ᵗⁿking fountain resembling a cross at the
       ᵗ the Broad Walk and commemorat-

ing the protection of Parsis, Indian Zoroastrians, under British colonial rule in India.
1. The Roman Empire included most of Britain from 43 to 410 C.E.

perched on the railing opposite chirped Septimus, Septimus, four or five times over and went on, drawing its notes out, to sing freshly and piercingly in Greek words how there is no crime and, joined by another sparrow, they sang in voices prolonged and piercing in Greek words,[2] from trees in the meadow of life beyond a river where the dead walk,[3] how there is no death.

There was his hand; there the dead. White things were assembling behind the railings opposite. But he dared not look. Evans was behind the railings!

"What are you saying?" said Rezia suddenly, sitting down by him.

Interrupted again! She was always interrupting.

Away from people—they must get away from people, he said (jumping up), right away over there, where there were chairs beneath a tree and the long slope of the park dipped like a length of green stuff with a ceiling cloth of blue and pink smoke high above, and there was a rampart of far irregular houses hazed in smoke, the traffic hummed in a circle, and on the right, duncoloured animals stretched long necks over the Zoo[4] palings, barking, howling. There they sat down under a tree.

"Look," she implored him, pointing at a little troop of boys carrying cricket stumps,[5] and one shuffled, spun round on his heel and shuffled, as if he were acting a clown at the music hall.

"Look," she implored him, for Dr. Holmes had told her to make him notice real things, go to a music hall, play cricket—that was the very game, Dr. Holmes said, a nice out-of-door game, the very game for her husband.

"Look," she repeated.

Look the unseen bade him, the voice which now communicated with him who was the greatest of mankind, Septimus, lately taken from life to death, the Lord who had come to renew society, who lay like a coverlet, a snow blanket smitten only by the sun, for ever unwasted, suffering for ever, the scapegoat, the eternal sufferer, but he did not want it, he moaned, putting from him with a wave of his hand that eternal suffering, that eternal loneliness.

"Look," she repeated, for he must not talk aloud to himself out of doors.

"Oh look," she implored him. But what was there to look at? A few sheep. That was all.

The way to Regent's Park Tube[6] station—could they tell her the way to Regent's Park Tube station—Maisie Johnson wanted to know. She was only up from Edinburgh[7] two days ago.

"Not this way—over there!" Rezia exclaimed, waving her aside, lest she should see Septimus.

Both seemed queer, Maisie Johnson thought. Everything seemed very queer. In London for the first time, come to take up a post at her uncle's in Leadenhall Street,[8] and now walking through Regent's Park in the morning, this couple on the chairs gave her quite a turn; the young woman seeming foreign, the man looking queer; so that should she be very old she would still

---

2. Woolf wrote of having a similar experience during a 1904 breakdown, in her 1922 memoir "Old Bloomsbury."

3. Cf. the River Styx, separating the living from the realm of the dead in the mythical Greek underworld.

4. In Regent's Park.

5. Upright sticks that, with cross-pieces called bails, form the wicket defended by the batsman in cricket.

6. Underground (subway).

7. Colloquially, one travels "up" to London even if, as in this case, one is actually traveling south from Scotland's capital.

8. Street in east London.

remember and make it jangle again among her memories how she had walked through Regent's Park on a fine summer's morning fifty years ago. For she was only nineteen and had got her way at last, to come to London; and now how queer it was, this couple she had asked the way of, and the girl started and jerked her hand, and the man—he seemed awfully odd; quarrelling, perhaps; parting for ever, perhaps; something was up, she knew; and now all these people (for she returned to the Broad Walk), the stone basins, the prim flowers, the old men and women, invalids most of them in Bath chairs—all seemed, after Edinburgh, so queer. And Maisie Johnson, as she joined that gently trudging, vaguely gazing, breeze-kissed company—squirrels perching and preening, sparrow fountains fluttering for crumbs, dogs busy with the railings, busy with each other, while the soft warm air washed over them and lent to the fixed unsurprised gaze with which they received life some-thing whimsical and mollified—Maisie Johnson positively felt she must cry Oh! (for that young man on the seat had given her quite a turn. Something was up, she knew.)

Horror! horror! she wanted to cry. (She had left her people; they had warned her what would happen.)

Why hadn't she stayed at home? she cried, twisting the knob of the iron railing.

That girl, thought Mrs. Dempster (who saved crusts for the squirrels and often ate her lunch in Regent's Park), don't know a thing yet; and really it seemed to her better to be a little stout, a little slack, a little moderate in one's expectations. Percy drank. Well, better to have a son, thought Mrs. Dempster. She had had a hard time of it, and couldn't help smiling at a girl like that. You'll get married, for you're pretty enough, thought Mrs. Demp-ster. Get married, she thought, and then you'll know. Oh, the cooks, and so on. Every man has his ways. But whether I'd have chosen quite like that if I could have known, thought Mrs. Dempster, and could not help wishing to whisper a word to Maisie Johnson; to feel on the creased pouch of her worn old face the kiss of pity. For it's been a hard life, thought Mrs. Dempster. What hadn't she given to it? Roses; figure; her feet too. (She drew the knobbed lumps beneath her skirt.)

Roses, she thought sardonically. All trash, m'dear. For really, what with eating, drinking, and mating, the bad days and good, life had been no mere matter of roses, and what was more, let me tell you, Carrie Dempster had no wish to change her lot with any woman's in Kentish Town![9] But, she implored, pity. Pity, for the loss of roses. Pity she asked of Maisie Johnson, standing by the hyacinth beds.

Ah, but that aeroplane! Hadn't Mrs. Dempster always longed to see for-eign parts? She had a nephew, a missionary. It soared and shot. She always went on the sea at Margate,[1] not out o' sight of land, but she had no patience with women who were afraid of water. It swept and fell. Her stom-ach was in her mouth. Up again. There's a fine young feller aboard of it, Mrs. Dempster wagered, and away and away it went, fast and fading, away and away the aeroplane shot; soaring over Greenwich[2] and all the masts; over the little island of grey churches, St. Paul's[3] and the rest till, on either

9. Working-class neighborhood in north London near Hampstead Heath.
1. Seaside town in the county of Kent, west of London.
2. London borough south of the Thames.
3. St. Paul's Cathedral, the tallest building in London in 1923.

side of London, fields spread out and dark brown woods where adventurous thrushes hopping boldly, glancing quickly, snatched the snail and tapped him on a stone, once, twice, thrice.

Away and away the aeroplane shot, till it was nothing but a bright spark; an aspiration; a concentration; a symbol (so it seemed to Mr. Bentley, vigorously rolling his strip of turf at Greenwich) of man's soul; of his determination, thought Mr. Bentley, sweeping round the cedar tree, to get outside his body, beyond his house, by means of thought, Einstein,[4] speculation,[5] mathematics, the Mendelian theory[6]—away the aeroplane shot.

Then, while a seedy-looking nondescript man carrying a leather bag stood on the steps of St. Paul's Cathedral, and hesitated, for within was what balm, how great a welcome, how many tombs with banners waving over them, tokens of victories not over armies, but over, he thought, that plaguy spirit of truth seeking which leaves me at present without a situation, and more than that, the cathedral offers company, he thought, invites you to membership of a society; great men belong to it; martyrs have died for it; why not enter in, he thought, put this leather bag stuffed with pamphlets before an altar, a cross, the symbol of something which has soared beyond seeking and questing and knocking of words together and has become all spirit, disembodied, ghostly— why not enter in? he thought and while he hesitated out flew the aeroplane over Ludgate Circus.[7]

It was strange; it was still. Not a sound was to be heard above the traffic. Unguided it seemed; sped of its own free will. And now, curving up and up, straight up, like something mounting in ecstasy, in pure delight, out from behind poured white smoke looping, writing a T, an O, an F.

"What are they looking at?" said Clarissa Dalloway to the maid who opened her door.

The hall of the house was cool as a vault. Mrs. Dalloway raised her hand to her eyes, and, as the maid shut the door to, and she heard the swish of Lucy's skirts, she felt like a nun who has left the world and feels fold round her the familiar veils and the response to old devotions. The cook whistled in the kitchen. She heard the click of the typewriter. It was her life, and, bending her head over the hall table, she bowed beneath the influence, felt blessed and purified, saying to herself, as she took the pad with the telephone message on it, how moments like this are buds on the tree of life, flowers of darkness they are, she thought (as if some lovely rose had blossomed for her eyes only); not for a moment did she believe in God; but all the more, she thought, taking up the pad, must one repay in daily life to servants, yes, to dogs and canaries, above all to Richard her husband, who was the foundation of it—of the gay sounds, of the green lights, of the cook even whistling, for Mrs. Walker was Irish and whistled all day long—one must pay back from this secret deposit of exquisite moments, she thought, lifting the pad, while Lucy stood by her, trying to explain how

"Mr. Dalloway, ma'am"—

4. German-born theoretical physicist Albert Einstein (1879–1955) won the 1921 Nobel Prize in Physics.
5. Risky buying and selling for profit.
6. Laws of genetics studied by Austrian monk Gregor Mendel (1822–1884) in his work with pea plants.
7. London intersection west of St. Paul's Cathedral.

Clarissa read on the telephone pad, "Lady Bruton wishes to know if Mr. Dalloway will lunch with her to-day."

"Mr. Dalloway, ma'am, told me to tell you he would be lunching out."

"Dear!" said Clarissa, and Lucy shared as she meant her to her disappointment (but not the pang); felt the concord between them; took the hint; thought how the gentry love; gilded her own future with calm; and, taking Mrs. Dalloway's parasol, handled it like a sacred weapon which a Goddess, having acquitted herself honourably in the field of battle, sheds, and placed it in the umbrella stand.

"Fear no more," said Clarissa. Fear no more the heat o' the sun;[8] for the shock of Lady Bruton asking Richard to lunch without her made the moment in which she had stood shiver, as a plant on the river-bed feels the shock of a passing oar and shivers: so she rocked: so she shivered.

Millicent Bruton, whose lunch parties were said to be extraordinarily amusing, had not asked her. No vulgar jealousy could separate her from Richard. But she feared time itself, and read on Lady Bruton's face, as if it had been a dial cut in impassive stone, the dwindling of life; how year by year her share was sliced; how little the margin that remained was capable any longer of stretching, of absorbing, as in the youthful years, the colours, salts, tones of existence, so that she filled the room she entered, and felt often as she stood hesitating one moment on the threshold of her drawing-room, an exquisite suspense, such as might stay a diver before plunging while the sea darkens and brightens beneath him, and the waves which threaten to break, but only gently split their surface, roll and conceal and encrust as they just turn over the weeds with pearl.

She put the pad on the hall table. She began to go slowly upstairs, with her hand on the bannisters, as if she had left a party, where now this friend now that had flashed back her face, her voice; had shut the door and gone out and stood alone, a single figure against the appalling night, or rather, to be accurate, against the stare of this matter-of-fact June morning; soft with the glow of rose petals for some, she knew, and felt it, as she paused by the open staircase window which let in blinds flapping, dogs barking, let in, she thought, feeling herself suddenly shrivelled, aged, breastless, the grinding, blowing, flowering of the day, out of doors, out of the window, out of her body and brain which now failed, since Lady Bruton, whose lunch parties were said to be extraordinarily amusing, had not asked her.

Like a nun withdrawing, or a child exploring a tower, she went upstairs, paused at the window, came to the bathroom. There was the green linoleum and a tap dripping. There was an emptiness about the heart of life; an attic room. Women must put off their rich apparel. At midday they must disrobe. She pierced the pincushion and laid her feathered yellow hat on the bed. The sheets were clean, tight stretched in a broad white band from side to side. Narrower and narrower would her bed be. The candle was half burnt down and she had read deep in Baron Marbot's *Memoirs*.[9] She had read late at night of the retreat from Moscow. For the House sat so long that Richard insisted, after her illness, that she must sleep undisturbed. And really she preferred to read of the retreat from Moscow. He knew it. So

---

8. See p. 288 and n. 9.
9. Memoirs by French general Jean-Baptiste Antoine Marcellin, baron de Marbot (1782–1854), describe the disastrous Russian campaign undertaken in the winter of 1812 by Napoleon Bonaparte (1769–1821).

the room was an attic; the bed narrow; and lying there reading, for she slept badly, she could not dispel a virginity preserved through childbirth which clung to her like a sheet. Lovely in girlhood, suddenly there came a moment—for example on the river beneath the woods at Clieveden—when, through some contraction of this cold spirit, she had failed him. And then at Constantinople,[1] and again and again. She could see what she lacked. It was not beauty; it was not mind. It was something central which permeated; something warm which broke up surfaces and rippled the cold contact of man and woman, or of women together. For *that* she could dimly perceive. She resented it, had a scruple picked up Heaven knows where, or, as she felt, sent by Nature (who is invariably wise); yet she could not resist sometimes yielding to the charm of a woman, not a girl, of a woman confessing, as to her they often did, some scrape, some folly. And whether it was pity, or their beauty, or that she was older, or some accident—like a faint scent, or a violin next door (so strange is the power of sounds at certain moments), she did undoubtedly then feel what men felt. Only for a moment; but it was enough. It was a sudden revelation, a tinge like a blush which one tried to check and then, as it spread, one yielded to its expansion, and rushed to the farthest verge and there quivered and felt the world come closer, swollen with some astonishing significance, some pressure of rapture, which split its thin skin and gushed and poured with an extraordinary alleviation over the cracks and sores! Then, for that moment, she had seen an illumination; a match burning in a crocus; an inner meaning almost expressed. But the close withdrew; the hard softened. It was over—the moment. Against such moments (with women too) there contrasted (as she laid her hat down) the bed and Baron Marbot and the candle half-burnt. Lying awake, the floor creaked; the lit house was suddenly darkened, and if she raised her head she could just hear the click of the handle released as gently as possible by Richard, who slipped upstairs in his socks and then, as often as not, dropped his hot-water bottle and swore! How she laughed!

But this question of love (she thought, putting her coat away), this falling in love with women. Take Sally Seton; her relation in the old days with Sally Seton. Had not that, after all, been love?

She sat on the floor—that was her first impression of Sally—she sat on the floor with her arms round her knees, smoking a cigarette. Where could it have been? The Mannings? The Kinloch-Jones's? At some party (where, she could not be certain), for she had a distinct recollection of saying to the man she was with, "Who is *that*?" And he had told her, and said that Sally's parents did not get on (how that shocked her—that one's parents should quarrel!). But all that evening she could not take her eyes off Sally. It was an extraordinary beauty of the kind she most admired, dark, large-eyed, with that quality which, since she hadn't got it herself, she always envied—a sort of abandonment, as if she could say anything, do anything; a quality much commoner in foreigners than in Englishwomen. Sally always said she had French blood in her veins, an ancestor had been with Marie Antoinette,[2] had his head cut off, left a ruby ring. Perhaps that summer she came to stay at Bourton, walking in quite unexpectedly without a penny in her pocket,

1. Now Istanbul, Turkey. "Clieveden": forest on the banks of the Thames.
2. Queen of France and wife of Louis XVI (1755–1793), guillotined during the French Revolution.

one night after dinner, and upsetting poor Aunt Helena to such an extent that she never forgave her. There had been some quarrel at home. She literally hadn't a penny that night when she came to them—had pawned a brooch to come down. She had rushed off in a passion. They sat up till all hours of the night talking. Sally it was who made her feel, for the first time, how sheltered the life at Bourton was. She knew nothing about sex—nothing about social problems. She had once seen an old man who had dropped dead in a field—she had seen cows just after their calves were born. But Aunt Helena never liked discussion of anything (when Sally gave her William Morris,[3] it had to be wrapped in brown paper). There they sat, hour after hour, talking in her bedroom at the top of the house, talking about life, how they were to reform the world. They meant to found a society to abolish private property, and actually had a letter written, though not sent out. The ideas were Sally's, of course—but very soon she was just as excited—read Plato in bed before breakfast; read Morris; read Shelley[4] by the hour.

Sally's power was amazing, her gift, her personality. There was her way with flowers, for instance. At Bourton they always had stiff little vases all the way down the table. Sally went out, picked hollyhocks, dahlias—all sorts of flowers that had never been seen together—cut their heads off, and made them swim on the top of water in bowls. The effect was extraordinary—coming in to dinner in the sunset (Of course Aunt Helena thought it wicked to treat flowers like that.) Then she forgot her sponge, and ran along the passage naked. That grim old housemaid, Ellen Atkins, went about grumbling—"Suppose any of the gentlemen had seen?" Indeed she did shock people. She was untidy, Papa said.

The strange thing, on looking back, was the purity, the integrity, of her feeling for Sally. It was not like one's feeling for a man. It was completely disinterested, and besides, it had a quality which could only exist between women, between women just grown up. It was protective, on her side; sprang from a sense of being in league together, a presentiment of something that was bound to part them (they spoke of marriage always as a catastrophe), which led to this chivalry, this protective feeling which was much more on her side than Sally's. For in those days she was completely reckless; did the most idiotic things out of bravado; bicycled round the parapet on the terrace; smoked cigars. Absurd, she was—very absurd. But the charm was overpowering, to her at least, so that she could remember standing in her bedroom at the top of the house holding the hot-water can in her hands and saying aloud, "She is beneath this roof. . . . She is beneath this roof!"

No, the words meant absolutely nothing to her now. She could not even get an echo of her old emotion. But she could remember going cold with excitement, and doing her hair in a kind of ecstasy (now the old feeling began to come back to her, as she took out her hairpins, laid them on the dressing-table, began to do her hair), with the rooks flaunting up and down in the pink evening light, and dressing, and going downstairs, and feeling as she crossed the hall "if it were now to die 'twere now to be most happy." That was her feeling—Othello's feeling,[5] and she felt it, she was convinced,

---

3. I.e., a book by the English designer, writer, and socialist (1834–1896).
4. Percy Bysshe Shelley (1792–1822), English

Romantic poet. Plato (ca. 429–347 B.C.E.), Greek philosopher.
5. From Shakespeare's *Othello* 2.1.87–88.

as strongly as Shakespeare meant Othello to feel it, all because she was coming down to dinner in a white frock to meet Sally Seton!

She was wearing pink gauze—was that possible? She *seemed*, anyhow, all light, glowing, like some bird or air ball[6] that has flown in, attached itself for a moment to a bramble. But nothing is so strange when one is in love (and what was this except being in love?) as the complete indifference of other people. Aunt Helena just wandered off after dinner; Papa read the paper. Peter Walsh might have been there, and old Miss Cummings; Joseph Breitkopf certainly was, for he came every summer, poor old man, for weeks and weeks, and pretended to read German with her, but really played the piano and sang Brahms[7] without any voice.

All this was only a background for Sally. She stood by the fireplace talking, in that beautiful voice which made everything she said sound like a caress, to Papa, who had begun to be attracted rather against his will (he never got over lending her one of his books and finding it soaked on the terrace), when suddenly she said, "What a shame to sit indoors!" and they all went out on to the terrace and walked up and down. Peter Walsh and Joseph Breitkopf went on about Wagner. She and Sally fell a little behind. Then came the most exquisite moment of her whole life passing a stone urn with flowers in it. Sally stopped; picked a flower; kissed her on the lips. The whole world might have turned upside down! The others disappeared; there she was alone with Sally. And she felt that she had been given a present, wrapped up, and told just to keep it, not to look at it—a diamond, something infinitely precious, wrapped up, which, as they walked (up and down, up and down), she uncovered, or the radiance burnt through, the revelation, the religious feeling!—when old Joseph and Peter faced them:

"Star-gazing?" said Peter.

It was like running one's face against a granite wall in the darkness! It was shocking; it was horrible!

Not for herself. She felt only how Sally was being mauled already, maltreated; she felt his hostility; his jealousy; his determination to break into their companionship. All this she saw as one sees a landscape in a flash of lightning—and Sally (never had she admired her so much!) gallantly taking her way unvanquished. She laughed. She made old Joseph tell her the names of the stars, which he liked doing very seriously. She stood there: she listened. She heard the names of the stars.

"Oh this horror!" she said to herself, as if she had known all along that something would interrupt, would embitter her moment of happiness.

Yet, after all, how much she owed to him later. Always when she thought of him she thought of their quarrels for some reason—because she wanted his good opinion so much, perhaps. She owed him words: "sentimental," "civilised"; they started up every day of her life as if he guarded her. A book was sentimental; an attitude to life sentimental. "Sentimental," perhaps she was to be thinking of the past. What would he think, she wondered, when he came back?

That she had grown older? Would he say that, or would she see him thinking when he came back, that she had grown older? It was true. Since her illness she had turned almost white.

6. Toy balloon.
7. Johannes Brahms (1837–1897), German Romantic composer.

Laying her brooch on the table, she had a sudden spasm, as if, while she mused, the icy claws had had the chance to fix in her. She was not old yet. She had just broken into her fifty-second year. Months and months of it were still untouched. June, July, August! Each still remained almost whole, and, as if to catch the falling drop, Clarissa (crossing to the dressing-table) plunged into the very heart of the moment, transfixed it, there—the moment of this June morning on which was the pressure of all the other mornings, seeing the glass, the dressing-table, and all the bottles afresh, collecting the whole of her at one point (as she looked into the glass), seeing the delicate pink face of the woman who was that very night to give a party; of Clarissa Dalloway; of herself.

How many million times she had seen her face, and always with the same imperceptible contraction! She pursed her lips when she looked in the glass. It was to give her face point. That was her self—pointed; dartlike; definite. That was her self when some effort, some call on her to be her self, drew the parts together, she alone knew how different, how incompatible and composed so for the world only into one centre, one diamond, one woman who sat in her drawing-room and made a meeting-point, a radiancy no doubt in some dull lives, a refuge for the lonely to come to, perhaps; she had helped young people, who were grateful to her; had tried to be the same always, never showing a sign of all the other sides of her—faults, jealousies, vanities, suspicions, like this of Lady Bruton not asking her to lunch; which, she thought (combing her hair finally), is utterly base! Now, where was her dress?

Her evening dresses hung in the cupboard. Clarissa, plunging her hand into the softness, gently detached the green dress and carried it to the window. She had torn it. Some one had trod on the skirt. She had felt it give at the Embassy party at the top among the folds. By artificial light the green shone, but lost its colour now in the sun. She would mend it. Her maids had too much to do. She would wear it to-night. She would take her silks, her scissors, her—what was it?—her thimble, of course, down into the drawing-room, for she must also write, and see that things generally were more or less in order.

Strange, she thought, pausing on the landing, and assembling that diamond shape, that single person, strange how a mistress knows the very moment, the very temper of her house! Faint sounds rose in spirals up the well of the stairs; the swish of a mop; tapping; knocking; a loudness when the front door opened; a voice repeating a message in the basement; the chink of silver on a tray, clean silver for the party. All was for the party.

(And Lucy, coming into the drawing-room with her tray held out, put the giant candlesticks on the mantelpiece, the silver casket[8] in the middle, turned the crystal dolphin towards the clock. They would come; they would stand; they would talk in the mincing tones which she could imitate, ladies and gentlemen. Of all, her mistress was loveliest—mistress of silver, of linen, of china, for the sun, the silver, doors off their hinges, Rumpelmayer's men, gave her a sense, as she laid the paper-knife[9] on the inlaid table, of something achieved. Behold! Behold! she said, speaking to her old friends in the baker's shop, where she had first seen service at Caterham,[1] prying into the glass. She was Lady Angela, attending Princess Mary, when in came Mrs. Dalloway.)

---

8. Small box.
9. A slim knife used, e.g., for slitting open letters.

1. Town south of London in the county of Surrey.

"Oh Lucy," she said, "the silver does look nice!"

"And how," she said, turning the crystal dolphin to stand straight, "how did you enjoy the play last night?" "Oh, they had to go before the end!" she said. "They had to be back at ten!" she said. "So they don't know what happened," she said. "That does seem hard luck," she said (for her servants stayed later, if they asked her). "That does seem rather a shame," she said, taking the old bald-looking cushion in the middle of the sofa and putting it in Lucy's arms, and giving her a little push, and crying:

"Take it away! Give it to Mrs. Walker with my compliments! Take it away!" she cried.

And Lucy stopped at the drawing-room door, holding the cushion, and said, very shyly, turning a little pink, Couldn't she help to mend that dress?

But, said Mrs. Dalloway, she had enough on her hands already, quite enough of her own to do without that.

"But, thank you, Lucy, oh, thank you," said Mrs. Dalloway, and thank you, thank you, she went on saying (sitting down on the sofa with her dress over her knees, her scissors, her silks), thank you, thank you, she went on saying in gratitude to her servants generally for helping her to be like this, to be what she wanted, gentle, generous-hearted. Her servants liked her. And then this dress of hers—where was the tear? and now her needle to be threaded. This was a favourite dress, one of Sally Parker's, the last almost she ever made, alas, for Sally had now retired, living at Ealing,[2] and if ever I have a moment, thought Clarissa (but never would she have a moment any more), I shall go and see her at Ealing. For she was a character, thought Clarissa, a real artist. She thought of little out-of-the-way things; yet her dresses were never queer. You could wear them at Hatfield;[3] at Buckingham Palace. She had worn them at Hatfield; at Buckingham Palace.

Quiet descended on her, calm, content, as her needle, drawing the silk smoothly to its gentle pause, collected the green folds together and attached them, very lightly, to the belt. So on a summer's day waves collect, overbalance, and fall; collect and fall; and the whole world seems to be saying "that is all" more and more ponderously, until even the heart in the body which lies in the sun on the beach says too, That is all. Fear no more, says the heart. Fear no more, says the heart, committing its burden to some sea, which sighs collectively for all sorrows, and renews, begins, collects, lets fall. And the body alone listens to the passing bee; the wave breaking; the dog barking, far away barking and barking.

"Heavens, the front-door bell!" exclaimed Clarissa, staying her needle. Roused, she listened.

"Mrs. Dalloway will see me," said the elderly man in the hall. "Oh yes, she will see *me*," he repeated, putting Lucy aside very benevolently, and running upstairs ever so quickly. "Yes, yes, yes," he muttered as he ran upstairs. "She will see me. After five years in India,[4] Clarissa will see me."

"Who can—what can," asked Mrs. Dalloway (thinking it was outrageous to be interrupted at eleven o'clock on the morning of the day she was giving a party), hearing a step on the stairs. She heard a hand upon the door. She

2. District in west London.
3. Hertfordshire estate.
4. I.e., after five years working in India as a colonial administrator. Peter Walsh's position there would have become more complicated following the 1919 Amritsar Massacre. It created strong anti-British sentiment and led to the Government of India Act, which established a national parliament, and the beginning of Mohandas Gandhi's campaign of civil disobedience (1920).

made to hide her dress, like a virgin protecting chastity, respecting privacy. Now the brass knob slipped. Now the door opened, and in came—for a single second she could not remember what he was called! so surprised she was to see him, so glad, so shy, so utterly taken aback to have Peter Walsh come to her unexpectedly in the morning! (She had not read his letter.)

"And how are you?" said Peter Walsh, positively trembling; taking both her hands; kissing both her hands. She's grown older, he thought, sitting down. I shan't tell her anything about it, he thought, for she's grown older. She's looking at me, he thought, a sudden embarrassment coming over him, though he had kissed her hands. Putting his hand into his pocket, he took out a large pocket-knife and half opened the blade.

Exactly the same, thought Clarissa; the same queer look; the same check suit; a little out of the straight his face is, a little thinner, dryer, perhaps, but he looks awfully well, and just the same.

"How heavenly it is to see you again!" she exclaimed. He had his knife out. That's so like him, she thought.

He had only reached town last night, he said; would have to go down into the country at once; and how was everything, how was everybody—Richard? Elizabeth?

"And what's all this?" he said, tilting his pen-knife towards her green dress.

He's very well dressed, thought Clarissa; yet he always criticises *me*.

Here she is mending her dress; mending her dress as usual, he thought; here she's been sitting all the time I've been in India; mending her dress; playing about; going to parties; running to the House and back and all that, he thought, growing more and more irritated, more and more agitated, for there's nothing in the world so bad for some women as marriage, he thought; and politics; and having a Conservative husband, like the admirable Richard. So it is, so it is, he thought, shutting his knife with a snap.

"Richard's very well. Richard's at a Committee,"[5] said Clarissa.

And she opened her scissors, and said, did he mind her just finishing what she was doing to her dress, for they had a party that night?

"Which I shan't ask you to," she said. "My dear Peter!" she said.

But it was delicious to hear her say that—my dear Peter! Indeed, it was all so delicious—the silver, the chairs; all so delicious!

Why wouldn't she ask him to her party? he asked.

Now of course, thought Clarissa, he's enchanting! perfectly enchanting! Now I remember how impossible it was ever to make up my mind—and why did I make up my mind—not to marry him? she wondered, that awful summer?

"But it's so extraordinary that you should have come this morning!" she cried, putting her hands, one on top of another, down on her dress.

"Do you remember," she said, "how the blinds used to flap at Bourton?"

"They did," he said; and he remembered breakfasting alone, very awkwardly, with her father; who had died; and he had not written to Clarissa. But he had never got on well with old Parry, that querulous, weak-kneed old man, Clarissa's father, Justin Parry.

"I often wish I'd got on better with your father," he said.

---

5. Group of members of Parliament charged with overseeing a particular issue. "The House": the House of Commons, the lower house of Parliament. "Conservative": member of the Conservative Party, the less reforming of the (usually) two major political parties.

"But he never liked any one who—our friends," said Clarissa; and could have bitten her tongue for thus reminding Peter that he had wanted to marry her.

Of course I did, thought Peter; it almost broke my heart too, he thought; and was overcome with his own grief, which rose like a moon looked at from a terrace, ghastly beautiful with light from the sunken day. I was more unhappy than I've ever been since, he thought. And as if in truth he were sitting there on the terrace he edged a little towards Clarissa; put his hand out; raised it; let it fall. There above them it hung, that moon. She too seemed to be sitting with him on the terrace, in the moonlight.

"Herbert has it now," she said. "I never go there now," she said.

Then, just as happens on a terrace in the moonlight, when one person begins to feel ashamed that he is already bored, and yet as the other sits silent, very quiet, sadly looking at the moon, does not like to speak, moves his foot, clears his throat, notices some iron scroll on a table leg, stirs a leaf, but says nothing—so Peter Walsh did now. For why go back like this to the past? he thought. Why make him think of it again? Why make him suffer, when she had tortured him so infernally? Why?

"Do you remember the lake?" she said, in an abrupt voice, under the pressure of an emotion which caught her heart, made the muscles of her throat stiff, and contracted her lips in a spasm as she said "lake." For she was a child, throwing bread to the ducks, between her parents, and at the same time a grown woman coming to her parents who stood by the lake, holding her life in her arms which, as she neared them, grew larger and larger in her arms, until it became a whole life, a complete life, which she put down by them and said, "This is what I have made of it! This!" And what had she made of it? What, indeed? sitting there sewing this morning with Peter.

She looked at Peter Walsh; her look, passing through all that time and that emotion, reached him doubtfully; settled on him tearfully; and rose and fluttered away, as a bird touches a branch and rises and flutters away. Quite simply she wiped her eyes.

"Yes," said Peter. "Yes, yes, yes," he said, as if she drew up to the surface something which positively hurt him as it rose. Stop! Stop! he wanted to cry. For he was not old; his life was not over; not by any means. He was only just past fifty. Shall I tell her, he thought, or not? He would like to make a clean breast of it all. But she is too cold, he thought; sewing, with her scissors; Daisy would look ordinary beside Clarissa. And she would think me a failure, which I am in their sense, he thought; in the Dalloways' sense. Oh yes, he had no doubt about that; he was a failure, compared with all this—the inlaid table, the mounted paper-knife, the dolphin and the candlesticks, the chair-covers and the old valuable English tinted prints—he was a failure! I detest the smugness of the whole affair, he thought; Richard's doing, not Clarissa's; save that she married him. (Here Lucy came into the room, carrying silver, more silver, but charming, slender, graceful she looked, he thought, as she stooped to put it down.) And this has been going on all the time! he thought; week after week; Clarissa's life; while I—he thought; and at once everything seemed to radiate from him; journeys; rides; quarrels; adventures; bridge parties; love affairs; work; work, work! and he took out his knife quite openly—his old horn-handled knife which Clarissa could swear he had had these thirty years—and clenched his fist upon it.

What an extraordinary habit that was, Clarissa thought; always playing with a knife. Always making one feel, too, frivolous; empty-minded; a mere silly chatterbox, as he used. But I too, she thought, and, taking up her needle, summoned, like a Queen whose guards have fallen asleep and left her unprotected (she had been quite taken aback by this visit—it had upset her) so that any one can stroll in and have a look at her where she lies with the brambles curving over her, summoned to her help the things she did; the things she liked; her husband; Elizabeth; her self, in short, which Peter hardly knew now, all to come about her and beat off the enemy.

"Well, and what's happened to you?" she said. So before a battle begins, the horses paw the ground; toss their heads; the light shines on their flanks; their necks curve. So Peter Walsh and Clarissa, sitting side by side on the blue sofa, challenged each other. His powers chafed and tossed in him. He assembled from different quarters all sorts of things; praise; his career at Oxford; his marriage, which she knew nothing whatever about; how he had loved; and altogether done his job.

"Millions of things!" he exclaimed, and, urged by the assembly of powers which were now charging this way and that and giving him the feeling at once frightening and extremely exhilarating of being rushed through the air on the shoulders of people he could no longer see, he raised his hands to his forehead.

Clarissa sat very upright; drew in her breath.

"I am in love," he said, not to her however, but to some one raised up in the dark so that you could not touch her but must lay your garland down on the grass in the dark.

"In love," he repeated, now speaking rather dryly to Clarissa Dalloway; "in love with a girl in India." He had deposited his garland. Clarissa could make what she would of it.

"In love!" she said. That he at his age should be sucked under in his little bow-tie by that monster! And there's no flesh on his neck; his hands are red; and he's six months older than I am! her eye flashed back to her; but in her heart she felt, all the same, he is in love. He has that, she felt; he is in love.

But the indomitable egotism which for ever rides down the hosts opposed to it, the river which says on, on, on; even though, it admits, there may be no goal for us whatever, still on, on; this indomitable egotism charged her cheeks with colour; made her look very young; very pink; very bright-eyed as she sat with her dress upon her knee, and her needle held to the end of green silk, trembling a little. He was in love! Not with her. With some younger woman, of course.

"And who is she?" she asked.

Now this statue must be brought from its height and set down between them.

"A married woman, unfortunately," he said; "the wife of a Major in the Indian Army."

And with a curious ironical sweetness he smiled as he placed her in this ridiculous way before Clarissa.

(All the same, he is in love, thought Clarissa.)

"She has," he continued, very reasonably, "two small children; a boy and a girl; and I have come over to see my lawyers about the divorce."

There they are! he thought. Do what you like with them, Clarissa! There they are! And second by second it seemed to him that the wife of the Major in the Indian Army[6] (his Daisy) and her two small children became more and more lovely as Clarissa looked at them; as if he had set light to a grey pellet on a plate and there had risen up a lovely tree in the brisk sea-salted air of their intimacy (for in some ways no one understood him, felt with him, as Clarissa did)—their exquisite intimacy.

She flattered him; she fooled him, thought Clarissa; shaping the woman, the wife of the Major in the Indian Army, with three strokes of a knife. What a waste! What a folly! All his life long Peter had been fooled like that; first getting sent down from Oxford;[7] next marrying the girl on the boat going out to India; now the wife of a Major in the Indian Army—thank Heaven she had refused to marry him! Still, he was in love; her old friend, her dear Peter, he was in love.

"But what are you going to do?" she asked him. Oh the lawyers and solicitors, Messrs. Hooper and Grateley of Lincoln's Inn,[8] they were going to do it, he said. And he actually pared his nails with his pocket-knife.

For Heaven's sake, leave your knife alone! she cried to herself in irrepressible irritation; it was his silly unconventionality, his weakness; his lack of the ghost of a notion what any one else was feeling that annoyed her, had always annoyed her; and now at his age, how silly!

I know all that, Peter thought; I know what I'm up against, he thought, running his finger along the blade of his knife, Clarissa and Dalloway and all the rest of them; but I'll show Clarissa—and then to his utter surprise, suddenly thrown by those uncontrollable forces thrown through the air, he burst into tears; wept; wept without the least shame, sitting on the sofa, the tears running down his cheeks.

And Clarissa had leant forward, taken his hand, drawn him to her, kissed him,—actually had felt his face on hers before she could down the brandishing of silver flashing—plumes like pampas grass in a tropic gale in her breast, which, subsiding, left her holding his hand, patting his knee and, feeling as she sat back extraordinarily at her ease with him and light-hearted, all in a clap it came over her, If I had married him, this gaiety would have been mine all day!

It was all over for her. The sheet was stretched and the bed narrow. She had gone up into the tower alone and left them blackberrying in the sun. The door had shut, and there among the dust of fallen plaster and the litter of birds' nests how distant the view had looked, and the sounds came thin and chill (once on Leith Hill,[9] she remembered), and Richard, Richard! she cried, as a sleeper in the night starts and stretches a hand in the dark for help. Lunching with Lady Bruton, it came back to her. He has left me; I am alone for ever, she thought, folding her hands upon her knee.

Peter Walsh had got up and crossed to the window and stood with his back to her, flicking a bandanna handkerchief from side to side. Masterly and dry and desolate he looked, his thin shoulder-blades lifting his coat slightly; blowing his nose violently. Take me with you, Clarissa thought impulsively, as if he were starting directly upon some great voyage; and then, next moment, it was as if the five acts of a play that had been very exciting and moving were

---

6. British Army stationed in India.
7. Compelled to leave the university as a punishment.
8. One of the Inns of Court, or legal societies,
that admitted people to the bar to practice law.
9. The highest point in southeast England, in the county of Surrey, famous for its early summer flowers.

now over and she had lived a lifetime in them and had run away, had lived with Peter, and it was now over.

Now it was time to move, and, as a woman gathers her things together, her cloak, her gloves, her opera-glasses, and gets up to go out of the theatre into the street, she rose from the sofa and went to Peter.

And it was awfully strange, he thought, how she still had the power, as she came tinkling, rustling, still had the power as she came across the room, to make the moon, which he detested, rise at Bourton on the terrace in the summer sky.

"Tell me," he said, seizing her by the shoulders. "Are you happy, Clarissa? Does Richard—"

The door opened.

"Here is my Elizabeth," said Clarissa, emotionally, histrionically, perhaps.

"How d'y do?" said Elizabeth coming forward.

The sound of Big Ben striking the half-hour struck out between them with extraordinary vigour, as if a young man, strong, indifferent, inconsiderate, were swinging dumb-bells this way and that.

"Hullo, Elizabeth!" cried Peter, stuffing his handkerchief into his pocket, going quickly to her, saying "Good-bye, Clarissa" without looking at her, leaving the room quickly, and running downstairs and opening the hall door.

"Peter! Peter!" cried Clarissa, following him out on to the landing. "My party to-night! Remember my party to-night!" she cried, having to raise her voice against the roar of the open air, and, overwhelmed by the traffic and the sound of all the clocks striking, her voice crying "Remember my party to-night!" sounded frail and thin and very far away as Peter Walsh shut the door.

Remember my party, remember my party, said Peter Walsh as he stepped down the street, speaking to himself rhythmically, in time with the flow of the sound, the direct downright sound of Big Ben striking the half-hour. (The leaden circles dissolved in the air.) Oh these parties, he thought; Clarissa's parties. Why does she give these parties, he thought. Not that he blamed her or this effigy of a man in a tail-coat with a carnation in his button-hole coming towards him. Only one person in the world could be as he was, in love. And there he was, this fortunate man, himself, reflected in the plate-glass window of a motor-car manufacturer in Victoria Street. All India lay behind him; plains, mountains; epidemics of cholera; a district twice as big as Ireland; decisions he had come to alone—he, Peter Walsh; who was now really for the first time in his life, in love. Clarissa had grown hard, he thought; and a trifle sentimental into the bargain, he suspected, looking at the great motor-cars capable of doing—how many miles on how many gallons? For he had a turn for mechanics; had invented a plough in his district, had ordered wheelbarrows from England, but the coolies[1] wouldn't use them, all of which Clarissa knew nothing whatever about.

The way she said "Here is my Elizabeth!"—that annoyed him. Why not "Here's Elizabeth" simply? It was insincere. And Elizabeth didn't like it either. (Still the last tremors of the great booming voice shook the air round him; the half-hour; still early; only half-past eleven still.) For he understood young people; he liked them. There was always something cold in Clarissa, he

---

1. Manual laborers in British colonies, usually from the lower classes.

thought. She had always, even as a girl, a sort of timidity, which in middle age becomes conventionality, and then it's all up, it's all up, he thought, looking rather drearily into the glassy depths, and wondering whether by calling at that hour he had annoyed her; overcome with shame suddenly at having been a fool; wept; been emotional; told her everything, as usual, as usual.

As a cloud crosses the sun, silence falls on London; and falls on the mind. Effort ceases. Time flaps on the mast. There we stop; there we stand. Rigid, the skeleton of habit alone upholds the human frame. Where there is nothing, Peter Walsh said to himself; feeling hollowed out, utterly empty within. Clarissa refused me, he thought. He stood there thinking, Clarissa refused me.

Ah, said St. Margaret's,[2] like a hostess who comes into her drawing-room on the very stroke of the hour and finds her guests there already. I am not late. No, it is precisely half-past eleven, she says. Yet, though she is perfectly right, her voice, being the voice of the hostess, is reluctant to inflict its individuality. Some grief for the past holds it back; some concern for the present. It is half-past eleven, she says, and the sound of St. Margaret's glides into the recesses of the heart and buries itself in ring after ring of sound, like something alive which wants to confide itself, to disperse itself, to be, with a tremor of delight, at rest—like Clarissa herself, thought Peter Walsh, coming down the stairs on the stroke of the hour in white. It is Clarissa herself, he thought, with a deep emotion, and an extraordinarily clear, yet puzzling, recollection of her, as if this bell had come into the room years ago, where they sat at some moment of great intimacy, and had gone from one to the other and had left, like a bee with honey, laden with the moment. But what room? What moment? And why had he been so profoundly happy when the clock was striking? Then, as the sound of St. Margaret's languished, he thought, She has been ill, and the sound expressed languor and suffering. It was her heart, he remembered; and the sudden loudness of the final stroke tolled for death that surprised in the midst of life, Clarissa falling where she stood, in her drawing room. No! No! he cried. She is not dead! I am not old, he cried, and marched up Whitehall,[3] as if there rolled down to him, vigorous, unending, his future.

He was not old, or set, or dried in the least. As for caring what they said of him—the Dalloways, the Whitbreads, and their set, he cared not a straw—not a straw (though it was true he would have, some time or other, to see whether Richard couldn't help him to some job). Striding, staring, he glared at the statue of the Duke of Cambridge.[4] He had been sent down from Oxford—true. He had been a Socialist, in some sense a failure—true. Still the future of civilisation lies, he thought, in the hands of young men like that; of young men such as he was, thirty years ago; with their love of abstract principles; getting books sent out to them all the way from London to a peak in the Himalayas; reading science; reading philosophy. The future lies in the hands of young men like that, he thought.

A patter like the patter of leaves in a wood came from behind, and with it a rustling, regular thudding sound, which as it overtook him drummed his thoughts, strict in step, up Whitehall, without his doing. Boys in uniform,

2. Bells of the parish church for the Houses of Parliament, situated on the grounds of Westminster Abbey.
3. Street in Westminster and site of government buildings.
4. Equestrian statue of Prince George, duke of Cambridge (1819–1904), commander in chief of the army and grandson of King George III.

carrying guns, marched with their eyes ahead of them, marched, their arms stiff, and on their faces an expression like the letters of a legend written round the base of a statue praising duty, gratitude, fidelity, love of England.

It is, thought Peter Walsh, beginning to keep step with them, a very fine training. But they did not look robust. They were weedy for the most part, boys of sixteen, who might, tomorrow, stand behind bowls of rice, cakes of soap on counters. Now they wore on them unmixed with sensual pleasure or daily preoccupations the solemnity of the wreath which they had fetched from Finsbury Pavement to the empty tomb.[5] They had taken their vow. The traffic respected it; vans were stopped.

I can't keep up with them, Peter Walsh thought, as they marched up Whitehall, and sure enough, on they marched, past him, past every one, in their steady way, as if one will worked legs and arms uniformly, and life, with its varieties, its irreticences, had been laid under a pavement of monuments and wreaths and drugged into a stiff yet staring corpse by discipline. One had to respect it; one might laugh; but one had to respect it, he thought. There they go, thought Peter Walsh, pausing at the edge of the pavement; and all the exalted statues, Nelson, Gordon, Havelock, the black, the spectacular images of great soldiers[6] stood looking ahead of them, as if they too had made the same renunciation (Peter Walsh felt he too had made it, the great renunciation), trampled under the same temptations, and achieved at length a marble stare. But the stare Peter Walsh did not want for himself in the least; though he could respect it in others. He could respect it in boys. They don't know the troubles of the flesh yet, he thought, as the marching boys disappeared in the direction of the Strand[7]—all that I've been through, he thought, crossing the road, and standing under Gordon's statue, Gordon whom as a boy he had worshipped; Gordon standing lonely with one leg raised and his arms crossed,—poor Gordon, he thought.

And just because nobody yet knew he was in London, except Clarissa, and the earth, after the voyage, still seemed an island to him, the strangeness of standing alone, alive, unknown, at half-past eleven in Trafalgar Square overcame him. What is it? Where am I? And why, after all, does one do it? he thought, the divorce seeming all moonshine. And down his mind went flat as a marsh, and three great emotions bowled over him; understanding; a vast philanthropy; and finally, as if the result of the others, an irrepressible, exquisite delight; as if inside his brain by another hand strings were pulled, shutters moved, and he, having nothing to do with it, yet stood at the opening of endless avenues, down which if he chose he might wander. He had not felt so young for years.

He had escaped! was utterly free—as happens in the downfall of habit when the mind, like an unguarded flame, bows and bends and seems about to blow from its holding. I haven't felt so young for years! thought Peter, escaping (only of course for an hour or so) from being precisely what he was, and feeling like a child who runs out of doors, and sees, as he runs, his

5. The boys, probably members of the London Cadets, have come from east London, near the Armoury House, to place a wreath at the Cenotaph, a World War I memorial.
6. Monumental statues in Trafalgar Square commemorating the 1805 battle in which the British defeated Napoleon's navy. The statue of the hero of the battle, Horatio Nelson (1758–

1805), appears on top of Nelson's Column. The statue of Henry Havelock (1795–1857), killed while serving in India, stands on the southeast plinth of the square. The statue of army officer Charles George Gordon (1833–1885), killed while serving in the Sudan, would be removed in 1943. The silhouetted statues all appear black.
7. Street running east from Trafalgar Square.

old nurse waving at the wrong window. But she's extraordinarily attractive, he thought, as, walking across Trafalgar Square in the direction of the Haymarket,[8] came a young woman who, as she passed Gordon's statue, seemed, Peter Walsh thought (susceptible as he was), to shed veil after veil, until she became the very woman he had always had in mind; young, but stately; merry, but discreet, black,[9] but enchanting.

Straightening himself and stealthily fingering his pocket-knife he started after her to follow this woman, this excitement, which seemed even with its back turned to shed on him a light which connected them, which singled him out, as if the random uproar of the traffic had whispered through hollowed hands his name, not Peter, but his private name which he called himself in his own thoughts. "You," she said, only "you," saying it with her white gloves and her shoulders. Then the thin long cloak which the wind stirred as she walked past Dent's shop in Cockspur Street[1] blew out with an enveloping kindness, a mournful tenderness, as of arms that would open and take the tired—

But she's not married; she's young; quite young, thought Peter, the red carnation he had seen her wear as she came across Trafalgar Square burning again in his eyes and making her lips red. But she waited at the kerbstone. There was a dignity about her. She was not worldly, like Clarissa; not rich, like Clarissa. Was she, he wondered as she moved, respectable? Witty, with a lizard's flickering tongue, he thought (for one must invent, must allow oneself a little diversion), a cool waiting wit, a darting wit; not noisy.

She moved; she crossed; he followed her. To embarrass her was the last thing he wished. Still if she stopped he would say "Come and have an ice," he would say, and she would answer, perfectly simply, "Oh yes."

But other people got between them in the street, obstructing him, blotting her out. He pursued; she changed. There was colour in her cheeks; mockery in her eyes; he was an adventurer, reckless, he thought, swift, daring, indeed (landed as he was last night from India) a romantic buccaneer, careless of all these damned proprieties, yellow dressing-gowns, pipes, fishing-rods, in the shop windows; and respectability and evening parties and spruce old men wearing white slips beneath their waistcoats. He was a buccaneer.[2] On and on she went, across Piccadilly, and up Regent Street, ahead of him, her cloak, her gloves, her shoulders combining with the fringes and the laces and the feather boas in the windows to make the spirit of finery and whimsy which dwindled out of the shops on to the pavement, as the light of a lamp goes wavering at night over hedges in the darkness.

Laughing and delightful, she had crossed Oxford Street and Great Portland Street[3] and turned down one of the little streets, and now, and now, the great moment was approaching, for now she slackened, opened her bag, and with one look in his direction, but not at him, one look that bade farewell, summed up the whole situation and dismissed it triumphantly, for ever, had fitted her key, opened the door, and gone! Clarissa's voice saying, Remember

8. Street to the west of Trafalgar Square, running northwest toward Piccadilly Circus.
9. With a dark complexion or black hair, i.e., not of African descent.
1. Street connecting Trafalgar Square with Haymarket. Instead of turning here, Walsh follows the young woman up Regent Street (which runs parallel to Haymarket), crosses Piccadilly, and

continues north toward Regent's Park. "Dent's shop": headquarters of the company that constructed Big Ben.
2. Pirate.
3. Walsh follows north along Regent Street, crosses Oxford Street, and then turns into a street near Great Portland Street, which leads into Regent's Park.

my party, Remember my party, sang in his ears. The house was one of those flat red houses with hanging flower-baskets of vague impropriety. It was over.

Well, I've had my fun; I've had it, he thought, looking up at the swinging baskets of pale geraniums. And it was smashed to atoms—his fun, for it was half made up, as he knew very well; invented, this escapade with the girl; made up, as one makes up the better part of life, he thought—making oneself up; making her up; creating an exquisite amusement, and something more. But odd it was, and quite true; all this one could never share—it smashed to atoms.

He turned; went up the street, thinking to find somewhere to sit, till it was time for Lincoln's Inn—for Messrs. Hooper and Grateley. Where should he go? No matter. Up the street, then, towards Regent's Park. His boots on the pavement struck out "no matter"; for it was early, still very early.

It was a splendid morning too. Like the pulse of a perfect heart, life struck straight through the streets. There was no fumbling—no hesitation. Sweeping and swerving, accurately, punctually, noiselessly, there, precisely at the right instant, the motor-car stopped at the door. The girl, silk-stockinged, feathered, evanescent, but not to him particularly attractive (for he had had his fling), alighted. Admirable butlers, tawny chow dogs, halls laid in black and white lozenges[4] with white blinds blowing, Peter saw through the opened door and approved of. A splendid achievement in its own way, after all, London; the season; civilisation. Coming as he did from a respectable Anglo-Indian family[5] which for at least three generations had administered the affairs of a continent (it's strange, he thought, what a sentiment I have about that, disliking India, and empire, and army as he did), there were moments when civilisation, even of this sort, seemed dear to him as a personal possession; moments of pride in England; in butlers; chow dogs; girls in their security. Ridiculous enough, still there it is, he thought. And the doctors and men of business and capable women all going about their business, punctual, alert, robust, seemed to him wholly admirable, good fellows, to whom one would entrust one's life, companions in the art of living, who would see one through. What with one thing and another, the show was really very tolerable; and he would sit down in the shade and smoke.

There was Regent's Park. Yes. As a child he had walked in Regent's Park—odd, he thought, how the thought of childhood keeps coming back to me—the result of seeing Clarissa, perhaps; for women live much more in the past than we do, he thought. They attach themselves to places; and their fathers—a woman's always proud of her father. Bourton was a nice place, a very nice place, but I could never get on with the old man, he thought. There was quite a scene one night—an argument about something or other, what, he could not remember. Politics presumably.

Yes, he remembered Regent's Park; the long straight walk; the little house where one bought air-balls to the left; an absurd statue with an inscription[6] somewhere or other. He looked for an empty seat. He did not want to be bothered (feeling a little drowsy as he did) by people asking him the time. An elderly grey nurse, with a baby asleep in its perambulator—that was the best he could do for himself; sit down at the far end of the seat by that nurse.

---

4. Diamondlike shapes.
5. A person of British heritage born in India.
6. Possibly the Matilda drinking fountain, with a statue of a milkmaid.

She's a queer-looking girl, he thought, suddenly remembering Elizabeth as she came into the room and stood by her mother. Grown big; quite grown-up, not exactly pretty; handsome rather; and she can't be more than eighteen. Probably she doesn't get on with Clarissa. "There's my Elizabeth"— that sort of thing—why not "Here's Elizabeth" simply?—trying to make out, like most mothers, that things are what they're not. She trusts to her charm too much, he thought. She overdoes it.

The rich benignant cigar smoke eddied coolly down his throat; he puffed it out again in rings which breasted the air bravely for a moment; blue, circular—I shall try and get a word alone with Elizabeth to-night, he thought— then began to wobble into hour-glass shapes and taper away; odd shapes they take, he thought. Suddenly he closed his eyes, raised his hand with an effort, and threw away the heavy end of his cigar. A great brush swept smooth across his mind, sweeping across it moving branches, children's voices, the shuffle of feet, and people passing, and humming traffic, rising and falling traffic. Down, down he sank into the plumes and feathers of sleep, sank, and was muffled over.

The grey nurse resumed her knitting as Peter Walsh, on the hot seat beside her, began snoring. In her grey dress, moving her hands indefatigably yet quietly, she seemed like the champion of the rights of sleepers, like one of those spectral presences which rise in twilight in woods made of sky and branches. The solitary traveller, haunter of lanes, disturber of ferns, and devastator of great hemlock plants, looking up, suddenly sees the giant figure at the end of the ride.

By conviction an atheist perhaps, he is taken by surprise with moments of extraordinary exaltation. Nothing exists outside us except a state of mind, he thinks; a desire for solace, for relief, for something outside these miserable pigmies, these feeble, these ugly, these craven men and women. But if he can conceive of her, then in some sort she exists, he thinks, and advancing down the path with his eyes upon sky and branches he rapidly endows them with womanhood; sees with amazement how grave they become; how majestically, as the breeze stirs them, they dispense with a dark flutter of the leaves charity, comprehension, absolution, and then, flinging themselves suddenly aloft, confound the piety of their aspect with a wild carouse.

Such are the visions which proffer great cornucopias full of fruit to the solitary traveller, or murmur in his ear like sirens lolloping away on the green sea waves, or are dashed in his face like bunches of roses, or rise to the surface like pale faces which fishermen flounder through floods to embrace.

Such are the visions which ceaselessly float up, pace beside, put their faces in front of, the actual thing; often overpowering the solitary traveller and taking away from him the sense of the earth, the wish to return, and giving him for substitute a general peace, as if (so he thinks as he advances down the forest ride) all this fever of living were simplicity itself; and myriads of things merged in one thing; and this figure, made of sky and branches as it is, had risen from the troubled sea (he is elderly, past fifty now) as a shape might be sucked up out of the waves to shower down from her magnificent hands compassion, comprehension, absolution. So, he thinks, may I never go back to the lamplight; to the sitting-room; never finish my book; never knock out my pipe; never ring for Mrs. Turner to clear away; rather let me walk straight on to this great figure, who will, with a

toss of her head, mount me on her streamers and let me blow to nothingness with the rest.

Such are the visions. The solitary traveller is soon beyond the wood; and
there, coming to the door with shaded eyes, possibly to look for his return,
with hands raised, with white apron blowing, is an elderly woman who
seems (so powerful is this infirmity) to seek, over a desert, a lost son; to
search for a rider destroyed; to be the figure of the mother whose sons have
been killed in the battles of the world. So, as the solitary traveller advances
down the village street where the women stand knitting and the men dig in
the garden, the evening seems ominous; the figures still; as if some august
fate, known to them, awaited without fear, were about to sweep them into
complete annihilation.

Indoors among ordinary things, the cupboard, the table, the window-sill
with its geraniums, suddenly the outline of the landlady, bending to remove
the cloth, becomes soft with light, an adorable emblem which only the recollection of cold human contacts forbids us to embrace. She takes the marmalade; she shuts it in the cupboard.

"There is nothing more to-night, sir?"

But to whom does the solitary traveller make reply?

So the elderly nurse knitted over the sleeping baby in Regent's Park. So
Peter Walsh snored.

He woke with extreme suddenness, saying to himself, "The death of the
soul."

"Lord, Lord!" he said to himself out loud, stretching and opening his eyes.
"The death of the soul." The words attached themselves to some scene, to
some room, to some past he had been dreaming of. It became clearer; the
scene, the room, the past he had been dreaming of.

It was at Bourton that summer, early in the 'nineties, when he was so passionately in love with Clarissa. There were a great many people there, laughing and talking, sitting round a table after tea and the room was bathed in
yellow light and full of cigarette smoke. They were talking about a man who
had married his housemaid, one of the neighbouring squires, he had forgotten
his name. He had married his housemaid, and she had been brought to Bourton to call—an awful visit it had been. She was absurdly over-dressed, "like a
cockatoo," Clarissa had said, imitating her, and she never stopped talking. On
and on she went, on and on. Clarissa imitated her. Then somebody said—
Sally Seton it was—did it make any real difference to one's feelings to know
that before they'd married she had had a baby? (In those days, in mixed company, it was a bold thing to say.) He could see Clarissa now, turning bright
pink; somehow contracting; and saying, "Oh, I shall never be able to speak to
her again!" Whereupon the whole party sitting round the tea-table seemed to
wobble. It was very uncomfortable.

He hadn't blamed her for minding the fact, since in those days a girl
brought up as she was, knew nothing, but it was her manner that annoyed
him; timid; hard; something arrogant; unimaginative; prudish. "The death
of the soul." He had said that instinctively, ticketing the moment as he used
to do—the death of her soul.

Every one wobbled; every one seemed to bow, as she spoke, and then to
stand up different. He could see Sally Seton, like a child who has been in
mischief, leaning forward, rather flushed, wanting to talk, but afraid, and

Clarissa did frighten people. (She was Clarissa's greatest friend, always about the place, totally unlike her, an attractive creature, handsome, dark, with the reputation in those days of great daring and he used to give her cigars, which she smoked in her bedroom. She had either been engaged to somebody or quarrelled with her family and old Parry disliked them both equally, which was a great bond.) Then Clarissa, still with an air of being offended with them all, got up, made some excuse, and went off, alone. As she opened the door, in came that great shaggy dog which ran after sheep. She flung herself upon him, went into raptures. It was as if she said to Peter—it was all aimed at him, he knew—"I know you thought me absurd about that woman just now; but see how extraordinarily sympathetic I am; see how I love my Rob!"

They had always this queer power of communicating without words. She knew directly he criticised her. Then she would do something quite obvious to defend herself, like this fuss with the dog—but it never took him in, he always saw through Clarissa. Not that he said anything, of course; just sat looking glum. It was the way their quarrels often began.

She shut the door. At once he became extremely depressed. It all seemed useless—going on being in love; going on quarrelling; going on making it up, and he wandered off alone, among outhouses, stables, looking at the horses. (The place was quite a humble one; the Parrys were never very well off; but there were always grooms and stable-boys about—Clarissa loved riding—and an old coachman—what was his name?—an old nurse, old Moody, old Goody, some such name they called her, whom one was taken to visit in a little room with lots of photographs, lots of bird-cages.)

It was an awful evening! He grew more and more gloomy, not about that only; about everything. And he couldn't see her; couldn't explain to her; couldn't have it out. There were always people about—she'd go on as if nothing had happened. That was the devilish part of her—this coldness, this woodenness, something very profound in her, which he had felt again this morning talking to her; an impenetrability. Yet Heaven knows he loved her. She had some queer power of fiddling on one's nerves, turning one's nerves to fiddle-strings, yes.

He had gone in to dinner rather late, from some idiotic idea of making himself felt, and had sat down by old Miss Parry—Aunt Helena—Mr. Parry's sister, who was supposed to preside. There she sat in her white Cashmere shawl, with her head against the window—a formidable old lady, but kind to him, for he had found her some rare flower, and she was a great botanist, marching off in thick boots with a black collecting-box slung between her shoulders. He sat down beside her, and couldn't speak. Everything seemed to race past him; he just sat there, eating. And then half-way through dinner he made himself look across at Clarissa for the first time. She was talking to a young man on her right. He had a sudden revelation. "She will marry that man," he said to himself. He didn't even know his name.

For of course it was that afternoon, that very afternoon, that Dalloway had come over; and Clarissa called him "Wickham"; that was the beginning of it all. Somebody had brought him over; and Clarissa got his name wrong. She introduced him to everybody as Wickham.[7] At last he said "My name is Dalloway!"—that was his first view of Richard—a fair young man, rather

7. Cf. George Wickham, the villainous suitor in *Pride and Prejudice* (1813) by English novelist Jane Austen (1775–1817).

awkward, sitting on a deck-chair, and blurting out "My name is Dalloway!" Sally got hold of it; always after that she called him "My name is Dalloway!"

He was a prey to revelations at that time. This one—that she would marry Dalloway—was blinding—overwhelming at the moment. There was a sort of—how could he put it?—a sort of ease in her manner to him; something maternal; something gentle. They were talking about politics. All through dinner he tried to hear what they were saying.

Afterwards he could remember standing by old Miss Parry's chair in the drawing-room. Clarissa came up, with her perfect manners, like a real hostess, and wanted to introduce him to some one—spoke as if they had never met before, which enraged him. Yet even then he admired her for it. He admired her courage; her social instinct; he admired her power of carrying things through. "The perfect hostess," he said to her, whereupon she winced all over. But he meant her to feel it. He would have done anything to hurt her after seeing her with Dalloway. So she left him. And he had a feeling that they were all gathered together in a conspiracy against him—laughing and talking—behind his back. There he stood by Miss Parry's chair as though he had been cut out of wood, he talking about wild flowers. Never, never had he suffered so infernally! He must have forgotten even to pretend to listen; at last he woke up; he saw Miss Parry looking rather disturbed, rather indignant, with her prominent eyes fixed. He almost cried out that he couldn't attend because he was in Hell! People began going out of the room. He heard them talking about fetching cloaks; about its being cold on the water, and so on. They were going boating on the lake by moonlight—one of Sally's mad ideas. He could hear her describing the moon. And they all went out. He was left quite alone.

"Don't you want to go with them?" said Aunt Helena—old Miss Parry!—she had guessed. And he turned round and there was Clarissa again. She had come back to fetch him. He was overcome by her generosity—her goodness.

"Come along," she said. "They're waiting."

He had never felt so happy in the whole of his life! Without a word they made it up. They walked down to the lake. He had twenty minutes of perfect happiness. Her voice, her laugh, her dress (something floating, white, crimson), her spirit, her adventurousness; she made them all disembark and explore the island; she startled a hen; she laughed; she sang. And all the time, he knew perfectly well, Dalloway was falling in love with her; she was falling in love with Dalloway; but it didn't seem to matter. Nothing mattered. They sat on the ground and talked—he and Clarissa. They went in and out of each other's minds without any effort. And then in a second it was over. He said to himself as they were getting into the boat, "She will marry that man," dully, without any resentment; but it was an obvious thing. Dalloway would marry Clarissa.

Dalloway rowed them in. He said nothing. But somehow as they watched him start, jumping on to his bicycle to ride twenty miles through the woods, wobbling off down the drive, waving his hand and disappearing, he obviously did feel, instinctively, tremendously, strongly, all that; the night; the romance; Clarissa. He deserved to have her.

For himself, he was absurd. His demands upon Clarissa (he could see it now) were absurd. He asked impossible things. He made terrible scenes. She would have accepted him still, perhaps, if he had been less absurd. Sally thought so. She wrote him all that summer long letters; how they had talked of him; how she had praised him, how Clarissa burst into tears! It was an extraordinary summer—all letters, scenes, telegrams—arriving at Bourton early in the morning, hanging about till the servants were up; appalling *tête-à-têtes* with old Mr. Parry at breakfast; Aunt Helena formidable but kind; Sally sweeping him off for talks in the vegetable garden; Clarissa in bed with headaches.

The final scene, the terrible scene which he believed had mattered more than anything in the whole of his life (it might be an exaggeration—but still so it did seem now) happened at three o'clock in the afternoon of a very hot day. It was a trifle that led up to it—Sally at lunch saying something about Dalloway, and calling him "My name is Dalloway"; whereupon Clarissa suddenly stiffened, coloured, in a way she had, and rapped out sharply, "We've had enough of that feeble joke." That was all; but for him it was precisely as if she had said, "I'm only amusing myself with you; I've an understanding with Richard Dalloway." So he took it. He had not slept for nights. "It's got to be finished one way or the other," he said to himself. He sent a note to her by Sally asking her to meet him by the fountain at three. "Something very important has happened," he scribbled at the end of it.

The fountain was in the middle of a little shrubbery, far from the house, with shrubs and trees all round it. There she came, even before the time, and they stood with the fountain between them, the spout (it was broken) dribbling water incessantly. How sights fix themselves upon the mind! For example, the vivid green moss.

She did not move. "Tell me the truth, tell me the truth," he kept on saying. He felt as if his forehead would burst. She seemed contracted, petrified. She did not move. "Tell me the truth," he repeated, when suddenly that old man Breitkopf popped his head in carrying the *Times*, stared at them; gaped; and went away. They neither of them moved. "Tell me the truth," he repeated. He felt that he was grinding against something physically hard; she was unyielding. She was like iron, like flint, rigid up the backbone. And when she said, "It's no use. It's no use. This is the end"—after he had spoken for hours, it seemed, with the tears running down his cheeks—it was as if she had hit him in the face. She turned, she left him, went away.

"Clarissa!" he cried. "Clarissa!" But she never came back. It was over. He went away that night. He never saw her again.

It was awful, he cried, awful, awful!

Still, the sun was hot. Still, one got over things. Still, life had a way of adding day to day. Still, he thought, yawning and beginning to take notice—Regent's Park had changed very little since he was a boy, except for the squirrels—still, presumably there were compensations—when little Elise Mitchell, who had been picking up pebbles to add to the pebble collection which she and her brother were making on the nursery mantelpiece, plumped her handful down on the nurse's knee and scudded off again full tilt into a lady's legs. Peter Walsh laughed out.

But Lucrezia Warren Smith was saying to herself, It's wicked; why should I suffer? she was asking, as she walked down the broad path. No; I can't stand it any longer, she was saying, having left Septimus, who wasn't Septimus any longer, to say hard, cruel, wicked things, to talk to himself, to talk to a dead man, on the seat over there; when the child ran full tilt into her, fell flat, and burst out crying.

That was comforting rather. She stood her upright, dusted her frock, kissed her.

But for herself she had done nothing wrong; she had loved Septimus; she had been happy; she had had a beautiful home, and there her sisters lived still, making hats. Why should *she* suffer?

The child ran straight back to its nurse, and Rezia saw her scolded, comforted, taken up by the nurse who put down her knitting, and the kind-looking man gave her his watch to blow open[8] to comfort her—but why should *she* be exposed? Why not left in Milan? Why tortured? Why?

Slightly waved by tears the broad path, the nurse, the man in grey, the perambulator, rose and fell before her eyes. To be rocked by this malignant torturer was her lot. But why? She was like a bird sheltering under the thin hollow of a leaf, who blinks at the sun when the leaf moves; starts at the crack of a dry twig. She was exposed; she was surrounded by the enormous trees, vast clouds of an indifferent world, exposed; tortured; and why should she suffer? Why?

She frowned; she stamped her foot. She must go back again to Septimus since it was almost time for them to be going to Sir William Bradshaw. She must go back and tell him, go back to him sitting there on the green chair under the tree, talking to himself, or to that dead man Evans, whom she had only seen once for a moment in the shop. He had seemed a nice quiet man; a great friend of Septimus's, and he had been killed in the War. But such things happen to every one. Every one has friends who were killed in the War. Every one gives up something when they marry. She had given up her home. She had come to live here, in this awful city. But Septimus let himself think about horrible things, as she could too, if she tried. He had grown stranger and stranger. He said people were talking behind the bedroom walls. Mrs. Filmer thought it odd. He saw things too—he had seen an old woman's head in the middle of a fern. Yet he could be happy when he chose. They went to Hampton Court[9] on top of a bus, and they were perfectly happy. All the little red and yellow flowers were out on the grass, like floating lamps he said, and talked and chattered and laughed, making up stories. Suddenly he said, "Now we will kill ourselves," when they were standing by the river, and he looked at it with a look which she had seen in his eyes when a train went by, or an omnibus—a look as if something fascinated him; and she felt he was going from her and she caught him by the arm. But going home he was perfectly quiet—perfectly reasonable. He would argue with her about killing themselves; and explain how wicked people were; how he could see them making up lies as they passed in the street. He knew all their thoughts, he said; he knew everything. He knew the meaning of the world, he said. Then when they got back he could hardly walk. He lay on the sofa and made her hold his hand to prevent him from falling down, down, he cried, into the flames! and saw faces laughing at him, calling him horrible disgusting names, from the walls, and hands pointing round the screen. Yet they were quite alone. But he began to talk aloud, answering people, arguing, laughing, crying, getting very excited and making her write things down. Perfect nonsense it was; about death; about Miss Isabel Pole. She could stand it no longer. She would go back.

---

8. Perhaps Walsh opens the cover on his pocket watch and pretends that the child has blown it open.

9. Royal palace on the Thames in western London, near Richmond.

She was close to him now, could see him staring at the sky, muttering, clasping his hands. Yet Dr. Holmes said there was nothing the matter with him. What then had happened—why had he gone, then, why, when she sat by him, did he start, frown at her, move away, and point at her hand, take her hand, look at it terrified?

Was it that she had taken off her wedding ring? "My hand has grown so thin," she said. "I have put it in my purse," she told him.

He dropped her hand. Their marriage was over, he thought, with agony, with relief. The rope was cut; he mounted; he was free, as it was decreed that he, Septimus, the lord of men, should be free; alone (since his wife had thrown away her wedding ring; since she had left him), he, Septimus, was alone, called forth in advance of the mass of men to hear the truth, to learn the meaning, which now at last, after all the toils of civilisation—Greeks, Romans, Shakespeare, Darwin,[1] and now himself—was to be given whole to. . . . "To whom?" he asked aloud. "To the Prime Minister," the voices which rustled above his head replied. The supreme secret must be told to the Cabinet; first that trees are alive; next there is no crime; next love, universal love, he muttered, gasping, trembling, painfully drawing out these profound truths which needed, so deep were they, so difficult, an immense effort to speak out, but the world was entirely changed by them for ever.

No crime; love; he repeated, fumbling for his card and pencil, when a Skye terrier snuffed his trousers and he started in an agony of fear. It was turning into a man! He could not watch it happen! It was horrible, terrible to see a dog become a man! At once the dog trotted away.

Heaven was divinely merciful, infinitely benignant. It spared him, pardoned his weakness. But what was the scientific explanation (for one must be scientific above all things)? Why could he see through bodies, see into the future, when dogs will become men? It was the heat wave presumably, operating upon a brain made sensitive by eons of evolution. Scientifically speaking, the flesh was melted off the world. His body was macerated until only the nerve fibres were left. It was spread like a veil upon a rock.

He lay back in his chair, exhausted but upheld. He lay resting, waiting, before he again interpreted, with effort, with agony, to mankind. He lay very high, on the back of the world. The earth thrilled beneath him. Red flowers grew through his flesh; their stiff leaves rustled by his head. Music began clanging against the rocks up here. It is a motor horn down in the street, he muttered; but up here it cannoned from rock to rock, divided, met in shocks of sound which rose in smooth columns (that music should be visible was a discovery) and became an anthem, an anthem twined round now by a shepherd boy's piping (That's an old man playing a penny whistle by the public-house, he muttered) which, as the boy stood still came bubbling from his pipe, and then, as he climbed higher, made its exquisite plaint while the traffic passed beneath. This boy's elegy is played among the traffic, thought Septimus. Now he withdraws up into the snows, and roses hang about him—the thick red roses which grow on my bedroom wall, he reminded himself. The music stopped. He has his penny, he reasoned it out, and has gone on to the next public-house.

1. Charles Darwin (1809–1882), English scientist whose writings laid the foundation for the study of evolution.

But he himself remained high on his rock, like a drowned sailor on a rock. I leant over the edge of the boat and fell down, he thought I went under the sea. I have been dead, and yet am now alive, but let me rest still; he begged (he was talking to himself again—it was awful, awful!); and as, before waking, the voices of birds and the sound of wheels chime and chatter in a queer harmony, grow louder and louder and the sleeper feels himself drawing to the shores of life, so he felt himself drawing towards life, the sun growing hotter, cries sounding louder, something tremendous about to happen.

He had only to open his eyes; but a weight was on them; a fear. He strained; he pushed; he looked; he saw Regent's Park before him. Long streamers of sunlight fawned at his feet. The trees waved, brandished. We welcome, the world seemed to say; we accept; we create. Beauty, the world seemed to say. And as if to prove it (scientifically) wherever he looked at the houses, at the railings, at the antelopes stretching over the palings, beauty sprang instantly. To watch a leaf quivering in the rush of air was an exquisite joy. Up in the sky swallows swooping, swerving, flinging themselves in and out, round and round, yet always with perfect control as if elastics held them; and the flies rising and falling; and the sun spotting now this leaf, now that, in mockery, dazzling it with soft gold in pure good temper; and now and again some chime (it might be a motor horn) tinkling divinely on the grass stalks—all of this, calm and reasonable as it was, made out of ordinary things as it was, was the truth now; beauty, that was the truth now. Beauty was everywhere.

"It is time," said Rezia.

The word "time" split its husk; poured its riches over him; and from his lips fell like shells, like shavings from a plane, without his making them, hard, white, imperishable words, and flew to attach themselves to their places in an ode to Time; an immortal ode to Time. He sang. Evans answered from behind the tree. The dead were in Thessaly,[2] Evans sang, among the orchids. There they waited till the War was over, and now the dead, now Evans himself—

"For God's sake don't come!" Septimus cried out. For he could not look upon the dead.

But the branches parted. A man in grey was actually walking towards them. It was Evans! But no mud was on him; no wounds; he was not changed. I must tell the whole world, Septimus cried, raising his hand (as the dead man in the grey suit came nearer), raising his hand like some colossal figure who has lamented the fate of man for ages in the desert alone with his hands pressed to his forehead, furrows of despair on his cheeks, and now sees light on the desert's edge which broadens and strikes the iron-black figure (and Septimus half rose from his chair), and with legions of men prostrate behind him he, the giant mourner, receives for one moment on his face the whole—

"But I am so unhappy, Septimus," said Rezia trying to make him sit down.

The millions lamented; for ages they had sorrowed. He would turn round, he would tell them in a few moments, only a few moments more, of this relief, of this joy, of this astonishing revelation—

"The time, Septimus," Rezia repeated. "What is the time?"

---

2. Region of Greece also known as Aeolia.

He was talking, he was starting, this man must notice him. He was looking at them.

"I will tell you the time," said Septimus, very slowly, very drowsily, smiling mysteriously. As he sat smiling at the dead man in the grey suit the quarter struck—the quarter to twelve.

And that is being young, Peter Walsh thought as he passed them. To be having an awful scene—the poor girl looked absolutely desperate—in the middle of the morning. But what was it about, he wondered, what had the young man in the overcoat been saying to her to make her look like that; what awful fix had they got themselves into, both to look so desperate as that on a fine summer morning? The amusing thing about coming back to England, after five years, was the way it made, anyhow the first days, things stand out as if one had never seen them before; lovers squabbling under a tree; the domestic family life of the parks. Never had he seen London look so enchanting—the softness of the distances; the richness; the greenness; the civilisation, after India, he thought, strolling across the grass.

This susceptibility to impressions had been his undoing no doubt. Still at his age he had, like a boy or a girl even, these alternations of mood; good days, bad days, for no reason whatever, happiness from a pretty face, downright misery at the sight of a frump. After India of course one fell in love with every woman one met. There was a freshness about them; even the poorest dressed better than five years ago surely; and to his eye the fashions had never been so becoming; the long black cloaks; the slimness; the elegance; and then the delicious and apparently universal habit of paint. Every woman, even the most respectable, had roses blooming under glass; lips cut with a knife; curls of Indian ink; there was design, art, everywhere; a change of some sort had undoubtedly taken place. What did the young people think about? Peter Walsh asked himself.

Those five years—1918 to 1923—had been, he suspected, somehow very important. People looked different. Newspapers seemed different. Now for instance there was a man writing quite openly in one of the respectable weeklies about water-closets. That you couldn't have done ten years ago— written quite openly about water-closets[3] in a respectable weekly. And then this taking out a stick of rouge, or a powder-puff and making up in public. On board ship coming home there were lots of young men and girls—Betty and Bertie he remembered in particular—carrying on quite openly; the old mother sitting and watching them with her knitting, cool as a cucumber. The girl would stand still and powder her nose in front of every one. And they weren't engaged; just having a good time; no feelings hurt on either side. As hard as nails she was—Betty What'shername—; but a thorough good sort. She would make a very good wife at thirty—she would marry when it suited her to marry; marry some rich man and live in a large house near Manchester.[4]

Who was it now who had done that? Peter Walsh asked himself, turning into the Broad Walk,—married a rich man and lived in a large house near Manchester? Somebody who had written him a long, gushing letter quite lately about "blue hydrangeas." It was seeing blue hydrangeas that made her think of him and the old days—Sally Seton, of course! It was Sally Seton—the

---

3. Toilets.   4. Large industrial city in northern England.

last person in the world one would have expected to marry a rich man and live in a large house near Manchester, the wild, the daring, the romantic Sally!

But of all that ancient lot, Clarissa's friends—Whitbreads, Kinderleys, Cunninghams, Kinloch-Jones's—Sally was probably the best. She tried to get hold of things by the right end anyhow. She saw through Hugh Whitbread anyhow—the admirable Hugh—when Clarissa and the rest were at his feet.

"The Whitbreads?" he could hear her saying. "Who are the Whitbreads? Coal merchants. Respectable tradespeople."

Hugh she detested for some reason. He thought of nothing but his own appearance, she said. He ought to have been a Duke. He would be certain to marry one of the Royal Princesses. And of course Hugh had the most extraordinary, the most natural, the most sublime respect for the British aristocracy of any human being he had ever come across. Even Clarissa had to own that. Oh, but he was such a dear, so unselfish, gave up shooting to please his old mother—remembered his aunts' birthdays, and so on.

Sally, to do her justice, saw through all that. One of the things he remembered best was an argument one Sunday morning at Bourton about women's rights[5] (that antediluvian topic), when Sally suddenly lost her temper, flared up, and told Hugh that he represented all that was most detestable in British middle-class life. She told him that she considered him responsible for the state of "those poor girls in Piccadilly"[6]—Hugh, the perfect gentleman, poor Hugh!—never did a man look more horrified! She did it on purpose she said afterwards (for they used to get together in the vegetable garden and compare notes). "He's read nothing, thought nothing, felt nothing," he could hear her saying in that very emphatic voice which carried so much farther than she knew. The stable-boys had more life in them than Hugh, she said. He was a perfect specimen of the public school[7] type, she said. No country but England could have produced him. She was really spiteful, for some reason; had some grudge against him. Something had happened—he forgot what—in the smoking-room. He had insulted her—kissed her? Incredible! Nobody believed a word against Hugh of course. Who could? Kissing Sally in the smoking-room! If it had been some Honourable Edith or Lady Violet, perhaps; but not that ragamuffin Sally without a penny to her name, and a father or a mother gambling at Monte Carlo.[8] For of all the people he had ever met Hugh was the greatest snob—the most obsequious—no, he didn't cringe exactly. He was too much of a prig for that. A first-rate valet was the obvious comparison—somebody who walked behind carrying suit cases; could be trusted to send telegrams—indispensable to hostesses. And he'd found his job—married his Honourable Evelyn; got some little post at Court, looked after the King's cellars, polished the Imperial shoe-buckles, went about in knee-breeches and lace ruffles. How remorseless life is! A little job at Court!

He had married this lady, the Honourable Evelyn, and they lived hereabouts, so he thought (looking at the pompous houses overlooking the Park), for he had lunched there once in a house which had, like all Hugh's possessions, something that no other house could possibly have—linen cupboards it might have been. You had to go and look at them—you had to

5. Campaigns by suffragists led to the right to vote for British women thirty and older in 1918 and, in 1928, for women twenty-one and older. Thus the topic was hardly "antediluvian," i.e.,

antiquated or outdated.
6. Prostitutes.
7. Fee-paying secondary school (British).
8. City in Monaco with a famous casino.

spend a great deal of time always admiring whatever it was—linen cup-boards, pillow-cases, old oak furniture, pictures, which Hugh had picked up for an old song. But Mrs. Hugh sometimes gave the show away. She was one of those obscure mouse-like little women who admire big men. She was almost negligible. Then suddenly she would say something quite unexpected—something sharp. She had the relics of the grand manner perhaps. The steam coal was a little too strong for her—it made the atmosphere thick. And so there they lived, with their linen cupboards and their old masters and their pillow-cases fringed with real lace at the rate of five or ten thousand a year presumably, while he, who was two years older than Hugh, cadged for a job.[9]

At fifty-three he had to come and ask them to put him into some secre-tary's office, to find him some usher's job teaching little boys Latin, at the beck and call of some mandarin[1] in an office, something that brought in five hundred a year; for if he married Daisy, even with his pension, they could never do on less. Whitbread could do it presumably; or Dalloway. He didn't mind what he asked Dalloway. He was a thorough good sort; a bit limited; a bit thick in the head; yes; but a thorough good sort Whatever he took up he did in the same matter-of-fact sensible way; without a touch of imagination, without a spark of brilliancy, but with the inexplicable niceness of his type. He ought to have been a country gentleman—he was wasted on politics. He was at his best out of doors, with horses and dogs—how good he was, for instance, when that great shaggy dog of Clarissa's got caught in a trap and had its paw half torn off, and Clarissa turned faint and Dalloway did the whole thing; bandaged, made splints; told Clarissa not to be a fool. That was what she liked him for perhaps—that was what she needed. "Now, my dear, don't be a fool. Hold this—fetch that," all the time talking to the dog as if it were a human being.

But how could she swallow all that stuff about poetry? How could she let him hold forth about Shakespeare? Seriously and solemnly Richard Dallo-way got on his hind legs and said that no decent man ought to read Shake-speare's sonnets because it was like listening at keyholes (besides the relationship was not one that he approved). No decent man ought to let his wife visit a deceased wife's sister. Incredible! The only thing to do was to pelt him with sugared almonds—it was at dinner. But Clarissa sucked it all in; thought it so honest of him; so independent of him; Heaven knows if she didn't think him the most original mind she'd ever met!

That was one of the bonds between Sally, and himself. There was a gar-den where they used to walk, a walled-in place, with rose-bushes and giant cauliflowers—he could remember Sally tearing off a rose, stopping to exclaim at the beauty of the cabbage leaves in the moonlight (it was extraor-dinary how vividly it all came back to him, things he hadn't thought of for years), while she implored him, half laughing of course, to carry off Clar-issa, to save her from the Hughs and the Dalloways and all the other "per-fect gentlemen" who would "stifle her soul" (she wrote reams of poetry in those days), make a mere hostess of her, encourage her worldliness. But one must do Clarissa justice. She wasn't going to marry Hugh anyhow. She had a perfectly clear notion of what she wanted. Her emotions were all on the surface. Beneath, she was very shrewd—a far better judge of character than

9. Begged for employment.
1. Powerful, sometimes secretive or corrupt, civil servant.

Sally, for instance, and with it all, purely feminine; with that extraordinary gift, that woman's gift, of making a world of her own wherever she happened to be. She came into a room; she stood, as he had often seen her, in a doorway with lots of people round her. But it was Clarissa one remembered. Not that she was striking; not beautiful at all; there was nothing picturesque about her; she never said anything specially clever; there she was, however; there she was.

No, no, no! He was not in love with her any more! He only felt, after seeing her that morning, among her scissors and silks, making ready for the party, unable to get away from the thought of her; she kept coming back and back like a sleeper jolting against him in a railway carriage; which was not being in love, of course; it was thinking of her, criticising her, starting again, after thirty years, trying to explain her. The obvious thing to say of her was that she was worldly; cared too much for rank and society and getting on in the world—which was true in a sense; she had admitted it to him. (You could always get her to own up if you took the trouble; she was honest.) What she would say was that she hated frumps, fogies, failures, like himself presumably; thought people had no right to slouch about with their hands in their pockets; must do something, be something; and these great swells, these Duchesses, these hoary old Countesses one met in her drawing-room, unspeakably remote as he felt them to be from anything that mattered a straw, stood for something real to her. Lady Bexborough, she said once, held herself upright (so did Clarissa herself; she never lounged in any sense of the word; she was straight as a dart, a little rigid in fact). She said they had a kind of courage which the older she grew the more she respected. In all this there was a great deal of Dalloway, of course; a great deal of the public-spirited, British Empire, tariff-reform, governing-class spirit,[2] which had grown on her, as it tends to do. With twice his wits, she had to see things through his eyes—one of the tragedies of married life. With a mind of her own, she must always be quoting Richard—as if one couldn't know to a tittle what Richard thought by reading the *Morning Post*[3] of a morning! These parties for example were all for him, or for her idea of him (to do Richard justice he would have been happier farming in Norfolk). She made her drawing-room a sort of meeting-place; she had a genius for it. Over and over again he had seen her take some raw youth, twist him, turn him, wake him up; set him going. Infinite numbers of dull people conglomerated round her of course. But odd unexpected people turned up; an artist sometimes; sometimes a writer; queer fish in that atmosphere. And behind it all was that network of visiting, leaving cards, being kind to people; running about with bunches of flowers, little presents; So-and-so was going to France—must have an air-cushion; a real drain on her strength; all that interminable traffic that women of her sort keep up; but she did it genuinely, from a natural instinct.

Oddly enough, she was one of the most thorough-going sceptics he had ever met, and possibly (this was a theory he used to make up to account for her, so transparent in some ways, so inscrutable in others), possibly she said to herself, As we are a doomed race, chained to a sinking ship (her favourite reading as a girl was Huxley and Tyndall,[4] and they were fond of these nautical

---

2. Richard's views are typical of the Conservative Party. Tariff reform would have been intended to protect British goods.
3. Conservative daily newspaper.

4. Thomas Henry Huxley (1825–1895), English biologist, and John Tyndall (1820–1893), English physicist. The work of both scientists challenged Victorians' religious worldviews.

metaphors), as the whole thing is a bad joke, let us, at any rate, do our part; mitigate the sufferings of our fellow-prisoners (Huxley again); decorate the dungeon with flowers and air-cushions; be as decent as we possibly can. Those ruffians, the Gods, shan't have it all their own way,—her notion being that the Gods, who never lost a chance of hurting, thwarting and spoiling human lives were seriously put out if, all the same, you behaved like a lady. That phase came directly after Sylvia's death—that horrible affair. To see your own sister killed by a falling tree (all Justin Parry's fault—all his carelessness) before your very eyes, a girl too on the verge of life, the most gifted of them, Clarissa always said, was enough to turn one bitter. Later she wasn't so positive perhaps; she thought there were no Gods; no one was to blame; and so she evolved this atheist's religion of doing good for the sake of goodness.

And of course she enjoyed life immensely. It was her nature to enjoy (though goodness only knows, she had her reserves; it was a mere sketch, he often felt, that even he, after all these years, could make of Clarissa). Anyhow there was no bitterness in her; none of that sense of moral virtue which is so repulsive in good women. She enjoyed practically everything. If you walked with her in Hyde Park now it was a bed of tulips, now a child in a perambulator, now some absurd little drama she made up on the spur of the moment. (Very likely, she would have talked to those lovers, if she had thought them unhappy.) She had a sense of comedy that was really exquisite, but she needed people, always people, to bring it out, with the inevitable result that she frittered her time away, lunching, dining, giving these incessant parties of hers, talking nonsense, saying things she didn't mean, blunting the edge of her mind, losing her discrimination. There she would sit at the head of the table taking infinite pains with some old buffer who might be useful to Dalloway—they knew the most appalling bores in Europe—or in came Elizabeth and everything must give way to *her*. She was at a High School,[5] at the inarticulate stage last time he was over, a round-eyed, pale-faced girl, with nothing of her mother in her, a silent stolid creature, who took it all as a matter of course, let her mother make a fuss of her, and then said "May I go now?" like a child of four; going off, Clarissa explained, with that mixture of amusement and pride which Dalloway himself seemed to rouse in her, to play hockey. And now Elizabeth was "out,"[6] presumably; thought him an old fogy, laughed at her mother's friends. Ah well, so be it. The compensation of growing old, Peter Walsh thought, coming out of Regent's Park, and holding his hat in hand, was simply this; that the passions remain as strong as ever, but one has gained—at last!—the power which adds the supreme flavour to existence,—the power of taking hold of experience, of turning it round, slowly, in the light.

A terrible confession it was (he put his hat on again), but now, at the age of fifty-three one scarcely needed people any more. Life itself, every moment of it, every drop of it, here, this instant, now, in the sun, in Regent's Park, was enough. Too much indeed. A whole lifetime was too short to bring out, now that one had acquired the power, the full flavour; to extract every ounce of pleasure, every shade of meaning; which both were so much more

5. A fee-paying girls' day school.
6. I.e., introduced to society, presented at Court, and participating in the social life of a debutante.

solid than they used to be, so much less personal. It was impossible that he should ever suffer again as Clarissa had made him suffer. For hours at a time (pray God that one might say these things without being overheard!), for hours and days he never thought of Daisy.

Could it be that he was in love with her then, remembering the misery, the torture, the extraordinary passion of those days? It was a different thing altogether—a much pleasanter thing—the truth being, of course, that now *she* was in love with *him*. And that perhaps was the reason why, when the ship actually sailed, he felt an extraordinary relief, wanted nothing so much as to be alone; was annoyed to find all her little attentions—cigars, notes, a rug for the voyage—in his cabin. Every one if they were honest would say the same; one doesn't want people after fifty; one doesn't want to go on telling women they are pretty; that's what most men of fifty would say, Peter Walsh thought, if they were honest.

But then these astonishing accesses of emotion—bursting into tears this morning, what was all that about? What could Clarissa have thought of him? thought him a fool presumably, not for the first time. It was jealousy that was at the bottom of it—jealousy which survives every other passion of mankind, Peter Walsh thought, holding his pocket-knife at arm's length. She had been meeting Major Orde, Daisy said in her last letter; said it on purpose he knew; said it to make him jealous; he could see her wrinkling her forehead as she wrote, wondering what she could say to hurt him; and yet it made no difference; he was furious! All this pother of coming to England and seeing lawyers wasn't to marry her, but to prevent her from marrying anybody else. That was what tortured him, that was what came over him when he saw Clarissa so calm, so cold, so intent on her dress or whatever it was; realising what she might have spared him, what she had reduced him to—a whimpering, snivelling old ass. But women, he thought, shutting his pocketknife, don't know what passion is. They don't know the meaning of it to men. Clarissa was as cold as an icicle. There she would sit on the sofa by his side, let him take her hand, give him one kiss—Here he was at the crossing.

A sound interrupted him; a frail quivering sound, a voice bubbling up without direction, vigour, beginning or end, running weakly and shrilly and with an absence of all human meaning into

> ee um fah um so
> foo swee too eem oo—

the voice of no age or sex, the voice of an ancient spring spouting from the earth; which issued, just opposite Regent's Park Tube station from a tall quivering shape, like a funnel, like a rusty pump, like a wind-beaten tree for ever barren of leaves which lets the wind run up and down its branches singing

> ee um fah um so
> foo swee too eem oo

and rocks and creaks and moans in the eternal breeze.

Through all ages—when the pavement was grass, when it was swamp, through the age of tusk and mammoth, through the age of silent sunrise, the battered woman—for she wore a skirt—with her right hand exposed, her left clutching at her side, stood singing of love—love which has lasted a million years, she sang, love which prevails, and millions of years ago, her lover, who had been dead these centuries, had walked, she crooned, with her in May; but in the course of ages, long as summer days, and flaming, she remembered, with nothing but red asters, he had gone; death's enormous sickle had swept those tremendous hills, and when at last she laid her hoary and immensely aged head on the earth, now become a mere cinder of ice, she implored the Gods to lay by her side a bunch of purple heather, there on her high burial place which the last rays of the last sun caressed; for then the pageant of the universe would be over.

As the ancient song bubbled up opposite Regent's Park Tube station still the earth seemed green and flowery; still, though it issued from so rude a mouth, a mere hole in the earth, muddy too, matted with root fibres and tangled grasses, still the old bubbling burbling song, soaking through the knotted roots of infinite ages, and skeletons and treasure, streamed away in rivulets over the pavement and all along the Marylebone Road, and down towards Euston,[7] fertilising, leaving a damp stain.

Still remembering how once in some primeval May she had walked with her lover, this rusty pump, this battered old woman with one hand exposed for coppers the other clutching her side, would still be there in ten million years, remembering how once she had walked in May, where the sea flows now, with whom it did not matter—he was a man, oh yes, a man who had loved her. But the passage of ages had blurred the clarity of that ancient May day, the bright petalled flowers were hoar and silver frosted; and she no longer saw, when she implored him (as she did now quite clearly) "look in my eyes with thy sweet eyes intently," she no longer saw brown eyes, black whiskers or sunburnt face but only a looming shape, a shadow shape, to which, with the bird-like freshness of the very aged she still twittered "give me your hand and let me press it gently" (Peter Walsh couldn't help giving the poor creature a coin as he stepped into his taxi), "and if some one should see, what matter they?" she demanded; and her fist clutched at her side, and she smiled, pocketing her shilling, and all peering inquisitive eyes seemed blotted out, and the passing generations—the pavement was crowded with bustling middleclass people—vanished, like leaves, to be trodden under, to be soaked and steeped and made mould of by that eternal spring—

> ee um fah um so
> foo swee too eem oo

"Poor old woman," said Rezia Warren Smith, waiting to cross.

Oh poor old wretch!

Suppose it was a wet night? Suppose one's father, or somebody who had known one in better days had happened to pass, and saw one standing there in the gutter? And where did she sleep at night?

Cheerfully, almost gaily, the invincible thread of sound wound up into the air like the smoke from a cottage chimney, winding up clean beech trees and issuing in a tuft of blue smoke among the topmost leaves. "And if some one should see, what matter they?"

Since she was so unhappy, for weeks and weeks now, Rezia had given meanings to things that happened, almost felt sometimes that she must stop

---

7. Area in London east of Regent's Park, accessible by walking east along the Marylebone Road, which lies to the south of the park.

people in the street, if they looked good, kind people, just to say to them "I am unhappy"; and this old woman singing in the street "if some one should see, what matter they?" made her suddenly quite sure that everything was going to be right. They were going to Sir William Bradshaw; she thought his name sounded nice; he would cure Septimus at once. And then there was a brewer's cart, and the grey horses had upright bristles of straw in their tails; there were newspaper placards. It was a silly, silly dream, being unhappy.

So they crossed, Mr. and Mrs. Septimus Warren Smith, and was there, after all, anything to draw attention to them, anything to make a passer-by suspect here is a young man who carries in him the greatest message in the world, and is, moreover, the happiest man in the world, and the most miserable? Perhaps they walked more slowly than other people, and there was something hesitating, trailing, in the man's walk, but what more natural for a clerk, who has not been in the West End[8] on a weekday at this hour for years, than to keep looking at the sky, looking at this, that and the other, as if Portland Place were a room he had come into when the family are away, the chandeliers being hung in holland bags,[9] and the caretaker, as she lets in long shafts of dusty light upon deserted, queer-looking armchairs, lifting one corner of the long blinds, explains to the visitors what a wonderful place it is; how wonderful, but at the same time, he thinks, as he looks at chairs and tables, how strange.

To look at, he might have been a clerk, but of the better sort; for he wore brown boots; his hands were educated; so, too, his profile—his angular, big-nosed, intelligent, sensitive profile; but not his lips altogether, for they were loose; and his eyes (as eyes tend to be), eyes merely; hazel, large; so that he was, on the whole, a border case, neither one thing nor the other, might end with a house at Purley[1] and a motor car, or continue renting apartments in back streets all his life; one of those half-educated, self-educated men whose education is all learnt from books borrowed from public libraries, read in the evening after the day's work, on the advice of well-known authors consulted by letter.

As for the other experiences, the solitary ones, which people go through alone, in their bedrooms, in their offices, walking the fields and the streets of London, he had them; had left home, a mere boy, because of his mother; she lied; because he came down to tea for the fiftieth time with his hands unwashed; because he could see no future for a poet in Stroud;[2] and so, making a confidant of his little sister, had gone to London leaving an absurd note behind him, such as great men have written, and the world has read later when the story of their struggles has become famous.

London has swallowed up many millions of young men called Smith; thought nothing of fantastic Christian names like Septimus with which their parents have thought to distinguish them. Lodging off the Euston Road,[3] there were experiences, again experiences, such as change a face in two years from a pink innocent oval to a face lean, contracted, hostile. But of all this what could the most observant of friends have said except what

---

8. Entertainment and shopping district to the west of Portland Place, a street running south from the Regent's Park Tube station toward Oxford Street.
9. Bags made from smooth linen fabric often used as furniture covering.

1. Town south of London.
2. Town in Gloucestershire, west of London.
3. Road running east from the Regent's Park Tube station toward King's Cross, a busy train station.

a gardener says when he opens the conservatory door in the morning and finds a new blossom on his plant:—It has flowered; flowered from vanity, ambition, idealism, passion, loneliness, courage, laziness, the usual seeds, which all muddled up (in a room off the Euston Road), made him shy, and stammering, made him anxious to improve himself, made him fall in love with Miss Isabel Pole, lecturing in the Waterloo Road[4] upon Shakespeare.

Was he not like Keats?[5] she asked; and reflected how she might give him a taste of *Antony and Cleopatra*[6] and the rest; lent him books; wrote him scraps of letters; and lit in him such a fire as burns only once in a lifetime, without heat, flickering a red gold flame infinitely ethereal and insubstantial over Miss Pole; *Antony and Cleopatra*; and the Waterloo Road. He thought her beautiful, believed her impeccably wise; dreamed of her, wrote poems to her, which, ignoring the subject, she corrected in red ink; he saw her, one summer evening, walking in a green dress in a square. "It has flowered," the gardener might have said, had he opened the door; had he come in, that is to say, any night about this time, and found him writing; found him tearing up his writing; found him finishing a masterpiece at three o'clock in the morning and running out to pace the streets, and visiting churches, and fasting one day, drinking another, devouring Shakespeare, Darwin, *The History of Civilisation*, and Bernard Shaw.[7]

Something was up, Mr. Brewer knew; Mr. Brewer, managing clerk at Sibleys and Arrowsmiths,[8] auctioneers, valuers, land and estate agents; something was up, he thought, and, being paternal with his young men, and thinking very highly of Smith's abilities, and prophesying that he would, in ten or fifteen years, succeed to the leather arm-chair in the inner room under the skylight with the deed-boxes round him, "if he keeps his health," said Mr. Brewer, and that was the danger—he looked weakly; advised football, invited him to supper and was seeing his way to consider recommending a rise of salary, when something happened which threw out many of Mr. Brewer's calculations, took away his ablest young fellows, and eventually, so prying and insidious were the fingers of the European War, smashed a plaster cast of Ceres,[9] ploughed a hole in the geranium beds, and utterly ruined the cook's nerves at Mr. Brewer's establishment at Muswell Hill.[1]

Septimus was one of the first to volunteer. He went to France to save an England which consisted almost entirely of Shakespeare's plays and Miss Isabel Pole in a green dress walking in a square. There in the trenches the change which Mr. Brewer desired when he advised football was produced instantly; he developed manliness; he was promoted; he drew the attention, indeed the affection of his officer, Evans by name. It was a case of two dogs playing on a hearth-rug; one worrying a paper screw, snarling, snapping, giving a pinch, now and then, at the old dog's ear; the other lying somnolent, blinking at the fire, raising a paw, turning and growling good-temperedly. They had to be together, share with each other, fight with each other, quarrel with each other. But when Evans (Rezia who had only seen him once called

4. Road running south from the Thames. Miss Pole likely teaches classes for Morley College in the Old Vic Theater.
5. John Keats (1795–1821), English Romantic poet.
6. Tragedy by Shakespeare.
7. George Bernard Shaw (1856–1950), Irish play-

wright, journalist, and Fabian Socialist. "*The History of Civilisation*" (1857–61): two-volume study of human interaction with nature, by English writer Henry Thomas Buckle (1821–1862).
8. Fictional real estate company.
9. Roman goddess of agriculture.
1. Residential district in north London.

him "a quiet man," a sturdy red-haired man, undemonstrative in the company of women), when Evans was killed, just before the Armistice,[2] in Italy, Septimus, far from showing any emotion or recognising that here was the end of a friendship, congratulated himself upon feeling very little and very reasonably. The War had taught him. It was sublime. He had gone through the whole show, friendship, European War, death, had won promotion, was still under thirty and was bound to survive. He was right there. The last shells missed him. He watched them explode with indifference. When peace came he was in Milan, billeted in the house of an innkeeper with a courtyard, flowers in tubs, little tables in the open, daughters making hats, and to Lucrezia, the younger daughter, he became engaged one evening when the panic was on him—that he could not feel.

For now that it was all over, truce signed, and the dead buried, he had, especially in the evening, these sudden thunderclaps of fear. He could not feel. As he opened the door of the room where the Italian girls sat making hats, he could see them; could hear them; they were rubbing wires among coloured beads in saucers; they were turning buckram[3] shapes this way and that; the table was all strewn with feathers, spangles, silks, ribbons; scissors were rapping on the table; but something failed him; he could not feel. Still, scissors rapping, girls laughing, hats being made protected him; he was assured of safety; he had a refuge. But he could not sit there all night. There were moments of waking in the early morning. The bed was falling; he was falling. Oh for the scissors and the lamplight and the buckram shapes! He asked Lucrezia to marry him, the younger of the two, the gay, the frivolous, with those little artist's fingers that she would hold up and say "It is all in them." Silk, feathers, what not were alive to them.

"It is the hat that matters most," she would say, when they walked out together. Every hat that passed, she would examine; and the cloak and the dress and the way the woman held herself. Ill-dressing, over-dressing she stigmatised, not savagely, rather with impatient movements of the hands, like those of a painter who puts from him some obvious well-meant glaring imposture; and then, generously, but always critically, she would welcome a shopgirl who had turned her little bit of stuff gallantly, or praise, wholly, with enthusiastic and professional understanding, a French lady descending from her carriage, in chinchilla,[4] robes, pearls.

"Beautiful!" she would murmur, nudging Septimus, that he might see. But beauty was behind a pane of glass. Even taste (Rezia liked ices, chocolates, sweet things) had no relish to him. He put down his cup on the little marble table. He looked at people outside; happy they seemed, collecting in the middle of the street, shouting, laughing, squabbling over nothing. But he could not taste, he could not feel. In the teashop among the tables and the chattering waiters the appalling fear came over him—he could not feel. He could reason; he could read, Dante for example, quite easily ("Septimus, do put down your book," said Rezia, gently shutting the *Inferno*[5]), he could add up his bill; his brain was perfect; it must be the fault of the world then—that he could not feel.

---

2. Agreement ending World War I, November 11, 1918.
3. Linen or cotton fabric.
4. Soft gray fur from rodents native to South

America.
5. Description of hell in one of three parts of *The Divine Comedy*, by Italian poet Dante Alighieri (1265–1321).

"The English are so silent," Rezia said. She liked it, she said. She respected these Englishmen, and wanted to see London, and the English horses, and the tailor-made suits, and could remember hearing how wonderful the shops were, from an Aunt who had married and lived in Soho.[6]

It might be possible, Septimus thought, looking at England from the train window, as they left Newhaven;[7] it might be possible that the world itself is without meaning.

At the office they advanced him to a post of considerable responsibility. They were proud of him; he had won crosses. "You have done your duty; it is up to us—" began Mr. Brewer; and could not finish, so pleasurable was his emotion. They took admirable lodgings off the Tottenham Court Road.[8]

Here he opened Shakespeare once more. That boy's business of the intoxication of language—*Antony and Cleopatra*—had shrivelled utterly. How Shakespeare loathed humanity—the putting on of clothes, the getting of children, the sordidity of the mouth and the belly! This was now revealed to Septimus; the message hidden in the beauty of words. The secret signal which one generation passes, under disguise, to the next is loathing, hatred, despair. Dante the same. Aeschylus[9] (translated) the same. There Rezia sat at the table trimming hats. She trimmed hats for Mrs. Filmer's friends; she trimmed hats by the hour. She looked pale, mysterious, like a lily, drowned, under water, he thought.

"The English are so serious," she would say, putting her arms round Septimus, her cheek against his.

Love between man and woman was repulsive to Shakespeare. The business of copulation was filth to him before the end. But, Rezia said, she must have children. They had been married five years.

They went to the Tower together; to the Victoria and Albert Museum; stood in the crowd to see the King open Parliament.[1] And there were the shops—hat shops, dress shops, shops with leather bags in the window, where she would stand staring. But she must have a boy.

She must have a son like Septimus, she said. But nobody could be like Septimus; so gentle; so serious; so clever. Could she not read Shakespeare too? Was Shakespeare a difficult author? she asked.

One cannot bring children into a world like this. One cannot perpetuate suffering, or increase the breed of these lustful animals, who have no lasting emotions, but only whims and vanities, eddying them now this way, now that.

He watched her snip, shape, as one watches a bird hop, flit in the grass, without daring to move a finger. For the truth is (let her ignore it) that human beings have neither kindness, nor faith, nor charity beyond what serves to increase the pleasure of the moment. They hunt in packs. Their packs scour the desert and vanish screaming into the wilderness. They desert the fallen. They are plastered over with grimaces. There was Brewer at the office, with his waxed moustache, coral tie-pin, white slip, and pleasurable

6. London district known for its cosmopolitanism, entertainment, and sex industries.
7. Port city on the English Channel south of London.
8. Major London road running north through Bloomsbury, home to Woolf and her friends, toward the Euston Road.

9. Greek dramatist (ca. 525–426 B.C.E.).
1. The monarch traditionally gives a speech to begin the annual session of Parliament. "The Tower": the Tower of London, fortress and royal palace on the Thames, begun in 1078. "Victoria and Albert Museum": exhibition of applied arts opened in 1909.

emotions—all coldness and clamminess within,—his geraniums ruined in the War—his cook's nerves destroyed; or Amelia What'shername, handing round cups of tea punctually at five—a leering, sneering obscene little harpy; and the Toms and Berties[2] in their starched shirt fronts oozing thick drops of vice. They never saw him drawing pictures of them naked at their antics in his notebook. In the street, vans roared past him; brutality blared out on placards; men were trapped in mines; women burnt alive; and once a maimed file of lunatics being exercised or displayed for the diversion of the populace (who laughed aloud), ambled and nodded and grinned past him, in the Tottenham Court Road, each half apologetically, yet triumphantly, inflicting his hopeless woe. And would *he* go mad?

At tea Rezia told him that Mrs. Filmer's daughter was expecting a baby. *She* could not grow old and have no children! She was very lonely, she was very unhappy! She cried for the first time since they were married. Far away he heard her sobbing; he heard it accurately, he noticed it distinctly; he compared it to a piston thumping. But he felt nothing.

His wife was crying, and he felt nothing; only each time she sobbed in this profound, this silent, this hopeless way, he descended another step into the pit.

At last, with a melodramatic gesture which he assumed mechanically and with complete consciousness of its insincerity, he dropped his head on his hands. Now he had surrendered; now other people must help him. People must be sent for. He gave in.

Nothing could rouse him. Rezia put him to bed. She sent for a doctor—Mrs. Filmer's Dr. Holmes. Dr. Holmes examined him. There was nothing whatever the matter, said Dr. Holmes. Oh, what a relief! What a kind man, what a good man! thought Rezia. When he felt like that he went to the Music Hall, said Dr. Holmes. He took a day off with his wife and played golf. Why not try two tabloids of bromide[3] dissolved in a glass of water at bedtime? These old Bloomsbury houses, said Dr. Holmes, tapping the wall, are often full of very fine panelling, which the landlords have the folly to paper over. Only the other day, visiting a patient, Sir Somebody Something in Bedford Square[4]—

So there was no excuse; nothing whatever the matter, except the sin for which human nature had condemned him to death; that he did not feel. He had not cared when Evans was killed; that was worst; but all the other crimes raised their heads and shook their fingers and jeered and sneered over the rail of the bed in the early hours of the morning at the prostrate body which lay realising its degradation; how he had married his wife without loving her; had lied to her; seduced her; outraged Miss Isabel Pole, and was so pocked and marked with vice that women shuddered when they saw him in the street. The verdict of human nature on such a wretch was death.

Dr. Holmes came again. Large, fresh coloured, handsome, flicking his boots, looking in the glass, he brushed it all aside—headaches, sleeplessness, fears, dreams—nerve symptoms and nothing more, he said. If Dr. Holmes found himself even half a pound below eleven stone six, he asked his wife for another plate of porridge at breakfast. (Rezia would learn to cook porridge.) But, he continued, health is largely a matter in our own control. Throw

---

2. Diminutives of Thomas and Albert, common British names.

3. Potassium bromide, likely taken as a sedative.
4. Residential area in Bloomsbury.

yourself into outside interests; take up some hobby. He opened Shake-speare—*Antony and Cleopatra*; pushed Shakespeare aside. Some hobby, said Dr. Holmes, for did he not owe his own excellent health (and he worked as hard as any man in London) to the fact that he could always switch off from his patients on to old furniture? And what a very pretty comb, if he might say so, Mrs. Warren Smith was wearing!

When the damned fool came again, Septimus refused to see him. Did he indeed? said Dr. Holmes, smiling agreeably. Really he had to give that charming little lady, Mrs. Smith, a friendly push before he could get past her into her husband's bedroom.

"So you're in a funk," he said agreeably, sitting down by his patient's side. He had actually talked of killing himself to his wife, quite a girl, a foreigner, wasn't she? Didn't that give her a very odd idea of English husbands? Didn't one owe perhaps a duty to one's wife? Wouldn't it be better to do something instead of lying in bed? For he had had forty years' experience behind him; and Septimus could take Dr. Holmes's word for it—there was nothing whatever the matter with him. And next time Dr. Holmes came he hoped to find Smith out of bed and not making that charming little lady his wife anxious about him.

Human nature, in short, was on him—the repulsive brute, with the blood-red nostrils. Holmes was on him. Dr. Holmes came quite regularly every day. Once you stumble, Septimus wrote on the back of a postcard, human nature is on you. Holmes is on you. Their only chance was to escape, without letting Holmes know; to Italy—anywhere, anywhere, away from Dr. Holmes.

But Rezia could not understand him. Dr. Holmes was such a kind man. He was so interested in Septimus. He only wanted to help them, he said. He had four little children and he had asked her to tea, she told Septimus.

So he was deserted. The whole world was clamouring: Kill yourself, kill yourself, for our sakes. But why should he kill himself for their sakes? Food was pleasant; the sun hot; and this killing oneself, how does one set about it, with a table knife, uglily, with floods of blood,—by sucking a gaspipe? He was too weak; he could scarcely raise his hand. Besides, now that he was quite alone, condemned, deserted, as those who are about to die are alone, there was a luxury in it, an isolation full of sublimity; a freedom which the attached can never know. Holmes had won of course; the brute with the red nostrils had won. But even Holmes himself could not touch this last relic straying on the edge of the world, this outcast, who gazed back at the inhab-ited regions, who lay, like a drowned sailor, on the shore of the world.

It was at that moment (Rezia gone shopping) that the great revelation took place. A voice spoke from behind the screen. Evans was speaking. The dead were with him.

"Evans, Evans!" he cried.

Mr. Smith was talking aloud to himself, Agnes the servant girl cried to Mrs. Filmer in the kitchen. "Evans, Evans," he had said as she brought in the tray. She jumped, she did. She scuttled downstairs.

And Rezia came in, with her flowers, and walked across the room, and put the roses in a vase, upon which the sun struck directly, and it went laughing, leaping round the room.

She had had to buy the roses, Rezia said, from a poor man in the street. But they were almost dead already, she said, arranging the roses.

So there was a man outside; Evans presumably; and the roses, which Rezia said were half dead, had been picked by him in the fields of Greece.

"Communication is health; communication is happiness, communication—" he muttered.

"What are you saying, Septimus?" Rezia asked, wild with terror, for he was talking to himself.

She sent Agnes running for Dr. Holmes. Her husband, she said, was mad. He scarcely knew her.

"You brute! You brute!" cried Septimus, seeing human nature, that is Dr. Holmes, enter the room.

"Now what's all this about?" said Dr. Holmes in the most amiable way in the world. "Talking nonsense to frighten your wife?" But he would give him something to make him sleep. And if they were rich people, said Dr. Holmes, looking ironically round the room, by all means let them go to Harley Street;[5] if they had no confidence in him, said Dr. Holmes, looking not quite so kind.

It was precisely twelve o'clock; twelve by Big Ben; whose stroke was wafted over the northern part of London; blent with that of other clocks, mixed in a thin ethereal way with the clouds and wisps of smoke, and died up there among the seagulls—twelve o'clock struck as Clarissa Dalloway laid her green dress on her bed, and the Warren Smiths walked down Harley Street. Twelve was the hour of their appointment. Probably, Rezia thought, that was Sir William Bradshaw's house with the grey motor car in front of it. The leaden circles dissolved in the air.

Indeed it was—Sir William Bradshaw's motor car; low, powerful, grey with plain initials interlocked on the panel, as if the pomps of heraldry were incongruous, this man being the ghostly helper, the priest of science; and, as the motor car was grey, so to match its sober suavity, grey furs, silver grey rugs were heaped in it, to keep her ladyship warm while she waited. For often Sir William would travel sixty miles or more down into the country to visit the rich, the afflicted, who could afford the very large fee which Sir William very properly charged for his advice. Her ladyship waited with the rugs about her knees an hour or more, leaning back, thinking sometimes of the patient, sometimes, excusably, of the wall of gold, mounting minute by minute while she waited; the wall of gold that was mounting between them and all shifts and anxieties (she had borne them bravely; they had had their struggles) until she felt wedged on a calm ocean, where only spice winds blow; respected, admired, envied, with scarcely anything left to wish for, though she regretted her stoutness; large dinner-parties every Thursday night to the profession; an occasional bazaar to be opened; Royalty greeted; too little time, alas, with her husband, whose work grew and grew; a boy doing well at Eton;[6] she would have liked a daughter too; interests she had, however, in plenty; child welfare; the after-care of the epileptic, and photography, so that if there was a church building, or a church decaying, she bribed the sexton,[7] got the key and took photographs, which were scarcely to be distinguished from the work of professionals, while she waited.

Sir William himself was no longer young. He had worked very hard; he had won his position by sheer ability (being the son of a shopkeeper); loved his profession; made a fine figurehead at ceremonies and spoke well—all of which had by the time he was knighted given him a heavy look, a weary look

5. A popular street for doctors, running south from the Marylebone Road.
6. Eton College, aristocratic boys' school in southwest England.
7. Church officer responsible for its property and grounds.

(the stream of patients being so incessant, the responsibilities and privileges of his profession so onerous), which weariness, together with his grey hairs, increased the extraordinary distinction of his presence and gave him the reputation (of the utmost importance in dealing with nerve cases) not merely of lightning skill, and almost infallible accuracy in diagnosis but of sympathy; tact; understanding of the human soul. He could see the first moment they came into the room (the Warren Smiths they were called); he was certain directly he saw the man; it was a case of extreme gravity. It was a case of complete breakdown—complete physical and nervous breakdown, with every symptom in an advanced stage, he ascertained in two or three minutes (writing answers to questions, murmured discreetly, on a pink card).

How long had Dr. Holmes been attending him?

Six weeks.

Prescribed a little bromide? Said there was nothing the matter? Ah yes (those general practitioners! thought Sir William. It took half his time to undo their blunders. Some were irreparable).

"You served with great distinction in the War?"

The patient repeated the word "war" interrogatively.

He was attaching meanings to words of a symbolical kind. A serious symptom, to be noted on the card.

"The War?" the patient asked. The European War—that little shindy of schoolboys with gunpowder? Had he served with distinction? He really forgot. In the War itself he had failed.

"Yes, he served with the greatest distinction," Rezia assured the doctor; "he was promoted."

"And they have the very highest opinion of you at your office?" Sir William murmured, glancing at Mr. Brewer's very generously worded letter. "So that you have nothing to worry you, no financial anxiety, nothing?"

He had committed an appalling crime and been condemned to death by human nature.

"I have—I have," he began, "committed a crime—"

"He has done nothing wrong whatever," Rezia assured the doctor. If Mr. Smith would wait, said Sir William, he would speak to Mrs. Smith in the next room. Her husband was very seriously ill, Sir William said. Did he threaten to kill himself?

Oh, he did, she cried. But he did not mean it, she said. Of course not. It was merely a question of rest,[8] said Sir William; of rest, rest, rest; a long rest in bed. There was a delightful home down in the country where her husband would be perfectly looked after. Away from her? she asked. Unfortunately, yes; the people we care for most are not good for us when we are ill. But he was not mad, was he? Sir William said he never spoke of "madness"; he called it not having a sense of proportion. But her husband did not like doctors. He would refuse to go there. Shortly and kindly Sir William explained to her the state of the case. He had threatened to kill himself. There was no alternative. It was a question of law.[9] He would lie in bed in a beautiful house in the country. The nurses were admirable. Sir William would visit him once a week. If Mrs. Warren Smith was quite sure she had no more questions to ask—he never hurried

8. A period of inactivity was commonly prescribed to treat mental illness.

9. Suicide was illegal in Britain until 1961.

his patients—they would return to her husband. She had nothing more to ask—not of Sir William.

So they returned to the most exalted of mankind; the criminal who faced his judges; the victim exposed on the heights; the fugitive; the drowned sailor; the poet of the immortal ode; the Lord who had gone from life to death; to Septimus Warren Smith, who sat in the arm-chair under the skylight staring at a photograph of Lady Bradshaw in Court dress, muttering messages about beauty.

"We have had our little talk," said Sir William.

"He says you are very, very ill," Rezia cried.

"We have been arranging that you should go into a home," said Sir William.

"One of Holmes's homes?" sneered Septimus.

The fellow made a distasteful impression. For there was in Sir William, whose father had been a tradesman, a natural respect for breeding and clothing, which shabbiness nettled; again, more profoundly, there was in Sir William, who had never had time for reading, a grudge, deeply buried, against cultivated people who came into his room and intimated that doctors, whose profession is a constant strain upon all the highest faculties, are not educated men.

"One of _my_ homes, Mr. Warren Smith," he said, "where we will teach you to rest."

And there was just one thing more.

He was quite certain that when Mr. Warren Smith was well he was the last man in the world to frighten his wife. But he had talked of killing himself.

"We all have our moments of depression," said Sir William.

Once you fall, Septimus repeated to himself, human nature is on you. Holmes and Bradshaw are on you. They scour the desert. They fly screaming into the wilderness. The rack and the thumbscrew[1] are applied. Human nature is remorseless.

"Impulses came upon him sometimes?" Sir William asked, with his pencil on a pink card.

That was his own affair, said Septimus.

"Nobody lives for himself alone," said Sir William, glancing at the photograph of his wife in Court dress.

"And you have a brilliant career before you," said Sir William. There was Mr. Brewer's letter on the table. "An exceptionally brilliant career."

But if he confessed? If he communicated? Would they let him off then, his torturers?

"I—I—" he stammered.

But what was his crime? He could not remember it.

"Yes?" Sir William encouraged him. (But it was growing late.)

Love, trees, there is no crime—what was his message?

He could not remember it.

"I—I—" Septimus stammered.

"Try to think as little about yourself as possible," said Sir William kindly. Really, he was not fit to be about.

---

1. Instruments of torture.

Was there anything else they wished to ask him? Sir William would make all arrangements (he murmured to Rezia) and he would let her know between five and six that evening he murmured.

"Trust everything to me," he said, and dismissed them.

Never, never had Rezia felt such agony in her life! She had asked for help and been deserted! He had failed them! Sir William Bradshaw was not a nice man.

The upkeep of that motor car alone must cost him quite a lot, said Septimus, when they got out into the street.

She clung to his arm. They had been deserted.

But what more did she want?

To his patients he gave three-quarters of an hour; and if in this exacting science which has to do with what, after all, we know nothing about—the nervous system, the human brain—a doctor loses his sense of proportion, as a doctor he fails. Health we must have; and health is proportion; so that when a man comes into your room and says he is Christ (a common delusion), and has a message, as they mostly have, and threatens, as they often do, to kill himself, you invoke proportion; order rest in bed; rest in solitude; silence and rest; rest without friends, without books, without messages; six months' rest; until a man who went in weighing seven stone six comes out weighing twelve.[2]

Proportion, divine proportion, Sir William's goddess, was acquired by Sir William walking hospitals, catching salmon, begetting one son in Harley Street by Lady Bradshaw, who caught salmon herself and took photographs scarcely to be distinguished from the work of professionals. Worshipping proportion, Sir William not only prospered himself but made England prosper, secluded her lunatics, forbade childbirth, penalised despair; made it impossible for the unfit to propagate their views until they, too, shared his sense of proportion—his, if they were men, Lady Bradshaw's if they were women (she embroidered, knitted, spent four nights out of seven at home with her son), so that not only did his colleagues respect him, his subordinates fear him, but the friends and relations of his patients felt for him the keenest gratitude for insisting that these prophetic Christs and Christesses, who prophesied the end of the world, or the advent of God, should drink milk in bed, as Sir William ordered; Sir William with his thirty years' experience of these kinds of cases, and his infallible instinct, this is madness, this sense; in fact, his sense of proportion.

But Proportion has a sister, less smiling, more formidable, a Goddess even now engaged—in the heat and sands of India, the mud and swamp of Africa, the purlieus[3] of London, wherever in short the climate or the devil tempts men to fall from the true belief which is her own—is even now engaged in dashing down shrines, smashing idols, and setting up in their place her own stern countenance. Conversion is her name and she feasts on the wills of the weakly, loving to impress, to impose, adoring her own features stamped on the face of the populace. At Hyde Park Corner[4] on a tub she stands preaching; shrouds herself in white and walks penitentially disguised as brotherly

---

2. A stone is a measure of weight equal to fourteen pounds, hence an increase from 104 to 168 pounds.
3. Outskirts, borders, or slums.

4. Speaker's Corner, at the northeast corner of Hyde Park, where anyone may stand and talk on any subject.

love through factories and parliaments; offers help, but desires power; smites out of her way roughly the dissentient, or dissatisfied; bestows her blessing on those who, looking upward, catch submissively from her eyes the light of their own. This lady too (Rezia Warren Smith divined it) had her dwelling in Sir William's heart, though concealed, as she mostly is, under some plausible disguise; some venerable name; love, duty, self sacrifice. How he would work—how toil to raise funds, propagate reforms, initiate institutions! But conversion, fastidious Goddess, loves blood better than brick, and feasts most subtly on the human will. For example, Lady Bradshaw. Fifteen years ago she had gone under. It was nothing you could put your finger on; there had been no scene, no snap; only the slow sinking, water-logged, of her will into his. Sweet was her smile, swift her submission; dinner in Harley Street, number-ing eight or nine courses, feeding ten or fifteen guests of the professional classes, was smooth and urbane. Only as the evening wore on a very slight dulness, or uneasiness perhaps, a nervous twitch, fumble, stumble and con-fusion indicated, what it was really painful to believe—that the poor lady lied. Once, long ago, she had caught salmon freely: now, quick to minister to the craving which lit her husband's eye so oilily for dominion, for power, she cramped, squeezed, pared, pruned, drew back, peeped through; so that with-out knowing precisely what made the evening disagreeable, and caused this pressure on the top of the head (which might well be imputed to the profes-sional conversation, or the fatigue of a great doctor whose life, Lady Brad-shaw said, "is not his own but his patients'") disagreeable it was: so that guests, when the clock struck ten, breathed in the air of Harley Street even with rapture; which relief, however, was denied to his patients.

There in the grey room, with the pictures on the wall, and the valuable furniture, under the ground glass skylight, they learnt the extent of their transgressions; huddled up in armchairs, they watched him go through, for their benefit, a curious exercise with the arms, which he shot out, brought sharply back to his hip, to prove (if the patient was obstinate) that Sir Wil-liam was master of his own actions, which the patient was not. There some weakly broke down; sobbed, submitted; others, inspired by Heaven knows what intemperate madness, called Sir William to his face a damnable hum-bug; questioned, even more impiously, life itself. Why live? they demanded. Sir William replied that life was good. Certainly Lady Bradshaw in ostrich feathers hung over the mantelpiece, and as for his income it was quite twelve thousand a year. But to us, they protested, life has given no such bounty. He acquiesced. They lacked a sense of proportion. And perhaps, after all, there is no God? He shrugged his shoulders. In short, this living or not living is an affair of our own? But there they were mistaken. Sir William had a friend in Surrey where they taught, what Sir William frankly admitted was a difficult art—a sense of proportion. There were, moreover, family affection; honour; courage; and a brilliant career. All of these had in Sir William a reso-lute champion. If they failed him, he had to support police and the good of society, which, he remarked very quietly, would take care, down in Surrey,[5] that these unsocial impulses, bred more than anything by the lack of good blood, were held in control. And then stole out from her hiding-place and mounted her throne that Goddess whose lust is to override opposition, to

5. English county south of London.

stamp indelibly in the sanctuaries of others the image of herself. Naked, defenceless, the exhausted, the friendless received the impress of Sir William's will. He swooped; he devoured. He shut people up. It was this combination of decision and humanity that endeared Sir William so greatly to the relations of his victims.

But Rezia Warren Smith cried, walking down Harley Street, that she did not like that man.

Shredding and slicing, dividing and subdividing, the clocks of Harley Street nibbled at the June day, counselled submission, upheld authority, and pointed out in chorus the supreme advantages of a sense of proportion, until the mound of time was so far diminished that a commercial clock, suspended above a shop in Oxford Street, announced, genially and fraternally, as if it were a pleasure to Messrs. Rigby and Lowndes to give the information gratis, that it was half-past one.

Looking up, it appeared that each letter of their names stood for one of the hours; subconsciously one was grateful to Rigby and Lowndes for giving one time ratified by Greenwich;[6] and this gratitude (so Hugh Whitbread ruminated, dallying there in front of the shop window), naturally took the form later of buying off Rigby and Lowndes socks or shoes. So he ruminated. It was his habit. He did not go deeply. He brushed surfaces; the dead languages, the living, life in Constantinople, Paris, Rome; riding, shooting, tennis, it had been once. The malicious asserted that he now kept guard at Buckingham Palace, dressed in silk stockings and knee-breeches, over what nobody knew. But he did it extremely efficiently. He had been afloat on the cream of English society for fifty-five years. He had known Prime Ministers. His affections were understood to be deep. And if it were true that he had not taken part in any of the great movements of the time or held important office, one or two humble reforms stood to his credit; an improvement in public shelters was one; the protection of owls in Norfolk[7] another; servant girls had reason to be grateful to him; and his name at the end of letters to the *Times*,[8] asking for funds, appealing to the public to protect, to preserve, to clear up litter, to abate smoke, and stamp out immorality in parks, commanded respect.

A magnificent figure he cut too, pausing for a moment (as the sound of the half hour died away) to look critically, magisterially, at socks and shoes; impeccable, substantial, as if he beheld the world from a certain eminence, and dressed to match; but realised the obligations which size, wealth, health, entail, and observed punctiliously even when not absolutely necessary, little courtesies, old-fashioned ceremonies which gave a quality to his manner, something to imitate, something to remember him by, for he would never lunch, for example, with Lady Bruton, whom he had known these twenty years, without bringing her in his outstretched hand a bunch of carnations and asking Miss Brush, Lady Bruton's secretary, after her brother in South Africa, which, for some reason, Miss Brush, deficient though she was in every attribute of female charm, so much resented that she said "Thank you, he's doing very well in South Africa," when, for half a dozen years, he had been doing badly in Portsmouth.[9]

6. Greenwich Mean Time, international standard for deriving time since 1884, is calculated by the Royal Observatory, located on the prime meridian in the London borough of Greenwich. "Messrs. Rigby and Lowndes": fictional department store with a clock.
7. English county northeast of London.
8. Major London newspaper since the 1780s.
9. City on the English Channel with a naval base.

Lady Bruton herself preferred Richard Dalloway, who arrived at the next moment. Indeed they met on the doorstep.

Lady Bruton preferred Richard Dalloway of course. He was made of much finer material. But she wouldn't let them run down her poor dear Hugh. She could never forget his kindness—he had been really remarkably kind—she forgot precisely upon what occasion. But he had been—remarkably kind. Anyhow, the difference between one man and another does not amount to much. She had never seen the sense of cutting people up, as Clarissa Dalloway did—cutting them up and sticking them together again; not at any rate when one was sixty-two. She took Hugh's carnations with her angular grim smile. There was nobody else coming, she said. She had got them there on false pretences, to help her out of a difficulty—

"But let us eat first," she said.

And so there began a soundless and exquisite passing to and fro through swing doors of aproned white-capped maids, handmaidens not of necessity, but adepts in a mystery or grand deception practised by hostesses in Mayfair[1] from one-thirty to two, when, with a wave of the hand, the traffic ceases, and there rises instead this profound illusion in the first place about the food—how it is not paid for; and then that the table spreads itself voluntarily with glass and silver, little mats, saucers of red fruit; films of brown cream mask turbot;[2] in casseroles severed chickens swim; coloured, undomestic, the fire burns; and with the wine and the coffee (not paid for) rise jocund visions before musing eyes; gently speculative eyes; eyes to whom life appears musical, mysterious; eyes now kindled to observe genially the beauty of the red carnations which Lady Bruton (whose movements were always angular) had laid beside her plate, so that Hugh Whitbread, feeling at peace with the entire universe and at the same time completely sure of his standing, said, resting his fork,

"Wouldn't they look charming against your lace?"

Miss Brush resented this familiarity intensely. She thought him an underbred fellow. She made Lady Bruton laugh.

Lady Bruton raised the carnations, holding them rather stiffly with much the same attitude with which the General held the scroll in the picture behind her; she remained fixed, tranced. Which was she now, the General's great-grand-daughter? great-great-grand-daughter? Richard Dalloway asked himself. Sir Roderick, Sir Miles, Sir Talbot—that was it. It was remarkable how in that family the likeness persisted in the women. She should have been a general of dragoons[3] herself. And Richard would have served under her, cheerfully; he had the greatest respect for her; he cherished these romantic views about well-set-up old women of pedigree, and would have liked, in his good-humoured way, to bring some young hot-heads of his acquaintance to lunch with her; as if a type like hers could be bred of amiable tea-drinking enthusiasts! He knew her country. He knew her people. There was a vine, still bearing, which either Lovelace or Herrick[4]—she never read a word of poetry herself, but so the story ran—had sat under. Better wait to put before them the question that bothered her (about making an appeal to the public;

---

1. Posh neighborhood east of Hyde Park.
2. Large flat fish.
3. Cavalry soldiers.
4. English lyric poets Richard Lovelace (1617–

1657) and Robert Herrick (1591–1674), noted for their love poems and known as Cavalier poets because of their support for Charles I (1600–1649) in the English Civil War.

if so, in what terms and so on), better wait until they have had their coffee, Lady Bruton thought; and so laid the carnations down beside her plate.

"How's Clarissa?" she asked abruptly.

Clarissa always said that Lady Bruton did not like her. Indeed, Lady Bruton had the reputation of being more interested in politics than people; of talking like a man; of having had a finger in some notorious intrigue of the eighties, which was now beginning to be mentioned in memoirs. Certainly there was an alcove in her drawing-room, and a table in that alcove, and a photograph upon that table of General Sir Talbot Moore, now deceased, who had written there (one evening in the eighties) in Lady Bruton's presence, with her cognisance, perhaps advice, a telegram ordering the British troops to advance upon an historical occasion. (She kept the pen and told the story.) Thus, when she said in her offhand way "How's Clarissa?" husbands had difficulty in persuading their wives and indeed, however devoted, were secretly doubtful themselves, of her interest in women who often got in their husbands' way, prevented them from accepting posts abroad, and had to be taken to the seaside in the middle of the session to recover from influenza. Nevertheless her inquiry, "How's Clarissa?" was known by women infallibly, to be a signal from a well-wisher, from an almost silent companion, whose utterances (half a dozen perhaps in the course of a lifetime) signified recognition of some feminine comradeship which went beneath masculine lunch parties and united Lady Bruton and Mrs. Dalloway, who seldom met, and appeared when they did meet indifferent and even hostile, in a singular bond.

"I met Clarissa in the Park this morning," said Hugh Whitbread, diving into the casserole, anxious to pay himself this little tribute, for he had only to come to London and he met everybody at once; but greedy, one of the greediest men she had ever known, Milly Brush thought, who observed men with unflinching rectitude, and was capable of everlasting devotion, to her own sex in particular, being knobbed, scraped, angular, and entirely without feminine charm.

"D'you know who's in town?" said Lady Bruton suddenly bethinking her. "Our old friend, Peter Walsh."

They all smiled. Peter Walsh! And Mr. Dalloway was genuinely glad, Milly Brush thought; and Mr. Whitbread thought only of his chicken.

Peter Walsh! All three, Lady Bruton, Hugh Whitbread, and Richard Dalloway, remembered the same thing—how passionately Peter had been in love; been rejected; gone to India; come a cropper;[5] made a mess of things; and Richard Dalloway had a very great liking for the dear old fellow too. Milly Brush saw that; saw a depth in the brown of his eyes; saw him hesitate; consider; which interested her, as Mr. Dalloway always interested her, for what was he thinking, she wondered, about Peter Walsh?

That Peter Walsh had been in love with Clarissa; that he would go back directly after lunch and find Clarissa; that he would tell her, in so many words, that he loved her. Yes, he would say that.

Milly Brush once might almost have fallen in love with these silences; and Mr. Dalloway was always so dependable; such a gentleman too. Now, being forty, Lady Bruton had only to nod, or turn her head a little abruptly,

5. Failed badly.

and Milly Brush took the signal, however deeply she might be sunk in these reflections of a detached spirit, of an uncorrupted soul whom life could not bamboozle, because life had not offered her a trinket of the slightest value; not a curl, smile, lip, cheek, nose; nothing whatever; Lady Bruton had only to nod, and Perkins was instructed to quicken the coffee.

"Yes; Peter Walsh has come back," said Lady Bruton. It was vaguely flattering to them all. He had come back, battered, unsuccessful, to their secure shores. But to help him, they reflected, was impossible; there was some flaw in his character. Hugh Whitbread said one might of course mention his name to So-and-so. He wrinkled lugubriously, consequentially, at the thought of the letters he would write to the heads of Government offices about "my old friend, Peter Walsh," and so on. But it wouldn't lead to anything—not to anything permanent, because of his character.

"In trouble with some woman," said Lady Bruton. They had all guessed that *that* was at the bottom of it.

"However," said Lady Bruton, anxious to leave the subject, "we shall hear the whole story from Peter himself."

(The coffee was very slow in coming.)

"The address?" murmured Hugh Whitbread; and there was at once a ripple in the grey tide of service which washed round Lady Bruton day in, day out, collecting, intercepting, enveloping her in a fine tissue which broke concussions, mitigated interruptions, and spread round the house in Brook Street[6] a fine net where things lodged and were picked out accurately, instantly, by grey-haired Perkins, who had been with Lady Bruton these thirty years and now wrote down the address; handed it to Mr. Whitbread, who took out his pocketbook, raised his eyebrows, and slipping it in among documents of the highest importance, said that he would get Evelyn to ask him to lunch.

(They were waiting to bring the coffee until Mr. Whitbread had finished.)

Hugh was very slow, Lady Bruton thought. He was getting fat, she noticed. Richard always kept himself in the pink of condition.[7] She was getting impatient; the whole of her being was setting positively, undeniably, domineeringly brushing aside all this unnecessary trifling (Peter Walsh and his affairs) upon that subject which engaged her attention, and not merely her attention, but that fibre which was the ramrod of her soul, that essential part of her without which Millicent Bruton would not have been Millicent Bruton; that project for emigrating young people of both sexes born of respectable parents and setting them up with a fair prospect of doing well in Canada.[8] She exaggerated. She had perhaps lost her sense of proportion. Emigration was not to others the obvious remedy, the sublime conception. It was not to them (not to Hugh, or Richard, or even to devoted Miss Brush) the liberator of the pent[9] egotism, which a strong martial woman, well nourished, well descended, of direct impulses, downright feelings, and little introspective power (broad and simple—why could not every one be broad and simple? she asked) feels rise within her, once youth is past, and must eject upon some object—it may be Emigration, it may be Emancipation; but whatever it be, this object round which the essence of her soul is daily

6. In Mayfair.
7. I.e., in excellent health.
8. In response to Britain's supposedly "surplus" population and resultant worries about employ-

ment, Lady Bruton favors a project encouraging young people to emigrate to Canada, which had suffered great losses in World War I.
9. Unspoken or repressed.

secreted, becomes inevitably prismatic, lustrous, half looking-glass, half precious stone; now carefully hidden in case people should sneer at it; now proudly displayed. Emigration had become, in short, largely Lady Bruton.

But she had to write. And one letter to the *Times*, she used to say to Miss Brush, cost her more than to organise an expedition to South Africa (which she had done in the war). After a morning's battle beginning, tearing up, beginning again, she used to feel the futility of her own womanhood as she felt it on no other occasion, and would turn gratefully to the thought of Hugh Whitbread who possessed—no one could doubt it—the art of writing letters to the *Times*.

A being so differently constituted from herself, with such a command of language; able to put things as editors like them put; had passions which one could not call simply greed. Lady Bruton often suspended judgement upon men in deference to the mysterious accord in which they, but no woman, stood to the laws of the universe; knew how to put things; knew what was said; so that if Richard advised her, and Hugh wrote for her, she was sure of being somehow right. So she let Hugh eat his soufflé; asked after poor Evelyn; waited until they were smoking, and then said,

"Milly, would you fetch the papers?"

And Miss Brush went out, came back; laid papers on the table; and Hugh produced his fountain pen; his silver fountain pen, which had done twenty years' service, he said, unscrewing the cap. It was still in perfect order; he had shown it to the makers; there was no reason, they said, why it should ever wear out; which was somehow to Hugh's credit, and to the credit of the sentiments which his pen expressed (so Richard Dalloway felt) as Hugh began carefully writing capital letters with rings round them in the margin, and thus marvellously reduced Lady Bruton's tangles to sense, to grammar such as the editor of the *Times*, Lady Bruton felt, watching the marvellous transformation, must respect. Hugh was slow. Hugh was pertinacious. Richard said one must take risks. Hugh proposed modifications in defer-ence to people's feelings, which, he said rather tartly when Richard laughed, "had to be considered," and read out "how, therefore, we are of opinion that the times are ripe . . . the superfluous youth of our ever-increasing population . . . what we owe to the dead . . ." which Richard thought all stuff-ing and bunkum, but no harm in it, of course, and Hugh went on drafting sentiments in alphabetical order of the highest nobility, brushing the cigar ash from his waistcoat, and summing up now and then the progress they had made until, finally, he read out the draft of a letter which Lady Bruton felt certain was a masterpiece. Could her own meaning sound like that?

Hugh could not guarantee that the editor would put it in; but he would be meeting somebody at luncheon.

Whereupon Lady Bruton, who seldom did a graceful thing, stuffed all Hugh's carnations into the front of her dress, and flinging her hands out called him "My Prime Minister!" What she would have done without them both she did not know. They rose. And Richard Dalloway strolled off as usual to have a look at the General's portrait, because he meant, whenever he had a moment of leisure, to write a history of Lady Bruton's family.

And Millicent Bruton was very proud of her family. But they could wait, they could wait, she said, looking at the picture; meaning that her family, of military men, administrators, admirals, had been men of action, who had done their duty; and Richard's first duty was to his country, but it was a fine face, she said; and all the papers were ready for Richard down at Aldmixton whenever the time came; the Labour Government[1] she meant. "Ah, the news from India!" she cried.

And then, as they stood in the hall taking yellow gloves from the bowl on the malachite[2] table and Hugh was offering Miss Brush with quite unnecessary courtesy some discarded ticket or other compliment, which she loathed from the depths of her heart and blushed brick red, Richard turned to Lady Bruton, with his hat in his hand, and said,

"We shall see you at our party to-night?" whereupon Lady Bruton resumed the magnificence which letter-writing had shattered. She might come; or she might not come. Clarissa had wonderful energy. Parties terrified Lady Bruton. But then, she was getting old. So she intimated, standing at her doorway; handsome; very erect; while her chow stretched behind her, and Miss Brush disappeared into the background with her hands full of papers.

And Lady Bruton went ponderously, majestically, up to her room, lay, one arm extended, on the sofa. She sighed, she snored, not that she was asleep, only drowsy and heavy, drowsy and heavy, like a field of clover in the sunshine this hot June day, with the bees going round and about and the yellow butterflies. Always she went back to those fields down in Devonshire,[3] where she had jumped the brooks on Patty, her pony, with Mortimer and Tom, her brothers. And there were the dogs; there were the rats; there were her father and mother on the lawn under the trees, with the tea-things out, and the beds of dahlias, the hollyhocks, the pampas grass; and they, little wretches, always up to some mischief! stealing back through the shrubbery, so as not to be seen, all bedraggled from some roguery. What old nurse used to say about her frocks!

Ah dear, she remembered—it was Wednesday in Brook Street. Those kind good fellows, Richard Dalloway, Hugh Whitbread, had gone this hot day through the streets whose growl came up to her lying on the sofa. Power was hers, position, income. She had lived in the forefront of her time. She had had good friends; known the ablest men of her day. Murmuring London flowed up to her, and her hand, lying on the sofa back, curled upon some imaginary baton such as her grandfathers might have held, holding which she seemed, drowsy and heavy, to be commanding battalions marching to Canada, and those good fellows walking across London, that territory of theirs, that little bit of carpet, Mayfair.

And they went further and further from her, being attached to her by a thin thread (since they had lunched with her) which would stretch and stretch, get thinner and thinner as they walked across London; as if one's friends were attached to one's body, after lunching with them, by a thin thread, which (as she dozed there) became hazy with the sound of bells, striking the hour or ringing to service, as a single spider's thread is blotted with rain-drops, and, burdened, sags down. So she slept.

And Richard Dalloway and Hugh Whitbread hesitated at the corner of Conduit Street[4] at the very moment that Millicent Bruton, lying on the sofa, let the thread snap; snored. Contrary winds buffeted at the street corner.

---

1. I.e., whenever a Labour Government comes to power, Richard, a Conservative, might be voted out of office and thus become free to write her family history.
2. Deep green stone.

3. County in southwest England.
4. Street in Mayfair. Richard and Hugh appear to have walked east on Brook Street and then south on Bond Street to this intersection.

They looked in at a shop window; they did not wish to buy or to talk but to part, only with contrary winds buffeting the street corner, with some sort of lapse in the tides of the body, two forces meeting in a swirl, morning and afternoon, they paused. Some newspaper placard went up in the air, gallantly, like a kite at first, then paused, swooped, fluttered; and a lady's veil hung. Yellow awnings trembled. The speed of the morning traffic slackened, and single carts rattled carelessly down half-empty streets. In Norfolk, of which Richard Dalloway was half thinking, a soft warm wind blew back the petals; confused the waters; ruffled the flowering grasses. Haymakers, who had pitched beneath hedges to sleep away the morning toil, parted curtains of green blades; moved trembling globes of cow parsley to see the sky, the blue, the steadfast, the blazing summer sky.

Aware that he was looking at a silver two-handled Jacobean mug,[5] and that Hugh Whitbread admired condescendingly with airs of connoisseurship a Spanish necklace which he thought of asking the price of in case Evelyn might like it—still Richard was torpid; could not think or move. Life had thrown up this wreckage; shop windows full of coloured paste, and one stood stark with the lethargy of the old, stiff with the rigidity of the old, looking in. Evelyn Whitbread might like to buy this Spanish necklace—so she might. Yawn he must. Hugh was going into the shop.

"Right you are!" said Richard, following.

Goodness knows he didn't want to go buying necklaces with Hugh. But there are tides in the body. Morning meets afternoon. Borne like a frail shallop[6] on deep, deep floods, Lady Bruton's great-grandfather and his memoir and his campaigns in North America were whelmed and sunk. And Millicent Bruton too. She went under. Richard didn't care a straw what became of Emigration; about that letter, whether the editor put it in or not. The necklace hung stretched between Hugh's admirable fingers. Let him give it to a girl, if he must buy jewels—any girl, any girl in the street. For the worthlessness of this life did strike Richard pretty forcibly—buying necklaces for Evelyn. If he'd had a boy he'd have said, Work, work. But he had his Elizabeth; he adored his Elizabeth.

"I should like to see Mr. Dubonnet," said Hugh in his curt worldly way. It appeared that this Dubonnet had the measurements of Mrs. Whitbread's neck, or, more strangely still, knew her views upon Spanish jewellery and the extent of her possessions in that line (which Hugh could not remember). All of which seemed to Richard Dalloway awfully odd. For he never gave Clarissa presents, except a bracelet two or three years ago, which had not been a success. She never wore it. It pained him to remember that she never wore it. And as a single spider's thread after wavering here and there attaches itself to the point of a leaf, so Richard's mind, recovering from its lethargy, set now on his wife, Clarissa, whom Peter Walsh had loved so passionately; and Richard had had a sudden vision of her there at luncheon; of himself and Clarissa; of their life together; and he drew the tray of old jewels towards him, and taking up first this brooch then that ring, "How much is that?" he asked, but doubted his own taste. He wanted to open the drawing-room door and come in holding out something; a present for Clarissa. Only what? But Hugh was on his legs again. He was unspeakably

<hr/>

5. In the style of, or dating from, the reign of King James I (1603–25).
6. Small boat; dinghy.

pompous. Really, after dealing here for thirty-five years he was not going to be put off by a mere boy who did not know his business. For Dubonnet, it seemed, was out, and Hugh would not buy anything until Mr. Dubonnet chose to be in; at which the youth flushed and bowed his correct little bow. It was all perfectly correct. And yet Richard couldn't have said that to save his life! Why these people stood that damned insolence he could not conceive. Hugh was becoming an intolerable ass. Richard Dalloway could not stand more than an hour of his society. And, flicking his bowler hat by way of farewell, Richard turned at the corner of Conduit Street eager, yes, very eager, to travel that spider's thread of attachment between himself and Clarissa; he would go straight to her, in Westminster.

But he wanted to come in holding something. Flowers? Yes, flowers, since he did not trust his taste in gold; any number of flowers, roses, orchids, to celebrate what was, reckoning things as you will, an event; this feeling about her when they spoke of Peter Walsh at luncheon; and they never spoke of it; not for years had they spoken of it; which, he thought, grasping his red and white roses together (a vast bunch in tissue paper), is the greatest mistake in the world. The time comes when it can't be said; one's too shy to say it, he thought, pocketing his sixpence or two of change, setting off with his great bunch held against his body to Westminster to say straight out in so many words (whatever she might think of him), holding out his flowers, "I love you." Why not? Really it was a miracle thinking of the war, and thousands of poor chaps, with all their lives before them, shovelled together, already half forgotten; it was a miracle. Here he was walking across London to say to Clarissa in so many words that he loved her. Which one never does say, he thought. Partly one's lazy; partly one's shy. And Clarissa—it was difficult to think of her; except in starts, as at luncheon, when he saw her quite distinctly; their whole life. He stopped at the crossing; and repeated—being simple by nature, and undebauched, because he had tramped, and shot; being pertinacious and dogged, having championed the downtrodden and followed his instincts in the House of Commons; being preserved in his simplicity yet at the same time grown rather speechless, rather stiff—he repeated that it was a miracle that he should have married Clarissa; a miracle—his life had been a miracle, he thought; hesitating to cross. But it did make his blood boil to see little creatures of five or six crossing Piccadilly alone. The police ought to have stopped the traffic at once. He had no illusions about the London police. Indeed, he was collecting evidence of their malpractices; and those costermongers,[7] not allowed to stand their barrows in the streets; and prostitutes, good Lord, the fault wasn't in them, nor in young men either, but in our detestable social system and so forth; all of which he considered, could be seen considering, grey, dogged, dapper, clean, as he walked across the Park to tell his wife that he loved her.

For he would say it in so many words, when he came into the room. Because it is a thousand pities never to say what one feels, he thought, crossing the Green Park and observing with pleasure how in the shade of the trees whole families, poor families, were sprawling; children kicking up their legs; sucking milk; paper bags thrown about, which could easily be picked up (if people objected) by one of those fat gentlemen in livery;[8] for he

---

7. Street vendors who sell fruit from open carts.
8. In uniform, presumably that of park officials.

was of opinion that every park, and every square, during the summer months should be open to children (the grass of the park flushed and faded, lighting up the poor mothers of Westminster and their crawling babies, as if a yellow lamp were moved beneath). But what could be done for female vagrants like that poor creature, stretched on her elbow (as if she had flung herself on the earth, rid of all ties, to observe curiously, to speculate boldly, to consider the whys and the wherefores, impudent, loose-lipped, humorous), he did not know. Bearing his flowers like a weapon, Richard Dalloway approached her; intent he passed her; still there was time for a spark between them—she laughed at the sight of him, he smiled good-humouredly, considering the problem of the female vagrant; not that they would ever speak. But he would tell Clarissa that he loved her, in so many words. He had, once upon a time, been jealous of Peter Walsh; jealous of him and Clarissa. But she had often said to him that she had been right not to marry Peter Walsh; which, knowing Clarissa, was obviously true; she wanted support. Not that she was weak; but she wanted support.

As for Buckingham Palace (like an old prima donna facing the audience all in white) you can't deny it a certain dignity, he considered, nor despise what does, after all, stand to millions of people (a little crowd was waiting at the gate to see the King drive out) for a symbol, absurd though it is; a child with a box of bricks could have done better, he thought; looking at the memorial to Queen Victoria (whom he could remember in her horn spectacles driving through Kensington), its white mound, its billowing motherliness; but he liked being ruled by the descendant of Horsa;[9] he liked continuity; and the sense of handing on the traditions of the past. It was a great age in which to have lived. Indeed, his own life was a miracle; let him make no mistake about it; here he was, in the prime of life, walking to his house in Westminster to tell Clarissa that he loved her. Happiness is this, he thought.

It is this, he said, as he entered Dean's Yard.[1] Big Ben was beginning to strike, first the warning, musical; then the hour, irrevocable. Lunch parties waste the entire afternoon, he thought, approaching his door.

The sound of Big Ben flooded Clarissa's drawing-room, where she sat, ever so annoyed, at her writing-table; worried; annoyed. It was perfectly true that she had not asked Ellie Henderson to her party; but she had done it on purpose. Now Mrs. Marsham wrote "she had told Ellie Henderson she would ask Clarissa—Ellie so much wanted to come."

But why should she invite all the dull women in London to her parties? Why should Mrs. Marsham interfere? And there was Elizabeth closeted all this time with Doris Kilman. Anything more nauseating she could not conceive. Prayer at this hour with that woman. And the sound of the bell flooded the room with its melancholy wave; which receded, and gathered itself together to fall once more, when she heard, distractingly, something fumbling, something scratching at the door. Who at this hour? Three, good Heavens! Three already! For with overpowering directness and dignity the clock struck three; and she heard nothing else; but the door handle slipped round and in came Richard! What a surprise! In came Richard, holding out

9. Of Saxon heritage. The brothers Horsa and Hengist were said to have begun the Anglo-Saxon invasion of Britain in the fifth century c.e. "Kensington": London borough west of Hyde Park, where Kensington Gardens and Kensing-ton Palace are located.
1. Residential area that was once part of the gardens of Westminster Abbey belonging to its dean.

flowers. She had failed him, once at Constantinople; and Lady Bruton, whose lunch parties were said to be extraordinarily amusing, had not asked her. He was holding out flowers—roses, red and white roses. (But he could not bring himself to say he loved her; not in so many words.)

But how lovely, she said, taking his flowers. She understood; she understood without his speaking; his Clarissa. She put them in vases on the mantelpiece. How lovely they looked! she said. And was it amusing, she asked? Had Lady Bruton asked after her? Peter Walsh was back. Mrs. Marsham had written. Must she ask Ellie Henderson? That woman Kilman was upstairs.

"But let us sit down for five minutes," said Richard.

It all looked so empty. All the chairs were against the wall. What had they been doing? Oh, it was for the party; no, he had not forgotten, the party. Peter Walsh was back. Oh yes; she had had him. And he was going to get a divorce; and he was in love with some woman out there. And he hadn't changed in the slightest. There she was, mending her dress. . . .

"Thinking of Bourton," she said.

"Hugh was at lunch," said Richard. She had met him too! Well, he was getting absolutely intolerable. Buying Evelyn necklaces; fatter than ever; an intolerable ass.

"And it came over me 'I might have married you,'" she said, thinking of Peter sitting there in his little bow-tie; with that knife, opening it, shutting it. "Just as he always was, you know."

They were talking about him at lunch, said Richard. (But he could not tell her he loved her. He held her hand. Happiness is this, he thought.) They had been writing a letter to the *Times* for Millicent Bruton. That was about all Hugh was fit for.

"And our dear Miss Kilman?" he asked. Clarissa thought the roses absolutely lovely, first bunched together; now of their own accord starting apart.

"Kilman arrives just as we've done lunch," she said. "Elizabeth turns pink. They shut themselves up. I suppose they're praying."

Lord! He didn't like it; but these things pass over if you let them.

"In a mackintosh with an umbrella," said Clarissa.

He had not said "I love you"; but he held her hand. Happiness is this, is this, he thought.

"But why should I ask all the dull women in London to my parties?" said Clarissa. And if Mrs. Marsham gave a party, did *she* invite her guests?

"Poor Ellie Henderson," said Richard—it was a very odd thing how much Clarissa minded about her parties, he thought.

But Richard had no notion of the look of a room. However—what was he going to say?

If she worried about these parties he would not let her give them. Did she wish she had married Peter? But he must go.

He must be off, he said, getting up. But he stood for a moment as if he were about to say something; and she wondered what? Why? There were the roses.

"Some Committee?" she asked, as he opened the door.

"Armenians," he said; or perhaps it was "Albanians."[2]

<hr />

2. Armenians, a Christian minority in Turkey, were persecuted; 1.75 million were forced to emigrate between 1915 and 1921. Their plight is more likely to be the subject of Richard's meeting than that of the Albanians, who, after a period of unrest (1908–21), had their territorial security guaranteed by the League of Nations.

And there is a dignity in people; a solitude; even between husband and wife a gulf; and that one must respect, thought Clarissa, watching him open the door; for one would not part with it oneself, or take it, against his will, from one's husband, without losing one's independence, one's self-respect—something, after all, priceless.

He returned with a pillow and a quilt.

"An hour's complete rest after luncheon," he said. And he went.

How like him! He would go on saying "An hour's complete rest after luncheon" to the end of time, because a doctor had ordered it once. It was like him to take what doctors said literally; part of his adorable, divine simplicity, which no one had to the same extent; which made him go and do the thing while she and Peter frittered their time away bickering. He was already halfway to the House of Commons, to his Armenians, his Albanians, having settled her on the sofa, looking at his roses. And people would say, "Clarissa Dalloway is spoilt." She cared much more for her roses than for the Armenians. Hunted out of existence, maimed, frozen, the victims of cruelty and injustice (she had heard Richard say so over and over again)—no, she could feel nothing for the Albanians, or was it the Armenians? but she loved her roses (didn't that help the Armenians?)—the only flowers she could bear to see cut. But Richard was already at the House of Commons; at his Committee, having settled all her difficulties. But no; alas, that was not true. He did not see the reasons against asking Ellie Henderson. She would do it, of course, as he wished it. Since he had brought the pillows, she would lie down. . . . But—but—why did she suddenly feel, for no reason that she could discover, desperately unhappy? As a person who has dropped some grain of pearl or diamond into the grass and parts the tall blades very carefully, this way and that, and searches here and there vainly, and at last spies it there at the roots, so she went through one thing and another; no, it was not Sally Seton saying that Richard would never be in the Cabinet because he had a second-class brain (it came back to her); no, she did not mind that; nor was it to do with Elizabeth either and Doris Kilman; those were facts. It was a feeling, some unpleasant feeling, earlier in the day perhaps; something that Peter had said, combined with some depression of her own, in her bedroom, taking off her hat; and what Richard had said had added to it, but what had he said? There were his roses. Her parties! That was it! Her parties! Both of them criticised her very unfairly, laughed at her very unjustly, for her parties. That was it! That was it!

Well, how was she going to defend herself? Now that she knew what it was, she felt perfectly happy. They thought, or Peter at any rate thought, that she enjoyed imposing herself; liked to have famous people about her; great names; was simply a snob in short. Well, Peter might think so. Richard merely thought it foolish of her to like excitement when she knew it was bad for her heart. It was childish, he thought. And both were quite wrong. What she liked was simply life.

"That's what I do it for," she said, speaking aloud, to life.

Since she was lying on the sofa, cloistered, exempt, the presence of this thing which she felt to be so obvious became physically existent; with robes of sound from the street, sunny, with hot breath, whispering, blowing out the blinds. But suppose Peter said to her, "Yes, yes, but your parties—what's the sense of your parties?" all she could say was (and nobody could be expected to understand): They're an offering; which sounded horribly vague.

But who was Peter to make out that life was all plain sailing?—Peter always in love, always in love with the wrong woman? What's your love? she might say to him. And she knew his answer; how it is the most important thing in the world and no woman possibly understood it. Very well. But could any man understand what she meant either? about life? She could not imagine Peter or Richard taking the trouble to give a party for no reason whatever.

But to go deeper, beneath what people said (and these judgements, how superficial, how fragmentary they are!) in her own mind now, what did it mean to her, this thing she called life? Oh, it was very queer. Here was So-and-so in South Kensington; some one up in Bayswater;[3] and somebody else, say, in Mayfair. And she felt quite continuously a sense of their existence; and she felt what a waste; and she felt what a pity; and she felt if only they could be brought together; so she did it. And it was an offering; to combine, to create; but to whom?

An offering for the sake of offering, perhaps. Anyhow, it was her gift. Nothing else had she of the slightest importance; could not think, write, even play the piano. She muddled Armenians and Turks; loved success; hated discomfort; must be liked; talked oceans of nonsense: and to this day, ask her what the Equator was, and she did not know.

All the same, that one day should follow another; Wednesday, Thursday, Friday, Saturday, that one should wake up in the morning; see the sky; walk in the park; meet Hugh Whitbread; then suddenly in came Peter; then these roses; it was enough. After that, how unbelievable death was!—that it must end; and no one in the whole world would know how she had loved it all; how, every instant . . .

The door opened. Elizabeth knew that her mother was resting. She came in very quietly. She stood perfectly still. Was it that some Mongol[4] had been wrecked on the coast of Norfolk (as Mrs. Hilbery said), had mixed with the Dalloway ladies, perhaps, a hundred years ago? For the Dalloways, in general, were fair-haired; blue-eyed; Elizabeth, on the contrary, was dark; had Chinese eyes[5] in a pale face; an Oriental mystery; was gentle, considerate, still. As a child, she had had a perfect sense of humour; but now at seventeen, why, Clarissa could not in the least understand, she had become very serious; like a hyacinth, sheathed in glossy green, with buds just tinted, a hyacinth which has had no sun.

She stood quite still and looked at her mother; but the door was ajar, and outside the door was Miss Kilman, as Clarissa knew; Miss Kilman in her mackintosh, listening to whatever they said.

Yes, Miss Kilman stood on the landing, and wore a mackintosh; but had her reasons. First, it was cheap; second, she was over forty; and did not, after all, dress to please. She was poor, moreover; degradingly poor. Otherwise she would not be taking jobs from people like the Dalloways; from rich people, who liked to be kind. Mr. Dalloway, to do him justice, had been kind. But Mrs. Dalloway had not. She had been merely condescending. She came from the most worthless of all classes—the rich, with a smattering of culture. They had expensive things everywhere; pictures, carpets, lots of servants. She considered that she had a perfect right to anything that the Dalloways did for her.

---

3. London borough north of Hyde Park. South Kensington: borough south of Hyde Park.
4. Person from Mongolia, in Asia.

5. Almond-shaped, presumably, and suggestive to Britons at this time of an "oriental" mystery.

She had been cheated. Yes, the word was no exaggeration, for surely a girl has a right to some kind of happiness? And she had never been happy, what with being so clumsy and so poor. And then, just as she might have had a chance at Miss Dolby's school, the war came; and she had never been able to tell lies. Miss Dolby thought she would be happier with people who shared her views about the Germans. She had had to go. It was true that the family was of German origin; spelt the name Kiehlman in the eighteenth century; but her brother had been killed. They turned her out because she would not pretend that the Germans were all villains—when she had German friends, when the only happy days of her life had been spent in Germany! And after all, she could read history. She had had to take whatever she could get. Mr. Dalloway had come across her working for the Friends.[6] He had allowed her (and that was really generous of him) to teach his daughter history. Also she did a little Extension lecturing[7] and so on. Then Our Lord had come to her (and here she always bowed her head). She had seen the light two years and three months ago. Now she did not envy women like Clarissa Dalloway; she pitied them.

She pitied and despised them from the bottom of her heart, as she stood on the soft carpet, looking at the old engraving of a little girl with a muff.[8] With all this luxury going on, what hope was there for a better state of things? Instead of lying on a sofa—"My mother is resting," Elizabeth had said—she should have been in a factory; behind a counter; Mrs. Dalloway and all the other fine ladies!

Bitter and burning, Miss Kilman had turned in to a church two years three months ago. She had heard the Rev. Edward Whittaker preach; the boys sing; had seen the solemn lights descend, and whether it was the music, or the voices (she herself when alone in the evening found comfort in a violin; but the sound was excruciating; she had no ear), the hot and turbulent feelings which boiled and surged in her had been assuaged as she sat there, and she had wept copiously, and gone to call on Mr. Whittaker at his private house in Kensington. It was the hand of God, he said. The Lord had shown her the way. So now, whenever the hot and painful feelings boiled within her, this hatred of Mrs. Dalloway, this grudge against the world, she thought of God. She thought of Mr. Whittaker. Rage was succeeded by calm. A sweet savour filled her veins, her lips parted, and, standing formidable upon the landing in her mackintosh, she looked with steady and sinister serenity at Mrs. Dalloway, who came out with her daughter.

Elizabeth said she had forgotten her gloves. That was because Miss Kilman and her mother hated each other. She could not bear to see them together. She ran upstairs to find her gloves.

But Miss Kilman did not hate Mrs. Dalloway. Turning her large gooseberry-coloured eyes upon Clarissa, observing her small pink face, her delicate body, her air of freshness and fashion, Miss Kilman felt, Fool! Simpleton! You who have known neither sorrow nor pleasure; who have trifled your life away! And there rose in her an overmastering desire to overcome her; to unmask her. If she could have felled her it would have eased her. But it was not the body; it was the soul and its mockery that she wished to subdue; make feel her mastery. If only she could make her weep; could ruin her; humiliate her; bring

---

6. Religious Society of Friends, known as the Quakers.
7. Teaching students who are not part of a typical degree program.
8. A cylindrical warmer for both hands.

her to her knees crying, You are right! But this was God's will, not Miss Kilman's. It was to be a religious victory. So she glared; so she glowered.

Clarissa was really shocked. This a Christian—this woman! This woman had taken her daughter from her! She in touch with invisible presences! Heavy, ugly, commonplace, without kindness or grace, she know the meaning of life!

"You are taking Elizabeth to the Stores?"[9] Mrs. Dalloway said.

Miss Kilman said she was. They stood there. Miss Kilman was not going to make herself agreeable. She had always earned her living. Her knowledge of modern history was thorough in the extreme. She did out of her meagre income set aside so much for causes she believed in; whereas this woman did nothing, believed nothing; brought up her daughter—but here was Elizabeth, rather out of breath, the beautiful girl.

So they were going to the Stores. Odd it was, as Miss Kilman stood there (and stand she did, with the power and taciturnity of some prehistoric monster armoured for primeval warfare), how, second by second, the idea of her diminished, how hatred (which was for ideas, not people) crumbled, how she lost her malignity, her size, became second by second merely Miss Kilman, in a mackintosh, whom Heaven knows Clarissa would have liked to help.

At this dwindling of the monster, Clarissa laughed. Saying good-bye, she laughed.

Off they went together, Miss Kilman and Elizabeth, downstairs.

With a sudden impulse, with a violent anguish, for this woman was taking her daughter from her, Clarissa leant over the bannisters and cried out, "Remember the party! Remember our party to-night!"

But Elizabeth had already opened the front door; there was a van passing; she did not answer.

Love and religion! thought Clarissa, going back into the drawing-room, tingling all over. How detestable, how detestable they are! For now that the body of Miss Kilman was not before her, it overwhelmed her—the idea. The crudest things in the world, she thought, seeing them clumsy, hot, domineering, hypocritical, eavesdropping, jealous, infinitely cruel and unscrupulous, dressed in a mackintosh coat, on the landing; love and religion. Had she ever tried to convert any one herself? Did she not wish everybody merely to be themselves? And she watched out of the window the old lady opposite climbing upstairs. Let her climb upstairs if she wanted to; let her stop; then let her, as Clarissa had often seen her, gain her bedroom, part her curtains, and disappear again into the background. Somehow one respected that— that old woman looking out of the window, quite unconscious that she was being watched. There was something solemn in it—but love and religion would destroy that, whatever it was, the privacy of the soul. The odious Kilman would destroy it. Yet it was a sight that made her want to cry.

Love destroyed too. Everything that was fine, everything that was true went. Take Peter Walsh now. There was a man, charming, clever, with ideas about everything. If you wanted to know about Pope, say, or Addison,[1] or just to talk nonsense, what people were like, what things meant, Peter knew better than any one. It was Peter who had helped her; Peter who had lent her books. But look at the women he loved—vulgar, trivial, commonplace. Think of Peter in love—he came to see her after all these years, and what did he talk about?

---

9. I.e., the Army and Navy Stores in Victoria Street, founded as a cooperative society to supply cheap goods to military families.

1. Joseph Addison (1672–1719), English politician and writer.

Himself. Horrible passion! she thought. Degrading passion! she thought, thinking of Kilman and her Elizabeth walking to the Army and Navy Stores.

Big Ben struck the half-hour.

How extraordinary it was, strange, yes, touching, to see the old lady (they had been neighbours ever so many years) move away from the window, as if she were attached to that sound, that string. Gigantic as it was, it had something to do with her. Down, down, into the midst of ordinary things the finger fell making the moment solemn. She was forced, so Clarissa imagined, by that sound, to move, to go—but where? Clarissa tried to follow her as she turned and disappeared, and could still just see her white cap moving at the back of the bedroom. She was still there moving about at the other end of the room. Why creeds and prayers and mackintoshes? when, thought Clarissa, that's the miracle, that's the mystery; that old lady, she meant, whom she could see going from chest of drawers to dressing-table. She could still see her. And the supreme mystery which Kilman might say she had solved, or Peter might say he had solved, but Clarissa didn't believe either of them had the ghost of an idea of solving, was simply this: here was one room; there another. Did religion solve that, or love?

Love—but here the other clock, the clock which always struck two minutes after Big Ben, came shuffling in with its lap full of odds and ends, which it dumped down as if Big Ben were all very well with his majesty laying down the law, so solemn, so just, but she must remember all sorts of little things besides—Mrs. Marsham, Ellie Henderson, glasses for ices—all sorts of little things came flooding and lapping and dancing in on the wake of that solemn stroke which lay flat like a bar of gold on the sea. Mrs. Marsham, Ellie Henderson, glasses for ices. She must telephone now at once.

Volubly, troublously, the late clock sounded, coming in on the wake of Big Ben, with its lap full of trifles. Beaten up, broken up by the assault of carriages, the brutality of vans, the eager advance of myriads of angular men, of flaunting women, the domes and spires of offices and hospitals, the last relics of this lap full of odds and ends seemed to break, like the spray of an exhausted wave, upon the body of Miss Kilman standing still in the street for a moment to mutter "It is the flesh."

It was the flesh that she must control. Clarissa Dalloway had insulted her. That she expected. But she had not triumphed; she had not mastered the flesh. Ugly, clumsy, Clarissa Dalloway had laughed at her for being that; and had revived the fleshly desires, for she minded looking as she did beside Clarissa. Nor could she talk as she did. But why wish to resemble her? Why? She despised Mrs. Dalloway from the bottom of her heart. She was not serious. She was not good. Her life was a tissue of vanity and deceit. Yet Doris Kilman had been overcome. She had, as a matter of fact, very nearly burst into tears when Clarissa Dalloway laughed at her. "It is the flesh, it is the flesh," she muttered (it being her habit to talk aloud) trying to subdue this turbulent and painful feeling as she walked down Victoria Street. She prayed to God. She could not help being ugly; she could not afford to buy pretty clothes. Clarissa Dalloway had laughed—but she would concentrate her mind upon something else until she had reached the pillar-box.[2] At any rate she had got Elizabeth. But she would think of something else; she would think of Russia; until she reached the pillar-box.

---

2. Mailbox shaped like a pillar.

How nice it must be, she said, in the country, struggling, as Mr. Whittaker had told her, with that violent grudge against the world which had scorned her, sneered at her, cast her off, beginning with this indignity—the infliction of her unlovable body which people could not bear to see. Do her hair as she might, her forehead remained like an egg, bald, white. No clothes suited her. She might buy anything. And for a woman, of course, that meant never meeting the opposite sex. Never would she come first with any one. Sometimes lately it had seemed to her that, except for Elizabeth, her food was all that she lived for; her comforts; her dinner, her tea; her hot-water bottle at night. But one must fight; vanquish; have faith in God. Mr. Whittaker had said she was there for a purpose. But no one knew the agony! He said, pointing to the crucifix, that God knew. But why should she have to suffer when other women, like Clarissa Dalloway, escaped? Knowledge comes through suffering, said Mr. Whittaker.

She had passed the pillar-box, and Elizabeth had turned into the cool brown tobacco department of the Army and Navy Stores while she was still muttering to herself what Mr. Whittaker had said about knowledge coming through suffering and the flesh. "The flesh," she muttered.

What department did she want? Elizabeth interrupted her.

"Petticoats," she said abruptly, and stalked straight on to the lift.

Up they went. Elizabeth guided her this way and that; guided her in her abstraction as if she had been a great child, an unwieldy battleship. There were the petticoats, brown, decorous, striped, frivolous, solid, flimsy; and she chose, in her abstraction, portentously, and the girl serving thought her mad.

Elizabeth rather wondered, as they did up the parcel, what Miss Kilman was thinking. They must have their tea, said Miss Kilman, rousing, collecting herself. They had their tea.

Elizabeth rather wondered whether Miss Kilman could be hungry. It was her way of eating, eating with intensity, then looking, again and again, at a plate of sugared cakes on the table next them; then, when a lady and a child sat down and the child took the cake, could Miss Kilman really mind it? Yes, Miss Kilman did mind it. She had wanted that cake—the pink one. The pleasure of eating was almost the only pure pleasure left her, and then to be baffled even in that!

When people are happy, they have a reserve, she had told Elizabeth, upon which to draw, whereas she was like a wheel without a tyre (she was fond of such metaphors), jolted by every pebble, so she would say staying on after the lesson standing by the fire-place with her bag of books, her "satchel," she called it, on a Tuesday morning, after the lesson was over. And she talked too about the war. After all, there were people who did not think the English invariably right. There were books. There were meetings. There were other points of view. Would Elizabeth like to come with her to listen to So-and-so (a most extraordinary looking old man)? Then Miss Kilman took her to some church in Kensington and they had tea with a clergyman. She had lent her books. Law, medicine, politics, all professions are open to women of your generation, said Miss Kilman. But for herself, her career was absolutely ruined and was it her fault? Good gracious, said Elizabeth, no.

And her mother would come calling to say that a hamper had come from Bourton and would Miss Kilman like some flowers? To Miss Kilman she was always very, very nice, but Miss Kilman squashed the flowers all in a bunch, and hadn't any small talk, and what interested Miss Kilman bored her mother, and Miss Kilman and she were terrible together; and Miss Kilman swelled and looked very plain. But then Miss Kilman was frightfully clever. Elizabeth had never thought about the poor. They lived with everything they wanted,—her mother had breakfast in bed every day; Lucy carried it up; and she liked old women because they were Duchesses, and being descended from some Lord. But Miss Kilman said (one of those Tuesday mornings when the lesson was over), "My grandfather kept an oil and colour shop[3] in Kensington." Miss Kilman made one feel so small.

Miss Kilman took another cup of tea. Elizabeth, with her oriental bearing, her inscrutable mystery, sat perfectly upright; no, she did not want anything more. She looked for her gloves—her white gloves. They were under the table. Ah, but she must not go! Miss Kilman could not let her go! this youth, that was so beautiful, this girl, whom she genuinely loved! Her large hand opened and shut on the table.

But perhaps it was a little flat somehow, Elizabeth felt. And really she would like to go.

But said Miss Kilman, "I've not quite finished yet."

Of course, then, Elizabeth would wait. But it was rather stuffy in here.

"Are you going to the party to-night?" Miss Kilman said. Elizabeth supposed she was going; her mother wanted her to go. She must not let parties absorb her, Miss Kilman said, fingering the last two inches of a chocolate éclair.

She did not much like parties, Elizabeth said. Miss Kilman opened her mouth, slightly projected her chin, and swallowed down the last inches of the chocolate éclair, then wiped her fingers, and washed the tea round in her cup.

She was about to split asunder, she felt. The agony was so terrific. If she could grasp her, if she could clasp her, if she could make her hers absolutely and forever and then die; that was all she wanted. But to sit here, unable to think of anything to say; to see Elizabeth turning against her; to be felt repulsive even by her—it was too much; she could not stand it. The thick fingers curled inwards.

"I never go to parties," said Miss Kilman, just to keep Elizabeth from going. "People don't ask me to parties"—and she knew as she said it that it was this egotism that was her undoing; Mr. Whittaker had warned her; but she could not help it. She had suffered so horribly. "Why should they ask me?" she said. "I'm plain, I'm unhappy." She knew it was idiotic. But it was all those people passing—people with parcels who despised her, who made her say it. However, she was Doris Kilman. She had her degree. She was a woman who had made her way in the world. Her knowledge of modern history was more than respectable.

"I don't pity myself," she said. "I pity"—she meant to say "your mother" but no, she could not, not to Elizabeth. "I pity other people," she said, "more."

Like some dumb creature who has been brought up to a gate for an unknown purpose, and stands there longing to gallop away, Elizabeth Dalloway sat silent. Was Miss Kilman going to say anything more?

"Don't quite forget me," said Doris Kilman; her voice quivered. Right away to the end of the field the dumb creature galloped in terror.

The great hand opened and shut.

Elizabeth turned her head. The waitress came. One had to pay at the desk, Elizabeth said, and went off, drawing out, so Miss Kilman felt, the

3. Store selling oils, paints, and other supplies.

very entrails in her body, stretching them as she crossed the room, and then, with a final twist, bowing her head very politely, she went.

She had gone. Miss Kilman sat at the marble table among the éclairs, stricken once, twice, thrice by shocks of suffering. She had gone. Mrs. Dalloway had triumphed. Elizabeth had gone. Beauty had gone, youth had gone.

So she sat. She got up, blundered off among the little tables, rocking slightly from side to side, and somebody came after her with her petticoat, and she lost her way, and was hemmed in by trunks specially prepared for taking to India; next got among the accouchement[4] sets, and baby linen; through all the commodities of the world, perishable and permanent, hams, drugs, flowers, stationery, variously smelling, now sweet, now sour she lurched; saw herself thus lurching with her hat askew, very red in the face, full length in a looking-glass; and at last came out into the street.

The tower of Westminster Cathedral[5] rose in front of her, the habitation of God. In the midst of the traffic, there was the habitation of God. Doggedly she set off with her parcel to that other sanctuary, the Abbey,[6] where, raising her hands in a tent before her face, she sat beside those driven into shelter too; the variously assorted worshippers, now divested of social rank, almost of sex, as they raised their hands before their faces; but once they removed them, instantly reverent, middle class, English men and women, some of them desirous of seeing the wax works.[7]

But Miss Kilman held her tent before her face. Now she was deserted; now rejoined. New worshippers came in from the street to replace the strollers, and still, as people gazed round and shuffled past the tomb of the Unknown Warrior,[8] still she barred her eyes with her fingers and tried in this double darkness, for the light in the Abbey was bodiless, to aspire above the vanities, the desires, the commodities, to rid herself both of hatred and of love. Her hands twitched. She seemed to struggle. Yet to others God was accessible and the path to Him smooth. Mr. Fletcher, retired, of the Treasury, Mrs. Gorham, widow of the famous K.C.,[9] approached Him simply, and having done their praying, leant back, enjoyed the music (the organ pealed sweetly), and saw Miss Kilman at the end of the row, praying, praying, and, being still on the threshold of their underworld, thought of her sympathetically as a soul haunting the same territory, a soul cut out of immaterial substance; not a woman, a soul.

But Mr. Fletcher had to go. He had to pass her, and being himself neat as a new pin, could not help being a little distressed by the poor lady's disorder; her hair down; her parcel on the floor. She did not at once let him pass. But, as he stood gazing about him, at the white marbles, grey window panes, and accumulated treasures (for he was extremely proud of the Abbey), her largeness, robustness, and power as she sat there shifting her knees from time to time (it was so rough the approach to her God—so tough her desires) impressed him, as they had impressed Mrs. Dalloway (she could not get the thought of her out of her mind that afternoon), the Rev. Edward Whittaker, and Elizabeth too.

And Elizabeth waited in Victoria Street for an omnibus. It was so nice to be out of doors. She thought perhaps she need not go home just yet. It was

4. Childbirth.
5. Roman Catholic cathedral (1903) on Victoria Street, with a high bell tower.
6. Westminster Abbey, Anglican cathedral near Parliament.
7. Effigies of monarchs buried in the Abbey, such as Elizabeth I, located in the Abbey Museum.
8. The Tomb of the Unknown Warrior, in the Abbey's nave, commemorates the dead of World War I; it contains the body of an unidentified soldier, buried there on November 11, 1920.
9. King's Counsel, senior barrister or lawyer.

so nice to be out in the air. So she would get on to an omnibus. And already, even as she stood there, in her very well cut clothes, it was beginning. . . . People were beginning to compare her to poplar trees, early dawn, hyacinths, fawns, running water, and garden lilies, and it made her life a burden to her, for she so much preferred being left alone to do what she liked in the country, but they would compare her to lilies, and she had to go to parties, and London was so dreary compared with being alone in the country with her father and the dogs.

Buses swooped, settled, were off—garish caravans, glistening with red and yellow varnish. But which should she get on to? She had no preferences. Of course, she would not push her way. She inclined to be passive. It was expression she needed, but her eyes were fine, Chinese, oriental, and, as her mother said, with such nice shoulders and holding herself so straight, she was always charming to look at; and lately, in the evening especially, when she was interested, for she never seemed excited, she looked almost beautiful, very stately, very serene. What could she be thinking? Every man fell in love with her, and she was really awfully bored. For it was beginning. Her mother could see that—the compliments were beginning. That she did not care more about it—for instance for her clothes—sometimes worried Clarissa, but perhaps it was as well with all those puppies and guinea pigs about having distemper, and it gave her a charm. And now there was this odd friendship with Miss Kilman. Well, thought Clarissa about three o'clock in the morning, reading Baron Marbot for she could not sleep, it proves she has a heart.

Suddenly Elizabeth stepped forward and most competently boarded the omnibus, in front of everybody. She took a seat on top. The impetuous creature—a pirate—started forward, sprang away; she had to hold the rail to steady herself, for a pirate it was, reckless, unscrupulous, bearing down ruthlessly, circumventing dangerously, boldly snatching a passenger, or ignoring a passenger, squeezing eel-like and arrogant in between, and then rushing insolently all sails spread up Whitehall. And did Elizabeth give one thought to poor Miss Kilman who loved her without jealousy, to whom she had been a fawn in the open, a moon in a glade? She was delighted to be free. The fresh air was so delicious. It had been so stuffy in the Army and Navy Stores. And now it was like riding, to be rushing up Whitehall; and to each movement of the omnibus the beautiful body in the fawn-coloured coat responded freely like a rider, like the figurehead of a ship, for the breeze slightly disarrayed her; the heat gave her cheeks the pallor of white painted wood; and her fine eyes, having no eyes to meet, gazed ahead, blank, bright, with the staring incredible innocence of sculpture.

It was always talking about her own sufferings that made Miss Kilman so difficult. And was she right? If it was being on committees and giving up hours and hours every day (she hardly ever saw him in London) that helped the poor, her father did that, goodness knows,—if that was what Miss Kilman meant about being a Christian; but it was so difficult to say. Oh, she would like to go a little further. Another penny was it to the Strand? Here was another penny then. She would go up the Strand.

She liked people who were ill. And every profession is open to the women of your generation, said Miss Kilman. So she might be a doctor. She might be a farmer. Animals are often ill. She might own a thousand acres and have people under her. She would go and see them in their cottages. This was

Somerset House.[1] One might be a very good farmer—and that, strangely enough though Miss Kilman had her share in it, was almost entirely due to Somerset House. It looked so splendid, so serious, that great grey building. And she liked the feeling of people working. She liked those churches, like shapes of grey paper, breasting the stream of the Strand. It was quite different here from Westminster, she thought, getting off at Chancery Lane.[2] It was so serious; it was so busy. In short, she would like to have a profession. She would become a doctor, a farmer, possibly go into Parliament, if she found it necessary, all because of the Strand.

The feet of those people busy about their activities, hands putting stone to stone, minds eternally occupied not with trivial chatterings (comparing women to poplars—which was rather exciting, of course, but very silly), but with thoughts of ships, of business, of law, of administration, and with it all so stately (she was in the Temple), gay (there was the river), pious (there was the Church[3]), made her quite determined, whatever her mother might say, to become either a farmer or a doctor. But she was, of course, rather lazy.

And it was much better to say nothing about it. It seemed so silly. It was the sort of thing that did sometimes happen, when one was alone—buildings without architects' names, crowds of people coming back from the city having more power than single clergymen in Kensington, than any of the books Miss Kilman had lent her, to stimulate what lay slumbrous, clumsy, and shy on the mind's sandy floor to break surface, as a child suddenly stretches its arms; it was just that, perhaps, a sigh, a stretch of the arms, an impulse, a revelation, which has its effects for ever, and then down again it went to the sandy floor. She must go home. She must dress for dinner. But what was the time?—where was a clock?

She looked up Fleet Street.[4] She walked just a little way towards St. Paul's, shyly, like some one penetrating on tiptoe, exploring a strange house by night with a candle, on edge lest the owner should suddenly fling wide his bedroom door and ask her business, nor did she dare wander off into queer alleys, tempting bye-streets, any more than in a strange house open doors which might be bedroom doors, or sitting-room doors, or lead straight to the larder.[5] For no Dalloways came down the Strand daily; she was a pioneer, a stray, venturing, trusting.

In many ways, her mother felt, she was extremely immature, like a child still, attached to dolls, to old slippers; a perfect baby; and that was charming. But then, of course, there was in the Dalloway family the tradition of public service. Abbesses, principals, head mistresses, dignitaries, in the republic of women—without being brilliant, any of them, they were that. She penetrated a little further in the direction of St. Paul's. She liked the geniality, sisterhood, motherhood, brotherhood of this uproar. It seemed to her good. The noise was tremendous; and suddenly there were trumpets (the unemployed) blaring, rattling about in the uproar, military music; as if people were marching; yet had they been dying—had some woman breathed her last and whoever was watching, opening the window of the room where she had just brought off that act of supreme dignity, looked down on Fleet

---

1. Large 18th-century neoclassical building, between the Strand and the Thames Embankment, housing the national registry for births, marriages, and deaths.
2. A center of the legal profession.

3. The Temple Church, shared by two of the Inns of Court, at the foot of Chancery Lane, between Fleet Street and the Thames.
4. Center of the newspaper industry.
5. Room for storing provisions, especially meat.

Street, that uproar, that military music would have come triumphing up to him, consolatory, indifferent.

It was not conscious. There was no recognition in it of one's fortune, or fate, and for that very reason even to those dazed with watching for the last shivers of consciousness on the faces of the dying, consoling. Forgetfulness in people might wound, their ingratitude corrode, but this voice, pouring endlessly, year in year out, would take whatever it might be; this vow; this van; this life; this procession, would wrap them all about and carry them on, as in the rough stream of a glacier the ice holds a splinter of bone, a blue petal, some oak trees, and rolls them on.

But it was later than she thought. Her mother would not like her to be wandering off alone like this. She turned back down the Strand.

A puff of wind (in spite of the heat, there was quite a wind) blew a thin black veil over the sun and over the Strand. The faces faded; the omnibuses suddenly lost their glow. For although the clouds were of mountainous white so that one could fancy hacking hard chips off with a hatchet, with broad golden slopes, lawns of celestial pleasure gardens, on their flanks, and had all the appearance of settled habitations assembled for the conference of gods above the world, there was a perpetual movement among them. Signs were interchanged, when, as if to fulfil some scheme arranged already, now a summit dwindled, now a whole block of pyramidal size which had kept its station inalterably advanced into the midst or gravely led the procession to fresh anchorage. Fixed though they seemed at their posts, at rest in perfect unanimity, nothing could be fresher, freer, more sensitive superficially than the snow-white or gold-kindled surface; to change, to go, to dismantle the solemn assemblage was immediately possible; and in spite of the grave fixity, the accumulated robustness and solidity, now they struck light to the earth, now darkness.

Calmly and competently, Elizabeth Dalloway mounted the Westminster omnibus.

Going and coming, beckoning, signalling, so the light and shadow which now made the wall grey, now the bananas bright yellow, now made the Strand grey, now made the omnibuses bright yellow, seemed to Septimus Warren Smith lying on the sofa in the sitting-room; watching the watery gold glow and fade with the astonishing sensibility of some live creature on the roses, on the wall-paper. Outside the trees dragged their leaves like nets through the depths of the air; the sound of water was in the room and through the waves came the voices of birds singing. Every power poured its treasures on his head, and his hand lay there on the back of the sofa, as he had seen his hand lie when he was bathing, floating, on the top of the waves, while far away on shore he heard dogs barking and barking far away. Fear no more, says the heart in the body; fear no more.

He was not afraid. At every moment Nature signified by some laughing hint like that gold spot which went round the wall—there, there, there— her determination to show, by brandishing her plumes, shaking her tresses, flinging her mantle this way and that, beautifully, always beautifully, and standing close up to breathe through her hollowed hands Shakespeare's words, her meaning.

Rezia, sitting at the table twisting a hat in her hands, watched him; saw him smiling. He was happy then. But she could not bear to see him smiling. It was not marriage; it was not being one's husband to look strange like that, always to be starting, laughing, sitting hour after hour silent, or clutching her and telling her to write. The table drawer was full of those writings; about war, about Shakespeare; about great discoveries; how there is no death. Lately he had become excited suddenly for no reason (and both Dr. Holmes and Sir William Bradshaw said excitement was the worst thing for him), and waved his hands and cried out that he knew the truth! He knew everything! That man, his friend who was killed, Evans, had come, he said. He was singing behind the screen. She wrote it down just as he spoke it. Some things were very beautiful; others sheer nonsense. And he was always stopping in the middle, changing his mind; wanting to add something; hearing something new; listening with his hand up.

But she heard nothing.

And once they found the girl who did the room reading one of these papers in fits of laughter. It was a dreadful pity. For that made Septimus cry out about human cruelty—how they tear each other to pieces. The fallen, he said, they tear to pieces. "Holmes is on us," he would say, and he would invent stories about Holmes; Holmes eating porridge; Holmes reading Shakespeare—making himself roar with laughter or rage, for Dr. Holmes seemed to stand for something horrible to him. "Human nature," he called him. Then there were the visions. He was drowned, he used to say, and lying on a cliff with the gulls screaming over him. He would look over the edge of the sofa down into the sea. Or he was hearing music. Really it was only a barrel organ or some man crying in the street. But "Lovely!" he used to cry, and the tears would run down his cheeks, which was to her the most dreadful thing of all, to see a man like Septimus, who had fought, who was brave, crying. And he would lie listening until suddenly he would cry that he was falling down, down into the flames! Actually she would look for flames, it was so vivid. But there was nothing. They were alone in the room. It was a dream, she would tell him and so quiet him at last, but sometimes she was frightened too. She sighed as she sat sewing.

Her sigh was tender and enchanting, like the wind outside a wood in the evening. Now she put down her scissors; now she turned to take something from the table. A little stir, a little crinkling, a little tapping built up something on the table there, where she sat sewing. Through his eyelashes he could see her blurred outline; her little black body; her face and hands; her turning movements at the table, as she took up a reel, or looked (she was apt to lose things) for her silk. She was making a hat for Mrs. Filmer's married daughter, whose name was—he had forgotten her name.

"What is the name of Mrs. Filmer's married daughter?" he asked.

"Mrs. Peters," said Rezia. She was afraid it was too small, she said, holding it before her. Mrs. Peters was a big woman; but she did not like her. It was only because Mrs. Filmer had been so good to them. "She gave me grapes this morning," she said—that Rezia wanted to do something to show that they were grateful. She had come into the room the other evening and found Mrs. Peters, who thought they were out, playing the gramophone.

"Was it true?" he asked. She was playing the gramophone? Yes; she had told him about it at the time; she had found Mrs. Peters playing the gramophone.

He began, very cautiously, to open his eyes, to see whether a gramophone was really there. But real things—real things were too exciting. He must be cautious. He would not go mad. First he looked at the fashion papers on the lower shelf, then, gradually at the gramophone with the green trumpet. Nothing could be more exact. And so, gathering courage, he looked at the sideboard; the plate of bananas; the engraving of Queen Victoria and the Prince Consort;[6] at the mantelpiece, with the jar of roses. None of these things moved. All were still; all were real.

"She is a woman with a spiteful tongue," said Rezia.

"What does Mr. Peters do?" Septimus asked.

"Ah," said Rezia, trying to remember. She thought Mrs. Filmer had said that he travelled for some company. "Just now he is in Hull,"[7] she said.

"Just now!" She said that with her Italian accent. She said that herself. He shaded his eyes so that he might see only a little of her face at a time, first the chin, then the nose, then the forehead, in case it were deformed, or had some terrible mark on it. But no, there she was, perfectly natural, sewing, with the pursed lips that women have, the set, the melancholy expression, when sewing. But there was nothing terrible about it, he assured himself, looking a second time, a third time at her face, her hands, for what was frightening or disgusting in her as she sat there in broad daylight, sewing? Mrs. Peters had a spiteful tongue. Mr. Peters was in Hull. Why then rage and prophesy? Why fly scourged and outcast? Why be made to tremble and sob by the clouds? Why seek truths and deliver messages when Rezia sat sticking pins into the front of her dress, and Mr. Peters was in Hull? Miracles, revelations, agonies, loneliness, falling through the sea, down, down into the flames, all were burnt out, for he had a sense, as he watched Rezia trimming the straw hat for Mrs. Peters, of a coverlet of flowers.

"It's too small for Mrs. Peters," said Septimus.

For the first time for days he was speaking as he used to do! Of course it was—absurdly small, she said. But Mrs. Peters had chosen it.

He took it out of her hands. He said it was an organ grinder's monkey's hat.

How it rejoiced her that! Not for weeks had they laughed like this together, poking fun privately like married people. What she meant was that if Mrs. Filmer had come in, or Mrs. Peters or anybody they would not have understood what she and Septimus were laughing at.

"There," she said, pinning a rose to one side of the hat. Never had she felt so happy! Never in her life!

But that was still more ridiculous, Septimus said. Now the poor woman looked like a pig at a fair. (Nobody ever made her laugh as Septimus did.)

What had she got in her work-box? She had ribbons and beads, tassels, artificial flowers. She tumbled them out on the table. He began putting odd colours together—for though he had no fingers, could not even do up a parcel, he had a wonderful eye, and often he was right, sometimes absurd, of course, but sometimes wonderfully right.

"She shall have a beautiful hat!" he murmured, taking up this and that, Rezia kneeling by his side, looking over his shoulder. Now it was finished— that is to say the design; she must stitch it together. But she must be very, very careful, he said, to keep it just as he had made it.

So she sewed. When she sewed, he thought, she made a sound like a kettle on the hob;[8] bubbling, murmuring, always busy, her strong little pointed

---

6. Prince Albert of Saxe-Coburg-Gotha (1819–1861), husband of Queen Victoria.

7. Port city on the river Hull, near the North Sea.
8. Shelf at the back or side of the fireplace.

fingers pinching and poking; her needle flashing straight. The sun might go in and out, on the tassels, on the wallpaper, but he would wait, he thought, stretching out his feet, looking at his ringed sock at the end of the sofa; he would wait in this warm place, this pocket of still air, which one comes on at the edge of a wood sometimes in the evening, when, because of a fall in the ground, or some arrangement of the trees (one must be scientific above all, scientific), warmth lingers, and the air buffets the cheek like the wing of a bird.

"There it is," said Rezia, twirling Mrs. Peters' hat on the tips of her fingers. "That'll do for the moment. Later . . ." her sentence bubbled away drip, drip, drip, like a contented tap left running.

It was wonderful. Never had he done anything which made him feel so proud. It was so real, it was so substantial, Mrs. Peters' hat.

"Just look at it," he said.

Yes, it would always make her happy to see that hat. He had become himself then, he had laughed then. They had been alone together. Always she would like that hat.

He told her to try it on.

"But I must look so queer!" she cried, running over to the glass and looking first this side then that. Then she snatched it off again, for there was a tap at the door. Could it be Sir William Bradshaw? Had he sent already?

No! it was only the small girl with the evening paper.

What always happened, then happened—what happened every night of their lives. The small girl sucked her thumb at the door; Rezia went down on her knees; Rezia cooed and kissed; Rezia got a bag of sweets out of the table drawer. For so it always happened. First one thing, then another. So she built it up, first one thing and then another. Dancing, skipping, round and round the room they went. He took the paper. Surrey was all out,[9] he read. There was a heat wave. Rezia repeated: Surrey was all out. There was a heat wave, making it part of the game she was playing with Mrs. Filmer's grandchild, both of them laughing, chattering at the same time, at their game. He was very tired. He was very happy. He would sleep. He shut his eyes. But directly he saw nothing the sounds of the game became fainter and stranger and sounded like the cries of people seeking and not finding, and passing further and further away. They had lost him!

He started up in terror. What did he see? The plate of bananas on the sideboard. Nobody was there (Rezia had taken the child to its mother. It was bedtime). That was it: to be alone forever. That was the doom pronounced in Milan when he came into the room and saw them cutting out buckram shapes with their scissors; to be alone forever.

He was alone with the sideboard and the bananas. He was alone, exposed on this bleak eminence, stretched out—but not on a hill-top; not on a crag; on Mrs. Filmer's sitting-room sofa. As for the visions, the faces, the voices of the dead, where were they? There was a screen in front of him, with black bulrushes and blue swallows. Where he had once seen mountains, where he had seen faces, where he had seen beauty, there was a screen.

"Evans!" he cried. There was no answer. A mouse had squeaked, or a curtain rustled. Those were the voices of the dead. The screen, the coal-scuttle,

9. Headline indicating that the Surrey cricket team has ended its first innings in a match.

the sideboard remained to him. Let him then face the screen, the coal-scuttle and the sideboard . . . but Rezia burst into the room chattering.

Some letter had come. Everybody's plans were changed. Mrs. Filmer would not be able to go to Brighton[1] after all. There was no time to let Mrs. Williams know, and really Rezia thought it very, very annoying, when she caught sight of the hat and thought . . . perhaps . . . she . . . might just make a little. . . . Her voice died out in contented melody.

"Ah, damn!" she cried (it was a joke of theirs, her swearing), the needle had broken. Hat, child, Brighton, needle. She built it up; first one thing, then another, she built it up, sewing.

She wanted him to say whether by moving the rose she had improved the hat. She sat on the end of the sofa.

They were perfectly happy now, she said, suddenly, putting the hat down. For she could say anything to him now. She could say whatever came into her head. That was almost the first thing she had felt about him, that night in the café when he had come in with his English friends. He had come in, rather shyly, looking round him, and his hat had fallen when he hung it up. That she could remember: She knew he was English, though not one of the large Englishmen her sister admired, for he was always thin; but he had a beautiful fresh colour; and with his big nose, his bright eyes, his way of sitting a little hunched made her think, she had often told him, of a young hawk, that first evening she saw him, when they were playing dominoes, and he had come in—of a young hawk; but with her he was always very gentle. She had never seen him wild or drunk, only suffering sometimes through this terrible war, but even so, when she came in, he would put it all away. Anything, anything in the whole world, any little bother with her work, anything that struck her to say she would tell him, and he understood at once. Her own family even were not the same. Being older than she was and being so clever—how serious he was, wanting her to read Shakespeare before she could even read a child's story in English!—being so much more experienced, he could help her. And she too could help him.

But this hat now. And then (it was getting late) Sir William Bradshaw.

She held her hands to her head, waiting for him to say did he like the hat or not, and as she sat there, waiting, looking down, he could feel her mind, like a bird, falling from branch to branch, and always alighting, quite rightly; he could follow her mind, as she sat there in one of those loose lax poses that came to her naturally and, if he should say anything, at once she smiled, like a bird alighting with all its claws firm upon the bough.

But he remembered Bradshaw said, "The people we are most fond of are not good for us when we are ill." Bradshaw said, he must be taught to rest. Bradshaw said they must be separated.

"Must," "must," why "must"? What power had Bradshaw over him? "What right has Bradshaw to say 'must' to me?" he demanded.

"It is because you talked of killing yourself," said Rezia. (Mercifully, she could now say anything to Septimus.)

So he was in their power! Holmes and Bradshaw were on him! The brute with the red nostrils was snuffing into every secret place! "Must" it could say! Where were his papers? the things he had written?

---

1. Popular seaside resort town in Sussex, on England's south coast.

She brought him his papers, the things he had written, things she had written for him. She tumbled them out on to the sofa. They looked at them together. Diagrams, designs, little men and women brandishing sticks for arms, with wings—were they?—on their backs; circles traced round shillings and sixpences—the suns and stars; zigzagging precipices with mountaineers ascending roped together, exactly like knives and forks; sea pieces with little faces laughing out of what might perhaps be waves: the map of the world. Burn them! he cried. Now for his writings; how the dead sing behind rhododendron bushes; odes to Time; conversations with Shakespeare; Evans, Evans, Evans—his messages from the dead; do not cut down trees; tell the Prime Minister. Universal love: the meaning of the world. Burn them! he cried.

But Rezia laid her hands on them. Some were very beautiful, she thought. She would tie them up (for she had no envelope) with a piece of silk.

Even if they took him, she said, she would go with him. They could not separate them against their wills, she said.

Shuffling the edges straight, she did up the papers, and tied the parcel almost without looking, sitting beside him, he thought, as if all her petals were about her. She was a flowering tree; and through her branches looked out the face of a lawgiver, who had reached a sanctuary where she feared no one; not Holmes; not Bradshaw; a miracle, a triumph, the last and greatest. Staggering he saw her mount the appalling staircase, laden with Holmes and Bradshaw, men who never weighed less than eleven stone six, who sent their wives to Court, men who made ten thousand a year and talked of proportion; who different in their verdicts (for Holmes said one thing, Bradshaw another), yet judges they were; who mixed the vision and the sideboard; saw nothing clear, yet ruled, yet inflicted. "Must" they said. Over them she triumphed.

"There!" she said. The papers were tied up. No one should get at them. She would put them away.

And, she said, nothing should separate them. She sat down beside him and called him by the name of that hawk or crow which being malicious and a great destroyer of crops was precisely like him. No one could separate them, she said.

Then she got up to go into the bedroom to pack their things, but hearing voices downstairs and thinking that Dr. Holmes had perhaps called, ran down to prevent him coming up.

Septimus could hear her talking to Holmes on the staircase.

"My dear lady, I have come as a friend," Holmes was saying.

"No. I will not allow you to see my husband," she said.

He could see her, like a little hen, with her wings spread barring his passage. But Holmes persevered.

"My dear lady, allow me . . ." Holmes said, putting her aside (Holmes was a powerfully built man).

Holmes was coming upstairs. Holmes would burst open the door. Holmes would say "In a funk, eh?" Holmes would get him. But no; not Holmes; not Bradshaw. Getting up rather unsteadily, hopping indeed from foot to foot, he considered Mrs. Filmer's nice clean bread knife with "Bread" carved on the handle. Ah, but one mustn't spoil that. The gas fire? But it was too late now. Holmes was coming. Razors he might have got, but Rezia, who always did that sort of thing, had packed them. There remained only the window,

the large Bloomsbury-lodging house window, the tiresome, the troublesome, and rather melodramatic business of opening the window and throwing himself out. It was their idea of tragedy, not his or Rezia's (for she was
with him). Holmes and Bradshaw like that sort of thing. (He sat on the sill.)
But he would wait till the very last moment. He did not want to die. Life
was good. The sun hot. Only human beings—what did *they* want? Coming
down the staircase opposite an old man stopped and stared at him. Holmes
was at the door. "I'll give it you!" he cried, and flung himself vigorously,
violently down on to Mrs. Filmer's area railings.

"The coward!" cried Dr. Holmes, bursting the door open. Rezia ran to the
window, she saw; she understood. Dr. Holmes and Mrs. Filmer collided
with each other. Mrs. Filmer flapped her apron and made her hide her eyes
in the bedroom. There was a great deal of running up and down stairs. Dr.
Holmes came in—white as a sheet, shaking all over, with a glass in his
hand. She must be brave and drink something, he said (What was it? Something sweet), for her husband was horribly mangled, would not recover consciousness, she must not see him, must be spared as much as possible,
would have the inquest to go through, poor young woman. Who could have
foretold it? A sudden impulse, no one was in the least to blame (he told
Mrs. Filmer). And why the devil he did it, Dr. Holmes could not conceive.

It seemed to her as she drank the sweet stuff that she was opening long
windows, stepping out into some garden. But where? The clock was striking—
one, two, three: how sensible the sound was; compared with all this thumping and whispering; like Septimus himself. She was falling asleep. But the
clock went on striking, four, five, six and Mrs. Filmer waving her apron (they
wouldn't bring the body in here, would they?) seemed part of that garden; or
a flag. She had once seen a flag slowly rippling out from a mast when she
stayed with her aunt at Venice. Men killed in battle were thus saluted, and
Septimus had been through the War. Of her memories, most were happy.

She put on her hat, and ran through cornfields—where could it have
been?—on to some hill, somewhere near the sea, for there were ships, gulls,
butterflies, they sat on a cliff. In London too, there they sat, and, half
dreaming, came to her through the bedroom door, rain falling, whisper-
ings, stirrings among dry corn, the caress of the sea, as it seemed to her,
hollowing them in its arched shell and murmuring to her laid on shore,
strewn she felt, like flying flowers over some tomb.

"He is dead," she said, smiling at the poor old woman who guarded her
with her honest light-blue eyes fixed on the door. (They wouldn't bring him in
here, would they?) But Mrs. Filmer pooh-poohed. Oh no, oh no! They were
carrying him away now. Ought she not to be told? Married people ought to be
together, Mrs. Filmer thought. But they must do as the doctor said.

"Let her sleep," said Dr. Holmes, feeling her pulse. She saw the large outline of his body standing dark against the window. So that was Dr. Holmes.

One of the triumphs of civilisation, Peter Walsh thought. It is one of the triumphs of civilisation, as the light high bell of the ambulance sounded.
Swiftly, cleanly the ambulance sped to the hospital, having picked up
instantly, humanely, some poor devil; some one hit on the head, struck down
by disease, knocked over perhaps a minute or so ago at one of these crossings,
as might happen to oneself. That was civilisation. It struck him coming
back from the East—the efficiency, the organisation, the communal spirit

of London. Every cart or carriage of its own accord drew aside to let the ambulance pass. Perhaps it was morbid; or was it not touching rather, the respect which they showed this ambulance with its victim inside—busy men hurrying home yet instantly bethinking them as it passed of some wife; or presumably how easily it might have been them there, stretched on a shelf with a doctor and a nurse. . . . Ah, but thinking became morbid, sentimental, directly one began conjuring up doctors, dead bodies; a little glow of pleasure, a sort of lust too over the visual impression warned one not to go on with that sort of thing any more—fatal to art, fatal to friendship. True. And yet, thought Peter Walsh, as the ambulance turned the corner though the light high bell could be heard down the next street and still farther as it crossed the Tottenham Court Road, chiming constantly, it is the privilege of loneliness; in privacy one may do as one chooses. One might weep if no one saw. It had been his undoing—this susceptibility—in Anglo-Indian society; not weeping at the right time, or laughing either. I have that in me, he thought standing by the pillar-box, which could now dissolve in tears. Why, Heaven knows. Beauty of some sort probably, and the weight of the day, which beginning with that visit to Clarissa had exhausted him with its heat, its intensity, and the drip, drip, of one impression after another down into that cellar where they stood, deep, dark, and no one would ever know. Partly for that reason, its secrecy, complete and inviolable, he had found life like an unknown garden, full of turns and corners, surprising, yes; really it took one's breath away, these moments; there coming to him by the pillar-box opposite the British Museum[2] one of them, a moment, in which things came together; this ambulance; and life and death. It was as if he were sucked up to some very high roof by that rush of emotion and the rest of him, like a white shell-sprinkled beach, left bare. It had been his undoing in Anglo-Indian society—this susceptibility.

Clarissa once, going on top of an omnibus with him somewhere, Clarissa superficially at least, so easily moved, now in despair, now in the best of spirits, all aquiver in those days and such good company, spotting queer little scenes, names, people from the top of a bus, for they used to explore London and bring back bags full of treasures from the Caledonian market[3]— Clarissa had a theory in those days—they had heaps of theories, always theories, as young people have. It was to explain the feeling they had of dissatisfaction; not knowing people; not being known. For how could they know each other? You met every day, then not for six months, or years. It was unsatisfactory, they agreed, how little one knew people. But she said, sitting on the bus going up Shaftesbury Avenue, she felt herself everywhere; not "here, here, here"; and she tapped the back of the seat; but everywhere. She waved her hand, going up Shaftesbury Avenue.[4] She was all that. So that to know her, or any one, one must seek out the people who completed them; even the places. Odd affinities she had with people she had never spoken to, some woman in the street, some man behind a counter—even trees, or barns. It ended in a transcendental theory which, with her horror of death, allowed her to believe, or say that she believed (for all her scepticism), that since our apparitions, the part of us which appears, are so momentary compared with

---

2. National museum in Bloomsbury.
3. Street market held on Fridays in north London.

4. Road through the theater district, running northeast from Piccadilly Circus to Covent Garden.

the other, the unseen part of us, which spreads wide, the unseen might survive, be recovered somehow attached to this person or that, or even haunting certain places after death . . . perhaps—perhaps.

Looking back over that long friendship of almost thirty years her theory worked to this extent. Brief, broken, often painful as their actual meetings had been what with his absences and interruptions (this morning, for instance, in came Elizabeth, like a long-legged colt, handsome, dumb, just as he was beginning to talk to Clarissa) the effect of them on his life was immeasurable. There was a mystery about it. You were given a sharp, acute, uncomfortable grain—the actual meeting; horribly painful as often as not; yet in absence, in the most unlikely places, it would flower out, open, shed its scent, let you touch, taste, look about you, get the whole feel of it and understanding, after years of lying lost. Thus she had come to him; on board ship; in the Himalayas; suggested by the oddest things (so Sally Seton, generous, enthusiastic goose! thought of *him* when she saw blue hydrangeas). She had influenced him more than any person he had ever known. And always in this way coming before him without his wishing it, cool, lady-like, critical; or ravishing, romantic, recalling some field or English harvest. He saw her most often in the country, not in London. One scene after another at Bourton. . . .

He had reached his hotel. He crossed the hall, with its mounds of reddish chairs and sofas, its spike-leaved, withered-looking plants. He got his key off the hook. The young lady handed him some letters. He went upstairs—he saw her most often at Bourton, in the late summer, when he stayed there for a week, or fortnight even, as people did in those days. First on top of some hill there she would stand, hands clapped to her hair, her cloak blowing out, pointing, crying to them—she saw the Severn[5] beneath. Or in a wood, making the kettle boil—very ineffective with her fingers; the smoke curtseying, blowing in their faces; her little pink face showing through; begging water from an old woman in a cottage, who came to the door to watch them go. They walked always; the others drove. She was bored driving, disliked all animals, except that dog. They tramped miles along roads. She would break off to get her bearings, pilot him back across country; and all the time they argued, discussed poetry, discussed people, discussed politics (she was a Radical then); never noticing a thing except when she stopped, cried out at a view or a tree, and made him look with her; and so on again, through stubble fields, she walking ahead, with a flower for her aunt, never tired of walking for all her delicacy; to drop down on Bourton in the dusk. Then, after dinner, old Breitkopf would open the piano and sing without any voice, and they would lie sunk in arm-chairs, trying not to laugh, but always breaking down and laughing, laughing—laughing at nothing. Breitkopf was supposed not to see. And then in the morning, flirting up and down like a wagtail[6] in front of the house. . . .

Oh it was a letter from her! This blue envelope; that was her hand. And he would have to read it. Here was another of those meetings, bound to be painful! To read her letter needed the devil of an effort. "How heavenly it was to see him. She must tell him that." That was all.

---

5. The river Severn, in Gloucestershire.
6. Small bird with a characteristic tail-wagging motion.

But it upset him. It annoyed him. He wished she hadn't written it. Coming on top of his thoughts, it was like a nudge in the ribs. Why couldn't she let him be? After all, she had married Dalloway, and lived with him in perfect happiness all these years.

These hotels are not consoling places. Far from it. Any number of people had hung up their hats on those pegs. Even the flies, if you thought of it, had settled on other people's noses. As for the cleanliness which hit him in the face, it wasn't cleanliness, so much as bareness, frigidity; a thing that had to be. Some arid matron made her rounds at dawn sniffing, peering, causing blue-nosed[7] maids to scour, for all the world as if the next visitor were a joint of meat to be served on a perfectly clean platter. For sleep, one bed; for sitting in, one arm-chair; for cleaning one's teeth and shaving one's chin, one tumbler, one looking-glass. Books, letters, dressing-gown, slipped about on the impersonality of the horsehair like incongruous impertinences. And it was Clarissa's letter that made him see all this. "Heavenly to see you. She must say so!" He folded the paper; pushed it away; nothing would induce him to read it again!

To get that letter[8] to him by six o'clock she must have sat down and written it directly he left her; stamped it; sent somebody to the post. It was, as people say, very like her. She was upset by his visit. She had felt a great deal; had for a moment, when she kissed his hand, regretted, envied him even, remembered possibly (for he saw her look it) something he had said—how they would change the world if she married him perhaps; whereas, it was this; it was middle age; it was mediocrity; then forced herself with her indomitable vitality to put all that aside, there being in her a thread of life which for toughness, endurance, power to overcome obstacles, and carry her triumphantly through he had never known the like of. Yes; but there would come a reaction directly he left the room. She would be frightfully sorry for him; she would think what in the world she could do to give him pleasure (short always of the one thing) and he could see her with the tears running down her cheeks going to her writing-table and dashing off that one line which he was to find greeting him. . . . "Heavenly to see you!" And she meant it.

Peter Walsh had now unlaced his boots.

But it would not have been a success, their marriage. The other thing, after all, came so much more naturally.

It was odd; it was true; lots of people felt it. Peter Walsh, who had done just respectably, filled the usual posts adequately, was liked, but thought a little cranky, gave himself airs—it was odd that *he* should have had, especially now that his hair was grey, a contented look; a look of having reserves. It was this that made him attractive to women who liked the sense that he was not altogether manly. There was something unusual about him, or something behind him. It might be that he was bookish—never came to see you without taking up the book on the table (he was now reading, with his bootlaces trailing on the floor); or that he was a gentleman, which showed itself in the way he knocked the ashes out of his pipe, and in his manners of course to women. For it was very charming and quite ridiculous how easily some girl without a grain of sense could twist him round her finger. But at her own risk. That is to say, though he might be ever so easy, and indeed

7. Puritanical or prudish.
8. Multiple daily mail deliveries in the 1920s ensure that Clarissa could write a letter and Peter could receive it on the same day.

with his gaiety and good-breeding fascinating to be with, it was only up to a point. She said something—no, no; he saw through that. He wouldn't stand that—no, no. Then he could shout and rock and hold his sides together over some joke with men. He was the best judge of cooking in India. He was a man. But not the sort of man one had to respect—which was a mercy; not like Major Simmons, for instance; not in the least like that, Daisy thought, when, in spite of her two small children, she used to compare them.

He pulled off his boots. He emptied his pockets. Out came with his pocket-knife a snapshot of Daisy on the verandah; Daisy all in white, with a fox-terrier on her knee; very charming, very dark; the best he had ever seen of her. It did come, after all so naturally; so much more naturally than Clarissa. No fuss. No bother. No finicking and fidgeting. All plain sailing. And the dark, adorably pretty girl on the verandah exclaimed (he could hear her). Of course, of course she would give him everything! she cried (she had no sense of discretion) everything he wanted! she cried, running to meet him, whoever might be looking. And she was only twenty-four. And she had two children. Well, well!

Well indeed he had got himself into a mess at his age. And it came over him when he woke in the night pretty forcibly. Suppose they did marry? For him it would be all very well, but what about her? Mrs. Burgess, a good sort and no chatterbox, in whom he had confided, thought this absence of his in England, ostensibly to see lawyers might serve to make Daisy reconsider, think what it meant. It was a question of her position, Mrs. Burgess said; the social barrier; giving up her children. She'd be a widow with a past one of these days, draggling about in the suburbs, or more likely, indiscriminate (you know, she said, what such women get like, with too much paint). But Peter Walsh pooh-poohed all that. He didn't mean to die yet. Anyhow she must settle for herself; judge for herself, he thought, padding about the room in his socks, smoothing out his dress-shirt, for he might go to Clarissa's party, or he might go to one of the Halls, or he might settle in and read an absorbing book written by a man he used to know at Oxford. And if he did retire, that's what he'd do—write books. He would go to Oxford and poke about in the Bodleian.[9] Vainly the dark, adorably pretty girl ran to the end of the terrace; vainly waved her hand; vainly cried she didn't care a straw what people said. There he was, the man she thought the world of, the perfect gentleman, the fascinating, the distinguished (and his age made not the least difference to her), padding about a room in an hotel in Blooms-bury, shaving, washing, continuing, as he took up cans, put down razors, to poke about in the Bodleian, and get at the truth about one or two little matters that interested him. And he would have a chat with whoever it might be, and so come to disregard more and more precise hours for lunch, and miss engagements, and when Daisy asked him, as she would, for a kiss, a scene, fail to come up to the scratch[1] (though he was genuinely devoted to her)—in short it might be happier, as Mrs. Burgess said, that she should forget him, or merely remember him as he was in August 1922, like a figure standing at the cross roads at dusk, which grows more and more remote as the dog-cart[2] spins away, carrying her securely fastened to the back seat, though her arms are outstretched, and as she sees the figure dwindle and

9. Main library at Oxford University.
1. I.e., to meet the required standard.
2. An open carriage with two back-to-back seats, one facing forward for the driver and another facing towards the rear for the passenger.

disappear still she cries out how she would do anything in the world, any-thing, anything, anything. . . .

He never knew what people thought. It became more and more difficult for him to concentrate. He become absorbed; he became busied with his own concerns; now surly, now gay; dependent on women, absent-minded, moody, less and less able (so he thought as he shaved) to understand why Clarissa couldn't simply find them a lodging and be nice to Daisy; introduce her. And then he could just—just do what? just haunt and hover (he was at the moment actually engaged in sorting out various keys, papers), swoop and taste, be alone, in short, sufficient to himself; and yet nobody of course was more dependent upon others (he buttoned his waistcoat); it had been his undoing. He could not keep out of smoking-rooms, liked colonels, liked golf, liked bridge, and above all women's society, and the fineness of their companionship, and their faithfulness and audacity and greatness in loving which though it had its drawbacks seemed to him (and the dark, adorably pretty face was on top of the envelopes) so wholly admirable, so splendid a flower to grow on the crest of human life, and yet he could not come up to the scratch, being always apt to see round things (Clarissa had sapped something in him permanently), and to tire very easily of mute devotion and to want variety in love, though it would make him furious if Daisy loved anybody else, furious! for he was jealous, uncontrollably jealous by tem-perament. He suffered tortures! But where was his knife; his watch; his seals, his notecase, and Clarissa's letter which he would not read again but liked to think of, and Daisy's photograph? And now for dinner.

They were eating.

Sitting at little tables round vases, dressed or not dressed, with their shawls and bags laid beside them, with their air of false composure, for they were not used to so many courses at dinner, and confidence, for they were able to pay for it, and strain, for they had been running about London all day shopping, sightseeing; and their natural curiosity, for they looked round and up as the nice-looking gentleman in horn-rimmed spectacles came in, and their good nature, for they would have been glad to do any little service, such as lend a time-table or impart useful information, and their desire, pulsing in them, tugging at them subterraneously, somehow to establish connections if it were only a birthplace (Liverpool,[3] for example) in common or friends of the same name; with their furtive glances, odd silences, and sudden withdrawals into family jocularity and isolation; there they sat eating dinner when Mr. Walsh came in and took his seat at a little table by the curtain.

It was not that he said anything, for being solitary he could only address himself to the waiter; it was his way of looking at the menu, of pointing his forefinger to a particular wine, of hitching himself up to the table, of addressing himself seriously, not gluttonously to dinner, that won him their respect; which, having to remain unexpressed for the greater part of the meal, flared up at the table where the Morrises sat when Mr. Walsh was heard to say at the end of the meal, "Bartlett pears." Why he should have spoken so moderately yet firmly, with the air of a disciplinarian well within his rights which are founded upon justice, neither young Charles Morris, nor old Charles, neither Miss Elaine nor Mrs. Morris knew. But when he said, "Bartlett pears," sitting alone at his table, they felt that he counted on

3. Major port city in northwest England, on the Irish Sea.

their support in some lawful demand; was champion of a cause which immediately became their own, so that their eyes met his eyes sympathetically, and when they all reached the smoking-room simultaneously, a little talk between them became inevitable.

It was not very profound—only to the effect that London was crowded; had changed in thirty years; that Mr. Morris preferred Liverpool; that Mrs. Morris had been to the Westminster flower-show, and that they had all seen the Prince of Wales. Yet, thought Peter Walsh, no family in the world can compare with the Morrises; none whatever; and their relations to each other are perfect, and they don't care a hang for the upper classes, and they like what they like, and Elaine is training for the family business, and the boy has won a scholarship at Leeds, and the old lady (who is about his own age) has three more children at home; and they have two motor cars, but Mr. Morris still mends the boots on Sunday: it is superb, it is absolutely superb, thought Peter Walsh, swaying a little backwards and forwards with his liqueur glass in his hand among the hairy red chairs and ashtrays, feeling very well pleased with himself, for the Morrises liked him. Yes, they liked a man who said, "Bartlett pears." They liked him, he felt.

He would go to Clarissa's party. (The Morrises moved off; but they would meet again.) He would go to Clarissa's party, because he wanted to ask Richard what they were doing in India—the conservative duffers.[4] And what's being acted? And music. . . . Oh yes, and mere gossip.

For this is the truth about our soul, he thought, our self, who fish-like inhabits deep seas and plies among obscurities threading her way between the boles of giant weeds, over sun-flickered spaces and on and on into gloom, cold, deep, inscrutable; suddenly she shoots to the surface and sports on the wind-wrinkled waves; that is, has a positive need to brush, scrape, kindle herself, gossiping. What did the Government mean—Richard Dalloway would know—to do about India?

Since it was a very hot night and the paper boys went by with placards proclaiming in huge red letters that there was a heat-wave, wicker chairs were placed on the hotel steps and there, sipping, smoking, detached gentlemen sat. Peter Walsh sat there. One might fancy that day, the London day, was just beginning. Like a woman who had slipped off her print dress and white apron to array herself in blue and pearls, the day changed, put off stuff, took gauze, changed to evening, and with the same sigh of exhilaration that a woman breathes, tumbling petticoats on the floor, it too shed dust, heat, colour; the traffic thinned; motor cars, tinkling, darting, succeeded the lumber of vans; and here and there among the thick foliage of the squares an intense light hung. I resign, the evening seemed to say, as it paled and faded above the battlements and prominences, moulded, pointed, of hotel, flat, and block of shops, I fade, she was beginning, I disappear, but London would have none of it, and rushed her bayonets into the sky, pinioned her, constrained her to partnership in her revelry.

For the great revolution of Mr. Willett's summer time had taken place since Peter Walsh's last visit to England. The prolonged evening was new to him. It was inspiriting, rather. For as the young people went by with their despatch-boxes,[5] awfully glad to be free, proud too, dumbly, of stepping this

4. Incompetent people, fools.
5. Boxes for carrying important messages requiring quick delivery.

famous pavement, joy of a kind, cheap, tinselly, if you like, but all the same rapture, flushed their faces. They dressed well too; pink stockings; pretty shoes. They would now have two hours at the pictures. It sharpened, it refined them, the yellow-blue evening light; and on the leaves in the square shone lurid, livid—they looked as if dipped in sea water—the foliage of a submerged city. He was astonished by the beauty; it was encouraging too, for where the returned Anglo-Indian sat by rights (he knew crowds of them) in the Oriental Club[6] biliously summing up the ruin of the world, here was he, as young as ever; envying young people their summer time[7] and the rest of it, and more than suspecting from the words of a girl, from a housemaid's laughter—intangible things you couldn't lay your hands on—that shift in the whole pyramidal accumulation which in his youth had seemed immovable. On top of them it had pressed; weighed them down, the women especially, like those flowers Clarissa's Aunt Helena used to press between sheets of grey blotting-paper with Littré's dictionary[8] on top, sitting under the lamp after dinner. She was dead now. He had heard of her, from Clarissa, losing the sight of one eye. It seemed so fitting—one of nature's masterpieces—that old Miss Parry should turn to glass. She would die like some bird in a frost gripping her perch. She belonged to a different age, but being so entire, so complete, would always stand up on the horizon, stone-white, eminent, like a lighthouse marking some past stage on this adventurous, long, long voyage, this interminable (he felt for a copper[9] to buy a paper and read about Surrey and Yorkshire—he had held out that copper millions of times. Surrey was all out once more)—this interminable life. But cricket was no mere game. Cricket was important. He could never help reading about cricket. He read the scores in the stop press first, then how it was a hot day; then about a murder case. Having done things millions of times enriched them, though it might be said to take the surface off. The past enriched, and experience, and having cared for one or two people, and so having acquired the power which the young lack, of cutting short, doing what one likes, not caring a rap what people say and coming and going without any very great expectations (he left his paper on the table and moved off), which however (and he looked for his hat and coat) was not altogether true of him, not to-night, for here he was starting to go to a party, at his age, with the belief upon him that he was about to have an experience. But what?

Beauty anyhow. Not the crude beauty of the eye. It was not beauty pure and simple—Bedford Place leading into Russell Square.[1] It was straightness and emptiness of course; the symmetry of a corridor; but it was also windows lit up, a piano, a gramophone sounding; a sense of pleasure-making hidden, but now and again emerging when, through the uncurtained window, the window left open, one saw parties sitting over tables, young people slowly circling, conversations between men and women, maids idly looking out (a strange comment theirs, when work was done), stockings drying on top ledges, a parrot, a few plants. Absorbing, mysterious, of infinite richness, this life. And in the large square where the cabs shot and swerved so quick, there were loitering couples, dallying, embracing, shrunk up under the shower of a tree; that was moving; so silent, so absorbed, that one passed, discreetly,

6. Gentlemen's club for members of the East India Company.
7. Daylight Savings Time, introduced in Britain in 1916.

8. Four-volume French dictionary by Émile Littré (1801–1881).
9. Penny or halfpenny.
1. In Bloomsbury.

timidly, as if in the presence of some sacred ceremony to interrupt which would have been impious. That was interesting. And so on into the flare and glare.

His light overcoat blew open, he stepped with indescribable idiosyncrasy, leant a little forward, tripped, with his hands behind his back and his eyes still a little hawklike; he tripped through London, towards Westminster, observing.

Was everybody dining out, then? Doors were being opened here by a footman to let issue a high-stepping old dame, in buckled shoes, with three purple ostrich feathers in her hair. Doors were being opened for ladies wrapped like mummies in shawls with bright flowers on them, ladies with bare heads. And in respectable quarters with stucco pillars through small front gardens lightly swathed with combs in their hair (having run up to see the children), women came; men waited for them, with their coats blowing open, and the motor started. Everybody was going out. What with these doors being opened, and the descent and the start, it seemed as if the whole of London were embarking in little boats moored to the bank, tossing on the waters, as if the whole place were floating off in carnival. And Whitehall was skated over, silver beaten as it was, skated over by spiders, and there was a sense of midges[2] round the arc lamps; it was so hot that people stood about talking. And here in Westminster was a retired Judge, presumably, sitting four square at his house door dressed all in white. An Anglo-Indian presumably.

And here a shindy[3] of brawling women, drunken women; here only a policeman and looming houses, high houses, domed houses, churches, parliaments, and the hoot of a steamer on the river, a hollow misty cry. But it was her street, this, Clarissa's; cabs were rushing round the corner, like water round the piers of a bridge, drawn together, it seemed to him because they bore people going to her party, Clarissa's party.

The cold stream of visual impressions failed him now as if the eye were a cup that overflowed and let the rest run down its china walls unrecorded. The brain must wake now. The body must contract now, entering the house, the lighted house, where the door stood open, where the motor cars were standing, and bright women descending: the soul must brave itself to endure. He opened the big blade of his pocket-knife.

Lucy came running full tilt downstairs, having just nipped in to the drawing-room to smooth a cover, to straighten a chair, to pause a moment and feel whoever came in must think how clean, how bright, how beautifully cared for, when they saw the beautiful silver, the brass fire-irons, the new chair-covers, and the curtains of yellow chintz: she appraised each; heard a roar of voices; people already coming up from dinner; she must fly!

The Prime Minister[4] was coming, Agnes said: so she had heard them say in the dining-room, she said, coming in with a tray of glasses. Did it matter, did it matter in the least, one Prime Minister more or less? It made no difference at this hour of the night to Mrs. Walker among the plates, saucepans, cullenders, frying-pans, chicken in aspic,[5] ice-cream freezers, pared crusts of bread, lemons, soup tureens, and pudding basins which, however hard they washed up in the scullery seemed to be all on top of her, on the

2. Gnatlike insects.
3. Commotion.
4. Stanley Baldwin (1867–1947) was prime minister in 1923.
5. Meat-flavored jelly. "Cullenders": colanders.

kitchen table, on chairs, while the fire blared and roared, the electric lights glared, and still supper had to be laid. All she felt was, one Prime Minister more or less made not a scrap of difference to Mrs. Walker.

The ladies were going upstairs already, said Lucy; the ladies were going up, one by one, Mrs. Dalloway walking last and almost always sending back some message to the kitchen, "My love to Mrs. Walker," that was it one night. Next morning they would go over the dishes—the soup, the salmon; the salmon, Mrs. Walker knew, as usual underdone, for she always got nervous about the pudding and left it to Jenny; so it happened, the salmon was always under-done. But some lady with fair hair and silver ornaments had said, Lucy said, about the entrée, was it really made at home? But it was the salmon that bothered Mrs. Walker, as she spun the plates round and round, and pulled in dampers and pulled out dampers;[6] and there came a burst of laughter from the dining-room; a voice speaking; then another burst of laughter—the gen-tlemen enjoying themselves when the ladies had gone. The tokay, said Lucy running in. Mr. Dalloway had sent for the tokay, from the Emperor's cellars, the Imperial Tokay.[7]

It was borne through the kitchen. Over her shoulder Lucy reported how Miss Elizabeth looked quite lovely; she couldn't take her eyes off her; in her pink dress, wearing the necklace Mr. Dalloway had given her. Jenny must remember the dog, Miss Elizabeth's fox-terrier, which, since it bit, had to be shut up and might, Elizabeth thought, want something. Jenny must remem-ber the dog. But Jenny was not going upstairs with all those people about. There was a motor at the door already! There was a ring at the bell—and the gentlemen still in the dining-room, drinking tokay!

There, they were going upstairs; that was the first to come, and now they would come faster and faster, so that Mrs. Parkinson (hired for parties) would leave the hall door ajar, and the hall would be full of gentlemen wait-ing (they stood waiting, sleeking down their hair) while the ladies took their cloaks off in the room along the passage; where Mrs. Barnet helped them, old Ellen Barnet, who had been with the family for forty years, and came every summer to help the ladies, and remembered mothers when they were girls, and though very unassuming did shake hands; said "milady" very respectfully, yet had a humorous way with her, looking at the young ladies, and ever so tactfully helping Lady Lovejoy, who had some trouble with her underbodice. And they could not help feeling, Lady Lovejoy and Miss Alice, that some little privilege in the matter of brush and comb, was awarded them having known Mrs. Barnet—"thirty years, milady," Mrs. Barnet sup-plied her. Young ladies did not use to rouge, said Lady Lovejoy, when they stayed at Bourton in the old days. And Miss Alice didn't need rouge, said Mrs. Barnet, looking at her fondly. There Mrs. Barnet would sit, in the cloakroom, patting down the furs, smoothing out the Spanish shawls, tidy-ing the dressing-table, and knowing perfectly well, in spite of the furs and the embroideries, which were nice ladies, which were not. The dear old body, said Lady Lovejoy, mounting the stairs, Clarissa's old nurse.

And then Lady Lovejoy stiffened. "Lady and Miss Lovejoy," she said to Mr. Wilkins (hired for parties). He had an admirable manner, as he bent and straightened himself, bent and straightened himself and announced

6. Metal plates in stoves that regulate air flow and thus control the intensity of the fire.
7. Sweet Hungarian wine.

with perfect impartiality "Lady and Miss Lovejoy . . . Sir John and Lady Needham . . . Miss Weld . . . Mr. Walsh." His manner was admirable; his family life must be irreproachable, except that it seemed impossible that a being with greenish lips and shaven cheeks could ever have blundered into the nuisance of children.

"How delightful to see you!" said Clarissa. She said it to every one. How delightful to see you! She was at her worst—effusive, insincere. It was a great mistake to have come. He should have stayed at home and read his book, thought Peter Walsh; should have gone to a music hall; he should have stayed at home, for he knew no one.

Oh dear, it was going to be a failure; a complete failure, Clarissa felt it in her bones as dear old Lord Lexham stood there apologising for his wife who had caught cold at the Buckingham Palace garden party. She could see Peter out of the tail of her eye, criticising her, there, in that corner. Why, after all, did she do these things? Why seek pinnacles and stand drenched in fire? Might it consume her anyhow! Burn her to cinders! Better anything, better brandish one's torch and hurl it to earth than taper and dwindle away like some Ellie Henderson! It was extraordinary how Peter put her into these states just by coming and standing in a corner. He made her see herself; exaggerate. It was idiotic. But why did he come, then, merely to criticise? Why always take, never give? Why not risk one's one little point of view? There he was wandering off, and she must speak to him. But she would not get the chance. Life was that—humiliation, renunciation. What Lord Lexham was saying was that his wife would not wear her furs at the garden party because "my dear, you ladies are all alike"—Lady Lexham being seventy-five at least! It was delicious, how they petted each other, that old couple. She did like old Lord Lexham. She did think it mattered, her party, and it made her feel quite sick to know that it was all going wrong, all falling flat. Anything, any explosion, any horror was better than people wandering aimlessly, standing in a bunch at a corner like Ellie Henderson, not even caring to hold themselves upright.

Gently the yellow curtain with all the birds of Paradise[8] blew out and it seemed as if there were a flight of wings into the room, right out, then sucked back. (For the windows were open.) Was it draughty, Ellie Henderson wondered? She was subject to chills. But it did not matter that she should come down sneezing tomorrow; it was the girls with their naked shoulders she thought of, being trained to think of others by an old father, an invalid, late vicar of Bourton, but he was dead now; and her chills never went to her chest, never. It was the girls she thought of, the young girls with their bare shoulders, she herself having always been a wisp of a creature, with her thin hair and meagre profile; though now, past fifty, there was beginning to shine through some mild beam, something purified into distinction by years of self-abnegation but obscured again, perpetually, by her distressing gentility, her panic fear, which arose from three hundred pounds' income, and her weaponless state (she could not earn a penny) and it made her timid, and more and more disqualified year by year to meet well-dressed people who did this sort of thing every night of the season, merely telling their maids "I'll wear so and so," whereas Ellie Henderson ran out nervously and bought cheap pink flowers, half a dozen, and then

---

8. Birds native to New Guinea, notable for the beautiful plumage of the males.

threw a shawl over her old black dress. For her invitation to Clarissa's party had come at the last moment. She was not quite happy about it. She had a sort of feeling that Clarissa had not meant to ask her this year.

Why should she? There was no reason really, except that they had always known each other. Indeed, they were cousins. But naturally they had rather drifted apart, Clarissa being so sought after. It was an event to her, going to a party. It was quite a treat just to see the lovely clothes. Wasn't that Elizabeth, grown up, with her hair done in the fashionable way, in the pink dress? Yet she could not be more than seventeen. She was very, very handsome. But girls when they first came out didn't seem to wear white as they used. (She must remember everything to tell Edith.) Girls wore straight frocks, perfectly tight, with skirts well above the ankles. It was not becoming, she thought.

So, with her weak eyesight, Ellie Henderson craned rather forward, and it wasn't so much she who minded not having any one to talk to (she hardly knew anybody there), for she felt that they were all such interesting people to watch; politicians presumably; Richard Dalloway's friends; but it was Richard himself who felt that he could not let the poor creature go on standing there all the evening by herself.

"Well, Ellie, and how's the world treating *you?*" he said in his genial way, and Ellie Henderson, getting nervous and flushing and feeling that it was extraordinarily nice of him to come and talk to her, said that many people really felt the heat more than the cold.

"Yes, they do," said Richard Dalloway. "Yes."

But what more did one say?

"Hullo, Richard," said somebody, taking him by the elbow, and, good Lord, there was old Peter, old Peter Walsh. He was delighted to see him— ever so pleased to see him! He hadn't changed a bit. And off they went together walking right across the room, giving each other little pats, as if they hadn't met for a long time, Ellie Henderson thought, watching them go, certain she knew that man's face. A tall man, middle aged, rather fine eyes, dark, wearing spectacles, with a look of John Burrows. Edith would be sure to know.

The curtain with its flight of birds of Paradise blew out again. And Clarissa saw—she saw Ralph Lyon beat it back, and go on talking. So it wasn't a failure after all! it was going to be all right now—her party. It had begun. It had started. But it was still touch and go. She must stand there for the present. People seemed to come in a rush.

Colonel and Mrs. Garrod . . . Mr. Hugh Whitbread . . . Mr. Bowley . . . Mrs. Hilbery . . . Lady Mary Maddox . . . Mr. Quin . . . intoned Wilkin. She had six or seven words with each, and they went on, they went into the rooms; into something now, not nothing, since Ralph Lyon had beat back the curtain.

And yet for her own part, it was too much of an effort. She was not enjoying it. It was too much like being—just anybody, standing there; anybody could do it, yet this anybody she did a little admire, couldn't help feeling that she had, anyhow, made this happen, that it marked a stage, this post that she felt herself to have become, for oddly enough she had quite forgotten what she looked like, but felt herself a stake driven in at the top of her stairs. Every time she gave a party she had this feeling of being something not herself, and that every one was unreal in one way; much more real in another. It was, she thought, partly their clothes, partly being taken out of their ordinary ways, partly the background, it was possible to say things you couldn't say anyhow else, things that needed an effort; possible to go much deeper. But not for her; not yet anyhow.

"How delightful to see you!" she said. Dear old Sir Harry! He would know every one.

And what was so odd about it was the sense one had as they came up the stairs one after another, Mrs. Mount and Celia, Herbert Ainsty, Mrs. Dakers—oh and Lady Bruton!

"How awfully good of you to come!" she said, and she meant it—it was odd how standing there one felt them going on, going on, some quite old, some . . .

What name? Lady Rosseter? But who on earth was Lady Rosseter?

"Clarissa!" That voice! It was Sally Seton! Sally Seton! after all these years! She loomed through a mist. For she hadn't looked like *that*, Sally Seton, when Clarissa grasped the hot water can, to think of her under this roof, under this roof! Not like that!

All on top of each other, embarrassed, laughing, words tumbled out— passing through London; heard from Clara Haydon; what a chance of see-ing you! So I thrust myself in—without an invitation. . . .

One might put down the hot water can quite composedly. The lustre had gone out of her. Yet it was extraordinary to see her again, older, happier, less lovely. They kissed each other, first this cheek then that, by the drawing-room door, and Clarissa turned, with Sally's hand in hers, and saw her rooms full, heard the roar of voices, saw the candlesticks, the blowing cur-tains, and the roses which Richard had given her.

"I have five enormous boys," said Sally.

She had the simplest egotism, the most open desire to be thought first always, and Clarissa loved her for being still like that. "I can't believe it!" she cried, kindling all over with pleasure at the thought of the past.

But alas, Wilkins; Wilkins wanted her; Wilkins was emitting in a voice of commanding authority as if the whole company must be admonished and the hostess reclaimed from frivolity, one name:

"The Prime Minister," said Peter Walsh.

The Prime Minister? Was it really? Ellie Henderson marvelled. What a thing to tell Edith!

One couldn't laugh at him. He looked so ordinary. You might have stood him behind a counter and bought biscuits[9]—poor chap, all rigged up in gold lace. And to be fair, as he went his rounds, first with Clarissa then with Richard escorting him, he did it very well. He tried to look somebody. It was amusing to watch. Nobody looked at him. They just went on talking, yet it was perfectly plain that they all knew, felt to the marrow of their bones, this majesty passing; this symbol of what they all stood for, English society. Old Lady Bruton, and she looked very fine too, very stalwart in her lace, swam up, and they withdrew into a little room which at once became spied upon, guarded, and a sort of stir and rustle rippled through every one, openly: the Prime Minister!

Lord, lord, the snobbery of the English! thought Peter Walsh, standing in the corner. How they loved dressing up in gold lace and doing homage! There!

9. Thin, dry cookies.

That must be, by Jove it was, Hugh Whitbread, snuffing round the precincts of the great, grown rather fatter, rather whiter, the admirable Hugh!

He looked always as if he were on duty, thought Peter, a privileged, but secretive being, hoarding secrets which he would die to defend, though it was only some little piece of tittle-tattle dropped by a court footman, which would be in all the papers to-morrow. Such were his rattles, his baubles, in playing with which he had grown white, come to the verge of old age, enjoying the respect and affection of all who had the privilege of knowing this type of the English public school man.[1] Inevitably one made up things like that about Hugh; that was his style; the style of those admirable letters which Peter had read thousands of miles across the sea in the *Times*, and had thanked God he was out of that pernicious hubble-bubble if it were only to hear baboons chatter and coolies beat their wives. An olive-skinned youth from one of the Universities stood obsequiously by. Him he would patronise, initiate, teach how to get on. For he liked nothing better than doing kindnessses, making the hearts of old ladies palpitate with the joy of being thought of in their age, their affliction, thinking themselves quite forgotten, yet here was dear Hugh driving up and spending an hour talking of the past, remembering trifles, praising the homemade cake, though Hugh might eat cake with a Duchess any day of his life, and, to look at him, probably did spend a good deal of time in that agreeable occupation. The All-judging, the All-merciful, might excuse. Peter Walsh had no mercy. Villains there must be, and God knows the rascals who get hanged for battering the brains of a girl out in a train do less harm on the whole than Hugh Whitbread and his kindness. Look at him now, on tiptoe, dancing forward, bowing and scraping, as the Prime Minister and Lady Bruton emerged, intimating for all the world to see that he was privileged to say something, something private, to Lady Bruton as she passed. She stopped. She wagged her fine old head. She was thanking him presumably for some piece of servility. She had her toadies, minor officials in Government offices who ran about putting through little jobs on her behalf, in return for which she gave them luncheon. But she derived from the eighteenth century. She was all right.

And now Clarissa escorted her Prime Minister down the room, prancing, sparkling, with the stateliness of her grey hair. She wore ear-rings, and a silver-green mermaid's dress. Lolloping on the waves and braiding her tresses she seemed, having that gift still; to be; to exist; to sum it all up in the moment as she passed; turned, caught her scarf in some other woman's dress, unhitched it, laughed, all with the most perfect ease and air of a creature floating in its element. But age had brushed her; even as a mermaid might behold in her glass the setting sun on some very clear evening over the waves. There was a breath of tenderness; her severity, her prudery, her woodenness were all warmed through now, and she had about her as she said goodbye to the thick gold-laced man who was doing his best, and good luck to him, to look important, an inexpressible dignity; an exquisite cordiality; as if she wished the whole world well, and must now, being on the very verge and rim of things, take her leave. So she made him think. (But he was not in love.)

Indeed, Clarissa felt, the Prime Minister had been good to come. And, walking down the room with him, with Sally there and Peter there and Richard very pleased, with all those people rather inclined, perhaps, to envy, she

1. I.e., a man with an elite education from a British public school, analogous to an American private school.

had felt that intoxication of the moment, that dilatation of the nerves of the heart itself till it seemed to quiver, steeped, upright;—yes, but after all it was what other people felt, that; for, though she loved it and felt it tingle and sting, still these semblances, these triumphs (dear old Peter, for example, thinking her so brilliant), had a hollowness; at arm's length they were, not in the heart; and it might be that she was growing old but they satisfied her no longer as they used; and suddenly, as she saw the Prime Minister go down the stairs, the gilt rim of the Sir Joshua picture[2] of the little girl with a muff brought back Kilman with a rush; Kilman her enemy. That was satisfying; that was real. Ah, how she hated her—hot, hypocritical, corrupt; with all that power; Elizabeth's seducer; the woman who had crept in to steal and defile (Richard would say, What nonsense!). She hated her: she loved her. It was enemies one wanted, not friends—not Mrs. Durrant and Clara, Sir William and Lady Bradshaw, Miss Truelock and Eleanor Gibson (whom she saw coming upstairs). They must find her if they wanted her. She was for the party!

There was her old friend Sir Harry.

"Dear Sir Harry!" she said, going up to the fine old fellow who had produced more bad pictures than any other two Academicians in the whole of St. John's Wood[3] (they were always of cattle, standing in sunset pools absorbing moisture, or signifying, for he had a certain range of gesture, by the raising of one foreleg and the toss of the antlers, "the Approach of the Stranger"—all his activities, dining out, racing, were founded on cattle standing absorbing moisture in sunset pools).

"What are you laughing at?" she asked him. For Willie Titcomb and Sir Harry and Herbert Ainsty were all laughing. But no. Sir Harry could not tell Clarissa Dalloway (much though he liked her; of her type he thought her perfect, and threatened to paint her) his stories of the music hall stage. He chaffed her about her party. He missed his brandy. These circles, he said, were above him. But he liked her; respected her, in spite of her damnable, difficult upper-class refinement, which made it impossible to ask Clarissa Dalloway to sit on his knee. And up came that wandering will-o'-the-wisp,[4] that vagulous phosphorescence, old Mrs. Hilbery, stretching her hands to the blaze of his laughter (about the Duke and the Lady), which, as she heard it across the room, seemed to reassure her on a point which sometimes bothered her if she woke early in the morning and did not like to call her maid for a cup of tea; how it is certain we must die.

"They won't tell us their stories," said Clarissa.

"Dear Clarissa!" exclaimed Mrs. Hilbery. She looked tonight, she said, so like her mother as she first saw her walking in a garden in a grey hat.

And really Clarissa's eyes filled with tears. Her mother, walking in a garden! But alas, she must go.

For there was Professor Brierly, who lectured on Milton,[5] talking to little Jim Hutton (who was unable even for a party like this to compass both tie and waistcoat or make his hair lie flat), and even at this distance they were quarrelling, she could see. For Professor Brierly was a very queer fish. With all those degrees, honours, lectureships between him and the scribblers he suspected instantly an atmosphere not favourable to his queer compound;

---

2. Painting by English portraitist Sir Joshua Reynolds (1723–1792).
3. District in north London near Regent's Park.
4. Flitting phosphorescent light seen at night in marshes; colloquially, something misleading.
5. John Milton (1608–1674), English poet.

his prodigious learning and timidity; his wintry charm without cordiality, his innocence blent with snobbery; he quivered if made conscious by a lady's unkempt hair, a youth's boots, of an underworld, very creditable doubtless, of rebels, of ardent young people; of would-be geniuses, and intimated with a little toss of the head, with a sniff—Humph!—the value of moderation; of some slight training in the classics in order to appreciate Milton. Professor Brierly (Clarissa could see) wasn't hitting it off with little Jim Hutton (who wore red socks, his black being at the laundry) about Milton. She interrupted.

She said she loved Bach.[6] So did Hutton. That was the bond between them, and Hutton (a very bad poet) always felt that Mrs. Dalloway was far the best of the great ladies who took an interest in art. It was odd how strict she was. About music she was purely impersonal. She was rather a prig. But how charming to look at! She made her house so nice if it weren't for her Professors. Clarissa had half a mind to snatch him off and set him down at the piano in the back room. For he played divinely.

"But the noise!" she said. "The noise!"

"The sign of a successful party." Nodding urbanely, the Professor stepped delicately off.

"He knows everything in the whole world about Milton," said Clarissa.

"Does he indeed?" said Hutton, who would imitate the Professor throughout Hampstead;[7] the Professor on Milton; the Professor on moderation; the Professor stepping delicately off.

But she must speak to that couple, said Clarissa, Lord Gayton and Nancy Blow.

Not that *they* added perceptibly to the noise of the party. They were not talking (perceptibly) as they stood side by side by the yellow curtains. They would soon be off elsewhere, together; and never had very much to say in any circumstances. They looked; that was all. That was enough. They looked so clean, so sound, she with an apricot bloom of powder and paint, but he scrubbed, rinsed, with the eyes of a bird, so that no ball could pass him or stroke surprise him. He struck, he leapt, accurately, on the spot. Ponies' mouths quivered at the end of his reins. He had his honours, ancestral monuments, banners hanging in the church at home. He had his duties; his tenants; a mother and sisters; had been all day at Lords, and that was what they were talking about—cricket, cousins, the movies—when Mrs. Dalloway came up. Lord Gayton liked her most awfully. So did Miss Blow. She had such charming manners.

"It is angelic—it is delicious of you to have come!" she said. She loved Lords; she loved youth, and Nancy, dressed at enormous expense by the greatest artists in Paris, stood there looking as if her body had merely put forth, of its own accord, a green frill.

"I had meant to have dancing," said Clarissa.

For the young people could not talk. And why should they? Shout, embrace, swing, be up at dawn; carry sugar to ponies; kiss and caress the snouts of adorable chows; and then all tingling and streaming, plunge and swim. But the enormous resources of the English language, the power it bestows, after all, of communicating feelings (at their age, she and Peter would have been

6. Johann Sebastian Bach (1685–1750), German composer.

7. A preserved open area in north London, popular with artists.

arguing all the evening), was not for them. They would solidify young. They would be good beyond measure to the people on the estate, but alone, perhaps, rather dull.

"What a pity!" she said. "I had hoped to have dancing."

It was so extraordinarily nice of them to have come! But talk of dancing! The rooms were packed.

There was old Aunt Helena in her shawl. Alas, she must leave them— Lord Gayton and Nancy Blow. There was old Miss Parry, her aunt.

For Miss Helena Parry was not dead: Miss Parry was alive. She was past eighty. She ascended staircases slowly with a stick. She was placed in a chair (Richard had seen to it). People who had known Burma in the 'seventies were always led up to her. Where had Peter got to? They used to be such friends. For at the mention of India, or even Ceylon,[8] her eyes (only one was glass) slowly deepened, became blue, beheld, not human beings—she had no tender memories, no proud illusions about Viceroys, Generals, Mutinies[9]—it was orchids she saw, and mountain passes and herself carried on the backs of coolies in the 'sixties over solitary peaks; or descending to uproot orchids (startling blossoms, never beheld before) which she painted in water-colour; an indomitable Englishwoman, fretful if disturbed by the War, say, which dropped a bomb at her very door, from her deep meditation over orchids and her own figure journeying in the 'sixties in India—but here was Peter.

"Come and talk to Aunt Helena about Burma," said Clarissa.

And yet he had not had a word with her all the evening!

"We will talk later," said Clarissa, leading him up to Aunt Helena, in her white shawl, with her stick.

"Peter Walsh," said Clarissa.

That meant nothing.

Clarissa had asked her. It was tiring; it was noisy; but Clarissa had asked her. So she had come. It was a pity that they lived in London—Richard and Clarissa. If only for Clarissa's health it would have been better to live in the country. But Clarissa had always been fond of society.

"He has been in Burma," said Clarissa.

Ah. She could not resist recalling what Charles Darwin had said about her little book on the orchids of Burma.

(Clarissa must speak to Lady Bruton.)

No doubt it was forgotten now, her book on the orchids of Burma, but it went into three editions before 1870, she told Peter. She remembered him now. He had been at Bourton (and he had left her, Peter Walsh remembered, without a word in the drawing-room that night when Clarissa had asked him to come boating).

"Richard so much enjoyed his lunch party," said Clarissa to Lady Bruton.

"Richard was the greatest possible help," Lady Bruton replied. "He helped me to write a letter. And how are you?"

"Oh, perfectly well!" said Clarissa. (Lady Bruton detested illness in the wives of politicians.)

8. British colonial name for Sri Lanka. "Burma in the 'seventies": southeast Asian country now known as Myanmar, formerly part of the British Empire, which fought three wars to annex it, in 1824–26, 1852, and 1885.

9. Cf. the 1857 Indian Rebellion, or Indian Mutiny, of Indian troops against British colonial rule. "Viceroys": British governors of colonial territories.

"And there's Peter Walsh!" said Lady Bruton (for she could never think of anything to say to Clarissa; though she liked her. She had lots of fine qualities; but they had nothing in common—she and Clarissa. It might have been better if Richard had married a woman with less charm, who would have helped him more in his work. He had lost his chance of the Cabinet). "There's Peter Walsh!" she said, shaking hands with that agreeable sinner, that very able fellow who should have made a name for himself but hadn't (always in difficulties with women), and, of course, old Miss Parry. Wonderful old lady!

Lady Bruton stood by Miss Parry's chair, a spectral grenadier, draped in black, inviting Peter Walsh to lunch; cordial; but without small talk, remembering nothing whatever about the flora or fauna of India. She had been there, of course; had stayed with three Viceroys; thought some of the Indian civilians uncommonly fine fellows; but what a tragedy it was—the state of India! The Prime Minister had just been telling her (old Miss Parry huddled up in her shawl, did not care what the Prime Minister had just been telling her), and Lady Bruton would like to have Peter Walsh's opinion, he being fresh from the centre, and she would get Sir Sampson to meet him, for really it prevented her from sleeping at night, the folly of it, the wickedness she might say, being a soldier's daughter. She was an old woman now, not good for much. But her house, her servants, her good friend Milly Brush—did he remember her?—were all there only asking to be used if—if they could be of help, in short. For she never spoke of England, but this isle of men, this dear, dear land,[1] was in her blood (without reading Shakespeare), and if ever a woman could have worn the helmet and shot the arrow, could have led troops to attack, ruled with indomitable justice barbarian hordes and lain under a shield noseless in a church, or made a green grass mound on some primeval hillside, that woman was Millicent Bruton. Debarred by her sex and some truancy, too, of the logical faculty (she found it impossible to write a letter to the *Times*), she had the thought of Empire always at hand, and had acquired from her association with that armoured goddess[2] her ramrod bearing, her robustness of demeanour, so that one could not figure her even in death parted from the earth or roaming territories over which, in some spiritual shape, the Union Jack[3] had ceased to fly. To be not English even among the dead—no, no! Impossible!

But was it Lady Bruton (whom she used to know)? Was it Peter Walsh grown grey? Lady Rosseter asked herself (who had been Sally Seton). It was old Miss Parry certainly—the old aunt who used to be so cross when she stayed at Bourton. Never should she forget running along the passage naked, and being sent for by Miss Parry! And Clarissa! oh Clarissa! Sally caught her by the arm.

Clarissa stopped beside them.

"But I can't stay," she said. "I shall come later. Wait," she said, looking at Peter and Sally. They must wait, she meant, until all these people had gone.

"I shall come back," she said, looking at her old friends, Sally and Peter, who were shaking hands, and Sally, remembering the past no doubt, was laughing.

But her voice was wrung of its old ravishing richness; her eyes not aglow as they used to be, when she smoked cigars, when she ran down the passage to fetch her sponge bag, without a stitch of clothing on her, and Ellen Atkins

1. Cf. Shakespeare's play *Richard II* 2.1.57.
2. Cf. the Greek goddess Athena, often represented with armor.
3. British national flag.

asked, What if the gentlemen had met her? But everybody forgave her. She stole a chicken from the larder because she was hungry in the night; she smoked cigars in her bedroom; she left a priceless book in the punt.[4] But everybody adored her (except perhaps Papa). It was her warmth; her vitality—she would paint, she would write. Old women in the village never to this day forgot to ask after "your friend in the red cloak who seemed so bright." She accused Hugh Whitbread, of all people (and there he was, her old friend Hugh, talking to the Portuguese Ambassador), of kissing her in the smoking-room to punish her for saying that women should have votes. Vulgar men did, she said. And Clarissa remembered having to persuade her not to denounce him at family prayers—which she was capable of doing with her daring, her recklessness, her melodramatic love of being the centre of everything and creating scenes, and it was bound, Clarissa used to think, to end in some awful tragedy; her death; her martyrdom; instead of which she had married, quite unexpectedly, a bald man with a large buttonhole who owned, it was said, cotton mills at Manchester. And she had five boys!

She and Peter had settled down together. They were talking: it seemed so familiar—that they should be talking. They would discuss the past. With the two of them (more even than with Richard) she shared her past; the garden; the trees; old Joseph Breitkopf singing Brahms without any voice; the drawing-room wallpaper; the smell of the mats. A part of this Sally must always be; Peter must always be. But she must leave them. There were the Bradshaws, whom she disliked. She must go up to Lady Bradshaw (in grey and silver, balancing like a sea-lion at the edge of its tank, barking for invitations, Duchesses, the typical successful man's wife), she must go up to Lady Bradshaw and say . . .

But Lady Bradshaw anticipated her.

"We are shockingly late, dear Mrs. Dalloway, we hardly dared to come in," she said.

And Sir William, who looked very distinguished, with his grey hair and blue eyes, said yes; they had not been able to resist the temptation. He was talking to Richard about that Bill probably, which they wanted to get through the Commons. Why did the sight of him, talking to Richard, curl her up? He looked what he was, a great doctor. A man absolutely at the head of his profession, very powerful, rather worn. For think what cases came before him—people in the uttermost depths of misery; people on the verge of insanity; husbands and wives. He had to decide questions of appalling difficulty. Yet—what she felt was, one wouldn't like Sir William to see one unhappy. No; not that man.

"How is your son at Eton?" she asked Lady Bradshaw.

He had just missed his eleven,[5] said Lady Bradshaw, because of the mumps. His father minded even more than he did, she thought "being," she said, "nothing but a great boy himself."

Clarissa looked at Sir William, talking to Richard. He did not look like a boy—not in the least like a boy. She had once gone with some one to ask his advice. He had been perfectly right; extremely sensible. But Heavens—what a relief to get out to the street again! There was some poor wretch sobbing, she remembered, in the waiting-room. But she did not know what it was—about

4. Flat-bottomed, shallow boat.
5. His cricket team, made up of eleven players.

Sir William; what exactly she disliked. Only Richard agreed with her, "didn't like his taste, didn't like his smell." But he was extraordinarily able. They were talking about this Bill. Some case, Sir William was mentioning, lowering his voice. It had its bearing upon what he was saying about the deferred effects of shell shock.[6] There must be some provision in the Bill.

Sinking her voice, drawing Mrs. Dalloway into the shelter of a common femininity, a common pride in the illustrious qualities of husbands and their sad tendency to overwork, Lady Bradshaw (poor goose—one didn't dislike her) murmured how, "just as we were starting, my husband was called up on the telephone, a very sad case. A young man (that is what Sir William is telling Mr. Dalloway) had killed himself. He had been in the army." Oh! thought Clarissa, in the middle of my party, here's death, she thought.

She went on, into the little room where the Prime Minister had gone with Lady Bruton. Perhaps there was somebody there. But there was nobody. The chairs still kept the impress of the Prime Minister and Lady Bruton, she turned deferentially, he sitting four-square, authoritatively. They had been talking about India. There was nobody. The party's splendour fell to the floor, so strange it was to come in alone in her finery.

What business had the Bradshaws to talk of death at her party? A young man had killed himself. And they talked of it at her party—the Bradshaws, talked of death. He had killed himself—but how? Always her body went through it first, when she was told, suddenly, of an accident; her dress flamed, her body burnt. He had thrown himself from a window. Up had flashed the ground; through him, blundering, bruising, went the rusty spikes. There he lay with a thud, thud, thud in his brain, and then a suffocation of blackness. So she saw it. But why had he done it? And the Bradshaws talked of it at her party!

She had once thrown a shilling into the Serpentine, never anything more. But he had flung it away. They went on living (she would have to go back; the rooms were still crowded; people kept on coming). They (all day she had been thinking of Bourton, of Peter, of Sally), they would grow old. A thing there was that mattered; a thing, wreathed about with chatter, defaced, obscured in her own life, let drop every day in corruption, lies, chatter. This he had preserved. Death was defiance. Death was an attempt to communicate; people feeling the impossibility of reaching the centre which, mystically, evaded them; closeness drew apart; rapture faded, one was alone. There was an embrace in death.

But this young man who had killed himself—had he plunged holding his treasure? "If it were now to die, 'twere now to be most happy,"[7] she had said to herself once, coming down in white.

Or there were the poets and thinkers. Suppose he had had that passion, and had gone to Sir William Bradshaw, a great doctor yet to her obscurely evil, without sex or lust, extremely polite to women, but capable of some indescribable outrage—forcing your soul, that was it—if this young man had gone to him, and Sir William had impressed him, like that, with his power, might he not then have said (indeed she felt it now), Life is made intolerable; they make life intolerable, men like that?

6. Psychological disturbance caused by prolonged exposure to combat (at first thought to be a reaction to the sound of exploding bombshells). The War Office undertook an official inquiry into the subject and issued a report, printed in the *Times* in 1922, that recognized the complexity of the illness. The condition today is known as post-traumatic stress disorder.
7. Cf. p. 302 and n. 5.

Then (she had felt it only this morning) there was the terror; the over-whelming incapacity, one's parents giving it into one's hands, this life, to be lived to the end, to be walked with serenely; there was in the depths of her heart an awful fear. Even now, quite often if Richard had not been there read-ing the *Times*, so that she could crouch like a bird and gradually revive, send roaring up that immeasurable delight, rubbing stick to stick, one thing with another, she must have perished. But that young man had killed himself.

Somehow it was her disaster—her disgrace. It was her punishment to see sink and disappear here a man, there a woman, in this profound darkness, and she forced to stand here in her evening dress. She had schemed; she had pil-fered. She was never wholly admirable. She had wanted success. Lady Bexbor-ough and the rest of it. And once she had walked on the terrace at Bourton.

It was due to Richard; she had never been so happy. Nothing could be slow enough; nothing last too long. No pleasure could equal, she thought, straightening the chairs, pushing in one book on the shelf, this having done with the triumphs of youth, lost herself in the process of living, to find it, with a shock of delight, as the sun rose, as the day sank. Many a time had she gone, at Bourton when they were all talking, to look at the sky, or seen it between people's shoulders at dinner; seen it in London when she could not sleep. She walked to the window.

It held, foolish as the idea was, something of her own in it, this country sky, this sky above Westminster. She parted the curtains; she looked. Oh, but how surprising!—in the room opposite the old lady stared straight at her! She was going to bed. And the sky. It will be a solemn sky, she had thought, it will be a dusky sky, turning away its cheek in beauty. But there it was—ashen pale, raced over quickly by tapering vast clouds. It was new to her. The wind must have risen. She was going to bed, in the room oppo-site. It was fascinating to watch her, moving about, that old lady, crossing the room, coming to the window. Could she see her? It was fascinating, with people still laughing and shouting in the drawing-room, to watch that old woman, quite quietly, going to bed. She pulled the blind now. The clock began striking. The young man had killed himself; but she did not pity him; with the clock striking the hour, one, two, three, she did not pity him, with all this going on. There! the old lady had put out her light! the whole house was dark now with this going on, she repeated, and the words came to her, Fear no more the heat of the sun. She must go back to them. But what an extraordinary night! She felt somehow very like him—the young man who had killed himself. She felt glad that he had done it; thrown it away. The clock was striking. The leaden circles dissolved in the air. He made her feel the beauty; made her feel the fun. But she must go back. She must assemble. She must find Sally and Peter. And she came in from the little room.

"But where is Clarissa?" said Peter. He was sitting on the sofa with Sally. (After all these years he really could not call her "Lady Rosseter.") "Where's the woman gone to?" he asked. "Where's Clarissa?"

Sally supposed, and so did Peter for the matter of that, that there were people of importance, politicians, whom neither of them knew unless by sight in the picture papers, whom Clarissa had to be nice to, had to talk to. She was with them. Yet there was Richard Dalloway not in the Cabinet. He hadn't been a success, Sally supposed? For herself, she scarcely ever read the papers. She sometimes saw his name mentioned. But then—well, she lived a very solitary life, in the wilds, Clarissa would say, among great merchants, great manufacturers, men, after all, who did things. She had done things too!

"I have five sons!" she told him.

Lord, Lord, what a change had come over her! the softness of motherhood; its egotism too. Last time they met, Peter remembered, had been among the cauliflowers in the moonlight, the leaves "like rough bronze" she had said, with her literary turn; and she had picked a rose. She had marched him up and down that awful night, after the scene by the fountain; he was to catch the midnight train. Heavens, he had wept!

That was his old trick, opening a pocket-knife, thought Sally, always opening and shutting a knife when he got excited. They had been very, very intimate, she and Peter Walsh, when he was in love with Clarissa, and there was that dreadful, ridiculous scene over Richard Dalloway at lunch. She had called Richard "Wickham." Why not call Richard "Wickham"? Clarissa had flared up! and indeed they had never seen each other since, she and Clarissa, not more than half a dozen times perhaps in the last ten years. And Peter Walsh had gone off to India, and she had heard vaguely that he had made an unhappy marriage, and she didn't know whether he had any children, and she couldn't ask him, for he had changed. He was rather shrivelled-looking, but kinder, she felt, and she had a real affection for him, for he was connected with her youth, and she still had a little Emily Brontë[8] he had given her, and he was to write, surely? In those days he was to write.

"Have you written?" she asked him, spreading her hand, her firm and shapely hand, on her knee in a way he recalled.

"Not a word!" said Peter Walsh, and she laughed.

She was still attractive, still a personage, Sally Seton. But who was this Rosseter? He wore two camelias on his wedding day—that was all Peter knew of him. "They have myriads of servants, miles of conservatories,"[9] Clarissa wrote; something like that. Sally owned it with a shout of laughter.

"Yes, I have ten thousand a year"—whether before the tax was paid or after, she couldn't remember, for her husband, "whom you must meet," she said, "whom you would like," she said, did all that for her.

And Sally used to be in rags and tatters. She had pawned her grandmother's ring which Marie Antoinette had given her great-grandfather to come to Bourton.

Oh yes, Sally remembered; she had it still, a ruby ring which Marie Antoinette had given her great-grandfather. She never had a penny to her name in those days, and going to Bourton always meant some frightful pinch. But going to Bourton had meant so much to her—had kept her sane, she believed, so unhappy had she been at home. But that was all a thing of the past—all over now, she said. And Mr. Parry was dead; and Miss Parry was still alive. Never had he had such a shock in his life! said Peter. He had been quite certain she was dead. And the marriage had been, Sally supposed, a success? And that very handsome, very self-possessed young woman was Elizabeth, over there, by the curtains, in red.[1]

(She was like a poplar, she was like a river, she was like a hyacinth, Willie Titcomb was thinking. Oh how much nicer to be in the country and do

---

8. A book by the English novelist and poet (1818–1848).
9. Greenhouses.
1. Earlier described as pink.

what she liked! She could hear her poor dog howling, Elizabeth was certain.) She was not a bit like Clarissa, Peter Walsh said.

"Oh, Clarissa!" said Sally.

What Sally felt was simply this. She had owed Clarissa an enormous amount. They had been friends, not acquaintances, friends, and she still saw Clarissa all in white going about the house with her hands full of flowers—to this day tobacco plants made her think of Bourton. But—did Peter understand?—she lacked something. Lacked what was it? She had charm; she had extraordinary charm. But to be frank (and she felt that Peter was an old friend, a real friend—did absence matter? did distance matter? She had often wanted to write to him, but torn it up, yet felt he understood, for people understand without things being said, as one realises growing old, and old she was, had been that afternoon to see her sons at Eton, where they had the mumps), to be quite frank then, how could Clarissa have done it?—married Richard Dalloway? a sportsman, a man who cared only for dogs. Literally, when he came into the room he smelt of the stables. And then all this? She waved her hand.

Hugh Whitbread it was, strolling past in his white waistcoat, dim, fat, blind, past everything he looked, except self-esteem and comfort.

"He's not going to recognise *us*," said Sally, and really she hadn't the courage—so that was Hugh! the admirable Hugh!

"And what does he do?" she asked Peter.

He blacked the King's boots or counted bottles at Windsor,[2] Peter told her. Peter kept his sharp tongue still! But Sally must be frank, Peter said. That kiss now, Hugh's.

On the lips, she assured him, in the smoking-room one evening. She went straight to Clarissa in a rage. Hugh didn't do such things! Clarissa said, the admirable Hugh! Hugh's socks were without exception the most beautiful she had ever seen—and now his evening dress. Perfect! And had he children?

"Everybody in the room has six sons at Eton," Peter told her, except himself. He, thank God, had none. No sons, no daughters, no wife. Well, he didn't seem to mind, said Sally. He looked younger, she thought, than any of them.

But it had been a silly thing to do, in many ways, Peter said, to marry like that; "a perfect goose she was," he said, but, he said, "we had a splendid time of it," but how could that be? Sally wondered; what did he mean? and how odd it was to know him and yet not know a single thing that had happened to him. And did he say it out of pride? Very likely, for after all it must be galling for him (though he was an oddity, a sort of sprite, not at all an ordinary man), it must be lonely at his age to have no home, nowhere to go to. But he must stay with them for weeks and weeks. Of course he would; he would love to stay with them, and that was how it came out. All these years the Dalloways had never been once. Time after time they had asked them. Clarissa (for it was Clarissa of course) would not come. For, said Sally, Clarissa was at heart a snob—one had to admit it, a snob. And it was that that was between them, she was convinced. Clarissa thought she had married beneath her, her husband being—she was proud of it—a miner's son. Every penny they had he had earned. As a little boy (her voice trembled) he had carried great sacks.

(And so she would go on, Peter felt, hour after hour; the miner's son; people thought she had married beneath her; her five sons; and what was

2. Windsor Castle, a royal residence west of London.

the other thing—plants, hydrangeas, syringas, very, very rare hibiscus lilies that never grow north of the Suez Canal,[3] but she, with one gardener in a suburb near Manchester, had beds of them, positively beds! Now all that Clarissa had escaped, unmaternal as she was.)

A snob was she? Yes, in many ways. Where was she, all this time? It was getting late.

"Yet," said Sally, "when I heard Clarissa was giving a party, I felt I couldn't *not* come—must see her again (and I'm staying in Victoria Street, practically next door). So I just came without an invitation. But," she whispered, "tell me, do. Who is this?"

It was Mrs. Hilbery, looking for the door. For how late it was getting! And, she murmured, as the night grew later, as people went, one found old friends; quiet nooks and corners; and the loveliest views. Did they know, she asked, that they were surrounded by an enchanted garden? Lights and trees and wonderful gleaming lakes and the sky. Just a few fairy lamps,[4] Clarissa Dalloway had said, in the back garden! But she was a magician! It was a park. . . . And she didn't know their names, but friends she knew they were, friends without names, songs without words, always the best. But there were so many doors, such unexpected places, she could not find her way.

"Old Mrs. Hilbery," said Peter; but who was that? that lady standing by the curtain all the evening, without speaking? He knew her face; connected her with Bourton. Surely she used to cut up underclothes at the large table in the window? Davidson, was that her name?

"Oh, that is Ellie Henderson," said Sally. Clarissa was really very hard on her. She was a cousin, very poor. Clarissa *was* hard on people.

She was rather, said Peter. Yet, said Sally, in her emotional way, with a rush of that enthusiasm which Peter used to love her for, yet dreaded a little now, so effusive she might become—how generous to her friends Clarissa was! and what a rare quality one found it, and how sometimes at night or on Christmas Day, when she counted up her blessings, she put that friendship first. They were young; that was it. Clarissa was pure-hearted; that was it. Peter would think her sentimental. So she was. For she had come to feel that it was the only thing worth saying—what one felt. Cleverness was silly. One must say simply what one felt.

"But I do not know," said Peter Walsh, "what I feel."

Poor Peter, thought Sally. Why did not Clarissa come and talk to them? That was what he was longing for. She knew it. All the time he was thinking only of Clarissa, and was fidgeting with his knife.

He had not found life simple, Peter said. His relations with Clarissa had not been simple. It had spoilt his life, he said. (They had been so intimate—he and Sally Seton, it was absurd not to say it.) One could not be in love twice, he said. And what could she say? Still, it is better to have loved (but he would think her sentimental—he used to be so sharp). He must come and stay with them in Manchester. That is all very true, he said. All very true. He would love to come and stay with them, directly he had done what he had to do in London.

And Clarissa had cared for him more than she had ever cared for Richard. Sally was positive of that.

---

3. Canal in Egypt connecting the Mediterranean and the Red Seas.
4. Small colored lights often hung in trees for decoration.

"No, no, no!" said Peter (Sally should not have said that—she went too far). That good fellow—there he was at the end of the room, holding forth, the same as ever, dear old Richard. Who was he talking to? Sally asked, that very distinguished-looking man? Living in the wilds as she did, she had an insatiable curiosity to know who people were. But Peter did not know. He did not like his looks, he said, probably a Cabinet Minister. Of them all, Richard seemed to him the best, he said—the most disinterested.

"But what has he done?" Sally asked. Public work, she supposed. And were they happy together? Sally asked (she herself was extremely happy); for, she admitted, she knew nothing about them, only jumped to conclusions, as one does, for what can one know even of the people one lives with every day? she asked. Are we not all prisoners? She had read a wonderful play about a man who scratched on the wall of his cell,[5] and she had felt that was true of life—one scratched on the wall. Despairing of human relationships (people were so difficult), she often went into her garden and got from her flowers a peace which men and women never gave her. But no; he did not like cabbages; he preferred human beings, Peter said. Indeed, the young are beautiful, Sally said, watching Elizabeth cross the room. How unlike Clarissa at her age! Could he make anything of her? She would not open her lips. Not much, not yet, Peter admitted. She was like a lily, Sally said, a lily by the side of a pool. But Peter did not agree that we know nothing. We know everything, he said; at least he did.

But these two, Sally whispered, these two coming now (and really she must go, if Clarissa did not come soon), this distinguished-looking man and his rather common-looking wife who had been talking to Richard—what could one know about people like that?

"That they're damnable humbugs," said Peter, looking at them casually. He made Sally laugh.

But Sir William Bradshaw stopped at the door to look at a picture. He looked in the corner for the engraver's name. His wife looked too. Sir William Bradshaw was so interested in art.

When one was young, said Peter, one was too much excited to know people. Now that one was old, fifty-two[6] to be precise (Sally was fifty-five, in body, she said, but her heart was like a girl's of twenty); now that one was mature then, said Peter, one could watch, one could understand, and one did not lose the power of feeling, he said. No, that is true, said Sally. She felt more deeply, more passionately, every year. It increased, he said, alas, perhaps, but one should be glad of it—it went on increasing in his experience. There was some one in India. He would like to tell Sally about her. He would like Sally to know her. She was married, he said. She had two small children. They must all come to Manchester, said Sally—he must promise before they left.

There's Elizabeth, he said, she feels not half what we feel, not yet. But, said Sally, watching Elizabeth go to her father, one can see they are devoted to each other. She could feel it by the way Elizabeth went to her father.

For her father had been looking at her, as he stood talking to the Bradshaws, and he had thought to himself, Who is that lovely girl? And suddenly he realised that it was his Elizabeth, and he had not recognised her, she looked so lovely in her pink frock! Elizabeth had felt him looking at her as she talked to Willie Titcomb. So she went to him and they stood together,

---

5. Cf. Shakespeare's *Richard II* 5.5.19–21.
6. Earlier, fifty-three years old.

now that the party was almost over, looking at the people going, and the rooms getting emptier and emptier, with things scattered on the floor. Even Ellie Henderson was going, nearly last of all, though no one had spoken to her, but she had wanted to see everything, to tell Edith. And Richard and Elizabeth were rather glad it was over, but Richard was proud of his daughter. And he had not meant to tell her, but he could not help telling her. He had looked at her, he said, and he had wondered, Who is that lovely girl? and it was his daughter! That did make her happy. But her poor dog was howling.

"Richard has improved. You are right," said Sally. "I shall go and talk to him. I shall say good-night. What does the brain matter," said Lady Rosseter, getting up, "compared with the heart?"

"I will come," said Peter, but he sat on for a moment. What is this terror? what is this ecstasy? he thought to himself. What is it that fills me with extraordinary excitement?

It is Clarissa, he said.

For there she was.

1925

From A Room of One's Own

[SHAKESPEARE'S SISTER][1]

It was disappointing not to have brought back in the evening some important statement, some authentic fact. Women are poorer than men because— this or that. Perhaps now it would be better to give up seeking for the truth, and receiving on one's head an avalanche of opinion hot as lava, discoloured as dish-water. It would be better to draw the curtains; to shut out distractions; to light the lamp; to narrow the enquiry and to ask the historian, who records not opinions but facts, to describe under what conditions women lived, not throughout the ages, but in England, say in the time of Elizabeth.[2]

For it is a perennial puzzle why no woman wrote a word of that extraordinary literature when every other man, it seemed, was capable of song or sonnet. What were the conditions in which women lived, I asked myself; for fiction, imaginative work that is, is not dropped like a pebble upon the ground, as science may be; fiction is like a spider's web, attached ever so lightly perhaps, but still attached to life at all four corners. Often the attachment is scarcely perceptible; Shakespeare's plays, for instance, seem to hang there complete by themselves. But when the web is pulled askew, hooked up at the edge, torn in the middle, one remembers that these webs are not spun in midair by incorporeal creatures, but are the work of suffering human beings, and are attached to grossly material things, like health and money and the houses we live in.

I went, therefore, to the shelf where the histories stand and took down one of the latest, Professor Trevelyan's History of England.[3] Once more I

---

1. The selection is drawn from chapter 3 and from the conclusion to the final chapter. In chapter 2, Woolf has been to the library of the British Museum, trying in vain to find answers to questions about the different fates of men and women.
2. Elizabeth I (r. 1558–1603).
3. G. M. Trevelyan's History of England (1926) long held its place as the standard one-volume history of the country.

looked up Women, found "position of," and turned to the pages indicated. "Wife-beating," I read, "was a recognised right of man, and was practised without shame by high as well as low. . . . Similarly," the historian goes on, "the daughter who refused to marry the gentleman of her parents' choice was liable to be locked up, beaten and flung about the room, without any shock being inflicted on public opinion. Marriage was not an affair of personal affection, but of family avarice, particularly in the 'chivalrous' upper classes. . . . Betrothal often took place while one or both of the parties was in the cradle, and marriage when they were scarcely out of the nurses' charge." That was about 1470, soon after Chaucer's time. The next reference to the position of women is some two hundred years later, in the time of the Stuarts.[4] "It was still the exception for women of the upper and middle class to choose their own husbands, and when the husband had been assigned, he was lord and master, so far at least as law and custom could make him. Yet even so," Professor Trevelyan concludes, "neither Shakespeare's women nor those of authentic seventeenth-century memoirs, like the Verneys and the Hutchinsons,[5] seem wanting in personality and character." Certainly, if we consider it, Cleopatra must have had a way with her; Lady Macbeth, one would suppose, had a will of her own; Rosalind,[6] one might conclude, was an attractive girl. Professor Trevelyan is speaking no more than the truth when he remarks that Shakespeare's women do not seem wanting in personality and character. Not being a historian, one might go even further and say that women have burnt like beacons in all the works of all the poets from the beginning of time—Clytemnestra, Antigone, Cleopatra, Lady Macbeth, Phèdre, Cressida, Rosalind, Desdemona, the Duchess of Malfi, among the dramatists; then among the prose writers: Millamant, Clarissa, Becky Sharp, Anna Karenina, Emma Bovary, Madame de Guermantes[7]—the names flock to mind, nor do they recall women "lacking in personality and character." Indeed, if woman had no existence save in the fiction written by men, one would imagine her a person of the utmost importance, very various; heroic and mean; splendid and sordid; infinitely beautiful and hideous in the extreme; as great as a man, some think even greater.[8] But this is woman in fiction. In fact, as Professor Trevelyan points out, she was locked up, beaten and flung about the room.

4. I.e., during the reign of the British house of Stuart (1603–49, 1660–1714).
5. "The ideal family life of the period [1640–50] that ended in such tragic political division has been recorded once for all in the *Memoirs of the Verney Family*" (Trevelyan, *History of England*). Lucy Hutchinson (1620–after 1675) wrote the biography of her husband, Col. John Hutchinson (1615–1664); it was first published in 1806.
6. These three Shakespearean heroines are, respectively, in *Antony and Cleopatra*, *Macbeth*, and *As You Like It*.
7. Characters in, respectively, Aeschylus's *Agamemnon*; Sophocles' *Antigone*; Shakespeare's *Antony and Cleopatra* and *Macbeth*; Racine's *Phèdre*; Shakespeare's *Troilus and Cressida*, *As You Like It*, and *Othello*; Webster's *The Duchess of Malfi*; Congreve's *Way of the World*; Richardson's *Clarissa*; Thackeray's *Vanity Fair*; Tolstoy's *Anna Karenina*; Flaubert's *Madame Bovary*; and Proust's *A la Recherche du Temps Perdu* (*In Search of Lost Time*).
8. "It remains a strange and almost inexplicable fact that in Athena's city, where women were kept in almost Oriental suppression as odalisques or drudges, the stage should yet have produced figures like Clytemnestra and Cassandra, Atossa and Antigone, Phèdre and Medea, and all the other heroines who dominate play after play of the 'misogynist' Euripides. But the paradox of this world where in real life a respectable woman could hardly show her face alone in the street, and yet on the stage woman equals or surpasses man, has never been satisfactorily explained. In modern tragedy the same predominance exists. At all events, a very cursory survey of Shakespeare's work (similarly with Webster, though not with Marlowe or Jonson) suffices to reveal how this dominance, this initiative of women, persists from Rosalind to Lady Macbeth. So too in Racine; six of his tragedies bear their heroines' names; and what male characters of his shall we set against Hermione and Andromaque, Bérénice and Roxane, Phèdre and Athalie? So again with Ibsen; what men shall we match with Solveig and Nora, Hedda and Hilda Wangel and Rebecca West?"—F. L. Lucas, *Tragedy*, pp. 114–15 [Woolf's note].

A very queer, composite being thus emerges. Imaginatively she is of the highest importance; practically she is completely insignificant. She pervades poetry from cover to cover; she is all but absent from history. She dominates the lives of kings and conquerors in fiction; in fact she was the slave of any boy whose parents forced a ring upon her finger. Some of the most inspired words, some of the most profound thoughts in literature fall from her lips; in real life she could hardly read, could scarcely spell, and was the property of her husband.

It was certainly an odd monster that one made up by reading the historians first and the poets afterwards—a worm winged like an eagle; the spirit of life and beauty in a kitchen chopping up suet. But these monsters, however amusing to the imagination, have no existence in fact. What one must do to bring her to life was to think poetically and prosaically at one and the same moment, thus keeping in touch with fact—that she is Mrs Martin, aged thirty-six, dressed in blue, wearing a black hat and brown shoes; but not losing sight of fiction either—that she is a vessel in which all sorts of spirits and forces are coursing and flashing perpetually. The moment, however, that one tries this method with the Elizabethan woman, one branch of illumination fails; one is held up by the scarcity of facts. One knows nothing detailed, nothing perfectly true and substantial about her. History scarcely mentions her. And I turned to Professor Trevelyan again to see what history meant to him. I found by looking at his chapter headings that it meant—

"The Manor Court and the Methods of Open-field Agriculture . . . The Cistercians and Sheep-farming . . . The Crusades . . . The University . . . The House of Commons . . . The Hundred Years' War . . . The Wars of the Roses . . . The Renaissance Scholars . . . The Dissolution of the Monasteries . . . Agrarian and Religious Strife . . . The Origin of English Sea-power . . . The Armada . . ." and so on. Occasionally an individual woman is mentioned, an Elizabeth, or a Mary; a queen or a great lady. But by no possible means could middle-class women with nothing but brains and character at their command have taken part in any one of the great movements which, brought together, constitute the historian's view of the past. Nor shall we find her in any collection of anecdotes. Aubrey[9] hardly mentions her. She never writes her own life and scarcely keeps a diary; there are only a handful of her letters in existence. She left no plays or poems by which we can judge her. What one wants, I thought—and why does not some brilliant student at Newnham or Girton[1] supply it?—is a mass of information; at what age did she marry; how many children had she as a rule; what was her house like; had she a room to herself; did she do the cooking; would she be likely to have a servant? All these facts lie somewhere, presumably, in parish registers and account books; the life of the average Elizabethan woman must be scattered about somewhere, could one collect it and make a book of it. It would be ambitious beyond my daring, I thought, looking about the shelves for books that were not there, to suggest to the students of those famous colleges that they should re-write history, though I own that it often seems a little queer as it is, unreal, lop-sided; but

9. John Aubrey (1626–1697), English writer, especially of short biographies.
1. The two women's colleges at Cambridge, where Woolf first delivered a version of *A Room of One's Own*.

why should they not add a supplement to history? calling it, of course, by some inconspicuous name so that women might figure there without impropriety? For one often catches a glimpse of them in the lives of the great, whisking away into the background, concealing, I sometimes think, a wink a laugh, perhaps a tear. And, after all, we have lives enough of Jane Austen;[2] it scarcely seems necessary to consider again the influence of the tragedies of Joanna Baillie upon the poetry of Edgar Allan Poe;[3] as for myself, I should not mind if the homes and haunts of Mary Russell Mitford[4] were closed to the public for a century at least. But what I find deplorable, I continued, looking about the bookshelves again, is that nothing is known about women before the eighteenth century. I have no model in my mind to turn about this way and that. Here am I asking why women did not write poetry in the Elizabethan age, and I am not sure how they were educated; whether they were taught to write; whether they had sitting-rooms to themselves; how many women had children before they were twenty-one; what, in short, they did from eight in the morning till eight at night. They had no money evidently; according to Professor Trevelyan they were married whether they liked it or not before they were out of the nursery, at fifteen or sixteen very likely. It would have been extremely odd, even upon this showing, had one of them suddenly written the plays of Shakespeare, I concluded, and I thought of that old gentleman, who is dead now, but was a bishop, I think, who declared that it was impossible for any woman, past, present, or to come, to have the genius of Shakespeare. He wrote to the papers about it. He also told a lady who applied to him for information that cats do not as a matter of fact go to heaven, though they have, he added, souls of a sort. How much thinking those old gentlemen used to save one! How the borders of ignorance shrank back at their approach! Cats do not go to heaven. Women cannot write the plays of Shakespeare.

Be that as it may, I could not help thinking, as I looked at the works of Shakespeare on the shelf, that the bishop was right at least in this; it would have been impossible, completely and entirely, for any woman to have written the plays of Shakespeare in the age of Shakespeare. Let me imagine, since facts are so hard to come by, what would have happened had Shakespeare had a wonderfully gifted sister, called Judith,[5] let us say. Shakespeare himself went, very probably—his mother was an heiress—to the grammar school, where he may have learnt Latin—Ovid, Virgil and Horace—and the elements of grammar and logic. He was, it is well known, a wild boy who poached rabbits, perhaps shot a deer, and had, rather sooner than he should have done, to marry a woman in the neighbourhood, who bore him a child rather quicker than was right. That escapade sent him to seek his fortune in London. He had, it seemed, a taste for the theatre; he began by holding horses at the stage door. Very soon he got work in the theatre, became a successful actor, and lived at the hub of the universe, meeting everybody, knowing everybody, practising his art on the boards, exercising his wits in the streets, and even getting access to the palace of the queen. Meanwhile his extraordinarily gifted sister, let us suppose, remained at home. She was as adventurous, as imaginative, as agog to see the world as he was. But she was

---

2. English novelist (1775–1817).
3. American poet and fiction writer (1809–1849). Joanna Baillie: English poet and dramatist (1762–1851).
4. Poet and novelist (1787–1855), best-known for sketches of country life.
5. Shakespeare had a daughter named Judith.

not sent to school. She had no chance of learning grammar and logic, let alone of reading Horace and Virgil. She picked up a book now and then, one of her brother's perhaps, and read a few pages. But then her parents came in and told her to mend the stockings or mind the stew and not moon about with books and papers. They would have spoken sharply but kindly, for they were substantial people who knew the conditions of life for a woman and loved their daughter—indeed, more likely than not she was the apple of her father's eye. Perhaps she scribbled some pages up in an apple loft on the sly, but was careful to hide them or set fire to them. Soon, however, before she was out of her teens, she was to be betrothed to the son of a neighbouring wool-stapler.[6] She cried out that marriage was hateful to her, and for that she was severely beaten by her father. Then he ceased to scold her. He begged her instead not to hurt him, not to shame him in this matter of her marriage. He would give her a chain of beads or a fine petticoat, he said; and there were tears in his eyes. How could she disobey him? How could she break his heart? The force of her own gift alone drove her to it. She made up a small parcel of her belongings, let herself down by a rope one summer's night and took the road to London. She was not seventeen. The birds that sang in the hedge were not more musical than she was. She had the quickest fancy, a gift like her brother's, for the tune of words. Like him, she had a taste for the theatre. She stood at the stage door; she wanted to act, she said. Men laughed in her face. The manager—a fat, loose-lipped man—guffawed. He bellowed something about poodles dancing and women acting—no woman, he said, could possibly be an actress. He hinted—you can imagine what. She could get no training in her craft. Could she even seek her dinner in a tavern or roam the streets at midnight? Yet her genius was for fiction and lusted to feed abundantly upon the lives of men and women and the study of their ways. At last—for she was very young, oddly like Shakespeare the poet in her face, with the same grey eyes and rounded brows—at last Nick Greene the actor-manager took pity on her; she found herself with child by that gentleman and so—who shall measure the heat and violence of the poet's heart when caught and tangled in a woman's body?—killed herself one winter's night and lies buried at some cross-roads where the omnibuses now stop outside the Elephant and Castle.[7]

That, more or less, is how the story would run, I think, if a woman in Shakespeare's day had had Shakespeare's genius. But for my part, I agree with the deceased bishop, if such he was—it is unthinkable that any woman in Shakespeare's day should have had Shakespeare's genius. For genius like Shakespeare's is not born among labouring, uneducated, servile people. It was not born in England among the Saxons and the Britons. It is not born today among the working classes. How, then, could it have been born among women whose work began, according to Professor Trevelyan, almost before they were out of the nursery, who were forced to it by their parents and held to it by all the power of law and custom? Yet genius of a sort must have existed among women as it must have existed among the working classes. Now and again an Emily Brontë or a Robert Burns[8] blazes out and

6. A stapler is a dealer in staple goods (i.e., established goods in trade and marketing); hence a wool-stapler is a dealer in wool (one of the "staple" products of 16th-century England).
7. Suicides were buried at crossroads. The Ele-

phant and Castle was a tavern south of the river Thames, where roads went off to different parts of southern England.
8. Scottish poet (1759–1796).

proves its presence. But certainly it never got itself on to paper. When, however, one reads of a witch being ducked, of a woman possessed by devils, of a wise woman selling herbs, or even of a very remarkable man who had a mother, then I think we are on the track of a lost novelist, a suppressed poet, of some mute and inglorious[9] Jane Austen, some Emily Brontë who dashed her brains out on the moor or mopped and mowed about the highways crazed with the torture that her gift had put her to. Indeed, I would venture to guess that Anon, who wrote so many poems without signing them, was often a woman. It was a woman Edward Fitzgerald,[1] I think, suggested who made the ballads and the folk-songs, crooning them to her children, beguiling her spinning with them, or the length of the winter's night.

This may be true or it may be false—who can say?—but what is true in it, so it seemed to me, reviewing the story of Shakespeare's sister as I had made it, is that any woman born with a great gift in the sixteenth century would certainly have gone crazed, shot herself, or ended her days in some lonely cottage outside the village, half witch, half wizard, feared and mocked at. For it needs little skill in psychology to be sure that a highly gifted girl who had tried to use her gift for poetry would have been so thwarted and hindered by other people, so tortured and pulled asunder by her own contrary instincts, that she must have lost her health and sanity to a certainty. No girl could have walked to London and stood at a stage door and forced her way into the presence of actor-managers without doing herself a violence and suffering an anguish which may have been irrational—for chastity may be a fetish invented by certain societies for unknown reasons—but were none the less inevitable. Chastity had then, it has even now, a religious importance in a woman's life, and has so wrapped itself round with nerves and instincts that to cut it free and bring it to the light of day demands courage of the rarest. To have lived a free life in London in the sixteenth century would have meant for a woman who was poet and playwright a nervous stress and dilemma which might well have killed her. Had she survived, whatever she had written would have been twisted and deformed, issuing from a strained and morbid imagination. And undoubtedly, I thought, looking at the shelf where there are no plays by women, her work would have gone unsigned. That refuge she would have sought certainly. It was the relic of the sense of chastity that dictated anonymity to women even so late as the nineteenth century. Currer Bell, George Eliot, George Sand,[2] all the victims of inner strife as their writings prove, sought ineffectively to veil themselves by using the name of a man. Thus they did homage to the convention, which if not implanted by the other sex was liberally encouraged by them (the chief glory of a woman is not to be talked of, said Pericles,[3] himself a much-talked-of man), that publicity in women is detestable. Anonymity runs in their blood. The desire to be veiled still possesses them. They are not even now as concerned about the health of their fame as men are, and, speaking generally, will pass a tombstone or a signpost without feeling an irresistible desire to cut their names on it, as Alf, Bert or Chas must do in obedience to their instinct, which murmurs if it sees a fine woman go by, or even a dog,

9. An echo of Thomas Gray's "Elegy Written in a Country Churchyard" (1751), line 59: "Some mute inglorious Milton here may rest."
1. Poet and translator (1809–1883).

2. Male pseudonyms, respectively, of Charlotte Brontë, Marian Evans, and Amandine-Aurore-Lucie Dupin (1804–1876).
3. Athenian statesman (ca. 495–429 B.C.E.).

Ce chien est à moi.[4] And, of course, it may not be a dog, I thought, remembering Parliament Square, the Sieges Allee[5] and other avenues; it may be a piece of land or a man with curly black hair. It is one of the great advantages of being a woman that one can pass even a very fine negress without wishing to make an Englishwoman of her.

That woman, then, who was born with a gift of poetry in the sixteenth century, was an unhappy woman, a woman at strife against herself. All the conditions of her life, all her own instincts, were hostile to the state of mind which is needed to set free whatever is in the brain. But what is the state of mind that is most propitious to the act of creation, I asked. Can one come by any notion of the state that furthers and makes possible that strange activity? Here I opened the volume containing the Tragedies of Shakespeare. What was Shakespeare's state of mind, for instance, when he wrote *Lear* and *Antony and Cleopatra*? It was certainly the state of mind most favourable to poetry that there has ever existed. But Shakespeare himself said nothing about it. We only know casually and by chance that he "never blotted a line."[6] Nothing indeed was ever said by the artist himself about his state of mind until the eighteenth century perhaps. Rousseau[7] perhaps began it. At any rate, by the nineteenth century self-consciousness had developed so far that it was the habit for men of letters to describe their minds in confessions and autobiographies. Their lives also were written, and their letters were printed after their deaths. Thus, though we do not know what Shakespeare went through when he wrote *Lear*, we do know what Carlyle went through when he wrote the *French Revolution*; what Flaubert went through when he wrote *Madame Bovary*; what Keats was going through when he tried to write poetry against the coming of death and the indifference of the world.

And one gathers from this enormous modern literature of confession and self-analysis that to write a work of genius is almost always a feat of prodigious difficulty. Everything is against the likelihood that it will come from the writer's mind whole and entire. Generally material circumstances are against it. Dogs will bark; people will interrupt; money must be made; health will break down. Further, accentuating all these difficulties and making them harder to bear is the world's notorious indifference. It does not ask people to write poems and novels and histories; it does not need them. It does not care whether Flaubert finds the right word or whether Carlyle[8] scrupulously verifies this or that fact. Naturally, it will not pay for what it does not want. And so the writer, Keats,[9] Flaubert, Carlyle, suffers, especially in the creative years of youth, every form of distraction and discouragement. A curse, a cry of agony, rises from those books of analysis and confession. "Mighty poets in their misery dead"[1]—that is the burden of their song. If anything comes through in spite of all this, it is a miracle, and probably no book is born entire and uncrippled as it was conceived.

But for women, I thought, looking at the empty shelves, these difficulties were infinitely more formidable. In the first place, to have a room of her

---

4. This dog is mine (French).
5. Avenue of Victory, a busy thoroughfare in Berlin. "Parliament Square": London intersection.
6. Ben Jonson, *Timber* (1640): "I remember, the players have often mentioned it as an honour to Shakespeare that in his writing (whatsoever he' penned) he never blotted out a line."
7. Jean-Jacques Rousseau (1712–1778), early-

Romantic French (Swiss-born) philosopher and memoirist.
8. Thomas Carlyle (1795–1881), Scottish writer and historian. Gustave Flaubert (1821–1880), French novelist who believed the literary artist should find "the right word" (*le mot juste*).
9. John Keats (1795–1821), English poet.
1. From William Wordsworth's "Resolution and Independence" (1807), line 116.

own, let alone a quiet room or a sound-proof room, was out of the question, unless her parents were exceptionally rich or very noble, even up to the beginning of the nineteenth century. Since her pin money, which depended on the good will of her father, was only enough to keep her clothed, she was debarred from such alleviations as came even to Keats or Tennyson[2] or Carlyle, all poor men, from a walking tour, a little journey to France, from the separate lodging which, even if it were miserable enough, sheltered them from the claims and tyrannies of their families. Such material difficulties were formidable; but much worse were the immaterial. The indifference of the world which Keats and Flaubert and other men of genius have found so hard to bear was in her case not indifference but hostility. The world did not say to her as it said to them, Write if you choose; it makes no difference to me. The world said with a guffaw, Write? What's the good of your writing?

* * *

Young women, I would say, and please attend, for the peroration is beginning, you are, in my opinion, disgracefully ignorant. You have never made a discovery of any sort of importance. You have never shaken an empire or led an army into battle. The plays of Shakespeare are not by you, and you have never introduced a barbarous race to the blessings of civilisation. What is your excuse? It is all very well for you to say, pointing to the streets and squares and forests of the globe swarming with black and white and coffee-coloured inhabitants, all busily engaged in traffic and enterprise and love-making, we have had other work on our hands. Without our doing, those seas would be unsailed and those fertile lands a desert. We have borne and bred and washed and taught, perhaps to the age of six or seven years, the one thousand six hundred and twenty-three million human beings who are, according to statistics, at present in existence, and that, allowing that some had help, takes time.

There is truth in what you say—I will not deny it. But at the same time may I remind you that there have been at least two colleges for women in existence in England since the year 1866; that after the year 1880 a married woman was allowed by law to possess her own property; and that in 1919—which is a whole nine years ago—she was given a vote? May I also remind you that the most of the professions have been open to you for close on ten years now? When you reflect upon these immense privileges and the length of time during which they have been enjoyed, and the fact that there must be at this moment some two thousand women capable of earning over five hundred a year in one way or another, you will agree that the excuse of lack of opportunity, training, encouragement, leisure and money no longer holds good. Moreover, the economists are telling us that Mrs Seton has had too many children. You must, of course, go on bearing children, but, so they say, in twos and threes, not in tens and twelves.

Thus, with some time on your hands and with some book learning in your brains—you have had enough of the other kind, and are sent to college partly, I suspect, to be uneducated—surely you should embark upon another stage of your very long, very laborious and highly obscure career. A thousand pens are ready to suggest what you should do and what effect you will have. My own suggestion is a little fantastic, I admit; I prefer, therefore, to put it in the form of fiction.

2. Alfred, Lord Tennyson (1809–1892), English poet.

I told you in the course of this paper that Shakespeare had a sister; but do not look for her in Sir Sidney Lee's[3] life of the poet. She died young—alas, she never wrote a word. She lies buried where the omnibuses now stop, opposite the Elephant and Castle. Now my belief is that this poet who never wrote a word and was buried at the crossroads still lives. She lives in you and in me, and in many other women who are not here tonight, for they are washing up the dishes and putting the children to bed. But she lives; for great poets do not die; they are continuing presences; they need only the opportunity to walk among us in the flesh. This opportunity, as I think, it is now coming within your power to give her. For my belief is that if we live another century or so—I am talking of the common life which is the real life and not of the little separate lives which we live as individuals—and have five hundred a year each of us and rooms of our own; if we have the habit of freedom and the courage to write exactly what we think; if we escape a little from the common sitting-room and see human beings not always in their relation to each other but in relation to reality; and the sky, too, and the trees or whatever it may be in themselves; if we look past Milton's bogey,[4] for no human being should shut out the view; if we face the fact, for it is a fact, that there is no arm to cling to, but that we go alone and that our relation is to the world of reality and not only to the world of men and women, then the opportunity will come and the dead poet who was Shakespeare's sister will put on the body which she has so often laid down. Drawing her life from the lives of the unknown who were her forerunners, as her brother did before her, she will be born. As for her coming without that preparation, without that effort on our part, without that determination that when she is born again she shall find it possible to live and write her poetry, that we cannot expect, for that would be impossible. But I maintain that she would come if we worked for her, and that so to work, even in poverty and obscurity, is worth while.

1929

Professions for Women[1]

When your secretary invited me to come here, she told me that your Society is concerned with the employment of women and she suggested that I might tell you something about my own professional experiences. It is true I am a woman; it is true I am employed; but what professional experiences have I had? It is difficult to say. My profession is literature; and in that profession there are fewer experiences for women than in any other, with the exception of the stage—fewer, I mean, that are peculiar to women. For the road was cut many years ago—by Fanny Burney, by Aphra Behn, by Harriet Martineau,[2] by Jane Austen, by George Eliot—many famous women, and

3. Biographer and Shakespeare scholar (1859–1926), author of *Life of William Shakespeare* (1898).
4. Cf. Milton's unhappy first marriage, his campaign for freedom of divorce, and his deliberate subordination of Eve to Adam in *Paradise Lost*.
1. A paper read to the Women's Service League [Woolf's note]. Woolf here echoes her points in *A*

Room of One's Own about a woman's needing money (specifically, an annual income of five hundred British pounds) and a room in which to write.
2. Economist, moralist, journalist, and novelist (1802–1876). Burney (1752–1840), author of *Evelina* and other novels. Behn (1640–1689), writer of romances and plays.

many more unknown and forgotten, have been before me, making the path smooth, and regulating my steps. Thus, when I came to write, there were very few material obstacles in my way. Writing was a reputable and harmless occupation. The family peace was not broken by the scratching of a pen. No demand was made upon the family purse. For ten and sixpence one can buy paper enough to write all the plays of Shakespeare—if one has a mind that way. Pianos and models, Paris, Vienna, and Berlin, masters and mistresses, are not needed by a writer. The cheapness of writing paper is, of course, the reason why women have succeeded as writers before they have succeeded in the other professions.

But to tell you my story—it is a simple one. You have only got to figure to yourselves a girl in a bedroom with a pen in her hand. She had only to move that pen from left to right—from ten o'clock to one. Then it occurred to her to do what is simple and cheap enough after all—to slip a few of those pages into an envelope, fix a penny stamp in the corner, and drop the envelope into the red box at the corner. It was thus that I became a journalist; and my effort was rewarded on the first day of the following month—a very glorious day it was for me—by a letter from an editor containing a cheque for one pound ten shillings and sixpence. But to show you how little I deserve to be called a professional woman, how little I know of the struggles and difficulties of such lives, I have to admit that instead of spending that sum upon bread and butter, rent, shoes and stockings, or butcher's bills, I went out and bought a cat—a beautiful cat, a Persian cat, which very soon involved me in bitter disputes with my neighbours.

What could be easier than to write articles and to buy Persian cats with the profits? But wait a moment. Articles have to be about something. Mine, I seem to remember, was about a novel by a famous man. And while I was writing this review, I discovered that if I were going to review books I should need to do battle with a certain phantom. And the phantom was a woman, and when I came to know her better I called her after the heroine of a famous poem, The Angel in the House.[3] It was she who used to come between me and my paper when I was writing reviews. It was she who bothered and wasted my time and so tormented me that at last I killed her. You who come of a younger and happier generation may not have heard of her— you may not know what I mean by The Angel in the House. I will describe her as shortly as I can. She was intensely sympathetic. She was immensely charming. She was utterly unselfish. She excelled in the difficult arts of family life. She sacrificed herself daily. If there was chicken, she took the leg; if there was a draught she sat in it—in short she was so constituted that she never had a mind or a wish of her own, but preferred to sympathise always with the minds and wishes of others. Above all—I need not say it— she was pure. Her purity was supposed to be her chief beauty—her blushes, her great grace. In those days—the last of Queen Victoria—every house had its Angel. And when I came to write I encountered her with the very first words. The shadow of her wings fell on my page; I heard the rustling of her skirts in the room. Directly, that is to say, I took my pen in my hand to review that novel by a famous man, she slipped behind me and whispered: 'My dear, you are a young woman. You are writing about a book that has been written by a man. Be sympathetic; be tender; flatter; deceive; use all

3. By Coventry Patmore (1823–1896), published 1854–62.

the arts and wiles of our sex. Never let anybody guess that you have a mind of your own. Above all, be pure.' And she made as if to guide my pen. I now record the one act for which I take some credit to myself, though the credit rightly belongs to some excellent ancestors of mine who left me a certain sum of money—shall we say five hundred pounds a year?—so that it was not necessary for me to depend solely on charm for my living. I turned upon her and caught her by the throat. I did my best to kill her. My excuse, if I were to be had up in a court of law, would be that I acted in self-defence. Had I not killed her she would have killed me. She would have plucked the heart out of my writing. For, as I found, directly I put pen to paper, you cannot review even a novel without having a mind of your own, without expressing what you think to be the truth about human relations, morality, sex. And all these questions, according to the Angel of the House, cannot be dealt with freely and openly by women; they must charm, they must conciliate, they must—to put it bluntly—tell lies if they are to succeed. Thus, whenever I felt the shadow of her wing or the radiance of her halo upon my page, I took up the inkpot and flung it at her. She died hard. Her fictitious nature was of great assistance to her. It is far harder to kill a phantom than a reality. She was always creeping back when I thought I had despatched her. Though I flatter myself that I killed her in the end, the struggle was severe; it took much time that had better have been spent upon learning Greek grammar; or in roaming the world in search of adventures. But it was a real experience; it was an experience that was bound to befall all women writers at that time. Killing the Angel in the House was part of the occupation of a woman writer.

But to continue my story. The Angel was dead; what then remained? You may say that what remained was a simple and common object—a young woman in a bedroom with an inkpot. In other words, now that she had rid herself of falsehood, that young woman had only to be herself. Ah, but what is 'herself'? I mean, what is a woman? I assure you, I do not know. I do not believe that you know. I do not believe that anybody can know until she has expressed herself in all the arts and professions open to human skill. That indeed is one of the reasons why I have come here—out of respect for you, who are in process of showing us by your experiments what a woman is, who are in process of providing us, by your failures and successes, with that extremely important piece of information.

But to continue the story of my professional experiences. I made one pound ten and six by my first review; and I bought a Persian cat with the proceeds. Then I grew ambitious. A Persian cat is all very well, I said; but a Persian cat is not enough. I must have a motor-car. And it was thus that I became a novelist—for it is a very strange thing that people will give you a motor-car if you will tell them a story. It is a still stranger thing that there is nothing so delightful in the world as telling stories. It is far pleasanter than writing reviews of famous novels. And yet, if I am to obey your secretary and tell you my professional experiences as a novelist, I must tell you about a very strange experience that befell me as a novelist. And to understand it you must try first to imagine a novelist's state of mind. I hope I am not giving away professional secrets if I say that a novelist's chief desire is to be as unconscious as possible. He has to induce in himself a state of perpetual lethargy. He wants life to proceed with the utmost quiet and regularity. He wants to see the same faces, to read the same books, to do the same things day after day, month after month, while he is writing, so that nothing may break the illusion in which he is living—so that nothing may disturb or disquiet the mysterious nosings about, feelings round, darts, dashes, and sudden discoveries of that very shy and illusive spirit, the imagination. I suspect that this state is the same both for men and women. Be that as it may, I want you to imagine me writing a novel in a state of trance. I want you to figure to yourselves a girl sitting with a pen in her hand, which for minutes, and indeed for hours, she never dips into the inkpot. The image that comes to my mind when I think of this girl is the image of a fisherman lying sunk in dreams on the verge of a deep lake with a rod held out over the water. She was letting her imagination sweep unchecked round every rock and cranny of the world that lies submerged in the depths of our unconscious being. Now came the experience that I believe to be far commoner with women writers than with men. The line raced through the girl's fingers. Her imagination had rushed away. It had sought the pools, the depths, the dark places where the largest fish slumber. And then there was a smash. There was an explosion. There was foam and confusion. The imagination had dashed itself against something hard. The girl was roused from her dream. She was indeed in a state of the most acute and difficult distress. To speak without figure, she had thought of something, something about the body, about the passions which it was unfitting for her as a woman to say. Men, her reason told her, would be shocked. The consciousness of what men will say of a woman who speaks the truth about her passions had roused her from her artist's state of unconsciousness. She could write no more. The trance was over. Her imagination could work no longer. This I believe to be a very common experience with women writers—they are impeded by the extreme conventionality of the other sex. For though men sensibly allow themselves great freedom in these respects, I doubt that they realize or can control the extreme severity with which they condemn such freedom in women.

These then were two very genuine experiences of my own. These were two of the adventures of my professional life. The first—killing the Angel in the House—I think I solved. She died. But the second, telling the truth about my own experiences as a body, I do not think I solved. I doubt that any woman has solved it yet. The obstacles against her are still immensely powerful—and yet they are very difficult to define. Outwardly, what is simpler than to write books? Outwardly, what obstacles are there for a woman rather than for a man? Inwardly, I think, the case is very different; she has still many ghosts to fight, many prejudices to overcome. Indeed it will be a long time still, I think, before a woman can sit down to write a book without finding a phantom to be slain, a rock to be dashed against. And if this is so in literature, the freest of all professions for women, how is it in the new professions which you are now for the first time entering?

Those are the questions that I should like, had I time, to ask you. And indeed, if I have laid stress upon these professional experiences of mine, it is because I believe that they are, though in different forms, yours also. Even when the path is nominally open—when there is nothing to prevent a woman from being a doctor, a lawyer, a civil servant—there are many phantoms and obstacles, as I believe, looming in her way. To discuss and define them is I think of great value and importance; for thus only can the labour be shared, the difficulties be solved. But besides this, it is necessary also to discuss the ends and the aims for which we are fighting, for which we are doing battle with these formidable obstacles. Those aims cannot be taken for granted;

they must be perpetually questioned and examined. The whole position, as I see it—here in this hall surrounded by women practising for the first time in history I know not how many different professions—is one of extraordinary interest and importance. You have won rooms of your own in the house hitherto exclusively owned by men. You are able, though not without great labour and effort, to pay the rent. You are earning your five hundred pounds a year. But this freedom is only a beginning; the room is your own, but it is still bare. It has to be furnished; it has to be decorated; it has to be shared. How are you going to furnish it, how are you going to decorate it? With whom are you going to share it, and upon what terms? These, I think are questions of the utmost importance and interest. For the first time in history you are able to ask them; for the first time you are able to decide for yourselves what the answers should be. Willingly would I stay and discuss those questions and answers—but not tonight. My time is up; and I must cease.

1942

JAMES JOYCE
1882–1941

J ames Joyce was born in Dublin, son of a talented but feckless father, who is accurately described in Joyce's novel *A Portrait of the Artist as a Young Man* (1916) as having been "a medical student, an oarsman, a tenor, an amateur actor, a shouting politician, a small landlord, a small investor, a drinker, a good fellow, a storyteller, somebody's secretary, something in a distillery, a tax-gatherer, a bankrupt, and at present a praiser of his own past." The elder Joyce, like the father in Joyce's novel, drifted steadily down the financial and social scale, his family moving from house to house, each one less genteel and more shabby than the previous. James Joyce's primary education was Catholic, from the age of six to the age of nine at Clongowes Wood College and from eleven to sixteen at Belvedere College, as vividly recalled in *A Portrait of the Artist*. Both were Jesuit institutions and were normal roads to the priesthood. He then studied modern languages at University College, Dublin.

From a comparatively young age Joyce regarded himself as a rebel against the shabbiness and philistinism of Dublin. In his last year of school at Belvedere he began to reject his Catholic faith in favor of a literary mission that he saw as involving rebellion and exile. He refused to play any part in the nationalist or other popular activities of his fellow students, and he created some stir by his outspoken articles, one of which, on the Norwegian playwright Henrik Ibsen, appeared in London's *Fortnightly Review* when Joyce was eighteen. He taught himself Dano-Norwegian in order to read Ibsen and to write to him. When, on instructions of the faculty adviser, an article by Joyce, significantly titled "The Day of the Rabblement," was refused by the student magazine that had commissioned it, he had it printed privately. By 1902, when he received his A.B. degree, the young man was already committed to a career as exile and writer. For Joyce, as for his character Stephen Dedalus in *A Portrait of the Artist* and *Ulysses*, being a writer necessarily implied a self-imposed state of exile. To preserve his integrity, to avoid involvement

Dublin ca. 1899. Sackville Street, renamed O'Connell Street in 1924, was and still is the grand main street in Dublin. After he left for the Continent, Joyce imaginatively populated the city with such fictional characters as Stephen Dedalus, Leopold Bloom, and Molly Bloom. In Joyce's time, as seen in this picture, Dublin bustled with pedestrians, horse-drawn carriages, electric trams, and automobiles. Also visible are monuments to the British colonial system, most prominently Nelson's Pillar, dedicated in 1809 to the British naval hero Horatio Nelson and destroyed in 1966 by Irish republicans.

in popular causes, to devote himself to the life of the artist, he felt that he had to go abroad.

Joyce went to Paris after graduation, was recalled to Dublin by his mother's fatal illness, had a short spell there as a schoolteacher, then returned to the Continent in 1904 to teach English in Trieste and then in Zurich. He took with him Nora Barnacle, a woman from Galway with no interest in literature; her vivacity and wit charmed Joyce, and the two lived in devoted companionship until his death, although they were not married until 1931. In 1920 Joyce and Barnacle settled in Paris, where they lived until December 1940, when the war forced them to take refuge in Switzerland; he died in Zurich a few weeks later.

Proud, obstinate, absolutely convinced of his genius, given to fits of sudden gaiety and of sudden silence, Joyce was not always an easy person to get along with, yet he never lacked friends, and throughout his thirty-six years on the Continent he was always the center of a literary circle. Life was hard at first. In Trieste he had little money, and he did not improve matters by drinking heavily, a habit checked somewhat by his brother Stanislaus, who came out from Dublin to act (as Stanislaus put it much later) as his "brother's keeper." Joyce also suffered from eye diseases and, blind for brief periods, underwent twenty-five operations. In 1917 Edith Rockefeller McCormick and then the lawyer John Quinn, steered in Joyce's direction by Ezra Pound, helped out financially. A benefactor who would prove to be permanent was the English feminist and editor Harriet Shaw Weaver, who not only subsidized Joyce generously from 1917 to the end of his life but also occupied herself indefatigably with arrangements for publishing his work.

In spite of doing most of his writing in Trieste, Zurich, and Paris, Joyce paradoxically wrote only and always about Dublin. No writer has ever been more soaked in Dublin—its atmosphere, its history, its topography. He devised ways of expanding his accounts of the Irish capital, however, so that they became microcosms of human history, geography, and experience.

Joyce began his career by writing a series of stories that etched, with extraordinary clarity, aspects of Dublin life. These stories—published as *Dubliners* in 1914—are sharp, realistic sketches of what Joyce called the "paralysis" that beset the lives of people in then-provincial Ireland. The language is crisp, lucid, and detached, and the details are chosen and organized so meticulously that their symbolic meanings intensify as the events and images intersect. Some of the stories, such as "Araby," are built around what Joyce called an "epiphany," a dramatic but fleeting moment of revelation about the self or the world. Many end abruptly, without conventional narrative closure, or they lack overt connectives and transitions, leaving multiple possibilities in suspension. The last story in *Dubliners*, "The Dead," was not part of the original draft of the book but was added later, when Joyce was preoccupied with the nature of artistic objectivity. At a festive event, attended by guests whose portraits Joyce draws with precision and economy, a series of jolting events frees the protagonist, Gabriel, from his possessiveness and egotism. The view he attains at the end is the mood of supreme neutrality that Joyce saw as the beginning of artistic awareness. It is the view of art developed by Stephen Dedalus in *A Portrait of the Artist*.

Dubliners represents Joyce's first phase, in which he came to terms with the life he had rejected. Next he had to come to terms with the meaning of his emergence as a man dedicated to imaginative writing; the result was a novel about the youth and development of an artist, *A Portrait of the Artist as a Young Man* (1916). Joyce wove his autobiography into a work of fiction so finely chiseled and arranged, so stripped of anything superfluous, that each word contributes to the presentation of the theme: the parallel movement toward art and toward exile. A part of his first draft was published posthumously under the original title, *Stephen Hero* (1944), and a comparison between it and the final version, *A Portrait of the Artist*, shows the precision with which Joyce reworked and compressed his material for maximum effect.

From the beginning, Joyce had trouble getting his writing into print. The release of *Dubliners* was held up for many years while he fought with both English and Irish editors about words and phrases that they wished to eliminate. Censorship cuts were made to *A Portrait of the Artist* when it was first issued, in serial form, and three European publishers rejected it before it was finally accepted by an American firm. Joyce's next novel, *Ulysses* (1922), was banned in Britain and America on publication; its earlier serialization in an American magazine, *The Little Review* (March 1918–December 1920), had been stopped abruptly when the U.S. Post Office brought a charge of obscenity against the work. Fortunately Judge John Woolsey's history-making decision in a federal district court on December 6, 1933, resulted in the lifting of the ban and the free circulation of *Ulysses*, first in America and soon afterward in Britain.

Ulysses is an account of one day in the lives of Dubliners; it thus describes a limited number of events involving a limited number of people in a limited environment. Yet Joyce's ambition—which took him seven years to realize—is to give the events the depth and implication that can convey symbolic significance. The episodes in *Ulysses* correspond to incidents in Homer's ancient Greek epic *Odyssey*, although the Homeric names customarily given to the episodes, such as "Proteus," "Circe," and "Penelope," appear not in the book but in Joyce's schematic outline. Joyce regarded Odysseus, or Ulysses, as the most "complete" man in literature, shown in all his aspects—coward and hero, cautious and reckless, weak and strong, husband and philanderer, father and son, dignified and ridiculous; so he makes his hero, Leopold Bloom, an Irish Jew, into a modern Ulysses. The parallels between the Homeric archetypes and the modern-day characters and events create a host of interpretive complexities. They can seem tight or loose, deflating or ennobling, ironic or heroic, epic or mock-epic, depending on their specific application in a particular episode and, to some extent, on the propensities of the reader.

Joyce's final work, *Finnegans Wake* (1939), took more than fourteen years to write, and Joyce considered it his masterpiece, though some readers have found its dense, multilayered language impenetrable. For this work, Joyce invents a dream language in which words are combined, distorted, created from bits of other words fitted together, several meanings at once, often drawn from several languages, and fused in conveying a variety of ways to achieve whole clusters of meaning simultaneously. In *Ulysses* Joyce had made the symbolic aspect of the novel at least as important as the realistic aspect, but in *Finnegans Wake* he gave up realism altogether. This vast story of a symbolic Irishman's cosmic dream develops, by enormous reverberating puns, a continuous expansion of meaning, the elements in the puns deriving from every conceivable source in history, literature, mythology, and Joyce's personal experience.

Like his other novels, *Finnegans Wake* put Joyce's consummate craftsmanship at the service of a humanely comic vision. His innovations in organization, style, and narrative technique have influenced countless writers, but his works of fiction are unique.

Araby[1]

North Richmond Street, being blind, was a quiet street except at the hour when the Christian Brothers' School[2] set the boys free. An uninhabited house of two storeys stood at the blind end, detached from its neighbours in a square ground. The other houses of the street, conscious of decent lives within them, gazed at one another with brown imperturbable faces.

The former tenant of our house, a priest, had died in the back drawing-room. Air, musty from having been long enclosed, hung in all the rooms, and the waste room behind the kitchen was littered with old useless papers. Among these I found a few paper-covered books, the pages of which were curled and damp: *The Abbot*, by Walter Scott, *The Devout Communicant* and *The Memoirs of Vidocq*,[3] I liked the last best because its leaves were yellow. The wild garden behind the house contained a central apple-tree and a few straggling bushes under one of which I found the late tenant's rusty bicycle-pump. He had been a very charitable priest; in his will he had left all his money to institutions and the furniture of his house to his sister.

When the short days of winter came dusk fell before we had well eaten our dinners. When we met in the street the houses had grown sombre. The space of sky above us was the colour of ever-changing violet and towards it the lamps of the street lifted their feeble lanterns. The cold air stung us and we played

1. The third of the fifteen stories in *Dubliners*. This tale of the frustrated quest for beauty in the midst of drabness is both meticulously realistic in its handling of details of Dublin life and the Dublin scene, and also highly symbolic in that almost every image and incident suggests some particular aspect of the theme (e.g., the suggestion of the Holy Grail in the image of the chalice, mentioned in the fifth paragraph). Joyce was drawing on his own childhood recollections, and the uncle in the story is a reminiscence of Joyce's father. But in all the stories in *Dubliners* dealing with childhood, the child lives not with his parents but with an uncle and aunt—a symbol of that isolation and lack of proper relation between "consubstantial" (in the flesh) parents and children that is a major theme in Joyce's work.
2. The Joyce family moved to 17 North Richmond Street, Dublin, in 1894; and Joyce had earlier briefly attended the Christian Brothers' school a few doors away (the Christian Brothers are a Catholic religious community). The details of the house described here correspond exactly to those of number 17. "Blind": i.e., it was a dead-end street.
3. François Eugéne Vidocq (1775–1857) had an extraordinary career as soldier, thief, chief of the French detective force, and private detective. *The Abbot* is a historical novel dealing with Mary, Queen of Scots. *The Devout Communicant* is a Catholic religious manual.

till our bodies glowed. Our shouts echoed in the silent street. The career of our play brought us through the dark muddy lanes behind the houses where we ran the gantlet of the rough tribes from the cottages, to the back doors of the dark dripping gardens where odours arose from the ashpits, to the dark odorous stables where a coachman smoothed and combed the horse or shook music from the buckled harness. When we returned to the street light from the kitchen windows had filled the areas. If my uncle was seen turning the corner we hid in the shadow until we had seen him safely housed. Or if Mangan's sister came out on the doorstep to call her brother in to his tea we watched her from our shadow peer up and down the street. We waited to see whether she would remain or go in and, if she remained, we left our shadow and walked up to Mangan's steps resignedly. She was waiting for us, her figure defined by the light from the half-opened door. Her brother always teased her before he obeyed and I stood by the railings looking at her. Her dress swung as she moved her body and the soft rope of her hair tossed from side to side.

Every morning I lay on the floor in the front parlour watching her door. The blind was pulled down to within an inch of the sash so that I could not be seen. When she came out on the doorstep my heart leaped. I ran to the hall, seized my books and followed her. I kept her brown figure always in my eye and, when we came near the point at which our ways diverged, I quickened my pace and passed her. This happened morning after morning. I had never spoken to her, except for a few casual words, and yet her name was like a summons to all my foolish blood.

Her image accompanied me even in places the most hostile to romance. On Saturday evenings when my aunt went marketing I had to go to carry some of the parcels. We walked through the flaring streets, jostled by drunken men and bargaining women, amid the curses of labourers, the shrill litanies of shop-boys who stood on guard by the barrels of pigs' cheeks, the nasal chanting of street-singers, who sang a *come-all-you*[4] about O'Donovan Rossa, or a ballad about the troubles in our native land. These noises converged in a single sensation of life for me: I imagined that I bore my chalice safely through a throng of foes. Her name sprang to my lips at moments in strange prayers and praises which I myself did not understand. My eyes were often full of tears (I could not tell why) and at times a flood from my heart seemed to pour itself out into my bosom. I thought little of the future. I did not know whether I would ever speak to her or not or, if I spoke to her, how I could tell her of my confused adoration. But my body was like a harp and her words and gestures were like fingers running upon the wires.

One evening I went into the back drawing-room in which the priest had died. It was a dark rainy evening and there was no sound in the house. Through one of the broken panes I heard the rain impinge upon the earth, the fine incessant needles of water playing in the sodden beds. Some distant lamp or lighted window gleamed below me. I was thankful that I could see so little. All my senses seemed to desire to veil themselves and, feeling that I was about to slip from them, I pressed the palms of my hands together until they trembled, murmuring: *O love! O love!* many times.

At last she spoke to me. When she addressed the first words to me I was so confused that I did not know what to answer. She asked me was I going

---

4. Street ballad, so called from its opening words. This one was about the 19th-century Irish nationalist Jeremiah Donovan, popularly known as O'Donovan Rossa.

to *Araby*.[5] I forgot whether I answered yes or no. It would be a splendid bazaar, she said; she would love to go.

—And why can't you? I asked.

While she spoke she turned a silver bracelet round and round her wrist. She could not go, she said, because there would be a retreat that week in her convent.[6] Her brother and two other boys were fighting for their caps and I was alone at the railings. She held one of the spikes, bowing her head towards me. The light from the lamp opposite our door caught the white curve of her neck, lit up her hair that rested there and, falling, lit up the hand upon the railing. It fell over one side of her dress and caught the white border of a petticoat, just visible as she stood at ease.

—It's well for you, she said.

—If I go, I said, I will bring you something.

What innumerable follies laid waste my waking and sleeping thoughts after that evening! I wished to annihilate the tedious intervening days. I chafed against the work of school. At night in my bedroom and by day in the classroom her image came between me and the page I strove to read. The syllables of the word *Araby* were called to me through the silence in which my soul luxuriated and cast an Eastern enchantment over me. I asked for leave to go to the bazaar on Saturday night. My aunt was surprised and hoped it was not some Freemason affair.[7] I answered few questions in class. I watched my master's face pass from amiability to sternness; he hoped I was not beginning to idle. I could not call my wandering thoughts together. I had hardly any patience with the serious work of life which, now that it stood between me and my desire, seemed to me child's play, ugly monotonous child's play.

On Saturday morning I reminded my uncle that I wished to go to the bazaar in the evening. He was fussing at the hallstand, looking for the hat-brush, and answered me curtly:

—Yes, boy, I know.

As he was in the hall I could not go into the front parlour and lie at the window. I left the house in bad humour and walked slowly towards the school. The air was pitilessly raw and already my heart misgave me.

When I came home to dinner my uncle had not yet been home. Still it was early. I sat staring at the clock for some time and, when its ticking began to irritate me, I left the room. I mounted the staircase and gained the upper part of the house. The high cold empty gloomy rooms liberated me and I went from room to room singing. From the front window I saw my companions playing below in the street. Their cries reached me weakened and indistinct and, leaning my forehead against the cool glass, I looked over at the dark house where she lived. I may have stood there for an hour, seeing nothing but the brown-clad figure cast by my imagination, touched discreetly by the lamplight at the curved neck, at the hand upon the railings and at the border below the dress.

When I came downstairs again I found Mrs Mercer sitting at the fire. She was an old garrulous woman, a pawn-broker's widow, who collected used stamps for some pious purpose. I had to endure the gossip of the tea-table. The meal was prolonged beyond an hour and still my uncle did not

5. The bazaar, described by its "official catalogue" as a "Grand Oriental Fête," was actually held in Dublin on May 14–19, 1894.
6. I.e., her convent school. "Retreat": period of seclusion from ordinary activities devoted to religious exercises.
7. His aunt shares her church's distrust of the Freemasons, an old European secret society, reputedly anti-Catholic.

come. Mrs Mercer stood up to go: she was sorry she couldn't wait any longer, but it was after eight o'clock and she did not like to be out late, as the night air was bad for her. When she had gone I began to walk up and down the room, clenching my fists. My aunt said:

—I'm afraid you may put off your bazaar for this night of Our Lord.

At nine o'clock I heard my uncle's latchkey in the halldoor. I heard him talking to himself and heard the hallstand rocking when it had received the weight of his overcoat. I could interpret these signs. When he was midway through his dinner I asked him to give me the money to go to the bazaar. He had forgotten.

—The people are in bed and after their first sleep now, he said.

I did not smile. My aunt said to him energetically:

—Can't you give him the money and let him go? You've kept him late enough as it is.

My uncle said he was very sorry he had forgotten. He said he believed in the old saying: *All work and no play makes Jack a dull boy.* He asked me where I was going and, when I had told him a second time he asked me did I know *The Arab's Farewell to his Steed.*[8] When I left the kitchen he was about to recite the opening lines of the piece to my aunt.

I held a florin[9] tightly in my hand as I strode down Buckingham Street towards the station. The sight of the streets thronged with buyers and glaring with gas recalled to me the purpose of my journey. I took my seat in a third-class carriage of a deserted train. After an intolerable delay the train moved out of the station slowly. It crept onward among ruinous houses and over the twinkling river. At Westland Row Station a crowd of people pressed to the carriage doors; but the porters moved them back, saying that it was a special train for the bazaar. I remained alone in the bare carriage. In a few minutes the train drew up beside an improvised wooden platform. I passed out on to the road and saw by the lighted dial of a clock that it was ten minutes to ten. In front of me was a large building which displayed the magical name.

I could not find any sixpenny entrance and, fearing that the bazaar would be closed, I passed in quickly through a turnstile, handing a shilling to a weary-looking man. I found myself in a big hall girdled at half its height by a gallery. Nearly all the stalls were closed and the greater part of the hall was in darkness. I recognized a silence like that which pervades a church after a service. I walked into the centre of the bazaar timidly. A few people were gathered about the stalls which were still open. Before a curtain, over which the words *Café Chantant*[1] were written in coloured lamps, two men were counting money on a salver. I listened to the fall of the coins.

Remembering with difficulty why I had come I went over to one of the stalls and examined porcelain vases and flowered tea-sets. At the door of the stall a young lady was talking and laughing with two young gentlemen. I remarked their English accents and listened vaguely to their conversation.

—O, I never said such a thing!

—O, but you did!

---

8. Once-popular sentimental poem by Caroline Norton.

9. A silver coin, now obsolete, worth two shillings.

1. Singing café (French; literal trans.); a café that provided musical entertainment, popular early in the 20th century.

—O, but I didn't!

—Didn't she say that?

—Yes. I heard her.

—O, there's a . . . fib!

Observing me the young lady came over and asked me did I wish to buy anything. The tone of her voice was not encouraging; she seemed to have spoken to me out of a sense of duty. I looked humbly at the great jars that stood like eastern guards at either side of the dark entrance to the stall and murmured:

—No, thank you.

The young lady changed the position of one of the vases and went back to the two young men. They began to talk of the same subject. Once or twice the young lady glanced at me over her shoulder.

I lingered before her stall, though I knew my stay was useless, to make my interest in her wares seem the more real. Then I turned away slowly and walked down the middle of the bazaar. I allowed the two pennies to fall against the sixpence in my pocket. I heard a voice call from one end of the gallery that the light was out. The upper part of the hall was now completely dark.

Gazing up into the darkness I saw myself as a creature driven and derided by vanity; and my eyes burned with anguish and anger.

1905   1914

The Dead

Lily, the caretaker's daughter, was literally run off her feet. Hardly had she brought one gentleman into the little pantry behind the office on the ground floor and helped him off with his overcoat than the wheezy hall-door bell clanged again and she had to scamper along the bare hallway to let in another guest. It was well for her she had not to attend to the ladies also. But Miss Kate and Miss Julia had thought of that and had converted the bathroom upstairs into a ladies' dressing-room. Miss Kate and Miss Julia were there, gossiping and laughing and fussing, walking after each other to the head of the stairs, peering down over the banisters and calling down to Lily to ask her who had come.

It was always a great affair, the Misses Morkan's annual dance. Everybody who knew them came to it, members of the family, old friends of the family, the members of Julia's choir, any of Kate's pupils that were grown up enough and even some of Mary Jane's pupils too. Never once had it fallen flat. For years and years it had gone off in splendid style as long as anyone could remember; ever since Kate and Julia, after the death of their brother Pat, had left the house in Stoney Batter and taken Mary Jane, their only niece, to live with them in the dark gaunt house on Usher's Island, the upper part of which they had rented from Mr Fulham, the cornfactor[1] on the ground floor. That was a good thirty years ago if it was a day. Mary Jane, who was then a little girl in short clothes, was now the main prop of the household for she

---

1. Grain merchant.

had the organ in Haddington Road.[2] She had been through the Academy and gave a pupils' concert every year in the upper room of the Antient Concert Rooms.[3] Many of her pupils belonged to better-class families on the Kingstown and Dalkey line. Old as they were, her aunts also did their share. Julia, though she was quite grey, was still the leading soprano in Adam and Eve's, and Kate, being too feeble to go about much, gave music lessons to beginners on the old square piano in the back room. Lily, the caretaker's daughter, did housemaid's work for them. Though their life was modest they believed in eating well; the best of everything: diamond-bone sirloins, three-shilling tea and the best bottled stout.[4] But Lily seldom made a mistake in the orders so that she got on well with her three mistresses. They were fussy, that was all. But the only thing they would not stand was back answers.

Of course they had good reason to be fussy on such a night. And then it was long after ten o'clock and yet there was no sign of Gabriel and his wife. Besides they were dreadfully afraid that Freddy Malins might turn up screwed.[5] They would not wish for worlds that any of Mary Jane's pupils should see him under the influence; and when he was like that it was sometimes very hard to manage him. Freddy Malins always came late but they wondered what could be keeping Gabriel: and that was what brought them every two minutes to the banisters to ask Lily had Gabriel or Freddy come.

—O, Mr Conroy, said Lily to Gabriel when she opened the door for him, Miss Kate and Miss Julia thought you were never coming. Good-night, Mrs Conroy.

—I'll engage[6] they did, said Gabriel, but they forget that my wife here takes three mortal hours to dress herself.

He stood on the mat, scraping the snow from his goloshes, while Lily led his wife to the foot of the stairs and called out:

—Miss Kate, here's Mrs Conroy.

Kate and Julia came toddling down the dark stairs at once. Both of them kissed Gabriel's wife, said she must be perished alive and asked was Gabriel with her.

—Here I am as right as the mail, Aunt Kate! Go on up. I'll follow, called out Gabriel from the dark.

He continued scraping his feet vigorously while the three women went upstairs, laughing, to the ladies' dressing-room. A light fringe of snow lay like a cape on the shoulders of his overcoat and like toecaps on the toes of his goloshes; and, as the buttons of his overcoat slipped with a squeaking noise through the snow-stiffened frieze,[7] a cold fragrant air from out-of-doors escaped from crevices and folds.

—Is it snowing again, Mr Conroy? asked Lily.

She had preceded him into the pantry to help him off with his overcoat. Gabriel smiled at the three syllables she had given his surname and glanced at her. She was a slim, growing girl, pale in complexion and with hay-coloured hair. The gas in the pantry made her look still paler. Gabriel had

---

2. Haddington Road, like Adam and Eve's below, is a church.
3. Concert hall in Dublin. The academy was the Royal Irish Academy of Music.

4. A dark brown malt liquor, akin to beer.
5. Drunk.
6. Bet.
7. A kind of coarse woolen cloth.

known her when she was a child and used to sit on the lowest step nursing a rag doll.

—Yes, Lily, he answered, and I think we're in for a night of it.

He looked up at the pantry ceiling, which was shaking with the stamping and shuffling of feet on the floor above, listened for a moment to the piano and then glanced at the girl, who was folding his overcoat carefully at the end of a shelf.

—Tell me, Lily, he said in a friendly tone, do you still go to school?

—O no, sir, she answered. I'm done schooling this year and more.

—O, then, said Gabriel gaily, I suppose we'll be going to your wedding one of these fine days with your young man, eh?

The girl glanced back at him over her shoulder and said with great bitterness:

—The men that is now is only all palaver[8] and what they can get out of you.

Gabriel coloured as if he felt he had made a mistake and, without looking at her, kicked off his goloshes and flicked actively with his muffler at his patent-leather shoes.

He was a stout tallish young man. The high colour of his cheeks pushed upwards even to his forehead where it scattered itself in a few formless patches of pale red; and on his hairless face there scintillated restlessly the polished lenses and the bright gilt rims of the glasses which screened his delicate and restless eyes. His glossy black hair was parted in the middle and brushed in a long curve behind his ears where it curled slightly beneath the groove left by his hat.

When he had flicked lustre into his shoes he stood up and pulled his waistcoat down more tightly on his plump body. Then he took a coin rapidly from his pocket.

—O Lily, he said, thrusting it into her hands, it's Christmas-time, isn't it? Just . . . here's a little. . . .

He walked rapidly towards the door.

—O no, sir! cried the girl, following him. Really, sir, I wouldn't take it.

—Christmas-time! Christmas-time! said Gabriel, almost trotting to the stairs and waving his hand to her in deprecation.

The girl, seeing that he had gained the stairs, called out after him:

—Well, thank you, sir.

He waited outside the drawing-room door until the waltz should finish, listening to the skirts that swept against it and to the shuffling of feet. He was still discomposed by the girl's bitter and sudden retort. It had cast a gloom over him which he tried to dispel by arranging his cuffs and the bows of his tie. Then he took from his waistcoat pocket a little paper and glanced at the headings he had made for his speech. He was undecided about the lines from Robert Browning for he feared they would be above the heads of his hearers. Some quotation that they could recognise from Shakespeare or from the Melodies[9] would be better. The indelicate clacking of the men's heels and the shuffling of their soles reminded him that their grade of culture differed from his. He would only make himself ridiculous by quoting poetry to them which they could not understand. They would think that he

8. Empty and deceptive talk.
9. *Irish Melodies* by Dublin-born Thomas Moore (1779–1852), a collection of songs—including one called "O Ye Dead"—that was extremely popular in late 19th- and early 20th-century Ireland.

was airing his superior education. He would fail with them just as he had failed with the girl in the pantry. He had taken up a wrong tone. His whole speech was a mistake from first to last, an utter failure.

Just then his aunts and his wife came out of the ladies' dressing-room. His aunts were two small plainly dressed old women. Aunt Julia was an inch or so the taller. Her hair, drawn low over the tops of her ears, was grey; and grey also, with darker shadows, was her large flaccid face. Though she was stout in build and stood erect her slow eyes and parted lips gave her the appearance of a woman who did not know where she was or where she was going. Aunt Kate was more vivacious. Her face, healthier than her sister's, was all puckers and creases, like a shrivelled red apple, and her hair, braided in the same old-fashioned way, had not lost its ripe nut colour.

They both kissed Gabriel frankly. He was their favourite nephew, the son of their dead elder sister, Ellen, who had married T. J. Conroy of the Port and Docks.[1]

—Gretta tells me you're not going to take a cab back to Monkstown tonight, Gabriel, said Aunt Kate.

—No, said Gabriel, turning to his wife, we had quite enough of that last year, hadn't we? Don't you remember, Aunt Kate, what a cold Gretta got out of it? Cab windows rattling all the way, and the east wind blowing in after we passed Mention. Very jolly it was. Gretta caught a dreadful cold.

Aunt Kate frowned severely and nodded her head at every word.

—Quite right, Gabriel, quite right, she said. You can't be too careful.

—But as for Gretta there, said Gabriel, she'd walk home in the snow if she were let.

Mrs Conroy laughed.

—Don't mind him, Aunt Kate, she said. He's really an awful bother, what with green shades for Tom's eyes at night and making him do the dumb-bells, and forcing Eva to eat the stirabout.[2] The poor child! And she simply hates the sight of it! . . . O, but you'll never guess what he makes me wear now!

She broke out into a peal of laughter and glanced at her husband, whose admiring and happy eyes had been wandering from her dress to her face and hair. The two aunts laughed heartily too, for Gabriel's solicitude was a standing joke with them.

—Goloshes! said Mrs Conroy. That's the latest. Whenever it's wet underfoot I must put on my goloshes. To-night even he wanted me to put them on, but I wouldn't. The next thing he'll buy me will be a diving suit.

Gabriel laughed nervously and patted his tie reassuringly while Aunt Kate nearly doubled herself, so heartily did she enjoy the joke. The smile soon faded from Aunt Julia's face and her mirthless eyes were directed towards her nephew's face. After a pause she asked:

—And what are goloshes, Gabriel?

—Goloshes, Julia! exclaimed her sister. Goodness me, don't you know what goloshes are? You wear them over your . . . over your boots, Gretta, isn't it?

1. Board managing the Port of Dublin.
2. Porridge made by stirring oatmeal in boiling milk or water.
3. Originally the name of a troupe of entertainers imitating African Americans, founded by George Christy of New York. By Joyce's time the meaning had become extended to any group with blackened faces who sang what were known as Negro melodies to banjo accompaniment, interspersed with jokes.
4. The Gresham Hotel, still one of the best hotels in Dublin.

—Yes, said Mrs Conroy. Guttapercha things. We both have a pair now. Gabriel says everyone wears them on the continent.

—O, on the continent, murmured Aunt Julia, nodding her head slowly.

Gabriel knitted his brows and said, as if he were slightly angered:

—It's nothing very wonderful but Gretta thinks it very funny because she says the word reminds her of Christy Minstrels.[3]

—But tell me, Gabriel, said Aunt Kate, with brisk tact. Of course, you've seen about the room. Gretta was saying . . .

—O, the room is all right, replied Gabriel. I've taken one in the Gresham.[4]

—To be sure, said Aunt Kate, by far the best thing to do. And the children, Gretta, you're not anxious about them?

—O, for one night, said Mrs Conroy. Besides, Bessie will look after them.

—To be sure, said Aunt Kate again. What a comfort it is to have a girl like that, one you can depend on! There's that Lily, I'm sure I don't know what has come over her lately. She's not the girl she was at all.

Gabriel was about to ask his aunt some questions on this point but she broke off suddenly to gaze after her sister who had wandered down the stairs and was craning her neck over the banisters.

—Now, I ask you, she said, almost testily, where is Julia going? Julia! Julia! Where are you going?

Julia, who had gone halfway down one flight, came back and announced blandly:

—Here's Freddy.

At the same moment a clapping of hands and a final flourish of the pianist told that the waltz had ended. The drawing-room door was opened from within and some couples came out. Aunt Kate drew Gabriel aside hurriedly and whispered into his ear:

—Slip down, Gabriel, like a good fellow and see if he's all right, and don't let him up if he's screwed. I'm sure he's screwed. I'm sure he is.

Gabriel went to the stairs and listened over the banisters. He could hear two persons talking in the pantry. Then he recognised Freddy Malins' laugh. He went down the stairs noisily.

—It's such a relief, said Aunt Kate to Mrs Conroy, that Gabriel is here. I always feel easier in my mind when he's here. . . . Julia, there's Miss Daly and Miss Power will take some refreshment. Thanks for your beautiful waltz, Miss Daly. It made lovely time.

A tall wizen-faced man, with a stiff grizzled moustache and swarthy skin, who was passing out with his partner said:

—And may we have some refreshment, too, Miss Morkan?

—Julia, said Aunt Kate summarily, and here's Mr Browne and Miss Furlong. Take them in, Julia, with Miss Daly and Miss Power.

—I'm the man for the ladies, said Mr Browne, pursing his lips until his moustache bristled and smiling in all his wrinkles. You know, Miss Morkan, the reason they are so fond of me is—

He did not finish his sentence, but, seeing that Aunt Kate was out of earshot, at once led the three young ladies into the back room. The middle of the room was occupied by two square tables placed end to end, and on these Aunt Julia and the caretaker were straightening and smoothing a large cloth. On the sideboard were arrayed dishes and plates, and glasses and bundles of knives and forks and spoons. The top of the closed square piano served also as a sideboard for viands and sweets. At a smaller side-board in one corner two young men were standing, drinking hop-bitters.

Mr Browne led his charges thither and invited them all, in jest, to some ladies' punch, hot, strong and sweet. As they said they never took anything strong he opened three bottles of lemonade for them. Then he asked one of the young men to move aside, and, taking hold of the decanter, filled out for himself a goodly measure of whisky. The young men eyed him respectfully while he took a trial sip.

—God help me, he said, smiling, it's the doctor's orders.

His wizened face broke into a broader smile, and the three young ladies laughed in musical echo to his pleasantry, swaying their bodies to and fro, with nervous jerks of their shoulders. The boldest said:

—O, now, Mr Browne, I'm sure the doctor never ordered anything of the kind.

Mr Browne took another sip of his whisky and said, with sidling mimicry:

—Well, you see, I'm like the famous Mrs Cassidy, who is reported to have said: *Now, Mary Grimes, if I don't take it, make me take it, for I feel I want it.*

His hot face had leaned forward a little too confidentially and he had assumed a very low Dublin accent so that the young ladies, with one instinct, received his speech in silence. Miss Furlong, who was one of Mary Jane's pupils, asked Miss Daly what was the name of the pretty waltz she had played; and Mr Browne, seeing that he was ignored, turned promptly to the two young men who were more appreciative.

A red-faced young woman, dressed in pansy, came into the room, excit-edly clapping her hands and crying:

—Quadrilles.[5] Quadrilles!

Close on her heels came Aunt Kate, crying:

—Two gentlemen and three ladies, Mary Jane!

—O, here's Mr Bergin and Mr Kerrigan, said Mary Jane. Mr Kerrigan, will you take Miss Power? Miss Furlong, may I get you a partner, Mr Ber-gin. O, that'll just do now.

—Three ladies, Mary Jane, said Aunt Kate.

The two young gentlemen asked the ladies if they might have the plea-sure, and Mary Jane turned to Miss Daly.

—O, Miss Daly, you're really awfully good, after playing for the last two dances, but really we're so short of ladies to-night.

—I don't mind in the least, Miss Morkan.

—But I've a nice partner for you, Mr Bartell D'Arcy, the tenor. I'll get him to sing later on. All Dublin is raving about him.

—Lovely voice, lovely voice! said Aunt Kate.

As the piano had twice begun the prelude to the first figure Mary Jane led her recruits quickly from the room. They had hardly gone when Aunt Julia wandered slowly into the room, looking behind her at something.

—What is the matter, Julia? asked Aunt Kate anxiously. Who is it?

Julia, who was carrying in a column of table-napkins, turned to her sister and said, simply, as if the question had surprised her:

—It's only Freddy, Kate, and Gabriel with him.

---

5. A square dance usually performed by four couples.

In fact right behind her Gabriel could be seen piloting Freddy Malins across the landing. The latter, a young man of about forty, was of Gabriel's size and build, with very round shoulders. His face was fleshy and pallid, touched with colour only at the thick hanging lobes of his ears and at the wide wings of his nose. He had coarse features, a blunt nose, a convex and receding brow, tumid and protruded lips. His heavy-lidded eyes and the disorder of his scanty hair made him look sleepy. He was laughing heartily in a high key at a story which he had been telling Gabriel on the stairs and at the same time rubbing the knuckles of his left fist backwards and forwards into his left eye.

—Good-evening, Freddy, said Aunt Julia.

Freddy Malins bade the Misses Morkan good-evening in what seemed an offhand fashion by reason of the habitual catch in his voice and then, seeing that Mr Browne was grinning at him from the sideboard, crossed the room on rather shaky legs and began to repeat in an undertone the story he had just told to Gabriel.

—He's not so bad, is he? said Aunt Kate to Gabriel.

Gabriel's brows were dark but he raised them quickly and answered:

—O no, hardly noticeable.

—Now, isn't he a terrible fellow! she said. And his poor mother made him take the pledge[6] on New Year's Eve. But come on, Gabriel, into the drawing-room.

Before leaving the room with Gabriel she signalled to Mr Browne by frowning and shaking her forefinger in warning to and fro. Mr Browne nodded in answer and, when she had gone, said to Freddy Malins:

—Now, then, Teddy, I'm going to fill you out a good glass of lemonade just to buck you up.

Freddy Malins, who was nearing the climax of his story, waved the offer aside impatiently but Mr Browne, having first called Freddy Malins' attention to a disarray in his dress, filled out and handed him a full glass of lemonade. Freddy Malins' left hand accepted the glass mechanically, his right hand being engaged in the mechanical readjustment of his dress. Mr Browne, whose face was once more wrinkling with mirth, poured out for himself a glass of whisky while Freddy Malins exploded, before he had well reached the climax of his story, in a kink of high-pitched bronchitic laughter and, setting down his untasted and overflowing glass, began to rub the knuckles of his left fist backwards and forwards into his left eye, repeating words of his last phrase as well as his fit of laughter would allow him.

Gabriel could not listen while Mary Jane was playing her Academy piece, full of runs and difficult passages, to the hushed drawing-room. He liked music but the piece she was playing had no melody for him and he doubted whether it had any melody for the other listeners, though they had begged Mary Jane to play something. Four young men, who had come from the refreshment-room to stand in the door-way at the sound of the piano, had gone away quietly in couples after a few minutes. The only persons who seemed to follow the music were Mary Jane herself, her hands racing along the key-board or

---

6. Sign a solemn promise not to drink alcohol.

lifted from it at the pauses like those of a priestess in momentary impreca-
tion, and Aunt Kate standing at her elbow to turn the page.

Gabriel's eyes, irritated by the floor, which glittered with beeswax under the
heavy chandelier, wandered to the wall above the piano. A picture of the balcony scene in *Romeo and Juliet* hung there and beside it was a picture of the
two murdered princes in the Tower[7] which Aunt Julia had worked in red, blue
and brown wools when she was a girl. Probably in the school they had gone to
as girls that kind of work had been taught, for one year his mother had worked
for him as a birthday present a waistcoat of purple tabinet,[8] with little foxes'
heads upon it, lined with brown satin and having round mulberry buttons. It
was strange that his mother had had no musical talent though Aunt Kate used
to call her the brains carrier of the Morkan family. Both she and Julia had
always seemed a little proud of their serious and matronly sister. Her photograph stood before the pierglass.[9] She held an open book on her knees and was
pointing out something in it to Constantine who, dressed in a man-o'-war
suit,[1] lay at her feet. It was she who had chosen the names for her sons for
she was very sensible of the dignity of family life. Thanks to her, Constantine was now senior curate[2] in Balbriggan and, thanks to her, Gabriel himself had taken his degree in the Royal University. A shadow passed over his
face as he remembered her sullen opposition to his marriage. Some slight-
ing phrases she had used still rankled in his memory; she had once spoken
of Gretta as being country cute and that was not true of Gretta at all. It was
Gretta who had nursed her during all her last long illness in their house at
Monkstown.

He knew that Mary Jane must be near the end of her piece for she was
playing again the opening melody with runs of scales after every bar and
while he waited for the end the resentment died down in his heart. The
piece ended with a trill of octaves in the treble and a final deep octave in the
bass. Great applause greeted Mary Jane as, blushing and rolling up her music
nervously, she escaped from the room. The most vigorous clapping came from
the four young men in the doorway who had gone away to the refreshment-
room at the beginning of the piece but had come back when the piano had
stopped.

Lancers[3] were arranged. Gabriel found himself partnered with Miss
Ivors. She was a frank-mannered talkative young lady, with a freckled
face and prominent brown eyes. She did not wear a low-cut bodice and the
large brooch which was fixed in the front of her collar bore on it an Irish
device.

When they had taken their places she said abruptly:

—I have a crow to pluck with you.

—With me? said Gabriel.

She nodded her head gravely.

—What is it? asked Gabriel, smiling at her solemn manner.

—Who is G. C.? answered Miss Ivors, turning her eyes upon him.

Gabriel coloured and was about to knit his brows, as if he did not understand, when she said bluntly:

---

7. Probably Edward V and his brother Richard,
duke of York, reputedly murdered in 1483 by
their uncle and successor, Richard III.
8. Silk and wool fabric made chiefly in Ireland.
9. Large tall mirror.

1. Sailor suit, favorite wear for children of both
sexes early in the 20th century.
2. Clergyman appointed to assist a parish priest.
3. A sequence of five quadrilles (square dances).

—O, innocent Amy! I have found out that you write for *The Daily Express*. Now, aren't you ashamed of yourself?

—Why should I be ashamed of myself? asked Gabriel, blinking his eyes and trying to smile.

—Well, I'm ashamed of you, said Miss Ivors frankly. To say you'd write for a rag like that. I didn't think you were a West Briton.[4]

A look of perplexity appeared on Gabriel's face. It was true that he wrote a literary column every Wednesday in *The Daily Express*, for which he was paid fifteen shillings. But that did not make him a West Briton surely. The books he received for review were almost more welcome than the paltry cheque. He loved to feel the covers and turn over the pages of newly printed books. Nearly every day when his teaching in the college was ended he used to wander down the quays to the second-hand booksellers, to Hickey's on Bachelor's Walk, to Webb's, or Massey's on Aston's Quay, or to O'Clohissey's in the by-street. He did not know how to meet her charge. He wanted to say that literature was above politics. But they were friends of many years' standing and their careers had been parallel, first at the University and then as teachers: he could not risk a grandiose phrase with her. He continued blinking his eyes and trying to smile and murmured lamely that he saw nothing political in writing reviews of books.

When their turn to cross had come he was still perplexed and inattentive. Miss Ivors promptly took his hand in a warm grasp and said in a soft friendly tone:

—Of course, I was only joking. Come, we cross now.

When they were together again she spoke of the University question[5] and Gabriel felt more at ease. A friend of hers had shown her his review of Browning's poems. That was how she had found out the secret: but she liked the review immensely. Then she said suddenly:

—O, Mr Conroy, will you come for an excursion to the Aran Isles[6] this summer? We're going to stay there a whole month. It will be splendid out in the Atlantic. You ought to come. Mr Clancy is coming, and Mr Kilkelly and Kathleen Kearney. It would be splendid for Gretta too if she'd come. She's from Connach,[7] isn't she?

—Her people are, said Gabriel shortly.

—But you will come, won't you? said Miss Ivors, laying her warm hand eagerly on his arm.

—The fact is, said Gabriel, I have already arranged to go—

—Go where? asked Miss Ivors.

—Well, you know, every year I go for a cycling tour with some fellows and so—

—But where? asked Miss Ivors.

—Well, we usually go to France or Belgium or perhaps Germany, said Gabriel awkwardly.

—And why do you go to France and Belgium, said Miss Ivors, instead of visiting your own land?

---

4. A pejorative term for one who denies a separate Irish nationality and sees Ireland as simply a western extension of Great Britain.
5. Namely, whether Ireland's elite Protestant universities should be open to Catholics.

6. Three small islands lying across the entrance to Galway Bay, on the west coast of Ireland.
7. Or Connaught, a rural region on the west coast of Ireland.

—Well, said Gabriel, it's partly to keep in touch with the languages and partly for a change.

—And haven't you your own language to keep in touch with—Irish? asked Miss Ivors.

—Well, said Gabriel, if it comes to that, you know, Irish is not my language.

Their neighbours had turned to listen to the cross-examination. Gabriel glanced right and left nervously and tried to keep his good humour under the ordeal which was making a blush invade his forehead.

—And haven't you your own land to visit, continued Miss Ivors, that you know nothing of, your own people, and your own country?

—O, to tell you the truth, retorted Gabriel suddenly, I'm sick of my own country, sick of it!

—Why? asked Miss Ivors.

Gabriel did not answer for his retort had heated him.

—Why? repeated Miss Ivors.

They had to go visiting together and, as he had not answered her, Miss Ivors said warmly:

—Of course, you've no answer.

Gabriel tried to cover his agitation by taking part in the dance with great energy. He avoided her eyes for he had seen a sour expression on her face. But when they met in the long chain he was surprised to feel his hand firmly pressed. She looked at him from under her brows for a moment quizzically[8] until he smiled. Then, just as the chain was about to start again, she stood on tiptoe and whispered into his ear:

—West Briton!

When the lancers were over Gabriel went away to a remote corner of the room where Freddy Malins' mother was sitting. She was a stout feeble old woman with white hair. Her voice had a catch in it like her son's and she stuttered slightly. She had been told that Freddy had come and that he was nearly all right. Gabriel asked her whether she had had a good crossing. She lived with her married daughter in Glasgow and came to Dublin on a visit once a year. She answered placidly that she had had a beautiful crossing and that the captain had been most attentive to her. She spoke also of the beautiful house her daughter kept in Glasgow, and of all the nice friends they had there. While her tongue rambled on Gabriel tried to banish from his mind all memory of the unpleasant incident with Miss Ivors. Of course the girl or woman, or whatever she was, was an enthusiast but there was a time for all things. Perhaps he ought not to have answered her like that. But she had no right to call him a West Briton before people, even in joke. She had tried to make him ridiculous before people, heckling him and staring at him with her rabbit's eyes.

He saw his wife making her way towards him through the waltzing couples. When she reached him she said into his ear:

—Gabriel, Aunt Kate wants to know won't you carve the goose as usual. Miss Daly will carve the ham and I'll do the pudding.

—All right, said Gabriel.

—She's sending in the younger ones first as soon as this waltz is over so that we'll have the table to ourselves.

—Were you dancing? asked Gabriel.

8. Teasingly.

—Of course I was. Didn't you see me? What words had you with Molly Ivors?

—No words. Why? Did she say so?

—Something like that. I'm trying to get that Mr D'Arcy to sing. He's full of conceit, I think.

—There were no words, said Gabriel moodily, only she wanted me to go for a trip to the west of Ireland and I said I wouldn't.

His wife clasped her hands excitedly and gave a little jump.

—O, do go, Gabriel, she cried. I'd love to see Galway again.

—You can go if you like, said Gabriel coldly.

She looked at him for a moment, then turned to Mrs Malins and said:

—There's a nice husband for you, Mrs Malins.

While she was threading her way back across the room Mrs Malins, without adverting to the interruption, went on to tell Gabriel what beautiful places there were in Scotland and beautiful scenery. Her son-in-law brought them every year to the lakes and they used to go fishing. Her son-in-law was a splendid fisher. One day he caught a fish, a beautiful big big fish, and the man in the hotel boiled it for their dinner.

Gabriel hardly heard what she said. Now that supper was coming near he began to think again about his speech and about the quotation. When he saw Freddy Malins coming across the room to visit his mother Gabriel left the chair free for him and retired into the embrasure[9] of the window. The room had already cleared and from the back room came the clatter of plates and knives. Those who still remained in the drawing-room seemed tired of dancing and were conversing quietly in little groups. Gabriel's warm trembling fingers tapped the cold pane of the window. How cool it must be outside! How pleasant it would be to walk out alone, first along by the river and then through the park! The snow would be lying on the branches of the trees and forming a bright cap on the top of the Wellington Monument.[1] How much more pleasant it would be there than at the supper-table!

He ran over the headings of his speech: Irish hospitality, sad memories, the Three Graces, Paris,[2] the quotation from Browning. He repeated to himself a phrase he had written in his review: *One feels that one is listening to a thought-tormented music.* Miss Ivors had praised the review. Was she sincere? Had she really any life of her own behind all her propagandism? There had never been any ill-feeling between them until that night. It unnerved him to think that she would be at the supper-table, looking up at him while he spoke with her critical quizzing eyes. Perhaps she would not be sorry to see him fail in his speech. An idea came into his mind and gave him courage. He would say, alluding to Aunt Kate and Aunt Julia: *Ladies and Gentlemen, the generation which is now on the wane among us may have had its faults but for my part I think it had certain qualities of hospitality, of humour, of humanity, which the new and very serious and hypereducated generation that is growing up around us seems to me to lack.* Very good: that

9. Opening for a window in a thick wall.
1. Tribute to Arthur Wellesley (1769–1852), 1st duke of Wellington, Dublin-born hero of the British army. The obelisk stands in Dublin's Phoenix Park.
2. In Greek mythology, Paris was selected by Zeus to choose which of three goddesses was the most beautiful. The Graces were three sister-goddesses—Aglaia, splendor; Euphrosyne, festivity; and Thalia, rejoicing—who together represented loveliness and joy. Gabriel is making a mental note to refer to his two aunts and Mary Jane in a complimentary way.

was one for Miss Ivors. What did he care that his aunts were only two ignorant old women?

A murmur in the room attracted his attention. Mr Browne was advancing
from the door, gallantly escorting Aunt Julia, who leaned upon his arm,
smiling and hanging her head. An irregular musketry of applause escorted
her also as far as the piano and then, as Mary Jane seated herself on the
stool, and Aunt Julia, no longer smiling, half turned so as to pitch her voice
fairly into the room, gradually ceased. Gabriel recognised the prelude. It
was that of an old song of Aunt Julia's—*Arrayed for the Bridal*.[3] Her voice,
strong and clear in tone, attacked with great spirit the runs which embel-
lish the air and though she sang very rapidly she did not miss even the
smallest of the grace notes. To follow the voice, without looking at the singer's face, was to feel and share the excitement of swift and secure flight.
Gabriel applauded loudly with all the others at the close of the song and
loud applause was borne in from the invisible supper-table. It sounded so
genuine that a little colour struggled into Aunt Julia's face as she bent to
replace in the music-stand the old leather-bound song-book that had her
initials on the cover. Freddy Malins, who had listened with his head perched
sideways to hear her better, was still applauding when everyone else had
ceased and talking animatedly to his mother who nodded her head gravely
and slowly in acquiescence. At last, when he could clap no more, he stood
up suddenly and hurried across the room to Aunt Julia whose hand he
seized and held in both his hands, shaking it when words failed him or the
catch in his voice proved too much for him.

—I was just telling my mother, he said, I never heard you sing so well,
never. No, I never heard your voice so good as it is to-night. Now! Would
you believe that now? That's the truth. Upon my word and honour that's the
truth. I never heard your voice sound so fresh and so . . . so clear and fresh,
never.

Aunt Julia smiled broadly and murmured something about compliments
as she released her hand from his grasp. Mr Browne extended his open
hand towards her and said to those who were near him in the manner of a
showman introducing a prodigy to an audience:

—Miss Julia Morkan, my latest discovery!

He was laughing very heartily at this himself when Freddy Malins turned
to him and said:

—Well, Browne, if you're serious you might make a worse discovery. All I
can say is I never heard her sing half so well as long as I am coming here.
And that's the honest truth.

—Neither did I, said Mr Browne. I think her voice has greatly improved.

Aunt Julia shrugged her shoulders and said with meek pride:

—Thirty years ago I hadn't a bad voice as voices go.

—I often told Julia, said Aunt Kate emphatically, that she was simply
thrown away in that choir. But she never would be said by me.

She turned as if to appeal to the good sense of the others against a refractory child while Aunt Julia gazed in front of her, a vague smile of reminiscence playing on her face.

---

3. This old song (beginning "Arrayed for the bridal, in beauty behold her") "is replete with long and complicated runs, requiring a sophisti-cated and gifted singer" (Bowen, *Musical Allu-*sions in the Works of James Joyce, 1974); the suggestion is that Aunt Julia was a really accom-plished singer.

—No, continued Aunt Kate, she wouldn't be said or led by anyone, slaving there in that choir night and day, night and day. Six o'clock on Christmas morning! And all for what?

—Well, isn't it for the honour of God, Aunt Kate? asked Mary Jane, twisting round on the piano-stool and smiling.

Aunt Kate turned fiercely on her niece and said:

—I know all about the honour of God, Mary Jane, but I think it's not at all honourable for the pope to turn out the women out of the choirs that have slaved there all their lives and put little whipper-snappers of boys over their heads. I suppose it is for the good of the Church if the pope does it. But it's not just, Mary Jane, and it's not right.

She had worked herself into a passion and would have continued in defence of her sister for it was a sore subject with her but Mary Jane, seeing that all the dancers had come back, intervened pacifically:

—Now, Aunt Kate, you're giving scandal to Mr Browne who is of the other persuasion.[4]

Aunt Kate turned to Mr Browne, who was grinning at this allusion to his religion, and said hastily:

—O, I don't question the pope's being right. I'm only a stupid old woman and I wouldn't presume to do such a thing. But there's such a thing as common everyday politeness and gratitude. And if I were in Julia's place I'd tell that Father Healy straight up to his face . . .

—And besides, Aunt Kate, said Mary Jane, we really are all hungry and when we are hungry we are all very quarrelsome.

—And when we are thirsty we are also quarrelsome, added Mr Browne.

—So that we had better go to supper, said Mary Jane, and finish the discussion afterwards.

On the landing outside the drawing-room Gabriel found his wife and Mary Jane trying to persuade Miss Ivors to stay for supper. But Miss Ivors, who had put on her hat and was buttoning her cloak, would not stay. She did not feel in the least hungry and she had already overstayed her time.

—But only for ten minutes, Molly, said Mrs Conroy. That won't delay you.

—To take a pick itself, said Mary Jane, after all your dancing.

—I really couldn't, said Miss Ivors.

—I am afraid you didn't enjoy yourself at all, said Mary Jane hopelessly.

—Ever so much, I assure you, said Miss Ivors, but you really must let me run off now.

—But how can you get home? asked Mrs Conroy.

—O, it's only two steps up the quay.

Gabriel hesitated a moment and said:

—If you will allow me, Miss Ivors, I'll see you home if you really are obliged to go.

But Miss Ivors broke away from them.

—I won't hear of it, she cried. For goodness sake go in to your suppers and don't mind me. I'm quite well able to take care of myself.

—Well, you're the comical girl, Molly, said Mrs Conroy frankly.

4. I.e., Protestant.

—*Beannacht libh,*[5] cried Miss Ivors, with a laugh, as she ran down the staircase.

Mary Jane gazed after her, a moody puzzled expression on her face, while Mrs Conroy leaned over the banisters to listen for the hall-door. Gabriel asked himself was he the cause of her abrupt departure. But she did not seem to be in ill humour: she had gone away laughing. He stared blankly down the staircase.

At that moment Aunt Kate came toddling out of the supper-room, almost wringing her hands in despair.

—Where is Gabriel? she cried. Where on earth is Gabriel? There's everyone waiting in there, stage to let, and nobody to carve the goose!

—Here I am, Aunt Kate! cried Gabriel, with sudden animation, ready to carve a flock of geese, if necessary.

A fat brown goose lay at one end of the table and at the other end, on a bed of creased paper strewn with sprigs of parsley, lay a great ham, stripped of its outer skin and peppered over with crust crumbs, a neat paper frill round its shin and beside this was a round of spiced beef. Between these rival ends ran parallel lines of side-dishes: two little minsters of jelly, red and yellow; a shallow dish full of blocks of blancmange[6] and red jam, a large green leaf-shaped dish with a stalk-shaped handle, on which lay bunches of purple raisins and peeled almonds, a companion dish on which lay a solid rectangle of Smyrna figs, a dish of custard topped with grated nutmeg, a small bowl full of chocolates and sweets wrapped in gold and silver papers and a glass vase in which stood some tall celery stalks. In the centre of the table there stood, as sentries to a fruit-stand which upheld a pyramid of oranges and American apples, two squat old-fashioned decanters of cut glass, one containing port and the other dark sherry. On the closed square piano a pudding in a huge yellow dish lay in waiting and behind it were three squads of bottles of stout and ale and minerals, drawn up according to the colours of their uniforms, the first two black, with brown and red labels, the third and smallest squad white, with transverse green sashes.

Gabriel took his seat boldly at the head of the table and, having looked to the edge of the carver, plunged his fork firmly into the goose. He felt quite at ease now for he was an expert carver and liked nothing better than to find himself at the head of a well-laden table.

—Miss Furlong, what shall I send you? he asked. A wing or a slice of the breast?

—Just a small slice of the breast.

—Miss Higgins, what for you?

—O, anything at all, Mr Conroy.

While Gabriel and Miss Daly exchanged plates of goose and plates of ham and spiced beef Lily went from guest to guest with a dish of hot floury potatoes wrapped in a white napkin. This was Mary Jane's idea and she had also suggested apple sauce for the goose but Aunt Kate had said that plain roast goose without apple sauce had always been good enough for her and she hoped she might never eat worse. Mary Jane waited on her pupils and saw that they got the best slices and Aunt Kate and Aunt Julia opened and carried across from the piano bottles of stout and ale for the gentlemen and bottles of

---

5. Blessing on you (Gaelic; literal trans.); goodbye.　　6. Sweet almond-flavored pudding.

minerals for the ladies. There was a great deal of confusion and laughter and noise, the noise of orders and counter-orders, of knives and forks, of corks and glass-stoppers. Gabriel began to carve second helpings as soon as he had finished the first round without serving himself. Everyone protested loudly so that he compromised by taking a long draught of stout for he had found the carving hot work. Mary Jane settled down quietly to her supper but Aunt Kate and Aunt Julia were still toddling round the table, walking on each other's heels, getting in each other's way and giving each other unheeded orders. Mr Browne begged of them to sit down and eat their suppers and so did Gabriel but they said there was time enough so that, at last, Freddy Malins stood up and, capturing Aunt Kate, plumped her down on her chair amid general laughter.

When everyone had been well served Gabriel said, smiling:

—Now, if anyone wants a little more of what vulgar people call stuffing let him or her speak.

A chorus of voices invited him to begin his own supper and Lily came forward with three potatoes which she had reserved for him.

—Very well, said Gabriel amiably, as he took another preparatory draught, kindly forget my existence, ladies and gentlemen, for a few minutes.

He set to his supper and took no part in the conversation with which the table covered Lily's removal of the plates. The subject of talk was the opera company which was then at the Theatre Royal. Mr Bartell D'Arcy, the tenor, a dark-complexioned young man with a smart moustache, praised very highly the leading contralto of the company but Miss Furlong thought she had a rather vulgar style of production. Freddy Malins said there was a negro chieftain singing in the second part of the Gaiety pantomime who had one of the finest tenor voices he had ever heard.

—Have you heard him? he asked Mr Bartell D'Arcy across the table.

—No, answered Mr Bartell D'Arcy carelessly.

—Because, Freddy Malins explained, now I'd be curious to hear your opinion of him. I think he has a grand voice.

—It takes Teddy to find out the really good things, said Mr Browne familiarly to the table.

—And why couldn't he have a voice too? asked Freddy Malins sharply. Is it because he's only a black?

Nobody answered this question and Mary Jane led the table back to the legitimate opera. One of her pupils had given her a pass for *Mignon*.[7] Of course it was very fine, she said, but it made her think of poor Georgina Burns. Mr Browne could go back farther still, to the old Italian companies that used to come to Dublin—Tietjens, Ilma de Murzka, Campanini, the great Trebelli, Giuglini, Ravelli, Aramburo. Those were the days, he said, when there was something like singing to be heard in Dublin. He told too of how the top gallery of the old Royal used to be packed night after night, of how one night an Italian tenor had sung five encores to *Let Me Like a Soldier Fall*,[8] introducing a high C every time, and of how the gallery boys would sometimes in their

7. Opera by Ambroise Thomas first produced in Paris in 1866 and in London in 1870.
8. This song, from the opera *Montana* by W. Wallace (it actually begins "Yes! let me like a soldier fall"), ends on middle C; it would be a piece of exhibitionism to end on a high C, as Joyce's father, who had a good voice, used to do. Joyce's brother Stanislaus remembered the song as insufferable rubbish. Mr. Browne is not to be taken seriously as a music critic.

enthusiasm unyoke the horses from the carriage of some great *prima donna* and pull her themselves through the streets to her hotel. Why did they never play the grand old operas now, he asked, *Dinorah, Lucrezia Borgia?*[9] Because they could not get the voices to sing them: that was why.

—O, well, said Mr Bartell D'Arcy, I presume there are as good singers today as there were then.

—Where are they? asked Mr Browne defiantly.

—In London, Paris, Milan, said Mr Bartell d'Arcy warmly. I suppose Caruso[1] for example, is quite as good, if not better than any of the men you have mentioned.

—Maybe so, said Mr Browne. But I may tell you I doubt it strongly.

—O, I'd give anything to hear Caruso sing, said Mary Jane.

—For me, said Aunt Kate, who had been picking a bone, there was only one tenor. To please me, I mean. But I suppose none of you ever heard of him.

—Who was he, Miss Morkan? asked Mr Bartell D'Arcy politely.

—His name, said Aunt Kate, was Parkinson. I heard him when he was in his prime and I think he had then the purest tenor voice that was ever put into a man's throat.

—Strange, said Mr Bartell d'Arcy. I never even heard of him.

—Yes, yes, Miss Morkan is right, said Mr Browne. I remember hearing of old Parkinson but he's too far back for me.

—A beautiful pure sweet mellow English tenor, said Aunt Kate with enthusiasm.

Gabriel having finished, the huge pudding was transferred to the table. The clatter of forks and spoons began again. Gabriel's wife served out spoonfuls of the pudding and passed the plates down the table. Midway down they were held up by Mary Jane, who replenished them with raspberry or orange jelly or with blancmange and jam. The pudding was of Aunt Julia's making and she received praises for it from all quarters. She herself said that it was not quite brown enough.

—Well, I hope, Miss Morkan, said Mr Browne, that I'm brown enough for you because, you know, I'm all brown.

All the gentlemen, except Gabriel, ate some of the pudding out of compliment to Aunt Julia. As Gabriel never ate sweets the celery had been left for him. Freddy Malins also took a stalk of celery and ate it with his pudding. He had been told that celery was a capital thing for the blood and he was just then under doctor's care. Mrs Malins, who had been silent all through the supper, said that her son was going down to Mount Melleray in a week or so. The table then spoke of Mount Melleray, how bracing the air was down there, how hospitable the monks were and how they never asked for a penny-piece from their guests.

—And do you mean to say, asked Mr Browne incredulously, that a chap can go down there and put up there as if it were a hotel and live on the fat of the land and then come away without paying a farthing?

—O, most people give some donation to the monastery when they leave, said Mary Jane.

9. An opera by Donizetti, first produced at La Scala, Milan, in 1833. *Dinorah* is an opera by Meyerbeer, first produced in Paris in 1859.

1. Enrico Caruso (1873–1921), the great Italian dramatic tenor.

—I wish we had an institution like that in our Church, said Mr Browne candidly.

He was astonished to hear that the monks never spoke, got up at two in the morning and slept in their coffins. He asked what they did it for.

—That's the rule of the order, said Aunt Kate firmly.

—Yes, but why? asked Mr Browne.

Aunt Kate repeated that it was the rule, that was all. Mr Browne still seemed not to understand. Freddy Malins explained to him, as best he could, that the monks were trying to make up for the sins committed by all the sinners in the outside world. The explanation was not very clear for Mr Browne grinned and said:

—I like that idea very much but wouldn't a comfortable spring bed do them as well as a coffin?

—The coffin, said Mary Jane, is to remind them of their last end.

As the subject had grown lugubrious it was buried in a silence of the table during which Mrs Malins could be heard saying to her neighbour in an indistinct undertone:

—They are very good men, the monks, very pious men.

The raisins and almonds and figs and apples and oranges and chocolates and sweets were now passed about the table and Aunt Julia invited all the guests to have either port or sherry. At first Mr Bartell D'Arcy refused to take either but one of his neighbours nudged him and whispered something to him upon which he allowed his glass to be filled. Gradually as the last glasses were being filled the conversation ceased. A pause followed, broken only by the noise of the wine and by unsettlings of chairs. The Misses Morkan, all three, looked down at the tablecloth. Someone coughed once or twice and then a few gentlemen patted the table gently as a signal for silence. The silence came and Gabriel pushed back his chair and stood up.

The patting at once grew louder in encouragement and then ceased altogether. Gabriel leaned his ten trembling fingers on the tablecloth and smiled nervously at the company. Meeting a row of upturned faces he raised his eyes to the chandelier. The piano was playing a waltz tune and he could hear the skirts sweeping against the drawing-room door. People, perhaps, were standing in the snow on the quay outside, gazing up at the lighted windows and listening to the waltz music. The air was pure there. In the distance lay the park where the trees were weighted with snow. The Wellington Monument wore a gleaming cap of snow that flashed westward over the white field of Fifteen Acres.

He began:

—Ladies and Gentlemen.

—It has fallen to my lot this evening, as in years past, to perform a very pleasing task but a task for which I am afraid my poor powers as a speaker are all too inadequate.

—No, no! said Mr Browne.

—But, however that may be, I can only ask you to-night to take the will for the deed and to lend me your attention for a few moments while I endeavour to express to you in words what my feelings are on this occasion.

—Ladies and Gentlemen. It is not the first time that we have gathered together under this hospitable roof, around this hospitable board. It is not the first time that we have been the recipients—or perhaps, I had better say, the victims—of the hospitality of certain good ladies.

He made a circle in the air with his arm and paused. Everyone laughed or smiled at Aunt Kate and Aunt Julia and Mary Jane who all turned crimson with pleasure. Gabriel went on more boldly:

—I feel more strongly with every recurring year that our country has no tradition which does it so much honour and which it should guard so jealously as that of its hospitality. It is a tradition that is unique as far as my experience goes (and I have visited not a few places abroad) among the modern nations. Some would say, perhaps, that with us it is rather a failing than anything to be boasted of. But granted even that, it is, to my mind, a princely failing, and one that I trust will long be cultivated among us. Of one thing, at least, I am sure. As long as this one roof shelters the good ladies aforesaid—and I wish from my heart it may do so for many and many a long year to come—the tradition of genuine warm-hearted courteous Irish hospitality, which our forefathers have handed down to us and which we in turn must hand down to our descendants, is still alive among us.

A hearty murmur of assent ran round the table. It shot through Gabriel's mind that Miss Ivors was not there and that she had gone away discourteously: and he said with confidence in himself:

—Ladies and Gentlemen.

—A new generation is growing up in our midst, a generation actuated by new ideas and new principles. It is serious and enthusiastic for these new ideas and its enthusiasm, even when it is misdirected, is, I believe, in the main sincere. But we are living in a sceptical and, if I may use the phrase, a thought-tormented age: and sometimes I fear that this new generation, educated or hypereducated as it is, will lack those qualities of humanity, of hospitality, of kindly humour which belonged to an older day. Listening to-night to the names of all those great singers of the past it seemed to me, I must confess, that we were living in a less spacious age. Those days might, without exaggeration, be called spacious days: and if they are gone beyond recall let us hope, at least, that in gatherings such as this we shall still speak of them with pride and affection, still cherish in our hearts the memory of those dead and gone great ones whose fame the world will not willingly let die.

—Hear, hear! said Mr Browne loudly.

—But yet, continued Gabriel, his voice falling into a softer inflection, there are always in gatherings such as this sadder thoughts that will recur to our minds: thoughts of the past, of youth, of changes, of absent faces that we miss here to-night. Our path through life is strewn with many such sad memories: and were we to brood upon them always we could not find the heart to go on bravely with our work among the living. We have all of us living duties and living affections which claim, and rightly claim, our strenuous endeavours.

—Therefore, I will not linger on the past. I will not let any gloomy moralising intrude upon us here to-night. Here we are gathered together for a brief moment from the bustle and rush of our everyday routine. We are met here as friends, in the spirit of good-fellowship, as colleagues, also to a certain extent, in the true spirit of *camaraderie*, and as the guests of—what shall I call them?—the Three Graces of the Dublin musical world.

The table burst into applause and laughter at this sally. Aunt Julia vainly asked each of her neighbours in turn to tell her what Gabriel had said.

—He says we are the Three Graces,[2] Aunt Julia, said Mary Jane.

Aunt Julia did not understand but she looked up, smiling, at Gabriel, who continued in the same vein:

—Ladies and Gentlemen.

—I will not attempt to play to-night the part that Paris played on another occasion. I will not attempt to choose between them. The task would be an invidious one and one beyond my poor powers. For when I view them in turn, whether it be our chief hostess herself, whose good heart, whose too good heart, has become a byword with all who know her, or her sister, who seems to be gifted with perennial youth and whose singing must have been a surprise and a revelation to us all to-night, or, last but not least, when I consider our youngest hostess, talented, cheerful, hard-working and the best of nieces, I confess, Ladies and Gentlemen, that I do not know to which of them I should award the prize.

Gabriel glanced down at his aunts and, seeing the large smile on Aunt Julia's face and the tears which had risen to Aunt Kate's eyes, hastened to his close. He raised his glass of port gallantly, while every member of the company fingered a glass expectantly, and said loudly:

—Let us toast them all three together. Let us drink to their health, wealth, long life, happiness and prosperity and may they long continue to hold the proud and self-won position which they hold in their profession and the position of honour and affection which they hold in our hearts.

All the guests stood up, glass in hand, and, turning towards the three seated ladies, sang in unison, with Mr Browne as leader:

> For they are jolly gay fellows,
> For they are jolly gay fellows,
> For they are jolly gay fellows,
> Which nobody can deny.

Aunt Kate was making frank use of her handkerchief and even Aunt Julia seemed moved. Freddy Malins beat time with his pudding-fork and the singers turned towards one another, as if in melodious conference, while they sang, with emphasis:

> Unless he tells a lie,
> Unless he tells a lie.

Then, turning once more towards their hostesses, they sang:

> For they are jolly gay fellows,
> For they are jolly gay fellows,
> For they are jolly gay fellows,
> Which nobody can deny.

The acclamation which followed was taken up beyond the door of the supper-room by many of the other guests and renewed time after time, Freddy Malins acting as officer with his fork on high.

---

2. See p. 421, n. 2.

The piercing morning air came into the hall where they were standing so that Aunt Kate said:

—Close the door, somebody. Mrs Malins will get her death of cold.

—Browne is out there, Aunt Kate, said Mary Jane.

—Browne is everywhere, said Aunt Kate, lowering her voice.

Mary Jane laughed at her tone.

—Really, she said archly, he is very attentive.

—He has been laid on here like the gas, said Aunt Kate in the same tone, all during the Christmas.

She laughed herself this time good-humouredly and then added quickly:

—But tell him to come in, Mary Jane, and close the door. I hope to goodness he didn't hear me.

At that moment the hall-door was opened and Mr Browne came in from the doorstep, laughing as if his heart would break. He was dressed in a long green overcoat with mock astrakhan cuffs and collar and wore on his head an oval fur cap. He pointed down the snow-covered quay from where the sound of shrill prolonged whistling was borne in.

—Teddy will have all the cabs in Dublin out, he said.

Gabriel advanced from the little pantry behind the office, struggling into his overcoat and, looking round the hall, said:

—Gretta not down yet?

—She's getting on her things, Gabriel, said Aunt Kate.

—Who's playing up there? asked Gabriel.

—Nobody. They're all gone.

—O no, Aunt Kate, said Mary Jane. Bartell D'Arcy and Miss O'Callaghan aren't gone yet.

—Someone is strumming at the piano, anyhow, said Gabriel.

Mary Jane glanced at Gabriel and Mr Browne and said with a shiver:

—It makes me feel cold to look at you two gentlemen muffled up like that. I wouldn't like to face your journey home at this hour.

—I'd like nothing better this minute, said Mr Browne stoutly, than a rattling fine walk in the country or a fast drive with a good spanking goer between the shafts.

—We used to have a very good horse and trap[3] at home, said Aunt Julia sadly.

—The never-to-be-forgotten Johnny, said Mary Jane, laughing.

Aunt Kate and Gabriel laughed too.

—Why, what was wonderful about Johnny? asked Mr Browne.

—The late lamented Patrick Morkan, our grandfather, that is, explained Gabriel, commonly known in his later years as the old gentleman, was a glue-boiler.[4]

—O, now, Gabriel, said Aunt Kate, laughing, he had a starch mill.

—Well, glue or starch, said Gabriel, the old gentleman had a horse by the name of Johnny. And Johnny used to work in the old gentleman's mill, walking round and round in order to drive the mill. That was all very well; but now comes the tragic part about Johnny. One fine day the old gentleman thought he'd like to drive out with the quality[5] to a military review in the park.

---

3. A two-wheeled horse-drawn carriage on springs.
4. Glue was made by boiling animal hides and hoofs.
5. People of rank or high social position.

—The Lord have mercy on his soul, said Aunt Kate compassionately.

—Amen, said Gabriel. So the old gentleman, as I said, harnessed Johnny and put on his very best tall hat and his very best stock collar and drove out in grand style from his ancestral mansion somewhere near Back Lane, I think.

Everyone laughed, even Mrs Malins, at Gabriel's manner and Aunt Kate said:

—O now, Gabriel, he didn't live in Back Lane, really. Only the mill was there.

—Out from the mansion of his forefathers, continued Gabriel, he drove with Johnny. And everything went on beautifully until Johnny came in sight of King Billy's statue[6] and whether he fell in love with the horse King Billy sits on or whether he thought he was back again in the mill, anyhow he began to walk round the statue.

Gabriel paced in a circle round the hall in his goloshes amid the laughter of the others.

—Round and round he went, said Gabriel, and the old gentleman, who was a very pompous old gentleman, was highly indignant. *Go on, sir! What do you mean, sir? Johnny! Johnny! Most extraordinary conduct! Can't understand the horse!*

The peals of laughter which followed Gabriel's imitation of the incident were interrupted by a resounding knock at the hall-door. Mary Jane ran to open it and let in Freddy Malins. Freddy Malins, with his hat well back on his head and his shoulders humped with cold, was puffing and steaming after his exertions.

—I could only get one cab, he said.

—O, we'll find another along the quay, said Gabriel.

—Yes, said Aunt Kate. Better not keep Mrs Malins standing in the draught.

Mrs Malins was helped down the front steps by her son and Mr Browne and, after many manœuvres, hoisted into the cab. Freddy Malins clambered in after her and spent a long time settling her on the seat, Mr Browne helping him with advice. At last she was settled comfortably and Freddy Malins invited Mr Browne into the cab. There was a good deal of confused talk, and then Mr Browne got into the cab. The cabman settled his rug over his knees, and bent down for the address. The confusion grew greater and the cabman was directed differently by Freddy Malins and Mr Browne, each of whom had his head out through a window of the cab. The difficulty was to know where to drop Mr Browne along the route and Aunt Kate, Aunt Julia and Mary Jane helped the discussion from the doorstep with cross-directions and contradictions and abundance of laughter. As for Freddy Malins he was speechless with laughter. He popped his head in and out of the window every moment, to the great danger of his hat, and told his mother how the discussion was progressing till at last Mr Browne shouted to the bewildered cabman above the din of everybody's laughter:

—Do you know Trinity College?

—Yes, sir, said the cabman.

---

6. Statue of King William III of England in front of Trinity College, Dublin. He defeated predominantly Irish Catholic forces in the 1690 Battle of the Boyne.

—Well, drive bang up against Trinity College gates, said Mr Browne, and then we'll tell you where to go. You understand now?

—Yes, sir, said the cabman.

—Make like a bird for Trinity College.

—Right, sir, cried the cabman.

The horse was whipped up and the cab rattled off along the quay amid a chorus of laughter and adieus.

Gabriel had not gone to the door with the others. He was in a dark part of the hall gazing up the staircase. A woman was standing near the top of the first flight, in the shadow also. He could not see her face but he could see the terracotta and salmonpink panels of her skirt which the shadow made appear black and white. It was his wife. She was leaning on the banisters, listening to something. Gabriel was surprised at her stillness and strained his ear to listen also. But he could hear little save the noise of laughter and dispute on the front steps, a few chords struck on the piano and a few notes of a man's voice singing.

He stood still in the gloom of the hall, trying to catch the air that the voice was singing and gazing up at his wife. There was grace and mystery in her attitude as if she were a symbol of something. He asked himself what is a woman standing on the stairs in the shadow, listening to distant music, a symbol of. If he were a painter he would paint her in that attitude. Her blue felt hat would show off the bronze of her hair against the darkness and the dark panels of her skirt would show off the light ones. *Distant Music* he would call the picture if he were a painter.

The hall-door was closed; and Aunt Kate, Aunt Julia and Mary Jane came down the hall, still laughing.

—Well, isn't Freddy terrible? said Mary Jane. He's really terrible.

Gabriel said nothing but pointed up the stairs towards where his wife was standing. Now that the hall-door was closed the voice and the piano could be heard more clearly. Gabriel held up his hand for them to be silent. The song seemed to be in the old Irish tonality and the singer seemed uncertain both of his words and of his voice. The voice, made plaintive by distance and by the singer's hoarseness, faintly illuminated the cadence of the air with words expressing grief:

> *O, the rain falls on my heavy locks*
> *And the dew wets my skin,*
> *My babe lies cold . . .*

—O, exclaimed Mary Jane. It's Bartell D'Arcy singing and he wouldn't sing all the night. O, I'll get him to sing a song before he goes.

—O do, Mary Jane, said Aunt Kate.

Mary Jane brushed past the others and ran to the staircase but before she reached it the singing stopped and the piano was closed abruptly.

—O, what a pity! she cried. Is he coming down, Gretta?

Gabriel heard his wife answer yes and saw her come down towards them. A few steps behind her were Mr Bartell D'Arcy and Miss O'Callaghan.

—O, Mr D'Arcy, cried Mary Jane, it's downright mean of you to break off like that when we were all in raptures listening to you.

—I have been at him all the evening, said Miss O'Callaghan, and Mrs Conroy too and he told us he had a dreadful cold and couldn't sing.

—O, Mr D'Arcy, said Aunt Kate, now that was a great fib to tell.

—Can't you see that I'm as hoarse as a crow? said Mr D'Arcy roughly.

He went into the pantry hastily and put on his overcoat. The others, taken aback by his rude speech, could find nothing to say. Aunt Kate wrinkled her brows and made signs to the others to drop the subject. Mr D'Arcy stood swathing his neck carefully and frowning.

—It's the weather, said Aunt Julia, after a pause.

—Yes, everybody has colds, said Aunt Kate readily, everybody.

—They say, said Mary Jane, we haven't had snow like it for thirty years; and I read this morning in the newspapers that the snow is general all over Ireland.

—I love the look of snow, said Aunt Julia sadly.

—So do I, said Miss O'Callaghan. I think Christmas is never really Christmas unless we have the snow on the ground.

—But poor Mr D'Arcy doesn't like the snow, said Aunt Kate, smiling.

Mr D'Arcy came from the pantry, full swathed and buttoned, and in a repentant tone told them the history of his cold. Everyone gave him advice and said it was a great pity and urged him to be very careful of his throat in the night air. Gabriel watched his wife who did not join in the conversation. She was standing right under the dusty fanlight and the flame of the gas lit up the rich bronze of her hair which he had seen her drying at the fire a few days before. She was in the same attitude and seemed unaware of the talk about her. At last she turned towards them and Gabriel saw that there was colour on her cheeks and that her eyes were shining. A sudden tide of joy went leaping out of his heart.

—Mr D'Arcy, she said, what is the name of that song you were singing?

—It's called *The Lass of Aughrim*,[7] said Mr D'Arcy, but I couldn't remember it properly. Why? Do you know it?

—*The Lass of Aughrim*, she repeated. I couldn't think of the name.

—It's a very nice air, said Mary Jane. I'm sorry you were not in voice tonight.

—Now, Mary Jane, said Aunt Kate, don't annoy Mr D'Arcy. I won't have him annoyed.

Seeing that all were ready to start she shepherded them to the door where good-night was said:

—Well, good-night, Aunt Kate, and thanks for the pleasant evening.

—Good-night, Gabriel. Good-night, Gretta!

—Good-night, Aunt Kate, and thanks ever so much. Good-night, Aunt Julia.

—O, good-night, Gretta, I didn't see you.

—Good-night, Mr D'Arcy. Good-night, Miss O'Callaghan.

—Good-night, Miss Morkan.

—Good-night, again.

—Good-night, all. Safe home.

—Good-night. Good-night.

The morning was still dark. A dull yellow light brooded over the houses and the river; and the sky seemed to be descending. It was slushy underfoot; and only streaks and patches of snow lay on the roofs, on the parapets of

7. An Irish version of a ballad about a girl deserted by her lover, whom she later tries to find, bringing the baby she had by him. Other versions are called "Love Gregory" and "Lord Gregory" (the name of the deserting lover), "The Lass of Lochryan," and "The Lass of Ocram."

the quay and on the area railings. The lamps were still burning redly in the murky air and, across the river, the palace of the Four Courts stood out menacingly against the heavy sky.

She was walking on before him with Mr Bartell D'Arcy, her shoes in a brown parcel tucked under one arm and her hands holding her skirt up from the slush. She had no longer any grace of attitude but Gabriel's eyes were still bright with happiness. The blood went bounding along his veins; and the thoughts went rioting through his brain, proud, joyful, tender, valorous.

She was walking on before him so lightly and so erect that he longed to run after her noiselessly, catch her by the shoulders and say something foolish and affectionate into her ear. She seemed to him so frail that he longed to defend her against something and then to be alone with her. Moments of their secret life together burst like stars upon his memory. A heliotrope[8] envelope was lying beside his breakfast-cup and he was caressing it with his hand. Birds were twittering in the ivy and the sunny web of the curtain was shimmering along the floor: he could not eat for happiness. They were standing on the crowded platform and he was placing a ticket inside the warm palm of her glove. He was standing with her in the cold, looking in through a grated window at a man making bottles in a roaring furnace. It was very cold. Her face, fragrant in the cold air, was quite close to his; and suddenly she called out to the man at the furnace:

—Is the fire hot, sir?

But the man could not hear her with the noise of the furnace. It was just as well. He might have answered rudely.

A wave of yet more tender joy escaped from his heart and went coursing in warm flood along his arteries. Like the tender fires of stars moments of their life together, that no one knew of or would ever know of, broke upon and illumined his memory. He longed to recall to her those moments, to make her forget the years of their dull existence together and remember only their moments of ecstasy. For the years, he felt, had not quenched his soul or hers. Their children, his writing, her household cares had not quenched all their souls' tender fire. In one letter that he had written to her then he had said: *Why is it that words like these seem to me so dull and cold? Is it because there is no word tender enough to be your name?*

Like distant music these words that he had written years before were borne towards him from the past. He longed to be alone with her. When the others had gone away, when he and she were in their room in the hotel, then they would be alone together. He would call her softly:

—Gretta!

Perhaps she would not hear at once: she would be undressing. Then something in his voice would strike her. She would turn and look at him. . . .

At the corner of Winetavern Street they met a cab. He was glad of its rattling noise as it saved him from conversation. She was looking out of the window and seemed tired. The others spoke only a few words, pointing out some building or street. The horse galloped along wearily under the murky morning sky, dragging his old rattling box after his heels, and Gabriel was again in a cab with her, galloping to catch the boat, galloping to their honeymoon.

8. Grayish purple.

As the cab drove across O'Connell[9] Bridge Miss O'Callaghan said:

—They say you never cross O'Connell Bridge without seeing a white horse.

—I see a white man this time, said Gabriel.

—Where? asked Mr Bartell D'Arcy.

Gabriel pointed to the statue, on which lay patches of snow. Then he nodded familiarly to it and waved his hand.

—Good-night, Dan, he said gaily.

When the cab drew up before the hotel Gabriel jumped out and, in spite of Mr Bartell D'Arcy's protest, paid the driver. He gave the man a shilling over his fare. The man saluted and said:

—A prosperous New Year to you, sir.

—The same to you, said Gabriel cordially.

She leaned for a moment on his arm in getting out of the cab and while standing at the curbstone, bidding the others good-night. She leaned lightly on his arm, as lightly as when she had danced with him a few hours before. He had felt proud and happy then, happy that she was his, proud of her grace and wifely carriage. But now, after the kindling again of so many memories, the first touch of her body, musical and strange and perfumed, sent through him a keen pang of lust. Under cover of her silence he pressed her arm closely to his side; and, as they stood at the hotel door, he felt that they had escaped from their lives and duties, escaped from home and friends and run away together with wild and radiant hearts to a new adventure.

An old man was dozing in a great hooded chair in the hall. He lit a candle in the office and went before them to the stairs. They followed him in silence, their feet falling in soft thuds on the thickly carpeted stairs. She mounted the stairs behind the porter, her head bowed in the ascent, her frail shoulders curved as with a burden, her skirt girt tightly about her. He could have flung his arms about her hips and held her still for his arms were trembling with desire to seize her and only the stress of his nails against the palms of his hands held the wild impulse of his body in check. The porter halted on the stairs to settle his guttering candle. They halted too on the steps below him. In the silence Gabriel could hear the falling of the molten wax into the tray and the thumping of his own heart against his ribs.

The porter led them along a corridor and opened a door. Then he set his unstable candle down on a toilet-table and asked at what hour they were to be called in the morning.

—Eight, said Gabriel.

The porter pointed to the tap of the electric-light and began a muttered apology but Gabriel out him short.

—We don't want any light. We have light enough from the street. And I say, he added, pointing to the candle, you might remove that handsome article, like a good man.

The porter took up his candle again, but slowly for he was surprised by such a novel idea. Then he mumbled good-night and went out. Gabriel shot the lock to.

A ghostly light from the street lamp lay in a long shaft from one window to the door. Gabriel threw his overcoat and hat on a couch and crossed the room towards the window. He looked down into the street in order that his

9. Daniel O'Connell (1775–1847), Irish nationalist, statesman, and orator. His statue stands by O'Connell Bridge in Dublin.

emotion might calm a little. Then he turned and leaned against a chest of drawers with his back to the light. She had taken off her hat and cloak and was standing before a large swinging mirror, unhooking her waist.[1] Gabriel paused for a few moments, watching her, and then said:

—Gretta!

She turned away from the mirror slowly and walked along the shaft of light towards him. Her face looked so serious and weary that the words would not pass Gabriel's lips. No, it was not the moment yet.

—You looked tired, he said.

—I am a little, she answered.

—You don't feel ill or weak?

—No, tired: that's all.

She went on to the window and stood there, looking out. Gabriel waited again and then, fearing that diffidence was about to conquer him, he said abruptly:

—By the way, Gretta!

—What is it?

—You know that poor fellow Malins? he said quickly.

—Yes. What about him?

—Well, poor fellow, he's a decent sort of chap after all, continued Gabriel in a false voice. He gave me back that sovereign I lent him and I didn't expect it really. It's a pity he wouldn't keep away from that Browne, because he's not a bad fellow at heart.

He was trembling now with annoyance. Why did she seem so abstracted? He did not know how he could begin. Was she annoyed, too, about something? If she would only turn to him or come to him of her own accord! To take her as she was would be brutal. No, he must see some ardour in her eyes first. He longed to be master of her strange mood.

—When did you lend him the pound? she asked, after a pause.

Gabriel strove to restrain himself from breaking out into brutal language about the sottish Malins and his pound. He longed to cry to her from his soul, to crush her body against his, to overmaster her. But he said:

—O, at Christmas, when he opened that little Christmas-card shop in Henry Street.

He was in such a fever of rage and desire that he did not hear her come from the window. She stood before him for an instant, looking at him strangely. Then, suddenly raising herself on tiptoe and resting her hands lightly on his shoulders, she kissed him.

—You are a very generous person, Gabriel, she said.

Gabriel, trembling with delight at her sudden kiss and at the quaintness of her phrase, put his hands on her hair and began smoothing it back, scarcely touching it with his fingers. The washing had made it fine and brilliant. His heart was brimming over with happiness. Just when he was wishing for it she had come to him of her own accord. Perhaps her thoughts had been running with his. Perhaps she had felt the impetuous desire that was in him and then the yielding mood had come upon her. Now that she had fallen to him so easily he wondered why he had been so diffident.

He stood, holding her head between his hands. Then, slipping one arm swiftly about her body and drawing her towards him, he said softly:

---

1. Shirtwaist; a tailored blouse.

—Gretta dear, what are you thinking about?

She did not answer nor yield wholly to his arm. He said again, softly:

—Tell me what it is, Gretta. I think I know what is the matter. Do I know?

She did not answer at once. Then she said in an outburst of tears:

—O, I am thinking about that song, *The Lass of Aughrim*.

She broke loose from him and ran to the bed and, throwing her arms across the bed-rail, hid her face. Gabriel stood stock-still for a moment in astonishment and then followed her. As he passed in the way of the cheval-glass[2] he caught sight of himself in full length, his broad, well-filled shirt-front, the face whose expression always puzzled him when he saw it in a mirror and his glimmering gilt-rimmed eyeglasses. He halted a few paces from her and said:

—What about the song? Why does that make you cry?

She raised her head from her arms and dried her eyes with the back of her hand like a child. A kinder note than he had intended went into his voice.

—Why, Gretta? he asked.

—I am thinking about a person long ago who used to sing that song.

—And who was the person long ago? asked Gabriel, smiling.

—It was a person I used to know in Galway when I was living with my grandmother, she said.

The smile passed away from Gabriel's face. A dull anger began to gather again at the back of his mind and the dull fires of his lust began to glow angrily in his veins.

—Someone you were in love with? he asked ironically.

—It was a young boy I used to know, she answered, named Michael Furey. He used to sing that song, *The Lass of Aughrim*. He was very delicate.

Gabriel was silent. He did not wish her to think that he was interested in this delicate boy.

—I can see him so plainly, she said after a moment. Such eyes as he had: big dark eyes! And such an expression in them—an expression!

—O then, you were in love with him? said Gabriel.

—I used to go out walking with him, she said, when I was in Galway.

A thought flew across Gabriel's mind.

—Perhaps that was why you wanted to go to Galway with that Ivors girl? he said coldly.

She looked at him and asked in surprise:

—What for?

Her eyes made Gabriel feel awkward. He shrugged his shoulders and said:

—How do I know! To see him perhaps.

She looked away from him along the shaft of light towards the window in silence.

—He is dead, she said at length. He died when he was only seventeen. Isn't it a terrible thing to die so young as that?

—What was he? asked Gabriel, still ironically.

—He was in the gasworks,[3] she said.

Gabriel felt humiliated by the failure of his irony and by the evocation of this figure from the dead, a boy in the gasworks. While he had been full of memories of their secret life together, full of tenderness and joy and desire, she had been comparing him in her mind with another. A shameful

2. Full-length mirror that can be tilted.
3. Factory where coal gas for heating and lighting is produced.

consciousness of his own person assailed him. He saw himself as a ludicrous figure, acting as a pennyboy for his aunts, a nervous well-meaning sentimentalist, orating to vulgarians and idealising his own clownish lusts, the pitiable fatuous fellow he had caught a glimpse of in the mirror. Instinctively he turned his back more to the light lest she might see the shame that burned upon his forehead.

He tried to keep up his tone of cold interrogation but his voice when he spoke was humble and indifferent.

—I suppose you were in love with this Michael Furey, Gretta, he said.

—I was great with him at that time, she said.

Her voice was veiled and sad. Gabriel, feeling now how vain it would be to try to lead her whither he had purposed, caressed one of her hands and said, also sadly:

—And what did he die of so young, Gretta? Consumption, was it?

—I think he died for me, she answered.

A vague terror seized Gabriel at this answer as if, at that hour when he had hoped to triumph, some impalpable and vindictive being was coming against him, gathering forces against him in its vague world. But he shook himself free of it with an effort of reason and continued to caress her hand. He did not question her again for he felt that she would tell him of herself. Her hand was warm and moist: it did not respond to his touch but he continued to caress it just as he had caressed her first letter to him that spring morning.

—It was in the winter, she said, about the beginning of the winter when I was going to leave my grandmother's and come up here to the convent. And he was ill at the time in his lodgings in Galway and wouldn't be let out and his people in Oughterard were written to. He was in decline, they said, or something like that. I never knew rightly.

She paused for a moment and sighed.

—Poor fellow, she said. He was very fond of me and he was such a gentle boy. We used to go out together, walking, you know, Gabriel, like the way they do in the country. He was going to study singing only for his health. He had a very good voice, poor Michael Furey.

—Well; and then? asked Gabriel.

—And then when it came to the time for me to leave Galway and come up to the convent he was much worse and I wouldn't be let see him so I wrote a letter saying I was going up to Dublin and would be back in the summer and hoping he would be better then.

She paused for a moment to get her voice under control and then went on:

—Then the night before I left I was in my grandmother's house in Nuns' Island, packing up, and I heard gravel thrown up against the window. The window was so wet I couldn't see so I ran downstairs as I was and slipped out the back into the garden and there was the poor fellow at the end of the garden, shivering.

—And did you not tell him to go back? asked Gabriel.

—I implored him to go home at once and told him he would get his death in the rain. But he said he did not want to live. I can see his eyes as well as well! He was standing at the end of the wall where there was a tree.

—And did he go home? asked Gabriel.

—Yes, he went home. And when I was only a week in the convent he died and he was buried in Oughterard where his people came from. O, the day I heard that, that he was dead!

She stopped, choking with sobs, and overcome by emotion, flung herself face downward on the bed, sobbing in the quilt. Gabriel held her hand for a moment longer, irresolutely, and then, shy of intruding on her grief, let it fall gently and walked quietly to the window.

She was fast asleep.

Gabriel, leaning on his elbow, looked for a few moments unresentfully on her tangled hair and half-open mouth, listening to her deep-drawn breath. So she had had that romance in her life: a man had died for her sake. It hardly pained him now to think how poor a part he, her husband, had played in her life. He watched her while she slept as though he and she had never lived together as man and wife. His curious eyes rested long upon her face and on her hair: and, as he thought of what she must have been then, in that time of her first girlish beauty, a strange friendly pity for her entered his soul. He did not like to say even to himself that her face was no longer beautiful but he knew that it was no longer the face for which Michael Furey had braved death.

Perhaps she had not told him all the story. His eyes moved to the chair over which she had thrown some of her clothes. A petticoat string dangled to the floor. One boot stood upright, its limp upper fallen down: the fellow of it lay upon its side. He wondered at his riot of emotions of an hour before. From what had it proceeded? From his aunt's supper, from his own foolish speech, from the wine and dancing, the merry-making when saying good-night in the hall, the pleasure of the walk along the river in the snow. Poor Aunt Julia! She, too, would soon be a shade with the shade of Patrick Morkan and his horse. He had caught that haggard look upon her face for a moment when she was singing *Arrayed for the Bridal*. Soon, perhaps, he would be sitting in that same drawing-room, dressed in black, his silk hat on his knees. The blinds would be drawn down and Aunt Kate would be sitting beside him, crying and blowing her nose and telling him how Julia had died. He would cast about in his mind for some words that might console her, and would find only lame and useless ones. Yes, yes: that would happen very soon.

The air of the room chilled his shoulders. He stretched himself cautiously along under the sheets and lay down beside his wife. One by one they were all becoming shades. Better pass boldly into that other world, in the full glory of some passion, than fade and wither dismally with age. He thought of how she who lay beside him had locked in her heart for so many years that image of her lover's eyes when he had told her that he did not wish to live.

Generous tears filled Gabriel's eyes. He had never felt like that himself towards any woman but he knew that such a feeling must be love. The tears gathered more thickly in his eyes and in the partial darkness he imagined he saw the form of a young man standing under a dripping tree. Other forms were near. His soul had approached that region where dwell the vast hosts of the dead. He was conscious of, but could not apprehend, their wayward and flickering existence. His own identity was fading out into a grey impalpable world: the solid world itself which these dead had one time reared and lived in was dissolving and dwindling.

A few light taps upon the pane made him turn to the window. It had begun to snow again. He watched sleepily the flakes, silver and dark, falling obliquely against the lamplight. The time had come for him to set out on his journey westward. Yes, the newspapers were right: snow was general all over Ireland. It was falling on every part of the dark central plain, on the treeless hills, falling softly upon the Bog of Allen[4] and, farther westward, softly falling into the dark mutinous Shannon waves. It was falling, too, upon every part of the lonely churchyard on the hill where Michael Furey lay buried. It lay thickly drifted on the crooked crosses and headstones, on the spears of the little gate, on the barren thorns. His soul swooned slowly as he heard the snow falling faintly through the universe and faintly falling, like the descent of their last end, upon all the living and the dead.

1914

A Portrait of the Artist as a Young Man

Like many first novels, *A Portrait of the Artist as a Young Man* has autobiographical roots. Growing up in late-nineteenth-century Dublin, the novel's protagonist, Stephen Dedalus, attends the same schools, suffers the same downward-spiraling family fortunes, and experiences the same Roman Catholic upbringing and Irish nationalist ferment as did the young James Joyce. But Stephen Dedalus and James Joyce are not identical. Joyce transmuted the "sluggish matter" of life into the "imperishable" life of art (to borrow Stephen's words), compressing and heightening events, reshaping both himself and other figures, and establishing internal resonances that form a distinct world at many different levels, including character (Stephen in relation to his family, teachers, friends, love interests), image (e.g., flight, birds, music), theme (e.g., self-definition, love, religious devotion), and plot (rise, climax, and denouement). Although Joyce often speaks through Stephen, his novel evokes Stephen's resemblances not only to Daedalus, the legendary Greek artist and heroic inventor whose name he bears, but also to Icarus, his winged son who flies too close to the sun and perishes in the sea.

A Portrait of the Artist as a Young Man traces Stephen Dedalus's growth from babyhood to boarding school, from adolescence to adulthood. In a sense, the novel tells the story of its own genesis, since by the end, the protagonist has become the sort of person who might be able to write the novel we have just finished reading. *A Portrait of the Artist* is thus the kind of work known by the German term *Künstlerroman*, a novel of the artist's development or education (a variation on the *Bildungsroman*, or a novel of maturation), a form that Joyce remakes for the twentieth century and after. In sharply etched and discontinuous episodes, Joyce's novel tracks the development of the young man's character, ideas, and convictions through his vexed and often rebellious responses to the key matrices of family and school, religion and politics, as well as the emergence of his sexuality through evolving responses to objects of desire. At first, the baby Stephen parrots the words and songs he is taught ("He was baby tuckoo"), but already by boarding school he has gained sufficient independence of mind to question unjust punishment. As he continues to mature, he subjects to increasingly fierce scrutiny the orthodoxies and institutions that surround him.

But rather than merely describe these changes in the central character, the book's narrative style enacts them: it alters as Stephen changes to evoke developments in his consciousness—an important innovation in the history of the novel. *A Portrait of the Artist* opens with a bare evocation of a young child's tactile experiences ("When you wet the bed first it is warm then it gets cold"). By the climactic fourth of the novel's five parts, its once spare language has become lush and rhapsodic, at times ironically so, as Stephen embraces his vocation as an artist ("On and on and on and on he strode, far out over the sands, singing wildly to the sea, crying to greet the advent of the life that had cried to him"). Joyce's free indirect discourse modulates third-person narration toward the first person, as if the prism of Stephen's

---

4. The name given to many separate peat bogs between the rivers Liffey (which runs through Dublin) and Shannon (which runs through the central plain of Ireland).

Clongowes Wood College. From age six to nine Joyce attended Clongowes Wood College, a Jesuit-run boys boarding school in County Kildare, until his father could no longer afford the tuition. The hero of *A Portrait of the Artist as a Young Man*, Stephen Dedalus, also attends Clongowes, one of Ireland's oldest Catholic schools. Joyce's novel vividly represents the sensory, emotional, and psychological experience of boyhood in and around the refurbished castle, residence of the Jesuit community.

mind were bending the narrative light that enters and leaves it. Matching Stephen's intellectual growth, the novel's long fifth part, set at the university, is written in an analytical style, and by book's end, third-person narration has disappeared altogether, replaced by Stephen's cryptic and self-critical diary entries; the novel's protagonist has assumed a double role, as both character in and narrator of his own story.

These shifts in narrative voice break with the tradition of the stable authorial narrator who tells a story from start to finish. No single style, no fixed angle of vision seems adequate any longer to human change and complexity. This narrative multiplicity—a kind of perspectival wandering or cubistic fragmentation—anticipates the still more dramatic explosion of narrative styles and points of view in the later sections of Joyce's next novel, *Ulysses*. The variety of discourses incorporated in *A Portrait of the Artist* also anticipates the linguistic riot of Joyce's later novel, ranging from baby babble to abstract reflections on scholastic philosophy, from the sensory detail of "cold and slimy" ditch water to earnest reflections on the pious life, and from a lengthy sermon on hell to supposedly unseemly details excised in censorship cuts in the novel's first serialized printing, such as visits to prostitutes and a joking exchange about farting. Some sections are lyrical—Stephen even composes a love poem in the highly intricate form of the villanelle; other sections are mostly in dialogue, such as the ferocious Christmas dinner argument over politics and religion; in the novel's mercurial narrative technique, still other sections mediate between these poles. In the novel's final part, Stephen develops a theory of art as moving from the lyrical form (the simplest, the personal expression of an instant of emotion) through the narrative form (no longer purely personal) to the dramatic (the highest and most nearly perfect form, where "the artist, like the God of creation, remains within or behind or beyond or above his handiwork, invisible, refined out of existence, indifferent, paring his fingernails"). Although *A Portrait of the Artist* favors the objectivity of the dramatic, the novel can be seen as encompassing all three modes.

Although *A Portrait of the Artist* is focused on a single character's mind, that mind is seen not in isolation but in its evolving responsiveness to the outside world, including powerful historical forces. Set largely in Dublin from the 1880s to the early twentieth century, the novel takes place against the backdrop of the political movement for at least a measure of autonomy from Britain, or Home Rule. Like many Irish people at the time, the young Stephen Dedalus sees Charles Stuart Parnell as a heroic leader in the cause of Irish nationalism. Parnell's tragic fall and death—after it was revealed that he was having an affair with a married woman and many Irish Catholic leaders condemned him—split the Irish public, a division reflected in the novel in Stephen's childhood household. Once at University College, in a tense conversation with an English dean of studies, Stephen reflects bitterly on the imposition by the English of their language on the Irish. This postcolonial consciousness helps explain Joyce's twisting and bending of the English language, his skepticism toward fixed point of view and narrative omniscience, his splintering of the novel form into multiplicities of style and viewpoint. But despite his nationalist sympathies, Stephen is leery of subordinating art to politics, and so resists attempts by his contemporaries to enlist his support for Irish political causes, or indeed any causes.

By turns ardently religious and fiercely anticlerical, Stephen must also work out his relation to the Catholicism in which he is reared and schooled, since, as a friend observes, his "mind is supersaturated with the religion" that he at times tries to disavow, his secular theories of art wound around kernels of medieval Catholic philosophy. Fashioning his version of the aestheticist ideal of art for art's sake, Stephen Dedalus, like his namesake, prepares to "fly" the "nets" that have constrained him: he would leave Ireland and its imagination-crippling obsessions with nationality and religion. Ironically, the novel that paints Stephen's portrait of development toward artistic independence is awash in the historical crosscurrents of Irish nationalism and Catholicism, out of which surges this counter-ideal of the unfettered artist, whose ultimate allegiance is to art itself.

A Portrait of the Artist as a Young Man*

Et ignotas animum dimittit in artes.[1]
Ovid, *Metamorphoses*. VIII. 188.

I

Once upon a time and a very good time it was there was a moocow coming down along the road and this moocow that was coming down along the road met a nicens little boy named baby tuckoo. . . . .

His father told him that story: his father looked at him through a glass:[2] he had a hairy face.

---

* First printed in book form in 1916, the text given here of *A Portrait of the Artist as a Young Man* (as collated by Hans Walter Gabler from the holograph, printings, and corrections) is from the 2007 Norton Critical Edition and the 1993 Garland edition. Line numbers at the top of the page are from those editions and are provided for ease of cross-reference.
1. And he applies his mind to unknown arts (Latin). This epigraph refers to the decision of Daedalus, the legendary artist and inventor, to begin work in the unknown realm of human flight. He fashions wings of wax and feathers so that he and his son, Icarus, can escape from an island prison, but because Icarus flies too close to the sun, the wax on his wings melts, and he falls into the sea. Their tale is part of the collection of mythological stories by the Roman poet Ovid (43 B.C.E.–17 C.E.).
2. Monocle.

He was baby tuckoo. The moocow came down the road where Betty Byrne lived: she sold lemon platt.[3]

> O, the wild rose blossoms
> On the little green place.

He sang that song. That was his song.

> O, the geen wothe botheth.[4]

When you wet the bed first it is warm then it gets cold. His mother put on the oilsheet.[5] That had the queer smell.

His mother had a nicer smell than his father. She played on the piano the sailor's hornpipe[6] for him to dance. He danced:

> Tralala lala
> Tralala tralaladdy
> Tralala lala
> Tralala lala.

Uncle Charles and Dante clapped. They were older than his father and mother but uncle Charles was older than Dante.

Dante had two brushes in her press.[7] The brush with the maroon velvet back was for Michael Davitt and the brush with the green velvet back was for Parnell.[8] Dante gave him a cachou[9] every time he brought her a piece of tissue paper.

The Vances lived in number seven. They had a different father and mother. They were Eileen's father and mother. When they were grown up he was going to marry Eileen.

He hid under the table. His mother said:

—O, Stephen will apologise.

Dante said:

—O, if not, the eagles will come and pull out his eyes.

> Pull out his eyes,
> Apologise,
> Apologise,
> Pull out his eyes.

> Apologise,
> Pull out his eyes,
> Pull out his eyes,
> Apologise.

◆ ◆ ◆

3. Braided stick of lemon candy.
4. Adapted from a song about a girl's death, "Lilly Dale" (1852), by the American minstrel composer H. S. Thompson. The song's chorus is: "Oh! Lilly, sweet Lilly, dear Lilly Dale, / Now the wild rose blossoms o'er her little green grave, / 'Neath the trees in the flow'ry vale."
5. Sheet of cloth waterproofed with oil.
6. Lively dance associated with sailors.

7. Cupboard or closet.
8. Irish nationalist politician (1846–1891). Michael Davitt (1846–1906): Irish nationalist political leader. In the 1880s both men were working to protect the rights of land tenants and to achieve Home Rule, or limited political autonomy, for Ireland.
9. Candy breath freshener made from cashews and licorice.

The wide playgrounds were swarming with boys. All were shouting and the prefects[1] urged them on with strong cries. The evening air was pale and chilly and after every charge and thud of the footballers the greasy leather orb[2] flew like a heavy bird through the grey light. He kept on the fringe[3] of his line, out of sight of his prefect, out of the reach of the rude feet, feigning to run now and then. He felt his body small and weak amid the throng of players and his eyes were weak and watery. Rody Kickham was not like that: he would be captain of the third line[4] all the fellows said.

Rody Kickham was a decent fellow but Nasty Roche was a stink. Rody Kickham had greaves in his number and a hamper in the refectory.[5] Nasty Roche had big hands. He called the Friday pudding[6] dog-in-the-blanket. And one day he had asked:

—What is your name?

Stephen had answered:

—Stephen Dedalus.

Then Nasty Roche had said:

—What kind of a name is that?

And when Stephen had not been able to answer Nasty Roche had asked:

—What is your father?

Stephen had answered:

—A gentleman.

Then Nasty Roche had asked:

—Is he a magistrate?[7]

He crept about from point to point on the fringe of his line, making little runs now and then. But his hands were bluish with cold. He kept his hands in the sidepockets of his belted grey suit. That was a belt round his jacket. And belt was also to give a fellow a belt.[8] One day a fellow had said to Cantwell:

—I'd give you such a belt in a second.

Cantwell had answered:

—Go and fight your match. Give Cecil Thunder a belt. I'd like to see you. He'd give you a toe in the rump for yourself.

That was not a nice expression. His mother had told him not to speak with the rough boys in the college.[9] Nice mother! The first day in the hall of the castle[1] when she had said good-bye she had put up her veil double to her nose to kiss him: and her nose and eyes were red. But he had pretended not to see that she was going to cry. She was a nice mother but she was not so nice when she cried. And his father had given him two fiveshilling pieces[2] for pocket money. And his father had told him if he wanted anything to write home to him and, whatever he did, never to peach on[3] a fellow. Then at the door of the

---

1. Older students with disciplinary authority.
2. Ball used in playing rugby or Gaelic football, a soccer-like game, revived in the 1880s.
3. Edge.
4. The youngest group of students, composed of those under thirteen years old. Those from thirteen to fifteen were in the lower line, and those from fifteen to eighteen were in the higher line.
5. I.e., shin guards in a numbered locker and a food container in the dining hall.
6. Dessert.

7. Well-paid members of the judiciary with the status of country gentlemen. Few were Catholics.
8. I.e., to hit him.
9. Clongowes Wood College, a prestigious, fashionable boys' school founded in 1814 by the Society of Jesus, a Catholic religious order of priest-educators, also known as the Jesuits.
1. The school's central building.
2. A generous sum, equal to more than $60 in today's U.S. currency (2016).
3. Inform against.

castle the rector had shaken hands with his father and mother, his soutane[4] fluttering in the breeze, and the car had driven off with his father and mother on it. They had cried to him from the car, waving their hands:

—Goodbye, Stephen, goodbye!

—Goodbye, Stephen, goodbye!

He was caught in the whirl of a scrimmage[5] and, fearful of the flashing eyes and muddy boots,[6] bent down to look through the legs. The fellows were struggling and groaning and their legs were rubbing and kicking and stamping. Then Jack Lawton's yellow boots dodged out the ball and all the other boots and legs ran after. He ran after them a little way and then stopped. It was useless to run on. Soon they would be going home for the holidays. After supper in the studyhall he would change the number pasted up inside his desk from seventyseven to seventysix.[7]

It would be better to be in the studyhall than out there in the cold. The sky was pale and cold but there were lights in the castle. He wondered from which window Hamilton Rowan had thrown his hat on the haha[8] and had there been flowerbeds at that time under the windows. One day when he had been called to the castle the butler had shown him the marks of the soldiers' slugs in the wood of the door and had given him a piece of shortbread that the community[9] ate. It was nice and warm to see the lights in the castle. It was like something in a book. Perhaps Leicester Abbey[1] was like that. And there were nice sentences in Doctor Cornwell's Spelling Book.[2] They were like poetry but they were only sentences to learn the spelling from.

> Wolsey[3] died in Leicester Abbey
> Where the abbots buried him.
> Canker is a disease of plants,
> Cancer one of animals.

It would be nice to lie on the hearthrug before the fire, leaning his head upon his hands, and think on those sentences. He shivered as if he had cold slimy water next his skin. That was mean of Wells to shoulder him into the square ditch because he would not swop his little snuffbox for Wells's seasoned hacking chestnut,[4] the conqueror of forty. How cold and slimy the water had been! A fellow had once seen a big rat jump plop into the scum. He shivered and longed to cry. It would be so nice to be at home. Mother was sitting at the fire with Dante waiting for Brigid to bring in the tea. She had her feet on the fender[5] and her jewelly slippers were so hot and they had such a lovely warm smell! Dante knew a lot of things. She had taught

4. Long buttoned gown, typically worn by Roman Catholic priests such as the rector, head of the school.

5. A contest for the ball.

6. Shoes for playing sports.

7. Days until Christmas.

8. A fence concealed by a trench, or a walled dry moat. Archibald Hamilton Rowan (1751–1834) was an Irish nationalist convicted of sedition and imprisoned in 1794; he escaped to France and purportedly confused his pursuers by throwing his hat into the haha at Clongowes Wood Castle.

9. Religious society composed of the priests living and working together at the school.

1. The Abbey of St. Mary Pré in England, to the northwest of London.

2. One of the grammar and spelling textbooks by James Cornwell (1812–1902), standard in Irish schools at the time.

3. English cardinal and archbishop of York (ca. 1470–1530), who could not convince the pope to annul Henry VIII's first marriage and died at Leicester Abbey.

4. Used in a game to strike another chestnut until it breaks. "Square ditch": cesspool for the water closet behind the dormitory. "Swop": swap.

5. Metal frame or screen used in front of a fire to keep coals from rolling into the room.

him where the Mozambique Channel[6] was and what was the longest river in America and what was the name of the highest mountain in the moon. Father Arnall knew more than Dante because he was a priest but both his father and uncle Charles said that Dante was a clever woman and a well-read woman. And when Dante made that noise after dinner and then put up her hand to her mouth: that was heartburn.

A voice cried far out on the playground:

—All in!

Then other voices cried from the lower and third lines:

—All in! All in!

The players closed around, flushed and muddy, and he went among them, glad to go in. Rody Kickham held the ball by its greasy lace. A fellow asked him to give it one last: but he walked on without even answering the fellow. Simon Moonan told him not to because the prefect was looking. The fellow turned to Simon Moonan and said:

—We all know why you speak. You are McGlade's suck.[7]

Suck was a queer word. The fellow called Simon Moonan that name because Simon Moonan used to tie the prefect's false sleeves[8] behind his back and the prefect used to let on to be angry. But the sound was ugly. Once he had washed his hands in the lavatory of the Wicklow Hotel[9] and his father pulled the stopper up by the chain after and the dirty water went down through the hole in the basin. And when it had all gone down slowly the hole in the basin had made a sound like that: suck. Only louder.

To remember that and the white look of the lavatory made him feel cold and then hot. There were two cocks[1] that you turned and water came out: cold and hot. He felt cold and then a little hot: and he could see the names printed on the cocks. That was a very queer thing.

And the air in the corridor chilled him too. It was queer and wettish. But soon the gas would be lit and in burning it made a light noise like a little song. Always the same: and when the fellows stopped talking in the play-room you could hear it.

It was the hour for sums. Father Arnall wrote a hard sum on the board and then he said:

—Now then, who will win? Go ahead, York! Go ahead, Lancaster.[2]

Stephen tried his best but the sum was too hard and he felt confused. The little silk badge with the white rose on it that was pinned on the breast of his jacket began to flutter. He was no good at sums but he tried his best so that York might not lose. Father Arnall's face looked very black but he was not in a wax: he was laughing. Then Jack Lawton cracked his fingers and Father Arnall looked at his copybook and said:

—Right. Bravo Lancaster! The red rose wins. Come on now, York! Forge ahead!

---

6. Channel between Mozambique, on the eastern side of Africa, and the island of Madagascar.
7. Sycophant, or a person who sucks up to another.
8. Pieces of cloth hanging from the shoulders of the gown worn by Jesuit priests.
9. Hotel on Wicklow Street, south of the river Liffey, in central Dublin.

1. I.e., handles for the taps.
2. York and Lancaster were the names of the opposing houses in the English War of the Roses (1445–1485), named after the emblem of each house, a red rose for Lancaster and a white rose for York. Ireland sided with York in the conflict, which Lancaster eventually won.

Jack Lawton looked over from his side. The little silk badge with the red rose on it looked very rich because he had a blue sailor top on. Stephen felt his own face red too, thinking of all the bets about who would get first place in elements,[3] Jack Lawton or he. Some weeks Jack Lawton got the card for first and some weeks he got the card for first. His white silk badge fluttered and fluttered as he worked at the next sum and heard Father Arnall's voice. Then all his eagerness passed away and he felt his face quite cool. He thought his face must be white because it felt so cool. He could not get out the answer for the sum but it did not matter. White roses and red roses: those were beautiful colours to think of. And the cards for first place and second place and third place were beautiful colours too: pink and cream and lavender. Lavender and cream and pink roses were beautiful to think of. Perhaps a wild rose might be like those colours: and he remembered the song about the wild rose blossoms on the little green place. But you could not have a green rose. But perhaps somewhere in the world you could.

The bell rang and then the classes began to file out of the rooms and along the corridors towards the refectory. He sat looking at the two prints of butter[4] on his plate but could not eat the damp bread. The tablecloth was damp and limp. But he drank off the hot weak tea which the clumsy scullion,[5] girt with a white apron, poured into his cup. He wondered whether the scullion's apron was damp too or whether all white things were cold and damp. Nasty Roche and Saurin drank cocoa that their people sent them in tins. They said they could not drink the tea; that it was hogwash. Their fathers were magistrates, the fellows said.

All the boys seemed to him very strange. They had all fathers and mothers and different clothes and voices. He longed to be at home and lay his head on his mother's lap. But he could not: and so he longed for the play and study and prayers to be over and to be in bed.

He drank another cup of hot tea and Fleming said:

—What's up? Have you a pain or what's up with you?

—I don't know, Stephen said.

—Sick in your breadbasket,[6] Fleming said, because your face looks white. It will go away.

—O yes, Stephen said.

But he was not sick there. He thought that he was sick in his heart if you could be sick in that place. Fleming was very decent to ask him. He wanted to cry. He leaned his elbows on the table and shut and opened the flaps of his ears. Then he heard the noise of the refectory every time he opened the flaps of his ears. It made a roar like a train at night. And when he closed the flaps the roar was shut off like a train going into a tunnel. That night at Dalkey[7] the train had roared like that and then, when it went into the tunnel, the roar stopped. He closed his eyes and the train went on, roaring and then stopping; roaring again, stopping. It was nice to hear it roar and stop and then roar out of the tunnel again and then stop.

---

3. A division of the third line in which students took classes in spelling, grammar, writing, arithmetic, geography, history, and Latin (according to Joyce scholar Don Gifford).
4. Pieces of butter shaped in a mold.

5. Lowest-ranking domestic servant.
6. I.e., with an upset stomach.
7. Village on the Irish Sea coast, southeast of Dublin.

Then the higher line fellows began to come down along the matting in the middle of the refectory, Paddy Rath and Jimmy Magee and the Spaniard who was allowed to smoke cigars and the little Portuguese who wore the woolly cap. And then the lower line tables and the tables of the third line. And every single fellow had a different way of walking.

He sat in a corner of the playroom pretending to watch a game of dominos and once or twice he was able to hear for an instant the little song of the gas.[8] The prefect was at the door with some boys and Simon Moonan was knotting his false sleeves. He was telling them something about Tullabeg.[9]

Then he went away from the door and Wells came over to Stephen and said:

Tell us, Dedalus, do you kiss your mother every night before you go to bed? Stephen answered:
—I do.

Wells turned to the other fellows and said:
—O, I say, here's a fellow says he kisses his mother every night before he goes to bed.

The other fellows stopped their game and turned round, laughing. Stephen blushed under their eyes and said:
—I do not.

Wells said:
—O, I say, here's a fellow says he doesn't kiss his mother before he goes to bed.

They all laughed again. Stephen tried to laugh with them. He felt his whole body hot and confused in a moment. What was the right answer to the question? He had given two and still Wells laughed. But Wells must know the right answer for he was in third of grammar.[1] He tried to think of Wells's mother but he did not dare to raise his eyes to Wells's face. He did not like Wells's face. It was Wells who had shouldered him into the square ditch the day before because he would not swop his little snuffbox for Wells's seasoned hacking chestnut, the conqueror of forty. It was a mean thing to do; all the fellows said it was. And how cold and slimy the water had been! And a fellow had once seen a big rat jump plop into the scum.

The cold slime of the ditch covered his whole body; and, when the bell rang for study and the lines filed out of the playrooms, he felt the cold air of the corridor and staircase inside his clothes. He still tried to think what was the right answer. Was it right to kiss his mother or wrong to kiss his mother? What did that mean, to kiss? You put your face up like that to say goodnight and then his mother put her face down. That was to kiss. His mother put her lips on his cheek; her lips were soft and they wetted his cheek; and they made a tiny little noise: kiss. Why did people do that with their two faces?

Sitting in the studyhall he opened the lid of his desk and changed the number pasted up inside from seventyseven to seventysix. But the Christmas vacation was very far away: but one time it would come because the earth moved round always.

8. I.e., the noise made by a gaslight.
9. Village west of Dublin that was the home of another Jesuit boys' school until 1886, when that school merged with Clongowes Wood College, and the school became the site of the Jesuit Novitiate in Ireland.
1. I.e., in the class just above Stephen's.

There was a picture of the earth on the first page of his geography:[2] a big ball in the middle of clouds. Fleming had a box of crayons and one night during free study he had coloured the earth green and the clouds maroon. That was like the two brushes in Dante's press, the brush with the green velvet back for Parnell and the brush with the maroon velvet back for Michael Davitt. But he had not told Fleming to colour them those colours. Fleming had done it himself.

He opened the geography to study the lesson; but he could not learn the names of places in America. Still they were all different places that had those different names. They were all in different countries and the countries were in continents and the continents were in the world and the world was in the universe.

He turned to the flyleaf[3] of the geography and read what he had written there: himself, his name and where he was.

Stephen Dedalus
Class of Elements
Clongowes Wood College
Sallins[4]
County Kildare
Ireland
Europe
The World
The Universe

That was in his writing: and Fleming one night for a cod[5] had written on the opposite page:

Stephen Dedalus is my name,
Ireland is my nation.
Clongowes is my dwellingplace
And heaven my expectation.

He read the verses backwards but then they were not poetry. Then he read the flyleaf from the bottom to the top till he came to his own name. That was he: and he read down the page again. What was after the universe? Nothing. But was there anything round the universe to show where it stopped before the nothing place began? It could not be a wall but there could be a thin thin line there all round everything. It was very big to think about everything and everywhere. Only God could do that. He tried to think what a big thought that must be but he could think only of God. God was God's name just as his name was Stephen. *Dieu* was the French for God and that was God's name too; and when anyone prayed to God and said *Dieu* then God knew at once that it was a French person that was praying. But though there were different names for God in all the different languages in the world and God understood what all the people who prayed said in their different languages still God remained always the same God and God's real name was God.

---

2. I.e., his geography textbook.
3. Blank pages at the beginning of a book.
4. Village near Clongowes Wood College in

County Kildare, just to the west of Dublin.
5. As a joke or prank.

It made him very tired to think that way. It made him feel his head very big. He turned over the flyleaf and looked wearily at the green round earth in the middle of the maroon clouds. He wondered which was right, to be for the green or for the maroon, because Dante had ripped the green velvet back off the brush that was for Parnell one day with her scissors and had told him that Parnell was a bad man. He wondered if they were arguing at home about that. That was called politics. There were two sides in it: Dante was on one side and his father and Mr Casey were on the other side but his mother and uncle Charles were on no side. Every day there was something in the paper about it.[6]

It pained him that he did not know well what politics meant and that he did not know where the universe ended. He felt small and weak. When would he be like the fellows in poetry and rhetoric?[7] They had big voices and big boots and they studied trigonometry. That was very far away. First came the vacation and then the next term and then vacation again and then again another term and then again the vacation. It was like a train going in and out of tunnels and that was like the noise of the boys eating in the refectory when you opened and closed the flaps of the ears. Term, vacation; tunnel, out; noise, stop. How far away it was! It was better to go to bed to sleep. Only prayers in the chapel and then bed. He shivered and yawned. It would be lovely in bed after the sheets got a bit hot. First they were so cold to get into. He shivered to think how cold they were first. But then they got hot and then he could sleep. It was lovely to be tired. He yawned again. Night prayers and then bed: he shivered and wanted to yawn. It would be lovely in a few minutes. He felt a warm glow creeping up from the cold shivering sheets, warmer and warmer till he felt warm all over, ever so warm; ever so warm and yet he shivered a little and still wanted to yawn.

The bell rang for night prayers and he filed out of the studyhall after the others and down the staircase and along the corridors to the chapel. The corridors were darkly lit and the chapel was darkly lit. Soon all would be dark and sleeping. There was cold night air in the chapel and the marbles[8] were the colour the sea was at night. The sea was cold day and night: but it was colder at night. It was cold and dark under the seawall[9] beside his father's house. But the kettle would be on the hob to make punch.[1]

The prefect of the chapel prayed above his head and his memory knew the responses:

> O Lord, open our lips
> And our mouth shall announce Thy praise.
> Incline unto our aid, O God!
> O Lord, make haste to help us![2]

There was a cold night smell in the chapel. But it was a holy smell. It was not like the smell of the old peasants who knelt at the back of the chapel at Sun-

6. There was a major controversy over Parnell's leadership of the Irish Parliamentary Party after the revelation, in 1889, of his affair with Katherine ("Kitty") O'Shea, the wife of a political colleague. Parnell split with the leadership of the party in late 1890, and the controversy continued until his death, in October 1891, reverberating long after that.
7. The two highest grades.

8. Walls or pillars painted to look like marble.
9. Wall forming a breakwater against the sea.
1. Hot alcoholic drink, usually made from wine and spices. "Hob": shelf at the back or side of the fireplace.
2. The opening lines of Matins, a daily religious service performed in the morning. The second and fourth lines are the responses.

day mass. That was a smell of air and rain and turf[3] and corduroy. But they were very holy peasants. They breathed behind him on his neck and sighed as they prayed. They lived in Clane,[4] a fellow said: there were little cottages there and he had seen a woman standing at the halfdoor of a cottage with a child in her arms as the cars[5] had come past from Sallins. It would be lovely to sleep for one night in that cottage before the fire of smoking turf, in the dark lit by the fire, in the warm dark, breathing the smell of the peasants, air and rain and turf and corduroy. But, O, the road there between the trees was dark! You would be lost in the dark. It made him afraid to think of how it was.

He heard the voice of the prefect of the chapel saying the last prayer. He prayed it too against the dark outside under the trees.

> *Visit, we beseech Thee, O Lord, this habitation and drive away from it all the snares of the enemy. May Thy holy angels dwell herein to preserve us in peace and may Thy blessing be always upon us through Christ, Our Lord. Amen.*[6]

His fingers trembled as he undressed himself in the dormitory. He told his fingers to hurry up. He had to undress and then kneel and say his own prayers and be in bed before the gas was lowered so that he might not go to hell when he died. He rolled his stockings off and put on his nightshirt quickly and knelt trembling at his bedside and repeated his prayers quickly quickly fearing that the gas would go down. He felt his shoulders shaking as he murmured:

> *God bless my father and my mother and spare them to me!*
> *God bless my little brothers and sisters and spare them to me!*
> *God bless Dante and uncle Charles and spare them to me!*

He blessed himself and climbed quickly into bed and, tucking the end of the nightshirt under his feet, curled himself together under the cold white sheets, shaking and trembling. But he would not go to hell when he died; and the shaking would stop. A voice bade the boys in the dormitory goodnight. He peered out for an instant over the coverlet and saw the yellow curtains round and before his bed that shut him off on all sides. The light was lowered quietly.

The prefect's shoes went away. Where? Down the staircase and along the corridors or to his room at the end? He saw the dark. Was it true about the black dog that walked there at night with eyes as big as carriagelamps? They said it was the ghost of a murderer. A long shiver of fear flowed over his body. He saw the dark entrance hall of the castle. Old servants in old dress were in the ironingroom above the staircase. It was long ago. The old servants were quiet. There was a fire there but the hall was still dark. A figure came up the staircase from the hall. He wore the white cloak of a marshal;[7] his face was pale and strange; he held his hand pressed to his side. He looked out of strange eyes at the old servants. They looked at him and saw their master's face and cloak and knew that he had received his deathwound. But only the dark was where they looked: only dark silent air. Their master had received

---

3. Slab of peat used as fuel.
4. Village very near Clongowes Wood College that used the college chapel as its parish church.
5. Horse-drawn carriages.
6. The last prayer before the end of Compline, the final daily religious service.
7. Maximilian Ulysses, Count von Browne (1705–

1757), a member of the family that owned Clongowes Wood before it became a boys' school, was a marshal in the Austrian army. He was killed at the Battle of Prague in the Seven Years' War; according to legend, on the day of his death his ghost appeared in his family's home.

his deathwound on the battlefield of Prague far away over the sea. He was standing on the field; his hand was pressed to his side; his face was pale and strange and he wore the white cloak of a marshal.

O how cold and strange it was to think of that! All the dark was cold and strange. There were pale strange faces there, great eyes like carriagelamps. They were the ghosts of murderers, the figures of marshals who had received their deathwound on battlefields far away over the sea. What did they wish to say that their faces were so strange?

Visit, we beseech Thee, O Lord, this habitation and drive away from it all. . . .

Going home for the holidays! That would be lovely: the fellows had told him. Getting up on the cars in the early wintry morning outside the door of the castle. The cars were rolling on the gravel. Cheers for the rector!

Hurray! Hurray! Hurray!

The cars drove past the chapel and all caps were raised. They drove merrily along the country roads. The drivers pointed with their whips to Bodenstown.[8] The fellows cheered. They passed the farmhouse of the Jolly Farmer.[9] Cheer after cheer after cheer. Through Clane they drove, cheering and cheered. The peasant women stood at the halfdoors, the men stood here and there. The lovely smell there was in the wintry air: the smell of Clane: rain and wintry air and turf smouldering and corduroy.

The train was full of fellows: a long long chocolate train with cream facings. The guards went to and fro opening, closing, locking, unlocking the doors. They were men in dark blue and silver; they had silvery whistles and their keys made a quick music: click, click: click, click.

And the train raced on over the flat lands and past the Hill of Allen.[1] The telegraphpoles were passing, passing. The train went on and on. It knew. There were coloured lanterns in the hall of his father's house and ropes of green branches. There were holly and ivy round the pierglass[2] and holly and ivy, green and red, twined round the chandeliers. There were red holly and green ivy round the old portraits on the walls. Holly and ivy for him and for Christmas.

Lovely. . . . . .

All the people. Welcome home, Stephen! Noises of welcome. His mother kissed him. Was that right? His father was a marshal now higher than a magistrate. Welcome home, Stephen!

Noises. . . . .

There was a noise of curtainrings running back along the rods, of water being splashed in the basins. There was a noise of rising and dressing and washing in the dormitory: a noise of clapping of hands as the prefect went up and down telling the fellows to look sharp. A pale sunlight showed the yellow curtains drawn back, the tossed beds. His bed was very hot and his face and body were very hot.

He got up and sat on the side of his bed. He was weak. He tried to pull on his stocking. It had a horrid rough feel. The sunlight was queer and cold.

Fleming said:

—Are you not well?

8. Town and parish in County Kildare.
9. Children's piano piece by German composer Robert Schumann (1810–1856).

1. Hill eight miles west of Sallins.
2. Large mirror, usually over a chimney.

He did not know; and Fleming said:

—Get back into bed. I'll tell McGlade you're not well.

—He's sick.

—Who is?

—Tell McGlade.

—Get back into bed.

—Is he sick?

A fellow held his arms while he loosened the stocking clinging to his foot and climbed back into the hot bed.

He crouched down between the sheets, glad of their tepid glow. He heard the fellows talk among themselves about him as they dressed for mass. It was a mean thing to do, to shoulder him into the square ditch, they were saying.

Then their voices ceased; they had gone. A voice at his bed said:

—Dedalus, don't spy on us,[3] sure you won't?

Wells's face was there. He looked at it and saw that Wells was afraid.

—I didn't mean to. Sure you won't?

His father had told him, whatever he did, never to peach on a fellow. He shook his head and answered no and felt glad. Wells said:

—I didn't mean to, honour bright. It was only for cod. I'm sorry.

The face and the voice went away. Sorry because he was afraid. Afraid that it was some disease. Canker was a disease of plants and cancer one of animals: or another different. That was a long time ago then out on the playgrounds in the evening light, creeping from point to point on the fringe of his line, a heavy bird flying low through the grey light. Leicester Abbey lit up. Wolsey died there. The abbots buried him themselves.

It was not Wells's face, it was the prefect's. He was not foxing.[4] No, no: he was sick really. He was not foxing. And he felt the prefect's hand on his forehead; and he felt his forehead warm and damp against the prefect's cold damp hand. That was the way a rat felt, slimy and damp and cold. Every rat had two eyes to look out of. Sleek slimy coats, little little feet tucked up to jump, black shiny eyes to look out of. They could understand how to jump. But the minds of rats could not understand trigonometry. When they were dead they lay on their sides. Their coats dried then. They were only dead things.

The prefect was there again and it was his voice that was saying that he was to get up, that Father Minister had said he was to get up and dress and go to the infirmary. And while he was dressing himself as quickly as he could the prefect said:

—We must pack off to Brother Michael because we have the collywobbles.[5] Terrible thing to have the collywobbles! How we wobble when we have the collywobbles!

He was very decent to say that. That was all to make him laugh. But he could not laugh because his cheeks and lips were all shivery: and then the prefect had to laugh by himself.

The prefect cried:

—Quick march! Hayfoot! Strawfoot![6]

3. Don't inform against us.
4. Pretending.
5. An upset stomach.

6. Reference to the practice of tying hay to the left foot and straw to the right foot in order to teach army recruits how to march.

They went together down the staircase and along the corridor and past the bath. As he passed the door he remembered with a vague fear the warm turfcoloured bogwater, the warm moist air, the noise of plunges, the smell of the towels, like medicine.

Brother Michael was standing at the door of the infirmary and from the door of the dark cabinet on his right came a smell like medicine. That came from the bottles on the shelves. The prefect spoke to Brother Michael and Brother Michael answered and called the prefect sir. He had reddish hair mixed with grey and a queer look. It was queer that he would always be a brother. It was queer too that you could not call him sir because he was a brother[7] and had a different kind of look. Was he not holy enough or why could he not catch up on the others?

There were two beds in the room and in one bed there was a fellow: and when they went in he called out:

—Hello! It's young Dedalus! What's up?

—The sky is up, Brother Michael said.

He was a fellow out of third of grammar and, while Stephen was undressing, he asked Brother Michael to bring him a round of buttered toast.

—Ah, do! he said.

—Butter you up! said Brother Michael. You'll get your walking papers[8] in the morning when the doctor comes.

—Will I? the fellow said. I'm not well yet.

Brother Michael repeated:

—You'll get your walking papers, I tell you.

He bent down to rake the fire. He had a long back like the long back of a tramhorse.[9] He shook the poker gravely and nodded his head at the fellow out of third of grammar.

Then Brother Michael went away and after a while the fellow out of third of grammar turned in towards the wall and fell asleep.

That was the infirmary. He was sick then. Had they written home to tell his mother and father? But it would be quicker for one of the priests to go himself to tell them. Or he would write a letter for the priest to bring.

Dear Mother

I am sick. I want to go home. Please come and take me home. I am in the infirmary.

Your fond son,
Stephen

How far away they were! There was cold sunlight outside the window. He wondered if he would die. You could die just the same on a sunny day. He might die before his mother came. Then he would have a dead mass in the chapel like the way the fellows had told him it was when Little had died. All the fellows would be at the mass, dressed in black, all with sad faces. Wells too would be there but no fellow would look at him. The rector would be there in a cope[1] of black and gold and there would be tall yellow candles on the altar and round the catafalque.[2] And they would carry the coffin out

---

7. I.e., a member of the Jesuit order but not an ordained priest.
8. Permission to leave the infirmary (after a more formal notice of dismissal).

9. Horse that draws the tram, a passenger carriage.
1. Long cloak or cape.
2. Platform holding a coffin at a funeral.

of the chapel slowly and he would be buried in the little graveyard of the community off the main avenue of limes.[3] And Wells would be sorry then for what he had done. And the bell would toll slowly.

He could hear the tolling. He said over to himself the song that Brigid had taught him.

> *Dingdong! The castle bell!*
> *Farewell, my mother!*
> *Bury me in the old churchyard*
> *Beside my eldest brother.*
> *My coffin shall be black,*
> *Six angels at my back,*
> *Two to sing and two to pray*
> *And two to carry my soul away.*[4]

How beautiful and sad that was! How beautiful the words were where they said *Bury me in the old churchyard!* A tremor passed over his body. How sad and how beautiful! He wanted to cry quietly but not for himself: for the words, so beautiful and sad, like music. The bell! The bell! Farewell! O farewell!

The cold sunlight was weaker and Brother Michael was standing at his bedside with a bowl of beeftea.[5] He was glad for his mouth was hot and dry. He could hear them playing on the playgrounds. It was after lunchtime. And the day was going on in the college just as if he were there.

Then Brother Michael was going away and the fellow out of third of grammar told him to be sure and come back and tell him all the news in the paper. He told Stephen that his name was Athy and that his father kept a lot of racehorses that were spiffing[6] jumpers and that his father would give a good tip to Brother Michael any time he wanted it because Brother Michael was very decent and always told him the news out of the paper they got every day up in the castle. There was every kind of news in the paper: accidents, shipwrecks, sports and politics.

—Now it is all about politics in the paper, he said. Do your people talk about that too?

—Yes, Stephen said.

—Mine too, he said.

Then he thought for a moment and said:

—You have a queer name, Dedalus, and I have a queer name too, Athy.[7] My name is the name of a town. Your name is like Latin.

Then he asked:

—Are you good at riddles?

Stephen answered:

—Not very good.

Then he said:

—Can you answer me this one? Why is the county Kildare like the leg of a fellow's breeches?

Stephen thought what could be the answer and then said:

—I give it up.

---

3. Linden trees.
4. A nursery rhyme.
5. Beef bouillon.

6. Excellent.
7. A town in County Kildare, southwest of Dublin.

—Because there is a thigh in it, he said. Do you see the joke? Athy is the town in the county Kildare and a thigh is the other thigh.

O, I see, Stephen said.

That's an old riddle, he said.

After a moment he said:

—I say!

—What? asked Stephen.

—You know, he said, you can ask that riddle another way?

—Can you? said Stephen.

—The same riddle, he said. Do you know the other way to ask it?

—No, said Stephen.

—Can you not think of the other way? he said.

He looked at Stephen over the bedclothes as he spoke. Then he lay back on the pillow and said:

—There is another way but I won't tell you what it is.

Why did he not tell it? His father, who kept the racehorses, must be a magistrate too like Saurin's father and Nasty Roche's father. He thought of his own father, of how he sang songs while his mother played and of how he always gave him a shilling when he asked for sixpence[8] and he felt sorry for him that he was not a magistrate like the other boys' fathers. Then why was he sent to that place with them? But his father had told him that he would be no stranger there because his granduncle had presented an address to the liberator[9] there fifty years before. You could know the people of that time by their old dress. It seemed to him a solemn time: and he wondered if that was the time when the fellows in Clongowes wore blue coats with brass buttons and yellow waistcoats and caps of rabbit-skin and drank beer like grownup people and kept greyhounds of their own to course the hares with.

He looked at the window and saw that the daylight had grown weaker. There would be cloudy grey light over the playgrounds. There was no noise on the playgrounds. The class must be doing the themes or perhaps Father Arnall was reading a legend[1] out of the book.

It was queer that they had not given him any medicine. Perhaps Brother Michael would bring it back when he came. They said you got stinking stuff to drink when you were in the infirmary. But he felt better now than before. It would be nice getting better slowly. You could get a book then. There was a book in the library about Holland. There were lovely foreign names in it and pictures of strangelooking cities and ships. It made you feel so happy.

How pale the light was at the window! But that was nice. The fire rose and fell on the wall. It was like waves. Someone had put coal on and he heard voices. They were talking. It was the noise of the waves. Or the waves were talking among themselves as they rose and fell.

He saw the sea of waves, long dark waves rising and falling, dark under the moonless night. A tiny light twinkled at the pierhead[2] where the ship was entering: and he saw a multitude of people gathered by the waters' edge

---

8. Since one shilling was equal to twelve pence, twice as much.

9. Daniel O'Connell (1775–1847), the most prominent Irish leader in the early 19th century. He earned this nickname by leading the movement to force the British government, in 1829, to pass Catholic emancipation, which granted full political and civil liberties to Catholics in Britain and Ireland, including the right to hold public office.

1. A story of a saint's life. "Themes": writing exercises or essays.

2. The end of a pier nearest the sea.

to see the ship that was entering their harbour. A tall man stood on the deck, looking out towards the flat dark land: and by the light at the pierhead he saw his face, the sorrowful face of Brother Michael.

He saw him lift his hand towards the people and heard him say in a loud voice of sorrow over the waters:

—He is dead. We saw him lying upon the catafalque.

A wail of sorrow went up from the people.

—Parnell! Parnell! He is dead![3]

They fell upon their knees, moaning in sorrow.

And he saw Dante in a maroon velvet dress and with a green velvet mantle[4] hanging from her shoulders walking proudly and silently past the people who knelt by the waters' edge.

◆   ◆   ◆

A great fire, banked high and red, flamed in the grate and under the ivy-twined branches of the chandelier the Christmas table was spread. They had come home a little late and still dinner was not ready: but it would be ready in a jiffy, his mother had said. They were waiting for the door to open and for the servants to come in, holding the big dishes covered with their heavy metal covers.

All were waiting: uncle Charles, who sat far away in the shadow of the window, Dante and Mr Casey, who sat in the easychairs at either side of the hearth, Stephen, seated on a chair between them, his feet resting on the toasted boss.[5] Mr Dedalus looked at himself in the pierglass above the mantelpiece, waxed out his moustache ends and then, parting his coattails, stood with his back to the glowing fire: and still, from time to time, he withdrew a hand from his coattail to wax out one of his moustache ends. Mr Casey leaned his head to one side and, smiling, tapped the gland of his neck with his fingers. And Stephen smiled too for he knew now that it was not true that Mr Casey had a purse of silver in his throat. He smiled to think how the silvery noise which Mr Casey used to make had deceived him. And when he had tried to open Mr Casey's hand to see if the purse of silver was hidden there he had seen that the fingers could not be straightened out: and Mr Casey had told him that he had got those three cramped fingers making a birthday present for Queen Victoria.[6]

Mr Casey tapped the gland of his neck and smiled at Stephen with sleepy eyes: and Mr Dedalus said to him:

—Yes. Well now, that's all right. O, we had a good walk, hadn't we, John? Yes . . . . . . I wonder if there's any likelihood of dinner this evening. Yes . . . . . O, well now, we got a good breath of ozone round the Head[7] today. Ay, bedad.[8]

He turned to Dante and said:

—You didn't stir out at all, Mrs Riordan?

Dante frowned and said shortly:

—No.

3. Parnell died in England on October 6, 1891; his body was brought back to Ireland, to Kingstown (or Dun Laoghire), on October 11, and from there to Dublin City Hall to lie in state.
4. Loose sleeveless cloak.
5. Stuffed footstool made warm by the fire.
6. By picking oakum, the loosely twisted fibers of old rope (according to Don Gifford). This task was a form of hard labor, to which Mr. Casey has been sentenced because of his activity as an Irish revolutionary.
7. Bray Head, a headland on the coast south of the village of Bray, 12 miles south of Dublin. "Ozone": fresh air.
8. An emphatic assertion.

Mr Dedalus dropped his coattails and went over to the sideboard. He brought forth a great stone jar of whisky from the locker and filled the decanter slowly, bending now and then to see how much he had poured in. Then replacing the jar in the locker he poured out a little of the whisky into two glasses, added a little water and came with them back to the fireplace.

—A thimbleful, John, he said. Just to whet your appetite.

Mr Casey took the glass, drank, and placed it near him on the mantel-piece. Then he said:

—Well, I can't help thinking of our friend Christopher manufacturing. . . .

He broke into a fit of laughter and coughing and added:

— . . . manufacturing that champagne[9] for those fellows.

Mr Dedalus laughed loudly.

—Is it Christy? he said. There's more cunning in one of those warts on his bald head than in a pack of jack foxes.[1]

He inclined his head, closed his eyes, and, licking his lips profusely, began to speak with the voice of the hotel keeper.

—And he has such a soft mouth when he's speaking to you, don't you know. He's very moist and watery about the dewlaps,[2] God bless him.

Mr Casey was still struggling through his fit of coughing and laughter. Stephen, seeing and hearing the hotel keeper through his father's face and voice, laughed.

Mr Dedalus put up his eyeglass and, staring down at him, said quietly and kindly:

—What are you laughing at, you little puppy, you?

The servants entered and placed the dishes on the table. Mrs Dedalus followed and the places were arranged.

—Sit over, she said.

Mr Dedalus went to the end of the table and said:

—Now, Mrs Riordan, sit over. John, sit you down, my hearty.

He looked round to where uncle Charles sat and said:

—Now then, sir, there's a bird here waiting for you.

When all had taken their seats he laid his hand on the cover and then said quickly, withdrawing it:

—Now, Stephen.

Stephen stood up in his place to say the grace before meals:

> Bless us, O Lord, and these Thy gifts which through
> Thy bounty we are about to receive through Christ
> Our Lord. Amen.

All blessed themselves and Mr Dedalus with a sigh of pleasure lifted from the dish the heavy cover pearled around the edge with glistening drops.

Stephen looked at the plump turkey which had lain, trussed and skewered, on the kitchen table. He knew that his father had paid a guinea for it in Dunn's of D'Olier Street[3] and that the man had prodded it often at the breastbone to show how good it was: and he remembered the man's voice when he had said:

---

9. Likely a euphemism for explosives.
1. Male foxes.
2. Folds of loose skin at the throat.

3. Fashionable store for food in central Dublin. "Guinea": a gold coin worth one pound, one shilling.

—Take that one, sir. That's the real Ally Daly,[4]

Why did Mr Barrett in Clongowes call his pandybat[5] a turkey? It was not like a turkey. But Clongowes was far away: and the warm heavy smell of turkey and ham and celery rose from the plates and dishes and the great fire was banked high and red in the grate and the green ivy and red holly made you feel so happy and when dinner was ended the big plumpudding would be carried in, studded with peeled almonds and sprigs of holly, with bluish fire running around it[6] and a little green flag flying from the top.

It was his first Christmas dinner and he thought of his little brothers and sisters who were waiting in the nursery, as he had often waited, till the pudding came. The deep low collar and the Eton jacket[7] made him feel queer and oldish: and that morning when his mother had brought him down to the parlour, dressed for mass, his father had cried. That was because he was thinking of his own father. And uncle Charles had said so too.

Mr Dedalus covered the dish and began to eat hungrily. Then he said:

—Poor old Christy, he's nearly lopsided now with roguery.

—Simon, said Mrs Dedalus, you haven't given Mrs Riordan any sauce.

Mr Dedalus seized the sauceboat.

—Haven't I? he cried. Mrs Riordan, pity the poor blind.

Dante covered her plate with her hands and said:

—No, thanks.

Mr Dedalus turned to uncle Charles.

—How are you off, sir?

—Right as the mail, Simon.

—You, John?

—I'm all right. Go on yourself.

—Mary? Here, Stephen, here's something to make your hair curl.

He poured sauce freely over Stephen's plate and set the boat again on the table. Then he asked uncle Charles was it tender. Uncle Charles could not speak because his mouth was full but he nodded that it was.

—That was a good answer our friend made to the canon. What? said Mr Dedalus.

—I didn't think he had that much in him, said Mr Casey.

—*I'll pay you your dues, father, when you cease turning the house of God into a pollingbooth.*

—A nice answer, said Dante, for any man calling himself a catholic to give to his priest.

—They have only themselves to blame, said Mr Dedalus suavely. If they took a fool's advice they would confine their attention to religion.

—It is religion, Dante said. They are doing their duty in warning the people.

—We go to the house of God, Mr Casey said, in all humility to pray to our Maker and not to hear election addresses.

—It is religion, Dante said again. They are right. They must direct their flocks.

—And preach politics from the altar, is it? asked Mr Dedalus.

—Certainly, said Dante. It is a question of public morality. A priest would not be a priest if he did not tell his flock what is right and what is wrong.

Mrs Dedalus laid down her knife and fork, saying:

---

4. The real thing, or the best.
5. Reinforced leather strap used to strike students' hands as punishment.
6. The brandy dressing has been set alight.

7. Short black jacket, named after the typical attire of the younger boys at Eton, a British public school.

—For pity' sake[8] and for pity sake let us have no political discussion on this day of all days in the year.

—Quite right, ma'am, said uncle Charles. Now, Simon, that's quite enough now. Not another word now.

—Yes, yes, said Mr Dedalus quickly.

He uncovered the dish boldly and said:

—Now then, who's for more turkey?

Nobody answered. Dante said:

—Nice language for any catholic to use!

—Mrs Riordan, I appeal to you, said Mrs Dedalus, to let the matter drop now.

Dante turned on her and said:

—And am I to sit here and listen to the pastors of my church being flouted?

—Nobody is saying a word against them, said Mr Dedalus, so long as they don't meddle in politics.

—The bishops and priests of Ireland have spoken, said Dante, and they must be obeyed.

—Let them leave politics alone, said Mr Casey, or the people may leave their church alone.

—You hear? said Dante turning to Mrs Dedalus.

—Mr Casey! Simon! said Mrs Dedalus. Let it end now.

—Too bad! Too bad! said uncle Charles.

—What? cried Mr Dedalus. Were we to desert him at the bidding of the English people?[9]

—He was no longer worthy to lead, said Dante. He was a public sinner.

—We are all sinners and black sinners, said Mr Casey coldly.

—*Woe be to the man by whom the scandal cometh!* said Mrs Riordan. *It would be better for him that a millstone were tied about his neck and that he were cast into the depths of the sea rather than that he should scandalise one of these, my least little ones.* That is the language of the Holy Ghost.[1]

—And very bad language, if you ask me, said Mr Dedalus coolly.

—Simon! Simon! said uncle Charles. The boy.

—Yes, yes, said Mr Dedalus. I meant about the. . . . I was thinking about the bad language of that railway porter. Well now, that's all right. Here, Stephen, show me your plate, old chap. Eat away now. Here.

He heaped up the food on Stephen's plate and served uncle Charles and Mr Casey to large pieces of turkey and splashes of sauce. Mrs Dedalus was eating little and Dante sat with her hands in her lap. She was red in the face. Mr Dedalus rooted with the carvers at the end of the dish and said:

—There's a tasty bit here we call the pope's nose.[2] If any lady or gentleman. . . . .

He held a piece of fowl up on the prong of the carvingfork. Nobody spoke. He put it on his own plate, saying:

8. Here, Joyce's spelling mimics pronunciation, eliding the possessive "s" before a noun beginning with an "s" (as later in "for God' sake"); the second "pity" also omits the apostrophe.

9. After the scandal over Parnell's affair with a married woman, the English prime minister, William Gladstone (1809–1898), informed the Irish Parliamentary Party, in November 1890, that as long as Parnell remained its leader, his English Liberal Party could form no alliance with it over Home Rule. In December the IPP voted to remove Parnell from leadership, partly because many saw the situation as a choice between Parnell and Home Rule.

1. The third person, who with the Father and the Son, comprises the Holy Trinity. Mrs. Riordan quotes Luke 17.1–2.

2. Fatty rump of the turkey.

—Well, you can't say but you were asked. I think I had better eat it myself because I'm not well in my health lately.

He winked at Stephen and, replacing the dishcover, began to eat again.

There was a silence while he ate. Then he said:

—Well now, the day kept up fine after all. There were plenty of strangers down too.

Nobody spoke. He said again:

—I think there were more strangers down than last Christmas.

He looked round at the others whose faces were bent towards their plates and, receiving no reply, waited for a moment and said bitterly:

—Well, my Christmas dinner has been spoiled anyhow.

—There could be neither luck nor grace, Dante said, in a house where there is no respect for the pastors of the church.

Mr Dedalus threw his knife and fork noisily on his plate.

—Respect! he said. Is it for Billy with the lip or for the tub of guts up in Armagh?[3] Respect!

—Princes of the church, said Mr Casey with slow scorn.

—Lord Leitrim's coachman,[4] yes, said Mr Dedalus.

—They are the Lord's anointed, Dante said. They are an honour to their country.

—Tub of guts, said Mr Dedalus coarsely. He has a handsome face, mind you, in repose. You should see that fellow lapping up his bacon and cabbage of a cold winter's day. O Johnny!

He twisted his features into a grimace of heavy bestiality and made a lapping noise with his lips.

—Really, Simon, said Mrs Dedalus, you should not speak that way before Stephen. It's not right.

—O, he'll remember all this when he grows up, said Dante hotly, the language he heard against God and religion and priests in his own home.

—Let him remember too, cried Mr Casey to her from across the table, the language with which the priests and the priests' pawns broke Parnell's heart and hounded him into his grave. Let him remember that too when he grows up.

—Sons of bitches! cried Mr Dedalus. When he was down they turned on him to betray him and rend him like rats in a sewer. Lowlived dogs! And they look it! By Christ, they look it!

—They behaved rightly, cried Dante. They obeyed their bishops and their priests. Honour to them!

—Well, it is perfectly dreadful to say that not even for one day of the year, said Mrs Dedalus, can we be free from these dreadful disputes!

Uncle Charles raised his hands mildly and said:

—Come now, come now, come now! Can we not have our opinions whatever they are without this bad temper and this bad language? It is too bad surely.

Mrs Dedalus spoke to Dante in a low voice but Dante said loudly:

—I will not say nothing. I will defend my church and my religion when it is insulted and spit on by renegade catholics.

3. William J. Walsh (1841–1921), archbishop of Dublin, and Michael Logue (1840–1924), archbishop of Armagh, both denounced Parnell publicly.
4. I.e., an Irish person who tries to protect or col- ludes with an oppressor. The phrase refers to the (unsuccessful) attempt of an Irish coachman to protect William Sydney Clements, earl of Leitrim (1806–1878), an English landlord notorious for his treatment of Irish tenants, from assassination.

Mr Casey pushed his plate rudely into the middle of the table and, resting his elbows before him, said in a harsh voice to his host:

—Tell me, did I tell you that story about a very famous spit?

—You did not, John, said Mr Dedalus.

—Why then, said Mr Casey, it is a most instructive story. It happened not long ago in the county Wicklow where we are now.

He broke off and, turning towards Dante, said with quiet indignation:

—And I may tell you, ma'am, that I, if you mean me, am no renegade catholic. I am a catholic as my father was and his father before him and his father before him again when we gave up our lives rather than sell our faith.

—The more shame to you now, Dante said, to speak as you do.

—The story, John, said Mr Dedalus smiling. Let us have the story anyhow.

—Catholic indeed! repeated Dante ironically. The blackest protestant[5] in the land would not speak the language I have heard this evening.

Mr Dedalus began to sway his head to and fro, crooning like a country singer.

—I am no protestant, I tell you again, said Mr Casey flushing.

Mr Dedalus, still crooning and swaying his head, began to sing in a grunting nasal tone:

> O, come all you Roman catholics
> That never went to mass.[6]

He took up his knife and fork again in good humour and set to eating, saying to Mr Casey:

—Let us have the story, John. It will help us to digest.

Stephen looked with affection at Mr Casey's face which stared across the table over his joined hands. He liked to sit near him at the fire, looking up at his dark fierce face. But his dark eyes were never fierce and his slow voice was good to listen to. But why was he then against the priests? Because Dante must be right then. But he had heard his father say that she was a spoiled nun and that she had come out of the convent in the Alleghanies when her brothers had got the money from the savages for the trinkets and chainies.[7] Perhaps that made her severe against Parnell. And she did not like him to play with Eileen because Eileen was a protestant and when she was young she knew children that used to play with protestants and the protestants used to make fun of the litany of the Blessed Virgin. *Tower of Ivory*, they used to say, *House of Gold*![8] How could a woman be a tower of ivory or a house of gold? Who was right then? And he remembered the evening in the infirmary in Clongowes, the dark waters, the light at the pierhead and the moan of sorrow from the people when they had heard.

Eileen had long white hands. One evening when playing tig[9] she had put her hands over his eyes: long and white and thin and cold and soft. That was ivory: a cold white thing. That was the meaning of *Tower of Ivory*.

5. The most anti-Catholic Protestant.

6. Parody of the traditional opening of an Irish street song.

7. Damaged china. The implication is that Dante left her training as a nun in a convent in the Allegheny Mountains, in the eastern United States, because her brothers gave her money they earned from cheating Africans in trade.

8. Phrases applied to the Virgin Mary in the Litany of Our Lady, a prayer constructed in alternating sentences so that the clergy lead and the people respond.

9. Tag or hide-and-go-seek.

—The story is very short and sweet, Mr Casey said. It was one day down in Arklow, a cold bitter day, not long before the chief[1] died. May God have mercy on him!

He closed his eyes wearily and paused. Mr Dedalus took a bone from his plate and tore some meat from it with his teeth, saying:

—Before he was killed, you mean.

Mr Casey opened his eyes, sighed and went on:

—It was down in Arklow one day. We were down there at a meeting and after the meeting was over we had to make our way to the railway station through the crowd. Such booing and baaing, man, you never heard. They called us all the names in the world. Well there was one old lady, and a drunken old harridan[2] she was surely, that paid all her attention to me. She kept dancing along beside me in the mud bawling and screaming into my face: *Priesthunter! The Paris Funds! Mr Fox! Kitty O'Shea!*[3]

—And what did you do, John? asked Mr Dedalus.

—I let her bawl away, said Mr Casey. It was a cold day and to keep up my heart I had (saving your presence, ma'am) a quid of Tullamore[4] in my mouth and sure I couldn't say a word in any case because my mouth was full of tobacco juice.

—Well, John?

—Well. I let her bawl away to her heart's content *Kitty O'Shea* and the rest of it till at last she called that lady a name that I won't sully this Christmas board[5] nor your ears, ma'am, nor my own lips by repeating.

He paused. Mr Dedalus, lifting his head from the bone, asked:

And what did you do, John?

Do! said Mr Casey. She stuck her ugly old face up at me when she said it and I had my mouth full of tobacco juice. I bent down to her and *Phth!* says I to her like that.

He turned aside and made the act of spitting.

—*Phth!* says I to her like that, right into her eye.

He clapped a hand to his eye and gave a hoarse scream of pain.

—*O Jesus, Mary and Joseph!* says she. *I'm blinded! I'm blinded and drownded!*

He stopped in a fit of coughing and laughter, repeating:

—*I'm blinded entirely!*

Mr Dedalus laughed loudly and lay back in his chair while uncle Charles swayed his head to and fro.

Dante looked terribly angry and repeated while they laughed:

—Very nice! Ha! Very nice!

It was not nice about the spit in the woman's eye. But what was the name the woman had called Kitty O'Shea that Mr Casey would not repeat? He thought of Mr Casey walking through the crowds of people and making speeches from a wagonette. That was what he had been in prison for and he

1. Parnell. "Arklow": a town in County Wicklow south of Dublin.
2. Wild-looking old woman.
3. Katherine O'Shea, the married woman with whom Parnell had an affair. The diminuitive form of her name was considered an insult with sexual connotations. "Priesthunter": an insult meant to evoke both Parnell's anticlerical stance and those who had informed on clergy forbidden to hold ser-

vices by the Penal Laws. "The Paris Funds": money held by the Irish Parliamentary Party in Paris to prevent British confiscation, which was rumored to have funded Parnell's affair. "Mr. Fox": pseudonym used by Parnell in his communications with Mrs. O'Shea during their affair.
4. Chewing tobacco produced in a town with the same name, west of Dublin.
5. Feast or table.

remembered that one night Sergeant O'Neill had come to the house and had stood in the hall, talking in a low voice with his father and chewing nervously at the chinstrap of his cap. And that night Mr Casey had not gone to Dublin by train but a car had come to the door and he had heard his father say something about the Cabinteely road.[6]

He was for Ireland and Parnell and so was his father: and so was Dante too for one night at the band on the esplanade she had hit a gentleman on the head with her umbrella because he had taken off his hat when the band played *God save the Queen*[7] at the end.

Mr Dedalus gave a snort of contempt.

—Ah, John, he said. It is true for them. We are an unfortunate priestridden race and always were and always will be till the end of the chapter.

Uncle Charles shook his head, saying:

—A bad business! A bad business!

Mr Dedalus repeated:

—A priestridden Godforsaken race![8]

He pointed to the portrait of his grandfather on the wall to his right.

—Do you see that old chap up there, John? he said. He was a good Irishman when there was no money in the job. He was condemned to death as a whiteboy.[9] But he had a saying about our clerical friends, that he would never let one of them put his two feet under his mahogany.[1]

Dante broke in angrily:

—If we are a priestridden race we ought to be proud of it! They are the apple of God's eye. *Touch them not*, says Christ, *for they are the apple of My eye.*[2]

—And can we not love our country then? asked Mr Casey. Are we not to follow the man that was born to lead us?

—A traitor to his country! replied Dante. A traitor, an adulterer! The priests were right to abandon him. The priests were always the true friends of Ireland.

—Were they, faith? said Mr Casey.

He threw his fist on the table and, frowning angrily, protruded one finger after another.

—Didn't the bishops of Ireland betray us in the time of the union when bishop Lanigan presented an address of loyalty to the marquess Cornwallis? Didn't the bishops and priests sell the aspirations of this country in 1829 in return for catholic emancipation? Didn't they denounce the fenian movement from the pulpit and in the confession box? And didn't they dishonour the ashes of Terence Bellew MacManus?[3]

6. Little-used road that provided an indirect route to Dublin and thus might have helped Mr. Casey avoid arrest, about which Sergeant O'Neill may be warning him here.
7. The unofficial British national anthem.
8. A term often used at the time to mean a people or nation (rather than a group defined by skin color).
9. I.e., one of the late-eighteenth-century protesters for land and tax reform who made raids on livestock and farmhouses at night, during which they wore white shirts in order to be able to identify each other.
1. Under his dining-room table.
2. Cf. Zacharias 2.8–9.
3. All of Mr. Casey's questions refer to compromises made by Catholics that were not in the interest of Irish nationalism. "The union": the Act of Union (1800), which dissolved the Irish Parliament and merged it with the British Parliament. "Address of loyalty": complimentary address paid by James Lanigan, bishop of Ossory, to Charles, Marquess Cornwallis, in 1799, the year after Cornwallis had been instrumental in putting down the Irish Rebellion. "Catholic emancipation": laws enacted in 1829 that gave Catholics full civil liberties. "Fenian movement": Irish Republican Brotherhood, a militant nationalist group. Terence Bellew MacManus: Irish nationalist (1811/12–1861) who died in exile. When his body was brought back to Ireland, his funeral became a large nationalist demonstration.

His face was glowing with anger and Stephen felt the glow rise to his own cheek as the spoken words thrilled him. Mr Dedalus uttered a guffaw of coarse scorn.

—O, by God, he cried, I forgot little old Paul Cullen![4] Another apple of God's eye!

Dante bent across the table and cried to Mr Casey:

—Right! Right! They were always right! God and morality and religion come first.

Mrs Dedalus, seeing her excitement, said to her:

—Mrs Riordan, don't excite yourself answering them.

—God and religion before everything! Dante cried. God and religion before the world!

Mr Casey raised his clenched fist and brought it down on the table with a crash.

—Very well, then, he shouted hoarsely, if it comes to that, no God for Ireland!

—John! John! cried Mr Dedalus, seizing his guest by the coat sleeve.

Dante stared across the table, her cheeks shaking. Mr Casey struggled up from his chair and bent across the table towards her, scraping the air from before his eyes with one hand as though he were tearing aside a cobweb.

—No God for Ireland! he cried. We have had too much God in Ireland. Away with God!

—Blasphemer! Devil! screamed Dante, starting to her feet and almost spitting in his face.

Uncle Charles and Mr Dedalus pulled Mr Casey back into his chair again, talking to him from both sides reasonably. He stared before him out of his dark flaming eyes, repeating:

—Away with God, I say!

Dante shoved her chair violently aside and left the table, upsetting her napkinring which rolled slowly along the carpet and came to rest against the foot of an easychair. Mrs Dedalus rose quickly and followed her towards the door. At the door Dante turned round violently and shouted down the room, her cheeks flushed and quivering with rage:

—Devil out of hell! We won! We crushed him to death! Fiend!

The door slammed behind her.

Mr Casey, freeing his arms from his holders, suddenly bowed his head on his hands with a sob of pain.

—Poor Parnell! he cried loudly. My dead king!

He sobbed loudly and bitterly.

Stephen, raising his terrorstricken face, saw that his father's eyes were full of tears.

◆ ◆ ◆

The fellows talked together in little groups.

One fellow said:

—They were caught near the Hill of Lyons.

—Who caught them?

—Mr Gleeson and the minister.[5] They were on a car.

The same fellow added:

4. Archbishop of Dublin (1803–1878), who condemned the Fenian movement and refused permission for a lying-in-state for McManus.
5. Vice rector. "Hill of Lyons": hill situated between Clongowes Wood College and Dublin; the passage implies that the boys were attempting to run away to Dublin.

—A fellow in the higher line told me.

Fleming asked:

—But why did they run away, tell us?

—I know why, Cecil Thunder said. Because they had fecked[6] cash out of the rector's room.

—Who fecked it?

—Kickham's brother. And they all went shares in it.

But that was stealing. How could they have done that?

—A fat lot you know about it, Thunder! Wells said. I know why they scut.[7]

—Tell us why.

—I was told not to. Wells said.

—O, go on, Wells, all said. You might tell us. We won't let it out.

Stephen bent forward his head to hear. Wells looked round to see if anyone was coming. Then he said secretly:

—You know the altar wine they keep in the press in the sacristy?[8]

—Yes.

—Well, they drank that and it was found out who did it by the smell. And that's why they ran away, if you want to know.

And the fellow who had spoken first said:

—Yes, that's what I heard too from the fellow in the higher line.

The fellows were all silent. Stephen stood among them, afraid to speak, listening. A faint sickness of awe made him feel weak. How could they have done that? He thought of the dark silent sacristy. There were dark wooden presses there where the crimped surplices[9] lay quietly folded. It was not the chapel but still you had to speak under your breath. It was a holy place. He remembered the summer evening he had been there to be dressed as boat-bearer,[1] the evening of the procession to the little altar in the wood. A strange and holy place. The boy that held the censer[2] had swung it gently to and fro near the door with the silvery cap lifted by the middle chain to keep the coals lighting. That was called charcoal: and it had burned quietly as the fellow had swung it gently and had given off a weak sour smell. And then when all were vested he had stood holding out the boat to the rector and the rector had put a spoonful of incense in and it had hissed on the red coals.

The fellows were talking together in little groups here and there on the playground. The fellows seemed to him to have grown smaller: that was because a sprinter[3] had knocked him down the day before, a fellow out of second of grammar. He had been thrown by the fellow's machine lightly on the cinderpath[4] and his spectacles had been broken in three pieces and some of the grit of the cinders had gone into his mouth.

That was why the fellows seemed to him smaller and farther away and the goalposts so thin and far and the soft grey sky so high up. But there was no play on the football grounds for cricket was coming: and some said that Barnes would be the prof[5] and some said it would be Flowers. And all over the playgrounds they were playing rounders and bowling twisters and lobs.[6]

---

6. Stolen.

7. Ran away.

8. The room in a church in which the sacred vessels and robes of the clergy are kept.

9. Loose-fitting white clerical gowns with wide sleeves.

1. Assistant who carries the container of unlit incense.

2. Vessel in which incense is burned.

3. Fast-moving bicyclist.

4. Footpath made of cinders.

5. Captain of the cricket team.

6. Ways of bowling, or delivering the ball to the batsman, in cricket. "Rounders": an English game similar to baseball.

And from here and from there came the sounds of the cricket bats through the soft grey air. They said: pick, pack, pock, puck: like drops of water in a fountain slowly falling in the brimming bowl.

Athy, who had been silent, said quietly:

—You are all wrong.

All turned towards him eagerly.

—Why?

—Do you know?

—Who told you?

—Tell us, Athy.

Athy pointed across the playground to where Simon Moonan was walking by himself kicking a stone before him.

—Ask him, he said.

The fellows looked there and then said:

—Why him?

—Is he in it?

—Tell us, Athy. Go on. You might if you know.

Athy lowered his voice and said:

—Do you know why those fellows scut? I will tell you but you must not let on you know.

He paused for a moment and then said mysteriously:

—They were caught with Simon Moonan and Tusker Boyle in the square one night.

The fellows looked at him and asked:

—Caught?

—What doing?

Athy said:

—Smugging.[7]

All the fellows were silent: and Athy said:

—And that's why.

Stephen looked at the faces of the fellows but they were all looking across the playground. He wanted to ask somebody about it. What did that mean about the smugging in the square? Why did the five fellows out of the higher line run away for that? It was a joke, he thought. Simon Moonan had nice clothes and one night he had shown him a ball of creamy sweets that the fellows of the football fifteen had rolled down to him along the carpet in the middle of the refectory when he was at the door. It was the night of the match against the Bective Rangers and the ball was made just like a red and green apple only it opened and it was full of the creamy sweets. And one day Boyle had said that an elephant had two tuskers instead of two tusks and that was why he was called Tusker Boyle but some fellows called him Lady Boyle because he was always at his nails, paring them.

Eileen had long thin cool white hands too because she was a girl. They were like ivory; only soft. That was the meaning of *Tower of Ivory* but protestants could not understand it and made fun of it. One day he had stood beside her looking into the hotel grounds. A waiter was running up a trail of bunting[8] on the flagstaff and a fox terrier was scampering to and fro on the sunny lawn. She had put her hand into his pocket where his hand was and

---

7. Amorous homosexual behavior.   8. Cloth used for making flags.

he had felt how cool and thin and soft her hand was. She had said that pockets were funny things to have: and then all of a sudden she had broken away and had run laughing down the sloping curve of the path. Her fair hair had streamed out behind her like gold in the sun. *Tower of Ivory. House of Gold.* By thinking about things you could understand them.

But why in the square? You went there when you wanted to do something. It was all thick slabs of slate and water trickled all day out of tiny pinholes and there was a queer smell of stale water there. And behind the door of one of the closets there was a drawing in red pencil of a bearded man in a Roman dress with a brick in each hand and underneath was the name of the drawing:

Balbus was building a wall.[9]

Some fellow had drawn it there for a cod. It had a funny face but it was very like a man with a beard. And on the wall of another closet there was written in backhand in beautiful writing:

Julius Caesar wrote The Calico Belly.[1]

Perhaps that was why they were there because it was a place where some fellows wrote things for cod. But all the same it was queer what Athy said and the way he said it. It was not a cod because they had run away. He looked with the others in silence across the playground and began to feel afraid.

At last Fleming said:

—And we are all to be punished for what other fellows did?

—I won't come back, see if I do, Cecil Thunder said. Three days' silence in the refectory and sending us up for six and eight[2] every minute.

—Yes, said Wells. And old Barrett has a new way of twisting the note so that you can't open it and fold it again to see how many ferulae[3] you are to get. I won't come back too.

—Yes, said Cecil Thunder, and the prefect of studies[4] was in second of grammar this morning.

—Let us get up a rebellion, Fleming said. Will we?

All the fellows were silent. The air was very silent and you could hear the cricket bats but more slowly than before: pick, pock.

Wells asked:

—What is going to be done to them?

—Simon Moonan and Tusker are going to be flogged,[5] Athy said, and the fellows in the higher line got their choice of flogging or being expelled.

—And which are they taking? asked the fellow who had spoken first.

—All are taking expulsion except Corrigan, Athy answered. He's going to be flogged by Mr Gleeson.

—Is it Corrigan that big fellow? said Fleming. Why, he'd be able for two of Gleeson!

—I know why, Cecil Thunder said. He is right and the other fellows are wrong because a flogging wears off after a bit but a fellow that has been expelled from college is known all his life on account of it. Besides Gleeson won't flog him hard.

—It's best of his play not to, Fleming said.

---

9. Possibly a reference to Latin classes.
1. A pun on Caesar's *Commentarii de Bello Gallico* (*Commentaries on the Gallic War*).
2. Number of strokes given as punishment, three on each hand followed by four on each hand.
3. Strokes administered with a rod as punish-

ment.
4. Dean of studies, in charge of the classes and teachers and thus not a student, as is true when "prefect" is used more generally.
5. Beaten on the buttocks with a cane or rod.

—I wouldn't like to be Simon Moonan and Tusker, Cecil Thunder said. But I don't believe they will be flogged. Perhaps they will be sent up for twice nine.[6]

—No, no, said Athy. They'll both get it on the vital spot.

Wells rubbed himself and said in a crying voice:

—Please, sir, let me off!

Athy grinned and turned up the sleeves of his jacket, saying:

> *It can't be helped;*
> *It must be done.*
> *So down with your breeches*
> *And out with your bum.*

The fellows laughed; but he felt that they were a little afraid. In the silence of the soft grey air he heard the cricket bats from here and from there: pock. That was a sound to hear but if you were hit then you would feel a pain. The pandybat made a sound too but not like that. The fellows said it was made of whalebone and leather with lead inside: and he wondered what was the pain like. There were different kinds of pains for all the different kinds of sounds. A long thin cane would have a high whistling sound and he wondered what was that pain like. It made him shivery to think of it and cold: and what Athy said too. But what was there to laugh at in it? It made him shivery: but that was because you always felt like a shiver when you let down your trousers. It was the same in the bath when you undressed yourself. He wondered who had to let them down, the master or the boy himself. O how could they laugh about it that way?

He looked at Athy's rolledup sleeves and knuckly inky hands. He had rolled up his sleeves to show how Mr Gleeson would roll up his sleeves. But Mr Gleeson had round shiny cuffs and clean white wrists and fattish white hands and the nails of them were long and pointed. Perhaps he pared them too like Lady Boyle. But they were terribly long and pointed nails. So long and cruel they were though the white fattish hands were not cruel but gentle. And though he trembled with cold and fright to think of the cruel long nails and of the high whistling sound of the cane and of the chill you felt at the end of your shirt when you undressed yourself yet he felt a feeling of queer quiet pleasure inside him to think of the white fattish hands, clean and strong and gentle. And he thought of what Cecil Thunder had said: that Mr Gleeson would not flog Corrigan hard. And Fleming had said he would not because it was best of his play not to. But that was not why.

A voice from far out on the playgrounds cried:

—All in!

And other voices cried:

—All in! All in!

During the writing lesson he sat with his arms folded, listening to the slow scraping of the pens. Mr Harford went to and fro making little signs in red pencil and sometimes sitting beside the boy to show him how to hold the pen. He had tried to spell out the headline[7] for himself though he knew already what it was for it was the last in the book. *Zeal without prudence is like a ship adrift.* But the lines of the letters were like fine invisible threads

---

6. Nine strokes on each hand.
7. Line at the top of the page for the students to copy, as part of their handwriting lesson.

and it was only by closing his right eye tight tight and staring out of the left eye that he could make out the full curves of the capital.

But Mr Harford was very decent and never got into a wax.[8] All the other masters got into dreadful waxes. But why were they to suffer for what fellows in the higher line did? Wells had said that they had drunk some of the altar wine out of the press in the sacristy and that it had been found out who had done it by the smell. Perhaps they had stolen a monstrance[9] to run away with it and sell it somewhere. That must have been a terrible sin, to go in quietly there at night, to open the dark press and steal the flashing gold thing into which God was put on the altar in the middle of flowers and candles at bene-diction[1] while the incense went up in clouds at both sides as the fellow swung the censer and Dominic Kelly sang the first part by himself in the choir. But God was not in it of course when they stole it. But still it was a strange and a great sin even to touch it. He thought of it with deep awe; a terrible and strange sin: it thrilled him to think of it in the silence when the pens scraped lightly. But to drink the altar wine out of the press and be found out by the smell was a sin too: but it was not terrible and strange. It only made you feel a little sickish on account of the smell of the wine. Because on the day when he had made his first holy communion in the chapel he had shut his eyes and opened his mouth and put out his tongue a little: and when the rector had stooped down to give him the holy communion he had smelt a faint winy smell off the rector's breath after the wine of the mass. The word was beauti-ful: wine. It made you think of dark purple because the grapes were dark purple that grew in Greece outside houses like white temples. But the faint smell off the rector's breath had made him feel a sick feeling on the morning of his first communion. The day of your first communion was the happiest day of your life. And once a lot of generals had asked Napoleon what was the happiest day of his life. They thought he would say the day he won some great battle or the day he was made an emperor. But he said:

—Gentlemen, the happiest day of my life was the day on which I made my first holy communion.

Father Arnall came in and the Latin lesson began and he remained still, leaning on the desk with his arms folded. Father Arnall gave out the theme-books and he said that they were scandalous and that they were all to be writ-ten out again with the corrections at once. But the worst of all was Fleming's theme because the pages were stuck together by a blot: and Father Arnall held it up by a corner and said it was an insult to any master to send him up such a theme. Then he asked Jack Lawton to decline[2] the noun *mare* and Jack Lawton stopped at the ablative singular and could not go on with the plural.

—You should be ashamed of yourself, said Father Arnall sternly. You, the leader of the class!

Then he asked the next boy and the next and the next. Nobody knew. Father Arnall became very quiet, more and more quiet as each boy tried to answer and could not. But his face was blacklooking and his eyes were star-ing though his voice was so quiet. Then he asked Fleming and Fleming said

---

8. Fit of anger.
9. Vessel holding the consecrated Eucharist for the view of the congregation during the Benedic-tion.
1. A part of the Catholic mass (religious service) involving blessing, in this case the Blessed Sacra-

ment, in which the Eucharist is displayed to the congregation.
2. To state the six grammatical cases (e.g., nom-inative, objective, possessive) for a noun—here, the Latin word for "sea." The ablative is the last case in the list.

that that word had no plural. Father Arnall suddenly shut the book and shouted at him:

—Kneel out there in the middle of the class. You are one of the idlest boys I ever met. Copy out your themes again the rest of you.

Fleming moved heavily out of his place and knelt between the two last benches. The other boys bent over their theme-books and began to write. A silence filled the classroom and Stephen, glancing timidly at Father Arnall's dark face, saw that it was a little red from the wax he was in.

Was that a sin for Father Arnall to be in a wax or was he allowed to get into a wax when the boys were idle because that made them study better or was he only letting on to be in a wax? It was because he was allowed because a priest would know what a sin was and would not do it. But if he did it one time by mistake what would he do to go to confession? Perhaps he would go to confession to the minister. And if the minister did it he would go to the rector: and the rector to the provincial: and the provincial to the general of the jesuits.[3] That was called the order: and he had heard his father say that they were all clever men. They could all have become highup people in the world if they had not become jesuits. And he wondered what Father Arnall and Paddy Barrett would have become and what Mr McGlade and Mr Gleeson would have become if they had not become jesuits. It was hard to think what because you would have to think of them in a different way with different coloured coats and trousers and with beards and moustaches and different kinds of hats.

The door opened quietly and closed. A quick whisper ran through the class: the prefect of studies. There was an instant of dead silence and then the loud crack of a pandybat on the last desk. Stephen's heart leapt up in fear.

—Any boys want flogging here, Father Arnall? cried the prefect of studies. Any lazy idle loafers that want flogging in this class?

He came to the middle of the class and saw Fleming on his knees.

—Hoho! he cried. Who is this boy? Why is he on his knees? What is your name, boy?

—Fleming, sir.

—Hoho, Fleming! An idler of course. I can see it in your eye. Why is he on his knees, Father Arnall?

—He wrote a bad Latin theme, Father Arnall said, and he missed all the questions in grammar.

—Of course he did! cried the prefect of studies. Of course he did! A born idler! I can see it in the corner of his eye.

He banged his pandybat down on the desk and cried:

—Up, Fleming! Up, my boy!

Fleming stood up slowly.

—Hold out! cried the prefect of studies.

Fleming held out his hand. The pandybat came down on it with a loud smacking sound: one, two, three, four, five, six.

—Other hand!

The pandybat came down again in six loud quick smacks.

—Kneel down! cried the prefect of studies.

Fleming knelt down squeezing his hands under his armpits, his face contorted with pain, but Stephen knew how hard his hands were because

---

3. The hierarchy of the Jesuits: the provincial is the highest authority in Ireland, and the general in Rome is the head of the order, but in reality confession need not be given to a higher-ranking priest.

Fleming was always rubbing rosin[4] into them. But perhaps he was in great pain for the noise of the pandies was terrible. Stephen's heart was beating and fluttering.

—At your work, all of you! shouted the prefect of studies. We want no lazy idle loafers here, lazy idle little schemers. At your work, I tell you. Father Dolan will be in to see you every day. Father Dolan will be in tomorrow.

He poked one of the boys in the side with the pandybat, saying:

—You, boy! When will Father Dolan be in again?

—Tomorrow, sir, said Tom Furlong's voice.

—Tomorrow and tomorrow and tomorrow,[5] said the prefect of studies. Make up your minds for that. Every day Father Dolan. Write away. You, boy, who are you?

Stephen's heart jumped suddenly.

—Dedalus, sir.

—Why are you not writing like the others?

—I . . . . . my . . .

—He could not speak with fright.

—Why is he not writing, Father Arnall?

—He broke his glasses, said Father Arnall, and I exempted him from work.

—Broke? What is this I hear? What is this your name is? said the prefect of studies.

—Dedalus, sir.

—Out here, Dedalus. Lazy little schemer. I see schemer in your face. Where did you break your glasses?

Stephen stumbled into the middle of the class, blinded by fear and haste.

—Where did you break your glasses? repeated the prefect of studies.

—The cinderpath, sir.

—Hoho! The cinderpath! cried the prefect of studies. I know that trick.

Stephen lifted his eyes in wonder and saw for a moment Father Dolan's whitegrey not young face, his baldy whitegrey head with fluff at the sides of it, the steel rims of his spectacles and his nocoloured eyes looking through the glasses. Why did he say that he knew that trick?

—Lazy idle little loafer! cried the prefect of studies. Broke my glasses! An old schoolboy trick! Out with your hand this moment!

Stephen closed his eyes and held out in the air his trembling hand with the palm upwards. He felt the prefect of studies touch it for a moment at the fingers to straighten it and then the swish of the sleeve of the soutane as the pandybat was lifted to strike. A hot burning stinging tingling blow like the loud crack of a broken stick made his trembling hand crumple together like a leaf in the fire: and at the sound and the pain scalding tears were driven into his eyes. His whole body was shaking with fright, his arm was shaking and his crumpled burning livid hand shook like a loose leaf in the air. A cry sprang to his lips, a prayer to be let off. But though the tears scalded his eyes and his limbs quivered with pain and fright he held back the hot tears and the cry that scalded his throat.

—Other hand! shouted the prefect of studies.

Stephen drew back his maimed and quivering right arm and held out his left hand. The soutane sleeve swished again as the pandybat was lifted and a

4. Solid resin obtained by distilling turpentine.
5. Cf. Macbeth's response to his wife's death in Shakespeare's *Macbeth* (5.5.18).

loud crashing sound and a fierce maddening tingling burning pain made his hand shrink together with the palms and fingers in a livid quivering mass. The scalding water burst forth from his eyes and, burning with shame and agony and fear, he drew back his shaking arm in terror and burst out into a whine of pain. His body shook with a palsy of fright and in shame and rage he felt the scalding cry come from his throat and the scalding tears falling out of his eyes and down his flaming cheeks.

—Kneel down! cried the prefect of studies.

Stephen knelt down quickly pressing his beaten hands to his sides. To think of them beaten and swollen with pain all in a moment made him feel so sorry for them as if they were not his own but someone else's that he felt so sorry for. And as he knelt, calming the last sobs in his throat and feeling the burning tingling pain pressed in to his sides, he thought of the hands which he had held out in the air with the palms up and of the firm touch of the prefect of studies when he had steadied the shaking fingers and of the beaten swollen reddened mass of palm and fingers that shook helplessly in the air.

—Get at your work, all of you, cried the prefect of studies from the door. Father Dolan will be in every day to see if any boy, any lazy idle little loafer wants flogging. Every day. Every day.

The door closed behind him.

The hushed class continued to copy out the themes. Father Arnall rose from his seat and went among them, helping the boys with gentle words and telling them the mistakes they had made. His voice was very gentle and soft. Then he returned to his seat and said to Fleming and Stephen:

—You may return to your places, you two.

Fleming and Stephen rose and, walking to their seats, sat down. Stephen, scarlet, with shame, opened a book quickly with one weak hand and bent down upon it, his face close to the page.

It was unfair and cruel: because the doctor had told him not to read without glasses and he had written home to his father that morning to send him a new pair. And Father Arnall had said that he need not study till the new glasses came. Then to be called a schemer before the class and to be pandied when he always got the card for first or second and was the leader of the Yorkists![6] How could the prefect of studies know that it was a trick? He felt the touch of the prefect's fingers as they had steadied his hand and at first he had thought that he was going to shake hands with him because the fingers were soft and firm: but then in an instant he had heard the swish of the soutane sleeve and the crash. It was cruel and unfair to make him kneel in the middle of the class then: and Father Arnall had told them both that they might return to their places without making any difference between them. He listened to Father Arnall's low and gentle voice as he corrected the themes. Perhaps he was sorry now and wanted to be decent. But it was unfair and cruel. The prefect of studies was a priest but that was cruel and unfair. And his whitegrey face and the nocoloured eyes behind the steelrimmed spectacles were cruel looking because he had steadied the hand first with his firm soft fingers and that was to hit it better and louder.

—It's a stinking mean thing, that's what it is, said Fleming in the corridor as the classes were passing out in file to the refectory, to pandy a fellow for what is not his fault.

6. Team named after the House of York. See p. 446, n. 2.

—You really broke your glasses by accident, didn't you? Nasty Roche asked.

Stephen felt his heart filled by Fleming's words and did not answer.

—Of course he did! said Fleming. I wouldn't stand it. I'd go up and tell the rector on him.

—Yes, said Cecil Thunder eagerly, and I saw him lift the pandybat over his shoulder and he's not allowed to do that.

—Did they hurt much? Nasty Roche asked.

—Very much, Stephen said.

—I wouldn't stand it, Fleming repeated, from Baldyhead or any other Baldyhead. It's a stinking mean low trick, that's what it is. I'd go up straight up to the rector and tell him about it after dinner.

—Yes, do. Yes, do, said Cecil Thunder.

—Yes, do. Yes, go up and tell the rector on him, Dedalus, said Nasty Roche, because he said that he'd come in tomorrow again to pandy you.

—Yes, yes. Tell the rector, all said.

And there were some fellows out of second of grammar listening and one of them said:

—The senate and the Roman people declared that Dedalus had been wrongly punished.[7]

It was wrong; it was unfair and cruel: and, as he sat in the refectory, he suffered time after time in memory the same humiliation until he began to wonder whether it might not really be that there was something in his face which made him look like a schemer and he wished he had a little mirror to see. But there could not be; and it was unjust and cruel and unfair.

He could not eat the blackish fish fritters they got on Wednesdays in lent[8] and one of his potatoes had the mark of the spade in it. Yes, he would do what the fellows had told him. He would go up and tell the rector that he had been wrongly punished. A thing like that had been done before by somebody in history, by some great person whose head was in the books of history. And the rector would declare that he had been wrongly punished because the senate and the Roman people always declared that the man who did that had been wrongly punished. Those were the great men whose names were in Richmal Magnall's Questions. History was all about those men and what they did and that was what Peter Parley's Tales about Greece and Rome were all about.[9] Peter Parley himself was on the first page in a picture. There was a road over a heath with grass at the side and little bushes: and Peter Parley had a broad hat like a protestant minister and a big stick and he was walking fast along the road to Greece and Rome.

It was easy what he had to do. All he had to do was when the dinner was over and he came out in his turn to go on walking but not out to the corridor but up the staircase on the right that led to the castle. He had nothing to do but that: to turn to the right and walk fast up the staircase and in half a minute he would be in the low dark narrow corridor that led through the castle to the rector's room. And every fellow had said that it was unfair, even the fellow out of second of grammar who had said that about the senate and the Roman people.

---

7. Statement made in the form of decrees of the Roman senate.

8. Period of forty days' penitence and dietary restriction before Easter.

9. Instructional books for children (1832–33) by

Samuel Goodrich (1793–1860). "Richmal Magnall's Questions": *Historical and Miscellaneous Questions for the Use of Young People* (1800), by Richmal Mangnall (1769–1820), whose name is misspelled.

What would happen? He heard the fellows of the higher line stand up at the top of the refectory and heard their steps as they came down the matting: Paddy Rath and Jimmy Magee and the Spaniard and the Portuguese and the fifth was big Corrigan who was going to be flogged by Mr Gleeson. That was why the prefect of studies had called him a schemer and pandied him for nothing: and, straining his weak eyes, tired with the tears, he watched big Corrigan's broad shoulders and big hanging black head passing in the file. But he had done something and besides Mr Gleeson would not flog him hard: and he remembered how big Corrigan looked in the bath. He had skin the same colour as the turfcoloured bogwater in the shallow end of the bath and when he walked along the side his feet slapped loudly on the wet tiles and at every step his thighs shook a little because he was fat.

The refectory was half empty and the fellows were still passing out in file. He could go up the staircase because there was never a priest or a prefect outside the refectory door. But he could not go. The rector would side with the prefect of studies and think it was a schoolboy trick and then the prefect of studies would come in every day the same only it would be worse because he would be dreadfully waxy at any fellow going up to the rector about him. The fellows had told him to go but they would not go themselves. They had forgotten all about it. No, it was best to forget all about it: and perhaps the prefect of studies had only said he would come in. No, it was best to hide out of the way because when you were small and young you could often escape that way.

The fellows at his table stood up. He stood up and passed out among them in the file. He had to decide. He was coming near the door. If he went on with the fellows he could never go up to the rector because he could not leave the playground for that. And if he went and was pandied all the same all the fellows would make fun and talk about young Dedalus going up to the rector to tell on the prefect of studies.

He was walking down along the matting and he saw the door before him. It was impossible: he could not. He thought of the baldy head of the prefect of studies with the cruel no-coloured eyes looking at him and he heard the voice of the prefect of studies asking him twice what his name was. Why could he not remember the name when he was told the first time? Was he not listening the first time or was it to make fun out of the name? The great men in the history had names like that and nobody made fun of them. It was his own name that he should have made fun of if he wanted to make fun. Dolan: it was like the name of a woman that washed clothes.

He had reached the door and, turning quickly to the right, walked up the stairs: and, before he could make up his mind to come back, he had entered the low dark narrow corridor that led to the castle. And as he crossed the threshold of the door of the corridor he saw, without turning his head to look, that all the fellows were looking after him as they went filing by.

He passed along the narrow dark corridor, passing little doors that were the doors of the rooms of the community. He peered in front of him and right and left through the gloom and thought that those must be portraits. It was dark and silent and his eyes were weak and tired with tears so that he could not see. But he thought they were the portraits of the saints and great men of the order who were looking down on him silently as he passed: saint Ignatius Loyola holding an open book and pointing to the words *Ad Majorem Dei*

Gloriam[1] in it, saint Francis Xavier[2] pointing to his chest, Lorenzo Ricci[3] with his berretta on his head like one of the prefects of the lines, the three patrons of holy youth, saint Stanislaus Kostka, saint Aloysius Gonzaga and blessed John Berchmans,[4] all with young faces because they died when they were young, and Father Peter Kenny[5] sitting in a chair wrapped in a big cloak.

He came out on the landing above the entrance hall and looked about him. That was where Hamilton Rowan had passed and the marks of the soldiers' slugs were there. And it was there that the old servants had seen the ghost in the white cloak of a marshal.

An old servant was sweeping at the end of the landing. He asked him where was the rector's room and the old servant pointed to the door at the far end and looked after him as he went on to it and knocked.

There was no answer. He knocked again more loudly and his heart jumped when he heard a muffled voice say:

—Come in!

He turned the handle and opened the door and fumbled for the handle of the green baize[6] door inside. He found it and pushed it open and went in.

He saw the rector sitting at a desk writing. There was a skull on the desk and a strange solemn smell in the room like the old leather of chairs.

His heart was beating fast on account of the solemn place he was in and the silence of the room: and he looked at the skull and at the rector's kind-looking face.

—Well, my little man, said the rector. What is it?

Stephen swallowed down the thing in his throat and said:

—I broke my glasses, sir.

The rector opened his mouth and said:

—O!

Then he smiled and said:

—Well, if we broke our glasses we must write home for a new pair.

—I wrote home, sir, said Stephen, and Father Arnall said I am not to study till they come.

—Quite right! said the rector.

Stephen swallowed down the thing again and tried to keep his legs and his voice from shaking.

—But, sir. . . .

—Yes?

—Father Dolan came in today and pandied me because I was not writing my theme.

The rector looked at him in silence and he could feel the blood rising to his face and the tears about to rise to his eyes.

The rector said:

—Your name is Dedalus, isn't it?

—Yes, sir.

—And where did you break your glasses?

---

1. To the Greater Glory of God (Latin), the motto of the Jesuit order, founded by Spanish theologian St. Ignatius of Loyola (1491–1556).
2. Disciple of Loyola (1506–1552).
3. Jesuit general (1703–1775), who wears the hat of a cardinal.
4. Jesuit saints from the late 16th and early 17th centuries who died in their youth.
5. Peter Kenney (1779–1841), Jesuit priest and founder of Clongowes Wood College (his name is misspelled).
6. Coarse woolen cloth often used for linings and curtains.

—On the cinderpath, sir. A fellow was coming out of the bicycle house and I fell and they got broken. I don't know the fellow's name.

The rector looked at him again in silence. Then he smiled and said:

—O, well, it was a mistake. I am sure Father Dolan did not know.

—But I told him I broke them, sir, and he pandied me.

—Did you tell him that you had written home for a new pair? the rector asked.

—No, sir.

—O, well then, said the rector, Father Dolan did not understand. You can say that I excuse you from your lessons for a few days.

Stephen said quickly for fear his trembling would prevent him:

—Yes, sir, but Father Dolan said he will come in tomorrow to pandy me again for it.

—Very well, the rector said. It is a mistake and I shall speak to Father Dolan myself. Will that do now?

Stephen felt the tears wetting his eyes and murmured:

—O yes, sir, thanks.

The rector held his hand across the side of the desk where the skull was and Stephen, placing his hand in it for a moment, felt a cool moist palm.

—Good day now, said the rector, withdrawing his hand and bowing.

—Good day, sir, said Stephen.

He bowed and walked quietly out of the room, closing the doors carefully and slowly.

But when he had passed the old servant on the landing and was again in the low narrow dark corridor he began to walk faster and faster. Faster and faster he hurried on through the gloom, excitedly. He bumped his elbow against the door at the end and, hurrying down the staircase, walked quickly through the two corridors and out into the air.

He could hear the cries of the fellows on the playgrounds. He broke into a run and, running quicker and quicker, ran across the cinderpath and reached the third line playground, panting.

The fellows had seen him running. They closed round him in a ring, pushing one against another to hear.

—Tell us! Tell us!

—What did he say?

—Did you go in?

—What did he say?

—Tell us! Tell us!

He told them what he had said and what the rector had said and, when he had told them, all the fellows flung their caps spinning up into the air and cried:

—Hurroo!

They caught their caps and sent them up again spinning skyhigh and cried again:

—Hurroo! Hurroo!

They made a cradle of their locked hands and hoisted him up among them and carried him along till he struggled to get free. And when he had escaped from them they broke away in all directions, flinging their caps again into the air and whistling as they went spinning up and crying:

—Hurroo!

And they gave three groans for Baldyhead Dolan and three cheers for Conmee and they said he was the decentest rector that was ever in Clongowes.

The cheers died away in the soft grey air. He was alone. He was happy and free: but he would not be anyway proud with Father Dolan. He would be very quiet and obedient: and he wished that he could do something kind for him to show him that he was not proud.

The air was soft and grey and mild and evening was coming. There was the smell of evening in the air, the smell of the fields in the country where they digged up turnips to peel them and eat them when they went out for a walk to Major Barton's, the smell there was in the little wood beyond the pavilion where the gallnuts[7] were.

The fellows were practising long shies and bowling lobs and slow twisters.[8] In the soft grey silence he could hear the bump of the balls: and from here and from there through the quiet air the sound of the cricket bats: pick, pack, pock, puck: like drops of water in a fountain falling softly in the brimming bowl.

II

Uncle Charles smoked such black twist[9] that at last his outspoken nephew suggested to him to enjoy his morning smoke in a little outhouse[1] at the end of the garden.

—Very good, Simon. All serene, Simon, said the old man tranquilly. Anywhere you like. The outhouse will do me nicely: it will be more salubrious.

—Damn me, said Mr Dedalus frankly, if I know how you can smoke such villainous awful tobacco. It's like gunpowder, by God.

—It's very nice, Simon, replied the old man. Very cool and mollifying.

Every morning, therefore, uncle Charles repaired to his outhouse but not before he had creased and brushed scrupulously his back hair and brushed and put on his tall hat. While he smoked the brim of his tall hat and the bowl of his pipe were just visible beyond the jambs of the outhouse door. His arbour, as he called the reeking outhouse which he shared with the cat and the garden tools, served him also as a soundingbox: and every morning he hummed contentedly one of his favourite songs: O, *twine me a bower* or *Blue eyes and golden hair* or *The Groves of Blarney*[2] while the grey and blue coils of smoke rose slowly from his pipe and vanished in the pure air.

During the first part of the summer in Blackrock[3] uncle Charles was Stephen's constant companion. Uncle Charles was a hale old man with a well tanned skin, rugged features and white side whiskers. On week days he did messages between the house in Carysfort Avenue[4] and those shops in the main street of the town with which the family dealt. Stephen was glad to go with him on these errands for uncle Charles helped him very liberally to handfuls of whatever was exposed in open boxes and barrels outside the counter. He would seize a handful of grapes and sawdust or three or four American apples and thrust them generously into his grandnephew's hand

---

7. Growth on a tree, especially an oak, caused by insects. "Major Barton's": estate near the school.
8. Ways of throwing and bowling the ball in cricket.
9. Strong tobacco twisted into a cord.

1. Shed.
2. All popular Irish songs or ballads.
3. Southern Dublin suburb.
4. Street in Blackrock.

while the shopman smiled uneasily; and on Stephen's feigning reluctance to take them, he would frown and say:

—Take them, sir. Do you hear me, sir? They're good for your bowels.

When the order list had been booked the two would go on to the park where an old friend of Stephen's father, Mike Flynn, would be found seated on a bench, waiting for them. Then would begin Stephen's run round the park. Mike Flynn would stand at the gate near the railway station, watch in hand, while Stephen ran round the track in the style Mike Flynn favoured, his head high lifted, his knees well lifted and his hands held straight down by his sides. When the morning practice was over the trainer would make his comments and sometimes illustrate them by shuffling along for a yard or so comically in an old pair of blue canvas shoes. A small ring of wonder-struck children and nursemaids would gather to watch him and linger even when he and uncle Charles had sat down again and were talking athletics and politics. Though he had heard his father say that Mike Flynn had put some of the best runners of modern times through his hands Stephen often glanced with mistrust at his trainer's flabby stubblecovered face, as it bent over the long stained fingers through which he rolled his cigarette, and with pity at the mild lustreless blue eye which would look up suddenly from the task and gaze vaguely into the bluer distance while the long swollen fingers ceased their rolling and grains and fibres of tobacco fell back into the pouch.

On the way home uncle Charles would often pay a visit to the chapel and, as the font was above Stephen's reach, the old man would dip his hand and then sprinkle the water briskly about Stephen's clothes and on the floor of the porch. While he prayed he knelt on his red handkerchief and read above his breath from a thumbblackened prayerbook wherein catchwords[5] were printed at the foot of every page. Stephen knelt at his side respecting, though he did not share, his piety. He often wondered what his granduncle prayed for so seriously. Perhaps he prayed for the souls in purgatory or for the grace of a happy death: or perhaps he prayed that God might send him back a part of the big fortune he had squandered in Cork.[6]

On Sundays Stephen with his father and his granduncle took their constitutional. The old man was a nimble walker in spite of his corns and often ten or twelve miles of the road were covered. The little village of Stillorgan was the parting of the ways. Either they went to the left towards the Dublin mountains or along the Goatstown road and thence into Dundrum, coming home by Sandyford.[7] Trudging along the road or standing in some grimy wayside publichouse[8] his elders spoke constantly of the subjects nearest their hearts, of Irish politics, of Munster[9] and of the legends of their own family, to all of which Stephen lent an avid ear. Words which he did not understand he said over and over to himself till he had learned them by heart: and through them he had glimpses of the real world about him. The hour when he too would take his part in the life of that world seemed drawing near and in secret he began to make ready for the great part which he felt awaited him the nature of which he only dimly apprehended.

---

5. Words printed at the end of a page to indicate the last item on that page.
6. Main city of County Cork, in southern Ireland.
7. All places within a few miles of Blackrock.
8. Pub.
9. Southern province of Ireland.

His evenings were his own; and he pored over a ragged translation of *The Count of Monte Cristo*.[1] The figure of that dark avenger stood forth in his mind for whatever he had heard or divined in childhood of the strange and terrible. At night he built up on the parlour table an image of the wonderful island cave out of transfers and paper flowers and coloured tissue paper and strips of the silver and golden paper in which chocolate is wrapped. When he had broken up this scenery, weary of its tinsel, there would come to his mind the bright picture of Marseilles, of sunny trellisses and of Mercedes.[2] Outside Blackrock, on the road that led to the mountains, stood a small whitewashed house in the garden of which grew many rosebushes: and in this house, he told himself, another Mercedes lived. Both on the outward and on the homeward journey he measured distance by this landmark: and in his imagination he lived through a long train of adventures, marvellous as those in the book itself, towards the close of which there appeared an image of himself, grown older and sadder, standing in a moonlit garden with Mercedes who had so many years before slighted his love, and with a sadly proud gesture of refusal, saying:

—Madam, I never eat muscatel grapes.[3]

He became the ally of a boy named Aubrey Mills and founded with him a gang of adventurers in the avenue. Aubrey carried a whistle dangling from his buttonhole and a bicycle lamp attached to his belt while the others had short sticks thrust daggerwise through theirs. Stephen, who had read of Napoleon's plain style of dress, chose to remain unadorned and thereby heightened for himself the pleasure of taking counsel with his lieutenant before giving orders. The gang made forays into the gardens of old maids or went down to the castle[4] and fought a battle on the shaggy weedgrown rocks, coming home after it weary stragglers with the stale odours of the foreshore in their nostrils and the rank oils of the seawrack[5] upon their hands and in their hair.

Aubrey and Stephen had a common milkman and often they drove out in the milkcar to Carrickmines[6] where the cows were at grass. While the men were milking the boys would take turns in riding the tractable mare round the field. But when autumn came the cows were driven home from the grass: and the first sight of the filthy cowyard at Stradbrook[7] with its foul green puddles and clots of liquid dung and steaming brantroughs[8] sickened Stephen's heart. The cattle which had seemed so beautiful in the country on sunny days revolted him and he could not ever look at the milk they yielded.

The coming of September did not trouble him this year for he knew he was not to be sent back to Clongowes. The practice in the park came to an end when Mike Flynn went into hospital. Aubrey was at school and had only an hour or two free in the evening. The gang fell asunder and there were no more nightly forays or battles on the rocks. Stephen sometimes went round with the car which delivered the evening milk: and these chilly drives blew

---

1. Adventure novel (1844) by French novelist Alexandre Dumas père (1802–1870), in which the hero, Edmond Dantès, escapes from prison and attempts to exact revenge and regain his beloved, Mercedes.
2. The heroine of the novel. "Marseilles": French port city on the Mediterranean.
3. Grapes used to make sweet wine. Here, Stephen borrows one of Dantès's statements from the novel.
4. One of the Martello towers built on Dublin Bay during the Napoleonic Wars (1803–06) to defend Ireland against invasion by the French.
5. Coarse seaweed cast on the shore.
6. Village south of Blackrock.
7. Area southeast of Blackrock.
8. Troughs of bran, presumably to feed the cattle.

away his memory of the filth of the cowyard and he felt no repugnance at seeing the cowhairs and hayseeds on the milkman's coat. Whenever the car drew up before a house he waited to catch a glimpse of a well scrubbed kitchen or of a softly lighted hall and to see how the servant would hold the jug and how she would close the door. He thought it should be a pleasant life enough, driving along the roads every evening to deliver milk, if he had warm gloves and a fat bag of gingernuts[9] in his pocket to eat from. But the same foreknowledge which had sickened his heart and made his limbs sag suddenly as he raced round the park, the same intuition which had made him glance with mistrust at his trainer's flabby stubblecovered face as it bent heavily over his long stained fingers, dissipated any vision of the future. In a vague way he understood that his father was in trouble and that this was the reason why he himself had not been sent back to Clongowes. For some time he had felt the slight changes in his house; and these changes in what he had deemed unchangeable were so many slight shocks to his boyish conception of the world. The ambition which he felt astir at times in the darkness of his soul sought no outlet. A dusk like that of the outer world obscured his mind as he heard the mare's hoofs clattering along the tramtrack on the Rock Road[1] and the great can swaying and rattling behind him.

He returned to Mercedes and, as he brooded upon her image, a strange unrest crept into his blood. Sometimes a fever gathered within him and led him to rove alone in the evening along the quiet avenues. The peace of the gardens and the kindly lights in the windows poured a tender influence into his restless heart. The noise of children at play annoyed him and their silly voices made him feel, even more keenly than he had felt at Clongowes, that he was different from others. He did not want to play. He wanted to meet in the real world the unsubstantial image which his soul so constantly beheld. He did not know where to seek it or how: but a premonition which led him on told him that this image would, without any overt act of his, encounter him. They would meet quietly as if they had known each other and had made their tryst, perhaps at one of the gates or in some more secret place. They would be alone, surrounded by darkness and silence: and in that moment of supreme tenderness he would be transfigured. He would fade into something impalpable under her eyes and then, in a moment, he would be transfigured. Weakness and timidity and inexperience would fall from him in that magic moment.

◆ ◆ ◆

Two great yellow caravans[2] had halted one morning before the door and men had come tramping into the house to dismantle it. The furniture had been hustled out through the front garden which was strewn with wisps of straw and rope ends and into the huge vans at the gate. When all had been safely stowed the vans had set off noisily down the avenue: and from the window of the railway carriage, in which he had sat with his redeyed mother, Stephen had seen them lumbering heavily along the Merrion Road.[3]

---

9. Gingerbread-nut, a small round cake.
1. Track for horse-drawn transportation on the road running northwest from Blackrock toward Dublin.

2. Covered, horse-drawn carriages or carts.
3. Part of the main road to Dublin and a continuation of the Rock Road.

The parlour fire would not draw that evening and Mr Dedalus rested the poker against the bars of the grate to attract the flame. Uncle Charles dozed in a corner of the half furnished uncarpeted room and near him the family portraits leaned against the wall. The lamp on the table shed a weak light over the boarded floor, muddied by the feet of the vanmen. Stephen sat on a footstool beside his father listening to a long and incoherent monologue. He understood little or nothing of it at first but he became slowly aware that his father had enemies and that some fight was going to take place. He felt, too, that he was being enlisted for the fight, that some duty was being laid upon his shoulders. The sudden flight from the comfort and revery of Blackrock, the passage through the gloomy foggy city, the thought of the bare cheerless house in which they were now to live made his heart heavy: and again an intuition or foreknowledge of the future came to him. He understood also why the servants had often whispered together in the hall and why his father had often stood on the hearthrug, with his back to the fire, talking loudly to uncle Charles who urged him to sit down and eat his dinner.

—There's a crack of the whip left in me yet, Stephen, old chap, said Mr Dedalus, poking at the dull fire with fierce energy. We're not dead yet, sonny. No, by the Lord Jesus (God forgive me) nor half dead.

Dublin was a new and complex sensation. Uncle Charles had grown so witless that he could no longer be sent out on errands and the disorder in settling in the new house left Stephen freer than he had been in Blackrock. In the beginning he contented himself with circling timidly round the neighbouring square or, at most, going half way down one of the side streets: but when he had made a skeleton map of the city in his mind he followed boldly one of its central lines until he reached the customhouse.[4] He passed unchallenged among the docks and along the quays wondering at the multitude of corks that lay bobbing on the surface of the water in a thick yellow scum, at the crowds of quay porters and the rumbling carts and the illdressed bearded policeman. The vastness and strangeness of the life suggested to him by the bales of merchandise stacked along the walls or swung aloft out of the holds of steamers wakened again in him the unrest which had sent him wandering in the evening from garden to garden in search of Mercedes. And amid this new bustling life he might have fancied himself in another Marseilles but that he missed the bright sky and the sunwarmed trellisses of the wineshops. A vague dissatisfaction grew up within him as he looked on the quays and on the river and on the lowering skies and yet he continued to wander up and down day after day as if he really sought someone that eluded him.

He went once or twice with his mother to visit their relatives: and, though they passed a jovial array of shops lit up and adorned for Christmas, his mood of embittered silence did not leave him. The causes of his embitterment were many, remote and near. He was angry with himself for being young and the prey of restless foolish impulses, angry also with the change of fortune which was reshaping the world about him into a vision of squalor and insincerity. Yet his anger lent nothing to the vision. He chronicled with patience what he saw, detaching himself from it and tasting its mortifying flavour in secret.

He was sitting on the backless chair in his aunt's kitchen. A lamp with a reflector hung on the japanned[5] wall of the fireplace and by its light his

---

4. The Custom House (1791), an impressive public building on the bank of the river Liffey at the end of Gardiner Street, the main road to which

Stephen refers here.
5. Finished with a hard black gloss.

aunt was reading the evening paper that lay on her knees. She looked a long time at a smiling picture that was set in it and said musingly:

—The beautiful Mabel Hunter![6]

A ringletted girl stood on tiptoe to peer at the picture and said softly:

—What is she in, mud?

—In the pantomime,[7] love.

The child leaned her ringletted head against her mother's sleeve, gazing on the picture and murmured, as if fascinated:

—The beautiful Mabel Hunter!

As if fascinated, her eyes rested long upon those demurely taunting eyes and she murmured again devotedly:

—Isn't she an exquisite creature?

And the boy who came in from the street, stamping crookedly under his stone[8] of coal, heard her words. He dropped his load promptly on the floor and hurried to her side to see. But she did not raise her easeful head to let him see. He mauled the edges of the paper with his reddened and blackened hands, shouldering her aside and complaining that he could not see.

He was sitting in the narrow breakfast room high up in the old darkwindowed house. The firelight flickered on the wall and beyond the window a spectral dusk was gathering upon the river. Before the fire an old woman was busy making tea and, as she bustled at her task, she told in a low voice of what the priest and the doctor had said. She told too of certain changes that she had seen in her of late and of her odd ways and sayings. He sat listening to the words and following the ways of adventure that lay open in the coals, arches and vaults and winding galleries and jagged caverns.

Suddenly he became aware of something in the doorway. A skull appeared suspended in the gloom of the doorway. A feeble creature like a monkey was there, drawn thither by the sound of voices at the fire. A whining voice came from the door, asking:

—Is that Josephine?

The old bustling woman answered cheerily from the fireplace:

—No, Ellen. It's Stephen.

—O. . . . O, good evening, Stephen.

He answered the greeting and saw a silly smile break out over the face in the doorway.

—Do you want anything, Ellen? asked the old woman at the fire.

But she did not answer the question and said:

—I thought it was Josephine. I thought you were Josephine, Stephen.

And, repeating this several times, she fell to laughing feebly.

He was sitting in the midst of a children's party at Harold's Cross.[9] His silent watchful manner had grown upon him and he took little part in the games. The children, wearing the spoils of their crackers,[1] danced and romped noisily and, though he tried to share their merriment, he felt himself a gloomy figure amid the gay cocked hats and sunbonnets.

But when he had sung his song and withdrawn into a snug corner of the room he began to taste the joy of his loneliness. The mirth, which in the beginning of the evening had seemed to him false and trivial, was like a

---

6. Probably an actress of the day.
7. Popular form of holiday entertainment consisting of music, dance, and topical jokes held together by a loose plotline, usually drawn from a fairy tale or classic story.

8. Measure of weight equal to fourteen pounds.
9. Inner suburb of Dublin.
1. Paper packets containing candy or party favors that burst apart when pulled at both ends.

soothing air to him, passing gaily by his senses, hiding from other eyes the feverish agitation of his blood while through the circling of the dancers and amid the music and laughter her glances travelled to his corner, flattering, taunting, searching, exciting his heart.

In the hall the children who had stayed latest were putting on their things: the party was over. She had thrown a shawl about her and, as they went together towards the tram, sprays of her fresh warm breath flew gaily above her cowled[2] head and her shoes tapped blithely on the glassy road.

It was the last tram. The lank brown horses knew it and shook their bells to the clear night in admonition. The conductor talked with the driver, both nodding often in the green light of the lamp. On the empty seats of the tram were scattered a few coloured tickets. No sound of footsteps came up or down the road. No sound broke the peace of the night save when the lank brown horses rubbed their noses together and shook their bells.

They seemed to listen, he on the upper step and she on the lower. She came up to his step many times and went down to hers again between their phrases and once or twice stood close beside him for some moments on the upper step, forgetting to go down, and then went down. His heart danced upon her movements like a cork upon a tide. He heard what her eyes said to him from beneath their cowl and knew that in some dim past, whether in life or in revery, he had heard their tale before. He saw her urge her vanities, her fine dress and sash and long black stockings, and knew that he had yielded to them a thousand times. Yet a voice within him spoke above the noise of his dancing heart, asking him would he take her gift to which he had only to stretch out his hand. And he remembered the day when he and Eileen had stood looking into the hotel grounds, watching the waiters running up a trail of bunting on the flagstaff and the foxterrier scampering to and fro on the sunny lawn, and how, all of a sudden, she had broken out into a peal of laughter and had run down the sloping curve of the path. Now, as then, he stood listlessly in his place, seemingly a tranquil watcher of the scene before him.

—She too wants me to catch hold of her, he thought. That's why she came with me to the tram. I could easily catch hold of her when she comes up to my step: nobody is looking. I could hold her and kiss her.

But he did neither: and, when he was sitting alone in the deserted tram, he tore his ticket into shreds and stared gloomily at the corrugated footboard.

The next day he sat at his table in the bare upper room for many hours. Before him lay a new pen, a new bottle of ink and a new emerald exercise.[3] From force of habit he had written at the top of the first page the initial letters of the jesuit motto: A. M. D. G.[4] On the first line of the page appeared the title of the verses he was trying to write: To E— C—. He knew it was right to begin so for he had seen similar titles in the collected poems of Lord Byron.[5] When he had written this title and drawn an ornamental line underneath he fell into a daydream and began to draw diagrams on the cover of the book. He saw himself sitting at his table in Bray[6] the morning after the discussion at the Christmas dinnertable, trying to write a poem about Par-

2. Covered with a cowl, a hooded, usually sleeveless cloak.
3. Blank notebook used for school assignments.
4. *Ad Majorem Dei Gloriam* ("To the Greater Glory of God" [Latin]), a Jesuit motto usually writ-ten at the beginning of school exercises.
5. George Gordon, Lord Byron (1788–1824), English Romantic poet.
6. Town in County Wicklow, on the coast, about 12 miles southeast of Dublin.

nell on the back of one of his father's second moiety notices.[7] But his brain had then refused to grapple with the theme and, desisting, he had covered the page with the names and addresses of certain of his classmates:

> Roderick Kickham
> John Lawton
> Anthony MacSwiney
> Simon Moonan

Now it seemed as if he would fail again but, by dint of brooding on the incident, he thought himself into confidence. During this process all those elements which he deemed common and insignificant fell out of the scene. There remained no trace of the tram itself nor of the trammen[8] nor of the horses: nor did he and she appear vividly. The verses told only of the night and the balmy breeze and the maiden lustre of the moon. Some undefined sorrow was hidden in the hearts of the protagonists as they stood in silence beneath the leafless trees and when the moment of farewell had come the kiss, which had been withheld by one, was given by both. After this the letters L. D. S.[9] were written at the foot of the page and, having hidden the book, he went into his mother's bedroom and gazed at his face for a long time in the mirror of her dressingtable.

But his long spell of leisure and liberty was drawing to its end. One evening his father came home full of news which kept his tongue busy all through dinner. Stephen had been awaiting his father's return for there had been mutton hash[1] that day and he knew that his father would make him dip his bread in the gravy. But he did not relish the hash for the mention of Clongowes had coated his palate with a scum of disgust.

—I walked bang into him, said Mr Dedalus for the fourth time, just at the corner of the square.

—Then I suppose, said Mrs Dedalus, he will be able to arrange it. I mean, about Belvedere.[2]

—Of course he will, said Mr Dedalus. Don't I tell you he's provincial of the order[3] now?

—I never liked the idea of sending him to the christian brothers[4] myself, said Mrs Dedalus.

—Christian brothers be damned! said Mr Dedalus. Is it with Paddy Stink and Mickey Mud?[5] No, let him stick to the jesuits in God's name since he began with them. They'll be of service to him in after years. Those are the fellows that can get you a position.

—And they're a very rich order, aren't they, Simon?

—Rather. They live well, I tell you. You saw their table at Clongowes. Fed up, by God, like gamecocks.[6]

Mr Dedalus pushed his plate over to Stephen and bade him finish what was on it.

7. Notices demanding payment for a moiety, or second half, of a bill, possibly here as part of bankruptcy.
8. I.e., the men who drive the tram.
9. *Laus Deo Semper* ("Praise to God Always" [Latin]), a Jesuit motto usually written at the end of school exercises.
1. Chopped-up pieces of cooked sheep's meat rewarmed with gravy.
2. Belvedere College, a boys' day school run by the Jesuits.
3. See p. 471, n. 3.
4. The Irish Christian Brothers, a lay order of the Catholic Church, provided education to those who could not afford school fees and ran less prestigious schools than the Jesuits.
5. Derogatory names for Irish people, indicating a lower social and economic status.
6. Roosters bred, trained, and fed for cockfighting.

—Now then, Stephen, he said. You must put your shoulder to the wheel, old chap. You've had a fine long holiday.

—O, I'm sure he'll work very hard now, said Mrs Dedalus. Especially when he has Maurice with him.

—O, Holy Paul, I forgot about Maurice, said Mr Dedalus. Here, Maurice! Come here, you thickheaded ruffian! Do you know I'm going to send you to a college where they'll teach you to spell c.a.t: cat. And I'll buy you a nice little penny handkerchief to keep your nose dry. Won't that be grand fun?

Maurice grinned at his father and then at his brother. Mr Dedalus screwed his glass into his eye and stared hard at both his sons. Stephen mumbled his bread[7] without answering his father's gaze.

—By the bye, said Mr Dedalus at length, the rector, or provincial, rather, was telling me that story about you and Father Dolan. You're an impudent thief, he said.

—O, he didn't, Simon!

—Not he! said Mr Dedalus. But he gave me a great account of the whole affair. We were chatting, you know, and one word borrowed another. And, by the way, who do you think he told me will get that job in the corporation?[8] But I'll tell you that after. Well, as I was saying, we were chatting away quite friendly and he asked me did our friend here wear glasses still and then he told me the whole story.

—And was he annoyed, Simon?

—Annoyed! Not he! *Manly little chap!* he said.

Mr Dedalus imitated the mincing nasal tone of the provincial.

—Father Dolan and I, when I told them all at dinner about it, Father Dolan and I had a great laugh over it. *You better mind yourself; Father Dolan*, said I, *or young Dedalus will send you up for twice nine.* We had a famous laugh together over it. Ha! Ha! Ha!

Mr Dedalus turned to his wife and interjected in his natural voice:

—Shows you the spirit in which they take the boys there. O, a jesuit for your life, for diplomacy!

He reassumed the provincial's voice and repeated:

—*I told them all at dinner about it and Father Dolan and I and all of us we all had a hearty laugh together over it. Ha! Ha! Ha!*

◆ ◆ ◆

The night of the Whitsuntide[9] play had come and Stephen from the window of the dressingroom looked out on the small grassplot across which lines of Chinese lanterns were stretched. He watched the visitors come down the steps from the house and pass into the theatre. Stewards[1] in evening dress, old Belvedereans, loitered in groups about the entrance to the theatre and ushered in the visitors with ceremony. Under the sudden glow of a lantern he could recognize the smiling face of a priest.

The Blessed Sacrament had been removed from the tabernacle[2] and the first benches had been driven back so as to leave the dais of the altar and

---

7. Chewed ineffectually, or turned over and over in his mouth.

8. The Dublin Corporation, the government bureaucracy in Dublin, now known as the City Council.

9. The week beginning with Whitsunday, or Pentecost (the seventh Sunday after Easter), which

marks the descent of the Holy Spirit on the apostles.

1. People serving as ushers for the evening.

2. Container in which the Host is usually kept but from which it has been removed temporarily, so that it is not accidentally desecrated during the play in the chapel.

the space before it free. Against the walls stood companies of barbells and Indian clubs;[3] the dumbbells were piled in one corner: and in the midst of countless hillocks of gymnasium shoes and sweaters and singlets in untidy brown parcels there stood the stout leatherjacketed vaulting horse[4] waiting its turn to be carried up on to the stage. A large bronze shield, tipped with silver, leaned against the panel of the altar also waiting its turn to be carried up on to the stage and set in the middle of the winning team at the end of the gymnastic display.

Stephen, though in deference to his reputation for essay-writing he had been elected secretary to the gymnasium, had no part in the first section of the programme: but in the play which formed the second section he had the chief part, that of a farcical pedagogue. He had been cast for it on account of his stature and grave manners for he was now at the end of his second year at Belvedere and in number two.[5]

A score of the younger boys in white knickers and singlets came pattering down from the stage, through the vestry[6] and into the chapel. The vestry and chapel were peopled with eager masters and boys. The plump bald sergeantmajor was testing with his foot the springboard of the vaulting horse. The lean young man in a long overcoat, who was to give a special display of intricate club swinging, stood near watching with interest, his silvercoated clubs peeping out of his deep side-pockets. The hollow rattle of the wooden dumbbells was heard as another team made ready to go up on the stage: and in another moment the excited prefect was hustling the boys through the vestry like a flock of geese, flapping the wings of his soutane nervously and crying to the laggards to make haste. A little troop of Neapolitan peasants[7] were practising their steps at the end of the chapel, some arching their arms above their heads, some swaying their baskets of paper violets and curtseying. In a dark corner of the chapel at the gospel side of the altar[8] a stout old lady knelt amid her copious black skirts. When she stood up a pinkdressed figure, wearing a curly golden wig and an oldfashioned straw sunbonnet, with black pencilled eyebrows and cheeks delicately rouged and powdered, was discovered. A low murmur of curiosity ran round the chapel at the discovery of this girlish figure. One of the prefects, smiling and nodding his head, approached the dark corner and, having bowed to the stout old lady, said pleasantly:

—Is this a beautiful young lady or a doll that you have here, Mrs Tallon?

Then, bending down to peer at the smiling painted face under the leaf of the bonnet, he exclaimed:

—No! Upon my word I believe it's little Bertie Tallon after all!

Stephen at his post by the window heard the old lady and the priest laugh together and heard the boys' murmur of admiration behind him as they pressed forward to see the little boy who had to dance the sunbonnet dance by himself. A movement of impatience escaped him. He let the edge of the blind fall and, stepping down from the bench on which he had been standing, walked out of the chapel.

---

3. Bottle-shaped clubs.
4. Leather-covered, saddle-shaped wooden object over which vaulting takes place in gymnastics.
5. In his second-to-last year of studies at the college.
6. Room next to the chapel in which the vestments, or ritual robes, are kept. "Singlets": under-shirts or jerseys.
7. Students dressed like peasants from Naples, Italy.
8. The left side of the altar (as the congregation faces it), where the Gospels are read, as opposed to the right side, where the Epistles are read.

He passed out of the schoolhouse and halted under the shed that flanked the garden. From the theatre opposite came the muffled noise of the audience and sudden brazen clashes of the soldiers band. The light spread upwards from the glass roof making the theatre seem a festive ark, anchored amid the hulks of houses, her frail cables of lanterns looping her to her moorings. A sidedoor of the theatre opened suddenly and a shaft of light flew across the grassplots. A sudden burst of music issued from the ark, the prelude of a waltz: and when the sidedoor closed again the listener could hear the faint rhythm of the music. The sentiment of the opening bars, their languor and supple movement, evoked the incommunicable emotion which had been the cause of all his day's unrest and of his impatient movement of a moment before. His unrest issued from him like a wave of sound: and on the tide of flowing music the ark was journeying, trailing her cables of lanterns in her wake. Then a noise like dwarf artillery broke the movement. It was the clapping that greeted the entry of the dumbbell team on the stage.

At the far end of the shed near the street a speck of pink light showed in the darkness and as he walked towards it he became aware of a faint aromatic odour. Two boys were standing in the shelter of the doorway, smoking, and before he reached them he had recognised Heron by his voice.

—Here comes the noble Dedalus! cried a high throaty voice. Welcome to our trusty friend!

This welcome ended in a soft peal of mirthless laughter as Heron salaamed[9] and then began to poke the ground with his cane.

—Here I am, said Stephen, halting and glancing from Heron to his friend.

The latter was a stranger to him but in the darkness, by the aid of the glowing cigarette tips, he could make out a pale dandyish face, over which a smile was travelling slowly, a tall overcoated figure and a hard hat. Heron did not trouble himself about an introduction but said instead:

—I was just telling my friend Wallis what a lark it would be tonight if you took off the rector in the part of the schoolmaster. It would be a ripping good joke.

Heron made a poor attempt to imitate for his friend Wallis the rector's pedantic bass and then, laughing at his failure, asked Stephen to do it.

—Go on, Dedalus, he urged. You can take him off rippingly. *He that will not hear the churcha let him be to theea as the heathena and the publicana.*[1]

The imitation was prevented by a mild expression of anger from Wallis in whose mouthpiece the cigarette had become too tightly wedged.

—Damn this blankety blank holder, he said, taking it from his mouth and smiling and frowning upon it tolerantly. It's always getting stuck like that. Do you use a holder?

—I don't smoke, answered Stephen.

—No, said Heron, Dedalus is a model youth. He doesn't smoke and he doesn't go to bazaars[2] and he doesn't flirt and he doesn't damn anything or damn all.

Stephen shook his head and smiled in his rival's flushed and mobile face, beaked like a bird's. He had often thought it strange that Vincent Heron had a bird's face as well as a bird's name. A shock of pale hair lay on the forehead

---

9. Greeted ceremoniously, probably with a low bow.
1. Echoing Matthew 18.17.

2. Fairs with many stalls selling a variety of goods, usually to benefit a charitable organization. (Cf. Joyce's story "Araby.")

like a ruffled crest: the forehead was narrow and bony and a thin hooked nose stood out between the closeset prominent eyes which were light and inexpressive. The rivals were school friends. They sat together in class, knelt together in the chapel, talked together after beads[3] over their lunches. As the fellows in number one[4] were undistinguished dullards Stephen and Heron had been during the year the virtual heads of the school. It was they who went up to the rector together to ask for a free day or to get a fellow off.

—O, by the way, said Heron suddenly, I saw your governor going in.

The smile waned on Stephen's face. Any allusion made to his father by a fellow or by a master put his calm to rout in a moment. He waited in timorous silence to hear what Heron might say next. Heron, however, nudged him expressively with his elbow and said:

—You're a sly dog, Dedalus!

—Why so? said Stephen.

—You'd think butter wouldn't melt in your mouth, said Heron. But I'm afraid you're a sly dog.

—Might I ask you what you are talking about? said Stephen urbanely.

—Indeed you might, answered Heron. We saw her, Wallis, didn't we? And deucedly pretty she is too. And so inquisitive! *And what part does Stephen take, Mr Dedalus? And will Stephen not sing, Mr Dedalus?* Your governor was staring at her through that eyeglass of his for all he was worth so that I think the old man has found you out too. I wouldn't care a bit, by Jove. She's ripping, isn't she, Wallis?

—Not half bad, answered Wallis quietly as he placed his holder once more in a corner of his mouth.

A shaft of momentary anger flew through Stephen's mind at these indelicate allusions in the hearing of a stranger. For him there was nothing amusing in a girl's interest and regard. All day he had thought of nothing but their leavetaking on the steps of the tram at Harold's Cross, the stream of moody emotions it had made to course through him and the poem he had written about it. All day he had imagined a new meeting with her for he knew that she was to come to the play. The old restless moodiness had again filled his heart as it had done on the night of the party but had not found an outlet in verse. The growth and knowledge of two years of boyhood stood between then and now, forbidding such an outlet: and all day the stream of gloomy tenderness within him had started forth and returned upon itself in dark courses and eddies, wearying him in the end until the pleasantry of the prefect and the painted little boy had drawn from him a movement of impatience.

—So you may as well admit, Heron went on, that we've fairly found you out this time. You can't play the saint on me any more, that's one sure five.[5]

A soft peal of mirthless laughter escaped from his lips and, bending down as before, he struck Stephen lightly across the calf of the leg with his cane, as if in jesting reproof.

Stephen's moment of anger had already passed. He was neither flattered nor confused but simply wished the banter to end. He scarcely resented what had seemed to him at first a silly indelicateness for he knew that the adventure in his mind stood in no danger from their words: and his face mirrored his rival's false smile.

3. I.e., after using rosary beads to say prayers, a part of the college's daily schedule.

4. In their last year at the college.

5. A certainty.

—Admit! repeated Heron, striking him again with his cane across the calf of the leg.

The stroke was playful but not so lightly given as the first one had been. Stephen felt the skin tingle and glow slightly and almost painlessly; and bowing submissively, as if to meet his companion's jesting mood, began to recite the *Confiteor*.[6] The episode ended well for both Heron and Wallis laughed indulgently at the irreverence.

The confession came only from Stephen's lips and, while they spoke the words, a sudden memory had carried him to another scene called up, as if by magic, at the moment when he had noted the faint cruel dimples at the corners of Heron's smiling lips and had felt the familiar stroke of the cane against his calf and had heard the familiar word of admonition:
—Admit!

It was towards the close of his first term in the college when he was in number six.[7] His sensitive nature was still smarting under the lashes of an undivined and squalid way of life. His soul was still disquieted and cast down by the dull phenomenon of Dublin. He had emerged from a two years' spell of revery to find himself in the midst of a new scene, every event and figure of which affected him intimately, disheartened him or allured him and, whether alluring or disheartening, filled him always with unrest and bitter thoughts. All the leisure that his school life left him was passed in the company of subversive writers whose gibes and violence of speech set up a ferment in his brain before they passed out of it into his crude writings.

The essay was for him the chief labour of his week and every Tuesday, as he marched from home to the school, he read his fate in the incidents of the way, pitting himself against some figure ahead of him and quickening his pace to outstrip it before a certain goal was reached or planting his steps scrupulously in the spaces of the patchwork of the footpath and telling himself that he would be first and not first in the weekly essay.

On a certain Tuesday the course of his triumphs was rudely broken. Mr Tate, the English master, pointed his finger at him and said bluntly:
—This fellow has heresy in his essay.

A hush fell on the class. Mr Tate did not break it but dug with his hand between his crossed thighs while his heavily starched linen creaked about his neck and wrists. Stephen did not look up. It was a raw spring morning and his eyes were still smarting and weak. He was conscious of failure and of detection, of the squalor of his own mind and home, and felt against his neck the raw edge of his turned and jagged collar.

A short loud laugh from Mr Tate set the class more at ease.
—Perhaps you didn't know that, he said.
—Where? asked Stephen.

Mr Tate withdrew his delving hand and spread out the essay.
—Here. It's about the Creator and the soul. Rrm . . . rrm . . . . . rrm . . . Ah! *without a possibility of ever approaching nearer.* That's heresy.

Stephen murmured:
—I meant *without a possibility of ever reaching.*

It was a submission and Mr Tate, appeased, folded up the essay and passed it across to him, saying:

6. Literally, "I confess" (Latin), a prayer for forgiveness at the beginning of the Catholic mass.

7. In his sixth-to-last year at the college.

—O . . . Ah! *ever reaching.* That's another story.

But the class was not so soon appeased. Though nobody spoke to him of the affair after class he could feel about him a vague general malignant joy.

A few nights after this public chiding he was walking with a letter along the Drumcondra Road[8] when he heard a voice cry:

—Halt!

He turned and saw three boys of his own class coming towards him in the dusk. It was Heron who had called out and, as he marched forward between his two attendants, he cleft the air before him with a thin cane, in time to their steps. Boland, his friend, marched beside him, a large grin on his face, while Nash came on a few steps behind, blowing from the pace and wagging his great red head.

As soon as the boys had turned into Clonliffe Road[9] together they began to speak about books and writers, saying what books they were reading and how many books there were in their fathers' bookcases at home. Stephen listened to them in some wonderment for Boland was the dunce and Nash the idler of the class. In fact after some talk about their favourite writers Nash declared for Captain Marryat[1] who, he said, was the greatest writer.

—Fudge! said Heron. Ask Dedalus. Who is the greatest writer, Dedalus?

Stephen noted the mockery in the question and said:

—Of prose, do you mean?

—Yes.

—Newman,[2] I think.

—Is it Cardinal Newman? asked Boland.

—Yes, answered Stephen.

The grin broadened on Nash's freckled face as he turned to Stephen and said:

—And do you like Cardinal Newman, Dedalus?

—O, many people say that Newman has the best prose style, Heron said to the other two in explanation. Of course, he's not a poet.

—And who is the best poet, Heron? asked Boland.

—Lord Tennyson,[3] of course, answered Heron.

—O, yes, Lord Tennyson, said Nash. We have all his poetry at home in a book.

At this Stephen forgot the silent vows he had been making and burst out:

—Tennyson a poet! Why, he's only a rhymester!

—O, get out! said Heron. Everyone knows that Tennyson is the greatest poet.

—And who do you think is the greatest poet? asked Boland, nudging his neighbour.

—Byron, of course, answered Stephen.

Heron gave the lead and all three joined in a scornful laugh.

—What are you laughing at? asked Stephen.

—You, said Heron. Byron the greatest poet! He's only a poet for uneducated people.

---

8. Main road from Dublin toward the northern suburb of Drumcondra.

9. Important road that runs east from Drumcondra Road toward Dublin Bay.

1. Frederick Marryat (1792–1848), English naval officer and author of adventure novels about life at sea.

2. John Henry, Cardinal Newman (1801–1890), English Protestant clergyman who converted to Catholicism and wrote extensively about his beliefs.

3. Alfred, Lord Tennyson (1809–1892), Victorian poet laureate of England.

—He must be a fine poet! said Boland.

—You may keep your mouth shut, said Stephen, turning on him boldly. All you know about poetry is what you wrote up on the slates in the yard and were going to be sent to the loft for.

Boland, in fact, was said to have written on the slates in the yard a couplet about a classmate of his who often rode home from the college on a pony:

> As Tyson was riding into Jerusalem
> He fell and hurt his Alec Kafoozelum.[4]

This thrust put the two lieutenants to silence but Heron went on:

—In any case Byron was a heretic and immoral too.

—I don't care what he was, cried Stephen hotly.

—You don't care whether he was a heretic or not? said Nash.

—What do you know about it? shouted Stephen. You never read a line of anything in your life except a trans[5] or Boland either.

—I know that Byron was a bad man, said Boland.

—Here. Catch hold of this heretic, Heron called out.

In a moment Stephen was a prisoner.

—Tate made you buck up the other day, Heron went on, about the heresy in your essay.

—I'll tell him tomorrow, said Boland.

—Will you? said Stephen. You'd be afraid to open your lips.

—Afraid?

—Ay. Afraid of your life.

—Behave yourself! cried Heron, cutting at Stephen's legs with his cane.

It was the signal for their onset. Nash pinioned his arms behind while Boland seized a long cabbage stump which was lying in the gutter. Struggling and kicking under the cuts of the cane and the blows of the knotty stump Stephen was borne back against a barbed wire fence.

—Admit that Byron was no good.

—No.

—Admit.

—No.

—Admit.

—No. No.

At last after a fury of plunges he wrenched himself free. His tormentors set off towards Jones's Road,[6] laughing and jeering at him, while he, half blinded with tears, stumbled on, clenching his fists madly and sobbing.

While he was still repeating the *Confiteor* amid the indulgent laughter of his hearers and while the scenes of that malignant episode were still passing sharply and swiftly before his mind he wondered why he bore no malice now to those who had tormented him. He had not forgotten a whit of their cowardice and cruelty but the memory of it called forth no anger from him. All the descriptions of fierce love and hatred which he had met in books had seemed to him therefore unreal. Even that night as he stumbled homewards along Jones's Road he had felt that some power was divesting him of that sudden-woven anger as easily as a fruit is divested of her soft ripe peel.

---

4. Variation on an anonymous ballad.
5. A translation or crib.

6. Road leading back toward central Dublin.

He remained standing with his two companions at the end of the shed, listening idly to their talk or to the bursts of applause in the theatre. She was sitting there among the others, perhaps waiting for him to appear. He tried to recall her appearance but could not. He could remember only that she had worn a shawl about her head like a cowl and that her dark eyes had invited and unnerved him. He wondered had he been in her thoughts as she had been in his. Then in the dark and unseen by the other two he rested the tips of the fingers of one hand upon the palm of the other hand, scarcely touching it and yet pressing upon it lightly. But the pressure of her fingers had been lighter and steadier: and suddenly the memory of their touch traversed his brain and body like an invisible warm wave.

A boy came towards them, running along under the shed. He was excited and breathless.

—O, Dedalus, he cried, Doyle is in a great bake about you.[7] You're to go in at once and get dressed for the play. Hurry up, you better.

—He's coming now, said Heron to the messenger with a haughty drawl, when he wants to.

The boy turned to Heron and repeated:

—But Doyle is in an awful bake.

—Will you tell Doyle with my best compliments that I damned his eyes? answered Heron.

—Well, I must go now, said Stephen who cared little for such points of honour.

—I wouldn't, said Heron, damn me if I would. That's no way to send for one of the senior boys. In a bake, indeed! I think it's quite enough that you're taking a part in his bally[8] old play.

This spirit of quarrelsome comradeship which he had observed lately in his rival had not seduced Stephen from his habits of quiet obedience. He mistrusted the turbulence and doubted the sincerity of such comradeship which seemed to him a sorry anticipation of manhood. The question of honour here raised was, like all such questions, trivial to him. While his mind had been pursuing its intangible phantoms and turning in irresolution from such pursuit he had heard about him the constant voices of his father and of his masters, urging him to be a gentleman above all things and urging him to be a good catholic above all things. These voices had now come to be hollowsounding in his ears. When the gymnasium had been opened he had heard another voice urging him to be strong and manly and healthy and when the movement towards national revival had begun to be felt in the college yet another voice had bidden him be true to his country and help to raise up her fallen language and tradition.[9] In the profane[1] world, as he foresaw, a worldly voice would bid him raise up his father's fallen state by his labours and, meanwhile, the voice of his schoolcomrades urged him to be a decent fellow, to shield others from blame or to beg them off and to do his best to get free days for the school. And it was the din of all these hollowsounding voices that made him halt irresolutely in the pursuit of phantoms. He gave them ear only

7. Very angry at you.
8. A euphemism for "bloody"; darn.
9. I.e., to revive Ireland's Gaelic heritage through the work of groups like the Gaelic League and the

Gaelic Athletic Association, founded at the end of the nineteenth century.
1. Secular.

for a time but he was happy only when he was far from them, beyond their call, alone or in the company of phantasmal comrades.

In the vestry a plump freshfaced jesuit and an elderly man, in shabby blue clothes, were dabbling in a case of paints and chalks. The boys who had been painted walked about or stood still awkwardly, touching their faces in a gingerly fashion with their furtive fingertips. In the middle of the vestry a young jesuit, who was then on a visit to the college, stood rocking himself rhythmically from the tips of his toes to his heels and back again, his hands thrust well forward into his sidepockets. His small head set off with glossy red curls and his newly shaven face agreed well with the spotless decency of his soutane and with his spotless shoes.

As he watched this swaying form and tried to read for himself the legend of the priest's mocking smile there came into Stephen's memory a saying which he had heard from his father before he had been sent to Clongowes, that you could always tell a jesuit by the style of his clothes. At the same moment he thought he saw a likeness between his father's mind and that of this smiling welldressed priest: and he was aware of some desecration of the priest's office or of the vestry itself, whose silence was now routed by loud talk and joking and its air pungent with the smells of the gasjets and the grease.

While his forehead was being wrinkled and his jaws painted black and blue by the elderly man he listened distractedly to the voice of the plump young jesuit which bade him speak up and make his points clearly. He could hear the band playing *The Lily of Killarney*[2] and knew that in a few moments the curtain would go up. He felt no stage fright but the thought of the part he had to play humiliated him. A remembrance of some of his lines made a sudden flush rise to his painted cheeks. He saw her serious alluring eyes watching him from among the audience and their image at once swept away his scruples, leaving his will compact. Another nature seemed to have been lent him: the infection of the excitement and youth about him entered into and transformed his moody mistrustfulness. For one rare moment he seemed to be clothed in the real apparel of boyhood: and, as he stood in the wings among the other players, he shared the common mirth amid which the drop scene was hauled upwards by two ablebodied priests with violent jerks and all awry.

A few moments after he found himself on the stage amid the garish gas and the dim scenery, acting before the innumerable faces of the void. It surprised him to see that the play which he had known at rehearsals for a disjointed lifeless thing had suddenly assumed a life of its own. It seemed now to play itself, he and his fellow actors aiding it with their parts. When the curtain fell on the last scene he heard the void filled with applause and, through a rift in the side scene, saw the simple body before which he had acted magically deformed, the void of faces breaking at all points and falling asunder into busy groups.

He left the stage quickly and rid himself of his mummery[3] and passed out through the chapel into the college garden. Now that the play was over his nerves cried for some further adventure. He hurried onwards as if to overtake it. The doors of the theatre were all open and the audience had emptied out. On the lines which he had fancied the moorings of an ark a few

2. Overture to the opera of that title (1862), by German-born English composer Julius Benedict (1804–1885).
3. Costume.

lanterns swung in the night breeze, flickering cheerlessly. He mounted the steps from the garden in haste, eager that some prey should not elude him, and forced his way through the crowd in the hall and past the two jesuits who stood watching the exodus and bowing and shaking hands with the visitors. He pushed onward nervously, feigning a still greater haste and faintly conscious of the smiles and stares and nudges which his powdered head left in its wake.

When he came out on the steps he saw his family waiting for him at the first lamp. In a glance he noted that every figure of the group was familiar and ran down the steps angrily.

—I have to leave a message down in George's Street,[4] he said to his father quickly. I'll be home after you.

Without waiting for his father's questions he ran across the road and began to walk at breakneck speed down the hill. He hardly knew where he was walking. Pride and hope and desire like crushed herbs in his heart sent up vapours of maddening incense before the eyes of his mind. He strode down the hill amid the tumult of suddenrisen vapours of wounded pride and fallen hope and baffled desire. They streamed upwards before his anguished eyes in dense and maddening fumes and passed away above him till at last the air was clear and cold again.

A film still veiled his eyes but they burned no longer. A power, akin to that which had often made anger or resentment fall from him, brought his steps to rest. He stood still and gazed up at the sombre porch of the morgue and from that to the dark cobbled laneway at its side. He saw the word *Lotts* on the wall of the lane and breathed slowly the rank heavy air.

—That is horse piss and rotted straw, he thought. It is a good odour to breathe. It will calm my heart. My heart is quite calm now. I will go back.

◆   ◆   ◆

Stephen was once again seated beside his father in the corner of a railway carriage at Kingsbridge.[5] He was travelling with his father by the night mail[6] to Cork. As the train steamed out of the station he recalled his childish wonder of years before and every event of his first day in Clongowes. But he felt no wonder now. He saw the darkening lands slipping past him, the silent telegraphpoles passing his window swiftly every four seconds, the little glimmering stations, manned by a few silent sentries, flung by the mail behind her and twinkling for a moment in the darkness like fiery grains flung backwards by a runner.

He listened without sympathy to his father's evocation of Cork and of scenes of his youth, a tale broken by sighs or draughts from his pocket flask whenever the image of some dead friend appeared in it or whenever the evoker remembered suddenly the purpose of his actual visit. Stephen heard but could feel no pity. The images of the dead were all strange to him save that of uncle Charles, an image which had lately been fading out of memory. He knew, however, that his father's property was going to be sold by auction and in the manner of his own dispossession he felt the world give the lie rudely to his phantasy.

4. Street leading from Belvedere College south-east toward central Dublin.
5. A Dublin railway station.

6. Train that carries mail across the country at night.

At Maryborough[7] he fell asleep. When he awoke the train had passed out of Mallow[8] and his father was stretched asleep on the other seat. The cold light of the dawn lay over the country, over the unpeopled fields and the closed cottages. The terror of sleep fascinated his mind as he watched the silent country or heard from time to time his father's deep breath or sudden sleepy movement. The neighbourhood of unseen sleepers filled him with strange dread as though they could harm him; and he prayed that the day might come quickly. His prayer, addressed neither to God nor saint, began with a shiver, as the chilly morning breeze crept through the chink of the carriage door to his feet, and ended in a trail of foolish words which he made to fit the insistent rhythm of the train: and silently, at intervals of four seconds, the telegraphpoles held the galloping notes of the music between punctual bars. This furious music allayed his dread and, leaning against the windowledge, he let his eyelids close again.

They drove in a jingle[9] across Cork while it was still early morning and Stephen finished his sleep in a bedroom of the Victoria Hotel.[1] The bright warm sunlight was streaming through the window and he could hear the din of traffic. His father was standing before the dressingtable, examining his hair and face and moustache with great care, craning his neck across the waterjug and drawing it back sideways to see the better. While he did so he sang softly to himself with quaint accent and phrasing:

> 'Tis youth and folly
> Makes young men marry,
> So here, my love, I'll
> No longer stay.
> What can't be cured, sure,
> Must be injured, sure,
> So I'll go to
> Amerikay.
>
> My love she's handsome,
> My love she's honey:
> She's like good whisky
> When it is new;
> But when 'tis old
> And growing cold
> It fades and dies like
> The mountain dew.

The consciousness of the warm sunny city outside his window and the tender tremors with which his father's voice festooned the strange sad happy air drove off all the mists of the night's ill humour from Stephen's brain. He got up quickly to dress and, when the song had ended, said:

—That's much prettier than any of your other come-all-yous.[2]

—Do you think so? asked Mr Dedalus.

—I like it, said Stephen.

—It's a pretty old air, said Mr Dedalus, twirling the points of his moustache. Ah, but you should have heard Mick Lacy sing it! Poor Mick Lacy!

---

7. A town approximately 50 miles from Dublin.
8. A town approximately 145 miles from Dublin and 20 miles from Cork.
9. Covered, two-wheeled, horse-drawn car.

1. The most fashionable hotel in Cork at the time.
2. Popular Irish street ballads, which often begin with these words.

He had little turns for it, grace notes he used to put in that I haven't got. That was the boy could sing a *come-all-you*, if you like.

Mr Dedalus had ordered drisheens[3] for breakfast and during the meal he crossexamined the waiter for local news. For the most part they spoke at cross purposes when a name was mentioned, the waiter having in mind its present holder and Mr Dedalus his father or perhaps his grandfather.

—Well, I hope they haven't moved the Queen's College[4] anyhow, said Mr Dedalus, for I want to show it to this youngster of mine.

Along the Mardyke[5] the trees were in bloom. They entered the grounds of the college and were led by the garrulous porter across the quadrangle. But their progress across the gravel was brought to a halt after every dozen or so paces by some reply of the porter's.

—Ah, do you tell me so? And is poor Pottlebelly dead?

—Yes, sir. Dead, sir.

During these halts Stephen stood awkwardly behind the two men, weary of the subject and waiting restlessly for the slow march to begin again. By the time they had crossed the quadrangle his restlessness had risen to fever. He wondered how his father, whom he knew for a shrewd suspicious man, could be duped by the servile manners of the porter: and the lively southern speech which had entertained him all the morning now irritated his ears.

They passed into the anatomy theatre where Mr Dedalus, the porter aiding him, searched the desks for his initials. Stephen remained in the background, depressed more than ever by the darkness and silence of the theatre and by the air it wore of jaded and formal study. On the desk before him he read the word *Foetus* cut several times in the dark stained wood. The sudden legend startled his blood: he seemed to feel the absent students of the college about him and to shrink from their company. A vision of their life, which his father's words had been powerless to evoke, sprang up before him out of the word cut in the desk. A broadshouldered student with a moustache was cutting in the letters with a jackknife, seriously. Other students stood or sat near him laughing at his handiwork. One jogged his elbow. The big student turned on him, frowning. He was dressed in loose grey clothes and had tan boots.

Stephen's name was called. He hurried down the steps of the theatre so as to be as far away from the vision as he could be and, peering closely at his father's initials, hid his flushed face.

But the word and the vision capered before his eyes as he walked back across the quadrangle and towards the college gate. It shocked him to find in the outer world a trace of what he had deemed till then a brutish and individual malady of his own mind. His recent monstrous reveries came thronging into his memory. They too had sprung up before him, suddenly and furiously, out of mere words. He had soon given in to them and allowed them to sweep across and abase his intellect, wondering always where they came from, from what den of monstrous images, and always weak and humble towards others, restless and sickened of himself when they had swept over him.

—Ay, bedad! And there's the Groceries[6] sure enough! cried Mr Dedalus. You often heard me speak of the Groceries, didn't you, Stephen. Many's the

3. Sausages made from sheep's blood and milk.
4. One of three Queen's Colleges in Ireland, established in 1845 to provide higher education for Catholics, and now known as University College, Cork.
5. A promenade in the western part of the city.
6. A pub that also sold groceries.

time we went down there when our names had been marked, a crowd of us, Harry Peard and little Jack Mountain and Bob Dyas and Maurice Moriarty, the Frenchman, and Tom O'Grady and Mick Lacy that I told you of this morning and Joey Corbet and poor little goodhearted Johnny Keevers of the Tantiles.

The leaves of the trees along the Mardyke were astir and whispering in the sunlight. A team of cricketers passed, agile young men in flannels and blazers, one of them carrying the long green wicketbag.[7] In a quiet bystreet a German band of five players in faded uniforms and with battered brass instruments was playing to an audience of street arabs[8] and leisurely messenger boys. A maid in a white cap and apron was watering a box of plants on a sill which shone like a slab of limestone in the warm glare. From another window open to the air came the sound of a piano, scale after scale rising into the treble.

Stephen walked on at his father's side, listening to stories he had heard before, hearing again the names of the scattered and dead revellers who had been the companions of his father's youth. And a faint sickness sighed in his heart. He recalled his own equivocal position in Belvedere, a free boy,[9] a leader afraid of his own authority, proud and sensitive and suspicious, battling against the squalor of his life and against the riot of his mind. The letters cut in the stained wood of the desk stared upon him, mocking his bodily weakness and futile enthusiasms and making him loathe himself for his own mad and filthy orgies. The spittle in his throat grew bitter and foul to swallow and the faint sickness climbed to his brain so that for a moment he closed his eyes and walked on in darkness.

He could still hear his father's voice.

—When you kick out for yourself, Stephen, (as I daresay you will one of those days) remember, whatever you do, to mix with gentlemen. When I was a young fellow I tell you I enjoyed myself. I mixed with fine decent fellows. Everyone of us could do something. One fellow had a good voice, another fellow was a good actor, another could sing a good comic song, another was a good oarsman or a good racketplayer, another could tell a good story and so on. We kept the ball rolling anyhow and enjoyed ourselves and saw a bit of life and we were none the worse of it either. But we were all gentlemen, Stephen, (at least I hope we were) and bloody good honest Irishmen too. That's the kind of fellows I want you to associate with, fellows of the right kidney. I'm talking to you as a friend, Stephen. I don't believe in playing the stern father. I don't believe a son should be afraid of his father. No, I treat you as your grandfather treated me when I was a young chap. We were more like brothers than father and son. I'll never forget the first day he caught me smoking. I was standing at the end of the South Terrace one day with some maneens[1] like myself and sure we thought we were grand fellows because we had pipes stuck in the corners of our mouths. Suddenly the governor passed. He didn't say a word or stop even. But the next day, Sunday, we were out for a walk together and when we were coming home he took out his cigar case and said: *By the bye, Simon, I didn't know you smoked:* or something like that.—Of course I tried to carry it off as best I could. *If you want*

---

7. Bag used to carry the parts of the wicket, the structure in cricket at which the bowler aims the ball and which is defended by the batsman.

8. Poor children from the slums.
9. Student on full scholarship.
1. Little men (moderately derisive Irish dialect).

a good smoke, he said, *try one of these cigars. An American captain made me a present of them last night in Queenstown.*[2]

Stephen heard his father's voice break into a laugh which was almost a sob.

—He was the handsomest man in Cork at that time, by God he was! The women used to stand to look after him in the street.

He heard the sob passing loudly down his father's throat and opened his eyes with a nervous impulse. The sunlight breaking suddenly on his sight turned the sky and clouds into a fantastic world of sombre masses with lake-like spaces of dark rosy light. His very brain was sick and powerless. He could scarcely interpret the letters of the signboards of the shops. By his monstrous way of life he seemed to have put himself beyond the limits of reality. Nothing moved him or spoke to him from the real world unless he heard in it an echo of the infuriated cries within him. He could respond to no earthly or human appeal, dumb and insensible to the call of summer and gladness and companionship, wearied and dejected by his father's voice. He could scarcely recognise as his his own thoughts, and repeated slowly to himself:

—I am Stephen Dedalus. I am walking beside my father whose name is Simon Dedalus. We are in Cork, in Ireland. Cork is a city. Our room is in the Victoria Hotel. Victoria and Stephen and Simon. Simon and Stephen and Victoria. Names.

The memory of his childhood suddenly grew dim. He tried to call forth some of its vivid moments but could not. He recalled only names: Dante, Parnell, Clane, Clongowes. A little boy had been taught geography by an old woman who kept two brushes in her wardrobe. Then he had been sent away from home to a college. In the college he had made his first communion and eaten slim jim[3] out of his cricket cap and watched the firelight leaping and dancing on the wall of a little bedroom in the infirmary and dreamed of being dead, of mass being said for him by the rector in a black and gold cope, of being buried then in the little graveyard of the community off the main avenue of limes. But he had not died then. Parnell had died. There had been no mass for the dead in the chapel and no procession. He had not died but he had faded out like a film in the sun. He had been lost or had wandered out of existence for he no longer existed. How strange to think of him passing out of existence in such a way, not by death but by fading out in the sun or by being lost and forgotten somewhere in the universe! It was strange to see his small body appear again for a moment: a little boy in a grey belted suit. His hands were in his sidepockets and his trousers were tucked in at the knees by elastic bands.

On the evening of the day on which the property was sold Stephen followed his father meekly about the city from bar to bar. To the sellers in the market, to the barmen and barmaids, to the beggars who importuned him for a lob[4] Mr Dedalus told the same tale, that he was an old Corkonian, that he had been trying for thirty years to get rid of his Cork accent up in Dublin and that Peter Pickackafox beside him was his eldest son but that he was only a Dublin jackeen.[5]

They had set out early in the morning from Newcombe's coffeehouse where Mr Dedalus' cup had rattled noisily against its saucer and Stephen had

---

2. Port city southeast of Cork; now known as Cobh.
3. Candy made of long strips of marshallow
coated in powdered sugar.
4. Penny.
5. A brazen, lower-class person.

tried to cover that shameful sign of his father's drinkingbout of the night before by moving his chair and coughing. One humiliation had succeeded another: the false smiles of the market sellers, the curvettings and oglings[6] of the barmaids with whom his father flirted, the compliments and encouraging words of his father's friends. They had told him that he had a great look of his grandfather and Mr Dedalus had agreed that he was an ugly likeness. They had unearthed traces of a Cork accent in his speech and made him admit that the Lee was a much finer river than the Liffey.[7] One of them in order to put his Latin to the proof had made him translate short passages from Dilectus[8] and asked him whether it was correct to say: *Tempora mutantur nos et mutamur in illis* or *Tempora mutantur et nos mutamur in illis.*[9] Another, a brisk old man, whom Mr Dedalus called Johnny Cashman, had covered him with confusion by asking him to say which were prettier, the Dublin girls or the Cork girls.

—He's not that way built, said Mr Dedalus. Leave him alone. He's a levelheaded thinking boy who doesn't bother his head about that kind of nonsense.

—Then he's not his father's son, said the little old man.

—I don't know, I'm sure, said Mr Dedalus, smiling complacently.

—Your father, said the little old man to Stephen, was the boldest flirt in the city of Cork in his day. Do you know that?

Stephen looked down and studied the tiled floor of the bar into which they had drifted.

—Now don't be putting ideas into his head, said Mr Dedalus. Leave him to his Maker.

—Yerra, sure I wouldn't put any ideas into his head. I'm old enough to be his grandfather. And I am a grandfather, said the little old man to Stephen. Do you know that?

—Are you? asked Stephen.

—Bedad I am, said the little old man. I have two bouncing grandchildren out at Sunday's Well.[1] Now then! What age do you think I am? And I remember seeing your grandfather in his red coat riding out to hounds. That was before you were born.

—Ay, or thought of, said Mr Dedalus.

—Bedad I did! repeated the little old man. And, more than that, I can remember even your greatgrandfather, old John Stephen Dedalus, and a fierce old fireeater he was. Now then! There's a memory for you!

—That's three generations—four generations, said another of the company. Why, Johnny Cashman, you must be nearing the century.

—Well, I'll tell you the truth, said the little old man. I'm just twentyseven years of age.

—We're as old as we feel, Johnny, said Mr Dedalus. And just finish what you have there and we'll have another. Here, Tim or Tom or whatever your name is, give us the same again here. By God, I don't feel more than eighteen myself. There's that son of mine there not half my age and I'm a better man than he is any day of the week.

---

6. Amorous looks or stares. "Curvettings": flirtatious movements designed to attract attention.
7. The central river in Dublin; Lee is the central river in Cork.
8. A book of Latin quotations often used in schools.

9. The meaning of both quotations: circumstances change and we change with them or because of them.
1. Western suburb of Cork.

—Draw it mild[2] now, Dedalus. I think it's about time for you to take a back seat, said the gentleman who had spoken before.

—No, by God! asserted Mr Dedalus. I'll sing a tenor song against him or I'll vault a fivebarred gate[3] against him or I'll run with him after the hounds across the country as I did thirty years ago along with the Kerry Boy and the best man for it.

—But he'll beat you here, said the little old man, tapping his forehead and raising his glass to drain it.

—Well, I hope he'll be as good a man as his father. That's all I can say, said Mr Dedalus.

—If he is, he'll do, said the little old man.

—And thanks be to God, Johnny, said Mr Dedalus, that we lived so long and did so little harm.

—But did so much good, Simon, said the little old man gravely. Thanks be to God we lived so long and did so much good.

Stephen watched the three glasses being raised from the counter as his father and his two cronies drank to the memory of their past. An abyss of fortune or of temperament sundered him from them. His mind seemed older than theirs: it shone coldly on their strifes and happiness and regrets like a moon upon a younger earth. No life or youth stirred in him as it had stirred in them. He had known neither the pleasure of companionship with others nor the vigour of rude male health nor filial piety. Nothing stirred within his soul but a cold and cruel and loveless lust. His childhood was dead or lost and with it his soul capable of simple joys: and he was drifting amid life like the barren shell of the moon.

> Art thou pale for weariness
> Of climbing heaven and gazing on the earth
> Wandering companionless . . . . ?

He repeated to himself the lines of Shelley's fragment.[4] Its alternation of sad human ineffectiveness with vast inhuman cycles of activity chilled him: and he forgot his own human and ineffectual grieving.

◆ ◆ ◆

Stephen's mother and his brother and one of his cousins waited at the corner of quiet Foster Place[5] while he and his father went up the steps and along the colonnade where the highland sentry[6] was parading. When they had passed into the great hall and stood at the counter Stephen drew forth his orders on the governor of the bank of Ireland for thirty and three pounds; and these sums, the moneys of his exhibition[7] and essay prize, were paid over to him rapidly by the teller in notes and in coin respectively. He bestowed them in his pockets with feigned composure and suffered the friendly teller, to whom his father chatted, to take his hand across the broad counter and wish him a brilliant career in after life. He was impatient of their voices and could not keep his feet at rest. But the teller still deferred

2. Calm down.
3. According to Don Gifford, a gate at least 6 feet high and thus a formidable obstacle.
4. First lines of "To the Moon" by English Romantic poet Percy Bysshe Shelley (1792–1822).
5. Street in central Dublin near the Bank of Ireland.
6. A guard presumably from the Scottish Highlands.
7. Award for his performance on the annual national secondary school examinations.

the serving of others to say that he was living in changed times and that there was nothing like giving a boy the best education that money could buy. Mr Dedalus lingered in the hall gazing about him and up at the roof and telling Stephen, who urged him to come out, that they were standing in the house of commons of the old Irish parliament.[8]

—God help us! he said piously. To think of the men of those times, Stephen, Hely Hutchinson and Flood and Henry Grattan and Charles Kendal Bushe,[9] and the noblemen we have now, leaders of the Irish people at home and abroad. Why, by God, they wouldn't be seen dead in a ten acre field with them. No, Stephen, old chap, I'm sorry to say that they are only as I roved out one fine May morning in the merry month of sweet July.[1]

A keen October wind was blowing round the bank. The three figures standing at the edge of the muddy path had pinched cheeks and watery eyes. Stephen looked at his thinly clad mother and remembered that a few days before he had seen a mantle priced at twenty guineas in the window of Barnardo's.[2]

—Well, that's done, said Mr Dedalus.

—We had better go to dinner, said Stephen. Where?

—Dinner? said Mr Dedalus. Well, I suppose we had better, what?

—Some place that's not too dear, said Mrs Dedalus.

—Underdone's?[3]

—Yes. Some quiet place.

—Come along, said Stephen quickly. It doesn't matter about the dearness.

He walked on before them with short nervous steps, smiling. They tried to keep up with him, smiling also at his eagerness.

—Take it easy like a good young fellow, said his father. We're not out for the half mile, are we?

For a swift season of merrymaking the money of his prizes ran through Stephen's fingers. Great parcels of groceries and delicacies and dried fruits arrived from the city. Every day he drew up a bill of fare for the family and every night led a party of three or four to the theatre to see *Ingomar* or *The Lady of Lyons*.[4] In his coat pockets he carried squares of Vienna chocolate for his guests while his trousers' pockets bulged with masses of silver and copper coins. He bought presents for everyone, overhauled his room, wrote out resolutions, marshalled his books up and down their shelves, pored upon all kinds of price lists, drew up a form of commonwealth for the household by which every member of it held some office, opened a loan bank for his family and pressed loans on willing borrowers so that he might have the pleasure of making out receipts and reckoning the interests on the sums lent. When he could do no more he drove up and down the city in trams. Then the season of pleasure came to an end. The pot of pink enamel paint gave out and the wainscot of his bedroom remained with its unfinished and illplastered coat.

8. In the building of the Bank of Ireland, which had formerly housed the Irish Parliament, dissolved in the Act of Union (1800) with England.
9. Irish statesmen and orators: John Hely-Hutchinson (1724–1794), Henry Flood (1732–1791), Henry Grattan (1746–1820), and Charles Kendal Bushe (1767–1843).
1. Allusion to the opening lines of many Irish street ballads, which are usually fictional; the phrase is used by Mr. Dedalus to indicate that the leaders of the day should not be believed.
2. An expensive fur in the window of a shop on Grafton Street, in a fashionable shopping district.
3. Joking nickname for a restaurant.
4. Play (1838) by English novelist and playwright Edward Bulwer-Lytton (1803–1873). "Ingomar": *Ingomar the Barbarian* (1851), a play by English actress and playwright Maria Lovell (1803–1877).

His household returned to its usual way of life. His mother had no further occasion to upbraid him for squandering his money. He too returned to his old life at school and all his novel enterprises fell to pieces. The commonwealth fell, the loan bank closed its coffers and its books on a sensible[5] loss, the rules of life which he had drawn about himself fell into desuetude.

How foolish his aim had been! He had tried to build a breakwater of order and elegance against the sordid tide of life without him and to dam up, by rules of conduct and active interests and new filial relations, the powerful recurrence of the tides within him. Useless. From without as from within the waters had flowed over his barriers: their tides began once more to jostle fiercely above the crumbled mole.[6]

He saw clearly too his own futile isolation. He had not gone one step nearer the lives he had sought to approach nor bridged the restless shame and rancour that divided him from father and mother and brother and sister. He felt that he was hardly of the one blood with them but stood to them rather in the mystical kinship of fosterage, fosterchild and fosterbrother.

He burned to appease the fierce longings of his heart before which everything else was idle and alien. He cared little that he was in mortal sin,[7] that his life had grown to be a tissue of subterfuges and falsehood. Beside the savage desire within him to realise the enormities which he brooded on nothing was sacred. He bore cynically with the shameful details of his secret riots in which he exulted to defile with patience whatever image had attracted his eyes. By day and by night he moved among distorted images of the outer world. A figure that had seemed to him by day demure and innocent came towards him by night through the winding darkness of sleep, her face transfigured by a lecherous cunning, her eyes bright with brutish joy. Only the morning pained him with its dim memory of dark orgiastic riot, its keen and humiliating sense of transgression.

He returned to his wanderings. The veiled autumnal evenings led him from street to street as they had led him years before along the quiet avenues of Blackrock. But no vision of trim front gardens or of kindly lights in the windows poured a tender influence upon him now. Only at times, in the pauses of his desire, when the luxury that was wasting him gave room to a softer languor, the image of Mercedes traversed the background of his memory. He saw again the small white house and the garden of rosebushes on the road that led to the mountains and he remembered the sadly proud gesture of refusal which he was to make there, standing with her in the moonlit garden after years of estrangement and adventure. At those moments the soft speeches of Claude Melnotte[8] rose to his lips and eased his unrest. A tender premonition touched him of the tryst he had then looked forward to and, in spite of the horrible reality which lay between his hope of then and now, of the holy encounter he had then imagined at which weakness and timidity and inexperience were to fall from him.

Such moments passed and the wasting fires of lust sprang up again. The verses passed from his lips and the inarticulate cries and the unspoken brutal words rushed forth from his brain to force a passage. His blood was in revolt.

---

5. I.e., perceptible or significant.
6. Stone pier.
7. A sin so grave that it is not pardonable and

causes spiritual death, in this case the sin of lust.
8. Hero of *The Lady of Lyons*.

He wandered up and down the dark slimy streets peering into the gloom of lanes and doorways, listening eagerly for any sound. He moaned to himself like some baffled prowling beast. He wanted to sin with another of his kind, to force another being to sin with him and to exult with her in sin. He felt some dark presence moving irresistibly upon him from the darkness, a presence subtle and murmurous as a flood filling him wholly with itself. Its murmur besieged his ears like the murmur of some multitude in sleep; its subtle streams penetrated his being. His hands clenched convulsively and his teeth set together as he suffered the agony of its penetration. He stretched out his arms in the street to hold fast the frail swooning form that eluded him and incited him: and the cry that he had strangled for so long in his throat issued from his lips. It broke from him like a wail of despair from a hell of sufferers and died in a wail of furious entreaty, a cry for an iniquitous abandonment, a cry which was but the echo of an obscene scrawl which he had read on the oozing wall of a urinal.

He had wandered into a maze of narrow and dirty streets. From the foul laneways he heard bursts of hoarse riot and wrangling and the drawling of drunken singers. He walked onward, undismayed, wondering whether he had strayed into the quarter of the jews.[9] Women and girls dressed in long vivid gowns traversed the street from house to house. They were leisurely and perfumed. A trembling seized him and his eyes grew dim. The yellow gasflames arose before his troubled vision against the vapoury sky, burning as if before an altar. Before the doors and in the lighted halls groups were gathered, arrayed as for some rite. He was in another world: he had awakened from a slumber of centuries.

He stood still in the middle of the roadway, his heart clamouring against his bosom in a tumult. A young woman dressed in a long pink gown laid her hand on his arm to detain him and gazed into his face. She said gaily:

—Good night, Willie dear!

Her room was warm and lightsome. A huge doll[1] sat with her legs apart in the copious easychair beside the bed. He tried to bid his tongue speak that he might seem at ease, watching her as she undid her gown, noting the proud conscious movements of her perfumed head.

As he stood silent in the middle of the room she came over to him and embraced him gaily and gravely. Her round arms held him firmly to her and he, seeing her face lifted to him in serious calm and feeling the warm calm rise and fall of her breast, all but burst into hysterical weeping. Tears of joy and relief shone in his delighted eyes and his lips parted though they would not speak.

She passed her tinkling hand through his hair, calling him a little rascal.

—Give me a kiss, she said.

His lips would not bend to kiss her. He wanted to be held firmly in her arms, to be caressed slowly, slowly, slowly. In her arms he felt that he had suddenly become strong and fearless and sure of himself. But his lips would not bend to kiss her.

With a sudden movement she bowed his head and joined her lips to his and he read the meaning of her movements in her frank uplifted eyes. It was too much for him. He closed his eyes, surrendering himself to her, body and

---

9. Not the Jewish neighborhood of Dublin, but rather the red-light district.

1. A pretty woman, in this case a prostitute.

mind, conscious of nothing in the world but the dark pressure of her softly parting lips. They pressed upon his brain as upon his lips as though they were the vehicle of a vague speech; and between them he felt an unknown and timid pressure, darker than the swoon of sin, softer than sound or odour.

III

The swift December dusk had come tumbling clownishly after its dull day and as he stared through the dull square of the window of the schoolroom he felt his belly crave for its food. He hoped there would be stew for dinner, turnips and carrots and bruised potatoes and fat mutton pieces to be ladled out in thick peppered flourfattened sauce. Stuff it into you, his belly counselled him.

It would be a gloomy secret night. After early nightfall the yellow lamps would light up here and there the squalid quarter of the brothels. He would follow a devious course up and down the streets, circling always nearer and nearer in a tremor of fear and joy, until his feet led him suddenly round a dark corner. The whores would be just coming out of their houses making ready for the night, yawning lazily after their sleep and settling the hairpins in their clusters of hair. He would pass by them calmly waiting for a sudden movement of his own will or a sudden call to his sinloving soul from their soft perfumed flesh. Yet as he prowled in quest of that call his senses, stultified only by his desire, would note keenly all that wounded and shamed them, his eyes a ring of porter[2] froth on a clothless table or a photograph of two soldiers standing to attention or a gaudy playbill, his ears the drawling jargon of greeting:

—Hello, Bertie, any good in your mind?
—Is that you, pigeon?
—Number ten. Fresh Nelly is waiting on you.
—Good night, husband! Coming in to have a short time?

The equation on the page of his scribbler[3] began to spread out a widening tail, eyed and starred like a peacock's: and when the eyes and stars of its indices had been eliminated began slowly to fold itself together again. The indices appearing and disappearing were eyes opening and closing; the eyes opening and closing were stars being born and being quenched. The vast cycle of starry life bore his weary mind outward to its verge and inward to its centre, a distant music accompanying him outward and inward. What music? The music came nearer and he recalled the words, the words of Shelley's fragment upon the moon wandering companionless, pale for weariness. The stars began to crumble and a cloud of fine stardust fell through space.

The dull light fell more faintly upon the page whereon another equation began to unfold itself slowly and to spread abroad its widening tail. It was his own soul going forth to experience, unfolding itself sin by sin, spreading abroad the balefire[4] of its burning stars and folding back upon itself, fading slowly, quenching its own lights and fires. They were quenched: and the cold darkness filled chaos.

A cold lucid indifference reigned in his soul. At his first violent sin he had felt a wave of vitality pass out of him and had feared to find his body or his

2. A type of beer.
3. A notebook.

4. A large open-air fire.

soul maimed by the excess. Instead the vital wave had carried him on its bosom out of himself and back again when it receded: and no part of body or soul had been maimed but a dark peace had been established between them. The chaos in which his ardour extinguished itself was a cold indifferent knowledge of himself. He had sinned mortally not once but many times and he knew that, while he stood in danger of eternal damnation for the first sin alone, by every succeeding sin he multiplied his guilt and his punishment. His days and works and thoughts could make no atonement for him, the fountains of sanctifying grace having ceased to refresh his soul. At most by an alms given to a beggar, whose blessing he fled from, he might hope wearily to win for himself some measure of actual grace.[5] Devotion had gone by the board. What did it avail to pray when he knew that his soul lusted after its own destruction? A certain pride, a certain awe, withheld him from offering to God even one prayer at night though he knew it was in God's power to take away his life while he slept and hurl his soul hellward ere he could beg for mercy. His pride in his own sin, his loveless awe of God told him that his offence was too grievous to be atoned for in whole or in part by a false homage to the Allseeing and Allknowing.

—Well now, Ennis, I declare you have a head and so has my stick! Do you mean to say that you are not able to tell me what a surd[6] is?

The blundering answer stirred the embers of his contempt of his fellows. Towards others he felt neither shame nor fear. On Sunday mornings as he passed the churchdoor he glanced coldly at the worshippers who stood bareheaded, four deep, outside the church, morally present at the mass which they could neither see nor hear. Their dull piety and the sickly smell of the cheap hairoil with which they had anointed their heads repelled him from the altar they prayed at. He stooped to the evil of hypocrisy with others, sceptical of their innocence which he could cajole so easily.

On the wall of his bedroom hung an illuminated scroll, the certificate of his prefecture in the college of the sodality of the Blessed Virgin Mary.[7] On Saturday mornings when the sodality met in the chapel to recite the little office[8] his place was a cushioned kneelingdesk at the right of the altar from which he led his wing of boys through the responses. The falsehood of his position did not pain him. If at moments he felt an impulse to rise from his post of honour and, confessing before them all his unworthiness, to leave the chapel, a glance at their faces restrained him. The imagery of the psalms of prophecy soothed his barren pride. The glories of Mary held his soul captive: spikenard[9] and myrrh and frankincense, symbolising the preciousness of God's gifts to her soul, rich garments, symbolising her royal lineage, her emblems, the lateflowering plant and lateblossoming tree, symbolising the agelong gradual growth of her cultus[1] among men. When it fell to him to read the lesson towards the close of the office he read it in a veiled voice, lulling his conscience to its music:

> *Quasi cedrus exaltata sum in Libanon et quasi cupressus in monte Sion. Quasi palma exaltata sum in Cades et quasi plantatio rosae in*

5. Under Catholic doctrine, actual grace is granted by God for the performance of good deeds but disappears with the act; in contrast, sanctifying grace is the habitual grace of the soul but is lost because of mortal sin.
6. An irrational number.

7. Association of lay people that meets regularly for devotional purposes, in this case to honor the Virgin Mary.
8. Collection of biblical passages.
9. Northern Indian plant related to valerian.
1. Worship.

Jericho. Quasi uliva speciosa in campis et quasi platanus exaltata sum juxta aquam in plateis. Sicut cinnamomum et balsamum aromatizans odorem dedi et quasi myrrha electa dedi suavitatem odoris.[2]

His sin, which had covered him from the sight of God, had led him nearer to the refuge of sinners. Her eyes seemed to regard him with mild pity; her holiness, a strange light glowing faintly upon her frail flesh, did not humiliate the sinner who approached her. If ever he was impelled to cast sin from him and to repent the impulse that moved him was the wish to be her knight. If ever his soul, reentering her dwelling shyly after the frenzy of his body's lust had spent itself, was turned towards her whose emblem is the morning star, *bright and musical, telling of heaven and infusing peace,*[3] it was when her names were murmured softly by lips whereon there still lingered foul and shameful words, the savour itself of a lewd kiss.

That was strange. He tried to think how it could be but the dusk, deepening in the schoolroom, covered over his thought. The bell rang. The master marked the sums and cuts[4] to be done for the next lesson and went out. Heron, beside Stephen, began to hum tunelessly:

My excellent friend Bombados.[5]

Ennis, who had gone to the yard, came back, saying:
—The boy from the house is coming up for the rector.
A tall boy behind Stephen rubbed his hands and said:
—That's game ball.[6] We can scut the whole hour. He won't be in till after half two. Then you can ask him questions on the catechism,[7] Dedalus.

Stephen, leaning back and drawing idly on his scribbler, listened to the talk about him which Heron checked from time to time by saying:
—Shut up, will you. Don't make such a bally racket!

It was strange too that he found an arid pleasure in following up to the end the rigid lines of the doctrines of the church and penetrating into obscure silences only to hear and feel the more deeply his own condemnation. The sentence of saint James which says that he who offends against one commandment becomes guilty of all[8] had seemed to him first a swollen phrase until he had begun to grope in the darkness of his own state. From the evil seed of lust all other deadly sins[9] had sprung forth: pride in himself and contempt of others, covetousness in using money for the purchase of unlawful pleasure, envy of those whose vices he could not reach to and calumnious murmuring against the pious, gluttonous enjoyment of food, the dull glowering anger amid which he brooded upon his longing, the swamp of spiritual and bodily sloth in which his whole being had sunk.

As he sat in his bench gazing calmly at the rector's shrewd harsh face his mind wound itself in and out of the curious questions proposed to it. If a man had stolen a pound in his youth and had used that pound to amass a

2. I was exalted like a cedar of Lebanon and as a cypress tree on Mount Sion. I was exalted like a palm tree in Cades, and as a rose plant in Jericho. As a fair olive tree in the plains, and as a plane tree by the water in the streets was I exalted. I gave a sweet smell like cinnamon and aromatical balm: I yielded a sweet odor like the best myrrh (Latin, derived from Ecclesiasticus 24.17–20).
3. From "The Glories of Mary for the Sake of Her Son," in the *Discourses to Mixed Congregations* (1849), by Cardinal Newman.
4. Mathematics schoolwork, most likely geometry.
5. Line probably from a pantomime.
6. The final ball of a game, the deciding factor.
7. Treatise for religious instruction, written in the form of questions and answers.
8. Cf. James 2.10.
9. The seven deadly sins are lust, pride, covetousness, envy, gluttony, anger, and sloth.

huge fortune how much was he obliged to give back, the pound he had stolen only or the pound together with the compound interest accruing upon it or all his huge fortune? If a layman in giving baptism pour the water before saying the words is the child baptised? Is baptism with a mineral water valid? How comes it that while the first beatitude promises the kingdom of heaven to the poor of heart the second beatitude promises also to the meek that they shall possess the land?[1] Why was the sacrament of the eucharist[2] instituted under the two species of bread and wine if Jesus Christ be present body and blood, soul and divinity, in the bread alone and in the wine alone? Does a tiny particle of the consecrated bread contain all the body and blood of Jesus Christ or a part only of the body and blood? If the wine change into vinegar and the host crumble into corruption after they have been consecrated is Jesus Christ still present under their species as God and as man?

—Here he is! Here he is!

A boy from his post at the window had seen the rector come from the house. All the catechisms were opened and all heads bent upon them silently. The rector entered and took his seat on the dais.[3] A gentle kick from the tall boy in the bench behind urged Stephen to ask a difficult question.

The rector did not ask for a catechism to hear the lesson from. He clasped his hands on the desk and said:

—The retreat will begin on Wednesday afternoon in honour of saint Francis Xavier whose feast day is Saturday.[4] The retreat will go on from Wednesday to Friday. On Friday confessions will be heard all the afternoon after beads. If any boys have special confessors perhaps it will be better for them not to change. Mass will be on Saturday morning at nine o'clock and general communion for the whole college. Saturday will be a free day. Sunday of course. But Saturday and Sunday being free days some boys might be inclined to think that Monday is a free day also. Beware of making that mistake. I think you, Lawless, are likely to make that mistake.

—I, sir? Why, sir?

A little wave of quiet mirth broke forth over the class of boys from the rector's grim smile. Stephen's heart began slowly to fold and fade with fear like a withering flower.

The rector went on gravely:

—You are all familiar with the story of the life of saint Francis Xavier, I suppose, the patron of your college. He came of an old and illustrious Spanish family and you remember that he was one of the first followers of saint Ignatius. They met in Paris where Francis Xavier was professor of philosophy at the university. This young and brilliant nobleman and man of letters entered heart and soul into the ideas of our glorious founder and you know that he, at his own desire, was sent by saint Ignatius to preach to the Indians. He is called, as you know, the apostle of the Indies. He went from country to country in the east, from Africa to India, from India to Japan, baptising the people. He is said to have baptised as many as ten thousand idolaters in one month. It is said that his right arm had grown powerless from having been raised so often over the heads of those whom he baptised. He wished then to

---

1. Jesus began the Sermon on the Mount with the beatitudes, or declarations of blessings, including, "Blessed are the poor in spirit: for theirs is the kingdom of heaven. Blessed are the meek: for they shall possess the land" (Matthew 5.3–4).
2. The consecrated elements of Communion, in which the bread is believed to be Jesus Christ's body and the wine to be his blood.
3. Raised table or platform on which distinguished persons sit.
4. December 3, feast day of St. Francis Xavier (see p. 476).

go to China to win still more souls for God but he died of fever on the island of Sancian.[5] A great saint, saint Francis Xavier! A great soldier of God!

The rector paused and then, shaking his clasped hands before him, went on:

—He had the faith in him that moves mountains. Ten thousand souls won for God in a single month! That is a true conqueror, true to the motto of our order *ad majorem Dei gloriam*![6] A saint who has great power in heaven, remember: power to intercede for us in our grief, power to obtain whatever we pray for if it be for the good of our souls, power above all to obtain for us the grace to repent if we be in sin. A great saint, saint Francis Xavier! A great fisher of souls![7]

He ceased to shake his clasped hands and, resting them against his forehead, looked right and left of them keenly at his listeners out of his dark stern eyes.

In the silence their dark fire kindled the dusk into a tawny glow. Stephen's heart had withered up like a flower of the desert that feels the simoom[8] coming from afar.

◆ ◆ ◆

Remember only thy last things and thou shalt not sin for ever—words taken, my dear little brothers in Christ, from the book of Ecclesiastes, seventh chapter, fortieth verse.[9] In the name of the Father and of the Son and of the Holy Ghost. Amen.

Stephen sat in the front bench of the chapel. Father Arnall sat at a table to the left of the altar. He wore about his shoulders a heavy cloak; his pale face was drawn and his voice broken with rheum. The figure of his old master, so strangely rearisen, brought back to Stephen's mind his life at Clongowes: the wide playgrounds, swarming with boys, the square ditch, the little cemetery off the main avenue of limes where he had dreamed of being buried, the firelight on the wall of the infirmary where he lay sick, the sorrowful face of Brother Michael. His soul, as these memories came back to him, became again a child's soul.

—We are assembled here today, my dear little brothers in Christ, for one brief moment far away from the busy bustle of the outer world to celebrate and to honour one of the greatest of saints, the apostle of the Indies, the patron saint also of your college, saint Francis Xavier. Year after year for much longer than any of you, my dear little boys, can remember or than I can remember the boys of this college have met in this very chapel to make their annual retreat before the feast day of their patron saint. Time has gone on and brought with it its changes. Even in the last few years what changes can most of you not remember? Many of the boys who sat in those front benches a few short years ago are perhaps now in distant lands, in the burning tropics or immersed in professional duties or in seminaries or voyaging over the vast expanse of the deep or, it may be, already called by the great God to another life and to the rendering up of their stewardship. And still as the years roll by, bringing with them changes for good and bad, the memory of the great saint is honoured by the boys of his college who make every year

5. Shangchuan, an island off the Chinese coast.
6. See p. 476, n. 1.
7. Cf. Jesus's remark to his disciples, "Come, follow me, and I will make you fishers of men" (Matthew 4.19).
8. Hot, dry wind carrying sand.
9. From Ecclesiasticus 7.40, not Ecclesiastes.

their annual retreat on the days preceding the feast day set apart by our holy mother the church to transmit to all the ages the name and fame of one of the greatest sons of catholic Spain.

Now what is the meaning of this word *retreat* and why is it allowed on all hands to be a most salutary practice for all who desire to lead before God and in the eyes of men a truly christian life? A retreat, my dear boys, signifies a withdrawal for a while from the cares of our life, the cares of this workaday world, in order to examine the state of our conscience, to reflect on the mysteries of holy religion and to understand better why we are here in this world. During these few days I intend to put before you some thoughts concerning the four last things. They are, as you know from your catechism, death, judgment, hell and heaven. We shall try to understand them fully during these few days so that we may derive from the understanding of them a lasting benefit to our souls. And remember, my dear boys, that we have been sent into this world for one thing and for one thing alone: to do God's holy will and to save our immortal souls. All else is worthless. One thing alone is needful, the salvation of one's soul. What doth it profit a man to gain the whole world if he suffer the loss of his immortal soul?[1] Ah, my dear boys, believe me there is nothing in this wretched world that can make up for such a loss.

I will ask you therefore, my dear boys, to put away from your minds during these few days all worldly thoughts, whether of study or pleasure or ambition, and to give all your attention to the state of your souls. I need hardly remind you that during the days of the retreat all boys are expected to preserve a quiet and pious demeanour and to shun all loud unseemly pleasure. The elder boys, of course, will see that this custom is not infringed and I look especially to the prefects and officers of the sodality of Our Blessed Lady and of the sodality of the holy angels to set a good example to their fellowstudents.

Let us try therefore to make this retreat in honour of saint Francis with our whole heart and our whole mind. God's blessing will then be upon all your year's studies. But, above and beyond all, let this retreat be one to which you can look back in after years when maybe you are far from this college and among very different surroundings, to which you can look back with joy and thankfulness and give thanks to God for having granted you this occasion of laying the first foundation of a pious honourable zealous christian life. And if, as may so happen, there be at this moment in these benches any poor soul which has had the unutterable misfortune to lose God's holy grace and to fall into grievous sin I fervently trust and pray that this retreat may be the turningpoint in the life of that soul. I pray to God through the merits of His zealous servant Francis Xavier that such a soul may be led to sincere repentance and that the holy communion on saint Francis' day of this year may be a lasting covenant between God and that soul. For just and unjust, for saint and sinner alike, may this retreat be a memorable one.

Help me, my dear little brothers in Christ. Help me by your pious attention, by your own devotion, by your outward demeanour. Banish from your minds all worldly thoughts and think only of the last things, death, judgment, hell and heaven. He who remembers these things, says Ecclesiastes, shall not sin for ever. He who remembers the last things will act and think

---

1. Drawn from Matthew 16.26.

with them always before his eyes. He will live a good life and die a good death, believing and knowing that, if he has sacrificed much in this earthly life, it will be given to him a hundredfold and a thousandfold more in the life to come, in the kingdom without end—a blessing, my dear boys, which I wish you from my heart; one and all, in the name of the Father and of the Son and of the Holy Ghost. Amen.

As he walked home with silent companions a thick log seemed to compass his mind. He waited in stupor of mind till it should lift and reveal what it had hidden. He ate his dinner with surly appetite and, when the meal was over and the greasestrewn plates lay abandoned on the table, he rose and went to the window, clearing the thick scum from his mouth with his tongue and licking it from his lips. So he had sunk to the state of a beast that licks his chaps[2] after meat. This was the end: and a faint glimmer of fear began to pierce the fog of his mind. He pressed his face against the pane of the window and gazed out into the darkening street. Forms passed this way and that way through the dull light. And that was life. The letters of the name of Dublin lay heavily upon his mind, pushing one another surlily hither and thither with slow boorish insistence. His soul was fattening and congealing into a gross grease, plunging ever deeper in its dull fear into a sombre threatening dusk, while the body that was his stood, listless and dishonoured, gazing out of darkened eyes, helpless, perturbed and human for a bovine god to stare upon.

The next day brought death and judgment, stirring his soul slowly from its listless despair. The faint glimmer of fear became a terror of spirit as the hoarse voice of the preacher blew death into his soul. He suffered its agony. He felt the deathchill touch the extremities and creep onward towards the heart, the film of death veiling the eyes, the bright centres of the brain extinguished one by one like lamps, the last sweat oozing upon the skin, the powerlessness of the dying limbs, the speech thickening and wandering and failing, the heart throbbing faintly and more faintly, all but vanquished, the breath, the poor timid breath, the poor helpless human spirit, sobbing and sighing, gurgling and rattling in the throat. No help! No help! He, he himself, his body to which he had yielded was dying. Into the grave with it! Nail it down into a wooden box, the corpse. Carry it out of the house on the shoulders of hirelings. Thrust it out of men's sight into a long hole in the ground, into the grave, to rot, to feed the mass of its creeping worms and to be devoured by scuttling plumpbellied rats.

And while the friends were still standing in tears by the bedside the soul of the sinner was judged. At the last moment of consciousness the whole earthly life passed before the vision of the soul and, ere it had time to reflect, the body had died and the soul stood terrified before the judgment-seat. God, who had long been merciful, would then be just. He had long been patient, pleading with the sinful soul, giving it time to repent, sparing it yet awhile. But that time had gone. Time was to sin and to enjoy, time was to scoff at God and at the warnings of His holy church, time was to defy His majesty, to disobey His commands, to hoodwink one's fellow men, to commit sin after sin and sin after sin and to hide one's corruption from the sight of men. But that time was over. Now it was God's turn: and He was not to be hoodwinked or deceived. Every sin would then come forth from its

2. Chops.

lurkingplace, the most rebellious against the divine will and the most degrading to our poor corrupt nature, the tiniest imperfection and the most heinous atrocity. What did it avail then to have been a great emperor, a great general, a marvellous inventor, the most learned of the learned? All were as one before the judgmentseat of God. He would reward the good and punish the wicked. One single instant was enough for the trial of a man's soul. One single instant after the body's death, the soul had been weighed in the balance. The particular judgment was over and the soul had passed to the abode of bliss or to the prison of purgatory or had been hurled howling into hell.

Nor was that all. God's justice had still to be vindicated before men: after the particular there still remained the general judgment. The last day had come. The doomsday[3] was at hand. The stars of heaven were falling upon the earth like the figs cast by the figtree which the wind has shaken. The sun, the great luminary of the universe, had become as sackcloth of hair. The moon was bloodred. The firmament was as a scroll rolled away. The archangel Michael,[4] the prince of the heavenly host, appeared glorious and terrible against the sky. With one foot on the sea and one foot on the land he blew from the archangelical trumpet the brazen death of time. The three blasts of the angel filled all the universe. Time is, time was but time shall be no more. At the last blast the souls of universal humanity throng towards the valley of Jehoshaphat,[5] rich and poor, gentle and simple, wise and foolish, good and wicked. The soul of every human being that has ever existed, the souls of all those who shall yet be born, all the sons and daughters of Adam, all are assembled on that supreme day. And lo the supreme judge is coming! No longer the lowly Lamb of God, no longer the meek Jesus of Nazareth, no longer the Man of Sorrows, no longer the Good Shepherd, He is seen now coming upon the clouds, in great power and majesty, attended by nine choirs of angels, angels and archangels, principalities, powers and virtues, thrones and dominations, cherubim and seraphim,[6] God Omnipotent, God Everlasting. He speaks: and His voice is heard even at the farthest limits of space, even in the bottomless abyss. Supreme Judge, from His sentence there will be and can be no appeal. He calls the just to His side bidding them enter into the kingdom, the eternity of bliss prepared for them. The unjust He casts from Him, crying in His offended majesty: *Depart from me, ye cursed, into everlasting fire which was prepared for the devil and his angels.*[7] O what agony then for the miserable sinners! Friend is torn apart from friend, children from their parents, husbands from their wives. The poor sinner holds out his arms to those who were dear and near to him in this earthly world, to those whose simple piety perhaps he made a mock of, to those who counselled him and tried to lead him on the right path, to a kind brother, to a loving sister, to the mother and father who loved him so dearly. But it is too late: the just turn away from the wretched damned souls which now appear before the eyes of all in their hideous and evil character. O you hypocrites, O you whited sepulchres, O you who present a smooth smiling face to the world

---

3. Time also known as the last day and the day of judgment, the end of the world as humans understand it, on which God will judge all the living and the resurrected dead.
4. Chief angel, usually represented in a militant pose. Cf. Revelation 10.1–6, which suggests his stance in the sentence that follows.

5. Valley east of Jerusalem, mentioned in Joel 3.2 as the place where judgment will occur.
6. List of the hierarchy of the nine choirs (or groups) of angels, in ascending order, although thrones and dominations are reversed.
7. From Matthew 25.41.

while your soul within is a foul swamp of sin, how will it fare with you in that terrible day?

And this day will come, shall come, must come: the day of death and the day of judgment. It is appointed unto man to die and after death the judgment. Death is certain. The time and manner are uncertain, whether from long disease or from some unexpected accident: the Son of God cometh at an hour when you little expect Him. Be therefore ready every moment, seeing that you may die at any moment. Death is the end of us all. Death and judgment, brought into the world by the sin of our first parents, are the dark portals that close our earthly existence, the portals that open into the unknown and the unseen, portals through which every soul must pass, alone, unaided save by its good works, without friend or brother or parents or master to help it, alone and trembling. Let that thought be ever before our minds and then we cannot sin. Death, a cause of terror to the sinner, is a blessed moment for him who has walked in the right path, fulfilling the duties of his station[8] in life, attending to his morning and evening prayers, approaching the holy sacrament frequently and performing good and merciful works. For the pious and believing catholic, for the just man, death is no cause of terror. Was it not Addison,[9] the great English writer, who, when on his deathbed, sent for the wicked young earl of Warwick[1] to let him see how a christian can meet his end? He it is and he alone, the pious and believing christian, who can say in his heart:

> O grave, where is thy victory?
> O death, where is thy sting?[2]

Every word of it was for him. Against his sin, foul and secret, the whole wrath of God was aimed. The preacher's knife had probed deeply into his diseased conscience and he felt now that his soul was festering in sin. Yes, the preacher was right. God's turn had come. Like a beast in its lair his soul had lain down in its own filth but the blasts of the angel's trumpet had driven him forth from the darkness of sin into the light. The words of doom cried by the angel shattered in an instant his presumptuous peace. The wind of the last day blew through his mind; his sins, the jeweleyed harlots of his imagination, fled before the hurricane, squeaking like mice in their terror and huddled under a mane of hair.

As he crossed the square, walking homeward, the light laughter of a girl reached his burning ears. The frail gay sound smote his heart more strongly than a trumpetblast, and, not daring to lift his eyes, he turned aside and gazed, as he walked, into the shadow of the tangled shrubs. Shame rose from his smitten heart and flooded his whole being. The image of Emma appeared before him and, under her eyes, the flood of shame rushed forth anew from his heart. If she knew to what his mind had subjected her or how his brutelike lust had torn and trampled upon her innocence! Was that boyish love? Was that chivalry? Was that poetry? The sordid details of his orgies stank under his very nostrils: the sootcoated packet of pictures which he had hidden in the flue of the fireplace and in the presence of whose shameless or

8. Position.
9. Joseph Addison, English writer and politician (1672–1719), who served as chief secretary for Ireland under English rule.
1. Addison's stepson, according to English writer

Samuel Johnson's *Lives of the English Poets* (1779–1781).
2. "The Dying Christian to His Soul" (lines 17–18), by English poet Alexander Pope (1688–1744). Cf. 1 Corinthians 15.55.

bashful wantonness he lay for hours sinning in thought and deed: his monstrous dreams, peopled by apelike creatures and by harlots with gleaming jewel eyes: the foul long letters he had written in the joy of guilty confession and carried secretly for days and days only to throw them under cover of night among the grass in the corner of a field or beneath some hingeless door or in some niche in the hedges where a girl might come upon them as she walked by and read them secretly. Mad! Mad! Was it possible he had done these things? A cold sweat broke out upon his forehead as the foul memories condensed within his brain.

When the agony of shame had passed from him he tried to raise his soul from its abject powerlessness. God and the Blessed Virgin were too far from him: God was too great and stern and the Blessed Virgin too pure and holy. But he imagined that he stood near Emma in a wide land and, humbly and in tears, bent and kissed the elbow of her sleeve.

In a wide land under a tender lucid evening sky, a cloud drifting westward amid a pale green sea of heaven, they stood together; children that had erred. Their error had offended deeply God's majesty, though it was the error of two children, but it had not offended her whose beauty *is not like earthly beauty, dangerous to look upon, but like the morning star which is its emblem, bright and musical.*[3] The eyes were not offended which she turned upon them nor reproachful. She placed their hands together, hand in hand, and said, speaking to their hearts:

—Take hands, Stephen and Emma. It is a beautiful evening now in heaven. You have erred but you are always my children. It is one heart that loves another heart. Take hands together, my dear children, and you will be happy together and your hearts will love each other.

The chapel was flooded by the dull scarlet light that filtered through the lowered blinds: and through the fissure between the last blind and the sash a shaft of wan light entered like a spear and touched the embossed brasses of the candlesticks upon the altar that gleamed like the battleworn mail armour of angels.

Rain was falling on the chapel, on the garden, on the college. It would rain for ever, noiselessly. The water would rise inch by inch, covering the grass and shrubs, covering the trees and houses, covering the monuments and the mountain tops. All life would be choked off, noiselessly: birds, men, elephants, pigs, children: noiselessly floating corpses amid the litter of the wreckage of the world. Forty days and forty nights the rain would fall till the waters covered the face of the earth.[4]

It might be. Why not?

—*Hell has enlarged its soul and opened its mouth without any limits*—words taken, my dear little brothers in Christ Jesus, from the book of Isaias, fifth chapter, fourteenth verse.[5] In the name of the Father and of the Son and of the Holy Ghost. Amen.

The preacher took a chainless watch from a pocket within his soutane and, having considered its dial for a moment in silence, placed it silently before him on the table.

He began to speak in a quiet tone.

3. Partly quoted already; see p. 507, n. 3.
4. Allusion to the biblical flood. Cf. Genesis 6–8.
5. Also spelled Isaiah (5.14), quoted here.

—Adam and Eve, my dear boys, were, as you know, our first parents and you will remember that they were created by God in order that the seats in heaven left vacant by the fall of Lucifer and his rebellious angels might be filled again. Lucifer,[6] we are told, was a son of the morning, a radiant and mighty angel; yet he fell: he fell and there fell with him a third part of the host of heaven: he fell and was hurled with his rebellious angels into hell. What his sin was we cannot say. Theologians consider that it was the sin of pride, the sinful thought conceived in an instant: *non serviam: I will not serve.*[7] That instant was his ruin. He offended the majesty of God by the sinful thought of one instant and God cast him out of heaven into hell for ever.

Adam and Eve were then created, by God and placed in Eden, that lovely garden in the plain of Damascus resplendent with sunlight and colour, teeming with luxuriant vegetation. The fruitful earth gave them her bounty: beasts and birds were their willing servants: they knew not the ills our flesh is heir to, disease and poverty and death: all that a great and generous God could do for them was done. But there was one condition imposed on them by God: obedience to His word. They were not to eat of the fruit of the forbidden tree.

Alas, my dear little boys, they too fell. The devil, once a shining angel, a son of the morning, now a foul fiend came to them in the shape of a serpent, the subtlest of all the beasts of the field. He envied them. He, the fallen great one, could not bear to think that man, a being of clay, should possess the inheritance which he by his sin had forfeited for ever. He came to the woman, the weaker vessel, and poured the poison of his eloquence into her ear, promising her (O, the blasphemy of that promise!) that if she and Adam ate of the forbidden fruit they would become as gods, nay as God Himself. Eve yielded to the wiles of the archtempter. She ate the apple and gave it also to Adam who had not the moral courage to resist her. The poison tongue of Satan had done its work. They fell.

And then the voice of God was heard in that garden, calling His creature man to account: and Michael, prince of the heavenly host, with a sword of flame in his hand appeared before the guilty pair and drove them forth from Eden into the world, the world of sickness and striving, of cruelty and disappointment, of labour and hardship, to earn their bread in the sweat of their brow. But even then how merciful was God! He took pity on our poor degraded first parents and promised that in the fulness of time He would send down from heaven One who would redeem them, make them once more children of God and heirs to the kingdom of heaven: and that One, that Redeemer of fallen man, was to be God's onlybegotten Son, the Second Person of the Most Blessed Trinity, the Eternal Word.

He came. He was born of a virgin pure, Mary the virgin mother. He was born in a poor cowhouse in Judea and lived as a humble carpenter for thirty years until the hour of His mission had come. And then, filled with love for men, He went forth and called to men to hear the new gospel.

Did they listen? Yes, they listened but would not hear. He was seized and bound like a common criminal, mocked at as a fool, set aside to give place to a public robber, scourged with five thousand lashes, crowned with a crown of thorns, hustled through the streets by the jewish rabble and the Roman

6. Rebel archangel who fell from heaven, thus   7. Cf. Jeremiah 2.20.
becoming Satan. Cf. Isaiah 14.12.

soldiery, stripped of His garments and hanged upon a gibbet and His side was pierced with a lance and from the wounded body of Our Lord water and blood issued continually.

Yet even then, in that hour of supreme agony, Our Merciful Redeemer had pity for mankind. Yet even there, on the hill of Calvary, He founded the holy catholic church against which, it is promised, the gates of hell shall not prevail. He founded it upon the rock of ages and endowed it with His grace, with sacraments and sacrifice, and promised that if men would obey the word of His church they would still enter into eternal life but if, after all that had been done for them, they still persisted in their wickedness there remained for them an eternity of torment: hell.

The preacher's voice sank. He paused, joined his palms for an instant, parted them. Then he resumed:

—Now let us try for a moment to realise, as far as we can, the nature of that abode of the damned which the justice of an offended God has called into existence for the eternal punishment of sinners. Hell is a strait[8] and dark and foulsmelling prison, an abode of demons and lost souls, filled with fire and smoke. The straitness of this prison house is expressly designed by God to punish those who refused to be bound by His laws. In earthly prisons the poor captive has at least some liberty of movement, were it only within the four walls of his cell or in the gloomy yard of his prison. Not so in hell. There, by reason of the great number of the damned, the prisoners are heaped together in their awful prison the walls of which are said to be four thousand miles thick: and the damned are so utterly bound and helpless that, as a blessed saint, saint Anselm, writes in his book on similitudes,[9] they are not even able to remove from the eye a worm that gnaws it.

They lie in exterior darkness. For, remember, the fire of hell gives forth no light. As, at the command of God, the fire of the Babylonian furnace[1] lost its heat but not its light so, at the command of God, the fire of hell, while retaining the intensity of its heat, burns eternally in darkness, it is a neverending storm of darkness, dark flames and dark smoke of burning brimstone,[2] amid which the bodies are heaped one upon another without even a glimpse of air. Of all the plagues with which the land of the Pharaohs was smitten one plague alone, that of darkness, was called horrible.[3] What name, then, shall we give to the darkness of hell which is to last not for three days alone but for all eternity?

The horror of this strait and dark prison is increased by its awful stench. All the filth of the world, all the offal and scum of the world, we are told, shall run there as to a vast reeking sewer when the terrible conflagration of the last day has purged the world. The brimstone too which burns there in such prodigious quantity fills all hell with its intolerable stench: and the bodies of the damned themselves exhale such a pestilential odour that, as saint Bonaventure[4] says, one of them alone would suffice to infect the whole world. The very air of this world, that pure element, becomes foul and unbreathable when it has been long enclosed. Consider then what must be the foulness of the air of hell. Imagine some foul and putrid corpse that has lain rotting and

8. Narrow.
9. Saint Anselm of Canterbury (1033–1099) wrote theological treatises, but not one on similitudes, or allegories.
1. Cf. Daniel 3.19–27.

2. Sulfur.
3. Ten instances of divine punishment of the Egyptians recounted in Exodus 7–12.
4. Franciscan monk and writer (ca. 1221–1274).

decomposing in the grave, a jellylike mass of liquid corruption. Imagine such a corpse a prey to flames, devoured by the fire of burning brimstone and giving off dense choking fumes of nauseous loathsome decomposition. And then imagine this sickening stench, multiplied a millionfold and a millionfold again from the millions upon millions of fetid carcases massed together in the reeking darkness, a huge and rotting human fungus. Imagine all this and you will have some idea of the horror of the stench of hell.

But this stench is not, horrible though it is, the greatest physical torment to which the damned are subjected. The torment of fire is the greatest torment to which the tyrant has ever subjected his fellowcreatures. Place your finger for a moment in the flame of a candle and you will feel the pain of fire. But our earthly fire was created by God for the benefit of man, to maintain in him the spark of life and to help him in the useful arts whereas the fire of hell is of another quality and was created by God to torture and punish the unrepentant sinner. Our earthly fire also consumes more or less rapidly according as the object which it attacks is more or less combustible so that human ingenuity has even succeeded in inventing chemical preparations to check or frustrate its action. But the sulphureous brimstone which burns in hell is a substance which is specially designed to burn for ever and for ever with unspeakable fury. Moreover our earthly fire destroys at the same time as it burns so that the more intense it is the shorter is its duration: but the fire of hell has this property that it preserves that which it burns and though it rages with incredible intensity it rages for ever.

Our earthly fire again, no matter how fierce or widespread it may be, is always of a limited extent: but the lake of fire in hell is boundless, shoreless and bottomless. It is on record that the devil himself, when asked the question by a certain soldier, was obliged to confess that if a whole mountain were thrown into the burning ocean of hell it would be burned up in an instant like a piece of wax. And this terrible fire will not afflict the bodies of the damned only from without but each lost soul will be a hell unto itself, the boundless fire raging in its very vitals. O, how terrible is the lot of those wretched beings! The blood seethes and boils in the veins, the brains are boiling in the skull, the heart in the breast glowing and bursting, the bowels a redhot mass of burning pulp, the tender eyes flaming like molten balls.

And yet what I have said as to the strength and quality and boundlessness of this fire is as nothing when compared to its intensity, an intensity which it has as being the instrument chosen by divine design for the punishment of soul and body alike. It is a fire which proceeds directly from the ire of God, working not of its own activity but as an instrument of divine vengeance. As the waters of baptism cleanse the soul with the body so do the fires of punishment torture the spirit with the flesh. Every sense of the flesh is tortured and every faculty of the soul therewith: the eyes with impenetrable utter darkness, the nose with noisome odours, the ears with yells and howls and execrations,[5] the taste with foul matter, leprous corruption, nameless suffocating filth, the touch with redhot goads and spikes, with cruel tongues of flame. And through the several torments of the senses the immortal soul is tortured eternally in its very essence amid the leagues upon leagues of glowing fires kindled in the abyss by the offended majesty of the Omnipotent God and fanned into

5. Curses.

everlasting and ever increasing fury by the breath of the anger of the Godhead.

Consider finally that the torment of this infernal prison is increased by the company of the damned themselves. Evil company on earth is so noxious that even the plants, as if by instinct, withdraw from the company of whatsoever is deadly or hurtful to them. In hell all laws are overturned: there is no thought of family or country, of ties or relationship. The damned howl and scream at one another, their torture and rage intensified by the presence of beings tortured and raging like themselves. All sense of humanity is forgotten. The yells of the suffering sinners fill the remotest corners of the vast abyss. The mouths of the damned are full of blasphemies against God and of hatred for their fellow sufferers and of curses against those souls which were their accomplices in sin. In olden times it was the custom to punish the parricide, the man who had raised his murderous hand against his father, by casting him into the depths of the sea in a sack in which were placed a cock, a monkey and a serpent. The intention of those lawgivers who framed such a law, which seems cruel in our times, was to punish the criminal by the company of hateful and hurtful beasts. But what is the fury of those dumb beasts compared with the fury of execration which bursts from the parched lips and aching throats of the damned in hell when they behold in their companions in misery those who aided and abetted them in sin, those whose words sowed the first seeds of evil thinking and evil living in their minds, those whose immodest suggestions led them on to sin, those whose eyes tempted and allured them from the path of virtue. They turn upon those accomplices and upbraid them and curse them. But they are helpless and hopeless: it is too late now for repentance.

Last of all consider the frightful torment to those damned souls, tempters and tempted alike, of the company of the devils. These devils will afflict the damned in two ways, by their presence and by their reproaches. We can have no idea of how horrible these devils are. Saint Catherine of Siena[6] once saw a devil and she has written that, rather than look again for one single instant on such a frightful monster, she would prefer to walk until the end of her life along a track of red coals. These devils, who were once beautiful angels, have become as hideous and ugly as they once were beautiful. They mock and jeer at the lost souls whom they dragged down to ruin. It is they, the foul demons, who are made in hell the voices of conscience. Why did you sin? Why did you lend an ear to the temptings of fiends? Why did you turn aside from your pious practices and good works? Why did you not shun the occasions of sin? Why did you not leave that evil companion? Why did you not give up that lewd habit, that impure habit? Why did you not listen to the counsels of your confessor? Why did you not, even after you had fallen the first or the second or the third or the fourth or the hundredth time, repent of your evil ways and turn to God who only waited for your repentance to absolve you of your sins? Now the time for repentance has gone by. Time is, time was but time shall be no more! Time was to sin in secrecy, to indulge in that sloth and pride, to covet the unlawful, to yield to the promptings of your lower nature, to live like the beasts of the field, nay worse than the beasts of the field for they, at least, are but brutes and have not reason to guide them: time was but time shall be no more. God spoke to you by so

6. Christian saint and mystic (1347–1380).

many voices but you would not hear. You would not crush out that pride and anger in your heart, you would not restore those illgotten goods, you would not obey the precepts of your holy church nor attend to your religious duties, you would not abandon those wicked companions, you would not avoid those dangerous temptations. Such is the language of those fiendish tormentors, words of taunting and of reproach, of hatred and of disgust. Of disgust, yes! For even they, the very devils, when they sinned sinned by such a sin as alone was compatible with such angelical natures, a rebellion of the intellect: and they, even they, the foul devils must turn away, revolted and disgusted, from the contemplation of those unspeakable sins by which degraded man outrages and defiles the temple of the Holy Ghost, defiles and pollutes himself.[7]

O, my dear little brothers in Christ, may it never be our lot to hear that language! May it never be our lot, I say! In the last day of terrible reckoning I pray fervently to God that not a single soul of those who are in this chapel today may be found among those miserable beings whom the Great Judge shall command to depart for ever from His sight, that not one of us may ever hear ringing in his ears the awful sentence of rejection: *Depart from me, ye cursed, into everlasting fire which was prepared for the devil and his angels!*

He came down the aisle of the chapel, his legs shaking and the scalp of his head trembling as though it had been touched by ghostly fingers. He passed up the staircase and into the corridor along the walls of which the overcoats and waterproofs[8] hung like gibbeted malefactors,[9] headless and dripping and shapeless. And at every step he feared that he had already died, that his soul had been wrenched forth of the sheath of his body, that he was plunging headlong through space.

He could not grip the floor with his feet and sat heavily at his desk, opening one of his books at random and poring over it. Every word for him! It was true. God was almighty. God could call him now, call him as he sat at his desk, before he had time to be conscious of the summons. God had called him. Yes? What? Yes? His flesh shrank together as it felt the approach of the ravenous tongues of flames, dried up as it felt about it the swirl of stifling air. He had died. Yes. He was judged. A wave of fire swept through his body: the first. Again a wave. His brain began to glow. Another. His brain was simmering and bubbling within the cracking tenement of the skull. Flames burst forth from his skull like a corolla,[1] shrieking like voices:

—Hell! Hell! Hell! Hell! Hell!

Voices spoke near him:

—On hell.

—I suppose he rubbed it into you well.

—You bet he did. He put us all into a blue funk.[2]

—That's what you fellows want; and plenty of it to make you work.

He leaned back weakly in his desk. He had not died. God had spared him still. He was still in the familiar world of the school. Mr Tate and Vincent Heron stood at the window, talking, jesting, gazing out at the bleak rain, moving their heads.

—I wish it would clear up. I had arranged to go for a spin on the bike with some fellows out by Malahide.[3] But the roads must be kneedeep.

---

7. Cf. 1 Corinthians 6.18–19, in which the body is referred to as the temple of the Holy Spirit.
8. Garments made waterproof, usually by treatment with rubber; raincoats.
9. Hanged evildoers.
1. Crown.
2. Deep dread.
3. Village north of Dublin.

—It might clear up, sir.

The voices that he knew so well, the common words, the quiet of the classroom when the voices paused and the silence was filled by the sound of softly browsing cattle as the other boys munched their lunches tranquilly, lulled his aching soul.

There was still time. O Mary, refuge of sinners, intercede for him! O Virgin Undefiled, save him from the gulf of death!

The English lesson began with the hearing of the history. Royal persons, favourites, intriguers, bishops passed like mute phantoms behind their veil of names. All had died: all had been judged. What did it profit a man to gain the whole world if he lost his soul? At last he had understood: and human life lay around him, a plain of peace whereon antlike men laboured in brotherhood, their dead sleeping under quiet mounds. The elbow of his companion touched him and his heart was touched: and when he spoke to answer a question of his master he heard his own voice full of the quietude of humility and contrition.

His soul sank back deeper into depths of contrite peace, no longer able to suffer the pain of dread and sending forth, as she sank, a faint prayer. Ah yes, he would still be spared; he would repent in his heart and be forgiven: and then those above, those in heaven, would see what he would do to make up for the past: a whole life, every hour of life. Only wait.

—All, God! All, all!

A messenger came to the door to say that confessions were being heard in the chapel. Four boys left the room; and he heard others passing down the corridor. A tremulous chill blew round his heart, no stronger than a little wind, and yet, listening and suffering silently, he seemed to have laid an ear against the muscle of his own heart, feeling it close and quail, listening to the flutter of its ventricles.

No escape. He had to confess, to speak out in words what he had done and thought, sin after sin. How? How?

—Father, I . . .

The thought slid like a cold shining rapier into his tender flesh: confession. But not there in the chapel of the college. He would confess all, every sin of deed and thought, sincerely: but not there among his school companions. Far away from there in some dark place he would murmur out his own shame: and he besought God humbly not to be offended with him if he did not dare to confess in the college chapel: and in utter abjection of spirit he craved forgiveness mutely of the boyish hearts about him.

Time passed.

He sat again in the front bench of the chapel. The daylight without was already failing and, as it fell slowly through the dull red blinds, it seemed that the sun of the last day was going down and that all souls were being gathered for the judgment.—*I am cast away from the sight of Thine eyes:* words taken, my dear little brothers in Christ, from the Book of Psalms, thirtieth chapter, twentythird verse.[4] In the name of the Father and of the Son and of the Holy Ghost. Amen.

The preacher began to speak in a quiet friendly tone. His face was kind and he joined gently the fingers of each hand, forming a frail cage by the union of their tips.

---

4. Cf. Psalms 31.22 in the King James Bible.

—This morning we endeavoured, in our reflection upon hell, to make what our holy founder calls in his book of spiritual exercises, the composition of place.[5] We endeavoured, that is, to imagine with the senses of the mind, in our imagination, the material character of that awful place and of the physical torments which all who are in hell endure. This evening we shall consider for a few moments the nature of the spiritual torments of hell.

Sin, remember, is a twofold enormity. It is a base consent to the promptings of our corrupt nature, to the lower instincts, to that which is gross and beastlike; and it is also a turning away from the counsel of our higher nature, from all that is pure and holy, from the Holy God Himself. For this reason mortal sin is punished in hell by two different forms of punishment, physical and spiritual.

Now of all these spiritual pains by far the greatest is the pain of loss, so great, in fact, that in itself it is a torment greater than all the others. Saint Thomas,[6] the greatest doctor of the church, the angelic doctor, as he is called, says that the worst damnation consists in this that the understanding of man is totally deprived of divine light and his affection obstinately turned away from the goodness of God. God, remember, is a being infinitely good and therefore the loss of such a being must be a loss infinitely painful. In this life we have not a very clear idea of what such a loss must be but the damned in hell, for their greater torment, have a full understanding of that which they have lost and understand that they have lost it through their own sins and have lost it for ever. At the very instant of death the bonds of the flesh are broken asunder and the soul at once flies towards God. The soul tends towards God as towards the center of her existence. Remember, my dear little boys, our souls long to be with God. We come from God, we live by God, we belong to God: we are His, inalienably His. God loves with a divine love every human soul and every human soul lives in that love. How could it be otherwise? Every breath that we draw, every thought of our brain, every instant of life proceed from God's inexhaustible goodness. And if it be pain for a mother to be parted from her child, for a man to be exiled from hearth and home, for friend to be sundered from friend, O think what pain, what anguish it must be for the poor soul to be spurned from the presence of the supremely good and loving Creator Who has called that soul into existence from nothingness and sustained it in life and loved it with an immeasurable love. This, then, to be separated for ever from its greatest good, from God, and to feel the anguish of that separation, knowing full well that it is unchangeable, this is the greatest torment which the created soul is capable of bearing, *poena damni*, the pain of loss.[7]

The second pain which will afflict the souls of the damned in hell is the pain of conscience. Just as in dead bodies worms are engendered by putrefaction so in the souls of the lost there arises a perpetual remorse from the putrefaction of sin, the sting of conscience, the worm, as Pope Innocent the Third[8] calls it, of the triple sting. The first sting inflicted by this cruel worm will be the memory of past pleasures. O what a dreadful memory will that be! In the lake of alldevouring flame the proud king will remember the

---

5. Cf. *The Spiritual Exercises* (1548), by St. Ignatius of Loyola, in which he recommends meditating on a physical object.
6. St. Thomas Aquinas (ca. 1224–1274), whose

writings are central to Catholic thought.
7. Translation of the preceding Latin phrase for the punishment of the damned.
8. Pope from 1198 to 1216.

pomps of his court, the wise but wicked man his libraries and instruments of research, the lover of artistic pleasures his marbles and pictures and other art treasures, he who delighted in the pleasures of the table his gorgeous feasts, his dishes prepared with such delicacy, his choice wines; the miser will remember his hoard of gold, the robber his illgotten wealth, the angry and revengeful and merciless murderers their deeds of blood and violence in which they revelled, the impure and adulterous the unspeakable and filthy pleasures in which they delighted. They will remember all this and loathe themselves and their sins. For how miserable will all those pleasures seem to the soul condemned to suffer in hellfire for ages and ages. How they will rage and fume to think that they have lost the bliss of heaven for the dross of earth, for a few pieces of metal, for vain honours, for bodily comforts, for a tingling of the nerves. They will repent indeed: and this is the second sting of the worm of conscience, a late and fruitless sorrow for sins committed. Divine justice insists that the understanding of those miserable wretches be fixed continually on the sins of which they were guilty and, moreover, as saint Augustine[9] points out, God will impart to them His own knowledge of sin so that sin will appear to them in all its hideous malice as it appears to the eyes of God Himself. They will behold their sins in all their foulness and repent but it will be too late and then they will bewail the good occasions which they neglected. This is the last and deepest and most cruel sting of the worm of conscience. The conscience will say: You had time and opportunity to repent and would not. You were brought up religiously by your parents. You had the sacraments and graces and indulgences[1] of the church to aid you. You had the minister of God to preach to you, to call you back when you had strayed, to forgive you your sins, no matter how many, how abominable, if only you had confessed and repented. No. You would not. You flouted the ministers of holy religion, you turned your back on the confessional, you wallowed deeper and deeper in the mire of sin. God appealed to you, threatened you, entreated you to return to Him. O what shame, what misery! The ruler of the universe entreated you, a creature of clay, to love Him Who made you and to keep His law. No. You would not. And now, though you were to flood all hell with your tears if you could still weep, all that sea of repentance would not gain for you what a single tear of true repentance shed during your mortal life would have gained for you. You implore now a moment of earthly life wherein to repent: in vain. That time is gone: gone for ever.

Such is the threefold sting of conscience, the viper which gnaws the very heart's core of the wretches in hell so that filled with hellish fury they curse themselves for their folly and curse the evil companions who have brought them to such ruin and curse the devils who tempted them in life and now mock them and torture them in eternity and even revile and curse the Supreme Being Whose goodness and patience they scorned and slighted but Whose justice and power they cannot evade.

The next spiritual pain to which the damned are subjected is the pain of extension. Man, in this earthly life, though he be capable of many evils, is not capable of them all at once inasmuch as one evil corrects and counteracts another just as one poison frequently corrects another. In hell on the

---

9. Early church father and writer (354–430).
1. In Catholic doctrine, remission of punishment for sin.

contrary one torment, instead of counteracting another, lends it still greater force: and moreover as the internal faculties are more perfect than the external senses so are they more capable of suffering. Just as every sense is afflicted with a fitting torment so is every spiritual faculty; the fancy[2] with horrible images, the sensitive faculty with alternate longing and rage, the mind and understanding with an interior darkness more terrible even than the exterior darkness which reigns in that dreadful prison. The malice, impotent though it be, which possesses these demon souls is an evil of boundless extension, of limitless duration, a frightful state of wickedness which we can scarcely realise unless we bear in mind the enormity of sin and the hatred God bears to it.

Opposed to this pain of extension and yet coexistent with it we have the pain of intensity. Hell is the center of all evils and, as you know, things are more intense at their centers than at their remotest points. There are no contraries or admixtures of any kind to temper or soften in the least the pains of hell. Nay, things which are good in themselves become evil in hell. Company, elsewhere a source of comfort to the afflicted, will be there a continual torment: knowledge, so much longed for as the chief good of the intellect, will there be hated worse than ignorance: light, so much coveted by all creatures from the lord of creation down to the humblest plant in the forest, will be loathed intensely. In this life our sorrows are either not very long or not very great because nature either overcomes them by habits or puts an end to them by sinking under their weight. But in hell the torments cannot be overcome by habit for while they are of terrible intensity they are at the same time of continual variety, each pain, so to speak, taking fire from another and reendowing that which has enkindled it with a still fiercer flame. Nor can nature escape from these intense and various tortures by succumbing to them for the soul in hell is sustained and maintained in evil so that its suffering may be the greater. Boundless extension of torment, incredible intensity of suffering, unceasing variety of torture—this is what the divine majesty, so outraged by sinners, demands, this is what the holiness of heaven, slighted and set aside for the lustful and low pleasures of the corrupt flesh, requires, this is what the blood of the innocent Lamb of God, shed for the redemption of sinners, trampled upon by the vilest of the vile, insists upon.

Last and crowning torture of all the tortures of that awful place is the eternity of hell. Eternity! O dread and dire word, Eternity! What mind of man can understand it? And, remember, it is an eternity of pain. Even though the pains of hell were not so terrible as they are yet they would become infinite as they are destined to last for ever. But while they are everlasting they are at the same time, as you know, intolerably intense, unbearably extensive. To bear even the sting of an insect for all eternity would be a dreadful torment. What must it be then to bear the manifold tortures of hell for ever. For ever! For all eternity! Not for a year or for an age but for ever. Try to imagine the awful meaning of this. You have often seen the sand on the seashore. How fine are its tiny grains! And how many of those tiny little grains go to make up the small handful which a child grasps in its play. Now imagine a mountain of that sand, a million miles high, reaching from the earth to the farthest heavens, and a million miles broad, extending to

---

2. I.e., the imagination.

remotest space, and a million miles in thickness: and imagine such an enormous mass of countless particles of sand multiplied as often as there are leaves in the forest, drops of water in the mighty ocean, feathers on birds, scales on fish, hairs on animals, atoms in the vast expanse of the air: and imagine that at the end of every million years a little bird came to that mountain and carried away in its beak a tiny grain of that sand. How many millions upon millions of centuries would pass before that bird had carried away even a square foot of that mountain, how many eons upon eons of ages before it had carried away all. Yet at the end of that immense stretch of time not even one instant of eternity could be said to have ended. At the end of all those billions and trillions of years eternity would have scarcely begun. And if that mountain rose again after it had been all carried away and if the bird came again and carried it all away again grain by grain: and if it so rose and sank as many times as there are stars in the sky, atoms in the air, drops of water in the sea, leaves on the trees, feathers upon birds, scales upon fish, hairs upon animals, at the end of all those innumerable risings and sinkings of that immeasurably vast mountain not one single instant of eternity could be said to have ended: even then, at the end of such a period, after that eon of time the mere thought of which makes our very brain reel dizzily, eternity would have scarcely begun.

A holy saint (one of our own fathers I believe it was) was once vouchsafed a vision of hell. It seemed to him that he stood in the midst of a great hall, dark and silent save for the ticking of a great clock. The ticking went on unceasingly; and it seemed to this saint that the sound of the ticking was the ceaseless repetition of the words: ever, never; ever, never. Ever to be in hell, never to be in heaven; ever to be shut off from the presence of God, never to enjoy the beatific vision;[3] ever to be eaten with flames, gnawed by vermin, goaded with burning spikes, never to be free from those pains; ever to have the conscience upbraid one, the memory enrage, the mind filled with darkness and despair, never to escape; ever to curse and revile the foul demons who gloat fiendishly over the misery of their dupes, never to behold the shining raiment[4] of the blessed spirits; ever to cry out of the abyss of fire to God for an instant, a single instant of respite from such awful agony, never to receive, even for an instant, God's pardon; ever to suffer, never to enjoy; ever to be damned, never to be saved; ever, never; ever, never. O what a dreadful punishment! An eternity of endless agony, of endless bodily and spiritual torment, without one ray of hope, without one moment of cessation, of agony limitless in extent, limitless in intensity, of torment infinitely lasting, infinitely varied, of torture that sustains eternally that which it eternally devours, of anguish that everlastingly preys upon the spirit while it racks the flesh, an eternity, every instant of which is itself an eternity, and that eternity an eternity of woe. Such is the terrible punishment decreed for those who die in mortal sin by an almighty and a just God.

Yes, a just God! Men, reasoning always as men, are astonished that God should mete out an everlasting and infinite punishment in the fires of hell for a single grievous sin. They reason thus because, blinded by the gross illusion of the flesh and the darkness of human understanding, they are unable to comprehend the hideous malice of mortal sin. They reason thus because they are unable to comprehend that even venial sin[5] is of such a foul and

---

3. Immediate sight of God in heaven.
4. Clothing.

5. A lesser offense, believed to open the soul to the possibility of mortal sin.

hideous nature that even if the omnipotent Creator could end all the evil and misery in the world, the wars, the diseases, the robberies, the crimes, the deaths, the murders, on condition that He allowed a single venial sin to pass unpunished, a single venial sin, a lie, an angry look, a moment of wilful sloth, He, the great omnipotent God could not do so because sin, be it in thought or deed, is a transgression of His law and God would not be God if He did not punish the transgressor.

A sin, an instant of rebellious pride of the intellect, made Lucifer and a third part of the cohorts of angels fall from their glory. A sin, an instant of folly and weakness, drove Adam and Eve out of Eden and brought death and suffering into the world. To retrieve the consequences of that sin the onlybegotten Son of God came down to earth, lived and suffered and died a most painful death, hanging for three hours on the cross.

O, my dear little brethren in Christ Jesus, will we then offend that good Redeemer and provoke His anger? Will we trample again upon that torn and mangled corpse? Will we spit upon that face so full of sorrow and love? Will we too, like the cruel jews and the brutal soldiers, mock that gentle and compassionate Saviour Who trod alone for our sakes the awful winepress of sorrow? Every word of sin is a wound in His tender side. Every sinful act is a thorn piercing His head. Every impure thought, deliberately yielded to, is a keen lance transfixing that sacred and loving heart. No, no. It is impossible for any human being to do that which offends so deeply the divine majesty, that which is punished by an eternity of agony, that which crucifies again the Son of God and makes a mockery of Him.

I pray to God that my poor words may have availed today to confirm in holiness those who are in a state of grace, to strengthen the wavering, to lead back to the state of grace the poor soul that has strayed if any such be among you. I pray to God, and do you pray with me, that we may repent of our sins. I will ask you now, all of you, to repeat after me the act of contrition, kneeling here in this humble chapel in the presence of God. He is there in the tabernacle burning with love for mankind, ready to comfort the afflicted. Be not afraid. No matter how many or how foul the sins if only you repent of them they will be forgiven you. Let no worldly shame hold you back. God is still the merciful Lord Who wishes not the eternal death of the sinner but rather that he be converted and live.

He calls you to Him. You are His. He made you out of nothing. He loved you as only a God can love. His arms are open to receive you even though you have sinned against Him. Come to Him, poor sinner, poor vain and erring sinner. Now is the acceptable time. Now is the hour.

The priest rose and turning towards the altar knelt upon the step before the tabernacle in the fallen gloom. He waited till all in the chapel had knelt and every least noise was still. Then raising his head he repeated the act of contrition,[6] phrase by phrase, with fervour. The boys answered him phrase by phrase. Stephen, his tongue cleaving to his palate, bowed his head, praying with his heart.

> —O my God!—
> —O my God!—
> —I am heartily sorry—
> —I am heartily sorry—
> —for having offended Thee—

6. Prayer expressing sorrow for having sinned and revulsion for those sins. Its words follow.

—for having offended Thee—
—and I detest my sins—
—and I detest my sins—
—above every other evil—
—above every other evil—
—because they displease Thee, my God—
—because they displease Thee, my God—
—Who art so deserving—
—Who art so deserving—
—of all my love—
—of all my love—
—and I firmly purpose—
—and I firmly purpose—
—by Thy holy grace—
—by Thy holy grace—
—never more to offend Thee—
—never more to offend Thee—
—and to amend my life—
—and to amend my life—

◆ ◆ ◆

He went up to his room after dinner in order to be alone with his soul: and at every step his soul seemed to sigh: at every step his soul mounted with his feet, sighing in the ascent, through a region of viscid[7] gloom.

He halted on the landing before the door and then, grasping the porcelain knob, opened the door quickly. He waited in fear, his soul pining within him, praying silently that death might not touch his brow as he passed over the threshold, that the fiends that inhabit darkness might not be given power over him. He waited still at the threshold as at the entrance to some dark cave. Faces were there; eyes: they waited and watched.

—We knew perfectly well of course that though it was bound to come to the light he would find considerable difficulty in endeavouring to try to induce himself to try to endeavour to ascertain the spiritual plenipotentiary[8] and so we knew of course perfectly well—

Murmuring faces waited and watched; murmurous voices filled the dark shell of the cave. He feared intensely in spirit and in flesh but, raising his head bravely, he strode into the room firmly. A doorway, a room, the same room, same window. He told himself calmly that those words had absolutely no sense which had seemed to rise murmurously from the dark. He told himself that it was simply his room with the door open.

He closed the door and, walking swiftly to the bed, knelt beside it and covered his face with his hands. His hands were cold and damp and his limbs ached with chill. Bodily unrest and chill and weariness beset him, routing his thoughts. Why was he kneeling there like a child saying his evening prayers? To be alone with his soul, to examine his conscience, to meet his sins face to face, to recall their times and manners and circumstances, to weep over them. He could not weep. He could not summon them to his memory. He felt only an ache of soul and body, his whole being, memory, will, understanding, flesh, benumbed and weary.

---

7. Glutinous or sticky.   8. I.e., spiritual ambassador.

That was the work of devils, to scatter his thoughts and overcloud his conscience, assailing him at the gates of the cowardly and sincorrupted flesh: and, praying God timidly to forgive him his weakness, he crawled up on to the bed and, wrapping the blankets closely about him, covered his face again with his hands. He had sinned. He had sinned so deeply against heaven and before God that he was not worthy to be called God's child.

Could it be that he, Stephen Dedalus, had done those things? His conscience sighed in answer. Yes, he had done them, secretly, filthily, time after time, and, hardened in sinful impenitence, he had dared to wear the mask of holiness before the tabernacle itself while his soul within was a living mass of corruption. How came it that God had not struck him dead? The leprous company of his sins closed about him, breathing upon him, bending over him from all sides. He strove to forget them in an act of prayer, huddling his limbs closer together and binding down his eyelids: but the senses of the soul would not be bound and, though his eyes were shut fast, he saw the places where he had sinned and, though his ears were tightly covered, he heard. He desired with all his will not to hear or see. He desired till his frame shook under the strain of his desire and until the senses of his soul closed. They closed for an instant and then opened. He saw.

A field of stiff weeds and thistles and tufted nettlebunches. Thick among the tufts of rank stiff growth lay battered canisters and clots and coils of solid excrement. A faint marshlight struggled upwards from air the ordure through the bristling greygreen weeds. An evil smell, faint and foul as the light, curled upwards sluggishly out of the canisters and from the stale crusted dung.

Creatures were in the field; one, three, six: creatures were moving in the field, hither and thither. Goatish creatures with human faces, hornybrowed, lightly bearded and grey as india-rubber.[9] The malice of evil glittered in their hard eyes, as they moved hither and thither, trailing their long tails behind them. A rictus of cruel malignity lit up greyly their old bony faces. One was clasping about his ribs a torn flannel waistcoat, another complained monotonously as his beard stuck in the tufted weeds. Soft language issued from their spittleless lips as they swished in slow circles round and round the field, winding hither and thither through the weeds, dragging their long tails amid the rattling canisters. They moved in slow circles, circling closer and closer, to enclose, to enclose, soft language issuing from their lips, their long swishing tails besmeared with stale shite, thrusting upwards their terrific faces . . . . .

Help!

He flung the blankets from him madly to free his face and neck. That was his hell. God had allowed him to see the hell reserved for his sins: stinking, bestial, malignant, a hell of lecherous goatish fiends. For him! For him!

He sprang from the bed, the reeking odour pouring down his throat, clogging and revolting his entrails. Air! The air of heaven! He stumbled towards the window, groaning and almost fainting with sickness. At the washstand a convulsion seized him within: and, clasping his cold forehead wildly, he vomited profusely in agony.

When the fit had spent itself he walked weakly to the window and, lifting the sash, sat in a corner of the embrasure[1] and leaned his elbow upon the sill. The rain had drawn off; and amid the moving vapours from point to

9. Natural rubber produced from trees and often used for erasers.
1. Opening in the wall for the window.

point of light the city was spinning about herself a soft cocoon of yellowish haze. Heaven was still and faintly luminous and the air sweet to breathe, as in a thicket drenched with showers: and amid peace and shimmering lights and quiet fragrances he made a covenant with his heart.

He prayed:

—*He once had meant to come on earth in heavenly glory but we sinned: and then He could not safely visit us but with a shrouded majesty and a bedimmed radiance for He was God. So He came Himself in weakness not in power and He sent thee, a creature in His stead, with a creature's comeliness and lustre suited to our state. And now thy very face and form, dear mother, speak to us of the Eternal; not like earthly beauty, dangerous to look upon, but like the morning star which is thy emblem, bright and musical, breathing purity, telling of heaven and infusing peace. O harbinger of day! O light of the pilgrim! Lead us still as thou hast led. In the dark night, across the bleak wilderness guide us on to our Lord Jesus, guide us home.*[2]

His eyes were dimmed with tears and, looking humbly up to heaven, he wept for the innocence he had lost.

When evening had fallen he left the house and the first touch of the damp dark air and the noise of the door as it closed behind him made ache again his conscience, lulled by prayer and tears. Confess! Confess! It was not enough to lull the conscience with a tear and a prayer. He had to kneel before the minister of the Holy Ghost and tell over his hidden sins truly and repentantly. Before he heard again the footboard of the housedoor trail over the threshold as it opened to let him in, before he saw again the table in the kitchen set for supper he would have knelt and confessed. It was quite simple.

The ache of conscience ceased and he walked onward swiftly through the dark streets. There were so many flagstones on the footpath of that street and so many streets in that city and so many cities in the world. Yet eternity had no end. He was in mortal sin. Even once was a mortal sin. It could happen in an instant. But how so quickly? By seeing or by thinking of seeing. The eyes see the thing, without having wished first to see. Then in an instant it happens. But does that part of the body understand or what? The serpent, the most subtle beast of the field. It must understand when it desires in one instant and then prolongs its own desire instant after instant, sinfully. It feels and understands and desires. What a horrible thing! Who made it to be like that, a bestial part of the body able to understand bestially and desire bestially? Was that then he or an inhuman thing moved by a lower soul than his soul? His soul sickened at the thought of a torpid snaky life feeding itself out of the tender marrow of his life and fattening upon the slime of lust. O why was that so? O why?

He cowered in the shadow of the thought, abasing himself in the awe of God Who had made all things and all men. Madness. Who could think such a thought? And, cowering in darkness and abject, he prayed mutely to his angel guardian to drive away with his sword the demon that was whispering to his brain.

The whisper ceased and he knew then clearly that his own soul had sinned in thought and word and deed wilfully through his own body. Confess! He had to confess every sin. How could he utter in words to the priest what he had done? Must, must. Or how could he explain without dying of shame? Or

---

2. Cf. Cardinal Newman's "Glories of Mary" (see p. 505, n. 3).

how could he have done such things without shame? A madman, a loathsome madman! Confess! O he would indeed to be free and sinless again! Perhaps the priest would know. O dear God!

He walked on and on through illlit streets, fearing to stand still for a moment lest it might seem that he held back from what awaited him, fearing to arrive at that towards which he still turned with longing. How beautiful must be a soul in the state of grace when God looked upon it with love!

Frowsy[3] girls sat along the curbstones before their baskets. Their dank hair hung trailed over their brows. They were not beautiful to see as they crouched in the mire. But their souls were seen by God; and if their souls were in a state of grace they were radiant to see: and God loved them, seeing them.

A wasting breath of humiliation blew bleakly over his soul to think of how he had fallen, to feel that those souls were dearer to God than his. The wind blew over him and passed on to the myriads and myriads of other souls on whom God's favour shone now more and now less, stars now brighter and now dimmer, sustained and failing. And the glimmering souls passed away, sustained and failing, merged in a moving breath. One soul was lost; a tiny soul: his. It flickered once and went out, forgotten, lost. The end: black cold void waste.

Consciousness of place came ebbing back to him slowly over a vast tract of time unlit, unfelt, unlived. The squalid scene composed itself around him; the common accents, the burning gasjets in the shops, odours of fish and spirits and wet sawdust, moving men and women. An old woman was about to cross the street, an oilcan in her hand. He bent down and asked her was there a chapel near.

—A chapel, sir? Yes, sir. Church Street chapel.

—Church?

She shifted the can to her other hand and directed him: and, as she held out her reeking withered right hand under its fringe of shawl, he bent lower towards her, saddened and soothed by her voice.

—Thank you.

—You are quite welcome, sir.

The candles on the high altar had been extinguished but the fragrance of incense still floated down the dim nave. Bearded workmen with pious faces were guiding a canopy out through a sidedoor, the sacristan aiding them with quiet gestures and words. A few of the faithful still lingered, praying before one of the sidealtars or kneeling in the benches near the confessionals. He approached timidly and knelt at the last bench in the body, thankful for the peace and silence and fragrant shadow of the church. The board on which he knelt was narrow and worn and those who knelt near him were humble followers of Jesus. Jesus too had been born in poverty and had worked in the shop of a carpenter, cutting boards and planing them, and had first spoken of the kingdom of God to poor fishermen, teaching all men to be meek and humble of heart.

He bowed his head upon his hands, bidding his heart be meek and humble that he might be like those who knelt beside him and his prayer as acceptable as theirs. He prayed beside them but it was hard. His soul was foul with sin and he dared not ask forgiveness with the simple trust of those whom Jesus, in the mysterious ways of God, had called first to His side, the carpenters, the

3. With a dirty, neglected appearance.

fishermen, poor and simple people following a lowly trade, handling and shaping the wood of trees, mending their nets with patience.

A tall figure came down the aisle and the penitents stirred: and, at the last moment glancing up swiftly, he saw a long grey beard and the brown habit of a capuchin.[4] The priest entered the box and was hidden. Two penitents rose and entered the confessional at either side. The wooden slide[5] was drawn back and the faint murmur of a voice troubled the silence.

His blood began to murmur in his veins, murmuring like a sinful city summoned from its sleep to hear its doom. Little flakes of fire fell and powdery ashes fell softly, alighting on the houses of men. They stirred, waking from sleep, troubled by the heated air.

The slide was shot back. The penitent emerged from the side of the box. The farther slide was drawn. A woman entered quietly and deftly where the first penitent had knelt. The faint murmur began again.

He could still leave the chapel. He could stand up, put one foot before the other and walk out softly and then run, run, run swiftly through the dark streets. He could still escape from the shame. O what shame! His face was burning with shame. Had it been any terrible crime but that one sin! Had it been murder! Little fiery flakes fell and touched him at all points, shameful thoughts, shameful words, shameful acts. Shame covered him wholly like fine glowing ashes falling continually. To say it in words! His soul, stifling and helpless, would cease to be.

The slide was shot back. A penitent emerged from the farther side of the box. The near slide was drawn. A penitent entered where the other penitent had come out. A soft whispering noise floated in vaporous cloudlets out of the box. It was the woman: soft whispering cloudlets, soft whispering vapour, whispering and vanishing.

He beat his breast with his fist humbly, secretly under cover of the wooden armrest. He would be at one with others and with God. He would love his neighbour. He would love God Who had made and loved him. He would kneel and pray with others and be happy. God would look down on him and on them and would love them all.

It was easy to be good. God's yoke was sweet and light. It was better never to have sinned, to have remained always a child, for God loved little children and suffered them to come to Him. It was a terrible and a sad thing to sin. But God was merciful to poor sinners who were truly sorry. How true that was! That was indeed goodness.

The slide was shot to suddenly. The penitent came out. He was next. He stood up in terror and walked blindly into the box.

At last it had come. He knelt in the silent gloom and raised his eyes to the white crucifix suspended above him. God could see that he was sorry. He would tell all his sins. His confession would be long, long. Everybody in the chapel would know then what a sinner he had been. Let them know. It was true. But God had promised to forgive him if he was sorry. He was sorry. He clasped his hands and raised them towards the white form,

<hr>

4. A Capuchin monk. The division of the order of St. Francis is named for the cowl that is part of the monks' standard brown robes.
5. Either of the pieces of wood covering the screen that separates the priest, in the center compartment of the confessional, from the compartments to either side of him, in which penitents sit and confess in turn. When the slide is drawn back so that it reveals the screen, confession may begin.

praying with his darkened eyes, praying with all his trembling body, swaying his head to and fro like a lost creature, praying with whimpering lips.
—Sorry! Sorry! O sorry!

The slide clicked back and his heart bounded in his breast. The face of
an old priest was at the grating, averted from him, leaning upon a hand. He
made the sign of the cross and prayed of the priest to bless him for he had
sinned. Then, bowing his head, he repeated the *Confiteor* in fright. At the
words *my most grievous fault* he ceased, breathless.

—How long is it since your last confession, my child?

—A long time, father.

—A month, my child?

—Longer, father.

—Three months, my child?

—Longer, father.

—Six months?

—Eight months, father.

He had begun. The priest asked:

—And what do you remember since that time?

He began to confess his sins: masses missed, prayers not said, lies.

—Anything else, my child?

Sins of anger, envy of others, gluttony, vanity, disobedience.

—Anything else, my child?

Sloth.

—Anything else, my child?

There was no help. He murmured:

—I. . . . committed sins of impurity, father.

The priest did not turn his head.

—With yourself, my child?

—And . . . with others.

—With women, my child?

—Yes, father.

—Were they married women, my child?

He did not know. His sins trickled from his lips, one by one, trickled in
shameful drops from his soul festering and oozing like a sore, a squalid
stream of vice. The last sins oozed forth, sluggish, filthy. There was no more
to tell. He bowed his head, overcome.

The priest was silent. Then he asked:

—How old are you, my child?

—Sixteen, father.

The priest passed his hand several times over his face. Then, resting his
forehead against his hand, he leaned towards the grating and, with eyes
still averted, spoke slowly. His voice was weary and old.

—You are very young, my child, he said, and let me implore of you to give
up that sin. It is a terrible sin. It kills the body and it kills the soul. It is the
cause of many crimes and misfortunes. Give it up, my child, for God'[6] sake.
It is dishonourable and unmanly. You cannot know where that wretched
habit will lead you or where it will come against you. As long as you commit
that sin, my poor child, you will never be worth one farthing[7] to God. Pray

---

6. On Joyce's eliding the possessive "s," see p. 458, n. 8.
7. A quarter of a penny; thus, figuratively, a very small amount.

to our mother Mary to help you. She will help you, my child. Pray to Our Blessed Lady when that sin comes into your mind. I am sure you will do that, will you not? You repent of all those sins. I am sure you do. And you will promise God now that by His holy grace you will never offend Him any more by that wicked sin. You will make that solemn promise to God, will you not?

—Yes, father.

The old and weary voice fell like sweet rain upon his quaking parching heart. How sweet and sad!

—Do so, my poor child. The devil has led you astray. Drive him back to hell when he tempts you to dishonour your body in that way—the foul spirit who hates Our Lord. Promise God now that you will give up that sin, that wretched wretched sin.

Blinded by his tears and by the light of God's mercifulness he bent his head and heard the grave words of absolution spoken and saw the priest's hand raised above him in token of forgiveness.[8]

—God bless you, my child. Pray for me.

He knelt to say his penance, praying in a corner of the dark nave: and his prayers ascended to heaven from his purified heart like perfume streaming upwards from a heart of white rose.

The muddy streets were gay. He strode homeward, conscious of an invisible grace pervading and making light his limbs. In spite of all he had done it. He had confessed and God had pardoned him. His soul was made fair and holy once more, holy and happy.

It would be beautiful to die if God so willed. It was beautiful to live if God so willed, to live in grace a life of peace and virtue and forbearance with others.

He sat by the fire in the kitchen, not daring to speak for happiness. Till that moment he had not known how beautiful and peaceful life could be. The green square of paper pinned round the lamp cast down a tender shade. On the dresser was a plate of sausages and white pudding[9] and on the shelf there were eggs. They would be for the breakfast in the morning after the communion in the college chapel. White pudding and eggs and sausages and cups of tea. How simple and beautiful was life after all! And life lay all before him.

In a dream he fell asleep. In a dream he rose and saw that it was morning. In a waking dream he went through the quiet morning towards the college.

The boys were all there, kneeling in their places. He knelt among them, happy and shy. The altar was heaped with fragrant masses of white flowers: and in the morning light the pale flames of the candles among the white flowers were clear and silent as his own soul.

He knelt before the altar with his classmates, holding the altar cloth with them over a living rail of hands. His hands were trembling: and his soul trembled as he heard the priest pass with the ciborium[1] from communicant to communicant.

—*Corpus Domini nostri.*

Could it be? He knelt there sinless and timid: and he would hold upon his tongue the host and God would enter his purified body.

8. I.e., making a gesture of benediction.
9. Sausage made of oatmeal and suet.

1. Cup in which the consecrated wafers of the Eucharist are carried for Communion.

—*In vitam eternam. Amen.*

Another life! A life of grace and virtue and happiness! It was true. It was not a dream from which he would wake. The past was past.

—*Corpus Domini nostri.*[2]

The ciborium had come to him.

IV

Sunday was dedicated to the mystery of the Holy Trinity, Monday to the Holy Ghost, Tuesday to the Guardian Angels, Wednesday to saint Joseph, Thursday to the Most Blessed Sacrament of the Altar, Friday to the Suffering Jesus, Saturday to the Blessed Virgin Mary.

Every morning he hallowed himself anew in the presence of some holy image or mystery. His day began with an heroic offering of its every moment of thought or action for the intentions of the sovereign pontiff[3] and with an early mass. The raw morning air whetted his resolute piety; and often as he knelt among the few worshippers at the sidealtar, following with his interleaved[4] prayerbook the murmur of the priest, he glanced up for an instant towards the vested figure standing in the gloom between the two candles which were the old and the new testaments and imagined that he was kneeling at mass in the catacombs.[5]

His daily life was laid out in devotional areas. By means of ejaculations[6] and prayers he stored up ungrudgingly for the souls in purgatory centuries of days and quarantines[7] and years; yet the spiritual triumph which he felt in achieving with ease so many fabulous ages of canonical penances did not wholly reward his zeal of prayer since he could never know how much temporal punishment he had remitted by way of suffrage for the agonising souls: and, fearful lest in the midst of the purgatorial fire, which differed from the infernal only in that it was not everlasting, his penance might avail no more than a drop of moisture, he drove his soul daily through an increasing circle of works of supererogation.[8]

Every part of his day, divided by what he regarded now as the duties of his station in life, circled about its own centre of spiritual energy. His life seemed to have drawn near to eternity; every thought, word and deed, every instance of consciousness could be made to revibrate radiantly in heaven: and at times his sense of such immediate repercussion was so lively that he seemed to feel his soul in devotion pressing like fingers the keyboard of a great cash register and to see the amount of his purchase start forth immediately in heaven not as a number but as a frail column of incense or as a slender flower.

The rosaries too which he said constantly (for he carried his beads loose in his trousers' pockets that he might tell[9] them as he walked the streets) transformed themselves into coronals[1] of flowers of such vague unearthly

2. The body of our Lord (Latin). "*In vitam eternam*": Unto life eternal. Phrases spoken by the priest as he administers Communion.
3. The pope. "Mystery": something incomprehensible to human intelligence. "Heroic offering": act of offering all one's good works to God for the sake of another's spiritual well-being.
4. With other pieces of paper, in this case devotional material, between its pages.

5. Underground tombs used by early persecuted Christians to hold religious services.
6. Short, exclamatory, emotional prayers.
7. Periods of forty days. Stephen is performing penance for the sake of souls in purgatory.
8. Good works that go beyond the required standard.
9. Use the rosary to say prayers.
1. Wreaths or garlands, usually for the head.

texture that they seemed to him as hueless and odourless as they were nameless. He offered up each of his three daily chaplets[2] that his soul might grow strong in each of the three theological virtues, in faith in the Father Who had created him, in hope in the Son Who had redeemed him and in love of the Holy Ghost Who had sanctified him: and this thrice triple prayer he offered to the Three Persons through Mary in the name of her joyful and sorrowful and glorious mysteries.

On each of the seven days of the week he further prayed that one of the seven gifts of the Holy Ghost[3] might descend upon his soul and drive out of it day by day the seven deadly sins which had defiled it in the past: and he prayed for each gift on its appointed day, confident that it would descend upon him, though it seemed to him strange at times that wisdom and understanding and knowledge were so distinct in their nature that each should be prayed for apart from the others. Yet he believed that at some future stage of his spiritual progress this difficulty would be removed when his sinful soul had been raised up from its weakness and enlightened by the Third Person of the Most Blessed Trinity. He believed this all the more and with trepidation because of the divine gloom and silence wherein dwelt the unseen Paraclete,[4] Whose symbols were a dove and a mighty wind, to sin against Whom was a sin beyond forgiveness, the eternal, mysterious, secret Being to Whom, as God, the priests offered up mass once a year, robed in the scarlet of the tongues of fire.[5]

The imagery through which the nature and kinship of the Three Persons of the Trinity were darkly shadowed forth in the books of devotion which he read (the Father contemplating from all eternity as in a mirror His Divine Perfections and thereby begetting eternally the Eternal Son and the Holy Spirit proceeding out of Father and Son from all eternity) were easier of acceptance by his mind by reason of their august incomprehensibility than was the simple fact that God had loved his soul from all eternity, for ages before he had been born into the world, for ages before the world itself had existed. He had heard the names of the passions of love and hate pronounced solemnly on the stage and in the pulpit, had found them set forth solemnly in books, and had wondered why his soul was unable to harbour them for any time or to force his lips to utter their names with conviction. A brief anger had often invested him but he had never been able to make it an abiding passion and had always felt himself passing out of it as if his very body were being divested with ease of some outer skin or peel. He had felt a subtle, dark and murmurous presence penetrate his being and fire him with a brief iniquitous lust: it too had slipped beyond his grasp leaving his mind lucid and indifferent. This, it seemed, was the only love and that the only hate his soul would harbour.

But he could no longer disbelieve in the reality of love since God Himself had loved his individual soul with divine love from all eternity. Gradually, as his soul was enriched with spiritual knowledge, he saw the whole world forming one vast symmetrical expression of God's power and love. Life became a divine gift for every moment and sensation of which, were it even the sight of a single leaf hanging on the twig of a tree, his soul should praise

2. A third of a rosary.
3. Cf. Isaiah 11.2: wisdom, understanding, counsel, fortitude, knowledge, piety, and fear of the Lord.
4. The Holy Spirit.
5. The red robes of the priests at Pentecost, or Whitsunday, represent the descent of the Holy Spirit in the form of tongues of fire (cf. Acts 2.3).

and thank the Giver. The world for all its solid substance and complexity no longer existed for his soul save as a theorem of divine power and love and universality. So entire and unquestionable was this sense of the divine meaning in all nature granted to his soul that he could scarcely understand why it was in any way necessary that he should continue to live. Yet that also was part of the divine purpose and he dared not question its use, he above all others who had sinned so deeply and so foully against the divine purpose. Meek and abased by this consciousness of the one eternal omnipresent perfect reality his soul took up again her burden of pieties, masses and prayers and sacraments and mortifications:[6] and only then for the first time since he had brooded on the great mystery of love did he feel within him a warm movement like that of some newly born life or virtue of the soul itself. The attitude of rapture in sacred art, the raised and parted hands, the parted lips and eyes as of one about to swoon, became for him an image of the soul in prayer, humiliated and faint before her Creator.

But he had been forewarned of the dangers of spiritual exaltation and did not allow himself to desist from even the least or lowliest devotion, striving also by constant mortification to undo the sinful past rather than to achieve a saintliness fraught with peril. Each of his senses was brought under a rigorous discipline. In order to mortify the sense of sight he made it his rule to walk in the street with downcast eyes, glancing neither to right nor left and never behind him. His eyes shunned every encounter with the eyes of women. From time to time also he balked them by a sudden effort of the will, as by lifting them suddenly in the middle of an unfinished sentence and closing the book. To mortify his hearing he exerted no control over his voice which was then breaking, neither sang nor whistled and made no attempt to flee from noises which caused him painful nervous irritation such as the sharpening of knives on the knifeboard, the gathering of cinders on the fireshovel and the twigging[7] of the carpet. To mortify his smell was more difficult as he found in himself no instinctive repugnance to bad odours, whether they were the odours of the outdoor world such as those of dung and tar or the odours of his own person among which he had made many curious comparisons and experiments. He found in the end that the only odour against which his sense of smell revolted was a certain stale fishy stink like that of longstanding urine: and whenever it was possible he subjected himself to this unpleasant odour. To mortify the taste he practised strict habits at table, observed to the letter all the fasts of the church and sought by distraction to divert his mind from the savours of different foods. But it was to the mortification of touch that he brought the most assiduous ingenuity of inventiveness. He never consciously changed his position in bed, sat in the most uncomfortable positions, suffered patiently every itch and pain, kept away from the fire, remained on his knees all through the mass except at the gospels,[8] left parts of his neck and face undried so that the air might sting them and, whenever he was not saying his beads, carried his arms stiffly at his sides like a runner and never in his pockets or clasped behind him.

He had no temptations to sin mortally. It surprised him however to find that at the end of his course of intricate piety and selfrestraint he was so

6. Practices meant to bring bodily appetites under control through austerity, discomfort, self-inflicted pain.
7. Beating, or brushing, with a stiff, short broom.
8. The part of mass during which everyone is expected to stand.

easily at the mercy of childish and unworthy imperfections. His prayers and fasts availed him little for the suppression of anger at hearing his mother sneeze or at being disturbed in his devotions. It needed an immense effort of his will to master the impulse which urged him to give outlet to such irritation. Images of the outbursts of trivial anger which he had often noted among his masters, their twitching mouths, closeshut lips and flushed cheeks, recurred to his memory, discouraging him, for all his practice of humility, by the comparison. To merge his life in the common tide of other lives was harder for him than any fasting or prayer and it was his constant failure to do this to his own satisfaction which caused in his soul at last a sensation of spiritual dryness together with a growth of doubts and scruples. His soul traversed a period of desolation in which the sacraments themselves seemed to have turned into dried up sources. His confession became a channel for the escape of scrupulous and unrepented imperfections. His actual reception of the eucharist did not bring him the same dissolving moments of virginal selfsurrender as did those spiritual communions made by him sometimes at the close of some visit to the Blessed Sacrament.[9] The book which he used for these visits was an old neglected book written by saint Alphonsus Liguori with fading characters and sere foxpapered leaves.[1] A faded world of fervent love and virginal responses seemed to be evoked for his soul by the reading of its pages in which the imagery of the canticles[2] was interwoven with the communicant's prayers. An inaudible voice seemed to caress the soul, telling her names and glories, bidding her arise as for espousal and come away, bidding her look forth, a spouse, from Amana[3] and from the mountains of the leopards; and the soul seemed to answer with the same inaudible voice, surrendering herself:

Inter ubera mea commorabitur.[4]

This idea of surrender had a perilous attraction for his mind now that he felt his soul beset once again by the insistent voices of the flesh which began to murmur to him again during his prayers and meditations. It gave him an intense sense of power to know that he could, by a single act of consent, in a moment of thought, undo all that he had done. He seemed to feel a flood slowly advancing towards his naked feet and to be waiting for the first faint timid noiseless wavelet to touch his fevered skin. Then, almost at the instant of that touch, almost at the verge of sinful consent, he found himself standing far away from the flood upon a dry shore, saved by a sudden act of the will or a sudden ejaculation: and, seeing the silver line of the flood far away and beginning again its slow advance towards his feet, a new thrill of power and satisfaction shook his soul to know that he had not yielded nor undone all.

When he had eluded the flood of temptation many times in this way he grew troubled and wondered whether the grace which he had refused to lose was not being filched from him little by little. The clear certitude of his own immunity grew dim and to it succeeded a vague fear that his soul had really fallen unawares. It was with difficulty that he won back his old con-

---

9. Visits to the church to pray alone, between masses.
1. Discolored pages. "St. Alphonsus Liguori": Italian bishop, musician, and theologian (1696–1787).
2. The songs of the Bible, such as the Song of

Solomon in the King James Bible or the Canticle of Canticles in the Douay Bible.
3. Biblical mountain in or near Lebanon.
4. He shall lie between my breasts (Latin), a phrase from the Canticle of Canticles 1.13, meant to express the Church's love for Christ.

sciousness of his state of grace by telling himself that he had prayed to God at every temptation and that the grace which he had prayed for must have been given to him inasmuch as God was obliged to give it. The very frequency and violence of temptations showed him at last the truth of what he had heard about the trials of the saints. Frequent and violent temptations were a proof that the citadel of the soul had not fallen and that the devil raged to make it fall.

Often when he had confessed his doubts and scruples, some momentary inattention at prayer, a movement of trivial anger in his soul or a subtle wilfulness in speech or act, he was bidden by his confessor to name some sin of his past life before absolution was given him. He named it with humility and shame and repented of it once more. It humiliated and shamed him to think that he would never be freed from it wholly, however holily he might live or whatever virtues or perfections he might attain. A restless feeling of guilt would always be present with him: he would confess and repent and be absolved, confess and repent again and be absolved again, fruitlessly. Perhaps that first hasty confession wrung from him by the fear of hell had not been good? Perhaps, concerned only for his imminent doom, he had not had sincere sorrow for his sin? But the surest sign that his confession had been good and that he had had sincere sorrow for his sin was, he knew, the amendment of his life.

—I have amended my life, have I not? he asked himself.

◆　◆　◆

The director stood in the embrasure of the window, his back to the light, leaning an elbow on the brown crossblind and, as he spoke and smiled, slowly dangling and looping the cord of the other blind. Stephen stood before him, following for a moment with his eyes the waning of the long summer daylight above the roofs or the slow deft movements of the priestly fingers. The priest's face was in total shadow but the waning daylight from behind him touched the deeply grooved temples and the curves of the skull. Stephen followed also with his ears the accents and intervals of the priest's voice as he spoke gravely and cordially of indifferent themes, the vacation which had just ended, the colleges of the order abroad, the transference of masters. The grave and cordial voice went on easily with its tale and in the pauses Stephen felt bound to set it on again with respectful questions. He knew that the tale was a prelude and his mind waited for the sequel. Ever since the message of summons had come for him from the director his mind had struggled to find the meaning of the message: and during the long restless time he had sat in the college parlour waiting for the director to come in his eyes had wandered from one sober picture to another around the walls and his mind had wandered from one guess to another until the meaning of the summons had almost become clear. Then just as he was wishing that some unforeseen cause might prevent the director from coming he had heard the handle of the door turning and the swish of a soutane.

The director had begun to speak of the dominican and franciscan orders and of the friendship between saint Thomas and saint Bonaventure. The capuchin dress, he thought, was rather too . . . .

Stephen's face gave back the priest's indulgent smile and, not being anxious to give an opinion, he made a slight dubitative movement with his lips.

—I believe, continued the director, that there is some talk now among the capuchins themselves of doing away with it and following the example of the other franciscans.[5]

—I suppose they would retain it in the cloister, said Stephen.

—O certainly, said the director. For the cloister it is all right but for the street I really think it would be better to do away with it, don't you?

—It must be troublesome, I imagine.

—Of course it is: of course. Just imagine, when I was in Belgium I used to see them out cycling in all kinds of weather with this thing up about their knees! It was really ridiculous. *Les jupes*,[6] they call them in Belgium.

The vowel was so modified as to be indistinct.

—What do they call them?

—*Les jupes*.

—O.

Stephen smiled again in answer to the smile which he could not see on the priest's shadowed face, its image or spectre only passing rapidly across his mind as the low discreet accent fell upon his ear. He gazed calmly before him at the waning sky, glad of the cool of the evening and of the faint yellow glow which hid the tiny flame kindling upon his cheek.

The names of articles of dress worn by women or of certain soft and delicate stuffs used in their making brought always to his mind a delicate and sinful perfume. As a boy he had imagined the reins by which horses are driven as slender silken bands and it had shocked him to feel at Stradbrooke[7] the greasy leather of harness. It had shocked him too when he had felt for the first time beneath his tremulous fingers the brittle texture of a woman's stocking for, retaining nothing of all he read save that which seemed to him an echo or a prophecy of his own state, it was only amid softworded phrases or within rosesoft stuffs that he dared to conceive of the soul or body of a woman moving with tender life.

But the phrase on the priest's lips was disingenuous for he knew that a priest should not speak lightly on that theme. The phrase had been spoken lightly with design and he felt that his face was being searched by the eyes in the shadow. Whatever he had heard or read of the craft of jesuits he had put aside frankly as not borne out by his own experience. His masters, even when they had not attracted him, had seemed to him always intelligent and serious priests, athletic and highspirited prefects. He thought of them as men who washed their bodies briskly with cold water and wore clean cold linen. During all the years he had lived among them in Clongowes and in Belvedere he had received only two pandies and, though these had been dealt him in the wrong, he knew that he had often escaped punishment. During all those years he had never heard from any of his masters a flippant word: it was they who had taught him christian doctrine and urged him to live a good life and, when he had fallen into grievous sin, it was they who had led him back to grace. Their presence had made him diffident of himself when he was a muff[8] in Clongowes and it had made him diffident of himself also while he had held his equivocal position in Belvedere. A constant sense of this had remained with him up to the last year of his school

5. The larger order of monks to which the Capuchins belong.
6. Skirts (French).

7. Stradbrook, an area southeast of Blackrock.
8. Beginner or novice.

life. He had never once disobeyed or allowed turbulent companions to seduce him from his habit of quiet obedience: and, even when he doubted some statement of a master, he had never presumed to doubt openly. Lately some of their judgments had sounded a little childish in his ears and had made him feel a regret and pity as though he were slowly passing out of an accustomed world and were hearing its language for the last time. One day when some boys had gathered round a priest under the shed near the chapel he had heard the priest say:

—I believe that Lord Macaulay[9] was a man who probably never committed a mortal sin in his life, that is to say, a deliberate mortal sin.[1]

Some of the boys had then asked the priest if Victor Hugo[2] were not the greatest French writer. The priest had answered that Victor Hugo had never written half so well when he had turned against the church as he had written when he was a catholic.

—But there are many eminent French critics, said the priest, who consider that even Victor Hugo, great as he certainly was, had not so pure a French style as Louis Veuillot.[3]

The tiny flame which the priest's allusion had kindled upon Stephen's cheek had sunk down again and his eyes were still fixed calmly on the colourless sky. But an unresting doubt flew hither and thither before his mind. Masked memories passed quickly before him: he recognized scenes and persons yet he was conscious that he had failed to perceive some vital circumstance in them. He saw himself walking about the grounds watching the sports in Clongowes and eating slim jim out of his cricketcap. Some jesuits were walking round the cycletrack in the company of ladies. The echoes of certain expressions used in Clongowes sounded in remote caves of his mind.

His ears were listening to these distant echoes amid the silence of the parlour when he became aware that the priest was addressing him in a different voice.

—I sent for you today, Stephen, because I wished to speak to you on a very important subject.

—Yes, sir.

—Have you ever felt that you had a vocation?

Stephen parted his lips to answer yes and then withheld the word suddenly. The priest waited for the answer and added:

—I mean have you ever felt within yourself, in your soul, a desire to join the order. Think.

—I have sometimes thought of it, said Stephen.

The priest let the blindcord fall to one side and, uniting his hands, leaned his chin gravely upon them, communing with himself.

—In a college like this, he said at length, there is one boy or perhaps two or three boys whom God calls to the religious life. Such a boy is marked off from his companions by his piety, by the good example he shows to others. He is looked up to by them; he is chosen perhaps as prefect by his fellow sodalists. And you, Stephen, have been such a boy in this college, prefect of Our Blessed Lady's sodality. Perhaps you are the boy in this college whom God designs to call to Himself.

---

9. Thomas Babington Macaulay, Baron Macaulay (1800–1859), English essayist, historian, and poet.

1. Mortal sin is, by definition, deliberate.
2. French novelist and poet (1802–1885).
3. French journalist (1813–1883).

A strong note of pride reinforcing the gravity of the priest's voice made Stephen's heart quicken in response.

—To receive that call, Stephen, said the priest, is the greatest honour that the Almighty God can bestow upon a man. No king or emperor on this earth has the power of the priest of God. No angel or archangel in heaven, no saint, not even the Blessed Virgin herself has the power of a priest of God: the power of the keys, the power to bind and to loose from sin,[4] the power of exorcism, the power to cast out from the creatures of God the evil spirits that have power over them, the power, the authority, to make the great God of Heaven come down upon the altar and take the form of bread and wine. What an awful power, Stephen!

A flame began to flutter again on Stephen's cheek as he heard in this proud address an echo of his own proud musings. How often had he seen himself as a priest wielding calmly and humbly the awful power of which angels and saints stood in reverence! His soul had loved to muse in secret on this desire. He had seen himself, a young and silentmannered priest, entering a confessional swiftly, ascending the altarsteps, incensing, genuflecting, accomplishing the vague acts of the priesthood which pleased him by reason of their semblance of reality and of their distance from it. In that dim life which he had lived through in his musings he had assumed the voices and gestures which he had noted with various priests. He had bent his knee sideways like such a one, he had shaken the thurible[5] only slightly like such a one, his chasuble[6] had swung open like that of such another as he had turned to the altar again after having blessed the people. And above all it had pleased him to fill the second place[7] in those dim scenes of his imagining. He shrank from the dignity of celebrant because it displeased him to imagine that all the vague pomp should end in his own person or that the ritual should assign to him so clear and final an office. He longed for the minor sacred offices, to be vested with the tunicle of subdeacon[8] at high mass, to stand aloof from the altar, forgotten by the people, his shoulders covered with a humeral veil,[9] holding the paten[1] within its folds, or when the sacrifice had been accomplished, to stand as deacon in a dalmatic[2] of cloth of gold on the step below the celebrant, his hand joined and his face towards the people, and sing the chant *Ite, missa est.*[3] If ever he had seen himself celebrant it was as in the pictures of the mass in his child's massbook, in a church without worshippers, save for the angel of the sacrifice, at a bare altar and served by an acolyte[4] scarcely more boyish than himself. In vague sacrificial or sacramental acts alone his will seemed drawn to go forth to encounter reality: and it was partly the absence of an appointed rite which had always constrained him to inaction whether he had allowed silence to cover his anger or pride or had suffered only an embrace he longed to give.

He listened in reverent silence now to the priest's appeal and through the words he heard even more distinctly a voice bidding him approach, offering

---

4. The power to hear confession and give or withhold absolution.
5. Container in which incense is burned.
6. Sleeveless outer vestment worn by the priest during mass.
7. The office of deacon, the assistant to the priest during mass.
8. The short outer vestment worn by the assistant to the deacon.
9. Cloth, worn by the subdeacon over his shoul-

ders at mass, with which he covers the sacred vessels when handling them.
1. Plate used to hold the consecrated Host at mass.
2. Wide-sleeved vestment open on both sides and worn by the deacon at mass.
3. Go, the mass is ended (Latin). The words with which the deacon or celebrant concludes the mass.
4. Person who assists a priest.

him secret knowledge and secret power. He would know then what was the sin of Simon Magus[5] and what the sin against the Holy Ghost[6] for which there was no forgiveness. He would know obscure things, hidden from others, from those who were conceived and born children of wrath. He would know the sins, the sinful longings and sinful thoughts and sinful acts, of others, hearing them murmured into his ear in the confessional under the shame of a darkened chapel by the lips of women and of girls: but rendered immune mysteriously at his ordination by the imposition of hands his soul would pass again uncontaminated to the white peace of the altar. No touch of sin would linger upon the hands with which he would elevate and break the host; no touch of sin would linger on his lips in prayer to make him eat and drink damnation to himself, not discerning the body of the Lord.[7] He would hold his secret knowledge and secret power, being as sinless as the innocent: and he would be a priest for ever according to the order of Melchisedech.[8]

—I will offer up my mass tomorrow morning, said the director, that Almighty God may reveal to you His holy will. And let you, Stephen, make a novena[9] to your patron saint, the first martyr,[1] who is very powerful with God, that God may enlighten your mind. But you must be quite sure, Stephen, that you have a vocation because it would be terrible if you found afterwards that you had none. Once a priest always a priest, remember. Your catechism tells you that the sacrament of Holy Orders is one of those which can be received only once because it imprints on the soul an indelible spiritual mark which can never be effaced. It is before you must weigh well, not after. It is a solemn question, Stephen, because on it may depend the salvation of your eternal soul. But we will pray to God together.

He held open the heavy halldoor and gave his hand as if already to a companion in the spiritual life. Stephen passed out on to the wide platform above the steps and was conscious of the caress of mild evening air. Towards Findlater's church a quartet of young men were striding along with linked arms, swaying their heads and stepping to the agile melody of their leader's concertina.[2] The music passed in an instant, as the first bars of sudden music always did, over the fantastic fabrics of his mind, dissolving them painlessly and noiselessly as a sudden wave dissolves the sandbuilt turrets of children. Smiling at the trivial air he raised his eyes to the priest's face and, seeing in it a mirthless reflection of the sunken day, detached his hand slowly which had acquiesced faintly in that companionship.

As he descended the steps the impression which effaced his troubled self-communion was that of a mirthless mask reflecting a sunken day from the threshold of the college. The shadow, then, of the life of the college passed gravely over his consciousness. It was a grave and ordered and passionless life that awaited him, a life without material cares. He wondered how he would pass the first night in the novitiate[3] and with what dismay he would wake the first morning in the dormitory. The troubling odour of the long

---

5. The sin of simony, offering money in exchange for spiritual power.
6. A mysterious sin, the blasphemy of the spirit, was to deny the divine force of good works.
7. I.e., not recognizing Christ's presence in the wafer of the Eucharist.
8. Cf. Hebrews 5.6–7. Figuratively, any modern Catholic priest.

9. Period of nine days devoted to special prayer for a particular purpose.
1. St. Stephen, his namesake, the first Christian martyr, was stoned for blasphemy.
2. Portable accordionlike musical instrument.
3. Probationary period undertaken before entry into a religious order.

corridors of Clongowes came back to him and he heard the discreet murmur of the burning gasflames. At once from every part of his being unrest began to irradiate. A feverish quickening of his pulses followed and a din of meaningless words drove his reasoned thoughts hither and thither confusedly. His lungs dilated and sank as if he were inhaling a warm moist unsustaining air and he smelt again the warm moist air which hung in the bath in Clongowes above the sluggish turfcoloured water.

Some instinct, waking at these memories, stronger than education or piety, quickened within him at every near approach to that life, an instinct subtle and hostile, and armed him against acquiescence. The chill and order of the life repelled him. He saw himself rising in the cold of the morning and filing down with the others to early mass and trying vainly to struggle with his prayers against the fainting sickness of his stomach. He saw himself sitting at dinner with the community of a college. What then had come of that deeprooted shyness of his which had made him loth to eat or drink under a strange roof? What had come of the pride of his spirit which had always made him conceive himself as a being apart in every order?

The Reverend Stephen Dedalus, S. J.[4]

His name in that new life leaped into characters before his eyes and to it there followed a mental sensation of an undefined face or colour of a face. The colour faded and became strong like a changing glow of pallid brick red. Was it the raw reddish glow he had so often seen on wintry mornings on the shaven gills[5] of the priests? The face was eyeless and sourfavoured and devout, shot with pink tinges of suffocated anger. Was it not a mental spectre of the face of one of the jesuits whom some of the boys called Lantern Jaws and others Foxy Campbell?

He was passing at that moment before the jesuit house in Gardiner Street and wondered vaguely which window would be his if he ever joined the order. Then he wondered at the vagueness of his wonder, at the remoteness of his own soul from what he had hitherto imagined her sanctuary, at the frail hold which so many years of order and obedience had of him when once a definite and irrevocable act of his threatened to end for ever, in time and in eternity, his freedom. The voice of the director urging upon him the proud claims of the church and the mystery and power of the priestly office repeated itself idly in his memory. His soul was not there to hear and greet it and he knew now that the exhortation he had listened to had already fallen into an idle formal tale. He would never swing the thurible before the tabernacle as priest. His destiny was to be elusive of social or religious orders. The wisdom of the priest's appeal did not touch him to the quick. He was destined to learn his own wisdom apart from others or to learn the wisdom of others himself wandering among the snares of the world.

The snares of the world were its ways of sin. He would fall. He had not yet fallen but he would fall silently, in an instant. Not to fall was too hard, too hard: and he felt the silent lapse of his soul, as it would be at some instant to come, falling, falling but not yet fallen, still unfallen but about to fall.

He crossed the bridge over the stream of the Tolka[6] and turned his eyes coldly for an instant towards the faded blue shrine of the Blessed Virgin which stood fowlwise on a pole in the middle of a hamshaped encampment

---

4. Society of Jesus, initials denoting that one is a Jesuit.

5. Flesh under the jaws and ears.
6. River in Dublin.

of poor cottages. Then, bending to the left, he followed the lane which led up to his house. The faint sour stink of rotted cabbages came towards him from the kitchen gardens on the rising ground above the river. He smiled to think that it was this disorder, the misrule and confusion of his father's house and the stagnation of vegetable life, which was to win the day in his soul. Then a short laugh broke from his lips as he thought of that solitary farmhand in the kitchen gardens behind their house whom they had nick-named the man with the hat. A second laugh, taking rise from the first after a pause, broke from him involuntarily as he thought of how the man with the hat worked, considering in turn the four points of the sky and then regret-fully plunging his spade in the earth.

He pushed open the latchless door of the porch and passed through the naked hallway into the kitchen. A group of his brothers and sisters was sit-ting round the table. Tea was nearly over and only the last of the second watered tea[7] remained in the bottoms of the small glassjars and jampots which did service for teacups. Discarded crusts and lumps of sugared bread, turned brown by the tea which had been poured over them, lay scattered on the table. Little wells of tea lay here and there on the board and a knife with a broken ivory handle was stuck through the pith of a ravaged turnover.

The sad quiet greyblue glow of the dying day came through the window and the open door, covering over and allaying quietly a sudden instinct of remorse in Stephen's heart. All that had been denied them had been freely given to him, the eldest: but the quiet glow of evening showed him in their faces no sign of rancour.

He sat near them at the table and asked where his father and mother were. One answered:

—Goneboro toboro lookboro atboro aboro houseboro.

Still another removal! A boy named Fallon in Belvedere had often asked him with a silly laugh why they moved so often. A frown of scorn darkened quickly his forehead as he heard again the silly laugh of the questioner.

He asked:

—Why are we on the move again, if it's a fair question?

The same sister answered:

—Becauseboro theboro landboro lordboro willboro putboro usboro out-boro.

The voice of his youngest brother from the farther side of the fireplace began to sing the air *Oft in the Stilly Night.*[8] One by one the others took up the air until a full choir of voices was singing. They would sing so for hours, melody after melody, glee after glee, till the last pale light died down on the horizon, till the first dark nightclouds came forth and night fell.

He waited for some moments, listening, before he too took up the air with them. He was listening with pain of spirit to the overtone of weariness behind their frail fresh innocent voices. Even before they set out on life's journey they seemed weary already of the way.

He heard the choir of voices in the kitchen echoed and multiplied through an endless reverberation of the choirs of endless generations of children: and heard in all the echoes an echo also of the recurring note of weariness and pain. All seemed weary of life even before entering upon it. And he

---

7. Tea brewed by using tea leaves a second time; a sign of poverty.

8. By the Irish poet and songwriter Thomas Moore (1779–1852).

remembered that Newman had heard this note also in the broken lines of Virgil *giving utterance, like the voice of Nature herself, to that pain and weariness yet hope of better things which has been the experience of her children in every time.*[9]

◆ ◆ ◆

He could wait no longer.

From the door of Byron's publichouse to the gate of Clontarf[1] chapel, from the gate of Clontarf chapel to the door of Byron's publichouse and then back again to the chapel and then back again to the publichouse he had paced slowly at first planting his steps scrupulously in the spaces of the patchwork of the footpath, then timing their fall to the fall of verses. A full hour had passed since his father had gone in with Dan Crosby, the tutor, to find out from him something about the university.[2] For a full hour he had paced up and down, waiting: but he could wait no longer.

He set off abruptly for the Bull,[3] walking rapidly lest his father's shrill whistle might call him back; and in a few moments he had rounded the curve at the police barrack and was safe.

Yes, his mother was hostile to the idea as he had read from her listless silence. Yet her mistrust pricked him more keenly than his father's pride and he thought coldly how he had watched the faith which was fading down in his soul aging and strengthening in her eyes. A dim antagonism gathered force within him and darkened his mind as a cloud against her disloyalty: and when it passed cloudlike leaving his mind serene and dutiful towards her again he was made aware dimly and without regret of a first noiseless sundering of their lives.

The university! So he had passed beyond the challenge of the sentries who had stood as guardians of his boyhood and had sought to keep him among them, that he might be subject to them and serve their ends. Pride after satisfaction uplifted him like long slow waves. The end he had been born to serve yet did not see had led him to escape by an unseen path: and now it beckoned to him once more and a new adventure was about to be opened to him. It seemed to him that he heard notes of fitful music leaping upwards a tone and downwards a diminished fourth, upwards a tone and downwards a major third, like triplebranching flames leaping fitfully, flame after flame, out of a midnight wood. It was an elfin prelude, endless and formless: and, as it grew wilder and faster, the flames leaping out of time, he seemed to hear from under the boughs and grasses wild creatures racing, their feet pattering like rain upon the leaves. Their feet passed in pattering tumult over his mind, the feet of hares and rabbits, the feet of harts[4] and hinds and antelopes, until he heard them no more and remembered only a proud cadence from Newman: *Whose feet are as the feet of harts and underneath the everlasting arms.*[5]

The pride of that dim image brought back to his mind the dignity of the office he had refused. All through his boyhood he had mused upon that which he had so often thought to be his destiny and when the moment had

9. From Cardinal Newman's *Essay in Aid of a Grammar of Assent* (1870).

1. Area on Dublin Bay northeast of the city center.

2. I.e., University College, Dublin.

3. Seawall from Clontarf into Dublin Bay.

4. Male deer, especially red deer.

5. From Cardinal Newman's *Idea of a University Defined and Illustrated* (1852).

come for him to obey the call he had turned aside, obeying a wayward instinct. Now time lay between: the oils of ordination would never anoint his body. He had refused. Why?

He turned seaward from the road at Dollymount[6] and as he passed on to the thin wooden bridge he felt the planks shaking with the tramp of heavily shod feet. A squad of christian brothers was on its way back from the Bull and had begun to pass, two by two, across the bridge. Soon the whole bridge was trembling and resounding. The uncouth faces passed him two by two, stained yellow or red or livid by the sea and, as he strove to look at them with ease and indifference, a faint stain of personal shame and commiseration rose to his own face. Angry with himself he tried to hide his face from their eyes by gazing down sideways into the shallow swirling water under the bridge but he still saw a reflection therein of their topheavy silk hats and humble tapelike collars and loosely hanging clerical clothes.

—Brother Hickey.

Brother Quaid.

Brother MacArdle.

Brother Keogh.

Their piety would be like their names, like their faces, like their clothes: and it was idle for him to tell himself that their humble and contrite hearts, it might be, paid a far richer tribute of devotion than his had ever been, a gift tenfold more acceptable than his elaborate adoration. It was idle for him to move himself to be generous towards them, to tell himself that if he ever came to their gates, stripped of his pride, beaten and in beggar's weeds, that they would be generous towards him, loving him as themselves. Idle and embittering, finally, to argue, against his own dispassionate certitude, that the commandment of love bade us not to love our neighbour as ourselves with the same amount and intensity of love but to love him as ourselves with the same kind of love.

He drew forth a phrase from his treasure and spoke it softly to himself:

—A day of dappled seaborne clouds.[7]

The phrase and the day and the scene harmonised in a chord. Words. Was it their colours? He allowed them to glow and fade, hue after hue: sunrise gold, the russet and green of apple orchards, azure of waves, the greyfringed fleece of clouds. No, it was not their colours: it was the poise and balance of the period itself. Did he then love the rhythmic rise and fall of words better than their associations of legend and colour? Or was it that, being as weak of sight as he was shy of mind, he drew less pleasure from the reflection of the glowing sensible world through the prism of a language manycoloured and richly storied than from the contemplation of an inner world of individual emotions mirrored perfectly in a lucid supple periodic prose?[8]

He passed from the trembling bridge on to firm land again. At that instant, as it seemed to him, the air was chilled; and looking askance towards the water he saw a flying squall darkening and crisping suddenly the tide. A faint click at his heart, a faint throb in his throat told him once more of how his flesh dreaded the cold infrahuman[9] odour of the sea: yet he did not strike

6. Area to the north of Clontarf.
7. From *The Testimony of the Rocks* (1857), a theological treatise by Scottish writer Hugh Miller (1802–1856), though "seaborne" has been substituted for "breeze-borne."

8. Characterized by long (periodic) sentences that, with balanced subordinate clauses, delay completion of the thought until the end.
9. Below the human level.

across the downs on his left but held straight on along the spine of rocks that pointed against the river's mouth.

A veiled sunlight lit up faintly the grey sheet of water where the river was embayed.[1] In the distance along the course of the slowflowing Liffey slender masts flecked the sky and, more distant still, the dim fabric of the city lay prone in haze. Like a scene on some vague arras,[2] old as man's weariness, the image of the seventh city of Christendom was visible to him across the timeless air, no older nor more weary nor less patient of subjection than in the days of the thingmote.[3]

Disheartened, he raised his eyes towards the slowdrifting clouds, dappled and seaborne. They were voyaging across the deserts of the sky, a host of nomads on the march, voyaging high over Ireland, westward bound. The Europe they had come from lay out there beyond the Irish Sea, Europe of strange tongues and valleyed and woodbegirt[4] and citadelled and of entrenched and marshalled races. He heard a confused music within him as of memories and names which he was almost conscious of but could not capture even for an instant; then the music seemed to recede, to recede, to recede: and from each receding trail of nebulous music there fell always one longdrawn calling note, piercing like a star the dusk of silence. Again! Again! Again! Again! A voice from beyond the world was calling.

—Hello, Stephanos![5]

—Here comes The Dedalus!

—Ao! . . . Eh, give it over, Dwyer, I'm telling you or I'll give you a stuff in the kisser[6] for yourself. . . . Ao!

—Good man, Towser! Duck him!

—Come along, Dedalus! Bous Stephanoumenos! Bous Stephaneforos![7]

—Duck him! Guzzle him now, Towser!

—Help! Help! . . . Ao!

He recognised their speech collectively before he distinguished their faces. The mere sight of that medley of wet nakedness chilled him to the bone. Their bodies, corpsewhite or suffused with a pallid golden light or rawly tanned by the sun, gleamed with the wet of the sea. Their divingstone, poised on its rude supports and rocking under their plunges, and the rough-hewn stones of the sloping breakwater over which they scrambled in their horseplay gleamed with cold wet lustre. The towels with which they smacked their bodies were heavy with cold seawater: and drenched with cold brine was their matted hair.

He stood still in deference to their calls and parried their banter with easy words. How characterless they looked: Shuley without his deep unbuttoned collar, Ennis without his scarlet belt with the snaky clasp and Connolly without his Norfolk coat with the flapless sidepockets! It was a pain to see them and a swordlike pain to see the signs of adolescence that made repellent their pitiable nakedness. Perhaps they had taken refuge in number and noise from the secret dread in their souls. But he, apart from them and in silence, remembered in what dread he stood of the mystery of his own body.

1. Shaped into a bay.
2. Tapestry.
3. Mound in the center of Dublin that served as the meeting place for the council of law that ruled Dublin during the Scandinavian occupation (ca. 852–1014).

4. Surrounded by woods.
5. Wreath, crown, or garland (Greek).
6. A blow to the face or mouth.
7. Ox as wreath bearer for the sacrifice (Greek). "Bous Stephanoumenos": the ox soul of Stephen (Greek).

—Stephanos Dedalos! Bous Stephanoumenos! Bous Stephaneforos!

Their banter was not new to him and now, as always, it flattered his mild proud sovereignty. Now, as never before, his strange name seemed to him a prophecy. So timeless seemed the grey warm air, so fluid and impersonal his own mood, that all ages were as one to him. A moment before the ghost of the ancient kingdom of the Danes had looked forth through the vesture of the hazewrapped city. Now, at the name of the fabulous artificer,[8] he seemed to hear the noise of dim waves and to see a winged form flying above the waves and slowly climbing the air. What did it mean? Was it a quaint device opening a page of some medieval book of prophecies and symbols, a hawk-like man flying sunward above the sea, a prophecy of the end he had been born to serve and had been following through the mists of childhood and boyhood, a symbol of the artist forging anew in his workshop out of the sluggish matter of the earth a new soaring impalpable imperishable being?

His heart trembled; his breath came faster and a wild spirit passed over his limbs as though he were soaring sunward. His heart trembled in an ecstasy of fear and his soul was in flight. His soul was soaring in an air beyond the world and the body he knew was purified in a breath and delivered of incertitude and made radiant and commingled with the element of the spirit. An ecstasy of flight made radiant his eyes and wild his breath and tremulous and wild and radiant his windswept limbs.

—One! Two! . . . Look out!

—O, Cripes, I'm drownded!

—One! Two! Three and away!

—Me next! Me next!

—One! . . . Uk!

—Stephaneforos!

His throat ached with a desire to cry aloud, the cry of a hawk or eagle on high, to cry piercingly of his deliverance to the winds. This was the call of life to his soul not the dull gross voice of the world of duties and despair, not the inhuman voice that had called him to the pale service of the altar. An instant of wild flight had delivered him and the cry of triumph which his lips withheld cleft his brain.

—Stephaneforos!

What were they now but cerements[9] shaken from the body of death—the fear he had walked in night and day, the incertitude that had ringed him round, the shame that had abased him within and without—cerements, the linens of the grave?

His soul had arisen from the grave of boyhood, spurning her graveclothes. Yes! Yes! Yes! He would create proudly out of the freedom and power of his soul, as the great artificer whose name he bore, a living thing, new and soaring and beautiful, impalpable, imperishable.

He started up nervously from the stoneblock for he could no longer quench the flame in his blood. He felt his cheeks aflame and his throat throbbing with song. There was a lust of wandering in his feet that burned to set out for the ends of the earth. On! On! his heart seemed to cry. Evening would deepen above the sea, night fall upon the plains, dawn glimmer before the wanderer and show him strange fields and hills and faces. Where?

8. Daedalus, legendary father of Icarus, whose name in Greek means "artificer."

9. Shrouds, or waxed wrappings for the dead.

He looked northward towards Howth.[1] The sea had fallen below the line of seawrack on the shallow side of the breakwater and already the tide was running out fast along the foreshore. Already one long oval bank of sand lay warm and dry amid the wavelets. Here and there warm isles of sand gleamed above the shallow tide: and about the isles and around the long bank and amid the shallow currents of the beach were lightclad gayclad figures wading and delving.

In a few moments he was barefoot, his stockings folded in his pockets and his canvas shoes dangling by their knotted laces over his shoulders: and, picking a pointed salteaten stick out of the jetsam among the rocks, he clambered down the slope of the breakwater.

There was a long rivulet in the strand: and, as he waded slowly up its course, he wondered at the endless drift of seaweed. Emerald and black and russet and olive, it moved beneath the current, swaying and turning. The water of the rivulet was dark with endless drift and mirrored the highdrifting clouds. The clouds were drifting above him silently and silently the seatangle was drifting below him; and the grey warm air was still: and a new wild life was singing in his veins.

Where was his boyhood now? Where was the soul that had hung back from her destiny, to brood alone upon the shame of her wounds and in her house of squalor and subterfuge to queen it in faded cerements and in wreaths that withered at the touch? Or where was he?

He was alone. He was unheeded, happy and near to the wild heart of life. He was alone and young and wilful and wildhearted, alone amid a waste of wild air and brackish waters and the seaharvest of shells and tangle and veiled grey sunlight and gayclad lightclad figures of children and girls and voices childish and girlish in the air.

A girl stood before him in midstream: alone and still, gazing out to sea. She seemed like one whom magic had changed into the likeness of a strange and beautiful seabird. Her long slender bare legs were delicate as a crane's and pure save where an emerald trail of seaweed had fashioned itself as a sign upon the flesh. Her thighs, fuller and softhued as ivory, were bared almost to the hips where the white fringes of her drawers[2] were like featherings of soft white down. Her slateblue skirts were kilted boldly about her waist and dovetailed behind her. Her bosom was as a bird's, soft and slight; slight and soft as the breast of some darkplumaged dove. But her long fair hair was girlish; and girlish, and touched with the wonder of mortal beauty, her face.

She was alone and still, gazing out to sea; and when she felt his presence and the worship of his eyes her eyes turned to him in quiet sufferance of his gaze, without shame or wantonness. Long, long she suffered his gaze and then quietly withdrew her eyes from his and bent them towards the stream, gently stirring the water with her foot hither and thither. The first faint noise of gently moving water broke the silence, low and faint and whispering, faint as the bells of sleep; hither and thither, hither and thither: and a faint flame trembled on her cheek.

—Heavenly God! cried Stephen's soul in an outburst of profane joy.

He turned away from her suddenly and set off across the strand. His cheeks were aflame; his body was aglow; his limbs were trembling. On and

---

1. Hill that forms the northeast headland of Dublin Bay.

2. Underwear.

on and on and on he strode, far out over the sands, singing wildly to the sea, crying to greet the advent of the life that had cried to him.

Her image had passed into his soul for ever and no word had broken the holy silence of his ecstasy. Her eyes had called him and his soul had leaped at the call. To live, to err, to fall, to triumph, to recreate life out of life! A wild angel had appeared to him, the angel of mortal youth and beauty, an envoy from the fair courts of life, to throw open before him in an instant of ecstasy the gates of all the ways of error and glory. On and on and on and on!

He halted suddenly and heard his heart in the silence. How far had he walked? What hour was it?

There was no human figure near him nor any sound borne to him over the air. But the tide was near the turn and already the day was on the wane. He turned landward and ran towards the shore and, running up the sloping beach, reckless of the sharp shingle,[3] found a sandy nook amid a ring of tufted sandknolls and lay down there that the peace and silence of the evening might still the riot of his blood.

He felt above him the vast indifferent dome and the calm processes of the heavenly bodies: and the earth beneath him, the earth that had borne him, had taken him to her breast.

He closed his eyes in the languor of sleep. His eyelids trembled as if they felt the vast cyclic movement of the earth and her watchers, trembled as if they felt the strange light of some new world. His soul was swooning into some new world, fantastic, dim, uncertain as under sea, traversed by cloudy shapes and beings. A world, a glimmer or a flower? Glimmering and trembling, trembling and unfolding, a breaking light, an opening flower, it spread in endless succession to itself, breaking in full crimson and unfolding and fading to palest rose, leaf by leaf and wave of light by wave of light, flooding all the heavens with its soft flushes, every flush deeper than other.

Evening had fallen when he woke and the sand and arid grasses of his bed glowed no longer. He rose slowly and, recalling the rapture of his sleep, sighed at its joy.

He climbed to the crest of the sandhill and gazed about him. Evening had fallen. A rim of the young moon cleft the pale waste of sky like the rim of a silver hoop embedded in grey sand: and the tide was flowing in fast to the land with a low whisper of her waves, islanding a few last figures in distant pools.

V

He drained his third cup of watery tea to the dregs and set to chewing the crusts of fried bread that were scattered near him, staring into the dark pool of the jar. The yellow dripping[4] had been scooped out like a boghole[5] and the pool under it brought back to his memory the dark turfcoloured water of the bath in Clongowes. The box of pawntickets at his elbow had just been rifled and he took up idly one after another in his greasy fingers the blue and white dockets, scrawled and sanded and creased and bearing the name of the pledger as Daly or MacEvoy.[6]

---

3. Loose pebbles collected on the shore.
4. Melted fat that has dripped from roasted meat and is then used cold.
5. Natural hole with a swampy bottom.

6. Aliases used by the Dedalus family to pawn their belongings. "Dockets": pawn tickets. "Pledger": person who pawns something.

—1 Pair Buskins[7]
   1 D. Coat
   3 Articles and White
   1 Man's Pants

Then he put them aside and gazed thoughtfully at the lid of the box, speckled with lousemarks, and asked vaguely:

—How much is the clock fast now?

His mother straightened the battered alarmclock that was lying on its side in the middle of the kitchen mantelpiece until its dial showed a quarter to twelve and then laid it once more on its side.

—An hour and twentyfive minutes, she said. The right time now is twenty past ten. The dear knows[8] you might try to be in time for your lectures.

—Fill out[9] the place for me to wash, said Stephen.

—Katey, fill out the place for Stephen to wash.

—Boody, fill out the place for Stephen to wash.

—I can't. I'm going for blue.[1] Fill it out, you, Maggie.

When the enamelled basin had been fitted into the well of the sink and the old washingglove flung on the side of it he allowed his mother to scrub his neck and root into the folds of his ears and into the interstices at the wings of his nose.

—Well, it's a poor case, she said, when a university student is so dirty that his mother has to wash him.

—But it gives you pleasure, said Stephen calmly.

An earsplitting whistle was heard from upstairs and his mother thrust a damp overall into his hands, saying:

—Dry yourself and hurry out for the love of goodness.

A second shrill whistle, prolonged angrily, brought one of the girls to the foot of the staircase.

—Yes, father?

—Is your lazy bitch of a brother gone out yet?

—Yes, father.

—Sure?

—Yes, father.

—Hm!

The girl came back making signs to him to be quick and go out quietly by the back. Stephen laughed and said:

—He has a curious idea of genders if he thinks a bitch is masculine.

—Ah, it's a scandalous shame for you, Stephen, said his mother, and you'll live to rue the day you set your foot in that place. I know how it has changed you.

—Good morning, everybody, said Stephen smiling and kissing the tips of his fingers in adieu.

The lane behind the terrace was waterlogged and as he went down it slowly, choosing his steps amid heaps of wet rubbish, he heard a mad nun screeching in the nuns' madhouse[2] beyond the wall:

—Jesus! O Jesus! Jesus!

---

7. Boots reaching up the calf, usually to the knee.
8. God knows.
9. Set up.

1. Working as hard as possible (according to Don Gifford).
2. St. Vincent's Lunatic Asylum, run by the Sisters of Charity, in Fairview, in northeast Dublin.

He shook the sound out of his ears by an angry toss of his head and hurried on, stumbling through the mouldering[3] offal, his heart already bitten by an ache of loathing and bitterness. His father's whistle, his mother's mutterings, the screech of an unseen maniac were to him now so many voices offending and threatening to humble the pride of his youth. He drove their echoes even out of his heart with an execration: but as he walked down the avenue and felt the grey morning light falling about him through the dripping trees and smelt the strange wild smell of the wet leaves and bark his soul was loosed of her miseries.

The rainladen trees of the avenue evoked in him, as always, memories of the girls and women in the plays of Gerhart Hauptmann:[4] and the memory of their pale sorrows and the fragrance falling from the wet branches mingled in a mood of quiet joy. His morning walk across the city had begun: and he foreknew that as he passed the sloblands of Fairview[5] he would think of the cloistral silverveined prose of Newman, that as he walked along the North Strand Road, glancing idly at the windows of the provision shops, he would recall the dark humour of Guido Cavalcanti[6] and smile, that as he went by Baird's stonecutting works in Talbot Place[7] the spirit of Ibsen[8] would blow through him like a keen wind, a spirit of wayward boyish beauty, and that passing a grimy marine dealer's shop beyond the Liffey he would repeat the song by Ben Jonson which begins:

I was not wearier where I lay.[9]

His mind when wearied of its search for the essence of beauty amid the spectral words of Aristotle[1] or Aquinas turned often for its pleasure to the dainty songs of the Elizabethans.[2] His mind, in the vesture of a doubting monk, stood often in shadow under the windows of that age, to hear the grave and mocking music of the lutenists or the frank laughter of waistcoateers until a laugh too low, a phrase, tarnished by time, of chambering[3] and false honour stung his monkish pride and drove him on from his lurkingplace.

The lore which he was believed to pass his days brooding upon so that it had rapt him from the companionships of youth was only a garner of slender sentences from Aristotle's poetics and psychology and a *Synopsis Philosophiae Scholasticae ad mentem divi Thomae.*[4] His thinking was a dusk of doubt and selfmistrust lit up at moments by the lightnings of intuition, but lightnings of so clear a splendour that in those moments the world perished about his feet as if it had been fireconsumed: and thereafter his tongue grew heavy and he met the eyes of others with unanswering eyes for he felt that the spirit of beauty had folded him round like a mantle and that in revery at least he had been acquainted with nobility. But when this brief pride of silence upheld him no longer he was glad to find himself still in the midst

3. Rotting or decaying.
4. German dramatist (1862–1946).
5. Tidal flats created by the flow of the Tolka into Dublin Bay.
6. Italian poet (ca. 1259–1300).
7. Engineering firm located behind the Custom House in central Dublin, north of the Liffey. Stephen has walked southwest through the city toward Trinity College.
8. Norwegian dramatist (1828–1906).
9. From *The Vision of Delight* (1617), by English playwright Ben Jonson (1572–1637).
1. Greek philosopher (384–322 B.C.E.).
2. Poets during the reign of Queen Elizabeth I (1558–1603).
3. Sexually promiscuous behavior. "Waistcoateers": lower-class prostitutes.
4. *A Synopsis of Scholastic Philosophy for the Understanding of St. Thomas* (Latin). "Garner": collection. "Aristotle's poetics and psychology": the Greek philosopher's *Poetics* and his writing in *De Anima* (*Of the Soul*) and *De Sensu* (*Of the Senses*).

of common lives, passing on his way amid the squalor and noise and sloth of the city fearlessly and with a light heart.

Near the hoardings[5] on the canal he met the consumptive[6] man with the doll's face and the brimless hat coming towards him down the slope of the bridge with little steps, tightly buttoned into his chocolate overcoat and holding his furled umbrella a span or two from him like a diviningrod.[7] It must be eleven, he thought, and peered into a dairy to see the time. The clock in the dairy told him that it was five minutes to five but, as he turned away, he heard a clock somewhere near him but unseen beating eleven strokes in swift precision. He laughed as he heard it for it made him think of MacCann; and he saw him a squat figure in a shooting jacket and breeches and with a fair goatee standing in the wind at Hopkins' corner[8] and heard him say:

—Dedalus, you're an antisocial being, wrapped up in yourself. I'm not. I'm a democrat: and I'll work and act for social liberty and equality among all classes and sexes in the United States of the Europe of the future.

Eleven! Then he was late for that lecture too. What day of the week was it? He stopped at a newsagent's to read the headline of a placard. Thursday. Ten to eleven; English: eleven to twelve; French: twelve to one; physics. He fancied to himself the English lecture and felt, even at that distance, restless and helpless. He saw the heads of his classmates meekly bent as they wrote in their notebooks the points they were bidden to note, nominal definitions, essential definitions[9] and examples or dates of birth and death, chief works, a favourable and an unfavourable criticism side by side. His own head was unbent for his thoughts wandered abroad and whether he looked around the little class of students or out of the window across the desolate gardens of the green an odour assailed him of cheerless cellardamp and decay. Another head than his, right before him in the first benches, was poised squarely above its bending fellows like the head of a priest appealing without humility to the tabernacle for the humble worshippers about him. Why was it that when he thought of Cranly he could never raise before his mind the entire image of his body but only the image of the head and face? Even now against the grey curtain of the morning he saw it before him like the phantom of a dream, the face of a severed head or deathmask, crowned on the brows by its stiff black upright hair as by an iron crown. It was a priestlike face, priestlike in its pallor, in the wide-winged nose, in the shadowings below the eyes and along the jaws, priestlike in the lips that were long and bloodless and faintly smiling: and Stephen, remembering swiftly how he had told Cranly of all the tumults and unrest and longings in his soul, day after day and night by night only to be answered by his friend's listening silence, would have told himself that it was the face of a guilty priest who heard confessions of those whom he had not power to absolve but that he felt again in memory the gaze of its dark womanish eyes.

Through this image he had a glimpse of a strange dark cavern of speculation but at once turned away from it feeling that it was not yet the hour to enter it. But the nightshade[1] of his friend's listlessness seemed to be diffusing in the air around him a tenuous and deadly exhalation: and he found himself

5. Board fences on which advertisements are posted.

6. Suffering from tuberculosis.

7. Rod used to search for water underground, by observing its point, which supposedly moves in response to unseen forces.

8. Corner of Lower Sackville Street and Eden Quay, where Hopkins and Hopkins, a jewelry and metalsmith shop, was located.

9. Descriptions of effect and descriptions of cause, from Aristotle's *Posterior Analytics*.

1. Poisonous flowering plant.

glancing from one casual word to another on his right or left in stolid wonder that they had been so silently emptied of instantaneous sense until every mean shop legend[2] bound his mind like the words of a spell and his soul shrivelled up sighing with age as he walked on in a lane among heaps of dead language. His own consciousness of language was ebbing from his brain and trickling into the very words themselves which set to band and disband themselves in wayward rhythms:

> *The ivy whines upon the wall*
> *And whines and twines upon the wall*
> *The ivy whines upon the wall*
> *The yellow ivy on the wall*
> *Ivy, ivy up the wall.*

Did any one ever hear such drivel? Lord Almighty! Who ever heard of ivy whining on a wall? Yellow ivy: that was all right. Yellow ivory also. And what about ivory ivy?

The word now shone in his brain, clearer and brighter than any ivory sawn from the mottled tusks of elephants. *Ivory, ivoire, avorio, ebur.*[3] One of the first examples that he had learnt in Latin had run: *India mittit ebur:*[4] and he recalled the shrewd northern face of the rector who had taught him to construe the Metamorphoses of Ovid in a courtly English, made whimsical by the mention of porkers and potsherds and chines of bacon.[5] He had learnt what little he knew of the laws of Latin verse from a ragged book written by a Portuguese priest:

Contrahit orator, variant in carmine vates.[6]

The crises and victories and secessions in Roman history were handed on to him in the trite words *in tanto discrimine*[7] and he had tried to peer into the social life of the city of cities through the words *implere ollam denario-rum* which the rector had rendered sonorously as the filling of a pot with denaries.[8] The pages of his timeworn Horace[9] never felt cold to the touch even when his own fingers were cold: they were human pages: and fifty years before they had been turned by the human fingers of John Duncan Inverarity and by his brother William Malcolm Inverarity. Yes, those were noble names on the dusky flyleaf and, even for so poor a Latinist as he, the dusky verses were as fragrant as though they had lain all those years in myrtle and lavender and vervain:[1] but yet it wounded him to think that he would never be but a shy guest at the feast of the world's culture and that the monkish learning, in terms of which he was striving to forge out an esthetic philosophy, was held no higher by the age he lived in than the subtle and curious jargons of heraldry and falconry.

The grey block of Trinity[2] on his left, set heavily in the city's ignorance like a great dull stone set in a cumbrous ring, pulled his mind downward: and while he was striving this way and that to free his feet from the fetters

---

2. Sign bearing the name of a store.
3. Translations of "ivory" into French, Italian, and Latin.
4. India sends ivory (Latin).
5. I.e., little pigs and broken pottery and pigs' backbones.
6. The orator summarizes, the poet elaborates in song (Latin). From the *Prosodia*, by the Portu-

guese Jesuit Emmanuel Alvarez (1526–1582).
7. In such a great crisis (Latin).
8. This is the rector's translation of the preceding Latin phrase. "Denaries": Roman coins.
9. Roman poet (65–8 B.C.E.).
1. Herb often used for medical or magical purposes.
2. I.e., Trinity College, a Protestant institution.

of the reformed conscience[3] he came upon the droll statue of the national poet of Ireland.[4]

He looked at it without anger: for, though sloth of the body and of the soul crept over it like unseen vermin, over the shuffling feet and up the folds of the cloak and around the servile head, it seemed humbly conscious of its indignity. It was a Firbolg in the borrowed cloak of a Milesian;[5] and he thought of his friend Davin, the peasant student. It was a jesting name between them but the young peasant bore with it lightly, saying:

—Go on, Stevie. I have a hard head, you tell me. Call me what you will.

The homely version of his christian name on the lips of his friend had touched Stephen pleasantly when first heard for he was as formal in speech with others as they were with him. Often, as he sat in Davin's rooms in Grantham Street,[6] wondering at his friend's wellmade boots that flanked the wall pair by pair and repeating for his friend's simple ear the verses and cadences of others which were the veils of his own longing and dejection, the rude Firbolg mind of his listener had drawn his mind towards it and flung it back again, drawing it by a quiet inbred courtesy of attention or by a quaint turn of old English speech or by the force of its delight in rude bodily skill (for Davin had sat at the feet of Michael Cusack, the Gael[7]), repelling swiftly and suddenly by a grossness of intelligence or by a bluntness of feeling or by a dull stare of terror in the eyes the terror of soul of a starving Irish village in which the curfew[8] was still a nightly fear.

Side by side with his memory of the deeds of prowess of his uncle Mat Davin, the athlete,[9] the young peasant worshipped the sorrowful legend of Ireland. The gossip of his fellowstudents which strove to render the flat life of the college significant at any cost loved to think of him as a young fenian.[1] His nurse had taught him Irish and shaped the rude imagination by the broken lights of Irish myth. He stood towards this myth upon which no individual mind had ever drawn out a line of beauty and to its unwieldy tales that divided against themselves as they moved down the cycles[2] in the same attitude as towards the Roman catholic religion, the attitude of a dullwitted loyal serf. Whatsoever of thought or of feeling came to him from England or by way of English culture his mind stood armed against in obedience to a password: and of the world that lay beyond England he knew only the foreign legion of France in which he spoke of serving.

Coupling this ambition with the young man's diffident humour Stephen had often called him one of the tame geese:[3] and there was even a point of irritation in the name pointed against that very reluctance of speech and deed in his friend which seemed so often to stand between Stephen's mind, eager of speculation, and the hidden ways of Irish life.

3. Attitudes characteristic of English Protestantism (post-Reformation).

4. Thomas Moore (1779–1852).

5. Half-legendary civilized invader of Ireland. "Firbolg": half-legendary primitive inhabitants of Ireland.

6. Street in Dublin to the west of University College.

7. Founder (1847–1906) of the Gaelic Athletic Association, one of the movements meant to revive Ireland's Celtic heritage.

8. Governmental order to return home and extinguish lights by a certain time, mandated by the Coercion Acts passed in England.

9. Maurice Davin (1842–1927), another founder of the Gaelic Athletic Association and one of several brothers who held records in running and jumping in the 1870s.

1. Member of the Irish Republican Brotherhood, founded in 1858 and dedicated to militant nationalism.

2. Groups of Irish epic legends.

3. A person who lacks the courage to leave Ireland, in contrast to the so-called wild geese, Irish Catholic soldiers who left the country to serve in foreign armies, after William III reconquered Ireland in 1691.

One night the young peasant, his spirit stung by the violent or luxurious language in which Stephen escaped from the cold silence of intellectual revolt, had called up before Stephen's mind a strange vision. The two were walking slowly towards Davin's rooms through the dark narrow streets of the poorer jews.

—A thing happened to myself, Stevie, last autumn coming on winter and I never told it to a living soul and you are the first person now I ever told it to. I disremember if it was October or November. It was October because it was before I came up here to join the matriculation class.[4]

Stephen had turned his smiling eyes towards his friend's face, flattered by his confidence and won over to sympathy by the speaker's simple accent.

—I was away all that day from my own place, over in Buttevant[5] (I don't know if you know where that is) at a hurling match[6] between the Croke's Own Boys and the Fearless Thurles and by God, Stevie, that was the hard fight. My first cousin Fonsy Davin was stripped to his buff that day minding cool[7] for the Limericks but he was up with the forwards half the time and shouting like mad. I never will forget that day. One of the Crokes made a woful wipe at him one time with his camaun[8] and I declare to God he was within an aim's ace of getting it at the side of the temple. O, honest to God, if the crook of it caught him that time he was done for.

—I am glad he escaped, Stephen had said with a laugh, but surely that's not the strange thing that happened you?

—Well, I suppose that doesn't interest you but leastways there was such noise after the match that I missed the train home and I couldn't get any kind of a yoke[9] to give me a lift for, as luck would have it, there was a mass meeting that same day over in Castletownroche[1] and all the cars in the country were there. So there was nothing for it only to stay the night or to foot it out. Well, I started to walk and on I went and it was coming on night when I got into the Ballyhoura hills, that's better than ten miles from Kilmallock[2] and there's a long lonely road after that. You wouldn't see the sign of a christian house along the road or hear a sound. It was pitch dark almost. Once or twice I stopped by the way under a bush to redden[3] my pipe and only for the dew was thick I'd have stretched out there and slept. At last after a bend of the road I spied a little cottage with a light in the window. I went up and knocked at the door. A voice asked who was there and I answered I was over at the match in Buttevant and was walking back and that I'd be thankful for a glass of water. After a while a young woman opened the door and brought me out a big mug of milk. She was half undressed as if she was going to bed when I knocked and she had her hair hanging: and I thought by her figure and by something in the look of her eyes that she must be carrying a child. She kept me in talk a long while at the door and I thought it strange because her breast and her shoulders were bare. She asked me was I tired and would I like to stop the night there. She said she was all alone in the house and that her husband had gone that morning to Queenstown with his sister to see her

---

4. Students in their first year of study.
5. Town in County Cork, southwest of Dublin.
6. An Irish game, revived by the Gaelic Athletic Association, that resembles both field hockey and lacrosse, with fifteen players on each team.
7. Keeping goal. "Stripped to his buff": shirtless.
8. The bladed stick used in hurling.

9. A general term for a vehicle or a person operating one.
1. Town in County Cork.
2. Small market town north of Buttevant. Davin was walking north.
3. I.e., to light.

off. And all the time she was talking, Stevie, she had her eyes fixed on my face and she stood so close to me I could hear her breathing. When I handed her back the mug at last she took my hand to draw me in over the threshold and said: *Come in and stay the night here. You've no call to be frightened. There's no-one in it but ourselves.* . . . . I didn't go in, Stevie. I thanked her and went on my way again, all in a fever. At the first bend of the road I looked back and she was standing in the door.

The last words of Davin's story sang in his memory and the figure of the woman in the story stood forth reflected in other figures of the peasant women whom he had seen standing in the doorways at Clane as the college cars drove by, as a type of her race and his own, a batlike soul waking to the consciousness of itself in darkness and secrecy and loneliness and, through the eyes and voice and gesture of a woman without guile, calling the stranger to her bed.

A hand was laid on his arm and a young voice cried:

—Ah, gentleman, your own girl, sir! The first handsel[4] today, gentleman. Buy that lovely bunch. Will you, gentleman?

The blue flowers which she lifted towards him and her young blue eyes seemed to him at that instant images of guilelessness: and he halted till the image had vanished and he saw only her ragged dress and damp coarse hair and hoydenish[5] face.

—Do, gentleman! Don't forget your own girl, sir!

—I have no money, said Stephen.

—Buy them lovely ones, will you, sir? Only a penny.

—Did you hear what I said? asked Stephen, bending towards her. I told you I had no money. I tell you again now.

—Well, sure, you will some day, sir, please God, the girl answered after an instant.

—Possibly, said Stephen, but I don't think it likely.

He left her quickly, fearing that her intimacy might turn to gibing and wishing to be out of the way before she offered her ware to another, a tourist from England or a student of Trinity. Grafton Street[6] along which he walked prolonged that moment of discouraged poverty. In the roadway at the head of the street a slab was set to the memory of Wolfe Tone[7] and he remembered having been present with his father at its laying. He remembered with bitterness that scene of tawdry tribute. There were four French delegates in a brake and one, a plump smiling young man, held, wedged on a stick, a card on which were printed the words: *Vive l'Irlande!*[8]

But the trees in Stephen's Green[9] were fragrant of rain and the rainsodden earth gave forth its mortal odour, a faint incense rising upward through the mould from many hearts. The soul of the gallant venal city which his elders had told him of had shrunk with time to a faint mortal odour rising from the earth and he knew that in a moment when he entered the sombre college he would be conscious of a corruption other than that of Buck Egan and Burnchapel Whaley.[1]

---

4. First, good-luck sale.
5. With the characteristics of a hoyden, a rude, badly mannered girl.
6. Fashionable shopping street in Dublin.
7. Irish nationalist (1763–1798), imprisoned after leading a French army into Ireland to fight for independence during the 1798 Rebellion. A memorial to him was erected in 1898.

8. Long live Ireland (French).
9. Public park in the center of Dublin.
1. Combined reference to men with reputations for extreme behavior, including corruption and black masses: John "Bully" Egan (1750–1810), Richard "Burnchapel" Whaley (ca. 1700–1769), and his son, Thomas "Buck" Whaley (1766–1800).

It was too late to go upstairs to the French class. He crossed the hall and took the corridor to the left which led to the physics theatre. The corridor was dark and silent but not unwatchful. Why did he feel that it was not unwatchful? Was it because he had heard that in Buck Whaley's time there was a secret staircase there? Or was the jesuit house extraterritorial[2] and was he walking among aliens? The Ireland of Tone and of Parnell seemed to have receded in space.

He opened the door of the theatre and halted in the chilly grey light that struggled through the dusty windows. A figure was crouching before the large grate and by its leanness and greyness he knew that it was the dean of studies lighting the fire. Stephen closed the door quietly and approached the fireplace.

—Good morning, sir! Can I help you?

The priest looked up quickly and said:

—One moment now, Mr Dedalus, and you will see. There is an art in lighting a fire. We have the liberal arts and we have the useful arts. This is one of the useful arts.

—I will try to learn it, said Stephen.

—Not too much coal, said the dean, working briskly at his task, that is one of the secrets.

He produced four candle butts from the sidepockets of his soutane and placed them deftly among the coals and twisted papers. Stephen watched him in silence. Kneeling thus on the flagstone to kindle the fire and busied with the disposition of his wisps of paper and candle butts he seemed more than ever a humble server making ready the place of sacrifice in an empty temple, a levite[3] of the Lord. Like a levite's robe of plain linen the faded worn soutane draped the kneeling figure of one whom the canonicals or the bell-bordered ephod[4] would irk and trouble. His very body had waxed old in lowly service of the Lord—in tending the fire upon the altar, in bearing tidings secretly, in waiting upon worldlings, in striking swiftly when bidden—and yet had remained ungraced by aught[5] of saintly or of prelatic beauty. Nay, his very soul had waxed old in that service without growing towards light and beauty or spreading abroad a sweet odour of her sanctity—a mortified will no more responsive to the thrill of its obedience than was to the thrill of love or combat his aging body, spare and sinewy, greyed with a silverpointed down.

The dean rested back on his hunkers[6] and watched the sticks catch. Stephen, to fill the silence, said:

—I am sure I could not light a fire.

—You are an artist, are you not, Mr Dedalus? said the dean, glancing up and blinking his pale eyes. The object of the artist is the creation of the beautiful. What the beautiful is is another question.

He rubbed his hands slowly and drily over the difficulty.

—Can you solve that question now? he asked.

—Aquinas, answered Stephen, says *Pulcra sunt quae visa placent.*[7]

—This fire before us, said the dean, will be pleasing to the eye. Will it therefore be beautiful?

---

2. Possessing an allegiance to somewhere outside Ireland—in this case, presumably to the Vatican.
3. Under Mosaic law, a subordinate priest or assistant.
4. An elaborate robe for a priest.

5. Anything.
6. On his heels, in a squatting position.
7. Those things are beautiful that please the eye (Latin), a statement based on one by Aquinas in his *Summa Theologica.*

—In so far as it is apprehended by the sight, which I suppose means here esthetic intellection, it will be beautiful. But Aquinas also says *Bonum est in quod tendit appetitus.*[8] In so far as it satisfies the animal craving for warmth fire is a good. In hell however it is an evil.

—Quite so, said the dean, you have certainly hit the nail on the head.

He rose nimbly and went towards the door, set it ajar and said:

—A draught is said to be a help in these matters.

As he came back to the hearth, limping slightly but with a brisk step, Stephen saw the silent soul of a jesuit look out at him from the pale loveless eyes. Like Ignatius he was lame but in his eyes burned no spark of Ignatius' enthusiasm. Even the legendary craft of the company,[9] a craft subtler and more secret than its fabled books of secret subtle wisdom, had not fired his soul with the energy of apostleship. It seemed as if he used the shifts and lore and cunning of the world, as bidden to do, for the greater glory of God, without joy in their handling or hatred of that in them which was evil but turning them, with a firm gesture of obedience, back upon themselves: and for all this silent service it seemed as if he loved not at all the master and little, if at all, the ends he served. *Similiter atque senis baculus,*[1] he was, as the founder would have had him, like a staff in an old man's hand, to be left in a corner, to be leaned on in the road at nightfall or in stress of weather, to lie with a lady's nosegay on a garden seat, to be raised in menace.

The dean returned to the hearth and began to stroke his chin.

—When may we expect to have something from you on the esthetic question? he asked.

—From me! said Stephen in astonishment. I stumble on an idea once a fortnight if I am lucky.

—These questions are very profound, Mr Dedalus, said the dean. It is like looking down from the cliffs of Moher[2] into the depths. Many go down into the depths and never come up. Only the trained diver can go down into those depths and explore them and come to the surface again.

—If you mean speculation, sir, said Stephen, I also am sure that there is no such thing as free thinking inasmuch as all thinking must be bound by its own laws.

—Ha!

—For my purpose I can work on at present by the light of one or two ideas of Aristotle and Aquinas.

—I see. I quite see your point.

—I need them only for my own use and guidance until I have done something for myself by their light. If the lamp smokes or smells I shall try to trim it. If it does not give light enough I shall sell it and buy or borrow another.

—Epictetus[3] also had a lamp, said the dean, which was sold for a fancy price after his death. It was the lamp he wrote his philosophical dissertations by. You know Epictetus?

—An old gentleman, said Stephen coarsely, who said that the soul is very like a bucketful of water.

8. The good is in that which is desired (Latin). Another statement from Aquinas.
9. I.e., the Jesuits.
1. Similar to an old man's walking staff (Latin), a phrase from St. Ignatius's *Constitution of the*

Society of Jesus.
2. Dramatic cliffs on the west coast of Ireland, in County Clare.
3. Greek Stoic philosopher (ca. 55–ca. 135 C.E.).

—He tells us in his homely way, the dean went on, that he put an iron lamp before a statue of one of the gods and that a thief stole the lamp. What did the philosopher do? He reflected that it was in the character of a thief to steal and determined to buy an earthen lamp next day instead of the iron lamp.

A smell of molten tallow came up from the dean's candle butts and fused itself in Stephen's consciousness with the jingle of the words, bucket and lamp and lamp and bucket. The priest's voice too had a hard jingling tone. Stephen's mind halted by instinct, checked by the strange tone and the imagery and by the priest's face which seemed like an unlit lamp or a reflector hung in a false focus. What lay behind it or within it? A dull torpor of the soul or the dullness of the thundercloud, charged with intellection and capable of the gloom of God?

—I meant a different kind of lamp, sir, said Stephen.

—Undoubtedly, said the dean.

—One difficulty, said Stephen, in esthetic discussion is to know whether words are being used according to the literary tradition or according to the tradition of the marketplace.[4] I remember a sentence of Newman's in which he says of the Blessed Virgin that she was detained in the full company of the saints. The use of the word in the marketplace is quite different. *I hope I am not detaining you.*

—Not in the least, said the dean politely.

—No, no, said Stephen smiling, I mean . . . .

—Yes, yes: I see, said the dean quickly, I quite catch the point: *detain.*

He thrust forward his under jaw and uttered a dry short cough.

—To return to the lamp, he said, the feeding of it is also a nice problem. You must choose the pure oil and you must be careful when you pour it in not to overflow it, not to pour in more than the funnel can hold.

—What funnel? asked Stephen.

—The funnel through which you pour the oil into your lamp.

—That? said Stephen. Is that called a funnel? Is it not a tundish?[5]

—What is a tundish?

—That. The . . . the funnel.

—Is that called a tundish in Ireland? asked the dean. I never heard the word in my life.

—It is called a tundish in Lower Drumcondra,[6] said Stephen laughing, where they speak the best English.

—A tundish! said the dean reflectively. That is a most interesting word. I must look that word up. Upon my word I must.

His courtesy of manner rang a little false and Stephen looked at the English convert with the same eyes as the elder brother in the parable may have turned on the prodigal.[7] A humble follower in the wake of clamorous conversions, a poor Englishman in Ireland, he seemed to have entered on the stage of jesuit history when that strange play of intrigue and suffering and envy and struggle and indignity had been all but given through—a latecomer, a tardy spirit.[8] From what had he set out? Perhaps he had been born and bred

---

4. I.e, colloquially.
5. An English, not an Irish, word for a funnel commonly used in brewing.
6. Northern suburb of Dublin.

7. Cf. Luke 15.11–32, which recounts the story of the younger prodigal son, who is loved by his father despite his wasteful ways.
8. A late convert.

among serious dissenters,[9] seeing salvation in Jesus only and abhorring the vain pomps of the establishment. Had he felt the need of an implicit faith amid the welter of sectarianism and the jargon of its turbulent schisms, six principle men, peculiar people, seed and snake baptists, supralapsarian dogmatists?[1] Had he found the true church all of a sudden in winding up to the end like a reel of cotton some finespun line of reasoning upon insufflation or the imposition of hands or the procession of the Holy Ghost?[2] Or had Lord Christ touched him and bidden him follow, like that disciple who had sat at the receipt of custom, as he sat by the door of some zincroofed chapel, yawning and telling over his church pence?

The dean repeated the word yet again.

—Tundish! Well now, that is interesting!

—The question you asked me a moment ago seems to me more interesting. What is that beauty which the artist struggles to express from lumps of earth, said Stephen coldly.

The little word seemed to have turned a rapier point of his sensitiveness against this courteous and vigilant foe. He felt with a smart of dejection that the man to whom he was speaking was a countryman of Ben Jonson. He thought:

—The language in which we are speaking is his before it is mine. How different are the words *home, Christ, ale, master* on his lips and on mine! I cannot speak or write these words without unrest of spirit. His language, so familiar and so foreign, will always be for me an acquired speech. I have not made or accepted its words. My voice holds them at bay. My soul frets in the shadow of his language.

—And to distinguish between the beautiful and the sublime, the dean added. To distinguish between moral beauty and material beauty. And to inquire what kind of beauty is proper to each of the various arts. These are some interesting points we might take up.

Stephen, disheartened suddenly by the dean's firm dry tone, was silent. The dean also was silent: and through the silence a distant noise of many boots and confused voices came up the staircase.

—In pursuing these speculations, said the dean conclusively, there is however the danger of perishing of inanition.[3] First you must take your degree. Set that before you as your first aim. Then, little by little, you will see your way. I mean, in every sense, your way in life and in thinking. It may be uphill pedalling at first. Take Mr Moonan. He was a long time before he got to the top. But he got there.

—I may not have his talent, said Stephen quietly.

—You never know, said the dean brightly. We never can say what is in us. I most certainly should not be despondent. *Per aspera ad astra.*[4]

He left the hearth quickly and went towards the landing to oversee the arrival of the first arts' class.

Leaning against the fireplace Stephen heard him greet briskly and impartially every student of the class and could almost see the frank smiles of the

9. Protestants who were not members of the Church of England.
1. All dissenting Baptist sects.
2. Part of the doctrine of the Trinity, which holds that the Holy Ghost proceeds from the Father and the Son. "Insufflation": breathing spiritual life into a person. "Imposition of hands": the laying-on of hands, which symbolizes the expulsion of evil, as at baptism.
3. Condition of being empty or exhausted; starvation.
4. Through difficulty to the stars (Latin).

coarser students. A desolating pity began to fall like a dew upon his easily embittered heart for this faithful servingman of the knightly Loyola, for this halfbrother of the clergy, more venal than they in speech, more steadfast of soul than they, one whom he would never call his ghostly father: and he thought how this man and his companions had earned the name of world-lings at the hands not of the unworldly only but of the worldly also for having pleaded, during all their history, at the bar of God's justice for the souls of the lax and the lukewarm and the prudent.

The entry of the professor was signalled by a few rounds of Kentish fire[5] from the heavy boots of those students who sat on the highest tier of the gloomy theatre under the grey cobwebbed windows. The calling of the roll began and the responses to the names were given out in all tones until the name of Peter Byrne was reached.

—Here!

A deep bass note in response came from the upper tier, followed by coughs of protest along the other benches.

The professor paused in his reading and called the next name:

—Cranly!

No answer.

—Mr Cranly!

A smile flew across Stephen's face as he thought of his friend's studies.

—Try Leopardstown![6] said a voice from the bench behind.

Stephen glanced up quickly but Moynihan's snoutish face outlined on the grey light was impassive. A formula was given out. Amid the rustling of the notebooks Stephen turned back again and said:

—Give me some paper for God' sake.

—Are you as bad as that? asked Moynihan with a broad grin.

He tore a sheet from his scribbler and passed it down, whispering:

—In case of necessity any layman or woman can do it.

The formula which he wrote obediently on the sheet of paper, the coiling and uncoiling calculations of the professor, the spectrelike symbols of force and velocity fascinated and jaded Stephen's mind. He had heard some say that the old professor was an atheist freemason.[7] O the grey dull day! It seemed a limbo of painless patient consciousness through which souls of mathematicians might wander, projecting long slender fabrics from plane to plane of ever rarer and paler twilight, radiating swift eddies to the last verges of a universe ever vaster, farther and more impalpable.

—So we must distinguish between elliptical and ellipsoidal. Perhaps some of you gentlemen may be familiar with the works of Mr W. S. Gilbert. In one of his songs he speaks of the billiard sharp who is condemned to play:

> On a cloth untrue
> With a twisted cue
> And elliptical billiard balls.[8]

He means a ball having the form of the ellipsoid of the principal axes of which I spoke a moment ago.

Moynihan leaned down towards Stephen's ear and murmured:

---

5. Extended applause or foot stomping.
6. Horseracing track in south Dublin.
7. A contradiction, since Freemasonry (membership in the fraternal society) requires a belief in God.
8. Lyrics from the comic operetta *The Mikado* (1885), by W. S. Gilbert (1836–1911) and Arthur Sullivan (1842–1900).

—What price ellipsoidal balls! Chase me, ladies, I'm in the cavalry!

His fellowstudent's rude humour ran like a gust through the cloister of Stephen's mind, shaking into gay life limp priestly vestments that hung upon the walls, setting them to sway and caper in a sabbath of misrule. The forms of the community emerged from the gustblown vestments, the dean of studies, the portly florid bursar[9] with his cap of grey hair, the president, the little priest with feathery hair who wrote devout verses, the squat peasant form of the professor of economics, the tall form of the young professor of mental science discussing on the landing a case of conscience with his class like a giraffe cropping high leafage among a herd of antelopes, the grave troubled prefect of the sodality, the plump roundheaded professor of Italian with his rogue's eyes. They came ambling and stumbling, tumbling and capering, kilting[1] their gowns for leap frog, holding one another back, shaken with deep false laughter, smacking one another behind and laughing at their rude malice, calling to one another by familiar nicknames, protesting with sudden dignity at some rough usage, whispering two and two behind their hands.

The professor had gone to the glass cases on the sidewall from a shelf of which he took down a set of coils, blew away the dust from many points and, bearing it carefully to the table, held a finger on it while he proceeded with his lecture. He explained that the wires in modern coils were of a compound called platinoid lately discovered by F. W. Martino.[2]

He spoke clearly the initials and surname of the discoverer. Moynihan whispered from behind:

—Good old Fresh Water Martin!

—Ask him, Stephen whispered back with weary humour, if he wants a subject for electrocution. He can have me.

Moynihan, seeing the professor bend over the coils, rose in his bench and, clacking noiselessly the fingers of his right hand, began to call with the voice of a slobbering urchin:

—Please, teacher! Please, teacher! This boy is after saying a bad word, teacher.

—Platinoid, the professor said solemnly, is preferred to German silver because it has a lower coefficient of resistance variation by changes of temperature. The platinoid wire is insulated and the covering of silk that insulates it is wound double on the ebonite[3] bobbins just where my finger is. If it were wound single an extra current would be induced in the coils. The bobbins are saturated in hot paraffinwax . . .

A sharp Ulster[4] voice said from the bench below Stephen:

—Are we likely to be asked questions on applied science?

The professor began to juggle gravely with the terms pure science and applied science. A heavybuilt student wearing gold spectacles stared with some wonder at the questioner. Moynihan murmured from behind in his natural voice:

—Isn't MacAlister a devil for his pound of flesh?

Stephen looked down coldly on the oblong skull beneath him overgrown with tangled twinecoloured hair. The voice, the accent, the mind of the questioner offended him and he allowed the offence to carry him towards wilful unkindness, bidding his mind think that the student's father would have

---

9. Treasurer of a college.
1. Tucking up.
2. Probably Fernando Wood Martin (1863–1933), an American chemist who developed the

alloy platinoid.
3. Compound of rubber and sulfur.
4. The Protestant-dominated northeastern area of Ireland.

done better had he sent his son to Belfast[5] to study and have saved something on the trainfare by so doing.

The oblong skull beneath did not turn to meet this shaft of thought and yet the shaft came back to its bowstring: for he saw in a moment the student's wheypale face.

—That thought is not mine, he said to himself quickly. It came from the comic Irishman in the bench behind. Patience. Can you say with certitude by whom the soul of your race was bartered and its elect betrayed—by the questioner or by the mocker? Patience. Remember Epictetus. It is probably in his character to ask such a question at such a moment in such a tone and to pronounce the word *science* as a monosyllable.

The droning voice of the professor continued to wind itself slowly round and round the coils it spoke of, doubling, trebling, quadrupling its somnolent energy as the coil multiplied its ohms of resistance.

Moynihan's voice called from behind in echo to a distant bell:

—Closing time, gents!

The entrance hall was crowded and loud with talk. On a table near the door were two photographs in frames and between them a long roll of paper bearing an irregular tail of signatures. MacCann went briskly to and fro among the students, talking rapidly, answering rebuffs and leading one after another to the table. In the inner hall the dean of studies stood talking to a young professor, stroking his chin gravely and nodding his head.

Stephen, checked by the crowd at the door, halted irresolutely. From under the wide falling leaf of a soft hat Cranly's dark eyes were watching him.

—Have you signed? Stephen asked.

Cranly closed his long thinlipped mouth, communed with himself an instant and answered:

—*Ego habeo.*[6]

—What is it for?

—*Quod?*[7]

—What is it for?

Cranly turned his pale face to Stephen and said blandly and bitterly:

—*Per pax universalis.*[8]

Stephen pointed to the Czar's photograph[9] and said:

—He has the face of a besotted Christ.

The scorn and anger in his voice brought Cranly's eyes back from a calm survey of the walls of the hall.

—Are you annoyed? he asked.

—No, answered Stephen.

—Are you in bad humour?

—No.

—*Credo ut vos sanguinarius mendax estis,* said Cranly, *quia facies vostra monstrat ut vos in damno malo humore estis.*[1]

Moynihan, on his way to the table, said in Stephen's ear:

—MacCann is in tiptop form. Ready to shed the last drop. Brandnew world. No stimulants and votes for the bitches.

---

5. City in Ulster (a province in the north of Ireland), where Queen's University is located.
6. I have (Latin).
7. What? (Latin).
8. For universal peace (Latin).
9. Photograph of the czar of Russia, Nicholas II

(1868–1918), as well as one of his wife, Czarina Alexandra Feodorovna (1872–1918).
1. I believe that you are a bloody liar because your face shows that you are in a damned bad humor (Latin).

Stephen smiled at the manner of this confidence and, when Moynihan had passed, turned again to meet Cranly's eyes.

—Perhaps you can tell me, he said, why he pours his soul so freely into my ear. Can you?

A dull scowl appeared on Cranly's forehead. He stared at the table where Moynihan had bent to write his name on the roll, and then said flatly:

—A sugar![2]

—*Quis est malo humore*, said Stephen, *ego ant vos?*[3]

Cranly did not take up the taunt. He brooded sourly on his judgment and repeated with the same flat force:

—A flaming bloody sugar, that's what he is!

It was his epitaph for all dead friendships and Stephen wondered whether it would ever be spoken in the same tone over his memory. The heavy lumpish phrase sank slowly out of hearing like a stone through a quagmire. Stephen saw it sink as he had seen many an other, feeling its heaviness depress his heart. Cranly's speech, unlike that of Davin, had neither rare phrases of Elizabethan English nor quaintly turned versions of Irish idioms. Its drawl was an echo of the quays of Dublin given back by a bleak decaying seaport, its energy an echo of the sacred eloquence of Dublin given back flatly by a Wicklow pulpit.[4]

The heavy scowl faded from Cranly's face as MacCann marched briskly towards them from the other side of the hall.

—Here you are! said MacCann cheerily.

—Here I am! said Stephen.

—Late as usual. Can you not combine the progressive tendency[5] with a respect for punctuality?

—That question is out of order, said Stephen. Next business.

His smiling eyes were fixed on a silverwrapped tablet of milk chocolate which peeped out of the propagandist's breastpocket. A little ring of listeners closed round to hear the war of wits. A lean student with olive skin and lank black hair thrust his face between the two, glancing from one to the other at each phrase and seeming to try to catch each flying phrase in his open moist mouth. Cranly took a small grey handball from his pocket and began to examine it closely, turning it over and over.

—Next business? said MacCann. Hom!

He gave a loud cough of laughter, smiled broadly and tugged twice at the strawcoloured goatee which hung from his blunt chin.

—The next business is to sign the testimonial.

—Will you pay me anything if I sign? asked Stephen.

—I thought you were an idealist, said MacCann.

The gipsylike student looked about him and addressed the onlookers in an indistinct bleating voice.

—By hell, that's a queer notion. I consider that notion to be a mercenary notion.

His voice faded into silence. No heed was paid to his words. He turned his olive face, equine in expression, towards Stephen, inviting him to speak again.

---

2. Euphemism for "a shit."
3. Who is in a bad mood, me or you? (Latin).
4. I.e., 18th-century Irish oratory that has degenerated in contemporary Dublin speech.
5. Socialist views.

MacCann began to speak with fluent energy of the Czar's rescript, of Stead,[6] of general disarmament, arbitration in cases of international disputes, of the signs of the times, of the new humanity and the new gospel of life which would make it the business of the community to secure as cheaply as possible the greatest possible happiness of the greatest possible number.[7]

The gipsy student responded to the close of the period by crying:

—Three cheers for universal brotherhood!

—Go on, Temple, said a stout ruddy student near him. I'll stand you a pint after.

—I'm a believer in universal brotherhood, said Temple, glancing about him out of his dark oval eyes. Marx is only a bloody cod.[8]

Cranly gripped his arm tightly to check his tongue, smiling uneasily, and repeated:

—Easy, easy, easy!

Temple struggled to free his arm but continued, his mouth flecked by a thin foam:

—Socialism was founded by an Irishman and the first man in Europe who preached the freedom of thought was Collins. Two hundred years ago. He denounced priestcraft. The philosopher of Middlesex. Three cheers for John Anthony Collins![9]

A thin voice from the verge of the ring replied:

—Pip! pip!

Moynihan murmured beside Stephen's ear:

—And what about John Anthony's poor little sister:

> Lottie Collins[1] lost her drawers;
> Won't you kindly lend her yours?

Stephen laughed and Moynihan, pleased with the result, murmured again:

—We'll have five bob each way[2] on John Anthony Collins.

—I am waiting for your answer, said MacCann briefly.

—The affair doesn't interest me in the least, said Stephen wearily. You knew that well. Why do you make a scene about it?

—Good! said MacCann, smacking his lips. You are a reactionary then?

—Do you think you impress me, Stephen asked, when you flourish your wooden sword?

—Metaphors! said MacCann bluntly. Come to facts.

Stephen blushed and turned aside. MacCann stood his ground and said with hostile humour:

—Minor poets, I suppose, are above such trivial questions as the question of universal peace.

Cranly raised his head and held the handball between the two students by way of a peaceoffering, saying:

—*Pax super totum sanguinarium globum.*[3]

---

6. William Thomas Stead (1849–1912), English journalist. "Czar's rescript": plan for world peace issued by Czar Nicholas II in 1899.
7. Goal of the utilitarian philosophy elaborated by Jeremy Bentham (1748–1832) and later supported by many social democrats.
8. Fool.

9. Anthony Collins (1676–1729), English theologian and freethinker.
1. English music-hall performer in the 1890s.
2. Five shillings on his finishing one way and five on another, as in betting on a horse race.
3. Peace over the whole bloody globe (Latin).

Stephen, moving away the bystanders, jerked his shoulder angrily in the direction of the Czar's image, saying:

—Keep your icon. If we must have a Jesus let us have a legitimate Jesus.

—By hell, that's a good one! said the gipsy student to those about him. That's a fine expression. I like that expression immensely.

He gulped down the spittle in his throat as if he were gulping down the phrase and, fumbling at the peak of his tweed cap, turned to Stephen, saying:

—Excuse me, sir, what do you mean by that expression you uttered just now?

Feeling himself jostled by the students near him, he said to them:

—I am curious to know now what he meant by that expression.

He turned again to Stephen and said in a whisper:

—Do you believe in Jesus? I believe in man. Of course, I don't know if you believe in man. I admire you, sir. I admire the mind of man independent of all religions. Is that your opinion about the mind of Jesus?

—Go on, Temple, said the stout ruddy student returning, as was his wont, to his first idea, that pint is waiting for you.

—He thinks I'm an imbecile, Temple explained to Stephen, because I'm a believer in the power of mind.

Cranly linked his arms into those of Stephen and his admirer and said:

—*Nos ad manum ballum jocabimus.*[4]

Stephen, in the act of being led away, caught sight of MacCann's flushed bluntfeatured face.

—My signature is of no account, he said politely. You are right to go your way. Leave me to go mine.

—Dedalus, said MacCann crisply, I believe you're a good fellow but you have yet to learn the dignity of altruism and the responsibility of the human individual.

A voice said:

—Intellectual crankery is better out of this movement than in it.

Stephen, recognising the harsh tone of MacAlister's voice, did not turn in the direction of the voice. Cranly pushed solemnly through the throng of students, linking Stephen and Temple like a celebrant attended by his ministers on his way to the altar.

Temple bent eagerly across Cranly's breast and said:

—Did you hear MacAlister what he said? That youth is jealous of you. Did you see that? I bet Cranly didn't see that. By hell, I saw that at once.

As they crossed the inner hall the dean of studies was in the act of escaping from the student with whom he had been conversing. He stood at the foot of the staircase, a foot on the lowest step, his threadbare soutane gathered about him for the ascent with womanish care, nodding his head often and repeating:

—Not a doubt of it, Mr Hackett! Very true! Not a doubt of it!

In the middle of the hall the prefect of the college sodality was speaking earnestly, in a soft querulous voice, with a boarder. As he spoke he wrinkled a little his freckled brow and bit, between his phrases, at a tiny bone pencil.

—I hope the matric men will all come. The first arts men are pretty sure. Second arts too. We must make sure of the newcomers.[5]

---

4. Let's go play handball (Latin).
5. Students in their first, second, and third years of study. "Matric": matriculation.

Temple bent again across Cranly, as they were passing through the doorway, and said in a swift whisper:

—Do you know that he is a married man? He was a married man before they converted him. He has a wife and children somewhere. By hell, I think that's the queerest notion I ever heard! Eh?

His whisper trailed off into sly cackling laughter. The moment they were through the doorway Cranly seized him rudely by the neck and shook him, saying:

—You flaming floundering fool! I'll take my dying bible there isn't a bigger bloody ape, do you know, than you in the whole flaming bloody world!

Temple wriggled in his grip, laughing still with sly content, while Cranly repeated flatly at every rude shake:

—A flaming flaring bloody idiot!

They crossed the weedy garden together. The president, wrapped in a heavy loose cloak, was coming towards them along one of the walks, reading his office. At the end of the walk he halted before turning and raised his eyes. The students saluted, Temple fumbling as before at the peak of his cap. They walked forward in silence. As they neared the alley Stephen could hear the thuds of the players' hands and the wet smacks of the ball and Davin's voice crying out excitedly at each stroke.

The three students halted round the box on which Davin sat to follow the game. Temple, after a few moments, sidled across to Stephen and said:

—Excuse me, I wanted to ask you do you believe that Jean Jacques Rousseau[6] was a sincere man?

Stephen laughed outright. Cranly, picking up the broken stave[7] of a cask from the grass at his foot, turned swiftly and said sternly:

—Temple, I declare to the living God if you say another word, do you know, to anybody on any subject I'll kill you *super spottum*.[8]

—He was like you, I fancy, said Stephen, an emotional man.

—Blast him, curse him! said Cranly broadly. Don't talk to him at all. Sure you might as well be talking, do you know, to a flaming chamberpot as talking to Temple. Go home, Temple. For God' sake go home.

—I don't care a damn about you, Cranly, answered Temple, moving out of reach of the uplifted stave and pointing at Stephen. He's the only man I see in this institution that has an individual mind.

—Institution! Individual! cried Cranly. Go home, blast you, for you're a hopeless bloody man.

—I'm an emotional man, said Temple. That's quite rightly expressed. And I'm proud that I'm an emotionalist.

He sidled out of the alley, smiling slily. Cranly watched him with a blank expressionless face.

—Look at him! he said. Did you ever see such a go-by-the-wall?[9]

His phrase was greeted by a strange laugh from a student who lounged against the wall, his peaked cap down on his eyes. The laugh, pitched in a high key and coming from a so muscular frame, seemed like the whinny of an elephant. The student's body shook all over and, to ease his mirth, he rubbed both his hands delightedly over his groins.

—Lynch is awake, said Cranly.

6. French (Swiss-born) philosopher (1712–1778).
7. One of the pieces of wood that, when hooped together, form a cask or barrel.
8. On the spot (simplified Latin).
9. Slippery person.

Lynch, for answer, straightened himself and thrust forward his chest.

—Lynch puts out his chest, said Stephen, as a criticism of life.

Lynch smote himself sonorously on the chest and said:

—Who has anything to say about my girth?

Cranly took him at the word and the two began to tussle. When their faces had flushed with the struggle they drew apart, panting. Stephen bent down towards Davin who, intent on the game, had paid no heed to the talk of the others.

—And how is my little tame goose? he asked. Did he sign too?

Davin nodded and said:

—And you, Stevie?

Stephen shook his head.

—You're a terrible man, Stevie, said Davin, taking the short pipe from his mouth. Always alone.

—Now that you have signed the petition for universal peace, said Stephen, I suppose you will burn that little copybook I saw in your room.

As Davin did not answer Stephen began to quote:

—Long pace, fianna! Right incline, fianna! Fianna, by numbers, salute, one, two![1]

—That's a different question, said Davin. I'm an Irish nationalist, first and foremost. But that's you all out. You're a born sneerer, Stevie.

—When you make the next rebellion with hurleysticks,[2] said Stephen, and want the indispensable informer, tell me. I can find you a few in this college.

—I can't understand you, said Davin. One time I hear you talk against English literature. Now you talk against the Irish informers. What with your name and your ideas. . . . Are you Irish at all?

—Come with me now to the office of arms[3] and I will show you the tree of my family, said Stephen.

—Then be one of us, said Davin. Why don't you learn Irish? Why did you drop out of the league class[4] after the first lesson?

—You know one reason why, answered Stephen.

Davin tossed his head and laughed.

—O, come now, he said. Is it on account of that certain young lady and Father Moran? But that's all in your own mind, Stevie. They were only talking and laughing.

Stephen paused and laid a friendly hand upon Davin's shoulder.

—Do you remember, he said, when we knew each other first. The first morning we met you asked me to show you the way to the matriculation class, putting a very strong stress on the first syllable. You remember? Then you used to address the jesuits as father,[5] you remember? I ask myself about you: *Is he as innocent as his speech?*

—I'm a simple person, said Davin. You know that. When you told me that night in Harcourt Street those things about your private life, honest to God, Stevie, I was not able to eat my dinner. I was quite bad. I was awake a long time that night. Why did you tell me those things?

1. Military drill instructions from the Fenian handbook. The word "fenian" is derived from "fianna," Irish for "warriors."
2. Bladed sticks used in the game of hurling.
3. Office in Dublin Castle housing coats of arms and family genealogies.
4. Gaelic League class in the Irish, or Gaelic, language.
5. As opposed to "sir," unsophisticated form of address by those from the country.

—Thanks, said Stephen. You mean I am a monster.

—No, said Davin, but I wish you had not told me.

A tide began to surge beneath the calm surface of Stephen's friendliness.

—This race and this country and this life produced me, he said. I shall express myself as I am.

—Try to be one of us, repeated Davin. In your heart you are an Irishman but your pride is too powerful.

—My ancestors threw off their language and took on another, Stephen said. They allowed a handful of foreigners to subject them. Do you fancy I am going to pay in my own life and person debts they made? What for?

—For our freedom, said Davin.

—No honourable and sincere man, said Stephen, has given up to you his life and his youth and his affections from the days of Tone to those of Parnell but you sold him to the enemy or failed him in need or reviled him and left him for another. And you invite me to be one of you. I'd see you damned first.

—They died for their ideals, Stevie, said Davin. Our day will come yet,[6] believe me.

Stephen, following his own thought, was silent for an instant.

—The soul is born, he said vaguely, first in those moments I told you of. It has a slow and dark birth, more mysterious than the birth of the body. When the soul of a man is born in this country there are nets flung at it to hold it back from flight. You talk to me of nationality, language, religion. I shall try to fly by those nets.

Davin knocked the ashes from his pipe.

—Too deep for me, Stevie, he said. But a man's country comes first. Ireland first, Stevie. You can be a poet or a mystic after.

—Do you know what Ireland is? asked Stephen with cold violence. Ireland is the old sow that eats her farrow.[7]

Davin rose from his box and went towards the players, shaking his head sadly. But in a moment his sadness left him and he was hotly disputing with Cranly and the two players who had finished their game. A match of four was arranged, Cranly insisting, however, that his ball should be used. He let it rebound twice or thrice to his hand and then struck it strongly and swiftly towards the base of the alley, exclaiming in answer to its thud:

—Your soul![8]

Stephen stood with Lynch till the score began to rise. Then he plucked him by the sleeve to come away. Lynch obeyed, saying:

—Let us eke[9] go, as Cranly has it.

Stephen smiled at this sidethrust. They passed back through the garden and out through the hall where the doddering porter was pinning up a notice in the frame. At the foot of the steps they halted and Stephen took a packet of cigarettes from his pocket and offered it to his companion.

—I know you are poor, he said.

—Damn your yellow insolence, answered Lynch.

This second proof of Lynch's culture made Stephen smile again.

—It was a great day for European culture, he said, when you made up your mind to swear in yellow.[1]

6. A Fenian motto.
7. Litter of pigs.
8. I.e., damn your soul!

9. An archaism meaning "also," habitually misused by Cranly in lieu of "e'en" or "even."
1. Personal substitution for "bloody."

They lit their cigarettes and turned to the right. After a pause Stephen began:

—Aristotle has not defined pity and terror.[2] I have. I say . . .

Lynch halted and said bluntly:

—Stop! I won't listen! I am sick. I was out last night on a yellow drunk with Horan and Goggins.

Stephen went on:

—Pity is the feeling which arrests the mind in the presence of whatsoever is grave and constant in human sufferings and unites it with the human sufferer. Terror is the feeling which arrests the mind in the presence of whatsoever is grave and constant in human sufferings and unites it with the secret cause.

—Repeat, said Lynch.

Stephen repeated the definitions slowly.

—A girl got into a hansom[3] a few days ago, he went on, in London. She was on her way to meet her mother whom she had not seen for many years. At the corner of a street the shaft of a lorry shivered[4] the window of the hansom in the shape of a star. A long fine needle of the shivered glass pierced her heart. She died on the instant. The reporter called it a tragic death. It is not. It is remote from terror and pity according to the terms of my definitions.

The tragic emotion, in fact, is a face looking two ways, towards terror and towards pity, both of which are phases of it. You see I use the word *arrest*. I mean that the tragic emotion is static. Or rather the dramatic emotion is. The feelings excited by improper art are kinetic, desire or loathing. Desire urges us to possess, to go to something, loathing urges us to abandon, to go from something. These are kinetic emotions. The arts which excite them, pornographical or didactic,[5] are therefore improper arts. The esthetic emotion (I use the general term) is therefore static. The mind is arrested and raised above desire and loathing.

—You say that art must not excite desire, said Lynch. I told you that one day I wrote my name in pencil on the backside of the Venus of Praxiteles in the Museum.[6] Was that not desire?

—I speak of normal natures, said Stephen. You also told me that when you were a boy in that charming carmelite school[7] you ate pieces of dried cowdung.

Lynch broke again into a whinny of laughter and again rubbed both his hands over his groins but without taking them from his pockets.

—O, I did! I did! he cried.

Stephen turned towards his companion and looked at him for a moment boldly in the eyes. Lynch, recovering from his laughter, answered his look from his humbled eyes. The long slender flattened skull beneath the long pointed cap brought before Stephen's mind the image of a hooded reptile. The eyes, too, were reptilelike in glint and gaze. Yet at that instant, humbled and alert in their look, they were lit by one tiny human point, the window of a shrivelled soul, poignant and selfembittered.

---

2. Terms used by Aristotle in his *Poetics* to describe the effects of tragedy.
3. Horse-drawn cab.
4. Part of a truck, or moving van, broke the glass into shards.
5. Instructional.

6. The National Museum in Kildare Street contained a plaster cast of this statue by the Greek sculptor Praxiteles (4th century B.C.E.).
7. Run by Carmelite nuns, known for their discipline.

—As for that, Stephen said in polite parenthesis, we are all animals. I also am an animal.

—You are, said Lynch.

—But we are just now in a mental world, Stephen continued. The desire and loathing excited by improper esthetic means are really not esthetic emotions not only because they are kinetic in character but also because they are not more than physical. Our flesh shrinks from what it dreads and responds to the stimulus of what it desires by a purely reflex action of the nervous system. Our eyelid closes before we are aware that the fly is about to enter our eye.

—Not always, said Lynch critically.

—In the same way, said Stephen, your flesh responded to the stimulus of a naked statue but it was, I say, simply a reflex action of the nerves. Beauty expressed by the artist cannot awaken in us an emotion which is kinetic or a sensation which is purely physical. It awakens, or ought to awaken, or induces, or ought to induce, an esthetic stasis, an ideal pity or an ideal terror, a stasis called forth, prolonged and at last dissolved by what I call the rhythm of beauty.

—What is that exactly? asked Lynch.

—Rhythm, said Stephen, is the first formal esthetic relation of part to part in any esthetic whole or of an esthetic whole to its part or parts or of any part to the esthetic whole of which it is a part.

—If that is rhythm, said Lynch, let me hear what you call beauty: and, please remember, though I did eat a cake of cowdung once, that I admire only beauty.

Stephen raised his cap as if in greeting. Then, blushing slightly, he laid his hand on Lynch's thick tweed sleeve.

—We are right, he said, and the others are wrong. To speak of these things and to try to understand their nature and, having understood it, to try slowly and humbly and constantly to express, to press out again, from the gross earth or what it brings forth, from sound and shape and colour which are the prison gates of our soul, an image of the beauty we have come to understand—that is art.

They had reached the canal bridge[8] and, turning from their course, went on by the trees. A crude grey light, mirrored in the sluggish water, and a smell of wet branches over their heads seemed to war against the course of Stephen's thought.

—But you have not answered my question, said Lynch. What is art? What is the beauty it expresses?

—That was the first definition I gave you, you sleepyheaded wretch, said Stephen, when I began to try to think out the matter for myself. Do you remember the night? Cranly lost his temper and began to talk about Wicklow bacon.

—I remember, said Lynch. He told us about them flaming fat devils of pigs.

—Art, said Stephen, is the human disposition of sensible or intelligible matter for an esthetic end. You remember the pigs and forget that. You are a distressing pair, you and Cranly.

Lynch made a grimace at the raw grey sky and said:

8. Bridge over the canal in the southeast part of Dublin.

—If I am to listen to your esthetic philosophy give me at least another ciga-rette. I don't care about it. I don't even care about women. Damn you and damn everything. I want a job of five hundred a year. You can't get me one.

Stephen handed him the packet of cigarettes. Lynch took the last one that remained, saying simply:

—Proceed!

—Aquinas, said Stephen, says that is beautiful the apprehension of which pleases.

Lynch nodded.

—I remember that, he said. *Pulcra sunt quae visa placent.*

—He uses the word *visa,* said Stephen, to cover esthetic apprehension of all kinds, whether through sight or hearing or through any other avenue of apprehension. This word, though it is vague, is clear enough to keep away good and evil which excite desire and loathing. It means certainly a stasis and not a kinesis. How about the true? It produces also a stasis of the mind. You would not write your name in pencil across the hypothenuse of a right-angled triangle.

—No, said Lynch. Give me the hypothenuse of the Venus of Praxiteles.

—Static therefore, said Stephen. Plato, I believe, said that beauty is the splendour of truth.[9] I don't think that it has a meaning but the true and the beautiful are akin. Truth is beheld by the intellect which is appeased by the most satisfying relations of the intelligible: beauty is beheld by the imagination which is appeased by the most satisfying relations of the sen-sible. The first step in the direction of truth is to understand the frame and scope of the intellect itself, to comprehend the act itself of intellection. Aris-totle's entire system of philosophy rests upon his book of psychology and that, I think, rests on his statement that the same attribute cannot at the same time and in the same connection belong to and not belong to the same sub-ject.[1] The first step in the direction of beauty is to understand the frame and scope of the imagination, to comprehend the act itself of esthetic apprehen-sion. Is that clear?

—But what is beauty? asked Lynch impatiently. Out with another defini-tion. Something we see and like! Is that the best you and Aquinas can do?

—Let us take woman, said Stephen.

—Let us take her! said Lynch fervently.

—The Greek, the Turk, the Chinese, the Copt, the Hottentot,[2] said Ste-phen, all admire a different type of female beauty. That seems to be a maze out of which we cannot escape. I see however two ways out. One is this hypothesis: that every physical quality admired by men in women is in direct connection with the manifold functions of women for the propagation of the species. It may be so. The world, it seems, is drearier than even you, Lynch, imagined. For my part I dislike that way out. It leads to eugenics[3] rather than to esthetic. It leads you out of the maze into a new gaudy lectureroom where MacCann, with one hand on *The Origin of Species*[4] and the other hand on the new testament, tells you that you admired the great flanks of Venus

9. This formulation echoes a remark by French novelist Gustave Flaubert (1821–1880) in a March 18, 1857, letter.
1. An idea derived from Aristotle's *Metaphysics.*
2. Derogatory term for the Khoikhoi people of southern Africa. "Copt": native Egyptian Christian.
3. The science of propagating desirable human traits through reproduction.
4. Scientific treatise (1859) by the English natu-ralist Charles Darwin (1809–1882), which pre-sented his theory of natural selection.

because you felt that she would bear you burly offspring and admired her great breasts because you felt that she would give good milk to her children and yours.

—Then MacCann is a sulphuryellow[5] liar, said Lynch energetically.

—There remains another way out, said Stephen laughing.

—To wit? said Lynch.

—This hypothesis, Stephen began.

A long dray laden with old iron came round the corner of Sir Patrick Dun's hospital[6] covering the end of Stephen's speech with the harsh roar of jangled and rattling metal. Lynch closed his ears and gave out oath after oath till the dray had passed. Then he turned on his heel rudely. Stephen turned also and waited for a few moments till his companion's illhumour had had its vent.

—This hypothesis, Stephen repeated, is the other way out: that, though the same object may not seem beautiful to all people, all people who admire a beautiful object find in it certain relations which satisfy and coincide with the stages themselves of all esthetic apprehension. These relations of the sensible, visible to you through one form and to me through another, must be therefore the necessary qualities of beauty. Now, we can return to our old friend saint Thomas for another pennyworth of wisdom.

Lynch laughed.

—It amuses me vastly, he said, to hear you quoting him time after time like a jolly round friar. Are you laughing in your sleeve?

—MacAlister, answered Stephen, would call my esthetic theory applied Aquinas. So far as this side of esthetic philosophy extends Aquinas will carry me all along the line. When we come to the phenomenon of artistic conception, artistic gestation and artistic reproduction I require a new terminology and a new personal experience.

—Of course, said Lynch. After all Aquinas, in spite of his intellect, was exactly a good round friar. But you will tell me about the new personal experience and new terminology some other day. Hurry up and finish the first part.

—Who knows? said Stephen smiling. Perhaps Aquinas would understand me better than you. He was a poet himself. He wrote a hymn for Maundy Thursday.[7] It begins with the words *Pange lingua gloriosi*.[8] They say it is the highest glory of the hymnal. It is an intricate and soothing hymn. I like it: but there is no hymn that can be put beside that mournful and majestic processional song, the *Vexilla Regis*[9] of Venantius Fortunatus.

Lynch began to sing softly and solemnly in a deep bass voice:

> *Impleta sunt quae concinit*
> *David fideli carmine*
> *Dicendo nationibus*
> *Regnavit a ligno Deus.*[1]

—That's great! he said, well pleased. Great music!

---

5. Another substitution, meant to evoke an intensification of the word "bloody."

6. Hospital near the canal in Dublin. "Dray": a cart used to carry heavy loads.

7. The Thursday before Good Friday.

8. Sing, my tongue, the Savior's glory (Latin), beginning of a hymn commemorating Christ's institution of the sacrament of the Eucharist.

9. The Banners of the King (Latin), partial title of another hymn.

1. The prophetic songs of David were fulfilled when he said to the nations that God ruled from a tree (i.e., the cross) (Latin). From "Vexilla Regis," a 6th-century hymn.

They turned into Lower Mount Street. A few steps from the corner a fat young man, wearing a silk neckcloth, saluted them and stopped.

—Did you hear the results of the exams? he asked. Griffin was plucked. Halpin and O'Flynn are through the home civil. Moonan got fifth place in the Indian. O'Shaughenessy got fourteenth.[2] The Irish fellows in Clarke's gave them a feed last night. They all ate curry.

His pallid bloated face expressed benevolent malice and, as he had advanced through his tidings of success, his small fatencircled eyes vanished out of sight and his weak wheezing voice out of hearing.

In reply to a question of Stephen's his eyes and his voice came forth again from their lurkingplaces.

—Yes. MacCullagh and I, he said. He's taking pure mathematics and I'm taking constitutional history. There are twenty subjects. I'm taking botany too. You know I'm a member of the field club.[3]

He drew back from the other two in a stately fashion and placed a plump woollengloved hand on his breast from which muttered wheezing laughter at once broke forth.

—Bring us a few turnips and onions the next time you go out said Stephen drily, to make a stew.

The fat student laughed indulgently and said:

—We are all highly respectable people in the field club. Last Saturday we went out to Glenmalure,[4] seven of us.

—With women, Donovan? said Lynch.

Donovan again laid his hand on his chest and said:

—Our end is the acquisition of knowledge.

Then he said quickly:

—I hear you are writing some essay about esthetics.

Stephen made a vague gesture of denial.

—Goethe and Lessing,[5] said Donovan, have written a lot on that subject, the classical school and the romantic school and all that. The *Laocoon*[6] interested me very much when I read it. Of course it is idealistic, German, ultraprofound.

Neither of the others spoke. Donovan took leave of them urbanely.

—I must go, he said softly and benevolently. I have a strong suspicion, amounting almost to a conviction, that my sister intended to make pancakes today for the dinner of the Donovan family.

—Goodbye, Stephen said in his wake. Don't forget the turnips for me and my mate.

Lynch gazed after him, his lip curling in slow scorn till his face resembled a devil's mask:

—To think that that yellow pancakeeating excrement can get a good job, he said at length, and I have to smoke cheap cigarettes!

They turned their faces towards Merrion Square and went on for a little in silence.

---

2. Place in the examinations to enter the British civil service. "Was plucked": failed. "Through the home civil": passed the examination for the domestic (U.K.) civil service. "The Indian": examination for service in the British Empire's administration in India.
3. Extracurricular club for studying botany, not a formal part of the curriculum.
4. Valley in County Wicklow, south of Dublin.

5. Johann Wolfgang von Goethe (1749–1832) and Gotthold Ephraim Lessing (1729–1781), German writers.
6. Lessing's 1766 treatise, a meditation on a famous classical statue of Laocoön and his sons being strangled by sea serpents, distinguishes between literature as a temporal art and sculpture as a spatial art.

—To finish what I was saying about beauty, said Stephen, the most satisfying relations of the sensible must therefore correspond to the necessary phases of artistic apprehension. Find these and you find the qualities of universal beauty. Aquinas says: *ad pulcritudinem tria requiruntur, integritas, consonantia, claritas.*[7] I translate it so: *Three things are needed for beauty, wholeness, harmony and radiance.* Do these correspond to the phases of apprehension? Are you following?

—Of course, I am, said Lynch. If you think I have an excrementitious intelligence run after Donovan and ask him to listen to you.

   Stephen pointed to a basket which a butcher's boy had slung inverted on his head.

—Look at that basket, he said.

—I see it, said Lynch.

—In order to see that basket, said Stephen, your mind first of all separates the basket from the rest of the visible universe which is not the basket. The first phase of apprehension is a bounding line drawn about the object to be apprehended. An esthetic image is presented to us either in space or in time. What is audible is presented in time, what is visible is presented in space. But temporal or spatial the esthetic image is first luminously apprehended as selfbounded and selfcontained upon the immeasurable background of space or time which is not it. You apprehend it as *one* thing. You see it as one whole. You apprehend its wholeness. That is *integritas*.

—Bull's eye! said Lynch laughing. Go on.

—Then, said Stephen, you pass from point to point, led by its formal lines; you apprehend it as balanced part against part within its limits; you feel the rhythm of its structure. In other words the synthesis of immediate perception is followed by the analysis of apprehension. Having first felt that it is *one* thing you feel now that it is a *thing*. You apprehend it as complex, multiple, divisible, separable, made up of its parts, the result of its parts and their sum, harmonious. That is *consonantia*.

—Bull's eye again! said Lynch wittily. Tell me now what is *claritas* and you win the cigar.

—The connotation of the word, Stephen said, is rather vague. Aquinas uses a term which seems to be inexact. It baffled me for a long time. It would lead you to believe that he had in mind symbolism or idealism, the supreme quality of beauty being a light from some other world, the idea of which the matter is but the shadow, the reality of which it is but the symbol. I thought he might mean that *claritas* is the artistic discovery and representation of the divine purpose in anything or a force of generalisation which would make the esthetic image a universal one, make it outshine its proper conditions. But that is literary talk. I understand it so. When you have apprehended that basket as one thing and have then analysed it according to its form and apprehended it as a thing you make the only synthesis which is logically and esthetically permissible. You see that it is that thing which it is and no other thing. The radiance of which he speaks is the scholastic *quidditas*, the *whatness* of a thing. This supreme quality is felt by the artist when the esthetic image is first conceived in his imagination. The mind in that mysterious instant Shelley likened beautifully to a fading coal.[8] The instant wherein

---

7. Abbreviated paraphrase from Aquinas's *Summa Theologica.*
8. In "A Defence of Poetry" (1821) Shelley writes, "the mind in creation is as a fading coal, which some invisible influence, like an inconstant wind, awakens to transitory brightness; this power arises from within."

that supreme quality of beauty, the clear radiance of the esthetic image, is apprehended luminously by the mind which has been arrested by its wholeness and fascinated by its harmony is the luminous silent stasis of esthetic pleasure, a spiritual state very like to that cardiac condition which the Italian physiologist Luigi Galvani, using a phrase almost as beautiful as Shelley's, called the enchantment of the heart.[9]

Stephen paused and, though his companion did not speak, felt that his words had called up around them a thoughtenchanted silence.

—What I have said, he began again, refers to beauty in the wider sense of the word, in the sense which the word has in the literary tradition. In the marketplace it has another sense. When we speak of beauty in the second sense of the term our judgment is influenced in the first place by the art itself and by the form of that art. The image, it is clear, must be set between the mind or senses of the artist himself and the mind or senses of others. If you bear this in memory you will see that art necessarily divides itself into three forms progressing from one to the next. These forms are: the lyrical form, the form wherein the artist presents his image in immediate relation to himself; the epical form, the form wherein he presents his image in mediate relation to himself and to others; the dramatic form, the form wherein he presents his image in immediate relation to others.

—That you told me a few nights ago, said Lynch, and we began the famous discussion.

—I have a book at home, said Stephen, in which I have written down questions which are more amusing than yours were. In finding the answers to them I found the theory of esthetic which I am trying to explain. Here are some questions I set myself: *Is a chair finely made tragic or comic? Is the portrait of Mona Lisa good if I desire to see it? Is the bust of sir Philip Crampton[1] lyrical, epical or dramatic? Can excrement or a child or a louse be a work of art? If not, why not?*

—Why not, indeed? said Lynch laughing.

—*If a man hacking in fury at a block of wood*, Stephen continued, *make there an image of a cow is that image a work of art? If not, why not?*

—That's a lovely one, said Lynch laughing again. That has the true scholastic stink.

—Lessing, said Stephen, should not have taken a group of statues to write of. The art, being inferior, does not present the forms I spoke of distinguished clearly one from another. Even in literature, the highest and most spiritual art, the forms are often confused. The lyrical form is in fact the simplest verbal gesture of an instant of emotion, a rhythmical cry such as ages ago cheered on the man who pulled at the oar or dragged stones up a slope. He who utters it is more conscious of the instant of emotion than of himself as feeling emotion. The simplest epical form is seen emerging out of lyrical literature when the artist prolongs and broods upon himself as the centre of an epical event and this form progresses till the centre of emotional gravity is equidistant from the artist himself and from others. The narrative is no longer purely personal. The personality of the artist passes into the narration itself, flowing round and round the persons and the action like a vital sea. This progress you will see easily in that old English ballad *Turpin*

9. Description by the scientist (1737–1798) of the temporary pause in a frog's heartbeart when a needle was inserted into its spine.

1. Famous Dublin surgeon (1777–1858), whose bust once decorated a drinking fountain near Trinity College.

Hero[2] which begins in the first person and ends in the third person. The dramatic form is reached when the vitality which has flowed and eddied round each person fills every person with such vital force that he or she assumes a proper and intangible esthetic life. The personality of the artist at first a cry or a cadence or a mood and then a fluid and lambent narrative finally refines itself out of existence, impersonalises itself, so to speak. The esthetic image in the dramatic form is life purified in and reprojected from the human imagination. The mystery of esthetic like that of material creation is accomplished. The artist, like the God of the creation, remains within or behind or beyond or above his handiwork, invisible, refined out of existence, indifferent, paring his fingernails.[3]

—Trying to refine them also out of existence, said Lynch.

A fine rain began to fall from the high veiled sky and they turned into the duke's lawn to reach the national library[4] before the shower came.

—What do you mean, Lynch asked surlily, by prating about beauty and the imagination in this miserable Godforsaken island? No wonder the artist retired within or behind his handiwork after having perpetrated this country.

The rain fell faster. When they passed through the passage beside Kildare house they found many students sheltering under the arcade of the library. Cranly leaning against a pillar was picking his teeth with a sharpened match, listening to some companions. Some girls stood near the entrance door. Lynch whispered to Stephen:

—Your beloved is here.

Stephen took his place silently on the step below the group of students, heedless of the rain which fell fast, turning his eyes towards her from time to time. She too stood silently among her companions. She has no priest to flirt with, he thought with conscious bitterness, remembering how he had seen her last. Lynch was right. His mind, emptied of theory and courage, lapsed back into a listless peace.

He heard the students talking among themselves. They spoke of two friends who had passed the final medical examination, of the chances of getting places on ocean liners, of poor and rich practices.

—That's all a bubble. An Irish country practice is better.

—Hynes was two years in Liverpool and he says the same. A frightful hole he said it was. Nothing but midwifery cases. Half a crown cases.[5]

—Do you mean to say it is better to have a job here in the country than in a rich city like that? I know a fellow. . . .

—Hynes has no brains. He got through by stewing, pure stewing.[6]

—Don't mind him. There's plenty of money to be made in a big commercial city.

—Depends on the practice.

—*Ego credo ut vita pauperum est simpliciter atrox, simpliciter sanguinarius atrox, in Liverpoolio.*[7]

Their voices reached his ears as if from a distance in interrupted pulsation. She was preparing to go away with her companions.

2. About the 18th-century robber Dick Turpin.
3. Drawing on Flaubert's letter of March 18, 1857, which asserts (in translation from the French): "The artist must be in his work like God in the created world, invisible and all powerful, felt everywhere but unable to be seen."
4. The National Library is in the same complex of buildings as the National Museum and Leinster House, formerly the residence of the duke of Leinster and adjoining the small lawn to which Stephen refers.
5. Charity cases, or instances in which the doctor was paid two shillings, sixpence for a delivery.
6. Dogged study.
7. I believe that the life of the poor is simply frightful, simply bloody frightful, in Liverpool (simplified, joking Latin).

The quick light shower had drawn off, tarrying in clusters of diamonds among the shrubs of the quadrangle where an exhalation was breathed forth by the blackened earth. Their trim boots prattled as they stood on the steps of the colonnade talking quietly and gaily, glancing at the clouds, holding their umbrellas at cunning angles against the few last raindrops, closing them again, holding their skirts demurely.

And if he had judged her harshly? If her life were a simple rosary of hours, her life simple and strange as a bird's life, gay in the morning, restless all day, tired at sundown? Her heart simple and wilful as a bird's heart?

◆ ◆ ◆

Towards dawn he awoke. O what sweet music! His soul was all dewy wet. Over his limbs in sleep pale cool waves of light had passed. He lay still, as if his soul lay amid cool waters, conscious of faint sweet music. His mind was waking slowly to a tremulous morning knowledge, a morning inspiration. A spirit filled him, pure as the purest water, sweet as dew, moving as music. But how faintly it was inbreathed, how passionlessly as if the seraphim themselves were breathing upon him! His soul was waking slowly, fearing to awake wholly. It was that windless hour of dawn when madness wakes and strange plants open to the light and the moth flies forth silently.

An enchantment of the heart! The night had been enchanted. In dream or vision he had known the ecstasy of seraphic life.[8] Was it an instant of enchantment only or long hours and days and years and ages?

The instant of inspiration seemed now to be reflected from all sides at once from a multitude of cloudy circumstance of what had happened or of what might have happened. The instant flashed forth like a point of light and now from cloud on cloud of vague circumstance confused form was veiling softly its afterglow. O! In the virgin womb of the imagination the word was made flesh. Gabriel the seraph had come to the virgin's chamber.[9] An afterglow deepened within his spirit, whence the white flame had passed, deepening to a rose and ardent light. That rose and ardent light was her strange wilful heart, strange that no man had known or would know, wilful from before the beginning of the world: and lured by that ardent roselike glow the choirs of the seraphim were falling from heaven.

> Are you not weary of ardent ways.
> Lure of the fallen seraphim?
> Tell no more of enchanted days.

The verses passed from his mind to his lips and, murmuring them over, he felt the rhythmic movement of a villanelle[1] pass through them. The roselike glow sent forth its rays of rhyme; ways, days, blaze, praise, raise. Its rays burned up the world, consumed the hearts of men and angels: the rays from the rose that was her wilful heart.

> Your eyes have set man's heart ablaze
> And you have had your will of him.
> Are you not weary of ardent ways?

8. Life of the seraphim, the highest-ranking angels.
9. In other words, the archangel Gabriel had come to announce to Mary the coming birth of Jesus (Luke 1.26–28). In John 1.14, "the Word was made flesh."
1. Poetic form in which the first and third lines of the first stanza are repeated, alternately, as a refrain in the subsequent stanzas and, together, form the last two lines of the poem.

And then? The rhythm died away, ceased, began again to move and beat. And then? Smoke, incense ascending from the altar of the world.

> *Above the flame the smoke of praise*
> *Goes up from ocean rim to rim.*
> *Tell no more of enchanted days.*

Smoke went up from the whole earth, from the vapoury oceans, smoke of her praise. The earth was like a swinging swaying smoking censer, a ball of incense, an ellipsoidal ball. The rhythm died out at once; the cry of his heart was broken. His lips began to murmur the first verses over and over; then went on stumbling through half verses, stammering and baffled; then stopped. The heart's cry was broken.

The veiled windless hour had passed and behind the panes of the naked window the morning light was gathering. A bell beat faintly very far away. A bird twittered; two birds, three. The bell and the birds ceased: and the dull white light spread itself east and west, covering the world, covering the rose-light in his heart.

Fearing to lose all he raised himself suddenly on his elbow to look for paper and pencil. There was neither on the table; only the soup plate he had eaten the rice from for supper and the candlestick with its tendrils of tallow and its paper socket, singed by the last flame. He stretched his arm wearily towards the foot of the bed, groping with his hand in the pockets of the coat that hung there. His fingers found a pencil and then a cigarette packet. He lay back and, tearing open the packet, placed the last cigarette on the window ledge and began to write out the stanzas of the villanelle in small neat letters on the rough cardboard surface.

Having written them out he lay back on the lumpy pillow, murmuring them again. The lumps of knotted flock[2] under his head reminded him of the lumps of knotted horsehair in the sofa of her parlour on which he used to sit, smiling or serious, asking himself why he had come, displeased with her and with himself, confounded by the print of the Sacred Heart above the untenanted[3] sideboard. He saw her approach him in a lull of the talk and beg him to sing one of his curious songs. Then he saw himself sitting at the old piano, striking chords softly from its speckled keys and singing, amid the talk which had risen again in the room, to her who leaned beside the mantelpiece a dainty song of the Elizabethans, a sad and sweet loth to depart, the victory chant of Agincourt, the happy air of Greensleeves.[4] While he sang and she listened, or feigned to listen, his heart was at rest but when the quaint old songs had ended and he heard again the voices in the room he remembered his own sarcasm: the house where young men are called by their christian names a little too soon.

At certain instants her eyes seemed about to trust him but he had waited in vain. She passed now dancing lightly across his memory as she had been that night at the carnival ball. Her white dress a little lifted, a white spray nodding in her hair. She danced lightly in the round. She was dancing towards him and, as she came, her eyes were a little averted and a faint glow was on her

---

2. Tufts of wool, used here to stuff the pillow.
3. Empty. "Sacred Heart": Jesus's heart, representing his divine love.
4. A 16th-century English ballad in which the singer complains to his beloved, the Lady

Greensleeves, "you do me wrong / To cast me off discourteously." "Agincourt": battle (1415) during the Hundred Years' War in which the English defeated the French, commemorated in various songs.

cheek. At the pause in the chain of hands her hand had lain in his an instant, a soft merchandise.[5]

—You are a great stranger now.

—Yes. I was born to be a monk.

—I am afraid you are a heretic.

—Are you much afraid?

For answer she had danced away from him along the chain of hands, dancing lightly and discreetly, giving herself to none. The white spray nodded to her dancing and when she was in shadow the glow was deeper on her cheek.

A monk! His own image started forth a profaner of the cloister, a heretic franciscan, willing and willing not to serve, spinning like Gherardino da Borgo San Donnino[6] a lithe web of sophistry and whispering in her ear.

No, it was not his image. It was the image of the young priest in whose company he had seen her last, looking at him out of dove's eyes, toying with the pages of her Irish phrasebook.

—Yes, yes, the ladies are coming round to us. I can see it every day. The ladies are with us. The best helpers the language has.

—And the church, Father Moran?

—The church too. Coming round too. The work is going ahead there too. Don't fret about the church.

Bah! he had done well to leave the room in disdain. He had done well not to salute her on the steps of the library. He had done well to leave her to flirt with her priest, to toy with a church which was the scullerymaid of christendom.

Rude brutal anger routed the last lingering instant of ecstasy from his soul. It broke up violently her fair image and flung the fragments on all sides. On all sides distorted reflections of her image started from his memory: the flowergirl in the ragged dress with damp coarse hair and a hoyden's face who had called herself his own girl and begged his handsel,[7] the kitchengirl in the next house who sang over the clatter of her plates with the drawl of a country singer the first bars of *By Killarney's Lakes and Fells*,[8] a girl who had laughed gaily to see him stumble when the iron grating in the footpath near Cork Hill had caught the broken sole of his shoe, a girl he had glanced at, attracted by her small ripe mouth as she passed out of Jacob's biscuit factory,[9] who had cried to him over her shoulder:

—Do you like what you seen of me, straight hair and curly eyebrows?

And yet he felt that, however he might revile and mock her image, his anger was also a form of homage. He had left the classroom in disdain that was not wholly sincere, feeling that perhaps the secret of her race lay behind those dark eyes upon which her long lashes flung a quick shadow. He had told himself bitterly as he walked through the streets that she was a figure of the womanhood of her country, a batlike soul waking to the consciousness of itself in darkness and secrecy and loneliness, tarrying a while, loveless and sinless, with her mild lover and leaving him to whisper of innocent transgressions in the latticed[1] ear of a priest. His anger against her found vent in coarse railing at her paramour, whose name and voice and features offended

---

5. Possession.
6. Franciscan monk (d. 1276) imprisoned for life because of his heretical treatise predicting the imminent end of the Roman Catholic Church.
7. See notes on p. 554.
8. Song idealizing the Irish countryside by Irish composer and singer Michael William Balfe (1808–1870).
9. Bakery just west of Stephen's Green.
1. Screened by the lattice dividing the priest from the penitent in the confessional.

his baffled pride: a priested peasant, with a brother a policeman in Dublin and a brother a potboy in Moycullen.[2] To him she would unveil her soul's shy nakedness, to one who was but schooled in the discharging of a formal rite rather than to him, a priest of the eternal imagination, transmuting the daily bread of experience into the radiant body of everliving life.[3]

The radiant image of the eucharist united again in an instant his bitter and despairing thoughts, their cries arising unbroken in a hymn of thanksgiving.

> *Our broken cries and mournful lays*
> *Rise in one eucharistic hymn.*
> *Are you not weary of ardent ways?*
>
> *While sacrificing hands upraise*
> *The chalice flowing to the brim.*
> *Tell no more of enchanted days.*

He spoke the verses aloud from the first lines till the music and rhythm suffused his mind, turning it to quiet indulgence; then copied them painfully to feel them the better by seeing them; then lay back on his bolster.

The full morning light had come. No sound was to be heard: but he knew that all around him life was about to awaken in common noises, hoarse voices, sleepy prayers. Shrinking from that life he turned towards the wall, making a cowl of the blanket and staring at the great overblown scarlet flowers of the tattered wallpaper. He tried to warm his perishing joy in their scarlet glow, imagining a roseway from where he lay upwards to heaven all strewn with scarlet flowers. Weary! Weary! He too was weary of ardent ways.

A gradual warmth, a languorous weariness passed over him descending along his spine from his closely cowled head. He felt it descend and, seeing himself as he lay, smiled. Soon he would sleep.

He had written verses for her again after ten years. Ten years before she had worn her shawl cowlwise about her head, sending sprays of her warm breath into the night air, tapping her foot upon the glassy road. It was the last tram; the lank brown horses knew it and shook their bells to the clear night in admonition. The conductor talked with the driver, both nodding often in the green light of the lamp. They stood on the steps of the tram, he on the upper, she on the lower. She came up to his step many times between their phrases and went down again and once or twice remained beside him forgetting to go down and then went down. Let be! Let be!

Ten years from that wisdom of children to his folly. If he sent her the verses? They would be read out at breakfast amid the tapping of eggshells. Folly indeed! The brothers would laugh and try to wrest the page from each other with their strong hard fingers. The suave priest, her uncle, seated in his armchair, would hold the page at arm's length, read it smiling and approve of the literary form.

No, no: that was folly. Even if he sent her the verses she would not show them to others. No, no: she could not.

He began to feel that he had wronged her. A sense of her innocence moved him almost to pity her, an innocence he had never understood till he had

2. A boy serving pub drinks in a village in County Galway, in western Ireland.
3. Cf. the conversion in the Eucharist of the bread into the body of Christ, in the Catholic doctrine of transubstantiation.

come to the knowledge of it through sin, an innocence which she too had not understood while she was innocent or before the strange humiliation of her nature[4] had first come upon her. Then first her soul had begun to live as his soul had when he had first sinned: and a tender compassion filled his heart as he remembered her frail pallor and her eyes, humbled and saddened by the dark shame of womanhood.

While his soul had passed from ecstasy to languor where had she been? Might it be, in the mysterious ways of spiritual life, that her soul at those same moments had been conscious of his homage? It might be.

A glow of desire kindled again his soul and fired and fulfilled all his body. Conscious of his desire she was waking from odorous sleep, the temptress of his villanelle. Her eyes, dark and with a look of languor, were opening to his eyes. Her nakedness yielded to him, radiant, warm, odorous and lavish-limbed, enfolded him like a shining cloud, enfolded him like water with a liquid life: and like a cloud of vapour or like waters circumfluent in space the liquid letters of speech, symbols of the element of mystery, flowed forth over his brain.

> Are you not weary of ardent ways?
> Lure of the fallen seraphim.
> Tell no more of enchanted days.
>
> Your eyes have set man's heart ablaze
> And you have had your will of him.
> Are you not weary of ardent ways?
>
> Above the flame the smoke of praise
> Goes up from ocean rim to rim.
> Tell no more of enchanted days.
>
> Our broken cries and mournful lays
> Rise in one eucharistic hymn.
> Are you not weary of ardent ways?
>
> While sacrificing hands upraise
> The chalice flowing to the brim.
> Tell no more of enchanted days.
>
> And still you hold our longing gaze
> With languorous look and lavish limb.
> Are you not weary of ardent ways?
> Tell no more of enchanted days.

◆ ◆ ◆

What birds were they?

He stood on the steps of the library to look at them, leaning wearily on his ashplant.[5] They flew round and round the jutting shoulder of a house in Molesworth Street.[6] The air of the late March evening made clear their

---

4. Her menstrual period.
5. Sapling of the ash tree, used as a walking stick.

6. Street running west from the quadrangle between the National Library and the National Museum on Kildare Street.

flight, their dark darting quivering bodies flying clearly against the sky as against a limphung cloth of smoky tenuous blue.

He watched their flight: bird after bird: a dark flash, a swerve, a flash again, a dart aside, a curve, a flutter of wings. He tried to count them before all their darting quivering bodies passed: six, ten, eleven: and wondered were they odd or even in number. Twelve, thirteen: for two came wheeling down from the upper sky. They were flying high and low but ever round and round in straight and curving lines and ever flying from left to right, circling about a temple of air.

He listened to their cries: like the squeak of mice behind the wainscot: a shrill twofold note. But the notes were long and shrill and whirring, unlike the cry of vermin, falling a third or a fourth and trilled as the flying beaks clove the air. Their cry was shrill and clear and fine and falling like threads of silken light unwound from whirring spools.

The inhuman clamour soothed his ears in which his mother's sobs and reproaches murmured insistently and the dark frail quivering bodies wheeling and fluttering and swerving round an airy temple of the tenuous sky soothed his eyes which still saw the image of his mother's face.

Why was he gazing upwards from the steps of the porch, hearing their shrill twofold cry, watching their flight? For an augury of good or evil? A phrase of Cornelius Agrippa[7] flew through his mind and then there flew hither and thither shapeless thoughts from Swedenborg[8] on the correspondence of birds to things of the intellect and of how the creatures of the air have their knowledge and know their times and seasons because they, unlike man, are in the order of their life and have not perverted that order by reason.

And for ages men had gazed upward as he was gazing at birds in flight. The colonnade above him made him think vaguely of an ancient temple and the ashplant on which he leaned wearily of the curved stick of an augur.[9] A sense of fear of the unknown moved in the heart of his weariness, a fear of symbols and portents, of the hawklike man whose name he bore soaring out of his captivity on osierwoven[1] wings, of Thoth, the god of writers, writing with a reed upon a tablet and bearing on his narrow ibis head the cusped moon.[2]

He smiled as he thought of the god's image for it made him think of a bottlenosed judge in a wig, putting commas into a document which he held at arm's length and he knew that he would not have remembered the god's name but that it was like an Irish oath. It was folly. But was it for this folly that he was about to leave for ever the house of prayer and prudence into which he had been born and the order of life out of which he had come?

They came back with shrill cries over the jutting shoulder of the house, flying darkly against the fading air. What birds were they? He thought that they must be swallows who had come back from the south. Then he was to go

7. Heinrich Cornelius Agrippa von Nettesheim (1486–1535), German occult philosopher who discusses divination from the flight of birds.
8. Emanuel Swedenborg (1688–1772), Swedish mystical philosopher of correspondences between natural and spiritual realities.
9. A person skilled in reading the future, espe-

cially a Roman official who read omens associated with birds.
1. Woven from branches of a flexible willow plant often used in basketwork.
2. Thoth, the Egyptian god of writing and learning, was often represented as a man with the head of an ibis crowned with a lunar crescent.

away? for they were birds ever going and coming, building ever an unlasting home under the eaves of men's houses and ever leaving the homes they had built to wander.

> Bend down your faces, Oona and Aleel.
> I gaze upon them as the swallow gazes
> Upon the nest under the eave before
> He wander the loud waters.[3]

A soft liquid joy like the noise of many waters flowed over his memory and he felt in his heart the soft peace of silent spaces of fading tenuous sky above the waters, of oceanic silence, of swallows flying through the seadusk over the flowing waters.

A soft liquid joy flowed through the words where the soft long vowels hurtled noiselessly and fell away, lapping and flowing back and ever shaking the white bells of their waves in mute chime and mute peal and soft low swooning cry: and he felt that the augury he had sought in the wheeling darting birds and in the pale space of sky above him had come forth from his heart like a bird from a turret quietly and swiftly.

Symbol of departure or of loneliness? The verses crooned in the ear of his memory composed slowly before his remembering eyes the scene of the hall on the night of the opening of the national theatre.[4] He was alone at the side of the balcony, looking out of jaded eyes at the culture of Dublin in the stalls and at the tawdry scenecloths and human dolls framed by the garish lamps of the stage. A burly policeman sweated behind him and seemed at every moment about to act. The catcalls and hisses and mocking cries ran in rude gusts round the hall from his scattered fellowstudents.

—A libel on Ireland!

—Made in Germany![5]

—Blasphemy!

—We never sold our faith!

—No Irish woman ever did it!

—We want no amateur atheists.

—We want no budding buddhists.[6]

A sudden soft hiss fell from the windows above him and he knew that the electric lamps had been switched on in the readers' room. He turned into the pillared hall, now calmly lit, went up the staircase and passed in through the clicking turnstile.

Cranly was sitting over near the dictionaries. A thick book, opened at the frontispiece, lay before him on the wooden rest. He leaned back in his chair, inclining his ear like that of a confessor to the face of the medical student who was reading to him a problem from the chess page of a journal. Stephen sat down at his right and the priest at the other side of the table closed his copy of *The Tablet*[7] with an angry snap and stood up.

Cranly gazed after him blandly and vaguely. The medical student went on in a softer voice:

3. Spoken by the dying title character of *The Countess Cathleen* (1892), who, in the play by the Irish poet and playwright W. B. Yeats (1865–1939), sells her soul to the devil to save peasants facing starvation.

4. In May 1899 *The Countess Cathleen*, the first production by the Irish Literary Theatre, drew public protests on religious and political grounds.

5. Germany, associated with Protestantism, was then seen as flooding the world market with cheap goods.

6. An insult aimed at the interest that Yeats and other Irish literary figures had in Eastern religions and the occult.

7. Conservative Catholic weekly newspaper.

—Pawn to king's fourth.[8]

—We had better go, Dixon, said Stephen in warning. He has gone to complain.

Dixon folded the journal and rose with dignity, saying:

—Our men retired in good order.

—With guns and cattle, added Stephen, pointing to the titlepage of Cranly's book on which was printed *Diseases of the Ox.*

As they passed through a lane of the tables Stephen said:

—Cranly, I want to speak to you.

Cranly did not answer or turn. He laid his book on the counter and passed out, his wellshod feet sounding flatly on the floor. On the staircase he paused and gazing absently at Dixon repeated:

—Pawn to king's bloody fourth.

—Put it that way if you like, Dixon said.

He had a quiet toneless voice and urbane manners and on a finger of his plump clean hand he displayed at moments a signet ring.

As they crossed the hall a man of dwarfish stature came towards them. Under the dome of his tiny hat his unshaven face began to smile with pleasure and he was heard to murmur. The eyes were melancholy as those of a monkey.

—Good evening, captain, said Cranly, halting.

—Good evening, gentlemen, said the stubblegrown monkeyish face.

Warm weather for March, said Cranly. They have the windows open upstairs.

Dixon smiled and turned his ring. The blackish monkey-puckered face pursed its human mouth with gentle pleasure and its voice purred:

Delightful weather for March. Simply delightful.

There are two nice young ladies upstairs, captain, tired of waiting, Dixon said.

Cranly smiled and said kindly:

The captain has only one love: sir Walter Scott.[9] Isn't that so, captain?

—What are you reading now, captain? Dixon asked. *The Bride of Lammermoor?*[1]

—I love old Scott, the flexible lips said. I think he writes something lovely. There is no writer can touch sir Walter Scott.

He moved a thin shrunken brown hand gently in the air in time to his praise and his thin quick eyelids beat often over his sad eyes.

Sadder to Stephen's ear was his speech: a genteel accent, low and moist, marred by errors:[2] and listening to it he wondered was the story true and was the thin blood that flowed in his shrunken frame noble and come of an incestuous love?

The park trees were heavy with rain and rain fell still and ever in the lake, lying grey like a shield. A game of swans[3] flew there and the water and the shore beneath were fouled with their greenwhite slime. They embraced softly impelled by the grey rainy light, the wet silent trees, the shieldlike witnessing lake, the swans. They embraced without joy or passion, his arm about his sister's neck. A grey woollen cloak was wrapped athwart from her shoulder to her waist: and her fair head was bent in willing shame. He had

---

8. A standard opening move in chess.
9. Scottish novelist (1771–1832).
1. Novel by Scott (1819).

2. Grammatical mistakes.
3. Flock kept for pleasure.

loose redbrown hair and tender shapely strong freckled hands. Face? There was no face seen. The brother's face was bent upon her fair rainfragrant hair. The hand freckled and strong and shapely and caressing was Davin's hand.

He frowned angrily upon his thought and on the shrivelled mannikin[4] who had called it forth. His father's gibes at the Bantry gang[5] leaped out of his memory. He held them at a distance and brooded uneasily on his own thought again. Why were they not Cranly's hands? Had Davin's simplicity and innocence stung him more secretly?

He walked on across the hall with Dixon, leaving Cranly to take leave elaborately of the dwarf.

Under the colonnade Temple was standing in the midst of a little group of students. One of them cried:

—Dixon, come over till you hear. Temple is in grand form.

Temple turned on him his dark gipsy eyes.

—You're a hypocrite, O'Keeffe, he said. And Dixon's a smiler. By hell, I think that's a good literary expression.

He laughed slily, looking in Stephen's face, repeating:

—By hell, I'm delighted with that name. A smiler.

A stout student who stood below them on the steps said:

—Come back to the mistress, Temple. We want to hear about that.

—He had, faith, Temple said. And he was a married man too. And all the priests used to be dining there. By hell, I think they all had a touch.[6]

—We shall call it riding a hack to spare the hunter,[7] said Dixon.

—Tell us, Temple, O'Keeffe said. How many quarts of porter have you in you?

—All your intellectual soul is in that phrase, O'Keeffe, said Temple with open scorn.

He moved with a shambling gait round the group and spoke to Stephen.

—Did you know that the Forsters are the kings of Belgium?[8] he asked.

Cranly came out through the door of the entrance hall, his hat thrust back on the nape of his neck and picking his teeth with care.

—And here's the wiseacre,[9] said Temple. Do you know that about the Forsters?

He paused for an answer. Cranly dislodged a figseed from his teeth on the point of his rude toothpick and gazed at it intently.

—The Forster family, Temple said, is descended from Baldwin the First, king of Flanders. He was called the Forester. Forester and Forster are the same name. A descendant of Baldwin the first, captain Francis Forster, settled in Ireland and married the daughter of the last chieftain of Clanbrassil. Then there are the Blake Forsters. That's a different branch.[1]

—From Baldhead, king of Flanders, Cranly repeated, rooting again deliberately at his gleaming uncovered teeth.

—Where did you pick up all that history? O'Keeffe asked.

4. Or manikin, deprecating term suggesting little man or dwarf.
5. Anti-Parnell politicians from this town in County Cork.
6. Sex.
7. Riding a horse typically used for work instead of a more valuable one.

8. They are not. This is perhaps a play on the desire to find aristocratic Irish genealogies.
9. A person who believes himself to be wise but is usually foolish.
1. More nonsensical claims to aristocratic lineage.

—I know all the history of your family too, Temple said, turning to Stephen. Do you know what Giraldus Cambrensis[2] says about your family?

—Is he descended from Baldwin too? asked a tall consumptive student with dark eyes.

—Baldhead, Cranly repeated, sucking at a crevice in his teeth.

—*Pernobilis et pervetusta familia*,[3] Temple said to Stephen.

The stout student who stood below them on the steps farted briefly. Dixon turned towards him saying in a soft voice:

—Did an angel speak?

Cranly turned also and said vehemently but without anger:

—Goggins, you're the flamingest dirty devil I ever met, do you know.

—I had it on my mind to say that, Goggins answered firmly. It did no-one any harm, did it?

—We hope, Dixon said suavely, that it was not of the kind known to science as a *paulo post futurum*.[4]

—Didn't I tell you he was a smiler? said Temple, turning right and left. Didn't I give him that name?

—You did. We're not deaf, said the tall consumptive.

Cranly still frowned at the stout student below him. Then, with a snort of disgust, he shoved him violently down the steps.

—Go away from here, he said rudely. Go away, you stinkpot. And you are a stinkpot.

Goggins skipped down on to the gravel and at once returned to his place with good humour. Temple turned back to Stephen and asked:

—Do you believe in the law of heredity?

—Are you drunk or what are you or what are you trying to say? asked Cranly, facing round on him with an expression of wonder.

—The most profound sentence ever written, Temple said with enthusiasm, is the sentence at the end of the zoology. Reproduction is the beginning of death.

He touched Stephen timidly at the elbow and said eagerly:

—Do you feel how profound that is because you are a poet?

Cranly pointed his long forefinger.

—Look at him! he said with scorn to the others. Look at Ireland's hope!

They laughed at his words and gesture. Temple turned on him bravely, saying:

—Cranly, you're always sneering at me. I can see that. But I am as good as you are any day. Do you know what I think about you now as compared with myself?

—My dear man, said Cranly urbanely, you are incapable, do you know, absolutely incapable of thinking.

—But do you know, Temple went on, what I think of you and of myself compared together?

—Out with it, Temple! the stout student cried from the steps. Get it out in bits!

Temple turned right and left, making sudden feeble gestures as he spoke.

---

2. Welsh historian (ca. 1146–1223) who wrote about Ireland.
3. From a noble and venerable family (Latin).

4. Latin name for the future perfect tense of Greek verbs, used for events that will happen immediately.

—I'm a ballocks,[5] he said, shaking his head in despair. I am. And I know I am. And I admit it that I am.

Dixon patted him lightly on the shoulder and said mildly:

—And it does you every credit, Temple.

—But he, Temple said, pointing to Cranly. He is a ballocks too like me. Only he doesn't know it. And that's the only difference I see.

A burst of laughter covered his words. But he turned again to Stephen and said with a sudden eagerness:

—That word is a most interesting word. That's the only English dual number.[6] Did you know?

—Is it? Stephen said vaguely.

He was watching Cranly's firmfeatured suffering face, lit up now by a smile of false patience. The gross name had passed over it like foul water poured over an old stone image, patient of injuries: and, as he watched him, he saw him raise his hat in salute and uncover the black hair that stood up stiffly from his forehead like an iron crown.

She passed out from the porch of the library and bowed across Stephen in reply to Cranly's greeting. He also? Was there not a slight flush on Cranly's cheek? Or had it come forth at Temple's words? The light had waned. He could not see.

Did that explain his friend's listless silence, his harsh comments, the sudden intrusions of rude speech with which he had shattered so often Stephen's ardent wayward confessions? Stephen had forgiven freely for he had found this rudeness also in himself towards himself. And he remembered an evening when he had dismounted from a borrowed creaking bicycle to pray to God in a wood near Malahide.[7] He had lifted up his arms and spoken in ecstasy to the sombre nave of the trees, knowing that he stood on holy ground and in a holy hour. And when two constabularymen had come into sight round a bend in the gloomy road he had broken off his prayer to whistle loudly an air from the last pantomime.

He began to beat the frayed end of his ashplant against the base of a pillar. Had Cranly not heard him? Yet he could wait. The talk about him ceased for a moment: and a soft hiss fell again from a window above. But no other sound was in the air and the swallows whose flight he had followed with idle eyes were sleeping.

She had passed through the dusk. And therefore the air was silent save for one soft hiss that fell. And therefore the tongues about him had ceased their babble. Darkness was falling.

Darkness falls from the air.[8]

A trembling joy, lambent[9] as a faint light, played like a fairy host around him. But why? Her passage through the darkening air or the verse with its black vowels and its opening sound, rich and lutelike?

He walked away slowly towards the deeper shadows at the end of the colonnade, beating the stone softly with his stick to hide his revery from the

---

5. Or bollocks, a stupid, blundering man; literally, testicles.
6. The special form of a plural used to indicate two of something.
7. Village on the Irish Sea north of Dublin.

8. Misquotation of "Brightness falls from the air," a line from "A Litany in Time of Plague" (1592), by English poet Thomas Nashe (1567–1601), as Stephen later recalls.
9. Softly shining.

students whom he had left: and allowed his mind to summon back to itself the age of Dowland and Byrd and Nash.[1]

Eyes, opening from the darkness of desire, eyes that dimmed the breaking east. What was their languid grace but the softness of chambering? And what was their shimmer but the shimmer of the scum that mantled the cesspool of the court of a slobbering Stuart.[2] And he tasted in the language of memory ambered wines,[3] dying fallings of sweet airs,[4] the proud pavan:[5] and saw with the eyes of memory kind gentlewomen in Covent Garden[6] wooing from their balconies with sucking mouths and the poxfouled wenches of the taverns and young wives that, gaily yielding to their ravishers, clipped[7] and clipped again.

The images he had summoned gave him no pleasure. They were secret and enflaming but her image was not entangled by them. That was not the way to think of her. It was not even the way in which he thought of her. Could his mind then not trust itself? Old phrases, sweet only with a disinterred sweetness like the figseeds Cranly rooted out of his gleaming teeth.

It was not thought nor vision though he knew vaguely that her figure was passing homeward through the city. Vaguely first and then more sharply he smelt her body. A conscious unrest seethed in his blood. Yes, it was her body that he smelt: a wild and languid smell: the tepid limbs over which his music had flowed desirously and the secret soft linen upon which her flesh distilled odour and a dew.

A louse crawled over the nape of his neck and, putting his thumb and forefinger deftly beneath his loose collar, he caught it. He rolled its body, tender yet brittle as a grain of rice, between thumb and finger for an instant before he let it fall from him and wondered would it live or die. There came to his mind a curious phrase from Cornelius a Lapide[8] which said that the lice born of human sweat were not created by God with the other animals on the sixth day. But the tickling of the skin of his neck made his mind raw and red. The life of his body, illclad, illfed, louseeaten, made him close his eyelids in a sudden spasm of despair: and in the darkness he saw the brittle bright bodies of lice falling from the air and turning often as they fell. Yes: and it was not darkness that fell from the air. It was brightness.

He had not even remembered rightly Nash's line. All the images it had awakened were false. His mind bred vermin. His thoughts were lice born of the sweat of sloth.

He came back quickly along the colonnade towards the group of students. Well then let her go and be damned to her. She could love some clean athlete who washed himself every morning to the waist and had black hair on his chest. Let her.

Cranly had taken another dried fig from the supply in his pocket and was eating it slowly and noisily. Temple sat on the pediment of a pillar, leaning back, his cap pulled down on his sleepy eyes. A squat young man came out of the porch, a leather portfolio tucked under his armpit. He

---

1. Like Nashe, English poets and composers from the Elizabethan and Jacobean eras (1558–1625): John Dowland (ca. 1563–1626) and William Byrd (1543–1623).
2. King James I, who reigned (1603–25) after Elizabeth I.
3. Having the fragrance of ambergris.

4. Songs. Cf. the "dying fall" in Shakespeare's *Twelfth Night* 1.1.4.
5. A stately Elizabethan dance.
6. Entertainment district in central London developed in the 1630s.
7. Had sexual intercourse.
8. Flemish Jesuit priest (1567–1637).

marched towards the group, striking the flags[9] with the heels of his boots and with the ferrule[1] of his heavy umbrella. Then, raising the umbrella in salute, he said to all:

Good evening, sirs.

He struck the flags again and tittered while his head trembled with a slight nervous movement. The tall consumptive student and Dixon and O'Keeffe were speaking in Irish and did not answer him. Then, turning to Cranly, he said:

—Good evening, particularly to you.

He moved the umbrella in indication and tittered again. Cranly, who was still chewing the fig, answered with loud movements of his jaws.

—Good? Yes. It is a good evening.

The squat student looked at him seriously and shook his umbrella gently and reprovingly.

—I can see, he said, that you are about to make obvious remarks.

—Um, Cranly answered, holding out what remained of the halfchewed fig and jerking it towards the squat student's mouth in sign that he should eat.

The squat student did not eat it but, indulging his special humour, said gravely, still tittering and prodding his phrase with his umbrella:

—Do you intend that . . .

He broke off, pointed bluntly to the munched pulp of the fig and said loudly:

—I allude to that.

—Um, Cranly said as before.

—Do you intend that now, the squat student said, as *ipso facto*[2] or, let us say, as so to speak?

Dixon turned aside from his group, saying:

—Goggins was waiting for you, Glynn. He has gone round to the Adelphi[3] to look for you and Moynihan. What have you there? he asked, tapping the portfolio under Glynn's arm.

—Examination papers, Glynn answered. I give them monthly examinations to see that they are profiting by my tuition.

He also tapped the portfolio and coughed gently and smiled.

—Tuition! said Cranly rudely. I suppose you mean the barefooted children that are taught by a bloody ape like you. God help them!

He bit off the rest of the fig and flung away the butt.

—I suffer little children to come unto me,[4] Glynn said amiably.

—A bloody ape, Cranly repeated with emphasis, and a blasphemous bloody ape!

Temple stood up and, pushing past Cranly, addressed Glynn:

—That phrase you said now, he said, is from the new testament about suffer the children to come to me.

—Go to sleep again, Temple, said O'Keeffe.

—Very well, then, Temple continued, still addressing Glynn, and if Jesus suffered the children to come why does the church send them all to hell if they die unbaptised? Why is that?

9. Flagstones.
1. Metal cap at the end of a stick.
2. By that fact (Latin).

3. Hotel near the National Library.
4. Cf. Mark 10.14.

—Were you baptised yourself, Temple? the consumptive student asked.

—But why are they sent to hell if Jesus said they were all to come? Temple said, his eyes searching in Glynn's eyes.

Glynn coughed and said gently, holding back with difficulty the nervous titter in his voice and moving his umbrella at every word:

—And, as you remark, if it is thus I ask emphatically whence comes this thusness.

—Because the church is cruel like all old sinners, Temple said.

—Are you quite orthodox on that point, Temple? Dixon said suavely.

—Saint Augustine says that about unbaptised children going to hell, Temple answered, because he was a cruel old sinner too.

—I bow to you, Dixon said, but I had the impression that limbo[5] existed for such cases.

—Don't argue with him, Dixon, Cranly said brutally. Don't talk to him or look at him. Lead him home with a sugan[6] the way you'd lead a bleating goat.

—Limbo! Temple cried. That's a fine invention too. Like hell.

—But with the unpleasantness left out, Dixon said.

He turned smiling to the others and said:

—I think I am voicing the opinions of all present in saying so much.

—You are, Glynn said in a firm tone. On that point Ireland is united.

He struck the ferrule of his umbrella on the stone floor of the colonnade.

—Hell, Temple said. I can respect that invention of the grey spouse of Satan.[7] Hell is Roman, like the walls of the Romans, strong and ugly. But what is limbo?

—Put him back into the perambulator, Cranly, O'Keeffe called out.

Cranly made a swift step towards Temple, halted, stamping his foot and crying as if to a fowl:

—Hoosh!

Temple moved away nimbly.

—Do you know what limbo is? he cried. Do you know what we call a notion like that in Roscommon?[8]

—Hoosh! Blast you! Cranly cried, clapping his hands.

—Neither my arse nor my elbow! Temple cried out scornfully. And that's what I call limbo.

—Give us that stick here, Cranly said.

He snatched the ashplant roughly from Stephen's hand and sprang down the steps: but Temple, hearing him move in pursuit, fled through the dusk like a wild creature, nimble and fleetfooted. Cranly's heavy boots were heard loudly charging across the quadrangle and then returning heavily, foiled and spurning the gravel at each step.

His step was angry and with an angry abrupt gesture he thrust the stick back into Stephen's hand. Stephen felt that his anger had another cause but, feigning patience, touched his arm slightly and said quietly:

—Cranly, I told you I wanted to speak to you. Come away.

Cranly looked at him for a few moments and asked:

—Now?

—Yes, now, Stephen said. We can't speak here. Come away.

---

5. Region bordering hell for unbaptized infants and for the just people who died before the coming of Christ.

6. Rope made of twisted straw (Irish).

7. I.e., sin.

8. A town and a county to the west of Dublin.

They crossed the quadrangle together without speaking. The birdcall from *Siegfried*[9] whistled softly followed them from the steps of the porch. Cranly turned: and Dixon, who had whistled, called out:

—Where are you fellows off to? What about that game, Cranly?

They parleyed in shouts across the still air about a game of billiards[1] to be played in the Adelphi hotel. Stephen walked on alone and out into the quiet of Kildare Street. Opposite Maple's hotel he stood to wait, patient again. The name of the hotel, a colourless polished wood, and its colourless quiet front stung him like a glance of polite disdain. He stared angrily back at the softly lit drawingroom of the hotel in which he imagined the sleek lives of the patricians of Ireland housed in calm. They thought of army commissions and land agents: peasants greeted them along the roads in the country: they knew the names of certain French dishes and gave orders to jarvies[2] in high-pitched provincial voices which pierced through their skintight accents.

How could he hit their conscience or how cast his shadow over the imagination of their daughters, before their squires begat upon them, that they might breed a race less ignoble than their own? And under the deepened dusk he felt the thoughts and desires of the race to which he belonged flitting like bats across the dark country lanes, under trees by the edges of streams and near the poolmottled bogs. A woman had waited in the doorway as Davin had passed by at night and, offering him a cup of milk, had all but wooed him to her bed: for Davin had the mild eyes of one that could be secret. But him no woman's eyes had wooed.

His arm was taken in a strong grip and Cranly's voice said:

—Let us eke go.

They walked southward in silence. Then Cranly said:

—That blithering idiot Temple! I swear to Moses, do you know, that I'll be the death of that fellow one time.

But his voice was no longer angry and Stephen wondered was he thinking of her greeting to him under the porch.

They turned to the left and walked on as before. When they had gone on so for some time Stephen said:

—Cranly, I had an unpleasant quarrel this evening.

—With your people? Cranly asked.

—With my mother.

—About religion?

—Yes, Stephen answered.

After a pause Cranly asked:

—What age is your mother?

—Not old, Stephen said. She wishes me to make my easter duty.[3]

—And will you?

—I will not, Stephen said.

—Why not? Cranly said.

—I will not serve, answered Stephen.

—That remark was made before,[4] Cranly said calmly.

9. An 1876 opera by the German composer Richard Wagner (1813–1883).
1. Game similar to American pool but played on a table without pockets. "Parleyed": discussed the terms of.
2. Drivers of hackney coaches, horse-drawn carriages available for hire.
3. To receive Communion on or around Easter Sunday.
4. I.e., when Lucifer said it as he fell from heaven. See p. 513, n. 6 and n. 7.

—It is made behind now, said Stephen hotly.

Cranly pressed Stephen's arm, saying:

—Go easy, my dear man. You're an excitable bloody man, do you know.

He laughed nervously as he spoke and, looking up into Stephen's face with moved and friendly eyes, said:

—Do you know that you are an excitable man?

—I daresay I am, said Stephen, laughing also.

Their minds, lately estranged, seemed suddenly to have been drawn closer, one to the other.

—Do you believe in the eucharist? Cranly asked.

—I do not, Stephen said.

—Do you disbelieve then?

—I neither believe in it nor disbelieve in it, Stephen answered.

—Many persons have doubts, even religious persons, yet they overcome them or put them aside, Cranly said. Are your doubts on that point too strong?

—I do not wish to overcome them, Stephen answered.

Cranly, embarrassed for a moment, took another fig from his pocket and was about to eat it when Stephen said:

—Don't, please. You cannot discuss this question with your mouth full of chewed fig.

Cranly examined the fig by the light of a lamp under which he halted. Then he smelt it with both nostrils, bit a tiny piece, spat it out and threw the fig rudely into the gutter. Addressing it as it lay, he said:

—Depart from me, ye cursed, into everlasting fire!

Taking Stephen's arm he went on again and said:

—Do you not fear that those words may be spoken to you on the day of judgment?

—What is offered me on the other hand? Stephen asked. An eternity of bliss in the company of the dean of studies?

—Remember, Cranly said, that he would be glorified.

—Ay, Stephen said somewhat bitterly. Bright, agile, impassible and, above all, subtle.

—It is a curious thing, do you know, Cranly said dispassionately, how your mind is supersaturated with the religion in which you say you disbelieve. Did you believe in it when you were at school? I bet you did.

—I did, Stephen answered.

—And were you happier then? Cranly asked softly. Happier than you are now, for instance?

—Often happy, Stephen said, and often unhappy. I was someone else then.

—How someone else? What do you mean by that statement?

—I mean, said Stephen, that I was not myself as I am now, as I had to become.

—Not as you are now, not as you had to become, Cranly repeated. Let me ask you a question. Do you love your mother?

Stephen shook his head slowly.

—I don't know what your words mean, he said simply.

—Have you never loved anyone? Cranly asked.

—Do you mean women?

—I am not speaking of that, Cranly said in a colder tone. I ask you if you ever felt love towards anyone or anything.

Stephen walked on beside his friend, staring gloomily at the footpath.

—I tried to love God, he said at length. It seems now I failed. It is very difficult. I tried to unite my will with the will of God instant by instant. In that I did not always fail. I could perhaps do that still . . . . .

Cranly cut him short by asking:

—Has your mother had a happy life?

—How do I know? Stephen said.

—How many children had she?

—Nine or ten, Stephen answered. Some died.

—Was your father. . . . Cranly interrupted himself for an instant: and then said: I don't want to pry into your family affairs. But was your father what is called well-to-do? I mean when you were growing up?

—Yes, Stephen said.

—What was he? Cranly asked after a pause.

Stephen began to enumerate glibly his father's attributes.

—A medical student, an oarsman, a tenor, an amateur actor, a shouting politician, a small landlord, a small investor, a drinker, a good fellow, a storyteller, somebody's secretary, something in a distillery, a taxgatherer, a bankrupt and at present a praiser of his own past.

Cranly laughed, tightening his grip on Stephen's arm, and said:

—The distillery is damn good.

—Is there anything else you want to know? Stephen asked.

—Are you in good circumstances at present?

—Do I look it? Stephen asked bluntly.

—So then, Cranly went on musingly, you were born in the lap of luxury.

He used the phrase broadly and loudly as he often used technical expressions as if he wished his hearer to understand that they were used by him without conviction.

—Your mother must have gone through a good deal of suffering, he said then. Would you not try to save her from suffering more even if. . . . or would you?

—If I could, Stephen said. That would cost me very little.

—Then do so, Cranly said. Do as she wishes you to do. What is it for you? You disbelieve in it. It is a form: nothing else. And you will set her mind at rest.

He ceased and, as Stephen did not reply, remained silent. Then, as if giving utterance to the process of his own thought, he said:

—Whatever else is unsure in this stinking dunghill of a world a mother's love is not. Your mother brings you into the world, carries you first in her body. What do we know about what she feels? But whatever she feels, it, at least, must be real. It must be. What are our ideas or ambitions? Play. Ideas! Why, that bloody bleating goat Temple has ideas. MacCann has ideas too. Every jackass going the roads thinks he has ideas.

Stephen, who had been listening to the unspoken speech behind the words, said with assumed carelessness:

—Pascal, if I remember rightly, would not suffer his mother to kiss him as he feared the contact of her sex.[5]

—Pascal was a pig, said Cranly.

—Aloysius Gonzaga,[6] I think, was of the same mind, Stephen said.

---

5. A possibly apocryphal story about the conservative Catholicism of the French philosopher Blaise Pascal (1623–1662).

6. Young saint and patron of Clongowes Wood College (1568–1591).

—And he was another pig then, said Cranly.

—The church calls him a saint, Stephen objected.

—I don't care a flaming damn what anyone calls him, Cranly said rudely and flatly. I call him a pig.

Stephen, preparing the words neatly in his mind, continued:

—Jesus too seems to have treated his mother with scant courtesy in public but Suarez, a jesuit theologian and Spanish gentleman,[7] has apologised for him.

—Did the idea ever occur to you, Cranly asked, that Jesus was not what he pretended to be?

—The first person to whom that idea occurred, Stephen answered, was Jesus himself.

—I mean, Cranly said, hardening in his speech, did the idea ever occur to you that he was himself a conscious hypocrite, what he called the jews of his time, a whited sepulchre?[8] Or, to put it more plainly, that he was a blackguard?[9]

—That idea never occurred to me, Stephen answered. But I am curious to know are you trying to make a convert of me or a pervert[1] of yourself?

He turned towards his friend's face and saw there a raw smile which some force of will strove to make finely significant.

Cranly asked suddenly in a plain sensible tone:

—Tell me the truth. Were you at all shocked by what I said?

—Somewhat, Stephen said.

—And why were you shocked, Cranly pressed on in the same tone, if you feel sure that our religion is false and that Jesus was not the son of God?

—I am not at all sure of it, Stephen said. He is more like a son of God than a son of Mary.

—And is that why you will not communicate,[2] Cranly asked, because you are not sure of that too, because you feel that the host too may be the body and blood of the son of God and not a wafer of bread? And because you fear that it may be?

—Yes, Stephen said quietly. I feel that and I also fear it.

—I see, Cranly said.

Stephen, struck by his tone of closure, reopened the discussion at once by saying:

I fear many things: dogs, horses, firearms, the sea, thunderstorms, machinery, the country roads at night.

But why do you fear a bit of bread?

I imagine, Stephen said, that there is a malevolent reality behind those things I say I fear.

Do you fear then, Cranly asked, that the God of the Roman Catholics would strike you dead and damn you if you made a sacrilegious communion?

The God of the Roman catholics could do that now, Stephen said. I fear more than that the chemical action which would be set up in my soul by a

---

7. Francisco Suarez (1548–1617) claimed that Jesus's words to Mary—"Woman, what have I to do with thee?" (John 2.4)—were actually polite.

8. Coming into conflict with the Jewish sect of the Pharisees, Jesus compared them and the scribes to "whited sepulchers," beautiful on the outside but unclean and filled with bones (Matthew 23.27).

9. Scoundrel.

1. Here, someone who turns away from religious faith.

2. Receive Communion.

false homage to a symbol behind which are massed twenty centuries of authority and veneration.

—Would you, Cranly asked, in extreme danger commit that particular sacrilege? For instance, if you lived in the penal days?[3]

—I cannot answer for the past, Stephen replied. Possibly not.

—Then, said Cranly, you do not intend to become a protestant?

—I said that I had lost the faith, Stephen answered, but not that I had lost selfrespect. What kind of liberation would that be to forsake an absurdity which is logical and coherent and to embrace one which is illogical and incoherent?

They had walked on towards the township of Pembroke[4] and now, as they went on slowly along the avenues, the trees and the scattered lights in the villas soothed their minds. The air of wealth and repose diffused about them seemed to comfort their neediness. Behind a hedge of laurel a light glimmered in the window of a kitchen and the voice of a servant was heard singing as she sharpened knives. She sang in short broken bars *Rosie O'Grady*.[5]

Cranly stopped to listen, saying:

—*Mulier cantat.*[6]

The soft beauty of the Latin word touched with an enchanting touch the dark of the evening, with a touch fainter and more persuading than the touch of music or of a woman's hand. The strife of their minds was quelled. The figure of woman as she appears in the liturgy of the church passed silently through the darkness: a whiterobed figure, small and slender as a boy and with a falling girdle.[7] Her voice, frail and high as a boy's, was heard intoning from a distant choir the first words of a woman which pierce the gloom and clamour of the first chanting of the passion:

—*Et tu cum Jesu Galilaeo eras.*[8]

And all hearts were touched and turned to her voice, shining like a young star, shining clearer as the voice intoned the proparoxyton[9] and more faintly as the cadence died.

The singing ceased. They went on together, Cranly repeating in strongly stressed rhythm the end of the refrain:

> *And when we are married*
> *O, how happy we'll be*
> *For I love sweet Rosie O'Grady*
> *And Rosie O'Grady loves me.*

—There's real poetry for you, he said. There's real love.

He glanced sideways at Stephen with a strange smile and said:

—Do you consider that poetry? Or do you know what the words mean?

—I want to see Rosie first, said Stephen.

—She's easy to find, Cranly said.

His hat had come down on his forehead. He shoved it back: and in the shadow of the trees Stephen saw his pale face, framed by the dark, and his

---

3. The English penal laws were in effect in Ireland from the 1690s to the 1820s, disenfranchising, dispossessing, and religiously suppressing the Roman Catholic majority.
4. Township on the southeastern outskirts of Dublin.
5. Popular song by music-hall singer Maude Nugent (1877–1958).
6. A woman is singing (Latin).
7. With her belt around her hips rather than her waist.
8. Thou also wast with Jesus of Galilee (Matthew 26.69), part of the mass usually sung on the Sunday before Easter.
9. A word accented on the third-to-last syllable.

large dark eyes. Yes. His face was handsome: and his body was strong and hard. He had spoken of a mother's love. He felt then the sufferings of women, the weaknesses of their bodies and souls: and would shield them with a strong and resolute arm and bow his mind to them.

Away then: it is time to go. A voice spoke softly to Stephen's lonely heart, bidding him go and telling him that his friendship was coming to an end. Yes: he would go. He could not strive against another. He knew his part.

—Probably I shall go away, he said.

—Where? Cranly asked.

—Where I can, Stephen said.

—Yes, Cranly said. It might be difficult for you to live here now. But is it that that makes you go?

I have to go, Stephen answered.

Because, Cranly continued, you need not look upon yourself as driven away if you do not wish to go or as a heretic or an outlaw. There are many good believers who think as you do. Would that surprise you? The church is not the stone building nor even the clergy and their dogmas. It is the whole mass of those born into it. I don't know what you wish to do in life. Is it what you told me the night we were standing outside Harcourt Street station?

Yes, Stephen said, smiling in spite of himself at Cranly's way of remembering thoughts in connection with places. The night you spent half an hour wrangling with Doherty about the shortest way from Sallygap to Larras.[1]

—Pothead! Cranly said with calm contempt. What does he know about the way from Sallygap to Larras? Or what does he know about anything for that matter? And the big slobbering washingpot head of him!

He broke out into a loud long laugh.

—Well? Stephen said. Do you remember the rest?

—What you said, is it? Cranly asked. Yes, I remember it. To discover the mode of life or of art whereby your spirit could express itself in unfettered freedom.

Stephen raised his hat in acknowledgment.

—Freedom! Cranly repeated. But you are not free enough yet to commit a sacrilege. Tell me, would you rob?

—I would beg first, Stephen said.

—And if you got nothing would you rob?

—You wish me to say, Stephen answered, that the rights of property are provisional and that in certain circumstances it is not unlawful to rob. Everyone would act in that belief. So I will not make you that answer. Apply to the jesuit theologian Juan Mariana de Talavera[2] who will also explain to you in what circumstances you may lawfully kill your king and whether you had better hand him his poison in a goblet or smear it for him upon his robe or his saddlebow.[3] Ask me rather would I suffer others to rob me or, if they did, would I call down upon them what I believe is called the chastisement of the secular arm.

—And would you?

—I think, Stephen said, it would pain me as much to do so as to be robbed.

---

1. The shortest route from Sallygap, in the Wicklow Mountains south of Dublin, to Larras was over the mountains.

2. Spanish Jesuit theologian (1536–1623).
3. Arched front part of a saddle.

—I see, Cranly said.

He produced his match and began to clean the crevice between two teeth. Then he said carelessly:

—Tell me, for example, would you deflower a virgin?

—Excuse me, Stephen said politely. Is that not the ambition of most young gentlemen?

—What then is your point of view? Cranly asked.

His last phrase, soursmelling as the smoke of charcoal and disheartening, excited Stephen's brain over which its fumes seemed to brood.

—Look here, Cranly, he said. You have asked me what I would do and what I would not do. I will tell you what I will do and what I will not do. I will not serve that in which I no longer believe whether it call itself my home, my fatherland or my church: and I will try to express myself in some mode of life or art as freely as I can and as wholly as I can, using for my defence the only arms I allow myself to use, silence, exile and cunning.

Cranly seized his arm and steered him round so as to lead him back towards Leeson Park.[4] He laughed almost slily and pressed Stephen's arm with an elder's affection.

—Cunning indeed! he said. Is it you? You poor poet, you!

—And you made me confess to you, Stephen said, thrilled by his touch, as I have confessed to you so many other things, have I not?

—Yes, my child,[5] Cranly said, still gaily.

—You made me confess the fears that I have. But I will tell you also what I do not fear. I do not fear to be alone or to be spurned for another or to leave whatever I have to leave. And I am not afraid to make a mistake, even a great mistake, a lifelong mistake and perhaps as long as eternity too.

Cranly, now grave again, slowed his pace and said:

—Alone, quite alone. You have no fear of that. And you know what that word means? Not only to be separate from all others but to have not even one friend.

—I will take the risk, said Stephen.

—And not to have any one person, Cranly said, who would be more than a friend, more even than the noblest and truest friend a man ever had.

His words seemed to have struck some deep chord in his own nature. Had he spoken of himself, of himself as he was or wished to be? Stephen watched his face for some moments in silence. A cold sadness was there. He had spoken of himself, of his own loneliness which he feared.

—Of whom are you speaking? Stephen asked at length.

Cranly did not answer.

◆　◆　◆

20 *March:* Long talk with Cranly on the subject of my revolt. He had his grand manner on. I supple and suave. Attacked me on the score of love for one's mother. Tried to imagine his mother: cannot. Told me once, in a moment of thoughtlessness, his father was sixtyone when he was born. Can see him. Strong farmer type. Pepper and salt suit. Square feet. Unkempt grizzled beard. Probably attends coursing matches.[6] Pays his dues regularly

---

4. This would lead them to Leeson Street and then back to Stephen's Green.
5. Words usually spoken by a priest to a penitent in the confessional.
6. Greyhound races in which the dogs pursue live game, usually hares.

but not plentifully to Father Dwyer of Larras. Sometimes talks to girls after nightfall. But his mother? Very young or very old? Hardly the first. If so, Cranly would not have spoken as he did. Old then. Probably: and neglected. Hence Cranly's despair of soul: the child of exhausted loins.

21 March, morning: Thought this in bed last night but was too lazy and free to add it. Free, yes. The exhausted loins are those of Elizabeth and Zachary. Then is he the precursor. Item: he eats chiefly belly bacon and dried figs. Read locusts and wild honey. Also, when thinking of him, saw always a stern severed head or deathmask as if outlined on a grey curtain or veronica. Decollation they call it in the fold. Puzzled for the moment by saint John at the Latin gate. What do I see? A decollated precursor trying to pick the lock.[7]

21 March, night: Free. Soul free and fancyfree. Let the dead bury the dead. Ay. And let the dead marry the dead.[8]

22 March: In company with Lynch followed a sizable hospital nurse. Lynch's idea. Dislike it. Two lean hungry greyhounds walking after a heifer.

23 March: Have not seen her since that night. Unwell? Sits at the fire perhaps with mamma's shawl on her shoulders. But not peevish. A nice bowl of gruel? Won't you now?

24 March: Began with a discussion with my mother. Subject: B. V. M.[9] Handicapped by my sex and youth. To escape held up relations between Jesus and Papa against those between Mary and her son. Said religion is not a lying-in hospital.[1] Mother indulgent. Said I have a queer mind and have read too much. Not true. Have read little and understood less. Then she said I would come back to faith because I had a restless mind. This means to leave church by backdoor of sin and reenter through the skylight of repentance. Cannot repent. Told her so and asked for sixpence. Got threepence.

Then went to college. Other wrangle with little roundhead rogue's eye Ghezzi.[2] This time about Bruno the Nolan.[3] Began in Italian and ended in pidgin English. He said Bruno was a terrible heretic. I said he was terribly burned. He agreed to this with some sorrow. Then gave me recipe for what he calls *risotto alla bergamasca*.[4] When he pronounces a soft *o* he protrudes his full carnal lips as if he kissed the vowel. Has he? And could he repent? Yes, he could: and cry two round rogue's tears, one from each eye.

Crossing Stephen's, that is, my green, remembered that his countrymen and not mine had invented what Cranly the other night called our religion. A quartet of them, soldiers of the ninetyseventh infantry regiment, sat at the foot of the cross and tossed up dice for the overcoat of the crucified.

Went to library. Tried to read three reviews. Useless. She is not out yet. Am I alarmed? About what? That she will never be out again. Blake wrote:

7. All these items link Cranly to John the Baptist. "Exhausted loins": Elizabeth and Zachary, John the Baptist's parents, were old (Luke 7.1). "Locusts and wild honey": his food in exile (Matthew 3.4; Mark 1.6). "Severed head": he was beheaded at the wish of Salomé (Matthew 14.6–11). "Veronica": cloth bearing the image of Jesus's face, which appeared after St. Veronica used it to wipe his face on his way to the cross and which Stephen compares to the severed head of John the Baptist. "Decollation": the act of being beheaded. "Saint John at the Latin gate": John the Apostle, who escaped from the Romans at this site and might thus be said to have had the lock picked for him by John the Baptist.
8. A citation of and then a play on Luke 9.60.
9. Blessed Virgin Mary.
1. Maternity hospital.
2. The Italian lecturer at University College.
3. Giordano Bruno of Nola (1548–1600), Italian philosopher who was burned at the stake as a heretic.
4. Rice dish made as it is in Bergamo (Italian), an Italian town northeast of Milan.

> *I wonder if William Bond will die.*
> *For assuredly he is very ill.*[5]

Alas, poor William!

I was once at a diorama in Rotunda.[6] At the end were pictures of big nobs.[7] Among them William Ewart Gladstone, just then dead. Orchestra played *O Willie, we have missed you.*[8]

A race of clodhoppers.[9]

25 March, morning: A troubled night of dreams. Want to get them off my chest.

A long curving gallery. From the floor ascend pillars of dark vapours. It is peopled by the images of fabulous kings, set in stone. Their hands are folded upon their knees in token of weariness and their eyes are darkened for the errors of men go up before them for ever as dark vapours.

Strange figures advance from a cave. They are not as tall as men. One does not seem to stand quite apart from another. Their faces are phosphorescent, with darker streaks. They peer at me and their eyes seem to ask me something. They do not speak.

30 March: This evening Cranly was in the porch of the library, proposing a problem to Dixon and her brother. A mother let her child fall into the Nile. Still harping on the mother. A crocodile seized the child. Mother asked it back. Crocodile said all right if she told him what he was going to do with the child, eat it or not eat it.

This mentality, Lepidus would say, is indeed bred out of your mud by the operation of your sun.[1]

And mine? Is it not too? Then into Nilemud with it!

1 April: Disapprove of this last phrase.

2 April: Saw her drinking tea and eating cakes in Johnston, Mooney and O'Brien's. Rather lynxeyed[2] Lynch saw her as we passed. He tells me Cranly was invited there by brother. Did he bring his crocodile? Is he the shining light now? Well, I discovered him. I protest I did. Shining quietly behind a bushel of Wicklow bran.

3 April: Met Davin at the cigar shop opposite Findlater's church.[3] He was in a black sweater and had a hurleystick. Asked me was it true I was going away and why. Told him the shortest way to Tara was via Holyhead.[4] Just then my father came up. Introduction. Father polite and observant. Asked Davin if he might offer him some refreshment. Davin could not, was going to a meeting. When we came away father told me he had a good honest eye. Asked me why I did not join a rowing club. I pretended to think it over. Told me then how he broke Pennyfeather's heart.[5] Wants me to read law.[6] Says I was cut out for that. More mud, more crocodiles.

---

5. From "William Bond" by English poet William Blake (1757–1827). The preceding lines are "I wonder whether the Girls are mad, / And I wonder whether they mean to kill."

6. Group of buildings at the end of Sackville (now O'Connell) Street, used for various public purposes. "Diorama": scenic representation by translucent pictures, before films were available.

7. Distinguished persons.

8. Cf. the song (1854) of this title by American songwriter Stephen Collins Foster (1826–1864). "Willie" refers to English prime minister William Gladstone (1809–1898) and the other Williams in this passage.

9. People who plow the land and thus, figuratively, clumsy, boorish country folk.

1. Drawing on this character's remark in Shakespeare's *Antony and Cleopatra* 2.7.25–26.

2. Keen-sighted.

3. Presbyterian church at the corner of Rutland (now Parnell) Square North and Frederick Street North.

4. The Welsh port across the Irish Sea from Ireland. "Tara": the ancient seat of the High Kings of Ireland. The phrase suggests that the best way to gain recognition is by exile.

5. Colloquial expression of disappointment.

6. I.e., to study law.

5 April: Wild spring. Scudding clouds. O life! Dark stream of swirling bog-water on which appletrees have cast down their delicate flowers. Eyes of girls among the leaves. Girls demure and romping. All fair or auburn: no dark ones. They blush better. Houp-la!

6 April: Certainly she remembers the past. Lynch says all women do. Then she remembers the time of her childhood—and mine if I was ever a child. The past is consumed in the present and the present is living only because it brings forth the future. Statues of women, if Lynch be right, should always be fully draped, one hand of the woman feeling regretfully her own hinder parts.

6 April: later: Michael Robartes remembers forgotten beauty[7] and, when his arms wrap her round, he presses in his arms the loveliness which has long faded from the world. Not this. Not at all. I desire to press in my arms the loveliness which has not yet come into the world.

10 April: Faintly, under the heavy night, through the silence of the city which has turned from dreams to dreamless sleep as a weary lover whom no caresses move, the sound of hoofs upon the road. Not so faintly now as they come near the bridge; and in a moment as they pass the darkened windows the silence is cloven by alarm as by an arrow. They are heard now far away, hoofs that shine amid the heavy night as gems, hurrying beyond the sleeping fields to what journey's end—what heart?—bearing what tidings?

11 April: Read what I wrote last night. Vague words for a vague emotion. Would she like it? I think so. Then I should have to like it also.

13 April: That tundish has been on my mind for a long time. I looked it up and find it is English and good old blunt English too. Damn the dean of studies and his funnel! What did he come here for to teach us his own language or to learn it from us. Damn him one way or the other!

14 April: John Alphonsus Mulrennan has just returned from the west of Ireland (European and Asiatic papers please copy). He told us he met an old man there in a mountain cabin. Old man had red eyes and short pipe. Old man spoke Irish. Mulrennan spoke Irish. Then old man and Mulrennan spoke English. Mulrennan spoke to him about universe and stars. Old man sat, listened, smoked, spat. Then said:

—Ah, there must be terrible queer creatures at the latter end of the world.

I fear him. I fear his redrimmed horny eyes. It is with him I must struggle all through this night till day come, till he or I lie dead, gripping him by the sinewy throat till. . . . Till what? Till he yield to me? No. I mean him no harm.

15 April: Met her today pointblank in Grafton Street. The crowd brought us together. We both stopped. She asked me why I never came, said she had heard all sorts of stories about me. This was only to gain time. Asked me was I writing poems. About whom? I asked her. This confused her more and I felt sorry and mean. Turned off that valve at once and opened the spiritual-heroic refrigerating apparatus, invented and patented in all countries by Dante Alighieri.[8] Talked rapidly of myself and my plans. In the midst of it unluckily I made a sudden gesture of a revolutionary nature. I must have looked like a fellow throwing a handful of peas up into the air. People began to look at us. She shook hands a moment after and, in going away, said she hoped I would do what I said.

---

7. Title of a poem (1899) by W. B. Yeats quoted in the remainder of the sentence but then reversed.

8. Italian poet (1265–1321) whose work idealized his beloved Beatrice.

Now I call that friendly, don't you?

Yes. I liked her today. A little or much? Don't know. I liked her—and it seems a new feeling to me. Then, in that case, all the rest, all that I thought I thought and all that I felt I felt, all the rest before now, in fact. . . . . . O, give it up, old chap! Sleep it off!

16 April: Away! Away!

The spell of arms and voices: the white arms of roads, their promise of close embraces and the black arms of tall ships that stand against the moon, their tale of distant nations. They are held out to say: We are alone. Come. And the voices say with them: We are your kinsmen. And the air is thick with their company as they call to me, their kinsman, making ready to go, shaking the wings of their exultant and terrible youth.

26 April: Mother is putting my new secondhand clothes in order. She prays now, she says, that I may learn in my own life and away from home and friends what the heart is and what it feels. Amen. So be it. Welcome, O life! I go to encounter for the millionth time the reality of experience and to forge in the smithy of my soul the uncreated conscience of my race.

27 April: Old father, old artificer,[9] stand me now and ever in good stead.

Dublin 1904
Trieste 1914

1916

Ulysses

Ulysses From the vantage point of the twenty-first century, *Ulysses* (1922) is often singled out as the greatest novel of the twentieth century, and so it may be hard to understand the scandal it aroused upon publication. After parts of it first appeared serially in the American journal *The Little Review* from 1918 and the English journal *The Egoist* in 1919, instances in the novel of coarse language, masturbation, and other sexual content led to legal prosecution and to the banning of *Ulysses* as obscene in both the United States and the United Kingdom until the 1930s. New York district judge John M. Woolsey's 1933 ruling that the book, "in spite of its unusual frankness," was not pornographic but an "amazing *tour de force*" set an important precedent in obscenity law. In his perceptive appraisal of *Ulysses*, Woolsey explained Joyce's sexual frankness by saying that the novelist had attempted "to show exactly how the minds of his characters operate" and "to tell fully what his characters think about," conveying "the screen of consciousness with its ever-shifting kaleidoscopic impressions"—that is, not only each character's observations of the present but also the residue of "past impressions, some recent and some drawn up by association from the domain of the subconscious."

Ulysses opens at eight o'clock in the morning of June 16, 1904. Stephen Dedalus (the same character as in *A Portrait of the Artist as a Young Man*, but two years after the last glimpse of him there) has been summoned back to Dublin by his mother's fatal illness. The first three episodes of *Ulysses* concentrate on Stephen, the aloof, uncompromising artist, but the fourth introduces the novel's central character, Leopold Bloom. A somewhat frustrated and confused Jewish outsider in Irish society, Bloom emerges as a humane champion of kindness and justice. We follow closely his every activity: attending a funeral, transacting business, eating lunch, walking through the Dublin streets, worrying about his wife's infidelity with Blazes Boylan, even defecating and masturbating—and at each point the contents of his mind, including retrospect and anticipation, are revealed. Finally, late at night, Bloom and

---

9. Daedalus, the father of Icarus. On the term "race," see p. 464, n. 8.

Stephen, who have been just missing each other all day, get together, Stephen having had too much to drink. Bloom is moved by a paternal feeling toward Stephen, in part because his own son, Rudy, died in infancy, and in a symbolic way Stephen takes Rudy's place; Bloom follows Stephen during subsequent adventures in the role of fatherly protector. The climax of the book comes when Stephen, far gone in drink, and Bloom, worn out with fatigue, succumb to a series of hallucinations, during which their unconscious minds surface in dramatic form and their personalities are disclosed with extraordinary frankness. Then Bloom takes the unresponsive Stephen home and gives him a meal. After Stephen's departure Bloom retires to bed, while his wife, Molly, lying in bed, ends the novel with a long monologue in which she recalls her romantic and other experiences.

On the level of realistic description, *Ulysses* pulses with life and can be enjoyed for its evocation of early twentieth-century Dublin. On the psychological level, it profoundly and movingly reveals the personalities and consciousnesses of Leopold Bloom, Stephen Dedalus, and Molly Bloom. It explores the paradoxes of human loneliness and sociability (Bloom is both Jew and Dubliner, both exile and citizen), and it examines problems in the relations between parent and child, between the generations, and between the sexes. On the level of style, it shimmers with linguistic virtuosity, with many an episode written in a distinctive way that reflects its subject—e.g., headlines intruding in a chapter set in a newspaper office (the "Aeolus" episode); the sentimental language of women's magazines dominating a chapter set on a beach where girls are playing ("Nausicaa"); and the pastiche of styles of English literature from its Anglo-Saxon birth to the twentieth century in a chapter set in a maternity hospital ("Oxen of the Sun"). Through its use of themes from Homer, Dante, Shakespeare, and from other works of literature, and from philosophy and history, the book weaves a subtle pattern of allusion and suggestion.

Those who come to *Ulysses* with narrative expectations drawn from Victorian novels or even twentieth-century novelists such as Conrad and Lawrence will find much that is at first puzzling. In the novel's stream-of-consciousness method, also known as interior monologue, Joyce presents the consciousness of his characters directly, often without authorial comment. Past and present mingle in the texture of the prose because they mingle in the texture of consciousness; this interweaving can be indicated by puns, by sudden breaks in style or subject matter, or by other devices for keeping the reader constantly in sight of the shifting, multilayered nature of human awareness.

"Penelope" is the last of the eighteen episodes that make up *Ulysses*. It is two o'clock in the morning on June 17, 1904, and Bloom has returned home and joined his wife, Molly, in bed. His return both parallels and differs from Odysseus's return after twenty years' absence to Ithaca, in book 23 of Homer's *Odyssey*, in which he slays all the suitors who have occupied his house and attempted to woo his patient and faithful wife, Penelope. In Joyce's novel, the "Penelope" episode shifts the narrative focus of *Ulysses* from Stephen's and Bloom's male voices to the female voice of Molly Bloom, whose thoughts appear as an interior monologue, unpunctuated until the very end. In this episode, as also at the diaristic end of *A Portrait of the Artist as a Young Man*, there is no third-person narrator. The monologue, often called "Molly Bloom's soliloquy," unfolds in eight flowing, run-on sentences, including the final sentence (or paragraph) printed below, which culminates at the book's end in a resonant affirmation, a memory of her response to Bloom's marriage proposal and ultimately to life itself: "and yes I said yes I will Yes."

In this excerpt, Molly, lying head to toe in bed with the sleeping Bloom, contemplates her relationships with men and often shifts from one "he" to another, from past to present, reality to fantasy, without explicitly marking the change in reference. Although she intermittently tries to quiet her mind ("let me see if I can doze off 1 2 3 4 5"), her thoughts often rapidly tumble forward over memories and hopes and worries, sometimes slowing down to linger over a single point. She revisits the

details of her adulterous tryst that afternoon with Blazes Boylan, laments an insufficiently appreciative Bloom's shortcomings as a lover, and fantasizes about finding
romantic and sexual fulfillment. She worries about Stephen's family life, spinning out
both maternal and erotic fantasies about him, and she remembers the conception and
death of her son, Rudy, a deeply felt loss ten years earlier that has stymied her and
Bloom's sexual relationship. She also recalls her girlhood in the colorful, culturally
diverse Gibraltar. Reflecting on men and women, she contemplates the differences in
their anatomies, sexual natures, freedoms and constraints, and capacities to bring
world peace. She decides to give Bloom one more chance to prove himself sexually,
and if he cannot pass her test, she will tell him about her affair with Boylan (in Homer's *Odyssey*, Penelope also tests the returning Odysseus to prove he is who he claims
to be; her final tests involve knowledge of their bed's construction). Finally, Molly
returns to the memory of the day she first gave fully of herself to Bloom, when they lay
together on Howth Hill and Bloom proposed to her and she agreed to marry him, a
memory infiltrated by and layered with memories of other love interests. All these
thoughts and remembrances highlight the differences between Molly and the novel's
two other main characters, since Molly's thoughts are neither as abstract as Stephen's
nor as concrete as Bloom's, but combine elements of the two, as well as a measure of
frank sexuality. Joyce provides an exquisitely detailed and textured portrait of the intricate movements of human consciousness, perhaps more so than can be found in any
previous literary work, as Molly swings from the imaginative to the mundane, from
regret and longing to a rhapsodic embrace of the world in all its multifariousness, her
vital and passionate voice bringing *Ulysses* to a resounding culmination.

From Ulysses

FROM [PENELOPE]

no thats no way for him[1] has he no manners nor no refinement nor no nothing in his nature slapping us behind like that on my bottom because I didnt
call him Hugh the ignoramus that doesnt know poetry from a cabbage thats
what you get for not keeping them in their proper place pulling off his shoes
and trousers there on the chair before me so barefaced without even asking
permission and standing out that vulgar way in the half of a shirt they wear
to be admired like a priest or a butcher or those old hypocrites in the time
of Julius Caesar[2] of course hes right enough in his way to pass the time as a
joke sure you might as well be in bed with what with a lion God Im sure hed
have something better to say for himself an old Lion would[3] O well I suppose its because they were so plump and tempting in my short petticoat he
couldnt resist they excite myself sometimes its well for men all the amount
of pleasure they get off a womans body were so round and white for them
always I wished I was one myself for a change just to try with that thing they
have swelling upon you so hard and at the same time so soft when you touch
it my uncle John has a thing long I heard those cornerboys saying passing
the corner of Marrowbone lane my aunt Mary has a thing hairy because it
was dark and they knew a girl was passing it didnt make me blush why
should it either its only nature and he puts his thing long into my aunt

1. Blazes Boylan.
2. Perhaps Julius Caesar's assassins. Toga-
wearing Marcus Brutus, together with other conspirators, killed his close friend Caesar and then
stood before the public professing his love for

him, as dramatized in Shakespeare's *Julius Caesar*
(3.1–2).
3. Penelope calls Odysseus "my lord, my lion
heart" in Homer's *Odyssey*.

Marys hairy etcetera and turns out to be you put the handle in a sweeping-brush[4] men again all over they can pick and choose what they please a married woman or a fast widow or a girl for their different tastes like those houses round behind Irish street[5] no but were to be always chained up theyre not going to be chaining me up no damn fear once I start I tell you for stupid husbands jealousy why cant we all remain friends over it instead of quarrelling her husband found it out what they did together well naturally and if he did can he undo it hes coronado anyway whatever he does and then he going to the other mad extreme about the wife in Fair Tyrants[6] of course the man never even casts a 2nd thought on the husband or wife either its the woman he wants and he gets her what else were we given all those desires for Id like to know I cant help it if Im young still can I its a wonder Im not an old shrivelled hag before my time living with him[7] so cold never embracing me except sometimes when hes asleep the wrong end of me not knowing I suppose who he has any man thatd kiss a womans bottom Id throw my hat at him after that hed kiss anything unnatural where we havent 1 atom of any kind of expression in us all of us the same 2 lumps of lard before ever Id do that to a man pfooh the dirty brutes the mere thought is enough I kiss the feet of you senorita theres some sense in that didnt he kiss our halldoor[8] yes he did what a madman nobody understands his cracked ideas but me still of course a woman wants to be embraced 20 times a day almost to make her look young no matter by who so long as to be in love or loved by somebody if the fellow you want isnt there sometimes by the Lord God I was thinking would I go around by the quays there some dark evening where nobodyd know me and pick up a sailor off the sea thatd be hot on for it and not care a pin whose I was only to do it off up in a gate somewhere or one of those wildlooking gipsies in Rathfarnham had their camp pitched near the Bloomfield laundry to try and steal our things if they could I only sent mine there a few times for the name model laundry[9] sending me back over and over some old ones odd stockings that blackguardlooking fellow with the fine eyes peeling a switch attack me in the dark and ride me up against the wall without a word or a murderer anybody what they do themselves the fine gentlemen in their silk hats that K. C. lives up somewhere this way coming out of Hardwicke lane[1] the night he gave us the fish supper on account of winning over the boxing match of course it was for me he gave it I knew him by his gaiters[2] and the walk and when I turned round a minute after just to see there was a woman after coming out of it too some filthy prostitute then he goes home to his wife after that only I suppose the half of those sailors are rotten again with disease O move over your big carcass out of that for the love of Mike listen to him the winds that waft my sighs to

4. Molly recalls a dirty riddle about Uncle John putting his "thing long" into Aunt Mary's "thing hairy," which actually turns out to be about putting a handle in a sweeping brush. "Marrowbone Lane": a street in southeastern Dublin.
5. I.e., Irish Town in Gibraltar, which Molly implies was the location of prostitutes' houses.
6. Supposed title of a novel by James Lovebirch, who published under this pseudonym in the early twentieth century but is not known to have written anything with this title. "Coronado": tonsured (Spanish), but Molly probably means "cornudo," or cuckolded.
7. Leopold Bloom.
8. Customary Jewish gesture of kissing or touch-ing the mezuzah, a parchment inscribed with religious text and attached to the doorpost of the house. Since there appears to be no parchment affixed to the Blooms' door, it seems that Bloom has secularized the custom. "I kiss the feet of you senorita" [for señorita]: translation of a Spanish expression of courtesy or thanks.
9. Model Laundry, Bloomfield Steam Laundry Company, Ltd., in Rathfarnham, a village four miles south of the Dublin city center.
1. A street to the east of the Blooms' house in Dublin. "K. C.": King's Counsel, a senior barrister, or lawyer.
2. Coverings of cloth or leather for the ankle and lower leg.

thee so well he may sleep and sigh the great Suggester Don Poldo de la Flora[3] if he knew how he came out on the cards this morning hed have something to sigh for a dark man in some perplexity between 2 7s[4] too in prison for Lord knows what he does that I dont know and Im to be slooching around down in the kitchen to get his lordship his breakfast while hes rolled up like a mummy will I indeed did you ever see me running Id just like to see myself at it show them attention and they treat you like dirt I dont care what anybody says itd be much better for the world to be governed by the women in it you wouldnt see women going and killing one another and slaughtering when do you ever see women rolling around drunk like they do or gambling every penny they have and losing it on horses yes because a woman whatever she does she knows where to stop sure they wouldnt be in the world at all only for us they dont know what it is to be a woman and a mother how could they where would they all of them be if they hadnt all a mother to look after them what I never had thats why I suppose hes[5] running wild now out at night away from his books and studies and not living at home on account of the usual rowy[6] house I suppose well its a poor case that those that have a fine son like that theyre not satisfied and I none was he[7] not able to make one it wasnt my fault we came together when I was watching the two dogs up in her behind in the middle of the naked street that disheartened me altogether I suppose I oughtnt to have buried him[8] in that little woolly jacket I knitted crying as I was but give it to some poor child but I knew well Id never have another our 1st death too it was we were never the same since O Im not going to think myself into the glooms about that any more I wonder why he[9] wouldnt stay the night I felt all the time it was somebody strange he[1] brought in instead of roving around the city meeting God knows who night-walkers and pickpockets his poor mother wouldnt like that if she was alive ruining himself for life perhaps still its a lovely hour so silent I used to love coming home after dances the air of the night they have friends they can talk to weve none either he wants what he wont get or its some woman ready to stick her knife in you I hate that in women no wonder they treat us the way they do we are a dreadful lot of bitches I suppose its all the troubles we have makes us so snappy Im not like that he could easy have slept in there on the sofa in the other room I suppose he was as shy as a boy he being so young hardly 20 of me in the next room hed have heard me on the chamber arrah[2] what harm Dedalus I wonder its like those names in Gibraltar Dela-paz Delagracia they had the devils queer names there father Vial plana of Santa Maria that gave me the rosary Rosales y O'Reilly in the Calle las Siete Revueltas and Pisimbo and Mrs Opisso in Governor street[3] O what a

3. Molly once pretended to be engaged to a Span-ish nobleman named Don Miguel de la Flora, and here she combines his name with her husband's first name, Leopold. "Flora," which means flower, also corresponds to Leopold's last name, Bloom. "The winds that waft my sighs to thee": title of a song by lyricist H. W. Challis and composer Wil-liam V. Wallace.
4. Molly has been telling fortunes with cards, and in her reading, Bloom is represented by the king of clubs ("a dark man"), and his position between two sevens indicates perplexity about how he can "benefit by his own integrity."
5. Stephen Dedalus.
6. Characterized by rows, or arguments.
7. Leopold Bloom.
8. The Blooms' son, Rudy, who was born on

December 29, 1893, and died eleven days later.
9. Stephen Dedalus.
1. Leopold Bloom.
2. Well, indeed (Irish). "On the chamber": on the chamber pot.
3. Mrs. Catherine Opisso, dressmaker whose shop was on Governor's Street in Gibraltar. "Dela-paz Delagracia": de la Paz and de Gracia are com-mon Spanish surnames. "Father Vial plana of Santa Maria": according to Don Gifford, the Rev-erend J. Vilaplana was associated with the Roman Catholic Cathedral Church of St. Mary the Crowned, but this association does not appear in the directory in Gibraltar until 1912. "Calle las Siete Revueltas": Street of the Seven Turnings (Spanish), known in English-speaking Gibraltar as City Mill Lane. "Pisimbo": reference unknown.

name Id go and drown myself in the first river if I had a name like her O my and all the bits of streets Paradise ramp and Bedlam ramp and Rodgers ramp and Crutchetts ramp and the devils gap steps[4] well small blame to me if I am a harumscarum[5] I know I am a bit I declare to God I dont feel a day older than then I wonder could I get my tongue round any of the Spanish como esta usted muy bien gracias y usted[6] see I havent forgotten it all I thought I had only for the grammar a noun is the name of any person place or thing pity I never tried to read that novel cantankerous Mrs Rubio lent me by Valera with the questions in it all upside down[7] the two ways I always knew wed go away in the end I can tell him[8] the Spanish and he tell me the Italian then hell see Im not so ignorant what a pity he didnt stay Im sure the poor fellow was dead tired and wanted a good sleep badly I could have brought him in his breakfast in bed with a bit of toast so long as I didnt do it on the knife for bad luck[9] or if the woman was going her rounds with the watercress and something nice and tasty there are a few olives in the kitchen he might like I never could bear the look of them in Abrines I could do the criada[1] the room looks all right since I changed it the other way you see something was telling me all the time Id have to introduce myself not knowing me from Adam very funny wouldnt it Im his wife or pretend we were in Spain with, him half awake without a Gods notion where he is dos huevos estrellados senor[2] Lord the cracked things come into my head sometimes itd be great fun supposing he stayed with us why not theres the room upstairs empty and Millys[3] bed in the back room he could do his writing and studies at the table in there for all the scribbling he does at it and if he wants to read in bed in the morning like me as hes making the breakfast for 1 he can make it for 2 Im sure Im not going to take in lodgers off the street for him if he takes a gesabo[4] of a house like this Id love to have a long talk with an intelligent welleducated person Id have to get a nice pair of red slippers like those Turks with the fez used to sell or yellow and a nice semitransparent morning gown that I badly want or a peachblossom dressing jacket like the one long ago in Walpoles only 8/6 or 18/6[5] I'll just give him one more chance Ill get up early in the morning Im sick of Cohens[6] old bed in any case I might go over to the markets to see all the vegetables and cabbages and tomatoes and carrots and all kinds of splendid fruits all coming in lovely and fresh who knows whod be the 1st man Id meet theyre out looking for it in the morning Mamy Dillon used to say they are and the night too that was her massgoing Id love a big juicy pear now to melt in your mouth like when I used to be in the longing way then Ill throw him up his eggs and tea in the moustachecup[7] she gave him to make his mouth bigger I suppose hed like my nice cream too I

---

4. Ravine that separates the upper slopes of Gibraltar from the southern plateau. "Paradise ramp and Bedlam ramp and Rodgers ramp and Crutchetts ramp": all stairway streets that slope up the Rock in Gibraltar.
5. A reckless person.
6. Basic Spanish conversation: "How are you?" "Very well, thank you. And you?"
7. In Spanish, question marks appear upside down at the beginning of the sentence and right side up at the end. "Mrs Rubio": Molly's family's housekeeper in Gibraltar. "Valera": Juan Valera y Alcalá Galiano (1824–1905), Spanish novelist.
8. Stephen Dedalus.
9. Using a knife instead of a spoon was considered bad luck.
1. Servant (Spanish). "Abrines": name of a bak-

ery in Gibraltar.
2. Two fried eggs, sir (Spanish).
3. The Blooms' teenage daughter, who is away learning photography.
4. According to Gifford, "a vaguely pejorative term, as in 'the whole gesabo,' meaning the whole show or mess."
5. Eight shillings, six pence, or eighteen shillings, six pence. "Fez": hat in the form of a flat-topped cone, usually made of wool or felt. Walpole Brothers was a store selling cloth in Dublin.
6. David Cohen, a boot and shoe salesman, from whom Molly's father purchased the bed in Gibraltar before they moved to Dublin.
7. Cup with a partial cover meant to protect a mustache during drinking.

know what Ill do Ill go about rather gay not too much singing a bit now and then mi fa pieta Masetto then Ill start dressing myself to go out presto non son più forte[8] Ill put on my best shift and drawers let him have a good eyeful out of that to make his micky stand for him Ill let him know if thats what he wanted that his wife is fucked yes and damn well fucked too up to my neck nearly not by him 5 or 6 times handrunning theres the mark of his spunk on the clean sheet I wouldnt bother to even iron it out that ought to satisfy him if you dont believe me feel my belly unless I made him stand there and put him into me Ive a mind to tell him every scrap and make him do it in front of me serve him right its all his own fault if I am an adulteress as the thing in the gallery said O much about it if thats all the harm ever we did in this vale of tears[9] God knows its not much doesnt everybody only they hide it I suppose thats what a woman is supposed to be there for or He wouldn't have made us the way He did so attractive to men then if he wants to kiss my bottom Ill drag open my drawers and bulge it right out in his face as large as life he can stick his tongue 7 miles up my hole as hes there my brown part then Ill tell him I want £ 1 or perhaps 30/[1] Ill tell him I want to buy underclothes then if he gives me that well he wont be too bad I dont want to soak it all out of him like other women do I could often have written out a fine cheque for myself and write his name on it for a couple of pounds a few times he forgot to lock it up besides he wont spend it Ill let him do it off on me behind provided he doesnt smear all my good drawers O I suppose that cant be helped Ill do the indifferent 1 or 2 questions Ill know by the answers when hes like that he cant keep a thing back I know every turn in him Ill tighten my bottom well and let out a few smutty words smell-rump or lick my shit or the first mad thing comes into my head then Ill suggest about yes O wait now sonny my turn is coming Ill be quite gay and friendly over it O but I was forgetting this bloody pest of a thing[2] pfooh you wouldnt know which to laugh or cry were such a mixture of plum and apple[3] no Ill have to wear the old things so much the better itll be more pointed hell never know whether he did it or not there thats good enough for you any old thing at all then Ill wipe him off me just like a business his omission[4] then Ill go out Ill have him eying up at the ceiling where is she gone now make him want me thats the only way a quarter after[5] what an unearthly hour I suppose theyre just getting up in China now combing out their pigtails for the day well soon have the nuns ringing the angelus[6] theyve nobody coming in to spoil their sleep except an odd priest or two for his night office the alarmclock next door at cockshout clattering the brains out of itself let me see if I can doze off 1 2 3 4 5 what kind of flowers are those they invented

8. Quick, my strength is failing (Italian). "Mi fa pieta Masetto": I'm sorry for Masetto (Italian). Lines from the opera *Don Giovanni* (1787) by Austrian composer Wolfgang Amadeus Mozart (1756–1791), which Molly practices in her capacity as a professional singer.
9. Phrase from Psalms 84.6 (or Psalm 83 in the Douay Bible). "As the thing in the gallery said": during a performance of the play *The Wife of Scarli* (1897), which Molly attended and which she recalls earlier in "Penelope," a man sitting in the gallery hissed at the protagonist, calling her "a woman adulteress." The play—an English version by G. A. Greene of an Italian drama, *Tristi amore*, by Giuseppe Giacosa (1847–1906)—appears to condone the title character's adultery by making her husband an unsympathetic character.
1. Thirty shillings; i.e., one pound, ten shillings.
2. Her menstrual period.
3. A mixture of good and bad things. In slang usage, a plum is a desirable thing, and the apple is the apple plucked by Eve that caused the fall of humankind.
4. I.e., Bloom's emission, or ejaculation.
5. A clock rings a quarter after the hour: it is now 2:15 A.M., and Molly ruminates on the activities of various people at this hour.
6. Devotional exercise commemorating the Incarnation, announced by the ringing of a bell.

like the stars the wallpaper in Lombard street[7] was much nicer the apron he gave me was like that[8] something only I only wore it twice better lower this lamp and try again so as I can get up early Ill go to Lambes there beside Findlaters[9] and get them to send us some flowers to put about the place in case he brings him[1] home tomorrow today I mean no no Fridays an unlucky day first I want to do the place up someway the dust grows in it I think while Im asleep then we can have music and cigarettes I can accompany him first I must clean the keys of the piano with milk whatll I wear shall I wear a white rose or those fairy cakes in Liptons[2] I love the smell of a rich big shop at 7 1/2 d a lb or the other ones with the cherries in them and the pinky sugar 11 d a couple of lbs[3] of course a nice plant for the middle of the table Id get that cheaper in wait wheres this I saw them not long ago I love flowers Id love to have the whole place swimming in roses God of heaven theres nothing like nature the wild mountains then the sea and the waves rushing then the beautiful country with fields of oats and wheat and all kinds of things and all the fine cattle going about that would do your heart good to see rivers and lakes and flowers all sorts of shapes and smells and colours springing up even out of the ditches primroses and violets nature it is as for them saying theres no God I wouldnt give a snap of my two fingers for all their learning why dont they go and create something I often asked him atheists or whatever they call themselves go and wash the cobbles[4] off themselves first then they go howling for the priest and they dying and why why because theyre afraid of hell on account of their bad conscience ah yes I know them well who was the first person in the universe before there was anybody that made it all who ah that they dont know neither do I so there you are they might as well try to stop the sun from rising tomorrow the sun shines for you he said the day we were lying among the rhododendrons on Howth head[5] in the grey tweed suit and his straw hat the day I got him to propose to me yes first I gave him the bit of seedcake out of my mouth and it was leapyear like now yes 16 years ago my God after that long kiss I near lost my breath yes he said I was a flower of the mountain yes so we are flowers all a womans body yes that was one true thing he said in his life and the sun shines for you today yes that was why I liked him because I saw he understood or felt what a woman is and I knew I could always get round him and I gave him all the pleasure I could leading him on till he asked me to say yes and I wouldnt answer first only looked out over the sea and the sky I was thinking of so many things he didnt know of Mulvey and Mr Stanhope and Hester and father and old captain Groves and the sailors playing all birds fly and I say stoop[6] and

7. A street in Dublin where the Blooms had their first house, which Molly remembers fondly.
8. The apron Bloom gave her when they lived at Lombard Street.
9. Alexander Findlater and Company, Ltd., the tea, wine, and spirits store on Sackville Street Upper in Dublin. "Lambes": the fruit and flower shop next to Findlater's store.
1. Bloom brings Stephen.
2. Lipton's Ltd., a grocery store in Dublin. "Shall I wear a white rose": lyrics from the song "Shall I Wear a White Rose or Shall I Wear a Red?" by H. S. Clarke and E. B. Farmer, quoted by Molly earlier in the episode. "Fairy cakes": cupcakes.
3. Eleven pence for two pounds. "7 1/2d a lb": seven and a half pence per pound.

4. Lumps or blemishes (dialect English).
5. Headland on Dublin Bay, about 9 miles northeast of Dublin, where Leopold and Molly were picnicking on September 10, 1888, the day he proposed to her. Bloom recalls the same moment with the seedcake in "Lestrygonians."
6. A game, which probably depends, like "all birds fly," on the players' ability to obey commands. "Mulvey": Lieutenant Jack Mulvey, Molly's first suitor, whom she recalls at length earlier in the episode. "Mr. Stanhope and Hester": a girlhood friend of Molly's and the friend's husband. "Father": Molly's father, Major Brian Cooper Tweedy of the Royal Dublin Fusiliers. "Old captain Groves": a friend of Molly's father.

washing up dishes they called it on the pier and the sentry in front of the governors house with the thing round his white helmet poor devil half roasted and the Spanish girls laughing in their shawls and their tall combs and the auctions in the morning[7] the Greeks and the jews and the Arabs and the devil knows who else from all the ends of Europe and Duke street and the fowl market all clucking outside Larby Sharons and the poor donkeys slipping half asleep and the vague fellows in the cloaks asleep in the shade on the steps and the big wheels of the carts of the bulls and the old castle[8] thousands of years old yes and those handsome Moors all in white and turbans like kings asking you to sit down in their little bit of a shop and Ronda with the old windows of the posadas glancing eyes a lattice hid for her lover to kiss the iron and the wineshops half open at night and the castanets and the night we missed the boat at Algeciras[9] the watchman going about serene with his lamp and O that awful deepdown torrent O and the sea the sea crimson sometimes like fire and the glorious sunsets and the figtrees in the Alameda gardens[1] yes and all the queer little streets and pink and blue and yellow houses and the rosegardens and the jessamine and geraniums and cactuses and Gibraltar as a girl where I was a Flower of the mountain yes when I put the rose in my hair like the Andalusian girls used[2] or shall I wear a red[3] yes and how he kissed me under the Moorish wall[4] and I thought well as well him[5] as another and then I asked him with my eyes to ask again yes and then he asked me would I yes to say yes my mountain flower and first I put my arms around him yes and drew him down to me so he could feel my breasts all perfume yes and his heart was going like mad and yes I said yes I will Yes.

Trieste-Zurich-Paris,
  1914–1921.

1922

7. The daily auction in Commercial Square in Gibraltar. "The thing round his white helmet": a band marking the sentry as a military policeman.
8. The Moorish castle on the Rock of Gibraltar, built in 725 C.E. "Poor donkeys": donkeys were used for carrying supplies up the slopes of the Rock. "Carts of the bulls": carts used for transporting animals for bullfighting.
9. Town in Spain on the opposite side of the Bay of Algeciras from Gibraltar. "Ronda": a town in southern Spain about 40 miles northeast of Gibraltar, with well-preserved Moorish architecture. "Eyes a lattice hid": lyrics from the song "In Old Madrid," with words by Clifton Bingham (1859–1913) and music by Henry Trotere (1855–1912). "For her lover to kiss the iron": according to Gifford, "a Spanish colloquialism for a conventional gesture of courtship, since the ground-floor windows of Spanish town houses were usually defended by iron grilles."
1. Garden promenade on Gibraltar.
2. Girls from Andalusia, the southern region of Spain ruled by Muslims, or Moors, in the Middle Ages but also including Christians and Jews.
3. More lyrics from the song "Shall I Wear a White Rose or Shall I Wear a Red?"
4. Wall at the center of the plateau on the upper slopes of the Rock of Gibraltar and the site of Molly's first kiss from Lieutenant Mulvey, which she recalls earlier in the episode: "he was the first man kissed me under the Moorish wall."
5. Leopold Bloom.

D. H. LAWRENCE
1885–1930

David Herbert Lawrence was born in the midland mining village of Eastwood, Nottinghamshire. His father was a miner; his mother, better educated than her husband and self-consciously genteel, fought, all her married life, to lift her children out of the working class. Lawrence was aware from a young age of the struggle between his parents, and allied himself with his mother's delicacy and refinement, resenting his father's coarse and sometimes drunken behavior. In his early novel *Sons and Lovers* (1913), against a background of paternal coarseness conflicting with maternal refinement, Lawrence sets the theme of the demanding mother who has given up the prospect of achieving a true emotional life with her husband and turns to her sons with a stultifying and possessive love. Many years later, Lawrence came to feel that he had failed to appreciate his father's vitality and wholeness, even if they were distorted by the culture in which he lived.

Spurred on by his mother, Lawrence escaped from the mining world through education. He won a scholarship to Nottingham high school and later, after working first as a clerk and then as an elementary-school teacher, studied for two years at University College, Nottingham, where he obtained his teacher's certificate. Meanwhile he was reading on his own a great deal of literature and some philosophy and was working on his first novel. Publishing a group of poems in 1909, his first short story and his first novel, *The White Peacock*, in 1910, he was regarded in London literary circles as a promising young writer. He taught school from 1908 to 1912 in Croydon, a southern suburb of London, but he gave this up after falling in love with Frieda von Richthofen Weekley, the German wife of a professor at Nottingham. They went to Germany together and married in 1914, after Frieda's divorce.

Abroad with Frieda, Lawrence finished *Sons and Lovers*, at which he had been working off and on for years. The war brought them back to England, where Frieda's German origins and Lawrence's pacifist objection to the war gave him trouble with the authorities. More and more—especially after the almost immediate banning, for indecency, of his next novel, *The Rainbow*, in 1915—Lawrence came to feel that the forces of modern civilization were arrayed against him. As soon as he could leave England after the war, he sought refuge in Italy, Australia, Mexico, then again in Italy, and finally in the south of France, often desperately ill, restlessly searching for an ideal, or at least a tolerable, community in which to live. He died of tuberculosis in the south of France at the age of forty-four.

In his poetry and his fiction, Lawrence seeks to express the deep-rooted, the elemental, the instinctual in people and nature. He is at constant war with the mechanical and artificial, with the constraints and hypocrisies that civilization imposes. Because he had new things to say and a new way of saying them, he was not easily or quickly appreciated. Although his early novels are more conventional in style and treatment, from the publication of *The Rainbow* the critics turned away in bewilderment and condemnation. The rest of his life, during which he produced about a dozen more novels and many poems, short stories, sketches, and miscellaneous articles, was, in his own words, "a savage enough pilgrimage," marked by incessant struggle and by periods of frustration and despair. Phrases such as "supreme impulse" and "quickening spontaneous emotion" were characteristic of Lawrence's belief in intuition, in the dark forces of the inner self, that must not be allowed to be swamped by the rational faculties but must be brought into a harmonious relation with them.

The genteel culture of Lawrence's mother came more and more to represent death for Lawrence. In much of his later work, and especially in some of his short stories, he sets the deadening restrictiveness of conventional middle-class living against the forces of liberation that are often represented by an outsider—a peasant, a gypsy, a worker, a primitive of some kind, someone free by circumstance or personal effort. The recurring theme of his short stories—which contain some of his best work—is the distortion of love by possessiveness or gentility or a false romanticism or a false conception of the life of the artist and the achievement of a living relation between a man and a woman against the pressure of class-feeling or tradition or habit or prejudice.

In his two masterpieces, *The Rainbow* and *Women in Love* (both of which developed out of what was originally conceived as a single novel to be called *The Sisters*), Lawrence probes, with both subtlety and power, into various aspects of relationship— the relationship between humans and their environment, the relationship between the generations, the relationship between man and woman, the relationship between instinct and intellect, and above all the proper basis for the marriage relationship as he conceived it. Lawrence's view of marriage as a struggle, bound up with the deepest rhythms and most profound instincts, derived from his own relationship with his strong-minded wife. He explores this and other kinds of human relationships with a combination of uncanny psychological precision and intense poetic feeling. His novels have an acute surface realism, a sharp sense of time and place, and brilliant topographical detail; at the same time their high symbolism, both of the total pattern of action and of incidents and objects within it, establishes a formal and emotional rhythm.

In poetry as in fiction, Lawrence sought out new modes of expression. He began writing in traditional verse forms but, especially after 1912, came to feel that poetry had to be unshackled from habit and fixed form if it is to make contact with what he called the "insurgent naked throb of the instant moment." Harkening back to the experiments of the American poet Walt Whitman and anticipating the more "open" and "organic" forms of the later twentieth century, Lawrence claimed poetry must be spontaneous, flexible, alive, "direct utterance from the instant, whole man," and should express the "pulsating, carnal self" ("The Poetry of the Present," 1919). To convey the dynamism of animals and people, the emotional intensity of human relationships, his poems repeat and develop symbols or layer clauses in ritualistic cadences or unfold parallels with ancient myths. Vehemently autobiographical, the vital and even ecstatic encounters with nature, sex, and raw feeling in his poems assert the primacy of the unconscious and instinctual self, from which he felt the cerebral-intellectual self had alienated the English middle classes.

In the late 1950s the critic A. Alvarez judged: "The only native English poet of any importance to survive the First World War was D. H. Lawrence." Although there are complex reasons for the posthumous critical triumph of this writer who was so much reviled in his lifetime, there is also a simple and striking reason that must not be forgotten. Lawrence had vision; he responded intensely to life; he had a keen ear and a piercing eye for vitality and color and sound, for landscape—be it of England or Italy or New Mexico—for the individuality and concreteness of things in nature, and for the individuality and concreteness of people. His travel sketches are as impressive in their way as his novels and poems; he seizes both on the symbolic incident and on the concrete reality, and each is interpreted in terms of the other. He looked at the world freshly, with his own eyes, avoiding formulas and clichés; and he forged for himself a kind of utterance that, at his best, was able to convey powerfully and vividly what his original vision showed him. A restless pilgrim, he had uncanny perceptions into the depths of physical things and an uncompromising honesty in his view of human beings and the world.

Odour of Chrysanthemums

I

The small locomotive engine, Number 4, came clanking, stumbling down from Selston with seven full wagons. It appeared round the corner with loud threats of speed, but the colt that it startled from among the gorse,[1] which still flickered indistinctly in the raw afternoon, out-distanced it at a canter. A woman, walking up the railway line to Underwood, drew back into the hedge, held her basket aside, and watched the footplate of the engine advancing. The trucks[2] thumped heavily past, one by one, with slow inevitable move-ment, as she stood insignificantly trapped between the jolting black wagons and the hedge; then they curved away towards the coppice[3] where the with-ered oak leaves dropped noiselessly, while the birds, pulling at the scarlet hips beside the track, made off into the dusk that had already crept into the spinney.[4] In the open, the smoke from the engine sank and cleaved to the rough grass. The fields were dreary and forsaken, and in the marshy strip that led to the whimsey,[5] a reedy pit-pond, the fowls had already abandoned their run among the alders, to roost in the tarred fowl-house. The pit-bank loomed up beyond the pond, flames like red sores licking its ashy sides, in the afternoon's stagnant light. Just beyond rose the tapering chimneys and the clumsy black headstocks of Brinsley Colliery.[6] The two wheels were spinning fast up against the sky, and the winding engine rapped out its little spasms. The miners were being turned up.

The engine whistled as it came into the wide bay of railway lines beside the colliery, where rows of trucks stood in harbour.

Miners, single, trailing and in groups, passed like shadows diverging home. At the edge of the ribbed level of sidings squat a low cottage, three steps down from the cinder track. A large bony vine clutched at the house, as if to claw down the tiled roof. Round the bricked yard grew a few wintry primroses. Beyond, the long garden sloped down to a bush-covered brook course. There were some twiggy apple trees, winter-crack trees, and ragged cabbages. Beside the path hung disheveled pink chrysanthemums, like pink cloths hung on bushes. A woman came stooping out of the felt-covered fowl-house, half-way down the garden. She closed and padlocked the door, then drew herself erect, having brushed some bits from her white apron.

She was a tall woman of imperious mien, handsome, with definite black eyebrows. Her smooth black hair was parted exactly. For a few moments she stood steadily watching the miners as they passed along the railway: then she turned towards the brook course. Her face was calm and set, her mouth was closed with disillusionment. After a moment she called:

"John!" There was no answer. She waited, and then said distinctly:

"Where are you?"

"Here!" replied a child's sulky voice from among the bushes. The woman looked piercingly through the dusk.

"Are you at that brook?" she asked sternly.

1. Common prickly bush with yellow flowers.
2. Open freight cars.
3. A wood of small trees or shrubs.
4. Thicket.

5. Machine for raising ore or water from a mine.
6. Coal mine. "Headstocks" support revolving parts of a machine.

For answer the child showed himself before the raspberry-canes that rose like whips. He was a small, sturdy boy of five. He stood quite still, defiantly.

"Oh!" said the mother, conciliated. "I thought you were down at that wet brook—and you remember what I told you——"

The boy did not move or answer.

"Come, come on in," she said more gently, "it's getting dark. There's your grandfather's engine coming down the line!"

The lad advanced slowly, with resentful, taciturn movement. He was dressed in trousers and waistcoat of cloth that was too thick and hard for the size of the garments. They were evidently cut down from a man's clothes.

As they went slowly towards the house he tore at the ragged wisps of chrysanthemums and dropped the petals in handfuls along the path.

"Don't do that—it does look nasty," said his mother. He refrained, and she, suddenly pitiful, broke off a twig with three or four wan flowers and held them against her face. When mother and son reached the yard her hand hesitated, and instead of laying the flower aside, she pushed it in her apron-band. The mother and son stood at the foot of the three steps looking across the bay of lines at the passing home of the miners. The trundle of the small train was imminent. Suddenly the engine loomed past the house and came to a stop opposite the gate.

The engine-driver, a short man with round grey beard, leaned out of the cab high above the woman.

"Have you got a cup of tea?" he said in a cheery, hearty fashion.

It was her father. She went in, saying she would mash.[7] Directly, she returned.

"I didn't come to see you on Sunday," began the little grey-bearded man.

"I didn't expect you," said his daughter.

The engine-driver winced; then, reassuming his cheery, airy manner, he said:

"Oh, have you heard then? Well, and what do you think——?"

"I think it is soon enough," she replied.

At her brief censure the little man made an impatient gesture, and said coaxingly, yet with dangerous coldness:

"Well, what's a man to do? It's no sort of life for a man of my years, to sit at my own hearth like a stranger. And if I'm going to marry again it may as well be soon as late—what does it matter to anybody?"

The woman did not reply, but turned and went into the house. The man in the engine-cab stood assertive, till she returned with a cup of tea and a piece of bread and butter on a plate. She went up the steps and stood near the footplate of the hissing engine.

"You needn't 'a' brought me bread an' butter," said her father. "But a cup of tea"—he sipped appreciatively—"it's very nice." He sipped for a moment or two, then: "I hear as Walter's got another bout[8] on," he said.

"When hasn't he?" said the woman bitterly.

"I heerd tell of him in the 'Lord Nelson' braggin' as he was going to spend that b—— afore he went: half a sovereign[9] that was."

"When?" asked the woman.

7. Steep the tea.
8. Session; i.e., bout of drinking.
9. Gold coin worth twenty shillings. Half a sov-

ereign is worth ten. Lord Nelson is the name of a public house (pub).

"A' Sat'day night—I know that's true."

"Very likely," she laughed bitterly. "He gives me twenty-three shillings."

"Aye, it's a nice thing, when a man can do nothing with his money but make a beast of himself!" said the grey-whiskered man. The woman turned her head away. Her father swallowed the last of his tea and handed her the cup.

"Aye," he sighed, wiping his mouth. "It's a settler,[1] it is——"

He put his hand on the lever. The little engine strained and groaned, and the train rumbled towards the crossing. The woman again looked across the metals. Darkness was settling over the spaces of the railway and trucks: the miners, in grey somber groups, were still passing home. The winding engine pulsed hurriedly, with brief pauses. Elizabeth Bates looked at the dreary flow of men, then she went indoors. Her husband did not come.

The kitchen was small and full of firelight; red coals piled glowing up the chimney mouth. All the life of the room seemed in the white, warm hearth and the steel fender reflecting the red fire. The cloth was laid for tea; cups glinted in the shadows. At the back, where the lowest stairs protruded into the room, the boy sat struggling with a knife and a piece of white wood. He was almost hidden in the shadow. It was half-past four. They had but to await the father's coming to begin tea. As the mother watched her son's sullen little struggle with the wood, she saw herself in his silence and pertinacity; she saw the father in her child's indifference to all but himself. She seemed to be occupied by her husband. He had probably gone past his home, slunk past his own door, to drink before he came in, while his dinner spoiled and wasted in waiting. She glanced at the clock, then took the potatoes to strain them in the yard. The garden and fields beyond the brook were closed in uncertain darkness. When she rose with the saucepan, leaving the drain steaming into the night behind her, she saw the yellow lamps were lit along the high road that went up the hill away beyond the space of the railway lines and the field.

Then again she watched the men trooping home, fewer now and fewer.

Indoors the fire was sinking and the room was dark red. The woman put her saucepan on the hob,[2] and set a batter-pudding near the mouth of the oven. Then she stood unmoving. Directly, gratefully, came quick young steps to the door. Someone hung on the latch a moment, then a little girl entered and began pulling off her outdoor things, dragging a mass of curls, just ripening from gold to brown, over her eyes with her hat.

Her mother chid her for coming late from school, and said she would have to keep her at home the dark winter days.

"Why, mother, it's hardly a bit dark yet. The lamp's not lighted, and my father's not home."

"No, he isn't. But it's a quarter to five! Did you see anything of him?"

The child became serious. She looked at her mother with large, wistful blue eyes.

"No, mother, I've never seen him. Why? Has he come up an' gone past, to Old Brinsley? He hasn't, mother, 'cos I never saw him."

"He'd watch that," said the mother bitterly, "he'd take care as you didn't see him. But you may depend upon it, he's seated in the 'Prince o' Wales.'[3] He wouldn't be this late."

1. Crushing (or final) blow.
2. Part of the fireplace.

3. Name of a pub.

The girl looked at her mother piteously.

"Let's have our teas, mother, should we?" said she.

The mother called John to table. She opened the door once more and looked out across the darkness of the lines. All was deserted: she could not hear the winding-engines.

"Perhaps," she said to herself, "he's stopped to get some ripping[4] done."

They sat down to tea. John, at the end of the table near the door, was almost lost in the darkness. Their faces were hidden from each other. The girl crouched against the fender[5] slowly moving a thick piece of bread before the fire. The lad, his face a dusky mark on the shadow, sat watching her who was transfigured in the red glow.

"I do think it's beautiful to look in the fire," said the child.

"Do you?" said her mother. "Why?"

"It's so red, and full of little caves—and it feels so nice, and you can fair smell it."

"It'll want mending directly," replied her mother, "and then if your father comes he'll carry on and say there never is a fire when a man comes home sweating from the pit. A public-house is always warm enough."

There was silence till the boy said complainingly: "Make haste, our Annie."

"Well, I am doing! I can't make the fire do it no faster, can I?"

"She keeps wafflin' it about so's to make 'er slow," grumbled the boy.

"Don't have such an evil imagination, child," replied the mother.

Soon the room was busy in the darkness with the crisp sound of crunching. The mother ate very little. She drank her tea determinedly, and sat thinking. When she rose her anger was evident in the stern unbending of her head. She looked at the pudding in the fender, and broke out:

"It is a scandalous thing as a man can't even come home to his dinner! If it's crozzled[6] up to a cinder I don't see why I should care. Past his very door he goes to get to a public-house, and here I sit with his dinner waiting for him——"

She went out. As she dropped piece after piece of coal on the red fire, the shadows fell on the walls, till the room was almost in total darkness.

"I canna see," grumbled the invisible John. In spite of herself, the mother laughed.

"You know the way to your mouth," she said. She set the dust pan outside the door. When she came again like a shadow on the hearth, the lad repeated, complaining sulkily:

"I canna see."

"Good gracious!" cried the mother irritably, "you're as bad as your father if it's a bit dusk!"

Nevertheless, she took a paper spill from a sheaf on the mantelpiece and proceeded to light the lamp that hung from the ceiling in the middle of the room. As she reached up, her figure displayed itself just rounding with maternity.

"Oh, mother——!" exclaimed the girl.

"What?" said the woman, suspended in the act of putting the lamp-glass over the flame. The copper reflector shone handsomely on her, as she stood with uplifted arm, turning to face her daughter.

---

4. Taking out or cutting away coal or stone (a mining and quarrying term).

5. Frame that keeps coals in the fireplace.

6. Curled.

"You've got a flower in your apron!" said the child, in a little rapture at this unusual event.

"Goodness me!" exclaimed the woman, relieved. "One would think the house was afire." She replaced the glass and waited a moment before turning up the wick. A pale shadow was seen floating vaguely on the floor.

"Let me smell!" said the child, still rapturously, coming forward and putting her face to her mother's waist.

"Go along, silly!" said the mother, turning up the lamp. The light revealed their suspense so that the woman felt it almost unbearable. Annie was still bending at her waist. Irritably, the mother took the flowers out from her apron-band.

"Oh, mother—don't take them out!" Annie cried, catching her hand and trying to replace the sprig.

"Such nonsense!" said the mother, turning away. The child put the pale chrysanthemums to her lips, murmuring:

"Don't they smell beautiful!"

Her mother gave a short laugh.

"No," she said, "not to me. It was chrysanthemums when I married him, and chrysanthemums when you were born, and the first time they ever brought him home drunk, he'd got brown chrysanthemums in his button-hole."

She looked at the children. Their eyes and their parted lips were wondering. The mother sat rocking in silence for some time. Then she looked at the clock.

"Twenty minutes to six!" In a tone of fine bitter carelessness she continued: "Eh, he'll not come now till they bring him. There he'll stick! But he needn't come rolling in here in his pit-dirt, for *I* won't wash him. He can lie on the floor——Eh, what a fool I've been, what a fool! And this is what I came here for, to this dirty hole, rats and all, for him to slink past his very door. Twice last week—he's begun now——"

She silenced herself and rose to clear the table.

While for an hour or more the children played, subduedly intent, fertile of imagination, united in fear of the mother's wrath, and in dread of their father's home-coming, Mrs Bates sat in her rocking chair making a "singlet" of thick cream-coloured flannel, which gave a dull wounded sound as she tore off the grey edge. She worked at her sewing with energy, listening to the children, and her anger wearied itself, lay down to rest, opening its eyes from time to time and steadily watching, its ears raised to listen. Sometimes even her anger quailed and shrank, and the mother suspended her sewing, tracing the footsteps that thudded along the sleepers[7] outside; she would lift her head sharply to bid the children "hush," but she recovered herself in time, and the footsteps went past the gate, and the children were not flung out of their play-world.

But at last Annie sighed, and gave in. She glanced at her wagon of slippers, and loathed the game. She turned plaintively to her mother.

"Mother!"—but she was inarticulate.

John crept out like a frog from under the sofa. His mother glanced up.

"Yes," she said, "just look at those shirt-sleeves!"

---

7. Railroad ties.

The boy held them out to survey them, saying nothing. Then somebody called in a hoarse voice away down the line, and suspense bristled in the room, till two people had gone by outside, talking.

"It is time for bed," said the mother.

"My father hasn't come," wailed Annie plaintively. But her mother was primed with courage.

"Never mind. They'll bring him when he does come—like a log." She meant there would be no scene. "And he may sleep on the floor till he wakes himself. I know he'll not go to work to-morrow after this!"

The children had their hands and faces wiped with a flannel. They were very quiet. When they had put on their night-dresses, they said their prayers, the boy mumbling. The mother looked down at them, at the brown silken bush of intertwining curls in the nape of the girl's neck, at the little black head of the lad, and her heart burst with anger at their father, who caused all three such distress. The children hid their faces in her skirts for comfort.

When Mrs Bates came down, the room was strangely empty, with a tension of expectancy. She took up her sewing and stitched for some time without raising her head. Meantime her anger was tinged with fear.

II

The clock struck eight and she rose suddenly, dropping her sewing on her chair. She went to the stair-foot door, opened it, listening. Then she went out, locking the door behind her.

Something scuffled in the yard, and she started, though she knew it was only the rats with which the place was over-run. The night was very dark. In the great bay of railway lines, bulked with trucks, there was no trace of light, only away back she could see a few yellow lamps at the pit-top, and the red smear of the burning pit-bank on the night. She hurried along the edge of the track, then, crossing the converging lines, came to the stile by the white gates, whence she emerged on the road. Then the fear which had led her shrank. People were walking up to New Brinsley; she saw the lights in the houses; twenty yards farther on were the broad windows of the "Prince of Wales," very warm and bright, and the loud voices of men could be heard distinctly. What a fool she had been to imagine that anything had happened to him! He was merely drinking over there at the "Prince of Wales." She faltered. She had never yet been to fetch him, and she never would go. So she continued her walk towards the long straggling line of houses, standing back on the highway. She entered a passage between the dwellings.

"Mr Rigley?—Yes! Did you want him? No, he's not in at this minute."

The raw-boned woman leaned forward from her dark scullery[8] and peered at the other, upon whom fell a dim light through the blind of the kitchen window.

"Is it Mrs Bates?" she asked in a tone tinged with respect.

"Yes. I wondered if your Master was at home. Mine hasn't come yet."

"'Asn't 'e! Oh, Jack's been 'ome an' 'ad 'is dinner an' gone out. 'E's just gone for 'alf an hour afore bed-time. Did you call at the 'Prince of Wales'?"

"No——"

8. Back kitchen.

"No, you didn't like——! It's not very nice." The other woman was indulgent. There was an awkward pause. "Jack never said nothink about—about your Master," she said.

"No!—I expect he's stuck in there!"

Elizabeth Bates said this bitterly, and with recklessness. She knew that the woman across the yard was standing at her door listening, but she did not care. As she turned:

"Stop a minute! I'll just go an' ask Jack if 'e knows anythink," said Mrs Rigley.

"Oh no—I wouldn't like to put——!"

"Yes, I will, if you'll just step inside an' see as th' childer doesn't come downstairs and set theirselves afire."

Elizabeth Bates, murmuring a remonstrance, stepped inside. The other woman apologised for the state of the room.

The kitchen needed apology. There were little frocks and trousers and childish undergarments on the squab[9] and on the floor, and a litter of playthings everywhere. On the black American cloth[1] of the table were pieces of bread and cake, crusts, slops, and a teapot with cold tea.

"Eh, ours is just as bad," said Elizabeth Bates, looking at the woman, not at the house. Mrs Rigley put a shawl over her head and hurried out, saying:

"I shanna be a minute."

The other sat, noting with faint disapproval the general untidiness of the room. Then she fell to counting the shoes of various sizes scattered over the floor. There were twelve. She sighed and said to herself: "No wonder!"—glancing at the litter. There came the scratching of two pairs of feet on the yard, and the Rigleys entered. Elizabeth Bates rose. Rigley was a big man, with very large bones. His head looked particularly bony. Across his temple was a blue scar, caused by a wound got in the pit, a wound in which the coal dust remained blue like tattooing.

"'Asna 'e come whoam yit?" asked the man, without any form of greeting, but with deference and sympathy. "I couldna say wheer he is—'e's non ower theer!"—he jerked his head to signify the "Prince of Wales."

"'E's 'appen gone up to th' Yew,"[2] said Mrs Rigley.

There was another pause. Rigley had evidently something to get off his mind:

"Ah left 'im finishin' a stint," he began. "Loose-all[3] 'ad bin gone about ten minutes when we com'n away, an' I shouted: 'Are ter comin', Walt?' an' 'e said: 'Go on, Ah shanna be but a'ef a minnit,' so we com'n ter th' bottom, me an' Bowers, thinkin' as 'e wor just behint, an' 'ud come up i' th' next bantle[4]——"

He stood perplexed, as if answering a charge of deserting his mate. Elizabeth Bates, now again certain of disaster, hastened to reassure him:

"I expect 'e's gone up to th' 'Yew Tree,' as you say. It's not the first time. I've fretted myself into a fever before now. He'll come home when they carry him."

"Ay, isn't it too bad!" deplored the other woman.

"I'll just step up to Dick's an' see if 'e *is* theer," offered the man, afraid of appearing alarmed, afraid of taking liberties.

9. Couch.
1. Oilcloth.
2. I.e., the Yew Tree (a pub).

3. Signal for end of work.
4. Group.

"Oh, I wouldn't think of bothering you that far," said Elizabeth Bates, with emphasis, but he knew she was glad of his offer.

As they stumbled up the entry, Elizabeth Bates heard Rigley's wife run across the yard and open her neighbour's door. At this, suddenly all the blood in her body seemed to switch away from her heart.

"Mind!" warned Rigley. "Ah've said many a time as Ah'd fill up them ruts in this entry, sumb'dy 'll be breakin' their legs yit."

She recovered herself and walked quickly along with the miner.

"I don't like leaving the children in bed, and nobody in the house," she said.

"No, you dunna!" he replied courteously. They were soon at the gate of the cottage.

"Well, I shanna be many minnits. Dunna you be frettin' now, 'e'll be all right," said the butty.[5]

"Thank you very much, Mr Rigley," she replied.

"You're welcome!" he stammered, moving away. "I shanna be many minnits."

The house was quiet. Elizabeth Bates took off her hat and shawl, and rolled back the rug. When she had finished, she sat down. It was a few minutes past nine. She was startled by the rapid chuff of the winding-engine at the pit, and the sharp whirr of the brakes on the rope as it descended. Again she felt the painful sweep of her blood, and she put her hand to her side, saying aloud: "Good gracious!—it's only the nine o'clock deputy[6] going down," rebuking herself.

She sat still, listening. Half an hour of this, and she was wearied out.

"What am I working myself up like this for?" she said pitiably to herself, "I s'll only be doing myself some damage."

She took out her sewing again.

At a quarter to ten there were footsteps. One person! She watched for the door to open. It was an elderly woman, in a black bonnet and a black woollen shawl—his mother. She was about sixty years old, pale, with blue eyes, and her face all wrinkled and lamentable. She shut the door and turned to her daughter-in-law peevishly.

"Eh, Lizzie, whatever shall we do, whatever shall we do!" she cried.

Elizabeth drew back a little, sharply.

"What is it, mother?" she said.

The elder woman seated herself on the sofa.

"I don't know, child, I can't tell you!"—she shook her head slowly. Elizabeth sat watching her, anxious and vexed.

"I don't know," replied the grandmother, sighing very deeply. "There's no end to my troubles, there isn't. The things I've gone through, I'm sure it's enough——!" She wept without wiping her eyes, the tears running.

"But, mother," interrupted Elizabeth, "what do you mean? What is it?"

The grandmother slowly wiped her eyes. The fountains of her tears were stopped by Elizabeth's directness. She wiped her eyes slowly.

"Poor child! Eh, you poor thing!" she moaned. "I don't know what we're going to do, I don't—and you as you are—it's a thing, it is indeed!"

Elizabeth waited.

5. Workmate, "buddy." Among English miners it means a supervisor intermediary between the employers and the men.
6. Minor coal-mine official.

"Is he dead?" she asked, and at the words her heart swung violently, though she felt a slight flush of shame at the ultimate extravagance of the question. Her words sufficiently frightened the old lady, almost brought her to herself.

"Don't say so, Elizabeth! We'll hope it's not as bad as that; no, may the Lord spare us that, Elizabeth. Jack Rigley came just as I was sittin' down to a glass afore going to bed, an' 'e said: ''Appen you'll go down th' line, Mrs. Bates. Walt's had an accident. 'Appen you'll go an' sit wi' 'er till we can get him home.' I hadn't time to ask him a word afore he was gone. An' I put my bonnet on an' come straight down, Lizzie. I thought to myself: 'Eh, that poor blessed child, if anybody should come an' tell her of a sudden, there's no knowin' what'll 'appen to 'er.' You mustn't let it upset you, Lizzie—or you know what to expect. How long is it, six months—or is it five, Lizzie? Ay!"—the old woman shook her head—"time slips on, it slips on! Ay!"

Elizabeth's thoughts were busy elsewhere. If he was killed—would she be able to manage on the little pension and what she could earn?—she counted up rapidly. If he was hurt—they wouldn't take him to the hospital—how tiresome he would be to nurse!—but perhaps she'd be able to get him away from the drink and his hateful ways. She would—while he was ill. The tears offered to come to her eyes at the picture. But what sentimental luxury was this she was beginning? She turned to consider the children. At any rate she was absolutely necessary for them. They were her business.

"Ay!" repeated the old woman, "it seems but a week or two since he brought me his first wages. Ay—he was a good lad, Elizabeth, he was, in his way. I don't know why he got to be such a trouble, I don't. He was a happy lad at home, only full of spirits. But there's no mistake he's been a handful of trouble, he has! I hope the Lord'll spare him to mend his ways. I hope so, I hope so. You've had a sight o' trouble with him, Elizabeth, you have indeed. But he was a jolly enough lad wi' me, he was, I can assure you. I don't know how it is. . . ."

The old woman continued to muse aloud, a monotonous irritating sound, while Elizabeth thought concentratedly, startled once, when she heard the winding-engine chuff quickly, and the brakes skirr with a shriek. Then she heard the engine more slowly, and the brakes made no sound. The old woman did not notice. Elizabeth waited in suspense. The mother-in-law talked, with lapses into silence.

"But he wasn't your son, Lizzie, an' it makes a difference. Whatever he was, I remember him when he was little, an' I learned to understand him and to make allowances. You've got to make allowances for them——"

It was half-past ten, and the old woman was saying: "But it's trouble from beginning to end; you're never too old for trouble, never too old for that——" when the gate banged back, and there were heavy feet on the steps.

"I'll go, Lizzie, let me go," cried the old woman, rising. But Elizabeth was at the door. It was a man in pit-clothes.

"They're bringin' 'im, Missis," he said. Elizabeth's heart halted a moment. Then it surged on again, almost suffocating her.

"Is he—is it bad?" she asked.

The man turned away, looking at the darkness:

"The doctor says 'e'd been dead hours. 'E saw 'im i' th' lamp-cabin."

The old woman, who stood just behind Elizabeth, dropped into a chair, and folded her hands, crying: "Oh, my boy, my boy!"

"Hush!" said Elizabeth, with a sharp twitch of a frown. "Be still, mother, don't waken th' children: I wouldn't have them down for anything!"

The old woman moaned softly, rocking herself. The man was drawing away. Elizabeth took a step forward.

"How was it?" she asked.

"Well, I couldn't say for sure," the man replied, very ill at ease. "'E wor finishin' a stint an' th' butties 'ad gone, an' a lot o' stuff come down atop 'n 'im."

"And crushed him?" cried the widow, with a shudder.

"No," said the man, "it fell at th' back of 'im. 'E wor under th' face an' it niver touched 'im. It shut 'im in. It seems 'e wor smothered."

Elizabeth shrank back. She heard the old woman behind her cry:

"What?—what did 'e say it was?"

The man replied, more loudly: "'E wor smothered!"

Then the old woman wailed aloud, and this relieved Elizabeth.

"Oh, mother," she said, putting her hand on the old woman, "don't waken th' children, don't waken th' children."

She wept a little, unknowing, while the old mother rocked herself and moaned. Elizabeth remembered that they were bringing him home, and she must be ready. "They'll lay him in the parlour," she said to herself, standing a moment pale and perplexed.

Then she lighted a candle and went into the tiny room. The air was cold and damp, but she could not make a fire, there was no fireplace. She set down the candle and looked round. The candlelight glittered on the lustre-glasses, on the two vases that held some of the pink chrysanthemums, and on the dark mahogany. There was a cold, deathly smell of chrysanthemums in the room. Elizabeth stood looking at the flowers. She turned away, and calculated whether there would be room to lay him on the floor, between the couch and the chiffonier. She pushed the chairs aside. There would be room to lay him down and to step round him. Then she fetched the old red table-cloth, and another old cloth, spreading them down to save her bit of carpet. She shivered on leaving the parlour; so, from the dresser drawer she took a clean shirt and put it at the fire to air. All the time her mother-in-law was rocking herself in the chair and moaning.

"You'll have to move from there, mother," said Elizabeth. "They'll be bringing him in. Come in the rocker."

The old mother rose mechanically, and seated herself by the fire, continuing to lament. Elizabeth went into the pantry for another candle, and there, in the little pent-house under the naked tiles, she heard them coming. She stood still in the pantry doorway, listening. She heard them pass the end of the house, and come awkwardly down the three steps, a jumble of shuffling footsteps and muttering voices. The old woman was silent. The men were in the yard.

Then Elizabeth heard Matthews, the manager of the pit, say: "You go in first, Jim. Mind!"

The door came open, and the two women saw a collier backing into the room, holding one end of a stretcher, on which they could see the nailed pit-boots of the dead man. The two carriers halted, the man at the head stooping to the lintel of the door.

"Wheer will you have him?" asked the manager, a short, white-bearded man.

Elizabeth roused herself and came from the pantry carrying the unlighted candle.

"In the parlour," she said.

"In there, Jim!" pointed the manager, and the carriers backed round into the tiny room. The coat with which they had covered the body fell off as they awkwardly turned through the two doorways, and the women saw their man, naked to the waist, lying stripped for work. The old woman began to moan in a low voice of horror.

"Lay th' stretcher at th' side," snapped the manager, "an' put 'im on th' cloths. Mind now, mind! Look you now——!"

One of the men had knocked off a vase of chrysanthemums. He stared awkwardly, then they set down the stretcher. Elizabeth did not look at her husband. As soon as she could get in the room, she went and picked up the broken vase and the flowers.

"Wait a minute!" she said.

The three men waited in silence while she mopped up the water with a duster.

"Eh, what a job, what a job, to be sure!" the manager was saying, rubbing his brow with trouble and perplexity. "Never knew such a thing in my life, never! He'd no business to ha' been left. I never knew such a thing in my life! Fell over him clean as a whistle, an' shut him in. Not four foot of space, there wasn't—yet it scarce bruised him."

He looked down at the dead man, lying prone, half naked, all grimed with coal-dust.

"'Sphyxiated,' the doctor said. It *is* the most terrible job I've ever known. Seems as if it was done o' purpose. Clean over him, an' shut 'im in, like a mouse-trap"—he made a sharp, descending gesture with his hand.

The colliers standing by jerked aside their heads in hopeless comment.

The horror of the thing bristled upon them all.

Then they heard the girl's voice upstairs calling shrilly: "Mother, mother—who is it? Mother, who is it?"

Elizabeth hurried to the foot of the stairs and opened the door:

"Go to sleep!" she commanded sharply. "What are you shouting about? Go to sleep at once—there's nothing——"

Then she began to mount the stairs. They could hear her on the boards, and on the plaster floor of the little bedroom. They could hear her distinctly:

"What's the matter now?—what's the matter with you, silly thing?"—her voice was much agitated, with an unreal gentleness.

"I thought it was some men come," said the plaintive voice of the child. "Has he come?"

"Yes, they've brought him. There's nothing to make a fuss about. Go to sleep now, like a good child."

They could hear her voice in the bedroom, they waited whilst she covered the children under the bedclothes.

"Is he drunk?" asked the girl, timidly, faintly.

"No! No—he's not! He—he's asleep."

"Is he asleep downstairs?"

"Yes—and don't make a noise."

There was silence for a moment, then the men heard the frightened child again:

"What's that noise?"

"It's nothing, I tell you, what are you bothering for?"

The noise was the grandmother moaning. She was oblivious of everything, sitting on her chair rocking and moaning. The manager put his hand on her arm and bade her "Sh—sh!!"

The old woman opened her eyes and looked at him. She was shocked by this interruption, and seemed to wonder.

"What time is it?" the plaintive thin voice of the child, sinking back unhappily into sleep, asked this last question.

"Ten o'clock," answered the mother more softly. Then she must have bent down and kissed the children.

Matthews beckoned to the men to come away. They put on their caps and took up the stretcher. Stepping over the body, they tiptoed out of the house. None of them spoke till they were far from the wakeful children.

When Elizabeth came down she found her mother alone on the parlour floor, leaning over the dead man, the tears dropping on him.

"We must lay him out," the wife said. She put on the kettle, then returning knelt at the feet, and began to unfasten the knotted leather laces. The room was clammy and dim with only one candle, so that she had to bend her face almost to the floor. At last she got off the heavy boots and put them away.

"You must help me now," she whispered to the old woman. Together they stripped the man.

When they arose, saw him lying in the naïve dignity of death, the women stood arrested in fear and respect. For a few moments they remained still, looking down, the old mother whimpering. Elizabeth felt countermanded.[7] She saw him, how utterly inviolable he lay in himself. She had nothing to do with him. She could not accept it. Stooping, she laid her hand on him, in claim. He was still warm, for the mine was hot where he had died. His mother had his face between her hands, and was murmuring incoherently. The old tears fell in succession as drops from wet leaves; the mother was not weeping, merely her tears flowed. Elizabeth embraced the body of her husband, with cheek and lips. She seemed to be listening, inquiring, trying to get some connection. But she could not. She was driven away. He was impregnable.

She rose, went into the kitchen where she poured warm water into a bowl, brought soap and flannel and a soft towel. "I must wash him," she said.

Then the old mother rose stiffly, and watched Elizabeth as she carefully washed his face, carefully brushing his big blond moustache from his mouth with the flannel. She was afraid with a bottomless fear, so she ministered to him. The old woman, jealous, said:

"Let me wipe him!"—and she kneeled on the other side drying slowly as Elizabeth washed, her big black bonnet sometimes brushing the dark head of her daughter-in-law. They worked thus in silence for a long time. They never forgot it was death, and the touch of the man's dead body gave them strange emotions, different in each of the women; a great dread possessed them both, the mother felt the lie was given to her womb, she was denied; the wife felt the utter isolation of the human soul, the child within her was a weight apart from her.

At last it was finished. He was a man of handsome body, and his face showed no traces of drink. He was blond, full-fleshed, with fine limbs. But he was dead.

7. Contradicted.

"Bless him," whispered his mother, looking always at his face, and speaking out of sheer terror. "Dear lad—bless him!" She spoke in a faint, sibilant ecstasy of fear and mother love.

Elizabeth sank down again to the floor, and put her face against his neck, and trembled and shuddered. But she had to draw away again. He was dead, and her living flesh had no place against his. A great dread and weariness held her: she was so unavailing. Her life was gone like this.

"White as milk he is, clear as a twelve-month baby, bless him, the darling!" the old mother murmured to herself. "Not a mark on him, clear and clean and white, beautiful as ever a child was made," she murmured with pride. Elizabeth kept her face hidden.

"He went peaceful, Lizzie—peaceful as sleep. Isn't he beautiful, the lamb? Ay—he must ha' made his peace, Lizzie. 'Appen he made it all right, Lizzie, shut in there. He'd have time. He wouldn't look like this if he hadn't made his peace. The lamb, the dear lamb. Eh, but he had a hearty laugh. I loved to hear it. He had the heartiest laugh, Lizzie, as a lad——"

Elizabeth looked up. The man's mouth was fallen back, slightly open under the cover of the moustache. The eyes, half shut, did not show glazed in the obscurity. Life with its smoky burning gone from him, had left him apart and utterly alien to her. And she knew what a stranger he was to her. In her womb was ice of fear, because of this separate stranger with whom she had been living as one flesh. Was this what it all meant—utter, intact separateness, obscured by heat of living? In dread she turned her face away. The fact was too deadly. There had been nothing between them, and yet they had come together, exchanging their nakedness repeatedly. Each time he had taken her, they had been two isolated beings, far apart as now. He was no more responsible than she. The child was like ice in her womb. For as she looked at the dead man, her mind, cold and detached, said clearly: "Who am I? What have I been doing? I have been fighting a husband who did not exist. *He* existed all the time. What wrong have I done? What was that I have been living with? There lies the reality, this man." And her soul died in her for fear: she knew she had never seen him, he had never seen her, they had met in the dark and had fought in the dark, not knowing whom they met or whom they fought. And now she saw, and turned silent in seeing. For she had been wrong. She had said he was something he was not; she had felt familiar with him. Whereas he was apart all the while, living as she never lived, feeling as she never felt.

In fear and shame she looked at his naked body, that she had known falsely. And he was the father of her children. Her soul was torn from her body and stood apart. She looked at his naked body and was ashamed, as if she had denied it. After all, it was itself. It seemed awful to her. She looked at his face, and she turned her own face to the wall. For his look was other than hers, his way was not her way. She had denied him what he was—she saw it now. She had refused him as himself. And this had been her life, and his life. She was grateful to death, which restored the truth. And she knew she was not dead.

And all the while her heart was bursting with grief and pity for him. What had he suffered? What stretch of horror for this helpless man! She was rigid with agony. She had not been able to help him. He had been cruelly injured, this naked man, this other being, and she could make no reparation. There were the children—but the children belonged to life. This dead man had nothing to do with them. He and she were only channels through which life had flowed to issue in the children. She was a mother—but how awful she knew it now to have been a wife. And he, dead now, how awful he must have felt it to be a husband. She felt that in the next world he would be a stranger to her. If they met there, in the beyond, they would only be ashamed of what had been before. The children had come, for some mysterious reason, out of both of them. But the children did not unite them. Now he was dead, she knew how eternally he was apart from her, how eternally he had nothing more to do with her. She saw this episode of her life closed. They had denied each other in life. Now he had withdrawn. An anguish came over her. It was finished then: it had become hopeless between them long before he died. Yet he had been her husband. But how little!

"Have you got his shirt, 'Lizabeth?"

Elizabeth turned without answering, though she strove to weep and behave as her mother-in-law expected. But she could not, she was silenced. She went into the kitchen and returned with the garment.

"It is aired," she said, grasping the cotton shirt here and there to try. She was almost ashamed to handle him; what right had she or anyone to lay hands on him; but her touch was humble on his body. It was hard work to clothe him. He was so heavy and inert. A terrible dread gripped her all the while: that he could be so heavy and utterly inert, unresponsive, apart. The horror of the distance between them was almost too much for her—it was so infinite a gap she must look across.

At last it was finished. They covered him with a sheet and left him lying, with his face bound. And she fastened the door of the little parlour, lest the children should see what was lying there. Then, with peace sunk heavy on her heart, she went about making tidy the kitchen. She knew she submitted to life, which was her immediate master. But from death, her ultimate master, she winced with fear and shame.

1911, 1914

The Horse Dealer's Daughter

"Well, Mabel, and what are you going to do with yourself?" asked Joe, with foolish flippancy. He felt quite safe himself. Without listening for an answer, he turned aside, worked a grain of tobacco to the tip of his tongue, and spat it out. He did not care about anything, since he felt safe himself.

The three brothers and the sister sat round the desolate breakfast-table, attempting some sort of desultory consultation. The morning's post had given the final tap to the family fortunes, and all was over. The dreary dining-room itself, with its heavy mahogany furniture, looked as if it were waiting to be done away with.

But the consultation amounted to nothing. There was a strange air of ineffectuality about the three men, as they sprawled at table, smoking and reflecting vaguely on their own condition. The girl was alone, a rather short, sullen-looking young woman of twenty-seven. She did not share the same life as her brothers. She would have been good-looking, save for the impressive fixity of her face, "bull-dog," as her brothers called it.

There was a confused tramping of horses' feet outside. The three men all sprawled round in their chairs to watch. Beyond the dark holly bushes that separated the strip of lawn from the high-road, they could see a cavalcade of shire horses swinging out of their own yard, being taken for exercise. This was the last time. These were the last horses that would go through their hands. The young men watched with critical, callous look. They were all frightened at the collapse of their lives, and the sense of disaster in which they were involved left them no inner freedom.

Yet they were three fine, well-set fellows enough. Joe, the eldest, was a man of thirty-three, broad and handsome in a hot, flushed way. His face was red, he twisted his black moustache over a thick finger, his eyes were shallow and restless. He had a sensual way of uncovering his teeth when he laughed, and his bearing was stupid. Now he watched the horses with a glazed look of helplessness in his eyes, a certain stupor of downfall.

The great draught horses swung past. They were tied head to tail, four of them, and they heaved along to where a lane branched off from the high-road, planting their great hoofs floutingly in the fine black mud, swinging their great rounded haunches sumptuously, and trotting a few sudden steps as they were led into the lane, round the corner. Every movement showed a massive, slumbrous strength, and a stupidity which held them in subjection. The groom at the head looked back, jerking the leading rope. And the cavalcade moved out of sight up the lane, the tail of the last horse, bobbed up tight and stiff, held out taut from the swinging great haunches as they rocked behind the hedges in a motion-like sleep.

Joe watched with glazed hopeless eyes. The horses were almost like his own body to him. He felt he was done for now. Luckily he was engaged to a woman as old as himself, and therefore her father, who was steward of a neighbouring estate, would provide him with a job. He would marry and go into harness. His life was over, he would be a subject animal now.

He turned uneasily aside, the retreating steps of the horses echoing in his ears. Then, with foolish restlessness, he reached for the scraps of bacon-rind from the plates, and making a faint whistling sound, flung them to the terrier that lay against the fender. He watched the dog swallow them, and waited till the creature looked into his eyes. Then a faint grin came on his face, and in a high, foolish voice he said:

"You won't get much more bacon, shall you, you little b——?"

The dog faintly and dismally wagged its tail, then lowered its haunches, circled round, and lay down again.

There was another helpless silence at the table. Joe sprawled uneasily in his seat, not willing to go till the family conclave was dissolved. Fred Henry, the second brother, was erect, clean-limbed, alert. He had watched the passing of the horses with more *sang-froid*.[1] If he was an animal, like Joe, he was an animal which controls, not one which is controlled. He was master of any horse, and he carried himself with a well-tempered air of mastery. But he was not master of the situations of life. He pushed his coarse brown moustache upwards, off his lip, and glanced irritably at his sister, who sat impassive and inscrutable.

"You'll go and stop with Lucy for a bit, shan't you?" he asked. The girl did not answer.

___

1. Literally, "cold blood" (French); here, calm detachment.

"I don't see what else you can do," persisted Fred Henry.

"Go as a skivvy,"[2] Joe interpolated laconically.

The girl did not move a muscle.

"If I was her, I should go in for training for a nurse," said Malcolm, the youngest of them all. He was the baby of the family, a young man of twenty-two, with a fresh, jaunty *museau.*[3]

But Mabel did not take any notice of him. They had talked at her and round her for so many years, that she hardly heard them at all.

The marble clock on the mantelpiece softly chimed the half-hour, the dog rose uneasily from the hearth-rug and looked at the party at the breakfast-table. But still they sat in an ineffectual conclave.

"Oh, all right," said Joe suddenly, apropos of nothing. "I'll get a move on."

He pushed back his chair, straddled his knees with a downward jerk, to get them free, in horsey fashion, and went to the fire. Still he did not go out of the room; he was curious to know what the others would do or say. He began to charge his pipe, looking down at the dog and saying in a high, affected voice:

"Going wi' me? Going wi' me are ter? Tha'rt goin' further than tha counts on just now, dost hear?"

The dog faintly wagged his tail, the man stuck out his jaw and covered his pipe with his hands, and puffed intently, losing himself in the tobacco, looking down all the while at the dog with an absent brown eye. The dog looked up at him in mournful distrust. Joe stood with his knees stuck out, in real horsey fashion.

"Have you had a letter from Lucy?" Fred Henry asked of his sister.

"Last week," came the neutral reply.

"And what does she say?"

There was no answer.

"Does she *ask* you to go and stop there?" persisted Fred Henry.

"She says I can if I like."

"Well, then, you'd better. Tell her you'll come on Monday."

This was received in silence.

"That's what you'll do then, is it?" said Fred Henry, in some exasperation.

But she made no answer. There was a silence of futility and irritation in the room. Malcolm grinned fatuously.

"You'll have to make up your mind between now and next Wednesday," said Joe loudly, "or else find yourself lodgings on the kerbstone."

The face of the young woman darkened, but she sat on immutable.

"Here's Jack Ferguson!" exclaimed Malcolm, who was looking aimlessly out of the window.

"Where?" exclaimed Joe loudly.

"Just gone past."

"Coming in?"

Malcolm craned his neck to see the gate.

"Yes," he said.

There was a silence. Mabel sat on like one condemned, at the head of the table. Then a whistle was heard from the kitchen. The dog got up and barked sharply. Joe opened the door and shouted:

---

2. Servant girl.   3. Muzzle (French); here, face.

"Come on."

After a moment a young man entered. He was muffled up in overcoat and a purple woollen scarf, and his tweed cap, which he did not remove, was pulled down on his head. He was of medium height, his face was rather long and pale, his eyes looked tired.

"Hello, Jack! Well, Jack!" exclaimed Malcolm and Joe. Fred Henry merely said: "Jack."

"What's doing?" asked the newcomer, evidently addressing Fred Henry.

"Same. We've got to be out by Wednesday. Got a cold?"

"I have—got it bad, too."

"Why don't you stop in?"

"*Me* stop in? When I can't stand on my legs, perhaps I shall have a chance." The young man spoke huskily. He had a slight Scotch accent.

"It's a knock-out, isn't it," said Joe, boisterously, "if a doctor goes round croaking with a cold. Looks bad for the patients, doesn't it?"

The young doctor looked at him slowly.

"Anything the matter with *you*, then?" he asked sarcastically.

"Not as I know of. Damn your eyes, I hope not. Why?"

"I thought you were very concerned about the patients, wondered if you might be one yourself."

"Damn it, no, I've never been patient to no flaming doctor, and hope I never shall be," returned Joe.

At this point Mabel rose from the table, and they all seemed to become aware of her existence. She began putting the dishes together. The young doctor looked at her, but did not address her. He had not greeted her. She went out of the room with the tray, her face impassive and unchanged.

"When are you off then, all of you?" asked the doctor.

"I'm catching the eleven-forty," replied Malcolm. "Are you goin' down wi' th' trap, Joe?"

"Yes, I've told you I'm going down wi' th' trap, haven't I?"

"We'd better be getting her in then. So long Jack, if I don't see you before I go," said Malcolm, shaking hands.

He went out, followed by Joe, who seemed to have his tail between his legs.

"Well, this is the devil's own," exclaimed the doctor, when he was left alone with Fred Henry. "Going before Wednesday, are you?"

"That's the orders," replied the other.

"Where, to Northampton?"

"That's it."

"The devil!" exclaimed Ferguson, with quiet chagrin.

And there was silence between the two.

"All settled up, are you?" asked Ferguson.

"About."

There was another pause.

"Well, I shall miss yer, Freddy, boy," said the young doctor.

"And I shall miss thee, Jack," returned the other.

"Miss you like hell," mused the doctor.

Fred Henry turned aside. There was nothing to say. Mabel came in again, to finish clearing the table.

"What are *you* going to do, then, Miss Pervin?" asked Ferguson. "Going to your sister's, are you?"

Mabel looked at him with her steady, dangerous eyes, that always made him uncomfortable, unsettling his superficial ease.

"No," she said.

"Well, what in the name of fortune *are* you going to do? Say what you mean to do," cried Fred Henry, with futile intensity.

But she only averted her head, and continued her work. She folded the white table-cloth, and put on the chenille cloth.

"The sulkiest bitch that ever trod!" muttered her brother.

But she finished her task with perfectly impassive face, the young doctor watching her interestedly all the while. Then she went out.

Fred Henry stared after her, clenching his lips, his blue eyes fixing in sharp antagonism, as he made a grimace of sour exasperation.

"You could bray[4] her into bits, and that's all you'd get out of her," he said, in a small, narrowed tone.

The doctor smiled faintly.

"What's she *going* to do, then?" he asked.

"Strike me if *I* know!" returned the other.

There was a pause. Then the doctor stirred.

"I'll be seeing you tonight, shall I?" he said to his friend.

"Ay—where's it to be? Are we going over to Jessdale?"

"I don't know. I've got such a cold on me. I'll come round to the 'Moon and Stars,'[5] anyway."

"Let Lizzie and May miss their night for once, eh?"

"That's it—if I feel as I do now."

"All's one——"

The two young men went through the passage and down to the back door together. The house was large, but it was servantless now, and desolate. At the back was a small bricked house-yard and beyond that a big square, gravelled fine and red, and having stables on two sides. Sloping, dank, winter-dark fields stretched away on the open sides.

But the stables were empty. Joseph Pervin, the father of the family, had been a man of no education, who had become a fairly large horse dealer. The stables had been full of horses, there was a great turmoil and come-and-go of horses and of dealers and grooms. Then the kitchen was full of servants. But of late things had declined. The old man had married a second time, to retrieve his fortunes. Now he was dead and everything was gone to the dogs,[6] there was nothing but debt and threatening.

For months, Mabel had been servantless in the big house, keeping the home together in penury for her ineffectual brothers. She had kept house for ten years. But previously it was with unstinted means. Then, however brutal and coarse everything was, the sense of money had kept her proud, confident. The men might be foul-mouthed, the women in the kitchen might have had reputations, her brothers might have illegitimate children. But so long as there was money, the girl felt herself established, and brutally proud, reserved.

No company came to the house, save dealers and coarse men. Mabel had no associates of her own sex, after her sister went away. But she did not mind. She went regularly to church, she attended to her father. And she lived in the

---

4. Grind.
5. Name of a public house (pub).
6. Gone wrong (slang).

memory of her mother, who had died when she was fourteen, and whom she had loved. She had loved her father, too, in a different way, depending upon him, and feeling secure in him, until at the age of fifty-four, he married again. And then she had set hard against him. Now he had died and left them all hopelessly in debt.

She had suffered badly during the period of poverty. Nothing, however, could shake the curious, sullen, animal pride that dominated each member of the family. Now, for Mabel, the end had come. Still she would not cast about her. She would follow her own way just the same. She would always hold the keys of her own situation. Mindless and persistent, she endured from day to day. Why should she think? Why should she answer anybody? It was enough that this was the end, and there was no way out. She need not pass any more darkly along the main street of the small town, avoiding every eye. She need not demean herself any more, going into the shops and buying the cheapest food. This was at an end. She thought of nobody, not even of herself. Mindless and persistent, she seemed in a sort of ecstasy to be coming nearer to her fulfilment, her own glorification, approaching her dead mother, who was glorified.

In the afternoon, she took a little bag, with shears and sponge and a small scrubbing-brush, and went out. It was a grey, wintry day, with saddened, dark green fields and an atmosphere blackened by the smoke of foundries not far off. She went quickly, darkly along the causeway, heeding nobody, through the town to the churchyard.

There she always felt secure, as if no one could see her, although as a matter of fact she was exposed to the stare of everyone who passed along under the churchyard wall. Nevertheless, once under the shadow of the great looming church, among the graves, she felt immune from the world, reserved within the thick churchyard wall as in another country.

Carefully she clipped the grass from the grave, and arranged the pinky-white, small chrysanthemums in the tin cross. When this was done, she took an empty jar from a neighbouring grave, brought water, and carefully, most scrupulously sponged the marble headstone and the coping-stone.

It gave her sincere satisfaction to do this. She felt in immediate contact with the world of her mother. She took minute pains, went through the park in a state bordering on pure happiness, as if in performing this task she came into a subtle, intimate connection with her mother. For the life she followed here in the world was far less real than the world of death she inherited from her mother.

The doctor's house was just by the church. Ferguson, being a mere hired assistant, was slave to the country-side. As he hurried now to attend to the out-patients in the surgery, glancing across the graveyard with his quick eye, he saw the girl at her task at the grave. She seemed so intent and remote, it was like looking into another world. Some mystical element was touched in him. He slowed down as he walked, watching her as if spellbound.

She lifted her eyes, feeling him looking. Their eyes met. And each looked away again at once, each feeling, in some way, found out by the other. He lifted his cap and passed on down the road. There remained distinct in his consciousness, like a vision, the memory of her face, lifted from the tombstone in the churchyard, and looking at him with slow, large, portentous eyes. It *was* portentous, her face. It seemed to mesmerise him. There was a heavy power in her eyes which laid hold of his whole being, as if he had drunk some powerful drug. He had been feeling weak and done before. Now the life came back into him, he felt delivered from his own fretted, daily self.

He finished his duties at the surgery as quickly as might be, hastily filling up the bottles of the waiting people with cheap drugs. Then, in perpetual haste, he set off again to visit several cases in another part of his round, before tea-time. At all times he preferred to walk if he could, but particularly when he was not well. He fancied the motion restored him.

The afternoon was falling. It was grey, deadened, and wintry, with a slow, moist, heavy coldness sinking in and deadening all the faculties. But why should he think or notice? He hastily climbed the hill and turned across the dark green fields, following the black cinder-track. In the distance, across a shallow dip in the country, the small town was clustered like smouldering ash, a tower, a spire, a heap of low, raw, extinct houses. And on the nearest fringe of the town, sloping into the dip, was Oldmeadow, the Pervins' house. He could see the stables and the outbuildings distinctly, as they lay towards him on the slope. Well, he would not go there many more times! Another resource would be lost to him, another place gone: the only company he cared for in the alien, ugly little town he was losing. Nothing but work, drudgery, constant hastening from dwelling to dwelling among the colliers and the iron-workers. It wore him out, but at the same time he had a craving for it. It was a stimulant to him to be in the homes of the working people, moving, as it were, through the innermost body of their life. His nerves were excited and gratified. He could come so near, into the very lives of the rough, inarticulate, powerfully emotional men and women. He grumbled, he said he hated the hellish hole. But as a matter of fact it excited him, the contact with the rough, strongly-feeling people was a stimulant applied direct to his nerves.

Below Oldmeadow, in the green, shallow, soddened hollow of fields, lay a square, deep pond. Roving across the landscape, the doctor's quick eye detected a figure in black passing through the gate of the field, down towards the pond. He looked again. It would be Mabel Pervin. His mind suddenly became alive and attentive.

Why was she going down there? He pulled up on the path on the slope above, and stood staring. He could just make sure of the small black figure moving in the hollow of the failing day. He seemed to see her in the midst of such obscurity, that he was like a clairvoyant, seeing rather with the mind's eye than with ordinary sight. Yet he could see her positively enough, whilst he kept his eye attentive. He felt, if he looked away from her, in the thick, ugly falling dusk, he would lose her altogether.

He followed her minutely as she moved, direct and intent, like something transmitted rather than stirring in voluntary activity, straight down the field towards the pond. There she stood on the bank for a moment. She never raised her head. Then she waded slowly into the water.

He stood motionless as the small black figure walked slowly and deliberately towards the centre of the pond, very slowly, gradually moving deeper into the motionless water, and still moving forward as the water got up to her breast. Then he could see her no more in the dusk of the dead afternoon.

"There!" he exclaimed. "Would you believe it?"

And he hastened straight down, running over the wet, soddened fields, pushing through the hedges, down into the depression of callous wintry obscurity. It took him several minutes to come to the pond. He stood on the bank, breathing heavily. He could see nothing. His eyes seemed to penetrate the dead water. Yes, perhaps that was the dark shadow of her black clothing beneath the surface of the water.

He slowly ventured into the pond. The bottom was deep, soft clay, he sank in, and the water clasped dead cold round his legs. As he stirred he could smell the cold, rotten clay that fouled up into the water. It was objectionable in his lungs. Still, repelled and yet not heeding, he moved deeper into the pond. The cold water rose over his thighs, over his loins, upon his abdomen. The lower part of his body was all sunk in the hideous cold element. And the bottom was so deeply soft and uncertain, he was afraid of pitching with his mouth underneath. He could not swim, and was afraid.

He crouched a little, spreading his hands under the water and moving them round, trying to feel for her. The dead cold pond swayed upon his chest. He moved again, a little deeper, and again, with his hands underneath, he felt all around under the water. And he touched her clothing. But it evaded his fingers. He made a desperate effort to grasp it.

And so doing he lost his balance and went under, horribly, suffocating in the foul earthy water, struggling madly for a few moments. At last, after what seemed an eternity, he got his footing, rose again into the air and looked around. He gasped, and knew he was in the world. Then he looked at the water. She had risen near him. He grasped her clothing, and drawing her nearer, turned to take his way to land again.

He went very slowly, carefully, absorbed in the slow progress. He rose higher, climbing out of the pond. The water was now only about his legs; he was thankful, full of relief to be out of the clutches of the pond. He lifted her and staggered on to the bank, out of the horror of wet, grey clay.

He laid her down on the bank. She was quite unconscious and running with water. He made the water come from her mouth, he worked to restore her. He did not have to work very long before he could feel the breathing begin again in her; she was breathing naturally. He worked a little longer. He could feel her live beneath his hands; she was coming back. He wiped her face, wrapped her in his overcoat, looked round into the dim, dark grey world, then lifted her and staggered down the bank and across the fields.

It seemed an unthinkably long way, and his burden so heavy he felt he would never get to the house. But at last he was in the stable-yard, and then in the house-yard. He opened the door and went into the house. In the kitchen he laid her down on the hearth-rug and called. The house was empty. But the fire was burning in the grate.

Then again he kneeled to attend to her. She was breathing regularly, her eyes were wide open and as if conscious, but there seemed something missing in her look. She was conscious in herself, but unconscious of her surroundings.

He ran upstairs, took blankets from a bed, and put them before the fire to warm. Then he removed her saturated, earthy-smelling clothing, rubbed her dry with a towel, and wrapped her naked in the blankets. Then he went into the dining room, to look for spirits. There was a little whisky. He drank a gulp himself, and put some into her mouth.

The effect was instantaneous. She looked full into his face, as if she had been seeing him for some time, and yet had only just become conscious of him.

"Dr. Ferguson?" she said.

"What?" he answered.

He was divesting himself of his coat, intending to find some dry clothing upstairs. He could not bear the smell of the dead, clayey water, and he was mortally afraid for his own health.

"What did I do?" she asked.

"Walked into the pond," he replied. He had begun to shudder like one sick, and could hardly attend to her. Her eyes remained full on him, he seemed to be going dark in his mind, looking back at her helplessly. The shuddering became quieter in him, his life came back to him, dark and unknowing, but strong again.

"Was I out of my mind?" she asked, while her eyes were fixed on him all the time.

"Maybe, for the moment," he replied. He felt quiet, because his strength had come back. The strange fretful strain had left him.

"Am I out of my mind now?" she asked.

"Are you?" he reflected a moment. "No," he answered truthfully. "I don't see that you are." He turned his face aside. He was afraid now, because he felt dazed, and felt dimly that her power was stronger than his, in this issue. And she continued to look at him fixedly all the time. "Can you tell me where I shall find some dry things to put on?" he asked.

"Did you dive into the pond for me?" she asked.

"No," he answered. "I walked in. But I went in overhead as well."

There was silence for a moment. He hesitated. He very much wanted to go upstairs to get into dry clothing. But there was another desire in him. And she seemed to hold him. His will seemed to have gone to sleep, and left him, standing there slack before her. But he felt warm inside himself. He did not shudder at all, though his clothes were sodden on him.

"Why did you?" she asked.

"Because I didn't want you to do such a foolish thing," he said.

"It wasn't foolish," she said, still gazing at him as she lay on the floor, with a sofa cushion under her head. "It was the right thing to do. *I* knew best, then."

"I'll go and shift these wet things," he said. But still he had not the power to move out of her presence, until she sent him. It was as if she had the life of his body in her hands, and he could not extricate himself. Or perhaps he did not want to.

Suddenly she sat up. Then she became aware of her own immediate condition. She felt the blankets about her, she knew her own limbs. For a moment it seemed as if her reason were going. She looked round, with wild eye, as if seeking something. He stood still with fear. She saw her clothing lying scattered.

"Who undressed me?" she asked, her eyes resting full and inevitable on his face.

"I did," he replied, "to bring you round."

For some moments she sat and gazed at him awfully, her lips parted.

"Do you love me, then?" she asked.

He only stood and stared at her, fascinated. His soul seemed to melt.

She shuffled forward on her knees, and put her arms round him, round his legs, as he stood there, pressing her breasts against his knees and thighs, clutching him with strange, convulsive certainty, pressing his thighs against her, drawing him to her face, her throat, as she looked up at him with flaring, humble eyes of transfiguration, triumphant in first possession.

"You love me," she murmured, in strange transport, yearning and triumphant and confident. "You love me. I know you love me, I know."

And she was passionately kissing his knees, through the wet clothing, passionately and indiscriminately kissing his knees, his legs, as if unaware of everything.

He looked down at the tangled wet hair, the wild, bare, animal shoulders. He was amazed, bewildered, and afraid. He had never thought of loving her. He had never wanted to love her. When he rescued her and restored her, he was a doctor, and she was a patient. He had had no single personal thought of her. Nay, this introduction of the personal element was very distasteful to him, a violation of his professional honour. It was horrible to have her there embracing his knees. It was horrible. He revolted from it, violently. And yet—and yet—he had not the power to break away.

She looked at him again, with the same supplication of powerful love, and that same transcendent, frightening light of triumph. In view of the delicate flame which seemed to come from her face like a light, he was powerless. And yet he had never intended to love her. He had never intended. And something stubborn in him could not give way.

"You love me," she repeated, in a murmur of deep, rhapsodic assurance. "You love me."

Her hands were drawing him, drawing him down to her. He was afraid, even a little horrified. For he had, really, no intention of loving her. Yet her hands were drawing him towards her. He put out his hand quickly to steady himself, and grasped her bare shoulder. A flame seemed to burn the hand that grasped her soft shoulder. He had no intention of loving her: his whole will was against his yielding. It was horrible. And yet wonderful was the touch of her shoulders, beautiful the shining of her face. Was she perhaps mad? He had a horror of yielding to her. Yet something in him ached also.

He had been staring away at the door, away from her. But his hand remained on her shoulder. She had gone suddenly very still. He looked down at her. Her eyes were now wide with fear, with doubt, the light was dying from her face, a shadow of terrible greyness was returning. He could not bear the touch of her eyes' question upon him, and the look of death behind the question.

With an inward groan he gave way, and let his heart yield towards her. A sudden gentle smile came on his face. And her eyes, which never left his face, slowly, slowly filled with tears. He watched the strange water rise in her eyes, like some slow fountain coming up. And his heart seemed to burn and melt away in his breast.

He could not bear to look at her any more. He dropped on his knees and caught her head with his arms and pressed her face against his throat. She was very still. His heart, which seemed to have broken, was burning with a kind of agony in his breast. And he felt her slow, hot tears wetting his throat. But he could not move.

He felt the hot tears wet his neck and the hollows of his neck, and he remained motionless, suspended through one of man's eternities. Only now it had become indispensable to him to have her face pressed close to him; he could never let her go again. He could never let her head go away from the close clutch of his arm. He wanted to remain like that for ever, with his heart hurting him in a pain that was also life to him. Without knowing, he was looking down on her damp, soft brown hair.

Then, as it were suddenly, he smelt the horrid stagnant smell of that water. And at the same moment she drew away from him and looked at him. Her eyes were wistful and unfathomable. He was afraid of them, and he fell to kissing her, not knowing what he was doing. He wanted her eyes not to have that terrible, wistful, unfathomable look.

When she turned her face to him again, a faint delicate flush was glowing, and there was again dawning that terrible shining of joy in her eyes, which really terrified him, and yet which he now wanted to see, because he feared the look of doubt still more.

"You love me?" she said, rather faltering.

"Yes." The word cost him a painful effort. Not because it wasn't true. But because it was too newly true, the *saying* seemed to tear open again his newly-torn heart. And he hardly wanted it to be true, even now.

She lifted her face to him, and he bent forward and kissed her on the mouth, gently, with the one kiss that is an eternal pledge. And as he kissed her his heart strained again in his breast. He never intended to love her. But now it was over. He had crossed over the gulf to her, and all that he had left behind had shrivelled and become void.

After the kiss, her eyes again slowly filled with tears. She sat still, away from him, with her face drooped aside, and her hands folded in her lap. The tears fell very slowly. There was complete silence. He too sat there motionless and silent on the hearth-rug. The strange pain of his heart that was broken seemed to consume him. That he should love her? That this was love! That he should be ripped open in this way! Him, a doctor! How they would all jeer if they knew! It was agony to him to think they might know.

In the curious naked pain of the thought he looked again to her. She was sitting there drooped into a muse. He saw a tear fall, and his heart flared hot. He saw for the first time that one of her shoulders was quite uncovered, one arm bare, he could see one of her small breasts; dimly, because it had become almost dark in the room.

"Why are you crying?" he asked, in an altered voice.

She looked up at him, and behind her tears the consciousness of her situation for the first time brought a dark look of shame to her eyes.

"I'm not crying, really," she said, watching him, half frightened.

He reached his hand, and softly closed it on her bare arm.

"I love you! I love you!" he said in a soft, low vibrating voice, unlike himself.

She shrank, and dropped her head. The soft, penetrating grip of his hand on her arm distressed her. She looked up at him.

"I want to go," she said. "I want to go and get you some dry things."

"Why?" he said. "I'm all right."

"But I want to go," she said. "And I want you to change your things."

He released her arm, and she wrapped herself in the blanket, looking at him, rather frightened. And still she did not rise.

"Kiss me," she said wistfully.

He kissed her, but briefly, half in anger.

Then, after a second, she rose nervously, all mixed up in the blanket. He watched her in her confusion as she tried to extricate herself and wrap herself up so that she could walk. He watched her relentlessly, as she knew. And as she went, the blanket trailing, and as he saw a glimpse of her feet and her white leg, he tried to remember her as she was when he had wrapped her in the blanket. But then he didn't want to remember, because she had been nothing to him then, and his nature revolted from remembering her as she was when she was nothing to him.

A tumbling muffled noise from within the dark house startled him. Then he heard her voice: "There are clothes." He rose and went to the foot of the stairs, and gathered up the garments she had thrown down. Then he came back to the fire, to rub himself down and dress. He grinned at his own appearance when he had finished.

The fire was sinking, so he put on coal. The house was now quite dark, save for the light of a street-lamp that shone in faintly from beyond the holly trees. He lit the gas with matches he found on the mantelpiece. Then he emptied the pockets of his own clothes, and threw all his wet things in a heap into the scullery. After which he gathered up her sodden clothes, gently, and put them in a separate heap on the copper-top in the scullery.

It was six o'clock on the clock. His own watch had stopped. He ought to go back to the surgery. He waited, and still she did not come down. So he went to the foot of the stairs and called:

"I shall have to go."

Almost immediately he heard her coming down. She had on her best dress of black voile, and her hair was tidy, but still damp. She looked at him—and in spite of herself, smiled.

"I don't like you in those clothes," she said.

"Do I look a sight?" he answered.

They were shy of one another.

"I'll make you some tea," she said.

"No, I must go."

"Must you?" And she looked at him again with the wide, strained, doubtful eyes. And again, from the pain of his breast, he knew how he loved her. He went and bent to kiss her, gently, passionately, with his heart's painful kiss.

"And my hair smells so horrible," she murmured in distraction. "And I'm so awful, I'm so awful! Oh no, I'm too awful." And she broke into bitter, heart-broken sobbing. "You can't want to love me, I'm horrible."

"Don't be silly, don't be silly," he said, trying to comfort her, kissing her, holding her in his arms. "I want you, I want to marry you, we're going to be married, quickly, quickly—to-morrow if I can."

But she only sobbed terribly, and cried:

"I feel awful. I feel awful. I feel I'm horrible to you."

"No, I want you, I want you," was all he answered, blindly, with that terrible intonation which frightened her almost more than her horror lest he should *not* want her.

1922

Why the Novel Matters

We have curious ideas of ourselves. We think of ourselves as a body with a spirit in it, or a body with a soul in it, or a body with a mind in it. *Mens sana in corpore sano.*[1] The years drink up the wine, and at last throw the bottle away, the body, of course, being the bottle.

1. A healthy mind in a healthy body (Latin).

It is a funny sort of superstition. Why should I look at my hand, as it so cleverly writes these words, and decide that it is a mere nothing compared to the mind that directs it? Is there really any huge difference between my hand and my brain? Or my mind? My hand is alive, it flickers with a life of its own. It meets all the strange universe in touch, and learns a vast number of things, and knows a vast number of things. My hand, as it writes these words, slips gaily along, jumps like a grasshopper to dot an *i*, feels the table rather cold, gets a little bored if I write too long, has its own rudiments of thought, and is just as much *me* as is my brain, my mind, or my soul. Why should I imagine that there is a *me* which is more *me* than my hand is? Since my hand is absolutely alive, me alive.

Whereas, of course, as far as I am concerned, my pen isn't alive at all. My pen *isn't me* alive. Me alive ends at my finger tips.

Whatever is me alive is me. Every tiny bit of my hands is alive, every little freckle and hair and fold of skin. And whatever is me alive is me. Only my finger-nails, those ten little weapons between me and an inanimate universe, they cross the mysterious Rubicon[2] between me alive and things like my pen, which are not alive, in my own sense.

So, seeing my hand is all alive, and me alive, wherein is it just a bottle, or a jug, or a tin can, or a vessel of clay, or any of the rest of that nonsense? True, if I cut it it will bleed, like a can of cherries. But then the skin that is cut, and the veins that bleed, and the bones that should never be seen, they are all just as alive as the blood that flows. So the tin can business, or vessel of clay, is just bunk.

And that's what you learn, when you're a novelist. And that's what you are very liable *not* to know, if you're a parson, or a philosopher, or a scientist, or a stupid person. If you're a parson, you talk about souls in heaven. If you're a novelist, you know that paradise is in the palm of your hand, and on the end of your nose, because both are alive; and alive, and man alive, which is more than you can say, for certain, of paradise. Paradise is after life, and I for one am not keen on anything that is *after* life. If you are a philosopher, you talk about infinity, and the pure spirit which knows all things. But if you pick up a novel, you realise immediately that infinity is just a handle to this self-same jug of a body of mine; while as for knowing, if I find my finger in the fire, I know that fire burns, with a knowledge so emphatic and vital, it leaves Nirvana[3] merely a conjecture. Oh, yes, my body, me alive, *knows*, and knows intensely. And as for the sum of all knowledge, it can't be anything more than an accumulation of all the things I know in the body, and you, dear reader, know in the body.

These damned philosophers, they talk as if they suddenly went off in steam, and were then much more important than they are when they're in their shirts. It is nonsense. Every man, philosopher included, ends in his own finger-tips. That's the end of his man alive. As for the words and thoughts and sighs and aspirations that fly from him, they are so many tremulations in the ether, and not alive at all. But if the tremulations reach another man alive, he may receive them into his life, and his life may take on a new colour, like a

---

2. When Julius Caesar crossed the river Rubicon (near Rimini, Italy) in 49 B.C.E., in defiance of the Senate, he indicated his intention of advancing against Pompey and thus involving the country in civil war. Hence to "cross the Rubicon" means to

take an important and irrevocable decision.
3. In Buddhist theology, the extinction of the self and its desires and the attainment of perfect beatitude.

chameleon creeping from a brown rock on to a green leaf. All very well and good. It still doesn't alter the fact that the so-called spirit, the message or teaching of the philosopher or the saint, isn't alive at all, but just a tremulation upon the ether, like a radio message. All this spirit stuff is just tremulations upon the ether. If you, as man alive, quiver from the tremulation of the ether into new life, that is because you are man alive, and you take sustenance and stimulation into your alive man in a myriad ways. But to say that the message, or the spirit which is communicated to you, is more important than your living body, is nonsense. You might as well say that the potato at dinner was more important.

Nothing is important but life. And for myself, I can absolutely see life nowhere but in the living. Life with a capital L is only man alive. Even a cabbage in the rain is cabbage alive. All things that are alive are amazing. And all things that are dead are subsidiary to the living. Better a live dog than a dead lion. But better a live lion than a live dog. *C'est la vie!*

It seems impossible to get a saint, or a philosopher, or a scientist, to stick to this simple truth. They are all, in a sense, renegades. The saint wishes to offer himself up as spiritual food for the multitude. Even Francis of Assisi[4] turns himself into a sort of angel-cake, of which anyone may take a slice. But an angel-cake is rather less than man alive. And poor St Francis might well apologise to his body, when he is dying: "Oh, pardon me, my body, the wrong I did you through the years!" It was no wafer,[5] for others to eat.

The philosopher, on the other hand, because he can think, decides that nothing but thoughts matter. It is as if a rabbit, because he can make little pills, should decide that nothing but little pills matter. As for the scientist, he has absolutely no use for me so long as I am man alive. To the scientist, I am dead. He puts under the microscope a bit of dead me, and calls it me. He takes me to pieces, and says first one piece, and then another piece, is me. My heart, my liver, my stomach have all been scientifically me, according to the scientist; and nowadays I am either a brain, or nerves, or glands, or something more up-to-date in the tissue line.

Now I absolutely flatly deny that I am a soul, or a body, or a mind, or an intelligence, or a brain, or a nervous system, or a bunch of glands, or any of the rest of these bits of me. The whole is greater than the part. And therefore, I, who am man alive, am greater than my soul, or spirit, or body, or mind, or consciousness, or anything else that is merely a part of me. I am a man, and alive. I am man alive, and as long as I can, I intend to go on being man alive.

For this reason I am a novelist. And being a novelist, I consider myself superior to the saint, the scientist, the philosopher, and the poet, who are all great masters of different bits of man alive, but never get the whole hog.

The novel is the one bright book of life. Books are not life. They are only tremulations on the ether. But the novel as a tremulation can make the whole man alive tremble. Which is more than poetry, philosophy, science, or any other book-tremulation can do.

The novel is the book of life. In this sense, the Bible is a great confused novel. You may say, it is about God. But it is really about man alive. Adam, Eve, Sarai, Abraham, Isaac, Jacob, Samuel, David, Bath-Sheba, Ruth, Esther, Solomon, Job, Isaiah, Jesus, Mark, Judas, Paul, Peter: what is it but man

4. Roman Catholic saint (1181 or 1182–1226).
5. The Host, consumed as Christ's body in Roman Catholic Communion.

alive, from start to finish? Man alive, not mere bits. Even the Lord is another man alive, in a burning bush, throwing the tablets of stone at Moses's head.

I do hope you begin to get my idea, why the novel is supremely important, as a tremulation on the ether. Plato makes the perfect ideal being tremble in me. But that's only a bit of me. Perfection is only a bit, in the strange makeup of man alive. The Sermon on the Mount[6] makes the selfless spirit of me quiver. But that, too, is only a bit of me. The Ten Commandments set the old Adam shivering in me, warning me that I am a thief and a murderer, unless I watch it. But even the old Adam is only a bit of me.

I very much like all these bits of me to be set trembling with life and the wisdom of life. But I do ask that the whole of me shall tremble in its wholeness, some time or other.

And this, of course, must happen in me, living.

But as far as it can happen from a communication, it can only happen when a whole novel communicates itself to me. The Bible—but *all* the Bible—and Homer, and Shakespeare: these are the supreme old novels. These are all things to all men. Which means that in their wholeness they affect the whole man alive, which is the man himself, beyond any part of him. They set the whole tree trembling with a new access of life, they do not just stimulate growth in one direction.

I don't want to grow in any one direction any more. And, if I can help it, I don't want to stimulate anybody else into some particular direction. A particular direction ends in a *cul-de-sac*. We're in a *cul-de-sac* at present.

I don't believe in any dazzling revelation, or in any supreme Word. "The grass withereth, the flower fadeth, but the Word of the Lord shall stand for ever."[7] That's the kind of stuff we've drugged ourselves with. As a matter of fact, the grass withereth, but comes up all the greener for that reason, after the rains. The flower fadeth, and therefore the bud opens. But the Word of the Lord, being man-uttered and a mere vibration on the ether, becomes staler and staler, more and more boring, till at last we turn a deaf ear and it ceases to exist, far more finally than any withered grass. It is grass that renews its youth like the eagle, not any Word.

We should ask for no absolutes, or absolute. Once and for all and for ever, let us have done with the ugly imperialism of any absolute. There is no absolute good, there is nothing absolutely right. All things flow and change, and even change is not absolute. The whole is a strange assembly of apparently incongruous parts, slipping past one another.

Me, man alive, I am a very curious assembly of incongruous parts. My yea! of today is oddly different from my yea! of yesterday. My tears of to-morrow will have nothing to do with my tears of a year ago. If the one I love remains unchanged and unchanging, I shall cease to love her. It is only because she changes and startles me into change and defies my inertia, and is herself staggered in her inertia by my changing, that I can continue to love her. If she stayed put, I might as well love the pepper pot.

In all this change, I maintain a certain integrity. But woe betide me if I try to put my finger on it. If I say of myself, I am this, I am that!—then, if I stick to it, I turn into a stupid fixed thing like a lamp-post. I shall never know wherein lies my integrity, my individuality, my me. I *can* never know it. It is useless to talk about my ego. That only means that I have made up an *idea*

---

6. See Matthew 5.7. 7. Isaiah 40.8.

of myself, and that I am trying to cut myself out to pattern. Which is no good. You can cut your cloth to fit your coat, but you can't clip bits off your living body, to trim it down to your idea. True, you can put yourself into ideal corsets. But even in ideal corsets, fashions change.

Let us learn from the novel. In the novel, the characters can do nothing but *live*. If they keep on being good, according to pattern, or bad, according to pattern, or even volatile, according to pattern, they cease to live, and the novel falls dead. A character in a novel has got to live, or it is nothing.

We, likewise, in life have got to live, or we are nothing.

What we mean by living is, of course, just as indescribable as what we mean by *being*. Men get ideas into their heads, of what they mean by Life, and they proceed to cut life out to pattern. Sometimes they go into the desert to seek God, sometimes they go into the desert to seek cash, sometimes it is wine, woman, and song, and again it is water, political reform, and votes. You never know what it will be next: from killing your neighbour with hideous bombs and gas that tears the lungs, to supporting a Foundlings' Home[8] and preaching infinite Love, and being co-respondent in a divorce.

In all this wild welter, we need some sort of guide. It's no good inventing Thou Shalt Nots!

What then? Turn truly, honourably to the novel, and see wherein you are man alive, and wherein you are dead man in life. You may love a woman as man alive, and you may be making love to a woman as sheer dead man in life. You may eat your dinner as man alive, or as a mere masticating corpse. As man alive you may have shot at your enemy. But as a ghastly simulacrum of life you may be firing bombs into men who are neither your enemies nor your friends, but just things you are dead to. Which is criminal, when the things happen to be alive.

To be alive, to be man alive, to be whole man alive: that is the point. And at its best, the novel, and the novel supremely, can help you. It can help you not to be dead man in life. So much of a man walks about dead and a carcass in the street and house, to-day: so much of women is merely dead. Like a pianoforte with half the notes mute.

But the novel you can see, plainly, when the man goes dead, the woman goes inert. You can develop an instinct for life, if you will, instead of a theory of right and wrong, good and bad.

In life, there is right and wrong, good and bad, all the time. But what is right in one case is wrong in another. And in the novel you see one man becoming a corpse, because of his so-called goodness, another going dead because of his so-called wickedness. Right and wrong is an instinct: but an instinct of the whole consciousness in a man, bodily, mental, spiritual at once. And only in the novel are *all* things given full play, or at least, they may be given full play, when we realize that life itself, and not inert safety, is the reason for living. For out of the full play of all things emerges the only thing that is anything, the wholeness of a man, the wholeness of a woman, man live, and live woman.

1936

8. Orphanage.

Love on the Farm[1]

What large, dark hands are those at the window
Grasping in the golden light
Which weaves its way through the evening wind
    At my heart's delight?

5   Ah, only the leaves! But in the west
I see a redness suddenly come
Into the evening's anxious breast—
    'Tis the wound of love goes home!

The woodbine° creeps abroad   *honeysuckle*
10   Calling low to her lover:
    The sunlit flirt who all the day
    Has poised above her lips in play
    And stolen kisses, shallow and gay
    Of pollen, now has gone away—
15   She woos the moth with her sweet, low word;
And when above her his moth-wings hover
Then her bright breast she will uncover
And yield her honey-drop to her lover.

Into the yellow, evening glow
20   Saunters a man from the farm below;
Leans, and looks in at the low-built shed
Where the swallow has hung her marriage bed.
    The bird lies warm against the wall.
    She glances quick her startled eyes
25   Towards him, then she turns away
    Her small head, making warm display
    Of red upon the throat. Her terrors sway
    Her out of the nest's warm, busy ball,
    Whose plaintive cry is heard as she flies
30   In one blue stoop from out the sties°   *pens for animals*
    Into the twilight's empty hall.
Oh, water-hen, beside the rushes
Hide your quaintly scarlet blushes,
Still your quick tail, lie still as dead,
35   Till the distance folds over his ominous tread!

The rabbit presses back her ears,
Turns back her liquid, anguished eyes
And crouches low; then with wild spring
Spurts from the terror of *his* oncoming;
40   To be choked back, the wire ring
Her frantic effort throttling:
    Piteous brown ball of quivering fears!
Ah, soon in his large, hard hands she dies,

---

1. Called "Cruelty and Love" when first published in 1913 and "Love on the Farm" when it appeared in *Collected Poems* (1928).

And swings all loose from the swing of his walk!
45 Yet calm and kindly are his eyes
And ready to open in brown surprise
Should I not answer to his talk
Or should he my tears surmise.

I hear his hand on the latch, and rise from my chair
50 Watching the door open; he flashes bare
His strong teeth in a smile, and flashes his eyes
In a smile like triumph upon me; then careless-wise
He flings the rabbit soft on the table board
And comes towards me: ah! the uplifted sword
55 Of his hand against my bosom! and oh, the broad
Blade of his glance that asks me to applaud
His coming! With his hand he turns my face to him
And caresses me with his fingers that still smell grim
Of the rabbit's fur! God, I am caught in a snare!
60 I know not what fine wire is round my throat;
I only know I let him finger there
My pulse of life, and let him nose like a stoat°   *weasel*
Who sniffs with joy before he drinks the blood.

And down his mouth comes to my mouth! and down
65 His bright dark eyes come over me, like a hood
Upon my mind! his lips meet mine, and a flood
Of sweet fire sweeps across me, so I drown
Against him, die, and find death good.

1913, 1928

Piano[1]

Softly, in the dusk, a woman is singing to me;
Taking me back down the vista of years, till I see
A child sitting under the piano, in the boom of the tingling strings
And pressing the small, poised feet of a mother who smiles as she sings.

5 In spite of myself, the insidious mastery of song
Betrays me back, till the heart of me weeps to belong
To the old Sunday evenings at home, with winter outside
And hymns in the cozy parlour, the tinkling piano our guide.

So now it is vain for the singer to burst into clamour
10 With the great black piano appassionato.° The glamour   *played with passion*
Of childish days is upon me, my manhood is cast
Down in the flood of remembrance, I weep like a child for the past.

1918

---

1. For an earlier version of this poem, see "Poems in Process," in the NAEL Archive.

Bavarian Gentians

Not every man has gentians in his house
in soft September, at slow, sad Michaelmas.[1]

Bavarian gentians, big and dark, only dark
darkening the daytime torchlike with the smoking blueness of Pluto's[2]
    gloom,
5 ribbed and torchlike, with their blaze of darkness spread blue
down flattening into points, flattened under the sweep of white day
torch-flower of the blue-smoking darkness, Pluto's dark-blue daze,
black lamps from the halls of Dis, burning dark blue,
giving off darkness, blue darkness, as Demeter's pale lamps give off light,
10 lead me then, lead me the way.

Reach me a gentian, give me a torch
let me guide myself with the blue, forked torch of this flower
down the darker and darker stairs, where blue is darkened on blueness
even where Persephone goes, just now, from the frosted September
15 to the sightless realm where darkness was awake upon the dark
and Persephone herself is but a voice
or a darkness invisible enfolded in the deeper dark
of the arms Plutonic, and pierced with the passion of dense gloom,
among the splendour of torches of darkness, shedding darkness on the lost
    bride and her groom.

1923

Snake

A snake came to my water-trough
On a hot, hot day, and I in pyjamas for the heat,
To drink there.

In the deep, strange-scented shade of the great dark
    carob-tree°   *Mediterranean evergreen*
5 I came down the steps with my pitcher
And must wait, must stand and wait, for there he was at the trough before
    me.

He reached down from a fissure in the earth-wall in the gloom
And trailed his yellow-brown slackness soft-bellied down, over the edge of
    the stone trough
And rested his throat upon the stone bottom,
10 And where the water had dripped from the tap, in a small clearness,

1. September 29, the feast celebrating the Archangel Michael.
2. God of the underworld in classical mythology.
Also called Dis, he abducted Persephone, daughter of the goddess of agriculture, Demeter. Persephone was allowed to return to the earth every
spring, but had to descend again to Hades in the
autumn, "the frosted September" (line 14). Demeter and Persephone were central figures in ancient
fertility myths, where Persephone's annual
descent and return were linked with the death
and rebirth of vegetation.

He sipped with his straight mouth,
Softly drank through his straight gums, into his slack long body,
Silently.

Someone was before me at my water-trough,
15 And I, like a second comer, waiting.

He lifted his head from his drinking, as cattle do,
And looked at me vaguely, as drinking cattle do,
And flickered his two-forked tongue from his lips, and mused a moment,
And stooped and drank a little more,
20 Being earth-brown, earth-golden from the burning bowels of
        the earth
On the day of Sicilian July, with Etna° smoking.   *the volcano*

The voice of my education said to me
He must be killed,
For in Sicily the black, black snakes are innocent, the gold are venomous.

25 And voices in me said, If you were a man
You would take a stick and break him now, and finish him off.

But must I confess how I liked him,
How glad I was he had come like a guest in quiet, to drink at my water-
        trough
And depart peaceful, pacified, and thankless
30 Into the burning bowels of this earth?

Was it cowardice, that I dared not kill him?
Was it perversity, that I longed to talk to him?
Was it humility, to feel so honoured?
I felt so honoured.

35 And yet those voices:
If you were not afraid, you would kill him!

And truly I was afraid, I was most afraid,
But even so, honoured still more
That he should seek my hospitality
40 From out the dark door of the secret earth.

He drank enough
And lifted his head, dreamily, as one who has drunken,
And flickered his tongue like a forked night on the air, so black;
Seeming to lick his lips,
45 And looked around like a god, unseeing, into the air,
And slowly turned his head,
And slowly, very slowly, as if thrice adream
Proceeded to draw his slow length curving round
And climb the broken bank of my wall-face.

50 And as he put his head into that dreadful hole,
And as he slowly drew up, snake-easing his shoulders, and entered farther,

A sort of horror, a sort of protest against his withdrawing into that horrid
    black hole,
Deliberately going into the blackness, and slowly drawing himself after,
Overcame me now his back was turned.

55   I looked round, I put down my pitcher,
I picked up a clumsy log
And threw it at the water-trough with a clatter.

I think it did not hit him;
But suddenly that part of him that was left behind convulsed in undignified
    haste,
60   Writhed like lightning, and was gone
Into the black hole, the earth-lipped fissure in the wall-front
At which, in the intense still noon, I stared with fascination.

And immediately I regretted it.
I thought how paltry, how vulgar, what a mean act!
65   I despised myself and the voices of my accursed human education.

And I thought of the albatross,[1]
And I wished he would come back, my snake.

For he seemed to me again like a king,
Like a king in exile, uncrowned in the underworld,
70   Now due to be crowned again.

And so, I missed my chance with one of the lords
Of life.
And I have something to expiate;
A pettiness.

1923

How Beastly the Bourgeois Is

How beastly the bourgeois is
especially the male of the species—

Presentable, eminently presentable—
shall I make you a present of him?

5   Isn't he handsome? Isn't he healthy? Isn't he a fine specimen?
Doesn't he look the fresh clean englishman, outside?
Isn't it god's own image? tramping his thirty miles a day
after partridges, or a little rubber ball?
wouldn't you like to be like that, well off, and quite the thing?

---

1. In Coleridge's *Rime of the Ancient Mariner.*

10   Oh, but wait!
Let him meet a new emotion, let him be faced with another man's need,
let him come home to a bit of moral difficulty, let life face him with a new
      demand on his understanding
and then watch him go soggy, like a wet meringue.
Watch him turn into a mess, either a fool or a bully.
15   Just watch the display of him, confronted with a new demand on his
      intelligence,
a new life-demand.

How beastly the bourgeois is
especially the male of the species—
Nicely groomed, like a mushroom
20   standing there so sleek and erect and eyeable—
and like a fungus, living on the remains of bygone life
sucking his life out of the dead leaves of greater life than his own.

And even so, he's stale, he's been there too long.
Touch him, and you'll find he's all gone inside
25   just like an old mushroom, all wormy inside, and hollow
under a smooth skin and an upright appearance.

Full of seething, wormy, hollow feelings
rather nasty—
How beastly the bourgeois is!

30   Standing in their thousands, these appearances, in damp England
what a pity they can't all be kicked over
like sickening toadstools, and left to melt back, swiftly
into the soil of England.

                                       1929

The Ship of Death[1]

I

Now it is autumn and the falling fruit
and the long journey towards oblivion.

The apples falling like great drops of dew
to bruise themselves an exit from themselves.

5   And it is time to go, to bid farewell
to one's own self, and find an exit
from the fallen self.

---

1. Lawrence is remembering "the sacred treasures of the dead, the little bronze ship of death
that should bear him over to the other world," found in Etruscan tombs and described in his
book *Etruscan Places* (1932).

II

Have you built your ship of death, O have you?
O build your ship of death, for you will need it.

10   The grim frost is at hand, when the apples will fall
thick, almost thundrous, on the hardened earth.

And death is on the air like a smell of ashes!
Ah! can't you smell it?

And in the bruised body, the frightened soul
15   finds itself shrinking, wincing from the cold
that blows upon it through the orifices.

III

And can a man his own quietus make
with a bare bodkin?[2]

With daggers, bodkins, bullets, man can make
20   a bruise or break of exit for his life;
but is that a quietus, O tell me, is it quietus?

Surely not so! for how could murder, even self-murder
ever a quietus make?

IV

O let us talk of quiet that we know,
25   that we can know, the deep and lovely quiet
of a strong heart at peace!

How can we this, our own quietus, make?

V

Build then the ship of death, for you must take
the longest journey, to oblivion.

30   And die the death, the long and painful death
that lies between the old self and the new.

Already our bodies are fallen, bruised, badly bruised,
already our souls are oozing through the exit
of the cruel bruise.

35   Already the dark and endless ocean of the end
is washing in through the breaches of our wounds,
already the flood is upon us.

2. Cf. Shakespeare's *Hamlet* 3.1.70–76: "For who would bear the whips and scorns of time, / . . . When he himself might his quietus make / With a bare bodkin?" ("Bodkin": dagger.)

Oh build your ship of death, your little ark
and furnish it with food, with little cakes, and wine
40   for the dark flight down oblivion.

VI

Piecemeal the body dies, and the timid soul
has her footing washed away, as the dark flood rises.

We are dying, we are dying, we are all of us dying
and nothing will stay the death-flood rising within us
45   and soon it will rise on the world, on the outside world.

We are dying, we are dying, piecemeal our bodies are dying
and our strength leaves us,
and our soul cowers naked in the dark rain over the flood,
cowering in the last branches of the tree of our life.

VII

50   We are dying, we are dying, so all we can do
is now to be willing to die, and to build the ship
of death to carry the soul on the longest journey.

A little ship, with oars and food
and little dishes, and all accoutrements
55   fitting and ready for the departing soul.

Now launch the small ship, now as the body dies
and life departs, launch out, the fragile soul
in the fragile ship of courage, the ark of faith
with its store of food and little cooking pans
60   and change of clothes,
upon the flood's black waste
upon the waters of the end
upon the sea of death, where still we sail
darkly, for we cannot steer, and have no port.

65   There is no port, there is nowhere to go
only the deepening blackness darkening still
blacker upon the soundless, ungurgling flood
darkness at one with darkness, up and down
and sideways utterly dark, so there is no direction any more
70   and the little ship is there; yet she is gone.
She is not seen, for there is nothing to see her by.
She is gone! gone! and yet
somewhere she is there.
Nowhere!

VIII

75 And everything is gone, the body is gone
completely under, gone, entirely gone.
The upper darkness is heavy as the lower,
between them the little ship
is gone
80 she is gone.

It is the end, it is oblivion.

IX

And yet out of eternity a thread
separates itself on the blackness,
a horizontal thread
85 that fumes a little with pallor upon the dark.

Is it illusion? or does the pallor fume
A little higher?
Ah wait, wait, for there's the dawn,
the cruel dawn of coming back to life
90 out of oblivion.

Wait, wait, the little ship
drifting, beneath the deathly ashy grey
of a flood-dawn.

Wait, wait! even so, a flush of yellow
95 and strangely, O chilled wan soul, a flush of rose.

A flush of rose, and the whole thing starts again.

X

The flood subsides, and the body, like a worn sea-shell
emerges strange and lovely.
And the little ship wings home, faltering and lapsing
100 on the pink flood,
and the frail soul steps out, into her house again
filling the heart with peace.

Swings the heart renewed with peace
even of oblivion.

105 Oh build your ship of death, oh build it!
for you will need it.
For the voyage of oblivion awaits you.

1929–30   1933

T. S. ELIOT

1888–1965

Thomas Stearns Eliot was born in St. Louis, Missouri, of New England stock. He entered Harvard in 1906 and was influenced there by the anti-Romanticism of Irving Babbitt and the philosophical and critical interests of George Santayana, as well as by the enthusiastic study of Renaissance literature and of South Asian religions. He wrote his Harvard dissertation on the English idealist philosopher F. H. Bradley, whose emphasis on the private nature of individual experience, "a circle enclosed on the outside," influenced Eliot's poetry considerably. He also studied literature and philosophy in France and Germany before going to England shortly after the outbreak of World War I in 1914. He studied Greek philosophy at Oxford, taught school in London, and then obtained a position with Lloyds Bank. In 1915 he married an English writer, Vivienne Haigh-Wood, but the marriage was not a success. She suffered from poor emotional and physical health. The strain told on Eliot, too. By November 1921 distress and worry had brought him to the verge of a nervous breakdown, and on medical advice he went to recuperate in a Swiss sanitorium. Two months later he returned, pausing in Paris long enough to give his early supporter and adviser Ezra Pound the manuscript of *The Waste Land*. Eliot left his wife in 1933, and she was eventually committed to a psychiatric hospital, where she died in 1947. Ten years later he was happily remarried to his secretary, Valerie Fletcher.

Eliot started writing literary and philosophical reviews soon after settling in London and was assistant editor of *The Egoist* magazine from 1917 to 1919. In 1922 he founded the influential quarterly *The Criterion*, which he edited until it ceased publication in 1939. His poetry first appeared in 1915, when, at Pound's urging, "The Love Song of J. Alfred Prufrock" was printed in *Poetry* magazine (Chicago), and a few other short poems were published in the short-lived periodical *Blast*. His first published collection of poems was *Prufrock and Other Observations* (1917); two other small collections followed in 1919 and 1920; in 1922 *The Waste Land* appeared, first in *The Criterion* in October, then in *The Dial* (in America) in November, and finally in book form. Meanwhile he was also publishing collections of his critical essays. In 1925 he joined the London publishing firm Faber & Gwyer, and he was made a director when the firm was renamed Faber & Faber. He became a British subject and joined the Church of England in 1927.

"Our civilization comprehends great variety and complexity, and this variety and complexity, playing upon a refined sensibility, must produce various and complex results. The poet must become more and more comprehensive, more allusive, more indirect, in order to force, to dislocate if necessary, language into his meaning." This remark, from Eliot's essay "The Metaphysical Poets" (1921), gives one clue to his poetic method from "Prufrock" through *The Waste Land*. When he settled in London he saw poetry in English as exhausted, with no verbal excitement or original craftsmanship. He sought to make poetry more subtle, more suggestive, and at the same time more precise. Like the imagists, he emphasized the necessity of clear and precise images. From the philosopher poet T. E. Hulme and from Pound, he learned to fear what was seen as Romantic self-indulgence and vagueness, and to regard the poetic medium rather than the poet's personality as the important factor. At the same time the "hard, dry" images advocated by Hulme were not enough for him; he wanted wit, allusiveness, irony. He saw in the Metaphysical poets how wit and passion could be combined, and he saw in the French symbolists, such as Charles Baudelaire, Stéphane Mallarmé, Paul Verlaine, and Arthur Rimbaud, how an image could be both absolutely precise in what it referred to physically and endlessly suggestive in its meanings because of its relationship to other images. The combination of precision, symbolic suggestion, and ironic mockery in the poetry of the late-nineteenth-century French poet Jules Laforgue attracted and influenced him, as did Laforgue's verse technique that Eliot described in an interview as "rhyming lines of irregular length, with the rhymes coming in irregular places." He also found in the Jacobean dramatists, such as Thomas Middleton, Cyril Tourneur, and John Webster, a flexible blank verse with overtones of colloquial movement, a way of counterpointing the accent of conversation and the note of terror. Eliot's fluency in French and German, his study of Western and non-Western literary and religious texts in their original languages, his rigorous knowledge of philosophy, his exacting critical intellect, his keen sensitivity to colloquial rhythm and idiom, his ability to fuse anguished emotional states with sharply etched intellectual satire—all of these contributed to his crafting one of the twentieth century's most distinctive and influential bodies of poetry.

Hulme's protests against the Romantic concept of poetry reinforced what Eliot had learned from Babbitt at Harvard; yet for all his severity with poets such as Percy Shelley and Walt Whitman, for all his cultivation of a classical viewpoint and his insistence on order and discipline rather than on mere self-expression in art, one side of Eliot's poetic genius is Romantic. The symbolist influence on his imagery, his elegiac lamentation over loss and fragmentation, his interest in the evocative and the suggestive, lines such as "And fiddled whisper music on those strings / And bats with baby faces in the violet light / Whistled, and beat their wings," and recurring images such as the hyacinth girl and the rose garden show what could be called a Romantic element in his poetry. But it is combined with a dry ironic allusiveness, a play of wit and satire, and a colloquial element, which are not normally found in poets of the Romantic tradition.

Eliot's real novelty—and the cause of much bewilderment when his poems first appeared—was his deliberate elimination of all merely connective and transitional passages, his building up of the total pattern of meaning through the immediate juxtaposition of images without overt explanation of what they are doing, together with his use of oblique references to other works of literature (some of them quite obscure to most readers of his time). "Prufrock" presents a symbolic landscape where the meaning emerges from the mutual interaction of the images, and that meaning is enlarged by echoes, often ironic, of Hesiod and Dante and Shakespeare. *The Waste Land* is a series of scenes and images with no author's voice intervening to tell us where we are but with the implications developed through multiple contrasts and through analogies with older literary works often referred to in a distorted quotation or half-concealed allusion. Furthermore, the works referred to are not necessarily central in the Western literary tradition: besides Dante and Shakespeare there are pre-Socratic philosophers; major and minor seventeenth-century poets and dramatists; works of anthropology, history, and philosophy; texts of Buddhism and Hinduism; even popular songs and vaudeville. Ancient and modern voices, high and low art, Western and non-Western languages clash, coincide, jostle alongside one another. In a culture where the poet's public might lack a common cultural heritage, a shared knowledge of works of the past, Eliot felt it necessary to accumulate his own body of references. In this his use of earlier literature differs from, say, John Milton's. Both poets are difficult for the modern reader, who needs editorial assistance in recognizing and understanding many of the allusions—but Milton was drawing on a body of knowledge common to educated people in his day. Nevertheless, this aspect of Eliot can be exaggerated; his imagery and the movement of his verse set the tone he requires, establish the area of meaning to be developed, so that even a reader ignorant of most of the literary allusions can often get the feel of the poem and achieve some understanding of what it says.

Eliot's early poetry, until at least the middle 1920s, is mostly concerned in one way or another with the Waste Land, with aspects of cultural decay in the modern Western world. After his formal acceptance of Anglican Christianity, a penitential note appears in much of his verse, a note of quiet searching for spiritual peace, with considerable allusion to biblical, liturgical, and mystical religious literature and to Dante. *Ash Wednesday* (1930), a poem in six parts, much less fiercely concentrated in style than the earlier poetry, explores with gentle insistence a mood both penitential and questioning. The Ariel poems (so called because published in Faber's Ariel pamphlet series) present or explore aspects of religious doubt or discovery or revelation, sometimes, as in "Journey of the Magi," drawing on biblical incident. In *Four Quartets* (of which the first, "Burnt Norton," appeared in the *Collected Poems* of 1936, though all four were not completed until 1943, when they were published together), Eliot further explored essentially religious moods, dealing with the relation between time and eternity and the cultivation of that selfless passivity that can yield the moment of timeless revelation in the midst of time. The mocking irony, the savage humor, the collage of quotations, the deliberately startling juxtaposition of the sordid and the romantic give way in these later poems to a quieter poetic idiom that is less jagged and more abstract, less fragmentary and more formally patterned.

As a critic Eliot worked out in his reading of older literature what he needed as a poet to hold and to admire. He lent the growing weight of his authority to a shift in literary taste that replaced Milton with John Donne as the great seventeenth-century English poet and replaced Alfred, Lord Tennyson in the nineteenth century with Gerard Manley Hopkins. Rewriting English literary history, he saw the late-seventeenth-century "dissociation of sensibility"—the segregation of intellect and emotion—as determining the course of English poetry throughout the eighteenth and nineteenth centuries. This theory also explained what he was aiming at in his own poetry: the reestablishment of that *unified* sensibility he found in Donne and other early seventeenth-century poets and dramatists, who were able, he suggests in "The Metaphysical Poets," to "feel their thought as immediately as the odour of a rose." His view of tradition, his dislike of the poetic exploitation of the author's personality, his advocacy of what he called "orthodoxy," made him suspicious of what he considered eccentric geniuses such as William Blake and D. H. Lawrence. On the other side, his dislike of the grandiloquent and his insistence on complexity and on the mingling of the formal with the conversational made him distrust Milton's influence on English poetry. He considered himself a "classicist in literature, royalist in politics, and Anglo-Catholic in religion" (*For Lancelot Andrewes*, 1928), in favor of order against chaos, tradition against eccentricity, authority against rampant individualism; yet his own poetry is in many respects untraditional and certainly highly individual in tone. His conservative and even authoritarian habit of mind, his anti-Semitic remarks and missionary zeal, alienated some who admire—and some whose own poetry has been much influenced by—his poetry.

Eliot's plays address, directly or indirectly, religious themes. *Murder in the Cathedral* (1935) deals in an appropriately ritual manner with the killing of Archbishop Thomas à Becket, using a chorus and presenting its central speech as a sermon by the archbishop. *The Family Reunion* (1939) deals with the problem of guilt and redemption in a modern upper-class English family; combining choric devices from Greek tragedy with a poetic idiom subdued to the accents of drawing-room conversation. In his three later plays, all written in the 1950s, *The Cocktail Party*, *The Confidential Clerk*, and *The Elder Statesman*, he achieved popular success by casting a serious religious theme in the form of a sophisticated modern social comedy, using a verse that is so conversational in movement that when spoken in the theater it does not sound like verse at all.

Critics differ on the degree to which Eliot succeeded in his last plays in combining box-office success with dramatic effectiveness. But there is no disagreement on his importance as one of the great renovators of poetry in English, whose influence on a whole generation of poets, critics, and intellectuals was enormous. His range as a poet is limited, and his interest in the great middle ground of human experience (as distinct from the extremes of saint and sinner) deficient; but when in 1948 he was awarded the rare honor of the Order of Merit by King George VI and also gained the Nobel Prize in literature, his positive qualities were widely and fully recognized—his poetic cunning, his fine craftsmanship, his original accent, his historical importance as *the* poet of the modern symbolist-Metaphysical tradition.

The Love Song of J. Alfred Prufrock

> *S'io credesse che mia risposta fosse*
> *a persona che mai tornasse al mondo,*
> *questa fiamma staria senza più scosse.*
> *Ma per ciò che giammai di questo fondo*
> *non tornò vivo alcun, s'i'odo il vero,*
> *senza tema d'infamia ti rispondo.*[1]

Let us go then, you and I,
When the evening is spread out against the sky
Like a patient etherised upon a table;
Let us go, through certain half-deserted streets,
5   The muttering retreats
Of restless nights in one-night cheap hotels
And sawdust restaurants with oyster shells:
Streets that follow like a tedious argument
Of insidious intent
10   To lead you to an overwhelming question . . .
Oh, do not ask, 'What is it?'
Let us go and make our visit.

In the room the women come and go
Talking of Michelangelo.

15   The yellow fog that rubs its back upon the window-panes,
The yellow smoke that rubs its muzzle on the window-panes
Licked its tongue into the corners of the evening,
Lingered upon the pools that stand in drains,
Let fall upon its back the soot that falls from chimneys,
20   Slipped by the terrace, made a sudden leap,
And seeing that it was a soft October night,
Curled once about the house, and fell asleep.

And indeed there will be time[2]
For the yellow smoke that slides along the street,
25   Rubbing its back upon the window-panes;
There will be time, there will be time
To prepare a face to meet the faces that you meet;

1. "If I thought that my reply would be to one who would ever return to the world, this flame would stay without further movement; but since none has ever returned alive from this depth, if what I hear is true, I answer you without fear of infamy" (Dante, *Inferno* 27.61–66). Guido da Montefeltro, shut up in his flame (the punishment given to false counselors), tells the shame of his evil life to Dante because he believes Dante will never return to earth to report it.
2. Cf. Andrew Marvell, "To His Coy Mistress," line 1: "Had we but world enough, and time."

There will be time to murder and create,
And time for all the works and days of hands[3]
30 That lift and drop a question on your plate;
Time for you and time for me,
And time yet for a hundred indecisions,
And for a hundred visions and revisions,
Before the taking of a toast and tea.

35 In the room the women come and go
Talking of Michelangelo.

And indeed there will be time
To wonder, 'Do I dare?' and, 'Do I dare?'
Time to turn back and descend the stair,
40 With a bald spot in the middle of my hair—
(They will say: 'How his hair is growing thin!')
My morning coat, my collar mounting firmly to the chin,
My necktie rich and modest, but asserted by a simple pin—
(They will say: 'But how his arms and legs are thin!')
45 Do I dare
Disturb the universe?
In a minute there is time
For decisions and revisions which a minute will reverse.

For I have known them all already, known them all—
50 Have known the evenings, mornings, afternoons,
I have measured out my life with coffee spoons;
I know the voices dying with a dying fall[4]
Beneath the music from a farther room.
     So how should I presume?

55 And I have known the eyes already, known them all—
The eyes that fix you in a formulated phrase,
And when I am formulated, sprawling on a pin,
When I am pinned and wriggling on the wall,
Then how should I begin
60 To spit out all the butt-ends of my days and ways?
     And how should I presume?

And I have known the arms already, known them all—
Arms that are braceleted and white and bare
(But in the lamplight, downed with light brown hair!)
65 Is it perfume from a dress
That makes me so digress?
Arms that lie along a table, or wrap about a shawl.
     And should I then presume?
     And how should I begin?

•   •   •   •   •

3. *Works and Days* is a poem about the farming
year by the Greek poet Hesiod (8th century
B.C.E.). Eliot contrasts useful agricultural labor
with the futile "works and days of hands"
engaged in meaningless social gesturing.
4. Cf. Shakespeare's *Twelfth Night* 1.1.4: "That
strain again, it had a dying fall."

70 Shall I say, I have gone at dusk through narrow streets
And watched the smoke that rises from the pipes
Of lonely men in shirt-sleeves, leaning out of windows? . . .
I should have been a pair of ragged claws
Scuttling across the floors of silent seas,[5]

•   •   •   •   •

75 And the afternoon, the evening, sleeps so peacefully!
Smoothed by long fingers,
Asleep . . . tired . . . or it malingers,
Stretched on the floor, here beside you and me.
Should I, after tea and cakes and ices,
80 Have the strength to force the moment to its crisis?
But though I have wept and fasted, wept and prayed,
Though I have seen my head (grown slightly bald) brought in upon a
    platter,[6]
I am no prophet—and here's no great matter;
I have seen the moment of my greatness flicker,
85 And I have seen the eternal Footman hold my coat, and snicker,
And in short, I was afraid.

And would it have been worth it, after all,
After the cups, the marmalade, the tea,
Among the porcelain, among some talk of you and me,
90 Would it have been worth while,
To have bitten off the matter with a smile,
To have squeezed the universe into a ball[7]
To roll it toward some overwhelming question,
To say: 'I am Lazarus,[8] come from the dead,
95 Come back to tell you all, I shall tell you all'—
If one, settling a pillow by her head,
    Should say: 'That is not what I meant at all.
    That is not it, at all.'

And would it have been worth it, after all,
100 Would it have been worth while,
After the sunsets and the dooryards and the sprinkled streets,
After the novels, after the teacups, after the skirts that trail along the
    floor—
And this, and so much more?—
It is impossible to say just what I mean!
105 But as if a magic lantern threw the nerves in patterns on a screen:
Would it have been worth while
If one, settling a pillow or throwing off a shawl,
And turning toward the window, should say:
    'That is not it at all,
110 That is not what I meant, at all.'

•   •   •   •   •

---

5. I.e., he would have been better as a crab on the ocean bed.
6. Like that of John the Baptist. See Mark 6.17–28 and Matthew 14.3–11.
7. Cf. "To His Coy Mistress," lines 41–44: "Let us roll all our strength and all / Our sweetness up into one ball, / And tear our pleasures with rough strife / Thorough the iron gates of life."
8. One Lazarus was raised by Jesus from the dead (John 11.1–44). In a parable, a different Lazarus is a beggar who goes to heaven, in contrast to a rich man who goes to hell. The rich man wishes

No! I am not Prince Hamlet, nor was meant to be;
Am an attendant lord, one that will do
To swell a progress,[9] start a scene or two,
Advise the prince; no doubt, an easy tool,
115   Deferential, glad to be of use,
Politic, cautious, and meticulous;
Full of high sentence,[1] but a bit obtuse;
At times, indeed, almost ridiculous—
Almost, at times, the Fool.

120   I grow old . . . I grow old . . .
I shall wear the bottoms of my trousers rolled.

Shall I part my hair behind? Do I dare to eat a peach?
I shall wear white flannel trousers, and walk upon the beach.
I have heard the mermaids, singing, each to each.

125   I do not think that they will sing to me.

I have seen them riding seaward on the waves
Combing the white hair of the waves blown back
When the wind blows the water white and black.

We have lingered in the chambers of the sea
130   By sea-girls wreathed with seaweed red and brown
Till human voices wake us, and we drown.

1910–11   1915, 1917

Sweeney among the Nightingales

ὤμοι, πέπληγμαι καιρίαν πληγὴν ἔσω[1]

Apeneck Sweeney spreads his knees
Letting his arms hang down to laugh,
The zebra stripes along his jaw
Swelling to maculate° giraffe.   *spotted, stained*

5   The circles of the stormy moon
Slide westward toward the River Plate,[2]
Death and the Raven[3] drift above
And Sweeney guards the hornèd gate.[4]

Lazarus could return from the dead to warn the living, but his wish is refused (Luke 16.19–31).
9. In the Elizabethan sense of a state journey made by a royal or noble person. Elizabethan plays sometimes showed such "progresses" crossing the stage.
1. In its older meanings: "opinions," "sententiousness." Cf. Chaucer's *General Prologue* to *The Canterbury Tales*, line 308.
1. "Alas, I am struck with a mortal blow within"

(Aeschylus, *Agamemnon*, line 1343); the voice of Agamemnon heard crying out from the palace as he is murdered by his wife, Clytemnestra.
2. Or Rio de la Plata, an estuary on the South American coast between Argentina and Uruguay, formed by the Uruguay and Paraná rivers.
3. The constellation Corvus.
4. The gates of horn, in Hades, through which true dreams come to the upper world.

Gloomy Orion and the Dog
10 Are veiled;[5] and hushed the shrunken seas;
The person in the Spanish cape
Tries to sit on Sweeney's knees

Slips and pulls the table cloth
Overturns a coffee-cup,
15 Reorganized upon the floor
She yawns and draws a stocking up;

The silent man in mocha brown
Sprawls at the window-sill and gapes;
The waiter brings in oranges
20 Bananas figs and hothouse grapes;

The silent vertebrate in brown
Contracts and concentrates, withdraws;
Rachel *née* Rabinovitch
Tears at the grapes with murderous paws;

25 She and the lady in the cape
Are suspect, thought to be in league;
Therefore the man with heavy eyes
Declines the gambit, shows fatigue,

Leaves the room and reappears
30 Outside the window, leaning in,
Branches of wistaria
Circumscribe a golden grin;

The host with someone indistinct
Converses at the door apart,
35 The nightingales are singing near
The Convent of the Sacred Heart,

And sang within the bloody wood
When Agamemnon cried aloud[6]
And let their liquid sittings fall
40 To stain the stiff dishonoured shroud.

1918, 1919

5. For Sweeney and his female friend, the gate
of vision is blocked and the great myth-making
constellations—"Orion and the Dog"—are
"veiled."
6. Agamemnon is murdered not in a "bloody
wood" but in his bath. Eliot here telescopes
Agamemnon's murder with the wood where, in

Greek myth, Philomela was raped by her sister's
husband, Tereus (she was subsequently turned
into a nightingale), and also with the ancient
"bloody wood" of Nemi, where the old priest was
slain by his successor (as described in the first
chapter of Sir James Frazer's *Golden Bough*).

The Waste Land

In the essay "*Ulysses*, Order, and Myth" (1923), Eliot hinted at the ambitions of *The Waste Land* when he declared that others would follow James Joyce "in manipulating a continuous parallel between contemporaneity and antiquity. . . . It is simply a way of controlling, of ordering, of giving a shape and a significance to the immense panorama of futility and anarchy which is contemporary history. . . . It is, I seriously believe, a step toward making the modern world possible in art." Eliot labeled this new technique "the mythical method."

He gave another clue to the theme and structure of *The Waste Land* in a general note, in which he stated that "not only the title, but the plan and a good deal of the symbolism of the poem were suggested by Miss Jessie L. Weston's book on the Grail legend: *From Ritual to Romance* [1920]." He further acknowledged a general indebtedness to Sir James Frazer's *Golden Bough* (thirteen volumes, 1890–1915), "especially the . . . volumes *Adonis, Attis, Osiris*," in which Frazer deals with ancient vegetation myths and fertility ceremonies. Drawing on material from Frazer and other anthropologists, Weston traces the relationship of these myths and rituals to Christianity and especially to the legend of the Holy Grail. She finds an archetypal fertility myth in the story of the Fisher King, whose death, infirmity, or impotence (there are many forms of the myth) brought drought and desolation to the land and failure of the power to reproduce themselves among both humans and beasts. This symbolic Waste Land can be revived only if a "questing knight" goes to the Chapel Perilous, situated in the heart of it, and there asks certain ritual questions about the Grail (or Cup) and the Lance—originally fertility symbols, female and male, respectively. The proper asking of these questions revives the king and restores fertility to the land. The relation of this original Grail myth to fertility cults and rituals found in many different civilizations, and represented by stories of a god who dies and is later resurrected (e.g., Tammuz, Adonis, Attis), shows their common origin in a response to the cyclical movement of the seasons, with vegetation dying in winter to be resurrected again in the spring. Christianity, according to Weston, gave its own spiritual meaning to the myth; it "did not hesitate to utilize the already existing medium of instruction, but boldly identified the Deity of Vegetation, regarded as Life Principle, with the God of the Christian Faith." The Fisher King is related to the use of the fish symbol in early Christianity. Weston states "with certainty that the Fish is a Life symbol of immemorial antiquity, and that the title of Fisher has, from the earliest ages, been associated with the Deities who were held to be specially connected with the origin and preservation of Life." Eliot, following Weston, thus uses a great variety of mythological and religious material, both Western and Eastern, to paint a symbolic picture of the modern Waste Land and the need for regeneration. He vividly presents the terror of that desiccated life—its loneliness, emptiness, and irrational apprehensions—as well as its misuse of sexuality, but he paradoxically ends the poem with a benediction. The mass death and social collapse of World War I inform the poem's vision of a Waste Land strewn with corpses, wreckage, and ruin. Another significant general source for the poem is the German composer Richard Wagner's operas *Götterdämmerung* (*Twilight of the Gods*), *Parsifal*, *Das Rheingold*, and *Tristan und Isolde*.

The poem as published owes a great deal to the severe pruning by Ezra Pound; the original manuscript, with Pound's excisions and comments, provides fascinating information about the genesis and development of the poem, and was reproduced in facsimile in 1971, edited by Eliot's widow, Valerie Eliot. Reprinted below is the text as first published in book form in December 1922, including Eliot's notes, which are supplemented by the present editors' notes.

The Waste Land

"NAM Sibyllam quidem Cumis ego ipse oculis meis vidi in ampulla pendere, et cum illi pueri dicerent: Σίβυλλα τί θέλεις; respondebat illa: ἀποθανεῖν θέλω."[1]

FOR EZRA POUND
il miglior fabbro[2]

I. The Burial of the Dead[3]

April is the cruellest month, breeding
Lilacs out of the dead land, mixing
Memory and desire, stirring
Dull roots with spring rain.
5   Winter kept us warm, covering
Earth in forgetful snow, feeding
A little life with dried tubers.
Summer surprised us, coming over the Starnbergersee[4]
With a shower of rain; we stopped in the colonnade,
10   And went on in sunlight, into the Hofgarten,[5]
And drank coffee, and talked for an hour.
Bin gar keine Russin, stamm' aus Litauen, echt deutsch.[6]
And when we were children, staying at the archduke's,
My cousin's, he took me out on a sled,
15   And I was frightened. He said, Marie,
Marie, hold on tight. And down we went.
In the mountains, there you feel free.
I read, much of the night, and go south in the winter.

What are the roots that clutch, what branches grow
20   Out of this stony rubbish? Son of man,[7]
You cannot say, or guess, for you know only
A heap of broken images, where the sun beats,
And the dead tree gives no shelter, the cricket no relief,[8]

1. From the *Satyricon* of Petronius (1st century C.E.): "For once I myself saw with my own eyes the Sibyl at Cumae hanging in a cage, and when the boys said to her 'Sibyl, what do you want?' she replied, 'I want to die.'" (The Greek may be transliterated, "Síbylla tí théleis?" and "apothanéin thélo.") The Cumaean Sibyl was the most famous of the Sibyls, the prophetic old women of Greek mythology; she guided Aeneas through Hades in Virgil's *Aeneid*. She had been granted immortality by Apollo, but because she forgot to ask for perpetual youth, she shrank into withered old age and her authority declined.
2. The better craftsman (Italian); a tribute originally paid to the Provençal poet Arnaut Daniel in Dante's *Purgatorio* 26.117. Ezra Pound (1885–1972), American expatriate poet who was a key figure in the modern movement in poetry, helped Eliot massively revise the manuscript.
3. The title comes from the Anglican burial service.
4. Lake a few miles south of Munich, where the "mad" King Ludwig II of Bavaria drowned in 1886 in mysterious circumstances. This romantic, melancholy king passionately admired Rich-

ard Wagner and especially Wagner's opera *Tristan und Isolde*, which plays a significant part in The Waste Land. Ludwig's suffering of "death by water" in the Starnbergersee thus evokes a cluster of themes central to the poem. Eliot had met King Ludwig's second cousin Countess Marie Larisch and talked with her. Although he had probably not read the countess's book *My Past*, which discusses King Ludwig at length, he got information about her life and times from her in person, and the remarks made in lines 8–18 are hers.
5. A small public park in Munich.
6. I am not Russian at all; I come from Lithuania, a true German (German).
7. Cf. Ezekiel II, i [Eliot's note]. God, addressing Ezekiel, continues: "stand upon thy feet, and I will speak unto thee."
8. Cf. Ecclesiastes XII, v [Eliot's note]. The verse Eliot cites is part of the preacher's picture of the desolation of old age, "when they shall be afraid of that which is high, and fears shall be in the way and the almond tree shall flourish, and the grasshopper shall be a burden, and desire shall fail."

And the dry stone no sound of water. Only
25 There is shadow under this red rock,[9]
(Come in under the shadow of this red rock),
And I will show you something different from either
Your shadow at morning striding behind you
Or your shadow at evening rising to meet you;
30 I will show you fear in a handful of dust.

> Frisch weht der Wind
> Der Heimat zu,
> Mein Irisch Kind,
> Wo weilest du?[1]

35 "You gave me hyacinths first a year ago;
"They called me the hyacinth girl."
—Yet when we came back, late, from the Hyacinth[2] garden,
Yours arms full, and your hair wet, I could not
Speak, and my eyes failed, I was neither
40 Living nor dead, and I knew nothing,
Looking into the heart of light, the silence.
Oed' und leer das Meer.[3]

Madame Sosostris,[4] famous clairvoyante,
Had a bad cold, nevertheless
45 Is known to be the wisest woman in Europe,
With a wicked pack of cards.[5] Here, said she,
Is your card, the drowned Phoenician Sailor,[6]
(Those are pearls that were his eyes. Look!)

---

9. Cf. Isaiah 32.2: the "righteous king" "shall be . . . as rivers of water in a dry place, as the shadow of a great rock in a weary land."

1. V. [see] *Tristan und Isolde*, I, verses 5–8 [Eliot's note]. In Wagner's opera a sailor recalls the girl he has left behind: "Fresh blows the wind to the homeland; my Irish child, where are you waiting?"

2. Name of a young man loved and accidentally killed by Apollo in Greek mythology; from his blood sprang the flower named for him, inscribed with "AI," a cry of grief.

3. Id. [Ibid] III, verse 24 [Eliot's note]. In act 3 of *Tristan und Isolde*, Tristan lies dying. He is waiting for Isolde to come to him from Cornwall, but a shepherd, appointed to watch for her sail, can report only, "Waste and empty is the sea." *Oed'* (or *Öd'*) was originally misspelled *Od'*.

4. A mock Egyptian name (suggested to Eliot by "Sesostris, the Sorceress of Ecbatana," the name assumed by a character in Aldous Huxley's novel *Crome Yellow* [1921] who dresses up as a gypsy to tell fortunes at a fair).

5. I.e., the deck of Tarot cards. The four suits of the Tarot pack, discussed by Jessie Weston in *From Ritual to Romance*, are the cup, lance, sword, and dish—the life symbols found in the Grail story. Weston noted that "today the Tarot has fallen somewhat into disrepute, being principally used for purposes of divination." Some of the cards mentioned in lines 46–56 are discussed by Eliot in his note to this passage:

"I am not familiar with the exact constitution of the Tarot pack of cards, from which I have obviously departed to suit my own convenience. The Hanged Man, a member of the traditional pack, fits my purpose in two ways: because he is associated in my mind with the Hanged God of Frazer, and because I associate him with the hooded figure in the passage of the disciples to Emmaus in part V. The Phoenician Sailor and the Merchant appear later; also the 'crowds of people,' and Death by Water is executed in part IV. The Man with Three Staves (an authentic member of the Tarot pack) I associate, quite arbitrarily, with the Fisher King himself."

6. See part IV. Phlebas the Phoenician and Mr. Eugenides, the Smyrna merchant—both of whom appear later in the poem—are different phases of the same symbolic character, here identified as the "Phoenician Sailor." Mr. Eugenides exports "currants" (line 210); the drowned Phlebas floats in the "current" (line 315). Line 48 draws from Ariel's song in Shakespeare's *The Tempest* (1.2.400–08) to the shipwrecked Ferdinand, who was "sitting on a bank / Weeping again the King my father's wrack," when "this music crept by me on the waters." The song is about the supposed drowning of Ferdinand's father, Alonso. *The Waste Land* contains many references to *The Tempest*. Ferdinand is associated with Phlebas and Mr. Eugenides and, therefore, with the "drowned Phoenician Sailor."

Here is Belladonna,[7] the Lady of the Rocks,
50 The lady of situations.
Here is the man with three staves, and here the Wheel,[8]
And here is the one-eyed merchant,[9] and this card,
Which is blank, is something he carries on his back,
Which I am forbidden to see. I do not find
55 The Hanged Man.[1] Fear death by water.
I see crowds of people, walking round in a ring.
Thank you. If you see dear Mrs. Equitone,
Tell her I bring the horoscope myself:
One must be so careful these days.

60 Unreal City.[2]
Under the brown fog of a winter dawn,
A crowd flowed over London Bridge, so many,[3]
I had not thought death had undone so many.
Sighs, short and infrequent, were exhaled,[4]
65 And each man fixed his eyes before his feet.
Flowed up the hill and down King William Street,
To where Saint Mary Woolnoth kept the hours
With a dead sound on the final stroke of nine.[5]
There I saw one I knew, and stopped him, crying: "Stetson![6]
70 "You who were with me in the ships at Mylae![7]
"That corpse you planted last year in your garden,
"Has it begun to sprout?[8] Will it bloom this year?
"Or has the sudden frost disturbed its bed?
"Oh keep the Dog far hence, that's friend to men,
75 "Or with his nails he'll dig it up again![9]
"You! hypocrite lecteur!—mon semblable—mon frère!"[1]

---

7. Beautiful lady (Italian). The word also suggests Madonna (the Virgin Mary) and, therefore, the Madonna of the Rocks (as in Leonardo da Vinci's painting); the rocks symbolize the Church. Belladonna is also an eye cosmetic and a poison—the deadly nightshade.
8. I.e., the wheel of fortune, whose turning represents the reversals of human life.
9. I.e., Mr. Eugenides, "one-eyed" because the figure is in profile on the card. Unlike the man with three staves and the wheel, which are Tarot cards, he is Eliot's creation.
1. On his card in the Tarot pack he is shown hanging by one foot from a T-shaped cross. He symbolizes the self-sacrifice of the fertility god who is killed so that his resurrection may restore fertility to land and people.
2. Cf. Baudelaire: "Fourmillante cité, cité pleine de rêves, / Où le spectre en plein jour raccroche le passant" [Eliot's note]. The lines are quoted from "Les Sept Vieillards" ("The Seven Old Men") of Les Fleurs du Mal (The Flowers of Evil), by the French poet Charles Baudelaire (1821–1867): "Swarming city, city full of dreams, / Where the specter in broad daylight accosts the passerby." The word rêve was originally misspelled rève.
3. Cf. Inferno III, 55–57 [Eliot's note]. The note goes on to quote Dante's lines, which may be translated: "So long a train of people, / that I should never have believed / That death had undone so many." Dante, just outside the gate of hell, has seen "the wretched souls of those who lived without disgrace and without praise."
4. Cf. Inferno IV, 25–27 [Eliot's note]. In Limbo, the first circle of hell, Dante has found

the virtuous heathens, who lived before Christianity and are, therefore, eternally unable to achieve their desire of seeing God. Dante's lines, cited by Eliot, mean "Here, so far as I could tell by listening, / there was no lamentation except sighs, / which caused the eternal air to tremble."
5. A phenomenon which I have often noticed [Eliot's note]. St. Mary Woolnoth is a church in the City of London (the financial district); the crowd is flowing across London Bridge to work in the City. According to the Bible, Jesus died at the ninth hour.
6. Presumably representing the "average businessman."
7. The Battle of Mylae (260 B.C.E.) in the First Punic War, which, in some measure like World War I, was fought for economic reasons.
8. A distortion of the fertility god's ritual death, which heralded rebirth.
9. Cf. the Dirge in Webster's White Devil [Eliot's note]. In the play by John Webster (d. 1625), the dirge, sung by Cornelia, has the lines "But keep the wolf far thence, that's foe to men, / For with his nails he'll dig them up again." Eliot makes the "wolf" into a "dog," which is not a foe but a friend to humans.
1. V. Baudelaire, Preface to Fleurs du Mal [Eliot's note]. The passage is the last line of the introductory poem "Au Lecteur" ("To the Reader"), in Baudelaire's Fleurs du Mal; it may be translated: "Hypocrite reader!—my likeness—my brother!" "Au Lecteur" describes humans as sunk in stupidity, sin, and evil, but the worst in "each man's foul menagerie of sin" is boredom, the "monstre délicat"—"You know him; reader."

II. A Game of Chess[2]

The Chair she sat in, like a burnished throne,[3]
Glowed on the marble, where the glass
Held up by standards wrought with fruited vines
80 From which a golden Cupidon peeped out
(Another hid his eyes behind his wing)
Doubled the flames of sevenbranched candelabra
Reflecting light upon the table as
The glitter of her jewels rose to meet it,
85 From satin cases poured in rich profusion;
In vials of ivory and coloured glass
Unstoppered, lurked her strange synthetic perfumes,
Unguent, powdered, or liquid—troubled, confused
And drowned the sense in odours; stirred by the air
90 That freshened from the window, these ascended
In fattening the prolonged candle-flames,
Flung their smoke into the laquearia,[4]
Stirring the pattern on the coffered ceiling.
Huge sea-wood fed with copper
95 Burned green and orange, framed by the coloured stone,
In which sad light a carved dolphin swam.
Above the antique mantel was displayed
As though a window gave upon the sylvan scene[5]
The change of Philomel,[6] by the barbarous king
100 So rudely forced; yet there the nightingale
Filled all the desert with inviolable voice
And still she cried, and still the world pursues,
"Jug Jug"[7] to dirty ears.
And other withered stumps of time
105 Were told upon the walls; staring forms
Leaned out, leaning, hushing the room enclosed.
Footsteps shuffled on the stair.
Under the firelight, under the brush, her hair
Spread out in fiery points
110 Glowed into words, then would be savagely still.

"My nerves are bad tonight. Yes, bad. Stay with me.
"Speak to me. Why do you never speak. Speak.
"What are you thinking of? What thinking? What?
"I never know what you are thinking. Think."

2. The title suggests two plays by Thomas Middleton (1580–1627): *A Game at Chess* and, more significant, *Women Beware Women*, which has a scene in which a mother-in-law is distracted by a game of chess while her daughter-in-law is seduced: every move in the chess game represents a move in the seduction.
3. Cf. *Antony and Cleopatra*, II, ii, 1. 190 [Eliot's note]. In Shakespeare's play, Enobarbus's famous description of the first meeting of Antony and Cleopatra begins, "The barge she sat in, like a burnish'd throne, / Burn'd on the water." Eliot's language in the opening lines of part 2 echoes ironically Enobarbus's speech.
4. Laquearia. V. *Aeneid*, I, 726 [Eliot's note]. *Laquearia* means "a paneled ceiling," and Eliot's note quotes the passage in the *Aeneid* that was

his source for the word. The passage may be translated: "Blazing torches hang from the gold-paneled ceiling [*laquearibus aureis*], and torches conquer the night with flames." Virgil is describing the banquet given by Dido, queen of Carthage, for Aeneas, with whom she fell in love.
5. Sylvan scene. V. Milton, *Paradise Lost*, IV, 140 [Eliot's note]. The phrase is part of the first description of Eden, seen through Satan's eyes.
6. V. Ovid, *Metamorphoses*, VI, Philomela [Eliot's note]. Philomela was raped by "the barbarous king" Tereus, husband of her sister, Procne. Philomela was then transformed into a nightingale. Eliot's note for line 100 refers ahead to his elaboration of the nightingale's song.
7. Conventional representation of nightingale's song in Elizabethan poetry.

115 I think we are in rats' alley[8]
Where the dead men lost their bones.

"What is that noise?"
                    The wind under the door.[9]
"What is that noise now? What is the wind doing?"
120   Nothing again nothing.
                              "Do

"You know nothing? Do you see nothing? Do you remember
"Nothing?"

      I remember
125 Those are pearls that were his eyes.[1]
"Are you alive, or not? Is there nothing in your head?"
                                                   But

O O O O that Shakespeherian Rag[2]—
It's so elegant
130 So intelligent

"What shall I do now? What shall I do?"
"I shall rush out as I am, and walk the street
"With my hair down, so. What shall we do tomorrow?
"What shall we ever do?"
135   The hot water at ten.
And if it rains, a closed car at four.
And we shall play a game of chess,[3]
Pressing lidless eyes and waiting for a knock upon the door.

When Lil's husband got demobbed,[4] I said—
140 I didn't mince my words, I said to her myself,
HURRY UP PLEASE ITS TIME[5]
Now Albert's coming back, make yourself a bit smart.
He'll want to know what you done with that money he gave you
To get yourself some teeth. He did, I was there.
145 You have them all out, Lil, and get a nice set,
He said, I swear, I can't bear to look at you.
And no more can't I, I said, and think of poor Albert,
He's been in the army four years, he wants a good time,
And if you dont give it him, there's others will, I said.
150 Oh is there, she said. Something o' that, I said.
Then I'll know who to thank, she said, and give me a straight look.
HURRY UP PLEASE ITS TIME

8. Cf. Part III, l. 195 [Eliot's note].
9. Cf. Webster: "Is the wind in that door still?" [Eliot's note]. In John Webster's The Devil's Law Case (3.2.162), a physician asks this question on finding that the victim of a murderous attack is still breathing, meaning "Is he still alive?"
1. Cf. Part I, l. 37, 48 [Eliot's note].
2. American ragtime song; a hit of Ziegfeld's Follies in 1912. The chorus is "That Shakespear-ian Rag, most intelligent, very elegant."
3. Cf. the game of chess in Middleton's Women Beware Women [Eliot's note]. The significance of this chess game is discussed in the first note to part 2.
4. British slang for "demobilized" (discharged from the army after World War I).
5. The traditional call of the British bartender at closing time.

If you dont like it you can get on with it, I said,
Others can pick and choose if you can't.
155 But if Albert makes off, it wont be for lack of telling.
You ought to be ashamed, I said, to look so antique.
(And her only thirty-one.)
I can't help it, she said, pulling a long face,
It's them pills I took, to bring it off, she said.
160 (She's had five already, and nearly died of young George.)
The chemist⁶ said it would be alright, but I've never been the same.
You *are* a proper fool, I said.
Well, if Albert wont leave you alone, there it is, I said,
What you get married for if you dont want children?
165 HURRY UP PLEASE ITS TIME
Well, that Sunday Albert was home, they had a hot gammon,°   *ham, bacon*
And they asked me in to dinner, to get the beauty of it hot—
HURRY UP PLEASE ITS TIME
HURRY UP PLEASE ITS TIME
170 Goonight Bill. Goonight Lou. Goonight May. Goonight.
Ta ta. Goonight. Goonight.
Good night, ladies, good night, sweet ladies, good night, good night.⁷

III. The Fire Sermon⁸

The river's tent is broken: the last fingers of leaf
Clutch and sink into the wet bank. The wind
175 Crosses the brown land, unheard. The nymphs are departed.
Sweet Thames, run softly, till I end my song,⁹
The river bears no empty bottles, sandwich papers,
Silk handkerchiefs, cardboard boxes, cigarette ends
Or other testimony of summer nights. The nymphs are departed.
180 And their friends, the loitering heirs of city directors;
Departed, have left no addresses.
By the waters of Leman I sat down and wept,¹ . . .
Sweet Thames, run softly till I end my song,
Sweet Thames, run softly, for I speak not loud or long.
185 But at my back in a cold blast I hear²
The rattle of the bones, and chuckle spread from ear to ear.

A rat crept softly through the vegetation
Dragging its slimy belly on the bank
While I was fishing in the dull canal
190 On a winter evening round behind the gashouse
Musing upon the king my brother's wreck

---

6. Pharmacist. "To bring it off": to cause an abortion.
7. Cf. the mad Ophelia's departing words (Shakespeare, *Hamlet* 4.5.69–70). Ophelia, too, met "death by water." Cf. also the popular song lyric "Good night ladies, we're going to leave you now."
8. The Buddha preached the Fire Sermon, against the fires of lust and other passions that destroy people and prevent their regeneration.
9. V. Spenser, *Prothalamion* [Eliot's note]. Eliot's line is the refrain from Edmund Spenser's marriage song, which is also set by the river Thames

in London.
1. Cf. Psalms 137.1, in which the exiled Hebrews mourn for their homeland: "By the rivers of Babylon, there we sat down, yea, we wept, when we remembered Zion." Lake Leman is another name for Lake Geneva, in Switzerland; Eliot wrote *The Waste Land* in Lausanne, by that lake. The noun *leman* is an archaic word meaning lover.
2. An ironic distortion of Andrew Marvell's "To His Coy Mistress," lines 21–22: "But at my back I always hear / Time's wingèd chariot hurrying near." Cf. lines 196–97.

And on the king my father's death before him,[3]
White bodies naked on the low damp ground
And bones cast in a little low dry garret,
195 Rattled by the rat's foot only, year to year.
But at my back from time to time I hear
The sound of horns and motors,[4] which shall bring
Sweeney to Mrs. Porter in the spring.[5]
O the moon shone bright on Mrs. Porter
200 And on her daughter
They wash their feet in soda water[6]
Et O ces voix d'enfants, chantant dans la coupole![7]

Twit twit twit
Jug jug jug jug jug jug
205 So rudely forc'd.
Tereu[8]

Unreal City
Under the brown fog of a winter noon
Mr. Eugenides, the Smyrna[9] merchant
210 Unshaven, with a pocket full of currants
C.i.f.[1] London: documents at sight,
Asked me in demotic° French   *colloquial*
To luncheon at the Cannon Street Hotel
Followed by a weekend at the Metropole.[2]

215 At the violet hour, when the eyes and back
Turn upward from the desk, when the human engine waits
Like a taxi throbbing waiting,
I Tiresias,[3] though blind, throbbing between two lives,
Old man with wrinkled female breasts, can see
220 At the violet hour, the evening hour that strives

3. Cf. *The Tempest*, I, ii [Eliot's note]. See line 48.
4. Cf. Marvell, *To His Coy Mistress* [Eliot's note].
5. Cf. Day, *Parliament of Bees:* "When of the sudden, listening, you shall hear, / A noise of horns and hunting, which shall bring / Actaeon to Diana in the spring, / Where all shall see her naked skin" [Eliot's note]. Actaeon was changed to a stag and hunted to death after he saw Diana, the goddess of chastity, bathing with her nymphs. John Day (1574–ca. 1640), English poet.
6. I do not know the origin of the ballad from which these lines are taken; it was reported to me from Sydney, Australia [Eliot's note]. One of the less bawdy versions of the song, which was popular among Australian troops in World War I, went as follows: "O the moon shines bright on Mrs. Porter / And on the daughter / Of Mrs. Porter. / They wash their feet in soda water / And so they oughter / To keep them clean."
7. V. Verlaine, *Parsifal* [Eliot's note]: "And O those children's voices singing in the dome!" The sonnet by the French poet Paul Verlaine (1844–1896) describes Parsifal, the questing knight, resisting all sensual temptations to keep himself pure for the Grail and heal the Fisher King; Wagner's Parsifal had his feet washed before entering the castle of the Grail.
8. A reference to Tereus, who "rudely forc'd"

Philomela; it was also a word for a nightingale's song in Elizabethan poetry. Cf. the song from John Lyly's *Campaspe* (1584): "Oh, 'tis the ravished nightingale. / Jug, jug, jug, jug, tereu! she cries." Cf. also lines 100ff.
9. Now Izmir, a seaport in western Turkey; here associated with Carthage and the ancient Phoenician and Syrian merchants, who spread the old mystery cults.
1. The currants were quoted at a price "carriage and insurance free to London"; and the Bill of Lading etc. were to be handed to the buyer upon payment of the sight draft [Eliot's note]. Another gloss of C.i.f. is "cost, insurance and freight."
2. Luxury hotel in the seaside resort of Brighton. Cannon Street Hotel, near the station that was then chief terminus for travelers to the Continent, was a favorite meeting place for business-people going or coming from abroad; it was also a locale for homosexual liaisons.
3. Tiresias, although a mere spectator and not indeed a "character," is yet the most important personage in the poem, uniting all the rest. Just as the one-eyed merchant, seller of currants, melts into the Phoenician Sailor, and the latter is not wholly distinct from Ferdinand Prince of Naples, so all the women are one woman, and the two sexes meet in Tiresias. What Tiresias *sees*, in fact,

Homeward, and brings the sailor home from sea,[4]
The typist home at teatime, clears her breakfast, lights
Her stove, and lays out food in tins.
Out of the window perilously spread
225 Her drying combinations° touched by the sun's last rays,   *undergarments*
On the divan are piled (at night her bed)
Stockings, slippers, camisoles, and stays.°   *corset*
I Tiresias, old man with wrinkled dugs
Perceived the scene, and foretold the rest—
230 I too awaited the expected guest.
He, the young man carbuncular,° arrives,   *pimply*
A small house agent's clerk, with one bold stare,
One of the low on whom assurance sits
As a silk hat on a Bradford[5] millionaire.
235 The time is now propitious, as he guesses,
The meal is ended, she is bored and tired,
Endeavours to engage her in caresses
Which still are unreproved, if undesired.
Flushed and decided, he assaults at once;
240 Exploring hands encounter no defence;
His vanity requires no response,
And makes a welcome of indifference.
(And I Tiresias have foresuffered all
Enacted on this same divan or bed;
245 I who have sat by Thebes[6] below the wall
And walked among the lowest of the dead.)
Bestows one final patronising kiss,
And gropes his way, finding the stairs unlit . . .

She turns and looks a moment in the glass,
250 Hardly aware of her departed lover;
Her brain allows one half-formed thought to pass:
"Well now that's done: and I'm glad it's over."
When lovely woman stoops to folly and
Paces about her room again, alone,

---

is the substance of the poem. The whole passage from Ovid is of great anthropological interest [Eliot's note]. The note then quotes, from the Latin text of Ovid's *Metamorphoses*, the story of Tiresias's change of sex: "[The story goes that once Jove, having drunk a great deal,] jested with Juno. He said, 'Your pleasure in love is really greater than that enjoyed by men.' She denied it; so they decided to seek the opinion of the wise Tiresias, for he knew both aspects of love. For once, with a blow of his staff, he had committed violence on two huge snakes as they copulated in the green forest; and—wonderful to tell—was turned from a man into a woman and thus spent seven years. In the eighth year he saw the same snakes again and said: 'If a blow struck at you is so powerful that it changes the sex of the giver, I will now strike at you again.' With these words she struck the snakes, and again became a man. So he was appointed arbitrator in the playful quarrel, and supported Jove's statement. It is said that Saturnia [i.e., Juno] was quite disproportionately upset, and condemned the arbitrator to perpetual blindness.

But the almighty father (for no god may undo what has been done by another god), in return for the sight that was taken away, gave him the power to know the future and so lightened the penalty paid by the honor."
4. This may not appear as exact as Sappho's lines, but I had in mind the "longshore" or "dory" fisherman, who returns at nightfall [Eliot's note]. Sappho's poem addressed Hesperus, the evening star, as the star that brings everyone home from work to evening rest; her poem is here distorted by Eliot. There is also an echo of the 19th-century Scottish writer Robert Louis Stevenson's "Requiem," line 221: "Home is the sailor, home from sea."
5. Either the Yorkshire woolen manufacturing town, where many fortunes were made in World War I, or the pioneer oil town of Bradford, Pennsylvania, the home of one of Eliot's wealthy Harvard contemporaries, T. E. Hanley.
6. For many generations, Tiresias lived in Thebes, where he witnessed the tragic fates of Oedipus and Creon; he prophesied in the marketplace by the wall of Thebes.

255 She smoothes her hair with automatic hand,
And puts a record on the gramophone.[7]

"This music crept by me upon the waters"[8]
And along the Strand, up Queen Victoria Street.
O City, City, I can sometimes hear
260 Beside a public bar in Lower Thames Street,
The pleasant whining of a mandoline
And a clatter and a chatter from within
Where fishmen lounge at noon: where the walls
Of Magnus Martyr hold
265 Inexplicable splendour of Ionian white and gold.[9]

The river sweats[1]
Oil and tar
The barges drift
With the turning tide
270 Red sails
Wide
To leeward, swing on the heavy spar.
The barges wash
Drifting logs
275 Down Greenwich reach
Past the Isle of Dogs.[2]
            Weialala leia
            Wallala leialala

Elizabeth and Leicester[3]
280 Beating oars
The stern was formed
A gilded shell
Red and gold
The brisk swell
285 Rippled both shores

7. V. Goldsmith, the song in *The Vicar of Wakefield* [Eliot's note]. Olivia, a character in Oliver Goldsmith's 1766 novel, sings the following song when she returns to the place where she was seduced: "When lovely woman stoops to folly / And finds too late that men betray / What charm can soothe her melancholy, / What art can wash her guilt away? / The only art her guilt to cover, / To hide her shame from every eye, / To give repentance to her lover / And wring his bosom—is to die."
8. V. *The Tempest*, as above [Eliot's note]. Cf. line 48. The line is from Ferdinand's speech, continuing after "weeping again the King my father's wrack."
9. The interior of St. Magnus Martyr is to my mind one of the finest among [Sir Christopher] Wren's interiors. See *The Proposed Demolition of Nineteen City Churches*: (P. S. King & Son, Ltd.) [Eliot's note]. In these lines the "pleasant" music, the "fishmen" resting after labor, and the splendor of the church interior suggest a world of true values, where work and relaxation are both real and take place in a context of religious meaning.
1. The Song of the (three) Thames-daughters

begins here. From line 292 to 306 inclusive they speak in turn. V. *Götterdämmerung*, III, i: the Rhinedaughters [Eliot's note]. Eliot parallels the Thames-daughters with the Rhinemaidens in Wagner's opera *Götterdämmerung* (*The Twilight of the Gods*), who lament that, with the gold of the Rhine stolen, the beauty of the river is gone. The refrain in lines 277–78 is borrowed from Wagner.
2. Greenwich is a borough in London on the south side of the Thames; opposite is the Isle of Dogs (a peninsula).
3. The fruitless love of Queen Elizabeth and the earl of Leicester (Robert Dudley) is recalled in Eliot's note: "V. [J. A.] Froude, *Elizabeth*, Vol. I, ch. iv, letter of De Quadra to Philip of Spain: 'In the afternoon we were in a barge, watching the games on the river. (The queen) was alone with Lord Robert and myself on the poop, when they began to talk nonsense, and went so far that Lord Robert at last said, as I was on the spot there was no reason why they should not be married if the queen pleased.'" Queen Elizabeth I was born in the old Greenwich House, by the river, where Greenwich Hospital now stands.

Southwest wind
Carried down stream
The peal of bells
White towers
290   Weialala leia
         Wallala leialala

"Trams and dusty trees.
Highbury bore me. Richmond and Kew
Undid me.[4] By Richmond I raised my knees
295 Supine on the floor of a narrow canoe."

"My feet are at Moorgate,[5] and my heart
Under my feet. After the event
He wept. He promised 'a new start.'
I made no comment. What should I resent?"

300 "On Margate[6] Sands.
I can connect
Nothing with nothing.
The broken fingernails of dirty hands.
My people humble people who expect
305 Nothing."
         la la

To Carthage then I came[7]

Burning burning burning burning[8]
O Lord Thou pluckest me out[9]
310 O Lord Thou pluckest

burning

IV. Death by Water[1]

Phlebas the Phoenician, a fortnight dead,
Forgot the cry of gulls, and the deep sea swell

4. Cf. *Purgatorio*, V, 133 [Eliot's note]. The *Purgatorio* lines, which Eliot here parodies, may be translated: "Remember me, who am La Pia. / Siena made me, Maremma undid me." "Highbury": a residential London suburb. "Richmond": a pleasant part of London westward up the Thames, with boating and riverside hotels. "Kew": adjoining Richmond, has the famous Kew Gardens.
5. Underground (i.e., subway) station Eliot used daily while working at Lloyds Bank.
6. Popular seaside resort on the Thames estuary.
7. V. St. Augustine's *Confessions*: "to Carthage then I came, where a caldron of unholy loves sang all about mine ears" [Eliot's note]. The passage from the *Confessions* quoted here occurs in St. Augustine's account of his youthful life of lust. Cf. line 92 and its note.
8. The complete text of the Buddha's Fire Sermon (which corresponds in importance to the Sermon on the Mount) from which these words are taken, will be found translated in the late Henry Clarke Warren's *Buddhism in Translation* (Harvard Oriental Series). Mr. Warren was one of the great pioneers of Buddhist studies in the occident [Eliot's note]. In the sermon, the Buddha instructs his priests that all things "are on fire. . . . The eye . . . is on fire; forms are on fire; eye-consciousness is on fire; impressions received by the eye are on fire; and whatever sensation, pleasant, unpleasant, or indifferent, originates in dependence on impressions received by the eye, that also is on fire. And with what are these on fire? With the fire of passion, say I, with the fire of hatred, with the fire of infatuation." For Jesus's Sermon on the Mount, see Matthew 5–7.
9. From St. Augustine's *Confessions* again. The collocation of these two representatives of eastern and western asceticism, as the culmination of this part of the poem, is not an accident [Eliot's note].
1. This section has been interpreted as signifying death by water without resurrection or as symbolizing the sacrificial death that precedes rebirth.

And the profit and loss.
315   A current under sea
Picked his bones in whispers. As he rose and fell
He passed the stages of his age and youth
Entering the whirlpool.
                        Gentile or Jew
320 O you who turn the wheel and look to windward,
Consider Phlebas, who was once handsome and tall as you.

V. What the Thunder Said[2]

After the torchlight red on sweaty faces
After the frosty silence in the gardens
After the agony in stony places
325 The shouting and the crying
Prison and palace and reverberation
Of thunder of spring over distant mountains
He who was living is now dead[3]
We who were living are now dying
330 With a little patience

Here is no water but only rock
Rock and no water and the sandy road
The road winding above among the mountains
Which are mountains of rock without water
335 If there were water we should stop and drink
Amongst the rock one cannot stop or think
Sweat is dry and feet are in the sand
If there were only water amongst the rock
Dead mountain mouth of carious° teeth that cannot spit   decayed
340 Here one can neither stand nor lie nor sit
There is not even silence in the mountains
But dry sterile thunder without rain
There is not even solitude in the mountains
But red sullen faces sneer and snarl
345 From doors of mudcracked houses
                        If there were water
          And no rock
          If there were rock
          And also water
350   And water
          A spring
          A pool among the rock
          If there were the sound of water only
          Not the cicada[4]
355   And dry grass singing
          But sound of water over a rock

2. In the first part of Part V three themes are employed: the journey to Emmaus, the approach to the Chapel Perilous (see Miss Weston's book), and the present decay of eastern Europe [Eliot's note]. On the journey to Emmaus, the resurrected Jesus walks alongside and converses with two disciples, who think he is a stranger until he reveals his identity (Luke 24.13–14).
3. These lines allude to Jesus's agony in the Garden of Gethsemane, his trial, and his crucifixion.
4. Cf. Ecclesiastes' prophecy "the grasshopper shall be a burden, and desire shall fail." Cf. also line 23 and its note.

Where the hermit-thrush[5] sings in the pine trees
Drip drop drip drop drop drop drop
But there is no water

360 Who is the third who walks always beside you?[6]
When I count, there are only you and I together
But when I look ahead up the white road
There is always another one walking beside you
Gliding wrapt in a brown mantle, hooded
365 I do not know whether a man or a woman
—But who is that on the other side of you?

What is that sound high in the air[7]
Murmur of maternal lamentation
Who are those hooded hordes swarming
370 Over endless plains, stumbling in cracked earth
Ringed by the flat horizon only
What is the city over the mountains
Cracks and reforms and bursts in the violet air
Falling towers
375 Jerusalem Athens Alexandria
Vienna London
Unreal

A woman drew her long black hair out tight
And fiddled whisper music on those strings
380 And bats with baby faces in the violet light
Whistled, and beat their wings
And crawled head downward down a blackened wall
And upside down in air were towers
Tolling reminiscent bells, that kept the hours
385 And voices singing out of empty cisterns and exhausted wells.

In this decayed hole among the mountains
In the faint moonlight, the grass is singing
Over the tumbled graves, about the chapel
There is the empty chapel, only the wind's home.[8]
390 It has no windows, and the door swings,
Dry bones can harm no one.

5. This is *Turdus aonalaschkae pallasii*, the hermit-thrush which I have heard in Quebec County. Chapman says (*Handbook of Birds of Eastern North America*) "it is most at home in secluded woodland and thickety retreats. . . . Its notes are not remarkable for variety or volume, but in purity and sweetness of tone and exquisite modulation they are unequaled." Its "water-dripping song" is justly celebrated [Eliot's note].
6. The following lines were stimulated by the account of one of the Antarctic expeditions (I forget which, but I think one of Shackleton's): it was related that the party of explorers, at the extremity of their strength, had the constant delusion that there was *one more member* than could actually be counted [Eliot's note]. This reminiscence is associated with Jesus's unrecognized presence on the way to Emmaus.
7. Eliot's note for lines 367–77 is: "Cf. Herman Hesse, *Blick ins Chaos* ["A Glimpse into Chaos"]." The note then quotes a passage from the German text, which is translated: "Already half of Europe, already at least half of Eastern Europe, on the way to Chaos, drives drunk in sacred infatuation along the edge of the precipice, sings drunkenly, as though hymn singing, as Dmitri Karamazov [in Dostoyevsky's *Brothers Karamazov*] sang. The offended bourgeois laughs at the songs; the saint and the seer hear them with tears."
8. Suggesting the moment of near despair before the Chapel Perilous, when the questing knight sees nothing there but decay. This illusion of nothingness is the knight's final test.

Only a cock stood on the rooftree
Co co   rico   co co   rico[9]
In a flash of lightning. Then a damp gust
395 Bringing rain

Ganga[1] was sunken, and the limp leaves
Waited for rain, while the black clouds
Gathered far distant, over Himavant.[2]
The jungle crouched, humped in silence.
400 Then spoke the thunder
Da[3]
Datta: what have we given?
My friend, blood shaking my heart
The awful daring of a moment's surrender
405 Which an age of prudence can never retract
By this, and this only, we have existed
Which is not to be found in our obituaries
Or in memories draped by the beneficent spider[4]
Or under seals broken by the lean solicitor°   *lawyer*
410 In our empty rooms
Da
Dayadhvam: I have heard the key[5]
Turn in the door once and turn once only
We think of the key, each in his prison
415 Thinking of the key, each confirms a prison
Only at nightfall, æthereal rumours
Revive for a moment a broken Coriolanus[6]
Da
Damyata: The boat responded
420 Gaily, to the hand expert with sail and oar
The sea was calm, your heart would have responded
Gaily, when invited, beating obedient
To controlling hands

9. The crowing of the cock signals the departure of ghosts and evil spirits. Cf. *Hamlet* 1.1.157ff. In Matthew 26, 34, and 74 the cock crows after Peter betrays Jesus three times.
1. Sanskrit name for the major sacred river in India.
2. I.e., snowy mountain (Sanskrit); usually applied to the Himalayas.
3. Datta, dayadhvam, damyata (Give, sympathize, control). The fable of the meaning of the Thunder is found in the *Brihadaranyaka—Upanishad*, 5, 1. A translation is found in Deussen's *Sechzig Upanishads des Veda*, p. 489 [Eliot's note]. In the Old Indian fable "The Three Great Disciplines," the Creator God Prajapati utters the enigmatic syllable *DA* to three groups. Lesser gods, naturally unruly, interpret it as "Control yourselves" (*Damyata*); humans, naturally greedy, as "Give" (*Datta*); demons, naturally cruel, as "Be compassionate" (*Dayadhvam*); "That very thing is repeated even today by the heavenly voice, in the form of thunder as 'DA' 'DA' 'DA,' which means 'Control yourselves,' 'Give,' and 'Have compassion.' Therefore one should practice these three things: self-control, giving, and mercy." The Upanishads are ancient philosophical dialogues in Sanskrit. They are primary texts for an early form of Hinduism sometimes called Brahminism.
4. Cf. Webster, *The White Devil*, V, vi: ". . . they'll remarry / Ere the worm pierce your winding-sheet, ere the spider / Make a thin curtain for your epitaphs" [Eliot's note].
5. Cf. *Inferno*, XXXIII, 46 [Eliot's note]. In this passage from the *Inferno*, Ugolino recalls his imprisonment in the tower with his children, where they starved to death: "And I heard below the door of the horrible tower being nailed shut." Eliot's note for this line goes on to quote F. H. Bradley, *Appearance and Reality*, p. 346: "'My external sensations are no less private to myself than are my thoughts or my feelings. In either case my experience falls within my own circle, a circle closed on the outside; and, with all its elements alike, every sphere is opaque to the others which surround it. . . . In brief, regarded as an existence which appears in a soul, the whole world for each is peculiar and private to that soul.'" Eliot wrote his doctoral thesis on Bradley's philosophy.
6. Coriolanus, who acted out of pride rather than duty, exemplifies a man locked in the prison of himself. He led the enemy against his native city out of injured pride (cf. Shakespeare's *Coriolanus*).

The Twentieth and Twenty-First Centuries

Les Demoiselles d'Avignon, Pablo Picasso, 1907

This masterpiece by Spanish expatriate painter Pablo Picasso helped unleash the experimental energies of modern art. The painting breaks with formal traditions of one-point perspective and human modeling, violently fracturing space in jagged planes. At the same time it defies conventions of sexual decorum in the visual arts, confronting the viewer with five naked prostitutes in a brothel. The masklike faces, particularly of the women to the right, echo African art; they suggest the crucial role non-Western art will play in the development of modernism. The abstract faces, angular forms, and formally fragmented bodies intimate the revolutionary techniques of analytic cubism that Picasso and his French collaborator Georges Braque would develop in Paris from 1907 to 1914.

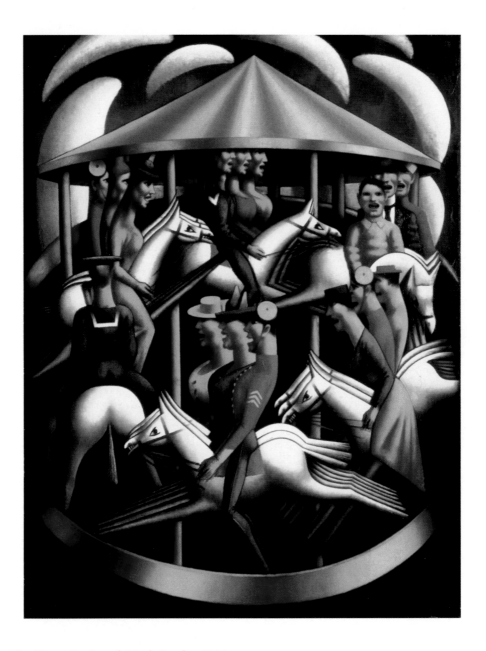

The Merry-Go-Round, Mark Gertler, 1916

Painted in the midst of World War I, *The Merry-Go-Round* explores the insufferable condition of life on the home front and on the battlefields. Its circularity describes the frustration of the deadlock on the Western Front, while its mingling of automatized soldiers and women conveys the sense of psychological menace pervading civilian society. The grinning puppetlike figures and the fun-fair setting convey an atmosphere of ghastly levity, in which war becomes a game. Glaring artificial colors contribute to the impression of a violent and confined world, where even nature is mechanical.

Over the Top, 1st Artists' Rifles at Marcoing, 30th December 1917,
John Northcote Nash, 1918

John Nash enlisted in the Artists' Rifles in 1916 and survived several attempts at going "over the top" before his appointment as a War Artist two years later. In this painting he powerfully recollects the futile danger of an attack near Cambrai in 1917. A line of soldiers clambers out of a crude, wound-red trench to trudge through snow toward an unseen enemy. Several men are killed immediately, then fall prostrate or fall back into the ready-made grave of their recent refuge. Years later Nash recalled that the advance had from the outset been doomed, "was in fact pure murder," designed to divert attention from a bombing raid elsewhere. Of the eighty men who set out, only twelve, including Nash, returned.

Tube Shelter Perspective, 1941, Henry Moore

In their disparate treatments of space and community, the works on these two pages powerfully demonstrate the antithetic atmospheres of war and peace. Moore took up sketching during World War I because of a scarcity of sculpting material. His impression of crowds sheltering in the London Underground during an air raid, ranged in parallel lines down a seemingly endless tunnel, evokes the involuntary intimacy of strangers—forced into proximity, yet still isolated and anonymous. *Family Group,* by contrast, expresses a postwar moment of relative security, when the birth of Moore's only daughter coincided with the government's promotion of traditional family values, and Moore's return to sculpture found a ready market for large-scale public art. Two parents, infants on their knees, sit in a cozy circle, their bodies merging in a physical expression of unity. The holes within the sculpture recall the wartime tunnel, transforming it from a void that swallows masses of people to a harmonious space controlled by the bodies.

Family Group, 1947, Henry Moore

Painting, Francis Bacon, 1946

Bacon's nightmarish association of the slaughterhouse with the emblems of political and religious power conjures both the suffering and the hypocrisy of the twentieth century. The bust of a man, his face overshadowed by an open umbrella, surrounded by microphones, the whole superimposed upon a butcher's display, evokes the discrepancy between rhetoric and means of power. While the umbrella offers a ludicrous symbol of respectability, the visual parallels between man and meat draw attention to the brutal foundations of political influence. The man's broad shoulders resemble the squared outline of the carcass behind him. The red and white of his face, and his exposed teeth, suggest the flesh and bone of the beef. Incongruous religious references, in the cruciform spread of the carcass and the churchlike decorations on the walls, augment the painting's insinuations of corruption.

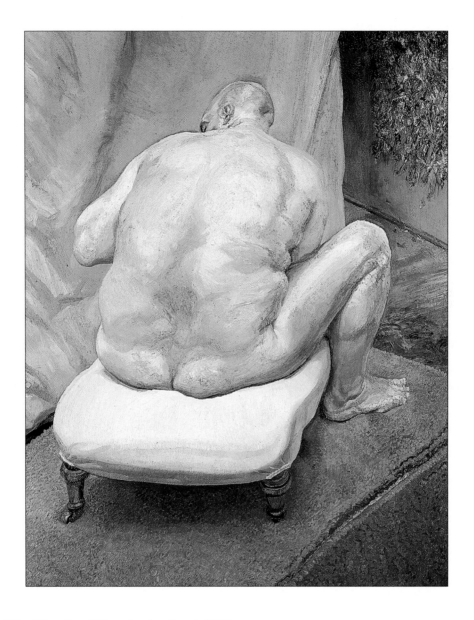

Naked Man, Back View, Lucian Freud, 1993

Freud's nudes study the details of the human body with an unflinching fascination that is modern in its refusal to censor or sentimentalize. Bowery, Freud's model, was a two-hundred-pound nightclub performer, famous for the gorgeous and outrageous costumes he used to reinvent himself in public. Yet Freud, recalling their first encounter, remembered the shape of his lower limbs rather than his outfit, observing that "his calves went right down to his feet, almost avoiding the whole business of ankles altogether." His depiction of Bowery in the nude strongly evokes the magnificence and the vulnerability of a body better known for its sartorial transformations.

Yinka Shonibare, *Nelson's Ship in a Bottle,* May 24, 2010–December 31, 2011

Commissioned as a temporary addition to London's Trafalgar Square, Anglo-Nigerian artist Yinka Shonibare's work is a scaled replica of the ship that carried Admiral Horatio Nelson (whose statue ascends nearby) to victory over Napoleon at the Battle of Trafalgar in 1805—except that Shonibare playfully corks the ship in a massive, dreamy bottle and refashions the sails out of brightly colored cloth. This textile, frequently seen in his work, is often considered authentically African. But in the cross-cultural irony he relishes, its designs were originally Indonesian, its production English and Dutch, for sale to West Africans. Nelson's victory enabled the British colonization of Africa but also ultimately the reverse colonization of Britain's cultural landscape by people like Shonibare, a self-described "postcolonial hybrid."

I sat upon the shore

425 Fishing[7] with the arid plain behind me
    Shall I at least set my lands in order?[8]

    London Bridge is falling down falling down falling down[9]
    Poi s'ascose nel foco che gli affina[1]
    Quando fiam uti chelidon[2]—O swallow swallow[3]
430 *Le Prince d'Aquitaine à la tour abolie*[4]
    These fragments I have shored against my ruins
    Why then Ile fit you. Hieronymo's mad againe.[5]
    Datta. Dayadhvam. Damyata.

Shantih   shantih   shantih[6]

1921   1922

The Hollow Men

Mistah Kurtz—he dead[1]
A penny for the Old Guy[2]

I

    We are the hollow men
    We are the stuffed men
    Leaning together
    Headpiece filled with straw. Alas!
5 Our dried voices, when
    We whisper together
    Are quiet and meaningless
    As wind in dry glass
    Or rats' feet over broken glass
10 In our dry cellar[3]

---

7. V. Weston: *From Ritual to Romance*; chapter on the Fisher King [Eliot's note].
8. Cf. Isaiah 38.1: "Thus saith the Lord, Set thine house in order, for thou shalt die, and not live."
9. One of the later lines of this nursery rhyme is "Take the key and lock her up, my fair lady."
1. V. *Purgutorio*, XXVI, 148 [Eliot's note]. The note goes on to quote lines 145–148 of the *Purgatorio*, in which the Provençal poet Arnaut Daniel addresses Dante: "'Now I pray you, by that virtue which guides you to the summit of the stairway, be mindful in due time of my pain.'" Then (in the line Eliot quotes here) "he hid himself in the fire which refines them."
2. V. *Pervigilium Veneris*. Cf. Philomela in parts II and III [Eliot's note]. The Latin phrase in the text, originally misquoting *uti* as *ceu*, means, "When shall I be as the swallow?" It comes from the late Latin poem *"Pervigilium Veneris"* ("Vigil of Venus"): "When will my spring come? When shall I be as the swallow that I may cease to be silent? I have lost the Muse in silence, and Apollo regards me not."
3. Cf. A. C. Swinburne's "Itylus," which begins, "Swallow, my sister, O sister swallow, / How can thine heart be full of spring?" and Tennyson's lyric in *The Princess*: "O Swallow, Swallow, flying, flying south."

4. V. Gerard de Nerval, Sonnet *El Desdichado* [Eliot's note]. The French line may be translated: "The Prince of Aquitaine in the ruined tower." One of the cards in the Tarot pack is "the tower struck by lightning."
5. V. Kyd's *Spanish Tragedy* [Eliot's note]. Subtitled *Hieronymo's Mad Againe*, Kyd's play (1594) is an early example of the Elizabethan tragedy of revenge. Hieronymo, driven mad by the murder of his son, has his revenge when he is asked to write a court entertainment. He replies, "Why then Ile fit you!" (i.e., accommodate you), and assigns the parts in the entertainment so that, in the course of the action, his son's murderers are killed.
6. Shantih. Repeated as here, a formal ending to an Upanishad. "The Peace which passeth understanding" is a feeble translation of the content of this word [Eliot's note]. On the Upanishads see the note to line 401 above.
1. From Joseph Conrad's *Heart of Darkness* (see p. 71).
2. Every year on Nov. 5, British children build bonfires, on which they burn a scarecrow effigy of the traitor Guido [Guy] Fawkes, who in 1605 attempted to blow up the Parliament buildings. For some days before this, they ask people in the streets for pennies with which to buy fireworks.
3. Cf. *The Waste Land*, lines 115 and 195.

Shape without form, shade without colour,
Paralysed force, gesture without motion;

Those who have crossed
With direct eyes, to death's other Kingdom
15   Remember us—if at all—not as lost
Violent souls, but only
As the hollow men
The stuffed men.

II

Eyes I dare not meet in dreams
20   In death's dream kingdom[4]
These do not appear:
There, the eyes are
Sunlight on a broken column
There, is a tree swinging
25   And voices are
In the wind's singing
More distant and more solemn
Than a fading star.

Let me be no nearer
30   In death's dream kingdom
Let me also wear
Such deliberate disguises
Rat's coat, crowskin, crossed staves
In a field[5]
35   Behaving as the wind behaves
No nearer—

Not that final meeting
In the twilight kingdom[6]

III

This is the dead land
40   This is cactus land
Here the stone images[7]
Are raised, here they receive
The supplication of a dead man's hand
Under the twinkle of a fading star.

45   Is it like this
In death's other kingdom
Waking alone

4. At the end of Dante's *Purgatorio* and in *Paradiso* 4, he cannot meet the gaze of Beatrice (see Eliot's 1929 essay "Dante"). In some printings, Part II ends with an additional line: "With eyes I dare not meet in dreams."
5. The traditional British scarecrow is made from two sticks tied in the form of a cross (the vertical one stuck in the ground), dressed in cast-off clothes, and sometimes draped with dead vermin.
6. Perhaps a reference to Dante's meeting with Beatrice after he has crossed the river Lethe. There reminded of his sins, he is allowed to proceed to Paradise (*Purgatorio* 30).
7. Cf. *The Waste Land*, line 22.

At the hour when we are
Trembling with tenderness
50 Lips that would kiss
Form prayers to broken stone.

IV

The eyes are not here
There are no eyes here
In this valley of dying stars
55 In this hollow valley
This broken jaw of our lost kingdoms

In this last of meeting places
We grope together
And avoid speech
60 Gathered on this beach of the tumid river[8]

Sightless, unless
The eyes reappear
As the perpetual star
Multifoliate rose[9]
65 Of death's twilight kingdom
The hope only
Of empty men.

V

Here we go round the prickly pear
Prickly pear prickly pear
70 *Here we go round the prickly pear*
At five o'clock in the morning.[1]

Between the idea
And the reality
Between the motion
75 And the act[2]
Falls the Shadow[3]
                    For Thine is the Kingdom[4]

Between the conception
And the creation
80 Between the emotion
And the response
Falls the Shadow
                    Life is very long

8. Dante's Acheron, which encircles hell, and the Congo of Conrad's *Heart of Darkness*.
9. The image of heaven in Dante's *Paradiso* 32.
1. Parodic version of the children's rhyme ending "Here we go round the mulberry bush / On a cold and frosty morning."
2. Cf. Shakespeare's *Julius Caesar* 2.1.63–65: "Between the acting of a dreadful thing / And the first motion, all the interim is / Like a phantasma or a hideous dream."
3. Cf. Ernest Dowson's "*Non sum qualis eram bonae sub regno Cynarae*," lines 1–2: "Last night, ah, yesternight, betwixt her lips and mine / There fell thy shadow, Cynara!"
4. Cf. The Lord's Prayer.

Between the desire
85 And the spasm
Between the potency
And the existence
Between the essence
And the descent
90 Falls the Shadow
For Thine is the Kingdom

For Thine is
Life is
For Thine is the

95 *This is the way the world ends*
This is the way the world ends
This is the way the world ends
Not with a bang but a whimper.

1924–25   1925

Journey of the Magi[1]

'A cold coming we had of it,
Just the worst time of the year
For a journey, and such a long journey:
The ways deep and the weather sharp,
5 The very dead of winter.'[2]
And the camels galled, sore-footed, refractory,
Lying down in the melting snow.
There were times we regretted
The summer palaces on slopes, the terraces,
10 And the silken girls bringing sherbet.
Then the camel men cursing and grumbling
And running away, and wanting their liquor and women,
And the night-fires going out, and the lack of shelters,
And the cities hostile and the towns unfriendly
15 And the villages dirty and charging high prices:
A hard time we had of it.
At the end we preferred to travel all night,
Sleeping in snatches,
With the voices singing in our ears, saying
20 That this was all folly.

Then at dawn we came down to a temperate valley,
Wet, below the snow line, smelling of vegetation;
With a running stream and a water mill beating the darkness,

1. One of the wise men who came from the east to Jerusalem to do homage to the infant Jesus (Matthew 2.1–12) is recalling in old age the meaning of the experience.
2. Adapted from a passage in a 1622 Christmas sermon by Bishop Lancelot Andrewes: "A cold coming they had of it at this time of the year, just the worst time of the year to take a journey, and specially a long journey in. The ways deep, the weather sharp, the days short, the sun farthest off, *in solstitio brumali,* 'the very dead of winter.'"

And three trees on the low sky[3]
25 And an old white horse galloped away in the meadow.
Then we came to a tavern with vine-leaves over the lintel,
Six hands at an open door dicing for pieces of silver,
And feet kicking the empty wine-skins.
But there was no information, and so we continued
30 And arrived at evening, not a moment too soon
Finding the place; it was (you may say) satisfactory.

    All this was a long time ago, I remember,
And I would do it again, but set down
This set down
35 This: were we led all that way for
Birth or Death? There was a Birth, certainly,
We had evidence and no doubt. I had seen birth and death,
But had thought they were different; this Birth was
Hard and bitter agony for us, like Death, our death.
40 We returned to our places, these Kingdoms,
But no longer at ease here, in the old dispensation,
With an alien people clutching their gods.
I should be glad of another death.

1927

From Four Quartets

Little Gidding[1]

I

Midwinter spring is its own season
Sempiternal° though sodden towards sundown,   *eternal, everlasting*
Suspended in time, between pole and tropic,
When the short day is brightest, with frost and fire,
5 The brief sun flames the ice, on pond and ditches,
In windless cold that is the heart's heat,
Reflecting in a watery mirror
A glare that is blindness in the early afternoon.
And glow more intense than blaze of branch, or brazier,

3. The "three trees" suggest the three crosses, with Jesus crucified on the center one; the men "dicing for pieces of silver" (line 27) suggest the soldiers dicing for Jesus's garments and Judas's betrayal of him for thirty pieces of silver; the empty wineskins recall one of Jesus's parables of old and new (Mark 2.22).

1. This is the last of Eliot's *Four Quartets*, four related poems each divided into five "movements" in a manner reminiscent of the structure of a quartet or a sonata and each dealing with some aspect of the relation of time and eternity, the meaning of history, the achievement of the moment of timeless insight. Although the *Four Quartets* constitute a unified sequence, they were

written separately and can be read as individual poems. "*Little Gidding* can be understood by itself, without reference to the preceding poems, which it yet so beautifully completes" (Helen Gardner, *The Composition of Four Quartets*). Each of the four is named after a place. Little Gidding is a village in Huntingdonshire, where, in 1625, Nicholas Ferrar established an Anglican religious community; the community was broken up in 1647, toward the end of the English Civil War, by the victorious Puritans; the chapel, however, was rebuilt in the 19th century and still exists. Eliot wrote the poem in 1942, when he was taking his turn as a nighttime fire watcher during the incendiary bombings of London in World War II.

10   Stirs the dumb spirit: no wind, but pentecostal fire[2]
      In the dark time of the year. Between melting and freezing
      The soul's sap quivers. There is no earth smell
      Or smell of living thing. This is the springtime
      But not in time's covenant. Now the hedgerow
15   Is blanched for an hour with transitory blossom
      Of snow, a bloom more sudden
      Than that of summer, neither budding nor fading,
      Not in the scheme of generation.
      Where is the summer, the unimaginable
      Zero summer?

20   If you came this way,
      Taking the route you would be likely to take
      From the place you would be likely to come from,
      If you came this way in may time, you would find the hedges
      White again, in May, with voluptuary sweetness.
25   It would be the same at the end of the journey,
      If you came at night like a broken king,[3]
      If you came by day not knowing what you came for,
      It would be the same, when you leave the rough road
      And turn behind the pig-sty to the dull façade
30   And the tombstone. And what you thought you came for
      Is only a shell, a husk of meaning
      From which the purpose breaks only when it is fulfilled
      If at all. Either you had no purpose
      Or the purpose is beyond the end you figured
35   And is altered in fulfilment. There are other places
      Which also are the world's end, some at the sea jaws,
      Or over a dark lake, in a desert or a city[4]—
      But this is the nearest, in place and time,
      Now and in England.

                      If you came this way,
40   Taking any route, starting from anywhere,
      At any time or at any season,
      It would always be the same: you would have to put off
      Sense and notion. You are not here to verify,
      Instruct yourself, or inform curiosity
45   Or carry report. You are here to kneel
      Where prayer has been valid. And prayer is more
      Than an order of words, the conscious occupation
      Of the praying mind, or the sound of the voice praying.
      And what the dead had no speech for, when living,
50   They can tell you, being dead: the communication
      Of the dead is tongued with fire beyond the language of the living.

2. On the Pentecost day after the death and resurrection of Jesus, there appeared to his apostles "cloven tongues like as of fire . . . And they were all filled with the Holy Ghost" (Acts 2).
3. King Charles I visited Ferrar's community more than once and is said to have paid his last visit in secret after his final defeat at the Battle of Naseby in the Civil War.

4. "The 'sea jaws' [Eliot] associated with Iona and St. Columba and with Lindisfarne and St. Cuthbert: the 'dark lake' with the lake of Glendalough and St Kevin's hermitage in County Wicklow: the desert with the hermits of the Thebaid and St. Antony: the city with Padua and the other St. Antony" (Gardner).

Here, the intersection of the timeless moment
Is England and nowhere. Never and always.

II

Ash on an old man's sleeve
55 Is all the ash the burnt roses leave.
Dust in the air suspended
Marks the place where a story ended.[5]
Dust inbreathed was a house—
The wall, the wainscot, and the mouse.
60 The death of hope and despair,
This is the death of air.[6]

There are flood and drouth
Over the eyes and in the mouth,
Dead water and dead sand
65 Contending for the upper hand.
The parched eviscerate soil
Gapes at the vanity of toil,
Laughs without mirth.
This is the death of earth.

70 Water and fire succeed
The town, the pasture, and the weed.
Water and fire deride
The sacrifice that we denied.
Water and fire shall rot
75 The marred foundations we forgot,
Of sanctuary and choir.
This is the death of water and fire.

In the uncertain hour before the morning[7]
Near the ending of interminable night
80 At the recurrent end of the unending
After the dark dove with the flickering tongue[8]
Had passed below the horizon of his homing
While the dead leaves still rattled on like tin
Over the asphalt where no other sound was
85 Between three districts whence the smoke arose
I met one walking, loitering and hurried
As if blown towards me like the metal leaves
Before the urban dawn wind unresisting.
And as I fixed upon the down-turned face
90 That pointed scrutiny with which we challenge

5. Eliot wrote to a friend: "During the Blitz [bombing] the accumulated debris was suspended in the London air for hours after a bombing. Then it would slowly descend and cover one's sleeves and coat with a fine white ash."
6. "The death of air," like that of "earth" and of "water and fire" in the succeeding stanzas, recalls the theory of the creative strife of the four elements propounded by Heraclitus (Greek philosopher of 4th and 5th centuries B.C.E.): "Fire lives in the death of air; water lives in the death of earth; and earth lives in the death of water."
7. The pattern of indentation in the left margin of lines 78–149, their movement and elevated diction, are meant to suggest the terza rima of Dante's *Divine Comedy*.
8. The German dive bomber.

The first-met stranger in the waning dusk
I caught the sudden look of some dead master
Whom I had known, forgotten, half recalled
Both one and many; in the brown baked features
95 The eyes of a familiar compound ghost[9]
Both intimate and unidentifiable.
    So I assumed a double part, and cried
And heard another's voice cry: 'What! are *you* here?'
Although we were not. I was still the same,
100 Knowing myself yet being someone other—
And he a face still forming; yet the words sufficed
To compel the recognition they preceded.
    And so, compliant to the common wind,
Too strange to each other for misunderstanding,
105 In concord at this intersection time
Of meeting nowhere, no before and after,
We trod the pavement in a dead patrol.
I said: 'The wonder that I feel is easy,
Yet ease is cause of wonder. Therefore speak:
110 I may not comprehend, may not remember.'
And he: 'I am not eager to rehearse
My thought and theory which you have forgotten.
These things have served their purpose: let them be.
So with your own, and pray they be forgiven
115 By others, as I pray you to forgive
Both bad and good. Last season's fruit is eaten
And the fullfed beast shall kick the empty pail.
For last year's words belong to last year's language
And next year's words await another voice.
120 But, as the passage now presents no hindrance
To the spirit unappeased and peregrine°   foreign, wandering
Between two worlds become much like each other,
So I find words I never thought to speak
In streets I never thought I should revisit
125 When I left my body on a distant shore.[1]
Since our concern was speech, and speech impelled us
To purify the dialect of the tribe[2]
And urge the mind to aftersight and foresight,
Let me disclose the gifts reserved for age
130 To set a crown upon your lifetime's effort.
First, the cold friction of expiring sense
Without enchantment, offering no promise
But bitter tastelessness of shadow fruit
As body and soul begin to fall asunder.
135 Second, the conscious impotence of rage[3]
At human folly, and the laceration

---

9. This encounter with a ghost "compounded" of W. B. Yeats and his fellow Irishman Jonathan Swift is modeled on Dante's meeting with Brunette Latini (*Inferno* 15), including a direct translation (line 98) of Dante's cry of horrified recognition: "*Siete voi qui, ser Brunetto?*" Cf. also Shakespeare's sonnet 86, line 9: "that affable familiar ghost."
1. Yeats died on Jan. 28, 1939, at Roquebrune in the south of France.
2. A rendering of the line "*Dormer un sens plus pur aux mots de la tribu*" in Stéphane Mallarmé's 1877 sonnet "Le Tombeau d'Edgar Poe" ("The Tomb of Edgar Poe").
3. Cf. Yeats's "The Spur": "You think it horrible that lust and rage / Should dance attendance upon my old age."

Of laughter at what ceases to amuse.[4]
And last, the rending pain of re-enactment
Of all that you have done, and been;[5] the shame
140   Of motives late revealed, and the awareness
Of things ill done and done to others' harm
Which once you took for exercise of virtue.
Then fools' approval stings, and honour stains.
From wrong to wrong the exasperated spirit
145   Proceeds, unless restored by that refining fire[6]
Where you must move in measure, like a dancer.'[7]
The day was breaking. In the disfigured street
He left me, with a kind of valediction,
And faded on the blowing of the horn.[8]

III

150   There are three conditions which often look alike
Yet differ completely, flourish in the same hedgerow:
Attachment to self and to things and to persons, detachment
From self and from things and from persons; and, growing between
    them, indifference
Which resembles the others as death resembles life,
155   Being between two lives—unflowering, between
The live and the dead nettle.[9] This is the use of memory:
For liberation—not less of love but expanding
Of love beyond desire, and so liberation
From the future as well as the past. Thus, love of a country
160   Begins as attachment to our own field of action
And comes to find that action of little importance
Though never indifferent. History may be servitude,
History may be freedom. See, now they vanish,
The faces and places, with the self which, as it could, loved them,
165   To become renewed, transfigured, in another pattern.

Sin is Behovely, but
All shall be well, and
All manner of thing shall be well.[1]
If I think, again, of this place,
170   And of people, not wholly commendable,
Of no immediate kin or kindness,

---

4. Cf. Yeats's "Swift's Epitaph" (translated from Swift's own Latin): "Savage indignation there / Cannot lacerate his breast."
5. Cf. Yeats's "Man and the Echo": "All that I have said and done, / Now that I am old and ill, / Turns into a question till / I lie awake night after night / And never get the answer right. / Did that play of mine send out / Certain men the English shot?"
6. Cf. *The Waste Land*, line 428 and its note; also the refining fire in Yeats's "Byzantium," lines 25–32.
7. Cf. Yeats's "Among School Children," line 64: "How can we know the dancer from the dance?"
8. Cf. *Hamlet* 1.2.157: "It faded on the crowing of the cock." The horn is the all-clear signal after an air raid (the dialogue has taken place between the dropping of the last bomb and the sounding of the

all clear). Eliot called the section that ends with this line "the nearest equivalent to a canto of the *Inferno* or *Purgatorio*" that he could achieve and spoke of his intention to present "a parallel, by means of contrast, between the *Inferno* and the *Purgatorio* . . . and a hallucinated scene after an air raid."
9. Eliot wrote to a friend: "The dead nettle is the family of flowering plants of which the White Archangel is one of the commonest and closely resembles the stinging nettle and is found in its company."
1. A quotation from the 14th-century English mystic Dame Julian of Norwich: "Sin is behovabil [inevitable and fitting], but all shall be well and all shall be well and all manner of thing shall be well."

But some of peculiar genius,
All touched by a common genius,
United in the strife which divided them;
175 If I think of a king at nightfall,[2]
Of three men, and more, on the scaffold
And a few who died forgotten
In other places, here and abroad,
And of one who died blind and quiet[3]
180 Why should we celebrate
These dead men more than the dying?
It is not to ring the bell backward
Nor is it an incantation
To summon the spectre of a Rose.
185 We cannot revive old factions
We cannot restore old policies
Or follow an antique drum.
These men, and those who opposed them
And those whom they opposed
190 Accept the constitution of silence
And are folded in a single party.
Whatever we inherit from the fortunate
We have taken from the defeated
What they had to leave us—a symbol:
195 A symbol perfected in death.
And all shall be well and
All manner of thing shall be well
By the purification of the motive
In the ground of our beseeching.[4]

IV

200 The dove[5] descending breaks the air
With flame of incandescent terror
Of which the tongues declare
The one discharge from sin and error.
The only hope, or else despair
205   Lies in the choice of pyre or pyre—
To be redeemed from fire by fire.

Who then devised the torment? Love.
Love is the unfamiliar Name
Behind the hands that wove
210 The intolerable shirt of flame[6]
Which human power cannot remove.

---

2. I.e., Charles I. He died "on the scaffold" in 1649, while his principal advisers, Archbishop Laud and Thomas Wentworth, earl of Strafford, were both executed earlier by the victorious parliamentary forces.
3. I.e., Milton, who sided with Cromwell against the king.
4. Dame Julian of Norwich was instructed in a vision that "the ground of our beseeching" is love.

5. Both a dive bomber and the Holy Spirit with its Pentecostal tongues of fire.
6. Out of love for her husband, Hercules, Deianira gave him the poisoned shirt of Nessus. She had been told that it would increase his love for her, but instead it so corroded his flesh that in his agony he mounted a funeral pyre and burned himself to death.

We only live, only suspire°   *breathe, sigh*
Consumed by either fire or fire.

V

What we call the beginning is often the end
215 And to make an end is to make a beginning.
The end is where we start from. And every phrase
And sentence that is right (where every word is at home,
Taking its place to support the others,
The word neither diffident nor ostentatious,
220 And easy commerce of the old and the new,
The common word exact without vulgarity,
The formal word precise but not pedantic,
The complete consort[7] dancing together)
Every phrase and every sentence is an end and a beginning,
225 Every poem an epitaph. And any action
Is a step to the block, to the fire, down the sea's throat
Or to an illegible stone: and that is where we start.
We die with the dying:
See, they depart, and we go with them.
230 We are born with the dead:
See, they return, and bring us with them.
The moment of the rose and the moment of the yew-tree[8]
Are of equal duration. A people without history
Is not redeemed from time, for history is a pattern
235 Of timeless moments. So, while the light fails
On a winter's afternoon, in a secluded chapel
History is now and England.

With the drawing of this Love and the voice of this Calling[9]

We shall not cease from exploration
240 And the end of all our exploring
Will be to arrive where we started
And know the place for the first time.
Through the unknown, remembered gate
When the last of earth left to discover
245 Is that which was the beginning;
At the source of the longest river
The voice of the hidden waterfall
And the children in the apple tree
Not known, because not looked for
250 But heard, half-heard, in the stillness
Between two waves of the sea[1]
Quick now, here, now, always—
A condition of complete simplicity

---

7. Company; also harmony of sounds.
8. Traditional symbol of death and grief.
9. This line is from the *Cloud of Unknowing,* an anonymous 14th-century mystical work.
1. The voices of the children in the apple tree symbolize the sudden moment of insight. Cf. the conclusion to "Burnt Norton" (the first of the *Four Quartets*), where the laughter of the children in the garden has a like meaning: "Sudden in a shaft of sunlight / Even while the dust moves / There rises the hidden laughter / Of children in the foliage / Quick now, here, now, always."

(Costing not less than everything)
255 And all shall be well and
All manner of thing shall be well
When the tongues of flame are in-folded
Into the crowned knot of fire
And the fire and the rose are one.

1942   1942, 1943

Tradition and the Individual Talent[1]

I

In English writing we seldom speak of tradition, though we occasionally apply
its name in deploring its absence. We cannot refer to 'the tradition' or to 'a
tradition'; at most, we employ the adjective in saying that the poetry of So-
and-so is 'traditional' or even 'too traditional.' Seldom, perhaps, does the word
appear except in a phrase of censure. If otherwise, it is vaguely approbative,
with the implication, as to the work approved, of some pleasing archaeological
reconstruction. You can hardly make the word agreeable to English ears without this comfortable reference to the reassuring science of archæology.

Certainly the word is not likely to appear in our appreciations of living or
dead writers. Every nation, every race, has not only its own creative, but its
own critical turn of mind; and is even more oblivious of the shortcomings
and limitations of its critical habits than of those of its creative genius. We
know, or think we know, from the enormous mass of critical writing that has
appeared in the French language the critical method or habit of the French;
we only conclude (we are such unconscious people) that the French are 'more
critical' than we, and sometimes even plume ourselves a little with the fact,
as if the French were the less spontaneous. Perhaps they are; but we might
remind ourselves that criticism is as inevitable as breathing, and that we
should be none the worse for articulating what passes in our minds when we
read a book and feel an emotion about it, for criticizing our own minds in
their work of criticism. One of the facts that might come to light in this process is our tendency to insist, when we praise a poet, upon those aspects of
his work in which he least resembles anyone else. In these aspects or parts
of his work we pretend to find what is individual, what is the peculiar essence
of the man. We dwell with satisfaction upon the poet's difference from his
predecessors, especially his immediate predecessors; we endeavour to find
something that can be isolated in order to be enjoyed. Whereas if we approach
a poet without this prejudice we shall often find that not only the best, but
the most individual parts of his work may be those in which the dead poets,
his ancestors, assert their immortality most vigorously. And I do not mean the
impressionable period of adolescence, but the period of full maturity.

Yet if the only form of tradition, of handing down, consisted in following
the ways of the immediate generation before us in a blind or timid adherence to its successes, 'tradition' should positively be discouraged. We have
seen many such simple currents soon lost in the sand; and novelty is better
than repetition. Tradition is a matter of much wider significance. It cannot

1. First published in *The Egoist* magazine (1919) and later collected in *The Sacred Wood* (1920).

be inherited, and if you want it you must obtain it by great labour. It involves, in the first place, the historical sense, which we may call nearly indispensable to any one who would continue to be a poet beyond his twenty-fifth year; and the historical sense involves a perception, not only of the pastness of the past, but of its presence; the historical sense compels a man to write not merely with his own generation in his bones, but with a feeling that the whole of the literature of Europe from Homer and within it the whole of the literature of his own country has a simultaneous existence and composes a simultaneous order. This historical sense, which is a sense of the timeless as well as of the temporal and of the timeless and of the temporal together, is what makes a writer traditional. And it is at the same time what makes a writer most acutely conscious of his place in time, of his own contemporaneity.

No poet, no artist of any art, has his complete meaning alone. His significance, his appreciation is the appreciation of his relation to the dead poets and artists. You cannot value him alone; you must set him, for contrast and comparison, among the dead. I mean this as a principle of aesthetic, not merely historical, criticism. The necessity that he shall conform, that he shall cohere, is not one-sided; what happens when a new work of art is created is something that happens simultaneously to all the works of art which preceded it. The existing monuments form an ideal order among themselves, which is modified by the introduction of the new (the really new) work of art among them. The existing order is complete before the new work arrives; for order to persist after the supervention of novelty, the *whole* existing order must be, if ever so slightly, altered; and so the relations, proportions, values of each work of art toward the whole are readjusted; and this is conformity between the old and the new. Whoever has approved this idea of order, of the form of European, of English literature will not find it preposterous that the past should be altered by the present as much as the present is directed by the past. And the poet who is aware of this will be aware of great difficulties and responsibilities.

In a peculiar sense he will be aware also that he must inevitably be judged by the standards of the past. I say judged, not amputated, by them; not judged to be as good as, or worse or better than, the dead; and certainly not judged by the canons of dead critics. It is a judgment, a comparison, in which two things are measured by each other. To conform merely would be for the new work not really to conform at all; it would not be new, and would therefore not be a work of art. And we do not quite say that the new is more valuable because it fits in; but its fitting in is a test of its value—a test, it is true, which can only be slowly and cautiously applied, for we are none of us infallible judges of conformity. We say: it appears to conform, and is perhaps individual, or it appears individual, and may conform; but we are hardly likely to find that it is one and not the other.

To proceed to a more intelligible exposition of the relation of the poet to the past: he can neither take the past as a lump, an indiscriminate bolus,[2] nor can he form himself wholly on one or two private admirations, nor can he form himself wholly upon one preferred period. The first course is inadmissible, the second is an important experience of youth, and the third is a

2. A round mass of anything: a large pill.

pleasant and highly desirable supplement. The poet must be very conscious of the main current, which does not at all flow invariably through the most distinguished reputations. He must be quite aware of the obvious fact that art never improves, but that the material of art is never quite the same. He must be aware that the mind of Europe—the mind of his own country—a mind which he learns in time to be much more important than his own private mind—is a mind which changes, and that this change is a development which abandons nothing *en route*, which does not superannuate either Shakespeare, or Homer, or the rock drawing of the Magdalenian[3] draftsmen. That this development, refinement perhaps, complication certainly, is not, from the point of view of the artist, any improvement. Perhaps not even an improvement from the point of view of the psychologist or not to the extent which we imagine; perhaps only in the end based upon a complication in economics and machinery. But the difference between the present and the past is that the conscious present is an awareness of the past in a way and to an extent which the past's awareness of itself cannot show.

Someone said: 'The dead writers are remote from us because we *know* so much more than they did.' Precisely, and they are that which we know.

I am alive to a usual objection to what is clearly part of my programme for the *métier*[4] poetry. The objection is that the doctrine requires a ridiculous amount of erudition (pedantry), a claim which can be rejected by appeal to the lives of poets in any pantheon. It will even be affirmed that much learning deadens or perverts poetic sensibility. While, however, we persist in believing that a poet ought to know as much as will not encroach upon his necessary receptivity and necessary laziness, it is not desirable to confine knowledge to whatever can be put into a useful shape for examinations, drawing-rooms, or the still more pretentious modes of publicity. Some can absorb knowledge, the more tardy must sweat for it. Shakespeare acquired more essential history from Plutarch[5] than most men could from the whole British Museum. What is to be insisted upon is that the poet must develop or procure the consciousness of the past and that he should continue to develop this consciousness throughout his career.

What happens is a continual surrender of himself as he is at the moment to something which is more valuable. The progress of an artist is a continual self-sacrifice, a continual extinction of personality.

There remains to define this process of depersonalisation and its relation to the sense of tradition. It is in this depersonalization that art may be said to approach the condition of science. I, therefore, invite you to consider, as a suggestive analogy, the action which takes place when a bit of finely filiated[6] platinum is introduced into a chamber containing oxygen and sulphur dioxide.

II

Honest criticism and sensitive appreciation are directed not upon the poet but upon the poetry. If we attend to the confused cries of the newspaper critics and the susurrus[7] of popular repetition that follows, we shall hear the

3. The most advanced culture of the European Paleolithic period (from discoveries at La Madeleine, France).
4. Vocation (French).
5. Greek biographer (1st century c.e.) of famous Greeks and Romans; from his work Shakespeare drew the plots of his Roman plays.
6. Drawn out like a thread.
7. Murmuring, buzzing (Latin).

names of poets in great numbers; if we seek not Blue-book[8] knowledge but the enjoyment of poetry, and ask for a poem, we shall seldom find it. I have tried to point out the importance of the relation of the poem to other poems by other authors, and suggested the conception of poetry as a living whole of all the poetry that has ever been written. The other aspect of this Impersonal theory of poetry is the relation of the poem to its author. And I hinted, by an analogy, that the mind of the mature poet differs from that of the immature one not precisely in any valuation of 'personality,' not being necessarily more interesting, or having 'more to say,' but rather by being a more finely perfected medium in which special, or very varied, feelings are at liberty to enter into new combinations.

The analogy was that of the catalyst.[9] When the two gases previously mentioned are mixed in the presence of a filament of platinum, they form sulphurous acid. This combination takes place only if the platinum is present; nevertheless the newly formed acid contains no trace of platinum, and the platinum itself is apparently unaffected; has remained inert, neutral, and unchanged. The mind of the poet is the shred of platinum. It may partly or exclusively operate upon the experience of the man himself; but, the more perfect the artist, the more completely separate in him will be the man who suffers and the mind which creates; the more perfectly will the mind digest and transmute the passions which are its material.

The experience, you will notice, the elements which enter the presence of the transforming catalyst, are of two lands: emotions and feelings. The effect of a work of art upon the person who enjoys it is an experience different in kind from any experience not of art. It may be formed out of one emotion, or may be a combination of several; and various feelings, inhering for the writer in particular words or phrases or images, may be added to compose the final result. Or great poetry may be made without the direct use of any emotion whatever composed out of feelings solely. Canto XV of the *Inferno* (Brunetto Latini)[1] is a working up of the emotion evident in the situation; but the effect, though single as that of any work of art, is obtained by considerable complexity of detail. The last quatrain gives an image, a feeling attaching to an image, which 'came,' which did not develop simply out of what precedes, but which was probably in suspension in the poet's mind until the proper combination arrived for it to add itself to.[2] The poet's mind is in fact a receptacle for seizing and storing up numberless feelings, phrases, images, which remain there until all the particles which can unite to form a new compound are present together.

If you compare several representative passages of the greatest poetry you see how great is the variety of types of combination, and also how completely any semi-ethical criterion of 'sublimity' misses the mark. For it is not the 'greatness,' the intensity, of the emotions, the components, but the intensity of the artistic process, the pressure, so to speak, under which the fusion takes place, that counts. The episode of Paolo and Francesca[3] employs a definite emotion, but the intensity of the poetry is something quite different

8. British government publication.
9. Substance that triggers a chemical change without being affected by the reaction.
1. In hell Dante meets his old master, Brunetto Latini, suffering eternal punishment for unnatural lust yet still loved and admired by Dante, who addresses him with affectionate courtesy.
2. Dante's strange interview with Brunetto is over, and Brunetto moves off to continue his punishment: "Then he turned round, and seemed like one of those / Who run for the green cloth [in the footrace] at Verona / In the field; and he seemed among them / Not the loser but the winner."
3. Illicit lovers whom Dante meets in the second circle of hell (*Inferno* 5) and at whose punishment and sorrows he swoons with pity.

from whatever intensity in the supposed experience it may give the impression of. It is no more intense, furthermore, than Canto XXVI,[4] the voyage of Ulysses, which has not the direct dependence upon an emotion. Great variety is possible in the process of transmutation of emotion: the murder of Agamemnon, or the agony of Othello,[5] gives an artistic effect apparently closer to a possible original than the scenes from Dante. In the *Agamemnon*, the artistic emotion approximates to the emotion of an actual spectator; in *Othello* to the emotion of the protagonist himself. But the difference between art and the event is always absolute; the combination which is the murder of Agamemnon is probably as complex as that which is the voyage of Ulysses. In either case there has been a fusion of elements. The ode of Keats contains a number of feelings which have nothing particular to do with the nightingale, but which the nightingale, partly, perhaps, because of its attractive name, and partly because of its reputation, served to bring together.

The point of view which I am struggling to attack is perhaps related to the metaphysical theory of the substantial unity of the soul: for my meaning is, that the poet has, not a 'personality' to express, but a particular medium, which is only a medium and not a personality, in which impressions and experiences combine in peculiar and unexpected ways. Impressions and experiences which are important for the man may take no place in the poetry, and those which become important in the poetry may play quite a negligible part in the man, the personality.

I will quote a passage which is unfamiliar enough to be regarded with fresh attention in the light—or darkness—of these observations:

> And now methinks I could e'en chide myself
> For doating on her beauty, though her death
> Shall be revenged after no common action.
> Does the silkworm expend her yellow labours
> For thee? For thee does she undo herself?
> Are lordships solid to maintain ladyships
> For the poor benefit of a bewildering minute?
> Why does yon fellow falsify highways,
> And put his life between the judge's lips,
> To refine such a thing—keeps horse and men
> To beat their valours for her? . . . [6]

In this passage (as is evident if it is taken in its context) there is a combination of positive and negative emotions: an intensely strong attraction toward beauty and an equally intense fascination by the ugliness which is contrasted with it and which destroys it. This balance of contrasted emotion is in the dramatic situation to which the speech is pertinent, but that situation alone is inadequate to it. This is, so to speak, the structural emotion, provided by the drama. But the whole effect, the dominant tone, is due to the fact that a number of floating feelings, having an affinity to this emotion by no means superficially evident, have combined with it to give us a new art emotion.

4. Of the *Inferno*. Ulysses, suffering in hell for "false counseling," tells Dante of his final voyage.
5. Shakespeare's character kills himself after being duped into jealously murdering his wife.

In Aeschylus's play *Agamemnon*, the title character is murdered by his wife, Clytemnestra.
6. From Cyril Tourneur's *Revenger's Tragedy* 3.4 (1607).

It is not in his personal emotions, the emotions provoked by particular events in his life, that the poet is in any way remarkable or interesting. His particular emotions may be simple, or crude, or flat. The emotion in his poetry will be a very complex thing, but not with the complexity of the emotions of people who have very complex or unusual emotions in life. One error, in fact, of eccentricity in poetry is to seek for new human emotions to express; and in this search for novelty in the wrong place it discovers the perverse. The business of the poet is not to find new emotions, but to use the ordinary ones and, in working them up into poetry, to express feelings which are not in actual emotions at all. And emotions which he has never experienced will serve his turn as well as those familiar to him. Consequently, we must believe that 'emotion recollected in tranquillity'[7] is an inexact formula. For it is neither emotion, nor recollection, nor, without distortion of meaning, tranquility. It is a concentration, and a new thing resulting from the concentration, of a very great number of experiences which to the practical and active person would not seem to be experiences at all; it is a concentration which does not happen consciously or of deliberation. These experiences are not 'recollected,' and they finally unite in an atmosphere which is 'tranquil' only in that it is a passive attending upon the event. Of course this is not quite the whole story. There is a great deal, in the writing of poetry, which must be conscious and deliberate. In fact, the bad poet is usually unconscious where he ought to be conscious, and conscious where he ought to be unconscious. Both errors tend to make him 'personal.' Poetry is not a turning loose of emotion, but an escape from emotion; it is not the expression of personality, but an escape from personality. But, of course, only those who have personality and emotions know what it means to want to escape from these things.

III

ὁ δὲ νοῦς ἴσως θειότερόν τι καὶ ἀπαθές ἐστιν.[8]

This essay proposes to halt at the frontier of metaphysics or mysticism, and confine itself to such practical conclusions as can be applied by the responsible person interested in poetry. To divert interest from the poet to the poetry is a laudable aim: for it would conduce to a juster estimation of actual poetry, good and bad. There are many people who appreciate the expression of sincere emotion in verse, and there is a smaller number of people who can appreciate technical excellence. But very few know when there is an expression of *significant* emotion, emotion which has its life in the poem and not in the history of the poet. The emotion of art is impersonal. And the poet cannot reach this impersonality without surrendering himself wholly to the work to be done. And he is not likely to know what is to be done unless he lives in what is not merely the present, but the present moment of the past, unless he is conscious, not of what is dead, but of what is already living.

1919, 1920

---

7. In his preface to *Lyrical Ballads* (2nd ed., 1800), Wordsworth writes that poetry "takes its origin from emotion recollected in tranquility."

8. Aristotle's "De Anima" ("On the Soul") 1.4: "The mind is doubtless something more divine and unimpressionable."

The Metaphysical Poets

By collecting these poems[1] from the work of a generation more often named than read, and more often read than profitably studied, Professor Grierson has rendered a service of some importance. Certainly the reader will meet with many poems already preserved in other anthologies, at the same time that he discovers poems such as those of Aurelian Townshend or Lord Herbert of Cherbury here included. But the function of such an anthology as this is neither that of Professor Saintsbury's admirable edition of Caroline poets nor that of the *Oxford Book of English Verse*. Mr. Grierson's book is in itself a piece of criticism and a provocation of criticism; and we think that he was right in including so many poems of Donne, elsewhere (though not in many editions) accessible, as documents in the case of 'metaphysical poetry.' The phrase has long done duty as a term of abuse or as the label of a quaint and pleasant taste. The question is to what extent the so-called metaphysicals formed a school (in our own time we should say a 'movement'), and how far this so-called school or movement is a digression from the main current.

Not only is it extremely difficult to define metaphysical poetry, but difficult to decide what poets practise it and in which of their verses. The poetry of Donne (to whom Marvell and Bishop King are sometimes nearer than any of the other authors) is late Elizabethan, its feeling often very close to that of Chapman. The 'courtly' poetry is derivative from Jonson, who borrowed liberally from the Latin; it expires in the next century with the sentiment and witticism of Prior. There is finally the devotional verse of Herbert, Vaughan, and Crashaw (echoed long after by Christina Rossetti and Francis Thompson); Crashaw, sometimes more profound and less sectarian than the others, has a quality which returns through the Elizabethan period to the early Italians. It is difficult to find any precise use of metaphor, simile, or other conceit, which is common to all the poets and at the same time important enough as an element of style to isolate these poets as a group. Donne, and often Cowley, employ a device which is sometimes considered characteristically 'metaphysical'; the elaboration (contrasted with the condensation) of a figure of speech to the furthest stage to which ingenuity can carry it. Thus Cowley develops the commonplace comparison of the world to a chess-board through long stanzas (*To Destiny*), and Donne, with more grace, in *A Valediction*,[2] the comparison of two lovers to a pair of compasses. But elsewhere we find, instead of the mere explication of the content of a comparison, a development by rapid association of thought which requires considerable agility on the part of the reader.

> *On a round ball*
> *A workeman that hath copies by, can lay*
> *An Europe, Afrique, and an Asia,*
> *And quickly make that, which was nothing, All,*
> > *So doth each teare,*
> > *Which thee doth weare,*

---

1. *Metaphysical Lyrics and Poems of the Seventeenth Century: Donne to Butler* (1921), selected and edited, with an essay, by Herbert J. C. Grierson. Eliot's essay was originally a review of this book in the London *Times Literary Supplement*.
2. I.e., "A Valediction: Forbidding Mourning."

> *A globe, yea world by that impression grow,*
> *Till thy tears mixt with mine doe overflow*
> *This world, by waters sent from thee, my heaven dissolved so.*[3]

Here we find at least two connexions which are not implicit in the first figure, but are forced upon it by the poet: from the geographer's globe to the
tear, and the tear to the deluge. On the other hand, some of Donne's most
successful and characteristic effects are secured by brief words and sudden
contrasts:

> *A bracelet of bright hair about the bone,*[4]

where the most powerful effect is produced by the sudden contrast of associations of 'bright hair' and of 'bone'. This telescoping of images and multiplied associations is characteristic of the phrase of some of the dramatists of
the period which Donne knew: not to mention Shakespeare, it is frequent in
Middleton, Webster, and Tourneur, and is one of the sources of the vitality of
their language.

Johnson, who employed the term 'metaphysical poets', apparently having
Donne, Cleveland, and Cowley chiefly in mind, remarks of them that 'the
most heterogeneous ideas are yoked by violence together'[5] The force of this
impeachment lies in the failure of the conjunction, the fact that often the
ideas are yoked but not united; and if we are to judge of styles of poetry by
their abuse, enough examples, may be found in Cleveland to justify Johnson's condemnation. But a degree of heterogeneity of material compelled
into unity by the operation of the poet's mind is omnipresent in poetry. We
need not select for illustration such a line as:

> *Notre âme est un trois-mâts cherchant son Icarie;*[6]

we may find it in some of the best lines of Johnson himself (*The Vanity of
Human Wishes*):

> *His fate was destined to a barren strand,*
> *A petty fortress, and a dubious hand;*
> *He left a name at which the world grew pale,*
> *To point a moral, or adorn a tale.*

where the effect is due to a contrast of ideas, different in degree but the same
in principle, as that which Johnson mildly reprehended. And in one of the
finest poems of the age (a poem which could not have been written in any
other age), the *Exequy* of Bishop King, the extended comparison is used with
perfect success: the idea and the simile become one, in the passage in which
the Bishop illustrates his impatience to see his dead wife, under the figure of
a journey:

> *Stay for me there; I will not faile*
> *To meet thee in that hollow Vale.*
> *And think not much of my delay;*
> *I am already on the way,*

---

3. Donne's "A Valediction: Of Weeping," lines
10–18.
4. "The Relic," line 6.
5. See Samuel Johnson's *Cowley.*
6. From Charles Baudelaire's "Le Voyage": "Our
soul is a three-masted ship searching for her Icarie"; Icarie is an imaginary utopia in *Voyage en
Icarie* (1840), a novel by the French socialist Eti-
enne Cabet.

> *And follow thee with all the speed*
> *Desire can make, or sorrows breed.*
> *Each minute is a short degree,*
> *And ev'ry hour a step towards thee,*
> *At night when I betake to rest,*
> *Next morn I rise nearer my West*
> *Of life, almost by eight houres sail,*
> *Than when sleep breath'd his drowsy gale. . . .*
> *But heark! My Pulse, like a soft Drum*
> *Beats my approach, tells Thee I come;*
> *And slow howere my marches be,*
> *I shall at last sit down by Thee.*

(In the last few lines there is that effect of terror which is several times attained by one of Bishop King's admirers, Edgar Poe.) Again, we may justly take these quatrains from Lord Herbert's Ode,[7] stanzas which would, we think, be immediately pronounced to be of the metaphysical school:

> *So when from hence we shall be gone,*
> *And be no more, nor you, nor I,*
> *As one another's mystery,*
> *Each shall be both, yet both but one.*
>
> *This said, in her up-lifted face,*
> *Her eyes, which did that beauty crown,*
> *Were like two stars, that having faln down,*
> *Look up again to find their place:*
>
> *While such a moveless silent peace*
> *Did seize on their becalmed sense,*
> *One would have thought some influence*
> *Their ravished spirits did possess.*

There is nothing in these lines (with the possible exception of the stars, a simile not at once grasped, but lovely and justified) which fits Johnson's general observations on the metaphysical poets in his essay on Cowley. A good deal resides in the richness of association which is at the same time borrowed from and given to the word 'becalmed'; but the meaning is clear, the language simple and elegant. It is to be observed that the language of these poets is as a rule simple and pure; in the verse of George Herbert this simplicity is carried as far as it can go—a simplicity emulated without success by numerous modern poets. The *structure* of the sentences, on the other hand, is sometimes far from simple, but this is not a vice; it is a fidelity to thought and feeling. The effect, at its best, is far less artificial than that of an ode by Gray. And as this fidelity induces variety of thought and feeling, so it induces variety of music. We doubt whether, in the eighteenth century, could be found two poems in nominally the same metre, so dissimilar as Marvell's *Coy Mistress* and Crashaw's *Saint Teresa*; the one producing an effect of great speed

---

7. Edward, Lord Herbert of Cherbury (1583–1648), brother of George Herbert. The "Ode" is his "Ode upon a Question moved, whether Love should continue forever?"

by the use of short syllables, and the other an ecclesiastical solemnity by the use of long ones:

> Love, thou art absolute sole lord
> Of life and death.

If so shrewd and sensitive (though so limited) a critic as Johnson failed to define metaphysical poetry by its faults, it is worth while to inquire whether we may not have more success by adopting the opposite method: by assuming that the poets of the seventeenth century (up to the Revolution)[8] were the direct and normal development of the precedent age; and, without prejudicing their case by the adjective 'metaphysical', consider whether their virtue was not something permanently valuable, which subsequently disappeared, but ought not to have disappeared. Johnson has hit, perhaps by accident, on one of their peculiarities, when he observes that 'their attempts were always analytic'; he would not agree that, after the dissociation, they put the material together again in a new unity.

It is certain that the dramatic verse of the later Elizabethan and early Jacobean poets expresses a degree, of development of sensibility which is not found in any of the prose, good as it often is. If we except Marlowe, a man of prodigious intelligence, these dramatists were directly or indirectly (it is at least a tenable theory) affected by Montaigne.[9] Even if we except also Jonson and Chapman, these two were probably erudite, and were notably men who incorporated their erudition into their sensibility: their mode of feeling was directly and freshly altered by their reading and thought. In Chapman especially there is a direct sensuous apprehension of thought, or a recreation of thought into feeling, which is exactly what we find in Donne:

> in this one thing, all the discipline
> Of manners and of manhood is contained;
> A man to join himself with th' Universe
> In his main sway, and make in all things fit
> One with that All, and go on, round as it;
> Not plucking from the whole his wretched part,
> And into straits, or into nought revert,
> Wishing the complete Universe might be
> Subject to such a rag of it as he;
> But to consider great Necessity.[1]

We compare this with some modern passage:

> No, when the fight begins within himself,
> A man's worth something. God stoops o'er his head,
> Satan looks up between his feet—both tug—
> He's left, himself, i' the middle; the soul wakes
> And grows. Prolong that battle through his life![2]

It is perhaps somewhat less fair, though very tempting (as both poets are concerned with the perpetuation of love by offspring), to compare with the

---

8. Of 1688; when James II was replaced by William and Mary.
9. Michel de Montaigne (1533–1592), French essayist.

1. From The Revenge of Bussy d'Ambois (4.1.137–46).
2. Robert Browning, "Bishop Blougram's Apology," lines 693–97.

stanzas already quoted from Lord Herbert's Ode the following from Tennyson:

> One walked between his wife and child,
> With measured footfall firm and mild,
> And now and then he gravely smiled.
>   The prudent partner of his blood
>   Leaned on him, faithful, gentle, good,
>   Wearing the rose of womanhood.
> And in their double love secure,
> The little maiden walked demure,
> Pacing with downward eyelids pure.
>   These three made unity so sweet,
>   My frozen heart began to beat,
>   Remembering its ancient heat.[3]

The difference is not a simple difference of degree between poets. It is something which had happened to the mind of England between the time of Donne or Lord Herbert of Cherbury and the time of Tennyson and Browning; it is the difference between the intellectual poet and the reflective poet. Tennyson and Browning are poets, and they think; but they do not feel their thought as immediately as the odour of a rose. A thought to Donne was an experience; it modified his sensibility. When a poet's mind is perfectly equipped for its work, it is constantly amalgamating disparate experience; the ordinary man's experience is chaotic, irregular, fragmentary. The latter falls in love, or reads Spinoza,[4] and these two experiences have nothing to do with each other, or with the noise of the typewriter or the smell of cooking; in the mind of the poet these experiences are always forming new wholes.

We may express the difference by the following theory: The poets of the seventeenth century, the successors of the dramatists of the sixteenth, possessed a mechanism of sensibility which could devour any kind of experience. They are simple, artificial, difficult, or fantastic, as their predecessors were; no less nor more than Dante, Guido Cavalcanti, Guinicelli, or Cino.[5] In the seventeenth century a dissociation of sensibility set in, from which we have never recovered; and this dissociation, as is natural, was aggravated by the influence of the two most powerful poets of the century, Milton and Dryden. Each of these men performed certain poetic functions so magnificently well that the magnitude of the effect concealed the absence of others. The language went on and in some respects improved; the best verse of Collins, Gray, Johnson, and even Goldsmith satisfies some of our fastidious demands better than that of Donne or Marvell or King. But while the language became more refined, the feeling became more crude. The feeling, the sensibility, expressed in the _Country Churchyard_[6] (to say nothing of Tennyson and Browning) is cruder than that in the _Coy Mistress._

The second effect of the influence of Milton and Dryden followed from the first, and was therefore slow in manifestation. The sentimental age began early in the eighteenth century, and continued. The poets revolted against

---

3. "The Two Voices," lines 412–23.
4. 17th-century Dutch philosopher.
5. These last three poets, all of whom lived in the 13th century, were members of the Tuscan school of lyric love poets. Guido Guinicelli was hailed by

Dante in the _Purgatorio_ as "father of Italian poets." Cino da Pistoia was a friend of Dante and Petrarch.
6. I.e., "An Elegy Written in a Country Churchyard," by Thomas Gray (1716–1771).

the ratiocinative, the descriptive; they thought and felt by fits, unbalanced; they reflected. In one or two passages of Shelley's *Triumph of Life*, in the second *Hyperion*, there are traces of a struggle toward unification of sensibility. But Keats and Shelley died, and Tennyson and Browning ruminated.

After this brief exposition of a theory—too brief, perhaps, to carry conviction—we may ask, what would have been the fate of the 'metaphysical' had the current of poetry descended in a direct line from them, as it descended in a direct line to them? They would not, certainly, be classified as metaphysical. The possible interests of a poet are unlimited; the more intelligent he is the better; the more intelligent he is the more likely that he will have interests: our only condition is that he turn them into poetry, and not merely meditate on them poetically. A philosophical theory which has entered into poetry is established, for its truth or falsity in one sense ceases to matter, and its truth in another sense is proved. The poets in question have, like other poets, various faults. But they were, at best, engaged in the task of trying to find the verbal equivalent for states of mind and feeling. And this means both that they are more mature, and that they wear better, than later poets of certainly not less literary ability.

It is not a permanent necessity that poets should be interested in philosophy, or in any other subject. We can only say that it appears likely that poets in our civilization, as it exists at present, must be *difficult*. Our civilization comprehends great variety and complexity, and this variety and complexity, playing upon a refined sensibility, must produce various and complex results. The poet must become more and more comprehensive, more allusive, more indirect, in order to force, to dislocate if necessary, language into his meaning. (A brilliant and extreme statement of this view, with which it is not requisite to associate oneself, is that of M Jean Epstein, *La Poésie d'aujourd'hui*.[7] Hence we get something which looks very much like the conceit—we get, in fact, a method curiously similar to that of the 'metaphysical poets', similar also in its use of obscure words and of simple phrasing.

> *O géraniums diaphanes, guerroyeurs sortilèges,*
> *Sacrilèges monomanes!*
> *Emballages, dévergondages, douches! O pressoirs*
> *Des vendanges des grands soirs!*
> *Layettes aux abois,*
> *Thyrses au fond des bois!*
> *Transfusions, représailles,*
> *Relevailles, compresses et l'éternal potion,*
> *Angélus! n'en pouvoir plus*
> *De débâcles nuptiales! de débâcles nuptiales!*[8]

The same poet could write also simply:

> *Elle est bien loin, elle pleure,*
> *Le grand vent se lamente aussi . . .* [9]

---

7. Poetry of today (French).
8. From *Derniers Vers* (*Last Poems*, 1890) 10, by Jules Laforgue (1860–1887): "O transparent geraniums, warrior incantations, / Monomaniac sacrileges! / Packing materials, shamelessnesses, shower baths! O wine presses / Of great evening vintages! / Hard-pressed baby linen, / Thyrsis in the depths of the woods! / Transfusions, reprisals, / Churchings, compresses, and the eternal potion, / Angelus! no longer to be borne [are] / Catastrophic marriages! catastrophic marriages!"
9. From *Derniers Vers* 11, "Sur une Défunte" ("On a Dead Woman"): "She is far away, she weeps / The great wind mourns also."

Jules Laforgue, and Tristan Corbière[1] in many of his poems, are nearer to the 'school of Donne' than any modern English poet. But poets more classical than they have the same essential quality of transmuting ideas into sensations, of transforming an observation into a state of mind.

> Pour l'enfant, amoureux de cartes et d'estampes,
> L'univers est égal à son vaste appétit.
> Ah, que le monde est grand à la clarté des lampes!
> Aux yeux du souvenir que le monde est petit![2]

In French literature the great master of the seventeenth century—Racine—and the great master of the nineteenth—Baudelaire—are in some ways more like each other than they are like anyone else. The greatest two masters of diction are also the greatest two psychologists, the most curious explorers of the soul. It is interesting to speculate whether it is not a misfortune that two of the greatest masters of diction in our language, Milton and Dryden, triumph with a dazzling disregard of the soul. If we continued to produce Miltons and Drydens it might not so much matter, but as things are it is a pity that English poetry has remained so incomplete. Those who object to the 'artificiality' of Milton or Dryden sometimes tell us to 'look into our hearts and write.'[3] But that is not looking deep enough; Racine or Donne looked into a good deal more than the heart. One must look into the cerebral cortex, the nervous system, and the digestive tracts.

May we not conclude, then, that Donne, Crashaw, Vaughan, Herbert and Lord Herbert, Marvell, King, Cowley at his best, are in the direct current of English poetry, and that their faults should be reprimanded by this standard rather than coddled by antiquarian affection? They have been enough praised in terms which are implicit limitations because they are 'metaphysical' or 'witty,' 'quaint' or 'obscure,' though at their best they have not these attributes more than other serious poets. On the other hand, we must not reject the criticism of Johnson (a dangerous person to disagree with) without having mastered it, without having assimilated the Johnsonian canons of taste. In reading the celebrated passage in his essay on Cowley we must remember that by wit he clearly means something more serious than we usually mean to-day; in his criticism of their versification we must remember in what a narrow discipline he was trained, but also how well trained; we must remember that Johnson tortures chiefly the chief offenders, Cowley and Cleveland. It would be a fruitful work, and one requiring a substantial book, to break up the classification of Johnson (for there has been none since) and exhibit these poets in all their difference of kind and of degree, from the massive music of Donne to the faint, pleasing tinkle of Aurelian Townshend—whose *Dialogue between a Pilgrim and Time* is one of the few regrettable omissions from the excellent anthology of Professor Grierson.

1921

---

1. French symbolist poet (1845–1875).
2. From Charles Baudelaire's "Le Voyage": "For the child, in love with maps and prints, / The universe matches his vast appetite. / Ah, how big the world is by lamplight! How small the world is to the eyes of memory!"
3. An adaptation of the last line of the first sonnet of *Astrophil and Stella*, by Sir Philip Sidney (1554–1586).

KATHERINE MANSFIELD
1888–1923

Kathleen Mansfield Beauchamp was born in Wellington, New Zealand, daughter of a respected businessman who was later knighted. In 1903 the family moved to London, where Kathleen and her sisters entered Queen's College, the first institution in England founded expressly for the higher education of women. The family returned to New Zealand, leaving the girls in London, but the Beauchamps brought their daughters home in 1906. By this time Kathleen had written a number of poems, sketches, and stories; and after experimenting with different pen names, she adopted that of Katherine Mansfield. She was restless and ambitious and chafed against the narrowness of middle-class life in New Zealand, at that time still very much a new country in the shadow of the British Empire.

In July 1908 Mansfield left again for London; she never returned to New Zealand. In 1909 she suddenly married G. C. Bowden, a teacher of singing and elocution, but left him the same evening. Shortly afterward she became pregnant by another man and went to Germany to await the birth, but she had a miscarriage there. Her experiences in Germany are told in carefully observed sketches full of ironic detail in her first published book, *In a German Pension* (1911).

In 1910 she briefly resumed life with Bowden, who put her in touch with A. R. Orage, editor of the avant-garde periodical *The New Age*. There she published a number of her stories and sketches. At the end of 1911 she met the critic John Middleton Murry, editor of the modernist magazine *Rhythm*, and eventually married him. She developed intense but conflicted friendships with D. H. Lawrence, Virginia Woolf, and other writers of the day. During all this time Mansfield experimented in technique and refined her art, attempting within the short story to illuminate the ambivalences and complexities of friendship and family, gender and class. The death in World War I, in October 1915, of her much-loved younger brother sent her imagination back to their childhood days in New Zealand and in doing so gave a fresh charge and significance to her writing. Using her newly developed style with an ever greater subtlety and sensitivity, she now produced her best stories, including "Prelude," "Daughters of the Late Colonel," "At the Bay," and "The Garden Party." With the publication of *The Garden Party and Other Stories* in February 1922, Mansfield's place as a master of the modern short story was ensured. But she was gravely ill with tuberculosis and died suddenly at the age of thirty-four in Fontainebleau, France, where she had gone to try to find a cure by adopting the methods of the controversial mystic George Ivanovich Gurdjieff.

Mansfield produced her best and most characteristic work in her last years, when she combined incident, image, symbol, and structure in a way comparable with, yet interestingly different from, James Joyce's method in *Dubliners*, the two writers sharing an influence in the precise and understated art of the Russian writer Anton Chekhov. "Daughters of the Late Colonel," a story of two middle-aged sisters and their devotion to a tyrannical father, shows her working characteristically through suggestion rather than explicit development to illuminate a late-Victorian world, with the subdued elegiac sense of female lives wasted in the service of an outmoded patriarchal order, although the story's ironic surface is restrained comedy. The meaning is achieved most of all through the atmosphere, built up by the accumulation of small strokes, none of which seems more than a shrewdly observed realistic detail. Mansfield also manipulates time masterfully: she makes particularly effective use of the unobtrusive flashback, where we find ourselves in an earlier phase of the action without quite knowing how we got there but fully aware of its relevance to the total action and atmosphere.

The Daughters of the Late Colonel

I

The week after was one of the busiest weeks of their lives. Even when they went to bed it was only their bodies that lay down and rested; their minds went on, thinking things out, talking things over, wondering, deciding, trying to remember where . . .

Constantia lay like a statue, her hands by her sides, her feet just overlapping each other, the sheet up to her chin. She stared at the ceiling.

'Do you think father would mind if we gave his top-hat to the porter?'

'The porter?' snapped Josephine. 'Why ever the porter? What a very extraordinary idea!'

'Because,' said Constantia slowly, 'he must often have to go to funerals. And I noticed at—at the cemetery that he only had a bowler.' She paused. 'I thought then how very much he'd appreciate a top-hat. We ought to give him a present, too. He was always very nice to father.'

'But,' cried Josephine, flouncing on her pillow and staring across the dark at Constantia, 'father's head!' And suddenly, for one awful moment, she nearly giggled. Not, of course, that she felt in the least like giggling. It must have been habit. Years ago, when they had stayed awake at night talking, their beds had simply heaved. And now the porter's head, disappearing, popped out, like a candle, under father's hat. . . . The giggle mounted, mounted; she clenched her hands; she fought it down; she frowned fiercely at the dark and said 'Remember' terribly sternly.

'We can decide tomorrow,' she sighed.

Constantia had noticed nothing; she sighed.

'Do you think we ought to have our dressing-gowns dyed as well?'

'Black?' almost shrieked Josephine.

'Well, what else?' said Constantia. 'I was thinking—it doesn't seem quite sincere, in a way, to wear black out of doors and when we're fully dressed, and then when we're at home—'

'But nobody sees us,' said Josephine. She gave the bedclothes such a twitch that both her feet became uncovered and she had to creep up the pillows to get them well under again.

'Kate does,' said Constantia. 'And the postman very well might.'

Josephine thought of her dark-red slippers, which matched her dressing-gown, and of Constantia's favourite indefinite green ones which went with hers. Black! Two black dressing-gowns and two pairs of black woolly slippers, creeping off to the bathroom like black cats.

'I don't think it's absolutely necessary,' said she.

Silence. Then Constantia said, 'We shall have to post the papers with the notice in them tomorrow to catch the Ceylon mail. . . . How many letters have we had up till now?'

'Twenty-three.'

Josephine had replied to them all, and twenty-three times when she came to 'We miss our dear father so much' she had broken down and had to use her handkerchief, and on some of them even to soak up a very light-blue tear with an edge of blotting-paper. Strange! She couldn't have put it on—but twenty-three times. Even now, though, when she said over to herself sadly 'We miss our dear father *so* much,' she could have cried if she'd wanted to.

'Have you got enough stamps?' came from Constantia.

'Oh, how can I tell?' said Josephine crossly. 'What's the good of asking me that now?'

'I was just wondering,' said Constantia mildly.

Silence again. There came a little rustle, a scurry, a hop.

'A mouse,' said Constantia.

'It can't be a mouse because there aren't any crumbs,' said Josephine.

'But it doesn't know there aren't,' said Constantia.

A spasm of pity squeezed her heart. Poor little thing! She wished she'd left a tiny piece of biscuit on the dressing-table. It was awful to think of it not finding anything. What would it do?

'I can't think how they manage to live at all,' she said slowly.

'Who?' demanded Josephine.

And Constantia said more loudly than she meant to, 'Mice.'

Josephine was furious. 'Oh, what nonsense, Con!' she said. 'What have mice got to do with it? You're asleep.'

'I don't think I am,' said Constantia. She shut her eyes to make sure. She was.

Josephine arched her spine, pulled up her knees, folded her arms so that her fists came under her ears, and pressed her cheek hard against the pillow.

II

Another thing which complicated matters was they had Nurse Andrews staying on with them that week. It was their own fault; they had asked her. It was Josephine's idea. On the morning—well, on the last morning, when the doctor had gone, Josephine had said to Constantia, 'Don't you think it would be rather nice if we asked Nurse Andrews to stay on for a week as our guest?'

'Very nice,' said Constantia.

'I thought,' went on Josephine quickly, 'I should just say this afternoon, after I've paid her, 'My sister and I would be very pleased, after all you've done for us, Nurse Andrews, if you would stay on for a week as our guest.' I'd have to put that in about being our guest in case—'

'Oh, but she could hardly expect to be paid!' cried Constantia.

'One never knows,' said Josephine sagely.

Nurse Andrews had, of course, jumped at the idea. But it was a bother. It meant they had to have regular sit-down meals at the proper times, whereas if they'd been alone they could just have asked Kate if she wouldn't have minded bringing them a tray wherever they were. And meal-times now that the strain was over were rather a trial.

Nurse Andrews was simply fearful about butter. Really they couldn't help feeling that about butter, at least, she took advantage of their kindness. And she had that maddening habit of asking for just an inch more bread to finish what she had on her plate, and then, at the last mouthful, absent-mindedly—of course it wasn't absent-mindedly—taking another helping. Josephine got very red when this happened, and she fastened her small, bead-like eyes on the tablecloth as if she saw a minute strange insect creeping through the web of it. But Constantia's long, pale face lengthened and set, and she gazed away—away—far over the desert, to where that line of camels unwound like a thread of wool. . . .

'When I was with Lady Tukes,' said Nurse Andrews, 'she had such a dainty little contrayvance for the buttah. It was a silvah cupid balanced on the—on the bordah of a glass dish, holding a tayny fork. And when you wanted some buttah you simply pressed his foot and he bent down and speared you a piece. It was quite a gayme.'

Josephine could hardly bear that. But 'I think those things are very extravagant' was all she said.

'But whey?' asked Nurse Andrews, beaming through her eyeglasses. 'No one, surely, would take more buttah than one wanted—would one?'

'Ring, Con,' cried Josephine. She couldn't trust herself to reply.

And proud young Kate, the enchanted princess, came in to see what the old tabbies wanted now. She snatched away their plates of mock something or other and slapped down a white terrified blancmange.[1]

'Jam, please, Kate,' said Josephine kindly.

Kate knelt and burst open the sideboard, lifted the lid of the jam-pot, saw it was empty, put it on the table, and stalked off.

'I'm afraid,' said Nurse Andrews a moment later, 'there isn't any.'

'Oh, what a bother!' said Josephine. She bit her lip. 'What had we better do?'

Constantia looked dubious. 'We can't disturb Kate again,' she said softly.

Nurse Andrews waited, smiling at them both. Her eyes wandered, spying at everything behind her eyeglasses. Constantia in despair went back to her camels. Josephine frowned heavily—concentrated. If it hadn't been for this idiotic woman she and Con would, of course, have eaten their blancmange without. Suddenly the idea came.

'I know,' she said. 'Marmalade. There's some marmalade in the sideboard. Get it, Con.'

'I hope,' laughed Nurse Andrews—and her laugh was like a spoon tinkling against a medicine glass—'I hope it's not very bittah marmalayde.'

III

But, after all, it was not long now, and then she'd be gone for good. And there was no getting over the fact that she had been very kind to father. She had nursed him day and night at the end. Indeed, both Constantia and Josephine felt privately she had rather overdone the not leaving him at the very last. For when they had gone in to say goodbye Nurse Andrews had sat beside his bed the whole time, holding his wrist and pretending to look at her watch. It couldn't have been necessary. It was so tactless, too. Supposing father had wanted to say something—something private to them. Not that he had. Oh, far from it! He lay there, purple, a dark, angry purple in the face, and never even looked at them when they came in. Then, as they were standing there, wondering what to do, he had suddenly opened one eye. Oh, what a difference it would have made, what a difference to their memory of him, how much easier to tell people about it, if he had only opened both! But no—one eye only. It glared at them a moment and then . . . went out.

---

1. A gelatinous dessert.

IV

It had made it very awkward for them when Mr Farolles, of St John's, called the same afternoon.

'The end was quite peaceful, I trust?' were the first words he said as he glided towards them through the dark drawing-room.

'Quite,' said Josephine faintly. They both hung their heads. Both of them felt certain that eye wasn't at all a peaceful eye.

'Won't you sit down?' said Josephine.

'Thank you, Miss Pinner,' said Mr Farolles gratefully. He folded his coattails and began to lower himself into father's armchair, but just as he touched it he almost sprang up and slid into the next chair instead.

He coughed. Josephine clasped her hands; Constantia looked vague.

'I want you to feel, Miss Pinner,' said Mr Farolles, 'and you, Miss Constantia, that I'm trying to be helpful. I want to be helpful to you both, if you will let me. These are the times,' said Mr Farolles, very simply and earnestly, 'when God means us to be helpful to one another.'

'Thank you very much, Mr Farolles,' said Josephine and Constantia.

'Not at all,' said Mr Farolles gently. He drew his kid gloves through his fingers and leaned forward. 'And if either of you would like a little Communion, either or both of you, here and now, you have only to tell me. A little Communion is often very help—a great comfort,' he added tenderly.

But the idea of a little Communion terrified them. What! In the drawing room by themselves—with no—no altar or anything! The piano would be much too high, thought Constantia, and Mr Farolles could not possibly lean over it with the chalice. And Kate would be sure to come bursting in and interrupt them, thought Josephine. And supposing the bell rang in the middle? It might be somebody important—about their mourning. Would they get up reverently and go out, or would they have to wait . . . in torture?

'Perhaps you will send round a note by your good Kate if you would care for it later,' said Mr Farolles.

'Oh yes, thank you very much!' they both said.

Mr Farolles got up and took his black straw hat from the round table.

'And about the funeral,' he said softly. 'I may arrange that—as your dear father's old friend and yours, Miss Pinner—and Miss Constantia?'

Josephine and Constantia got up too.

'I should like it to be quite simple,' said Josephine firmly, 'and not too expensive. At the same time, I should like—'

'A good one that will last,' thought dreamy Constantia, as if Josephine were buying a nightgown. But of course Josephine didn't say that. 'One suitable to our father's position.' She was very nervous.

'I'll run round to our good friend Mr Knight,' said Mr Farolles soothingly. 'I will ask him to come and see you. I am sure you will find him very helpful indeed.'

V

Well, at any rate, all that part of it was over, though neither of them could possibly believe that father was never coming back. Josephine had had a moment of absolute terror at the cemetery, while the coffin was lowered, to think that she and Constantia had done this thing without asking his permission. What would father say when he found out? For he was bound to find out sooner or later. He always did. 'Buried. You two girls had me buried?' She heard his stick thumping. Oh, what would they say? What possible excuse could they make? It sounded such an appallingly heartless thing to do. Such a wicked advantage to take of a person because he happened to be helpless at the moment. The other people seemed to treat it all as a matter of course. They were strangers; they couldn't be expected to understand that father was the very last person for such a thing to happen to. No, the entire blame for it all would fall on her and Constantia. And the expense, she thought, stepping into the tight-buttoned cab. When she had to show him the bills. What would he say then?

She heard him absolutely roaring, 'And do you expect me to pay for this gimcrack excursion of yours?'

'Oh,' groaned poor Josephine aloud, 'we shouldn't have done it, Con!'

And Constantia, pale as a lemon in all that blackness, said in a frightened whisper, 'Done what, Jug?'

'Let them bu-bury father like that,' said Josephine, breaking down and crying into her new, queer-smelling mourning handkerchief.

'But what else could we have done?' asked Constantia wonderingly. 'We couldn't have kept him unburied. At any rate, not in a flat that size.'

Josephine blew her nose; the cab was dreadfully stuffy.

'I don't know,' she said forlornly. 'It is all so dreadful. I feel we ought to have tried to, just for a time at least. To make perfectly sure. One thing's certain'—and her tears sprang out again—'father will never forgive us for this—never!'

VI

Father would never forgive them. That was what they felt more than ever when, two mornings later, they went into his room to go through his things. They had discussed it quite calmly. It was even down on Josephine's list of things to be done. Go through father's things and settle about them. But that was a very different matter from saying after breakfast:

'Well, are you ready, Con?'

'Yes, Jug—when you are.'

'Then I think we'd better get it over.'

It was dark in the hall. It had been a rule for years never to disturb father in the morning, whatever happened. And now they were going to open the door without knocking even. . . . Constantia's eyes were enormous at the idea; Josephine felt weak in the knees.

'You—you go first,' she gasped, pushing Constantia.

But Constantia said, as she always had said on those occasions, 'No, Jug, that's not fair. You're the eldest.'

Josephine was just going to say—what at other times she wouldn't have owned to for the world—what she kept for her very last weapon, 'But you're the tallest,' when they noticed that the kitchen door was open, and there stood Kate. . . .

'Very stiff,' said Josephine, grasping the door-handle and doing her best to turn it. As if anything ever deceived Kate!

It couldn't be helped. That girl was . . . Then the door was shut behind them, but—but they weren't in father's room at all. They might have suddenly walked through the wall by mistake into a different flat altogether. Was the door just behind them? They were too frightened to look. Josephine knew that if it was it was holding itself tight shut; Constantia felt that, like the doors in dreams, it hadn't any handle at all. It was the coldness which made it so awful. Or the whiteness—which? Everything was covered. The blinds were down, a cloth hung over the mirror, a sheet hid the bed, a huge fan of white paper filled the fireplace. Constantia timidly put out her hand; she almost expected a snowflake to fall. Josephine felt a queer tingling in her nose, as if her nose was freezing. Then a cab klop-klopped over the cobbles below, and the quiet seemed to shake into little pieces.

'I had better pull up a blind,' said Josephine bravely.

'Yes, it might be a good idea,' whispered Constantia.

They only gave the blind a touch, but it flew up and the cord flew after, rolling round the blind-stick, and the little tassel tapped as if trying to get free. That was too much for Constantia.

'Don't you think—don't you think we might put it off for another day?' she whispered.

'Why?' snapped Josephine, feeling, as usual, much better now that she knew for certain that Constantia was terrified. 'It's got to be done. But I do wish you wouldn't whisper, Con.'

'I didn't know I was whispering,' whispered Constantia.

'And why do you keep on staring at the bed?' said Josephine, raising her voice almost defiantly. 'There's nothing on the bed.'

'Oh, Jug, don't say so!' said poor Connie. 'At any rate, not so loudly.'

Josephine felt herself that she had gone too far. She took a wide swerve over to the chest of drawers, put out her hand, but quickly drew it back again.

'Connie!' she gasped, and she wheeled round and leaned with her back against the chest of drawers.

'Oh, Jug—what?'

Josephine could only glare. She had the most extraordinary feeling that she had just escaped something simply awful. But how could she explain to Constantia that father was in the chest of drawers? He was in the top drawer with his handkerchiefs and neckties, or in the next with his shirts and pyjamas, or in the lowest of all with his suits. He was watching there, hidden away—just behind the door-handle—ready to spring.

She pulled a funny old-fashioned face at Constantia, just as she used to in the old days when she was going to cry.

'I can't open,' she nearly wailed.

'No, don't, Jug,' whispered Constantia earnestly. 'It's much better not to. Don't let's open anything. At any rate, not for a long time.'

'But—but it seems so weak,' said Josephine, breaking down.

'But why not be weak for once, Jug?' argued Constantia, whispering quite fiercely. 'If it is weak.' And her pale stare flew from the locked writing-table—so safe—to the huge glittering wardrobe, and she began to breathe in a queer, panting way. 'Why shouldn't we be weak for once in our lives, Jug? It's quite excusable. Let's be weak—be weak, Jug. It's much nicer to be weak than to be strong.'

And then she did one of those amazingly bold things that she'd done about twice before in their lives: she marched over to the wardrobe, turned the key, and took it out of the lock. Took it out of the lock and held it up to Josephine, showing Josephine by her extraordinary smile that she knew what she'd done—she'd risked deliberately father being in there among his overcoats.

If the huge wardrobe had lurched forward, had crashed down on Constantia, Josephine wouldn't have been surprised. On the contrary, she would have thought it the only suitable thing to happen. But nothing happened. Only the room seemed quieter than ever, and bigger flakes of cold air fell on Josephine's shoulders and knees. She began to shiver.

'Come, Jug,' said Constantia, still with that awful callous smile; and Josephine followed just as she had that last time, when Constantia had pushed Benny into the round pond.

VII

But the strain told on them when they were back in the dining-room. They sat down, very shaky, and looked at each other.

'I don't feel I can settle to anything,' said Josephine, 'until I've had something. Do you think we could ask Kate for two cups of hot water?'

'I really don't see why we shouldn't,' said Constantia carefully. She was quite normal again. 'I won't ring. I'll go to the kitchen door and ask her.'

'Yes, do,' said Josephine, sinking down into a chair. 'Tell her, just two cups, Con, nothing else—on a tray.'

'She needn't even put the jug on, need she?' said Constantia, as though Kate might very well complain if the jug had been there.

'Oh, no, certainly not! The jug's not at all necessary. She can pour it direct out of the kettle,' cried Josephine, feeling that would be a labour-saving indeed.

Their cold lips quivered at the greenish brims. Josephine curved her small red hands round the cup; Constantia sat up and blew on the wavy stream, making it flutter from one side to the other.

'Speaking of Benny,' said Josephine.

And though Benny hadn't been mentioned Constantia immediately looked as though he had.

'He'll expect us to send him something of father's, of course. But it's so difficult to know what to send to Ceylon.'

'You mean things get unstuck so on the voyage,' murmured Constantia.

'No, lost,' said Josephine sharply. 'You know there's no post. Only runners.'

Both paused to watch a black man in white linen drawers running through the pale fields for dear life, with a large brown-paper parcel in his hands. Josephine's black man was tiny; he scurried along glistening like an ant. But there was something blind and tireless about Constantia's tall, thin fellow, which made him, she decided, a very unpleasant person indeed. . . . On the veranda, dressed all in white and wearing a cork helmet, stood Benny. His right hand shook up and down, as father's did when he was impatient. And behind him, not in the least interested, sat Hilda, the unknown sister-in-law. She swung in a cane rocker and flicked over the leaves of the *Tatler*.

'I think his watch would be the most suitable present,' said Josephine.

Constantia looked up; she seemed surprised.

'Oh, would you trust a gold watch to a native?'

'But of course I'd disguise it,' said Josephine. 'No one would know it was a watch.' She liked the idea of having to make a parcel such a curious shape that no one could possibly guess what it was. She even thought for a moment of hiding the watch in a narrow cardboard corset-box that she'd kept by her for a long time, waiting for it to come in for something. It was such beautiful firm cardboard. But, no, it wouldn't be appropriate for this occasion. It had lettering on it: *Medium Women's 28. Extra Firm Busks.* It would be almost too much of a surprise for Benny to open that and find father's watch inside.

'And of course it isn't as though it would be going—ticking, I mean,' said Constantia, who was still thinking of the native love of jewelery. 'At least,' she added, 'it would be very strange if after all that time it was.'

VIII

Josephine made no reply. She had flown off on one of her tangents. She had suddenly thought of Cyril. Wasn't it more usual for the only grandson to have the watch? And then dear Cyril was so appreciative and a gold watch meant so much to a young man. Benny, in all probability, had quite got out of the habit of watches; men so seldom wore waistcoats in those hot climates. Whereas Cyril in London wore them from year's end to year's end. And it would be so nice for her and Constantia, when he came to tea, to know it was there. 'I see you've got on grandfather's watch, Cyril.' It would be somehow so satisfactory.

Dear boy! What a blow his sweet, sympathetic little note had been! Of course they quite understood; but it was most unfortunate.

'It would have been such a point, having him,' said Josephine.

'And he would have enjoyed it so,' said Constantia, not thinking what she was saying.

However, as soon as he got back he was coming to tea with his aunties. Cyril to tea was one of their rare treats.

'Now, Cyril, you mustn't be frightened of our cakes. Your Auntie Con and I bought them at Buszard's this morning. We know what a man's appetite is. So don't be ashamed of making a good tea.'

Josephine cut recklessly into the rich dark cake that stood for her winter gloves or the soling and heeling of Constantia's only respectable shoes. But Cyril was most unmanlike in appetite.

'I say, Aunt Josephine, I simply can't. I've only just had lunch, you know.'

'Oh, Cyril, that can't be true! It's after four,' cried Josephine. Constantia sat with her knife poised over the chocolate-roll.

'It is, all the same,' said Cyril. 'I had to meet a man at Victoria,[2] and he kept me hanging about till . . . there was only time to get lunch and to come on here. And he gave me—phew'—Cyril put his hand to his forehead—'a terrific blow-out,'[3] he said.

It was disappointing—today of all days. But still he couldn't be expected to know.

'But you'll have a meringue, won't you, Cyril?' said Aunt Josephine. 'These meringues were bought specially for you. Your dear father was so fond of them. We were sure you are, too.'

'I *am*, Aunt Josephine,' cried Cyril ardently. 'Do you mind if I take half to begin with?'

'Not at all, dear boy; but we mustn't let you off with that.'

2. London railroad station, connecting with the 3. Feast.
Channel ports.

'Is your dear father still so fond of meringues?' asked Auntie Con gently. She winced faintly as she broke through the shell of hers.

'Well, I don't quite know, Auntie Con,' said Cyril breezily.

At that they both looked up.

'Don't know?' almost snapped Josephine. 'Don't know a thing like that about your own father, Cyril?'

'Surely,' said Auntie Con softly.

Cyril tried to laugh it off. 'Oh, well,' he said, 'it's such a long time since—' He faltered. He stopped. Their faces were too much for him.

'Even *so*,' said Josephine.

And Auntie Con looked.

Cyril put down his teacup. 'Wait a bit,' he cried. 'Wait a bit, Aunt Josephine. What am I thinking of?'

He looked up. They were beginning to brighten. Cyril slapped his knee.

'Of course,' he said, 'it was meringues. How could I have forgotten? Yes, Aunt Josephine, you're perfectly right. Father's most frightfully keen on meringues.'

They didn't only beam. Aunt Josephine went scarlet with pleasure; Auntie Con gave a deep, deep sigh.

'And now, Cyril, you must come and see father,' said Josephine. 'He knows you were coming today.'

'Right,' said Cyril, very firmly and heartily. He got up from his chair; suddenly he glanced at the clock.

'I say, Auntie Con, isn't your clock a bit slow? I've got to meet a man at— at Paddington[4] just after five. I'm afraid I shan't be able to stay very long with grandfather.'

'Oh, he won't expect you to stay *very* long!' said Aunt Josephine.

Constantia was still gazing at the clock. She couldn't make up her mind if it was fast or slow. It was one or the other, she felt almost certain of that. At any rate, it had been.

Cyril still lingered. 'Aren't you coming along, Auntie Con?'

'Of course,' said Josephine, 'we shall all go. Come on, Con.'

IX

They knocked at the door, and Cyril followed his aunts into grandfather's hot, sweetish room.

'Come on,' said Grandfather Pinner. 'Don't hang about. What is it? What've you been up to?'

He was sitting in front of a roaring fire, clasping his stick. He had a thick rug over his knees. On his lap there lay a beautiful pale yellow silk handkerchief.

'It's Cyril, father,' said Josephine shyly. And she took Cyril's hand and led him forward.

'Good afternoon, grandfather,' said Cyril, trying to take his hand out of Aunt Josephine's. Grandfather Pinner shot his eyes at Cyril in the way he was famous for. Where was Auntie Con? She stood on the other side of Aunt Josephine; her long arms hung down in front of her; her hands were clasped. She never took her eyes off grandfather.

---

4. London railroad station, serving the west of England and Wales.

'Well,' said Grandfather Pinner, beginning to thump, 'what have you got to tell me?'

What had he, what had he got to tell him? Cyril felt himself smiling like a perfect imbecile. The room was stifling, too.

But Aunt Josephine came to his rescue. She cried brightly, 'Cyril says his father is still very fond of meringues, father dear.'

'Eh?' said Grandfather Pinner, curving his hand like a purple meringue-shell over one ear.

Josephine repeated, 'Cyril says his father is still very fond of meringues.'

'Can't hear,' said old Colonel Pinner. And he waved Josephine away with his stick, then pointed with his stick to Cyril. 'Tell me what she's trying to say,' he said.

(My God!) 'Must I?' said Cyril, blushing and staring at Aunt Josephine.

'Do, dear,' she smiled. 'It will please him so much.'

'Come on, out with it!' cried Colonel Pinner testily, beginning to thump again.

And Cyril leaned forward and yelled, 'Father's still very fond of meringues.'

At that Grandfather Pinner jumped as though he had been shot.

'Don't shout!' he cried. 'What's the matter with the boy? Meringues! What about 'em?'

'Oh, Aunt Josephine, must we go on?' groaned Cyril desperately.

'It's quite all right, dear boy,' said Aunt Josephine, as though he and she were at the dentist's together. 'He'll understand in a minute.' And she whispered to Cyril, 'He's getting a bit deaf, you know.' Then she leaned forward and really bawled at Grandfather Pinner, 'Cyril only wanted to tell you, father dear, that his father is still very fond of meringues.'

Colonel Pinner heard that time, heard and brooded, looking Cyril up and down.

'What an esstrordinary thing!' said old Grandfather Pinner. 'What an esstrordinary thing to come all this way here to tell me!'

And Cyril felt it *was*.

'Yes, I shall send Cyril the watch,' said Josephine.

'That would be very nice,' said Constantia. 'I seem to remember last time he came there was some little trouble about the time.'

X

They were interrupted by Kate bursting through the door in her usual fashion, as though she had discovered some secret panel in the wall.

'Fried or boiled?' asked the bold voice.

Fried or boiled? Josephine and Constantia were quite bewildered for the moment. They could hardly take it in.

'Fried or boiled what, Kate?' asked Josephine, trying to begin to concentrate.

Kate gave a loud sniff. 'Fish.'

'Well, why didn't you say so immediately?' Josephine reproached her gently. 'How could you expect us to understand, Kate? There are a great many things in this world, you know, which are fried or boiled.' And after such a display of courage she said quite brightly to Constantia, 'Which do you prefer, Con?'

'I think it might be nice to have it fried,' said Constantia. 'On the other hand, of course boiled fish is very nice. I think I prefer both equally well . . . Unless you . . . In that case—'

'I shall fry it,' said Kate, and she bounced back, leaving their door open and slamming the door of her kitchen.

Josephine gazed at Constantia; she raised her pale eyebrows until they rippled away into her pale hair. She got up. She said in a very lofty, imposing way, 'Do you mind following me into the drawing-room, Constantia? I've something of great importance to discuss with you.'

For it was always to the drawing-room they retired when they wanted to talk over Kate.

Josephine closed the door meaningly. 'Sit down, Constantia,' she said, still very grand. She might have been receiving Constantia for the first time. And Con looked round vaguely for a chair, as though she felt indeed quite a stranger.

'Now the question is,' said Josephine, bending forward, 'whether we shall keep her or not.'

'That is the question,' agreed Constantia.

'And this time,' said Josephine firmly, 'we must come to a definite decision.'

Constantia looked for a moment as though she might begin going over all the other times, but she pulled herself together and said, 'Yes, Jug.'

'You see, Con,' explained Josephine, 'everything is so changed now.' Constantia looked up quickly. 'I mean,' went on Josephine, 'we're not dependent on Kate as we were.' And she blushed faintly. 'There's not father to cook for.'

'That is perfectly true,' agreed Constantia. 'Father certainly doesn't want any cooking now, whatever else—'

Josephine broke in sharply, 'You're not sleepy, are you, Con?'

'Sleepy, Jug?' Constantia was wide-eyed.

'Well, concentrate more,' said Josephine sharply, and she returned to the subject. 'What it comes to is, if we did'—and this she barely breathed, glancing at the door—'give Kate notice'—she raised her voice again—'we could manage our own food.'

'Why not?' cried Constantia. She couldn't help smiling. The idea was so exciting. She clasped her hands. 'What should we live on, Jug?'

'Oh, eggs in various forms!' said Jug, lofty again. 'And, besides, there are all the cooked foods.'

'But I've always heard,' said Constantia, 'they are considered so very expensive.'

'Not if one buys them in moderation,' said Josephine. But she tore herself away from this fascinating bypath and dragged Constantia after her.

'What we've got to decide now, however, is whether we really do trust Kate or not.'

Constantia leaned back. Her flat little laugh flew from her lips.

'Isn't it curious, Jug,' said she, 'that just on this one subject I've never been able to quite make up my mind?'

XI

She never had. The whole difficulty was to prove anything. How did one prove things, how could one? Suppose Kate had stood in front of her and deliberately made a face. Mightn't she very well have been in pain? Wasn't it impossible, at any rate, to ask Kate if she was making a face at her? If Kate answered 'No'—and of course she would say 'No'—what a position! How undignified! Then again Constantia suspected, she was almost certain that Kate went to her chest of drawers when she and Josephine were out, not to take things but to spy. Many times she had come back to find her amethyst cross in the most unlikely places, under her lace ties or on top of her evening Bertha.[5] More than once she had laid a trap for Kate. She had arranged things in a special order and then called Josephine to witness.

'You see, Jug?'

'Quite, Con.'

'Now we shall be able to tell.'

But, oh dear, when she did go to look, she was as far off from a proof as ever! If anything was displaced, it might so very well have happened as she closed the drawer; a jolt might have done it so easily.

'You come, Jug, and decide. I really can't. It's too difficult.'

But after a pause and a long glare Josephine would sigh. 'Now you've put the doubt into my mind, Con, I'm sure I can't tell myself.'

'Well, we can't postpone it again,' said Josephine. 'If we postpone it this time—'

XII

But at that moment in the street below a barrel-organ struck up. Josephine and Constantia sprang to their feet together.

'Run, Con,' said Josephine. 'Run quickly. There's sixpence on the—'

Then they remembered. It didn't matter. They would never have to stop the organ-grinder again. Never again would she and Constantia be told to make that monkey take his noise somewhere else. Never would sound that loud, strange bellow when father thought they were not hurrying enough. The organ-grinder might play there all day and the stick would not thump.

It never will thump again,
It never will thump again,

played the barrel-organ.

What was Constantia thinking? She had such a strange smile; she looked different. She couldn't be going to cry.

'Jug, Jug,' said Constantia softly, pressing her hands together. 'Do you know what day it is? It's Saturday. It's a week today, a whole week.'

A week since father died,
A week since father died,

cried the barrel-organ. And Josephine, too, forgot to be practical and sensible; she smiled faintly, strangely. On the Indian carpet there fell a square of sunlight, pale red; it came and went and came—and stayed, deepened—until it shone almost golden.

'The sun's out,' said Josephine, as though it really mattered.

---

5. Detachable lace collar for low-necked dresses.

A perfect fountain of bubbling notes shook from the barrel-organ, round, bright notes, carelessly scattered.

Constantia lifted her big, cold hands as if to catch them, and then her hands fell again. She walked over to the mantelpiece to her favourite Buddha. And the stone and gilt image, whose smile always gave her such a queer feeling, almost a pain and yet a pleasant pain, seemed today to be more than smiling. He knew something; he had a secret. 'I know something that you don't know,' said her Buddha. Oh, what was it, what could it be? And yet she had always felt there was . . . something.

The sunlight pressed through the windows, thieved its way in, flashed its light over the furniture and the photographs. Josephine watched it. When it came to mother's photograph, the enlargement over the piano, it lingered as though puzzled to find so little remained of mother, except the ear-rings shaped like tiny pagodas and a black feather boa. Why did the photographs of dead people always fade so? wondered Josephine. As soon as a person was dead their photograph died too. But, of course, this one of mother was very old. It was thirty-five years old. Josephine remembered standing on a chair and pointing out that feather boa to Constantia and telling her that it was a snake that had killed their mother in Ceylon. . . . Would everything have been different if mother hadn't died? She didn't see why. Aunt Florence had lived with them until they had left school, and they had moved three times and had their yearly holiday and . . . and there'd been changes of servants, of course.

Some little sparrows, young sparrows they sounded, chirped on the window-ledge. *Yeep—eyeep—yeep.* But Josephine felt they were not sparrows, not on the window-ledge. It was inside her, that queer little crying noise. *Yeep–eyeep—yeep.* Ah, what was it crying, so weak and forlorn?

If mother had lived, might they have married? But there had been nobody for them to marry. There had been father's Anglo-Indian friends before he quarreled with them. But after that she and Constantia never met a single man except clergymen. How did one meet men? Or even if they'd met them, how could they have got to know men well enough to be more than strangers? One read of people having adventures, being followed, and so on. But nobody had ever followed Constantia and her. Oh yes, there had been one year at Eastbourne[6] a mysterious man at their boarding-house who had put a note on the jug of hot water outside their bedroom door! But by the time Connie had found it the steam had made the writing too faint to read; they couldn't even make out to which of them it was addressed. And he had left next day. And that was all. The rest had been looking after father and at the same time keeping out of father's way. But now? But now? The thieving sun touched Josephine gently. She lifted her face. She was drawn over to the window by gentle beams. . . .

Until the barrel-organ stopped playing Constantia stayed before the Buddha, wondering, but not as usual, not vaguely. This time her wonder was like longing. She remembered the times she had come in here, crept out of bed in her nightgown when the moon was full, and lain on the floor with her arms outstretched, as though she was crucified. Why? The big, pale moon had made her do it. The horrible dancing figures on the carved screen had leered at her and she hadn't minded. She remembered too how,

---

6. Seaside resort on Sussex coast.

whenever they were at the seaside, she had gone off by herself and got as close to the sea as she could, and sung something, something she had made up, while she gazed all over that restless water. There had been this other life, running out, bringing things home in bags, getting things on approval, discussing them with Jug, and taking them back to get more things on approval, and arranging father's trays and trying not to annoy father. But it all seemed to have happened in a kind of tunnel. It wasn't real. It was only when she came out of the tunnel into the moonlight or by the sea or into a thunderstorm that she really felt herself. What did it mean? What was it she was always wanting? What did it all lead to? Now? Now?

She turned away from the Buddha with one of her vague gestures. She went over to where Josephine was standing. She wanted to say something to Josephine, something frightfully important, about—about the future and what . . .

'Don't you think perhaps—' she began.

But Josephine interrupted her. 'I was wondering if now—' she murmured. They stopped; they waited for each either.

'Go on, Con,' said Josephine.

'No, no, Jug; after you,' said Constantia.

'No, say what you were going to say. You began,' said Josephine.

'I . . . I'd rather hear what you were going to say first,' said Constantia.

'Don't be absurd, Con.'

'Really, Jug.'

'Connie!'

'Oh, *Jug!*'

A pause. Then Constantia said faintly, 'I can't say what I was going to say, Jug, because I've forgotten what it was . . . that I was going to say.'

Josephine was silent for a moment. She stared at a big cloud where the sun had been. Then she replied shortly, 'I've forgotten too.'

1920   1922

The Garden Party[1]

And after all the weather was ideal. They could not have had a more perfect day for a garden party if they had ordered it. Windless, warm, the sky without a cloud. Only the blue was veiled with a haze of light gold, as it is sometimes in early summer. The gardener had been up since dawn, mowing the lawns and sweeping them, until the grass and the dark flat rosettes where the daisy plants had been seemed to shine. As for the roses, you could not help feeling they understood that roses are the only flowers that impress people at garden parties; the only flowers that everybody is certain of knowing. Hundreds, yes, literally hundreds, had come out in a single night; the green bushes bowed down as though they had been visited by archangels.

Breakfast was not yet over before the men came to put up the marquee.

---

1. This story draws on an incident from Mansfield's life. In March 1907 her mother gave a garden party in their Wellington house, but a street accident befell a neighbor living in a poor quarter nearby.

'Where do you want the marquee put, mother?'

'My dear child, it's no use asking me. I'm determined to leave everything to you children this year. Forget I am your mother. Treat me as an honoured guest.'

But Meg could not possibly go and supervise the men. She had washed her hair before breakfast, and she sat drinking her coffee in a green turban, with a dark wet curl stamped on each cheek. Jose, the butterfly, always came down in a silk petticoat and a kimono jacket.

'You'll have to go, Laura; you're the artistic one.'

Away Laura flew, still holding her piece of bread-and-butter. It's so delicious to have an excuse for eating out of doors, and besides, she loved having to arrange things; she always felt she could do it so much better than anybody else.

Four men in their shirt-sleeves stood grouped together on the garden path. They carried staves covered with rolls of canvas, and they had big tool-bags slung on their backs. They looked impressive. Laura wished now that she had not got the bread-and-butter, but there was nowhere to put it, and she couldn't possibly throw it away. She blushed and tried to look severe and even a little bit short-sighted as she came up to them.

'Good morning,' she said, copying her mother's voice. But that sounded so fearfully affected that she was ashamed, and stammered like a little girl, 'Oh—er—have you come—is it about the marquee?'

'That's right, miss,' said the tallest of the men, a lanky, freckled fellow, and he shifted his tool-bag, knocked back his straw hat and smiled down at her. 'That's about it.'

His smile was so easy, so friendly that Laura recovered. What nice eyes he had, small, but such a dark blue! And now she looked at the others, they were smiling too. 'Cheer up, we won't bite,' their smile seemed to say. How very nice workmen were! And what a beautiful morning! She mustn't mention the morning; she must be business-like. The marquee.

'Well, what about the lily-lawn? Would that do?'

And she pointed to the lily-lawn with the hand that didn't hold the bread-and-butter. They turned, they stared in the direction. A little fat chap thrust out his under-lip, and the tall fellow frowned.

'I don't fancy it,' said he. 'Not conspicuous enough. You see, with a thing like a marquee,' and he turned to Laura in his easy way, 'you want to put it somewhere where it'll give you a bang slap in the eye, if you follow me.'

Laura's upbringing made her wonder for a moment whether it was quite respectful of a workman to talk to her of bangs slap in the eye. But she did quite follow him.

'A corner of the tennis-court,' she suggested. 'But the band's going to be in one corner.'

'H'm, going to have a band, are you?' said another of the workmen. He was pale. He had a haggard look as his dark eyes scanned the tennis-court. What was he thinking?

'Only a very small band,' said Laura gently. Perhaps he wouldn't mind so much if the band was quite small. But the tall fellow interrupted.

'Look here, miss, that's the place. Against those trees. Over there. That'll do fine.'

Against the karakas. Then the karaka-trees would be hidden. And they were so lovely, with their broad, gleaming leaves, and their clusters of yellow fruit. They were like trees you imagined growing on a desert island, proud, solitary, lifting their leaves and fruits to the sun in a kind of silent splendour. Must they be hidden by a marquee?

They must. Already the men had shouldered their staves and were making for the place. Only the tall fellow was left. He bent down, pinched a sprig of lavender, put his thumb and forefinger to his nose and snuffed up the smell. When Laura saw that gesture she forgot all about the karakas in her wonder at him caring for things like that—caring for the smell of lavender. How many men that she knew would have done such a thing? Oh, how extraordinarily nice workmen were, she thought. Why couldn't she have workmen for friends rather than the silly boys she danced with and who came to Sunday night supper? She would get on much better with men like these.

It's all the fault, she decided, as the tall fellow drew something on the back of an envelope, something that was to be looped up or left to hang, of these absurd class distinctions. Well, for her part, she didn't feel them. Not a bit, not an atom . . . And now there came the chock-chock of wooden hammers. Some one whistled, some one sang out, 'Are you right there, matey?' 'Matey!' The friendliness of it, the—the—Just to prove how happy she was, just to show the tall fellow how at home she felt, and how she despised stupid conventions, Laura took a big bite of her bread-and-butter as she stared at the little drawing. She felt just like a work-girl.

'Laura, Laura, where are you? Telephone, Laura!' a voice cried from the house.

'Coming!' Away she skimmed, over the lawn, up the path, up the steps, across the veranda, and into the porch. In the hall her father and Laurie were brushing their hats ready to go to the office.

'I say, Laura,' said Laurie very fast, 'you might just give a squiz[2] at my coat before this afternoon. See if it wants pressing.'

'I will,' said she. Suddenly she couldn't stop herself. She ran at Laurie and gave him a small, quick squeeze. 'Oh, I do love parties, don't you?' gasped Laura.

'Ra-ther,' said Laurie's warm, boyish voice, and he squeezed his sister too, and gave her a gentle push. 'Dash off to the telephone, old girl.'

The telephone. 'Yes, yes; oh yes. Kitty? Good morning, dear. Come to lunch? Do, dear. Delighted of course. It will only be a very scratch meal—just the sandwich crusts and broken meringue-shells and what's left over. Yes, isn't it a perfect morning? Your white? Oh, I certainly should. One moment—hold the line. Mother's calling.' And Laura sat back. 'What, mother? Can't hear.'

Mrs Sheridan's voice floated down the stairs. 'Tell her to wear that sweet hat she had on last Sunday.'

'Mother says you're to wear that sweet hat you had on last Sunday. Good. One o'clock. Bye-bye.'

Laura put back the receiver, flung her arms over her head, took a deep breath, stretched and let them fall. 'Huh,' she sighed, and the moment after the sigh she sat up quickly. She was still, listening. All the doors in the house seemed to be open. The house was alive with soft, quick steps and running voices. The green baize[3] door that led to the kitchen regions swung open and shut with a muffled thud. And now there came a long, chuckling absurd sound. It was the heavy piano being moved on its stiff castors. But the air! If

2. Glance.

3. Coarse woolen.

you stopped to notice, was the air always like this? Little faint winds were playing chase in at the tops of the windows, out at the doors. And there were two tiny spots of sun, one on the inkpot, one on a silver photograph frame, playing too. Darling little spots. Especially the one on the inkpot lid. It was quite warm. A warm little silver star. She could have kissed it.

The front door bell pealed, and there sounded the rustle of Sadie's print skirt on the stairs. A man's voice murmured; Sadie answered, careless, 'I'm sure I don't know. Wait. I'll ask Mrs Sheridan.'

'What is it, Sadie?' Laura came into the hall.

'It's the florist, Miss Laura.'

It was, indeed. There, just inside the door, stood a wide, shallow tray full of pots of pink lilies. No other kind. Nothing but lilies—canna lilies, big pink flowers, wide open, radiant, almost frighteningly alive on bright crimson stems.

'O-oh, Sadie!' said Laura, and the sound was like a little moan. She crouched down as if to warm herself at that blaze of lilies; she felt they were in her fingers, on her lips, growing in her breast.

'It's some mistake,' she said faintly. 'Nobody ever ordered so many. Sadie, go and find mother.'

But at that moment Mrs Sheridan joined them.

'It's quite right,' she said calmly. 'Yes, I ordered them. Aren't they lovely?' She pressed Laura's arm. 'I was passing the shop yesterday, and I saw them in the window. And I suddenly thought for once in my life I shall have enough canna lilies. The garden party will be a good excuse.'

'But I thought you said you didn't mean to interfere,' said Laura. Sadie had gone. The florist's man was still outside at his van. She put her arm round her mother's neck and gently, very gently, she bit her mother's ear.

'My darling child, you wouldn't like a logical mother, would you? Don't do that. Here's the man.'

He carried more lilies still, another whole tray.

'Bank them up, just inside the door, on both sides of the porch, please,' said Mrs Sheridan. 'Don't you agree, Laura?'

'Oh, I *do* mother.'

In the drawing-room Meg, Jose and good little Hans had at last succeeded in moving the piano.

'Now, if we put this chesterfield against the wall and move everything out of the room except the chairs, don't you think?'

'Quite.'

'Hans, move these tables into the smoking-room, and bring a sweeper to take these marks off the carpet and—one moment, Hans—' Jose loved giving orders to the servants, and they loved obeying her. She always made them feel they were taking part in some drama. 'Tell mother and Miss Laura to come here at once.'

'Very good, Miss Jose.'

She turned to Meg. 'I want to hear what the piano sounds like, just in case I'm asked to sing this afternoon. Let's try over "This Life is Weary."'

Pom! Ta-ta-ta *Tee*-ta! The piano burst out so passionately that Jose's face changed. She clasped her hands. She looked mournfully and enigmatically at her mother and Laura as they came in.

> This Life is *Wee*-ary,
>   A Tear—a Sigh.
> A Love that *Chan*-ges,
>   This Life is *Wee*-ary,
> A Tear—a Sigh.
> A Love that *Chan*-ges,
> And then . . . Good-bye!

But at the word 'Good-bye,' and although the piano sounded more desperate than ever, her face broke into a brilliant, dreadfully unsympathetic smile.

'Aren't I in good voice, mummy?' she beamed.

> This Life is *Wee*-ary,
> Hope comes to Die.
> A Dream—a *Wa*-kening.

But now Sadie interrupted them. 'What is it, Sadie?'

'If you please, m'm, cook says have you got the flags[4] for the sandwiches?'

'The flags for the sandwiches, Sadie?' echoed Mrs Sheridan dreamily. And the children knew by her face that she hadn't got them. 'Let me see.' And she said to Sadie firmly, 'Tell cook I'll let her have them in ten minutes.'

Sadie went.

'Now, Laura,' said her mother quickly. 'Come with me into the smoking-room. I've got the names[5] somewhere on the back of an envelope. You'll have to write them out for me. Meg, go upstairs this minute and take that wet thing off your head. Jose, run and finish dressing this instant. Do you hear me, children, or shall I have to tell your father when he comes home to-night? And—and, Jose, pacify cook if you do go into the kitchen, will you? I'm terrified of her this morning.'

The envelope was found at last behind the dining-room clock, though how it had got there Mrs Sheridan could not imagine.

'One of you children must have stolen it out of my bag, because I remember vividly—cream cheese and lemon-curd. Have you done that?'

'Yes.'

'Egg and—' Mrs Sheridan held the envelope away from her. 'It looks like mice. It can't be mice, can it?'

'Olive, pet,' said Laura, looking over her shoulder.

'Yes, of course, olive. What a horrible combination it sounds. Egg and olive.'

They were finished at last, and Laura took them off to the kitchen. She found Jose there pacifying the cook, who did not look at all terrifying.

'I have never seen such exquisite sandwiches,' said Jose's rapturous voice. 'How many kinds did you say there were, cook? Fifteen?'

'Fifteen, Miss Jose.'

'Well, cook, I congratulate you.'

Cook swept up crusts with the long sandwich knife and smiled broadly.

---

4. Little paper flags stuck in a plate of small triangular sandwiches indicating what is inside the sandwiches on each plate—an English custom adopted by the New Zealand middle class as a sign of gentility.
5. I.e., the names of the sandwich fillings to be written on each flag.

'Godber's has come,' announced Sadie, issuing out of the pantry. She had seen the man pass the window.

That meant the cream puffs had come. Godber's were famous for their cream puffs. Nobody ever thought of making them at home.

'Bring them in and put them on the table, my girl,' ordered cook.

Sadie brought them in and went back to the door. Of course Laura and Jose were far too grown-up to really care about such things. All the same, they couldn't help agreeing that the puffs looked very attractive. Very. Cook began arranging them, shaking off the extra icing sugar.

'Don't they carry one back to all one's parties?' said Laura.

'I suppose they do,' said practical Jose, who never liked to be carried back. 'They look beautifully light and feathery, I must say.'

'Have one each, my dears,' said cook in her comfortable voice. 'Yer ma won't know.'

Oh, impossible. Fancy cream puffs so soon after breakfast. The very idea made one shudder. All the same, two minutes later Jose and Laura were licking their fingers with that absorbed inward look that only comes from whipped cream.

'Let's go into the garden, out by the back way,' suggested Laura. 'I want to see how the men are getting on with the marquee. They're such awfully nice men.'

But the back door was blocked by cook, Sadie, Godber's man and Hans.

Something had happened.

'Tuk-tuk-tuk,' clucked cook like an agitated hen. Sadie had her hand clapped to her cheek as though she had toothache. Hans's face was screwed up in the effort to understand. Only Godber's man seemed to be enjoying himself; it was his story.

'What's the matter? What's happened?'

'There's been a horrible accident,' said cook. 'A man killed.'

'A man killed! Where? How? When?'

But Godber's man wasn't going to have his story snatched from under his very nose.

'Know those little cottages just below here, miss?' Know them? Of course, she knew them. 'Well, there's a young chap living there, name of Scott, a carter. His horse shied at a traction-engine, corner of Hawke Street this morning, and he was thrown out on the back of his head. Killed.'

'Dead!' Laura stared at Godber's man.

'Dead when they picked him up,' said Godber's man with relish. 'They were taking the body home as I come up here.' And he said to the cook, 'He's left a wife and five little ones.'

'Jose, come here.' Laura caught hold of her sister's sleeve and dragged her through the kitchen to the other side of the green baize door. There she paused and leaned against it. 'Jose!' she said, horrified, 'however are we going to stop everything?'

'Stop everything, Laura!' cried Jose in astonishment. 'What do you mean?'

'Stop the garden party, of course.' Why did Jose pretend?

But Jose was still more amazed. 'Stop the garden party? My dear Laura, don't be so absurd. Of course we can't do anything of the kind. Nobody expects us to. Don't be so extravagant.'

'But we can't possibly have a garden party with a man dead just outside the front gate.'

That really was extravagant, for the little cottages were in a lane to themselves at the very bottom of a steep rise that led up to the house. A broad road ran between. True, they were far too near. They were the greatest possible eyesore, and they had no right to be in that neighbourhood at all. They were little mean dwellings painted a chocolate brown. In the garden patches there was nothing but cabbage stalks, sick hens and tomato cans. The very smoke coming out of their chimneys was poverty-stricken. Little rags and shreds of smoke, so unlike the great silvery plumes that uncurled from the Sheridans' chimneys. Washerwomen lived in the lane and sweeps and a cobbler, and a man whose house-front was studded all over with minute bird-cages. Children swarmed. When the Sheridans were little they were forbidden to set foot there because of the revolting language and of what they might catch. But since they were grown up, Laura and Laurie on their prowls sometimes walked through. It was disgusting and sordid. They came out with a shudder. But still one must go everywhere; one must see everything. So through they went.

'And just think of what the band would sound like to that poor woman,' said Laura.

'Oh, Laura!' Jose began to be seriously annoyed. 'If you're going to stop a band playing every time some one has an accident, you'll lead a very strenuous life. I'm every bit as sorry about it as you. I feel just as sympathetic.' Her eyes hardened. She looked at her sister just as she used to when they were little and fighting together. 'You won't bring a drunken workman back to life by being sentimental,' she said softly.

'Drunk! Who said he was drunk?' Laura turned furiously on Jose. She said, just as they had used to say on those occasions, 'I'm going straight up to tell mother.'

'Do, dear,' cooed Jose.

'Mother, can I come into your room?' Laura turned the big glass door-knob.

'Of course, child. Why, what's the matter? What's given you such a colour?' And Mrs Sheridan turned round from her dressing-table. She was trying on a new hat.

'Mother, a man's been killed,' began Laura.

'Not in the garden?' interrupted her mother.

'No, no!'

'Oh, what a fright you gave me!' Mrs Sheridan sighed with relief, and took off the big hat and held it on her knees.

'But listen, mother,' said Laura. Breathless, half-choking, she told the dreadful story. 'Of course, we can't have our party, can we?' she pleaded. 'The band and everybody arriving. They'd hear us, mother; they're nearly neighbours!'

To Laura's astonishment her mother behaved just like Jose; it was harder to bear because she seemed amused. She refused to take Laura seriously.

'But, my dear child, use your common sense. It's only by accident we've heard of it. If some one had died there normally—and I can't understand how they keep alive in those poky little holes—we should still be having our party, shouldn't we?'

Laura had to say 'yes' to that, but she felt it was all wrong. She sat down on her mother's sofa and pinched the cushion frill.

'Mother, isn't it really terribly heartless of us?' she asked.

'Darling!' Mrs Sheridan got up and came over to her, carrying the hat. Before Laura could stop her she had popped it on. 'My child!' said her mother, 'the hat is yours. It's made for you. It's much too young for me. I have never seen you look such a picture. Look at yourself!' And she held up her hand-mirror.

'But, mother,' Laura began again. She couldn't look at herself; she turned aside.

This time Mrs Sheridan lost patience just as Jose had done.

'You are being very absurd, Laura,' she said coldly. 'People like that don't expect sacrifices from us. And it's not very sympathetic to spoil everybody's enjoyment as you're doing now.'

'I don't understand,' said Laura, and she walked quickly out of the room into her own bedroom. There, quite by chance, the first thing she saw was this charming girl in the mirror, in her black hat trimmed with gold daisies, and a long black velvet ribbon. Never had she imagined she could look like that. Is mother right? she thought. And now she hoped her mother was right. Am I being extravagant? Perhaps it was extravagant. Just for a moment she had another glimpse of that poor woman and those little children, and the body being carried into the house. But it all seemed blurred, unreal, like a picture in the newspaper. I'll remember it again after the party's over, she decided. And somehow that seemed quite the best plan . . .

Lunch was over by half past one. By half past two they were all ready for the fray. The green-coated band had arrived and was established in a corner of the tennis-court.

'My dear!' trilled Kitty Maitland, 'aren't they too like frogs for words? You ought to have arranged them round the pond with the conductor in the middle on a leaf.'

Laurie arrived and hailed them on his way to dress. At the sight of him Laura remembered the accident again. She wanted to tell him. If Laurie agreed with the others, then it was bound to be all right. And she followed him into the hall.

'Laurie!'

'Hallo!' He was half-way upstairs, but when he turned round and saw Laura he suddenly puffed out his cheeks and goggled his eyes at her. 'My word, Laura! You do look stunning,' said Laurie. 'What an absolutely topping hat!'

Laura said faintly 'Is it?' and smiled up at Laurie, and didn't tell him after all.

Soon after that people began coming in streams. The band struck up; the hired waiters ran from the house to the marquee. Wherever you looked there were couples strolling, bending to the flowers, greeting, moving on over the lawn. They were like bright birds that had alighted in the Sheridans' garden for this one afternoon, on their way to—where? Ah, what happiness it is to be with people who all are happy, to press hands, press cheeks, smile into eyes.

'Darling Laura, how well you look!'

'What a becoming hat, child!'

'Laura, you look quite Spanish. I've never seen you look so striking.'

And Laura, glowing, answered softly, 'Have you had tea? Won't you have an ice? The passion-fruit ices really are rather special.' She ran to her father and begged him. 'Daddy darling, can't the band have something to drink?'

And the perfect afternoon slowly ripened, slowly faded, slowly its petals closed.

'Never a more delightful garden party . . .' 'The greatest success . . .' 'Quite the most . . .'

Laura helped her mother with the goodbyes. They stood side by side in the porch till it was all over.

'All over, all over, thank heaven,' said Mrs Sheridan. 'Round up the others, Laura. Let's go and have some fresh coffee. I'm exhausted. Yes, it's been very successful. But oh, these parties, these parties! Why will you children insist on giving parties!' And they all of them sat down in the deserted marquee.

'Have a sandwich, daddy dear. I wrote the flag.'

'Thanks.' Mr Sheridan took a bite and the sandwich was gone. He took another. 'I suppose you didn't hear of a beastly accident that happened today?' he said.

'My dear,' said Mrs Sheridan, holding up her hand, 'we did. It nearly ruined the party. Laura insisted we should put it off.'

'Oh, mother!' Laura didn't want to be teased about it.

'It was a horrible affair all the same,' said Mr Sheridan. 'The chap was married too. Lived just below in the lane, and leaves a wife and half a dozen kiddies, so they say.'

An awkward little silence fell. Mrs Sheridan fidgeted with her cup. Really, it was very tactless of father . . .

Suddenly she looked up. There on the table were all those sandwiches, cakes, puffs, all un-eaten, all going to be wasted. She had one of her brilliant ideas.

'I know,' she said. 'Let's make up a basket. Let's send that poor creature some of this perfectly good food. At any rate, it will be the greatest treat for the children. Don't you agree? And she's sure to have neighbours calling in and so on. What a point to have it all ready prepared. Laura!' She jumped up. 'Get me the big basket out of the stairs cupboard.'

'But, mother, do you really think it's a good idea?' said Laura.

Again, how curious, she seemed to be different from them all. To take scraps from their party. Would the poor woman really like that?

'Of course! What's the matter with you today? An hour or two ago you were insisting on us being sympathetic, and now—'

Oh well! Laura ran for the basket. It was filled, it was heaped by her mother.

'Take it yourself, darling,' said she. 'Run down just as you are. No, wait, take the arum lilies too. People of that class are so impressed by arum lilies.'

'The stems will ruin her lace frock,' said practical Jose.

So they would. Just in time. 'Only the basket, then. And, Laura!'—her mother followed her out of the marquee—'don't on any account—'

'What mother?'

No, better not put such ideas into the child's head! 'Nothing! Run along.'

It was just growing dusky as Laura shut their garden gates. A big dog ran by like a shadow. The road gleamed white, and down below in the hollow the little cottages were in deep shade. How quiet it seemed after the afternoon. Here she was going down the hill to somewhere where a man lay dead, and she couldn't realize it. Why couldn't she? She stopped a minute. And it seemed to her that kisses, voices, tinkling spoons, laughter, the smell of crushed grass were somehow inside her. She had no room for anything else. How strange! She looked up at the pale sky, and all she thought was, 'Yes, it was the most successful.'

Now the broad road was crossed. The lane began, smoky and dark. Women in shawls and men's tweed caps hurried by. Men hung over the palings; the children played in the doorways. A low hum came from the mean little cottages. In some of them there was a flicker of light, and a shadow, crab-like, moved across the window. Laura bent her head and hurried on. She wished now she had put on a coat. How her frock shone! And the big hat with the velvet streamer—if only it was another hat! Were the people looking at her? They must be. It was a mistake to have come; she knew all along it was a mistake. Should she go back even now?

No, too late. This was the house. It must be. A dark knot of people stood outside. Beside the gate an old, old woman with a crutch sat in a chair, watching. She had her feet on a newspaper. The voices stopped as Laura drew near. The group parted. It was as though she was expected, as though they had known she was coming here.

Laura was terribly nervous. Tossing the velvet ribbon over her shoulder, she said to a woman standing by, 'Is this Mrs Scott's house?' and the woman, smiling queerly, said, 'It is, my lass.'

Oh, to be away from this! She actually said, 'Help me, God,' as she walked up the tiny path and knocked. To be away from those staring eyes, or to be covered up in anything, one of those women's shawls even. I'll just leave the basket and go, she decided. I shan't even wait for it to be emptied.

Then the door opened. A little woman in black showed in the gloom.

Laura said, 'Are you Mrs Scott?' But to her horror the woman answered, 'Walk in please, miss,' and she was shut in the passage.

'No,' said Laura, 'I don't want to come in. I only want to leave this basket. Mother sent—'

The little woman in the gloomy passage seemed not to have heard her. 'Step this way, please, miss,' she said in an oily voice, and Laura followed her.

She found herself in a wretched little low kitchen, lighted by a smoky lamp. There was a woman sitting before the fire.

'Em,' said the little creature who had let her in. 'Em! It's a young lady.' She turned to Laura. She said meaningly, 'I'm her sister, Miss. You'll excuse 'er, won't you?'

'Oh, but of course!' said Laura. 'Please, please don't disturb her. I—I only want to leave—'

But at that moment the woman at the fire turned round. Her face, puffed up, red, with swollen eyes and swollen lips, looked terrible. She seemed as though she couldn't understand why Laura was there. What did it mean? Why was this stranger standing in the kitchen with a basket? What was it all about? And the poor face puckered up again.

'All right, my dear,' said the other. 'I'll thenk the young lady.'

And again she began, 'You'll excuse her, miss, I'm sure,' and her face, swollen too, tried an oily smile.

Laura only wanted to get out, to get away. She was back in the passage. The door opened. She walked straight through into the bedroom where the dead man was lying.

'You'd like a look at 'im, wouldn't you?' said Em's sister, and she brushed past Laura over to the bed. 'Don't be afraid, my lass,'—and now her voice sounded fond and sly, and fondly she drew down the sheet—''e looks a picture. There's nothing to show. Come along, my dear.'

Laura came.

There lay a young man, fast asleep—sleeping so soundly, so deeply, that he was far, far away from them both. Oh, so remote, so peaceful. He was dreaming. Never wake him up again. His head was sunk in the pillow, his eyes were closed; they were blind under the closed eyelids. He was given up to his dream. What did garden parties and baskets and lace frocks matter to him? He was far from all those things. He was wonderful, beautiful. While they were laughing and while the band was playing, this marvel had come to the lane. Happy . . . happy . . . All is well, said that sleeping face. This is just as it should be. I am content.

But all the same you had to cry, and she couldn't go out of the room without saying something to him. Laura gave a loud childish sob.

'Forgive my hat,' she said.

And this time she didn't wait for Em's sister. She found her way out of the door, down the path, past all those dark people. At the corner of the lane she met Laurie.

He stepped out of the shadow. 'Is that you, Laura?'

'Yes.'

'Mother was getting anxious. Was it all right?'

'Yes, quite. Oh, Laurie!' She took his arm, she pressed up against him.

'I say, you're not crying, are you?' asked her brother.

Laura shook her head. She was.

Laurie put his arm round her shoulder. 'Don't cry,' he said in his warm, loving voice. 'Was it awful?'

'No,' sobbed Laura. 'It was simply marvellous. But, Laurie—' She stopped, she looked at her brother. 'Isn't life,' she stammered, 'isn't life—' But what life was she couldn't explain. No matter. He quite understood.

'*Isn't* it, darling?' said Laurie.

1921   1922

JEAN RHYS
1890–1979

J ean Rhys was born Ella Gwendolen Rees Williams on the small island of Dominica in the West Indies. Her father was a Welsh doctor; her mother, a Creole (that is, a white West Indian) descended from wealthy, slave-holding plantation owners. Rhys was educated at a convent school in Roseau, Dominica, before, at the age of seventeen, leaving the island to attend the Perse School in Cambridge, England; she returned to her birthplace only once, in 1936. Her feelings toward her Caribbean background and childhood were mixed: she deeply appreciated the rich sensations and cross-racial engagements of her tropical experience; haunted by the knowledge of her violent heritage, however, she carried a heavy burden of historical guilt. As a West Indian she felt estranged from mainstream European culture and identified with the suffering of African Caribbeans, yet as a white Creole she grew up feeling out of place amid the predominantly black population of Dominica.

After studying briefly at the Academy of Dramatic Art in London, Rhys worked as a traveling chorus girl, mannequin, film extra, and—during World War I—volunteer cook. In 1919 she left England to marry the first of three husbands, and for many years she lived abroad, mainly in Paris, where she began to write the stories of her first book, *The Left Bank: Sketches and Studies of Present-Day Bohemian Paris* (1927). It was published with an introduction by the established novelist and poet Ford Madox Ford, who was for a time her lover. Ford grasped the link between Rhys's vulnerability as a person and her strength as a writer; he perceived her "terrifying insight . . . and passion for stating the case of the underdog." Rhys declared, "I have only ever written about myself," and indeed much of her writing is semiautobiographical. Her fiction frequently depicts single, economically challenged women, rootless outsiders living in bohemian London or Paris. Her early sketches were followed by her first novel, *Postures* (1928, reprinted as *Quartet* in 1969), in part an account of her affair with Ford; *After Leaving Mr. Mackenzie* (1930), about sexual betrayal; *Voyage in the Dark* (1934), the story of a nineteen-year-old chorus girl in London who has come from Dominica; and *Good Morning, Midnight* (1939), another first-person narrative of a lonely drifter, this time in Paris.

For many years Rhys published nothing more, dropping out of sight and often living in poverty, until, following the enthusiastic reception of a radio adaptation of *Good Morning, Midnight* in 1957, she began to work in earnest on her masterpiece, *Wide Sargasso Sea* (1966). In this novel, set in Jamaica and Dominica in the 1830s and 1840s, Rhys returns to her Caribbean childhood and, in a brilliant act of imaginative sympathy, creates a West Indian prehistory for the first Mrs. Rochester, the madwoman in the attic of Charlotte Brontë's *Jane Eyre*. Altogether Rhys worked on the novel for twenty-one years, amid bouts of depression, loneliness, and alcoholism, but its immediate acclaim gave her the recognition she had so long been denied. She continued to publish works of fiction and autobiography, and in the year before her death received the Commander of the Order of the British Empire.

Like *Wide Sargasso Sea*, some of Rhys's published short stories draw on her Caribbean youth. Books, narratives, and fiction itself figure prominently in some of these stories. In "The Day They Burned the Books," set in the West Indies, a white girl who only partly understands the painful entanglements of class, race, and prejudice tells how a lower-class Englishman has accumulated a trove of books he values for their cultural prestige, while his mulatto wife, embittered by her husband's racism, comes to despise them as emblems of British imperial oppression. In "On Not Shooting Sitting Birds," the narrator recalls an awkward date when she was twenty-two years old and tried to impress a snooty young Englishman with a story from her childhood in Dominica. Tailoring her story within a story to fit ideas about Englishmen in novels she has read, the narrator finds herself trapped in a lie.

Rhys is one of the great prose stylists of the twentieth century, her language spare yet lyrical, her sentences exactingly written and rewritten to suggest the most in the fewest possible words. Her writing is almost painfully alert to sensory detail, sensitive to the fears and longings of marginalized people, and fierce in its unmasking of the social and psychic consequences of cruelty and injustice.

The Day They Burned the Books

My friend Eddie was a small, thin boy. You could see the blue veins in his wrists and temples. People said that he had consumption[1] and wasn't long for this world. I loved, but sometimes despised him.

---

1. Wasting of the body associated with tuberculosis.

His father, Mr Sawyer, was a strange man. Nobody could make out what he was doing in our part of the world at all. He was not a planter or a doctor or a lawyer or a banker. He didn't keep a store. He wasn't a schoolmaster or a government official. He wasn't—that was the point—a gentleman. We had several resident romantics who had fallen in love with the moon on the Caribbees[2]—they were all gentlemen and quite unlike Mr Sawyer who hadn't an 'h' in his composition.[3] Besides, he detested the moon and everything else about the Caribbean and he didn't mind telling you so.

He was agent for a small steamship line which in those days linked up Venezuela and Trinidad[4] with the smaller islands, but he couldn't make much out of that. He must have a private income, people decided, but they never decided why he had chosen to settle in a place he didn't like and to marry a coloured woman. Though a decent, respectable, nicely educated coloured woman, mind you.

Mrs Sawyer must have been very pretty once but, what with one thing and another, that was in days gone by.

When Mr Sawyer was drunk—this often happened—he used to be very rude to her. She never answered him.

'Look at the nigger showing off,' he would say; and she would smile as if she knew she ought to see the joke but couldn't. 'You damned, long-eyed, gloomy half-caste,[5] you don't smell right,' he would say; and she never answered, not even to whisper, 'You don't smell right to me, either.'

The story went that once they had ventured to give a dinner party and that when the servant, Mildred, was bringing in coffee, he had pulled Mrs Sawyer's hair. 'Not a wig, you see,' he bawled. Even then, if you can believe it, Mrs Sawyer had laughed and tried to pretend that it was all part of the joke, this mysterious, obscure, sacred English joke.

But Mildred told the other servants in the town that her eyes had gone wicked, like a soucriant's[6] eyes, and that afterwards she had picked up some of the hair he pulled out and put it in an envelope, and that Mr Sawyer ought to look out (hair is obeah[7] as well as hands).

Of course, Mrs Sawyer had her compensations. They lived in a very pleasant house in Hill Street. The garden was large and they had a fine mango tree, which bore prolifically. The fruit was small, round, very sweet and juicy—a lovely, red-and-yellow colour when it was ripe. Perhaps it was one of the compensations, I used to think.

Mr Sawyer built a room on to the back of this house. It was unpainted inside and the wood smelt very sweet. Bookshelves lined the walls. Every time the Royal Mail steamer[8] came in it brought a package for him, and gradually the empty shelves filled.

Once I went there with Eddie to borrow *The Arabian Nights*.[9] That was on a Saturday afternoon, one of those hot, still afternoons when you felt that everything had gone to sleep, even the water in the gutters. But

---

2. Or Caribbees: old term for the group of islands in the southeastern West Indies, now called the Lesser Antilles.
3. I.e., his pronunciation marks him as lower-class.
4. Formerly British, Caribbean island off northeast Venezuela.
5. Offensive term for a person of mixed racial descent.
6. Female vampire, in Caribbean legend.

7. A charm or fetish used in Afro-Caribbean witchcraft or sorcery.
8. Ship, owned by the Royal Mail Steam Packet Company, that ferried mail from London to the West Indies beginning in 1841.
9. Also called *The Thousand and One Nights*, a collection of old stories, largely Persian, Arabian, and Indian in origin.

Mrs Sawyer was not asleep. She put her head in at the door and looked at us, and I knew that she hated the room and hated the books.

It was Eddie with the pale blue eyes and straw-coloured hair—the living image of his father, though often as silent as his mother—who first infected me with doubts about 'home', meaning England. He would be so quiet when others who had never seen it—none of us had ever seen it—were talking about its delights, gesticulating freely as we talked—London, the beautiful, rosy-cheeked ladies, the theatres, the shops, the fog, the blazing coal fires in winter, the exotic food (whitebait[1] eaten to the sound of violins), strawberries and cream—the word 'strawberries' always spoken with a guttural and throaty sound which we imagined to be the proper English pronunciation.

'I don't like strawberries,' Eddie said on one occasion.

'You *don't like* strawberries?'

'No, and I don't like daffodils either. Dad's always going on about them. He says they lick the flowers here into a cocked hat[2] and I bet that's a lie.'

We were all too shocked to say, 'You don't know a thing about it.' We were so shocked that nobody spoke to him for the rest of the day. But I for one admired him. I also was tired of learning and reciting poems in praise of daffodils, and my relations with the few 'real' English boys and girls I had met were awkward. I had discovered that if I called myself English they would snub me haughtily: 'You're not English; you're a horrid colonial.' 'Well, I don't much want to be English,' I would say. 'It's much more fun to be French or Spanish or something like that—and, as a matter of fact, I am a bit.' Then I was too killingly funny, quite ridiculous. Not only a horrid colonial, but also ridiculous. Heads I win, tails you lose—that was the English. I had thought about all this, and thought hard, but I had never dared to tell anybody what I thought and I realized that Eddie had been very bold.

But he was bold, and stronger than you would think. For one thing, he never felt the heat; some coldness in his fair skin resisted it. He didn't burn red or brown, he didn't freckle much.

Hot days seemed to make him feel especially energetic. 'Now we'll run twice round the lawn and then you can pretend you're dying of thirst in the desert and that I'm an Arab chieftain bringing you water.'

'You must drink slowly,' he would say, 'for if you're very thirsty and you drink quickly you die.'

So I learnt the voluptuousness of drinking slowly when you are very thirsty—small mouthful by small mouthful, until the glass of pink, iced Coca-Cola was empty.

Just after my twelfth birthday Mr Sawyer died suddenly, and as Eddie's special friend I went to the funeral, wearing a new white dress. My straight hair was damped with sugar and water the night before and plaited into tight little plaits, so that it should be fluffy for the occasion.

When it was all over everybody said how nice Mrs Sawyer had looked, walking like a queen behind the coffin and crying her eyeballs out at the right moment, and wasn't Eddie a funny boy? He hadn't cried at all.

After this Eddie and I took possession of the room with the books. No one else ever entered it, except Mildred to sweep and dust in the mornings, and gradually the ghost of Mr Sawyer pulling Mrs Sawyer's hair faded, though this

1. Young of a small fish, such as herring, considered a delicacy when cooked whole.
2. From *knocked into a cocked hat*: make them look terrible by comparison. Daffodils are common in English poetry, but do not grow in the West Indies.

took a little time. The blinds were always halfway down and going in out of the sun was like stepping into a pool of brown-green water. It was empty except for the bookshelves, a desk with a green baize[3] top and a wicker rocking-chair.

'My room,' Eddie called it. 'My books,' he would say, 'my books.'

I don't know how long this lasted. I don't know whether it was weeks after Mr Sawyer's death or months after, that I see myself and Eddie in the room. But there we are and there, unexpectedly, are Mrs Sawyer and Mildred. Mrs Sawyer's mouth tight, her eyes pleased. She is pulling all the books out of the shelves and piling them into two heaps. The big, fat glossy ones—the good-looking ones, Mildred explains in a whisper—lie in one heap. The *Encyclopaedia Britannica, British Flowers, Birds and Beasts*, various histories, books with maps, Froude's *English in the West Indies*[4] and so on—they are going to be sold. The unimportant books, with paper covers or damaged covers or torn pages, lie in another heap. They are going to be burnt—yes, burnt.

Mildred's expression was extraordinary as she said that—half hugely delighted, half shocked, even frightened. And as for Mrs Sawyer—well, I knew bad temper (I had often seen it), I knew rage, but this was hate. I recognized the difference at once and stared at her curiously. I edged closer to her so that I could see the titles of the books she was handling.

It was the poetry shelf. *Poems*, Lord Byron, *Poetical Works*, Milton, and so on. Vlung, vlung, vlung—all thrown into the heap that were to be sold. But a book by Christina Rossetti, though also bound in leather, went into the heap that was to be burnt, and by a flicker in Mrs Sawyer's eyes I knew that worse than men who wrote books were women who wrote books—infinitely worse. Men could be mercifully shot; women must be tortured.

Mrs Sawyer did not seem to notice that we were there, but she was breathing free and easy and her hands had got the rhythm of tearing and pitching. She looked beautiful, too—beautiful as the sky outside which was a very dark blue, or the mango tree, long sprays of brown and gold.

When Eddie said 'no', she did not even glance at him.

'No,' he said again in a high voice. 'Not that one. I was reading that one.'

She laughed and he rushed at her, his eyes starting out of his head, shrieking, 'Now I've got to hate you too. Now I hate you too.'

He snatched the book out of her hand and gave her a violent push. She fell into the rocking-chair.

Well, I wasn't going to be left out of all this, so I grabbed a book from the condemned pile and dived under Mildred's outstretched arm.

Then we were both in the garden. We ran along the path, bordered with crotons.[5] We pelted down the path though they did not follow us and we could hear Mildred laughing—kyah, kyah, kyah, kyah. As I ran I put the book I had taken into the loose front of my brown holland dress. It felt warm and alive.

When we got into the street we walked sedately, for we feared the black children's ridicule. I felt very happy, because I had saved this book and it was my book and I would read it from the beginning to the triumphant words 'The End'. But I was uneasy when I thought of Mrs Sawyer.

'What will she do?' I said.

'Nothing,' Eddie said. 'Not to me.'

---

3. Feltlike fabric.
4. Published in 1888 by the English historian

James Anthony Froude (1818–1894).
5. Tropical plants.

He was white as a ghost in his sailor suit, a blue-white even in the setting sun, and his father's sneer was clamped on his face.

'But she'll tell your mother all sorts of lies about you,' he said. 'She's an awful liar. She can't make up a story to save her life, but she makes up lies about people all right.'

'My mother won't take any notice of her,' I said. Though I was not at all sure.

'Why not? Because she's . . . because she isn't white?'

Well, I knew the answer to that one. Whenever the subject was brought up—people's relations and whether they had a drop of coloured blood or whether they hadn't—my father would grow impatient and interrupt. 'Who's white?' he would say. 'Damned few.'

So I said, 'Who's white? Damned few.'

'You can go to the devil,' Eddie said. 'She's prettier than your mother. When she's asleep her mouth smiles and she has your curling eyelashes and quantities and quantities and *quantities* of hair.'

'Yes,' I said truthfully. 'She's prettier than my mother.'

It was a red sunset that evening, a huge, sad, frightening sunset.

'Look, let's go back,' I said. 'If you're sure she won't be vexed with you, let's go back. It'll be dark soon.'

At his gate he asked me not to go. 'Don't go yet, don't go yet.'

We sat under the mango tree and I was holding his hand when he began to cry. Drops fell on my hand like the water from the dripstone in the filter[6] in our yard. Then I began to cry too and when I felt my own tears on my hand I thought, 'Now perhaps we're married.'

'Yes, certainly, now we're married,' I thought. But I didn't say anything. I didn't say a thing until I was sure he had stopped. Then I asked, 'What's your book?'

'It's *Kim*,'[7] he said. 'But it got torn. It starts at page twenty now. What's the one you took?'

'I don't know, it's too dark to see,' I said.

When I got home I rushed into my bedroom and locked the door because I knew that this book was the most important thing that had ever happened to me and I did not want anybody to be there when I looked at it.

But I was very disappointed, because it was in French and seemed dull. *Fort Comme La Mort*,[8] it was called. . . .

1960

On Not Shooting Sitting Birds[1]

There is no control over memory. Quite soon you find yourself being vague about an event which seemed so important at the time that you thought you'd never forget it. Or unable to recall the face of someone whom you could have sworn was there for ever. On the other hand, trivial and mean-

6. Dripstone is a sandstone used as a filter to clean water for household use.
7. Novel (1901) by the English writer Rudyard Kipling (1865–1936), about an Irish orphan boy growing up in India.
8. *Strong as Death*, 1889 novel by the French writer Guy de Maupassant (1850–1893).
1. Game-bird hunters traditionally consider the shooting of sitting (rather than flying) birds shockingly unsportsmanlike.

ingless memories may stay with you for life. I can still shut my eyes and see Victoria grinding coffee on the pantry steps, the glass bookcase and the books in it, my father's pipe-rack, the leaves of the sandbox tree, the wallpaper of the bedroom in some shabby hotel, the hairdresser in Antibes.[2] It's in this way that I remember buying the pink milanese[3] silk underclothes, the assistant who sold them to me and coming into the street holding the parcel.

I had started out in life trusting everyone and now I trusted no one. So I had few acquaintances and no close friends. It was perhaps in reaction against the inevitable loneliness of my life that I'd find myself doing bold, risky, even outrageous things without hesitation or surprise. I was usually disappointed in these adventures and they didn't have much effect on me, good or bad, but I never quite lost the hope of something better or different.

One day, I've forgotten now where, I met this young man who smiled at me and when we had talked a bit I agreed to have dinner with him in a couple of days' time. I went home excited, for I'd liked him very much, and began to plan what I should wear. I had a dress I quite liked, an evening cloak, shoes, stockings, but my underclothes weren't good enough for the occasion, I decided. Next day I went out and bought the milanese silk chemise[4] and drawers.

So there we were seated at a table having dinner with a bedroom very obvious in the background. He was younger than I'd thought and stiffer and I didn't like him much after all. He kept eyeing me in such a wary, puzzled way. When we had finished our soup and the waiter had taken the plates away, he said: 'But you're a lady, aren't you?' exactly as he might have said, 'But you're really a snake or a crocodile, aren't you?'

'Oh no, not that you'd notice,' I said, but this didn't work. We looked glumly at each other across the gulf that had yawned between us.

Before I came to England I'd read many English novels and I imagined I knew all about the thoughts and tastes of various sorts of English people. I quickly decided that to distract or interest this man I must talk about shooting.

I asked him if he knew the West Indies at all. He said no, he didn't and I told him a long story of having been lost in the Dominican forest when I was a child. This wasn't true. I'd often been in the woods but never alone. 'There are no parrots now,' I said, 'or very few. There used to be. There's a Dominican parrot in the zoo—have you ever seen it?—a sulky bird, very old I think. However, there are plenty of other birds and we do have shooting parties. Perdrix are very good to eat, but ramiers[5] are rather bitter.'

Then I began describing a fictitious West Indian shooting party and all the time I talked I was remembering the real thing. An old shotgun leaning up in one corner of the room, the round table in the middle where we would sit to make cartridges, putting the shot in, ramming it down with a wad of paper. Gunpowder? There was that too, for I remember the smell. I suppose the boys were trusted to be careful.

The genuine shooting party consisted of my two brothers, who shared the shotgun, some hangers-on and me at the end of the procession, for then I couldn't bear to be left out of anything. As soon as the shooting was about to start I would stroll away casually and when I was out of sight run as hard

2. Resort town on the south coast of France.
3. Made in Milan, Italy.
4. Loose-fitting undergarment hanging straight from the shoulders.
5. Pigeons of the eastern Caribbean.

as I could, crouch down behind a bush and put my fingers in my ears. It wasn't that I was sorry for the birds, but I hated and feared the noise of the gun. When it was all over I'd quietly join the others. I must have done this unobtrusively or probably my brothers thought me too insignificant to worry about, for no one ever remarked on my odd behaviour or teased me about it.

On and on I went, almost believing what I was saying, when he interrupted me. 'Do you mean to say that your brothers shot sitting birds?' His voice was cold and shocked.

I stared at him. How could I convince this man that I hadn't the faintest idea whether my brothers shot sitting birds or not? How could I explain now what really happened? If I did he'd think me a liar. Also a coward and there he'd be right, for I was afraid of many things, not only the sound of gunfire. But by this time I wasn't sure that I liked him at all so I was silent and felt my face growing as stiff and unsmiling as his.

It was a most uncomfortable dinner. We both avoided looking at the bedroom and when the last mouthful was swallowed he announced that he was going to take me home. The way he said this rather puzzled me. Then I told myself that probably he was curious to see where I lived. Neither of us spoke in the taxi except to say, 'Well, goodnight.' 'Goodnight.'

I felt regretful when it came to taking off my lovely pink chemise, but I could still think: Some other night perhaps, another sort of man.

I slept at once.

1976

STEVIE SMITH
1902–1971

Stevie Smith's real name was Florence Margaret Smith, but she was nicknamed "Stevie" after a famous jockey because of her small stature. She was born in Hull, Yorkshire, but at the age of three went with her mother and sister to live with an aunt in Palmer's Green, a suburb north of London. She worked as a secretary at the magazine-publishing firm of Newnes, Pearson, while continuing to live with her aunt, to whom she was devoted. When her aunt grew old and infirm, Smith gave up her job to look after her, although she herself was often in ill health. At the same time, she managed to lead a lively social life in London and was known for the vividness and range of her conversation.

Smith brought out her first novel, *Novel on Yellow Paper* (1936), at the suggestion of a publisher who rejected a collection of poems. This was followed by her first volume of poetry, *A Good Time Was Had by All* (1937), and in due course by eight further poetry collections and two more novels.

Smith's work is utterly original, fitting into no category and showing none of the characteristic influences of the age. Her poetry sometimes seems to be light verse, and it draws on nursery rhyme and often employs simple language, but its humor can shade into dread, its whimsy into metaphysical pondering. She illustrated many of her poems with line drawings (she called them "doodles") that reinforce the effect of mock-naïveté. This stance is akin to the cunning innocence of the fool or the trickster, and can be seen, in part, as a gendered deflection and subversion of masculine cultural norms. Her diction ranges from the matter-of-fact to the archaic, from colloquialism ("Poor chap"), slang ("you ass"), and nonsense ("Our Bog Is Dood") to didacticism ("My point which upon this has been obscured") and foreign phrases ("Sunt Leones"). Her verse moves from free conversational rhythms to traditional verse patterns, on occasion becoming—to ironic effect—almost doggerel. Her tone can be satiric, solemn, or both at once. A poem such as "Not Waving but Drowning" belies the apparent guilelessness of Smith's art. Like the dying man's ambiguous gesture here, her poetry waves to us, with its songlike lyricism and comedy, and yet also reveals much about "drowning"—about death, suicide, and other painful human issues. A religious skeptic, Smith said she was always in danger of falling into belief, and her poetry shows her to be fascinated by theological speculation, the language of the Bible, and religious experience.

Sunt Leones[1]

The lions who ate the Christians on the sands of the arena
By indulging native appetites played what has now been seen a
Not entirely negligible part
In consolidating at the very start
5   The position of the Early Christian Church.
Initiatory rites are always bloody
And the lions, it appears
From contemporary art, made a study
Of dyeing Coliseum sands a ruddy
10 Liturgically sacrificial hue
And if the Christians felt a little blue—
Well people being eaten often do.
Theirs was the death, and theirs the crown undying,[2]
A state of things which must be satisfying.
15 My point which up to this has been obscured
Is that it was the lions who procured
By chewing up blood gristle flesh and bone
The martyrdoms on which the Church has grown.
I only write this poem because I thought it rather looked
20 As if the part the lions played was being overlooked.
By lions' jaws great benefits and blessings were begotten
And so our debt to Lionhood must never be forgotten.

1937

---

1. There be lions (Latin). Christians were attacked and eaten by lions in the public games held in the Colosseum during the Roman Empire.

2. I.e., of martyrdom, in heaven. The Christian liturgy, or system of worship, prescribes certain colors for certain festivals (line 10).

Our Bog Is Dood

Our Bog is dood, our Bog is dood,
They lisped in accents mild,
But when I asked them to explain
They grew a little wild.
5   How do you know your Bog is dood
My darling little child?

We know because we wish it so
That is enough, they cried,
And straight within each infant eye
10 Stood up the flame of pride,
And if you do not think it so
You shall be crucified.

Then tell me, darling little ones,
What's dood, suppose Bog is?
15 Just what we think, the answer came,
Just what we think it is.
They bowed their heads. Our Bog is ours
And we are wholly his.

But when they raised them up again
20 They had forgotten me
Each one upon each other glared
In pride and misery
For what was dood, and what their Bog
They never could agree.

25 Oh sweet it was to leave them then,
And sweeter not to see,
And sweetest of all to walk alone
Beside the encroaching sea,
The sea that soon should drown them all,
30 That never yet drowned me.

1950

Not Waving but Drowning

Nobody heard him, the dead man,
But still he lay moaning:
I was much further out than you thought
And not waving but drowning.

5   Poor chap, he always loved larking
And now he's dead
It must have been too cold for him his heart gave way,
They said.

Oh, no no no, it was too cold always
10   (Still the dead one lay moaning)
I was much too far out all my life
And not waving but drowning.

1957

Thoughts About the Person from Porlock[1]

Coleridge received the Person from Porlock
And ever after called him a curse,
Then why did he hurry to let him in?
He could have hid in the house.

5   It was not right of Coleridge in fact it was wrong
(But often we all do wrong)
As the truth is I think he was already stuck
With Kubla Khan.

He was weeping and wailing: I am finished, finished,
10   I shall never write another word of it,
When along comes the Person from Porlock
And takes the blame for it.

It was not right, it was wrong,
But often we all do wrong.

              •   •   •

15   May we inquire the name of the Person from Porlock?
Why, Porson, didn't you know?
He lived at the bottom of Porlock Hill
So had a long way to go,

He wasn't much in the social sense
20   Though his grandmother was a Warlock,
One of the Ruthlandshire ones I fancy
And nothing to do with Porlock.

And he lived at the bottom of the hill as I said
And had a cat named Flo,
25   And had a cat named Flo.

I long for the Person from Porlock
To bring my thoughts to an end,
I am becoming impatient to see him
I think of him as a friend,

30   Often I look out of the window
Often I run to the gate
I think, He will come this evening,
I think it is rather late.

I am hungry to be interrupted
35   Forever and ever amen
O Person from Porlock come quickly
And bring my thoughts to an end.

1. In the prefatory note to his poem "Kubla Khan" (1816), Samuel Taylor Coleridge wrote that he had dreamed the poem's vision under the effects of opium, and that, on awakening, he immediately started to write the poem. "At this moment," Coleridge says (referring to himself in the third person), "he was unfortunately called out by a person on business from Porlock, and detained by him above an hour"; afterward, trying to finish the poem, Coleridge found, "to his no small surprise and mortification," that the vision had vanished "like the images on the surface of a stream."

⚫ ⚫ ⚫

I felicitate the people who have a Person from Porlock
To break up everything and throw it away
40 Because then there will be nothing to keep them
And they need not stay.

⚫ ⚫ ⚫

Why do they grumble so much?
He comes like a benison
They should be glad he has not forgotten them
45 They might have had to go on.

⚫ ⚫ ⚫

These thoughts are depressing I know. They are depressing,
I wish I was more cheerful, it is more pleasant,
Also it is a duty, we should smile as well as submitting
To the purpose of One Above who is experimenting

50 With various mixtures of human character which goes best,
All is interesting for him it is exciting, but not for us.
There I go again, Smile, smile, and get some work to do
Then you will be practically unconscious without positively having to go.

1962

Pretty

Why is the word pretty so underrated?
In November the leaf is pretty when it falls
The stream grows deep in the woods after rain
And in the pretty pool the pike stalks

5 He stalks his prey, and this is pretty too,
The prey escapes with an underwater flash
But not for long, the great fish has him now
The pike is a fish who always has his prey

And this is pretty. The water rat is pretty
10 His paws are not webbed, he cannot shut his nostrils
As the otter can and the beaver, he is torn between
The land and water, Not "torn," he does not mind.

The owl hunts in the evening and it is pretty
The lake water below him rustles with ice
15 There is frost coming from the ground, in the air mist
All this is pretty, it could not be prettier.

Yes, it could always be prettier, the eye abashes
It is becoming an eye that cannot see enough,
Out of the wood the eye climbs. This is prettier
20 A field in the evening, tilting up.

The field tilts to the sky. Though it is late
The sky is lighter than the hill field
All this looks easy but really it is extraordinary
Well, it is extraordinary to be so pretty.

25   And it is careless, and that is always pretty
This field, this owl, this pike, this pool are careless,
As Nature is always careless and indifferent
Who sees, who steps, means nothing, and this is pretty.

So a person can come along like a thief—pretty!—
30   Stealing a look, pinching the sound and feel,
Lick the icicle broken from the bank
And still say nothing at all, only cry pretty.

Cry pretty, pretty, pretty and you'll be able
Very soon not even to cry pretty
35   And so be delivered entirely from humanity
This is prettiest of all, it is very pretty.

1966

GEORGE ORWELL
1903–1950

"George Orwell" was the pseudonym of Eric Blair, who was born in the village of Motihari in Bengal, India, where his father was a British civil servant. He was sent to private school in England and won a scholarship to Eton, the foremost "public school" (i.e., private boarding school) in the country. At these schools he became conscious of the difference between his own background and the wealthy backgrounds of many of his schoolmates. On leaving school he joined the Imperial Police in Burma (both Burma—now called Myanmar—and India were then still part of the British Empire). His service in Burma from 1922 to 1927 produced a sense of guilt about British colonialism and a feeling that he had to make some personal expiation for it. This he would later do with an anticolonial novel, *Burmese Days* (1934), and essays such as "Shooting an Elephant" (1936), which subordinates lingering colonial attitudes to fiercely anti-imperial insights. He returned to England determined to be a writer and adopted his pseudonym as one way of escaping from the class position in which his elite education placed him. He went to Paris to try to earn a living by teaching while he made his first attempts at writing. His extremely difficult time in Paris was followed by a spell as a tramp in England, and he vividly recorded both experiences in his first book, *Down and Out in Paris and London* (1933). Orwell did not have to suffer the dire poverty that he seems to have courted (he had influential friends who would have been glad to help him); he wanted, however, to learn firsthand about the life of the poor, both out of humane curiosity and because, as he wrote, if he did so "part of my guilt would drop from me."

The Road to Wigan Pier (1937) discusses the experiences Orwell shared with unemployed miners in the north of England. The book pleased neither the left nor the right, for by now Orwell was showing what was to become his characteristic independence of mind on political and social questions: he wrote of what he knew firsthand to be true and was contemptuous of ideologies. He never joined a political party but regarded himself as a man of the uncommitted and independent left.

When the Spanish Civil War broke out in 1936 after General Franco raised his military rebellion against the elected government, Orwell went there as a reporter and stayed to fight on the Republican side, rising to the rank of second lieutenant and suffering a throat wound. His *Homage to Catalonia* (1938) strongly criticized the Communist part in the civil war and showed from his own experience how the Communist Party in Spain was out to destroy anarchists, Trotskyists, and any others on the Republican side who were suspected of not toeing the Stalinist line; it aroused great indignation on the left in Britain and elsewhere, for many leftists believed that they should solidly support the Soviet Union and the Communist Party as the natural leaders in the struggle against international fascism. Orwell never wavered in his belief that while profound social change was necessary and desirable in capitalist countries of the West, the so-called socialism established in Soviet Russia was a perversion of socialism and a wicked tyranny. In *Animal Farm* (1945) he wrote a fable showing how such a perversion of socialism could develop, while in *Nineteen-Eighty-Four* (1949), when he was an embittered man dying of tuberculosis, he wrote a savagely powerful novel depicting a totalitarian future, where the government uses the language of socialism to cover a tyranny that systematically destroys the human spirit. In that vision of hell on Earth, language has become one of the principal instruments of oppression. The Ministry of Truth is concerned with the transmission of untruth, and the white face of its pyramidal structure proclaims in "Newspeak" the three slogans of the party: "WAR IS PEACE / FREEDOM IS SLAVERY / IGNORANCE IS STRENGTH." Three years before Orwell formulated "Newspeak," "doublespeak," and "Big Brother is watching you," he had explored in one of his most influential essays, "Politics and the English Language," the decay of language and the ways in which that decay might be resisted. The fifty years that have passed since he wrote the piece have only confirmed the accuracy of its diagnosis and the value of its prescription.

Orwell was an outstanding journalist, and the essays he wrote regularly for the left-wing British journal *Tribune* and other periodicals include some of his best work. His independent eye made him both a permanent misfit politically and a brilliantly original writer.

Shooting an Elephant

In Moulmein, in Lower Burma, I was hated by large numbers of people—the only time in my life that I have been important enough for this to happen to me. I was sub-divisional police officer of the town, and in an aimless, petty kind of way anti-European feeling was very bitter. No one had the guts to raise a riot, but if a European woman went through the bazaars alone somebody would probably spit betel[1] juice over her dress. As a police officer I was an obvious target and was baited whenever it seemed safe to do so. When a nimble Burman tripped me up on the football field and the referee (another Burman) looked the other way, the crowd yelled with hideous laughter. This happened more than once. In the end the sneering yellow faces of young men that met me everywhere, the insults hooted after me when I was at a safe

---

1. Leaf and seed of a plant chewed as a stimulant in Burma and other Eastern countries.

distance, got badly on my nerves. The young Buddhist priests were the worst of all. There were several thousands of them in the town and none of them seemed to have anything to do except stand on street corners and jeer at Europeans.

All this was perplexing and upsetting. For at that time I had already made up my mind that imperialism was an evil thing and the sooner I chucked up my job and got out of it the better. Theoretically—and secretly, of course—I was all for the Burmese and all against their oppressors, the British. As for the job I was doing, I hated it more bitterly than I can perhaps make clear. In a job like that you see the dirty work of Empire at close quarters. The wretched prisoners huddling in the stinking cages of the lock-ups, the grey, cowed faces of the long-term convicts, the scarred buttocks of the men who had been flogged with bamboos—all these oppressed me with an intolerable sense of guilt. But I could get nothing into perspective. I was young and ill-educated and I had had to think out my problems in the utter silence that is imposed on every Englishman in the East. I did not even know that the British Empire is dying, still less did I know that it is a great deal better than the younger empires that are going to supplant it. All I knew was that I was stuck between my hatred of the empire I served and my rage against the evil-spirited little beasts who tried to make my job impossible. With one part of my mind I thought of the British Raj as an unbreakable tyranny, as something clamped down, *in saecula saeculorum*,[2] upon the will of prostrate peoples; with another part I thought that the greatest joy in the world would be to drive a bayonet into a Buddhist priest's guts. Feelings like these are the normal by-products of imperialism; ask any Anglo-Indian official, if you can catch him off duty.

One day something happened which in a roundabout way was enlightening. It was a tiny incident in itself, but it gave me a better glimpse than I had had before of the real nature of imperialism—the real motives for which despotic governments act. Early one morning the sub-inspector at a police station the other end of the town rang me up on the phone and said that an elephant was ravaging the bazaar. Would I please come and do something about it? I did not know what I could do, but I wanted to see what was happening and I got on to a pony and started out. I took my rifle, an old .44 Winchester and much too small to kill an elephant, but I thought the noise might be useful *in terrorem*.[3] Various Burmans stopped me on the way and told me about the elephant's doings. It was not, of course, a wild elephant, but a tame one which had gone "must."[4] It had been chained up as tame elephants always are when their attack of "must" is due, but on the previous night it had broken its chain and escaped. Its mahout,[5] the only person who could manage it when it was in that state, had set out in pursuit, but he had taken the wrong direction and was now twelve hours' journey away, and in the morning the elephant had suddenly reappeared in the town. The Burmese population had no weapons and were quite helpless against it. It had already destroyed somebody's bamboo hut, killed a cow and raided some fruit-stalls and devoured the stock; also it had met the municipal rubbish van, and, when the driver jumped out and took to his heels, had turned the van over and inflicted violence upon it.

2. For ever and ever (Latin). "Raj": rule (Hindi).
3. To frighten it (Latin).
4. A state of sexual frenzy to which certain animals are subject at irregular intervals.
5. Elephant driver (Hindi).

The Burmese sub-inspector and some Indian constables were waiting for me in the quarter where the elephant had been seen. It was a very poor quarter, a labyrinth of squalid bamboo huts, thatched with palm-leaf, winding all over a steep hillside. I remember that it was a cloudy stuffy morning at the beginning of the rains. We began questioning the people as to where the elephant had gone, and, as usual, failed to get any definite information. That is invariably the case in the East; a story always sounds clear enough at a distance, but the nearer you get to the scene of events the vaguer it becomes. Some of the people said that the elephant had gone in one direction, some said that he had gone in another, some professed not even to have heard of any elephant. I had almost made up my mind that the whole story was a pack of lies, when we heard yells a little distance away. There was a loud, scandalised cry of "Go away, child! Go away this instant!" and an old woman with a switch in her hand came round the corner of a hut, violently shooing away a crowd of naked children. Some more women followed, clicking their tongues and exclaiming; evidently there was something there that the children ought not to have seen. I rounded the hut and saw a man's dead body sprawling in the mud. He was an Indian, a black Dravidian coolie,[6] almost naked, and he could not have been dead many minutes. The people said that the elephant had come suddenly upon him round the comer of the hut, caught him with its trunk, put its foot on his back and ground him into the earth. This was the rainy season and the ground was soft, and his face had scored a trench a foot deep and a couple of yards long. He was lying on his belly with arms crucified and head sharply twisted to one side. His face was coated with mud, the eyes wide open, the teeth bared and grinning with an expression of unendurable agony. (Never tell me, by the way, that the dead look peaceful. Most of the corpses I have seen looked devilish.) The friction of the great beast's foot had stripped the skin from his back as neatly as one skins a rabbit. As soon as I saw the dead man I sent an orderly to a friend's house nearby to borrow an elephant rifle. I had already sent back the pony, not wanting it to go mad with fright and throw me if it smelled the elephant.

The orderly came back in a few minutes with a rifle and five cartridges, and meanwhile some Burmans had arrived and told us that the elephant was in the paddy fields below, only a few hundred yards away. As I started forward practically the whole population of the quarter flocked out of their houses and followed me. They had seen the rifle and were all shouting excitedly that I was going to shoot the elephant. They had not shown much interest in the elephant when he was merely ravaging their homes, but it was different now that he was going to be shot. It was a bit of fun to them, as it would be to an English crowd; besides, they wanted the meat. It made me vaguely uneasy. I had no intention of shooting the elephant—I had merely sent for the rifle to defend myself if necessary—and it is always unnerving to have a crowd following you. I marched down the hill, looking and feeling a fool, with the rifle over my shoulder and an ever-growing army of people jostling at my heels. At the bottom, when you got away from the huts, there was a metalled road and beyond that a miry waste of paddy fields a thousand yards across, not yet ploughed but soggy from the first rains and dotted with coarse grass. The elephant was standing eighty yards from the road, his left side towards us. He took not the slightest notice of the crowd's approach. He was tearing up

6. Hired laborer (disputed origin). "Dravidian": a South Asian people.

bunches of grass, beating them against his knees to clean them and stuffing them into his mouth.

I had halted on the road. As soon as I saw the elephant I knew with perfect certainty that I ought not to shoot him. It is a serious matter to shoot a working elephant—it is comparable to destroying a huge and costly piece of machinery—and obviously one ought not to do it if it can possibly be avoided. And at that distance, peacefully eating, the elephant looked no more dangerous than a cow. I thought then and I think now that his attack of "must" was already passing off; in which case he would merely wander harmlessly about until the mahout came back and caught him. Moreover, I did not in the least want to shoot him. I decided that I would watch him for a little while to make sure that he did not turn savage again, and then go home.

But at that moment I glanced round at the crowd that had followed me. It was an immense crowd, two thousand at the least and growing every minute. It blocked the road for a long distance on either side. I looked at the sea of yellow faces above the garish clothes—faces all happy and excited over this bit of fun, all certain that the elephant was going to be shot. They were watching me as they would watch a conjuror about to perform a trick. They did not like me, but with the magical rifle in my hands I was momentarily worth watching. And suddenly I realised that I should have to shoot the elephant after all. The people expected it of me and I had got to do it; I could feel their two thousand wills pressing me forward, irresistibly. And it was at this moment, as I stood there with the rifle in my hands, that I first grasped the hollowness, the futility of the white man's dominion in the East. Here was I, the white man with his gun, standing in front of the unarmed native crowd—seemingly the leading actor of the piece; but in reality I was only an absurd puppet pushed to and fro by the will of those yellow faces behind. I perceived in this moment that when the white man turns tyrant it is his own freedom that he destroys. He becomes a sort of hollow, posing dummy, the conventionalised figure of a sahib.[7] For it is the condition of his rule that he shall spend his life in trying to impress the "natives" and so in every crisis he has got to do what the "natives" expect of him. He wears a mask, and his face grows to fit it. I had got to shoot the elephant. I had committed myself to doing it when I sent for the rifle. A sahib has got to act like a sahib; he has got to appear resolute, to know his own mind and do definite things. To come all that way, rifle in hand, with two thousand people marching at my heels, and then to trail feebly away, having done nothing—no, that was impossible. The crowd would laugh at me. And my whole life, every white man's life in the East, was one long struggle not to be laughed at.

But I did not want to shoot the elephant. I watched him beating his bunch of grass against his knees, with that preoccupied grandmotherly air that elephants have. It seemed to me that it would be murder to shoot him. At that age I was not squeamish about killing animals, but I had never shot an elephant and never wanted to. (Somehow it always seems worse to kill a *large* animal.) Besides, there was the beast's owner to be considered. Alive, the elephant was worth at least a hundred pounds; dead, he would only be worth the value of his tusks—five pounds, possibly. But I had got to act quickly. I turned to some experienced-looking Burmans who had been there when we arrived, and asked them how the elephant had been behaving. They

---

7. White gentleman (Urdu).

all said the same thing: he took no notice of you if you left him alone, but he might charge if you went too close to him.

It was perfectly clear to me what I ought to do. I ought to walk up to within, say, twenty-five yards of the elephant and test his behaviour. If he charged I could shoot, if he took no notice of me it would be safe to leave him until the mahout came back. But also I knew that I was going to do no such thing. I was a poor shot with a rifle and the ground was soft mud into which one would sink at every step. If the elephant charged and I missed him, I should have about as much chance as a toad under a steam-roller. But even then I was not thinking particularly of my own skin, only the watchful yellow faces behind. For at that moment, with the crowd watching me, I was not afraid in the ordinary sense, as I would have been if I had been alone. A white man mustn't be frightened in front of "natives"; and so, in general, he isn't frightened. The sole thought in my mind was that if anything went wrong those two thousand Burmans would see me pursued, caught, trampled on and reduced to a grinning corpse like that Indian up the hill. And if that happened it was quite probable that some of them would laugh. That would never do. There was only one alternative. I shoved the cartridges into the magazine and lay down on the road to get a better aim.

The crowd grew very still, and a deep, low, happy sigh, as of people who see the theatre curtain go up at last, breathed from innumerable throats. They were going to have their bit of fun after all. The rifle was a beautiful German thing with cross-hair sights. I did not then know that in shooting an elephant one should shoot to cut an imaginary bar running from ear-hole to ear-hole. I ought therefore, as the elephant was sideways on, to have aimed straight at his ear-hole; actually I aimed several inches in front of this, thinking the brain would be further forward.

When I pulled the trigger I did not hear the bang or feel the kick—one never does when a shot goes home—but I heard the devilish roar of glee that went up from the crowd. In that instant, in too short a time, one would have thought, even for the bullet to get there, a mysterious, terrible change had come over the elephant. He neither stirred nor fell, but every line of his body had altered. He looked suddenly stricken, shrunken, immensely old, as though the frightful impact of the bullet had paralysed him without knocking him down. At last, after what seemed a long time—it might have been five seconds, I dare say—he sagged flabbily to his knees. His mouth slobbered. An enormous senility seemed to have settled upon him. One could have imagined him thousands of years old. I fired again into the same spot. At the second shot he did not collapse but climbed with desperate slowness to his feet and stood weakly upright, with legs sagging and head drooping. I fired a third time. That was the shot that did for him. You could see the agony of it jolt his whole body and knock the last remnant of strength from his legs. But in falling he seemed for a moment to rise, for as his hind legs collapsed beneath him he seemed to tower upwards like a huge rock toppling, his trunk reaching skyward like a tree. He trumpeted, for the first and only time. And then down he came, his belly towards me, with a crash that seemed to shake the ground even where I lay.

I got up. The Burmans were already racing past me across the mud. It was obvious that the elephant would never rise again, but he was not dead. He was breathing very rhythmically with long rattling gasps, his great mound of a side painfully rising and falling. His mouth was wide open—I could see far down into caverns of pale pink throat. I waited a long time for him to die, but his breathing did not weaken. Finally I fired my two remaining shots into the spot where I thought his heart must be. The thick blood welled out of him like red velvet, but still he did not die. His body did not even jerk when the shots hit him, the tortured breathing continued without a pause. He was dying, very slowly and in great agony, but in some world remote from me where not even a bullet could damage him further. I felt that I had got to put an end to that dreadful noise. It seemed dreadful to see the great beast lying there, powerless to move and yet powerless to die, and not even to be able to finish him. I sent back for my small rifle and poured shot after shot into his heart and down his throat. They seemed to make no impression. The tortured gasps continued as steadily as the ticking of a clock.

In the end I could not stand it any longer and went away. I heard later that it took him half an hour to die. Burmans were arriving with dahs[8] and baskets even before I left, and I was told they had stripped his body almost to the bones by the afternoon.

Afterwards, of course, there were endless discussions about the shooting of the elephant. The owner was furious, but he was only an Indian and could do nothing. Besides, legally I had done the right thing, for a mad elephant has to be killed, like a mad dog, if its owner fails to control it. Among the Europeans opinion was divided. The older men said I was right, the younger men said it was a damn shame to shoot an elephant for killing a coolie, because an elephant was worth more than any damn Coringhee[9] coolie. And afterwards I was very glad that the coolie had been killed; it put me legally in the right and it gave me a sufficient pretext for shooting the elephant. I often wondered whether any of the others grasped that I had done it solely to avoid looking a fool.

1936

Politics and the English Language

Most people who bother with the matter at all would admit that the English language is in a bad way, but it is generally assumed that we cannot by conscious action do anything about it. Our civilisation is decadent, and our language—so the argument runs—must inevitably share in the general collapse. It follows that any struggle against the abuse of language is a sentimental archaism, like preferring candles to electric light or hansom cabs to aeroplanes. Underneath this lies the half-conscious belief that language is a natural growth and not an instrument which we shape for our own purposes.

Now, it is clear that the decline of a language must ultimately have political and economic causes: it is not due simply to the bad influence of this or that individual writer. But an effect can become a cause, reinforcing the original cause and producing the same effect in an intensified form, and so on indefinitely. A man may take to drink because he feels himself to be a failure, and then fail all the more completely because he drinks. It is rather the same thing that is happening to the English language. It becomes ugly

8. Short heavy swords (Burmese).
9. From the seaport Coringa, on the east coast of Madras in British India.

and inaccurate because our thoughts are foolish, but the slovenliness of our language makes it easier for us to have foolish thoughts. The point is that the process is reversible. Modern English, especially written English, is full of bad habits which spread by imitation and which can be avoided if one is willing to take the necessary trouble. If one gets rid of these habits one can think more clearly, and to think clearly is a necessary first step towards political regeneration: so that the fight against bad English is not frivolous and is not the exclusive concern of professional writers. I will come back to this presently, and I hope that by that time the meaning of what I have said here will have become clearer. Meanwhile, here are five specimens of the English language as it is now habitually written.

These five passages have not been picked out because they are especially bad—I could have quoted far worse if I had chosen—but because they illustrate various of the mental vices from which we now suffer. They are a little below the average, but are fairly representative samples. I number them so that I can refer back to them when necessary:

1. I am not, indeed, sure whether it is not true to say that the Milton who once seemed not unlike a seventeenth-century Shelley had not become, out of an experience ever more bitter in each year, more alien (sic)[1] the founder of that Jesuit sect which nothing could induce him to tolerate.

Professor Harold Laski (Essay in *Freedom of Expression*).

2. Above all, we cannot play ducks and drakes with a native battery of idioms which prescribes such egregious collocations of vocables as the Basic *put up with* for *tolerate* or *put at a loss* for *bewilder*.

Professor Lancelot Hogben (*Interglossa*).

3. On the one side we have the free personality: by definition it is not neurotic, for it has neither conflict nor dream. Its desires, such as they are, are transparent, for they are just what institutional approval keeps in the forefront of consciousness; another institutional pattern would alter their number and intensity; there is little in them that is natural, irreducible, or culturally dangerous. But *on the other side*, the social bond itself is nothing but the mutual reflection of these self-secure integrities. Recall the definition of love. Is not this the very picture of a small academic? Where is there a place in this hall of mirrors for either personality or fraternity?

Essay on psychology in *Politics* (New York).

4. All the "best people" from the gentlemen's clubs, and all the frantic Fascist captains, united in common hatred of Socialism and bestial horror of the rising tide of the mass revolutionary movement, have turned to acts of provocation, to foul incendiarism, to medieval legends of poisoned wells, to legalise their own destruction to proletarian organisations, and rouse the agitated petty-bourgeoisie to chauvinistic fervour on behalf of the fight against the revolutionary way out of the crisis.

Communist pamphlet.

---

1. Thus (Latin), i.e., that's the way it was written.

5. If a new spirit *is* to be infused into this old country, there is one thorny and contentious reform which must be tackled, and that is the humanisation and galvanisation of the BBC[2] Timidity here will bespeak canker and atrophy of the soul. The heart of Britain may be sound and of strong beat, for instance, but the British lion's roar at present is like that of Bottom in Shakespeare's *Midsummer Night's Dream*—as gentle as any sucking dove. A virile new Britain cannot continue indefinitely to be traduced in the eyes, or rather ears, of the world by the effete languors of Langham Place, brazenly masquerading as "standard English." When the Voice of Britain is heard at nine o'clock, better far and infinitely less ludicrous to hear aitches[3] honestly dropped than the present priggish, inflated, inhibited, school-ma'amish arch braying of blameless bashful mewing maidens!

Letter in *Tribune*.

Each of these passages has faults of its own, but, quite apart from avoidable ugliness, two qualities are common to all of them. The first is staleness of imagery: the other is lack of precision. The writer either has a meaning and cannot express it, or he inadvertently says something else, or he is almost indifferent as to whether his words mean anything or not. This mixture of vagueness and sheer incompetence is the most marked characteristic of modern English prose, and especially of any kind of political writing. As soon as certain topics are raised, the concrete melts into the abstract and no one seems able to think of turns of speech that are not hackneyed: prose consists less and less of *words* chosen for the sake of their meaning, and more of *phrases* tacked together like the sections of a prefabricated henhouse. I list below, with notes and examples, various of the tricks by means of which the work of prose construction is habitually dodged:

Dying metaphors. A newly invented metaphor assists thought by evoking a visual image, while on the other hand a metaphor which is technically "dead" (e.g., *iron resolution*) has in effect reverted to being an ordinary word and can generally be used without loss of vividness. But in between these two classes there is a huge dump of worn-out metaphors which have lost all evocative power and are merely used because they save people the trouble of inventing phrases for themselves. Examples are: *Ring the changes on, take up the cudgels for, toe the line, ride roughshod over, stand shoulder to shoulder with, play into the hands of, no axe to grind, grist to the mill, fishing in troubled waters, rift within the lute, on the order of the day, Achilles' heel, swan song, hotbed.* Many of these are used without knowledge of their meaning (What is a "rift," for instance?), and incompatible metaphors are frequently mixed, a sure sign that the writer is not interested in what he is saying. Some metaphors now current have been twisted out of their original meaning without those who use them even being aware of the fact. For example, *toe the line* is sometimes written *tow the line.* Another example is *the hammer and the anvil,* now always used with the implication that the anvil gets the worst of it. In real life it is always the anvil that breaks the hammer, never

---

2. British Broadcasting Corporation.
3. I.e., *h* sounds, which are not aspirated in the colloquial speech of some English accents. During—and for some time after—World War II, few programs had a larger audience than the evening nine o'clock news. Langham Place is the location of the BBC's main offices in London.

the other way about: a writer who stopped to think what he was saying would be aware of this, and would avoid perverting the original phrase.

Operators, or verbal false limbs. These save the trouble of picking out appropriate verbs and nouns, and at the same time pad each sentence with extra syllables which give it an appearance of symmetry. Characteristic phrases are: *render inoperative, militate against, prove unacceptable, make contact with, be subjected to, give rise to, give grounds for, have the effect of, play a leading part (rôle) in, make itself felt, take effect, exhibit a tendency to, serve the purpose of,* etc etc. The keynote is the elimination of simple verbs. Instead of being a single word, such as *break, stop, spoil, mend, kill,* a verb becomes a *phrase,* made up of a noun or adjective tacked on to some general-purposes verb such as *prove, serve, form, play, render.* In addition, the passive voice is wherever possible used in preference to the active, and noun constructions are used instead of gerunds (*by examination of* instead of *by examining*). The range of verbs is further cut down by means of the *-ise* and *de-* formations, and banal statements are given an appearance of profundity by means of the *not un*formation. Simple conjunctions and prepositions are replaced by such phrases as *with respect to, having regard to, the fact that, by dint of, in view of, in the interests of, on the hypothesis that*; and the ends of sentences are saved from anticlimax by such resounding commonplaces as *greatly to be desired, cannot be left out of account, a development to be expected in the near future, deserving of serious consideration, brought to a satisfactory conclusion,* and so on and so forth.

Pretentious diction. Words like *phenomenon, element, individual* (as noun), *objective, categorical, effective, virtual, basic, primary, promote, constitute, exhibit, exploit, utilise, eliminate, liquidate,* are used to dress up simple statements and give an air of scientific impartiality to biassed judgements. Adjectives like *epoch-making, epic, historic, unforgettable, triumphant, age-old, inevitable, inexorable, veritable,* are used to dignify the sordid processes of international politics, while writing that aims at glorifying war usually takes on an archaic colour, its characteristic words being: *realm, throne, chariot, mailed fist, trident, sword, shield, buckler, banner, jackboot, clarion.* Foreign words and expressions such as *cul de sac, ancien régime, deus ex machina, mutatis mutandis, status quo, Gleichschaltung, Weltanschauung,*[4] are used to give an air of culture and elegance. Except for the useful abbreviations *i.e., e.g.,* and *etc.,* there is no real need for any of the hundreds of foreign phrases now current in English. Bad writers, and especially scientific, political and sociological writers, are nearly always haunted by the notion that Latin or Greek words are grander than Saxon ones, and unnecessary words like *expedite, ameliorate, predict, extraneous, deracinated, clandestine, sub-aqueous* and hundreds of others constantly gain ground from their Anglo-Saxon opposite numbers.[5] The jargon peculiar to Marxist writing (*hyena, hangman, cannibal,*

4. Respectively: dead end (French), former system of government (French), the god from the machine (Latin), with the necessary changes (Latin), the existing state of things (Latin), standardization of political institutions among authoritarian states (German), and philosophy of life (German).

5. An interesting illustration of this is the way in which the English flower names which were in use till very recently are being ousted by Greek ones, *snapdragon* becoming *antirrhinum, forget-me-not* becoming *myosotis,* etc. It is hard to see any practical reason for this change of fashion: it is probably due to an instinctive turning-away from the more homely word and a vague feeling that the Greek word is scientific [Orwell's note].

petty bourgeois, these gentry, lacquey, flunkey, mad dog, White Guard, etc.) consists largely of words and phrases translated from Russian, German or French; but the normal way of coining a new word is to use a Latin or Greek root with the appropriate affix and, where necessary, the *-ise* formation. It is often easier to make up words of this kind (*deregionalise, impermissible, extra-marital, non-fragmentatory* and so forth) than to think up the English words that will cover one's meaning. The result, in general, is an increase in slovenliness and vagueness.

Meaningless words. In certain lands of writing, particularly in art criticism and literary criticism, it is normal to come across long passages which are almost completely lacking in meaning.[6] Words like *romantic, plastic, values, human, dead, sentimental, natural, vitality,* as used in art criticism, are strictly meaningless, in the sense that they not only do not point to any discoverable object, but are hardly even expected to do so by the reader. When one critic writes, "The outstanding features of Mr X's work is its living quality," while another writes, "The immediately striking thing about Mr X's work is its peculiar deadness," the reader accepts this as a simple difference of opinion. If words like *black* and *white* were involved, instead of the jargon words *dead* and *living,* he would see at once that language was being used in an improper way. Many political words are similarly abused. The word *Fascism* has now no meaning except in so far as it signifies "something not desirable." The words *democracy, socialism, freedom, patriotic, realistic, justice,* have each of them several different meanings which cannot be reconciled with one another. In the case of a word like *democracy,* not only is there no agreed definition, but the attempt to make one is resisted from all sides. It is almost universally felt that when we call a country democratic we are praising it: consequently the defenders of every kind of régime claim that it is a democracy, and fear that they might have to stop using the word if it were tied down to any one meaning. Words of this kind are often used in a consciously dishonest way. That is, the person who uses them has his own private definition, but allows his hearer to think he means something quite different. Statements like *Marshal Pétain*[7] was a true patriot, The Soviet press is the freest in the world, The Catholic Church is opposed to persecution, are almost always made with intent to deceive. Other words used in variable meanings, in most cases more or less dishonestly, are: *class, totalitarian, science, progressive, reactionary, bourgeois, equality.*

Now that I have made this catalogue of swindles and perversions, let me give another example of the kind of writing that they lead to. This time it must of its nature be an imaginary one. I am going to translate a passage of good English into modern English of the worst sort. Here is a well-known verse from *Ecclesiastes:*

> I returned, and saw under the sun, that the race is not to the swift, nor the battle to the strong, neither yet bread to the wise, nor yet riches to men of understanding, nor yet favour to men of skill; but time and chance happeneth to them all.

6. Example: "Comfort's catholicity of perception and image, strangely Whitmanesque in range, almost the exact opposite in aesthetic compulsion, continues to evoke that trembling atmospheric accumulative hinting at a cruel, an inexorably serene timelessness . . . Wrey Gardiner scores by aiming at simple bullseyes with precision. Only they are not so simple, and through this contented sadness runs more than the surface bitter-sweet of resignation." (*Poetry Quarterly.*) [Orwell's note].
7. French army officer (1856–1951), head of the Vichy government that collaborated with Germany in World War II.

Here it is in modern English:

> Objective consideration of contemporary phenomena compels the conclusion that success or failure in competitive activities exhibits no tendency to be commensurate with innate capacity, but that a considerable element of the unpredictable must invariably be taken into account.

This is a parody, but not a very gross one. Exhibit 3, above, for instance, contains several patches of the same kind of English. It will be seen that I have not made a full translation. The beginning and ending of the sentence follow the original meaning fairly closely, but in the middle the concrete illustrations—race, battle, bread—dissolve into the vague phrase "success or failure in competitive activities". This had to be so, because no modern writer of the kind I am discussing—no one capable of using phrases like "objective consideration of contemporary phenomena"—would ever tabulate his thoughts in that precise and detailed way. The whole tendency of modern prose is away from concreteness. Now analyse these two sentences a little more closely. The first contains 49 words but only 60 syllables, and all its words are those of everyday life. The second contains 38 words of 90 syllables: 18 of its words are from Latin roots, and one from Greek. The first sentence contains six vivid images, and only one phrase ("time and chance") that could be called vague. The second contains not a single fresh, arresting phrase, and in spite of its 90 syllables it gives only a shortened version of the meaning contained in the first. Yet without a doubt it is the second kind of sentence that is gaining ground in modern English. I do not want to exaggerate. This kind of writing is not yet universal, and outcrops of simplicity will occur here and there in the worst-written page. Still, if you or I were told to write a few lines on the uncertainty of human fortunes, we should probably come much nearer to my imaginary sentence than to the one from *Ecclesiastes*.

As I have tried to show, modern writing at its worst does not consist in picking out words for the sake of their meaning and inventing images in order to make the meaning clearer. It consists in gumming together long strips of words which have already been set in order by someone else, and making the results presentable by sheer humbug. The attraction of this way of writing is that it is easy. It is easier—even quicker, once you have the habit—to say *In my opinion it is a not unjustifiable assumption that* than to say *I think*. If you use ready-made phrases, you not only don't have to hunt about for words; you also don't have to bother with the rhythms of your sentences, since these phrases are generally so arranged as to be more or less euphonious. When you are composing in a hurry—when you are dictating to a stenographer, for instance, or making a public speech—it is natural to fall into a pretentious, latinised style. Tags like *a consideration which we should do well to bear in mind* or *a conclusion to which all of us would readily assent* will save many a sentence from coming down with a bump. By using stale metaphors, similes and idioms, you save much mental effort, at the cost of leaving your meaning vague, not only for your reader but for yourself. This is the significance of mixed metaphors. The sole aim of a metaphor is to call up a visual image. When these images clash—as in *The Fascist octopus has sung its swan song, the jackboot is thrown into the melting-pot*—it can be taken as certain that the writer is not seeing a mental image of the objects he is naming; in other words he is not really thinking. Look again at the examples I gave at the beginning of this essay. Professor Laski (1) uses five negatives in 53 words. One of these is superfluous, making nonsense of the whole passage, and in addition there is the slip *alien* for akin, making further nonsense, and several avoidable pieces of clumsiness which increase the general vagueness. Professor Hogben (2) plays ducks and drakes with a battery which is able to write prescriptions, and, while disapproving of the everyday phrase *put up with*, is unwilling to look *egregious* up in the dictionary and see what it means. (3), if one takes an uncharitable attitude towards it, is simply meaningless: probably one could work out its intended meaning by reading the whole of the article in which it occurs. In (4) the writer knows more or less what he wants to say, but an accumulation of stale phrases chokes him like tea-leaves blocking a sink. In (5) words and meaning have almost parted company. People who write in this manner usually have a general emotional meaning—they dislike one thing and want to express solidarity with another—but they are not interested in the detail of what they are saying. A scrupulous writer, in every sentence that he writes, will ask himself at least four questions, thus: What am I trying to say? What words will express it? What image or idiom will make it clearer? Is this image fresh enough to have an effect? And he will probably ask himself two more: Could I put it more shortly? Have I said anything that is avoidably ugly? But you are not obliged to go to all this trouble. You can shirk it by simply throwing your mind open and letting the ready-made phrases come crowding in. They will construct your sentences for you—even think your thoughts for you, to a certain extent—and at need they will perform the important service of partially concealing your meaning even from yourself. It is at this point that the special connection between politics and the debasement of language becomes clear.

In our time it is broadly true that political writing is bad writing. Where it is not true, it will generally be found that the writer is some kind of rebel, expressing his private opinions, and not a "party line." Orthodoxy, of whatever colour, seems to demand a lifeless, imitative style. The political dialects to be found in pamphlets, leading articles, manifestos, White Papers and the speeches of Under-Secretaries[8] do, of course, vary from party to party, but they are all alike in that one almost never finds in them a fresh, vivid, homemade turn of speech. When one watches some tired hack on the platform mechanically repeating the familiar phrases—*bestial atrocities, iron heel, blood-stained tyranny, free peoples of the world, stand shoulder to shoulder*—one often has a curious feeling that one is not watching a live human being but some kind of dummy: a feeling which suddenly becomes stronger at moments when the light catches the speaker's spectacles and turns them into blank discs which seem to have no eyes behind them. And this is not altogether fanciful. A speaker who uses that kind of phraseology has gone some distance towards turning himself into a machine. The appropriate noises are coming out of his larynx, but his brain is not involved as it would be if he were choosing his words for himself. If the speech he is making is one that he is accustomed to make over and over again, he may be almost unconscious of what he is saying, as one is when one utters the responses in church. And this reduced state of consciousness, if not indispensable, is at any rate favourable to political conformity.

In our time, political speech and writing are largely the defence of the indefensible. Things like the continuance of British rule in India,[9] the Russian purges and deportations, the dropping of the atom bombs on Japan, can indeed be defended, but only by arguments which are too brutal for most people to face, and which do not square with the professed aims of political

---

8. Senior British civil servants. "White Papers": official documents, each on a particular topic, issued by the British government.
9. This ended in 1947.

parties. Thus political language has to consist largely of euphemism, question-begging and sheer cloudy vagueness. Defenceless villages are bombarded from the air, the inhabitants driven out into the countryside, the cattle machine-gunned, the huts set on fire with incendiary bullets: this is called *pacification*. Millions of peasants are robbed of their farms and sent trudging along the roads with no more than they can carry: this is called *transfer of population* or *rectification of frontiers*. People are imprisoned for years without trial, or shot in the back of the neck or sent to die of scurvy in Arctic lumber camps: this is called *elimination of unreliable elements*. Such phraseology is needed if one wants to name things without calling up mental pictures of them. Consider for instance some comfortable English professor defending Russian totalitarianism. He cannot say outright, "I believe in killing off your opponents when you can get good results by doing so." Probably, therefore, he will say something like this:

> While freely conceding that the Soviet régime exhibits certain features which the humanitarian may be inclined to deplore, we must, I think, agree that a certain curtailment of the right to political opposition is an unavoidable concomitant of transitional periods, and that the rigours which the Russian people have been called upon to undergo have been amply justified in the sphere of concrete achievement.

The inflated style is itself a kind of euphemism. A mass of Latin words falls upon the facts like soft snow, blurring the outlines and covering up all the details. The great enemy of clear language is insincerity. When there is a gap between one's real and one's declared aims, one turns as it were instinctively to long words and exhausted idioms, like a cuttlefish squirting out ink. In our age there is no such thing as "keeping out of politics." All issues are political issues, and politics itself is a mass of lies, evasions, folly, hatred and schizophrenia. When the general atmosphere is bad, language must suffer. I should expect to find—this is a guess which I have not sufficient knowledge to verify—that the German, Russian and Italian languages have all deteriorated in the last ten or fifteen years, as a result of dictatorship.

But if thought corrupts language, language can also corrupt thought. A bad usage can spread by tradition and imitation, even among people who should and do know better. The debased language that I have been discussing is in some ways very convenient. Phrases like a *not unjustifiable assumption, leaves much to be desired, would serve no good purpose, a consideration which we should do well to bear in mind*, are a continuous temptation, a packet of aspirins always at one's elbow. Look back through this essay, and for certain you will find that I have again and again committed the very faults I am protesting against. By this morning's post I have received a pamphlet dealing with conditions in Germany. The author tells me that he "felt impelled" to write it. I open it at random, and here is almost the first sentence that I see: "(The Allies) have an opportunity not only of achieving a radical transformation of Germany's social and political structure in such a way as to avoid a nationalistic reaction in Germany itself, but at the same time of laying the foundations of a co-operative and unified Europe." You see, he "feels impelled" to write—feels, presumably, that he has something new to say—and yet his words, like cavalry horses answering the bugle, group themselves automatically into the familiar dreary pattern. This invasion of one's mind by ready-made phrases (*lay the foundations, achieve a radical transformation*) can only be prevented if one is constantly on guard against them, and every such phrase anaesthetises a portion of one's brain.

I said earlier that the decadence of our language is probably curable. Those who deny this would argue, if they produced an argument at all, that language merely reflects existing social conditions, and that we cannot influence its development by any direct tinkering with words and constructions. So far as the general tone or spirit of a language goes, this may be true, but it is not true in detail. Silly words and expressions have often disappeared, not through any evolutionary process but owing to the conscious action of a minority. Two recent examples were *explore every avenue* and *leave no stone unturned*, which were killed by the jeers of a few journalists. There is a long list of fly-blown metaphors which could similarly be got rid of if enough people would interest themselves in the job; and it should also be possible to laugh the *not un*formation out of existence,[1] to reduce the amount of Latin and Greek in the average sentence, to drive out foreign phrases and strayed scientific words, and, in general, to make pretentiousness unfashionable. But all these are minor points. The defence of the English language implies more than this, and perhaps it is best to start by saying what it does *not* imply.

To begin with, it has nothing to do with archaism, with the salvaging of obsolete words and turns of speech, or with the setting-up of a "standard English" which must never be departed from. On the contrary, it is especially concerned with the scrapping of every word or idiom which has outworn its usefulness. It has nothing to do with correct grammar and syntax, which are of no importance so long as one makes one's meaning clear, or with the avoidance of Americanisms, or with having what is called a "good prose style." On the other hand it is not concerned with fake simplicity and the attempt to make written English colloquial. Nor does it even imply in every case preferring the Saxon word to the Latin one, though it does imply using the fewest and shortest words that will cover one's meaning. What is above all needed is to let the meaning choose the word, and not the other way about. In prose, the worst thing one can do with words is to surrender to them. When you think of a concrete object, you think wordlessly, and then, if you want to describe the thing you have been visualising, you probably hunt about till you find the exact words that seem to fit it. When you think of something abstract you are more inclined to use words from the start, and unless you make a conscious effort to prevent it, the existing dialect will come rushing in and do the job for you, at the expense of blurring or even changing your meaning. Probably it is better to put off using words as long as possible and get one's meaning as clear as one can through pictures or sensations. Afterwards one can choose—not simply *accept*—the phrases that will best cover the meaning, and then switch round and decide what impression one's words are likely to make on another person. This last effort of the mind cuts out all stale or mixed images, all prefabricated phrases, needless repetitions, and humbug and vagueness generally. But one can often be in doubt about the effect of a word or a phrase, and one needs rules that one can rely on when instinct fails. I think the following rules will cover most cases:

   i. Never use a metaphor, simile or other figure of speech which you are used to seeing in print.

   ii. Never use a long word where a short one will do.

---

1. One can cure oneself of the *not un-* formation by memorising this sentence: *A not unblack dog was chasing a not unsmall rabbit across a not ungreen field* [Orwell's note].

iii. If it is possible to cut a word out, always cut it out.

iv. Never use the passive where you can use the active.

v. Never use a foreign phrase, a scientific word or a jargon word if you can think of an everyday English equivalent.

vi. Break any of these rules sooner than say anything outright barbarous.

These rules sound elementary, and so they are, but they demand a deep change of attitude in anyone who has grown used to writing in the style now fashionable. One could keep all of them and still write bad English, but one could not write the kind of stuff that I quoted in those five specimens at the beginning of this article.

I have not here been considering the literary use of language, but merely language as an instrument for expressing and not for concealing or preventing thought. Stuart Chase and others have come near to claiming that all abstract words are meaningless, and have used this as a pretext for advocating a kind of political quietism. Since you don't know what Fascism is, how can you struggle against Fascism? One need not swallow such absurdities as this, but one ought to recognise that the present political chaos is connected with the decay of language, and that one can probably bring about some improvement by starting at the verbal end. If you simplify your English, you are freed from the worst follies of orthodoxy. You cannot speak any of the necessary dialects, and when you make a stupid remark its stupidity will be obvious, even to yourself. Political language—and with variations this is true of all political parties, from Conservatives to Anarchists—is designed to make lies sound truthful and murder respectable, and to give an appearance of solidity to pure wind. One cannot change this all in a moment, but one can at least change one's own habits, and from time to time one can even, if one jeers loudly enough, send some worn-out and useless phrase—some *jackboot, Achilles' heel, hotbed, melting pot, acid test, veritable inferno* or other lump of verbal refuse—into the dustbin where it belongs.

1946, 1947

SAMUEL BECKETT
1906–1989

Samuel Beckett was born near Dublin. Like W. B. Yeats, George Bernard Shaw, and Oscar Wilde, he came from an Anglo-Irish Protestant family. He received a B.A. from Trinity College, Dublin, and after teaching English at the École Normale Supérieure in Paris for two years, returned to Trinity College to take his M.A. in 1931. A year later he gave up teaching to write, and having produced an insightful essay on the early stages of James Joyce's *Finnegans Wake*, Beckett also worked as Joyce's amanuensis (secretary) and translator. In 1937 he settled permanently in Paris. There, during World War II, he joined an underground group in the anti-Nazi resistance and, after the group was betrayed, barely escaped into unoccupied France. From the mid-1940s he generally wrote in French and subsequently translated some of his work into an eloquent, Irish-inflected English. His early novels—*Murphy* (1938; Eng. trans., 1957);

Watt (1953); and the trilogy, *Molloy* (1951; 1955), *Malone Dies* (1951; 1956), and *The Unnameable* (1953; 1958)—have been hailed as masterpieces and precursors of postmodern fiction; but he is best known for his plays, especially *Waiting for Godot* (1952; 1954) and *Endgame* (1957; 1958). He received the Nobel Prize in Literature in 1969.

Not much happens in a Beckett play; there is little characterization, little plot, and little incident. Characters engage in dialogue or dialectical monologues that go nowhere. There is no progression, no development, no resolution. Rambling exchanges and repetitive actions enact the lack of a fixed center, of meaning, of purpose, in the lives depicted. Yet the characters persist in their habitual, almost ritualistic, activities; they go on talking, even if only to themselves. In spite of the reiterated theme of nonexistence, the characters go on existing—if minimally: a stream of discourse, of thought and will, a consciousness questioning its own meaning and purpose. In *Waiting for Godot* the main characters wait for an arrival that is constantly deferred. They inhabit a bleak landscape seemingly confined to one road, one tree; they talk of moving on, yet never leave. In *Endgame* the main characters—irritable and peevish— live inside a room with two small, high windows, outside of which everything may or may not be dead. Two of their parents live inside garbage cans and appear only from the shoulders up. Subsequent plays restrict the acting space to smaller spaces, such as

Waiting for Godot at the Théâtre Hebertot in Paris, 1956. Like the 1953 premiere in French and 1955 in English, the Paris revival of *Waiting for Godot* had a spare, minimalist set. Pozzo (far right) holds a whip and a rope that goes around Lucky's neck, while Lucky holds a bag, picnic basket, folding stool, and greatcoat. The play's central characters, Vladimir and Estragon, look on in puzzlement.

urns or a mound in which the actor is buried; characters are physically confined or disabled, until *Not I* (1973) presents the most minimal embodiment of human consciousness available to theatrical representation: a disembodied mouth.

Beckett focuses his work on fundamental questions of existence and nonexistence, the mind and the body, the self as known from within and as seen from the outside or in retrospect. Joyce's artistic integrity and stream of consciousness technique influenced him, but the minimalism of Beckett's plays and fiction contrast with the maximalism of Joyce's *Ulysses* and *Finnegans Wake*. "I realised that Joyce had gone as far as one could in the direction of knowing more, in control of one's material," he told the biographer James Knowlson. "I realised my own way was in impoverishment, in lack of knowledge and in taking away, in subtracting rather than adding."

The daring minimalism of *Waiting for Godot*—its radically diminished setting, clownish characters, and circular plot—is often seen as having transformed serious theater for the second half of the twentieth century. Because Act II of the play largely repeats Act I, with subtle variations, the Irish critic Vivian Mercier famously called *Waiting for Godot* "a play in which nothing happens, twice." As they wait for an appointment with the mysteriously indeterminate Godot, the play's central characters, Vladimir and Estragon, nicknamed Didi and Gogo, haplessly amuse, comfort, and annoy each other. The play implicitly contrasts their affable, if vexed, friendship with the master-slave relation between another pair of characters who appear twice on the scene: the sometimes brutal Pozzo and the ironically named Lucky, whipped and driven like an animal by his master. As in subsequent Beckett plays, this one juxtaposes vaudeville, slapstick, and other comic traditions with stark insight into the meaningless void beneath our feet, however we may try to cover it up by speech and action. Blinded and humbled by the second act, Pozzo cries out, "one day we were born, one day we shall die," adding, "They give birth astride of a grave, the light gleams an instant, then it's night once more." Combining such bleak pathos with horseplay, banter, pranks, juggling, and crude puns, *Waiting for Godot* shares its tragicomic quality with absurdist drama, which disrupts the conventions of realist drama, draws attention to its own fictionality, and refuses to provide hierarchies of significance. Reduced to bare essentials, desperately seeking ways to pass the time during their seemingly interminable wait, the characters in *Waiting for Godot*—though often behaving as if bumbling protagonists of a farce—raise unsettling questions about meaning and absurdity, power and dependency, time and repetition, language and death.

Waiting for Godot

A Tragicomedy in Two Acts

CHARACTERS

ESTRAGON   POZZO
VLADIMIR   A BOY
LUCKY

Act 1

A country road. A tree.
Evening.

> [ESTRAGON, *sitting on a low mound, is trying to take off his boot. He pulls at it with both hands, panting. He gives up, exhausted, rests, tries again. As before.*]
>
> [*Enter* VLADIMIR.]

ESTRAGON [*giving up again*]   Nothing to be done.

VLADIMIR [*advancing with short, stiff strides, legs wide apart*]   I'm beginning to come round to that opinion. All my life I've tried to put it from
me, saying, Vladimir, be reasonable, you haven't yet tried everything.
And I resumed the struggle. [*He broods, musing on the struggle. Turning
to* ESTRAGON.] So there you are again.

ESTRAGON   Am I?

VLADIMIR   I'm glad to see you back. I thought you were gone for ever.

ESTRAGON   Me too.

VLADIMIR   Together again at last! We'll have to celebrate this. But how?
[*He reflects.*] Get up till I embrace you.

ESTRAGON [*irritably*]   Not now, not now.

VLADIMIR [*hurt, coldly*]   May one enquire where His Highness spent the
night?

ESTRAGON   In a ditch.

VLADIMIR [*admiringly*]   A ditch! Where?

ESTRAGON [*without gesture*]   Over there.

VLADIMIR   And they didn't beat you?

ESTRAGON   Beat me? Certainly they beat me.

VLADIMIR   The same lot as usual?

ESTRAGON   The same? I don't know.

VLADIMIR   When I think of it . . . all these years . . . but for me . . . where
would you be . . . [*Decisively.*] You'd be nothing more than a little heap
of bones at the present minute, no doubt about it.

ESTRAGON   And what of it?

VLADIMIR [*gloomily*]   It's too much for one man. [*Pause. Cheerfully.*] On
the other hand what's the good of losing heart now, that's what I say.
We should have thought of it a million years ago, in the nineties.[1]

ESTRAGON   Ah stop blathering and help me off with this bloody thing.

VLADIMIR   Hand in hand from the top of the Eiffel Tower, among the
first.[2] We were respectable in those days. Now it's too late. They wouldn't
even let us up. [ESTRAGON *tears at his boot.*] What are you doing?

ESTRAGON   Taking off my boot. Did that never happen to you?

VLADIMIR   Boots must be taken off every day, I'm tired telling you that.
Why don't you listen to me?

ESTRAGON [*feebly*]   Help me!

VLADIMIR   It hurts?

ESTRAGON [*angrily*]   Hurts! He wants to know if it hurts!

VLADIMIR [*angrily*]   No one ever suffers but you. I don't count. I'd like to
hear what you'd say if you had what I have.

ESTRAGON   It hurts?

VLADIMIR [*angrily*]   Hurts! He wants to know if it hurts!

ESTRAGON [*pointing*]   You might button it all the same.

VLADIMIR [*stooping*]   True. [*He buttons his fly.*] Never neglect the little
things of life.

ESTRAGON   What do you expect, you always wait till the last moment.

VLADIMIR [*musingly*]   The last moment . . . [*He meditates.*] Hope deferred
maketh the something sick, who said that?[3]

1. I.e., the 1890s. "It": suicide.
2. I.e., they should have jumped from the Eiffel
Tower, completed in 1889; it was the tallest
human-built structure in the world until 1930.

3. "Hope deferred maketh the heart sick: but
when the desire cometh, it is a tree of life" (Proverbs 13.12).

ESTRAGON   Why don't you help me?

VLADIMIR   Sometimes I feel it coming all the same. Then I go all queer. [*He takes off his hat, peers inside it, feels about inside it, shakes it, puts it on again.*] How shall I say? Relieved and at the same time . . . [*He searches for the word.*] . . . appalled. [*With emphasis.*] AP-PALLED. [*He takes off his hat again, peers inside it.*] Funny. [*He knocks on the crown as though to dislodge a foreign body, peers into it again, puts it on again.*] Nothing to be done. [ESTRAGON *with a supreme effort succeeds in pulling off his boot. He peers inside it, feels about inside it, turns it upside down, shakes it, looks on the ground to see if anything has fallen out, finds nothing, feels inside it again, staring sightlessly before him.*] Well?

ESTRAGON   Nothing.

VLADIMIR   Show.

ESTRAGON   There's nothing to show.

VLADIMIR   Try and put it on again.

ESTRAGON [*examining his foot*]   I'll air it for a bit.

VLADIMIR   There's man all over for you, blaming on his boots the faults of his feet. [*He takes off his hat again, peers inside it, feels about inside it, knocks on the crown, blows into it, puts it on again.*] This is getting alarming. [*Silence. Vladimir deep in thought, Estragon pulling at his toes.*] One of the thieves was saved.[4] [*Pause.*] It's a reasonable percentage. [*Pause.*] Gogo.

ESTRAGON   What?

VLADIMIR   Suppose we repented.

ESTRAGON   Repented what?

VLADIMIR   Oh . . . [*He reflects.*] We wouldn't have to go into the details.

ESTRAGON   Our being born?

[VLADIMIR *breaks into a hearty laugh which he immediately stifles, his hand pressed to his pubis, his face contorted.*]

VLADIMIR   One daren't even laugh any more.

ESTRAGON   Dreadful privation.

VLADIMIR   Merely smile. [*He smiles suddenly from ear to ear, keeps smiling, ceases as suddenly.*] It's not the same thing. Nothing to be done. [*Pause.*] Gogo.

ESTRAGON [*irritably*]   What is it?

VLADIMIR   Did you ever read the Bible?

ESTRAGON   The Bible . . . [*He reflects.*] I must have taken a look at it.

VLADIMIR   Do you remember the Gospels?

ESTRAGON   I remember the maps of the Holy Land. Coloured they were. Very pretty. The Dead Sea[5] was pale blue. The very look of it made me thirsty. That's where we'll go, I used to say, that's where we'll go for our honeymoon. We'll swim. We'll be happy.

VLADIMIR   You should have been a poet.

ESTRAGON   I was. [*Gesture towards his rags.*] Isn't that obvious?

[*Silence.*]

VLADIMIR   Where was I . . . How's your foot?

ESTRAGON   Swelling visibly.

VLADIMIR   Ah yes, the two thieves. Do you remember the story?

ESTRAGON   No.

---

4. I.e., one of the thieves crucified at the same time as Jesus. Cf. Luke 23.32–43.
5. The salt lake, or inland sea, between Israel and Jordan. "Gospels": the four books of the Bible written by the four Evangelists—Matthew, Mark, Luke, and John.

VLADIMIR   Shall I tell it to you?

ESTRAGON   No.

VLADIMIR   It'll pass the time. [*Pause.*] Two thieves, crucified at the same time as our Saviour. One—

ESTRAGON   Our what?

VLADIMIR   Our Saviour. Two thieves. One is supposed to have been saved and the other . . . [*he searches for the contrary of saved*] . . . damned.

ESTRAGON   Saved from what?

VLADIMIR   Hell.

ESTRAGON   I'm going.

[*He does not move.*]

VLADIMIR   And yet . . . [*pause*] . . . how is it—this is not boring you I hope— how is it that of the four Evangelists only one speaks of a thief being saved. The four of them were there—or thereabouts—and only one speaks of a thief being saved. [*Pause.*] Come on, Gogo, return the ball, can't you, once in a way?

ESTRAGON [*with exaggerated enthusiasm*]   I find this really most extraordinarily interesting.

VLADIMIR   One out of four. Of the other three two don't mention any thieves at all and the third says that both of them abused him.[6]

ESTRAGON   Who?

VLADIMIR   What?

ESTRAGON   What's all this about? Abused who?

VLADIMIR   The Saviour.

ESTRAGON   Why?

VLADIMIR   Because he wouldn't save them.

ESTRAGON   From hell?

VLADIMIR   Imbecile! From death.

ESTRAGON   I thought you said hell.

VLADIMIR   From death, from death.

ESTRAGON   Well what of it?

VLADIMIR   Then the two of them must have been damned.

ESTRAGON   And why not?

VLADIMIR   But one of the four says that one of the two was saved.

ESTRAGON   Well? They don't agree and that's all there is to it.

VLADIMIR   But all four were there. And only one speaks of a thief being saved. Why believe him rather than the others?

ESTRAGON   Who believes him?

VLADIMIR   Everybody. It's the only version they know.

ESTRAGON   People are bloody ignorant apes.

[*He rises painfully, goes limping to extreme left, halts, gazes into distance off with his hand screening his eyes, turns, goes to extreme right, gazes into distance,* VLADIMIR *watches him, then goes and picks up the boot, peers into it, drops it hastily.*]

VLADIMIR   Pah!

[*He spits.* ESTRAGON *moves to center, halts with his back to auditorium.*]

ESTRAGON   Charming spot. [*He turns, advances to front, halts facing auditorium.*] Inspiring prospects. [*He turns to* VLADIMIR.] Let's go.

---

6. Verbally attacked him, or used foul language toward him. "The other three": Matthew, Mark, and John. In fact, all the Gospels mention the thieves. John calls them "two others," and both Matthew and Mark say that the thieves verbally attacked Jesus. Cf. John 19.18, Matthew 27.38–44, and Mark 15.27–32.

VLADIMIR   We can't.
ESTRAGON   Why not?
VLADIMIR   We're waiting for Godot.
ESTRAGON [*despairingly*]   Ah! [*Pause.*] You're sure it was here?
VLADIMIR   What?
ESTRAGON   That we were to wait.
VLADIMIR   He said by the tree. [*They look at the tree.*] Do you see any others?
ESTRAGON   What is it?
VLADIMIR   I don't know. A willow.[7]
ESTRAGON   Where are the leaves?
VLADIMIR   It must be dead.
ESTRAGON   No more weeping.
VLADIMIR   Or perhaps it's not the season.
ESTRAGON   Looks to me more like a bush.
VLADIMIR   A shrub.
ESTRAGON   A bush.
VLADIMIR   A—. What are you insinuating? That we've come to the wrong place?
ESTRAGON   He should be here.
VLADIMIR   He didn't say for sure he'd come.
ESTRAGON   And if he doesn't come?
VLADIMIR   We'll come back tomorrow.
ESTRAGON   And then the day after tomorrow.
VLADIMIR   Possibly.
ESTRAGON   And so on.
VLADIMIR   The point is—
ESTRAGON   Until he comes.
VLADIMIR   You're merciless.
ESTRAGON   We came here yesterday.
VLADIMIR   Ah no, there you're mistaken.
ESTRAGON   What did we do yesterday?
VLADIMIR   What did we do yesterday?
ESTRAGON   Yes.
VLADIMIR   Why . . . [*Angrily.*] Nothing is certain when you're about.
ESTRAGON   In my opinion we were here.
VLADIMIR [*looking round*]   You recognize the place?
ESTRAGON   I didn't say that.
VLADIMIR   Well?
ESTRAGON   That makes no difference.
VLADIMIR   All the same . . . that tree . . . [*turning towards auditorium*] that bog . . .
ESTRAGON   You're sure it was this evening?
VLADIMIR   What?
ESTRAGON   That we were to wait.
VLADIMIR   He said Saturday. [*Pause.*] I think.
ESTRAGON   You think.
VLADIMIR   I must have made a note of it. [*He fumbles in his pockets, bursting with miscellaneous rubbish.*]
ESTRAGON [*very insidious*]   But what Saturday? And is it Saturday? Is it not rather Sunday? [*Pause.*] Or Monday? [*Pause.*] Or Friday?

7. A tree often associated with sadness or grief.

VLADIMIR [*looking wildly about him, as though the date was inscribed in the landscape*] It's not possible!

ESTRAGON Or Thursday?

VLADIMIR What'll we do?

ESTRAGON If he came yesterday and we weren't here you may be sure he won't come again today.

VLADIMIR But you say we were here yesterday.

ESTRAGON I may be mistaken. [*Pause.*] Let's stop talking for a minute, do you mind?

VLADIMIR [*feebly*] All right. [ESTRAGON *sits down on the mound.* VLADIMIR *paces agitatedly to and fro, halting from time to time to gaze into distance off.* ESTRAGON *falls asleep.* VLADIMIR *halts finally before* ESTRAGON.] Gogo! . . . Gogo! . . . GOGO!
  [ESTRAGON *wakes with a start.*]

ESTRAGON [*restored to the horror of his situation*] I was asleep! [*Despairingly.*] Why will you never let me sleep?

VLADIMIR I felt lonely.

ESTRAGON I had a dream.

VLADIMIR Don't tell me!

ESTRAGON I dreamt that—

VLADIMIR DON'T TELL ME!

ESTRAGON [*gesture towards the universe*] This one is enough for you? [*Silence.*] It's not nice of you, Didi. Who am I to tell my private nightmares to if I can't tell them to you?

VLADIMIR Let them remain private. You know I can't bear that.

ESTRAGON [*coldly*] There are times when I wonder if it wouldn't be better for us to part.

VLADIMIR You wouldn't go far.

ESTRAGON That would be too bad, really too bad. [*Pause.*] Wouldn't it, Didi, be really too bad? [*Pause.*] When you think of the beauty of the way. [*Pause.*] And the goodness of the wayfarers. [*Pause. Wheedling.*] Wouldn't it, Didi?

VLADIMIR Calm yourself.

ESTRAGON [*voluptuously*] Calm . . . calm . . . The English say cawm. [*Pause.*] You know the story of the Englishman in the brothel?

VLADIMIR Yes.

ESTRAGON Tell it to me.

VLADIMIR Ah stop it!

ESTRAGON An Englishman having drunk a little more than usual proceeds to a brothel. The bawd asks him if he wants a fair one, a dark one or a red-haired one.[8] Go on.

VLADIMIR STOP IT!
  [*Exit* VLADIMIR *hurriedly.* ESTRAGON *gets up and follows him as far as the limit of the stage. Gestures of* ESTRAGON *like those of a spectator encouraging a pugilist.*[9] *Enter* VLADIMIR. *He brushes past* ESTRAGON, *crosses the stage with bowed head.* ESTRAGON *takes a step towards him, halts.*]

8. In one version of the rest of the bawdy story, the Englishman replies that he wants a boy. Taken aback, the bawd threatens to call a policeman, to which the Englishman replies, "Oh, no, they're too gritty." In another version, he is shown through a series of doors, marked by hair color and size of private parts, and finally selects one marked "Grands Cons" (in French slang, literally, large vaginas; figuratively, big idiots). Confirming him as *con*, or idiot, his choice lands him back on the street.
9. I.e., a boxer.

ESTRAGON [*gently*]   You wanted to speak to me? [*Silence.* ESTRAGON *takes a step forward.*] You had something to say to me? [*Silence. Another step forward.*] Didi . . .

VLADIMIR [*without turning*]   I've nothing to say to you.

ESTRAGON [*step forward*]   You're angry? [*Silence. Step forward.*] Forgive me. [*Silence. Step forward.* ESTRAGON *lays his hand on* VLADIMIR's *shoulder.*] Come, Didi. [*Silence.*] Give me your hand. [VLADIMIR *half turns.*] Embrace me! [VLADIMIR *stiffens.*] Don't be stubborn! [VLADIMIR *softens. They embrace.* ESTRAGON *recoils.*] You stink of garlic!

VLADIMIR   It's for the kidneys. [*Silence.* ESTRAGON *looks attentively at the tree.*] What do we do now?

ESTRAGON   Wait.

VLADIMIR   Yes, but while waiting.

ESTRAGON   What about hanging ourselves?

VLADIMIR   Hmm. It'd give us an erection.

ESTRAGON [*highly excited*]   An erection!

VLADIMIR   With all that follows. Where it falls mandrakes grow. That's why they shriek when you pull them up.[1] Did you not know that?

ESTRAGON   Let's hang ourselves immediately!

VLADIMIR   From a bough? [*They go towards the tree.*] I wouldn't trust it.

ESTRAGON   We can always try.

VLADIMIR   Go ahead.

ESTRAGON   After you.

VLADIMIR   No no, you first.

ESTRAGON   Why me?

VLADIMIR   You're lighter than I am.

ESTRAGON   Just so!

VLADIMIR   I don't understand.

ESTRAGON   Use your intelligence, can't you?
       [VLADIMIR *uses his intelligence.*]

VLADIMIR [*finally*]   I remain in the dark.

ESTRAGON   This is how it is. [*He reflects.*] The bough . . . the bough . . . [*Angrily.*] Use your head, can't you?

VLADIMIR   You're my only hope.

ESTRAGON [*with effort*]   Gogo light—bough not break—Gogo dead. Didi heavy—bough break—Didi alone. Whereas—

VLADIMIR   I hadn't thought of that.

ESTRAGON   If it hangs you it'll hang anything.

VLADIMIR   But am I heavier than you?

ESTRAGON   So you tell me. I don't know. There's an even chance. Or nearly.

VLADIMIR   Well? What do we do?

ESTRAGON   Don't let's do anything. It's safer.

VLADIMIR   Let's wait and see what he says.

ESTRAGON   Who?

VLADIMIR   Godot.

ESTRAGON   Good idea.

VLADIMIR   Let's wait till we know exactly how we stand.

---

1. The mandrake is a plant with a forked root that resembles the human body, which, according to medieval European folklore, was said to grow from the semen ejaculated by hanged men and to shriek when uprooted. Hearing the shriek was said to be fatal, or to make the listener go mad.

ESTRAGON   On the other hand it might be better to strike the iron before
it freezes.[2]

VLADIMIR   I'm curious to hear what he has to offer. Then we'll take it or
leave it.

ESTRAGON   What exactly did we ask him for?

VLADIMIR   Were you not there?

ESTRAGON   I can't have been listening.

VLADIMIR   Oh . . . Nothing very definite.

ESTRAGON   A kind of prayer.

VLADIMIR   Precisely.

ESTRAGON   A vague supplication.

VLADIMIR   Exactly.

ESTRAGON   And what did he reply?

VLADIMIR   That he'd see.

ESTRAGON   That he couldn't promise anything.

VLADIMIR   That he'd have to think it over.

ESTRAGON   In the quiet of his home.

VLADIMIR   Consult his family.

ESTRAGON   His friends.

VLADIMIR   His agents.

ESTRAGON   His correspondents.

VLADIMIR   His books.

ESTRAGON   His bank account.

VLADIMIR   Before taking[3] a decision.

ESTRAGON   It's the normal thing.

VLADIMIR   Is it not?

ESTRAGON   I think it is.

VLADIMIR   I think so too.
   [Silence.]

ESTRAGON [anxious]   And we?

VLADIMIR   I beg your pardon?

ESTRAGON   I said, And we?

VLADIMIR   I don't understand.

ESTRAGON   Where do we come in?

VLADIMIR   Come in?

ESTRAGON   Take your time.

VLADIMIR   Come in? On our hands and knees.

ESTRAGON   As bad as that?

VLADIMIR   Your Worship wishes to assert his prerogatives?

ESTRAGON   We've no rights any more?
   [Laugh of VLADIMIR, stifled as before, less the smile.]

VLADIMIR   You'd make me laugh if it wasn't prohibited.

ESTRAGON   We've lost our rights?

VLADIMIR [distinctly]   We got rid of them.
   [Silence. They remain motionless, arms dangling, heads sunk, sagging
   at the knees.]

ESTRAGON [feebly]   We're not tied? [Pause.] We're not—

VLADIMIR   Listen!
   [They listen, grotesquely rigid.]

ESTRAGON   I hear nothing.

2. Cf. the proverb "Strike while the iron is hot."   3. I.e., making.

VLADIMIR   Hsst! [*They listen.* ESTRAGON *loses his balance, almost falls. He clutches the arm of* VLADIMIR, *who totters. They listen, huddled together.*] Nor I.

    [*Sighs of relief. They relax and separate.*]

ESTRAGON   You gave me a fright.

VLADIMIR   I thought it was he.

ESTRAGON   Who?

VLADIMIR   Godot.

ESTRAGON   Pah! The wind in the reeds.

VLADIMIR   I could have sworn I heard shouts.

ESTRAGON   And why would he shout?

VLADIMIR   At his horse.

    [*Silence.*]

ESTRAGON [*violently*]   I'm hungry!

VLADIMIR   Do you want a carrot?

ESTRAGON   Is that all there is?

VLADIMIR   I might have some turnips.

ESTRAGON   Give me a carrot. [VLADIMIR *rummages in his pockets, takes out a turnip and gives it to* ESTRAGON *who takes a bite out of it. Angrily.*] It's a turnip!

VLADIMIR   Oh pardon! I could have sworn it was a carrot. [*He rummages again in his pockets, finds nothing but turnips.*] All that's turnips. [*He rummages.*] You must have eaten the last. [*He rummages.*] Wait, I have it. [*He brings out a carrot and gives it to* ESTRAGON.] There, dear fellow, [ESTRAGON *wipes the carrot on his sleeve and begins to eat it.*] Make it last, that's the end of them.

ESTRAGON [*chewing*]   I asked you a question.

VLADIMIR   Ah.

ESTRAGON   Did you reply?

VLADIMIR   How's the carrot?

ESTRAGON   It's a carrot.

VLADIMIR   So much the better, so much the better. [*Pause.*] What was it you wanted to know?

ESTRAGON   I've forgotten. [*Chews.*] That's what annoys me. [*He looks at the carrot appreciatively, dangles it between finger and thumb.*] I'll never forget this carrot. [*He sucks the end of it meditatively.*] Ah yes, now I remember.

VLADIMIR   Well?

ESTRAGON [*his mouth full, vacuously*]   We're not tied?

VLADIMIR   I don't hear a word you're saying.

ESTRAGON [*chews, swallows*]   I'm asking you if we're tied.

VLADIMIR   Tied?

ESTRAGON   Ti-ed.

VLADIMIR   How do you mean tied?

ESTRAGON   Down.

VLADIMIR   But to whom? By whom?

ESTRAGON   To your man.

VLADIMIR   To Godot? Tied to Godot! What an idea! No question of it. [*Pause.*] For the moment.

ESTRAGON   His name is Godot?

VLADIMIR   I think so.

ESTRAGON   Fancy that. [*He raises what remains of the carrot by the stub of leaf, twirls it before his eyes.*] Funny, the more you eat the worse it gets.

VLADIMIR With me it's just the opposite.

ESTRAGON In other words?

VLADIMIR I get used to the muck as I go along.

ESTRAGON [*after prolonged reflection*] Is that the opposite?

VLADIMIR Question of temperament.

ESTRAGON Of character.

VLADIMIR Nothing you can do about it.

ESTRAGON No use struggling.

VLADIMIR One is what one is.

ESTRAGON No use wriggling.

VLADIMIR The essential doesn't change.

ESTRAGON Nothing to be done. [*He proffers the remains of the carrot to* VLADIMIR.] Like to finish it?

[*A terrible cry, close at hand.* ESTRAGON *drops the carrot. They remain motionless, then together make a sudden rush towards the wings.* ESTRAGON *stops halfway, runs back, picks up the carrot, stuffs it in his pocket, runs to rejoin* VLADIMIR *who is waiting for him, stops again, runs back, picks up his boot, runs to rejoin* VLADIMIR. *Huddled together, shoulders hunched, cringing away from the menace, they wait.*]

[*Enter* POZZO *and* LUCKY. POZZO *drives* LUCKY *by means of a rope passed round his neck, so that* LUCKY *is the first to enter, followed by the rope which is long enough to let him reach the middle of the stage before* POZZO *appears.* LUCKY *carries a heavy bag, a folding stool, a picnic basket and a greatcoat,*[4] POZZO *a whip.*]

POZZO [*off*] On! [*Crack of whip.* POZZO *appears. They cross the stage.* LUCKY *passes before* VLADIMIR *and* ESTRAGON *and exit.* POZZO *at the sight of* VLADIMIR *and* ESTRAGON *stops short. The rope tautens.* POZZO *jerks at it violently.*] Back!

[*Noise of* LUCKY *falling with all his baggage.* VLADIMIR *and* ESTRAGON *turn towards him, half wishing half fearing to go to his assistance.* VLADIMIR *takes a step towards Lucky,* ESTRAGON *holds him back by the sleeve.*]

VLADIMIR Let me go!

ESTRAGON Stay where you are!

POZZO Be careful! He's wicked. [VLADIMIR *and* ESTRAGON *turn towards* POZZO.] With strangers.

ESTRAGON [*undertone*] Is that him?

VLADIMIR Who?

ESTRAGON [*trying to remember the name*] Er . . .

VLADIMIR Godot?

ESTRAGON Yes.

POZZO I present myself: Pozzo.

VLADIMIR [*to* ESTRAGON] Not at all!

ESTRAGON He said Godot.

VLADIMIR Not at all!

ESTRAGON [*timidly, to* POZZO] You're not Mr. Godot, Sir?

POZZO [*terrifying voice*] I am Pozzo! [*Silence.*] Pozzo! [*Silence.*] Does that name mean nothing to you? [*Silence.*] I say does that name mean nothing to you?

[VLADIMIR *and* ESTRAGON *look at each other questioningly.*]

ESTRAGON [*pretending to search*] Bozzo . . . Bozzo . . .

4. An overcoat.

VLADIMIR [*ditto*]   Pozzo . . . Pozzo . . .

POZZO   PPPOZZZO!

ESTRAGON   Ah! Pozzo . . . let me see . . . Pozzo . . .

VLADIMIR   Is it Pozzo or Bozzo?

ESTRAGON   Pozzo . . . no . . . I'm afraid I . . . no . . . I don't seem to . . . [POZZO *advances threateningly.*]

VLADIMIR [*conciliating*]   I once knew a family called Cozzo. The mother had the clap.[5]

ESTRAGON [*hastily*]   We're not from these parts, Sir.

POZZO [*halting*]   You are human beings none the less. [*He puts on his glasses.*] As far as one can see. [*He takes off his glasses.*] Of the same species as myself. [*He bursts into an enormous laugh.*] Of the same species as Pozzo! Made in God's image!

VLADIMIR   Well you see—

POZZO [*peremptory*]   Who is Godot?

ESTRAGON   Godot?

POZZO   You took me for Godot.

VLADIMIR   Oh no, Sir, not for an instant, Sir.

POZZO   Who is he?

VLADIMIR   Oh he's a . . . he's a kind of acquaintance.

ESTRAGON   Nothing of the kind, we hardly know him.

VLADIMIR   True . . . we don't know him very well . . . but all the same . . .

ESTRAGON   Personally I wouldn't even know him if I saw him.

POZZO   You took me for him.

ESTRAGON [*recoiling before* POZZO]   That's to say . . . you understand . . . the dusk . . . the strain . . . waiting . . . I confess . . . I imagined . . . for a second . . .

POZZO   Waiting? So you were waiting for him?

VLADIMIR   Well you see—

POZZO   Here? On my land?

VLADIMIR   We didn't intend any harm.

ESTRAGON   We meant well.

POZZO   The road is free to all.

VLADIMIR   That's how we looked at it.

POZZO   It's a disgrace. But there you are.

ESTRAGON   Nothing we can do about it.

POZZO [*with magnanimous gesture*]   Let's say no more about it. [*He jerks the rope.*] Up pig! [*Pause.*] Every time he drops he falls asleep. [*Jerks the rope.*] Up hog! [*Noise of* LUCKY *getting up and picking up his baggage.* POZZO *jerks the rope.*] Back! [*Enter* LUCKY *backwards.*] Stop! [LUCKY *stops.*] Turn! [LUCKY *turns. To* VLADIMIR *and* ESTRAGON, *affably.*] Gentlemen, I am happy to have met you. [*Before their incredulous expression.*] Yes yes, sincerely happy. [*He jerks the rope.*] Closer! [LUCKY *advances.*] Stop! [LUCKY *stops.*] Yes, the road seems long when one journeys all alone for . . . [*he consults his watch*] . . . yes . . . [*he calculates*] . . . yes, six hours, that's right, six hours on end, and never a soul in sight. [*To* LUCKY.] Coat! [LUCKY *puts down the bag, advances, gives the coat, goes back to his place, takes up the bag.*] Hold that! [POZZO *holds out the whip.* LUCKY *advances and, both his hands being occupied, takes the whip in his mouth, then goes back to his place.* POZZO *begins to put on*

5. A venereal disease, usually gonorrhea (slang).

his coat, stops.] Coat! [LUCKY *puts down the bag, basket and stool, helps* POZZO *on with his coat, goes back to his place and takes up bag, basket and stool.*] Touch of autumn in the air this evening. [POZZO *finishes buttoning his coat, stoops, inspects himself, straightens up.*] Whip! [LUCKY *advances, stoops,* POZZO *snatches the whip from his mouth,* LUCKY *goes back to his place.*] Yes, gentlemen, I cannot go for long without the society of my likes [*he puts on his glasses and looks at the two likes*] even when the likeness is an imperfect one. [*He takes off his glasses.*] Stool! [LUCKY *puts down bag and basket, advances, opens stool, puts it down, goes back to his place, takes up bag and basket.*] Closer! [LUCKY *puts down bag and basket, advances, moves stool, goes back to his place, takes up bag and basket.* POZZO *sits down, places the butt of his whip against* LUCKY'S *chest and pushes.*] Back! [LUCKY *takes a step back.*] Further! [LUCKY *takes another step back.*] Stop! [LUCKY *stops. To* VLADIMIR *and* ESTRAGON.] That is why, with your permission, I propose to dally with you a moment, before I venture any further. Basket! [LUCKY *advances, gives the basket, goes back to his place.*] The fresh air stimulates the jaded appetite. [*He opens the basket, takes out a piece of chicken and a bottle of wine.*] Basket! [LUCKY *advances, picks up the basket and goes back to his place.*] Further! [LUCKY *takes a step back.*] He stinks. Happy days!

> [*He drinks from the bottle, puts it down and begins to eat. Silence.* VLADIMIR *and* ESTRAGON, *cautiously at first, then more boldly, begin to circle about* LUCKY, *inspecting him up and down.* POZZO *eats his chicken voraciously, throwing away the bones after having sucked them.* LUCKY *sags slowly, until bag and basket touch the ground, then straightens up with a start and begins to sag again. Rhythm of one sleeping on his feet.*]

ESTRAGON   What ails him?

VLADIMIR   He looks tired.

ESTRAGON   Why doesn't he put down his bags?

VLADIMIR   How do I know? [*They close in on him.*] Careful!

ESTRAGON   Say something to him.

VLADIMIR   Look!

ESTRAGON   What?

VLADIMIR [*pointing*]   His neck!

ESTRAGON [*looking at the neck*]   I see nothing.

VLADIMIR   Here.

> [ESTRAGON *goes over beside* VLADIMIR.]

ESTRAGON   Oh I say!

VLADIMIR   A running sore![6]

ESTRAGON   It's the rope.

VLADIMIR   It's the rubbing.

ESTRAGON   It's inevitable.

VLADIMIR   It's the knot.

ESTRAGON   It's the chafing.

> [*They resume their inspection, dwell on the face.*]

VLADIMIR [*grudgingly*]   He's not bad looking.

ESTRAGON [*shrugging his shoulders, wry face*]   Would you say so?

VLADIMIR   A trifle effeminate.

ESTRAGON   Look at the slobber.

VLADIMIR   It's inevitable.

---

6. A wound producing a discharge (hence, figuratively, constant irritation).

ESTRAGON   Look at the slaver.[7]
VLADIMIR   Perhaps he's a halfwit.
ESTRAGON   A cretin.
VLADIMIR [*looking closer*]   Looks like a goiter.[8]
ESTRAGON [*ditto*]   It's not certain.
VLADIMIR   He's panting.
ESTRAGON   It's inevitable.
VLADIMIR   And his eyes!
ESTRAGON   What about them?
VLADIMIR   Goggling out of his head.
ESTRAGON   Looks at his last gasp to me.
VLADIMIR   It's not certain. [*Pause.*] Ask him a question.
ESTRAGON   Would that be a good thing?
VLADIMIR   What do we risk?
ESTRAGON [*timidly*]   Mister . . .
VLADIMIR   Louder.
ESTRAGON [*louder*]   Mister . . .
POZZO   Leave him in peace! [*They turn towards* POZZO *who, having finished eating, wipes his mouth with the back of his hand.*] Can't you see he wants to rest? Basket! [*He strikes a match and begins to light his pipe.* ESTRAGON *sees the chicken bones on the ground and stares at them greedily. As* LUCKY *does not move* POZZO *throws the match angrily away and jerks the rope.*] Basket! [LUCKY *starts, almost falls, recovers his senses, advances, puts the bottle in the basket and goes back to his place.* ESTRAGON *stares at the bones.* POZZO *strikes another match and lights his pipe.*] What can you expect, it's not his job. [*He pulls at his pipe, stretches out his legs.*] Ah! That's better.
ESTRAGON [*timidly*]   Please Sir . . .
POZZO   What is it, my good man?
ESTRAGON   Er . . . you've finished with the . . . er . . . you don't need the . . . er . . . bones, Sir?
VLADIMIR [*scandalized*]   You couldn't have waited?
POZZO   No no, he does well to ask. Do I need the bones? [*He turns them over with the end of his whip.*] No, personally I do not need them any more. [ESTRAGON *takes a step towards the bones.*] But . . . [ESTRAGON *stops short.*] . . . but in theory the bones go to the carrier. He is therefore the one to ask. [ESTRAGON *turns towards* LUCKY, *hesitates.*] Go on, go on, don't be afraid, ask him, he'll tell you.
       [ESTRAGON *goes towards* LUCKY, *stops before him.*]
ESTRAGON   Mister . . . excuse me, Mister . . .
POZZO   You're being spoken to, pig! Reply! [*To* ESTRAGON.] Try him again.
ESTRAGON   Excuse me, Mister, the bones, you won't be wanting the bones?
       [LUCKY *looks long at* ESTRAGON.]
POZZO [*in raptures*]   Mister! [LUCKY *bows his head.*] Reply! Do you want them or don't you? [*Silence of* LUCKY. *To* ESTRAGON.] They're yours. [ESTRAGON *makes a dart at the bones, picks them up and begins to gnaw them.*] I don't like it. I've never known him refuse a bone before. [*He looks anxiously at* LUCKY.] Nice business it'd be if he fell sick on me! [*He puffs at his pipe.*]

---

7. Saliva running out of the mouth.   8. A swelling of the thyroid gland, in the neck.

VLADIMIR [*exploding*] It's a scandal!
> [*Silence. Flabbergasted,* ESTRAGON *stops gnawing, looks at* POZZO *and* VLADIMIR *in turn.* POZZO *outwardly calm.* VLADIMIR *embarrassed.*]

POZZO [*to* VLADIMIR] Are you alluding to anything in particular?

VLADIMIR [*stutteringly resolute*] To treat a man . . . [*Gesture towards* LUCKY] . . . like that . . . I think that . . . no . . . a human being . . . no . . . it's a scandal!

ESTRAGON [*not to be outdone*] A disgrace! [*He resumes his gnawing.*]

POZZO You are severe. [*To* VLADIMIR.] What age are you, if it's not a rude question? [*Silence.*] Sixty? Seventy? [*To* ESTRAGON.] What age would you say he was?

ESTRAGON Eleven.

POZZO I am impertinent. [*He knocks out his pipe against the whip, gets up.*] I must be getting on. Thank you for your society. [*He reflects.*] Unless I smoke another pipe before I go. What do you say? [*They say nothing.*] Oh I'm only a small smoker, a very small smoker, I'm not in the habit of smoking two pipes one on top of the other, it makes [*hand to heart, sighing*] my heart go pit-a-pat. [*Silence.*] It's the nicotine, one absorbs it in spite of one's precautions. [*Sighs.*] You know how it is. [*Silence.*] But perhaps you don't smoke? Yes? No? It's of no importance. [*Silence.*] But how am I to sit down now, without affectation, now that I have risen? Without appearing to—how shall I say—without appearing to falter. [*To* VLADIMIR.] I beg your pardon? [*Silence.*] Perhaps you didn't speak? [*Silence.*] It's of no importance. Let me see . . . [*He reflects.*]

ESTRAGON Ah! That's better. [*He puts the bones in his pocket.*]

VLADIMIR Let's go.

ESTRAGON So soon?

POZZO One moment! [*He jerks the rope.*] Stool! [*He points with his whip.* LUCKY *moves the stool.*] More! There! [*He sits down.* LUCKY *goes back to his place.*] Done it! [*He fills his pipe.*]

VLADIMIR [*vehemently*] Let's go!

POZZO I hope I'm not driving you away. Wait a little longer, you'll never regret it.

ESTRAGON [*scenting charity*] We're in no hurry.

POZZO [*having lit his pipe*] The second is never so sweet . . . [*he takes the pipe out of his mouth, contemplates it*] . . . as the first I mean. [*He puts the pipe back in his mouth.*] But it's sweet just the same.

VLADIMIR I'm going.

POZZO He can no longer endure my presence. I am perhaps not particularly human, but who cares? [*To* VLADIMIR.] Think twice before you do anything rash. Suppose you go now while it is still day, for there is no denying it is still day. [*They all look up at the sky.*] Good. [*They stop looking at the sky.*] What happens in that case—[*he takes the pipe out of his mouth, examines it*]—I'm out—[*he relights his pipe*]—in that case—[*puff*]—in that case—[*puff*]—what happens in that case to your appointment with this . . . Godet . . . Godot . . . Godin . . . anyhow you see who I mean, who has your future in his hands . . . [*pause*] . . . at least your immediate future?

VLADIMIR Who told you?

POZZO He speaks to me again! If this goes on much longer we'll soon be old friends.

ESTRAGON   Why doesn't he put down his bags?

POZZO   I too would be happy to meet him. The more people I meet the happier I become. From the meanest creature one departs wiser, richer, more conscious of one's blessings. Even you . . . [*he looks at them ostentatiously in turn to make it clear they are both meant*] . . . even you, who knows, will have added to my store.

ESTRAGON   Why doesn't he put down his bags?

POZZO   But that would surprise me.

VLADIMIR   You're being asked a question.

POZZO [*delighted*]   A question! Who? What? A moment ago you were calling me Sir, in fear and trembling. Now you're asking me questions. No good will come of this!

VLADIMIR [*to* ESTRAGON]   I think he's listening.

ESTRAGON [*circling about* LUCKY]   What?

VLADIMIR   You can ask him now. He's on the alert.

ESTRAGON   Ask him what?

VLADIMIR   Why he doesn't put down his bags.

ESTRAGON   I wonder.

VLADIMIR   Ask him, can't you?

POZZO [*who has followed these exchanges with anxious attention, fearing lest the question get lost*]   You want to know why he doesn't put down his bags, as you call them.

VLADIMIR   That's it.

POZZO [*to* ESTRAGON]   You are sure you agree with that?

ESTRAGON   He's puffing like a grampus.[9]

POZZO   The answer is this. [*To* ESTRAGON.] But stay still, I beg of you, you're making me nervous!

VLADIMIR   Here.

ESTRAGON   What is it?

VLADIMIR   He's about to speak.

> [ESTRAGON *goes over beside* VLADIMIR. *Motionless, side by side, they wait.*]

POZZO   Good. Is everybody ready? Is everybody looking at me? [*He looks at* LUCKY, *jerks the rope.* LUCKY *raises his head.*] Will you look at me, pig! [LUCKY *looks at him.*] Good. [*He puts the pipe in his pocket, takes out a little vaporizer and sprays his throat, puts back the vaporizer in his pocket, clears his throat, spits, takes out the vaporizer again, sprays his throat again, puts back the vaporizer in his pocket.*] I am ready. Is everybody listening? Is everybody ready? [*He looks at them all in turn, jerks the rope.*] Hog! [LUCKY *raises his head.*] I don't like talking in a vacuum. Good. Let me see. [*He reflects.*]

ESTRAGON   I'm going.

POZZO   What was it exactly you wanted to know?

VLADIMIR   Why he—

POZZO [*angrily*]   Don't interrupt me! [*Pause. Calmer.*] If we all speak at once we'll never get anywhere. [*Pause.*] What was I saying? [*Pause. Louder.*] What was I saying?

> [VLADIMIR *mimics one carrying a heavy burden,* POZZO *looks at him, puzzled.*]

9. A dolphin.

ESTRAGON [*forcibly*]   Bags. [*He points at* LUCKY.] Why? Always hold. [*He sags, panting.*] Never put down. [*He opens his hands, straightens up with relief.*] Why?

POZZO   Ah! Why couldn't you say so before? Why he doesn't make himself comfortable? Let's try and get this clear. Has he not the right to? Certainly he has. It follows that he doesn't want to. There's reasoning for you. And why doesn't he want to? [*Pause.*] Gentlemen, the reason is this.

VLADIMIR [*to* ESTRAGON]   Make a note of this.

POZZO   He wants to impress me, so that I'll keep him.

ESTRAGON   What?

POZZO   Perhaps I haven't got it quite right. He wants to mollify me, so that I'll give up the idea of parting with him. No, that's not exactly it either.

VLADIMIR   You want to get rid of him?

POZZO   He wants to cod[1] me, but he won't.

VLADIMIR   You want to get rid of him?

POZZO   He imagines that when I see how well he carries I'll be tempted to keep him on in that capacity.

ESTRAGON   You've had enough of him?

POZZO   In reality he carries like a pig. It's not his job.

VLADIMIR   You want to get rid of him?

POZZO   He imagines that when I see him indefatigable I'll regret my decision. Such is his miserable scheme. As though I were short of slaves! [*All three look at* LUCKY.] Atlas, son of Jupiter![2] [*Silence.*] Well, that's that I think. Anything else?
    [*Vaporizer.*]

VLADIMIR   You want to get rid of him?

POZZO   Remark that I might just as well have been in his shoes and he in mine. If chance had not willed otherwise. To each one his due.

VLADIMIR   You waagerrim?

POZZO   I beg your pardon?

VLADIMIR   You want to get rid of him?

POZZO   I do. But instead of driving him away as I might have done, I mean instead of simply kicking him out on his arse, in the goodness of my heart I am bringing him to the fair, where I hope to get a good price for him. The truth is you can't drive such creatures away. The best thing would be to kill them.
    [*LUCKY weeps.*]

ESTRAGON   He's crying!

POZZO   Old dogs have more dignity. [*He proffers his handkerchief to* ESTRAGON.] Comfort him, since you pity him. [ESTRAGON *hesitates.*] Come on. [ESTRAGON *takes the handkerchief.*] Wipe away his tears, he'll feel less forsaken.
    [ESTRAGON *hesitates.*]

VLADIMIR   Here, give it to me, I'll do it.
    [ESTRAGON *refuses to give the handkerchief. Childish gestures.*]

---

1. To fool (Irish slang).
2. In classical mythology, his father was the Titan Iapetus, not Jupiter, the chief god of the Roman pantheon. Atlas had to hold the heavens on his shoulders.

POZZO Make haste, before he stops. [ESTRAGON *approaches* LUCKY *and makes to wipe his eyes.* LUCKY *kicks him violently in the shins.* ESTRAGON *drops the handkerchief, recoils, staggers about the stage howling with pain.*] Hanky!

    [LUCKY *puts down bag and basket, picks up handkerchief and gives it to* POZZO, *goes back to his place, picks up bag and basket.*]

ESTRAGON Oh the swine! [*He pulls up the leg of his trousers.*] He's crippled me!

POZZO I told you he didn't like strangers.

VLADIMIR [*to* ESTRAGON] Show. [ESTRAGON *shows his leg. To* POZZO, *angrily*] He's bleeding!

POZZO It's a good sign.

ESTRAGON [*on one leg*] I'll never walk again!

VLADIMIR [*tenderly*] I'll carry you. [*Pause.*] If necessary.

POZZO He's stopped crying. [*To* ESTRAGON.] You have replaced him as it were. [*Lyrically.*] The tears of the world are a constant quantity. For each one who begins to weep, somewhere else another stops. The same is true of the laugh. [*He laughs.*] Let us not then speak ill of our generation, it is not any unhappier than its predecessors. [*Pause.*] Let us not speak well of it either. [*Pause.*] Let us not speak of it at all. [*Pause. Judiciously.*] It is true the population has increased.

VLADIMIR Try and walk.

    [ESTRAGON *takes a few limping steps, stops before* LUCKY *and spits on him, then goes and sits down on the mound.*]

POZZO Guess who taught me all these beautiful things. [*Pause. Pointing to* LUCKY.] My Lucky!

VLADIMIR [*looking at the sky*] Will night never come?

POZZO But for him all my thoughts, all my feelings, would have been of common things. [*Pause. With extraordinary vehemence.*] Professional worries! [*Calmer.*] Beauty, grace, truth of the first water,[3] I knew they were all beyond me. So I took a knook.[4]

VLADIMIR [*startled from his inspection of the sky*] A knook?

POZZO That was nearly sixty years ago . . . [*he consults his watch*] . . . yes, nearly sixty. [*Drawing himself up proudly.*] You wouldn't think it to look at me, would you? Compared to him I look like a young man, no? [*Pause.*] Hat! [LUCKY *puts down the basket and takes off his hat. His long white hair falls about his face. He puts his hat under his arm and picks up the basket.*] Now look. [POZZO *takes off his hat.*[5] *He is completely bald. He puts on his hat again.*] Did you see?

VLADIMIR And now you turn him away? Such an old and faithful servant!

ESTRAGON Swine!

    [POZZO *more and more agitated.*]

VLADIMIR After having sucked all the good out of him you chuck him away like a . . . like a banana skin. Really . . .

POZZO [*groaning, clutching his head*] I can't bear it . . . any longer . . . the way he goes on . . . you've no idea . . . it's terrible . . . he must go . . .

---

3. Of the highest order.
4. Invented word, apparently referring to Lucky's position as servant; it may echo the Rus-

sian word *knout*, or "whip."
5. All four wear bowlers [Beckett's note].

[*he waves his arms*] . . . I'm going mad . . . [*he collapses, his head in his hands*] . . . I can't bear it . . . any longer . . .

    [*Silence. All look at* POZZO.]

VLADIMIR He can't bear it.

ESTRAGON Any longer.

VLADIMIR He's going mad.

ESTRAGON It's terrible.

VLADIMIR [*to* LUCKY] How dare you! It's abominable! Such a good master! Crucify him like that! After so many years! Really!

POZZO [*sobbing*] He used to be so kind . . . so helpful . . . and entertaining . . . my good angel . . . and now . . . he's killing me.

ESTRAGON [*to* VLADIMIR] Does he want to replace him?

VLADIMIR What?

ESTRAGON Does he want someone to take his place or not?

VLADIMIR I don't think so.

ESTRAGON What?

VLADIMIR I don't know.

ESTRAGON Ask him.

POZZO [*calmer*] Gentlemen, I don't know what came over me. Forgive me. Forget all I said. [*More and more his old self.*] I don't remember exactly what it was, but you may be sure there wasn't a word of truth in it. [*Drawing himself up, striking his chest.*] Do I look like a man that can be made to suffer? Frankly? [*He rummages in his pockets.*] What have I done with my pipe?

VLADIMIR Charming evening we're having.

ESTRAGON Unforgettable.

VLADIMIR And it's not over.

ESTRAGON Apparently not.

VLADIMIR It's only beginning.

ESTRAGON It's awful.

VLADIMIR Worse than the pantomime.[6]

ESTRAGON The circus.

VLADIMIR The music-hall.[7]

ESTRAGON The circus.

POZZO What can I have done with that briar?

ESTRAGON He's a scream. He's lost his dudeen.[8] [*Laughs noisily.*]

VLADIMIR I'll be back. [*He hastens towards the wings.*]

ESTRAGON End of the corridor, on the left.

VLADIMIR Keep my seat. [*Exit* VLADIMIR.]

POZZO [*on the point of tears*] I've lost my Kapp and Peterson![9]

ESTRAGON [*convulsed with merriment*] He'll be the death of me!

POZZO You didn't see by any chance—. [*He misses* VLADIMIR.] Oh! He's gone! Without saying goodbye! How could he! He might have waited!

ESTRAGON He would have burst.

POZZO Oh! [*Pause.*] Oh well then of course in that case . . .

ESTRAGON Come here.

---

6. A kind of theater involving music and slapstick comedy, usually based on fairy tales and performed for children around Christmastime in Britain, Ireland, France, and elsewhere.

7. Vaudeville, or popular entertainment includ-

ing comedy, singing, and dancing.

8. A short clay pipe (Irish). "Briar": a pipe made from briar wood.

9. A brand of pipe from Dublin's most famous tobacco shop.

POZZO   What for?

ESTRAGON   You'll see.

POZZO   You want me to get up?

ESTRAGON   Quick! [POZZO *gets up and goes over beside* ESTRAGON. ESTRAGON *points off.*] Look!

POZZO [*having put on his glasses*]   Oh I say!

ESTRAGON   It's all over.

> [*Enter* VLADIMIR, *somber. He shoulders* LUCKY *out of his way, kicks over the stool, comes and goes agitatedly.*]

POZZO   He's not pleased.

ESTRAGON [*to* VLADIMIR]   You missed a treat. Pity.

> [VLADIMIR *halts, straightens the stool, comes and goes, calmer.*]

POZZO   He subsides. [*Looking round.*] Indeed all subsides. A great calm descends. [*Raising his hand.*] Listen! Pan sleeps.[1]

VLADIMIR   Will night never come?

> [*All three look at the sky.*]

POZZO   You don't feel like going until it does?

ESTRAGON   Well you see—

POZZO   Why it's very natural, very natural. I myself in your situation, if I had an appointment with a Godin . . . Godet . . . Godot . . . anyhow you see who I mean, I'd wait till it was black night before I gave up. [*He looks at the stool.*] I'd very much like to sit down, but I don't quite know how to go about it.

ESTRAGON   Could I be of any help?

POZZO   If you asked me perhaps.

ESTRAGON   What?

POZZO   If you asked me to sit down.

ESTRAGON   Would that be a help?

POZZO   I fancy so.

ESTRAGON   Here we go. Be seated, Sir, I beg of you.

POZZO   No no, I wouldn't think of it! [*Pause. Aside.*] Ask me again.

ESTRAGON   Come come, take a seat I beseech you, you'll get pneumonia.

POZZO   You really think so?

ESTRAGON   Why it's absolutely certain.

POZZO   No doubt you are right. [*He sits down.*] Done it again! [*Pause.*] Thank you, dear fellow. [*He consults his watch.*] But I must really be getting along, if I am to observe my schedule.

VLADIMIR   Time has stopped.

POZZO [*cuddling his watch to his ear*]   Don't you believe it, Sir, don't you believe it. [*He puts his watch back in his pocket.*] Whatever you like, but not that.

ESTRAGON [*to* POZZO]   Everything seems black to him today.

POZZO   Except the firmament.[2] [*He laughs, pleased with this witticism.*] But I see what it is, you are not from these parts, you don't know what our twilights can do. Shall I tell you? [*Silence.* ESTRAGON *is fiddling with his boot again,* VLADIMIR *with his hat.*] I can't refuse you. [*Vaporizer.*] A little attention, if you please. [VLADIMIR *and* ESTRAGON *continue*

---

1. Greek god of shepherds, flocks, fields, and herds. His appearance was said to create terror similar to that of a stampeding herd, and the word "panic" is derived from his name. Thus, his sleep here may connote an absence of panic.
2. The sky or the heavens.

their fiddling, LUCKY *is half asleep.* POZZO *cracks his whip feebly.*] What's the matter with this whip? [*He gets up and cracks it more vigorously, finally with success.* LUCKY *jumps.* VLADIMIR'S *hat,* ESTRAGON'S *boot,* LUCKY'S *hat, fall to the ground.* POZZO *throws down the whip.*] Worn out, this whip. [*He looks at* VLADIMIR *and* ESTRAGON.] What was I saying?

VLADIMIR   Let's go.

ESTRAGON   But take the weight off your feet, I implore you, you'll catch your death.

POZZO   True. [*He sits down. To* ESTRAGON.] What is your name?

ESTRAGON   Adam.

POZZO [*who hasn't listened*]   Ah yes! The night. [*He raises his head.*] But be a little more attentive, for pity's sake, otherwise we'll never get anywhere. [*He looks at the sky.*] Look! [*All look at the sky except* LUCKY *who is dozing off again.* POZZO *jerks the rope.*] Will you look at the sky, pig! [LUCKY *looks at the sky.*] Good, that's enough. [*They stop looking at the sky.*] What is there so extraordinary about it? Qua sky.[3] It is pale and luminous like any sky at this hour of the day. [*Pause.*] In these latitudes. [*Pause.*] When the weather is fine. [*Lyrical.*] An hour ago [*he looks at his watch, prosaic*] roughly [*lyrical*] after having poured forth even since [*he hesitates, prosaic*] say ten o'clock in the morning [*lyrical*] tirelessly torrents of red and white light it begins to lose its effulgence, to grow pale [*gesture of the two hands lapsing by stages*] pale, ever a little paler, a little paler until [*dramatic pause, ample gesture of the two hands flung wide apart*] pppfff! finished! it comes to rest. But—[*hand raised in admonition*]—but behind this veil of gentleness and peace night is charging [*vibrantly*] and will burst upon us [*snaps his fingers.*] pop! like that! [*His inspiration leaves him.*] just when we least expect it. [*Silence. Gloomily.*] That's how it is on this bitch of an earth.

   [*Long silence.*]

ESTRAGON   So long as one knows.

VLADIMIR   One can bide one's time.

ESTRAGON   One knows what to expect.

VLADIMIR   No further need to worry.

ESTRAGON   Simply wait.

VLADIMIR   We're used to it. [*He picks up his hat, peers inside it, shakes it, puts it on.*]

POZZO   How did you find me? [VLADIMIR *and* ESTRAGON *look at him blankly.*] Good? Fair? Middling? Poor? Positively bad?

VLADIMIR [*first to understand*]   Oh very good, very very good.

POZZO [*to* ESTRAGON]   And you, Sir?

ESTRAGON   Oh tray bong, tray tray tray bong.[4]

POZZO [*fervently*]   Bless you, gentlemen, bless you! [*Pause.*] I have such need of encouragement! [*Pause.*] I weakened a little towards the end, you didn't notice?

VLADIMIR   Oh perhaps just a teeny weeny little bit.

---

3. As sky—that is, in the capacity of sky.
4. A play on the French phrase *"oui très bon,"* meaning "yes, very good." "Oui! Tray bong!" was also the title of a popular music-hall song performed at the end of the 19th century by Charles Chaplin Sr. (1863–1901).

ESTRAGON   I thought it was intentional.

POZZO   You see my memory is defective.
        [*Silence.*]

ESTRAGON   In the meantime nothing happens.

POZZO   You find it tedious?

ESTRAGON   Somewhat.

POZZO [*to* VLADIMIR]   And you, Sir?

VLADIMIR   I've been better entertained.
        [*Silence.* POZZO *struggles inwardly.*]

POZZO   Gentlemen, you have been . . . civil to me.

ESTRAGON   Not at all!

VLADIMIR   What an idea!

POZZO   Yes yes, you have been correct. So that I ask myself is there any-
    thing I can do in my turn for these honest fellows who are having such
    a dull, dull time.

ESTRAGON   Even ten francs[5] would be a help.

VLADIMIR   We are not beggars!

POZZO   Is there anything I can do, that's what I ask myself, to cheer them
    up? I have given them bones, I have talked to them about this and that,
    I have explained the twilight, admittedly. But is it enough, that's what
    tortures me, is it enough?

ESTRAGON   Even five.

VLADIMIR [*to* ESTRAGON, *indignantly*]   That's enough!

ESTRAGON   I couldn't accept less.

POZZO   Is it enough? No doubt. But I am liberal. It's my nature. This eve-
    ning. So much the worse for me. [*He jerks the rope.* LUCKY *looks at him.*]
    For I shall suffer, no doubt about that. [*He picks up the whip.*] What do
    you prefer? Shall we have him dance, or sing, or recite, or think, or—

ESTRAGON   Who?

POZZO   Who! You know how to think, you two?

VLADIMIR   He thinks?

POZZO   Certainly. Aloud. He even used to think very prettily once, I could
    listen to him for hours. Now . . . [*He shudders.*] So much the worse for
    me. Well, would you like him to think something for us?

ESTRAGON   I'd rather he'd dance, it'd be more fun.

POZZO   Not necessarily.

ESTRAGON   Wouldn't it, Didi, be more fun?

VLADIMIR   I'd like well to hear him think.

ESTRAGON   Perhaps he could dance first and think afterwards, if it isn't
    too much to ask him.

VLADIMIR [*to* POZZO]   Would that be possible?

POZZO   By all means, nothing simpler. It's the natural order. [*He laughs
    briefly.*]

VLADIMIR   Then let him dance.
        [*Silence.*]

POZZO   Do you hear, hog?

ESTRAGON   He never refuses?

POZZO   He refused once. [*Silence.*] Dance, misery!

---

5. Ten French francs were then worth about 3 dollars.

[LUCKY *puts down bag and basket, advances towards front, turns to* POZZO. LUCKY *dances. He stops.*]

ESTRAGON   Is that all?

POZZO   Encore!

[LUCKY *executes the same movements, stops.*]

ESTRAGON   Pooh! I'd do as well myself. [*He imitates* LUCKY, *almost falls.*] With a little practice.

POZZO   He used to dance the farandole, the fling, the brawl, the jig, the fandango and even the hornpipe.[6] He capered. For joy. Now that's the best he can do. Do you know what he calls it?

ESTRAGON   The Scapegoat's Agony.

VLADIMIR   The Hard Stool.

POZZO   The Net. He thinks he's entangled in a net.

VLADIMIR [*squirming like an aesthete*]   There's something about it . . .

[LUCKY *makes to return to his burdens.*]

POZZO   Woaa!

[LUCKY *stiffens.*]

ESTRAGON   Tell us about the time he refused.

POZZO   With pleasure, with pleasure. [*He fumbles in his pockets.*] Wait. [*He fumbles.*] What have I done with my spray? [*He fumbles.*] Well now isn't that . . . [*He looks up, consternation on his features. Faintly.*] I can't find my pulverizer![7]

ESTRAGON [*faintly*]   My left lung is very weak! [*He coughs feebly. In ringing tones.*] But my right lung is as sound as a bell!

POZZO [*normal voice*]   No matter! What was I saying. [*He ponders.*] Wait. [*Ponders.*] Well now isn't that . . . [*He raises his head.*] Help me!

ESTRAGON   Wait!

VLADIMIR   Wait!

POZZO   Wait!

[*All three take off their hats simultaneously, press their hands to their foreheads, concentrate.*]

ESTRAGON [*triumphantly*]   Ah!

VLADIMIR   He has it.

POZZO [*impatient*]   Well?

ESTRAGON   Why doesn't he put down his bags?

VLADIMIR   Rubbish!

POZZO   Are you sure?

VLADIMIR   Damn it haven't you already told us?

POZZO   I've already told you?

ESTRAGON   He's already told us?

VLADIMIR   Anyway he has put them down.

ESTRAGON [*glance at* LUCKY]   So he has. And what of it?

VLADIMIR   Since he has put down his bags it is impossible we should have asked why he does not do so.

POZZO   Stoutly reasoned!

ESTRAGON   And why has he put them down?

POZZO   Answer us that.

VLADIMIR   In order to dance.

---

6. All lively dances, associated, respectively, with Provence, the Scottish Highlands, France, Ireland, Spain, and England.
7. I.e., his vaporizer.

ESTRAGON   True!

POZZO   True!

[*Silence. They put on their hats.*]

ESTRAGON   Nothing happens, nobody comes, nobody goes, it's awful!

VLADIMIR [*to* POZZO]   Tell him to think.

POZZO   Give him his hat.

VLADIMIR   His hat?

POZZO   He can't think without his hat.

VLADIMIR [*to* ESTRAGON]   Give him his hat.

ESTRAGON   Me! After what he did to me! Never!

VLADIMIR   I'll give it to him. [*He does not move.*]

ESTRAGON [*to* POZZO]   Tell him to go and fetch it.

POZZO   It's better to give it to him.

VLADIMIR   I'll give it to him.

[*He picks up the hat and tenders it at arm's length to* LUCKY, *who does not move.*]

POZZO   You must put it on his head.

ESTRAGON [*to* POZZO]   Tell him to take it.

POZZO   It's better to put it on his head.

VLADIMIR   I'll put it on his head.

[*He goes round behind* LUCKY, *approaches him cautiously, puts the hat on his head and recoils smartly.* LUCKY *does not move. Silence.*]

ESTRAGON   What's he waiting for?

POZZO   Stand back! [VLADIMIR *and* ESTRAGON *move away from* LUCKY. POZZO *jerks the rope,* LUCKY *looks at* POZZO.] Think, pig! [*Pause.* LUCKY *begins to dance.*] Stop! [LUCKY *stops.*] Forward! [LUCKY *advances.*] Stop! [LUCKY *stops.*] Think!

[*Silence.*]

LUCKY   On the other hand with regard to—

POZZO   Stop! [LUCKY *stops.*] Back! [LUCKY *moves back.*] Stop! [LUCKY *stops.*] Turn! [LUCKY *turns towards auditorium.*] Think!

LUCKY   Given the existence as uttered forth in the public, works of Puncher and Wattmann[8] of a personal God quaquaquaqua[9] with white beard quaquaquaqua outside time without extension who from the heights of divine apathia divine athambia divine aphasia[1] loves us dearly with some exceptions for reasons unknown but time will tell and

[VLADIMIR   suffers like the divine Miranda[2] with those who for reasons

and   unknown but time will tell are plunged in torment plunged

ESTRAGON   in fire whose fire flames if that continues and who can

all   doubt it will fire the firmament that is to say blast hell to

attention,   heaven so blue still and calm so calm with a calm which even

POZZO   though intermittent is better than nothing but not so fast

dejected   and considering what is more that as a result of the labors

---

8. Made-up scholars' names.
9. Repetition of the Latin word *qua*, meaning "in the capacity of," or "as being," in philosophy.
1. Partial or total loss of speech. "Apathia": apathy, or the absence of emotion. "Athambia": absence of fear or surprise. All Greek words, of

which only "aphasia" is common in English.
2. The heroine of Shakespeare's *The Tempest* (1611), who empathizes with the victims of a shipwreck: "O, I have suffered / With those that I saw suffer!" (1.2.5–6).

and disgusted.]

[VLADIMIR *and* ESTRAGON *begin to protest,* POZZO'S *sufferings increase.*]

[VLADIMIR *and* ESTRAGON *attentive again,* POZZO *more and more agitated and groaning.*]

[VLADIMIR *and* ESTRAGON *protest violently.* POZZO *jumps up, pulls on the rope.* General *outcry.* LUCKY *pulls*

left unfinished crowned by the Acacacacademy of Anthropopopometry of Essy-in-Possy[3] of Testew and Cunard[4] it is established beyond all doubt all other doubt than that which clings to the labors of men that as a result of the labors unfinished of Testew and Cunard it is established as hereinafter but not so fast for reasons unknown that as a result of the public works of Puncher and Wattmann it is established beyond all doubt that in view of the labors of Fartov and Belcher[5] left unfinished for reasons unknown of Testew and Cunard left unfinished it is established what many deny that man in Possy of Testew and Cunard that man in Essy that man in short that man in brief in spite of the strides of alimentation[6] and defecation wastes and pines wastes and pines and concurrently simultaneously what is more for reasons unknown in spite of the strides of physical culture the practice of sports such as tennis football running cycling swimming flying floating riding gliding conating camogie[7] skating tennis of all kinds dying flying sports of all sorts autumn summer winter winter tennis of all kinds hockey of all sorts penicillin and succedanea[8] in a word I resume flying gliding golf over nine and eighteen holes tennis of all sorts in a word for reasons unknown in Feckham Peckham Fulham Clapham[9] namely concurrently simultaneously what is more for reasons unknown but time will tell fades away I resume Fulham Clapham in a word the dead loss per head since the death of Bishop Berkeley[1] being to the tune of one inch four ounce per head approximately by and large more or less to the nearest decimal good measure round figures stark naked in the stockinged feet in Connemara[2] in a word for reasons unknown no matter what matter the facts are there and considering what is more much more grave that in the light of the labors lost of Steinweg and Peterman[3] it appears what is more much more grave that in the light the light the light of the labors lost of Steinweg and Peterman that in the plains in the mountains by the seas by the rivers running water running fire the air is the same and then the earth namely the air and then the earth in the great cold the great dark the air and the earth abode of stones in the great cold alas alas in the year of their Lord six hundred and

---

3. A fictitious place, with a name that echoes the Latin words "*esse*" (to be) and "*posse*" (to be able to). "Acacacademy": a play on the words "academy" and "*caca*," a children's word for excrement in French. "Anthropopopometry": that is, anthropometry, the measurement of the human body.
4. Made-up scholars' names, playing on words for male and female sexual organs.
5. Made-up scholars' names, with puns on bodily functions.
6. Nourishment, or feeding.
7. Women's version of Irish sport of hurling,

played with sticks and a ball. "Conating": attempting or desiring (a word created by Beckett from "*conation*").
8. Substitutes.
9. The last three names are neighborhoods in south London, the first a vulgar pun ("fuck 'em").
1. George Berkeley (1685–1753), Irish philosopher and bishop, who theorized that objects exist only insofar as they are perceived.
2. A region in western Ireland.
3. Made-up scholars' names.

on the rope, something the air the earth the sea the earth abode of
staggers, stones in the great deeps the great cold on sea on land and
shouts his in the air I resume for reasons unknown in spite of the
text. All tennis the facts are there but time will tell I resume alas
three throw alas on on in short in fine on on abode of stones who can
themselves doubt it I resume but not so fast I resume the skull fading
on LUCKY fading fading and concurrently simultaneously what is more
who for reasons unknown in spite of the tennis on on the beard
struggles the flames the tears the stones so blue so calm alas alas on
and shouts on the skull the skull the skull the skull in Connemara in
his text.] spite of the tennis the labors abandoned left unfinished
graver still abode of stones in a word I resume alas alas
abandoned unfinished the skull the skull in Connemara in
spite of the tennis the skull alas the stones Cunard [*mêlée,
final vociferations*] tennis . . . the stones . . . so calm . . .
Cunard . . . unfinished . . .

POZZO   His hat!

[VLADIMIR *seizes* LUCKY's *hat. Silence of* LUCKY. *He falls. Silence. Panting of the victors.*]

ESTRAGON   Avenged!

[VLADIMIR *examines the hat, peers inside it.*]

POZZO   Give me that! [*He snatches the hat from* VLADIMIR, *throws it on the ground, tramples on it.*] There's an end to his thinking!

VLADIMIR   But will he be able to walk?

POZZO   Walk or crawl! [*He kicks* LUCKY.] Up pig!

ESTRAGON   Perhaps he's dead.

VLADIMIR   You'll kill him.

POZZO   Up scum! [*He jerks the rope.*] Help me!

VLADIMIR   How?

POZZO   Raise him up!

[VLADIMIR *and* ESTRAGON *hoist* LUCKY *to his feet, support him an instant, then let him go. He falls.*]

ESTRAGON   He's doing it on purpose!

POZZO   You must hold him. [*Pause.*] Come on, come on, raise him up.

ESTRAGON   To hell with him!

VLADIMIR   Come on, once more.

ESTRAGON   What does he take us for?

[*They raise* LUCKY, *hold him up.*]

POZZO   Don't let him go! [VLADIMIR *and* ESTRAGON *totter.*] Don't move!

POZZO [*fetches bag and basket and brings them towards* LUCKY.] Hold him tight! [*He puts the bag in* LUCKY's *hand.* LUCKY *drops it immediately.*] Don't let him go! [*He puts back the bag in* LUCKY's *hand. Gradually, at the feel of the bag,* LUCKY *recovers his senses and his fingers finally close round the handle.*] Hold him tight! [*As before with basket.*] Now! You can let him go. [VLADIMIR *and* ESTRAGON *move away from* LUCKY *who totters, reels, sags, but succeeds in remaining on his feet, bag and basket in his hands.* POZZO *steps back, cracks his whip.*] Forward! [LUCKY *totters forward.*] Back! [LUCKY *totters back.*] Turn! [LUCKY *turns.*] Done it! He can walk. [*Turning to* VLADIMIR *and* ESTRAGON.] Thank you, gentlemen, and let me . . . [*he fumbles in his pockets*] . . . let me wish you . . . [*fumbles.*] . . . wish you . . . [*fumbles.*] . . . what have I done with my watch? [*fumbles.*] A genuine half-hunter, gentlemen, with deadbeat escapement![4] [*Sobbing.*] Twas my granpa gave it to me! [*He searches on the ground,* VLADIMIR *and* ESTRAGON *likewise.* POZZO *turns over with his foot the remains of* LUCKY'S *hat.*] Well now isn't that just—

VLADIMIR   Perhaps it's in your fob.[5]

POZZO   Wait! [*He doubles up in an attempt to apply his ear to his stomach, listens. Silence.*] I hear nothing. [*He beckons them to approach,* VLADIMIR *and* ESTRAGON *go over to him, bend over his stomach.*] Surely one should hear the tick-tick.

VLADIMIR   Silence!
        [*All listen, bent double.*]

ESTRAGON   I hear something.

POZZO   Where?

VLADIMIR   It's the heart.

POZZO [*disappointed*]   Damnation!

VLADIMIR   Silence!

ESTRAGON   Perhaps it has stopped.
        [*They straighten up.*]

POZZO   Which of you smells so bad?

ESTRAGON   He has stinking breath and I have stinking feet.

POZZO   I must go.

ESTRAGON   And your half-hunter?

POZZO   I must have left it at the manor.
        [*Silence.*]

ESTRAGON   Then adieu.

POZZO   Adieu.

VLADIMIR   Adieu.

POZZO   Adieu.
        [*Silence. No one moves.*]

VLADIMIR   Adieu.

POZZO   Adieu.

ESTRAGON   Adieu.
        [*Silence.*]

POZZO   And thank you.

VLADIMIR   Thank *you.*

POZZO   Not at all.

ESTRAGON   Yes yes.

POZZO   No no.

VLADIMIR   Yes yes.

ESTRAGON   No no.
        [*Silence.*]

POZZO   I don't seem to be able . . . [*long hesitation*] . . . to depart.

ESTRAGON   Such is life.
        [POZZO *turns, moves away from* LUCKY *towards the wings, paying out the rope as he goes.*]

VLADIMIR   You're going the wrong way.

---

4. A check-and-release mechanism in watches; here, "deadbeat" because it does not work. "Half-hunter": a kind of pocket watch with a hinged metal cover, in the center of which is a small glass window allowing the hands to be seen.
5. A small front pocket for a watch.

POZZO   I need a running start. [*Having come to the end of the rope, i.e. off stage, he stops, turns and cries.*] Stand back! [VLADIMIR *and* ESTRAGON *stand back, look towards* POZZO. *Crack of whip.*] On! On!

ESTRAGON   On!

VLADIMIR   On!

> [LUCKY *moves off.*]

POZZO   Faster! [*He appears, crosses the stage preceded by* LUCKY. VLADIMIR *and* ESTRAGON *wave their hats. Exit* LUCKY.] On! On! [*On the point of disappearing in his turn he stops and turns. The rope tautens. Noise of* LUCKY *falling off.*] Stool! [VLADIMIR *fetches stool and gives it to* POZZO *who throws it to* LUCKY.] Adieu!

VLADIMIR }
ESTRAGON }[*waving*]   Adieu! Adieu!

POZZO   Up! Pig! [*Noise of* LUCKY *getting up.*] On! [*Exit* POZZO.] Faster! On! Adieu! Pig! Yip! Adieu!

> [*Long silence.*]

VLADIMIR   That passed the time.

ESTRAGON   It would have passed in any case.

VLADIMIR   Yes, but not so rapidly.

> [*Pause.*]

ESTRAGON   What do we do now?

VLADIMIR   I don't know.

ESTRAGON   Let's go.

VLADIMIR   We can't.

ESTRAGON   Why not?

VLADIMIR   We're waiting for Godot.

ESTRAGON [*despairingly*]   Ah!

> [*Pause.*]

VLADIMIR   How they've changed!

ESTRAGON   Who?

VLADIMIR   Those two.

ESTRAGON   That's the idea, let's make a little conversation.

VLADIMIR   Haven't they?

ESTRAGON   What?

VLADIMIR   Changed.

ESTRAGON   Very likely. They all change. Only we can't.

VLADIMIR   Likely! It's certain. Didn't you see them?

ESTRAGON   I suppose I did. But I don't know them.

VLADIMIR   Yes you do know them.

ESTRAGON   No I don't know them.

VLADIMIR   We know them, I tell you. You forget everything. [*Pause. To himself.*] Unless they're not the same . . .

ESTRAGON   Why didn't they recognize us then?

VLADIMIR   That means nothing. I too pretended not to recognize them. And then nobody ever recognizes us.

ESTRAGON   Forget it. What we need—ow! [VLADIMIR *does not react.*] Ow!

VLADIMIR [*to himself*]   Unless they're not the same . . .

ESTRAGON   Didi! It's the other foot! [*He goes hobbling towards the mound.*]

VLADIMIR   Unless they're not the same . . .

BOY [*off*]   Mister!

> [ESTRAGON *halts. Both look towards the voice.*]

ESTRAGON   Off we go again.
VLADIMIR   Approach, my child.
        [*Enter* BOY, *timidly. He halts.*]
BOY   Mister Albert . . . ?
VLADIMIR   Yes.
ESTRAGON   What do you want?
VLADIMIR   Approach!
        [*The* BOY *does not move.*]
ESTRAGON [*forcibly*]   Approach when you're told, can't you?
        [*The* BOY *advances timidly, halts.*]
VLADIMIR   What is it?
BOY   Mr. Godot . . .
VLADIMIR   Obviously . . . [*Pause.*] Approach.
ESTRAGON [*violently*]   Will you approach! [*The* BOY *advances timidly.*] What
   kept you so late?
VLADIMIR   You have a message from Mr. Godot?
BOY   Yes Sir.
VLADIMIR   Well, what is it?
ESTRAGON   What kept you so late?
        [*The* BOY *looks at them in turn, not knowing to which he should reply.*]
VLADIMIR [*to* ESTRAGON]   Let him alone.
ESTRAGON [*violently*]   You let me alone. [*Advancing, to the* BOY.] Do you
   know what time it is?
BOY [*recoiling*]   It's not my fault, Sir.
ESTRAGON   And whose is it? Mine?
BOY   I was afraid, Sir.
ESTRAGON   Afraid of what? Of us? [*Pause.*] Answer me!
VLADIMIR   I know what it is, he was afraid of the others.
ESTRAGON   How long have you been here?
BOY   A good while, Sir.
VLADIMIR   You were afraid of the whip?
BOY   Yes Sir.
VLADIMIR   The roars?
BOY   Yes Sir.
VLADIMIR   The two big men.
BOY   Yes Sir.
VLADIMIR   Do you know them?
BOY   No Sir.
VLADIMIR   Are you a native of these parts? [*Silence.*] Do you belong to these
   parts?
BOY   Yes Sir.
ESTRAGON   That's all a pack of lies. [*Shaking the* BOY *by the arm.*] Tell us
   the truth!
BOY [*trembling*]   But it is the truth, Sir!
VLADIMIR   Will you let him alone! What's the matter with you? [ESTRAGON
   releases the BOY, *moves away, covering his face with his hands.* VLADIMIR
   and the BOY *observe him.* ESTRAGON *drops his hands. His face is convulsed.*]
   What's the matter with you?
ESTRAGON   I'm unhappy.
VLADIMIR   Not really! Since when?
ESTRAGON   I'd forgotten.

VLADIMIR   Extraordinary the tricks that memory plays!
> [ESTRAGON *tries to speak, renounces, limps to his place, sits down and begins to take off his boots. To* BOY]

Well?

BOY   Mr. Godot—

VLADIMIR   I've seen you before, haven't I?

BOY   I don't know, Sir.

VLADIMIR   You don't know me?

BOY   No Sir.

VLADIMIR   It wasn't you came yesterday?

BOY   No Sir.

VLADIMIR   This is your first time?

BOY   Yes Sir.
> [*Silence.*]

VLADIMIR   Words words. [*Pause.*] Speak.

BOY [*in a rush*]   Mr. Godot told me to tell you he won't come this evening but surely tomorrow.
> [*Silence.*]

VLADIMIR   Is that all?

BOY   Yes Sir.
> [*Silence.*]

VLADIMIR   You work for Mr. Godot?

BOY   Yes Sir.

VLADIMIR   What do you do?

BOY   I mind the goats, Sir.

VLADIMIR   Is he good to you?

BOY   Yes Sir.

VLADIMIR   He doesn't beat you?

BOY   No Sir, not me.

VLADIMIR   Whom does he beat?

BOY   He beats my brother, Sir.

VLADIMIR   Ah, you have a brother?

BOY   Yes Sir.

VLADIMIR   What does he do?

BOY   He minds the sheep, Sir.[6]

VLADIMIR   And why doesn't he beat you?

BOY   I don't know, Sir.

VLADIMIR   He must be fond of you.

BOY   I don't know, Sir.
> [*Silence.*]

VLADIMIR   Does he give you enough to eat? [*The* BOY *hesitates.*] Does he feed you well?

BOY   Fairly well, Sir.

VLADIMIR   You're not unhappy? [*The* BOY *hesitates.*] Do you hear me?

BOY   Yes Sir.

VLADIMIR   Well?

BOY   I don't know, Sir.

VLADIMIR   You don't know if you're unhappy or not?

---

6. Cf. the parable in Matthew 25, in which the goats (the damned) are punished and the sheep (the saved) are blessed.

BOY   No Sir.

VLADIMIR   You're as bad as myself. [*Silence.*] Where do you sleep?

BOY   In the loft, Sir.

VLADIMIR   With your brother?

BOY   Yes Sir.

VLADIMIR   In the hay?

BOY   Yes Sir.
      [*Silence.*]

VLADIMIR   All right, you may go.

BOY   What am I to tell Mr. Godot, Sir?

VLADIMIR   Tell him . . . [*he hesitates.*] . . . tell him you saw us. [*Pause.*]
   You did see us, didn't you?

BOY   Yes Sir.
      [*He steps back, hesitates, turns and exits running. The light suddenly
      fails. In a moment it is night. The moon rises at back, mounts in the
      sky, stands still, shedding a pale light on the scene.*]

VLADIMIR   At last! [ESTRAGON *gets up and goes towards* VLADIMIR, *a boot in
   each hand. He puts them down at edge of stage, straightens and contemplates the moon.*] What are you doing?

ESTRAGON   Pale for weariness.

VLADIMIR   Eh?

ESTRAGON   Of climbing heaven and gazing on the likes of us.

VLADIMIR   Your boots, what are you doing with your boots?

ESTRAGON   [*turning to look at the boots*]   I'm leaving them there. [*Pause.*]
   Another will come, just as . . . as . . . as me, but with smaller feet, and
   they'll make him happy.

VLADIMIR   But you can't go barefoot!

ESTRAGON   Christ did.

VLADIMIR   Christ! What has Christ got to do with it? You're not going to
   compare yourself to Christ!

ESTRAGON   All my life I've compared myself to him.

VLADIMIR   But where he lived it was warm, it was dry!

ESTRAGON   Yes. And they crucified quick.
      [*Silence.*]

VLADIMIR   We've nothing more to do here.

ESTRAGON   Nor anywhere else.

VLADIMIR   Ah Gogo, don't go on like that. Tomorrow everything will be
   better.

ESTRAGON   How do you make that out?

VLADIMIR   Did you not hear what the child said?

ESTRAGON   No.

VLADIMIR   He said that Godot was sure to come tomorrow. [*Pause.*] What
   do you say to that?

ESTRAGON   Then all we have to do is to wait on here.

VLADIMIR   Are you mad? We must take cover. [*He takes* ESTRAGON *by the
   arm.*] Come on.
      [*He draws* ESTRAGON *after him.* ESTRAGON *yields, then resists.
      They halt.*]

ESTRAGON   [*looking at the tree*]   Pity we haven't got a bit of rope.

VLADIMIR   Come on. It's cold.
      [*He draws* ESTRAGON *after him. As before.*]

ESTRAGON   Remind me to bring a bit of rope tomorrow.
VLADIMIR   Yes. Come on.
      [*He draws him after him. As before.*]
ESTRAGON   How long have we been together all the time now?
VLADIMIR   I don't know. Fifty years maybe.
ESTRAGON   Do you remember the day I threw myself into the Rhône?[7]
VLADIMIR   We were grape harvesting.
ESTRAGON   You fished me out.
VLADIMIR   That's all dead and buried.
ESTRAGON   My clothes dried in the sun.
VLADIMIR   There's no good harking back on that. Come on.
      [*He draws him after him. As before.*]
ESTRAGON   Wait!
VLADIMIR   I'm cold!
ESTRAGON   Wait! [*He moves away from* VLADIMIR.] I sometimes wonder if
   we wouldn't have been better off alone, each one for himself. [*He crosses
   the stage and sits down on the mound.*] We weren't made for the same
   road.
VLADIMIR [*without anger*]   It's not certain.
ESTRAGON   No, nothing is certain.
      [VLADIMIR *slowly crosses the stage and sits down beside* ESTRAGON.]
VLADIMIR   We can still part, if you think it would be better.
ESTRAGON   It's not worth while now.
      [*Silence.*]
VLADIMIR   No, it's not worth while now.
      [*Silence.*]
ESTRAGON   Well, shall we go?
VLADIMIR   Yes, let's go.
      [*They do not move.*]
                    Curtain.

                    Act 2

Next day. Same time.
Same place.

      [ESTRAGON'*s boots front center, heels together, toes splayed.* LUCKY'*s hat at
      same place.*]

      [*The tree has four or five leaves.*]

      [*Enter* VLADIMIR *agitatedly. He halts and looks long at the tree, then
      suddenly begins to move feverishly about the stage. He halts before the
      boots, picks one up, examines it, sniffs it, manifests disgust, puts it
      back carefully. Comes and goes. Halts extreme right and gazes into
      distance off, shading his eyes with his hand. Comes and goes. Halts
      extreme left, as before. Comes and goes. Halts suddenly and begins to
      sing loudly.*]
VLADIMIR   A dog came in—
      [*Having begun too high he stops, clears his throat, resumes:*]
            A dog came in the kitchen

---

7. A major river in southeastern France.

And stole a crust of bread.
Then cook up with a ladle[8]
And beat him till he was dead.

Then all the dogs came running
And dug the dog a tomb—

[*He stops, broods, resumes:*]
Then all the dogs came running
And dug the dog a tomb
And wrote upon the tombstone
For the eyes of dogs to come:

A dog came in the kitchen
And stole a crust of bread.
Then cook up with a ladle
And beat him till he was dead.

Then all the dogs came running
And dug the dog a tomb—

[*He stops, broods, resumes:*]
Then all the dogs came running
And dug the dog a tomb—

[*He stops, broods. Softly.*]
And dug the dog a tomb . . .

[*He remains a moment silent and motionless, then begins to move feverishly about the stage. He halts before the tree, comes and goes, before the boots, comes and goes, halts extreme right, gazes into distance, extreme left, gazes into distance. Enter* ESTRAGON *right, barefoot, head bowed. He slowly crosses the stage.* VLADIMIR *turns and sees him.*]

VLADIMIR You again! [ESTRAGON *halts but does not raise his head.* VLADIMIR *goes towards him.*] Come here till I embrace you.

ESTRAGON Don't touch me!

[VLADIMIR *holds back, pained.*]

VLADIMIR Do you want me to go away? [*Pause.*] Gogo! [*Pause.* VLADIMIR *observes him attentively.*] Did they beat you? [*Pause.*] Gogo! [ESTRAGON *remains silent, head bowed.*] Where did you spend the night?

ESTRAGON Don't touch me! Don't question me! Don't speak to me! Stay with me!

VLADIMIR Did I ever leave you?

ESTRAGON You let me go.

VLADIMIR Look at me. [ESTRAGON *does not raise his head. Violently.*] Will you look at me!

[ESTRAGON *raises his head. They look long at each other, then suddenly embrace, clapping each other on the back. End of the embrace.* ESTRAGON, *no longer supported, almost falls.*]

ESTRAGON What a day!

---

8. I.e., the cook took up a ladle. Vladimir sings a round song.

VLADIMIR   Who beat you? Tell me.

ESTRAGON   Another day done with.

VLADIMIR   Not yet.

ESTRAGON   For me it's over and done with, no matter what happens. [*Silence.*] I heard you singing.

VLADIMIR   That's right, I remember.

ESTRAGON   That finished me. I said to myself, He's all alone, he thinks I'm gone for ever, and he sings.

VLADIMIR   One is not master of one's moods. All day I've felt in great form. [*Pause.*] I didn't get up in the night, not once!

ESTRAGON [*sadly*]   You see, you piss better when I'm not there.

VLADIMIR   I missed you . . . and at the same time I was happy. Isn't that a queer thing?

ESTRAGON [*shocked*]   Happy?

VLADIMIR   Perhaps it's not quite the right word.

ESTRAGON   And now?

VLADIMIR   Now? . . . [*Joyous.*] There you are again . . . [*Indifferent.*] There we are again . . . [*Gloomy.*] There I am again.

ESTRAGON   You see, you feel worse when I'm with you. I feel better alone too.

VLADIMIR [*vexed*]   Then why do you always come crawling back?

ESTRAGON   I don't know.

VLADIMIR   No, but I do. It's because you don't know how to defend yourself. I wouldn't have let them beat you.

ESTRAGON   You couldn't have stopped them.

VLADIMIR   Why not?

ESTRAGON   There was ten of them.

VLADIMIR   No, I mean before they beat you. I would have stopped you from doing whatever it was you were doing.

ESTRAGON   I wasn't doing anything.

VLADIMIR   Then why did they beat you?

ESTRAGON   I don't know.

VLADIMIR   Ah no, Gogo, the truth is there are things escape you that don't escape me, you must feel it yourself.

ESTRAGON   I tell you I wasn't doing anything.

VLADIMIR   Perhaps you weren't. But it's the way of doing it that counts, the way of doing it, if you want to go on living.

ESTRAGON   I wasn't doing anything.

VLADIMIR   You must be happy too, deep down, if you only knew it.

ESTRAGON   Happy about what?

VLADIMIR   To be back with me again.

ESTRAGON   Would you say so?

VLADIMIR   Say you are, even if it's not true.

ESTRAGON   What am I to say?

VLADIMIR   Say, I am happy.

ESTRAGON   I am happy.

VLADIMIR   So am I.

ESTRAGON   So am I.

VLADIMIR   We are happy.

ESTRAGON   We are happy. [*Silence.*] What do we do now, now that we are happy?

VLADIMIR Wait for Godot. [ESTRAGON *groans. Silence.*] Things have changed here since yesterday.

ESTRAGON And if he doesn't come.

VLADIMIR [*after a moment of bewilderment*] We'll see when the time comes. [*Pause.*] I was saying that things have changed here since yesterday.

ESTRAGON Everything oozes.

VLADIMIR Look at the tree.

ESTRAGON It's never the same pus from one second to the next.[9]

VLADIMIR The tree, look at the tree.

[ESTRAGON *looks at the tree.*]

ESTRAGON Was it not there yesterday?

VLADIMIR Yes of course it was there. Do you not remember? We nearly hanged ourselves from it. But you wouldn't. Do you not remember?

ESTRAGON You dreamt it.

VLADIMIR Is it possible you've forgotten already?

ESTRAGON That's the way I am. Either I forget immediately or I never forget.

VLADIMIR And Pozzo and Lucky, have you forgotten them too?

ESTRAGON Pozzo and Lucky?

VLADIMIR He's forgotten everything!

ESTRAGON I remember a lunatic who kicked the shins off me. Then he played the fool.

VLADIMIR That was Lucky.

ESTRAGON I remember that. But when was it?

VLADIMIR And his keeper, do you not remember him?

ESTRAGON He gave me a bone.

VLADIMIR That was Pozzo.

ESTRAGON And all that was yesterday, you say?

VLADIMIR Yes of course it was yesterday.

ESTRAGON And here where we are now?

VLADIMIR Where else do you think? Do you not recognize the place?

ESTRAGON [*suddenly furious*] Recognize! What is there to recognize? All my lousy life I've crawled about in the mud! And you talk to me about scenery! [*Looking wildly about him.*] Look at this muckheap! I've never stirred from it!

VLADIMIR Calm yourself, calm yourself.

ESTRAGON You and your landscapes! Tell me about the worms!

VLADIMIR All the same, you can't tell me that this [*gesture*] bears any resemblance to . . . [*he hesitates.*] . . . to the Mâcon country[1] for example. You can't deny there's a big difference.

ESTRAGON The Mâcon country! Who's talking to you about the Mâcon country?

VLADIMIR But you were there yourself, in the Mâcon country.

ESTRAGON No I was never in the Mâcon country! I've puked my puke of a life away here, I tell you! Here! In the Cackon country![2]

VLADIMIR But we were there together, I could swear to it! Picking grapes for a man called . . . [*he snaps his fingers*] . . . can't think of the name

---

9. Cf. "You can never step into the same river twice," a statement on flux by the ancient Greek philosopher Heraclitus (active ca. 500 B.C.E.).
1. A wine-producing area in the Burgundy region of eastern France.
2. Punning on *caca*, children's word in French for excrement.

of the man, at a place called . . . [*snaps his fingers*] . . . can't think of the name of the place, do you not remember?

ESTRAGON [*a little calmer*]   It's possible. I didn't notice anything.

VLADIMIR   But down there everything is red!

ESTRAGON [*exasperated*]   I didn't notice anything, I tell you!
    [*Silence.* VLADIMIR *sighs deeply.*]

VLADIMIR   You're a hard man to get on with, Gogo.

ESTRAGON   It'd be better if we parted.

VLADIMIR   You always say that and you always come crawling back.

ESTRAGON   The best thing would be to kill me, like the other.

VLADIMIR   What other? [*Pause.*] What other?

ESTRAGON   Like billions of others.

VLADIMIR [*sententious*]   To every man his little cross. [*He sighs.*] Till he dies. [*Afterthought.*] And is forgotten.

ESTRAGON   In the meantime let us try and converse calmly, since we are incapable of keeping silent.

VLADIMIR   You're right, we're inexhaustible.

ESTRAGON   It's so we won't think.

VLADIMIR   We have that excuse.

ESTRAGON   It's so we won't hear.

VLADIMIR   We have our reasons.

ESTRAGON   All the dead voices.

VLADIMIR   They make a noise like wings.

ESTRAGON   Like leaves.

VLADIMIR   Like sand.

ESTRAGON   Like leaves.
    [*Silence.*]

VLADIMIR   They all speak at once.

ESTRAGON   Each one to itself.
    [*Silence.*]

VLADIMIR   Rather they whisper.

ESTRAGON   They rustle.

VLADIMIR   They murmur.

ESTRAGON   They rustle.
    [*Silence.*]

VLADIMIR   What do they say?

ESTRAGON   They talk about their lives.

VLADIMIR   To have lived is not enough for them.

ESTRAGON   They have to talk about it.

VLADIMIR   To be dead is not enough for them.

ESTRAGON   It is not sufficient.
    [*Silence.*]

VLADIMIR   They make a noise like feathers.

ESTRAGON   Like leaves.

VLADIMIR   Like ashes.

ESTRAGON   Like leaves.
    [*Long silence.*]

VLADIMIR   Say something!

ESTRAGON   I'm trying.
    [*Long silence.*]

VLADIMIR [*in anguish*]   Say anything at all!

ESTRAGON What do we do now?
VLADIMIR Wait for Godot.
ESTRAGON Ah!
    [*Silence.*]
VLADIMIR This is awful!
ESTRAGON Sing something.
VLADIMIR No no! [*He reflects.*] We could start all over again perhaps.
ESTRAGON That should be easy.
VLADIMIR It's the start that's difficult.
ESTRAGON You can start from anything.
VLADIMIR Yes, but you have to decide.
ESTRAGON True.
    [*Silence.*]
VLADIMIR Help me!
ESTRAGON I'm trying.
    [*Silence.*]
VLADIMIR When you seek you hear.
ESTRAGON You do.
VLADIMIR That prevents you from finding.
ESTRAGON It does.
VLADIMIR That prevents you from thinking.
ESTRAGON You think all the same.
VLADIMIR No no, impossible.
ESTRAGON That's the idea, let's contradict each other.
VLADIMIR Impossible.
ESTRAGON You think so?
VLADIMIR We're in no danger of ever thinking any more.
ESTRAGON Then what are we complaining about?
VLADIMIR Thinking is not the worst.
ESTRAGON Perhaps not. But at least there's that.
VLADIMIR That what?
ESTRAGON That's the idea, let's ask each other questions.
VLADIMIR What do you mean, at least there's that?
ESTRAGON That much less misery.
VLADIMIR True.
ESTRAGON Well? If we gave thanks for our mercies?
VLADIMIR What is terrible is to *have* thought.
ESTRAGON But did that ever happen to us?
VLADIMIR Where are all these corpses from?
ESTRAGON These skeletons.
VLADIMIR Tell me that.
ESTRAGON True.
VLADIMIR We must have thought a little.
ESTRAGON At the very beginning.
VLADIMIR A charnel-house! A charnel-house![3]
ESTRAGON You don't have to look.
VLADIMIR You can't help looking.
ESTRAGON True.
VLADIMIR Try as one may.

---

3. A vault for the bodies or bones of the dead.

ESTRAGON   I beg your pardon?

VLADIMIR   Try as one may.

ESTRAGON   We should turn resolutely towards Nature.

VLADIMIR   We've tried that.

ESTRAGON   True.

VLADIMIR   Oh it's not the worst, I know.

ESTRAGON   What?

VLADIMIR   To have thought.

ESTRAGON   Obviously.

VLADIMIR   But we could have done without it.

ESTRAGON   Que voulez-vous?[4]

VLADIMIR   I beg your pardon?

ESTRAGON   Que voulez-vous.

VLADIMIR   Ah! que voulez-vous. Exactly.
    [*Silence.*]

ESTRAGON   That wasn't such a bad little canter.

VLADIMIR   Yes, but now we'll have to find something else.

ESTRAGON   Let me see. [*He takes off his hat, concentrates.*]

VLADIMIR   Let me see. [*He takes off his hat, concentrates. Long silence.*] Ah!
    [*They put on their hats, relax.*]

ESTRAGON   Well?

VLADIMIR   What was I saying, we could go on from there.

ESTRAGON   What were you saying when?

VLADIMIR   At the very beginning.

ESTRAGON   The very beginning of WHAT?

VLADIMIR   This evening . . . I was saying . . . I was saying . . .

ESTRAGON   I'm not a historian.

VLADIMIR   Wait . . . we embraced . . . we were happy . . . happy . . . what
    do we do now that we're happy . . . go on waiting . . . waiting . . . let me
    think . . . it's coming . . . go on waiting . . . now that we're happy . . . let
    me see . . . ah! The tree!

ESTRAGON   The tree?

VLADIMIR   Do you not remember?

ESTRAGON   I'm tired.

VLADIMIR   Look at it.
    [*They look at the tree.*]

ESTRAGON   I see nothing.

VLADIMIR   But yesterday evening it was all black and bare. And now it's
    covered with leaves.

ESTRAGON   Leaves?

VLADIMIR   In a single night.

ESTRAGON   It must be the Spring.

VLADIMIR   But in a single night!

ESTRAGON   I tell you we weren't here yesterday. Another of your night-
    mares.

VLADIMIR   And where were we yesterday evening according to you?

ESTRAGON   How would I know? In another compartment. There's no lack
    of void.

4. What do you want? (formal French).

VLADIMIR [*sure of himself*]   Good. We weren't here yesterday evening. Now what did we do yesterday evening?

ESTRAGON   Do?

VLADIMIR   Try and remember.

ESTRAGON   Do . . . I suppose we blathered.

VLADIMIR [*controlling himself*]   About what?

ESTRAGON   Oh . . . this and that I suppose, nothing in particular. [*With assurance.*] Yes, now I remember, yesterday evening we spent blathering about nothing in particular. That's been going on now for half a century.

VLADIMIR   You don't remember any fact, any circumstance?

ESTRAGON [*weary*]   Don't torment me, Didi.

VLADIMIR   The sun. The moon. Do you not remember?

ESTRAGON   They must have been there, as usual.

VLADIMIR   You didn't notice anything out of the ordinary?

ESTRAGON   Alas!

VLADIMIR   And Pozzo? And Lucky?

ESTRAGON   Pozzo?

VLADIMIR   The bones.

ESTRAGON   They were like fishbones.

VLADIMIR   It was Pozzo gave them to you.

ESTRAGON   I don't know.

VLADIMIR   And the kick.

ESTRAGON   That's right, someone gave me a kick.

VLADIMIR   It was Lucky gave it to you.

ESTRAGON   And all that was yesterday?

VLADIMIR   Show your leg.

ESTRAGON   Which?

VLADIMIR   Both. Pull up your trousers. [ESTRAGON *gives a leg to* VLADIMIR, *staggers.* VLADIMIR *takes the leg. They stagger.*] Pull up your trousers.

ESTRAGON   I can't.

  [VLADIMIR *pulls up the trousers, looks at the leg, lets it go.* ESTRAGON *almost falls.*]

VLADIMIR   The other. [ESTRAGON *gives the same leg.*] The other, pig! [ESTRAGON *gives the other leg. Triumphantly.*] There's the wound! Beginning to fester!

ESTRAGON   And what about it?

VLADIMIR [*letting go the leg*]   Where are your boots?

ESTRAGON   I must have thrown them away.

VLADIMIR   When?

ESTRAGON   I don't know.

VLADIMIR   Why?

ESTRAGON [*exasperated*]   I don't know why I don't know!

VLADIMIR   No, I mean why did you throw them away?

ESTRAGON [*exasperated*]   Because they were hurting me!

VLADIMIR [*triumphantly, pointing to the boots*]   There they are! [ESTRAGON *looks at the boots.*] At the very spot where you left them yesterday!

  [ESTRAGON *goes towards the boots, inspects them closely.*]

ESTRAGON   They're not mine.

VLADIMIR [*stupefied*]   Not yours!

ESTRAGON   Mine were black. These are brown.

VLADIMIR   You're sure yours were black?

ESTRAGON   Well they were a kind of grey.

VLADIMIR   And these are brown. Show.

ESTRAGON [*picking up a boot*]   Well they're a kind of green.

VLADIMIR   Show. [ESTRAGON *hands him the boot.* VLADIMIR *inspects it, throws it down angrily.*] Well of all the—

ESTRAGON   You see, all that's a lot of bloody—

VLADIMIR   Ah! I see what it is. Yes, I see what's happened.

ESTRAGON   All that's a lot of bloody—

VLADIMIR   It's elementary. Someone came and took yours and left you his.

ESTRAGON   Why?

VLADIMIR   His were too tight for him, so he took yours.

ESTRAGON   But mine were too tight.

VLADIMIR   For you. Not for him.

ESTRAGON [*having tried in vain to work it out*]   I'm tired! [*Pause.*] Let's go.

VLADIMIR   We can't.

ESTRAGON   Why not?

VLADIMIR   We're waiting for Godot.

ESTRAGON   Ah! [*Pause. Despairing.*] What'll we do, what'll we do!

VLADIMIR   There's nothing we can do.

ESTRAGON   But I can't go on like this!

VLADIMIR   Would you like a radish?

ESTRAGON   Is that all there is?

VLADIMIR   There are radishes and turnips.

ESTRAGON   Are there no carrots?

VLADIMIR   No. Anyway you overdo it with your carrots.

ESTRAGON   Then give me a radish. [VLADIMIR *fumbles in his pockets, finds nothing but turnips, finally brings out a radish and hands it to* ESTRAGON *who examines it, sniffs it.*] It's black!

VLADIMIR   It's a radish.

ESTRAGON   I only like the pink ones, you know that!

VLADIMIR   Then you don't want it?

ESTRAGON   I only like the pink ones!

VLADIMIR   Then give it back to me. [ESTRAGON *gives it back.*]

ESTRAGON   I'll go and get a carrot. [*He does not move.*]

VLADIMIR   This is becoming really insignificant.

ESTRAGON   Not enough.

[*Silence.*]

VLADIMIR   What about trying them.

ESTRAGON   I've tried everything.

VLADIMIR   No, I mean the boots.

ESTRAGON   Would that be a good thing?

VLADIMIR   It'd pass the time. [ESTRAGON *hesitates.*] I assure you, it'd be an occupation.

ESTRAGON   A relaxation.

VLADIMIR   A recreation.

ESTRAGON   A relaxation.

VLADIMIR   Try.

ESTRAGON   You'll help me?

VLADIMIR   I will of course.

ESTRAGON   We don't manage too badly, eh Didi, between the two of us?

VLADIMIR   Yes yes. Come on, we'll try the left first.

ESTRAGON   We always find something, eh Didi, to give us the impression
we exist?

VLADIMIR [*impatiently*]   Yes yes, we're magicians. But let us persevere in
what we have resolved, before we forget. [*He picks up a boot.*] Come on,
give me your foot. [ESTRAGON *raises his foot.*] The other, hog! [ESTRAGON
raises the other foot.] Higher! [*Wreathed together they stagger about the
stage.* VLADIMIR *succeeds finally in getting on the boot.*] Try and walk.
[ESTRAGON *walks.*] Well?

ESTRAGON   It fits.

VLADIMIR [*taking string from his pocket*]   We'll try and lace it.

ESTRAGON [*vehemently*]   No no, no laces, no laces!

VLADIMIR   You'll be sorry. Let's try the other. [*As before.*] Well?

ESTRAGON [*grudgingly*]   It fits too.

VLADIMIR   They don't hurt you?

ESTRAGON   Not yet.

VLADIMIR   Then you can keep them.

ESTRAGON   They're too big.

VLADIMIR   Perhaps you'll have socks some day.

ESTRAGON   True.

VLADIMIR   Then you'll keep them?

ESTRAGON   That's enough about these boots.

VLADIMIR   Yes, but—

ESTRAGON [*violently*]   Enough! [*Silence.*] I suppose I might as well sit
down. [*He looks for a place to sit down, then goes and sits down on the
mound.*]

VLADIMIR   That's where you were sitting yesterday evening.

ESTRAGON   If I could only sleep.

VLADIMIR   Yesterday you slept.

ESTRAGON   I'll try. [*He resumes his foetal posture, his head between his
knees.*]

VLADIMIR   Wait. [*He goes over and sits down beside* ESTRAGON *and begins
to sing in a loud voice.*]

Bye bye bye bye
Bye bye—

ESTRAGON [*looking up angrily*]   Not so loud!

VLADIMIR [*softly*]

Bye bye bye bye
Bye bye bye bye
Bye bye bye bye
Bye bye . . .

[ESTRAGON *sleeps.* VLADIMIR *gets up softly, takes off his coat and lays it
across* ESTRAGON'S *shoulders, then starts walking up and down, swinging his arms to keep himself warm.* ESTRAGON *wakes with a start, jumps
up, casts[5] about wildly.* VLADIMIR *returns to him, puts his arms round
him.*]

5. Looks.

There . . . there . . . Didi is there . . . don't be afraid . . .

ESTRAGON   Ah!

VLADIMIR   There . . . there . . . it's all over.

ESTRAGON   I was falling—

VLADIMIR   It's all over, it's all over.

ESTRAGON   I was on top of a—

VLADIMIR   Don't tell me! Come, we'll walk it off.
[*He takes* ESTRAGON *by the arm and walks him up and down until* ESTRAGON *refuses to go any further.*]

ESTRAGON   That's enough. I'm tired.

VLADIMIR   You'd rather be stuck there doing nothing?

ESTRAGON   Yes.

VLADIMIR   Please yourself.
[*He releases* ESTRAGON, *picks up his coat and puts it on.*]

ESTRAGON   Let's go.

VLADIMIR   We can't.

ESTRAGON   Why not?

VLADIMIR   We're waiting for Godot.

ESTRAGON   Ah! [VLADIMIR *walks up and down.*] Can you not stay still?

VLADIMIR   I'm cold.

ESTRAGON   We came too soon.

VLADIMIR   It's always at nightfall.

ESTRAGON   But night doesn't fall.

VLADIMIR   It'll fall all of a sudden, like yesterday.

ESTRAGON   Then it'll be night.

VLADIMIR   And we can go.

ESTRAGON   Then it'll be day again. [*Pause. Despairing.*] What'll we do, what'll we do!

VLADIMIR   [*halting, violently*]   Will you stop whining! I've had about my bellyful of your lamentations!

ESTRAGON   I'm going.

VLADIMIR   [*seeing* LUCKY's *hat*]   Well!

ESTRAGON   Farewell.

VLADIMIR   Lucky's hat. [*He goes towards it.*] I've been here an hour and never saw it. [*Very pleased.*] Fine!

ESTRAGON   You'll never see me again.

VLADIMIR   I knew it was the right place. Now our troubles are over. [*He picks up the hat, contemplates it, straightens it.*] Must have been a very fine hat. [*He puts it on in place of his own which he hands to* ESTRAGON.] Here.

ESTRAGON   What?

VLADIMIR   Hold that.

[ESTRAGON *takes* VLADIMIR's *hat.* VLADIMIR *adjusts* LUCKY's *hat on his head.* ESTRAGON *puts on* VLADIMIR's *hat in place of his own which he hands to* VLADIMIR. VLADIMIR *takes* ESTRAGON's *hat.* ESTRAGON *adjusts* VLADIMIR's *hat on his head.* VLADIMIR *puts on* ESTRAGON's *hat in place of* LUCKY's *which he hands to* ESTRAGON. ESTRAGON *takes* LUCKY's *hat.* VLADIMIR *adjusts* ESTRAGON's *hat on his head.* ESTRAGON *puts on* LUCKY's *hat in place of* VLADIMIR's *which he hands to* VLADIMIR. VLADI-MIR *takes his hat,* ESTRAGON *adjusts* LUCKY's *hat on his head.* VLADIMIR *puts on his hat in place of* ESTRAGON's *which he hands to* ESTRAGON. ESTRAGON *takes his hat.* VLADIMIR *adjusts his hat on his head.* ESTRAGON

puts on his hat in place of LUCKY's *which he hands to* VLADIMIR. VLADI-
MIR *takes* LUCKY's *hat.* ESTRAGON *adjusts his hat on his head.* VLADIMIR
puts on LUCKY's *hat in place of his own which he hands to* ESTRAGON.
ESTRAGON *takes* VLADIMIR's *hat.* VLADIMIR *adjusts* LUCKY's *hat on his
head.* ESTRAGON *hands* VLADIMIR's *hat back to* VLADIMIR *who takes it
and hands it back to* ESTRAGON *who takes it and hands it back to* VLAD-
IMIR *who takes it and throws it down.*]

How does it fit me?

ESTRAGON How would I know?

VLADIMIR No, but how do I look in it? [*He turns his head coquettishly to
and fro, minces like a mannequin.*[6]]

ESTRAGON Hideous.

VLADIMIR Yes, but not more so than usual?

ESTRAGON Neither more nor less.

VLADIMIR Then I can keep it. Mine irked me. [*Pause.*] How shall I say?
[*Pause.*] It itched me. [*He takes off* LUCKY's *hat, peers into it, shakes it,
knocks on the crown, puts it on again.*]

ESTRAGON I'm going.

    [*Silence.*]

VLADIMIR Will you not play?

ESTRAGON Play at what?

VLADIMIR We could play at Pozzo and Lucky.

ESTRAGON Never heard of it.

VLADIMIR I'll do Lucky, you do Pozzo. [*He imitates* LUCKY *sagging under
the weight of his baggage.* ESTRAGON *looks at him with stupefaction.*] Go
on.

ESTRAGON What am I to do?

VLADIMIR Curse me!

ESTRAGON [*after reflection*] Naughty!

VLADIMIR Stronger!

ESTRAGON Gonococcus! Spirochete![7]

    [VLADIMIR *sways back and forth, doubled in two.*]

VLADIMIR Tell me to think.

ESTRAGON What?

VLADIMIR Say, Think, pig!

ESTRAGON Think, pig!

    [*Silence.*]

VLADIMIR I can't!

ESTRAGON That's enough of that.

VLADIMIR Tell me to dance.

ESTRAGON I'm going.

VLADIMIR Dance, hog! [*He writhes. Exit* ESTRAGON *left, precipitately.*] I
can't! [*He looks up, misses* ESTRAGON.] Gogo! [*He moves wildly about the
stage. Enter* ESTRAGON *left, panting. He hastens towards* VLADIMIR, *falls
into his arms.*] There you are again at last!

ESTRAGON I'm accursed!

VLADIMIR Where were you? I thought you were gone for ever.

ESTRAGON They're coming!

---

6. A person employed to model clothes.
7. One of a group of bacteria, usually the one
that causes syphilis. "Gonococcus": the bacte-
rium that causes gonorrhea.

VLADIMIR   Who?

ESTRAGON   I don't know.

VLADIMIR   How many?

ESTRAGON   I don't know.

VLADIMIR [*triumphantly*]   It's Godot! At last! Gogo! It's Godot! We're saved! Let's go and meet him! [*He drags* ESTRAGON *towards the wings.* ESTRAGON *resists, pulls himself free, exits right.*] Gogo! Come back! [VLADIMIR *runs to extreme left, scans the horizon. Enter* ESTRAGON *right, he hastens towards* VLADIMIR, *falls into his arms.*] There you are again again!

ESTRAGON   I'm in hell!

VLADIMIR   Where were you?

ESTRAGON   They're coming there too!

VLADIMIR   We're surrounded! [ESTRAGON *makes a rush towards back.*] Imbecile! There's no way out there. [*He takes* ESTRAGON *by the arm and drags him towards front. Gesture towards front.*] There! Not a soul in sight! Off you go! Quick! [*He pushes* ESTRAGON *towards auditorium.* ESTRAGON *recoils in horror.*] You won't? [*He contemplates auditorium.*] Well I can understand that. Wait till I see. [*He reflects.*] Your only hope left is to disappear.

ESTRAGON   Where?

VLADIMIR   Behind the tree. [ESTRAGON *hesitates.*] Quick! Behind the tree. [ESTRAGON *goes and crouches behind the tree, realizes he is not hidden, comes out from behind the tree.*] Decidedly this tree will not have been the slightest use to us.

ESTRAGON [*calmer*]   I lost my head. Forgive me. It won't happen again. Tell me what to do.

VLADIMIR   There's nothing to do.

ESTRAGON   You go and stand there. [*He draws* VLADIMIR *to extreme right and places him with his back to the stage.*] There, don't move, and watch out. [VLADIMIR *scans horizon, screening his eyes with his hand.* ESTRAGON *runs and takes up same position extreme left. They turn their heads and look at each other.*] Back to back like in the good old days. [*They continue to look at each other for a moment, then resume their watch. Long silence.*] Do you see anything coming?

VLADIMIR [*turning his head.*]   What?

ESTRAGON [*louder*]   Do you see anything coming?

VLADIMIR   No.

ESTRAGON   Nor I.

    [*They resume their watch. Silence.*]

VLADIMIR   You must have had a vision.

ESTRAGON [*turning his head*]   What?

VLADIMIR [*louder*]   You must have had a vision.

ESTRAGON   No need to shout!

    [*They resume their watch. Silence.*]

VLADIMIR ⎫
ESTRAGON ⎭ [*turning simultaneously*]   Do you—

VLADIMIR   Oh pardon!

ESTRAGON   Carry on.

VLADIMIR   No no, after you.

ESTRAGON   No no, you first.

VLADIMIR   I interrupted you.

ESTRAGON   On the contrary.
    [*They glare at each other angrily.*]
VLADIMIR   Ceremonious ape!
ESTRAGON   Punctilious pig!
VLADIMIR   Finish your phrase, I tell you!
ESTRAGON   Finish your own!
    [*Silence. They draw closer, halt.*]
VLADIMIR   Moron!
ESTRAGON   That's the idea, let's abuse each other.
    [*They turn, move apart, turn again and face each other.*]
VLADIMIR   Moron!
ESTRAGON   Vermin!
VLADIMIR   Abortion!
ESTRAGON   Morpion![8]
VLADIMIR   Sewer-rat!
ESTRAGON   Curate!
VLADIMIR   Cretin!
ESTRAGON [*with finality*]   Crritic!
VLADIMIR   Oh! [*He wilts, vanquished, and turns away.*]
ESTRAGON   Now let's make it up.
VLADIMIR   Gogo!
ESTRAGON   Didi!
VLADIMIR   Your hand!
ESTRAGON   Take it!
VLADIMIR   Come to my arms!
ESTRAGON   Your arms?
VLADIMIR   My breast!
ESTRAGON   Off we go!
    [*They embrace. They separate. Silence.*]
VLADIMIR   How time flies when one has fun!
    [*Silence.*]
ESTRAGON   What do we do now?
VLADIMIR   While waiting.
ESTRAGON   While waiting.
    [*Silence.*]
VLADIMIR   We could do our exercises.
ESTRAGON   Our movements.
VLADIMIR   Our elevations.
ESTRAGON   Our relaxations.
VLADIMIR   Our elongations.
ESTRAGON   Our relaxations.
VLADIMIR   To warm us up.
ESTRAGON   To calm us down.
VLADIMIR   Off we go.
    [VLADIMIR *hops from one foot to the other.* ESTRAGON *imitates him.*]
ESTRAGON [*stopping*]   That's enough. I'm tired.
VLADIMIR [*stopping*]   We're not in form. What about a little deep breathing?
ESTRAGON   I'm tired breathing.
VLADIMIR   You're right. [*Pause.*] Let's just do the tree, for the balance.

8. Crab louse (a common French word, now obsolete in English).

ESTRAGON   The tree?
[VLADIMIR *does the tree, staggering about on one leg.*]
VLADIMIR [*stopping*]   Your turn.
[ESTRAGON *does the tree, staggers.*]
ESTRAGON   Do you think God sees me?
VLADIMIR   You must close your eyes.
[ESTRAGON *closes his eyes, staggers worse.*]
ESTRAGON [*stopping, brandishing his fists, at the top of his voice*]   God
have pity on me!
VLADIMIR [*vexed*]   And me?
ESTRAGON   On me! On me! Pity! On me!
[*Enter* POZZO *and* LUCKY. POZZO *is blind.* LUCKY *burdened as before.
Rope as before, but much shorter, so that* POZZO *may follow more easily.*
LUCKY *wearing a different hat. At the sight of* VLADIMIR *and* ESTRAGON
he stops short. POZZO, *continuing on his way, bumps into him.*]
VLADIMIR   Gogo!
POZZO [*clutching on to* LUCKY *who staggers*]   What is it? Who is it?
[LUCKY *falls, drops everything and brings down* POZZO *with him. They
lie helpless among the scattered baggage.*]
ESTRAGON   Is it Godot?
VLADIMIR   At last! [*He goes towards the heap.*] Reinforcements at last!
POZZO   Help!
ESTRAGON   Is it Godot?
VLADIMIR   We were beginning to weaken. Now we're sure to see the eve-
ning out.
POZZO   Help!
ESTRAGON   Do you hear him?
VLADIMIR   We are no longer alone, waiting for the night, waiting for
Godot, waiting for . . . waiting. All evening we have struggled, unas-
sisted. Now it's over. It's already tomorrow.
POZZO   Help!
VLADIMIR   Time flows again already. The sun will set, the moon rise, and
we away . . . from here.
POZZO   Pity!
VLADIMIR   Poor Pozzo!
ESTRAGON   I knew it was him.
VLADIMIR   Who?
ESTRAGON   Godot.
VLADIMIR   But it's not Godot.
ESTRAGON   It's not Godot?
VLADIMIR   It's not Godot.
ESTRAGON   Then who is it?
VLADIMIR   It's Pozzo.
POZZO   Here! Here! Help me up!
VLADIMIR   He can't get up.
ESTRAGON   Let's go.
VLADIMIR   We can't.
ESTRAGON   Why not?
VLADIMIR   We're waiting for Godot.
ESTRAGON   Ah!
VLADIMIR   Perhaps he has another bone for you.

ESTRAGON   Bone?
VLADIMIR   Chicken. Do you not remember?
ESTRAGON   It was him?
VLADIMIR   Yes.
ESTRAGON   Ask him.
VLADIMIR   Perhaps we should help him first.
ESTRAGON   To do what?
VLADIMIR   To get up.
ESTRAGON   He can't get up?
VLADIMIR   He wants to get up.
ESTRAGON   Then let him get up.
VLADIMIR   He can't.
ESTRAGON   Why not?
VLADIMIR   I don't know.
        [POZZO *writhes, groans, beats the ground with his fists.*]
ESTRAGON   We should ask him for the bone first. Then if he refuses we'll
    leave him there.
VLADIMIR   You mean we have him at our mercy?
ESTRAGON   Yes.
VLADIMIR   And that we should subordinate our good offices to certain
    conditions?
ESTRAGON   What?
VLADIMIR   That seems intelligent all right. But there's one thing I'm
    afraid of.
POZZO   Help!
ESTRAGON   What?
VLADIMIR   That Lucky might get going all of a sudden. Then we'd be bal-
    locksed.[9]
ESTRAGON   Lucky?
VLADIMIR   The one that went for you yesterday.
ESTRAGON   I tell you there was ten of them.
VLADIMIR   No, before that, the one that kicked you.
ESTRAGON   Is he there?
VLADIMIR   As large as life. [*Gesture towards* LUCKY.] For the moment he is
    inert. But he might run amuck any minute.
POZZO   Help!
ESTRAGON   And suppose we gave him a good beating the two of us?
VLADIMIR   You mean if we fell on him in his sleep?
ESTRAGON   Yes.
VLADIMIR   That seems a good idea all right. But could we do it? Is he
    really asleep? [*Pause.*] No, the best would be to take advantage of Pozzo's
    calling for help—
POZZO   Help!
VLADIMIR   To help him—
ESTRAGON   *We* help *him*?
VLADIMIR   In anticipation of some tangible return.
ESTRAGON   And suppose he—
VLADIMIR   Let us not waste our time in idle discourse! [*Pause. Vehe-
    mently.*] Let us do something, while we have the chance! It is not every

9. Screwed (slang); from "bollocks," or testicles.

day that we are needed. Not indeed that we personally are needed. Others would meet the case equally well, if not better. To all mankind they were addressed, those cries for help still ringing in our ears! But at this place, at this moment of time, all mankind is us, whether we like it or not. Let us make the most of it, before it is too late! Let us represent worthily for once the foul brood to which a cruel fate consigned us! What do you say? [ESTRAGON *says nothing.*] It is true that when with folded arms we weigh the pros and cons we are no less a credit to our species. The tiger bounds to the help of his congeners[1] without the least reflexion, or else he slinks away into the depths of the thickets. But that is not the question. What are we doing here, *that* is the question. And we are blessed in this, that we happen to know the answer. Yes, in this immense confusion one thing alone is clear. We are waiting for Godot to come—

ESTRAGON   Ah!

POZZO   Help!

VLADIMIR   Or for night to fall. [*Pause.*] We have kept our appointment and that's an end to that. We are not saints, but we have kept our appointment. How many people can boast as much?

ESTRAGON   Billions.

VLADIMIR   You think so?

ESTRAGON   I don't know.

VLADIMIR   You may be right.

POZZO   Help!

VLADIMIR   All I know is that the hours are long, under these conditions, and constrain us to beguile them with proceedings which—how shall I say—which may at first sight seem reasonable, until they become a habit. You may say it is to prevent our reason from foundering. No doubt. But has it not long been straying in the night without end of the abyssal depths? That's what I sometimes wonder. You follow my reasoning?

ESTRAGON [*aphoristic for once*]   We are all born mad. Some remain so.

POZZO   Help! I'll pay you!

ESTRAGON   How much?

POZZO   One hundred francs![2]

ESTRAGON   It's not enough.

VLADIMIR   I wouldn't go so far as that.

ESTRAGON   You think it's enough?

VLADIMIR   No, I mean so far as to assert that I was weak in the head when I came into the world. But that is not the question.

POZZO   Two hundred!

VLADIMIR   We wait. We are bored. [*He throws up his hand.*] No, don't protest, we are bored to death, there's no denying it. Good. A diversion comes along and what do we do? We let it go to waste. Come, let's get to work! [*He advances towards the heap, stops in his stride.*] In an instant all will vanish and we'll be alone once more, in the midst of nothingness! [*He broods.*]

POZZO   Two hundred!

1. Members of his kind.
2. Then worth about 30 dollars.

VLADIMIR   We're coming!
    [*He tries to pull* POZZO *to his feet, fails, tries again, stumbles, falls, tries to get up, fails.*]
ESTRAGON   What's the matter with you all?
VLADIMIR   Help!
ESTRAGON   I'm going.
VLADIMIR   Don't leave me! They'll kill me!
POZZO   Where am I?
VLADIMIR   Gogo!
POZZO   Help!
VLADIMIR   Help!
ESTRAGON   I'm going.
VLADIMIR   Help me up first, then we'll go together.
ESTRAGON   You promise?
VLADIMIR   I swear it!
ESTRAGON   And we'll never come back?
VLADIMIR   Never!
ESTRAGON   We'll go to the Pyrenees.[3]
VLADIMIR   Wherever you like.
ESTRAGON   I've always wanted to wander in the Pyrenees.
VLADIMIR   You'll wander in them.
ESTRAGON [*recoiling*]   Who farted?
VLADIMIR   Pozzo.
POZZO   Here! Here! Pity!
ESTRAGON   It's revolting!
VLADIMIR   Quick! Give me your hand!
ESTRAGON   I'm going. [*Pause. Louder.*] I'm going.
VLADIMIR   Well I suppose in the end I'll get up by myself. [*He tries, fails.*] In the fullness of time.
ESTRAGON   What's the matter with you?
VLADIMIR   Go to hell.
ESTRAGON   Are you staying there?
VLADIMIR   For the time being.
ESTRAGON   Come on, get up, you'll catch a chill.
VLADIMIR   Don't worry about me.
ESTRAGON   Come on, Didi, don't be pig-headed!
    [*He stretches out his hand which* VLADIMIR *makes haste to seize.*]
VLADIMIR   Pull!
    [ESTRAGON *pulls, stumbles, falls. Long silence.*]
POZZO   Help!
VLADIMIR   We've arrived.
POZZO   Who are you?
VLADIMIR   We are men.
    [*Silence.*]
ESTRAGON   Sweet mother earth!
VLADIMIR   Can you get up?
ESTRAGON   I don't know.
VLADIMIR   Try.
ESTRAGON   Not now, not now.
    [*Silence.*]

---

3. Mountain range along the border between France and Spain.

POZZO   What happened?

VLADIMIR [*violently*]   Will you stop it, you! Pest! He can think of nothing but himself!

ESTRAGON   What about a little snooze?

VLADIMIR   Did you hear him? He wants to know what happened!

ESTRAGON   Don't mind him. Sleep.
        [*Silence.*]

POZZO   Pity! Pity!

ESTRAGON [*with a start*]   What is it?

VLADIMIR   Were you asleep?

ESTRAGON   I must have been.

VLADIMIR   It's this bastard Pozzo at it again.

ESTRAGON   Make him stop it. Kick him in the crotch.

VLADIMIR [*striking Pozzo*]   Will you stop it! Crablouse! [POZZO *extricates himself with cries of pain and crawls away. He stops, saws the air blindly, calling for help.* VLADIMIR, *propped on his elbow, observes his retreat.*] He's off! [POZZO *collapses.*] He's down!

ESTRAGON   What do we do now?

VLADIMIR   Perhaps I could crawl to him.

ESTRAGON   Don't leave me!

VLADIMIR   Or I could call to him.

ESTRAGON   Yes, call to him.

VLADIMIR   Pozzo! [*Silence.*] Pozzo! [*Silence.*] No reply.

ESTRAGON   Together.

VLADIMIR }
ESTRAGON } Pozzo! Pozzo!

VLADIMIR   He moved.

ESTRAGON   Are you sure his name is Pozzo?

VLADIMIR [*alarmed*]   Mr. Pozzo! Come back! We won't hurt you!
        [*Silence.*]

ESTRAGON   We might try him with other names.

VLADIMIR   I'm afraid he's dying.

ESTRAGON   It'd be amusing.

VLADIMIR   What'd be amusing?

ESTRAGON   To try him with other names, one after the other. It'd pass the time. And we'd be bound to hit on the right one sooner or later.

VLADIMIR   I tell you his name is Pozzo.

ESTRAGON   We'll soon see. [*He reflects.*] Abel! Abel!

POZZO   Help!

ESTRAGON   Got it in one!

VLADIMIR   I begin to weary of this motif.

ESTRAGON   Perhaps the other is called Cain.[4] Cain! Cain!

POZZO   Help!

ESTRAGON   He's all humanity. [*Silence.*] Look at the little cloud.

VLADIMIR [*raising his eyes*]   Where?

ESTRAGON   There. In the zenith.[5]

VLADIMIR   Well? [*Pause.*] What is there so wonderful about it?
        [*Silence.*]

ESTRAGON   Let's pass on now to something else, do you mind?

4. The older son of Adam and Eve, who murdered his brother, Abel. Cf. Genesis 4.1–15.
5. The point of the sky directly overhead.

VLADIMIR I was just going to suggest it.

ESTRAGON But to what?

VLADIMIR Ah!

[*Silence.*]

ESTRAGON Suppose we got up to begin with?

VLADIMIR No harm trying.

[*They get up.*]

ESTRAGON Child's play.

VLADIMIR Simple question of will-power.

ESTRAGON And now?

POZZO Help!

ESTRAGON Let's go.

VLADIMIR We can't.

ESTRAGON Why not?

VLADIMIR We're waiting for Godot.

ESTRAGON Ah! [*Despairing.*] What'll we do, what'll we do!

POZZO Help!

VLADIMIR What about helping him?

ESTRAGON What does he want?

VLADIMIR He wants to get up.

ESTRAGON Then why doesn't he?

VLADIMIR He wants us to help him to get up.

ESTRAGON Then why don't we? What are we waiting for?

[*They help* POZZO *to his feet, let him go. He falls.*]

VLADIMIR We must hold him. [*They get him up again.* POZZO *sags between them, his arms round their necks.*] Feeling better?

POZZO Who are you?

VLADIMIR Do you not recognize us?

POZZO I am blind.

[*Silence.*]

ESTRAGON Perhaps he can see into the future.[6]

VLADIMIR Since when?

POZZO I used to have wonderful sight—but are you friends?

ESTRAGON [*laughing noisily*] He wants to know if we are friends!

VLADIMIR No, he means friends of his.

ESTRAGON Well?

VLADIMIR We've proved we are, by helping him.

ESTRAGON Exactly. Would we have helped him if we weren't his friends?

VLADIMIR Possibly.

ESTRAGON True.

VLADIMIR Don't let's quibble about that now.

POZZO You are not highwaymen?

ESTRAGON Highwaymen! Do we look like highwaymen?

VLADIMIR Damn it can't you see the man is blind!

ESTRAGON Damn it so he is. [*Pause.*] So he says.

POZZO Don't leave me!

VLADIMIR No question of it.

ESTRAGON For the moment.

---

6. Perhaps a reference to Tiresias, a figure in Greek mythology and literature who, although blind, possessed the gift of prophecy.

POZZO   What time is it?

VLADIMIR [*inspecting the sky*]   Seven o'clock . . . eight o'clock . . .

ESTRAGON   That depends what time of year it is.

POZZO   Is it evening?

[*Silence.* VLADIMIR *and* ESTRAGON *scrutinize the sunset.*]

ESTRAGON   It's rising.

VLADIMIR   Impossible.

ESTRAGON   Perhaps it's the dawn.

VLADIMIR   Don't be a fool. It's the west over there.

ESTRAGON   How do you know?

POZZO [*anguished*]   Is it evening?

VLADIMIR   Anyway it hasn't moved.

ESTRAGON   I tell you it's rising.

POZZO   Why don't you answer me?

ESTRAGON   Give us a chance.

VLADIMIR [*reassuring*]   It's evening, Sir, it's evening, night is drawing nigh. My friend here would have me doubt it and I must confess he shook me for a moment. But it is not for nothing I have lived through this long day and I can assure you it is very near the end of its repertory. [*Pause.*] How do you feel now?

ESTRAGON   How much longer are we to cart him around? [*They half release him, catch him again as he falls.*] We are not caryatids![7]

VLADIMIR   You were saying your sight used to be good, if I heard you right.

POZZO   Wonderful! Wonderful, wonderful sight!

[*Silence.*]

ESTRAGON [*irritably*]   Expand! Expand!

VLADIMIR   Let him alone. Can't you see he's thinking of the days when he was happy. [*Pause.*] *Memoria praeteritorum bonorum*[8]—that must be unpleasant.

ESTRAGON   We wouldn't know.

VLADIMIR   And it came on you all of a sudden?

POZZO   Quite wonderful!

VLADIMIR   I'm asking you if it came on you all of a sudden.

POZZO   I woke up one fine day as blind as Fortune.[9] [*Pause.*] Sometimes I wonder if I'm not still asleep.

VLADIMIR   And when was that?

POZZO   I don't know.

VLADIMIR   But no later than yesterday—

POZZO [*violently*]   Don't question me! The blind have no notion of time. The things of time are hidden from them too.

VLADIMIR   Well just fancy that! I could have sworn it was just the opposite.

ESTRAGON   I'm going.

POZZO   Where are we?

VLADIMIR   I couldn't tell you.

---

7. Female figures serving as support columns in classical buildings.

8. The memory of past good (Latin, quoting the *Summa Theologica Secunda* 2.2.36.1, by theologian and philosopher Thomas Aquinas [1225–1274]).

9. The Roman goddess of chance or luck, sometimes depicted as blindfolded.

POZZO   It isn't by any chance the place known as the Board?[1]

VLADIMIR   Never heard of it.

POZZO   What is it like?

VLADIMIR [*looking round*]   It's indescribable. It's like nothing. There's nothing. There's a tree.

POZZO   Then it's not the Board.

ESTRAGON [*sagging*]   Some diversion!

POZZO   Where is my menial?

VLADIMIR   He's about somewhere.

POZZO   Why doesn't he answer when I call?

VLADIMIR   I don't know. He seems to be sleeping. Perhaps he's dead.

POZZO   What happened exactly?

ESTRAGON   Exactly!

VLADIMIR   The two of you slipped. [*Pause.*] And fell.

POZZO   Go and see is he hurt.

VLADIMIR   We can't leave you.

POZZO   You needn't both go.

VLADIMIR [*to* ESTRAGON]   You go.

ESTRAGON   After what he did to me? Never!

POZZO   Yes yes, let your friend go, he stinks so. [*Silence.*] What is he waiting for?

VLADIMIR   What you waiting for?

ESTRAGON   I'm waiting for Godot.
         [*Silence.*]

VLADIMIR   What exactly should he do?

POZZO   Well to begin with he should pull on the rope, as hard as he likes so long as he doesn't strangle him. He usually responds to that. If not he should give him a taste of his boot, in the face and the privates as far as possible.

VLADIMIR [*to* ESTRAGON]   You see, you've nothing to be afraid of. It's even an opportunity to revenge yourself.

ESTRAGON   And if he defends himself?

POZZO   No no, he never defends himself.

VLADIMIR   I'll come flying to the rescue.

ESTRAGON   Don't take your eyes off me. [*He goes towards* LUCKY.]

VLADIMIR   Make sure he's alive before you start. No point in exerting yourself if he's dead.

ESTRAGON [*bending over* LUCKY]   He's breathing.

VLADIMIR   Then let him have it.
         [*With sudden fury* ESTRAGON *starts kicking* LUCKY, *hurling abuse at him as he does so. But he hurts his foot and moves away, limping and groaning.* LUCKY *stirs.*]

ESTRAGON   Oh the brute!
         [*He sits down on the mound and tries to take off his boot. But he soon desists and disposes himself for sleep, his arms on his knees and his head on his arms.*]

POZZO   What's gone wrong now?

VLADIMIR   My friend has hurt himself.

POZZO   And Lucky?

---

1. The stage, or the profession of acting, is often called "the boards."

VLADIMIR   So it is he?

POZZO   What?

VLADIMIR   It is Lucky?

POZZO   I don't understand.

VLADIMIR   And you are Pozzo?

POZZO   Certainly I am Pozzo.

VLADIMIR   The same as yesterday?

POZZO   Yesterday?

VLADIMIR   We met yesterday. [*Silence.*] Do you not remember?

POZZO   I don't remember having met anyone yesterday. But tomorrow I won't remember having met anyone today. So don't count on me to enlighten you.

VLADIMIR   But—

POZZO   Enough! Up pig!

VLADIMIR   You were bringing him to the fair to sell him. You spoke to us. He danced. He thought. You had your sight.

POZZO   As you please. Let me go! [VLADIMIR *moves away.*] Up! [LUCKY *gets up, gathers up his burdens.*]

VLADIMIR   Where do you go from here?

POZZO   On. [LUCKY, *laden down, takes his place before* POZZO.] Whip! [LUCKY *puts everything down, looks for whip, finds it, puts it into* POZZO's *hand, takes up everything again.*] Rope!

　　　[LUCKY *puts everything down, puts end of rope into* POZZO's *hand, takes up everything again.*]

VLADIMIR   What is there in the bag?

POZZO   Sand. [*He jerks the rope.*] On!

VLADIMIR   Don't go yet.

POZZO   I'm going.

VLADIMIR   What do you do when you fall far from help?

POZZO   We wait till we can get up. Then we go on. On!

VLADIMIR   Before you go tell him to sing.

POZZO   Who?

VLADIMIR   Lucky.

POZZO   To sing?

VLADIMIR   Yes. Or to think. Or to recite.

POZZO   But he is dumb.

VLADIMIR   Dumb!

POZZO   Dumb. He can't even groan.

VLADIMIR   Dumb! Since when?

POZZO [*suddenly furious*]   Have you not done tormenting me with your accursed time! It's abominable! When! When! One day, is that not enough for you, one day he went dumb, one day I went blind, one day we'll go deaf, one day we were born, one day we shall die, the same day, the same second, is that not enough for you? [*Calmer.*] They give birth astride of a grave, the light gleams an instant, then it's night once more. [*He jerks the rope.*] On!

　　　[*Exeunt*[2] POZZO *and* LUCKY. VLADIMIR *follows them to the edge of the stage, looks after them. The noise of falling, reinforced by mimic of* VLADIMIR, *announces that they are down again. Silence.* VLADIMIR

---

2. [They] exit (Latin).

goes towards ESTRAGON, *contemplates him a moment, then shakes him awake.*]

ESTRAGON [*wild gestures, incoherent words. Finally.*] Why will you never let me sleep?

VLADIMIR I felt lonely.

ESTRAGON I was dreaming I was happy.

VLADIMIR That passed the time.

ESTRAGON I was dreaming that—

VLADIMIR [*violently*] Don't tell me! [*Silence.*] I wonder is he really blind.

ESTRAGON Blind? Who?

VLADIMIR Pozzo.

ESTRAGON Blind?

VLADIMIR He told us he was blind.

ESTRAGON Well what about it?

VLADIMIR It seemed to me he saw us.

ESTRAGON You dreamt it. [*Pause.*] Let's go. We can't. Ah! [*Pause.*] Are you sure it wasn't him?

VLADIMIR Who?

ESTRAGON Godot.

VLADIMIR But who?

ESTRAGON Pozzo.

VLADIMIR Not at all! [*Less sure.*] Not at all! [*Still less sure.*] Not at all!

ESTRAGON I suppose I might as well get up. [*He gets up painfully.*] Ow! Didi!

VLADIMIR I don't know what to think any more.

ESTRAGON My feet! [*He sits down again and tries to take off his boots.*] Help me!

VLADIMIR Was I sleeping, while the others suffered? Am I sleeping now? Tomorrow, when I wake, or think I do, what shall I say of today? That with Estragon my friend, at this place, until the fall of night, I waited for Godot? That Pozzo passed, with his carrier, and that he spoke to us? Probably. But in all that what truth will there be? [ESTRAGON, *having struggled with his boots in vain, is dozing off again.* VLADIMIR *looks at him.*] He'll know nothing. He'll tell me about the blows he received and I'll give him a carrot. [*Pause.*] Astride of a grave and a difficult birth. Down in the hole, lingeringly, the grave-digger puts on the forceps.[3] We have time to grow old. The air is full of our cries. [*He listens.*] But habit is a great deadener. [*He looks again at* ESTRAGON.] At me too someone is looking, of me too someone is saying, He is sleeping, he knows nothing, let him sleep on. [*Pause.*] I can't go on! [*Pause.*] What have I said?

[*He goes feverishly to and fro, halts finally at extreme left, broods. Enter* BOY *right. He halts. Silence.*]

BOY Mister . . . [VLADIMIR *turns.*] Mister Albert . . .

VLADIMIR Off we go again. [*Pause.*] Do you not recognize me?

BOY No Sir.

VLADIMIR It wasn't you came yesterday.

BOY No Sir.

VLADIMIR This is your first time.

---

3. An instrument used in obstetrics to pull the baby out of the birth canal.

BOY   Yes Sir.
　　　[*Silence.*]
VLADIMIR   You have a message from Mr. Godot.
BOY   Yes Sir.
VLADIMIR   He won't come this evening.
BOY   No Sir.
VLADIMIR   But he'll come tomorrow.
BOY   Yes Sir.
VLADIMIR   Without fail.
BOY   Yes Sir.
　　　[*Silence.*]
VLADIMIR   Did you meet anyone?
BOY   No Sir.
VLADIMIR   Two other . . . [*he hesitates.*] . . . men?
BOY   I didn't see anyone, Sir.
　　　[*Silence.*]
VLADIMIR   What does he do, Mr. Godot? [*Silence.*] Do you hear me?
BOY   Yes Sir.
VLADIMIR   Well?
BOY   He does nothing, Sir.
　　　[*Silence.*]
VLADIMIR   How is your brother?
BOY   He's sick, Sir.
VLADIMIR   Perhaps it was he came yesterday.
BOY   I don't know, Sir.
　　　[*Silence.*]
VLADIMIR [*softly*]   Has he a beard, Mr. Godot?
BOY   Yes Sir.
VLADIMIR   Fair or . . . [*he hesitates.*] . . . or black?
BOY   I think it's white, Sir.
　　　[*Silence.*]
VLADIMIR   Christ have mercy on us!
　　　[*Silence.*]
BOY   What am I to tell Mr. Godot, Sir?
VLADIMIR   Tell him . . . [*he hesitates*] . . . tell him you saw me and that . . .
　　　[*he hesitates*] . . . that you saw me. [*Pause.* VLADIMIR *advances, the* BOY
　　　recoils. VLADIMIR *halts, the* BOY *halts. With sudden violence.*] You're sure
　　　you saw me, you won't come and tell me tomorrow that you never saw me!
　　　[*Silence.* VLADIMIR *makes a sudden spring forward, the* BOY *avoids him
　　　and exits running. Silence. The sun sets, the moon rises. As in Act 1.*
　　　VLADIMIR *stands motionless and bowed.* ESTRAGON *wakes, takes off his
　　　boots, gets up with one in each hand and goes and puts them down cen-
　　　ter front, then goes towards* VLADIMIR.]
ESTRAGON   What's wrong with you?
VLADIMIR   Nothing.
ESTRAGON   I'm going.
VLADIMIR   So am I.
ESTRAGON   Was I long asleep?
VLADIMIR   I don't know.
　　　[*Silence.*]
ESTRAGON   Where shall we go?
VLADIMIR   Not far.

ESTRAGON Oh yes, let's go far away from here.

VLADIMIR We can't.

ESTRAGON Why not?

VLADIMIR We have to come back tomorrow.

ESTRAGON What for?

VLADIMIR To wait for Godot.

ESTRAGON Ah! [*Silence.*] He didn't come?

VLADIMIR No.

ESTRAGON And now it's too late.

VLADIMIR Yes, now it's night.

ESTRAGON And if we dropped him? [*Pause.*] If we dropped him?

VLADIMIR He'd punish us. [*Silence. He looks at the tree.*] Everything's dead but the tree.

ESTRAGON [*looking at the tree*] What is it?

VLADIMIR It's the tree.

ESTRAGON Yes, but what kind?

VLADIMIR I don't know. A willow.

[ESTRAGON *draws* VLADIMIR *towards the tree. They stand motionless before it. Silence.*]

ESTRAGON Why don't we hang ourselves?

VLADIMIR With what?

ESTRAGON You haven't got a bit of rope?

VLADIMIR No.

ESTRAGON Then we can't.

[*Silence.*]

VLADIMIR Let's go.

ESTRAGON Wait, there's my belt.

VLADIMIR It's too short.

ESTRAGON You could hang onto my legs.

VLADIMIR And who'd hang on to mine?

ESTRAGON True.

VLADIMIR Show all the same. [ESTRAGON *loosens the cord that holds up his trousers which, much too big for him, fall about his ankles. They look at the cord.*] It might do at a pinch. But is it strong enough?

ESTRAGON We'll soon see. Here.

[*They each take an end of the cord and pull. It breaks. They almost fall.*]

VLADIMIR Not worth a curse.

[*Silence.*]

ESTRAGON You say we have to come back tomorrow?

VLADIMIR Yes.

ESTRAGON Then we can bring a good bit of rope.

VLADIMIR Yes.

[*Silence.*]

ESTRAGON Didi.

VLADIMIR Yes.

ESTRAGON I can't go on like this.

VLADIMIR That's what you think.

ESTRAGON If we parted? That might be better for us.

VLADIMIR We'll hang ourselves tomorrow. [*Pause.*] Unless Godot comes.

ESTRAGON And if he comes?

VLADIMIR   We'll be saved.

> [VLADIMIR *takes off his hat* (LUCKY's), *peers inside it, feels about inside it, shakes it, knocks on the crown, puts it on again.*]

ESTRAGON   Well? Shall we go?

VLADIMIR   Pull on your trousers.

ESTRAGON   What?

VLADIMIR   Pull on your trousers.

ESTRAGON   You want me to pull off my trousers?

VLADIMIR   Pull ON your trousers.

ESTRAGON [*realizing his trousers are down*]   True. [*He pulls up his trousers.*]

VLADIMIR   Well? Shall we go?

ESTRAGON   Yes, let's go.

> [*They do not move.*]

Curtain.

1952; 1954

W. H. AUDEN
1907–1973

Wystan Hugh Auden was born in York, England, the son of a doctor and of a former nurse. He was educated at private schools and Christ Church, Oxford. After graduation from Oxford he traveled abroad, taught school in England from 1930 to 1935, and later worked for a government film unit. His sympathies in the 1930s were with the left, like those of most intellectuals of his age, and he went to Spain during its civil war, intending to serve as an ambulance driver on the left-wing Republican side. To his surprise he felt so disturbed by the sight of the many Roman Catholic churches gutted and looted by the Republicans that he returned to England without fulfilling his ambition. He traveled in Iceland and China before moving to the United States in 1939; in 1946 he became an American citizen. He taught at a number of American colleges and was professor of poetry at Oxford from 1956 to 1960. Most of his later life was shared between residences in New York City and in Europe—first in southern Italy, then in Austria.

Auden was the most prominent of the young English poets who, in the late 1920s and early 1930s, saw themselves bringing new techniques and attitudes to English poetry. Stephen Spender, C. Day Lewis, and Louis MacNeice were other liberal and leftist poets in this loosely affiliated group. Auden learned metrical and verbal techniques from Gerard Manley Hopkins and Wilfred Owen, and from T. S. Eliot he took a conversational and ironic tone, an acute inspection of cultural decay. Thomas Hardy's metrical variety, formal irregularity, and fusion of panoramic and intimate perspectives also proved a useful example, and Auden admired W. B. Yeats's "serious reflective" poems of "personal and public interest," though he later came to disavow Yeats's grand aspirations and rhetoric. Auden's English studies at Oxford familiarized him with the rhythms and long alliterative line of Anglo-Saxon poetry. He learned, too, from popular and folk culture, particularly the songs of the English music hall and, later, American blues singers.

The Depression that hit America in 1929 hit England soon afterward, and Auden and his contemporaries looked out at an England of industrial stagnation and mass unemployment, seeing not Eliot's metaphorical Waste Land but a more literal Waste Land of poverty and "depressed areas." Auden's early poetry diagnoses the ills of his country. This diagnosis, conducted in a verse that combines irreverence with craftsmanship, draws on both Freud and Marx to show England now as a nation of neurotic invalids, now as the victim of an antiquated economic system. The intellectual liveliness and nervous force of this work made a great impression, even though the compressed, elliptical, impersonal style created difficulties of interpretation.

Gradually Auden sought to clarify his imagery and syntax, and in the late 1930s he produced "Lullaby," "Musée des Beaux Arts," "In Memory of W. B. Yeats," and other poems of finely disciplined movement, pellucid clarity, and deep yet unsentimental feeling. Some of the poems he wrote at this time, such as "Spain" and "September 1, 1939," aspire to a visionary perspective on political and social change; but as Auden became increasingly skeptical of poetry in the grand manner, of poetry as revelation or as a tool for political change, he removed these poems from his canon. (He came to see as false his claim in "September 1, 1939" that "We must love one another or die.") "Poetry is not magic," he said in the essay "Writing," but a form of truth telling that should "disenchant and disintoxicate." As he continued to remake his style during World War II, he created a voice that, in contrast not only to Romanticism but also to the authoritarianism devastating Europe, was increasingly flat, ironic, and conversational. He never lost his ear for popular speech or his ability to combine elements from popular art with technical formality. He daringly mixed the grave and the flippant, vivid detail and allegorical abstraction. He always experimented, particularly in ways of bringing together high artifice and a colloquial tone.

The poems of Auden's last phase are increasingly personal in tone and combine an air of offhand informality with remarkable technical skill in versification. He turned out, as if effortlessly, poems in numerous verse forms, including sestinas, sonnets, ballads, canzones, syllabics, haiku, the blues, even limericks. As he became evermore mistrustful of a prophetic role for the poet, he embraced the ordinary—the hours of the day, the rooms of a house, a changeable landscape. He took refuge in love and friendship, particularly the love and friendship he shared with the American writer Chester Kallmann. Like Eliot, Auden became a member of the Church of England, and the emotions of his late poetry—sometimes comic, sometimes solemn—were grounded in an ever deepening but rarely obtrusive religious feeling. In the last year of his life he returned to England to live in Oxford, feeling the need to be part of a university community as a protection against loneliness. Auden is now generally recognized as one of the masters of twentieth-century English poetry, a thoughtful, seriously playful poet, combining extraordinary intelligence and immense craftsmanship.

A note on the texts: Auden heavily revised his poems, sometimes omitting stanzas (as in "Spain" and "In Memory of W. B. Yeats") or even entire poems ("Spain" and "September 1, 1939"). The texts below are reprinted as they first appeared in book form and again in his *Selected Poems: A New Edition*, ed. Edward Mendelson (1989).

Petition[1]

    Sir, no man's enemy, forgiving all
    But will his negative inversion, be prodigal:
    Send to us power and light, a sovereign touch[2]
    Curing the intolerable neural itch,
5   The exhaustion of weaning, the liar's quinsy,°   *tonsillitis*

---

1. This title, by which the poem is widely known, is from Auden's later collections. Many of his early poems first appeared without titles.

2. The king's touch was often regarded as miraculous cure for disease (cf. *sovereign* as an adjective, meaning "supreme, all-dominating").

And the distortions of ingrown virginity.
Prohibit sharply the rehearsed response
And gradually correct the coward's stance;
Cover in time with beams those in retreat
10 That, spotted, they turn though the reverse were great;
Publish each healer that in city lives
Or country houses at the end of drives;
Harrow the house of the dead; look shining at
New styles of architecture, a change of heart.

Oct. 1929   1930

On This Island[1]

Look, stranger, at this island now
The leaping light for your delight discovers,
Stand stable here
And silent be,
5 That through the channels of the ear
May wander like a river
The swaying sound of the sea.

Here at the small field's ending pause
Where the chalk wall falls to the foam, and its tall ledges
10 Oppose the pluck
And knock of the tide,
And the shingle scrambles after the suck-
ing surf, and the gull lodges
A moment on its sheer side.

15 Far off like floating seeds the ships
Diverge on urgent voluntary errands;
And the full view
Indeed may enter
And move in memory as now these clouds do,
20 That pass the harbour mirror
And all the summer through the water saunter.

Nov. 1935   1936

Lullaby[1]

Lay your sleeping head, my love,
Human on my faithless arm;
Time and fevers burn away
Individual beauty from
5 Thoughtful children, and the grave
Proves the child ephemeral:

1. The title is from Auden's later collections.
1. Title from Auden's later collections.

But in my arms till break of day
Let the living creature lie,
Mortal, guilty, but to me
10   The entirely beautiful.

Soul and body have no bounds:
To lovers as they lie upon
Her tolerant enchanted slope
In their ordinary swoon,
15   Grave the vision Venus° sends   *Roman goddess of love*
Of supernatural sympathy,
Universal love and hope;
While an abstract insight wakes
Among the glaciers and the rocks
20   The hermit's sensual ecstasy.

Certainty, fidelity
On the stroke of midnight pass
Like vibrations of a bell,
And fashionable madmen raise
25   Their pedantic boring cry:
Every farthing[2] of the cost,
All the dreaded cards foretell,
Shall be paid, but from this night
Not a whisper, not a thought,
30   Not a kiss nor look be lost.

Beauty, midnight, vision dies:
Let the winds of dawn that blow
Softly round your dreaming head
Such a day of sweetness show
35   Eye and knocking heart may bless,
Find the mortal world enough;
Noons of dryness see you fed
By the involuntary powers,
Nights of insult let you pass
40   Watched by every human love.

Jan. 1937   1937, 1940

Spain[1]

Yesterday all the past. The language of size
Spreading to China along the trade-routes; the diffusion
     Of the counting-frame and the cromlech;[2]
Yesterday the shadow-reckoning in the sunny climates.

2. A quarter-penny, at one time the smallest and least valuable British coin.

1. The Spanish Civil War, which began in 1936 as a rebellion by General Franco's right-wing army against the left-wing, elected Spanish government, was viewed by British liberal intellectuals as a testing struggle between fascism and democracy. Written while the war was raging, this poem appeared separately in 1937, the proceeds of its sale going to Medical Aid for Spain. In 1940 Auden retitled the poem "Spain 1937," deleted lines 69–76, and made other changes; later he removed the poem from his canon.

2. Ancient stone circle.

5   Yesterday the assessment of insurance by cards,
The divination of water; yesterday the invention
      Of cartwheels and clocks, the taming of
Horses. Yesterday the bustling world of the navigators.

Yesterday the abolition of fairies and giants,
10   The fortress like a motionless eagle eyeing the valley,
      The chapel built in the forest;
Yesterday the carving of angels and alarming gargoyles;

The trial of heretics among the columns of stone;
Yesterday the theological feuds in the taverns
15   And the miraculous cure at the fountain;
Yesterday the Sabbath of witches; but to-day the struggle.

Yesterday the installation of dynamos and turbines,
The construction of railways in the colonial desert;
      Yesterday the classic lecture
20   On the origin of Mankind. But to-day the struggle.

Yesterday the belief in the absolute value of Greek,
The fall of the curtain upon the death of a hero;
      Yesterday the prayer to the sunset
And the adoration of madmen. But to-day the struggle.

25   As the poet whispers, startled among the pines,
Or where the loose waterfall sings compact, or upright
      On the crag by the leaning tower:
"O my vision. O send me the luck of the sailor."

And the investigator peers through his instruments
30   At the inhuman provinces, the virile bacillus
      Or enormous Jupiter finished:
"But the lives of my friends. I inquire. I inquire."

And the poor in their fireless lodgings, dropping the sheets
Of the evening paper: "Our day is our loss, O show us
35   History the operator, the
Organiser, Time the refreshing river."

And the nations combine each cry, invoking the life
That shapes the individual belly and orders
      The private nocturnal terror:
40   "Did you not found the city state of the sponge,

"Raise the vast military empires of the shark
And the tiger, establish the robin's plucky canton?°   *district*
      Intervene. O descend as a dove or
A furious papa or a mild engineer,[3] but descend."

---

3. Auden plays on the idea of a deus ex machina, literally a god from a machine, who appears suddenly in a play to resolve an impasse. "Dove": in the Bible, the form taken by the Holy Spirit when descending to Earth.

45 And the life, if it answers at all, replies from the heart
And the eyes and the lungs, from the shops and squares of the city
  "O no, I am not the mover;
Not to-day; not to you. To you, I'm the

"Yes-man, the bar-companion, the easily-duped;
50 I am whatever you do. I am your vow to be
  Good, your humorous story.
I am your business voice. I am your marriage.

"What's your proposal? To build the just city? I will.
I agree. Or is it the suicide pact, the romantic
55   Death? Very well, I accept, for
I am your choice, your decision. Yes, I am Spain."

Many have heard it on remote peninsulas,
On sleepy plains, in the aberrant fishermen's islands
  Or the corrupt heart of the city,
60 Have heard and migrated like gulls or the seeds of a flower.

They clung like burrs to the long expresses that lurch
Through the unjust lands, through the night, through the alpine
  tunnel;
  They floated over the oceans;
They walked the passes. All presented their lives.

65 On that arid square, that fragment nipped off from hot
Africa, soldered so crudely to inventive Europe;
  On that tableland scored by rivers,
Our thoughts have bodies; the menacing shapes of our fever

Are precise and alive. For the fears which made us respond
70 To the medicine ad. and the brochure of winter cruises
  Have become invading battalions;
And our faces, the institute-face, the chain-store, the ruin

Are projecting their greed as the firing squad and the bomb.
Madrid is the heart. Our moments of tenderness blossom
75   As the ambulance and the sandbag;
Our hours of friendship into a people's army.

To-morrow, perhaps the future. The research on fatigue
And the movements of packers; the gradual exploring of all the
  Octaves of radiation;
80 To-morrow the enlarging of consciousness by diet and breathing.

To-morrow the rediscovery of romantic love,
The photographing of ravens; all the fun under
  Liberty's masterful shadow;
To-morrow the hour of the pageant-master and the musician,

85 The beautiful roar of the chorus under the dome;
To-morrow the exchanging of tips on the breeding of terriers,

The eager election of chairmen
By the sudden forest of hands. But to-day the struggle.

To-morrow for the young the poets exploding like bombs,
90 The walks by the lake, the weeks of perfect communion;
       To-morrow the bicycle races
Through the suburbs on summer evenings. But to-day the struggle.

To-day the deliberate increase in the chances of death,
The conscious acceptance of guilt in the necessary murder;[4]
95   To-day the expending of powers
On the flat ephemeral pamphlet and the boring meeting.

To-day the makeshift consolations: the shared cigarette,
The cards in the candlelit barn, and the scraping concert,
       The masculine jokes; to-day the
100 Fumbled and unsatisfactory embrace before hurting.

The stars are dead. The animals will not look.
We are left alone with our day, and the time is short, and
       History to the defeated
May say Alas but cannot help nor pardon.

Mar. 1937   1937

As I Walked Out One Evening[1]

As I walked out one evening,
    Walking down Bristol Street,
The crowds upon the pavement
    Were fields of harvest wheat.

5 And down by the brimming river
    I heard a lover sing
Under an arch of the railway:
    "Love has no ending.

"I'll love you, dear, I'll love you
10   Till China and Africa meet
And the river jumps over the mountain
    And the salmon sing in the street.

"I'll love you till the ocean
    Is folded and hung up to dry
15 And the seven stars[2] go squawking
    Like geese about the sky.

---

4. After these two lines were criticized by George Orwell, Auden revised them to read "the inevitable increase" and "the fact of murder."

1. Title from Auden's later collections.
2. The constellation of the Pleiades, supposed by the ancients to be seven sisters.

"The years shall run like rabbits
    For in my arms I hold
The Flower of the Ages
20   And the first love of the world."

But all the clocks in the city
    Began to whirr and chime:
"O let not Time deceive you,
    You cannot conquer Time.

25   "In the burrows of the Nightmare
    Where Justice naked is,
Time watches from the shadow
    And coughs when you would kiss.

"In headaches and in worry
30   Vaguely life leaks away,
And Time will have his fancy
    To-morrow or to-day.

"Into many a green valley
    Drifts the appalling[3] snow;
35   Time breaks the threaded dances
    And the diver's brilliant bow.

"O plunge your hands in water,
    Plunge them in up to the wrist;
Stare, stare in the basin
40   And wonder what you've missed.

"The glacier knocks in the cupboard,
    The desert sighs in the bed,
And the crack in the tea-cup opens
    A lane to the land of the dead.

45   "Where the beggars raffle the banknotes
    And the Giant is enchanting to Jack,
And the Lily-white Boy is a Roarer
    And Jill goes down on her back.[4]

"O look, look in the mirror,
50   O look in your distress;
Life remains a blessing
    Although you cannot bless.

"O stand, stand at the window
    As the tears scald and start;
55   You shall love your crooked neighbour
    With your crooked heart."

---

3. Literally, making white.
4. The giant of "Jack and the Bean Stalk" is trying to seduce Jack; the "lily-white Boy" (presumably pure) becomes a boisterous reveler; Jill, of "Jack and Jill," is seduced.

It was late, late in the evening,
    The lovers they were gone;
    The clocks had ceased their chiming
60   And the deep river ran on.

Nov. 1937

1938, 1940

Musée des Beaux Arts[1]

About suffering they were never wrong,
The Old Masters: how well they understood
Its human position; how it takes place
While someone else is eating or opening a window or just walking
    dully along;
5 How, when the aged are reverently, passionately waiting
For the miraculous birth, there always must be
Children who did not specially want it to happen, skating
On a pond at the edge of the wood:
They never forgot
10 That even the dreadful martyrdom must run its course
Anyhow in a corner, some untidy spot
Where the dogs go on with their doggy life and the torturer's horse
Scratches its innocent behind on a tree.

In Brueghel's *Icarus*,[2] for instance: how everything turns away
15 Quite leisurely from the disaster; the ploughman may
Have heard the splash, the forsaken cry,
But for him it was not an important failure; the sun shone
As it had to on the white legs disappearing into the green
Water; and the expensive delicate ship that must have seen
20 Something amazing, a boy falling out of the sky,
Had somewhere to get to and sailed calmly on.

Dec. 1938

1940

In Memory of W. B. Yeats[1]

(d. January 1939)

I

He disappeared in the dead of winter:
The brooks were frozen, the air-ports almost deserted,
And snow disfigured the public statues;

1. Museum of Fine Arts (French).
2. *The Fall of Icarus*, by the Flemish painter Pieter Brueghel (ca. 1525–1569), in the Musées Royaux des Beaux Arts in Brussels. In one corner of Brueghel's painting, Icarus's legs are seen disappearing into the sea, his wings having melted when he flew too close to the sun. Auden also alludes to other paintings by Brueghel: the nativity scene in *The Numbering at Bethlehem*, skaters in *Winter Landscape with Skaters and a Bird Trap*, and possibly animals in *The Massacre of the Innocents*.
1. The Irish poet William Butler Yeats, born in 1865, died on January 29, 1939, in Roquebrune (southern France).

The mercury sank in the mouth of the dying day.
5   O all the instruments agree
The day of his death was a dark cold day.

Far from his illness
The wolves ran on through the evergreen forests,
The peasant river was untempted by the fashionable quays;
10   By mourning tongues
The death of the poet was kept from his poems.

But for him it was his last afternoon as himself,
An afternoon of nurses and rumours;
The provinces of his body revolted,
15   The squares of his mind were empty,
Silence invaded the suburbs,
The current of his feeling failed: he became his admirers.

Now he is scattered among a hundred cities
And wholly given over to unfamiliar affections;
20   To find his happiness in another kind of wood[2]
And be punished under a foreign code of conscience.
The words of a dead man
Are modified in the guts of the living.

But in the importance and noise of to-morrow
25   When the brokers are roaring like beasts on the floor of the Bourse,[3]
And the poor have the sufferings to which they are fairly accustomed,
And each in the cell of himself is almost convinced of his freedom;
A few thousand will think of this day
As one thinks of a day when one did something slightly unusual.

30   O all the instruments agree
The day of his death was a dark cold day.

II

You were silly like us: your gift survived it all;
The parish of rich women,[4] physical decay,
Yourself; mad Ireland hurt you into poetry.
35   Now Ireland has her madness and her weather still,
For poetry makes nothing happen: it survives
In the valley of its saying where executives
Would never want to tamper; it flows south
From ranches of isolation and the busy griefs,
40   Raw towns that we believe and die in; it survives,
A way of happening, a mouth.

2. Cf. the beginning of Dante's *Inferno:* "In the middle of the journey of our life I came to myself in a dark wood where the straight way was lost" (1.1–3).

3. The French stock exchange.
4. Several wealthy women, including Lady Augusta Gregory (1852–1932), provided financial help to Yeats.

III[5]

Earth, receive an honoured guest;
William Yeats is laid to rest:
Let the Irish vessel lie
45 Emptied of its poetry.

Time that is intolerant
Of the brave and innocent,
And indifferent in a week
To a beautiful physique,

50 Worships language and forgives
Everyone by whom it lives;
Pardons cowardice, conceit,
Lays its honours at their feet.

Time that with this strange excuse
55 Pardoned Kipling[6] and his views,
And will pardon Paul Claudel,[7]
Pardons him for writing well.

In the nightmare of the dark
All the dogs of Europe bark,[8]
60 And the living nations wait,
Each sequestered in its hate;

Intellectual disgrace
Stares from every human face,
And the seas of pity lie
65 Locked and frozen in each eye.

Follow, poet, follow right
To the bottom of the night,
With your unconstraining voice
Still persuade us to rejoice;

70 With the farming of a verse
Make a vineyard of the curse,
Sing of human unsuccess
In a rapture of distress;

In the deserts of the heart
75 Let the healing fountain start,
In the prison of his days
Teach the free man how to praise.

Feb. 1939

1939, 1940

---

5. The stanza pattern of this section echoes that of Yeats's late poem "Under Ben Bulben." Auden later omitted the section's second, third, and fourth stanzas.
6. The British writer Rudyard Kipling (1865–1936) championed imperialism.
7. French author (1868–1955) with extremely conservative politics. Yeats was at times antidemocratic and appeared to favor dictatorship.
8. World War II began in September 1939.

The Unknown Citizen

To JS/07/M/378
This Marble Monument is Erected by the State

He was found by the Bureau of Statistics to be
One against whom there was no official complaint,
And all the reports on his conduct agree
That, in the modern sense of an old-fashioned word, he was a saint,
5   For in everything he did he served the Greater Community.
Except for the War till the day he retired
He worked in a factory and never got fired,
But satisfied his employers, Fudge Motors Inc.
Yet he wasn't a scab or odd in his views,
10   For his Union reports that he paid his dues,
(Our report on his Union shows it was sound)
And our Social Psychology workers found
That he was popular with his mates and liked a drink.
The Press are convinced that he bought a paper every day
15   And that his reactions to advertisements were normal in every way.
Policies taken out in his name prove that he was fully insured,
And his Health-card shows he was once in hospital but left it cured.
Both Producers Research and High-Grade Living declare
He was fully sensible to the advantages of the Installment Plan
20   And had everything necessary to the Modern Man;
A gramophone, a radio, a car and a frigidaire.
Our researchers into Public Opinion are content
That he held the proper opinions for the time of year;
When there was peace, he was for peace; when there was war, he went.
25   He was married and added five children to the population,
Which our Eugenist[1] says was the right number for a parent of his
      generation,
And our teachers report that he never interfered with their education.
Was he free? Was he happy? The question is absurd:
Had anything been wrong, we should certainly have heard.

Mar. 1939   1939, 1940

September 1, 1939[1]

I sit in one of the dives
On Fifty-Second Street[2]
Uncertain and afraid
As the clever hopes expire
5   Of a low dishonest decade:
Waves of anger and fear
Circulate over the bright

---

1. An expert in eugenics, a pseudoscience for the genetic "improvement" of humans.
1. The date of Germany's invasion of Poland and the outbreak of World War II.
2. In New York City, where Auden was living.

And darkened lands of the earth,
Obsessing our private lives;
10 The unmentionable odour of death
Offends the September night.

Accurate scholarship can
Unearth the whole offence
From Luther[3] until now
15 That has driven a culture mad,
Find what occurred at Linz,[4]
What huge imago[5] made
A psychopathic god:
I and the public know
20 What all schoolchildren learn,
Those to whom evil is done
Do evil in return.

Exiled Thucydides[6] knew
All that a speech can say
25 About Democracy,
And what dictators do,
The elderly rubbish they talk
To an apathetic grave;
Analysed all in his book,
30 The enlightenment driven away,
The habit-forming pain,
Mismanagement and grief:
We must suffer them all again.

Into this neutral air
35 Where blind skyscrapers use
Their full height to proclaim
The strength of Collective Man,
Each language pours its vain
Competitive excuse:
40 But who can live for long
In an euphoric dream;
Out of the mirror they stare,
Imperialism's face
And the international wrong.

45 Faces along the bar
Cling to their average day:
The lights must never go out,
The music must always play,
All the conventions conspire
50 To make this fort assume

---

3. Martin Luther (1483–1546), founder of the Protestant Reformation.
4. Austrian city where Hitler spent his childhood.
5. Psychoanalytic term for the unconscious representation of a parental figure.
6. Greek general (d. ca. 401 B.C.E.) and historian of the Peloponnesian War, exiled from Athens because he failed to prevent the Spartans from seizing a colony.

The furniture of home;
Lest we should see where we are,
Lost in a haunted wood,
Children afraid of the night
55 Who have never been happy or good.

The windiest militant trash
Important Persons shout
Is not so crude as our wish:
What mad Nijinsky wrote
60 About Diaghilev[7]
Is true of the normal heart;
For the error bred in the bone
Of each woman and each man
Craves what it cannot have,
65 Not universal love
But to be loved alone.

From the conservative dark
Into the ethical life
The dense commuters come,
70 Repeating their morning vow,
"I *will* be true to the wife,
I'll concentrate more on my work,"
And helpless governors wake
To resume their compulsory game:
75 Who can release them now,
Who can reach the deaf,
Who can speak for the dumb?[8]

All I have is a voice
To undo the folded lie,
80 The romantic lie in the brain
Of the sensual man-in-the-street
And the lie of Authority
Whose buildings grope the sky:
There is no such thing as the State
85 And no one exists alone;
Hunger allows no choice
To the citizen or the police;
We must love one another or die.[9]

Defenceless under the night
90 Our world in stupor lies;
Yet, dotted everywhere,
Ironic points of light
Flash out wherever the Just
Exchange their messages:

7. The Russian dancer and choreographer Vaslav Nijinsky (1890–1950) wrote that his former lover, the ballet impresario Sergey Diaghilev (1872–1929), "does not want universal love, but to be loved alone."

8. Proverbs 31.8.
9. Auden later revised this line, which struck him as "dishonest." In one version of the poem the line reads: "We must love one another and die." Another version leaves out the entire stanza.

95   May I, composed like them
      Of Eros° and of dust,   *Greek god of desire*
      Beleaguered by the same
      Negation and despair,
      Show an affirming flame.

Sept. 1939   1939, 1940

In Praise of Limestone[1]

If it form the one landscape that we the inconstant ones
    Are consistently homesick for, this is chiefly
Because it dissolves in water. Mark these rounded slopes
    With their surface fragrance of thyme and beneath
5   A secret system of caves and conduits; hear these springs
    That spurt out everywhere with a chuckle
Each filling a private pool for its fish and carving
    Its own little ravine whose cliffs entertain
The butterfly and the lizard; examine this region
10   Of short distances and definite places:
What could be more like Mother or a fitter background
    For her son, for the nude young male who lounges
Against a rock displaying his dildo,° never doubting   *penis*
    That for all his faults he is loved, whose works are but
15 Extensions of his power to charm? From weathered outcrop
    To hill-top temple, from appearing waters to
Conspicuous fountains, from a wild to a formal vineyard,
    Are ingenious but short steps that a child's wish
To receive more attention than his brothers, whether
20   By pleasing or teasing, can easily take.

Watch, then, the band of rivals as they climb up and down
    Their steep stone gennels[2] in twos and threes, sometimes
Arm in arm, but never, thank God, in step; or engaged
    On the shady side of a square at midday in
25 Voluble discourse, knowing each other too well to think
    There are any important secrets, unable
To conceive a god whose temper-tantrums are moral
    And not to be pacified by a clever line
Or a good lay: for, accustomed to a stone that responds,
30   They have never had to veil their faces in awe
Of a crater whose blazing fury could not be fixed;
    Adjusted to the local needs of valleys
Where everything can be touched or reached by walking,
    Their eyes have never looked into infinite space

1. Inspired by the limestone landscape outside Florence, Italy, where Auden and his longtime companion Chester Kallman (1921–1975) were staying; the poem also recalls the poet's native Yorkshire. In a letter to Elizabeth Mayer, Auden wrote: "I hadn't realised till I came how like Italy is to my 'Mutterland', the Pennines [hills in the north of England]. Am in fact starting on a poem, 'In Praise of Limestone', the theme of which is that rock creates the only truly human landscape."
2. Narrow passages between houses (Yorkshire dialect) or, as here, rocks.

35 Through the lattice-work of a nomad's comb; born lucky,
        Their legs have never encountered the fungi
    And insects of the jungle, the monstrous forms and lives
        With which we have nothing, we like to hope, in common.
    So, when one of them goes to the bad, the way his mind works
40   Remains comprehensible: to become a pimp
    Or deal in fake jewelry or ruin a fine tenor voice
        For effects that bring down the house could happen to all
    But the best and the worst of us . . .
                                    That is why, I suppose,
        The best and worst never stayed here long but sought
45 Immoderate soils where the beauty was not so external,
        The light less public and the meaning of life
    Something more than a mad camp. "Come!" cried the granite wastes,
        "How evasive is your humor, how accidental
    Your kindest kiss, how permanent is death." (Saints-to-be
50   Slipped away sighing.) "Come!" purred the clays and gravels
    "On our plains there is room for armies to drill; rivers
        Wait to be tamed and slaves to construct you a tomb
    In the grand manner: soft as the earth is mankind and both
        Need to be altered." (Intendant Caesars rose and
55 Left, slamming the door.) But the really reckless were fetched
        By an older colder voice, the oceanic whisper:
    "I am the solitude that asks and promises nothing;
        That is how I shall set you free. There is no love;
    There are only the various envies, all of them sad."

60 They were right, my dear, all those voices were right
    And still are; this land is not the sweet home that it looks,
        Nor its peace the historical calm of a site
    Where something was settled once and for all: A backward
        And dilapidated province, connected
65 To the big busy world by a tunnel, with a certain
        Seedy appeal, is that all it is now? Not quite:
    It has a worldly duty which in spite of itself
        It does not neglect, but calls into question
    All the Great Powers assume; it disturbs our rights. The poet,
70   Admired for his earnest habit of calling
    The sun the sun, his mind Puzzle, is made uneasy
        By these solid statues which so obviously doubt
    His antimythological myth; and these gamins,°   urchins
        Pursuing the scientist down the tiled colonnade
75 With such lively offers, rebuke his concern for Nature's
        Remotest aspects: I, too, am reproached, for what
    And how much you know. Not to lose time, not to get caught,
        Not to be left behind, not, please! to resemble
    The beasts who repeat themselves, or a thing like water
80   Or stone whose conduct can be predicted, these
    Are our Common Prayer[3] whose greatest comfort is music
        Which can be made anywhere, is invisible,
    And does not smell. In so far as we have to look forward
        To death as a fact, no doubt we are right: But if

3. *The Book of Common Prayer* is the liturgical book of the Anglican Church.

85 Sins can be forgiven, if bodies rise from the dead,
    These modifications of matter into
  Innocent athletes and gesticulating fountains,
    Made solely for pleasure, make a further point:
  The blessed will not care what angle they are regarded from,
90   Having nothing to hide. Dear, I know nothing of
  Either, but when I try to imagine a faultless love
    Or the life to come, what I hear is the murmur
  Of underground streams, what I see is a limestone landscape.

May 1948   1948, 1951

The Shield of Achilles[1]

          She looked over his shoulder
            For vines and olive trees,
          Marble well-governed cities,
            And ships upon untamed seas,
5   But there on the shining metal
            His hands had put instead
          An artificial wilderness
            And a sky like lead.

          A plain without a feature, bare and brown,
10   No blade of grass, no sign of neighborhood,
          Nothing to eat and nowhere to sit down,
            Yet, congregated on its blankness, stood
            An unintelligible multitude,
          A million eyes, a million boots in line,
15   Without expression, waiting for a sign.

          Out of the air a voice without a face
            Proved by statistics that some cause was just
          In tones as dry and level as the place:
            No one was cheered and nothing was discussed;
20   Column by column in a cloud of dust
          They marched away enduring a belief
          Whose logic brought them, somewhere else, to grief.

          She looked over his shoulder
            For ritual pieties,
25   White flower-garlanded heifers,
            Libation and sacrifice,[2]
          But there on the shining metal

1. In Homer's *Iliad* Achilles, the chief Greek hero in the war with Troy, lends his armor to his great friend Patroclus and loses it when Patroclus is killed by Hector. While Achilles is mourning the death of his friend, his mother, the goddess Thetis, goes to Mt. Olympus to beg Hephaestos, the god of fire, to forge new armor for Achilles. The splendid shield of Achilles that Hephaestos then makes is described in book 18 (lines 478–608). On it he depicts the earth, the heavens, the sea, and the planets; a city in peace (with a wedding and a trial) and a city at war; scenes from country life, animal life, and the joyful life of young men and women. The ocean, as the outer border, flows around all these scenes.
2. Cf. John Keats's "Ode on a Grecian Urn" (1820): "Who are these coming to the sacrifice? / To what green altar, O mysterious priest, / Lead'st thou that heifer lowing at the skies, / And all her silken flanks with garlands dressed?" "Libation": sacrifice of wine or other liquid.

Where the altar should have been,
She saw by his flickering forge-light
30   Quite another scene.

Barbed wire enclosed an arbitrary spot
    Where bored officials lounged (one cracked a joke)
And sentries sweated, for the day was hot:
    A crowd of ordinary decent folk
35   Watched from without and neither moved nor spoke
As three pale figures were led forth and bound
To three posts driven upright in the ground.

The mass and majesty of this world, all
    That carries weight and always weighs the same,
40 Lay in the hands of others; they were small
    And could not hope for help and no help came:
    What their foes liked to do was done, their shame
Was all the worst could wish; they lost their pride
And died as men before their bodies died.

45   She looked over his shoulder
            For athletes at their games,
        Men and women in a dance
            Moving their sweet limbs
        Quick, quick, to music,
50   But there on the shining shield
        His hands had set no dancing-floor
            But a weed-choked field.

A ragged urchin, aimless and alone,
    Loitered about that vacancy; a bird
55 Flew up to safety from his well-aimed stone:
    That girls are raped, that two boys knife a third,
    Were axioms to him, who'd never heard
Of any world where promises were kept
Or one could weep because another wept.

60   The thin-lipped armorer,
            Hephaestos, hobbled away;
        Thetis of the shining breasts
            Cried out in dismay
        At what the god had wrought
65   To please her son, the strong
        Iron-hearted man-slaying Achilles
            Who would not live long.

1952   1952, 1955

[Poetry as Memorable Speech][1]

Of the many definitions of poetry, the simplest is still the best: 'memorable speech.' That is to say, it must move our emotions, or excite our intellect, for only that which is moving or exciting is memorable, and the stimulus is the audible spoken word and cadence, to which in all its power of suggestion and incantation we must surrender, as we do when talking to an intimate friend. We must, in fact, make exactly the opposite kind of mental effort to that we make in grasping other verbal uses, for in the case of the latter the aura of suggestion round every word through which, like the atom radiating lines of force through the whole of space and time, it becomes ultimately a sign for the sum of all possible meanings, must be rigorously suppressed and its meaning confined to a single dictionary one. For this reason the exposition of a scientific theory is easier to read than to hear. No poetry, on the other hand, which when mastered is not better heard than read is good poetry.

All speech has rhythm, which is the result of the combination of the alternating periods of effort and rest necessary to all living things, and the laying of emphasis on what we consider important; and in all poetry there is a tension between the rhythm due to the poet's personal values, and those due to the experiences of generations crystallised into habits of language such as the English tendency to alternate weak and accented syllables, and conventional verse forms like the hexameter, the heroic pentameter, or the French Alexandrine. Similes, metaphors of image or idea, and auditory metaphors such as rhyme, assonance, and alliteration help further to clarify and strengthen the pattern and internal relations of the experience described.

Poetry, in fact, bears the same kind of relation to Prose, using prose simply in the sense of all those uses of words that are not poetry, that algebra bears to arithmetic. The poet writes of personal or fictitious experiences, but these are not important in themselves until the reader has realised them in his own consciousness.

> Soldier from the war returning,
> Spoiler of the taken town[2]

It is quite unimportant, though it is the kind of question not infrequently asked, who the soldier is, what regiment he belongs to, what war he had been fighting in, etc. The soldier is you or me, or the man next door. Only when it throws light on our own experience, when these lines occur to us as we see, say, the unhappy face of a stockbroker in the suburban train, does poetry convince us of its significance. The test of a poet is the frequency and diversity of the occasions on which we remember his poetry.

Memorable speech then. About what? Birth, death, the Beatific Vision,[3] the abysses of hatred and fear, the awards and miseries of desire, the unjust walking the earth and the just scratching miserably for food like hens, triumphs, earthquakes, deserts of boredom and featureless anxiety, the Golden Age promised or irrevocably past, the gratifications and terrors of childhood, the

---

1. Excerpted from Auden and John Garrett's introduction to their anthology of verse, *The Poet's Tongue*.
2. Beginning lines of a poem (in which "war" is plural) by the English poet A. E. Housman (1859–1936).
3. A sight of the glories of heaven.

impact of nature on the adolescent, the despairs and wisdoms of the mature, the sacrificial victim, the descent into Hell, the devouring and the benign mother? Yes, all of these, but not these only. Everything that we remember no matter how trivial: the mark on the wall, the joke at luncheon, word games, these, like the dance of a stoat[4] or the raven's gamble, are equally the subject of poetry.

We shall do poetry a great disservice if we confine it only to the major experiences of life:

> The soldier's pole is fallen,
> Boys and girls are level now with men,
> And there is nothing left remarkable
> Beneath the visiting moon.
>
> They had a royal wedding.
> All his courtiers wished him well.
> The horses pranced and the dancers danced.
> O Mister it was swell.
>
> And masculine is found to be
> Hadria the Adriatic Sea.[5]

have all their rightful place, and full appreciation of one depends on full appreciation of the others.

A great many people dislike the idea of poetry as they dislike over-earnest people, because they imagine it is always worrying about the eternal verities.

Those, in Mr Spender's[6] words, who try to put poetry on a pedestal only succeed in putting it on the shelf. Poetry is no better and no worse than human nature; it is profound and shallow, sophisticated and naïve, dull and witty, bawdy and chaste in turn.

In spite of the spread of education and the accessibility of printed matter, there is a gap between what is commonly called 'highbrow' and 'lowbrow' taste, wider perhaps than it has ever been.

The industrial revolution broke up the agricultural communities, with their local conservative cultures, and divided the growing population into two classes: those whether employers or employees who worked and had little leisure, and a small class of shareholders who did no work, had leisure but no responsibilities or roots, and were therefore preoccupied with themselves. Literature has tended therefore to divide into two streams, one providing the first with a compensation and escape, the other the second with a religion and a drug. The Art for Art's sake[7] of the London drawing-rooms of the '90's, and towns like Burnley and Rochdale,[8] are complementary.

Nor has the situation been much improved by the increased leisure and educational opportunities which the population to-day as a whole possess. Were leisure all, the unemployed would have created a second Athens.

---

4. Weasel.
5. A mnemonic to help remember that Hadria, Latin for the Adriatic Sea, is masculine, despite its typically feminine ending. The first quotation is a remembered version of Cleopatra's speech after Antony dies in Shakespeare's *Antony and Cleopatra* (4.16.67–70). The middle quotation is from the popular song "King of Borneo" (1929) by American singer and songwriter Frank Crumit (1889–1943).
6. Stephen Spender (1909–1995), English poet.
7. Phrase associated with aestheticism.
8. Once industrial mill towns in Lancashire, England.

Artistic creations may be produced by individuals, and because their work is only appreciated by a few it does not necessarily follow that it is not good; but a universal art can only be the product of a community united in sympathy, sense of worth, and aspiration; and it is improbable that the artist can do his best except in such a society.

＊　＊　＊

The 'average' man says: 'When I get home I want to spend my time with my wife or in the nursery; I want to get out on to the links[9] or go for a spin in the car, not to read poetry. Why should I? I'm quite happy without it.' We must be able to point out to him that whenever, for example, he makes a good joke he is creating poetry, that one of the motives behind poetry is curiosity, the wish to know what we feel and think, and how, as E. M. Forster[1] says, can I know what I think till I see what I say, and that curiosity is the only human passion that can be indulged in for twenty-four hours a day without satiety.

The psychologist maintains that poetry is a neurotic symptom, an attempt to compensate by phantasy for a failure to meet reality. We must tell him that phantasy is only the beginning of writing; that, on the contrary, like psychology, poetry is a struggle to reconcile the unwilling subject and object; in fact, that since psychological truth depends so largely on context, poetry, the parabolic[2] approach, is the only adequate medium for psychology.

The propagandist, whether moral or political, complains that the writer should use his powers over words to persuade people to a particular course of action, instead of fiddling while Rome burns.[3] But Poetry is not concerned with telling people what to do, but with extending our knowledge of good and evil, perhaps making the necessity for action more urgent and its nature more clear, but only leading us to the point where it is possible for us to make a rational and moral choice.

＊　＊　＊

1935

---

9. Ground on which golf is played.
1. English novelist (1879–1970).
2. I.e., akin to parable.

3. The Roman emperor Nero (37–68) reputedly fiddled while Rome burned.

DYLAN THOMAS
1914–1953

Dylan Thomas was born in Swansea, Wales, and educated at Swansea Grammar School. After working for a time as a newspaper reporter, he was "discovered" as a poet in 1933 through a poetry contest in a popular newspaper. The following year his *Eighteen Poems* caused considerable excitement because of their powerfully suggestive obscurity and the strange violence of their imagery. It looked as though a new kind of visionary Romanticism had been restored to English poetry after the deliberately muted ironic tones of T. S. Eliot and his followers. Over time it became clear that Thomas was also a master of poetic craft, not merely a shouting rhapsodist. His verbal panache played against strict verse forms, such as the villanelle ("Do Not Go Gentle into That Good Night"). "I am a painstaking, conscientious, involved and devious craftsman in words," he wrote in his "Poetic Manifesto." His images were carefully ordered in a patterned sequence, and his major theme was the unity of all life, the continuing *process* of life and death and new life that linked the generations. Thomas saw the workings of biology as a magical transformation producing unity out of diversity, and again and again in his poetry he sought a poetic ritual to celebrate this unity ("The force that through the green fuse drives the flower / Drives my green age"). He saw men and women locked in cycles of growth, love, procreation, new growth, death, and new life again. Hence each image engenders its opposite in what he called "my dialectical method": "Each image holds within it the seed of its own destruction." Thomas derives his closely woven, sometimes self-contradictory images from the Bible, Welsh folklore and preaching, and Freud. In his poems of reminiscence and autobiographical emotion, such as "Poem in October," he communicates more immediately through compelling use of lyrical feeling and simple natural images. His autobiographical work *Portrait of the Artist as a Young Dog* (1940) and his radio play *Under Milk Wood* (1954) reveal a vividness of observation and a combination of violence and tenderness in expression that show he could handle prose as excitingly as verse.

Thomas was a brilliant talker, an alcoholic, a reckless and impulsive man whose short life was packed with emotional ups and downs. His poetry readings in the United States between 1950 and 1953 were enormous successes, in spite of his sometimes reckless antics. He died suddenly in New York of what was diagnosed as "an insult to the brain," precipitated by alcohol. He played the part of the wild bohemian poet, and while some thought this behavior wonderful, others deplored it. He was a stirring reader of his own and others' poems, and many people who do not normally read poetry were drawn to Thomas's by the magic of his own reading. After his premature death a reaction set in: some critics declared that he had been overrated as a poet because of his sensational life. The "Movement" poets, such as Philip Larkin, repudiated his rhetorical extravagance. Even so, Thomas is still considered an original poet of great power and beauty.

The Force That Through the Green Fuse Drives the Flower

> The force that through the green fuse drives the flower
> Drives my green age; that blasts the roots of trees
> Is my destroyer.
> And I am dumb to tell the crooked rose
> 5 My youth is bent by the same wintry fever.
>
> The force that drives the water through the rocks
> Drives my red blood; that dries the mouthing streams
> Turns mine to wax.
> And I am dumb to mouth unto my veins
> 10 How at the mountain spring the same mouth sucks.
>
> The hand that whirls the water in the pool[1]
> Stirs the quicksand; that ropes the blowing wind

1. The hand of the angel who troubles the water of the pool Bethesda, thus rendering it curative, in John 5.1–4.

Hauls my shroud sail.
And I am dumb to tell the hanging man
15   How of my clay is made the hangman's lime.[2]

The lips of time leech to the fountain head;
Love drips and gathers, but the fallen blood
Shall calm her sores.

And I am dumb to tell a weather's wind
20   How time has ticked a heaven round the stars.

And I am dumb to tell the lover's tomb
How at my sheet goes the same crooked worm.

1933

The Hunchback in the Park

The hunchback in the park
A solitary mister
Propped between trees and water
From the opening of the garden lock
5   That lets the trees and water enter
Until the Sunday sombre bell at dark[1]

Eating bread from a newspaper
Drinking water from the chained cup
That the children filled with gravel
10   In the fountain basin where I sailed my ship
Slept at night in a dog kennel
But nobody chained him up.

Like the park birds he came early
Like the water he sat down
15   And Mister they called Hey mister
The truant boys from the town
Running when he had heard them clearly
On out of sound

Past lake and rockery°   rock garden
20   Laughing when he shook his paper
Hunchbacked in mockery
Through the loud zoo of the willow groves
Dodging the park keeper
With his stick that picked up leaves.

25   And the old dog sleeper
Alone between nurses and swans

2. Quicklime was sometimes poured into the graves of public hangmen's victims to accelerate decomposition.

1. The bell indicates the park's closing for the night.

While the boys among willows
Made the tigers jump out of their eyes
To roar on the rockery stones
30   And the groves were blue with sailors

Made all day until bell time
A woman figure without fault
Straight as a young elm
Straight and tall from his crooked bones
35   That she might stand in the night
After the locks and chains

All night in the unmade park
After the railings and shrubberies
The birds the grass the trees the lake
40   And the wild boys innocent as strawberries
Had followed the hunchback
To his kennel in the dark.

1941   1946

Poem in October

It was my thirtieth year to heaven
Woke to my hearing from harbour and neighbour wood
And the mussel pooled and the heron
Priested shore
5   The morning beckon
With water praying and call of seagull and rook[1]
And the knock of sailing boats on the net webbed wall
Myself to set foot
That second
10   In the still sleeping town and set forth.

My birthday began with the water-
Birds and the birds of the winged trees flying my name
Above the farms and the white horses
And I rose
15   In rainy autumn
And walked abroad in a shower of all my days.
High tide and the heron dived when I took the road
Over the border
And the gates
20   Of the town closed as the town awoke.

A springful of larks in a rolling
Cloud and the roadside bushes brimming with whistling
Blackbirds and the sun of October
Summery
25   On the hill's shoulder,

---

1. A large type of crow.

Here were fond climates and sweet singers suddenly
Come in the morning where I wandered and listened
       To the rain wringing
        Wind blow cold
30   In the wood faraway under me.

      Pale rain over the dwindling harbour
And over the sea wet church the size of a snail
       With its horns through mist and the castle
        Brown as owls
35   But all the gardens
Of spring and summer were blooming in the tall tales
Beyond the border and under the lark full cloud.
       There could I marvel
        My birthday
40   Away but the weather turned around.

      It turned away from the blithe country
And down the other air and the blue altered sky
       Streamed again a wonder of summer
        With apples
45   Pears and red currants
And I saw in the turning so clearly a child's
Forgotten mornings when he walked with his mother
       Through the parables
        Of sun light
50   And the legends of the green chapels

      And the twice told fields of infancy
That his tears burned my cheeks and his heart moved in mine.
       These were the woods the river and sea
        Where a boy
55   In the listening
Summertime of the dead whispered the truth of his joy
To the trees and the stones and the fish in the tide.
       And the mystery
        Sang alive
60   Still in the water and singingbirds.

      And there could I marvel my birthday
Away but the weather turned around. And the true
       Joy of the long dead child sang burning
        In the sun.
65   It was my thirtieth
Year to heaven stood there then in the summer noon
Though the town below lay leaved with October blood.
       O may my heart's truth
        Still be sung
70   On this high hill in a year's turning.

1944   1946

Fern Hill[1]

Now as I was young and easy under the apple boughs
About the lilting house and happy as the grass was green,
    The night above the dingle[2] starry,
      Time let me hail and climb
5   Golden in the heydays of his eyes,
And honoured among wagons I was prince of the apple towns
And once below a time I lordly had the trees and leaves
      Trail with daisies and barley
    Down the rivers of the windfall light.

10 And as I was green and carefree, famous among the barns
About the happy yard and singing as the farm was home,
    In the sun that is young once only,
      Time let me play and be
    Golden in the mercy of his means,
15 And green and golden I was huntsman and herdsman, the calves
Sang to my horn, the foxes on the hills barked clear and cold,
      And the sabbath rang slowly
    In the pebbles of the holy streams.

All the sun long it was running, it was lovely, the hay
20 Fields high as the house, the tunes from the chimneys, it was air
    And playing, lovely and watery
      And fire green as grass.
    And nightly under the simple stars
As I rode to sleep the owls were bearing the farm away,
25 All the moon long I heard, blessed among stables, the night-jars[3]
      Flying with the ricks,° and the horses   *haystacks*
      Flashing into the dark.

And then to awake, and the farm, like a wanderer white
With the dew, come back, the cock on his shoulder: it was all
30   Shining, it was Adam and maiden,[4]
      The sky gathered again
    And the sun grew round that very day.
So it must have been after the birth of the simple light
In the first, spinning place, the spellbound horses walking warm
35   Out of the whinnying green stable
      On to the fields of praise.

And honoured among foxes and pheasants by the gay house
Under the new made clouds and happy as the heart was long,
    In the sun born over and over,
40   I ran my heedless ways,
    My wishes raced through the house high hay

---

1. Name of the Welsh farmhouse, home of his
aunt Ann Jones, where Thomas spent summer
holidays as a boy.

2. Deep dell or hollow, usually wooded.
3. Species of bird.
4. Cf. Genesis 1.

And nothing I cared, at my sky blue trades, that time allows
In all his tuneful turning so few and such morning songs
    Before the children green and golden
45   Follow him out of grace,

Nothing I cared, in the lamb white days, that time would take me
Up to the swallow thronged loft by the shadow of my hand,
    In the moon that is always rising,
        Nor that riding to sleep
50   I should hear him fly with the high fields
And wake to the farm forever fled from the childless land.
Oh as I was young and easy in the mercy of his means,
        Time held me green and dying
    Though I sang in my chains like the sea.

1945   1946

Do Not Go Gentle into That Good Night

Do not go gentle into that good night,
Old age should burn and rave at close of day;
Rage, rage against the dying of the light.

Though wise men at their end know dark is right,
5 Because their words had forked no lightning they
Do not go gentle into that good night.

Good men, the last wave by, crying how bright
Their frail deeds might have danced in a green bay,
Rage, rage against the dying of the light.

10 Wild men who caught and sang the sun in flight,
And learn, too late, they grieved it on its way,
Do not go gentle into that good night.

Grave men, near death, who see with blinding sight
Blind eyes could blaze like meteors and be gay,
15 Rage, rage against the dying of the light.

And you, my father, there on the sad height,
Curse, bless, me now with your fierce tears, I pray.
Do not go gentle into that good night.
Rage, rage against the dying of the light.

1951   1952

Voices from World War II

I n December 1939, a few months after the start of World War II, a leading article in the *Times Literary Supplement* urged poets to do their duty: "it is for the poets to sound the trumpet call. . . . The monstrous threat to belief and freedom which we are fighting should urge new psalmists to fresh songs of deliverance." The biblical diction reveals the underlying expectation that the poets of 1940 would come forward, like those of 1914, to sanctify the cause with images of sacrifice derived from Jesus Christ's precedent and precept: "greater love hath no man than this, that a man lay down his life for his friends." Far from taking up trumpets, the poets responded bitterly—C. Day Lewis with the poem "Where Are the War Poets?":

> They who in folly or mere greed
> Enslaved religion, markets, laws,
> Borrow our language now and bid
> Us to speak up in freedom's cause.
>
> It is the logic of our times,
> No subject for immortal verse—
> That we who lived by honest dreams
> Defend the bad against the worse.

With few exceptions the British poets of the 1930s had been born shortly before the outbreak of World War I, and those who were to be the poets of World War II were born during that earlier conflict. They grew up not, as Rupert Brooke, in the sunlit peace of Georgian England but amid wars and rumors of wars. They lived through the Great Depression and the rise of fascism. Introduced to the horrors of the last war—increased to mythic proportions by their fathers, uncles, and elder brothers—they were continually reminded of it by a flood of best-selling battle memoirs: Edmund Blunden's *Undertones of War* (1928), Robert Graves's *Goodbye to All That* (1929), Siegfried Sassoon's *Memoirs of an Infantry Officer* (1930) and *Sherston's Progress* (1936), and David Jones's *In Parenthesis* (1937). By then another myth, that of the Next War, was taking even more terrifying shape. Western intellectuals' last hope for the 1930s rested with the ragged troops of the left-wing Spanish Republic in their civil war against the right-wing Spanish army that had mutinied in 1936 against the country's elected government. Democracy and fascism were at last in the open, fighting a war that many thought would determine not simply the future of Spain but the future of Europe. With the final defeat of the Spanish Republicans in 1938, the Next War ceased to be a myth so much as an all-but-inescapable certainty.

World War I had been fought, for the most part, on the land, and its emblem in popular mythology was the trench. After the indiscriminate killing of civilians in a bombing raid—by German aircraft—on the Spanish town of Guernica in 1937, the emblem of the Next War was the bomb, the fire from heaven. Horrified by pictures of children bombed by Franco's fascist forces in the Spanish Civil War, Virginia Woolf was moved on the eve of World War II to write her long pacifist polemic, *Three Guineas* (1938). Subjecting nationalism to fierce irony and indicting the masculinist assertion of power, Woolf appealed for a cosmopolitanism in which one's country is the "whole world." In her diary she summed up what she considered her role as writer and intellectual in wartime: "Thinking is my fighting."

On September 1, 1939, Germany, in pursuit of imperial ambitions and without warning, launched a savage attack on Poland by land and air. Two days later Britain and France declared war on Germany. By the end of the month, Germany and its

The dome of St. Paul's Cathedral, 1940. Despite some direct hits, St. Paul's stands in the midst of smoke and flames caused by the German Air Force's nightly bombing, or blitz, of London and other major British cities. On December 29, more than ten thousand incendiary bombs fell on the capital.

ally Russia had, between them, defeated and partitioned Poland. Russia then attacked Finland, and in April 1940 Germany invaded Denmark and Norway. For Britain and France the period of inactivity that came to be known as "The Phoney War" ended in May, when the German Army overran Luxembourg and invaded the Netherlands and Belgium; their armored columns raced for the English Channel. Cut off, the British forces were evacuated by sea, with heavy losses, from Dunkirk, and in June, France signed an armistice with Germany. In August, as prelude to an invasion, the German *Luftwaffe* (Air Force) attacked England. Over the months that followed, the fighter pilots of the Royal Air Force (RAF) challenged the enemy bombers' nightly blitz of London and other major cities. The Battle of Britain, as it came to be called, cost the *Luftwaffe* twenty-three hundred planes, and the RAF, nine hundred. The losses forced the Germans to postpone their plans for invasion.

In 1941, Woolf imagined the coming fury, which would be a factor in her suicide. At the end of Woolf's novel *Between the Acts*, the village pageant of English history is over, and Mr. Streatfield's speech of thanks is interrupted: "A zoom severed it. Twelve aeroplanes in perfect formation like a flight of wild duck came overhead." The following year Edith Sitwell depicted the blitz in "Still Falls the Rain," as did T. S. Eliot in part 2 of "Little Gidding." The Battle of Britain, however, was not the only battle, and British poets were already responding to war on land and at sea as well as in the air. The dominant mood of their poetry is strikingly unlike that from and about the trenches of the Western Front. Just as the heroics of 1914 were impossible in 1940 (although there was no lack of heroism), so too was the antipropagandist indignation of a Siegfried Sassoon. Now that everybody knew about the Battle of the Somme, the bombing of Guernica, London, and Dresden, who could be surprised by evidence of "Man's inhumanity to man"? In the draft preface to his poems, one of the more influential poetic manifestos of the twentieth century, Wilfred Owen had written: "All a poet can do today is warn. That is why the true poets must be truthful." His warnings and those of his contemporaries had been uttered in vain, but the poets and novelists of World War II knew they must be truthful, true to their wartime experience of boredom and brutality, true to their humanity, and above all resistant to the murderous inhumanity of the machines.

VIRGINIA WOOLF

I n 1938, the year before the outbreak of full-blown war, when battles were already raging in Spain and Hitler's nazism and Mussolini's fascism were extending their reach in Europe and Africa, Virginia Woolf wrote *Three Guineas* (see the introduction to Woolf [1882–1941] and the selection of her works earlier in this volume). In this long essay on war and gender, nationalism, and pacifism, she identifies the foundations of conflict in patriarchy and in the intimate connections among different forms of domination. Although Woolf doesn't believe that women are inherently pacifist, she argues that they must stand as ironic outsiders to the nationalism and militarism often mobilized, ostensibly, in their defense.

"This morning I got a packet of photographs from Spain, all of dead children, killed by bombs." So Woolf wrote to her nephew Julian Bell, on November 14, 1936. Within a year her nephew himself was dead, killed while driving an ambulance for the anti-fascist Republican forces in Spain. These war photographs and Bell's death, together with the pressure of the impending conflagration, spurred Woolf's meditation on war in relation to gender inequities and social power. The epistolary essay is written in the form of a freewheeling but hard-edged reply to a male correspondent who had asked her three years earlier, "How in your opinion are we to prevent war?" He had also invited her to join a society for war's prevention. Refusing his overture, she argues for the feminist cosmopolitan who has the courage to say, "as a woman I have no country. As a woman I want no country. As a woman my country is the whole world."

From Three Guineas

[AS A WOMAN I HAVE NO COUNTRY]

* * *

To begin with an elementary distinction: a society is a conglomeration of people joined together for certain aims; while you, who write in your own person with your own hand are single. You the individual are a man whom we have reason to respect; a man of the brotherhood, to which, as biography proves, many brothers have belonged. Thus Anne Clough,[1] describing her brother, says: "Arthur is my best friend and adviser. . . . Arthur is the comfort and joy of my life; it is for him, and from him, that I am incited to seek after all that is lovely and of good report." To which William Wordsworth, speaking of his sister but answering the other as if one nightingale called to another in the forests of the past, replies:

---

1. British promoter of women's education and the first principal of Newnham College, Cambridge (1820–1892). Her brother was Arthur Clough (1819–1861), English poet.

> The Blessing of my later years
> Was with me when a Boy:
> She gave me eyes, she gave me ears;
> And humble cares, and delicate fears;
> A heart, the fountain of sweet tears;
> And love, and thought, and joy.[2]

Such was, such perhaps still is, the relationship of many brothers and sisters in private, as individuals. They respect each other and help each other and have aims in common. Why then, if such can be their private relationship, as biography and poetry prove, should their public relationship, as law and history prove, be so very different? And here, since you are a lawyer, with a lawyer's memory, it is not necessary to remind you of certain decrees of English law from its first records to the year 1919 by way of proving that the public, the society relationship of brother and sister has been very different from the private. The very word "society" sets tolling in memory the dismal bells of a harsh music: shall not, shall not, shall not. You shall not learn; you shall not earn; you shall not own; you shall not—such was the society relationship of brother to sister for many centuries. And though it is possible, and to the optimistic credible, that in time a new society may ring a carillon[3] of splendid harmony, and your letter heralds it, that day is far distant. Inevitably we ask ourselves, is there not something in the conglomeration of people into societies that releases what is most selfish and violent, least rational and humane in the individuals themselves? Inevitably we look upon society, so kind to you, so harsh to us, as an ill-fitting form that distorts the truth; deforms the mind; fetters the will. Inevitably we look upon societies as conspiracies that sink the private brother, whom many of us have reason to respect, and inflate in his stead a monstrous male, loud of voice, hard of fist, childishly intent upon scoring the floor of the earth with chalk marks, within whose mystic boundaries human beings are penned, rigidly, separately, artificially; where, daubed red and gold, decorated like a savage with feathers he goes through mystic rites and enjoys the dubious pleasures of power and dominion while we, "his" women, are locked in the private house without share in the many societies of which his society is composed. For such reasons compact as they are of many memories and emotions—for who shall analyse the complexity of a mind that holds so deep a reservoir of time past within it?—it seems both wrong for us rationally and impossible for us emotionally to fill up your form and join your society. For by so doing we should merge our identity in yours; follow and repeat and score still deeper the old worn ruts in which society, like a gramophone whose needle has stuck, is grinding out with intolerable unanimity "Three hundred millions spent upon arms." We should not give effect to a view which our own experience of "society" should have helped us to envisage. Thus, Sir, while we respect you as a private person and prove it by giving you a guinea[4] to spend as you choose, we believe that we can help you most effectively by refusing to join your society; by working for our common ends—justice and equality and liberty for all men and women—outside your society, not within.

---

2. From "The Sparrows' Nest" by English poet William Wordsworth (1770–1850). His sister was Dorothy Wordsworth (1771–1855).
3. Melody played on bells.
4. A guinea is a gold coin worth a pound and a shilling; its name links it to the West African coast (a region once called Guinea) and the slave trade in which the coin originated. It was often the standard fee for subscription to a society.

But this, you will say, if it means anything, can only mean that you, the daughters of educated men, who have promised us your positive help, refuse to join our society in order that you may make another of your own. And what sort of society do you propose to found outside ours, but in co-operation with it, so that we may both work together for our common ends? That is a question which you have every right to ask, and which we must try to answer in order to justify our refusal to sign the form you send. Let us then draw rapidly in outline the kind of society which the daughters of educated men might found and join outside your society but in co-operation with its ends. In the first place, this new society, you will be relieved to learn, would have no honorary treasurer, for it would need no funds. It would have no office, no committee, no secretary; it would call no meetings; it would hold no conferences. If name it must have, it could be called the Outsiders' Society. That is not a resonant name, but it has the advantage that it squares with facts—the facts of history, of law, of biography; even, it may be, with the still hidden facts of our still unknown psychology. It would consist of educated men's daughters working in their own class—how indeed can they work in any other?[5] and by their own methods for liberty, equality and peace. Their first duty, to which they would bind themselves not by oath, for oaths and ceremonies have no part in a society which must be anonymous and elastic before everything, would be not to fight with arms. This is easy for them to observe, for in fact, as the papers inform us, "the Army Council have no intention of opening recruiting for any women's corps."[6] The country ensures it. Next they would refuse in the event of war to make munitions or nurse the wounded. Since in the last war both these activities were mainly discharged by the daughters of working men, the pressure upon them here too would be slight, though probably disagreeable. On the other hand the next duty to which they would pledge themselves is one of considerable difficulty, and calls not only for courage and initiative, but for the special knowledge of the educated man's daughter. It is, briefly, not to incite their brothers to fight, or to dissuade them, but to maintain an attitude of complete indifference. But the attitude expressed by the word "indifference" is so complex and of such importance that it needs even here further definition. Indifference in the first place must be given a firm footing upon fact. As it is a fact that she cannot understand what instinct compels him, what glory, what interest, what manly satisfaction fighting provides for him— "without war there would be no outlet for the manly qualities which fighting develops"—as fighting thus is a sex characteristic which she cannot share, the counterpart some claim of the maternal instinct which he cannot share, so is it an instinct which she cannot judge. The outsider therefore must leave him free to deal with this instinct by himself, because liberty of opinion must be respected, especially when it is based upon an instinct which is as foreign to her as centuries of tradition and education can make it.[7] This is a fundamen-

5. In a lengthy note, Woolf describes the benefits to women of the working class and the educated class who dedicate themselves to improving the social and economic standing of their class. She warns against glamorizing the working class. "The average housewife," reports a newspaper article Woolf cites, "washed an acre of dirty dishes, a mile of glass and three miles of clothes and scrubbed miles of floor yearly" (*Daily Telegraph*, Sept. 29, 1937).
6. "It was stated yesterday at the War Office that

the Army Council have no intention of opening recruiting for any women's corps." (*The Times*, October 22, 1937 [p. 13]). This marks a prime distinction between the sexes. Pacifism is enforced upon women. Men are still allowed liberty of choice [Woolf's note].
7. The following quotation shows, however, that if sanctioned the fighting instinct easily develops. "The eyes deeply sunk into the sockets, the features acute, the amazon keeps herself very straight on the stirrups at the head of her squadron. . . .

tal and instinctive distinction upon which indifference may be based. But the outsider will make it her duty not merely to base her indifference upon instinct, but upon reason. When he says, as history proves that he has said, and may say again, "I am fighting to protect our country" and thus seeks to rouse her patriotic emotion, she will ask herself, "What does 'our country' mean to me an outsider?" To decide this she will analyse the meaning of patriotism in her own case. She will inform herself of the position of her sex and her class in the past. She will inform herself of the amount of land, wealth and property in the possession of her own sex and class in the present—how much of "England" in fact belongs to her. From the same sources she will inform herself of the legal protection which the law has given her in the past and now gives her. And if he adds that he is fighting to protect her body, she will reflect upon the degree of physical protection that she now enjoys when the words "Air Raid Precaution" are written on blank walls. And if he says that he is fighting to protect England from foreign rule, she will reflect that for her there are no "foreigners," since by law she becomes a foreigner if she marries a foreigner. And she will do her best to make this a fact, not by forced fraternity, but by human sympathy. All these facts will convince her reason (to put it in a nutshell) that her sex and class has very little to thank England for in the past; not much to thank England for in the present; while the security of her person in the future is highly dubious. But probably she will have imbibed, even from the governess, some romantic notion that Englishmen, those fathers and grandfathers whom she sees marching in the picture of history, are "superior" to the men of other countries. This she will consider it her duty to check by comparing French historians with English; German with French; the testimony of the ruled—the Indians or the Irish, say—with the claims made by their rulers. Still some "patriotic" emotion, some ingrained belief in the intellectual superiority of her own country over other countries may remain. Then she will compare English painting with French painting; English music with German music; English literature with Greek literature, for translations abound. When all these comparisons have been faithfully made by the use of reason, the outsider will find herself in possession of very good reasons for her indifference. She will find that she has no good reason to ask her brother to fight on her behalf to protect "our" country. "'Our country,'" she will say, "throughout the greater part of its history has treated me as a slave; it has denied me education or any share in its possessions. 'Our' country still ceases to be mine if I marry a foreigner. 'Our' country denies me the means of protecting myself, forces me to pay others a very large sum annually to protect me, and is so little able, even so, to protect me that Air Raid precautions are written on the wall. Therefore if you insist upon fighting to protect

---

Five English parliamentaries look at this woman with the respectful and a bit restless admiration one feels for a 'fauve' of an unknown species. . . .

—Come nearer Amalia—orders the commandant. She pushes her horse towards us and salutes her chief with the sword.

—Sergeant Amalia Bonilla—continues the chief of the squadron—how old are you?—Thirty-six.—Where were you born?—In Granada.—Why have you joined the army?—My two daughters were militiawomen. The younger has been killed in the Alto de Leon. I thought I had to supersede her and avenge her.—And how many enemies have you killed to avenge her?—You know it, commandant, five. The sixth is not sure.—No, but you have taken his horse. The amazon Amalia rides in fact a magnificent dapple-grey horse, with glossy hair, which flatters like a parade horse. . . . This woman who has killed five men—but who feels not sure about the sixth—was for the envoys of the House of Commons an excellent introducer to the Spanish War." (*The Martyrdom of Madrid, Inedited Witnesses,* by Louis Delaprée, pp. 34, 5, 6. Madrid, 1937.) [Louis Delaprée (1902–1936) was a French journalist killed covering the Spanish Civil War; Woolf's note].

me, or 'our' country, let it be understood, soberly and rationally between us, that you are fighting to gratify a sex instinct which I cannot share; to procure benefits which I have not shared and probably will not share; but not to gratify my instincts, or to protect either myself or my country. For," the outsider will say, "in fact, as a woman, I have no country. As a woman I want no country. As a woman my country is the whole world." And if, when reason has said its say, still some obstinate emotion remains, some love of England dropped into a child's ears by the cawing of rooks in an elm tree, by the splash of waves on a beach, or by English voices murmuring nursery rhymes, this drop of pure, if irrational, emotion she will make serve her to give to England first what she desires of peace and freedom for the whole world.

Such then will be the nature of her "indifference" and from this indifference certain actions must follow. She will bind herself to take no share in patriotic demonstrations; to assent to no form of national self-praise; to make no part of any claque[8] or audience that encourages war; to absent herself from military displays, tournaments, tattoos, prize-givings and all such ceremonies as encourage the desire to impose "our" civilization or "our" dominion upon other people. The psychology of private life, moreover, warrants the belief that this use of indifference by the daughters of educated men would help materially to prevent war. For psychology would seem to show that it is far harder for human beings to take action when other people are indifferent and allow them complete freedom of action, than when their actions are made the centre of excited emotion. The small boy struts and trumpets outside the window: implore him to stop; he goes on; say nothing; he stops. That the daughters of educated men then should give their brothers neither the white feather of cowardice nor the red feather of courage, but no feather at all; that they should shut the bright eyes that rain influence, or let those eyes look elsewhere when war is discussed—that is the duty to which outsiders will train themselves in peace before the threat of death inevitably makes reason powerless.

Such then are some of the methods by which the society, the anonymous and secret Society of Outsiders would help you, Sir, to prevent war and to ensure freedom.

*　　*　　*

1938

8. Group of subservient followers.

PABLO PICASSO

Guernica

(p. 842)

Picasso painted the starkly black-white-and-gray, mural-size depiction of anguished and shattered human and animal figures after the German bombing and destruction of a Basque village in his native Spain in 1937. The attack by the warplanes in support of General Franco's Nationalist forces during the Civil War foreshadowed the widespread bombing of civilians in World War II. At the left of the painting, a woman mourns a dead child under a standing bull. At the center is a horse stabbed through by a spear and partly covered with newsprint; above the animal shines an eyelike light, and below it is the shattered body of a soldier. From the right, two female figures enter the room, one carrying a candle that contrasts with the harsh lightbulb, while a terrified person at the far right is surrounded by fire. The painting helped spread awareness of the Spanish Civil War's ravages, traveling to a large number of cities, including London, where it arrived in 1938 under the patronage in part of the novelists Virginia Woolf and E. M. Forster.

Guernica, 1937, Pablo Picasso.

EDITH SITWELL

E dith Sitwell's father was an eccentric English baronet; her mother, the daughter of an earl. Sitwell (1887–1964), an eccentrically gifted poet, objected to the subdued rural descriptions and reflections of the Georgian poets (of whom Rupert Brooke was the most popular) and reacted in favor of a highly abstract verbal experimentation that exploited the sounds and rhythms and suggestions of words and phrases, often with remarkable pyrotechnic display. She edited and contributed to the six "cycles" of *Wheels* (1916–21), an annual anthology of modern poems in which she displayed her verbal and rhythmic virtuosity and encouraged others to follow her example. Her sequence *Façade* (1922), with its cunning exploration of rhymes and rhythms, was set to music by the composer Sir William Walton, whose sympathetic treatment of the words enhanced their impact. The 1923 performance in London's Aeolian Hall was a sensation: Sitwell intoned the poems from behind a screen, and Walton conducted the orchestra.

But Sitwell was more than a manipulator of surfaces. Throughout her poetry she hints at profounder meanings, sometimes with mocking laughter, sometimes with anguish, and in her later work she attacks the pettiness and philistinism of high society. In still later poems, influenced by William Blake, W. B. Yeats, and her friend Dylan Thomas, Sitwell wished to achieve, she said in her autobiography, "a greater expressiveness, a greater formality, and a return to rhetoric," rejecting "the outcry for understatement, for quietness, for neutral tints in poetry." These poems, such as "Still Falls the Rain," are much concerned with the horrors of war, the varieties of human suffering produced by modern civilization, and the healing powers of a faith in God, combined with a sense of the richness and variety of nature.

Still Falls the Rain

The Raids, 1940.[1] Night and Dawn

Still falls the Rain—
Dark as the world of man, black as our loss—
Blind as the nineteen hundred and forty nails
Upon the Cross.

5   Still falls the Rain
With a sound like the pulse of the heart that is changed to the
    hammer-beat
In the Potter's Field,[2] and the sound of the impious feet
On the Tomb:
           Still falls the Rain
In the Field of Blood where the small hopes breed and the human brain
10 Nurtures its greed, that worm with the brow of Cain.[3]

---

1. During the Battle of Britain, the German Air Force carried out many raids on London, often with incendiary bombs (see lines 27 and 30).
2. Cf. Matthew 27.3–8: "Then Judas, which betrayed [Jesus], when he saw that he was condemned, repented himself, and brought back the 30 pieces of silver to the chief priests and elders, saying, I have sinned in that I betrayed innocent blood. But they said, What is that to us? see thou to it. And he cast down the pieces of silver into the sanctuary, and departed; and he went away and hanged himself. And the chief priests took the pieces of silver . . . and bought with them the potter's field, to bury strangers in. Wherefore that field was called, The field of blood, unto this day."
3. The first murderer in the Bible (Genesis 4).

Still falls the Rain
At the feet of the Starved Man hung upon the Cross.
Christ that each day, each night, nails there, have mercy on us—
On Dives and on Lazarus.[4]
15 Under the Rain the sore and the gold are as one.

Still falls the Rain—
Still falls the Blood from the Starved Man's wounded Side:
He bears in His Heart all wounds,—those of the light that died,
The last faint spark
20 In the self-murdered heart, the wounds of the sad uncomprehending dark,
The wounds of the baited bear,[5]—
The blind and weeping bear whom the keepers beat
On his helpless flesh . . . the tears of the hunted hare.

Still falls the Rain—
25 Then—O Ile leape up to my God: who pulles me doune—
See, see where Christ's blood streames in the firmament:[6]
It flows from the Brow we nailed upon the tree
Deep to the dying, to the thirsting heart
That holds the fires of the world,—dark-smirched with pain
30 As Caesar's laurel crown.[7]

Then sounds the voice of One who like the heart of man
Was once a child who among beasts has lain—
"Still do I love, still shed my innocent light, my Blood, for thee."

1942

4. In Jesus's parable the rich man Dives was sent to hell, while the leprous beggar Lazarus went to heaven (Luke 16.19–31). This is not the same Lazarus who was raised from the dead.
5. A medieval and Elizabethan sport in which dogs fought a bear chained to a post.
6. Faustus's cry at the end of Marlowe's *Doctor Faustus* (1604), when he realizes that he has been damned for his pact with Mephistopheles.
7. Traditionally worn by victorious generals, and perhaps here associated with Jesus's crown of thorns (Matthew 27.29).

HENRY REED

H enry Reed (1914–1986) was born and educated in Birmingham, at the King Edward VI School and at Birmingham University, where he gained a first-class degree in classics (having taught himself Greek) and began an M.A. thesis on Thomas Hardy. After leaving the university in 1934, he tried teaching, like other British writers of the 1930s, but, like most of them, hated it and left to make his way as a freelance writer and critic. During World War II he served—"or rather *studied*," as he put it—in the Royal Army Ordnance Corps for a year. A notable mimic, he entertained friends with a comic imitation of a sergeant instructing new recruits. After a few performances he noticed that the words of the weapon-training instructor, couched in the style of the military manual, fell into certain rhythmic patterns. His fascination with these patterns eventually informed his *Lessons of the War*, the first of which, "Naming of Parts," is probably the most anthologized poem prompted by World War II.

From 1942 to 1945, Reed worked as a cryptographer and translator at the Government Code and Cypher School at Bletchley. In the evenings he wrote much of his first radio play—an adaptation of Melville's *Moby-Dick*—and many of the poems to be published in *A Map of Verona* (1946). After the war, he produced a number of other successful—and often funny—radio plays, verse translations of the Italian poet Giacomo Leopardi (1798–1837), and more poems. Many of the best of these were found in manuscript at his death, and with the posthumous publication of his *Collected Poems* (1991), he emerged as a writer whose lifelong quest for lasting homosexual love—which he never found—led him through Edenic landscapes of desire, like the setting of "Naming of Parts."

From Lessons of the War

To Alan Michell

Vixi duellis nuper idoneus
Et militavi non sine gloria[1]

1. Naming of Parts

Today we have naming of parts. Yesterday,
We had daily cleaning. And tomorrow morning,
We shall have what to do after firing. But today,
Today we have naming of parts. Japonica[2]
5   Glistens like coral in all of the neighbouring gardens,
     And today we have naming of parts.

This is the lower sling swivel. And this
Is the upper sling swivel, whose use you will see,
When you are given your slings. And this is the piling swivel,
10 Which in your case you have not got. The branches
Hold in the gardens their silent, eloquent gestures,
     Which in our case we have not got.

This is the safety-catch, which is always released
With an easy flick of the thumb. And please do not let me
15 See anyone using his finger. You can do it quite easy
If you have any strength in your thumb. The blossoms
Are fragile and motionless, never letting anyone see
     Any of them using their finger.

And this you can see is the bolt. The purpose of this
20 Is to open the breech, as you see. We can slide it
Rapidly backwards and forwards: we call this
Easing the spring.[3] And rapidly backwards and forwards
The early bees are assaulting and fumbling the flowers:
     They call it easing the Spring.

25 They call it easing the Spring: it is perfectly easy
If you have any strength in your thumb; like the bolt,
And the breech, and the cocking-piece, and the point of balance,
Which in our case we have not got; and the almond-blossom
Silent in all of the gardens and the bees going backwards and forwards,
30   For today we have naming of parts.

1945

1. "Lately I have lived in the midst of battles, creditably enough, / and have soldiered, not without glory" (Horace's *Odes* 3.26.1–2, with the *p* of *puellis*—girls—turned upside down to produce *duellis*—battles; an emendation that encap-sulates the theme of the *Lessons*).
2. A shrub with brilliant scarlet flowers.
3. Ejecting the bullets from the magazine of a rifle takes the pressure off the magazine spring.

KEITH DOUGLAS

K eith Douglas (1920–1944) was born in Tunbridge Wells, the son of a regular
army officer who had won the Military Cross in World War I and who, in 1927,
deserted his wife and son. Like Byron, whose army officer father died in the poet's
youth, Douglas developed an almost obsessive interest in warfare. At the age of ten
he wrote a poem about the Battle of Waterloo, and later, at Christ's Hospital School
in London, he divided his leisure time among developing his precocious talents as
poet and artist, riding, playing rugby football, and participating enthusiastically in
the Officer Cadet Corps. At Merton College, Oxford, he was tutored by Edmund
Blunden, a distinguished soldier poet of World War I. In 1940 Douglas enlisted in a
cavalry regiment that was soon obliged to exchange its horses for tanks, and in
August 1942 he went into battle against German field marshal Rommel's Africa
Corps in the Egyptian desert. Forced to remain in reserve behind the lines, Douglas
commandeered a truck and, disobeying orders, drove off to join his regiment.

His subsequent achievement as a poet and as the author of a brilliant memoir
of the desert campaign, *Alamein to Zem Zem* (published in 1966), was to celebrate
the last stand of the chivalric hero. His poem "Aristocrats" ends perhaps with a
distant echo of Roland's horn, sounded in the Pass of Roncevalles at the end of
the twelfth-century French epic *La Chanson de Roland* (*The Song of Roland*).
Douglas's poem succeeds where most of the would-be heroic poems of 1914 and
1915 fail. Sharply focused, it acknowledges both the stupidity and the chivalry,
the folly and the glamor of cavalrymen on mechanical mounts, dueling in the
desert. Douglas's language, spare and understated, responsive to his theme, fuses
ancient and modern: his heroes are "gentle"—like Chaucer's "verray parfit gentil
knight" in *The Canterbury Tales*—and at the same time "obsolescent."

Douglas survived the desert campaign, but was killed on the Normandy beaches
on June 9, 1944, three days after the D-Day landings.

Vergissmeinnicht[1]

Three weeks gone and the combatants gone
returning over the nightmare ground
we found the place again, and found
the soldier sprawling in the sun.

5   The frowning barrel of his gun
overshadowing. As we came on
that day, he hit my tank with one
like the entry of a demon.

Look. Here in the gunpit spoil
10   the dishonoured picture of his girl
who has put: *Steffi. Vergissmeinnicht*
in a copybook gothic script.

We see him almost with content,
abased, and seeming to have paid
15   and mocked at by his own equipment
that's hard and good when he's decayed.

---

1. Forget me not (German).

But she would weep to see today
how on his skin the swart° flies move;   *black*
the dust upon the paper eye
20   and the burst stomach like a cave.

For here the lover and killer are mingled
who had one body and one heart.
And death who had the soldier singled
has done the lover mortal hurt.

Tunisia, 1943   1944

Aristocrats[1]

"I think I am becoming a God"[2]

The noble horse with courage in his eye
clean in the bone, looks up at a shellburst:
away fly the images of the shires[3]
but he puts the pipe back in his mouth.

5   Peter was unfortunately killed by an 88.[4]
it took his leg away, he died in the ambulance.
I saw him crawling on the sand; he said
It's most unfair, they've shot my foot off.

How can I live among this gentle
10   obsolescent breed of heroes, and not weep?
Unicorns, almost,
for they are falling into two legends
in which their stupidity and chivalry
are celebrated. Each, fool and hero, will be an immortal.

15   The plains were their cricket pitch[5]
and in the mountains the tremendous drop fences[6]
brought down some of the runners. Here then
under the stones and earth they dispose themselves,
I think with their famous unconcern.
20   It is not gunfire I hear but a hunting horn.[7]

Enfidaville, Tunisia, 1943   1946

1. Another version of this poem is entitled "Sportsmen."
2. The dying words of Roman emperor Vespasian were supposedly "Alas! I suppose I am turning into a god."
3. Counties. Cf. Wilfred Owen's "Anthem for Doomed Youth," line 8 (p. 160).
4. A German gun that fired an 88-millimeter projectile.
5. Field on which the game of cricket is played.
6. Fences in a steeplechase horse race.
7. Lt. Col. J. D. Player, killed in Tunisia, Enfidaville, February 1943, left £3,000 to the Beaufort Hunt, and directed that the incumbent of the living in his gift [i.e., the church whose vicar he was entitled to appoint] should be a 'man who approves of hunting, shooting, and all manly sports, which are the backbone of the nation.' [Douglas's note on one of the manuscripts of "Aristocrats." Player was in fact killed in April.]

Nation, Race, and Language

A rmies and navies, cannons and guns helped spread and consolidate British rule across vast areas of the earth's surface, but so too did the English language. Over many years, in various parts of the world, the language of the British Empire displaced or commingled with indigenous languages. Then the twentieth century witnessed the decolonization and devolution of the British Empire—from early-century Ireland; to mid-century South Asia, Africa, and the Caribbean; to late-century Hong Kong. Those under colonial rule were often made to feel inferior because they had "a different complexion or slightly flatter noses," as Conrad's Marlow puts it in *Heart of Darkness*. When large numbers of nonwhite immigrants arrived in England after World War II, they were likely to find themselves stigmatized and discriminated against because of their race. Imaginative writers from the former colonies, as well as immigrants to Britain and their children, have thus had to wrestle with questions of nation, race, and language. Should they write stories, plays, and poems in the language and traditions of the colonizer, or should they repudiate English and return to their indigenous languages? Is English an enabling tool by which peoples of different races and nationalities can express their identities, or is it contaminated by a colonial history and racist mentality that it insidiously perpetuates? If English is chosen for imaginative writing, should it be the Standard English of the imperial center or an English inflected by contact with indigenous languages—creole, patois, or pidgin? Since the power of the United States has sustained the global reach of English long after the withdrawal of British colonial armies and administrators, debates over such questions have persisted in many parts of the world where English still thrives in the aftermath of a dead empire.

Postwar immigrants to Britain from its former colonies have also brought these once faraway issues home to the "mother country." On June 21, 1948, the first shipload of Caribbean immigrants, 492 passengers onboard the *Empire Windrush*, arrived at Tilbury Docks, near London. Many other black and Asian immigrants from the Caribbean, from Asia, and from Africa soon followed, diversifying Britain until peoples of ethnic minorities made up 12.9 percent of the total population in 2011. Between the 1948 British Nationality Act, which allowed British subjects to immigrate, and the 1968 measure limiting immigration to citizens of British (that is, white) family origin, hundreds of thousands of blacks and Asians were "colonizin / Englan in reverse," in Jamaican poet Louise Bennett's witty phrase.

Assuming they would be welcomed as full-fledged British subjects, many of these immigrants, arriving in search of jobs and educational opportunities, were surprised by the racial discrimination they encountered. Bearing with them the dream England of Shakespeare, public monuments, and English civilization—encapsulated in Jamaican poet Claude McKay's poem "Old England"—many of these immigrants were refused housing because of their race and consigned to jobs below their skill level. In "Englan Is a Bitch," black British poet Linton Kwesi Johnson relates the job woes of one such hapless immigrant. The British Pakistani writer Hanif Kureishi writes of being made to feel painfully embarrassed over his South Asian ethnicity. It is in this context that Salman Rushdie asserts the British Indian's right to lay claim to full membership in British society and to British, Indian, and a variety of transnational literary inheritances. From a "black" perspective, Daljit Nagra retells the *History of the English-Speaking Peoples*, as Winston Churchill titled his monumental chronicle, to make room for an Asian Briton's ambivalent participation in that history, as an insider-outsider who reinhabits an English literary canon centered on Shakespeare. Bernardine Evaristo goes back even further in time in *The Emperor's Babe*, to the

The *Windrush* arrives, June 21, 1948. The *Empire Windrush* brought 492 passengers from Kingston, Jamaica, to Tilbury Docks, near London. Since Britain had just passed the 1948 British Nationality Act that granted citizenship to colonial subjects, West Indians sailed to Britain, many in search of job opportunities. Although they met with discrimination upon arrival, a large number of the Caribbean migrants stayed, becoming the first members of what is sometimes called "the *Windrush* generation."

third century C.E., when African diasporic people like her were already living in Roman Londinium, contrary to the widespread misconception that Britain was racially homogeneous before 1948. Unmoored from the "calypso ways" of her native Guyana and feeling displaced in England's "misty greyness," immigrant poet Grace Nichols nevertheless declares, "Wherever I hang me knickers—that's my home." In her view, the new creolized English tongue she and other African Caribbeans have created after losing their African languages is a kind of linguistic home: "from the root of the old one / a new one has sprung."

Such issues of nation, race, and language have a deep history in Britain's colonies, and not only its far-flung possessions in the global South. Irish immigrants to Britain had long found themselves discriminated against as racial "others." In Ireland itself, the British, having tried to subdue the local people for centuries, outlawed the use of the Irish language (or Gaelic). Because of Ireland's long and bloody colonial history and the flowering there of cultural nationalism, early-twentieth-century Irish writers were already expressing a powerful ambivalence toward English as both a vital literary inheritance and the language of colonial subjugation. Recalling the sixteenth- and seventeenth-century English "wars of extermination" against the Irish, W. B. Yeats acknowledges a historical hatred of the English but then reminds himself that, as an English-language writer, "I owe my soul to Shakespeare, to Spenser and to Blake, perhaps to William Morris, and to the English language in which I think, speak and write, that everything I love has come to me through English; my hatred tortures me with love, my love with hate" (see his "Introduction," excerpted in this volume). In *A Portrait of the Artist as a Young Man*, James Joyce's autobiographical persona, Stephen Dedalus, reflects on his conversation with an academic dean, an Englishman: "The language in which we are speaking is his before it is mine. . . . I

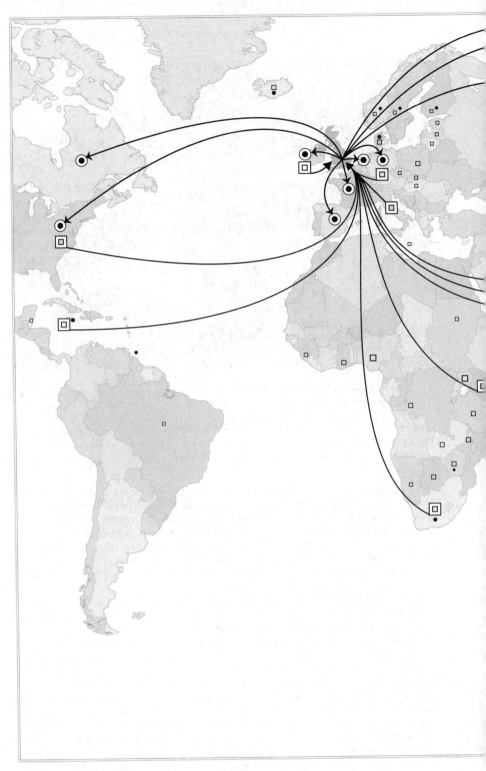

Having extended its dominion to nearly a quarter of the Earth's population and land area by 1914, the British Empire shrank following World War II and hundreds of thousands of people migrated from the former colonies to Britain. Immigrants from Asia, Africa, the Caribbean, and elsewhere diversified the United Kingdom. In 2011, ethnic minorities

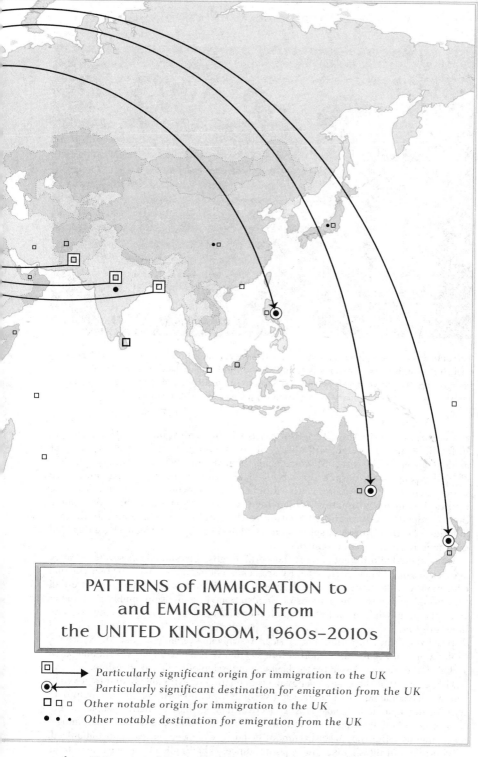

PATTERNS of IMMIGRATION to and EMIGRATION from the UNITED KINGDOM, 1960s–2010s

made up 12.9 percent of the total population, of whom 6.9 percent were Asian, 3 percent black, 2 percent mixed, and 1 percent "other." Most of the emigration has been in search of employment opportunities.

London, 1968. Young Asian immigrants with suitcases at a London airport. Holders of British nationality, Asians—mostly from Pakistan, India, Bangladesh, as well as Asian refugees from Africa—began new lives in Britain in the 1950s and 1960s, before tighter restrictions stemmed primary immigration from Commonwealth countries.

cannot speak or write these [English] words without unrest of spirit. His language, so familiar and so foreign, will always be for me an acquired speech. I have not made or accepted its words. My voice holds them at bay. My soul frets in the shadow of his language." Yet despite this vexed relation to the language, Yeats and Joyce wrote some of the most innovative English-language poetry and fiction of the twentieth century, ultimately influencing the very language that had so troubled them. Indeed, their conflicted relation to the English language and its literary inheritance—that "unrest of spirit" in its shadow—may, paradoxically, have impelled their massive literary achievements.

Transplanted to different parts of the world, English has sometimes seemed strange and estranging. When African and Caribbean schoolchildren with British colonial educations tried to write poems, as Kamau Brathwaite and other writers have attested, they would follow the conventions of English poetry, composing iambic pentameter verse about snowfall or daffodils, which they had never seen. English language and literature thus risked alienating colonized peoples from their local environments and distinctive cultural histories. The African Caribbean–Canadian poet M. NourbeSe Philip writes of English as a "mother tongue" that is also a strangely violent and patriarchal "father tongue," used for the brutal suppression of her slave ancestors.

The feeling that the English language is alienating, inextricably bound to colonialism, has led some nativist writers, such as the Kenyan novelist Ngũgĩ wa Thiong'o, to reject it outright. If language is a "collective memory bank," then a people cannot recover its colonially suppressed identity and history without returning to an indigenous language. But the novelist Salman Rushdie, who often writes in an Indianized, or "chutnified," English, takes the opposite stance: "The English language ceased to be the sole possession of the English some time ago," he asserts. English has become a local language even in parts of the world, such as India, where it was once imposed by colonial rulers. Rushdie and other cosmopolitan writers reject the assumption that the English language has an inherent relationship to only one kind of national or racial experience. "The English language is nobody's special property," asserts the Caribbean poet Derek Walcott. In her bravura, rap-inflected performance of poetic "acrobatics," Patience Agbabi demonstrates a black Briton's rights to the repossession of an imperial tongue.

For the colonial, postcolonial, or immigrant writer who embraces English, the question remains, Which English? The imported Standard or a local vernacular? Or if both, should they be intermingled or kept apart? At one end of the spectrum are writers, such as V. S. Naipaul, who think Standard English, perhaps slightly altered, can bespeak a postcolonial experience of race, identity, and history. At the other end are vernacular writers who feel that the language of the center cannot do justice to their experience at the margins of empire. Louise Bennett, for example, gives voice to everyday Jamaican experience in her witty and wily use of Jamaican Creole, or patois; she mocks its denigration as a "corruption of the English language," pointing out that Standard English is itself but an amalgam of dialects and foreign languages. "It was in language that the slave was perhaps most successfully imprisoned by his master," Kamau Brathwaite has written, "and it was in his (mis-)use of it that he perhaps most effectively rebelled." Linton Kwesi Johnson graphically emphasizes his resistance to the norms of Standard English by his phonetic (mis-)spelling of English words.

Between the Standard English writer and the vernacular writer range a host of fiction writers, such as Chinua Achebe, Caryl Phillips, and Zadie Smith, and poets, such as Walcott, Brathwaite, and Nichols, who switch between standard and "dialect" within or across individual works, creating juxtapositions, tensions, and new relationships between languages that have traditionally been kept hierarchically discrete. They linguistically embody their interstitial experience of living in between metropolis and margin, canon and creole, schoolbooks and the street.

Whether using slightly or heavily creolized English, or a medley of the two, writers from across the world—Barbadians and Bengalis and black Britons—have employed a diverse array of distinctive idioms, dialects, and creoles to defy imperial norms, express emerging cultural identities, and inaugurate rich new possibilities for literature in English.

CLAUDE McKAY

Claude McKay (1890–1948) was born into a poor farm-working family in Sunny Ville, Clarendon Parish, Jamaica, and spent the first half of his life on the British Caribbean island. He was apprenticed to a cabinetmaker and then a wheelwright and served for less than a year as a police constable in Kingston. An English linguist and folklorist, Walter Jekyll, encouraged him to write in Jamaican dialect, or Creole. Drawing on the example of the Scottish-dialect poet Robert Burns, McKay harnessed the Jamaican idiom in poems collected in two books published in 1912, *Constab Ballads* and *Songs of Jamaica*, including "Old England," a seemingly reverent imaginative journey, in a new literary language, to the imperial "homeland." The first major poet to make effective literary use of Jamaican English, he influenced many later African Caribbean poets who went further, such as Louise Bennett.

For his poetry McKay won a prize that enabled him to travel to the United States and study at Alabama's Tuskegee Institute and at Kansas State College, before moving to Harlem in 1914. Switching in his poetry from Jamaican to Standard English, he helped precipitate the Harlem Renaissance with his *Harlem Shadows* (1922), which included sonnets addressing the vexed racial experience of a Caribbean immigrant. For most of the 1920s and into the mid-1930s, McKay, identifying with the radical left, lived and wrote novels and short stories mainly in England, France, and Morocco. He died in poverty in Chicago, where he taught in his last years for a

Catholic youth organization. His sonnet "If We Must Die," written in response to the American antiblack riots of the summer of 1919, became a World War II rallying cry after Winston Churchill read it, without attribution, to the British people.

Old England

I've longin' in me dept's of heart dat I can conquer not,
'Tis a wish dat I've been havin' from since I could form a t'o't,°   *thought*
'Tis to sail athwart the ocean an' to hear de billows roar,
When dem ride aroun' de steamer,° when dem beat on   *steamship*
    England's shore.

5 Just to view de homeland England, in de streets of London walk,
An' to see de famous sights dem 'bouten which dere's so much talk,
An' to watch de fact'ry chimneys pourin' smoke up to de sky,
An' to see de matches-children, dat I hear 'bout, passin' by.[1]

I would see Saint Paul's Cathedral,[2] an' would hear some of de great
10 Learnin' comin' from de bishops, preachin' relics of old fait';
I would ope me mout' wid wonder at de massive organ soun',
An' would 'train me eyes to see de beauty lyin' all aroun'.

I'd go to de City Temple,[3] where de old fait' is a wreck,
An' de parson is a-preachin' views dat most folks will not tek;
15 I'd go where de men of science meet togeder in deir hall,
To give light unto de real truths, to obey king Reason's call.

I would view Westminster Abbey,[4] where de great of England sleep,
An' de solemn marble statues o'er deir ashes vigil keep;
I would see immortal Milton an' de wul'-famous Shakespeare,
20 Past'ral Wordswort', gentle Gray,[5] an' all de great souls buried dere.

I would see de ancient chair where England's kings deir crowns put on,
Soon to lay dem by again when all de vanity is done;
An' I'd go to view de lone spot where in peaceful solitude
Rests de body of our Missis Queen,[6] Victoria de Good.

25 An' dese places dat I sing of now shall afterwards impart
All deir solemn sacred beauty to a weary searchin' heart;
So I'll rest glad an' contented in me min'° for evermore,   *mind*
When I sail across de ocean back to my own native shore.

1912

1. Cf. the short story "The Little-Match Seller," by the Danish writer Hans Christian Andersen (1805–1875), and the poem "The Little Match Girl," by the Scottish writer William McGonagall (1830?–1902), both about a poor match-selling girl who freezes to death on New Year's Eve.
2. In London, cathedral of the Anglican bishop.
3. Victorian church in central London.
4. London church where monarchs are crowned and the famous, including poets, are buried.
5. Thomas Gray (1716–1771), English poet and author of "Elegy Written in a Country Churchyard."
6. So-called in Jamaica, Victoria reigned during the emancipation of slaves in 1837.

If We Must Die

If we must die, let it not be like hogs
Hunted and penned in an inglorious spot,
While round us bark the mad and hungry dogs,
Making their mock at our accursed lot.
5　If we must die, O let us nobly die,
So that our precious blood may not be shed
In vain; then even the monsters we defy
Shall be constrained to honor us though dead!
O kinsmen! we must meet the common foe!
10　Though far outnumbered let us show us brave,
And for their thousand blows deal one deathblow!
What though before us lies the open grave?
Like men we'll face the murderous, cowardly pack,
Pressed to the wall, dying, but fighting back!

1919, 1922

LOUISE BENNETT

Louise Bennett (1919–2006), the preeminent West Indian poet of Creole verse, was born and grew up in Kingston, Jamaica, in the British West Indies, her mother a dressmaker, her father a baker. After she had published her first book of poetry, *Dialect Verses* (1942), she attended London's Royal Academy of Dramatic Art. As "Miss Lou" she won a mass following in the Caribbean through her vibrant stage performances of her poetry and of folk song; her weekly "dialect" poems published from 1943 in Jamaica's national newspaper, the *Gleaner*; her radio show, "Miss Lou's Views" (1966–82); and her children's television program, "Ring Ding" (1970–82).

Bennett helped dismantle the view that Jamaican English is a corruption of Standard English, a prejudice she lambasted in radio monologues such as "Jamaica Language" and in poems such as "Dry-Foot Bwoy," which humorously juxtaposes a metaphor-rich Creole with a hollowly imitative British English. From a young age she felt that the humor, wit, and vigor of Creole were largely untapped possibilities for writing and performing poetry, even though this commitment to Jamaican English prevented her from being recognized as a poet until after the black cultural revolution of the late 1960s and 1970s. In her poetry she often assumes the perspective of a West Indian trickster, such as the woman who cunningly subverts gender and geographic hierarchies in "Jamaica Oman [Woman]." Bennett makes wily and ebullient use of received forms, employing the ironic possibilities of dramatic monologue, the contrasts and inversions afforded by the ballad stanza, and the time-tested wisdom and pith of Jamaican proverbs. Both on the page and in her recorded performances, Bennett's vital characters and robust imagination help win over readers unfamiliar with Jamaican English, who can join in the laughing seriousness of poems such as "Colonization in Reverse," which ironically inverts Britain's xenophobic apprehension at the postwar influx of Jamaican immigrants, while also casting a suspicious eye on some Jamaicans' reverse exploitation of their exploiters. No one is safe from the multiple ironies and carnivalesque irreverence of Bennett's verse.

Jamaica Language[1]

Listen, na!

My Aunty Roachy seh dat it bwile[2] her temper an really bex[3] her fi true anytime she hear anybody a style we Jamaican dialec as "corruption of the English language." For if dat be de case, den dem shoulda call English Language corruption of Norman French an Latin an all dem tarra[4] language what dem seh dat English is derived from.

Oonoo[5] hear de wud? "Derived." English is a derivation but Jamaica Dialec is corruption! What a unfairity!

Aunty Roachy seh dat if Jamaican Dialec is corruption of de English Language, den it is also a corruption of de African Twi Language to, a oh!

For Jamaican Dialec did start when we English forefahders did start musanboun[6] we African ancestors fi stop talk fi-dem African Language altogedder an learn fi talk so-so[7] English, because we English forefahders couldn understan what we African ancestors-dem wasa seh to dem one anodder when dem wasa talk eena dem African Language to dem one annodder!

But we African ancestors-dem pop[8] we English forefahders-dem. Yes! Pop dem an disguise up de English Language fi projec fi-dem African Language in such a way dat we English forefahders-dem still couldn understan what we African ancestors-dem wasa talk bout when dem wasa talk to dem one annodder!

Yes, bwoy!

So till now, aldoah plenty a we Jamaica Dialec wuds-dem come from English wuds, yet, still an for all, de talkin is so-so Jamaican, an when we ready we can meck it soun like it no got no English at all eena it! An no so-so English-talkin smaddy cyaan[9] understan weh we a seh if we doan want dem to understan weh we a seh, a oh!

An we fix up we dialec wud fi soun like whatsoever we a talk bout, look like! For instance, when we seh sinting "kooroo-kooroo"[1] up, yuh know seh dat it mark-up mark-up. An if we seh one house "rookoo-rookoo"[2] up, it is plain to see dat it ole an shaky-shaky. An when we seh smaddy "boogoo-yagga," everybody know seh dat him outa-order; an if we seh dem "boonoonoonoos,"[3] yuh know seh dat dem nice an we like dem. Mmmm.

Aunty Roachy seh dat Jamaica Dialec is more direc an to de point dan English. For all like how English smaddy would seh "Go away," Jamaican jus seh "Gweh!" An de only time we use more wuds dan English is when we want fi meck someting soun strong: like when dem seh sinting "batter-batter" up, it soun more expressive dan if yuh seh "it is battered." But most of all we fling weh all de bangarang an trimmins[4]-dem an only lef what wantin, an dat's why when English smaddy seh "I got stuck by a prickle" Jamaican jus seh "Macca[5] jook me"!

---

1. Originally broadcast sometime between 1979 and 1981, this radio monologue has been reprinted from *Aunty Roachy Seh* (1993), ed. Mervyn Morris.
2. Boils.
3. Vexes.
4. Other.
5. You (plural).
6. Compel.
7. Only.

8. Outwitted.
9. Can't. "Smaddy": people.
1. Rough; rocky. "Sinting": something.
2. Unsteady.
3. Beautiful; wonderful (term of endearment). "Boogoo-yagga": ill-mannered.
4. Miscellaneous trash and trimmings.
5. A prickly plant.

So fi-we Jamaica Language is not no English Language corruption at all, a oh! An we no haffi shame a it, like one gal who did go a Englan go represent we Jamaican folk-song "One shif me got" as "De sole underwear garment I possess," and go sing "Mumma, Mumma, dem ketch Puppa" as "Mother, Mother, they apprehended Father"!

Ay ya yie!

1979–81   1993

Dry-Foot Bwoy[1]

Wha wrong wid Mary dry-foot bwoy?
Dem gal got him fi mock,°   *The girls are mocking him*
An when me meet him tarra night
De bwoy gi me a shock!

5   Me tell him seh him auntie an
Him cousin dem sen howdy[2]
An ask him how him getting awn.
Him seh, 'Oh, jolley, jolley!'

Me start fi feel so sorry fi
10   De po bad-lucky soul,
Me tink him come a foreign lan
Come ketch bad foreign cole!

Me tink him got a bad sore-troat,
But as him chat-chat gwan
15   Me fine out seh is foreign twang
De bwoy wasa put awn![3]

For me notice dat him answer
To nearly all me seh
Was 'Actually', 'What', 'Oh deah!'
20   An all dem sinting deh.°   *All of them things there*

Me gi a joke, de gal dem laugh;
But hear de bwoy, 'Haw-haw!
I'm sure you got that bally-dash°   *nonsense, balderdash*
Out of the cinema!'

25   Same time me laas me temper, an
Me holler, 'Bwoy, kirout!°   *clear out*
No chat to me wid no hot pittata
Eena yuh mout!'

Him tan° up like him stunted, den   *stand*
30   Hear him no, 'How silley!

---

1. Thin-legged (inexperienced) boy.
2. I told him that his auntie and his cousins sent [or send] greetings.

3. But as he kept talking I realized his foreign accent was put on.

I don't think that I really
Understand you, actually.'

Me seh, 'Yuh understan me, yaw!
No yuh name Cudjoe Scoop?
35   Always visit Nana kitchen an
Gi laugh fi gungoo soup!⁴

'An now all yuh can seh is "actually"?
Bwoy, but tap!
Wha happen to dem sweet Jamaica
40   Joke yuh use fi pop?'

Him get bex° and walk tru de door,   *vexed*
Him head eena de air;
De gal-dem bawl out affa him,⁵
'Not going? What! Oh deah!'

45   An from dat night till tedeh, mah,
Dem all got him fi mock.
Miss Mary dry-foot bwoy!
Cyaan get over de shock!

1957

Colonization in Reverse

What a joyful news, Miss Mattie;
Ah feel like me heart gwine burs—
Jamaica people colonizin
Englan in reverse.¹

5   By de hundred, by de tousan,
From country an from town,
By de ship-load, by de plane-load,
Jamaica is Englan boun.

Dem a pour out a Jamaica;
10   Everybody future plan
Is fi get a big-time job
An settle in de motherlan.

What a islan! What a people!
Man an woman, ole an young
15   Jussa pack dem bag an baggage
An tun history upside dung!°   *down*

---

4. Chastising the boy for his pretensions, the speaker reminds him that he is African Jamaican. Cudjoe and Nana are African names used in Jamaica. "Gungoo": congo pea.
5. The girls went crying after him.

1. Encouraged by the postwar labor shortage in England and the scarcity of work at home, three hundred thousand West Indians migrated to Britain from 1948 to 1962.

Some people doan like travel,
But fi show dem loyalty
Dem all a open up cheap-fare-
20   To-Englan agency;

An week by week dem shippin off
Dem countryman like fire
Fi immigrate an populate
De seat a de Empire.

25   Oonoo° se how life is funny,   *you (plural)*
Oonoo see de tunabout?
Jamaica live fi box bread
Out a English people mout.

For when dem catch a Englan
30   An start play dem different role
Some will settle down to work
An some will settle fi de dole.°   *for unemployment benefits*

Jane seh de dole is not too bad
Because dey payin she
35   Two pounds a week fi seek a job
Dat suit her dignity.

Me seh Jane will never fine work
At de rate how she dah look
For all day she stay pon Aunt Fan couch
40   An read love-story book.

What a devilment a Englan!
Dem face war an brave de worse;
But ah wonderin how dem gwine stan
Colonizin in reverse.

1957

Jamaica Oman[1]

Jamaica oman cunny, sah!°   *cunning, sir*
Is how dem jinnal so?°   *how are they so tricky?*
Look how long dem liberated
An de man dem never know!

5   Look how long Jamaica oman
—Modder, sister, wife, sweetheart—
Outa road an eena yard° deh pon   *home*
A dominate her part!

1. Woman.

From Maroon Nanny[2] teck her body
10 Bounce bullet back pon man,
To when nowadays gal-pickney° tun   *girl-child*
Spellin-Bee champion.

From de grass root to de hill-top,
In profession, skill an trade,
15 Jamaica oman teck her time
Dah mount an meck de grade.

Some backa man a push, some side-a
Man a hole him han,
Some a lick sense eena man head,
20 Some a guide him pon him plan!

Neck an neck an foot an foot wid man
She buckle hole° her own;   *she take hold*
While man a call her 'so-so rib'
Oman a tun backbone![3]

25 An long before Oman Lib[4] bruck out
Over foreign lan
Jamaica female wasa work
Her liberated plan!

Jamaica oman know she strong,
30 She know she tallawah,°   *sturdy*
But she no want her pickney° dem   *children*
Fi start call her 'Puppa'.°   *Papa*

So de cunny Jamma° oman   *Jamaican*
Gwan like pants-suit is a style,
35 An Jamaica man no know she wear
De trousiz all de while!

So Jamaica oman coaxin
Fambly budget from explode
A so Jamaica man a sing
40 'Oman a heaby load!'[5]

But de cunny Jamma oman
Ban her belly,[6] bite her tongue,
Ketch water, put pot pon fire
An jus dig her toe a grung.[7]

45 For 'Oman luck deh a dungle',[8]
Some rooted more dan some,

---

2. Jamaican national hero who led the Maroons, fugitive slaves, in battle during the 18th century. Bullets reputedly ricocheted off her and killed her enemies.
3. Eve is said to have come from Adam's rib (Genesis 2.21–22).
4. Women's liberation movement.

5. A folk song often sung while working in the fields.
6. Binds her belly (a practice associated with grief; also a suggestion of belt tightening, as in hunger).
7. And just digs her toes into the ground.
8. I.e., woman's luck will be rediscovered (proverbial). "Dungle": garbage dump.

But as long as fowl a scratch dungle heap
Oman luck mus come!

Lickle by lickle man start praise her,
50   Day by day de praise a grow;
So him praise her, so it sweet her,
For she wonder if him know.

1975

KAMAU BRATHWAITE

As a poet and historian, Kamau Brathwaite (b. 1930) has been the most prominent West Indian spokesman for "the literature of reconnection": he has sought to recover and revalue the African inheritance in the Caribbean—a religious, linguistic, and cultural legacy seen as embarrassing or taboo through most of the twentieth century. In *History of the Voice*, a lecture first delivered in 1979, Brathwaite argues that African Caribbeans, their ancestors uprooted by slavery, were further cut off from their specific history and their local environment by Standard English models of language and literature. He proposes "nation language," a creolized English saturated with African words, rhythms, even grammar, as a crucial tool for writers to recuperate African Caribbean history and experience. His own poetry draws on West Indian syncopations, orality, and musical traditions, but also adapts imported models, such as the modernist dislocations of persona, rhythm, and tone in T. S. Eliot's verse.

He was born Lawson Edward Brathwaite in Bridgetown, Barbados, at the eastern edge of the West Indies. His undergraduate studies in history were at Cambridge University; his graduate studies, at the University of Sussex. He worked as an education officer for the Ministry of Education in Ghana (1955–62) and taught history at the University of the West Indies, before taking a position in comparative literature at New York University in 1991. His many books of poetry include a work of epic scope and scale, *The Arrivants: A New World Trilogy* (1973), which gathers *Rights of Passage* (1967), *Masks* (1968), and *Islands* (1969).

[Nation Language][1]

What I am going to talk about this morning is language from the Caribbean, the process of using English in a different way from the "norm". English in a new sense as I prefer to call it. English in an ancient sense. English in a very traditional sense. And sometimes not English at all, but *language*.

I start my thoughts, taking up from the discussion that developed after Dennis Brutus's[2] very excellent presentation. Without logic, and through instinct, the people who spoke with Dennis from the floor yesterday brought

1. First printed separately in 1984, Brathwaite's lecture *History of the Voice* was slightly modified and incorporated in his essay collection *Roots* (1986, 1993), from which this selection is excerpted.
2. South African poet (1924–2009).

up the question of language. * * * In his case, it was English, and English as spoken by Africans, and the native languages as spoken by Africans.

We in the Caribbean have a similar kind of plurality: we have English, which is the imposed language on much of the archipelago. English is an imperial language, as are French, Dutch, and Spanish. We have what we call creole English, which is a mixture of English and an adaptation that English took in the new environment of the Caribbean when it became mixed with the other imported languages. We have also what is called *nation language*, which is the kind of English spoken by the people who were brought to the Caribbean, not the official English now, but the language of slaves and labourers, the servants who were brought in by the conquistadors. Finally, we have the remnants of ancestral languages still persisting in the Caribbean. There is Amerindian, which is active in certain parts of Central America but not in the Caribbean because the Amerindians are a destroyed people, and their languages were practically destroyed. We have Hindi, spoken by some of the more traditional East Indians who live in the Caribbean, and there are also varieties of Chinese. And, miraculously, there are survivals of African languages still persisting in the Caribbean. So we have that spectrum—that prism—of languages similar to the kind of structure that Dennis described for South Africa. Now, I have to give you some kind of background to the development of these languages, the historical development of this plurality, because I can't take it for granted that you know and understand the history of the Caribbean.

The Caribbean is a set of islands stretching out from Florida in a mighty curve. You must know of the Caribbean at least from television, at least now with hurricane David[3] coming right into it. The islands stretch out on an arc of some two thousand miles from Florida through the Atlantic to the South American coast, and they were originally inhabited by Amerindian people, Taino, Siboney, Carib, Arawak. In 1492, Columbus "discovered" (as it is said) the Caribbean, and with that discovery came the intrusion of European culture and peoples and a fragmentation of the original Amerindian culture. We had Europe "nationalizing" itself into Spanish, French, English and Dutch so that people had to start speaking (and *thinking*) in four metropolitan languages rather than possibly a single native language. Then, with the destruction of the Amerindians, which took place within 30 years of Columbus' discovery (one million dead a year), it was necessary for the Europeans to import new labour bodies into the Caribbean. And the most convenient form of labour was the labour on the very edge of the trade winds—the labour on the edge of the *slave* trade winds, the labour on the edge of the hurricane, the labour on the edge of West Africa—. And so the peoples of Ashanti,[4] Congo, Nigeria, from all that mighty coast of western Africa were imported into the Caribbean. And we had the arrival in that area of a new language structure. It consisted of many languages, but basically they had a common semantic and stylistic form. What these languages had to do, however, was to submerge themselves, because officially the conquering peoples—the Spaniards, the English, the French, and the Dutch— did not wish to hear people speaking Ashanti or any of the Congolese languages. So there was a submergence of this imported language. Its status became one of inferiority. Similarly, its speakers were slaves. They were

---

3. A hurricane that killed over 2,000 people in the Caribbean in August 1979.
4. Region in present-day central Ghana.

conceived of as inferiors—nonhuman, in fact—. But this very submergence served an interesting intercultural purpose, because although people continued to speak English as it was spoken in Elizabethan times and on through the Romantic and Victorian ages, that English was, nonetheless, still being influenced by the underground language, the submerged language that the slaves had brought. And that underground language was itself constantly transforming itself into new forms. It was moving from a purely African form to a form that was African, but which was adapting to the new environment and to the cultural imperatives of the European languages. And it was influencing the way in which the French, Dutch, and Spanish spoke their own languages. So there was a very complex process taking place which is now beginning to surface in our literature.

In the Caribbean, as in South Africa (and in any area of cultural imperialism for that matter), the educational system did not recognize the presence of these various languages. What our educational system did was to recognize and maintain the language of the conquistador—the language of the planter, the language of the official, the language of the Anglican preacher—. It insisted that not only would English be spoken in the anglophone Caribbean, but that the educational system would carry the contours of an English heritage. Hence, as Dennis said, Shakespeare, George Eliot, Jane Austen—British literature and literary forms, the models that were intimate to Great Britain, that had very little to do, really, with the environment and the reality of the Caribbean—were dominant in the Caribbean educational system. People were forced to learn things that had no relevance to themselves. Paradoxically, in the Caribbean (as in many other "cultural disaster" areas), the people educated in this system came to know more, even today, about English kings and queens than they do about our own national heroes, our own slave rebels—the people who helped to build and to destroy our society—. We are more excited by English literary models, by the concept of, say, Sherwood Forest and Robin Hood, than we are by Nanny of the Maroons,[5] a name some of us didn't even know until a few years ago. And in terms of what we write, our perceptual models, we are more conscious (in terms of sensibility) of the falling of snow for instance—the models are all there for the falling of the snow—than of the force of the hurricanes that take place every year. In other words, we haven't got the syllables, the syllabic intelligence, to describe the hurricane, which is our own experience; whereas we can describe the imported alien experience of the snowfall. It is that kind of situation that we are in.

Now the creole adaptation to all this is the child who, instead of writing in an essay "The snow was falling on the fields of Shropshire"[6] (which is what our children literally were writing until a few years ago, below drawings they made of white snow fields and the corn-haired people who inhabited such a landscape), wrote "The snow was falling on the cane fields." The child had not yet reached the obvious statement that it wasn't snow at all, but rain that was probably falling on the cane fields. She was trying to have both cultures at the same time. But that is creolization.

5. The Maroons were Africans and escaped slaves who, after running away or participating in successful rebellions, set up autonomous societies throughout plantation America in marginal and certainly inaccessible areas outside European influence. . . . Nanny of the Maroons, an ex-Ashanti (?) Queen Mother, is regarded as one of the greatest of the Jamaican freedom fighters [Brathwaite's note].

6. Region of western England on the Welsh border, written about by the English poet A. E. Housman (1859–1936).

What is even more important, as we develop this business of emergent language in the Caribbean, is the actual rhythm and the syllables, the very body work, in a way, of the language. What English has given us as a model for poetry, and to a lesser extent, prose (but poetry is the basic tool here), is the pentameter: "The curfew tolls the knell of parting day."[7] There have, of course, been attempts to break it. And there were other dominant forms like, for example, *Beowulf* (c. 750), *The Seafarer*,[8] and what Langland (1322?–1400) had produced:

> For trewthe telleth that love. is triacle of hevene;
> May no synne be on him sene. that useth that spise,
> And alle his werkes he wrougte. with love as him liste.

Or, from *Piers the Plowman* (which does not make it into *Palgrave's Golden Treasury*,[9] but which we all had to "do" at school) the haunting prologue:

> In a somer seson. whan soft was the sonne
> I shope me into shroudes. as I a shepe were

Which has recently inspired our own Derek Walcott to his first major nation language effort:

> In idle August, while the sea soft,
> and leaves of brown islands stick to the rim
> of this Caribbean, I blow out the light
> by the dreamless face of Maria Concepcion
> to ship as a seaman on the schooner Flight.[1]

But by the time we reach Chaucer (1345–1400), the pentameter prevails. Over in the New World, the Americans—Walt Whitman—tried to bridge or to break the pentameter through a cosmic movement, a large movement of sound. Cummings tried to fragment it. And Marianne Moore attacked it with syllabics.[2] But basically the pentameter remained, and it carries with it a certain kind of experience, which is not the experience of a hurricane. The hurricane does not roar in pentameter. And that's the problem: how do you get a rhythm that approximates the natural experience, the environmental experience. We have been trying to break out of the entire pentametric model in the Caribbean and to move into a system that more closely and intimately approaches our own experience. So that is what we are talking about now.

It is nation language in the Caribbean that, in fact, largely ignores the pentameter. Nation language is the language that is influenced very strongly by the African model, the African aspect of our New World/Caribbean heritage. English it may be in terms of its lexicon, but it is not English in terms of its syntax. And English it certainly is not in terms of its rhythm and timbre, its own sound explosion. In its contours, it is not English, even though the words, as you hear them, would be English to a greater or lesser degree. And this brings us back to the question that some of you raised yester-

7. The opening line of "Elegy Written in a Country Churchyard," by the English poet Thomas Gray (1716–1771).
8. Poem in Old English.
9. Collection of songs and lyric poems published in London. *Piers the Plowman*: Middle English poem believed to have been written by William

Langland (ca. 1330–1387).
1. Beginning of "The Schooner *Flight*," by the Saint Lucian poet Derek Walcott (1930–2017).
2. Verses based on the number of syllables, not accents, in a line. E. E. Cummings (1894–1962), American poet. Marianne Moore (1887–1972), American poet.

day: can English be a revolutionary language? And the lovely answer that came back was: it is not English that is the agent. It is not language, but people, who make revolutions.

I think, however, that language does really have a role to play here, certainly in the Caribbean. But it is an English that is not the standard, imported, educated English, but that of the submerged, surrealist experience and sensibility, which has always been there and which is now increasingly coming to the surface and influencing the perception of contemporary Caribbean people. It is what I call, as I say, *nation language.* I use the term in contrast to *dialect.* The word dialect has been bandied about for a long time, and it carries very pejorative overtones. Dialect is thought of as "bad" English. Dialect is "inferior" English. Dialect is the language when you want to make fun of someone. Caricature speaks in dialect. Dialect has a long history coming from the plantation where people's dignity was distorted through their languages and the descriptions that the dialect gave to them. Nation language, on the other hand, is the submerged area of that dialect that is much more closely allied to the African aspect of experience in the Caribbean. It may be in English, but often it is in an English which is like a howl, or a shout, or a machine-gun, or the wind, or a wave. It is also like the blues. And sometimes it is English and African at the same time.

✻ ✻ ✻

The mainstream poets who were moving from standard English to nation language were influenced basically, I think (again the models are important), by T. S. Eliot. What T. S. Eliot did for Caribbean poetry and Caribbean literature was to introduce the notion of the speaking voice, the conversational tone.[3] That is what really attracted us to Eliot. And you can see how the Caribbean poets introduced here have been influenced by him, although they eventually went on to create their own environmental expression.

✻ ✻ ✻

1979–81   1984, 1986

---

3. For those of us who really made the breakthrough, it was Eliot's actual voice—or rather his recorded voice, property of the British Council (Barbados)—reading "Preludes," "The Love Song of J. Alfred Prufrock," *The Waste Land,* and later the *Four Quartets*—not the texts—which turned us on. In that dry deadpan delivery, the "riddims" of St. Louis (though we did not know the source then) were stark and clear for those of us who at the same time were listening to the dislocations of Bird, Dizzy, and Klook. And it is interesting that, on the whole, the establishment could not stand Eliot's voice—and far less jazz [Brathwaite's note]. Bird: American jazz musician Charlie "Bird" Parker (1920–1955). Dizzy: American jazz trumpeter Dizzy Gillespie (1917–1993). Klook: American jazz drummer Kenny Clarke (1914–1985).

Calypso[1]

1

The stone had skidded arc'd and bloomed into islands:
Cuba and San Domingo
Jamaica and Puerto Rico
Grenada Guadeloupe Bonaire[2]

5   curved stone hissed into reef
wave teeth fanged into clay
white splash flashed into spray
Bathsheba Montego Bay[3]

bloom of the arcing summers . . .

2

10   The islands roared into green plantations
ruled by silver sugar cane
sweat and profit
cutlass profit
islands ruled by sugar cane

15   And of course it was a wonderful time
a profitable hospitable well-worth-your-time
when captains carried receipts for rices
letters spices wigs
opera glasses swaggering asses
20   debtors vices pigs

O it was a wonderful time
an elegant benevolent redolent time—
and young Mrs. P.'s quick irrelevant crime
at four o'clock in the morning . . .

3

25   But what of black Sam
with the big splayed toes
and the shoe black shiny skin?

He carries bucketfulls of water
'cause his Ma's just had another daughter.

30   And what of John with the European name
who went to school and dreamt of fame
his boss one day called him a fool
and the boss hadn't even been to school . . .

1. Type of folk song originating in Trinidad, often involving commentary on current events and improvised wordplay with syncopated rhythms. This poem is from *Rights of Passage*, the first of three books collected as *The Arrivants*.
2. Caribbean islands. The first two stanzas sug-gest a creation myth in which the islands are formed in a rock-skipping game called ducks and drakes.
3. Jamaican city and tourist resort. "Bathsheba": seaside resort in Barbados.

4

Steel drum steel drum
35   hit the hot calypso dancing
hot rum hot rum
who goin' stop this bacchanalling?[4]

For we glance the banjo
dance the limbo
40   grow our crops by maljo[5]

have loose morals
gather corals
father our neighbour's quarrels

perhaps when they come
45   with their cameras and straw
hats: sacred pink tourists from the frozen Nawth

we should get down to those
white beaches
where if we don't wear breeches

50   it becomes an island dance
Some people doin' well
while others are catchin' hell

o the boss gave our Johnny the sack
though we beg him please
55   please to take 'im back

so the boy now nigratin' overseas . . .

1967

4. From *Bacchanalia*: festival of Bacchus, the Roman god of wine, celebrated with song, dancing, and revelry.

5. Evil eye (Trinidadian dialect; from the French *mal yeux*, "evil eyes").

NGŨGĨ WA THIONG'O

Ngũgĩ wa Thiong'o (b. 1938) was born in Limuru, Kenya, where his father was a peasant farmer. He was educated at the Alliance High School in Kikuyu, Kenya; Makerere University in Kampala, Uganda; and Leeds University in England. In the late 1960s, while teaching at University College, Nairobi, Kenya, he was one of the prime movers behind the abolition of the college's English department, arguing for its replacement by a Department of African Literature and Languages (two departments were formed, one of literature, the other of language). His novels include *Weep Not, Child* (1964), about the 1950s Mau Mau rebellion against British rule in Kenya, *A Grain of Wheat* (1967), about the war's aftermath, and *Petals of Blood* (1977), about the failure of the East African state, and he has written plays and novels in his native Gĩkũyũ, also sharply critical of post-independence Kenya, such as the novel *Matigarima Njiruungi* (1986). In 1982, after his imprisonment in Kenya and the banning of his books there, Ngũgĩ left to teach abroad, most recently at New York University.

At the beginning of *Decolonising the Mind* (1986), Ngũgĩ declares the book "my farewell to English as a vehicle for any of my writings. From now on it is Gĩkũyũ and Kiswahili all the way." Although Ngũgĩ has subsequently modified this position, he lays out starkly the case against English language and literature as tools of colonialism, which continue to have insidious effects long after formal decolonization. As the student of a British colonial education, Ngũgĩ came to feel that, because of the close relation between language and cultural memory, the imposition of English language and literature severs colonized peoples from their cultural experience—an experience best recovered and explored in indigenous languages.

From Decolonising the Mind

From *The Language of African Literature*

III

I was born into a large peasant family: father, four wives and about twenty-eight children. I also belonged, as we all did in those days, to a wider extended family and to the community as a whole.

We spoke Gĩkũyũ[1] as we worked in the fields. We spoke Gĩkũyũ in and outside the home. I can vividly recall those evenings of story-telling around the fireside. It was mostly the grown-ups telling the children but everybody was interested and involved. We children would re-tell the stories the following day to other children who worked in the fields picking the pyrethrum flowers,[2] tea-leaves or coffee beans of our European and African landlords.

The stories, with mostly animals as the main characters, were all told in Gĩkũyũ. Hare, being small, weak but full of innovative wit and cunning, was our hero. We identified with him as he struggled against the brutes of prey like lion, leopard, hyena. His victories were our victories and we learnt that the apparently weak can outwit the strong. We followed the animals in their struggle against hostile nature—drought, rain, sun, wind—a confrontation often forcing them to search for forms of co-operation. But we were also interested in their struggles amongst themselves, and particularly between the beasts and the victims of prey. These twin struggles, against nature and other animals, reflected real-life struggles in the human world.

Not that we neglected stories with human beings as the main characters. There were two types of characters in such human-centred narratives: the species of truly human beings with qualities of courage, kindness, mercy, hatred of evil, concern for others; and a man-eat-man two-mouthed species with qualities of greed, selfishness, individualism and hatred of what was good for the larger co-operative community. Co-operation as the ultimate

---

1. Bantu language spoken in western Kenya by approximately five million people.

2. Flower used to produce a natural insecticide.

good in a community was a constant theme. It could unite human beings with animals against ogres and beasts of prey, as in the story of how dove, after being fed with castor-oil seeds, was sent to fetch a smith working far away from home and whose pregnant wife was being threatened by these man-eating two-mouthed ogres.

There were good and bad story-tellers. A good one could tell the same story over and over again, and it would always be fresh to us, the listeners. He or she could tell a story told by someone else and make it more alive and dramatic. The differences really were in the use of words and images and the inflexion of voices to effect different tones.

We therefore learnt to value words for their meaning and nuances. Language was not a mere string of words. It had a suggestive power well beyond the immediate and lexical meaning. Our appreciation of the suggestive magical power of language was reinforced by the games we played with words through riddles, proverbs, transpositions of syllables, or through nonsensical but musically arranged words. So we learnt the music of our language on top of the content. The language, through images and symbols, gave us a view of the world, but it had a beauty of its own. The home and the field were then our pre-primary school but what is important, for this discussion, is that the language of our evening teach-ins, and the language of our immediate and wider community, and the language of our work in the fields were one.

And then I went to school, a colonial school, and this harmony was broken. The language of my education was no longer the language of my culture. I first went to Kamaandura, missionary run, and then to another called Maanguuū run by nationalists grouped around the Gīkūyū Independent and Karinga Schools Association. Our language of education was still Gīkūyū. The very first time I was ever given an ovation for my writing was over a composition in Gīkūyū. So for my first four years there was still harmony between the language of my formal education and that of the Limuru peasant community.

It was after the declaration of a state of emergency over Kenya in 1952[3] that all the schools run by patriotic nationalists were taken over by the colonial regime and were placed under District Education Boards chaired by Englishmen. English became the language of my formal education. In Kenya, English became more than a language: it was *the* language, and all the others had to bow before it in deference.

Thus one of the most humiliating experiences was to be caught speaking Gīkūyū in the vicinity of the school. The culprit was given corporal punishment—three to five strokes of the cane on bare buttocks—or was made to carry a metal plate around the neck with inscriptions such as I AM STUPID or I AM A DONKEY. Sometimes the culprits were fined money they could hardly afford. And how did the teachers catch the culprits? A button was initially given to one pupil who was supposed to hand it over to whoever was caught speaking his mother tongue. Whoever had the button at the end of the day would sing who had given it to him and the ensuing process would bring out all the culprits of the day. Thus children were turned

---

3. The Mau Mau, militant African nationalists, led a revolt in 1952 that resulted in four years of British military operations and the deaths of more than 11,000 insurgents.

into witch-hunters and in the process were being taught the lucrative value of being a traitor to one's immediate community.

The attitude to English was the exact opposite: any achievement in spoken or written English was highly rewarded; prizes, prestige, applause; the ticket to higher realms. English became the measure of intelligence and ability in the arts, the sciences, and all the other branches of learning. English became *the* main determinant of a child's progress up the ladder of formal education.

As you may know, the colonial system of education in addition to its apartheid racial demarcation had the structure of a pyramid: a broad primary base, a narrowing secondary middle, and an even narrower university apex. Selections from primary into secondary were through an examination, in my time called Kenya African Preliminary Examination, in which one had to pass six subjects ranging from Maths to Nature Study and Kiswahili.[4] All the papers were written in English. Nobody could pass the exam who failed the English language paper no matter how brilliantly he had done in the other subjects. I remember one boy in my class of 1954 who had distinctions in all subjects except English, which he had failed. He was made to fail the entire exam. He went on to become a turn boy[5] in a bus company. I who had only passes but a credit in English got a place at the Alliance High School, one of the most elitist institutions for Africans in colonial Kenya. The requirements for a place at the University, Makerere University College,[6] were broadly the same: nobody could go on to wear the undergraduate red gown, no matter how brilliantly they had performed in all the other subjects unless they had a credit—not even a simple pass!—in English. Thus the most coveted place in the pyramid and in the system was only available to the holder of an English language credit card. English was the official vehicle and the magic formula to colonial elitedom.

Literary education was now determined by the dominant language while also reinforcing that dominance. Orature (oral literature) in Kenyan languages stopped. In primary school I now read simplified Dickens and Stevenson alongside Rider Haggard. Jim Hawkins, Oliver Twist, Tom Brown—not Hare, Leopard and Lion—were now my daily companions in the world of imagination.[7] In secondary school, Scott and G. B. Shaw vied with more Rider Haggard, John Buchan, Alan Paton, Captain W. E. Johns.[8] At Makerere I read English: from Chaucer to T. S. Eliot with a touch of Graham Greene.[9]

Thus language and literature were taking us further and further from ourselves to other selves, from our world to other worlds.

✳   ✳   ✳

4. Swahili, a Bantu language that is the most widely understood language in Africa.
5. I.e., the person who operates a turnstile.
6. University in Kampala, Uganda, that was connected with the University of London in the 1950s and 1960s.
7. The English novelist Charles Dickens (1812–1870) wrote *Oliver Twist*. Jim Hawkins is the hero of *Treasure Island*, by the Scottish fiction writer and essayist Robert Louis Stevenson (1850–1894). The English novelist Rider Haggard (1856–1925) wrote African adventure stories. *Tom Brown's Schooldays* is by the English novelist Thomas Hughes (1822–1896).
8. Sir Walter Scott (1771–1832), Scottish novelist. George Bernard Shaw (1856–1950), Anglo-Irish dramatist. John Buchan (1875–1940), Scottish author of adventure stories. Alan Paton (1903–1988), South African novelist. William Earl Johns (1893–1968), English author of children's fiction.
9. Geoffrey Chaucer (ca. 1343–1400), English poet. T. S. Eliot (1888–1965), Anglo-American poet. Graham Greene (1904–1991), English novelist. "Read": here "majored in."

IV

* * *

Language carries culture, and culture carries, particularly through orature and literature, the entire body of values by which we come to perceive our-selves and our place in the world. How people perceive themselves affects how they look at their culture, at their politics and at the social production of wealth, at their entire relationship to nature and to other beings. Lan-guage is thus inseparable from ourselves as a community of human beings with a specific form and character, a specific history, a specific relationship to the world.

V

So what was the colonialist imposition of a foreign language doing to us chil-dren?

The real aim of colonialism was to control the people's wealth: what they produced, how they produced it, and how it was distributed; to control, in other words, the entire realm of the language of real life. Colonialism imposed its control of the social production of wealth through military con-quest and subsequent political dictatorship. But its most important area of domination was the mental universe of the colonised, the control, through culture, of how people perceived themselves and their relationship to the world. Economic and political control can never be complete or effective without mental control. To control a people's culture is to control their tools of self-definition in relationship to others.

For colonialism this involved two aspects of the same process: the destruc-tion or the deliberate undervaluing of a people's culture, their art, dances, religions, history, geography, education, orature and literature, and the conscious elevation of the language of the coloniser. The domination of a people's language by the languages of the colonising nations was crucial to the domination of the mental universe of the colonised.

* * *

IX

I started writing in Gĩkũyũ language in 1977 after seventeen years of involve-ment in Afro-European literature, in my case Afro-English literature. * * * Wherever I have gone, particularly in Europe, I have been confronted with the question: why are you now writing in Gĩkũyũ? Why do you now write in an African language? In some academic quarters I have been confronted with the rebuke, 'Why have you abandoned us?' It was almost as if, in choos-ing to write in Gĩkũyũ, I was doing something abnormal. But Gĩkũyũ is my mother tongue! The very fact that what common sense dictates in the literary practice of other cultures is being questioned in an African writer is a mea-sure of how far imperialism has distorted the view of African realities. It has turned reality upside down: the abnormal is viewed as normal and the normal is viewed as abnormal. Africa actually enriches Europe: but Africa is made to believe that it needs Europe to rescue it from poverty. Africa's natural and human resources continue to develop Europe and America: but Africa is made to feel grateful for aid from the same quarters that still sit on the back of the continent. Africa even produces intellectuals who now rationalise this upside-down way of looking at Africa.

I believe that my writing in Gĩkũyũ language, a Kenyan language, an African language, is part and parcel of the anti-imperialist struggles of Kenyan and African peoples. In schools and universities our Kenyan languages— that is the languages of the many nationalities which make up Kenya—were associated with negative qualities of backwardness, underdevelopment, humiliation and punishment. We who went through that school system were meant to graduate with a hatred of the people and the culture and the values of the language of our daily humiliation and punishment. I do not want to see Kenyan children growing up in that imperialist-imposed tradition of contempt for the tools of communication developed by their communities and their history. I want them to transcend colonial alienation.

※　※　※

We African writers are bound by our calling to do for our languages what Spenser, Milton and Shakespeare did for English; what Pushkin and Tolstoy[1] did for Russian; indeed what all writers in world history have done for their languages by meeting the challenge of creating a literature in them, which process later opens the languages for philosophy, science, technology and all the other areas of human creative endeavours.

1986

1. Aleksandr Pushkin (1799–1837), Russian poet, and Leo Tolstoy (1828–1910), Russian novelist.

M. NOURBESE PHILIP

Marlene Nourbese Philip (b. 1947), publishing recently as M. NourbeSe Philip, was born on the island of Tobago and raised on the island of Trinidad. She received her B.Sc. in Economics at the University of the West Indies (1968), before completing a master's degree in political science (1970) and law degree (1973) at the University of Western Ontario. She practiced law for seven years in Toronto, where she still lives, before turning full-time to writing poetry, novels, essays, and plays. Her book-length poem *Zong!* (2008) reexamines a famous eighteenth-century case of slaves thrown overboard for insurance savings. Her poem "Discourse on the Logic of Language," from her third book of poetry, *She Tries Her Tongue, Her Silence Softly Breaks* (1989), considers the estrangement of the postcolonial and female subject within the imposed colonial language of English. She experiments with typography, wordplay, multiple voices and discourses to give visible form to this linguistic imprisonment—and to her witty and violent attempts at subversion.

Discourse on the Logic of Language

WHEN IT WAS BORN, THE MOTHER HELD HER NEWBORN CHILD CLOSE: SHE BEGAN THEN TO LICK IT ALL OVER. THE CHILD WHIMPERED A LITTLE, BUT AS THE MOTHER'S TONGUE MOVED FASTER AND STRONGER OVER ITS BODY, IT GREW SILENT—THE MOTHER TURNING IT THIS WAY AND THAT UNDER HER TONGUE, UNTIL SHE HAD TONGUED IT CLEAN OF THE CREAMY WHITE SUBSTANCE COVERING ITS BODY.

English
is my mother tongue.
A mother tongue is not
not a foreign lan lan lang
language
l/anguish
    anguish
—a foreign anguish.

English is
my father tongue.
A father tongue is
a foreign language,
therefore English is
a foreign language
not a mother tongue.

What is my mother
tongue
my mammy tongue
my mummy tongue
my momsy tongue
my modder tongue
my ma tongue?

I have no mother
tongue
no mother to tongue
no tongue to mother
to mother
tongue
me

I must therefore be tongue
dumb
dumb-tongued
dub[1]-tongued
damn dumb
tongue

EDICT I

*Every owner of slaves
shall, wherever possible,
ensure that his slaves
belong to as many ethno-
linguistic groups as
possible. If they cannot
speak to each other,
they cannot then foment
rebellion and revolution.*

---

1. Type of African Caribbean performance poetry, named after "dub music," or remixed reggae-style music.

Those parts of the brain chiefly responsible for speech are named after two learned nineteenth century doctors, the eponymous Doctors Wernicke and Broca[2] respectively.

Dr. Broca believed the size of the brain determined intelligence; he devoted much of his time to 'proving' that white males of the Caucasian race had larger brains than, and where therefore superior to, women, Blacks and other peoples of colour.

Understanding and recognition of the spoken word takes place in Wernicke's area—the left temporal lobe, situated next to the auditory cortex; from there relevant information passes to Broca's area—situated in the left frontal cortex—which then forms the response and passes it on to the motor cortex. The motor cortex controls the muscles of speech.

2. Pierre Paul Broca (1824–1880), French physician; Carl Wernicke (1848–1905), German physician.

THE MOTHER THEN PUT HER FINGERS INTO HER CHILD'S MOUTH—GENTLY FORCING IT OPEN; SHE TOUCHES HER TONGUE TO THE CHILD'S TONGUE, AND HOLDING THE TINY MOUTH OPEN, SHE BLOWS INTO IT—HARD. SHE WAS BLOWING WORDS—HER WORDS, HER MOTHER'S WORDS, THOSE OF HER MOTHER'S MOTHER, AND ALL THEIR MOTHERS BEFORE—INTO HER DAUGHTER'S MOUTH.

but I have
a dumb tongue
tongue dumb
father tongue
and english is
my mother tongue
is
my father tongue
is a foreign lan lan lang
language
l/anguish
  anguish
a foreign anguish
is english—
another tongue
my mother
    mammy
    mummy
    moder
    mater
    macer
    moder[3]
tongue
mothertongue

tongue mother
tongue me
mothertongue me
mother me
touch me
with the tongue of your
lan lan lang
language
l/anguish
  anguish
english
is a foreign anguish

EDICT II

Every slave caught speaking his native language shall be severely punished. Where necessary, removal of the tongue is recommended. The offending organ, when removed, should be hung on high in a central place, so that all may see and tremble.

3. Mother (archaic Scots, Swedish, etc.). "Mater": mother (Latin). "Macer": lean, poor (Latin).

A tapering, blunt-tipped, muscular, soft and fleshy organ describes
(a) the penis.
(b) the tongue.
(c) neither of the above.
(d) both of the above.

In man the tongue is
(a) the principal organ of taste.
(b) the principal organ of articulate speech.
(c) the principal organ of oppression and exploitation.
(d) all of the above.

The tongue
(a) is an interwoven bundle of striated muscle running in three planes.
(b) is fixed to the jawbone.
(c) has an outer covering of a mucous membrane covered with papillae.
(d) contains ten thousand taste buds, none of which is sensitive to the taste
    of foreign words.

Air is forced out of the lungs up the throat to the larynx where it causes the
vocal cords to vibrate and create sound. The metamorphosis from sound to
intelligible word requires
(a) the lip, tongue and jaw all working together.
(b) a mother tongue.
(c) the overseer's whip.
(d) all of the above or none.

1989

SALMAN RUSHDIE

In these excerpts from two essays in his collection *Imaginary Homelands*, fiction writer Salman Rushdie (b. 1947; see the headnote to him and see his story "The Prophet's Hair," later in this volume) claims both Britishness and the English language for immigrant writers in England. Lured by a dream-England, such writers have often been disappointed by exclusionary racial attitudes in their new homeland. Transplanted and culturally plural, they write out of multiple literary inheritances, including the literature of exile and displacement. Rushdie counters the nativist view of English as an imperial yoke that must be thrown off: he recounts the spread of English as a world language, describes its indigenization by the non-English, and claims it as a vital and expressive South Asian literary language, with its own history and tradition.

[The British Indian Writer and a Dream-England]

❊   ❊   ❊

So if I am to speak for Indian writers in England I would say this, para-phrasing G. V. Desani's H. Hatterr: The migrations of the fifties and sixties happened. 'We are. We are here.'[1] And we are not willing to be excluded from any part of our heritage; which heritage includes both a Bradford-born Indian kid's right to be treated as a full member of British society, and also the right of any member of this post-diaspora community to draw on its roots for its art, just as all the world's community of displaced writers has always done. (I'm thinking, for instance, of Grass's Danzig-become-Gdansk, of Joyce's abandoned Dublin, of Isaac Bashevis Singer and Maxine Hong Kingston and Milan Kundera[2] and many others. It's a long list.)

Let me override at once the faintly defensive note that has crept into these last few remarks. The Indian writer, looking back at India, does so through guilt-tinted spectacles. (I am of course, once more, talking about myself.) I am speaking now of those of us who emigrated . . . and I suspect that there are times when the move seems wrong to us all, when we seem, to ourselves, post-lapsarian men and women. We are Hindus who have crossed the black water; we are Muslims who eat pork.[3] And as a result—as my use of the Christian notion of the Fall indicates—we are now partly of the West. Our identity is at once plural and partial. Sometimes we feel that we straddle two cultures; at other times, that we fall between two stools. But however ambiguous and shifting this ground may be, it is not an infer-tile territory for a writer to occupy. If literature is in part the business of finding new angles at which to enter reality, then once again our distance, our long geographical perspective, may provide us with such angles. Or it may be that that is simply what we must think in order to do our work.

❊   ❊   ❊

England's Indian writers are by no means all the same type of animal. Some of us, for instance, are Pakistani. Others Bangladeshi. Others West, or East, or even South African. And V. S. Naipaul,[4] by now, is something else entirely. This word 'Indian' is getting to be a pretty scattered concept. Indian writers in England include political exiles, first-generation migrants, affluent expatriates whose residence here is frequently temporary, natural-ized Britons, and people born here who may never have laid eyes on the subcontinent. Clearly, nothing that I say can apply across all these catego-ries. But one of the interesting things about this diverse community is that, as far as Indo-British fiction is concerned, its existence changes the ball

---

1. From *All About H. Hatterr* (1948) by the Indian novelist G. V. Desani (1909–2000).
2. Czech novelist (b. 1929). "Grass's Danzig-become-Gdansk": Polish city known until the end of World War II as Danzig (its German name) and known today as Gdansk; the city features promi-nently in a trilogy by the German novelist Günter Grass (1927–2015). "Joyce's abandoned Dublin": birthplace of the Irish writer James Joyce (1882–1941) and the setting for much of his work, although Joyce spent most of his adult life outside

Dublin, in Paris, Trieste, and Zurich. "Isaac Bashevis Singer": Polish American writer (1904–1991). "Maxine Hong Kingston": Chinese Ameri-can writer (b. 1940).
3. Inverting, that is, the Muslim prohibition against eating pork as unclean and the Hindu prohibition against crossing the ocean ("black water").
4. Trinidad-born English writer of Indian descent (b. 1932).

game, because that fiction is in future going to come as much from addresses in London, Birmingham and Yorkshire as from Delhi or Bombay.

One of the changes has to do with attitudes towards the use of English. Many have referred to the argument about the appropriateness of this language to Indian themes. And I hope all of us share the view that we can't simply use the language in the way the British did; that it needs remaking for our own purposes. Those of us who do use English do so in spite of our ambiguity towards it, or perhaps because of that, perhaps because we can find in that linguistic struggle a reflection of other struggles taking place in the real world, struggles between the cultures within ourselves and the influences at work upon our societies. To conquer English may be to complete the process of making ourselves free.

But the British Indian writer simply does not have the option of rejecting English, anyway. His children, her children, will grow up speaking it, probably as a first language; and in the forging of a British Indian identity the English language is of central importance. It must, in spite of everything, be embraced. (The word 'translation' comes, etymologically, from the Latin for 'bearing across'. Having been borne across the world, we are translated men. It is normally supposed that something always gets lost in translation; I cling, obstinately, to the notion that something can also be gained.)

To be an Indian writer in this society is to face, every day, problems of definition. What does it mean to be 'Indian' outside India? How can culture be preserved without becoming ossified? How should we discuss the need for change within ourselves and our community without seeming to play into the hands of our racial enemies? What are the consequences, both spiritual and practical, of refusing to make any concessions to Western ideas and practices? What are the consequences of embracing those ideas and practices and turning away from the ones that came here with us? These questions are all a single, existential question: How are we to live in the world?

I do not propose to offer, prescriptively, any answers to these questions; only to state that these are some of the issues with which each of us will have to come to terms.

To turn my eyes outwards now, and to say a little about the relationship between the Indian writer and the majority white culture in whose midst he lives, and with which his work will sooner or later have to deal:

In common with many Bombay-raised middle-class children of my generation, I grew up with an intimate knowledge of, and even sense of friendship with, a certain kind of England: a dream-England composed of Test Matches at Lord's presided over by the voice of John Arlott, at which Freddie Trueman bowled unceasingly and without success at Polly Umrigar;[5] of Enid Blyton and Billy Bunter, in which we were even prepared to smile indulgently at portraits such as 'Hurree Jamset Ram Singh', 'the dusky nabob of Bhanipur'.[6] I wanted to come to England. I couldn't wait. And to be fair, England has done all right

---

5. Pahlan Ratanji Umrigar (1926–2006), Indian cricket player. "Test Matches at Lord's": cricket matches played at Lord's Cricket Ground in London. "John Arlott": English cricket commentator and writer (1914–1991). "Freddie Trueman": Fred Trueman (1931–2006), English cricket player.
6. Character who speaks stereotypically comic English in the "Famous Five" series of children's books by English author Enid Blyton (1897–1968), whose work has been criticized for its racism. "Billy Bunter": key character in the Greyfriars School stories published from 1908 to 1940 in the boys' weekly magazine *The Magnet* by Charles Hamilton (1876–1961), writing under the pen name Frank Richards.

by me; but I find it a little difficult to be properly grateful. I can't escape the view that my relatively easy ride is not the result of the dream-England's famous sense of tolerance and fair play, but of my social class, my freak fair skin and my 'English' English accent. Take away any of these, and the story would have been very different. Because of course the dream-England is no more than a dream.

Sadly, it's a dream from which too many white Britons refuse to awake. Recently, on a live radio programme, a professional humorist asked me, in all seriousness, why I objected to being called a wog.[7] He said he had always thought it a rather charming word, a term of endearment. 'I was at the zoo the other day,' he revealed, 'and a zoo keeper told me that the wogs were best with the animals; they stuck their fingers in their ears and wiggled them about and the animals felt at home.' The ghost of Hurree Jamset Ram Singh walks among us still.

As Richard Wright[8] found long ago in America, black and white descriptions of society are no longer compatible. Fantasy, or the mingling of fantasy and naturalism, is one way of dealing with these problems. It offers a way of echoing in the form of our work the issues faced by all of us: how to build a new, 'modern' world out of an old, legend-haunted civilization, an old culture which we have brought into the heart of a newer one. But whatever technical solutions we may find, Indian writers in these islands, like others who have migrated into the north from the south, are capable of writing from a kind of double perspective: because they, we, are at one and the same time insiders and outsiders in this society. This stereoscopic vision is perhaps what we can offer in place of 'whole sight'.

* * *

Art is a passion of the mind. And the imagination works best when it is most free. Western writers have always felt free to be eclectic in their selection of theme, setting, form; Western visual artists have, in this century, been happily raiding the visual storehouses of Africa, Asia, the Philippines. I am sure that we must grant ourselves an equal freedom.

Let me suggest that Indian writers in England have access to a second tradition, quite apart from their own racial history. It is the culture and political history of the phenomenon of migration, displacement, life in a minority group. We can quite legitimately claim as our ancestors the Huguenots,[9] the Irish, the Jews; the past to which we belong is an English past, the history of immigrant Britain. Swift, Conrad, Marx are as much our literary forebears as Tagore or Ram Mohan Roy.[1] America, a nation of immigrants, has created great literature out of the phenomenon of cultural transplantation, out of examining the ways in which people cope with a new world; it may be that by discovering what we have in common with those who preceded us into this country, we can begin to do the same.

I stress this is only one of many possible strategies. But we are inescapably international writers at a time when the novel has never been a more

---

7. A derogatory term for a foreigner.
8. American fiction writer and essayist (1908–1960).
9. Protestants who emigrated from France in the 16th and 17th centuries because of religious persecution.
1. Bengali intellectual and social and religious

reformer (1772–1833). Jonathan Swift (1667–1745), Anglo-Irish writer. Joseph Conrad (1857–1924), Polish novelist who lived in England and wrote in English. Karl Marx (1818–1883), German social theorist who spent much of his adult life in England. Rabindranath Tagore (1861–1941), Bengali poet.

international form (a writer like Borges speaks of the influence of Robert Louis Stevenson on his work; Heinrich Böll[2] acknowledges the influence of Irish literature; cross-pollination is everywhere); and it is perhaps one of the more pleasant freedoms of the literary migrant to be able to choose his parents. My own—selected half consciously, half not—include Gogol, Cervantes, Kafka, Melville, Machado de Assis;[3] a polyglot family tree, against which I measure myself, and to which I would be honoured to belong.

There's a beautiful image in Saul Bellow's latest novel, *The Dean's December*.[4] The central character, the Dean, Corde, hears a dog barking wildly somewhere. He imagines that the barking is the dog's protest against the limit of dog experience. 'For God's sake,' the dog is saying, 'open the universe a little more!' And because Bellow is, of course, not really talking about dogs, or not only about dogs, I have the feeling that the dog's rage, and its desire, is also mine, ours, everyone's. 'For God's sake, open the universe a little more!'

1982

[English Is an Indian Literary Language]

I'll begin from an obvious starting place. English is by now the world language. It achieved this status partly as a result of the physical colonization of a quarter of the globe by the British, and it remains ambiguous but central to the affairs of just about all the countries to whom it was given, along with mission schools, trunk roads[1] and the rules of cricket, as a gift of the British colonizers.

But its present-day pre-eminence is not solely—perhaps not even primarily—the result of the British legacy. It is also the effect of the primacy of the United States of America in the affairs of the world. This second impetus towards English could be termed a kind of linguistic neo-colonialism, or just plain pragmatism on the part of many of the world's governments and educationists, according to your point of view.

As for myself, I don't think it is always necessary to take up the anti-colonial—or is it post-colonial?—cudgels against English. What seems to me to be happening is that those peoples who were once colonized by the language are now rapidly remaking it, domesticating it, becoming more and more relaxed about the way they use it—assisted by the English language's enormous flexibility and size, they are carving out large territories for themselves within its frontiers.

To take the case of India, only because it's the one with which I'm most familiar. The debate about the appropriateness of English in post-British India has been raging ever since 1947;[2] but today, I find, it is a debate which has meaning only for the older generation. The children of independent

2. German writer (1917–1985). Jorge Luis Borges (1899–1986), Argentinean writer. Robert Louis Stevenson (1850–1894), Scottish writer.
3. Joaquim María Machado de Assis (1839–1908), Brazilian writer. Nikolai Gogol (1809–1852), Russian writer. Miguel de Cervantes Saavedra (1547–1616), Spanish writer. Franz Kafka (1883–1924), Czech writer. Herman Melville (1819–1891), American writer.
4. Novel (1982) by Bellow (1915–2005), American novelist.
1. Main roads, such as the Grand Trunk Road, the immense highway between Calcutta and Amritsar constructed during the British Raj.
2. When the British relinquished control of India.

India seem not to think of English as being irredeemably tainted by its colonial provenance. They use it as an Indian language, as one of the tools they have to hand.

(I am simplifying, of course, but the point is broadly true.)

There is also an interesting North–South divide in Indian attitudes to English. In the North, in the so-called 'Hindi belt', where the capital, Delhi, is located, it is possible to think of Hindi as a future national language; but in South India, which is at present suffering from the attempts of central government to *impose* this national language on it, the resentment of Hindi is far greater than of English. After spending quite some time in South India, I've become convinced that English is an essential language in India, not only because of its technical vocabularies and the international communication which it makes possible, but also simply to permit two Indians to talk to each other in a tongue which neither party hates.

Incidentally, in West Bengal, where there is a State-led move against English, the following graffito, a sharp dig at the State's Marxist chief minister, Jyoti Basu, appeared on a wall, in English: it said, 'My son won't learn English; your son won't learn English; but Jyoti Basu will send his son abroad to learn English.'

One of the points I want to make is that what I've said indicates, I hope, that Indian society and Indian literature have a complex and developing relationship with the English language. * * *

English literature has its Indian branch. By this I mean the literature of the English language. This literature is also Indian literature. There is no incompatibility here. If history creates complexities, let us not try to simplify them.

So: English is an Indian literary language, and by now, thanks to writers like Tagore, Desani, Chaudhuri, Mulk Raj Anand, Raja Rao, Anita Desai[3] and others, it has quite a pedigree.

＊　＊　＊

In my own case, I have constantly been asked whether I am British, or Indian. The formulation 'Indian-born British writer' has been invented to explain me. But, as I said last night, my new book deals with Pakistan. So what now? 'British-resident Indo-Pakistani writer'? You see the folly of trying to contain writers inside passports.

One of the most absurd aspects of this quest for national authenticity is that—as far as India is concerned, anyway—it is completely fallacious to suppose that there is such a thing as a pure, unalloyed tradition from which to draw. The only people who seriously believe this are religious extremists. The rest of us understand that the very essence of Indian culture is that we possess a mixed tradition, a *mélange* of elements as disparate as ancient Mughal[4] and contemporary Coca-Cola American. To say nothing of Muslim, Buddhist, Jain,[5] Christian, Jewish, British, French, Portuguese, Marxist, Maoist, Trotskyist, Vietnamese, capitalist, and of course Hindu elements. Eclecticism, the ability to take from the world what seems fitting and to

3. Rabindranath Tagore (1861–1941), Bengali poet; G. V. Desani (1909–2000), Nirad C. Chaudhuri (1897–1999), Mulk Raj Anand (1905–2004), Raja Rao (1909–2006), Anita Desai (b. 1937):

Indian fiction and nonfiction writers.
4. Dynasty of Muslim emperors who reigned in India, 1526–1858.
5. Jainism is one of India's oldest religions.

leave the rest, has always been a hallmark of the Indian tradition, and today it is at the centre of the best work being done both in the visual arts and in literature.

* * *

As far as Eng. Lit. itself is concerned, I think that if *all* English literatures could be studied together, a shape would emerge which would truly reflect the new shape of the language in the world, and we could see that Eng. Lit. has never been in better shape, because the world language now also possesses a world literature, which is proliferating in every conceivable direction.

The English language ceased to be the sole possession of the English some time ago. * * *

1983

GRACE NICHOLS

Born and raised in British Guiana (now Guyana), Grace Nichols (b. 1950) worked as a freelance journalist after receiving a diploma in communications from the University of Guyana. She left the Caribbean for England in 1977.

In "Epilogue" and other poems, Nichols memorializes the uprooting of Africans and their languages when slavery brought these peoples to the West Indies, where a new tongue grew "from the root of the old one." The new tongue melded English with African and European languages, and despite the stigma that once attached to it, Nichols celebrates it as a vibrant medium for literature. Like Louise Bennett, she writes of black immigrants' reverse colonization of the English language and of English society. In *The Fat Black Woman's Poems* (1984) and other of her subsequent volumes, the speaker—appropriating and reversing cultural stereotypes—transforms London's landscape by virtue of her robust physical, verbal, and cultural presence.

Epilogue

I have crossed an ocean
I have lost my tongue
from the root of the old one
a new one has sprung

1983

The Fat Black Woman Goes Shopping

Shopping in London winter
is a real drag for the fat black woman

going from store to store
in search of accommodating clothes
5 and de weather so cold

Look at the frozen thin mannequins
fixing her with grin
and de pretty face salesgals
exchanging slimming glances
10 thinking she don't notice

Lord is aggravating

Nothing soft and bright and billowing
to flow like breezy sunlight
when she walking

15 The fat black woman curses in Swahili/Yoruba
and nation language[1] under her breathing
all this journeying and journeying

The fat black woman could only conclude
that when it come to fashion
20 the choice is lean

Nothing much beyond size 14

1984

Wherever I Hang

I leave me people, me land, me home
For reasons, I not too sure
I forsake de sun
And de humming-bird splendour
5 Had big rats in de floorboard
So I pick up me new-world-self
And come, to this place call England
At first I feeling like I in dream—
De misty greyness
10 I touching de walls to see if they real
They solid to de seam
And de people pouring from de underground system[1]
Like beans
And when I look up to de sky
15 I see Lord Nelson[2] high—too high to lie

1. Term for creolized English coined by West Indian poet Kamau Brathwaite (b. 1930). "Swahili": East African language. "Yoruba": Nigerian language.
1. The London subway system.
2. British Admiral Horatio Nelson (1758–1805), whose naval victories are commemorated by a tall column surmounted by his statue in Trafalgar Square, London. There are also monuments to him in the Caribbean, where he spent much of his career.

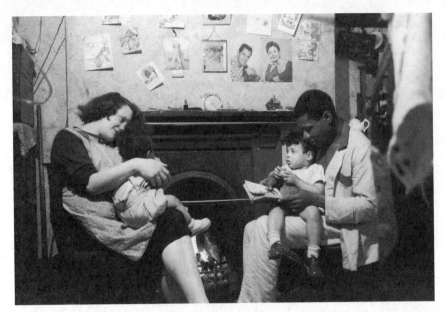

An interracial family at home by the fire, 1955. A foundry worker who left Jamaica in 1947 sits with his Welsh wife and their children in their one-room home in Birmingham. During this period of large-scale immigration into the United Kingdom, when interracial marriage was uncommon, white Britons held widely divergent views toward people of color, with approximately equal numbers said to be tolerant, prejudiced, or mildly prejudiced. Many immigrants found that they were discriminated against and forced to take lower-scale jobs than they were trained for.

"Stop the Coloured Invasion" protest amid the lions of Trafalgar Square, London, January 1, 1959. After the British Nationality Act of 1948, citizens of the British colonies were allowed to enter and work in the United Kingdom without a visa. As people of African and Asian descent arrived from the British Empire and Commonwealth in the 1950s and 1960s, some whites denounced the policies that permitted immigration. As a result, laws permitting entry were tightened in the 1960s, and politicians such as Member of Parliament Enoch Powell fomented anxieties that immigration was destroying Britain and would lead to civil strife.

And is so I sending home photos of myself
Among de pigeons and de snow
And is so I warding off de cold
And is so, little by little
20 I begin to change my calypso ways
Never visiting nobody
Before giving them clear warning
And waiting me turn in queue°   *in line*
Now, after all this time
25 I get accustom to de English life
But I still miss back-home side
To tell you de truth
I don't know really where I belaang

Yes, divided to de ocean
30 Divided to de bone

Wherever I hang me knickers—that's my home.

1989

LINTON KWESI JOHNSON

Born in Jamaica in 1952, Linton Kwesi Johnson immigrated to England at the age of eleven. He grew up in Brixton, South London, where he was shocked by the racist hostility. After he graduated with a B.A. in sociology from Goldsmiths, University of London, he began to publish collections of poetry, beginning with *Voices of the Living and the Dead* (1974). His influential recordings of his poetry set to reggae music, such as his first album *Dread Beat an' Blood* (1977), reached a wide audience. In 2002 he became the second living poet published in the Penguin Modern Classics series.

Building on the example of poets such as Claude McKay and Louise Bennett but more fiercely assailing the norms of Standard English, Johnson represents black British speech in words spelled phonetically, sentences without punctuation, and rhythms surging with reggae and other African diasporic musical traditions. In stylized versions of the voices of working-class immigrants to Britain, poems such as "Inglan Is a Bitch" chronicle their relentless struggle with racism, violence, discrimination, incarceration, and police brutality. Although both Johnson's poem and Claude McKay's "Old England" draw on African Caribbean speech, McKay's buoyantly idealized London could hardly differ more from the grimly repressive London of "Inglan Is a Bitch."

Inglan Is a Bitch

wen mi jus come to Landan toun
mi use to work pan di andahgroun
but workin pan di andahgroun
yu dont get fi know your way aroun

little

5 Inglan is a bitch
dere's no escapin it
Inglan is a bitch
dere's no runin whe fram it

mi get a likkle° jab in a big otell   *little*
10 an awftah a while, mi woz doin quite well
dem staat mi awf as a dish-washah
but wen mi tek a stack, mi noh tun clack-watchah!¹

Inglan is a bitch
dere's no escapin it
15 Inglan is a bitch
noh baddah try fi hide fram it

wen dem gi you di likkle wage packit°   *check*
fus dem rab it wid dem big tax rackit°   *fraud*
yu haffi struggle fi mek enz meet
20 an wen yu goh a yu bed yu jus cant sleep

Inglan is a bitch
dere's no escapin it
Inglan is a bitch fi true
a noh lie mi a tell, a true

25 me use to work dig ditch wen it cowl noh bitch°   *cold, no shit*
mi did° strang like a mule, but, bwoy, mi did fool   *was*
den awftah a while mi jus stap dhu owevahtime
den awftah a while mi jus phu dung° mi tool   *put down*

Inglan is a bitch
30 dere's no escapin it
Inglan is a bitch
yu haffi know how fi suvive in it

well mi dhu° day wok an mi dhu nite wok   *did*
mi dhu clean wok and mi dhu dutty° wok   *dirty*
35 dem seh dat black man is very lazy
but if yu si how mi wok yu woodah seh mi crazy

Inglan is a bitch
dere's no escapin it
Inglan is a bitch
40 yu bettah face up to it

dem have a likkle facktri up inna Brackly
inna disya facktri all dem dhu is pack crackry
fi di laas fifteen years dem get mi laybah
now awftah fifteen years mi fall out a fayvah

---

1. But when I started to make money, I didn't turn into a clock-watcher (i.e., lazy worker).

45 Inglan is a bitch
dere's no escapin it
Inglan is a bitch
dere's no runin whe fram it

mi know dem have wok, wok in abundant
50 yet still, dem mek mi redundant°   *they laid me off*
now, at fifty-five mi getin quite ole
yet still, dem sen mi fi goh draw dole°   *welfare payments*

Inglan is a bitch
dere's no escapin it
55 Inglan is a bitch fi true
is whe wi a goh dhu bout it?

1980

HANIF KUREISHI

I n his essay "The Rainbow Sign" (excerpted below), Hanif Kureishi (b. 1954; see the headnote to him and his story "My Son the Fanatic," later in this volume) recalls the difficulties of coming of age in a country that hadn't yet come to grips with black and Asian immigrants from its former colonies. As a boy, he was made to feel ashamed of his Pakistani background and wanted to identify with Englishness. At the same time, he witnessed the racial exclusions and violence against Pakistani and other recent immigrants in the name of Englishness. Though horrified by neo-Nazi attitudes, the young Kureishi also felt uncomfortable with separatist and fundamentalist attitudes on the part of those who demonized whites and non-Muslims. He began to explore ways of belonging that confound simplistic conceptions of race, identity, and nationhood.

[You Will Always Be a Paki]

One: England

I was born in London of an English mother and Pakistani father. My father, who lives in London, came to England from Bombay in 1947 to be educated by the old colonial power. He married here and never went back to India. The rest of his large family, his brothers, their wives, his sisters, moved from Bombay to Karachi, in Pakistan, after partition.[1]

Frequently during my childhood, I met my Pakistani uncles when they came to London on business. They were important, confident people who took me to hotels, restaurants and test matches,[2] often in taxis. But I had no idea of what the subcontinent was like or how my numerous uncles,

1. Division of the South Asian subcontinent into the nations of India and Pakistan (and later, Bangladesh) in 1947, after independence from British colonial rule.
2. Important international cricket matches.

aunts and cousins lived there. When I was nine or ten a teacher purpose-fully placed some pictures of Indian peasants in mud huts in front of me and said to the class: 'Hanif comes from India.' I wondered: did my uncles ride on camels? Surely not in their suits? Did my cousins, so like me in other ways, squat down in the sand like little Mowglis,[3] half-naked and eat-ing with their fingers?

In the mid-1960s, Pakistanis were a risible subject in England, derided on television and exploited by politicians. They had the worst jobs, they were uncomfortable in England, some of them had difficulties with the language. They were despised and out of place.

From the start I tried to deny my Pakistani self. I was ashamed. It was a curse and I wanted to be rid of it. I wanted to be like everyone else. I read with understanding a story in a newspaper about a black boy who, when he noticed that burnt skin turned white, jumped into a bath of boiling water.

At school, one teacher always spoke to me in a 'Peter Sellers' Indian accent.[4] Another refused to call me by my name, calling me Pakistani Pete instead. So I refused to call the teacher by *his* name and used his nickname instead. This led to trouble; arguments, detentions, escapes from school over hedges and, eventually, suspension. This played into my hands; this couldn't have been better.

With a friend I roamed the streets and fields all day; I sat beside streams; I stole yellow lurex trousers[5] from a shop and smuggled them out of the house under my school trousers; I hid in woods reading hard books; and I saw the film *Zulu*[6] several times.

✳   ✳   ✳

And then, in the evening, B.B.[7] took me to meet with the other lads. We climbed the park railings and strolled across to the football pitch, by the goalposts. This is where the lads congregated to hunt down Pakistanis and beat them. Most of them I was at school with. The others I'd grown up with. I knew their parents. They knew my father.

I withdrew, from the park, from the lads, to a safer place, within myself. I moved into what I call my 'temporary' period. I was only waiting now to get away, to leave the London suburbs, to make another kind of life, somewhere else, with better people.

In this isolation, in my bedroom where I listened to the Pink Floyd, the Beatles and the John Peel show,[8] I started to write down the speeches of politicians, the words which helped create the neo-Nazi attitudes I saw around me. This I called 'keeping the accounts'.

In 1965, Enoch Powell[9] said: 'We should not lose sight of the desirability of achieving a steady flow of voluntary repatriation for the elements which are proving unsuccessful or unassimilable.'

3. The child reared by wolves in the stories in *The Jungle Book* (1894) by the English novelist Rudyard Kipling (1865–1936).
4. English comic actor (1925–1980), who played Indian characters in the films *The Millionairess* (1960) and *The Party* (1968).
5. Pants made from fabric with metallic threads.
6. Film (1964) depicting a battle in 1879 between the British Army and the Zulu tribe in South Africa.
7. A friend.
8. Show on Radio 1, the British Broadcasting Corporation's pop music station, which popular-ized the countercultural music of the late 1960s and early 1970s. Peel (1939–2004) was a disc jockey on the station from 1967 until 2004.
9. Anti-immigrant British politician (1912–1998).

In 1967, Duncan Sandys[1] said: 'The breeding of millions of half-caste children would merely produce a generation of misfits and create national tensions.'

I wasn't a misfit; I could join the elements of myself together. It was the others, they wanted misfits; they wanted you to embody within yourself their ambivalence.

Also in 1967, Enoch Powell—who once said he would love to have been Viceroy of India—quoted a constituent of his as saying that because of the Pakistanis 'this country will not be worth living in for our children'.

And Powell said, more famously: 'As I look ahead I am filled with foreboding. Like the Roman, "I seem to see the River Tiber foaming with much blood".'[2]

As Powell's speeches appeared in the papers, graffiti in support of him appeared in the London streets. Racists gained confidence. People insulted me in the street. Someone in a café refused to eat at the same table with me. The parents of a girl I was in love with told her she'd get a bad reputation by going out with darkies.

Powell allowed himself to become a figurehead for racists. He helped create racism in Britain and was directly responsible not only for the atmosphere of fear and hatred, but through his influence, for individual acts of violence against Pakistanis.

Television comics used Pakistanis as the butt of their humour. Their jokes were highly political: they contributed to a way of seeing the world. The enjoyed reduction of racial hatred to a joke did two things: it expressed a collective view (which was sanctioned by its being on the BBC), and it was a celebration of contempt in millions of living rooms in England. I was afraid to watch TV because of it; it was too embarrassing, too degrading.

Parents of my friends, both lower-middle-class and working-class, often told me they were Powell supporters. Sometimes I heard them talking, heatedly, violently, about race, about 'the Pakis'. I was desperately embarrassed and afraid of being identified with these loathed aliens. I found it almost impossible to answer questions about where I came from. The word 'Pakistani' had been made into an insult. It was a word I didn't want used about myself. I couldn't tolerate being myself.

The British complained incessantly that the Pakistanis wouldn't assimilate. This meant they wanted the Pakistanis to be exactly like them. But of course even then they would have rejected them.

The British were doing the assimilating: they assimilated Pakistanis to their world view. They saw them as dirty, ignorant and less than human—worthy of abuse and violence.

At this time I found it difficult to get along with anyone. I was frightened and hostile. I suspected that my white friends were capable of racist insults. And many of them did taunt me, innocently. I reckoned that at least once every day since I was five years old I had been racially abused. I became incapable of distinguishing between remarks that were genuinely intended to hurt and those intended as 'humour'.

1. Conservative British politician (1908–1987) and head of the Commonwealth Relations Office, who opposed immigration from Britain's former colonies.
2. From Enoch Powell's "Rivers of Blood" speech (1968), warning against unchecked immigration from the Commonwealth and citing the prophecy of war from book 6 of the Roman poet Virgil's *Aeneid* (1st century B.C.E.).

*   *   *

I saw racism as unreason and prejudice, ignorance and a failure of sense; it was Fanon's 'incomprehension'.[3] That the men I wanted to admire had liberated themselves only to take to unreason, to the abdication of intelligence, was shocking to me. And the separatism, the total loathing of the white man as innately corrupt, the 'All whites are devils' view,[4] was equally unacceptable. I had to live in England, in the suburbs of London, with whites. My mother was white. I wasn't ready for separate development. I'd had too much of that already.

*   *   *

I saw the taking up of Islam as an aberration, a desperate fantasy of worldwide black brotherhood; it was a symptom of extreme alienation. It was also an inability to seek a wider political view or cooperation with other oppressed groups—or with the working class as a whole—since alliance with white groups was necessarily out of the question.

*   *   *

Two: Pakistan

*   *   *

I was having a little identity crisis. I'd been greeted so warmly in Pakistan, I felt so excited by what I saw, and so at home with all my uncles, I wondered if I were not better off here than there.[5] And when I said, with a little unnoticed irony, that I was an Englishman, people laughed. They fell about. Why would anyone with a brown face, Muslim name and large well-known family in Pakistan want to lay claim to that cold little decrepit island off Europe where you always had to spell your name? Strangely, anti-British remarks made me feel patriotic, though I only felt patriotic when I was away from England.

But I couldn't allow myself to feel too Pakistani. I didn't want to give in to that falsity, that sentimentality. As someone said to me at a party, provoked by the fact I was wearing jeans: we are Pakistanis, but you, you will always be a Paki—emphasising the slang derogatory name the English used against Pakistanis, and therefore the fact that I couldn't rightfully lay claim to either place.

*   *   *

1986

---

3. Cf. "Racism and Culture" (1956), an essay by Frantz Fanon (1925–1961), psychologist and theorist of decolonization. Fanon writes that "the end of race prejudice begins with a sudden incomprehension," a mental shift in which the target of prejudice recognizes that racism is unreasonable and ineffective and refuses to condone it.
4. Elijah Muhammad (1897–1975), African American leader of the Nation of Islam, condemned whites as "blue-eyed devils."
5. I.e., in Pakistan rather than in England.

BERNARDINE EVARISTO

B orn in London in 1959, the daughter of an English mother and Nigerian father, Bernardine Evaristo was educated at the Rose Bruford College of Speech and Drama and at the University of London, and was a founding member of the London-based Theatre of Black Women. The author of a number of books in prose and verse, she made her reputation with two novels-in-verse exploring hybrid identities and histories: the semiautobiographical *Lara* (1997), which traces its mixed-race heroine's English, Nigerian, Brazilian, and Irish roots, and *The Emperor's Babe* (2001), for which "Amo Amas Amat" is the prologue.

Set in a teeming multicultural London in the year 211 C.E., when Britain was a far-flung colony at the periphery of the Roman Empire, *The Emperor's Babe* tells the story of Zuleika, the hip, restless, playful daughter of Sudanese immigrants. Married at a young age to an often absent nobleman, she eventually has an affair with visiting Septimius Severus—a historical figure, an emperor of African origin who ruled over Rome and died in Britain's York. Delving into Britain's deep past, Evaristo's novel-in-verse humorously provincializes London, representing it not as the energizing hub of empire but, in the Roman scheme of things, as an underdeveloped backwater. Against the idea that Britain was racially or culturally homogeneous before the arrival of post-war, *Windrush*-era immigrants, Evaristo represents it as already richly multicultural in ancient times. In her verbal amalgamations, she zigzags from street slang to high diction and among multiple foreign tongues, highlighting the multinational roots of the English language. Both historical and humorously anachronistic, the poem's linguistic mix is emblematic of both the ancient and the contemporary cultural hybridization of Britain.

From The Emperor's Babe

Amo Amas Amat[1]

Who do you love? Who *do* you love,
when the man you married goes off

for months on end, quelling rebellions
at the frontiers, or playing hot-shot senator in Rome;

5   his flashy villa on the Palatine Hill,[2] home
to another woman, I hear,

one who has borne him offspring.
My days are spent roaming this house,

its vast mosaic walls full of the scenes on Olympus,
10   for my husband loves melodrama.

They say his mistress is an actress,
a flaxen-Fräulein type, from Germania Superior.[3]

---

1. I love, you love, he/she loves (Latin conjugations).
2. Historic center of ancient Rome.

3. Province of the Roman Empire (now parts of Switzerland, France, and Germany). "Fräulein": unmarried woman (German).

Oh, everyone envied me, *Illa Bella Negreeta!*[4]
born in the back of a shop on Gracechurch Street,[5]

15 who got hitched to a Roman nobleman,
whose parents sailed out of Khartoum[6] on a barge,

no burnished throne, no poop of beaten gold,
but packed with vomiting brats

and cows releasing warm turds
20 on to their bare feet. Thus perfumed,

they made it to Londinium on a donkey,
with only a thin purse and a fat dream.

Here in the drizzle of this wild west town
Dad wandered the streets looking for work,

25 but there was no room at the inn,
so he set up shop on the kerb

and sold sweet cakes which Mum made.
(He's told me this story a mille° times.)   *thousand (Latin)*

Now he owns several shops, selling everything
30 from vino to shoes, veggies to tools,

and he employs all sorts to work in them,
a Syrian, Tunisian, Jew, Persian,

hopefuls just off the olive barge from Gaul,[7]
in fact anyone who'll work for pebbles.

35 When Felix came after me, Dad was in ecstasy,
father-in-law to Lucius Aurelius Felix, no less.

I was spotted at the baths of Cheapside,[8]
just budding, and my fate was sealed

by a man thrice my age and thrice my girth,
40 all at sweet eleven—even then Dad

thought I was getting past it.
Then I was sent off to a snooty Roman bitch

called Clarissa for decorum classes,
learnt how to talk, eat and fart,

---

4. *The Beautiful Negress!* (Italian).
5. A main road in modern London, site of the early Roman settlement called "Londinium" established around 43 C.E.
6. Now capital of Sudan.

7. Large region of Western Europe, including most of modern-day France, under Roman rule from 58 B.C.E. to 486 C.E.
8. Street in London.

45 how to get my amo amas amat right, and ditch
my second-generation plebby creole.[9]

Zuleika accepta est.
Zuleika delicata est.[1]
Zuleika bloody goody-two-shoes est.

50 But I dreamt of creating mosaics,
of remaking my town with bright stones and glass.

But no! Numquam!° It's not allowed.   *Never!*
Sure, Felix brings me presents, when he deigns

to come west. I've had Chinese silk, a marble
55 figurine from Turkey, gold earrings

shaped like dolphins, and I have the deepest
fondness for my husband, of course,

sort of, though he spills over me like dough
and I'm tempted to call Cook mid coitus

60 to come trim his sides so that he fits me.
Then it's puff and *Ciao, baby!*

Solitudoh, solitudee, solitudargh!

2001

9. A hybrid language. "Plebby": vulgar (from "ple-   1. Zuleika is accepted. Zuleika is delicate (Latin).
beian," or lower-class).

PATIENCE AGBABI

orn in 1965 in London to Nigerian parents, Patience Agbabi became a foster child. Later describing herself as "bi-cultural," she grew up in a white English family in Sussex and Wales while maintaining a close relationship with her birth parents, with whom she also lived from time to time. In high school she was thrilled by the General Prologue to Chaucer's *Canterbury Tales*, which she later recast for a contemporary, multiracial Britain as *Telling Tales* (2014). She earned a B.A. in English with honors at Oxford and an M.A. in creative writing from the University of Sussex.

Hailed as a "performance" or "spoken word" poet, Agbabi composes for both the stage and the page. In "Prologue," from her second book of poems, *Transformatrix* (2000), as in her other work, Agbabi's language and the forms she uses amalgamate high literary art with oral and musical traditions. The poem adapts the insistent rhyme, syncopated rhythms, and self-reflexive wordplay of hip-hop. Dotted with literary terms and techniques, it also draws on the ancient *ars poetica* tradition—poems as instruction manuals for writing poetry. Partly rap boast and partly literary manifesto, Agbabi's exuberantly hybrid art remakes and renews the disparate sources it welds together.

Prologue

Give me a word
any word
let it roll across your tongue
like a dolly mixture.°   *British candy*
5   Open your lips
say it loud
let each syllable vibrate
like a transistor.
Say it again again again again again
10   till it's a tongue twister
till its meaning is in tatters
till its meaning equals sound
now write it down,
letter by letter
15   loop the loops
till you form a structure.
Do it again again again again again
till it's a word picture.
Does this inspire?
20   Is your consciousness on fire?
Then let me take you higher.[1]

Give me a noun
give me a verb
and I'm in motion
25   cos I'm on a mission
to deliver information
so let me take you to the fifth dimension.
No fee, it's free,
you only gotta pay attention.
30   So sit back, relax,
let me take you back
to when you learnt to walk, talk,
learnt coordination
and communication,
35   mama
dada.
If you rub two words together you get friction
cut them in half, you get a fraction.
If you join two words you get multiplication.
40   My school of mathematics
equals verbal acrobatics
so let's make conversation.

Give me a preposition
give me an interjection
45   give me inspiration.
In the beginning was creation

1. "I Want to Take You Higher" is the title of a song (1969) by Sly and the Family Stone.

I'm not scared of revelations
cos I've done my calculations.
I've got high hopes
50 on the tightrope,
I just keep talking.
I got more skills than I got melanin
I'm fired by adrenaline
if you wanna know what rhyme it is
55 it's feminine.
Cos I'm Eve on an Apple Mac
this is a rap attack
so rich in onomatopoeia
I'll take you higher than the ozone layer.
60 So give me Word for Windows
give me 'W' times three
cos I'm on a mission
to deliver information
that is gravity defying
65 and I'll keep on trying
till you lose your fear of flying.

Give me a pronoun
give me a verb
and I'm living in syntax.
70 You only need two words to form a sentence.
I am I am I am I am I am
bicultural and sometimes clinical,
my mother fed me rhymes through the umbilical,
I was born waxing lyrical.
75 I was raised on Watch with Mother[2]
The Rime of the Ancient Mariner[3]
and Fight the Power.[4]
Now I have the perfect tutor
in my postmodern suitor,
80 I'm in love with my computer.
But let me shut down
before I touch down.

Give me a word
give me a big word
85 let me manifest
express in excess
the M I X
of my voice box.
Now I've eaten the apple
90 I'm more subtle than a snake is.
I wanna do poetic things in poetic places.
Give me poetry unplugged
so I can counter silence.
Give me my poetic licence

---

2. British children's TV series (1953–73).
3. Long poem (1798) by the English Romantic
poet Samuel Taylor Coleridge (1772–1834).

4. Song (1989) by the American hip-hop group
Public Enemy.

95 and I'll give you metaphors that top eclipses
I'll give megabytes and megamixes.

Give me a stage and I'll cut form on it
give me a page and I'll perform on it.

Give me a word
100 any word.

2000

DALJIT NAGRA

*L*ook, *We Have Coming to Dover!* (2007) is Daljit Nagra's first, Forward Prize–winning collection of poems, its title alluding to Matthew Arnold and W. H. Auden and inflecting an iconic British site with Indianized English. Nagra was born in 1966 in Yiewsley, west London, to Sikh Punjabi parents who had come to England in the 1950s. He grew up in Britain between Punjabi and English cultures, and his work, including the poems in *Tippoo Sultan's Incredible White Man Eating Tiger Toy Machine!!!* (2011) and *British Museum* (2017), as well as an English retelling of the *Ramayana* (2013), weaves together his disparate inheritances.

His poem "A Black History of the English-Speaking Peoples"—a title that ironically recalls Winston Churchill's monumental *History of the English-Speaking Peoples*—meditates on Shakespeare's Globe from an Asian British perspective. Although some of Nagra's poetry is in an ebulliently performative Indian English, this poem and others are written in a Standard English richly threaded with literary allusions. Nagra lovingly and mockingly echoes poets who helped forge the language and forms of his poetry, writers such as Shakespeare, Tennyson, Walcott, and Auden (whose anvil-like stanza form Nagra adapts from the poem "Spain"). He writes in this high literary English as an insider-outsider: he self-consciously extends a literary canon that goes back to Shakespeare, even as he recalls, from within the heart of the former empire, Britain's sometimes exploitative and racist history. Combining insider and rebel, perpetuator and opponent, mimic and insurgent, Nagra acknowledges his complicity in colonialism even as he disavows it, resists the empire even as he renovates its language and literary traditions.

A Black History of the English-Speaking Peoples[1]

I

A king's invocations at the Globe Theatre[2]
spin me from my stand to a time when boyish

---

1. Cf. *A History of the English-Speaking Peoples* (1956–58), a history in four volumes of Great Britain and its former possessions by Winston Churchill (1874–1965). As an ethnic descriptor, "black" in the British context has sometimes been used to include people not only of African but also of South Asian descent.
2. London theater associated with Shakespeare, built in 1599, destroyed by fire in 1613, rebuilt the following year, closed in 1642, and reconstructed near the original site in 1997.

bravado and cannonade
and plunder were enough to woo the regal seat.

5   That the stuff of Elizabethan art and a nation
of walled gardens in a local one-upmanship
   would tame the four-cornered
world for Empire's dominion seems inconceivable.

Between the birth and the fire and rebirth of the Globe
10   the visions of Albion[3] led to a Rule Britannia
   of trade-winds-and-Gulf-Stream
all-conquering fleets that aroused theatres

for lectures on Hottentots[4] and craniology,[5]
whilst Eden was paraded in Kew.[6]
15   Between *Mayflower* and *Windrush*[7]
(with each *necessary murder*[8]) the celebrated

embeddings of imperial gusto where jungles
were surmounted so the light of learning be spread
   to help sobbing suttees[9]
20   give up the ghost of a husband's flaming pyre.

II

So much for yesterday,[1] but today's time-honoured
televised clashes repeat the flag of a book burning[2]
   and May Day's Mohican
Churchill[3] and all that shock and awe[4]

25   that brings me back to Mr Wanamaker's[5] Globe.
An American's thatched throwback to the king
   of the canon! I watch the actor
as king, from the cast of masterful Robeson.[6]

The crowd, too, seem a hotchpotch from the pacts
30   and sects of our ebb and flow.[7] My forbears played

3. Ancient name for the island of Great Britain. Cf. *Visions of the Daughters of Albion* (1793) by the English poet William Blake (1757–1827).
4. Derogatory term for the native Khoikhoi people of southern Africa.
5. Study of the shape and size of the skulls of different human races.
6. West London suburb. Kew Gardens massively expanded its global collection of plants in the Victorian era.
7. Ship that in 1948 brought the first large group of West Indian immigrants to Britain. *Mayflower*: ship that in 1620 brought the first English Puritan emigrants to Massachusetts.
8. Phrase that, like the poem's stanza form, is taken from "Spain" (1937) by W. H. Auden (1907–1973) (see p. 810, above).
9. Indian widows who immolated themselves on their husbands' funeral pyres before Britain banned the practice in the 19th century.

1. Cf. the refrain of "Yesterday" in Auden's "Spain" (lines 1ff.) (p. 810, above).
2. British Muslim protesters were televised burning Salman Rushdie's *Satanic Verses* (1988).
3. During May Day demonstrations in London in 2000, a statue of Winston Churchill was given a Mohawk ("Mohican") hairdo made of turf.
4. U.S. military doctrine widely cited during the U.S.-led invasion of Iraq in 2003.
5. Sam Wanamaker (1919–1993), American expatriate film director and actor who re-created the Globe Theatre.
6. Paul Robeson (1898–1976), American singer, actor, and civil rights advocate acclaimed for his performances as Othello.
7. Cf. King Lear addressing his daughter Cordelia: "and we'll wear out, / In a walled prison, packs and sects of great ones, / That ebb and flow by the moon" (*King Lear* 5.3.17–19).

their part for the Empire's quid°   *one pound sterling*
pro quo by assisting the rule and divide[8] of their ilk.

Did such relations bear me to this stage?
Especially with Macaulay[9] in mind, who claimed the passing
35   of the imperial sceptre would highlight
the imperishable empire of our arts . . . [1]

So does the red of Macaulay's map run through
my blood? Am I a noble scruff who hopes a proud
        academy might canonise
40   his poems for their faith in canonical allusions?

Is my voice phoney over these oft-heard beats?
Well if my voice feels vexatious, what can I but pray
        that it reign Bolshie[2]
through puppetry and hypocrisy full of gung-ho fury!

III

45   The heyday Globe incited brave new verse[3]
modelled on the past, where time's frictions
        courted Shakespeare's corruptions
for tongue's mastery of the pageant subject. Perhaps

the Globe should be my muse! I'm happy digging
50   for my England's good garden[4] to bear again.
        My garden's only a state
of mind, where it's easy aligning myself with a 'turncoat'

T. E. Lawrence[5] and a *half-naked fakir*[6] and always
the groundling. Perhaps to aid the succession
55   of this language of the world,
for the poet weeding the roots, for the debate

in ourselves, now we're bound to the wheels
of global power,[7] we should tend the manorial

8. The British Empire employed a "divide and rule" strategy to weaken local powers in India.
9. Thomas Babington Macaulay (1800–1859), British historian and politician who mandated English language instruction in Indian schools.
1. In a 1833 speech calling for the education of Indians in English ways, Macaulay said: "The scepter may pass away from us. . . . But . . . [t]here is an empire exempt from all natural causes of decay. Those triumphs are the pacific triumphs of reason over barbarism: that empire is the imperishable empire of our arts and our morals, our literature and our laws."
2. British slang for Bolshevik, Russian revolutionary communist; hence, disobedient, uncooperative.
3. Cf. *Brave New World* (1931), a dystopian novel set in London by English writer Aldous Huxley (1894–1963), its title taken from Miranda's speech in Shakespeare's *The Tempest* (5.1.205).
4. Cf. *Richard II* (2.1.42, 50): "This other Eden, demi-paradise / . . . This blessed plot, this earth, this realm, this England."
5. British military officer (1888–1935) who, dressing like and identifying with his Arab partners, led a revolt against the Ottoman Empire during World War I; he became known as Lawrence of Arabia.
6. Condensed version of Churchill's insulting reference to Mahatma Gandhi (1869–1948), leader of the Indian Independence movement.
7. Cf. *King Lear* 4.7.46–47: "I am bound / Upon a wheel of fire."

slime[8]—that legacy
60 offending the outcasts who fringe our circles.

IV

Who believes a bleached yarn? Would we openly
admit the Livingstone[9] spirit turned Kurtz,[1] our flag
is a union of black and blue
flapping in the anthems of haunted rain . . . ?

65 Coming clean would surely give us greater distance
than this king at the Globe, whose head seems cluttered
with golden-age bumph,[2]
whose suffering ends him agog at the stars.

V

I applaud and stroll toward Westminster,[3]
70 yet softly tonight the waters of Britannia bobble
with flotillas of tea and white gold
cotton and sugar and the sweetness-and-light[4]

blood lettings and ultimately red-faced Suez.[5]
And how swiftly the tide removes from the scene
75 the bagpipe clamouring
garrisons with the field-wide scarlet soldiery

and the martyr's cry: *Every man die at his post!*[6]
Till what's ahead are the upbeat lovers who gaze
from the London Eye[7]
80 at multinationals lying along the sanitised Thames.

2011

---

8. "Some slave is rotting in this manorial lake," exclaims St. Lucian poet Derek Walcott (1930–2017) in his poem "Ruins of a Great House" (1962), which meditates on the decay of empire by invoking the stench of "rotting lime."
9. David Livingstone (1813–1873), Scottish medical missionary and explorer in Africa.
1. Fictional European ivory trader who rules a society of central African natives as a demigod in Joseph Conrad's *Heart of Darkness* (see p. 71).
2. I.e., superfluous documents; toilet paper.
3. London area with Westminster Abbey, Buckingham Palace, and the Houses of Parliament.
4. Phrase for the beauty and intelligence of culture that English poet Matthew Arnold (1822–1888) borrowed from Irish poet Jonathan Swift (1667–1745).
5. Egyptian seaport city where an invasion by Britain, France, and Israel failed in 1956, a failure seen as a turning point in the decline of the British Empire.
6. From "The Defence of Lucknow" (1879) by English poet Alfred, Lord Tennyson (1809–1892), which celebrates the defenders of the British Residency in the Indian city of Lucknow that fell under siege during the Indian Rebellion of 1857.
7. Tallest Ferris wheel in Europe, on the south bank of the River Thames.

DORIS LESSING
1919–2013

B orn in Persia (now Iran) to British parents, Doris Lessing (née Tayler) lived in
southern Rhodesia (now Zimbabwe) from 1924 to 1949, before settling in
England. Her five-novel sequence with the general title Children of Violence
(beginning with *Martha Quest*, 1952) combines psychological autobiography with
powerful explorations of the relationship between blacks and whites in southern
Africa. Her combination of psychological introspection, political analysis, social
documentary, and feminism gives a characteristic tone to her novels and short stories. These elements are effectively combined in her novel *The Golden Notebook*
(1962), which explores with unexhibitionist frankness the sexual problems of an
independent woman while at the same time probing the political conscience of an
ex-communist and the needs and dilemmas of a creative writer. In the early 1970s,
influenced by the writings of the renegade psychologist R. D. Laing and by the principles of Sufism (the mystical, ecstatic dimension of Islam), Lessing's realistic investigations of social issues took a different turn. In *Briefing for a Descent into Hell*
(1971) and *The Memoirs of a Survivor* (1974), she explores myth and fantasy, restrained
within a broadly realist context. In a series of novels with the general title *Canopus in
Argos: Archives* (written between 1979 and 1983), she draws on her reading of the Old
and New Testaments, the Apocrypha, and the Koran and borrows conventions from
science fiction to describe the efforts of a superhuman, extraterrestrial race to guide
human history. The novels convey the scope of human suffering in the twentieth
century with a rare imaginative power. On completion of this novel sequence, Lessing
took the unusual step of publishing two pseudonymous novels (now known jointly as
The Diaries of Jane Somers, 1983–84), in which she reverted to the realist mode with
which she was most widely associated. *The Good Terrorist* (1985) is also written in the
style of documentary realism, but *The Fifth Child* (1988) combines elements of realism and fantasy, exploring the effect on a happy family of the birth of a genetically
abnormal, nonhuman child.

Her work from the early 1990s on included two candid volumes of autobiography,
Under My Skin (1994) and *Walking in the Shade* (1997); the four short novels that
comprise *The Grandmothers* (2003); *The Cleft* (2007); a clutch of other novels; and
a series of short stories. Some of these stories—which deal with racial and social
dilemmas as well as with loneliness, the claims of politics, the problems of aging
(especially for women), the conflict between the generations, and a whole spectrum
of problems of alienation and isolation—have a particular pungency and force.
Winner of the Nobel Prize in Literature in 2007, Lessing was very much a writer of
her time, deeply involved with the changing patterns of thought, feeling, and culture during the last sixty years. She consistently explored and tested the boundaries of realist technique, without resort to formal experimentalism. Published just on
the cusp of second-wave feminism, the story reprinted here, "To Room Nineteen," is
a psychologically penetrating study of a woman who finds ultimate fulfillment in
neither her marriage nor her children and, feeling trapped by traditional gender roles,
seeks solitude in—to echo the title of Virginia Woolf's feminist classic about gender,
space, and identity—a room of her own.

To Room Nineteen

This is a story, I suppose, about a failure in intelligence: the Rawlings' marriage was grounded in intelligence.

They were older when they married than most of their married friends: in their well-seasoned late twenties. Both had had a number of affairs, sweet rather than bitter; and when they fell in love—for they did fall in love—had known each other for some time. They joked that they had saved each other "for the real thing." That they had waited so long (but not too long) for this real thing was to them a proof of their sensible discrimination. A good many of their friends had married young, and now (they felt) probably regretted lost opportunities; while others, still unmarried, seemed to them arid, self-doubting, and likely to make desperate or romantic marriages.

Not only they, but others, felt they were well matched: their friends' delight was an additional proof of their happiness. They had played the same roles, male and female, in this group or set, if such a wide, loosely connected, constantly changing constellation of people could be called a set. They had both become, by virtue of their moderation, their humour, and their abstinence from painful experience people to whom others came for advice. They could be, and were, relied on. It was one of those cases of a man and a woman linking themselves whom no one else had ever thought of linking, probably because of their similarities. But then everyone exclaimed: Of course! How right! How was it we never thought of it before!

And so they married amid general rejoicing, and because of their foresight and their sense for what was probable, nothing was a surprise to them.

Both had well-paid jobs. Matthew was a subeditor on a large London newspaper, and Susan worked in an advertising firm. He was not the stuff of which editors or publicised journalists are made, but he was much more than "a subeditor," being one of the essential background people who in fact steady, inspire and make possible the people in the limelight. He was content with this position. Susan had a talent for commercial drawing. She was humorous about the advertisements she was responsible for, but she did not feel strongly about them one way or the other.

Both, before they married, had had pleasant flats, but they felt it unwise to base a marriage on either flat, because it might seem like a submission of personality on the part of the one whose flat it was not. They moved into a new flat in South Kensington on the clear understanding that when their marriage had settled down (a process they knew would not take long, and was in fact more a humorous concession to popular wisdom than what was due to themselves) they would buy a house and start a family.

And this is what happened. They lived in their charming flat for two years, giving parties and going to them, being a popular young married couple, and then Susan became pregnant, she gave up her job, and they bought a house in Richmond. It was typical of this couple that they had a son first, then a daughter, then twins, son and daughter. Everything right, appropriate, and what everyone would wish for, if they could choose. But people did feel these two had chosen; this balanced and sensible family was no more than what was due to them because of their infallible sense for *choosing* right.

And so they lived with their four children in their gardened house in Richmond and were happy. They had everything they had wanted and had planned for.

And yet . . .

Well, even this was expected, that there must be a certain flatness. . . .

Yes, yes, of course, it was natural they sometimes felt like this. Like what?

Their life seemed to be like a snake biting its tail. Matthew's job for the sake of Susan, children, house, and garden—which caravanserai[1] needed a well-paid job to maintain it. And Susan's practical intelligence for the sake of Matthew, the children, the house and the garden—which unit would have collapsed in a week without her.

But there was no point about which either could say: "For the sake of *this* is all the rest." Children? But children can't be a centre of life and a reason for being. They can be a thousand things that are delightful, interesting, satisfying, but they can't be a wellspring to live from. Or they shouldn't be. Susan and Matthew knew that well enough.

Matthew's job? Ridiculous. It was an interesting job, but scarcely a reason for living. Matthew took pride in doing it well; but he could hardly be expected to be proud of the newspaper: the newspaper he read, *his* newspaper, was not the one he worked for.

Their love for each other? Well, that was nearest it. If this wasn't a centre, what was? Yes, it was around this point, their love, that the whole extraordinary structure revolved. For extraordinary it certainly was. Both Susan and Matthew had moments of thinking so, of looking in secret disbelief at this thing they had created: marriage, four children, big house, garden, charwomen,[2] friends, cars . . . and this *thing*, this entity, all of it had come into existence, been blown into being out of nowhere, because Susan loved Matthew and Matthew loved Susan. Extraordinary. So that was the central point, the wellspring.

And if one felt that it simply was not strong enough, important enough, to support it all, well whose fault was that? Certainly neither Susan's nor Matthew's. It was in the nature of things. And they sensibly blamed neither themselves nor each other.

On the contrary, they used their intelligence to preserve what they had created from a painful and explosive world: they looked around them, and took lessons. All around them, marriages collapsing, or breaking, or rubbing along (even worse, they felt). They must not make the same mistakes, they must not.

They had avoided the pitfall so many of their friends had fallen into—of buying a house in the country *for the sake of the children*; so that the husband became a weekend husband, a weekend father, and the wife always careful not to ask what went on in the town flat which they called (in joke) a bachelor flat. No, Matthew was a full-time husband, a full-time father, and at nights, in the big married bed in the big married bedroom (which had an attractive view of the river) they lay beside each other talking and he told her about his day, and what he had done, and whom he had met; and she told him about her day (not as interesting, but that was not her fault) for both knew of the hidden resentments and deprivations of the woman who

---

1. Inn with large courtyard, in West Asia.   2. Household workers.

has lived her own life—and above all, has earned her own living—and is now dependent on a husband for outside interests and money.

Nor did Susan make the mistake of taking a job for the sake of her independence, which she might very well have done, since her old firm, missing her qualities of humour, balance, and sense, invited her often to go back. Children needed their mother to a certain age, that both parents knew and agreed on; and when these four healthy wisely brought-up children were of the right age, Susan would work again, because she knew, and so did he, what happened to women of fifty at the height of their energy and ability, with grown-up children who no longer needed their full devotion.

So here was this couple, testing their marriage, looking after it, treating it like a small boat full of helpless people in a very stormy sea. Well, of course, so it was. . . . The storms of the world were bad, but not too close—which is not to say they were selfishly felt: Susan and Matthew were both well-informed and responsible people. And the inner storms and quicksands were understood and charted. So everything was all right. Everything was in order. Yes, things were under control.

So what did it matter if they felt dry, flat? People like themselves, fed on a hundred books (psychological, anthropological, sociological) could scarcely be unprepared for the dry, controlled wistfulness which is the distinguishing mark of the intelligent marriage. Two people, endowed with education, with discrimination, with judgement, linked together voluntarily from their will to be happy together and to be of use to others—one sees them everywhere, one knows them, one even is that thing oneself: sadness because so much is after all so little. These two, unsurprised, turned towards each other with even more courtesy and gentle love: this was life, that two people, no matter how carefully chosen, could not be everything to each other. In fact, even to say so, to think in such a way, was banal, they were ashamed to do it.

It was banal, too, when one night Matthew came home late and confessed he had been to a party, taken a girl home and slept with her. Susan forgave him, of course. Except that forgiveness is hardly the word. Understanding, yes. But if you understand something, you don't forgive it, you are the thing itself: forgiveness is for what you *don't* understand. Nor had he *confessed*—what sort of word is that?

The whole thing was not important. After all, years ago they had joked: Of course I'm not going to be faithful to you, no one can be faithful to one other person for a whole lifetime. (And there was the word *faithful*—stupid, all these words, stupid, belonging to a savage old world.) But the incident left both of them irritable. Strange, but they were both bad-tempered, annoyed. There was something unassimilable about it.

Making love splendidly after he had come home that night, both had felt that the idea that Myra Jenkins, a pretty girl met at a party, could be even relevant was ridiculous. They had loved each other for over a decade, would love each other for years more. Who, then, was Myra Jenkins?

Except, thought Susan, unaccountably bad-tempered, she was (is?) the first. In ten years. So either the ten years' fidelity was not important, or she isn't. (No, no, there is something wrong with this way of thinking, there must be.) But if she isn't important, presumably it wasn't important either when Matthew and I first went to bed with each other that afternoon whose delight even now (like a very long shadow at sundown) lays a long, wand-like finger over us. (Why did I say sundown?) Well, if what we felt that afternoon was not important, nothing is important, because if it hadn't been for what we felt, we wouldn't be Mr and Mrs Rawlings with four children, etc., etc. The whole thing is *absurd*—for him to have come home and told me was absurd. For him not to have told me was absurd. For me to care, or for that matter not to care, is absurd . . . and who is Myra Jenkins? Why, no one at all.

There was only one thing to do, and of course these sensible people did it: they put the thing behind them, and consciously, knowing what they were doing, moved forward into a different phase of their marriage, giving thanks for past good fortune as they did so.

For it was inevitable that the handsome, blond, attractive, manly man, Matthew Rawlings, should be at times tempted (oh, what a word!) by the attractive girls at parties she could not attend because of the four children; and that sometimes he would succumb (a word even more repulsive, if possible) and that she, a good-looking woman in the big well-tended garden at Richmond, would sometimes be pierced as by an arrow from the sky with bitterness. Except that bitterness was not in order, it was out of court. Did the casual girls touch the marriage? They did not. Rather it was they who knew defeat because of the handsome Matthew Rawlings' marriage body and soul to Susan Rawlings.

In that case why did Susan feel (though luckily not for longer than a few seconds at a time) as if life had become a desert, and that nothing mattered, and that her children were not her own?

Meanwhile her intelligence continued to assert that all was well. What if her Matthew did have an occasional sweet afternoon, the odd affair? For she knew quite well, except in her moments of aridity, that they were very happy, that the affairs were not important.

Perhaps that was the trouble? It was in the nature of things that the adventures and delights could no longer be hers, because of the four children and the big house that needed so much attention. But perhaps she was secretly wishing, and even knowing that she did, that the wildness and the beauty could be his. But he was married to her. She was married to him. They were married inextricably. And therefore the gods could not strike him with the real magic, not really. Well, was it Susan's fault that after he came home from an adventure he looked harassed rather than fulfilled? (In fact, that was how she knew he had been *unfaithful*, because of his sullen air, and his glances at her, similar to hers at him: What is it that I share with this person that shields all delight from me?) But none of it by anybody's fault. (But what did they feel ought to be somebody's fault?) Nobody's fault, nothing to be at fault, no one to blame, no one to offer or to take it . . . and nothing wrong, either, except that Matthew never was really struck, as he wanted to be, by joy; and that Susan was more and more often threatened by emptiness. (It was usually in the garden that she was invaded by this feeling: she was coming to avoid the garden, unless the children or Matthew were with her.) There was no need to use the dramatic words, unfaithful, forgive, and the rest: intelligence forbade them. Intelligence barred, too, quarrelling, sulking, anger, silences of withdrawal, accusations and tears. Above all, intelligence forbids tears.

A high price has to be paid for the happy marriage with the four healthy children in the large white gardened house.

And they were paying it, willingly, knowing what they were doing. When they lay side by side or breast to breast in the big civilised bedroom overlooking the wild sullied river, they laughed, often, for no particular reason;

but they knew it was really because of these two small people, Susan and Matthew, supporting such an edifice on their intelligent love. The laugh comforted them; it saved them both, though from what, they did not know.

They were now both fortyish. The older children, boy and girl were ten and eight, at school. The twins, six, were still at home. Susan did not have nurses or girls to help her: childhood is short; and she did not regret the hard work. Often enough she was bored, since small children can be boring; she was often very tired; but she regretted nothing. In another decade, she would turn herself back into being a woman with a life of her own.

Soon the twins would go to school, and they would be away from home from nine until four. These hours, so Susan saw it, would be the preparation for her own slow emancipation away from the role of hub-of-the-family into woman-with-her-own-life. She was already planning for the hours of freedom when all the children would be "off her hands." That was the phrase used by Matthew and by Susan and by their friends, for the moment when the youngest child went off to school. "They'll be off your hands, darling Susan, and you'll have time to yourself." So said Matthew, the intelligent husband, who had often enough commended and consoled Susan, standing by her in spirit during the years when her soul was not her own, as she said, but her children's.

What it amounted to was that Susan saw herself as she had been at twenty-eight, unmarried; and then again somewhere about fifty, blossoming from the root of what she had been twenty years before. As if the essential Susan were in abeyance, as if she were in cold storage. Matthew said something like this to Susan one night: and she agreed that it was true—she did feel something like that. What, then, was this essential Susan? She did not know. Put like that it sounded ridiculous, and she did not really feel it. Anyway, they had a long discussion about the whole thing before going off to sleep in each other's arms.

So the twins went off to their school, two bright affectionate children who had no problems about it, since their older brother and sister had trodden this path so successfully before them. And now Susan was going to be alone in the big house, every day of the school term, except for the daily woman who came in to clean.

It was now, for the first time in this marriage, that something happened which neither of them had foreseen.

This is what happened. She returned, at nine-thirty, from taking the twins to the school by car, looking forward to seven blissful hours of freedom. On the first morning she was simply restless, worrying about the twins "naturally enough" since this was their first day away at school. She was hardly able to contain herself until they came back. Which they did happily, excited by the world of school, looking forward to the next day. And the next day Susan took them, dropped them, came back, and found herself reluctant to enter her big and beautiful home because it was as if something was waiting for her there that she did not wish to confront. Sensibly, however, she parked the car in the garage, entered the house, spoke to Mrs Parkes the daily woman about her duties, and went up to her bedroom. She was possessed by a fever which drove her out again, downstairs, into the kitchen, where Mrs Parkes was making cake and did not need her, and into the garden. There she sat on a bench and tried to calm herself, looking at trees, at a brown glimpse of the river. But she was filled with tension, like a panic: as if an enemy was in the garden with her. She spoke to herself severely, thus: All this is quite natural. First, I spent twelve years of my adult life working, *living my own life*. Then I married, and from the moment I became pregnant for the first time I signed myself over, so to speak, to other people. To the children. Not for one moment in twelve years have I been alone, had time to myself. So now I have to learn to be myself again. That's all.

And she went indoors to help Mrs Parkes cook and clean, and found some sewing to do for the children. She kept herself occupied every day. At the end of the first term she understood she felt two contrary emotions. First: secret astonishment and dismay that during those weeks when the house was empty of children she had in fact been more occupied (had been careful to keep herself occupied) than ever she had been when the children were around her needing her continual attention. Second: that now she knew the house would be full of them, and for five weeks, she resented the fact she would never be alone. She was already looking back at those hours of sewing, cooking (but by herself), as at a lost freedom which would not be hers for five long weeks. And the two months of term which would succeed the five weeks stretched alluringly open to her—freedom. But what freedom—when in fact she had been so careful *not* to be free of small duties during the last weeks? She looked at herself, Susan Rawlings, sitting in a big chair by the window in the bedroom, sewing shirts or dresses, which she might just as well have bought. She saw herself making cakes for hours at a time in the big family kitchen: yet usually she bought cakes. What she saw was a woman alone, that was true, but she had not felt alone. For instance, Mrs Parkes was always somewhere in the house. And she did not like being in the garden at all, because of the closeness there of the enemy—irritation, restlessness, emptiness, whatever it was, which keeping her hands occupied made less dangerous for some reason.

Susan did not tell Matthew of these thoughts. They were not sensible. She did not recognize herself in them. What should she say to her dear friend and husband Matthew? "When I go into the garden, that is, if the children are not there, I feel as if there is an enemy there waiting to invade me." "What enemy, Susan darling?" "Well I don't know, really. . . ." "Perhaps you should see a doctor?"

No, clearly this conversation should not take place. The holidays began and Susan welcomed them. Four children, lively, energetic, intelligent, demanding: she was never, not for a moment of her day, alone. If she was in a room, they would be in the next room, or waiting for her to do something for them; or it would soon be time for lunch or tea, or to take one of them to the dentist. Something to do: five weeks of it, thank goodness.

On the fourth day of these so welcome holidays, she found she was storming with anger at the twins, two shrinking beautiful children who (and this is what checked her) stood hand in hand looking at her with sheer dismayed disbelief. This was their calm mother, shouting at them. And for what? They had come to her with some game, some bit of nonsense. They looked at each other, moved closer for support, and went off hand in hand, leaving Susan holding on to the windowsill of the living room, breathing deep, feeling sick. She went to lie down, telling the older children she had a headache. She heard the boy Harry telling the little ones: "It's all right, Mother's got a headache." She heard that *It's all right* with pain.

That night she said to her husband: "Today I shouted at the twins, quite unfairly." She sounded miserable, and he said gently: "Well, what of it?"

"It's more of an adjustment than I thought, their going to school."

"But Susie, Susie darling. . . ." For she was crouched weeping on the bed. He comforted her: "Susan, what is all this about? You shouted at them? What of it? If you shouted at them fifty times a day it wouldn't be more than the little devils deserve." But she wouldn't laugh. She wept. Soon he comforted her with his body. She became calm. Calm, she wondered what was wrong with her, and why she should mind so much that she might, just once, have behaved unjustly with the children. What did it matter? They had forgotten it all long ago: Mother had a headache and everything was all right.

It was a long time later that Susan understood that that night, when she had wept and Matthew had driven the misery out of her with his big solid body, was the last time, ever in their married life, that they had been—to use their mutual language—with each other. And even that was a lie, because she had not told him of her real fears at all.

The five weeks passed, and Susan was in control of herself, and good and kind, and she looked forward to the end of the holidays with a mixture of fear and longing. She did not know what to expect. She took the twins off to school (the elder children took themselves to school) and she returned to the house determined to face the enemy wherever he was, in the house, or the garden or—where?

She was again restless, she was possessed by restlessness. She cooked and sewed and worked as before, day after day, while Mrs Parkes remonstrated: "Mrs Rawlings, what's the need for it? I can do that, it's what you pay me for."

And it was so irrational that she checked herself. She would put the car into the garage, go up to her bedroom, and sit, hands in her lap, forcing herself to be quiet. She listened to Mrs Parkes moving around the house. She looked out into the garden and saw the branches shake the trees. She sat defeating the enemy, restlessness. Emptiness. She ought to be thinking about her life, about herself. But she did not. Or perhaps she could not. As soon as she forced her mind to think about Susan (for what else did she want to be alone for?) it skipped off to thoughts of butter or school clothes. Or it thought of Mrs Parkes. She realised that she sat listening for the movements of the cleaning woman, following her every turn, bend, thought. She followed her in her mind from kitchen to bathroom, from table to oven, and it was as if the duster, the cleaning cloth, the saucepan, were in her own hand. She would hear herself saying: No, not like that, don't put that there. . . . Yet she did not give a damn what Mrs Parkes did, or if she did it at all. Yet she could not prevent herself from being conscious of her, every minute. Yes, this was what was wrong with her: she needed, when she was alone, to be really alone, with no one near. She could not endure the knowledge that in ten minutes or in half an hour Mrs Parkes would call up the stairs: "Mrs Rawlings, there's no silver polish. Madam, we're out of flour."

So she left the house and went to sit in the garden where she was screened from the house by trees. She waited for the demon to appear and claim her, but he did not.

She was keeping him off, because she had not, after all, come to an end of arranging herself.

She was planning how to be somewhere where Mrs Parkes would not come after her with a cup of tea, or a demand to be allowed to telephone (always irritating since Susan did not care who she telephoned or how often), or just a nice talk about something. Yes, she needed a place, or a state of affairs, where it would not be necessary to keep reminding herself: In ten minutes I must telephone Matthew about . . . and at half past three I must leave early for the children because the car needs cleaning. And at ten o'clock tomorrow I must remember. . . . She was possessed with resentment that the seven hours of freedom in every day (during weekdays in the school term) were not free, that never, not for one second, ever, was she free from the pressure of time, from having to remember this or that. She could never forget herself; never really let herself go into forgetfulness.

Resentment. It was poisoning her. (She looked at this emotion and thought it was absurd. Yet she felt it.) She was a prisoner. (She looked at this thought too, and it was no good telling herself it was a ridiculous one.) She must tell Matthew—but what? She was filled with emotions that were utterly ridiculous, that she despised, yet that nevertheless she was feeling so strongly she could not shake them off.

The school holidays came round, and this time they were for nearly two months, and she behaved with a conscious controlled decency that nearly drove her crazy. She would lock herself in the bathroom, and sit on the edge of the bath, breathing deep, trying to let go into some kind of calm. Or she went up into the spare room, usually empty, where no one would expect her to be. She heard the children calling "Mother, Mother," and kept silent, feeling guilty. Or she went to the very end of the garden, by herself, and looked at the slow-moving brown river; she looked at the river and closed her eyes and breathed slow and deep, taking it into her being, into her veins.

Then she returned to the family, wife and mother, smiling and responsible, feeling as if the pressure of these people—four lively children and her husband—were a painful pressure on the surface of her skin, a hand pressing on her brain. She did not once break down into irritation during these holidays, but it was like living out a prison sentence, and when the children went back to school, she sat on a white stone seat near the flowing river, and she thought: It is not even a year since the twins went to school, since *they were off my hands* (What on earth did I think I meant when I used that stupid phrase?) and yet I'm a different person. I'm simply not myself. I don't understand it.

Yet she had to understand it. For she knew that this structure—big white house, on which the mortgage still cost four hundred a year, a husband, so good and kind and insightful, four children, all doing so nicely, and the garden where she sat, and Mrs Parkes the cleaning woman—all this depended on her, and yet she could not understand why, or even what it was she contributed to it.

She said to Matthew in their bedroom: "I think there must be something wrong with me."

And he said: "Surely not, Susan? You look marvelous—you're as lovely as ever."

She looked at the handsome blond man, with his clear, intelligent, blue-eyed face, and thought: Why is it I can't tell him? Why not? And she said: "I need to be alone more than I am."

At which he swung his slow blue gaze at her, and she saw what she had been dreading: Incredulity. Disbelief. And fear. An incredulous blue stare from a stranger who was her husband, as close to her as her own breath.

He said: "But the children are at school and off your hands."

She said to herself: I've got to force myself to say: Yes, but do you realise that I never feel free? There's never a moment I can say to myself: There's nothing I have to remind myself about, nothing I have to do in half an hour, or an hour, or two hours. . . .

But she said: "I don't feel well."

He said: "Perhaps you need a holiday."

She said, appalled: "But not without you, surely?" For she could not imagine herself going off without him. Yet that was what he meant. Seeing her face, he laughed, and opened his arms, and she went into them, thinking: Yes, yes, but why can't I say it? And what is it I have to say?

She tried to tell him, about never being free. And he listened and said: "But Susan, what sort of freedom can you possibly want—short of being dead! Am I ever free? I go to the office, and I have to be there at ten—all right, half past ten, sometimes. And I have to do this or that, don't I? Then I've got to come home at a certain time—I don't mean it, you know I don't—but if I'm not going to be back home at six I telephone you. When can I ever say to myself: I have nothing to be responsible for in the next six hours?"

Susan, hearing this, was remorseful. Because it was true. The good marriage, the house, the children, depended just as much on his voluntary bondage as it did on hers. But why did he not feel bound? Why didn't he chafe and become restless? No, there was something really wrong with her and this proved it.

And that word *bondage*—why had she used it? She had never felt marriage, or the children, as bondage. Neither had he, or surely they wouldn't be together lying in each other's arms content after twelve years of marriage.

No, her state (whatever it was) was irrelevant, nothing to do with her real good life with her family. She had to accept the fact that after all, she was an irrational person and to live with it. Some people had to live with crippled arms, or stammers, or being deaf. She would have to live knowing she was subject to a state of mind she could not own.

Nevertheless, as a result of this conversation with her husband, there was a new regime next holidays.

The spare room at the top of the house now had a cardboard sign saying: PRIVATE! DO NOT DISTURB! on it. (This sign had been drawn in coloured chalks by the children, after a discussion between the parents in which it was decided this was psychologically the right thing.) The family and Mrs Parkes knew this was "Mother's Room" and that she was entitled to her privacy. Many serious conversations took place between Matthew and the children about not taking Mother for granted. Susan overheard the first, between father and Harry, the older boy, and was surprised at her irritation over it. Surely she could have a room somewhere in that big house and retire into it without such a fuss being made? Without it being so solemnly discussed? Why couldn't she simply have announced: "I'm going to fit out the little top room for myself, and when I'm in it I'm not to be disturbed for anything short of fire"? Just that, and finished; instead of long earnest discussions. When she heard Harry and Matthew explaining it to the twins with Mrs Parkes coming in—"Yes, well, a family sometimes gets on top of a woman"—she had to go right away to the bottom of the garden until the devils of exasperation had finished their dance in her blood.

But now there was a room, and she could go there when she liked, she used it seldom: she felt even more caged there than in her bedroom. One day she had gone up there after a lunch for ten children she had cooked and served because Mrs Parkes was not there, and had sat alone for a while looking into the garden. She saw the children stream out from the kitchen and stand looking up at the window where she sat behind the curtains. They were all—her children and their friends—discussing Mother's Room. A few minutes later, the chase of children in some game came pounding up the stairs, but ended as abruptly as if they had fallen over a ravine, so sudden was the silence. They had remembered she was there, and had gone silent in a great gale of "Hush! Shhhhh! Quiet, you'll disturb her. . . ." And they went tiptoeing downstairs like criminal conspirators. When she came down to make tea for them, they all apologised. The twins put their arms around her, from front and back, making a human cage of loving limbs, and promised it would never occur again. "We forgot, Mummy, we forgot all about it!"

What it amounted to was that Mother's Room, and her need for privacy, had become a valuable lesson in respect for other people's rights. Quite soon Susan was going up to the room only because it was a lesson it was a pity to drop. Then she took sewing up there, and the children and Mrs Parkes came in and out: it had become another family room.

She sighed, and smiled, and resigned herself—she made jokes at her own expense with Matthew over the room. That is, she did from the self she liked, she respected. But at the same time, something inside her howled with impatience, with rage. . . . And she was frightened. One day she found herself kneeling by her bed and praying: "Dear God, keep it away from me, keep him away from me." She meant the devil, for she now thought of it, not caring if she were irrational, as some sort of demon. She imagined him, or it, as a youngish man, or perhaps a middle-aged man pretending to be young. Or a man young-looking from immaturity? At any rate, she saw the young-looking face which, when she drew closer, had dry lines about mouth and eyes. He was thinnish, meagre in build. And he had a reddish complexion, and ginger hair. That was he—a gingery, energetic man, and he wore a reddish hairy jacket, unpleasant to the touch.

Well, one day she saw him. She was standing at the bottom of the garden, watching the river ebb past, when she raised her eyes and saw this person, or being, sitting on the white stone bench. He was looking at her, and grinning. In his hand was a long crooked stick, which he had picked off the ground, or broken off the tree above him. He was absent-mindedly, out of an absent-minded or freakish impulse of spite, using the stick to stir around in the coils of a blindworm or a grass snake (or some kind of snakelike creature: it was whitish and unhealthy to look at, unpleasant). The snake was twisting about, flinging its coils from side to side in a kind of dance of protest against the teasing prodding stick.

Susan looked at him thinking: Who is the stranger? What is he doing in our garden? Then she recognised the man around whom her terrors had crystallised. As she did so, he vanished. She made herself walk over to the bench. A shadow from a branch lay across thin emerald grass, moving jerkily over its roughness, and she could see why she had taken it for a snake, lashing and twisting. She went back to the house thinking: Right, then, so I've seen him with my own eyes, so I'm not crazy after all—there *is* a danger because I've seen him. He is lurking in the garden and sometimes even in the house, and he wants *to get into me and to take me over.*

She dreamed of having a room or a place, anywhere, where she could go and sit, by herself, no one knowing where she was.

Once, near Victoria, she found herself outside a news agent that had Rooms to Let advertised. She decided to rent a room, telling no one. Sometimes she could take the train in to Richmond and sit alone in it for an hour or two. Yet how could she? A room would cost three or four pounds a week, and she earned no money, and how could she explain to Matthew that she needed such a sum? What for? It did not occur to her that she was taking it for granted she wasn't going to tell him about the room.

Well, it was out of the question, having a room; yet she knew she must.

One day, when a school term was well established, and none of the children had measles or other ailments, and everything seemed in order, she did the shopping early, explained to Mrs Parkes she was meeting an old school friend, took the train to Victoria, searched until she found a small quiet hotel, and asked for a room for the day. They did not let rooms by the day, the manageress said, looking doubtful, since Susan so obviously was not the kind of woman who needed a room for unrespectable reasons. Susan made a long explanation about not being well, being unable to shop without frequent rests for lying down. At last she was allowed to rent the room provided she paid a full night's price for it. She was taken up by the manageress and a maid, both concerned over the state of her health . . . which must be pretty bad if, living at Richmond (she had signed her name and address in the register), she needed a shelter at Victoria.

The room was ordinary and anonymous, and was just what Susan needed. She put a shilling in the gas fire, and sat, eyes shut, in a dingy armchair with her back to a dingy window. She was alone. She was alone. She was alone. She could feel pressures lifting off her. First the sounds of traffic came very loud; then they seemed to vanish; she might even have slept a little. A knock on the door: it was Miss Townsend the manageress, bringing her a cup of tea with her own hands, so concerned was she over Susan's long silence and possible illness.

Miss Townsend was a lonely woman of fifty, running this hotel with all the rectitude expected of her, and she sensed in Susan the possibility of understanding companionship. She stayed to talk. Susan found herself in the middle of a fantastic story about her illness, which got more and more improbable as she tried to make it tally with the large house at Richmond, well-off husband, and four children. Suppose she said instead: Miss Townsend, I'm here in your hotel because I need to be alone for a few hours, above all *alone and with no one knowing where I am.* She said it mentally, and saw, mentally, the look that would inevitably come on Miss Townsend's elderly maiden's face. "Miss Townsend, my four children and my husband are driving me insane, do you understand that? Yes, I can see from the gleam of hysteria in your eyes that comes from loneliness controlled but only just contained that I've got everything in the world you've ever longed for. Well, Miss Townsend, I don't want any of it. You can have it, Miss Townsend. I wish I was absolutely alone in the world, like you. Miss Townsend, I'm besieged by seven devils, Miss Townsend, Miss Townsend, let me stay here in your hotel where the devils can't get me. . . ." Instead of saying all this, she described her anaemia, agreed to try Miss Townsend's remedy for it, which was raw liver, minced, between whole-meal bread, and said yes, perhaps it would be better if she stayed at home and let a friend do shopping for her. She paid her bill and left the hotel, defeated.

At home Mrs Parkes said she didn't really like it, no, not really, when Mrs Rawlings was away from nine in the morning until five. The teacher had telephoned from school to say Joan's teeth were paining her, and she hadn't known what to say; and what was she to make for the children's tea, Mrs Rawlings hadn't said.

All this was nonsense, of course. Mrs Parkes's complaint was that Susan had withdrawn herself spiritually, leaving the burden of the big house on her.

Susan looked back at her day of "freedom" which had resulted in her becoming a friend to the lonely Miss Townsend, and in Mrs Parkes's remonstrances. Yet she remembered the short blissful hour of being alone, really alone. She was determined to arrange her life, no matter what it cost, so that she could have that solitude more often. An absolute solitude, where no one knew her or cared about her.

But how? She thought of saying to her old employer: I want you to back me up in a story with Matthew that I am doing part-time work for you. The truth is that . . . but she would have to tell him a lie too, and which lie? She could not say: I want to sit by myself three or four times a week in a rented room. And besides, he knew Matthew, and she could not really ask him to tell lies on her behalf, apart from his being bound to think it meant a lover.

Suppose she really took a part-time job, which she could get through fast and efficiently, leaving time for herself. What job? Addressing envelopes? Canvassing?

And there was Mrs Parkes, working widow, who knew exactly what she was prepared to give to the house, who knew by instinct when her mistress withdrew in spirit from her responsibilities. Mrs Parkes was one of the servers of this world, but she needed someone to serve. She had to have Mrs Rawlings, her madam, at the top of the house or in the garden, so that she could come and get support from her: "Yes, the bread's not what it was when I was a girl. . . . Yes, Harry's got a wonderful appetite, I wonder where he puts it all. . . . Yes, it's lucky the twins are so much of a size, they can wear each other's shoes, that's a saving in these hard times. . . . Yes, the cherry jam from Switzerland is not a patch on the jam from Poland, and three times the price. . . ." And so on. That sort of talk Mrs Parkes must have, every day, or she would leave, not knowing herself why she left.

Susan Rawlings, thinking these thoughts, found that she was prowling through the great thicketed garden like a wild cat: she was walking up the stairs, down the stairs, through the rooms, into the garden, along the brown running river, back, up through the house, down again. . . . It was a wonder Mrs Parkes did not think it strange. But on the contrary, Mrs Rawlings could do what she liked, she could stand on her head if she wanted, provided she was *there*. Susan Rawlings prowled and muttered through her house, hating Mrs Parkes, hating poor Miss Townsend, dreaming of her hour of solitude in the dingy respectability of Miss Townsend's hotel bedroom, and she knew quite well she was mad. Yes, she was mad.

She said to Matthew that she must have a holiday. Matthew agreed with her. This was not as things had been once—how they had talked in each other's arms in the marriage bed. He had, she knew, diagnosed her finally as *unreasonable*. She had become someone outside himself that he had to manage. They were living side by side in this house like two tolerably friendly strangers.

Having told Mrs Parkes, or rather, asked for her permission, she went off on a walking holiday in Wales. She chose the remotest place she knew of. Every morning the children telephoned her before they went off to school, to encourage and support her, just as they had over Mother's Room. Every evening she telephoned them, spoke to each child in turn, and then to Matthew. Mrs Parkes, given permission to telephone for instructions or advice, did so every day at lunchtime. When, as happened three times, Mrs Rawlings was out on the mountainside, Mrs Parkes asked that she should ring back at such and such a time, for she would not be happy in what she was doing without Mrs Rawlings' blessing.

Susan prowled over wild country with the telephone wire holding her to her duty like a leash. The next time she must telephone, or wait to be telephoned, nailed her to her cross. The mountains themselves seemed trammelled by her unfreedom. Everywhere on the mountains, where she met no one at all, from breakfast time to dusk, excepting sheep, or a shepherd, she came face to face with her own craziness which might attack her in the broadest valleys, so that they seemed too small; or on a mountaintop from which she could see a hundred other mountains and valleys, so that they seemed too low, too small, with the sky pressing down too close. She would stand gazing at a hillside brilliant with ferns and bracken, jeweled with running water, and see nothing but her devil, who lifted inhuman eyes at her from where he leaned negligently on a rock, switching at his ugly yellow boots with a leafy twig.

She returned to her home and family, with the Welsh emptiness at the back of her mind like a promise of freedom.

She told her husband she wanted to have an *au pair* girl.[3]

They were in their bedroom, it was late at night, the children slept. He sat, shirted and slippered, in a chair by the window, looking out. She sat brushing her hair and watching him in the mirror. A time-hallowed scene in the connubial bedroom. He said nothing, while she heard the arguments coming into his mind, only to be rejected because every one was *reasonable*.

"It seems strange to get one now, after all, the children are in school most of the day. Surely the time for you to have help was when you were stuck with them day and night. Why don't you ask Mrs Parkes to cook for you? She's even offered to—I can understand if you are tired of cooking for six people. But you know that an *au pair* girl means all kinds of problems, it's not like having an ordinary char[4] in during the day. . . ."

Finally he said carefully: "Are you thinking of going back to work?"

"No," she said, "no, not really," She made herself sound vague, rather stupid. She went on brushing her black hair and peering at herself so as to be oblivious of the short uneasy glances her Matthew kept giving her. "Do you think we can't afford it?" she went on vaguely, not at all the old efficient Susan who knew exactly what they could afford.

"It's not that," he said, looking out of the window at dark trees, so as not to look at her. Meanwhile she examined a round, candid, pleasant face with clear dark brows and clear grey eyes. A sensible face. She brushed thick healthy black hair and thought: Yet that's the reflection of a madwoman. How

3. Live-in foreigner who serves a family in exchange for learning its language.   4. Charwoman.

very strange! Much more to the point if what looked back at me was the gin-gery green-eyed demon with his dry meagre smile. . . . Why wasn't Matthew agreeing? After all, what else could he do? She was breaking her part of the bargain and there was no way of forcing her to keep it: that her spirit, her soul, should live in this house, so that the people in it could grow like plants in water, and Mrs Parkes remain content in their service. In return for this, he would be a good loving husband, and responsible towards the children. Well, nothing like this had been true of either of them for a long time. He did his duty, perfunctorily; she did not even pretend to do hers. And he had become like other husbands, with his real life in his work and the people he met there, and very likely a serious affair. All this was her fault.

At last he drew heavy curtains, blotting out the trees, and turned to force her attention: "Susan, are you really sure we need a girl?" But she would not meet his appeal at all: She was running the brush over her hair again and again, lifting fine black clouds in a small hiss of electricity. She was peering in and smiling as if she were amused at the clinging hissing hair that fol-lowed the brush.

"Yes, I think it would be a good idea on the whole," she said, with the cunning of a madwoman evading the real point.

In the mirror she could see her Matthew lying on his back, his hands behind his head, staring upwards, his face sad and hard. She felt her heart (the old heart of Susan Rawlings) soften and call out to him. But she set it to be indifferent.

He said: "Susan, the children?" It was an appeal that *almost* reached her. He opened his arms, lifting them from where they had lain by his sides, palms up, empty. She had only to run across and fling herself into them, onto his hard, warm chest, and melt into herself, into Susan. But she could not. She would not see his lifted arms. She said vaguely: "Well, surely it'll be even better for them? We'll get a French or a German girl and they'll learn the language."

In the dark she lay beside him, feeling frozen, a stranger. She felt as if Susan had been spirited away. She disliked very much this woman who lay here, cold and indifferent beside a suffering man, but she could not change her.

Next morning she set about getting a girl, and very soon came Sophie Traub from Hamburg, a girl of twenty, laughing, healthy, blue-eyed, intend-ing to learn English. Indeed, she already spoke a good deal. In return for a room—"Mother's Room"—and her food, she undertook to do some light cooking, and to be with the children when Mrs Rawlings asked. She was an intelligent girl and understood perfectly what was needed. Susan said: "I go off sometimes, for the morning or for the day—well, sometimes the children run home from school, or they ring up, or a teacher rings up. I should be here, really. And there's the daily woman. . . ." And Sophie laughed her deep fruity *Fräulein's* laugh, showed her fine white teeth and her dimples, and said: "You want some person to play mistress of the house sometimes, not so?"

"Yes, that is just so," said Susan, a bit dry, despite herself, thinking in secret fear how easy it was, how much nearer to the end she was than she thought. Healthy Fräulein Traub's instant understanding of their position proved this to be true.

The *au pair* girl, because of her own common sense, or (as Susan said to herself with her new inward shudder) because she had been *chosen* so well by Susan, was a success with everyone, the children liking her, Mrs Parkes forgetting almost at once that she was German, and Matthew finding her "nice to have around the house." For he was now taking things as they came, from the surface of life, withdrawn both as a husband and a father from the household.

One day Susan saw how Sophie and Mrs Parkes were talking and laughing in the kitchen, and she announced that she would be away until teatime. She knew exactly where to go and what she must look for. She took the District Line to South Kensington, changed to the Circle, got off at Paddington, and walked around looking at the smaller hotels until she was satisfied with one which had FRED'S HOTEL painted on windowpanes that needed cleaning. The façade was a faded shiny yellow, like unhealthy skin. A door at the end of a passage said she must knock; she did, and Fred appeared. He was not at all attractive, not in any way, being fattish, and run-down, and wearing a tasteless striped suit. He had small sharp eyes in a white creased face, and was quite prepared to let Mrs Jones (she chose the farcical name deliberately, staring him out) have a room three days a week from ten until six. Provided of course that she paid in advance each time she came? Susan produced fifteen shillings (no price had been set by him) and held it out, still fixing him with a bold unblinking challenge she had not known until then she could use at will. Looking at her still, he took up a ten-shilling note from her palm between thumb and forefinger, fingered it; then shuffled up two half crowns, held out his own palm with these bits of money displayed thereon, and let his gaze lower broodingly at them. They were standing in the passage, a red-shaded light above, bare boards beneath, and a strong smell of floor polish rising about them. He shot his gaze up at her over the still-extended palm, and smiled as if to say: What do you take me for? "I shan't," said Susan, "be using this room for the purposes of making money." He still waited. She added another five shillings, at which he nodded and said: "You pay, and I ask no questions." "Good," said Susan. He now went past her to the stairs, and there waited a moment: the light from the street door being in her eyes, she lost sight of him momentarily. Then she saw a sober-suited, white-faced, white-balding little man trotting up the stairs like a waiter, and she went after him. They proceeded in utter silence up the stairs of this house where no questions were asked—Fred's Hotel, which could afford the freedom for its visitors that poor Miss Townsend's hotel could not. The room was hideous. It had a single window, with thin green brocade curtains, a three-quarter bed that had a cheap green satin bedspread on it, a fireplace with a gas fire and a shilling meter by it, a chest of drawers, and a green wicker armchair.

"Thank you," said Susan, knowing that Fred (if this was Fred, and not George, or Herbert or Charlie) was looking at her not so much with curiosity, an emotion he would not own to, for professional reasons, but with a philosophical sense of what was appropriate. Having taken her money and shown her up and agreed to everything, he was clearly disapproving of her for coming here. She did not belong here at all, so his look said. (But she knew, already, how very much she did belong: the room had been waiting for her to join it.) "Would you have me called at five o'clock, please?" and he nodded and went downstairs.

It was twelve in the morning. She was free. She sat in the armchair, she simply sat, she closed her eyes and sat and let herself be alone. She was alone and no one knew where she was. When a knock came on the door she was annoyed, and prepared to show it: but it was Fred himself, it was five o'clock and he was calling her as ordered. He flicked his sharp little eyes over the room—bed, first. It was undisturbed. She might never have been in the room at all. She thanked him, said she would be returning the day after tomorrow, and left. She was back home in time to cook supper, to put the children to bed, to cook a second supper for her husband and herself later. And to welcome Sophie back from the pictures where she had gone with a friend. All these things she did cheerfully, willingly. But she was thinking all the time of the hotel room, she was longing for it with her whole being.

Three times a week. She arrived promptly at ten, looked Fred in the eyes, gave him twenty shillings, followed him up the stairs, went into the room, and shut the door on him with gentle firmness. For Fred, disapproving of her being here at all, was quite ready to let friendship, or at least acquaintance-ship, follow his disapproval, if only she would let him. But he was content to go off on her dismissing nod, with the twenty shillings in his hand.

She sat in the armchair and shut her eyes.

What did she *do* in the room? Why, nothing at all. From the chair, when it had rested her, she went to the window, stretching her arms, smiling, treasuring her anonymity, to look out. She was no longer Susan Rawlings, mother of four, wife of Matthew, employer of Mrs Parkes and of Sophie Traub, with these and those relations with friends, schoolteachers, trades-men. She no longer was mistress of the big white house and garden, owning clothes suitable for this and that activity or occasion. She was Mrs Jones, and she was alone, and she had no past and no future. Here I am, she thought, after all these years of being married and having children and playing those roles of responsibility—and I'm just the same. Yet there have been times I thought that nothing existed of me except the roles that went with being Mrs Matthew Rawlings. Yes, here I am, and if I never saw any of my family again, here I would still be . . . how very strange that is! And she leaned on the sill, and looked into the street, loving the men and women who passed, because she did not know them. She looked at the downtrod-den buildings over the street, and at the sky, wet and dingy, or sometimes blue, and felt she had never seen buildings or sky before. And then she went back to the chair, empty, her mind a blank. Sometimes she talked aloud, saying nothing—an exclamation, meaningless, followed by a com-ment about the floral pattern on the thin rug, or a stain on the green satin coverlet. For the most part, she wool-gathered—what word is there for it?—brooded, wandered, simply went dark, feeling emptiness run deliciously through her veins like the movement of her blood.

This room had become more her own than the house she lived in. One morning she found Fred taking her a flight higher than usual. She stopped, refusing to go up, and demanded her usual room, Number 19. "Well, you'll have to wait half an hour then," he said. Willingly she descended to the dark disinfectant-smelling hall, and sat waiting until the two, man and woman, came down the stairs, giving her swift indifferent glances before they hur-ried out into the street, separating at the door. She went up to the room, *her* room, which they had just vacated. It was no less hers, though the windows were set wide open, and a maid was straightening the bed as she came in.

After these days of solitude, it was both easy to play her part as mother and wife, and difficult—because it was so easy: she felt an impostor. She felt as if her shell moved here, with her family, answering to Mummy, Mother,

Susan, Mrs Rawlings. She was surprised no one saw through her, that she wasn't turned out of doors, as a fake. On the contrary, it seemed the children loved her more; Matthew and she "got on" pleasantly, and Mrs Parkes was happy in her work under (for the most part, it must be confessed) Sophie Traub. At night she lay beside her husband, and they made love again, apparently just as they used to, when they were really married. But she, Susan, or the being who answered so readily and improbably to the name of Susan, was not there: she was in Fred's Hotel, in Paddington, waiting for the easing hours of solitude to begin.

Soon she made a new arrangement with Fred and with Sophie. It was for five days a week. As for the money, five pounds, she simply asked Matthew for it. She saw that she was not even frightened he might ask what for: he would give it to her, she knew that, and yet it was terrifying it could be so, for this close couple, these partners, had once known the destination of every shilling they must spend. He agreed to give her five pounds a week. She asked for just so much, not a penny more. He sounded indifferent about it. It was as if he were paying her, she thought: *paying her off*—yes, that was it. Terror came back for a moment, when she understood this, but she stilled it: things had gone too far for that. Now, every week, on Sunday nights, he gave her five pounds, turning away from her before their eyes could meet on the transaction. As for Sophie Traub, she was to be somewhere in or near the house until six at night, after which she was free. She was not to cook, or to clean, she was simply to be there. So she gardened or sewed, and asked friends in, being a person who was bound to have a lot of friends. If the children were sick, she nursed them. If teachers telephoned, she answered them sensibly. For the five daytimes in the school week, she was altogether the mistress of the house.

One night in the bedroom, Matthew asked: "Susan, I don't want to interfere—don't think that, please—but are you sure you are well?"

She was brushing her hair at the mirror. She made two more strokes on either side of her head, before she replied: "Yes, dear, I am sure I am well."

He was again lying on his back, his big blond head on his hands, his elbows angled up and part-concealing his face. He said: "Then Susan, I have to ask you this question, though you must understand, I'm not putting any sort of pressure on you." (Susan heard the word pressure with dismay, because this was inevitable, of course she could not go on like this.) "Are things going to go on like this?"

"Well," she said, going vague and bright and idiotic again, so as to escape: "Well, I don't see why not."

He was jerking his elbows up and down, in annoyance or in pain, and, looking at him, she saw he had got thin, even gaunt; and restless angry movements were not what she remembered of him. He said: "Do you want a divorce, is that it?"

At this, Susan only with the greatest difficulty stopped herself from laughing: she could hear the bright bubbling laughter she *would* have emitted, had she let herself. He could only mean one thing: she had a lover, and that was why she spent her days in London, as lost to him as if she had vanished to another continent.

Then the small panic set in again: she understood that he hoped she did have a lover, he was begging her to say so, because otherwise it would be too terrifying.

She thought this out, as she brushed her hair, watching the fine black stuff fly up to make its little clouds of electricity, hiss, hiss, hiss. Behind her head, across the room, was a blue wall. She realised she was absorbed in watching the black hair making shapes against the blue. She should be answering him. "Do *you* want a divorce, Matthew?"

He said: "That surely isn't the point, is it?"

"You brought it up, I didn't," she said, brightly, suppressing meaningless tinkling laughter.

Next day she asked Fred: "Have enquiries been made for me?"

He hesitated, and she said: "I've been coming here a year now. I've made no trouble, and you've been paid every day. I have a right to be told."

"As a matter of fact, Mrs Jones, a man did come asking."

"A man from a detective agency?"

"Well, he could have been, couldn't he?"

"I was asking you . . . well, what did you tell him?"

"I told him a Mrs Jones came every weekday from ten until five or six and stayed in Number Nineteen by herself."

"Describing me?"

"Well Mrs Jones, I had no alternative. Put yourself in my place."

"By rights I should deduct what that man gave you for the information."

He raised shocked eyes: she was not the sort of person to make jokes like this! Then he chose to laugh: a pinkish wet slit appeared across his white crinkled face: his eyes positively begged her to laugh, otherwise he might lose some money. She remained grave, looking at him.

He stopped laughing and said: "You want to go up now?"—returning to the familiarity, the comradeship, of the country where no questions are asked, on which (and he knew it) she depended completely.

She went up to sit in her wicker chair. But it was not the same. Her husband had searched her out. (The world had searched her out.) The pressures were on her. She was here with his connivance. He might walk in at any moment, here, into Room 19. She imagined the report from the detective agency: "A woman calling herself Mrs Jones, fitting the description of your wife (etc., etc., etc.), stays alone all day in room No. 19. She insists on this room, waits for it if it is engaged. As far as the proprietor knows she receives no visitors there, male or female." A report something on these lines, Matthew must have received.

Well of course he was right: things couldn't go on like this. He had put an end to it all simply by sending the detective after her.

She tried to shrink herself back into the shelter of the room, a snail pecked out of its shell and trying to squirm back. But the peace of the room had gone. She was trying consciously to revive it, trying to let go into the dark creative trance (or whatever it was) that she had found there. It was no use, yet she craved for it, she was as ill as a suddenly deprived addict.

Several times she returned to the room, to look for herself there, but instead she found the unnamed spirit of restlessness, a prickling fevered hunger for movement, an irritable self-consciousness that made her brain feel as if it had coloured lights going on and off inside it. Instead of the soft dark that had been the room's air, were now waiting for her demons that made her dash blindly about, muttering words of hate; she was impelling herself from point to point like a moth dashing itself against a windowpane, sliding to the bottom, fluttering off on broken wings, then crashing into the invisible barrier again. And again and again. Soon she was exhausted, and she told Fred that for a while she would not be needing the room, she was going on holiday. Home she went, to the big white house by the river. The middle of a weekday, and she felt guilty at returning to her own home when not expected. She stood unseen, looking in at the kitchen window. Mrs Parkes, wearing a discarded floral overall of Susan's, was stooping to slide something into the oven. Sophie, arms folded, was leaning her back against a cupboard and laughing at some joke made by a girl not seen before by Susan—a dark foreign girl, Sophie's visitor. In an armchair Molly, one of the twins, lay curled, sucking her thumb and watching the grownups. She must have some sickness, to be kept from school. The child's listless face, the dark circles under her eyes, hurt Susan: Molly was looking at the three grownups working and talking in exactly the same way Susan looked at the four through the kitchen window: she was remote, shut off from them.

But then, just as Susan imagined herself going in, picking up the little girl, and sitting in an armchair with her, stroking her probably heated forehead, Sophie did just that: she had been standing on one leg, the other knee flexed, its foot set against the wall. Now she let her foot in its ribbon-tied red shoe slide down the wall, and stood solid on two feet, clapping her hands before and behind her, and sang a couple of lines in German, so that the child lifted her heavy eyes at her and began to smile. Then she walked, or rather skipped, over to the child, swung her up, and let her fall into her lap at the same moment she sat herself. She said "Hopla! Hopla! Molly . . ." and began stroking the dark untidy young head that Molly laid on her shoulder for comfort.

Well. . . . Susan blinked the tears of farewell out of her eyes, and went quietly up the house to her bedroom. There she sat looking at the river through the trees. She felt at peace, but in a way that was new to her. She had no desire to move, to talk, to do anything at all. The devils that had haunted the house, the garden, were not there; but she knew it was because her soul was in Room 19 in Fred's Hotel; she was not really here at all. It was a sensation that should have been frightening: to sit at her own bedroom window, listening to Sophie's rich young voice sing German nursery songs to her child, listening to Mrs Parkes clatter and move below, and to know that all this had nothing to do with her: she was already out of it.

Later, she made herself go down and say she was home: it was unfair to be here unannounced. She took lunch with Mrs Parkes, Sophie, Sophie's Italian friend Maria, and her daughter Molly, and felt like a visitor.

A few days later, at bedtime, Matthew said: "Here's your five pounds," and pushed them over at her. Yet he must have known she had not been leaving the house at all.

She shook her head, gave it back to him, and said, in explanation, not in accusation: "As soon as you knew where I was, there was no point."

He nodded, not looking at her. He was turned away from her: thinking, she knew, how best to handle this wife who terrified him.

He said: "I wasn't trying to . . . it's just that I was worried."

"Yes, I know."

"I must confess that I was beginning to wonder . . ."

"You thought that I had a lover?"

"Yes, I am afraid I did."

She knew that he wished she had. She sat wondering how to say: "For a year now I've been spending all my days in a very sordid hotel room. It's the place where I'm happy. In fact, without it I don't exist." She heard herself saying this, and understood how terrified he was that she might. So instead she said: "Well, perhaps you're not far wrong."

Probably Matthew would think the hotel proprietor lied: he would want to think so.

"Well," he said, and she could hear his voice spring up, so to speak, with relief: "in that case I must confess I've got a bit of an affair on myself."

She said, detached and interested: "Really? Who is she?" and saw Matthew's startled look because of this reaction.

"It's Phil. Phil Hunt."

She had known Phil Hunt well in the old unmarried days. She was thinking: No, she won't do, she's too neurotic and difficult. She's never been happy yet. Sophie's much better: Well Matthew will see that himself, as sensible as he is.

This line of thought went on in silence, while she said aloud: "It's no point in telling you about mine, because you don't know him."

Quick, quick, invent, she thought. Remember how you invented all that nonsense for Miss Townsend.

She began slowly, careful not to contradict herself: "His name is Michael"— (*Michael What?*)—"Michael Plant." (What a silly name!) "He's rather like you—in looks, I mean." And indeed, she could imagine herself being touched by no one but Matthew himself. "He's a publisher." (Really? Why?) "He's got a wife already and two children."

She brought out this fantasy, proud of herself.

Matthew said: "Are you two thinking of marrying?"

She said, before she could stop herself: "Good God, *no!*"

She realised, if Matthew wanted to marry Phil Hunt, that this was too emphatic, but apparently it was all right, for his voice sounded relieved as he said: "It is a bit impossible to imagine oneself married to anyone else, isn't it?" With which he pulled her to him, so that her head lay on his shoulder. She turned her face into the dark of his flesh, and listened to the blood pounding through her ears saying: I am alone, I am alone, I am alone.

In the morning Susan lay in bed while he dressed.

He had been thinking things out in the night, because now he said: "Susan, why don't we make a foursome?"

Of course, she said to herself, of course he would be bound to say that. If one is sensible, if one is reasonable, if one never allows oneself a base thought or an envious emotion, naturally one says: Let's make a foursome!

"Why not?" she said.

"We could all meet for lunch. I mean, it's ridiculous, you sneaking off to filthy hotels, and me staying late at the office, and all the lies everyone has to tell."

What on earth did I say his name was?—she panicked, then said: "I think it's a good idea, but Michael is away at the moment. When he comes back though—and I'm sure you two would like each other."

"He's away, is he? So that's why you've been . . ." Her husband put his hand to the knot of his tie in a gesture of male coquetry she would not before have associated with him; and he bent to kiss her cheek with the expression that goes with the words: Oh you naughty little puss! And she felt its answering look, naughty and coy, come onto her face.

Inside she was dissolving in horror at them both, at how far they had both sunk from honesty of emotion.

So now she was saddled with a lover, and he had a mistress! How ordinary, how reassuring, how jolly! And now they would make a foursome of it, and go about to theatres and restaurants. After all, the Rawlings could well afford that sort of thing, and presumably the publisher Michael Plant could afford to do himself and his mistress quite well. No, there was nothing to stop the four of them developing the most intricate relationship of civilised tolerance, all enveloped in a charming afterglow of autumnal passion. Perhaps they would all go off on holidays together? She had known people who did. Or perhaps Matthew would draw the line there? Why should he, though, if he was capable of talking about "foursomes" at all?

She lay in the empty bedroom, listening to the car drive off with Matthew in it, off to work. Then she heard the children clattering off to school to the accompaniment of Sophie's cheerfully ringing voice. She slid down into the hollow of the bed, for shelter against her own irrelevance. And she stretched out her hand to the hollow where her husband's body had lain, but found no comfort there: he was not her husband. She curled herself up in a small tight ball under the clothes: she could stay here all day, all week, indeed, all her life.

But in a few days she must produce Michael Plant, and—but how? She must presumably find some agreeable man prepared to impersonate a publisher called Michael Plant. And in return for which she would—what? Well, for one thing they would make love. The idea made her want to cry with sheer exhaustion. Oh no, she had finished with all that—the proof of it was that the words "make love," or even imagining it, trying hard to revive no more than the pleasures of sensuality, let alone affection, or love, made her want to run away and hide from the sheer effort of the thing. . . . Good Lord, why make love at all? Why make love with anyone? Or if you are going to make love, what does it matter who with? Why shouldn't she simply walk into the street, pick up a man and have a roaring sexual affair with him? Why not? Or even with Fred? What difference did it make?

But she had let herself in for it—an interminable stretch of time with a lover, called Michael, as part of a gallant civilised foursome. Well, she could not, and she would not.

She got up, dressed, went down to find Mrs Parkes, and asked her for the loan of a pound, since Matthew, she said, had forgotten to leave her money. She exchanged with Mrs Parkes variations on the theme that husbands are all the same, they don't think, and without saying a word to Sophie, whose voice could be heard upstairs from the telephone, walked to the underground, travelled to South Kensington, changed to the Inner Circle, got out at Paddington, and walked to Fred's Hotel. There she told Fred that she wasn't going on holiday after all, she needed the room. She would have to wait an hour, Fred said. She went to a busy tearoom-cum-restaurant around the corner, and sat watching the people flow in and out the door that kept swinging open and shut, watched them mingle and merge and separate, felt her being flow into them, into their movement. When the hour was up she left a half crown for her pot of tea, and left the place without looking back at it, just as she had left her house, the big, beautiful white house, without another look, but silently dedicating it to Sophie. She returned to Fred, received the key of No. 19, now free, and ascended the grimy stairs slowly, letting floor after floor fall away below her, keeping her eyes lifted, so that floor after floor descended jerkily to her level of vision, and fell away out of sight.

No. 19 was the same. She saw everything with an acute, narrow, checking glance: the cheap shine of the satin spread, which had been replaced carelessly after the two bodies had finished their convulsions under it; a trace of powder on the glass that topped the chest of drawers; an intense green shade in a fold of the curtain. She stood at the window, looking down, watching people pass and pass and pass until her mind went dark from the constant movement. Then she sat in the wicker chair, letting herself go slack. But she had to be careful, because she did not want, today, to be surprised by Fred's knock at five o'clock.

The demons were not here. They had gone forever, because she was buying her freedom from them. She was slipping already into the dark fructifying dream that seemed to caress her inwardly, like the movement of her blood . . . but she had to think about Matthew first. Should she write a letter for the coroner? But what should she say? She would like to leave him with the look on his face she had seen this morning—banal, admittedly, but at least confidently healthy. Well, that was impossible, one did not look like that with a wife dead from suicide. But how to leave him believing she was dying because of a man—because of the fascinating publisher Michael Plant? Oh, how ridiculous! How absurd! How humiliating! But she decided not to trouble about it, simply not to think about the living. If he wanted to believe she had a lover, he would believe it. And he *did* want to believe it. Even when he had found out that there was no publisher in London called Michael Plant, he would think: Oh poor Susan, she was afraid to give me his real name.

And what did it matter whether he married Phil Hunt or Sophie? Though it ought to be Sophie, who was already the mother of those children . . . and what hypocrisy to sit here worrying about the children, when she was going to leave them because she had not got the energy to stay.

She had about four hours. She spent them delightfully, darkly, sweetly, letting herself slide gently, gently, to the edge of the river. Then, with hardly a break in her consciousness, she got up, pushed the thin rug against the door, made sure the windows were tight shut, put two shillings in the meter, and turned on the gas. For the first time since she had been in the room she lay on the hard bed that smelled stale, that smelled of sweat and sex.

She lay on her back on the green satin cover, but her legs were chilly. She got up, found a blanket folded in the bottom of the chest of drawers, and carefully covered her legs with it. She was quite content lying there, listening to the faint soft hiss of the gas that poured into the room, into her lungs, into her brain, as she drifted off into the dark river.

1963

PHILIP LARKIN
1922–1985

Philip Larkin was born in Coventry; was educated at its King Henry VIII School and at St. John's College, Oxford; and was for many years librarian of the Hull University Library. He wrote the poems of his first book, *The North Ship* (1945), under W. B. Yeats's strong enchantment. Although this influence persisted in the English poet's formal skill and subdued visionary longings, Larkin began to read Thomas Hardy seriously after World War II, and Hardy's rugged language, local settings, and ironic tone helped counter Yeats's influence. "After that," Larkin said, "Yeats came to seem so artificial—all that crap about masks and Crazy Jane and all the rest. It all rang so completely unreal." Also rejecting the international modernism of Eliot and Pound because of its mythical allusions, polyglot discourse, and fragmentary syntax, Larkin reclaimed a more direct, personal, formally regular model of poetry, supposedly rooted in a native English tradition of Wordsworth, Hardy, A. E. Housman, Wilfred Owen, and W. H. Auden. Even so, his poetry is not so thoroughly antimodernist as are his declarations: witness his imagist precision and alienated personae, his blending of revulsion and attraction toward modernity.

Larkin was the dominant figure in what came to be known as "the Movement," a group of university poets that included Kingsley Amis, Donald Davie, and Thom Gunn, gathered together in Robert Conquest's landmark anthology of 1956, *New Lines*. Their work was seen as counteracting not only the extravagances of modernism but also the influence of Dylan Thomas's high-flown, apocalyptic rhetoric: like Larkin, these poets preferred a civil grammar and rational syntax over prophecy, suburban realities over mythmaking.

No other poet presents the welfare-state world of postimperial Britain so vividly, so unsparingly, and so tenderly. "Poetry is an affair of sanity, of seeing things as they are," Larkin said; "I don't want to transcend the commonplace, I love the commonplace life. Everyday things are lovely to me." Eschewing the grandiose, he writes poetry that, in its everyday diction and melancholy wryness, worldly subjects and regular meters, affirms rather than contravenes the restrictions of ordinary life. Love's failure, the erosion of religious and national abutments, the loneliness of age and death—Larkin does not avert his poetic gaze from these bleak realities. As indicated by the title of his 1955 collection *The Less Deceived*, disillusionment, drabness, and resignation color these poems. Yet Larkin's drearily mundane world often gives way to muted promise, his speakers' alienation to possible communion, his skepticism to encounters even with the sublime. At the end of "High Windows," the characteristically ironic and self-deprecating speaker glimpses both radiant presence and total absence in the sunlit glass: "And beyond it, the deep blue air, that shows / Nothing, and is nowhere, and is endless."

Like Hardy, Larkin also wrote novels—*Jill* (1946) and *A Girl in Winter* (1947)—and his poems have a novelist's sense of place and skill in the handling of direct speech. He also edited a controversial anthology, *The Oxford Book of Twentieth-Century English Verse* (1973), which attempted to construct a modern native tradition in England. But his most significant legacy was his poetry, although his output was limited to four volumes. Out of "the commonplace life" he fashioned uncommon poems—some of the most emotionally complex, rhythmically polished, and intricately rhymed poems of the second half of the twentieth century.

Church Going

Once I am sure there's nothing going on
I step inside, letting the door thud shut.
Another church: matting, seats, and stone,
And little books; sprawlings of flowers, cut
For Sunday, brownish now; some brass and stuff
Up at the holy end; the small neat organ;
And a tense, musty, unignorable silence,
Brewed God knows how long. Hatless, I take off
My cycle-clips in awkward reverence,

Move forward, run my hand around the font.
From where I stand, the roof looks almost new—
Cleaned, or restored? Someone would know: I don't.
Mounting the lectern, I peruse a few
Hectoring large-scale verses,[1] and pronounce
"Here endeth" much more loudly than I'd meant.
The echoes snigger briefly. Back at the door
I sign the book, donate an Irish sixpence,[2]
Reflect the place was not worth stopping for.

Yet stop I did: in fact I often do,
And always end much at a loss like this,
Wondering what to look for; wondering, too,
When churches fall completely out of use
What we shall turn them into, if we shall keep
A few cathedrals chronically on show,
Their parchment, plate and pyx[3] in locked cases,
And let the rest rent-free to rain and sheep.
Shall we avoid them as unlucky places?

Or, after dark, will dubious women come
To make their children touch a particular stone;
Pick simples° for a cancer; or on some   *medicinal herbs*
Advised night see walking a dead one?
Power of some sort or other will go on
In games, in riddles, seemingly at random;
But superstition, like belief, must die,
And what remains when disbelief has gone?
Grass, weedy pavement, brambles, buttress, sky,

A shape less recognisable each week,
A purpose more obscure. I wonder who
Will be the last, the very last, to seek
This place for what it was; one of the crew
That tap and jot and know what rood-lofts[4] were?
Some ruin-bibber, randy for antique,
Or Christmas-addict, counting on a whiff

---

1. I.e., Bible verses printed in large type for reading aloud.
2. An Irish sixpence has no value in England.
3. Box in which Communion wafers are kept.
4. Galleries on top of carved screens separating the nave of a church from the choir.

Of gown-and-bands and organ-pipes and myrrh?[5]
45   Or will he be my representative,

Bored, uninformed, knowing the ghostly silt
Dispersed, yet tending to this cross of ground[6]
Through suburb scrub because it held unspilt
So long and equably what since is found
50   Only in separation—marriage, and birth,
And death, and thoughts of these—for which was built
This special shell? For, though I've no idea
What this accoutred frowsty barn is worth,
It pleases me to stand in silence here;

55   A serious house on serious earth it is,
In whose blent air all our compulsions meet,
Are recognised, and robed as destinies.
And that much never can be obsolete,
Since someone will forever be surprising
60   A hunger in himself to be more serious,
And gravitating with it to this ground,
Which, he once heard, was proper to grow wise in,
If only that so many dead lie round.

1954   1955

MCMXIV[1]

Those long uneven lines
Standing as patiently
As if they were stretched outside
The Oval or Villa Park,[2]
5   The crowns of hats, the sun
On moustached archaic faces
Grinning as if it were all
An August Bank Holiday[3] lark;

And the shut shops, the bleached,
10   Established names on the sunblinds,
The farthings and sovereigns,[4]
And dark-clothed children at play
Called after kings and queens,
The tin advertisements
15   For cocoa and twist,° and the pubs   *tobacco*
Wide open all day;

And the countryside not caring:
The place-names all hazed over

---

5. Gum resin used in the making of incense; one of three presents given by the three wise men to the infant Jesus. "Gown-and-bands": gown and decorative collar worn by clergypeople.
6. Most Christian churches were built in the shape of a cross.
1. 1914, in Roman numerals, as incised on stone memorials to the dead of World War I.

2. Respectively, London cricket ground and Birmingham football ground.
3. Nationwide public holiday observed, when this poem was written (and in 1914), on the first Monday in August.
4. At that time the least valuable and the most valuable British coins.

With flowering grasses, and fields
20 Shadowing Domesday lines[5]
Under wheat's restless silence;
The differently-dressed servants
With tiny rooms in huge houses,
The dust behind limousines;

25 Never such innocence,
Never before or since,
As changed itself to past
Without a word—the men
Leaving the gardens tidy,
30 The thousands of marriages
Lasting a little while longer:
Never such innocence again.

1960   1964

Talking in Bed

Talking in bed ought to be easiest,
Lying together there goes back so far,
An emblem of two people being honest.

Yet more and more time passes silently.
5 Outside, the wind's incomplete unrest
Builds and disperses clouds about the sky,

And dark towns heap up on the horizon.
None of this cares for us. Nothing shows why
At this unique distance from isolation

10 It becomes still more difficult to find
Words at once true and kind,
Or not untrue and not unkind.

1960   1964

Ambulances

Closed like confessionals,[1] they thread
Loud noons of cities, giving back
None of the glances they absorb.
Light glossy grey, arms on a plaque,[2]
5 They come to rest at any kerb:
All streets in time are visited.

5. The still-visible boundaries of medieval farmers' long and narrow plots, ownership of which is recorded in William the Conqueror's *Domesday Book* (1085–86).

1. Enclosed stalls in Roman Catholic churches in which priests hear confession.
2. Many officially chartered British entities, such as hospitals, display the royal coat of arms.

Then children strewn on steps or road,
Or women coming from the shops
Past smells of different dinners, see
10 A wild white face that overtops
Red stretcher-blankets momently
As it is carried in and stowed,

And sense the solving emptiness
That lies just under all we do,
15 And for a second get it whole,
So permanent and blank and true.
The fastened doors recede. *Poor soul,*
They whisper at their own distress;

For borne away in deadened air
20 May go the sudden shut of loss
Round something nearly at an end,
And what cohered in it across
The years, the unique random blend
Of families and fashions, there

25 At last begin to loosen. Far
From the exchange of love to lie
Unreachable inside a room
The traffic parts to let go by
Brings closer what is left to come,
30 And dulls to distance all we are.

1961   1964

High Windows

When I see a couple of kids
And guess he's fucking her and she's
Taking pills or wearing a diaphragm,
I know this is paradise

5 Everyone old has dreamed of all their lives—
Bonds and gestures pushed to one side
Like an outdated combine harvester,[1]
And everyone young going down the long slide

To happiness, endlessly. I wonder if
10 Anyone looked at me, forty years back,
And thought, *That'll be the life;*
No God any more, or sweating in the dark

About hell and that, or having to hide
What you think of the priest. He

---

1. Farm machine for harvesting grain.

15   *And his lot will all go down the long slide*
     Like free bloody birds. And immediately

     Rather than words comes the thought of high windows:
     The sun-comprehending glass,
     And beyond it, the deep blue air, that shows
20   Nothing, and is nowhere, and is endless.

1967   1974

Sad Steps[1]

     Groping back to bed after a piss
     I part thick curtains, and am startled by
     The rapid clouds, the moon's cleanliness.

     Four o'clock: wedge-shadowed gardens lie
5   Under a cavernous, a wind-picked sky.
     There's something laughable about this,

     The way the moon dashes through clouds that blow
     Loosely as cannon-smoke to stand apart
     (Stone-coloured light sharpening the roofs below)

10   High and preposterous and separate—
     Lozenge° of love! Medallion of art!   *diamondlike shape*
     O wolves of memory! Immensements! No,

     One shivers slightly, looking up there.
     The hardness and the brightness and the plain
15   Far-reaching singleness of that wide stare

     Is a reminder of the strength and pain
     Of being young; that it can't come again,
     But is for others undiminished somewhere.

1968   1974

Homage to a Government

     Next year we are to bring the soldiers home
     For lack of money,[1] and it is all right.
     Places they guarded, or kept orderly,
     Must guard themselves, and keep themselves orderly.
5   We want the money for ourselves at home
     Instead of working. And this is all right.

     It's hard to say who wanted it to happen,
     But now it's been decided nobody minds.

1. Cf. Sir Philip Sidney's *Astrophil and Stella* 31: "With how sad steps, O Moon, thou climb'st the skies."

1. In 1968 Harold Wilson's Labour government decided to withdraw troops east of the Suez Canal, mainly in the Persian Gulf and Southeast Asia.

The places are a long way off, not here,
10   Which is all right, and from what we hear
The soldiers there only made trouble happen.
Next year we shall be easier in our minds.

Next year we shall be living in a country
That brought its soldiers home for lack of money.
15   The statues will be standing in the same
Tree-muffled squares, and look nearly the same.
Our children will not know it's a different country.
All we can hope to leave them now is money.

Jan. 10, 1969   1974

The Explosion

On the day of the explosion
Shadows pointed towards the pithead:°   *mine entrance*
In the sun the slagheap° slept.   *pile of scrap, refuse*

Down the lane came men in pitboots
5   Coughing oath-edged talk and pipe-smoke,
Shouldering off the freshened silence.

One chased after rabbits; lost them;
Came back with a nest of lark's eggs;
Showed them; lodged them in the grasses.

10   So they passed in beards and moleskins,[1]
Fathers, brothers, nicknames, laughter,
Through the tall gates standing open.

At noon, there came a tremor; cows
Stopped chewing for a second; sun,
15   Scarfed as in a heat-haze, dimmed.

The dead go on before us, they
Are sitting in God's house in comfort,
We shall see them face to face—

Plain as lettering in the chapels
20   It was said, and for a second
Wives saw men of the explosion

Larger than in life they managed—
Gold as on a coin, or walking
Somehow from the sun towards them,

25   One showing the eggs unbroken.

1970   1974

1. Clothes of heavy fabric.

This Be The Verse[1]

They fuck you up, your mum and dad.
    They may not mean to, but they do.
They fill you with the faults they had
    And add some extra, just for you.

5   But they were fucked up in their turn
        By fools in old-style hats and coats,
    Who half the time were soppy-stern
        And half at one another's throats.

    Man hands on misery to man.
10   It deepens like a coastal shelf.[2]
    Get out as early as you can,
        And don't have any kids yourself.

Apr.? 1971   1974

Aubade[1]

I work all day, and get half-drunk at night.
Waking at four to soundless dark, I stare.
In time the curtain-edges will grow light.
Till then I see what's really always there:
5   Unresting death, a whole day nearer now,
Making all thought impossible but how
And where and when I shall myself die.
Arid interrogation: yet the dread
Of dying, and being dead,
10   Flashes afresh to hold and horrify.

The mind blanks at the glare. Not in remorse
—The good not done, the love not given, time
Torn off unused—nor wretchedly because
An only life can take so long to climb
15   Clear of its wrong beginnings, and may never;
But at the total emptiness for ever,
The sure extinction that we travel to
And shall be lost in always. Not to be here,
Not to be anywhere,
20   And soon; nothing more terrible, nothing more true.

This is a special way of being afraid
No trick dispels. Religion used to try,
That vast moth-eaten musical brocade
Created to pretend we never die,

---

1. Cf. the elegy "Requiem," by Robert Louis Stevenson (1850–1894), of which the final verse reads, "This be the verse you grave for me: / Here he lies where he longed to be, / Home is the sailor, *home from sea, / And the hunter home from the hill.*"
2. I.e., continental shelf.
1. Music or poem announcing dawn.

25 And specious stuff that says *No rational being*
Can fear a thing it will not feel, not seeing
That this is what we fear—no sight, no sound,
No touch or taste or smell, nothing to think with,
Nothing to love or link with,
30 The anaesthetic from which none come round.

And so it stays just on the edge of vision,
A small unfocused blur, a standing chill
That slows each impulse down to indecision.
Most things may never happen: this one will,
35 And realisation of it rages out
In furnace-fear when we are caught without
People or drink. Courage is no good:
It means not scaring others. Being brave
Lets no one off the grave.
40 Death is no different whined at than withstood.

Slowly light strengthens, and the room takes shape.
It stands plain as a wardrobe, what we know,
Have always known, know that we can't escape,
Yet can't accept. One side will have to go.
45 Meanwhile telephones crouch, getting ready to ring
In locked-up offices, and all the uncaring
Intricate rented world begins to rouse.
The sky is white as clay, with no sun.
Work has to be done.
50 Postmen like doctors go from house to house.

1977   1977

NADINE GORDIMER
1923–2014

Nadine Gordimer's fiction has given imaginative and moral shape to the recent history of South Africa. From the time of the publication of her first book, *The Lying Days* (1953), she charted the changing patterns of response and resistance to apartheid by exploring the place of the European in Africa, selecting representative themes and governing motifs for novels and short stories, and shifting her ideological focus from a liberal to a more radical position. In recognition of this achievement, of having borne untiring and lucid narrative witness, Gordimer was awarded the 1991 Nobel Prize in Literature.

Born to Jewish immigrant parents in the South African mining town of Springs, Gordimer began writing early, from the beginning taking as her subject the pathologies and everyday realities of a racially divided society. Her decision to remain in Johannesburg through the years of political repression reflected her commitment to her subject and to her vision of a postapartheid future. After apartheid was dismantled in 1994, Gordimer continued to live and write in South Africa, and her late novels, such as *The House Gun* (1998), *The Pickup* (2001), and *Get a Life* (2006), retain an uncompromising focus on the inhabitants of a racially fractured culture.

In her nonfiction, Gordimer self-consciously places her writing within a tradition of European realism, most notably that defined by the Hungarian philosopher and critic Georg Lukács (1885–1971). Her aim—as shown in her incisive and highly acclaimed novels of the 1970s, *The Conservationist* (1974) and *Burger's Daughter* (1979)—was to evoke by way of the personal and of the precisely observed particular a broader political and historical totality. This method gives her characters, and the stories in which they reside, their representativeness. As Gordimer famously said, "politics is character in South Africa." Yet throughout the long years of political polarization in that country and the banning of three of her own books, Gordimer distanced herself from polemics and retained a firm humanist belief in what she variously described as the objectivity and the inwardness of the writer. Although she referred to an engagement with political reality as imperative and explores permutations of the question of engagement in novels such as *Burger's Daughter* and *July's People* (1981), she nevertheless asserted the autonomy of the writer's perspective, "the last true judgment." Narrative for Gordimer helped define and clarify historical experience. Her keen sense of history as formation, and as demanding a continual rewriting, has ensured that her novels can be read as at once contemporary in their reference and symbolic of broader social and historical patterns, as in the paranoia surrounding the case of the buried black body on a white farm in *The Conservationist*, or in the psychosocial portrait of Rosa Burger in *Burger's Daughter*.

Gordimer drew criticism both for her apparent lack of attention to feminism in favor of race issues and for the wholeness and unfashionable completeness of her novels—their plottedness, meticulous scene paintings, fully realized characters. However, the searching symbolism and complexity of her narratives generally work against such judgments. As the following short story shows, a prominent feature of her writing is to give a number of different perspectives on a situation, in some cases most poignantly those of apartheid's supporters, and in this way to represent the broader anatomy of a diseased politics and, more generally, of the human being in history.

The Moment before the Gun Went Off

Marais Van der Vyver shot one of his farm labourers, dead. An accident, there are accidents with guns every day of the week—children playing a fatal game with a father's revolver in the cities where guns are domestic objects, nowadays, hunting mishaps like this one, in the country—but these won't be reported all over the world. Van der Vyver knows his will be. He knows that the story of the Afrikaner farmer—regional Party leader and Commandant of the local security commando—shooting a black man who worked for him will fit exactly *their* version of South Africa, it's made for them. They'll be able to use it in their boycott and divestment campaigns, it'll be another piece of evidence in their truth about the country. The papers at home will quote the story as it has appeared in the overseas press, and in the back-and-forth he and the black man will become those crudely drawn figures on anti-apartheid banners, units in statistics of white brutality against the blacks quoted at the United Nations—he, whom they will gleefully be able to call "a leading member" of the ruling Party.

People in the farming community understand how he must feel. Bad enough to have killed a man, without helping the Party's, the government's, the country's enemies, as well. They see the truth of that. They know, reading the Sunday papers, that when Van der Vyver is quoted saying he is "terribly shocked," he will "look after the wife and children," none of those Americans and English, and none of those people at home who want to destroy the white man's power will believe him. And how they will sneer when he even says of the farm boy (according to one paper, if you can trust any of those reporters), "He was my friend, I always took him hunting with me." Those city and overseas people don't know it's true: farmers usually have one particular black boy they like to take along with them in the lands; you could call it a kind of friend, yes, friends are not only your own white people, like yourself, you take into your house, pray with in church and work with on the Party committee. But how can those others know that? They don't want to know it. They think all blacks are like the big-mouth agitators in town. And Van der Vyver's face, in the photographs, strangely opened by distress—everyone in the district remembers Marais Van der Vyver as a little boy who would go away and hide himself if he caught you smiling at him, and everyone knows him now as a man who hides any change of expression round his mouth behind a thick, soft moustache, and in his eyes by always looking at some object in hand, leaf of a crop fingered, pen or stone picked up, while concentrating on what he is saying, or while listening to you. It just goes to show what shock can do; when you look at the newspaper photographs you feel like apologising, as if you had stared in on some room where you should not be.

There will be an inquiry; there had better be, to stop the assumption of yet another case of brutality against farm workers, although there's nothing in doubt—an accident, and all the facts fully admitted by Van der Vyver. He made a statement when he arrived at the police station with the dead man in his bakkie.[1] Captain Beetge knows him well, of course; he gave him brandy. He was shaking, this big, calm, clever son of Willem Van der Vyver, who inherited the old man's best farm. The black was stone dead, nothing to be done for him. Beetge will not tell anyone that after the brandy Van der Vyver wept. He sobbed, snot running onto his hands, like a dirty kid. The Captain was ashamed, for him, and walked out to give him a chance to recover himself.

Marais Van der Vyver left his house at three in the afternoon to cull a buck from the family of kudu[2] he protects in the bush areas of his farm. He is interested in wildlife and sees it as the farmers' sacred duty to raise game as well as cattle. As usual, he called at his shed workshop to pick up Lucas, a twenty-year-old farmhand who had shown mechanical aptitude and whom Van der Vyver himself had taught to maintain tractors and other farm machinery. He hooted, and Lucas followed the familiar routine, jumping onto the back of the truck. He liked to travel standing up there, spotting game before his employer did. He would lean forward, braced against the cab below him.

Van der Vyver had a rifle and .300 ammunition beside him in the cab. The rifle was one of his father's, because his own was at the gunsmith's in

1. Pickup truck.
2. Large African antelope. The males have long, spirally twisted horns.

town. Since his father died (Beetge's sergeant wrote "passed on") no one had used the rifle and so when he took it from a cupboard he was sure it was not loaded. His father had never allowed a loaded gun in the house; he himself had been taught since childhood never to ride with a loaded weapon in a vehicle. But this gun was loaded. On a dirt track, Lucas thumped his fist on the cab roof three times to signal: look left. Having seen the white-ripple-marked flank of a kudu, and its fine horns raking through disguising bush, Van der Vyver drove rather fast over a pot-hole. The jolt fired the rifle. Upright, it was pointing straight through the cab roof at the head of Lucas. The bullet pierced the roof and entered Lucas's brain by way of his throat.

That is the statement of what happened. Although a man of such standing in the district, Van der Vyver had to go through the ritual of swearing that it was the truth. It has gone on record, and will be there in the archive of the local police station as long as Van der Vyver lives, and beyond that, through the lives of his children, Magnus, Helena and Karel—unless things in the country get worse, the example of black mobs in the towns spreads to the rural areas and the place is burned down as many urban police stations have been. Because nothing the government can do will appease the agitators and the whites who encourage them. Nothing satisfies them, in the cities: blacks can sit and drink in white hotels, now, the Immorality Act[3] has gone, blacks can sleep with whites. . . . It's not even a crime any more.

Van der Vyver has a high barbed security fence round his farmhouse and garden which his wife, Alida, thinks spoils completely the effect of her artificial stream with its tree-ferns beneath the jacarandas.[4] There is an aerial soaring like a flag-pole in the back yard. All his vehicles, including the truck in which the black man died, have aerials that swing their whips when the driver hits a pot-hole: they are part of the security system the farmers in the district maintain, each farm in touch with every other by radio, twenty-four hours out of twenty-four. It has already happened that infiltrators from over the border have mined remote farm roads, killing white farmers and their families out on their own property for a Sunday picnic. The pot-hole could have set off a land-mine, and Van der Vyver might have died with his farm boy. When neighbours use the communications system to call up and say they are sorry about "that business" with one of Van der Vyver's boys, there goes unsaid: it could have been worse.

It is obvious from the quality and fittings of the coffin that the farmer has provided money for the funeral. And an elaborate funeral means a great deal to blacks; look how they will deprive themselves of the little they have, in their lifetime, keeping up payments to a burial society so they won't go in boxwood to an unmarked grave. The young wife is pregnant (of course) and another little one, wearing red shoes several sizes too large, leans under her jutting belly. He is too young to understand what has happened, what he is witnessing that day, but neither whines nor plays about; he is solemn without knowing why. Blacks expose small children to everything, they don't protect them from the sight of fear and pain the way whites do theirs. It is the young wife who rolls her head and cries like a child, sobbing on the breast of this relative and that.

---

3. South African government act prohibiting sexual relations between whites and other races.
4. Tropical trees with blue flowers.

All present work for Van der Vyver or are the families of those who work; and in the weeding and harvest seasons, the women and children work for him, too, carried—wrapped in their blankets, on a truck, singing—at sunrise to the fields. The dead man's mother is a woman who can't be more than in her late thirties (they start bearing children at puberty) but she is heavily mature in a black dress between her own parents, who were already working for old Van der Vyver when Marais, like their daughter, was a child. The parents hold her as if she were a prisoner or a crazy woman to be restrained. But she says nothing, does nothing. She does not look up; she does not look at Van der Vyver, whose gun went off in the truck, she stares at the grave. Nothing will make her look up; there need be no fear that she will look up; at him. His wife, Alida, is beside him. To show the proper respect, as for any white funeral, she is wearing the navy-blue-and-cream hat she wears to church this summer. She is always supportive, although he doesn't seem to notice it; this coldness and reserve—his mother says he didn't mix well as a child— she accepts for herself but regrets that it has prevented him from being nominated, as he should be, to stand as the Party's parliamentary candidate for the district. He does not let her clothing, or that of anyone else gathered closely, make contact with him. He, too, stares at the grave. The dead man's mother and he stare at the grave in communication like that between the black man outside and the white man inside the cab the moment before the gun went off.

The moment before the gun went off was a moment of high excitement shared through the roof of the cab, as the bullet was to pass, between the young black man outside and the white farmer inside the vehicle. There were such moments, without explanation, between them, although often around the farm the farmer would pass the young man without returning a greeting, as if he did not recognize him. When the bullet went off what Van der Vyver saw was the kudu stumble in fright at the report and gallop away. Then he heard the thud behind him, and past the window saw the young man fall out of the vehicle. He was sure he had leapt up and toppled—in fright, like the buck. The farmer was almost laughing with relief, ready to tease, as he opened his door, it did not seem possible that a bullet passing through the roof could have done harm.

The young man did not laugh with him at his own fright. The farmer carried him in his arms, to the truck. He was sure, sure he could not be dead. But the young black man's blood was all over the farmer's clothes, soaking against his flesh as he drove.

How will they ever know, when they file newspaper clippings, evidence, proof, when they look at the photographs and see his face—guilty! guilty! they are right!—how will they know, when the police stations burn with all the evidence of what has happened now, and what the law made a crime in the past. How could they know that *they do not know.* Anything. The young black callously shot through the negligence of the white man was not the farmer's boy; he was his son.

1991

A. K. RAMANUJAN
1929–1993

B orn in Mysore, India, Attipat Krishnaswami Ramanujan grew up amid the different languages that later informed his life's work as poet, translator, and linguist: he spoke Kannada in the streets, Tamil with his mother, and English with his father, a mathematics professor at Mysore University. Educated there and at Deccan College, he traveled for graduate studies to Indiana University, staying on in the United States to teach at the University of Chicago from 1961. He was the recipient of a MacArthur Fellowship, and in 1976 the Indian government honored him with the Padma Shri for distinguished service to the nation.

Ramanujan affirmed that "cultural traditions in India are indissolubly plural and often conflicting," and his poetry—in its texture and subject matter—embodies this complex intercultural mingling within India and across much of the contemporary world. His poems reflect the influence of modern English-language poets, such as W. B. Yeats, Ezra Pound, William Carlos Williams, and Wallace Stevens, while also drawing on the vivid and structural use of metaphor, the flowing imagery and syntax, the spare diction and paradoxes of ancient and medieval poetry of south India. A poem such as the wittily entitled "Elements of Composition" recalls a traditional Indian vision of identity as embedded in endlessly fluid, concentrically arranged contexts at the same time that it suggests a postmodern vision of the self as decentered, composite, and provisional. "India does not have one past," Ramanujan emphasized, "but many pasts," and the same is true of the self whose multiple pasts he composes and decomposes in his poetry.

Self-Portrait

I resemble everyone
but myself, and sometimes see
in shop-windows,
    despite the well-known laws
5   of optics,
the portrait of a stranger,
date unknown,
often signed in a corner
by my father.

1966

Elements of Composition

Composed as I am, like others,
   of elements on certain well-known lists,
father's seed and mother's egg

936

gathering earth, air, fire, mostly
5   water, into a mulberry mass,
moulding calcium,

carbon, even gold, magnesium and such,
    into a chattering self tangled
in love and work,

10   scary dreams, capable of eyes that can see,
        only by moving constantly,
the constancy of things

like Stonehenge or cherry trees;

add uncle's eleven fingers
15   making shadow-plays of rajas°   *Indian kings or princes*
and cats, hissing,

becoming fingers again, the look
    of panic on sister's face
an hour before

20   her wedding, a dated newspaper map
    of a place one has never seen, maybe
no longer there

after the riots, downtown Nairobi,[1]
    that a friend carried in his passport
25   as others would

a woman's picture in their wallets;

add the lepers of Madurai,°   *city in south India*
    male, female, married,
with children,

30   lion faces, crabs for claws,
        clotted on their shadows
under the stone-eyed

goddesses of dance, mere pillars,
    moving as nothing on earth
35   can move—

I pass through them
    as they pass through me
taking and leaving

affections, seeds, skeletons,

1. Capital of Kenya; in the rioting that ensued after a coup in 1978, many Asian-owned shops were looted and burned. (South Asians formed much of Nairobi's merchant class during and after the era of British colonial rule.)

40 millennia of fossil records
    of insects that do not last
a day,

body-prints of mayflies,
    a legend half-heard
45 in a train

of the half-man searching
    for an ever-fleeing
other half[2]

through Muharram tigers,[3]
50   hyacinths in crocodile waters,
and the sweet

twisted lives of epileptic saints,

and even as I add,
    I lose, decompose
55 into my elements,

into other names and forms,
    past, and passing, tenses
without time,

caterpillar on a leaf, eating,
60   being eaten.[4]

                                1986

2. In an essay Ramanujan compares the Hindu myth of the god that "splits himself into male and female" to "the androgynous figure in Plato's *Symposium*, halved into male and female segments which forever seek each other and crave union."
3. During the first month of the Islamic calendar, Muharram processions, often including dancers in tiger masks, commemorate the martyrdom of Muhammad's grandson, Husein.
4. According to a poem in the ancient Sanskrit *Taittiriya Upanishad*, "What eats is eaten, / and what's eaten, eats / in turn" (Ramanujan's translation, in his essay "Some Thoughts on 'Non-Western' Classics").

THOM GUNN
1929–2004

The son of a London journalist, Thomson Gunn was educated at University College School, London, then Trinity College, Cambridge, and Stanford University, where he studied under the antimodernist, classically inclined poet Yvor Winters. In a poem addressed to Winters, he wrote: "You keep both Rule and Energy in view, / Much power in each, most in the balanced two." The poems of Gunn's *Fighting Terms* (1954) and *The Sense of Movement* (1957) aimed for the same balance. They were influenced by the seventeenth-century English poet John Donne and the twentieth-century French philosopher Jean-Paul Sartre and introduced a modern Metaphysical poet able to give powerfully concrete expression to abstract ideas. Along with Philip Larkin, he was seen as a member of "the Movement"—English poets who preferred inherited verse forms to either modernist avant-gardism or high-flown Romanticism. In the second half of *My Sad Captains* (1961), he began to move away from the will-driven heroes and the tight-fitting stanzas of his early work into more tentative explorations of experience and more supple syllabic or open verse forms. "Most of my poems are ambivalent," he said. Moving from England to San Francisco, he experimented with LSD and moved also from poems presumably addressed to women to poems frankly homosexual. *The Man with Night Sweats* (1992) ends with a sequence of poems remarkable for their unflinching directness, compassion, and grace about the deaths of friends from AIDS. Gunn was a poet of rare intelligence and power in all his protean changes.

Black Jackets

> In the silence that prolongs the span
> Rawly of music when the record ends,
> The red-haired boy who drove a van
> In weekday overalls but, like his friends,
>
> 5   Wore cycle boots and jacket here
> To suit the Sunday hangout he was in,
>   Heard, as he stretched back from his beer,
> Leather creak softly round his neck and chin.
>
>   Before him, on a coal-black sleeve
> 10   Remote exertion had lined, scratched, and burned
>   Insignia that could not revive
> The heroic fall or climb where they were earned.
>
>   On the other drinkers bent together,
> Concocting selves for their impervious kit,
> 15   He saw it as no more than leather
> Which, taut across the shoulders grown to it,
>
>   Sent through the dimness of a bar
> As sudden and anonymous hints of light
>   As those that shipping give, that are
> 20   Now flickers in the Bay, now lost in night.
>
>   He stretched out like a cat, and rolled
> The bitterish taste of beer upon his tongue,
>   And listened to a joke being told:
> The present was the things he stayed among.
>
> 25   If it was only loss he wore,
> He wore it to assert, with fierce devotion,
>   Complicity and nothing more.
> He recollected his initiation,

And one especially of the rites.
30 For on his shoulders they had put tattoos:
The group's name on the left, The Knights,
And on the right the slogan Born To Lose.

1961

My Sad Captains

One by one they appear in
the darkness: a few friends, and
a few with historical
names. How late they start to shine!
5 but before they fade they stand
perfectly embodied, all

the past lapping them like a
cloak of chaos. They were men
who, I thought, lived only to
10 renew the wasteful force they
spent with each hot convulsion.
They remind me, distant now.

True, they are not at rest yet,
but now that they are indeed
15 apart, winnowed from failures,
they withdraw to an orbit
and turn with disinterested
hard energy, like the stars.

1961

From the Wave

It mounts at sea, a concave wall
    Down-ribbed with shine,
And pushes forward, building tall
    Its steep incline.

5 Then from their hiding rise to sight
    Black shapes on boards
Bearing before the fringe of white
    It mottles towards.

Their pale feet curl, they poise their weight
10   With a learn'd skill.
It is the wave they imitate
    Keeps them so still.

The marbling bodies have become
        Half wave, half men,
15 Grafted it seems by feet of foam
        Some seconds, then,

Late as they can, they slice the face
        In timed procession:
Balance is triumph in this place,
20   Triumph possession.

The mindless heave of which they rode
        A fluid shelf
Breaks as they leave it, falls and, slowed,
        Loses itself.

25 Clear, the sheathed bodies slick as seals
        Loosen and tingle;
And by the board the bare foot feels
        The suck of shingle.

They paddle in the shallows still;
30   Two splash each other;
Then all swim out to wait until
        The right waves gather.

                                            1971

Still Life

        I shall not soon forget
        The greyish-yellow skin
        To which the face had set:
        Lids tight: nothing of his,
5   No tremor from within,
        Played on the surfaces.

        He still found breath, and yet
        It was an obscure knack.
        I shall not soon forget
10   The angle of his head,
        Arrested and reared back
        On the crisp field of bed,

        Back from what he could neither
        Accept, as one opposed,
15   Nor, as a life-long breather,
        Consentingly let go,
        The tube his mouth enclosed
        In an astonished O.

                                            1992

The Missing

Now as I watch the progress of the plague,°   *AIDS*
The friends surrounding me fall sick, grow thin,
And drop away. Bared, is my shape less vague
—Sharply exposed and with a sculpted skin?

5   I do not like the statue's chill contour,
Not nowadays. The warmth investing me
Led outward through mind, limb, feeling, and more
In an involved increasing family.

Contact of friend led to another friend,
10   Supple entwinement through the living mass
Which for all that I knew might have no end,
Image of an unlimited embrace.

I did not just feel ease, though comfortable:
Aggressive as in some ideal of sport,
15   With ceaseless movement thrilling through the whole,
Their push kept me as firm as their support.

But death—Their deaths have left me less defined:
It was their pulsing presence made me clear.
I borrowed from it, I was unconfined,
20   Who tonight balance unsupported here,

Eyes glaring from raw marble, in a pose
Languorously part-buried in the block,
Shins perfect and no calves, as if I froze
Between potential and a finished work.

25   —Abandoned incomplete, shape of a shape,
In which exact detail shows the more strange,
Trapped in unwholeness, I find no escape
Back to the play of constant give and change.

Aug. 1987   1992

DEREK WALCOTT
1930—2017

Derek Walcott was born on the island of Saint Lucia in the British West Indies, where he had a Methodist upbringing in a largely Roman Catholic society. He was educated at St. Mary's College in Saint Lucia and the University of the West Indies in Jamaica. He then moved to Trinidad, where he worked as a book reviewer, art critic, playwright, and artistic director of a theater workshop.

From the early 1980s on he also taught at a number of American colleges and universities, especially Boston University; in 1992 he received the Nobel Prize in Literature.

As a black poet writing from within both the English literary tradition and the history of a colonized people, Walcott self-mockingly referred to his split allegiances to his African Caribbean and his European inheritances as those of a "schizophrenic," a "mongrel," a "mulatto of style." His background was indeed racially and culturally mixed: his grandmothers were of African descent; his grandfathers were white, a Dutchman and an Englishman. Schooled in the Standard English that is the official language of Saint Lucia, Walcott also grew up speaking the predominantly French Creole (or patois) that is the primary language of everyday life (the island had traded hands fourteen times in colonial wars between the British and the French). In his poetry this cross-cultural inheritance is sometimes the source of pain and ambivalence, as when in "A Far Cry from Africa" he refers to himself as being "poisoned with the blood of both." At other times it fuels a celebratory integration of multiple forms, visions, and energies, as in parts of his long poem *Omeros*, which transposes elements of Homeric epic from the Aegean to the Caribbean.

Even as a schoolboy Walcott knew he was not alone in his effort to sort through his vexed postcolonial affiliations. From a young age he felt a special affinity with Irish writers such as W. B. Yeats, James Joyce, and J. M. Synge, whom he saw as fellow colonials—"They were the niggers of Britain"—with the same paradoxical hatred for the British Empire and worship of the English language. He repeatedly asked how the postcolonial poet can both grieve the agonizing harm of British colonialism and appreciate the empire's literary gift. Walcott also acknowledged other English and American writers—T. S. Eliot, Ezra Pound, Hart Crane, W. H. Auden, and Robert Lowell—as enabling influences.

Over the course of his prolific career, Walcott adapted various European literary archetypes (e.g., the Greek character Philoctetes) and forms (epic, quatrains, terza rima, English meters). He ascribed his rigorous concern with craft to his youthful Protestantism. At once disciplined and flamboyant as a poet, he insisted on the specifically Caribbean opulence of his art: "I come from a place that likes grandeur; it likes large gestures; it is not inhibited by flourish; it is a rhetorical society; it is a society of physical performance; it is a society of style." Although much of his poetry is in a rhetorically elevated Standard English, Walcott adapted the calypso rhythms of a lightly creolized English in "The Schooner *Flight*," and he braided together West Indian English, Standard English, and French patois in *Omeros*. He had a great passion for metaphor, by which he deftly wove imaginative connections across cultural and racial boundaries. His plays, written in an accurate and energetic language, are similarly infused with the spirit of syncretism, vividly conjoining Caribbean and European motifs, images, and idioms.

A Far Cry from Africa

A wind is ruffling the tawny pelt
Of Africa. Kikuyu,[1] quick as flies,
Batten upon the bloodstreams of the veldt.[2]
Corpses are scattered through a paradise.
5   Only the worm, colonel of carrion, cries:
"Waste no compassion on these separate dead!"
Statistics justify and scholars seize

---

1. An east African ethnic group whose members, as Mau Mau fighters, conducted an eight-year campaign of violent resistance against British colonial settlers in Kenya in the 1950s.
2. Open country, neither cultivated nor forest (Afrikaans).

The salients of colonial policy.
What is that to the white child hacked in bed?
10   To savages, expendable as Jews?

Threshed out by beaters,[3] the long rushes break
In a white dust of ibises whose cries
Have wheeled since civilization's dawn
From the parched river or beast-teeming plain.
15   The violence of beast on beast is read
As natural law, but upright man
Seeks his divinity by inflicting pain.
Delirious as these worried beasts, his wars
Dance to the tightened carcass of a drum,
20   While he calls courage still that native dread
Of the white peace contracted by the dead.
Again brutish necessity wipes its hands
Upon the napkin of a dirty cause, again
A waste of our compassion, as with Spain,[4]
25   The gorilla wrestles with the superman.
I who am poisoned with the blood of both,
Where shall I turn, divided to the vein?
I who have cursed
The drunken officer of British rule, how choose
30   Between this Africa and the English tongue I love?
Betray them both, or give back what they give?
How can I face such slaughter and be cool?
How can I turn from Africa and live?

1956, 1962

From The Schooner Flight

1 Adios, Carenage[1]

In idle August, while the sea soft,
and leaves of brown islands stick to the rim
of this Caribbean, I blow out the light
by the dreamless face of Maria Concepcion
5   to ship as a seaman on the schooner Flight.
Out in the yard turning grey in the dawn,
I stood like a stone and nothing else move
but the cold sea rippling like galvanize
and the nail holes of stars in the sky roof,
10   till a wind start to interfere with the trees.
I pass me dry neighbour sweeping she yard
as I went downhill, and I nearly said:
"Sweep soft, you witch, 'cause she don't sleep hard,"
but the bitch look through me like I was dead.

---

3. In big-game hunting, natives are hired to beat the brush, driving birds—such as ibises—and other animals into the open.

4. The Spanish Civil War (1936–39).
1. Waterfront where schooners are cleaned and repaired. "Adios": good-bye (Spanish).

15 A route taxi pull up, park-lights still on.
The driver size up my bags with a grin:
"This time, Shabine, like you really gone!"
I ain't answer the ass, I simply pile in
the back seat and watch the sky burn
20 above Laventille[2] pink as the gown
in which the woman I left was sleeping,
and I look in the rearview and see a man
exactly like me, and the man was weeping
for the houses, the streets, the whole fucking island.

25 Christ have mercy on all sleeping things!
From that dog rotting down Wrightson Road
to when I was a dog on these streets;
if loving these islands must be my load,
out of corruption my soul takes wings,
30 But they had started to poison my soul
with their big house, big car, big-time bohbohl,[3]
coolie, nigger, Syrian, and French Creole,
so I leave it for them and their carnival—
I taking a sea-bath, I gone down the road.
35 I know these islands from Monos to Nassau,[4]
a rusty head sailor with sea-green eyes
that they nickname Shabine, the patois° for   spoken dialect
any red nigger, and I, Shabine, saw
when these slums of empire was paradise.
40 I'm just a red nigger who love the sea,
I had a sound colonial education,
I have Dutch, nigger, and English in me,
and either I'm nobody, or I'm a nation.

But Maria Concepcion was all my thought
45 watching the sea heaving up and down
as the port side of dories, schooners, and yachts
was painted afresh by the strokes of the sun
signing her name with every reflection;
I knew when dark-haired evening put on
50 her bright silk at sunset, and, folding the sea,
sidled under the sheet with her starry laugh,
that there'd be no rest, there'd be no forgetting.
Is like telling mourners round the graveside
about resurrection, they want the dead back,
55 so I smile to myself as the bow rope untied
and the *Flight* swing seaward: "Is no use repeating
that the sea have more fish. I ain't want her
dressed in the sexless light of a seraph,°   angel
I want those round brown eyes like a marmoset,[5] and
60 till the day when I can lean back and laugh,
those claws that tickled my back on sweating

2. Hillside slum outside Port of Spain, Trinidad.
3. Or *bobol*: corrupt practices or fraud, organized by people in positions of power (Eastern
Caribbean English).

4. Capital of the Bahamas. "Monos": island off
the northwest coast of Trinidad.
5. South American monkey.

Sunday afternoons, like a crab on wet sand."
As I worked, watching the rotting waves come
past the bow that scissor the sea like silk,
65   I swear to you all, by my mother's milk,
by the stars that shall fly from tonight's furnace,
that I loved them, my children, my wife, my home;
I loved them as poets love the poetry
that kills them, as drowned sailors the sea.

70   You ever look up from some lonely beach
and see a far schooner? Well, when I write
this poem, each phrase go be soaked in salt;
I go draw and knot every line as tight
as ropes in this rigging; in simple speech
75   my common language go be the wind,
my pages the sails of the schooner *Flight*.

1979

The Season of Phantasmal Peace

Then all the nations of birds lifted together
the huge net of the shadows of this earth
in multitudinous dialects, twittering tongues,
stitching and crossing it. They lifted up
5   the shadows of long pines down trackless slopes,
the shadows of glass-faced towers down evening streets,
the shadow of a frail plant on a city sill—
the net rising soundless as night, the birds' cries soundless, until
there was no longer dusk, or season, decline, or weather,
10   only this passage of phantasmal light
that not the narrowest shadow dared to sever.

And men could not see, looking up, what the wild geese drew,
what the ospreys trailed behind them in silvery ropes
that flashed in the icy sunlight; they could not hear
15   battalions of starlings waging peaceful cries,
bearing the net higher, covering this world
like the vines of an orchard, or a mother drawing
the trembling gauze over the trembling eyes
of a child fluttering to sleep;
                         it was the light
20   that you will see at evening on the side of a hill
in yellow October, and no one hearing knew
what change had brought into the raven's cawing,
the killdeer's screech, the ember-circling chough°   *bird in crow family*
such an immense, soundless, and high concern
25   for the fields and cities where the birds belong,
except it was their seasonal passing, Love,
made seasonless, or, from the high privilege of their birth,
something brighter than pity for the wingless ones
below them who shared dark holes in windows and in houses,

30 and higher they lifted the net with soundless voices
above all change, betrayals of falling suns,
and this season lasted one moment, like the pause
between dusk and darkness, between fury and peace,
but, for such as our earth is now, it lasted long.

1981

From Omeros[1]

Book One

Chapter III

III

"Mais qui ça qui rivait-'ous, Philoctete?"[2]
                                    "Moin blessé."[3]
"But what is wrong wif you, Philoctete?"
                                    "I am blest
wif this wound, Ma Kilman[4] *qui pas ka guérir pièce.*

Which will never heal."
                        "Well, you must take it easy.
5   Go home and lie down, give the foot a lickle°   *little (West Indian English)*
        rest."
Philoctete, his trouser-legs rolled, stares out to sea

from the worn rumshop window. The itch in the sore
tingles like the tendrils of the anemone,
and the puffed blister of Portuguese man-o'-war.°   *jellyfish*

10 He believed the swelling came from the chained ankles
of his grandfathers. Or else why was there no cure?
That the cross he carried was not only the anchor's

but that of his race, for a village black and poor
as the pigs that rooted in its burning garbage,
15 then were hooked on the anchors of the abattoir.°   *slaughterhouse*

Ma Kilman was sewing. She looked up and saw his face
squinting from the white of the street. He was waiting
to pass out on the table. This went on for days.

---

1. Modern Greek version of the name Homer. Homer's *Iliad* and *Odyssey* are, along with Dante's *Divine Comedy*, from which Walcott adapts the terza rima stanza, and James Joyce's *Ulysses* (1922) major influences on this Caribbean epic, which moves across centuries and geographies, from Saint Lucia to Africa to Ireland.
2. Pronounced *fee-lock-TET*; a name shared with Philoctetes, who, in the *Iliad* and Sophocles' eponymous play, is abandoned on an island on the way to the Trojan War after receiving a snakebite. The wound never heals and continu-

ally torments Philoctetes, who moans uncontrollably. Later the gods decide that the war cannot be won without him, and the Greek soldiers have to go back to the island and beg him to return with them to battle.
3. French patois, punningly mistranslated below, since *blessé* actually means "wounded."
4. The owner of the No Pain Café, Ma Kilman serves in the poem as a sibyl (female prophet) and an obeah woman (one practicing a kind of West Indian sorcery).

The ice turned to warm water near the self-hating
20 gesture of clenching his head tight in both hands. She
heard the boys in blue uniforms, going to school,

screaming at his elbow: "Pheeloh! Pheelosophee!"
A mummy embalmed in Vaseline and alcohol.
In the Egyptian silence she muttered softly:

25 "It have a flower somewhere, a medicine, and ways
my grandmother would boil it. I used to watch ants
climbing her white flower-pot. But, God, in which place?"

Where was this root? What senna,° what tepid   *medicinal herb*
  tisanes,°   *medicinal beverages*
could clean the branched river of his corrupted blood,
30 whose sap was a wounded cedar's? What did it mean,

this name that felt like a fever? Well, one good heft
of his garden-cutlass would slice the damned name clean
from its rotting yam. He said, *"Merci."*° Then he left.   *Thank you (French)*

Book Six

Chapter XLIX

I

She bathed him in the brew of the root.[1] The basin
was one of those cauldrons from the old sugar-mill,
with its charred pillars, rock pasture, and one grazing

horse, looking like helmets that have tumbled downhill
5   from an infantry charge. Children rang them with stones.
Wildflowers sprung in them when the dirt found a seam.

She had one in her back yard, close to the crotons,°   *tree or shrub*
agape in its crusted, agonized O: the scream
of centuries. She scraped its rusted scabs, she scoured

10 the mouth of the cauldron, then fed a crackling pyre
with palms and banana-trash. In the scream she poured
tin after kerosene tin, its base black from fire,

of seawater and sulphur. Into this she then fed
the bubbling root and leaves. She led Philoctete
15 to the gurgling lava. Trembling, he entered

his bath like a boy. The lime leaves leeched to his wet
knuckled spine like islands that cling to the basin
of the rusted Caribbean. An icy sweat

---

1. Ma Kilman is bathing Philoctete to heal his wound.

glazed his scalp, but he could feel the putrescent shin
20 drain in the seethe like sucked marrow, he felt it drag
the slime from his shame. She rammed him back to his place

as he tried climbing out with: *"Not yet!"* With a rag
sogged in a basin of ice she rubbed his squeezed face
the way boys enjoy their mother's ritual rage,

25 and as he surrendered to her, the foul flower
on his shin whitened and puckered, the corolla
closed its thorns like the sea-egg. What else did it cure?

II

The bow leapt back to the palm of the warrior.
The yoke of the wrong name lifted from his shoulders.
30 His muscles loosened like those of a brown river

that was dammed with silt, and then silkens its boulders
with refreshing strength. His ribs thudded like a horse
cantering on a beach that bursts into full gallop

while a boy yanks at its rein with terrified "Whoas!"
35 The white foam unlocked his coffles, his ribbed shallop
broke from its anchor, and the water, which he swirled

like a child, steered his brow into the right current,
as calm as *In God We Troust*[2] to that other world,
and his flexed palm enclosed an oar with the identi-

40 ical closure of a mouth around its own name,
the way a sea-anemone closes slyly
into a secrecy many mistake for shame.

Centuries weigh down the head of the swamp-lily,
its tribal burden arches the sea-almond's° spine,   *a tree*
45 in barracoon[3] back yards the soul-smoke still passes,

but the wound has found her own cure. The soft days spin
the spittle of the spider in webbed glasses,
as she drenches the burning trash to its last flame,

and the embers steam and hiss to the schoolboys' cries
50 when he'd weep in the window for their tribal shame.
A shame for the loss of words, and a language tired

of accepting that loss, and then all accepted.
That was why the sea stank from the frothing urine
of surf, and fish-guts reeked from the government shed,

2. Near the poem's beginning, the character Achille chisels this misspelled phrase into his canoe and then decides, "Leave it! Is God' spelling and mine" (1.1.2).
3. Barracks for housing convicts or slaves.

₅₅ and why God pissed on the village for months of rain.
But now, quite clearly the tears trickled down his face
like rainwater down a cracked carafe from Choiseul,[4]

as he stood like a boy in his bath with the first clay's
innocent prick! So she threw Adam a towel.
₆₀ And the yard was Eden. And its light the first day's.

1990

4. A village in Saint Lucia.

TED HUGHES
1930–1998

Ted Hughes was born in Yorkshire, the son of one of seventeen men from a regiment of several hundred to return from the battle of Gallipoli in World War I, a tragedy that imprinted the imagination of the poet. He was educated at Mexborough Grammar School and Pembroke College, Cambridge, where in his last year he changed his course of study from English to archaeology and anthropology, pursuing his interest in the mythic structures that were later to inform his poetry. In 1956 he married the American-born poet Sylvia Plath, who committed suicide in 1963. As poets they explored the world of raw feeling and sensation, a world that Hughes's poems tended to view through the eye of the predator, Plath's through the eye of the victim.

In contrast to the rational lucidity and buttoned-up forms of Philip Larkin and other English poets of "the Movement," Hughes fashions a mythical consciousness in his poems, embodied in violent metaphors, blunt syntax, harsh alliterative clusters, bunched stresses, incantatory repetitions, insistent assonances, and a dark brooding tone. His early books, *The Hawk in the Rain* (1957) and *Lupercal* (1960), show the influence of D. H. Lawrence's *Birds, Beasts and Flowers* (1923), and Hughes's electrifying descriptions of jaguars, thrushes, and pike similarly generate metaphors that relate such creatures to forces underlying all animal and human experience. With *Crow* (1970) and *Gaudete* (1977) he abandoned at once the semblance of realism and the traditional metrical patterning of his early work, in the belief that "the very sound of metre calls up the ghosts of the past and it is difficult to sing one's own tune against that choir. It is easier to speak a language that raises no ghosts." Returning from the wilder shores of myth, Hughes showed in *Moortown* (1979), *Remains of Elmet* (1979), *River* (1983), and *Flowers and Insects* (1989) that he could render the natural world with a delicacy and tenderness as arresting as his earlier ferocity. In *Tales from Ovid* (1997) he brilliantly re-created—rather than translated—twenty-four passages from the Roman poet Ovid's *Metamorphoses*. In the poems of his last volume, *Birthday Letters* (1998), all but two of which are addressed to Plath, Hughes broke a silence of thirty-five years to lift the curtain on the tragic drama of their marriage. That same year he was appointed a member of the Order of Merit, having served as poet laureate of the United Kingdom since 1984. His *Collected Poems* was published in 2003.

Wind

This house has been far out at sea all night,
The woods crashing through darkness, the booming hills,
Winds stampeding the fields under the window
Floundering black astride and blinding wet

5   Till day rose; then under an orange sky
The hills had new places, and wind wielded
Blade-light, luminous and emerald,
Flexing like the lens of a mad eye.

At noon I scaled along the house-side as far as
10   The coal-house door. I dared once to look up—
Through the brunt wind that dented the balls of my eyes
The tent of the hills drummed and strained its guyrope,

The fields quivering, the skyline a grimace,
At any second to bang and vanish with a flap:
15   The wind flung a magpie away and a black-
Back gull bent like an iron bar slowly. The house

Rang like some fine green goblet in the note
That any second would shatter it. Now deep
In chairs, in front of the great fire, we grip
20   Our hearts and cannot entertain book, thought,

Or each other. We watch the fire blazing,
And feel the roots of the house move, but sit on,
Seeing the window tremble to come in,
Hearing the stones cry out under the horizons.

1957

Relic

I found this jawbone at the sea's edge:
There, crabs, dogfish, broken by the breakers or tossed
To flap for half an hour and turn to a crust
Continue the beginning. The deeps are cold:
5   In that darkness camaraderie does not hold:

Nothing touches but, clutching, devours. And the jaws,
Before they are satisfied or their stretched purpose
Slacken, go down jaws; go gnawn bare. Jaws
Eat and are finished and the jawbone comes to the beach:
10   This is the sea's achievement; with shells,
Vertebrae, claws, carapaces, skulls.

Time in the sea eats its tail, thrives, casts these
Indigestibles, the spars of purposes
That failed far from the surface. None grow rich

15   In the sea. This curved jawbone did not laugh
But gripped, gripped and is now a cenotaph.[1]

1960

Pike

Pike, three inches long, perfect
Pike in all parts, green tigering the gold.
Killers from the egg: the malevolent aged grin.
They dance on the surface among the flies.

5   Or move, stunned by their own grandeur,
Over a bed of emerald, silhouette
Of submarine delicacy and horror.
A hundred feet long in their world.

In ponds, under the heat-struck lily pads—
10 Gloom of their stillness:
Logged on last year's black leaves, watching upwards.
Or hung in an amber cavern of weeds

The jaws' hooked clamp and fangs
Not to be changed at this date;
15 A life subdued to its instrument;
The gills kneading quietly, and the pectorals.

Three we kept behind glass,
Jungled in weed: three inches, four,
And four and a half: fed fry° to them—   *young fish*
20 Suddenly there were two. Finally one

With a sag belly and the grin it was born with.
And indeed they spare nobody.
Two, six pounds each, over two feet long,
High and dry and dead in the willow-herb—

25 One jammed past its gills down the other's gullet:
The outside eye stared: as a vice locks—
The same iron in this eye
Though its film shrank in death.

A pond I fished, fifty yards across,
30 Whose lilies and muscular tench[1]
Had outlasted every visible stone
Of the monastery that planted them—

Stilled legendary depth:
It was as deep as England. It held
35 Pike too immense to stir, so immense and old
That past nightfall I dared not cast

---

1. Monument to the dead.   1. Variety of freshwater fish.

But silently cast and fished
With the hair frozen on my head
For what might move, for what eye might move.
40   The still splashes on the dark pond,

Owls hushing the floating woods
Frail on my ear against the dream
Darkness beneath night's darkness had freed,
That rose slowly towards me, watching.

1959, 1960

Out

1 The Dream Time

My father sat in his chair recovering
From the four-year mastication° by gunfire and mud,   *grinding; chewing*
Body buffeted wordless, estranged by long soaking
In the colors of mutilation.
                    His outer perforations
5   Were valiantly healed, but he and the hearth-fire, its blood-flicker
On biscuit-bowl and piano and table leg,
Moved into strong and stronger possession
Of minute after minute, as the clock's tiny cog
Labored and on the thread of his listening
10 Dragged him bodily from under
The mortised° four-year strata of dead Englishmen   *firmly fixed*
He belonged with. He felt his limbs clearing
With every slight, gingerish movement. While I, small and four,
Lay on the carpet as his luckless double,
15 His memory's buried, immovable anchor,
Among jawbones and blown-off boots, tree-stumps, shell-cases and craters,
Under rain that goes on drumming its rods and thickening
Its kingdom, which the sun has abandoned, and where nobody
Can ever again move from shelter.

2

20 The dead man in his cave beginning to sweat;
The melting bronze visor of flesh
Of the mother in the baby-furnace—

Nobody believes, it
Could be nothing, all
25 Undergo smiling at
The lulling of blood in
Their ears, their ears, their ears, their eyes
Are only drops of water and even the dead man suddenly
Sits up and sneezes—Atishoo!
30 Then the nurse wraps him up, smiling,
And, though faintly, the mother is smiling,
And it's just another baby.

As after being blasted to bits
The reassembled infantryman
35 Tentatively totters out, gazing around with the eyes
Of an exhausted clerk.

3 Remembrance Day[1]

The poppy is a wound, the poppy is the mouth
Of the grave, maybe of the womb searching—

A canvas-beauty puppet on a wire
40 Today whoring everywhere. It is years since I wore one.

It is more years
The shrapnel that shattered my father's paybook

Gripped me, and all his dead
Gripped him to a time

45 He no more than they could outgrow, but, cast into one, like iron,
Hung deeper than refreshing of ploughs

In the woe-dark under my mother's eye—
One anchor

Holding my juvenile neck bowed to the dunkings of the Atlantic.
50 So goodbye to that bloody-minded flower.

You dead bury your dead.
Goodbye to the cenotaphs° on my mother's breasts.   *empty tombs*

Goodbye to all the remaindered charms of my father's survival.
Let England close. Let the green sea-anemone close.

1967

Theology

No, the serpent did not
Seduce Eve to the apple.
All that's simply
Corruption of the facts.

5 Adam ate the apple.
Eve ate Adam.
The serpent ate Eve.
This is the dark intestine.

---

1. Holiday (November 11) commemorating soldiers who lost their lives in battle. The practice of
wearing red poppies in honor of lost soldiers
recalls John McCrae's poem "In Flanders Fields"
(1915), which depicts the flowers growing between
the graves on a battlefield.

The serpent, meanwhile,
10   Sleeps his meal off in Paradise—
     Smiling to hear
     God's querulous calling.

1967

Crow's Last Stand

Burning
          burning
                    burning[1]
                         there was finally something
5   The sun could not burn, that it had rendered
     Everything down to—a final obstacle
     Against which it raged and charred

     And rages and chars

     Limpid° among the glaring furnace clinkers°   *clear / coal remains*
10   The pulsing blue tongues and the red and the yellow
     The green lickings of the conflagration

     Limpid and black—

     Crow's eye-pupil, in the tower of its scorched fort.

1970

Daffodils

     Remember how we[1] picked the daffodils?
     Nobody else remembers, but I remember.
     Your daughter came with her armfuls, eager and happy,
     Helping the harvest. She has forgotten.
5   She cannot even remember you. And we sold them.
     It sounds like sacrilege, but we sold them.
     Were we so poor? Old Stoneman, the grocer,
     Boss-eyed, his blood-pressure purpling to beetroot
     (It was his last chance,
10   He would die in the same great freeze as you),
     He persuaded us. Every Spring
     He always bought them, sevenpence a dozen,
     'A custom of the house'.

---

1. Cf. "Burning burning burning burning," line 308 of T. S. Eliot's *Waste Land*, where it is quoted from the Buddha's Fire Sermon.

1. Hughes is addressing his first wife, the American poet Sylvia Plath (1932–1963).

Besides, we still weren't sure we wanted to own
15   Anything. Mainly we were hungry
To convert everything to profit.
Still nomads—still strangers
To our whole possession. The daffodils
Were incidental gilding of the deeds,[2]
20   Treasure trove. They simply came,
And they kept on coming.
As if not from the sod but falling from heaven.
Our lives were still a raid on our own good luck.
We knew we'd live for ever. We had not learned
25   What a fleeting glance of the everlasting
Daffodils are. Never identified
The nuptial flight of the rarest ephemera[3]—
Our own days!
            We thought they were a windfall.
Never guessed they were a last blessing.
30   So we sold them. We worked at selling them
As if employed on somebody else's
Flower-farm. You bent at it
In the rain of that April—your last April.
We bent there together, among the soft shrieks
35   Of their jostled stems, the wet shocks shaken
Of their girlish dance-frocks—
Fresh-opened dragonflies, wet and flimsy,
Opened too early.

We piled their frailty lights on a carpenter's bench,
40   Distributed leaves among the dozens—
Buckling blade-leaves, limber, groping for air, zinc-silvered—
Propped their raw butts in bucket water,
Their oval, meaty butts,
And sold them, sevenpence a bunch—

45   Wind-wounds, spasms from the dark earth,
With their odourless metals,
A flamy purification of the deep grave's stony cold
As if ice had a breath—

We sold them, to wither.
50   The crop thickened faster than we could thin it.
Finally, we were overwhelmed
And we lost our wedding-present scissors.

Every March since they have lifted again
Out of the same bulbs, the same
55   Baby-cries from the thaw,
Ballerinas too early for music, shiverers
In the draughty wings of the year.
On that same groundswell of memory, fluttering

---

2. Document establishing legal possession of a
house.

3. Insect that lives only a few days.

They return to forget you stooping there
60   Behind the rainy curtains of a dark April,
Snipping their stems.

But somewhere your scissors remember. Wherever they are.
Here somewhere, blades wide open,
April by April
65   Sinking deeper
Through the sod—an anchor, a cross of rust.

1998

HAROLD PINTER
1930–2008

Harold Pinter was one of the most original and challenging of the many important playwrights to have emerged in Britain in the last half-century. He was born and educated in East London, studied briefly at the Academy of Dramatic Art, and from the age of nineteen to the age of twenty-seven acted in a repertory company. His first play (in one act), *The Room*, was written and produced in 1957 and was followed immediately by *The Dumb Waiter* and *The Birthday Party*, his first real success. In addition to his prize-winning work for theater and television, he wrote a number of screenplays based on novels such as Marcel Proust's *A la Recherche du Temps Perdu* (*In Search of Lost Time*), John Fowles's *The French Lieutenant's Woman*, and Margaret Atwood's *The Handmaid's Tale*; his screenplays were collected and published in three volumes in 2000. In 2005 he was awarded the Nobel Prize in Literature. In the last years of his life, he devoted himself to political activism and to writing poetry.

Pinter's early work shows the influence of Samuel Beckett and of absurdist drama, notably that of the French playwright Eugène Ionesco, but his vision rapidly established itself as more naturalistic (though no less alarming) than theirs. His territory is typically a room (refuge, prison cell, trap) symbolic of its occupants' world. Into this, and into their ritualized relationship with its rules and taboos, comes a stranger on to whom—as on to a screen—the occupants project their deepest desires, guilts, neuroses. The breakdown that follows is mirrored in the breakdown of language. Pinter, who had a poet's ear for the rhythms of spoken English, is a master of the pauses, double entendres, and silences that communicate a secondary level of meaning often opposed to the first. He said of language:

> The speech we hear is an indication of that which we don't hear. It is a necessary avoidance, a violent, sly, and anguished or mocking smoke screen which keeps the other in its true place. When true silence falls we are left with echo but are nearer nakedness. One way of looking at speech is to say that it is a constant stratagem to cover nakedness.

The critic Lois Gordon has well said that "one way of looking at Pinter's plays is to say that they are dramatic stratagems that uncover nakedness."

The Dumb Waiter

SCENE: *A basement room. Two beds, flat against the back wall. A serving hatch, closed, between the beds. A door to the kitchen and lavatory, left. A door to a passage, right.*

BEN *is lying on a bed, left, reading a paper.* GUS *is sitting on a bed, right, tying his shoelaces, with difficulty. Both are dressed in shirts, trousers and braces.*

Silence.

GUS *ties his laces, rises, yawns and begins to walk slowly to the door, left. He stops, looks down, and shakes his foot.*

BEN *lowers his paper and watches him.* GUS *kneels and unties his shoelace and slowly takes off the shoe. He looks inside it and brings out a flattened matchbox. He shakes it and examines it. Their eyes meet.* BEN *rattles his paper and reads.* GUS *puts the matchbox in his pocket and bends down to put on his shoe. He ties his lace, with difficulty.* BEN *lowers his paper and watches him.* GUS *walks to the door, left, stops, and shakes the other foot. He kneels, unties his shoelace, and slowly takes off the shoe. He looks inside it and brings out a flattened cigarette packet. He shakes it and examines it. Their eyes meet.* BEN *rattles his paper and reads.* GUS *puts the packet in his pocket, bends down, puts on his shoe and ties the lace.*

He wanders off, left.

BEN *slams the paper down on the bed and glares after him. He picks up the paper and lies on his back, reading.*

Silence.

A lavatory chain is pulled twice off left, but the lavatory does not flush.

Silence.

GUS *re-enters, left, and halts at the door, scratching his head.*

BEN *slams down the paper.*

BEN Kaw!
   [*He picks up the paper.*]
What about this? Listen to this!
   [*He refers to the paper.*]
A man of eighty-seven wanted to cross the road. But there was a lot of traffic, see? He couldn't see how he was going to squeeze through. So he crawled under a lorry.[1]

GUS He what?

BEN He crawled under a lorry. A stationary lorry.

GUS No?

BEN The lorry started and ran over him.

GUS Go on!

BEN That's what it says here.

GUS Get away.

BEN It's enough to make you want to puke, isn't it?

GUS Who advised him to do a thing like that?

BEN A man of eighty-seven crawling under a lorry!

1. Truck.

GUS It's unbelievable.

BEN It's down here in black and white.

GUS Incredible.

> [*Silence.*
>
> GUS *shakes his head and exits.* BEN *lies back and reads.*
>
> *The lavatory chain is pulled once off left, but the lavatory does not flush.*
>
> BEN *whistles at an item in the paper.*
>
> GUS *re-enters.*]

I want to ask you something.

BEN What are you doing out there?

GUS Well, I was just—

BEN What about the tea?

GUS I'm just going to make it.

BEN Well, go on, make it.

GUS Yes, I will. [*He sits in a chair. Ruminatively.*] He's laid on some very nice crockery this time, I'll say that. It's sort of striped. There's a white stripe.

> [BEN *reads.*]

It's very nice. I'll say that.

> [BEN *turns the page.*]

You know, sort of round the cup. Round the rim. All the rest of it's black, you see. Then the saucer's black, except for right in the middle, where the cup goes, where it's white.

> [BEN *reads.*]

Then the plates are the same, you see. Only they've got a black stripe—the plates—right across the middle. Yes, I'm quite taken with the crockery.

BEN [*Still reading.*] What do you want plates for? You're not going to eat.

GUS I've brought a few biscuits.

BEN Well, you'd better eat them quick.

GUS I always bring a few biscuits. Or a pie. You know I can't drink tea without anything to eat.

BEN Well, make the tea then, will you? Time's getting on.

> [GUS *brings out the flattened cigarette packet and examines it.*]

GUS You got any cigarettes? I think I've run out.

> [*He throws the packet high up and leans forward to catch it.*]

I hope it won't be a long job, this one.

> [*Aiming carefully, he flips the packet under his bed.*]

Oh, I wanted to ask you something.

BEN [*Slamming his paper down.*] Kaw!

GUS What's that?

BEN A child of eight killed a cat!

GUS Get away.

BEN It's a fact. What about that, eh? A child of eight killing a cat!

GUS How did he do it?

BEN It was a girl.

GUS How did she do it?

BEN She—

> [*He picks up the paper and studies it.*]

It doesn't say.

GUS Why not?

BEN   Wait a minute. It just says—Her brother, aged eleven, viewed the incident from the toolshed.

GUS   Go on!

BEN   That's bloody ridiculous.

        [*Pause.*]

GUS   I bet he did it.

BEN   Who?

GUS   The brother.

BEN   I think you're right.

        [*Pause.*]

    [*Slamming down the paper.*] What about that, eh? A kid of eleven killing a cat and blaming it on his little sister of eight! It's enough to—

        [*He breaks off in disgust and seizes the paper.* GUS *rises.*]

GUS   What time is he getting in touch?

        [BEN *reads.*]

    What time is he getting in touch?

BEN   What's the matter with you? It could be any time. Any time.

GUS   [*Moves to the foot of* BEN's *bed.*] Well, I was going to ask you something.

BEN   What?

GUS   Have you noticed the time that tank takes to fill?

BEN   What tank?

GUS   In the lavatory.

BEN   No. Does it?

GUS   Terrible.

BEN   Well, what about it?

GUS   What do you think's the matter with it?

BEN   Nothing.

GUS   Nothing?

BEN   It's got a deficient ballcock, that's all.

GUS   A deficient what?

BEN   Ballcock.

GUS   No? Really?

BEN   That's what I should say.

GUS   Go on! That didn't occur to me.

        [GUS *wanders to his bed and presses the mattress.*]

    I didn't have a very restful sleep today, did you? It's not much of a bed. I could have done with another blanket too. [*He catches sight of a picture on the wall.*] Hello, what's this? [*Peering at it.*] "The First Eleven."[2] Cricketers. You seen this, Ben?

BEN   [*Reading.*] What?

GUS   The first eleven.

BEN   What?

GUS   There's a photo here of the first eleven.

BEN   What first eleven?

GUS   [*Studying the photo.*] It doesn't say.

BEN   What about that tea?

GUS   They all look a bit old to me.

        [GUS *wanders downstage, looks out front, then all about the room.*]

---

2. A school's top team of cricketers.

I wouldn't like to live in this dump. I wouldn't mind if you had a window, you could see what it looked like outside.

BEN What do you want a window for?

GUS Well, I like to have a bit of a view, Ben. It whiles away the time.
[*He walks about the room.*]
I mean, you come into a place when it's still dark, you come into a room you've never seen before, you sleep all day, you do your job, and then you go away in the night again.
[*Pause.*]
I like to get a look at the scenery. You never get the chance in this job.

BEN You get your holidays, don't you?

GUS Only a fortnight.

BEN [*Lowering the paper.*] You kill me. Anyone would think you're working every day. How often do we do a job? Once a week? What are you complaining about?

GUS Yes, but we've got to be on tap though, haven't we? You can't move out of the house in case a call comes.

BEN You know what your trouble is?

GUS What?

BEN You haven't got any interests.

GUS I've got interests.

BEN What? Tell me one of your interests.
[*Pause.*]

GUS I've got interests.

BEN Look at me. What have I got?

GUS I don't know. What?

BEN I've got my woodwork. I've got my model boats. Have you ever seen me idle? I'm never idle. I know how to occupy my time, to its best advantage. Then when a call comes, I'm ready.

GUS Don't you ever get a bit fed up?

BEN Fed up? What with?
[*Silence.*
BEN *reads.* GUS *feels in the pocket of his jacket, which hangs on the bed.*]

GUS You got any cigarettes? I've run out.
[*The lavatory flushes off left.*]
There she goes.
[GUS *sits on his bed.*]
No, I mean, I say the crockery's good. It is. It's very nice. But that's about all I can say for this place. It's worse than the last one. Remember that last place we were in? Last time, where was it? At least there was a wireless there. No, honest. He doesn't seem to bother much about our comfort these days.

BEN When are you going to stop jabbering?

GUS You'd get rheumatism in a place like this, if you stay long.

BEN We're not staying long. Make the tea, will you? We'll be on the job in a minute.
[GUS *picks up a small bag by his bed and brings out a packet of tea. He examines it and looks up.*]

GUS Eh, I've been meaning to ask you.

BEN What the hell is it now?

GUS Why did you stop the car this morning, in the middle of that road?

BEN   [*Lowering the paper.*] I thought you were asleep.

GUS   I was, but I woke up when you stopped. You did stop, didn't you?
     [*Pause.*]
In the middle of that road. It was still dark, don't you remember? I looked
out. It was all misty. I thought perhaps you wanted to kip[3] but you were
sitting up dead straight, like you were waiting for something.

BEN   I wasn't waiting for anything.

GUS   I must have fallen asleep again. What was all that about then? Why
did you stop?

BEN   [*Picking up the paper.*] We were too early.

GUS   Early? [*He rises.*] What do you mean? We got the call, didn't we, saying we were to start right away. We did. We shoved out on the dot. So
how could we be too early?

BEN   [*Quietly.*] Who took the call, me or you?

GUS   You.

BEN   We were too early.

GUS   Too early for what?
     [*Pause.*]
You mean someone had to get out before we got in?
     [*He examines the bedclothes.*]
I thought these sheets didn't look too bright. I thought they ponged[4] a bit.
I was too tired to notice when I got in this morning. Eh, that's taking a bit
of a liberty, isn't it? I don't want to share my bed-sheets. I told you things
were going down the drain. I mean, we've always had clean sheets laid on
up till now. I've noticed it.

BEN   How do you know those sheets weren't clean?

GUS   What do you mean?

BEN   How do you know they weren't clean? You've spent the whole day in
them, haven't you?

GUS   What, you mean it might be my pong? [*He sniffs sheets.*] Yes. [*He sits
slowly on bed.*] It could be my pong, I suppose. It's difficult to tell. I don't
really know what I pong like, that's the trouble.

BEN   [*Referring to the paper.*] Kaw!

GUS   Eh, Ben.

BEN   Kaw!

GUS   Ben.

BEN   What?

GUS   What town are we in? I've forgotten.

BEN   I've told you. Birmingham.

GUS   Go on!
     [*He looks with interest about the room.*]
That's in the Midlands. The second biggest city in Great Britain. I'd never
have guessed.
     [*He snaps his fingers.*]
Eh, it's Friday today, isn't it? It'll be Saturday tomorrow.

BEN   What about it?

GUS   [*Excited.*] We could go and watch the Villa.[5]

BEN   They're playing away.

---

3. Nap.
4. Smelled.

5. Aston Villa, popularly known as "the Villa,"
Birmingham's soccer team.

GUS   No, are they? Caarr! What a pity.

BEN   Anyway, there's no time. We've got to get straight back.

GUS   Well, we have done in the past, haven't we? Stayed over and watched a game, haven't we? For a bit of relaxation.

BEN   Things have tightened up, mate. They're tightened up.

> [GUS *chuckles to himself.*]

GUS   I saw the Villa get beat in a cup tie once. Who was it against now? White shirts. It was one-all at half time. I'll never forget it. Their opponents won by a penalty. Talk about drama. Yes, it was a disputed penalty. Disputed. They got beat two–one, anyway, because of it. You were there yourself.

BEN   Not me.

GUS   Yes, you were there. Don't you remember that disputed penalty?

BEN   No.

GUS   He went down just inside the area. Then they said he was just acting. I didn't think the other bloke touched him myself. But the referee had the ball on the spot.

BEN   Didn't touch him! What are you talking about? He laid him out flat!

GUS   Not the Villa. The Villa don't play that sort of game.

BEN   Get out of it.

> [*Pause.*]

GUS   Eh, that must have been here, in Birmingham.

BEN   What must?

GUS   The Villa. That must have been here.

BEN   They were playing away.

GUS   Because you know who the other team was? It was the Spurs. It was Tottenham Hotspur.[6]

BEN   Well, what about it?

GUS   We've never done a job in Tottenham.

BEN   How do you know?

GUS   I'd remember Tottenham.

> [BEN *turns on his bed to look at him.*]

BEN   Don't make me laugh, will you?

> [BEN *turns back and reads.* GUS *yawns and speaks through his yawn.*]

GUS   When's he going to get in touch?

> [*Pause.*]

Yes, I'd like to see another football match. I've always been an ardent football fan. Here, what about coming to see the Spurs tomorrow?

BEN   [*Tonelessly.*] They're playing away.

GUS   Who are?

BEN   The Spurs.

GUS   Then they might be playing here.

BEN   Don't be silly.

GUS   If they're playing away they might be playing here. They might be playing the Villa.

BEN   [*Tonelessly.*] But the Villa are playing away.

> [*Pause. An envelope slides under the door, right.* GUS *sees it. He stands, looking at it.*]

---

6. A professional soccer team; Tottenham is in north London.

GUS Ben.
BEN Away. They're all playing away.
GUS Ben, look here.
BEN What?
GUS Look.
    [BEN *turns his head and sees the envelope. He stands.*]
BEN What's that?
GUS I don't know.
BEN Where did it come from?
GUS Under the door.
BEN Well, what is it?
GUS I don't know.
    [*They stare at it.*]
BEN Pick it up.
GUS What do you mean?
BEN Pick it up!
    [GUS *slowly moves towards it, bends and picks it up.*]
  What is it?
GUS An envelope.
BEN Is there anything on it?
GUS No.
BEN Is it sealed?
GUS Yes.
BEN Open it.
GUS What?
BEN Open it!
    [GUS *opens it and looks inside.*]
  What's in it?
    [GUS *empties twelve matches into his hand.*]
GUS Matches.
BEN Matches?
GUS Yes.
BEN Show it to me.
    [GUS *passes the envelope.* BEN *examines it.*]
  Nothing on it. Not a word.
GUS That's funny, isn't it?
BEN It came under the door?
GUS Must have done.
BEN Well, go on.
GUS Go on where?
BEN Open the door and see if you catch anyone outside.
GUS Who, me?
BEN Go on!
    [GUS *stares at him, puts the matches in his pocket, goes to his bed and brings a revolver from under the pillow. He goes to the door, opens it, looks out and shuts it.*]
GUS No one.
    [*He replaces the revolver.*]
BEN What did you see?
GUS Nothing.
BEN They must have been pretty quick.
    [GUS *takes the matches from pocket and looks at them.*]

GUS   Well, they'll come in handy.

BEN   Yes.

GUS   Won't they?

BEN   Yes, you're always running out, aren't you?

GUS   All the time.

BEN   Well, they'll come in handy then.

GUS   Yes.

BEN   Won't they?

GUS   Yes, I could do with them. I could do with them too.

BEN   You could, eh?

GUS   Yes.

BEN   Why?

GUS   We haven't any.

BEN   Well, you've got some now, haven't you?

GUS   I can light the kettle now.

BEN   Yes, you're always cadging matches. How many have you got there?

GUS   About a dozen.

BEN   Well, don't lose them. Red too. You don't even need a box.

        [GUS *probes his ear with a match.*]

[*Slapping his hand.*] Don't waste them! Go on, go and light it.

GUS   Eh?

BEN   Go and light it.

GUS   Light what?

BEN   The kettle.

GUS   You mean the gas.

BEN   Who does?

GUS   You do.

BEN   [*His eyes narrowing.*] What do you mean, I mean the gas?

GUS   Well, that's what you mean, don't you? The gas.

BEN   [*Powerfully.*] If I say go and light the kettle I mean go and light the kettle.

GUS   How can you light a kettle?

BEN   It's a figure of speech! Light the kettle. It's a figure of speech!

GUS   I've never heard it.

BEN   Light the kettle! It's common usage!

GUS   I think you've got it wrong.

BEN   [*Menacing.*] What do you mean?

GUS   They say put on the kettle.

BEN   [*Taut.*] Who says?

        [*They stare at each other, breathing hard.*]

[*Deliberately.*] I have never in all my life heard anyone say put on the kettle.

GUS   I bet my mother used to say it.

BEN   Your mother? When did you last see your mother?

GUS   I don't know, about—

BEN   Well, what are you talking about your mother for?

        [*They stare.*]

Gus, I'm not trying to be unreasonable. I'm just trying to point out something to you.

GUS   Yes, but—

BEN   Who's the senior partner here, me or you?

GUS   You.

BEN   I'm only looking after your interests, Gus. You've got to learn, mate.

GUS   Yes, but I've never heard—

BEN   [*Vehemently.*] Nobody says light the gas! What does the gas light?

GUS   What does the gas—?

BEN   [*Grabbing him with two hands by the throat, at arm's length.*] THE
KETTLE, YOU FOOL!
[GUS *takes the hands from his throat.*]

GUS   All right, all right.
[*Pause.*]

BEN   Well, what are you waiting for?

GUS   I want to see if they light.

BEN   What?

GUS   The matches.
[*He takes out the flattened box and tries to strike.*]
No.
[*He throws the box under the bed.*
BEN *stares at him.*
GUS *raises his foot.*]
Shall I try it on here?
[BEN *stares.* GUS *strikes a match on his shoe. It lights.*]
Here we are.

BEN   [*Wearily.*] Put on the bloody kettle, for Christ's sake.
[BEN *goes to his bed, but, realizing what he has said, stops and half turns.
They look at each other.* GUS *slowly exits, left.* BEN *slams his paper down
on the bed and sits on it, head in hands.*]

GUS   [*Entering.*] It's going.

BEN   What?

GUS   The stove.
[GUS *goes to his bed and sits.*]
I wonder who it'll be tonight.
[*Silence.*]
Eh, I've been wanting to ask you something.

BEN   [*Putting his legs on the bed.*] Oh, for Christ's sake.

GUS   No. I was going to ask you something.
[*He rises and sits on* BEN's *bed.*]

BEN   What are you sitting on my bed for?
[GUS *sits.*]
What's the matter with you? You're always asking me questions. What's
the matter with you?

GUS   Nothing.

BEN   You never used to ask me so many damn questions. What's come
over you?

GUS   No, I was just wondering.

BEN   Stop wondering. You've got a job to do. Why don't you just do it and
shut up?

GUS   That's what I was wondering about.

BEN   What?

GUS   The job.

BEN   What job?

GUS   [*Tentatively.*] I thought perhaps you might know something.
[BEN *looks at him.*]
I thought perhaps you—I mean—have you got any idea—who it's going
to be tonight?

BEN   Who what's going to be?

[*They look at each other.*]
GUS [*At length.*] Who it's going to be.
[*Silence.*]
BEN Are you feeling all right?
GUS Sure.
BEN Go and make the tea.
GUS Yes, sure.
[GUS *exits, left,* BEN *looks after him. He then takes his revolver from under the pillow and checks it for ammunition.* GUS *re-enters.*]
The gas has gone out.
BEN Well, what about it?
GUS There's a meter.[7]
BEN I haven't got any money.
GUS Nor have I.
BEN You'll have to wait.
GUS What for?
BEN For Wilson.
GUS He might not come. He might just send a message. He doesn't always come.
BEN Well, you'll have to do without it, won't you?
GUS Blimey.
BEN You'll have a cup of tea afterwards. What's the matter with you?
GUS I like to have one before.
[BEN *holds the revolver up to the light and polishes it.*]
BEN You'd better get ready anyway.
GUS Well, I don't know, that's a bit much, you know, for my money.
[*He picks up a packet of tea from the bed and throws it into the bag.*]
I hope he's got a shilling, anyway, if he comes. He's entitled to have. After all, it's his place, he could have seen there was enough gas for a cup of tea.
BEN What do you mean, it's his place?
GUS Well, isn't it?
BEN He's probably only rented it. It doesn't have to be his place.
GUS I know it's his place. I bet the whole house is. He's not even laying on any gas now either.
[GUS *sits on his bed.*]
It's his place all right. Look at all the other places. You go to this address, there's a key there, there's a teapot, there's never a soul in sight—[*He pauses.*] Eh, nobody ever hears a thing, have you ever thought of that? We never get any complaints, do we, too much noise or anything like that? You never see a soul, do you?—except the bloke who comes. You ever noticed that? I wonder if the walls are soundproof. [*He touches the wall above his bed.*] Can't tell. All you do is wait, eh? Half the time he doesn't even bother to put in an appearance, Wilson.
BEN Why should he? He's a busy man.
GUS [*Thoughtfully.*] I find him hard to talk to, Wilson. Do you know that, Ben?
BEN Scrub round it, will you?
[*Pause.*]
GUS There are a number of things I want to ask him. But I can never get round to it, when I see him.
[*Pause.*]

7. One that controls the supply of gas and must be fed with shilling coins.

I've been thinking about the last one.

BEN   What last one?

GUS   That girl.

    [BEN *grabs the paper, which he reads.*]

[*Rising, looking down at* BEN.] How many times have you read that paper?

    [BEN *slams the paper down and rises.*]

BEN   [*Angrily.*] What do you mean?

GUS   I was just wondering how many times you'd—

BEN   What are you doing, criticizing me?

GUS   No, I was just—

BEN   You'll get a swipe round your earhole if you don't watch your step.

GUS   Now look here, Ben—

BEN   I'm not looking anywhere! [*He addresses the room.*] How many times have I—! A bloody liberty!

GUS   I didn't mean that.

BEN   You just get on with it, mate. Get on with it, that's all.

    [BEN *gets back on the bed.*]

GUS   I was just thinking about that girl, that's all.

    [GUS *sits on his bed.*]

She wasn't much to look at, I know, but still. It was a mess though, wasn't it? What a mess. Honest, I can't remember a mess like that one. They don't seem to hold together like men, women. A looser texture, like. Didn't she spread, eh? She didn't half spread. Kaw! But I've been meaning to ask you.

    [BEN *sits up and clenches his eyes.*]

Who clears up after we've gone? I'm curious about that. Who does the clearing up? Maybe they don't clear up. Maybe they just leave them there, eh? What do you think? How many jobs have we done? Blimey, I can't count them. What if they never clear anything up after we've gone.

BEN   [*Pityingly.*] You mutt. Do you think we're the only branch of this organization? Have a bit of common. They got departments for everything.

GUS   What, cleaners and all?

BEN   You birk!

GUS   No, it was that girl made me start to think—

    [*There is a loud clatter and racket in the bulge of wall between the beds, of something descending. They grab their revolvers, jump up and face the wall. The noise comes to a stop. Silence. They look at each other.* BEN *gestures sharply towards the wall.* GUS *approaches the wall slowly. He bangs it with his revolver. It is hollow.* BEN *moves to the head of his bed, his revolver cocked.* GUS *puts his revolver on his bed and pats along the bottom of the centre panel. He finds a rim. He lifts the panel. Disclosed is a serving-hatch, a "dumb waiter." A wide box is held by pulleys.* GUS *peers into the box. He brings out a piece of paper.*]

BEN   What is it?

GUS   You have a look at it.

BEN   Read it.

GUS   [*Reading.*] Two braised steak and chips. Two sago puddings. Two teas without sugar.

BEN   Let me see that. [*He takes the paper.*]

GUS   [*To himself.*] Two teas without sugar.

BEN   Mmnn.

GUS   What do you think of that?

BEN   Well—

    [*The box goes up,* BEN *levels his revolver.*]

GUS   Give us a chance! They're in a hurry, aren't they?

    [BEN *rereads the note.* GUS *looks over his shoulder.*]

That's a bit—that's a bit funny, isn't it?

BEN   [*Quickly.*] No, it's not funny. It probably used to be a café here, that's all. Upstairs. These places change hands very quickly.

GUS   A café?

BEN   Yes.

GUS   What, do you mean this was the kitchen, down here?

BEN   Yes, they change hands overnight, these places. Go into liquidation. The people who run it, you know, they don't find it a going concern, they move out.

GUS   You mean the people who ran this place didn't find it a going concern and moved out?

BEN   Sure.

GUS   WELL, WHO'S GOT IT NOW?

    [*Silence.*]

BEN   What do you mean, who's got it now?

GUS   Who's got it now? If they moved out, who moved in?

BEN   Well, that all depends—

    [*The box descends with a clatter and bang.* BEN *levels his revolver.* GUS *goes to the box and brings out a piece of paper.*]

GUS   [*Reading.*] Soup of the day. Liver and onions. Jam tart.

    [*A pause.* GUS *looks at* BEN. BEN *takes the note and reads it. He walks slowly to the hatch.* GUS *follows.* BEN *looks into the hatch but not up it.* GUS *puts his hand on* BEN's *shoulder.* BEN *throws it off.* GUS *puts his finger to his mouth. He leans on the hatch and swiftly looks up it.* BEN *flings him away in alarm.* BEN *looks at the note. He throws his revolver on the bed and speaks with decision.*]

BEN   We'd better send something up.

GUS   Eh?

BEN   We'd better send something up.

GUS   Oh! Yes. Yes. Maybe you're right.

    [*They are both relieved at the decision.*]

BEN   [*Purposefully.*] Quick! What have you got in that bag?

GUS   Not much.

    [GUS *goes to the hatch and shouts up it.*]

Wait a minute!

BEN   Don't do that!

    [GUS *examines the contents of the bag and brings them out, one by one.*]

GUS   Biscuits. A bar of chocolate. Half a pint of milk.

BEN   That all?

GUS   Packet of tea.

BEN   Good.

GUS   We can't send the tea. That's all the tea we've got.

BEN   Well, there's no gas. You can't do anything with it, can you?

GUS   Maybe they can send us down a bob.[8]

BEN   What else is there?

---

8. A shilling (i.e., to insert in the gas meter).

GUS   [*Reaching into bag.*] One Eccles cake.[9]

BEN   One Eccles cake?

GUS   Yes.

BEN   You never told me you had an Eccles cake.

GUS   Didn't I?

BEN   Why only one? Didn't you bring one for me?

GUS   I didn't think you'd be keen.

BEN   Well, you can't send up one Eccles cake, anyway.

GUS   Why not?

BEN   Fetch one of those plates.

GUS   All right.
       [GUS *goes towards the door, left, and stops.*]
    Do you mean I can keep the Eccles cake then?

BEN   Keep it?

GUS   Well, they don't know we've got it, do they?

BEN   That's not the point.

GUS   Can't I keep it?

BEN   No, you can't. Get the plate.
       [GUS *exits, left.* BEN *looks in the bag. He brings out a packet of crisps.*[1]
       Enter GUS *with a plate.*]
    [*Accusingly, holding up the crisps.*] Where did these come from?

GUS   What?

BEN   Where did these crisps come from?

GUS   Where did you find them?

BEN   [*Hitting him on the shoulder.*] You're playing a dirty game, my lad!

GUS   I only eat those with beer!

BEN   Well, where were you going to get the beer?

GUS   I was saving them till I did.

BEN   I'll remember this. Put everything on the plate.
       [*They pile everything on to the plate. The box goes up without the
       plate.*]
    Wait a minute!
           [*They stand.*]

GUS   It's gone up.

BEN   It's all your stupid fault, playing about!

GUS   What do we do now?

BEN   We'll have to wait till it comes down.
       [BEN *puts the plate on the bed, puts on his shoulder holster, and starts
       to put on his tie.*]
    You'd better get ready.
       [GUS *goes to his bed, puts on his tie, and starts to fix his holster.*]

GUS   Hey, Ben.

BEN   What?

GUS   What's going on here?
       [*Pause.*]

BEN   What do you mean?

GUS   How can this be a café?

BEN   It used to be a café.

---

9. A small cake originally made in the Lancashire town of Eccles.
1. Potato chips.

GUS   Have you seen the gas stove?

BEN   What about it?

GUS   It's only got three rings.

BEN   So what?

GUS   Well, you couldn't cook much on three rings, not for a busy place like this.

BEN   [*Irritably.*] That's why the service is slow!

    [BEN *puts on his waistcoat.*]

GUS   Yes, but what happens when we're not here? What do they do then? All these menus coming down and nothing going up. It might have been going on like this for years.

    [BEN *brushes his jacket.*]

What happens when we go?

    [BEN *puts on his jacket.*]

They can't do much business.

    [*The box descends. They turn about.* GUS *goes to the hatch and brings out a note.*]

GUS   [*Reading.*] Macaroni Pastitsio. Ormitha Macarounada.

BEN   What was that?

GUS   Macaroni Pastitsio. Ormitha Macarounada.

BEN   Greek dishes.

GUS   No.

BEN   That's right.

GUS   That's pretty high class.

BEN   Quick before it goes up.

    [GUS *puts the plate in the box.*]

GUS   [*Calling up the hatch.*] Three McVitie and Price! One Lyons Red Label! One Smith's Crisps![2] One Eccles cake! One Fruit and Nut!

BEN   Cadbury's.[3]

GUS   [*Up the hatch.*] Cadbury's!

BEN   [*Handing the milk.*] One bottle of milk.

GUS   [*Up the hatch.*] One bottle of milk! Half a pint! [*He looks at the label.*] Express Dairy! [*He puts the bottle in the box.*]

    [*The box goes up.*]

Just did it.

BEN   You shouldn't shout like that.

GUS   Why not?

BEN   It isn't done.

    [BEN *goes to his bed.*]

Well, that should be all right, anyway, for the time being.

GUS   You think so, eh?

BEN   Get dressed, will you? It'll be any minute now.

    [GUS *puts on his waistcoat.* BEN *lies down and looks up at the ceiling.*]

GUS   This is some place. No tea and no biscuits.

BEN   Eating makes you lazy, mate. You're getting lazy, you know that? You don't want to get slack on your job.

GUS   Who me?

BEN   Slack, mate, slack.

---

2. Brands, respectively, of cookies, tea, and potato chips.
3. A brand of chocolate bar.

GUS   Who me? Slack?

BEN   Have you checked your gun? You haven't even checked your gun. It
looks disgraceful, anyway. Why don't you ever polish it?
[GUS *rubs his revolver on the sheet.* BEN *takes out a pocket mirror and
straightens his tie.*]

GUS   I wonder where the cook is. They must have had a few, to cope with
that. Maybe they had a few more gas stoves. Eh! Maybe there's another
kitchen along the passage.

BEN   Of course there is! Do you know what it takes to make an Ormitha
Macarounada?

GUS   No, what?

BEN   An Ormitha—! Buck your ideas up, will you?

GUS   Takes a few cooks, eh?
[GUS *puts his revolver in its holster.*]
The sooner we're out of this place the better.
[*He puts on his jacket.*]
Why doesn't he get in touch? I feel like I've been here years. [*He takes his
revolver out of its holster to check the ammunition.*] We've never let him
down though, have we? We've never let him down. I was thinking only
the other day, Ben. We're reliable, aren't we?
[*He puts his revolver back in its holster.*]
Still, I'll be glad when it's over tonight.
[*He brushes his jacket.*]
I hope the bloke's not going to get excited tonight, or anything. I'm feeling
a bit off. I've got a splitting headache.
[*Silence.*
   The box descends. BEN *jumps up.*
   GUS *collects the note.*]
[*Reading.*] One Bamboo Shoots, Water Chestnuts, and Chicken. One Char
Siu and Beansprouts.

BEN   Beansprouts?

GUS   Yes.

BEN   Blimey.

GUS   I wouldn't know where to begin.
[*He looks back at the box. The packet of tea is inside it. He picks it
up.*]
They've sent back the tea.

BEN   [*Anxious.*] What'd they do that for?

GUS   Maybe it isn't teatime.
[*The box goes up. Silence.*]

BEN   [*Throwing the tea on the bed, and speaking urgently.*] Look here.
We'd better tell them.

GUS   Tell them what?

BEN   That we can't do it, we haven't got it.

GUS   All right then.

BEN   Lend us your pencil. We'll write a note.
[GUS, *turning for a pencil, suddenly discovers the speaking tube, which
hangs on the right wall of the hatch facing his bed.*]

GUS   What's this?

BEN   What?

GUS   This.

BEN   [*Examining it.*] This? It's a speaking tube.

GUS   How long has that been there?

BEN   Just the job. We should have used it before, instead of shouting up there.

GUS   Funny I never noticed it before.

BEN   Well, come on.

GUS   What do you do?

BEN   See that? That's a whistle.

GUS   What, this?

BEN   Yes, take it out. Pull it out.

> [GUS *does so.*]

That's it.

GUS   What do we do now?

BEN   Blow into it.

GUS   Blow?

BEN   It whistles up there if you blow. Then they know you want to speak. Blow.

> [GUS *blows. Silence.*]

GUS   [*Tube at mouth.*] I can't hear a thing.

BEN   Now you speak! Speak into it!

> [GUS *looks at* BEN, *then speaks into the tube.*]

GUS   The larder's bare!

BEN   Give me that!

> [*He grabs the tube and puts it to his mouth.*]

[*Speaking with great deference.*] Good evening. I'm sorry to—bother you, but we just thought we'd better let you know that we haven't got anything left. We sent up all we had. There's no more food down here.

> [*He brings the tube slowly to his ear.*]

What?

> [*To mouth.*]

What?

> [*To ear. He listens. To mouth.*]

No, all we had we sent up.

> [*To ear. He listens. To mouth.*]

Oh, I'm very sorry to hear that.

> [*To ear. He listens. To* GUS.]

The Eccles cake was stale.

> [*He listens. To* GUS.]

The chocolate was melted.

> [*He listens. To* GUS.]

The milk was sour.

GUS   What about the crisps?

BEN   [*Listening.*] The biscuits were mouldy.

> [*He glares at* GUS. *Tube to mouth.*]

Well, we're sorry about that.

> [*Tube to ear.*]

What?

> [*To mouth.*]

What?

> [*To ear.*]

Yes. Yes.

> [*To mouth.*]

Yes certainly. Right away.

[*To ear. The voice has ceased. He hangs up the tube.*]
[*Excitedly.*] Did you hear that?

GUS What?

BEN You know what he said? Light the kettle! Not put on the kettle! Not light the gas! But light the kettle!

GUS How can we light the kettle?

BEN What do you mean?

GUS There's no gas.

BEN [*Clapping hand to head.*] Now what do we do?

GUS What did he want us to light the kettle for?

BEN For tea. He wanted a cup of tea.

GUS *He* wanted a cup of tea! What about me? I've been wanting a cup of tea all night!

BEN [*Despairingly.*] What do we do now?

GUS What are we supposed to drink?

[BEN *sits on his bed, staring.*]

What about us?

[BEN *sits.*]

I'm thirsty too. I'm starving. And he wants a cup of tea. That beats the band, that does.

[BEN *lets his head sink on his chest.*]

I could do with a bit of sustenance myself. What about you? You look as if you could do with something too.

[GUS *sits on his bed.*]

We send him up all we've got and he's not satisfied. No, honest, it's enough to make the cat laugh. Why did you send him up all that stuff? [*Thoughtfully.*] Why did I send it up?

[*Pause.*]

Who knows what he's got upstairs? He's probably got a salad bowl. They must have something up there. They won't get much from down here. You notice they didn't ask for any salads? They've probably got a salad bowl up there. Cold meat, radishes, cucumbers. Watercress. Roll mops.

[*Pause.*]

Hardboiled eggs.

[*Pause.*]

The lot. They've probably got a crate of beer too. Probably eating my crisps with a pint of beer now. Didn't have anything to say about those crisps, did he? They do all right, don't worry about that. You don't think they're just going to sit there and wait for stuff to come up from down here, do you? That'll get them nowhere.

[*Pause.*]

They do all right.

[*Pause.*]

And he wants a cup of tea.

[*Pause.*]

That's past a joke, in my opinion.

[*He looks over at* BEN, *rises, and goes to him.*]

What's the matter with you? You don't look too bright. I feel like an Alka-Seltzer myself.

[BEN *sits up.*]

BEN [*In a low voice.*] Time's getting on.

GUS I know. I don't like doing a job on an empty stomach.

BEN   [*Wearily.*] Be quiet a minute. Let me give you your instructions.

GUS   What for? We always do it the same way, don't we?

BEN   Let me give you your instructions.

> [GUS *sighs and sits next to* BEN *on the bed. The instructions are stated and repeated automatically.*]

When we get the call, you go over and stand behind the door.

GUS   Stand behind the door.

BEN   If there's a knock on the door you don't answer it.

GUS   If there's a knock on the door I don't answer it.

BEN   But there won't be a knock on the door.

GUS   So I won't answer it.

BEN   When the bloke comes in—

GUS   When the bloke comes in—

BEN   Shut the door behind him.

GUS   Shut the door behind him.

BEN   Without divulging your presence.

GUS   Without divulging my presence.

BEN   He'll see me and come towards me.

GUS   He'll see you and come towards you.

BEN   He won't see you.

GUS   [*Absently.*] Eh?

BEN   He won't see you.

GUS   He won't see me.

BEN   But he'll see me.

GUS   He'll see you.

BEN   He won't know you're there.

GUS   He won't know you're there.

BEN   He won't know *you're* there.

GUS   He won't know I'm there.

BEN   I take out my gun.

GUS   You take out your gun.

BEN   He stops in his tracks.

GUS   He stops in his tracks.

BEN   If he turns round—

GUS   If he turns round—

BEN   You're there.

GUS   I'm here.

> [BEN *frowns and presses his forehead.*]

You've missed something out.

BEN   I know. What?

GUS   I haven't taken my gun out, according to you.

BEN   You take your gun out—

GUS   After I've closed the door.

BEN   After you've closed the door.

GUS   You've never missed that out before, you know that?

BEN   When he sees you behind him—

GUS   Me behind him—

BEN   And me in front of him—

GUS   And you in front of him—

BEN   He'll feel uncertain—

GUS   Uneasy.

BEN   He won't know what to do.
GUS   So what will he do?
BEN   He'll look at me and he'll look at you.
GUS   We won't say a word.
BEN   We'll look at him.
GUS   He won't say a word.
BEN   He'll look at us.
GUS   And we'll look at him.
BEN   Exactly.
          [*Pause.*]
GUS   What do we do if it's a girl?
BEN   We do the same.
GUS   Exactly the same?
BEN   Exactly.
          [*Pause.*]
GUS   We don't do anything different?
BEN   We do exactly the same.
GUS   Oh.
          [GUS *rises, and shivers.*]
    Excuse me.
          [*He exits through the door on the left.* BEN *remains sitting on the bed, still.*
              The lavatory chain is pulled once off left, but the lavatory does not flush.
              Silence.
              GUS *re-enters and stops inside the door, deep in thought. He looks at* BEN, *then walks slowly across to his own bed. He is troubled. He stands, thinking. He turns and looks at* BEN. *He moves a few paces towards him.*]
    [*Slowly in a low, tense voice.*] Why did he send us matches if he knew there was no gas?
          [*Silence.*
              BEN *stares in front of him.* GUS *crosses to the left side of* BEN, *to the foot of his bed, to get to his other ear.*]
    Ben. Why did he send us matches if he knew there was no gas?
          [BEN *looks up.*]
    Why did he do that?
BEN   Who?
GUS   Who sent us those matches?
BEN   What are you talking about?
          [GUS *stares down at him.*]
GUS   [*Thickly.*] Who is it upstairs?
BEN   [*Nervously.*] What's one thing to do with another?
GUS   Who is it, though?
BEN   What's one thing to do with another?
          [BEN *fumbles for his paper on the bed.*]
GUS   I asked you a question.
BEN   Enough!
GUS   [*With growing agitation.*] I asked you before. Who moved in? I asked you. You said the people who had it before moved out. Well, who moved in?
BEN   [*Hunched.*] Shut up.
GUS   I told you, didn't I?
BEN   [*Standing.*] Shut up!

GUS   [*Feverishly.*] I told you before who owned this place, didn't I? I told you.
>   [BEN *hits him viciously on the shoulder.*]
>   I told you who ran this place, didn't I?
>   [BEN *hits him viciously on the shoulder.*]
>   [*Violently.*] Well, what's he playing all these games for? That's what I want to know. What's he doing it for?

BEN   What games?

GUS   [*Passionately, advancing.*] What's he doing it for? We've been through our tests, haven't we? We got right through our tests, years ago, didn't we? We took them together, don't you remember, didn't we? We've proved ourselves before now, haven't we? We've always done our job. What's he doing all this for? What's the idea? What's he playing these games for?
>   [*The box in the shaft comes down behind them. The noise is this time accompanied by a shrill whistle, as it falls.* GUS *rushes to the hatch and seizes the note.*]
>   [*Reading.*] Scampi!
>   [*He crumples the note, picks up the tube, takes out the whistle, blows and speaks.*]
>   WE'VE GOT NOTHING LEFT! NOTHING! DO YOU UNDERSTAND?
>   [BEN *seizes the tube and flings* GUS *away. He follows* GUS *and slaps him hard, back-handed, across the chest.*]

BEN   Stop it! You maniac!

GUS   But you heard!

BEN   [*Savagely.*] That's enough! I'm warning you!
>   [*Silence.
>   BEN hangs the tube. He goes to his bed and lies down. He picks up his paper and reads.
>   Silence.
>   The box goes up.
>   They turn quickly, their eyes meet. BEN turns to his paper.
>   Slowly GUS goes back to his bed, and sits.
>   Silence.
>   The hatch falls back into place.
>   They turn quickly, their eyes meet. BEN turns back to his paper.
>   Silence.
>   BEN throws his paper down.*]

BEN   Kaw!
>   [*He picks up the paper and looks at it.*]
>   Listen to this!
>   [*Pause.*]
>   What about that, eh?
>   [*Pause.*]
>   Kaw!
>   [*Pause.*]
>   Have you ever heard such a thing?

GUS   [*Dully.*] Go on!

BEN   It's true.

GUS   Get away.

BEN   It's down here in black and white.

GUS   [*Very low.*] Is that a fact?

BEN   Can you imagine it.

GUS   It's unbelievable.

BEN   It's enough to make you want to puke, isn't it?

GUS [*Almost inaudible.*] Incredible.
>   [BEN *shakes his head. He puts the paper down and rises. He fixes the revolver in his holster.*
>   GUS *stands up. He goes towards the door on the left.*]

BEN Where are you going?

GUS I'm going to have a glass of water.
>   [*He exits.* BEN *brushes dust off his clothes and shoes. The whistle in the speaking tube blows. He goes to it, takes the whistle out and puts the tube to his ear. He listens. He puts it to his mouth.*]

BEN Yes.
>   [*To ear. He listens. To mouth.*]

Straight away. Right.
>   [*To ear. He listens. To mouth.*]

Sure we're ready.
>   [*To ear. He listens. To mouth.*]

Understood. Repeat. He has arrived and will be coming in straight away. The normal method to be employed. Understood.
>   [*To ear. He listens. To mouth.*]

Sure we're ready.
>   [*To ear. He listens. To mouth.*]

Right.
>   [*He hangs the tube up.*]

Gus!
>   [*He takes out a comb and combs his hair, adjusts his jacket to diminish the bulge of the revolver. The lavatory flushes off left.* BEN *goes quickly to the door, left.*]

Gus!
>   [*The door right opens sharply.* BEN *turns, his revolver leveled at the door.* GUS *stumbles in.*
>   *He is stripped of his jacket, waistcoat, tie, holster, and revolver.*
>   *He stops, body stooping, his arms at his sides.*
>   *He raises his head and looks at* BEN.
>   *A long silence.*
>   *They stare at each other.*]

CURTAIN

1960

CHINUA ACHEBE
1930–2013

The most celebrated African novelist is Chinua Achebe, whose work transformed the landscape of African fiction, both in his own continent and in the Western imagination. While steadfastly refusing to sentimentalize the people and traditions of Nigeria, his writings effectively challenged many entrenched impressions of African life and culture, replacing simplistic stereotypes with portrayals of a complex society still suffering from the legacy of colonial oppression.

Achebe was born in Ogidi, an Igbo-speaking town in eastern Nigeria, and educated—in English—at church schools and University College, Ibadan, where he subsequently taught (briefly) before joining the Nigerian Broadcasting Corporation in Lagos. He was director of external broadcasting from 1961 to 1966, and then launched a publishing company with Christopher Okigbo, a poet soon to die in the Nigerian Civil War (1967–70). After the war Achebe taught in the United States, before returning for a time to the University of Nigeria at Nsukka. In 1990 Achebe joined the faculty of Bard College and, in 2009, of Brown University.

A volume of Achebe's poems was joint winner of the Commonwealth Poetry Prize in 1972. He also wrote short stories and essays, including an attack on political corruption in his homeland, *The Trouble with Nigeria* (1983), and reflections on growing up in colonial Nigeria, *The Education of a British-Protected Child* (2009). He was best known for his novels, however, especially *Things Fall Apart* (1958), written with an insider's understanding of the African world and its history and depicting the destruction of an individual, a family, and a culture at the moment of colonial incursion. The British asserted their authority over the Igbo in Nigeria through trade, religion, politics, and military might. In *Things Fall Apart*, Achebe represents the process of colonization from the vantage point of villagers who are puzzled, intrigued, co-opted, enraged, divided against themselves, or killed. The turn-of-the-nineteenth-century imperial onslaught seems all the more bewildering and violent because the novel has immersed the reader in this village's finely calibrated cultural practices in religion and government, athletics and storytelling, agriculture and the family. The Africans in the novel speak a resonantly proverbial language that operates as an image of all the beautiful and traditional structures transformed irrevocably by colonialism. Achebe's other novels include *No Longer at Ease* (1960), *Arrow of God* (1964), *A Man of the People* (1966), and *Anthills of the Savannah* (1987). Helping to rebut Western preconceptions of African primitivism, Achebe's rich portraits of African culture advanced his ambition to help his "society regain belief in itself and put away the complexes of the years of denigration and self-abasement" produced by the distortions of colonialism. He said he wanted his novels to teach his African "readers that their past—with all its imperfections—was not one long night of savagery from which the first Europeans acting on God's behalf delivered them."

Written in the aftermath of the Nigerian Civil War, Achebe's short story printed here, ironically named "Civil Peace," represents a society coming out of the devastation of the continent's first major post-independence civil conflict. Despite his many losses, Jonathan Iwegbu benevolently welcomes the blessings of survival. Through Achebe's meticulous and terse characterization, Jonathan emerges as a man who humbly affirms life, while shrewdly observing and assessing those around him and his future prospects. Achebe builds dramatic tension when robbers threaten Jonathan and his family in a dramatic scene that blends terror with comedy. As one of his characters says of wartime in another of Achebe's stories, "Girls at War": "It was a tight, blockaded and desperate world but none the less a world—with some goodness and some badness and plenty of heroism, which, however, happened most times far, far below the eye-level" of self-important people. Achebe's attention to extraordinarily ordinary characters like Jonathan Iwegbu, though they exist far below eye level, helped him fulfill his lifelong ambition of reversing the dehumanizing preconceptions long affixed to Africans. In "Civil Peace," Achebe deftly interweaves Standard English with pidgin dialogue, economically evokes a society at a moment of historic transition, and sharply draws his characters with wit and compassion, thereby demonstrating in miniature some of the gifts that made him one of the most acclaimed fiction writers of the postcolonial world.

Civil Peace

Jonathan Iwegbu counted himself extraordinarily lucky. 'Happy survival!' meant so much more to him than just a current fashion of greeting old friends in the first hazy days of peace. It went deep to his heart. He had come out of the war[1] with five inestimable blessings—his head, his wife Maria's head and the heads of three out of their four children. As a bonus he also had his old bicycle—a miracle too but naturally not to be compared to the safety of five human heads.

The bicycle had a little history of its own. One day at the height of the war it was commandeered 'for urgent military action'. Hard as its loss would have been to him he would still have let it go without a thought had he not had some doubts about the genuineness of the officer. It wasn't his disreputable rags, nor the toes peeping out of one blue and one brown canvas shoes, nor yet the two stars of his rank done obviously in a hurry in biro,[2] that troubled Jonathan; many good and heroic soldiers looked the same or worse. It was rather a certain lack of grip and firmness in his manner. So Jonathan, suspecting he might be amenable to influence, rummaged in his raffia[3] bag and produced the two pounds with which he had been going to buy firewood which his wife, Maria, retailed to camp officials for extra stock-fish and corn meal, and got his bicycle back. That night he buried it in the little clearing in the bush where the dead of the camp, including his own youngest son, were buried. When he dug it up again a year later after the surrender all it needed was a little palm-oil[4] greasing. 'Nothing puzzles God,' he said in wonder.

He put it to immediate use as a taxi and accumulated a small pile of Biafran money[5] ferrying camp officials and their families across the four-mile stretch to the nearest tarred road. His standard charge per trip was six pounds and those who had the money were only glad to be rid of some of it in this way. At the end of a fortnight he had made a small fortune of one hundred and fifteen pounds.

Then he made the journey to Enugu[6] and found another miracle waiting for him. It was unbelievable. He rubbed his eyes and looked again and it was still standing there before him. But, needless to say, even that monumental blessing must be accounted also totally inferior to the five heads in the family. This newest miracle was his little house in Ogui Overside.[7] Indeed nothing puzzles God! Only two houses away a huge concrete edifice some wealthy contractor had put up just before the war was a mountain of rubble. And here was Jonathan's little zinc house[8] of no regrets built with mud blocks quite intact! Of course the doors and windows were missing and five sheets off the roof. But what was that? And anyhow he had returned to Enugu early enough to pick up bits of old zinc and wood and soggy sheets

1. The Nigerian Civil War, or Biafran War (1967–70), in which the predominantly Igbo (or Ibo) portion of eastern Nigeria declared itself the independent Republic of Biafra and was put down by the federal government, dominated by the Hausa-Fulani and Yoruba ethnic groups and backed by international support. Perhaps as many as one million Igbo people died as a result of the conflict.
2. In ballpoint pen.

3. Soft fiber made from the leaves of an African palm tree.
4. Oil produced from the palm tree.
5. I.e., money from the now-defunct Republic of Biafra.
6. An industrial city in southeastern Nigeria and the Biafran capital during the civil war.
7. Area outside the city of Enugu.
8. House made from corrugated sheet metal, galvanized with zinc, typically used in roofing.

of cardboard lying around the neighbourhood before thousands more came out of their forest holes looking for the same things. He got a destitute carpenter with one old hammer, a blunt plane and a few bent and rusty nails in his tool bag to turn this assortment of wood, paper and metal into door and window shutters for five Nigerian shillings or fifty Biafran pounds. He paid the pounds, and moved in with his overjoyed family carrying five heads on their shoulders.

His children picked mangoes near the military cemetery and sold them to soldiers' wives for a few pennies—real pennies this time—and his wife started making breakfast akara balls[9] for neighbours in a hurry to start life again. With his family earnings he took his bicycle to the villages around and bought fresh palm-wine[1] which he mixed generously in his rooms with the water which had recently started running again in the public tap down the road, and opened up a bar for soldiers and other lucky people with good money.

At first he went daily, then every other day and finally once a week, to the offices of the Coal Corporation where he used to be a miner, to find out what was what. The only thing he did find out in the end was that that little house of his was even a greater blessing than he had thought. Some of his fellow ex-miners who had nowhere to return at the end of the day's waiting just slept outside the doors of the offices and cooked what meal they could scrounge together in Bournvita tins.[2] As the weeks lengthened and still nobody could say what was what Jonathan discontinued his weekly visits altogether and faced his palm-wine bar.

But nothing puzzles God. Came the day of the windfall when after five days of endless scuffles in queues and counter-queues in the sun outside the Treasury he had twenty pounds counted into his palms as ex-gratia[3] award for the rebel money he had turned in. It was like Christmas for him and for many others like him when the payments began. They called it (since few could manage its proper official name) *egg-rasher.*

As soon as the pound notes were placed in his palm Jonathan simply closed it tight over them and buried fist and money inside his trouser pocket. He had to be extra careful because he had seen a man a couple of days earlier collapse into near-madness in an instant before that oceanic crowd because no sooner had he got his twenty pounds than some heartless ruffian picked it off him. Though it was not right that a man in such an extremity of agony should be blamed yet many in the queues that day were able to remark quietly on the victim's carelessness, especially after he pulled out the innards of his pocket and revealed a hole in it big enough to pass a thief's head. But of course he had insisted that the money had been in the other pocket, pulling it out too to show its comparative wholeness. So one had to be careful.

Jonathan soon transferred the money to his left hand and pocket so as to leave his right free for shaking hands should the need arise, though by fixing his gaze at such an elevation as to miss all approaching human faces he made sure that the need did not arise, until he got home.

---

9. Bean cakes or fritters made from black-eyed peas.
1. Wine made by fermenting the sap of palm trees.

2. Cans that had contained powdered mix for a brand of chocolate malted drink.
3. Given as a favor.

He was normally a heavy sleeper but that night he heard all the neighbourhood noises die down one after another. Even the night watchman who knocked the hour on some metal somewhere in the distance had fallen silent after knocking one o'clock. That must have been the last thought in Jonathan's mind before he was finally carried away himself. He couldn't have been gone for long, though, when he was violently awakened again.

'Who is knocking?' whispered his wife lying beside him on the floor.

'I don't know,' he whispered back breathlessly.

The second time the knocking came it was so loud and imperious that the rickety old door could have fallen down.

'Who is knocking?' he asked then, his voice parched and trembling.

'Na tief-man[4] and him people,' came the cool reply. 'Make you hopen de door.' This was followed by the heaviest knocking of all.

Maria was the first to raise the alarm, then he followed and all their children.

'Police-o! Thieves-o! Neighbours-o! Police-o! We are lost! We are dead! Neighbours, are you asleep? Wake up! Police-o!'

This went on for a long time and then stopped suddenly. Perhaps they had scared the thief away. There was total silence. But only for a short while.

'You done finish?' asked the voice outside. 'Make we help you small. Oya,[5] everybody!'

'Police-o! Tief-man-o! Neighbours-o! we done loss-o! Police-o! . . .'

There were at least five other voices besides the leader's.

Jonathan and his family were now completely paralysed by terror. Maria and the children sobbed inaudibly like lost souls. Jonathan groaned continuously.

The silence that followed the thieves' alarm vibrated horribly. Jonathan all but begged their leader to speak again and be done with it.

'My frien,' said he at long last, 'we don try our best for call dem but I tink say dem all done sleep-o . . . So wetin[6] we go do now? Sometaim you wan call soja?[7] Or you wan make we call dem for you? Soja better pass[8] police. No be so?'

'Na so!' replied his men. Jonathan thought he heard even more voices now than before and groaned heavily. His legs were sagging under him and his throat felt like sand-paper.

'My frien, why you no de talk again. I de ask you say you wan make we call soja?'

'No'.

'Awrighto. Now make we talk business. We no be bad tief. We no like for make trouble. Trouble done finish. War done finish and all the katakata wey de for inside.[9] No Civil War again. This time na Civil Peace. No be so?'

'Na so!' answered the horrible chorus.

---

4. Thief. "Na": it is (Nigerian pidgin, as in the ensuing glosses).
5. Let's get to it.
6. What.
7. Soldier.
8. Than.
9. Trouble it brought.

'What do you want from me? I am a poor man. Everything I had went with this war. Why do you come to me? You know people who have money. We . . .'

'Awright! We know say you no get plenty money. But we sef no get even anini.[1] So derefore make you open dis window and give us one hundred pound and we go commot.[2] Orderwise we de come for inside now to show you guitar-boy like dis . . .'[3]

A volley of automatic fire rang through the sky. Maria and the children began to weep aloud again.

'Ah, missisi de cry again. No need for dat. We done talk say we na good tief. We just take our small money and go nwayorly.[4] No molest. Abi[5] we de molest?'

'At all!' sang the chorus.

'My friends,' began Jonathan hoarsely. 'I hear what you say and I thank you. If I had one hundred pounds . . .'

'Lookia my frien, no be play we come play for your house. If we make mistake and step for inside you no go like am-o.[6] So derefore . . .'

'To God who made me; if you come inside and find one hundred pounds, take it and shoot me and shoot my wife and children. I swear to God. The only money I have in this life is this twenty-pounds *egg-rasher* they gave me today . . .'

'OK. Time de go. Make you open dis window and bring the twenty pound. We go manage am[7] like dat.'

There were now loud murmurs of dissent among the chorus: 'Na lie de man de lie; e get plenty money . . . Make we go inside and search properly well . . . Wetin[8] be twenty pound? . . .'

'Shurrup!' rang the leader's voice like a lone shot in the sky and silenced the murmuring at once. 'Are you dere? Bring the money quick!'

'I am coming,' said Jonathan fumbling in the darkness with the key of the small wooden box he kept by his side on the mat.

At the first sign of light as neighbours and others assembled to commiserate with him he was already strapping his five-gallon demijohn[9] to his bicycle carrier and his wife, sweating in the open fire, was turning over akara balls in a wide clay bowl of boiling oil. In the corner his eldest son was rinsing out dregs of yesterday's palm wine from old beer bottles.

'I count it as nothing,' he told his sympathizers, his eyes on the rope he was tying. 'What is *egg-rasher*? Did I depend on it last week? Or is it greater than other things that went with the war? I say, let *egg-rasher* perish in the flames! Let it go where everything else has gone. Nothing puzzles God.'

1971

---

1. A farthing, a disused coin worth less than a penny.
2. Get out of here.
3. I.e., hold (and fire) guns like guitar players.
4. Gently, quietly, without protest.
5. Is it.
6. It ("am" used in place of pronoun, "-o" for emphasis, a dire warning).
7. Him.
8. What.
9. A large bottle with a round body and narrow neck, usually encased in woven wicker.

ALICE MUNRO
b. 1931

A lice Munro is one of the leading short-story writers of her generation. Her fiction combines spareness and realism—an uncompromising look at a panorama of faltering lives—with magisterial vision and expansiveness. Munro's signature approach to the short story, in which she uses a deceptively simple style to produce complex, layered, and emotionally potent effects, has influenced many of her English-language contemporaries, both within and outside Canada. In addition to one novel, *Lives of Girls and Women* (1972), she has published numerous collections of short stories, including *Dance of the Happy Shades* (1968), *Something I've Been Meaning to Tell You* (1974), *The Moons of Jupiter* (1982), *Friend of My Youth* (1990), *The Love of a Good Woman* (1998), *Hateship, Friendship, Courtship, Loveship, Marriage* (2001), *Runaway* (2004), *Carried Away* (2006), *The View from Castle Rock* (2006), *Too Much Happiness* (2009), and *Dear Life* (2012). She won the Man Booker International Prize in 2009 and the Nobel Prize in Literature in 2013.

Many of Munro's stories are written in the first person, often from the perspective of women whose voices and experiences suggest the author's history. She was born Alice Anne Laidlaw to a poor family in Wingham, Ontario, and her parents' struggles within a variety of rural occupations continued throughout her childhood. She began writing in her teens and in 1949 enrolled in the University of Western Ontario; she left the university two years later to marry and raise three daughters. She typically sets her stories in small towns where poverty stamps itself on all facets of life, and where women confront—often in a spirit that combines resignation with stubborn resistance—the triple binds of economic, gender, and cultural confinement. Through a precise and particular emphasis on setting and character, Munro evokes rural Canadian life in the decades following midcentury, when modernity and the promise of the future are often crowded out by a hardening sense of the past.

In an early writing, Munro describes an approach to the outside world that effectively captures her sense of the mystery within the ordinary—the hallmark of her realist style: "It seems as if there are feelings that have to be translated into a next-door language, which might blow them up and burst them altogether; or else they have to be let alone. The truth about them is always suspected, never verified, the light catches but doesn't define them. . . . Yet there is the feeling—I have the feeling—that at some level these things open; fragments, moments, suggestions, open, full of power." This aura of openness and suggestion, conveyed through "next-door language," gives Munro's stories their haunting aspect, their quality of movement, rippling and widening from the small-scale to the magnificent. The story included here, "Walker Brothers Cowboy," exemplifies her ability to imbue "fragments, moments, suggestions" with fullness and power, as we view through a young girl's eyes both the pathos and the degradation of men and women whose lives have fallen into a potentially deadening cycle of promise and decay.

Walker Brothers Cowboy[1]

After supper my father says, "Want to go down and see if the Lake's still there?" We leave my mother sewing under the dining-room light, making clothes for me against[2] the opening of school. She has ripped up for this purpose an old suit and an old plaid wool dress of hers, and she has to cut and match very cleverly and also make me stand and turn for endless fittings, sweaty, itching from the hot wool, ungrateful. We leave my brother in bed in the little screened porch at the end of the front veranda, and sometimes he kneels on his bed and presses his face against the screen and calls mournfully, "Bring me an ice-cream cone!" but I call back, "You will be asleep," and do not even turn my head.

Then my father and I walk gradually down a long, shabby sort of street, with Silverwoods Ice Cream signs standing on the sidewalk, outside tiny, lighted stores. This is in Tuppertown, an old town on Lake Huron,[3] an old grain port. The street is shaded, in some places, by maple trees whose roots have cracked and heaved the sidewalk and spread out like crocodiles into the bare yards. People are sitting out, men in shirtsleeves and undershirts and women in aprons—not people we know but if anybody looks ready to nod and say, "Warm night," my father will nod too and say something the same. Children are still playing. I don't know them either because my mother keeps my brother and me in our own yard, saying he is too young to leave it and I have to mind him. I am not so sad to watch their evening games because the games themselves are ragged, dissolving. Children, of their own will, draw apart, separate into islands of two or one under the heavy trees, occupying themselves in such solitary ways as I do all day, planting pebbles in the dirt or writing in it with a stick.

Presently we leave these yards and houses behind; we pass a factory with boarded-up windows, a lumberyard whose high wooden gates are locked for the night. Then the town falls away in a defeated jumble of sheds and small junkyards, the sidewalk gives up and we are walking on a sandy path with burdocks, plantains, humble nameless weeds all around. We enter a vacant lot, a kind of park really, for it is kept clear of junk and there is one bench with a slat missing on the back, a place to sit and look at the water. Which is generally gray in the evening, under a lightly overcast sky, no sunsets, the horizon dim. A very quiet, washing noise on the stones of the beach. Further along, towards the main part of town, there is a stretch of sand, a water slide, floats bobbing around the safe swimming area, a lifeguard's rickety throne. Also a long dark-green building, like a roofed veranda, called the Pavilion, full of farmers and their wives, in stiff good clothes, on Sundays. That is the part of the town we used to know when we lived at Dungannon and came here three or four times a summer, to the Lake. That, and the docks where we would go and look at the grain boats, ancient, rusty, wallowing, making us wonder how they got past the breakwater let alone to Fort William.

Tramps hang around the docks and occasionally on these evenings wander up the dwindling beach and climb the shifting, precarious path boys

---

1. Refers to a traveling salesman for a Canadian company, which is probably modeled on the American direct marketer Watkins Products.
2. In time for.

3. One of the Great Lakes, bordering on Ontario and eastern Michigan. Place-names are both real and invented.

have made, hanging on to dry bushes, and say something to my father which, being frightened of tramps, I am too alarmed to catch. My father says he is a bit hard up himself. "I'll roll you a cigarette if it's any use to you," he says, and he shakes tobacco out carefully on one of the thin butterfly papers, flicks it with his tongue, seals it and hands it to the tramp, who takes it and walks away. My father also rolls and lights and smokes one cigarette of his own.

He tells me how the Great Lakes came to be. All where Lake Huron is now, he says, used to be flat land, a wide flat plain. Then came the ice, creeping down from the North, pushing deep into the low places. Like *that*—and he shows me his hand with his spread fingers pressing the rock-hard ground where we are sitting. His fingers make hardly any impression at all and he says, "Well, the old ice cap had a lot more power behind it than this hand has." And then the ice went back, shrank back towards the North Pole where it came from, and left its fingers of ice in the deep places it had gouged, and ice turned to lakes and there they were today. They were *new*, as time went. I try to see that plain before me, dinosaurs walking on it, but I am not able even to imagine the shore of the Lake when the Indians were there, before Tuppertown. The tiny share we have of time appalls me, though my father seems to regard it with tranquillity. Even my father, who sometimes seems to me to have been at home in the world as long as it has lasted, has really lived on this earth only a little longer than I have, in terms of all the time there has been to live in. He has not known a time, any more than I, when automobiles and electric lights did not at least exist. He was not alive when this century started. I will be barely alive—old, old—when it ends. I do not like to think of it. I wish the Lake to be always just a lake, with the safe-swimming floats marking it, and the breakwater and the lights of Tuppertown.

My father has a job, selling for Walker Brothers. This is a firm that sells almost entirely in the country, the back country. Sunshine, Boylesbridge, Turnaround—that is all his territory. Not Dungannon where we used to live, Dungannon is too near town and my mother is grateful for that. He sells cough medicine, iron tonic, corn plasters, laxatives, pills for female disorders, mouthwash, shampoo, liniment, salves, lemon and orange and raspberry concentrate for making refreshing drinks, vanilla, food coloring, black and green tea, ginger, cloves, and other spices, rat poison. He has a song about it, with these two lines:

> And have all liniments and oils,
> For everything from corns to boils. . . .

Not a very funny song, in my mother's opinion. A peddler's song, and that is what he is, a peddler knocking at backwoods kitchens. Up until last winter we had our own business, a fox farm. My father raised silver foxes and sold their pelts to the people who make them into capes and coats and muffs. Prices fell, my father hung on hoping they would get better next year, and they fell again, and he hung on one more year and one more and finally it was not possible to hang on anymore, we owed everything to the feed company. I have heard my mother explain this, several times, to Mrs. Oliphant, who is the only neighbor she talks to. (Mrs. Oliphant also has come down in the world, being a schoolteacher who married the janitor.) We poured all we had into it, my mother says, and we came out with nothing. Many people could say the same thing, these days, but my mother has no time for the national calamity, only ours. Fate has flung us onto a street of poor people (it does not matter that we were poor before; that was a different sort of poverty), and the only way to take this, as she sees it, is with dignity, with bitterness, with no reconciliation. No bathroom with a claw-footed tub and a flush toilet is going to comfort her, nor water on tap and sidewalks past the house and milk in bottles, not even the two movie theatres and the Venus Restaurant and Woolworths so marvellous it has live birds singing in its fan-cooled corners and fish as tiny as fingernails, as bright as moons, swimming in its green tanks. My mother does not care.

In the afternoons she often walks to Simon's Grocery and takes me with her to help carry things. She wears a good dress, navy blue with little flowers, sheer, worn over a navy-blue slip. Also a summer hat of white straw, pushed down on the side of the head, and white shoes I have just whitened on a newspaper on the back steps. I have my hair freshly done in long damp curls which the dry air will fortunately soon loosen, a stiff large hair ribbon on top of my head. This is entirely different from going out after supper with my father. We have not walked past two houses before I feel we have become objects of universal ridicule. Even the dirty words chalked on the sidewalk are laughing at us. My mother does not seem to notice. She walks serenely like a lady shopping, like a *lady* shopping, past the housewives in loose belt-less dresses torn under the arms. With me her creation, wretched curls and flaunting hair bow, scrubbed knees and white socks—all I do not want to be. I loathe even my name when she says it in public, in a voice so high, proud, and ringing, deliberately different from the voice of any other mother on the street.

My mother will sometimes carry home, for a treat, a brick of ice cream— pale Neapolitan; and because we have no refrigerator in our house we wake my brother and eat it at once in the dining room, always darkened by the wall of the house next door. I spoon it up tenderly, leaving the chocolate till last, hoping to have some still to eat when my brother's dish is empty. My mother tries then to imitate the conversations we used to have at Dungan-non, going back to our earliest, most leisurely days before my brother was born, when she would give me a little tea and a lot of milk in a cup like hers and we would sit out on the step facing the pump, the lilac tree, the fox pens beyond. She not able to keep from mentioning those days. "Do you remember when we put you in your sled and Major pulled you?" (Major our dog, that we had to leave with neighbors when we moved.) "Do you remember your sandbox outside the kitchen window?" I pretend to remember far less than I do, wary of being trapped into sympathy or any unwanted emotion.

My mother has headaches. She often has to lie down. She lies on my brother's narrow bed in the little screened porch, shaded by heavy branches. "I look up at that tree and I think I am at home," she says.

"What you need," my father tells her, "is some fresh air and a drive in the country." He means for her to go with him, on his Walker Brothers route.

That is not my mother's idea of a drive in the country.

"Can I come?"

"Your mother might want you for trying on clothes."

"I'm beyond sewing this afternoon," my mother says.

"I'll take her then. Take both of them, give you a rest."

What is there about us that people need to be given a rest from? Never mind. I am glad enough to find my brother and make him go to the toilet and get us both into the car, our knees unscrubbed, my hair unringleted. My father brings from the house his two heavy brown suitcases, full of bottles, and sets them on the back seat. He wears a white shirt, brilliant in the sunlight, a tie, light trousers belonging to his summer suit (his other suit is black, for funerals, and belonged to my uncle before he died), and a creamy straw hat. His salesman's outfit, with pencils clipped in the shirt pocket. He goes back once again, probably to say goodbye to my mother, to ask her if she is sure she doesn't want to come, and hear her say, "No. No thanks, I'm better just to lie here with my eyes closed." Then we are backing out of the driveway with the rising hope of adventure, just the little hope that takes you over the bump into the street, the hot air starting to move, turning into a breeze, the houses growing less and less familiar as we follow the shortcut my father knows, the quick way out of town. Yet what is there waiting for us all afternoon but hot hours in stricken farmyards, perhaps a stop at a country store and three ice-cream cones or bottles of pop, and my father singing? The one he made up about himself has a title—"The Walker Brothers Cowboy"—and it starts out like this:

> Old Ned Fields, he now is dead,
> So I am ridin' the route instead. . . .

Who is Ned Fields? The man he has replaced, surely, and if so he really is dead; yet my father's voice is mournful-jolly, making his death some kind of nonsense, a comic calamity. "Wisht I was back on the Rio Grande,[4] plungin' through the dusky sand." My father sings most of the time while driving the car. Even now, heading out of town, crossing the bridge and taking the sharp turn onto the highway, he is humming something, mumbling a bit of a song to himself, just tuning up, really, getting ready to improvise, for out along the highway we pass the Baptist Camp, the Vacation Bible Camp, and he lets loose:

> Where are the Baptists, where are the Baptists,
>   where are all the Baptists today?
> They're down in the water, in Lake Huron water,
>   with their sins all a-gittin' washed away.

My brother takes this for straight truth and gets up on his knees trying to see down to the Lake. "I don't see any Baptists," he says accusingly. "Neither do I, son," says my father. "I told you, they're down in the Lake."

No roads paved when we left the highway. We have to roll up the windows because of dust. The land is flat, scorched, empty. Bush lots at the back of the farms hold shade, black pine-shade like pools nobody can ever get to. We bump up a long lane and at the end of it what could look more unwelcoming, more deserted than the tall unpainted farmhouse with grass growing uncut right up to the front door, green blinds down, and a door upstairs opening on nothing but air? Many houses have this door, and I have never yet been able to find out why. I ask my father and he says they are for walking in your sleep. *What?* Well, if you happen to be walking in your sleep and you want

---

4. River that begins in Colorado and flows south, becoming the border between Mexico and the United States.

to step outside. I am offended, seeing too late that he is joking, as usual, but my brother says sturdily, "If they did that they would break their necks."

The 1930s. How much this kind of farmhouse, this kind of afternoon seem to me to belong to that one decade in time, just as my father's hat does, his bright flared tie, our car with its wide running board (an Essex, and long past its prime). Cars somewhat like it, many older, none dustier, sit in the farmyards. Some are past running and have their doors pulled off, their seats removed for use on porches. No living things to be seen, chickens or cattle. Except dogs. There are dogs lying in any kind of shade they can find, dreaming, their lean sides rising and sinking rapidly. They get up when my father opens the car door, he has to speak to them. "Nice boy, there's a boy, nice old boy." They quiet down, go back to their shade. He should know how to quiet animals, he has held desperate foxes with tongs around their necks. One gentling voice for the dogs and another, rousing, cheerful, for calling at doors. "Hello there, missus, it's the Walker Brothers man and what are you out of today?" A door opens, he disappears. Forbidden to follow, forbidden even to leave the car, we can just wait and wonder what he says. Sometimes trying to make my mother laugh, he pretends to be himself in a farm kitchen, spreading out his sample case. "Now then, missus, are you troubled with parasitic life? Your children's scalps, I mean. All those crawly little things we're too polite to mention that show up on the heads of the best of families? Soap alone is useless, kerosene is not too nice a perfume, but I have here—" Or else, "Believe me, sitting and driving all day the way I do I *know* the value of these fine pills. Natural relief. A problem common to old folks too, once their days of activity are over—How about you, Grandma?" He would wave the imaginary box of pills under my mother's nose and she would laugh finally, unwillingly. "He doesn't say that really, does he?" I said, and she said no of course not, he was too much of a gentleman.

One yard after another, then, the old cars, the pumps, dogs, views of gray barns and falling-down sheds and unturning windmills. The men, if they are working in the fields, are not in any fields that we can see. The children are far away, following dry creek beds or looking for blackberries, or else they are hidden in the house, spying at us through cracks in the blinds. The car seat has grown slick with our sweat. I dare my brother to sound the horn, wanting to do it myself but not wanting to get the blame. He knows better. We play I Spy, but it is hard to find many colors. Gray for the barns and sheds and toilets and houses, brown for the yard and fields, black or brown for the dogs. The rusting cars show rainbow patches, in which I strain to pick out purple or green; likewise I peer at doors for shreds of old peeling paint, maroon or yellow. We can't play with letters, which would be better, because my brother is too young to spell. The game disintegrates anyway. He claims my colors are not fair, and wants extra turns.

In one house no door opens, though the car is in the yard. My father knocks and whistles, calls, "Hullo there! Walker Brothers man!" but there is not a stir of reply anywhere. This house has no porch, just a bare, slanting slab of cement on which my father stands. He turns around, searching the barnyard, the barn whose mow must be empty because you can see the sky through it, and finally he bends to pick up his suitcases. Just then a window is opened upstairs, a white pot appears on the sill, is tilted over and its contents splash down the outside wall. The window is not directly above my father's head, so only a stray splash would catch him. He picks up his suitcases with no particular hurry and walks, no longer whistling, to the car. "Do you know what that was?" I say to my brother. *"Pee."* He laughs and laughs.

My father rolls and lights a cigarette before he starts the car. The window has been slammed down, the blind drawn, we never did see a hand or face. "Pee, pee," sings my brother ecstatically. "Somebody dumped down pee!" "Just don't tell your mother that," my father says. "She isn't liable to see the joke." "Is it in your song?" my brother wants to know. My father says no but he will see what he can do to work it in.

I notice in a little while that we are not turning in any more lanes, though it does not seem to me that we are headed home. "Is this the way to Sunshine?" I ask my father, and he answers, "No, ma'am, it's not." "Are we still in your territory?" He shakes his head. "We're going *fast*," my brother says approvingly, and in fact we are bouncing along through dry puddle-holes so that all the bottles in the suitcases clink together and gurgle promisingly.

Another lane, a house, also unpainted, dried to silver in the sun.

"I thought we were out of your territory."

"We are."

"Then what are we going in here for?"

"You'll see."

In front of the house a short, sturdy woman is picking up washing, which had been spread on the grass to bleach and dry. When the car stops she stares at it hard for a moment, bends to pick up a couple more towels to add to the bundle under her arm, comes across to us and says in a flat voice, neither welcoming nor unfriendly, "Have you lost your way?"

My father takes his time getting out of the car. "I don't think so," he says. "I'm the Walker Brothers man."

"George Golley is our Walker Brothers man," the woman says, "and he was out here no more than a week ago. Oh, my Lord God," she says harshly, "it's you."

"It was, the last time I looked in the mirror," my father says.

The woman gathers all the towels in front of her and holds on to them tightly, pushing them against her stomach as if it hurt. "Of all the people I never thought to see. And telling me you were the Walker Brothers man."

"I'm sorry if you were looking forward to George Golley," my father says humbly.

"And look at me, I was prepared to clean the henhouse. You'll think that's just an excuse but it's true. I don't go round looking like this every day." She is wearing a farmer's straw hat, through which pricks of sunlight penetrate and float on her face, a loose, dirty print smock, and canvas shoes. "Who are those in the car, Ben? They're not yours?"

"Well, I hope and believe they are," my father says, and tells our names and ages. "Come on, you can get out. This is Nora, Miss Cronin. Nora, you better tell me, is it still Miss, or have you got a husband hiding in the woodshed?"

"If I had a husband that's not where I'd keep him, Ben," she says, and they both laugh, her laugh abrupt and somewhat angry. "You'll think I got no manners, as well as being dressed like a tramp," she says. "Come on in out of the sun. It's cool in the house."

We go across the yard ("Excuse me taking you in this way but I don't think the front door has been opened since Papa's funeral, I'm afraid the hinges might drop off"), up the porch steps, into the kitchen, which really is cool, high-ceilinged, the blinds of course down, a simple, clean, thread-bare room with waxed worn linoleum, potted geraniums, drinking-pail and dipper, a round table with scrubbed oilcloth. In spite of the cleanness, the wiped and swept surfaces, there is a faint sour smell—maybe of the dishrag or the tin dipper or the oilcloth, or the old lady, because there is one, sitting in an easy chair under the clock shelf. She turns her head slightly in our direction and says, "Nora? Is that company?"

"Blind," says Nora in a quick explaining voice to my father. Then, "You won't guess who it is, Momma. Hear his voice."

My father goes to the front of her chair and bends and says hopefully, "Afternoon, Mrs. Cronin."

"Ben Jordan," says the old lady with no surprise. "You haven't been to see us in the longest time. Have you been out of the country?"

My father and Nora look at each other.

"He's married, Momma," says Nora cheerfully and aggressively. "Married and got two children and here they are." She pulls us forward, makes each of us touch the old lady's dry, cool hand while she says our names in turn. Blind! This is the first blind person I have ever seen close up. Her eyes are closed, the eyelids sunk away down, showing no shape of the eyeball, just hollows. From one hollow comes a drop of silver liquid, a medicine, or a miraculous tear.

"Let me get into a decent dress," Nora says. "Talk to Momma. It's a treat for her. We hardly ever see company, do we, Momma?"

"Not many makes it out this road," says the old lady placidly. "And the ones that used to be around here, our old neighbors, some of them have pulled out."

"True everywhere," my father says.

"Where's your wife then?"

"Home. She's not too fond of the hot weather, makes her feel poorly."

"Well." This is a habit of country people, old people, to say "well," meaning, "Is that so?" with a little extra politeness and concern.

Nora's dress, when she appears again—stepping heavily on Cuban heels down the stairs in the hall—is flowered more lavishly than anything my mother owns, green and yellow on brown, some sort of floating sheer crêpe, leaving her arms bare. Her arms are heavy, and every bit of her skin you can see is covered with little dark freckles like measles. Her hair is short, black, coarse and curly, her teeth very white and strong. "It's the first time I knew there was such a thing as green poppies," my father says, looking at her dress.

"You would be surprised all the things you never knew," says Nora, sending a smell of cologne far and wide when she moves and displaying a change of voice to go with the dress, something more sociable and youthful. "They're not poppies anyway, they're just flowers. You go and pump me some good cold water and I'll make these children a drink." She gets down from the cupboard a bottle of Walker Brothers Orange syrup.

"You telling me you were the Walker Brothers man!"

"It's the truth, Nora. You go and look at my sample cases in the car if you don't believe me. I got the territory directly south of here."

"Walker Brothers? Is that a fact? You selling for Walker Brothers?"

"Yes, ma'am."

"We always heard you were raising foxes over Dungannon way."

"That's what I was doing, but I kind of run out of luck in that business."

"So where're you living? How long've you been out selling?"

"We moved into Tuppertown. I been at it, oh, two, three months. It keeps the wolf from the door. Keeps him as far away as the back fence."

Nora laughs. "Well, I guess you count yourself lucky to have the work. Isabel's husband in Brantford, he was out of work the longest time. I thought if he didn't find something soon I was going to have them all land in here to feed, and I tell you I was hardly looking forward to it. It's all I can manage with me and Momma."

"Isabel married," my father says. "Muriel married too?"

"No, she's teaching school out West. She hasn't been home for five years. I guess she finds something better to do with her holidays. I would if I was her." She gets some snapshots out of the table drawer and starts showing him. "That's Isabel's oldest boy, starting school. That's the baby sitting in her carriage. Isabel and her husband. Muriel. That's her roommate with her. That's a fellow she used to go around with, and his car. He was working in a bank out there. That's her school, it has eight rooms. She teaches Grade Five." My father shakes his head. "I can't think of her any way but when she was going to school, so shy I used to pick her up on the road—I'd be on my way to see you—and she would not say one word, not even to agree it was a nice day."

"She's got over that."

"Who are you talking about?" says the old lady.

"Muriel. I said she's got over being shy."

"She was here last summer."

"No, Momma, that was Isabel. Isabel and her family were here last summer. Muriel's out West."

"I meant Isabel."

Shortly after this the old lady falls asleep, her head on the side, her mouth open. "Excuse her manners," Nora says. "It's old age." She fixes an afghan over her mother and says we can all go into the front room where our talking won't disturb her.

"You two," my father says. "Do you want to go outside and amuse yourselves?"

Amuse ourselves how? Anyway, I want to stay. The front room is more interesting than the kitchen, though barer. There is a gramophone and a pump organ and a picture on the wall of Mary, Jesus' mother—I know that much—in shades of bright blue and pink with a spiked band of light around her head. I know that such pictures are found only in the homes of Roman Catholics and so Nora must be one. We have never known any Roman Catholics at all well, never well enough to visit in their houses. I think of what my grandmother and my Aunt Tena, over in Dungannon, used to always say to indicate that somebody was a Catholic. *So-and-so digs with the wrong foot,* they would say. *She digs with the wrong foot.* That was what they would say about Nora.[5]

---

5. Relations between Protestants and Catholics within the Irish population in southern Ontario were often strained.

Nora takes a bottle, half full, out of the top of the organ and pours some of what is in it into the two glasses that she and my father have emptied of the orange drink.

"Keep it in case of sickness?" my father says.

"Not on your life," says Nora. "I'm never sick. I just keep it because I keep it. One bottle does me a fair time, though, because I don't care for drinking alone. Here's luck!" She and my father drink and I know what it is. Whisky. One of the things my mother has told me in our talks together is that my father never drinks whisky. But I see he does. He drinks whisky and he talks of people whose names I have never heard before. But after a while he turns to a familiar incident. He tells about the chamberpot that was emptied out the window. "Picture me there," he says, "hollering my heartiest. *Oh, lady, it's your Walker Brothers man, anybody home?*" He does himself hollering, grinning absurdly, waiting, looking up in pleased expectation, and then—oh, ducking, covering his head with his arms, looking as if he begged for mercy (when he never did anything like that, I was watching), and Nora laughs, almost as hard as my brother did at the time.

"That isn't true! That's not a word true!"

"Oh, indeed it is, ma'am. We have our heroes in the ranks of Walker Brothers. I'm glad you think it's funny," he says sombrely.

I ask him shyly, "Sing the song."

"What song? Have you turned into a singer on top of everything else?"

Embarrassed, my father says, "Oh, just this song I made up while I was driving around, it gives me something to do, making up rhymes."

But after some urging he does sing it, looking at Nora with a droll, apologetic expression, and she laughs so much that in places he has to stop and wait for her to get over laughing so he can go on, because she makes him laugh too. Then he does various parts of his salesman's spiel. Nora when she laughs squeezes her large bosom under her folded arms. "You're crazy," she says. "That's all you are." She sees my brother peering into the gramophone and she jumps up and goes over to him. "Here's us sitting enjoying ourselves and not giving you a thought, isn't it terrible?" she says. "You want me to put a record on, don't you? You want to hear a nice record? Can you dance? I bet your sister can, can't she?"

I say no. "A big girl like you and so good-looking and can't dance!" says Nora. "It's high time you learned. I bet you'd make a lovely dancer. Here, I'm going to put on a piece I used to dance to and even your daddy did, in his dancing days. You didn't know your daddy was a dancer, did you? Well, he is a talented man, your daddy!"

She puts down the lid and takes hold of me unexpectedly around the waist, picks up my other hand, and starts making me go backwards. "This is the way, now, this is how they dance. Follow me. This foot, see. One and one-two. One and one-two. That's fine, that's lovely, don't look at your feet! Follow me, that's right, see how easy? You're going to be a lovely dancer! One and one-two. One and one-two. Ben, see your daughter dancing!" *Whispering while you cuddle near me, Whispering so no one can hear me . . .* [6]

Round and round the linoleum, me proud, intent, Nora laughing and moving with great buoyancy, wrapping me in her strange gaiety, her smell

6. From the popular song "Whispering," whose original 1920 release was one of the first records to sell a million copies.

of whisky, cologne, and sweat. Under the arms her dress is damp, and little drops form along her upper lip, hang in the soft black hairs at the corners of her mouth. She whirls me around in front of my father—causing me to stumble, for I am by no means so swift a pupil as she pretends—and lets me go, breathless.

"Dance with me, Ben."

"I'm the world's worst dancer, Nora, and you know it."

"I certainly never thought so."

"You would now."

She stands in front of him, arms hanging loose and hopeful, her breasts, which a moment ago embarrassed me with their warmth and bulk, rising and falling under her loose flowered dress, her face shining with the exercise, and delight.

"Ben."

My father drops his head and says quietly, "Not me, Nora."

So she can only go and take the record off. "I can drink alone but I can't dance alone," she says. "Unless I am a whole lot crazier than I think I am."

"Nora," says my father, smiling. "You're not crazy."

"Stay for supper."

"Oh, no. We couldn't put you to the trouble."

"It's no trouble. I'd be glad of it."

"And their mother would worry. She'd think I'd turned us over in a ditch."

"Oh, well. Yes."

"We've taken a lot of your time now."

"Time," says Nora bitterly. "Will you come by ever again?"

"I will if I can," says my father.

"Bring the children. Bring your wife."

"Yes, I will," says my father. "I will if I can."

When she follows us to the car he says, "You come to see us too, Nora. We're right on Grove Street, left-hand side going in, that's north, and two doors this side—east—of Baker Street."

Nora does not repeat these directions. She stands close to the car in her soft, brilliant dress. She touches the fender, making an unintelligible mark in the dust there.

On the way home my father does not buy any ice cream or pop, but he does go into a country store and get a package of licorice, which he shares with us. She digs with the wrong foot, I think, and the words seem sad to me as never before, dark, perverse. My father does not say anything to me about not mentioning things at home, but I know, just from the thoughtfulness, the pause when he passes the licorice, that there are things not to be mentioned. The whisky, maybe the dancing. No worry about my brother, he does not notice enough. At most he might remember the blind lady, the picture of Mary.

"Sing," my brother commands my father, but my father says gravely, "I don't know, I seem to be fresh out of songs. You watch the road and let me know if you see any rabbits."

So my father drives and my brother watches the road for rabbits and I feel my father's life flowing back from our car in the last of the afternoon, darkening and turning strange, like a landscape that has an enchantment on it, making it kindly, ordinary and familiar while you are looking at it, but changing it, once your back is turned, into something you will never know, with all kinds of weathers, and distances you cannot imagine.

When we get closer to Tuppertown the sky becomes gently overcast, as always, nearly always, on summer evenings by the Lake.

1968

GEOFFREY HILL
1932–2016

Geoffrey Hill, born in the Worcestershire village of Bromsgrove, educated at its high school and at Keble College, Oxford, was a professor of English at Leeds University, a lecturer at Cambridge, and a professor at Boston University. In 2010 he was elected Professor of Poetry at Oxford. As a boy he was drawn to the Metaphysical poets' "fusion of intellectual strength with simple, sensuous, and passionate immediacy," and his own poems offer something of the same fusion. What he said of "Annunciations: 2" might have been said of many of his poems: "But I want the poem to have this dubious end; because I feel dubious; and the whole business is dubious." He was a religious poet but a poet of religious doubt—a skeptic confronting the extremes of human experience, "man's inhumanity to man," on the cross and in the concentration camps—or delight in the abundance of the natural world: pain and pleasure alike rendered with a Keatsian richness and specificity, a modernist allusiveness and syntactic contortion. Distinctively resonant as is the voice of Hill's poems, they are consistently impersonal. Even when the poet's earlier self is conflated with that of historical figures, subjectivity is dissolved in the objective projection of a historical imagination of great range and power. The Holocaust poem "September Song" elegizes a victim of the Nazi concentration camps born the day after the poet was born, implicitly contrasting their divergent fates. Hill was at once one of the most ambitious, most difficult, and most rewarding contemporary poets writing in English.

In Memory of Jane Fraser

When snow like sheep lay in the fold°   *shelter for sheep*
And winds went begging at each door,
And the far hills were blue with cold,
And a cold shroud lay on the moor,

5   She kept the siege. And every day
We watched her brooding over death
Like a strong bird above its prey.
The room filled with the kettle's breath.

Damp curtains glued against the pane
10 Sealed time away. Her body froze
As if to freeze us all, and chain
Creation to a stunned repose.

She died before the world could stir.
In March the ice unloosed the brook
15 And water ruffled the sun's hair.
Dead cones upon the alder shook.

1959

Requiem for the Plantagenet Kings[1]

For whom the possessed sea littered, on both shores,
Ruinous arms; being fired, and for good,
To sound the constitution of just wars,
Men, in their eloquent fashion, understood.

5 Relieved of soul, the dropping-back of dust,
Their usage, pride, admitted within doors;
At home, under caved chantries,[2] set in trust,
With well-dressed alabaster and proved spurs
They lie; they lie; secure in the decay
10 Of blood, blood-marks, crowns hacked and coveted,
Before the scouring fires of trial-day
Alight on men; before sleeked groin, gored head,
Budge through the clay and gravel, and the sea
Across daubed rock evacuates its dead.

1959

September Song[1]

born 19.6.32—deported 24.9.42

Undesirable you may have been, untouchable
you were not. Not forgotten
or passed over at the proper time.

As estimated, you died. Things marched,
5 sufficient, to that end.
Just so much Zyklon and leather, patented
terror, so many routine cries.

(I have made
an elegy for myself it
10 is true)[2]

1. Dynastic succession of 12th- to 15th-century English kings, beginning with Henry II, who was followed in turn by Richard I, John, Henry III, Edward I, Edward II, Edward III, and Richard II. They ruled not only over England but also over much of France ("on both shores"). The last Plantagenet king was Richard III, who was killed at the Battle of Bosworth on Aug. 22, 1485.
2. Chapels endowed for priests to sing Masses for the souls of those who founded them. Many chantries have cavelike ceilings of vaulted stone and contain effigies—sometimes in alabaster—of their founders.
1. The poem is about the gassing of Jews in German extermination camps; Zyklon-B was the gas used. Hill's fellow poet Jon Silkin has drawn attention to the kind of wit involved in the subtitle, "where the natural event of birth is placed, simply, beside the human and murderous 'deported' as if the latter were of the same order and inevitability for the victim"; he discusses, too, "the irony of conjuncted meanings between 'undesirable' (touching on both sexual desire and racism) and 'untouchable,' which exploits a similar ambiguity but reverses the emphases" and is "unusually dense *and* simple."
2. As the critic Christopher Ricks pointed out, Hill was born on 18.6.32 (June 18, 1932).

September fattens on vines. Roses
flake from the wall. The smoke
of harmless fires drifts to my eyes.

This is plenty. This is more than enough.

1968

Broken Hierarchies

When to depict rain—heavy rain—it stands
in dense verticals diagonally lashed,
chalk-white yet with the chalk translucent;

the roadway sprouts ten thousand flowerets,
5   storm-paddies instantly reaped, replenished,
and again cut down:

the holding burden of a wisteria
drape amid drape, the sodden
copia° of all things flashing and drying: *abundance*

10   first here after the storm these butterflies
fixed on each jinking° run,   *zigzagging*
probing, priming, then leaping back,

a babble of silent tongues;
and the flint church also choiring
15   into dazzle

. . .

like Appalachian music, those
aureate° stark sounds   *golden*
plucked or bowed, a wild patience

replete with loss,
20   the twankled dulcimer,
scrawny rich fiddle gnawing;

a man's low voice that looms out of the drone:
the humming bird that is not
of these climes; and the great

25   wanderers like the albatross;
the ocean, ranging-in, laying itself
down on our alien shore.

2006

V. S. NAIPAUL
b. 1932

Widely regarded as the most accomplished novelist from the English-speaking Caribbean, Vidiadhar Surajprasad Naipaul was born to a family of Indian descent in Trinidad and educated at Queen's Royal College, Port of Spain, and at University College, Oxford. After settling in England, he became editor of the *Caribbean Voices* program for the British Broadcasting Corporation (1954–56) and fiction reviewer for the *New Statesman* (1957–61). The recipient of many prestigious prizes and awards, he won the Booker Prize in 1971 for *In a Free State*, was knighted in 1990, and received the Nobel Prize in Literature in 2001. He continues to live in England.

Naipaul's first three books, *The Mystic Masseur* (1957), *The Suffrage of Elvira* (1958), and *Miguel Street* (short stories, 1959), are comedies of manners, set in a Trinidad viewed with an exile's acute and ironic eye. These early works present a starkly satiric vision, but a more modulated tone appears in Naipaul's first major novel, partly based on his father's experience, *A House for Mr. Biswas* (1961). Following the declining fortunes of its gentle hero from cradle to grave, this tragicomic novel traces the disintegration of a traditional way of life on something approaching an epic scale. Subsequent novels, including *The Mimic Men* (1967), *Guerrillas* (1973), *The Enigma of Arrival* (1987), and *Half a Life* (2001), have continued to explore the desperate and destructive conditions facing individuals as they struggle with cultures in complicated states of transition and development. Because of his often bitter, even withering critiques of so-called Third World states and societies, he is controversial among readers of postcolonial fiction.

Naipaul has also produced essays on a variety of themes, including a travel narrative about the southern United States, *A Turn in the South* (1988), another about African belief, *The Masque of Africa* (2010), and two studies—what he calls "cultural explorations"—of Islam: *Among the Believers: An Islamic Journey* (1981) and *Beyond Belief: Islamic Excursions among the Converted Peoples* (1998). Like his novels, these writings range widely, carrying readers to Africa, England, the Indian subcontinent, the Middle East, South and North America. With the years, Naipaul's vision of the human condition has grown darker and more pessimistic, as he brilliantly lays bare the insensitivities and disconnections that bedevil relations among individuals, races, and nations.

Such tremendous disjunctions and dire consequences are revealed in "One Out of Many," the second of three stories that, with two linking diary entries, make up *In a Free State*, a bleakly ironic yet emotionally engaging study of what it means to be enslaved and what it means to be free. The story—its title playing on the American motto "*E pluribus unum*" ("from many, one")—follows the fortunes of Santosh, an Indian immigrant to the United States, whose sense of self changes dramatically in relation to various liberating and imprisoning spaces, various ethnic, cultural, and sexual others. In contrast to narratives of immigration as empowerment, the story represents the promise of more freedom, more status, more economic opportunity in America as coming at the price of an intensified isolation and alienation. As in the literary journeys of other innocents abroad, Santosh's immersion in America satirically reveals as much about the culture he assumes as about the culture he leaves behind.

One Out of Many

I am now an American citizen and I live in Washington, capital of the world. Many people, both here and in India, will feel that I have done well. But.

I was so happy in Bombay. I was respected, I had a certain position. I worked for an important man. The highest in the land came to our bachelor chambers and enjoyed my food and showered compliments on me. I also had my friends. We met in the evenings on the pavement below the gallery of our chambers. Some of us, like the tailor's bearer[1] and myself, were domestics who lived in the street. The others were people who came to that bit of pavement to sleep. Respectable people; we didn't encourage riff-raff.

In the evenings it was cool. There were few passers-by and, apart from an occasional double-decker bus or taxi, little traffic. The pavement was swept and sprinkled, bedding brought out from daytime hiding-places, little oil-lamps lit. While the folk upstairs chattered and laughed, on the pavement we read newspapers, played cards, told stories and smoked. The clay pipe passed from friend to friend; we became drowsy. Except of course during the monsoon,[2] I preferred to sleep on the pavement with my friends, although in our chambers a whole cupboard below the staircase was reserved for my personal use.

It was good after a healthy night in the open to rise before the sun and before the sweepers came. Sometimes I saw the street lights go off. Bedding was rolled up; no one spoke much; and soon my friends were hurrying in silent competition to secluded lanes and alleys and open lots to relieve themselves. I was spared this competition; in our chambers I had facilities.[3]

Afterwards for half an hour or so I was free simply to stroll. I liked walking beside the Arabian Sea, waiting for the sun to come up. Then the city and the ocean gleamed like gold. Alas for those morning walks, that sudden ocean dazzle, the moist salt breeze on my face, the flap of my shirt, that first cup of hot sweet tea from a stall, the taste of the first leaf-cigarette.

Observe the workings of fate. The respect and security I enjoyed were due to the importance of my employer. It was this very importance which now all at once destroyed the pattern of my life.

My employer was seconded[4] by his firm to Government service and was posted to Washington. I was happy for his sake but frightened for mine. He was to be away for some years and there was nobody in Bombay he could second me to. Soon, therefore, I was to be out of a job and out of the chambers. For many years I had considered my life as settled. I had served my apprenticeship, known my hard times. I didn't feel I could start again. I despaired. Was there a job for me in Bombay? I saw myself having to return to my village in the hills, to my wife and children there, not just for a holiday but for good. I saw myself again becoming a porter during the tourist season, racing after the buses as they arrived at the station and shouting with forty or fifty others for luggage. Indian luggage, not this lightweight American stuff! Heavy metal trunks!

I could have cried. It was no longer the sort of life for which I was fitted. I had grown soft in Bombay and I was no longer young. I had acquired possessions, I was used to the privacy of my cupboard. I had become a city man, used to certain comforts.

1. Servant.
2. Rainy season.

3. I.e., a toilet.
4. Temporarily transferred.

My employer said, "Washington is not Bombay, Santosh. Washington is expensive. Even if I was able to raise your fare, you wouldn't be able to live over there in anything like your present style."

But to be barefoot in the hills, after Bombay! The shock, the disgrace! I couldn't face my friends. I stopped sleeping on the pavement and spent as much of my free time as possible in my cupboard among my possessions, as among things which were soon to be taken from me.

My employer said, "Santosh, my heart bleeds for you."

I said, "Sahib,[5] if I look a little concerned it is only because I worry about you. You have always been fussy, and I don't see how you will manage in Washington."

"It won't be easy. But it's the principle. Does the representative of a poor country like ours travel about with his cook? Will that create a good impression?"

"You will always do what is right, sahib."

He went silent.

After some days he said, "There's not only the expense, Santosh. There's the question of foreign exchange. Our rupee[6] isn't what it was."

"I understand, sahib. Duty is duty."

A fortnight later, when I had almost given up hope, he said, "Santosh, I have consulted Government. You will accompany me. Government has sanctioned, will arrange accommodation. But no expenses. You will get your passport and your P form. But I want you to think, Santosh. Washington is not Bombay."

I went down to the pavement that night with my bedding.

I said, blowing down my shirt, "Bombay gets hotter and hotter."

"Do you know what you are doing?" the tailor's bearer said. "Will the Americans smoke with you? Will they sit and talk with you in the evenings? Will they hold you by the hand and walk with you beside the ocean?"

It pleased me that he was jealous. My last days in Bombay were very happy.

I packed my employer's two suitcases and bundled up my own belongings in lengths of old cotton. At the airport they made a fuss about my bundles. They said they couldn't accept them as luggage for the hold because they didn't like the responsibility. So when the time came I had to climb up to the aircraft with all my bundles. The girl at the top, who was smiling at everybody else, stopped smiling when she saw me. She made me go right to the back of the plane, far from my employer. Most of the seats there were empty, though, and I was able to spread my bundles around and, well, it was comfortable.

It was bright and hot outside, cool inside. The plane started, rose up in the air, and Bombay and the ocean tilted this way and that. It was very nice. When we settled down I looked around for people like myself, but I could see no one among the Indians or the foreigners who looked like a domestic. Worse, they were all dressed as though they were going to a wedding and, brother, I soon saw it wasn't they who were conspicuous. I was in my ordinary Bombay clothes, the loose long-tailed shirt, the wide-waisted pants held up with a piece of string. Perfectly respectable domestic's wear, neither dirty nor clean, and in Bombay no one would have looked. But now on the plane I felt heads turning whenever I stood up.

<hr>

5. Master (Urdu).   6. Indian currency, at this time worth ten cents.

I was anxious. I slipped off my shoes, tight even without the laces, and drew my feet up. That made me feel better. I made myself a little betel-nut[7] mixture and that made me feel better still. Half the pleasure of betel, though, is the spitting; and it was only when I had worked up a good mouthful that I saw I had a problem. The airline girl saw too. That girl didn't like me at all. She spoke roughly to me. My mouth was full, my cheeks were bursting, and I couldn't say anything. I could only look at her. She went and called a man in uniform and he came and stood over me. I put my shoes back on and swallowed the betel juice. It made me feel quite ill.

The girl and the man, the two of them, pushed a little trolley of drinks down the aisle. The girl didn't look at me but the man said, "You want a drink, chum?" He wasn't a bad fellow. I pointed at random to a bottle. It was a kind of soda drink, nice and sharp at first but then not so nice. I was worrying about it when the girl said, "Five shillings sterling or sixty cents U.S." That took me by surprise. I had no money, only a few rupees. The girl stamped, and I thought she was going to hit me with her pad when I stood up to show her who my employer was.

Presently my employer came down the aisle. He didn't look very well. He said, without stopping, "Champagne, Santosh? Already we are overdoing?" He went on to the lavatory. When he passed back he said, "Foreign exchange, Santosh! Foreign exchange!" That was all. Poor fellow, he was suffering too.

The journey became miserable for me. Soon, with the wine I had drunk, the betel juice, the movement and the noise of the aeroplane, I was vomiting all over my bundles, and I didn't care what the girl said or did. Later there were more urgent and terrible needs. I felt I would choke in the tiny, hissing room at the back. I had a shock when I saw my face in the mirror. In the fluorescent light it was the colour of a corpse. My eyes were strained, the sharp air hurt my nose and seemed to get into my brain. I climbed up on the lavatory seat and squatted. I lost control of myself. As quickly as I could I ran back out into the comparative openness of the cabin and hoped no one had noticed. The lights were dim now; some people had taken off their jackets and were sleeping. I hoped the plane would crash.

The girl woke me up. She was almost screaming. "It's you, isn't it? Isn't it?"

I thought she was going to tear the shirt off me. I pulled back and leaned hard on the window. She burst into tears and nearly tripped on her sari as she ran up the aisle to get the man in uniform.

Nightmare. And all I knew was that somewhere at the end, after the airports and the crowded lounges where everybody was dressed up, after all those takeoffs and touchdowns, was the city of Washington. I wanted the journey to end but I couldn't say I wanted to arrive at Washington. I was already a little scared of that city, to tell the truth. I wanted only to be off the plane and to be in the open again, to stand on the ground and breathe and to try to understand what time of day it was.

At last we arrived. I was in a daze. The burden of those bundles! There were more closed rooms and electric lights. There were questions from officials.

"Is he diplomatic?"[8]

"He's only a domestic," my employer said.

"Is that his luggage? What's in that pocket?"

---

7. Evergreen plant, the leaves of which are chewed in the East with areca-nut parings, as a mild stimulant.

8. I.e., in the Diplomatic Corps.

I was ashamed.

"Santosh," my employer said.

I pulled out the little packets of pepper and salt, the sweets, the envelopes with scented napkins, the toy tubes of mustard. Airline trinkets. I had been collecting them throughout the journey, seizing a handful, whatever my condition, every time I passed the galley.

"He's a cook," my employer said.

"Does he always travel with his condiments?"

"Santosh, Santosh," my employer said in the car afterwards, "in Bombay it didn't matter what you did. Over here you represent your country. I must say I cannot understand why your behaviour has already gone so much out of character."

"I am sorry, sahib."

"Look at it like this, Santosh. Over here you don't only represent your country, you represent me."

For the people of Washington it was late afternoon or early evening, I couldn't say which. The time and the light didn't match, as they did in Bombay. Of that drive I remember green fields, wide roads, many motor cars travelling fast, making a steady hiss, hiss, which wasn't at all like our Bombay traffic noise. I remember big buildings and wide parks; many bazaar areas; then smaller houses without fences and with gardens like bush, with the *hubshi*[9] standing about or sitting down, more usually sitting down, everywhere. Especially I remember the *hubshi*. I had heard about them in stories and had seen one or two in Bombay. But I had never dreamt that this wild race existed in such numbers in Washington and were permitted to roam the streets so freely. O father, what was this place I had come to?

I wanted, I say, to be in the open, to breathe, to come to myself, to reflect. But there was to be no openness for me that evening. From the aeroplane to the airport building to the motor car to the apartment block to the elevator to the corridor to the apartment itself, I was forever enclosed, forever in the hissing, hissing sound of air-conditioners.

I was too dazed to take stock of the apartment. I saw it as only another halting place. My employer went to bed at once, completely exhausted, poor fellow. I looked around for my room. I couldn't find it and gave up. Aching for the Bombay ways, I spread my bedding in the carpeted corridor just outside our apartment door. The corridor was long: doors, doors. The illuminated ceiling was decorated with stars of different sizes; the colours were grey and blue and gold. Below that imitation sky I felt like a prisoner.

Waking, looking up at the ceiling, I thought just for a second that I had fallen asleep on the pavement below the gallery of our Bombay chambers. Then I realized my loss. I couldn't tell how much time had passed or whether it was night or day. The only clue was that newspapers now lay outside some doors. It disturbed me to think that while I had been sleeping, alone and defenceless, I had been observed by a stranger and perhaps by more than one stranger.

I tried the apartment door and found I had locked myself out. I didn't want to disturb my employer. I thought I would get out into the open, go for a walk. I remembered where the elevator was. I got in and pressed the button. The elevator dropped fast and silently and it was like being in the aeroplane again. When the elevator stopped and the blue metal door slid open I saw plain con-

<hr />

9. Derogatory Indian term for African blacks (Hindustani).

crete corridors and blank walls. The noise of machinery was very loud. I knew I was in the basement and the main floor was not far above me. But I no longer wanted to try; I gave up ideas of the open air. I thought I would just go back up to the apartment. But I hadn't noted the number and didn't even know what floor we were on. My courage flowed out of me. I sat on the floor of the elevator and felt the tears come to my eyes. Almost without noise the elevator door closed, and I found I was being taken up silently at great speed.

The elevator stopped and the door opened. It was my employer, his hair uncombed, yesterday's dirty shirt partly unbuttoned. He looked frightened.

"Santosh, where have you been at this hour of morning? Without your shoes."

I could have embraced him. He hurried me back past the newspapers to our apartment and I took the bedding inside. The wide window showed the early morning sky, the big city; we were high up, way above the trees.

I said, "I couldn't find my room."

"Government sanctioned," my employer said. "Are you sure you've looked?"

We looked together. One little corridor led past the bathroom to his bedroom; another, shorter corridor led to the big room and the kitchen. There was nothing else.

"Government sanctioned," my employer said, moving about the kitchen and opening cupboard doors. "Separate entrance, shelving. I have the correspondence." He opened another door and looked inside. "Santosh, do you think it is possible that this is what Government meant?"

The cupboard he had opened was as high as the rest of the apartment and as wide as the kitchen, about six feet. It was about three feet deep. It had two doors. One door opened into the kitchen; another door, directly opposite, opened into the corridor.

"Separate entrance," my employer said. "Shelving, electric light, power point, fitted carpet."

"This must be my room, sahib."

"Santosh, some enemy in Government has done this to me."

"Oh no, sahib. You mustn't say that. Besides, it is very big. I will be able to make myself very comfortable. It is much bigger than my little cubbyhole in the chambers. And it has a nice flat ceiling. I wouldn't hit my head."

"You don't understand, Santosh. Bombay is Bombay. Here if we start living in cupboards we give the wrong impression. They will think we all live in cupboards in Bombay."

"O sahib, but they can just look at me and see I am dirt."

"You are very good, Santosh. But these people are malicious. Still, if you are happy, then I am happy."

"I am very happy, sahib."

And after all the upset, I was. It was nice to crawl in that evening, spread my bedding and feel protected and hidden. I slept very well.

In the morning my employer said, "We must talk about money, Santosh. Your salary is one hundred rupees a month. But Washington isn't Bombay. Everything is a little bit more expensive here, and I am going to give you a Dearness Allowance. As from today you are getting one hundred and fifty rupees."

"Sahib."

"And I'm giving you a fortnight's pay in advance. In foreign exchange. Seventy-five rupees. Ten cents to the rupee, seven hundred and fifty cents. Seven fifty U.S. Here, Santosh. This afternoon you go out and have a little walk and enjoy. But be careful. We are not among friends, remember."

So at last, rested, with money in my pocket, I went out in the open. And of course the city wasn't a quarter as frightening as I had thought. The buildings weren't particularly big, not all the streets were busy, and there were many lovely trees. A lot of the *hubshi* were about, very wild-looking some of them, with dark glasses and their hair frizzed out, but it seemed that if you didn't trouble them they didn't attack you.

I was looking for a café or a tea-stall where perhaps domestics congregated. But I saw no domestics, and I was chased away from the place I did eventually go into. The girl said, after I had been waiting some time, "Can't you read? We don't serve hippies or bare feet here."

O father! I had come out without my shoes. But what a country, I thought, walking briskly away, where people are never allowed to dress normally but must forever wear their very best! Why must they wear out shoes and fine clothes for no purpose? What occasion are they honouring? What waste, what presumption! Who do they think is noticing them all the time?

And even while these thoughts were in my head I found I had come to a roundabout with trees and a fountain where—and it was like a fulfilment in a dream, not easy to believe—there were many people who looked like my own people. I tightened the string around my loose pants, held down my flapping shirt and ran through the traffic to the green circle.

Some of the *hubshi* were there, playing musical instruments and looking quite happy in their way. There were some Americans sitting about on the grass and the fountain and the kerb. Many of them were in rough, friendly-looking clothes; some were without shoes; and I felt I had been over hasty in condemning the entire race. But it wasn't these people who had attracted me to the circle. It was the dancers. The men were bearded, barefooted and in saffron robes, and the girls were in saris and canvas shoes that looked like our own Bata shoes.[1] They were shaking little cymbals and chanting and lifting their heads up and down and going round in a circle, making a lot of dust. It was a little bit like a Red Indian dance in a cowboy movie, but they were chanting Sanskrit words in praise of Lord Krishna.[2]

I was very pleased. But then a disturbing thought came to me. It might have been because of the half-caste[3] appearance of the dancers; it might have been their bad Sanskrit pronunciation and their accent. I thought that these people were now strangers, but that perhaps once upon a time they had been like me. Perhaps, as in some story, they had been brought here among the *hubshi* as captives a long time ago and had become a lost people, like our own wandering gipsy folk, and had forgotten who they were. When I thought that, I lost my pleasure in the dancing; and I felt for the dancers the sort of distaste we feel when we are faced with something that should be kin but turns out not to be, turns out to be degraded, like a deformed man, or like a leper, who from a distance looks whole.

I didn't stay. Not far from the circle I saw a café which appeared to be serving bare feet. I went in, had a coffee and a nice piece of cake and bought a pack of cigarettes; matches they gave me free with the cigarettes. It was all right, but then the bare feet began looking at me, and one bearded fellow came and sniffed loudly at me and smiled and spoke some sort of gibberish, and then some others of the bare feet came and sniffed at me. They weren't unfriendly, but I didn't appreciate the behaviour; and it was

1. I.e., from the Bata Shoe Company.
2. Great Hindu deity.
3. Mixed-race, usually in India, descended from

or born to an Indian mother and a European father.

a little frightening to find, when I left the place, that two or three of them appeared to be following me. They weren't unfriendly, but I didn't want to take any chances. I passed a cinema; I went in. It was something I wanted to do anyway. In Bombay I used to go once a week.

And that was all right. The movie had already started. It was in English, not too easy for me to follow, and it gave me time to think. It was only there, in the darkness, that I thought about the money I had been spending. The prices had seemed to me very reasonable, like Bombay prices. Three for the movie ticket, one fifty in the café, with tip. But I had been thinking in rupees and paying in dollars. In less than an hour I had spent nine days' pay.

I couldn't watch the movie after that. I went out and began to make my way back to the apartment block. Many more of the *hubshi* were about now and I saw that where they congregated the pavement was wet, and dangerous with broken glass and bottles. I couldn't think of cooking when I got back to the apartment. I couldn't bear to look at the view. I spread my bedding in the cupboard, lay down in the darkness and waited for my employer to return.

When he did I said, "Sahib, I want to go home."

"Santosh, I've paid five thousand rupees to bring you here. If I send you back now, you will have to work for six or seven years without salary to pay me back."

I burst into tears.

"My poor Santosh, something has happened. Tell me what has happened."

"Sahib, I've spent more than half the advance you gave me this morning. I went out and had a coffee and cake and then I went to a movie."

His eyes went small and twinkly behind his glasses. He bit the inside of his top lip, scraped at his moustache with his lower teeth, and he said, "You see, you see. I told you it was expensive."

I understood I was a prisoner. I accepted this and adjusted. I learned to live within the apartment, and I was even calm.

My employer was a man of taste and he soon had the apartment looking like something in a magazine, with books and Indian paintings and Indian fabrics and pieces of sculpture and bronze statues of our gods. I was careful to take no delight in it. It was of course very pretty, especially with the view. But the view remained foreign and I never felt that the apartment was real, like the shabby old Bombay chambers with the cane chairs, or that it had anything to do with me.

When people came to dinner I did my duty. At the appropriate time I would bid the company goodnight, close off the kitchen behind its folding screen and pretend I was leaving the apartment. Then I would lie down quietly in my cupboard and smoke. I was free to go out; I had my separate entrance. But I didn't like being out of the apartment. I didn't even like going down to the laundry room in the basement.

Once or twice a week I went to the supermarket on our street. I always had to walk past groups of *hubshi* men and children. I tried not to look, but it was hard. They sat on the pavement, on steps and in the bush around their redbrick houses, some of which had boarded-up windows. They appeared to be very much a people of the open air, with little to do; even in the mornings some of the men were drunk.

Scattered among the *hubshi* houses were others just as old but with gas-lamps that burned night and day in the entrance. These were the houses of the Americans. I seldom saw these people; they didn't spend much time on the street. The lighted gas-lamp was the American way of saying that though a house looked old outside it was nice and new inside. I also felt that it was like a warning to the *hubshi* to keep off.

Outside the supermarket there was always a policeman with a gun. Inside, there were always a couple of *hubshi* guards with truncheons, and, behind the cashiers, some old *hubshi* beggar men in rags. There were also many young *hubshi* boys, small but muscular, waiting to carry parcels, as once in the hills I had waited to carry Indian tourists' luggage.

These trips to the supermarket were my only outings, and I was always glad to get back to the apartment. The work there was light. I watched a lot of television and my English improved. I grew to like certain commercials very much. It was in these commercials I saw the Americans whom in real life I so seldom saw and knew only by their gas-lamps. Up there in the apartment, with a view of the white domes and towers and greenery of the famous city, I entered the homes of the Americans and saw them cleaning those homes. I saw them cleaning floors and dishes. I saw them buying clothes and cleaning clothes, buying motor cars and cleaning motor cars. I saw them cleaning, cleaning.

The effect of all this television on me was curious. If by some chance I saw an American on the street I tried to fit him or her into the commercials; and I felt I had caught the person in an interval between his television duties. So to some extent Americans have remained to me, as people not quite real, as people temporarily absent from television.

Sometimes a *hubshi* came on the screen, not to talk of *hubshi* things, but to do a little cleaning of his own. That wasn't the same. He was too different from the *hubshi* I saw on the street and I knew he was an actor. I knew that his television duties were only make-believe and that he would soon have to return to the street.

One day at the supermarket, when the *hubshi* girl took my money, she sniffed and said, "You always smell sweet, baby."

She was friendly, and I was at last able to clear up that mystery, of my smell. It was the poor country weed I smoked. It was a peasant taste of which I was slightly ashamed, to tell the truth; but the cashier was encouraging. As it happened, I had brought a quantity of the weed with me from Bombay in one of my bundles, together with a hundred razor blades, believing both weed and blades to be purely Indian things. I made an offering to the girl. In return she taught me a few words of English. "Me black and beautiful"[4] was the first thing she taught me. Then she pointed to the policeman with the gun outside and taught me: "He pig."

My English lessons were taken a stage further by the *hubshi* maid who worked for someone on our floor in the apartment block. She too was attracted by my smell, but I soon began to feel that she was also attracted by my smallness and strangeness. She herself was a big woman, broad in the face, with high cheeks and bold eyes and lips that were full but not pendulous. Her largeness disturbed me; I found it better to concentrate on her face. She misunderstood; there were times when she frolicked with me in a violent way. I didn't like it, because I couldn't fight her off as well as I would have liked and because in spite of myself I was fascinated by her appearance. Her smell mixed with the perfumes she used could have made me forget myself.

She was always coming into the apartment. She disturbed me while I was watching the Americans on television. I feared the smell she left behind.

4. Cf. the 1960s slogan "Black is Beautiful."

Sweat, perfume, my own weed: the smells lay thick in the room, and I prayed to the bronze gods my employer had installed as living-room ornaments that I would not be dishonoured. Dishonoured, I say; and I know that this might seem strange to people over here, who have permitted the *hubshi* to settle among them in such large numbers and must therefore esteem them in certain ways. But in our country we frankly do not care for the *hubshi*. It is written in our books, both holy and not so holy, that it is indecent and wrong for a man of our blood to embrace the *hubshi* woman. To be dishonoured in this life, to be born a cat or a monkey or a *hubshi* in the next!

But I was falling. Was it idleness and solitude? I was found attractive: I wanted to know why. I began to go to the bathroom of the apartment simply to study my face in the mirror. I cannot easily believe it myself now, but in Bombay a week or a month could pass without my looking in the mirror; then it wasn't to consider my looks but to check whether the barber had cut off too much hair or whether a pimple was about to burst. Slowly I made a discovery. My face was handsome. I had never thought of myself in this way. I had thought of myself as unnoticeable, with features that served as identification alone.

The discovery of my good looks brought its strains. I became obsessed with my appearance, with a wish to see myself. It was like an illness. I would be watching television, for instance, and I would be surprised by the thought: are you as handsome as that man? I would have to get up and go to the bathroom and look in the mirror.

I thought back to the time when these matters hadn't interested me, and I saw how ragged I must have looked, on the aeroplane, in the airport, in that café for bare feet, with the rough and dirty clothes I wore, without doubt or question, as clothes befitting a servant. I was choked with shame. I saw, too, how good people in Washington had been, to have seen me in rags and yet to have taken me for a man.

I was glad I had a place to hide. I had thought of myself as a prisoner. Now I was glad I had so little of Washington to cope with: the apartment, my cupboard, the television set, my employer, the walk to the supermarket, the *hubshi* woman. And one day I found I no longer knew whether I wanted to go back to Bombay. Up there, in the apartment, I no longer knew what I wanted to do.

I became more careful of my appearance. There wasn't much I could do. I bought laces for my old black shoes, socks, a belt. Then some money came my way. I had understood that the weed I smoked was of value to the *hubshi* and the bare feet; I disposed of what I had, disadvantageously as I now know, through the *hubshi* girl at the supermarket. I got just under two hundred dollars. Then, as anxiously as I had got rid of my weed, I went out and bought some clothes.

I still have the things I bought that morning. A green hat, a green suit. The suit was always too big for me. Ignorance, inexperience; but I also remember the feeling of presumption. The salesman wanted to talk, to do his job. I didn't want to listen. I took the first suit he showed me and went into the cubicle and changed. I couldn't think about size and fit. When I considered all that cloth and all that tailoring I was proposing to adorn my simple body with, that body that needed so little, I felt I was asking to be destroyed. I changed back quickly, went out of the cubicle and said I would take the green suit. The salesman began to talk; I cut him short; I asked for a hat. When I got back to the apartment I felt quite weak and had to lie down for a while in my cupboard.

I never hung the suit up. Even in the shop, even while counting out the precious dollars, I had known it was a mistake. I kept the suit folded in the box with all its pieces of tissue paper. Three or four times I put it on and walked about the apartment and sat down on chairs and lit cigarettes and crossed my legs, practising. But I couldn't bring myself to wear the suit out of doors. Later I wore the pants, but never the jacket. I never bought another suit; I soon began wearing the sort of clothes I wear today, pants with some sort of zippered jacket.

Once I had had no secrets from my employer; it was so much simpler not to have secrets. But some instinct told me now it would be better not to let him know about the green suit or the few dollars I had, just as instinct had already told me I should keep my growing knowledge of English to myself.

Once my employer had been to me only a presence. I used to tell him then that beside him I was as dirt. It was only a way of talking, one of the courtesies of our language, but it had something of truth. I meant that he was the man who adventured in the world for me, that I experienced the world through him, that I was content to be a small part of his presence. I was content, sleeping on the Bombay pavement with my friends, to hear the talk of my employer and his guests upstairs. I was more than content, late at night, to be identified among the sleepers and greeted by some of those guests before they drove away.

Now I found that, without wishing it, I was ceasing to see myself as part of my employer's presence, and beginning at the same time to see him as an outsider might see him, as perhaps the people who came to dinner in the apartment saw him. I saw that he was a man of my own age, around thirty-five; it astonished me that I hadn't noticed this before. I saw that he was plump, in need of exercise, that he moved with short, fussy steps; a man with glasses, thinning hair, and that habit, during conversation, of scraping at his moustache with his teeth and nibbling at the inside of his top lip; a man who was frequently anxious, took pains over his work, was subjected at his own table to unkind remarks by his office colleagues; a man who looked as uneasy in Washington as I felt, who acted as cautiously as I had learned to act.

I remember an American who came to dinner. He looked at the pieces of sculpture in the apartment and said he had himself brought back a whole head from one of our ancient temples; he had got the guide to hack it off.

I could see that my employer was offended. He said, "But that's illegal."

"That's why I had to give the guide two dollars. If I had a bottle of whisky he would have pulled down the whole temple for me."

My employer's face went blank. He continued to do his duties as host but he was unhappy throughout the dinner. I grieved for him.

Afterwards he knocked on my cupboard. I knew he wanted to talk. I was in my underclothes but I didn't feel underdressed, with the American gone. I stood in the door of my cupboard; my employer paced up and down the small kitchen; the apartment felt sad.

"Did you hear that person, Santosh?"

I pretended I hadn't understood, and when he explained I tried to console him. I said, "Sahib, but we know these people are Franks[5] and barbarians."

"They are malicious people, Santosh. They think that because we are a poor country we are all the same. They think an official in Government is just the

_____
5. Here, foreigners of Western origin.

same as some poor guide scraping together a few rupees to keep body and soul together, poor fellow."

I saw that he had taken the insult only in a personal way, and I was disappointed. I thought he had been thinking of the temple.

A few days later I had my adventure. The *hubshi* woman came in, moving among my employer's ornaments like a bull. I was greatly provoked. The smell was too much; so was the sight of her armpits. I fell. She dragged me down on the couch, on the saffron spread which was one of my employer's nicest pieces of Punjabi folk-weaving. I saw the moment, helplessly, as one of dishonour. I saw her as Kali,[6] goddess of death and destruction, coal-black, with a red tongue and white eyeballs and many powerful arms. I expected her to be wild and fierce; but she added insult to injury by being very playful, as though, because I was small and strange, the act was not real. She laughed all the time. I would have liked to withdraw, but the act took over and completed itself. And then I felt dreadful.

I wanted to be forgiven, I wanted to be cleansed, I wanted her to go. Nothing frightened me more than the way she had ceased to be a visitor in the apartment and behaved as though she possessed it. I looked at the sculpture and the fabrics and thought of my poor employer, suffering in his office somewhere.

I bathed and bathed afterwards. The smell would not leave me. I fancied that the woman's oil was still on that poor part of my poor body. It occurred to me to rub it down with half a lemon. Penance and cleansing; but it didn't hurt as much as I expected, and I extended the penance by rolling about naked on the floor of the bathroom and the sitting-room and howling. At last the tears came, real tears, and I was comforted.

It was cool in the apartment; the air-conditioning always hummed; but I could see that it was hot outside, like one of our own summer days in the hills. The urge came upon me to dress as I might have done in my village on a religious occasion. In one of my bundles I had a dhoti[7]-length of new cotton, a gift from the tailor's bearer that I had never used. I draped this around my waist and between my legs, lit incense sticks, sat down cross-legged on the floor and tried to meditate and become still. Soon I began to feel hungry. That made me happy; I decided to fast.

Unexpectedly my employer came in. I didn't mind being caught in the attitude and garb of prayer; it could have been so much worse. But I wasn't expecting him till late afternoon.

"Santosh, what has happened?"

Pride got the better of me. I said, "Sahib, it is what I do from time to time."

But I didn't find merit in his eyes. He was far too agitated to notice me properly. He took off his lightweight fawn jacket, dropped it on the saffron spread, went to the refrigerator and drank two tumblers of orange juice, one after the other. Then he looked out at the view, scraping at his moustache.

"Oh, my poor Santosh, what are we doing in this place? Why do we have to come here?"

I looked with him. I saw nothing unusual. The wide window showed the colours of the hot day: the pale-blue sky, the white, almost colourless, domes of famous buildings rising out of dead-green foliage; the untidy roofs of apartment blocks where on Saturday and Sunday mornings people sun-

6. Great Hindu deity.   7. Loincloth (Hindi).

bathed; and, below, the fronts and backs of houses on the tree-lined street down which I walked to the supermarket.

My employer turned off the air-conditioning and all noise was absent from the room. An instant later I began to hear the noises outside: sirens far and near. When my employer slid the window open the roar of the disturbed city rushed into the room. He closed the window and there was near-silence again. Not far from the supermarket I saw black smoke, uncurling, rising, swiftly turning colourless. This was not the smoke which some of the apartment blocks gave off all day. This was the smoke of a real fire.

"The *hubshi* have gone wild, Santosh. They are burning down Washington."

I didn't mind at all. Indeed, in my mood of prayer and repentance, the news was even welcome. And it was with a feeling of release that I watched and heard the city burn that afternoon and watched it burn that night. I watched it burn again and again on television; and I watched it burn in the morning. It burned like a famous city and I didn't want it to stop burning. I wanted the fire to spread and spread and I wanted everything in the city, even the apartment block, even the apartment, even myself, to be destroyed and consumed. I wanted escape to be impossible; I wanted the very idea of escape to become absurd. At every sign that the burning was going to stop I felt disappointed and let down.

For four days my employer and I stayed in the apartment and watched the city burn. The television continued to show us what we could see and what, whenever we slid the window back, we could hear. Then it was over. The view from our window hadn't changed. The famous buildings stood; the trees remained. But for the first time since I had understood that I was a prisoner I found that I wanted to be out of the apartment and in the streets.

The destruction lay beyond the supermarket. I had never gone into this part of the city before, and it was strange to walk in those long wide streets for the first time, to see trees and houses and shops and advertisements, everything like a real city, and then to see that every signboard on every shop was burnt or stained with smoke, that the shops themselves were black and broken, that flames had burst through some of the upper windows and scorched the red bricks. For mile after mile it was like that. There were *hubshi* groups about, and at first when I passed them I pretended to be busy, minding my own business, not at all interested in the ruins. But they smiled at me and I found I was smiling back. Happiness was on the faces of the *hubshi*. They were like people amazed they could do so much, that so much lay in their power. They were like people on holiday. I shared their exhilaration.

The idea of escape was a simple one, but it hadn't occurred to me before. When I adjusted to my imprisonment I had wanted only to get away from Washington and to return to Bombay. But then I had become confused. I had looked in the mirror and seen myself, and I knew it wasn't possible for me to return to Bombay to the sort of job I had had and the life I had lived. I couldn't easily become part of someone else's presence again. Those evening chats on the pavement, those morning walks: happy times, but they were like the happy times of childhood: I didn't want them to return.

I had taken, after the fire, to going for long walks in the city. And one day, when I wasn't even thinking of escape, when I was just enjoying the sights and my new freedom of movement, I found myself in one of those leafy streets where private houses had been turned into business premises. I saw a fellow countryman superintending the raising of a signboard on his gallery. The signboard told me that the building was a restaurant, and I assumed that the man in charge was the owner. He looked worried and slightly ashamed, and he smiled at me. This was unusual, because the Indians I had seen on the streets of Washington pretended they hadn't seen me; they made me feel that they didn't like the competition of my presence or didn't want me to start asking them difficult questions.

I complimented the worried man on his signboard and wished him good luck in his business. He was a small man of about fifty and he was wearing a double-breasted suit with old-fashioned wide lapels. He had dark hollows below his eyes and he looked as though he had recently lost a little weight. I could see that in our country he had been a man of some standing, not quite the sort of person who would go into the restaurant business. I felt at one with him. He invited me in to look around, asked my name and gave his. It was Priya.

Just past the gallery was the loveliest and richest room I had ever seen. The wallpaper was like velvet; I wanted to pass my hand over it. The brass lamps that hung from the ceiling were in a lovely cut-out pattern and the bulbs were of many colours. Priya looked with me, and the hollows under his eyes grew darker, as though my admiration was increasing his worry at his extravagance. The restaurant hadn't yet opened for customers and on a shelf in one corner I saw Priya's collection of good-luck objects: a brass plate with a heap of uncooked rice, for prosperity; a little copybook and a little diary pencil, for good luck with the accounts; a little clay lamp, for general good luck.

"What do you think, Santosh? You think it will be all right?"

"It is bound to be all right, Priya."

"But I have enemies, you know, Santosh. The Indian restaurant people are not going to appreciate me. All mine, you know, Santosh. Cash paid. No mortgage or anything like that. I don't believe in mortgages. Cash or nothing."

I understood him to mean that he had tried to get a mortgage and failed, and was anxious about money.

"But what are you doing here, Santosh? You used to be in Government or something?"

"You could say that, Priya."

"Like me. They have a saying here. If you can't beat them, join them. I joined them. They are still beating me." He sighed and spread his arms on the top of the red wall-seat. "Ah, Santosh, why do we do it? Why don't we renounce and go and meditate on the riverbank?" He waved about the room. "The yemblems[8] of the world, Santosh. Just yemblems."

I didn't know the English word he used, but I understood its meaning; and for a moment it was like being back in Bombay, exchanging stories and philosophies with the tailor's bearer and others in the evening.

"But I am forgetting, Santosh. You will have some tea or coffee or something?"

I shook my head from side to side to indicate that I was agreeable, and he called out in a strange harsh language to someone behind the kitchen door.

"Yes, Santosh. Yem-*blems!*" And he sighed and slapped the red seat hard.

A man came out from the kitchen with a tray. At first he looked like a fellow countryman, but in a second I could tell he was a stranger.

8. Emblems.

"You are right," Priya said, when the stranger went back to the kitchen. "He is not of Bharat. He is a Mexican. But what can I do? You get fellow countrymen, you fix up their papers and everything. And then? Then they run away. Run-run-runaway. Crooks this side, crooks that side, I can't tell you. Listen, Santosh. I was in cloth business before. Buy for fifty rupees that side, sell for fifty dollars this side. Easy. But then. Caftan, everybody wants caftan. Caftan-aftan, I say, I will settle your caftan. I buy one thousand, Santosh. Delays India-side,[9] of course. They come one year later. Nobody wants caftan then. We're not organized, Santosh. We don't do enough consumer research. That's what the fellows at the embassy tell me. But if I do consumer research, when will I do my business? The trouble, you know, Santosh, is that this shopkeeping is not in my blood. The damn thing goes *against* my blood. When I was in cloth business I used to hide sometimes for shame when a customer came in. Sometimes I used to pretend I was a shopper myself. Consumer research! These people make us dance, Santosh. You and I, we will renounce. We will go together and walk beside Potomac and meditate."

I loved his talk. I hadn't heard anything so sweet and philosophical since the Bombay days. I said, "Priya, I will cook for you, if you want a cook."

"I feel I've known you a long time, Santosh. I feel you are like a member of my own family. I will give you a place to sleep, a little food to eat and a little pocket money, as much as I can afford."

I said, "Show me the place to sleep."

He led me out of the pretty room and up a carpeted staircase. I was expecting the carpet and the new paint to stop somewhere, but it was nice and new all the way. We entered a room that was like a smaller version of my employer's apartment.

"Built-in cupboards and everything, you see, Santosh."

I went to the cupboard. It had a folding door that opened outward. I said, "Priya, it is too small. There is room on the shelf for my belongings. But I don't see how I can spread my bedding inside here. It is far too narrow."

He giggled nervously. "Santosh, you are a joker. I feel that we are of the same family already."

Then it came to me that I was being offered the whole room. I was stunned.

Priya looked stunned too. He sat down on the edge of the soft bed. The dark hollows under his eyes were almost black and he looked very small in his double-breasted jacket. "This is how they make us dance over here, Santosh. You say staff quarters and they say staff quarters. This is what they mean."

For some seconds we sat silently, I fearful, he gloomy, meditating on the ways of this new world.

Someone called from downstairs, "Priya!"

His gloom gone, smiling in advance, winking at me, Priya called back in an accent of the country, "Hi, Bab!"

I followed him down.

"Priya," the American said, "I've brought over the menus."

He was a tall man in a leather jacket, with jeans that rode up above thick white socks and big rubber-soled shoes. He looked like someone about to run in a race. The menus were enormous; on the cover there was a drawing

---

9. In India. "Caftan": long loose tunic or shirt (Turkish).

of a fat man with a moustache and a plumed turban, something like the man in the airline advertisements.

"They look great, Bab."

"I like them myself. But what's that, Priya? What's that shelf doing there?"

Moving like the front part of a horse, Bab walked to the shelf with the rice and the brass plate and the little clay lamp. It was only then that I saw that the shelf was very roughly made.

Priya looked penitent and it was clear he had put the shelf up himself. It was also clear he didn't intend to take it down.

"Well, it's yours," Bab said. "I suppose we had to have a touch of the East somewhere. Now, Priya—"

"Money-money-money, is it?" Priya said, racing the words together as though he was making a joke to amuse a child. "But, Bab, how can *you ask me* for money? Anybody hearing you would believe that this restaurant is mine. But this restaurant isn't mine, Bab. This restaurant is yours."

It was only one of our courtesies, but it puzzled Bab and he allowed himself to be led to other matters.

I saw that, for all his talk of renunciation and business failure, and for all his jumpiness, Priya was able to cope with Washington. I admired this strength in him as much as I admired the richness of his talk. I didn't know how much to believe of his stories, but I liked having to guess about him. I liked having to play with his words in my mind. I liked the mystery of the man. The mystery came from his solidity. I knew where I was with him. After the apartment and the green suit and the *hubshi* woman and the city burning for four days, to be with Priya was to feel safe. For the first time since I had come to Washington I felt safe.

I can't say that I moved in. I simply stayed. I didn't want to go back to the apartment even to collect my belongings. I was afraid that something might happen to keep me a prisoner there. My employer might turn up and demand his five thousand rupees. The *hubshi* woman might claim me for her own; I might be condemned to a life among the *hubshi*. And it wasn't as if I was leaving behind anything of value in the apartment. The green suit I was even happy to forget. But.

Priya paid me forty dollars a week. After what I was getting, three dollars and seventy-five cents, it seemed a lot; and it was more than enough for my needs. I didn't have much temptation to spend, to tell the truth. I knew that my old employer and the *hubshi* woman would be wondering about me in their respective ways and I thought I should keep off the streets for a while. That was no hardship; it was what I was used to in Washington. Besides, my days at the restaurant were pretty full; for the first time in my life I had little leisure.

The restaurant was a success from the start, and Priya was fussy. He was always bursting into the kitchen with one of those big menus in his hand, saying in English, "Prestige job, Santosh, prestige." I didn't mind. I liked to feel I had to do things perfectly; I felt I was earning my freedom. Though I was in hiding, and though I worked every day until midnight, I felt I was much more in charge of myself than I had ever been.

Many of our waiters were Mexicans, but when we put turbans on them they could pass. They came and went, like the Indian staff. I didn't get on with these people. They were frightened and jealous of one another and very treacherous. Their talk amid the biryanis and the pillaus¹ was all of papers and green cards. They were always about to get green cards or they had been cheated out of green cards or they had just got green cards. At first I didn't know what they were talking about. When I understood I was more than depressed.

I understood that because I had escaped from my employer I had made myself illegal in America. At any moment I could be denounced, seized, jailed, deported, disgraced. It was a complication. I had no green card; I didn't know how to set about getting one; and there was no one I could talk to.

I felt burdened by my secrets. Once I had none; now I had so many. I couldn't tell Priya I had no green card. I couldn't tell him I had broken faith with my old employer and dishonoured myself with a *hubshi* woman and lived in fear of retribution. I couldn't tell him that I was afraid to leave the restaurant and that nowadays when I saw an Indian I hid from him as anxiously as the Indian hid from me. I would have felt foolish to confess. With Priya, right from the start, I had pretended to be strong; and I wanted it to remain like that. Instead, when we talked now, and he grew philosophical, I tried to find bigger causes for being sad. My mind fastened on to these causes, and the effect of this was that my sadness became like a sickness of the soul.

It was worse than being in the apartment, because now the responsibility was mine and mine alone. I had decided to be free, to act for myself. It pained me to think of the exhilaration I had felt during the days of the fire; and I felt mocked when I remembered that in the early days of my escape I had thought I was in charge of myself.

The year turned. The snow came and melted. I was more afraid than ever of going out. The sickness was bigger than all the causes. I saw the future as a hole into which I was dropping. Sometimes at night when I awakened my body would burn and I would feel the hot perspiration break all over.

I leaned on Priya. He was my only hope, my only link with what was real. He went out; he brought back stories. He went out especially to eat in the restaurants of our competitors.

He said, "Santosh, I never believed that running a restaurant was a way to God. But it is true. I eat like a scientist. Every day I eat like a scientist. I feel I have already renounced."

This was Priya. This was how his talk ensnared me and gave me the bigger causes that steadily weakened me. I became more and more detached from the men in the kitchen. When they spoke of their green cards and the jobs they were about to get I felt like asking them: Why? Why?

And every day the mirror told its own tale. Without exercise, with the sickening of my heart and my mind, I was losing my looks. My face had become pudgy and sallow and full of spots; it was becoming ugly. I could have cried for that, discovering my good looks only to lose them. It was like a punishment for my presumption, the punishment I had feared when I bought the green suit.

Priya said, "Santosh, you must get some exercise. You are not looking well. Your eyes are getting like mine. What are you pining for? Are you pining for Bombay or your family in the hills?"

But now, even in my mind, I was a stranger in those places.

---

1. "Biryanis" and "pillaus": Indian dishes.

Priya said one Sunday morning, "Santosh, I am going to take you to see a Hindi movie today. All the Indians of Washington will be there, domestics and everybody else."

I was very frightened. I didn't want to go and I couldn't tell him why. He insisted. My heart began to beat fast as soon as I got into the car. Soon there were no more houses with gas-lamps in the entrance, just those long wide burnt-out *hubshi* streets, now with fresh leaves on the trees, heaps of rubble on bulldozed, fenced-in lots, boarded-up shop windows, and old smoke-stained signboards announcing what was no longer true. Cars raced along the wide roads; there was life only on the roads. I thought I would vomit with fear.

I said, "Take me back, *sahib*."

I had used the wrong word. Once I had used the word a hundred times a day. But then I had considered myself a small part of my employer's presence, and the word was not servile; it was more like a name, like a reassuring sound, part of my employer's dignity and therefore part of mine. But Priya's dignity could never be mine; that was not our relationship. Priya I had always called Priya; it was his wish, the American way, man to man. With Priya the word was servile. And he responded to the word. He did as I asked; he drove me back to the restaurant. I never called him by his name again.

I was good-looking; I had lost my looks. I was a free man; I had lost my freedom.

One of the Mexican waiters came into the kitchen late one evening and said, "There is a man outside who wants to see the chef."

No one had made this request before, and Priya was at once agitated. "Is he an American? Some enemy has sent him here. Sanitary-anitary, health-ealth, they can inspect my kitchens at any time."

"He is an Indian," the Mexican said.

I was alarmed. I thought it was my old employer; that quiet approach was like him. Priya thought it was a rival. Though Priya regularly ate in the restaurants of his rivals he thought it unfair when they came to eat in his. We both went to the door and peeked through the glass window into the dimly lit dining-room.

"Do you know that person, Santosh?"

"Yes, sahib."

It wasn't my old employer. It was one of his Bombay friends, a big man in Government, whom I had often served in the chambers. He was by himself and seemed to have just arrived in Washington. He had a new Bombay haircut, very close, and a stiff dark suit, Bombay tailoring. His shirt looked blue, but in the dim multi-coloured light of the dining-room everything white looked blue. He didn't look unhappy with what he had eaten. Both his elbows were on the curry-spotted tablecloth and he was picking his teeth, half closing his eyes and hiding his mouth with his cupped left hand.

"I don't like him," Priya said. "Still, big man in Government and so on. You must go to him, Santosh."

But I couldn't go.

"Put on your apron, Santosh. And that chef's cap. Prestige. You must go, Santosh."

Priya went out to the dining-room and I heard him say in English that I was coming.

I ran up to my room, put some oil on my hair, combed my hair, put on my best pants and shirt and my shining shoes. It was so, as a man about town rather than as a cook, I went to the dining-room.

The man from Bombay was as astonished as Priya. We exchanged the old courtesies, and I waited. But, to my relief, there seemed little more to say. No difficult questions were put to me; I was grateful to the man from Bombay for his tact. I avoided talk as much as possible. I smiled. The man from Bombay smiled back. Priya smiled uneasily at both of us. So for a while we were, smiling in the dim blue-red light and waiting.

The man from Bombay said to Priya, "Brother, I just have a few words to say to my old friend Santosh."

Priya didn't like it, but he left us.

I waited for those words. But they were not the words I feared. The man from Bombay didn't speak of my old employer. We continued to exchange courtesies. Yes, I was well and he was well and everybody else we knew was well; and I was doing well and he was doing well. That was all. Then, secretively, the man from Bombay gave me a dollar. A dollar, ten rupees, an enormous tip for Bombay. But, from him, much more than a tip: an act of graciousness, part of the sweetness of the old days. Once it would have meant so much to me. Now it meant so little. I was saddened and embarrassed. And I had been anticipating hostility!

Priya was waiting behind the kitchen door. His little face was tight and serious, and I knew he had seen the money pass. Now, quickly, he read my own face, and without saying anything to me he hurried out into the dining-room.

I heard him say in English to the man from Bombay, "Santosh is a good fellow. He's got his own room with bath and everything. I am giving him a hundred dollars a week from next week. A thousand rupees a week. This is a first-class establishment."

A thousand chips a week! I was staggered. It was much more than any man in Government got, and I was sure the man from Bombay was also staggered, and perhaps regretting his good gesture and that precious dollar of foreign exchange.

"Santosh," Priya said, when the restaurant closed that evening, "that man was an enemy. I knew it from the moment I saw him. And because he was an enemy I did something very bad, Santosh."

"Sahib."

"I lied, Santosh. To protect you. I told him, Santosh, that I was going to give you seventy-five dollars a week after Christmas."

"Sahib."

"And now I have to make that lie true. But, Santosh, you know that is money we can't afford. I don't have to tell you about overheads and things like that. Santosh, I will give you sixty."

I said, "Sahib, I couldn't stay on for less than a hundred and twenty-five."

Priya's eyes went shiny and the hollows below his eyes darkened. He giggled and pressed out his lips. At the end of that week I got a hundred dollars. And Priya, good man that he was, bore me no grudge.

Now here was a victory. It was only after it happened that I realized how badly I had needed such a victory, how far, gaining my freedom, I had begun to accept death not as the end but as the goal. I revived. Or rather, my senses revived. But in this city what was there to feed my senses? There were no walks to be taken, no idle conversations with understanding friends. I could buy new clothes. But then? Would I just look at myself in the mirror? Would I go walking, inviting passers-by to look at me and my clothes? No, the whole business of clothes and dressing up only threw me back into myself.

There was a Swiss or German woman in the cake-shop some doors away, and there was a Filipino woman in the kitchen. They were neither of them attractive, to tell the truth. The Swiss or German could have broken my back with a slap, and the Filipino, though young, was remarkably like one of our older hill women. Still, I felt I owed something to the senses, and I thought I might frolic with these women. But then I was frightened of the responsibility. Goodness, I had learned that a woman is not just a roll and a frolic but a big creature weighing a hundred-and-so-many pounds who is going to be around afterwards.

So the moment of victory passed, without celebration. And it was strange, I thought, that sorrow lasts and can make a man look forward to death, but the mood of victory fills a moment and then is over. When my moment of victory was over I discovered below it, as if waiting for me, all my old sickness and fears: fear of my illegality, my former employer, my presumption, the *hubshi* woman. I saw then that the victory I had had was not something I had worked for, but luck; and that luck was only fate's cheating, giving an illusion of power.

But that illusion lingered, and I became restless. I decided to act, to challenge fate. I decided I would no longer stay in my room and hide. I began to go out walking in the afternoons. I gained courage; every afternoon I walked a little farther. It became my ambition to walk to that green circle with the fountain where, on my first day out in Washington, I had come upon those people in Hindu costumes, like domestics abandoned a long time ago, singing their Sanskrit gibberish and doing their strange Red Indian dance. And one day I got there.

One day I crossed the road to the circle and sat down on a bench. The *hubshi* were there, and the bare feet, and the dancers in saris and the saffron robes. It was mid-afternoon, very hot, and no one was active. I remembered how magical and inexplicable that circle had seemed to me the first time I saw it. Now it seemed so ordinary and tired: the roads, the motor cars, the shops, the trees, the careful policemen: so much part of the waste and futility that was our world. There was no longer a mystery. I felt I knew where everybody had come from and where those cars were going. But I also felt that everybody there felt like me, and that was soothing. I took to going to the circle every day after the lunch rush and sitting until it was time to go back to Priya's for the dinners.

Late one afternoon, among the dancers and the musicians, the *hubshi* and the bare feet, the singers and the police, I saw her. The *hubshi* woman. And again I wondered at her size; my memory had not exaggerated. I decided to stay where I was. She saw me and smiled. Then, as if remembering anger, she gave me a look of great hatred; and again I saw her as Kali, many-armed, goddess of death and destruction. She looked hard at my face; she considered my clothes. I thought: is it for this I bought these clothes? She got up. She was very big and her tight pants made her much more appalling. She moved towards me. I got up and ran. I ran across the road and then, not looking back, hurried by devious ways to the restaurant.

Priya was doing his accounts. He always looked older when he was doing his accounts, not worried, just older, like a man to whom life could bring no further surprises. I envied him.

"Santosh, some friend brought a parcel for you."

It was a big parcel wrapped in brown paper. He handed it to me, and I thought how calm he was, with his bills and pieces of paper, and the pen with which he made his neat figures, and the book in which he would write every day until that book was exhausted and he would begin a new one.

I took the parcel up to my room and opened it. Inside there was a cardboard box; and inside that, still in its tissue paper, was the green suit.

I felt a hole in my stomach. I couldn't think. I was glad I had to go down almost immediately to the kitchen, glad to be busy until midnight. But then I had to go up to my room again, and I was alone. I hadn't escaped; I had never been free. I had been abandoned. I was like nothing; I had made myself nothing. And I couldn't turn back.

In the morning Priya said, "You don't look very well, Santosh."

His concern weakened me further. He was the only man I could talk to and I didn't know what I could say to him. I felt tears coming to my eyes. At that moment I would have liked the whole world to be reduced to tears. I said, "Sahib, I cannot stay with you any longer."

They were just words, part of my mood, part of my wish for tears and relief. But Priya didn't soften. He didn't even look surprised. "Where will you go, Santosh?"

How could I answer his serious question?

"Will it be different where you go?"

He had freed himself of me. I could no longer think of tears. I said, "Sahib, I have enemies."

He giggled. "You are a joker, Santosh. How can a man like yourself have enemies? There would be no profit in it. *I* have enemies. It is part of your happiness and part of the equity of the world that you cannot have enemies. That's why you can run-run-runaway." He smiled and made the running gesture with his extended palm.

So, at last, I told him my story. I told him about my old employer and my escape and the green suit. He made me feel I was telling him nothing he hadn't already known. I told him about the *hubshi* woman. I was hoping for some rebuke. A rebuke would have meant that he was concerned for my honour, that I could lean on him, that rescue was possible.

But he said, "Santosh, you have no problems. Marry the *hubshi*. That will automatically make you a citizen. Then you will be a free man."

It wasn't what I was expecting. He was asking me to be alone forever. I said, "Sahib, I have a wife and children in the hills at home."

"But this is your home, Santosh. Wife and children in the hills, that is very nice and that is always there. But that is over. You have to do what is best for you here. You are alone here. *Hubshi-ubshi*, nobody worries about that here, if that is your choice. This isn't Bombay. Nobody looks at you when you walk down the street. Nobody cares what you do."

He was right. I was a free man; I could do anything I wanted. I could, if it were possible for me to turn back, go to the apartment and beg my old employer for forgiveness. I could, if it were possible for me to become again what I once was, go to the police and say, "I am an illegal immigrant here. Please deport me to Bombay." I could run away, hang myself, surrender, confess, hide. It didn't matter what I did, because I was alone. And I didn't know what I wanted to do. It was like the time when I felt my senses revive and I wanted to go out and enjoy and I found there was nothing to enjoy.

To be empty is not to be sad. To be empty is to be calm. It is to renounce. Priya said no more to me; he was always busy in the mornings. I left him and went up to my room. It was still a bare room, still like a room that in half an hour could be someone else's. I had never thought of it as mine. I was frightened of its spotless painted walls and had been careful to keep them spotless. For just such a moment.

I tried to think of the particular moment in my life, the particular action, that had brought me to that room. Was it the moment with the *hubshi* woman, or was it when the American came to dinner and insulted my employer? Was it the moment of my escape, my sight of Priya in the gallery, or was it when I looked in the mirror and bought the green suit? Or was it much earlier, in that other life, in Bombay, in the hills? I could find no one moment; every moment seemed important. An endless chain of action had brought me to that room. It was frightening; it was burdensome. It was not a time for new decisions. It was time to call a halt.

I lay on the bed watching the ceiling, watching the sky. The door was pushed open. It was Priya.

"My goodness, Santosh! How long have you been here? You have been so quiet I forgot about you."

He looked about the room. He went into the bathroom and came out again.

"Are you all right, Santosh?"

He sat on the edge of the bed and the longer he stayed the more I realized how glad I was to see him. There was this: when I tried to think of him rushing into the room I couldn't place it in time; it seemed to have occurred only in my mind. He sat with me. Time became real again. I felt a great love for him. Soon I could have laughed at his agitation. And later, indeed, we laughed together.

I said, "Sahib, you must excuse me this morning. I want to go for a walk. I will come back about tea time."

He looked hard at me, and we both knew I had spoken truly.

"Yes, yes, Santosh. You go for a good long walk. Make yourself hungry with walking. You will feel much better."

Walking, through streets that were now so simple to me, I thought how nice it would be if the people in Hindu costumes in the circle were real. Then I might have joined them. We would have taken to the road; at midday we would have halted in the shade of big trees; in the late afternoon the sinking sun would have turned the dust clouds to gold; and every evening at some village there would have been welcome, water, food, a fire in the night. But that was a dream of another life. I had watched the people in the circle long enough to know that they were of their city; that their television life awaited them; that their renunciation was not like mine. No television life awaited me. It didn't matter. In this city I was alone and it didn't matter what I did.

As magical as the circle with the fountain the apartment block had once been to me. Now I saw that it was plain, not very tall, and faced with small white tiles. A glass door; four tiled steps down; the desk to the right, letters and keys in the pigeonholes; a carpet to the left, upholstered chairs, a low table with paper flowers in the vase; the blue door of the swift, silent elevator. I saw the simplicity of all these things. I knew the floor I wanted. In the corridor, with its illuminated star-decorated ceiling, an imitation sky, the colours were blue, grey and gold. I knew the door I wanted. I knocked.

The *hubshi* woman opened. I saw the apartment where she worked. I had never seen it before and was expecting something like my old employer's apartment, which was on the same floor. Instead, for the first time, I saw something arranged for a television life.

I thought she might have been angry. She looked only puzzled. I was grateful for that.

I said to her in English, "Will you marry me?"

And there, it was done.

"It is for the best, Santosh," Priya said, giving me tea when I got back to the restaurant. "You will be a free man. A citizen. You will have the whole world before you."

I was pleased that he was pleased.

So I am now a citizen, my presence is legal, and I live in Washington. I am still with Priya. We do not talk together as much as we did. The restaurant is one world, the parks and green streets of Washington are another, and every evening some of these streets take me to a third. Burnt-out brick houses, broken fences, overgrown gardens; in a levelled lot between the high brick walls of two houses, a sort of artistic children's playground which the *hubshi* children never use; and then the dark house in which I now live.

Its smells are strange, everything in it is strange. But my strength in this house is that I am a stranger. I have closed my mind and heart to the English language, to newspapers and radio and television, to the pictures of *hubshi* runners and boxers and musicians on the wall. I do not want to understand or learn any more.

I am a simple man who decided to act and see for himself, and it is as though I have had several lives. I do not wish to add to these. Some afternoons I walk to the circle with the fountain. I see the dancers but they are separated from me as by glass. Once, when there were rumours of new burnings, someone scrawled in white paint on the pavement outside my house: *Soul Brother.* I understand the words; but I feel, brother to what or to whom? I was once part of the flow, never thinking of myself as a presence. Then I looked in the mirror and decided to be free. All that my freedom has brought me is the knowledge that I have a face and have a body, that I must feed this body and clothe this body for a certain number of years. Then it will be over.

1971

TOM STOPPARD
b. 1937

Tom Stoppard was born Tomas Straussler in the former Czechoslovakia. His family emigrated to Singapore in 1939 to escape the Nazis and moved to India in 1941 to escape the Japanese. His father stayed behind and was killed in the invasion of Singapore. Tom and his mother went to England in 1946; on her remarriage he took his stepfather's name of Stoppard. After leaving Pocklington School in Yorkshire at seventeen, he became a journalist, wrote a novel, and in 1962 had two short plays broadcast on the radio. The British theater had been dominated for a decade by realistic "kitchen sink" dramas when Stoppard's *Rosencrantz and Guildenstern Are Dead* (1966) appeared and was hailed as a major theatrical event. Critics recognized a debt to *Waiting for Godot*, but where Samuel Beckett had focused on the hopelessness of his two abandoned characters, Stoppard celebrates the gaiety and perverse vitality that can be generated from despair.

He frequently uses plays by other playwrights as launching pads for his own: Rosencrantz and Guildenstern step out of the shadows of Shakespeare's *Hamlet*; *The Real Inspector Hound* (1968) parodies Agatha Christie's classic country-house murder-mystery play, *The Mousetrap*; and the plot of *Travesties* (1974) is entwined with that of Oscar Wilde's *The Importance of Being Earnest*. Past and present are again entwined, though not intertextually, in his masterpiece, *Arcadia* (1993), which explores the nature of Nature, classical and Romantic theories of landscape gardening, literary history and historians, truth and time. As is appropriate for a play with a double time frame (early nineteenth century spliced with late twentieth century), *Arcadia* has the intricate movement of a grandfather clock, its characters and their concerns interacting with finely geared precision. Appropriately again, the classical mechanism is driven by a Romantic power source: sex—"the attraction which Newton left out."

Newton's classical mechanics posited an order underlying a seemingly disordered world. He saw its "laws" operating via cause-and-effect mechanisms, leading to determinism: given adequate information, one could predict future events. His near-contemporary, however, the wittily named heroine of Stoppard's play, Thomasina [*Tom 'as seen a*] Coverly, has seen another future, one ordered by disorder, what is now known as "chaos theory." (Stoppard found the seed of his play in James Gleick's *Chaos: The Making of a New Science*.) The opposition of order and disorder, past and future (our present), provides the structuring principle of *Arcadia*.

Its action takes place in a large room in a large English country house. Here in 1809 Thomasina, a mathematically and scientifically precocious thirteen-year-old, is being tutored by Septimus, whose friend the poet Lord Byron visits long enough to shoot a hare and, perhaps, another visiting poet, Ezra Chater, in a duel. The opposition of science and poetry is repeated, more than a century and a half later, in the second scene and the same room, when a twentieth-century member of the Coverly family, Valentine, a graduate student "chaotician," tells a visiting literary biographer and theoretician, Hannah Jarvis, about his researches in the new science. The analytically inclined Hannah and a rival, romantically inclined literary critic, Bernard Nightingale, are each embarked on a quest for the truth of Byron's role (if any) in the death of Ezra Chater.

The five principal characters of *Arcadia* are, thus, each engaged in the quest for knowledge. While truth, the whole truth scientific and humanistic, eludes the questers, the interwoven themes of the play reach their resolution in a final scene of astonishing technical virtuosity. After three scenes set in the past and three in the present, the seventh and longest brings past and present—the Romantic age and the postmodern—together. Characters from both periods are on stage simultaneously, all wearing Regency costume (the modern ones for a fancy-dress ball). The scene is at once "chaotic" and supremely ordered, ending—like so many Renaissance and later comedies—with a dance. Here, on the verge of tragedy, humanist and mathematician/scientist from each period join hands and start to waltz. As the Russian Yevgeny Yevtushenko put it in a war poem called "Weddings," even on the verge of tragedy, "you can't not dance."

Stoppard's late plays include *Indian Ink* (1993); *The Invention of Love* (1997), which brings together in one galaxy A. E. Housman, Oscar Wilde, and a sparkling constellation of Victorian worthies; *The Coast of Utopia* (2002), an epic trilogy that follows the trajectory of romantics and revolutionaries in the twilight of Czarist Russia; *Rock 'n' Roll* (2006), which explores the importance of rock music for the democratic resistance in communist Czechoslovakia; and *The Hard Problem* (2015), about the problem of consciousness. Stoppard shared an Oscar for the screenplay of *Shakespeare in Love* (1998) and has also written for radio and television, alternating—sometimes in the same work—between a serious handling of political themes and arabesques of exuberant fantasy. As he says: "I never quite know whether I want to be a serious artist or a siren." He has succeeded in being both, often—as in *Arcadia*—at the same time.

Stoppard was knighted in 1997 and three years later was appointed a member of the Order of Merit.

Arcadia[1]

CHARACTERS (IN ORDER OF APPEARANCE)

THOMASINA COVERLY, *aged thirteen, later sixteen*

SEPTIMUS HODGE, *her tutor, aged twenty-two, later twenty-five*

JELLABY, *a butler, middle-aged*

EZRA CHATER, *a poet, aged thirty-one*

RICHARD NOAKES, *a landscape architect, middle-aged*

LADY CROOM, *middle thirties*

CAPT. BRICE, RN,[2] *middle thirties*

HANNAH JARVIS, *an author, late thirties*

CHLOË COVERLY, *aged eighteen*

BERNARD NIGHTINGALE, *a don,[3] late thirties*

VALENTINE COVERLY, *aged twenty-five to thirty*

GUS COVERLY, *aged fifteen*

AUGUSTUS COVERLY, *aged fifteen*

Act One

SCENE ONE

A room on the garden front of a very large country house in Derbyshire in April 1809. Nowadays, the house would be called a stately home. The upstage wall is mainly tall, shapely, uncurtained windows, one or more of which work as doors. Nothing much need be said or seen of the exterior beyond. We come to learn that the house stands in the typical English park of the time. Perhaps we see an indication of this, perhaps only light and air and sky.

---

1. A mountainous region of central Peloponnese, Greece; scene of idealized and idyllic country life in the pastoral poetry of ancient Greece, notably that of Theocritus, and Italy, notably that of Vir-

gil; its shepherds are called "Arcades."
2. Royal Navy.
3. University teacher.

The room looks bare despite the large table which occupies the centre of it. The table, the straight-backed chairs and, the only other item of furniture, the architect's stand or reading stand, would all be collectable pieces now but here, on an uncarpeted wood floor, they have no more pretension than a schoolroom, which is indeed the main use of this room at this time. What elegance there is, is architectural, and nothing is impressive but the scale. There is a door in each of the side walls. These are closed, but one of the french windows[4] is open to a bright but sunless morning.

There are two people, each busy with books and paper and pen and ink, separately occupied. The pupil is THOMASINA COVERLY, *aged 13. The tutor is* SEPTIMUS HODGE, *aged 22. Each has an open book. Hers is a slim mathematics primer.[5] His is a handsome thick quarto,[6] brand new, a vanity production,[7] with little tapes to tie when the book is closed. His loose papers, etc, are kept in a stiff-backed portfolio which also ties up with tapes.*

Septimus has a tortoise which is sleepy enough to serve as a paperweight.

Elsewhere on the table there is an old-fashioned theodolite[8] and also some other books stacked up.

THOMASINA Septimus, what is carnal embrace?[9]

SEPTIMUS Carnal embrace is the practice of throwing one's arms around a side of beef.

THOMASINA Is that all?

SEPTIMUS No . . . a shoulder of mutton, a haunch of venison well hugged,[1] an embrace of grouse . . . *caro, carnis,* feminine; flesh.[2]

THOMASINA Is it a sin?

SEPTIMUS Not necessarily, my lady, but when carnal embrace is sinful it is a sin of the flesh, QED.[3] We had *caro* in our Gallic Wars[4]—'The Britons live on milk and meat'—'*lacte et carne vivunt*'. I am sorry that the seed fell on stony ground.[5]

THOMASINA That was the sin of Onan,[6] wasn't it, Septimus?

SEPTIMUS Yes. He was giving his brother's wife a Latin lesson and she was hardly the wiser after it than before. I thought you were finding a proof for Fermat's last theorem.[7]

THOMASINA It is very difficult, Septimus. You will have to show me how.

SEPTIMUS If I knew how, there would be no need to ask *you*. Fermat's last theorem has kept people busy for a hundred and fifty years, and I hoped it would keep *you* busy long enough for me to read Mr Chater's poem in praise of love with only the distraction of its own absurdities.

THOMASINA Our Mr Chater has written a poem?

4. Glass-paneled door in the outside wall of a house, serving as a window and a door.

5. Textbook.

6. Book, larger-than-average size, made from sheets folded over twice.

7. Published at author's expense.

8. Surveyor's measuring instrument, a telescope mounted on a tripod.

9. Sexual intercourse.

1. Wordplay on *well-hung*.

2. I.e., *caro* is the adjective form and *carnis* is the genetive singular form of the feminine-gendered Latin noun meaning "flesh."

3. Initials indicating a problem has been solved: *quod erat demonstrandum* ("as has been demonstrated," Latin).

4. Julius Caesar's history of his wars in Gaul (France), *De Bello Gallico.*

5. Cf. Matthew 13.3–8: Christ's parable of the sower who "went forth to sow."

6. Cf. Genesis 38.9. Thomasina mischievously confuses the sower's seed with the semen Onan "spilled . . . on the ground" rather than impregnate his brother's wife.

7. Famous problem proposed by the French mathematician Pierre de Fermat (1601–1665) and described by Septimus on p. 1024. See also p. 1026. Often held to be unprovable, Fermat's last theorem was proved by Professor Andrew Wiles a few months after *Arcadia* was first performed.

SEPTIMUS   He believes he has written a poem, yes. I can see that there might be more carnality in your algebra than in Mr Chater's 'Couch of Eros'.[8]

THOMASINA   Oh, it was not my algebra. I heard Jellaby telling cook that Mrs Chater was discovered in carnal embrace in the gazebo.

SEPTIMUS   [Pause]   Really? With whom, did Jellaby happen to say?
    [THOMASINA considers this with a puzzled frown.]

THOMASINA   What do you mean, with whom?

SEPTIMUS   With what? Exactly so. The idea is absurd. Where did this story come from?

THOMASINA   Mr Noakes.

SEPTIMUS   Mr Noakes!

THOMASINA   Papa's landskip[9] architect. He was taking bearings in the garden when he saw—through his spyglass—Mrs Chater in the gazebo in carnal embrace.

SEPTIMUS   And do you mean to tell me that Mr Noakes told the butler?

THOMASINA   No. Mr Noakes told Mr Chater. *Jellaby* was told by the groom, who overheard Mr Noakes telling Mr Chater, in the stable yard.

SEPTIMUS   Mr Chater being engaged in closing the stable door.[1]

THOMASINA   What do you mean, Septimus?

SEPTIMUS   So, thus far, the only people who know about this are Mr Noakes the landskip architect, the groom, the butler, the cook and, of course, Mrs Chater's husband, the poet.

THOMASINA   And Arthur who was cleaning the silver, and the bootboy. And now you.

SEPTIMUS   Of course. What else did he say?

THOMASINA   Mr Noakes?

SEPTIMUS   No, not Mr Noakes. Jellaby. You heard Jellaby telling the cook.

THOMASINA   Cook hushed him almost as soon as he started. Jellaby did not see that I was being allowed to finish yesterday's upstairs'[2] rabbit pie before I came to my lesson. I think you have not been candid with me, Septimus. A gazebo is not, after all, a meat larder.

SEPTIMUS   I never said my definition was complete.

THOMASINA   Is carnal embrace kissing?

SEPTIMUS   Yes.

THOMASINA   And throwing one's arms around Mrs Chater?

SEPTIMUS   Yes. Now, Fermat's last theorem—

THOMASINA   I thought as much. I hope you are ashamed.

SEPTIMUS   I, my lady?

THOMASINA   If *you* do not teach me the true meaning of things, who will?

SEPTIMUS   Ah. Yes, I am ashamed. Carnal embrace is sexual congress, which is the insertion of the male genital organ into the female genital organ for purposes of procreation and pleasure. Fermat's last theorem, by contrast, asserts that when x, y and z are whole numbers each raised to power of n, the sum of the first two can never equal the third when n is greater than 2.
    [Pause.]

8. Greek god of love.
9. Landscape.
1. Proverbial saying that continues "after the horse has bolted."

2. As prepared for Lord and Lady Croom and their guests ("upstairs," as distinct from the servants "below stairs").

THOMASINA Eurghhh!

SEPTIMUS Nevertheless, that is the theorem.

THOMASINA It is disgusting and incomprehensible. Now when I am grown to practise it myself I shall never do so without thinking of you.

SEPTIMUS Thank you very much, my lady. Was Mrs Chater down this morning?

THOMASINA No. Tell me more about sexual congress.

SEPTIMUS There is nothing more to be said about sexual congress.

THOMASINA Is it the same as love?

SEPTIMUS Oh no, it is much nicer than that.

[*One of the side doors leads to the music room. It is the other side door which now opens to admit* JELLABY, *the butler.*]

I am teaching, Jellaby.

JELLABY Beg your pardon, Mr Hodge, Mr Chater said it was urgent you receive his letter.

SEPTIMUS Oh, very well. [SEPTIMUS *takes the letter.*] Thank you. [*And to dismiss* JELLABY.] Thank you.

JELLABY [*Holding his ground.*] Mr Chater asked me to bring him your answer.

SEPTIMUS My answer?

[*He opens the letter. There is no envelope as such, but there is a 'cover' which, folded and sealed, does the same service.*

SEPTIMUS *tosses the cover negligently aside and reads.*]

Well, my answer is that as is my custom and my duty to his lordship I am engaged until a quarter to twelve in the education of his daughter. When I am done, and if Mr Chater is still there, I will be happy to wait upon him in—[*He checks the letter.*]—in the gunroom.

JELLABY I will tell him so, thank you, sir.

[SEPTIMUS *folds the letter and places it between the pages of 'The Couch of Eros'.*]

THOMASINA What is for dinner, Jellaby?

JELLABY Boiled ham and cabbages, my lady, and a rice pudding.

THOMASINA Oh, goody.

[JELLABY *leaves.*]

SEPTIMUS Well, so much for Mr Noakes. He puts himself forward as a gentleman, a philosopher of the picturesque,[3] a visionary who can move mountains and cause lakes, but in the scheme of the garden he is as the serpent.[4]

THOMASINA When you stir your rice pudding, Septimus, the spoonful of jam spreads itself round making red trails like the picture of a meteor in my astronomical atlas. But if you stir backward, the jam will not come together again. Indeed, the pudding does not notice and continues to turn pink just as before. Do you think this is odd?

SEPTIMUS No.

THOMASINA Well, I do. You cannot stir things apart.

SEPTIMUS No more you can, time must needs run backward, and since it will not, we must stir our way onward mixing as we go, disorder out of disorder into disorder until pink is complete, unchanging and unchangeable,

3. Italianate landscape associated with the writers and landscape gardeners of the early-nineteenth-century Romantic movement.
4. Noakes spies on and spoils the happiness of the lovers in the gazebo, as the serpent in the Garden of Eden poisoned the bliss of Adam and Eve (Genesis 3).

and we are done with it for ever.[5] This is known as free will or self-determination.

> [*He picks up the tortoise and moves it a few inches as though it had strayed, on top of some loose papers, and admonishes it.*]

Sit!

THOMASINA Septimus, do you think God is a Newtonian?[6]

SEPTIMUS An Etonian?[7] Almost certainly, I'm afraid. We must ask your brother to make it his first enquiry.

THOMASINA No, Septimus, a Newtonian. Septimus! Am I the first person to have thought of this?

SEPTIMUS No.

THOMASINA I have not said yet.

SEPTIMUS 'If everything from the furthest planet to the smallest atom of our brain acts according to Newton's law of motion, what becomes of free will?'

THOMASINA No.

SEPTIMUS God's will.

THOMASINA No.

SEPTIMUS Sin.

THOMASINA [*Derisively.*] No!

SEPTIMUS Very well.

THOMASINA If you could stop every atom in its position and direction, and if your mind could comprehend all the actions thus suspended, then if you were really, *really* good at algebra you could write the formula for all the future; and although nobody can be so clever to do it, the formula must exist just as if one could.

SEPTIMUS [*Pause.*] Yes. [*Pause.*] Yes, as far as I know, you are the first person to have thought of this. [*Pause. With an effort.*] In the margin of his copy of *Arithmetica*, Fermat wrote that he had discovered a wonderful proof of his theorem but, the margin being too narrow for his purpose, did not have room to write it down. The note was found after his death, and from that day to this—

THOMASINA Oh! I see now! The answer is perfectly obvious.

SEPTIMUS This time you may have overreached yourself.

> [*The door is opened, somewhat violently.* CHATER *enters.*] Mr Chater! Perhaps my message miscarried. I will be at liberty at a quarter to twelve, if that is convenient.

CHATER It is not convenient, sir. My business will not wait.

SEPTIMUS Then I suppose you have Lord Croom's opinion that your business is more important than his daughter's lesson.

CHATER I do not, but, if you like, I will ask his lordship to settle the point.

SEPTIMUS [*Pause.*] My lady, take Fermat into the music room. There will be an extra spoonful of jam if you find his proof.

THOMASINA There is no proof, Septimus. The thing that is perfectly obvious is that the note in the margin was a joke to make you all mad.

> [THOMASINA *leaves.*]

---

5. Evidence offered, with no awareness of its significance, of the then-undiscovered second law of thermodynamics.
6. Believer in the scientific theories of Isaac Newton (1642–1727).
7. Alumnus of the famous English public (i.e., in the United States, private) school, Eton, which Thomasina's brother Augustus will later attend.

SEPTIMUS Now, sir, what is this business that cannot wait?

CHATER I think you know it, sir. You have insulted my wife.

SEPTIMUS Insulted her? That would deny my nature, my conduct, and the admiration in which I hold Mrs Chater.

CHATER I have heard of your admiration, sir! You insulted my wife in the gazebo yesterday evening!

SEPTIMUS You are mistaken. I made love to your wife in the gazebo. She asked me to meet her there, I have her note somewhere, I dare say I could find it for you, and if someone is putting it about that I did not turn up, by God, sir, it is a slander.

CHATER You damned lecher! You would drag down a lady's reputation to make a refuge for your cowardice. It will not do! I am calling you out![8]

SEPTIMUS Chater! Chater, Chater, Chater! My dear friend!

CHATER You dare to call me that. I demand satisfaction!

SEPTIMUS Mrs Chater demanded satisfaction and now you are demanding satisfaction. I cannot spend my time day and night satisfying the demands of the Chater family. As for your wife's reputation, it stands where it ever stood.

CHATER You blackguard!

SEPTIMUS I assure you. Mrs Chater is charming and spirited, with a pleasing voice and a dainty step, she is the epitome of all the qualities society applauds in her sex—and yet her chief renown is for a readiness that keeps her in a state of tropical humidity as would grow orchids in her drawers in January.

CHATER Damn you, Hodge, I will not listen to this! Will you fight or not?

SEPTIMUS [Definitively.] Not! There are no more than two or three poets of the first rank now living, and I will not shoot one of them dead over a perpendicular poke in a gazebo with a woman whose reputation could not be adequately defended with a platoon of musketry deployed by rota.

CHATER Ha! You say so! Who are the others? In your opinion?—no— no—!—this goes very ill, Hodge. I will not be flattered out of my course. You say so, do you?

SEPTIMUS I do. And I would say the same to Milton[9] were he not already dead. Not the part about his wife, of course—

CHATER But among the living? Mr Southey?[1]

SEPTIMUS Southey I would have shot on sight.

CHATER [Shaking his head sadly.] Yes, he has fallen off. I admired 'Thalaba' quite, but 'Madoc', [He chuckles.] oh dear me!—but we are straying from the business here—you took advantage of Mrs Chater, and if that were not bad enough, it appears every stableboy and scullery maid on the strength—

SEPTIMUS Damn me! Have you not listened to a word I said?

CHATER I have heard you, sir, and I will not deny I welcome your regard, God knows one is little appreciated if one stands outside the coterie of hacks and placemen[2] who surround Jeffrey and the Edinburgh—[3]

8. Challenging you to a duel.
9. John Milton (1608–1674), English poet.
1. Robert Southey (1774–1843), English poet, author of the long poems Thalaba and Madoc.
2. Clique of those who write only for money or social advantage.
3. Frances Lord Jeffrey (1773–1850), cofounder and editor of the Edinburgh Review (1802–29), was a stern but generally perceptive literary critic.

SEPTIMUS   My dear Chater, they judge a poet by the seating plan of Lord Holland's table![4]

CHATER   By heaven, you are right! And I would very much like to know the name of the scoundrel who slandered my verse drama 'Maid of Turkey' in the *Piccadilly Recreation*, too!

SEPTIMUS   'The Maid of Turkey'! I have it by my bedside! When I cannot sleep I take up 'The Maid of Turkey' like an old friend!

CHATER   [*Gratified.*]   There you are! And the scoundrel wrote he would not give it to his dog for dinner were it covered in bread sauce and stuffed with chestnuts. When Mrs Chater read that, she wept, sir, and would not give herself to me for a fortnight—which recalls me to my purpose—

SEPTIMUS   The new poem, however, will make your name perpetual—

CHATER   Whether it do or not—

SEPTIMUS   It is not a question, sir. No coterie can oppose the acclamation of the reading public. 'The Couch of Eros' will take the town.

CHATER   Is that your estimation?

SEPTIMUS   It is my intent.

CHATER   Is it, is it? Well, well! I do not understand you.

SEPTIMUS   You see I have an early copy—sent to me for review. I say review, but I speak of an extensive appreciation of your gifts and your rightful place in English literature.

CHATER   Well, I must say. That is certainly . . . You have written it?

SEPTIMUS   [*Crisply.*]   Not yet.

CHATER   Ah. And how long does . . . ?

SEPTIMUS   To be done right, it first requires a careful re-reading of your book, of both your books, several readings, together with outlying works[5] for an exhibition of deference or disdain as the case merits. I make notes, of course, I order my thoughts, and finally, when all is ready and I am *calm in my mind* . . .

CHATER   [*Shrewdly.*]   Did Mrs Chater know of this before she—before you—

SEPTIMUS   I think she very likely did.

CHATER   [*Triumphantly.*]   There is nothing that woman would not do for me! Now you have an insight to her character. Yes, by God, she is a wife to me, sir!

SEPTIMUS   For that alone, I would not make her a widow.

CHATER   Captain Brice once made the same observation!

SEPTIMUS   Captain Brice did?

CHATER   Mr Hodge, allow me to inscribe your copy in happy anticipation. Lady Thomasina's pen will serve us.

SEPTIMUS   Your connection with Lord and Lady Croom you owe to your fighting her ladyship's brother?

CHATER   No! It was all nonsense, sir—a canard![6] But a fortunate mistake, sir. It brought me the patronage of a captain of His Majesty's Navy and the brother of a countess. I do not think Mr Walter Scott[7] can say as much, and here I am, a respected guest at Sidley Park.

---

4. Henry Richard Vassall Fox, Lord Holland (1773–1840), British politician, exerted considerable influence on literature and politics through the hospitality that Holland House offered the brilliant and distinguished people of his day.

5. Other writers' books.
6. Malicious, false gossip.
7. Best-selling Scottish poet and, later, novelist (1771–1832).

SEPTIMUS Well, sir, you can say you have received satisfaction.

[CHATER *is already inscribing the book, using the pen and ink-pot on the table.* NOAKES *enters through the door used by* CHATER. *He carries rolled-up plans.* CHATER, *inscribing, ignores* NOAKES. NOAKES *on seeing the occupants, panics.*]

NOAKES Oh!

SEPTIMUS Ah, Mr Noakes—my muddy-mettled[8] rascal! Where's your spyglass?

NOAKES I beg your leave—I thought her ladyship—excuse me—

[*He is beating an embarrassed retreat when he becomes rooted by* CHATER'S *voice.* CHATER *reads his inscription in ringing tones.*]

CHATER 'To my friend Septimus Hodge, who stood up[9] and gave his best on behalf of the Author—Ezra Chater, at Sidley Park, Derbyshire, April 10th, 1809.' [*Giving the book to* SEPTIMUS.] There, sir—something to show your grandchildren!

SEPTIMUS This is more than I deserve, this is handsome, what do you say, Noakes?

[*They are interrupted by the appearance, outside the windows, of* LADY CROOM *and* CAPTAIN EDWARD BRICE, RN.[1] *Her first words arrive through the open door.*]

LADY CROOM Oh, no! Not the gazebo!

[*She enters, followed by* BRICE *who carries a leatherbound sketch book.*]

Mr Noakes! What is this I hear?

BRICE Not only the gazebo, but the boat-house, the Chinese bridge, the shrubbery—

CHATER By God, sir! Not possible!

BRICE Mr Noakes will have it so.

SEPTIMUS Mr Noakes, this is monstrous!

LADY CROOM I am glad to hear it from *you*, Mr Hodge.

THOMASINA [*Opening the door from the music room.*] May I return now?

SEPTIMUS [*Attempting to close the door.*] Not just yet—

LADY CROOM Yes, let her stay. A lesson in folly is worth two in wisdom.

[BRICE *takes the sketch book to the reading stand, where he lays it open. The sketch book is the work of* MR NOAKES, *who is obviously an admirer of Humphry Repton's 'Red Books'.[2] The pages, drawn in watercolours, show 'before' and 'after' views of the landscape, and the pages are cunningly cut to allow the latter to be superimposed over portions of the former, though Repton did it the other way round.*]

BRICE Is Sidley Park to be an Englishman's garden or the haunt of Corsican brigands?

SEPTIMUS Let us not hyperbolize, sir.

BRICE It is rape, sir!

NOAKES [*Defending himself.*] It is the modern style.

CHATER [*Under the same misapprehension as* SEPTIMUS.] Regrettable, of course, but so it is.

[THOMASINA *has gone to examine the sketch book.*]

---

8. Dirty-minded.
9. Cf. Septimus's "perpendicular poke in a gazebo" (p. 1027).
1. See p. 1022, n. 2.
2. Repton (1752–1818), a landscape architect, presented his designs in so-called Red Books showing "before" and "after" views of his clients' grounds. Noakes is proposing to Gothicize the classical English landscape of Sidley Park.

LADY CROOM   Mr Chater, you show too much submission. Mr Hodge. I appeal to you.
SEPTIMUS   Madam, I regret the gazebo, I sincerely regret the gazebo—and the boat-house up to a point—but the Chinese bridge, fantasy!—and the shrubbery I reject with contempt! Mr Chater!—would you take the word of a jumped-up jobbing gardener[3] who sees carnal embrace in every nook and cranny of the landskip!
THOMASINA   Septimus, they are not speaking of carnal embrace, are you, Mama?
LADY CROOM   Certainly not. What do you know of carnal embrace?
THOMASINA   Everything, thanks to Septimus. In my opinion, Mr Noakes's scheme for the garden is perfect. It is a Salvator![4]
LADY CROOM   What does she mean?
NOAKES [Answering the wrong question.]   Salvator Rosa, your ladyship, the painter. He is indeed the very exemplar of the picturesque style.
BRICE   Hodge, what is this?
SEPTIMUS   She speaks from innocence not from experience.
BRICE   You call it innocence? Has he ruined you, child?
   [Pause.]
SEPTIMUS   Answer your uncle!
THOMASINA [To SEPTIMUS.]   How is a ruined child different from a ruined castle?
SEPTIMUS   On such questions I defer to Mr Noakes.
NOAKES [Out of his depth.]   A ruined castle is picturesque, certainly.
SEPTIMUS   That is the main difference. [To BRICE.] I teach the classical authors. If I do not elucidate their meaning, who will?
BRICE   As her tutor you have a duty to keep her in ignorance.
LADY CROOM   Do not dabble in paradox, Edward, it puts you in danger of fortuitous wit. Thomasina, wait in your bedroom.
THOMASINA [Retiring.]   Yes, mama. I did not intend to get you into trouble, Septimus. I am very sorry for it. It is plain that there are some things a girl is allowed to understand, and these include the whole of algebra, but there are others, such as embracing a side of beef, that must be kept from her until she is old enough to have a carcass of her own.
LADY CROOM   One moment.
BRICE   What is she talking about?
LADY CROOM   Meat.
BRICE   Meat?
LADY CROOM   Thomasina, you had better remain. Your knowledge of the picturesque obviously exceeds anything the rest of us can offer. Mr Hodge, ignorance should be like an empty vessel waiting to be filled at the well of truth—not a cabinet of vulgar curios.[5] Mr Noakes—now at last it is your turn—
NOAKES   Thank you, your ladyship—
LADY CROOM   Your drawing is a very wonderful transformation. I would not have recognized my own garden but for your ingenious book—is it not?—look! Here is the Park as it appears to us now, and here as it

3. Presumptuously conceited odd-job gardener.
4. Salvator Rosa (1615–1673), Italian painter.
5. Strange objects.

might be when Mr Noakes has done with it. Where there is the familiar pastoral refinement of an Englishman's garden, here is an eruption of gloomy forest and towering crag, of ruins where there was never a house, of water dashing against rocks where there was neither spring nor a stone I could not throw the length of a cricket pitch.[6] My hyacinth dell is become a haunt for hobgoblins, my Chinese bridge, which I am assured is superior to the one at Kew,[7] and for all I know at Peking, is usurped by a fallen obelisk overgrown with briars—

NOAKES [*Bleating.*]   Lord Little has one very similar—

LADY CROOM   I cannot relieve Lord Little's misfortunes by adding to my own. Pray, what is this rustic hovel that presumes to superpose itself on my gazebo?

NOAKES   That is the hermitage,[8] madam.

LADY CROOM   I am bewildered.

BRICE   It is all irregular, Mr Noakes.

NOAKES   It is, sir. Irregularity is one of the chiefest principles of the picturesque style—

LADY CROOM   But Sidley Park is already a picture, and a most amiable picture too. The slopes are green and gentle. The trees are companionably grouped at intervals that show them to advantage. The rill[9] is a serpentine ribbon unwound from the lake peaceably contained by meadows on which the right amount of sheep are tastefully arranged—in short, it is nature as God intended, and I can say with the painter, '*Et in Arcadia ego!*'[1] 'Here I am in Arcadia,' Thomasina.

THOMASINA   Yes, mama, if you would have it so.

LADY CROOM   Is she correcting my taste or my translation?

THOMASINA   Neither are beyond correction, mama, but it was your geography caused the doubt.

LADY CROOM   Something has occurred with the girl since I saw her last, and surely that was yesterday. How old are you this morning?

THOMASINA   Thirteen years and ten months, mama.

LADY CROOM   Thirteen years and ten months. She is not due to be pert for six months at the earliest, or to have notions of taste for much longer. Mr Hodge, I hold you accountable. Mr Noakes, back to you—

NOAKES   Thank you, my—

LADY CROOM   You have been reading too many novels by Mrs Radcliffe, that is my opinion. This is a garden for *The Castle of Otranto* or *The Mysteries of Udolpho*—[2]

CHATER   *The Castle of Otranto*, my lady, is by Horace Walpole.

NOAKES [*Thrilled.*]   Mr Walpole the gardener?!

LADY CROOM   Mr Chater, you are a welcome guest at Sidley Park but while you are one, *The Castle of Otranto* was written by whomsoever I say it was, otherwise what is the point of being a guest or having one?

[*The distant popping of guns heard.*]

---

6. Area, twenty-two yards long, between cricketers' "wickets."
7. Site of London's Royal Botanical Gardens.
8. Hermit's residence.
9. Stream.
1. Latin phrase, inscribed on a tomb in a painting by the French artist Nicolas Poussin (1594–1665). Lady Groom translates it more or less

literally, but the speaker is often taken—as Septimus does below—to be Death.
2. Ann Radcliffe (1764–1823) wrote Gothic novels, the most famous of which is *The Mysteries of Udolpho* (1794). Horace Walpole (1717–1797), author of *The Castle of Otranto* (1764), also pioneered the Gothic style of picturesque landscaping.

Well, the guns have reached the brow[3]—I will speak to his lordship on the subject, and we will see by and by—[*She stands looking out.*] Ah!—your friend has got down a pigeon, Mr Hodge. [*Calls out.*] Bravo, sir!

SEPTIMUS   The pigeon, I am sure, fell to your husband or to your son, your ladyship—my schoolfriend was never a sportsman.

BRICE [*Looking out.*]   Yes, to Augustus!—bravo, lad!

LADY CROOM [*Outside.*]   Well, come along! Where are my troops?

[BRICE, NOAKES *and* CHATER *obediently follow her,* CHATER *making a detour to shake* SEPTIMUS's *hand fervently.*]

CHATER   My dear Mr Hodge!

[CHATER *leaves also. The guns are heard again, a little closer.*]

THOMASINA   Pop, pop, pop . . . I have grown up in the sound of guns like the child of a siege. Pigeons and rooks in the close season,[4] grouse on the heights from August, and the pheasants to follow—partridge, snipe, woodcock, and teal—pop—pop—pop, and the culling of the herd. Papa has no need of the recording angel, his life is written in the game book.[5]

SEPTIMUS   A calendar of slaughter. 'Even in Arcadia, there am I!'

THOMASINA   Oh, phooey to Death!

[*She dips a pen and takes it to the reading stand.*]

I will put in a hermit, for what is a hermitage without a hermit? Are you in love with my mother, Septimus?

SEPTIMUS   You must not be cleverer than your elders. It is not polite.

THOMASINA   Am I cleverer?

SEPTIMUS   Yes. Much.

THOMASINA   Well, I am sorry, Septimus. [*She pauses in her drawing and produces a small envelope from her pocket.*] Mrs Chater came to the music room with a note for you. She said it was of scant importance, and that therefore I should carry it to you with the utmost safety, urgency and discretion. Does carnal embrace addle the brain?

SEPTIMUS [*Taking the letter.*]   Invariably. Thank you. That is enough education for today.

THOMASINA   There. I have made him like the Baptist in the wilderness.[6]

SEPTIMUS   How picturesque.

[LADY CROOM *is heard calling distantly for* THOMASINA *who runs off into the garden, cheerfully, an uncomplicated girl.*

SEPTIMUS *opens Mrs Chater's note. He crumples the envelope and throws it away. He reads the note, folds it and inserts it into the pages of* 'The Couch of Eros'.]

SCENE TWO

The lights come up on the same room, on the same sort of morning, in the present day, as is instantly clear from the appearance of HANNAH JARVIS; *and from nothing else.*

Something needs to be said about this. The action of the play shuttles back and forth between the early nineteenth century and the present day, always in this same room. Both periods must share the state of the room, without the additions and subtractions which would normally be expected. The general

---

3. Top of the hill.
4. Closed to hunters.
5. For recording a sportsman's or sportswoman's kill.

6. Thomasina's hermit looks like John the Baptist (cf. Luke 1.4), who lived many years in the desert.

appearance of the room should offend neither period. In the case of props—
books, paper, flowers, etc., there is no absolute need to remove the evidence of
one period to make way for another. However, books, etc., used in both peri-
ods should exist in both old and new versions. The landscape outside, we are
told, has undergone changes. Again, what we see should neither change nor
contradict.

On the above principle, the ink and pens etc., of the first scene can remain.
Books and papers associated with Hannah's research, in Scene Two, can have
been on the table from the beginning of the play. And so on. During the course
of the play the table collects this and that, and where an object from one scene
would be an anachronism in another (say a coffee mug) it is simply deemed to
have become invisible. By the end of the play the table has collected an inven-
tory of objects.

HANNAH *is leafing through the pages of Mr Noakes's sketch book. Also to*
hand, opened and closed, are a number of small volumes like diaries (these
turn out to be Lady Croom's 'garden books'). After a few moments, HANNAH
takes the sketch book to the windows, comparing the view with what has been
drawn, and then she replaces the sketch book on the reading stand.

She wears nothing frivolous. Her shoes are suitable for the garden, which is
where she goes now after picking up the theodolite from the table. The room
is empty for a few moments.

One of the other doors opens to admit CHLOË *and* BERNARD. *She is the*
daughter of the house and is dressed casually. BERNARD, *the visitor, wears a suit*
and a tie. His tendency is to dress flamboyantly, but he has damped it down for
the occasion, slightly. A peacock-coloured display handkerchief boils over in his
breast pocket. He carries a capacious leather bag which serves as a briefcase.

CHLOË   Oh! Well, she *was* here . . .
BERNARD   Ah . . . the french window . . .
CHLOË   Yes. Hang on.
       [CHLOË *steps out through the garden door and disappears from view.*
       BERNARD *hangs on. The second door opens and* VALENTINE *looks in.*]
VALENTINE   Sod.[7]
       [VALENTINE *goes out again, closing the door.* CHLOË *returns, carrying a*
       pair of rubber boots. She comes in and sits down and starts exchanging
       her shoes for the boots, while she talks.]
CHLOË   The best thing is, you wait here, save you tramping around. She
    spends a good deal of time in the garden, as you may imagine.
BERNARD   Yes. Why?
CHLOË   Well, she's writing a history of the garden, didn't you know?
BERNARD   No, I knew she was working on the Croom papers but . . .
CHLOË   Well, it's not exactly a history of the garden either. I'll let Hannah
    explain it. The trench you nearly drove into is all to do with it. I was
    going to say make yourself comfortable but that's hardly possible, every-
    thing's been cleared out, it's en route[8] to the nearest lavatory.
BERNARD   Everything is?
CHLOË   No, this room is. They drew the line at chemical 'Ladies'.[9]
BERNARD   Yes, I see. Did you say Hannah?

---

7. Angry expletive.
8. On the way to.

9. They would not allow portable toilets for women in the garden.

CHLOË   Hannah, yes. Will you be all right?
[*She stands up wearing the boots.*]
I won't be . . . [*But she has lost him.*] Mr Nightingale?

BERNARD   [*Waking up.*]   Yes. Thank you. Miss Jarvis is Hannah Jarvis the author?

CHLOË   Yes. Have you read her book?

BERNARD   Oh, yes. Yes.

CHLOË   I bet she's in the hermitage, can't see from here with the marquee . . . [1]

BERNARD   Are you having a garden party?

CHLOË   A dance for the district, our annual dressing up and general drunkenness. The wrinklies won't have it in the house, there was a teapot we once had to bag back from Christie's[2] in the nick of time, so anything that can be destroyed, stolen or vomited on has been tactfully removed; tactlessly, I should say—
[*She is about to leave.*]

BERNARD   Um—look—would you tell her—would you mind not mentioning my name just yet?

CHLOË   Oh. All right.

BERNARD [*Smiling.*]   More fun to surprise her. Would you mind?

CHLOË   No. But she's bound to ask . . . Should I give you another name, just for the moment?

BERNARD   Yes, why not?

CHLOË   Perhaps another bird, you're not really a Nightingale.
[*She leaves again.* BERNARD *glances over the books on the table. He puts his briefcase down. There is the distant pop-pop of a shotgun. It takes* BERNARD *vaguely to the window. He looks out. The door he entered by now opens and* GUS *looks into the room.* BERNARD *turns and sees him.*]

BERNARD   Hello.
[GUS *doesn't speak. He never speaks. Perhaps he cannot speak. He has no composure, and faced with a stranger, he caves in and leaves again. A moment later the other door opens again and* VALENTINE *crosses the room, not exactly ignoring* BERNARD *and yet ignoring him.*]

VALENTINE   Sod, sod, sod, sod, sod, sod . . . [*As many times as it takes him to leave by the opposite door, which he closes behind him. Beyond it, he can be heard shouting.* Chlo! Chlo! BERNARD's *discomfort increases. The same door opens and* VALENTINE *returns. He looks at* BERNARD.]

BERNARD   She's in the garden looking for Miss Jarvis.

VALENTINE   Where is everything?

BERNARD   It's been removed for the, er . . .

VALENTINE   The dance is all in the tent, isn't it?

BERNARD   Yes, but this is the way to the nearest toilet.

VALENTINE   I need the commode.[3]

BERNARD   Oh. Can't you use the toilet?

VALENTINE   It's got all the game books in it.

BERNARD   Ah. The toilet has or the commode has?

VALENTINE   Is anyone looking after you?

---

1. Large tent.
2. Rescue from Christie's, famous London firm of auctioneers.
3. Lavatory bowl enclosed in a chair or box with a cover.

BERNARD   Yes. Thank you. I'm Bernard Nigh—I've come to see Miss Jarvis. I wrote to Lord Croom but unfortunately I never received a reply, so I—

VALENTINE   Did you type it?

BERNARD   Type it?

VALENTINE   Was your letter typewritten?

BERNARD   Yes.

VALENTINE   My father never replies to typewritten letters.

[*He spots a tortoise which has been half-hidden on the table.*]

Oh! Where have you been hiding, Lightning? [*He picks up the tortoise.*]

BERNARD   So I telephoned yesterday and I think I spoke to you—

VALENTINE   To me? Ah! Yes! Sorry! You're doing a talk about—someone—and you wanted to ask Hannah—something—

BERNARD   Yes. As it turns out. I'm hoping Miss Jarvis will look kindly on me.

VALENTINE   I doubt it.

BERNARD   Ah, you know about research?

VALENTINE   I know Hannah.

BERNARD   Has she been here long?

VALENTINE   Well in possession,[4] I'm afraid. My mother had read her book, you see. Have you?

BERNARD   No. Yes. Her book. Indeed.

VALENTINE   She's terrifically pleased with herself.

BERNARD   Well, I dare say if I wrote a bestseller—

VALENTINE   No, for reading it. My mother basically reads gardening books.

BERNARD   She must be delighted to have Hannah Jarvis writing a book about her garden.

VALENTINE   Actually it's about hermits.

[GUS *returns through the same door, and turns to leave again.*]

It's all right, Gus—what do you want?—

[*But* GUS *has gone again.*]

Well . . . I'll take Lightning for his run.

BERNARD   Actually, we've met before. At Sussex,[5] a couple of years ago, a seminar . . .

VALENTINE   Oh. Was I there?

BERNARD   Yes. One of my colleagues believed he had found an unattributed short story by D. H. Lawrence,[6] and he analysed it on his home computer, most interesting, perhaps you remember the paper?

VALENTINE   Not really. But I often sit with my eyes closed and it doesn't necessarily mean I'm awake.

BERNARD   Well, by comparing sentence structures and so forth, this chap showed that there was a ninety per cent chance that the story had indeed been written by the same person as *Women in Love*. To my inexpressible joy, one of your maths mob was able to show that on the same statistical basis there was a ninety per cent chance that Lawrence also wrote the *Just William* books and much of the previous day's *Brighton and Hove Argus*.[7]

---

4. In a position of power.
5. Sussex University at Brighton.
6. English novelist and short-story writer (1885–1930), author of *Women in Love* (1920).

7. A local newspaper. "*Just William* books": series of "schoolboy" novels by the best-selling children's author Richmal Crompton (1890–1969).

VALENTINE [*Pause.*] Oh, Brighton. Yes. I was there. [*And looking out.*] Oh—here she comes, I'll leave you to talk. By the way, is yours the red Mazda?

BERNARD Yes.

VALENTINE If you want a tip I'd put it out of sight through the stable arch before my father comes in. He won't have anyone in the house with a Japanese car. Are you queer?

BERNARD No, actually.

VALENTINE Well, even so.

[VALENTINE *leaves, closing the door.* BERNARD *keeps staring at the closed door. Behind him,* HANNAH *comes to the garden door.*]

HANNAH Mr Peacock?

[BERNARD *looks round vaguely then checks over his shoulder for the missing Peacock, then recovers himself and turns on the Nightingale bonhomie.*]

BERNARD Oh . . . hello! Hello. Miss Jarvis, of course. Such a pleasure. I was thrown for a moment—the photograph doesn't do you justice.

HANNAH Photograph?

[*Her shoes have got muddy and she is taking them off.*]

BERNARD On the book. I'm sorry to have brought you indoors, but Lady Chloë kindly insisted she—

HANNAH No matter—you would have muddied your shoes.

BERNARD How thoughtful. And how kind of you to spare me a little of your time.

[*He is overdoing it. She shoots him a glance.*]

HANNAH Are you a journalist?

BERNARD [*Shocked.*] No!

HANNAH [*Resuming.*] I've been in the ha-ha,[8] very squelchy.

BERNARD [*Unexpectedly.*] Ha-*hah!*

HANNAH What?

BERNARD A theory of mine. Ha-hah, not ha-ha. If you were strolling down the garden and all of a sudden the ground gave way at your feet, you're not going to go 'ha-ha', you're going to jump back and go 'ha-hah!', or more probably, 'Bloody 'ell!' . . . though personally I think old Murray was up the pole[9] on that one—in France, you know, 'ha-ha' is used to denote a strikingly ugly woman, a much more likely bet for something that keeps the cows off the lawn.

[*This is not going well for* BERNARD *but he seems blithely unaware.* HANNAH *stares at him for a moment.*]

HANNAH Mr Peacock, what can I do for you?

BERNARD Well, to begin with, you can call me Bernard, which is my name.

HANNAH Thank you.

[*She goes to the garden door to bang her shoes together and scrape off the worst of the mud.*]

BERNARD The book!—the book is a revelation! To see Caroline Lamb[1] through your eyes is really like seeing her for the first time. I'm ashamed

8. Ditch with a wall on its inner side below ground level, forming a boundary to a lawn without interrupting the view from the house.
9. James Murray (1837–1915), editor of the original *Oxford English Dictionary*. Bernard thinks him misguided—"up the [greasy] pole" (slang)—in the pronunciation of "ha-ha" recommended in his *OED*.
1. Novelist (1785–1828), best-known as the mistress of Lord Byron (1788–1824).

to say I never read her fiction, and how right you are, it's extraordinary stuff—Early Nineteenth is my period as much as anything is.

HANNAH   You teach?

BERNARD   Yes. And write, like you, like we all, though I've never done anything which has sold like *Caro*.[2]

HANNAH   I don't teach.

BERNARD   No. All the more credit to you. To rehabilitate a forgotten writer, I suppose you could say that's the main reason for an English don.[3]

HANNAH   Not to teach?

BERNARD   Good God, no, let the brats sort it out for themselves. Anyway, many congratulations. I expect someone will be bringing out Caroline Lamb's oeuvre[4] now?

HANNAH   Yes, I expect so.

BERNARD   How wonderful! Bravo! Simply as a document shedding reflected light on the character of Lord Byron, it's bound to be—

HANNAH   Bernard. You did say Bernard, didn't you?

BERNARD   I did.

HANNAH   I'm putting my shoes on again.

BERNARD   Oh. You're not going to go out?

HANNAH   No, I'm going to kick you in the balls.

BERNARD   Right. Point taken. Ezra Chater.

HANNAH   Ezra Chater.

BERNARD   Born Twickenham, Middlesex, 1778, author of two verse narratives, 'The Maid of Turkey', 1808, and 'The Couch of Eros', 1809. Nothing known after 1809, disappears from view.

HANNAH   I see. And?

BERNARD [*Reaching for his bag.*]   There is a Sidley Park connection.
        [*He produces 'The Couch of Eros' from the bag. He reads the inscription.*]

'To my friend Septimus Hodge, who stood up and gave his best on behalf of the Author—Ezra Chater, at Sidley Park, Derbyshire, April 10th, 1809.'
        [*He gives her the book.*]
I am in your hands.

HANNAH   'The Couch of Eros'. Is it any good?

BERNARD   Quite surprising.

HANNAH   You think there's a book in him?

BERNARD   No, no—a monograph perhaps for the *Journal of English Studies*. There's almost nothing on Chater, not a word in the *DNB*,[5] of course—by that time he'd been completely forgotten.

HANNAH   Family?

BERNARD   Zilch. There's only one other Chater in the British Library database.

HANNAH   Same period?

BERNARD   Yes, but he wasn't a poet like our Ezra, he was a botanist who described a dwarf dahlia in Martinique[6] and died there after being bitten by a monkey.

HANNAH   And Ezra Chater?

---

2. Title of Hannah's biography. Cf. p. 1021.
3. See p. 1022, n. 3.
4. A writer's body of work.

5. British *Dictionary of National Biography*.
6. One of the Windward Islands of the Caribbean.

BERNARD   He gets two references in the periodical index, one for each book, in both cases a substantial review in the *Piccadilly Recreation*, a thrice weekly folio sheet, but giving no personal details.

HANNAH   And where was this [*the book*]?

BERNARD   Private collection. I've got a talk to give next week, in London, and I think Chater is interesting, so anything on him, or this Septimus Hodge, Sidley Park, any leads at all . . . I'd be most grateful.
    [*Pause.*]

HANNAH   Well! This is a new experience for me. A grovelling academic.

BERNARD   Oh, I say.

HANNAH   Oh, but it is. All the academics who reviewed my book patronized it.

BERNARD   Surely not.

HANNAH   Surely yes. The Byron gang unzipped their flies and patronized all over it. Where is it you don't bother to teach, by the way?

BERNARD   Oh, well, Sussex, actually.

HANNAH   Sussex. [*She thinks a moment.*] Nightingale. Yes; a thousand words in the *Observer*[7] to see me off the premises with a pat on the bottom. You must know him.

BERNARD   As I say, I'm in your hands.

HANNAH   Quite. Say please, then.

BERNARD   Please.

HANNAH   Sit down, do.

BERNARD   Thank you.
    [*He takes a chair. She remains standing. Possibly she smokes; if so, perhaps now. A short cigarette-holder sounds right, too. Or brown-paper cigarillos.*]

HANNAH   How did you know I was here?

BERNARD   Oh, I didn't. I spoke to the son on the phone but he didn't mention you by name . . . and then he forgot to mention me.

HANNAH   Valentine. He's at Oxford,[8] technically.

BERNARD   Yes, I met him. Brideshead Regurgitated.[9]

HANNAH   My fiancé.
    [*She holds his look.*]

BERNARD [*Pause.*]   I'll take a chance. You're lying.

HANNAH [*Pause*]   Well done, Bernard.

BERNARD   Christ.

HANNAH   He calls me his fiancée.

BERNARD   Why?

HANNAH   It's a joke.

BERNARD   You turned him down?

HANNAH   Don't be silly, do I look like the next Countess of—

BERNARD   No, no—a freebie. The joke that consoles. My tortoise Lightning, my fiancée Hannah.

HANNAH   Oh. Yes. You have a way with you, Bernard. I'm not sure I like it.

BERNARD   What's he doing, Valentine?

HANNAH   He's a postgrad. Biology.

---

7. British Sunday newspaper.
8. University, attended by Sebastian Flyte, anti-hero of Evelyn Waugh's satirical novel of British upper-class life, *Brideshead Revisited* (1945).
9. Vomited up.

BERNARD   No, he's a mathematician.

HANNAH   Well, he's doing grouse.[1]

BERNARD   Grouse?

HANNAH   Not actual grouse. Computer grouse.

BERNARD   Who's the one who doesn't speak?

HANNAH   Gus.

BERNARD   What's the matter with him?

HANNAH   I didn't ask.

BERNARD   And the father sounds like a lot of fun.

HANNAH   Ah yes.

BERNARD   And the mother is the gardener. What's going on here?

HANNAH   What do you mean?

BERNARD   I nearly took her head off—she was standing in a trench at the time.

HANNAH   Archaeology. The house had a formal Italian garden until about 1740. Lady Croom is interested in garden history. I sent her my book—it contains, as you know if you've read it—which I'm not assuming, by the way—a rather good description of Caroline's garden at Brocket Hall. I'm here now helping Hermione.

BERNARD [Impressed]   Hermione.

HANNAH   The records are unusually complete and they have never been worked on.

BERNARD   I'm beginning to admire you.

HANNAH   Before was bullshit?

BERNARD   Completely. Your photograph does you justice, I'm not sure the book does.

[She considers him. He waits, confident.]

HANNAH   Septimus Hodge was the tutor.

BERNARD [Quietly.]   Attagirl.

HANNAH   His pupil was the Croom daughter. There was a son at Eton. Septimus lived in the house: the pay book specifies allowances for wine and candles. So, not quite a guest but rather more than a steward.[2] His letter of self-recommendation is preserved among the papers. I'll dig it out for you. As far as I remember he studied mathematics and natural philosophy at Cambridge. A scientist, therefore, as much as anything.

BERNARD   I'm impressed. Thank you. And Chater?

HANNAH   Nothing.

BERNARD   Oh. Nothing at all?

HANNAH   I'm afraid not.

BERNARD   How about the library?

HANNAH   The catalogue was done in the 1880s. I've been through the lot.

BERNARD   Books or catalogue?

HANNAH   Catalogue.

BERNARD   Ah. Pity.

HANNAH   I'm sorry.

BERNARD   What about the letters? No mention?

---

1. Valentine is researching changes in the Sidley   2. Chief servant.
Park population of the grouse, a game bird.

HANNAH   I'm afraid not. I've been very thorough in your period because, of course, it's my period too.

BERNARD   Is it? Actually, I don't quite know what it is you're . . .

HANNAH   The Sidley hermit.

BERNARD   Ah. Who's he?

HANNAH   He's my peg[3] for the nervous breakdown of the Romantic Imagination. I'm doing landscape and literature 1750 to 1834.

BERNARD   What happened in 1834?

HANNAH   My hermit died.

BERNARD   Of course.

HANNAH   What do you mean, of course?

BERNARD   Nothing.

HANNAH   Yes, you do.

BERNARD   No, no . . . However, Coleridge[4] also died in 1834.

HANNAH   So he did. What a stroke of luck. [*Softening.*] Thank you, Bernard.

[*She goes to the reading stand and opens Noakes's sketch book.*]
Look—there he is.

[BERNARD *goes to look.*]

BERNARD   Mmm.

HANNAH   The only known likeness of the Sidley hermit.

BERNARD   Very biblical.[5]

HANNAH   Drawn in by a later hand, of course. The hermitage didn't yet exist when Noakes did the drawings.

BERNARD   Noakes . . . the painter?

HANNAH   Landscape gardener. He'd do these books for his clients, as a sort of prospectus. [*She demonstrates.*] Before and after, you see. This is how it all looked until, say, 1810—smooth, undulating, serpentine— open water, clumps of trees, classical boat-house—

BERNARD   Lovely. The real England.

HANNAH   You can stop being silly now, Bernard. English landscape was invented by gardeners imitating foreign painters who were evoking classical authors. The whole thing was brought home in the luggage from the grand tour. Here, look—Capability Brown doing Claude, who was doing Virgil.[6] Arcadia! And here, superimposed by Richard Noakes, untamed nature in the style of Salvator Rosa. It's the Gothic novel expressed in landscape. Everything but vampires. There's an account of my hermit in a letter by your illustrious namesake.

BERNARD   Florence?[7]

HANNAH   What?

BERNARD   No. You go on.

HANNAH   Thomas Love Peacock.[8]

BERNARD   Ah yes.

---

3. On which to hang the argument of a book about the Romantic Imagination.
4. Samuel Taylor Coleridge (1722–1834), English Romantic poet.
5. See p. 1032, n. 6.
6. Hannah sees Lancelot "Capability" Brown (1715–1783), England's most celebrated landscape designer, imitating ("doing") Claude Lorrain (1600–1682), French landscape painter, who was imitating Virgil's *Georgics*, poems cele-

brating the country/pastoral life of an idealized Arcadia.
7. Florence Nightingale (1820–1910), English nurse considered the founder of modern nursing (Bernard has temporarily forgotten his alias).
8. English novelist and poet (1785–1866), author of *Headlong* [not *Heading*] *Hall* (1816), and onetime "Examiner" (investigator) with the British East India Company in India.

HANNAH   I found it in an essay on hermits and anchorites[9] published in
the *Cornhill Magazine* in the 1860s . . . [*She fishes for the magazine
itself among the books on the table, and finds it.*] . . . 1862 . . . Peacock
calls him [*She quotes from memory.*] 'Not one of your village simpletons
to frighten the ladies, but a savant[1] among idiots, a sage of lunacy.'

BERNARD   An oxy-moron,[2] so to speak.

HANNAH [*Busy*]   Yes. What?

BERNARD   Nothing.

HANNAH [*Having found the place.*]   Here we are. 'A letter we have seen,
written by the author of *Heading Hall* nearly thirty years ago, tells of
a visit to the Earl of Croom's estate, Sidley Park—'

BERNARD   Was the letter to Thackeray?[3]

HANNAH [*Brought up short.*]   I don't know. Does it matter?

BERNARD   No. Sorry.

[*But the gaps he leaves for her are false promises—and she is not quick
enough. That's how it goes.*]

Only, Thackeray edited the *Cornhill* until '63 when, as you know, he
died. His father had been with the East India Company where Peacock,
of course, had held the position of Examiner, so it's quite possible that if
the essay were by Thackeray, the *letter* . . . Sorry. Go on.

Of course, the East India Library in Blackfriars has most of Peacock's
letters, so it would be quite easy to . . . Sorry. Can I look?

[*Silently she hands him the* Cornhill.]

Yes, it's been topped and tailed, of course. It might be worth . . . Go on.
I'm listening . . .

[*Leafing through the essay, he suddenly chuckles.*] Oh yes, it's Thackeray
all right . . .

[*He slaps the book shut.*] Unbearable . . .

[*He hands it back to her.*] What were you saying?

HANNAH   Are you always like this?

BERNARD   Like what?

HANNAH   The point is, the Crooms, of course, had the hermit under their
noses for twenty years so hardly thought him worth remarking. As I'm
finding out. The Peacock letter is still the main source, unfortunately.
When I read this [*the magazine in her hand*], well, it was one of those
moments that tell you what your next book is going to be. The hermit of
Sidley Park was my . . .

BERNARD   Peg.

HANNAH   Epiphany.

BERNARD   Epiphany, that's it.

HANNAH   The hermit was *placed* in the landscape exactly as one might
place a pottery gnome. And there he lived out his life as a garden ornament.

BERNARD   Did he do anything?

HANNAH   Oh, he was very busy. When he died, the cottage was stacked
solid with paper. Hundreds of pages. Thousands. Peacock says he was
suspected of genius. It turned out, of course, he was off his head. He'd

---

9. In medieval Europe, hermits who voluntarily
lived out their lives enclosed in tiny cells within
the walls of local churches.
1. Learned man.
2. Phrase that seems to contradict itself ("sage

of lunacy"), here prompting Bernard's pun on
"moron" (meaning "idiot").
3. William Makepeace Thackeray (1811–1863),
English novelist and poet.

covered every sheet with cabalistic[4] proofs that the world was coming to an end. It's perfect, isn't it? A perfect symbol, I mean.

BERNARD   Oh, yes. Of what?

HANNAH   The whole Romantic sham, Bernard! It's what happened to the Enlightenment, isn't it? A century of intellectual rigour turned in on itself. A mind in chaos suspected of genius. In a setting of cheap thrills and false emotion. The history of the garden says it all, beautifully. There's an engraving of Sidley Park in 1730 that makes you want to weep. Paradise in the age of reason. By 1760 everything had gone— the topiary, pools and terraces, fountains, an avenue of limes—the whole sublime geometry was ploughed under by Capability Brown. The grass went from the doorstep to the horizon and the best box hedge in Derbyshire was dug up for the ha-ha so that the fools could pretend they were living in God's countryside. And then Richard Noakes came in to bring God up to date. By the time he'd finished it looked like this [*the sketch book*]. The decline from thinking to feeling, you see.

BERNARD   [*A judgement.*]   That's awfully good.

[HANNAH *looks at him in case of irony but he is professional.*]

No, that'll stand up.

HANNAH   Thank you.

BERNARD   Personally I like the ha-ha. Do you like hedges?

HANNAH   I don't like sentimentality.

BERNARD   Yes, I see. Are you sure? You seem quite sentimental over geometry. But the hermit is very very good. The genius[5] of the place.

HANNAH   [*Pleased.*]   That's my title!

BERNARD   Of course.

HANNAH   [*Less pleased.*]   Of course?

BERNARD   Of course. Who was he when he wasn't being a symbol?

HANNAH   I don't know.

BERNARD   Ah.

HANNAH   I mean, yet.

BERNARD   Absolutely. What did they do with all the paper? Does Peacock say?

HANNAH   Made a bonfire.

BERNARD   Ah, well.

HANNAH   I've still got Lady Croom's garden books to go through.

BERNARD   Account books or journals?

HANNAH   A bit of both. They're gappy but they span the period.

BERNARD   Really? Have you come across Byron at all? As a matter of interest.

HANNAH   A first edition of 'Childe Harold' in the library, and *English Bards*, I think.[6]

BERNARD   Inscribed?

HANNAH   No.

BERNARD   And he doesn't pop up in the letters at all?

HANNAH   Why should he? The Crooms don't pop up in his.

---

4. Coded.
5. With a pun on the meaning "attendant spirit of a person or a place."

6. Two of Byron's long poems: *English Bards and Scotch Reviewers* (1809) and *Childe Harold's Pilgrimage* (1812).

BERNARD [*Casually.*] That's true, of course. But Newstead[7] isn't so far away. Would you mind terribly if I poked about a bit? Only in the papers you've done with, of course.

[HANNAH *twigs*[8] *something.*]

HANNAH Are you looking into Byron or Chater?

[CHLOË *enters in stockinged feet through one of the side doors, laden with an armful of generally similar leather-covered ledgers. She detours to collect her shoes.*]

CHLOË Sorry—just cutting through—there's tea in the pantry if you don't mind mugs—

BERNARD How kind.

CHLOË Hannah will show you.

BERNARD Let me help you.

CHLOË No, it's all right—

[BERNARD *opens the opposite door for her.*]

Thank you—I've been saving Val's game books. Thanks.

[BERNARD *closes the door.*]

BERNARD Sweet girl.

HANNAH Mmm.

BERNARD Oh, really?

HANNAH Oh really what?

[CHLOË'S *door opens again and she puts her head round it.*]

CHLOË Meant to say, don't worry if father makes remarks about your car, Mr Nightingale, he's got a thing about—[*and the Nightingale now being out of the bag*] ooh—ah, how was the surprise?—not yet, eh? Oh, well— sorry—tea, anyway—so sorry if I—[*Embarrassed, she leaves again, closing the door. Pause.*]

HANNAH You absolute shit.

[*She heads off to leave.*]

BERNARD The thing is, there's a Byron connection too.

[HANNAH *stops and faces him.*]

HANNAH I don't care.

BERNARD You should. The Byron gang are going to get their dicks caught in their zip.

HANNAH [*Pause.*] Oh really?

BERNARD If we collaborate.

HANNAH On what?

BERNARD Sit down, I'll tell you.

HANNAH I'll stand for the moment.

BERNARD This copy of 'The Couch of Eros' belonged to Lord Byron.

HANNAH It belonged to Septimus Hodge.

BERNARD Originally, yes. But it was in Byron's library which was sold to pay his debts when he left England for good in 1816. The sales catalogue is in the British Library. 'Eros' was lot 74A and was bought by the bookseller and publisher John Nightingale of Opera Court, Pall Mall . . . whose name survives in the firm of Nightingale and Matlock, the present Nightingale being my cousin.

[*He pauses.* HANNAH *hesitates and then sits down at the table.*]

I'll just give you the headlines. 1939, stock removed to Nightingale country house in Kent. 1945, stock returned to bookshop. Meanwhile,

---

7. Newstead Abbey, Byron's family home.   8. Suddenly notices or realizes.

overlooked box of early nineteenth-century books languish in country house cellar until house sold to make way for the Channel Tunnel rail-link.[9] 'Eros' discovered with sales slip from 1816 attached—photocopy available for inspection.

[*He brings this from his bag and gives it to* HANNAH *who inspects it.*]

HANNAH   All right. It was in Byron's library.

BERNARD   A number of passages have been underlined.

[HANNAH *picks up the book and leafs through it.*]

All of them, and only them—no, no, look at me, not at the book—all the underlined passages, word for word, were used as quotations in the review of 'The Couch of Eros' in the *Piccadilly Recreation* of April 30th 1809. The reviewer begins by drawing attention to his previous notice in the same periodical of 'The Maid of Turkey'.

HANNAH   The reviewer is obviously Hodge. 'My friend Septimus Hodge who stood up and gave his best on behalf of the Author.'

BERNARD   That's the point. The *Piccadilly* ridiculed both books.

HANNAH   [*Pause.*]   Do the reviews read like Byron?

BERNARD   [*Producing two photocopies from his case.*]   They read a damn sight more like Byron than Byron's review of Wordsworth the previous year.

[HANNAH *glances over the photocopies.*]

HANNAH   I see. Well, congratulations. Possibly. Two previously unknown book reviews by the young Byron. Is that it?

BERNARD   No. Because of the tapes, three documents survived undisturbed in the book.

[*He has been carefully opening a package produced from his bag. He has the originals. He holds them carefully one by one.*]

'Sir—we have a matter to settle. I wait on you in the gun room. E. Chater, Esq.'

'My husband has sent to town for pistols. Deny what cannot be proven— for Charity's sake—I keep my room this day.' Unsigned.

'Sidley Park, April 11th 1809. Sir—I call you a liar, a lecher, a slanderer in the press and a thief of my honour. I wait upon your arrangements for giving me satisfaction as a man and a poet. E. Chater, Esq.'

[*Pause.*]

HANNAH   Superb. But inconclusive. The book had seven years to find its way into Byron's possession. It doesn't connect Byron with Chater, or with Sidley Park. Or with Hodge for that matter. Furthermore, there isn't a hint in Byron's letters and this kind of scrape is the last thing he would have kept quiet about.

BERNARD   *Scrape?*

HANNAH   He would have made a comic turn out of it.

BERNARD   Comic turn, fiddlesticks! [*He pauses for effect.*] He killed Chater!

HANNAH   [*A raspberry.*]   Oh, really!

BERNARD   Chater was thirty-one years old. The author of two books. Nothing more is heard from him after 'Eros'. He disappears completely after April 1809. And Byron—Byron had just published his satire, *English Bards and Scotch Reviewers,* in March. He was just getting a name. Yet he

9. High-speed railway line linking London with the tunnel that crosses the English Channel.

sailed for Lisbon[1] as soon as he could find a ship, and stayed abroad for two years. Hannah, *this is fame.* Somewhere in the Croom papers there will be *something*—

HANNAH   There isn't, I've looked.

BERNARD   But you were looking for something else! It's not going to jump out at you like 'Lord Byron remarked wittily at breakfast!'

HANNAH   Nevertheless his presence would be unlikely to have gone unremarked. But there is nothing to suggest that Byron was here, and I don't believe he ever was.

BERNARD   All right, but let me have a look.

HANNAH   You'll queer my pitch.[2]

BERNARD   Dear girl, I know how to handle myself—

HANNAH   And don't call me dear girl. If I find anything on Byron, or Chater, or Hodge, I'll pass it on. Nightingale, Sussex.

[*Pause. She stands up.*]

BERNARD   Thank you. I'm sorry about that business with my name.

HANNAH   Don't mention it . . .

BERNARD   What was Hodge's college,[3] by the way?

HANNAH   Trinity.

BERNARD   Trinity?

HANNAH   Yes. [*She hesitates.*] Yes. Byron's old college.

BERNARD   How old was Hodge?

HANNAH   I'd have to look it up but a year or two older than Byron. Twenty-two . . .

BERNARD   Contemporaries at Trinity?

HANNAH   [*Wearily.*]   Yes, Bernard, and no doubt they were both in the cricket eleven when Harrow played Eton at Lords![4]

[BERNARD *approaches her and stands close to her.*]

BERNARD   [*Evenly.*]   Do you mean that Septimus Hodge was at school with Byron?

HANNAH   [*Falters slightly.*]   Yes . . . he must have been . . . as a matter of fact.

BERNARD   Well, you silly cow.

[*With a large gesture of pure happiness,* BERNARD *throws his arms around* HANNAH *and gives her a great smacking kiss on the cheek.* CHLOË *enters to witness the end of this.*]

CHLOË   Oh—erm . . . I thought I'd bring it to you.

[*She is carrying a small tray with two mugs on it.*]

BERNARD   I have to go and see about my car.

HANNAH   Going to hide it?

BERNARD   Hide it? I'm going to sell it! Is there a pub I can put up at in the village?

[*He turns back to them as he is about to leave through the garden.*]

Aren't you glad I'm here?

[*He leaves.*]

CHLOË   He said he knew you.

HANNAH   He couldn't have.

---

1. Capital of Portugal.
2. Spoil my chances.
3. At Cambridge University.
4. Contemporaries also at Harrow School,

Byron and Hodge could have been in the same team (of eleven players) that played against Eton at Lords cricket ground in London.

CHLOË   No, perhaps not. He said he wanted to be a surprise, but I suppose that's different. I thought there was a lot of sexual energy there, didn't you?

HANNAH   What?

CHLOË   Bouncy on his feet, you see, a sure sign. Should I invite him for you?

HANNAH   To what? No.

CHLOË   You can invite him—that's better. He can come as your partner.

HANNAH   Stop it. Thank you for the tea.

CHLOË   If you don't want him, I'll have him. Is he married?

HANNAH   I haven't the slightest idea. Aren't you supposed to have a pony?

CHLOË   I'm just trying to fix you up, Hannah.

HANNAH   Believe me, it gets less important.

CHLOË   I mean for the dancing. He can come as Beau Brummel.[5]

HANNAH   I don't want to dress up and I don't want a dancing partner, least of all Mr Nightingale. I don't dance.

CHLOË   Don't be such a prune. You were kissing him, anyway.

HANNAH   He was kissing me, and only out of general enthusiasm.

CHLOË   Well, don't say I didn't give you first chance. My genius brother will be much relieved. He's in love with you, I suppose you know.

HANNAH [Angry.]   That's a joke!

CHLOË   It's not a joke to him.

HANNAH   Of course it is—not even a joke—how can you be so ridiculous?
[GUS enters from the garden, in his customary silent awkwardness.]

CHLOË   Hello, Gus, what have you got?
[GUS has an apple, just picked, with a leaf or two still attached. He offers the apple to HANNAH.][6]

HANNAH [Surprised.]   Oh! . . . Thank you!

CHLOË [Leaving.]   Told you.
[CHLOË closes the door on herself.]

HANNAH   Thank you. Oh dear.

SCENE THREE

The schoolroom. The next morning. Present are: THOMASINA, SEPTIMUS, JELLABY. We have seen this composition before: THOMASINA at her place at the table; SEPTIMUS reading a letter which has just arrived; JELLABY waiting, having just delivered the letter.

'The Couch of Eros' is in front of SEPTIMUS, open, together with sheets of paper on which he has been writing. His portfolio is on the table. Plautus (the tortoise) is the paperweight. There is also an apple on the table now, the same apple from all appearances.

SEPTIMUS [With his eyes on the letter.]   Why have you stopped?
[THOMASINA is studying a sheet of paper, a 'Latin unseen' lesson.[7] She is having some difficulty.]

5. George Bryan Brummel (1778–1840), known as "Beau" because of his elegant clothes.
6. Cf. Genesis 3.1–6, specifically Eve's gift of an apple to Adam in the Garden of Eden; cf. also the golden apple of discord given by Paris to the goddess Aphrodite in Greek legend.
7. Latin passage that a student is required to translate: here, the Roman historian Plutarch's description of Cleopatra in her barge, on which Shakespeare based a famous speech by Enobarbus (Antony and Cleopatra 2.2.196ff.) Below, Septimus pretends Shakespeare's lines are his own translation.

THOMASINA *Solio insessa . . . in igne . . .* seated on a throne . . . in the fire . . . and also on a ship . . . *sedebat regina . . .* sat the queen . . .

SEPTIMUS There is no reply, Jellaby. Thank you.

    [*He folds the letter up and places it between the leaves of 'The Couch of Eros'.*]

JELLABY I will say so, sir.

THOMASINA . . . the wind smelling sweetly . . . *purpureis velis . . .* by, with or from purple sails—

SEPTIMUS [*To* JELLABY] I will have something for the post, if you would be so kind.

JELLABY [*Leaving.*] Yes sir.

THOMASINA . . . was like as to—something—by, with or from lovers—oh, Septimus!—*musica tibiarum imperabat . . .* music of pipes commanded . . .

SEPTIMUS 'Ruled' is better.

THOMASINA . . . the silver oars—exciting the ocean—as if—as if—amorous—

SEPTIMUS That is very good.

    [*He picks up the apple. He picks off the twig and leaves, placing these on the table. With a pocket knife he cuts a slice of apple, and while he eats it, cuts another slice which he offers to Plautus.*]

THOMASINA *Regina reclinabat . . .* the queen—was reclining—*praeter descriptionem*—indescribably—in a golden tent . . . like Venus and yet more—

SEPTIMUS Try to put some poetry into it.

THOMASINA How can I if there is none in the Latin?

SEPTIMUS Oh, a critic!

THOMASINA Is it Queen Dido?[8]

SEPTIMUS No.

THOMASINA Who is the poet?

SEPTIMUS Known to you.

THOMASINA Known to me?

SEPTIMUS Not a Roman.

THOMASINA Mr Chater?

SEPTIMUS Your translation is quite like Chater.

    [SEPTIMUS *picks up his pen and continues with his own writing.*]

THOMASINA I know who it is, it is your friend Byron.

SEPTIMUS Lord Byron, if you please.

THOMASINA Mama is in love with Lord Byron.

SEPTIMUS [*Absorbed.*] Yes. Nonsense.

THOMASINA It is not nonsense. I saw them together in the gazebo.

    [SEPTIMUS's *pen stops moving, he raises his eyes to her at last.*]

Lord Byron was reading to her from his satire, and mama was laughing, with her head in her best position.

SEPTIMUS She did not understand the satire, and was showing politeness to a guest.

THOMASINA She is vexed with papa for his determination to alter the park, but that alone cannot account for her politeness to a guest. She came

8. Legendary queen of Carthage who, in Virgil's *Aeneid*, is abandoned by her lover Aeneas and commits suicide.

downstairs hours before her custom. Lord Byron was amusing at breakfast. He paid you a tribute, Septimus.

SEPTIMUS   Did he?

THOMASINA   He said you were a witty fellow, and he had almost by heart an article you wrote about—well, I forget what, but it concerned a book called 'The Maid of Turkey' and how you would not give it to your dog for dinner.

SEPTIMUS   Ah. Mr Chater was at breakfast, of course.

THOMASINA   He was, not like certain lazybones.

SEPTIMUS   He does not have Latin to set and mathematics to correct.
   [*He takes Thomasina's lesson book from underneath Plautus and tosses it down the table to her.*]

THOMASINA   Correct? What was incorrect in it? [*She looks into the book.*] Alpha minus?[9] Pooh! What is the minus for?

SEPTIMUS   For doing more than was asked.

THOMASINA   You did not like my discovery?

SEPTIMUS   A fancy is not a discovery.

THOMASINA   A gibe is not a rebuttal.
   [SEPTIMUS *finishes what he is writing. He folds the pages into a letter. He has sealing wax and the means to melt it. He seals the letter and writes on the cover. Meanwhile—*]

You are churlish with me because mama is paying attention to your friend. Well, let them elope, they cannot turn back the advancement of knowledge. I think it is an excellent discovery. Each week I plot your equations dot for dot, xs against ys in all manner of algebraical relation, and every week they draw themselves as commonplace geometry, as if the world of forms were nothing but arcs and angles. God's truth, Septimus, if there is an equation for a curve like a bell, there must be an equation for one like a bluebell, and if a bluebell, why not a rose? Do we believe nature is written in numbers?

SEPTIMUS   We do.

THOMASINA   Then why do your equations only describe the shapes of manufacture?

SEPTIMUS   I do not know.

THOMASINA   Armed thus, God could only make a cabinet.

SEPTIMUS   He has mastery of equations which lead into infinities where we cannot follow.

THOMASINA   What a faint-heart! We must work outward from the middle of the maze. We will start with something simple. [*She picks up the apple leaf.*] I will plot this leaf and deduce its equation. You will be famous for being my tutor when Lord Byron is dead and forgotten.
   [SEPTIMUS *completes the business with his letter. He puts the letter in his pocket.*]

SEPTIMUS [*Firmly.*]   Back to Cleopatra.[1]

THOMASINA   Is it Cleopatra?—I hate Cleopatra!

SEPTIMUS   You hate her? Why?

THOMASINA   Everything is turned to love with her. New love, absent love, lost love—I never knew a heroine that makes such noodles of our sex. It

9. A grade of A-minus.
1. Queen of Egypt (69–30 B.C.E.), mistress of the Roman Mark Antony.

only needs a Roman general to drop anchor outside the window and away goes the empire like a christening mug into a pawn shop. If Queen Elizabeth had been a Ptolemy history would have been quite different—we would be admiring the pyramids of Rome and the great Sphinx of Verona.[2]

SEPTIMUS   God save us.

THOMASINA   But instead, the Egyptian noodle made carnal embrace with the enemy who burned the great library of Alexandria without so much as a fine for all that is overdue. Oh, Septimus!—can you bear it? All the lost plays of the Athenians! Two hundred at least by Aeschylus, Sophocles, Euripides—thousands of poems—Aristotle's own library brought to Egypt by the noodle's ancestors![3] How can we sleep for grief?

SEPTIMUS   By counting our stock. Seven plays from Aeschylus, seven from Sophocles, *nineteen* from Euripides, my lady! You should no more grieve for the rest than for a buckle lost from your first shoe, or for your lesson book which will be lost when you are old. We shed as we pick up, like travellers who must carry everything in their arms, and what we let fall will be picked up by those behind. The procession is very long and life is very short. We die on the march. But there is nothing outside the march so nothing can be lost to it. The missing plays of Sophocles will turn up piece by piece, or be written again in another language. Ancient cures for diseases will reveal themselves once more. Mathematical discoveries glimpsed and lost to view will have their time again. You do not suppose, my lady, that if all of Archimedes[4] had been hiding in the great library of Alexandria, we would be at a loss for a corkscrew? I have no doubt that the improved steam-driven heat-engine which puts Mr Noakes into an ecstasy that he and it and the modern age should all coincide, was described on papyrus. Steam and brass were not invented in Glasgow. Now, where are we? Let me see if I can attempt a free translation for you. At Harrow I was better at this than Lord Byron.

[*He takes the piece of paper from her and scrutinizes it, testing one or two Latin phrases speculatively before committing himself.*]

Yes—'The barge she sat in, like a burnished throne . . . burned on the water . . . the—something—the poop was beaten gold, purple the sails, and—what's this?—oh yes,—so perfumed that—

THOMASINA [*Catching on and furious.*]   Cheat!

SEPTIMUS [*Imperturbably.*]   '—the winds were lovesick with them . . .'

THOMASINA   Cheat!

SEPTIMUS   '. . . the oars were silver which to the tune of flutes kept stroke . . .'

THOMASINA [*Jumping to her feet.*]   Cheat! Cheat! Cheat!

SEPTIMUS [*As though it were too easy to make the effort worthwhile.*]   '. . . and made the water which they beat to follow faster, as *amorous* of their strokes. For her own person, it beggared all description—she did lie in her pavilion—'

[THOMASINA, *in tears of rage, is hurrying out through the garden.*]

THOMASINA   I hope you die!

---

2. In Italy. I.e., if Queen Elizabeth I of England (1533–1603) had been Cleopatra (a member of the Ptolemy family), says Thomasina, Egypt would have overthrown the Roman Empire.
3. The plays of Aeschylus (525–456 B.C.E.), Sophocles (ca. 496–406 B.C.E.), and Euripides (ca. 484–406 B.C.E.) and the library of the phi-

losopher Aristotle (384–322 B.C.E.) had been brought to Egypt from Greece by Cleopatra's forebears.
4. All the writings of the Greek scientist Archimedes (ca. 287–212 B.C.E.), who invented the Archimedean screw to raise water.

[*She nearly bumps into* BRICE *who is entering. She runs out of sight.* BRICE *enters.*]

BRICE   Good God, man, what have you told her?

SEPTIMUS   Told her? Told her what?

BRICE   Hodge!

[SEPTIMUS *looks outside the door, slightly contrite about* THOMASINA, *and sees that* CHATER *is skulking out of view.*]

SEPTIMUS   Chater! My dear fellow! Don't hang back—come in, sir!

[CHATER *allows himself to be drawn sheepishly into the room, where* BRICE *stands on his dignity.*]

CHATER   Captain Brice does me the honour—I mean to say, sir, whatever you have to say to me, sir, address yourself to Captain Brice.[5]

SEPTIMUS   How unusual. [*To* BRICE.] Your wife did not appear yesterday, sir. I trust she is not sick?

BRICE   My wife? I have no wife. What the devil do you mean, sir?

[SEPTIMUS *makes to reply, but hesitates, puzzled. He turns back to* CHATER.]

SEPTIMUS   I do not understand the scheme, Chater. Whom do I address when I want to speak to Captain Brice?

BRICE   Oh, slippery, Hodge—slippery!

SEPTIMUS [*To* CHATER]   By the way, Chater—[*He interrupts himself and turns back to* BRICE, *and continues as before.*] by the way, Chater, I have amazing news to tell you. Someone has taken to writing wild and whirling letters in your name. I received one not half an hour ago.

BRICE [*Angrily.*]   Mr Hodge! Look to your honour, sir! If you cannot attend to me without this foolery, nominate your second who might settle the business as between gentlemen. No doubt your friend Byron would do you the service.

[SEPTIMUS *gives up the game.*]

SEPTIMUS   Oh yes, he would do me the service. [*His mood changes, he turns to* CHATER.] Sir—I repent your injury. You are an honest fellow with no more malice in you than poetry.

CHATER [*Happily.*]   Ah well!—that is more like the thing! [*Overtaken by doubt.*] Is he apologizing?

BRICE   There is still the injury to his conjugal[6] property, Mrs Chater's—

CHATER   Tush,[7] sir!

BRICE   As you will—her tush. Nevertheless—

[*But they are interrupted by* LADY CROOM, *also entering from the garden.*]

LADY CROOM   Oh—excellently found! Mr Chater, this will please you very much. Lord Byron begs a copy of your new book. He dies to read it and intends to include your name in the second edition of his *English Bards and Scotch Reviewers.*

CHATER   *English Bards and Scotch Reviewers,* your ladyship, is a doggerel aimed at Lord Byron's seniors and betters. If he intends to include me, he intends to insult me.

---

5. Brice has done Chater "the honour" of agreeing to act as his "second" (supporter) in the duel to which Chater has challenged Septimus. Dueling etiquette required the two seconds to arrange the time, place, and choice of weapons.
6. Marital.
7. Expression of mild irritation, which Brice turns into a vulgar joke.

LADY CROOM   Well, of course he does, Mr Chater. Would you rather be thought not worth insulting? You should be proud to be in the company of Rogers and Moore and Wordsworth—[8] ah! 'The Couch of Eros!' [*For she has spotted Septimus's copy of the book on the table.*]

SEPTIMUS   That is my copy, madam.

LADY CROOM   So much the better—what are a friend's books for if not to be borrowed?

> [*Note: 'The Couch of Eros' now contains the three letters, and it must do so without advertising the fact. This is why the volume has been described as a substantial quarto.*]

Mr Hodge, you must speak to your friend[9] and put him out of his affectation of pretending to quit us. I will not have it. He says he is determined on the Malta packet sailing out of Falmouth! His head is full of Lisbon and Lesbos,[1] and his portmanteau[1] of pistols, and I have told him it is not to be thought of. The whole of Europe is in a Napoleonic fit,[2] all the best ruins will be closed, the roads entirely occupied with the movement of armies, the lodgings turned to billets[3] and the fashion for godless republicanism not yet arrived at its natural reversion. He says his aim is poetry. One does not aim at poetry with pistols. At poets, perhaps. I charge you to take command of his pistols, Mr Hodge! He is not safe with them. His lameness, he confessed to me, is entirely the result of his habit from boyhood of shooting himself in the foot.[4] What is that *noise*?

> [*The noise is a badly played piano in the next room. It has been going on for some time since* THOMASINA *left.*]

SEPTIMUS   The new Broadwood pianoforte,[5] madam. Our music lessons are at an early stage.

LADY CROOM   Well, restrict your lessons to the *piano* side of the instrument and let her loose on the *forte* when she has learned something.

> [LADY CROOM, *holding the book, sails out back into the garden.*]

BRICE   Now! If that was not God speaking through Lady Croom, he never spoke through anyone!

CHATER [*Awed.*]   Take command of Lord Byron's pistols!

BRICE   You hear Mr Chater, sir—how will you answer him?

> [SEPTIMUS *has been watching* LADY CROOM's *progress up the garden. He turns back*].

SEPTIMUS   By killing him. I am tired of him.

CHATER [*Startled.*]   Eh?

BRICE [*Pleased.*]   Ah!

SEPTIMUS   Oh, damn your soul, Chater! Ovid[6] would have stayed a lawyer and Virgil a farmer if they had known the bathos[7] to which love would descend in your sportive satyrs and noodle nymphs![8] I am at your service with a half-ounce ball[9] in your brain. May it satisfy you—behind

---

8. Samuel Rogers (1763–1855), English poet; Thomas Moore (1779–1852), Irish poet, and friend and biographer of Byron; William Wordsworth (1770–1850), English poet.
9. Lord Byron.
1. Suitcase. "Packet": mail boat, which also carried passengers. "Lesbos": Greek island.
2. France, under Napoleon, was fighting the Peninsula War (1804–14) against Great Britain, Portugal, and Spanish guerrillas in the Iberian Peninsula.

3. Accommodation for troops.
4. Byron was born with a clubfoot.
5. An early form of the piano, its name combining the Italian words for soft and loud, respectively.
6. Roman poet (43 B.C.E.–17? C.E.)
7. Rhetorical descent from the exalted to the commonplace.
8. Your lustful men and foolish young women.
9. Bullet.

the boat-house at daybreak—shall we say five o'clock? My compliments to Mrs Chater—have no fear for her, she will not want for protection while Captain Brice has a guinea[1] in his pocket, he told her so himself.

BRICE   You lie, sir!

SEPTIMUS   No, sir. Mrs Chater, perhaps.

BRICE   You lie, or you will answer to me!

SEPTIMUS [*Wearily.*]   Oh, very well—I can fit you in at five minutes after five. And then it's off to the Malta packet out of Falmouth. You two will be dead, my penurious[2] schoolfriend will remain to tutor Lady Thomasina, and I trust everybody including Lady Croom will be satisfied!

[SEPTIMUS *slams the door behind him.*]

BRICE   He is all bluster and bladder. Rest assured, Chater, I will let the air out of him.

[BRICE *leaves by the other door.* CHATER's *assurance lasts only a moment. When he spots the flaw . . .* [3]]

CHATER   Oh! But . . .

[*He hurries out after* BRICE.]

SCENE FOUR

HANNAH *and* VALENTINE. *She is reading aloud. He is listening. Lightning, the tortoise, is on the table and is not readily distinguishable from Plautus. In front of* VALENTINE *is Septimus's portfolio, recognizably so but naturally somewhat faded. It is open. Principally associated with the portfolio (although it may contain sheets of blank paper also) are three items: a slim maths primer; a sheet of drawing paper on which there is a scrawled diagram and some mathematical notations, arrow marks, etc.; and Thomasina's mathematics lesson book, i.e. the one she writes in, which* VALENTINE *is leafing through as he listens to* HANNAH *reading from the primer.*

HANNAH   'I, Thomasina Coverly, have found a truly wonderful method whereby all the forms of nature must give up their numerical secrets and draw themselves through number alone. This margin being too mean for my purpose, the reader must look elsewhere for the New Geometry of Irregular Forms discovered by Thomasina Coverly.'

[*Pause. She hands* VALENTINE *the text book.* VALENTINE *looks at what she has been reading.*

From the next room, a piano is heard, beginning to play quietly, unintrusively, improvisationally.]

Does it mean anything?

VALENTINE   I don't know. I don't know what it means, except mathematically.

HANNAH   I meant mathematically.

VALENTINE [*Now with the lesson book again.*]   It's an iterated algorithm.[4]

HANNAH   What's that?

VALENTINE   Well, it's . . . Jesus . . . it's an algorithm that's been . . . iterated. How'm I supposed to . . . ? [*He makes an effort.*] The left-hand pages are graphs of what the numbers are doing on the right-hand

1. British gold coin with a value (in the 19th century) of 21 shillings.
2. Penniless.
3. Brice, as Chater's "second," could duel with

Septimus only if Chater were dead or wounded.
4. Mathematical procedure for computing results through a series of repeated operations.

pages. But all on different scales. Each graph is a small section of the previous one, blown up. Like you'd blow up a detail of a photograph, and then a detail of the detail, and so on, forever. Or in her case, till she ran out of pages.

HANNAH   Is it difficult?

VALENTINE   The maths isn't difficult. It's what you did at school. You have some x-and-y equation. Any value for x gives you a value for y. So you put a dot where it's right for both x and y. Then you take the next value for x which gives you another value for y, and when you've done that a few times you join up the dots and that's your graph of whatever the equation is.

HANNAH   And is that what she's doing?

VALENTINE   No. Not exactly. Not at all. What she's doing is, every time she works out a value for y, she's using *that* as her next value for x. And so on. Like a feedback. She's feeding the solution back into the equation, and then solving it again. Iteration, you see.

HANNAH   And that's surprising, is it?

VALENTINE   Well, it is a bit. It's the technique I'm using on my grouse numbers, and it hasn't been around for much longer than, well, call it twenty years.
        [*Pause.*]

HANNAH   Why would she be doing it?

VALENTINE   I have no idea.
        [*Pause.*]
    I thought you were doing the hermit.

HANNAH   I am. I still am. But Bernard, damn him . . . Thomasina's tutor turns out to have interesting connections. Bernard is going through the library like a bloodhound. The portfolio was in a cupboard.

VALENTINE   There's a lot of stuff around. Gus loves going through it. No old masters or anything . . .

HANNAH   The maths primer she was using belonged to him—the tutor; he wrote his name in it.

VALENTINE   [*Reading.*]   'Septimus Hodge.'

HANNAH   Why were these things saved, do you think?

VALENTINE   Why should there be a reason?

HANNAH   And the diagram, what's it of?

VALENTINE   How would I know?

HANNAH   Why are you cross?

VALENTINE   I'm not cross. [*Pause.*] When your Thomasina was doing maths it had been the same maths for a couple of thousand years. Classical. And for a century after Thomasina. Then maths left the real world behind, just like modern art really. Nature was classical, maths was suddenly Picassos. But now nature is having the last laugh. The freaky stuff is turning out to be the mathematics of the natural world.

HANNAH   This feedback thing?

VALENTINE   For example.

HANNAH   Well, could Thomasina have—

VALENTINE   [*Snaps.*]   No, of course she bloody couldn't!

HANNAH   All right, you're not cross. What did you mean you were doing the same thing she was doing? [*Pause.*] What *are* you doing?

VALENTINE   Actually I'm doing it from the other end. She started with an equation and turned it into a graph. I've got a graph—real data—and I'm trying to find the equation which would give you the graph if you used it the way she's used hers. Iterated it.

HANNAH   What for?

VALENTINE   It's how you look at population changes in biology. Goldfish in a pond, say. This year there are x goldfish. Next year there'll be y goldfish. Some get born, some get eaten by herons, whatever. Nature manipulates the x and turns it into y. Then y goldfish is your starting population for the following year. Just like Thomasina. Your value for y becomes your next value for x. The question is: what is being done to x? What is the manipulation? Whatever it is, it can be written down as mathematics. It's called an algorithm.

HANNAH   It can't be the same every year.

VALENTINE   The details change, you can't keep tabs on everything, it's not nature in a box. But it isn't necessary to know the details. When they are all put together, it turns out the population is obeying a mathematical rule.

HANNAH   The goldfish are?

VALENTINE   Yes. No. The numbers. It's not about the behaviour of fish. It's about the behaviour of numbers. This thing works for any phenomenon which eats its own numbers—measles epidemics, rainfall averages, cotton prices, it's a natural phenomenon in itself. Spooky.

HANNAH   Does it work for grouse?

VALENTINE   I don't know yet. I mean, it does undoubtedly, but it's hard to show. There's more noise with grouse.

HANNAH   Noise?

VALENTINE   Distortions. Interference. Real data is messy. There's a thousand acres of moorland that had grouse on it, always did till about 1930. But nobody counted the grouse. They shot them. So you count the grouse they shot. But burning the heather interferes, it improves the food supply. A good year for foxes interferes the other way, they eat the chicks. And then there's the weather. It's all very, very noisy out there. Very hard to spot the tune. Like a piano in the next room, it's playing your song, but unfortunately it's out of whack, some of the strings are missing, and the pianist is tone deaf and drunk—I mean, the *noise*! Impossible!

HANNAH   What do you do?

VALENTINE   You start guessing what the tune might be. You try to pick it out of the noise. You try this, you try that, you start to get something— it's half-baked but you start putting in notes which are missing or not quite the right notes . . . and bit by bit . . . [*He starts to dumdi-da to the tune of 'Happy Birthday'.*] Dumdi-dum-dum, dear Val-en-tine, dumdi-dum-dum to you—the lost algorithm!

HANNAH [*Soberly.*]   Yes, I see. And then what?

VALENTINE   I publish.

HANNAH   Of course. Sorry. Jolly good.

VALENTINE   That's the theory. Grouse are bastards compared to goldfish.

HANNAH   Why did you choose them?

VALENTINE   The game books. My true inheritance. Two hundred years of real data on a plate.

HANNAH Somebody wrote down everything that's shot?

VALENTINE Well, that's what a game book is. I'm only using from 1870, when butts and beaters[5] came in.

HANNAH You mean the game books go back to Thomasina's time?

VALENTINE Oh yes. Further. [*And then getting ahead of her thought.*] No—really. I promise you. I *promise* you. Not a schoolgirl living in a country house in Derbyshire in eighteen-something!

HANNAH Well, what was she doing?

VALENTINE She was just playing with the numbers. The truth is, she wasn't doing anything.

HANNAH She must have been doing something.

VALENTINE Doodling. Nothing she understood.

HANNAH A monkey at a typewriter?[6]

VALENTINE Yes. Well, a piano.

[HANNAH *picks up the algebra book and reads from it.*]

HANNAH '. . . a method whereby all the forms of nature must give up their numerical secrets and draw themselves through number alone.' This feedback, is it a way of making pictures of forms in nature? Just tell me if it is or it isn't.

VALENTINE [*Irritated.*] To *me* it is. Pictures of turbulence—growth—change—creation—it's not a way of drawing an elephant, for God's sake!

HANNAH I'm sorry.

[*She picks up an apple leaf from the table. She is timid about pushing the point.*]

So you couldn't make a picture of this leaf by iterating a whatsit?

VALENTINE [*Off-hand.*] Oh yes, you could do that.

HANNAH [*Furiously.*] Well, tell me! Honestly, I could kill you!

VALENTINE If you knew the algorithm and fed it back say ten thousand times, each time there'd be a dot somewhere on the screen. You'd never know where to expect the next dot. But gradually you'd start to see this shape, because every dot will be inside the shape of this leaf. It wouldn't *be* a leaf, it would be a mathematical object. But yes. The unpredictable and the predetermined unfold together to make everything the way it is. It's how nature creates itself, on every scale, the snowflake and the snowstorm. It makes me so happy. To be at the beginning again, knowing almost nothing. People were talking about the end of physics. Relativity and quantum[7] looked as if they were going to clean out the whole problem between them. A theory of everything. But they only explained the very big and the very small. The universe, the elementary particles. The ordinary-sized stuff which is our lives, the things people write poetry about—clouds—daffodils—waterfalls—and what happens in a cup of coffee when the cream goes in—these things are full of mystery, as mysterious to us as the heavens were to the Greeks. We're better at predicting events at the edge of the galaxy or inside the nucleus of an atom than whether it'll rain on auntie's garden party three Sundays from now. Because the problem turns out to be different. We can't even

---

5. "Butts": concealed stands (blinds) for shooting birds. "Beaters": people employed to drive the birds toward the guns.

6. Refers to a once-popular belief that, given sufficient time, a monkey jabbing typewriter keys at random would eventually produce the complete plays of Shakespeare.

7. Twentieth-century advances in physics made by Albert Einstein (1879–1955) and others. Valentine continues with a simplified description of chaos theory.

predict the next drip from a dripping tap when it gets irregular. Each drip sets up the conditions for the next, the smallest variation blows prediction apart, and the weather is unpredictable the same way, will always be unpredictable. When you push the numbers through the computer you can see it on the screen. The future is disorder. A door like this has cracked open five or six times since we got up on our hind legs. It's the best possible time to be alive, when almost everything you thought you knew is wrong.

[Pause.]

HANNAH   The weather is fairly predictable in the Sahara.

VALENTINE   The scale is different but the graph goes up and down the same way. Six thousand years in the Sahara looks like six months in Manchester, I bet you.

HANNAH   How much?

VALENTINE   Everything you have to lose.

HANNAH [Pause.]   No.

VALENTINE   Quite right. That's why there was corn in Egypt.[8]

[Hiatus. The piano is heard again.]

HANNAH   What is he playing?

VALENTINE   I don't know. He makes it up.

HANNAH   Chloë called him 'genius'.

VALENTINE   It's what my mother calls him—only she means it. Last year some expert had her digging in the wrong place for months to find something or other—the foundations of Capability Brown's boat-house—and Gus put her right first go.

HANNAH   Did he ever speak?

VALENTINE   Oh yes. Until he was five. You've never asked about him. You get high marks here for good breeding.

HANNAH   Yes, I know. I've always been given credit for my unconcern.

[BERNARD enters in high excitement and triumph.]

BERNARD   English Bards and Scotch Reviewers. A pencilled superscrip-tion.[9] Listen and kiss my cycle-clips!

[He is carrying the book. He reads from it.]

'O harbinger of Sleep, who missed the press[1]
And hoped his drone might thus escape redress!
The wretched Chater, bard of Eros' Couch,
For his narcotic[2] let my pencil vouch!'

You see, you have to turn over every page.

HANNAH   Is it his[3] handwriting?

BERNARD   Oh, come on.

HANNAH   Obviously not.

BERNARD   Christ, what do you want?

HANNAH   Proof.

VALENTINE   Quite right. Who are you talking about?

BERNARD   Proof? Proof? You'd have to be there, you silly bitch!

VALENTINE [Mildly.]   I say, you're speaking of my fiancée.

8. Cf. Exodus 42.1.
9. Note.
1. O herald . . . who published his poem too late
to be included in the first edition of Byron's
work.
2. Sleep-inducing drug.
3. Byron's.

HANNAH Especially when I have a present for you. Guess what I found. [*Producing the present for* BERNARD.] Lady Croom writing from London to her husband. Her brother, Captain Brice, married a Mrs Chater. In other words, one might assume, a widow.
     [BERNARD *looks at the letter.*]

BERNARD I *said* he was dead. What year? 1810! Oh my God, 1810! Well *done*, Hannah! Are you going to tell me it's a different Mrs Chater?

HANNAH Oh no. It's her all right. Note her Christian name.

BERNARD Charity. Charity . . . 'Deny what cannot be proven for Charity's sake!'

HANNAH Don't kiss me!

VALENTINE She won't let anyone kiss her.

BERNARD You see! They wrote—they scribbled—they put it on paper. It was their employment. Their diversion. Paper is what they had. And there'll be more. There is always more. We can find it!

HANNAH Such passion. First Valentine, now you. It's moving.

BERNARD The aristocratic friend of the tutor—under the same roof as the poor sod whose book he savaged—the first thing he does is seduce Chater's wife. All is discovered. There is a duel. Chater dead, Byron fled! P.S. guess what?, the widow married her ladyship's brother! Do you honestly think no one wrote a word? How could they not! It dropped from sight but we will write it again!

HANNAH You can, Bernard. I'm not going to take any credit, I haven't done anything.
     [*The same thought has clearly occurred to* BERNARD. *He becomes instantly po-faced.*][4]

BERNARD Well, that's—very fair—generous—

HANNAH Prudent. Chater could have died of anything, anywhere.
     [*The po-face is forgotten.*]

BERNARD But he fought a duel with Byron!

HANNAH You haven't established it was fought. You haven't established it was Byron. For God's sake, Bernard, you haven't established Byron was even here!

BERNARD I'll tell you your problem. No guts.

HANNAH Really?

BERNARD By which I mean a visceral belief in yourself. Gut instinct. The part of you which doesn't reason. The certainty for which there is no back-reference. Because time is reversed. Tock, tick goes the universe and then recovers itself, but it was enough, you were in there and you bloody *know*.

VALENTINE Are you talking about Lord Byron, the poet?

BERNARD No, you fucking idiot, we're talking about Lord Byron the chartered[5] accountant.

VALENTINE [*Unoffended.*] Oh well, *he* was here all right, the poet.
     [*Silence.*]

HANNAH How do you know?

VALENTINE He's in the game book. I think he shot a hare. I read through the whole lot once when I had mumps—some quite interesting people—

---

4. Pompously serious.   5. Certified.

HANNAH   Where's the book?

VALENTINE   It's not one I'm using—too early, of course—

HANNAH   1809.

VALENTINE   They've always been in the commode. Ask Chloë.

> [HANNAH *looks to* BERNARD. BERNARD *has been silent because he has been incapable of speech. He seems to have gone into a trance, in which only his mouth tries to work.* HANNAH *steps over to him and gives him a demure kiss on the cheek. It works.* BERNARD *lurches out into the garden and can be heard croaking for 'Chloë . . . Chloë!']*

VALENTINE   My mother's lent him her bicycle. Lending one's bicycle is a form of safe sex, possibly the safest there is. My mother is in a flutter about Bernard, and he's no fool. He gave her a first edition of Horace Walpole, and now she's lent him her bicycle.

> [*He gathers up the three items [the primer, the lesson book and the diagram] and puts them into the portfolio.]*

Can I keep these for a while?

HANNAH   Yes, of course.

> [*The piano stops.* GUS *enters hesitantly from the music room.]*

VALENTINE   [*To* GUS.]   Yes, finished . . . coming now. [*To* HANNAH.] I'm trying to work out the diagram.

> [GUS *nods and smiles, at* HANNAH *too, but she is preoccupied.]*

HANNAH   What I don't understand is . . . why nobody did this feedback thing before—it's not like relativity, you don't have to be Einstein.

VALENTINE   You couldn't see to look before. The electronic calculator was what the telescope was for Galileo.[6]

HANNAH   Calculator?

VALENTINE   There wasn't enough time before. There weren't enough *pencils!* [*He flourishes Thomasina's lesson book.*] This took her I don't know how many days and she hasn't scratched the paintwork. Now she'd only have to press a button, the same button over and over. Iteration. A few minutes. And what I've done in a couple of months, with only a *pencil* the calculations would take me the rest of my life to do again—thousands of pages—tens of thousands! And so boring!

HANNAH   Do you mean—?

> [*She stops because* GUS *is plucking* VALENTINE's *sleeve.*]

Do you mean—?

VALENTINE   All right, Gus, I'm coming.

HANNAH   Do you mean that was the only problem? Enough time? And paper? And the boredom?

VALENTINE   We're going to get out the dressing-up box.

HANNAH [*Driven to raising her voice.*]   *Val!* Is that what you're saying?

VALENTINE [*Surprised by her. Mildly.*]   No, I'm saying you'd have to have a reason for doing it.

> [GUS *runs out of the room, upset.*]

[*Apologetically.*] He hates people shouting.

HANNAH   I'm sorry.

> [VALENTINE *starts to follow* GUS.]

But anything else?

VALENTINE   Well, the other thing is, you'd have to be insane.

---

6. Galileo Galilei (1564–1642), Italian astronomer.

[VALENTINE *leaves.*

HANNAH *stays, thoughtful. After a moment, she turns to the table and picks up the* Cornhill Magazine. *She looks into it briefly, then closes it, and leaves the room, taking the magazine with her.*

The empty room.

The light changes to early morning. From a long way off, there is a pistol shot. A moment later there is the cry of dozens of crows disturbed from the unseen trees.]

Act Two

SCENE FIVE

BERNARD *is pacing around, reading aloud from a handful of typed sheets.* VALENTINE *and* CHLOË *are his audience.* VALENTINE *has his tortoise and is eating a sandwich from which he extracts shreds of lettuce to offer the tortoise.*

BERNARD   'Did it happen? Could it happen?

Undoubtedly it could. Only three years earlier the Irish poet Tom Moore appeared on the field of combat to avenge a review by Jeffrey of the *Edinburgh*. These affairs were seldom fatal and sometimes farcical but, potentially, the duellist stood in respect to the law no differently from a murderer. As for the murderee, a minor poet like Ezra Chater could go to his death in a Derbyshire glade as unmissed and unremembered as his contemporary and namesake, the minor botanist who died in the forests of the West Indies, lost to history like the monkey that bit him. On April 16th 1809, a few days after he left Sidley Park, Byron wrote to his solicitor John Hanson: 'If the consequences of my leaving England were ten times as ruinous as you describe, I have no alternative; there are circumstances which render it absolutely indispensable, and quit the country I must immediately.' To which, the editor's note in the Collected Letters reads as follows: 'What Byron's urgent reasons for leaving England were at this time has never been revealed.' The letter was written from the family seat, Newstead Abbey, Nottinghamshire. A long day's ride to the northwest lay Sidley Park, the estate of the Coverlys—a far grander family, raised by Charles II to the Earldom of Croom . . .'

[HANNAH *enters briskly, a piece of paper in her hand.*]

HANNAH   Bernard . . . ! Val . . .

BERNARD   Do you mind?

[HANNAH *puts her piece of paper down in front of* VALENTINE.]

CHLOË [*Angrily.*]   Hannah!

HANNAH   What?

CHLOË   She's so *rude!*

HANNAH [*Taken aback.*]   What? Am I?

VALENTINE   Bernard's reading us his lecture.

HANNAH   Yes, I know. [*Then recollecting herself.*] Yes—yes—that *was* rude. I'm sorry, Bernard.

VALENTINE [*With the piece of paper.*]   What is this?

HANNAH [*To* BERNARD.]   Spot on—the India Office Library. [*To* VALENTINE.] Peacock's letter in holograph,[7] I got a copy sent—

---

7. Handwriting.

CHLOË *Hannah!* Shut up!

HANNAH [*Sitting down.*] Yes, sorry.

BERNARD It's all right, I'll read it to myself.

CHLOË *No.*

[HANNAH *reaches for the Peacock letter and takes it back.*]

HANNAH Go on, Bernard. Have I missed anything? Sorry.

[BERNARD *stares at her balefully but then continues to read.*]

BERNARD 'The Byrons of Newstead in 1809 comprised an eccentric widow and her undistinguished son, the "lame brat", who until the age of ten when he came into the title, had been carted about the country from lodging to lodging by his vulgar hectoring monster of a mother—' [HANNAH's *hand has gone up.*]—overruled—'and who four months past his twenty-first birthday was master of nothing but his debts and his genius. Between the Byrons and the Coverlys there was no social equality and none to be expected. The connection, undisclosed to posterity until now, was with Septimus Hodge, Byron's friend at Harrow and Trinity College—' [HANNAH's *hand goes up again.*]—sustained—[*He makes an instant correction with a silver pencil.*] 'Byron's contemporary at Harrow and Trinity College, and now tutor in residence to the Croom daughter, Thomasina Coverly. Byron's letters tell us where he was on April 8th and on April 12th. He was at Newstead. But on the 10th he was at Sidley Park, as attested by the game book preserved there: "April 10th 1809—forenoon. High cloud, dry, and sun between times, wind southeasterly. Self—Augustus—Lord Byron. Fourteen pigeon, one hare (Lord B.)." But, as we know now, the drama of life and death at Sidley Park was not about pigeons but about sex and literature.'

VALENTINE Unless you were the pigeon.

BERNARD I don't have to do this. I'm paying you a compliment.

CHLOË Ignore him, Bernard—go on, get to the duel.

BERNARD Hannah's not even paying attention.

HANNAH Yes I am, it's all going in. I often work with the radio on.

BERNARD Oh thanks!

HANNAH Is there much more?

CHLOË *Hannah!*

HANNAH No, it's fascinating. I just wondered how much more there was. I need to ask Valentine about this [*letter.*]—sorry, Bernard, go on, this will keep.

VALENTINE Yes—sorry, Bernard.

CHLOË Please, Bernard!

BERNARD Where was I?

VALENTINE Pigeons.

CHLOË Sex.

HANNAH Literature.

BERNARD Life and death. Right. 'Nothing could be more eloquent of that than the three documents I have quoted: the terse demand to settle a matter in private; the desperate scribble of "my husband has sent for pistols"; and on April 11th, the gauntlet thrown down by the aggrieved and cuckolded author Ezra Chater. The covers[8] have not survived. What is certain is that all three letters were in Byron's possession when his

8. Envelopelike wrappers of letters. "Cuckolded": whose wife is adulterous.

books were sold in 1816—preserved in the pages of "The Couch of Eros" which seven years earlier at Sidley Park Byron had borrowed from Septimus Hodge.'

HANNAH   Borrowed?

BERNARD   I will be taking questions at the end. Constructive comments will be welcome. Which is indeed my reason for trying out in the provinces before my London opening[9] under the auspices of the Byron Society prior to publication. By the way, Valentine, do you want a credit?—'the game book recently discovered by'?

VALENTINE   It was never lost, Bernard.

BERNARD   'As recently pointed out by.' I don't normally like giving credit where it's due, but with scholarly articles as with divorce, there is a certain cachet[1] in citing a member of the aristocracy. I'll pop it in ad lib[2] for the lecture, and give you a mention in the press release. How's that?

VALENTINE   Very kind.

HANNAH   Press release? What happened to the *Journal of English Studies*?

BERNARD   That comes later with the apparatus,[3] and in the recognized tone—very dry, very modest, absolutely gloat-free, and yet unmistakably 'Eat your heart out, you dozy bastards'. But first, it's 'Media Don,[4] book early to avoid disappointment'. Where was I?

VALENTINE   Game book.

CHLOË   Eros.

HANNAH   Borrowed.

BERNARD   Right. '—borrowed from Septimus Hodge. Is it conceivable that the letters were already in the book when Byron borrowed it?'

VALENTINE   Yes.

CHLOË   Shut up, Val.

VALENTINE   Well, it's conceivable.

BERNARD   'Is it *likely* that Hodge would have lent Byron the book without first removing the three private letters?'

VALENTINE   Look, sorry—I only meant, Byron could have borrowed the book without asking.

HANNAH   That's true.

BERNARD   Then why wouldn't Hodge get them back?

HANNAH   I don't know, I wasn't there.

BERNARD   That's right, you bloody weren't.

CHLOË   Go on, Bernard.

BERNARD   'It is the third document, the challenge itself, that convinces. Chater "as a man and a poet", points the finger at his "slanderer in the press". Neither as a man nor a poet did Ezra Chater cut such a figure as to be habitually slandered or even mentioned in the press. It is surely indisputable that the slander was the review of "The Maid of Turkey" in the *Piccadilly Recreation*. Did Septimus Hodge have any connection with the London periodicals? No. Did Byron? Yes! He had reviewed Wordsworth two years earlier, he was to review Spencer[5] two years later. And do we have any clue as to Byron's opinion of Chater the poet? Yes!

---

9. New plays in Britain are frequently first performed outside London in preparation for more-sophisticated audiences in the capital.
1. Distinction.
2. Short for *ad libitum* (Latin): as an extempora-

neous aside.
3. In the later version with footnotes.
4. Professor in the media spotlight.
5. William Robert Spencer (1769–1834), poet and wit.

Who but Byron could have written the four lines pencilled into Lady Croom's copy of *English Bards and Scotch Reviewers*'—

HANNAH   Almost anybody.

BERNARD   Darling—

HANNAH   Don't call me darling.

BERNARD   Dickhead, then, is it likely that the man Chater calls his friend Septimus Hodge is the same man who screwed his wife and kicked the shit out of his last book?

HANNAH   Put it like that, almost certain.

CHLOË [*Earnestly.*]   You've been deeply wounded in the past, haven't you, Hannah?

HANNAH   Nothing compared to listening to this. Why is there nothing in Byron's letters about the *Piccadilly* reviews?

BERNARD   Exactly. Because he killed the author.

HANNAH   But the first one, 'The Maid of Turkey', was the year before. Was he clairvoyant?

CHLOË   Letters get lost.

BERNARD   Thank you! Exactly! There is a platonic[6] letter which confirms everything—lost but ineradicable, like radio voices rippling through the universe for all eternity. "My dear Hodge—here I am in Albania and you're the only person in the whole world who knows why. Poor C! I never wished him any harm—except in the *Piccadilly*, of course—it was the woman who bade me eat,[7] dear Hodge!—what a tragic business, but thank God it ended well for poetry. Yours ever, B.—PS. Burn this."

VALENTINE   How did Chater find out the reviewer was Byron?

BERNARD [*Irritated.*]   I don't know, I wasn't there, was I? [*Pause. To* HANNAH.] You wish to say something?

HANNAH   Moi?[8]

CHLOË   I know. Byron told Mrs Chater in bed. Next day he dumped her so she grassed on him, and pleaded date rape.

BERNARD [*Fastidiously.*]   Date rape? What do you mean, date rape?

HANNAH   April the tenth.

[BERNARD *cracks. Everything becomes loud and overlapped as* BERNARD *threatens to walk out and is cajoled into continuing.*]

BERNARD   Right!—forget it!

HANNAH   Sorry—

BERNARD   No—I've had nothing but sarcasm and childish interruptions—

VALENTINE   What did I do?

BERNARD   No credit for probably the most sensational literary discovery of the century—

CHLOË   I think you're jolly unfair—they're jealous, Bernard—

HANNAH   I won't say another word—

VALENTINE   Yes, go on, Bernard—we promise.

BERNARD [*Finally.*]   Well, only if you stop *feeding tortoises*!

VALENTINE   Well, it's his lunch time.

BERNARD   And on condition that I am afforded the common courtesy of a scholar among scholars—

---

6. Nonexistent ideal.
7. Cf. Genesis 3.12.

8. Me? (French).

HANNAH   Absolutely mum till you're finished—

BERNARD   After which, any comments are to be couched in terms of accepted academic—

HANNAH   Dignity—you're right, Bernard.

BERNARD   —respect.

HANNAH   Respect. Absolutely. The language of scholars. Count on it.

[*Having made a great show of putting his pages away,* BERNARD *reassembles them and finds his place, glancing suspiciously at the other three for signs of levity.*]

BERNARD   Last paragraph. 'Without question, Ezra Chater issued a challenge to *somebody*. If a duel was fought in the dawn mist of Sidley Park in April 1809, his opponent, on the evidence, was a critic with a gift for ridicule and a taste for seduction. Do we need to look far? Without question, Mrs Chater was a widow by 1810. If we seek the occasion of Ezra Chater's early and unrecorded death, do we need to look far? Without question, Lord Byron, in the very season of his emergence as a literary figure, quit the country in a cloud of panic and mystery, and stayed abroad for two years at a time when Continental travel was unusual and dangerous. If we seek his reason—*do we need to look far?*'

[*No mean performer, he is pleased with the effect of his peroration. There is a significant silence.*]

HANNAH   Bollocks.[9]

CHLOË   Well, I think it's true.

HANNAH   You've left out everything which doesn't fit. Byron had been banging on[1] for months about leaving England—there's a letter in *February*—

BERNARD   But he didn't go, did he?

HANNAH   And then he didn't sail until the beginning of July!

BERNARD   Everything moved more slowly then. Time was different. He was two weeks in Falmouth waiting for wind or something—

HANNAH   Bernard, I don't know why I'm bothering—you're arrogant, greedy and reckless. You've gone from a glint in your eye to a sure thing in a hop, skip and a jump. You deserve what you get and I think you're mad. But I can't help myself, you're like some exasperating child pedalling its tricycle towards the edge of a cliff, and I have to do something. So listen to me. If Byron killed Chater in a duel I'm Marie of Romania.[2] You'll end up with so much *fame* you won't leave the house without a paper bag over your head.

VALENTINE   Actually, Bernard, as a scientist, your theory is incomplete.

BERNARD   But I'm not a scientist.

VALENTINE   [*Patiently.*]   No, *as a scientist*—

BERNARD   [*Beginning to shout.*]   I have yet to hear a proper argument.

HANNAH   Nobody would kill a man and then pan his book. I mean, not in that order. So he must have borrowed the book, written the review, *posted it*, seduced Mrs Chater, fought a duel and departed, all in the space of two or three days. Who would do that?

BERNARD   Byron.

9. Nonsense (slang).
1. Talking (slang).
2. Cf. Dorothy Parker's poem "Comment," lines

3–4: "And love is a thing that can never go wrong; / And I am Marie of Roumania."

HANNAH   It's hopeless.

BERNARD   You've never understood him, as you've shown in your novel-ette.[3]

HANNAH   In my what?

BERNARD   Oh, sorry—did you think it was a work of historical revision-ism? Byron the spoilt child promoted beyond his gifts by the spirit of the age! And Caroline the closet intellectual shafted by a male society!

VALENTINE   I read that somewhere—

HANNAH   It's his review.

BERNARD   And bloody well said, too!

[*Things are turning a little ugly and* BERNARD *seems in a mood to push them that way.*]

You got them backwards, darling. Caroline was Romantic waffle on wheels with no talent, and Byron was an eighteenth-century Rationalist[4] touched by genius. And he killed Chater.

HANNAH [*Pause.*]   If it's not too late to change my mind, I'd like you to go ahead.

BERNARD   I intend to. Look to the mote in your own eye![5]—you even had the wrong bloke on the dust-jacket!

HANNAH   Dust-jacket?

VALENTINE   What about my computer model? Aren't you going to men-tion it?

BERNARD   It's inconclusive.

VALENTINE [*To* HANNAH.]   The *Piccadilly* reviews aren't a very good fit with Byron's other reviews, you see.

HANNAH [*To* BERNARD.]   What do you mean, the wrong bloke?

BERNARD [*Ignoring her.*]   The other reviews aren't a very good fit for each other, are they?

VALENTINE   No, but differently. The parameters—[6]

BERNARD [*Jeering.*]   Parameters! You can't stick Byron's head in your lap-top! Genius isn't like your average grouse.

VALENTINE [*Casually.*]   Well, it's all trivial anyway.

BERNARD   What is?

VALENTINE   Who wrote what when . . .

BERNARD   Trivial?

VALENTINE   Personalities.

BERNARD   I'm sorry—did you say trivial?

VALENTINE   It's a technical term.[7]

BERNARD   Not where I come from, it isn't.

VALENTINE   The questions you're asking don't matter, you see. It's like arguing who got there first with the calculus. The English say Newton, the Germans say Leibnitz.[8] But it doesn't *matter*. Personalities. What matters is the calculus. Scientific progress. Knowledge.

BERNARD   Really? Why?

VALENTINE   Why what?

BERNARD   Why does scientific progress matter more than personalities?

VALENTINE   Is he serious?

3. Sentimental short novel.
4. Person whose opinions are based on pure rea-soning. "Waffle": gossip.
5. Cf. Matthew 7.3.

6. Distinguishing or defining characteristics.
7. From mathematics.
8. Gottfried Wilhelm, Baron von Leibnitz (1646–1716), German philosopher and mathematician.

HANNAH   No, he's trivial. Bernard—

VALENTINE [*Interrupting, to* BERNARD.]   Do yourself a favour, you're on a loser.

BERNARD   Oh, you're going to zap me with penicillin and pesticides. Spare me that and I'll spare you the bomb and aerosols. But don't confuse progress with perfectibility. A great poet is always timely. A great philosopher is an urgent need. There's no rush for Isaac Newton. We were quite happy with Aristotle's cosmos. Personally, I preferred it. Fifty-five crystal spheres geared to God's crankshaft is my idea of a satisfying universe. I can't think of anything more trivial than the speed of light. Quarks, quasars—big bangs, black holes—who gives a shit? How did you people[9] con us out of all that status? All that money? And why are you so pleased with yourselves?

CHLOË   Are you against penicillin, Bernard?

BERNARD   Don't feed the animals.[1] [*Back to* VALENTINE.]   I'd push the lot of you over a cliff myself. Except the one in the wheelchair.[2] I think I'd lose the sympathy vote before people had time to think it through.

HANNAH [*Loudly.*]   What the hell do you mean, the dust-jacket?

BERNARD [*Ignoring her.*]   If knowledge isn't self-knowledge it isn't doing much, mate. Is the universe expanding? Is it contracting? Is it standing on one leg and singing 'When Father Painted the Parlour'? Leave me out. I can expand my universe without you. 'She walks in beauty, like the night of cloudless climes and starry skies, and all that's best of dark and bright meet in her aspect and her eyes.'[3] There you are, he wrote it after coming home from a party. [*With offensive politeness.*] What is it that you're doing with grouse, Valentine, I'd love to know?

[VALENTINE *stands up and it is suddenly apparent that he is shaking and close to tears.*]

VALENTINE [*To* CHLOË.]   He's not against penicillin, and he knows I'm not against poetry. [*To* BERNARD.] I've given up on the grouse.

HANNAH   You haven't, Valentine!

VALENTINE [*Leaving.*]   I can't do it.

HANNAH   *Why?*

VALENTINE   Too much noise. There's just too much *bloody noise*!

[*On which,* VALENTINE *leaves the room.* CHLOË, *upset and in tears, jumps up and briefly pummels* BERNARD *ineffectually with her fists.*]

CHLOË   You bastard, Bernard!

[*She follows* VALENTINE *out. Pause.*]

HANNAH   Well, I think that's everybody. You can leave now, give Gus a kick on your way out.

BERNARD   Yes, I'm sorry about that. It's no fun when it's not among pros, is it?

HANNAH   No.

BERNARD   Oh, well . . . [*He begins to put his lecture sheets away in his briefcase, and is thus reminded . . .*] do you want to know about your book jacket? 'Lord Byron and Caroline Lamb at the Royal Academy'? Ink study by Henry Fuseli?[4]

---

9. Scientists.
1. Don't encourage them; i.e., don't keep the discussion going.
2. Stephen Hawking (b. 1942), physicist.

3. Lord Byron, "She walks in beauty," lines 1–4.
4. Swiss-born artist (1741–1825) who lived and worked in England.

HANNAH What about it?

BERNARD It's not them.

HANNAH [*She explodes.*] Who says!?

> [BERNARD *brings the* Byron Society Journal *from his briefcase.*]

BERNARD This Fuseli expert in the *Byron Society Journal*. They sent me the latest . . . as a distinguished guest speaker.

HANNAH But of course it's them! Everyone knows—

BERNARD Popular tradition only. [*He is finding the place in the journal.*] Here we are. 'No earlier than 1820'. He's analysed it. [*Offers it to her.*] Read at your leisure.

HANNAH [*She sounds like* BERNARD *jeering.*] Analysed it?

BERNARD Charming sketch, of course, but Byron was in Italy . . .

HANNAH But, Bernard—I *know* it's them.

BERNARD How?

HANNAH How? It just *is*. 'Analysed it', my big toe!

BERNARD Language!

HANNAH He's wrong.

BERNARD Oh, gut instinct, you mean?

HANNAH [*Flatly.*] He's wrong.

> [BERNARD *snaps shut his briefcase.*]

BERNARD Well, it's all trivial, isn't it? Why don't you come?

HANNAH Where?

BERNARD With me.

HANNAH To London? What for?

BERNARD What for.

HANNAH Oh, your lecture.

BERNARD No, no, bugger that. Sex.

HANNAH Oh . . . No. Thanks . . . [*Then, protesting.*] Bernard!

BERNARD You should try it. It's very underrated.

HANNAH Nothing against it.

BERNARD Yes, you have. You should let yourself go a bit. You might have written a better book. Or at any rate the right book.

HANNAH Sex and literature. Literature and sex. Your conversation, left to itself, doesn't have many places to go. Like two marbles rolling around a pudding basin. One of them is always sex.

BERNARD Ah well, yes. Men all over.

HANNAH No doubt. Einstein—relativity and sex. Chippendale—[5]sex and furniture. Galileo—'Did the earth move?' What the hell is it with you people? Chaps sometimes wanted to marry me, and I don't know a worse bargain. Available sex against not being allowed to fart in bed. What do you mean the right book?

BERNARD It takes a romantic to make a heroine of Caroline Lamb. You were cut out for Byron.

> [*Pause.*]

HANNAH So, cheerio.

BERNARD Oh, I'm coming back for the dance, you know. Chloë asked me.

HANNAH She meant well, but I don't dance.

BERNARD No, no—I'm going with her.

HANNAH Oh, I see. I don't, actually.

---

5. Thomas Chippendale (1718–1779), famous English cabinetmaker.

BERNARD I'm her date. Sub rosa.[6] Don't tell Mother.

HANNAH She doesn't want her mother to know?

BERNARD No—*I* don't want her mother to know. This is my first experience of the landed aristocracy. I tell you, I'm boggle-eyed.

HANNAH Bernard!—you haven't seduced that girl?

BERNARD Seduced her? Every time I turned round she was up a library ladder.

In the end I gave in. That reminds me—I spotted something between her legs that made me think of you.

[*He instantly receives a sharp stinging slap on the face but manages to remain completely unperturbed by it. He is already producing from his pocket a small book. His voice has hardly hesitated.*]

The Peaks Traveller and Gazetteer—James Godolphin 1832—unillustrated, I'm afraid. [*He has opened the book to a marked place.*] Sidley Park in Derbyshire, property of the Earl of Croom . . .'

HANNAH [*Numbly.*] The world is going to hell in a handcart.

BERNARD 'Five hundred acres including forty of lake—the Park by Brown and Noakes has pleasing features in the horrid style—viaduct, grotto,[7] etc—a hermitage occupied by a lunatic since twenty years without discourse or companion save for a pet tortoise, Plautus by name, which he suffers children to touch on request.' [*He holds out the book for her.*] A tortoise. They must be a feature.

[*After a moment* HANNAH *takes the book.*]

HANNAH Thank you.

[VALENTINE *comes to the door.*]

VALENTINE The station taxi is at the front . . .

BERNARD Yes . . . thanks . . . Oh—did Peacock come up trumps?[8]

HANNAH For some.

BERNARD Hermit's name and CV?

[*He picks up and glances at the Peacock letter.*]

'My dear Thackeray . . .' God, I'm good.

[*He puts the letter down.*]

Well, wish me luck—[*Vaguely to* VALENTINE] Sorry about . . . you know . . . [*and to* HANNAH] and about your . . .

VALENTINE Piss off, Bernard.

BERNARD Right.

[BERNARD *goes.*]

HANNAH Don't let Bernard get to you. It's only performance art, you know. Rhetoric, they used to teach it in ancient times, like PT.[9] It's not about being right, they had philosophy for that. Rhetoric was their chat show. Bernard's indignation is a sort of aerobics for when he gets on television.

VALENTINE I don't care to be rubbished by the dustbin man.[1]

[*He has been looking at the letter.*] The what of the lunatic?

[HANNAH *reclaims the letter and reads it for him.*]

HANNAH 'The testament of the lunatic serves as a caution against French fashion . . . for it was Frenchified mathematick that brought him to the

6. Secretly (Latin).
7. Artificial cave or cavern. "Horrid": Gothic. "Viaduct": bridgelike structure designed to carry a road over a valley, river, etc.
8. Give you what you wanted.

9. Physical training. "Performance art": nontraditional art form that involves presentation to an audience and sometimes involves acting.
1. Garbage collector.

melancholy certitude of a world without light or life . . . as a wooden stove that must consume itself until ash and stove are as one, and heat is gone from the earth.'

VALENTINE [*Amused, surprised.*]   Huh!

HANNAH   'He died aged two score years and seven, hoary as Job[2] and meagre as a cabbage-stalk, the proof of his prediction even yet unyielding to his labours for the restitution of hope through good English algebra.'

VALENTINE   That's it?

HANNAH [*Nods.*]   Is there anything in it?

VALENTINE   In what? We are all doomed? [*Casually.*] Oh yes, sure—it's called the second law of thermodynamics.

HANNAH   Was it known about?

VALENTINE   By poets and lunatics from time immemorial.

HANNAH   Seriously.

VALENTINE   No.

HANNAH   Is it anything to do with . . . you know, Thomasina's discovery?

VALENTINE   She didn't discover anything.

HANNAH   Her lesson book.

VALENTINE   No.

HANNAH   A coincidence, then?

VALENTINE   What is?

HANNAH [*Reading.*]   'He died aged two score years and seven.' That was in 1834. So he was born in 1787. So was the tutor. He says so in his letter to Lord Croom when he recommended himself for the job: 'Date of birth—1787.' The hermit was born in the same year as Septimus Hodge.

VALENTINE [*Pause.*]   Did Bernard bite you in the leg?[3]

HANNAH   Don't you see? I thought my hermit was a perfect symbol. An idiot in the landscape. But this is better. The Age of Enlightenment banished into the Romantic wilderness! The genius of Sidley Park living on in a hermit's hut!

VALENTINE   You don't *know* that.

HANNAH   Oh, but I do. I do. Somewhere there will be *something* . . . if only I can find it.

SCENE SIX

The room is empty.

A reprise: early morning—a distant pistol shot—the sound of the crows.

JELLABY *enters the dawn-dark room with a lamp. He goes to the windows and looks out. He sees something. He returns to put the lamp on the table, and then opens one of the french windows and steps outside.*

JELLABY [*Outside.*]   Mr Hodge!
    [SEPTIMUS *comes in, followed by* JELLABY, *who closes the garden door.* SEPTIMUS *is wearing a greatcoat.*]

SEPTIMUS   Thank you, Jellaby. I was expecting to be locked out. What time is it?

2. As old as Job, who, according to the Bible, lived to be 140. "Two score years and seven": forty-seven.

3. Like a mad dog, whose bite transmits madness (rabies).

JELLABY Half past five.

SEPTIMUS That is what I have. Well!—what a bracing experience!

[*He produces two pistols from inside his coat and places them on the table.*]

The dawn, you know. Unexpectedly lively. Fishes, birds, frogs . . . rabbits . . . [*he produces a dead rabbit from inside his coat.*] and very beautiful. If only it did not occur so early in the day. I have brought Lady Thomasina a rabbit. Will you take it?

JELLABY It's dead.

SEPTIMUS Yes. Lady Thomasina loves a rabbit pie.

[JELLABY *takes the rabbit without enthusiasm. There is a little blood on it.*]

JELLABY You were missed, Mr Hodge.

SEPTIMUS I decided to sleep last night in the boat-house. Did I see a carriage leaving the Park?

JELLABY Captain Brice's carriage, with Mr and Mrs Chater also.

SEPTIMUS Gone?!

JELLABY Yes, sir. And Lord Byron's horse was brought round at four o'clock.

SEPTIMUS Lord Byron too!

JELLABY Yes, sir. The house has been up and hopping.

SEPTIMUS But I have his rabbit pistols! What am I to do with his rabbit pistols?

JELLABY You were looked for in your room.

SEPTIMUS By whom?

JELLABY By her ladyship.

SEPTIMUS In my room?

JELLABY I will tell her ladyship you are returned.

[*He starts to leave.*]

SEPTIMUS Jellaby! Did Lord Byron leave a book for me?

JELLABY A book?

SEPTIMUS He had the loan of a book from me.

JELLABY His lordship left nothing in his room, sir, not a coin.[4]

SEPTIMUS Oh. Well, I'm sure he would have left a coin if he'd had one. Jellaby—here is a half-guinea for you.

JELLABY Thank you very much, sir.

SEPTIMUS What has occurred?

JELLABY The servants are told nothing, sir.

SEPTIMUS Come, come, does a half-guinea buy nothing any more?

JELLABY [*Sighs.*] Her ladyship encountered Mrs Chater during the night.

SEPTIMUS Where?

JELLABY On the threshold of Lord Byron's room.

SEPTIMUS Ah. Which one was leaving and which entering?

JELLABY Mrs Chater was leaving Lord Byron's room.

SEPTIMUS And where was Mr Chater?

JELLABY Mr Chater and Captain Brice were drinking cherry brandy. They had the footman to keep the fire up until three o'clock. There was a loud altercation upstairs, and—

[LADY CROOM *enters the room.*]

---

4. Guests staying in country houses were expected to leave tips for the servants.

LADY CROOM Well, Mr Hodge.

SEPTIMUS My lady.

LADY CROOM All this to shoot a hare?

SEPTIMUS A rabbit. [*She gives him one of her looks.*] No, indeed, a hare, though very rabbit-like—

[JELLABY *is about to leave.*]

LADY CROOM My infusion.[5]

JELLABY Yes, my lady.

[*He leaves.* LADY CROOM *is carrying two letters. We have not seen them before. Each has an envelope which has been opened. She flings them on the table.*]

LADY CROOM How dare you!

SEPTIMUS I cannot be called to account for what was written in private and read without regard to propriety.

LADY CROOM Addressed to me!

SEPTIMUS Left in my room, in the event of my death—

LADY CROOM Pah!—what earthly use is a love letter from beyond the grave?

SEPTIMUS As much, surely, as from this side of it. The second letter, however, was not addressed to your ladyship.

LADY CROOM I have a mother's right to open a letter addressed by you to my daughter, whether in the event of your life, your death, or your imbecility. What do you mean by writing to her of rice pudding when she has just suffered the shock of violent death in our midst?

SEPTIMUS Whose death?

LADY CROOM Yours, you wretch!

SEPTIMUS Yes, I see.

LADY CROOM I do not know which is the madder of your ravings. One envelope full of rice pudding, the other of the most insolent familiarities regarding several parts of my body, but have no doubt which is the more intolerable to me.

SEPTIMUS Which?

LADY CROOM Oh, aren't we saucy when our bags are packed! Your friend has gone before you, and I have despatched the harlot Chater and her husband—and also my brother for bringing them here. Such is the sentence, you see, for choosing unwisely in your acquaintance. Banishment. Lord Byron is a rake and a hypocrite, and the sooner he sails for the Levant[6] the sooner he will find society congenial to his character.

SEPTIMUS It has been a night of reckoning.

LADY CROOM Indeed, I wish it had passed uneventfully with you and Mr Chater shooting each other with the decorum due to a civilized house. You have no secrets left, Mr Hodge. They spilled out between shrieks and oaths and tears. It is fortunate that a lifetime's devotion to the sporting gun has halved my husband's hearing to the ear he sleeps on.

SEPTIMUS I'm afraid I have no knowledge of what has occurred.

LADY CROOM Your trollop[7] was discovered in Lord Byron's room.

SEPTIMUS Ah. Discovered by Mr Chater?

LADY CROOM Who else?

5. Tea.
6. Lands in the eastern part of the Mediterranean. "Rake": sexually promiscuous man.
7. Loose woman (Mrs. Chater).

SEPTIMUS   I am very sorry, madam, for having used your kindness to bring my unworthy friend to your notice. He will have to give an account of himself to me, you may be sure.

[*Before* LADY CROOM *can respond to this threat,* JELLABY *enters the room with her 'infusion'. This is quite an elaborate affair: a pewter tray on small feet on which there is a kettle suspended over a spirit lamp. There is a cup and saucer and the silver 'basket' containing the dry leaves for the tea.* JELLABY *places the tray on the table and is about to offer further assistance with it.*]

LADY CROOM   I will do it.

JELLABY   Yes, my lady. [*To* SEPTIMUS.] Lord Byron left a letter for you with the valet,[8] sir.

SEPTIMUS   Thank you.

[SEPTIMUS *takes the letter off the tray.* JELLABY *prepares to leave.* LADY CROOM *eyes the letter.*]

LADY CROOM   When did he do so?

JELLABY   As he was leaving, your ladyship.

[JELLABY *leaves.* SEPTIMUS *puts the letter into his pocket.*]

SEPTIMUS   Allow me.

[*Since she does not object, he pours a cup of tea for her. She accepts it.*]

LADY CROOM   I do not know if it is proper for you to receive a letter written in my house from someone not welcome in it.

SEPTIMUS   Very improper, I agree. Lord Byron's want of delicacy is a grief to his friends, among whom I no longer count myself. I will not read his letter until I have followed him through the gates.

[*She considers that for a moment.*]

LADY CROOM   That may excuse the reading but not the writing.

SEPTIMUS   Your ladyship should have lived in the Athens of Pericles![9] The philosophers would have fought the sculptors for your idle hour!

LADY CROOM [*Protesting.*]   Oh, really! . . . [*Protesting less.*] Oh really . . .

[SEPTIMUS *has taken Byron's letter from his pocket and is now setting fire to a corner of it using the little flame from the spirit lamp.*]

Oh . . . really . . .

[*The paper blazes in* SEPTIMUS's *hand and he drops it and lets it burn out on the metal tray.*]

SEPTIMUS   Now there's a thing—a letter from Lord Byron never to be read by a living soul. I will take my leave, madam, at the time of your desiring it.

LADY CROOM   To the Indies?[1]

SEPTIMUS   The Indies! Why?

LADY CROOM   To follow the Chater, of course. She did not tell you?

SEPTIMUS   She did not exchange half-a-dozen words with me.

LADY CROOM   I expect she did not like to waste the time. The Chater sails with Captain Brice.

SEPTIMUS   Ah. As a member of the crew?

LADY CROOM   No, as wife to Mr Chater, plant-gatherer to my brother's expedition.

SEPTIMUS   I knew he was no poet. I did not know it was botany under the false colours.

---

8. Manservant.
9. Athenian military commander, statesman, and

patron of the arts (ca. 495–429 B.C.E.).
1. West Indies.

LADY CROOM   He is no more a botanist. My brother paid fifty pounds to have him published, and he will pay a hundred and fifty to have Mr Chater picking flowers in the Indies for a year while the wife plays mistress of the Captain's quarters. Captain Brice has fixed his passion on Mrs Chater, and to take her on voyage he has not scrupled to deceive the Admiralty, the Linnean Society and Sir Joseph Banks, botanist to His Majesty at Kew.[2]

SEPTIMUS   Her passion is not as fixed as his.

LADY CROOM   It is a defect of God's humour that he directs our hearts everywhere but to those who have a right to them.

SEPTIMUS   Indeed, madam. [*Pause.*] But is Mr Chater deceived?

LADY CROOM   He insists on it, and finds the proof of his wife's virtue in his eagerness to defend it. Captain Brice is *not* deceived but cannot help himself. He would die for her.

SEPTIMUS   I think, my lady, he would have Mr Chater die for her.

LADY CROOM   Indeed, I never knew a woman worth the duel, or the other way about. Your letter to me goes very ill with your conduct to Mrs Chater, Mr Hodge. I have had experience of being betrayed before the ink is dry, but to be betrayed before the pen is even dipped, and with the village notice-board, what am I to think of such a performance?

SEPTIMUS   My lady, I was alone with my thoughts in the gazebo, when Mrs Chater ran me to ground, and I being in such a passion, in an agony of unrelieved desire—

LADY CROOM   Oh . . . !

SEPTIMUS   —I thought in my madness that the Chater with her skirts over her head would give me the momentary illusion of the happiness to which I dared not put a face.
        [*Pause.*]

LADY CROOM   I do not know when I have received a more unusual compliment, Mr Hodge. I hope I am more than a match for Mrs Chater with her head in a bucket. Does she wear drawers?

SEPTIMUS   She does.

LADY CROOM   Yes, I have heard that drawers are being worn now. It is unnatural for women to be got up like jockeys. I cannot approve.
        [*She turns with a whirl of skirts and moves to leave.*]
    I know nothing of Pericles or the Athenian philosophers. I can spare them an hour, in my sitting room when I have bathed. Seven o'clock. Bring a book.
        [*She goes out.* SEPTIMUS *picks up the two letters, the ones he wrote, and starts to burn them in the flame of the spirit lamp.*]

SCENE SEVEN

VALENTINE *and* CHLOË *are at the table.* GUS *is in the room.*

    CHLOË *is reading from two Saturday newspapers. She is wearing workaday period clothes, a Regency dress,[3] no hat.*

---

2. See p. 1031, n. 7. "Admiralty": headquarters of the British Navy. "Linnean Society": Britain's leading botanical association. Sir Joseph Banks (1743–1820), naturalist and patron of the sciences.

3. Fashionable in the "Regency" period, 1811–20, when George, Prince of Wales, was regent, ruling England after his father, George III, had been judged insane.

VALENTINE *is pecking at a portable computer. He is wearing unkempt Regency clothes, too.*

The clothes have evidently come from a large wicker laundry hamper, from which GUS *is producing more clothes to try on himself. He finds a Regency coat and starts putting it on.*

The objects on the table now include two geometrical solids, pyramid and cone, about twenty inches high, of the type used in a drawing lesson; and a pot of dwarf dahlias (which do not look like modern dahlias).

CHLOË 'Even in Arcadia—Sex, Literature and Death at Sidley Park'. Picture of Byron.

VALENTINE Not of Bernard?

CHLOË 'Byron Fought Fatal Duel, Says Don' . . . Valentine, do you think I'm the first person to think of this?

VALENTINE No.

CHLOË I haven't said yet. The future is all programmed like a computer—that's a proper theory, isn't it?

VALENTINE The deterministic[4] universe, yes.

CHLOË Right. Because everything including us is just a lot of atoms bouncing off each other like billiard balls.

VALENTINE Yes. There was someone, forget his name, 1820s, who pointed out that from Newton's laws you could predict everything to come—I mean, you'd need a computer as big as the universe but the formula would exist.

CHLOË But it doesn't work, does it?

VALENTINE No. It turns out the maths is different.

CHLOË No, it's all because of sex.

VALENTINE Really?

CHLOË That's what I think. The universe is deterministic all right, just like Newton said, I mean it's trying to be, but the only thing going wrong is people fancying people who aren't supposed to be in that part of the plan.

VALENTINE Ah. The attraction that Newton left out. All the way back to the apple in the garden.[5] Yes. [*Pause.*] Yes, I think you're the first person to think of this.

[HANNAH *enters, carrying a tabloid paper, and a mug of tea.*]

HANNAH Have you seen this? 'Bonking[6] Byron Shot Poet'.

CHLOË [*Pleased.*] Let's see.

[HANNAH *gives her the paper, smiles at* GUS.]

VALENTINE He's done awfully well, hasn't he? How did they all know?

HANNAH Don't be ridiculous. [*To* CHLOË.] Your father wants it back.

CHLOË All right.

HANNAH What a fool.

CHLOË Jealous. I think it's brilliant. [*She gets up to go. To* GUS.] Yes, that's perfect, but not with trainers. Come on, I'll lend you a pair of flatties,[7] they'll look period on you—

HANNAH Hello, Gus. You all look so romantic.

[GUS *following* CHLOË *out, hesitates, smiles at her.*]

4. Predetermined (see Valentine and Chloë's discussion below).
5. Of Eden; cf. Genesis 3. Also the apple whose fall from the tree alerted Isaac Newton to the law of gravity.
6. Fucking (slang).
7. Flat-soled shoes. "Trainers": sneakers.

CHLOË [*Pointedly.*] Are you coming?
> [*She holds the door for* GUS *and follows him out, leaving a sense of her disapproval behind her.*]

HANNAH The important thing is not to give two monkeys for what young people think about you.
> [*She goes to look at the other newspapers.*]

VALENTINE [*Anxiously.*] You don't think she's getting a thing about[8] Bernard, do you?

HANNAH I wouldn't worry about Chloë, she's old enough to vote on her back. 'Byron Fought Fatal Duel, Says Don'. Or rather—[*Sceptically.*] 'Says Don!'

VALENTINE It may all prove to be true.

HANNAH It can't prove to be true, it can only not prove to be false yet.

VALENTINE [*Pleased.*] Just like science.

HANNAH If Bernard can stay ahead of getting the rug pulled till he's dead, he'll be a success.

VALENTINE *Just* like science . . . The ultimate fear is of posterity . . .

HANNAH Personally I don't think it'll take that long.

VALENTINE . . . and then there's the afterlife. An afterlife would be a mixed blessing. 'Ah—Bernard Nightingale, I don't believe you know Lord Byron.' It must be heaven up there.

HANNAH You can't believe in an afterlife, Valentine.

VALENTINE Oh, you're going to disappoint me at last.

HANNAH Am I? Why?

VALENTINE Science and religion.

HANNAH No, no, been there, done that, boring.

VALENTINE Oh, Hannah. Fiancée. Have pity. Can't we have a trial marriage and I'll call it off in the morning?

HANNAH [*Amused.*] I don't know when I've received a more unusual proposal.

VALENTINE [*Interested.*] Have you had many?

HANNAH That would be telling.

VALENTINE Well, why not? Your classical reserve is only a mannerism; and neurotic.

HANNAH Do you want the room?

VALENTINE You get nothing if you give nothing.

HANNAH I ask nothing.

VALENTINE No, stay.
> [VALENTINE *resumes work at his computer.* HANNAH *establishes herself among her references at 'her' end of the table. She has a stack of pocket-sized volumes, Lady Croom's 'garden books'.*]

HANNAH What are you doing? Valentine?

VALENTINE The set of points on a complex plane[9] made by—

HANNAH Is it the grouse?

VALENTINE Oh, the grouse. The damned grouse.

HANNAH You mustn't give up.

VALENTINE Why? Didn't you agree with Bernard?

HANNAH Oh, that. It's *all* trivial—your grouse, my hermit, Bernard's Byron. Comparing what we're looking for misses the point. It's wanting to

---

8. An infatuation for.
9. The "complex numbers" of mathematics laid out in a two-dimensional plane.

know that makes us matter. Otherwise we're going out the way we came in. That's why you can't believe in the afterlife, Valentine. Believe in the after, by all means, but not the life. Believe in God, the soul, the spirit, the infinite, believe in angels if you like, but not in the great celestial get-together for an exchange of views. If the answers are in the back of the book I can wait, but what a drag. Better to struggle on knowing that failure is final. [*She looks over* VALENTINE'*s shoulder at the computer screen. Reacting.*] Oh!, but . . . how beautiful!

VALENTINE   The Coverly set.[1]

HANNAH   The Coverly set! My goodness, Valentine!

VALENTINE   Lend me a finger.

[*He takes her finger and presses one of the computer keys several times.*] See? In an ocean of ashes, islands of order. Patterns making themselves out of nothing.

I can't show you how deep it goes. Each picture is a detail of the previous one, blown up. And so on. For ever. Pretty nice, eh?

HANNAH   Is it important?

VALENTINE   Interesting. Publishable.

HANNAH   Well done!

VALENTINE   Not me. It's Thomasina's. I just pushed her equations through the computer a few million times further than she managed to do with her pencil.

[*From the old portfolio he takes Thomasina's lesson book and gives it to* HANNAH. *The piano starts to be heard.*]

You can have it back now.

HANNAH   What does it mean?

VALENTINE   Not what you'd like it to.

HANNAH   Why not?

VALENTINE   Well, for one thing, she'd be famous.

HANNAH   No, she wouldn't. She was dead before she had time to be famous . . .

VALENTINE   She died?

HANNAH   . . . burned to death.

VALENTINE [*Realizing.*]   Oh . . . the girl who died in the fire!

HANNAH   The night before her seventeenth birthday. You can see where the dormer[2] doesn't match. That was her bedroom under the roof. There's a memorial in the Park.

VALENTINE [*Irritated.*]   I know—it's my house.

[VALENTINE *turns his attention back to his computer.* HANNAH *goes back to her chair. She looks through the lesson book.*]

HANNAH   Val, Septimus was her tutor—he and Thomasina would have—

VALENTINE   You do yours.

[*Pause. Two researchers.*

LORD AUGUSTUS, *fifteen years old, wearing clothes of 1812, bursts in through the non-music room door. He is laughing. He dives under the table. He is chased into the room by* THOMASINA, *aged sixteen and furious. She spots* AUGUSTUS *immediately.*]

---

1. Graphic representation of Thomasina's "rabbit equation" (see p. 1076).

2. Vertical window that projects from a sloping roof.

THOMASINA   You swore! You crossed your heart!

[AUGUSTUS *scampers out from under the table and* THOMASINA *chases him around it.*]

AUGUSTUS   I'll tell mama! I'll tell mama!

THOMASINA   You beast!

[*She catches* AUGUSTUS *as* SEPTIMUS *enters from the other door, carrying a book, a decanter*[3] *and a glass, and his portfolio.*]

SEPTIMUS   Hush! What is this? My lord! Order, order!

[THOMASINA *and* AUGUSTUS *separate.*]

  I am obliged.[4]

[SEPTIMUS *goes to his place at the table. He pours himself a glass of wine.*]

AUGUSTUS   Well, good day to you, Mr Hodge!

[*He is smirking about something.*

  THOMASINA *dutifully picks up a drawing book and settles down to draw the geometrical solids.*

SEPTIMUS *opens his portfolio.*]

SEPTIMUS   Will you join us this morning, Lord Augustus? We have our drawing lesson.

AUGUSTUS   I am a master of it at Eton, Mr Hodge, but we only draw naked women.

SEPTIMUS   You may work from memory.

THOMASINA   Disgusting!

SEPTIMUS   We will have silence now, if you please.

[*From the portfolio* SEPTIMUS *takes Thomasina's lesson book and tosses it to her; returning homework. She snatches it and opens it.*]

THOMASINA   No marks?! Did you not like my rabbit equation?

SEPTIMUS   I saw no resemblance to a rabbit.

THOMASINA   It eats its own progeny.[5]

SEPTIMUS [*Pause.*]   I did not see that.

[*He extends his hand for the lesson book. She returns it to him.*]

THOMASINA   I have not room to extend it.

[SEPTIMUS *and* HANNAH *turn the pages doubled by time.* AUGUSTUS *indolently starts to draw the models.*]

HANNAH   Do you mean the world is saved after all?

VALENTINE   No, it's still doomed. But if this is how it started, perhaps it's how the next one will come.

HANNAH   From good English algebra?

SEPTIMUS   It will go to infinity or zero, or nonsense.

THOMASINA   No, if you set apart the minus roots they square back to sense.

[SEPTIMUS *turns the pages.*

  THOMASINA *starts drawing the models.*

  HANNAH *closes the lesson book and turns her attention to her stack of 'garden books'.*]

VALENTINE   Listen—you know your tea's getting cold.

HANNAH   I like it cold.

---

3. Glass bottle (with a stopper) from which wine is served.
4. Thank you.

5. See p. 1053. VALENTINE: "She's feeding the solution back into the equation."

VALENTINE [*Ignoring that.*]   I'm telling you something. Your tea gets cold by itself, it doesn't get hot by itself. Do you think that's odd?

HANNAH   No.

VALENTINE   Well, it is odd. Heat goes to cold. It's a one-way street. Your tea will end up at room temperature. What's happening to your tea is happening to everything everywhere. The sun and the stars. It'll take a while but we're all going to end up at room temperature. When your hermit set up shop nobody understood this. But let's say you're right, in 18-whatever nobody knew more about heat than this scribbling nutter[6] living in a hovel in Derbyshire.

HANNAH   He was at Cambridge—a scientist.

VALENTINE   Say he was. I'm not arguing. And the girl was his pupil, she had a genius for her tutor.

HANNAH   Or the other way round.

VALENTINE   Anything you like. But not *this*! Whatever he thought he was doing to save the world with good English algebra it wasn't this!

HANNAH   Why? Because they didn't have calculators?

VALENTINE   No. Yes. Because there's an order things can't happen in. You can't open a door till there's a house.

HANNAH   I thought that's what genius was.

VALENTINE   Only for lunatics and poets.

    [*Pause.*]

HANNAH   'I had a dream which was not all a dream.

    The bright sun was extinguished, and the stars

    Did wander darkling in the eternal space,

    Rayless, and pathless, and the icy earth

    Swung blind and blackening in the moonless air . . .'[7]

VALENTINE   Your own?

HANNAH   Byron.

    [*Pause. Two researchers again.*]

THOMASINA   Septimus, do you think that I will marry Lord Byron?

AUGUSTUS   Who is he?

THOMASINA   He is the author of 'Childe Harold's Pilgrimage', the most poetical and pathetic and bravest hero of any book I ever read before, and the most modern and the handsomest, for Harold is Lord Byron himself to those who know him, like myself and Septimus. Well, Septimus?

SEPTIMUS [*Absorbed.*]   No.

    [*Then he puts her lesson book away into the portfolio and picks up his own book to read.*]

THOMASINA   Why not?

SEPTIMUS   For one thing, he is not aware of your existence.

THOMASINA   We exchanged many significant glances when he was at Sidley Park. I do wonder that he has been home almost a year from his adventures and has not written to me once.

SEPTIMUS   It is indeed improbable, my lady.

AUGUSTUS   Lord Byron?!—he claimed my hare, although my shot was the earlier! He said I missed by a hare's breadth. His conversation was very facetious. But I think Lord Byron will not marry you, Thom, for he was only lame and not blind.

---

6. Madman.

7. Byron, "Darkness," lines 1–5.

SEPTIMUS Peace! Peace until a quarter to twelve. It is intolerable for a tutor to have his thoughts interrupted by his pupils.

AUGUSTUS You are not *my* tutor, sir. I am visiting your lesson by my free will.

SEPTIMUS If you are so determined, my lord.

[THOMASINA *laughs at that, the joke is for her.* AUGUSTUS, *not included, becomes angry.*]

AUGUSTUS Your peace is nothing to me, sir. You do not rule over me.

THOMASINA [*Admonishing.*] Augustus!

SEPTIMUS I do not rule here, my lord. I inspire by reverence for learning and the exaltation of knowledge whereby man may approach God. There will be a shilling[8] for the best cone and pyramid drawn in silence by a quarter to twelve *at the earliest.*

AUGUSTUS You will not buy my silence for a shilling, sir. What I know to tell is worth much more than that.

[*And throwing down his drawing book and pencil, he leaves the room on his dignity, closing the door sharply. Pause.* SEPTIMUS *looks enquiringly at* THOMASINA.]

THOMASINA I told him you kissed me. But he will not tell.

SEPTIMUS When did I kiss you?

THOMASINA What! Yesterday!

SEPTIMUS Where?

THOMASINA On the lips!

SEPTIMUS In which country?

THOMASINA In the hermitage, Septimus!

SEPTIMUS On the lips in the hermitage! That? That was not a shilling kiss! I would not give sixpence to have it back. I had almost forgot it already.

THOMASINA Oh, cruel! Have you forgotten our compact?

SEPTIMUS God save me! Our compact?

THOMASINA To teach me to waltz! Sealed with a kiss, and a second kiss due when I can dance like mama!

SEPTIMUS Ah yes. Indeed. We were all waltzing like mice in London.

THOMASINA I must waltz, Septimus! I will be despised if I do not waltz! It is the most fashionable and gayest and boldest invention conceivable— started in Germany!

SEPTIMUS Let them have the waltz, they cannot have the calculus.

THOMASINA Mama has brought from town a whole book of waltzes for the Broadwood,[9] to play with Count Zelinsky.

SEPTIMUS I need not be told what I cannot but suffer. Count Zelinsky banging on the Broadwood without relief has me reading in waltz time.

THOMASINA Oh, stuff! What is your book?

SEPTIMUS A prize essay of the Scientific Academy in Paris. The author deserves your indulgence, my lady, for you are his prophet.

THOMASINA I? What does he write about? The waltz?

SEPTIMUS Yes. He demonstrates the equation of the propagation of heat in a solid body.[1] But in doing so he has discovered heresy—a natural contradiction of Sir Isaac Newton.

---

8. British coin (before decimalization of the currency in 1971) equal to twelve old pennies/ pence, or one-twentieth of a pound.
9. Brand of piano.

1. "Paris was the center of such studies: in 1807 Jean-Baptiste Fourier had written about heat flow. The French scientist most relevant is Sadi Carnot, founder of thermodynamics; but he was

THOMASINA   Oh!—he contradicts determinism?

SEPTIMUS   No! . . . Well, perhaps. He shows that the atoms do not go according to Newton.

> [*Her interest has switched in the mercurial way characteristic of her— she has crossed to take the book.*]

THOMASINA   Let me see—oh! In French?

SEPTIMUS   Yes. Paris is the capital of France.

THOMASINA   Show me where to read.

> [*He takes the book back from her and finds the page for her. Meanwhile, the piano music from the next room has doubled its notes and its emotion.*]

THOMASINA   Four-handed now! Mama is in love with the Count.

SEPTIMUS   He is a Count in Poland. In Derbyshire he is a piano tuner.

> [*She has taken the book and is already immersed in it. The piano music becomes rapidly more passionate, and then breaks off suddenly in mid-phrase. There is an expressive silence next door which makes* SEPTIMUS *raise his eyes. It does not register with* THOMASINA. *The silence allows us to hear the distant regular thump of the steam engine which is to be a topic. A few moments later* LADY CROOM *enters from the music room, seeming surprised and slightly flustered to find the schoolroom occupied. She collects herself, closing the door behind her. And remains watching, aimless and discreet, as though not wanting to interrupt the lesson.* SEPTIMUS *has stood, and she nods him back into his chair.*
>
> CHLOË, *in Regency dress, enters from the door opposite the music room. She takes in* VALENTINE *and* HANNAH *but crosses without pausing to the music room door.*]

CHLOË   Oh!—where's Gus?

VALENTINE   Dunno.

> [CHLOË *goes into the music room.*]

LADY CROOM [*Annoyed*]   Oh!—Mr Noakes's engine!

> [*She goes to the garden door and steps outside.*]
>
> CHLOË *re-enters.*]

CHLOË   Damn.

LADY CROOM [*Calls out.*]   Mr Noakes!

VALENTINE   He was there not long ago . . .

LADY CROOM   Halloo!

CHLOË   Well, he has to be in the photograph—is he dressed?

HANNAH   Is Bernard back?

CHLOË   No—he's late!

> [*The piano is heard again, under the noise of the steam engine.* LADY CROOM *steps back into the room.*
>
> CHLOË *steps outside the garden door. Shouts.*] Gus!

LADY CROOM   I wonder you can teach against such a disturbance and I am sorry for it, Mr Hodge.

> [CHLOË *comes back inside.*]

---

only sixteen in 1812. The essay is about the passing of heat from one body to another, which is why Septimus can humourously agree that it is 'about' the 'waltz'" (Jim Hunter, *Tom Stoppard*, 2000).

VALENTINE [*Getting up.*]   Stop ordering everybody about.

LADY CROOM   It is an unendurable noise.

VALENTINE   The photographer will wait.

> [*But, grumbling, he follows* CHLOË *out of the door she came in by, and closes the door behind them.* HANNAH *remains absorbed.*
>
> *In the silence, the rhythmic thump can be heard again.*]

LADY CROOM   The ceaseless dull overbearing monotony of it! It will drive me distracted. I may have to return to town to escape it.

SEPTIMUS   Your ladyship could remain in the country and let Count Zelinsky return to town where you would not hear him.

LADY CROOM   I mean Mr Noakes's engine! [*Semi-aside to* SEPTIMUS.] *Would you sulk? I will not have my daughter study sulking.*

THOMASINA [*Not listening.*]   What, mama?

> [THOMASINA *remains lost in her book.* LADY CROOM *returns to close the garden door and the noise of the steam engine subsides.*
>
> HANNAH *closes one of the 'garden books', and opens the next. She is making occasional notes.*
>
> *The piano ceases.*]

LADY CROOM [*To* THOMASINA.]   What are we learning today? [*Pause.*] Well, not manners.

SEPTIMUS   We are drawing today.

> [LADY CROOM *negligently examines what* THOMASINA *had started to draw.*]

LADY CROOM   Geometry. I approve of geometry.

SEPTIMUS   Your ladyship's approval is my constant object.

LADY CROOM   Well, do not despair of it. [*Returning to the window impatiently.*] Where is 'Culpability' Noakes?[2] [*She looks out and is annoyed.*] Oh!—he has gone for his hat so that he may remove it.

> [*She returns to the table and touches the bowl of dahlias.*
>
> HANNAH *sits back in her chair, caught by what she is reading.*]

For the widow's dowry of dahlias I can almost forgive my brother's marriage. We must be thankful the monkey bit the husband. If it had bit the wife the monkey would be dead and we would not be first in the kingdom to show a dahlia. [HANNAH, *still reading the garden book, stands up.*] I sent one potted to Chatsworth.[3] The Duchess was most satisfactorily put out[4] by it when I called at Devonshire House. Your friend was there lording it as a poet.

> [HANNAH *leaves through the door, following* VALENTINE *and* CHLOË.
>
> *Meanwhile,* THOMASINA *thumps the book down on the table.*]

THOMASINA   Well! Just as I said! Newton's machine which would knock our atoms from cradle to grave by the laws of motion is incomplete! Determinism leaves the road at every corner, as I knew all along, and the cause is very likely hidden in this gentleman's observation.

---

2. Noakes is called "culpable" (deserving of blame) for ruining the landscape designed by the "capable" Brown (so called because of his habit of saying a landscape had "capabilities," or potential). See p. 1040, n. 6.

3. Derbyshire "stately home" of the duke and duchess of Devonshire, whose London residence is Devonshire House.

4. Jealously annoyed.

LADY CROOM   Of what?

THOMASINA   The action of bodies in heat.

LADY CROOM   Is this geometry?

THOMASINA   This? No, I despise geometry!
[*Touching the dahlias she adds, almost to herself.*] The Chater would overthrow the Newtonian system in a weekend.

SEPTIMUS   Geometry, Hobbes assures us in the *Leviathan*,[5] is the only science God has been pleased to bestow on mankind.

LADY CROOM   And what does he mean by it?

SEPTIMUS   Mr Hobbes or God?

LADY CROOM   I am sure I do not know what either means by it.

THOMASINA   Oh, pooh to Hobbes! Mountains are not pyramids and trees are not cones. God must love gunnery and architecture if Euclid[6] is his only geometry. There is another geometry which I am engaged in discovering by trial and error, am I not, Septimus?

SEPTIMUS   Trial and error perfectly describes your enthusiasm, my lady.

LADY CROOM   How old are you today?

THOMASINA   Sixteen years and eleven months, mama, and three weeks.

LADY CROOM   Sixteen years and eleven months. We must have you married before you are educated beyond eligibility.[7]

THOMASINA   I am going to marry Lord Byron.

LADY CROOM   Are you? He did not have the manners to mention it.

THOMASINA   You have spoken to him?!

LADY CROOM   Certainly not.

THOMASINA   Where did you see him?

LADY CROOM   [*With some bitterness.*]   Everywhere.

THOMASINA   Did you, Septimus?

SEPTIMUS   At the Royal Academy where I had the honour to accompany your mother and Count Zelinsky.

THOMASINA   What was Lord Byron doing?

LADY CROOM   Posing.

SEPTIMUS   [*Tactfully.*]   He was being sketched during his visit . . . by the Professor of Painting . . . Mr Fuseli.[8]

LADY CROOM   There was more posing *at* the pictures than *in* them. His companion likewise reversed the custom of the Academy that the ladies viewing wear more than the ladies viewed—well, enough! Let him be hanged there for a Lamb.[9] I have enough with Mr Noakes, who is to a garden what a bull is to a china shop.
[*This as* NOAKES *enters.*]

THOMASINA   The Emperor of Irregularity!
[*She settles down to drawing the diagram which is to be the third item in the surviving portfolio.*]

LADY CROOM   Mr Noakes!

NOAKES   Your ladyship—

LADY CROOM   What have you done to me!

---

5. Philosophic treatise, published in 1651, by Thomas Hobbes (1588–1679).
6. Greek mathematician (flourished ca. 300 B.C.E.), famous for his *Elements*, a presentation of the geometry and other mathematics known in his day.
7. Suitability (as a partner in marriage).
8. See p. 1065, n. 4.
9. Cf. the old proverb "One might as well be hung for a sheep as a lamb."

NOAKES   Everything is satisfactory, I assure you. A little behind, to be
sure, but my dam will be repaired within the month—

LADY CROOM [*Banging the table*.]   Hush!
   [*In the silence, the steam engine thumps in the distance*.]
Can you hear, Mr Noakes?

NOAKES [*Pleased and proud*.]   The Improved Newcomen steam pump[1]—
the only one in England!

LADY CROOM   That is what I object to. If everybody had his own I would
bear my portion of the agony without complaint. But to have been singled out by the only Improved Newcomen steam pump in England, this
is hard, sir, this is not to be borne.

NOAKES   Your lady—

LADY CROOM   And for what? My lake is drained to a ditch for no purpose
I can understand, unless it be that snipe and curlew[2] have deserted
three counties so that they may be shot in our swamp. What you painted
as forest is a mean plantation, your greenery is mud, your waterfall is
wet mud, and your mount is an opencast mine for the mud that was
lacking in the dell.[3] [*Pointing through the window*.] What is that cowshed?

NOAKES   The hermitage, my lady?

LADY CROOM   It is a cowshed.

NOAKES   Madam, it is, I assure you, a very habitable cottage, properly
founded and drained, two rooms and a closet under a slate roof and a
stone chimney—

LADY CROOM   And who is to live in it?

NOAKES   Why, the hermit.

LADY CROOM   Where is he?

NOAKES   Madam?

LADY CROOM   You surely do not supply a hermitage without a hermit?

NOAKES   Indeed, madam—

LADY CROOM   Come, come, Mr Noakes. If I am promised a fountain I
expect it to come with water. What hermits do you have?

NOAKES   I have no hermits, my lady.

LADY CROOM   Not one? I am speechless.

NOAKES   I am sure a hermit can be found. One could advertise.

LADY CROOM   Advertise?

NOAKES   In the newspapers.

LADY CROOM   But surely a hermit who takes a newspaper is not a hermit
in whom one can have complete confidence.

NOAKES   I do not know what to suggest, my lady.

SEPTIMUS   Is there room for a piano?

NOAKES [*Baffled*.]   A piano?

LADY CROOM   We are intruding here—this will not do, Mr Hodge. Evidently, nothing is being learned. [*To* NOAKES.] Come along, sir!

THOMASINA   Mr Noakes—bad news from Paris!

NOAKES   Is it the Emperor Napoleon?

THOMASINA   No. [*She tears the page off her drawing block, with her 'diagram' on it*.] It concerns your heat engine. Improve it as you will, you

---

1. Thomas Newcomen had produced his first,
very inefficient, steam pump in 1712.

2. Two species of game birds.
3. Small valley.

can never get out of it what you put in. It repays eleven pence in the shilling at most. The penny is for this author's thoughts.

[*She gives the diagram to* SEPTIMUS *who looks at it.*]

NOAKES [*Baffled again.*] Thank you, my lady.

[NOAKES *goes out into the garden.*]

LADY CROOM [*To* SEPTIMUS.] Do you understand her?

SEPTIMUS No.

LADY CROOM Then this business is over. I was married at seventeen. *Ce soir il faut qu'on parle français, je te demande,*[4] Thomasina, as a courtesy to the Count. Wear your green velvet, please, I will send Briggs to do your hair. Sixteen and eleven months . . . !

[*She follows* NOAKES *out of view.*]

THOMASINA Lord Byron was with a lady?

SEPTIMUS Yes.

THOMASINA Huh!

[*Now* SEPTIMUS *retrieves his book from* THOMASINA. *He turns the pages, and also continues to study Thomasina's diagram. He strokes the tortoise absently as he reads.* THOMASINA *takes up pencil and paper and starts to draw* SEPTIMUS *with Plautus.*]

SEPTIMUS Why does it mean Mr Noakes's engine pays eleven pence in the shilling? Where does he say it?

THOMASINA Nowhere. I noticed it by the way. I cannot remember now.

SEPTIMUS Nor is he interested by determinism—

THOMASINA Oh . . . yes. Newton's equations go forwards and backwards, they do not care which way. But the heat equation cares very much, it goes only one way. That is the reason Mr Noakes's engine cannot give the power to drive Mr Noakes's engine.

SEPTIMUS Everybody knows that.

THOMASINA Yes, Septimus, they know it about engines!

SEPTIMUS [*Pause. He looks at his watch.*] A quarter to twelve. For your essay this week, explicate[5] your diagram.

THOMASINA I cannot, I do not know the mathematics.

SEPTIMUS Without mathematics, then.

[THOMASINA *has continued to draw. She tears the top page from her drawing pad and gives it to* SEPTIMUS.]

THOMASINA There. I have made a drawing of you and Plautus.

SEPTIMUS [*Looking at it.*] Excellent likeness. Not so good of me.

[THOMASINA *laughs, and leaves the room.*

AUGUSTUS *appears at the garden door. His manner cautious and diffident.*[6] SEPTIMUS *does not notice him for a moment.*

SEPTIMUS *gathers his papers together.*]

AUGUSTUS Sir . . .

SEPTIMUS My lord . . . ?

AUGUSTUS I gave you offence, sir, and I am sorry for it.

SEPTIMUS I took none, my lord, but you are kind to mention it.

AUGUSTUS I would like to ask you a question, Mr Hodge. [*Pause.*] You have an elder brother, I dare say, being a Septimus?[7]

SEPTIMUS Yes, my lord. He lives in London. He is the editor of a newspaper, the *Piccadilly Recreation.* [*Pause.*] Was that your question?

---

4. This evening I must ask you to speak French (French).
5. Explain.
6. Shy.
7. Latin for "seventh."

[AUGUSTUS, *evidently embarrassed about something, picks up the drawing of Septimus.*]

AUGUSTUS No. Oh . . . it is you? . . . I would like to keep it. [SEPTIMUS *inclines his head in assent.*] There are things a fellow cannot ask his friends. Carnal things. My sister has told me . . . my sister believes such things as I cannot, I assure you, bring myself to repeat.

SEPTIMUS You must not repeat them, then. The walk between here and dinner will suffice to put us straight, if we stroll by the garden. It is an easy business. And then I must rely on you to correct your sister's state of ignorance.

[*A commotion is heard outside*—BERNARD's *loud voice in a sort of agony.*]

BERNARD [*outside the door.*] Oh no—no—no—oh, bloody hell!—

AUGUSTUS Thank you, Mr Hodge, I will.

[*Taking the drawing with him,* AUGUSTUS *allows himself to be shown out through the garden door, and* SEPTIMUS *follows him.*

BERNARD *enters the room, through the door* HANNAH *left by.* VALENTINE *comes in with him, leaving the door open and they are followed by* HANNAH *who is holding the 'garden book.'*]

BERNARD Oh, no—no—

HANNAH I'm sorry, Bernard.

BERNARD Fucked by a dahlia! Do you think? Is it open and shut? Am I fucked? What does it really amount to? When all's said and done? Am I fucked? What do *you* think, Valentine? Tell me the truth.

VALENTINE You're fucked.

BERNARD Oh God! Does it mean that?

HANNAH Yes, Bernard, it does.

BERNARD I'm not sure. Show me where it says. I want to see it. No—read it—no, wait . . .

[BERNARD *sits at the table. He prepares to listen as though listening were an oriental art.*]

Right.

HANNAH [*Reading.*] 'October 1st, 1810. Today under the direction of Mr Noakes, a parterre[8] was dug on the south lawn and will be a handsome show next year, a consolation for the picturesque catastrophe of the second and third distances. The dahlia having propagated under glass with no ill effect from the sea voyage, is named by Captain Brice 'Charity' for his bride, though the honour properly belongs to the husband who exchanged beds with my dahlia, and an English summer for everlasting night in the Indies.'

[*Pause.*]

BERNARD Well, it's so round the houses, isn't it? Who's to say what it means?

HANNAH [*Patiently.*] It means that Ezra Chater of the Sidley Park connection is the same Chater who described a dwarf dahlia in Martinique in 1810 and died there, of a monkey bite.

BERNARD [*Wildly.*] Ezra wasn't a botanist! He was a poet!

HANNAH He was not much of either, but he was both.

VALENTINE It's not a disaster.

---

8. Level space in a garden occupied by an ornamental arrangement of flower beds.

BERNARD   Of course it's a disaster! I was on 'The Breakfast Hour'![9]

VALENTINE   It doesn't mean Byron didn't fight a duel, it only means Chater wasn't killed in it.

BERNARD   Oh, pull yourself together!—do you think I'd have been on 'The Breakfast Hour' if Byron had *missed*!

HANNAH   Calm down, Bernard. Valentine's right.

BERNARD [*Grasping at straws.*]   Do you think so? You mean the *Piccadilly* reviews? Yes, two completely unknown Byron essays—*and* my discovery of the lines he added to 'English Bards'. That counts for something.

HANNAH [*Tactfully.*]   Very possible—persuasive, indeed.

BERNARD   Oh, bugger persuasive! I've proved Byron was here and as far as I'm concerned he wrote those lines as sure as he shot that hare. If only I hadn't somehow . . . made it all about *killing Chater*. Why didn't you stop me?! It's bound to get out, you know—I mean this—this *gloss*[1] on my discovery—I mean how long do you think it'll be before some botanical pedant[2] blows the whistle on me?

HANNAH   The day after tomorrow. A letter in *The Times*.

BERNARD   You wouldn't.

HANNAH   It's a dirty job but somebody—

BERNARD   Darling. Sorry. Hannah—

HANNAH   —and, after all, it is my discovery.

BERNARD   Hannah.

HANNAH   Bernard.

BERNARD   Hannah.

HANNAH   Oh, shut up. It'll be very short, very dry, absolutely gloat-free. Would you rather it were one of your friends?

BERNARD [*Fervently.*]   Oh God, no!

HANNAH   And then in *your* letter to *The Times*—

BERNARD   Mine?

HANNAH   Well, of course. Dignified congratulations to a colleague, in the language of scholars, I trust.

BERNARD   Oh, eat shit, you mean?

HANNAH   Think of it as a breakthrough in dahlia studies.

[CHLOË *hurries in from the garden.*]

CHLOË   Why aren't you coming?!—Bernard! And you're not dressed! How long have you been back?

[BERNARD *looks at her and then at* VALENTINE *and realizes for the first time that* VALENTINE *is unusually dressed.*]

BERNARD   Why are you wearing those clothes?

CHLOË   Do be quick!

[*She is already digging into the basket and producing odd garments for* BERNARD.]

Just put anything on. We're all being photographed. Except Hannah.

HANNAH   I'll come and watch.

[VALENTINE *and* CHLOË *help* BERNARD *into a decorative coat and fix a lace collar round his neck.*]

CHLOË [*To* HANNAH.]   Mummy says have you got the theodolite?

VALENTINE   What are you supposed to be, Chlo? Bo-Peep?

---

9. Popular British TV program.
1. Explanatory comment.

2. Person excessively concerned with minor details.

CHLOË Jane Austen![3]

VALENTINE Of course.

HANNAH [*To* CHLOË.] Oh—it's in the hermitage! Sorry.

BERNARD I thought it wasn't till this evening. What photograph?

CHLOË The local paper, of course—they always come before we start.
We want a good crowd of us—Gus looks gorgeous—

BERNARD [*Aghast.*] The newspaper!

[*He grabs something like a bishop's mitre[4] from the basket and pulls it
down completely over his face.*]

[*Muffled.*] I'm ready!

[*And he staggers out with* VALENTINE *and* CHLOË, *followed by*
HANNAH.

*A light change to evening. The paper lanterns outside begin to glow.
Piano music from the next room.*

SEPTIMUS *enters with an oil lamp. He carries Thomasina's algebra
primer, and also her essay on loose sheets. He settles down to read at
the table. It is nearly dark outside, despite the lanterns.*

THOMASINA *enters, in a nightgown and barefoot, holding a candlestick. Her manner is secretive and excited.*]

SEPTIMUS My lady! What is it?

THOMASINA Septimus! Shush!

[*She closes the door quietly.*]

Now is our chance!

SEPTIMUS For what, dear God?

[*She blows out the candle and puts the candlestick on the table.*]

THOMASINA Do not act the innocent! Tomorrow I will be seventeen!

[*She kisses* SEPTIMUS *full on the mouth.*]

There!

SEPTIMUS Dear Christ!

THOMASINA Now you must show me, you are paid in advance.

SEPTIMUS [*Understanding.*] Oh!

THOMASINA The Count plays for us, it is God-given! I cannot be seventeen and not waltz.

SEPTIMUS But your mother—

THOMASINA While she swoons, we can dance. The house is all abed. I
heard the Broadwood. Oh, Septimus, teach me now!

SEPTIMUS Hush! I cannot now!

THOMASINA Indeed you can, and I am come barefoot so mind my toes.

SEPTIMUS I cannot because it is not a waltz.

THOMASINA It is not?

SEPTIMUS No, it is too quick for waltzing.

THOMASINA Oh! Then we will wait for him to play slow.

SEPTIMUS My lady—

THOMASINA Mr Hodge!

[*She takes a chair next to him and looks at his work.*]

Are you reading my essay? Why do you work here so late?

SEPTIMUS To save my candles.

THOMASINA You have my old primer.

3. English novelist (1775–1817). "Bo-Peep": Little
Bo-Peep, subject of an 18th-century nursery
rhyme.
4. Bishop's ceremonial headdress.

SEPTIMUS   It is mine again. You should not have written in it.
    [*She takes it, looks at the open page.*]
THOMASINA   It was a joke.
SEPTIMUS   It will make me mad as you promised. Sit over there. You will
    have us in disgrace.
    [THOMASINA *gets up and goes to the furthest chair.*]
THOMASINA   If mama comes I will tell her we only met to kiss, not to waltz.
SEPTIMUS   Silence or bed.
THOMASINA   Silence!
    [SEPTIMUS *pours himself some more wine. He continues to read her
    essay.*
       *The music changes to party music from the marquee. And there are
    fireworks—small against the sky, distant flares of light like exploding
    meteors.*

    HANNAH *enters. She has dressed for the party. The difference is not,
    however, dramatic. She closes the door and crosses to leave by the gar-
    den door. But as she gets there,* VALENTINE *is entering. He has a glass of
    wine in his hand.*]
HANNAH   Oh . . .
    [*But* VALENTINE *merely brushes past her, intent on something, and
    half-drunk.*]
VALENTINE [*To her.*]   Got it!
    [*He goes straight to the table and roots about in what is now a consid-
    erable mess of papers, books and objects.* HANNAH *turns back, puz-
    zled by his manner. He finds what he has been looking for—the
    'diagram'.*

    Meanwhile, SEPTIMUS, *reading Thomasina's essay, also studies the
    diagram.*
       SEPTIMUS *and* VALENTINE *study the diagram doubled by time.*]
VALENTINE   It's heat.
HANNAH   Are you tight,[5] Val?
VALENTINE   It's a diagram of heat exchange.
SEPTIMUS   So, we are all doomed!
THOMASINA [*Cheerfully.*]   Yes.
VALENTINE   Like a steam engine, you see—
    [HANNAH *fills Septimus's glass from the same decanter, and sips from it.*]
    She didn't have the maths, not remotely. She saw what things meant, way
    ahead, like seeing a picture.
SEPTIMUS   This is not science. This is story-telling.
THOMASINA   Is it a waltz now?
SEPTIMUS   No.
    [*The music is still modern.*]
VALENTINE   Like a film.
HANNAH   What did she see?
VALENTINE   That you can't run the film backwards. Heat was the first thing
    which didn't work that way. Not like Newton. A film of a pendulum, or a
    ball falling through the air—backwards, it looks the same.
HANNAH   The ball would be going the wrong way.

5. Drunk.

VALENTINE You'd have to know that. But with heat—friction—a ball breaking a window—

HANNAH Yes.

VALENTINE It won't work backwards.

HANNAH Who thought it did?

VALENTINE She saw why. You can put back the bits of glass but you can't collect up the heat of the smash. It's gone.

SEPTIMUS So the Improved Newtonian Universe must cease and grow cold. Dear me.

VALENTINE The heat goes into the mix.

[*He gestures to indicate the air in the room, in the universe.*]

THOMASINA Yes, we must hurry if we are going to dance.

VALENTINE And everything is mixing the same way, all the time, irreversibly . . .

SEPTIMUS Oh, we have time, I think.

VALENTINE . . . till there's no time left. That's what time means.

SEPTIMUS When we have found all the mysteries and lost all the meaning, we will be alone, on an empty shore.

THOMASINA Then we will dance. Is this a waltz?

SEPTIMUS It will serve.

[*He stands up.*]

THOMASINA [*Jumping up.*] Goody!

[SEPTIMUS *takes her in his arms carefully and the waltz lesson, to the music from the marquee, begins.*

BERNARD *in unconvincing Regency dress, enters carrying a bottle.*]

BERNARD Don't mind me, I left my jacket . . .

[*He heads for the area of the wicker basket.*]

VALENTINE Are you leaving?

[BERNARD *is stripping off his period coat. He is wearing his own trousers, tucked into knee socks and his own shirt.*]

BERNARD Yes, I'm afraid so.

HANNAH What's up, Bernard?

BERNARD Nothing I can go into—

VALENTINE Should I go?

BERNARD No, *I'm* going!

[VALENTINE *and* HANNAH *watch* BERNARD *struggling into his jacket and adjusting his clothes.*

SEPTIMUS, *holding* THOMASINA, *kisses her on the mouth. The waltz lesson pauses. She looks at him. He kisses her again, in earnest. She puts her arms round him.*]

THOMASINA Septimus . . .

[SEPTIMUS *hushes her. They start to dance again, with the slight awkwardness of a lesson.*

CHLOË *bursts in from the garden.*]

CHLOË I'll kill her! I'll *kill* her!

BERNARD Oh dear.

VALENTINE What the hell is it, Chlo?

CHLOË [*Venomously.*] Mummy!

BERNARD [*To* VALENTINE.] Your mother caught us in that cottage.

CHLOË She snooped!

BERNARD   I don't think so. She was rescuing a theodolite.

CHLOË   I'll come with you, Bernard.

BERNARD   No, you bloody won't.

CHLOË   Don't you want me to?

BERNARD   Of course not. What for? [*To* VALENTINE.] I'm sorry.

CHLOË [*In furious tears.*]   What are you saying sorry to *him* for?

BERNARD   Sorry to you too. Sorry one and all. Sorry, Hannah—sorry, Hermione—sorry, Byron—sorry, sorry, sorry, now can I go?

[CHLOË *stands stiffly, tearfully.*]

CHLOË   Well . . .

[THOMASINA *and* SEPTIMUS *dance.*]

HANNAH   What a bastard you are, Bernard.

[CHLOË *rounds on her.*]

CHLOË   And you mind your own business! What do you know about anything?

HANNAH   Nothing.

CHLOË [*To* BERNARD.]   It *was* worth it, though, wasn't it?

BERNARD   It was wonderful.

[CHLOË *goes out, through the garden door, towards the party.*]

HANNAH [*An echo.*]   Nothing.

VALENTINE   Well, you shit. I'd drive you but I'm a bit sloshed.

[VALENTINE *follows* CHLOË *out and can be heard outside calling 'Chlo! Chlo!'*]

BERNARD   A scrape.

HANNAH   Oh . . . [*She gives up.*] Bernard!

BERNARD   I look forward to *The Genius of the Place.* I hope you find your hermit. I think out front is the safest.

[*He opens the door cautiously and looks out.*]

HANNAH   Actually, I've got a good idea who he was, but I can't prove it.

BERNARD [*With a carefree expansive gesture.*]   Publish!

[*He goes out closing the door.*]

SEPTIMUS *and* THOMASINA *are now waltzing freely. She is delighted with herself.*]

THOMASINA   Am I waltzing?

SEPTIMUS   Yes, my lady.

[*He gives her a final twirl, bringing them to the table where he bows to her. He lights her candlestick.*

HANNAH *goes to sit at the table, playing truant from the party. She pours herself more wine. The table contains the geometrical solids, the computer, decanter, glasses, tea mug, Hannah's research books, Septimus's books, the two portfolios, Thomasina's candlestick, the oil lamp, the dahlia, the Sunday papers . . .*

GUS *appears in the doorway. It takes a moment to realize that he is not Lord Augustus; perhaps not until* HANNAH *sees him.*]

SEPTIMUS   Take your essay, I have given it an alpha[6] in blind faith. Be careful with the flame.

THOMASINA   I will wait for you to come.

SEPTIMUS   I cannot.

6. An A grade.

THOMASINA You may.
SEPTIMUS I may not.
THOMASINA You must.
SEPTIMUS I will not.
> [*She puts the candlestick and the essay on the table.*]

THOMASINA Then I will not go. Once more, for my birthday.
> [SEPTIMUS *and* THOMASINA *start to waltz together.*
>
> GUS *comes forward, startling* HANNAH.]

HANNAH Oh!—you made me jump.
> [GUS *looks resplendent. He is carrying an old and somewhat tattered stiff-backed folio fastened with a tape tied in a bow. He comes to* HANNAH *and thrusts this present at her.*]

Oh . . .
> [*She lays the folio down on the table and starts to open it. It consists only of two boards hinged, containing Thomasina's drawing.*]

'Septimus with Plautus'. [*To* GUS.] I was looking for that. Thank you.
> [GUS *nods several times. Then, rather awkwardly, he bows to her. A Regency bow, an invitation to dance.*]

Oh, dear, I don't really . . .
> [*After a moment's hesitation, she gets up and they hold each other, keeping a decorous distance between them, and start to dance, rather awkwardly.*
>
> SEPTIMUS *and* THOMASINA *continue to dance, fluently, to the piano.*]

END

1993

LES MURRAY
b. 1938

Leslie Allan Murray was born at Nabiac, on the north coast of New South Wales, Australia, and grew up on a dairy farm at nearby Bunyah. He was educated at Taree High School and the University of Sydney, where he studied modern languages. After military service with the Royal Australian Naval Reserve, he worked as a translator in the Australian National University, Canberra, and as an officer in the prime minister's department. Since 1971 he has been a full-time writer.

Remaining true to his roots in the Australian "outback" (despite the global shuttling expected of a major poet in the twenty-first century), Murray has emerged as a powerful celebrant of the natural world and agricultural work. His substantial *Collected Poems* (1998), dedicated "to the glory of God," bears witness to a staunch and highly individual Roman Catholicism. His celebration of nature includes human nature and reveals a sensibility generously attuned to the hopes and fears, hurts and happinesses of ordinary lives.

Murray seems intent on proving that the provincial farmer living at the margins of the former British Empire can write poetry as learned, authoritative, and technically virtuosic as any from the metropolitan center. The language of his poetry startles and amuses, reveling in the fecundity and elasticity of English. In poems of metaphorical lushness and sonic opulence, he plays on the eddying reflections of homonyms and rhymes, alliterations and consonances, to suggest a profound interconnectedness among things. As Derek Walcott has said of Murray's work: "There is no poetry in the English language so rooted in its sacredness, so broad-leafed in its pleasures, and yet so intimate and conversational."

Morse[1]

Tuckett. Bill Tuckett. Telegraph operator, Hall's Creek,
which is way out back of the Outback, but he stuck it,
quite likely liked it, despite heat, glare, dust and the lack
of diversion or doctors. Come disaster you trusted to luck,
5   ingenuity and pluck. This was back when nice people said pluck,
the sleevelink and green eyeshade epoch.[2]
                       Faced, though, like Bill Tuckett
with a man needing surgery right on the spot, a lot
would have done their dashes. It looked hopeless (dot dot dot)
Lift him up on the table, said Tuckett, running the key hot
10   till Head Office turned up a doctor who coolly instructed
up a thousand miles of wire, as Tuckett advanced slit by slit
with a safety razor blade, pioneering on into the wet,
copper-wiring the rivers off, in the first operation conducted
along dotted lines, with rum drinkers gripping the patient:
d-d-dash it, take care, Tuck!
15   And the vital spark stayed unshorted.
Yallah![3] breathed the camelmen. Tuckett, you did it, you did it!
cried the spattered la-de-dah jodhpur[4]-wearing Inspector of Stock.
We imagine, some weeks later, a properly laconic
convalescent averring Without you, I'd have kicked the bucket . . .

20   From Chungking to Burrenjuck,[5] morse keys have mostly gone silent
and only old men meet now to chit-chat in their electric
bygone dialect. The last letter many will forget
is dit-dit-dit-dah,[6] V for Victory. The coders' hero had speed,
resource and a touch. So ditditdit daah for Bill Tuckett.

1983

---

1. Morse code was used to transmit messages by sequences of dots and dashes (or *dits* and *dahs*) to represent letters and numbers.
2. I.e., the nineteenth century. "Sleevelink": cuff link.
3. God be praised! (Arabic).
4. Long breeches for riding, close-fitting from knee to ankle.
5. I.e., from southwest China to southeast Australia.
6. The first four notes of Beethoven's Fifth Symphony, also representing *V* for victory, the signal by which Morse code operators prefaced messages in World War II.

Corniche[1]

I work all day and hardly drink at all.[2]
I can reach down and feel if I'm depressed.
I adore the Creator because I made myself
and a few times a week a wire jags in my chest.

5 The first time, I'd been coming apart all year,
weeping, incoherent; cigars had given me up:
any road round a cliff edge I'd whimper along in low gear
then: cardiac horror. Masking my pulse's calm lub-dub.

It was the victim-sickness. Adrenaline howling in my head,
10 the black dog[2] was my brain. Come to drown me in my breath
was energy's black hole, depression, compere[4] of
        the predawn show
when, returned from a pee, you stew and welter in your death.

The rogue space rock is on course to snuff your world,
sure. But go acute, and its oncoming fills your day.
15 The brave die but once? I could go a hundred times a week,
clinging to my pulse with the world's edge inches away.

Laugh, who never shrank around wizened genitals there
or killed themselves to stop dying. The blow that never falls
batters you stupid. Only gradually do
20 you notice a slight scorn in you for what appals.

A self inside self, cool as conscience, one to be erased
in your final night, or faxed, still knows beneath
all the mute grand opera and uncaused effect—
that death which can be imagined is not true death.

                                                        1996

The Kitchen Grammars

The verb in a Sanscrit or Farsi[1]
or Latin or Japanese sentence
most frequently comes last,
as if the ingredients and spices
5 only after collection, measure and
even preservation might get cooked.
To all these cuisines renown attaches.

It's the opening of a Celtic[2] sentence
is a verb. And it was more fire and pot

---

1. Coastal road.
2. Cf. the opening of "Aubade," by the English
poet Philip Larkin (1922–1985): "I work all day,
and get half drunk at night."
3. I.e., depression.

4. Master of ceremonies.

1. Persian.
2. Ancient family of languages including Breton,
Welsh, Irish, and Gaelic.

10   for us very often than ingredients.
     Had we not fed our severed heads[3] on poetry
     final might have been our fame's starvation.
     Upholding cuisine for us are the French
     to be counting in scores and called Gallic.[4]

15   In English and many more, in Chinese
     the verb surrounds itself nucleus-fashion
     with its subjects and qualifiers.
     Down every slope of the wok they go
     to the spitting middle, to be sauced,
20   ladled, lidded, steamed, flipped back up,
     becoming verbs themselves often

     and the calm egg centres the meatloaf.

                                                    2006

3. Sometimes said to have been venerated by the ancient Celts.
4. Of Gaul, the Roman name for the region of France. In French, 20 ("score") is still a base number from 70 to 99.

SEAMUS HEANEY
1939–2013

Seamus Heaney was born into a Roman Catholic family in predominantly Prot-estant North Ireland (or Ulster), and he grew up on a farm in County Derry bordered on one side by a stream that marked the frontier with the largely Catho-lic Irish Republic (or Eire) to the south. He won scholarships first to St. Columb's College, a Catholic boarding school, and then to Queen's University in Belfast. There he became one of an extraordinary group of Northern Irish poets from both Protestant and Catholic backgrounds, including Michael Longley and Derek Mahon, who read, discussed, and spurred on one another's work. He taught at Queen's Uni-versity, before moving in 1972 to the Irish Republic, where he became a citizen and full-time writer. He was Boylston Professor of Rhetoric and Oratory at Har-vard and Professor of Poetry at Oxford, and in 1995 won the Nobel Prize in Lit-erature.

With "Digging," placed appropriately as the first poem of his first book, Heaney defined his territory. He dug into his memory, uncovering first his father and then, going deeper, his grandfather. This idea of poetry as an archaeological process of recovery took on a darker cast after the eruption of internecine violence—"the Troubles"—in Northern Ireland in 1969, culminating in the 1972 Bloody Sunday killing of thirteen Catholic civilians by British paratroopers during a civil rights march in Derry. Across several volumes, especially *North* (1975), Heaney wrote a series of grim "bog poems," about well-preserved Iron Age corpses discovered in the peat of Northern Europe and Ireland. In these poems he sees the bog as a "memory bank," or unconscious, that preserves everything thrown into it, including the vic-tims of ritual killings. He views contemporary violence through the lens of ancient myths, sacrifices, and feuds, an oblique approach that gives his poetry about the Troubles an unusual depth and resonance. He had discovered emblems for the violence in Northern Ireland in *The Bog People*, a book by the Danish archaeologist P. V. Glob, published in translation in 1969, "the year the killing started." Heaney wrote of it:

> It was chiefly concerned with preserved bodies of men and women found in the bogs of Jutland, naked, strangled or with their throats cut, disposed under the peat since early Iron Age times. The author . . . argues convincingly that a number of these, and in particular, the Tollund Man, whose head is now preserved near Aarhus in the museum of Silkeburg, were ritual sacrifices to the Mother Goddess, the goddess of the ground who needed new bridegrooms each winter to bed with her in her sacred place, in the spring. Taken in relation to the tradition of Irish political martyrdom for the cause whose icon is Kathleen Ni Houlihan [mythic figure emblematic of Mother Ireland], this is more than an archaic barbarous rite: it is an archetypal pattern. And the unforgettable photographs of these victims blended in my mind with photographs of atrocities, past and present, in the long rites of Irish political and religious struggles. ("Feeling into Words")

In the bog poems Heaney reflects on the poet's responsibilities to write about the dead, yet to do so without prettifying or exploiting them. He probes the vexed relations between lyric song and historical suffering, "beauty and atrocity": the need to be true to his calling as artist, but also to represent the irredeemable carnage of modern political violence—"the actual weight / of each hooded victim / slashed and dumped" ("The Grauballe Man"). The result is a tough-minded witnessing, an ethically scrupulous and self-aware mourning of collective loss and sectarian murder. (For more on the Troubles, see "Imagining Ireland" in the NAEL Archive.)

From the late 1970s Heaney elegized specific victims of the Troubles, such as his acquaintance Louis O'Neill, in "Casualty," as well as more personal losses, such as the natural death of his mother, in "Clearances." He also wrote poems about domestic love, such as "The Skunk" and "The Sharping Stone." Heaney was thus both a private poet—skillfully kneading grief, love, and wonder into poems about his family and his humble origins—and a public poet, affirming his affinities with the Catholic civil rights movement, which has struggled for centuries against British and Protestant domination. Even in his public poetry he refused slogans, journalistic reportage, and political pieties, scrutinizing instead the wellsprings of collective identity, the ambivalences of individual response to history. Responding obliquely to the destruction of the Twin Towers on September 11, 2001, he reworked a two-thousand-year-old Latin ode by Horace in "Anything Can Happen," and the bombings of the London underground (subway) on July 7, 2005, reverberate in *District and Circle* (2006).

An Irishman writing in the language of the British Empire, he translated Gaelic poetry and renewed specifically Irish traditions, such as the *aisling*, or vision poem, but he was also steeped in the English literary canon, drawing on British poetry from *Beowulf* (his prize-winning translation appears earlier in this anthology) to the works of William Wordsworth, Gerard Manley Hopkins, and Ted Hughes. Straddling a multiplicity of divisions, transubstantiating crisscross feelings into unexpected images and intricate sonorities, Heaney's work has been embraced by popular audiences for its accessible style and yet also admired by poets and academic critics for its lyric subtlety and rigorous technique.

Formally, Heaney's poetry ranges from strenuous free verse—the clipped lines and unrhymed quatrains of the bog poems—to more traditional forms, such as the modified terza rima of "Station Island" and the sonnet sequence "Clearances." His poems are earthy and matter-of-fact, saturated with the physical textures, sights, smells, and sounds of farm life, and they are also visionary, lit up by hope and spirit, enacting penitential pilgrimages and unbridled imaginings. That Heaney's poetry is both earthbound and airborne, free and formed, public and private helps explain why he is seen by many as the most gifted English-language poet of his generation.

Digging

Between my finger and my thumb
The squat pen rests; snug as a gun.

Under my window, a clean rasping sound
When the spade sinks into gravelly ground:
5 My father, digging. I look down

Till his straining rump among the flowerbeds
Bends low, comes up twenty years away
Stooping in rhythm through potato drills[1]
Where he was digging.

10 The coarse boot nestled on the lug, the shaft
Against the inside knee was levered firmly.
He rooted out tall tops, buried the bright edge deep
To scatter new potatoes that we picked
Loving their cool hardness in our hands.

15 By God, the old man could handle a spade.
Just like his old man.

My grandfather cut more turf[2] in a day
Than any other man on Toner's bog.
Once I carried him milk in a bottle
20 Corked sloppily with paper. He straightened up
To drink it, then fell to right away
Nicking and slicing neatly, heaving sods
Over his shoulder, going down and down
For the good turf. Digging.

25 The cold smell of potato mould, the squelch and slap
Of soggy peat, the curt cuts of an edge
Through living roots awaken in my head.
But I've no spade to follow men like them.

Between my finger and my thumb
30 The squat pen rests.
I'll dig with it.

1966

The Forge

All I know is a door into the dark.
Outside, old axles and iron hoops rusting;
Inside, the hammered anvil's short-pitched ring,
The unpredictable fantail of sparks

---

1. Small furrows in which seeds are sown.
2. Slabs of peat that, when dried, are a common domestic fuel in Ireland.

5 Or hiss when a new shoe toughens in water.
The anvil must be somewhere in the centre,
Horned as a unicorn, at one end square,
Set there immoveable: an altar
Where he expends himself in shape and music.
10 Sometimes, leather-aproned, hairs in his nose,
He leans out on the jamb, recalls a clatter
Of hoofs where traffic is flashing in rows;
Then grunts and goes in, with a slam and flick
To beat real iron out, to work the bellows.

1969

The Grauballe Man[1]

As if he had been poured
in tar, he lies
on a pillow of turf
and seems to weep

5 the black river of himself.
The grain of his wrists
is like bog oak,
the ball of his heel

like a basalt egg.
10 His instep has shrunk
cold as a swan's foot
or a wet swamp root.

His hips are the ridge
and purse of a mussel,
15 his spine an eel arrested
under a glisten of mud.

The head lifts,
the chin is a visor
raised above the vent
20 of his slashed throat

that has tanned and toughened.
The cured wound
opens inwards to a dark
elderberry place.

25 Who will say 'corpse'
to his vivid cast?
Who will say 'body'
to his opaque repose?

1. A body exhumed from a Danish bog and photographed in P. V. Glob's book *The Bog People*.

And his rusted hair,

30 a mat unlikely
as a foetus's.
I first saw his twisted face

in a photograph,
a head and shoulder
35 out of the peat,
bruised like a forceps baby,

but now he lies
perfected in my memory,
down to the red horn
40 of his nails,

hung in the scales
with beauty and atrocity:
with the Dying Gaul[2]
too strictly compassed

45 on his shield,
with the actual weight
of each hooded victim,
slashed and dumped.

1975

Punishment[1]

I can feel the tug
of the halter at the nape
of her neck, the wind
on her naked front.

5 It blows her nipples
to amber beads,
it shakes the frail rigging
of her ribs.

---

2. Roman marble reproduction of a Greek bronze sculpture depicting a wounded soldier of Gaul, whose matted hair identifies him as a Celt, in Rome's Capitoline Museum.

1. In 1951 the peat-stained body apparently of a young girl, who lived in the late 1st century C.E., was recovered from a bog in Windeby, Germany. As P. V. Glob describes her in *The Bog People*, she "lay naked in the hole in the peat, a bandage over the eyes and a collar round the neck. The band across the eyes was drawn tight and had cut into the neck and the base of the nose. We may feel sure that it had been used to close her eyes to this world. There was no mark of strangulation on the neck, so that it had not been used for that purpose." Her hair "had been shaved off with a razor on the left side of the head. . . . When the brain was removed the convolutions and folds of the surface could be clearly seen [Glob reproduces a photograph of her brain]. . . . This girl of only fourteen had had an inadequate winter diet. . . . To keep the young body under, some birch branches and a big stone were laid upon her." According to the Roman historian Tacitus, the Germanic peoples punished adulterous women by shaving off their hair and then scourging them out of the village or killing them. More recently, her "betraying sisters" were sometimes shaved, stripped, tarred, and handcuffed by the Irish Republican Army (IRA) to the railings of Belfast in punishment for keeping company with British soldiers.

I can see her drowned
10   body in the bog,
the weighing stone,
the floating rods and boughs.

Under which at first
she was a barked sapling
15   that is dug up
oak-bone, brain-firkin:°   *small cask*

her shaved head
like a stubble of black corn,
her blindfold a soiled bandage,
20   her noose a ring

to store
the memories of love.
Little adultress,
before they punished you

25   you were flaxen-haired,
undernourished, and your
tar-black face was beautiful.
My poor scapegoat,

I almost love you
30   but would have cast, I know,
the stones of silence.
I am the artful voyeur

of your brain's exposed
and darkened combs,°   *valleys*
35   your muscles' webbing
and all your numbered bones:

I who have stood dumb
when your betraying sisters,
cauled° in tar,   *wrapped, enclosed*
40   wept by the railings,

who would connive
in civilized outrage
yet understand the exact
and tribal, intimate revenge.

1975

Casualty

1

He would drink by himself
And raise a weathered thumb
Towards the high shelf,
Calling another rum
5   And blackcurrant, without
Having to raise his voice,
Or order a quick stout°   *strong dark beer*
By a lifting of the eyes
And a discreet dumb-show
10   Of pulling off the top;
At closing time would go
In waders and peaked cap
Into the showery dark,
A dole-kept[1] breadwinner
15   But a natural for work.
I loved his whole manner,
Sure-footed but too sly,
His deadpan sidling tact,
His fisherman's quick eye
20   And turned observant back.
Incomprehensible
To him, my other life.
Sometimes, on his high stool,
Too busy with his knife
25   At a tobacco plug
And not meeting my eye
In the pause after a slug°   *gulp of liquor*
He mentioned poetry.
We would be on our own
30   And, always politic
And shy of condescension,
I would manage by some trick
To switch the talk to eels
Or lore of the horse and cart
35   Or the Provisionals.[2]

But my tentative art
His turned back watches too:
He was blown to bits
Out drinking in a curfew
40   Others obeyed, three nights
After they shot dead
The thirteen men in Derry.
PARAS THIRTEEN, the walls said,
BOGSIDE NIL.[3] That Wednesday

---

1. I.e., receiving unemployment benefits.
2. The Provisional, paramilitary branch of the IRA.

3. This graffito records—in the form of a soccer match score—that the British Army's Parachute Regiment had killed thirteen people; the Roman

45 Everybody held
His breath and trembled.

2

It was a day of cold
Raw silence, wind-blown
Surplice and soutane:[4]
50 Rained-on, flower-laden
Coffin after coffin
Seemed to float from the door
Of the packed cathedral
Like blossoms on slow water.
55 The common funeral
Unrolled its swaddling band,[5]
Lapping, tightening
Till we were braced and bound
Like brothers in a ring.

60 But he would not be held
At home by his own crowd
Whatever threats were phoned,
Whatever black flags waved.
I see him as he turned
65 In that bombed offending place,
Remorse fused with terror
In his still knowable face,
His cornered outfaced stare
Blinding in the flash.

70 He had gone miles away
For he drank like a fish
Nightly, naturally
Swimming towards the lure
Of warm lit-up places,
75 The blurred mesh and murmur
Drifting among glasses
In the gregarious smoke.
How culpable was he
That last night when he broke
80 Our tribe's complicity?[6]
'Now you're supposed to be
An educated man,'
I hear him say. 'Puzzle me
The right answer to that one.'

Catholic inhabitants of Derry's Bogside district,
none. The IRA bombing occurred after the killing of Catholic demonstrators on Bloody Sunday, January 30, 1972.
4. Vestments worn by Roman Catholic priests.

5. Long cloth in which babies were once wrapped
to restrain and warm them.
6. The Roman Catholic community's agreement
to obey the curfew (of lines 39–40).

3

85 I missed his funeral,
Those quiet walkers
And sideways talkers
Shoaling out of his lane
To the respectable
90 Purring of the hearse . . .
They move in equal pace
With the habitual
Slow consolation
Of a dawdling engine,
95 The line lifted, hand
Over fist, cold sunshine
On the water, the land
Banked under fog: that morning
I was taken in his boat,
100 The screw° purling, turning   *propellor*
Indolent fathoms white,
I tasted freedom with him.
To get out early, haul
Steadily off the bottom,
105 Dispraise the catch, and smile
As you find a rhythm
Working you, slow mile by mile,
Into your proper haunt
Somewhere, well out, beyond . . .

110 Dawn-sniffing revenant,[7]
Plodder through midnight rain,
Question me again.

1979

The Skunk

Up, black, striped and damasked like the chasuble[1]
At a funeral mass, the skunk's tail
Paraded the skunk. Night after night
I expected her like a visitor.

5 The refrigerator whinnied into silence.
My desk light softened beyond the verandah.
Small oranges loomed in the orange tree.
I began to be tense as a voyeur.

After eleven years I was composing
10 Love-letters again, broaching the word 'wife'

7. One returned from the dead.
1. Sleeveless vestment worn by the priest celebrating Mass, its color regulated by the feast of the
day. "Damasked": woven with elaborate designs.

Like a stored cask, as if its slender vowel
Had mutated into the night earth and air

Of California. The beautiful, useless
Tang of eucalyptus spelt your absence.
15   The aftermath of a mouthful of wine
Was like inhaling you off a cold pillow.

And there she was, the intent and glamorous,
Ordinary, mysterious skunk,
Mythologized, demythologized,
20   Snuffing the boards five feet beyond me.

It all came back to me last night, stirred
By the sootfall of your things at bedtime,
Your head-down, tail-up hunt in a bottom drawer
For the black plunge-line nightdress.

1979

From Station Island[1]

12

Like a convalescent, I took the hand
stretched down from the jetty, sensed again
an alien comfort as I stepped on ground

to find the helping hand still gripping mine,
5   fish-cold and bony, but whether to guide
or to be guided I could not be certain

for the tall man in step at my side
seemed blind, though he walked straight as a rush
upon his ash plant,[2] his eyes fixed straight ahead.

10   Then I knew him in the flesh
out there on the tarmac° among the cars,   *blacktop surface*
wintered hard and sharp as a blackthorn bush.

His voice eddying with the vowels of all rivers[3]
came back to me, though he did not speak yet,
15   a voice like a prosecutor's or a singer's,

1. *Station Island* is a sequence of dream encounters with familiar ghosts, set on Station Island on Lough Derg in Co. Donegal. The island is also known as St. Patrick's Purgatory because of a tradition that Patrick was the first to establish the penitential vigil of fasting and praying which still constitutes the basis of the three-day pilgrimage. Each unit of the contemporary pilgrim's exercises is called a 'station,' and a large part of each station involves walking barefoot and praying round the 'beds,' stone circles which are said to be the remains of early medieval monastic cells [Heaney's note]. In this last section of the poem, the familiar ghost is that of Heaney's countryman James Joyce. Cf. the stanza form and encounter with a ghost in T. S. Eliot's "Little Gidding."
2. Walking stick made of ash, like the one carried by Stephen Dedalus in Joyce's *Portrait of the Artist as a Young Man* and *Ulysses*. Joyce was almost blind.
3. The Anna Livia Plurabelle episode of *Finnegans Wake* resounds with the names of many rivers.

cunning,[4] narcotic, mimic, definite
as a steel nib's downstroke, quick and clean,
and suddenly he hit a litter basket

with his stick, saying, "Your obligation
20   is not discharged by any common rite.
What you must do must be done on your own

so get back in harness. The main thing is to write
for the joy of it. Cultivate a work-lust
that imagines its haven like your hands at night

25   dreaming the sun in the sunspot of a breast.
You are fasted now, light-headed, dangerous.
Take off from here. And don't be so earnest,

let others wear the sackcloth and the ashes.[5]
Let go, let fly, forget.
30   You've listened long enough. Now strike your note."

It was as if I had stepped free into space
alone with nothing that I had not known
already. Raindrops blew in my face

as I came to. "Old father, mother's son,
35   there is a moment in Stephen's diary
for April the thirteenth, a revelation

set among my stars—that one entry
has been a sort of password in my ears,
the collect of a new epiphany,[6]

40   the Feast of the Holy Tundish."[7] "Who cares,"
he jeered, "any more? The English language
belongs to us. You are raking at dead fires,

a waste of time for somebody your age.
That subject° people stuff is a cod's° game,   *colonized / fool's*
45   infantile, like your peasant pilgrimage.

You lose more of yourself than you redeem
doing the decent thing. Keep at a tangent.
When they make the circle wide, it's time to swim

---

4. "The only arms I allow myself to use—silence, exile, and cunning" (Joyce, *A Portrait of the Artist as a Young Man*).
5. As worn by penitents in biblical times and later.
6. Manifestation of a superhuman being, as of the infant Jesus to the Magi (Matthew 2). In the Christian calendar, the Feast of the Epiphany is January 6. "Epiphany" was also Joyce's term for the "sudden revelation of the whatness of a

thing." "Collect": short prayer assigned to a particular day.
7. See the end of James Joyce's *Portrait of the Artist as a Young Man* [Heaney's note]: "13 April: That tundish [funnel] has been on my mind for a long time. I looked it up and find it English and good old blunt English too. Damn the dean of studies and his funnel! What did he come here for to teach us his own language or to learn it from us? Damn him one way or the other!"

out on your own and fill the element
50   with signatures on your own frequency,
echo soundings, searches, probes, allurements,

elver-gleams[8] in the dark of the whole sea."
The shower broke in a cloudburst, the tarmac
fumed and sizzled. As he moved off quickly

55   the downpour loosed its screens round his straight walk.

1984

Clearances

in memoriam M.K.H.,[1] 1911–1984

She taught me what her uncle once taught her:
How easily the biggest coal block split
If you got the grain and hammer angled right.

The sound of that relaxed alluring blow,
5   *Its co-opted and obliterated echo,*
Taught me to hit, taught me to loosen,

Taught me between the hammer and the block
To face the music. Teach me now to listen,
To strike it rich behind the linear black.

1

10   A cobble thrown a hundred years ago
Keeps coming at me, the first stone
Aimed at a great-grandmother's turncoat brow.[2]
The pony jerks and the riot's on.
She's crouched low in the trap
15   Running the gauntlet that first Sunday
Down the brae° to Mass at a panicked gallop.   *steep slope*
He whips on through the town to cries of 'Lundy!'[3]

Call her 'The Convert'. 'The Exogamous[4] Bride'.
Anyhow, it is a genre piece
20   Inherited on my mother's side
And mine to dispose with now she's gone.
Instead of silver and Victorian lace,
The exonerating, exonerated stone.

---

8. Gleams as of young eels.
1. Margaret Kathleen Heaney, the poet's mother.
2. Heaney's Protestant great-grandmother married a Catholic.
3. I.e., traitor. In 1688 the Irish colonel Robert

Lundy knew that Derry (or Londonderry) would
be invaded by the English, but failed to prepare
adequate defenses.
4. Married outside the group.

2

Polished linoleum shone there. Brass taps shone.
25 The china cups were very white and big—
An unchipped set with sugar bowl and jug.
The kettle whistled. Sandwich and teascone
Were present and correct. In case it run,
The butter must be kept out of the sun.
30 And don't be dropping crumbs. Don't tilt your chair.
Don't reach. Don't point. Don't make noise when you stir.

It is Number 5, New Row, Land of the Dead,
Where grandfather is rising from his place
With spectacles pushed back on a clean bald head
35 To welcome a bewildered homing daughter
Before she even knocks. 'What's this? What's this?'
And they sit down in the shining room together.

3

When all the others were away at Mass
I was all hers as we peeled potatoes.
40 They broke the silence, let fall one by one
Like solder weeping off the soldering iron:
Cold comforts set between us, things to share
Gleaming in a bucket of clean water.
And again let fall. Little pleasant splashes
45 From each other's work would bring us to our senses.

So while the parish priest at her bedside
Went hammer and tongs at the prayers for the dying
And some were responding and some crying
I remembered her head bent towards my head,
50 Her breath in mine, our fluent dipping knives—
Never closer the whole rest of our lives.

4

Fear of affectation made her affect
Inadequacy whenever it came to
Pronouncing words 'beyond her'. *Bertold Brek.*[5]
55 She'd manage something hampered and askew
Every time, as if she might betray
The hampered and inadequate by too
Well-adjusted a vocabulary.
With more challenge than pride, she'd tell me, 'You
60 Know all them things.' So I governed my tongue
In front of her, a genuinely well-
adjusted adequate betrayal
Of what I knew better. I'd *naw* and *aye*

---

5. Bertolt Brecht (1898–1956), German playwright.

And decently relapse into the wrong
65   Grammar which kept us allied and at bay.

5

The cool that came off sheets just off the line
Made me think the damp must still be in them
But when I took my corners of the linen
And pulled against her, first straight down the hem
70   And then diagonally, then flapped and shook
The fabric like a sail in a cross-wind,
They made a dried-out undulating thwack.
So we'd stretch and fold and end up hand to hand
For a split second as if nothing had happened
75   For nothing had that had not always happened
Beforehand, day by day, just touch and go,
Coming close again by holding back
In moves where I was x and she was o
Inscribed in sheets she'd sewn from ripped-out flour sacks.

6

80   In the first flush of the Easter holidays
The ceremonies during Holy Week
Were highpoints of our *Sons and Lovers*[6] phase.
The midnight fire. The paschal candlestick.[7]
Elbow to elbow, glad to be kneeling next
85   To each other up there near the front
Of the packed church, we would follow the text
And rubrics° for the blessing of the font.[8]   *rules*
As the hind longs for the streams, so my soul . . . [9]
Dippings. Towellings. The water breathed on.
90   The water mixed with chrism[1] and with oil.
Cruet[2] tinkle. Formal incensation
And the psalmist's outcry taken up with pride:
Day and night my tears have been my bread.[3]

7

In the last minutes he said more to her
95   Almost than in all their life together.
'You'll be in New Row on Monday night
And I'll come up for you and you'll be glad
When I walk in the door . . . Isn't that right?'
His head was bent down to her propped-up head.
100   She could not hear but we were overjoyed.
He called her good and girl. Then she was dead,
The searching for a pulsebeat was abandoned
And we all knew one thing by being there.

---

6. Novel (1913) by the English writer D. H. Lawrence (1885–1930) that largely centers on the oedipal relationship between a mother and son.
7. Large candle lit during a ceremony on Holy Saturday, which precedes Easter Sunday.
8. Receptacle for holy water.
9. Psalms 42.1.
1. Mixture of olive oil and balsam.
2. Small vessel for wine or water.
3. Psalms 42.3.

The space we stood around had been emptied
105 Into us to keep, it penetrated
Clearances that suddenly stood open.
High cries were felled and a pure change happened.

8

I thought of walking round and round a space
Utterly empty, utterly a source
110 Where the decked chestnut tree had lost its place
In our front hedge above the wallflowers.
The white chips jumped and jumped and skited[4] high.
I heard the hatchet's differentiated
Accurate cut, the crack, the sigh
115 And collapse of what luxuriated
Through the shocked tips and wreckage of it all.
Deep planted and long gone, my coeval[5]
Chestnut from a jam jar in a hole,
Its heft and hush become a bright nowhere,
120 A soul ramifying and forever
Silent, beyond silence listened for.

1987

The Sharping Stone[1]

In an apothecary's° chest of drawers,   *pharmacist's*
Sweet cedar that we'd purchased second hand,
In one of its weighty deep-sliding recesses
I found the sharping stone that was to be
5 Our gift to him. Still in its wrapping paper.
Like a baton of black light I'd failed to pass.

•

Airless cinder-depths. But all the same,
The way it lay there, it wakened something too . . .
I thought of us that evening on the logs,
10 Flat on our backs, the pair of us, parallel,
Supported head to heel, arms straight, eyes front,
Listening to the rain drip off the trees
And saying nothing, braced to the damp bark.
What possessed us? The bare, lopped loveliness
15 Of those two winter trunks, the way they seemed
Prepared for launching, at right angles across
A causeway of short fence-posts set like rollers.
Neither of us spoke. The puddles waited.
The workers had gone home, saws fallen silent.
20 And next thing down we lay, babes in the wood,
Gazing up at the flood-face of the sky
Until it seemed a flood was carrying us

4. Shot off obliquely.
5. Of the same age.

1. Whetstone for sharpening metal blades.

Out of the forest park, feet first, eyes front,
Out of November, out of middle age,
25   Together, out, across the Sea of Moyle.[2]

•

Sarcophage des époux.[3] In terra cotta.
Etruscan couple shown side by side,
Recumbent on left elbows, husband pointing
With his right arm and watching where he points,
30   Wife in front, her earrings in, her braids
Down to her waist, taking her sexual ease.
He is all eyes, she is all brow and dream,
Her right forearm and hand held out as if
Some bird she sees in her deep inward gaze
35   Might be about to roost there. Domestic
Love, the artist thought, warm tones and property,
The frangibility of terra cotta . . .
Which is how they figured on the colour postcard
(Louvre, Département des Antiquités)[4]
40   That we'd sent him once, then found among his things.

•

He loved inspired mistakes: his Spanish grandson's
English transliteration, thanking him
For a boat trip: 'That was a marvellous
Walk on the water, granddad.' And indeed
45   He walked on air himself, never more so
Than when he had been widowed and the youth
In him, the athlete who had wooed her—
Breasting tapes and clearing the high bars—
Grew lightsome once again. Going at eighty
50   On the bendiest roads, going for broke
At every point-to-point[5] and poker-school,
'He commenced his wild career' a second time
And not a bother on him. Smoked like a train
And took the power mower in his stride.
55   Flirted and vaunted. Set fire to his bed.
Fell from a ladder. Learned to microwave.

•

So set the drawer on freshets° of thaw water   *surges*
And place the unused sharping stone inside it:
To be found next summer on a riverbank
60   Where scythes once hung all night in alder trees
And mowers played dawn scherzos[6] on the blades,
Their arms like harpists' arms, one drawing towards,
One sweeping the bright rim of the extreme.

1996

2. Channel between the northwestern coast of County Antrim in Ireland and the southwestern coast of Scotland.
3. Coffin for a married couple (French).
4. Department of Antiquities, Louvre Museum, Paris, in which this Etruscan funerary statue, known as *The Cerveteri Couple*, is to be found.
5. Horse race over jumps.
6. Vigorous light and playful musical compositions.

Anything Can Happen

after Horace, Odes, 1, 34[1]

Anything can happen. You know how Jupiter[2]
Will mostly wait for clouds to gather head
Before he hurls the lightning? Well, just now
He galloped his thunder cart and his horses

5　　Across a clear blue sky. It shook the earth
And the clogged underearth, the River Styx,[3]
The winding streams, the Atlantic shore itself.
Anything can happen, the tallest towers

Be overturned, those in high places daunted,
10　　Those overlooked regarded. Stropped-beak[4] Fortune
Swoops, making the air gasp, tearing the crest off one,
Setting it down bleeding on the next.

Ground gives. The heaven's weight
Lifts up off Atlas like a kettle-lid.
15　　Capstones shift, nothing resettles right.
Telluric[5] ash and fire-spores boil away.

2001, 2006

A Kite for Aibhín[1]

After "L'aquilone" by Giovanni Pascoli (1855–1912)[2]

Air from another life and time and place,
Pale blue heavenly air is supporting
A white wing beating high against the breeze,

And yes, it is a kite! As when one afternoon
5　　All of us there trooped out
Among the briar hedges and stripped thorn,

I take my stand again, halt opposite
Anahorish[3] Hill to scan the blue,
Back in that field to launch our long-tailed comet.

10　　And now it hovers, tugs, veers, dives askew,
Lifts itself, goes with the wind until
It rises to loud cheers from us below.

1. Cf. *Odes* (23 B.C.E.), books of lyric poetry by the Roman poet and satirist Horace (65–8 B.C.E.). Although he follows aspects of Horace's poem, Heaney drops Horace's first stanza and adds a new final stanza.
2. Supreme Roman god, whose weapon was the thunderbolt.
3. In Greek mythology, a river in the underworld, over which the shades of the dead were ferried.

4. With a beak with a sharpened edge.
5. Of the earth or soil. "Atlas": one of the Titans in Greek mythology, he was condemned to hold up the heavens. "Capstones": stones that crown structures, typically walls.
1. Heaney's granddaughter (pronounced AY-veen).
2. Italian poet.
3. Town in south Derry.

Rises, and my hand is like a spindle
Unspooling, the kite a thin-stemmed flower
15 Climbing and carrying, carrying farther, higher

The longing in the breast and planted feet
And gazing face and heart of the kite flier
Until string breaks and—separate, elate—

The kite takes off, itself alone, a windfall.[4]

2010

4. Literally, fruit or wood blown from a tree.

MARGARET ATWOOD
b. 1939

Margaret Atwood was born in Ottawa, Canada, into a family with roots in Nova Scotia, but when she was seven her family moved to Toronto. She did not receive formal schooling until she was eleven, because her family spent a large part of every year in the northern wildernesses of Quebec and Ontario. There, her father, a forest entomologist, pursued his research on insects, while she immersed herself in both the woods and books. The Canadian wilderness is the setting of a number of her poems, novels, and stories, although her work has ranged among a variety of real and fictional locales, including the Caribbean island of *Bodily Harm* (1981) and the dystopian Boston of *The Handmaid's Tale* (1985). Atwood received her B.A. in English from Victoria College, University of Toronto, in 1961. The next year she earned an M.A. at Harvard, later returning for doctoral research she did not complete, though several volumes of her poetry were published during that time. Before 1972, when she became a full-time writer, Atwood taught at Canadian universities in Vancouver, Montreal, Alberta, and Toronto.

Atwood is the author of more than a dozen collections of poetry, and more than twenty volumes of imaginative prose—both novels and short fiction—as well as a large number of essays and critical works. Her earliest books include the poems collected in the self-published *Double Persephone* (1961), and then the conventionally published *The Circle Game* (1964), a collection that won the Governor General's Literary Award for Poetry. Precisely carved language, doubleness of vision, ironic inversions of expectations—these are among the qualities that have garnered attention for her poetry. A poem such as "Miss July Grows Older" suggests the complexity of Atwood's surprising and witty examinations of gender relations. It opens with an arresting question in the voice of a smart, wryly self-critical beauty queen who, hardly a passive object, has skillfully manipulated men: "How much longer can I get away / with being so fucking cute?" Atwood has said that poetry is "the heart of the language, the activity through which language is renewed and kept alive."

She has also said that, for her, "fiction is the guardian of the moral and ethical sense of the community." Although she continued to publish collections of poetry over several decades, it is Atwood's fiction that has made her perhaps Canada's best-known writer. Her first novel, *The Edible Woman* (1969), explores a woman's eating disorders long before the sexual politics of anorexia and bulimia were widely discussed. Several of her subsequent novels were short-listed for the Booker Prize, including her most famous work, *The Handmaid's Tale* (1985), about a woman's struggle against imprisonment within sharply hierarchical gender roles in a religious fundamentalist dystopia; *Cat's Eye* (1989), about power and cruelty in girlhood friendships; and *Alias Grace* (1996), a fictionalized narrative of a historical nineteenth-century female servant accused of murder. *The Blind Assassin* (2000), which nests various stories within one another, finally won Atwood the Booker Prize. In 2015 she completed a manuscript, *Scribbler Moon*, that will be held in secrecy for a hundred years before being published.

Since the publication of her early book of essays, *Survival* (1972), Atwood has helped bring attention and shape to Canadian literature. Early in that book, she hazards sweeping comparisons between Canadian literature and both "the sense of adventure or danger" in the literature of the United States (its key symbol being "The Frontier") and the "smugness and/or sense of security" in the literature of England ("The Island"). In her view, Canadian literature reflects a distinct experience. "Our stories are likely to be tales not of those who made it but of those who made it back, from the awful experience—the North, the snowstorm, the sinking ship—that killed everyone else. The survivor has no triumph or victory but the fact of his survival." Some of Atwood's fictional characters are survivors of the Canadian wilderness, including the young female protagonist of *Surfacing*, a novel published in the same year as *Survival*, who journeys deep into the wilderness in search of her lost father. The main character in *Cat's Eye* reviews and relives the psychological damage inflicted on her by female friendships and bullying during her childhood and teenage years in the forest.

In the short story "Death by Landscape," the central character, Lois, is also a survivor of loss and painful memories, of vexed female friendship and power relations lived out in the Canadian wilderness. Reflecting on coming of age at camp, Lois remembers the singing, the stratification, the role-playing as American Indians, but her main focus is her friendship with an American girl, Lucy, who imports into Canada her troubled home life. After a defining incident on a canoe trip, "Death by Landscape," like other of Atwood's novels and short fiction, becomes a narrative in part about the power of stories to give meaning, as well as their potential duplicity—about the power of narrative both to condemn and to explore, of language both to cripple and to liberate.

Death by Landscape

Now that the boys are grown up and Rob is dead, Lois has moved to a condominium apartment in one of the newer waterfront developments. She is relieved not to have to worry about the lawn, or about the ivy pushing its muscular little suckers into the brickwork, or the squirrels gnawing their way into the attic and eating the insulation off the wiring, or about strange noises. This building has a security system, and the only plant life is in pots in the solarium.

Lois is glad she's been able to find an apartment big enough for her pictures. They are more crowded together than they were in the house, but this arrangement gives the walls a European look: blocks of pictures, above and beside one another, rather than one over the chesterfield,[1] one over the fireplace, one in the front hall, in the old acceptable manner of sprinkling art around so it does not get too intrusive. This way has more of an impact. You know it's not supposed to be furniture.

---

1. Sofa.

None of the pictures is very large, which doesn't mean they aren't valuable. They are paintings, or sketches and drawings, by artists who were not nearly as well known when Lois began to buy them as they are now. Their work later turned up on stamps, or as silk-screen reproductions hung in the principals' offices of high schools, or as jigsaw puzzles, or on beautifully printed calendars sent out by corporations as Christmas gifts, to their less important clients. These artists painted mostly in the twenties and thirties and forties; they painted landscapes. Lois has two Tom Thomsons, three A. Y. Jacksons, a Lawren Harris. She has an Arthur Lismer, she has a J. E. H. MacDonald. She has a David Milne.[2] They are pictures of convoluted tree trunks on an island or pink wave-smoothed stone, with more islands behind; of a lake with rough, bright, sparsely wooded cliffs; of a vivid river shore with a tangle of bush and two beached canoes, one red, one grey; of a yellow autumn woods with the ice-blue gleam of a pond half-seen through the interlaced branches.

It was Lois who'd chosen them. Rob had no interest in art, although he could see the necessity of having something on the walls. He left all the decorating decisions to her, while providing the money, of course. Because of this collection of hers, Lois's friends—especially the men—have given her the reputation of having a good nose for art investments.

But this is not why she bought the pictures, way back then. She bought them because she wanted them. She wanted something that was in them, although she could not have said at the time what it was. It was not peace: she does not find them peaceful in the least. Looking at them fills her with a wordless unease. Despite the fact that there are no people in them or even animals, it's as if there is something, or someone, looking back out.

When she was thirteen, Lois went on a canoe trip. She'd only been on overnights before. This was to be a long one, into the trackless wilderness, as Cappie put it. It was Lois's first canoe trip, and her last.

Cappie was the head of the summer camp to which Lois had been sent ever since she was nine. Camp Manitou, it was called; it was one of the better ones, for girls, though not the best. Girls of her age whose parents could afford it were routinely packed off to such camps, which bore a generic resemblance to one another. They favoured Indian names and had hearty, energetic leaders, who were called Cappie or Skip or Scottie. At these camps you learned to swim well and sail, and paddle a canoe, and perhaps ride a horse or play tennis. When you weren't doing these things you could do Arts and Crafts and turn out dingy, lumpish clay ashtrays for your mother—mothers smoked more, then—or bracelets made of coloured braided string.

Cheerfulness was required at all times, even at breakfast. Loud shouting and the banging of spoons on the tables were allowed, and even encouraged, at ritual intervals. Chocolate bars were rationed, to control tooth decay and pimples. At night, after supper, in the dining hall or outside around a mosquito-infested campfire ring for special treats, there were singsongs. Lois can still remember all the words to "My Darling Clementine," and to "My Bonnie Lies Over the Ocean," with acting-out gestures: a rippling of the

---

2. All Canadian landscape painters: Tom Thomson (1877–1917), A. Y. Jackson (1882–1974), Lawren Harris (1885–1970), Arthur Lismer (1885–1969), J. E. H. MacDonald (1873–1932), and David Milne (1882–1953). Jackson, Harris, Lismer, and MacDonald were members of the Group of Seven, the first major national movement in Canadian art, and Thomson was associated with the group. Its work was usually expressionist in style.

hands for "the ocean," two hands together under the cheek for "lies." She will never be able to forget them, which is a sad thought.

Lois thinks she can recognize women who went to these camps, and were good at it. They have a hardness to their handshakes, even now; a way of standing, legs planted firmly and farther apart than usual; a way of sizing you up, to see if you'd be any good in a canoe—the front, not the back. They themselves would be in the back. They would call it the stern.

She knows that such camps still exist, although Camp Manitou does not. They are one of the few things that haven't changed much. They now offer copper enamelling, and functionless pieces of stained glass baked in electric ovens, though judging from the productions of her friends' grandchildren the artistic standards have not improved.

To Lois, encountering it in the first year after the war, Camp Manitou seemed ancient. Its log-sided buildings with the white cement in between the half-logs, its flagpole ringed with whitewashed stones, its weathered grey dock jutting out into Lake Prospect, with its woven rope bumpers and its rusty rings for tying up, its prim round flowerbed of petunias near the office door, must surely have been there always. In truth it dated only from the first decade of the century; it had been founded by Cappie's parents, who'd thought of camping as bracing to the character, like cold showers, and had been passed along to her as an inheritance, and an obligation.

Lois realized, later, that it must have been a struggle for Cappie to keep Camp Manitou going, during the Depression and then the war, when money did not flow freely. If it had been a camp for the very rich, instead of the merely well off, there would have been fewer problems. But there must have been enough Old Girls, ones with daughters, to keep the thing in operation, though not entirely shipshape: furniture was battered, painted trim was peeling, roofs leaked. There were dim photographs of these Old Girls dotted around the dining hall, wearing ample woollen bathing suits and showing their fat, dimpled legs, or standing, arms twined, in odd tennis outfits with baggy skirts.

In the dining hall, over the stone fireplace that was never used, there was a huge moulting stuffed moose head, which looked somehow carnivorous. It was a sort of mascot; its name was Monty Manitou. The older campers spread the story that it was haunted, and came to life in the dark, when the feeble and undependable lights had been turned off or, due to yet another generator failure, had gone out. Lois was afraid of it at first, but not after she got used to it.

Cappie was the same: you had to get used to her. Possibly she was forty, or thirty-five, or fifty. She had fawn-coloured hair that looked as if it was cut with a bowl. Her head jutted forward, jigging like a chicken's as she strode around the camp, clutching notebooks and checking things off in them. She was like their minister in church: both of them smiled a lot and were anxious because they wanted things to go well; they both had the same overwashed skins and stringy necks. But all this disappeared when Cappie was leading a singsong, or otherwise leading. Then she was happy, sure of herself, her plain face almost luminous. She wanted to cause joy. At these times she was loved, at others merely trusted.

There were many things Lois didn't like about Camp Manitou, at first. She hated the noisy chaos and spoon-banging of the dining hall, the rowdy singsongs at which you were expected to yell in order to show that you were enjoying yourself. Hers was not a household that encouraged yelling. She hated the necessity of having to write dutiful letters to her parents claiming she was having fun. She could not complain, because camp cost so much money.

She didn't much like having to undress in a roomful of other girls, even in the dim light, although nobody paid any attention, or sleeping in a cabin with seven other girls, some of whom snored because they had adenoids[3] or colds, some of whom had nightmares, or wet their beds and cried about it. Bottom bunks made her feel closed in, and she was afraid of falling out of top ones; she was afraid of heights. She got homesick, and suspected her parents of having a better time when she wasn't there than when she was, although her mother wrote to her every week saying how much they missed her. All this was when she was nine. By the time she was thirteen she liked it. She was an old hand by then.

Lucy was her best friend at camp. Lois had other friends in winter, when there was school and itchy woollen clothing and darkness in the afternoons, but Lucy was her summer friend.

She turned up the second year, when Lois was ten, and a Bluejay. (Chickadees, Bluejays, Ravens, and Kingfishers—these were the names Camp Manitou assigned to the different age groups, a sort of totemic clan system. In those days, thinks Lois, it was birds for girls, animals for boys: wolves, and so forth. Though some animals and birds were suitable and some were not. Never vultures, for instance; never skunks, or rats.)

Lois helped Lucy to unpack her tin trunk and place the folded clothes on the wooden shelves, and to make up her bed. She put her in the top bunk right above her, where she could keep an eye on her. Already she knew that Lucy was an exception, to a good many rules; already she felt proprietorial.

Lucy was from the United States, where the comic books came from, and the movies. She wasn't from New York or Hollywood or Buffalo, the only American cities Lois knew the names of, but from Chicago. Her house was on the lake shore and had gates to it, and grounds. They had a maid, all of the time. Lois's family only had a cleaning lady twice a week.

The only reason Lucy was being sent to *this* camp (she cast a look of minor scorn around the cabin, diminishing it and also offending Lois, while at the same time daunting her) was that her mother had been a camper here. Her mother had been a Canadian once, but had married her father, who had a patch over one eye, like a pirate. She showed Lois the picture of him in her wallet. He got the patch in the war. "Shrapnel," said Lucy. Lois, who was unsure about shrapnel, was so impressed she could only grunt. Her own two-eyed, unwounded father was tame by comparison.

"My father plays golf," she ventured at last.

"*Everyone* plays golf," said Lucy. "My *mother* plays golf."

Lois's mother did not. Lois took Lucy to see the outhouses and the swimming dock and the dining hall with Monty Manitou's baleful head, knowing in advance they would not measure up.

This was a bad beginning; but Lucy was good-natured, and accepted Camp Manitou with the same casual shrug with which she seemed to accept everything. She would make the best of it, without letting Lois forget that this was what she was doing.

However, there were things Lois knew that Lucy did not. Lucy scratched the tops off all her mosquito bites and had to be taken to the infirmary to be daubed with Ozonol.[4] She took her T-shirt off while sailing, and although the

3. Enlarged masses of lymphoid tissue at the top   4. First-aid ointment.
of the throat, blocking the nasal passages.

counsellor spotted her after a while and made her put it back on, she burnt spectacularly, bright red, with the X of her bathing-suit straps standing out in alarming white; she let Lois peel the sheets of whispery-thin burned skin off her shoulders. When they sang "Alouette" around the campfire, she did not know any of the French words. The difference was that Lucy did not care about the things she didn't know, whereas Lois did.

During the next winter, and subsequent winters, Lucy and Lois wrote to each other. They were both only children, at a time when this was thought to be a disadvantage, so in their letters they pretended to be sisters, or even twins. Lois had to strain a little over this, because Lucy was so blonde, with translucent skin and large blue eyes like a doll's, and Lois was nothing out of the ordinary— just a tallish, thinnish, brownish person with freckles. They signed their letters LL, with the L's entwined together like the monograms on a towel. (Lois and Lucy, thinks Lois. How our names date us. Lois Lane, Superman's girlfriend, enterprising female reporter; "I Love Lucy." Now we are obsolete, and it's little Jennifers, little Emilys, little Alexandras and Carolines and Tiffanys.)

They were more effusive in their letters than they ever were in person. They bordered their pages with X's and O's, but when they met again in the summers it was always a shock. They had changed so much, or Lucy had. It was like watching someone grow up in jolts. At first it would be hard to think up things to say.

But Lucy always had a surprise or two, something to show, some marvel to reveal. The first year she had a picture of herself in a tutu, her hair in a ballerina's knot on the top of her head; she pirouetted around the swimming dock, to show Lois how it was done, and almost fell off. The next year she had given that up and was taking horseback riding. (Camp Manitou did not have horses.) The next year her mother and father had been divorced, and she had a new stepfather, one with both eyes, and a new house, although the maid was the same. The next year, when they had graduated from Bluejays and entered Ravens, she got her period, right in the first week of camp. The two of them snitched some matches from their counsellor, who smoked illegally, and made a small fire out behind the farthest outhouse, at dusk, using their flashlights. They could set all kinds of fires by now; they had learned how in Campcraft. On this fire they burned one of Lucy's used sanitary napkins. Lois is not sure why they did this, or whose idea it was. But she can remember the feeling of deep satisfaction it gave her as the white fluff singed and the blood sizzled, as if some wordless ritual had been fulfilled.

They did not get caught, but then they rarely got caught at any of their camp transgressions. Lucy had such large eyes, and was such an accomplished liar.

This year Lucy is different again: slower, more languorous. She is no longer interested in sneaking around after dark, purloining cigarettes from the counsellor, dealing in black-market candy bars. She is pensive, and hard to wake in the mornings. She doesn't like her stepfather, but she doesn't want to live with her real father either, who has a new wife. She thinks her mother may be having a love affair with a doctor; she doesn't know for sure, but she's seen them smooching in his car, out on the driveway, when her stepfather wasn't there. It serves him right. She hates her private school. She has a boyfriend, who is sixteen and works as a gardener's assistant. This is how she met him: in the garden. She describes to Lois what it is like when he kisses her—rubbery at first, but then your knees go limp. She has been forbidden to see him, and threatened with boarding school. She wants to run away from home.

Lois has little to offer in return. Her own life is placid and satisfactory, but there is nothing much that can be said about happiness. "You're so lucky," Lucy tells her, a little smugly. She might as well say *boring* because this is how it makes Lois feel.

Lucy is apathetic about the canoe trip, so Lois has to disguise her own excitement. The evening before they are to leave, she slouches into the campfire ring as if coerced, and sits down with a sigh of endurance, just as Lucy does.

Every canoe trip that went out of camp was given a special send-off by Cappie and the section leader and counsellors, with the whole section in attendance. Cappie painted three streaks of red across each of her cheeks with a lipstick. They looked like three-fingered claw marks. She put a blue circle on her forehead with fountain-pen ink, and tied a twisted bandanna around her head and stuck a row of frazzle-ended feathers around it, and wrapped herself in a red-and-black Hudson's Bay blanket. The counsellors, also in blankets but with only two streaks of red, beat on tom-toms made of round wooden cheese boxes with leather stretched over the top and nailed in place. Cappie was Chief Cappeosota. They all had to say "How!" when she walked into the circle and stood there with one hand raised.

Looking back on this, Lois finds it disquieting. She knows too much about Indians: this is why. She knows, for instance, that they should not even be called Indians, and that they have enough worries without other people taking their names and dressing up as them. It has all been a form of stealing.

But she remembers, too, that she was once ignorant of this. Once she loved the campfire, the flickering of light on the ring of faces, the sound of the fake tom-toms, heavy and fast like a scared heartbeat; she loved Cappie in a red blanket and feathers, solemn, as a chief should be, raising her hand and saying, "Greetings, my Ravens." It was not funny, it was not making fun. She wanted to be an Indian. She wanted to be adventurous and pure, and aboriginal.

"You go on big water," says Cappie. This is her idea—all their ideas—of how Indians talk. "You go where no man has ever trod. You go many moons." This is not true. They are only going for a week, not many moons. The canoe route is clearly marked, they have gone over it on a map, and there are prepared campsites with names which are used year after year. But when Cappie says this—and despite the way Lucy rolls up her eyes—Lois can feel the water stretching out, with the shores twisting away on either side, immense and a little frightening.

"You bring back much wampum,"[5] says Cappie. "Do good in war, my braves, and capture many scalps." This is another of her pretences: that they are boys, and bloodthirsty. But such a game cannot be played by substituting the word "squaw." It would not work at all.

Each of them has to stand up and step forward and have a red line drawn across her cheeks by Cappie. She tells them they must follow in the paths of their ancestors (who most certainly, thinks Lois, looking out the window of her apartment and remembering the family stash of daguerreotypes[6] and sepia-coloured portraits on her mother's dressing table, the stiff-shirted, black-coated, grim-faced men and the beflounced women with their severe

---

5. Beads made from polished shells and used as money by Native peoples of North America.
6. Early photographs.

hair and their corseted respectability, would never have considered heading off onto an open lake, in a canoe, just for fun).

At the end of the ceremony they all stood and held hands around the circle, and sang taps. This did not sound very Indian, thinks Lois. It sounded like a bugle call at a military post, in a movie. But Cappie was never one to be much concerned with consistency, or with archaeology.

After breakfast the next morning they set out from the main dock, in four canoes, three in each. The lipstick stripes have not come off completely, and still show faintly pink, like healing burns. They wear their white denim sailing hats, because of the sun, and thin-striped T-shirts, and pale baggy shorts with the cuffs rolled up. The middle one kneels, propping her rear end against the rolled sleeping bags. The counsellors going with them are Pat and Kip. Kip is no-nonsense; Pat is easier to wheedle, or fool.

There are white puffy clouds and a small breeze. Glints come from the little waves. Lois is in the bow of Kip's canoe. She still can't do a J-stroke very well, and she will have to be in the bow or the middle for the whole trip. Lucy is behind her; her own J-stroke is even worse. She splashes Lois with her paddle, quite a big splash.

"I'll get you back," says Lois.

"There was a stable fly on your shoulder," Lucy says.

Lois turns to look at her, to see if she's grinning. They're in the habit of splashing each other. Back there, the camp has vanished behind the first long point of rock and rough trees. Lois feels as if an invisible rope has broken. They're floating free, on their own, cut loose. Beneath the canoe the lake goes down, deeper and colder than it was a minute before.

"No horsing around in the canoe," says Kip. She's rolled her T-shirt sleeves up to the shoulder; her arms are brown and sinewy, her jaw determined, her stroke perfect. She looks as if she knows exactly what she is doing.

The four canoes keep close together. They sing, raucously and with defiance; they sing "The Quartermaster's Store," and "Clementine," and "Alouette." It is more like bellowing than singing.

After that the wind grows stronger, blowing slantwise against the bows, and they have to put all their energy into shoving themselves through the water.

Was there anything important, anything that would provide some sort of reason or clue to what happened next? Lois can remember everything, every detail; but it does her no good.

They stopped at noon for a swim and lunch, and went on in the afternoon. At last they reached Little Birch, which was the first campsite for overnight. Lois and Lucy made the fire, while the others pitched the heavy canvas tents. The fireplace was already there, flat stones piled into a U. A burned tin can and a beer bottle had been left in it. Their fire went out, and they had to restart it. "Hustle your bustle," said Kip. "We're starving."

The sun went down, and in the pink sunset light they brushed their teeth and spat the toothpaste froth into the lake. Kip and Pat put all the food that wasn't in cans into a packsack and slung it into a tree, in case of bears.

Lois and Lucy weren't sleeping in a tent. They'd begged to be allowed to sleep out; that way they could talk without the others hearing. If it rained, they told Kip, they promised not to crawl dripping into the tent over everyone's legs: they would get under the canoes. So they were out on the point.

Lois tried to get comfortable inside her sleeping bag, which smelled of musty storage and of earlier campers, a stale salty sweetness. She curled herself up, with her sweater rolled up under her head for a pillow and her flashlight inside her sleeping bag so it wouldn't roll away. The muscles of her sore arms were making small pings, like rubber bands breaking.

Beside her Lucy was rustling around. Lois could see the glimmering oval of her white face.

"I've got a rock poking into my back," said Lucy.

"So do I," said Lois. "You want to go into the tent?" She herself didn't, but it was right to ask.

"No," said Lucy. She subsided into her sleeping bag. After a moment she said, "It would be nice not to go back."

"To camp?" said Lois.

"To Chicago," said Lucy. "I hate it there."

"What about your boyfriend?" said Lois. Lucy didn't answer. She was either asleep or pretending to be.

There was a moon, and a movement of the trees. In the sky there were stars, layers of stars that went down and down. Kip said that when the stars were bright like that instead of hazy it meant bad weather later on. Out on the lake there were two loons, calling to each other in their insane, mournful voices. At the time it did not sound like grief. It was just background.

The lake in the morning was flat calm. They skimmed along over the glassy surface, leaving V-shaped trails behind them; it felt like flying. As the sun rose higher it got hot, almost too hot. There were stable flies in the canoes, landing on a bare arm or leg for a quick sting. Lois hoped for wind.

They stopped for lunch at the next of the named campsites, Lookout Point. It was called this because, although the site itself was down near the water on a flat shelf of rock, there was a sheer cliff nearby and a trail that led up to the top. The top was the lookout, although what you were supposed to see from there was not clear. Kip said it was just a view.

Lois and Lucy decided to make the climb anyway. They didn't want to hang around waiting for lunch. It wasn't their turn to cook, though they hadn't avoided much by not doing it, because cooking lunch was no big deal, it was just unwrapping the cheese and getting out the bread and peanut butter, but Pat and Kip always had to do their woodsy act and boil up a billy tin[7] for their own tea.

They told Kip where they were going. You had to tell Kip where you were going, even if it was only a little way into the woods to get dry twigs for kindling. You could never go anywhere without a buddy.

"Sure," said Kip, who was crouching over the fire, feeding driftwood into it. "Fifteen minutes to lunch."

"Where are they off to?" said Pat. She was bringing their billy tin of water from the lake.

"Lookout," said Kip.

"Be careful," said Pat. She said it as an afterthought, because it was what she always said.

"They're old hands," Kip said.

Lois looks at her watch: it's ten to twelve. She is the watch-minder; Lucy is careless of time. They walk up the path, which is dry earth and rocks, big

---

7. Metal pail with a close-fitting lid and a wire handle, used for cooking over open fires.

rounded pinky-grey boulders or split-open ones with jagged edges. Spindly balsam and spruce trees grow to either side, the lake is blue fragments to the left. The sun is right overhead; there are no shadows anywhere. The heat comes up at them as well as down. The forest is dry and crackly.

It isn't far, but it's a steep climb and they're sweating when they reach the top. They wipe their faces with their bare arms, sit gingerly down on a scorching-hot rock, five feet from the edge but too close for Lois. It's a lookout all right, a sheer drop to the lake and a long view over the water, back the way they've come. It's amazing to Lois that they've travelled so far, over all that water, with nothing to propel them but their own arms. It makes her feel strong. There are all kinds of things she is capable of doing.

"It would be quite a dive off here," says Lucy.

"You'd have to be nuts," says Lois.

"Why?" says Lucy. "It's really deep. It goes straight down." She stands up and takes a step nearer the edge. Lois gets a stab in her midriff, the kind she gets when a car goes too fast over a bump. "Don't," she says.

"Don't what?" says Lucy, glancing around at her mischievously. She knows how Lois feels about heights. But she turns back. "I really have to pee," she says.

"You have toilet paper?" says Lois, who is never without it. She digs in her shorts pocket.

"Thanks," says Lucy.

They are both adept at peeing in the woods: doing it fast so the mosquitoes don't get you, the underwear pulled up between the knees, the squat with the feet apart so you don't wet your legs, facing downhill. The exposed feeling of your bum, as if someone is looking at you from behind. The etiquette when you're with someone else is not to look. Lois stands up and starts to walk back down the path, to be out of sight.

"Wait for me?" says Lucy.

Lois climbed down, over and around the boulders, until she could not see Lucy; she waited. She could hear the voices of the others, talking and laughing, down near the shore. One voice was yelling, "Ants! Ants!" Someone must have sat on an ant hill. Off to the side, in the woods, a raven was croaking, a hoarse single note.

She looked at her watch: it was noon. This is when she heard the shout.

She has gone over and over it in her mind since, so many times that the first, real shout has been obliterated, like a footprint trampled by other footprints. But she is sure (she is almost positive, she is nearly certain) that it was not a shout of fear. Not a scream. More like a cry of surprise, cut off too soon. Short, like a dog's bark.

"Lucy?" Lois said. Then she called "Lucy!" By now she was clambering back up, over the stones of the path. Lucy was not up there. Or she was not in sight.

"Stop fooling around," Lois said. "It's lunch-time." But Lucy did not rise from behind a rock or step out, smiling, from behind a tree. The sunlight was all around; the rocks looked white. "This isn't funny!" Lois said, and it wasn't, panic was rising in her, the panic of a small child who does not know where the bigger ones are hidden. She could hear her own heart. She looked quickly around; she lay down on the ground and looked over the edge of the cliff. It made her feel cold. There was nothing.

She went back down the path, stumbling; she was breathing too quickly; she was too frightened to cry. She felt terrible—guilty and dismayed, as if she had done something very bad, by mistake. Something that could never be repaired. "Lucy's gone," she told Kip.

Kip looked up from her fire, annoyed. The water in the billy can was boiling. "What do you mean, gone?" she said. "Where did she go?"

"I don't know," said Lois. "She's just gone."

No one had heard the shout, but then no one had heard Lois calling, either. They had been talking among themselves, by the water.

Kip and Pat went up to the lookout and searched and called, and blew their whistles. Nothing answered.

Then they came back down, and Lois had to tell exactly what had happened. The other girls all sat in a circle and listened to her. Nobody said anything. They all looked frightened, especially Pat and Kip. They were the leaders. You did not just lose a camper like this, for no reason at all.

"Why did you leave her alone?" said Kip.

"I was just down the path," said Lois. "I told you. She had to go to the bathroom." She did not say *pee* in front of people older than herself.

Kip looked disgusted.

"Maybe she just walked off into the woods and got turned around," said one of the girls.

"Maybe she's doing it on purpose," said another.

Nobody believed either of these theories.

They took the canoes and searched around the base of the cliff, and peered down into the water. But there had been no sound of falling rock; there had been no splash. There was no clue, nothing at all. Lucy had simply vanished.

That was the end of the canoe trip. It took them the same two days to go back that it had taken coming in, even though they were short a paddler. They did not sing.

After that, the police went in a motorboat, with dogs; they were the Mounties[8] and the dogs were German shepherds, trained to follow trails in the woods. But it had rained since, and they could find nothing.

Lois is sitting in Cappie's office. Her face is bloated with crying, she's seen that in the mirror. By now she feels numbed; she feels as if she has drowned. She can't stay here. It has been too much of a shock. Tomorrow her parents are coming to take her away. Several of the other girls who were on the canoe trip are also being collected. The others will have to stay, because their parents are in Europe, or cannot be reached.

Cappie is grim. They've tried to hush it up, but of course everyone in camp knows. Soon the papers will know too. You can't keep it quiet, but what can be said? What can be said that makes any sense? "Girl vanishes in broad daylight, without a trace." It can't be believed. Other things, worse things, will be suspected. Negligence, at the very least. But they have always taken such care. Bad luck will gather around Camp Manitou like a fog; parents will avoid it, in favour of other, luckier places. Lois can see Cappie thinking all this, even through her numbness. It's what anyone would think.

Lois sits on the hard wooden chair in Cappie's office, beside the old wooden desk, over which hangs the thumb-tacked bulletin board of normal camp routine, and gazes at Cappie through her puffy eyelids. Cappie is now smiling what is supposed to be a reassuring smile. Her manner is too casual: she's after something. Lois has seen this look on Cappie's face when she's

8. Royal Canadian Mounted Police.

been sniffing out contraband chocolate bars, hunting down those rumoured to have snuck out of their cabins at night.

"Tell me again," says Cappie, "from the beginning."

Lois has told her story so many times by now, to Pat and Kip, to Cappie, to the police, that she knows it word for word. She knows it, but she no longer believes it. It has become a story. "I told you," she said. "She wanted to go to the bathroom. I gave her my toilet paper. I went down the path, I waited for her. I heard this kind of shout . . ."

"Yes," says Cappie, smiling confidingly, "but before that. What did you say to one another?"

Lois thinks. Nobody has asked her this before. "She said you could dive off there. She said it went straight down."

"And what did you say?"

"I said you'd have to be nuts."

"Were you mad at Lucy?" says Cappie, in an encouraging voice.

"No," says Lois. "Why would I be mad at Lucy? I wasn't ever mad at Lucy." She feels like crying again. The times when she has in fact been mad at Lucy have been erased already. Lucy was always perfect.

"Sometimes we're angry when we don't know we're angry," says Cappie, as if to herself. "Sometimes we get really mad and we don't even know it. Sometimes we might do a thing without meaning to, or without knowing what will happen. We lose our tempers."

Lois is only thirteen, but it doesn't take her long to figure out that Cappie is not including herself in any of this. By we she means Lois. She is accusing Lois of pushing Lucy off the cliff. The unfairness of this hits her like a slap. "I didn't!" she says.

"Didn't what?" says Cappie softly. "Didn't what, Lois?"

Lois does the worst thing, she begins to cry. Cappie gives her a look like a pounce. She's got what she wanted.

Later, when she was grown up, Lois was able to understand what this interview had been about. She could see Cappie's desperation, her need for a story, a real story with a reason in it; anything but the senseless vacancy Lucy had left for her to deal with. Cappie wanted Lois to supply the reason, to be the reason. It wasn't even for the newspapers or the parents, because she could never make such an accusation without proof. It was for herself: something to explain the loss of Camp Manitou and of all she had worked for, the years of entertaining spoiled children and buttering up parents and making a fool of herself with feathers stuck in her hair. Camp Manitou was in fact lost. It did not survive.

Lois worked all this out, twenty years later. But it was far too late. It was too late even ten minutes afterwards, when she'd left Cappie's office and was walking slowly back to her cabin to pack. Lucy's clothes were still there, folded on the shelves, as if waiting. She felt the other girls in the cabin watching her with speculation in their eyes. *Could she have done it? She must have done it.* For the rest of her life, she has caught people watching her in this way.

Maybe they weren't thinking this. Maybe they were merely sorry for her. But she felt she had been tried and sentenced, and this is what has stayed with her: the knowledge that she had been singled out, condemned for something that was not her fault.

Lois sits in the living room of her apartment, drinking a cup of tea. Through the knee-to-ceiling window she has a wide view of Lake Ontario, with its skin of wrinkled blue-grey light, and of the willows of Centre Island shaken by a wind, which is silent at this distance, and on this side of the glass. When there isn't too much pollution she can see the far shore, the foreign shore; though today it is obscured.

Possibly she could go out, go downstairs, do some shopping; there isn't much in the refrigerator. The boys say she doesn't get out enough. But she isn't hungry, and moving, stirring from this space, is increasingly an effort.

She can hardly remember, now, having her two boys in the hospital, nursing them as babies; she can hardly remember getting married, or what Rob looked like. Even at the time she never felt she was paying full attention. She was tired a lot, as if she was living not one life but two: her own, and another, shadowy life that hovered around her and would not let itself be realized—the life of what would have happened if Lucy had not stepped sideways, and disappeared from time.

She would never go up north, to Rob's family cottage or to any place with wild lakes and wild trees and the calls of loons. She would never go anywhere near. Still, it was as if she was always listening for another voice, the voice of a person who should have been there but was not. An echo.

While Rob was alive, while the boys were growing up, she could pretend she didn't hear it, this empty space in sound. But now there is nothing much left to distract her.

She turns away from the window and looks at her pictures. There is the pinkish island, in the lake, with the intertwisted trees. It's the same landscape they paddled through, that distant summer. She's seen travelogues of this country, aerial photographs; it looks different from above, bigger, more hopeless: lake after lake, random blue puddles in dark green bush, the trees like bristles.

How could you ever find anything there, once it was lost? Maybe if they cut it all down, drained it all away, they might find Lucy's bones, some time, wherever they are hidden. A few bones, some buttons, the buckle from her shorts.

But a dead person is a body; a body occupies space, it exists somewhere. You can see it; you put it in a box and bury it in the ground, and then it's in a box in the ground. But Lucy is not in a box, or in the ground. Because she is nowhere definite, she could be anywhere.

And these paintings are not landscape paintings. Because there aren't any landscapes up there, not in the old, tidy European sense, with a gentle hill, a curving river, a cottage, a mountain in the background, a golden evening sky. Instead there's a tangle, a receding maze, in which you can become lost almost as soon as you step off the path. There are no backgrounds in any of these paintings, no vistas; only a great deal of foreground that goes back and back, endlessly, involving you in its twists and turns of tree and branch and rock. No matter how far back in you go, there will be more. And the trees themselves are hardly trees; they are currents of energy, charged with violent colour.

Who knows how many trees there were on the cliff just before Lucy disappeared? Who counted? Maybe there was one more, afterwards.

Lois sits in her chair and does not move. Her hand with the cup is raised halfway to her mouth. She hears something, almost hears it: a shout of recognition, or of joy.

She looks at the paintings, she looks into them. Every one of them is a picture of Lucy. You can't see her exactly, but she's there, in behind the pink stone island or the one behind that. In the picture of the cliff she is hidden by the clutch of fallen rocks towards the bottom, in the one of the river shore she is crouching beneath the overturned canoe. In the yellow autumn woods she's behind the tree that cannot be seen because of the other trees, over beside the blue sliver of pond; but if you walked into the picture and found the tree, it would be the wrong one, because the right one would be further on.

Everyone has to be somewhere, and this is where Lucy is. She is in Lois's apartment, in the holes that open inwards on the wall, not like windows but like doors. She is here. She is entirely alive.

1991

Miss July Grows Older

How much longer can I get away
with being so fucking cute?
Not much longer.
The shoes with bows, the cunning underwear
5 with slogans on the crotch—*Knock Here*,
and so forth—
will have to go, along with the cat suit.[1]
After a while you forget
what you really look like.
10 You think your mouth is the size it was.
You pretend not to care.

When I was young I went with my hair
hiding one eye, thinking myself daring;
off to the movies in my jaunty pencil
15 skirt and elastic cinch-belt,
chewed gum, left lipstick
imprints the shape of grateful, rubbery
sighs on the cigarettes of men
I hardly knew and didn't want to.
20 Men were a skill, you had to have
good hands, breathe into
their nostrils, as for horses. It was something I did well,
like playing the flute, although I don't.

In the forests of grey stems there are standing pools,
25 tarn-coloured,[2] choked with brown leaves.
Through them you can see an arm, a shoulder,
when the light is right, with the sky clouded.
The train goes past silos, through meadows,
the winter wheat on the fields like scanty fur.

30 I still get letters, although not many.
A man writes me, requesting true-life stories
about bad sex. He's doing an anthology.
He got my name off an old calendar,
the photo that's mostly bum and daisies,
35 back when my skin had the golden slick
of fresh-spread margarine.
Not rape, he says, but disappointment,

1. Close-fitting jumpsuit, typically covering the body from the neck to the feet. 2. I.e., the color of a small mountain lake.

more like a defeat of expectations.
Dear Sir, I reply, I never had any.
40 Bad sex, that is.
It was never the sex, it was the other things,
the absence of flowers, the death threats,
the eating habits at breakfast.
I notice I'm using the past tense.

45 Though the vaporous cloud of chemicals that enveloped you
like a glowing eggshell, an incense,
doesn't disappear: it just gets larger
and takes in more. You grow out
of sex like a shrunk dress
50 into your common senses, those you share
with whatever's listening. The way the sun
moves through the hours becomes important,
the smeared raindrops
on the window, buds
55 on the roadside weeds, the sheen
of spilled oil on a raw ditch
filling with muddy water.

Don't get me wrong: with the lights out
I'd still take on anyone,
60 if I had the energy to spare.
But after a while these flesh arpeggios get boring,
like Bach[3] over and over;
too much of one kind of glory.

When I was all body I was lazy.
65 I had an easy life, and was not grateful.
Now there are more of me.
Don't confuse me with my hen-leg elbows:
what you get is no longer
what you see.

1995

3. Johann Sebastian Bach (1685–1750), German composer. "Arpeggios": the notes of a musical chord played in rapid succession.

J. M. COETZEE
b. 1940

John Maxwell Coetzee was born in Cape Town, South Africa. His mother was a schoolteacher; his father, a lawyer who became a sheepherder after losing his job. When Coetzee was eight his family left the provinces, and he chronicles this and other parts of his childhood in third-person memoirs, *Boyhood: Scenes from a Provincial Life* (1997) and *Youth: Scenes from a Provincial Life II* (2002), followed up by a novelistic pseudo-biography of his adulthood, *Summertime* (2009). Coetzee was educated in Cape Town and then lived in London for a few years, working as a computer programmer, before earning his Ph.D. from the University of Texas at Austin, where he wrote a dissertation on the fiction of Samuel Beckett—a major influence, along with Kafka and Dostoyevsky, on Coetzee's fiction. He was appointed, first, assistant professor and, subsequently, Butler Professor of English at the State University of New York at Buffalo. In 1984 he returned to South Africa as professor of general literature at the University of Cape Town, and since 2002 he has lived in Australia. Coetzee is the first novelist to win the prestigious Booker Prize twice, and in 2003 he was awarded the Nobel Prize in Literature.

The central concern of Coetzee's fiction—the oppressive nature of colonialism—made its appearance with his first book, *Dusklands* (1974). This consists of two novellas, one set in the U.S. State Department during the Vietnam War, the other in southern Africa two hundred years earlier. The protagonists of these seemingly different stories—Eugene Dawn, an expert in psychological warfare, and Jacobus Coetzee, an explorer and pioneer—are engaged in similar projects, each leading to oppression and murder. Coetzee's subsequent novels include *In the Heart of the Country* (1977), a feminist anticolonial fable in the voice of a mad South African farmwoman; *Life & Times of Michael K* (1983), about a homeless man trying to survive in war-torn Africa; *Foe* (1986), a retelling of Daniel Defoe's *Robinson Crusoe* from the perspective of a female castaway; *The Master of Petersburg* (1994), a fictionalized account of Dostoyevsky's life; *Disgrace* (1999), about sexual harassment, rape, and race relations; *Elizabeth Costello: Eight Lessons* (2003), which blends essay and fiction; and *The Childhood of Jesus* (2013) and *The Schooldays of Jesus* (2016), which return to the allegorical mode of his earlier novels. His many essays and works of criticism have concerned censorship, the rights of animals, South African history, and other themes.

Coetzee is at once a passionate political novelist and an intensely literary one, both qualities emerging in his most compelling indictment of colonialism, *Waiting for the Barbarians* (1980). This novel takes its title and theme from a well-known poem by the Greek poet Constantine Cavafy (1863–1933), which ends (in Rae Dalven's translation):

> . . . night is here but the barbarians have not come.
> Some people arrived from the frontiers,
> And they said that there are no longer any barbarians.
> And now what shall become of us without any barbarians?
> Those people were a kind of solution.

In Coetzee's novel the rulers of the unnamed empire claim it is threatened by barbarians, but the barbarian threat is, at least in part, a fantasy concocted by the empire to hold itself together. The narrator is a magistrate in charge of a frontier post, poised uneasily between the harmless inhabitants of the region and the empire's ruthless officials, and unable to protect either the natives or himself from his brutal colleague, Colonel Joll. Imprisoned and stripped of his duties, the magistrate becomes increasingly skeptical of the empire's motives. When the imperial army arrives to subdue supposed insurgents, its vicious treatment of prisoners calls into question the relation of "civilization" to "barbarism" and demonstrates, in harrowing scenes of abuse and torture, the ethical dangers of one people's dominance over another. In this medley of realist particularism and allegorical parable, Coetzee leaves the landscape and time of the novel hauntingly unspecified, suggesting that colonialism's degradation and coercion, violence, and moral corruption can occur anywhere, at any time.

From Waiting for the Barbarians

First there is the sound of muskets far away, as diminutive as popguns.[1] Then from nearer by, from the ramparts themselves, come volleys of answering shots. There is a stampede of footsteps across the barracks yard. "The barbarians!" someone shouts; but I think he is wrong. Above all the clamour the great bell begins to peal.

Kneeling with an ear to the crack of the door I try to make out what is going on.

The noise from the square mounts from a hubbub to a steady roar in which no single voice can be distinguished. The whole town must be pouring out in welcome, thousands of ecstatic souls. Volleys of musket-shots keep cracking. Then the tenor of the roar changes, rises in pitch and excitement. Faintly above it come the brassy tones of bugles.

The temptation is too great. What have I to lose? I unlock the door. In glare so blinding that I must squint and shade my eyes, I cross the yard, pass through the gate, and join the rear of the crowd. The volleys and the roar of applause continue. The old woman in black beside me takes my arm to steady herself and stands on her toes. "Can you see?" she says. "Yes, I can see men on horseback," I reply; but she is not listening.

I can see a long file of horsemen who, amid flying banners, pass through the gateway and make their way to the centre of the square where they dismount. There is a cloud of dust over the whole square, but I see that they are smiling and laughing: one of them rides with his hands raised high in triumph, another waves a garland of flowers. They progress slowly, for the crowd presses around them, trying to touch them, throwing flowers, clapping their hands above their heads in joy, spinning round and round in private ecstasies. Children dive past me, scrambling through the legs of the grownups to be nearer to their heroes. Fusillade after fusillade comes from the ramparts, which are lined with cheering people.

One part of the cavalcade does not dismount. Headed by a stern-faced young corporal bearing the green and gold banner of the battalion, it passes through the press of bodies to the far end of the square and then begins a circuit of the perimeter, the crowd surging slowly in its wake. The word runs like fire from neighbour to neighbour: *"Barbarians!"*

The standard-bearer's horse is led by a man who brandishes a heavy stick to clear his way. Behind him comes another trooper trailing a rope; and at the end of the rope, tied neck to neck, comes a file of men, barbarians, stark naked, holding their hands up to their faces in an odd way as though one and all are suffering from toothache. For a moment I am puzzled by the posture, by the tiptoeing eagerness with which they follow their leader, till I catch a glint of metal and at once comprehend. A simple loop of wire runs through the flesh of each man's hands and through holes pierced in his cheeks. "It makes them meek as lambs," I remember being told by a soldier who had once seen the trick: "they think of nothing but how to keep very still." My heart grows sick. I know now that I should not have left my cell.

---

1. The magistrate, narrator of the novel, listens from the prison in which the empire has incarcerated him.

I have to turn my back smartly to avoid being seen by the two who, with their mounted escort, bring up the rear of the procession: the bareheaded young captain whose first triumph this is, and at his shoulder, leaner and darker after his months of campaigning, Colonel of Police Joll.

The circuit is made, everyone has a chance to see the twelve miserable captives, to prove to his children that the barbarians are real. Now the crowd, myself reluctantly in its wake, flows towards the great gate, where a half-moon of soldiers blocks its way until, compressed at front and rear, it cannot budge.

"What is going on?" I ask my neighbour.

"I don't know," he says, "but help me to lift him." I help him to lift the child he carries on his arm on to his shoulders. "Can you see?" he asks the child.

"Yes."

"What are they doing?"

"They are making those barbarians kneel. What are they going to do to them?"

"I don't know. Let's wait and see."

Slowly, titanically, with all my might, I turn and begin to squeeze my body out, "Excuse me . . . excuse me . . ." I say: "the heat—I'm going to be sick." For the first time I see heads turn, fingers point.

I ought to go back to my cell. As a gesture it will have no effect, it will not even be noticed. Nevertheless, for my own sake, as a gesture to myself alone, I ought to return to the cool dark and lock the door and bend the key and stop my ears to the noise of patriotic bloodlust and close my lips and never speak again. Who knows, perhaps I do my fellow-townsmen an injustice, perhaps at this very minute the shoemaker is at home tapping on his last, humming to himself to drown the shouting, perhaps there are housewives shelling peas in their kitchens, telling stories to occupy their restless children, perhaps there are farmers still going calmly about the repair of the ditches. If comrades like these exist, what a pity I do not know them! For me, at this moment, striding away from the crowd, what has become important above all is that I should neither be contaminated by the atrocity that is about to be committed nor poison myself with impotent hatred of its perpetrators. I cannot save the prisoners, therefore let me save myself. Let it at the very least be said, if it ever comes to be said, if there is ever anyone in some remote future interested to know the way we lived, that in this farthest outpost of the Empire of light there existed one man who in his heart was not a barbarian.

I pass through the barracks gate into my prison yard. At the trough in the middle of the yard I pick up an empty bucket and fill it. With the bucket held up before me, slopping water over its sides, I approach the rear of the crowd again. "Excuse me," I say, and push. People curse me, give way, the bucket tilts and splashes, I forge forward till in a minute I am suddenly clear in the frontmost rank of the crowd behind the backs of the soldiers who, holding staves between them, keep an arena clear for the exemplary spectacle.

Four of the prisoners kneel on the ground. The other eight, still roped together, squat in the shade of the wall watching, their hands to their cheeks.

The kneeling prisoners bend side by side over a long heavy pole. A cord runs from the loop of wire through the first man's mouth, under the pole, up to the second man's loop, back under the pole, up to the third loop, under the pole, through the fourth loop. As I watch a soldier slowly pulls the cord tighter and the prisoners bend further till finally they are kneeling with their faces touching the pole. One of them writhes his shoulders in pain and moans. The others are silent, their thoughts wholly concentrated on moving smoothly with the cord, not giving the wire a chance to tear their flesh.

Directing the soldier with little gestures of the hand is Colonel Joll. Though I am only one in a crowd of thousands, though his eyes are shaded as ever, I stare at him so hard with a face so luminous with query that I know at once he sees me.

Behind me I distinctly hear the word *magistrate*. Do I imagine it or are my neighbours inching away from me?

The Colonel steps forward. Stooping over each prisoner in turn he rubs a handful of dust into his naked back and writes a word with a stick of charcoal. I read the words upside down: ENEMY . . . ENEMY . . . ENEMY . . . ENEMY. He steps back and folds his hands. At a distance of no more than twenty paces he and I contemplate each other.

Then the beating begins. The soldiers use the stout green cane staves, bringing them down with the heavy slapping sounds of washing-paddles, raising red welts on the prisoners' backs and buttocks. With slow care the prisoners extend their legs until they lie flat on their bellies, all except the one who had been moaning and who now gasps with each blow.

The black charcoal and ochre dust begin to run with sweat and blood. The game, I see, is to beat them till their backs are washed clean.

I watch the face of a little girl who stands in the front rank of the crowd gripping her mother's clothes. Her eyes are round, her thumb is in her mouth: silent, terrified, curious, she drinks in the sight of these big naked men being beaten. On every face around me, even those that are smiling, I see the same expression: not hatred, not bloodlust, but a curiosity so intense that their bodies are drained by it and only their eyes live, organs of a new and ravening appetite.

The soldiers doing the beating grow tired. One stands with his hands on his hips panting, smiling, gesturing to the crowd. There is a word from the Colonel: all four of them cease their labour and come forward offering their canes to the spectators.

A girl, giggling and hiding her face, is pushed forward by her friends. "Go on, don't be afraid!" they urge her. A soldier puts a cane in her hand and leads her to the place. She stands confused, embarrassed, one hand still over her face. Shouts, jokes, obscene advice are hurled at her. She lifts the cane, brings it down smartly on the prisoner's buttocks, drops it, and scuttles to safety to a roar of applause.

There is a scramble for the canes, the soldiers can barely keep order, I lose sight of the prisoners on the ground as people press forward to take a turn or simply watch the beating from nearer. I stand forgotten with my bucket between my feet.

Then the flogging is over, the soldiers reassert themselves, the crowd scrambles back, the arena is reconstituted, though narrower than before.

Over his head, exhibiting it to the crowd, Colonel Joll holds a hammer, an ordinary four-pound hammer used for knocking in tent-pegs. Again his gaze meets mine. The babble subsides.

"No!" I hear the first word from my throat, rusty, not loud enough. Then again: "No!" This time the word rings like a bell from my chest. The soldier who blocks my way stumbles aside. I am in the arena holding up my hands to still the crowd: *"No! No! No!"*

When I turn to Colonel Joll he is standing not five paces from me, his arms folded. I point a finger at him. *"You!"* I shout. Let it all be said. Let him be the one on whom the anger breaks. "You are depraving these people!"

He does not flinch, he does not reply.

"You!" My arm points at him like a gun. My voice fills the square. There is utter silence; or perhaps I am too intoxicated to hear.

Something crashes into me from behind. I sprawl in the dust, gasp, feel the sear of old pain in my back. A stick thuds down on me. Reaching out to ward it off, I take a withering blow on my hand.

It becomes important to stand up, however difficult the pain makes it. I come to my feet and see who it is that is hitting me. It is the stocky man with the sergeant's stripes who helped with the beatings. Crouched at the knees, his nostrils flaring, he stands with his stick raised for the next blow. "Wait!" I gasp, holding out my limp hand. "I think you have broken it!" He strikes, and I take the blow on the forearm. I hide my arm, lower my head, and try to grope towards him and grapple. Blows fall on my head and shoulders. Never mind: all I want is a few moments to finish what I am saying now that I have begun. I grip his tunic and hug him to me. Though he wrestles, he cannot use his stick; over his shoulder I shout again.

"Not with that!" I shout. The hammer lies cradled in the Colonel's folded arms. "You would not use a hammer on a beast, not on a beast!" In a terrible surge of rage I turn on the sergeant and hurl him from me. Godlike strength is mine. In a minute it will pass: let me use it well while it lasts! "Look!" I shout. I point to the four prisoners who lie docilely on the earth, their lips to the pole, their hands clasped to their faces like monkeys' paws, oblivious of the hammer, ignorant of what is going on behind them, relieved that the offending mark has been beaten from their backs, hoping that the punishment is at an end. I raise my broken hand to the sky. "Look!" I shout. "We are the great miracle of creation! But from some blows this miraculous body cannot repair itself! How—!" Words fail me. "Look at these men!" I recommence. *"Men!"* Those in the crowd who can crane to look at the prisoners, even at the flies that begin to settle on their bleeding welts.

I hear the blow coming and turn to meet it. It catches me full across the face. "I am blind!" I think, staggering back into the blackness that instantly falls. I swallow blood; something blooms across my face, starting as a rosy warmth, turning to fiery agony. I hide my face in my hands and stamp around in a circle trying not to shout, trying not to fall.

What I wanted to say next I cannot remember. A miracle of creation—I pursue the thought but it eludes me like a wisp of smoke. It occurs to me that we crush insects beneath our feet, miracles of creation too, beetles, worms, cockroaches, ants, in their various ways.

I take my fingers from my eyes and a grey world re-emerges swimming in tears. I am so profoundly grateful that I cease to feel pain. As I am hustled, a man at each elbow, back through the murmuring crowd to my cell, I even find myself smiling.

That smile, that flush of joy, leave behind a disturbing residue. I know that they commit an error in treating me so summarily. For I am no orator. What would I have said if they had let me go on? That it is worse to beat a man's feet to pulp than to kill him in combat? That it brings shame on everyone when a girl is permitted to flog a man? That spectacles of cruelty corrupt the hearts of the innocent? The words they stopped me from uttering may have been very paltry indeed, hardly words to rouse the rabble. What, after all, do I stand for besides an archaic code of gentlemanly behaviour towards captured foes, and what do I stand against except the new science of degradation that kills people on their knees, confused and disgraced in their own eyes? Would I have dared to face the crowd to demand justice for these ridiculous barbarian prisoners with their backsides in the air? *Justice:* once that word is uttered, where will it all end? Easier to shout *No!* Easier to be beaten and made a martyr. Easier to lay my head on a block than to defend the cause of justice for the barbarians: for where can that argument lead but to laying down our arms and opening the gates of the town to the people whose land we have raped? The old magistrate, defender of the rule of law, enemy in his own way of the State, assaulted and imprisoned, impregnably virtuous, is not without his own twinges of doubt.

My nose is broken, I know, and perhaps also the cheekbone where the flesh was laid open by the blow of the stick. My left eye is swelling shut.

As the numbness wears off the pain begins to come in spasms a minute or two apart so intense that I can no longer lie still. At the height of the spasm I trot around the room holding my face, whining like a dog; in the blessed valleys between the peaks I breathe deeply, trying to keep control of myself, trying not to make too disgraceful an outcry. I seem to hear surges and lulls in the noise from the mob on the square but cannot be sure that the roar is not simply in my eardrums.

They bring me my evening meal as usual but I cannot eat. I cannot keep still, I have to walk back and forth or rock on my haunches to keep myself from screaming, tearing my clothes, clawing my flesh, doing whatever people do when the limit of their endurance is reached. I weep, and feel the tears stinging the open flesh. I hum the old song about the rider and the juniper bush over and over again, clinging to the remembered words even after they have ceased to make any sense. One, two, three, four . . . I count. It will be a famous victory, I tell myself, if you can last the night.

In the early hours of the morning, when I am so giddy with exhaustion that I reel on my feet, I finally give way and sob from the heart like a child: I sit in a corner against the wall and weep, the tears running from my eyes without stop. I weep and weep while the throbbing comes and goes according to its own cycles. In this position sleep bursts upon me like a thunderbolt. I am amazed to come to myself in the thin grey light of day, slumped in a corner, with not the faintest sense that time has passed. Though the throbbing is still there I find I can endure it if I remain still. Indeed, it has lost its strangeness. Soon, perhaps, it will be as much part of me as breathing.

So I lie quietly against the wall, folding my sore hand under my armpit for comfort, and fall into a second sleep, into a confusion of images among which I search out one in particular, brushing aside the others that fly at me like leaves. It is of the girl. She is kneeling with her back to me before the snowcastle or sandcastle she has built. She wears a dark blue robe. As I approach I see that she is digging away in the bowels of the castle.

She becomes aware of me and turns. I am mistaken, it is not a castle she has built but a clay oven. Smoke curls up from the vent at the back. She holds out her hands to me offering me something, a shapeless lump which I peer at unwillingly through a mist. Though I shake my head my vision will not clear.

She is wearing a round cap embroidered in gold. Her hair is braided in a heavy plait which lies over her shoulder: there is gold thread worked into the braid. "Why are you dressed in your best?" I want to say: "I have never seen you looking so lovely." She smiles at me: what beautiful teeth she has, what clear jet-black eyes! Also now I can see that what she is holding out to me is a loaf of bread, still hot, with a coarse steaming broken crust. A surge of gratitude sweeps through me. "Where did a child like you learn to bake so well in the desert?" I want to say. I open my arms to embrace her, and come to myself with tears stinging the wound on my cheek. Though I scrabble back at once into the burrow of sleep I cannot re-enter the dream or taste the bread that has made my saliva run.

•   •

Colonel Joll sits behind the desk in my office. There are no books or files; the room is starkly empty save for a vase of fresh flowers.

The handsome warrant officer whose name I do not know lifts the cedar-wood chest on to the desk and steps back.

Looking down to refer to his papers, the Colonel speaks. "Among the items found in your apartment was this wooden chest. I would like you to consider it. Its contents are unusual. It contains approximately three hundred slips of white poplar-wood, each about eight inches by two inches, many of them wound about with lengths of string.[2] The wood is dry and brittle. Some of the string is new, some so old that it has perished.

"If one loosens the string one finds that the slip splits open revealing two flat inner surfaces. These surfaces are written on in an unfamiliar script.

"I think you will concur with this description."

I stare into the black lenses. He goes on.

"A reasonable inference is that the wooden slips contain messages passed between yourself and other parties, we do not know when. It remains for you to explain what the messages say and who the other parties were."

He takes a slip from the chest and flicks it across the polished surface of the desk towards me.

I look at the lines of characters written by a stranger long since dead. I do not even know whether to read from right to left or from left to right. In the long evenings I spent poring over my collection I isolated over four hundred different characters in the script, perhaps as many as four hundred and fifty. I have no idea what they stand for. Does each stand for a single thing, a circle for the sun, a triangle for a woman, a wave for a lake; or does a circle merely stand for "circle", a triangle for "triangle", a wave for "wave"? Does each sign represent a different state of the tongue, the lips, the throat, the lungs, as they combine in the uttering of some multifarious unimaginable extinct barbarian language? Or are my four hundred characters nothing but scribal embellishments of an underlying repertory of twenty or thirty whose primitive forms I am too stupid to see?

"He sends greetings to his daughter," I say. I hear with surprise the thick nasal voice that is now mine. My finger runs along the line of characters from right to left. "Whom he says he has not seen for a long time. He hopes she is happy and thriving. He hopes the lambing season has been good. He has a gift for her, he says, which he will keep till he sees her again. He

---

2. Over the years the magistrate has conducted archaeological digs outside the city, unearthing these poplar slips and other artifacts.

sends his love. It is not easy to read his signature. It could be simply 'Your father' or it could be something else, a name."

I reach over into the chest and pick out a second slip. The warrant officer, who sits behind Joll with a little notebook open on his knee, stares hard at me, his pencil poised above the paper.

"This one reads as follows," I say: "'I am sorry I must send bad news. The soldiers came and took your brother away. I have been to the fort every day to plead for his return. I sit in the dust with my head bare. Yesterday for the first time they sent a man to speak to me. He says your brother is no longer here. He says he has been sent away. "Where?" I asked, but he would not say. Do not tell your mother, but join me in praying for his safety.'

"And now let us see what this next one says." The pencil is still poised, he has not written anything, he has not stirred. "'We went to fetch your brother yesterday. They showed us into a room where he lay on a table sewn up in a sheet.'" Slowly Joll leans back in his chair. The warrant officer closes his notebook and half-rises; but with a gesture Joll restrains him. "'They wanted me to take him away like that, but I insisted on looking first. "What if it is the wrong body you are giving me?" I said—"You have so many bodies here, bodies of brave young men." So I opened the sheet and saw that it was indeed he. Through each eyelid, I saw that there was a stitch, "Why have you done that?" I said. "It is our custom," he said. I tore the sheet wide open and saw bruises all over his body, and saw that his feet were swollen and broken. "What happened to him?" I said. "I do not know," said the man, "it is not on the paper; if you have questions you must go to the sergeant, but he is very busy." We have had to bury your brother here, outside their fort, because he was beginning to stink. Please tell your mother and try console her.'

"Now let us see what the next one says. See, there is only a single character. It is the barbarian character *war*, but it has other senses too. It can stand for *vengeance*, and, if you turn it upside down like this, it can be made to read *justice*. There is no knowing which sense is intended. That is part of barbarian cunning.

"It is the same with the rest of these slips." I plunge my good hand into the chest and stir. "They form an allegory. They can be read in many orders. Further, each single slip can be read in many ways. Together they can be read as a domestic journal, or they can be read as a plan of war, or they can be turned on their sides and read as a history of the last years of the Empire—the old Empire, I mean. There is no agreement among scholars about how to interpret these relics of the ancient barbarians. Allegorical sets like this one can be found buried all over the desert. I found this one not three miles from here in the ruins of a public building. Graveyards are another good place to look in, though it is not always easy to tell where barbarian burial sites lie. It is recommended that you simply dig at random: perhaps at the very spot where you stand you will come upon scraps, shards, reminders of the dead. Also the air: the air is full of sighs and cries. These are never lost: if you listen carefully, with a sympathetic ear, you can hear them echoing forever within the second sphere. The night is best: sometimes when you have difficulty in falling asleep it is because your ears have been reached by the cries of the dead which, like their writings, are open to many interpretations.

"Thank you. I have finished translating."

I have not failed to keep an eye on Joll through all this. He has not stirred again, save to lay a hand on his subordinate's sleeve at the moment when I referred to the Empire and he rose, ready to strike me.

If he comes near me I will hit him with all the strength in my body. I will not disappear into the earth without leaving my mark on them.

The Colonel speaks. "You have no idea how tiresome your behaviour is. You are the one and only official we have had to work with on the frontier who has not given us his fullest co-operation. Candidly, I must tell you I am not interested in these sticks." He waves a hand at the slips scattered on the desk. "They are very likely gambling-sticks. I know that other tribes on the border gamble with sticks.

"I ask you to consider soberly: what kind of future do you have here? You cannot be allowed to remain in your post. You have utterly disgraced yourself. Even if you are not eventually prosecuted—"

"I am waiting for you to prosecute me!" I shout. "When are you going to do it? When are you going to bring me to trial? When am I going to have a chance to defend myself?" I am in a fury. None of the speechlessness I felt in front of the crowd afflicts me. If I were to confront these men now, in public, in a fair trial, I would find the words to shame them. It is a matter of health and strength: I feel my hot words swell in my breast. But they will never bring a man to trial while he is healthy and strong enough to confound them. They will shut me away in the dark till I am a muttering idiot, a ghost of myself; then they will haul me before a closed court and in five minutes dispose of the legalities they find so tiresome.

"For the duration of the emergency, as you know," says the Colonel, "the administration of justice is out of the hands of civilians and in the hands of the Bureau." He sighs. "Magistrate, you seem to believe that we do not dare to bring you to trial because we fear you are too popular a figure in this town. I do not think you are aware of how much you forfeited by neglecting your duties, shunning your friends, keeping company with low people. There is no one I have spoken to who has not at some time felt insulted by your behaviour."

"My private life is none of their business!"

"Nevertheless, I may tell you that our decision to relieve you of your duties has been welcomed in most quarters. Personally I have nothing against you. When I arrived back a few days ago, I had decided that all I wanted from you was a clear answer to a simple question, after which you could have returned to your concubines a free man."

It strikes me suddenly that the insult may not be gratuitous, that perhaps for different reasons these two men might welcome it if I lost my temper. Burning with outrage, tense in every muscle, I guard my silence.

"However, you seem to have a new ambition," he goes on. "You seem to want to make a name for yourself as the One Just Man, the man who is prepared to sacrifice his freedom to his principles.

"But let me ask you: do you believe that that is how your fellow-citizens see you after the ridiculous spectacle you created on the square the other day? Believe me, to people in this town you are not the One Just Man, you are simply a clown, a madman. You are dirty, you stink, they can smell you a mile away. You look like an old beggar-man, a refuse-scavenger. They do not want you back in any capacity. You have no future here.

"You want to go down in history as a martyr, I suspect. But who is going to put you in the history books? These border troubles are of no significance. In a while they will pass and the frontier will go to sleep for another twenty years. People are not interested in the history of the back of beyond."

"There were no border troubles before you came," I say.

"That is nonsense," he says. "You are simply ignorant of the facts. You are living in a world of the past. You think we are dealing with small groups of peaceful nomads. In fact we are dealing with a well organized enemy. If you had travelled with the expeditionary force you would have seen that for yourself."

"Those pitiable prisoners you brought in—are *they* the enemy I must fear? Is that what you say? *You* are the enemy, Colonel!" I can restrain myself no longer. I pound the desk with my fist. "*You* are the enemy, *you* have made the war, and *you* have given them all the martyrs they need—starting not now but a year ago when you committed your first filthy barbarities here! History will bear me out!"

"Nonsense. There will be no history, the affair is too trivial." He seems impassive, but I am sure I have shaken him.

"You are an obscene torturer! You deserve to hang!"

"Thus speaks the judge, the One Just Man," he murmurs.

We stare into each other's eyes.

"Now," he says, squaring the papers before him: "I would like a statement on everything that passed between you and the barbarians on your recent and unauthorized visit to them."

"I refuse."

"Very well. Our interview is over." He turns to his subordinate. "He is your responsibility." He stands up, walks out. I face the warrant officer.

•   •

The wound on my cheek, never washed or dressed, is swollen and inflamed. A crust like a fat caterpillar has formed on it. My left eye is a mere slit, my nose a shapeless throbbing lump. I must breathe through my mouth.

I lie in the reek of old vomit obsessed with the thought of water. I have had nothing to drink for two days.

In my suffering there is nothing ennobling. Little of what I call suffering is even pain. What I am made to undergo is subjection to the most rudimentary needs of my body: to drink, to relieve itself, to find the posture in which it is least sore. When Warrant Officer Mandel and his man first brought me back here and lit the lamp and closed the door, I wondered how much pain a plump comfortable old man would be able to endure in the name of his eccentric notions of how the Empire should conduct itself. But my torturers were not interested in degrees of pain. They were interested only in demonstrating to me what it meant to live in a body, as a body, a body which can entertain notions of justice only as long as it is whole and well, which very soon forgets them when its head is gripped and a pipe is pushed down its gullet and pints of salt water are poured into it till it coughs and retches and flails and voids itself. They did not come to force the story out of me of what I had said to the barbarians and what the barbarians had said to me. So I had no chance to throw the high-sounding words I had ready in their faces. They came to my cell to show me the meaning of humanity, and in the space of an hour they showed me a great deal.

•   •

Nor is it a question of who endures longest. I used to think to myself, "They are sitting in another room discussing me. They are saying to each other, 'How much longer before he grovels? In an hour we will go back and see.'"

But it is not like that. They have no elaborated system of pain and deprivation to which they subject me. For two days I go without food and water. On the third day I am fed. "I am sorry," says the man who brings my food, "we forgot." It is not malice that makes them forget. My torturers have their own lives to lead. I am not the centre of their universe. Mandel's underling probably spends his days counting bags in the commissary or patrolling the earthworks, grumbling to himself about the heat. Mandel himself, I am sure, spends more time polishing his straps and buckles than he spends on me. When the mood takes him he comes and gives me a lesson in humanity. How long can I withstand the randomness of their attacks? And what will happen if I succumb, weep, grovel, while yet the attacks go on?

• •

They call me into the yard. I stand before them hiding my nakedness, nursing my sore hand, a tired old bear made tame by too much baiting. "Run," Mandel says. I run around the yard under the blazing sun. When I slacken he slaps me on the buttocks with his cane and I trot faster. The soldiers leave their siesta and watch from the shade, the scullery maids hang over the kitchen door, children stare through the bars of the gate. "I cannot!" I gasp. "My heart!" I stop, hang my head, clutch my chest. Everyone waits patiently while I recover myself. Then the cane prods me and I shamble on, moving no faster than a man walks.

Or else I do tricks for them. They stretch a rope at knee-height and I jump back and forth over it. They call the cook's little grandson over and give him one end to hold. "Keep it steady," they say, "we don't want him to trip." The child grips his end of the rope with both hands, concentrating on this important task, waiting for me to jump. I baulk. The point of the cane finds its way between my buttocks and prods. "Jump," Mandel murmurs. I run, make a little skip, blunder into the rope, and stand there. I smell of shit. I am not permitted to wash. The flies follow me everywhere, circling around the appetizing sore on my cheek, alighting if I stand still for a moment. The looping movement of my hand before my face to chase them away has become as automatic as the flick of a cow's tail. "Tell him he must do better next time," Mandel says to the boy. The boy smiles and looks away. I sit down in the dust to wait for the next trick. "Do you know how to skip?" he says to the boy. "Give the rope to the man and ask him to show you how to skip." I skip.

It cost me agonies of shame the first time I had to come out of my den and stand naked before these idlers or jerk my body about for their amusement. Now I am past shame. My mind is turned wholly to the menace of the moment when my knees turn to water or my heart grips me like a crab and I have to stand still; and each time I discover with surprise that after a little rest, after the application of a little pain, I can be made to move, to jump or skip or crawl or run a little further. Is there a point at which I will lie down and say, "Kill me—I would rather die than go on"? Sometimes I think I am approaching that point, but I am always mistaken.

There is no consoling grandeur in any of this. When I wake up groaning in the night it is because I am reliving in dreams the pettiest degradations. There is no way of dying allowed me, it seems, except like a dog in a corner.

• •

Then one day they throw open the door and I step out to face not two men but a squad standing to attention. "Here," says Mandel, and hands me a woman's calico smock. "Put it on."

"Why?"

"Very well, if you want to go naked, go naked."

I slip the smock over my head. It reaches halfway down my thighs. I catch a glimpse of the two youngest maids ducking back into the kitchen, dissolving in giggles.

My wrists are caught behind my back and tied. "The time has come, Magistrate," Mandel whispers in my ear. "Do your best to behave like a man." I am sure I can smell liquor on his breath.

They march me out of the yard. Under the mulberry trees, where the earth is purple with the juice of fallen berries, there is a knot of people waiting. Children are scrambling about on the branches. As I approach everyone falls silent.

A soldier tosses up the end of a new white hemp rope; one of the children in the tree catches it, loops it over a branch, and drops it back.

I know this is only a trick, a new way of passing the afternoon for men bored with the old torments. Nevertheless my bowels turn to water. "Where is the Colonel?" I whisper. No one pays any heed.

"Do you want to say something?" says Mandel. "Say whatever you wish. We give you this opportunity."

I look into his clear blue eyes, as clear as if there were crystal lenses slipped over his eyeballs. He looks back at me. I have no idea what he sees. Thinking of him, I have said the words *torture . . . torturer* to myself, but they are strange words, and the more I repeat them the more strange they grow, till they lie like stones on my tongue. Perhaps this man, and the man he brings along to help him with his work, and their Colonel, are torturers, perhaps that is their designation on three cards in a pay-office somewhere in the capital, though it is more likely that the cards call them security officers. But when I look at him I see simply the clear blue eyes, the rather rigid good looks, the teeth slightly too long where the gums are receding. He deals with my soul: every day he folds the flesh aside and exposes my soul to the light; he has probably seen many souls in the course of his working life; but the care of souls seems to have left no more mark on him than the care of hearts leaves on the surgeon.

"I am trying very hard to understand your feelings towards me," I say. I cannot help mumbling, my voice is unsteady, I am afraid and the sweat is dripping from me. "Much more than an opportunity to address these people, to whom I have nothing to say, would I appreciate a few words from you. So that I can come to understand why you devote yourself to this work. And can hear what you feel towards me, whom you have hurt a great deal and now seem to be proposing to kill."

Amazed I stare at this elaborate utterance as it winds its way out of me. Am I mad enough to intend a provocation?

"Do you see this hand?" he says. He holds his hand an inch from my face. "When I was younger"—he flexes the fingers—"I used to be able to poke this finger"—he holds up the index finger—"through a pumpkin-shell." He puts the tip of his finger against my forehead and presses. I take a step backwards.

They even have a cap ready for me, a salt-bag which they slip over my head and tie around my throat with a string. Through the mesh I watch them bring up the ladder and prop it against the branch. I am guided to it, my foot is set on the lowest rung, the noose is settled under my ear. "Now climb," says Mandel.

I turn my head and see two dim figures holding the end of the rope. "I can't climb with my hands tied," I say. My heart is hammering. "Climb," he says, steadying me by the arm. The rope tightens. "Keep it tight," he orders.

I climb, he climbs behind me, guiding me. I count ten rungs. Leaves brush against me. I stop. He grips my arm tighter. "Do you think we are playing?" he says. He talks through clenched teeth in a fury I do not understand. "Do you think I don't mean what I say?"

My eyes sting with sweat inside the bag. "No," I say, "I do not think you are playing." As long as the rope remains taut I know they are playing. If the rope goes slack, and I slip, I will die.

"Then what do you want to say to me?"

"I want to say that nothing passed between myself and the barbarians concerning military matters. It was a private affair. I went to return the girl to her family. For no other purpose."

"Is that all you want to say to me?"

"I want to say that no one deserves to die." In my absurd frock and bag, with the nausea of cowardice in my mouth, I say: "I want to live. As every man wants to live. To live and live and live. No matter what."

"That isn't enough." He lets my arm go. I teeter on my tenth rung, the rope saving my balance. "Do you see?" he says. He retreats down the ladder, leaving me alone.

Not sweat but tears.

There is a rustling in the leaves near me. A child's voice: "Can you see, uncle?"

"No."

"Hey, monkeys, come down!" calls someone from below. Through the taut rope I can feel the vibration of their movements in the branches.

So I stand for a long while, balancing carefully on the rung, feeling the comfort of the wood in the curve of my sole, trying not to waver, keeping the tension of the rope as constant as possible.

How long will a crowd of idlers be content to watch a man stand on a ladder? I would stand here till the flesh dropped from my bones, through storm and hail and flood, to live.

But now the rope tightens, I can even hear it rasp as it passes over the bark, till I must stretch to keep it from throttling me.

This is not a contest of patience, then: if the crowd is not satisfied the rules are changed. But of what use is it to blame the crowd? A scapegoat is named, a festival is declared, the laws are suspended: who would not flock to see the entertainment? What is it I object to in these spectacles of abasement and suffering and death that our new regime puts on but their lack of decorum? What will my own administration be remembered for besides moving the shambles from the marketplace to the outskirts of the town twenty years ago in the interests of decency? I try to call out something, a word of blind fear, a shriek, but the rope is now so tight that I am strangled, speechless. The blood hammers in my ears. I feel my toes lose their hold. I am swinging gently in the air, bumping against the ladder, flailing with my feet. The drumbeat in my ears becomes slower and louder till it is all I can hear.

I am standing in front of the old man, screwing up my eyes against the wind, waiting for him to speak. The ancient gun still rests between his horse's ears, but it is not aimed at me. I am aware of the vastness of the sky all around us, and of the desert.

I watch his lips. At any moment now he will speak: I must listen carefully to capture every syllable, so that later, repeating them to myself, poring over them, I can discover the answer to a question which for the moment has flown like a bird from my recollection.

I can see every hair of the horse's mane, every wrinkle of the old man's face, every rock and furrow of the hillside.

The girl, with her black hair braided and hanging over her shoulder in barbarian fashion, sits her horse behind him. Her head is bowed, she too is waiting for him to speak.

I sigh. "What a pity," I think. "It is too late now."

I am swinging loose. The breeze lifts my smock and plays with my naked body. I am relaxed, floating. In a woman's clothes.

What must be my feet touch the ground, though they are numb to all feeling. I stretch myself out carefully, at full length, light as a leaf. Whatever it is that has held my head so tightly slackens its grip. From inside me comes a ponderous grating. I breathe. All is well.

Then the hood comes off, the sun dazzles my eyes, I am hauled to my feet, everything swims before me, I go blank.

The word *flying* whispers itself somewhere at the edge of my consciousness. Yes, it is true, I have been flying.

I am looking into the blue eyes of Mandel. His lips move but I hear no words. I shake my head, and having once started find that I cannot stop.

"I was saying," he says, "*now we will show you another form of flying.*"

"He can't hear you," someone says. "He can hear," says Mandel. He slips the noose from my neck and knots it around the cord that binds my wrists. "Pull him up."

If I can hold my arms stiff, if I am acrobat enough to swing a foot up and hook it around the rope, I will be able to hang upside down and not be hurt: that is my last thought before they begin to hoist me. But I am as weak as a baby, my arms come up behind my back, and as my feet leave the ground I feel a terrible tearing in my shoulders as though whole sheets of muscle are giving way. From my throat comes the first mournful dry bellow, like the pouring of gravel. Two little boys drop out of the tree and, hand in hand, not looking back, trot off. I bellow again and again, there is nothing I can do to stop it, the noise comes out of a body that knows itself damaged perhaps beyond repair and roars its fright. Even if all the children of the town should hear me I cannot stop myself: let us only pray that they do not imitate their elders' games, or tomorrow there will be a plague of little bodies dangling from the trees. Someone gives me a push and I begin to float back and forth in an arc a foot above the ground like a great old moth with its wings pinched together, roaring, shouting. "He is calling his barbarian friends," someone observes. "That is barbarian language you hear." There is laughter.

1980

EAVAN BOLAND
b. 1944

avan Boland was born in Dublin, the youngest daughter of an Irish diplomat and a painter, but as recalled in "Fond Memory" and other poems, she was displaced as a six-year-old from Ireland to London, where her father was Irish ambassador, and then to New York, where he was his country's representative at the United Nations, before finally returning to Ireland in adolescence. She attended convent schools in these various locations. In Ireland she studied—and then taught—English at Trinity College, Dublin, and since then she has taught at University College, the University of Iowa, and Stanford University.

Boland said in a 1994 lecture, "I am an Irish poet. A woman poet. In the first category I enter the tradition of the English language at an angle. In the second, I enter my own tradition at an even more steep angle." The great puzzle of Boland's career has been how to embrace Irish identity while rejecting certain male-centered assumptions that have long dominated Irish literary culture. For Boland as a young woman writer, the frozen, mythical images of the Irish nation as an idealized woman—Mother Ireland, Dark Rosaleen, Cathleen Ni Houlihan—were inhibiting and insufficient. To bring into Irish verse a national narrative, a "herstory" that interweaves private life and public life, Boland seized on an alternative tradition to that of Irish male poets—namely, the example of American women poets such as Sylvia Plath and Adrienne Rich. Her eye for symbolic detail, her ear for musical structure, her use of form to mirror content have served her well in her effort to recover and vivify Irish women's historical experiences, including domestic labor, motherhood, famine, prostitution, and emigration.

Fond Memory

It was a school where all the children wore darned worsted;°   *woolen fabric*
where they cried—or almost all—when the Reverend Mother
announced at lunch-time that the King[1] had died

peacefully in his sleep. I dressed in wool as well,
5   ate rationed food, played English games and learned
how wise the Magna Carta was, how hard the Hanoverians[2]

had tried, the measure and complexity of verse,
the hum and score of the whole orchestra.
At three-o-clock I caught two buses home

10   where sometimes in the late afternoon
at a piano pushed into a corner of the playroom
my father would sit down and play the slow

---

1. King George VI of the United Kingdom died in 1952. Boland's father was a diplomat, and she spent much of her childhood in London.

2. Family of English monarchs who reigned from 1714 to 1901. "Magna Carta": charter of English liberties granted by King John in 1215.

lilts of Tom Moore[3] while I stood there trying
not to weep at the cigarette smoke stinging up
from between his fingers and—as much as I could think—

I thought this is my country, was, will be again,
this upward-straining song made to be
our safe inventory of pain. And I was wrong.

1987

The Dolls Museum in Dublin

The wounds are terrible. The paint is old.
The cracks along the lips and on the cheeks
cannot be fixed. The cotton lawn[1] is soiled.
The arms are ivory dissolved to wax.

5   Recall the Quadrille.[2] Hum the waltz.
Promenade on the yacht-club terraces.
Put back the lamps in their copper holders,
the carriage wheels on the cobbled quays.

And recreate Easter in Dublin.[3]
10   Booted officers. Their mistresses.
Sunlight criss-crossing College Green.
Steam hissing from the flanks of horses.

Here they are. Cradled and cleaned,
held close in the arms of their owners.
15   Their cold hands clasped by warm hands,
their faces memorized like perfect manners.

The altars are mannerly with linen.
The lilies are whiter than surplices.[4]
The candles are burning and warning:
20   Rejoice, they whisper. After sacrifice.

Horse-chestnuts hold up their candles.
The Green is vivid with parasols.
Sunlight is pastel and windless.
The bar of the Shelbourne[5] is full.

25   Laughter and gossip on the terraces.
Rumour and alarm at the barracks.
The Empire is summoning its officers.
The carriages are turning: they are turning back.

3. Irish poet and singer (1779–1852).
1. Usually fine linen, but also, as here, fine cotton.
2. A square dance and the music for it.
3. What became known as the "Easter Rising" began on Easter Monday, 1916, when over sixteen hundred Irish nationalists seized key points

in Dublin and an Irish Republic was proclaimed from the General Post Office. See W. B. Yeats's "Easter, 1916" (p. 221).
4. White linen vestments worn over cassocks.
5. Large Dublin hotel.

Past children walking with governesses,
30 Looking down, cossetting their dolls,
then looking up as the carriage passes,
the shadow chilling them. Twilight falls.

It is twilight in the dolls' museum. Shadows
remain on the parchment-coloured waists,
35 are bruises on the stitched cotton clothes,
are hidden in the dimples on the wrists.

The eyes are wide. They cannot address
the helplessness which has lingered in
the airless peace of each glass case:
40 to have survived. To have been stronger than

a moment. To be the hostages ignorance
takes from time and ornament from destiny. Both.
To be the present of the past. To infer the difference
with a terrible stare. But not feel it. And not know it.

1994

The Lost Land

I have two daughters.

They are all I ever wanted from the earth.

Or almost all.

I also wanted one piece of ground:

5 One city trapped by hills. One urban river.
An island in its element.

So I could say *mine. My own.*
And mean it.

Now they are grown up and far away

10 and memory itself
has become an emigrant,
wandering in a place
where love dissembles itself as landscape:

Where the hills
15 are the colours of a child's eyes,
where my children are distances, horizons:

At night,
on the edge of sleep,

I can see the shore of Dublin Bay.
20 Its rocky sweep and its granite pier.

Is this, I say
how they must have seen it,
backing out on the mailboat at twilight,

shadows falling
25 on everything they had to leave?
And would love forever?
And then

I imagine myself
at the landward rail of that boat
30 searching for the last sight of a hand.

I see myself
on the underworld side of that water,
the darkness coming in fast, saying
all the names I know for a lost land:

35 *Ireland. Absence. Daughter.*

1998

SALMAN RUSHDIE
b. 1947

The most influential novelist to have come from South Asia in the last seventy years is Ahmed Salman Rushdie, whose dynamic narratives—stories of magic, suffering, and the vitality of human beings in the grip of history—have helped generate the literary renaissance flowering in India today. "I come from Bombay," Rushdie has said, "and from a Muslim family, too. 'My' India has always been based on ideas of multiplicity, pluralism, hybridity: ideas to which the ideologies of the communalists are diametrically opposed. To my mind, the defining image of India is the crowd, and a crowd is by its very nature superabundant, heterogeneous, many things at once." Rushdie was educated at Cathedral School, Bombay (now Mumbai), and from the age of thirteen, at Rugby School, Warwickshire, and King's College, Cambridge. After living briefly in Pakistan, where his prosperous family had moved, Rushdie eventually settled in England, working as an actor and as a freelance advertising copywriter (1970–80).

His first novel, *Grimus* (1979), passed unnoticed, but his second, *Midnight's Children* (1981), announced the arrival of a major writer. Taking its title from those who were born—two months later than its author—around midnight on August 15, 1947, when the independent state of India was born, *Midnight's Children* is a work of prodigious prodigality, a cornucopia as richly fertile in character, incident, and language as the subcontinent that is its setting. The book's triumphant progress across the world culminated in its being judged "the Booker of Bookers," the best novel to have won Britain's premier fiction prize in its first twenty-five years. Rushdie has said that "we're all radio-active with history," and the books that have followed *Midnight's Children* have again shown a form of "magical realism"—learned from Latin American writers such as Jorge Luis Borges and Gabriel García Márquez—deployed in the service of a powerful political-historical imagination.

In 1988 Rushdie found himself at the perilous center of a real, rather than a magical-realist, political-historical storm. His novel *The Satanic Verses* provoked riots in India, Pakistan, and South Africa, and was judged by senior religious figures in Iran to have blasphemed the Prophet Muhammad (called by the offensive name "Mahound" in the novel), founder of the Muslim faith. A fatwa, or legal decree, calling for his death was pronounced. He was obliged to go into hiding, and for almost a decade lived under round-the-clock protection from British Secret Service agents, while governments argued for and against the lifting of the fatwa, and the author himself became symbolic of the vulnerability of the intellectual in the face of fundamentalism. The lifting of the fatwa in 1998 allowed Rushdie to reappear in public, but it is seen as irrevocable by some religious groups, and so his life has remained under constant threat. Al-Qaeda was among the groups that condemned his being knighted by Queen Elizabeth II in 2007. Rushdie has defended *The Satanic Verses* in the essay "In Good Faith" (1990), while defining the irreverently pluralistic vision behind his "mongrel" aesthetic—a vision that has repeatedly resulted in the burning or banning of his books by political nationalists and religious purists in South Asia and other parts of the world:

> If *The Satanic Verses* is anything, it is a migrant's-eye view of the world. It is written from the very experience of uprooting, disjuncture and metamorphosis (slow or rapid, painful or pleasurable) that is the migrant condition, and from which, I believe, can be derived a metaphor for all humanity.
>
> Standing at the centre of the novel is a group of characters most of whom are British Muslims, or not particularly religious persons of Muslim background, struggling with just the sort of great problems of hybridization and ghettoization, of reconciling the old and the new. Those who oppose the novel most vociferously today are of the opinion that intermingling with a different culture will inevitably weaken and ruin their own. I am of the opposite opinion. *The Satanic Verses* celebrates hybridity, impurity, intermingling, the transformation that comes of new and unexpected combinations of human beings, cultures, ideas, politics, movies, songs. It rejoices in mongrelization and fears the absolutism of the Pure. *Mélange*, hotchpotch, a bit of this and a bit of that is *how newness enters the world*. It is the great possibility that mass migration gives the world, and I have tried to embrace it. *The Satanic Verses* is for change-by-fusion, change-by-conjoining. It is a love-song to our mongrel selves.

An earlier story, published the same year as his groundbreaking *Midnight's Children*, had invoked the Prophet uncontroversially. Like *Midnight's Children*, the story "The Prophet's Hair" buoyantly fuses Standard English with an exuberantly Indianized English, peppered with words of Hindi, Persian, Sanskrit, and Arabic origin—among the many languages that have been used in the extraordinarily polyglot Indian subcontinent. Like *The Satanic Verses*, "The Prophet's Hair" risks playfulness, satire, caricature, and whimsy in its treatment of the religion of his youth (though Rushdie has indicated he was brought up not as a believer but within a relaxed Muslim climate, almost secularized by the variety of other religions surrounding it). The story is at once a moral fable in the tradition of *The Thousand and One Nights* and a magical-realist extravaganza, packed with incident, poetic detail ("water to which the cold of the night had given the cloudy consistency of wild honey"), and humor, all brilliantly interwoven at breakneck speed.

The Prophet's[1] Hair

Early in the year 19—, when Srinagar[2] was under the spell of a winter so fierce it could crack men's bones as if they were glass, a young man upon whose cold-pinked skin there lay, like a frost, the unmistakable sheen of wealth was to be seen entering the most wretched and disreputable part of the city, where the houses of wood and corrugated iron seemed perpetually on the verge of losing their balance, and asking in low, grave tones where he might go to engage the services of a dependably professional burglar. The young man's name was Atta, and the rogues in that part of town directed him gleefully into ever darker and less public alleys, until in a yard wet with the blood of a slaughtered chicken he was set upon by two men whose faces he never saw, robbed of the substantial bank-roll which he had insanely brought on his solitary excursion, and beaten within an inch of his life.

Night fell. His body was carried by anonymous hands to the edge of the lake, whence it was transported by shikara[3] across the water and deposited, torn and bleeding, on the deserted embankment of the canal which led to the gardens of Shalimar. At dawn the next morning a flower-vendor was rowing his boat through water to which the cold of the night had given the cloudy consistency of wild honey when he saw the prone form of young Atta, who was just beginning to stir and moan, and on whose now deathly pale skin the sheen of wealth could still be made out dimly beneath an actual layer of frost.

The flower-vendor moored his craft and by stooping over the mouth of the injured man was able to learn the poor fellow's address, which was mumbled through lips that could scarcely move; whereupon, hoping for a large tip, the hawker rowed Atta home to a large house on the shores of the lake, where a beautiful but inexplicably bruised young woman and her distraught, but equally handsome mother, neither of whom, it was clear from their eyes, had slept a wink from worrying, screamed at the sight of their Atta—who was the elder brother of the beautiful young woman—lying motionless amidst the funereally stunted winter blooms of the hopeful florist.

The flower-vendor was indeed paid off handsomely, not least to ensure his silence, and plays no further part in our story. Atta himself, suffering terribly from exposure as well as a broken skull, entered a coma which caused the city's finest doctors to shrug helplessly. It was therefore all the more remarkable that on the very next evening the most wretched and disreputable part of the city received a second unexpected visitor. This was Huma, the sister of the unfortunate young man, and her question was the same as her brother's, and asked in the same low, grave tones:

'Where may I hire a thief?'

---

1. The Prophet Muhammad, founder of the Muslim religion, was born in Mecca in about 570 and died in 632.

2. Capital of the state of Kashmir.
3. Long, swift Kashmiri boat.

The story of the rich idiot who had come looking for a burglar was already common knowledge in those insalubrious[4] gullies, but this time the young woman added: 'I should say that I am carrying no money, nor am I wearing any jewellery items. My father has disowned me and will pay no ransom if I am kidnapped; and a letter has been lodged with the Deputy Commissioner of Police, my uncle, to be opened in the event of my not being safe at home by morning. In that letter he will find full details of my journey here, and he will move Heaven and Earth to punish my assailants.'

Her exceptional beauty, which was visible even through the enormous welts and bruises disfiguring her arms and forehead, coupled with the oddity of her inquiries, had attracted a sizable group of curious onlookers, and because her little speech seemed to them to cover just about everything, no one attempted to injure her in any way, although there were some raucous comments to the effect that it was pretty peculiar for someone who was trying to hire a crook to invoke the protection of a high-up policeman uncle.

She was directed into ever darker and less public alleys until finally in a gully as dark as ink an old woman with eyes which stared so piercingly that Huma instantly understood she was blind motioned her through a doorway from which darkness seemed to be pouring like smoke. Clenching her fists, angrily ordering her heart to behave normally, Huma followed the old woman into the gloom-wrapped house.

The faintest conceivable rivulet of candlelight trickled through the darkness; following this unreliable yellow thread (because she could no longer see the old lady), Huma received a sudden sharp blow to the shins and cried out involuntarily, after which she at once bit her lip, angry at having revealed her mounting terror to whoever or whatever waited before her, shrouded in blackness.

She had, in fact, collided with a low table on which a single candle burned and beyond which a mountainous figure could be made out, sitting cross-legged on the floor. 'Sit, sit,' said a man's calm, deep voice, and her legs, needing no more flowery invitation, buckled beneath her at the terse command. Clutching her left hand in her right, she forced her voice to respond evenly:

'And you, sir, will be the thief I have been requesting?'

Shifting its weight very slightly, the shadow-mountain informed Huma that all criminal activity originating in this zone was well organised and also centrally controlled, so that all requests for what might be termed freelance work had to be channelled through this room.

He demanded comprehensive details of the crime to be committed, including a precise inventory of items to be acquired, also a clear statement of all financial inducements being offered with no gratuities excluded, plus, for filing purposes only, a summary of the motives for the application.

At this, Huma, as though remembering something, stiffened both in body and resolve and replied loudly that her motives were entirely a matter for

4. Unhealthy.

herself; that she would discuss details with no one but the thief himself; but that the rewards she proposed could only be described as 'lavish'.

'All I am willing to disclose to you, sir, since it appears that I am on the premises of some sort of employment agency, is that in return for such lavish rewards I must have the most desperate criminal at your disposal, a man for whom life holds no terrors, not even the fear of God.

'The worst of fellows, I tell you—nothing less will do!'

At this a paraffin storm-lantern was lighted, and Huma saw facing her a grey-haired giant down whose left cheek ran the most sinister of scars, a cicatrice in the shape of the letter *sín* in the Nastaliq[5] script. She was gripped by the insupportably nostalgic notion that the bogeyman of her childhood nursery had risen up to confront her, because her ayah[6] had always forestalled any incipient acts of disobedience by threatening Huma and Atta: 'You don't watch out and I'll send that one to steal you away—that Sheikh[7] Sín, the Thief of Thieves!'

Here, grey-haired but unquestionably scarred, was the notorious criminal himself—and was she out of her mind, were her ears playing tricks, or had he truly just announced that, given the stated circumstances, he himself was the only man for the job?

Struggling hard against the newborn goblins of nostalgia, Huma warned the fearsome volunteer that only a matter of extreme urgency and peril would have brought her unescorted into these ferocious streets.

'Because we can afford no last-minute backings-out,' she continued, 'I am determined to tell you everything, keeping back no secrets whatsoever. If, after hearing me out, you are still prepared to proceed, then we shall do everything in our power to assist you, and to make you rich.'

The old thief shrugged, nodded, spat. Huma began her story.

Six days ago, everything in the household of her father, the wealthy money-lender Hashim, had been as it always was. At breakfast her mother had spooned khichri[8] lovingly on to the moneylender's plate; the conversation had been filled with those expressions of courtesy and solicitude on which the family prided itself.

Hashim was fond of pointing out that while he was not a godly man he set great store by 'living honourably in the world'. In that spacious lakeside residence, all outsiders were greeted with the same formality and respect, even those unfortunates who came to negotiate for small fragments of Hashim's large fortune, and of whom he naturally asked an interest rate of over 70 per cent, partly, as he told his khichri-spooning wife, 'to teach these people the value of money; let them only learn that, and they will be cured of this fever of borrowing borrowing all the time—so you see that if my plans succeed, I shall put myself out of business!'

In their children, Atta and Huma, the moneylender and his wife had successfully sought to inculcate the virtues of thrift, plain dealing and a

---

5. A Persian cursive script, characterized by rounded forms and elongated horizontal strokes. "Cicatrice": scar of a healed wound.
6. Child's nurse (Anglo-Indian, from Portu-

guese).
7. Chief (Arabic).
8. Rice and lentils cooked together (Hindi).

healthy independence of spirit. On this, too, Hashim was fond of congratulating himself.

Breakfast ended; the family members wished one another a fulfilling day. Within a few hours, however, the glassy contentment of that household, of that life of porcelain delicacy and alabaster sensibilities, was to be shattered beyond all hope of repair.

The moneylender summoned his personal shikara and was on the point of stepping into it when, attracted, by a glint of silver, he noticed a small vial floating between the boat and his private quay. On an impulse, he scooped it out of the glutinous water.

It was a cylinder of tinted glass cased in exquisitely wrought silver, and Hashim saw within its walls a silver pendant bearing a single strand of human hair.

Closing his fist around this unique discovery, he muttered to the boatman that he'd changed his plans, and hurried to his sanctum,[9] where, behind closed doors, he feasted his eyes on his find.

There can be no doubt that Hashim the moneylender knew from the first that he was in possession of the famous relic of the Prophet Muhammad, that revered hair whose theft from its shrine at Hazratbal mosque the previous morning had created an unprecedented hue and cry in the valley.

The thieves—no doubt alarmed by the pandemonium, by the procession through the streets of endless ululating[1] crocodiles of lamentation, by the riots, the political ramifications and by the massive police search which was commanded and carried out by men whose entire careers now hung upon the finding of this lost hair—had evidently panicked and hurled the vial into the gelatine bosom of the lake.

Having found it by a stroke of great good fortune, Hashim's duty as a citizen was clear: the hair must be restored to its shrine, and the state to equanimity and peace.

But the moneylender had a different notion.

All around him in his study was the evidence of his collector's mania. There were enormous glass cases full of impaled butterflies from Gulmarg, three dozen scale models in various metals of the legendary cannon Zamzama, innumerable swords, a Naga spear, ninety-four terracotta camels of the sort sold on railway station platforms, many samovars,[2] and a whole zoology of tiny sandalwood animals, which had originally been carved to serve as children's bathtime toys.

'And after all,' Hashim told himself, 'the Prophet would have disapproved mightily of this relic-worship. He abhorred the idea of being deified! So, by keeping this hair from its distracted devotees, I perform—do I not?—a finer service than I would by returning it! Naturally, I don't want it for its religious value . . . I'm a man of the world, of this world. I see it purely as a secular object of great rarity and blinding beauty. In short, it's the silver vial I desire, more than the hair.

9. Private room.
1. Howling.

2. Apparatuses for making tea (Russian for "self-boilers").

'They say there are American millionaires who purchase stolen art masterpieces and hide them away—they would know how I feel. I must, must have it!'

Every collector must share his treasures with one other human being, and Hashim summoned—and told—his only son Atta, who was deeply perturbed but, having been sworn to secrecy, only spilled the beans when the troubles became too terrible to bear.

The youth excused himself and left his father alone in the crowded solitude of his collections. Hashim was sitting erect in a hard, straight-backed chair, gazing intently at the beautiful vial.

It was well known that the moneylender never ate lunch, so it was not until evening that a servant entered the sanctum to summon his master to the dining-table. He found Hashim as Atta had left him. The same, and not the same—for now the moneylender looked swollen, distended. His eyes bulged even more than they always had, they were red-rimmed, and his knuckles were white.

He seemed to be on the point of bursting! As though, under the influence of the misappropriated relic, he had filled up with some spectral fluid which might at any moment ooze uncontrollably from his every bodily opening.

He had to be helped to the table, and then the explosion did indeed take place.

Seemingly careless of the effect of his words on the carefully constructed and fragile constitution of the family's life, Hashim began to gush, to spume long streams of awful truths. In horrified silence, his children heard their father turn upon his wife, and reveal to her that for many years their marriage had been the worst of his afflictions. 'An end to politeness!' he thundered. 'An end to hypocrisy!'

Next, and in the same spirit, he revealed to his family the existence of a mistress; he informed them also of his regular visits to paid women. He told his wife that, far from being the principal beneficiary of his will, she would receive no more than the eighth portion which was her due under Islamic law. Then he turned upon his children, screaming at Atta for his lack of academic ability—'A dope! I have been cursed with a dope!'—and accusing his daughter of lasciviousness, because she went around the city barefaced, which was unseemly for any good Muslim girl to do. She should, he commanded, enter purdah[3] forthwith.

Hashim left the table without having eaten and fell into the deep sleep of a man who has got many things off his chest, leaving his children stunned, in tears, and the dinner going cold on the sideboard under the gaze of an anticipatory bearer.[4]

At five o'clock the next morning the moneylender forced his family to rise, wash and say their prayers. From then on, he began to pray five times daily for the first time in his life, and his wife and children were obliged to do likewise.

---

3. Area of certain traditional Indian houses in which Hindu or Muslim women live secluded from the sight of men outside their family circle.
4. Servant.

Before breakfast, Huma saw the servants, under her father's direction, constructing a great heap of books in the garden and setting fire to it. The only volume left untouched was the Qur'an,[5] which Hashim wrapped in a silken cloth and placed on a table in the hall. He ordered each member of his family to read passages from this book for at least two hours per day. Visits to the cinema were forbidden. And if Atta invited male friends to the house, Huma was to retire to her room.

By now, the family had entered a state of shock and dismay; but there was worse to come.

That afternoon, a trembling debtor arrived at the house to confess his inability to pay the latest instalment of interest owed, and made the mistake of reminding Hashim, in somewhat blustering fashion, of the Qur'an's strictures against usury. The moneylender flew into a rage and attacked the fellow with one of his large collection of bullwhips.

By mischance, later the same day a second defaulter came to plead for time, and was seen fleeing Hashim's study with a great gash in his arm, because Huma's father had called him a thief of other men's money and had tried to cut off the wretch's right hand with one of the thirty-eight kukri knives[6] hanging on the study walls.

These breaches of the family's unwritten laws of decorum alarmed Atta and Huma, and when, that evening, their mother attempted to calm Hashim down, he struck her on the face with an open hand. Atta leapt to his mother's defence and he, too, was sent flying.

'From now on,' Hashim bellowed, 'there's going to be some discipline around here!'

The moneylender's wife began a fit of hysterics which continued throughout that night and the following day, and which so provoked her husband that he threatened her with divorce, at which she fled to her room, locked the door and subsided into a raga[7] of sniffling. Huma now lost her composure, challenged her father openly, and announced (with that same independence of spirit which he had encouraged in her) that she would wear no cloth over her face; apart from anything else, it was bad for the eyes.

On hearing this, her father disowned her on the spot and gave her one week in which to pack her bags and go.

By the fourth day, the fear in the air of the house had become so thick that it was difficult to walk around. Atta told his shock-numbed sister: 'We are descending to gutter-level—but I know what must be done.'

That afternoon, Hashim left home accompanied by two hired thugs to extract the unpaid dues from his two insolvent clients. Atta went immediately to his father's study. Being the son and heir, he possessed his own key to the moneylender's safe. This he now used, and removing the little vial from its hiding-place, he slipped it into his trouser pocket and re-locked the safe door.

Now he told Huma the secret of what his father had fished out of Lake Dal, and exclaimed: 'Maybe I'm crazy—maybe the awful things that are happening

5. Or Koran, Muslims' sacred book: a collection of the Prophet Muhammad's oral revelations.
6. Curved knives broadening toward the point (Hindi).
7. Musical improvisation (Sanskrit).

have made me cracked—but I am convinced there will be no peace in our house until this hair is out of it.'

His sister at once agreed that the hair must be returned, and Atta set off in a hired shikara to Hazratbal mosque. Only when the boat had delivered him into the throng of the distraught faithful which was swirling around the desecrated shrine did Atta discover that the relic was no longer in his pocket. There was only a hole, which his mother, usually so attentive to household matters, must have overlooked under the stress of recent events.

Atta's initial surge of chagrin was quickly replaced by a feeling of profound relief.

'Suppose', he imagined, 'that I had already announced to the mullahs[8] that the hair was on my person! They would never have believed me now—and this mob would have lynched me! At any rate, it has gone, and that's a load off my mind.' Feeling more contented than he had for days, the young man returned home.

Here he found his sister bruised and weeping in the hall; upstairs, in her bedroom, his mother wailed like a brand-new widow. He begged Huma to tell him what had happened, and when she replied that their father, returning from his brutal business trip, had once again noticed a glint of silver between boat and quay, had once again scooped up the errant relic, and was consequently in a rage to end all rages, having beaten the truth out of her—then Atta buried his face in his hands and sobbed out his opinion, which was that the hair was persecuting them, and had come back to finish the job.

It was Huma's turn to think of a way out of their troubles.

While her arms turned black and blue and great stains spread across her forehead, she hugged her brother and whispered to him that she was determined to get rid of the hair *at all costs*—she repeated this last phrase several times.

'The hair', she then declared, 'was stolen from the mosque; so it can be stolen from this house. But it must be a genuine robbery, carried out by a bona-fide thief, not by one of us who are under the hair's thrall—by a thief so desperate that he fears neither capture nor curses.'

Unfortunately, she added, the theft would be ten times harder to pull off now that their father, knowing that there had already been one attempt on the relic, was certainly on his guard.

'Can you do it?'

Huma, in a room lit by candle and storm-lantern, ended her account with one further question: 'What assurances can you give that the job holds no terrors for you still?'

The criminal, spitting, stated that he was not in the habit of providing references, as a cook might, or a gardener, but he was not alarmed so easily, certainly not by any children's djinni[9] of a curse. Huma had to be content with this boast, and proceeded to describe the details of the proposed burglary.

'Since my brother's failure to return the hair to the mosque, my father has taken to sleeping with his precious treasure under his pillow. However, he

8. Muslims learned in Islamic theology and sacred law.

9. In Muslim demonology, a spirit (genie) with supernatural powers.

sleeps alone, and very energetically; only enter his room without waking him, and he will certainly have tossed and turned quite enough to make the theft a simple matter. When you have the vial, come to my room,' and here she handed Sheikh Sín a plan of her home, 'and I will hand over all the jewellery owned by my mother and myself. You will find . . . it is worth . . . that is, you will be able to get a fortune for it . . .'

It was evident that her self-control was weakening and that she was on the point of physical collapse.

'Tonight,' she burst out finally. 'You must come tonight!'

No sooner had she left the room than the old criminal's body was convulsed by a fit of coughing: he spat blood into an old vanaspati[1] can. The great Sheikh, the 'Thief of Thieves', had become a sick man, and every day the time drew nearer when some young pretender to his power would stick a dagger in his stomach. A lifelong addiction to gambling had left him almost as poor as he had been when, decades ago, he had started out in this line of work as a mere pickpocket's apprentice; so in the extraordinary commission he had accepted from the moneylender's daughter he saw his opportunity of amassing enough wealth at a stroke to leave the valley for ever, and acquire the luxury of a respectable death which would leave his stomach intact.

As for the Prophet's hair, well, neither he nor his blind wife had ever had much to say for prophets—that was one thing they had in common with the moneylender's thunderstruck clan.

It would not do, however, to reveal the nature of this, his last crime, to his four sons. To his consternation, they had all grown up to be hopelessly devout men, who even spoke of making the pilgrimage to Mecca some day. 'Absurd!' their father would laugh at them. 'Just tell me how you will go?' For, with a parent's absolutist love, he had made sure they were all provided with a lifelong source of high income by crippling them at birth, so that, as they dragged themselves around the city, they earned excellent money in the begging business.

The children, then, could look after themselves.

He and his wife would be off soon with the jewel-boxes of the moneylender's women. It was a timely chance indeed that had brought the beautiful bruised girl into his corner of the town.

That night, the large house on the shore of the lake lay blindly waiting, with silence lapping at its walls. A burglar's night: clouds in the sky and mists on the winter water. Hashim the moneylender was asleep, the only member of his family to whom sleep had come that night. In another room, his son Atta lay deep in the coils of his coma with a blood-clot forming on his brain, watched over by a mother who had let down her long greying hair to show her grief, a mother who placed warm compresses on his head with gestures redolent of impotence. In a third bedroom Huma waited, fully dressed, amidst the jewel-heavy caskets of her desperation.

---

1. Vegetable fat used as butter in India.

At last a bulbul[2] sang softly from the garden below her window and, creeping downstairs, she opened a door to the bird, on whose face there was a scar in the shape of the Nastaliq letter *sín*.

Noiselessly, the bird flew up the stairs behind her. At the head of the staircase they parted, moving in opposite directions along the corridor of their conspiracy without a glance at one another.

Entering the moneylender's room with professional ease, the burglar, Sín, discovered that Huma's predictions had been wholly accurate. Hashim lay sprawled diagonally across his bed, the pillow untenanted by his head, the prize easily accessible. Step by padded step, Sín moved towards the goal.

It was at this point that, in the bedroom next door, young Atta sat bolt upright in his bed, giving his mother a great fright, and without any warning—prompted by goodness knows what pressure of the blood-clot upon his brain—began screaming at the top of his voice:

'Thief! Thief! Thief!'

It seems probable that his poor mind had been dwelling, in these last moments, upon his own father; but it is impossible to be certain, because having uttered these three emphatic words the young man fell back upon his pillow and died.

At once his mother set up a screeching and a wailing and a keening and a howling so earsplittingly intense that they completed the work which Atta's cry had begun—that is, her laments penetrated the walls of her husband's bedroom and brought Hashim wide awake.

Sheikh Sín was just deciding whether to dive beneath the bed or brain the moneylender good and proper when Hashim grabbed the tiger-striped swordstick which always stood propped up in a corner beside his bed, and rushed from the room without so much as noticing the burglar who stood on the opposite side of the bed in the darkness. Sín stooped quickly and removed the vial containing the Prophet's hair from its hiding-place.

Meanwhile Hashim had erupted into the corridor, having unsheathed the sword inside his cane. In his right hand he held the weapon and was waving it about dementedly. His left hand was shaking the stick. A shadow came rushing towards him through the midnight darkness of the passageway and, in his somnolent anger, the moneylender thrust his sword fatally through its heart. Turning up the light, he found that he had murdered his daughter, and under the dire influence of this accident he was so overwhelmed by remorse that he turned the sword upon himself, fell upon it and so extinguished his life. His wife, the sole surviving member of the family, was driven mad by the general carnage and had to be committed to an asylum for the insane by her brother, the city's Deputy Commissioner of Police.

Sheikh Sín had quickly understood that the plan had gone awry.

Abandoning the dream of the jewel-boxes when he was but a few yards from its fulfilment, he climbed out of Hashim's window and made his escape during the appalling events described above. Reaching home before

2. Asian song thrush.

dawn, he woke his wife and confessed his failure. It would be necessary, he whispered, for him to vanish for a while. Her blind eyes never opened until he had gone.

The noise in the Hashim household had roused their servants and even managed to awaken the night-watchman, who had been fast asleep as usual on his charpoy[3] by the street-gate. They alerted the police, and the Deputy Commissioner himself was informed. When he heard of Huma's death, the mournful officer opened and read the sealed letter which his niece had given him, and instantly led a large detachment of armed men into the light-repellent gullies of the most wretched and disreputable part of the city.

The tongue of a malicious cat-burglar named Huma's fellow-conspirator; the finger of an ambitious bank-robber pointed at the house in which he lay concealed; and although Sín managed to crawl through a hatch in the attic and attempt a roof-top escape, a bullet from the Deputy Commissioner's own rifle penetrated his stomach and brought him crashing messily to the ground at the feet of Huma's enraged uncle.

From the dead thief's pocket rolled a vial of tinted glass, cased in filigree silver.

The recovery of the Prophet's hair was announced at once on All-India Radio. One month later, the valley's holiest men assembled at the Hazratbal mosque and formally authenticated the relic. It sits to this day in a closely guarded vault by the shores of the loveliest of lakes in the heart of the valley which was once closer than any other place on earth to Paradise.

But before our story can properly be concluded, it is necessary to record that when the four sons of the dead Sheikh awoke on the morning of his death, having unwittingly spent a few minutes under the same roof as the famous hair, they found that a miracle had occurred, that they were all sound of limb and strong of wind, as whole as they might have been if their father had not thought to smash their legs in the first hours of their lives. They were, all four of them, very properly furious, because the miracle had reduced their earning powers by 75 per cent, at the most conservative estimate; so they were ruined men.

Only the Sheikh's widow had some reason for feeling grateful, because although her husband was dead she had regained her sight, so that it was possible for her to spend her last days gazing once more upon the beauties of the valley of Kashmir.

1981

3. Light Indian bedstead.

IAN McEWAN
b. 1948

Born in Aldershot, southwest of London, Ian McEwan spent much of his childhood at military bases in Libya, Singapore, and other countries where his army officer father, a Scotsman, was stationed. He has attributed his early fascination with imaginative literature to his mother, though she, like McEwan's father, had left school when she was fourteen. When he was twelve years old, McEwan returned to Britain to attend a state-run boarding school. He received a B.A. in English at the University of Sussex in 1970, and the next year, an M.A. in creative writing at the University of East Anglia.

McEwan's first three books—the short-story collection *First Love, Last Rites* (1975), which included a number of works he had written for his master's degree; his second book of short fiction, *In Between the Sheets and Other Stories* (1978); and his first novel, *The Cement Garden* (1978)—launched his reputation as a technically brilliant storyteller with masterful command of suspenseful narration, precise imagery, and deft characterization. The salacious details and shocking incidents in these early works—incest between siblings, a penis pickled in a jar, a girl abused and dumped in a canal—also indicated a fascination with sexual perversity and predatory evil. But as McEwan continued to write a prodigious variety of plays, screenplays, and especially novels, the scope of his work widened. Some of his novels are primarily domestic, such as the exploration of a couple's guilt and anger after their three-year-old child has been abducted, in *The Child in Time* (1987), and others chiefly political, such as the Cold War espionage novels *The Innocent* (1990) and *Sweet Tooth* (2012). Some are set in contemporary times, such as the Booker Award–winning *Amsterdam* (1998), about a euthanasia pact, *Saturday* (2005), whose events unfold in the shadow of September 11, 2001, the legal novel *The Children Act* (2014), and the fetus-narrated *Nutshell* (2016), while others—in particular, the celebrated World War II–era novel *Atonement* (2001), which centers on the disastrous consequences of an overly imaginative girl's false accusation of rape—take place at pivotal historical moments.

Although some of his early works, such as the story "Solid Geometry" (1975), have mystical elements, his later novels, including *Solar* (2010), about the issue of climate change, are permeated with scientific rationalism. McEwan's narrative method— often crystalline in its detachment, clinical in its analysis—aligns with his empiricist and scientific bent, but it is often put in the service of understanding human psychology. McEwan has commented in an interview that "the creation of character and the mapping out of other minds and the invitation to the reader to step into those other minds seems to me very much the central project of exploring our condition." Among the minds explored in the novel *Enduring Love* (1997) are the hyperrational science writer, Joe Rose, who intricately examines his experience, and the mad stalker, Jed Parry, who falls obsessively in love with Joe during the novel's opening crisis, exemplifying a psychiatric disorder known as de Clérambault's syndrome.

Explaining in a 2007 interview the strongly visual dimension of his work, McEwan remarked that

> forty percent of the brain's processing is given over to the visual, and the visual region projects deep into other parts of the brain, of language and emotion. We are visual creatures and the novel, more than cinema, for me is ultimately a visual medium. . . . I like, myself, to be able to see a scene. And in the opening

scene of *Enduring Love*, for example, the most important element of that set piece was to make the details in the relationship, of all the different bits, the people running across a field towards a balloon that was in trouble, to make that clear.

McEwan went on to talk about the genesis of the scene, widely viewed as one of the most compelling in contemporary fiction. He had been looking for an opening that would "have a sense of urgency and visual clarity with something knocking the heart," and a hiking partner

> suddenly remembered he'd read in a paper of a balloon and a father and son who had tried to tether it and dropped to their deaths. I never could find the newspaper piece 'til long afterwards. But as soon as he told me, I thought— now that's it. And I need more than two people, I need six or seven around that balloon. What better enactment of morality? This notion that if we all hang on we can hold it down, but if one breaks rank then there's no point in being good anymore.

In the opening scene of *Enduring Love*, Joe the science writer has taken his wife, Clarissa, a scholar of John Keats's poetry, for a picnic in the English countryside. On seeing a runaway helium balloon that holds a terrified boy, he hastily joins several other men in an attempt to bring it down. As Joe struggles to hang onto the windswept balloon, the suspenseful narrative slows down time, minutely exploring the significance of this crisis moment. The balloon incident becomes the meeting ground for tensions between heroism and retreat, self-preservation and communal collaboration, selfless love for others and self-protective self-love, life and death. As in much contemporary fiction, such meanings proliferate without resolution, as the effects of the moment reverberate through the lives of everyone touched by the incident, leaving some shattered, others groping slowly toward self-understanding.

From Enduring Love

One

The beginning is simple to mark. We were in sunlight under a turkey oak, partly protected from a strong, gusty wind. I was kneeling on the grass with a corkscrew in my hand, and Clarissa was passing me the bottle—a 1987 Daumas Gassac. This was the moment, this was the pinprick on the time map: I was stretching out my hand, and as the cool neck and the black foil touched my palm, we heard a man's shout. We turned to look across the field and saw the danger. Next thing, I was running towards it. The transformation was absolute: I don't recall dropping the corkscrew, or getting to my feet, or making a decision, or hearing the caution Clarissa called after me. What idiocy, to be racing into this story and its labyrinths, sprinting away from our happiness among the fresh spring grasses by the oak. There was the shout again, and a child's cry, enfeebled by the wind that roared in the tall trees along the hedgerows. I ran faster. And there, suddenly, from different points around the field, four other men were converging on the scene, running like me.

I see us from three hundred feet up, through the eyes of the buzzard we had watched earlier, soaring, circling and dipping in the tumult of currents: five men running silently towards the centre of a hundred-acre field. I approached from the south-east, with the wind at my back. About two hundred yards to my left two men ran side by side. They were farm labourers who had been repairing the fence along the field's southern edge where it skirts the road. The same distance beyond them was the motorist, John Logan, whose car was banked on the grass verge with its door, or doors, wide open. Knowing what I know now, it's odd to evoke the figure of Jed Parry directly ahead of me, emerging from a line of beeches on the far side of the field a quarter of a mile away, running into the wind. To the buzzard Parry and I were tiny forms, our white shirts brilliant against the green, rushing towards each other like lovers, innocent of the grief this entanglement would bring. The encounter that would unhinge us was minutes away, its enormity disguised from us not only by the barrier of time but by the colossus in the centre of the field that drew us in with the power of a terrible ratio that set fabulous magnitude against the puny human distress at its base.

What was Clarissa doing? She said she walked quickly towards the centre of the field. I don't know how she resisted the urge to run. By the time it happened—the event I am about to describe, the fall—she had almost caught us up and was well placed as an observer, unencumbered by participation, by the ropes and the shouting, and by our fatal lack of co-operation. What I describe is shaped by what Clarissa saw too, by what we told each other in the time of obsessive re-examination that followed: the aftermath, an appropriate term for what happened in a field waiting for its early summer mowing. The aftermath, the second crop, the growth promoted by that first cut in May.

I'm holding back, delaying the information. I'm lingering in the prior moment because it was a time when other outcomes were still possible; the convergence of six figures in a flat green space has a comforting geometry from the buzzard's perspective, the knowable, limited plane of the snooker table.[1] The initial conditions, the force and the direction of the force, define all the consequent pathways, all the angles of collision and return, and the glow of the overhead light bathes the field, the baize[2] and all its moving bodies, in reassuring clarity. I think that while we were still converging, before we made contact, we were in a state of mathematical grace. I linger on our dispositions, the relative distances and the compass point—because as far as these occurrences were concerned, this was the last time I understood anything clearly at all.

What were we running towards? I don't think any of us would ever know fully. But superficially the answer was, a balloon. Not the nominal space that encloses a cartoon character's speech or thought, or, by analogy, the kind that's driven by mere hot air. It was an enormous balloon filled with helium, that elemental gas forged from hydrogen in the nuclear furnace of the stars, first step along the way in the generation of multiplicity and variety of matter in the universe, including our selves and all our thoughts.

We were running towards a catastrophe, which itself was a kind of furnace in whose heat identities and fates would buckle into new shapes. At the base of the balloon was a basket in which there was a boy, and by the basket, clinging to a rope, was a man in need of help.

Even without the balloon the day would have been marked for memory, though in the most pleasurable of ways, for this was a reunion after a separation of six weeks, the longest Clarissa and I had spent apart in our seven

---

1. A type of billiard table. 2. A type of cloth often used to cover tables.

years. On the way out to Heathrow I had made a detour into Covent Garden and found a semi legal place to park, close to Carluccio's.[3] I went in and put together a picnic whose centre-piece was a great ball of mozzarella which the assistant fished out of an earthenware vat with a wooden claw. I also bought black olives, mixed salad and focaccia. Then I hurried up Long Acre to Bertram Rota's[4] to take delivery of Clarissa's birthday present. Apart from the flat and our car, it was the most expensive single item I had ever bought. The rarity of this little book seemed to give off a heat I could feel through the thick brown wrapping paper as I walked back up the street.

Forty minutes later I was scanning the screens for arrival information. The Boston flight had only just landed and I guessed I had a half-hour wait. If one ever wanted proof of Darwin's contention that the many expressions of emotion in humans are universal, genetically inscribed, then a few minutes by the arrivals gate in Heathrow's Terminal Four should suffice. I saw the same joy, the same uncontrollable smile, in the faces of a Nigerian earth mama, a thin-lipped Scottish granny and a pale, correct Japanese businessman as they wheeled their trolleys in and recognised a figure in the expectant crowd. Observing human variety can give pleasure, but so too can human sameness. I kept hearing the same sighing sound on a downward note, often breathed through a name as two people pressed forward to go into their embrace. Was it a major second, or a minor third, or somewhere in between? Pa-pa! Yolan-ta! Ho-bi! Nz-e! There was also a rising note, crooned into the solemn, wary faces of babies by long-absent fathers or grandparents, cajoling, beseeching an immediate return of love. Hann-ah? Tom-ee? Let me in!

The variety was in the private dramas: a father and teenage son, Turkish perhaps, stood in a long silent clinch, forgiving each other, or mourning a loss, oblivious to the baggage trolleys jamming around them; identical twins, women in their fifties, greeted each other with clear distaste, just touching hands and kissing without making contact; a small American boy, hoisted on to the shoulders of a father he did not recognise, screamed to be put down, provoking a fit of temper in his tired mother.

But mostly it was smiles and hugs, and in thirty-five minutes I experienced more than fifty theatrical happy endings, each one with the appearance of being slightly less well acted than the one before, until I began to feel emotionally exhausted and suspected that even the children were being insincere. I was just wondering how convincing I myself could be now in greeting Clarissa when she tapped me on the shoulder, having missed me in the crowd and circled round. Immediately my detachment vanished, and I called out her name, in tune with all the rest.

Less than an hour later we were parked by a track that ran through beech woods in the Chiltern Hills, near Christmas Common.[5] While Clarissa changed her shoes I loaded a backpack with our picnic. We set off down our path arm in arm, still elated by our reunion; what was familiar about her— the size and feel of her hand, the warmth and tranquillity in her voice, the Celt's pale skin and green eyes—was also novel, gleaming in an alien light, reminding me of our very first meetings and the months we spent falling in

---

3. Food shop and café in central London. "Heathrow": airport west of London. "Covent Garden": London district.
4. A rare-book store. "Long Acre": a key street in Covent Garden.
5. Village in Oxfordshire. "Chiltern Hills": a range of chalk hills to the west of London.

love. Or, I imagined, I was another man, my own sexual competitor, come to steal her from me. When I told her she laughed and said I was the world's most complicated simpleton, and it was while we stopped to kiss and wondered aloud whether we should not have driven straight home to bed, that we glimpsed through the fresh foliage the helium balloon drifting dreamily across the wooded valley to our west. Neither the man nor the boy were visible to us. I remember thinking, but not saying, that it was a precarious form of transport when the wind, rather than the pilot, set the course. Then I thought that perhaps this was the very nature of its attraction. And instantly the idea went out of my mind.

We went through College Wood towards Pishill,[6] stopping to admire the new greenery on the beeches. Each leaf seemed to glow with an internal light. We talked about the purity of this colour, the beech leaf in spring, and how looking at it cleared the mind. As we walked into the wood the wind began to get up and the branches creaked like rusted machinery. We knew this route well. This was surely the finest landscape within an hour of central London. I loved the pitch and roll of the fields and their scatterings of chalk and flint, and the paths that dipped across them to sink into the darkness of the beech stands, certain neglected, badly drained valleys where thick iridescent mosses covered the rotting tree trunks and where you occasionally glimpsed a muntjak[7] blundering through the undergrowth.

For much of the time as we walked westwards we were talking about Clarissa's research—John Keats dying in Rome in the house at the foot of the Spanish Steps where he lodged with his friend Joseph Severn. Was it possible there were still three or four unpublished letters of Keats' in existence? Might one of them be addressed to Fanny Brawne?[8] Clarissa had reason to think so and had spent part of a sabbatical term travelling around Spain and Portugal, visiting houses known to Fanny Brawne and to Keats' sister Fanny. Now she was back from Boston where she had been working in the Houghton Library at Harvard, trying to trace correspondence from Severn's remote family connections. Keats' last known letter was written almost three months before he died to his old friend Charles Brown.[9] It's rather stately in tone, and typical in throwing out, almost as a parenthesis, a brilliant description of artistic creation—'the knowledge of contrast, feeling for light and shade, all that information (primitive sense) necessary for a poem are great enemies to the recovery of the stomach.' It's the one with the famous farewell, so piercing in its reticence and courtesy: 'I can scarcely bid you goodbye, even in a letter. I always made an awkward bow. God bless you! John Keats.' But the biographies agreed that Keats was in remission from tuberculosis when he wrote this letter, and remained so for a further ten days. He visited the Villa Borghese, and strolled down the Corso. He listened with pleasure to Severn playing Haydn,[1] he mischievously tipped his dinner out the window in protest at the quality of the cooking, and he even thought about starting a poem. If letters existed from this period why

6. Village in Oxfordshire in the Chiltern Hills.
7. Small deer.
8. Frances Brawne (1800–1865), fiancée of John Keats (1795–1821), English Romantic poet, who went to Italy with his friend the English painter Joseph Severn (1793–1879), in September 1820 to recover from tuberculosis. "The Spanish Steps": hillside staircase in Rome.
9. English writer and friend of Keats (1787–1842).
1. Franz Joseph Haydn (1732–1809), Austrian composer. "Villa Borghese": art museum with lavish gardens in Rome. "The Corso": street near the Villa Borghese.

would Severn or, more likely, Brown, have wanted to suppress them? Clarissa thought she had found the answer in a couple of references in correspondence between distant relations of Brown's written in the 1840s, but she needed more evidence, different sources.

'He knew he'd never see Fanny again,' Clarissa said. 'He wrote to Brown and said that to see her name written would be more than he could bear. But he never stopped thinking about her. He was strong enough those days in December, and he loved her so hard. It's easy to imagine him writing a letter he never intended to send.'

I squeezed her hand and said nothing. I knew little about Keats or his poetry, but I thought it possible that in his hopeless situation he would not have wanted to write precisely because he loved her so much. Lately I'd had the idea that Clarissa's interest in these hypothetical letters had something to do with our own situation, and with her conviction that love that did not find its expression in a letter was not perfect. In the months after we met, and before we bought the apartment, she had written me some beauties, passionately abstract in their exploration of the ways our love was different from and superior to any that had ever existed. Perhaps that's the essence of a love letter, to celebrate the unique. I had tried to match hers, but all that sincerity would permit me were the facts, and they seemed miraculous enough to me: a beautiful woman loved and wanted to be loved by a large, clumsy, balding fellow who could hardly believe his luck.

We stopped to watch the buzzard as we were approaching Maidensgrove.[2] The balloon may have re-crossed our path while we were in the woods that cover the valleys around the nature reserve. By the early afternoon we were on the Ridgeway Path walking north along the line of the escarpment.[3] Then we struck out along one of those broad fingers of land that project westwards from the Chilterns into the rich farmland below. Across the Vale of Oxford we could make out the outlines of the Cotswold Hills and beyond them, perhaps, the Brecon Beacons[4] rising in a faint blue mass. Our plan had been to picnic right out on the end where the view was best, but the wind was too strong by now. We went back across the field and sheltered among the oaks along the northern side. And it was because of these trees that we did not see the balloon's descent. Later I wondered why it had not been blown miles away. Later still I discovered that the wind at five hundred feet was not the same that day as the wind at ground level.

The Keats conversation faded as we unpacked our lunch. Clarissa pulled the bottle from the bag and held it by its base as she offered it to me. As I have said, the neck touched my palm as we heard the shout. It was a baritone, on a rising note of fear. It marked the beginning and, of course, an end. At that moment a chapter, no, a whole stage of my life closed. Had I known, and had there been a spare second or two, I might have allowed myself a little nostalgia. We were seven years into a childless marriage of love. Clarissa Mellon was also in love with another man, but with his two hundredth birthday coming up he was little trouble. In fact he helped in the combative exchanges which were part of our equilibrium, our way of talking about work. We lived in an

2. Village in Oxfordshire.
3. Abrupt face or cliff. "The Ridgeway Path": British National Trail along the Chiltern Hills.
4. Mountain range in South Wales. "The Vale of Oxford": valley containing Oxford. "Cotswold Hills": range of hills in west-central England to the west of Oxford.

art deco apartment block in north London with a below average share of worries—a money shortage for a year or so, an unsubstantiated cancer scare, the divorces and illnesses of friends, Clarissa's irritation with my occasional and manic bouts of dissatisfaction with my kind of work—but there was nothing that threatened our free and intimate existence.

What we saw when we stood from our picnic was this: a huge grey balloon, the size of a house, the shape of a tear drop, had come down in the field. The pilot must have been half way out of the passenger basket as it touched the ground. His leg had become entangled in a rope that was attached to an anchor. Now, as the wind gusted, and pushed and lifted the balloon towards the escarpment, he was being half dragged, half carried across the field. In the basket was a child, a boy of about ten. In a sudden lull, the man was on his feet, clutching at the basket, or at the boy. Then there was another gust, and the pilot was on his back, bumping over the rough ground, trying to dig his feet in for purchase, or lunging for the anchor behind him in order to secure it in the earth. Even if he had been able, he would not have dared disentangle himself from the anchor rope. He needed his weight to keep the balloon on the ground, and the wind could have snatched the rope from his hands.

As I ran I heard him shouting at the boy, urging him to leap clear of the basket. But the boy was tossed from one side to another as the balloon lurched across the field. He regained his balance and got a leg over the edge of the basket. The balloon rose and fell, thumping into a hummock, and the boy dropped backwards out of sight. Then he was up again, arms stretched out towards the man and shouting something in return—words or inarticulate fear, I couldn't tell.

I must have been a hundred yards away when the situation came under control. The wind had dropped, the man was on his feet, bending over the anchor as he drove it into the ground. He had unlooped the rope from his leg. For some reason, complacency, exhaustion or simply because he was doing what he was told, the boy remained where he was. The towering balloon wavered and tilted and tugged, but the beast was tamed. I slowed my pace, though I did not stop. As the man straightened, he saw us—or at least the farm workers and me—and he waved us on. He still needed help, but I was glad to slow to a brisk walk. The farm labourers were also walking now. One of them was coughing loudly. But the man with the car, John Logan, knew something we didn't and kept on running. As for Jed Parry, my view of him was blocked by the balloon that lay between us.

The wind renewed its rage in the treetops just before I felt its force on my back. Then it struck the balloon which ceased its innocent comical wagging and was suddenly stilled. Its only motion was a shimmer of strain that rippled out across its ridged surface as the contained energy accumulated. It broke free, the anchor flew up in a spray of dirt, and balloon and basket rose ten feet in the air. The boy was thrown back, out of sight. The pilot had the rope in his hands and was lifted two feet clear off the ground. If Logan had not reached him and taken hold of one of the many dangling lines the balloon would have carried the boy away. Instead, both men were now being pulled across the field, and the farm workers and I were running again.

I got there before them. When I took a rope the basket was above head height. The boy inside it was screaming. Despite the wind, I caught the smell of urine. Jed Parry was on a rope seconds after me, and the two farm workers,

Joseph Lacey and Toby Greene, caught hold just after him. Greene was having a coughing fit, but he kept his grip. The pilot was shouting instructions at us, but too frantically, and no one was listening. He had been struggling too long, and now he was exhausted and emotionally out of control. With five of us on the lines the balloon was secured. We simply had to keep steady on our feet and pull hand over hand to bring the basket down, and this, despite whatever the pilot was shouting, was what we began to do.

By this time we were standing on the escarpment. The ground dropped away sharply at a gradient of about twenty-five per cent, and then levelled out into a gentle slope towards the bottom. In winter this is a favourite tobogganning spot for local kids. We were all talking at once. Two of us, myself and the motorist, wanted to walk the balloon away from the edge. Someone thought the priority was to get the boy out. Someone else was calling for the balloon to be pulled down so that we could anchor it firmly. I saw no contradiction, for we could be pulling the balloon down as we moved back into the field. But the second opinion was prevailing. The pilot had a fourth idea, but no one knew or cared what it was.

I should make something clear. There may have been a vague communality of purpose, but we were never a team. There was no chance, no time. Coincidences of time and place, a predisposition to help had brought us together under the balloon. No one was in charge—or everyone was, and we were in a shouting match. The pilot, red-faced, bawling and sweating, we ignored. Incompetence came off him like heat. But we were beginning to bawl our own instructions too. I know that if I had been uncontested leader the tragedy would not have happened. Later I heard some of the others say the same thing about themselves. But there was not time, no opportunity for force of character to show. Any leader, any firm plan would have been preferable to none. No human society, from the hunter-gatherer to the post-industrial, has come to the attention of anthropologists that did not have its leaders and the led; and no emergency was ever dealt with effectively by democratic process.

It was not so difficult to bring the passenger basket down low enough for us to see inside. We had a new problem. The boy was curled up on the floor. His arms covered his face and he was gripping his hair tightly. 'What's his name?' we said to the red-faced man.

'Harry.'

'Harry!' we shouted. 'Come on Harry. Harry! Take my hand, Harry. Get out of there Harry!'

But Harry curled up tighter. He flinched each time we said his name. Our words were like stones thrown down at his body. He was in paralysis of will, a state known as learned helplessness, often noted in laboratory animals subjected to unusual stress; all impulses to problem-solving disappear, all instinct for survival drains away. We pulled the basket down to the ground and managed to keep it there, and we were just leaning in to try and lift the boy out when the pilot shouldered us aside and attempted to climb in. He said later that he told us what he was trying to do. We heard nothing but our own shouting and swearing. What he was doing seemed ridiculous, but his intentions, it turned out, were completely sensible. He wanted to deflate the balloon by pulling a cord that was tangled in the basket.

'Yer great pillock!'[5] Lacey shouted. 'Help us reach the lad out.'

5. Idiot.

I heard what was coming two seconds before it reached us. It was as though an express train were traversing the treetops, hurtling towards us. An airy, whining, whooshing sound grew to full volume in half a second. At the inquest the Met office[6] figures for wind speeds that day were part of the evidence, and there were some gusts, it was said, of seventy miles an hour. This must have been one, but before I let it reach us, let me freeze the frame—there's a security in stillness—to describe our circle.

To my right the ground dropped away. Immediately to my left was John Logan, a family doctor from Oxford, forty-two years old, married to a historian, with two children. He was not the youngest of our group, but he was the fittest. He played tennis to county level, and belonged to a mountaineering club. He had done a stint with a mountain rescue team in the Western Highlands.[7] Logan was a mild, reticent man apparently, otherwise he might have been able to force himself usefully on us as a leader. To his left was Joseph Lacey, sixty-three, farm labourer, odd job man, captain of his local bowls[8] team. He lived with his wife in Watlington, a small town at the foot of the escarpment. On his left was his mate, Toby Greene, fifty-eight, also a farm labourer, unmarried, living with his mother at Russell's Water.[9] Both men worked for the Stonor estate. Greene was the one with the smoker's cough. Next around the circle, trying to get into the basket, was the pilot, James Gadd, fifty-five, an executive in a small advertising company, who lived in Reading[1] with his wife and one of their grown-up children who was mentally handicapped. At the inquest Gadd was found to have breached half a dozen basic safety procedures which the coroner listed tonelessly. Gadd's ballooning licence was withdrawn. The boy in the basket was Harry Gadd, his grandson, ten years old, from Camberwell, London.[2] Facing me, with the ground sloping away to his left, was Jed Parry. He was twenty-eight, unemployed, living on an inheritance in Hampstead.

This was the crew. As far as we were concerned, the pilot had abdicated his authority. We were breathless, excited, determined on our separate plans, while the boy was beyond participating in his own survival. He lay in a heap, blocking out the world with his forearms. Lacey, Greene and I were attempting to fish him out, and now Gadd was climbing over the top of us. Logan and Parry were calling out their own suggestions. Gadd had placed one foot by his grandson's head, and Greene was cussing him when it happened. A mighty fist socked the balloon in two rapid blows, one-two, the second more vicious than the first. And the first was vicious. It jerked Gadd right out of the basket on to the ground, and it lifted the balloon five feet or so, straight into the air. Gadd's considerable weight was removed from the equation. The rope ran through my grip, scorching my palms, but I managed to keep hold, with two feet of line spare. The others kept hold too. The basket was right above our heads now, and we stood with arms upraised like Sunday bell ringers. Into our amazed silence, before the shouting could resume, the second punch came and knocked the balloon up and westwards. Suddenly we were treading the air with all our weight in the grip of our fists.

Those one or two ungrounded seconds occupy as much space in memory as might a long journey up an uncharted river. My first impulse was to hang

---

6. National Weather Service of the United Kingdom.
7. In Scotland.
8. Outdoor bowling game.

9. Oxfordshire hamlet.
1. Town west of London.
2. District in southeast London.

on in order to keep the balloon weighted down. The child was incapable, and was about to be borne away. Two miles to the west were high-voltage power lines. A child alone and needing help. It was my duty to hang on, and I thought we would all do the same.

Almost simultaneous with the desire to stay on the rope and save the boy, barely a neuronal pulse later, came other thoughts in which fear and instant calculations of logarithmic complexity were fused. We were rising, and the ground was dropping away as the balloon was pushed westwards. I knew I had to get my legs and feet locked round the rope. But the end of the line barely reached below my waist and my grip was slipping. My legs flailed in the empty air. Every fraction of a second that passed increased the drop, and the point must come when to let go would be impossible or fatal. And compared to me Harry was safe curled up in the basket. The balloon might well come down safely at the bottom of the hill. And perhaps my impulse to hang on was nothing more than a continuation of what I had been attempting moments before, simply a failure to adjust quickly.

And again, less than one adrenally incensed heartbeat later, another variable was added to the equation: someone let go, and the balloon and its hangers-on lurched upwards another several feet.

I didn't know, nor have I ever discovered, who let go first. I'm not prepared to accept that it was me. But everyone claims not to have been first. What is certain is that if we had not broken ranks, our collective weight would have brought the balloon to earth a quarter of the way down the slope a few seconds later as the gust subsided. But as I've said, there was no team, there was no plan, no agreement to be broken. No failure. So can we accept that it was right, every man for himself? Were we all happy afterwards that this was a reasonable course? We never had that comfort, for there was a deeper covenant, ancient and automatic, written in our nature. Co-operation—the basis of our earliest hunting successes, the force behind our evolving capacity for language, the glue of our social cohesion. Our misery in the aftermath was proof that we knew we had failed ourselves. But letting go was in our nature too. Selfishness is also written on our hearts. This is our mammalian conflict—what to give to the others, and what to keep for yourself. Treading that line, keeping the others in check, and being kept in check by them, is what we call morality. Hanging a few feet above the Chilterns escarpment, our crew enacted morality's ancient, irresolvable dilemma: us, or me.

Someone said *me*, and then there was nothing to be gained by saying *us*. Mostly, we are good when it makes sense. A good society is one that makes sense of being good. Suddenly, hanging there below the basket, we were a bad society, we were disintegrating. Suddenly the sensible choice was to look out for yourself. The child was not my child, and I was not going to die for it. The moment I glimpsed a body fall away—but whose?—and I felt the balloon lurch upwards, the matter was settled; altruism had no place. Being good made no sense. I let go and fell, I reckon, about twelve feet. I landed heavily on my side and got away with a bruised thigh. Around me—before or after, I'm not so sure—bodies were thumping to the ground. Jed Parry was unhurt. Toby Greene broke his ankle. Joseph Lacey, the oldest, who had done his National Service[3] with a paratroop regiment, did no more than wind himself.

3. Compulsory service in the armed forces, in effect for young men in Britain between 1939 and 1962.

By the time I got to my feet the balloon was fifty yards away, and one man was still dangling by his rope. In John Logan, husband, father, doctor and mountain rescue worker, the flame of altruism must have burned a little stronger. It didn't need much. When four of us let go, the balloon, with six hundred pounds shed, must have surged upwards. A delay of one second would have been enough to close his options. When I stood up and saw him, he was a hundred feet up, and rising, just where the ground itself was falling. He wasn't struggling, he wasn't kicking or trying to claw his way up. He hung perfectly still along the line of the rope, all his energies concentrated in his weakening grip. He was already a tiny figure, almost black against the sky. There was no sight of the boy. The balloon and its basket lifted away and westwards, and the smaller Logan became, the more terrible it was, so terrible it was funny, it was a stunt, a joke, a cartoon, and a frightened laugh heaved out of my chest. For this was preposterous, the kind of thing that happened to Bugs Bunny, or Tom, or Jerry, and for an instant, I thought it wasn't true, and that only I could see right through the joke, and that my utter disbelief would set reality straight and see Dr Logan safely to the ground.

I don't know whether the others were standing, or sprawling. Toby Greene was probably doubled up over his ankle. But I do remember the silence into which I laughed. No exclamations, no shouted instructions as before. Mute helplessness. He was two hundred yards away now, and perhaps three hundred feet above the ground. Our silence was a kind of acceptance, a death warrant. Or it was horrified shame, because the wind had dropped, and barely stirred against our backs. He had been on the rope so long that I began to think he might stay there until the balloon drifted down, or the boy came to his senses and found the valve that released the gas, or until some beam, or god, or some other impossible cartoon thing came and gathered him up. Even as I had that hope we saw him slip down right to the end of the rope. And still he hung there. For two seconds, three, four. And then he let go. Even then, there was a fraction of time when he barely fell, and I still thought there was a chance that a freak physical law, a furious thermal, some phenomenon no more astonishing than the one we were witnessing would intervene and bear him up. We watched him drop. You could see the acceleration. No forgiveness, no special dispensation for flesh, or bravery, or kindness. Only ruthless gravity. And from somewhere, perhaps from him, perhaps from some indifferent crow, a thin squawk cut through the stilled air. He fell as he had hung, a stiff little black stick. I've never seen such a terrible thing as that falling man.

Two

Best to slow down. Let's give the half minute after John Logan's fall careful consideration. What occurred simultaneously or in quick succession, what was said, how we moved or failed to move, what I thought—these elements need to be separated out. So much followed from this incident, so much branching and subdivision began in those early moments, such pathways of love and hatred blazed from this starting position, that a little reflection, even pedantry, can only help me here. The best description of a reality does not need to mimic its velocity. Whole books, whole research departments, are dedicated to the first half minute in the history of the universe. Vertiginous theories of chaos and turbulence are predicated upon the supremacy of initial conditions which need painstaking depiction.

I've already marked my beginning, the explosion of consequences, with the touch of a wine bottle and a shout of distress. But this pinprick is as notional as a point in Euclidean geometry, and though it seems right, I could have proposed the moment Clarissa and I planned to picnic after I had collected her from the airport, or when we decided on our route, or the field in which to have our lunch, and the time we chose to have it. There are always antecedent causes. A beginning is an artifice, and what recommends one over another is how much sense it makes of what follows. The cool touch of glass on skin and James Gadd's cry—these synchronous moments fix a transition, a divergence from the expected: from the wine we didn't taste (we drank it that night to numb ourselves) to the summons, from the delightful existence we shared and expected to continue, to the ordeal we were to endure in the time ahead.

When I let the wine bottle fall to run across the field towards the balloon and its bumping basket, towards Jed Parry and the others, I chose a branching in the paths that foreclosed a certain kind of easeful life. The struggle with the ropes, the breaking of ranks and the bearing away of Logan— these were the obvious, large-scale events that shaped our story. But I see now that in the moments immediately after his fall there were subtler elements exerting powerful sway over the future. The moment Logan hit the ground should have been the end of this story rather than one more beginning I could have chosen. The afternoon could have ended in mere tragedy.

In the second or two it took for Logan to reach the ground I had a sense of *déjà vu*, and I immediately knew its source. What came back to me was a nightmare I had occasionally in my twenties and thirties from which I used to shout myself awake. The setting varied, but the essentials never did. I found myself in a prominent place watching from far off the unfolding of a disaster—an earthquake, a fire in a skyscraper, a sinking ship, an erupting volcano. I could see helpless people, reduced by distance to an undifferentiated mass, scurrying about in panic, certain to die. The horror was in the contrast between their apparent size and the enormity of their suffering. Life was revealed as cheap; thousands of screaming individuals, no bigger than ants, were about to be annihilated and I could do nothing to help. I did not think about the dream then so much as experience its emotional wash—terror, guilt and helplessness were the components—and feel the nausea of a premonition fulfilled.

Down below us, where the escarpment levelled out, was a grassy field used for pasture, bounded by a line of pollarded[4] willows. Beyond them was a larger pasture where sheep and a few lambs were grazing. It was in the centre of this second field, in our full view, that Logan landed. My impression was that at the moment of impact the little stick figure flowed or poured outwards across the ground, like a drop of viscous fluid. But what we saw in the stillness, as though reconstituted, was the compact dot of his huddled figure. The nearest sheep, twenty feet away, barely looked up from its chewing.

Joseph Lacey was attending to his friend Toby Greene who could not stand. Right next to me was Jed Parry. Some way off behind us was James

4. With upper trunk and branches cut back.

Gadd. He was less interested than we were in Logan. He was shouting about his grandson who was being carried away in the balloon across the Vale of Oxford towards the line of pylons.[5] Gadd pushed past us and went a few paces down the hill, as if intending to go in pursuit. Such is his genetic investment, I remember thinking stupidly. Clarissa came up behind me and looped her arms around my waist and pressed her face into my back. What surprised me was she was already crying (I could feel the wetness on my shirt) whereas to me, sorrow seemed a long way off.

Like a self in a dream I was both first and third persons. I acted, and saw myself act. I had my thoughts, and I saw them drift across a screen. As in a dream, my emotional responses were non-existent or inappropriate. Clarissa's tears were no more than a fact, but I was pleased by the way my feet were anchored to the ground and set well apart, and the way my arms were folded across my chest. I looked out across the fields and the thought scrolled across: *that man is dead.* I felt a warmth spreading through me, a kind of self-love, and my folded arms hugged me tight. The corollary seemed to be: *and I am alive.* It was a random matter, who was alive or dead at any given time. I happened to be alive. This was when I noticed Jed Parry watching me. His long bony face was framed round a pained question. He looked wretched, like a dog about to be punished. In the second or so that this stranger's clear grey-blue eyes held mine I felt I could include him in the self-congratulatory warmth I felt in being alive. It even crossed my mind to touch him comfortingly on the shoulder. My thoughts were up there on the screen: *this man is in shock. He wants me to help him.*

Had I known what this glance meant to him at the time, and how he was to construe it later and build around it a mental life, I would not have been so warm. In his pained, interrogative look was that first bloom of which I was entirely ignorant. The euphoric calm I felt was simply a symptom of my shock. I honoured Parry with a friendly nod and, ignoring Clarissa at my back—I was a busy man, I would deal with them all one at a time—I said to him in what I thought was a deep and reassuring voice, 'It's all right.'

This flagrant untruth reverberated so pleasantly between my ribs that I almost said it again. Perhaps I did. I was the first one to have spoken since Logan hit the ground. I reached into my trouser pocket and withdrew, of all things to have out here at this time, a mobile phone. I read the fractional widening of the young man's eyes as respect. It was what I felt for myself anyway as I held the dense little slab in my palm, and with the thumb of the same hand jabbed three nines. I was in the world, equipped, capable, connected. When the emergency operator came on I asked for police and ambulance and gave a lucid, minimal account of the accident and the balloon drifting away with the boy, and our position and the nearest access by road. It was all I could do to hold my excitement in. I wanted to shout something—commands, exhortations, inarticulate vowel sounds. I was brittle, speedy, perhaps I looked happy.

When I turned off the phone Joseph Lacey said, 'He won't need no ambulance.'

Greene looked up from his ankle. 'They'll need that to take him away.'

---

5. Metal towers for overhead electrical lines.

I remembered. Of course. This was what I needed—something to do. I was wild by now, ready to fight, run, dance, you name it. 'He might not be dead,' I said. 'There's always a chance. We'll go down and take a look.'

As I was saying this I became aware of a tremor in my legs. I wanted to stride away down the slope, but I did not trust my balance. Uphill would be better. I said to Parry, 'You'll come.' I meant it as a suggestion, but it came out as a request, something I needed from him. He looked at me, unable to speak. Everything, every gesture, every word I spoke was being stored away, gathered and piled, fuel for the long winter of his obsession.

I unclasped Clarissa's arms from my waist and turned. It didn't occur to me that she was trying to hold me steady. 'Let's go down,' I said quietly. 'There may be something we can do.' I heard my softening of tone, the artful lowering of volume. I was in a soap opera. *Now he's talking to his woman.* It was intimacy, a tight two-shot.

Clarissa put her hand on my shoulder. She told me later that it crossed her mind to slap my face. 'Joe,' she whispered. 'You've got to slow down.'

'What's up?' I said in a louder voice. A man lay dying in a field and no one was stirring. Clarissa looked at me, and though her mouth looked set to frame the words, she wouldn't tell me why I should slow down. I turned away and called to the others who stood about on the grass waiting for me, so I thought, to tell them what to do. 'I'm going down to him. Is anyone coming?' I didn't wait for an answer, but set off down the hill, conscious of the watery looseness in my knees and taking short steps. Twenty seconds later I glanced back. No one had moved.

As I carried on down, the mania began to subside and I felt trapped and lonely in my decision. Also there was the fear, not quite in me, but there in the field, spread like a mist, and denser at the core. I was walking into it without choice now, because they were watching me, and to turn back would have meant climbing up the hill, a double humiliation. As the euphoria lifted, so the fear seeped in. The dead man I did not want to meet was waiting for me in the middle of the field. Even worse would be finding him alive and dying. Then I'd have to face him alone with my first aid techniques, like so many silly party tricks. He wouldn't be taken in. He would go ahead and die anyway, and his death would be in and on my hands. I wanted to turn and shout for Clarissa, but they were watching me, I knew, and I had blustered so much up there I was ashamed. This long descent was my punishment.

I reached the line of pollarded willows at the bottom of the hill, crossed a dry ditch and climbed through a barbed wire fence. By now I was out of their sight and I wanted to be sick. Instead, I urinated against a tree trunk. My hand was trembling badly. Afterwards I stood still, delaying the moment when I would have to set out across the field. Being out of view was physical relief, like being shaded from a desert sun. I was conscious of Logan's position, but even at this distance I didn't care to look.

The sheep that had hardly glanced up at the impact, stared and backed away into faltering runs as I strode among them. I was feeling slightly better. I kept Logan at the periphery of vision, but even so, I knew he was not flat on the ground. Something protruded at the centre of the field, some stumpy antenna of his present or previous self. Not until I was twenty yards away did I permit myself to see him. He was sitting upright, his back to me, as though meditating, or gazing in the direction in which the balloon and

Harry had drifted. There was calmness in his posture. I came closer, instinctively troubled to be approaching him unseen from behind, but glad I could not yet see his face. I still clung to the possibility that there was a technique, a physical law or process of which I knew nothing, that would permit him to survive. That he should sit there so quietly in the field, as though he were collecting himself after his terrible experience, gave me hope and made me clear my throat stupidly and say, knowing that no one else could hear me, 'Do you need help?' It was not so ridiculous at the time. I could see his hair curling over his shirt collar and sunburned skin along the tops of his ears. His tweed jacket was unmarked, though it drooped strangely, for his shoulders were narrower than they should have been. They were narrower than any adult's could be. From the base of the neck there was no lateral spread. The skeletal structure had collapsed internally to produce a head on a thickened stick. And seeing that, I became aware that what I had taken for calmness was *absence*. There was no one there. The quietness was that of the inanimate, and I understood again, because I had seen dead bodies before, why a pre-scientific age would have needed to invent the soul. It was no less clear than the illusion of the evening sun sinking through the sky. The closing down of countless interrelated neural and bio-chemical exchanges combined to suggest to a naked eye the illusion of the extinguished spark, or the simple departure of a single necessary element. However scientifically informed we count ourselves to be, fear and awe still surprise us in the presence of the dead. Perhaps it's life we're really wondering at.

✳   ✳   ✳

1997

ANNE CARSON
b. 1950

Anne Carson was born in Toronto, Canada, and grew up in Ontario; she received both her B.A. and her Ph.D. in classics from the University of Toronto. The recipient of a MacArthur Fellowship, she has taught classics at the universities of Calgary, Princeton, Emory, McGill, and Michigan. Along with poetry, she has published books of criticism on classical literature, translations from Greek, and novels-in-verse, *Autobiography of Red* (1998) and *Red Doc>* (2013).

In her poetry, Carson braids together the ruminative texture of the essay, the narrative propulsion of the novel, the self-analysis of autobiography, and the lapidary compression of lyric. In "The Glass Essay," a long poem that reflects on the dislocations of identity through time, love, and madness, she vividly narrates the end of a love affair, a visit with a difficult mother, and the degeneration of a father with Alzheimer's in a nursing home. Into this semiautobiographical tale she weaves commentary on the writings of the Brontë sisters, whose works function—like the classical texts she often incorporates into her poetry—as oblique and remote points of comparison for the poet's experience. Both personal and impersonal, Carson's poetry bridges the gap between private narrative and philosophical speculation, between self-excavation and literary-critical analysis. Tightly wound with crisp diction, studded with striking metaphors, etched with epigrams and ironies, her poems are both lucid in feeling and intense in thought. They are at one and the same time intellectually crystalline and emotionally volcanic.

From The Glass Essay

* * *

Well there are many ways of being held prisoner,
160   I am thinking as I stride over the moor.
As a rule after lunch mother has a nap

and I go out to walk.
The bare blue trees and bleached wooden sky of April
carve into me with knives of light.

165   Something inside it reminds me of childhood—
it is the light of the stalled time after lunch
when clocks tick

and hearts shut
and fathers leave to go back to work
170   and mothers stand at the kitchen sink pondering

something they never tell.
You remember too much,
my mother said to me recently.

Why hold onto all that? And I said,
175   Where can I put it down?
She shifted to a question about airports.

Crops of ice are changing to mud all around me
as I push on across the moor
warmed by drifts from the pale blue sun.

180   On the edge of the moor our pines
dip and coast in breezes
from somewhere else.

Perhaps the hardest thing about losing a lover is
to watch the year repeat its days.
185   It is as if I could dip my hand down

into time and scoop up
blue and green lozenges° of April heat   *diamond-shaped figures*
a year ago in another country.

I can feel that other day running underneath this one
190   like an old videotape—here we go fast around the last corner
up the hill to his house, shadows

of limes and roses blowing in the car window
and music spraying from the radio and him
singing and touching my left hand to his lips.

195   Law[1] lived in a high blue room from which he could see the sea.
Time in its transparent loops as it passes beneath me now
still carries the sound of the telephone in that room

and traffic far off and doves under the window
chuckling coolly and his voice saying,
200   You beauty. I can feel that beauty's

heart beating inside mine as she presses into his arms in the
       high blue room—
No, I say aloud. I force my arms down
through air which is suddenly cold and heavy as water

and the videotape jerks to a halt
205   like a glass slide under a drop of blood.
I stop and turn and stand into the wind,

which now plunges towards me over the moor.
When Law left I felt so bad I thought I would die.
This is not uncommon.

210   I took up the practice of meditation.
Each morning I sat on the floor in front of my sofa
and chanted bits of old Latin prayers.

De profundis clamavi ad te Domine.[2]
Each morning a vision came to me.
215   Gradually I understood that these were naked glimpses of my
       soul.

I called them Nudes.
Nude #1. Woman alone on a hill.
She stands into the wind.

It is a hard wind slanting from the north.
220   Long flaps and shreds of flesh rip off the woman's body and lift
and blow away on the wind, leaving

an exposed column of nerve and blood and muscle
calling mutely through lipless mouth.
It pains me to record this,

---

1. The speaker's lover.
2. Psalm 130: "Out of the depths have I cried unto thee, O Lord" (Latin).

225　I am not a melodramatic person.
　　 But soul is "hewn in a wild workshop"
　　 as Charlotte Brontë says of *Wuthering Heights*.[3]

　　 Charlotte's preface to *Wuthering Heights* is a publicist's
　　　　 masterpiece.
　　 Like someone carefully not looking at a scorpion
230　crouched on the arm of the sofa Charlotte

　　 talks firmly and calmly
　　 about the other furniture of Emily's workshop—about
　　 the inexorable spirit ("stronger than a man, simpler than
　　　　 a child"),

　　 the cruel illness ("pain no words can render"),
235　the autonomous end ("she sank rapidly, she made haste to
　　　　 leave us")
　　 and about Emily's total subjection

　　 to a creative project she could neither understand nor control,
　　 and for which she deserves no more praise nor blame
　　 than if she had opened her mouth

240　"to breathe lightning." The scorpion is inching down
　　 the arm of the sofa while Charlotte
　　 continues to speak helpfully about lightning

　　 and other weather we may expect to experience
　　 when we enter Emily's electrical atmosphere.
245　It is "a horror of great darkness" that awaits us there

　　 but Emily is not responsible. Emily was in the grip.
　　 "Having formed these beings she did not know what she had done,"
　　 says Charlotte (of Heathcliff and Earnshaw and Catherine).[4]

　　 Well there are many ways of being held prisoner.
250　The scorpion takes a light spring and lands on our left knee
　　 as Charlotte concludes, "On herself she had no pity."

　　 Pitiless too are the Heights, which Emily called Wuthering
　　 because of their "bracing ventilation"
　　 and "a north wind over the edge."

255　Whaching[5] a north wind grind the moor
　　 that surrounded her father's house on every side,
　　 formed of a kind of rock called millstone grit,

3. Novel by English author Emily Brontë (1818–1848). Her sister Charlotte (1815–1855) wrote an introduction to the 1850 edition, explaining how such a mild and modest woman could have created a work of such passionate imagination and apparent "coarseness." The speaker of "The Glass Essay" compares herself to Emily Brontë throughout the poem.
4. Three characters from *Wuthering Heights*.
5. Emily Brontë's idiosyncratic spelling of *watcher*, as the poem explains earlier. This excerpt is from its fourth section, also titled "Whacher."

taught Emily all she knew about love and its necessities—
an angry education that shapes the way her characters
260 use one another. "My love for Heathcliff," says Catherine,

"resembles the eternal rocks beneath—
a source of little visible delight, but necessary."
Necessary? I notice the sun has dimmed

and the afternoon air sharpening.
265 I turn and start to recross the moor towards home.
What are the imperatives

that hold people like Catherine and Heathcliff
together and apart, like pores blown into hot rock
and then stranded out of reach

270 of one another when it hardens? What kind of necessity
     is that?
The last time I saw Law was a black night in September.
Autumn had begun,

my knees were cold inside my clothes.
A chill fragment of moon rose.
275 He stood in my living room and spoke

without looking at me. Not enough spin on it,
he said of our five years of love.
Inside my chest I felt my heart snap into two pieces

which floated apart. By now I was so cold
280 it was like burning. I put out my hand
to touch his. He moved back.

I don't want to be sexual with you, he said. Everything gets
     crazy.
But now he was looking at me.
Yes, I said as I began to remove my clothes.

285 Everything gets crazy. When nude
I turned my back because he likes the back.
He moved onto me.

Everything I know about love and its necessities
I learned in that one moment
290 when I found myself

thrusting my little burning red backside like a baboon
at a man who no longer cherished me.
There was no area of my mind

not appalled by this action, no part of my body
295 that could have done otherwise.
But to talk of mind and body begs the question.

Soul is the place,
stretched like a surface of millstone grit between body and mind,
where such necessity grinds itself out.

300 Soul is what I kept watch on all that night.
Law stayed with me.
We lay on top of the covers as if it weren't really a night of
       sleep and time,

caressing and singing to one another in our made-up language
like the children we used to be.
305 That was a night that centred Heaven and Hell,

as Emily would say. We tried to fuck
but he remained limp, although happy. I came
again and again, each time accumulating lucidity,

until at last I was floating high up near the ceiling looking down
310 on the two souls clasped there on the bed
with their mortal boundaries

visible around them like lines on a map.
I saw the lines harden.
He left in the morning.

315 It is very cold
walking into the long scraped April wind.
At this time of year there is no sunset
just some movements inside the light and then a sinking away.

1995

PAUL MULDOON
b. 1951

Paul Muldoon was born in Portadown, County Armagh, Northern Ireland. His mother was a schoolteacher; his father, a farm laborer and mushroom grower. Paul grew up in, as he put it, "a little enclave of Roman Catholics living within the predominantly Protestant parish of Loughgall, the village where the Orange Order was founded in 1795" (a unionist, anti-Catholic fraternal organization). Despite inheriting strong Republican sympathies, he depicts the Catholic Church unsympathetically, even going so far as to state that there is "a very fine line between organized religion and organized crime." His skepticism toward the nationalist extremism of the Irish Republican Army is evident in the wryly psychoanalytic poem "Anseo," which traces an IRA fighter's violent ways back to the violence inflicted on him by a cruel primary school teacher.

Muldoon was educated at the primary school in Collegelands (where his mother taught); St. Patrick's College, Armagh; and Queen's University, Belfast, where he was tutored by Seamus Heaney and came to know other poets of the "Belfast Group," such as Derek Mahon and Michael Longley. He worked as a radio and television producer for the British Broadcasting Corporation in Belfast until, in the mid-1980s, he became a freelance writer and moved to the United States, where he teaches at Princeton University. He was elected the Oxford Professor of Poetry, a post he held from 1999 to 2004, and he was the poetry editor of *The New Yorker* from 2007 to 2017.

Muldoon's first published poems were written in Irish, and although he soon switched to English, Irish words and phrases, such as "Anseo," continued to appear in his work. Like other Irish poets, he has had to contend with the long shadow cast by W. B. Yeats. In "7, Middagh Street," Muldoon quotes Yeats's agonizing worry, in his late poem "Man and the Echo," that his art may have helped inspire the executed leaders of the Easter Rising of 1916: "Did that play of mine send out / Certain men the English shot?" In Muldoon's poem, the characteristically irreverent answer, spoken by W. H. Auden, is "'Certainly not'. // If Yeats had saved his pencil-lead / would certain men have stayed in bed?" Muldoon is more circumspect than Yeats about the power of art to alter the course of history. Informed by his postmodern skepticism about language, his approach to the Irish Troubles is also more oblique and ironic than that of his tutor, Seamus Heaney. In "Anseo" and "Turtles," among his many poems that eerily skew the form of the sonnet, he deploys multiple screens of irony to tell sly parables about the relation of language to history, of art to violence, especially of the Irish Troubles (for more on the Troubles, see the "Imagining Ireland" topic in the NAEL Archive).

As with many other Irish poets, the United States soon loomed large in Muldoon's imagination. Excited by American films, he adapted cinematic techniques in long, hectic, hallucinatory poems. Other poems, such as "Meeting the British," parallel the plight of Native Americans with that of Northern Irish Catholics. Still others, such as "The Loaf," vigorously play on refrain, rhyme, and other repetitive formal structures to recall the sad history of Irish laborers in the United States. His earliest literary influence was, he said, Robert Frost's "strong, classic, lyric line. But the most important thing . . . was his mischievous, sly, multi-layered quality under the surface." It would be hard to improve on that last sentence as a description of Muldoon's own style, the expression of an omnivorous imagination that—in "Milkweed and Monarch," for example—mixes sensations at his parents' Collegelands grave with geographically scattered memories into a kaleidoscopic pattern that is at once moving, musically satisfying, and a brilliant postmodern variation on the poetic form of the villanelle (with the repetition of its first and third lines).

Anseo

When the Master was calling the roll
At the primary school in Collegelands,[1]
You were meant to call back *Anseo*
And raise your hand
5   As your name occurred.
Anseo, meaning here, here and now,
All present and correct,

---

1. Village in Northern Ireland where Muldoon went to school and his mother taught.

Was the first word of Irish I spoke.
The last name on the ledger
10   Belonged to Joseph Mary Plunkett Ward[2]
And was followed, as often as not,
By silence, knowing looks,
A nod and a wink, the Master's droll
'And where's our little Ward-of-court?'[3]

15   I remember the first time he came back
The Master had sent him out
Along the hedges
To weigh up for himself and cut
A stick with which he would be beaten.
20   After a while, nothing was spoken;
He would arrive as a matter of course
With an ash-plant, a salley-rod.[4]
Or, finally, the hazel-wand
He had whittled down to a whip-lash,
25   Its twist of red and yellow lacquers
Sanded and polished,
And altogether so delicately wrought
That he had engraved his initials on it.

I last met Joseph Mary Plunkett Ward
30   In a pub just over the Irish border.
He was living in the open,
In a secret camp
On the other side of the mountain.
He was fighting for Ireland,
35   Making things happen.
And he told me, Joe Ward,
Of how he had risen through the ranks
To Quartermaster, Commandant:
How every morning at parade
42   His volunteers would call back *Anseo*
And raise their hands
As their names occurred.

1980

Meeting the British

We met the British in the dead of winter.
The sky was lavender

---

2. Named after Joseph Mary Plunkett (1887–1916), one of the rebel leaders of the Easter Rising of 1916, executed for his role in planning the rebellion against British rule.
3. A minor under the care of a court-appointed guardian.
4. Stick made from a willow tree. "Ash-plant": stick or whip made from a sapling of the ash tree.

and the snow lavender-blue.
I could hear, far below,

5   the sound of two streams coming together
(both were frozen over)

and, no less strange,
myself calling out in French

across that forest-
10 clearing. Neither General Jeffrey Amherst[1]

nor Colonel Henry Bouquet
could stomach our willow-tobacco.

As for the unusual
scent when the Colonel shook out his hand-

15 kerchief: *C'est la lavande,*
une fleur mauve comme le ciel.[2]

They gave us six fishhooks
and two blankets embroidered with smallpox.

1987

From 7, Middagh Street

From *Wystan*[1]

*   *   *

And were Yeats living at this hour
65 it should be in some ruined tower

not malachited Ballylee[2]
where he paid out to those below

one gilt-edged scroll from his pencil
as though he were part-Rapunzel

1. Commander-in-chief of British forces in the French and Indian War (1754–63); fought against France and its Native American allies. During Pontiac's Rebellion (1763–64), led by Ottawa chief Pontiac in the Great Lakes region, Amherst wrote to the British officer Colonel Bouquet, "Could it not be contrived to Send the *Small Pox* among those Disaffected Tribes of Indians?" Bouquet replied, "I will try to inocculate [i.e., infect] the Indians by means of Blanketts that may fall in their hands, taking care however not to get the disease myself," to which Amherst responded, "You will Do well to try to Innoculate the Indians by means of Blanketts, as well as to try Every other method that can serve to Extirpate this Execreble Race." Apparently as a result of this and similar plans of other British officers, many Native Americans in the area, never having been exposed to smallpox, were killed by the disease in 1763–64. Pontiac concluded a peace treaty with the British in July 1766.

2. It is lavender, a flower purple as the sky (French).

1. This long poem is spoken in various voices, including this selection from "Wystan," first name of the Anglo-American poet W. H. Auden (1907–1973), whose periodic Brooklyn Heights address is the title of the poem.

2. The ancient Norman tower that the Irish poet W. B. Yeats (1865–1939) purchased and lived in. "Malachited": of a deep green color.

70 and partly Delphic oracle.[3]
As for his crass, rhetorical

posturing, 'Did that play of mine
send out certain men (*certain* men?)

the English shot . . . ?[4]
75 the answer is 'Certainly not'.

If Yeats had saved his pencil-lead
would certain men have stayed in bed?

For history's a twisted root
with art its small, translucent fruit

80 and never the other way round.
The roots by which we were once bound

are severed here, in any case,
and we are all now dispossessed;

prince, poet, construction worker,
85 salesman, soda fountain jerker—

all equally isolated.
Each loads flour, sugar and salted

beef into a covered wagon
and strikes out for his Oregon,

90 each straining for the ghostly axe
of a huge, blond-haired lumberjack.

*   *   *

1987

Milkweed and Monarch

As he knelt by the grave of his mother and father
the taste of dill, or tarragon—
he could barely tell one from the other—

filled his mouth. It seemed as if he might smother.
5 Why should he be stricken
with grief, not for his mother and father,

3. In ancient Greece, a cave and shrine where a priestess supposedly under a god's influence gave riddling answers to questions brought by worshipers. "Rapunzel": fairy-tale character imprisoned in a tower who let down her long hair for her rescuer to climb.

4. From Yeats's poem "Man and the Echo" (see p. 240), in which he worries that his nationalist play *Cathleen ni Houlihan* (1902) helped inspire the violent Easter 1916 uprising against British rule.

but a woman slinking from the fur of a sea-otter
in Portland, Maine, or, yes, Portland, Oregon—
he could barely tell one from the other—

10 and why should he now savour
the tang of her, her little pickled gherkin,
as he knelt by the grave of his mother and father?

•

He looked about. He remembered her palaver°   *beguiling talk*
on how both earth and sky would darken—
15 "You could barely tell one from the other"—

while the Monarch butterflies passed over
in their milkweed-hunger:[1] "A wing-beat, some reckon,
may trigger off the mother and father

of all storms, striking your Irish Cliffs of Moher
20 with the force of a hurricane."
Then: "Milkweed and Monarch 'invented' each other."

•

He looked about. Cow's-parsley in a samovar.[2]
He'd mistaken his mother's name, "Regan", for "Anger":
as he knelt by the grave of his mother and father
25 he could barely tell one from the other.

1994

The Loaf

When I put my finger to the hole they've cut for a dimmer switch
in a wall of plaster stiffened with horsehair
it seems I've scratched a two-hundred-year-old itch

with a pink and a pink and a pinkie-pick.

5 When I put my ear to the hole I'm suddenly aware
of spades and shovels turning up the gain°   *volume*
all the way from Raritan to the Delaware[1]

with a clink and a clink and a clinky-click.

When I put my nose to the hole I smell the floodplain
10 of the canal after a hurricane
and the spots of green grass where thousands of Irish have lain

with a stink and a stink and a stinky-stick.

---

1. The monarch butterfly's larvae appear to eat only milkweed.
2. Russian tea urn.
1. The Delaware and Raritan Canal was hand-built by Irish immigrants between 1830 and 1834, providing a route from Philadelphia to New York City. During its construction, many Irish laborers died of Asiatic cholera. Muldoon's house in New Jersey was built around 1750.

When I put my eye to the hole I see one holding horse dung to the rain
in the hope, indeed, indeed,
15 of washing out a few whole ears of grain

with a wink and a wink and a winkie-wick.

And when I do at last succeed
in putting my mouth to the horsehair-fringed niche
I can taste the small loaf of bread he baked from that whole seed

20 *with a link and a link and a linky-lick.*

2002

Turtles

A cubit-wide turtle acting the bin[1] lid
by the side of the canal
conjures those Belfast[2] nights I lay awake, putting in a bid
for the police channel
5 as lid bangers gave the whereabouts
of armored cars and petrol° bombers lit one flare   *gasoline*
after another. So many of those former sentries and scouts
have now taken up the lyre[3]
I can't be sure of what is and what is not.
10 The water, for example, has the look of tin.
Nor am I certain, given their ability to smell the rot
once the rot sets in,
that turtles have not been enlisted by some police forces
to help them recover corpses.

2006

1. Garbage can. "Cubit": ancient measure of length approximately equal to the forearm, or between 18 and 22 inches.
2. Capital of Northern Ireland and a site, from the 1970s, of violent sectarian conflict (known as "the Troubles") between Protestants and Catholics.
3. Stringed instrument similar to a harp; a symbol of lyric poetry.

HILARY MANTEL
b. 1952

Hilary Mantel was born and grew up in villages in Derbyshire and Cheshire, in the north of England, near greater Manchester. Her parents were struggling Irish Catholic immigrants, a textile worker and a clerk. She was a deeply religious student at convent schools, though by the age of twelve, she had lost her faith. After she studied law at the London School of Economics and the University of Sheffield, she was first employed as a social work assistant at a geriatric hospital and, after a year, as a sales assistant selling dresses in a department store where she began to write. With her husband, a geologist, she lived in Botswana for five years (1977–82) and Saudi Arabia for four (1983–86). Her ongoing and severe endometriosis was first misdiagnosed as psychosomatic. She has described her struggle with the painful disease in a memoir, *Giving up the Ghost* (2003), and illness and alienation from the body have been frequent concerns in her fiction.

Mantel was the first English novelist and the first woman to become a two-time winner of Britain's most prestigious award for fiction, the Man Booker Prize. The awards were for her historical novels written from the perspective of Thomas Cromwell, Henry VIII's key counselor: *Wolf Hall* (2009) and *Bring up the Bodies* (2012), the first two books of a projected trilogy. By the time she received these prizes and the National Book Critics Circle Award, she had already published novels in various genres in a wide range of settings and time periods, from revolutionary France and eighteenth-century England to contemporary southern Africa and Saudi Arabia. Despite their variety, all these novels draw, perhaps not surprisingly, on facets of Mantel's life. Written in Saudi Arabia, her first two published novels, *Every Day Is Mother's Day* (1985) and *Vacant Possession* (1986), are black comedies that made use of her experience in social work. In the thriller *Eight Months on Ghazzah Street* (1988), cross-cultural tensions erupt after an Englishwoman moves to Saudi Arabia. The theological mystery *Fludd* (1989) casts a critical eye on Roman Catholicism in 1950s England. Although it wasn't published until 1992, *A Place of Greater Safety* was the first novel Mantel wrote—a historical novel centered on three figures in the French Revolution who, she has suggested, reflected her youthful idealism. *A Change of Climate* (1994) tells the tragic story of an English missionary couple in southern Africa. *An Experiment in Love* (1995) concerns strained friendships among classmates who end up together at the University of London. *The Giant, O'Brien* (1998) describes an unusually large Irishman (and endometriosis had greatly enlarged Mantel's body) who only briefly fascinates eighteenth-century England. *Beyond Black* (2005) concerns a medium with a powerful memory and perhaps novelistic imagination who travels with her manager through the English suburbs.

Despite the autobiographical traces in her work, Mantel is uncannily able to inhabit minds and social worlds vastly distant from her own, perhaps nowhere more so than in her Thomas Cromwell novels. As a result, she can bring to life a sixteenth-century counselor as a multidimensional character, though Cromwell had been represented by other writers as a cardboard villain. Even with his execution of Henry VIII's perceived enemies, including Thomas More and Anne Boleyn, the shrewd and wily strategist becomes sympathetic in Mantel's retelling. Having grown up in poverty with an abusive father, he makes himself—by virtue of cunning, intelligence, and exacting observation—one of the most powerful and consequential figures of the English Renaissance. The complexity of Mantel's characters, her brilliant use of dialogue, her deft construction of dramatic scenes, and her fascination with historical detail suggest the abiding impression that Shakespeare made on her in childhood. She has said that, having only been exposed to snippets of his work, "I almost exploded with joy when I found there was a whole fat book of plays."

The immense historical and cultural differences between the Tudor court in Mantel's historical novels and the world of her semiautobiographical short story "Sorry to Disturb"—Jeddah, Saudi Arabia, as experienced by a budding English novelist in the 1980s—is a measure of Mantel's range. Yet from Mantel's perspective, these worlds are not entirely unlike. She has compared the limits on free expression and the consequent reliance on rumor in both Tudor England and 1980s Saudi Arabia, and in Mantel's telling, women in both worlds find themselves confined and trapped, even under conditions of relative affluence. "Sorry to Disturb" revolves around the misunderstandings between an English narrator and a South Asian businessman who regularly visits her coffinlike apartment. At first it seems as if he might provide a welcome diversion, but their encounters become increasingly vexed as he projects on her certain ideas about the British and other Westerners. She finds herself wanting, as she puts it, to "bear out the national character he had given me," yet also to deflect his gender assumptions. The layering of English with Saudi and South Asian cultural worlds, of fictional narration with dialogue and diary entries, of realist social observation with surreal hints and evocative figurative language (insecticide falling "like bright mists, veils"), all contribute to the making of a rich story. Mantel's tale demonstrates her abiding ability to write her way into the vulnerability of the outsider, to illuminate the constraints endured by women in various centuries and cultures, and to vivify the lived experience of religious and cultural friction, whether in sixteenth-century England or in the contemporary Persian Gulf.

Sorry to Disturb

In those days, the doorbell didn't ring often, and if it did I would draw back into the body of the house. Only at a persistent ring would I creep over the carpets, and make my way to the front door with its spy hole. We were big on bolts and shutters, deadlocks and mortises, safety chains and windows that were high and barred. Through the spy hole I saw a distraught man in a crumpled, silver-gray suit: thirties, Asian. He had dropped back from the door, and was looking about him, at the closed and locked door opposite, and up the dusty marble stairs. He patted his pockets, took out a balled-up handkerchief, and rubbed it across his face. He looked so fraught that his sweat could have been tears. I opened the door.

At once he raised his hands as if to show he was unarmed, his handkerchief dropping like a white flag. "Madam!" Ghastly pale I must have looked, under the light that dappled the tiled walls with swinging shadows. But then he took a breath, tugged at his creased jacket, ran a hand through his hair and conjured up his business card. "Muhammad Ijaz. Import-Export. I am so sorry to disturb your afternoon. I am totally lost. Would you permit use of your telephone?"

I stood aside to let him in. No doubt I smiled. Given what would ensue, I must suppose I did. "Of course. If it's working today."

I walked ahead and he followed, talking; an important deal, he had almost closed it, visit to client in person necessary, time—he worked up his sleeve and consulted a fake Rolex—time running out; he had the address—again he patted his pockets—but the office is not where it should be. He spoke into the telephone in rapid Arabic, fluent, aggressive, his eyebrows shooting up, finally shaking his head; he put down the receiver, looked at it in regret; then up at me, with a sour smile. Weak mouth, I thought. Almost a handsome man, but not: slim, sallow, easily thrown. "I am in your debt, madam," he said. "Now I must dash."

I wanted to offer him a what—bathroom break? Comfort stop? I had no idea how to phrase it. The absurd phrase *wash and brushup* came into my mind. But he was already heading for the door—though from the way the call had concluded I thought they might not be so keen to see him, at his destination, as he was to see them. "This crazy city," he said. "They are always digging up the streets and moving them. I am so sorry to break in on your privacy." In the hall, he darted another glance around and up the stairs. "Only the British will ever help you." He skidded across the hall and prized open the outer door with its heavy ironwork screen; admitting, for a moment, the dull roar of traffic from Medina Road. The door swung back, he was gone. I closed the hall door discreetly, and melted into the oppressive hush. The air conditioner rattled away, like an old relative with a loose cough. The air was heavy with insecticide; sometimes I sprayed it as I walked, and it fell about me like bright mists, veils. I resumed my phrasebook and tape, Fifth Lesson: *I'm living in Jeddah.*[1] *I'm busy today. God give you strength!*

When my husband came home in the afternoon I told him: "A lost man was here. Pakistani. Businessman. I let him in to phone."

My husband was silent. The air conditioner hacked away. He walked into the shower, having evicted the cockroaches. Walked out again, dripping, naked, lay on the bed, stared at the ceiling. Next day I swept the business card into a bin.

In the afternoon the doorbell rang again. Ijaz had come back, to apologize, to explain, to thank me for rescuing him. I made him some instant coffee and he sat down and told me about himself.

It was then June 1983. I had been in Saudi Arabia for six months. My husband worked for a Toronto-based company of consulting geologists, and had been seconded[2] by them to the Ministry of Mineral Resources. Most of his colleagues were housed in family "compounds" of various sizes, but the single men and a childless couple like ourselves had to take what they could get. This was our second flat. The American bachelor who had occupied it before had been moved out in haste. Upstairs, in this block of four flats, lived a Saudi civil servant with his wife and baby; the fourth flat was empty; on the ground floor across the hall from us lived a Pakistani accountant who worked for a government minister, handling his personal finances. Meeting the womenfolk in the hall or on the stairs—one blacked-out head to toe, one partly veiled—the bachelor had livened up their lives by calling "Hello!" Or possibly "Hi there!"

There was no suggestion of further impertinence. But a complaint had been made, and he vanished, and we went to live there instead. The flat was small by Saudi standards. It had beige carpet and off-white wallpaper on which there was a faint crinkled pattern, almost indiscernible. The windows were guarded by heavy wooden shutters that you cranked down by turning a handle on the inside. Even with the shutters up it was dim and I needed the strip lights on all day. The rooms were closed off from each other by double doors of dark wood, heavy like coffin lids. It was like living in a funeral home, with samples stacked around you, and insect opportunists frying themselves on the lights.

He was a graduate of a Miami business school, Ijaz said, and his business, his main business just now, was bottled water. Had the deal gone through, yesterday? He was evasive—obviously, there was nothing simple about it. He waved a hand—give it time, give it time.

I had no friends in this city as yet. Social life, such as it was, centered on private houses; there were no cinemas, theaters or lecture halls. There were sports grounds, but women could not attend them. No "mixed gatherings"

---

1. Saudi Arabian port city on the Red Sea and modern commercial hub.   2. Temporarily assigned.

were allowed. The Saudis did not mix with foreign workers. They looked down on them as necessary evils, though white-skinned, English-speaking expatriates were at the top of the pecking order. Others—Ijaz, for example— were "Third Country Nationals," a label that exposed them to every kind of truculence, insult and daily complication. Indians and Pakistanis staffed the shops and small businesses. Filipinos worked on building sites. Men from Thailand cleaned the streets. Bearded Yemenis sat on the pavement outside lock-up shops, their skirts rucked up, their hairy legs thrust out, their flip-flops inches from the whizzing cars.

I am married, Ijaz said, and to an American; you must meet her. Maybe, he said, maybe you could do something for her, you know? What I foresaw at best was the usual Jeddah arrangement, of couples shackled together. Women had no motive power in this city; they had no driving licenses, and only the rich had drivers. So couples who wanted to visit must do it together. I didn't think Ijaz and my husband would be friends. Ijaz was too restless and nervy. He laughed at nothing. He was always twitching his collar and twisting his feet in their scuffed Oxfords,[3] always tapping the fake Rolex, always apologiz-ing. Our apartment is down by the port, he said, with my sister-in-law and my brother, but he's back in Miami just now, and my mother's here just now for a visit, and my wife from America, and my son and my daughter, aged six, aged eight. He reached for his wallet and showed me a strange-looking, steeple-headed little boy. "Saleem."

When he left, he thanked me again for trusting him to come into my house. Why, he said, he might have been anybody. But it is not the British way to think badly of needy strangers. At the door he shook my hand. That's that, I thought. Part of me thought, it had better be.

For one was always observed: overlooked, without precisely being seen, rec-ognized. My Pakistani neighbor Yasmin, to get between my flat and hers, would fling a scarf over her rippling hair, then peep around the door; with nervous, pecking movements she hopped across the marble, head swiveling from side to side, in case someone should choose that very moment to shoul-der through the heavy street door. Sometimes, irritated by the dust that blew under the door and banked up on the marble, I would go out into the hall with a long broom. My male Saudi neighbor would come down from the first floor on his way out to his car and step over my brushstrokes without looking at me, his head averted. He was according me invisibility, as a mark of respect to another man's wife.

I was not sure that Ijaz accorded me this respect. Our situation was anom-alous and ripe for misunderstanding: I had an afternoon caller. He probably thought that only the kind of woman who took a lot of risks with herself would let a stranger into her house. Yet I could not guess what he probably thought. Surely a Miami business school, surely his time in the West, had made my attitude seem more normal than not? His talk was relaxed now he knew me, full of feeble jokes that he laughed at himself; but then there was the jiggling of his foot, the pulling of his collar, the tapping of his fingers. I had noticed, listening to my tape, that his situation was anticipated in the Nineteenth Lesson: *I gave the address to my driver, but when we arrived, there wasn't any house at this address.* I hoped to show by my brisk friendliness

3. Dress shoes.

what was only the truth, that our situation could be simple, because I felt no attraction to him at all; so little that I felt apologetic about it. That is where it began to go wrong—my feeling that I must bear out the national character he had given me, and that I must not slight him or refuse a friendship, in case he thought it was because he was a Third Country National.

For his second visit, and his third, were an interruption, almost an irritation. Having no choice in that city, I had decided to cherish my isolation, coddle it. I was ill in those days, and subject to a fierce drug regime that gave me blinding headaches, made me slightly deaf and made me, though I was hungry, unable to eat. The drugs were expensive and had to be imported from England; my husband's company brought them in by courier. Word of this leaked out, and the company wives decided I was taking fertility drugs; but I did not know this, and my ignorance made our conversations peculiar and, to me, slightly menacing. Why were they always talking, on the occasions of forced company sociability, about women who'd had miscarriages but now had a bouncing babe in the buggy? An older woman confided that her two were adopted; I looked at them and thought Jesus, where from, the zoo? My Pakistani neighbour also joined in the cooing over the offspring that I would have shortly—she was in on the rumors, but I put her hints down to the fact that she was carrying her first child and wanted company. I saw her most mornings for an interval of coffee and chat, and I would rather steer her to talking about Islam, which was easy enough; she was an educated woman and keen to instruct. June 6th: "Spent two hours with my neighbor," says my diary, "widening the cultural gap."

Next day, my husband brought home air tickets and my exit visa for our first home leave, which was seven weeks away. Thursday, June 9th: "Found a white hair in my head." At home there was a general election, and we sat up through the night to listen to the results on the BBC World Service. When we turned out the light, the grocer's daughter jigged through my dreams to the strains of "Lillibulero."[4] Friday was a holiday, and we slept undisturbed till the noon prayer call. Ramadan[5] began. Wednesday, June 15th: "Read *The Twyborn Affair*[6] and vomited sporadically."

On the sixteenth our neighbors across the hall left for pilgrimage, robed in white. They rang our doorbell before they left: "Is there anything we can bring you from Mecca?"[7] June 19th saw me desperate for change, moving the furniture around the sitting room and recording "not much improvement." I write that I am prey to "unpleasant and intrusive thoughts," but I do not say what they are. I describe myself as "hot, sick and morose." By July 4th I must have been happier, because I listened to the *Eroica*[8] while doing the ironing. But on the morning of July 10th, I got up first, put the coffee on, and went into the sitting room to find that the furniture had been trying to move itself back. An armchair was leaning to the left, as if executing some tipsy dance; at one side its base rested on the carpet, but the other side was a foot in the air, and balanced finely on the rim of a flimsy wastepaper basket. Open-mouthed, I shot back into the bedroom; it

---

4. March associated with the English Civil War (1642–51).
5. Islamic holy month of fasting, introspection, and prayer. "Noon prayer": Muslims typically pray at five designated times each day
6. Novel (1979) by Australian writer Patrick

White (1912–1990).
7. Birthplace of Muhammad and Islam's holiest city. All able Muslims are expected to make pilgrimage to Mecca at some point in their lives.
8. Third symphony by German composer Ludwig van Beethoven (1770–1827).

was the Eid holiday,[9] and my husband was still half awake. I gibbered at him. Silent, he rose, put on his glasses, and followed me. He stood in the doorway of the sitting room. He looked around and told me without hesitation it had nothing to do with him. He walked into the bathroom. I heard him close the door, curse the cockroaches, switch on the shower. I said later, I must be walking in my sleep. Do you think that's it? Do you think I did it? July 12th: "Execution dream again."

The trouble was, Ijaz knew I was at home; how would I be going anywhere? One afternoon I left him standing in the hall, while he pressed and pressed the doorbell, and next time, when I let him in, he asked me where I had been; when I said, "Ah, sorry, I must have been with my neighbor," I could see he did not believe me, and he looked at me so sorrowfully that my heart went out to him. Jeddah fretted him, it galled him, and he missed, he said, America, he missed his visits to London, he must go soon, take a break; when was our leave, perhaps we might meet up? I explained I did not live in London, which surprised him; he seemed to suspect it was an evasion, like my failure to answer the door. "Because I could get an exit visa," he said again. "Meet up there. Without all this . . ." he gestured at the coffin-lid doors, the heavy, willful furniture.

He made me laugh that day, telling me about his first girlfriend, his American girlfriend whose nickname was Patches. It was easy to picture her, sassy and suntanned, astonishing him one day by pulling off her top, bouncing her bare breasts at him and putting an end to his wan virginity. The fear he felt, the terror of touching her . . . his shameful performance . . . recalling it, he knuckled his forehead. I was charmed, I suppose. How often does a man tell you these things? I told my husband, hoping to make him laugh, but he didn't. Often, to be helpful, I hoovered up the cockroaches before his return from the Ministry. He shed his clothes and headed off. I heard the splash of the shower. Nineteenth Lesson: *Are you married? Yes, my wife is with me, she's standing there in the corner of the room.* I imagined the cockroaches, dark and flailing in the dust bag.

I went back to the dining table, on which I was writing a comic novel. It was a secret activity I never mentioned to the company wives, and barely mentioned to myself. I scribbled under the strip light, until it was time to drive out for food shopping. You had to shop between sunset prayers and night prayers; if you mistimed it, then at the first prayer call the shops slammed down their shutters, trapping you inside, or outside in the wet heat of the car park. The malls were patrolled by volunteers from the Committee for the Propagation of Virtue and the Elimination of Vice.

At the end of July Ijaz brought his family for tea. Mary-Beth was a small woman but seemed swollen beneath the skin; spiritless, freckled, limp, she was a faded redhead who seemed huddled into herself, unused to conversation. A silent daughter with eyes like dark stars had been trussed up for the visit in a frilly white dress. At six, steeple-headed Saleem had lost his baby fat, and his movements were tentative, as if his limbs were snappable. His eyes were watchful; Mary-Beth hardly met my gaze at all. What had Ijaz told her? That he was taking her to see a woman who was something like he'd like her to be? It was an unhappy afternoon. I can only have got through it because I was buoyed by an uprush of anticipation; my bags were packed

9. Feast day marking the end of Ramadan.

for our flight home. A day earlier, when I had gone into the spare room where I kept my clothes, I had met another dismaying sight. The doors of the fitted wardrobe, which were large and solid like the other coffin lids, had been removed from their hinges; they had been replaced, but hung by the lower hinges only, so that their upper halves flapped like the wings of some ramshackle flying machine.

On August 1st we left King Abdulaziz International Airport in an electrical storm, and had a bumpy flight. I was curious about Mary-Beth's situation and hoped to see her again, though another part of me hoped that she and Ijaz would simply vanish.

I didn't return to Jeddah till the very end of November, having left my book with an agent. Just before our leave I had met my Saudi neighbor, a young mother taking a part-time literature course at the women's university. Education for women was regarded as a luxury, an ornament, a way for a husband to boast of his broadmindedness; Munira couldn't even begin to do her assignments, and I took to going up to her flat in the late mornings and doing them for her, while she sat on the floor in her négligée, watching Egyptian soaps on TV and eating sunflower seeds. We three women, Yasmin and Munira and I, had become midmorning friends; all the better for them to watch me, I thought, and discuss me when I'm gone. It was easier for Yasmin and me to go upstairs, because to come down Munira had to get kitted out in full veil and abaya;[1] again, that treacherous, hovering moment on the public territory of the staircase, where a man might burst through from the street and shout "Hi!" Yasmin was a delicate woman, like a princess in a Persian miniature; younger than myself, she was impeccably soignée,[2] finished with a flawless glaze of good manners and restraint. Munira was nineteen, with coarse, eager good looks, a pale skin, and a mane of hair that crackled with static and seemed to lead a vital, separate life; her laugh was a raucous cackle. She and Yasmin sat on cushions but gave me a chair; they insisted. They served Nescafé in my honor, though I would have preferred a sludgy local brew. I had learned the crude effectiveness of caffeine against migraine; some nights, sleepless, pacing, I careened off the walls, and only the dawn prayer call sent me to bed, still thinking furiously of books I might write.

Ijaz rang the doorbell on December 6th. He was so very pleased to see me after my long leave; beaming, he said, "Now you are more like Patches than ever." I felt a flare of alarm; nothing, nothing had been said about this before. I was slimmer, he said, and looked well—my prescription drugs had been cut down, and I had been exposed to some daylight, I supposed that was what was doing it. But, "No, there is something different about you," he said. One of the company wives had said the same. She thought, no doubt, that I had conceived my baby at last.

I led Ijaz into the sitting room, while he trailed me with compliments, and made the coffee. "Maybe it's my book," I said, sitting down. "You see, I've written a book . . ." My voice tailed off. This was not his world. No one read books in Jeddah. You could buy anything in the shops except alcohol or a bookcase. My neighbor Yasmin, though she was an English graduate, said she had never read a book since her marriage; she was too busy making supper parties

---

1. Full-body robe (Arabic).   2. Elegant (French).

every night. I have had a little success, I explained, or I hope for a little success, I have written a novel you see, and an agent has taken it on.

"It is a storybook? For children?"

"For adults."

"You did this during your vacation?"

"No, I was always writing it." I felt deceitful. I was writing it when I didn't answer the doorbell.

"Your husband will pay to have it published for you."

"No, with luck someone will pay me. A publisher. The agent hopes he can sell it."

"This agent, where did you meet him?"

I could hardly say, in the *Writers' & Artists' Yearbook*.[3] "In London. At his office."

"But you do not live in London," Ijaz said, as if laying down an ace. He was out to find something wrong with my story. "Probably he is no good. He may steal your money."

I saw of course that in his world, the term *agent* would cover some broad, unsavory categories. But what about "Import-Export," as written on his business cards? That didn't sound to me like the essence of probity. I wanted to argue; I was still upset about Patches; without warning, Ijaz seemed to have changed the terms of engagement between us. "I don't think so. I haven't given him money. His firm, it's well known." Their office is where? Ijaz sniffed, and I pressed on, trying to make my case; though why did I think that an office in William IV Street was a guarantee of moral worth? Ijaz knew London well. "Charing Cross tube?" He still looked affronted. "Near Trafalgar Square?"

Ijaz grunted. "You went to this premises alone?"

I couldn't placate him. I gave him a biscuit. I didn't expect him to understand what I was up to, but he seemed aggrieved that another man had entered my life. "How is Mary-Beth?" I asked.

"She has some kidney disease."

I was shocked. "Is it serious?"

He raised his shoulders; not a shrug, more a rotation of the joints, as if easing some old ache. "She must go back to America for treatment. It's okay. I'm getting rid of her anyway."

I looked away. I hadn't imagined this. "I'm sorry you're unhappy."

"You see really I don't know what's the matter with her," he said testily. "She is always miserable and moping."

"You know, this is not the easiest place for a woman to live."

But did he know? Irritated, he said, "She wanted a big car. So I got a big car. What more does she want me to do?"

December 6th: "Ijaz stayed too long," the diary says. Next day he was back. After the way he had spoken of his wife—and the way he had compared me to dear old Patches from his Miami days—I didn't think I should see him again. But he had hatched a scheme and he wasn't going to let it go. I should come to a dinner party with my husband and meet his family and some of his business contacts. He had been talking about this project before my leave and I knew he set great store by it. I wanted, if I could, to do him some good; he would appear to his customers to be more a man of the world if he could arrange an international gathering, if—let's be blunt—he could

---

3. British directory for aspiring writers.

produce some white friends. Now the time had come. His sister-in-law was already cooking, he said. I wanted to meet her; I admired these diaspora Asians, their polyglot enterprise, the way they withstood rebuffs, and I wanted to see if she was more Western or Eastern or what. "We have to arrange the transportation," Ijaz said. "I shall come Thursday, when your husband is here. Four o'clock. To give him directions." I nodded. No use drawing a map. They might move the streets again.

The meeting of December 8th was not a success. Ijaz was late, but didn't seem to know it. My husband dispensed the briefest host's courtesies, then sat down firmly in his armchair, which was the one that had tried to levitate. He seemed, by his watchful silence, ready to put an end to any nonsense, from furniture or guests or any other quarter. Sitting on the edge of the sofa, Ijaz flaked his baklava over his lap, he juggled with his fork and jiggled his coffee cup. After our dinner party, he said, almost the next day, he was flying to America on business. "I shall route via London. Just for some recreation. Just to relax, three–four days."

My husband must have stirred himself to ask if he had friends there. "Very old friend," Ijaz said, brushing crumbs to the carpet. "Living at Trafalgar Square. A good district. You know it?"

My heart sank; it was a physical feeling, of the months falling away from me, months in which I'd had little natural light. When Ijaz left—and he kept hovering on the threshold, giving further and better street directions—I didn't know what to say, so I went into the bathroom, kicked out the cockroaches and cowered under the stream of tepid water. Wrapped in a towel, I lay on the bed in the dark. I could hear my husband—I hoped it was he, and not the armchair—moving around in the sitting room. Sometimes in those days when I closed my eyes I felt that I was looking back into my own skull. I could see the hemispheres of my brain. They were convoluted and the color of putty.

The family apartment down by the port was filled with cooking smells and crammed with furniture. There were photographs on every surface, carpets laid on carpets. It was a hot night, and the air conditioners labored and hacked, spitting out water, coughing up lungfuls of mold spores, blights. The table linen was limp and heavily fringed, and I kept fingering these fringes, which felt like nylon fur, like the ears of a teddy bear; they comforted me, though I felt electric with tension. At the table a vast lumpen elder presided, a woman with a long chomping jaw; she was like Quentin Matsys's Ugly Duchess,[4] except in a spangled sari. The sister-in-law was a bright, brittle woman, who gave a sarcastic lilt to all her phrases. I could see why; it was evident, from her knowing looks, that Ijaz had talked about me, and set me up in some way; if he was proposing me as his next wife, I offered little improvement on the original. Her scorn became complete when she saw I barely touched the food at my elbow; I kept smiling and nodding, demurring and deferring, nibbling a parsley leaf and sipping my Fanta. I wanted to eat, but she might as well have offered me stones on a doily. Did Ijaz think, as the Saudis did, that Western marriages meant nothing? That they were entered impulsively and on impulse broken? Did he assume my husband was as keen

---

4. Satirical portrait by the Flemish artist Quentin Matsys (1466–1530), also referred to as *A Grotesque Old Woman*.

to offload me as he was to lose Mary-Beth? From his point of view the evening was not going well. He had expected two supermarket managers, he told us, important men with spending power; now night prayers were over, the traffic was on the move again, all down Palestine Road and along the Corniche[5] the traffic lights were turning green, from Thumb Street to the Pepsi flyover[6] the city was humming, but where were they? Sweat dripped from his face. Fingers jabbed the buttons of the telephone. "Okay, he is delayed? He has left? He is coming now?" He rapped down the receiver, then gazed at the phone as if willing it to chirp back at him, like some pet fowl. "Time means nothing here," he joked, pulling at his collar. The sister-in-law shrugged and turned down her mouth. She never rested, but passed airily through the room in peach chiffon, each time returning from the kitchen with another laden tray; out of sight, presumably, some oily skivvy[7] was weeping into the dishes. The silent elder put away a large part of the food, pulling the plates toward her and working through them systematically till the pattern showed beneath her questing fingers; you looked away, and when you looked back the plate was clean. Sometimes, the phone rang: "Okay, they're nearly here," Ijaz called. Ten minutes, and his brow furrowed again. "Maybe they're lost."

"Sure they're lost," sister-in-law sang. She sniggered; she was enjoying herself. Nineteenth Lesson, translate these sentences: *So long as he holds the map the wrong way up, he will never find the house. They started traveling this morning, but have still not arrived.* It seemed a hopeless business, trying to get anywhere, and the textbook confessed it. I was not really learning Arabic, of course, I was too impatient; I was leafing through the lessons, looking for phrases that might be useful if I could say them. We stayed long, long into the evening, waiting for the men who had never intended to come; in the end, wounded and surly, Ijaz escorted us to the door. I heard my husband take in a breath of wet air. "We'll never have to do it again," I consoled him. In the car, "You have to feel for him," I said. No answer.

December 13th: My diary records that I am oppressed by "the darkness, the ironing and the smell of drains." I could no longer play my *Eroica* tape as it had twisted itself up in the innards of the machine. In my idle moments I had summarized forty chapters of *Oliver Twist*[8] for the use of my upstairs neighbor. Three days later I was "horribly unstable and restless," and reading the *Lyttelton/Hart-Davis Letters.*[9] Later that week I was cooking with my neighbor Yasmin. I recorded "an afternoon of graying pain." All the same, Ijaz was out of the country and I realized I breathed easier when I was not anticipating the ring of the doorbell. December 16th, I was reading *The Philosopher's Pupil*[1] and visiting my own student upstairs. Munira took my forty chapter summaries, flicked through them, yawned, and switched on the TV. "What is a workhouse?" I tried to explain about the English poor law, but her expression glazed; she had never heard of poverty. She yelled out for her servant, an ear-splitting yell, and the girl—a beaten-down Indonesian—brought in Munira's daughter for my diversion. A heavy, solemn child, she was beginning to walk, or stamp, under her own power, her hands flailing for a hold on the furniture. She would fall on her bottom with a grunt, haul herself up

5. Coastal resort area of Jeddah.
6. Overpass.
7. Low-ranking female domestic servant.
8. Novel (1838) by English writer Charles Dickens (1812–1870).
9. Correspondence between English literature
teacher George Lyttelton (1883–1962) and former student Rupert Hart-Davis (1907–1999), published in six volumes between 1978 and 1984.
1. Novel (1983) by Irish-born English writer Iris Murdoch (1919–1999).

again by clutching the sofa; the cushions slid away from her, she tumbled backward, banged on the floor her large head with its corkscrew curls, and lay there wailing. Munira laughed at her: "White nigger, isn't it?" She didn't get her flat nose from my side, she explained. Or those fat lips either. It's my husband's people, but of course, they're blaming me.

January 2nd 1984: We went to a dark little restaurant off Khalid bin Wahlid Street, where we were seated behind a lattice screen in the "family area." In the main part of the room men were dining with each other. The business of eating out was more a gesture than a pleasure; you would gallop through the meal, because without wine and its rituals there was nothing to slow it, and the waiters, who had no concept that a man and woman might eat together for more than sustenance, prided themselves on picking up your plate as soon as you had finished and slapping down another, and rushing you back onto the dusty street. That dusty orange glare, perpetual, like the lighting of a bad sci-fi film; the constant snarl and rumble of traffic; I had become afraid of traffic accidents, which were frequent, and every time we drove out at night I saw the gaping spaces beneath bridges and fly-overs; they seemed to me like amphitheaters in which the traffic's casualties enacted, flickering, their final moments. Sometimes, when I set foot outside the apartment, I started to shake. I blamed it on the drugs I was taking; the dose had been increased again. When I saw the other wives they didn't seem to be having these difficulties. They talked about paddling pools and former lives they had led in Hong Kong. They got up little souk[2] trips to buy jewelry, so that sliding on their scrawny tanned arms their bracelets clinked and chimed, like ice cubes knocking together. On Valentine's Day we went to a cheese party; you had to imagine the wine. I was bubbling with happiness; a letter had come from William IV Street, to tell me my novel had been sold. Spearing his Edam[3] with a cocktail stick, my husband's boss loomed over me: "Hubby tells me you're having a book published. That must be costing him a pretty penny."

Ijaz, I assumed, was still in America. After all, he had his marital affairs to sort out, as well as business. He doesn't reappear in the diary till March 17th, St. Patrick's Day, when I recorded, "Phone call, highly unwelcome." For politeness, I asked how business was; as ever, he was evasive. He had something else to tell me: "I've got rid of Mary-Beth. She's gone."

"What about the children?"

"Saleem is staying with me. The girl, it doesn't matter. She can have her if she wants."

"Ijaz, look, I must say good-bye. I hear the doorbell." What a lie.

"Who is it?"

What, did he think I could see through the wall? For a second I was so angry I forgot there was only a phantom at the door. "Perhaps my neighbor," I said meekly.

"See you soon," Ijaz said.

I decided that night I could no longer bear it. I did not feel I could bear even one more cup of coffee together. But I had no means of putting an end to it, and for this I excused myself, saying I had been made helpless by the society around me. I was not able to bring myself to speak to Ijaz directly. I still had no power in me to snub him. But the mere thought of him made

2. Open-air marketplace.   3. Dutch cheese.

me squirm inside with shame, at my own general cluelessness, and at the sad little lies he had told to misrepresent his life, and the situation into which we had blundered; I thought of the sister-in-law, her peach chiffon and her curled lip.

Next day when my husband came home I sat him down and instigated a conversation. I asked him to write to Ijaz and ask him not to call on me anymore, as I was afraid that the neighbors had noticed his visits and might draw the wrong conclusion: which, as he knew, could be dangerous to us all. My husband heard me out. You need not write much, I pleaded, he will get the point. I should be able to sort this out for myself, but I am not allowed to, it is beyond my power, or it seems to be. I heard my own voice, jangled, grating; I was doing what I had wriggled so hard to avoid, I was sheltering behind the mores of this society, off-loading the problem I had created for myself in a way that was feminine, weak and spiteful.

My husband saw all this. Not that he spoke. He got up, took his shower. He lay in the rattling darkness, in the bedroom where the wooden shutters blocked out the merest chink of afternoon glare. I lay beside him. The evening prayer call woke me from my doze. My husband had risen to write the letter. I remember the snap of the lock as he closed it in his briefcase.

I have never asked him what he put in the letter, but whatever it was it worked. There was nothing—not a chastened note pushed under the door, nor a regretful phone call. Just silence. The diary continues but Ijaz exits from it. I read *Zuckerman Unbound, The Present & The Past,* and *The Bottle Factory Outing.*[4] The company's post office box went missing, with all the incoming mail in it. You would think a post box was a fixed thing and wouldn't go wandering of its own volition, but it was many days before it was found, at a distant post office, and I suppose a post box can move if furniture can. We drifted toward our next leave. May 10th, we attended a farewell party for an escapee whose contract was up. "Fell over while dancing and sprained my ankle." May 11th: With my ankle strapped up, "watched *The Texas Chainsaw Massacre*."[5]

I had much more time to serve in Jeddah. I didn't leave finally till the spring of 1986. By that time we had been rehoused twice more, shuttled around the city and finally outside it to a compound off the freeway. I never heard of my visitor again. The woman trapped in the flat on the corner of Al-Suror Street seems a relative stranger, and I ask myself what she should have done, how she could have managed it better. She should have thrown those drugs away, for one thing; they are nowadays a medication of last resort, because everybody knows they make you frightened, deaf and sick. But about Ijaz? She should never have opened the door in the first place. Discretion is the better part of valor; she's always said that. Even after all this time it's hard to grasp exactly what happened. I try to write it as it occurred but I find myself changing the names to protect the guilty. I wonder if Jeddah left me forever off-kilter in some way, tilted from the vertical and condemned to see life skewed. I can never be certain that doors will stay closed and on their hinges, and I do not know, when I turn out the lights at night, whether the house is quiet as I left it or the furniture is frolicking in the dark.

2009, 2014

4. Novels by American writer Philip Roth (b. 1933) and English writers Ivy Compton-Burnett (1884–1969) and Beryl Bainbridge (1932–2010). 5. 1974 American slasher film.

KAZUO ISHIGURO
b. 1954

"The big emotions loom powerfully in understatement," states Kazuo Ishiguro, and accordingly his novels are often restrained and indirect. Winner of the 2017 Nobel Prize for Literature, he is one of the most acclaimed contemporary novelists living in England, but he was born in Nagasaki, Japan, where his mother had survived the dropping of the atomic bomb. When he was five, his father's work as an oceanographer led the family to move to a small town in southern England. Ishiguro earned a B.A. in English and philosophy at the University of Kent and an M.A. in creative writing at the University of East Anglia.

Ishiguro's first two novels, *A Pale View of Hills* (1982) and *An Artist of the Floating World* (1986), were set largely in Japan in the aftermath of World War II, both of them cast in the monologue form that he would employ frequently in subsequent fiction. With every novel he has written since, Ishiguro has dramatically changed his work's setting, genre, or style. The location shifts to a grand English estate in his third novel, *The Remains of the Day* (1989), winner of the Booker Prize, subsequently made into a celebrated movie. It centers on the ruminations and regrets of an English butler named Stevens, so constrained by propriety, class, and duty that he has served a lord with fascist sympathies and has missed a chance for romantic fulfillment with a coworker. *The Unconsoled* (1995) marks a further departure from the crisp realism of the early novels, a dreamlike, elliptically narrated story about a pianist in an unnamed city. *When We Were Orphans* (2000) warps and fuses detective story with historical fiction in narrating a detective's quest to understand his parents' disappearance in 1930s Shanghai. Like *The Remains of the Day*, Ishiguro's *Never Let Me Go* (2005) is one of his best-known novels, also re-created as a film. But unlike his earlier work, it takes up and subtly remakes the genre of dystopian science fiction: English boarding school students gradually realize they are fated to play a part in a society that will use them up and brutally discard them. *The Buried Giant* (2015) is yet another leap for Ishiguro, this time into Arthurian fantasy set in medieval England. Along with his novels, Ishiguro has also written short stories, film scripts, plays, and songs.

Although his novels dart in different directions, some preoccupations recur. In his early years, Ishiguro devoted himself to songwriting, and he has traced his fiction to this perhaps surprising source: "My style as a novelist comes substantially from what I learnt writing songs. The intimate, first-person quality of a singer performing to an audience, for instance, carried over for me into novels. As did the need to approach meaning subtly, sometimes by nudging it into the spaces between the lines."

Some of Ishiguro's characters grapple with regret over misdeeds and lives unlived. "On the one hand," he remarked, "there is a need for honesty, on the other hand a need to deceive themselves—to preserve a sense of dignity, some sort of self-respect. What I want to suggest is that some sort of dignity and self-respect does come from that sort of honesty." His characters sometimes are racked by conflicting demands for self-understanding and self-pacifying consolation.

Ishiguro wrote the short story "A Village after Dark" when he was preparing to write his dreamlike novel *The Unconsoled*. It frustrates our usual expectations for plot development. As in a play by Samuel Beckett, little happens. And recalling Franz Kafka's fiction, the setting seems somewhere between dream and reality. The narrative withholds all but a few details of time and place. The narrator, Fletcher, seems a washed-up leader of some kind, but we do not learn anything about the particular ideas or the movement he once advanced. This narrative restraint places less focus on the subject of the story than on how it is told. Like many of Ishiguro's first-person narrators, Fletcher tells his own story in a way that soon raises questions about his reliability. Almost like a dream, the story seems to enact his guilt over his past: a forgotten romantic partner berates him for having ruined her life, and a fellow schoolboy accuses him of having bullied him. His accusers also partly absolve Fletcher of his misdeeds, and he tries in various ways to justify and defend himself. His regrets, self-deceptions, and vanity suggest the limits to human self-understanding. One way to approach this strange story is to consider which of its aspects lend themselves to rational and realistic understanding, and which evoke what he called the "universal language" or "grammar" of dreams. Of "memory and dream" Ishiguro has said, "you manipulate both according to your emotional needs at the time." As in much of his work, Ishiguro challenges us to rethink what we thought we knew about the conventions of fiction and about the relation between dream and reality, between memory and truth.

A Village after Dark

There was a time when I could travel England for weeks on end and remain at my sharpest—when, if anything, the travelling gave me an edge. But now that I am older I become disoriented more easily. So it was that on arriving at the village just after dark I failed to find my bearings at all. I could hardly believe I was in the same village in which not so long ago I had lived and come to exercise such influence.

There was nothing I recognized, and I found myself walking forever around twisting, badly lit streets hemmed in on both sides by the little stone cottages characteristic of the area. The streets often became so narrow I could make no progress without my bag or my elbow scraping one rough wall or another. I persevered nevertheless, stumbling around in the darkness in the hope of coming upon the village square—where I could at least orient myself—or else of encountering one of the villagers. When after a while I had done neither, a weariness came over me, and I decided my best course was just to choose a cottage at random, knock on the door, and hope it would be opened by someone who remembered me.

I stopped by a particularly rickety-looking door, whose upper beam was so low that I could see I would have to crouch right down to enter. A dim light was leaking out around the door's edges, and I could hear voices and laughter. I knocked loudly to insure that the occupants would hear me over their talk. But just then someone behind me said, "Hello."

I turned to find a young woman of around twenty, dressed in raggedy jeans and a torn jumper, standing in the darkness a little way away.

"You walked straight past me earlier," she said, "even though I called to you."

"Did I really? Well, I'm sorry. I didn't mean to be rude."

"You're Fletcher, aren't you?"

"Yes," I said, somewhat flattered.

"Wendy thought it was you when you went by our cottage. We all got very excited. You were one of that lot, weren't you? With David Maggis and all of them."

"Yes," I said, "but Maggis was hardly the most important one. I'm surprised you pick him out like that. There were other, far more important figures." I reeled off a series of names and was interested to see the girl nodding at each one in recognition. "But this must have all been before your time," I said. "I'm surprised you know about such things."

"It was before our time, but we're all experts on your lot. We know more about all that than most of the older ones who were here then. Wendy recognized you instantly just from your photos."

"I had no idea you young people had taken such an interest in us. I'm sorry I walked past you earlier. But you see, now that I'm older, I get a little disoriented when I travel."

I could hear some boisterous talk coming from behind the door. I banged on it again, this time rather impatiently, though I was not so eager to bring the encounter with the girl to a close.

She looked at me for a moment, then said, "All of you from those days are like that. David Maggis came here a few years ago. In '93, or maybe it was '94. He was like that. A bit vague. It must get to you after a while, travelling all the time."

"So Maggis was here. How interesting. You know, he wasn't one of the really important figures. You mustn't get carried away with such an idea. Incidentally, perhaps you could tell me who lives in this cottage." I thumped the door again.

"The Petersons," the girl said. "They're an old house. They'll probably remember you."

"The Petersons," I repeated, but the name meant nothing to me.

"Why don't you come to our cottage? Wendy was really excited. So were the rest of us. It's a real chance for us, actually talking to someone from those days."

"I'd very much like to do that. But first of all I'd better get myself settled in. The Petersons, you say."

I thumped the door again, this time quite ferociously. At last it opened, throwing warmth and light out into the street. An old man was standing in the doorway. He looked at me carefully, then asked, "It's not Fletcher, is it?"

"Yes, and I've just got into the village. I've been travelling for several days."

He thought about this for a moment, then said, "Well, you'd better come in."

I found myself in a cramped, untidy room full of rough wood and broken furniture. A log burning in the fireplace was the only source of light, by which I could make out a number of hunched figures sitting around the room. The old man led me to a chair beside the fire with a grudgingness that suggested it was the very one he had just vacated. Once I sat down, I found I could not easily turn my head to see my surroundings or the others in the room. But the warmth of the fire was very welcome, and for a moment I just stared into its flames, a pleasant grogginess drifting over me. Voices came from behind me, inquiring if I was well, if I had come far, if I was hungry, and I replied as best I could, though I was aware that my answers were barely adequate. Eventually, the questions ceased, and it occurred to me that my presence was creating a heavy awkwardness, but I was so grateful for the warmth and the chance to rest that I hardly cared.

Nonetheless, when the silence behind me had gone unbroken for several minutes, I resolved to address my hosts with a little more civility, and I turned in my chair. It was then, as I did so, that I was suddenly seized by an intense sense of recognition. I had chosen the cottage quite at random, but now I could see that it was none other than the very one in which I had spent my years in this village. My gaze moved immediately to the far corner—at this moment shrouded in darkness—to the spot that had been my corner, where once my mattress had been and where I had spent many tranquil hours browsing through books or conversing with whoever happened to drift in. On summer days, the windows, and often the door, were left open to allow a refreshing breeze to blow right through. Those were the days when the cottage was surrounded by open fields and there would come from outside the voices of my friends, lazing in the long grass, arguing over poetry or philosophy. These precious fragments of the past came back to me so powerfully that it was all I could do not to make straight for my old corner then and there.

Someone was speaking to me again, perhaps asking another question, but I hardly listened. Rising, I peered through the shadows into my corner, and could now make out a narrow bed, covered by an old curtain, occupying more or less the exact space where my mattress had been. The bed looked extremely inviting, and I found myself cutting into something the old man was saying.

"Look," I said, "I know this is a bit blunt. But, you see, I've come such a long way today. I really need to lie down, close my eyes, even if it's just for a few minutes. After that, I'm happy to talk all you like."

I could see the figures around the room shifting uneasily. Then a new voice said, rather sullenly, "Go ahead then. Have a nap. Don't mind us."

But I was already picking my way through the clutter toward my corner. The bed felt damp, and the springs creaked under my weight, but no sooner had I curled up with my back to the room than my many hours of travelling began to catch up with me. As I was drifting off, I heard the old man saying, "It's Fletcher, all right. God, he's aged."

A woman's voice said, "Should we let him go to sleep like that? He might wake in a few hours and then we'll have to stay up with him."

"Let him sleep for an hour or so," someone else said. "If he's still asleep after an hour, we'll wake him."

At this point, sheer exhaustion overtook me.

It was not a continuous or comfortable sleep. I drifted between sleep and waking, always conscious of voices behind me in the room. At some point, I was aware of a woman saying, "I don't know how I was ever under his spell. He looks such a ragamuffin now."

In my state of near-sleep, I debated with myself whether these words applied to me or, perhaps, to David Maggis, but before long sleep engulfed me once more.

When I next awoke, the room appeared to have grown both darker and colder. Voices were continuing behind me in lowered tones, but I could make no sense of the conversation. I now felt embarrassed at having gone to sleep in the way I had, and for a few further moments remained motionless with my face to the wall. But something about me must have revealed that I was awake, for a woman's voice, breaking off from the general conversation, said, "Oh, look, look." Some whispers were exchanged, then I heard the sound of someone coming toward my corner. I felt a hand placed gently on my shoulder, and looked up to find a woman kneeling over me. I did not turn my body sufficiently to see the room, but I got the impression that it was lit by dying embers, and the woman's face was visible only in shadow.

"Now, Fletcher," she said. "It's time we had a talk. I've waited a long time for you to come back. I've thought about you often."

I strained to see her more clearly. She was somewhere in her forties, and even in the gloom I noticed a sleepy sadness in her eyes. But her face failed to stir in me even the faintest of memories.

"I'm sorry," I said. "I have no recollection of you. But please forgive me if we met some time ago. I do get very disoriented these days."

"Fletcher," she said, "when we used to know one another, I was young and beautiful. I idolized you, and everything you said seemed like an answer. Now here you are, back again. I've wanted to tell you for many years that you ruined my life."

"You're being unfair. All right, I was mistaken about a lot of things. But I never claimed to have any answers. All I said in those days was that it was our duty, all of us, to contribute to the debate. We knew so much more about the issues than the ordinary people here. If people like us procrasti- nated, claiming we didn't yet know enough, then who was there to act? But I never claimed I had the answers. No, you're being unfair."

"Fletcher," she said, and her voice was oddly gentle, "you used to make love to me, more or less every time I wandered in here to your room. In this corner, we did all kinds of beautifully dirty things. It's odd to think how I could have once been so physically excited by you. And here you're just a foul-smelling bundle of rags now. But look at me—I'm still attractive. My face has got a bit lined, but when I walk in the village streets I wear dresses I've made specially to show off my figure. A lot of men want me still. But you, no woman would look at you now. A bundle of stinking rags and flesh."

"I don't remember you," I said. "And I've no time for sex these days. I've other things to worry about. More serious things. Very well, I was mistaken about a lot in those days. But I've done more than most to try and make amends. You see, even now I'm travelling. I've never stopped. I've travelled and travelled trying to undo what damage I may once have caused. That's more than can be said of some others from those days. I bet Maggis, for instance, hasn't worked nearly as hard to try and put things right."

The woman was stroking my hair.

"Look at you. I used to do this, run my fingers through your hair. Look at this filthy mess. I'm sure you're contaminated with all sorts of parasites." But she continued slowly to run her fingers through the dirty knots. I failed to feel anything erotic from this, as perhaps she wished me to do. Rather, her caresses felt maternal. Indeed, for a moment it was as though I had finally reached some cocoon of protectiveness, and I began once more to feel sleepy. But suddenly she stopped and slapped me hard on the forehead.

"Why don't you join the rest of us now? You've had your sleep. You've got a lot of explaining to do." With that she got up and left.

For the first time, I turned my body sufficiently to survey the room. I saw the woman making her way past the clutter on the floor, then sitting down in a rocking chair by the fireplace. I could see three other figures hunched around the dying fire. One I recognized to be the old man who had opened the door. The two others—sitting together on what looked like a wooden trunk—seemed to be women of around the same age as the one who had spoken to me.

The old man noticed that I had turned, and he indicated to the others that I was watching. The four of them proceeded to sit stiffly, not speaking. From the way they did this, it was clear that they had been discussing me thoroughly while I was asleep. In fact, as I watched them I could more or less guess the whole shape their conversation had taken. I could see, for instance, that they had spent some time expressing concern for the young girl I had met outside, and about the effect I might have on her peers.

"They're all so impressionable," the old man would have said. "And I heard her inviting him to visit them."

To which, no doubt, one of the women on the trunk would have said, "But he can't do much harm now. In our time, we were all taken in because all his kind—they were young and glamorous. But these days the odd one passing through from time to time, looking all decrepit and burned out like that—if anything, it goes to demystify all that talk about the old days. In any case, people like him have changed their position so much these days. They don't know themselves what they believe."

The old man would have shaken his head. "I saw the way that young girl was looking at him. All right, he looks a pitiful mess over there just now. But once his ego's fed a little, once he has the flattery of the young people, sees how they want to hear his ideas, then there'll be no stopping him. It'll be just like before. He'll have them all working for his causes. Young girls like that, there's so little for them to believe in now. Even a stinking tramp like this could give them a purpose."

Their conversation, all the time I slept, would have gone something very much like that. But now, as I observed them from my corner, they continued to sit in guilty silence, staring at the last of their fire. After a while, I rose to my feet. Absurdly, the four of them kept their gazes averted from me. I waited a few moments to see if any of them would say anything. Finally, I said, "All right, I was asleep earlier, but I've guessed what you were saying. Well, you'll be interested to know I'm going to do the very thing you feared. I'm going this moment to the young people's cottage. I'm going to tell them what to do with all their energy, all their dreams, their urge to achieve something of lasting good in this world. Look at you, what a pathetic bunch. Crouching in your cottage, afraid to do anything, afraid of me, of Maggis, of anyone else from those times. Afraid to do anything in the world out there, just because once we made a few mistakes. Well, those young people haven't yet sunk so low, despite all the lethargy you've been preaching at them down the years. I'll talk to them. I'll undo in half an hour all of your sorry efforts."

"You see," the old man said to the others. "I knew it would be this way. We ought to stop him, but what can we do?"

I crashed my way across the room, picked up my bag, and went out into the night.

The girl was still standing outside when I emerged. She seemed to be expecting me and with a nod began to lead the way.

The night was drizzly and dark. We twisted and turned along the narrow paths that ran between the cottages. Some of the cottages we passed looked so decayed and crumbling that I felt I could destroy one of them simply by running at it with all my weight.

The girl kept a few paces ahead, occasionally glancing back at me over her shoulder. Once she said, "Wendy's going to be so pleased. She was sure it was you when you went past earlier. By now, she'll have guessed she was right, because I've been away this long, and she'll have brought the whole crowd together. They'll all be waiting."

"Did you give David Maggis this sort of reception, too?"

"Oh, yes. We were really excited when he came."

"I'm sure he found that very gratifying. He always had an exaggerated sense of his own importance."

"Wendy says Maggis was one of the interesting ones, but that you were, well, important. She thinks you were really important."

I thought about this for a moment.

"You know," I said, "I've changed my mind on very many things. If Wendy's expecting me to say all the things I used to all those years ago, well, she's going to be in for a disappointment."

The girl did not seem to hear this, but continued to lead me purposefully through the clusters of cottages.

After a little while, I became aware of footsteps following a dozen or so paces behind us. At first, I assumed this was just some villager out walking and refrained from turning round. But then the girl halted under a street lamp and looked behind us. I was thus obliged also to stop and turn. A middle-aged man in a dark overcoat was coming toward us. As he approached, he held out his hand and shook mine, though without smiling.

"So," he said, "you're here."

I then realized I knew the man. We had not seen each other since we were ten years old. His name was Roger Button, and he had been in my class at the school I had attended for two years in Canada before my family returned to England. Roger Button and I had not been especially close, but, because he had been a timid boy, and because he, too, was from England, he had for a while followed me about. I had neither seen nor heard from him since that time. Now, as I studied his appearance under the street lamp, I saw the years had not been kind to him. He was bald, his face was pocked and lined, and there was a weary sag to his whole posture. For all that, there was no mistaking my old classmate.

"Roger," I said, "I'm just on my way to visit this young lady's friends. They've gathered together to receive me. Otherwise I'd have come and looked you up straightaway. As it was, I had it in my mind as the next thing to do, even before getting any sleep tonight. I was just thinking to myself, However late things finish at the young people's cottage, I'll go and knock on Roger's door afterward."

"Don't worry," said Roger Button as we all started to walk again. "I know how busy you are. But we ought to talk. Chew over old times. When you last saw me—at school, I mean—I suppose I was a rather feeble specimen. But, you know, that all changed when I got to fourteen, fifteen. I really toughened up. Became quite a leader type. But you'd long since left Canada. I always wondered what would have happened if we'd come across each other at fifteen. Things would have been rather different between us, I assure you."

As he said this, memories came flooding back. In those days, Roger Button had idolized me, and in return I had bullied him incessantly. However, there had existed between us a curious understanding that my bullying him was all for his own good; that when, without warning, I suddenly punched him in the stomach on the playground, or when, passing him in the corridor, I impulsively wrenched his arm up his back until he started to cry, I was doing so in order to help him toughen up. Accordingly, the principal effect such attacks had on our relationship was to keep him in awe of me. This all came back to me as I listened to the weary-looking man walking beside me.

"Of course," Roger Button went on, perhaps guessing my train of thought, "it might well be that if you hadn't treated me the way you did I'd never have become what I did at fifteen. In any case, I've often wondered how it would have been if we'd met just a few years later. I really was something to be reckoned with by then."

We were once again walking along the narrow twisted passages between cottages. The girl was still leading the way, but she was now walking much faster. Often we would only just manage to catch a glimpse of her turning some corner ahead of us, and it struck me that we would have to keep alert if we were not to lose her.

"Today, of course," Roger Button was saying, "I've let myself go a bit. But I have to say, old fellow, you seem to be in much worse shape. Compared with you, I'm an athlete. Not to put too fine a point on it, you're just a filthy old tramp now, really, aren't you? But, you know, for a long time after you left I continued to idolize you. Would Fletcher do this? What would Fletcher think if he saw me doing that? Oh, yes. It was only when I got to fifteen or so that I looked back on it all and saw through you. Then I was very angry, of course. Even now, I still think about it sometimes. I look back and think, Well, he was just a thoroughly nasty so-and-so. He had a little more weight and muscle at that age than I did, a little more confidence, and he took full advantage. Yes, it's very clear, looking back, what a nasty little person you were. Of course, I'm not implying you still are today. We all change. That much I'm willing to accept."

"Have you been living here long?" I asked, wishing to change the subject.

"Oh, seven years or so. Of course, they talk about you a lot around here. I sometimes tell them about our early association. 'But he won't remember me,' I always tell them. 'Why would he remember a skinny little boy he used to bully and have at his beck and call?' Anyway, the young people here, they talk about you more and more these days. Certainly, the ones who've never seen you tend to idealize you the most. I suppose you've come back to capitalize on all that. Still, I shouldn't blame you. You're entitled to try and salvage a little self-respect."

We suddenly found ourselves facing an open field, and we both halted. Glancing back, I saw that we had walked our way out of the village; the last of the cottages were some distance behind us. Just as I had feared, we had lost the young woman; in fact, I realized we had not been following her for some time.

At that moment, the moon emerged, and I saw we were standing at the edge of a vast grassy field—extending, I supposed, far beyond what I could see by the moon.

Roger Button turned to me. His face in the moonlight seemed gentle, almost affectionate.

"Still," he said, "it's time to forgive. You shouldn't keep worrying so much. As you see, certain things from the past will come back to you in the end. But then we can't be held accountable for what we did when we were very young."

"No doubt you're right," I said. Then I turned and looked around in the darkness. "But now I'm not sure where to go. You see, there were some young people waiting for me in their cottage. By now they'd have a warm fire ready for me and some hot tea. And some home-baked cakes, perhaps even a good stew. And the moment I entered, ushered in by that young lady we were following just now, they'd all have burst into applause. There'd be smiling, adoring faces all around me. That's what's waiting for me somewhere. Except I'm not sure where I should go."

Roger Button shrugged. "Don't worry, you'll get there easily enough. Except, you know, that girl was being a little misleading if she implied you could walk to Wendy's cottage. It's much too far. You'd really need to catch a bus. Even then, it's quite a long journey. About two hours, I'd say. But don't worry, I'll show you where you can pick up your bus."

With that, he began to walk back toward the cottages. As I followed, I could sense that the hour had got very late and my companion was anxious to get some sleep. We spent several minutes walking around the cottages again, and then he brought us out into the village square. In fact, it was so small and shabby it hardly merited being called a square; it was little more than a patch of green beside a solitary street lamp. Just visible beyond the pool of light cast by the lamp were a few shops, all shut up for the night. There was complete silence and nothing was stirring. A light mist was hovering over the ground.

Roger Button stopped before we had reached the green and pointed.

"There," he said. "If you stand there, a bus will come along. As I say, it's not a short journey. About two hours. But don't worry, I'm sure your young people will wait. They've so little else to believe in these days, you see."

"It's very late," I said. "Are you sure a bus will come?"

"Oh, yes. Of course, you may have to wait. But eventually a bus will come." Then he touched me reassuringly on the shoulder. "I can see it might get a little lonely standing out here. But once the bus arrives your spirits will rise, believe me. Oh, yes. That bus is always a joy. It'll be brightly lit up, and it's always full of cheerful people, laughing and joking and pointing out the window. Once you board it, you'll feel warm and comfortable, and the other passengers will chat with you, perhaps offer you things to eat or drink. There may even be singing—that depends on the driver. Some drivers encourage it, others don't. Well, Fletcher, it was good to see you."

We shook hands, then he turned and walked away. I watched him disappear into the darkness between two cottages.

I walked up to the green and put my bag down at the foot of the lamppost. I listened for the sound of a vehicle in the distance, but the night was utterly still. Nevertheless, I had been cheered by Roger Button's description of the bus. Moreover, I thought of the reception awaiting me at my journey's end—of the adoring faces of the young people—and felt the stirrings of optimism somewhere deep within me.

2001

HANIF KUREISHI
b. 1954

Born in Bromley, a suburb of London, to a Pakistani immigrant father and an English mother, Hanif Kureishi has much in common with the semiautobiographical protagonist of his first novel, *The Buddha of Suburbia* (1990):

> My name is Karim Amir, and I am an Englishman born and bred, almost. I am often considered to be a funny kind of Englishman, a new breed as it were, having emerged from two old histories. But I don't care—Englishman I am (though not proud of it), from the South London suburbs and going somewhere.

The biracial and bicultural Karim is troubled by his "odd mixture of continents and blood, of here and there, of belonging and not." Like Zadie Smith and other black and Asian British writers inspired by his work, Kureishi is the product of postwar migrations, from Britain's former colonies in the Caribbean, South Asia, Africa, and elsewhere, to the empire's heart. The problem of puzzling out issues of identity and race, belonging and estrangement in contemporary Britain is at the core of much of Kureishi's writing (see the essay on his growing up in London, excerpted in "Nation, Race, and Language," earlier in this volume).

Kureishi studied philosophy at King's College London, receiving his B.A. in 1977. He worked at theaters in various capacities, rising from usher to writer in residence at the Royal Court Theatre in London. Trying his hand at different kinds of writing, he won international acclaim when his first screenplays were made into movies. In *My Beautiful Laundrette* (1985), a Pakistani Briton takes over a run-down commercial laundromat and, with the help of a white friend who becomes his lover and partner, fights off racist attacks and turns the venture into a success. Kureishi's next film venture, *Sammy and Rosie Get Laid* (1987), is also set against the backdrop of the racial tensions of Margaret Thatcher's 1980s, featuring an open marriage between a Pakistani Briton and an Englishwoman. Pathbreaking explorations of the new multiracial Britain, these films figured prominently in discussions of race, multiculturalism, and national identity in subsequent decades. Since their release, other of Kureishi's writings have been made into films, including *London Kills Me* (1992), *The Mother* (2004), *Venus* (2006), *Weddings and Beheadings* (2007) and *Le Week-End* (2013). He has also published many essays, short stories, and novels, including *The Black Album* (1995), which explores the disenfranchisement and radicalization of young British Muslims and the book burnings of Salman Rushdie's *The Satanic Verses*, followed by *Intimacy* (1999), *Gabriel's Gift* (2001), *The Body* (2004), and *Something to Tell You* (2008), in which the London transit-system bombings of July 7, 2005 (killing 52 and wounding 700) touch most of the characters' lives. *The Last Word* (2014) satirizes a postcolonial novelist who turns out to be depraved.

Among Kureishi's works adapted into films is the short story "My Son the Fanatic," one of his many reflections on Muslim Britain long before the subject received widespread attention. In this story Parvez, who has worked for twenty years as a taxi driver in an unnamed English city, tries to ensure his son Ali's financial success as a future accountant. When his son suddenly dumps his Western movies, books, videos, clothes, and friends, Parvez is baffled. In the ensuing conflict between a partly assimilated Punjabi father, who drinks alcohol (forbidden in Islam) and befriends a prostitute, and a son who has adopted a strictly observant form of Islam and identifies with oppressed Muslims around the world, Kureishi's story gives narrative form to the collision between different ways of belonging among Britain's people of non-Western descent.

Writing about the screenplay, Kureishi commented: "It perplexed me that young people, brought up in secular Britain, would turn to a form of belief that denied them the pleasures of the society in which they lived. Islam was a particularly firm way of saying no to all sorts of things." He surmised that decades of racial exclusion and economic disappointment help explain the appeal of fundamentalist forms of Islam to the children of South Asian immigrants in Britain:

> It must not be forgotten, therefore, that the backgrounds to the lives of these young people includes colonialism—being made to feel inferior in your own country. And then, in Britain, racism; again, being made to feel inferior in your own country. . . . Yet all along it was taken for granted that 'belonging', which means, in a sense, not having to notice where you are, and more importantly, not being seen as different, would happen eventually. Where it hasn't, there is, in the children and grandchildren of the great postwar wave of immigrants, considerable anger and disillusionment. . . . The 'West' was a dream that didn't come true. But one cannot go home again. One is stuck. . . . If you feel excluded it might be tempting to exclude others.

Religious fundamentalists, in his view, wanted to exclude others (non-Muslims, gays, "unsubmissive women," etc.), just as they had been excluded. Never idealizing or sentimentalizing the new multiracial Britain, Kureishi has been one of its most incisive observers, helping at the same time to reimagine its future.

My Son the Fanatic

Surreptitiously the father began going into his son's bedroom. He would sit there for hours, rousing himself only to seek clues. What bewildered him was that Ali was getting tidier. Instead of the usual tangle of clothes, books, cricket bats, video games, the room was becoming neat and ordered; spaces began appearing where before there had been only mess.

Initially Parvez had been pleased: his son was outgrowing his teenage attitudes. But one day, beside the dustbin, Parvez found a torn bag which contained not only old toys, but computer discs, video tapes, new books and fashionable clothes the boy had bought just a few months before. Also without explanation, Ali had parted from the English girlfriend who used to come often to the house. His old friends had stopped ringing.

For reasons he didn't himself understand, Parvez wasn't able to bring up the subject of Ali's unusual behaviour. He was aware that he had become slightly afraid of his son, who, alongside his silences, was developing a sharp tongue. One remark Parvez did make, 'You don't play your guitar any more,' elicited the mysterious but conclusive reply, 'There are more important things to be done.'

Yet Parvez felt his son's eccentricity as an injustice. He had always been aware of the pitfalls which other men's sons had fallen into in England. And so, for Ali, he had worked long hours and spent a lot of money paying for his education as an accountant. He had bought him good suits, all the books he required and a computer. And now the boy was throwing his possessions out!

The TV, video and sound system followed the guitar. Soon the room was practically bare. Even the unhappy walls bore marks where Ali's pictures had been removed.

Parvez couldn't sleep; he went more to the whisky bottle, even when he was at work. He realised it was imperative to discuss the matter with someone sympathetic.

Parvez had been a taxi driver for twenty years. Half that time he'd worked for the same firm. Like him, most of the other drivers were Punjabis.[1] They preferred to work at night, the roads were clearer and the money better. They slept during the day, avoiding their wives. Together they led almost a boy's life in the cabbies' office, playing cards and practical jokes, exchanging lewd stories, eating together and discussing politics and their problems.

But Parvez had been unable to bring this subject up with his friends. He was too ashamed. And he was afraid, too, that they would blame him for the wrong turning his boy had taken, just as he had blamed other fathers whose sons had taken to running around with bad girls, truanting from school and joining gangs.

---

1. From the Punjab, a South Asian region including part of Pakistan and northwestern India.

For years Parvez had boasted to the other men about how Ali excelled at cricket, swimming and football, and how attentive a scholar he was, getting straight 'A's in most subjects. Was it asking too much for Ali to get a good job now, marry the right girl and start a family? Once this happened, Parvez would be happy. His dreams of doing well in England would have come true. Where had he gone wrong?

But one night, sitting in the taxi office on busted chairs with his two closest friends watching a Sylvester Stallone film, he broke his silence.

'I can't understand it!' he burst out. 'Everything is going from his room. And I can't talk to him any more. We were not father and son—we were brothers! Where has he gone? Why is he torturing me!'

And Parvez put his head in his hands.

Even as he poured out his account the men shook their heads and gave one another knowing glances. From their grave looks Parvez realised they understood the situation.

'Tell me what is happening!' he demanded.

The reply was almost triumphant. They had guessed something was going wrong. Now it was clear. Ali was taking drugs and selling his possessions to pay for them. That was why his bedroom was emptying.

'What must I do, then?'

Parvez's friends instructed him to watch Ali scrupulously and then be severe with him, before the boy went mad, overdosed or murdered someone.

Parvez staggered out into the early morning air, terrified they were right. His boy—the drug-addict killer!

To his relief he found Bettina sitting in his car.

Usually the last customers of the night were local 'brasses' or prostitutes. The taxi drivers knew them well, often driving them to liaisons. At the end of the girls' shifts, the men would ferry them home, though sometimes the women would join them for a drinking session in the office. Occasionally the drivers would go with the girls. 'A ride in exchange for a ride,' it was called.

Bettina had known Parvez for three years. She lived outside the town and on the long drive home, when she sat not in the passenger seat but beside him, Parvez had talked to her about his life and hopes, just as she talked about hers. They saw each other most nights.

He could talk to her about things he'd never be able to discuss with his own wife. Bettina, in turn, always reported on her night's activities. He liked to know where she was and with whom. Once he had rescued her from a violent client, and since then they had come to care for one another.

Though Bettina had never met the boy, she heard about Ali continually. That late night, when he told Bettina that he suspected Ali was on drugs, she judged neither the boy nor his father, but became businesslike and told him what to watch for.

'It's all in the eyes,' she said. They might be bloodshot; the pupils might be dilated; he might look tired. He could be liable to sweats, or sudden mood changes. 'Okay?'

Parvez began his vigil gratefully. Now he knew what the problem might be, he felt better. And surely, he figured, things couldn't have gone too far? With Bettina's help he would soon sort it out.

He watched each mouthful the boy took. He sat beside him at every opportunity and looked into his eyes. When he could he took the boy's hand, checking his temperature. If the boy wasn't at home Parvez was active, looking under the carpet, in his drawers, behind the empty wardrobe, sniffing, inspecting, probing. He knew what to look for: Bettina had drawn pictures of capsules, syringes, pills, powders, rocks.

Every night she waited to hear news of what he'd witnessed.

After a few days of constant observation, Parvez was able to report that although the boy had given up sports, he seemed healthy, with clear eyes. He didn't, as his father expected, flinch guiltily from his gaze. In fact the boy's mood was alert and steady in this sense: as well as being sullen, he was very watchful. He returned his father's long looks with more than a hint of criticism, of reproach even, so much so that Parvez began to feel that it was he who was in the wrong and not the boy!

'And there's nothing else physically different?' Bettina asked.

'No!' Parvez thought for a moment. 'But he is growing a beard.'

One night, after sitting with Bettina in an all-night coffee shop, Parvez came home particularly late. Reluctantly he and Bettina had abandoned their only explanation, the drug theory, for Parvez had found nothing resembling any drug in Ali's room. Besides, Ali wasn't selling his belongings. He threw them out, gave them away or donated them to charity shops.

Standing in the hall, Parvez heard his boy's alarm clock go off. Parvez hurried into his bedroom where his wife was still awake, sewing in bed. He ordered her to sit down and keep quiet, though she had neither stood up nor said a word. From this post, and with her watching him curiously, he observed his son through the crack in the door.

The boy went into the bathroom to wash. When he returned to his room Parvez sprang across the hall and set his ear at Ali's door. A muttering sound came from within. Parvez was puzzled but relieved.

Once this clue had been established, Parvez watched him at other times. The boy was praying. Without fail, when he was at home, he prayed five times a day.[2]

Parvez had grown up in Lahore,[3] where all the boys had been taught the Koran. To stop him falling asleep when he studied, the Maulvis[4] had attached a piece of string to the ceiling and tied it to Parvez's hair, so that if his head fell forward he would instantly awake. After this indignity Parvez had avoided all religions. Not that the other taxi drivers had more respect. In fact they made jokes about the local mullahs[5] walking around with their caps and beards, thinking they could tell people how to live, while their eyes roved over the boys and girls in their care.

Parvez described to Bettina what he had discovered. He informed the men in the taxi office. The friends, who had been so curious before, now became oddly silent. They could hardly condemn the boy for his devotions.

Parvez decided to take a night off and go out with the boy. They could talk things over. He wanted to hear how things were going at college; he wanted to tell him stories about their family in Pakistan. More than anything he yearned to understand how Ali had discovered the 'spiritual dimension', as Bettina described it.

To Parvez's surprise, the boy refused to accompany him. He claimed he had an appointment. Parvez had to insist that no appointment could be more important than that of a son with his father.

2. Prayer five times a day is one of the pillars of Islam.
3. Pakistani city in the Punjab region.
4. Muslim doctors of the law, teachers, or imams.
5. Muslim clerics.

The next day, Parvez went immediately to the street where Bettina stood in the rain wearing high heels, a short skirt and a long mac[6] on top, which she would open hopefully at passing cars.

'Get in, get in!' he said.

They drove out across the moors and parked at the spot where on better days, with a view unimpeded for many miles by nothing but wild deer and horses, they'd lie back, with their eyes half closed, saying 'This is the life.' This time Parvez was trembling. Bettina put her arms around him.

'What's happened?'

'I've just had the worst experience of my life.'

As Bettina rubbed his head Parvez told her that the previous evening he and Ali had gone to a restaurant. As they studied the menu, the waiter, whom Parvez knew, brought him his usual whisky and water. Parvez had been so nervous he had even prepared a question. He was going to ask Ali if he was worried about his imminent exams. But first, wanting to relax, he loosened his tie, crunched a popadom[7] and took a long drink.

Before Parvez could speak, Ali made a face.

'Don't you know it's wrong to drink alcohol?' he said.

'He spoke to me very harshly,' Parvez told Bettina. 'I was about to castigate the boy for being insolent, but managed to control myself.'

He had explained patiently to Ali that for years he had worked more than ten hours a day, that he had few enjoyments or hobbies and never went on holiday. Surely it wasn't a crime to have a drink when he wanted one?

'But it is forbidden,' the boy said.

Parvez shrugged. 'I know.'

'And so is gambling, isn't it?'

'Yes. But surely we are only human?'

Each time Parvez took a drink, the boy winced, or made a fastidious face as an accompaniment. This made Parvez drink more quickly. The waiter, wanting to please his friend, brought another glass of whisky. Parvez knew he was getting drunk, but he couldn't stop himself. Ali had a horrible look on his face, full of disgust and censure. It was as if he hated his father.

Halfway through the meal Parvez suddenly lost his temper and threw a plate on the floor. He had felt like ripping the cloth from the table, but the waiters and other customers were staring at him. Yet he wouldn't stand for his own son telling him the difference between right and wrong. He knew he wasn't a bad man. He had a conscience. There were a few things of which he was ashamed, but on the whole he had lived a decent life.

'When have I had time to be wicked?' he asked Ali.

In a low monotonous voice the boy explained that Parvez had not, in fact, lived a good life. He had broken countless rules of the Koran.

'For instance?' Parvez demanded.

Ali hadn't needed time to think. As if he had been waiting for this moment, he asked his father if he didn't relish pork pies.[8]

'Well . . .'

Parvez couldn't deny that he loved crispy bacon smothered with mushrooms and mustard and sandwiched between slices of fried bread. In fact he ate this for breakfast every morning.

---

6. Mackintosh, a rainproof coat.
7. South Asian spiced wafer of bread.

8. Pork is forbidden in Islam.

Ali then reminded Parvez that he had ordered his own wife to cook pork sausages, saying to her, 'You're not in the village now, this is England. We have to fit in!'

Parvez was so annoyed and perplexed by this attack that he called for more drink.

'The problem is this,' the boy said. He leaned across the table. For the first time that night his eyes were alive. 'You are too implicated in Western civilisation.'

Parvez burped; he thought he was going to choke. 'Implicated!' he said. 'But we live here!'

'The Western materialists hate us,' Ali said. 'Papa, how can you love something which hates you?'

'What is the answer then?' Parvez said miserably. 'According to you?'

Ali addressed his father fluently, as if Parvez were a rowdy crowd that had to be quelled and convinced. The Law of Islam would rule the world; the skin of the infidel would burn off again and again; the Jews and Christers would be routed. The West was a sink of hypocrites, adulterers, homosexuals, drug-takers and prostitutes.

As Ali talked, Parvez looked out of the window as if to check that they were still in London.

'My people have taken enough. If the persecution doesn't stop there will be jihad.[9] I, and millions of others, will gladly give our lives for the cause.'

'But why, why?' Parvez said.

'For us the reward will be in paradise.'

'Paradise!'

Finally, as Parvez's eyes filled with tears, the boy urged him to mend his ways.

'How is that possible?' Parvez asked.

'Pray,' Ali said. 'Pray beside me.'

Parvez called for the bill and ushered his boy out of the restaurant as soon as he was able. He couldn't take any more. Ali sounded as if he'd swallowed someone else's voice.

On the way home the boy sat in the back of the taxi, as if he were a customer.

'What has made you like this?' Parvez asked him, afraid that somehow he was to blame for all this. 'Is there a particular event which has influenced you?'

'Living in this country.'

'But I love England,' Parvez said, watching his boy in the mirror. 'They let you do almost anything here.'

'That is the problem,' he replied.

For the first time in years Parvez couldn't see straight. He knocked the side of the car against a lorry,[1] ripping off the wing mirror. They were lucky not to have been stopped by the police: Parvez would have lost his licence and therefore his job.

Getting out of the car back at the house, Parvez stumbled and fell in the mud, scraping his hands and ripping his trousers. He managed to haul himself up. The boy didn't even offer him his hand.

---

9. Religious struggle or duty, sometimes interpreted to mean religious war (Arabic).
1. Truck.

Parvez told Bettina he was now willing to pray, if that was what the boy wanted, if that would dislodge the pitiless look from his eyes.

'But what I object to,' he said, 'is being told by my own son that I am going to hell!'

What finished Parvez off was that the boy had said he was giving up accountancy. When Parvez had asked why, Ali had said sarcastically that it was obvious.

'Western education cultivates an anti-religious attitude.'

And, according to Ali, in the world of accountants it was usual to meet women, drink alcohol and practise usury.[2]

'But it's well-paid work,' Parvez argued. 'For years you've been preparing!'

Ali said he was going to begin to work in prisons, with poor Muslims who were struggling to maintain their purity in the face of corruption. Finally, at the end of the evening, as Ali was going to bed, he had asked his father why he didn't have a beard, or at least a moustache.[3]

'I feel as if I've lost my son,' Parvez told Bettina. 'I can't bear to be looked at as if I'm a criminal. I've decided what to do.'

'What is it?'

'I'm going to tell him to pick up his prayer mat and get out of my house. It will be the hardest thing I've ever done, but tonight I'm going to do it.'

'But you mustn't give up on him,' said Bettina. 'Many young people fall into cults and superstitious groups. It doesn't mean they'll always feel the same way.'

She said Parvez had to stick by his boy, giving him support, until he came through.

Parvez was persuaded that she was right, even though he didn't feel like giving his son more love when he had hardly been thanked for all he had already given.

Nevertheless, Parvez tried to endure his son's looks and reproaches. He attempted to make conversation about his beliefs. But if Parvez ventured any criticism, Ali always had a brusque reply. On one occasion Ali accused Parvez of 'grovelling' to the whites; in contrast, he explained, he was not 'inferior'; there was more to the world than the West, though the West always thought it was best.

'How is it you know that?' Parvez said. 'Seeing as you've never left England?'

Ali replied with a look of contempt.

One night, having ensured there was no alcohol on his breath, Parvez sat down at the kitchen table with Ali. He hoped Ali would compliment him on the beard he was growing but Ali didn't appear to notice.

The previous day Parvez had been telling Bettina that he thought people in the West sometimes felt inwardly empty and that people needed a philosophy to live by.

'Yes,' said Bettina. 'That's the answer. You must tell him what your philosophy of life is. Then he will understand that there are other beliefs.'

After some fatiguing consideration, Parvez was ready to begin. The boy watched him as if he expected nothing.

---

2. To charge interest on a loan, a practice forbidden in Islam.
3. In some strict interpretations of Islam, a beard is seen as compulsory for men.

Haltingly Parvez said that people had to treat one another with respect, particularly children their parents. This did seem, for a moment, to affect the boy. Heartened, Parvez continued. In his view this life was all there was and when you died you rotted in the earth. 'Grass and flowers will grow out of me, but something of me will live on—'

'How?'

'In other people. I will continue—in you.' At this the boy appeared a little distressed. 'And your grandchildren,' Parvez added for good measure. 'But while I am here on earth I want to make the best of it. And I want you to, as well!'

'What d'you mean by "make the best of it"?' asked the boy.

'Well,' said Parvez. 'For a start . . . you should enjoy yourself. Yes. Enjoy yourself without hurting others.'

Ali said that enjoyment was a 'bottomless pit'.

'But I don't mean enjoyment like that!' said Parvez. 'I mean the beauty of living!'

'All over the world our people are oppressed,' was the boy's reply.

'I know,' Parvez replied, not entirely sure who 'our people' were, 'but still—life is for living!'

Ali said, 'Real morality has existed for hundreds of years. Around the world millions and millions of people share my beliefs. Are you saying you are right and they are all wrong?'

Ali looked at his father with such aggressive confidence that Parvez could say no more.

One evening Bettina was sitting in Parvez's car, after visiting a client, when they passed a boy on the street.

'That's my son,' Parvez said suddenly. They were on the other side of town, in a poor district, where there were two mosques.

Parvez set his face hard.

Bettina turned to watch him. 'Slow down then, slow down!' she said. 'He's good-looking. Reminds me of you. But with a more determined face. Please, can't we stop?'

'What for?'

'I'd like to talk to him.'

Parvez turned the cab round and stopped beside the boy.

'Coming home?' Parvez asked. 'It's quite a way.'

The sullen boy shrugged and got into the back seat. Bettina sat in the front. Parvez became aware of Bettina's short skirt, gaudy rings and ice-blue eye shadow. He became conscious that the smell of her perfume, which he loved, filled the cab. He opened the window.

While Parvez drove as fast as he could, Bettina said gently to Ali, 'Where have you been?'

'The mosque,' he said.

'And how are you getting on at college? Are you working hard?'

'Who are you to ask me these questions?' he said, looking out of the window. Then they hit bad traffic and the car came to a standstill.

By now Bettina had inadvertently laid her hand on Parvez's shoulder. She said, 'Your father, who is a good man, is very worried about you. You know he loves you more than his own life.'

'You say he loves me,' the boy said.

'Yes!' said Bettina.

'Then why is he letting a woman like you touch him like that?'

If Bettina looked at the boy in anger, he looked back at her with twice as much cold fury.

She said, 'What kind of woman am I that deserves to be spoken to like that?'

'You know,' he said. 'Now let me out.'

'Never,' Parvez replied.

'Don't worry, I'm getting out,' Bettina said.

'No, don't!' said Parvez. But even as the car moved she opened the door, threw herself out and ran away across the road. Parvez shouted after her several times, but she had gone.

Parvez took Ali back to the house, saying nothing more to him. Ali went straight to his room. Parvez was unable to read the paper, watch television or even sit down. He kept pouring himself drinks.

At last he went upstairs and paced up and down outside Ali's room. When, finally, he opened the door, Ali was praying. The boy didn't even glance his way.

Parvez kicked him over. Then he dragged the boy up by his shirt and hit him. The boy fell back. Parvez hit him again. The boy's face was bloody. Parvez was panting. He knew that the boy was unreachable, but he struck him nonetheless. The boy neither covered himself nor retaliated; there was no fear in his eyes. He only said, through his split lip: 'So who's the fanatic now?'

1997

CAROL ANN DUFFY
b. 1955

Carol Ann Duffy was born in Glasgow, Scotland, to an Irish mother and a Scottish father in a working-class Catholic family. After moving as a child to Stafford, England, she was educated there at St. Joseph's Convent and at Stafford Girls' High School, before studying philosophy at the University of Liverpool. She worked in television, edited a poetry magazine, and taught creative writing in London's schools, and since 1996 she has lectured at Manchester Metropolitan University. In 2009 she was appointed Britain's poet laureate, the first woman and first Scot to hold the post.

A playwright as well as poet, Duffy is especially skillful in her use of dramatic monologue, fashioning and assuming the voices of mythological, historical, and fictive characters, such as Medusa or Lazarus's imaginary wife. Such poetic ventriloquism is well suited to her feminist revisions of myth and history: it enables her to dramatize a silenced or marginalized female perspective, wittily playing on the ironic contrast between the traditional version of a narrative and her own. The biblical story of Lazarus's resurrection, for example, looks different from the perspective of his wife, who upon his miraculous return from the dead scoffs: "I breathed / his stench."

The author of love poetry ("Valentine"), historical poetry ("The Christmas Truce"), and political satire as well as dramatic monologues, Duffy has a sharp eye for detail and uses it deftly in poems characterized by their sensuality, economy, and exuberance. Working in well-constructed stanzas, carefully pacing her rhythms, playing on half-rhymes, effectively conjuring the senses of touch, smell, and sight, she mobilizes the resources of traditional lyric and turns them to contemporary ends— the remaking of master narratives, the celebration of lesbian desire.

Warming Her Pearls

for Judith Radstone[1]

Next to my own skin, her pearls. My mistress
bids me wear them, warm them, until evening
when I'll brush her hair. At six, I place them
round her cool, white throat. All day I think of her,

5   resting in the Yellow Room, contemplating silk
or taffeta, which gown tonight? She fans herself
whilst I work willingly, my slow heat entering
each pearl. Slack on my neck, her rope.

She's beautiful. I dream about her
10   in my attic bed; picture her dancing
with tall men, puzzled by my faint, persistent scent
beneath her French perfume, her milky stones.

I dust her shoulders with a rabbit's foot,
watch the soft blush seep through her skin
15   like an indolent sigh. In her looking-glass
my red lips part as though I want to speak.

Full moon. Her carriage brings her home. I see
her every movement in my head . . . Undressing,
taking off her jewels, her slim hand reaching
20   for the case, slipping naked into bed, the way

she always does . . . And I lie here awake,
knowing the pearls are cooling even now
in the room where my mistress sleeps. All night
I feel their absence and I burn.

1987

1. British political activist and bookseller (1925–2001). According to Radstone's obituary in *The Guardian*, the poem was inspired by a conversation with Radstone about the practice of ladies' maids increasing the luster of their mistresses' pearls by wearing them beneath their clothes.

Valentine

Not a red rose or a satin heart.

I give you an onion.
It is a moon wrapped in brown paper.
It promises light
5   like the careful undressing of love.

Here.
It will blind you with tears
like a lover.
It will make your reflection
10   a wobbling photo of grief.

I am trying to be truthful.

Not a cute card or a kissogram.[1]

I give you an onion.
Its fierce kiss will stay on your lips,
15   possessive and faithful
as we are,
for as long as we are.

Take it.
Its platinum loops shrink to a wedding ring,
20   if you like.
Lethal.
Its scent will cling to your fingers,
cling to your knife.

1993

Medusa[1]

A suspicion, a doubt, a jealousy
grew in my mind,
which turned the hairs on my head to filthy snakes,
as though my thoughts
5   hissed and spat on my scalp.

My bride's breath soured, stank
in the grey bags of my lungs.
I'm foul mouthed now, foul tongued,
yellow fanged.

---

1. Telegram delivered by a young woman with a kiss.
1. In Greek mythology the mortal, snake-haired gorgon with the power to turn anyone who gazed upon her into stone. Looking at her reflection in a shield given him by Athena, Perseus cut off Medusa's head as she slept.

10   There are bullet tears in my eyes.
    Are you terrified?

    Be terrified.
    It's you I love,
    perfect man, Greek God, my own;
15   but I know you'll go, betray me, stray
    from home.
    So better by far for me if you were stone.

    I glanced at a buzzing bee,
    a dull grey pebble fell
20   to the ground.
    I glanced at a singing bird,
    a handful of dusty gravel
    spattered down.

    I looked at a ginger cat,
25   a housebrick
    shattered a bowl of milk.
    I looked at a snuffling pig,
    a boulder rolled
    in a heap of shit.

30   I stared in the mirror.
    Love gone bad
    showed me a Gorgon.
    I stared at a dragon.
    Fire spewed
35   from the mouth of a mountain.

    And here you come
    with a shield for a heart
    and a sword for a tongue
    and your girls, your girls.
40   Wasn't I beautiful?
    Wasn't I fragrant and young?

    Look at me now.

1999

Mrs Lazarus[1]

I had grieved. I had wept for a night and a day
over my loss, ripped the cloth I was married in
from my breasts, howled, shrieked, clawed
at the burial stones till my hands bled, retched
5   his name over and over again, dead, dead.

Gone home. Gutted the place. Slept in a single cot,
widow, one empty glove, white femur
in the dust, half. Stuffed dark suits

1. Lazarus was the man raised from the dead by Jesus (John 11).

into black bags, shuffled in a dead man's shoes,
10   noosed the double knot of a tie round my bare neck,

gaunt nun in the mirror, touching herself. I learnt
the Stations of Bereavement,[2] the icon of my face
in each bleak frame; but all those months
he was going away from me, dwindling
15   to the shrunk size of a snapshot, going,

going. Till his name was no longer a certain spell
for his face. The last hair on his head
floated out from a book. His scent went from the house.
The will was read. See, he was vanishing
20   to the small zero held by the gold of my ring.

Then he was gone. Then he was legend, language;
my arm on the arm of the schoolteacher—the shock
of a man's strength under the sleeve of his coat—
along the hedgerows. But I was faithful
25   for as long as it took. Until he was memory.

So I could stand that evening in the field
in a shawl of fine air, healed, able
to watch the edge of the moon occur to the sky
and a hare thump from a hedge; then notice
30   the village men running towards me, shouting,

behind them the women and children, barking dogs,
and I knew. I knew by the sly light
on the blacksmith's face, the shrill eyes
of the barmaid, the sudden hands bearing me
35   into the hot tang of the crowd parting before me.

He lived. I saw the horror on his face.
I heard his mother's crazy song. I breathed
his stench; my bridegroom in his rotting shroud,
moist and dishevelled from the grave's slack chew,
40   croaking his cuckold name, disinherited, out of his time.

1999

The Christmas Truce[1]

Christmas Eve in the trenches of France,
the guns were quiet.
The dead lay still in No Man's Land—
Freddie, Franz, Friedrich, Frank . . .
5   The moon, like a medal, hung in the clear, cold sky.

---

2. Allusion to the Stations of the Cross, a series of fourteen icons (pictures or carvings) corresponding to the stages of Jesus's crucifixion and over each of which a prayer is said.

1. Series of unofficial but widespread ceasefires between British and German forces along the Western Front around Christmas 1914.

Silver frost on barbed wire, strange tinsel,
sparkled and winked.
A boy from Stroud[2] stared at a star
to meet his mother's eyesight there.
10 An owl swooped on a rat on the glove of a corpse.

In a copse of trees behind the lines,
a lone bird sang.
A soldier-poet noted it down—*a robin
holding his winter ground*—
15 then silence spread and touched each man like a hand.

Somebody kissed the gold of his ring;
a few lit pipes;
most, in their greatcoats, huddled,
waiting for sleep.
20 The liquid mud had hardened at last in the freeze.

But it was Christmas Eve; *believe*; belief
thrilled the night air,
where glittering rime° on unburied sons   *frost*
treasured their stiff hair.
25 The sharp, clean, midwinter smell held memory.

On watch, a rifleman scoured the terrain—
no sign of life,
no shadows, shots from snipers,
nowt° to note or report.   *nothing (Northern English)*
30 The frozen, foreign fields were acres of pain.

Then flickering flames from the other side
danced in his eyes,
as Christmas Trees in their dozens shone,
candlelit on the parapets,
35 and they started to sing, all down the German lines.

Men who would drown in mud, be gassed, or shot,
or vaporised
by falling shells, or live to tell,
heard for the first time then—
40 *Stille Nacht. Heilige Nacht. Alles schläft, einsam wacht* . . . [3]

Cariad,° the song was a sudden bridge   *darling (Welsh)*
from man to man;
a gift to the heart from home,
or childhood, some place shared . . .
45 When it was done, the British soldiers cheered.

A Scotsman started to bawl *The First Noel*
and all joined in,
till the Germans stood, seeing

---

2. Town in southwest England.
3. Silent night. Holy night. All is calm, all is
bright . . . (original German of "Stille Nacht" or
"Silent Night").

across the divide,
50   the sprawled, mute shapes of those who had died.

All night, along the Western Front, they sang,
the enemies—
carols, hymns, folk songs, anthems,
in German, English, French;
55   each battalion choired in its grim trench.

So Christmas dawned, wrapped in mist,
to open itself
and offer the day like a gift
for Harry, Hugo, Hermann, Henry, Heinz . . .
60   with whistles, waves, cheers, shouts, laughs.

Frohe Weinachten,[4] *Tommy! Merry*
        Christmas, Fritz!
A young Berliner,
brandishing schnapps,
was the first from his ditch to climb.
65   A Shropshire[5] lad ran at him like a rhyme.

Then it was up and over, every man,
to shake the hand
of a foe as a friend,
or slap his back like a brother would;
70   exchanging gifts of biscuits, tea, Maconochie's stew,

Tickler's jam[6] . . . for cognac, sausages, cigars,
beer, sauerkraut;
or chase six hares, who jumped
from a cabbage-patch, or find a ball
75   and make of a battleground a football pitch.°   *soccer field*

I showed him a picture of my wife.
Ich zeigte ihm
ein Foto meiner Frau.
Sie sei schön, sagte er.[7]
80   *He thought her beautiful, he said.*

They buried the dead then, hacked spades
into hard earth
again and again, till a score of men
were at rest, identified, blessed.
85   *Der Herr ist mein Hirt*[8] . . . *my shepherd, I shall not want.*

And all that marvellous, festive day and night,
they came and went,

---

4. Merry Christmas (German).
5. County in the West of England. See also *A Shropshire Lad* (1896), collection of poems by English poet A. E. Housman (1859–1936).
6. English jam often eaten by British troops in the trenches. "Maconochie's stew": wartime food ration from Scotland.
7. I showed him a picture of my wife. He thought her beautiful, he said (German).
8. The Lord is my shepherd (German, Psalm 23).

the officers, the rank and file,
their fallen comrades side by side
90 beneath the makeshift crosses of midwinter graves . . .

. . . beneath the shivering, shy stars
and the pinned moon
and the yawn of History;
the high, bright bullets
95 which each man later only aimed at the sky.

2011

CARYL PHILLIPS
b. 1958

" I am of, and not of, this place," repeats Caryl Phillips in a collection of essays, *A New World Order* (2001). Born on the Caribbean island of Saint Kitts when it was still under British rule, he moved with his parents to England when he was only four months old and settled in the northern city of Leeds. Growing up black in a predominantly white working-class community, he was the first student from his high school to attend Oxford University. After earning his B.A. in English Literature in 1979, he began making his living as a playwright, writing scripts for radio, television, and film. The success of his first novel, *The Final Passage* (1985), about a young woman who moves from the Caribbean to London with her baby and husband, enabled him to devote more energy to writing the prize-winning novels that have distinguished him as one of Britain's leading writers. The protagonist of his second novel, *A State of Independence* (1986), reverses the migration, returning to the Caribbean after twenty years in England. Since 1990, Phillips has taught predominantly in the United States, at Amherst, Barnard, and Yale.

Ever since his first novels, the voluntary and forced movement of people has remained at the empathic core of his fiction. As he remarked in an interview, his preoccupations have been "diaspora, dispossession, historical fracture, people being uprooted and displaced." Further emphasizing the mobility, displacement, and dispossession of his characters, he continued: "I am writing stories about people who find themselves on cattle trucks, I am writing stories about people who find themselves in ships sailing to countries that they don't want to go to, I find myself writing about people who wake up in the morning and their father is gone."

Phillips is best known for his historical novels about the transatlantic slave trade and its aftermath in Britain, the Caribbean, and the United States. It is central to a series of books, including the novels *Higher Ground* (1989), *Cambridge* (1991), and *Crossing the River* (1993), as well as his nonfictional *The Atlantic Sound* (2000). Reimagining the humanity of characters who are enslaved and enslaving, selling and sold, free and in bondage, Phillips deftly interweaves multiple narratives and perspectives in his novels. Sometimes he juxtaposes the radically discontinuous viewpoints of characters whose lives are entangled yet strangely parallel. The dominant narrative voices in *Cambridge* are those of Emily Cartwright, the white daughter of a British plantation owner, horrified by what she sees on the plantation but still racist in her views, and of

Cambridge, the repeatedly enslaved and freed title character. Similarly, *Crossing the River* encompasses not only the story of a freed slave and his well-intentioned former owner but also the diary of an eighteenth-century owner of a slave ship.

In addition to novels that probe human psychology in the historical past, some of Phillips's fictions come closer to the present and range widely in subject matter. *The Nature of Blood* (1997) is centered on the experience of a Jewish survivor of a Nazi death camp but reaches back to the fifteenth-century Venice of Othello. *A Distant Shore* (2003) features the unlikely friendship between a white English schoolteacher and an African refugee. *Dancing in the Dark* (2005) reimagines the lives of two famous minstrel singers, Bert Williams and his partner George Walker. *Foreigners* (2007), ironically subtitled *Three English Lives*, fuses real and historical material to tell the story of three black migrants struggling and failing to make England their home. Like other of his fictions, *In the Falling Snow* (2009) explores the struggles of Caribbean migration in Britain, but *The Lost Child* (2015) was an unexpected departure, reimagining the orphan Heathcliff in Emily Brontë's novel *Wuthering Heights* (1847).

Although he has also written books that combine first-person essay, travelogue, and social critique, such as *The European Tribe* (1987) and *Colour Me English* (2011), Phillips prefers in his novels to be invisible, to live through his characters. In the short autobiographical story "Growing Pains," Phillips writes about his early development as a black child in England in a voice that is at once personal and distanced, intimate and in the third person. The story traces a writer's coming of age. It is wound around a series of encounters with stories by British, Russian, white American, African American, and other writers through which the boy-turned-young-man attempts to understand his identity and purpose. It is the story of one person's maturation, as he negotiates questions of race and class in a 1960s and '70s Britain still partly in denial about its emerging multiracialism. But in the youth's cross-cultural engagements with imaginary characters in far-flung places and times, it is also a story that showcases the expansiveness of the literary imagination.

Growing Pains

A LIFE IN TEN CHAPTERS

There are ten chapters to this story.

Chapter One

He lives in Leeds, in the North of England. His is a strange school for there is a broad white line in the middle of the playground. The boys and girls from the local housing estate have to play on one side of the line. His immigrant parents own their small house and so he is instructed to play on the other side of the line. He is the only black boy in the school. When the bell signals the end of playtime the two groups, one neatly dressed, the other group more discernibly scruffy, retreat into their separate buildings. The five-year-old boy is beginning to understand difference—in the form of *class*. The final lesson of the day is story time. The neatly dressed children sit cross-legged on the floor at the feet of their teacher, Miss Teale. She begins to read them a tale about 'Little Black Sambo'.[1] He can feel eyes upon him. He now wishes that

---

1. Illustrated children's book first published in 1899, featuring a highly racialized dark-skinned protagonist, by Scottish writer Helen Bannerman (1862–1946).

he was on the other side of the line with the scruffy children. Either that, or would the teacher please read them a different story?

Chapter Two

He is a seven-year-old boy, and he has changed schools. At this new school there are no girls. His teacher asks him to stay behind after the lesson has finished. He is told that he must take his story and show it to the teacher in the next classroom. He isn't sure if he is being punished, but slowly he walks the short way up the corridor and shows the story to the other teacher, Miss Holmes. She sits on the edge of her desk and reads it. Then Miss Holmes looks down at him, but at first no words are exchanged. And then she speaks. 'Well done. I'll hold on to this.'

Chapter Three

The eight-year-old boy seems to spend his whole day with his head stuck in books. His mother encourages him to get into the habit of going to the local library every Saturday, but he can only take out four books at a time and by Monday he has read them all. Two brothers up the street sometimes let him borrow their Enid Blyton paperbacks. The Famous Five adventure stories.[2] Julian, Dick, Anne, George and Timmy the dog are the first literary lives that he intimately engages with. However, he tells his mother that he does not understand why the boys' mother warms the Enid Blyton paperbacks in the oven when he returns them. The two brothers have mentioned something to him about germs. His mother is furious. She forbids him to borrow any more books from these two boys. He begins to lose touch with Julian, Dick, Anne, George and Timmy the dog.

Chapter Four

His parents have recently divorced. He is nine and he is spending the week-end with his father, who seems to have little real interest in his son. He senses that his father is merely fulfilling a duty, but the son needs his father's attention and so he writes a story. The story includes the words 'glistening' and 'glittering' which have a glamour that the son finds alluring. When the son eventually hands the story to his father, the father seems somewhat baf-fled by this offering. His father is an immigrant, this much he already under-stands. But it is only later that he realises that imaginative writing played no part in his father's colonial education as a subject of the British Empire. His father's rudimentary schooling never embraced poetic conceits such as those his son seems determined to indulge in. As the father hands back the story to his son, a gap begins to open up between the two of them.

Chapter Five

He is only ten years old when his father decides that it is fine to leave him all alone in his spartan flat while he goes to work the night shift at the local factory. There is no television. No radio. Nothing to seize his attention

2. Series of children's adventure novels by English writer Enid Blyton (1897–1968).

beyond the few comic books and soccer magazines that the son has brought with him from his mother's house. Then, late at night, alone in the huge double bed, he leans over and discovers a paperback in the drawer of the bedside table and he begins to read the book. It is a true story about a white American man who has made himself black in order that he might experience what it is like to be a colored man. The ten-year-old boy reads John Howard Griffin's *Black Like Me*[3] and, alone in his father's double bed, he tries hard not to be afraid. That night he leaves the lights on, and in the morning he is still awake as his exhausted father slides into bed next to him.

Chapter Six

At sixteen he has no girlfriend. The truth is, his brothers aside, he has few friends of any kind, and he seldom speaks with his father or stepmother. During the long summer holiday he locks himself away in his bedroom and he reads one large nineteenth-century novel after another. He learns how to lose himself in the world and lives of others, and in this way he does not have to think about the woeful state of his own life. At the moment he is reading *Anna Karenina*.[4] Towards the end of one afternoon his heart leaps, and he has to catch his breath. He puts the book down and whispers to himself, 'My God.' His stepmother calls him downstairs for dinner. He sits at the table in silence but he cannot eat. He stares at his brothers, at his father, at his stepmother. Do they not understand? Anna has thrown herself in front of a train.

Chapter Seven

He is eighteen and he has completed his first term at university. He cannot go back to his father's house and so he travels 150 miles north to his mother's place. Mother and son have not, of late, spent much time in each other's company. His mother does not understand that her eighteen-year-old son is now, according to him, a man. They argue, and he gets in the car and drives off in a fit of frustration. He stops the car in the local park and opens his book. However, he cannot get past the sheer audacity of the first sentence of James Baldwin's *Blues for Mister Charlie*.[5] 'And may every nigger like this nigger end like this nigger—face down in the weeds!' This eighteen-year-old 'man' is completely overwhelmed by Baldwin's brutal prose. He reads this one sentence over and over and over again. And then he closes the book and decides that he should go back and make up with his mother.

Chapter Eight

His tutor has asked to see him in his office. Dr Rabbitt informs the student that he has passed the first part of his degree in Psychology, Neurophysiology and Statistics, but he reassures the student that at nineteen there is still time for him to reconsider his choice of a degree. Does he really wish to pursue psychology? The student patiently explains that he wishes to

---

3. Nonfiction book (1961) describing a six-week period in 1959 in which Griffin (1920–1980), a white man from Dallas, Texas, darkened his skin and passed as a black man while traveling through the American South.

4. Novel (1878) by Russian writer Leo Tolstoy (1828–1910).

5. Play (1964) by American writer James Baldwin (1924–1987).

understand people, and that before university he was assiduously reading Jung and Freud for pleasure. His unmoved tutor takes some snuff, and then he rubs his beard. So you want to know about people, do you? He patiently explains to the student that William James was the first professor of psychology at Harvard, but it was his brother, Henry,[6] who really knew about people. The student looks at Dr Rabbitt, but he is unsure what to say. His tutor helps him to make the decision. 'Literature. If you want to know about people study English literature, not psychology.'

Chapter Nine

He is twenty, and for the first time since arriving in England as a four-month-old baby he has left the country. He has travelled to the United States, and crossed the huge exciting nation by Greyhound bus. After three weeks on the road, he knows that soon he will have to return to England and complete his final year of university. In California he goes into a bookstore. He buys a copy of a book that has on the cover a picture of a young man who looks somewhat like himself. He takes the book to the beach, and sits on a deckchair and begins to read. When he finishes Richard Wright's *Native Son*[7] it is almost dark, and the beach is deserted. But he now knows what he wishes to do with his life. And then, some time later, he is grateful to discover that mere ambition is fading and is being replaced by something infinitely more powerful; purpose.

Chapter Ten

He sits with his great-grandmother in the small village at the far end of St Kitts,[8] the island on which he was born twenty-eight years earlier. He has now published two novels, and on each publication day he has asked his editor to send a copy of the book to his great-grandmother. But she has never mentioned the books and so gingerly he now asks her if she ever received them? *Does* she have them? When she moves it is like watching a statue come to life. She reaches beneath the chair and slowly pulls out two brown cardboard bundles. The books are still in their packaging. She has opened the bundles, looked at the books, and then neatly replaced them. Again she opens the packaging. She fingers the books in the same way that he has seen her finger her bible. Then she looks at her great-grandson and smiles. 'I was the teacher's favourite,' she says. She was born in 1898 and so he realises that she is talking to him about life at the dawn of the twentieth century. 'And,' she continues, 'I missed a lot of school for I had to do all the errands.' Suddenly he understands what she means. She cannot read. He swallows deeply and lowers his eyes. How could he be clumsy enough to cause her this embarrassment? She carefully puts the books back in their cardboard packaging and tucks them back under the chair. She looks at her great-grandson. She doted on this boy for the first four months of his life. The great-grandson who disappeared to England. The great-grandson who all these years later now sends her stories from England.

2005

---

6. Henry James (1843–1916), American fiction writer.
7. Novel (1940) by American writer Richard
Wright (1908–1960).
8. Island in the West Indies.

SIMON ARMITAGE

b. 1963

Born in the village of Marsden in West Yorkshire, Simon Armitage writes poetry marked by his working-class upbringing in the rural north of England. After earning a B.A. in geography at Portsmouth University and an M.A. in social work at Manchester University, he became, like his father, a probation officer, though after six years he turned his attention from drug-rehabilitation programs to poetry. His first book of poems, *Zoom!*, was published in 1989, followed by a number of poetry collections, including *Paper Aeroplane: Selected Poems 1989–2014* (2014). His alliterative translations from Middle English of *Sir Gawain and the Green Knight* (2007) and *The Death of King Arthur* (2012) have been widely praised. He also published a dramatic retelling of Homer's *Odyssey* (2006), and he has written novels, plays, and memoirs, including one about a walking tour in northern England and another about his obsession with popular music. Scripts for television, film, and radio have also kept him in the public eye in Britain. He has taught at a number of universities—since 2011 at the University of Sheffield—and in 2015 he was elected the Oxford Professor of Poetry, a post in which his predecessors include Geoffrey Hill, Paul Muldoon, and Seamus Heaney.

Like Philip Larkin, Armitage writes lyric poems that take inspiration from the everyday rather than the exotic or the extreme. In a manifesto poem, he writes of not having parachuted from a plane or visited the Taj Mahal; instead, he has skipped stones and "felt each stone's inertia / spend itself against the water; then sink"; he has "held the wobbly head of a boy / at the day centre, and stroked his fat hands" ("It Ain't What You Do, It's What It Does to You"). A poem may be about something as simple as rolling a tire down a hill, though visionary wonder may spring from such mundane sources ("The Tyre"). His diction is pitched in a colloquial register, including slang and Northern English vernacular (e.g., *ginnels* and *dunch* in "Horses, M62"). But his poetry accumulates resonances through modulations of enjambment and syntax, deft deployments of internal and end rhyme, and astonishing figurative language (an old tire is compared to "gashed, rhinoceros, sea-lion skin / nursing a gallon of rain in its gut"). Revitalizing the traditional tools of the English-language lyric, Armitage can make a poem about the encounter between cars and horses on a motorway stop in its tracks ("Standstill. / Motor oil pulses. / Black blood.") or burst with a scattering force ("a riderless charge, // a flack of horseshoe and hoof"). Even as he seeks to engage the common reader, he is poet of uncommon formal virtuosity and versatility.

The Tyre

Just how it came to rest where it rested,
miles out, miles from the last farmhouse even,
was a fair question. Dropped by hurricane
or aeroplane perhaps for some reason,
5   put down as a cairn[1] or marker, then lost.
Tractor-size, six or seven feet across,
it was sloughed, unconscious, warm to the touch,

1. A mound of stones raised as a monument or marker.

its gashed, rhinoceros, sea-lion skin
nursing a gallon of rain in its gut.
10   Lashed to the planet with grasses and roots,
it had to be cut. Stood up it was drunk
or slugged, wanted nothing more than to slump,
to spiral back to its circle of sleep,
dream another year in its nest of peat.
15   We bullied it over the moor, drove it,
pushed from the back or turned it from the side,
unspooling a thread in the shape and form
of its tread, in its length and in its line,
rolled its weight through broken walls, felt the shock
20   when it met with stones, guided its sleepwalk
down to meadows, fields, onto level ground.
There and then we were one connected thing,
five of us, all hands steering a tall ship
or one hand fingering a coin or ring.

25   Once on the road it picked up pace, freewheeled,
then moved up through the gears, and wouldn't give
to shoulder-charges, kicks; resisted force
until to tangle with it would have been
to test bone against engine or machine,
30   to be dragged in, broken, thrown out again
minus a limb. So we let the thing go,
leaning into the bends and corners,
balanced and centred, riding the camber,[2]
carried away with its own momentum.
35   We pictured an incident up ahead:
life carved open, gardens in half, parted,
a man on a motorbike taken down,
a phone-box upended, children erased,
police and an ambulance in attendance,
40   scuff-marks and the smell of burning rubber,
the tyre itself embedded in a house
or lying in the gutter, playing dead.
But down in the village the tyre was gone,
and not just gone but unseen and unheard of,
45   not curled like a cat in the graveyard, not
cornered in the playground like a reptile,
or found and kept like a giant fossil.
Not there or anywhere. No trace. Thin air.

Being more in tune with the feel of things
50   than science and facts, we knew that the tyre
had travelled too fast for its size and mass,
and broken through some barrier of speed,
outrun the act of being driven, steered,
and at that moment gone beyond itself
55   towards some other sphere, and disappeared.

1997

2. Tilt built into a road at a curve, allowing vehicles to maintain speed.

Horses, M62[1]

Sprung from a field,
a team
of a dozen or so

is suddenly here and amongst,
5   silhouettes
in the butterscotch dusk.

One ghosts
between vans,
traverses three lanes,

10   its chess-piece head
fording the river of fumes;
one jumps the barricades

between carriageways;
a third slows
15   to a halt

then bends, nosing
the road, tonguing the surface
for salt.

Standstill.
20   Motor oil pulses.
Black blood.

Some trucker
swings down from his cab
to muster and drove;° but   *herd*

25   unbiddable, crossbred nags
they scatter
through ginnels°   *narrow passageways*

of coachwork° and chrome,   *car-body work*
and are distant, gone,
30   then a dunch°   *slight collision*

and here alongside
is a horse,
the writhing mat of its hide

pressed on the glass—
35   a tank of worms—
a flank

---

1. Highway in northern England connecting Liverpool and Hull.

of actual horse . . .
It bolts,
all arse and tail

40 through a valley
of fleet saloons.°   *station wagons*
Regrouped they clatter away,

then spooked by a horn
double back,
45 a riderless charge,

a flack° of horseshoe and hoof   *burst*
into the idling cars,
now eyeball, nostril, tooth

under the sodium glow,
50 biblical, eastbound,
against the flow.

2006

The English Astronaut

He splashed down in rough seas off Spurn Point.[1]
I watched through a coin-op telescope jammed
with a lollipop stick as a trawler fished him out
of the waves and ferried him back to Mission
5   Control on a trading estate near the Humber Bridge.[2]
He spoke with a mild voice: yes, it was good to be
home; he'd missed his wife, the kids, couldn't wait
for a shave and a hot bath. 'Are there any more
questions?' No, there were not.

10 I followed him in his Honda Accord to a Little
Chef on the A1[3], took the table opposite, watched
him order the all-day breakfast and a pot of tea.
'You need to go outside to do that,' said the
waitress when he lit a cigarette. He read the paper,
15 started the crossword, poked at the black pudding[4]
with his fork. Then he stared through the window
for long unbroken minutes at a time, but only at the
busy road, never the sky. And his face was not the
moon. And his hands were not the hands of a man
20 who had held between finger and thumb the blue
planet, and lifted it up to his watchmaker's eye.

2010

1. Narrow sandbar off the northeast coast of
England, near Hull.
2. Suspension bridge southwest of Hull. "Trading
estate": industrial park.

3. Longest highway in Britain, London to Edinburgh. "Little Chef": chain of British diners.
4. Type of blood sausage.

Beck[1]

It is all one chase.
Trace it back: the source
might be nothing more
than a teardrop
5   squeezed from a curlew's eye,
then follow it down
to the full-throated roar
at its mouth:
a dipper°   *small diving bird*
10 strolls the river
dressed for dinner
in a white bib.

The unbroken thread
of the beck
15 with its nose for the sea,
all flux and flex,
soft-soaping a pebble
for thousands of years,
or here
20 after hard rain
sawing the hillside in half
with its chain.
Or here,
where water unbinds
25 and hangs
at the waterfall's face,
and just for that one
stretched white moment
becomes lace.

2013

1. A mountain stream; an attention-getting gesture, such as a nod or wave.

KIRAN DESAI
b. 1971

Born in New Delhi to Indian parents, Kiran Desai emigrated from India to England in 1985, when she was fourteen years old, and then to the United States a year later. Her mother, Anita Desai (b. 1937), is an acclaimed fiction writer, whose own mother was a German Jew and whose father was Bengali. Kiran Desai received a B.A. from Bennington College in Vermont in 1993, before continuing to study creative writing at Hollins University in Virginia and Columbia University in New York City, where she received her M.F.A. in 1999. An Indian citizen, she emphasizes in interviews that, despite living in the United States, she sees "everything through the lens of being an Indian," working from the "precise emotional location" of being "part of the Indian diaspora."

Anthologizing an early story of Desai's, Salman Rushdie hailed her work as "welcome proof that India's encounter with the English language, far from proving abortive, continues to give birth to new children, endowed with lavish gifts." Desai's fiction alludes to, and builds on, Rushdie's carnivalesque humor, magically talented children, and fusion of folktale with historical fiction; V. S. Naipaul's bleak transnational portraits of postcolonial despair; and Gabriel García Márquez's family dramas and magical realist plots. As a writer with a global array of influences, when Desai won the Man Booker Prize in 2006 (as well as the National Book Critics Circle Award), she celebrated literature's boundary-traversing capacities:

> Literature is located beyond flags and anthems, simple ideas of loyalty. The vocabulary of immigration, of exile, of translation, inevitably overlaps with a realization of the multiple options for reinvention, of myriad perspectives, shifting truths, telling of lies—the great big wobbliness of it all. In a world obsessed with national boundaries and belonging, as a novelist working with a form also traditionally obsessed with place, it was a journey to come to this thought, that the less structured, the multiple, may be a possible location for fiction, perhaps a more valid ethical location in general.

The work for which Desai won the Man Booker, her expansive second novel, *The Inheritance of Loss* (2006), interleaves and layers plots in multiple locations, spanning India, England, and the United States, tracking a variety of characters in India and the Indian diaspora who live out the disparate impact of globalization and postcolonial history on the world's rich and its poor.

Desai's comic first novel, *Hullabaloo in the Guava Orchard* (1998), is more firmly situated in a single locale, a small town in northern India, south of the Himalayas, although even this relatively isolated place is traversed by modernity. Part folktale, part realist short story, "The Sermon on the Guava Tree," which was published separately but later incorporated into the novel, offers a glimpse into Desai's fruitful commingling of the English language and its literatures with the author's Indian heritage. A dreamy, indolent young man, Sampath Chawla, refusing his father's proddings toward material success, has taken refuge in a guava tree. His predictably middle-class father, the cartoonish Mr. Chawla, had found him a solid job at a post office, but once Sampath is fired, he climbs to the solitude of his leafy new home. In a 1998 interview, Desai commented on the story's origins:

> I started with a very small idea, really. I'd read a story in the *Times* of India and heard about a character from many people, a man who was a very famous hermit in India who really did climb up a tree, who lived in a tree for many, many years, until he died. He died last year, I believe. So I began to wonder what it was about someone like this who would do something as extreme as to spend his life in a tree. So it started really with that character, and then the story built up around it.

This bizarre situation takes a still stranger turn when Sampath, whose name means "wealth" or "good fortune" in Hindi, turns out to be not such a deadbeat after all, assuming unsuspected powers akin to those of an omniscient narrator. Telling his story, Desai ironically examines intergenerational and gender relations amid the small town's social panoply. Along with memorable characterization, good-humored satire, and realism interfused with folktale, Desai builds the story through the precise use of figurative language ("the breeze ran over the foliage the way a hand runs over an animal's dark fur to expose a silvery underside") and comic dialogue in Indianized

English ("You are the Number One most strange mother in the world"). Desai both expands and refines the array of characters, settings, plots, tropes, and themes to be found in contemporary literature in English.

The Sermon in the Guava Tree

The day that Sampath Chawla moved into a guava tree, his family—father, mother, grandmother, and sister Pinky—took up residence outside the local police station of the small town of Shahkot. They sat on the bench beneath the station's prize yellow rose creeper and waited for news. That is, the three women sat on the bench while Mr. Chawla walked around and around the building, making the policemen dizzy by shouting through every window he passed during his revolutions. If he himself were the police chief, he said, Sampath would be right this minute ensconced in his usual vegetable-like stupor among them.

"How is it you cannot find my son?" he shouted. Surely he had suffered quite enough already where Sampath was concerned. Look at how badly he had turned out! At school, he succeeded only at failing more reliably than anyone else. And then, instead of pulling up his socks and working hard at the job Mr. Chawla begged for him at the post office, he had gotten himself fired for his incompetence. "How could you do that?" his father had said. "You have done it on purpose so now you can spend all your time doing nothing." But Sampath had merely looked at him with a blank and hopeless expression. No doubt he would spend the rest of his days drooping about the house and dreaming in the tea stalls, or singing to himself in the public gardens. If they managed to find him again, that is. "You must find my son!" he shouted at the police chief.

The town made the most of the drama. Neighbors came by regularly for news, and everyone called out their support on their way back and forth from the marketplace. In some places there are people of quiet disposition and few words. But around Shahkot this was the very rare exception.

For one awful day it seemed as if Sampath had vanished forever. But the next morning the watchman of the university research forest, who had bicycled into town to bring his married sister some curd,[1] also brought the news that beyond the compound of the retired district judge a strange man had climbed a tree and not come back down. Nobody knew why. The man, he said, would answer no questions.

"If someone in this country is crazy enough to climb up a tree, you can be sure it is Sampath," said Mr. Chawla. "There is no doubting the matter."

Holding hands, the family ran together to the bus stop, their rubber slippers slapping against their heels. They caught the same bus Sampath had taken the day before, when who knows what compulsion had driven him far from his home up into the guava tree. Here, in the place where he had taken up residence, the Chawlas made their way down the crisscross of little paths leading into an old orchard that had once borne enough fruit for it to be shipped and sold in New Delhi. But the orchard had been abandoned long ago, the fruit turning sour and the branches growing into each other, and was used now only by an occasional goatherd grazing his flock.

1. Yogurt, or coagulated milk.

Searching for Sampath, the family clacked about the trees and shouted up into the leaves, the three women uttering his name with mournful wails, Mr. Chawla shouting like an Army major. At last, at the far corner of the farthest guava grove, right near the crumbling wall that bordered the forest, they discovered Sampath, sitting in his tree, his legs dangling beneath him. He had been watching their efforts with some alarm.

What on earth was he to say? He imagined himself declaring, "I am happy over here." Or asking, in a surprised fashion, "But why have you come to visit me?" He could answer their accusations with a defiant "But for some people it is normal to sit in trees." Or, serene with newfound dignity, he could say, "I am adopting a simple way of life. From now on I have no relatives." However, he did not like the thought of hurting anyone's feelings.

In the end, as it happened, he said nothing at all.

"What are you doing up there?" shouted Mr. Chawla. "Get down at once!" Sampath looked sturdily into the leafy world about him, trying to steady his wildly fluttering heart. He concentrated on the way the breeze ran over the foliage the way a hand runs over an animal's dark fur to expose a silvery underside.

Pinky felt a sudden surge of embarrassment for her brother. "Get out of the tree—the whole family is being shamed," she said bitterly.

His grandmother exclaimed, "Come down, Sampath, please. You are going to fall sick up there. Look at his thin yellow face! We had better go for the doctor."

Still he was silent.

Looking at her son, Mrs. Chawla felt her girlhood come rushing back to her, engulfing her in the memory of a time when a desperation she had sometimes felt rose and surrounded her like an enormous wall. "Let him be," she said.

"Let him be!" said Mr. Chawla. "Do families allow their sons to climb up trees? You are the Number One most strange mother in the world. Your son leaves home and climbs up a tree and you say, 'Let him be.' With you as his mother no wonder he has turned out like this. How can I keep normality within this family? I take it as a full-time job and yet it defies possibility. We must formulate a plan. Only monkeys climb up trees."

Sampath clutched at the branch he was sitting on and held on tight.

Monkeys climbed trees. Beetles lived in trees. Ants crawled up and down them. Birds sat in them. People used them for fruit and firewood, and underneath them they made each other's acquaintance in the few months between the time they got married and the time the babies arrived. But for someone to travel a considerable distance just to sit in a tree was preposterous. For that person to be sitting there a few days later was more preposterous still.

In desperation, the family called upon Dr. Banerjee, from the clinic in the bazaar, and, an energetic man, he arrived at once to view his patient. He had a mustache and round glasses and a degree from the medical school in Ranchi.[2] "Come down!" he shouted good-humoredly. "How do you expect me to examine you while you're sitting up in a tree?"

2. Capital of the state of Jharkand, in eastern India.

But, oh no, Sampath was no fool. He would not climb down to be caught and—who knows!—be put into a cage and driven off to the insane asylum on Alipur Road like the madman who had interrupted the ladies' home-economics class in the university and been lured and trapped by a single sweet. So, at the family's pleading, Dr. Banerjee, who prided himself on being a good sport, hoisted himself into the tree, stethoscope and blood-pressure pump about his neck. He climbed all the way up to Sampath so he could look into his eyes and ears, check his tongue, listen to his heart, take his blood pressure, and hit his knee with an expertly aimed karatelike move of his hand. Then he climbed down and got back into the scooter rickshaw he had arrived in. "He is a crazy person," he said, beaming, the mirth of the entire situation too much for him. "Nobody except for God can do anything about that." And he disappeared back into town.

The family went to see the doctor of Tibetan medicine who had been recommended by their neighbor Lakshmiji. "A variety of cures may be prescribed," he said. "For example, medicines derived from the scorpion, the sea scorpion, the sea dragon, and the sea mouse."

"What sea mouse? There is no such thing as sea mouse!" shouted Mr. Chawla, and he dragged the family from the dark little clinic to the homeopathic and Ayurvedic doctors, and then to the naturopath who lived all the way in Kajuwala.[3]

Dutifully, they pounded pellets into powders, brewed teas, and counted out the homeopathic pills that looked and smelled promising but wrought none of the miraculous changes they had been assured of.

Finally, they visited the holy man who lived outside the tea stall near the deer park. "Sorry to disturb you. Our son is afflicted."

"How is he afflicted?"

"He is suffering from madness."

"Is he shouting?"

"No."

"Having fits?"

"No."

"Is he tearing his hair out?"

"No."

"Is he biting his neighbors? Biting himself? Is he sleepwalking? Does he stick out his tongue and roll his eyes? Is he rude to strangers?"

"No. He eats and sleeps and takes good care of his hair. He doesn't shout and he doesn't bite himself. He has never been rude to strangers."

"Then he is not mad."

"But he is sitting up in a tree!"

"Arrange a marriage for him. Then you can rest in peace. You will have no further problems."

It is necessary at some point for every family to acquire a daughter-in-law.[4] This girl must come from a good family. She must have a pleasant personality—decent and not shameless and bold. This girl should keep her eyes lowered

3. Town in the Bikaner district of the northwestern Indian state of Rajasthan, on the border with Pakistan. "Ayurvedic": practicing a traditional Indian system of medicine.
4. Cf. the opening line of *Pride and Prejudice*

(1813) by English novelist Jane Austen (1775–1817): "It is a truth universally acknowledged, that a single man in possession of a good fortune, must be in want of a wife."

and, because she is embarrassed and shy, her head bowed, as well. Nobody wants a girl who stares people right in the face with big froggy eyes. She should be fair-complexioned, but if she is dark the dowry must include at least one of the following items: a television set, a refrigerator, a Godrej brand steel cupboard,[5] or a motor scooter. When this girl sings, her voice must bring tears of feeling to the eyes. When she dances, people should exclaim "Wah!" in astounded pleasure. It should be made clear that she will not dance and sing after marriage and shame the family. This girl should have passed all her examinations in the first division[6] but will listen respectfully as you lecture her on various subjects you yourself failed in secondary school. She must not stride, or kick up her legs like a horse. She must sit quietly, with knees together. She should talk just a little to show she can: one word, or maybe two after she has been coaxed and begged several times, "Just a few sentences. Just one sentence." Her mother should urge, "Eat something. Eat a laddoo.[7] My daughter made these with her own hands." And these laddoos must not be recognizable as coming from the sweetmeat shop down the road.

She must be able to eat with knife and fork, or at least with a spoon. She should not be fat. She should be pleasantly plump, with large hips and breasts but a small waist. Talk of husband and children should so overcome her with shyness and embarrassment that she should hide her face, pink as a rosebud, in the fold of her sari. Then, if she has fulfilled all the requirements for a sound character and impressive accomplishments, if her parents have agreed to meet all the necessary financial contributions, if the fortune-tellers have decided the stars are lucky and the planets are compatible, everyone can laugh with relief and tilt her face up by the chin and say she is exactly what the family have been looking for, that she will be a daughter to their household. This, after all, is the boy's family. They're entitled to their sense of pride.

But the family could find only one prospective daughter-in-law. She was scrawny and dark. "Like a crow," Mrs. Chawla said indignantly when the first photograph was shown to them by their old neighbor Lakshmiji, who was acting as marriage broker. "You are trying to marry poor Sampath to a crow."

"He is lucky to find anyone at all," said Mr. Chawla, who had given up all hope of motor scooters and wedding parties at the Hans Raj Hotel.

The girl arrived, along with her family, on the public bus. Apart from her family, the bus was full of singing ladies and gentlemen, pilgrims returning from a trip to the Krishna temple[8] in a neighboring town. The Chawla family watched as the bus veered off the road like a crazy beetle and moved toward them in a cloud of dust.

The bus driver had obligingly offered to drop off the family right at Sampath's orchard. A bride-to-be should not have to walk and grow dusty and be shown to disadvantage, he said sympathetically. He himself had a daughter to marry. "Yes, yes, let's take them directly to the boy," chorused the

---

5. Locker or cabinet made by a large Indian company headquartered in Mumbai.
6. I.e., in the highest-scoring group.

7. A ball-shaped, fried Indian sweet.
8. Hindu temple dedicated to the god Krishna, often worshiped as a god of joy and fertility.

other passengers, pausing to make this decision before resuming their hymn singing.

Despite the driver's kindness and the attention she had received with the help of a handkerchief, a little spit, and a large amount of talcum powder, the girl descended from the bus looking extremely dusty. The pilgrims, curious about what might happen during this unusual encounter between prospective marriage partners, tumbled out of the bus as well, in a messy and chaotic heap. They needed a break for lunch anyway, and a little private time behind some trees. Holding the prospective bride before them like a gift, the group moved toward the guava tree.

Sampath had always had a soft corner for the lady on the label of the coconut hair-oil bottle. He had spent a rather large amount of time in consideration of her mysterious smile upon the bathroom shelf. While squatting on the mildewed wooden platform taking his bucket baths, he had conducted a series of imagined encounters with her, complete with imagined conversations and imagined quarrels and reconciliations. She would meet him wreathed in the scent of the oil, with a smile as white as the gleaming inside of a coconut. A braid of hair had travelled downward from the top of the coconut lady's head and followed the undulations of the bottle. Sampath looked down at the veiled woman standing underneath his tree, and felt hot and horrified.

"Please come down and be introduced. You have sat in the tree long enough," said Mr. Chawla. Sampath thought he might faint.

"Climb up, daughter," the girl's father urged her. "Climb up. Come on. One step. Just a step."

The devotees raised the girl's rigid, unwilling form into the tree. "Up," they urged. Slowly she began to climb. She was encased in layers of shiny material like a large, expensive toffee. The cloth billowed about her, making her look absurdly stout. Her gold slippers slipped with every step. Her sari was pulled over her head and she held the edge of it between her teeth so as to keep as much of her face modestly covered as possible. It was clear this girl would not take well to life in a tree. It seemed an eternity before she neared Sampath. She paused and looked back down for further directions. Nobody knew quite what to expect, or how she should proceed. Even Mr. Chawla was at a loss as to what should happen next.

"Touch his feet!" someone finally shouted, in a moment of inspiration.

"Yes, touch his feet," the rest of the pilgrims cried, and, extending a single timid finger like a snail peeping from its shell, she gingerly poked at Sampath's toe. Her finger was as cold as ice, and moist. Sampath leaped up in horror. In an equal state of distress, the girl let out a faint cry. Losing her balance and her gold slippers, she tumbled indecorously out of the tree, accompanied by the more robust cries of the pilgrims and her family, who rushed at her with arms outstretched. But they failed to catch her as she fell, and she landed with a dull thump upon the ground.

The signs for marriage were not auspicious.

The devotees propped her against a tree and fanned her with a leafy branch. "What am I to do with this boy?" Mr. Chawla said, throwing his hands up in the air. "Tell me what I should do. The best education. A job. A wife. The world served to him on a platter, but, oh no, none of it is good enough for him. Mister here must run and sit in a tree. He is not in the least bit thankful for all that has been done for him."

The girl began to sneeze in tiny mouselike squeals. "Stop fanning her with that dirty branch!" someone shouted. "All the dust must have gone up her nose."

"Dust or no dust, it is yet one more inauspicious sign," another onlooker said.

Pinky felt terribly scornful of this third-rate woman who had responded to such a greatly consequential moment in her life by sneezing and whimpering. She gave her a good pinch from behind, hoping to see her jump, but the girl continued to squeak and sniffle. The talcum powder slid down her face in a milky river.

"What can I do?" Mr. Chawla asked of the crowd. "What am I to do with this boy?" He was sweating despite the pleasant breeze that rotated about them, laden with the scent of earth and burgeoning vegetation.

He was the head of a family and he liked it that way.

But oh! What good was it to be the head of a family when you had a son who ran and sat in a tree? Who slipped from beneath your fingers and shamed you?

"What am I to do?" he demanded of the devotees still milling about, to show them it was not for lack of effort and concern on his behalf that Sampath had ended up in such a pitiful state. He hit his forehead with the flat of his palm, for drama has a way of overriding the embarrassment of a situation that should be privately experienced.

The ladies and gentlemen from the bus felt a little sorry for him. "Yes, yes, how shameful," they muttered. "And coming from a decent family and all. Clearly the boy has been derailed."

They stared at Sampath, watching to see how his father's distress would affect him. Surely any son, even a son like Sampath, would respond to such a moving show of emotion. Sensitive to the atmosphere of expectation beneath him, Sampath looked down into their upturned eyes. He thought of his old school and the post office and entire roomfuls of people awaiting the answer to questions he had often not even heard. He wondered how it could be that he had never felt comfortable among people. "Go on with your own lives!" he wanted to shout. "Go on, go on! Leave me to mine."

But of course he could not say any such thing. In desperation he looked around him. Among the crowd of faces down below he recognized that of Mr. Singh, the brother-in-law of a neighbor in Shahkot. Mr. Singh, whose letters he had sometimes read in idle moments in the post office, steaming them open over glasses of tea or just prying them open, the humidity in the air having rendered the gum almost entirely ineffectual. Lazily, he had perused the contents of a large quantity of letters during his time at work. In a frantic plea for help, he shouted, "Mr. Singhji!"[9]

He remembered one particular letter sent by Mr. Singh to his father.

"Is your jewelry still safely buried beneath the tulsi[1] plant?"

Mr. Singh turned pale. "How do you know about my circumstances?" he asked.

Sampath caught sight of Mrs. Chopra. "How is that lump in your throat that travels up and down your windpipe, whispering threats and almost bursting right out of your chest?"

9. As a suffix attached to a name, "-ji" shows respect in many languages of the Indian subcontinent.

1. Species of basil cultivated by Hindus as a sacred plant.

"*Hai*,"[2] she gasped, "who told you?"

Encouraged now by his success, Sampath brightened a little. He jabbed his finger at a bald-headed man in the crowd, and said. "And you, sir, that secret oil you got from the doctor in Side Gully. Clearly it is not working. Try a good massage with mustard oil, and your hair will sprout as thick and as plentiful as grass in the Cherrapunji rain."[3]

The devotees drove back into Shahkot with the news. There was a man up in the guava tree, a remarkable man. He had known all sorts of things. The dacoits[4] were blackmailing poor Mr. Singh. Ratan Sinha had been using a special hair oil to no effect. An evil spirit had established itself in Mrs. Chopra's throat.

Clearly, there was more to this post-office clerk than to ordinary mortals. In his eyes they had detected a rare spirit.

It was at this point that Mr. Chawla had a realization—all of a sudden, with a tumble and rush of understanding, a realization so quick and so incredible in nature that his heart was caught in a state of constant pounding. Sampath might make his family's fortune. They could be rich! How many hermits were secretly wealthy? How many holy men were not at all the beggars they appeared to be? How many men of unfathomable wisdom possessed unfathomable bank accounts? What an opportunity had arisen out of nowhere. Already there was a change in the way people looked at Sampath; no longer did they snigger and smirk or make sympathetic noises with their tongues. Mr. Chawla kept his thoughts to himself and didn't say a word to anyone, but, in a sudden turnabout of policy, which both surprised and pleased his wife and his mother, who were already settling into the orchard as if it were their own long-lost home, he stopped berating Sampath for having climbed up the tree, and turned his attention to other matters.

Gradually, Sampath was provided with all sorts of comforts, and the more elaborate his living arrangements the happier he was. A cot was raised up into the tree and fastened with rope. A striped umbrella donated by a friendly servant of the retired judge was positioned over Sampath's head. He made a lovely picture seated there amid the greenery, reclining on his cot at a slight angle to the world; propped against numerous cushions tucked up, during chilly evenings, in a glamorous satin quilt covered with leopard skin spots. On his head he sported a tea-cozy-like[5] red woollen hat that had been knitted by his grandmother and raised to him on a stick. He was particularly fond of this hat, for it kept his head snug and warm at night when the breeze was chilly, and it kept the night rustlings, the crawling of little black beetles, ants, and moths, out of his ears as well.

"I'm comfortable," he announced to his family with a gesture of dismissal when he found everything to his satisfaction, leaving them for a minute bewildered, for they were yet to get used to this reversal in their relationship. How they had scolded him once upon a time for every little thing he had done. Now here he was waving at them as if he were a rajah[6] wishing to be left alone. When they were needed again, he summoned them with shouts,

2. Exclamation of grief or frustration (Hindi and Punjabi).
3. Of the town in eastern India near Bangladesh, subject to very heavy rainfall and believed to be the wettest place on earth. Mustard oil is widely used in northern India for many purposes.
4. Robbers.
5. I.e., like a quilted or knitted teapot cover.
6. Indian prince, chief, or noble.

starting right at dawn, when he desired his morning tea, and then a little later when he was ready for his bath, which required elaborate arrangements to be made by the family, who were, after all, willing to do quite a bit of work in this regard, for they had always been a clean family. Bucketfuls of hot water were raised to Sampath via a rope levering system designed especially for this purpose by his father.

When it came to his meals, Pinky's efforts in climbing up with bowls and dishes had ended more often in accidents than in success, with Sampath's dinner either in the grass or, worse, splattered and scalding over the poor bearer of food.

"This is absurd," said Mr. Chawla. "This isn't working." And he attached an old wooden crate to the elementary pulley system used to deliver Sampath's bathwater, and thereafter Sampath's meals were given to him simply by pulling on a rope and raising the crate. As the fluffy chapatis and puris[7] were made down below they were proffered up to him speared atop a bamboo stick, as were slices of pickle, bits of fruit, and other tasty tidbits.

Thus ensconced in his orchard bower, Sampath gave what came to be known as the Sermon in the Guava Tree, in which he responded to people's queries with such a mysterious charm and wit that they arrived in growing numbers to see him, making their way down the narrow path to stare with amazement at this skinny, long-legged apparition amid the leaves.

Among the first to make this trip were Miss Jyotsna and Mr. Gupta, his two colleagues from the post office.

"He must have gone through a thorough and complete transformation," said Miss Jyotsna. "Look how his face is being so different now."

Certainly it was a happier, calmer face. "*Namasteji*,"[8] said Sampath, greeting them cheerfully from his cot in the tree, his new position of power. Really, he thought, he was quite fond of them. They had always meant well, unlike many others he could name.

"Hello, Sampath," said Mr. Gupta. "Why did you not take me with you? I could have had a little rest from this one here." He pointed at Miss Jyotsna with a comic expression on his face.

"Any time you want a rest from her you should send her to the sari and shalwar kameez[9] shop," said Sampath, laughing. "You know how much this lady is loving clothes. . . . Oh, but maybe that is not such a good idea. Already she owes the Ladies' Fashion Shop a hundred and fifty-two rupees and eighty paise."[1]

Once when Miss Jyotsna had been summoned to the office of the head of the post office, Sampath had had the occasion to examine the contents of her purse: the lipstick and comb, the embroidered handkerchief, the receipts and safety pins, the toffees and little vials of homeopathic medicine.

Miss Jyotsna raised a trembling hand to her mouth. The blood rushed to her face. She had kept her debt to the sari shop a strict secret. What else could Sampath say about her? She had heard of the way he had stunned

---

7. Round, unleavened cakes, usually fried. "Chapatis": unleavened bread.
8. Hello, or welcome (Hindi).
9. Outfit of loose tunic and trousers.

1. One Indian rupee is equal to 100 paise (singular paisa). In 1990, 17 rupees were worth about one U.S. dollar; thus, she owes about nine dollars.

the devotees of the Krishna temple with his clairvoyance; now he had used his powers to examine her.

She nudged Mr. Gupta with her elbow. "Treat him with some respect," she said, surprising him with the strange new note of reverence in her voice. She was apparently awestruck by what she saw. And even the paan-shop[2] man, who had also come to visit, thinking that maybe he would sell a few paans while satisfying his curiosity, turned to give Mr. Gupta a dirty look, and said, "Clearly this fellow here is unversed in spiritual matters."

"But it is only Sampath," protested Mr. Gupta.

But clearly it was not only Sampath. It was Sampath of unfathomable wisdom, sitting in his tree abode.

The sweetshop man joined them after work, then two college students skipping a lecture, the washerman on his bicycle, and a pregnant lady who wished to know if her baby would be a boy or a girl. "Ah, yes," she said with satisfaction, to those standing about the tree with her, "he has the same expression as the Tajewala sage in samadhi.[3] Perhaps you have seen the photographs?"

"My son is keeping bad company," interrupted a distressed but spirited relative of Lakshmiji's who was dressed in a canary-yellow sari. "What is there to do?" she asked.

"Add lemons to milk and it will grow sour," answered Sampath in an exceptionally sociable and happy temper, mimicking the old men of Shahkot, who liked to sit at their gates on winter afternoons, basking in their socks and hats, while they lectured passersby. "But add some sugar, Madam, and wah! how good that milk will taste. These are things I do not have to tell you. You yourself know you behaved just like your son when you were young."

He impressed himself by how many details he had stowed away while reading in the post office. Why, he could just pull them out of some secret compartment in his brain the way a magician pulled rabbits from a hat. How admiringly the people below the tree were looking at him! Never before had he felt the sweet and unique pleasure of giving advice which now suffused his being and spread to shine about his face.

"By this, do you mean I should remove him from the presence of these undesirable characters?" Lakshmiji's relative asked.

"If you put a chicken on the fire and leave it, in a little while it will be no longer a chicken but ash and bones. Leave a kettle on the flames, the water will grow hot, and then, if someone does not lift it off, it will all boil away until there is nothing left. If your child is playing with a dead smelly mouse, you will not debate, 'Should I let him be, should I let him play.' No, straightaway you will throw away the mouse and take your child indoors to wash his hands."

Mr. Chawla and Pinky, who had just arrived from a trip to the market in time to hear this last sentence, looked at each other in disbelief when they saw how closely people listened to Sampath.

"Did you hear?" Mr. Chawla asked Pinky.

"Dead smelly mouse?" said Pinky, incredulous.

"If you do not weed," said Sampath, "your tomato plant will not flower."

Sampath's grandmother and Mrs. Chawla, flushed with pride, were already part of the crowd. They listened to every word that was being uttered, leaning

2. Shop selling cigarettes and paan, a preparation of betel leaf, areca nut, and lime chewed as a stimulant.

3. Highest state of meditation. "Tajewala": site of a dam on the Yamuna River in northern India.

forward to hear a round-faced man ask, "I am being overtaken by spiritual matters. How can I keep my mind on my responsibilities?"

"If you talk to a young girl as she stands before the mirror, it is like talking to a deaf person. And can you keep a moth from flying into the lantern by saying she should worry about her three children?"

"But are you saying I should forgo my duties to my wife and children?"

"Once my uncle had a rooster, and an insect laid its eggs in the flesh of its rear end. It knew the young ones would have a warm place to live in and plenty to eat before they were old enough to leave."

"Which is the better way to realize God? The way of devotion or the way of knowledge?"

The questions came fast and furious.

"Some people can only digest fish cooked in a light curry. Others are of a sour disposition and should not eat pickled fish. In the South they enjoy fish cooked with coconut water. I myself have a preference for pomfret in a sauce of chili and tamarind thickened with gram flour."[4]

"Where can I begin my search? What is the starting point?"

"POST-OFFICE CLERK CLIMBS TREE," Mr. Chawla read to his astounded family a little later in the week when the news had reached the local news bureau and was deemed worthy of attention. "Fleeing tedious duties at the Shahkot Post Office, a clerk has been reported to have settled in a large guava tree. According to popular speculation, he is one of an unusual spiritual nature, his childlike ways being coupled with unfathomable wisdom."

There it was—a modest column introducing Sampath to the world, along with news of a scarcity of groundnut and an epidemic of tree frogs, and the rumor that Coca-Cola might soon be arriving in India.[5]

1997

4. Flour made from ground chickpeas. "Pomfret": a type of fish. "Tamarind": sweet, acidic fruit.
5. The Coca-Cola Company was forced out of India in 1977 after it refused to reveal its secret formula to the government; it was permitted to return in 1993. "Groundnut": peanut.

ZADIE SMITH
b. 1975

The London-born daughter of an English father and a Jamaican mother, Zadie Smith was a product of the great postwar demographic change in Britain, the influx of black and Asian immigrants from the empire's former colonies. Her mother had grown up in Jamaica and, like many other West Indians, settled in Britain in the 1960s. Of her mixed heritage Smith has written, "When your personal multiplicity is printed on your face, in an almost too obviously thematic manner, in your DNA, in your hair and in the neither this nor that beige of your skin—well, anyone can see you come from Dream City," her tongue-in-cheek name for the space of hybridity. "It is a place of many voices, where the unified singular self is an illusion," where "everything is doubled, everything is various. You have no choice but to cross borders and speak in tongues." Springing from the experience of "personal multiplicity," Smith's fiction has vigorously crossed borders and spoken in a cacophony of tongues.

Smith grew up in what she has called "the big, colorful, working-class sea" of the Willesden area of north London that figures in her fiction. When she was studying English literature at the "smaller, posher pond" (her words) of Cambridge University (B.A., 1997), her fiction had already attracted the interest of major publishers. The result was her prize-winning first novel, *White Teeth* (2000). Before its publication, no work had captured with such humor and zest the multicultural jangle of different peoples, dialects, and styles in contemporary Britain. Less riotously comic, her second novel, *The Autograph Man* (2002), tracks the celebrity quest of a Chinese-Jewish Londoner named Alex-Li Tandem, mourning his father's death in a world made shallow by the commodification of culture, the arts, personality, and ethnicity. Her third novel, *On Beauty* (2005), shifts locales from London largely to the Boston environs, where Smith spent a year, and deliberately echoes English author E. M. Forster's *Howards End* (1910) in telling the story of two entangled families. *NW* (2012) returns to North London but in a more fractured, experimental style, while *Swing Time* (2016) extends across London, New York, and West Africa.

Smith may still be best known for her first novel, despite her subsequent successes. A year before *White Teeth* came out, she published the short story "The Waiter's Wife," the work given here that includes scenes and characters that also appear in the novel's third and fourth chapters. The story confects many of the formal ingredients that made her novel famous, including her wisecracking humor and rapid-fire dialogue, mimicry of an array of finely distinguished dialects and accents, and vibrant characterization of people from London's South Asian, black, and other communities. This is a world of often surprising interchanges between East and West, raucous debates about secularism and religion and gender, cross-cultural friendships and marriages that blur the dividing lines among Asians, Caribbeans, Jews, the English, and many others.

Reveling in cultural and human comminglings, *White Teeth* tells the intertwined stories of three London families, the Anglo-Jamaican Joneses, the Bengali Iqbals, and the Anglo-Jewish Chalfens. At the heart of this sprawling novel is the friendship between the white Englishman Archie Jones and the Bengali Muslim Samad Iqbal. Having met during their less than heroic tour of duty in World War II, they renew their odd-couple bond when Samad leaves Bangladesh for London in 1975, and over time their much younger wives, the gap-toothed Jamaican Clara and the fierce Bangladeshi immigrant Alsana, also begin a friendship. Although each character misconceives other cultures, Smith's focus is less on intercultural strife than on fluid if often bumpy relationships across ethnic divisions. The threat of racist attacks on Bangladeshis in 1970s London hovers in the background (right-wing "kids breaking the basement windows with their steel-capped boots"; Asian families "running to the cellars while windows were smashed"). But in the foreground is an irreversibly hybridized and multiracial Britain. In this world, pulsing with energy and humor and surprise, an underemployed Bengali waiter daydreams while listening to tourists mangle the names of curries; an observant Bengali Muslim woman finds herself sewing black plastic erotic costumes; two pregnant women—one African Caribbean and one South Asian—squeeze with a third woman onto a park bench and exchange thoughts on gender, marriage, and baby names.

In a synoptic passage worth quoting from *White Teeth*, Smith uncovers, in names, emblems of Britain's new cultural heterogeneity:

> This has been the century of strangers, brown, yellow, and white. This has been the century of the great immigrant experiment. It is only this late in the day that you can walk into a playground and find Isaac Leung by the fish pond, Danny Rahman in the football cage, Quang O'Rourke bouncing a basketball, and Irie Jones humming a tune. Children with first and last names on

a direct collision course. Names that secrete within them mass exodus, cramped boats and planes, cold arrivals, medical checkups. It is only this late in the day, and possibly only in Willesden, that you can find best friends Sita and Sharon, constantly mistaken for each other because Sita is white (her mother liked the name) and Sharon is Pakistani (her mother thought it best— less trouble).

This is an emerging world that needed the sharp ear, ironic eye, and dazzling wit of Zadie Smith to be named, embodied in plot, and given narrative form. Smith teases out the painful histories of postcolonial migration embedded in her characters' names, yet she also discloses the promise of new criss-crossings of identity, new transnational communities coming into being and yet to be born.

The Waiter's Wife

In the spring of 1975, Samad and Alsana Iqbal left Bangladesh and came to live in Whitechapel, London,[1] the other side of town from Archie and Clara Jones. Samad and Archie had a friendship dating back to the Second World War, back to the hot and claustrophobic Churchill tank in which they sat side by side for three months, close enough to smell each other and to recognize those scents thirty years later when Samad emerged from Gate 12, Heathrow,[2] with a young wife and a paisley patterned luggage set in tow. 'Long time no see,' Archie had said, reaching out to grasp his old friend's palm, but Samad converted the handshake into a hug almost immediately, 'Archibald Jones. Long time no bloody *smell*.'

They fell back into easy conversation, two old boys slipping swiftly into an acquaintance as comfortable as slippers while their wives stood either side of the bags noting they had this thing in common and no more: that they were young, much younger than the men they stood awkwardly beside. They looked an unlikely pair. Alsana was small and rotund, moon-faced and with thick fingers she hid in the folds of her cardigan. Clara was tall, striking, a black girl with a winning smile, wearing red shorts of a shortness that Alsana had never imagined possible, even in this country.

'Hot pants,' said Clara, shyly, in response to Alsana's wide eyes, 'I made dem myself.'

'I sew also,' Alsana replied, and they had a pleasant enough chat about seams and bobbins, materials and prices per yard, in a motorway service station over an indigestible lunch. 'The wives get on like a house on fire,' Archie had said merrily, giving Samad a nudge in the ribs. But this made them nervous, the two young wives, and after the ice-cream sundaes they sat in silence.

So some black people *are* friendly, thought Alsana after that first meeting was over. It was her habit to single one shining exception out of every minority she disliked; certain dentists, certain singers, certain film stars had been granted specialist treatment in the past and now Clara Jones was to be given Alsana's golden reprieve. Their relations were hesitant in the beginning—a few lunch dates here and there, the occasional coffee; neither wished to admit how much time they had on their hands though newly wed, or that Archie and

---

1. Poor district where people of Bangladeshi descent are the largest demographic group.　　2. London airport.

Samad were always together. It wasn't until the Iqbals moved north, two minutes from Archie and his favourite watering hole, that the women truly resigned themselves to their husbands' mutual appreciation society and started something of a rearguard action. Picnics, the movies, museums, swimming pools—just the two of them. But even when they became fairly close, it was impossible to forget what a peculiar couple they made on the bus, in the park.

It took the Iqbals a year to get to Willesden High Road: a year of mercilessly hard graft to make the momentous move from the wrong side of Whitechapel to the wrong side of Willesden.[3] A year's worth of Alsana banging away at the old Singer machine that sat in the kitchen, sewing together pieces of black plastic for a shop called Domination in Soho[4] (many were the nights Alsana would hold up a piece of clothing she had just made—following the plans she was given—and wonder what on earth it was). A year's worth of Samad softly inclining his head at exactly the correct deferential angle, pencil in his right hand, notepad in his left, listening to the appalling pronunciation of the British, Spanish, American, French, Australian:

Go Bye Ello Sag,[5] Please.

Chicken Jail Fret See[6] Wiv Chips, Fanks.

From six in the evening until four in the morning was work and the rest was sleep, sleep without pause, until daylight was as rare as a decent tip. For what is the point, Samad would think, pushing aside two mints and a receipt to find fifteen pence, what is the point of tipping a man the same amount you would throw in a fountain to chase a wish? But before the illegal thought of folding the fifteen pence discreetly in his napkin hand had a chance to give itself form, Mukhul, Ardashir Mukhul, who ran The Palace and whose wiry frame paced the restaurant, one benevolent eye on the customers, one ever-watchful eye on the staff—Ardashir Mukhul was upon him.

'Saaamaad,' he said in his cloying, oleaginous way, 'did you kiss the necessary backside this evening, Cousin?'

Samad and Ardashir were distant cousins, Samad the elder by six years. With what joy (pure bliss!) had Ardashir opened the letter last January, to find his older, cleverer, handsomer cousin could get no work as a food inspector in England and could he possibly . . .

'Fifteen pence, Cousin,' said Samad lifting his palm.

'Well, every little helps, every little helps,' said Ardashir, his dead-fish lips stretching into a stringy smile. 'Into the Piss-Pot with it.'

The Piss-Pot was a black cooking pot that sat on a plinth outside the staff toilets into which all tips were pooled and then split at the end of the night. For the younger, good-looking waiters like Shiva this was a great injustice. Shiva was the only Hindu on the staff, a tribute to his waitering skills that had triumphed over religious difference. He could make fifteen pounds in tips in an evening if the blubberous white divorcee in the corner was lonely enough, and he batted his long lashes at her effectively. He also made money from the polo-necked directors and producers (The Palace sat in the centre of London's Theatreland) who flattered the boy, watched his ass wiggle provocatively to the bar and back, and swore that the next time someone put

---

3. A better-off northwest area with a more heterogeneous population.
4. Area of central London with entertainment and sex industries.

5. Gobi aloo saag, curried potatoes and cauliflower with spinach.
6. Jalfrezi, a curry of onions and green chili.

A Passage to India[7] on the stage, the casting couch would be his. For Shiva then, the Piss-Pot system was simply daylight robbery. But for men like Samad, in his forties, and for the even older, like the white-haired Mohammed (Ardashir's great-uncle), who was eighty if he was a day, who had deep pathways dug into the sides of his mouth where he had smiled when he was young—for men like this the Piss-Pot could not be complained about. It was a boon if anything, and it made more sense to join the collective than pocket fifteen pence and risk being caught (and docked a week's tips).

'You're all on my back!' Shiva would snarl, when he had to relinquish five pounds at the end of the night and drop it into the pot. 'You all live off my back! Somebody get these losers off my back! That was my fiver[8] and now it's going to be split sixty-five-fucking-million ways as a hand out to these losers! What is this, communism?'

And the rest would avoid his glare, and busy themselves quietly with other things until one evening, one fifteen-pence evening, Samad said, 'Shut up, boy,' quietly, almost underneath his breath.

'You!' Shiva swung round to where Samad stood crushing a great tub of lentils for tomorrow's dhal.[9] 'You're the worst of them! You're the worst fucking waiter I've ever seen! You couldn't get a tip if you mugged the bastards! I hear you trying to talk to the customer about biology this, politics that—just serve the food, you idiot—you're a waiter, for fuck's sake, you're not Michael Parkinson.[1] *Did I hear you say Delhi—*' Shiva put his apron over his arm and began posturing around the kitchen (he was a pitiful mimic) '—*I was there myself, you know, Delhi University, it was most fascinating, yes—and I fought in the war, for England, yes—yes, yes, charming, charming—*' round and round the kitchen he went, bending his head and rubbing his hands over and over like Uriah Heep,[2] bowing and genuflecting to the head cook, to the old man arranging great hunks of meat in the walk-in freezer, to the young boy scrubbing the inside of the oven. 'Samad, *Samad . . .*' he said with what seemed infinite pity, then stopped abruptly, pulled the apron off and wrapped it round his waist, 'you're a sad bastard.'

Mohammed looked up from his pot-scrubbing and shook his head again and again. To no one in particular he said, 'These young people—what kind of talk? What happened to respect? What kind of talk is this?'

'And you, you can fuck off too—' said Shiva, brandishing a ladle in his direction, '—You old fool! You're not my father.'

'Second cousin of your mother's uncle,' a voice muttered from the back.

'Bollocks,' said Shiva. 'Bollocks[3] to that.'

He grabbed the mop and was heading off for the toilets, when he stopped by Samad and placed the broom inches from Samad's mouth.

'Kiss it,' he sneered: and then impersonating Ardashir's sluggish drawl, 'Who knows, Cousin, you might get a raise!'

And that's what it was like most nights; abuse from Shiva and others; condescension from Ardashir; never seeing Alsana; never seeing the sun; clutching fifteen pence and then releasing it; wanting desperately to be wearing a sign, a large white placard that said:

---

7. Novel (1924) by English author E. M. Forster (1879–1970), set in 1920s British India.
8. Five-pound note.
9. Long-cooked dish.
1. English host (b. 1935) of the long-running tele-

vision show *Parkinson* (1971–1982, 1998–2007).
2. Character in *David Copperfield* (1850), by Charles Dickens.
3. Nonsense; literally, testicles.

I AM NOT A WAITER. THAT IS, I AM A WAITER, BUT NOT JUST A WAITER. I HAVE BEEN A STUDENT, A SCIENTIST, A SOLDIER. MY WIFE IS CALLED ALSANA. WE LIVE IN EAST LONDON BUT WE WOULD LIKE TO MOVE NORTH. I AM A MUSLIM BUT ALLAH HAS FORSAKEN ME OR I HAVE FORSAKEN ALLAH. I'M NOT SURE. I HAVE AN ENGLISH FRIEND—ARCHIE—AND OTHERS. I AM FORTY-NINE BUT WOMEN STILL TURN IN THE STREET. SOMETIMES.

But no such placard existing, he had instead the urge, the need, to speak to every man, and like the Ancient Mariner[4] to explain, always to explain, to reassert something, anything. Wasn't that important? But then the heart-breaking disappointment—to find out that the inclining of one's head, poising of one's pen, these were important, so important. It was important to be a good waiter, to listen when someone said:

Lamb Dawn Sock[5] and Rice. Please. With Chips. Thank you.

And fifteen pence clinked on china. Thank you Sir. Thank you so very much.

One evening, shortly after he had put the down payment on the Willesden flat, Samad had waited till everyone left and then climbed the loudly carpeted stairs to Ardashir's office, for he had something to ask him.

'Cousin!' said Ardashir with a friendly grimace at the sight of Samad's body curling cautiously round the door. He knew that Samad had come to enquire about a pay increase, and he wanted his cousin to feel that he had at least considered the case in all his friendly judiciousness before he declined.

'Cousin, come in!'

'Good evening, Ardashir Mukhul,' said Samad, stepping fully into the room.

'Sit down, sit down,' said Ardashir warmly. 'No point standing on ceremony now, is there?'

Samad was glad this was so. He said as much. He took a moment to look with the necessary admiration around the room with its relentless flashes of gold, its thick pile carpet, its furnishings in various shades of yellow and green. One had to admire Ardashir's business sense. He had taken the simple idea of an Indian restaurant (small room, pink tablecloth, loud music, atrocious wallpaper, meals) and just made it bigger. He hadn't improved anything; it was the same old crap but bigger in a bigger building in the biggest tourist trap in London. Leicester Square. You had to admire it and admire the man, who now sat like a benign locust, his slender insectile body swamped in a black leather chair, leaning over the desk, all smiles, a parasite disguised as a philanthropist.

'Cousin, what can I do for you?'

Samad took a deep breath. The matter was . . . what was the matter? The house was the matter. Samad was moving out of East London (where one couldn't bring up children, indeed, one couldn't, not if one didn't wish them to come to bodily harm), from East London, with its National Front[6] gangs, to North London, north-west in fact, where things were more . . . more . . . liberal. Ardashir's eyes glazed over a little as Samad explained his situation. His skinny legs twitched beneath the desk, and in his fingers he manipulated a paperclip until it looked reasonably like an A. A for Ardashir.

4. Long-winded teller of his sad sea story in the ballad "The Rime of the Ancient Mariner" (1798) by English poet Samuel Taylor Coleridge (1772–1834).

5. Dhansak, a sweet and sour curry.
6. Whites-only, anti-immigrant British political party advocating compulsory repatriation of people of non-European descent.

'I need only a small wage increase to help me finance the move. To make things a little easier as we settle in. And Alsana, well, she is pregnant.'

Pregnant. Difficult. Ardashir realized the case called for extreme diplomacy.

'Don't mistake me, Samad, we are both intelligent, frank men and I think I can speak frankly . . . I know you're not a *fucking* waiter—' he whispered the expletive and smiled indulgently after it, as if it were a naughty, private thing that brought them closer together, 'I see your position . . . of course I do . . . but you must understand mine . . . If I made allowances for every relative I employ I'd be walking around like bloody Mr Gandhi. Without a pot to piss in. Spinning my thread by the light of the moon.[7] An example: at this very moment that wastrel Fat Elvis brother-in-law of mine, Hussein Ishmael—'

'The butcher?'

'The butcher, demands that I should raise the price I pay for his stinking meat! "But Ardashir, we are brothers-in-law!" he is saying to me. And I am saying to him, but Mohammed, this is *retail* . . .'

It was Samad's turn to glaze over. He thought of his wife, Alsana, who was not as meek as he had assumed when they married, to whom he must deliver the bad news: Alsana, who was prone to moments, even fits—yes, fits was not too strong a word—of rage. Cousins, aunts, brothers thought it a bad sign. They wondered if there wasn't some 'funny mental history' in Alsana's family, they sympathized with him the way you sympathize with a man who has bought a stolen car with more mileage on it than first thought. In his naivety Samad had simply assumed a woman so young would be . . . easy. But Alsana was not . . . no, she was not easy. It was, he supposed, the way with young women these days.

Ardashir came to the end of what he felt was his perfectly worded speech, sat back satisfied, and laid the *M* for Mukhul he had moulded next to the *A* for Ardashir that sat on his lap.

'Thank you, Sir,' said Samad. 'Thank you so very much.'

That evening there was an awful row. Alsana slung the sewing machine, with the black studded hot pants she was working on, to the floor.

'Useless! Tell me, Samad Miah, what is the point of moving here—nice house, yes very nice, very nice—but where is the food?'

'It is a nice area, we have friends here . . .'

'Who are they?' she slammed her little fist on to the kitchen table, sending the salt and pepper flying to collide spectacularly with each other in the air. 'I don't know them! You fight in an old, forgotten war with some Englishman . . . married to a black! Whose friends are they? These are the people my child will grow up around? Their children—half blacky-white? But tell me,' she shouted, returning to her favoured topic, 'where is our food?'

Theatrically, she threw open every cupboard in the kitchen, 'Where is it? Can we eat china?'

Two plates smashed to the floor. She patted her stomach to indicate her unborn child and pointed to the pieces, 'Hungry?'

---

7. The Indian spiritual and political leader Mohandas Karamchand Gandhi (1869–1948) advocated that Indians spin cloth every day in support of the movement for independence from Britain.

Samad, who had an equally melodramatic nature when prompted, yanked open the freezer and pulled out a mountain of meat which he piled in the middle of the room. His mother worked through the night preparing meals for her family, he said. His mother did not, he said, spend the household money, as Alsana did, on prepared meals, yogurts and tinned[8] spaghetti. Alsana punched him full square in the stomach.

'Samad Iqbal the traditionalist! Why don't I just squat in the street over a bucket and wash clothes? Eh? In fact, what about my clothes? Edible?'

As Samad clutched his winded belly, there in the kitchen she ripped to shreds every stitch she had on and added them to the pile of frozen lamb, spare cuts from the restaurant. She stood naked before him for a moment, the as yet small mound of her pregnancy in full view, then put on a long, brown coat and left the house.

But all the same, she reflected, slamming the door behind her, it was a nice area; she couldn't deny it as she stormed towards the high street, avoiding pavement trees where previously, in Whitechapel, she had avoided flung-out mattresses and the homeless. It would be good for the child. Alsana had a deep-seated belief that living near green spaces was morally beneficial to the young and there to her right was Gladstone Park, a sweeping horizon of green named after the Liberal prime minister[9] (Alsana was from a respected old Bengal family and had read her English History), and in the Liberal[1] tradition it was a park without fences, unlike the more affluent Queen's Park (Victoria's) with its pointed metal railings. Willesden was not as pretty as Queen's Park but it was a nice area. No denying it. No NF[2] kids breaking the basement windows with their steel-capped boots like in Whitechapel. Now she was pregnant she needed a little bit of peace and quiet. Though it was the same here in a way; they all looked at her strangely, this tiny Indian woman stalking the high street in a mackintosh,[3] her plentiful hair flying every which way. *Mali's Kebabs, Mr Cheungs, Raj's, Malkovich Bakeries*—she read the new, unfamiliar signs as she passed. She was shrewd. She saw what this was. 'Liberal? Hosh-kosh nonsense!' No one was more liberal than anyone else anywhere anyway. It was only that here, in Willesden, there wasn't enough of any one thing to gang up against any other thing and send it running to the cellars while windows were smashed.[4]

'Survival is what it is about!' she concluded out loud (she spoke to her baby: she liked to give it one sensible thought a day), making the bell above Crazy Shoes tinkle as she opened the door. Her niece Neena worked here. It was an old-fashioned cobbler's. Neena fixed heels back on to stilettos.

'Alsana, you look like dog shit,' Neena called over in Bengali. 'What is that horrible coat?'

'It's none of your business is what it is,' replied Alsana in English. 'I came to collect my husband's shoes not to chit-chat with Niece-Of-Shame.'

Neena was used to this, and now Alsana had moved to Willesden there would only be more of it. It used to come in longer sentences (such as, 'Niece, you have brought nothing but shame . . .'), but now because Alsana no longer had the time or energy to summon up the necessary shock each time, it had

---

8. Canned.
9. William Ewart Gladstone (1809–1898).
1. Gladstone's political party.
2. National Front.

3. Waterproof raincoat.
4. There were numerous racist attacks against Asian and black minorities in 1970s London.

become abridged to Niece-Of-Shame, an all-purpose tag that summed up the general feeling.

'See these soles?' said Neena, taking Samad's shoes off the shelf and handing Alsana the little blue ticket. 'They were so worn through, Aunty Alsi, I had to reconstruct them from the very base. From the base! What does he do in them? Run marathons?'

'He works,' replied Alsana tersely. 'And prays,' she added, for she liked to make a point of her respectability, and besides she was really very traditional, very religious, lacking nothing except the faith.

'And don't call me Aunty, I am only two years older than you.'

Alsana swept the shoes into a plastic carrier bag and turned to leave.

'I thought that praying was done on people's knees,' said Neena, laughing lightly.

'Both, both, asleep, waking, walking,' snapped Alsana, as she passed under the tinkly bell once more. 'We are never out of sight of the Creator.'

'How's the new house, then?' Neena called after her.

But she had gone. Neena shook her head and sighed as she watched her young aunt disappear down the road like a little brown bullet. Alsana. She was young and old at the same time, Neena reflected. She acted so sensible, so straight-down-the-line in her long sensible coat, but you got the feeling—

'Oi! Miss! There's shoes back here that need your attention!' came a voice from the storeroom.

'Keep your tits on,' said Neena.

At the corner of the road, Alsana popped behind the post office and removed her pinchy sandals in favour of Samad's shoes. (It was an oddity about Alsana. She was small but her feet were enormous, as if she had more growing to do.) In seconds she whipped her hair into an efficient bun, and wrapped her coat tighter around her to keep out the wind. Then she set off, past the library and up a long green road she had never walked along before. 'Survival is all, Little Iqbal,' she said to her bump once more. 'Survival.'

Clara was also pregnant. When their bumps became too large and cinema seats no longer accommodated them, the two women began to meet up for lunch in Kilburn Park,[5] often with the Niece-Of-Shame, the three of them squeezed on to a generous bench, Alsana pressing a thermos of PG Tips[6] into Clara's hand, without milk, with lemon. Unwrapping several layers of cling film to reveal today's peculiar delight: savoury dough-like balls, crumbly Indian sweets shot through with the colours of the kaleidoscope, thin pastry with spiced beef inside, salad with onion, she says to Clara: 'Eat up! Stuff yourself silly! They're in there, wallowing around in your belly, waiting for the menu. Woman, don't torture them! You want to starve the bumps?' for, despite appearances, there are six people on that bench (three living, three coming); one girl for Clara, two boys for Alsana.

Alsana says: 'Nobody's complaining, let's get that straight. A boy is good and two boys is bloody good. But I tell you, when I turned my head and saw the ultra-business thingummybob—'

'Ultrasound,' corrects Clara, through a mouthful of rice.

---

5. In northwest London.   6. A brand of tea.

'—Yes, I almost had the heart attack to finish me off! Two! Feeding one is enough!'

Clara laughs and says she can imagine Samad's face when he saw it.

'No dearie,'—Alsana is reproving, tucking her large feet underneath the folds of her sari, 'he didn't see anything. He wasn't there. I am not letting him see things like that. A woman has to have the private things—a husband needn't be involved in body-business, in a lady's . . . *parts.*'

Niece-Of-Shame, who is sitting between them, sucks her teeth.

'Bloody Hell, Alsi, he must have been involved in your parts sometime, or is this the immaculate bloody conception?'

'So rude,' says Alsana to Clara in a snooty, English way. 'Too old to be so rude and too young to know any better.' And then Clara and Alsana, with the accidental mirroring that happens when two people are sharing the same experience, both lay their hands on their bulges.

Neena, to redeem herself: 'Yeah, well how are you doing on names? Any ideas?'

Alsana is decisive. '*Magid* and *Millat.* Ems are good. Ems are strong. Mahatma,[7] Mohammed, that funny Mr Morecambe, from Morecambe and Wise[8]—letter you can trust.'

But Clara is more cautious, because naming seems to her a fearful responsibility, a godlike task for a mere mortal: 'I tink I like *Irie.* It patois.[9] Means everyting OK, cool, peaceful, you know?'

Alsana is mock-horrified before the sentence is finished, '"OK"? This is a name for a child? You might as well call her "Wouldsirlikeanypopadums-withthat?"[1] or "Niceweatherwearehaving"—'

'. . . and Archie likes *Sarah.* Well, dere not much you can argue wid Sarah, but dere's not much to get happy bout either. I suppose if it was good enough for the wife of Abraham . . .'

'Ibrahim,'[2] Alsana corrects, out of instinct more than Koranic pedantry. 'Popping out babies when she was a hundred years old, by the grace of Allah.'[3]

And then Neena, groaning at the turn the conversation is taking: 'Well I *like* Irie. It's funky. It's different.'

Alsana loves this: 'For pity's sake, what does Archibald know about *funky* and *different*? If I were you, dearie,' she says patting Clara's knee, 'I'd choose Sarah and let that be an end to it. Sometimes you have to let these men have it their way. Anything for a little—how do you say it in the English? For a little—' she puts her finger over tightly pursed lips, like a guard at the gate, '—*shush.*'

But in response Niece-Of-Shame bats her voluminous eyelashes, wraps her college scarf round her head like purdah,[4] and says, 'Oh yes, Auntie, yes, the little submissive Indian woman. You don't talk to him, he talks at you. You scream and shout at each other, but there's no communication. And in the end he wins anyway because he does whatever he likes when he likes. You don't even know where he is, what he does, what he *feels,* half the time. It's

7. Honorific used for Gandhi, meaning "great soul."
8. British television comedy duo with their own show (1961–1983).
9. Jamaican English, or Creole.
1. Papadums are a type of thin, crisp South Asian bread.
2. Alternate versions of the name of the founding patriarch in Judaism, Christianity, and Islam.
3. In the Qur'an (Koran) and the Bible, Sarah miraculously gives birth to Isaac when she is old.
4. Covering.

1975, Alsi. You can't conduct relationships like that any more. It's not like back home. There has to be communication between men and women in the West, they've got to listen to each other, otherwise . . .' Neena mimes a small mushroom cloud going off in her hand.

'What a load of the codswallop,'[5] says Alsana sonorously, closing her eyes, shaking her head. 'It is you who do not listen. By Allah, I will always give as good as I get. But you presume I *care* what he does. You presume I want to *know*. The truth is, for a marriage to survive you don't need all this talk, talk, talk; all this "I am this" and "I am really like this" like on the television, all this *revelation*—especially when your husband is old, when he is wrinkly and falling apart—you do not *want* to know what is slimy underneath the bed and rattling in the wardrobe.'

Neena frowns. Clara cannot raise serious objection, and the rice is handed around once more.

'Moreover,' says Alsana after a pause, folding her dimpled arms underneath her breasts, pleased to be holding forth on a subject close to this formidable bosom, 'when you are from families such as ours you should have learned that *silence*, what is *not* said, is the very *best* recipe for family life.'

'So let me get this straight,' says Neena, derisively. 'You're saying that a good dose of repression keeps a marriage healthy?'

And as if someone had pressed a button, Alsana is outraged: 'Repression! Nonsense silly-billy[6] word! I'm just talking about common sense. What is my husband? What is yours?' she says pointing to Clara. 'Twenty-five years they live before we are even born. What are they? What are they capable of? What blood do they have on their hands? What is sticky and smelly in their private areas? Who knows?' She throws her hands up, releasing the questions into the unhealthy Kilburn air, sending a troupe of sparrows up with them.

'What you don't understand, my Niece-Of-Shame, what none of your generation understand—'

'But Auntie,' begs Neena, raising her voice, because this is what she really wants to argue about—the largest sticking point between the two of them—Alsana's arranged marriage, 'how could you bear to marry someone you didn't know from Adam?'

In response, an infuriating wink. Alsana always likes to appear jovial at the very moment that her interlocutor becomes hot under the collar. 'Because, *Miss Smarty-pants*, it is by far the easier option. It was exactly because Eve did not know Adam from Adam that they got on so A-OK. Let me explain. Yes, I was married to Samad Iqbal the same evening of the very day I met him. Yes, I didn't know him from Adam. But I liked him well enough. We met in the breakfast room on a steaming Dhaka[7] day and he fanned me with *The Times*. I thought he had a good face, a sweet voice, and his backside was high and well formed for a man of his age. Very good. Now every time I learn something more about him I *like him less*. So you see, we were better off the way we were.'

Neena stamps her foot in exasperation at the skewed logic.

---

5. Nonsense (British slang).
6. Here, as elsewhere, Alsana mimics the reduplication (repeating words and forms) common in South Asian languages.
7. Capital of Bangladesh.

'—Besides, I will never know him well. Getting anything out of my husband is like trying to squeeze water out when you're stoned.'

Neena laughs despite herself, 'Water out of a stone.'

'Yes, yes. You think I'm so stupid. But I am wise about things like men. I tell you,' Alsana prepares to deliver her summation as she has seen it done many years previously by the young Dhaka lawyers with their slick side-partings, 'men are the last mystery. God is easy compared with men. Now, enough of the philosophy. Samosa?'[8]

She peels the lid off the plastic tub and sits fat, pretty and satisfied on her conclusion.

'Shame that you're having them,' says Neena to her aunt, lighting a fag. 'Boys, I mean. Shame that you're going to have boys.'

'What do you mean?'

This is Clara, who has secretly subscribed (a secret from Alsana and Archie) to a lending library of Neena's through which she has read, in a few short months, *The Female Eunuch* by Greer, *Sex, Race and Class* by Selma James and Jong's *Fear of Flying*,[9] all in a clandestine attempt, on Neena's part, to rid Clara of her 'false consciousness'.[1]

'I mean, I just think men have caused enough chaos this century. There's enough bloody men in the world. If I knew I was going to have a boy . . .' she pauses to prepare her two falsely conscious friends for this new concept, 'I'd have to seriously consider abortion.'

Alsana screams, claps her hands over one of her own ears and one of Clara's, and then almost chokes on a piece of aubergine[2] with the physical exertion. For some reason the remark simultaneously strikes Clara as funny: hysterically, desperately funny, miserably funny; and the Niece-Of-Shame sits between them, nonplussed, while the two egg-shaped women bend over themselves, one in laughter, the other in horror and near asphyxiation.

'Are you all right, ladies?' It is Sol Jozefowicz, the park keeper, standing in front of them, ready as always to be of aid.

'We are all going to burn in hell, Mr Jozefowicz, if you call that being all right . . .' explains Alsana, pulling herself together.

Niece-Of-Shame rolls her eyes: 'Speak for yourself.'

But Alsana is faster than any sniper when it comes to firing back: 'I do, I do—thankfully Allah has arranged it that way.'

'Good afternoon, Neena, good afternoon, Mrs Jones,' says Sol, offering a neat bow to each. 'Are you sure you are all right? Mrs Jones?'

Clara cannot stop the tears from squeezing out of the corners of her eyes. She cannot work out, at this moment, whether she is crying or laughing; the two states suddenly seem only a stone's throw from each other.

'I'm fine, fine. Sorry to have worried you, Mr Jozefowicz. Really, I'm fine.'

'I do not see what so very funny-funny,' mutters Alsana. 'The murder of innocents—is this funny?'

'Not in my experience, Mrs Iqbal, no,' says Sol Jozefowicz[3] in the collected manner in which he says everything, passing his handkerchief to Clara. It

---

8. Stuffed pastry.
9. Studies and a novel, published in 1970, 1974, and 1973, respectively, that influenced second-wave feminism.
1. Inability to see oppression and exploitation as they really are.
2. Eggplant.
3. Marked as Jewish by his first name (nickname for Solomon), Eastern European by his last.

strikes all three women—the way history will: embarrassingly, without warning, like a blush—what the park keeper's experience might have been. They fall silent.

'Well, as long as you ladies are fine, I'll be getting on,' says Sol, motioning that Clara can keep the handkerchief and replacing the hat he had removed in the old fashion. He bows his neat little bow once more, and sets off slowly anticlockwise round the park.

Once Sol is out of earshot Neena says: 'OK, Aunty Alsi. I apologize. I apologize . . . What more do you want?'

'Oh, every-bloody-thing,' says Alsana, her voice losing the fight, becoming vulnerable. 'The whole bloody universe made clear—in a little nutshell. I cannot understand a thing any more, and I am just beginning. You understand?'

She sighs, not waiting for an answer, not looking at Neena, but across the way at the hunched, disappearing figure of Sol winding in and out of the yew trees. 'You may be right about Samad . . . about many things . . . maybe there are no good men, not even the two in this belly . . . and maybe I do not talk enough with mine, maybe I have married a stranger . . . you might see the truth better than I . . . what do I know, a barefoot country girl who never went to the universities . . .'

'Oh, Alsi,' Neena keeps saying, weaving her regret in and out of Alsana's words like tapestry, feeling bad, 'you know I didn't mean it like that.'

'But I cannot be worrying-worrying all the time about the truth. I have to worry about the truth that can be lived with. And that is the difference between losing your marbles drinking the salty sea, or swallowing the stuff from the streams. My Niece-Of-Shame believes in the talking cure,[4] eh?' says Alsana, with something of a grin. 'Talk, talk, talk and it will be better. Be honest, slice open your heart and spread the red stuff around. But the past is made of more than words, dearie. We married old men, you see? These bumps,' Alsana pats them both, 'they will always have Daddy-long-legs for fathers. One leg in the present, one in the past. No talking will change this. Their roots will always be tangled.'

Just as he reaches the far gate, Sol Jozefowicz turns round to wave, and the three women wave back. And Clara feels a little theatrical, flying the park keeper's cream handkerchief above her head. As if she is seeing someone off on a train journey which crosses the border of two countries.

1999

---

4. Term from Freudian psychoanalysis.

CHIMAMANDA NGOZI ADICHIE
b. 1977

The novelist Chimamanda Ngozi Adichie may be most widely known for her TEDx talk, "We Should All Be Feminists," sampled by the American singer Beyoncé in her song "Flawless" (2013). Adichie protests that girls are taught to "shrink themselves," to limit their success and ambition, lest they threaten men's egos, while boys are raised in a "hard, small cage" of masculinity, wary of exposing their fears and uncertainties. Refusing to be confined by such norms, Adichie achieved early renown as a fiction writer, and in a short story like "Checking Out," about the fate of an undocumented Nigerian migrant in contemporary London, she exposes the vulnerability and humanity of a young man like Obinze. In this story, as in her novels, she narrates the enmeshment of private lives with the racial, gender, and cultural structures and histories that shape them.

Adichie was born in Enugu, Nigeria, raised a Roman Catholic in the university town of Nsukka, and lived in a house that was once the residence of a Nigerian Igbo writer of an earlier generation, Chinua Achebe—a novelist she has credited as her literary inspiration. Adichie's father was a professor of statistics at the University of Nigeria and her mother the university registrar. She tried to focus on medicine and pharmacy for a year and a half at the University of Nigeria but left for the United States at the age of nineteen to escape a medical career. She studied communication and political science at Drexel University and Eastern Connecticut University before earning master's degrees in creative writing at Johns Hopkins University and in African studies at Yale. She has held fellowships at Princeton and Harvard, and in 2008 was awarded a MacArthur Fellowship. In recent years she has divided her time between the United States and Nigeria.

Adichie's fiction has been praised for its vivid characterization, bold reach, and humane warmth. Her first novel, *Purple Hibiscus* (2003), begins with a nod to Achebe: "Things started to fall apart at home." But her novel explores tensions between Western and Igbo cultures from the perspective of a young woman, fifteen-year-old Kambili, coming of age against the backdrop of Nigeria's military coups. Her second novel, *Half of a Yellow Sun* (2006), pushes back in time to the Nigerian Civil War of the 1960s, reimagining the first of many such postcolonial conflicts in sub-Saharan Africa as endured by two sisters. But Adichie has also resisted what she calls the "war and hunger" representation of Africa in the West, arguing that, beyond such crises, millions of Africans live out "ordinary" experiences of love, pain, and loss, "just like everyone else." Her third novel, *Americanah* (2013), winner of the National Book Critics Circle Award, widened the expanse of her canvas, spanning Nigeria, England, and the United States in tracking the love lives and migrant hardships of her Nigerian protagonists, Ifemelu and Obinze, who fall in love as teenagers in Lagos. The title is a term for Nigerians who return from the United States with American affectations, and the book cannily observes constructions of race and gender in transnational contexts. Extending beyond Achebe's Nigerian-centered fiction, the book's intercontinental scope exemplifies what is sometimes called the "global novel."

Part of Obinze's story also appears in Adichie's "Checking Out," among her many tightly constructed short stories (an earlier collection is *The Thing Around Your Neck* [2009]). A reflective young man, Obinze has dreamed of relocating to the United States, but, deterred by heightened restrictions after 9/11, he winds up in London, where he struggles to make a new life for himself. Lacking legal credentials, at the mercy of unscrupulous and exploitative fellow Africans, Obinze gazes wistfully at the people around him near the London Underground: "His eyes would follow them, with a lost longing, and he would think, You can work, you are legal, you are visible, and you don't even know how fortunate you are." Although the mass media constantly circulate pictures and news of multitudes on the move, Adichie harnesses the power of fiction to take readers inside the hopes, disappointments, and musings of one such person. Granted, he is more fortunate than many. Elsewhere she has remarked: "Obinze's journey is about the ways in which we become different versions of ourselves. The generally known immigration story, especially for the African immigrant, is that of leaving war or poverty. But this is about another kind of immigration, of people who do not come from burned villages, but are seeking that sublime thing: choice." For Obinze, as for millions of migrants with similar dreams and aspirations, that sublime thing is far from being within easy reach.

Checking Out

In London, night came too soon. It hung in the morning air like a threat and then in the afternoon a blue-gray dusk descended, and the Victorian buildings all wore a mournful face. In those first weeks, the weightless menace of the cold startled Obinze, drying his nostrils, deepening his anxieties, making him urinate too often. He would walk fast, his hands swallowed up by the sleeves of the gray wool coat his cousin had lent him. Sometimes he would stop outside a tube station,[1] often by a flower or a newspaper vender, and watch the people brushing past. They walked so quickly, as if they had an important destination, a purpose to their lives. His eyes would follow them, with a lost longing, and he would think, You can work, you are legal, you are visible, and you don't even know how fortunate you are.

It was at a tube station that he met the Angolans who would arrange his marriage, exactly two years and three days after he had arrived in England; he kept count.

"We'll talk in the car," one of them had said over the phone. Their old black Mercedes was fussily maintained, the floor mats wavy from vacuuming, the leather seats shiny with polish. The two Angolans looked alike, with thick eyebrows that almost touched, and they were dressed alike, too, in leather jackets and long gold chains. Their tabletop hair, which sat on their heads like tall hats, surprised him, but perhaps having retro haircuts was part of their hip image. They spoke to him with the authority of people who had done this before, and also with a slight condescension; his fate, after all, was in their hands.

"We decided on Newcastle[2] because we know people there and London is too hot right now—too many marriages happening in London, yeah?—so we don't want trouble," one of them said. "Everything is going to work out. Just make sure you keep a low profile, yeah? Don't attract any attention to yourself until the marriage is done. Don't fight in the pub, yeah?"

"I've never been a very good fighter," Obinze said dryly, but the Angolans did not smile.

"You have the money?" the other one asked.

Obinze handed over two hundred pounds, all in twenty-pound notes that he had taken out of the cash machine over two days. It was a deposit, to prove

1. London Underground station. 2. City in northern England.

that he was serious. Later, after he met the girl, he would pay two thousand pounds.

"The rest has to be up front, yeah? We'll use some of it to do the running around and the rest goes to the girl. Man, you know we're not making anything from this. We usually ask for much more, but we're doing this for your cousin," the first one said.

Obinze did not believe them, even then. He met the girl, Cleotilde, a few days later, at a shopping center, in a McDonald's whose windows looked out onto the dank entrance of a tube station across the street. He sat at a table with the Angolans and watched people hurry past, wondering if one of them was she, while the Angolans whispered into their phones; perhaps they were arranging other marriages.

"Hello there!" she said.

She surprised him. He had expected someone with pockmarks smothered under heavy makeup, someone tough and knowing. But here she was, dewy and fresh, bespectacled, olive-skinned, almost childlike, smiling shyly at him and sucking a milkshake through a straw. She looked like a university freshman who was innocent or dumb, or both.

"I just want to be sure that you're sure about doing this," he told her. Then, worried that he might frighten her away, he added, "I'm very grateful, and it won't take too much from you—in a year I'll have my papers and we'll do the divorce. But I just wanted to meet you first and make sure you are O.K. to do this."

"Yes," she said.

He watched her, expecting more. She played with her straw, not meeting his eyes, and it took him a while to realize that she was reacting more to him than to the situation. She was attracted to him.

"I want to help my mom out. Things are tight at home," she said, a trace of a non-British accent underlining her words.

"She's with us, yeah," one of the Angolans said impatiently.

"Show him your details, Cleo," the other Angolan said.

His calling her Cleo rang false; Obinze sensed this from the slight surprise on her face. It was a forced intimacy: the Angolan had never called her Cleo before. Obinze wondered how the Angolans knew her. Did they have a list of young women with European Union passports who needed money? Cleotilde pushed at her hair, a mass of tight coils, and adjusted her glasses, as though preparing herself, then presented her passport and license. Obinze examined them. He would have thought her younger than twenty-three.

"Can I have your number?" Obinze asked.

"Just call us for anything," the Angolans said, almost at the same time. But Obinze wrote his number on a napkin and pushed it across to Cleotilde. The Angolans gave him a sly look.

The next day, on the phone, she told him that she had been living in London for six years, and was saving money to go to fashion school; the Angolans had told him that she lived in Portugal.

"Would you like to meet again?" he asked. "It will be much easier if we try to get to know each other a little."

"Yes," she said without hesitation.

They ate fish-and-chips in a pub, a thin crust of grime on the sides of the wooden table, while she talked about her love of fashion and asked him about Nigerian traditional dress. She seemed a little more mature this time; he noticed the shimmer on her cheeks, the more defined curl of her hair, and knew that she had made an effort with her appearance.

"What will you do after you get your papers?" she asked him. "Will you bring your girlfriend from Nigeria?"

He was touched by her obviousness. "I don't have a girlfriend."

"I've never been to Africa. I'd love to go." She said "Africa" wistfully, like an admiring foreigner, loading the word with exotic excitement. Her black Angolan father had left her white Portuguese mother when she was three, she told him, and she had not seen him since, nor had she ever been to Angola. She said this with a shrug and a cynical raise of her eyebrows, as though it had never bothered her, an effort so out of character, so jarring, that it showed him just how deeply it did bother her. There were difficulties in her life that he wanted to know more about, parts of her thick, shapely body that he longed to touch, but he was wary of complicating things. He would wait until after the wedding, until the business side of their relationship was finished. She seemed to understand this without their talking about it. And so, as they met in the following weeks, sometimes practicing how they would answer questions during their immigration interview and other times just talking about football,[3] there was, between them, the growing urgency of restrained desire. It was there in how close they stood, not touching, as they waited at the tube station, and in their teasing each other about his support of Arsenal and her support of Manchester United.[4] After he paid the Angolans the additional two thousand pounds, she told him that they had given her only five hundred.

"I'm just telling you. I know you don't have any more money. I want to do this for you," she said.

He wanted to kiss her, her upper lip pinker and shinier with lip gloss than the lower, to hold her, to tell her how deeply, irrepressibly grateful he was. She would never flaunt her power over him. One Eastern European woman, Iloba had told him, had asked a Nigerian man, an hour before their wedding, to give her a thousand pounds extra not to walk away. In a panic, the man had had to call all of his friends to raise the money.

When Obinze asked the Angolans how much they had given Cleotilde, they said, "Man, we gave you a good deal," in the tone of people who knew how much they were needed. It was they, after all, who took him to a lawyer, a low-voiced Nigerian in a swivel chair, who slid backward to reach a file cabinet as he said, "You can still get married, even though your visa is expired. In fact, getting married is now your only choice." It was they who provided water and gas bills, going back six months, with his name and a Newcastle address. And it was they who found a man who would "sort out" his driver's license, a man called Brown. Obinze met Brown at the train station in Barking;[5] he stood near the gate, amid the bustle of people, looking around and waiting for his phone to ring, since Brown had refused to give him a phone number.

"Are you waiting for somebody?" Brown asked, when he appeared. He was a slight man, his winter hat pulled down to his eyebrows.

"Yes. I'm Obinze," he said, feeling like a character in a spy novel. Brown led him to a quiet corner, handed over an envelope, and there it was, his

---

3. Soccer.
4. Soccer team, with Arsenal, in the English

Premier League.
5. Suburban town in east London.

license, with his photo. It had the genuine, slightly worn look of something owned for a year. A small plastic card, but it weighed down his pocket. A few days later, he walked with it into a London building that looked like a church, steepled and grave from the outside, but inside was shabby, harried, knotted with people. Signs were scrawled on whiteboards:

Births and deaths this way. Marriage registration this way.

Obinze, his expression carefully frozen in neutrality, handed the license over to the registrar behind the desk.

A woman was walking toward the door, talking loudly to her companion. "Look how crowded this place is," she said. "It's all sham marriages, all of them, now that Blunkett[6] is after them."

Perhaps she had come to register a death, and her words were merely the lonely lashings-out of grief, but he felt the familiar tightening of panic in his chest. The registrar was examining his license, taking too long. The seconds lengthened and curdled. *"All sham marriages, all of them,"* rang in Obinze's head. Finally, the registrar looked up and pushed across a form.

"Getting married, are we? Congratulations!" The words came out with the mechanical good cheer of frequent repetition.

"Thank you," Obinze said, and tried to unfreeze his face.

Behind the desk, a whiteboard was propped against a wall, with venues and dates of intended marriages scrawled in blue; a name at the bottom caught his eye. Okoli Okafor and Crystal Smith. Okoli Okafor had been his classmate in secondary school and at university, a quiet boy who had been teased for having a surname for a first name, who later joined a vicious cult at university, and then left Nigeria during one of the long strikes.[7]

The memory, clear as a beam of light, took Obinze back to a time when he still believed the universe would bend according to his will. Once, during his final year at university, the year that people danced in the streets because General Abacha[8] had died, his mother had said, "One day, I will look up and all the people I know will be dead or abroad." For a moment, he felt as if he had betrayed her by having his own plan: to get a postgraduate degree in America, to work in America, to live in America. Of course, he knew how unreasonable the American Consulate could be—the vice-chancellor, of all people, had once been refused a visa to attend a conference—but he had never doubted his plan. He would wonder, later, why he had been so sure. Perhaps it was because he had never just wanted to go abroad, as many others did; some people were now even going to South Africa, which amused him. It had always been America, only America. A longing nurtured and nursed over many years. An advertisement on NTA[9] for "Andrew Checking Out," which he had watched as a child, had given shape to his longings. "Men, I'm checkin' out," the character Andrew had said, staring cockily at the camera. "No good roads, no light, no water. Men, you can't even get a common bottle of soft drink!" While Andrew was checking out, General Buhari's[1] soldiers were flogging adults in the streets, lecturers were striking for better pay, and Obinze's

6. David Blunkett (b. 1947), former British politician who endorsed tighter immigration measures after the 9/11 terrorist attacks.
7. Faculty and staff labor strikes, some lasting months during the 1980s and 1990s.
8. General Sani Abacha (1943–1998), president of Nigeria after a military coup in 1993, responsible for human-rights abuses.
9. Nigerian Television Authority.
1. Muhammadu Buhari (b. 1942), who seized control of Nigeria in 1983 after a military coup, responded harshly to critics. He was deposed in 1985 but elected president in 2015.

mother decided that he could no longer have Fanta whenever he wanted but only on Sundays. America became a place where bottles of Fanta could be had without permission. Obinze would stand in front of the mirror and repeat Andrew's words: "Men, I'm checkin' out!" Later, when he sought out magazines and books and films and secondhand stories about America, his longing took on a minor mystical quality. He saw himself walking the streets of Harlem, discussing the merits of Mark Twain with his American friends, gazing at Mt. Rushmore. Days after he graduated from university, bloated with knowledge about America, he applied for a visa at the consulate in Lagos.

He already knew that the best interviewer was the man with the blond beard, and, as the line moved forward, he hoped that he would not be interviewed by the horror story, a pretty white woman famous for screaming into her microphone and insulting even grandmothers. Finally, it was his turn, and the blond-bearded man said, "Next person!" Obinze walked up and slid his forms underneath the glass. The man glanced at the forms and said, kindly, "Sorry, you don't qualify. Next person!" Obinze was stunned. He went three more times in the next few months. Each time, he was told, with barely a glance at his documents, "Sorry, you don't qualify," and each time he emerged from the air-conditioned cool of the consulate into the harsh sunlight stunned and unbelieving.

"It's the terrorism fears," his mother said. "The Americans are now averse to foreign young men."

She told him to find a job and try again in a year. But his job applications yielded nothing. He travelled to Lagos and to Port Harcourt and to Abuja to take assessment tests, which he found easy, and then attended interviews, answering questions fluidly, but only long silences followed. Some of his friends got jobs, people who did not have his second-class upper degree and who did not speak as well as he did. He wondered if employers could smell his America-pining on his breath, or sense how obsessively he still looked at the Web sites of American universities.

One day, his mother left him a note on the bathroom sink: "I have been invited to an academic conference in London. We should speak." He was puzzled. When she came home from her lecture, he was in the living room waiting for her.

"Mummy, *nno*,"[2] he said.

She acknowledged his greeting with a nod. "I'm going to put your name on my British visa application as my research assistant," she said quietly. "That should get you a six-month visa. You can stay with Nicholas in London. See what you can do with your life. Maybe you can get to America from there. I know that your mind is no longer here."

He stared at her.

"I understand this sort of thing is done nowadays," she said, sitting down on the sofa beside him, and trying to sound offhand, but in the uncommon briskness of her words he sensed her discomfort. She was a woman who asked no favors, who would not lie, who would not accept even a Christmas card from her students, because it might compromise her. Yet here she was, behaving as though truth-telling were a luxury that they could no longer afford. She had lied for him. If anyone else had lied for him, it would not have mattered as much or even at all, but she lied for him and he got a six-

2. Welcome (Igbo).

month visa to the United Kingdom. He felt, even before he left, like a failure. He did not contact her for months, while he stayed with his cousin Nicholas, in Essex.[3] He did not contact her because there was nothing to tell and he wanted to wait until he had something to tell. Throughout his stay in England, he had spoken to her only a few times, strained conversations during which he felt her wondering why he had made nothing of himself. But she never asked for details; she only waited to hear what he was willing to tell.

Everyone joked about people who went abroad to clean toilets, and so Obinze approached his first job with irony: he was indeed abroad cleaning toilets, wearing rubber gloves and carrying a pail, in an estate agent's office on the second floor of a London building. Each time he opened the swinging door of a stall, it seemed to sigh. The beautiful woman who cleaned the ladies' toilet was Ghanaian, about his age, with the shiniest dark skin he had ever seen. He sensed, in the way she spoke and carried herself, that she came from a background similar to his, a childhood cushioned by family, regular meals, and dreams in which there was no conception of cleaning toilets in London. She ignored his friendly gestures, saying only "Good evening" as formally as she could, but she was friendly with the Polish woman who cleaned the offices upstairs, and once he saw them in a deserted café, drinking tea and talking in low tones. He stood watching them for a while, a great grievance exploding in his mind. He was too close to what she was; he knew her nuances, while with the Polish woman she was free to reinvent herself, to be whoever she wanted to be.

The toilets were not bad—some urine outside the urinal, some unfinished flushing. So he was shocked, one evening, to walk into a stall and discover a mound of shit on the toilet lid, solid, tapering, centered as though it had been carefully arranged. It looked like a puppy curled on a mat. It was a performance. He thought about the famed repression of the English. There was, in this performance, something of an unbuttoning. A person who had been fired? Denied a promotion? Obinze stared at that mound of shit for a long time, feeling smaller and smaller as he did so, until it became a personal affront, a punch to his jaw. And all for three quid[4] an hour. He took off his gloves, placed them next to the mound of shit, and left the building.

Obinze had not remembered that Iloba now lived in London; he had last seen him days before graduation. Iloba was merely from his mother's home-town, but he had been so enthusiastic about their kinship that everyone on campus assumed that they were cousins. Iloba would often pull up a chair, smiling and uninvited, and join Obinze and his friends at a roadside bar, or appear at Obinze's door on Sunday afternoons. Once, Iloba had stopped Obinze on the General Studies quad, cheerfully calling out "Kinsman!" and then giving him a rundown of marriages and deaths of people from his mother's home town whom he hardly knew. "Udoakpuanyi died some weeks ago. Don't you know him? Their homestead is next to your mother's." Obinze nodded and made appropriate sounds, humoring Iloba, because Iloba's demeanor was always so pleasant and oblivious, his trousers always too tight and too short, showing his bony ankles; they had earned him the nickname Iloba Jump Up.

3. County northeast of London.   4. Pounds sterling.

Obinze got his phone number from Nicholas and called him.

"The Zed![5] Kinsman! You did not tell me you were coming to London!" Iloba said, using Obinze's old nickname. "How is your mother? What of your uncle, the one who married from Abagana? How is Nicholas?" Iloba sounded full of a simple happiness. There were people who were born with an inability to be tangled up in dark emotions, in complications, and Iloba was one of them. With such people, Obinze felt both admiration and boredom. When Obinze asked if Iloba might be able to help him find a National Insurance number, he would have understood a little resentment, a little churlishness—after all, he was contacting Iloba only because he needed something—but it surprised him how sincerely eager to help Iloba was.

"I would let you use mine, but I am working with it and it is risky," Iloba said.

"Where do you work?"

"In central London. Security. It's not easy, this country is not easy, but we are managing. I like the night shifts, because it gives me time to read for my course. I'm doing a master's in management at Birkbeck College."[6] Iloba paused. "The Zed, don't worry, we will put our heads together. Let me ask around and let you know."

Iloba called back two weeks later to say that he had found somebody. "His name is Vincent Obi. He is from Abia State.[7] A friend of mine did the connection. He wants to meet you tomorrow evening."

They met in Iloba's flat. A claustrophobic feel pervaded the concrete neighborhood with scarred walls and no trees. Everything seemed too small, too tight.

"Nice place," Obinze said, not because the flat was nice but because Iloba had a flat in London.

"I would have told you to come and stay with me, the Zed, but I live with two of my cousins." Iloba placed bottles of beer and a small plate of fried chin-chin[8] on the table. The ritual of hospitality raised a sharp homesickness in Obinze. He was reminded of going back to his mother's village with her at Christmas, aunties offering him plates of chin-chin.

Vincent Obi was a small round man, submerged in a large pair of jeans and an ungainly coat. As he and Obinze shook hands, they sized each other up. From the set of Vincent's shoulders and the abrasiveness of his manner, Obinze sensed that he had learned early on, as a matter of necessity, to solve his own problems. Obinze imagined Vincent's Nigerian life: a community secondary school full of barefoot children; a polytechnic paid for with the help of a number of uncles; a family of many children; and a crowd of dependents in his hometown who, whenever he visited, would expect large loaves of bread and pocket money carefully distributed to each of them. Obinze saw himself through Vincent's eyes: a university staff child who grew up eating butter and now needed his help. At first, Vincent affected a British accent, saying "innit"[9] too many times.

"This is business, innit, but I'm helping you. You can use my N.I. number and pay me forty per cent of what you make," Vincent said. "It's business, innit. If I don't get what we agree on, I will report you."

---

5. Obinze's nickname. The letter "z" is pronounced "zed" in Britain and most of its former colonies.
6. A constituent college of the University of London.
7. In southeastern Nigeria.
8. Deep-fried Nigerian snack.
9. Isn't it? (British slang).

"My brother," Obinze said. "That's a little too much. You know my situation. I don't have anything. Please try and come down."

"Thirty-five per cent is the best I can do. This is business." He lost his accent and now spoke Nigerian English. "Let me tell you, there are many people in your situation."

Iloba spoke in Igbo: "Vincent, my brother here is trying to save money and do his papers. Thirty-five is too much. Please just try and help us."

"You know that some people take half. Yes, he is in a situation, but all of us are in a situation. I am helping him, but this is business." Vincent's Igbo had a rural accent. He put the National Insurance card on the table and started to write his bank-account number on a piece of paper. That evening, as dusk fell, the sky muting to a pale violet, Obinze became Vincent.

The warehouse chief looked like the archetype of an Englishman that Obinze carried in his mind: tall and spare, sandy-haired and blue-eyed. But he was a smiling man, and in Obinze's imagination Englishmen were not smiling men. His name was Roy Snell. He vigorously shook Obinze's hand.

"So, Vincent, you're from Africa?" he asked, as he took Obinze around the warehouse, which was the size of a football field and alive with trucks being loaded, flattened cardboard boxes being folded into a deep pit, and men talking.

"Yes. I was born in Birmingham[1] and went back to Nigeria when I was six." It was the story that he and Iloba had agreed was most convincing.

"Why did you come back? How bad are things in Nigeria?"

"I just wanted to see if I could have a better life here."

Roy Snell nodded. He seemed like a person for whom the word "jolly" would always be apt. "You'll work with Nigel today—he's our youngest," he said, gesturing toward a man with a pale doughy body, spiky dark hair, and an almost cherubic face. "I think you'll like working here, Vinny Boy!" It had taken him five minutes to go from Vincent to Vinny Boy and, in the following months, when they played table tennis during lunch break, Roy would tell the men, "I've got to beat Vinny Boy for once!" And they would titter and repeat "Vinny Boy."

It amused Obinze how keenly the men flipped through their newspapers every morning, stopping at the photo of the big-breasted woman, examining it as though it were an article of great interest, different from the photo on that same page the previous day, the previous week. Their conversations, as they waited for their trucks to be loaded up, were always about cars and football and, most of all, women, each man telling stories that sounded similar to stories told the day before, the week before. Each time they mentioned knickers—"the bird flashed her knickers"—Obinze was even more amused, because knickers, in Nigerian English, were shorts rather than underwear, and he imagined these nubile women in ill-fitting khaki shorts, the kind he had worn as a junior student in secondary school.

Roy Snell's greeting every morning was a jab to his belly. "Vinny Boy! You all right? You all right?" he would ask. He always put Obinze's name up for the outside work that paid better, always asked if he wanted to work weekends, which was double time, always asked about girls. It was as if Roy held a special affection for him, which was both protective and kind.

1. Major city in central England.

"You haven't had a shag since you came to the U.K., have you, Vinny Boy? I could give you this bird's number," he said once.

"I have a girlfriend back home," Obinze said.

"So what's wrong with a little shag, then?"

A few men nearby laughed.

"My girlfriend has magical powers," Obinze said.

Roy found this funnier than Obinze thought it was. He laughed and laughed. "She's into witchcraft, is she? All right, then, no shags for you. I've always wanted to go to Africa, Vinny Boy. I think I'll take a holiday and go to Nigeria when you're back there for a visit. You can show me around, find me some Nigerian birds, Vinny Boy, but no witchcraft!"

"Yes, I could do that."

"Oh, I know you could! You look like you know what to do with the birds," Roy said, with another jab at Obinze's belly.

Roy often assigned Obinze to work with Nigel, perhaps because they were the youngest men in the warehouse. That first morning, Obinze noticed that the other men, drinking coffee from paper cups and checking the board to see who would be working with whom, were laughing at Nigel. Nigel had no eyebrows; the patches of slightly pink skin where his eyebrows should have been gave his plump face an unfinished, ghostly look.

"I got pissed[2] at the pub and my mates shaved off my eyebrows," Nigel told Obinze, almost apologetically, as they shook hands.

"No shagging for you until you grow your eyebrows back, mate," one of the men called out as Nigel and Obinze headed for the truck. Obinze secured the washing machines at the back, tightening the straps until they were snug, and then climbed in and studied the map to find the shortest routes to their delivery addresses. Nigel took bends sharply and muttered about how people drove these days. At a traffic light, he brought out a bottle of cologne from a bag he had placed at his feet, sprayed it on his neck, and then offered it to Obinze.

"No, thanks," Obinze said. Nigel shrugged. Days later, he offered it again. The truck interior was dense with the scent of his cologne and, from time to time, Obinze would take deep gulps of fresh air through the open window.

"You're just new from Africa. You haven't seen the London sights, have you, mate?" Nigel asked.

"No," Obinze said.

And so, after early deliveries in central London, Nigel would take him for a drive, showing him Buckingham Palace, the Houses of Parliament, Tower Bridge, all the while talking about his mother's arthritis, and about his girlfriend Haley's knockers. It took a while for Obinze to completely understand what Nigel said, because of his accent, each word twisted and stretched. Once Nigel said "male" and Obinze thought he had said "mile," and, when Obinze finally understood what Nigel meant, Nigel laughed and said, "You talk kind of posh, don't you? African posh."

One day, months into his job, after they had delivered a fridge to an address in Kensington,[3] Nigel said, of the elderly man who had come into the kitchen while they were installing it, "He's a real gent, he is." Nigel's tone was admiring, slightly cowed. The man had looked dishevelled and hungover, his hair tousled, his robe open at the chest, and he had said, archly, "You do know

---

2. Drunk.   3. Affluent district in west London.

how to put it all together," as though he did not think they did. It amazed Obinze that, because Nigel thought the man was a "real gent," he did not complain about the dirty kitchen, as he ordinarily would have done. If the man had spoken with a different accent, Nigel would have called him miserly for not giving them a tip.

They were approaching their next delivery address, in South London, and Obinze had just called the homeowner to say that they were almost there, when Nigel blurted out, "What do you say to a girl you like?"

"What do you mean?" Obinze asked.

"Truth is, I'm not really shagging Haley. I like her, but I don't know how to tell her. The other day, I went round her house and there was another bloke there." Nigel paused. Obinze tried to keep his face expressionless. "You look like you know what to say to the birds, mate," Nigel added.

"Just tell her you like her," Obinze said, thinking how seamlessly Nigel, at the warehouse with the other men, contributed stories about shagging Haley, and, once, about shagging her friend while Haley was away on holiday. "No games and no lines. Just say, 'Look, I like you and I think you're beautiful.'"

Nigel gave him a wounded glance. It was as if he had convinced himself that Obinze was skilled in the art of women; he expected some profundity, which Obinze wished, as he loaded a dishwasher onto a trolley and wheeled it to the door, that he had. An Indian woman opened the door, a portly, kindly housewife, who offered them tea. Many people offered tea or water. A sad-looking woman had once offered Obinze a small pot of homemade jam, and he had hesitated, but he sensed that whatever deep unhappiness she had would be compounded if he said no, and so he had taken the jam home, where it was still languishing in the fridge, unopened.

"Thank you, thank you," the Indian woman said, as Obinze and Nigel installed the new dishwasher and rolled away the old one.

At the door, she gave Nigel a tip. Nigel was the only driver who split the tips down the middle with Obinze; the others pretended not to remember to share. Once, when Obinze was working with another driver, an old Jamaican woman pushed ten pounds into his pocket when the driver wasn't looking. "Thank you, brother," she said, and it made him want to call his mother in Nsukka[4] and tell her about it.

One morning in early summer, Obinze arrived at the warehouse and knew right away that something was amiss. The men avoided his eyes, and Nigel turned swiftly—too swiftly—toward the toilet when he saw Obinze. They knew. They had somehow found out. They saw the headlines about asylum seekers draining the National Health Service, they thought of the hordes further crowding a crowded island, and now they knew that he was one of the damned, working with a name that was not his. Where was Roy Snell? Had he gone to call the police? Was it the police that you called? Obinze tried to remember details from the stories of people who had been caught and deported, but his mind was numb. He felt naked. He wanted to turn and run, but his body kept moving, against his will, toward the loading area. Then he sensed a movement behind him, quick and violent and too close, and, before he could turn around, a paper hat was pushed onto his head. It was Nigel, and with him a crowd of grinning men.

"Happy birthday, Vinny Boy!" they all said.

---

4. Town in southeastern Nigeria.

Obinze froze, frightened by the complete blankness of his mind. Then he realized what it was. Vincent's birthday. Roy must have told the men. Even he had not remembered to remember Vincent's date of birth.

"Oh!" was all he said, nauseated with relief.

Nigel asked him to come into the coffee room, where all the men were trooping in, passing around the muffins and Coke they had bought with their own money in honor of a birthday they believed was his. A realization brought tears to his eyes: he felt safe.

Obinze was mildly surprised when Vincent called him that night, because he had called him only once before, months ago, when he changed his bank and wanted to give him the new account number. He wondered whether to say "Happy birthday" to Vincent, whether the call was indeed related to his birthday.

"Vincent, *kedu*?"[5] he said.

"I want a raise."

Had Vincent learned that from a film? The words sounded contrived and comical. "I want forty-five per cent. I know you are working more now."

"Vincent, ahn-ahn.[6] How much am I making? You know I am saving money to do this marriage thing."

"Forty-five per cent," Vincent said, and hung up.

Obinze decided to ignore him. He knew Vincent's type; he would push to see how far he could go and then he would retreat. If Obinze called back and tried to negotiate, it might embolden Vincent to make more demands. But he would not risk losing Obinze's regular weekly deposit entirely.

And so when, a week later, in the morning bustle of drivers and trucks, Roy said, "Vinny Boy, step into my office for a minute," Obinze thought nothing of it. On Roy's desk was a newspaper, folded at the page with the photo of the big-breasted woman. Roy slowly put his cup of coffee on top of the newspaper. He seemed uncomfortable, and wouldn't look directly at Obinze.

"Somebody called yesterday," he told Obinze. "Said you're not who you say you are—that you're illegal and working with a Brit's name." There was a pause. Obinze was stung with surprise. Roy picked up the coffee cup again. "Why don't you just bring in your passport tomorrow and we'll clear it up, all right?"

Obinze mumbled the first words that came to him. "O.K. I'll bring my passport tomorrow." He walked out of the office knowing that he would never feel again what he had felt moments ago. Was Roy merely asking him to bring in his passport to make the dismissal easier for him, to give him an exit, or did Roy really believe that the caller had been lying? Why would anybody call about such a thing unless it was true? Obinze had never made as much of an effort as he did the rest of the day to seem normal, to tame the rage that was engulfing him. It was not the thought of the power that Vincent had over him that infuriated him but the recklessness with which Vincent had exercised it. He left the warehouse that evening for the final time, wishing more than anything that he had told Nigel and Roy his real name.

The Angolans told him that things had "gone up," or were "tough," opaque words that were supposed to explain each new request for more money.

5. What's up? (Igbo).   6. Or "ah-ah," expression of surprise (Igbo).

"This is not what we agreed to," Obinze would say, or "I don't have any extra cash right now," and they would reply, "Things have gone up, yeah," in a tone that he imagined was accompanied by a shrug. A silence would follow, a wordlessness over the phone line that told him that it was his problem, not theirs. "I'll pay it in by Friday," he would say, finally, before hanging up.

Nicholas gave Obinze a suit for the wedding. "It's a good Italian suit," he said. "It's small for me, so it should fit you." The trousers were big, and they bunched up when Obinze tightened his belt, but the jacket, also big, shielded the unsightly pleat of cloth at his waist. Not that he minded. He was so focussed on finally beginning his life that he would have swaddled his lower parts in a baby's napkin[7] if it had been required. He and Iloba met Cleotilde near City Center. She was standing under a tree with some friends, her hair pushed back with a white band, her eyes boldly lined in black; she looked like an older, sexier person. Her ivory dress was tight at the hips. He had paid for the dress. "I haven't got any proper going-out dress," she had said, in apology, when she called to tell him that she had nothing that looked convincingly bridal.

She hugged him. She looked nervous, and he tried to deflect his own nervousness by thinking about them together after this—how, in less than an hour, he would be free to walk with surer steps on Britain's streets, and free to kiss her.

"You have the rings?" Iloba asked her.

"Yes," Cleotilde said.

She and Obinze had bought them the week before, plain, cheap matching rings from a side-street shop, and she had looked so delighted, laughingly slipping different rings on and off her finger, that he wondered if she wished it were a real wedding.

"Fifteen minutes to go," Iloba said. He took pictures, his digital camera held away from his face, saying, "Move closer! O.K., one more!" His sprightly good spirits annoyed Obinze. On the train up to Newcastle the previous day, while Obinze had spent his time looking out the window, unable even to read, Iloba had talked and talked, until his voice became a distant murmur, perhaps because he was trying to keep Obinze from worrying too much. Now he talked to Cleotilde's friends with easy friendliness about the new Chelsea manager, about "Big Brother,"[8] as if they were all there for something ordinary and normal.

"Time to go," Iloba said. They walked toward the civic center. The afternoon was bright with sunshine. Obinze opened the door and stood aside for the others to go ahead, into the sterile hallway, where they paused to get their bearings, to be sure which way the registry office was. Two policemen stood behind the door, watching them with stony eyes. Obinze quieted his panic. There was nothing to worry about, nothing at all, he told himself; the civic center probably had policemen present as a matter of routine. But he sensed in the sudden smallness of the hallway, the sudden thickening of doom in the air, that something was wrong. Then another man approached him, his shirtsleeves rolled up, his cheeks so red that he looked as though he were wearing terrible makeup.

7. Diaper.
8. Reality TV show. "Chelsea manager": soccer coach of Chelsea, another Premier League team.

"Are you Obinze Maduewesi?" the red-cheeked man asked. In his hands was a sheaf of papers in which Obinze could see a photocopy of his passport.

"Yes," Obinze said quietly, and that word was an acknowledgment to the red-cheeked immigration officer, to Iloba, to Cleotilde, and to himself that it was over.

"Your visa is expired and you are not allowed to be present in the U.K.," the man said.

One of the policemen clamped handcuffs around his wrists. He felt himself watching the scene from far away, watching himself walk to the police car outside, and sink into the too-soft seat in the back. There had been so many times in the past when he had feared that this would happen, so many moments that had become one single blur of panic, and now it felt like the dull echo of an aftermath. Cleotilde flung herself on the ground and began to cry. She may never have visited her father's country, but he was convinced at that moment of her Africanness; how else would she have been able to fling herself to the ground with that perfect dramatic flourish? He wondered if her tears were for him or for herself, or for what might have been between them. She had no need to worry; the policemen barely glanced at her. It was he who felt the heaviness of the handcuffs during the drive to the police station, he who silently handed over his watch and his belt and his wallet and his phone. Nicholas's large trousers were slipping down his hips.

"Your shoes, too. Take off your shoes," the policeman said.

He took off his shoes. He was led to a cell. It was small, with brown walls, and metal bars so thick that his hand could not get around one. It reminded him of the chimpanzee cage at Nsukka's dismal, forgotten zoo. From the high ceiling, a single bulb burned. There was an emptying, echoing vastness in the tiny cell.

"Were you aware that your visa had expired?"

"Yes," Obinze said.

"Were you about to have a sham marriage?"

"No. Cleotilde and I have been dating for a while."

"I can arrange for a lawyer for you, but it's obvious you'll be deported," the immigration officer said evenly.

When the lawyer came, puffy-faced, dark arcs under his eyes, Obinze thought of all the films in which the state lawyer is distracted and exhausted. He came with a bag but did not open it, and he sat across from Obinze, holding nothing—no file, no paper, no pen. He was pleasant and sympathetic.

"The government has a strong case. We can appeal, but, to be honest, it will only delay the case. You will eventually be removed from the U.K.," he said, with the air of a man who had said those same words, in the same tone, more times than he wished to, or could, remember.

"I'm willing to go back to Nigeria," Obinze said. The last shred of his dignity was like a wrapper slipping off his waist that he was desperate to retie.

The lawyer looked surprised. "O.K., then," he said, and got up a little too hastily, as though grateful that his job had been made easier. Obinze watched him leave. He was going to check a box on a form that said that his client was willing to be removed. Removed. The word made Obinze feel inanimate. A thing to be removed. A thing without breath and mind. A thing.

2013

APPENDIXES

General Bibliography

This bibliography consists of a list of suggested general readings on English literature. Bibliographies for the authors in *The Norton Anthology of English Literature* are available online in the NAEL Archive (digital.wwnorton.com/englishlit10abc and digital.wwnorton.com/englishlit10def).

Suggested General Readings

Histories of England and of English Literature

Even the most distinguished of the comprehensive general histories written in past generations have come to seem outmoded. Innovative research in social, cultural, and political history has made it difficult to write a single coherent account of England from the Middle Ages to the present, let alone to accommodate in a unified narrative the complex histories of Scotland, Ireland, Wales, and the other nations where writing in English has flourished. Readers who wish to explore the historical matrix out of which the works of literature collected in this anthology emerged are advised to consult the studies of particular periods listed in the appropriate sections of this bibliography. The multivolume *Oxford History of England* and *New Oxford History of England* are useful, as are the three-volume *Peoples of the British Isles: A New History*, ed. Stanford Lehmberg, 1992; the nine-volume *Cambridge Cultural History of Britain*, ed. Boris Ford, 1992; the three-volume *Cambridge Social History of Britain, 1750–1950*, ed. F. M. L. Thompson, 1992; and the multivolume *Penguin History of Britain*, gen. ed. David Cannadine, 1996–. For Britain's imperial history, readers can consult the five-volume *Oxford History of the British Empire*, ed. Roger Louis, 1998–99, as well as *Gender and Empire*, ed. Philippa Levine, 2004. Given the cultural centrality of London, readers may find particular interest in *The London Encyclopaedia*, ed. Ben Weinreb et al., 3rd ed., 2008; Roy Porter, *London: A Social History*, 1994; and Jerry White, *London in the Nineteenth Century: "A Human Awful Wonder of God,"* 2007, and *London in the Twentieth Century: A City and Its People*, 2001.

Similar observations may be made about literary history. In the light of such initiatives as women's studies, new historicism, and postcolonialism, the range of authors deemed significant has expanded, along with the geographical and conceptual boundaries of literature in English. Attempts to capture in a unified account the great sweep of literature from *Beowulf* to the early twenty-first century have largely given way to studies of individual genres, carefully delimited time periods, and specific authors. For these more focused accounts, see the listings by period. Among the large-scale literary surveys, *The Cambridge Guide to Literature in English*, 3rd ed., 2006, is useful, as is the nine-volume *Penguin History of Literature*, 1993–94. *The Feminist Companion to Literature in English*, ed. Virginia Blain, Isobel Grundy, and Patricia Clements, 1990, is an important resource, and the editorial materials in *The Norton Anthology of Literature by Women*, 3rd ed., 2007, eds. Sandra M. Gilbert and Susan Gubar, constitute a concise history and set of biographies of women authors since the Middle Ages. *Annals of English Literature, 1475–1950*, rev. 1961, lists important publications year by year, together with the significant literary events for each year. Six volumes have been published in the *Oxford English Literary History*, gen. ed. Jonathan Bate, 2002–: Laura Ashe, *1000–1350: Conquest and Transformation*;

James Simpson, *1350–1547: Reform and Cultural Revolution*; Philip Davis, *1830–1880: The Victorians*; Chris Baldick, *1830–1880: The Modern Movement*; Randall Stevenson, *1960–2000: The Last of England?*; and Bruce King, *1948–2000: The Internationalization of English Literature*. See also *The Cambridge History of Medieval English Literature*, ed. David Wallace, 1999; *The Cambridge History of Early Medieval English Literature*, ed. Clare E. Lees, 2012; *The Cambridge History of Early Modern English Literature*, ed. David Loewenstein and Janel Mueller, 2003; *The Cambridge History of English Literature, 1660–1780*, ed. John Richetti, 2005; *The Cambridge History of English Romantic Literature*, ed. James Chandler, 2009; *The Cambridge History of Victorian Literature*, ed. Kate Flint, 2012; and *The Cambridge History of Twentieth-Century English Literature*, ed. Laura Marcus and Peter Nicholls, 2005.

Helpful treatments and surveys of English meter, rhyme, and stanza forms are Paul Fussell Jr., *Poetic Meter and Poetic Form*, rev. 1979; Donald Wesling, *The Chances of Rhyme: Device and Modernity*, 1980; Charles O. Hartman, *Free Verse: An Essay in Prosody*, 1983; John Hollander, *Rhyme's Reason: A Guide to English Verse*, rev. 1989; Derek Attridge, *Poetic Rhythm: An Introduction*, 1995; Robert Pinsky, *The Sounds of Poetry: A Brief Guide*, 1998; Mark Strand and Eavan Boland, eds., *The Making of a Poem: A Norton Anthology of Poetic Forms*, 2000; Helen Vendler, *Poems, Poets, Poetry*, 3rd ed., 2010; Virginia Jackson and Yopie Prins, eds., *The Lyric Theory Reader*, 2013; and Jonathan Culler, *Theory of the Lyric*, 2015.

On the development and functioning of the novel as a form, see Ian Watt, *The Rise of the Novel*, 1957; Gérard Genette, *Narrative Discourse: An Essay in Method*, 1980; *Theory of the Novel: A Historical Approach*, ed. Michael McKeon, 2000; McKeon, *The Origins of the English Novel, 1600–1740*, 15th anniversary ed., 2002; and *The Novel*, ed. Franco Moretti, 2 vols., 2006–07. *The Cambridge History of the English Novel*, eds. Robert L. Caserio and Clement Hawes, 2012; *A Companion to the English Novel*, eds. Stephen Arata et al., 2015; eight volumes have been published from *The Oxford History of the Novel in English*, 2011–16. On women novelists and readers, see Nancy Armstrong, *Desire and Domestic Fiction: A Political History of the Novel*, 1987; and Catherine Gallagher, *Nobody's Story: The Vanishing Acts of Women Writers in the Marketplace, 1670–1820*, 1994.

On the history of playhouse design, see Richard Leacroft, *The Development of the English Playhouse: An Illustrated Survey of Theatre Building in England from Medieval to Modern Times*, 1988. For a survey of the plays that have appeared on these and other stages, see Allardyce Nicoll, *British Drama*, rev. 1962; the eight-volume *Revels History of Drama in English*, gen. eds. Clifford Leech and T. W. Craik, 1975–83; and Alfred Harbage, *Annals of English Drama, 975–1700*, 3rd ed., 1989, rev. S. Schoenbaum and Sylvia Wagonheim; and the three volumes of *The Cambridge History of British Theatre*, eds. Jane Milling, Peter Thomson, and Joseph Donohue, 2004.

On some of the key intellectual currents that are at once reflected in and shaped by literature and contemporary literary criticism, Arthur O. Lovejoy's classic studies *The Great Chain of Being*, 1936, and *Essays in the History of Ideas*, 1948, remain valuable, along with such works as Georg Simmel, *The Philosophy of Money*, 1907; Lovejoy and George Boas, *Primitivism and Related Ideas in Antiquity*, 1935; Norbert Elias, *The Civilizing Process*, orig. pub. 1939, English trans. 1969; Simone de Beauvoir, *The Second Sex*, 1949; Frantz Fanon, *Black Skin, White Masks*, 1952, new trans. 2008; Ernst Cassirer, *The Philosophy of Symbolic Forms*, 4 vols., 1953–96; Ernst Kantorowicz, *The King's Two Bodies: A Study in Medieval Political Theology*, 1957, new ed. 1997; Hannah Arendt, *The Human Condition*, 1958; Richard Popkin, *The History of Skepticism from Erasmus to Descartes*, 1960; M. H. Abrams, *Natural Supernaturalism: Tradition and Revolution in Romantic Literature*, 1971; Michel Foucault, *Madness and Civilization: A History of Insanity in the Age of Reason*, Eng.

trans. 1965, and *The Order of Things: An Archaeology of the Human Sciences*, Eng. trans. 1970; Gaston Bachelard, *The Poetics of Space*, Eng. trans. 1969; Martin Jay, *The Dialectical Imagination: A History of the Frankfurt School and the Institute of Social Research, 1923–1950*, 1973, new ed. 1996; Hayden White, *Metahistory*, 1973; Roland Barthes, *The Pleasure of the Text*, Eng. trans. 1975; Jacques Derrida, *Of Grammatology*, Eng. trans. 1976, and *Dissemination*, Eng. trans. 1981; Richard Rorty, *Philosophy and the Mirror of Nature*, 1979; Gilles Deleuze and Félix Guattari, *A Thousand Plateaus*, 1980; Raymond Williams, *Keywords: A Vocabulary of Culture and Society*, rev. 1983; Pierre Bourdieu, *Distinction: A Social Critique of the Judgment of Taste*, Eng. trans. 1984; Michel de Certeau, *The Practice of Everyday Life*, Eng. trans. 1984; Hans Blumenberg, *The Legitimacy of the Modern Age*, Eng. trans. 1985; Jürgen Habermas, *The Philosophical Discourse of Modernity*, Eng. trans, 1987; Slavoj Žižek, *The Sublime Object of Ideology*, 1989; Homi Bhabha, *The Location of Culture*, 1994; Judith Butler, *The Psychic Life of Power: Theories in Subjection*, 1997; and Sigmund Freud, *Writings on Art and Literature*, ed. Neil Hertz, 1997.

Reference Works

The single most important tool for the study of literature in English is the *Oxford English Dictionary*, 2nd ed. 1989, 3rd ed. in process. The most current edition is available online to subscribers. The *OED* is written on historical principles: that is, it attempts not only to describe current word use but also to record the history and development of the language from its origins before the Norman conquest to the present. It thus provides, for familiar as well as archaic and obscure words, the widest possible range of meanings and uses, organized chronologically and illustrated with quotations. The *OED* can be searched as a conventional dictionary arranged a–z and also by subject, usage, region, origin, and timeline (the first appearance of a word). Beyond the *OED* there are many other valuable dictionaries, such as *The American Heritage Dictionary* (5th ed., 2016), *The Oxford Dictionary of Abbreviations*, *The Concise Oxford Dictionary of English Etymology*, *The Oxford Dictionary of English Grammar*, *A New Dictionary of Eponyms*, *The Oxford Essential Dictionary of Foreign Terms in English*, *The Oxford Dictionary of Idioms*, *The Concise Oxford Dictionary of Linguistics*, *The Oxford Guide to World English*, and *The Concise Oxford Dictionary of Proverbs*. Other valuable reference works include *The Cambridge Encyclopedia of the English Language*, 2nd ed., ed. David Crystal, 2003; *The Concise Oxford Companion to the English Language*; *Pocket Fowler's Modern English Usage*; and the numerous guides to specialized vocabularies, slang, regional dialects, and the like.

There is a steady flow of new editions of most major and many minor writers in English, along with a ceaseless outpouring of critical appraisals and scholarship. James L. Harner's *Literary Research Guide: An Annotated List of Reference Sources in English Literary Studies* (6th ed., 2009; online ed. available to subscribers at www.mlalrg.org/public) offers thorough, evaluative annotations of a wide range of sources. For the historical record of scholarship and critical discussion, *The New Cambridge Bibliography of English Literature*, ed. George Watson, 5 vols. (1969–77) and *The Cambridge Bibliography of English Literature*, 3rd ed., 5 vols. (1941–2000) are useful. The *MLA International Bibliography* (also online) is a key resource for following critical discussion of literatures in English. Ranging from 1926 to the present; it includes journal articles, essays, chapters from collections, books, and dissertations, and covers folklore, linguistics, and film. The *Annual Bibliography of English Language and Literature* (*ABELL*), compiled by the Modern Humanities Research Association, lists monographs, periodical articles, critical editions of literary works, book reviews, and collections of essays published anywhere in the world; unpublished doctoral dissertations are covered for the period 1920–99 (available online to subscribers and as part of Literature Online, http://literature.proquest.com/marketing/index.jsp).

For compact biographies of English authors, see the multivolume *Oxford Dictionary of National Biography* (*DNB*), ed. H. C. G. Matthew and Brian Harrison, 2004; since 2004 the *DNB* has been extended online with three annual updates. Handy reference books of authors, works, and various literary terms and allusions include many volumes in the *Cambridge Companion* and *Oxford Companion* series (e.g., *The Cambridge Companion to Narrative*, ed David Herman, 2007; *The Oxford Companion to English Literature*, ed. Dinah Birch, rev. 2016; *The Cambridge Companion to Allegory*, ed. Rita Copeland and Peter Struck, 2010; etc.). Likewise, *The Princeton Encyclopedia of Poetry and Poetics*, ed. Roland Greene and others, 4th ed., is available online to subscribers in ProQuest Ebook Central. Handbooks that define and illustrate literary concepts and terms are *The Penguin Dictionary of Literary Terms and Literary Theory*, ed. J. A. Cuddon and M. A. R. Habib, 5th ed., 2015; William Harmon, *A Handbook to Literature*, 12th ed., 2011; *Critical Terms for Literary Study*, ed. Frank Lentricchia and Thomas McLaughlin, rev. 1995; and M. H. Abrams and Geoffrey Harpham, *A Glossary of Literary Terms*, 11th ed., 2014. Also useful are Richard Lanham, *A Handlist of Rhetorical Terms*, 2nd ed., 2012; Arthur Quinn, *Figures of Speech: 60 Ways to Turn a Phrase*, 1995; and the *Barnhart Concise Dictionary of Etymology*, ed. Robert K. Barnhart, 1995; and George Kennedy, *A New History of Classical Rhetoric*, 2009.

On the Greek and Roman backgrounds, see *The Cambridge History of Classical Literature* (vol. 1: *Greek Literature*, 1982; vol. 2: *Latin Literature*, 1989), both available online; *The Oxford Companion to Classical Literature*, ed. M. C. Howatson, 3rd ed., 2011; Gian Biagio Conte, *Latin Literature: A History*, 1994; *The Oxford Classical Dictionary*, 4th ed., 2012; Richard Rutherford, *Classical Literature: A Concise History*, 2005; and Mark P. O. Morford, Robert J. Lenardon, and Michael Sham, *Classical Mythology*, 10th ed., 2013. The Loeb Classical Library of Greek and Roman texts is now available online to subscribers at www.loebclassics.com.

Digital resources in the humanities have vastly proliferated since the previous edition of *The Norton Anthology of English Literature* and are continuing to grow rapidly. The NAEL Archive (accessed at digital.wwnorton.com/englishlit10abc and digital.wwnorton.com/englishlit10def) is the gateway to an extensive array of annotated texts, images, and other materials especially gathered for the readers of this anthology. Among other useful electronic resources for the study of English literature are enormous digital archives, available to subscribers: Early English Books Online (EEBO), http://eebo.chadwyck.com/home; Literature Online, http://literature.proquest.com/marketing/index.jsp; and Eighteenth Century Collections Online (ECCO), www.gale.com/primary-sources/eighteenth-century-collections-online. There are also numerous free sites of variable quality. Many of the best of these are period or author specific and hence are listed in the period/author bibiliographies in the NAEL Archive. Among the general sites, one of the most useful and wide-ranging is Voice of the Shuttle (http://vos.ucsb.edu), which includes in its aggregation links to Bartleby.com and Project Gutenberg.

Literary Criticism and Theory

Nine volumes of the *Cambridge History of Literary Criticism* have been published, 1989– : *Classical Criticism*, ed. George A. Kennedy; *The Middle Ages*, ed. Alastair Minnis and Ian Johnson; *The Renaissance*, ed. Glyn P. Norton; *The Eighteenth Century*, ed. H. B. Nisbet and Claude Rawson; *Romanticism*, ed. Marshall Brown; *The Nineteenth Century ca. 1830–1914*, ed. M. A. R. Habib; *Modernism and the New Criticism*, ed. A. Walton Litz, Louis Menand, and Lawrence Rainey; *From Formalism to Poststructuralism*, ed. Raman Selden; and *Twentieth-Century Historical, Philosoph-*

ical, and Psychological Perspectives, ed. Christa Knellwolf and Christopher Norris. See also M. H. Abrams, *The Mirror and the Lamp: Romantic Theory and the Critical Tradition*, 1953; William K. Wimsatt and Cleanth Brooks, *Literary Criticism: A Short History*, 1957; René Wellek, *A History of Modern Criticism: 1750–1950*, 9 vols., 1955–93; Frank Lentricchia, *After the New Criticism*, 1980; and J. Hillis Miller, *On Literature*, 2002. Raman Selden, Peter Widdowson, and Peter Brooker have written *A Reader's Guide to Contemporary Literary Theory*, 5th ed., 2015. Other useful resources include *The Johns Hopkins Guide to Literary Theory and Criticism*, 2nd ed., 2004; *Literary Theory, an Anthology*, eds. Julie Rivkin and Michael Ryan, 1998; and *The Norton Anthology of Theory and Criticism*, 3rd ed., gen. ed. Vincent Leitch, 2018.

Modern approaches to English literature and literary theory were shaped by certain landmark works: William Empson, *Seven Types of Ambiguity*, 1930, 3rd ed. 1953, *Some Versions of Pastoral*, 1935, and *The Structure of Complex Words*, 1951; F. R. Leavis, *Revaluation*, 1936, and *The Great Tradition*, 1948; Lionel Trilling, *The Liberal Imagination*, 1950; T. S. Eliot, *Selected Essays*, 3rd ed. 1951, and *On Poetry and Poets*, 1957; Erich Auerbach, *Mimesis: The Representation of Reality in Western Literature*, 1953; William K. Wimsatt, *The Verbal Icon*, 1954; Northrop Frye, *Anatomy of Criticism*, 1957; Wayne C. Booth, *The Rhetoric of Fiction*, 1961, rev. ed. 1983; and W. J. Bate, *The Burden of the Past and the English Poet*, 1970. René Wellek and Austin Warren, *Theory of Literature*, rev. 1970, is a useful introduction to the variety of scholarly and critical approaches to literature up to the time of its publication. Jonathan Culler's *Literary Theory: A Very Short Introduction*, 1997, discusses recurrent issues and debates.

Beginning in the late 1960s, there was a significant intensification of interest in literary theory as a specific field. Certain forms of literary study had already been influenced by the work of the Russian linguist Roman Jakobson and the Russian formalist Viktor Shklovsky and, still more, by conceptions that derived or claimed to derive from Marx and Engels, but the full impact of these theories was not felt until what became known as the "theory revolution" of the 1970s and '80s. For Marxist literary criticism, see Georg Lukács, *Theory of the Novel*, 1920, trans. 1971; *The Historical Novel*, 1937, trans. 1983; and *Studies in European Realism*, trans. 1964; Walter Benjamin's essays from the 1920s and '30s represented in *Illuminations*, trans. 1986, and *Reflections*, trans. 1986; Mikhail Bakhtin's essays from the 1930s represented in *The Dialogic Imagination*, trans. 1981, and *Rabelais and His World*, 1941, trans. 1968; *Selections from the Prison Notebooks of Antonio Gramsci*, ed. and trans. Quintin Hoare and Geoffrey Smith, 1971; Raymond Williams, *Marxism and Literature*, 1977; Tony Bennett, *Formalism and Marxism*, 1979; Fredric Jameson, *The Political Unconscious: Narrative as a Socially Symbolic Act*, 1981; and Terry Eagleton, *Literary Theory: An Introduction*, 3rd ed., 2008, and *The Ideology of the Aesthetic*, 1990.

Structural linguistics and anthropology gave rise to a flowering of structuralist literary criticism; convenient introductions include Robert Scholes, *Structuralism in Literature: An Introduction*, 1974, and Jonathan Culler, *Structuralist Poetics*, 1975. Poststructuralist challenges to this approach are epitomized in such influential works as Jacques Derrida, *Writing and Difference*, 1967, trans. 1978, and Paul de Man, *Blindness and Insight: Essays in the Rhetoric of Contemporary Criticism*, 1971, 2nd ed., 1983. Poststructuralism is discussed in Jonathan Culler, *On Deconstruction*, 1982; Slavoj Žižek, *The Sublime Object of Ideology*, 1989; Fredric Jameson, *Postmodernism; or the Cultural Logic of Late Capitalism*, 1991; John McGowan, *Postmodernism and Its Critics*, 1991; and *Beyond Structuralism*, ed. Wendell Harris, 1996. A figure who greatly influenced both structuralism and poststructuralism is Roland Barthes, in *Mythologies*, trans. 1972, and *S/Z*, trans. 1974. Among other influential contributions to literary theory are the psychoanalytic approach in Harold Bloom, *The Anxiety of*

Influence, 1973; and the reader-response approach in Stanley Fish, *Is There a Text in This Class?: The Authority of Interpretive Communities*, 1980. For a retrospect on the theory decades, see Terry Eagleton, *After Theory*, 2003.

Influenced by these theoretical currents but not restricted to them, modern feminist literary criticism was fashioned by such works as Patricia Meyer Spacks, *The Female Imagination*, 1975; Ellen Moers, *Literary Women*, 1976; Elaine Showalter, *A Literature of Their Own*, 1977; and Sandra Gilbert and Susan Gubar, *The Madwoman in the Attic*, 1979. Subsequent studies include Jane Gallop, *The Daughter's Seduction: Feminism and Psychoanalysis*, 1982; Luce Irigaray, *This Sex Which Is Not One*, trans. 1985; Gayatri Chakravorty Spivak, *In Other Worlds: Essays in Cultural Politics*, 1987; Sandra Gilbert and Susan Gubar, *No Man's Land: The Place of the Woman Writer in the Twentieth Century*, 3 vols., 1988–94; Barbara Johnson, *A World of Difference*, 1989; Judith Butler, *Gender Trouble*, 1990; and the critical views sampled in Elaine Showalter, *The New Feminist Criticism*, 1985; *The Hélène Cixous Reader*, ed. Susan Sellers, 1994; *Feminist Literary Theory: A Reader*, ed. Mary Eagleton, 3rd ed., 2010; and *Feminisms: An Anthology of Literary Theory and Criticism*, eds. Robyn R. Warhol and Diane Price Herndl, 2nd ed., 1997; *The Cambridge Companion to Feminist Literary Theory*, ed. Ellen Rooney, 2006; *Feminist Literary Theory and Criticism*, ed. Sandra Gilbert and Susan Gubar, 2007; and *Feminist Literary Theory: A Reader*, ed. Mary Eagleton, 3rd ed., 2011.

Just as feminist critics used poststructuralist and psychoanalytic methods to place literature in conversation with gender theory, a new school emerged placing literature in conversation with critical race theory. Comprehensive introductions include *Critical Race Theory: The Key Writings That Formed the Movement*, eds. Kimberlé Crenshaw et al.; *The Routledge Companion to Race and Ethnicity*, ed. Stephen Caliendo and Charlton McIlwain, 2010; and *Critical Race Theory: An Introduction*, ed. Richard Delgado and Jean Stefancic, 3rd ed., 2017. For an important precursor in cultural studies, see Stuart Hall et al., *Policing the Crisis*, 1978. Seminal works include Henry Louis Gates, Jr., *The Signifying Monkey: A Theory of African-American Literature*, 1988; Patricia Williams, *The Alchemy of Race and Rights*, 1991; Toni Morrison, *Playing the Dark: Whiteness and the Literary Imagination*, 1992; Cornel West, *Race Matters*, 2001; and Gene Andrew Jarrett, *Representing the Race: A New Political History of African American Literature*, 2011. Helpful anthologies and collections of essays have emerged in recent decades, such as *The Oxford Companion to African American Literature*, eds., William L. Andrews, Frances Smith Foster, and Trudier Harris, 1997; also their *Concise Companion*, 2001; *The Cambridge Companion to Jewish American Literature*, eds. Hana Wirth-Nesher and Michael P. Kramer, 2003; *The Routledge Companion to Anglophone Caribbean Literature*, eds. Michael A. Bucknor and Alison Donnell, 2011; *The Routledge Companion to Latino/a Literature*, eds. Suzanne Bost and Frances R. Aparicio, 2013; *A Companion to African American Literature*, ed. Gene Andrew Jarrett, 2013; *The Routledge Companion to Asian American and Pacific Islander Literature*, ed. Rachel Lee, 2014; *The Cambridge Companion to Asian American Literature*, eds. Crystal Parikh and Daniel Y. Kim, 2015; and *The Cambridge Companion to British Black and Asian Literature (1945–2010)*, ed. Deirdre Osborne, 2016.

Gay literature and queer studies are represented in *Inside/Out: Lesbian Theories, Gay Theories*, ed. Diana Fuss, 1991; *The Lesbian and Gay Studies Reader*, eds. Henry Abelove, Michele Barale, and David Halperin, 1993; *The Columbia Anthology of Gay Literature: Readings from Western Antiquity to the Present Day*, ed. Byrne R. S. Fone, 1998; and by such books as Eve Sedgwick, *Between Men: English Literature and Male Homosocial Desire*, 1985, and *Epistemology of the Closet*, 1990; Diana Fuss, *Essentially Speaking: Feminism, Nature, and Difference*, 1989; Terry Castle, *The Apparitional Lesbian: Female Homosexuality and Modern Culture*, 1993; Leo Bersani, *Homos*, 1995; Gregory Woods, *A History of Gay Literature: The Male Tradition*,

1998; David Halperin, *How to Do the History of Homosexuality*, 2002; Judith Halberstam, *In a Queer Time and Place: Transgender Bodies, Subcultural Lives*, 2005; Heather Love, *Feeling Backward: Loss and the Politics of Queer History*, 2009; *The Cambridge History of Gay and Lesbian Literature*, eds. E. L. McCallum and Mikko Tuhkanen, 2014; and *The Cambridge Companion to Lesbian Literature*, ed. Jodie Medd, 2015.

New historicism is represented in Stephen Greenblatt, *Learning to Curse*, 1990; in the essays collected in *The New Historicism Reader*, ed. Harold Veeser, 1993; in *New Historical Literary Study: Essays on Reproducing Texts, Representing History*, eds. Jeffrey N. Cox and Larry J. Reynolds, 1993; and in Catherine Gallagher and Stephen Greenblatt, *Practicing New Historicism*, 2000. The related social and historical dimension of texts is discussed in Jerome McGann, *Critique of Modern Textual Criticism*, 1983; and *Scholarly Editing: A Guide to Research*, ed. D. C. Greetham, 1995. Characteristic of new historicism is an expansion of the field of literary interpretation still further in cultural studies; for a broad sampling of the range of interests, see Lawrence Grossberg, Cary Nelson, and Paula Treichler, eds., *Cultural Studies*, 1992; *The Cultural Studies Reader*, ed. Simon During, 3rd ed., 2007; and *A Cultural Studies Reader: History, Theory, Practice*, eds. Jessica Munns and Gita Rajan, 1996.

This expansion of the field is similarly reflected in postcolonial studies: see Frantz Fanon, *Black Skin, White Masks*, 1952, new trans. 2008, and *The Wretched of the Earth*, 1961, new trans. 2004; Edward Said, *Orientalism*, 1978, and *Culture and Imperialism*, 1993; *The Post-Colonial Studies Reader*, 2nd ed., 2006; and such influential books as Homi Bhabha, ed., *Nation and Narration*, 1990, and *The Location of Culture*, 1994; Robert J. C. Young, *Postcolonialism: An Historical Introduction*, 2001; Bill Ashcroft, Gareth Griffiths, and Helen Tiffin, *The Empire Writes Back: Theory and Practice in Post-Colonial Literatures*, 2nd ed. 2002; Elleke Boehmer, *Colonial and Postcolonial Literature*, 2nd ed. 2005; and *The Cambridge History of Postcolonial Literature*, ed. Ato Quayson, 2011; *The Cambridge Companion to the Postcolonial Novel*, ed. Ato Quayson, 2015; and *The Cambridge Companion to Postcolonial Poetry*, ed. Jahan Ramazani, 2017.

In the wake of the theory revolution, critics have focused on a wide array of topics, which can only be briefly surveyed here. One current of work, focusing on the history of emotion, is represented in Brian Massumi, *Parables for the Virtual*, 2002; Sianne Ngai, *Ugly Feelings*, 2005; *The Affect Theory Reader*, eds. Melissa Gregg and Gregory J. Seigworth, 2010; and Judith Butler, *Senses of the Subject*, 2015. A somewhat related current, examining the special role of traumatic memory in literature, is exemplified in Cathy Caruth, *Trauma: Explorations in Memory*, 1995; and Dominic LaCapra, *Writing History, Writing Trauma*, 2000. Work on the literary implications of cognitive science may be glimpsed in *Introduction to Cognitive Cultural Studies*, ed. Lisa Zunshine, 2010. Interest in quantitative approaches to literature was sparked by Franco Moretti, *Graphs, Maps, Trees: Abstract Models for Literary History*, 2005. For the growing field of digital humanities, see also Moretti, *Distant Reading*, 2013; *Defining Digital Humanities: A Reader*, eds. Melissa Terras, Julianne Nyhan, and Edward Vanhoutte, 2014; and *A New Companion to Digital Humanities*, eds. Susan Schreibman, Ray Siemens, and John Unsworth, 2nd ed., 2016. There has also been a flourishing of ecocriticism, or studies of literature and the environment, including *The Ecocriticism Reader: Landmarks in Literary Ecology*, eds. Cheryll Glotfelty and Harold Fromm, 1996; *Writing the Environment*, eds. Richard Kerridge and Neil Sammells, 1998; Jonathan Bate, *The Song of the Earth*, 2002; Lawrence Buell, *The Future of Environmental Criticism: Environmental Crisis and Literary Imagination*, 2005; Timothy Morton, *Ecology Without Nature*, 2009; and *The Oxford Handbook of Ecocriticism*, ed. Greg Garrard, 2014. Related are the emerging fields of animal studies and posthumanism, where key works include

Bruno Latour, *We Have Never Been Modern*, 1993; Steve Baker, *Postmodern Animal*, 2000; Jacques Derrida, *The Animal That Therefore I Am*, trans. 2008; Cary Wolfe, *Animal Rites: American Culture, the Discourse of Species, and Posthumanist Theory*, 2003, and *What is Posthumanism?* 2009; Kari Weil, *Thinking Animals: Why Animal Studies Now?* 2012; and Aaron Gross and Anne Vallely, eds. *Animals and the Human Imagination: A Companion to Animal Studies*, 2012; and *Critical Animal Studies: Thinking the Unthinkable*, ed. John Sorenson, 2014. The relationship between literature and law is central to such works as *Interpreting Law and Literature: A Hermeneutic Reader*, eds. Sanford Levinson and Steven Mailloux, 1988; *Law's Stories: Narrative and Rhetoric in the Law*, eds. Peter Brooks and Paul Gerwertz, 1998; and *Literature and Legal Problem Solving: Law and Literature as Ethical Discourse*, Paul J. Heald, 1998. Ethical questions in literature have been usefully explored by, among others, Geoffrey Galt Harpham in *Getting It Right: Language, Literature, and Ethics*, 1997, and Derek Attridge in *The Singularity of Literature*, 2004. Finally, approaches to literature, such as formalism and literary biography, that seemed superseded in the theoretical ferment of the late twentieth century, have had a powerful resurgence. A renewed interest in form is evident in Susan Stewart, *Poetry and the Fate of the Senses*, 2002; *Reading for Form*, eds. Susan J. Wolfson and Marshall Brown, 2007; and Caroline Levine, *Forms: Whole, Rhythm, Hierarchy, Network*, 2015. Interest in the history of the book was spearheaded by D. F. McKenzie's *Bibliography and the Sociology of Texts*, 1986; Jerome McGann's *The Textual Condition*, 1991; and Roger Chartier's *The Order of Books: Readers, Authors, and Libraries in Europe Between the Fourteenth and Eighteenth Centuries*, 1994. See also *The Cambridge History of the Book in Britain*, 7 vols., 1998–2017; and *The Practice and Representation of Reading in England*, eds. James Raven, Helen Small, and Naomi Tadmor, 2007; *The Book History Reader*, eds. David Finkelstein and Alistair McCleery, 2nd ed., 2006; and *The Cambridge Companion to the History of the Book*, ed. Leslie Howsam, 2014.

Anthologies representing a range of recent approaches include *Modern Criticism and Theory*, ed. David Lodge, 1988; *Contemporary Literary Criticism*, ed. Robert Con Davis and Ronald Schlieffer, 4th ed., 1998; and *The Norton Anthology of Theory and Criticism*, gen. ed. Vincent Leitch, 3rd ed., 2018.

Literary Terminology*

Using simple technical terms can sharpen our understanding and streamline our discussion of literary works. Some terms, such as the ones in section A, help us address the internal style, structure, form, and kind of works. Other terms, such as those in section B, provide insight into the material forms in which literary works have been produced.

In analyzing what they called "rhetoric," ancient Greek and Roman writers determined the elements of what we call "style" and "structure." Our literary terms are derived, via medieval and Renaissance intermediaries, from the Greek and Latin sources. In the definitions that follow, the etymology, or root, of the word is given when it helps illuminate the word's current usage.

Most of the examples are drawn from texts in this anthology.

Words **boldfaced** within definitions are themselves defined in this appendix. Some terms are defined within definitions; such words are *italicized*.

A. Terms of Style, Structure, Form, and Kind

accent (synonym "stress"): a term of **rhythm.** The special force devoted to the voicing of one syllable in a word over others. In the noun "accent," for example, the accent, or stress, is on the first syllable.

act: the major subdivision of a play, usually divided into **scenes.**

aesthetics (from Greek, "to feel, apprehend by the senses"): the philosophy of artistic meaning as a distinct mode of apprehending untranslatable truth, defined as an alternative to rational enquiry, which is purely abstract. Developed in the late eighteenth century by the German philosopher Immanuel Kant especially.

Alexandrine: a term of **meter.** In French verse a line of twelve syllables, and, by analogy, in English verse a line of six stresses. See **hexameter.**

allegory (Greek "saying otherwise"): saying one thing (the "vehicle" of the allegory) and meaning another (the allegory's "tenor"). Allegories may be momentary aspects of a work, as in **metaphor** ("John is a lion"), or, through extended metaphor, may constitute the basis of narrative, as in Bunyan's *Pilgrim's Progress*: this second meaning is the dominant one. See also **symbol** and **type.** Allegory is one of the most significant **figures of thought.**

alliteration (from Latin "litera," alphabetic letter): a **figure of speech.** The repetition of an initial consonant sound or consonant cluster in consecutive or closely positioned words. This pattern is often an inseparable part of the meter in Germanic languages, where the tonic, or accented **syllable,** is usually the first syllable. Thus all Old English poetry and some varieties of Middle English poetry use alliteration as part of their basic metrical practice. *Sir Gawain and the Green Knight*, line 1: "Sithen the sege and the assaut was sesed at Troye" (see vol. A, p. 204). Otherwise used for local effects; Stevie Smith, "Pretty," lines 4–5: "And in the pretty pool the pike stalks / He stalks his prey . . ." (see vol. F, p. 733).

*This appendix was devised and compiled by James Simpson with the collaboration of all the editors. We especially thank Professor Lara Bovilsky of the University of Oregon at Eugene, for her help.

allusion: Literary allusion is a passing but illuminating reference within a literary text to another, well-known text (often biblical or **classical**). Topical allusions are also, of course, common in certain modes, especially **satire.**

anagnorisis (Greek "recognition"): the moment of **protagonist's** recognition in a narrative, which is also often the moment of moral understanding.

anapest: a term of **rhythm.** A three-syllable foot following the rhythmic pattern, in English verse, of two unstressed (uu) syllables followed by one stressed (/). Thus, for example, "Illinois."

anaphora (Greek "carrying back"): a **figure of speech.** The repetition of words or groups of words at the beginning of consecutive sentences, clauses, or phrases. Blake, "London," lines 5–8: "In every cry of every Man, / In every Infant's cry of fear, / In every voice, in every ban . . ." (see vol. D, p. 141); Louise Bennett, "Jamaica Oman," lines 17–20: "Some backa man a push, some side-a / Man a hole him han, / Some a lick sense eena him head, / Some a guide him pon him plan!" (see vol. F, p. 860).

animal fable: a **genre.** A short narrative of speaking animals, followed by moralizing comment, written in a low style and gathered into a collection. Robert Henryson, "The Preaching of the Swallow" (see vol. A, p. 523).

antithesis (Greek "placing against"): a **figure of thought.** The juxtaposition of opposed terms in clauses or sentences that are next to or near each other. Milton, *Paradise Lost* 1.777–80: "They but now who seemed / In bigness to surpass Earth's giant sons / Now less than smallest dwarfs, in narrow room / Throng numberless" (see vol. B, p. 1514).

apostrophe (from Greek "turning away"): a **figure of thought.** An address, often to an absent person, a force, or a quality. For example, a poet makes an apostrophe to a Muse when invoking her for inspiration.

apposition: a term of **syntax.** The repetition of elements serving an identical grammatical function in one sentence. The effect of this repetition is to arrest the flow of the sentence, but in doing so to add extra semantic nuance to repeated elements. This is an especially important feature of Old English poetic style. See, for example, Caedmon's *Hymn* (vol. A, p. 31), where the phrases "heaven-kingdom's Guardian," "the Measurer's might," "his mind-plans," and "the work of the Glory-Father" each serve an identical syntactic function as the direct objects of "praise."

assonance (Latin "sounding to"): a **figure of speech.** The repetition of identical or near identical stressed vowel sounds in words whose final consonants differ, producing half-rhyme. Tennyson, "The Lady of Shalott," line 100: "His broad clear brow in sunlight glowed" (see vol. E, p. 149).

aubade (originally from Spanish "alba," dawn): a **genre.** A lover's dawn song or lyric bewailing the arrival of the day and the necessary separation of the lovers; Donne, "The Sun Rising" (see vol. B, p. 926). Larkin recasts the genre in "Aubade" (see vol. F, p. 930).

autobiography (Greek "self-life writing"): a **genre.** A narrative of a life written by the subject; Wordsworth, *The Prelude* (see vol. D, p. 362). There are subgenres, such as the spiritual autobiography, narrating the author's path to conversion and subsequent spiritual trials, as in Bunyan's *Grace Abounding*.

ballad stanza: a **verse form.** Usually a **quatrain** in alternating **iambic tetrameter** and **iambic trimeter** lines, rhyming abcb. See "Sir Patrick Spens" (vol. D, p. 36); Louise Bennett's poems (vol. F, pp. 857–61); Eliot, "Sweeney among the Nightingales" (vol. F, p. 657); Larkin, "This Be The Verse" (vol. F, p. 930).

ballade: a **verse form.** A form consisting usually of three stanzas followed by a four-line envoi (French, "send off"). The last line of the first stanza establishes a **refrain,** which is repeated, or subtly varied, as the last line of each stanza. The form was derived from French medieval poetry; English poets, from the fourteenth to the sixteenth centuries especially, used it with varying stanza forms. Chaucer, "Complaint to His Purse" (see vol. A, p. 363).

bathos (Greek "depth"): a **figure of thought.** A sudden and sometimes ridiculous descent of tone; Pope, *The Rape of the Lock* 3.157–58: "Not louder shrieks to pitying heaven are cast, / When husbands, or when lapdogs breathe their last" (see vol. C, p. 518).

beast epic: a **genre.** A continuous, unmoralized narrative, in prose or verse, relating the victories of the wholly unscrupulous but brilliant strategist Reynard the Fox over all adversaries. Chaucer arouses, only to deflate, expectations of the genre in *The Nun's Priest's Tale* (see vol. A, p. 344).

biography (Greek "life-writing"): a **genre.** A life as the subject of an extended narrative. Thus Izaak Walton, *The Life of Dr. Donne* (see vol. B, p. 976).

blank verse: a **verse form.** Unrhymed **iambic pentameter** lines. Blank verse has no stanzas, but is broken up into uneven units (verse paragraphs) determined by sense rather than form. First devised in English by Henry Howard, earl of Surrey, in his translation of two books of Virgil's *Aeneid* (see vol. B, p. 141), this very flexible verse type became the standard form for dramatic poetry in the seventeenth century, as in most of Shakespeare's plays. Milton and Wordsworth, among many others, also used it to create an English equivalent to **classical epic.**

blazon: strictly, a heraldic shield; in rhetorical usage, a **topos** whereby the individual elements of a beloved's face and body are singled out for **hyperbolic** admiration. Spenser, *Epithalamion*, lines 167–84 (see vol. B, p. 495). For an inversion of the **topos,** see Shakespeare, Sonnet 130 (vol. B, p. 736).

burlesque (French and Italian "mocking"): a work that adopts the **conventions** of a genre with the aim less of comically mocking the genre than of satirically mocking the society so represented (see **satire**). Thus Pope's *Rape of the Lock* (see vol. C, p. 507) does not mock **classical epic** so much as contemporary mores.

caesura (Latin "cut") (plural "caesurae"): a term of **meter.** A pause or breathing space within a line of verse, generally occurring between syntactic units; Louise Bennett, "Colonization in Reverse," lines 5–8: "By de hundred, by de tousan, / From country an from town, / By de ship-load, by de plane-load, / Jamaica is Englan boun" (see vol. F, p. 858), where the caesurae occur in lines 5 and 7.

canon (Greek "rule"): the group of texts regarded as worthy of special respect or attention by a given institution. Also, the group of texts regarded as definitely having been written by a certain author.

catastrophe (Greek "overturning"): the decisive turn in **tragedy** by which the plot is resolved and, usually, the **protagonist** dies.

catharsis (Greek "cleansing"): According to Aristotle, the effect of **tragedy** on its audience, through their experience of pity and terror, was a kind of spiritual cleansing, or catharsis.

character (Greek "stamp, impression"): a person, personified animal, or other figure represented in a literary work, especially in narrative and drama. The more a character seems to generate the action of a narrative, and the less he or she seems merely to serve a preordained narrative pattern, the "fuller," or more "rounded," a character is said to be. A "stock" character, common particularly in many comic genres, will perform a predictable function in different works of a given genre.

chiasmus (Greek "crosswise"): a **figure of speech.** The inversion of an already established sequence. This can involve verbal echoes: Pope, "Eloisa to Abelard," line 104, "The crime was common, common be the pain" (see vol. C, p. 529); or it can be purely a matter of syntactic inversion: Pope, *Epistle to Dr. Arbuthnot*, line 8: "They pierce my thickets, through my grot they glide" (see vol. C, p. 544).

classical, classicism, classic: Each term can be widely applied, but in English literary discourse, "classical" primarily describes the works of either Greek or Roman antiquity. "Classicism" denotes the practice of art forms inspired by classical antiquity, in particular the observance of rhetorical norms of **decorum** and balance, as opposed to following the dictates of untutored inspiration, as in Romanticism. "Classic" denotes an especially famous work within a given **canon.**

climax (Greek "ladder"): a moment of great intensity and structural change, especially in drama. Also a **figure of speech** whereby a sequence of verbally linked clauses is made, in which each successive clause is of greater consequence than its predecessor. Bacon, *Of Studies*: "Studies serve for pastimes, for ornaments, and for abilities. Their chief use for pastimes is in privateness and retiring; for ornament, is in discourse; and for ability, is in judgement" (see vol. B, p. 1223–24).

comedy: a **genre.** A term primarily applied to drama, and derived from ancient drama, in opposition to **tragedy.** Comedy deals with humorously confusing, sometimes ridiculous situations in which the ending is, nevertheless, happy. A comedy often ends in one or more marriages. Shakespeare, *Twelfth Night* (see vol. B, p. 741).

comic mode: Many genres (e.g., **romance, fabliau, comedy**) involve a happy ending in which justice is done, the ravages of time are arrested, and that which is lost is found. Such genres participate in a comic mode.

connotation: To understand connotation, we need to understand **denotation.** While many words can denote the same concept—that is, have the same basic meaning—those words can evoke different associations, or connotations. Contrast, for example, the clinical-sounding term "depression" and the more colorful, musical, even poetic phrase "the blues."

consonance (Latin "sounding with"): a **figure of speech.** The repetition of final consonants in words or stressed syllables whose vowel sounds are different. Herbert, "Easter," line 13: "Consort, both heart and lute . . ." (see vol. B, p. 1258).

convention: a repeatedly recurring feature (in either form or content) of works, occurring in combination with other recurring formal features, which constitutes a convention of a particular genre.

couplet: a **verse form.** In English verse two consecutive, rhyming lines usually containing the same number of stresses. Chaucer first introduced the **iambic pentameter** couplet into English (*Canterbury Tales*); the form was later used in many types of writing, including drama; imitations and translations of **classical epic** (thus *heroic couplet*); essays; and **satire** (see Dryden and Pope). The *distich* (Greek "two lines") is a couplet usually making complete sense; Aemilia Lanyer, *Salve Deus Rex Judaeorum*, lines 5–6: "Read it fair queen, though it defective be, / Your excellence can grace both it and me" (see vol. B, p. 981).

dactyl (Greek "finger," because of the finger's three joints): a term of **rhythm.** A three-syllable foot following the rhythmic pattern, in English verse, of one stressed followed by two unstressed syllables. Thus, for example, "Oregon."

decorum (Latin "that which is fitting"): a rhetorical principle whereby each formal aspect of a work should be in keeping with its subject matter and/or audience.

deixis (Greek "pointing"): relevant to **point of view.** Every work has, implicitly or explicitly, a "here" and a "now" from which it is narrated. Words that refer to or imply this point from which the voice of the work is projected (such as "here," "there," "this," "that," "now," "then") are examples of deixis, or "deictics." This technique is especially important in drama, where it is used to create a sense of the events happening as the spectator witnesses them.

denotation: A word has a basic, "prosaic" (factual) meaning prior to the associations it connotes (see **connotation**). The word "steed," for example, might call to mind a horse fitted with battle gear, to be ridden by a warrior, but its denotation is simply "horse."

denouement (French "unknotting"): the point at which a narrative can be resolved and so ended.

dialogue (Greek "conversation"): a **genre.** Dialogue is a feature of many genres, especially in both the **novel** and drama. As a genre itself, dialogue is used in philosophical traditions especially (most famously in Plato's *Dialogues*), as the representation of a conversation in which a philosophical question is pursued among various speakers.

diction, or **"lexis"** (from, respectively, Latin *dictio* and Greek *lexis*, each meaning "word"): the actual words used in any utterance—speech, writing, and, for our purposes here, literary works. The choice of words contributes significantly to the style of a given work.

didactic mode (Greek "teaching mode"): **Genres** in a didactic mode are designed to instruct or teach, sometimes explicitly (e.g., sermons, philosophical **discourses, georgic**), and sometimes through the medium of fiction (e.g., **animal fable, parable**).

diegesis (Greek for "narration"): a term that simply means "narration," but is used in literary criticism to distinguish one kind of story from another. In a *mimetic* story, the events are played out before us (see **mimesis**), whereas in diegesis someone recounts the story to us. Drama is for the most part *mimetic*, whereas the novel is for the most part diegetic. In novels the narrator is not, usually, part of the action of the narrative; s/he is therefore extradiegetic.

dimeter (Greek "two measure"): a term of **meter.** A two-stress line, rarely used as the meter of whole poems, though used with great frequency in single poems by Skelton, e.g., "The Tunning of Elinour Rumming" (see vol. B, p. 39). Otherwise used for single lines, as in Herbert, "Discipline," line 3: "O my God" (see vol. B, p. 1274).

discourse (Latin "running to and fro"): broadly, any nonfictional speech or writing; as a more specific genre, a philosophical meditation on a set theme. Thus Newman, *The Idea of a University* (see vol. E, p. 64).

dramatic irony: a feature of narrative and drama, whereby the audience knows that the outcome of an action will be the opposite of that intended by a **character.**

dramatic monologue (Greek "single speaking"): a **genre.** A poem in which the voice of a historical or fictional **character** speaks, unmediated by any narrator, to an implied though silent audience. See Tennyson, "Ulysses" (vol. E, p. 156); Browning, "The Bishop Orders His Tomb" (vol. E, p. 332); Eliot, "The Love Song of J. Alfred Prufrock" (vol. F, p. 654); Carol Ann Duffy, "Medusa" and "Mrs Lazarus" (vol. F, pp. 1211–13).

ecphrasis (Greek "speaking out"): a **topos** whereby a work of visual art is represented in a literary work. Auden, "Musée des Beaux Arts" (see vol. F, p. 815).

elegy: a **genre.** In **classical** literature elegy was a form written in elegiac **couplets** (a **hexameter** followed by a **pentameter**) devoted to many possible topics. In Ovidian elegy a lover meditates on the trials of erotic desire (e.g., Ovid's *Amores*). The **sonnet** sequences of both Sidney and Shakespeare exploit this genre, and, while it was still practiced in classical tradition by Donne ("On His Mistress" [see vol. B, p. 942]), by the later seventeenth century the term came to denote the poetry of loss, especially through the death of a loved person. See Tennyson, *In Memoriam* (vol. E, p. 173); Yeats, "In Memory of Major Robert Gregory" (vol. F, p. 223); Auden, "In Memory of W. B. Yeats" (see vol. F, p. 815); Heaney, "Clearances" (vol. F, p. 1104).

emblem (Greek "an insertion"): a **figure of thought.** A picture allegorically express-ing a moral, or a verbal picture open to such interpretation. Donne, "A Hymn to Christ," lines 1–2: "In what torn ship soever I embark, / That ship shall be my emblem of thy ark" (see vol. B, p. 966).

end-stopping: the placement of a complete syntactic unit within a complete poetic line, fulfilling the metrical pattern; Auden, "In Memory of W. B. Yeats," line 42: "Earth, receive an honoured guest" (see vol. F, p. 817). Compare **enjambment.**

enjambment (French "striding," encroaching): The opposite of **end-stopping,** enjamb-ment occurs when the syntactic unit does not end with the end of the poetic line and the fulfillment of the metrical pattern. When the sense of the line overflows its meter and, therefore, the line break, we have enjambment; Auden, "In Memory of W. B. Yeats," lines 44–45: "Let the Irish vessel lie / Emptied of its poetry" (see vol. F, p. 817).

epic (synonym, *heroic poetry*): a **genre.** An extended narrative poem celebrating mar-tial heroes, invoking divine inspiration, beginning in medias res (see **order**), written in a high style (including the deployment of **epic similes;** on high style, see **register**), and divided into long narrative sequences. Homer's *Iliad* and Virgil's *Aeneid* were the prime models for English writers of epic verse. Thus Milton, *Paradise Lost* (see vol. B, p. 1495); Wordsworth, *The Prelude* (see vol. D, p. 362); and Walcott, *Omeros* (see vol. F, p. 947). With its precise repertoire of stylistic resources, epic lent itself easily to **parodic** and **burlesque** forms, known as **mock epic;** thus Pope, *The Rape of the Lock* (see vol. C, p. 507).

epigram: a **genre.** A short, pithy poem wittily expressed, often with wounding intent. See Jonson, *Epigrams* (see vol. B, p. 1089).

epigraph (Greek "inscription"): a **genre.** Any formal statement inscribed on stone; also the brief formulation on a book's title page, or a quotation at the beginning of a poem, introducing the work's themes in the most compressed form possible.

epistle (Latin "letter"): a **genre.** The letter can be shaped as a literary form, involv-ing an intimate address often between equals. The *Epistles* of Horace provided a model for English writers from the sixteenth century. Thus Wyatt, "Mine own John Poins" (see vol. B, p. 131), or Pope, "An Epistle to a Lady" (vol. C, p. 655). Letters can be shaped to form the matter of an extended fiction, as the eighteenth-century epistolary **novel** (e.g., Samuel Richardson's *Pamela*).

epitaph: a **genre.** A pithy formulation to be inscribed on a funeral monument. Thus Ralegh, "The Author's Epitaph, Made by Himself" (see vol. B, p. 532).

epithalamion (Greek "concerning the bridal chamber"): a **genre.** A wedding poem, celebrating the marriage and wishing the couple good fortune. Thus Spenser, *Epi-thalamion* (see vol. B, p. 491).

epyllion (plural "epyllia") (Greek: "little epic"): a **genre.** A relatively short poem in the meter of epic poetry. See, for example, Marlowe, *Hero and Leander* (vol. B, p 660).

essay (French "trial, attempt"): a **genre.** An informal philosophical meditation, usually in prose and sometimes in verse. The journalistic periodical essay was developed in the early eighteenth century. Thus Addison and Steele, periodical essays (see vol. C, p. 462); Pope, *An Essay on Criticism* (see vol. C, p. 490).

euphemism (Greek "sweet saying"): a **figure of thought.** The figure by which something distasteful is described in alternative, less repugnant terms (e.g., "he passed away").

exegesis (Greek "leading out"): interpretation, traditionally of the biblical text, but, by transference, of any text.

exemplum (Latin "example"): an example inserted into a usually nonfictional writing (e.g., sermon or **essay**) to give extra force to an abstract thesis. Thus Johnson's example of "Sober" in his essay "On Idleness" (see vol. C, p. 732).

fabliau (French "little story," plural *fabliaux*): a **genre.** A short, funny, often bawdy narrative in low style (see **register**) imitated and developed from French models, most subtly by Chaucer; see *The Miller's Prologue and Tale* (vol. A, p. 282).

farce (French "stuffing"): a **genre.** A play designed to provoke laughter through the often humiliating antics of stock **characters.** Congreve's *The Way of the World* (see vol. C, p. 188) draws on this tradition.

figures of speech: Literary language often employs patterns perceptible to the eye and/or to the ear. Such patterns are called "figures of speech"; in classical rhetoric they were called "schemes" (from Greek *schema*, meaning "form, figure").

figures of thought: Language can also be patterned conceptually, even outside the rules that normally govern it. Literary language in particular exploits this licensed linguistic irregularity. Synonyms for figures of thought are "trope" (Greek "twisting," referring to the irregularity of use) and "conceit" (Latin "concept," referring to the fact that these figures are perceptible only to the mind). Be careful not to confuse **trope** with **topos** (a common error).

first-person narration: relevant to **point of view,** a narrative in which the voice narrating refers to itself with forms of the first-person pronoun ("I," "me," "my," etc., or possibly "we," "us," "our"), and in which the narrative is determined by the limitations of that voice. Thus Mary Wollstonecraft Shelley, *Frankenstein.*

frame narrative: Some narratives, particularly collections of narratives, involve a frame narrative that explains the genesis of, and/or gives a perspective on, the main narrative or narratives to follow. Thus Chaucer, *Canterbury Tales*; Mary Wollstonecraft Shelley, *Frankenstein*; or Conrad, *Heart of Darkness.*

free indirect style: relevant to **point of view,** a narratorial voice that manages, without explicit reference, to imply, and often implicitly to comment on, the voice of a **character** in the narrative itself. Virginia Woolf, "A Sketch of the Past," where the voice, although strictly that of the adult narrator, manages to convey the child's manner of perception: "—I begin: the first memory. This was of red and purple flowers on a black background—my mother's dress."

genre and mode: The **style,** structure, and, often, length of a work, when coupled with a certain subject matter, raise expectations that a literary work conforms to a certain **genre** (French "kind"). Good writers might upset these expectations, but they remain aware of the expectations and thwart them purposefully. Works in different genres may nevertheless participate in the same **mode,** a broader category designating the fundamental perspectives governing various genres of writing. For mode, see **tragic, comic, satiric,** and **didactic modes.** Genres are fluid, sometimes very fluid (e.g., the **novel**); the word "usually" should be added to almost every account of the characteristics of a given genre!

georgic (Greek "farming"): a **genre.** Virgil's *Georgics* treat agricultural and occasionally scientific subjects, giving instructions on the proper management of farms. Unlike **pastoral,** which treats the countryside as a place of recreational idleness among shepherds, the georgic treats it as a place of productive labor. For an English poem that critiques both genres, see Crabbe, "The Village" (vol. C, p. 1019).

hermeneutics (from the Greek god Hermes, messenger between the gods and humankind): the science of interpretation, first formulated as such by the German philosophical theologian Friedrich Schleiermacher in the early nineteenth century.

heroic poetry: see **epic.**

hexameter (Greek "six measure"): a term of **meter.** The hexameter line (a six-stress line) is the meter of **classical** Latin **epic;** while not imitated in that form for epic verse in English, some instances of the hexameter exist. See, for example, the last line of a Spenserian stanza, *Faerie Queene* 1.1.2: "O help thou my weake wit, and sharpen my dull tong" (vol. B, p. 253), or Yeats, "The Lake Isle of Innisfree," line 1: "I will arise and go now, and go to Innisfree" (vol. F, p. 215).

homily (Greek "discourse"): a **genre.** A sermon, to be preached in church; *Book of Homilies* (see vol. B, p. 165). Writers of literary fiction sometimes exploit the homily, or sermon, as in Chaucer, *The Pardoner's Tale* (see vol. A, p. 329).

homophone (Greek "same sound"): a **figure of speech.** A word that sounds identical to another word but has a different meaning ("bear" / "bare").

hyperbaton (Greek "overstepping"): a term of **syntax.** The rearrangement, or inversion, of the expected word order in a sentence or clause. Gray, "Elegy Written in a Country Churchyard," line 38: "If Memory o'er their tomb no trophies raise" (vol. C, p. 999). Poets can suspend the expected syntax over many lines, as in the first sentences of the *Canterbury Tales* (vol. A, p. 261) and of *Paradise Lost* (vol. B, p. 1495).

hyperbole (Greek "throwing over"): a **figure of thought.** Overstatement, exaggeration; Marvell, "To His Coy Mistress," lines 11–12: "My vegetable love should grow / Vaster than empires, and more slow" (see vol. B, p. 1347); Auden, "As I Walked Out One Evening," lines 9–12: "'I'll love you, dear, I'll love you / Till China and Africa meet / And the river jumps over the mountain / And the salmon sing in the street" (see vol. F, p. 813).

hypermetrical (adj.; Greek "over measured"): a term of **meter;** the word describes a breaking of the expected metrical pattern by at least one extra syllable.

hypotaxis, or **subordination** (respectively Greek and Latin "ordering under"): a term of **syntax.** The subordination, by the use of subordinate clauses, of different elements of a sentence to a single main verb. Milton, *Paradise Lost* 9.513–15: "As when a ship by skillful steersman wrought / Nigh river's mouth or foreland, where the wind / Veers oft, as oft so steers, and shifts her sail; So varied he" (vol. B, p. 1654). The contrary principle to **parataxis.**

iamb: a term of **rhythm.** The basic foot of English verse; two syllables following the rhythmic pattern of unstressed followed by stressed and producing a rising effect. Thus, for example, "Vermont."

imitation: the practice whereby writers strive ideally to reproduce and yet renew the **conventions** of an older form, often derived from **classical** civilization. Such a practice will be praised in periods of classicism (e.g., the eighteenth century) and repudiated in periods dominated by a model of inspiration (e.g., Romanticism).

irony (Greek "dissimulation"): a **figure of thought.** In broad usage, irony designates the result of inconsistency between a statement and a context that undermines the statement. "It's a beautiful day" is unironic if it's a beautiful day; if, however, the weather is terrible, then the inconsistency between statement and context is ironic. The effect is often amusing; the need to be ironic is sometimes produced by censorship of one kind or another. Strictly, irony is a subset of allegory: whereas allegory says one thing and means another, irony says one thing and means its opposite. For an extended example of irony, see Swift's "Modest Proposal." See also **dramatic irony.**

journal (French "daily"): a **genre.** A diary, or daily record of ephemeral experience, whose perspectives are concentrated on, and limited by, the experiences of single days. Thus Pepys, *Diary* (see vol. C, p. 86).

lai: a **genre.** A short narrative, often characterized by images of great intensity; a French term, and a form practiced by Marie de France (see vol. A, p. 160).

legend (Latin "requiring to be read"): a **genre.** A narrative of a celebrated, possibly historical, but mortal **protagonist.** To be distinguished from **myth.** Thus the "Arthurian legend" but the "myth of Proserpine."

lexical set: Words that habitually recur together (e.g., January, February, March, etc.; or red, white, and blue) form a lexical set.

litotes (from Greek "smooth"): a **figure of thought.** Strictly, understatement by denying the contrary; More, *Utopia:* "differences of no slight import" (see vol. B, p. 47). More loosely, understatement; Swift, "A Tale of a Tub": "Last week I saw a woman flayed, and you will hardly believe how much it altered her person for the worse" (see vol. C, p. 274). Stevie Smith, "Sunt Leones," lines 11–12: "And if the Christians felt a little blue— / Well people being eaten often do" (see vol. F, p. 729).

lullaby: a **genre.** A bedtime, sleep-inducing song for children, in simple and regular meter. Adapted by Auden, "Lullaby" (see vol. F, p. 809).

lyric (from Greek "lyre"): Initially meaning a song, "lyric" refers to a short poetic form, without restriction of meter, in which the expression of personal emotion, often by a voice in the first person, is given primacy over narrative sequence. Thus "The Wife's Lament" (see vol. A, p. 123); Yeats, "The Wild Swans at Coole" (see vol. F, p. 223).

masque: a **genre.** Costly entertainments of the Stuart court, involving dance, song, speech, and elaborate stage effects, in which courtiers themselves participated.

metaphor (Greek "carrying across," etymologically parallel to Latin "translation"): One of the most significant **figures of thought,** metaphor designates identification or implicit identification of one thing with another with which it is not literally identifiable. Blake, "London," lines 11–12: "And the hapless Soldier's sigh / Runs in blood down Palace walls" (see vol. D, p. 141).

meter: Verse (from Latin *versus*, turned) is distinguished from prose (from Latin *prorsus*, "straightforward") as a more compressed form of expression, shaped by metrical norms. **Meter** (Greek "measure") refers to the regularly recurring sound pattern of verse lines. The means of producing sound patterns across lines differ in different poetic traditions. Verse may be **quantitative,** or determined by the quantities of syllables (set patterns of long and short syllables), as in Latin and Greek poetry. It may be **syllabic,** determined by fixed numbers of syllables in the line, as in the verse of Romance languages (e.g., French and Italian). It may be **accentual,** determined by the number of accents, or stresses in the line, with variable numbers of syllables, as in Old English and some varieties of Middle English alliterative verse. Or it may be **accentual-syllabic,** determined by the numbers of accents, but possessing a regular pattern of stressed and unstressed syllables, so as to produce regular numbers of syllables per line. Since Chaucer, English verse has worked primarily within the many possibilities of accentual-syllabic meter. The unit of meter is the **foot.** In English verse the number of feet per line corresponds to the number of accents in a line. For the types and examples of different meters, see **monometer, dimeter, trimester, tetrameter, pentameter,** and **hexameter.** In the definitions below, "u" designates one unstressed syllable, and "/" one stressed syllable.

metonymy (Greek "change of name"): one of the most significant **figures of thought.** Using a word to **denote** another concept or other concepts, by virtue of habitual association. Thus "The Press," designating printed news media. Fictional names often work by associations of this kind. Closely related to **synecdoche.**

mimesis (Greek for "imitation"): A central function of literature and drama has been to provide a plausible imitation of the reality of the world beyond the literary work; mimesis is the representation and imitation of what is taken to be reality.

mise-en-abyme (French for "cast into the abyss"): Some works of art represent themselves in themselves; if they do so effectively, the represented artifact also represents itself, and so ad infinitum. The effect achieved is called "*mise-en-abyme*." Hoccleve's *Complaint*, for example, represents a depressed man reading about a depressed man. This sequence threatens to become a *mise-en-abyme*.

monometer (Greek "one measure"): a term of **meter.** An entire line with just one stress; *Sir Gawain and the Green Knight*, line 15, "most (u) grand (/)" (see vol. A, p. 204).

myth: a **genre.** The narrative of **protagonists** with, or subject to, superhuman powers. A myth expresses some profound foundational truth, often by accounting for the origin of natural phenomena. To be distinguished from **legend.** Thus the "Arthurian legend" but the "myth of Proserpine."

novel: an extremely flexible **genre** in both form and subject matter. Usually in prose, giving high priority to narration of events, with a certain expectation of length, novels are preponderantly rooted in a specific, and often complex, social world; sensitive to the realities of material life; and often focused on one **character** or a small circle of central characters. By contrast with chivalric **romance** (the main European narrative genre prior to the novel), novels tend to eschew the marvelous in favor of a recognizable social world and credible action. The novel's openness allows it to participate in all modes, and to be co-opted for a huge variety of subgenres. In English literature the novel dates from the late seventeenth century and has been astonishingly successful in appealing to a huge readership, particularly in the nineteenth and twentieth centuries. The English and Irish tradition of the novel includes, for example, Fielding, Austen, the Brontë sisters, Dickens, George Eliot, Conrad, Woolf, Lawrence, and Joyce, to name but a few very great exponents of the genre.

novella: a **genre.** A short **novel,** often characterized by imagistic intensity. Conrad, *Heart of Darkness* (see vol. F, p. 73).

occupatio (Latin "taking possession"): a **figure of thought.** Denying that one will discuss a subject while actually discussing it; also known as "praeteritio" (Latin "passing by"). See Chaucer, *Nun's Priest's Tale*, lines 414–32 (see vol. A, p. 353).

ode (Greek "song"): a **genre.** A **lyric** poem in elevated, or high style (see **register**), often addressed to a natural force, a person, or an abstract quality. The Pindaric ode in English is made up of **stanzas** of unequal length, while the Horatian ode has stanzas of equal length. For examples of both types, see, respectively, Wordsworth, "Ode: Intimations of Immortality" (vol. D, p. 348); and Marvell, "An Horatian Ode" (vol. B, p. 1356), or Keats, "Ode on Melancholy" (vol. D, p. 981). For a fuller discussion, see the headnote to Jonson's "Ode on Cary and Morison" (vol. B, p. 1102).

omniscient narrator (Latin "all-knowing narrator"): relevant to **point of view.** A narrator who, in the fiction of the narrative, has complete access to both the deeds and the thoughts of all **characters** in the narrative. Thus Thomas Hardy, "On the Western Circuit" (see vol. F, p. 36).

onomatopoeia (Greek "name making"): a **figure of speech.** Verbal sounds that imitate and evoke the sounds they denotate. Hopkins, "Binsey Poplars," lines 10–12 (about some felled trees): "O if we but knew what we do / When we delve [dig] or hew— / Hack and rack the growing green!" (see vol. E, p. 598).

order: A story may be told in different narrative orders. A narrator might use the sequence of events as they happened, and thereby follow what **classical** rhetoricians called the *natural order*; alternatively, the narrator might reorder the sequence of events, beginning the narration either in the middle or at the end of the sequence of events, thereby following an *artificial order*. If a narrator begins in the middle of events, he or she is said to begin *in medias res* (Latin "in the middle of the matter"). For a brief discussion of these concepts, see Spenser, *Faerie Queene*, "A Letter of the Authors" (vol. B, p. 249). Modern narratology makes a related distinction, between *histoire* (French "story") for the natural order that readers mentally reconstruct, and *discours* (French, here "narration") for the narrative as presented. See also **plot** and **story.**

ottava rima: a **verse form.** An eight-line stanza form, rhyming abababcc, using **iambic pentameter;** Yeats, "Sailing to Byzantium" (see vol. F, p. 230). Derived from the Italian poet Boccaccio, an eight-line stanza was used by fifteenth-century English poets for inset passages (e.g., Christ's speech from the Cross in Lydgate's *Testament*, lines 754–897). The form in this rhyme scheme was used in English poetry for long narrative by, for example, Byron (*Don Juan*; see vol. D, p. 669).

oxymoron (Greek "sharp blunt"): a **figure of thought.** The conjunction of normally incompatible terms; Milton, *Paradise Lost* 1.63: "darkness visible" (see vol. B, p. 1497).

panegyric: a **genre.** Demonstrative, or epideictic (Greek "showing"), rhetoric was a branch of **classical** rhetoric. Its own two main branches were the rhetoric of praise on the one hand and of vituperation on the other. Panegyric, or eulogy (Greek "sweet speaking"), or encomium (plural *encomia*), is the term used to describe the speeches or writings of praise.

parable: a **genre.** A simple story designed to provoke, and often accompanied by, **allegorical** interpretation, most famously by Christ as reported in the Gospels.

paradox (Greek "contrary to received opinion"): a **figure of thought.** An apparent contradiction that requires thought to reveal an inner consistency. Chaucer, "Troilus's Song," line 12: "O sweete harm so quainte" (see vol. A, p. 362).

parataxis, or **coordination** (respectively Greek and Latin "ordering beside"): a term of **syntax.** The coordination, by the use of coordinating conjunctions, of different main clauses in a single sentence. Malory, *Morte Darthur*: "So Sir Lancelot departed and took his sword under his arm, and so he walked in his mantel, that noble knight, and put himself in great jeopardy" (see vol. A, p. 539). The opposite principle to **hypotaxis.**

parody: a work that uses the **conventions** of a particular genre with the aim of comically mocking a **topos,** a genre, or a particular exponent of a genre. Shakespeare parodies the topos of **blazon** in Sonnet 130 (see vol. B, p. 736).

pastoral (from Latin *pastor,* "shepherd"): a **genre.** Pastoral is set among shepherds, making often refined **allusion** to other apparently unconnected subjects (sometimes politics) from the potentially idyllic world of highly literary if illiterate shepherds. Pastoral is distinguished from **georgic** by representing recreational rural idleness, whereas the georgic offers instruction on how to manage rural labor. English writers had classical models in the *Idylls* of Theocritus in Greek and Virgil's *Eclogues* in Latin. Pastoral is also called bucolic (from the Greek word for "herdsman"). Thus Spenser, *Shepheardes Calender* (see vol. B, p. 241).

pathetic fallacy: the attribution of sentiment to natural phenomena, as if they were in sympathy with human feelings. Thus Milton, *Lycidas,* lines 146–47: "With cowslips wan that hang the pensive head, / And every flower that sad embroidery wears" (see vol. B, p. 1472). For critique of the practice, see Ruskin (who coined the term), "Of the Pathetic Fallacy" (vol. E, p. 386).

pentameter (Greek "five measure"): a term of **meter.** In English verse, a five-stress line. Between the late fourteenth and the nineteenth centuries, this meter, frequently employing an iambic rhythm, was the basic line of English verse. Chaucer, Shakespeare, Milton, and Wordsworth each, for example, deployed this very flexible line as their primary resource; Milton, *Paradise Lost* 1.128: "O Prince, O Chief of many thronèd Powers" (see vol. B, p. 1499).

performative: Verbal expressions have many different functions. They can, for example, be descriptive, or constative (if they make an argument), or performative, for example. A performative utterance is one that makes something happen in the world by virtue of its utterance. "I hereby sentence you to ten years in prison," if uttered in the appropriate circumstances, itself performs an action; it makes something happen in the world. By virtue of its performing an action, it is called a "performative." See also **speech act.**

peripeteia (Greek "turning about"): the sudden reversal of fortune (in both directions) in a dramatic work.

periphrasis (Greek "declaring around"): a **figure of thought.** Circumlocution; the use of many words to express what could be expressed in few or one; Sidney, *Astrophil and Stella* 39.1–4 (vol. B, p. 593).

persona (Latin "sound through"): originally the mask worn in the Roman theater to magnify an actor's voice; in literary discourse persona (plural *personae*) refers to the narrator or speaker of a text, whose voice is coherent and whose person need have no relation to the person of the actual author of a text. Eliot, "The Love Song of J. Alfred Prufrock" (see vol. F, p. 654).

personification, or **prosopopoeia** (Greek "person making"): a **figure of thought.** The attribution of human qualities to nonhuman forces or objects; Keats, "Ode on a Grecian Urn," lines 1–2: "Thou still unvanish'd bride of quietness, / Thou foster-child of silence and slow time" (see vol. D, p. 979).

plot: the sequence of events in a story as narrated, as distinct from **story,** which refers to the sequence of events as we reconstruct them from the plot. See also **order.**

point of view: All of the many kinds of writing involve a point of view from which a text is, or seems to be, generated. The presence of such a point of view may be powerful and explicit, as in many novels, or deliberately invisible, as in much drama. In some genres, such as the **novel,** the narrator does not necessarily tell the story from a position we can predict; that is, the needs of a particular story, not the **conventions** of the genre, determine the narrator's position. In other genres, the narrator's position is fixed by convention; in certain kinds of love poetry, for example, the narrating voice is always that of a suffering lover. Not only does the point of view significantly inform the style of a work, but it also informs the structure of that work.

protagonist (Greek "first actor"): the hero or heroine of a drama or narrative.

pun: a **figure of thought.** A sometimes irresolvable doubleness of meaning in a single word or expression; Shakespeare, Sonnet 135, line 1: "Whoever hath her wish, thou hast thy *Will*" (see vol. B, p. 736).

quatrain: a **verse form.** A stanza of four lines, usually rhyming abcb, abab, or abba. Of many possible examples, see Crashaw, "On the Wounds of Our Crucified Lord" (see vol. B, p. 1296).

refrain: usually a single line repeated as the last line of consecutive stanzas, sometimes with subtly different wording and ideally with subtly different meaning as the poem progresses. See, for example, Wyatt, "Blame not my lute" (see vol. B, p. 128).

register: The register of a word is its stylistic level, which can be distinguished by degree of technicality but also by degree of formality. We choose our words from different registers according to context, that is, audience and/or environment. Thus a chemist in a laboratory will say "sodium chloride," a cook in a kitchen "salt." A formal register designates the kind of language used in polite society (e.g., "Mr. President"), while an informal or colloquial register is used in less formal or more relaxed social situations (e.g., "the boss"). In **classical** and medieval rhetoric, these registers of formality were called *high style* and *low style*. A *middle style* was defined as the style fit for narrative, not drawing attention to itself.

rhetoric: the art of verbal persuasion. **Classical** rhetoricians distinguished three areas of rhetoric: the forensic, to be used in law courts; the deliberative, to be used in political or philosophical deliberations; and the demonstrative, or epideictic, to be used for the purposes of public praise or blame. Rhetorical manuals covered all the skills required of a speaker, from the management of style and structure to delivery. These manuals powerfully influenced the theory of poetics as a separate branch of verbal practice, particularly in the matter of style.

rhyme: a **figure of speech.** The repetition of identical vowel sounds in stressed syllables whose initial consonants differ ("dead" / "head"). In poetry, rhyme often links the end of one line with another. *Masculine rhyme*: full rhyme on the final syllable of the line ("decays" / "days"). *Feminine rhyme*: full rhyme on syllables that are followed by unaccented syllables ("fountains" / "mountains"). *Internal rhyme*: full rhyme within a single line; Coleridge, *The Rime of the Ancient Mariner*, line 7: "The guests are met, the feast is set" (see vol. D, p. 448). *Rhyme riche*: rhyming on **homophones**; Chaucer, *General Prologue*, lines 17–18: "seeke" / "seke." *Off rhyme* (also known as *half rhyme*, *near rhyme*, or *slant rhyme*): differs from perfect rhyme in changing the vowel sound and/or the concluding consonants expected of perfect rhyme; Byron, "They say that Hope is Happiness," lines 5–7: "most" / "lost." *Pararhyme*: stressed vowel sounds differ but are flanked by identical or similar consonants; Owen, "Miners," lines 9–11: "simmer" / "summer" (see vol. F, p. 163).

rhyme royal: a **verse form.** A **stanza** of seven **iambic pentameter** lines, rhyming ababbcc; first introduced by Chaucer and called "royal" because the form was used by James I of Scotland for his *Kingis Quair* in the early fifteenth century. Chaucer, "Troilus's Song" (see vol. A, p. 362).

rhythm: Rhythm is not absolutely distinguishable from **meter.** One way of making a clear distinction between these terms is to say that rhythm (from the Greek "to flow") denotes the patterns of sound within the feet of verse lines and the combination of those feet. Very often a particular meter will raise expectations that a given rhythm will be used regularly through a whole line or a whole poem. Thus in English verse the pentameter regularly uses an iambic rhythm. Rhythm, however, is much more fluid than meter, and many lines within the same poem using a single meter will frequently exploit different rhythmic possibilities. For examples of different rhythms, see **iamb, trochee, anapest, spondee,** and **dactyl.**

romance: a **genre.** From the twelfth to the sixteenth century, the main form of European narrative, in either verse or prose, was that of chivalric romance. Romance, like the later **novel,** is a very fluid genre, but romances are often characterized by (i) a tripartite structure of social integration, followed by disintegration, involving moral tests and often marvelous events, itself the prelude to reintegration in a happy ending, frequently of marriage; and (ii) aristocratic social milieux. Thus *Sir Gawain and the Green Knight* (see vol. A, p. 204); Spenser's (unfinished) *Faerie Queene* (vol. B, p. 249). The immensely popular, fertile genre was absorbed, in both domesticated and undomesticated form, by the novel. For an adaptation of romance, see Chaucer, *Wife of Bath's Tale* (vol. A, p. 300).

sarcasm (Greek "flesh tearing"): a **figure of thought.** A wounding expression, often expressed ironically; Boswell, *Life of Johnson:* Johnson [asked if any man of the modern age could have written the **epic** poem *Fingal*] replied, "Yes, Sir, many men, many women, and many children" (see vol. C, p. 844).

satire (Latin for "a bowl of mixed fruits"): a **genre.** In Roman literature (e.g., Juvenal), the communication, in the form of a letter between equals, complaining of the ills of contemporary society. The genre in this form is characterized by a first-person narrator exasperated by social ills; the letter form; a high frequency of contemporary reference; and the use of invective in **low-style** language. Pope practices the genre thus in the *Epistle to Dr. Arbuthnot* (see vol. C, p. 543). Wyatt's "Mine own John Poins" (see vol. B, p. 131) draws ultimately on a gentler, Horatian model of the genre.

satiric mode: Works in a very large variety of genres are devoted to the more or less savage attack on social ills. Thus Swift's travel narrative *Gulliver's Travels* (see vol. C, p. 279), his **essay** "A Modest Proposal" (vol. C, p. 454), Pope's mock-**epic** *The Dunciad* (vol. C, p. 555), and Gay's *Beggar's Opera* (vol. C, p. 659), to look no further than the eighteenth century, are all within a satiric mode.

scene: a subdivision of an **act,** itself a subdivision of a dramatic performance and/ or text. The action of a scene usually occurs in one place.

sensibility (from Latin, "capable of being perceived by the senses"): as a literary term, an eighteenth-century concept derived from moral philosophy that stressed the social importance of fellow feeling and particularly of sympathy in social relations. The concept generated a literature of "sensibility," such as the sentimental **novel** (the most famous of which was Goethe's *Sorrows of the Young Werther* [1774]), or sentimental poetry, such as Cowper's passage on the stricken deer in *The Task* (see vol. C, p. 1024).

short story: a **genre.** Generically similar to, though shorter and more concentrated than, the **novel;** often published as part of a collection. Thus Mansfield, "The Daughters of the Late Colonel" (see vol. F, p. 698).

simile (Latin "like"): a **figure of thought.** Comparison, usually using the word "like" or "as," of one thing with another so as to produce sometimes surprising analogies. Donne, "The Storm," lines 29–30: "Sooner than you read this line did the gale, / Like shot, not feared till felt, our sails assail." Frequently used, in extended form, in **epic** poetry; Milton, *Paradise Lost* 1.338–46 (see vol. B, p. 1504).

soliloquy (Latin "single speaking"): a **topos** of drama, in which a **character,** alone or thinking to be alone on stage, speaks so as to give the audience access to his or her private thoughts. Thus Viola's soliloquy in Shakespeare, *Twelfth Night* 2.2.17–41 (vol. B, p. 758).

sonnet: a verse form. A form combining a variable number of units of rhymed lines to produce a fourteen-line poem, usually in rhyming **iambic pentameter** lines. In English there are two principal varieties: the Petrarchan sonnet, formed by an octave (an eight-line stanza, often broken into two **quatrains** having the same rhyme scheme, typically abba abba) and a sestet (a six-line stanza, typically cdecde or cdcdcd); and the Shakespearean sonnet, formed by three quatrains (abab cdcd efef) and a **couplet** (gg). The declaration of a sonnet can take a sharp turn, or "volta," often at the decisive formal shift from octave to sestet in the Petrarchan sonnet, or in the final couplet of a Shakespearean sonnet, introducing a trenchant counterstatement. Derived from Italian poetry, and especially from the poetry of Petrarch, the sonnet was first introduced to English poetry by Wyatt, and initially used principally for the expression of unrequited erotic love, though later poets used the form for many other purposes. See Wyatt, "Whoso list to hunt" (vol. B, p. 121); Sidney, *Astrophil and Stella* (vol. B, p. 586); Shakespeare, *Sonnets* (vol. B, p. 723); Wordsworth, "London, 1802" (vol. D, p. 357); McKay, "If We Must Die" (vol. F, p. 854); Heaney, "Clearances" (vol. F, p. 1104).

speech act: Words and deeds are often distinguished, but words are often (perhaps always) themselves deeds. Utterances can perform different speech acts, such as promising, declaring, casting a spell, encouraging, persuading, denying, lying, and so on. See also **performative.**

Spenserian stanza: a verse form. The stanza developed by Spenser for *The Faerie Queene*; nine **iambic** lines, the first eight of which are **pentameters,** followed by one **hexameter,** rhyming ababbcbcc. See also, for example, Shelley, *Adonais* (vol. D, p. 856), and Keats, *The Eve of St. Agnes* (vol. D, p. 961).

spondee: a term of **meter.** A two-syllable foot following the rhythmic pattern, in English verse, of two stressed syllables. Thus, for example, "Utah."

stanza (Italian "room"): groupings of two or more lines, though "stanza" is usually reserved for groupings of at least four lines. Stanzas are often joined by rhyme, often in sequence, where each group shares the same metrical pattern and, when rhymed, rhyme scheme. Stanzas can themselves be arranged into larger groupings. Poets often invent new **verse forms,** or they may work within established forms.

story: a narrative's sequence of events, which we reconstruct from those events as they have been recounted by the narrator (i.e., the **plot**). See also **order.**

stream of consciousness: usually a **first-person** narrative that seems to give the reader access to the narrator's mind as it perceives or reflects on events, prior to organizing those perceptions into a coherent narrative. Thus (though generated from a **third-person** narrative) Joyce, *Ulysses*, "Penelope" (see vol. F, p. 604).

style (from Latin for "writing instrument"): In literary works the manner in which something is expressed contributes substantially to its meaning. The expressions "sun," "mass of helium at the center of the solar system," "heaven's golden orb" all designate "sun," but do so in different manners, or styles, which produce different meanings. The manner of a literary work is its "style," the effect of which is its "tone." We often can intuit the tone of a text; from that intuition of tone we can analyze the stylistic resources by which it was produced. We can analyze the style of literary works through consideration of different elements of style; for example, **diction, figures of thought, figures of speech, meter and rhythm, verse form, syntax, point of view.**

sublime: As a concept generating a literary movement, the sublime refers to the realm of experience beyond the measurable, and so beyond the rational, produced especially by the terrors and grandeur of natural phenomena. Derived especially from the first-century Greek treatise *On the Sublime*, sometimes attributed to Longinus, the notion of the sublime was in the later eighteenth century a spur to Romanticism.

syllable: the smallest unit of sound in a pronounced word. The syllable that receives the greatest stress is called the *tonic* syllable.

symbol (Greek "token"): a **figure of thought.** Something that stands for something else, and yet seems necessarily to evoke that other thing. In Neoplatonic, and therefore Romantic, theory, to be distinguished from **allegory** thus: whereas allegory involves connections between vehicle and tenor agreed by convention or made explicit, the meanings of a symbol are supposedly inherent to it. For discussion, see Coleridge, "On Symbol and Allegory" (vol. D, p. 507).

synecdoche (Greek "to take with something else"): a **figure of thought.** Using a part to express the whole, or vice versa; e.g., "all hands on deck." Closely related to **metonymy.**

syntax (Greek "ordering with"): Syntax designates the rules by which sentences are constructed in a given language. Discussion of meter is impossible without some reference to syntax, since the overall effect of a poem is, in part, always the product of a subtle balance of meter and sentence construction. Syntax is also essential to the understanding of prose style, since prose writers, deprived of the full shaping possibilities of meter, rely all the more heavily on syntactic resources. A working command of syntactical practice requires an understanding of the parts of speech (nouns, verbs, adjectives, adverbs, conjunctions, pronouns, prepositions, and interjections), since writers exploit syntactic possibilities by using particular combinations and concentrations of the parts of speech.

taste (from Italian "touch"): Although medieval monastic traditions used eating and tasting as a metaphor for reading, the concept of taste as a personal ideal to be cultivated by, and applied to, the appreciation and judgment of works of art in general was developed in the eighteenth century.

tercet: a **verse form.** A stanza or group of three lines, used in larger forms such as **terza rima,** the **Petrarchan sonnet,** and the **villanelle.**

terza rima: a **verse form.** A sequence of rhymed **tercets** linked by rhyme thus: aba bcb cdc, etc. first used extensively by Dante in *The Divine Comedy,* the form was adapted in English **iambic pentameters** by Wyatt and revived in the nineteenth century. See Wyatt, "Mine own John Poins" (vol. B, p. 131); Shelley, "Ode to the West Wind" (vol. D, p. 806); and Morris, "The Defence of Guinevere" (vol. E, p. 560). For modern adaptations see Eliot, lines 78–149 (though unrhymed) of "Little Gidding" (vol. F, pp. 679–81); Heaney, "Station Island" (vol. F, p. 1102); Walcott, *Omeros* (vol. F, p. 947).

tetrameter (Greek "four measure"): a term of **meter.** A line with four stresses. Coleridge, *Christabel,* line 31: "She stole along, she nothing spoke" (see vol. D, p. 468).

theme (Greek "proposition"): In literary criticism the term designates what the work is about; the theme is the concept that unifies a given work of literature.

third-person narration: relevant to **point of view.** A narration in which the narrator recounts a narrative of **characters** referred to explicitly or implicitly by third-person pronouns ("he," she," etc.), without the limitation of a **first-person narration.** Thus Johnson, *The History of Rasselas.*

topographical poem (Greek "place writing"): a **genre.** A poem devoted to the meditative description of particular places. Thus Gray, "Ode on a Distant Prospect of Eton College" (see vol. C, p. 994).

topos (Greek "place," plural *topoi*): a commonplace in the content of a given kind of literature. Originally, in **classical** rhetoric, the topoi were tried-and-tested stimuli to literary invention: lists of standard headings under which a subject might be investigated. In medieval narrative poems, for example, it was commonplace to begin with a description of spring. Writers did, of course, render the commonplace uncommon, as in Chaucer's spring scene at the opening of *The Canterbury Tales* (see vol. A, p. 261).

tradition (from Latin "passing on"): A literary tradition is whatever is passed on or revived from the past in a single literary culture, or drawn from others to enrich a writer's culture. "Tradition" is fluid in reference, ranging from small to large referents: thus it may refer to a relatively small aspect of texts (e.g., the tradition of **iambic pentameter**), or it may, at the other extreme, refer to the body of texts that constitute a **canon.**

tragedy: a **genre.** A dramatic representation of the fall of kings or nobles, beginning in happiness and ending in catastrophe. Later transferred to other social milieux. The opposite of **comedy;** thus Shakespeare, *Othello* (see vol. B, p. 806).

tragic mode: Many genres (**epic** poetry, **legend**ary chronicles, **tragedy,** the **novel**) either do or can participate in a tragic mode, by representing the fall of noble **protagonists** and the irreparable ravages of human society and history.

tragicomedy: a **genre.** A play in which potentially tragic events turn out to have a happy, or **comic,** ending. Thus Shakespeare, *Measure for Measure.*

translation (Latin "carrying across"): the rendering of a text written in one language into another.

trimeter (Greek "three measure"): a term of **meter.** A line with three stresses. Herbert, "Discipline," line 1: "Throw away thy rod" (see vol. B, p. 1274).

triplet: a **verse form.** A **tercet** rhyming on the same sound. Pope inserts triplets among heroic **couplets** to emphasize a particular thought; see *Essay on Criticism,* 315–17 (vol. C, p. 497).

trochee: a term of **rhythm.** A two-syllable foot following the pattern, in English verse, of stressed followed by unstressed syllable, producing a falling effect. Thus, for example, "Texas."

type (Greek "impression, figure"): a **figure of thought.** In Christian allegorical interpretation of the Old Testament, pre-Christian figures were regarded as "types," or foreshadowings, of Christ or the Christian dispensation. *Typology* has been the source of much visual and literary art in which the parallelisms between old and new are extended to nonbiblical figures; thus the virtuous plowman in *Piers Plowman* becomes a type of Christ.

unities: According to a theory supposedly derived from Aristotle's *Poetics,* the events represented in a play should have unity of time, place, and action: that the play take up no more time than the time of the play, or at most a day; that the space of action should be within a single city; and that there should be no subplot. See Johnson, *The Preface to Shakespeare* (vol. C, p. 807).

vernacular (from Latin *verna,* "servant"): the language of the people, as distinguished from learned and arcane languages. From the later Middle Ages especially, the "vernacular" languages and literatures of Europe distinguished themselves from the learned languages and literatures of Latin, Greek, and Hebrew.

verse form: The terms related to **meter** and **rhythm** describe the shape of individual lines. Lines of verse are combined to produce larger groupings, called verse forms. These larger groupings are in the first instance **stanzas.** The combination of a certain meter and stanza shape constitutes the verse form, of which there are many standard kinds.

villanelle: a **verse form.** A fixed form of usually five **tercets** and a **quatrain** employing only two rhyme sounds altogether, rhyming aba for the tercets and abaa for the quatrain, with a complex pattern of two **refrains.** Derived from a French fixed form. Thomas, "Do Not Go Gentle into That Good Night" (see vol. F, p. 833).

wit: Originally a synonym for "reason" in Old and Middle English, "wit" became a literary ideal in the Renaissance as brilliant play of the full range of mental resources. For eighteenth-century writers, the notion necessarily involved pleasing expression, as in Pope's definition of true wit as "Nature to advantage dressed, / What oft was thought, but ne'er so well expressed" (*Essay on Criticism,* lines 297–98; see vol. C, p. 496–97). See also Johnson, *Lives of the Poets,* "Cowley," on "metaphysical wit" (see vol. C, p. 817). Romantic theory of the imagination deprived wit of its full range of apprehension, whence the word came to be restricted to its modern sense, as the clever play of mind that produces laughter.

zeugma (Greek "a yoking"): a **figure of thought.** A figure whereby one word applies to two or more words in a sentence, and in which the applications are surprising, either because one is unusual, or because the applications are made in very different ways; Pope, *Rape of the Lock* 3.7–8, in which the word "take" is used in two senses: "Here thou, great Anna! whom three realms obey, / Dost sometimes counsel take— and sometimes tea" (see vol. C, p. 515).

B: Publishing History, Censorship

By the time we read texts in published books, they have already been treated—that is, changed by authors, editors, and printers—in many ways. Although there are differences across history, in each period literary works are subject to pressures of many kinds, which apply before, while, and after an author writes. The pressures might be financial, as in the relations of author and patron; commercial, as in the marketing of books; and legal, as in, during some periods, the negotiation through official and unofficial censorship. In addition, texts in all periods undergo technological processes, as they move from the material forms in which an author produced them to the forms in which they are presented to readers. Some of the terms below designate important material forms in which books were produced, disseminated, and surveyed across the historical span of this anthology. Others designate the skills developed to understand these processes. The anthology's introductions to individual periods discuss the particular forms these phenomena took in different eras.

bookseller: In England, and particularly in London, commercial bookmaking and -selling enterprises came into being in the early fourteenth century. These were loose organizations of artisans who usually lived in the same neighborhoods (around St. Paul's Cathedral in London). A bookseller or dealer would coordinate the production of hand-copied books for wealthy patrons (see **patronage**), who would order books to be custom-made. After the introduction of **printing** in the late fifteenth century, authors generally sold the rights to their work to booksellers, without any further **royalties.** Booksellers, who often had their own shops, belonged to the **Stationers' Company.** This system lasted into the eighteenth century. In 1710, however, authors were for the first time granted **copyright,** which tipped the commercial balance in their favor, against booksellers.

censorship: The term applies to any mechanism for restricting what can be published. Historically, the reasons for imposing censorship are heresy, sedition, blasphemy, libel, or obscenity. External censorship is imposed by institutions having legislative sanctions at their disposal. Thus the pre-Reformation Church imposed the Constitutions of Archbishop Arundel of 1409, aimed at repressing the Lollard "heresy." After the Reformation, some key events in the history of censorship are as follows: 1547, when anti-Lollard legislation and legislation made by Henry VIII concerning treason by writing (1534) were abolished; the Licensing Order of 1643, which legislated that works be licensed, through the Stationers' Company, prior to publication; and 1695, when the last such Act stipulating prepublication licensing lapsed. Postpublication censorship continued in different periods for different reasons. Thus, for example, British publication of D. H. Lawrence's *Lady Chatterley's Lover* (1928) was obstructed (though unsuccessfully) in 1960, under the Obscene Publications Act of 1959. Censorship can also be international: although not published in Iran, Salman Rushdie's *Satanic Verses* (1988) was censored in that country, where the leader, Ayatollah Ruhollah Khomeini, proclaimed a fatwa (religious decree) promising the author's execution. Very often censorship is not imposed externally, however: authors or publishers can censor work in anticipation of what will incur the wrath of readers or the penalties of the law. Victorian and Edwardian publishers of **novels,** for example, urged authors to remove potentially offensive material, especially for serial publication in popular magazines.

codex: the physical format of most modern books and medieval manuscripts, consisting of a series of separate leaves gathered into quires and bound together, often with a cover. In late antiquity, the codex largely replaced the scroll, the standard form of written documents in Roman culture.

copy text: the particular text of a work used by a textual editor as the basis of an edition of that work.

copyright: the legal protection afforded to authors for control of their work's publication, in an attempt to ensure due financial reward. Some key dates in the history of copyright in the United Kingdom are as follows: 1710, when a statute gave authors the exclusive right to publish their work for fourteen years, and fourteen years more if the author were still alive when the first term had expired; 1842, when the period of authorial control was extended to forty-two years; and 1911, when the term was extended yet further, to fifty years after the author's death. In 1995 the period of protection was harmonized with the laws in other European countries to be the life of the author plus seventy years. In the United States no works first published before 1923 are in copyright. Works published since 1978 are, as in the United Kingdom, protected for the life of the author plus seventy years.

folio: the leaf formed by both sides of a single page. Each folio has two sides: a *recto* (the front side of the leaf, on the right side of a double-page spread in an open codex), and a *verso* (the back side of the leaf, on the left side of a double-page spread). Modern book pagination follows the pattern 1, 2, 3, 4, while medieval manuscript pagination follows the pattern 1r, 1v, 2r, 2v. "Folio" can also designate the size of a printed book. Books come in different shapes, depending originally on the number of times a standard sheet of paper is folded. One fold produces a large volume, a *folio* book; two folds produce a *quarto*, four an *octavo*, and six a very small *duodecimo*. Generally speaking, the larger the book, the grander and more expensive. Shakespeare's plays were, for example, first printed in quartos, but were gathered into a folio edition in 1623.

foul papers: versions of a work before an author has produced, if she or he has, a final copy (a "fair copy") with all corrections removed.

incunabulum (plural "incunabula"): any printed book produced in Europe before 1501. Famous incunabula include the Gutenberg Bible, printed in 1455.

manuscript (Latin, "written by hand"): Any text written physically by hand is a manuscript. Before the introduction of **printing** with moveable type in 1476, all texts in England were produced and reproduced by hand, in manuscript. This is an extremely labor-intensive task, using expensive materials (e.g., **vellum**, or **parchment**); the cost of books produced thereby was, accordingly, very high. Even after the introduction of printing, many texts continued to be produced in manuscript. This is obviously true of letters, for example, but until the eighteenth century, poetry written within aristocratic circles was often transmitted in manuscript copies.

paleography (Greek "ancient writing"): the art of deciphering, describing, and dating forms of handwriting.

parchment: animal skin, used as the material for handwritten books before the introduction of paper. See also **vellum.**

patronage, patron (Latin "protector"): Many technological, legal, and commercial supports were necessary before professional authorship became possible. Although some playwrights (e.g., Shakespeare) made a living by writing for the theater, other authors needed, principally, the large-scale reproductive capacities of **printing** and the security of **copyright** to make a living from writing. Before these conditions obtained, many authors had another main occupation, and most authors had to rely on patronage. In different periods, institutions or individuals offered material support, or patronage, to authors. Thus in Anglo-Saxon England, monasteries afforded the conditions of writing to monastic authors. Between the twelfth and the seventeenth centuries, the main source of patronage was the royal court. Authors offered patrons prestige and ideological support in return for financial support. Even as the conditions of professional authorship came into being at the beginning of the eighteenth century, older forms of direct patronage were not altogether displaced until the middle of the century.

periodical: Whereas journalism, strictly, applies to daily writing (from French *jour*, "day"), periodical writing appears at larger, but still frequent, intervals, characteristically in the form of the **essay.** Periodicals were developed especially in the eighteenth century.

printing: Printing, or the mechanical reproduction of books using moveable type, was invented in Germany in the mid-fifteenth century by Johannes Gutenberg; it quickly spread throughout Europe. William Caxton brought printing into England from the Low Countries in 1476. Much greater powers of reproduction at much lower prices transformed every aspect of literary culture.

publisher: the person or company responsible for the commissioning and publicizing of printed matter. In the early period of **printing**, publisher, printer, and bookseller were often the same person. This trend continued in the ascendancy of the **Stationers' Company,** between the middle of the sixteenth and the end of the seventeenth centuries. Toward the end of the seventeenth century, these three functions began to separate, leading to their modern distinctions.

quire: When medieval manuscripts were assembled, a few loose sheets of parchment or paper would first be folded together and sewn along the fold. This formed a quire (also known as a "gathering" or "signature"). Folded in this way, four large sheets of parchment would produce eight smaller manuscript leaves. Multiple quires could then be bound together to form a codex.

royalties: an agreed-upon proportion of the price of each copy of a work sold, paid by the publisher to the author, or an agreed-upon fee paid to the playwright for each performance of a play.

scribe: In **manuscript** culture, the scribe is the copyist who reproduces a text by hand.

scriptorium (plural "scriptoria"): a place for producing written documents and man-uscripts.

serial publication: generally referring to the practice, especially common in the nineteenth century, of publishing novels a few chapters at a time, in periodicals.

Stationers' Company: The Stationers' Company was an English guild incorporating various tradesmen, including printers, publishers, and booksellers, skilled in the pro-duction and selling of books. It was formed in 1403, received its royal charter in 1557, and served as a means both of producing and of regulating books. Authors would sell the manuscripts of their books to individual stationers, who incurred the risks and took the profits of producing and selling the books. The stationers entered their rights over given books in the Stationers' Register. They also regulated the book trade and held their monopoly by licensing books and by being empowered to seize unauthor-ized books and imprison resisters. This system of licensing broke down in the social unrest of the Civil War and Interregnum (1640–60), and it ended in 1695. Even after the end of licensing, the Stationers' Company continued to be an intrinsic part of the **copyright** process, since the 1710 copyright statute directed that copyright had to be registered at Stationers' Hall.

subscription: An eighteenth-century system of bookselling somewhere between direct **patronage** and impersonal sales. A subscriber paid half the cost of a book before pub-lication and half on delivery. The author received these payments directly. The sub-scriber's name appeared in the prefatory pages.

textual criticism: Works in all periods often exist in many subtly or not so subtly different forms. This is especially true with regard to manuscript textual reproduc-tion, but it also applies to printed texts. Textual criticism is the art, developed from the fifteenth century in Italy but raised to new levels of sophistication from the eighteenth century, of deciphering different historical states of texts. This art involves the analysis of textual **variants,** often with the aim of distinguishing authorial from scribal forms.

variants: differences that appear among different manuscripts or printed editions of the same text.

vellum: animal skin, used as the material for handwritten books before the intro-duction of paper. See also **parchment.**

watermark: the trademark of a paper manufacturer, impressed into the paper but largely invisible unless held up to light.

Geographic Nomenclature

The British Isles refers to the prominent group of islands off the northwest coast of Europe, especially to the two largest, **Great Britain** and **Ireland**. At present these comprise two sovereign states: **the Republic of Ireland**, and **the United Kingdom of Great Britain and Northern Ireland**—known for short as the **United Kingdom** or the **U.K.** Most of the smaller islands are part of the **U.K.** but a few, like the **Isle of Man** and the tiny **Channel Islands,** are largely independent. The **U.K.** is often loosely referred to as "**Britain**" or "**Great Britain**" and is sometimes called simply, if inaccurately, "**England.**" For obvious reasons, the latter usage is rarely heard among the inhabitants of the other countries of the **U.K.**—**Scotland, Wales,** and **Northern Ireland** (sometimes called **Ulster**). England is by far the most populous part of the kingdom, as well as the seat of its capital, London.

From the first to the fifth century C.E. most of what is now **England** and **Wales** was a province of the Roman Empire called **Britain** (in Latin, **Britannia**). After the fall of Rome, much of the island was invaded and settled by peoples from northern Germany and Denmark speaking what we now call Old English. These peoples are collectively known as the Anglo-Saxons, and the word **England** is related to the first element of their name. By the time of the Norman Conquest (1066) most of the kingdoms founded by the Anglo-Saxons and subsequent Viking invaders had coalesced into the kingdom of **England,** which, in the latter Middle Ages, conquered and largely absorbed the neighboring Celtic kingdom of **Wales.** In 1603 James VI of **Scotland** inherited the island's other throne as James I of **England,** and for the next hundred years—except for the two decades of Puritan rule—**Scotland** (both its English-speaking **Lowlands** and its Gaelic-speaking **Highlands**) and **England** (with **Wales**) were two kingdoms under a single king. In 1707 the Act of Union welded them together as **the United Kingdom of Great Britain. Ireland,** where English rule had begun in the twelfth century and been tightened in the sixteenth, was incorporated by the 1800–1801 Act of Union into **the United Kingdom of Great Britain and Ireland**. With the division of Ireland and the establishment of **the Irish Free State** after World War I, this name was modified to its present form, and in 1949 **the Irish Free State** became **the Republic of Ireland,** or **Éire**. In 1999 **Scotland** elected a separate parliament it had relinquished in 1707, and **Wales** elected an assembly it lost in 1409; neither Scotland nor Wales ceased to be part of the **United Kingdom.**

The **British Isles** are further divided into counties, which in **Great Britain** are also known as shires. This word, with its vowel shortened in pronunciation, forms the suffix in the names of many counties, such as **Yorkshire, Wiltshire, Somersetshire.**

The Latin names **Britannia (Britain), Caledonia (Scotland),** and **Hibernia (Ireland)** are sometimes used in poetic diction; so too is **Britain'**s ancient Celtic name, **Albion**. Because of its accidental resemblance to *albus* (Latin for "white"), **Albion** is especially associated with the chalk cliffs that seem to gird much of the English coast like defensive walls.

The British Empire took its name from **the British Isles** because it was created not only by the **English** but also by the **Irish, Scots,** and **Welsh,** as well as by civilians and servicemen from other constituent countries of the empire. Some of the empire's **overseas colonies,** or **crown colonies,** were populated largely by settlers of European origin and their descendants. These predominantly white **settler colonies,** such as **Canada, Australia,** and **New Zealand,** were allowed significant self-government in the nineteenth century and recognized as **dominions** in the early twentieth century. The **white dominions** became members of **the Commonwealth of Nations**, also called **the Commonwealth, the British Commonwealth**, and "**the Old Commonwealth**" at different times, an association of sovereign states under the symbolic leadership of the British monarch.

Other **overseas colonies** of the empire had mostly indigenous populations (or, in the Caribbean, the descendants of imported slaves, indentured servants, and others). These **colonies** were granted political independence after World War II, later than the **dominions**, and have often been referred to since as **postcolonial** nations. In South and Southeast Asia, **India** and **Pakistan** gained independence in 1947, followed by other countries including **Sri Lanka** (formerly **Ceylon**), **Burma** (now **Myanmar**), **Malaya** (now **Malaysia**), and **Singapore**. In West and East Africa, the **Gold Coast** was decolonized as **Ghana** in 1957, **Nigeria** in 1960, **Sierra Leone** in 1961, **Uganda** in 1962, **Kenya** in 1963, and so forth, while in southern Africa, the white minority government of **South Africa** was already independent in 1931, though majority rule did not come until 1994. In the Caribbean, **Jamaica** and **Trinidad and Tobago** won independence in 1962, followed by **Barbados** in 1966, and other islands of the British West Indies in the 1970s and '80s. Other regions with nations emerging out of British colonial rule included Central America (**British Honduras**, now **Belize**), South America (**British Guiana**, now **Guyana**), the Pacific islands (**Fiji**), and Europe (**Cyprus, Malta**). After decolonization, many of these nations chose to remain within a newly conceived **Commonwealth** and are sometimes referred to as "**New Commonwealth**" countries. Some nations, such as **Ireland, Pakistan**, and **South Africa**, withdrew from the **Commonwealth**, though **South Africa** and **Pakistan** eventually rejoined, and others, such as **Burma** (now **Myanmar**), gained independence outside the **Commonwealth**. Britain's last major overseas colony, **Hong Kong**, was returned to Chinese sovereignty in 1997, but while Britain retains only a handful of dependent territories, such as **Bermuda** and **Montserrat**, the scope of the **Commonwealth** remains vast, with 30 percent of the world's population.

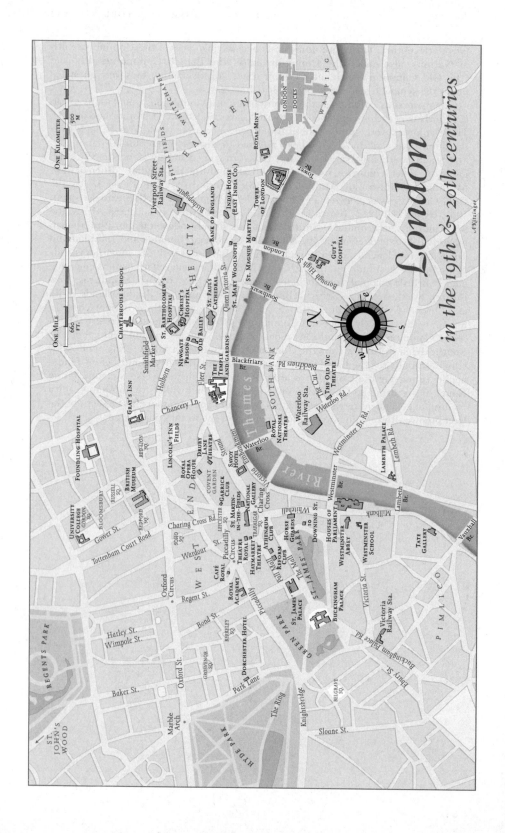

London in the 19th & 20th centuries

British Money

One of the most dramatic changes to the system of British money came in 1971. In the system previously in place, the pound consisted of 20 shillings, each containing 12 pence, making 240 pence to the pound. Since 1971, British money has been calculated on the decimal system, with 100 pence to the pound. Britons' experience of paper money did not change very drastically: as before, 5- and 10-pound notes constitute the majority of bills passing through their hands (in addition, 20- and 50- pound notes have been added). But the shift necessitated a whole new way of thinking about and exchanging coins and marked the demise of the shilling, one of the fundamental units of British monetary history. Many other coins, still frequently encountered in literature, had already passed. These include the groat, worth 4 pence (the word "groat" is often used to signify a trifling sum); the angel (which depicted the archangel Michael triumphing over a dragon), valued at 10 shillings; the mark, worth in its day two-thirds of a pound or 13 shillings 4 pence; and the sovereign, a gold coin initially worth 22 shillings 6 pence, later valued at 1 pound, last circulated in 1932. One prominent older coin, the guinea, was worth a pound and a shilling; though it has not been minted since 1813, a very few quality items or prestige awards (like the purse in a horse race) may still be quoted in guineas. (The table below includes some other well-known, obsolete coins.) Colloquially, a pound was (and is) called a quid; a shilling a bob; sixpence, a tanner; a copper could refer to a penny, a half-penny, or a farthing (¼ penny).

Old Currency	New Currency
1 pound note	1 pound coin (or note in Scotland)
10 shilling (half-pound note)	50 pence
5 shilling (crown)	
2½ shilling (half crown)	20 pence
2 shilling (florin)	10 pence
1 shilling	5 pence
6 pence	
2½ pence	1 penny
2 pence	
1 penny	
½ penny	
¼ penny (farthing)	

Throughout its tenure as a member of the European Union, Britain contemplated but did not make the change to the EU's common currency, the Euro. Many Britons strongly identify their country with its rich commercial history and tend to view their currency patriotically as a national symbol. Now, with the planned withdrawal of the United Kingdom from the EU, the pound seems here to stay.

Even more challenging than sorting out the values of obsolete coins is calculating for any given period the purchasing power of money, which fluctuates over time by its very nature. At the beginning of the twentieth century, 1 pound was worth about 5 American dollars, though those bought three to four times what they now do. Now, the pound buys anywhere from $1.20 to $1.50. As difficult as it is to generalize, it is clear that money used to be worth much more than it is currently. In Anglo-Saxon times, the most valuable circulating coin was the silver penny: four would buy a sheep. Beyond long-term inflationary trends, prices varied from times of plenty to those marked by poor harvests; from peacetime to wartime; from the country to the metropolis (life in London has always been very expensive); and wages varied according to the availability of labor (wages would sharply rise, for instance, during the devastating Black Death in the fourteenth century). The following chart provides a glimpse of some actual prices of given periods and their changes across time, though all the variables mentioned above prevent them from being definitive. Even from one year to the next, an added tax on gin or tea could drastically raise prices, and a lottery ticket could cost much more the night before the drawing than just a month earlier. Still, the prices quoted below do indicate important trends, such as the disparity of incomes in British society and the costs of basic commodities. In the chart on the following page, the symbol £ is used for pound, s. for shilling, d. for a penny (from Latin *denarius*); a sum would normally be written £2.19.3, i.e., 2 pounds, 19 shillings, 3 pence. (This is Leopold Bloom's budget for the day depicted in Joyce's novel *Ulysses* [1922]; in the new currency, it would be about £2.96.)

circa	1390	1590	1650	1750	1815	1875	1950
food and drink	gallon (8 pints) of ale, 1.5d.	tankard of beer, 5d.	coffee, 1d. a dish	"drunk for a penny, dead drunk for two-pence" (gin shop sign in Hogarth print)	ounce of laudanum, 3d.	pint of beer, 3d.	pint of Guinness stout, 11d.
	gallon (8 pints) of wine, 3 to 4d.	pound of beef, 2s. 5d.	chicken, 1s. 4d.	dinner at a steakhouse, 1s.	ham and potato dinner for two, 7s.	dinner in a good hotel, 5s.	pound of beef, 2s. 2d.
	pound of cinnamon, 1 to 3s.	pound of cinnamon, 10s. 6d.	pound of tea, £3 10s.	pound of tea, 16s.	bottle of French claret, 12s.	pound of tea, 2s.	dinner on railway car, 7s. 6d.
entertainment	no cost to watch a cycle play	admission to public theater, 1 to 3d.	falcon, £11 5s.	theater tickets, 1 to 5s.	admission to Covent Garden theater, 1 to 7s.	theater tickets, 6d. to 7s.	admission to Old Vic theater, 1s. 6d. to 10s. 6d.
	contributory admission to professional troupe theater	cheap seat in private theater, 6d.	billiard table, £25	admission to Vauxhall Gardens, 1s.	annual subscription to Almack's (exclusive club), 10 guineas	admission to Madam Tussaud's waxworks, 1s.	admission to Odeon cinema, Manchester, 1s 3d.
	maintenance for royal hounds at Windsor, .75d. a day	"to see a dead Indian" (quoted in *The Tempest*), 1.25d. (ten "doits")	three-quarter length portrait painting, £31	lottery ticket, £20 (shares were sold)	Jane Austen's piano, 30 guineas	annual fees at a gentleman's club, 7 to 10 guineas	tropical fish tank, £4 4s.

circa	1390	1590	1650	1750	1815	1875	1950
reading	cheap romance, 1s.	play quarto, 6d.	pamphlet, 1 to 6d.	issue of The Gentleman's Magazine, 6d.	issue of Edinburgh Review, 6s.	copy of the Times, 3d.	copy of the Times, 3d.
	a Latin Bible, 2 to £4	Shakespeare's First Folio (1623), £1	student Bible, 6s.	cheap edition of Milton, 2s.	membership in circulating library (3rd class), £1 4s. a year	illustrated edition of Through the Looking-glass, 6s.	issue of Eagle comics, 4.5d.
	payment for illuminating a liturgical book, £22 9s.	Foxe's Acts and Monuments, 24s.	Hobbes's Leviathan, 8s.	Johnson's Dictionary, folio, 2 vols., £4 10s.	1st edition of Austen's Pride and Prejudice, 18s.	1st edition of Trollope's The Way We Live Now, 2 vols., £1 1s.	Orwell's Nineteen Eighty-Four, paperback, 3s. 6d.
transportation	night's supply of hay for horse, 2d.	wherry (whole boat) across Thames, 1d.	day's journey, coach, 10s.	boat across Thames, 4d.	coach ride, outside, 2 to 3d. a mile; inside, 4 to 5d. a mile	15-minute journey in a London cab, 1s. 6d.	London tube fare, about 2d. a mile
	coach, £8	hiring a horse for a day, 12d.	coach horse, £30	coach fare, London to Edinburgh, £4 10s.	palanquin transport in Madras, 5s. a day	railway, 3rd class, London to Plymouth, 18s. 8d. (about 1d. a mile)	petrol, 3s. a gallon
	quality horse, £10	hiring a coach for a day, 10s.	fancy carriage, £170	transport to America, £5	passage, Liverpool to New York, £10	passage to India, 1st class, £50	midsize Austin sedan, £449 plus £188 4s. 2d. tax
clothes	clothing allowance for peasant, 3s. a year	shoes with buckles, 8d.	footman's frieze coat, 15s.	working woman's gown, 6s. 6d.	checked muslin, 7s. per yard	flannel for a cheap petticoat, 1s. 3d. a yard	woman's sun frock, £3 13s. 10d.

shoes for gentry wearer, 4d.	woman's gloves, £1 5s.	falconer's hat, 10s.	gentleman's suit, £8	hiring a dressmaker for a pelisse, 8s.	overcoat for an Eton schoolboy, £1 1s.	tweed sports jacket, £3 16s. 6d.
hat for gentry wearer, 10d.	fine cloak, £16	black cloth for mourning household of an earl, £100	very fine wig, £30	ladies silk stockings, 12s.	set of false teeth, £2 10s.	"Teddy boy" drape suit, £20
labor/incomes hiring a skilled building worker, 4d. a day	actor's daily wage during playing season, 1s.	agricultural laborer, 6s. 5d. a week	price of boy slave, £32	lowest-paid sailor on Royal Navy ship, 10s. 9d. a month	seasonal agricultural laborer, 14s. a week	minimum wage, agricultural laborer, £4 14s. per 47-hour week
wage for professional scribe, £2 3s. 4d. a year + cloak	household servant 2 to £5 a year + food, clothing	tutor to nobleman's children, £30 a year	housemaid's wage, £6 to £8 a year	contributor to *Quarterly Review*, 10 guineas per sheet	housemaid's wage, £10 to £25 a year	shorthand typist, £367 a year
minimum income to be called gentleman, £10 a year; for knighthood, 40 to £400	minimum income for eligibility for knighthood, £30 a year	Milton's salary as Secretary of Foreign Tongues, £288 a year	Boswell's allowance, £200 a year	minimum income for a "genteel" family, £100 a year	income of the "comfortable" classes, £800 and up a year	middle manager's salary, £1,480 a year
income from land of richest magnates, £3,500 a year	income from land of average earl, £4,000 a year	Earl of Bedford's income, £8,000 a year	Duke of Newcastle's income, £40,000 a year	Mr. Darcy's income, *Pride and Prejudice*, £10,000	Trollope's income, £4,000 a year	barrister's salary, £2,032 a year

The British Baronage

The English monarchy is in principle hereditary, though at times during the Middle Ages the rules were subject to dispute. In general, authority passes from father to eldest surviving son, to daughters in order of seniority if there is no son, to a brother if there are no children, and in default of direct descendants to collateral lines (cousins, nephews, nieces) in order of closeness. There have been breaks in the order of succession (1066, 1399, 1688), but so far as possible the usurpers have always sought to paper over the break with a legitimate, i.e., hereditary, claim. When a queen succeeds to the throne and takes a husband, he does not become king unless he is in the line of blood succession; rather, he is named prince consort, as Albert was to Victoria. He may father kings, but is not one himself.

The original Saxon nobles were the king's thanes, ealdormen, or earls, who provided the king with military service and counsel in return for booty, gifts, or landed estates. William the Conqueror, arriving from France, where feudalism was fully developed, considerably expanded this group. In addition, as the king distributed the lands of his new kingdom, he also distributed dignities to men who became known collectively as "the baronage." "Baron" in its root meaning signifies simply "man," and barons were the king's men. As the title was common, a distinction was early made between greater and lesser barons, the former gradually assuming loftier and more impressive titles. The first English "duke" was created in 1337; the title of "marquess," or "marquis" (pronounced "markwis"), followed in 1385, and "viscount" ("vyekount") in 1440. Though "earl" is the oldest title of all, an earl now comes between a marquess and a viscount in order of dignity and precedence, and the old term "baron" now designates a rank just below viscount. "Baronets" were created in 1611 as a means of raising revenue for the crown (the title could be purchased for about £1,000); they are marginal nobility and have never sat in the House of Lords.

Kings and queens are addressed as "Your Majesty," princes and princesses as "Your Highness," the other hereditary nobility as "My Lord" or "Your Lordship." Peers receive their titles either by inheritance (like Lord Byron, the sixth baron of that line) or from the monarch (like Alfred, Lord Tennyson, created 1st Baron Tennyson by Victoria). The children, even of a duke, are commoners unless they are specifically granted some other title or inherit their father's title from him. A peerage can be forfeited by act of attainder, as for example when a lord is convicted of treason; and, when forfeited, or lapsed for lack of a successor, can be bestowed on another family. Thus in 1605 Robert Cecil was made first earl of Salisbury in the third creation, the first creation dating from 1149, the second from 1337, the title having been in abeyance since 1539. Titles descend by right of succession and do not depend on tenure of land; thus, a title does not always indicate where a lord dwells or holds power. Indeed, noble titles do not always refer to a real place at all. At Prince Edward's marriage in 1999, the queen created him earl of Wessex, although the old kingdom of Wessex has had no political existence since the Anglo-Saxon period, and the name was all but forgotten until it was resurrected by Thomas Hardy as the setting of his novels. (This is perhaps but one of many ways in which the world of the aristocracy increasingly resembles the realm of literature.)

The king and queen	(These are all of the royal line.)
Prince and princess	
Duke and duchess	(These may or may not be of the royal
Marquess and marchioness	line, but are ordinarily remote from the succession.)
Earl and countess	
Viscount and viscountess	
Baron and baroness	
Baronet and lady	

Scottish peers sat in the parliament of Scotland, as English peers did in the parliament of England, till at the Act of Union (1707) Scottish peers were granted sixteen seats in the English House of Lords, to be filled by election. (In 1963, all Scottish lords were allowed to sit.) Similarly, Irish peers, when the Irish parliament was abolished in 1801, were granted the right to elect twenty-eight of their number to the House of Lords in Westminster. (Now that the Republic of Ireland is a separate nation, this no longer applies.) Women members (peeresses) were first allowed to sit in the House as nonhereditary Life Peers in 1958 (when that status was created for members of both genders); women first sat by their own hereditary right in 1963. Today the House of Lords still retains some power to influence or delay legislation, but its future is uncertain. In 1999, the hereditary peers (then amounting to 750) were reduced to 92 temporary members elected by their fellow peers. Holders of Life Peerages remain, as do senior bishops of the Church of England and high-court judges (the "Law Lords").

Below the peerage the chief title of honor is "knight." Knighthood, which is not hereditary, is generally a reward for services rendered. A knight (Sir John Black) is addressed, using his first name, as "Sir John"; his wife, using the last name, is "Lady Black"—unless she is the daughter of an earl or nobleman of higher rank, in which case she will be "Lady Arabella." The female equivalent of a knight bears the title of "Dame." Though the word *knight* itself comes from the Anglo-Saxon *cniht*, there is some doubt as to whether knighthood amounted to much before the arrival of the Normans. The feudal system required military service as a condition of land tenure, and a man who came to serve his king at the head of an army of tenants required a title of authority and badges of identity—hence the title of knighthood and the coat of arms. During the Crusades, when men were far removed from their land (or even sold it in order to go on crusade), more elaborate forms of fealty sprang up that soon expanded into orders of knighthood. The Templars, Hospitallers, Knights of the Teutonic Order, Knights of Malta, and Knights of the Golden Fleece were but a few of these companionships; not all of them were available at all times in England.

Gradually, with the rise of centralized government and the decline of feudal tenures, military knighthood became obsolete, and the rank largely honorific; sometimes, as under James I, it degenerated into a scheme of the royal government for making money. For hundreds of years after its establishment in the fourteenth century, the Order of the Garter was the only English order of knighthood, an exclusive courtly companionship. Then, during the late seventeenth, the eighteenth, and the nineteenth centuries, a number of additional orders were created, with names such as the Thistle, Saint Patrick, the Bath, Saint Michael, and Saint George, plus a number of special Victorian and Indian orders. They retain the terminology, ceremony, and dignity of knighthood, but the military implications are vestigial.

Although the British Empire now belongs to history, appointments to the Order of the British Empire continue to be conferred for services to that empire at home or abroad. Such honors (commonly referred to as "gongs") are granted by the monarch in her New Year's and Birthday lists, but the decisions are now made by the government in power. In recent years there have been efforts to popularize and democratize the dispensation of honors, with recipients including rock stars and actors. But this does not prevent large sectors of British society from regarding both knighthood and the peerage as largely irrelevant to modern life.

The Royal Lines of England and Great Britain

England

SAXONS AND DANES

Egbert, king of Wessex	802–839
Ethelwulf, son of Egbert	839–858
Ethelbald, second son of Ethelwulf	858–860
Ethelbert, third son of Ethelwulf	860–866
Ethelred I, fourth son of Ethelwulf	866–871
Alfred the Great, fifth son of Ethelwulf	871–899
Edward the Elder, son of Alfred	899–924
Athelstan the Glorious, son of Edward	924–940
Edmund I, third son of Edward	940–946
Edred, fourth son of Edward	946–955
Edwy the Fair, son of Edmund	955–959
Edgar the Peaceful, second son of Edmund	959–975
Edward the Martyr, son of Edgar	975–978 (murdered)
Ethelred II, the Unready, second son of Edgar	978–1016
Edmund II, Ironside, son of Ethelred II	1016–1016
Canute the Dane	1016–1035
Harold I, Harefoot, natural son of Canute	1035–1040
Hardecanute, son of Canute	1040–1042
Edward the Confessor, son of Ethelred II	1042–1066
Harold II, brother-in-law of Edward	1066–1066 (died in battle)

HOUSE OF NORMANDY

William I, the Conqueror	1066–1087
William II, Rufus, third son of William I	1087–1100 (shot from ambush)
Henry I, Beauclerc, youngest son of William I	1100–1135

HOUSE OF BLOIS

Stephen, son of Adela, daughter of William I	1135–1154

HOUSE OF PLANTAGENET

Henry II, son of Geoffrey Plantagenet by Matilda, daughter of Henry I	1154–1189
Richard I, Coeur de Lion, son of Henry II	1189–1199
John Lackland, son of Henry II	1199–1216
Henry III, son of John	1216–1272
Edward I, Longshanks, son of Henry III	1272–1307
Edward II, son of Edward I	1307–1327 (deposed)
Edward III of Windsor, son of Edward II	1327–1377
Richard II, grandson of Edward III	1377–1399 (deposed)

HOUSE OF LANCASTER

Henry IV, son of John of Gaunt, son of Edward III	1399–1413
Henry V, Prince Hal, son of Henry IV	1413–1422
Henry VI, son of Henry V	1422–1461 (deposed), 1470–1471 (deposed)

HOUSE OF YORK

Edward IV, great-great-grandson of Edward III	1461–1470 (deposed), 1471–1483
Edward V, son of Edward IV	1483–1483 (murdered)
Richard III, Crookback	1483–1485 (died in battle)

HOUSE OF TUDOR

Henry VII, married daughter of Edward IV	1485–1509
Henry VIII, son of Henry VII	1509–1547
Edward VI, son of Henry VIII	1547–1553
Mary I, "Bloody," daughter of Henry VIII	1553–1558
Elizabeth I, daughter of Henry VIII	1558–1603

HOUSE OF STUART

James I (James VI of Scotland)	1603–1625
Charles I, son of James I	1625–1649 (executed)

COMMONWEALTH & PROTECTORATE

Council of State	1649–1653
Oliver Cromwell, Lord Protector	1653–1658
Richard Cromwell, son of Oliver	1658–1660 (resigned)

HOUSE OF STUART (RESTORED)

Charles II, son of Charles I	1660–1685
James II, second son of Charles I	1685–1688

(INTERREGNUM, 11 DECEMBER 1688 TO 13 FEBRUARY 1689)

HOUSE OF ORANGE-NASSAU

William III of Orange, by	
Mary, daughter of Charles I	1689–1701
and Mary II, daughter of James II	–1694
Anne, second daughter of James II	1702–1714

Great Britain

HOUSE OF HANOVER

George I, son of Elector of Hanover and	
Sophia, granddaughter of James I	1714–1727
George II, son of George I	1727–1760
George III, grandson of George II	1760–1820
George IV, son of George III	1820–1830
William IV, third son of George III	1830–1837
Victoria, daughter of Edward, fourth son	
of George III	1837–1901

HOUSE OF SAXE-COBURG AND GOTHA

Edward VII, son of Victoria	1901–1910

HOUSE OF WINDSOR (NAME ADOPTED 17 JULY 1917)

George V, second son of Edward VII	1910–1936
Edward VIII, eldest son of George V	1936–1936 (abdicated)
George VI, second son of George V	1936–1952
Elizabeth II, daughter of George VI	1952–

Religions in Great Britain

In the late sixth century C.E., missionaries from Rome introduced Christianity to the Anglo-Saxons—actually, reintroduced it, since it had briefly flourished in the southern parts of the British Isles during the Roman occupation, and even after the Roman withdrawal had persisted in the Celtic regions of Scotland and Wales. By the time the earliest poems included in *The Norton Anthology of English Literature* were composed (i.e., the seventh century), therefore, there had been a Christian presence in the British Isles for hundreds of years. The conversion of the Germanic occupiers of England can, however, be dated only from 597. Our knowledge of the religion of pre-Christian Britain is sketchy, but it is likely that vestiges of Germanic polytheism assimilated into, or coexisted with, the practice of Christianity: fertility rites were incorporated into the celebration of Easter resurrection, rituals commemorating the dead into All-Hallows Eve and All Saints Day, and elements of winter solstice festivals into the celebration of Christmas. The most durable polytheistic remains are our days of the week, each of which except "Saturday" derives from the name of a Germanic pagan god, and the word "Easter," deriving, according to the Anglo-Saxon scholar Bede (d. 735), from the name of a Germanic pagan goddess, Eostre. In English literature such "folkloric" elements sometimes elicit romantic nostalgia. Geoffrey Chaucer's "Wife of Bath" looks back to a magical time before the arrival of Christianity in which the land was "fulfilled of fairye." Hundreds of years later, the seventeenth-century writer Robert Herrick honors the amalgamation of Christian and pagan elements in agrarian British culture in such poems as "Corinna's Gone A-Maying" and "The Hock Cart."

Medieval Christianity was fairly uniform, if complex, across Western Europe—hence called "catholic," or universally shared. The Church was composed of the so-called "regular" and "secular" orders, the regular orders being those who followed a rule in a community under an abbot or an abbess (i.e., monks, nuns, friars and canons), while the secular clergy of priests served parish communities under the governance of a bishop. In the unstable period from the sixth until the twelfth century, monasteries were the intellectual powerhouse of the Church. From the beginning of the thirteenth century, with the development of an urban Christian spirituality in Europe, friars dominated the recently invented institution of universities, as well as devoting themselves, in theory at least, to the urban poor.

The Catholic Church was also an international power structure. With its hierarchy of pope, cardinals, archbishops, and bishops, it offered a model of the centralized, bureaucratic state from the late eleventh century. That ecclesiastical power structure coexisted alongside a separate, often less centralized and feudal structure of lay authorities, with theoretically different and often competing spheres of social responsibilities. The sharing of lay and ecclesiastical authority in medieval England was sometimes a source of conflict. Chaucer's pilgrims are on their way to visit the memorial shrine to one victim of such exemplary struggle: Thomas à Becket, Archbishop of Canterbury, who opposed the policies of King Henry II, was assassinated by indirect suggestion of the king in 1170, and later made a saint. The Church, in turn, produced its own victims: Jews were subject to persecution in the late twelfth century in England, before being expelled in 1290. From the beginning of the fifteenth century, the English Church targeted Lollard heretics (see below) with capital punishment, for the first time.

As an international organization, the Church conducted its business in the universal language of Latin. Thus although in the period the largest segment of literate persons was made up of clerics, the clerical contribution to great literary writing in vernacular languages (e.g., French and English) was, so far as we know, relatively modest, with some great exceptions in the later Middle Ages (e.g., William Langland). Lay, vernacular writers of the period certainly reflect the importance of the Church as an institution and the pervasiveness of religion in the rituals that marked everyday life, as well as contesting institutional authority. From the late fourteenth century, indeed, England witnessed an active and articulate, proto-Protestant movement known as Lollardy, which attacked clerical hierarchy and promoted vernacular scriptures.

Beginning in 1517 the German monk Martin Luther, in Wittenberg, Germany, openly challenged many aspects of Catholic practice and by 1520 had completely repudiated the authority of the pope, setting in train the Protestant Reformation. Luther argued that the Roman Catholic Church had strayed far from the pattern of Christianity laid out in scripture. He rejected Catholic doctrines for which no biblical authority was to be found, such as the belief in Purgatory, and translated the Bible into German, on the grounds that the importance of scripture for all Christians made its translation into the vernacular tongue essential. Luther was not the first to advance such views— Lollard followers of the Englishman John Wycliffe had translated the Bible in the late fourteenth century. But Luther, protected by powerful German rulers, was able to speak out with impunity and convert others to his views, rather than suffer the persecution usually meted out to heretics. Soon other reformers were following in Luther's footsteps: of these, the Swiss Ulrich Zwingli and the French Jean Calvin would be especially influential for English religious thought.

At first England remained staunchly Catholic. Its king, Henry VIII, was so severe to heretics that the pope awarded him the title "Defender of the Faith," which British monarchs have retained to this day. In 1534, however, Henry rejected the authority of the pope to prevent his divorce from his queen, Catherine of Aragon, and his marriage to his mistress, Ann Boleyn. In doing so, Henry appropriated to himself ecclesiastical as well as secular authority. Thomas More, author of *Utopia*, was executed in 1535 for refusing to endorse Henry's right to govern the English church. Over the following six years, Henry consolidated his grip on the ecclesiastical establishment by dissolving the powerful, populous Catholic monasteries and redistributing their massive landholdings to his own lay followers. Yet Henry's church largely retained Catholic doctrine and liturgy. When Henry died and his young son, Edward, came to the throne in 1547, the English church embarked on a more Protestant path, a direction abruptly reversed when Edward died and his older sister Mary, the daughter of Catherine of Aragon, took the throne in 1553 and attempted to reintroduce Roman Catholicism. Mary's reign was also short, however, and her successor, Elizabeth I, the daughter of Ann Boleyn, was a Protestant. Elizabeth attempted to establish a "middle way" Christianity, compromising between Roman Catholic practices and beliefs and reformed ones.

The Church of England, though it laid claim to a national rather than pan-European authority, aspired like its predecessor to be the universal church of all English subjects. It retained the Catholic structure of parishes and dioceses and the Catholic hierarchy of bishops, though the ecclesiastical authority was now the Archbishop of Canterbury and the Church's "Supreme Governor" was the monarch. Yet disagreement and controversy persisted. Some members of the Church of England wanted to retain many of the ritual and liturgical elements of Catholicism. Others, the Puritans, advocated a more thoroughgoing reformation. Most Puritans remained within the Church of England, but a minority, the "Separatists" or "Congregationalists," split from the established church altogether. These dissenters no longer thought of the ideal church as an organization to which everybody belonged; instead, they conceived it as a more exclusive group of likeminded people, one not necessarily attached to a larger body of believers.

In the seventeenth century, the succession of the Scottish king James to the English throne produced another problem. England and Scotland were separate nations, and in the sixteenth century Scotland had developed its own national Presbyterian church, or "kirk," under the leadership of the reformer John Knox. The kirk retained fewer Catholic liturgical elements than did the Church of England, and its authorities, or "presbyters," were elected by assemblies of their fellow clerics, rather than appointed by the king. James I and his son Charles I, especially the latter, wanted to bring the Scottish kirk into conformity with Church of England practices. The Scots violently resisted these efforts, with the collaboration of many English Puritans, in a conflict that eventually developed into the English Civil War in the mid-seventeenth century. The effect of these disputes is visible in the poetry of such writers as John Milton, Robert Herrick, Henry Vaughan, and Thomas Traherne, and in the prose of Thomas Browne, Lucy Hutchinson, and Dorothy Waugh. Just as in the mid-sixteenth century, when a succession of monarchs with different religious commitments destabilized the church, so the seventeenth century endured spiritual whiplash. King Charles I's highly ritualistic Church of England was violently overturned by the Puritan victors in the Civil War—until 1660, after the death of the Puritan leader, Oliver Cromwell, when the Church of England was restored along with the monarchy.

The religious and political upheavals of the seventeenth century produced Christian sects that de-emphasized the ceremony of the established church and rejected as well its top-down authority structure. Some of these groups were ephemeral, but the Baptists (founded in 1608 in Amsterdam by the English expatriate John Smyth) and Quakers, or Society of Friends (founded by George Fox in the 1640s), flourished outside the established church, sometimes despite cruel persecution. John Bunyan, a Baptist, wrote the Christian allegory *Pilgrim's Progress* while in prison. Some dissenters, like the Baptists, shared the reformed reverence for the absolute authority of scripture but interpreted the scriptural texts differently from their fellow Protestants. Others, like the Quakers, favored, even over the authority of the Bible, the "inner light" or voice of individual conscience, which they took to be the working of the Holy Spirit in the lives of individuals.

The Protestant dissenters were not England's only religious minorities. Despite crushing fines and the threat of imprisonment, a minority of Catholics under Elizabeth and James openly refused to give their allegiance to the new church, and others remained secret adherents to the old ways. John Donne was brought up in an ardently Catholic family, and several other writers converted to Catholicism as adults—Ben Jonson for a considerable part of his career, Elizabeth Carey and Richard Crashaw permanently, and at profound personal cost. In the eighteenth century, Catholics remained objects of suspicion as possible agents of sedition, especially after the "Glorious Revolution" in 1688 deposed the Catholic James II in favor of the Protestant William and Mary. Anti-Catholic prejudice affected John Dryden, a Catholic convert, as well as the lifelong Catholic Alexander Pope. By contrast, the English colony of Ireland remained overwhelmingly Roman Catholic, the fervor of its religious commitment at least partly inspired by resistance to English occupation. Starting in the reign of Elizabeth, England shored up its own authority in Ireland by encouraging Protestant immigrants from Scotland to settle in the north of Ireland, producing a virulent religious divide the effects of which are still playing out today.

A small community of Jews had moved from France to London after 1066, when the Norman William the Conqueror came to the English throne. Although despised and persecuted by many Christians, they were allowed to remain as moneylenders to the Crown, until the thirteenth century, when the king developed alternative sources of credit. At this point, in 1290, the Jews were expelled from England. In 1655 Oliver Cromwell permitted a few to return, and in the late seventeenth and early eighteenth centuries the Jewish population slowly increased, mainly by immigration from Germany. In the mid-eighteenth century some prominent Jews had their children brought up as Christians so as to facilitate their full integration into English society: thus the nineteenth-century writer and politician Benjamin Disraeli, although he and his father were members of the Church of England, was widely considered a Jew insofar as his ancestry was Jewish.

In the late seventeenth century, as the Church of England reasserted itself, Catholics, Jews, and dissenting Protestants found themselves subject to significant legal restrictions. The Corporation Act, passed in 1661, and the Test Act, passed in 1673, excluded all who refused to take communion in the Church of England from voting, attending university, or working in government or in the professions. Members of religious minorities, as well as Church of England communicants, paid mandatory taxes in support of Church of England ministers and buildings. In 1689 the dissenters gained the right to worship in public, but Jews and Catholics were not permitted to do so.

During the eighteenth century, political, intellectual, and religious history remained closely intertwined. The Church of England came to accommodate a good deal of variety. "Low church" services resembled those of the dissenting Protestant churches, minimizing ritual and emphasizing the sermon; the "high church" retained more elaborate ritual elements, yet its prestige was under attack on several fronts. Many Enlightenment thinkers subjected the Bible to rational critique and found it wanting: the philosopher David Hume, for instance, argued that the "miracles" described therein were more probably lies or errors than real breaches of the laws of nature. Within the Church of England, the "broad church" Latitudinarians welcomed this rationalism, advocating theological openness and an emphasis on ethics rather than dogma. More radically, the Unitarian movement rejected the divinity of Christ while professing to accept his ethical teachings. Taking a different tack, the preacher John Wesley, founder of Methodism, responded to the rationalists' challenge with a newly fervent call to evangelism and personal discipline; his movement was particularly successful in Wales. Revolutions in America and France at the end of the century generated considerable millenarian excitement and fostered more new religious ideas, often in conjunction with a radical social agenda. Many important writers of the Romantic period were indebted to traditions of protestant dissent: Unitarian and rationalist protestant ideas influenced William Hazlitt, Anna Barbauld, Mary Wollstonecraft, and the young Samuel Taylor Coleridge. William Blake created a highly idiosyncratic poetic mythology loosely indebted to radical strains of Christian mysticism. Others were even more heterodox: Lord Byron and Robert Burns, brought up as Scots Presbyterians, rebelled fiercely, and Percy Shelley's writing of an atheistic pamphlet resulted in his expulsion from Oxford.

Great Britain never erected an American-style "wall of separation" between church and state, but in practice religion and secular affairs grew more and more distinct during the nineteenth century. In consequence, members of religious minorities no longer seemed to pose a threat to the commonweal. A movement to repeal the Test Act failed in the 1790s, but a renewed effort resulted in the extension of the franchise to dissenting Protestants in 1828 and to Catholics in 1829. The numbers of Roman Catholics in England were swelled by immigration from Ireland, but there were also some prominent English adherents. Among writers, the converts John Newman and Gerard Manley Hopkins are especially important. The political participation and social integration of Jews presented a thornier challenge. Lionel de Rothschild, repeatedly elected to represent London in Parliament during the 1840s and 1850s, was not permitted to take his seat there because he refused to take his oath of office "on the true faith of a Christian"; finally, in 1858, the Jewish Disabilities Act allowed him to omit these words. Only in 1871, however, were Oxford and Cambridge opened to non-Anglicans.

Meanwhile geological discoveries and Charles Darwin's evolutionary theories increasingly cast doubt on the literal truth of the Creation story, and close philological analysis of the biblical text suggested that its origins were human rather than divine. By the end of the nineteenth century, many writers were bearing witness to a world in which Christianity no longer seemed fundamentally plausible. In his poetry and prose, Thomas Hardy depicts a world devoid of benevolent providence. Matthew Arnold's poem "Dover Beach" is in part an elegy to lost spiritual assurance, as the "Sea of Faith" goes out like the tide: "But now I only hear / Its melancholy, long, withdrawing roar / Retreating." For Arnold, literature must replace religion as a source of spiritual truth, and intimacy between individuals substitute for the lost communal solidarity of the universal church.

The work of many twentieth-century writers shows the influence of a religious upbringing or a religious conversion in adulthood. T. S. Eliot and W. H. Auden embrace Anglicanism, William Butler Yeats spiritualism. James Joyce repudiates Irish Catholicism but remains obsessed with it. Yet religion, or lack of it, is a matter of individual choice and conscience, not social or legal mandate. In the past fifty years, church attendance has plummeted in Great Britain. Although 71 percent of the population still identified itself as "Christian" on the 2000 census, only about 7 percent of these regularly attend religious services of any denomination. Meanwhile, immigration from former British colonies has swelled the ranks of religions once uncommon in the British Isles—Muslim, Sikh, Hindu, Buddhist—though the numbers of adherents remain small relative to the total population.

PERMISSIONS ACKNOWLEDGMENTS

TEXT CREDITS

Chinua Achebe: "Civil Peace" from GIRLS AT WAR AND OTHER STORIES by Chinua Achebe, copyright © 1972, 1973 by Chinua Achebe. Used by permission of Doubleday, an imprint of the Knopf Doubleday Publishing Group, a division of Penguin Random House LLC. and The Wylie Agency LLC. All rights reserved.

Chimamanda Ngozi Adichie: "Checking Out" by Chimamanda Ngozi Adichie, originally published in *The New Yorker Magazine*, March 18, 2013. Copyright © 2013 by Chimamanda Ngozi Adichie. Used by Permission of The Wylie Agency LLC.

Patience Agbadi: "Prologue" from TRANSFORMATRIX by Patience Agbadi. Copyright © 2000 by Patience Agbadi. Reprinted by permission of Canongate Books Limited.

Simon Armitage: "The Tyre," "Horses, M62," "The English Astronaut," and "Beck" from PAPER AEROPLANES: SELECTED POEMS, 1989–2014 by Simon Armitage. Copyright © 2014 by Simon Armitage. Reprinted by permission of Faber and Faber Limited.

Margaret Atwood: "Miss July Grows Older" from MORNING IN THE BURNED HOUSE by Margaret Atwood. Copyright © 1995 by O.W. Toad and Margaret Atwood. Reprinted with permission of Houghton Mifflin Harcourt Publishing Company, McClelland & Stewart Ltd, a division of Penguin Random House Canada Limited, and Curtis Brown Group Ltd, London on behalf of Margaret Atwood. "Death by Landscape" from WILDERNESS TIPS by Margaret Atwood. Copyright © 1991 O. W. Toad Limited. Used with permission of Doubleday, an imprint of the Knopf Doubleday Publishing Group, a division of Penguin Random House LLC, and Emblem/McClelland & Stewart, a division of Penguin Random House Canada Limited. All rights reserved.

W. H. Auden: Introduction to THE POET'S TONGUE [Poetry as a Memorable Speech] by W. H. Auden. Copyright © 1935 and 1946 by W. H. Auden. Reprinted by permission of Curtis Brown. "Petition" ("Sir, no man's enemy") and from THE ENGLISH AUDEN by W. H. Auden, edited by Edward Mendelson. Copyright © 1934, 1940 and renewed 1962, 1968 by W. H. Auden. Reprinted by permission of Curtis Brown. "In Memory of W. B. Yeats," "Musée des Beaux Arts," "Spain 1937," "The Unknown Citizen," "September 1, 1939," "Lullaby," and "As I Walked Out One Evening," copyright © 1940 and renewed 1968 by W. H. Auden, "In Praise of Limestone," copyright © 1951 by W. H. Auden, "On This Island," copyright © 1937 and renewed 1965 by W. H. Auden, "The Shield of Achilles," copyright © 1952 by W. H. Auden, from W. H. AUDEN COLLECTED POEMS by W. H. Auden. Used by permission of Random House, an imprint and division of Penguin Random House LLC. All rights reserved. "Spain 1937," and "September 1, 1939," copyright © 1940 and copyright renewed 1968 by W. H. Auden; from SELECTED POEMS by W. H. Auden, edited by Edward Mendelson. Used by permission of Vintage Books, an imprint of the Knopf Doubleday Publishing Group, a division of Penguin Random House LLC, and Curtis Brown. All rights reserved.

Samuel Beckett: WAITING FOR GODOT. Copyright © 1952 by Les Éditions de Minuit. English text copyright © 1954 by Grove Press, Inc.; copyright © renewed 1982 by Samuel Beckett, now The Estate of Samuel Beckett. Used by permission of Grove/Atlantic, Inc., and Faber & Faber Limited.

Louise Bennett: "Jamaica Language" from AUNTY ROACHY SEH. "Dry-Foot Bwoy," "Jamaica Oman," "Colonization in Reverse" from SELECTED POEMS OF LOUISE BENNETT. Reprinted with permission of the Louise Bennett Coverley (LBC) Estate.

Eavan Boland: "Fond Memory" from AN ORIGIN LIKE WATER: COLLECTED POEMS 1967–1987 by Eavan Boland. Copyright © 1987 by Eavan Boland. "The Lost Land" from THE LOST LAND by Eavan Boland. Copyright © 1998 by Eavan Boland. "The Dolls Museum in Dublin" from IN A TIME OF VIOLENCE by Eavan Boland. Copyright © 1994 by Eavan Boland. Reprinted by permission of W. W. Norton & Company, Inc., and Carcanet Press Ltd.

Mary Borden: "Belgium" from THE FORBIDDEN ZONE by Mary Bordon. Copyright © 1929 by Mary Borden. "The Song of the Mud" from *The English Review*, August 1917. Copyright © 1917 by Mary Borden. Reprinted by permission of Patrick Aylmer.

Kamau Brathwaite: Extract from HISTORY OF THE VOICE by Kamau Brathwaite, published by New Beacon Books in 1994. Reprinted with the permission of the publisher. "Calypso" from THE ARRIVANTS, copyright © 1981. Reprinted by permission of Oxford University Press Limited.

May Wedderburn Cannan: "Rouen" from IN WAR TIME, POEMS. Reprinted by permission of James Cannan Slater.

Anne Carson: From "The Glass Essay" from GLASS, IRONY, AND GOD by Anne Carson. Copyright © 1995 by Anne Carson. Reprinted by permission of New Directions Publishing Corp. and The Random House Group Limited.

J. M. Coetzee: Excerpt from WAITING FOR THE BARBARIANS: A Novel by J. M. Coetzee. Copyright © 1980 by J. M. Coetzee. Used by permission of Viking Books, an imprint of Penguin Publishing Group, a division of Penguin Random House LLC and The Random House Group Ltd. All rights reserved.

Kiran Desai: "The Sermon in the Guava Tree" adapted from HULLABALOO IN THE GUAVA ORCHARD, copyright © 1998 by Kiran Desai. Used by permission of Grove/Atlantic, Inc. and Faber and Faber Limited.

H.D. (Hilda Doolittle): "Oread" and "Sea Rose" from COLLECTED POEMS, 1912–1944. Copyright © 1914 by Hilda Doolittle. Reprinted by permission of New Direction Publishing Corp. and Carcanet Press Limited.

Keith Douglas: "Vergissmeinnicht," and "Aristocrats" from THE COMPLETE POEMS OF KEITH DOUGLAS, edited by Desmond Graham (1978). Copyright © Marie J. Douglas, 1978. Reprinted by permission of Faber & Faber Ltd and Farrar, Straus and Giroux.

Carol Ann Duffy: "Warming Her Pearls" is taken from SELLING MANHATTAN by Carol Ann Duffy, published by Anvil Press Poetry in 1987. Copyright © Carol Ann Duffy. Reproduced by permission of the author c/o Rogers, Coleridge & White Ltd, 20 Powis Mews, London W11 1JN. "Medusa" and "Mrs. Lazarus" from THE WORLD'S WIFE by Carol Ann Duffy. Published by Picador. Copyright © 1999 by Carol Ann Duffy. "Valentine" from MEAN TIME by Carol Ann Duffy. Published by Anvil Press Poetry. Copyright © 1993 by Carol Ann Duffy. Excerpt from *The Christmas Truce* by Carol

IMAGE CREDITS

Pp. 2–3: Tate Gallery, London / Art Resource, NY; p. 4: Topical Press Agency / Stringer / Getty Images; p. 7: Public Domain / Wikipedia; p. 8: George Rinhart/Corbis via Getty Images; p. 9: Bettmann / Getty Images; p. 11: Bettmann / Corbis; p. 14: Jimmy Sime / Stringer / Getty Images; p. 15: Bettmann / Getty Images; p. 16: AP Photo / Matt Dunham; p. 73: New York Public Library; p. 136: (left) E. V. Kealey / Wikimedia Commons; p. 136: (right) E. V. Kealey / Wikimedia Commons; p. 138: Private Collection / The Stapleton Collection / Bridgeman Images; p. 139: © Bolton Museum and Art Gallery, Lancashire, UK / The Bridgeman Art Library International; p. 157: 'In the Trenches' (ink on paper), Rosenberg, Isaac (1890–1918) / British Library, London, UK / Bridgeman Images. © Isaac Rosenberg Estate, Courtesy Bernard Wynick.; p. 164: "Dulce et Decorum Est," *Poems, 1911–18* (ink on paper), Owen, Wilfred (1893–1918) / British Library, London, UK / Bridgeman Images. © The Wilfred Owen Literary Estate; p. 184: © Kettle's Yard, University of Cambridge / The Bridgeman Art Library International; p. 185: Edward Wadsworth; p. 198: Wyndham Lewis; p. 211: Front Cover of *The Tower* by W. B. Yeats, 1928 (colour litho), Moore, Thomas Sturge (1870–1944) / Private Collection / Photo @Christie's Images / Bridgeman Images; p. 283: Courtesy Adam Erwood, London Lamb, Jasmine Perrett, Anjaly Poruthorr, Manoj Vangala. Georgia Institute of Technology (Dr. Kathryn Crowther); p. 405: Library of Congress Prints and Photographs Division Washington, D.C. [LC-DIG-ppmsc-09876]; p. 441: Alain Le Garsmeur / Getty Images; p. 750: Lipnitzki / Roger Viollet / Getty Images; p. 835: Bettmann / Corbis; p. 842: *Guernica,* 1937 (oil on canvas), Picasso, Pablo (1881–1973) / Museo Nacional Centro de Arte Reina Sofia, Madrid, Spain / Bridgeman Images; p. 849: *Daily Herald* Archive / SSPL / Getty Images; p. 852: Bentley Archive / Popperfoto / Getty Images; p. 884: (top) Hulton-Deutsch / Corbis Historical / Getty Images; p. 884: (bottom) Keystone/Hulton Archive/Getty Images.

COLOR INSERT CREDITS

C1: The Museum of Modern Art / Licensed by Scala / Art Resource, NY / The Bridgeman Art Library; C2: Tate Gallery, London / Art Resource, NY; C3: Imperial War Museum, London, UK / Bridgeman Art Library; C4: Henry Moore Foundation; Tate Gallery, London / Art Resource, NY; C5: *Family Group,* 1945 and 1947 (bronze with brown patina), Moore, Henry Spencer (1898–1986). Private Collection / Photo © Christie's Images / © The Henry Moore Foundation. All Rights Reserved, DACS 2017 / www.henry-moore.org / Bridgeman Images; C6: The Estate of Francis Bacon / ARS, NY / DACS, London; Digital Image; The Museum of Modern Art / Licensed by Scala / Art Resource, NY; C7: Courtesy of Acquavella Galleries, Inc. © 1993 The Metropolitan Museum of Art, Purchase Lila Acheson Wallace Gift (1993.71); C8: Dan Kitwood / Getty Images.

Index

About suffering they were never wrong, 815
Achebe, Chinua, 978
'A cold coming we had of it, 676
A cubit-wide turtle acting the bin lid, 1179
Adam's Curse, 218
Adichie, Chimamanda Ngozi, 1249
Adlestrop, 142
Agbabi, Patience, 893
Ah, Are You Digging on My Grave? 62
Air from another life and time and place, 1109
All I know is a door into the dark, 1095
Ambulances, 926
Among School Children, 231
And were Yeats living at this hour, 1176
Anseo, 1174
Anthem for Doomed Youth, 162
Apologia Pro Poemate Meo, 162
Anything Can Happen, 1109
Anything can happen. You know how Jupiter, 1109
Apeneck Sweeney spreads his knees, 657
Apologia Pro Poemate Meo, 162
April is the cruellest month, breeding, 659
Araby, 407
Arcadia, 1022
Aristocrats, 847
Armitage, Simon, 1221
As he knelt by the grave of his mother and father, 1177
As if he had been poured, 1096
As I Walked Out One Evening, 813
A snake came to my water-trough, 644
As the Team's Head Brass, 144
As the team's head brass flashed out on the turn, 144
A sudden blow: the great wings beating still, 229
A suspicion, a doubt, a jealousy, 1211
A touch of cold in the Autumn night—, 196
Atwood, Margaret, 1110
Aubade, 930
Auden, W. H., 807
Autumn, 196
A wind is ruffling the tawny pelt, 943

Bavarian Gentians, 644
Beck, 1225

Beckett, Samuel, 749
Belgium, 145
Bennett, Louise, 855
Bent double, like old beggars under sacks, 164
Between my finger and my thumb, 1095
Black History of the English-Speaking Peoples, A, 896
Black Jackets, 939
Blast, 197
Blast 6, 201
Boland, Eavan, 1139
Borden, Mary, 145
Brathwaite, Kamau, 861
Break of Day in the Trenches, 156
[British Indian Writer and a Dream-England, The], 877
Broken Hierarchies, 997
Brooke, Rupert, 139
Burning, 955
Byzantium, 234

Calypso, 866
Cannan, May Wedderburn, 170
Casualty, 1099
Channel Firing, 59
Checking Out, 1250
Cherry Trees, The, 144
Christmas Eve in the trenches of France, 1212
Christmas Truce, The, 1213
Church Going, 924
Circus Animals' Desertion, The, 241
Civil Peace, 980
Clearances, 1104
Closed like confessionals, they thread, 926
Coat, A, 219
Coetzee, J. M., 1124
Coleridge received the Person from Porlock, 732
Colonization in Reverse, 858
Composed as I am, like others, 936
Conrad, Joseph, 67
Convergence of the Twain, The, 60
Corniche, 1092
Crazy Jane Talks with the Bishop, 235
Crow's Last Stand, 955

Daffodils, 955
Darkling Thrush, The, 53
Daughters of the Late Colonel, The, 698
Day They Burned the Books, The, 722
Dead, The, 411
Dead Man's Dump, 159
Death by Landscape, 1111
Decolonising the Mind, 868
Desai, Kiran, 1225
Dialogue of Self and Soul, A, 233
Digging, 1095
Disabled, 167
Discourse on the Logic of Language, 873
Dolls Museum in Dublin, The, 1140
Do Not Go Gentle into That Good Night, 833
Douglas, Keith, 846
Down by the Salley Gardens, 214
Down by the salley gardens my love and I did
    meet, 214
Downhill I came, hungry, and yet not starved,
    143
Drummer Hodge, 53
Dry-Foot Bwoy, 857
Duffy, Carol Ann, 1209
Dulce Et Decorum Est, 164
Dumb Waiter, The, 958
During Wind and Rain, 65

Early morning over Rouen, hopeful, high,
    courageous morning, 171
Easter, 1916, 221
Elements of Composition, 936
Eliot. T. S., 651
Emperor's Babe, The, 891
Enduring Love, 1155
English, 873
English Astronaut, The, 1224
[English Is an Indian Literary Language], 880
Entrance and exit wounds are silvered clean,
    176
Epilogue, 882
Epitaph on an Army of Mercenaries, 135
Evaristo, Bernardine, 891
Everyone Sang, 151
Everyone suddenly burst out singing, 151
Explosion, The, 929

Far Cry from Africa, A, 943
Fascination of What's Difficult, The, 219
Fat Black Woman Goes Shopping, The, 882
Feminist Manifesto, 205
Fern Hill, 832
Few Don'ts by an Imagiste, A, 192
Flint, F. S., 191
Fond Memory, 1139
Force That Through the Green Fuse Drives the
    Flower, The, 828
Forge, The, 1095
Forster, E. M., 248
For whom the possessed sea littered, on both
    shores, 996
Four Quartets, 677

From the Wave, 940
From Wynyard's Gap the livelong day, 55
Futility, 167

Garden Party, The, 711
General, The, 150
Give me a word, 894
Glass Essay, The, 1169
Glory of Women, 151
Goodbye to All That, 173
'Good-morning; good-morning!' the General
    said, 150
Gordimer, Nadine, 931
Grauballe Man, The, 1096
Graves, Robert, 172
Groping along the tunnel, step by step, 150
Groping back to bed after a piss, 928
Growing Pains, 1217
Guernica, 841
Gunn, Thom, 938
Gurney, Ivor, 153

Hap, 52
Hardy, Thomas, 34
Heaney, Seamus, 1093
Heart of Darkness, 71
He disappeared in the dead of winter, 815
He Never Expected Much, 66
He sat in a wheeled chair, waiting for dark,
    167
He's gone, and all our plans, 154
He splashed down in rough seas off Spurn
    Point, 1224
He stood among a crowd at Drumahair, 216
He was found by the Bureau of Statistics to
    be, 818
He would drink by himself, 1099
High Windows, 927
Hill, Geoffrey, 995
Hollow Men, The, 673
Homage to a Government, 928
Horse Dealer's Daughter, The, 626
Horses, M62, 1223
Housman, A. E., 131
How Beastly the Bourgeois Is, 646
How much longer can I get away, 1123
Hughes, Ted, 950
Hulme, T. E., 185, 195
Hunchback in the Park, The, 829

I, too, saw God through mud,—, 162
I can feel the tug, 1097
If but some vengeful god would call to me, 52
If I should die, think only this of me, 139
If it form the one landscape that we the
    inconstant ones, 821
I found this jawbone at the sea's edge, 951
If We Must Die, 854
If we must die, let it not be like hogs, 854
I had grieved. I had wept for a night and
    a day, 1212
I have crossed an ocean, 882

I have heard that hysterical women say, 236
I have met them at close of day, 221
I have two daughters, 1141
I know that I shall meet my fate, 226
I leant upon a coppice gate, 53
I leave me people, me land, me home, 883
I made my song a coat, 219
Imagisme, 191
I met the Bishop on the road, 235
In an apothecary's chest of drawers, 1107
In a solitude of the sea, 60
In a Station of the Metro, 196
Inglan Is a Bitch, 885
In idle August, while the sea soft, 944
In Memory of Jane Fraser, 995
In Memory of Major Robert Gregory, 223
In Memory of W. B. Yeats, 815
In Parenthesis, 178
In Praise of Limestone, 821
In the silence that prolongs the span, 939
In Time of 'The Breaking of Nations', 66
Introduction [*A General Introduction for My Work*], (Yeats), 242
I resemble everyone, 936
Irish Airman Foresees His Death, An, 226
I shall not soon forget, 941
Ishiguro, Kazuo, 1192
I sit in one of the dives, 818
I sought a theme and sought for it in vain, 241
It is all one chase, 1225
It mounts at sea, a concave wall, 940
It seemed that out of battle I escaped, 166
It was a school where all the children wore darned worsted, 1139
It was my thirtieth year to heaven, 830
I've longin' in me dept's of heart dat I can conquer not, 854
I walk through the long schoolroom questioning, 231
I will arise and go now, and go to Innisfree, 215
I work all day, and get half-drunk at night, 930
I work all day and hardly drink at all, 1092

Jamaica Language, 856
Jamaica Oman, 859
Jamaica oman cunny, sah!, 859
Johnson, Linton Kwesi, 885
Jones, David, 177
Journey of the Magi, 676
Joyce, James, 404
Just how it came to rest where it rested, 1221

Kitchen Grammars, The, 1092
Kite for Aibhín, A, 1109
Kureishi, Hanif, 887, 1200

Lake Isle of Innisfree, The, 215
Lapis Lazuli, 236
Larkin, Philip, 923
Lawrence, D. H., 611

Lay your sleeping head, my love, 809
Leda and the Swan, 229
Lessing, Doris, 900
Lessons of the War, 845
Let us go then, you and I, 654
Like a convalescent, I took the hand, 1102
Little Gidding, 677
Loaf, The, 1178
Long Live the Vortex!, 199
Look, stranger, at this island now, 809
Lost Land, The, 1141
Louse Hunting, 158
Loveliest of Trees, 132
Loveliest of trees, the cherry now, 132
Love on the Farm, 642
Love Song of J. Alfred Prufrock, The, 654
Loy, Mina, 204
Lullaby, 809

"Mais qui ça qui rivait-'ous, Philoctete?," 947
Man. In a cleft that's christened Alt, 240
Man and the Echo, 240
Mansfield, Katherine (Kathleen), 697
Mantel, Hilary, 1179
Man Who Dreamed of Faeryland, The, 216
Mark on the Wall, The, 272
McEwan, Ian, 1154
McKay, Claude, 853
MCMXIV, 925
Medusa, 1211
Meeting the British, 1175
Memoirs of an Infantry Officer, 152
Metaphysical Poets, The, 690
Midwinter spring is its own season, 677
Milkweed and Monarch, 1177
Miners, 163
Missing, The, 942
Miss July Grows Older, 1123
Modern Fiction, 277
Moment before the Gun Went Off, The, 932
Morse, 1091
Move him into the sun—, 167
Mrs. Dalloway, 282
Mrs Lazarus, 1212
Muldoon, Paul, 1173
Munro, Alice, 984
Murray, Les, 1090
Musée des Beaux Arts, 815
My father sat in his chair recovering, 953
My Sad Captains, 940
My Son the Fanatic, 1202
My Soul. I summon to the winding ancient stair, 233

Nagra, Daljit, 896
Naipaul, V. S., 998
[*Nation Language*], 861
Neutral Tones, 52
Next to my own skin, her pearls. My mistress, 1210
Next year we are to bring the soldiers home, 928

Ngũgĩ wa Thiong'o, 867
Nichols, Grace, 882
No, the serpent did not, 954
Nobody heard him, the dead man, 731
No Second Troy, 219
Not a red rose or a satin heart., 1211
Not every man has gentians in his house, 644
Not Waving but Drowning, 731
Now as I was young and easy under the apple boughs, 832
Now as I watch the progress of the plague, 942
Now it is autumn and the falling fruit, 647
Now that we're almost settled in our house, 223
Nudes—stark and glistening, 158

Odour of Chrysanthemums, 613
Old England, 854
'O 'Melia, my dear, this does everything crown!, 54
Omeros, 947
Once I am sure there's nothing going on, 924
Once more the storm is howling, and half hid, 227
One by one they appear in, 940
One Out of Many, 999
One We Knew, 58
Only a Boche, 140
Only a man harrowing clods, 66
On Not Shooting Sitting Birds, 726
On Passing the New Menin Gate, 151
On the day of the explosion, 929
On the Western Circuit, 36
On This Island, 809
Oread, 196
Orwell, George, 734
Other Boat, The, 249
Our Bog Is Dood, 730
Our Bog is dood, our Bog is dood, 730
Out, 953
Owen, Wilfred, 161
Owen's Letters to His Mother, 168
Owl, The, 143

Petition, 808
Philip, M. NourbeSe, 872
Phillips, Caryl, 1216
Piano, 643
Picasso, Pablo, 841
Pike, 952
Pike, three inches long, perfect, 952
Pinter, Harold, 957
Poem in October, 830
[Poetry as Memorable Speech], 825
Politics and the English Language, 740
Portrait of the Artist as a Young Man, A, 440
Pound, Ezra, 191, 195
Prayer for My Daughter, A, 227
Preface (Owen), 169
Preface to The Nigger of the "Narcissus" (Conrad), 69

Pretty, 733
Professions for Women, 400
Prologue, 894
Prophet's Hair, The, 1144
Punishment, 1097

Rain, 143
Rain, midnight rain, nothing but the wild rain, 143
Ramanujan, A. K., 936
Rear-Guard, The, 150
Recalling War, 176
Reed, Henry, 844
Relic, 951
Remember how we picked the daffodils?, 955
Requiem for the Plantagenet Kings, 996
Returning, We Hear the Larks, 158
Rhys, Jean, 721
Romanticism and Classicism, 186
Room of One's Own, A, 392
Rose, harsh rose, 197
Rosenberg, Isaac, 155
Rose of the World, The, 214
Rouen, 171
Ruined Maid, The, 54
Rushdie, Salman, 876, 1142

Sad Steps, 928
Sailing to Byzantium, 230
Sassoon, Siegfried, 148
Schooner Flight, The, 944
Sea Rose, 197
Season of Phantasmal Peace, The, 946
Second Coming, The, 227
Self-Portrait, 936
September 1913, 220
September 1, 1939, 818
September Song, 996
Sermon in the Guava Tree, The, 1227
Service, Robert, 140
7, Middagh Street, 1176
Sharping Stone, The, 1107
She looked over his shoulder, 823
She taught me what her uncle once taught her, 1104
She told how they used to form for the country dances—, 58
Shield of Achilles, The, 823
Ship of Death, The, 647
Shooting an Elephant, 735
Shopping in London winter, 882
Silent One, The, 155
Sir, no man's enemy, forgiving all, 808
Sitwell, Edith, 843
Skunk, The, 1101
Smith, Stevie, 728
Smith, Zadie, 1236
Snake, 644
Softly, in the dusk, a woman is singing to me, 643
Soldier, The, 139
Sombre the night is, 158

Song of the Mud, The, 147
Songs to Joannes, 208
Sorrow of Love, The, 215
Sorry to Disturb, 1181
Spain, 810
Spawn of Fantasies, 208
Sprung from a field, 1223
Station Island, 1102
Still Falls the Rain, 843
Still Life, 941
Stolen Child, The, 212
Stoppard, Tom, 1021
Strange Meeting, 166
Sunt Leones, 729
Swear by what the Sages spoke, 237
Sweeney among the Nightingales, 657

Talking in Bed, 926
Talking in bed ought to be easiest, 926
Terence, This Is Stupid Stuff, 134
That is no country for old men. The young, 230
That night your great guns, unawares, 59
The Bishop tells us: 'When the boys come back, 149
The brawling of a sparrow in the eaves, 215
The cherry trees bend over and are shedding, 144
The darkness crumbles away, 156
The lions who ate the Christians on the sands of the arena, 729
Then all the nations of birds lifted together, 946
The noble horse with courage in his eye, 847
Theology, 954
The plunging limbers over the shattered track, 159
There was a whispering in my hearth, 163
These, in the day when heaven was falling, 135
The stone had skidded arc'd and bloomed into islands, 866
The time you won your town the race, 133
The trees are in their autumn beauty, 223
The unpurged images of day recede, 234
The verb in a Sanscrit or Farsi, 1092
The wounds are terrible. The paint is old, 1140
'They', 149
They fuck you up, your mum and dad, 930
They sing their dearest songs—, 65
They throw in Drummer Hodge, to rest, 53
This Be the Verse, 930
This house has been far out at sea all night, 951
This is the song of the mud, 147
Thomas, Dylan, 827
Thomas, Edward, 142
Those long uneven lines, 925
Thoughts About the Person from Porlock, 732
Three Guineas, 836
Three weeks gone and the combatants gone, 846

To an Athlete Dying Young, 133
To His Love, 154
To Room Nineteen, 901
Tradition and the Individual Talent, 684
Trampwoman's Tragedy, A, 55
Tuckett. Bill Tuckett. Telegraph operator, Hall's Creek, 1091
Turning and turning in the widening gyre, 227
Turtles, 1179
Tyre, The, 1221

Ulysses, 602
Under Ben Bulben, 237
Under the Waterfall, 63
Undesirable you may have been, untouchable, 996
Unknown Citizen, The, 818
Up, black, striped and damasked like the chasuble, 1101

Valentine, 1211
Vergissmeinnicht, 846
Village after Dark, A, 1193
Voice, The, 64

Waiter's Wife, The, 1238
Waiting for Godot, 751
Waiting for the Barbarians, 1126
Walcott, Derek, 942
Walk, The, 64
Walker Brothers Cowboy, 985
Warming Her Pearls, 1210
Waste Land, The, 659
We are the hollow men, 673
We brought him in from between the lines: we'd better have let him lie, 140
Well, World, you have kept faith with me, 66
Well there are many ways of being held prisoner, 1169
We met the British in the dead of winter, 1175
wen mi jus come to Landan toun, 885
We sat together at one summer's end, 218
We stood by a pond that winter day, 52
What a joyful news, Miss Mattie, 858
What large, dark hands are those at the window, 642
What need you, being come to sense, 220
What passing-bells for these who die as cattle?, 161
Wha wrong wid Mary dry-foot bwoy?, 857
'Whenever I plunge my arm, like this, 63
When I put my finger to the hole they've cut for a dimmer switch, 1178
When I see a couple of kids, 927
When I Was One-and-Twenty, 132
When snow like sheep lay in the fold, 995
When the Master was calling the roll, 1174
When to depict rain—heavy rain—it stands, 997
When You Are Old, 216
When you are old and grey and full of sleep, 216

Where dips the rocky highland, 212
Wherever I Hang, 883
Whirl up, sea—, 196
Who died on the wires, and hung there, one of two—, 155
Who do you love? Who *do* you love, 891
Who dreamed that beauty passes like a dream? 214
Who Goes with Fergus? 216
Who will go drive with Fergus now, 216
Who will remember, passing through this Gate, 151
Why is the word pretty so underrated? 733
Why should I blame her that she filled my days, 219

Why the Novel Matters, 637
Wild Swans at Coole, The, 223
Wind, 951
Woman much missed, how you call to me, call to me, 64
Woolf, Virginia, 270, 836

Yeats, William Butler, 209
Yes, I remember Adlestrop—, 142
Yesterday all the past. The language of size, 810
You did not walk with me, 64
You love us when we're heroes, home on leave, 151
[*You Will Always Be a Paki*], 887

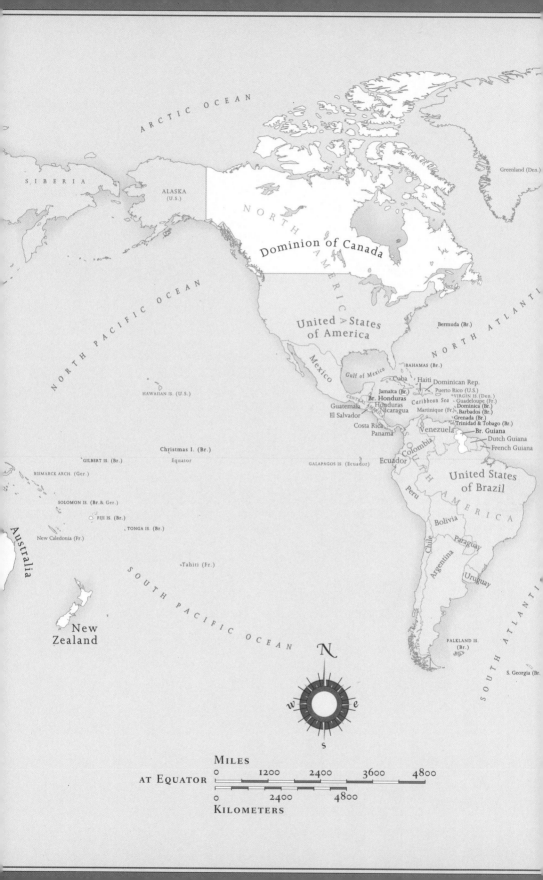